southeast asia
on a shoestring

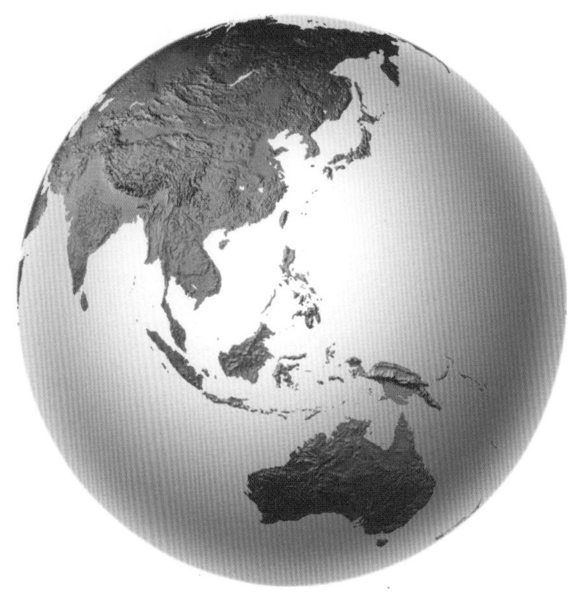

China Williams

Greg Bloom, Celeste Brash, Andrew Burke, Jayne D'Arcy, Shawn Low, Brandon Presser, Nick Ray, Daniel Robinson, Ryan Ver Berkmoes, Richard Waters

CHIANG MAI (p749)
Cycle around the old city, master the markets and study Thai cooking in this charming northern city
LUANG NAM THA (p399)
A centre for 'green' trekking, through jungle highlands and tribal communities
HANOI (p842)
Old Asia retrofitted for today, with medieval alleys and an embalmed Uncle Ho
BAGAN (p581)
Ancient Buddhist monuments crowd the landscape like a spiritual version of Manhattan
HALONG BAY (p861)
Sail among the thousands of humpbacked islands that freckle the emerald bay
LUANG PRABANG (p383)
A romantic ancient capital that is perfect for wandering and for dreams of a never-ending stay
BANGKOK (p710)
A city of excesses with thumping dance floors, low-key beer pubs, mega malls and teeming markets
TEMPLES OF ANGKOR (p95)
One of the world's greatest monuments, built for the god-kings of the Khmer empire
BATTAMBANG (p103)
Arrive by boat, wander around crumbling colonial villas and explore hilltop temples
PULAU WEH (p281)
Explore the underwater canyons and secluded beaches on this undisturbed island
KO TAO (p799)
Learn how to swim like a fish on this dive-centric island
MT KINABALU (p497)
Slog through the jungle to the granite-capped spires of this Borneo peak
KRABI (p815)
Scale craggy limestone peaks, paddle through gem-coloured waters and toast the sunset
BUKIT LAWANG (p279)
Snap an up-close encounter with semiwild orang-utans in a jungle sanctuary
PULAU PENANG (p461)
Chow through Malaysia's multicultural melange at hawker centres, morning markets and abundant restaurants
SINGAPORE (p669)
A sophisticated city for museum-hopping, shopping and hawker sampling
GUNUNG BROMO (p220)
Hike to the peak of this fuming volcano for sunrise over the towering moonscape
BALI (p222)
A beloved beach spot for surfing, sunning and slowing down
BHUTAN
INDIA
BANGLADESH
CHINA
MYANMAR (BURMA)
LAOS
THAILAND
VIETNAM
CAMBODIA
MALAYSIA
SINGAPORE
BRUNEI
INDONESIA
Hainan CHINA
Bay of Bengal
ANDAMAN SEA
Gulf of Tonkin
Gulf of Thailand
SOUTH CHINA SEA
JAVA SEA
INDIAN OCEAN
Paracel Islands
Christmas Island AUSTRALIA
Myitkyina
Mandalay
Sittwe
Bagan
Taunggyi
Kalaw
Inle Lake
Bago
Pathein
YANGON
Mergui (Myeik) Archipelago
Fansipan (3143m)
Sapa
HANOI
Haiphong
Halong Bay
Luang Nam Tha
Udomxai
Chiang Rai
Chiang Mai
Luang Prabang
VIENTIANE
Paksan
Vinh
Sukhothai
Udon Thani
Savannakhet
Hue
Danang
Hoi An
Ubon Ratchathani
Ayuthaya
Nakhon Ratchasima
Pakse
Kanchanaburi
BANGKOK
Temples of Angkor
Siem Reap
Pattaya
Battambang
Tonle Sap
Ko Chang
Nha Trang
Dalat
PHNOM PENH
Ho Chi Minh City
Vung Tau
Mekong
Ko Tao
Ko Pha-Ngan
Ko Samui
Phu Quoc
Surat Thani
Krabi
Nakhon Si Thammarat
Phuket
Hat Yai
Songkhla
Pulau Langkawi
Pulau Weh
Banda Aceh
Georgetown
Pulau Penang
Peninsular Malaysia
Ipoh
Taman Negara
Bukit Lawang
Medan
Berastagi
Danau Toba
KUALA LUMPUR
Melaka
Straits of Melaka
Pulau Tioman
Anambas Islands
Natuna Islands
Pulau Simeulue
Pulau Nias
Sumatra
Equator
Pekanbaru
Riau Islands
Kota Kinabalu
Mt Kinabalu (4095m)
BANDAR SERI BEGAWAN
Sabah
Niah
Sarawak
Kuching
Berau
Putussibau
Kalimantan
Kapuas
Pontianak
Samarinda
Balikpapan
Barito
Bukittinggi
Padang
Pulau Siberut
Singkep Islands
Jambi
Hari
Musi
Pulau Bangka
Mentawi Islands
Palembang
Pangkalanbun
Pulau Belitung
Banjarmasin
Bandarlampung
Sunda Strait
JAKARTA
Bogor
Bandung
Java
Semarang
Madura
Surabaya
Borobudur
Solo
Yogyakarta
Gunung Bromo
Malang
Bali Sea
Denpasar
Bali
Lombok
Sumbawa
Mataram
20°N
10°N
0°
10°S
100°E
110°E

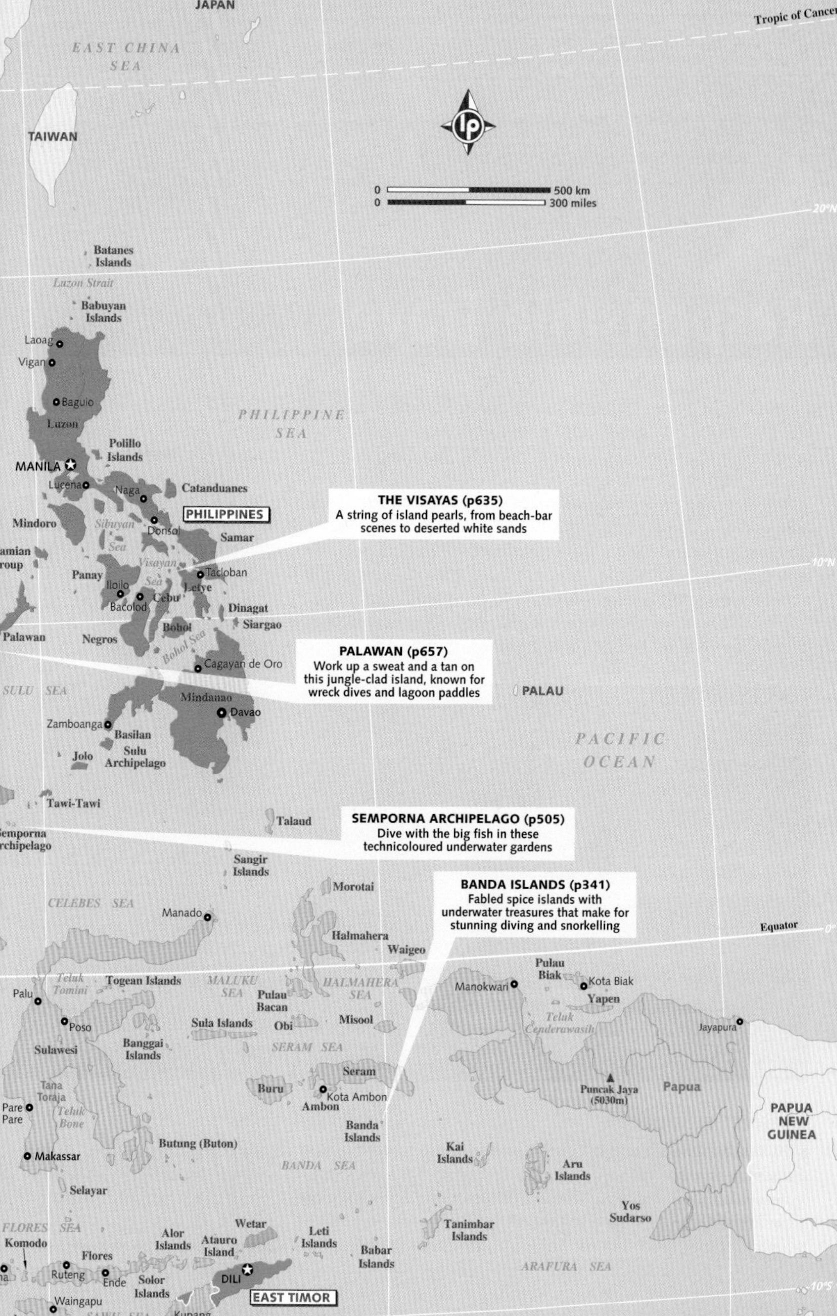

JAPAN
EAST CHINA SEA
Tropic of Cancer
TAIWAN
0 500 km
0 300 miles
20°N
Batanes Islands
Luzon Strait
Babuyan Islands
Laoag
Vigan
Baguio
Luzon
PHILIPPINE SEA
Polillo Islands
MANILA
Lucena
Naga
Catanduanes
THE VISAYAS (p635)
A string of island pearls, from beach-bar scenes to deserted white sands
PHILIPPINES
Mindoro
Sibuyan Sea
Donsol
Samar
Calamian Group
Visayan Sea
Tacloban
10°N
Panay
Iloilo
Leyte
Bacolod
Cebu
Dinagat
Siargao
Palawan
Negros
Bohol
Bohol Sea
PALAWAN (p657)
Work up a sweat and a tan on this jungle-clad island, known for wreck dives and lagoon paddles
Cagayan de Oro
SULU SEA
Mindanao
PALAU
Davao
Zamboanga
Basilan
PACIFIC OCEAN
Jolo
Sulu Archipelago
Tawi-Tawi
Talaud
SEMPORNA ARCHIPELAGO (p505)
Dive with the big fish in these technicoloured underwater gardens
Semporna Archipelago
Sangir Islands
BANDA ISLANDS (p341)
Fabled spice islands with underwater treasures that make for stunning diving and snorkelling
Morotai
CELEBES SEA
Manado
Halmahera
Equator
0°
Waigeo
Pulau Biak
Teluk Tomini
Togean Islands
MALUKU SEA
HALMAHERA SEA
Manokwari
Kota Biak
Palu
Pulau Bacan
Yapen
Poso
Sula Islands
Obi
Misool
Teluk Cenderawasih
Jayapura
Sulawesi
Banggai Islands
SERAM SEA
Seram
Buru
Puncak Jaya (5030m)
Papua
Tana Toraja
Kota Ambon
Ambon
PAPUA NEW GUINEA
Pare Pare
Teluk Bone
Banda Islands
Butung (Buton)
Makassar
Kai Islands
Aru Islands
BANDA SEA
Selayar
Yos Sudarso
FLORES SEA
Wetar
Leti Islands
Tanimbar Islands
Komodo
Alor Islands
Atauro Island
Babar Islands
Flores
Bima
Ruteng
Ende
Solor Islands
DILI
ARAFURA SEA
EAST TIMOR
10°S
Waingapu
Sumba
SAWU SEA
Kupang
West Timor
Rote
TIMOR SEA
Sawu
120°E
130°E
140°E
AUSTRALIA

STU SMUC

Responsible Travel

In Southeast Asia, tourism brings both blessings and curses. Small-scale tourism fosters family-owned businesses and promotes the preservation of cultural and environmental assets. From Cambodia's Angkor ruins to Thailand's coral reefs, tourists' dollars make their preservation a lucrative business.

But tourism also puts pressure on the host country's resources and hospitality. Whether clueless or callous, irresponsible tourism can adversely affect the local culture. Popular destinations rarely have the infrastructure to deal with the increased population's need for water, energy and waste removal. And then there are the one-on-one confrontations that occur due to cultural ignorance and economic disparity.

To ensure that your trip is a gift, not a burden, remember to be respectful of the local people, to be kind to the local environment and to be a conscientious consumer.

TRAVEL TIPS

- **Ask before you click** Learn to say 'May I take your picture?' in the local language.
- **Shop locally** Spend your money at family businesses.
- **Be money wise** Know how much things should cost; don't expect something for nothing, but don't let hustlers take advantage of you.
- **Learn the language** Take a language course or at least learn to say 'thank you' in every country you visit.
- **Protect the environment** Reduce your energy consumption and waste production. Tread lightly through natural areas. Don't buy souvenirs or eat meals produced from endangered species.
- **Respect the local culture** Observe local taboos and matters of etiquette.
- **Be informed** Learn about the country's history, current events and social problems.
- **Give back** Volunteer at an orphanage or wildlife sanctuary or help school children practise their English-language skills.

INTERNET RESOURCES

www.responsible-travel.org Common-sense advice on dealing with begging, bargaining and being green.
www.stay-another-day.org Searchable portal for sustainable-tourism activities in former Indochina.
www.sealang.net Academic resource for Southeast Asian languages.
www.atimes.com News and analysis of regional events.
www.panda.org WWF International's website covers environmental news and conservation projects.

Southeast Asia Highlights

Travellers and Lonely Planet staff and authors share their top experiences in Southeast Asia. Do you agree with their choices, or have we missed your favourites? Go to lonelyplanet.com and tell us your highlights.

JON ARMSTRONG

1 TRAFFIC

Everything – including the kitchen sink – is carried on a bike: entire families, dead pigs, piles of vegetables, boxes of Coca Cola. Crossing is a desperate dash across, hoping they will slow down.

lonelyplanet.com Member

SEAN CAFFREY

2 ANGKOR WAT

I am not a morning person at all but I would recommend anyone travelling through Cambodia to make the effort to rise for the sunrise over Angkor Wat (p95). Dark, looming temples silhouetted against a pink and crimson sky are mirrored perfectly in the ponds and moats, save only for the rippling interruption of a drifting water lily or hungry fish.

Sharyn Christie, Traveller, Australia

3 THE GIBBON EXPERIENCE

The Gibbon Experience (p405) is an adventurer's hidden delight. In Bokeo, in northern Laos, you will hike up the steepest hills to fly through the jungle on a wire cable in search of the black gibbon. Cables up to 200m high and 400m long see you squealing with glee, and you will then spend the night sleeping in a tree house. The Gibbon Experience is also an opportunity to help protect the rainforest and, if you're lucky, get a glimpse of gibbons in the wild.

Beware the leeches!

lonelyplanet.com Member

ANDERS BLOMQV

DALLAS STRIB

4 LONGTAIL BOATS

These rustic but elegant fishing boats, festooned with garlands, are handled effortlessly by the local fishermen. Now just imagine trying to climb into one. Most travellers aren't as graceful.

China Williams, Lonely Planet Author

MT KINABALU

You have to do it (p497). Forget about the cost, the pain in your knees, the price of beer at Laban Rata (hint, you don't want a hangover at this altitude) and your lame guide who insists on halting every five minutes. Forget about the 3am wake up, the freezing cold, your pounding head, and the people falling over in front of you as you haul yourself up the chain in the dark. When the sun comes up, all is revealed, and it is good. Very, very good. Head down to Poring Hot Springs (p499) and treat your weary bones to a private hot bath. And cheap beer.

Steve Waters, Lonely Planet Staff

6

KARL LEHMANN

JULIET COOMBE

5

INLE LAKE

Life here revolves around this rich, abundant lake (p565). Hire a boat and marvel at the fishermen with their one-legged rowing style, visit homes on stilts above the water, and watch farmers tend their floating fruit and vegetable gardens.

gotchagirl, Traveller

MANFRED GOTTSCHALK

7

HALONG BAY

If you can get out of bed after being lulled to sleep by the swaying boat, your morning on Halong Bay (p861) will truly be one for the books. The mountains meet the sea in this archipelago, with huge peaks rising all around you as you sail by. Every view is picture worthy, especially in the morning light. If you like rice for breakfast, you're really in luck.

Lucy Anne Kagan, Traveller, USA

RUSSELL MOUNTFORD

8 HAWKER FOOD

Offering mystery meats floating in a soup of herbs, unfamiliar vegetables, with textures from gelatinous to chewy, hawker stalls are an omnipresent adventure that allow you to exercise your tastebuds, make new friends, practise language skills and eat on the cheap.

Celeste Brash, Lonely Planet Author

9 MACRITCHIE RESERVOIR

Hidden in the bowels of Singapore is this patch of urban primary rainforest (p685) wrapped around a shimmering reservoir. Visitors can embark on a variety of trails and boardwalks that take them deep into the heart of the forest. The highlight is definitely the 250m suspension bridge hanging at a height of 25m – sure, it takes some hard work to get there, but standing in the middle of the bridge, your reward will be the stunning views of the landscape and the canopy of the rainforest below.

Shawn Low, Lonely Planet Author

MERVIN CH

CHRISTOPHER GROENHOU

10 HOI AN

After the chaos of Saigon, a few days in Hoi An (p881) was just what the doctor ordered. We cruised around the Old Town on beat up old bikes, made rice-paper rolls at the Red Bridge Cooking School (p883), explored the incredible market, and stuffed our faces with pork buns sold by street vendors. The town may be full of tourists, but there's a good reason why.

Blair Gatehouse, Lonely Planet Staff

SURFING

The dream of perfect barrels in remote locations is still alive and well in Indonesia. If you are prepared to strike out from the hot spots you will be rewarded with the trip of a lifetime. For me it was spending time with the locals that made surfing there such a special experience; teaching the young kids how to paddle in the shallows after another perfect sunset session is the memory that will last longer than the many perfect waves I scored.

John Viner, Lonely Planet Staff

11

PAUL KENNEDY

BANAUE RICE TERRACES

Imagine a giant staircase that surpasses that of a grand cruise ship. Mountains were fabricated into terraces of rice paddies (p628) – a true piece of art and hard work in the mountain ranges.

lonelyplanet.com Member

12

RICHARD I'ANSON

JOHN SONES

13

KIDS

East Timor's young population (p147) is no more evident than when school breaks for the day. Kids in white shirts and blue or brown skirts and shorts fill every inch of the roads, giggling and talking and making way for the occasional motorbike or minibus.

Jayne D'Arcy, Lonely Planet Author

DIVING EAST TIMOR

In stark contrast to the suburban feel of Dili is the teeming metropolis that lies under the water mere minutes from the capital. Expats have been submerging themselves in Timor's stunning underwater world since 2000, and the established dive-school scene is helping everyone get in on the secret (see p154).

Jayne D'Arcy,
Lonely Planet Author

14

MARK WEBSTER

WAYNE WALTO

15 JAME'ASR HASSANIL BOLKIAH MOSQUE

Not just a place of worship, the Jame'Asr Hassanil Bolkiah Mosque (p56) is a monument to power, wealth and benevolence. Built in 1992 to honour the 25th year of the current sultan's rule, this jaw-dropping concoction of domes and minarets is largest mosque in the sultanate, and the perfect target for an evening photo shoot. Not to be missed is the sea of gold-woven prayer rugs in the main hall. On the day of the mosque's grand opening, the sultan graciously offered every single attendee an ornate (and very expensive!) carpet.

Brandon Presser, Lonely Planet Author

ANDERS BLOMQVI

16 THAM KONG LO

Imagine floating through a 7.5km underworld in a rickety longtail boat, wrapped in darkness but for the torchlight of your boatman. Welcome to Kong Lo cave (p407), an Indiana Jones experience if ever there was one, except here there's no life vest, and no director yelling 'cut!'. Creepy but unlike anything else in Southeast Asia.

Richard Waters, Lonely Planet Author

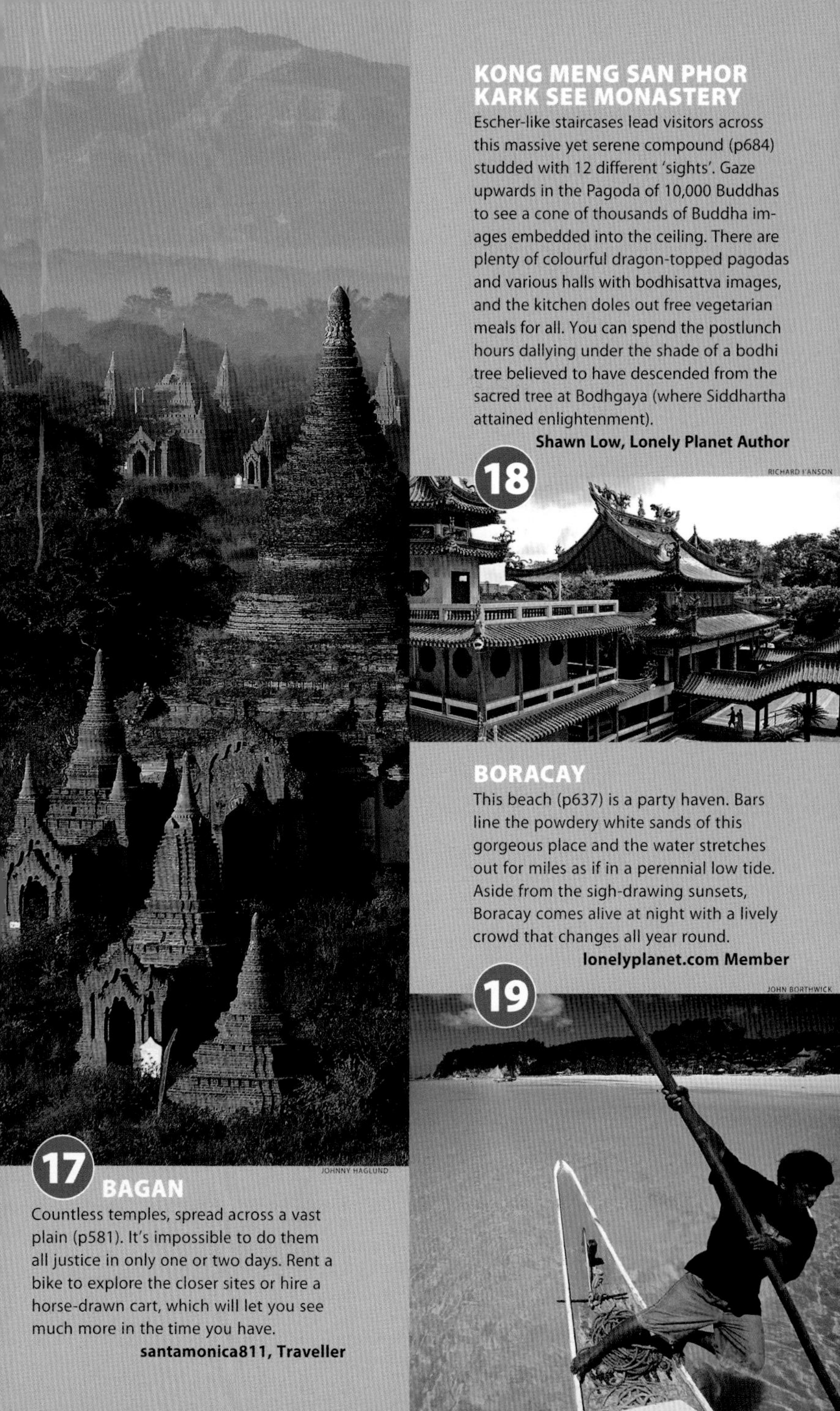

KONG MENG SAN PHOR KARK SEE MONASTERY

Escher-like staircases lead visitors across this massive yet serene compound (p684) studded with 12 different 'sights'. Gaze upwards in the Pagoda of 10,000 Buddhas to see a cone of thousands of Buddha images embedded into the ceiling. There are plenty of colourful dragon-topped pagodas and various halls with bodhisattva images, and the kitchen doles out free vegetarian meals for all. You can spend the postlunch hours dallying under the shade of a bodhi tree believed to have descended from the sacred tree at Bodhgaya (where Siddhartha attained enlightenment).

Shawn Low, Lonely Planet Author

18

RICHARD I'ANSON

BORACAY

This beach (p637) is a party haven. Bars line the powdery white sands of this gorgeous place and the water stretches out for miles as if in a perennial low tide. Aside from the sigh-drawing sunsets, Boracay comes alive at night with a lively crowd that changes all year round.

lonelyplanet.com Member

19

JOHN BORTHWICK

JOHNNY HAGLUND

17

BAGAN

Countless temples, spread across a vast plain (p581). It's impossible to do them all justice in only one or two days. Rent a bike to explore the closer sites or hire a horse-drawn cart, which will let you see much more in the time you have.

santamonica811, Traveller

NICK RAY

TRADITIONAL DANCE

Combining fluid grace with what's literally eye-popping discipline, dance performances in Bali (p244) are a must. Pull up a plastic chair in an open-air pavilion in Ubud, settle back with a cold Bintang and let yourself be carried away by the music and the movement.

Ryan Ver Berkmoes, Lonely Planet Author

21

PAUL KENN

20 KEP

I made a day trip to Kep (p124) for some sand and seafood. Soaking up the sun on the nearly deserted beach was wonderfully relaxing, but the real highlight was my lunchtime trip to the Crab Market. After watching groups of Cambodian women haggling over the eponymous crabs, I retired to a restaurant shack with a balcony overlooking the sea. And what a lunch I had! I gorged myself on piles and piles of fresh prawns fried with sprigs of Kampot pepper – all for the bargain price of US$5. A nap was inevitable after that…

Laura Stansfeld, Lonely Planet Staff

AUSTIN BU

22 ROOFTOP BARS IN BANGKOK

These rooftop bars (p726) really take your breath away even before you sip your drink. Peer over the ledge – the city is so far below and the usual deafening traffic noise sounds like a distant symphony.

China Williams, Lonely Planet Author

Contents

Laos 358

Malaysia 429

Myanmar (Burma) 533

Philippines 602

Destination Southeast Asia

The life-giving force of water has sculpted many of Southeast Asia's stunning landscapes, engaging cultures and collective psyches. It falls from the heavens during the monsoons to impregnate the fields and forests with a bounty found only in the tropics. The air takes its share becoming thick with moisture. The busy concrete cities and the sleepy wooden villages are always built near a water source: be it the sparkling sea where sinewy fisherman cast their nets at sunset or the muddy rivers criss-crossed by old dugouts. Even the staple crop of rice needs to be submerged in water for a portion of its life cycle.

The fluid qualities of water infuse the social landscape too. Road traffic flows like a river swollen with debris, as the big machines push aside the tatty motorcycles that cough up black smoke. The market crowds move through the aisles with the force of an invisible current, and the social interactions with humble noodle vendors or earnest students can be as refreshing as a tall, cold glass of beer.

Water and what it has wrought are the primary tourist attractions as well. The beaches are legendary amongst the sun-deprived, and encompass every idyll from the shallow coral-protected bays of the Malay peninsula to the powerful writhing seas of Indonesia and the Philippines and the languorous Vietnamese coastline. Inland there are scenic karst mountains, evidence of long-vanished seas that are now hollowed out by water's ceaseless sculpting powers.

The spirituality that washes over the land also requires this ingredient in its religious rituals. Muslims cleanse themselves five times a day before pressing their foreheads to the earth and presenting their supplications to God. The Buddhists celebrate the rains and the rivers with water-throwing festivals and candlelit offerings. The great Khmer empire grew and prospered in what was then a fecund corner of the world and built, as thanks to its god-kings, the magnificent Angkor temples embossed with the myths of oceans and sea serpents.

You may wonder what you'll do in this strange region, where water has shaped the landscape and identity. The answer is to swim in the warm seas, sweat in the hot sun, slurp down noodles floating in a salty broth and sip beer kept cool with ice cubes. The recipe for happiness is a simple and elemental one.

KAREN TRIST

Traditional longtail boats dock in the waters off Ko Phi Phi (p817), Thailand

HIGHLIGHTS

MOST AMAZING MONUMENTS

Temples of Angkor (Cambodia) – these incredible Hindu-Buddhist temples, built by the great Khmer empire, are among the world's greatest architectural feats (p95)

Bagan (Myanmar) – a deserted city of ancient temples rippling into the distance (p581)

Borobudur (Indonesia) – a stunning stupa ringed by mist and mountains (p210)

Hanoi (Vietnam) – an embalmed Ho Chi Minh gives this French-influenced city monumental status (p842)

Bangkok (Thailand) – a human-made mountain range of skyscrapers and dazzling coloured royal temples (p710)

BEST BEACHES & DIVE SPOTS

Bali (Indonesia) – synonymous with beach paradise thanks to the amazing dive spots of Pulau Menjangan and the white-sand coves near Ulu Watu (p222)

Ko Phi Phi (Thailand) – the prettiest little island you've ever seen, with dramatic limestone mountains jutting out of a sapphire sea (p817)

Boracay (Philippines) – long and leggy beaches, good-time bars and enough of a breeze to propel a windsurfer (p637)

Semporna Archipelago (Malaysia) – deep sea walls where turtles, sharks and rays hang out (p505)

Nha Trang (Vietnam) – party like a GI on Vietnam's good-times beach (p886)

BERNARD NAPTHINE

A Buddha watches over the ancient stupas of Borobudur (p210), Indonesia

JOHN ELK III

Akha women in Muang Sing (p401), Laos

BEST PLACES TO GET HIGH (ALTITUDE-WISE)

Mt Kinabalu (Malaysia) – make the blood-pumping scramble to the top of this looming granite spire for a spiritual sunrise (p497)

Cordillera Mountains (Philippines) – a vast range of jagged mountains with ancient rice terraces and superb trekking (p625)

Muang Sing (Laos) – a somnolent Thai Lu village surrounded by forested treks through the Nam Ha National Protected Area (p401)

Inle Lake (Myanmar) – an alpine lake of floating gardens, stilted villages and true tranquillity (p565)

Gunung Bromo (Indonesia) – an active volcano that is usually hiked at night for a sunrise view of its moonscape summit (p220)

BEST CULTURAL CONNECTIONS

Sapa (Vietnam) – a misty mountain market town for hill-tribe treks and country sojourns (p868)

Luang Prabang (Laos) – a romantic city of gleaming temples, crumbling French villas and the serpentine Mekong River (p383)

Kampot (Cambodia) – riverside charmer filled with ageing French architecture, a nearby hill station and pepper plantations (p121)

Chiang Mai (Thailand) – a culture-nerd's best friend known for kitchen demos and hill-tribe treks (p749)

Ubud (Indonesia) – a town amongst the rice paddies where Balinese culture occupies museums, classrooms and artists' studios (p237)

BEST OFF THE BEATEN PATH

Dili (East Timor) – a rapidly modernising city with reef dives in easy reach (p150)

Bukit Timah (Singapore) – a rainforest in the middle of a metropolis (p685)

Bario & Kelabit Highlands (Malaysia) – a Borneo hang-out with wobbly longhouses and jungle wonders (p523)

Myitkyina (Myanmar) – life in the slow lane along the fabled Ayeyarwady (p588)

Coron (Philippines) – a beach paradise with a pulse for wreck divers, kayakers and cove hunters (p660)

FOODIE CITIES

Pulau Penang (Malaysia) – eat from dawn till dusk from a buffet of Malaysia's culinary cultures: Chinese noodles, Indian curries and Malay desserts (p461)

Singapore – become a hawker centre expert in this city that knows how to nosh (p669)

Vientiane (Laos) – dine on a dime with the Mekong River as your backdrop and a collection of fiery Lao dishes by your side (p366)

Ho Chi Minh City (Vietnam) – graze through the markets, the *banh mi* (Vietnamese-style sandwiches) shops and the noodle hole-in-the-walls to savour Vietnam's zesty flavours (p901)

Chiang Rai (Thailand) – tailor your taste buds to northern Thai fare and home-grown coffee (p764)

AUN KOH

Singapore's cuisine (p687) is varied, cheap and delicious

Getting Started

It's easier than you think to amass enough know-how to tackle Southeast Asia. For an overview of regional practicalities, see the Southeast Asia Directory (p932) and then dive into the nitty-gritty details in each destination chapter. Give the Health chapter (p955) a scan for tips on vaccines, and pick up a few stock phrases in the Language chapter (p966).

WHEN TO GO

Southeast Asia is always hot and humid but there are degrees in temperature and wetness. The mainland countries (Myanmar, Laos, Cambodia, Thailand and Vietnam) tend to share similar weather patterns, enjoying a 'cool' season from roughly December to February (peak months for tourism) and a 'hot' season from March to May. The monsoons last from June to October, bringing sudden torrential downpours for an hour or two every day, which are followed just as suddenly by sunshine. The last or penultimate month in the monsoon season is usually the rainiest with all-day downpours. In Cambodia and Laos, travel in remote areas can be disrupted by flooded roads during the monsoon season, and ferries to some Thai islands go on abbreviated or suspended schedules during rough seas and low tourist demand.

See p936 for more climate information.

Along the Malay peninsula, two monsoons strike: from November to February, the east coast gets all the action; from May to October, the west coast gets soaked. The duration of monsoon season varies from year to year.

Indonesia also gets two monsoons; the best time to visit is from May to September. The rains start in September in Sumatra and head east, arriving in East Timor around November or December. April to June is the best time to visit East Timor.

The wet and dry seasons vary within the Philippines but, by and large, January and February are dry months. Typhoons can hit both the Philippines and Vietnam between June and November.

There are, of course, regional variations within each country; these are detailed in the respective country chapters' Directory sections.

Large festivals are also factors in plotting an arrival date. Businesses in certain countries tend to close during Muslim Ramadan and Chinese New Year, and everyone goes water-gun crazy during the Thai, Lao and Cambodian New Year in April. Check the Festivals & Events sections in specific country chapters for forthcoming events that might attract or impede a visit.

COSTS & MONEY

Western currencies enjoy a favourable exchange rate with many of the Southeast Asian currencies. If you travel and eat like a local, your daily budget could be a positively emaciated US$15 to US$35 a day.

This will vary on the country and the popularity of the destination. As a rule, beaches and big cities are expensive, while small towns tend to be cheaper. Food, especially street-stall meals, is rarely over US$1 a dish.

Travel within mainland Southeast Asia is generally affordable, but Indonesia tends to have wildly fluctuating petrol prices and, though cheaper than in year's past, air flights are more expensive than buses or/ferries and sometimes a necessity when jumping between Indonesian islands. Local transport won't stretch the budget but hiring taxis or chartered transport in most areas will require haggling and invariably the newly arrived tourist will pay more than a street-smart local.

HOW MUCH?

Bottle of beer US$1-3

Bus ticket US$4-15

Food-stall meal US$0.50-3

Guest-house bed US$4-15

Internet access per hour US$1-6

COMMON MONEY PIT

When you can't speak the language you have to rely on a middleman (or woman), usually a travel or booking agent, to make travel arrangements for you. That middle path comes at a cost. The trustworthy ones have obvious and nominal fees that pay for their efforts filling out forms and stamping various scraps of paper. But others will turn a cheap bus ride into a luxury-priced trip (and pocket the difference). When making travel arrangements, shop around to find the lowest commission rate and ultimately the best price.

What might be more bothersome than the price of goods is the 'walking ATM' syndrome where you feel like everyone wants a withdrawal. It isn't personal, but just simple economics. Remember that compared to the average worker in Southeast Asia, your pathetic bank account is the equivalent of a robber baron's. Many of the locals have never left their home towns, much less travelled to a foreign country.

For more information on money matters, see p941 or Money in individual country Directories.

LIFE ON THE ROAD

The shoestringer's life is an adventure in asceticism. By being cheap you see more of the local culture, learn how to live with the bare essentials and evolve into a grateful person, appreciative of the privileges and conveniences your nationality and economic class affords you.

The primary area of abstinence is in lodging, which is almost comical in its deprivation. Privacy, you'll soon discover, is a luxury. The walls are paper thin (letting in all of Southeast Asia's amplified noise), the mattresses are rock-hard and the bathroom is shared.

WHOOPS!

Greg Bloom

Public transport can be a contact sport in the Philippines. In Boracay I fell off a tricycle when the driver took a sudden swerve. Luckily only my pride was wounded. In Puerto Princesa I went flying out the back of the jeepney when the driver took off as I was disembarking, resulting in a badly scratched back and a broken laptop.

Your day might begin at a low-slung table parked roadside, where you order a cup of coffee from a woman who spends all day filtering coffee grounds and watching traffic. She thinks that you're hilarious with your knees poking above the table and your awkward attempts at language. The coffee is spiked with sweetened condensed milk and soon you're buzzing with caffeine and sugar. The empty seat beside you is filled by a curious local who wants to practise his English. He puts you through an informal interrogation: Where do you come from? How old are you? Are you married? With this out of the way, this stranger and you are now the dearest of friends according to local convention, and you might pose for a picture with him before parting ways, or join him for a tour of the town.

The next day you move to the next town because you've got a lot to see. Arriving at the destination station, the bus is flanked by touts all thirsty for your business. You haggle the price, which is almost always inflated due to an informal 'you're new in town' tax. The first guest house you visit has a shady yard with chickens scratching around in the dirt but the room is dank and noisy, so you thank the desk clerk and set off down the road. You use your budget senses to sniff out the best score in town, and in a few hours you're camped out in the shade with a steamy bowl of noodles and a sweaty bottle of beer. And you'll likely repeat the delightful process all over again.

CONDUCT

In general most Southeast Asians are glad to meet you, especially in small towns where foreigners are a rarity. Through our years of travel, we've met dozens of locals whose hobby is meeting and temporarily adopting travellers. In return all you have to do is charm the flip-flops off the locals, and that's relatively easy with a few pointers. For more guidance on how to avoid being a sore-thumb tourist, see p4 and the Culture sections in specific country chapters throughout this guidebook.

Here are some other helpful tips:

- Take a gift when visiting someone's home.
- Share your snacks or cigarettes with your neighbour on long bus rides.
- Tip here and there as daily wages are pitifully small.
- Smile while bargaining; your beauty will distract them from wanting to make a profit.
- Keep a thick skin and a sense of humour.

Dress

Except in the major urban cities, like Bangkok and Singapore, most locals dress modestly, especially in Muslim countries. To blend in a little better, cover to the shoulders and to the knees. And if you're hot, do as the locals do and walk in the shade instead of bearing your belly. Women who dare to wear more will help promote a healthier image of all Western women abroad.

Language

Try to learn a few stock phrases, like 'thank you', 'hello' and 'delicious' in every country you visit. Remember to smile – it expresses genuine appreciation and kindness when you lack sophisticated vocabulary.

SOUTH EAST ASIA ON THE CHEAP (IN FLARED PANTS) *Brian Thacker*

I recently travelled through Southeast Asia using the original 1975 Lonely Planet guidebook, to see how it holds up 35 years later. I stayed in the same hotels, ate at the same restaurants and followed the authors' advice on what to see and do. I was bit worried that hotels would now be highway overpasses or restaurants would now be KFCs, but I was happy to see that many places were still around (even if they haven't been in a Lonely Planet guide for years!).

I followed Tony and Maureen's original route from East Timor (which, back then, was Portuguese Timor) and finished up in the Palace Hotel in Singapore (now the Hotel Madras Eminence), in the same room that Tony and Maureen stayed in for a couple of months putting the entire guidebook together. It was wonderful to see that some things never change at all. In Ubud, Bali, the book recommended Canderi's restaurant where, 30 years ago 'the whole travelling population gathered to see Canderi perform miracles in her tiny kitchen'. Canderi is still cooking in that tiny kitchen today, but the whole travelling population isn't there anymore. Back then, Canderi was one of only two restaurants in a tiny village with no electricity. Today, there are hundreds of restaurants in Ubud, but Canderi still has the same menu and still has some of her old clientele, including her 108-year-old mother.

Other things have changed a lot. Today, Phuket has over 30,000 hotel beds, but just over 30 years ago there was nowhere to stay on the beach except for 'one beach restaurant that offers you a patch on the floor for three baht a night'.

There are also some once popular hidden gems from which the backpacker crowds have long since disappeared. Samosir Island in Sumatra, which was described as 'a most delightful island', was home to 'probably the nicest cheap accommodation in Asia' and 'the best fruit salad in South East Asia'. They are both still true, but there is hardly a backpacker in sight. The Tye Ann Hotel in Georgetown doesn't serve the 'best porridge' anymore though. That's because it's now Peter Siew & Tan Advocates & Solicitors.

Brian Thacker is the author of six travel books including Rule No 5: No Sex on the Bus *and* Sleeping Around. *You can read all about Brian Thacker's adventures travelling with the original Lonely Planet guidebook in* Tell Them To Get Lost, *due out in late 2010.*

Meals

Although meals in Southeast Asia appear informal, there are many unspoken rules that communicate appreciation and respect, which will vary with the situation. Try to figure out the country's table-side quirks beforehand or just ask as politely as possible if you're confused. In some situations you'll be the honoured guest and everyone will wait until you've been served before they begin to eat. In other cases you should show deference to the host or to the oldest person at the table. If eating with a Southeast Asian friend, it is always a nice gesture to pay for the meal. But if you're invited out with a large group, it is usually safe to let the host foot the bill.

Taboos

Southeast Asia is seriously foot-phobic. Feet for the most part should stay on the ground, not on chairs, tables or bags. Showing someone the bottom of your foot expresses the same insult as flipping them your middle finger. Remove your shoes when entering a home. Don't point your feet towards sacred images or people, and follow the locals' lead in sitting in a temple or mosque.

SOUTHEAST ASIA PLANNING CHECKLIST

What to Take

Take as little as possible because you're going to have to carry it everywhere, and try to get your pack small enough so that it will fit into the aircraft's overhead locker. The reward: the less junk in your trunk, the less of a target you are for touts and con artists.

Cash and credit cards Some small US dollar bills will be useful in places where ATMs are limited. Make sure the bills are crisp and clean as some money changers can be fickle. Take both a Visa and a MasterCard credit card in case merchants only accept one brand.

Clothes Bright lightweight, light-coloured, breathable clothes – leave the denim at home. Pack silk long johns and a fleece for cool climates, and remember rain gear. Line your pack with a plastic bag to keep the contents dry.

Earplugs These are a great sleep aid through your neighbours' drunken fight or the rooster's predawn alert.

Medicine Pack a first-aid kit and any speciality medicines from home. Most large cities have pharmacies and clinics with English-speaking staff. See p956 for advice on stocking a first-aid kit.

Odds and ends A sewing kit, padlock, Swiss army knife, money belt, safety pins, toilet paper, universal sink plug, small torch (flashlight) and travel adaptor can all come in handy.

Photocopies of important documents Definitely photocopy your passport, tickets, travellers-cheque serial numbers, and credit and ATM cards, and pack the copies separately from the originals. Leave a copy at home with a friend, just in case.

Repellent A heavy-duty spray helps fend off the mozzies.

Speciality gear If you plan to do serious (not occasional) camping, trekking or climbing, you should bring the equipment from home.

Toiletries Tampons and heavy-duty deodorant aren't so easy to come by, so stock up before leaving home. Also pack some biodegradable soap – it washes easily in cold water and is gentle on the environment.

USB drive A USB drive allows you to store photos and files. Also save a portable web browser on the drive so that you can protect your password at public machines.

What to Get There

In the large cities, you can buy every imaginable Western product, as well as medicines, and the following useful products are available at local markets:

Mosquito coils These coils are lit and placed at your feet to discourage a mozzie feast.

Sarong Can be used as a towel, mosquito net, sheet, head gear and general backpacker fashion.

Talcum powder Does wonders for heat rash and keeps you and your clothes smelling pretty, even when you've been sweating for months.

Tiger balm This all-purpose salve, available at pharmacies, relieves headaches, soothes mosquito bites and acts as a bug repellent.

TOP 10

THINGS WE LOVE ABOUT SOUTHEAST ASIA

1. The small shrines that decorate lowly noodle shops, crooks of trees and car dashboards.
2. The constant street activity of commerce, transport and average living.
3. The way the local guides can scramble up a steep mountain in flip-flops while smoking a cigarette.
4. The 'shirtless' masters, usually older Chinese men, who guard the cash registers at sweaty open-air restaurants.
5. The way the vegetable vendors don plastic bags as hats during a sudden downpour.
6. Taxi drivers who will turn you [illegible] down to try to figure out where y[illegible]nt to go.
7. The ladies who carry around small-scale kitchens on either end of a bamboo pole.
8. Shaking hands with a 101 schoolchildren you happened to meet on a jungle trail.
9. Picnicking families who wave you over like an honoured guest.
10. Your trip's scrapbook of photos filled with smiling strangers who befriended you for a day.

Taking Photographs

Southeast Asians are not shy in front of the camera – most outings with friends and family involve extensive photo shoots in front of pretty scenery or in group huddles. In fact they'll probably snap pictures of you before you're even focused. But it is always polite to ask permission before taking someone's picture, especially if you haven't yet introduced yourself. Also be aware that some minority tribes have spiritual beliefs that mean they are suspicious of photography.

Itineraries

BEACH BOUND, BABY!

From **Bangkok** (p710), make a beeline for the beach-bumming islands in the Gulf of Thailand: boisterous **Ko Samui** (p791), hippy **Ko Pha-Ngan** (p795) or dive-crazy **Ko Tao** (p799). Then follow the herd across to the Andaman coast to **Khao Lak** (p808), the base for live-aboard trips to world-class dive sites, polished **Phuket**, adrenaline-charged **Krabi** (p815), home to rock-climbing and cave exploring, (p810), beautiful **Ko Phi Phi** (p817), and laid-back **Ko Lanta** (p818). Rest awhile on the barely developed beaches of **Ko Tarutao National Marine Park** (p820).

Jump the Thailand–Malaysia border from **Satun** (p820) to the family-friendly beaches of **Pulau Langkawi** (p469). Then putter down to **Georgetown** (p461), for an urban antidote before bussing over to **Kota Bharu** (p482), the jumping-off point for the fabulous jungle islands of **Pulau Perhentian** (p481). Chase the coastline

HOW LONG?
1-2 months

WHEN TO GO?
Thailand, Malaysia & Philippines: Nov-May

Indonesia: Apr-Jul

BUDGET?
US$20-40 per day

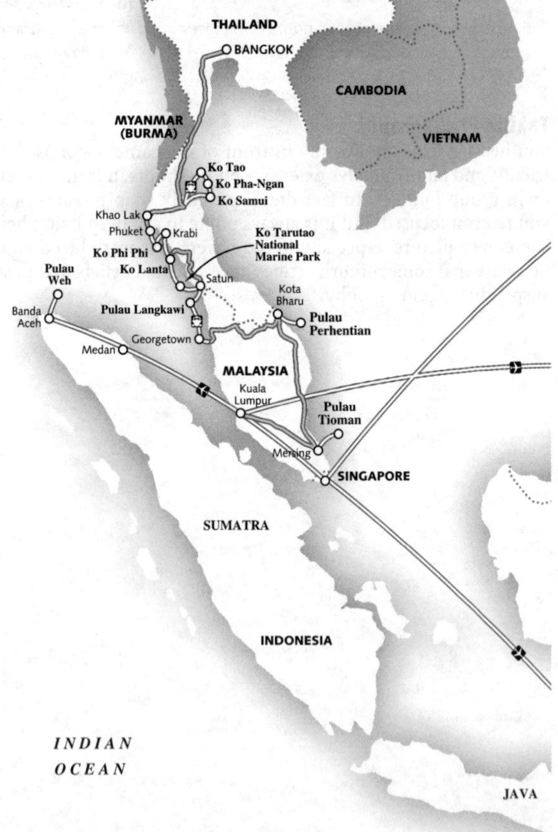

south to **Mersing** (p473), the mainland port for a dose of Malay village life on **Pulau Tioman** (p473), before returning to civilisation in **Kuala Lumpur** (p438).

From Kuala Lumpur you can fly to the 'other' Malaysia, on the island of Borneo, to sample the dive sites of the **Semporna Archipelago** (p505), accessible via **Semporna** (p505).

Still haven't found the perfect beach? From KL fly across the Strait of Melaka with a layover in **Medan** (p276) and then onward to Indonesia's **Banda Aceh** (p280) to **Pulau Weh** (p281), with its underwater canyons and coral. Pulau Weh is what Thai beaches used to be like 20 years ago.

Otherwise catapult yourself from **Singapore** (p669) to **Manila** (p611) in the Philippines with access to the island of **Palawan** (p657), a self-contained paradise hardly marred by modernity.

Wherever you end up be sure to visit the sun-worshipping temple of **Bali** (p222), and learn how to surf trouble free. Check out the uninterrupted R&R on **Lombok** (p286), then ferry to the celebrated **Gili Islands** (p292) for translucent water and technicolour reefs, or to **Sumbawa** (p300) for surf-able swells and a dramatic deserted coastline.

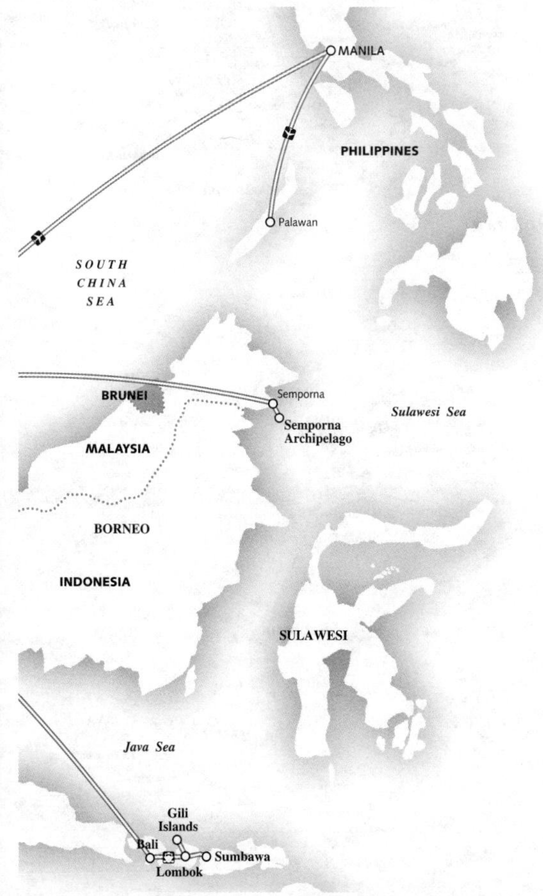

Mix socialising with sunbathing on the busy beaches of Thailand. Get dive certified on Ko Tao so you can go down on Thailand, Malaysian Borneo, Indonesia and Philippines. Tap into the village vibe in Malaysia. And don't forget to meet the paradise pin-up of Bali, still a bargain beach.

SPICE ISLANDS & VOLCANOES: ANGLING THROUGH THE ARCHIPELAGOS

Both Singapore (p669) and Kuala Lumpur (p438) have relatively cheap airfares for forays into the spice islands that adorn the equator.

It is a quick flight to Sumatra, landing in the not-so-spectacular town of **Medan** (p276) – a necessary transfer point for the bumpy bus ride to the orang-utan outpost in **Bukit Lawang** (p279) and volcano hiking in **Berastagi** (p274).

Buzz by plane from Medan to Java, touching down in the mayhem of **Jakarta** (p179). Follow the route through highland tea plantations to **Yogyakarta** (p203), Java's centre of batik, culture and busy markets. Day trip to the giant stupa of **Borobudur** (p210), or huff-and-puff your way to the top of nature's version of a stupa at **Gunung Bromo** (p220), an active volcano.

Leapfrog to **Denpasar** (p234), in blessed Bali, where you can nuzzle with sandy beaches (see Beach Bound, Baby! p30) or dive into Balinese culture in **Ubud** (p237). Skip across the islands for a dragon-spotting tour on **Komodo** (p302). Then catch a flight from the port town of **Labuanbajo** (p304) via Denpasar to **Sulawesi** (p328), a scorpion-shaped island filled with unique

HOW LONG?
1-2 months

WHEN TO GO?
Feb-Jun

BUDGET?
US$25-30 per day

tribal people. From Sulawesi's entry point of **Makassar** (p328) bus to **Tana Toraja** (p331), where funeral rituals take on a Carnival-like spectacle.

By now your Indonesian visa might soon expire so hop back to the Malay peninsula to catch a flight to **Kota Kinabalu** (p492) to slip and slither through Borneo's jungles. Buses deliver pilgrims to Kinabalu National Park, where towering **Mt Kinabalu** (p497) tickles the clouds. Pay a visit to **Sepilok** (p502), home to a sanctuary where orang-utans get back are reunited with to nature. Swing on over to **Kuching** (p508), a gateway to trekking in **Bako National Park** (p514), for wildlife trekking, or **Batang Rejang** (p516), a mighty riverine highway dotted by the traditional longhouses of indigenous people. Or fly to **Miri** (p521), which has air access to the remote **Bario** and **the Kelabit Highlands** (p523).

If you've had enough of nature, fly from Kota Kinabalu to manic **Manila** (p611) in the Philippines. Then bus north to the lush and toothy Cordillera region, with stops in laid-back **Sagada** (p627) and the hand-hewn rice terraces around **Banaue** (p628) and **Bontoc** (p628). Reward your aching travelling muscles with some island R&R by returning to Manila and hopping to **Boracay** (p637).

Bring your hiking boots because you'll be climbing mountains in these jungle-clad islands, formed by temperamental volcanoes and inhabited by ethnic minorities. You'll need more cash and time for this trip as bus travel can be slow and flights a little pricey.

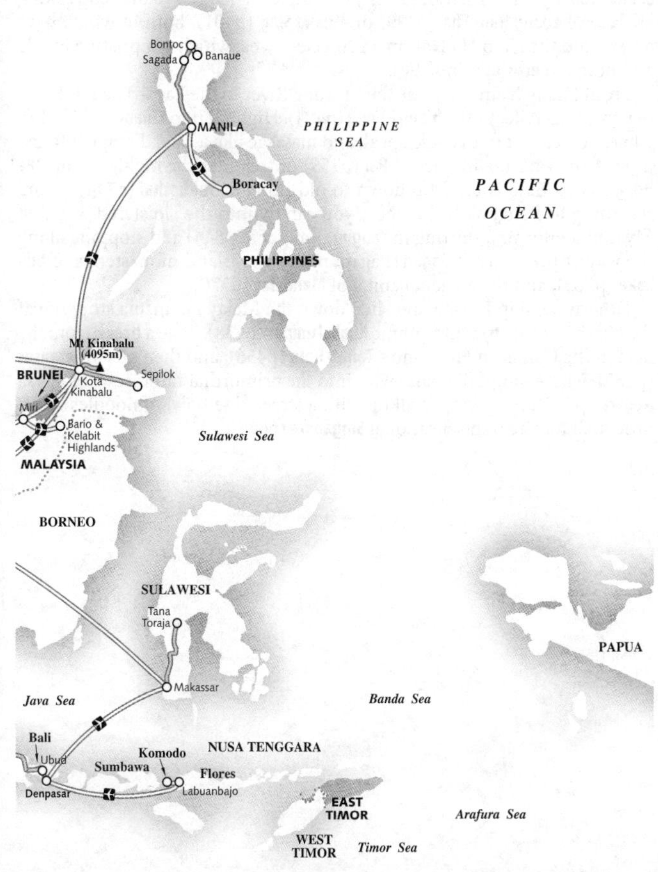

KINGDOMS & COLONIES: THE MAINLAND ROUTE

HOW LONG?
1-2 months

WHEN TO GO?
Just after the wet season (Nov-Jan) when the landscape is green

BUDGET?
US$20-35 per day

Tour trendy **Bangkok** (p710) and the old Thai capital of **Ayuthaya** (p738), and then break off of the tourist trail with a jungle escape to **Khao Yai National Park** (p773). Connect through **Nakhon Ratchasima** (p769) to visit the frontier Khmer temple at **Phimai** (p772) before making the pilgrimage to the centrepiece of Angkor Wat. From Nakhon Ratchasima catch a bus to the Thai–Cambodian border at **Aranya Prathet–Poipet** (p731) for the long pilgrimage to glorious **Angkor** (p95).

Bus to the shabby-genteel capital of **Phnom Penh** (p73) to learn about Cambodia's dramatic history. Sail the mighty Mekong River through the **Kaam Samnor–Vinh Xuong border** (p85) – a scenic gateway to Vietnam's high-energy **Ho Chi Minh City** (Saigon; p901). Push north along the stunning coastline with a detour to the hill station of **Dalat** (p894), then on to the old GI beach of **Nha Trang** (p886) and the antique streets of sartorial **Hoi An** (p881). Wander the leafy boulevards and visit a preserved Uncle Ho in **Hanoi** (p842). Shuffle into the mountain hill-tribe town of **Sapa** (p868) or float through the mountain-studded **Halong Bay** (p861).

Be air-lifted out of Vietnam's intensity to laid-back Laos, and head for **Luang Prabang** (p383), a tranquil city of temples. Then bus to the ecotrekking enclave of **Luang Nam Tha** (p399) or **Muang Sing** (p401), both of which have access into the Nam Ha National Protected Area, which is a pristine jungle and home to ethnic minorities.

From Luang Nam Tha, ride the Mekong River to the Laos–Thailand border crossing at **Huay Xai–Chiang Khong** (p404). Hightail it to **Chiang Mai** (p749), where you can learn to cook, speak and massage like a Thai. Escape into the mountains with the hippies in **Pai** (p759) or trek into the highlands in **Mae Hong Son** (p762). Then drop down to old ruins in **Sukhothai** (p744) before returning to Bangkok from where you can fly into the cloistered world of Myanmar (Burma), starting in **Yangon** (Rangoon; p544) and stopping along the way at the ruins of **Bagan** (Pagan; p581), the island monasteries of **Inle Lake** (p565), and the ancient capital of **Mandalay** (p570).

Otherwise, skip Burma and slide down the Malay peninsula stopping at the beaches, or fly to multi-ethnic **Kuala Lumpur** (p438). Take a break from the heat in the Cameron Highland's **Tanah Rata** (p456), and then bus to **Jerantut** (p485), where long-tail boats swim into the primordial rainforests of **Taman Negara** (p487). And wrap it all up with a street-side bowl of noodles and a little mall mayhem in sensational **Singapore** (p669).

This is the classic, guidebook-toting tour through Southeast Asia but we've given enough detours that you'll feel like you're escaping the 'Lonely Planet' bus...

FORGOTTEN CORNERS

HOW LONG?
2 weeks

WHEN TO GO?
Nov-Mar

BUDGET?
US$15-25 per day

If you've done all the highlights and the lowlights and are ready for the lesser-known lights then forge a path from **Bangkok** (p710) to the riverside charmer of **Nong Khai** (p779). You could cross the Mekong River here to **Vientiane** (p366) in Laos but for the less-common route follow the river road east toward **Nakhon Phanom** (p778), a little slice of Indochina in Siam. Cross into Laos at **Tha Khaek** (p407) and snake through the jumbled karst peaks on Route 8 to **Lak Sao** (p406).

Exploring odd corners means you'll rack up some long bus rides, one of them being the journey south to **Pakse** (p411). Detour to the cool waterfalls of **Bolaven Plateau** (p415) before splashing down in **Si Phan Don** (Four Thousand Islands; p417), where the Mekong becomes a tropical playground instead of a muddy workhorse. You're back on a tourist trail now and the sensible route leads to Cambodia via **Stung Treng** (p128). But take a detour to remote **Ratanakiri Province** (p128), which shelters the **Virachey National Park** (p130), a burgeoning ecotrekking destination. Slice through the interior of Cambodia to the backpacker beach of **Sihanoukville** (p116) or to the **Koh Kong Conservation Corridor** (p113), where a visit to an ethnic-minority village helps develop a sustainable industry for the fragile rainforest. And here you are at Thailand's door where you can cruise, depending on traffic, into Bangkok.

Village life is in full force in these rural corners of Thailand, Laos and Cambodia. You can play hide and seek with the Mekong River, bunk down in homestays, go elephant spotting and spend your money at a grass-roots level.

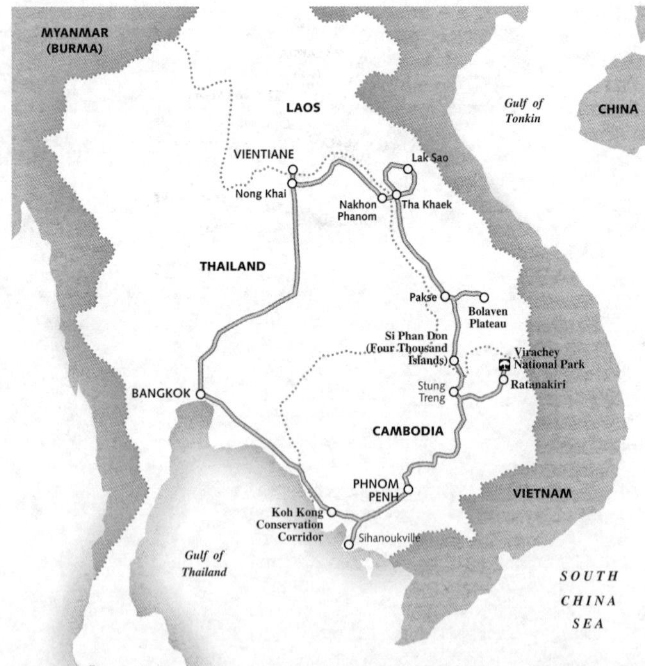

Snapshots

CURRENT EVENTS

During the boom times of last decade, Southeast Asia rode a steady wave of prosperity. Bangkok climbed a few notches closer to First World status. Laos woke up from its backwater slumber to find that China needed it for natural resources and for access to its neighbours, as modern highways ploughed through former opium pack-mule trails. Money was found aplenty in Vietnam's full-throttle economy and the country has today embraced such a youthful optimism that it is easy to forget about the old communist guard. Even Cambodia, which is consistently ranked high on Transparency International's corruption index, sampled the economic buffet with an ever-strengthening tourist economy.

Politically, the fireworks were in Thailand, where the 2006 coup opened a deep rift within the country's power structure, culminating in the 2008 closure of Bangkok's two airports and another 'silent' coup that removed the ruling and popularly elected party (again). The warring political factions have bruised Thailand's economy, tourist reputation and prospects for a peaceful future. And with the king in failing health, there will likely be more power-grabbing to come.

With Thailand's uncertain political future, Malaysia has started scooping up tourists thanks to the success of Air Asia, a no-frills airline based in the capital, Kuala Lumpur. Internally the multicultural country has been questioning the merits of the *bumiputra* system, in which the government favours ethnic Malays for government contracts and scholarships. Whether they reach an honest answer remains to be seen. Singapore is hustling to boost its population and build itself up bigger and better, though the global recession has taken its toll.

The Irrawaddy (www.irrawaddy.org), a print and online magazine, covers news and analysis of Myanmar and Southeast Asia.

Indonesia was tacking towards the middle path with its smooth 2009 elections, however in July of that year, suicide bombings at the JW Marriott and Ritz-Carlton hotels in Jakarta killed nine people and wounded 53, serving as a reminder that the nation is still plagued by terrorist activity. Following the attack, Indonesian forces started a manhunt for Noordin Mohamed Top, believed to be the organiser of the most recent bombings as well as similar attacks from 2003 to 2005 in Jakarta and Bali. Top allegedly led a radical splinter group of Jemaah Islamiyah and was believed to be the head of Al-Qaeda in Southeast Asia. After an unsuccessful house raid a month prior, authorities caught up with Top who was hiding out in Solo (Java) in September 2009. The nine-hour siege resulted in the shooting death of Top, who was found with firearms and 200kg of explosives.

The Philippines has been largely subdued through the scandal-ridden tenure of President Gloria-Macapagal Arroyo, though her administration is still dogged by the insurgency in the far southern island of Mindanao. Meanwhile, East Timor's transition to democracy remains transitional.

Amidst all this success is the ongoing sad tale of Myanmar, whose ruling military junta has been widely sanctioned by the international community for human rights abuses. In 2007, evidence of the military's crackdown on the so-called Saffron Revolution escaped to the world beyond, followed closely by Cyclone Nargis, which roared ashore in 2008 and ripped away lives and livelihoods. The government insisted upon tending to its own humanitarian crisis: outside aid groups were held up by a lack of visas and the Myanmar military's refusal to allow foreign planes to deliver aid while, according to the UN, one million people waited for help. This was followed shortly thereafter by another episode condemned by human rights groups, including Amnesty International: the alleged violation of Aung San Suu Kyi's terms of house arrest, a sentence awarded to her after she won the country's only legitimate elections.

In Cambodia, the UN-backed trials of the surviving Khmer Rouge members have been excruciatingly slow. It has taken three years to begin prosecution of one defendant and the recently resigned co-prosecutor told the press that the tribunal remains underfunded and hampered by political interference.

HISTORY

Early Kingdoms

The mainland Southeast Asia countries owe much of their early historical happenings to the more dominant kingdoms of China and India. As early as 150 BC, China and India interacted with the scattered Southeast Asian communities for trade and tribute. Vietnam, within short reach of China, was a subject, student and reluctant offspring of its more powerful neighbour for over 1000 years. India, on the other hand, conquered by spiritual means, spreading Hinduism, Buddhism and later Islam across the region, and influencing art and architecture.

Several highly organised states emerged in the region as a result of contact with India. From the 7th to the 9th centuries AD, the Srivijaya empire controlled all shipping through the Java Sea from its capital at Palembang in southeast Sumatra. The Srivijaya capital was also a religious centre for Mahayana Buddhism (Greater Vehicle Buddhism; see p46) and attracted scholars as well as merchants.

The Indonesian island of Java is home to a 'missing link', an early human ancestor approximately 1.8 million years old, that suggests the first humans might have migrated out of Asia instead of Africa.

But the region's most famous fallen empire emerged in the interior of present-day Cambodia. The Khmer empire ruled the land for four centuries, consuming territory and labour to build unparalleled and enduring Hindu-Buddhist monuments to its god-kings. Eventually the Khmer empire included most of what is now Thailand, Laos and Cambodia. Its economy was based on agriculture, and a sophisticated irrigation system cultivated vast tracts of land around Tonlé Sap (Great Lake). Attacks from emerging city-states on the Thai frontier contributed to the decline of the empire and the abandonment of the Angkor capital.

The Classical Period, Arrival of Europeans & Imperialism

As the larger powers withered, Southeast Asia entered an age of cultural definition and international influence. Regional kingdoms created distinctive works of art and literature, and joined the international sphere as important ports. The Thais expanded into the dying Khmer empire and exerted control over parts of Cambodia, Laos and Myanmar. Starting around 1331, the Hindu kingdom of Majapahit united the Indonesian archipelago from Sumatra to New Guinea and dominated the trade routes between India and China. The kingdom's reign continued until the advent of Islamic kingdoms and the emergence of the port town of Melaka on the Malay peninsula in 1402. Melaka's prosperity soon attracted European interest, and it fell first to the Portuguese in 1511, then the Dutch and finally the English.

Initially these European nations were only interested in controlling shipping in the region, usually brokering agreements and alliances with local authorities. Centred on Java and Sumatra, the Dutch monopolised European commerce with Asia for 200 years. The Spanish, French and later the English had civilisation and proselytising on their minds. Spain occupied the loosely related tribes of the Philippine archipelago, Britain steadily rolled through India, Myanmar and the Malay peninsula, while the Dutch grasped Indonesia to cement a presence in the region. And France, with a foothold in Vietnam, usurped Cambodia and Laos to form Indochina.

Although its sphere of influence was diminished, Thailand was the only Southeast Asian nation to remain independent. One reason for this was that England and France agreed to leave Thailand as a 'buffer' between their two colonies. Credit is also frequently given to the Thai kings who Westernised the country and played competing European powers against each other.

Independence & the Modern Day

The 20th century and WWII signalled an end to European domination in Southeast Asia. As European power receded, the Japanese expanded control throughout the region, invading Thailand, Malaysia and Indonesia. After the war, the power vacuums in formerly colonised countries provided leverage for a region-wide independence movement. Vietnam and Indonesia clamoured most violently for freedom, resulting in long-term wars with their respective colonial powers. For the latter half of the 20th century, Vietnam fought almost uninterrupted conflicts against foreign powers. After the French were defeated by communist nationals, Vietnam faced another enemy, the USA, which hoped to contain the spread of communism within the region. Cambodia's civil war ended in one of the worst nightmares of modern times, with the ascension of the Khmer Rouge. The revolutionary army evacuated the cities, separated families into labour camps and closed the country off from the rest of the world. An estimated 1.7 million people were killed by the regime during its brief four-year term (1975–79).

Many of the newly liberated countries struggled to unite a land mass that shared only a colonial legacy. Dictatorships in Myanmar, Indonesia and the Philippines thwarted the populace's hopes for representative governments and civil liberties. Civilian rioters, minority insurgents and communist guerrillas further provoked the unstable governments, and the internal chaos was usually agitated by the major superpowers: China, the Soviet Union and the USA.

The classic introduction to regional history is Milton Osborne's *Southeast Asia: An Introductory History*.

With the thawing of the Cold War, several raging national economies in the 1990s, and the onset of the new millennium, Southeast Asia enjoyed renewed stability and vitality. Today Singapore has become the shining star, while Thailand and Malaysia boast an affluent, educated middle class. Vietnam, Laos and Cambodia are now wide open to foreign trade, regional cooperation and tourism. Vietnam is racing through the milestones of development with almost unprecedented speed, boosted by a new generation of young people flush with disposable income and unscarred by the war with the USA. Development cash from China has turned Laos into its northern neighbour's backyard battery, by supplying hydroelectric power and natural resources to Chinese factories. On the mainland, only Myanmar remains cloistered and oppressed today.

Indonesia and the Philippines rode the first wave of postcolonial development, but have since stalled with the attendant industrialised problems of unemployment, corruption and urban pollution. The global recession has thus far had little effect on these countries, who were already struggling with their own downturns, meaning that their economies only have one direction left in which to go.

THE CULTURE

The most remarkable and unifying aspect of the diverse Southeast Asian societies is the importance placed on acting in a group. Social harmony is ensured by the concept of 'face' – that is, avoiding embarrassment of yourself or others. This is translated into everyday life by not showing anger or frustration and by avoiding serious debates that could cause offence. When the bus breaks down, the passengers calmly file out into the sun and wait for

COMMON MYTHS BUSTED

Think you've already got this Southeast Asian nut cracked? Here's the real deal on some common misconceptions:

- Indonesia isn't a repressive Muslim state. The country prides itself on its ethnic, linguistic and religious diversity. Sharia is not enforced nationally but is in some localities, like the province of Aceh, which is a delightful and welcoming place for foreigners, including women.
- Singapore is far from a sterile 'Disneyland'. It is a fantastic fusion of the best of Asia (food, street activity, friendliness) and the West (working infrastructure, coherent traffic patterns, obedience to simple rules of civility).
- Malaysia isn't boring. It has fewer touts than Thailand and more local English speakers to chew the proverbial fat with.

the repairs without causing a scene – in this way an undercurrent of peace is brought to a chaotic situation.

See the Culture sections in specific country chapters in this book for notes on each country's culture and lifestyle.

Lifestyle

The setting may vary – from the hulking megacities of Singapore, Bangkok and Jakarta to rural villages in Laos – but Southeast Asia moves through time with the underlying architecture of an agricultural village, no matter how big or small the town or how distant the rice fields. Families tend to stick together, pitching in to run the family noodle shop or helping Grandma do her market shopping. Because of the tropical temperature, most family life spreads out into the public space, replacing a sense of privacy with community. Babies get lots of group mothering, neighbours do lots of gossiping, and possessions are often shared or pooled, depending on the affluence of the community. In addition to blood, religion binds the society and the family with daily obligations of prayers in Muslim communities or spirit offerings in Buddhist countries.

Thailand is getting fatter. In a 2008 study, it was revealed that one in six Thais is overweight.

In the villages, life revolves around the harvest, a calendar set by the rains, the sun and the moon. In these old-fashioned corners, the food markets and the mosque or temple are the 'happening' parts of town.

More and more, the trappings of a modern and decidedly Western world are moving in and replacing the open-air markets and providing the new middle class with new things to consume. In the cities, the young dare to be different to their parents by adopting the latest fashions, texting their friends and scooting around town till all hours of the night. These countries are becoming transient, with the young people leaving the villages for jobs elsewhere. Their children may grow up separated from the rhythms of an agrarian society, feeling more comfortable in a shopping mall than a rice field. Fully entrenched in a middle-class world, Singaporeans often enjoy holidays to rural villages, where they can reconnect with a romantic version of the past.

Polish up your karaoke skills because Southeast Asians love to sing with a microphone.

Population

Each country in Southeast Asia has a dominant ruling class, typically the national ethnicity. It is believed that many of the mainland Southeast Asian peoples are descendants of Austronesian, Tai and Mon-Khmer peoples who migrated south from China. Countries with a high percentage of homogeneity include Vietnam, Cambodia, Brunei, Thailand and Singapore. More demographically diverse countries include Myanmar, the Philippines, Indonesia and East Timor, which doesn't have a majority ethnicity.

Many of the Southeast Asian countries share varying percentages of minority groups in isolated pockets or cultural islands. Ethnic Chinese filtered into the region as merchants and labourers, establishing distinct neighbourhoods within their host communities. Depending on the diaspora, most small towns have a Chinese-run business district. In places such as Malaysia and Singapore, the Chinese influence has formed a distinct entity, frequently termed Straits Chinese that merges Chinese and Malay customs. While most countries derive cultural and commercial strength from Chinese immigrants, in times of economic hardship ethnic Chinese are frequently targets of abuse because of their prosperity; this is especially the case in Malaysia and Indonesia. Ethnic Indians from the southern provinces of Tamil Nadu have also settled along the Malay peninsula and remain a distinct group.

High up in the mountains that run through Myanmar, Laos, Thailand and Vietnam, a diverse mix of minority groups, collectively referred to as hill tribes, maintain prehistoric traditions and wear elaborate tribal costumes. Believed to have migrated from the Himalaya or southern China, hill-tribe communities such as the Akha, Karen and Mon, thanks to the geography, have been relatively isolated from foreign influences. They were considered a nuisance by lowland governments until hill-tribe trekking became a widespread tourist attraction. Myanmar represents the largest concentration of hill tribes. In the outer areas of Indonesia, such as Kalimantan, Papua, Sulawesi and Sumba, indigenous people practise customs that have entered the global imagination through the pages of *National Geographic*.

East Timor is a young nation in two ways: it gained independence in 2002 and 50% of its population is under 18 years old.

Food

Southeast Asia's tropical climate creates a year-round bounty. Rice and fish are the primary staples and are often revered in various harvest festivals and local legends. A penchant for chillies is another hallmark, with almost every cuisine claiming a variation on a chilli condiment, including *sambal* in Indonesia and Malaysia and *naam phrik* in Thailand.

Traces of Southeast Asia's cultural parents – India and China – can be detected in the individual nations' cuisines. Myanmar has many Indian-inspired curries as do Thailand and Malaysia. Roti, an Indian flat bread, often accompanies curry dishes in Malaysia. The Chinese donated noodle soups, which have assumed various aliases: *laksa* in Malaysia and Singapore, *pho* in Vietnam or *kŭaytĭaw* in Thailand. Noodle soups are the quintessential comfort food, eaten in the morning, after a night carousing, or at midday when pressed for time. Culinary imports also came from the French, who left behind recipes for crusty baguettes and thick coffees in former Indochina.

Vietnam has perfected the cuisine of its culinary professor. Where Chinese food can be bland and oily, Vietnamese dishes are light and refreshing. A quintessential Vietnamese dish is the spring roll stuffed with shrimp, mint, basil leaves and cucumber that are sold at roadside stands.

Green Mangoes & Lemon Grass: Southeast Asia's Best Recipes from Bangkok to Bali, by Wendy Hutton, Charmaine Solomon and Masano Kawana, presents an edible journey through the region.

Thailand and Laos share many common dishes, often competing for the honour of spiciest cuisine. Green papaya salad is a mainstay of the two – the Thais like theirs with peanuts and dried shrimp; the Lao version uses fermented fish sauce and inland crab. In Laos and in neighbouring Thai provinces, the local people eat 'sticky rice' (a shorter grain than the standard fluffy white rice), which is eaten with the hands, usually rolled into balls and dipped into spicy sauces.

As dictated by the strictures of Islam, Muslim communities in Malaysia and Indonesia don't eat pork. Indonesians traditionally eat with their fingers – hence the rice is a little stickier than in mainland Southeast Asia. Perfecting the delicate shovelling motion is a true traveller accomplishment.

Filipino cooking is a mixture of Malay, Spanish and Chinese influences blended with typical Filipino exuberance. *Adobo,* a Spanish-inspired stew with local modifications, has come to symbolise Filipino cuisine.

In a postcolonial age, Singapore displays its position as a cosmopolitan crossroads with its development of Pacific Rim fusion cuisine while at the same time it stays true to its ancestral heritages with an amazing amount of cheap and delicious hawker food.

Art

Southeast Asia's most notable artistic endeavours are religious in nature, and distinctively depict the deities of Hinduism and Buddhism.

Both an artistic and architectural wonder, the temples of Angkor in Cambodia define much of the region's artistic output. Hindu temples include elaborate sculptured murals that pay homage to the Hindu gods Brahma (represented as a four-headed, four-armed figure) and Shiva (styled either in an embrace with his consort or as an ascetic), while also recording historical events and creation myths. Many of the temples were later altered to include images of Buddha after the kingdom converted to Buddhism.

'the temples of Angkor in Cambodia define much of the region's artistic output'

Statues of Buddha reflect the individual countries' artistic interpretations of an art form governed by highly symbolic strictures. Across mainland Southeast Asia, the Buddha is depicted sitting, standing and reclining – all representations of moments in his life that act as visual parables or sermons. In Vietnam, representations of the Buddha are more reminiscent of Chinese religious art. *Naga* (mythical serpent beings) are found decorating many temple railings in the region; they represent the life-giving power of water and played a role in protecting the meditating Buddha.

In Indonesia, Malaysia, Brunei and the Philippines, Islamic art and architecture intermingle with Hindu and animist traditions. Every town in Malaysia has a grand mosque with an Arabic minaret and Moorish tile work. Indonesia is also home to Borobudur, a Buddhist monument that complements the temples of Angkor in its splendour. Hand-loomed silk and wood carvings also define a country's or ethnic people's handicrafts tradition.

The literary epic of the Ramayana serves as cultural fodder for traditional art, dance and shadow puppetry throughout the region. In this fantastic tale, Prince Rama (an incarnation of the Hindu god Vishnu) falls in love with beautiful Sita and wins her hand in marriage by completing the challenge of stringing a magic bow. Before the couple can live in peace, Rama is banished from his kingdom and his wife is kidnapped by Ravana. With the help of the monkey king, Hanuman, Sita is rescued, but a great battle ensues. Rama and his allies defeat Ravana and restore peace and goodness to the land.

ART HOUSE BUZZ

The 2009 Cannes Film Festival was awash with Southeast Asian film directors. Winner of the festival's best director award was Filipino Brillante Mendoza with *Kinatay* (Butchered; 2009), a violent tale about the kidnapping, rape and murder of a prostitute by police. Mendoza had made a previous appearance in Cannes with *Serbis* (Service; 2008), which was set in a XXX-movie theatre. Thailand's leading new-wave director, Pen-Ek Ratanaruang visited the festival with his latest movie *Nang Mai* (Nymph; 2009). Ho Tzu Nyen, a Singaporean visual artist, won an award for *Here* (2009), which was set in a mental hospital. *Karaoke* (2009), by Chris Chong, was the first Malaysian movie in more than 10 years to be invited to Cannes. The movie depicts the return of a city boy to his home village, set in a palm-oil plantation.

Other regional directors are often spotlighted at the annual film festivals in Bangkok, Singapore and Jakarta.

ENVIRONMENT

The Land

Diverse and fertile, this tropical landmass spans the easternmost range of the Himalaya, which reaches through northern Myanmar, Thailand, Laos and Vietnam; the rich flood plains of the Mekong River; and the scattered archipelagos of Indonesia and the Philippines, formed by crashing tectonic plates and exploding volcanoes.

Much of the landmass of Southeast Asia is covered with a thick layer of limestone, the erosion of which yields distinctive towers known as karsts that jut out of the Andaman Sea to the southwest of Thailand, in Vietnam's Halong Bay or in parts of central Laos.

Indonesia and the Philippines, the world's largest island chains, together contain more than 20,000 islands, some of them uninhabited. The Philippines has 11 active volcanoes; Indonesia has at least 120. Although the fiery exhausts destroy homes and forests, the ashen remains of the earth's inner core creates fertile farmland – a constant cycle of destruction and rebirth.

More regulative than the seasonal temperature is the seasonal deposit of rain. When the rains come, the rivers transform from sluggish mud pits to watery bulldozers that sweep towards the sea. In the wet season, the dry deciduous forests of central mainland Southeast Asia spring to life. Also classified as monsoon forests, they occur in regions with a dry season of at least three months, and most trees shed their leaves in an attempt to conserve water.

The tropical rainforests of the Malay peninsula, Sumatra and Borneo get two monsoon seasons, and like sponges they soak up the moisture to feed their dense canopies. Rainforests occur in areas where rain falls more than nine months a year.

Living as a parasite in the thick jungles, the leafless plant rafflesia sprouts what looks like a cabbage head, which opens some nine months later to reveal one of the world's largest flowers – and an unrivalled putrid scent. Other plant species include a huge variety of bamboo and orchids. One of the region's most famous exports, teak, grows in the monsoon forests of Myanmar.

www.ecologyasia.com profiles the region's flora and fauna.

Coastal areas of Southeast Asia are famous around the world for their blonde sandy beaches and protective barriers of coral reefs. Part of the region's coastline is protected by the Gulf of Thailand, a shallow body water taming the greater ocean. But the real power of the sea can be felt in Indonesia, where the Indian Ocean hammers at the landmass, creating barrel waves and destructive walls of water. The land's primary defence against ocean invasions is the mangrove forest or dune forest, which both grow along the high-tide line, and consist of palms, hibiscus, casuarinas and other tree varieties that can withstand high winds and waves.

Wildlife

Tigers, elephants, monkeys, and Sumatran and Javan rhinoceroses once reigned over the region's forests. Today these animals are facing extinction due to habitat loss and poaching. Of the 'celebrity' species, monkeys and, to a lesser extent, elephants are the forest dwellers visitors are most likely to meet, although most encounters are in domesticated settings. Found in Sumatra and Kalimantan, the orang-utan is the only great ape species found outside of Africa.

Bornean Sun Bear Conservation Centre (www.sunbears.wildlifedirect.org) works to save the dwindling population of sun bears often killed for their gall bladder.

There are numerous bird species in Southeast Asia: Indonesia's Papua alone has more than 600 species; Thailand has more than 1000, making up an estimated 10% of the world's total. Parts of Southeast Asia are flyover zones for migratory species, and their arrival often heralds the approach of the monsoons. The Borneo rainforests boast a stunning array of birdlife, from the turkey-sized hornbill, to ground-dwelling pheasants. Many parts of the Indonesian jungle are so thick and remote that scientists have yet to explore and catalogue the resident flora and fauna.

The Mekong River is an expanding area of scientific study. Thousands of previously unidentified species of flora and fauna have been discovered in the last decade in the Mekong region, considered to boast a biodiversity that rivals the Amazon. The Irrawaddy dolphin is something of a tourist attraction; although it is actually an ocean species, it tends to inhabit brackish rivers.

The Mekong River flows through six countries and is home to the Mekong giant catfish, the world's largest freshwater fish.

Some species of tropical reptile have successfully adapted to the human environment. Geckos are frequently spotted catching bugs around fluorescent lights. The shy tookay is more frequently heard than seen: in rural areas this type of lizard croaks its name again and again. But perhaps the star of the Southeast Asian animal theatre is the komodo dragon, the world's largest lizard, which is found on the Indonesian island of Komodo and a few neighbouring islands. The monitor lizard, a smaller cousin, hangs out in the cool shade of the region's jungles.

National Parks

In recent years there has been an increase in the amount of land set aside across Southeast Asia as national parks and wildlife sanctuaries, but these protected areas are often undermined by logging interests (often illicit) and inadequate funding for conservation enforcement.

Thailand leads the conservation path with an astonishing 13% of land and sea under protection. Indonesia and Malaysia also boast fairly extensive national park systems. Laos remains one of the most environmentally undisturbed countries in the region, though this is changing as natural resource extraction increases.

Southeast Asia's national parks play an ever-increasing role in the region's tourism industry. Some parks are relatively undisturbed with little infrastructure, but in parks such as those of Thailand's marine islands, development and profit often outstrip environmental protection.

Environmental Issues

Environmental degradation is immediately tangible in Southeast Asia: smoke fills the air as the forests are cleared for more beach bungalows or small-scale farms; major cities are choked with smog and pollution; the waterways are clogged with plastic bags and soft-drink cans; and raw sewage is dumped into turquoise waters. Southeast Asia also faces huge challenges from its growing population and increased energy consumption. A recent study by the Asian Development Bank determined that Southeast Asia could suffer more serious economic losses than the global average if carbon emissions continue to rise.

LAND

The final half of the 20th century saw massive deforestation in Southeast Asia through logging and slash-and-burn agriculture. Indonesia, which contains 10% of the world's remaining tropical forests, is estimated to be losing up to 2% of its forest cover per year. This is the highest deforestation rate in the world, a superlative that has earned Indonesia a listing in the *Guinness World Records* in 2008 and 2009. Forests in all of the Southeast Asian countries are disappearing at extreme rates and their destruction is the region's biggest contributor to carbon emissions – 80% of Indonesia's carbon emissions come from deforestation (mainly conversion into palm-oil plantations), according to an Asian Development Bank study.

STORMY WEATHER

Tropical Storm Ketsana swept through the region as we were going to press, causing major damage to Manila and the Philippines before slamming into the central coast of Vietnam, causing widespread flooding in Hoi An and the Central Highlands. It then moved over northern Cambodia and southern Laos causing localised flooding. Always check local weather forecasts when travelling during typhoon season. Note that infrastructure may have been affected in the aforementioned countries and this may lengthen some journey times given in this book.

The few remaining natural areas are suffering high species loss, primarily due to poaching. Local people often augment subsistence farming with hunting of endangered animals for the lucrative wildlife trade. Thailand is one of the primary conduits through which live wildlife and harvested wildlife parts (which are often prized for perceived health and stamina benefits) travel to overseas markets in China, the USA and Europe. Favoured species include the sun bear, tigers and the pangolins (a type of anteater). The number of plant species lost is probably higher, but precise figures are unavailable because science has yet to catalogue all that the forests have to offer.

WATER

Southeast Asia's coral reefs are regarded as some of the world's most diverse and include a 6-million-sq-km area known as the Coral Triangle, which stretches all the way from Malaysia to the Solomon Islands. The Coral Triangle contains 75% of the world's coral species, 45% of reef-fish species and 90% of the world's marine-turtle species. Reefs around the region provide livelihood for the local people, from small-scale fishing to tourism. But the environmental pressures, such as overfishing, dynamiting and cyanide fishing, sediment run-off from coastal development, as well as the threat of climate change, have put immense pressure on these fragile ecosystems. According to a 2002 study by the World Resources Institute, the 1997–98 El Niño event caused the damage or destruction of 18% of Southeast Asia's reefs.

'The Coral Triangle contains 75% of the world's coral species, 45% of reef-fish species and 90% of the world's marine-turtle species'

In recent years, some of the governments of Southeast Asia have made efforts to preserve their reefs, by establishing marine parks and other protected zones; however, enforcement is somewhat spotty and the contributing factors to reef decline are complicated and often sanctioned for their economic benefits.

Mangrove forests along the coasts have also suffered. Countries such as the Philippines, Thailand, Myanmar and Cambodia have each been clearing mangrove forests for prawn farming and tourism development. Many scientists believe that the disastrous effects of the 2004 Boxing Day tsunami and 2008's Cyclone Nargis could have been reduced if the mangrove forests had been intact to absorb the tidal surges.

As the region continues to urbanise, the pressures on the environment will grow – indeed, the pace of building commercial enterprises often exceeds municipal infrastructure such as sewage treatment and garbage removal that would mitigate environmental degradation.

Along the Mekong River, hydroelectric dams are significantly altering the river's ecosystem, from sediment transport to fish migration, as well as water levels downstream. Recent dams in southwest China have already cut off an estimated 50% of the upper river's sediment input, and there are apparently plans to dam the entire length of the Mekong in Yúnnán and in parts of Laos and Cambodia.

RELIGION

The dominant religions of Southeast Asia have absorbed many of the traditional animistic beliefs of spirits, ancestor worship, and fortune-telling through astrology. Southeast Asia's connection to the realm of magic and miracles commands more respect, even among intellectual circles, than the remnants of paganism in Western Christianity: Thais erect spirit houses in front of their homes, ethnic Chinese set out daily offerings to their ancestors, and Vietnamese consult fortune-tellers for life advice.

Buddhism

The sedate smile of the Buddhist statues that decorate the landscapes and temples reflects the nature of the religion in Southeast Asia. Religious devotion within the Buddhist countries is highly individualistic and omnipresent with many daily rituals rooted in the indigenous ancestor worship.

Buddhism began with the story of an Indian prince named Siddhartha Gautama in the 6th century BC, who left his life of privilege at the age of 29 on a quest to find the truth. After years of experimentation and ascetic practices, he meditated under a Bodhi Tree for 49 days, reaching final emancipation and breaking the cycle of birth, death and rebirth. He returned as Buddha, the 'Awakened One', to teach the 'middle way' between extremes. Passion, desire, love and hate are regarded as extremes in Asia, so Buddhism counsels that constant patience, detachment, and renouncing desire for worldly pleasures and expectations brings peace and liberation from suffering.

Get an insight into the Buddhist cultures with the book *Buddhism for Beginners,* by Thubten Chodron.

Thailand, Cambodia, Laos and Myanmar practise Theravada Buddhism (Teaching of the Elders), which travelled to the region via Sri Lanka. Vietnam adopted Mahayana (Greater Vehicle) Buddhism, which is also found in Tibet, China and Japan. One of the major theological differences between the two types of Buddhism lies in the outcome of a devout life. In Theravada, followers strive to obtain nirvana (release from the cycle of existence), which is accomplished over the course of many reincarnations, the final one of which is as a member of the monastic order. In Mahayana, a layperson can become a bodhisattva (one who has almost reached nirvana but renounces it in order to help others attain it) within a single lifetime. The artistic expressions of temple architecture and sculpture create the greatest cultural differences between the Theravada Buddhist countries; similarly, religious art and temples in Vietnam favour Chinese influences over those of their Theravada neighbours.

Islam

Islam in Southeast Asia bears much of the region's hallmark passivity, lacking the fervour that results from religious persecution. Trade played an important role in the introduction of the religion to the region, with Southeast Asians converting to Islam to join a brotherhood of spice traders and to escape the inflexible caste system of the previous Hindu empires. The mystical Sufi sect of Islam also played an important role in spreading Islamic belief through Malaysia, Indonesia, parts of the Philippines and southern Thailand.

Living Faith: Inside the Muslim World of Southeast Asia, by Steve Raymer, is a beautiful pictorial essay on Islam outside the Arab world.

Revealed by the Prophet Mohammed in the 7th century, and meaning 'Submission' in Arabic, Islam states that the duty of every Muslim is to submit to Allah (God). This profession of faith is the first of the five pillars of Islam; the other four are to pray five times a day, give alms to the poor, fast during Ramadan and make the pilgrimage to Mecca.

A type of Sharia (Islamic law) is in effect in the Indonesian province of Aceh, and in some areas of Java and Sulawesi. It is also in effect in Malaysia, but it is only enforced for Muslim Malays. Traditionally, Southeast Asian

Muslim women were never cloistered, but headscarves have proliferated in recent years. While the traditional Muslim cultures retain many animistic beliefs and practices, there are periodic attempts to purge Islam of its pagan past, especially in Indonesia.

Muslim independence movements affecting southern Thailand and the southern Philippines are considered to be more economic than jihadist; typically the movements are in the poorest parts of their respective countries, and are virtually ignored by the majority government.

Christianity

Catholicism was introduced to Vietnam by the French, to the Philippines by the Spanish and to East Timor by the Portuguese. Parts of Indonesia are Christian, mainly Protestant, due to the efforts of Western missionary groups. In each of these converted groups there will be remnants of the original animistic beliefs and an almost personal emphasis on preferred aspects of the liturgy or the ideology. The local adaptations can often be so pronounced that Westerners of the same faith might still observe the practice as foreign.

The finale to the Christmas season in the Philippines is the celebration of the Santo Niño de Cebu, celebrating Cebu's patron saint, a depiction of the infant Christ much like the Infant of Prague.

Hinduism

Hinduism ruled the spiritual lives of Southeast Asians more than 1500 years ago, and the great Hindu empires of Angkor and Srivijaya built grand monuments to their pantheon of gods. The primary representations of the multiple faces of the one omnipresent god are Brahma, the creator; Vishnu, the preserver; and Shiva, the destroyer or reproducer. All three gods are usually shown with four arms, but Brahma has the added advantage of four heads to represent his all-seeing presence. Although Buddhism and Islam have filtered across the continent, Hinduism has managed to survive on the island of Bali. Within the last 100 years, the influx of Indian labourers to Southeast Asia has bolstered the religion's followers. Buddhism still retains many aspects of Hinduism and still regards the Hindu deities with respect.

Brunei Darussalam

HIGHLIGHTS

- **Bandar Seri Begawan** (p54) Wandering through Southeast Asia's smallest and most serene capital: a collection of wobbly wooden stilt villages, government offices and several intriguing museums.
- **Mosques** (p56) Ogling a sea of gold-woven prayer rugs under dozens of glittering domes and sky-scraping minarets at the Omar Ali Saifuddien Mosque and the Jame'Asr Hassanil Bolkiah Mosque.
- **Local Cuisine** (p61) Diving mouth-first into the country's unique dining scene, sampling the gamut of tasty Bruneian dishes.
- **Empire Hotel** (p57) Unleashing your inner sultan during a lavish weekend at this gold-encrusted palace.
- **Gadong** (p58) Discovering Brunei's version of nightlife at the bustling shopping malls.
- **Off the beaten track** (p59) Trudge through untouched acres of pristine rainforest in Ulu Temburong National Park.

FAST FACTS

- **Budget** B$25 to B$40 a day
- **Capital** Bandar Seri Begawan (BSB)
- **Costs** budget bed B$10 to B$20, street stall grub B$3, local bus ride B$1
- **Country code** ☎ 673
- **Languages** Malay, English
- **Money** US$1 = B$1.41 (Brunei dollar)
- **Phrases** *selamat pagi* (good morning), *selamat petang* (good afternoon), *selamat jalan* (goodbye), *terima kasih* (thank you)
- **Population** 398,000
- **Time** GMT + eight hours
- **Visas** see p63 for information

TRAVEL HINT

Prebooking accommodation online (or by phone) can yield significant discounts, especially at the Empire Hotel.

OVERLAND ROUTES

Brunei is a great rest stop if you are travelling between the Malaysian states of Sabah and Sarawak.

Welcome to the smallest chapter in Lonely Planet's illustrious Southeast Asia travel tome. And it's with good reason that Brunei earns the least amount of words – this bite-size nation is only famous for two reasons: money and oil. If it weren't for the vast riches it pumps out in hydrocarbons every year, it is doubtful whether this 'little country that could' would still be independent.

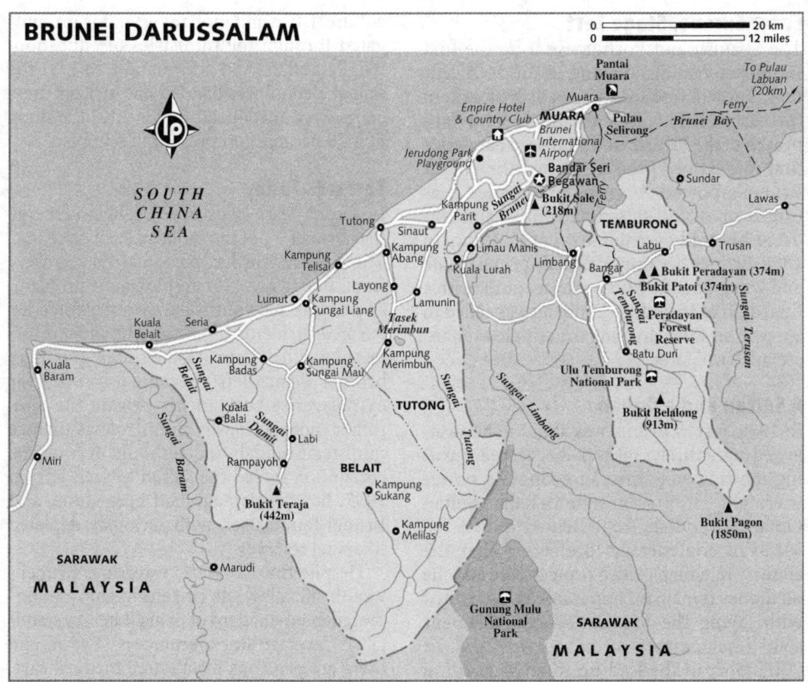

For many visitors, Brunei is just a convenient stop and an extra stamp in the passport, but for centuries this was the hub of the entire region, controlling the whole of Borneo and territory as far away as the Philippines. The country's culture and heritage are still deeply bound up in those proud times, and exploring its history is the best way to understand the unique national character.

Those with a bit more time on their hands will discover that Brunei's oil deposits sit beneath a truly beautiful land: virgin rainforests, bronze beaches, rolling hills and scenic lakes. Money may not buy happiness, but it apparently keeps 'Borneo's green heart' shining a brilliant emerald.

CURRENT EVENTS

Rumours of depleting oil resources have been circulating for the last decade; but the sultanate still appears to be going strong. Efforts to diversify Brunei's international appeal are underway, however tourists haven't quite taken the bait as of yet. Adapting to a global climate seems paramount at the moment – younger Bruneians are eager to marry what's hip to the nation's deep-seeded beliefs. Names of popular recording artists and actors are memorised with the same alacrity as the minutia of Bruneian lore. See p51 to learn more about the latest trends in the sultanate.

HISTORY

In the Beginning

The earliest recorded references to Brunei's presence relate to China's trading connections with 'Pu-ni' in the 6th century, during the Tang dynasty. Prior to the region's embrace of Islam, Brunei was within the boundaries of the Sumatran Srivijaya Empire, then the Majapahit Empire of Java. By the 15th and 16th centuries, the so-called Golden Age of Sultan Bolkiah (the fifth sultan), Brunei Darussalam had become a considerable power itself in the region, with its thalassocratic rule extending throughout Borneo and into the Philippines.

Enter Europe, Stage Left

The Spanish and Portuguese were the first European visitors, arriving in the 16th century, but failed to make inroads by force. In the early 19th century the more subtle approach of the British, in the guise of Sarawak's first raja, James Brooke, spelled the end of Brunei's power. A series of 'treaties' was forced upon the sultan as Brooke consolidated his hold over the town of Kuching. In 1888 Brunei became a British protectorate and was gradually whittled away until, with a final dash of absurdity, Limbang was ceded to Sarawak in 1890, dividing the crippled sultanate into two parts.

A Sultan and a Queen

In 1929, just as Brunei was about to be swallowed up entirely, oil was discovered, turning the tiny state into an economic power overnight. The present sultan's father, Sultan Omar Saifuddien, kept Brunei out of the Malayan confederacy, preferring that the country remain a British protectorate and the oil money remain on home soil. He's credited with laying the foundations for Brunei's solid development.

In 1962, in the lead up to amalgamation with the new state of Malaysia, the British pressured the sultan to hold elections. The opposition Ra'ayat Party, which wanted to keep Brunei independent and make the sultan a constitutional monarch within a democracy, won an overwhelming victory. When the sultan refused to allow the new government into power, an armed rebellion broke out, supported by the Indonesian government. The uprising was quickly crushed with British military backing, and the 'Abode of Peace' has been under emergency laws ever since.

Independence

Saifuddien abdicated in 1967, leaving the throne to his popular son and heir, Sultan Hassanal Bolkiah. Early in 1984 he reluctantly led his tightly ruled country into complete independence from Britain. As a former public-school boy and graduate of Sandhurst Royal Military Academy, the sultan rather enjoyed British patronage and the country still has close ties to Britain.

After independence Brunei veered towards Islamic fundamentalism, adopting a national ideology known as Melayu Islam Beraja (MIB). This institutionalised dogma stresses Malay culture, Islam and monarchy, and is promulgated through the ministries of education, religious affairs and information. In 1991 the sale of alcohol was banned and stricter dress codes were introduced, and in 1992 the study of MIB became compulsory in schools.

Towards Today

In recent years signs have begun to emerge that Brunei is not the model state it once was. The government has recognised a relatively small but growing unemployment problem, and disaffected youths have been blamed for isolated incidents of crime. The most disaffected youth of them all, the sultan's younger brother Prince Jefri, became a byword for extravagance both in his private life and, rather more seriously, in his role as finance minister. Scandals and rumours of financial corruption forced the sultan to sack Jefri in 1997, but the damage had been done, and Brunei found itself with seriously depleted financial reserves.

Despite the economic wavering, Brunei's wealth still allows its citizens to enjoy an unprecedented standard of living. Literacy stands at 94%, average life expectancy is 77 years, and there are pensions for all, free medical care, free schooling, free sport and leisure centres, cheap loans, subsidies for many purchases (including cars), short working weeks, no income tax and the highest minimum wages in the region. The sultan even marked his 60th birthday in 2006 by awarding civil servants their first pay rise in 20 years. Economic diversification and new deep-sea explorations for oil aim to keep the cash rolling in and, as long as it does, the people of Brunei should stay happy with their lot.

THE CULTURE

Brunei is the most observant Islamic country in Southeast Asia. Religion aside, visitors might be surprised to find just how friendly and forward-thinking the typical Bruneian can be. Bruneians readily embrace globalisation and strive to strike a balance between international trends and their stringent local rules. As an interesting sidenote, criminal indiscretions, like petty theft, are handled by the so-called English Court, while the Muslim Court controls personal matters like divorce – and ne'er the two courts shall meet.

People of Malay heritage and indigenous Kedayan, Tutong, Belait, Bisayah, Dusun

A DJ'S SPIN ON BRUNEI

Jenny Malai Ali, a well-known radio personality, gives us her spin on what makes Brunei really tick. Born in Brunei to a British mother and Bruneian father, Jenny has lived all over the world, returning to Brunei several years ago to settle down and start a family. We stopped by the radio station for a chat – here's what she had to say:

'Hm...where to begin!? Well, I love Brunei and I think it's quite an appealing place for a visitor, even if they don't have oodles of time to explore. Obviously we're a small country, so there aren't a million things to see, but we have all of the creature comforts one would want, not to mention genuine Bruneian hospitality.

'It's funny though, as much as I love it here, Brunei really is a land of strange contradictions. We are all so proud to be Bruneian, but we readily embrace the country's imminent globalisation. Everyone adds a faux French prefix like Le or D' to their establishment's name, and the hippest restaurants serve American or Japanese food – sushi is so 'in' right now. We're really into food here, namely because alcohol is prohibited...

'Right now we are entering an MTV generation – we love acronyms and catchy bumper stickers. Teenagers dress to be noticed and everyone buys cars they can't afford. Actually, there are a lot of people living an alternative lifestyle – quite a few lesbians and transgender individuals – but I think that's more a function of living in a sexually repressed society. It's hard sometimes – you can't even hold hands with your partner.

'Bruneians are obsessed with the internet – chatting, Facebook-ing, etc – but blogging has really taken our country by storm. Bloggers are our local heroes. If you're interested, I'd check out www.ranoadidas.com, he's an adopted member of the royal family, and the writer of www.anakbrunei.blogspot.com is a former government employee – he's quite patriotic.

'Ultimately, we desperately want to be a modern Islamic nation, but for some reason we haven't quite pulled it off. We have a beautiful country – a scenic shoreline and an untouched rainforest – but every time we build something, like Jerudong for example, it doesn't quite work out! Dubai's pulled it off – I don't know why we aren't there yet...but we'll get there...'

Jenny Malai Ali is well-known TV presenter and radio personality. She lives in Bandar Seri Begawan with her husband and son.

and Murut peoples make up approximately 67% of the 398,000 inhabitants. Iban, Kelabit and other tribes contribute to around 6%, and people of Chinese heritage account for 15% of the population. Westerners, Thais, Filipinos, Indonesians, Indians and Bangladeshis – generally the population of temporary workers – make up the rest.

RELIGION

Although Brunei is a strict Muslim country, with a Ministry of Religious Affairs that fosters and promotes Islam, only 67% of the population is actually Muslim. Buddhists and Christians make up 13% and 10% of the population respectively, and 10% of people have kept their indigenous beliefs.

ARTS

Traditional arts have all but disappeared in modern Brunei. In its heyday the sultanate was a source of brassware in the form of gongs, cannons and household vessels (such as kettles and betel containers) that were prized throughout Borneo and beyond. The lost-wax technique used to cast bronze declined with the old fortunes of the Brunei sultanate. Brunei's silversmiths were also celebrated. *Jong sarat* sarongs, using gold thread, are still prized for ceremonial occasions, and the art of weaving has survived.

ENVIRONMENT

The Land

Brunei consists of two areas, separated by the Limbang district of Sarawak, and covers a total area of just 5765 sq km. The western part of Brunei contains the main towns: Bandar Seri Begawan (BSB), the oil town of Seria (where the sultanate's billionth barrel was filled in 1991) and the commercial town of Kuala Belait. The eastern slice of the country, the rural Temburong district, is much less developed. Away from the coast, Brunei is mainly jungle, with approximately 78% of the country still covered by forest.

Wildlife

Wildlife species found in Brunei are similar to those found in the rest of Borneo. Proboscis monkeys, gibbons, hornbills, deer, monitor lizards, crocodiles and the rare clouded leopard live in the rainforest.

National Parks

Brunei has several recreational parks and forest reserves, as well as one national park – the superb Ulu Temburong National Park, a 500-sq-km swath of protected primary rainforest.

TRANSPORT

GETTING THERE & AWAY

Air

Brunei International Airport (☎ 233 2531, flight enquiries 233 1747) is about 4km out of the centre of Bandar Seri Begawan.

Royal Brunei Airlines (☎ 221 2222; www.bruneiair.com) flies to 20 major cities scattered throughout Asia, Australia, the Middle East and Europe. Stopover flights go to London and Frankfurt for connections throughout Europe and further afield.

Four other airlines offer services to regional destinations. They include **Philippines Airlines** (code PAL; www.philippineairlines.com), **Malaysia Airlines** (code MAS; ☎ 222 4141; www.malaysiaairlines.com), **Thai Airways** (code TG; ☎ 224 2991; www.thaiair.com) and **Singapore Airlines** (code SQ; ☎ 224 4901; www.singaporeair.com).

Boat

Most boats to/from BSB operate from the Serasa Ferry Terminal, in Muara, about 25km northeast of the city (B$2/RM6 bus ride or a B$40 taxi ride to/from BSB). Arrive 45 minutes before your boat just in case there's a line at customs. There are regular ferries between Muara and Pulau Labuan in Sabah, Malaysia (B$15, 1½ hours, six departures between 7.30am and 4.40pm).

> **DEPARTURE TAX**
>
> The departure tax at Brunei International Airport is B$5 for flights to Sabah and Sarawak and B$12 to west Malaysia, Singapore and all other destinations. It must be paid in Brunei dollars.

From Pulau Labuan there are two ferries a day onward to Kota Kinabalu, Sabah. Passengers are charged B$1 departure tax at the ferry terminal.

Bus

In the last few years express buses have started to link Brunei's capital, Bandar Seri Begawan, with Miri (Sarawak, Malaysia), Pontianak (Kalimantan, Indonesia) and Kota Kinabalu (Sabah, Malaysia). Buses to Kuching were not in operation during our visit, but they will be starting soon. A one-way ticket to KK costs B$45, it's B$80 to Pontianak. Direct buses leave from opposite Kianggeh Market in central BSB (just down street from the central bus station). Boat service between Malaysian Borneo and Brunei can be much more convenient than travelling overland between Sabah and Sarawak – crossing through Brunei will add 10 stamps in your passport (and you're likely to wait in line for each one!). See opposite for detailed border information, especially if you are planning to use a private vehicle.

Car

Car rentals are much more economical than taxi service. See below for information about rental car operators (almost all are located in BSB or at the airport).

GETTING AROUND

Transport around Brunei is by bus, rental car or taxi. The public bus system is easy and reliable, but only operates in and around Bandar Seri Begawan between 6am and 6pm daily. Taxis are a fine way of exploring central BSB; however, for longer distances it is more cost-effective to rent a vehicle or take a bus. Boats to Bangar (B$6, 45 minutes, about one departure per hour from 7am to 4.30pm) operate from the jetty along Jl Residency. Boats generally don't depart until they've got enough passengers to warrant the trip, so you'll probably have to wait. Temburong has a limited road network, and taxis are the only way to get around independently.

Intra-Brunei buses connect BSB's central bus station on Jl Cator to the towns of Seria (B$6, two hours) and Kuala Belait ($7, 2½ hours). However, if you are making your way between BSB and Sarawak it is quicker to take a direct bus to Miri. Seria and KB aren't the most interesting destinations if you're on a tight travel schedule...

Hiring a car is the most cost-effective way of exploring Brunei. All-inclusive rentals start at around B$130 per day; surcharges may apply if the car is taken into Sarawak. Petrol is cheap (fun fact: there are only Shell stations in Brunei) and the main roads are in good condition; some back roads require a 4WD. An International Driving Permit is required for driving in Brunei, and remember, Bruneians drive on the left side of the road.

If you will be driving your own vehicle, note that the usage of mobile phones while driving is strictly prohibited and punishable

BRUNEI BORDER CROSSINGS

Fancy a stopover in Brunei to check off another country on your list? Before you make the trip, check out www.mfa.gov.bn/visainformation/visaarrangements.htm or www.immigration.gov.bn/002/html/melawat.html for the most up-to-date information about visas (also listed p63). The sites list all countries that do not require visas or that can obtain them upon arrival. Automatic entry permits are awarded in increments of 14 or 30 days depending on your nationality (Americans score 90 days). Countries not on the list must apply for their visas in advance (Israeli citizens are barred from entering Brunei). Visitors that require a visa can get a 72-hour transit pass if they are arriving by air and their onward destination is different from their origin.

Brunei has five other entry points besides the airport: Sungai Tujuh (Miri–Brunei), Kuala Lurah (Brunei–Limbang), Puni (Limbang–Temburong), Labu (Temburong–Lawas) and Serasa Ferry Terminal (Muara Port). Crossings open at 6am and close around 10pm, but note that the Puni border closes for noon prayer on Friday, and traffic at Kuala Lurah has been known to cause three-hour delays, so plan accordingly.

The Serasa Ferry Terminal in Muara links passengers to Pualu Labuan (Sabah), Limbang (Sarawak) and Lawas (Sarawak). Car ferry service is in the works and will provide service to Menumbok on mainland Sabah.

When travelling overland from Miri (Sarawak) to Kota Kinabalu (Sabah) you'll rack up a whopping 10 chops in your passport (make sure you have a couple of blank pages!):

- Exit Malaysia at Sungai Tujuh (Miri)
- Enter Brunei at Sungai Tujuh (Belait)
- Exit Brunei at Kuala Lurah
- Enter Malaysia at Kuala Lurah (Limbang, Sarawak)
- Exit Malaysia at Tedungan
- Enter Brunei at Puni
- Exit Brunei at Labu
- Enter Malaysia at Lawas
- Exit Sarawak
- Enter Sabah at Sindumin
- Continue on to Kota Kinabalu

In the last few years regular bus service from Miri to Bandar and Bandar to Kota Kinabalu has made this adventure through the jungle of red tape a lot easier on the nerves. Note that if you are passing through with your own transportation, there are proper border-control posts almost everywhere now. By the time you read this the border post in Lawas (as you enter from Temburong) should be open, leaving only the Puni immigration (in Temburong as you enter from Limbang) as one that is by the roadside. A bridge also is being built across the Trusan River in Lawas (but it may be another year before it opens), so when that's done there will be only one ferry crossing left.

Oh, and while travelling between Bandar and Temburong don't forget to carry your passport as you'll technically be passing through Malaysian waters.

by hefty fines. Cameras and radars monitor phone usage, speed limits and buckled belts, so even if you don't see a cop, you could still find yourself with a hefty bill when returning your rental.

Rental operators in BSB include the following (all are located at the airport):

Avis (off Map p55; ☎ 242 6345)
Budget-U-Drive (off Map p55; ☎ 234 5573)
Hertz (off Map p55; ☎ 245 2244)

BANDAR SERI BEGAWAN

pop 258,000

If you come to Bandar Seri Begawan expecting some kind of lavish mini-Dubai, think again – Brunei may fancy itself as an oil state, but there's no nouveau-riche ostentation here, and the country's capital is as polite and unassuming as its people, wearing its wealth almost prosaically in places. For visitors on a layover, BSB's wide, quiet streets will form the entirety of their Bruneian experience. And while there's plenty to keep you occupied for a couple of days, the city itself is unlikely to inspire any great devotion. However, if you take the time to slow down and talk with the locals, you may find that there's more than meets the eye in this modest metropolis.

ORIENTATION

The central core of BSB is an easily navigable grid facing south towards the busy Sungai Brunei (Brunei River). Stilt villages sprawl on the opposite side of the shore and are connected to the centre by bridges and water taxis. Buildings in central Bandar are fairly spread out and there isn't a lot of shade, so hats and sunscreen are advised. Although the downtown is relatively quiet, there are plenty of sights, restaurants and shops, many of which are located around the Yayasan Complex. The main bus station is also located near the waterfront on Jl Cator. The international airport is 5km outside of the city centre.

INFORMATION

Bookshops

Paul & Elizabeth Book Services (☎ 222 0958; 2nd fl, Block B, Yayasan Complex, Jl Pretty) Stock a small range of English-language paperbacks, including a repository of ancient Lonely Planet guides!

Internet Access

Paul & Elizabeth Cyber Café (☎ 222 0958; 2nd fl, Block B, Yayasan Complex, Jl Pretty; per hr B$1; 🕑 8am-9.30pm) On the 2nd floor overlooking the central atrium in the northern building of the complex. Decent connections, bad soundtrack.

Internet Resources

For more detailed information about your visit to Brunei, visit www.tourismbrunei.com. Lately, blogging has become quite popular – check out p51 for local perspectives on the sultanate.

Medical Services

Jerudong Park Medical Centre (☎ 261 1433; Tutong-Muara Hwy; 🕑 24hr) Private medical facility with high standards of care.

RIPAS Hospital (☎ 224 2424; Jl Tutong; 🕑 24hr) A fully equipped, modern hospital across the Edinburgh Bridge on the western side of Sungai Kedayan.

Money

HSBC (☎ 225 2222; cnr Jl Sultan & Jl Pemancha; 🕑 9am-3.30pm Mon-Fri, to 11am Sat) Charges B$15 to change most travellers cheques and has an ATM.

Rupiah Express (ground fl, Britannia House, 1 Jl Cator; 🕑 8am-5.30pm Mon-Sat, to 3pm Sun) Exchanges cash only.

Post

Main post office (cnr Jl Sultan & Jl Elizabeth Dua; 🕑 8.30am-4.30pm Mon-Thu & Sat, 8.30am-11.30am & 2-4pm Fri) Be sure to stop in to the adjoining Stamp Gallery (same hours as post office).

Tourist Information

At the time of research there was no tourist information centre in Bandar's CBD; however, word on the street is that a visitors centre and adjoining art gallery will be opening in the Old Custom Building along the riverfront. See p62 for information about Brunei's tourism board.

SIGHTS

Royal Regalia Museum

A celebration of the sultan and all the trappings of Bruneian royalty, the **Royal Regalia Museum** (☎ 222 8358; Jl Sultan; admission free; 🕑 8.30am-4.30pm Sun-Thu, 9-11am Fri) belongs at the top of any Brunei itinerary. The first floor is dominated by a re-creation of the sultan's coronation day parade, while on the mezzanine floor of the museum you'll

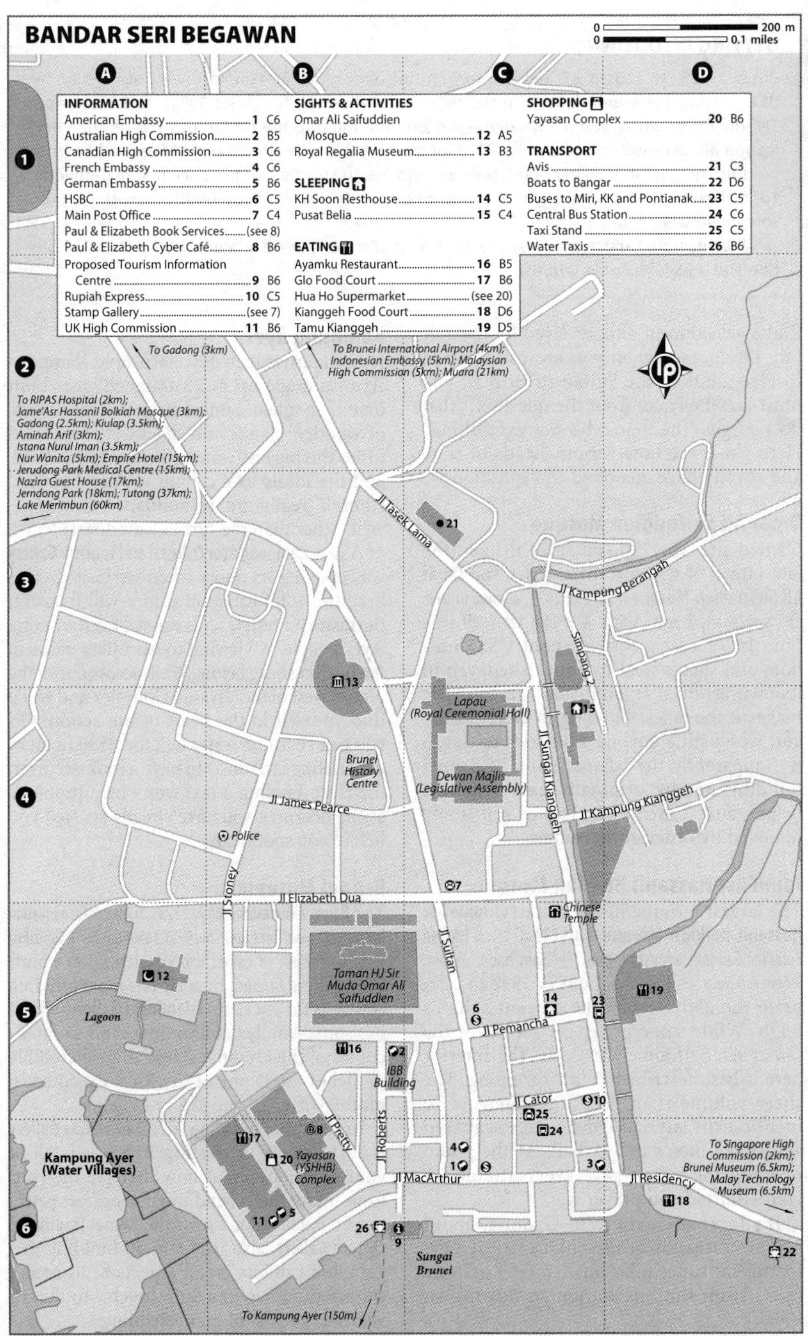
BANDAR SERI BEGAWAN
0 200 m
0 0.1 miles
A
B
C
D
1
2
3
4
5
6
INFORMATION
American Embassy 1 C6
Australian High Commission 2 B5
Canadian High Commission 3 C6
French Embassy 4 C6
German Embassy 5 B6
HSBC 6 C5
Main Post Office 7 C4
Paul & Elizabeth Book Services (see 8)
Paul & Elizabeth Cyber Café 8 B6
Proposed Tourism Information Centre 9 B6
Rupiah Express 10 C5
Stamp Gallery (see 7)
UK High Commission 11 B6
SIGHTS & ACTIVITIES
Omar Ali Saifuddien Mosque 12 A5
Royal Regalia Museum 13 B3
SLEEPING
KH Soon Resthouse 14 C5
Pusat Belia 15 C4
EATING
Ayamku Restaurant 16 B5
Glo Food Court 17 B6
Hua Ho Supermarket (see 20)
Kianggeh Food Court 18 D6
Tamu Kianggeh 19 D5
SHOPPING
Yayasan Complex 20 B6
TRANSPORT
Avis 21 C3
Boats to Bangar 22 D6
Buses to Miri, KK and Pontianak 23 C5
Central Bus Station 24 C6
Taxi Stand 25 C5
Water Taxis 26 B6
To Gadong (3km)
To Brunei International Airport (4km); Indonesian Embassy (5km); Malaysian High Commission (5km); Muara (21km)
To RIPAS Hospital (2km); Jame'Asr Hassanil Bolkiah Mosque (3km); Gadong (2.5km); Kiulap (3.5km); Aminah Arif (3km); Istana Nurul Iman (3.5km); Nur Wanita (5km); Empire Hotel (15km); Jerudong Park Medical Centre (15km); Nazira Guest House (17km); Jerndong Park (18km); Tutong (37km); Lake Merimbun (60km)
Jl Tasek Lama
Jl Kampung Berangah
Simpang 2
Lapau (Royal Ceremonial Hall)
Dewan Majlis (Legislative Assembly)
Jl Sungai Kianggeh
Brunei History Centre
Jl James Pearce
Jl Kampung Kianggeh
Police
Jl Stoney
Jl Elizabeth Dua
Chinese Temple
Jl Sultan
Taman HJ Sir Muda Omar Ali Saifuddien
Lagoon
Jl Pemancha
IBB Building
Jl Pretty
Jl Cator
Jl Roberts
Kampung Ayer (Water Villages)
Yayasan (YSHHB) Complex
Jl MacArthur
Jl Residency
To Singapore High Commission (2km); Brunei Museum (6.5km); Malay Technology Museum (6.5km)
Sungai Brunei
To Kampung Ayer (150m)

GETTING INTO TOWN

Buses 23, 24, 36 and 38 will get you to/from the airport, about 4km northwest of the city, for B$1. Leaving the terminal, keep to the right and walk south for about 300m to the bus stop. Tell the driver where you are headed – if it's on the route to the central bus station then he'll let you off. Taxis will charge around B$20 for trips between the airport and city centre (the price goes up by at least B$5 after 6pm); taxis are unmetered so agree on the price before getting in. For a cheaper alternative, many hotels offer free or inexpensive pick-up service from the airport, so enquire when you book.

All boats from Labuan and most from Limbang (Sarawak) arrive at Muara Port – it's a B$2 bus ride and a B$40 taxi ride into BSB.

find a selection of gifts received by the sultan. Of course, when you are called upon to give a gift to the Sultan of Brunei, you must inevitably confront the question: what do you give the man who has everything? Here you'll see how various heads of state and royalty have answered this question.

Omar Ali Saifuddien Mosque

Named after the 28th sultan of Brunei (the late father of the current sultan), the **Omar Ali Saifuddien Mosque** (☎ 222 2623; admission free; 🕑 8am-noon, 2-3pm, 5-6pm & 8-9pm Sat-Wed) was built in 1958 at a cost of about US$5 million, and stands next to Sungai Kedayan in its own artificial lagoon. The 44m minaret makes it the tallest building in central BSB, and woe betide anyone who tries to outdo it – apparently the Islamic Bank of Brunei building nearby originally exceeded this height, and consequently had its top storey removed by order of the sultan.

Jame'Asr Hassanil Bolkiah Mosque

The largest mosque in the country, **Jame'Asr Hassanil Bolkiah Mosque** (☎ 223 8741; Jl Hassan Bolkiah, Gadong; admission free; 🕑 8am-noon, 2-3pm, 5-6pm & 8-9pm Sat-Wed) was built in 1992 to celebrate the 25th year of the current sultan's reign. While some prefer the facade of the Omar Ali Saifuddien Mosque, the interior here is best described as jaw-dropping. The sheer volume is in itself amazing, not to mention the myriad woven rugs scattered across the men's prayer hall. At the grand opening the sultan gave every attendee a gold-embroidered prayer rug.

It's located en route to Gadong, about 2.5km northwest of the city centre. To get to the mosque, take bus 22 or 1 (Circle Line) from the bus station in downtown BSB.

Kampung Ayer

Housing an estimated 20,000 people, Kampung Ayer is made up of 28 water villages built on either side of Sungai Brunei. This jumble of wooden planks and shacks is considered to be the biggest water village in the world, and the locals love calling it 'Asia's Venice' (there's really no resemblance though – well, other than the turbid water part).

A new **Kampong Ayer Cultural and Tourism Gallery** was opening its doors when we visited. This brand-new information centre will focus on the history, lifestyle and crafts of the Kampong Ayer people. A viewing tower offers views of the bustling burg below. Walk across one of the planks west of the Yayasan Complex and you'll find yourself in the heart of the action. Or, you can charter a water taxi for B$30 (a bit of negotiating is a must) to have a look-see from the river. Finding a taxi won't be a problem, as the boatmen will have already spotted you before you spot them.

Brunei Museum

The **Brunei Museum** (☎ 222 3235; Jl Kota Batu; admission free; 🕑 9.30am-5pm Sun-Thu, 9-11.30am & 2.30-4.30pm Fri) is 6.5km east of central BSB, sitting on a bluff overlooking Sungai Brunei. The main building contains the excellent **Islamic Art Gallery**, which has some wonderful illuminated (decorated) copies of the Quran, as well as an incredible model of the Dome of the Rock executed in mother-of-pearl and abalone shell.

In the same building, the **Oil and Gas Gallery** is surprisingly interesting. It answers all of your questions about how they get the stuff from under the ground to your nearest petrol pump. Finally, don't miss the **Brunei Traditional Culture Gallery**, also in the main building. It's got good exhibits on all aspects of Bruneian culture, from circumcision (ouch!) to the invigorating sport of grass-sledding.

Descend the stairs from the car park behind the museum, then turn right to reach the **Malay Technology Museum** (admission free; 9.30am-5pm Sun-Thu, 9-11.30am & 2.30-4.30pm Fri). A pair of rooms here have interesting life-sized re-creations of stilt houses with accompanying information on traditional cultures.

To get to the museum, take bus 39 from the bus terminal in downtown BSB.

Istana Nurul Iman

The best way to measure the grandeur of a structure is by counting the bathrooms. The sultan's **Istana Nurul Iman** (Jl Tutong) has 257 – making it the largest residential palace in the world. With a price tag of over US$350 million, this 1788-room behemoth is, if you can believe it, more than four times the size of the Palace of Versailles and three times larger than Buckingham Palace.

Designed by Filipino architect Leandro Locsin, the design aesthetics of the palace draw heavily on an airport terminal concept. From an art-historical perspective it feels more like a Monet – from far away it's quite a sight, but from up close the whole thing doesn't really make sense.

Those who want to get inside the palace will have to time their visit with the Hari Raya festivities at the end of Ramadan – the sultan only opens the palace doors for three days in September, shaking hands and giving out goodies to his faithful locals.

SLEEPING

A sleepover in the sultanate is a pricier endeavour than in nearby Malaysia. Most of Brunei's accommodation abides by the old 'special price for you' market mantra, meaning that rack rates are usually much higher than what you'll actually pay. Unlike other Southeast Asian countries, the best lodging deals can usually be scouted on the internet.

Pusat Belia (Youth Centre; 222 2900, 876 5515; Jl Sungai Kianggeh; dm B$10;) No backpacker comforts here: this is the kind of classic youth hostel that should remind you of school trips or summer camps, and it still caters to exactly that kind of local clientele. The single-sex four-bed bunkrooms are basic but adequate, with rather iffy bathrooms; reception is only sporadically staffed, but hang around and someone should find you.

KH Soon Resthouse (222 2052; http://khsoon-resthouse.tripod.com; 140 Jl Pemancha; s/d B$35/39, with shared bathroom B$30/35;) It's quite a step up in price from the hostel to this simple Chinese-run place, but you don't get a whole lot for your extra 20 bucks apart from more space, better service and plenty of local information. Still, it's the only other budget option anywhere near the centre, and the bus station's almost right opposite.

Nazira Guest House (261 2053; hmarzuqo@brunet.bn; Spg 730-34 Kampong Jerudong; r from B$40;) Located near the Jerudong area, about 15 minutes from central BSB, Nazira is a homey (albeit slightly musty) option set along a residential block. Fully furnished apartments are also available.

EATING

Eat: the only thing Bruneians like to do more than shop. Most of Bandar's top noshes are located beyond the small city centre. See p61 for more on local cuisine.

SPLURGE

our pick Imagine a zillion-tonne hunk of Italian marble dipped in gold and tossed into the rainforest – you've just pictured the fanciful **Empire Hotel & Country Club** (241 8888; www.theempirehotel.com; Muara-Tutong Hwy, Kampung Jerudong; r incl breakfast from B$250;). Built on the same scale as a Las Vegas casino, the resort was commissioned by Prince Jefri as – get this – lodging for guests of the royal family. Construction costs were estimated at a whopping US$1.1 billion, an astronomical sum considering the Petronas Towers in KL cost US$1.9 billion to build! The property was quickly transformed into an upscale resort in order to recover some of the construction costs (they still have a long way to go). Among the resort's spoils are two camel-shaped lamps made from pure Baccarat crystal, topped with solid gold accoutrements. They cost over US$500,000 each, and one of them lives in the Emperor Suite (B$22,000 per night), home to the world's most opulent indoor swimming pool. Rooms for more conservative wallets have hand-woven carpets, gold-plated power points and enormous bathrooms with marble floors.

Food Courts, Markets & Hawker Stalls

Informal eating is the cornerstone of BSB's food scene, and every major shopping centre has its own air-conditioned food court. The Yayasan Complex and Gadong's Mall shopping centre are some of the larger specimens.

our pick **Kianggeh Food Court** (Jl Residency; dishes B$2; breakfast, lunch & dinner) Take in the sunset views over Kampung Ayer while devouring scrumptious local dishes like savoury satay sticks and a big bowl of *soto* with chicken and yellow noodles. Swing by in the morning for some flaky *roti canai*.

Glo Food Court (2nd fl, Yayasan Complex; dishes from B$3; lunch & dinner) Strut past plastic aquariums full of the daily catch and choose from an array of food stalls – each one with plate polaroids for the uninitiated. Grab a chair amongst the cafeteria-style seating and enjoy your cheap grub while taking in the views of the royal barge.

Self-caterers can walk across the canal to the local-produce market, **Tamu Kianggeh** (Kianggeh Market; Jl Sungai Kianggeh; breakfast, lunch & dinner), for a handful of fresh snacks. The large **Hua Ho Supermarket** (☎ 223 1120; Yayasan Complex; 10am-10pm) is a good place for self-catering and has a bunch of Bruneian treats.

Restaurants

Ayamku Restaurant (Jl Pemancha; meals from B$3.50; lunch & dinner) Brunei's answer to KFC is one of the cheapest places in town to get a meal. You can get a big piece of fried chicken, some rice and a drink for about B$3. And, the chicken is surprisingly good.

Aminah Arif (☎ 223 6198; Unit 2-3 Block B Rahman Bldg, Spg 88, Kiulap; meals B$22; breakfast, lunch & dinner) Aminah Arif is synonymous with *ambuyat* (see p61) – Brunei's signature dish. If you're up for trying a bowl of wiggly white goo, then this is the place. Aminah's daughter has opened up her own restaurant, Seri Balai Food House, next door, and uses the same family recipe.

Nur Wanita (☎ 242 6789; Unit 10 Block B, Kiarong Complex; dishes B$4-10; lunch & dinner) A fantastic new restaurant in the Kiarong area, this chic venue serves authentic dishes from northern Thailand. It's exceptionally popular during lunch when nearby office monkeys swing by to transport their taste buds.

SHOPPING

Shopping is definitely Brunei's national sport. Seriously – we might as well label this section 'Entertainment'. Locals bop through the shopping malls scouting out the best deals while bemoaning the fact that their micronation doesn't have enough variety. Things can get pretty hectic at the markets – the combination of food and shopping (Brunei's two biggest delights) can be a total bloodbath!

Escape the oppressive heat at ritzy Yayasan Complex located in the city centre near the mosque. Here you'll find everything from the big brand names (Versace, Guess etc) and a variety of high-end local boutiques selling fabrics and jewellery. There are several great places to eat (see left), and don't miss the Hua Ho Department Store, with its cache of traditional Brunei treats in the basement (p61).

The country's only traffic jam occurs nightly in Gadong, a suburb of BSB, as locals eagerly clog the streets while trying to find a parking space. This is Brunei's main shopping district and features several large complexes including Centrepoint and the Mall. And, just for the record, Brunei's only McDonald's is in Gadong. The Kuilap area, next door, also has a couple of window-shopping-worthy malls, including Seri Q-Lap, which houses Brunei's most popular Cineplex.

GETTING THERE & AWAY

Bandar Seri Begawan is Brunei's capital city and air hub. See p52 for information about getting to/from BSB. For details about travelling around Brunei, see p52.

GETTING AROUND

Bus

The government bus network covers most sights in and around the city, and the Serasa Ferry Terminal. Routes for local buses are displayed at the central bus station, beneath the multistorey car park on Jl Cator, and numbers are displayed on each bus. Apart from the 40-minute Muara express service (B$2), all fares are B$1. Buses to the Gadong area run every 15 minutes, other routes are less frequent (there's usually one bus per hour to the Serasa terminal in Muara). Public transport operates daily between 6.30am and 6pm.

Some useful routes:

Airport Buses 23, 24, 36 and 38.

Brunei Museum and Malay Technology Museum Bus 39.

Gadong Buses 1, 22 and 55.

Jame'Asr Hassanal Bolkiah Mosque Buses 1 and 22.

Jerudong Park Playground Buses 55 and 57.

Muara Buses 37, 38 and 39.

Car & Taxi

Hiring a car is a good way to explore Brunei – and there's definitely some gratification in saying you did a cross-country road trip (in under two hours!). Prices start at around B$130 per day. Rental agencies can arrange pick-ups/drop-offs at your hotel. Drivers can also be arranged for an additional fee. See p52 for additional information about renting a car.

If you're planning to stay within the city centre, then taxis are a fine option. Always negotiate your price before setting off. Trips around town cost around B$10, it's about B$35 to the Serasa Ferry Terminal in Muara, and rates can climb by 50% after 6pm.

AROUND BRUNEI

The sights strewn beyond the capital make a strong case for spending more than a day in Brunei.

JERUDONG

Jerudong's two white elephants – being the Empire Hotel (p57) and the Jerudong Park Playground – should rank high on your to-do list if you want to uncover the real Brunei.

Perhaps the biggest birthday gift ever, **Jerudong Park Playground** (☎ 261 1894; Jerudong; admission & unlimited rides B$15, or admission B$1 & individual rides B$3; 🕑 5pm-midnight Wed-Fri & Sun, to 2am Sat) is a sprawling amusement park that was once a private playground for the royal family. Today, it's in a semidormant state – most of the rides have been sold to other amusements and those that remain are 'closed for maintenance'. This gives the park a rather bizarre air – a mix of locals and tourists meander around slightly aimlessly, looking at the defunct attractions with a mixture of awe and bewilderment, like inhabitants of the *Planet of the Apes* discovering a post-apocalyptic Manhattan.

It's easy to get to the playground with Buses 55 or 57 from the bus station, but the last bus leaves at 5.30pm and getting back to town can be a problem. Major hotels have shuttle services for about B$20 per person. A taxi back to BSB will cost about B$35.

TUTONG & BELAIT

The Tutong and Belait districts form the bulk of the big western section of Brunei. Most travellers merely pass through the region en route between Miri (Sarawak) and BSB, as there are only a couple of mildly diverting attractions for those who have several days to spare. Buses ply the coastal highway, but if you want to see the sights the best way is to take a tour or rent a car.

Brunei's largest lake, **Tasek Merimbun**, is a unique black-water habitat that has been dyed a distinctive tea colour by the tannin from falling leaves. The area supports a wide variety of birds, mammals and snakes.

In Seria, check out the flashy **Oil & Gas Discovery Centre** (☎ 337 7200; www.shell.com.bn/ogdc; off Jl Tengah; adult/child/teenager B$5/1/2; 🕑 9am-5pm Tue-Thu, 10am-noon & 2-6pm Fri, 10am-6pm Sat & Sun), which aims to put an 'edutainment' spin on the industry, appealing particularly to young science buffs.

TEMBURONG

While Malaysia has plundered its cache of lush jungle in order to keep its economy afloat, Brunei has surfed the waves of 'black gold', leaving its rainforest completely untouched. Temburong, the smaller of Brunei's puzzle-piece-like land claims, is plunged deep in the heart of neighbouring Sarawak like an emerald dagger.

Three-street **Bangar** is the district 'capital' and gateway to the jungle-clad region. At the time of research there were plans underway to resurrect a tourism office near the pier. Spend the night at **Bangar Guest House** (Jl Batang Duri; r B$20; ❄), a great find located several kilometres beyond the town. Rooms are immaculate and there's always service with a smile.

Fifteen kilometres southeast of Bangar and protected within the **Peradayan Forest Reserve** (admission free) are the peaks of **Bukit Patoi** and **Bukit Peradayan**, which can be reached along walking tracks (bring your own water and trail food). For those who can't be bothered with the trouble or the expense of Ulu Temburong National Park, this is a fine and easy alternative.

Beautiful **Ulu Temburong National Park** is tucked inside the larger Batu Apoi Forest Reserve, a wild expanse of primary rainforest that covers most of southern Temburong. The main attraction at the park is the 60m canopy **walkway**, which is reached by a 1200-step climb up a shiny brass tower. The apparatus itself looks like a carpenter's scaffolding, but the views from the walkway are breathtaking (if you can get over the vertigo as the tower wobbles in the wind). The only accommodation in the park is the **Ulu Ulu Resort** (www.uluuluresort.com), managed by Sunshine Borneo Tours & Travel (p63). Accommodation prices start at B$248 and include transportation and guide treks. Day trips start at around B$180.

To reach Temburong from Bandar Seri Begawan, there are boats to Bangar (B$6, 45 minutes, about once per hour from 7am to early afternoon) which operate from the jetty just east of the Kianggeh Food Court, along Jl Residency. The last boat back to BSB departs Bangar at 4pm.

BRUNEI DIRECTORY

ACCOMMODATION

There are about 2800 rooms in Brunei spread across 35 establishments. Accommodation in Brunei is significantly more expensive than in neighbouring Malaysia. Most prices are quoted net, inclusive of 10% service charge. See p57 for more information about sleeping in the sultanate.

ACTIVITIES

Jungle trekking is popular at Ulu Temburong National Park and the nearby Peradayan Forest Reserve. Trekkers can stride through undisturbed rainforest and up jungle-covered hills. The scenic coastline sports several swim-friendly beaches.

BOOKS

If you're after a more in-depth look at travel in Brunei, grab yourself a copy of Lonely Planet's *Malaysia, Singapore & Brunei* guidebook.

Other reads include *History of Brunei* (2002) by Graham Saunders, a thorough, up-to-date history of the sultanate from its beginnings to modern times; *Time and the River* (2000) by Prince Mohamed Bolkiah, which describes the changes to the country as seen through the eyes of the sultan's youngest brother; *By God's Will: A Portrait of the Sultan of Brunei* (1989) by Lord Chalfont, taking a measured look at the sultan and his dominion; and *New World Hegemony in the Malay World* (2000) by Geoffrey C Gunn, which gives an insight into the more contemporary political issues for Brunei and the region.

BUSINESS HOURS

Government offices are open from 7.45am to 12.15pm and 1.30pm to 4.30pm (closed on Friday and Sunday); private-business offices are generally open from 8am to 5pm Monday to Friday and from 8am to noon on Saturday. Banks are generally open from 9am to 4pm weekdays and from 9am to 11am on Saturday. Most shops in the central area of Bandar Seri Begawan open daily around 10am and are closed by 6pm. Shops and shopping malls generally open around 9am or 10pm and close around 9.30pm (some may close earlier on Sunday). Hours are usually shorter during the fasting month of Ramadan.

CLIMATE

Brunei has a warm to hot climate year-round, with heavy (albeit variable) rainfall that peaks from September to January. See the BSB climate chart, p936.

CUSTOMS

Duty-free allowances for persons over 17 years of age are 200 cigarettes or 250g of tobacco, 60ml of perfume and 250ml of eau de toilette. Non-Muslims may import two bottles of liquor and 12 cans of beer, which must be declared upon arrival.

The importation of drugs carries the death penalty.

DRIVING LICENCE

An International Driving Permit (IDP) is required to drive in Brunei.

EMBASSIES & CONSULATES

Embassies & Consulates in Brunei

Countries with diplomatic representation in Bandar Seri Begawan:

Australia (Map p55; ☎ 222 9435; www.bruneidarussalam.embassy.gov.au; Jl Pemancha)
Canada (Map p55; ☎ 222 0043; www.dfait-maeci.gc.ca/Brunei; Bldg 1 Jl MacArthur)
France (Map p55; ☎ 222 0960; www.ambafrance-bn.org; Unit 301-305 51-55 Kompleks Jl Sultan, Jl Sultan)
Germany (Map p55; ☎ 222 5547; www.bandar-seri-begawan.diplo.de; 2nd fl, Unit 2.01, Block D, Yayasan Complex)
Indonesia (off Map p55; ☎ 233 0180; www.indonesia.org.bn; 4498 Simpang 528, Jl Muara, Kampung Sungai Hanching Baru)
Malaysia (off Map p55; ☎ 238 1095; mmalbrnei@kln.gov.my; 61 Simpang 396, Jl Kebangsaan, Kampung Sungai Akar)
Singapore (off Map p55; ☎ 226 2741; www.mfa.gov.sg/brunei/; 8 Simpang 74, Jl Subok)

MAKAN: THE BRUNEIAN REMIX

If there's one word you should learn during a visit to Brunei, it's *makan,* meaning 'eat' in Bahasa Malaysia. *Makan* isn't just a word, it's a way of life (namely because the locals joke that there's nothing else to do!). This micronation really knows how to chow down:

Ambuyat

If Brunei had a national dish, it would be *ambuyat.* Remember that kid in kindergarten who used to eat paste? Well, this comes pretty darn close. Made from the pith of the sago tree, which is ground to a powder and mixed with water, this glutinous mass was popularised during WWII, when the Japanese invaded Borneo and cut off the rice supply.

To eat *ambuyat,* begin by jabbing your chopsticks into the bowl of quivering white goo. Now these aren't your usual chopsticks – Bruneian chopsticks are attached at the top (so don't snap them in two!) making it easier to curl up the gelatinous globs before dunking the contents into a flavourful sauce. *Ambuyat* itself doesn't have a taste – it's the sauce that gives it its zing. Shrimp-and-chilli mixes are the most popular, although you can technically dip the dish in anything you'd like (we've heard of people using vanilla ice cream!). After your *ambuyat* is sufficiently drenched, place the dripping mass in your mouth and swallow – don't chew – just let it slide down your throat…

Ambuyat is widely available throughout Brunei – stop by the infamous Aminah Arif or Seri Balai (p58), both well known throughout the country for perfecting their recipes.

Snacks

Three meals a day? Hardly! Bruneians will always find an excuse for a quick nosh, and, as a result, they've perfected some delicious 'tween-meal treats. *Chakoi* is our favourite – it's the Bornean version of a *churro* chopped into bite-sized bits. Go for the *kawin chakoi* (*kawin* means marriage), which is flavoured with a scrumptious mix of butter and kaya. The Hua Ho supermarket in Yayasan serves up some of the best *chakoi* in town – it's lightly fried and always made to order – a generous helping costs a wallet-busting B$1.

If you are invited to a Bruneian home, you'll probably be served *buahulu* with your tea. This simple dessert is made from eggs, flour and sugar. *Kuripit sagu,* a biscuit-like version of *buahulu,* is jazzed up with mild coconut flavours.

Wash it all down with *cendol* (pronounced 'chendol'), a murky coconut beverage with floating bits of green and brown (kinda like boba tea, although not as sweet). The taste is undefinable (you'll agree with us when you try it) but it's surprisingly refreshing after a long day of sightseeing. Ask around for *cendol Temburong* – a special provincial brew available only around Ramadan.

UK (Map p55; ☎ 222 2231; http://ukinbruni.fco.gov.uk/en; 2nd fl, Block D, Yayasan Complex)
US (Map p55; ☎ 222 0384; amembassy_bsb@state.gov; 3rd fl, Teck Guan Plaza, Jl Sultan)

EMERGENCIES

Ambulance (☎ 991)
Fire (☎ 995)
Police (☎ 993)

FESTIVALS & EVENTS

See Holidays (right).

GAY & LESBIAN TRAVELLERS

Homosexual acts are illegal in Brunei; those caught can be subject to 10 years of imprisonment and a fine of up to B$30,000.

HOLIDAYS

Brunei has many of the same holidays as Malaysia next door, based on the Islamic calendar but including Chinese New Year, Christmas Day and New Year's Day.

Brunei National Day 23 February; parades and processions in downtown BSB to celebrate Brunei's independence.
Hari Raya Aidiladha Variable February/March
Muslim New Year (Hizrah) Variable
Royal Brunei Armed Forces Day 31 May
Prophet's Birthday Variable (in Malaysia and Brunei only)
Sultan of Brunei's Birthday 15 July; a lively event marked by fireworks, processions and yet more parades in downtown BSB and around Brunei. Festivities continue through the entire month of July.

Hari Raya Aidilfitri Variable around September/October; the sultan opens the palace to visitors.

School holidays occur from mid-November to the beginning of January, and for a week at the end of March, the last two weeks of June and the second week of September.

INTERNET ACCESS

All upmarket hotels have internet connections and a veritable blanket of wi-fi has begun to cover central BSB.

INTERNET RESOURCES

For additional information on Brunei, check out the following websites:

www.brudirect.com Up-to-date news and current affairs.

www.brunei.gov.bn Brunei's government website.

LEGAL MATTERS

The sale of alcohol is illegal in Brunei, and drinking in public is strictly prohibited. See p61 for information about homosexuality. See p60 for customs limitations.

MAPS

A tome of maps printed by Brunei Press, known simply as *Brunei Darussalam Street Directory,* is the best source for any of your road queries. Most hotels in central Bandar Seri Begawan have cartoon maps highlighting the city's main attractions.

MONEY

The official currency is the Brunei dollar (B$), available in denominations of $1, $5, $10, $50, $100, $500 and $1000. Singapore dollars can be used within Brunei (exchanged at an equal rate), however Brunei dollars will usually not be accepted as legal tender in Singapore.

There is no sales tax in Brunei. Tipping after a meal is not widely practiced in Brunei. Major credit cards (Visa, MasterCard and American Express) are widely accepted.

EXCHANGE RATES

Exchange rates at the time of press:

Country	Unit	Brunei dollars (B$)
Australia	A$1	1.24
Canada	C$1	1.31
Euro zone	€1	2.06
Japan	¥100	1.57
Malaysia	RM10	4.08
New Zealand	NZ$1	1.02
UK	£1	2.25
USA	US$1	1.41

POST

Post offices are open from 8am to 4.30pm Monday to Thursday and Saturday, and 8am to 11am and 2pm to 4pm Friday (closed Sunday).

RESPONSIBLE TRAVEL

Bruneians are scrupulous about keeping their cities and towns relatively clean, due to some rigid social standards. It's out in the fragile rainforest that visitors can play their part. Just remember the golden rule when it comes to walking or trekking: if you carry it in, carry it out. This applies to easily forgotten items such as foil, plastic wrapping and tissues. Never bury your rubbish – it may be out of sight, but it won't be out of reach of animals.

Bruneians are also quite conservative in terms of dress. Though you don't have to adopt Islamic dress code when travelling here, it is best to dress somewhat conservatively as a mark of respect to the locals. Sleeveless T-shirts and ripped jeans are inappropriate for men, and bikini tops and shorts are unacceptable for women.

TELEPHONE

To call Brunei from outside the country, the country code is ☎ 673; from Brunei, the international access code is ☎ 00. Within Brunei there are no area codes.

Hello card ('hallo kad'), Netcard ('netcad') and Payless are most common phonecards and can be purchased from most retail stores in denominations of B$5, B$10, B$20 and B$50. These can be used in public booths to make international calls. Most hotels have IDD phones with reasonable local rates.

Prepaid SIM cards from DST and b.mobile, the two major mobile service providers, are available for purchase from authorised dealers in popular shopping areas.

Note that if you have a Malaysian SIM card, it will not work within Brunei unless you use a special dial-out access code. Access rates are astronomical.

TOURIST INFORMATION

At the time of research, Brunei did not have a tourist information centre; however, the government's tourism authority, known simply as **Brunei Tourism** (☎ 238 2822; info@tourismbrunei.com; Ministry of Industry & Primary Resources, Jl Menteri Besar), has put together a wonderful website (www.tourismbrunei.com) with oodles of information on accommodation, sights, local festivals and transport, and photographs and maps.

Plans are underway to open a small visitors centre in central BSB.

TOURS

It's a cinch to get around Bandar on your own steam, but we recommend linking up with a tour to visit attractions beyond the capital.

Borneo Guide (☎ 876 6796; www.borneoguide.com; Block B 1st fl, Warisan Mat Mat, Gadong) Excellent service and a variety of eco-programs around Brunei and Borneo.

Freme Travel Services (☎ 223 4280; www.freme.com; 403B-407B Wisma Jaya, Jl Pemancha) Offers a variety of tours, including the city and Kampung Ayer, and trips to Ulu Temburong and Pulau Selirong.

Mona Florafauna Tours (☎ 223 0761; www.i-s-d-s.com/mona; 209 1st fl, Kiaw Lian Bldg, Jl Pemancha) Specialises in outdoor and wildlife tours around Brunei.

Sunshine Borneo Tours & Travel (☎ 244 6509; www.exploreborneo.com; No 2, Simpang 146, Jl Kiarong) Runs tours of the city and at the Ulu Ulu Resort in Temburong.

TRAVELLERS WITH DISABILITIES

The streets of BSB are easier to negotiate than those of neighbouring Malaysia and most other countries of Southeast Asia, however ramps for wheelchairs, and public transport that allows ready access for the mobility impaired, are unfortunately still lacking. On the plus side, most hotels in the capital have lifts.

VISAS

All visitors must have a valid passport or internationally recognised travel document valid for at least six months beyond the date of entry into Brunei.

Everything you need to know about entering Brunei can be found in the Brunei Border Crossing boxed text, p53.

There are 49 nationalities that do not require a visa to visit Brunei. Citizens of Malaysia, Singapore, the UK, Luxembourg, Ireland, Denmark, Austria, Belgium, Finland, the Netherlands, Germany, Sweden, Italy, France, Spain, Slovenia, Greece, Cyprus, Malta, the Czech Republic, Portugal, Hungary, Estonia, Slovakia, Lithuania, Poland, Latvia, South Korea, Norway, New Zealand, Iran, Oman, the UAE and Iceland do not require a visa for visits of 30 days or less. Indonesia, Thailand, Philippines, Canada, Japan, Switzerland, Maldives, Vietnam, Laos, Myanmar, Cambodia, Peru and Ukraine nationals get 14 days or less. US citizens get 90 days before having to renew their visa. Citizens from Australia, Bahrain and Kuwait entering by air can get a 30-day multi-entry visa on arrival for B$30; China and Qatar qualify for 14 days (also B$30). Israeli nationals are barred from entering Brunei.

WOMEN TRAVELLERS

As Brunei is a conservative Muslim society, dressing modestly is highly advised. Muslim women usually do not shake hands with men, thus a hand may not be extended to travellers of the opposite gender.

Cambodia

HIGHLIGHTS

- **Angkor Wat** (p95) Clamber through spell-binding galleries and then cycle to the Bayon's mysterious stone faces.
- **Battambang** (p103) Explore lush rural countryside by moto or bicycle, climbing hill-top temples and riding the bamboo train.
- **Sihanoukville** (p116) Discover brilliant beaches, uninhabited tropical islands, superb seafood and a happening night scene.
- **Kampot** (p121) Slow down and relax in this French-accented riverside town, in the shadow of Bokor.
- **Peam Krasaop Wildlife Sanctuary** (p114) Discover Koh Kong province's magnificent saltwater mangrove forests.
- **Off the beaten track** (p114) Take an outboard out to Koh Kong Island's pristine west coast.

FAST FACTS

- **Budget** US$15 to US$20 a day
- **Capital** Phnom Penh
- **Costs** guest house in Siem Reap US$3 to US$10, four-hour bus ride US$5, draught beer US$0.50 to US$1
- **Country code** ☎ 855
- **Languages** Khmer, English, French, Mandarin
- **Money** US$1 = 4176r (riel)
- **Phrases** *sua s'dei* (hello), *lia suhn hao-y* (goodbye), *aw kohn* (thank you), *somh toh* (I'm sorry)
- **Population** 15 million
- **Time** GMT + seven hours
- **Visas** US$20 for one month; issued at airports and land borders

TRAVEL HINT

Do as the locals do and buy a *krama* (checked scarf) – indispensable for protection from sun and dust, great as a towel and lots more…

OVERLAND ROUTES

Take a well-trodden land route from Bangkok and HCMC, or break the mould and enter Cambodia from northeastern Thailand, Vietnam's central highlands or Laos.

Ascend to the realm of the gods at Angkor Wat, a spectacular symbiosis of spirituality, symbolism, symmetry and the sublime. Descend into hell and come face to face with the horrors of the Khmer Rouge at Tuol Sleng. Welcome to Cambodia, a country with a history both inspiring and depressing, an enchanting land where Angkor Wat, the ultimate expression of Khmer genius, comes bundled with trauma, poverty, corruption and deforestation.

Siem Reap and Phnom Penh may be the most popular destinations but both, in many ways, are a bubble. Head to the provinces around Tonlé Sap to experience the rhythm of rural life and the timeless beauty of rice paddies and swaying sugar palms.

Fringed by beaches and tropical islands, the south coast is undeveloped but unlikely to stay that way. Inland lie the wild Cardamom Mountains, a vast emerald wilderness whose rainforests are emerging as a gateway to ecotourism adventures.

The mighty Mekong River, giver of life, is home to some of Southeast Asia's last remaining freshwater dolphins. Cyclists can explore the river's banks as it meanders through colonial towns and traditional communities. Meanwhile, the northeast is a world unto itself, its wild and mountainous landscapes sheltering Cambodia's ethnic minorities and remote natural attractions.

Despite having Angkor Wat – the eighth wonder of the world – in its backyard, Cambodia's greatest treasure is its people. The Khmers have been to hell and back but thanks to an unbreakable spirit and infectious optimism, they have prevailed with their spirits – and smiles – largely intact.

CURRENT EVENTS

Compare Cambodia today – stable and at peace – with the dark abyss into which it plunged under the Khmer Rouge and the picture looks pretty good, but compare it to its more successful neighbours, its huge (and growing) income disparities, the galloping inflation that's pauperising the poor, the all-pervasive corruption *and* the ecological devastation, and it is somewhat easy to be pessimistic.

The veneer of democracy is perilously thin. Elections come around every five years, but the Cambodian People's Party (CPP) continues to dominate politics through its control of the military, officials at all levels of government and the state-owned media, according to US democracy-monitoring group Freedom House. In the 2008 Corruption Perceptions Index issued by **Transparency International** (www.transparency.org), Cambodia ranked 166 out of 180 countries.

Indeed, corruption has become a way of life. UK-based NGO, Global Witness, reports that rule of, by and for the people has been displaced by kleptocracy, meritocracy by kickbacks and connections, and environmental protection by murky development deals. International donors tend to tread lightly when it comes to making demands for specific reforms.

Evictions and land grabs continue apace, with the powerful getting richer, with ever flashier SUVs, and the poor – rural and urban – finding themselves dispossessed. In recent years several communities have been kicked off valuable Phnom Penh real estate and dumped unceremoniously in arid (or flooded) fields, miles from the city. Refugees within their own country, these people's fate remains uncertain. In mid-2009, **Amnesty International** (www.amnesty.org) condemned the eviction of 60 poor families with strong claims to title from Group 78, an area along Phnom Penh's waterfront.

The UN-backed **Khmer Rouge trials** (www.cambodiatribunal.org) stumble along amid allegations of political interference and corruption. It is by no means certain that the wheels of justice will turn fast enough to prevent the surviving Khmer Rouge leaders from dying peacefully of old age, though as we go to press, one major Khmer Rouge figure – Tuol Sleng chief Duch – is finally in the dock.

But despite the political situation and recent galloping inflation, life *is* improving for many Cambodians. The economy is booming, largely thanks to tourism and foreign investment – not all of it on the up-and-up – and at least until the economic crisis of late 2008, investors – many of them Korean, Chinese and Russian – were pouring money into the country. However, much of this progress has been made despite the government, not because of it. In the end it is predominantly thanks to the ingenuity and adaptability of the long-suffering Khmer people that they continue to succeed against the odds.

HISTORY

Cambodia's history is inextricably linked with that of its neighbours. In recent centuries Vietnam and Thailand have been richer and more powerful, but during the Angkorian period, the Khmer empire was the regional power, its culture dominant and its creativity unrivalled.

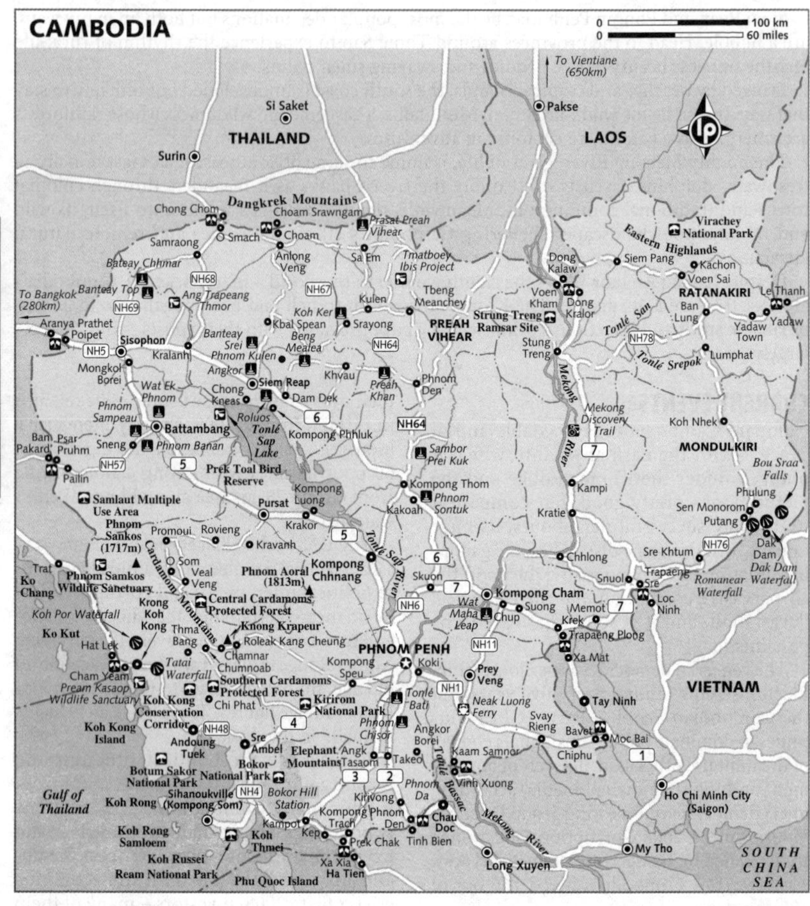

Funan & Chenla

The Indianisation of Cambodia began in the 1st century AD as traders plying the sea route from the Bay of Bengal to southern China brought Indian ideas and technologies to what is now southern Vietnam. The largest of the era's nascent kingdoms, known to the Chinese as Funan, embraced the worship of the Hindu deities Shiva and Vishnu and, at the same time, Buddhism, and was crucial in the transmission of Indian culture to the interior of Cambodia.

From the 6th to 8th centuries Cambodia seems to have been ruled by a collection of competing kingdoms. Chinese annals refer to 'Water Chenla', apparently the area around the modern-day town of Takeo, and 'Land Chenla', further north along the Mekong and around Sambor Prei Kuk.

The Rise & Fall of Angkor

The Angkorian era lasted from AD 802 to 1432, encompassing periods of conquest, turmoil and retreat, revival and decline, and fits of remarkable productivity.

In 802, Jayavarman II (reigned c 802–50) proclaimed himself a *devaraja* (god-king). He instigated an uprising against Javanese domination of southern Cambodia and, through alliances and conquests, brought the country under his control, becoming the first monarch to rule most of what we now call Cambodia.

The Angkorian empire was made possible by *baray* (reservoirs) and irrigation works sophisticated and massive enough to support Angkor's huge population. The first records of such works date from the time of Indravarman I (r 877–89), whose rule was marked by the flourishing of Angkorian art, including the construction of temples in the Roluos area.

In the late 9th century Yasovarman I (r 889–910) moved the capital to Angkor, creating a new centre for worship, scholarship and the arts. After a period of turmoil and conflict, Suryavarman II (r 1113–1150) unified the kingdom and embarked on another phase of territorial expansion, waging successful but costly wars against both Vietnam and Champa (an Indianised kingdom that occupied what is now southern and central Vietnam). His devotion to the Hindu deity Vishnu inspired him to commission Angkor Wat.

The tables soon turned. Champa struck back in 1177 with a naval expedition up the Mekong, taking Angkor by surprise and putting the king to death. But the following year a cousin of Suryavarman II – soon crowned Jayavarman VII (r 1181 to c 1219) – rallied the Khmers and defeated the Chams in another epic naval battle. A devout follower of Mahayana Buddhism, it was he who built the city of Angkor Thom.

Scholars believe that Angkor's decline was already on the horizon when Angkor Wat was built – and that the reasons were partly environmental. The 1000-sq-km irrigation network had begun silting up due to deforestation and erosion, and the latest climate data from tree rings indicates that two prolonged droughts also played a role.

During the twilight years of the empire, religious conflict and internecine rivalries were rife. The Thais made repeated incursions into Angkor, sacking the city in 1351 and again in 1431, and making off with thousands of intellectuals, artisans and dancers from the royal court whose profound impact on Thai culture can be seen to this day.

From 1600 until the arrival of the French, Cambodia was ruled by a series of weak kings whose intrigues often involved seeking the protection of either Thailand or Vietnam – granted, of course, at a price.

French Colonialism

The era of yo-yoing between Thai and Vietnamese masters came to a close in 1864, when French gunboats intimidated King Norodom I (r 1860–1904) into signing a treaty of protectorate. An exception in the annals of colonialism, the French presence really did protect the country at a time when it was in danger of being swallowed by its more powerful neighbours. In 1907 the French pressured Thailand into returning the northwest provinces of Battambang, Siem Reap and Sisophon, bringing Angkor under Cambodian control for the first time in more than a century.

Led by King Sihanouk (r 1941–55 and 1993–2004), Cambodia declared independence on 9 November 1953.

Independence & Civil War

The period after 1953 was one of peace and prosperity, and a time of creativity and optimism – Cambodia's golden years. Phnom Penh grew in size and stature and the temples of Angkor were the leading tourist destination in Southeast Asia. Dark clouds were circling, however, as the war in Vietnam began sucking in neighbouring countries.

As the 1960s drew to a close, the North Vietnamese and the Viet Cong were using Cambodian territory in their battle against South Vietnam and US forces, prompting devastating American bombing and a land invasion into eastern Cambodia.

In March 1970 Sihanouk, now serving as prime minister, was overthrown by General Lon Nol, and took up residence in Beijing. Here he set up a government-in-exile that allied itself with an indigenous Cambodian revolutionary movement that Sihanouk had dubbed the Khmer Rouge. Violence engulfed large parts of the country.

Khmer Rouge Rule

Upon taking Phnom Penh on 17 April 1975 – two weeks before the fall of Saigon (see p836) – the Khmer Rouge implemented one of the most radical and brutal restructurings of a society ever attempted. Its goal was to transform Cambodia – renamed Democratic Kampuchea – into a giant peasant-dominated

MUST READ

First They Killed My Father (2001) was written by Luong Ung and covers the destruction of an urban Cambodian family through execution and disease during the Khmer Rouge period.

DID YOU KNOW?

The UN allowed the Khmer Rouge to occupy the Cambodian seat at the UN General Assembly until 1991, meaning the murderers represented their victims for 12 years.

agrarian cooperative, untainted by anything that had come before. Within days, the entire populations of Phnom Penh and provincial towns, including the sick, elderly and infirm, were forced to march into the countryside and work as slaves for 12 to 15 hours a day. Intellectuals were systematically wiped out – having glasses or speaking a foreign language was reason enough to be killed. The advent of Khmer Rouge rule was proclaimed Year Zero.

Leading the Khmer Rouge was Saloth Sar, better known as Pol Pot. As a young man, he won a scholarship to study in Paris, where he began developing the radical Marxist ideas that later metamorphosed into extreme Maoism. Under his rule, Cambodia became a vast slave labour camp. Meals consisted of little more than watery rice porridge twice a day, meant to sustain men, women and children through a back-breaking day in the fields. Disease stalked the work camps, malaria and dysentery striking down whole families.

Khmer Rouge rule was brought to an end by the Vietnamese, who liberated the almost-empty city of Phnom Penh on 7 January 1979. It is still not known exactly how many Cambodians died during the three years, eight months and 20 days of Khmer Rouge rule. The most accepted estimate is that at least 1.7 million people perished at the hands of Pol Pot and his followers. The **Documentation Center of Cambodia** (www.dccam.org) documents the horrific events of the period.

A Sort of Peace

As Vietnamese tanks neared Phnom Penh in early 1979, the Khmer Rouge fled westward with as many civilians as it could seize, taking refuge in the mountains along the Thai border. The Vietnamese installed a new government led by several former Khmer Rouge officers, including current Prime Minister Hun Sen, who had defected to Vietnam in 1977. In the dislocation that followed liberation, little rice was planted or harvested, leading to a massive famine.

The civil war continued throughout the 1980s. In February 1991 all parties – including the Khmer Rouge – signed the Paris Peace Accords, according to which the UN Transitional Authority in Cambodia (UNTAC) would rule the country for two years. Although UNTAC is still heralded as one of the UN's success stories – elections with a 90% turnout were held in 1993 – the Khmer Rouge soon re-established a guerrilla network throughout Cambodia. UNTAC is also remembered for causing a significant increase in prostitution and AIDS.

The last Khmer Rouge hold-outs, including Ta Mok, were not defeated until the capture of Anlong Veng and Prasat Preah Vihear by government forces in the spring of 1998. Pol Pot cheated justice by dying a sorry death near Anlong Veng during that year, and was cremated on a pile of old tyres.

When the mercurial King Sihanouk – who resumed his tenure as monarch in 1993 – abdicated in 2004, the throne passed to his low-profile son, King Sihamoni, who has brought renewed credibility to the monarchy. In the July 2008 parliamentary elections, the Cambodian People's Party (CPP) of Prime Minister Hun Sen – a political survivor if there ever was one – won 72 out of 123 seats in parliament.

THE CULTURE

The National Psyche

On the surface Cambodia appears to be a nation of smiling, happy people, but a deeper look reveals a patchwork of light and dark, old and new, rich and poor, love and hate, life and death. The hellish abyss into which Cambodia was sucked by the Khmer Rouge left an entire people profoundly traumatised; only the generation that grew up after the war seems to have escaped the lingering sadness. Whenever you hear Pol Pot's name, there'll be stories of endless personal tragedy, of dead brothers, mothers and babies.

Angkor is everywhere: on the flag, the national beer, hotel and guest-house signage, cigarettes – it's *the* symbol of Cambodian nationhood and a source of fierce pride. No matter how bad things are, the Cambodians built Angkor and it doesn't get better than that.

Lifestyle

For untold centuries, life in Cambodia has centred on family, food and faith.

Extended families stick together, solving problems collectively, pooling resources and gathering to celebrate festivals and mourn deaths. Ties remain strong despite the fact that increasing numbers of young people are migrating to the cities in search of opportunity.

Food is extremely important to Cambodians as they have tasted what it is like to be without. Famine stalked the country in the late 1970s and, even today, there are serious food shortages in times of drought or inflation. For country folk – still the vast majority of the population – survival depends on what they can grow, and the harvest cycle dictates the rhythm of rural life.

Faith is a rock in the lives of many older Cambodians, and Buddhism helped them to survive the terrible years and then rebuild their lives after the Khmer Rouge. See below for more on religion in Cambodia.

Population

About 15 million people live in Cambodia. According to official statistics, around 96% are ethnic Khmers, making the country the most homogeneous in Southeast Asia. In reality though, anywhere between 10% and 20% of the population is of Cham, Chinese or Vietnamese origin. Cambodia's diverse Khmer Leu (Upper Khmer) or Chunchiet (minorities), who live in the country's mountainous regions, probably number between 60,000 and 70,000.

The official language is Khmer, spoken by 95% of the population. There's also a smattering of French, and a rapidly growing number of English speakers. The median age is just 22; life expectancy is 62 years.

RELIGION

The vast majority of Khmers (95%) follow the Theravada branch of Buddhism. Hinduism is threaded into the theology, with Hindu symbolism evident in ceremonies, legends and the statues in the middle of roundabouts.

Under the Khmer Rouge, the majority of Cambodia's Buddhist monks were murdered and nearly all of the country's wats (more than 3000) were damaged or destroyed. In the late 1980s, Buddhism once again became the state religion.

Other religions found in Cambodia are: Islam, practised by the Cham community; animism, practised among the hill tribes; and Christianity, which is making inroads via missionaries and Christian NGOs.

ARTS

The Khmer Rouge regime not only killed the living bearers of Khmer culture, it also destroyed cultural artefacts, statues, musical instruments, books and anything else that served as a reminder of a past it was trying to efface. The Angkorian temples were spared as symbols of Khmer glory and empire, but little else, apart from Phnom Penh's showcase Royal Palace, survived. Despite this, Cambodia is witnessing a resurgence of traditional arts, as well as a growing interest in cross-cultural fusion.

Cambodia's royal ballet is a tangible link with the glory of Angkor – think of all those dancing *apsaras* (heavenly nymphs). Cambodian music, too, goes back at least as far as Angkor. To get some sense of the music that Jayavarman VII liked, check out the bas-reliefs at Angkor Wat.

Throughout the mid-20th century a vibrant Cambodian pop-music scene developed, but it was killed off by the Khmer Rouge. After the war, overseas Khmers established a pop industry in the USA and some Cambodian-Americans, raised on a diet of rap, are now returning to their homeland. The Los Angeles–based sextet Dengue Fever, inspired by 1960s Cambodian pop and psychedelic rock, is the ultimate fusion band.

The people of Cambodia were producing masterfully sensuous sculptures – much more than mere copies of Indian forms – in the age of Funan and Chenla. The Banteay Srei style of the late 10th century is regarded as a high point in the evolution of Southeast Asian art.

ENVIRONMENT

The Land

Modern-day Cambodia covers 181,035 sq km, making it a little more than half the size of Vietnam. It has 435km of coastline along the island-specked Gulf of Thailand.

Cambodia's two dominant geographical features are the mighty Mekong and Tonlé

MUST SEE

The Killing Fields (1984) is a poignant film about American journalist Sydney Schanberg and his Cambodian assistant both during and after the Khmer Rouge takeover.

DID YOU KNOW?

During the wet season (June to October), the Mekong River rises dramatically, forcing the Tonlé Sap river to flow northwest into Tonlé Sap (Great Lake). During this period, the lake swells from around 3000 sq km to almost 13,000 sq km, and from the air Cambodia looks like one almighty puddle. As the Mekong falls during dry season, the Tonlé Sap river reverses its flow, and the lake's floodwaters drain back into the Mekong. This unique process makes Tonlé Sap one of the world's richest sources of freshwater fish.

Sap, Southeast Asia's largest lake. The rich sediment deposited during the annual wet-season flooding has made central Cambodia incredibly fertile.

In Cambodia's southwest quadrant, much of the land mass is covered by the Cardamom Mountains and, near Kampot, the Elephant Mountains. Along Cambodia's northern border with Thailand, the plains collide with the Dangkrek Mountains, a striking sandstone escarpment more than 300km long and up to 550m high.

In the northeastern corner of the country, in the provinces of Ratanakiri and Mondulkiri, the plains give way to the Eastern Highlands, a remote region of densely forested mountains and high plateaus.

Wildlife

It's estimated that 212 species of mammal live in Cambodia. Creatures under serious threat include the Asian elephant, tiger, kouprey (a wild ox), banteng (another wild ox), gaur, Asian golden cat, Asiatic wild dog, black gibbon, clouded leopard, fishing cat, marbled cat, sun bear, wild water buffalo and pangolin.

A whopping 720 bird species find a congenial home in Cambodia, thanks in large part to its year-round water resources, especially the marshes around the Tonlé Sap. The Sam Veasna Center (p95) runs birdwatching trips.

Cambodia has some of the last remaining freshwater Irrawaddy dolphins (p126), while the Mekong giant catfish, which can weigh up to 300kg, is critically endangered due to habitat loss and overfishing.

About 240 species of reptile can be found here. Four types of snake are especially dangerous: the cobra, king cobra, banded krait and Russell's viper.

The surest way to see Cambodian animals up close is to drop by the Phnom Tamao Wildlife Sanctuary (p86) near Phnom Penh or the Angkor Centre for Conservation of Biodiversity (p101) near Siem Reap.

National Parks

The good news is that national parks, wildlife sanctuaries, protected landscapes and multiple-use areas now cover 43,000 sq km, or around 25% of Cambodia's surface area. The bad news is that the government does not have the resources – or, in some cases, the will – to actually protect these areas beyond drawing lines on a map.

Cambodia's most important national parks – all of them threatened by development and/or deforestation – are Bokor (p123), Botum Sakor (p115), Kirirom (p86), Ream (p117) and Virachey (p130).

Environmental Issues

The greatest threat to Cambodia's globally important ecosystems is illegal logging, carried out to provide charcoal and timber, and to clear land for cash-crop plantations. The environmental watchdog **Global Witness** (www.globalwitness.org) publishes meticulously documented exposés on corrupt military and civilian officials and their well-connected business partners.

In the short term, deforestation is contributing to worsening floods along the Mekong, but the long-term implications of deforestation are mind-boggling. Siltation, combined with overfishing and pollution, may lead to the eventual death of the lake – a catastrophe for future generations of Cambodians.

TRANSPORT

GETTING THERE & AWAY

Air

Cambodia's two major international airports, Phnom Penh and Siem Reap, have frequent flights to destinations all over eastern Asia. Some airlines offer open-jaw tickets, which can save some time and money. All phone numbers are in Phnom Penh (☎ 023) unless otherwise stated.

Air Asia (code FD or AK; ☎ 356011; www.airasia.com) Flights to Kuala Lumpur, plus Phnom Penh to Bangkok.
Asiana Airlines (code OZ; http://flyasiana.com/english; Phnom Penh ☎ 890441 Siem Reap ☎ 063-965206) Flights to Seoul.
Bangkok Airways (code PG; ☎ Phnom Penh 722545, Siem Reap 063-965422; www.bangkokair.com) At press time still had a monopoly on Siem Reap to Bangkok flights and was handling Siem Reap Airways services.
China Airlines (code CI; ☎ 223525; www.china-airlines.com) Phnom Penh to Taipei.
China Eastern Airlines (code MU; ☎ 063-965229 in Siem Reap; www.flychinaeastern.com) Links Siem Reap with Kunmíng.
China Southern Airlines (code CZ; ☎ 430877; www.cs-air.com/en) Links Phnom Penh with Guangzhou.
Dragonair (code KA; ☎ 424300; www.dragonair.com) Flights to Hong Kong.
Eva Air (code BR; ☎ 210303; www.evaair.com) Phnom Penh to Taipei.
Jetstar Asia (code 3K; ☎ Phnom Penh 220909, Siem Reap 063-964388; www.jetstarasia.com) Cheapest flights to Singapore.
Korean Air (code KE; ☎ Phnom Penh 224047, Siem Reap 063-964881; www.koreanair.com) Flights to Seoul.
Lao Airlines (code QV; ☎ Phnom Penh 216563, Siem Reap 063-963283; www.laos-airlines.com) Flights to Vientiane, Luang Prabang & Pakse.
Malaysia Airlines (code MH; ☎ Phnom Penh 426688, Siem Reap 063-964135; www.malaysiaairlines.com) Flights to Kuala Lumpur.
Shanghai Airlines (code FM; ☎ 723999; www.shanghai-air.com) Links Phnom Penh with Shanghai.
SilkAir (code MI; ☎ Phnom Penh 426808, Siem Reap 063-964993; www.silkair.com) Lots of flights to Singapore, some via Danang in Vietnam.
Thai Airways International (code TG; ☎ 214359; www.thaiair.com) Links Phnom Penh with Bangkok.
Vietnam Airlines (code VN; ☎ Phnom Penh 363396, Siem Reap 063-964488; www.vietnamairlines.com) Has flights to Ho Chi Minh City, Hanoi, Vientiane and Luang Prabang so offers useful Indochina loop options.

Land

Cambodia shares one border crossing with Laos (Dong Kralor–Dong Kalaw, north of Stung Treng; see p128) and five with Thailand, though only the crossings at Poipet (Poipet–Aranya Prathet; see p109) and Krong Koh Kong (Cham Yeam–Hat Lek; see p114) see significant traffic. The three other crossings are southwest of Battambang near Pailin (Psar Pruhm–Ban Pakard; see p108), north of Anlong Veng (Choam–Chong Sa Ngam; see p112) and northeast of Banteay Chhmar (O Smach–Chong Chom; see p110).

Seven crossings with Vietnam are currently open to tourists. In addition to the main Phnom Penh–Ho Chi Minh City route along the NH1 (Bavet–Moc Bai; see p85), you can also cross on the Mekong (Kaam Samnor–Vinh Xuong; see p85), east of Kompong Cham (Trapaeng Plong–Xa Mat, p125, and Trapaeng Sre–Loc Ninh, p132), east of Ban Lung (O Yadaw–Le Thanh; see p131), south of Takeo (Phnom Den–Tinh Bien; see p85) and southeast of Kep (Prek Chak–Xa Xia; see p126).

See p140 for details on Cambodian visas and border scams. For the very latest lowdown on border crossings, see www.talesofasia.com and www.travelfish.org.

AIRPORT TAXES

There's a tax of US$25 on all international flights out of Cambodia. The airport tax for domestic flights is US$6.

GETTING AROUND

It's highly advisable to avoid intercity travel at dusk and after dark as roads lack lighting, and blind overtaking/passing at high speeds is rampant. Come late afternoon, settle in for a mellow evening and prepare for an early getaway (public transport starts shortly after sun-up).

Air

The only scheduled domestic flights link Phnom Penh with Siem Reap, and the majority of these are operated by Bangkok Airways (see left).

Bicycle

Cambodia is a great country for adventurous cyclists, in part because travelling at gentle speeds allows for lots of interaction with locals. Cycling around the temples of Angkor is a truly awesome experience as it really gives you a sense of the size and scale of the complex. Adventure mountain biking is also likely to take off in the Cardamom Mountains.

The majority of Cambodia is pancake flat or only moderately hilly. Safety, however, is a considerable concern on paved roads as trucks, buses and cars travel barrel along at high speed.

Boat

For details on the fast boats from Phnom Penh to Siem Reap see p84, and for details on the leisurely boats linking Siem Reap with Battambang, see p106.

Bus

About a dozen bus companies serve all populated parts of the country. The largest and often least expensive is **Phnom Penh Sorya** (www.ppsoryatransport.com); many expats' favourite is Capitol Tour. Comfort levels and prices vary, and a few companies charge foreigners more than they do locals, so it pays to shop around. Booking bus tickets through guest houses and hotels is convenient but incurs a commission.

Car & Motorcycle

Guest houses and hotels can arrange hire cars with a driver for US$25 to US$60 a day, plus petrol and lodging, and food for the driver.

While major national highways (NH) are a too heavily trafficked for happy motorcycling, many of Cambodia's less travelled tracks are perfect for two-wheeled exploration. However, forays on motorcycles into the remote and diabolical roads of the northwest and northeast should only be attempted by experienced riders. In all cases, proceed cautiously as outside of Phnom Penh and Siem Reap, medical facilities are as rudimentary as ambulances are rare.

See below for details of motorbike and motorcycle rental.

Local Transport

A few *cyclos* (pedicabs) can still be seen on the streets of Phnom Penh and Battambang, but they have been almost completely replaced by motos (or *motodups*), unmarked motorbike taxis that you flag down and hop on the back of.

It used to be that moto prices were rarely agreed to in advance, but with the increase in visitor numbers a lot of optimistic drivers have gotten into the habit of overcharging foreigners. For short hops, expect to pay between 2000r and US$1, more at night; local prices appear in many towns' Getting There & Away sections in this book.

Chartering a moto for the day costs between US$7 and US$10, but can cost more if a greater distance is involved or the driver speaks English.

> **WARNING**
>
> Since singed flesh doesn't smell very nice and, in the tropical humidity, takes a long time to heal, get in the habit of climbing off a moto to your left, stepping clear of the scorching exhaust pipe.

In many towns (Siem Reap is an exception), 100cc and 125cc motorbikes can be hired for US$5 to US$8 a day; 250cc bikes, where available, cost about double that. No one will ask you for a driver's licence – except, occasionally, the police. Make sure you have a strong lock and always leave the bike in guarded parking, if possible.

The vehicle known in Cambodia as a túk-túk is, technically speaking, a *remorque-moto* (in Khmer, a remork), ie a roofed, two-wheeled trailer hitched to the back of a motorbike (a true Thai túk-túk has a one-piece body). Fares are roughly double those of motos, though in some places you pay per passenger. Still, for two or more people a túk-túk can be cheaper than a moto – and much more comfortable if you've got luggage or it's raining.

Some guest houses and hotels rent out bicycles for US$1 to US$2 per day. If you'll be doing lots of cycling, bring along a bike helmet, which can also provide some protection on a moto.

Local taxis can be ordered via guest houses and hotels in Phnom Penh, Siem Reap and Sihanoukville.

Share Taxi, Minibus & Pick-up

Share taxis (usually jacked-up old Toyota Camrys) are faster, more flexible in terms of departure times and a bit more expensive than buses. They're also a lot more crowded. In addition to the driver, each one carries six or seven passengers – that's two in the front seat and four in the back, with a seventh passenger sometimes squished between the driver and his door! Pay double the regular fare and you get the front seat all to yourself; pay six fares and you've got yourself a private taxi. Haggle patiently, with a smile, to ensure fair prices.

Minibuses, which usually stick to sealed roads, are even more jam-packed, which is why they're a bit cheaper than share taxis – that, and the fact that some are driven by maniacs.

Pick-ups, which are favoured by peasants with oversized luggage, some of it alive, continue to take on the worst roads in Cambodia. Squeeze in the air-con cab or, if you feel like a tan and a mouthful of dust, sit out back. They leave when seriously full. Bring a *krama* (scarf), sun screen and, in the wet season, rain gear.

PHNOM PENH

☎ 023 / pop 1.3 million

Oh Phnom Penh. It's exotic, it's chaotic, it's beguiling, it's distressing, it's compulsive, it's repulsive. Every day brings wildly different experiences – some a shock to the senses, others that bring a smile; some that confound all logic, others that wrench the emotions. Many cities are captivating, but Phnom Penh is unique in its capacity to both charm and chill to the bone.

Phnom Penh has been to hell and back. The glamorous 'pearl of Asia' during Sihanouk's '60s, it was evacuated under the Khmer Rouge, only to rise from the ashes of civil war. Today Cambodia's capital is going places – and no, we're not talking about the ever-more-taxing traffic. Tastefully renovated French colonial buildings, skyscrapers and satellite cities are the new Phnom Penh – but all this is worlds away from the struggle for survival faced by most residents.

Many travellers hit the road after the obligatory sightseeing circuit is completed, but the hidden charms of Phnom Penh are best discovered at leisure.

ORIENTATION

Phnom Penh is easy to navigate thanks to its numbered, New York–style grid system. Generally, odd-numbered streets run north–south (the numbers getting higher as you move west), and even-numbered streets run east–west (the numbers getting higher as you move south).

To the east, Phnom Penh is bordered by the Tonlé Sap, Tonlé Bassac and Mekong rivers. The city centre is delineated by Wat Phnom to the north, Independence Monument to the south and the Olympic Stadium to the west.

The main thoroughfares, Monivong Blvd and Norodom Blvd – with Psar Thmei (Central Market) between them – run almost parallel to each other north to south, while Sihanouk Blvd cuts across the city centre, running east–west. The riverfront Sisowath Quay is where most visitors gravitate, but the main attractions are scattered throughout the city. Thanks to an almost-right-angle turn, Samdech Sothearos Blvd links the Royal Palace with Mao Tse Toung Blvd.

The river is traversed by the Chruoy Changvar (Japanese Friendship) Bridge to the northeast and the Monivong (Vietnam) Bridge to the south.

INFORMATION

Bookshops

D's Books (Map p78; www.ds-books.com; 79 St 240 & 7 St 178) The largest chain of second-hand bookshops in the capital.

Monument Books (Map p78; ☎ 217617; 111 Norodom Blvd) The best-stocked bookshop in town, with almost every Cambodia-related book available. Also has an airport branch.

Emergency

Ambulance (☎ 119)

Fire (☎ 118)

Police & Medical (☎ 117)

Tourist police (☎ 724793)

Internet Access

Internet cafes are everywhere and usually charge US$0.50 to US$1 per hour. Many hotels, plus some cafes and restaurants, offer free wi-fi connections.

Medical Services

Calmette Hospital (Map p78; ☎ 426948; 3 Monivong Blvd) A reputable hospital.

International SOS Medical Centre (Map p78; ☎ 216911; www.internationalsos.com; 161 St 51; 🕒 8am-5.30pm Mon-Fri, 8am-noon Sat, emergency 24hr; 161 St 51) International standards for health and teeth.

GETTING INTO TOWN

From Phnom Penh International Airport you can catch a moto to your hotel for US$2. Túk-túks charge US$5 and taxis have a fixed fare of US$9.

Nearly all buses, taxis and pick-ups drop off around Psar Thmei (New Market, also known as Central Market), from where it is a short moto ride (2000r) to any hotel or guest house. Boats arriving from Vietnam or Siem Reap dock on Sisowath Quay and St 104, where moto-madness awaits.

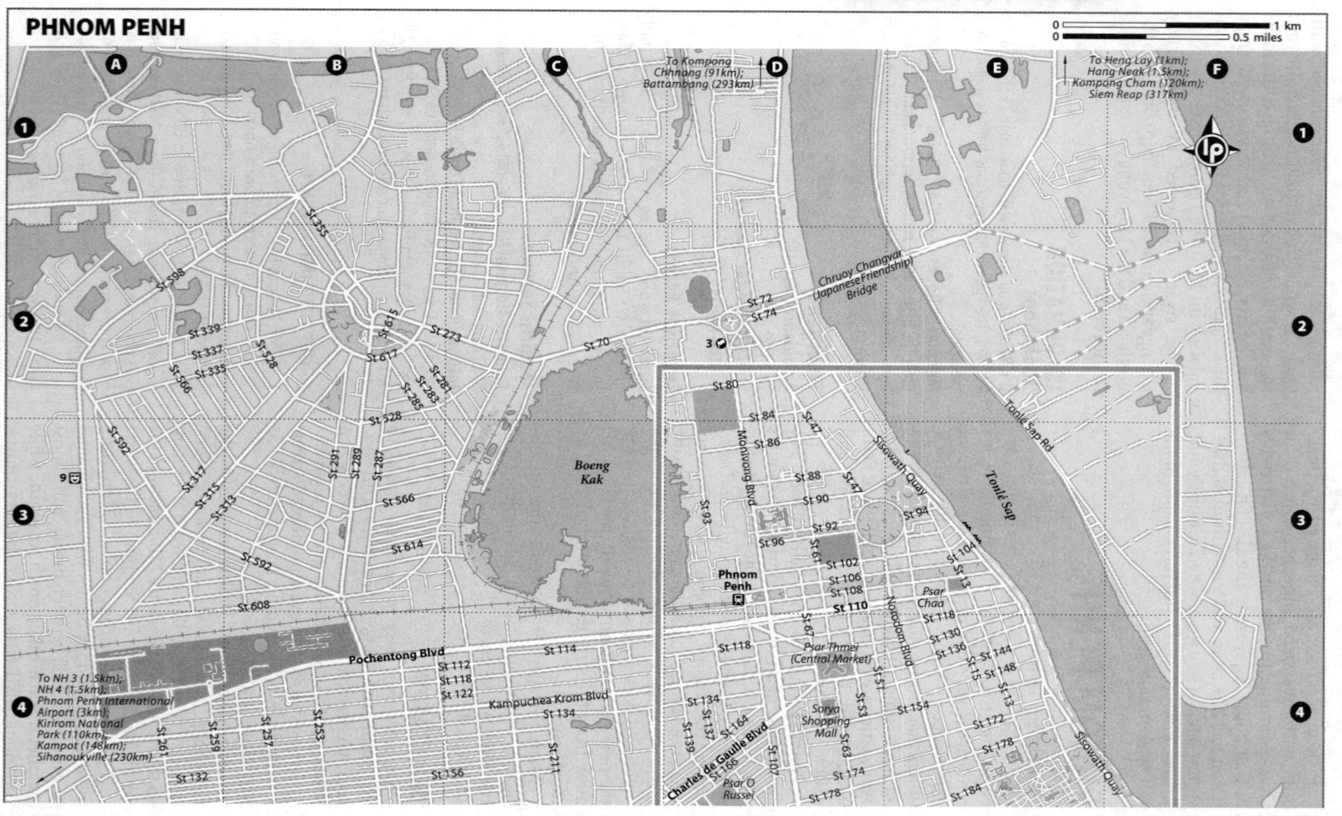
PHNOM PENH
0 1 km
0 0.5 miles
To Kompong Chhnang (91km); Battambang (293km)
To Heng Lay (1km); Hang Neak (1.5km); Kompong Cham (120km); Siem Reap (317km)
To NH 3 (1.5km); NH 4 (1.5km); Phnom Penh International Airport (3km); Kirirom National Park (110km); Kampot (148km); Sihanoukville (230km)
Chruoy Changvar (Japanese Friendship) Bridge
Tonlé Sap
Tonlé Sap Rd
Sisowath Quay
Boeng Kak
Phnom Penh
Psar Chaa
Psar Thmei (Central Market)
Sorya Shopping Mall
Psar O Russei
Monivong Blvd
Norodom Blvd
Charles de Gaulle Blvd
Pochentong Blvd
Kampuchea Krom Blvd
St 355
St 598
St 339
St 337
St 335
St 566
St 528
St 615
St 617
St 273
St 281
St 283
St 285
St 70
St 72
St 74
St 592
St 317
St 315
St 313
St 291
St 289
St 287
St 614
St 608
St 80
St 84
St 86
St 47
St 88
St 90
St 92
St 93
St 94
St 96
St 61
St 102
St 104
St 106
St 108
St 110
St 13
St 118
St 130
St 136
St 144
St 148
St 15
St 67
St 51
St 53
St 63
St 154
St 172
St 174
St 178
St 184
St 134
St 137
St 139
St 164
St 166
St 107
St 114
St 112
St 122
St 211
St 156
St 132
St 261
St 259
St 257
St 253

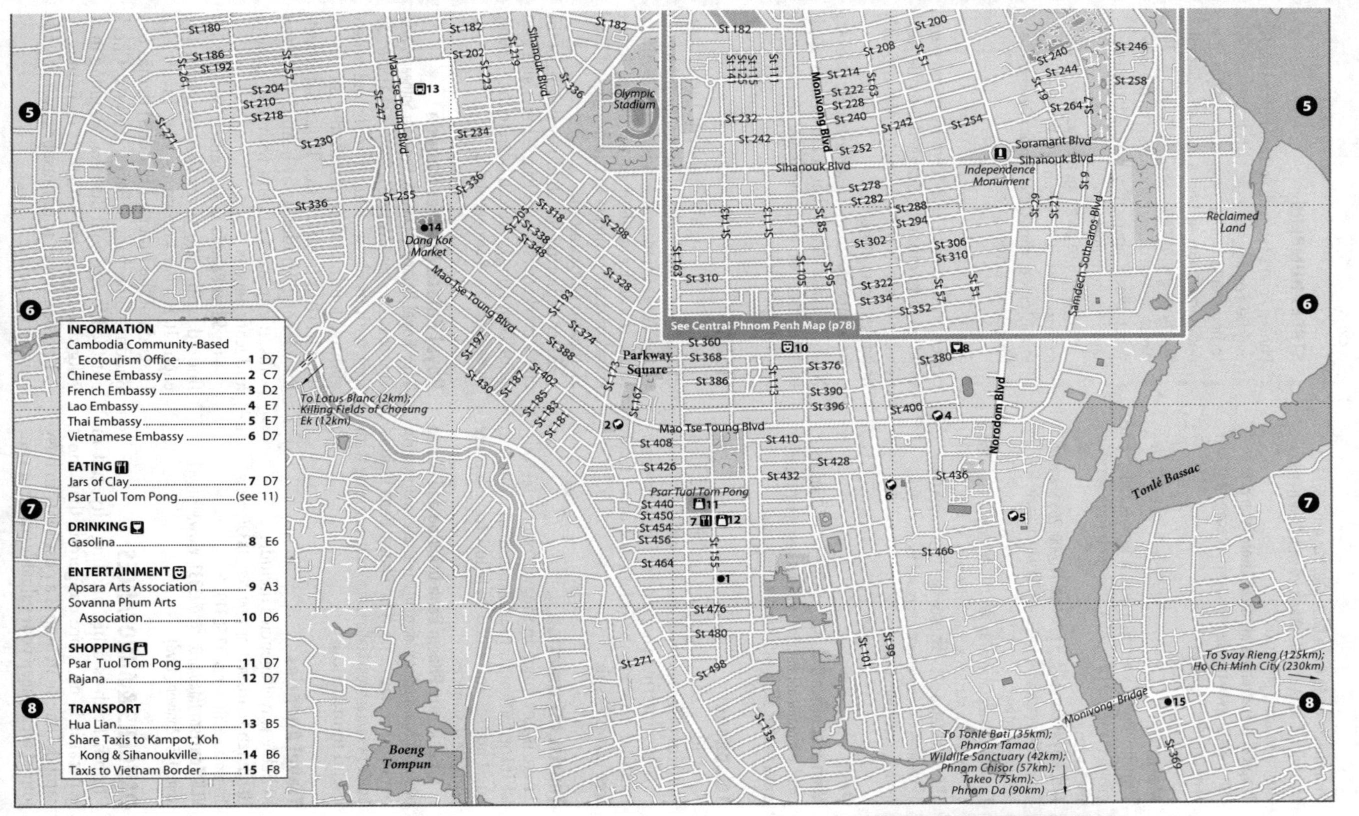
INFORMATION
Cambodia Community-Based Ecotourism Office 1 D7
Chinese Embassy 2 C7
French Embassy 3 D2
Lao Embassy 4 E7
Thai Embassy 5 E7
Vietnamese Embassy 6 D7
EATING
Jars of Clay 7 D7
Psar Tuol Tom Pong (see 11)
DRINKING
Gasolina 8 E6
ENTERTAINMENT
Apsara Arts Association 9 A3
Sovanna Phum Arts Association 10 D6
SHOPPING
Psar Tuol Tom Pong 11 D7
Rajana 12 D7
TRANSPORT
Hua Lian 13 B5
Share Taxis to Kampot, Koh Kong & Sihanoukville 14 B6
Taxis to Vietnam Border 15 F8
See Central Phnom Penh Map (p78)
Olympic Stadium
Independence Monument
Soramarit Blvd
Sihanouk Blvd
Monivong Blvd
Norodom Blvd
Mao Tse Toung Blvd
Samdech Sothearos Blvd
Dang Kor Market
Parkway Square
Psar Tuol Tom Pong
Reclaimed Land
Tonlé Bassac
Boeng Tompun
Monivong Bridge
To Lotus Blanc (2km); Killing Fields of Choeung Ek (12km)
To Svay Rieng (125km); Ho Chi Minh City (230km)
To Tonlé Bati (35km); Phnom Tamao Wildlife Sanctuary (42km); Phnom Chisor (57km); Takeo (75km); Phnom Da (90km)

Pharmacie de la Gare (Map p78; ☎ 430205; 81 Monivong Blvd) A reliable pharmacy with French- and English-speaking pharmacists.
Tropical & Travellers Medical Clinic (Map p78; ☎ 366802; www.travellersmedicalclinic.com; 88 St 108) Well-regarded British-run clinic.

Money

Phnom Penh's airport has a few ATMs. The city has plenty of banks and exchange services, including:
ANZ Royal Bank (Map p78; ☎ 726900; 265 Sisowath Quay) Offers cash advances and ATM withdrawals. Has multiple locations.
Canadia Bank (Map p78; ☎ 215286; 265 St 110) Cash advances with MasterCard and Visa, plus an ATM.
SBC Bank (Map p78; ☎ 990688; 315 Sisowath Quay; 8am-8pm) Convenient hours and location, plus represents Western Union.

Post

Main post office (Map p78; St 13; 7am-7pm) Located in a grand old building, this has increasingly reliable postal services along with pricey express mail.

Telephone

Roadside stalls displaying mobile-telephone prefixes offer cheap domestic calls.

Many internet shops offer low-cost international calls via the internet – or virtually free using Skype.

Tourist Information

There is not much in the way of official tourist information in the Cambodian capital so guest houses and clued-in fellow travellers are your best sources.

Check out **Phnom Penh Drinking and Dining** (www.cambodiapocketguide.com) for the lowdown on bars and restaurants. The **Phnom Penh Visitors' Guide** (www.canbypublications.com) is brimming with useful information.

Travel Agencies

Reliable travel agencies include:
Hanuman Tourism (Map p78; ☎ 218396; www.hanumantourism.com; 12 St 310)
VLK Tourism (Map p78; ☎ 723331; www.vlktravel.com; 195 Monivong Blvd)

DANGERS & ANNOYANCES

Phnom Penh is a big bustling city, but in general it is no more dangerous than most capitals. Bag snatching is a possibility in busy tourist areas; keep your valuables close or concealed, and in case of a drive-by be prepared to let go rather than be dragged into the road, especially if you're on a moto. Avoid poorly lit back streets at night.

Be aware of common-sense traffic rules (eg No Left Turn signs) that seem to only apply to foreigners or you may have to pay some on-the-spot fines.

> **STREET NUMBERS**
>
> Phnom Penh's sequentially numbered streets may be a paragon of logic, but when it comes to house numbering, utter chaos reigns. It's not uncommon to find a row of adjacent buildings numbered, say, 13A, 34, 7, 26. Worse, several different buildings on the same street, blocks apart, may have adopted the same house number!
>
> When you're given an address, try to get a cross-street, such as 'on St 240 near St 51'. In this guide, check the Phnom Penh maps for relevant cross-streets.

SIGHTS

Phnom Penh's sights highlight the contradictions of Cambodia. The stunning legacy of the Angkorian god-kings at the National Museum and grandeur of the Royal Palace stand in stark contrast to the horrors of Tuol Sleng and Choeung Ek.

After exploring the shadowy depths of the city's markets (such as Psar Thmei and Psar Tuol Tom Pong), you can head to the thriving riverfront for a sunset stroll.

Royal Palace & Silver Pagoda

The **Royal Palace** (Map p78; Samdech Sothearos Blvd; admission US$3, camera/video US$2/5; 7.30-11am & 2.30-5pm), with its classic Khmer roofs and ornate gilding, dominates the diminutive skyline of the riverfront, where the Tonlé Sap meets the Mekong. Hidden away behind protective walls, it's an oasis of calm with lush gardens and leafy havens.

The **Silver Pagoda** is so named because it's floored with 5000 silver tiles weighing 1kg each. It is also known as Wat Preah Keo (Pagoda of the Emerald Buddha) thanks to a Buddha statue made of Baccarat crystal. Check out the life-size gold Buddha, weighing in at 90kg, and decorated with 9584 diamonds.

Legs and upper arms must be covered while visiting the palace.

National Museum

A millennium's worth of masterful Khmer artwork, including the world's finest collection of Angkor-era sculpture, spills out from open-air galleries into the inviting inner courtyard of the **National Museum of Cambodia** (Map p78; St 13; admission US$3, camera/video US$1/3; 8am-5pm). The Angkor-era collection includes a giant pair of wrestling monkeys, an exquisite frieze from Banteay Srei, and a sublime statue of Jayavarman VII meditating.

No photography is allowed except in the courtyard.

Tuol Sleng Museum

Once a centre of learning, Tuol Svay Prey High School was taken over by Pol Pot's security forces in 1975, who transformed the classrooms into torture chambers and renamed the facility Security Prison 21 (S-21). At the height of its activity, some 100 victims were killed every day.

Like the Nazis, the Khmer Rouge leaders were meticulous in keeping records of their barbarism and each prisoner who passed through S-21 was photographed. When the Vietnamese army liberated Phnom Penh in early 1979, there were only seven prisoners alive at S-21, all of whom had used their skills – such as painting or photography – to stay alive. Today the long corridors of **Tuol Sleng Museum** (Map p78; St 113; admission US$2, video US$5; 8-5.30pm) display haunting photographs of the victims, their faces staring back eerily from the past.

For more information on Tuol Sleng and the Cambodian genocide, visit the websites of the **Documentation Center of Cambodia** (DC-Cam; www.dccam.org) or Yale University's **Cambodian Genocide Program** (www.yale.edu/cgp).

Killing Fields of Choeung Ek

Most of the 17,000 detainees held at the S-21 prison were executed at **Choeung Ek** (off Map pp74-5; admission US$3; 7am-5.30pm), 14km southwest of Phnom Penh. Prisoners were often bludgeoned to death to avoid wasting precious bullets. When wandering through this peaceful, shady former orchard it is hard to imagine the brutality that unfolded here, but the memorial stupa soon brings it home, displaying more than 8000 skulls of victims and their ragged clothes. See p67 for more on the Khmer Rouge.

Round-trip transport out here will cost US$5 by moto or about US$20 by taxi.

> **READING UP**
>
> For a greater insight into the methodical machine of death that was Tuol Sleng, pick up *Voices from S-21* by David Chandler, a chilling yet incisive description of life in the prison, pieced together from accounts from the tortured – and the torturers.

Other Sights

Occupying the city's highest point (don't get too excited, it's just a 27m-high mound), **Wat Phnom** (Map p78; admission US$1), meaning Hill Temple, is a quiet, shady and incense-infused respite. It is highly revered among locals, who flock here to pray for good luck. Legend has it that in the year 1373, the first temple was built by a lady named Penh to house four Buddha statues that she found floating in the Mekong. Penh's statue is in a shrine dedicated to her behind the *vihara* (temple sanctuary).

Beware of the monkeys as they have been known to bite – and a bite would mean rabies shots as a precaution. Sambo the elephant is available for rides; after his shift he lumbers down the riverfront and stops at various restaurants to collect bananas.

Wat Ounalom (Map p78) is the headquarters of Cambodian Buddhism. The site is peaceful but unexceptional. One eyebrow hair of Buddha himself is held in a stupa behind the main building.

Soaring over the city's largest roundabout is the grand **Independence Monument** (Map p78; cnr Norodom & Sihanouk Blvds), built in 1958 to commemorate Cambodia's 1953 independence from France and now also a memorial to Cambodia's war dead. Modelled on the central tower of Angkor Wat, it was given fancy new lighting in 2008.

ACTIVITIES

Boat Excursions

A variety of private operators offering boat rides up and down the Mekong are stationed along Sisowath Quay. Sunset cruises start at US$10 per hour.

Cooking Classes

You can delve into the secrets of Khmer cuisine by taking a **cooking class** (012-524801; www.cambodia-cooking-class.com; 67 St 240; half/full day

CENTRAL PHNOM PENH
0 500 m
0 0.2 miles
A
B
C
D
1
2
3
4
5
6
Boeng Kak
Phnom Penh
Monivong Blvd
Pochentong Blvd
Kampuchea Krom Blvd
Charles de Gaulle Blvd
Norodom Blvd
Sisowath Quay
Tonlé Sap Rd
Tonlé Sap
Psar Chaa
Psar Thmei (Central Market)
Sorya Shopping Mall
Psar O Russei
National Museum Entrance
Royal Palace & Silver Pagoda Entrance
Sihanouk Blvd
Soramarit Blvd
Samdech Sothearos Blvd
National Assembly
St 80
St 82
St 84
St 86
St 88
St 90
St 92
St 94
St 96
St 102
St 104
St 106
St 108
St 110
St 114
St 118
St 130
St 134
St 136
St 144
St 148
St 154
St 164
St 166
St 172
St 174
St 178
St 182
St 184
St 198
St 200
St 208
St 214
St 222
St 228
St 232
St 240
St 242
St 244
St 246
St 250
St 252
St 254
St 258
St 260
St 264
St 276
St 278
St 280
St 282
St 288
St 292
St 294
St 300
St 302
St 304
St 306
St 310
St 320
St 322
St 330
St 334
St 348
St 350
St 352
St 7
St 9
St 13
St 15
St 19
St 21
St 29
St 39
St 47
St 51
St 53
St 55
St 57
St 61
St 63
St 67
St 75
St 85
St 93
St 95
St 105
St 107
St 109
St 111
St 113
St 115
St 125
St 135
St 137
St 139
St 141
St 143
St 163

INFORMATION

- American Embassy 1 B2
- ANZ Royal Bank 2 C3
- Australian Embassy 3 C5
- Calmette Hospital 4 A1
- Canadia Bank 5 B2
- Canadian Embassy (see 3)
- Cooperation Committee for Cambodia 6 B4
- D's Books (see 74)
- D's Books 7 C4
- Filipino Embassy 8 C5
- German Embassy 9 B5
- Hanuman Tourism 10 C6
- Indonesian Embassy 11 C4
- International SOS Medical Centre 12 C5
- Main Post Office 13 C2
- Malaysian Embassy 14 C5
- Monument Books 15 C5
- Pharmacie de la Gare 16 A2
- SBC Bank 17 D3
- Singaporean Embassy 18 C5
- Tropical & Travellers Medical Clinic 19 B2
- UK Embassy 20 A1
- VLK Tourism 21 A3

SIGHTS & ACTIVITIES

- Himawari Hotel 22 D4
- Hotel Cambodiana (see 22)
- Independence Monument 23 C5
- National Museum of Cambodia 24 C4
- Royal Palace 25 D4
- Seeing Hands Massage 26 C2
- Silver Pagoda 27 D4
- Tuol Sleng Museum 28 A6
- Wat Ounalom 29 C3
- Wat Phnom 30 B2

SLEEPING

- Blue Dog Guesthouse 31 C5
- Boddhi Tree Umma 32 A6
- Dragon Guesthouse 33 A4
- Grand View Guesthouse 34 A1
- Last Home 35 C3
- Narin Guesthouse 36 A5
- Number 10 Lakeside Guesthouse (see 37)
- Number 9 Guesthouse 37 A1
- Okay Guesthouse 38 D4
- Paragon Hotel 39 C3
- Royal Guesthouse 40 C3
- Sky Park Guesthouse 41 A5
- Spring Guesthouse 42 A5
- Sunday Guesthouse 43 A5
- Tat Guesthouse 44 A5
- Top Banana Guesthouse 45 C5
- Waterview Guesthouse 46 C2

EATING

- Bayon Market 47 A3
- Bites 48 A4
- Boat Noodle Restaurant 49 D6
- Boddhi Tree Umma (see 32)
- Cantina 50 D3
- Chiang Mai Riverside 51 C3
- El Mundo Café (see 51)
- Friends 52 C3
- Frizz Restaurant 53 C4
- Goldfish River Restaurant 54 C2
- Happy Herb's Pizza (see 50)
- Kandal House (see 51)
- Khmer Borane Restaurant 55 D3
- Kiwi Bakery 56 C2
- Lazy Gecko Café 57 A1
- Le Rit's (see 10)
- Lucky Supermarket 58 B5
- Mama's Restaurant 59 A4
- Mount Everest 60 C5
- Nature & Sea 61 C5
- Pho Fortune 62 D3
- Psar O Russei 63 A4
- Psar Ta Pang 64 B3
- Psar Thmei (Central Market) 65 B3
- Romdeng 66 B4
- Sam Doo Restaurant 67 A3
- Seven Bright Restaurant 68 C2
- Sher-e-Punjab 69 C3
- Sorya Shopping Centre Food Court 70 B3

DRINKING

- Equinox 71 C5
- Flavour 72 C5
- Fly Lounge 73 C3
- Foreign Correspondents' Club 74 D3
- Green Vespa 75 C2
- Gym Bar 76 C4
- Heart of Darkness 77 B3
- Pontoon Lounge 78 C2
- Rising Sun 79 D3
- Riverhouse Lounge 80 C2
- Salt Lounge 81 C3
- Talkin To A Stranger 82 D5
- Zeppelin Café 83 B4

ENTERTAINMENT

- Memphis Pub 84 C2
- Riverside Bar & Bistro 85 C3

SHOPPING

- Colours of Cambodia (see 74)
- NCDP Handicrafts 86 B2
- Night Market 87 C2
- Nyemo (see 10)
- Psar Thmei (Central Market) (see 65)
- Tabitha 88 C6

TRANSPORT

- Boats to Siem Reap & Chau Doc 89 C2
- Capitol Tour 90 A4
- GST 91 B3
- Lucky! Lucky! 92 B4
- Mekong Express 93 C2
- New! New! (see 92)
- Phnom Penh Sorya Transport (PPST) 94 B3
- Share Taxis, Pick-ups & Minibuses 95 B3
- Tourist Boat Dock 96 C2
- Virak Buntham Express 97 C2

US$12.50/20; half day 9am-1pm, full day 9am-5pm, closed Sun) at Frizz Restaurant (p81).

Massage

'You want massage?' While it's tempting and sounds innocent enough, most Phnom Penh massages involve truly wandering hands – yes, many are of the naughty variety. For a real, rewarding rub, drop by the highly skilled blind masseurs of **Seeing Hands Massage** (Map p78; ☎ 012-680934; 12 St 13; per hr US$5.50). A visit can help you ease those aches and pains – and helps the masseurs stay self-sufficient.

Quad Biking

Nature Cambodia (☎ 012-676381; www.nature-cambodia.com, in French; near Choeung Ek; 1½ hr/half day US$15/35) offers quad biking (ATV trips) in the countryside around Phnom Penh. The quads are automatic, so easy to handle for beginners, and prices are pretty affordable. Despite its proximity to the capital, this is rural Cambodia and very beautiful. Longer trips and jeep tours are also available. Follow the signs to Choeung Ek and it is about 300m before the entrance.

Swimming

Dying for a dip? Don't plunge into Boeng Kak lake, no matter what you've been smoking. Several upmarket hotels offer the chance to escape the heat in a proper swimming pool. Enjoyable options include:

Himawari Hotel (Map p78; ☎ 214555; 313 Sisowath Quay; admission US$10)

Hotel Cambodiana (Map p78; ☎ 424888; 313 Sisowath Quay; admission US$8)

CAMBODIA

DID YOU KNOW?

In 2005 the Phnom Penh municipal government privatised the Killing Fields of Choeung Ek. The city is being paid an undisclosed sum (reported by the BBC to be US$15,000 a year) by a Japanese company, which will manage the site for 30 years and charge admission fees. This arrangement has enraged relatives of victims, who feel the government has sold the memory of their murdered loved ones for a quick profit.

FESTIVALS & EVENTS

The Chinese New Year (p135) and most national holidays (p136) are celebrated with vigour in Phnom Penh. Festivals that are focused primarily on the capital city include:

Royal Ploughing Ceremony This ritual agricultural festival takes place in early May in front of the National Museum. The noses of the royal oxen are said to predict the success of the forthcoming harvest.

Bon Om Tuk (Water Festival) Cambodians flock to the riverfront in late October or November to watch almost 400 boats compete in races on Tonlé Sap. The population of Phnom Penh doubles during this time.

SLEEPING

There's no real Khao San Rd area in Phnom Penh, although some may find this a relief. The Boeng Kak lakefront and the area west of Monivong Blvd have emerged as the most popular backpacker haunts. Boeng Kak's wooden guest houses are perched over water on stilts, a sort of Ko Pha-Ngan without the Gulf of Thailand, but are slated for eventual redevelopment, while the less atmospheric backstreets around Monivong west house hotel-like guest houses with a few more creature comforts. The riverfront is a smarter, if slightly more expensive, alternative.

Monivong West Area

Dragon Guesthouse (Map p78; ☎ 012-239066; 238 St 107; r US$6-12; ❄ 💻) A friendly little guest house, where all rooms include cable TV and bathroom. Free wi-fi with air-con rooms, plus a lively balcony restaurant.

Spring Guesthouse (Map p78; ☎ 222155; 34 St 111; r US$7-12; ❄ 💻) An unfortunate typo on their card says 'bland new building', but it's all about interior comfort and this place has bright, spotless rooms, complete with cable TV.

our pick **Sunday Guesthouse** (Map p78; ☎ 211623; 97 St 141; r US$7-16; ❄ 💻) Rooms are looking pretty smart here and they include wi-fi, which makes for a pretty good deal. The friendly English-speaking staff can help with travel arrangements.

Sky Park Guesthouse (Map p78; ☎ 992718; 78 St 111; r US$8-20; ❄ 💻) High-rise Sky Park is a real bargain for such cleanliness and comfort. Air-con starts at US$12, all rooms have cable TV and hot water, and there's even a lift. Wi-fi is available for a fee.

Other options include:

Narin Guesthouse (Map p78; ☎ 982554; touchnarin@hotmail.com; 50 St 125; r US$3-10; ❄) A long-running family place, Narin still offers some real budget deals, but rooms are quite basic.

Tat Guesthouse (Map p78; ☎ 986620; 52 St 125; r US$3-10; ❄) A friendly, family-run place with cheap and cheerful rooms, plus a breezy rooftop restaurant.

Boeng Kak Area

Despite some solid structures going up in recent years, this rickety area is still slated for redevelopment some time in the future. 'Tis a shame, as the guest houses here have a unique ambience, with wooden chill-out areas stretching over the water. They also offer very basic rooms at extremely cheap prices – though bugs are thrown in for free. Valuables should be kept in lockers, as most rooms aren't very secure.

In case some of the atmospheric lakeside places manage to survive the wrecking ball, make sure you check out: **Number 9 Guesthouse** (Map p78; ☎ 012-766225; St 93; r US$3-10; ❄), the original lakefront guest house, is still a popular place thanks to its blooming plants and billowing hammocks; **Number 10 Lakeside Guesthouse** (Map p78; ☎ 012-725032; 10 St 93; r US$3-10) has a good range of rooms, a mellow waterfront deck and even a boozy boat docked offshore; and **Grand View Guesthouse** (Map p78; ☎ 430766; St 93; r US$5-12; ❄ 💻) is a tall, skinny structure, which offers unrivalled views of Boeng Kak lake.

Central Phnom Penh

Top Banana Guesthouse (Map p78; ☎ 012-885572; www.topbanana.biz; cnr St 51 & St 278; r US$6-15; ❄ 💻) In a great location on a popular corner opposite Wat Langka, this place has a rooftop chill-out area. Cheap rooms have a shared bathroom; more expensive rooms include brisk air-con.

Royal Guesthouse (Map p78; ☎ 218026; 91 St 154; r US$6-12; ❄ 💻) This old timer recently had a major facelift, giving it a whole new lease of life with smart rooms, sparkling bathrooms and tasteful decoration.

Last Home (Map p78; ☎ 012-831702; 21 St 172; r US$7-20; ❄) Tucked away behind Wat Ounalom, the Last Home has a loyal following among regular visitors. Added extras include cable TV and newish bathrooms.

Paragon Hotel (Map p78; ☎ 222607; 219 Sisowath Quay; r US$15-38; ❄ 💻) Set on a lively stretch of the riverfront, this hotel is excellent value for those used to Saigon prices (read: more expensive than PP). All rooms have TV and minibar, plus smart showers. Wi-fi for a fee.

One area that is worth seeking out for those wanting a modicum more comfort is the so-called 'Golden Mile', a strip of hotels on St 278 that all feature 'Golden' in their name. There is little to choose between them, as most offer air-con, cable TV, fridge, hot water and free laundry for US$13/15 a single/double.

Other options:

Blue Dog Guesthouse (Map p78; ☎ 012-658075; 13 St 51; r US$5-13; ❄) A new place offering good-value rooms in an old house very near the St 278 action.

Okay Guesthouse (Map p78; ☎ 012-920556; St 258; r US$7-12; ❄) OK indeed thanks to a popular restaurant, appealing garden and reasonable rooms.

Boddhi Tree Umma (Map p78; www.boddhitree.com; 50 St 113; r US$12-32; ❄ 💻) Some might be spooked by the location opposite Tuol Sleng, but it's a wonderfully atmospheric place with a great garden restaurant (see p82).

Waterview Guesthouse (Map p78; ☎ 215375; waterview.gh@gmail.com; 151 Sisowath Quay; r US$15-30; ❄ 📶) Smart new riverfront guest house with clean and comfortable rooms, some with balconies.

EATING

Some travellers get in the habit of hunkering down on their guest-house balcony, encouraged by proprietors who talk up the dangers of Phnom Penh. Don't do it! Phnom Penh is home to fantastic flavours so make for the markets to dip into cheap Cambodian chow or delve into the city's impressive range of cosmopolitan eateries.

Unless stated otherwise, restaurants are open for breakfast, lunch and dinner.

Khmer

After dark, Khmer eateries scattered across town turn on their Angkor Beer signs, beckoning locals in for fine fare and generous jugs of draft beer. Don't be shy – the food is great and the atmosphere lively. A typical meal will cost just US$2 and a jug of beer is about the same.

The best markets for dining are **Psar Thmei** (Map p78; 🕑 breakfast & lunch), **Psar Tuol Tom Pong** (Map pp74-5; 🕑 breakfast & lunch) and **Psar O Russei** (Map p78; 🕑 breakfast & lunch), which is handy given these are also great shopping venues (see p84). Most dishes cost a reasonable 3000r to 5000r. There are also several areas around the city with open-air food stalls during the early evening – try **Psar Ta Pang** (Map p78; cnr St 51 & St 136; 🕑 dinner) for excellent *bobor* (rice porridge) and tasty desserts.

If the market stalls look a little raw, consider the air-conditioned alternative, **Sorya Shopping Centre Food Court** (Map p78; St 63 & St 154; meals 5000r), located on the 4th floor. *Soup chhnang dei* (cook-your-own soup) is a big thing with Cambodians and a great idea for group dining.

Seven Bright Restaurant (Map p78; ☎ 012-833555; St 13; mains US$1.50-5; 🕑 7am-10pm) This was once Gerard Depardieu's hotel lobby, at least in the Matt Dillon movie *City of Ghosts*. Good Khmer food, likeable location and occasional live music.

Khmer Borane Restaurant (Map p78; ☎ 012-290092; 389 Sisowath Quay; mains US$1.50-5; 🕑 11am-11pm) A great little restaurant for traditional Khmer recipes; choose from *trey kor* (steamed fish with sugar palm) or *lok lak* (fried diced beef with a traditional dip).

Goldfish River Restaurant (Map p78; Sisowath Quay; mains US$2-5; 🕑 7am-10pm) Sitting on stilts over the Tonlé Sap, the menu here offers authentic Cambodian food. Crab with black pepper, and squid with fresh peppercorns are highlights.

Frizz Restaurant (Map p78; ☎ 220953; 67 St 240; mains US$2-5) Cast aside the German sounding name, as this place serves up wonderfully aromatic Khmer cuisine. It also operates cooking classes (p77) for those wanting to learn its secrets.

Other Asian

Boat Noodle Restaurant (Map p78; ☎ 012-200426; St 294; mains 4000-15,000r; 🕑 10am-10pm) This old wooden house, in a leafy garden that brims with water features, offers some of the best value Thai and Cambodian food in town.

Bites (Map p78; 240 St 107; mains US$1-2.50; 🕑 7am-10pm) This is a clean little restaurant in a popular budget area of town that mixes Malaysian, some Padang dishes and international extras.

CAMBODIA

TOP FIVE: GOOD CAUSE DINING

These fantastic eateries act as training centres for young staff and help fund worthy causes in the capital.

- **Friends** (Map p78; ☎ 426748; www.friends-international.org; 215 St 13; dishes US$1.50-7; 🕐 11am-9pm) One of Phnom Penh's best-loved restaurants, this place serves up tasty tapas, heavenly smoothies and creative cocktails. It also offers former street children a head start in the hospitality industry.
- **Lazy Gecko Café** (Map p78; ☎ 012-1912935; 23B St 93; mains US$2-5; 🕐 8am-11pm) Boasting 'homemade hummus just like when mum was dating that chap from Cyprus', this fun place serves international dishes and supports a local orphanage.
- **Le Rit's** (Map p78; ☎ 213160; 14 St 310; breakfast from US$3, set lunch US$5; 🕐 7am-5pm Mon-Sat) The three-course lunch and dinners here are a relaxing experience in the well-groomed garden. Proceeds help disadvantaged women re-enter the workplace.
- **Romdeng** (Map p78; ☎ 092-219565; 74 St 174; mains US$4-7; 🕐 lunch & dinner Mon-Sat) Set in a gorgeous colonial villa with a small pool, the elegant Romdeng specialises in Cambodian country fare, including deep-fried spiders.
- **Lotus Blanc** (off Map pp74-5; ☎ 995660; Stung Mean Chey; set menu US$6; 🕐 12pm-2pm Mon-Fri) This suburban restaurant acts as a training centre for youths who previously scoured the city dump. Run by the French NGO Pour un Sourire d'Enfant (For the Smile of a Child), it serves classy Western and Khmer cuisine.

Chiang Mai Riverside (Map p78; 227 Sisowath Quay; mains US$2-5) Easily overlooked along the ever-glitzier riverfront strip, the Thai food here is delicious and inexpensive. Fish cakes, spicy *laap* (Lao-style salad of meat or fish with lime juice, garlic, spring onions, mint and chilli) and creative curries.

Sam Doo Restaurant (Map p78; ☎ 218773; 56 Kampuchea Krom Blvd; mains US$2-10; 🕐 7am-2pm) Chinese-Khmers swear this has the best food in town. Try the delicious dim sum or signature fried rice.

Sher-e-Punjab (Map p78; ☎ 992901; 16 St 130; mains US$2-10) One of the most reliable Indian restaurants in town. The tandoori dishes here are particularly good as is the chicken manchorian.

Or try these:

Pho Fortune (Map p78; ☎ 012-871753; 11 St 178; mains from US$2-4) Good *pho,* the noodle soup that drives Vietnam forward.

Mount Everest (Map p78; ☎ 213821; 98 Sihanouk Blvd; curries US$2-6) One of the oldest curry houses in town. The menu includes popular Indian and Nepalese dishes.

International

Boddhi Tree Umma (Map p78; 50 St 113; mains US$1.50-6; 🕐 7am-9pm) The lush garden is the perfect place to seek solace and silence after Tuol Sleng, across the road. Includes fusion flavours, Asian dishes, innovative shakes and tempting desserts. Rooms are also available here (see p81).

Kandal House (Map p78; 239 Sisowath Quay; mains US$2-4) A blink-and-you'll-miss-it place on the riverfront, the menu includes home-made pastas, salads and soups, plus a smattering of Asian favourites. Chilled Anchor draft available in pints.

El Mundo Café (Map p78; 219 Sisowath Quay; mains US$2-5; 🕐 6.30am-10.30pm) A mellow riverfront establishment that some say has the best coffee in town. The menu includes a good range of global food, ice cream and pastries.

Cantina (Map p78; 347 Sisowath Quay; mains US$2-5; 🕐 11am-11pm Sun-Fri) The place for tostadas, fajitas and other Mexican favourites, all freshly prepared. It's also a lively bar with professional margaritas and top tequilas.

Nature & Sea (Map p78; 78 St 51; mains US$2-6; 🕐 8am-10pm) Perched on a rooftop above the lively St 278 strip, this is a place to escape the moto madness below. Delicious health shakes, plus savoury whole-wheat pancakes and fresh sea fish in five styles.

Happy Herb's Pizza (Map p78; ☎ 362349; 345 Sisowath Quay; pizzas US$4-7; 🕐 8am-11pm) No, happy doesn't mean it comes with free toppings, it means pizza à la ganja. The nonmarijuana pizzas are also pretty good, but don't get you a free trip.

More international offerings:

Mama's Restaurant (Map p78; St 111; mains 3000-8000r) The cheapest of the international eateries in town, the menu ranges from shepherd's pie to French and even African specials.

Jars of Clay (Map pp74-5; ☎ 300281; 39 St 155; cakes US$1, mains US$2-3; ⌚ 9am-5.30pm Tue-Sat) If the Russian Market (Psar Tuol Tom Pong) becomes too much, this little cafe is a great escape. Home-baked cakes, light bites and thirst-quenching drinks.

Self-Catering

Inexpensive restaurants are often cheaper than self-catering, but for midday snacks or treats from home, supermarkets are perfect. Baguettes are widely available and the open-air markets have heaps of fresh fruit and vegetables.

Bayon Market (Map p78; 133 Monivong Blvd) Small in size, big on selection.

Lucky Supermarket (Map p78; 160 Sihanouk Blvd; ⌚ 7am-9pm) The leading supermarket chain in town, with a professional deli counter.

Kiwi Bakery (Map p78; ☎ 215784; 199 Sisowath Quay) Located on the riverfront strip this is one of the best Cambodian-owned bakeries in town, with cakes from several continents.

Another trick is to call at the bakeries of five-star hotels after 6pm, when cakes are half price.

DRINKING

If it survives the developer's wrecking ball, the Boeng Kak lakeside is a great place for a sunset drink. Laze in a hammock and watch the sun burn red – very romantic. But there is a whole lot more to Phnom Penh nightlife, including some tempting half-price happy hours.

There is quite a 'girlie bar' scene in Phnom Penh, with dozens of places dotted about town. They are pretty welcoming to both guys and girls, although 'I love you long time' should be taken with a pinch of salt.

Foreign Correspondents' Club (FCC; Map p78; ☎ 724014; 363 Sisowath Quay; ⌚ 7am-midnight) Occupying a grand old building with striking views the Tonlé Sap and the National Museum, this Phnom Penh institution is a good place for happy hour (5pm to 7pm), when drinks are half price. There is also food from four corners of the globe.

Green Vespa (Map p78; 95 Sisowath Quay; ⌚ 6.30am-late) Like your local back home, this inviting little place has a huge drinks selection, top pub grub, cracking music and some devilish promotions.

Talkin to a Stranger (Map p78; ☎ 012-798530; 21B St 294; ⌚ 5pm-late Mon-Fri) A popular garden bar with a loyal following thanks to the congenial hosts and their killer cocktails. Regular events include quiz nights and live music.

Flavour (Map p78; 21B St 278; ⌚ 7am-late) Located on the corner of up-and-coming 278 St, this place was always destined to be popular and, with cheap draft beer, has rapidly become a darling of the NGO crowd.

Equinox (Map p78; 3A St 278; ⌚ 11am-late) Close by Flavour (above), this place has a welcoming outdoor bar, plus a balcony hideaway upstairs and a happy hour from 5pm to 8pm.

Zeppelin Café (Map p78; 109 St 51; ⌚ 5pm-late) Who says vinyl is dead? It lives on here thanks to this old-skool rock bar with a serious '60s and '70s music collection.

Gym Bar (Map p78; 42 St 178; ⌚ 11am-late) The only workout going on here is raising glasses, as this is the top sports bar in town. You won't see a better selection of big screens in this part of the world.

Fly Lounge (Map p78; 21 St 148; ⌚ 5pm-late) A new bar that is turning heads. Enter the cocktail lounge, chill out amid cushions and drapes in the middle, and then take a swim in the indoor pool in the small nightclub at the back.

Riverhouse Lounge (Map p78; cnr St 110 & Sisowath Quay; ⌚ 4pm-2am) Almost a club as much as a pub, this atmospheric lounge bar has DJs and live music throughout the week. It's chic and cool, but look out for promotions to keep it cheap.

Pontoon Lounge (Map p78; Tonlé Sap river, end of St 108; ⌚ 4pm-late) Currently *the* in place around town, Pontoon floats in the waters of Tonlé Sap. There are DJs and events throughout the week and the dance floor is rammed.

Heart of Darkness (Map p78; 26 St 51; ⌚ 8pm-late) More the Heart of Business these days, this rowdy nightclub remains a place to see and be seen thanks to the flamboyant Angkor theme.

Other fine establishments with liquid menus:

Gasolina (Map pp74-5; ☎ 012-373009; 56-58 St 57; ⌚ 7am-midnight Tue-Sun) This Latin bar is housed in a spacious villa with a huge garden. Salsa lessons are held on Tuesday, Wednesday and Thursday nights.

Rising Sun (Map p78; 20 St 178; ⌚ 7am-late) Hole-in-the-wall place with excellent pub grub.

Salt Lounge (Map p78; 217 St 136; ⌚ 6pm-late) Sleek, modern and minimalist, this cool cocktail bar is the most gay-friendly in town.

ENTERTAINMENT

For the ins and outs of the entertainment scene, check the latest issues of **AsiaLIFE Phnom Penh** (www.asialifecambodia.com) or **Bayon Pearnik** (www.bayonpe arnik.com).

Dance

Apsara Arts Association (Map pp74-5; ☎ 990621; 71 St 598) Hosts performances of classical dance and folk dance (US$5) every Saturday at 7.30pm. Visitors are also welcome mornings and afternoons from Monday to Saturday to see the students train.

Sovanna Phum Arts Association (Map pp74-5; ☎ 987564; 111 St 360) Impressive traditional shadow-puppet performances (US$5) and classical-dance shows are held here at 7.30pm on Friday and Saturday nights.

Live Music

Memphis Pub (Map p78; 3 St 118; 5pm-1am) The leading live-music venue, with live rock'n'roll from Tuesday to Saturday nights.

Riverside Bar & Bistro (Map p78; ☎ 213898; cnr St 148 & Sisowath Quay; 7am-1am) A popular riverfront bar-restaurant, it often has bands jamming away in the back at weekends.

SHOPPING

Bargains, and bargaining sessions, await in Phnom Penh's lively markets – so put on your haggling hat and enter the fray. **Psar Tuol Tom Pong** (Map pp74-5; cnr St 440 & 163), nicknamed the Russian Market (not to be confused with Psar O Russei), is packed to the rafters with genuine, and not so genuine, Colombia, Gap and other branded clothing at pretty tempting prices. There's also beautiful Cambodian silk, pirated DVDs, CDs and software, and handicrafts. Most market stalls are open between 6.30am and 5.30pm.

A landmark building in the capital, the art deco **Psar Thmei** (Map p78) is often referred to as the Central Market thanks to its location and size. The huge domed hall resembles a Babylonian ziggurat and some claim that it ranks as one of the largest domes in the world. It houses an array of stalls selling jewellery, clothing and curios, and the food section is enormous with produce spilling onto the streets. It is currently undergoing a much-needed facelift with French funding.

Phnom Penh also has its very own **night market** (Map p78; Sisowath Quay; Fri-Sun), which is located at the riverfront end of Sts 106 and 108. It's mainly souvenirs, silks and knick-knacks.

GETTING THERE & AWAY

Air

See p70 for a list of airlines that serve Phnom Penh.

Boat

Speedboats to Siem Reap (US$35, five to six hours) depart daily at 7am from the **tourist-boat dock** (Sisowath Quay), but the tickets are hardly a bargain compared with the bus (opposite).

GOOD CAUSE SHOPPING

These stores sell high-quality silk items and handicrafts to provide the disabled and disenfranchised with valuable training for future employment, plus a regular flow of income:

- **Colours of Cambodia** (Map p78; 373 Sisowath Quay; 9am-6pm) Tucked away underneath Foreign Correspondents' Club (p83), this is a popular fair-trade gift shop that supports NGO craft projects. Lines include silk, wood carvings, T-shirts and jewellery.
- **NCDP Handicrafts** (Map p78; ☎ 213734; 3 Norodom Blvd; 8am-6pm) Run by the National Centre for Disabled Persons (NCDP), the collection here includes exquisite silk scarves, throws, bags and cushions.
- **Nyemo** (Map p78; 33 St 310; 7.30am-4.30pm) Nyemo's focus is on quality silk and soft toys for children, and helps disadvantaged women return to work.
- **Rajana** (Map pp74-5; www.rajanacrafts.org; 170 St 450; 10am-6pm) This place promotes fair wages and training, and offers a beautiful selection of cards, some quirky metalware products, quality jewellery and bamboo crafts. Near the Russian Market.
- **Tabitha** (Map p78; St 51; 7am-6pm) A leading NGO shop with a good collection of silk bags, tableware, bedroom decorations and children's toys. Proceeds go towards rural-community development, such as well drilling.

GETTING TO VIETNAM

Bavet to Moc Bai

The quickest and cheapest way to get to Ho Chi Minh City is to catch an international bus (US$12, six hours). Several companies offer direct services, including Capitol Tour, Mekong Express, Phnom Penh Sorya Transport and Sapaco. There is no change required at the Bavet–Moc Bai border crossing (open from 7am to 10pm), 170km east of Phnom Penh. For information on crossing this border in the other direction, see p914.

Kaam Samnor to Vinh Xuong

The most scenic way to get to Vietnam is to sail the Mekong, crossing the frontier at Kaam Samnor, about 100km southeast of Phnom Penh. Boats can either be picked up in Phnom Penh or – more cheaply – at Neak Luong, a ferry crossing on NH1 that's 60km southeast of the capital and is served by plenty of buses, minibuses and share taxis.

From Phnom Penh, **Ly Kim Hong** (☎ Phnom Penh 016-243767, Neak Luong 099-937229; US$18) departs at 7.30am, while **Hang Chau** (☎ 017-336307; slow/fast US$15/22) sets sail at noon. The more upmarket **Blue Cruiser** (☎ 016-824343; US$35) pulls out at 1.30pm. Fast boats take about four hours, including a slow border check.

From Neak Luong, **Ly Kim Hong** (☎ Phnom Penh 016-243767, Neak Luong 099-937229) runs smallish ferries to the border (US$4, two hours) and Chau Doc (US$8); departure is at 9am or 9.30am. You can also hire a 40HP open motorboat (US$30, 70 minutes) with room for five. The company's Neak Luong dock is on the western shore of the Mekong a few hundred metres south of the ferry landing, behind an almost anonymous house.

From Vinh Xuong, local Vietnamese transport waits to transfer you to Chau Doc, an hour away. For information on crossing this border in the other direction see p921.

Phnom Den to Tinh Bien

NH2 runs 58km from Takeo – linked to Phnom Penh by frequent buses – to the Phnom Den border crossing. Transport options from Takeo include early morning minibuses (5000r), share taxis and motos (US$8). Phnom Penh Sorya Transport runs buses from Psar Thmei. It may be necessary (or quicker) to change to a moto or túk-túk at Kirivong, 8km from the frontier. After walking across the border, motos and taxis can take you to Chau Doc, though beware: we've heard stories of overcharging and scams at bogus bus stations. See p921 for information on doing the trip in the opposite direction.

For information on taking the Mekong to Vietnam, see above.

Bus

An excellent bus network connects Phnom Penh with towns in all but the most remote parts of the country. See specific city and town listings for details on price and journey times. Departures are from bus-company offices.

Some of the leading companies:

Capitol Tour (Map p78; ☎ 217627; 14 St 182) Services to Battambang, Poipet, Siem Reap and Sihanoukville. Plus Ho Chi Minh City.
GST (Map p78; ☎ 012-895550; Psar Thmei) Services to Battambang, Poipet, Siem Reap, Sihanoukville and Sisophon.
Hua Lian (Map pp74-5; ☎ 880761; 217 Monireth Blvd) Far-flung services including to Ban Lung and Sen Monorom in the northeast.
Mekong Express (Map p78; ☎ 427518; 87 Sisowath Quay) Upmarket services to Battambang and Siem Reap, plus Ho Chi Minh City.
Phnom Penh Sorya Transport (PPST; Map p78; ☎ 210359; Psar Thmei) Long-running company serving most provincial destinations.
Virak Buntham Express (Map p78; ☎ 012-322302; St 106) Buses to Krong Koh Kong.

Car & Motorcycle

Guest houses and travel agencies can arrange a car and driver from US$25 to US$60 a day, depending on the destination. See p86 for motorcycle rental details.

Share Taxi, Pick-up & Minibus

With buses so cheap, comfortable and safe, share taxis, pick-ups and minibuses offer few advantages besides flexible departure

CAMBODIA

times. For Kampot, Krong Koh Kong and Sihanoukville minibuses, pick-ups and taxis leave from Psar Dang Kor (Map pp74–5), while for most other places they leave from the northwest corner of Psar Thmei (Map p78). Vehicles travelling to the Vietnam border leave from Chbah Ampeau taxi park (Map pp74–5).

GETTING AROUND

Bicycle

Bicycles can be hired from some guest houses and hotels from US$1 a day.

Moto, Túk-túk & Cyclo

Motos are everywhere, and drivers can often be recognised by their baseball caps. The ones near the tourist areas often speak a good level of street English; others will adamantly nod that they know the destination when they clearly have no clue, so if you don't want to end up in the 'burbs, pay attention and give directions if necessary. Short rides around the city cost 2000r, and US$1 to venture out a little further. At night these prices double. To charter one for a day, expect to pay US$6 to US$8. Túk-túks usually charge double the price of a moto, possibly more if you pile on the passengers.

Cyclos – a dying breed in Phnom Penh, if not in New York and London – cost about the same as motos. Arrange a *cyclo* tour through the **Cyclo Centre** (☎ 991178; www.cyclo.org.uk), dedicated to supporting *cyclo* drivers in Phnom Penh.

Motorcycle

Exploring Phnom Penh and the surrounding areas on a motorbike can be a very liberating experience – provided you are used to chaotic traffic conditions. Motorcycle theft is a problem and if the bike goes bye-bye you'll be liable, so use a hefty padlock. The following places rent bikes! bikes! (100cc to 250cc) from US$4 and US$10 per day:

Lucky! Lucky! (Map p78; ☎ 212788; 413 Monivong Blvd)

New! New! (Map p78; ☎ 012-855488; 417 Monivong Blvd)

Taxi

Phnom Penh now has metered taxis and they are cheap at just US$1 per kilometre. Call **Global Meter Taxi** (☎ 011-311888) as the fleet is small.

AROUND PHNOM PENH

PHNOM TAMAO WILDLIFE SANCTUARY

This **sanctuary** (http://wildlifealliance.org; admission US$5) for rescued animals is home to gibbons, sun bears, elephants, tigers, deer and a bird enclosure. All were taken from poachers or abusive owners and receive care and shelter here as part of a sustainable breeding program.

Getting to Phnom Tamao, about 45km south of Phnom Penh, requires your own wheels or a moto (around US$8). Take NH2 for about 38km, then turn right at the sign. From here, head straight down the sandy track.

TONLÉ BATI

Tonlé Bati (admission US$3) is home to two Angkorian-era temples and a popular lakeside picnic area. Set among flowers and wavering palms, **Ta Prohm** and its bas-reliefs, which depict stories of birth, infidelity and murder, are more evocative than the diminutive **Yeay Peau**. Ta Prohm was built by King Jayavarman VII on the site of a 6th-century Khmer shrine.

Tonlé Bati is 33km south of Phnom Penh, 2km off NH2. Buses going to Takeo (6000r) can drop you here; then find a moto to the temples.

PHNOM CHISOR

Some spectacular views of the countryside are on offer from the summit of Phnom Chisor, although the landscape screams Gobi Desert during the dry season. A laterite-and-brick **temple** (admission US$2; 🕑 7am-6pm), dating from the 11th-century, with carved sandstone lintels, guards the hilltop's eastern face. From atop the temple's southern stairs, the sacred pool of **Tonlé Om** is visible below.

To get to Phnom Chisor, 57km south of Phnom Penh, follow the directions for Tonlé Bati (above), but stay on the bus (8500r) a little longer until the signposted turn-off.

KIRIROM NATIONAL PARK

Set amid elevated pine forests, **Kirirom National Park** (admission $5), 112km southwest of Phnom Penh, offers some winding walking trails that lead to cascading waterfalls (in the wet season). Hiking up **Phnom Dat Chivit** (End of the World Mountain; 2hr) will take you to a cliff with amazing views of the distant Cardamom Mountains.

The Kirirom area is home to a community-based tourism project, the **Chambok Ecotourism Site** (☎ 012-355272; www.geocities.com/chambokcbet), which offers hiking, birdwatching, animal tracking, a visit to a bat cave, ox-cart rides (US$2.50) and bicycle rental (per day US$1.25). If you'd like to stay overnight, **homestays** (per person US$3, plus US$2 per home-cooked meal) are an option. Proceeds go back into the community.

Getting to Kirirom is not easy if you don't have wheels. Sihanoukville buses can let you off at the Kirirom turn-off, but you'll have to find a moto for the remaining 25km west.

SIEM REAP & THE TEMPLES OF ANGKOR

☎ 063 / pop 119,500

Siem Reap is the life-support system for the temples of Angkor, the eighth wonder of the world. Although in a state of slumber from the late 1960s until a few years ago, the town has woken up with a jolt and is now one of the regional hot spots for wining and dining, shopping and schmoozing.

Angkor is a place to be savoured, not rushed, and Siem Reap is the perfect base from which to plan your adventures.

GETTING AROUND

Bicycles are a great way to get to and around the temples, which are linked by flat roads in good shape. Just make sure you glug water at every opportunity. A **Grand Circuit** and a **Little Circuit** are marked on the Temples of Angkor map (pp96–7). See p94 for details on bike rental.

Another 'active transport' option is to head back to basics by hoofing it. Distances obviously limit what you can see on foot but exploring Angkor Thom's walls or walking to and from Angkor Wat are both feasible. Of course, just don't forget to buy an entrance ticket.

Motos (US$8 to US$10 per day, more for distant sites), zippy and inexpensive, are the most popular form of transport around the temples. Drivers accost visitors from the moment they set foot in Siem Reap – you can also find one through your guest house or get recommendations from fellow travellers – but these fellows often end up being friendly and knowledgeable.

Túk-túks (US$12 to US$15 a day, more for distant sites) take a little longer than motos but offer protection from the rain and sun and – if you're so inclined – can be very romantic.

Even more protection is offered by motorcars, though these tend to isolate you from the sights, sounds and smells. Hiring a car in Siem Reap (eg through your guest house) should cost about US$30 for a whole day of cruising around Angkor. Cars cost about US$45 to Kbal Spean and Banteay Srei, US$70 to Roluos and Beng Mealea, and US$90 out to Beng Mealea and Koh Ker.

As in days of old, you can travel by elephant between the south gate of Angkor Thom and the Bayon (US$15; available 8am to 11am) and, for sunset, from the base to the summit of Phnom Bakheng (US$20; available from about 4pm). The elephants are owned by the **Angkor Village** (☎ 963561; www.angkorvillage.com) and are well looked after.

SIEM REAP

At its heart, Siem Reap remains a charming town with rural qualities. Old French shophouses, shady tree-lined boulevards and a gentle winding river are attractive remnants of the past, while five-star hotels, air-conditioned buses and international restaurants point to a glitzy future.

Orientation

Siem Reap's focal point is a right triangle delineated by Psar Chaa (Phsa Chas; meaning 'Old Market') and Sivatha Blvd, the main commercial thoroughfare. From there, Sivatha Blvd heads north to east–west Achar Mean St (Tep Vong St) and to NH6, which leads west to the airport (7km) and east to the bus station (3km). Travelling due north takes you to Angkor Wat (6km) and Angkor Thom (8km). Like Phnom Penh, Siem Reap's street numbering is haphazard, to say the least.

Information

BOOKSHOPS

Some of the cheapest books on Angkor are hawked by local kids and amputees around temples – buying one is a decent way of assisting the disadvantaged. Purveyors of used books in English and other languages include **Blue Apsara Bookshop** (Map p88; ☎ 012-601483; 8am-11pm).

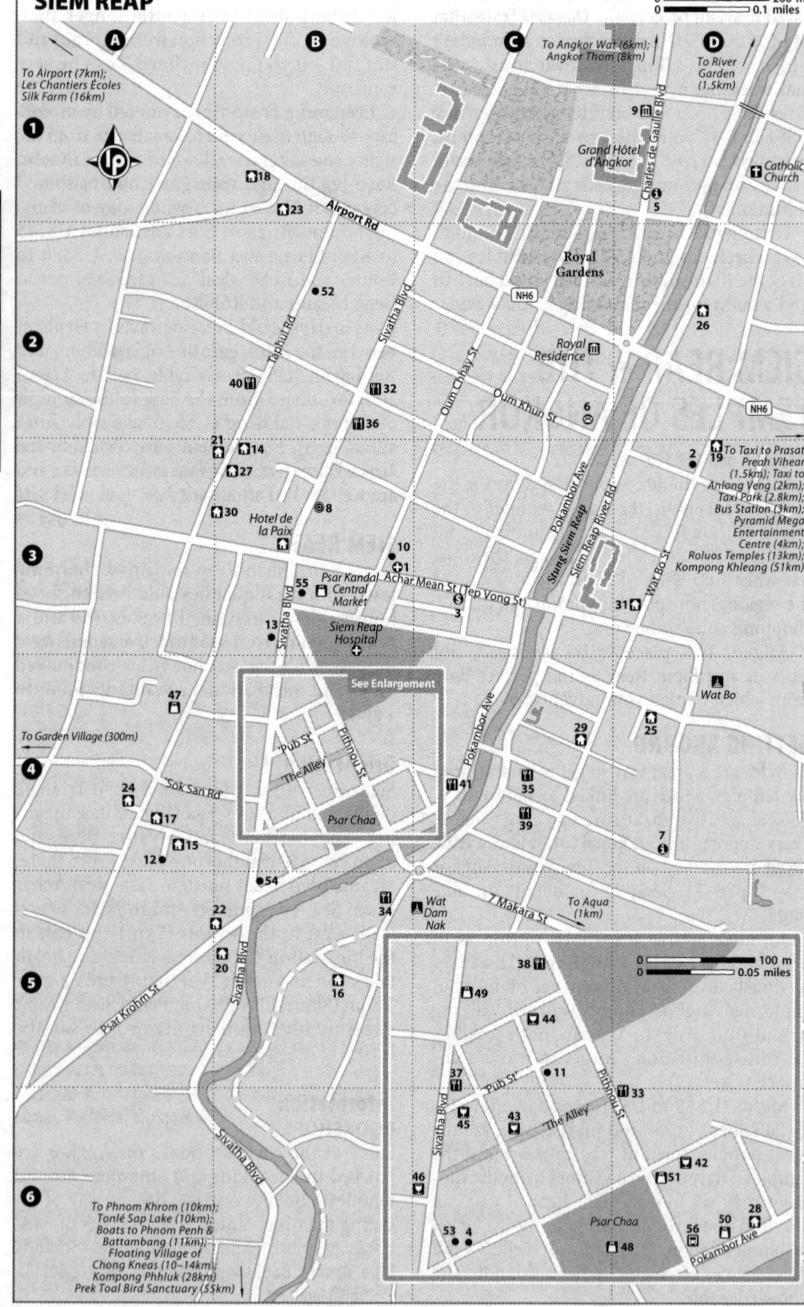
SIEM REAP
To Airport (7km); Les Chantiers Écoles Silk Farm (16km)
To Angkor Wat (6km); Angkor Thom (8km)
To River Garden (1.5km)
Airport Rd
Taphul Rd
Sivatha Blvd
Oum Chhay St
Grand Hôtel d'Angkor
Charles de Gaulle Blvd
Catholic Church
Royal Gardens
NH6
Royal Residence
Oum Khun St
Pokambor Ave
Stung Siem Reap
Siem Reap River Rd
Wat Bo St
To Taxi to Prasat Preah Vihear (1.5km); Taxi to Anlong Veng (2km); Taxi Park (2.8km); Bus Station (3km); Pyramid Mega Entertainment Centre (4km); Roluos Temples (13km); Kompong Khleang (51km)
Hotel de la Paix
Psar Kandal Central Market
Achar Mean St (Tep Vong St)
Siem Reap Hospital
See Enlargement
'Pub St'
'The Alley'
Pithnou St
Psar Chaa
Wat Bo
To Garden Village (300m)
'Sok San Rd'
Wat Dam Nak
7 Makara St
To Aqua (1km)
Psar Krohm St
To Phnom Khrom (10km); Tonlé Sap Lake (10km); Boats to Phnom Penh & Battambang (11km); Floating Village of Chong Kneas (10–14km); Kompong Phhluk (28km) Prek Toal Bird Sanctuary (55km)
Pokambor Ave

INFORMATION
Angkor Hospital for Children 1 B3
Angkor World Travel 2 D3
ANZ Royal Bank 3 C3
Blue Apsara Bookshop 4 C6
EMS .... (see 6)
Khmer Angkor Tour Guide Association 5 D1
Main Post Office 6 C2
Sam Veasna Center for Wildlife Conservation 7 D4
Tourism Information Office .... (see 5)
Wow Web 8 B3

SIGHTS & ACTIVITIES
Angkor National Museum 9 D1
Angkor Palm Restaurant .... (see 33)
Centre for Friends Without A Border 10 B3
Le Tigre de Papier 11 C5
Les Chantiers Écoles 12 A4
Sam Veasna Center for Wildlife Conservation .... (see 7)
Seeing Hands Massage 4 .... 13 B3

SLEEPING
Baca Villa 14 B3
EI8HT Rooms 15 A4
Golden Banana 16 B5
Golden Temple Villa 17 A4
Jasmine Lodge 18 B1
Mahogany Guesthouse 19 D3
Mandalay Inn 20 B5
Mommy's Guesthouse 21 B3
Popular Guesthouse 22 B5
Prince Mekong Villa 23 B1
Red Lodge 24 A4
Rithy Rin Villa 25 D4
Rosy Guesthouse 26 D2
Sala Baï Hotel School 27 B3
Shadow of Angkor Guesthouse 28 D6
Soria Moria Hotel 29 C4
Villa Siem Reap 30 B3
World Lounge Guesthouse 31 D3

EATING
Angkor Market 32 B2
Angkor Palm Restaurant 33 D6
BBQ Restaurants 34 B5
Butterflies Garden Restaurant 35 C4
Curry Walla 36 B2
Food Stalls 37 C5
Happy Herb's Pizza 38 C5
Le Tigre de Papier .... (see 11)
Singing Tree Café 39 C4
Sugar Palm 40 B2
Swenson's Ice Cream 41 C4

DRINKING
Angkor What? .... (see 11)
Laundry Bar 42 D6
Linga Bar 43 C6
Miss Wong 44 C5
Molly Malone's 45 C6
X Bar 46 C6

ENTERTAINMENT
Apsara Dances .... (see 29)

SHOPPING
Angkor Night Market 47 A4
Artisans Angkor .... (see 12)
Psar Chaa 48 D6
Rajana 49 C5
Rehab Craft 50 D6
Senteurs d'Angkor 51 D6

TRANSPORT
Bike Rental Shop 52 B2
Capitol Tours 53 C6
GST 54 B5
Mekong Express 55 B3
Neak Kror Horm 56 D6

CAMBODIA

EMERGENCY

Ambulance (☎ 119)
Fire (☎ 118)
Police (☎ 117)
Tourist police (Map pp96-7; ☎ 012-969991) At the main Angkor ticket checkpoint.

INTERNET ACCESS

Internet shops are everywhere, with the greatest concentration along Sivatha Blvd and around Psar Chaa. More and more restaurants and guest houses are offering free wi-fi.

Wow Web (Map p88; Sivatha Blvd; per hr 3000r; 24hr) Siem Reap's largest internet cafe.

MEDICAL SERVICES

Angkor Hospital for Children (Map p88; ☎ 963409; http://angkorhospital.org; Achar Mean St; 24hr) A paediatric hospital supported by NGOs that's free for anyone under 16, tourists included. Often crowded. Nonemergency hours are 7am to 5pm Monday to Friday and 7am to noon Saturday.

Royal Angkor International Hospital (Map pp96-7; ☎ 761888; www.royalangkorhospital.com; NH6; 24hr) A modern, international-standard facility affiliated with the Bangkok Hospital Medical Center. Call for an ambulance or to arrange a house call by a doctor.

MONEY

There are ATMs at the airport and in banks and minimarts all over central Siem Reap, especially along Sivatha Blvd.

ANZ Royal Bank (Map p88; ☎ 969700; Achar Mean St) Has an ATM and runs the exchange counter at the airport.

POST

Main post office (Map p88; Pokambor Ave) Services are more reliable these days, but it doesn't hurt to see your stamps franked.

EMS (☎ 963446) Express international postal service.

TRAVEL AGENCY

Angkor World Travel (Map p88; ☎ 966669; nkhtour@yahoo.com; 711 Wat Bo St; 8am-8pm) Also handles visa extensions.

TOURIST INFORMATION

Unbelievably, Siem Reap still lacks a helpful tourist office for independent travellers. Guest houses and fellow travellers are the best sources of general information.

Hotels, pubs and restaurants can supply you with the free **Siem Reap Angkor Visitors Guide** (www.canbypublications.com) and two handy booklets produced by **Pocket Guide Cambodia** (www.cambodiapo cketguide.com).

Dangers & Annoyances

Siem Reap is a pretty safe city, even at night. However, if you rent a bike don't keep your bag in the basket, as it will be easy pickings for a drive-by snatch. There are all sorts of commission scams involving guest houses and well-remunerated bus and moto drivers.

CAMBODIA

GETTING INTO TOWN

From the airport, an official moto/taxi/van costs US$2/7/8; túk-túks (US$4 or US$5) are available on the road outside the terminal's parking area.

Fast boats from Phnom Penh and Battambang dock at Chong Kneas, about 11km south of town. A moto into Siem Reap should cost about US$3. Some travellers are taken aback by the sight of their name on a board being furiously waved by a driver – guest houses in Phnom Penh pass on or sell names to guest houses in Siem Reap!

From the bus station, 3km east of the centre, a moto/túk-túk to the city centre should cost about US$1/2. If you're arriving on a bus service sold by a guest house, the bus will head straight to a partner guest house.

Sights

A worthwhile introduction to the glories of the Khmer empire, the state-of-the-art, if pricey, **Angkor National Museum** (Map p88; ☎ 966601; www.angkornationalmuseum.com; 968 Charles de Gaulle Blvd; adult/child under 1.2m US$12/6, audio guide US$3; 🕒 9am-8pm) does an admirable job clarifying Angkor's history, religious significance, and cultural and political context. Displays include 1400 exquisite stone carvings and artefacts. The museum is accessible for people with disabilities.

The **Centre for Friends Without a Border** (Map p88; ☎ 963409; www.fwab.org; Oum Chhay St; 🕒 8am-noon & 1-6pm Mon-Fri, 8am-noon Sat), which opened in late 2008, is a supremely elegant photography gallery; proceeds go to the adjacent Angkor Hospital for Children.

Tucked down a side road, **Les Chantiers Écoles** (Map p88; 🕒 7am-5pm Mon-Fri & Sat morning) teaches traditional Khmer artisanship, including lacquer-making, and wood- and stone-carving to impoverished youngsters; tours of the workshops are possible when school is in session. On the premises is an exquisite shop, Artisans Angkor (p93).

To see the entire silk-making process, from mulberry trees and silk worms to spinning and weaving, visit Les Chantiers Écoles' **silk farm** (off Map p88; 🕒 7.30am-5.30pm), 16km west of town. Shuttle buses leave Les Chantiers Écoles at 9.30am and 1.30pm for a three-hour tour.

The **War Museum** (Map pp96-7; ☎ 012-873666; admission US$3; 🕒 7.30am-5.30pm), 1km north of the Royal Angkor International Hospital, off NH6, displays old mines, rusty Soviet tanks, a Russian-built Mi-8 helicopter and a Chinese-built MiG-19 in a peaceful garden – all bear silent witness to decades of bloodshed.

At the **National Centre for Khmer Ceramics Revival** (Map pp96-7; ☎ 761519; www.khmerceramics.com; NH6; 🕒 8am-6pm), you can see ceramics being turned, decorated and fired using the traditional techniques that were almost lost because of the Khmer Rouge. Situated about 5km west of the town centre and 500m east of the airport turn-off.

The **Cambodian Cultural Village** (Map pp96-7; ☎ 963836; www.cambodianculturalvillage.com; NH6; Khmer/foreigner/child under 12 US$4/11/2; 🕒 8am-7pm Mon-Thu, 8am-8.30pm Fri-Sun) tries to represent all of Cambodia in a whirlwind tour of recreated houses and villages. It may be kitschy and overpriced, but it's very popular with Cambodians, and the dance and music performances will delight children.

On the main road to Angkor Wat, on the grounds of the Siem Reap School for Deaf or Blind, is the **Tonlé Sap Exhibition** (Map pp96-7; 🕒 8am-noon & 1.30-5.30pm), a low-tech but interesting exhibition about the Tonlé Sap ecosystem. Like the adjacent Massage by Blind (below), it is run by the NGO Krousar Thmey.

Modern-day pagodas offer an interesting contrast to the ancient structures of Angkor. On the left fork of the road to Angkor Wat, **Wat Thmei** (Map pp96-7; 🕒 6am-6.30pm), built in 1992, has a memorial stupa containing the skulls and bones of people killed here when the site – once a Chinese school – served as a Khmer Rouge prison. Some of the young monks are keen to practise their English.

Activities

Places offering genuine massages – great relaxation if your feet are feeling frumpy or your back is in knots after all those Angkorian staircases – can be found around Psar Chaa and along Sivatha Blvd. For a work over that will benefit Khmers with disabilities, try **Massage by Blind** (Map pp96-7; per hr US$7; 🕒 9am-9pm), next to the Tonlé Sap Exhibition out towards Angkor, or **Seeing Hands Massage 4** (Map p88; ☎ 012-786894; 324 Sivatha Blvd; per hr fan/air-con $5/7; 🕒 8am-10pm), down a short alley.

A few luxury hotels offer pay-by-the-day access to their swimming pools. Otherwise head to **Aqua** (Map pp96-7; ☎ 092-276799; 7 Makara St; admission US$2.50), a lively little British-run bar-restaurant with a large pool. Situated 1.2km east of Psar Chaa.

Cooking Courses

Cooking classes are a great way to discover the secrets of Cambodian cuisine. Some options:

Angkor Palm Restaurant (Map p88; ☎ 761436; www.angkorpalm.com; Pithnou St; 1/2/3 dishes US$10/15/20) Informal cooking classes from 11am to 3pm.

Cooks in Túk-túks (Map pp96-7; ☎ 963400; www.therivergarden.info; US$25; 10am-1pm) At the River Garden resort (p92). Includes a túk-túk trip to Psar Leu to buy ingredients. Book ahead.

Le Tigre de Papier (Map p88; ☎ 760930; www.letigredepapier.com; Pub St; US$12; 10am-1pm) Great value – and 75% of the profits are donated to worthy causes.

Sleeping

Siem Reap now has more guest houses and hotels (around 200) than there are temples around Angkor – and that's a lot. While accommodation is spread throughout town, three areas hold the bulk of budget choices: the Psar Chaa area; the area north of Achar Mean St; and the east bank of the river. Lots of midrange and top-end hostelries, some of them brand new, line NH6, especially west towards the airport, with more snazzy places north of town towards the temples.

PSAR CHAA AREA

The area south of Achar Mean St, around lively Psar Chaa and west across Sivatha Blvd, has an excellent selection of budget and midrange hostelries.

Red Lodge (Map p88; ☎ 012-963795; www.red-lodgeangkor.com; r US$7-12;) The welcome at this place, which is hidden in a maze of backstreets, is warm and low-key, and the 11 rooms are quiet, spacious and spotless. Free munchies and hot drinks. Reservations are not accepted.

> **DID YOU KNOW?**
>
> The name Siem Reap actually means 'Siamese Defeated' – hardly the most tactful name for a major city near Thailand!

Popular Guesthouse (Map p88; ☎ 963578; chum@camnet.com.kh; Psar Krohm St; r US$8-18;) Popular by name, popular by nature; this sprawling guest house has an all-wood lobby and more than 70 well-tended rooms.

Golden Temple Villa (Map p88; ☎ 012-943459; www.goldentemplevilla.com; r with fan/air-con from US$9/15;) Readers love this place thanks to its funky decor and fun outlook. It's surrounded by a lush garden and has free internet.

Mandalay Inn (Map p88; ☎ 761622; www.mandalayinn.com; Psar Krohm St; r US$9-20;) Burmese hospitality meets Khmer smiles at this smart lodging, with 33 spotless rooms plus free wi-fi and a rooftop gym.

our pick **Shadow of Angkor Guesthouse** (Map p88; ☎ 964774; www.shadowofangkor.com; 353 Pokambor Ave; r US$15-25;) In a grand old French-era building overlooking the river, this friendly, 15-room place offers affordable air-con and free internet.

our pick **EI8HT Rooms** (Map p88; ☎ 969788; www.ei8htrooms.com; r US$20-24;) A smart, gay-friendly guest house with boutique touches, bright silks, DVD players and free internet. Actually 12 rooms now.

NORTH OF ACHAR MEAN ST

Luxury properties tend to be located east of Sivatha Blvd while budget and midrange places are mainly to the west, especially on and around Taphul Rd.

Garden Village (Map pp96-7; ☎ 012-217373; gardenvillage@asia.com; dm US$1, r US$3-12;) This old-fashioned backpacker hang-out offers some of the cheapest beds in town and is a good place to meet travellers. Options among its 70 rooms include eight-bed dorms and US$3 cubicles with shared bathroom. At the rooftop bar beers cost just US$0.50 – nice!

Mommy's Guesthouse (Map p88; ☎ 012-941755; mommy_guesthouse@yahoo.com; r US$4-15;) A family-run, shoes-off affair, this 13-room villa has large rooms with air-con, as well as cheap digs with unheated showers. Homey and welcoming. Situated 30m west of 131 Taphul Rd.

Baca Villa (Map p88; ☎ 965328; www.baca-villa.com; 26 Taphul Rd; r US$8-15;) A Dutch-owned guest house whose 15 rooms are bright, cheerful and comfortable. Sometimes has barbecues out in the garden.

our pick **Sala Baï Hotel School** (Map p88; ☎ 963329; www.salabai.com; 135 Taphul Rd; r US$15-30;) At this four-room training hotel, run by a French NGO, the super staff are ever-helpful and the

CAMBODIA

rooms have some nice extra touches. Open from mid-October to mid-July except for a week around Khmer New Year (April).

Villa Siem Reap (Map p88; ☎ 761036; www.thevillasiemreap.com; Taphul Rd; r US$18-50;) Down-to-earth, Aussie-style service makes this place a popular choice. Runs well-regarded tours.

EAST BANK

This area is quieter than Psar Chaa, with plenty of charm near the river.

World Lounge Guesthouse (Map p88; ☎ 966490; 189 Wat Bo St; r US$4-10;) Painted devil-red so you can't miss it, this welcoming, 21-room guest house has plain rooms decorated in the same fire-engine shade as the exterior, narrow hallways and free internet.

Rithy Rin Villa (Map p88; ☎ 012-677645; rithyrin_villa@yahoo.com; r with fan US$5-10, with air-con US$15-20;) A large modern villa in a quiet part of town, the Rithy Rin is a friendly spot with a good range of big, unadorned rooms, all with pastel walls and TV. Air-con rooms come with fridge and hot water.

Mahogany Guesthouse (Map p88; ☎ 760909; mahoganyguesthouse@online.com.kh; Wat Bo St; r with fan/air-con US$8/15;) With thick mahogany floors, this weathered house – a guest house since the UNTAC days of 1992 – has 15 rooms, all with hot water. A bit of sprucing up, and the addition of TVs and fridges, is planned.

Rosy Guesthouse (Map p88; ☎ 965059; www.rosyguesthouse.com; Stung Siem Reap Rd; r US$8-20;) A British-owned establishment whose 15 sensibly priced rooms come with TV and DVD; the four cheapest are tiny and have shared bathrooms. Has a bustling pub downstairs.

our pick Golden Banana (Map p88; ☎ 012-885366; www.golden-banana.com; r US$23-70;) A mellow place with three sections: 20 B&B rooms set in a banana and bamboo garden; a 10-room boutique hotel; and a mainly gay, 16-room boutique resort. Situated 50m along a paved, well-lit alley. Has wi-fi.

Soria Moria Hotel (Map p88; ☎ 964768; www.thesoriamoria.com; Wat Bo St; r US$40-75;) A Norwegian-owned place with attractive rooms and a rooftop sun deck with spa, jacuzzi and bar. Promotes local causes to help the community.

FURTHER AFIELD

Earthwalkers (Map pp96-7; ☎ 012-967901; www.earthwalkers.no; dm US$5, s/d from US$12/15;) A 20-room backpacker hostel with dorm beds as well as super-clean singles and doubles.

Jasmine Lodge (Map p88; ☎ 760697; www.jasminelodge.com; NH6 west; r US$6-22;) A friendly and fun little guest house, the Jasmine has cheapies with private bathrooms and a range of smarter options. The elevated bar-restaurant includes a pool table. Has free wi-fi.

Prince Mekong Villa (Map p88; ☎ 012-437972; www.princemekong.com; s/d incl breakfast from US$8/10;) Satisfied guests buzz about the range of services provided here: good travel info, wi-fi (US$1 per hour), free laundry and free bicycles.

our pick River Garden (Map pp96-7; ☎ 963400; www.therivergarden.info; r US$44-88;) Set amid an enchanting, junglelike garden, this wood-built resort has 11 atmospheric rooms, wi-fi and cooking courses. Situated 1.5km north of NH6.

Eating

Guest houses boast of extensive menus mixing Khmer classics with comfort food, but hit town to experience a gastronomic extravaganza of Khmer and international flavours – most places won't break the bank and you can keep on rolling for a night on the town. The following establishments represent only a tiny fraction of what's on offer.

Siem Reap's culinary heart is the Psar Chaa area, whose focal point – 'The Alley' – is literally wall-to-wall with good Cambodian restaurants, many family owned. Cheap eats can be found at the **food stalls** (Sivatha Blvd; mains 4000r to 5000r; 4pm-3am) around Pub St's western end.

For self-caterers, markets have fruits and vegies. **Angkor Market** (Map p88; Sivatha Blvd; 7.30am-10pm) can supply international treats such as olive oil and cheeses.

our pick BBQ Restaurants (Map p88; main 7000r; 5pm-11pm or later) Hugely popular with Khmers, this row of no-frills eateries specialises in BBQ beef with *prahoc* (fermented fish) sauce.

Swenson's Ice Cream (Map p88; ☎ 966424; Pokambor Ave; cone US$1.25; 9am-9pm) The best ice cream in town. Inside the Angkor Trade Center shopping mall.

our pick Angkor Palm Restaurant (Map p88; ☎ 761436; Pithnou St; mains US$2-5; 11am-11pm) This award-winning restaurant offers the authentic taste of Cambodia. The *amoc* (baked fish in banana leaf) is legendary; the combo platter (US$7.50) comprises six different dishes. Also offers cooking courses (see p91).

Singing Tree Café (Map p88; ☎ 965210; www.singingtreecafe.com; mains US$2.50-7; ⏲ Tue-Sun) This garden eco-cafe serves scrumptious muffins, coffee and health food, and doubles as a yoga studio and handicrafts gallery. Has free internet access and wi-fi, as well as information on volunteering.

Curry Walla (Map p88; ☎ 965451; Sivatha Blvd; mains US$2.75-6; ⏲ 10am-11pm) For vegie and non-vegie Punjabi Indian food, this place is hard to beat.

Le Tigre de Papier (Map p88; ☎ 012-265811; www.letigredepapier.com; Pub St; Khmer mains US$3-6.50; ⏲ 24hr) Established spot with a wood-fired oven and a great menu of Italian, French and Khmer food. Has cooking classes (p91).

Happy Herb's Pizza (Map p88; ☎ 012-838134; Pithnou St; pizzas US$3-7; ⏲ 7am-11pm) The Siem Reap outpost of a Phnom Penh institution (p82), the 'happy' in question is a somewhat illegal herb that leaves diners on a high. Nonhappy pizzas also available.

Butterflies Garden Restaurant (Map p88; ☎ 761211; www.butterfliesofangkor.com; mains US$3-7; ⏲ 8am-10pm) In a blooming garden aflutter with butterflies, this place serves Khmer flavours (including vegie and vegan) with an international touch. Supports good causes.

Sugar Palm (Map p88; ☎ 964838; Taphul Rd; mains US$4-6; ⏲ 11.30am-3pm & 5.30-10pm) Set in a beautiful wooden house, this is an excellent place to sample traditional flavours infused with herbs and spices.

our pick **Madame Butterfly** (Map pp96-7; ☎ 016-909607; NH6; mains US$4.50-14; ⏲ 5.30-10.30pm or 11pm) One of Siem Reap's oldest houses has been sumptuously decorated with antiques, fine silks and billowing drapes. The menu is Khmer, Asian, French and vegie. Upstairs is especially romantic.

Drinking

Siem Reap rocks. The Psar Chaa area is a good hunting ground, and one street is now known as 'Pub St' – dive in, crawl out.

Laundry Bar (Map p88; Psar Chaa area; ⏲ 1pm-3am) One of the most alluring bars in town thanks to discerning decor, low lighting and a laid-back soundtrack. Happy hour is 5.30pm to 9pm.

Molly Malone's (Map p88; ☎ 963533; www.mollymalonescambodia.com; Pub St; ⏲ 7am-midnight) Siem Reap's first Irish pub brings the sparkle of the Emerald Isle to the Psar Chaa area. Occasionally hosts live bands. Has a guest house.

Linga Bar (Map p88; ☎ 012-246912; www.lingabar.com; 'The Alley'; ⏲ 10am-about 1am) This chic gay bar, colourful, cool and contemporary, has a relaxed atmosphere and a cracking cocktail list.

Miss Wong (Map p88; ☎ 092-428332; ⏲ 6pm-1am or later) A congenial, gay-friendly bar with decor that channels 1920s Shanghai. Tucked away on a side street one block north of Pub St.

Angkor What? (Map p88; ☎ 012-490755; Pub St; ⏲ 6pm-late) Siem Reap's original bar is still serving up serious hangovers every night. The happy hour (to 8pm) lightens the mood for later when everyone's bouncing along to indie anthems, sometimes on the tables.

X Bar (Map p88; ☎ 092-207842; Sivatha St; ⏲ 2pm-5am) Overlooking Pub St, this is *the* late-late hang-out in town. A big rooftop place with wicker chairs and a thatched roof; amenities include a huge TV screen for movies and sports, and pool tables.

One wonder-of-the-world pays homage to another at the glitzy new **Pyramid Mega Entertainment Centre** (Map pp96-7; ☎ 967778; www.pyramid-megaclub.com; NH6), whose **disco** (admission free; ⏲ 7pm-3am or 4am) has a state-of-the-art sound system. Situated about 4km west of town; locals pay 3000r by moto.

Entertainment

Children perform **apsara dances** at 7pm on Fridays at the Soria Moria Hotel (opposite); free with a set menu (US$6/8 for Khmer/Western food).

Shopping

Siem Reap has an excellent selection of fine Cambodian-made handicrafts. **Psar Chaa** (Map p88) is well stocked with anything you may want to buy in Cambodia, and lots you don't. There are bargains to be had if you haggle patiently and with good humour. The **Angkor Night Market** (Map p88; www.angkornightmarket.com; near Sivatha Blvd; ⏲ 4pm-midnight) is packed with silks, handicrafts and souvenirs.

A number of shops support Cambodians with disabilities and the disenfranchised:

Artisans Angkor (Map p88; ☎ 963330; www.artisansdangkor.com; ⏲ 7.30am-7.30pm) One of the best places in Cambodia for quality souvenirs and gifts – everything from silk clothing and accessories to elegant reproductions of Angkorian-era statuary.

Senteurs d'Angkor (Map p88; ☎ 964801; www.senteursdangkor.com; Pithnou St; ⏲ 7am-10pm) Has a wide-ranging collection of silk, stone carvings, beauty products, massage oils, spices, coffees and teas.

Rajana (Map p88; ☎ 965344; www.rajanacrafts.org; Sivatha Blvd; 8am-10pm Mon-Sat, 2-10pm Sun) Sells fair-trade silk, silver jewellery and hand-made cards.

Rehab Craft (Map p88; ☎ 965104; www.camnet.com.kh/rehabcraft; Pokambor St 9am-9pm) Specialises in quality products made of silk and coconut palm wood. Also has original T-shirts.

Getting There & Away

AIR

Siem Reap International Airport (Map pp96-7; www.cambodia-airports.com), an efficient, modern facility 7km west of the centre, is well connected to most neighbouring Asian countries. There are plans to resume flights to Sihanoukville. For details on airlines serving Siem Reap, see p70.

BOAT

Boats for the superb trip to Battambang (see p106) and the rather faster ride to Phnom Penh (US$35) depart at 7am from the new dock at Chong Kneas (off Map p88), 11km south of town. Tickets are sold at guest houses, hotels and travel agencies; pick-up at your hotel or guest house is at 6am or 6.30am.

BUS

All buses depart from the **bus station** (Map pp96–7), which is 3km east of town and about 200m south of NH6. Tickets are available at guest houses, hotels, bus offices, travel agencies and ticket kiosks. Some bus companies send a minibus around to pick up passengers at their place of lodging. Most departures to Phnom Penh are between 7am and 12.30pm; buses to other destinations generally leave early in the morning. Coming into Siem Reap, be prepared for a rugby scrum of moto eager drivers when you get off the bus.

Bus companies that serve Siem Reap:

Angkor Express (Map pp96-7; ☎ 092-523229; bus station)

Capitol Tours (Map p88; ☎ 963883; Psar Chaa area; 6am-8pm) Preferred by many NGO workers.

GST (☎ 092-905016; Sivatha Blvd Map p88, bus station Map pp96-7) No luxuries and reasonable prices.

Mekong Express (Map p88; ☎ 963662; 14A Sivatha Blvd) For a more upmarket service.

Neak Kror Horm (Map p88; ☎ 964924; Pithnou St; 6am-8.30pm)

Phnom Penh Sorya (Map pp96-7; ☎ 012-235618, 092-181800; bus station) Known for its reliable, no-frills service and extensive network.

Tickets to Phnom Penh (six hours), via NH6, cost US$5 to US$11, depending on the level of service (air-con, comfy seats, a toilet, a host), whether foreigners are charged more than locals, and whether there's hotel pick-up. Many companies charge the same price to Kompong Thom as they do to Phnom Penh.

Several companies offer direct services to Kompong Cham (US$6, five or six hours), Battambang (US$6, five hours), Sisophon and Poipet (US$5 to US$6, four hours). GST has a 1.30pm bus to Anlong Veng (US$5, four or five hours).

SHARE TAXI, PICK-UP & MOTO

Share taxis to most destinations stop along NH6 at a point just north of the bus station. Destinations include Phnom Penh (US$10, 4½ hours), Kompong Thom (US$5, two hours), Sisophon (US$5, 2¼ hours) and Poipet (US$7, four hours).

To travel to Banteay Chhmar, head to Sisophon and catch transport from there. For details on getting to Anlong Veng, see p109.

To get to Prasat Preah Vihear (via either Anlong Veng or Koh Ker), catch a share taxi (US$15, five or six hours) or pick-up (in cab/out back US$12.50/10) along NH6 about 1km west of the bus station turn-off (Map pp96–7), ie about 100m east of the ANZ Royal Bank, in front of the Prohm Meas Guesthouse.

Getting Around

For details on ways to explore the temples of Angkor, see p87.

Short moto trips around the centre of town cost 2000r or 3000r (US$1 at night). A túk-túk should be about double that, more with lots of people.

Places that rent out bicycles include the **Bike Rental Shop** (Map p88; ☎ 012-689068; Taphul Rd; city/mountain bike per day US$1.50/2; 6am-9pm), facing the Angkorland Hotel. Various guest houses, including Baca Villa (p91) and the Soria Moria Hotel (p92), rent out **White Bicycles** (www.thewhitebicycles.org; per day US$2), the proceeds of which go to local development projects.

Hiring a moto with a driver costs US$8 to US$10 for the whole day, while a túk-túk is about US$15.

Motorbike hire is prohibited in Siem Reap.

AROUND SIEM REAP

Cambodia Landmine Museum

Popular with travellers thanks to its informative displays on one of the country's post-war curses, the nonprofit **Cambodia Landmine**

Museum (off Map pp96-7; ☎ 012-598951; www.cambodialandminemuseum.org; admission US$1; 7am-6pm) has a mock minefield where visitors can search for (deactivated!) mines. Situated about 25km from Siem Reap and 6km south of Banteay Srei temple. For transport options to the museum and Banteay Srei, see p87.

Floating Villages

The commune of **Chong Kneas** – which groups seven of the Tonlé Sap's 170 floating villages – has become so popular with tourists that it's now something of a floating scam, at least insofar as hiring a boat (a cheeky US$15 or more per person for 1½ hours) is concerned. The small, floating **Gecko Environment Centre** (www.tsbr-ed.org; admission free; 7am-4pm) has displays on the Tonlé Sap's remarkable annual cycle. By moto, the 11km trip from Siem Reap to the Chong Kneas docks costs US$3.

More memorable than Chong Kneas, but somewhat harder to reach, is the friendly village of **Kompong Phhluk**, an other-worldly place built on soaring stilts. In the wet season you can explore the nearby flooded forest by canoe. To get here, either catch a boat (US$50 return) at overpriced Chong Kneas or come via the small town of Roluos by a two-hour combination of road (about US$7 return by moto) and boat (US$18 to US$20 for eight people).

Frankly, the best way to get to both villages is on a tour. A variety of Siem Reap outfits offer day trips, including Villa Siem Reap guest house (p92), which charges US$17.50 to Chong Kneas (three hours) and US$25 to Kompong Phhluk (full day).

Birdwatching & Ecotours

The respected **Sam Veasna Center for Wildlife Conservation** (SVC; ☎ office 963710, bookings 012-520828; www.samveasna.org), based in Siem Reap 250m east of Wat Bo St, runs birdwatching and ecotourism trips that benefit local communities to several globally important sites managed by the **Wildlife Conservation Society** (www.wcs.org). Book at least three days ahead for overnight trips and 24 to 48 hours ahead for day trips.

Nearest Siem Reap – at the northwestern tip of Tonlé Sap – is the 210-sq-km **Prek Toal Bird Reserve**, a seasonally inundated forest unmatched anywhere in Southeast Asia for its dry-season populations of endangered water birds, which include Lesser and Greater Adjutants, milky storks and spot-billed pelicans. An all-day SVC excursion to this ornithologist's fantasyland costs US$98 per person – this includes land and lake transport, meals, fees and guides, making it a very reasonable deal.

Also accessible on an SVC day trip from Siem Reap is the **Ang Trapeng Thmor Reserve**, a wetland bird sanctuary 100km northwest of Siem Reap that's home to the extremely rare Sarus crane, depicted on bas-reliefs at Bayon, and 200 other bird species. Overnight stays are possible.

Villa Siem Reap Tours (Map p88; ☎ 761036; www.thevillasiemreap.com; Taphul Rd) offers 'Day-in-the-Life' village tours (US$30) that let visitors participate in rural activities such as harvesting rice, thatching a roof, making bamboo-leaf wall panels and planting vegies. **Buffalo Trails** (☎ 012-297506; www.buffalotrails-cambodia.com; tours US$25-40) offers sustainable countryside tours.

TEMPLES OF ANGKOR

The ultimate fusion of creative ambition and spiritual devotion, the temples of Angkor are a source of inspiration and profound pride to all Khmers. No traveller to the region will want to miss their extravagant beauty and spine-tingling grandeur.

Some visitors assume they will be templed-out within a day or two, but soon discover the fascinating diversity in design and decoration, which changed significantly from one god-king to another. Come face to face (quite literally) with the Bayon, one of the world's weirdest structures; experience the excitement of the first European explorers at Ta Prohm, where nature runs riot; or follow the sacred River of a Thousand Lingas (Kbal Spean) like pilgrims of old – if any one of these holy sites were elsewhere in the region, it would have top billing. One day at Angkor? Sacrilege! Don't even consider it.

For details on options for getting to and around the temples, see p87.

Angkor Wat

Angkor Wat (Map pp96–7) is the heart and soul of Cambodia. The largest religious structure in the world, it is the Khmers' national symbol, the epicentre of their civilisation and a source of fierce national pride. Unlike the other Angkor monuments, it was never abandoned to the elements and has been in virtually continuous use since it was built.

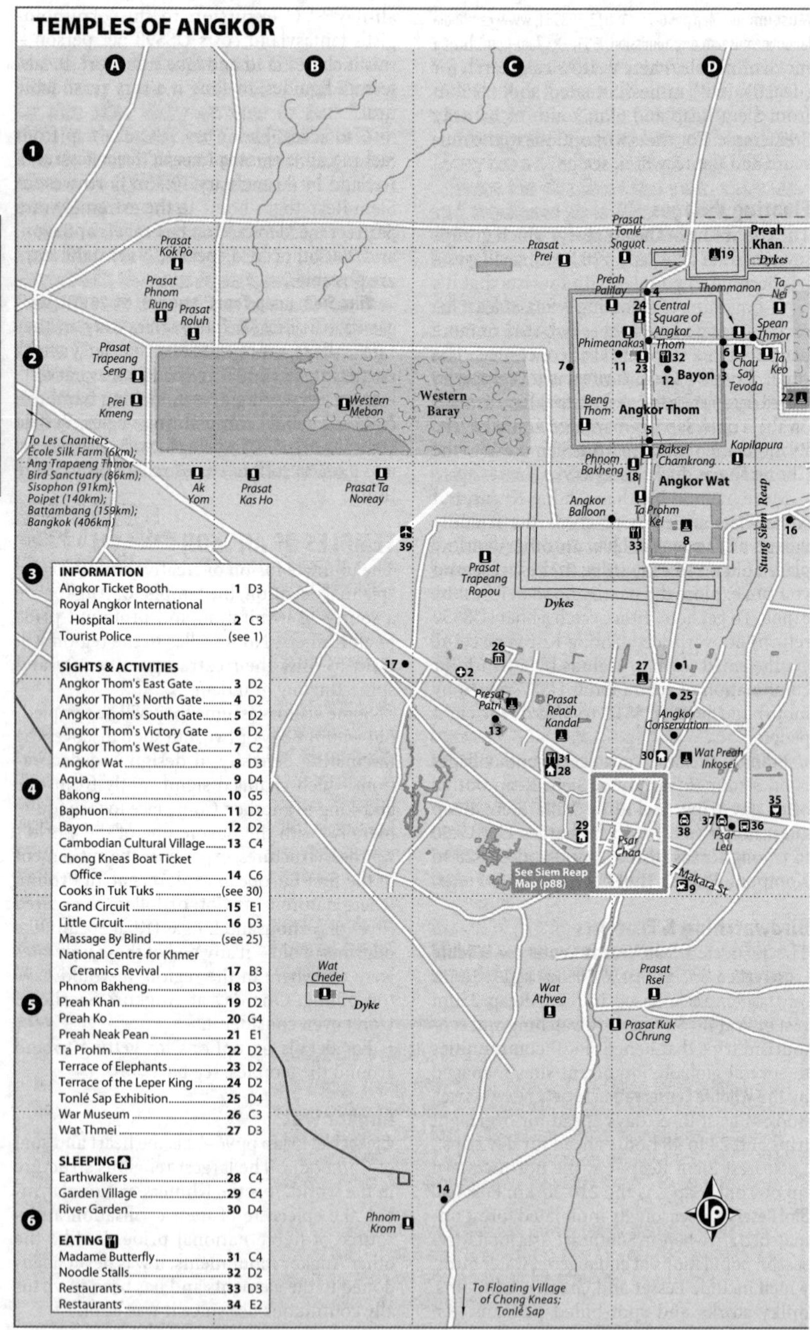

TEMPLES OF ANGKOR
A
B
C
D
1
2
3
4
5
6
Prasat Kok Po
Prasat Phnom Rung
Prasat Roluh
Prasat Trapeang Seng
Prei Kmeng
To Les Chantiers Ecole Silk Farm (6km); Ang Trapaeng Thmor Bird Sanctuary (86km); Sisophon (91km); Poipet (140km); Battambang (159km); Bangkok (406km)
Western Mebon
Western Baray
Ak Yom
Prasat Kas Ho
Prasat Ta Noreay
Prasat Tonlé Snguot
Prasat Prei
Preah Khan
Dykes
Preah Palilay
Thommanon
Ta Nei
Central Square of Angkor Thom
Phimeanakas
Spean Thmor
Ta Keo
Chau Say Tevoda
Bayon
Beng Thom
Angkor Thom
Baksei Chamkrong
Kapilapura
Phnom Bakheng
Angkor Wat
Angkor Balloon
Ta Prohm Kel
Stung Siem Reap
Prasat Trapeang Ropou
Dykes
Presat Patri
Prasat Reach Kandal
Angkor Conservation
Wat Preah Inkosei
Psar Chaa
See Siem Reap Map (p88)
Psar Leu
Makara St
Wat Chedei
Dyke
Prasat Rsei
Wat Athvea
Prasat Kuk O Chrung
Phnom Krom
To Floating Village of Chong Kneas; Tonlé Sap
INFORMATION
Angkor Ticket Booth 1 D3
Royal Angkor International Hospital 2 C3
Tourist Police (see 1)
SIGHTS & ACTIVITIES
Angkor Thom's East Gate 3 D2
Angkor Thom's North Gate 4 D2
Angkor Thom's South Gate 5 D2
Angkor Thom's Victory Gate 6 D2
Angkor Thom's West Gate 7 C2
Angkor Wat 8 D3
Aqua 9 D4
Bakong 10 G5
Baphuon 11 D2
Bayon 12 D2
Cambodian Cultural Village 13 C4
Chong Kneas Boat Ticket Office 14 C6
Cooks in Tuk Tuks (see 30)
Grand Circuit 15 E1
Little Circuit 16 D3
Massage By Blind (see 25)
National Centre for Khmer Ceramics Revival 17 B3
Phnom Bakheng 18 D3
Preah Khan 19 D2
Preah Ko 20 G4
Preah Neak Pean 21 E1
Ta Prohm 22 D2
Terrace of Elephants 23 D2
Terrace of the Leper King 24 D2
Tonlé Sap Exhibition 25 D4
War Museum 26 C3
Wat Thmei 27 D3
SLEEPING
Earthwalkers 28 C4
Garden Village 29 C4
River Garden 30 D4
EATING
Madame Butterfly 31 C4
Noodle Stalls 32 D2
Restaurants 33 D3
Restaurants 34 E2

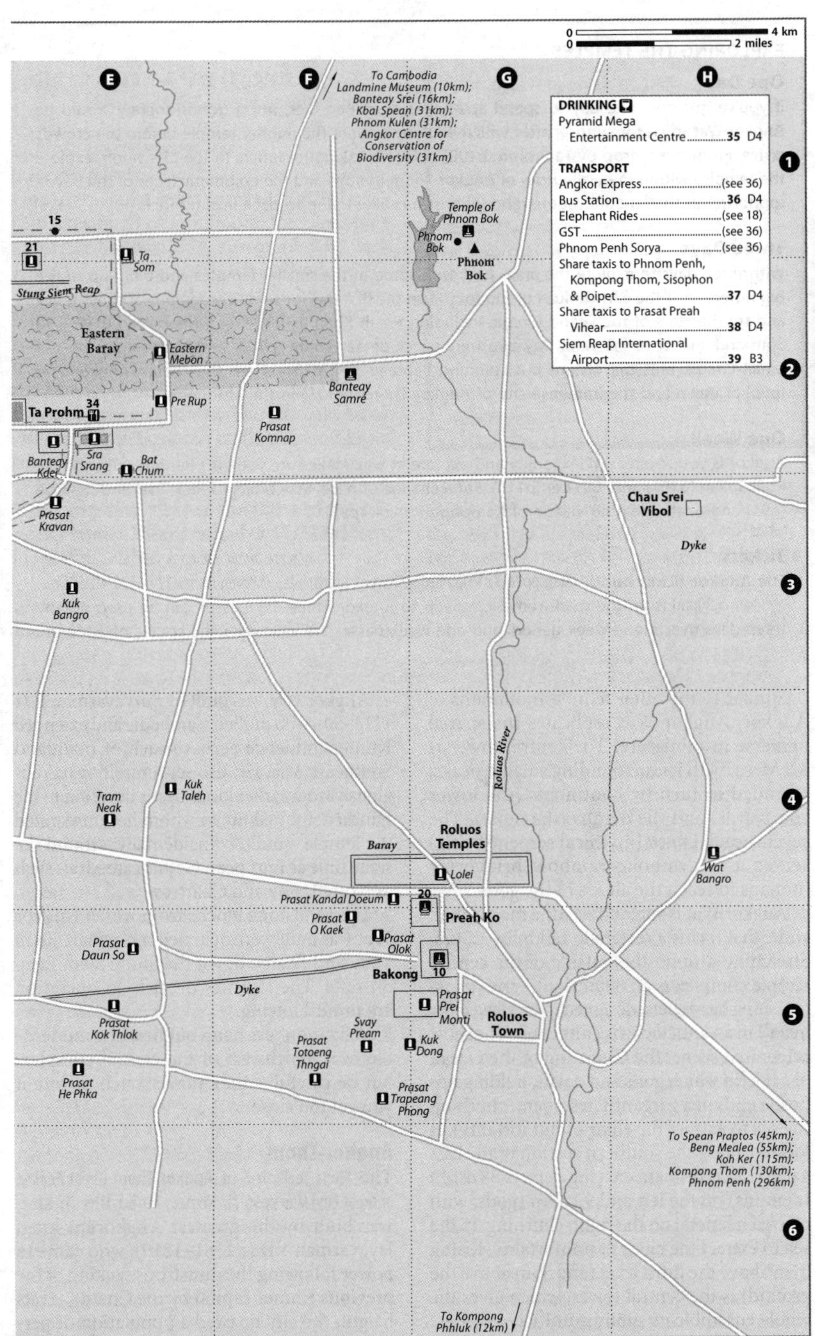
0 4 km
0 2 miles
E
F
G
H
1
2
3
4
5
6
To Cambodia Landmine Museum (10km); Banteay Srei (16km); Kbal Spean (31km); Phnom Kulen (31km); Angkor Centre for Conservation of Biodiversity (31km)
DRINKING
Pyramid Mega Entertainment Centre 35 D4
TRANSPORT
Angkor Express (see 36)
Bus Station 36 D4
Elephant Rides (see 18)
GST (see 36)
Phnom Penh Sorya (see 36)
Share taxis to Phnom Penh, Kompong Thom, Sisophon & Poipet 37 D4
Share taxis to Prasat Preah Vihear 38 D4
Siem Reap International Airport 39 B3
Temple of Phnom Bok
Phnom Bok
Phnom Bok
15
21
Ta Som
Stung Siem Reap
Eastern Baray
Eastern Mebon
Pre Rup
Banteay Samré
Ta Prohm
34
Prasat Komnap
Banteay Kdei
Sra Srang
Bat Chum
Prasat Kravan
Chau Srei Vibol
Dyke
Kuk Bangro
Roluos River
Kuk Taleh
Tram Neak
Baray
Roluos Temples
Lolei
Wat Bangro
20
Prasat Kandal Doeum
Preah Ko
Prasat O Kaek
Prasat Olok
Prasat Daun So
Bakong
10
Dyke
Prasat Prei Monti
Roluos Town
Prasat Kok Thlok
Svay Pream
Prasat Totoeng Thngai
Kuk Dong
Prasat He Phka
Prasat Trapeang Phong
To Spean Praptos (45km); Beng Mealea (55km); Koh Ker (115m); Kompong Thom (130km); Phnom Penh (296km)
To Kompong Phhluk (12km)

CAMBODIA

EXPLORING THE TEMPLES

One Day

If you've got only one day to spend at Angkor, then bad luck, but a good itinerary would be Angkor Wat (p95) for sunrise, after which you can explore the mighty temple before the crowds arrive. From there drop by Ta Prohm (p100) before breaking for lunch. In the afternoon, explore the temples within the walled city of Angkor Thom (below) and the enigmatic faces of the Bayon (opposite) in the late afternoon light. Biggest mistake: trying to pack in too much.

Three Days

With three days to explore the area, start with some of the smaller temples and build up to the big hitters. Visit the early Roluos group (p101) on the first day for some chronological consistency and try the stars of the Grand Circuit, including Preah Khan (p100), Preah Neak Pean (p101), Ta Som and sunset at Pre Rup. Day two might include Ta Prohm (p100) and the temples on the Small Circuit, plus the distant but stunning Banteay Srei (p101). Then the climax: Angkor Wat (p95) at dawn and the immense city of Angkor Thom (below) in the afternoon.

One Week

Angkor is your oyster – relax, enjoy and explore at will. Make sure you visit Beng Mealea (p102), Kbal Spean (p101) and Koh Ker (p110). For a change of pace, take boats to Prek Toal Bird Reserve (p95) and/or the floating village of Kompong Phhluk (p95).

Tickets

The **Angkor ticket booth** (Map pp96-7; 1-day/3-day/1-week tourist pass/children under 12 US$20/40/60/free; 5am-5.30pm) is on the road from Siem Reap to Angkor. Three-day passes can be used on any three days over a one-week period, and one-week passes are valid over the course of a month.

Similar to the other temple-mountains of Angkor, Angkor Wat replicates the spatial universe in miniature. The central tower is Mt Meru, with its surrounding smaller peaks, bounded in turn by continents (the lower courtyards) and the oceans (the moat). The seven-headed *naga* (mythical serpent-being) serves as a symbolic rainbow bridge for humans to reach the abode of the gods.

Angkor Wat is surrounded by a moat, 190m wide, that forms a rectangle 1.5km by 1.3km. Stretching around the outside of the central temple complex is an 800m-long series of astonishing bas-reliefs, designed to be viewed (or 'read') in an anticlockwise direction. The most celebrated scene, the Churning of the Ocean of Milk (in which gods and devils, holding opposite ends of a gargantuan serpent, churn up the sea to extract the elixir of immortality), is located along the southern section of the east gallery. This brilliant carving depicts 88 *asura* (demons) on the left and 92 *deva* (gods; with crested helmets) on the right, churning up the sea to extract the elixir of immortality. Rising 31m above the third level (and 55m above the ground) is the central tower, which gives the whole ensemble its sublime unity.

Angkor Wat was built by Suryavarman II (r 1113–50), who unified Cambodia and extended Khmer influence across much of mainland Southeast Asia. He also set himself apart religiously from earlier kings by his devotion to the Hindu deity Vishnu, to whom he consecrated the temple – built, coincidentally, around the same time as European Gothic cathedrals such as Notre Dame and Chartres.

The sandstone blocks from which Angkor Wat was built were quarried more than 50km away and floated down the Stung Siem Reap on rafts. The logistics of such an operation are mind-blowing.

Wild monkeys hang out near the modern-day wat, northwest of the central complex, but be careful – they may scratch or bite if you get too close.

Angkor Thom

The fortified city of **Angkor Thom** (Great Angkor, or Great City; Map pp96-7), some 10 sq km in size, was built by the greatest Angkorian king, Jayavarman VII (r 1181–1219), who came to power following the disastrous sacking of the previous Khmer capital by the Chams. At its height, the city boasted a population of per-

Tickets issued after 5pm (for sunset viewing) are valid the next day. Tickets are not valid for Phnom Kulen or Beng Mealea. Get caught ticketless in a temple and you'll be fined US$100 to US$300.

Try to be patient with the hordes of children selling food, drinks and souvenirs, as they're only doing what their families have asked them to do to survive. You'll find that their ice-cold bottled water and fresh pineapples are heavenly in the heat.

Eating

There are dozens of local **noodle stalls** (Map pp96-7) just north of the Bayon, and a village with a cluster of **restaurants** (Map pp96-7) about 2km east of Ta Prohm. Angkor Wat has full-blown cafes and restaurants.

Guides

The **Khmer Angkor Tour Guide Association** (Map p88; ☎ 964347, 012-963461; www.khmerangkortourguide.com; Charles de Gaulle Blvd; 7-11am & 2-5pm), based in the Tourism Information Office, can arrange certified tour guides in 10 languages (per day US$25 to US$35), túk-túks (US$12 for eight hours) and cars/minibuses (per day US$30/40).

Tours

One of the best ways to see Angkor's many temples – especially some of the more distant ones – is to take an organised excursion. Ask other travellers for recommendations, or keep an eye out for the tours offered by **Paneman** (www.paneman.org), **Terre Cambodge** (www.terrecambodge.com) and **Journeys Within** (www.journeys-within.com), or the Villa Siem Reap (p92) and River Garden (p92) guest houses.

haps one million, at a time when London was a scrawny town of 50,000. The city's houses, public buildings and palaces, constructed of wood because the right to dwell in brick or stone was reserved for the gods, decayed long ago, leaving us with just a skeleton of extravagantly beautiful religious structures.

The city has five 20m-high gates, one each in the northern, western and southern walls and two in the eastern wall, one of them – due east of the Terrace of Elephants – the Victory Gate. Decorated with stone elephant trunks, they are crowned by four gargantuan faces of Avalokiteshvara (the Bodhisattva of Compassion) facing the cardinal directions. In front of each gate stand statues of 54 gods (to the left of the causeway) and 54 demons (to the right of the causeway), a motif taken from the story of the Churning of the Ocean of Milk.

BAYON

The **Bayon** (Map pp96-7) epitomises the creative genius and inflated ego of Cambodia's legendary king, Jayavarman VII. Its 54 gothic towers are famously decorated with 216 enormous, coldly smiling faces of Avalokiteshvara that – so they say – bear more than a passing resemblance to the great king himself. These huge visages glare down from every angle, exuding power and control with a hint of humanity – precisely the blend required to hold sway over such a vast empire, ensuring that disparate and far-flung populations yielded to the monarch's magnanimous will.

The Bayon is decorated with 1.2km of extraordinary bas-reliefs which incorporate more than 11,000 figures. The famous carvings on the outer wall of the first level vividly depict everyday life in 12th-century Cambodia.

BAPHUON

Some have called this the 'world's largest jigsaw puzzle'. Before the civil war the **Baphuon** (Map pp96-7; observation platform 7am-3pm Mon-Fri) was painstakingly taken apart piece-by-piece by a team of archaeologists, but their meticulous records were destroyed during the Khmer Rouge madness. Now, after years of excruciating research, this temple is finally being restored. Grandly reopened in 2008, its central structure is still closed to visitors – you can glimpse inside from the observation platform.

About 200m northwest of Bayon, the Baphuon is a pyramidal representation of mythical Mt Meru, which marked the centre of the city that existed before Angkor Thom. Construction probably began under Suryavarman I and was later completed by Udayadityavarman II (r 1049–65). On the western side, the retaining wall of the second level was fashioned – apparently in the 15th or 16th century – into a reclining Buddha 60m in length.

TERRACE OF THE ELEPHANTS

The 350m-long **Terrace of the Elephants** (Map pp96-7) – decorated with parading elephants towards both ends – was used as a giant viewing stand for public ceremonies and served as a base for the king's grand audience hall. As you stand here, try to imagine the pomp and grandeur of the Khmer empire at its height, with infantry, cavalry, horse-drawn chariots and, of course, elephants parading across the Central Square in a colourful procession, pennants and standards aloft. Looking on is the god-king, crowned with a gold diadem, shaded by multi-tiered parasols and attended by mandarins and handmaidens.

TERRACE OF THE LEPER KING

This 7m-high **terrace** (Map pp96-7), which once supported a pavilion made of lightweight materials, is topped by a (replica) statue once believed to be that of a leprous king. Researchers now believe it's Yama, the god of death, and that this site served as a royal crematorium.

The terrace's front retaining walls are decorated with at least five tiers of meticulously executed carvings of seated *apsaras* (celestial nymphs), kings with princesses adorned with beautiful rows of pearls, and short double-edged swords. At the base on the southern side, there is narrow access to a hidden terrace that was covered up (and thus protected from the elements) when the outer structure was built. The figures, including *nagas,* look as fresh as if they had been carved yesterday.

Around Angkor Thom

PHNOM BAKHENG

The first of a succession of Angkor temples designed to represent mythical Mt Meru, this hill's main draw is the sunset view of Angkor Wat, though late afternoons here have turned into something of a circus, with hundreds of shutterbugs jockeying for space. Built by Yasovarman I (r 889–910), the **temple** (Map pp96–7) has five tiers, with seven levels (including the base and the summit). At the base there are – or were – 44 towers; each of the five tiers had 12 towers.

Phnom Bakheng is about 400m south of Angkor Thom. For information on elephant rides, see p87.

READING UP

The definitive guidebook to Angkor was long *A Guide to the Angkor Monuments* by Maurice Glaize, first published in French in 1944. It's hard to find, but you can download an English version for free at www.theangkorguide.com.

Among the modern titles, *Angkor: An Introduction to the Temples* by Dawn Rooney is the most popular. Complete with illustrations and photographs, it's a useful companion around Angkor. Another popular title is *Angkor: Heart of an Asian Empire* by Bruno Dagens, with the emphasis more on the discovery and restoration of Angkor; it's lavishly illustrated and dripping with interesting asides.

TA PROHM

If Angkor Wat and the Bayon are testimony to the genius of the ancient Khmers, the 12th-century Mahayana Buddhist temple of **Ta Prohm** (Map pp96–7) reminds us equally of the awesome fecundity and power of the jungle. Looking much the way most Angkor monuments did when European explorers first set eyes upon them, this temple – built from 1186 by Jayavarman VII – is cloaked in dappled shadow, its crumbling towers and walls locked in the muscular embrace of centuries-old trees. Bas-reliefs on bulging walls are carpeted with moss and creeping plants, shrubs sprout from the roofs of monumental porches, and many of the corridors are impassable, clogged with jumbled piles of delicately carved blocks. Indiana Jones would feel right at home – in fact Ta Prohm was used as a set for shooting both *Tomb Raider* and *Two Brothers*.

PREAH KHAN

One of the largest complexes at Angkor, **Preah Khan** (Sacred Sword; Map pp96-7), constructed by Jayavarman VII, once housed more than 1000 teachers and may have been a Buddhist university. The temple itself – a cruciform maze of vaulted corridors, fine carvings and lichen-clad stonework – is within a rectangular wall of around 700m by 800m. The southern corridor is a wonderfully atmospheric jumble of vines and stones, while near the eastern entrance stands a curious two-storey structure that would look at home in Greece.

Unless wet season conditions preclude it, try to enter via the historic east gate so the complex unfolds before you as its architects intended, rather than via the west gate, which is all-too-conveniently right on the main road.

PREAH NEAK PEAN

Another late-12th-century work of – no surprises here – Jayavarman VII, this petite **temple** (Map pp96–7) has a large square pool surrounded by four smaller square pools, with a circular 'island' in the middle. Water once flowed into the four peripheral pools via four ornamental spouts, in the form of an elephant's head, a horse's head, a lion's head and a human head.

Roluos Temples

About 13km east of Siem Reap along NH6, Roluos (then called Hariharalaya) served as the capital of Indravarman I (r 877–89). While the temples here can't compete with the major monuments, they are among the earliest large, stone temples built by the Khmers and mark the dawn of the country's classical art; it's worth visiting them early on in your visit for a chronological insight into the evolution of Khmer architectural ingenuity.

Preah Ko (Map pp96–7) is a direct link to the earlier brick structures of the pre-Angkorian Chenla period, and is comprised of six brick *prasat* (towers) decorated with carved sandstone and plaster reliefs. Erected in the late 9th century, it has elaborate inscriptions in Sanskrit on the doorposts of each tower and some of the best surviving examples of Angkorian plasterwork.

The grandest of Angkor's very early temples, **Bakong** (Map pp96–7) – dedicated to Shiva – consists of a five-tiered sandstone central pyramid (a representation of Mt Meru) flanked by eight towers of brick and sandstone.

DID YOU KNOW?

Much of Thailand's culture is linked to the Cambodian artisans, dancers, scholars and fighters with whom the Thais made off after they sacked Angkor in 1432. Have a peek at the bas-reliefs at Bayon and you'll see something that looks much like the 'Thai' kickboxing of today. The history of Angkor remains a seriously sensitive topic between the two cultures, fuelling a bitter rivalry that's lasted centuries.

Further Afield

BANTEAY SREI

Considered by many to be the jewel in the crown of Angkorian art, **Banteay Srei** (off Map pp96–7) – a Hindu temple dedicated to Shiva – is cut from stone of a pinkish hue and includes some of the finest stone carving anywhere on earth. Begun in AD 967, it is one of the few temples around Angkor not to be commissioned by a king, but by a Brahman, perhaps a tutor to Jayavarman V.

Banteay Srei, located 21km northeast of Bayon and about 32km from Siem Reap, can be visited along with Kbal Spean (below) and the Cambodia Landmine Museum (p94).

KBAL SPEAN

Kbal Spean (off Map pp96–7) is a spectacularly carved riverbed set deep in the jungle about 50km (one hour) northeast of Angkor. More commonly referred to in English as the 'River of a Thousand Lingas', it's a 2km uphill walk to the carvings. From there you can work your way back down to the waterfall to cool off. Carry plenty of water.

At the nearby **Angkor Centre for Conservation of Biodiversity** (ACCB; off Map pp96-7; ☎ 099-604017, 011-426856; www.accb-cambodia.org), trafficked animals are nursed back to health. Free tours generally begin at 1pm daily except Sunday.

PHNOM KULEN

The most sacred mountain in Cambodia, the 487m **Phnom Kulen** (off Map pp96–7) is where Jayavarman II proclaimed himself a *devaraja* (god-king) in AD 802, giving birth to the Khmer empire. A popular place of pilgrimage during weekends and festivals, the views it affords are absolutely tremendous.

Phnom Kulen is 50km from Siem Reap and 15km from Banteay Srei. The private road charges an outrageous US$20 toll per foreign visitor; none of this goes towards preserving the site. You may be able to avoid the toll by walking up on the old pilgrims' path.

DID YOU KNOW?

Banteay Srei means 'Citadel of the Women'; it is said that it must have been built by women because the elaborate carvings are too fine for the hand of a man.

BENG MEALEA

Built by Suryavarman II to the same floor plan as Angkor Wat, **Beng Mealea** (off Map pp96-7; admission US$5) is Angkor's ultimate Indiana Jones experience. Nature has well and truly run riot here – jumbled stones lie like forgotten jewels swathed in lichen, and the galleries are strangled by ivy and vines.

Beng Mealea is about 65km northeast of Siem Reap on a sealed toll road. It can be visited on the way to Koh Ker (p110).

NORTHWESTERN CAMBODIA

Offering a blend of highway accessibility and outback adventure, Northwestern Cambodia stretches from the Cardamom Mountains north to the Dangkrek Mountains, with Tonlé Sap lake in the middle. For details of Siem Reap and the temples of Angkor, see p87.

PURSAT

☎ 052 / pop 57,500

Known for its marble carvers and oranges, this mellow town makes an ideal base for a day trip to the floating village of Kompong Luong (right). Rough roads head from here into the untamed Cardamoms.

Orientation & Information

Pursat's main commercial street, St 3, is two blocks west of St 1, which runs along the riverfront. Both are perpendicular to NH5, where all the buses stop.

Acleda Bank (NH5) Has an ATM.

Pheng Ky Computer (St 1; per hr 3000r; 6am-8pm) Internet access, three blocks north of NH5.

Sights & Activities

For a pleasant stroll, walk north along St 1, cross the river on the vertiginous, Khmer Rouge–era cement **dam**, and then head south along the east bank of the river, where you'll come upon a number of **marble-carving workshops**.

Pursat's own **bamboo trains** – much less tourist-oriented than their Battambang cousins (p105) – stop at the train crossing 800m south of NH5, on the road to Kravanh. A three- or four-hour private excursion costs US$10, or you can hop on with the locals; departures are most frequent in the morning.

Sleeping & Eating

Sopheak Mongkol Guesthouse (☎ 012-584548; NH5; r with 1/2 beds US$4/6) A real cheapie – the 18 rooms, though TV-equipped, are barely larger than a bed and the bathrooms lack sinks. But it's friendly and a hub of activity.

New Toun Sour Hotel (Hotel Thmey Thansour; ☎ 951506; St 2; r US$6-15;) Its lobby chock full of carved wooden doodads, this hotel – popular with the NGO crowd – has 41 large, pleasant rooms.

Mlop Pursat (☎ 012-928586; St 1; soup 3500r; 6-11am or noon) Serves, in its shady garden, Pursat's best breakfast soup.

Community Villa (☎ 951483; mains 8000-22,000r; 7am-10pm) Run by a Cambodian NGO that gives job skills to at-risk young people, this place serves Khmer dishes, including ginger fish; salads; and the best pancakes and *tukalok* (fruit shakes; 2000r) in town. Situated two blocks north of NH5 just off St 2.

The recently rebuilt **market** (St 1) has both daytime eateries and a night market, as well as the usual fruit and vegie stalls.

Getting There & Away

Dozens of buses pass through Pursat daily, shuttling between Poipet (30,000r), Sisophon and Battambang (10,000r, 1½ hours) to the northwest, and Kompong Chhnang, Kompong Cham (35,000r) and Phnom Penh (US$5, three hours) to the southeast. Buses stop along NH5, many about 200m west of the bridge near the Phnom Penh Sorya office. Rith Mony has an early-morning bus to Siem Reap (35,000r).

Share taxis to Phnom Penh (30,000r) can be found on NH5 just east of the bridge; those to Battambang (15,000r) stop in front of the old train station.

The **Phnom Pech Hotel** (☎ 951515; St 1) rents out bicycles (per day US$2.50) and motorbikes (per day US$10).

KOMPONG LUONG

pop 10,000

Kompong Luong has all the amenities you'd expect to find in a large fishing village – cafes, mobile-phone shops, chicken coops, ice-making factories, a pagoda, a church – except that here everything floats! The result is an ethnic-Vietnamese Venice without the dry land. In the dry season, when water levels drop and the Tonlé Sap shrinks, the entire aquapolis is towed, boat by boat, a few kilometres north.

Kompong Luong is between 39km and 44km east of Pursat, depending on the time of year. From Pursat, transport options include moto (return US$7) and private taxi (about US$30 return). At the dock (just south of the new red-and-white telecom tower), the official tourist rate to charter a four-passenger wooden motorboat around Kompong Luong is US$10 per hour.

NORTHERN CARDAMOM MOUNTAINS

The **Central Cardamoms Protected Forest** (CCPF) and adjacent wildlife sanctuaries are slowly opening up to ecotourism, with Pursat (opposite) as the area's northern gateway. This part of Cambodia is still pretty wild: roads are heavily rutted, bridges have holes big enough for a car tyre to fall through, and some areas are still being de-mined. For details on accessing the Cardamoms from the south, see p113.

Conservation International (CI; www.conservation.org) provides technical and financial support to the CCPF's armed enforcement ranger teams, some of whose rough-and-ready ranger stations (eg Kravanh and Rovieng, one and two hours southwest of Pursat, respectively) now welcome overnight visitors. Surrounded by confiscated Toyota Camrys crammed to the gills with raw luxury timber, these have the feel of a remote military outpost and offer only very basic amenities. To stay at a ranger station, contact CI's **Ouk Kimsan** (☎ 012-256777; oukkimsan@yahoo.com) or **Seng Bunra** (☎ 012-835352; sbunra@conservation.org). Enjoyed your stay out here? Write and tell us what you think!

Promoui, the main town in the Phnom Samkos Wildlife Sanctuary (3338 sq km; highest point 1717m), is 125km and 4½ hours from Pursat over a ruinous road. The town has three **guest houses** (r US$5-10) and motos you can hire for forays into the forest.

From Promoui, an even worse track heads south to **O Som** (where there's a ranger station) and **Veal Veng** (where there are several guest houses) – by now you're well and truly out in the sticks. In the dry season, it *may* be possible to hire a moto from Promoui to all the way to the south coast and the Koh Kong Conservation Corridor (p113). In the wet season – fuggedaboutit.

In Pursat, pick-ups to Promoui leave from the **old market** (St 6), a car park two blocks north of NH5.

BATTAMBANG

☎ 053 / pop 140,000

The elegant riverside town of Battambang is home to Cambodia's best-preserved French-period architecture. The stunning boat trip from Siem Reap lures travellers here, but it's the remarkably chilled atmosphere that keeps them lingering. Battambang is an excellent base for exploring nearby temples (see p106) and villages that offer a real slice of rural Cambodia.

Orientation & Information

The focal point of Battambang's city centre, on the west bank of Stung Sangker, is Psar Nat (Meeting Market). The liveliest street on the up-and-coming East Bank is Old NH5.

ANZ Royal (St 1) One of several banks on the periphery of Psar Nat. Has an ATM.

Emergency Surgical Centre for War Victims (☎ 370065; emergency@online.com.kh; 24hr for emergencies) This 106-bed surgical hospital *cannot* help with tropical diseases or routine illness but may be able to save your life if you need emergency surgery, eg because of a traffic accident or appendicitis.

KCT Internet Café (per hr 1500r; 7am-9pm) Internet access.

Polyclinique Visal Sokh (☎ 952401; NH5; 24hr) For minor medical problems, including snake bites, malaria and rabies shots.

Vietnamese Consulate (☎ 952894; St 3; 8-11am & 2-4pm Mon-Fri) Issues 15-day Vietnamese visas (US$35) in 15 minutes; one-month visas (US$40) take two or three days.

Dangers & Annoyances

We've heard reports of persistent locals asking foreigners to come teach English to needy kids – or, in lieu of actually teaching, to make a donation. They then pocket the cash.

Sights

Much of Battambang's special charm lies in its early-20th-century French architecture. Some of the finest **colonial buildings** are along the waterfront (St 1), especially just south of **Psar Nat**, itself quite an impressive structure. There are also some old **French shop houses** along St 3, eg just east of the train station.

CAMBODIA

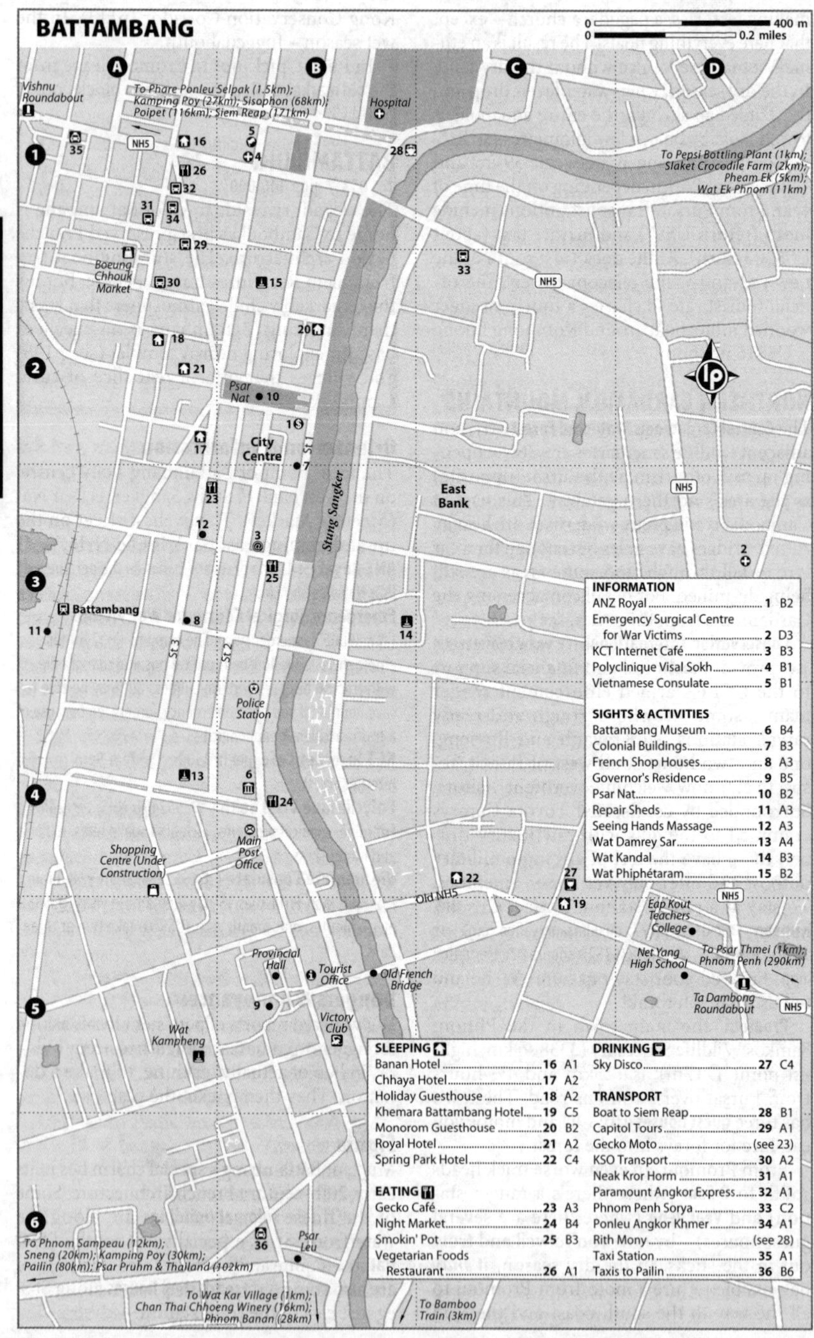
BATTAMBANG
0 400 m
0 0.2 miles
A
B
C
D
1
2
3
4
5
6
Vishnu Roundabout
To Phare Ponleu Selpak (1.5km); Kamping Poy (27km); Sisophon (68km); Poipet (116km); Siem Reap (171km)
Hospital
NH5
To Pepsi Bottling Plant (1km); Slaket Crocodile Farm (2km); Pheam Ek (5km); Wat Ek Phnom (11km)
Boeung Chhouk Market
Psar Nat
City Centre
St 1
St 2
St 3
Stung Sangker
East Bank
Battambang
Police Station
Main Post Office
Shopping Centre (Under Construction)
Old NH5
Eap Kout Teachers College
Net Yang High School
To Psar Thmei (1km); Phnom Penh (290km)
Ta Dambong Roundabout
Provincial Hall
Tourist Office
Old French Bridge
Victory Club
Wat Kampheng
Psar Leu
To Phnom Sampeau (12km); Sneng (20km); Kamping Poy (30km); Pailin (80km); Psar Pruhm & Thailand (102km)
To Wat Kar Village (1km); Chan Thai Chhoeng Winery (16km); Phnom Banan (28km)
To Bamboo Train (3km)
INFORMATION
ANZ Royal 1 B2
Emergency Surgical Centre for War Victims 2 D3
KCT Internet Café 3 B3
Polyclinique Visal Sokh 4 B1
Vietnamese Consulate 5 B1
SIGHTS & ACTIVITIES
Battambang Museum 6 B4
Colonial Buildings 7 B3
French Shop Houses 8 A3
Governor's Residence 9 B5
Psar Nat 10 B2
Repair Sheds 11 A3
Seeing Hands Massage 12 A3
Wat Damrey Sar 13 A4
Wat Kandal 14 B3
Wat Phiphétaram 15 B2
SLEEPING
Banan Hotel 16 A1
Chhaya Hotel 17 A2
Holiday Guesthouse 18 A2
Khemara Battambang Hotel 19 C5
Monorom Guesthouse 20 B2
Royal Hotel 21 A2
Spring Park Hotel 22 C4
EATING
Gecko Café 23 A3
Night Market 24 B4
Smokin' Pot 25 B3
Vegetarian Foods Restaurant 26 A1
DRINKING
Sky Disco 27 C4
TRANSPORT
Boat to Siem Reap 28 B1
Capitol Tours 29 A1
Gecko Moto (see 23)
KSO Transport 30 A2
Neak Kror Horm 31 A1
Paramount Angkor Express 32 A1
Phnom Penh Sorya 33 C2
Ponleu Angkor Khmer 34 A1
Rith Mony (see 28)
Taxi Station 35 A1
Taxis to Pailin 36 B6

The two-storey **Governor's Residence**, with its balconies and wooden shutters, is another handsome legacy of very early 1900s.

The worthwhile **Battambang Museum** (St 1; admission US$1; 8-11am & 2-5pm Mon-Fri) displays Angkorian lintels and statuary from all over the province, including Phnom Banan.

A number of the monks at **Wat Phiphétaram**, **Wat Damrey Sar** and **Wat Kandal** speak English and are glad for a chance to practise; they're often around in the late afternoon.

Around the old train station – where the time is always 8.02 – and along the tracks just south of there, you can explore a treasure trove of crumbling, French-era **repair sheds**, warehouses and rolling stock.

Activities

Battambang's ingenious **bamboo train** (*norry* or *nori*) is actually an ultralight bamboo frame powered by a 6HP gasoline engine – the whole contraption runs along the warped, French-era, single-track rail line. When two click-clacking bamboo trains meet, the less-loaded one is quickly disassembled to let the other one pass. Hiring a private bamboo train from O Dambong (on the east bank 3.7km south of the old French bridge) to O Sra Lav costs US$8; it's much cheaper to take a share-*norry* with locals transporting veggies, charcoal or wood to market. Not to be missed, especially since a planned rail line upgrade will put an end to this delightful transport system.

Phare Ponleu Selpak (952424; www.phareps.org; performance adult/child US$8/4, dinner US$6), a multi-arts centre for disadvantaged children, puts on internationally acclaimed *cirque nouveau* ('new circus') performances, often preceded by dinner (book a day ahead). For dates, see the website or check the sheets posted in hotels and cafes. To get there from the Vishnu Roundabout on NH5, head west for 900m and then turn right (north) and go 600m.

At **Seeing Hands Massage** (092-379903; per hr US$6; 7am-10pm), trained blind masseurs offer soothing work-overs.

Sleeping

CITY CENTRE

Most of the city's veteran hotels are within a few bustling blocks of Psar Nat. The rival Royal and the Chhaya Hotels dominate the backpacker market and can help arrange guides and transport.

Chhaya Hotel (952170; www.chhayahotel.com; 118 St 3; r with fan/air-con from US$4/10) This veteran backpackers' establishment, sprawling and a bit shambolic, has 84 Spartan but serviceable rooms.

Royal Hotel (016-912034; royalasiahotelbb@yahoo.com; r with fan/air-con from US$5/10) Long popular with independent travellers (and for good reason), the 45-room Royal is clean, friendly and very central.

Holiday Guesthouse (017-440448; r with fan/air-con from US$5/10) On a quiet side street just two blocks from the market, this place has 17 spacious rooms with practical wood furnishings. The affiliated, 78-room Holiday Hotel will soon open up around the corner.

Monorom Guesthouse (012-921374; 75 St 1; r with fan/air-con US$5/12) The no-frills rooms at this big, riverfront establishment are a touch fusty, but the price is right for such a central spot.

Banan Hotel (953242; bananhotel@yahoo.com; NH5; r US$15-30) A modern hotel that combines three-star comfort with Khmer-style wooden decor. The 30 rooms come with all the mod-cons.

EAST BANK

Spring Park Hotel (730999; spparkhotel@yahoo.com; Old NH5; r with fan/air-con from US$6/11) Has 94 comfortable rooms, all with either a proper shower stall or a bathtub. Excellent value all around.

Khemara Battambang Hotel (732727; Old NH5; US$12-25) The 32 three-star rooms tastefully mix Khmer and modern design.

Eating

Cheap dining is available in and around Psar Nat (eg in the space between the two market buildings). There's a **night market** (St 1; approx 3pm-midnight) along the river facing the Battambang Museum. A lively restaurant scene is developing on the East Bank, especially along Old NH5.

our pick **Vegetarian Foods Restaurant** (012-642234; mains 1500-3000r; 6am-approx 11am) Some of the most delicious vegetarian dishes in Cambodia, including rice soup and home-made soy milk. Open for breakfast and brunch.

Smokin' Pot (012-821400; vannacksmokinpot@yahoo.com; mains 4500-10,000r; 7am-approx 11pm) This cheery, laid-back restaurant serves good Khmer, Thai and Western food – burgers and fried beef with ginger are favourites. Offers cooking classes (US$8) every morning.

Gecko Café (☎ 092-719985; www.geckocafecambodia.com; St 3; mains US$2.75-5; ⌚ 8am-1pm) A mellow, atmospheric, American-owned bar that occupies the corner balcony of an old French shop house.

Drinking

Sky Disco (☎ 012-862777; ⌚ 8pm-1am) Sky Disco is Battambang's hottest dance venue, with Khmer love ballads in the early evening and house music later on.

Getting There & Away

Battambang is 290km northwest of Phnom Penh.

BOAT

The river boat to Siem Reap (US$18, 6½ to nine or more hours; departure at 7am) – Cambodia's most enchanting boat trip! – squeezes through narrow waterways and passes by protected wetlands that are a birdwatcher's paradise. The service is operated on alternate days by **Angkor Express** (☎ 012-601287) and **Chann Na** (☎ 012-354344). In the dry season, passengers have to be driven to a navigable section of the river. Try to sit as far from the noisy motor as possible.

BUS

Battambang does not have a central bus station. Rather, bus companies have offices and stops on or near NH5 – these include **Capitol Tours** (☎ 953040), **KSO Transport** (☎ 012-320737), **Neak Kror Horm** (☎ 953838), **Phnom Penh Sorya** (☎ 092-181804; NH5), **Paramount Angkor Express** (☎ 092-575572), **Ponleu Angkor Khmer** (☎ 092-517792) and **Rith Mony** (☎ 012-823885). All companies serve Phnom Penh (US$5 to US$8, five hours), Pursat (US$2.50, two hours), Sisophon (US$2 to US$3, one hour) and Poipet (US$3 to US$4, three hours). Capitol Tours and Neak Kror Horm both have buses to Bangkok (US$13 to US$15) and Siem Reap (US$5); Paramount Angkor Express also runs buses to Siem Reap (US$5). Phnom Penh Sorya has a direct service to Kompong Cham (US$9).

TAXI

At the **taxi station** (NH5), share taxis to Poipet (US$5), Sisophon (US$3.75) and Siem Reap (US$7.50) leave from the north side while taxis to Pursat (US$3.75) and Phnom Penh (US$10) leave from the southeast corner.

Getting Around

A moto ride in town costs 1000r to 3000r, a bit more at night.

Hiring a moto driver who speaks English or French costs US$6 to US$8 for a half-day in and around town and US$12 for an all-day trip out of the city.

Gecko Moto (☎ 089 924260; www.geckocafecambodia.com; St 3; ⌚ 8am-7pm) rents out 100cc/250cc motorbikes for US$7/12 a day. The Chhaya Hotel (p105) charges US$5/7 a day for an old/new motorbike; the Royal Hotel (p105) charges US$8.

Bicycles (US$2 a day at Gecko Moto or the Royal Hotel) are a great way to get around and can be ridden along either bank of the river in either direction.

AROUND BATTAMBANG

Before you head out to see Battambang's surrounds, try to link up with an English-speaking moto driver as it really adds to the experience. Possible itineraries include a loop via Phnom Sampeau and Phnom Banan, perhaps with a bamboo train ride (p105) on the way back.

Admission to Phnom Sampeau, Phnom Banan and Wat Ek Phnom is US$2. If you purchase a ticket – sold by the Tourist Police, who have a booth at each site – at one of the three phnoms, it's valid all day at the other two.

A full-day trip by moto/túk-túk to several sites is about US$12/19.

Phnom Sampeau

At the summit of this fabled limestone outcrop, 12km southwest of Battambang (towards Pailin), a complex of **temples** affords gorgeous views. Some of the macaques that live here, dining on bananas left as offerings, are pretty cantankerous.

Between the summit and the mobile-phone antenna, a deep canyon descends steeply through a natural arch to a 'lost world' of stalactites, creeping vines and bats. Nearby, two government artillery pieces still point west towards **Phnom Krapeu** (Crocodile Mountain), a one-time Khmer Rouge stronghold.

About halfway up the hill, a turn-off leads 250m up to the **Killing Caves of Phnom Sampeau**. An enchanted staircase, flanked by greenery, leads into a cavern where a golden reclining Buddha lies peacefully next to a glass-walled memorial filled with the bones and skulls of some of the people bludgeoned to death by Khmer Rouge cadres, before being thrown through the overhead skylight.

Return travel from Battambang by moto/túk-túk costs US$7/10.

Phnom Banan

Exactly 358 stone steps lead up a shaded slope to 11th-century **Prasat Banan**, 28km south of Battambang, whose five towers are reminiscent of the layout of Angkor Wat. Indeed, locals claim it was the inspiration for Angkor Wat! The views are well worth the climb.

From the temple, a narrow stone staircase leads south down the hill to three caves, two of which are not mined and can thus be visited with a torch-/flashlight-equipped local guide.

On the main road from Battambang to Phnom Banan (about midway between the two), in an area famous for its hot red chillies, you can visit Cambodia's only winery, **Chan Thai Chhoeng** (☎ 012-665238).

Return travel from Battambang by moto/túk-túk costs US$8/12.

Wat Ek Phnom

This atmospheric, partly collapsed, 11th-century **temple** is 11km north of Battambang. A lintel showing the Churning of the Ocean of Milk can be seen above the east entrance to the central temple, whose upper flanks hold some fine bas-reliefs. This is a great place for a shady picnic. Return travel from Battambang by moto/túk-túk costs US$6/10.

On the way from Battambang by bicycle or moto, it's possible to visit a 1960s **Pepsi bottling plant** (1.2km north of Battambang's ferry landing), frozen in time since 1975, and, 1km further out, the **Slaket crocodile farm**.

POIPET

☎ 054 / pop 45,000

Long the armpit of Cambodia, notorious for its squalor, sleaze and scams, Poipet (poi-*peh*) has recently applied some thick make-up and deodorant, at least in the border-adjacent casino zone. The Khmers' gentle side is little in evidence here but don't worry – the rest of the country does not carry on like this.

There's a **Canadia Bank** (NH5) 1km east of the roundabout and an **ANZ Bank** (NH5) 500m further east. ANZ Bank has ATMs at the border. Internet shops can be found along NH5.

Sleeping

Cheap guest houses, some of them brothels, are strung out along NH5 and around the bus station. If you have no choice but to overnight here, **Huy Kea Hotel** (☎ 012-346333; NH5; r 200B-500B; ❄), convenient to the border, the bus station and the market, has clean rooms for various prices.

Getting There & Away

Poipet is 48km west of Sisophon and 153km west of Siem Reap.

As of this writing, transport out of Poipet for foreigners (but not locals) is the official monopoly of **Oudom Rithy Tour & Transport** (☎ 012-722735), which has become notorious for hounding travellers, scaring off independent taxi drivers and using a variety of excuses (some of them true) to convince new arrivals to head straight to a bus station they control; often, a 'free shuttle' is laid on. Once there, your only option is to pay inflated prices. Poipet is famous for its audacious scams but the novelty of this one is that it's a recognised government concession.

BUS

All buses depart from the bus station (Tourist Lounge; NH5), controlled by Oudom Rithy. It's supposed to move to a site east of Poipet but, as of this writing, was still in town; from the border roundabout, go 1.3km east along NH5 and then 200m north.

Bus companies – including **Capitol Tour** (☎ 012-774361), **Phnom Penh Sorya** (☎ 092-181802) and **GST** (☎ 012-727771) – have roadside offices along NH5 near the turn-off to the bus station. Destinations include Sisophon (100B, 40 minutes), Siem Reap (200B; five hours), Battambang (150B to 200B, 2½ to three hours), Kompong Cham (450B, 10 hours) and Phnom Penh (300B, eight hours). All departures are between 6.15am and 8am; if you're heading east, your only options after that are a taxi or a hotel. Companies with mid-afternoon services to Bangkok (300B) include Capitol.

TAXI

Six-person share taxis – some of them Thai right-hand-drives that provide front-seat passengers the 'thrill' of seeing oncoming traffic before the driver can – are available all day long along NH5 about 1.3km east of the roundabout (near the bus station turn-off).

GETTING TO THAILAND: PSAR PRUHM TO DAN LEM

This out-of-the-way crossing is 102km southwest of Battambang and 22km northwest of Pailin. To enter Thailand here you *must* be able to produce an onward ticket out of Thailand; travellers report that e-tickets are being accepted.

In Battambang, taxis leave for Pailin and the border from the west side of Psar Leu (at the southern end of St 3) but be prepared – in the wet season NH57 often becomes an unholy mess. A share taxi to Pailin town (two hours in the dry season, double that in the wet) costs 25,000r; pick-ups are US$5/2.50 inside/out-back. An onward share taxi from Pailin to the frontier (which is open from 7am to 5pm) costs US$2.

On the Thai side, you can avoid being overcharged for transport to Chanthaburi (one hour) by hopping on a moto (50B) to the nearby *sŏrng tăaou* (pick-up) station. From Chanthaburi's bus station there are buses to Bangkok.

See p785 for information on doing the trip in the reverse direction.

Destinations include Sisophon (100B, 40 minutes), Siem Reap (250B, three hours), Battambang (US$5 to 200B, two hours) and Phnom Penh (500B). At the bus station, the Oudom Rithy monopoly (p107) charges higher prices for four-passenger share taxis, surpassing even its own posted fee schedule when it can get away with it.

SISOPHON

☎054 / pop 98,800

This town, strategically situated at northwest Cambodia's great crossroads, the intersection of NH5 and NH6, is the perfect base for a trip to the Angkorian temples of Banteay Chhmar (right). It's also a good transfer point for those heading to Phnom Penh via Battambang. Several internet places can be found along NH6 east of NH5.

Roeung Rong Hotel (☎092-260515; NH5; r US$5-11; ❄) is a family-run place just west of the NH5–NH6 intersection, with 24 simple but decent rooms. The karaoke brothel out back is kept separate from the hotel.

Long-haul buses and most share taxis stop at the bus station, about 400m south of NH6 (a new bus station is being built near the old one). Companies including **Capitol Tour** (☎012-525782), **Paramount Angkor Express** (☎092-575571) and **Angkor Khmer Transport** (☎092-185059) serve Poipet (100B), Siem Reap (US$6 to US$7.50), Battambang (100B), Phnom Penh (US$6 to US$8.50) and Bangkok (US$15). Buses heading west depart between 6.30am and 10.30am; buses to Poipet and Bangkok leave in the early afternoon.

Share taxis link the bus station with Phnom Penh (US$10, five hours), Siem Reap (US$5) and Battambang (100B, one hour); a private taxi to Siem Reap costs US$25. Share taxis to Poipet (100r, 40 minutes) stop on NH5 across the street from the Roeung Rong Hotel. For details on getting to Banteay Chhmar, see below.

BANTEAY CHHMAR

The 12th-century temple complex of **Banteay Chhmar** (www.globalheritagefund.org; admission US$5) is renowned for its intricate carvings, including two multi-armed Avalokiteshvaras and a bas-relief that dramatically depicts naval warfare between the Khmers (on the left) and the Chams (on the right).

A pioneering community-based **homestay project** (☎012-435660, 092-599115; cbtbanteaychhmar@yahoo.com; r US$7) makes it possible to stay in and around Banteay Chhmar. Rooms come with mosquito nets, fans that run when there's electricity (6pm to 10pm) and downstairs bathrooms. Bikes can be rented for US$1.50 a day.

In Sisophon, share taxis to Banteay Chhmar (61km via a terrible road) leave from near Psar Thmei, on NH69 1km north of NH6. A moto from Sisophon to Banteay Chhmar should cost about US$12 return. There's no public transport from Banteay Chhmar northeast to Samraong, though the road is in great shape.

ANLONG VENG

For almost a decade this dusty town served as the military headquarters of the most notorious leaders of Democratic Kampuchea. For those with a keen interest in contemporary Cambodian history, the Khmer Rouge sites around Anlong Veng are an important – if troubling and enigmatic – part of the picture.

There are no ATMs or internet shops.

Khmer Rouge Sites

Pol Pot's military enforcer, Ta Mok, was responsible for thousands of deaths in successive purges during the terrible years of Democratic Kampuchea. Widely known as 'The Butcher', he was arrested in 1999 and died in July 2006 while awaiting trial for genocide and crimes against humanity. **Ta Mok's house** (admission incl English tour US$2), a Spartan structure decorated with childish murals, is on a peaceful lakeside site 2km north of the roundabout and then a few hundred metres east.

Ta Mok's grave, next to a modest pagoda, is 7km further north in Tumnup Leu. Further north still, about 2km before the frontier, look out for a group of **statues** – hewn entirely from the surrounding rock by the Khmer Rouge – depicting a woman and two uniformed Khmer Rouge soldiers.

A few hundred metres before the frontier, under a rusted corrugated iron roof, is the **cremation site of Pol Pot**, who was hastily burned in 1998 (shortly before the Khmer Rouge's final surrender) on a pile of old tyres and rubbish – a fittingly inglorious end, some say.

From the frontier smugglers' market, a dirt road heads east between minefields, parallel to the escarpment. After about 4km you come to another **Ta Mok residence**, the cement shell of the Khmer Rouge's **radio station** and **Peuy Ta Mok** (Ta Mok's Cliff), where domestic tourists come to enjoy spectacular views of Cambodia's northern plains.

From here a half-hour moto ride takes you to the **house of Khieu Samphan**, the Khmer Rouge's one-time head-of-state, which is buried in the jungle on the bank of a stream. From there it's a few hundred metres along an overgrown road to **Pol Pot's house**, a modest complex that includes a low brick building, the courtyard of which hides an underground bunker.

Sleeping

Bot Huddom Guesthouse (Bot Uddom; ☎ 011-500507; r with fan/air-con US$6/15; ❄) About 300m east of the Dove of Peace roundabout, this establishment has 12 spacious, well-kept rooms with massive hardwood beds.

Getting There & Around

Anlong Veng is located 118km north of Siem Reap (along the recently improved NH67), 16km south of the Choam border crossing, 80km northeast of Samraong and 90km west of Sa Em (the turn-off to Prasat Preah Vihear).

A share taxi to Siem Reap (US$6.50, two to 2½ hours) is available a few hundred metres south of the roundabout (in Siem Reap, departures are from the northwest corner of Psar Leu, across NH6 from the Canadia Bank); a private taxi is US$39. **GST** (☎ 092-905026) has a 7am bus to Siem Reap (US$5, four or five hours).

There are no buses or share taxis from Anlong Veng to Samraong or Sa Em, though you may be able to snag the occasional pick-up. A bum-busting moto ride to either destination costs about US$20.

A moto circuit to the border costs US$6 (US$12 including a tour out to Pol Pot's house; left).

PREAH VIHEAR PROVINCE

Bordering Thailand and Laos to the north, vast Preah Vihear province – much of it heavily forested and extremely remote – is home to three of Cambodia's most impressive legacies of the Angkorian era, including stunning Prasat Preah Vihear, high atop the Dangkrek escarpment. The infrastructure is among the kingdom's worst, so while tortuous roads ensure long, dirty journeys, they also guarantee rich rewards for adventure addicts and a degree of solitude at the temples.

GETTING TO THAILAND: POIPET TO ARANYA PRATHET

This is by far Cambodia's most popular land crossing with Thailand. From the roundabout at the western terminus of NH5 (paved at long last!), go through **passport control** (⌚ 7am-8pm) and walk through the casino zone. On the Thai side you can catch a túk-túk (80B) for the 6km ride to Aranya Prathet, where buses go to Bangkok's northern bus station (Morchit; about 160B, four hours). Two 3rd-class trains a day go to Bangkok's Hualamphong station (five to 5½ hours). We've heard repeated reports of fake bus tickets being sold at the border.

For information on crossing this border in the other direction, see p731.

CAMBODIA

Preah Khan

Covering almost 5 sq km, **Preah Khan** (admission US$5) is the largest temple enclosure constructed during the Angkorian period – quite a feat when you consider the competition. Originally dedicated to Hindu deities, it was reconsecrated to Mahayana Buddhist worship by Jayavarman VII in the late 12th and early 13th centuries. Thanks to its back-of-the-beyond location, the site is astonishingly quiet and peaceful.

At the eastern end of the 3km-long *baray* (reservoir) is a small pyramid temple called **Prasat Damrei** (Elephant Temple), with several impressive carvings of *devadas* (goddesses). At the *baray's* western end stands **Prasat Preah Stung**, known to locals as Prasat Muk Buon (Temple of the Four Faces) because of its four Bayon-style faces.

GETTING THERE & AWAY

There's no public transport to Preah Khan, so your best bet is to hire a moto or a pick-up truck in Kompong Thom (120km, five hours), Phnom Den (on NH64, 35km east of the temple) or Tbeng Meanchey (four or five hours). If you've got more cash, you might consider chartering a 4WD. Only *very* experienced bikers should attempt to get to Preah Khan on rental motorcycles, as conditions are extremely tough from every side.

Preah Khan is not accessible in the wet season.

Koh Ker

Abandoned to the forests of the north, **Koh Ker** (admission US$10), capital of the Angkorian empire from AD 928 to AD 944, was long one of Cambodia's most inaccessible temple complexes. However, this has now changed thanks to recent de-mining and the opening of a new toll road from Dam Dek (via Beng Mealea) that puts Koh Ker (pronounced kah-*kei*) within day-trip distance of Siem Reap.

Most visitors start at **Prasat Krahom** (Red Temple), the stone archways and galleries of which lean hither and thither; impressive stone carvings grace lintels, doorposts and slender window columns.

The principal monument is Mayan-looking **Prasat Thom** (Prasat Kompeng), a 55m-wide, 40m-high sandstone-faced pyramid whose seven tiers offer spectacular views across the forest. At press time it was closed for safety reasons.

Some of the largest Shiva *linga* (phallic symbols) in Cambodia can be seen inside four temples about 1km northeast of Prasat Thom.

In the quiet village of Srayong, 2km south from the toll plaza, the family-run **Ponloeu Preah Chan Guesthouse** (☎ 012-489058; r US$5) has 12 small rooms, only one of which has its own plumbing.

GETTING THERE & AWAY

Koh Ker is 127km northeast of Siem Reap (2½ hours by car) and 72km west of Tbeng Meanchey (two hours). From Siem Reap, hiring a private car for a day trip to Koh Ker costs US$80. From Tbeng Meanchey, a private taxi costs US$70 return, a moto US$15.

Tbeng Meanchey

☎ 064 / pop 21,600

Tbeng Meanchey (pronounced 'tbai man-*chey*'), often referred to by locals as Preah Vihear (not to be confused with Prasat Preah Vihear), is a sprawling and dusty-red (or muddy-red, depending on the season) town. It makes a good staging post for the long haul to Prasat Preah Vihear, 110 punishing kilometres north.

The centre of town, insofar as there is one, is around the taxi park and the market, Psar Kompong Pranak. **Acleda Bank**, a block south of the market, has an ATM.

GETTING TO THAILAND: O SMACH TO CHONG CHOM

The crossing from O Smach to Chong Chom, 165km north of Siem Reap, is not the easiest frontier post to get to. Share taxis (four hours via Kralanh and NH68) and a bus (US$7) link Siem Reap – but not Banteay Chhmar, Sisophon or Anlong Veng – with Samraong (via NH68), the backwater capital of Oddar Meanchey province. From there you can hire a moto (250B) or a private taxi (1200B) for the punishing drive to O Smach (40km, 1½ to two hours) and its frontier casino zone. On the Thai side it's easy – *sŏrng tăaou* (pick-ups) and motos take arrivals to the stop for buses to Surin (70km, 1½ to two hours). For information on crossing this border in the other direction, see p776.

Facing the taxi park, **Monyroit Guesthouse** (☎ 012-789955; r with fan/air-con US$7/17; ❄) is a new, three-storey place with 12 spacious rooms with lots of windows.

For details on public transport to/from Kompong Thom, 157km to the south via the execrable NH64, see p112. For details on transport to Prasat Preah Vihear, 110km to the northwest, see right.

Prasat Preah Vihear

The most dramatically situated of all the Angkorian monuments, 800m-long, 730m-high **Prasat Preah Vihear** (admission 10,000r) consists of a series of four cruciform *gopura* (sanctuaries) decorated with exquisite carvings (keep an eye on the lintels). Starting at the monumental stairway up the steep slope, a walk south takes you to the Gopura of the Third Level, with its early rendition of the Churning of the Ocean of Milk and finally – at the edge of the cliff – the Central Sanctuary. The stupendous views of Cambodia's northern plains make this a fantastic spot for a picnic.

No wonder then that some Thais would like to get their hands on Prasat Preah Vihear, despite the fact that Cambodian sovereignty was confirmed by the International Court of Justice in 1962. In mid-2008, for reasons not unrelated to domestic Thai politics, Prasat Preah Vihear's recognition by Unesco as a World Heritage Site – in Cambodia – sparked off border tensions that saw Thai troops occupy disputed land near the temple, and armed clashes in which soldiers on both sides were killed.

Before the stand-off, visitors could visit Prasat Preah Vihear from Thailand, crossing into Cambodia with a special no-visa day pass (US$10). At press time, however, the border remained closed and negotiations were stalled over the question of what to call the temple (the Thais insist that all official documents include the Thai name, Phra Viharn). Check the political situation before heading up here.

Kor Muy (Koh Muy), the village at the base of the hill, has several very basic guest houses, including the **Raksaleap Guesthouse** (☎ 092-224838; r 30,000r), whose nine rooms have shared bathrooms. Visiting Prasat Preah Vihear from the Cambodian side is getting easier as Chinese engineers upgrade the road from Koh Ker. In the wet season, though, it's still a long, muddy slog.

> **MINE YOUR STEP**
>
> Ensure you stick to well-marked paths as the Khmer Rouge laid huge numbers of landmines around Prasat Preah Vihear as late as 1998.

From Tbeng Meanchey, 110km to the south along a miserable road made worse by the recent passage of military hardware, you can either take a morning share taxi (US$10, 4½ hours) or hire a private taxi. Share taxis and pick-ups often only go as far as Sa Em (Sra Em), 27km south of Prasat Preah Vihear; from there, it's a 30-minute moto ride (US$3) to Kor Muy at the base of the escarpment. Then you have two options: hire a moto (US$5 return); or take a 5km, two-hour walk up the steep road (bring plenty of water).

For details on transport from Siem Reap, see p94.

Precious few vehicles travel between Sa Em and Anlong Veng so your only option may be to hire a moto (US$20).

KOMPONG THOM

☎ 062 / pop 66,000

Kompong Thom is on NH6, midway between Phnom Penh (165km) and Siem Reap (150km). On the river's south bank about 600m west of the bridge, next to the **French governor's residence**, is the most extraordinary sight: hundreds of chirping bats live in three old mahogany trees, spending the day suspended upside-down like winged fruit.

The **Acleda Bank** (NH6), just north of the bridge, has an ATM. There's an **internet cafe** (Prachea Thepatay St; per hr 4000r; 🕒 11.30am-10pm) just west of the Arunras Hotel (below).

The neat **Mittapheap Hotel** (☎ 961213; NH6; r US$5-10; ❄), just north of the bridge, has 23 comfortable rooms at the right price. The **Arunras Hotel** (☎/fax 961294; 46 Sereipheap Blvd; r with fan/air-con US$6/15; ❄), in a seven-storey corner building, dominates the local accommodation scene, with 58 smart, good-value rooms.

Dozens of buses on the Phnom Penh–Siem Reap route pass through Kompong Thom and can easily be flagged down near the Arunras Hotel. Share taxis, which leave from the taxi park (one block east of the Arunras Hotel), are faster and cost US$5 to either Phnom Penh (2½ hours) or Siem Reap (2½ hours); minibuses cost just 15,000r.

Heading north towards Tbeng Meanchey (often referred to as Preah Vihear), pick-ups (20,000/15,000r inside/on the back, four to five hours) are the most common form of transport, though when NH64 is in decent condition share taxis also do the run.

Moto drivers can be found across NH6 from the Arunras Hotel. Count on paying US$6 to US$8 per day, plus petrol.

Bicycles can be rented at **Piseth Bike Rental** (St 103; per day US$3; 6am-5pm), a block north of the bridge.

SAMBOR PREI KUK

Cambodia's most impressive group of pre-Angkorian monuments, **Sambor Prei Kuk** (admission US$3), encompasses more than 100 mainly brick temples scattered through the forest. Originally called Isanapura, it served as the capital of Chenla during the reign of the early-7th-century King Isanavarman and continued to be an important learning centre during the Angkorian era.

Sambor Prei Kuk has a serene and soothing atmosphere. The main temple area consists of three complexes, each enclosed by the remains of two concentric walls. The principle group, **Prasat Sambor**, is dedicated to Gambhireshvara, one of Shiva's many incarnations (the other groups are dedicated to Shiva himself). **Prasat Yeay Peau** (Prasat Yeai Poeun) feels lost in the forest, its eastern gateway both held up and torn asunder by an ancient tree.

Just past the ticket booth, the **Isanborei Crafts Shop** sells a worthwhile English brochure (2000r) and high-quality craft items. Nearby are several small eateries.

From Kompong Thom, a moto ride out here (under an hour) should cost US$8 or US$10 (US$13 including Phnom Santuk).

> **GETTING TO THAILAND: CHOAM TO CHONG SA NGAM**
>
> This crossing is 16km north of Anlong Veng (10,000r by moto) and 134km north of Siem Reap. From Anlong Veng, a modern sealed road heads up the Dangkrek escarpment to a spiffy new Thai border complex, in mothballs because the Cambodians say it's on their territory. Head instead to the old crossing, a few hundred metres east next to the smugglers' market. On the Thai side, it should be possible to find a *sŏrng tăaou* to Phusing and from there a bus to Kantharalak. You might also suss out transport to Si Saket.
>
> See p776 for information on doing the trip in the reverse direction.

SOUTH COAST

Cambodia's south coast is an alluring mix of clear blue water, castaway islands, pristine mangrove forests, time-worn colonial towns and jungle-clad mountains, where tigers and elephants lurk. Adventurers will find this region of Cambodia just as rewarding as sun seekers will.

KRONG KOH KONG

☎ 035 / pop 29,300

Once Cambodia's Wild West, its frontier economy dominated by smuggling, prostitution and gambling, Krong Koh Kong is striding towards respectability as backpackers and ecotourists scare the sleaze away. The town serves as the gateway to the Koh Kong Conservation Corridor (opposite).

Orientation & Information

Krong Koh Kong's commercial heart is three blocks east of the river, between the intersection of St 3 and St 8, marked by a roundabout, and Psar Leu (the market).

Baht, US dollars and riel are all accepted here, despite what scammers at the border might say. **Acleda Bank** (cnr St 5 & St 3) has an ATM that accepts Visa cards. There are **internet cafes** (per hr 6000r) in the Asian Hotel (opposite) and along the westernmost block of St 2. In a medical emergency, evacuation across the border to Thailand is possible 24 hours a day.

Sleeping

Some places pay moto drivers a commission, leading to a whole lot of shenanigans.

Sunset Lounge (☎ 393907; St 1; r 150B) Attached to the Sunset Bar (opposite), this shambolic backpacker's crash pad has five small rooms and a bathroom at the end of the corridor.

Neptune Guesthouse (☎ 011-984512; r from US$3) Has nine very basic rooms, most with (sinkless) bathroom, that come with plank beds, mosquito nets and bare neon lights.

Rasmey Buntam Guesthouse (☎ 016-506167; r 150-500B;) A decent 18-room place with

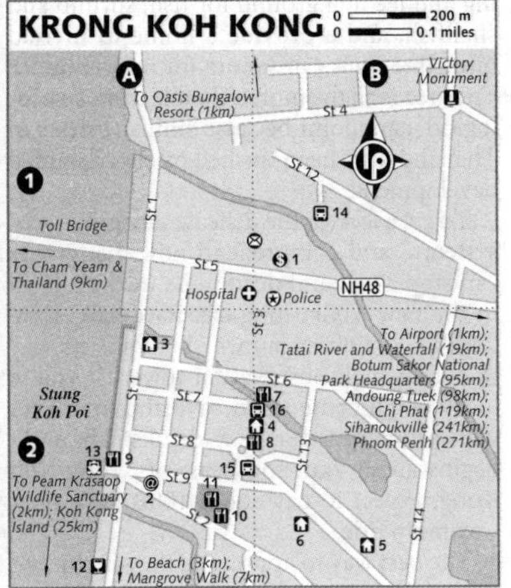

INFORMATION
Acleda Bank 1 B1
Internet Cafe .... (see 3)
Internet Cafes 2 A2

SLEEPING
Asian Hotel 3 A2
Dugout Hotel 4 B2
Neptune Guesthouse 5 B2
Rasmey Buntam Guesthouse 6 B2
Sunset Lounge .... (see 12)

EATING
Baan Peakmai 7 B2
Dessert Shop 8 A2
Food Stalls 9 A2
Fruit Stalls 10 A2
Psar Leu 11 A2

DRINKING
Sunset Bar 12 A2

TRANSPORT
Boat Dock 13 A2
Bun Thou Express .... (see 16)
Bus & Taxi Station 14 B1
Phnom Penh Sorya 15 A2
Rith Mony 16 B2
Virak-Buntham .... (see 16)

so many colourful tiles you'll think you're in Tunisia.

OUR PICK **Dugout Hotel** (☎ 016-650325; thedugouthotel@yahoo.com; St 3; r with fan/air-con 300/400B) A clean, quiet establishment smack in the centre of town. Five of the 11 rooms are arrayed around a 6.5m pool.

Asean Hotel (☎ 936667; http://aseanhotel.netkhmer.com; St 1; r US$15-20;) The 46 comfortable rooms have proper bathrooms and endearingly tacky wall lamps. A solid choice.

Eating & Drinking

There are cheap **food stalls** near the boat dock and around the perimeter of Psar Leu – have a look along St 2 and north of the market along St 3. **Fruit stalls** (St 2) can be found near the southeast corner of Psar Leu (the market).

Dessert shop (cnr St 3 & St 8; 6-11pm) Serves Cambodian after-dinner favourites such as *hon dov* (beans, rice and milk; 1000r) and *son dea kev* (the local version of a snow cone).

Baan Peakmai (☎ 393906; St 6; mains 60-150B; 7.30am-11pm) A relaxing Thai-style garden restaurant whose monster menu of Thai, Cambodian and Western dishes includes several dozen vegetarian choices.

Sunset Bar (☎ 393907; St 1; 8am-9pm or last customer) Nestled in a row of fishers' houses, this mellow riverfront bar – an ideal spot to watch the sun go down – is great for frank and funny travel tips. It's hidden down an alleyway – look for the 'bar' sign.

CAMBODIA

Getting There & Away

Phnom Penh Sorya (☎ 012-429809), **Bun Thou Express** (☎ 085-607727), **Rith Mony** (☎ 015-404085; St 3) and **Virak-Buntham** (☎ 012-322302; St 3) run early morning buses to Phnom Penh (US$5 to US$8, 4½ hours). Travel to Sihanoukville (US$8 with Phnom Penh Sorya) may involve a change at Plauv Bombek Sre Ambel, at the junction of NH48 and NH4. Also on offer are direct services to Thailand's Ko Chang (500B or US$14) and Bangkok (700B or US$20).

On the northeast edge of town, Krong Koh Kong's unpaved **bus and taxi station** (St 12) has a tin-roofed waiting area. Buses pick up passengers in town so the only reason to come out here is to find share taxis – most numerous in the morning – to Andoung Tuek (An Daung Toeuk; US$5), which is the jumping-off point for Chi Phat, Sihanoukville (change at the NH48–NH4 junction; US$10) and Phnom Penh (US$10).

For details on getting to sites along the Koh Kong Conservation Corridor, see p114.

The Neptune Guesthouse (opposite) rents out bicycles (per day US$1).

KOH KONG CONSERVATION CORRIDOR

Stretching along both sides of NH48 from Krong Koh Kong to the Gulf of Kompong Som (the bay north of Sihanoukville), the **Koh Kong Conservation Corridor** encompasses many of Cambodia's most outstanding natural sites,

GETTING TO THAILAND: CHAM YEAM TO HAT LEK

To get from Krong Koh Kong to the border crossing at Cham Yeam–Hat Lek, a private taxi costs 250B to 300B (plus the 48B bridge toll) while a moto costs 100B (plus the 12B toll). Walk across to the Thai side, where minibuses can take you to Trat for connections to Bangkok or Ko Chang. For information on crossing this border in the other direction, see p785.

including the most extensive mangrove forests on mainland Southeast Asia, and the southern reaches of the fabled 20,000-sq-km **Cardamom Mountains**, an area of breathtaking beauty and astonishing biodiversity that's just opening up to travellers. The potential for ecotourism is huge – akin, some say, to that of Costa Rica.

Getting There & Around

Krong Koh Kong's **boat dock** (cnr St 1 & St 9) is the best place to hire open-top fibreglass outboards to Peam Krasaop Wildlife Sanctuary (US$20/40 for up to three/eight people), Koh Kong Island via Peam Krasaop (US$40/80), Tatai Waterfall via Peam Krasaop (US$160) and Koh Por Waterfall (US$40/80). It's best to set out early in the morning as the sea tends to get choppy in the afternoon. Bring sunscreen, a hat and plenty of bottled water.

Buses, minibuses and share taxis travelling between Krong Koh Kong and points east, including Phnom Penh and Sihanoukville, stop along NH48 (eg at Andoung Tuek).

Within Krong Koh Kong, the Neptune Guesthouse (p112) rents out 125cc motorbikes for US$3 a day and 250cc bikes for US$15 a day.

Koh Por Waterfall

Upriver from Krong Koh Kong, this waterfall pours over a stone shelf in a lovely jungle gorge, though the site's tranquillity has recently been threatened by a new road. The best way to get there is by motorboat from Krong Koh Kong.

Peam Krasaop Wildlife Sanctuary

Anchored to alluvial islands – some no larger than a house – this 260-sq-km sanctuary's millions of magnificent mangroves protect the coast from erosion, serve as a vital breeding and feeding ground for fish, shrimp and shellfish, and a provide a home to myriad birds (see www.ramsar.org for information). The area is all the more valuable from an ecological standpoint because similar forests in Thailand have been trashed by short-sighted development.

To get a feel for the delicate mangrove ecosystem – and comprehend how mangroves can stop a tsunami dead in its tracks – head to the new, 600m-long **mangrove walk** (admission US$1; 6.30am-6pm), which wends its way to a 15m-high observation tower. If you're lucky you'll come upon cavorting monkeys with a fondness for fizzy drinks. The walk begins about 7km southeast of Krong Koh Kong; expect to pay about 100B for a one-way moto ride.

The best way to appreciate the sanctuary's sublime beauty is from a motorboat hired in Krong Koh Kong (see left). Endangered Irrawaddy dolphins can sometimes be seen early in the morning (6.30am or 7am) around the entrance to the Stung Koh Poi estuary.

Koh Kong Island

The west coast of Cambodia's largest island shelters seven pristine beaches fringed with coconut palms and lush vegetation, just as you'd expect in a true tropical paradise. At the sixth beach from the north, a narrow channel leads to a *Gilligan's Island*–style lagoon.

The island, about 25km south of Krong Koh Kong, is not part of any national park and thus has few protections against rampant development, which rumour has it will soon arrive.

Tatai River & Waterfall

As you drive east from Krong Koh Kong along NH48, after about 19km you come to the **Tatai River** (Stung Tatai). Nearby, surrounded by thick jungle, is **Tatai Waterfall**, whose waters run off smooth rocks and plunge into a series of pools. From Krong Koh Kong, you can either take a moto or a (pricey) motorboat.

Central Cardamoms Protected Forest

Encompassing 4013 sq km of dense rainforest, most of the Central Cardamoms Protected Forest (CCPF) is completely inaccessible except on foot. The enforcement rangers and military policemen who protect the CCPF from illegal hunting and logging are based in seven strategically positioned ranger stations, including one in **Thma Bang** (☎ 012-256777; oukkimsan@yahoo.com) – about two hours by road from Krong Koh Kong – that accepts paying guests (US$8 per person) who don't mind very basic overnight amenities. Bring warm clothes as temperatures can drop as low as 10°C. It may also be possible to hire guides for treks and accompany rangers on an overnight or three-day patrol.

The northern CCPF (p103) is accessible from Pursat.

Botum Sakor National Park

Occupying almost the entirety of a 35km-wide peninsula, this 1834-sq-km national park, encircled by mangroves and beaches, is home to a profusion of wildlife, including elephants (about 20 of them, according to recent camera-trap evidence), tigers, deer, leopards and sun bears. It's not yet geared up for tourism but at the sleepy **park headquarters** (☎ 015-374797), on NH48 about 3.5km west of Andoung Tuek, it should be possible to arrange a hike with a ranger (per day US$5), or a boat excursion.

In Andoung Tuek the **Botum Sakor Guesthouse** (☎ 016-732731; r with/without bathroom 25,000/20,000r) has six extremely basic rooms with bright pink mosquito nets and some dodgy wiring.

Chi Phat

Once notorious for its loggers and poachers, the river village of Chi Phat is now home to a pioneering **community-based ecotourism project** (CBET; www.mountainbikingcardamoms.com), which offers hardy travellers a unique opportunity to explore the Cardamoms ecosystem while contributing to its protection. Visitors can take day treks through the jungle, go sunrise birdwatching by boat, mountain bike to several sets of rapids and look for monkeys and hornbills with a former poacher as a guide (guide per day US$6 to US$10).

CAMBODIA

SENG BUNRA

When Seng Bunra, Cambodia country director for Conservation International (CI; www.conservation.org), was growing up in Kandal province, about 50km from Phnom Penh, he got to know the ecosystems around his village the way everyone did: as beneficiaries of nature's bounty. 'The people in my village, they got fish from the lake and the river; animals, fruit and wood for houses from the forest,' he explains. 'I went to the forest with my father, sometimes hunting, sometimes fishing, sometimes for fun.

'In the Pol Pot time, I was a "buffalo kid". The buffalos lived in the forest so I also lived in the forest, just bring rice and salt from the village. We can catch fish, kill animals, put out traps for birds, and then we can cook them with rice. I also was a poacher', he laughs, 'but not much, just for eating'.

At the age of 20, in 1985, Mr Seng began studying fisheries management, and in 1990 went to work for the Fisheries Administration in a remote part of Koh Kong province. 'The salary, I remember, was only 6000r per month', he recalls. 'But chicken rice in Phnom Penh cost 3000r – my salary was only enough to buy two chicken rice every month!'

These days CI and Mr Seng face a variety of even more daunting challenges. 'I don't want to say that development destroys, but with some development projects, people end up destroying nature. Development is easy – people just build this, cut that, destroy some place to do a new thing. But when we want to get nature back we can't.

'My first goal at CI is to protect and secure the Cardamom Mountains for the next generation', he explains. 'In mainland Southeast Asia, the Cardamom Mountains are the last true rainforest wilderness. Tourism can play a very important role in preserving the Cardamom Mountains because, first, it allows local people to generate income and improve their livelihoods without destroying the forest and, second, because if tourists show reverence for the forest, the local people will feel ashamed to engage in illegal activity.

'I want to see the Cardamoms become a magnet for tourism. It's a very, very beautiful area, the last wilderness rainforest in Cambodia, similar to some parts of the Amazon. I've never been in Amazon,' he admits, smiling, 'but my friend in Brazil says so!' He continues: 'You can see hornbills, Siamese crocodiles, Asian arowana and many kinds of gibbon and monkey. I want to send a message: please come!'

Basic accommodation options in Chi Phat include five CBET-member **guest houses** (per person US$5) and 10 **homestays** (per person US$3).

Chi Phat is on the Preak Piphot River 21km upstream from Andoung Tuek, which is on NH48 98km east of Krong Koh Kong and 191km from Phnom Penh and is served by all buses to/from Krong Koh Kong. The project's **Chi Phat office** (☎ 092-720925) can coordinate your visit and arrange for a motorboat from the Andoung Tuek bridge (US$40 for a 15-person wooden boat, US$50 for a seven-person speedboat each way). A much cheaper option is to take the daily cargo boat (US$2, two hours), which departs from Andoung Tuek's eastern shore (under the bridge) sometime between noon and 2pm, and from Chi Phat at 8am or 8.30am.

SIHANOUKVILLE

☎ 034 / pop 155,000

Surrounded by white-sand beaches and as-yet undeveloped tropical islands, Sihanoukville (Kompong Som) is Cambodia's premier seaside resort. The city's lively bars and sands remain pretty laid-back, offering bliss and relaxation by day, drinking and chilling by night.

Orientation

The scruffy city centre, where the bus station and most businesses are, is spread out along and north of Ekareach St. The main beach areas, Serendipity and Occheuteal, are about 2km to the south; Victory Beach is 2.5km to the northwest.

Information

Internet cafes (per hr 4000r) are sprinkled along the Road to Serendipity and, in the city centre, along Ekareach St near Sophamongkol St.

Laundry costs 3000r per kilo at places around Serendipity.

Ana Travel (☎ 933729; www.anainternet.com; 235 Ekareach St; 7am-10pm) A travel agency that handles visa extensions.

ANZ Royal Bank (215 Ekareach St) One of several ATM-equipped banks in the city centre along Ekareach St.

Casablanca Books (Road to Serendipity; 8am-9pm, until 11pm in high season) Next to Mick & Craig's (opposite), this bookshop sells new and used English paperbacks.

CT Clinic (☎ 934222; ct_clinic@yahoo.com; 47 Boray Kamakor St; 24hr for emergencies) The best medical clinic in town. Can administer rabies shots and snake serum.

Eco-Trek Tours (☎ 012-987073; ecotrektourscambodia@yahoo.com; Road to Serendipity; 8am-9pm or later) A travel agency whose offerings include snorkelling trips (US$15), island excursions and outings to Ream National Park (half/whole day US$20/30).

Utopia Information Centre (☎ 933791; www.welcometocambodia.com; Road to Serendipity) Books day trips to the islands and Ream National Park (US$20).

Vietnamese Consulate (☎ 934039; 310 Ekareach St; 8am-noon & 2-4pm Mon-Sat) Issues some of the world's speediest Vietnamese visas (US$35/37 for 15 days/one month), often on-the-spot. Bring a passport photo.

Dangers & Annoyances

Theft is common, so don't leave valuables on the beach unattended or motorbikes without a hefty padlock. At night, both men and women should avoid walking alone along dark, isolated beaches and roads, including Occheuteal Beach around and southeast of Chiva's Shack and poorly lit areas of Ekareach St.

Sights & Activities

BEACHES

Sihanoukville's sandy beaches are in a state of flux as developers move in and murky leases are signed to cash in on the tourism boom. The best all-rounder is 4km-long **Occheuteal Beach**, lined (at least for now) with ramshackle restaurants, and whose northwestern end – a tiny, rocky strip – has emerged as a happy, easy-going travellers' hang-out known as **Serendipity Beach**. South of Occheuteal (on the other side of the small headland), gloriously quiet **Otres Beach** is a seemingly infinite strip of almost-empty white sand that may face development.

Northwest of Serendipity, all but a tiny stretch of pretty 1.5km-long **Sokha Beach** now belongs to the exclusive Sokha Beach Resort. **Independence Beach** is a good stretch of clean sand but is now being aggressively developed. A bit north of tiny, secluded **Koh Pos Beach**, a bridge to **Koh Pos** (Snake Island), 800m offshore, is being built as part of a Russian resort project. The original backpacker beach, **Victory Beach**, now under Russian management, is clean, orderly and pretty much devoid of buzz.

ISLANDS & DIVING

The reefs around Sihanoukville, while less dramatic than those in Indonesia or Thailand, are rich in corals, sponges and all sorts of swimming creatures, including dolphins.

Some of the finest diving is around the islands of **Koh Tang** and **Koh Prins**, which require an overnight trip, though there's also excellent diving – and some delicious sand – closer in, near coral-rich **Koh Rong Samloem** (two hours by boat).

More than a dozen tropical islands dot the waters off Sihanoukville. Some have gorgeous, blissfully empty beaches, and on several you'll find rustic bungalows (US$10 to US$25). Among the islands that are great for overnighting are **Koh Russei** (Bamboo Island; one hour by boat), 15km-long **Koh Rong** (two hours) and – perhaps Sihanoukville's best getaway – 10km-long **Koh Rong Samloem** (EcoSea Dive ☎ 012-654104, www.ecoseadive.com; Lazy Beach ☎ 016-214211, www.lazybeachcambodia.com). Trips to the islands can be arranged through various travel agencies, dive shops and guest houses.

Reliable dive operators:

Chez Claude (☎ 934100; www.bestcambodia.com; above 2 Thnou St) Claude has been exploring the waters off Sihanoukville since 1992 and specialises in longer trips to distant reefs.

Dive Shop (☎ 933664; www.diveshopcambodia.com; Road to Serendipity; 7am-8pm) Cambodia's second PADI five-star dive centre.

EcoSea Dive (☎ 012-654104; www.ecoseadive.com; 225 Ekareach St) Offers PADI and SSI courses and one-/two-day dive packages (US$45/65) Also has offices on the Road to Serendipity and at Serendipity Beach.

Scuba Nation Diving Center (☎ 012-604680; www.divecambodia.com; Serendipity St) A PADI five-star dive centre offering National Geographic diver certification.

MASSAGE

NGO-trained blind and disabled masseurs deftly ease away the tension at **Seeing Hands Massage 3** (☎ 012-799016; 95 Ekareach St; per hr US$5; 8am-9pm;) and **Starfish Bakery & Café** (☎ 012-952011; 62 7 Makara St; per hr US$6; 9am-6pm).

COOKING

Traditional Khmer Cooking (☎ 092-738615; khmercookery@hotmail.com; 335 Ekareach St; per person US$30; 10am Mon-Sat) teaches traditional culinary techniques in classes with no more than eight participants. Reserve a day ahead.

REAM NATIONAL PARK

Also known as Preah Sihanouk National Park, this park – now seriously endangered by commercial development – comprises 150 sq km of primary forests and is an excellent place to see wildlife. Fascinating **jungle walks** (per person US$6) led by rangers – most, but not all, speak English – are easy to arrange (hiking unaccompanied is not allowed) at the **park headquarters** (☎ 016-767686, 012-875096; 7am-sunset), across the road from the airport. Ranger-led **boat trips** (1-5 people US$45) on the Prek Toeuk Sap Estuary and its mangrove channels are another option. Sihanoukville travel agencies offer day trips out here.

The park is 18km east of Sihanoukville. A return trip by moto should cost US$8 to US$10.

Sleeping

SERENDIPITY BEACH

The area between Serendipity Beach and the Golden Lions Traffic Circle, including the Road to Serendipity, is now the city's main travellers' hang-out. You pay a premium to stay right on the water, although Occheuteal Beach has some ultra-low-budget rooms for hard-core backpackers. Inland from Occheuteal Beach, 23 Tola St and 1 Kanda St offer an assortment of midrange hotels and guest houses.

Utopia (☎ 934319; www.utopiagathering.com; cnr Road to Serendipity & 14 Milthona St; dm Jun–mid-Nov/ mid-Nov–May free/US$2) A backpackers' party bar whose dorm beds could hardly be cheaper.

Chiva's Shack (☎ 012-360911; Occheuteal Beach; r US$2-6) One of the cheapest options right on the water, this aptly named party zone has 45 very basic rooms with thin plank walls, foam mattresses and shared bathrooms. Loud till late.

ourpick **Monkey Republic** (☎ 012-490290; monkeyrepubliccambodia@yahoo.co.uk; Road to Serendipity; r US$7-8) The epitome of what all backpacker accommodation should be: cool, friendly, laid-back, and with plenty of banana trees. Bungalows are simple, but the lofty chill-out zone is a smooth touch.

Mick & Craig's (☎ 012-727740; www.mickandcraigs.com; Road to Serendipity; r US$6-12) A popular restaurant with 17 simple rooms, in the heart of Serendipity's dining and nightlife strip.

Thida's Inn (☎ 012-981918; Serendipity St; r with fan/air-con from US$8/18) Welcoming and clean, this 10-room place is a short walk up the hill from the beach.

Coasters (☎ 933776; www.cambodia-beach.com; Serendipity St; d US$10-15, with air-con & hot water US$25-35;) Many of the 17 solid rooms and bungalows have verandahs for some quality contemplation time. The bar and restaurant run right to the water's edge.

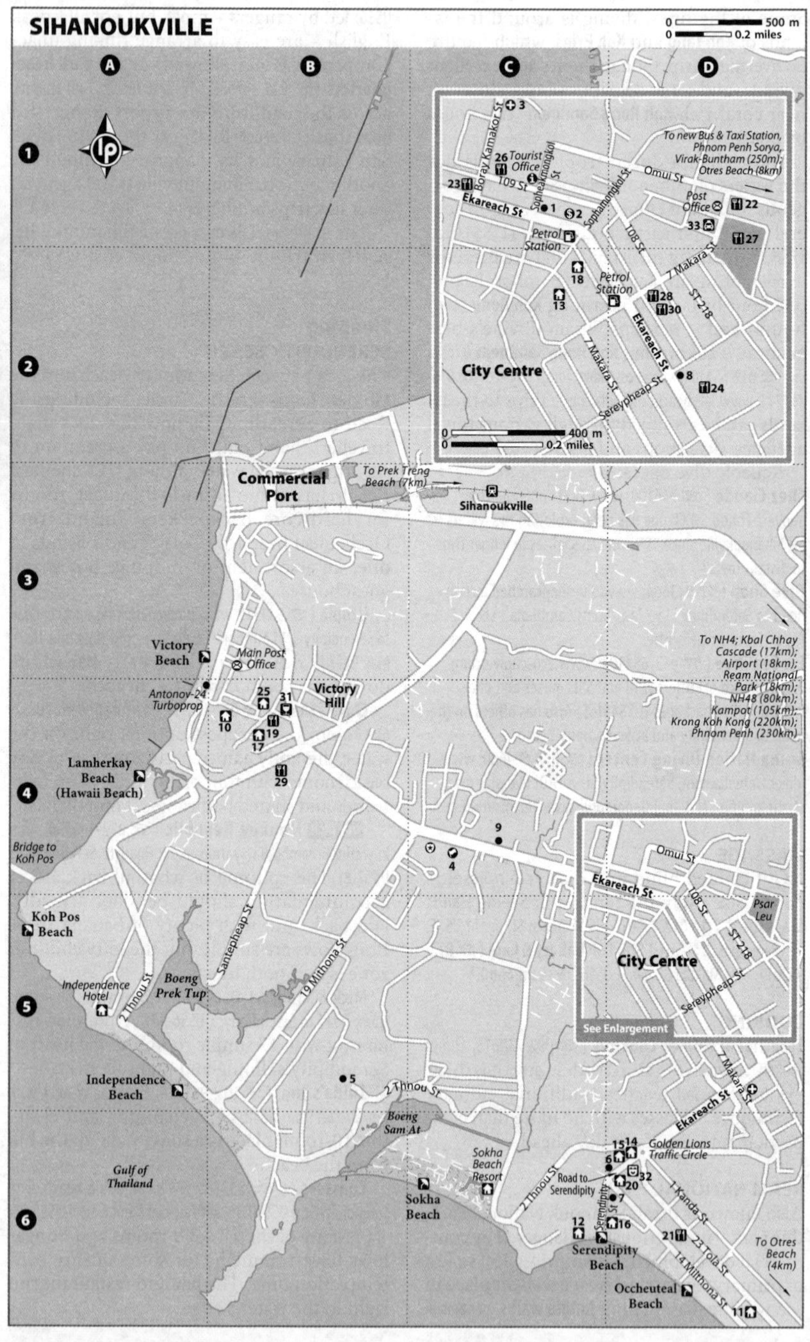
SIHANOUKVILLE
0 500 m
0 0.2 miles
A
B
C
D
1
2
3
4
5
6
To new Bus & Taxi Station, Phnom Penh Sorya, Virak-Buntham (250m); Otres Beach (8km)
Boray Kamakor St
Tourist Office
Sopheakmongkol St
Sophamongkol St
109 St
Omui St
Ekareach St
Post Office
Petrol Station
108 St
7 Makara St
ST 218
City Centre
Sereypheap St
0 400 m
0 0.2 miles
Commercial Port
To Prek Treng Beach (7km)
Sihanoukville
Victory Beach
Main Post Office
Antonov-24 Turboprop
Victory Hill
Lamherkay Beach (Hawaii Beach)
To NH4; Kbal Chhay Cascade (17km); Airport (18km); Ream National Park (18km); NH48 (80km); Kampot (105km); Krong Koh Kong (220km); Phnom Penh (230km)
Bridge to Koh Pos
Koh Pos Beach
Santepheap St
19 Mithona St
Independence Hotel
2 Thnou St
Boeng Prek Tup
Psar Leu
See Enlargement
Independence Beach
2 Thnou St
Boeng Sam At
Gulf of Thailand
Sokha Beach Resort
Sokha Beach
Golden Lions Traffic Circle
Road to Serendipity
Serendipity St
1 Kanda St
23 Tola St
14 Mithona St
Serendipity Beach
Occheuteal Beach
To Otres Beach (4km)

INFORMATION
Ana Travel 1 C1
ANZ Royal Bank 2 C1
Casablanca Books (see 14)
CT Clinic 3 C1
EcoSea Dive (see 2)
Eco-Trek Tours (see 14)
Internet Cafes (see 1)
Internet Cafes (see 15)
Utopia Information Centre (see 20)
Vietnamese Consulate 4 C4

SIGHTS & ACTIVITIES
Chez Claude 5 B5
Dive Shop (see 15)
EcoSea Dive 6 D6
EcoSea Dive (see 12)
Scuba Nation Diving Center 7 D6
Seeing Hands Massage 3 8 D2
Starfish Bakery & Café (see 30)
Traditional Khmer Cooking 9 C4

SLEEPING
Ana Guesthouse (see 1)
Beach Road Hotel (see 32)
Bungalow Village 10 B4
Chiva's Shack 11 D6
Coasters 12 C6
Geckozy Guesthouse 13 C2
House of Malibu (see 12)
Mick & Craig's 14 D6
Monkey Republic 15 D6
New Sea View Villa 16 D6
Rainy Season Guesthouse 17 B4
Small Hotel 18 C2
Sunset Garden Guesthouse 19 B4
Thida's Inn (see 7)
Utopia 20 D6

EATING
Angelo's 21 D6
Food Stalls 22 D1
Fruit & Veggie Stalls 23 C1
Holy Cow 24 D2
Koh Lin 25 B4
New Sea View Villa (see 16)
Night Market 26 C1
Psar Leu 27 D1
Samudera Supermarket 28 D2
Snake House 29 B4
Starfish Bakery & Café 30 D2

DRINKING
Chiva's Shack (see 11)
Mojo Bar 31 B4
Monkey Republic (see 14)
Utopia (see 20)

ENTERTAINMENT
Bungalow Village (see 10)
Top-Cat Cinema 32 D6

TRANSPORT
Share Taxis to Kampot 33 D1

Beach Road Hotel (☎ 016-433901; www.beachroad-hotel.com; Road to Serendipity; r with fan/air-con from US$15/20;) A bright, new establishment whose 27 modern rooms – more are being added – are clean and well kept.

New Sea View Villa (☎ 092-759753; www.sihanoukville-hotel.com; Serendipity Beach; d with fan/air-con from US$17/20) Has 15 spacious, clean rooms just 50m from the beach. A favourite with in-the-know expats.

VICTORY HILL

Once the main backpacker zone, the area between Victory Hill (Weather Station Hill) and Victory Beach is now the 'alternative' place to stay, and has some great deals.

Rainy Season Guesthouse (☎ 092-583372; rainyseasoncambodia@yahoo.com; r US$5) Named after an album by the American singer-songwriter Elliot Murphy, this French-run guest house throws in breakfast, so the rooms are really almost free.

Sunset Garden Guesthouse (☎ 012-562004; d US$5-12;) This spotless, family-run hostelry, in an Italianate house between Victory Hill and Victory Beach, has 18 spacious, spotless rooms.

Bungalow Village (☎ 012-490293; bungalowvillage@hotmail.com; r US$6-15) Set in a shaded hillside garden, this complex, just 200m from the beach, has an old-fashioned chill-out zone and 10 basic bungalows.

TOWN CENTRE

Given we're all here for the beach, the town centre is not the most exotic place to stay – but it's mighty convenient if you're travelling by bus.

Geckozy Guesthouse (☎ 012-495825; www.geckozy-guesthouse.com; r US$5-7) Located on a quiet side street, the place has six basic rooms in an old wooden house.

Ana Guesthouse (☎ 933729; www.anainternet.com; 235 Ekareach St; r US$5-7) Has five simply furnished rooms with high ceilings, small windows and an internet cafe downstairs.

our pick Small Hotel (☎ 012-716385; thesmallhotel@yahoo.com; r US$10-15;) Neat and organised in the best Scandinavian tradition, this super-welcoming guest house has a cheerful lounge and 11 spotless rooms.

Eating

Sihanoukville's centre of culinary gravity has shifted to the Serendipity area, but up on Victory Hill, the main drag still has a range of good-value restaurants. Unless stated otherwise, all restaurants listed here are open for breakfast, lunch and dinner.

SERENDIPITY BEACH

The Road to Serendipity is home to some of Sihanoukville's liveliest eateries, including restaurants attached to Mick & Craig's (p117) and Monkey Republic (p117). For romance, nothing beats dining on freshly barbecued seafood right on the water, either at Serendipity Beach or – more cheaply – in one of the shacks lining adjacent Occheuteal Beach, all with comfy satellite chairs, low tables with candles, and enthusiastic sellers. A string of outdoor restaurants along 23 Tola St, including **Angelo's** (☎ 092-738651), serve excellent grilled fish (eg barracuda), seafood (eg prawns), chicken, ribs and steak. Expats rave about the excellent Western dishes and superb set menu (US$7.50) at **New Sea View Villa** (☎ 017-420270).

VICTORY HILL

This area, though no longer the backpacker haven it once was, is worth a visit for its eateries.

Koh Lin (☎ 092-295011; mains 6000r-18,000r; ⌚ 9am-11pm) Serves Cambodian, Vietnamese and French bistro classics at five candle-lit tables. Dessert options include profiteroles, crème caramel and crêpes.

Snake House (☎ 012-673805; www.snake-house.com, in Russian; mains US$3.50-9.50; ⌚ 8am-11pm) Serves authentic Russian dishes, sushi and seafood. Diners at this unique establishment sit at glass-topped tables with live serpents inside (the snakes are kept here to produce antivenenes). Also has a bar, a guest house and a crocodile farm (US$3, free for diners) – one false step and the crocs will eat as well as you did.

CITY CENTRE

For Sihanoukville's cheapest dining, head to the row of **food stalls** (cnr 7 Makara St & Omui St) near Psar Leu (Phsa Leu; the recently rebuilt market) or to the **night market** (109 St; ⌚ from mid-afternoon). For self-caterers, there are **fruit and veggie stalls** (⌚ 6am-9pm) around Psar Leu and at the southern end of Boray Kamakor St. **Samudera Supermarket** (☎ 933441; 64 7 Makara St; ⌚ 7am-9pm) has a good selection of Western favourites, including cheese and wine.

Holy Cow (☎ 012-478510; 83 Ekareach St; mains US$2.50-4.50; ⌚ 9.30am-11pm) Options at this chic, funky cafe-restaurant include pasta, sandwiches on home-made bread, and two vegan desserts, both of which involve chocolate.

our pick Starfish Bakery & Café (☎ 012-952011; behind 62 7 Makara St; mains US$3-4; ⌚ 7am-6pm) This attractive, NGO-run garden cafe serves filling Western breakfasts, light lunches (sandwiches, quiche, tortillas, salads) and teatime treats such as brownies and apple tarts. Vegie options are legion. There's a nonprofit craft shop, Rajana, upstairs.

Drinking

Many of Sihanoukville's liveliest nightspots are along Serendipity Beach and the Road to Serendipity. Occheuteal Beach is lined with laid-back beach bars, some of which rock on until the early hours. Despite the arrival of girlie bars and the threat of demolition, Victory Hill's main drag still has some of its old-time backpacker vibe, as well as a certain French flair – check it out now or it may be gone.

Among the nightspots worth a look:

Monkey Republic (☎ 012-490290; Road to Serendipity) The bar and upstairs chill-out area are ideal for meeting other travellers.

Utopia (☎ 934319; www.utopiagathering.com; cnr Road to Serendipity & 14 Milthona St; ⌚ 24hr, may be closed 3-7am Jun-Nov) Home to the 24-hour party people, with draught beer for US$0.50, a backpackers' night bar from 10pm and DJs on Saturday nights.

Chiva's Shack (☎ 012-360911; Occheuteal Beach; ⌚ 24hr) This veteran establishment has made a name for itself with full-moon parties, fire throwers, happy pizzas and some delicious cocktails.

Mojo Bar (☎ 016-307704; Victory Hill; ⌚ 9am-1am or later) An unpretentious, rough-hewn bar with 35 kinds of rum, as well as jam sessions on Thursdays.

Entertainment

Top-Cat Cinema (☎ 011-617799; Road to Serendipity; tickets US$3; ⌚ screenings 5pm, 7pm, 9pm & 11pm; ❄) Hugely popular, this place screens movies on an 8m hi-definition screen.

Bungalow Village (☎ 012-490293; Victory Hill; ⌚ Mon, Wed, Fri & Sat Nov-May or Nov-Jun) Screens outdoor films in the dry season.

Getting There & Away

Eight bus companies, including **Phnom Penh Sorya** (☎ 933888; bus station), link the new bus and taxi station (Omui St), about 700m north-east of the intersection of Ekareach St and 7 Makara St, with Phnom Penh (US$4.25 to US$7.75, four hours); departures are frequent from 7am to about 2pm. Cramped share taxis to Phnom Penh cost US$7 per person, or US$50 for the whole car. Minibuses to Phnom Penh, packed to the gills with 18 passengers, cost 15,000r.

Virak-Buntham (☎ 011-558988) has buses to Krong Koh Kong (US$14, four hours), with stops along NH48 (eg at Andoung Tuek), and also to Bangkok (US$35, 11 hours).

Share taxis to Kampot (US$5, two hours) leave from an open lot across 7 Makara St from Psar Leu. For details on the G'day Mate minibus to Kampot, see p123.

NH4 to Phnom Penh is busy, boring and dangerous, so taking this route by motorcycle isn't recommended.

Rumour has it that there may soon be ferry service to Vietnam's Phu Quoc Island.

Getting Around

At the time of research, a cartel of taxi and moto drivers controls local transport from the bus and share-taxi station. Bargaining is futile – if you don't agree to the posted price (about double the usual rate) no one will take you. Walk out to Ekareach St, though, and you will find plenty of freelance motos and túk-túks.

Sihanoukville's moto drivers are notorious for overcharging, especially when the US Navy has a ship in port, so haggle hard – with a smile – before setting out. From the city centre, expect to pay US$1 to Serendipity, Occheuteal and Victory Beaches, and Victory Hill. Serendipity to Victory Hill costs US$1.50; Serendipity to Otres Beach costs US$1.50 to US$2.

Túk-túks generally charge about US$1 or US$1.50 per person for travel between the city centre and the beaches.

Motorbikes can be rented from many guest houses for US$4 to US$6 a day. For fund-raising purposes, the police sometimes 'crack down' on foreigners driving without a Cambodian driver's license but most rental places get advance tip-offs.

Bicycles can be hired from many guest houses for about US$1.50 a day. Mick & Craig's (p117) is a good source of information on cycling options.

KAMPOT

☎033 / pop 33,000

There is something about this little charmer that encourages visitors to linger. It might be the lovely riverside setting or the ageing French buildings, or it could be the great little guest houses and burgeoning bar scene. Whatever the magic ingredient, this is the perfect base from which to explore nearby caves and tackle Bokor National Park.

Information

Commercial activity is centred around 7 Makara St. Guest houses are the best source of travel information, and Boddhi Villa guest house (right) can supply details on options for volunteering.

Canadia Bank (Ekareach St) Has an ATM.

Kampot Network (7 Makara St; per hr 3000r; 6am-8pm or 9pm) One of several internet cafes along 7 Makara St.

Kepler's Kampot Books (8am-8pm) Second-hand books.

Sights & Activities

This is not a town where you come and do, but a place to come and feel. Sit on the riverbank and watch the sun set beneath the mountains, or stroll among the town's fine **French shophouses** (in the triangle delineated by 7 Makara St, the central roundabout and the post office).

Visitors are welcome to observe students at the **Kampot Traditional Music School** (8-11am & 7-9pm Mon-Fri), which trains orphaned and disabled children in traditional music and dance.

Blind masseurs offer soothing bliss at **Seeing Hands Massage 5** (☎012-328465; per hr US$4; 6am-10pm) and **Kampot Massage by the Blind** (☎012-662114; River Rd; per hr US$4; 8am-11pm).

Tours

One of the best ways to explore Kampot province is to take a group day trip. Popular destinations include Kep or Phnoms Chhnork and Sorsia (US$15 including a visit to a pepper plantation) and Bokor National Park (p123). A sunset river cruise (US$3) and a cycling tour are also options. Reliable tour operators:

Long Villa Tours (☎012-297193; longvillaguest house@yahoo.com; 75 St 713; 7.30am-8.30pm) Based at Long Villa Guesthouse (below).

Sok Lim Tours (☎012-719872, 012-801348; www.soklimtours.com) Kampot's largest and most experienced tour operator.

Wild Orchid Adventure Tours (☎092-226996) Based at Orchid Guesthouse.

Sleeping

Long Villa Guesthouse (☎012-210820; longvillaguesthouse@yahoo.com; 75 St 713; s US$4, d US$5-13;) A family-run travellers' sanctuary with 15 smallish, good-value rooms.

Orchid Guest House (☎092-226996; orchidguesthousekampot@yahoo.com; s US$4-6, d US$12-15;) Set in a manicured garden full of (what else?) orchids, this hostelry has 11 comfortable rooms and a fish pond out back.

Blissful Guesthouse (☎011-273101; www.blissfulguesthouse.com; r US$4-8) Surrounded by a lovely garden, this atmospheric wooden house has 10 slightly shabby rooms, three with shared bathroom. A good place to dine and to meet travellers.

Bodhi Villa (☎012-728884; bodhivilla@mac.com; dm US$2, r US$5-10) Situated 2km towards Tek Chhouu Falls from town (a few hundred metres upriver from the rail bridge), this happy hideaway – with four rooms and four

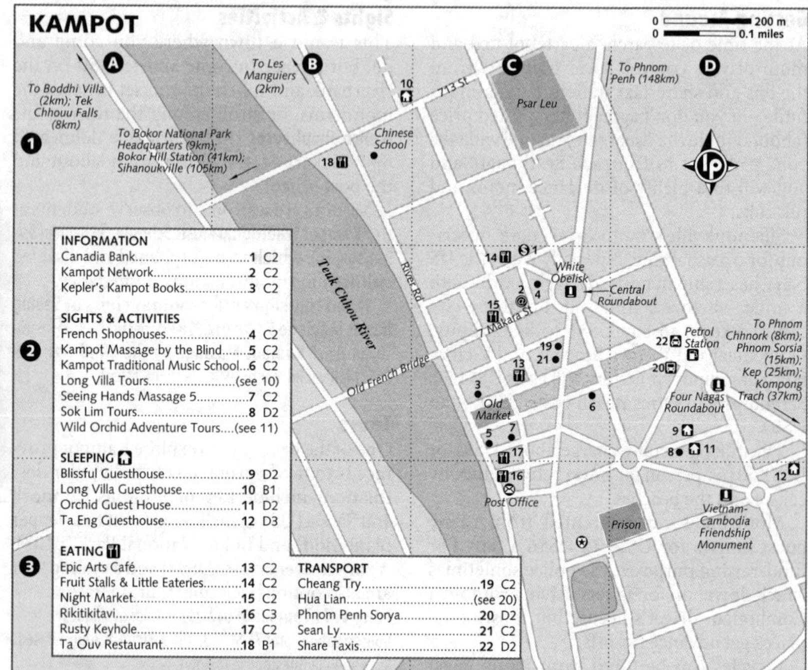

bungalows – is tucked away behind a luxuriant garden on the banks of the river and is a good base for water sports. A moto from town should cost 4000r (more at night).

Ta Eng Guesthouse (☎ 012-330058; 36 St 726; r US$5-8) On a street lined with 1960s row houses, this veteran guest house – Kampot's first – has 10 well-kept rooms. The gracious owner speaks French and some English.

Eating & Drinking

Quite a few restaurants line River Rd south of the old French bridge. There are **fruit stalls & little eateries** (⏲ 7am-10pm) next to the Canadia Bank and, nearby, a **night market** (7 Makara St) with both mains and desserts. Blissful Guesthouse (p121) has a popular restaurant and bar.

Ta Ouv Restaurant (☎ 932422; River Rd; mains US$2-4; ⏲ 10am-2pm & 6-10pm) Built on stilts over the river, this corrugated-iron pavilion is ideal for an unpretentious, romantic sunset meal. The extensive menu includes vegie dishes and fresh seafood (crab with peppercorns is a favourite).

Epic Arts Café (www.epicarts.org.uk; mains US$2-4; ⏲ 7am-6pm) A great place for breakfast, home-made cakes or tea, this mellow eatery is staffed by the hearing-impaired and young people with disabilities. Has free wi-fi and sometimes hosts dance performances. Profits fund arts workshops for Cambodians with disabilities.

Rusty Keyhole (☎ 092-758536; River Rd; mains 9000r-24,000r) This laid-back patio bar serves good-value Khmer and Western grub, including sandwiches and barbecued beef, chicken, ribs and shrimp.

Rikitikitavi (☎ 012-235102; River Rd; mains US$5.75-8.75; ⏲ 7am-10pm) A stylish river-view restaurant known for its Kampot pepper chicken, slow-cooked curry, sandwiches, salads, apple pie and vegie options. Serves wine by the glass. Also rents rooms.

Getting There & Away

Kampot is 105km from Sihanoukville and 148km from Phnom Penh.

Two bus companies, **Phnom Penh Sorya Transport** and **Hua Lian** (☎ 012-939917), sell tickets next to Sokhoda Restaurant (facing the Total petrol station). Buses to Phnom Penh (US$4 to US$5, four hours) via Kep (US$2, one hour) depart between 7.15am and 12.30pm. Across the street you can catch share taxis (25,000r), packed-to-the-gills minibuses (15,000r) and private taxis (US$45) to Phnom Penh.

Share taxis to Sihanoukville cost US$4, minibuses are US$3, and a private taxi is US$25 to US$30. Safe, reliable minibuses run by **G'day Mate** (☎ 012-707859) link Kampot with Sihanoukville (US$7.50) every morning; guest houses can arrange tickets.

A moto/túk-túk to Kep should cost about US$7/10 and a private taxi from US$15 to US$20.

Getting Around

Bicycles can be hired from guest houses, including Long Villa (p121; per day US$1).

Two excellent, adjacent shops rent out motorbikes (also available from Kampot, Long Villa and Orchid guest houses), motorcycles and cars:

Cheang Try (☎ 012-974698; 🕑 6am-9pm) Small bikes cost US$3 a day; new 125cc Hondas are US$5 a day; guided motorbike tours cost US$10 to US$15 a day. The owner speaks good English.

Sean Ly (☎ 012-944687; 🕑 7am-9pm) Rents 125cc bikes for US$3 a day (US$5 for a new one) and 250cc trail bikes for US$10.

AROUND KAMPOT

Picnic platforms, eateries and some refreshing rapids make **Tek Chhouu Falls**, 8km from Kampot, hugely popular with locals. A moto costs US$3 each way.

The limestone hills east towards Kep are honeycombed with fantastic caves, some of which can be explored with the help of local kids and a reliable torch (flashlight). The temple cave of **Phnom Chhnork** (Phnom Chngouk; admission US$1), surrounded by blazingly beautiful countryside, is a real gem. Known for its 7th-century (Funan-era) brick temple, it is 8km from Kampot; for a return moto/túk-túk ride count on paying about US$10/15. Also interesting is **Phnom Sorsia** (admission free), 15km southeast of Kampot, which has several natural caves and a gaudily painted modern temple.

DID YOU KNOW?

In the years before the Cambodian civil war took its toll, no self-respecting French restaurant in Paris would be without Kampot pepper on the table.

BOKOR NATIONAL PARK

One of Cambodia's most alluring protected areas, the 1581-sq-km **Bokor National Park** (Preah Monivong National Park; admission US$5) is famed for its abandoned French hill station, refreshingly cool climate and lush primary rainforest. At the park entrance, an informative (if low-budget) **visitors centre** has displays about Bokor's fauna and the challenges of protecting the area's ecosystems in the face of encroachment, poaching, illegal logging and the Kamchay hydropower project. Threatened animals that live in the park include the tiger (recently photographed by camera traps), leopard, Indian elephant, Asiatic black bear, Malayan sun bear, pileated gibbon, pig-tailed macaque, slow loris and pangolin. Unfortunately, illegal logging in the 1990s cost the park its shot at World Heritage status.

Bokor Hill Station

In the early 1920s the French – ever eager to escape the lowland heat – established a hill station atop Phnom Bokor (1080m), a plateau known for its dramatic vistas of the coastal plain – and for frequent pea-soup fogs. A grand, four-storey hotel-casino, the **Bokor Palace**, opened in 1925, but the entire holiday village, including the **Catholic church** and the **post office**, was abandoned to the howling winds in 1972 when Khmer Rouge forces infiltrated the area.

The hill station became a ghost town, its once-grand buildings turned into eerie, windowless shells. Over time they became carpeted with a bright-orange lichen that gives them an other-worldly cast. Appropriate, then, that the foggy showdown that ends the Matt Dillon crime thriller *City of Ghosts* (2002) was filmed here. Other Phnom Bokor sights include lichen-caked **Wat Sampeau Moi Roi** (Five Boats Wat), from which a peaceful 11km trail (which takes three hours) leads to two-tiered **Popokvil Falls**, best seen in the wet season as it's disappointingly drippy at other times.

In early 2008 the powerful, politically connected Sokimex company began a 30-month project to re-establish a luxury resort atop Phnom Bokor. Details are hazy but word has it that they plan to restore the Bokor Palace to its former glory and even build a golf course, though how golfers are supposed to make par – or even find the ball – in the fog is anyone's guess.

Trekking in the national park has huge but almost completely unrealised potential. The park charges US$20 a day for the services of an experienced but non-English-speaking **ranger** (☎ 015-819666; bokornp@camintel.com). Bring your own protection against mosquitoes, sun and rain.

SLEEPING

Near the old hill station, the **Preah Monivong 'Bokor' National Park Training & Research Facility** (☎ 015-819666; bokornp@camintel.com; dm US$5, r US$20-30) has simply decorated rooms with hot water and up to four beds. Bring warm clothes and a torch (flashlight) as electricity goes off at 9pm.

GETTING THERE & AWAY

The visitors centre of Bokor National Park (p123), at the bottom of the hill, is 9km west of Kampot. Until the new Sokimex road is finished, the only way to get up to Bokor Hill Station is to take either a steep trek (US$40 to US$50 including overnight accommodation on top) or a motorised tour (US$40 per person for a day trip) up the potholed remains of the road built by the French in the early 1920s; both can be arranged by travel agents in Kampot (p121) unless the road is closed (as it sometimes is without notice). Prices are likely to drop significantly when the road is finished and palms no longer need to be greased.

KEP

☎ 036 / pop 13,300

Kep is the comeback kid. Ravaged by the civil war and pillaged during the famine of 1979–80, it remained a virtual ghost town until it was rediscovered by Phnom Penh's SUV class a few years back. Founded by the French elite in 1908, the town is once again thriving and the seaside is as tranquil as ever, with lapping seas and swaying palms. The beach itself, though, is a touch scrappy, as it was never a natural sandy bay. Before the war, white sand was shipped in from Sihanoukville to keep up appearances!

Sights

Scores of Kep's luxurious **mid-20th-century villas** are blackened shells, relics of a once-great civilisation that met a sudden and violent end. On top of the hill northwest of Kep Beach you can visit a **palace** (admission US$1) built by King Sihanouk in the early 1990s, perhaps with thoughts of retiring here. In the interior of the Kep peninsula, **Kep National Park** is in a sad state, with little protection against illegal logging and no guest facilities.

Offshore, the legendarily rustic **Koh Tonsay** (Rabbit Island) is considered to have the nicest beaches of any Kep-area island (except Vietnam's Phu Quoc). You can overnight at several family-run clusters of rudimentary bungalows. Boats from Kep's boat dock cost US$20 return for up to 10 people (guest houses and moto drivers tend to charge US$5 per person) and take around 20 minutes one way. If you'd like to be picked up the next day make this clear when you book or you may be charged US$5 per person to get back – as a general rule, travellers stranded on islands are in a pretty weak bargaining position.

Sleeping

our pick **Rega-Kep Guesthouse** (☎ 012-301017; regahome@camintel.com; r with fan/air-con US$7/11) This new guest house, near the Koh Tonsay boat dock, has 15 cosy rooms set around a tropical courtyard. Excellent value considering Kep prices.

Kep Seaside Guesthouse (☎ ☎ 012-684241; sengbunly@bnckh.com; r with fan/air-con from US$7/15; ❄) So close to the shore you can hear the waves (though there isn't exactly a sandy beach here), this three-storey place – dormitory-like in appearance – has 25 clean, simply furnished rooms, with more being added. Often fills up with domestic tourists, especially on weekends and holidays.

Botanica Guesthouse (☎ 016-562775; www.kep-botanica.com; r US$8-10) A Belgian-owned place with five bungalows set in a flowery garden. About 2km north of the northern roundabout towards Kampot.

Vanna Bungalow (☎ 015-462938; www.vannabungalows.com; r with fan/air-con from US$10/20; ❄) This charming, family-run place has 17 tasteful bungalows set amid pleasant gardens. The sunset sea views from the restaurant verandah are mind-blowing.

Eating

Dining in Kep is all about fresh, grilled seafood. For the best deals head to the Crab Market, a row of wooden waterfront shacks. All of Kep's guest houses and hotels have restaurants.

our pick **Kimly Restaurant** (☎ 012-435096; mains US$5-10; ⏲ 9am-10pm) Considered the best of the Crab Market eateries, mouth-watering

CAMBODIA

specialities here include prawns and fresh crab with sprigs of Kampot pepper.

Getting There & Away

Kep is 25km from Kampot and 41km from the Prek Chak–Xa Xia border crossing to Vietnam (see p126). Phnom Penh Sorya Transport and Hua Lin buses link the town with Kampot (US$2, one hour), Kompong Trach and Phnom Penh (US$4 to US$5).

A moto/túk-túk to Kampot costs about US$7/10; private taxis are US$15 to US$20. Drivers hang out at the northern end of Kep Beach.

AROUND KEP

For an enchanting mixture of dramatic natural beauty and Buddhist piety, it's hard to beat **Wat Kiri Sela** (Phnom Kompong Trach, Wat Kirisan; admission US$1), 23km northeast of Kep. Built at the foot of a karst formation riddled with over 100 caverns and passageways, this Buddhist temple is linked by an underground passage to the centre of the hill, where the vine-draped cliffs of a hidden valley unfold before you. This is the sort of place where you'd hardly be surprised to see a dinosaur munching on foliage or, à la *Jurassic Park*, chewing on a lawyer. Friendly local kids with torches (flashlights), eager to put their evening-school English to use, are happy to serve as guides; make sure your tip covers the cost of batteries.

To get to Wat Kiri Sela from Kep, you can take a moto/túk-túk (US$3/5) or grab a Phnom Penh–bound bus or minibus (both US$2). From the town of Kompong Trach, take the dirt road opposite the Acleda Bank for 2km.

NORTHEASTERN CAMBODIA

The northeast, with its remote pine forests and rainforests, ethnic minorities and growing ecotourism sector, is a veritable smorgasbord of Cambodia's best – you can see rare Mekong dolphins one day and bamboo-munching highland elephants the next.

KOMPONG CHAM

☎ 042 / pop 45,400

This quiet Mekong city, an important trading post during the French period, serves as the gateway to Cambodia's northeast.

> **GETTING TO VIETNAM: TRAPAENG PLONG TO XA MAT**
>
> Krek (Kraek), on NH7 55km southeast of Kompong Cham, is served by the buses linking Kompong Cham with both Kratie and Sen Monorom. From there, take a moto 13km south along NH72 to snoozy **Trapaeng Plong** (7am-5pm), marked by a candy-striped road barrier and a few tin shacks. On the Vietnamese side, Xa Mat, motos and taxis go to Tay Ninh, 45km to the south. For information on crossing this border in the other direction, see p839.

Preah Bat Sihanouk St, home to several hotels and eateries, runs along the riverfront. Psar Thmei (New Market) is a few blocks inland (west); Preah Monivong Blvd is one block further west.

ANZ Royal Bank (Preah Monivong Blvd) is one of several banks with an ATM. You can check emails at **Sophary Internet** (cnr Preah Bat Sihanouk St & Vithei Pasteur; per hr 3000r; 7am-9pm).

Sights & Activities

Wat Nokor (admission US$2), about 1km west of town, is an 11th-century Mahayana Buddhist shrine of sandstone and laterite set slap-bang in the centre of an active and slightly kitsch Theravada wat. Equally tranquil is a bike ride or walk on the car-less rural island of **Koh Paen**, which is connected to town in the dry season by an elaborate bamboo bridge (during the wet season there's a ferry).

Phnom Pros (Man Hill) and its counterpart **Phnom Sre** (Woman Hill), located about 7km northwest of town (towards Phnom Penh), offer fine views of the countryside. Inquisitive monkeys populate the trees. A moto/túk-túk costs about US$5/10 return (depending on wait time), including a stop at Wat Nokor.

Sleeping

There are several hotels along the riverfront.

Bophea Guesthouse (☎ 012-857919; Vithei Pasteur; r US$3-5) This 10-room place is bare bones – but then what do you expect for these prices? Cheaper rooms have a shared bathroom. A block in from the riverfront.

Mekong Hotel (☎ 941536; Preah Bat Sihanouk St; r with fan/air-con US$6/12;) It's hard to beat this hotel, with its prime riverfront location, corridors wide enough for a footy match and 68

GETTING TO VIETNAM: PREK CHAK TO XA XIA

The cheapest way to get from Kampot or Kep to the **Prek Chak border crossing** (6am-5.30pm) is to take a Phnom Penh-bound bus to Kompong Trach and then a moto (about US$3) for the last 18km. In Kampot, tour agencies and guest houses can arrange a direct moto (US$10, one hour), share taxi (US$5, one hour) or private taxi (US$25). From pricier Kep, a moto/túk-túk (a taxi may be hard to find) should cost about US$8/15.

Coming to Prek Chak, taxis have been known to drop off passengers before the border in order to force them to overpay for an onward moto – make sure yours stops right at the Cambodian border barrier.

Some motos can take you from the Cambodian side to the Vietnamese border post, 300m past the Cambodian one, and then all the way to the Vietnamese town of Ha Tien (7km) for US$2 to US$3 (more for an English-speaking driver).

For information on crossing this border in the other direction, see p921.

good-value rooms with satellite TV. Ask for a Mekong view.

Eating & Drinking

Psar Thmei has **fruit stalls** in its northwest and southeast corners. After the sun goes down there's a **night market** along the river opposite the Mekong Hotel (p125).

Two Dragons Restaurant (☎ 011-888745; Ang Duong St; mains US$2-3; 4am-8pm) Incredibly popular with Khmers, this place serves early breakfasts, exotic dishes such as ginger-fried eel, and ever-changing off-the-menu specials. Situated 50m south of the roundabout on NH7 (just west of the bridge on-ramp).

Mekong Crossing (☎ 012-432427; Preah Bat Sihanouk St; mains US$2-4; 6am-9pm or 10pm) This old favourite serves an enticing mix of Khmer curries and Western favourites like burgers and sandwiches. By night it doubles as a bar and draws local expats.

Getting There & Around

Phnom Penh Sorya (☎ 092-181810) and **GST** (☎ 012-734052), both with offices on Preah Monivong Blvd, run direct buses to Phnom Penh (US$4, three hours), Siem Reap (US$7, five hours) via Kompong Thom (US$6, 2½ hours), Battambang (US$10) via Udong, and Stung Treng (US$10, six to eight hours) via Snuol (junction for travel to Mondulkiri province and Kratie (US$4 to US$6, four hours). **Neak Kror Horm** (☎ 012-557474) is a bit cheaper on some routes.

You can catch a share taxi to Phnom Penh (15,000r to 20,000r, 2½ hours) on the northeast side of the market.

The Mekong Hotel (p125) rents bicycles for US$2 a day.

KRATIE

☎ 072 / pop 79,000

The best place in Cambodia to glimpse Southeast Asia's remaining freshwater Irrawaddy dolphins, Kratie (pronounced 'kra-*cheh*') is a lively riverside town with a rich legacy of French-era architecture (such as that around the market) and some of the best Mekong sunsets in Cambodia. A thriving travel hub, it's the natural place to break the overland journey between Kompong Cham and Laos – or to pick up the Mekong Discovery Trail (p129).

Information

Kratie is laid out on a grid, with Rue Preah Suramarit running along the river and, at right angles, numbered streets heading inland. The market is one block inland between St 8 and St 10. Red Sun Falling cafe (opposite) and guest houses are pretty switched on when it comes to the kind of information travellers need.

Canadia Bank (Preah Mohaksat Iranie Kosomak near St 11) Should have an ATM by the time you read this.

Ly Kheang Web (St 10; per hr 4000r; 7am-9.30pm) Reliable internet.

Sights & Activities

About 15km north of town at **Kampi**, endangered **freshwater Irrawaddy dolphins** (Mekong River dolphins) often break the great river's silent surface for a breath of fresh air. It costs US$2 to visit the site, plus US$2 or US$3 per person for a boat, depending on the number of passengers. A return moto ride costs US$5 or US$6, depending on how long the driver has to wait and whether you stop off at **Phnom Sombok**, a 70m-high hill with an active wat and fine Mekong views, especially at sunset.

Cycling is also an option. The riverside road towards Chhlong makes for a nice bike ride; see p128 for information on bike hire.

Sleeping

You Hong Guesthouse (☎ 012-957003; youhong_kratie@yahoo.com; 91 St 8; r US$3-5; 💻) A great little shoes-off guest house overlooking the bustling market. Below the 11 simple rooms, there's a lively little bar-restaurant plastered wall-to-wall with travel info.

Sok Sen Guesthouse (☎ 012-732185; St 13; r US$4-6) On a quiet corner three blocks from the river, the 3m-by-3m cubicles have windows that look out onto a narrow patio, and basic but liveable tile bathrooms. US$6 rooms come with TV.

Oudom Sambath Hotel (☎ 971502, fax 971503; 439 Rue Preah Suramarit; r with fan/air-con from US$5/15; ❄) A large, well-kept riverfront property with spacious rooms. Excellent value, especially if you're a fan fan.

Heng Heng II Hotel (☎ 012-929943; hengheng2hotel@yahoo.com; Rue Preah Suramarit; r with fan/air-con US$7/15; ❄) A friendly, newish place whose 23 decent rooms have cable TV.

Eating & Drinking

Along the riverfront, **food stalls** (Rue Preah Suramarit) sell two famous Kratie specialities: *krolan* (sticky rice, beans and coconut milk steamed inside a bamboo tube; 7000r per kg), displayed on tables that look like miniature church organs; and *nehm* (tangy raw, spiced river fish wrapped in edible fresh leaves that are in turn wrapped in a cube of banana leaves; US$5 per kg).

Also on the riverfront, you can have a cheap dinner at the **night market** (Rue Preah Suramarit).

Red Sun Falling (☎ 012-476528; Rue Preah Suramarit; mains 6000r-14,000r) One of the liveliest little spots in town, with a relaxed cafe ambience, used books for sale and Asian and Western meals, including home-made brownies. By night it's a bar.

Getting There & Away

Buses depart Kratie from along the riverfront around St 8 and St 10. **GST Express** (in Heng Heng's restaurant), **Phnom Penh Sorya** (☎ 092-181806), **Rith Mony** (☎ 012-991663; on the riverbank next to the port building) and **Thong Ly** (☎ 011-787772; next to Red Sun Falling) run buses to Phnom Penh (25,000r, six to seven hours) via Snuol (connection point for Mondulkiri; US$2) and Kompong Cham (20,000r, three to four hours); Stung

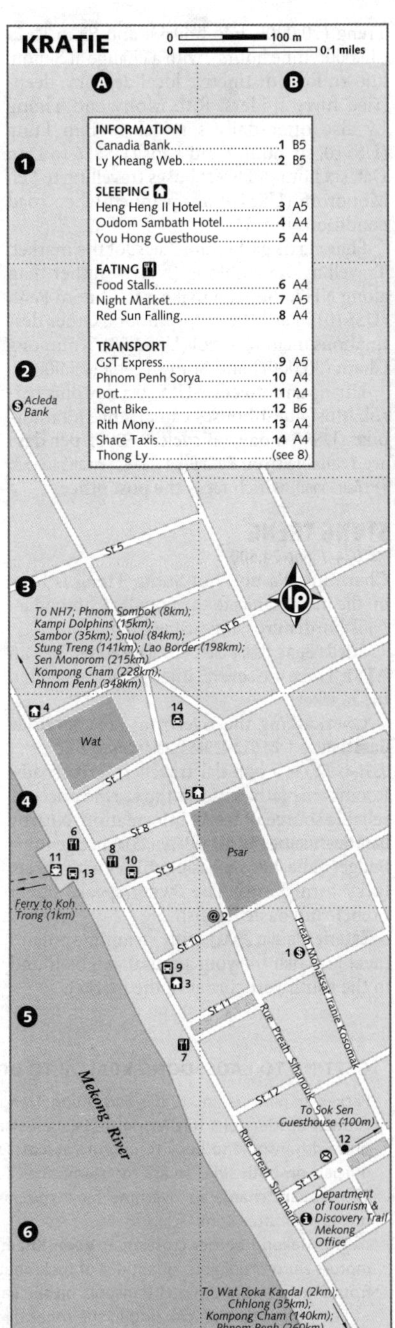

Treng (20,000r, two hours); and Siem Reap (45,000r, nine hours), with a change at Skuon, known for a distinctive local delicacy: deep-fried furry spiders. Rith Mony and Thong Ly also offer daily services to Ban Lung (US$10, six hours) and Laos (US$16 to Don Dat, six hours). Direct buses travelling to Sen Monorom (US$10) are planned when road conditions improve.

Share taxis gather northeast of the market. Travelling via Chhlong (NH73) rather than along NH7, they can make it to Phnom Penh (US$10) in as little as four hours. Other destinations include Snuol (US$2.50), Kompong Cham (30,000r) and Stung Treng (25,000r).

Hiring a moto costs US$10 a day plus petrol. Most guest houses can arrange a motorbike (US$6 a day). Bicycles (6000r per day) are available from **Rent Bike** (124 Rue Preah Sihanouk; 6am-6pm), which faces the post office.

STUNG TRENG

☎ 074 / pop 24,500

Charming it's not, but Stung Treng is back on the map thanks to the popular Cambodia–Laos border crossing just 60km north.

Acleda Bank (half a block east of the market) has an ATM. There are several internet places around the market.

Overlooking the riverfront area, **Riverside Guesthouse** (☎ 012-439454; taingpow@yahoo.com; r US$3-4;) is a popular travellers' crossroads. Rooms are pretty basic, but so are the prices. A reliable source of travel information. Nearby **Dara Guesthouse** (☎ 011-693429; r 15,000r), a genuine budget oldie, has six basic cubicles with cheap, tacky furnishings. The owner speaks fluent French and basic English.

Eateries (mains 2500r) with steaming pots of meat and fish for your perusal can be found in the southwest corner of the market.

Rith Mony (☎ 092-619441; next to Riverside Guesthouse), **Phnom Penh Sorya** (two blocks inland from the river) and **GST** (diagonally across the intersection from Phnom Penh Sorya) all have 7am buses to Phnom Penh (40,000r, nine hours) via Kratie (20,000r, two hours) and Kompong Cham (32,000r, six hours). Rith Mony has a 3pm bus to Ban Lung (US$5).

From the riverfront taxi park, share taxis and minibuses go to Phnom Penh (50,000r, eight hours), Kompong Cham (45,000r, six hours) and Ban Lung (30,000r, 3½ hours).

RATANAKIRI PROVINCE

Remote Ratanakiri province offers outdoor enthusiasts some of Cambodia's most adventurous options: swim in clear volcanic lakes, shower under waterfalls, ride an elephant or trek in vast Virachey National Park – it's all here. Many of the locals belong to minority peoples such as the Jarai, Tampuen, Brau and Kreung.

Prepare to do battle with the red dust of Ratanakiri, which will leave you with orange hair and a fake tan in the dry season and sliding around in a rust-coloured slurry in the wet.

Ban Lung

☎ 075 / pop 25,000

Ratanakiri's low-density, low-pressure capital is a functional base for romps around the region. Check out Cambodia's finest swimming hole – in fact, a volcanic crater known as Yeak Laom – or take the plunge under a waterfall to cleanse your skin and soothe your soul. Members of highland minorities, woven baskets on their backs, come from nearby villages to buy and sell at the market.

INFORMATION

The main commercial street stretches from the roundabout on NH78 south to the market.

GETTING TO LAOS: DONG KRALOR TO DONG KALAW

Packed minibuses link Kratie and Stung Treng with **Dong Kralor** (Dom Kralor; 6am-6pm) and Laotian destinations further north. Laotian visas are *not* available at the border and neither is onward transport so book through to at least Don Det (US$12 from Stung Treng). Expect border officials on both sides to ask for 'stamp fees' (US$1 to US$2, depending on how rich you look). The Laotians charge an 'overtime' fee if you pass through after 'working hours', ie on weekends, holidays or after 4pm.

The Mekong border crossing at **Voen Kham** (Voen Khao) is pretty much defunct – outboard motors slurp prodigious quantities of fuel – but if cost is no object you can charter a speedboat from Stung Treng. Onward transport on the Lao side needs to be arranged in advance.

For information on crossing in the other direction, see p421.

Acleda Bank Has an ATM.
Redland Internet Café (per hr US$2; 7am-8pm)
Tourist Information Center (974125; 7.30-11.30am & 2-5pm Mon-Fri) Has brochures on Ratanakiri.

SIGHTS & ACTIVITIES

Boeng Yeak Laom

One of the most serene and sublimely beautiful sites in all of Cambodia, this clear blue **crater lake** (admission US$1), surrounded by dark green jungle, is sacred to the indigenous minority peoples. It's a great place to take a dip – Cambodians do it fully clothed. The NGO-run **Cultural & Environmental Centre** (012-981226; admission by donation; 8am-5.30pm), 500m around the lake from the little eateries, displays traditional Tampuen crafts. The adjacent kiosk sells authentic Tampuen crafts and rents inner tubes (3000r).

Boeng Yeak Laom is a walkable 4km east of Ban Lung; turn right at the statue of the minority family. Motos cost about US$3 return, more if the driver has to wait around.

Waterfalls

There are three waterfalls within 10km of Ban Lung. For a power shower, head to **Chaa Ong Waterfall** (admission 2000r), which is set in a scenic rocky jungle gorge, allowing you to clamber straight under the falls. **Ka Tieng Waterfall** (admission free) is perhaps the most fun, as there are some vines on the far side that are strong enough to swing on. Another beautiful waterfall in the neighbourhood is **Kinchaan Waterfall** (admission 2000r).

Directions are signposted 3km west of town on the road to Stung Treng but hook up with a local as they're difficult to find. Admission to each is 2000r.

Trekking

Overnight trekking has really started to take off around Ratanakiri but make sure you link up with a guide who is culturally and ecologically sensitive. Popular routes take in minority villages, including Kreung villages near the road to Ta Veng and Jarai villages up in Andong Meas district. Only official ecorangers can take you into Virachey National Park (p130). With deforestation continuing apace, last year's lush forest may be this year's barren expanse of smouldering tree stumps.

Day hikes, elephant rides, kayaking and overnight treks are offered by a number of guest houses and tour companies:

Dutch Couple (17 571682; www.ecotourismcambodia.info; Oct-Aug) A new ecotourism outfit.
Highland Tour Association (089-954001; highland.tour@yahoo.com.kh; 7am-approximately 9pm) A group of Cambodian guides that runs day trips (per person US$10 to US$15) and overnight treks.
Parrot Tours (012-764714; sitha_guide@yahoo.com) Sitha Nan is a national-park-trained guide with expert local knowledge. Based at A'Dam Restaurant (below).

SLEEPING

In addition to the following options, there are a number of guest houses between the roundabout on NH78 and the market.

Tribal Guesthouse (974074; r US$3-15;) The only thing that's tribal here is some of the decor but the 42 rooms are decent and offer good value.

Star Hotel (012-958322; r with fan/air-con US$5/10;) Run by the irrepressible Mr Leng, this tiled structure, originally built as a private house, has 12 spacious rooms and a '90s-style all-wood lounge area. Excellent value.

Lake View Lodge (092-785259; ratanakiri@gmail.com; r US$5-13;) Overlooking the lake in a quiet villa once owned by the vice-governor, this backpacker pad has eight wood-panelled rooms with high ceilings.

EATING

Ban Lung's cheapest food is around the market. Guest houses offer some good dining options; **Star Hotel** (mains 12,000r-25,000r) is great for a beer or *phnom pleung* (literally, 'hill of fire').

A'Dam Restaurant (012-411115; mains US$2-2.50; 11am-3pm & 5.30pm-midnight) An animated bar

MEKONG DISCOVERY TRAIL

This 190km network of **walking and cycling trails** (www.mekongdiscoverytrail.com), which links Kratie with Stung Treng and the Lao border, can be followed for a few hours or several days, with overnights in village homestays (see the website for details). The most accessible bit of the trail – a 9km circuit – is on **Koh Trong**, a river island accessible by a short ferry ride (for a pedestrian/bicycle 1000/500r; leaves when full from about 6am to 5pm) from Kratie's **port** (Rue Preah Suramarit).

City bicycles can be rented in Kratie and Stung Treng and may soon be available on Koh Trong.

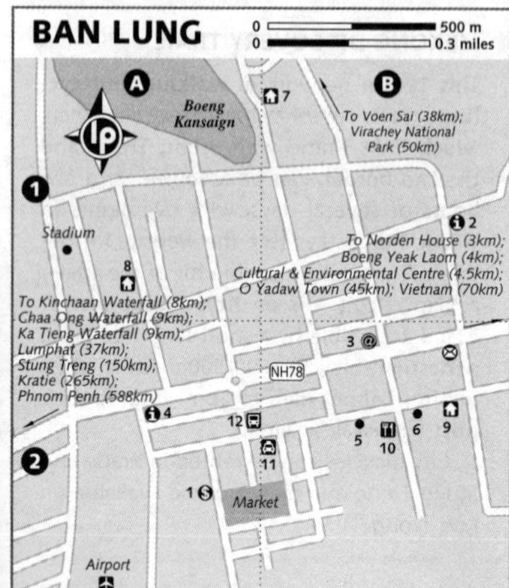

INFORMATION
Acleda Bank....1 A2
Eco-Tourism Information Center....2 B1
Redland Internet Café....3 B2
Tourist Information Center....4 A2

SIGHTS & ACTIVITIES
Dutch Couple....5 B2
Highland Tour Association....6 B2
Parrot Tours....(see 10)
Virachey National Park Headquarters....(see 2)

SLEEPING
Lake View Lodge....7 B1
Star Hotel....8 A1
Tribal Guesthouse....9 B2

EATING
A'Dam Restaurant....10 B2
Star Hotel....(see 8)

TRANSPORT
Ly Heng Express....(see 12)
Taxi Park....11 B2
Thong Ly....12 A2

by night, this mellow restaurant warmly welcomes locals, expats and travellers.

GETTING THERE & AWAY

Ban Lung is 588km northeast of Phnom Penh and 150km east of Stung Treng.

Thong Ly (☎ 092-278933) has full-size buses to Stung Treng (US$8, 4½ hours), Kratie (US$10, six hours), Kompong Cham (US$11.50, eight hours) and Phnom Penh (US$11.50, 12 hours). Prices rise in the wet season.

Fast minibuses operated by **Ly Heng Express** (☎ 023-350612) go to Kratie (US$12.50, three to four hours), Kompong Cham (US$15, seven to eight hours) and Phnom Penh (US$15, 10 hours). Travel times are longer in the wet season. In Phnom Penh, departures are from the Hua Lian office (p85).

Share taxis go from the taxi park to Kratie (US$10 to US$12.50), Phnom Penh (US$15 to US$17.50, seven hours) and Kompong Cham (US$15 to $17.50). Pick-ups are slightly cheaper if you ride out back.

Heading south to Sen Monorom in Mondulkiri, via Koh Nhek and Lumphat and the wilderness between them by dirt bike is not for the faint-hearted – or anyone without many years of off-road motorcycle experience.

Parrot Tours (p129) rents motorbikes for US$8 a day.

AROUND RATANAKIRI PROVINCE

Voen Sai

The *chunchiet* (ethnic minorities) of Ratanakiri province bury their dead amid the ancient jungle, carving wooded effigies of the deceased – some holding sunglasses and mobile phones – to stand guard over the graves. In **Voen Sai**, 38km (1½ hours by car or motorbike or, in the wet season, 4WD) northwest of Ban Lung, you can hire a long-tailed motorboat (US$15 for up to three people) for a 40-minute upriver ride to **Kachon**, where you can visit a **Tampuen cemetery** (admission US$1). The boat also drops by an orderly Chinese village, five minutes downriver from Voen Sai, and a nearby Lao village.

A number of Ban Lung tour agencies offer trekking in this area, including visits to a highly sensitive gibbon protected area 3km beyond Itup (I Tub) village, which is 9km north of the Voen Sai ferry. Unfortunately, if they're not conducted properly, such excursions can disturb the gibbons and disrupt the scientists' research. A sustainable ecotour of the area is planned but in the meantime if you choose to trek here, insist that your guide respects local cultures and steer clear of the gibbon protected area (there are plenty of other places to see primates).

Virachey National Park

Cambodia's most developed ecotrekking program takes visitors deep into 3325-sq-km **Virachey National Park** (admission US$5), an ecological gem in the country's far northeastern tip that's so remote it has yet to be fully explored. The park's forests and grasslands are home to elephants, gibbons and an amazing variety of birds, including hornbills and vultures. The area was once traversed by the Ho Chi Minh Trail (p900) and war relics are still lying around – don't touch!

The park offers two- to eight-day treks – at least one itinerary is available year-round – led by English-speaking ecorangers and designed to benefit local minority communities. Travel is on foot or by mountain bike, inflatable kayak, boat and/or motorbike (helmet provided). Per person prices drop the larger the group: including transport, accommodation and food, a two-day (one-night) trek costs US$64/57 per person with one/eight participants, while a four-day trek costs US$185/133. Bookings must be made by email, fax, phone or in person at least a day or two ahead via the park's official **Eco-Tourism Information Center** (☎ 974176, 012-1726817, fax 974013; virachey@camintel.com; 🕒 8-11.30am & 2-3pm Mon-Fri) in Ban Lung.

MONDULKIRI PROVINCE

Mondulkiri ('Meeting of the Hills') is a world apart from the rest of Cambodia, with not a rice paddy or sugar palm in sight. Home to the hardy Phnong (Bunong) people and their noble elephants, this upland area is a seductive mix of grassy hills, pine groves and rainforests of jade green. Conservationists, including the **WWF** (www.panda.org), have grand plans for the sparsely populated province but are facing off against loggers, poachers, prospectors and well-connected speculators.

Sen Monorom

☎ 073 / pop 7000 / elev 800m

Sen Monorom, the best base for exploring Mondulkiri, has the feel of a remote outpost town. Many Phnong people from nearby villages come to Sen Monorom to trade – the distinctive baskets they carry on their backs makes them easy to spot.

INFORMATION

Middle of Somewhere (right), as good an urban landmark as any, is half-a-block downhill (southeast) from the seldom-used dirt airstrip, which runs parallel to the main road through town.

Acleda Bank Situated about 1km towards Phnom Penh from the centre. Has an ATM.

Green House (☎ 017-905659; www.thewaytomondulkiri.com, in French; internet per hr US$1.50) Internet access and a lively open-air bar by night. Next to Middle of Somewhere.

Middle of Somewhere (☎ 012-474879; www.bunongcenter.org; 🕒 6am-9pm) This NGO-run 'drop-in centre' for Phnong people is the best source of information on sustainable tourism, village homestays and elephant rides. Sells authentic Phnong baskets, beads, musical instruments and cotton textiles. Internet access is planned.

SIGHTS & ACTIVITIES

Not much happens in Sen Monorom itself but there's plenty to see and do nearby.

The Phnong people have used elephants for jungle transport for countless generations. The **Elephant Valley Project** (☎ 011-694131; jackhighwood@yahoo.co.uk) – run by the NGO **Elephants Livelihood Initiative Environment** (www.elie-cambodia.org) – offers amateur mahout (elephant driver or keeper) training, elephant rides to a waterfall and overnight treks for US$50 per day (half that for kids), including transport, accommodation (in bungalows) and food; profits fund veterinary care for Mondulkiri's 61 working elephants (there are also hundreds of wild elephants). Middle of Somewhere has details and can make reservations.

Trips out to **Phnong villages**, including **elephant rides** (US$20) and overnight treks, and to waterfalls can be arranged via Middle of Somewhere, Long Vibol Guesthouse, Arun Reah II Hill Lodge (1km southwest of the town centre, towards Phnom Penh) and Green House.

Head to the observation deck of **Phnom Bai Chuw** (Raw Rice Mountain), 6km northwest of Sen Monorom (accessible on foot or by moto), for a jaw-dropping view of the emerald forest, known to locals as **Samot Cheur** (Ocean of Trees).

> **GETTING TO VIETNAM: O YADAW TO LE THANH**
>
> Opened to tourists in 2008, this **crossing** (🕒 7am-5pm) is 70km east of Ban Lung. From Ban Lung, pick-ups (inside/outside 15,000r/10,000r) and share taxis (about US$5) go to O Yadaw, a district town 25km west of the frontier. From there, your best bet is to hitch a paid ride with a cargo truck (don't count on being able to find a moto). On the Vietnamese side of the frontier, the road is nicely paved and motos await to take you to Duc Co (20km), where there are buses (15,000d) to Pleiku. For information on crossing in the other direction, see p898.

CAMBODIA

CAMBODIA

GETTING TO VIETNAM: TRAPAENG SRE TO LOC NINH

To get to this **crossing** (7am-5pm), seldom used by foreigners, catch a moto (US$5) in the much-maligned junction town of Snuol for an 18km trip southeast along NH74, which is little more than a rutted dirt track. Snuol, on nicely paved NH7, is linked by bus, share taxi and minibus with Sen Monorom, Kratie and Kompong Cham. On the Vietnamese side, the nearest town is Binh Long, 40km to the south. For information on crossing in the other direction, see p839.

SLEEPING

Pech Kiri Guesthouse (012-932102; r US$5-15) Once the only guest house in town, this laid-back place has a large garden, a new wing out back and bargain bungalows. From Middle of Somewhere, walk a block-and-a-half downhill and head right.

Phnom Meas Guesthouse (012-929562; r US$5-10) About 1km northeast of the centre, next to Long Vibol, the 'Golden Hill' has curious upstairs-downstairs huts, simply furnished garden bungalows and lots of potted plants.

our pick Long Vibol Guesthouse (012-944647; r US$5-20) An attractive wood-built resort with 20 rooms set amid a lush garden, with staff who are knowledgeable about the area. Situated on the main road through town 1km northeast of the centre.

Oeurn Sakona Hotel (012-950680; r US$5-20;) This modern place has 48 comfortable rooms with chintzy lamps and some over-the-top hardwood furniture in the lobby. Two blocks down the hill from Middle of Somewhere.

DRINKING

Middle of Somewhere (012-474879; 6am-9pm) Serves as a very informal cafe, with drinks, snacks and cakes. A favourite hang-out of all the local NGO folk.

GETTING THERE & AWAY

By the time you read this, the once-hellish road to Sen Monorom (NH76) should be passable year-round, making it possible to establish all-season bus- and share-taxi services to/from Phnom Penh (six hours), Kratie and Kompong Cham.

As we go to press, your only option may be to jam into one of the pick-up trucks that hang out one block west of Psar Thmei; destinations include Snuol (US$5), a junction on NH7 where you can catch buses, minibuses and pick-ups (all US$2) to Kratie (a share taxi, if you can find one, should cost US$2.50); Kompong Cham (US$10); and Phnom Penh (US$10). Riding inside the cab costs 50% more. Departures are generally very early in the morning.

Heading north to Ban Lung (p128), in Ratanakiri, via Koh Nhek and Lumphat on a motorcycle is only for hard-core bikers with oodles of off-road experience.

GETTING AROUND

Motorbike rental (US$8 to US$10 a day) can be arranged through Long Vibol Guesthouse, which can also organise a car. Renting a pick-up costs US$80 a day plus petrol (less in the dry season).

Around Sen Monorom

The real joy of the Mondulkiri Province is exploring by motorcycle or on foot at your own pace.

Monorom Falls, in the forest a walkable 3km northwest of town, is the closest thing to a public swimming pool for Sen Monorom. Motos take people out here for about US$2 return.

Two-tiered **Bou Sraa Waterfall**, 35km east of Sen Monorom along a good toll road, is famous throughout the country. Hire a moto for the day (US$15) or charter a car (US$60) for a group.

CAMBODIA DIRECTORY

ACCOMMODATION

In popular tourist destinations, budget guest houses generally charge US$5 to US$8 for a room with a cold-water bathroom; a few very basic places – some with share showers – have rooms for US$3. In much of rural Cambodia, the standard rate for the cheapest proper hotel room is US$5, usually with a bathroom and satellite TV.

Accommodation is fullest – and prices highest – from mid-November to March. Discounts are most in evidence during the wet season (June to October). All rooms quoted in this chapter have bathrooms unless stated otherwise.

Homestays, often part of a **community-based ecotourism project** (www.ccben.org), are a good way to meet the local people and learn about Cambodian life.

ACTIVITIES

Cambodia is emerging as an ecotourism destination and now offers cycling along the Mekong Discovery Trail (p129) and in places such as the temples of Angkor (p87), rainforest trekking in the Cardamom Mountains (p114) and Ratanakiri (p129), elephant riding in Mondulkiri (p131) and Ratanakiri (p129), scuba-diving and snorkelling near Sihanoukville (p116) and birdwatching with the Sam Veasna Center (p95).

BOOKS

For the full story on travelling in Cambodia, pick up Lonely Planet's *Cambodia* guide.

A great selection of books on Cambodia can be found in the better bookshops in Phnom Penh and Siem Reap. Markets and street sellers with disabilities offer cheap knock-offs of most titles, but we know you wouldn't dream of buying a pirated Lonely Planet guide. Be warned: if this is a photocopy it may self-destruct in five seconds!

The best introduction to the history of Cambodia is David P Chandler's *A History of Cambodia,* which covers the ups and downs of the Khmers over two millennia. Also by Chandler is *Brother Number One,* the menacing biography of Pol Pot, however Philip Short's biography *Pol Pot: The History of a Nightmare* is more detailed and a riveting read.

When the War was Over by Elizabeth Becker is an insight into life in the last days of Pol Pot's regime and its aftermath by one of the few journalists to visit Democratic Kampuchea back in 1978.

In *The Gate,* François Bizot recounts being kidnapped by the Khmer Rouge and interrogated by Comrade Duch, the head of Tuol Sleng prison, who is now on trial. Bizot is believed to be the only foreigner to have survived being captured.

WARNING

The Ho Chi Minh Trail (p900) once passed through the hills of Mondulkiri and was bombed by the Americans – never touch unexploded ordnance.

Sideshow: Kissinger, Nixon and the Destruction of Cambodia by William Shawcross (1979) is the definitive account of the secret American war of the early 1970s.

The classic travel literature option is Norman Lewis' *A Dragon Apparent* (1951), an account of his 1950 foray into an Indochina that was soon to disappear.

See p100 for books on Angkor.

BUSINESS HOURS

Most Cambodians get up very early and it's not unusual to see people out exercising at 5.30am when you're heading home – ahem, sorry, getting up.

Government offices, open from Monday to Friday and on Saturday mornings, theoretically begin the working day at 7.30am, break for a siesta from 11.30am to 2pm, and end the day at 5pm. However, it's a safe bet that few staffers will be around early in the morning or after 3.30pm or 4pm as their real income is earned elsewhere (government jobs are notoriously poorly paid – teachers, for instance, earn just US$30 a month).

Local markets *(psar)* operate seven days a week and usually open and close with the sun, running from 6.30am to 5.30pm. Shops in cities and larger towns tend to be open from about 8am until 7pm Monday to Saturday, and most are open on Sundays too.

Banking hours vary slightly, but you can reckon on core weekday hours of between 8.30am and 3pm. Most are also open Saturday mornings.

Local restaurants are generally open from about 6.30am until 9pm and international restaurants until a little later.

Any exceptions to these hours are listed in individual reviews.

CLIMATE

The climate of Cambodia is governed by two seasons, which set the rhythm of rural life. The dry season runs from about mid-November to May, with temperatures increasing from February; from June to early November, there are strong winds, high humidity and heavy rains. Even during the wet season, it rarely rains in the morning – most precipitation falls in the afternoon and, even then, only sporadically. If you're planning to explore more remote areas though, the wet season makes for tough, messy travel. See the climate charts on p936 for more information.

SCAMS

Cambodia is legendary for its inventive (and often well-connected) scammers. There's no need to be alarmed, but it helps to arrive with an idea of their repertoire.

The scam action often starts right at the Cambodian frontier – or, in many cases (eg Poipet), before you even get there – with shameless overcharging for visas (see p140). In fact, you may encounter your first Cambodia-related scam in Bangkok – remember, if that bus fare to Siem Reap sounds too good to be true, it probably is, and may involve arriving very late at night and being deposited at a substandard, overpriced guest house.

Upon setting foot on Cambodian territory, you are likely to meet your first moto drivers' cartel. These seemingly aggressive fellows – often quite friendly once you get to know them – are intent on convincing you (or forcing you, by making sure there's a dearth of other options) to pay over-the-odds to get to the nearest town.

Many frontier moto drivers will offer to help you to 'change money' – at rip-off rates or as part of a con. Remember, if you have US dollars (or, near Thailand, baht), there's absolutely no need to buy riels at the border (see p138). If you do want to exchange currency, never go to the exchange place 'recommended' by a moto driver, even if it bills itself as 'official'.

Both at borders and at some inland bus stations (eg Sihanoukville), members of moto cartels with semi-official monopoly status (local officials enjoy benefits from letting them operate) will make a determined effort to overcharge for rides. In parallel, they'll try to steer you to guest houses and hotels that pay them fat commissions. Don't believe age-old lines such as 'that place is closed' – if you want to go to a specific establishment, insist on being taken there (smiling also usually helps, as it does with everything in Cambodia).

CUSTOMS

A 'reasonable amount' of duty-free items is allowed into the country. Travellers arriving by air might bear in mind that alcohol and cigarettes are on sale at well below duty-free prices on the streets of Phnom Penh. It is illegal to take antiquities out of the country.

DANGERS & ANNOYANCES

Mines & Mortars

Cambodia remains is one of the most heavily mined countries in the world, especially in the west and northwest, and many mined areas are unmarked, so remember the golden rule – stick to well-marked paths in remote areas! *Never, ever* touch any unexploded ordnance (UXO) you come across, including mortars and artillery shells.

If you find yourself in a mined area, retrace your steps only if you can clearly see your footprints. If not, stay where you are and call for help. If someone is injured in a minefield, do not rush in to help even if they are in terrible pain – find someone who knows how to enter a mined area safely.

Theft & Street Crime

Cambodia is generally a safe place to travel as long as you exercise common sense. Hold-ups are rare but petty theft is a problem in the major cities and – especially – at beaches. Late at night, walking alone in unlit areas is not advisable, particularly for unaccompanied women – there's no need to be paranoid, just cautious.

In the major cities, drive-by bag snatchings happen and are especially dangerous when you're riding a moto as you can fall and hit your head. Shoulder bags are an attractive target, so on a moto hold them tightly in front of you so that thieves – who come up from behind – don't have a strap to slash (they sometimes miss the strap and end up stabbing the rider). Never put a bag or purse in the front basket of a motorbike or bicycle.

DRIVING LICENCE

The Cambodian police do not recognise foreign driver's licences or international driving permits so, in theory at least, you need a Cambodian licence to operate a motorcycle or car. With the right connections (ask around in Phnom Penh, Siem Reap, Sihanoukville or Battambang) and some cash in the right hands it's easy enough to arrange a local licence.

EMBASSIES & CONSULATES

Among the embassies in Phnom Penh:

Australia & Canada (Map p78; ☎ 023-213 470; www.cambodia.embassy.gov.au; 11 St 254)

China (Map pp74-5; ☎ 023-720920; www.fmprc.gov.cn; 156 Mao Tse Toung Blvd)
France (Map pp74-5; ☎ 023-430020; www.ambafrance-kh.org, in French; 1 Monivong Blvd)
Germany (Map p78; ☎ 023-216381; www.phnom-penh.diplo.de; 76-78 St 214)
Indonesia (Map p78; ☎ 023-216148; www.kbriphnompenh.org; 90 Norodom Blvd)
Laos (Map pp74-5; ☎ 023-982632; 15-17 Mao Tse Toung Blvd)
Malaysia (Map p78; ☎ 023-216177; www.kln.gov.my/perwakilan/phnompenh; 5 St 242)
Myanmar (Map pp74-5; ☎ 023-213663/4; www.mofa.gov.mm; 181 Norodom Blvd)
Singapore (Map p78; ☎ 023-221875; www.mfa.gov.sg/phnompenh; 129 Norodom Blvd)
Thailand (Map pp74-5; ☎ 023-726306; www.mfa.go.th; 196 Norodom Blvd)
UK (Map p78; ☎ 023-427124; http://ukincambodia.fco.gov.uk; 27 St 75)
USA (Map p78; ☎ 023-728000; http://cambodia.usembassy.gov; 1 St 96)
Vietnam (Map pp74-5; ☎ 023-726274; www.vietnamembassy-cambodia.org/en; 436 Monivong Blvd; 🕒 8.30-11.30am & 2.30-5pm Mon-Fri). There are handy consulates in Sihanoukville (p116) – issuing the fastest Vietnamese visa in Southeast Asia – and Battambang (p103).

For information on visas, see p140.

EMERGENCIES

Ambulance (☎ 119)
Fire (☎ 118)
Police & Medical (☎ 117)
Tourist police (☎ 724793)

FESTIVALS & EVENTS

Cambodia's festivals take place according to the lunar calendar so the dates vary from year to year.

Chinese New Year The big Chinese community goes wild for the new year in late January or early to mid-February, with dragon dances filling many of Phnom Penh's streets. As it's also Tet, the Vietnamese live it up too.
Chaul Chnam Held in mid-April, this is a three-day celebration of Khmer New Year. Khmers worship in wats to wash away sins, and plaster each other with water and talc.
Visakha Puja Celebrated collectively as Buddha's birth, enlightenment and *parinibbana* (passing in nirvana), this festival's activities are centred on wats. The festival falls on the eighth day of the fourth moon (that's May or June to you and me) and is best observed at Angkor Wat, where there are candlelit processions of monks.
P'chum Ben This festival falls between mid-September and early October, and is a kind of All Souls' Day, when respects are paid to the dead through offerings made at wats.
Bon Om Tuk This festival is held in early November to celebrate the epic victory of Jayavarman VII over the Chams in 1177 and the reversal of the Tonlé Sap river. This is one of the most important festivals in the Khmer calendar and a wonderful, if hectic, time to be in Phnom Penh.

FOOD & DRINK

Food

Some traditional Cambodian dishes are similar to those of neighbouring Thailand (though not as spicy), others closer to Chinese and Vietnamese cooking. The French left their mark, too.

Amoc (baked fish with coconut and lemongrass in banana leaf), Cambodia's national dish, is sublime, and *kyteow* (a rice-noodle soup packed with a punch), otherwise known as Cambodia in a bowl, will keep you going throughout the day.

Rice and *prahoc* – a fermented fish paste that your nose will recognise at a hundred paces – form the backbone of Khmer cuisine. Built around these are flavours that give the cuisine its kick: secret roots, pungent herbs and aromatic tubers. Together they give salads, snacks, soups and stews an aroma and taste that smacks of Cambodia.

Cambodian meals almost always include *samlor* (soup). *Samlor machou banle* is a popular hot-and-sour fish soup with pineapple and a splash of spices. Other popular soups include *samlor chapek* (ginger-flavoured pork soup), *samlor machou bawng kawng* (prawn soup similar to the popular Thai *tôm yam*) and *samlor ktis* (fish soup with coconut and pineapple).

Most fish eaten in Cambodia is freshwater, and *trey aing* (grilled fish) is a Cambodian speciality (*aing* means 'grilled' and can be applied to many dishes). Fish is traditionally eaten as pieces wrapped in lettuce or spinach leaves and dipped into a fish sauce known as

WE DARE YOU! THE TOP FIVE

Try these Cambodian treats:

- crickets
- duck embryo
- durian (the best ones come from Kampot province)
- *prahoc* (fermented fish paste)
- grilled tarantulas

CAMBODIA

TRAVEL YOUR TASTE BUDS

You're going to encounter food that's unusual, strange, maybe even immoral – or just plain weird. The fiercely omnivorous Cambodians find nothing strange in eating insects, algae, offal or fish bladders. They'll dine on a duck embryo, brew up some brains or snack on some spiders. They'll peel live frogs to grill on a barbecue or down the wine of a cobra to increase their virility. To the Khmers, there's nothing 'strange' about anything that will sustain the body. They'll try anything once, even a burger.

For obvious reasons, please avoid eating endangered species.

tuk trey, similar to Vietnam's *nuoc mam* but with ground peanuts added.

Drink

Don't drink tap water. Guzzle locally produced bottled water (from 500r per litre), available everywhere, or ecofriendly fresh coconut milk, sold by machete-wielding street vendors. Ice is made from treated water in local factories so relax and enjoy it. Don't be surprised if wait staff try to put it in your beer or wine.

Soft drinks and coffee are found everywhere and a free pot of Chinese-style tea will usually appear as soon as you sit down in local restaurants.

Excellent fruit smoothies, known locally as *tukalok,* are omnipresent in Cambodia. Look out for stalls with fruit and a blender. If you don't want heaps of sugar and condensed milk, or an egg, keep an eye on the preparatory stages.

The most popular beer is the local Angkor, but Anchor (*an*-tshor), Beer Lao, Tiger, San Miguel, Stella Artois, Carlsberg and Heineken also grace many a menu. Cans sell for around US$1 to US$1.50, with local draughts sometimes available for US$0.50.

In Phnom Penh, foreign wines and spirits are sold at bargain prices. 'Muscle wines', something like Red Bull meets absinthe, with names such as Commando Bear Beverage and Brace of Loma, are popular with Khmers. They contain enough unknown substances to contravene the Geneva Chemical Weapons Convention and should only be approached with extreme caution.

GAY & LESBIAN TRAVELLERS

While Cambodian culture is tolerant of homosexuality, the scene is nothing like that of neighbouring Thailand. Phnom Penh and Siem Reap have the best of the action. As with heterosexual couples, passionate public displays of affection are considered a basic no-no, so it's prudent – and respectful – not to flaunt your sexuality. That said, people of the same sex often hold hands in Cambodian society, so it's unlikely to raise eyebrows.

Utopia (www.utopia-asia.com) features gay travel information and contacts.

HOLIDAYS

Banks, government ministries and embassies close down for public holidays, so plan ahead during these times. Holidays are moved to the next working day if they fall on a weekend, and some people take a day or two extra during major festivals. See p135 for festivals that move with the lunar calendar.

International New Year's Day 1 January
Victory Over the Genocide Regime 7 January
International Women's Day 8 March
International Labour Day 1 May
King's Birthday 13 to 15 May
Queen Mother's Birthday 18 June
Constitution Day 24 September
King's Coronation Day 29 October
King Father's Birthday 31 October
Independence Day 9 November
International Human Rights Day 10 December

INSURANCE

Do not visit Cambodia without medical insurance. Anyone who has a serious injury or illness while in Cambodia may require emergency evacuation to Bangkok – US$10,000 to US$20,000 without insurance, free if you've got a policy costing the equivalent of a bottle of beer a day.

INTERNET ACCESS

Internet access is spreading rapidly and there are internet shops in all but the most remote provincial capitals. Charges range from 2000r to US$2 per hour. In this chapter, guest houses and hotels that offer access to an online computer are indicated by an internet icon ( ).

Some hotels, guest houses and cafes offer wi-fi, though connections are easiest to find in Phnom Penh and Siem Reap. Some reviews mention that wi-fi is available, but new establishments are going online all the time.

INTERNET RESOURCES

See p138 for websites with tips on responsible tourism.

Andy Brouwer (http://andybrouwer.co.uk) A great gateway to all things Cambodian; includes comprehensive links and regular Cambodian travel articles.
Angkor.com (http://angkor.com) Loads of useful links.
Canby Publications (www.canbypublications.com) By the publishers of the popular *Visitors Guide* brochure series.
Earthwalkers (www.earthwalkers.no/kft.htm) Fun online Khmer language tutorial with helpful pictures and phonetics. A great introduction.
Heritage Watch (www.heritagewatchinternational.org) Works to safeguard Cambodia's architectural heritage and promotes 'heritage-friendly' tourism.
Lonely Planet (www.lonelyplanet.com) Summaries on travelling to Cambodia, the Thorn Tree travellers' forum and travel news.
Ministry of Tourism (www.mot.gov.kh) Website of Cambodia's Ministry of Tourism.
Mr Pumpy (www.mrpumpy.net) Information on cycling through Cambodia, written with candour and humour.
Tales of Asia (www.talesofasia.com) Up-to-the-minute overland travel information.

LEGAL MATTERS

Paedophilia is a serious crime in Cambodia, and many Western countries have enacted legislation to make offences committed overseas punishable at home. See also p138.

Narcotics, including marijuana, are not legal in Cambodia and police are beginning to take a harder line – the days of free bowls in guest houses are long gone. However, marijuana is traditionally used in some Khmer food, so its presence lingers on.

The legal age for voting is 18, for driving a motorbike 16 and for driving a car 18. There doesn't seem to be a minimum drinking age.

Bribery has reached epidemic proportions.

HOW TO AVOID A BAD TRIP

Watch out for *yama* (known as *yaba* in Thailand), which ominously shares its name with the Hindu god of death. Known as ice or crystal meth back home, it's not the usual diet pills but instead home-made meta-amphetamines often laced with toxic substances, such as mercury and lithium. It is more addictive than many users would like to admit, provoking reactions such as powerful hallucinations, sleep deprivation and psychosis.

Also note that most of what is sold as cocaine in Cambodia is actually pure heroin and far stronger than any smack you'll find on the streets back home. Bang this up your nose and you're in serious trouble – several backpackers die each year.

MAPS

Unless you're looking to head into the wilds on the back of a dirt bike, you won't require additional maps to those in this guidebook. If you need one, the best all-rounder is Gecko's *Cambodia Road Map* at 1:750,000 scale.

MEDIA

Magazines & Newspapers

Cambodia has two daily newspapers in English, the *Cambodia Daily* (www.cambodiadaily.com) and the *Phnom Penh Post* (www.phnompenhpost.com). Free local travel mags include *AsiaLIFE Phnom Penh* (www.asialifecambodia.com) and *Bayon Pearnik* (www.bayonpe arnik.com).

Radio & TV

On FM radio, 24 hours a day, you can hear the BBC World Service (100 MHz in Phnom Penh and 99.25 MHz in Siem Reap), Radio Australia (101.5 MHz in Phnom Penh and Siem Reap) and Radio France Internationale (94.5 MHz or 92 MHz in five cities).

Many guest houses and hotels have satellite TV, offering access to BBC World, CNN, Star Sports, HBO and more.

MONEY

Cambodia's currency is the riel, abbreviated in this book by a lower-case r written after the amount. Riel notes (there are no coins) come in denominations of 50r, 100r, 200r, 500r, 1000r, 2000r, 5000r, 10,000r, 20,000r, 50,000r and 100,000r, though you rarely see the highest-denomination bills.

Throughout this chapter, each establishment's prices are in the currency quoted to the average punter. This is usually in US dollars or riel, but in the far west it is often in Thai baht (though recent border tensions have made the Thai currency unpopular). While this may seem inconsistent, this is the way it's done and the sooner you get used to thinking comparatively in riel, dollars or baht, the easier travelling will be.

ATMs

ATMs compatible with international credit cards (Visa and MasterCard), operated by banks such as Acleda (Visa cards only), ANZ Royal, Canadia and Union Commercial, can be found in all major cities and a growing number of provincial towns and border crossings with Thailand.

Bargaining

Bargaining is expected in local markets, when travelling by share taxi or moto and, sometimes, when taking a room. The Khmers are not ruthless hagglers so a persuasive smile and a little friendly quibbling is usually enough to get a good price.

See right for tips on appropriate bargaining etiquette.

Cash

The US dollar is accepted everywhere in Cambodia – indeed, US cash is what you'll get from ATMs – so if you've got US dollars (or, in the west, Thai baht) there's no need to buy riel at the border (don't believe the touts!). Avoid ripped banknotes, which Cambodians often refuse. Those with cash in another major currency can change it in major centres.

If you pay in dollars or baht, change is often given in riel, which is handy since small-denomination riel notes can be useful when paying for things such as moto rides and coconuts. When calculating change, the US dollar is usually rounded off to 4000r.

Credit Cards

Visa and MasterCard cash advances are available at a growing number of ATMs (see above). Credit cards are accepted at some hotels, restaurants, shops, airlines and travel agents but they sometimes pass the charges on to the customer.

Travellers Cheques

Travellers cheques aren't much use when venturing beyond the main tourist centres. Most banks charge a commission of 2%, and dish out US dollars rather than riel. Some hotels and travel agents will cash travellers cheques after banking hours.

PHOTOGRAPHY

Many internet cafes will burn CDs from digital images using USB connections. Digital memory is widely available in Cambodia.

EXCHANGE RATES

Exchange rates at the time this book went to press:

Country	Unit	Riel (r)
Australia	A$1	3698
Canada	C$1	3913
Euro zone	€1	6124
Japan	¥100	4652
Laos	10,000 kip	4906
New Zealand	NZ$1	3026
Thailand	10B	1253
UK	UK£1	6682
USA	US$1	4176
Vietnam	10,000d	2340

POST

The postal service is hit-and-miss, with Phnom Penh's main post office (Map p78) – where you'll find a poste restante service – the most reliable. At the counter, make sure postcards and letters are franked before they vanish from your sight. Courier services include EMS, which has offices at all major post offices.

RESPONSIBLE TRAVEL

Cambodia continues to experience unprecedented growth in tourism and this inevitably brings the bad along with the good. Your goal is a simple one: minimise the negatives and maximise the positives.

Child exploitation and sexual abuse are now taken very seriously in Cambodia. If you see suspicious behaviour of tourists with local children, it's your duty to report it to the **ChildSafe Hotline** (☎ 012-311112; www.childsafe-international.org) or to the national **police hotline** (☎ 023-997 919). Tourism establishments that sport the ChildSafe logo have staff trained to protect vulnerable children and, where necessary, intervene.

Cambodians dress very modestly and are offended by skimpily dressed foreigners. Just look at the Cambodians frolicking in the sea – most are fully dressed. Wearing bikinis on the beach is fine but cover up elsewhere. Topless or nude bathing is a definite no-no.

When bargaining for goods in a market or for a ride on a moto, remember the aim is not to get the lowest price, but one that's acceptable to both you and the seller. Coming on too strong or arguing over a few hundred riel does nothing to foster Cambodians' positive feelings towards travellers. Be thankful that in

Cambodia there's still room for discussion, so try not to abuse it – and don't forget to smile.

On the topic of money, Cambodia is an extremely poor country and begging is common in Phnom Penh and Siem Reap. Try not to become numb to the pleas as there's no social-security network and no government support. Amputees may also find themselves stigmatised by mainstream society and unable to make ends meet any other way. If you do give – an act viewed positively by Buddhists – keep the denominations small so expectations don't grow too big. Many amputees sell books on the street and buying from them may encourage others to become more self-sufficient. Please don't give cash to children as they rarely get to keep it – giving them some food is preferable. A great option in Phnom Penh, Siem Reap and Sihanoukville is to shop or eat in establishments whose profits benefit street children, people with disabilities and vulnerable women – check out the restaurants listed on p82, and the shops on p84 and p93 for more details.

Looting from Cambodia's ancient temples has been a huge problem over the past couple of decades. Avoid buying old stone carvings. Classy reproductions are available in Phnom Penh and Siem Reap, complete with export certificates.

Finally, don't forget what the Cambodians have been through in the protracted years of war, genocide and famine. Support local Cambodian-owned businesses; if anyone deserves to profit from the new-found interest in this wonderful country, it's surely the long-suffering Khmers. You might also want to pick up a copy of the pamphlet published by **Stay Another Day Cambodia** (www.stay-another-day.org), which has a list of sustainable-tourism initiatives, or you could check out the **Cambodia Community-Based Ecotourism Network** (www.ccben.org), which supplies details on community-based ecotourism initiatives that improve the lives of local people.

STUDYING

Travellers can indulge in Khmer cooking lessons in Phnom Penh (p81), Siem Reap (p91), Sihanoukville (p117) and Battambang (p105).

TELEPHONE

Landline area codes appear under the name of each city but in many areas service is spotty. Mobile (cell) phones, whose 'area codes' start with 01 or 09, are hugely popular with both individuals and commercial enterprises. Only Cambodians can purchase SIM cards but given the outrageous cost of roaming, you might want to procure one from a local. For listings of businesses and government offices, check out www.yellowpages-cambodia.com.

Brightly numbered mobile-phone stalls offer inexpensive domestic calls – look for signs displaying mobile phone prefixes (012 etc) – are found on every town's kerbs. The cheapest international calls are via the internet and cost as little as 100r to 500r per minute, though in places with broadband you can Skype for the price of an internet connection (usually 2000r to 4000r per hour). International calls from mobile-phone shops cost about 1000r per minute.

DOMESTIC TELEPHONE CODES

Banteay Meanchey	☎ 054
Battambang	☎ 053
Kampot	☎ 033
Kandal	☎ 024
Kep	☎ 036
Kompong Cham	☎ 042
Kompong Chhnang	☎ 026
Kompong Speu	☎ 025
Kompong Thom	☎ 062
Kratie	☎ 072
Koh Kong	☎ 035
Mondulkiri	☎ 073
Oddar Meanchey	☎ 065
Phnom Penh	☎ 023
Preah Vihear	☎ 064
Prey Veng	☎ 043
Pursat	☎ 052
Ratanakiri	☎ 075
Siem Reap	☎ 063
Sihanoukville	☎ 034
Stung Treng	☎ 074
Svay Rieng	☎ 044
Takeo	☎ 032

TOILETS

Although the occasional squat toilet turns up now and then, particularly in the most budget of budget guest houses, toilets are usually of the sit-down variety. In remote regions you'll find that hygiene conditions deteriorate somewhat. Generally, if there's a wastepaper basket next to the toilet, that is where the toilet paper goes, as many sewerage systems cannot handle toilet paper. Toilet paper is seldom provided, so keep a stash with you.

Should nature call in rural areas, don't let modesty drive you into the bushes: there may be landmines not far from the road or track.

TOURIST INFORMATION

Guest houses, free local magazines and your fellow travellers are generally more useful information sources than tourist offices, which, to the extent that they do anything at all, tend to deal more with provincial tourism policy than with informing travellers.

Cambodia has no official tourist offices abroad.

TOURS

It can seem as though every English-speaking moto driver in the country is a tour guide, and many of them do make excellent travel companions.

Organised city tours of Phnom Penh and its surrounds are promoted by numerous guest houses. Guest houses and dive shops in Sihanoukville offer boat tours to nearby tropical islands, as do some places in Kep and Krong Koh Kong. Organised day trips to Bokor National Park are a popular option in Kampot. In the northeast, guest houses in Mondulkiri offer elephant treks and village home-stay trips, while in Ratanakiri it's possible to trek through vast Virachey National Park. Even Siem Reap is at last getting in on the act, with some guest houses offering trips to the remote temples of Preah Vihear Province. The Siem Reap–based Sam Veasna Center (p95) offers superb birdwatching trips.

TRAVELLERS WITH DISABILITIES

Although Cambodia has one of the world's highest rates of limb loss (primarily due to mines), the country is not designed for people with impaired mobility. Few buildings have lifts (elevators), sidewalks and roads are riddled with potholes, and the staircases and rock jumbles of many Angkorian temples are daunting even for the able-bodied. Transport-wise, chartering is the way to go and is a fairly affordable option. Also affordable is hired help if you require it, and Khmers are generally very helpful should you need a hand.

VISAS

For most nationalities, one-month tourist visas (US$20; passport-sized photo required) are available on arrival at Phnom Penh and Siem Reap airports and at all land border crossings. Unfortunately, except at the airports and the land crossings with Vietnam, overcharging is rampant, and uniformed Cambodian border officials – and touts who work with them – are often very creative in manoeuvring travellers into paying more than official rates.

At the notorious Poipet–Aranya Prathet crossing (p109) and at Cham Yeam–Hat Lek (near Krong Koh Kong; p114), visitors are told they must pay for their visa in baht, with fees – based on prehistoric exchange rates – set at 1000B (US$29) to 1200B (US$35), plus 100B for a photo. A few valiant travellers insist on paying US$20 in US dollars, a move that may be crowned with at least partial success provided you make your case directly to the uniformed officials at the Cambodian Visa Service, which is inside Cambodia, ie past Thai immigration. Whatever you do, don't lose your cool. Ignore the Thai-side touts who will swear up and down that visas are not issued at the frontier. The 'Cambodian consulate' on the Thai side of Poipet is a scam.

You can avoid some of the hassles by getting a one-month e-visa (US$25) from www.mfaic.gov.kh. It takes three business days to issue and is valid for entry to Cambodia at the Phnom Penh and Siem Reap airports and, by land, at Bavet (p85), Poipet (p109) and Cham Yeam (p114).

Tourist visas can only be extended once (guest houses and travel agents in Phnom Penh, Siem Reap and Sihanoukville can tell you where) so if you're planning a longer stay, ask for a one-month business visa (US$25) when you arrive. Extensions for one/three/six/12 months cost about US$40/75/150/250 and take three or four business days; bring a passport photo. It may be cheaper do a 'visa run' to Thailand, getting a fresh visa when you cross back into Cambodia. Overstayers are charged US$5 per day at the point of exit.

The Thais issue free 30-day visas to qualifying passport holders at all border crossings but, at least at Psar Pruhm–Ban Pakard (p108; near Pailin), have recently been very strict about verifying that travellers have an onward ticket out of Thailand. Vietnamese visas are available in Phnom Penh, Sihanoukville (the quickest) and Battambang. Lao visas are issued in Phnom Penh.

VOLUNTEERING

Some of the many nongovernmental organisations (NGOs) working in Cambodia welcome volunteers, though they may require a commitment of at least several months.

Cambodian Children's Painting Project (www.artcambodia.org) Provides Sihanoukville beach children with a safe environment. Minimum volunteer period: one month.

City Dump Project (☎ 017-996435; www.bogieandbacall-cambodia.com/charity) Weekly trips to bring food to children who live at Phnom Penh's city dump.

Kampot Interact (www.kampotinteract.org) Has details on volunteer projects in and around Kampot. Some listings may not be up-to-date.

Lazy Gecko Café (Map p78; ☎ 012-1912935; 23B St 93, Phnom Penh) Drop in to see how you can help with Jeannie's Orphanage.

Ockenden Cambodia (www.ockenden-cambodia.org) Works at grassroots level to empower communities and improve vulnerable peoples' quality of life.

Sustainable Cambodia (www.sustainablecambodia.org) Minimum commitment: five months.

Village Focus International (www.villagefocus.org) Can find placements for volunteers interested in helping vulnerable communities.

Volunteer in Cambodia (www.volunteerincambodia.org) English teaching.

WOMEN TRAVELLERS

Women will generally find Cambodia a safe and hassle-free country to travel in. As is the case anywhere in the world, walking or cycling alone late at night can be dodgy, and if you're planning to head off the beaten track it's a good idea to find a travelling companion – this is true for men, too.

Khmer women dress fairly conservatively and it's best to follow suit, particularly when visiting wats and P hnom Penh's Royal Palace. In general, long-sleeved shirts and long trousers or skirts are preferable. In a skirt and hitting the town on a moto? Do as Khmer women do and sit side-saddle.

Tampons and sanitary napkins are widely available in major cities and provincial capitals, as is the contraceptive pill.

WORKING

Job opportunities are limited in Cambodia, partly because Cambodians need the jobs more than foreigners and partly because the foreigners working here are usually professionals recruited overseas. The easiest option is teaching English in Phnom Penh, as experience isn't a prerequisite at the smaller schools. Places to look for work include the classifieds sections of the *Phnom Penh Post* and the *Cambodia Daily,* and the notice board at guest houses and restaurants in Phnom Penh.

East Timor

HIGHLIGHTS

- **Diving Dili** (p151) Enjoy being in one of the few cities in the world where the reef is just steps away from the urban centre.
- **Atauro Island** (p155) Snorkel and relax day-trip-style, or stay awhile at Tua Kóin, a true ecoresort.
- **Maubisse** and **Mt Ramelau** (p158) See coffee plantations and misty valleys give way to sweeping views of the south and north coasts.
- **Tutuala** (p157) Peek over at Jaco Island from the open-air thatched huts on Walu beach.
- **Balibo** (p158) Make the pilgrimage to Balibo's 'Flag House', where five Australia-based journalists were killed in 1975.
- **Off the beaten track** (p159) Chill out in Oecussi, a barely visited and incredibly laid back enclave wedged between West Timor and stunning reefs.

FAST FACTS

- **Budget** US$20 to US$50 a day
- **Capital** Dili
- **Costs** guest-house room US$10, 1.5L bottle of water US$0.50, beer US$2.50, noodle dish from a local eatery US$1 to US$2, shore dive US$40
- **Country code** ☎ 670
- **Languages** Tetun, Portuguese, Indonesian, English
- **Money** US$ (US dollar)
- **Phrases** *olá* (hello), *adeus* (goodbye), *obrigadu/a* (m/f; thank you), *kolisensa* (excuse me)
- **Population** 1.1 million
- **Time** GMT + nine hours
- **Visas** US$30 on arrival

TRAVEL HINT

Roads around East Timor are diabolical: a 30km trip can take hours. Since everything will probably take longer than you expect, ask for your full 30-day visa on arrival, then go with the flow.

OVERLAND ROUTES

Overland travel is possible between East Timor and Indonesian West Timor: it's three to four hours from Dili to the border.

Almost everyone wants East Timor (Timor-Leste in the locally preferred Portuguese) to be a success story. The Timorese people have survived 500 years of Portuguese and Indonesian rule and finally it's their turn to shine but, 10 years after the overwhelming vote for independence, visitors to the country will discover the sun is only just beginning to rise.

Life is a daily struggle for most Timorese; food, water and electricity are all in short supply for much of the year. In the districts you'll face the same issues as the locals, including that of limited transport options.

However, tourism infrastructure is appearing, and some of the best mountains, beaches and towns have decent accommodation options, many with a focus on sustainability (locally run with solar and hydro power).

What East Timor needs from travellers is their time (as well as money). In exchange, you'll be well rewarded with outstanding diving, incredible mountain-top views, isolated beaches and welcoming smiles.

When you first arrive, hang out in Dili and get to know the expats. Some have called East Timor home for the past decade, and plenty have no plans to leave. They're a great source of information and will prepare you well for the adventures ahead.

CURRENT EVENTS

Just when East Timor dips off the world's radar, something new jolts it back to international headline status, and it's usually not good news. Over the past few years a series of violent events (communal conflict, violence between the army and police and an assumed attempted coup) have left both its citizens and its many foreign observers wondering: what's next? When do the good times start?

Visitors to East Timor will notice that for some at least, the good times *have* started. Timorese are running once expat-operated organisations and businesses, something that's especially evident in the tourism industry. A stalwart group of expats remains, with some members making Timor their home, and newcomers still arrive daily. However, each violent outburst seems to lead to Dili's fences getting higher and homes being secured with yet more razor wire, and the UN's presence in the country has, since 1999, risen and fallen and then risen again.

Fretilin, which led the struggle for independence during the entire Indonesian occupation, suffered from divisions after the UN backed away from propping up the government in 2005. Prime Minister Mari Alkatiri sacked one third of the army in March 2006 and, in the ensuing months of rioting, more than 150,000 people fled their homes. Relative peace only returned after public demonstrations forced Alkatiri to resign, and the UN force in East Timor was beefed up again.

In 2007, after a year as acting prime minister, José Ramos-Horta was elected president of East Timor with 70% of the vote. Unfortunately the vote for prime minister was not as clear-cut. Xanana Gusmão's National Congress for the Reconstruction of East Timor (CNRT) came second to Fretilin, winning 24% of the votes to Fretilin's 29%. However, CNRT quickly formed a coalition with other parties and Gusmão was sworn in as prime minister in August. Angry Fretilin supporters rioted, causing damage around the country and boosting the numbers of the more than 100,000 people already living in crowded internally displaced persons camps.

In February 2008, Ramos-Horta was shot and injured near his home during an alleged attempted coup led by former naval commander and East Timorese defence force (F-FDTL) major Alfreido Reinado. Reinado, who had been playing a cat-and-mouse game with Australian forces since escaping from jail in 2006 (in one instance he and his followers almost super-humanly flitted through the mountain towns in the west of the country, leaving the pursuing Australian forces bewildered), was killed at the scene by Ramos-Horta's security, though questions still remain about his motive for being there.

HISTORY

Portugal Settles In

Little is known of Timor before AD 1500, although Chinese and Javanese traders visited the island from at least the 13th century, and possibly as early as the 7th century. These traders searched the coastal settlements for aromatic sandalwood, which was valued for its use in making furniture and incense, and beeswax, used for making candles. Portuguese traders arrived between 1509 and 1511, but it wasn't until 1642 that the Topasses (descendents of Dominicans from nearby islands) established the first Portuguese settlement at Lifau in Oecussi and set about converting the Timorese to Catholicism.

To counter the Portuguese, the Dutch established a base at Kupang in western Timor in 1653. The Portuguese appointed an

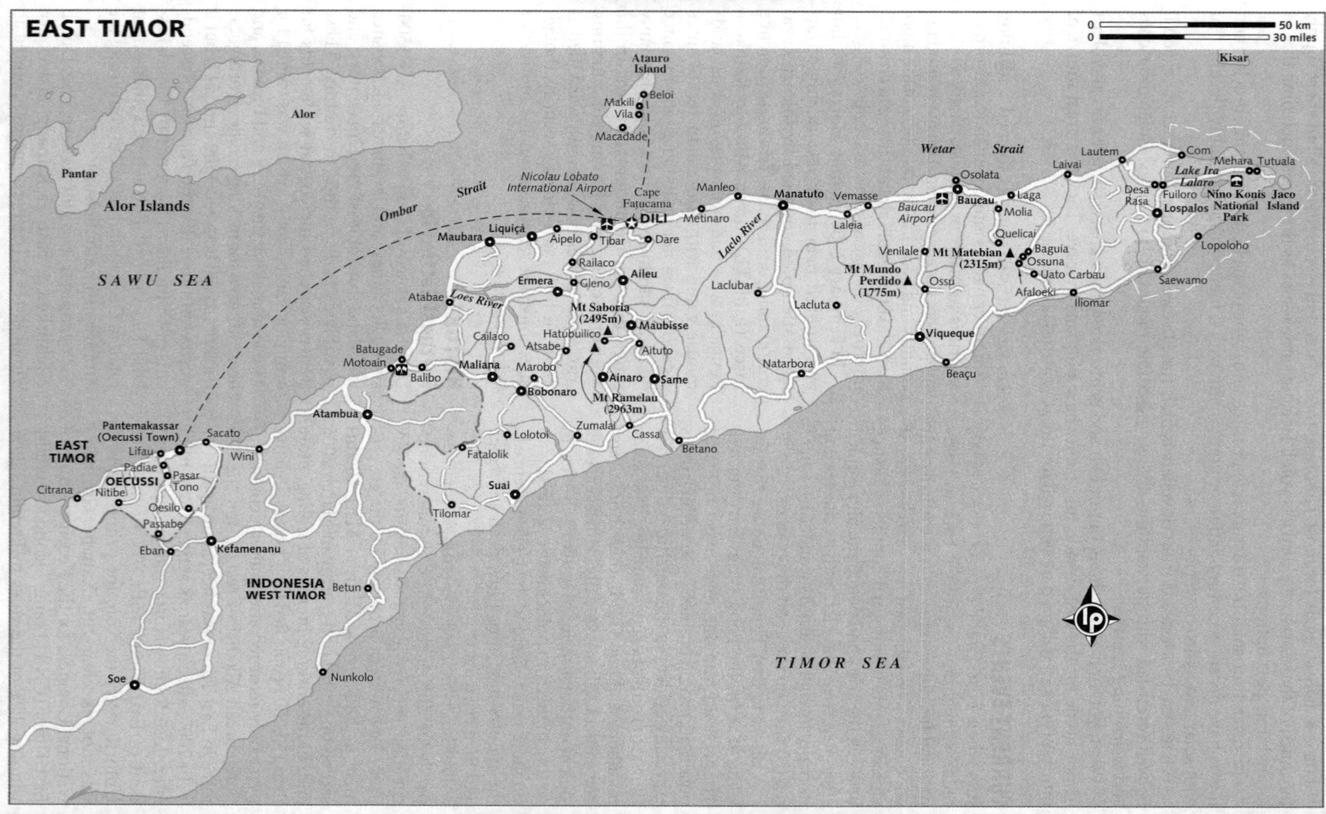
EAST TIMOR
0 50 km
0 30 miles
Kisar
Atauro Island
Beloi
Makili
Vila
Macadade
Alor
Pantar
Alor Islands
Ombar Strait
Nicolau Lobato International Airport
Cape Fatucama
DILI
Wetar Strait
Lautem
Com
Mehara
Tutuala
Lake Ira Lalaro
Nino Konis Santana National Park
Jaco Island
Laivai
Desa
Rasa
Fuiloro
Lospalos
Lopoloho
Osolata
Baucau
Laga
Molia
Baucau Airport
Manleo
Metinaro
Manatuto
Vemasse
Laleia
Laclo River
Quelicai
Baguia
Ossuna
Uato Carbau
Afaloeki
Iliomar
Saewamo
Venilale
Mt Matebian (2315m)
Mt Mundo Perdido (1775m)
Ossu
Viqueque
Beaçu
Laclubar
Lacluta
Natarbora
Maubara
Liquiçá
Aipelo
Tibar
Dare
Railaco
Aileu
Ermera
Gleno
SAWU SEA
Atabae
Loes River
Mt Saboria (2495m)
Maubisse
Hatubuilico
Aituto
Cailaco
Atsabe
Batugade
Motoain
Balibo
Maliana
Marobo
Bobonaro
Ainaro
Same
Mt Ramelau (2963m)
Atambua
Zumalai
Cassa
Betano
Lolotoi
Fatalolik
Suai
Tilomar
Pantemakassar (Oecussi Town)
EAST TIMOR
Sacato
Lifau
Wini
Padiae
Pasar
Tono
OECUSSI
Citrana
Nitibe
Oesilo
Passabe
Eban
Kefamenanu
INDONESIA WEST TIMOR
Betun
Soe
Nunkolo
TIMOR SEA

administrator to Lifau in 1656, but the Topasses went on to become a law unto themselves, driving out the Portuguese governor in 1705.

By 1749 the Topasses controlled central Timor and marched on Kupang, but the Dutch won the ensuing battle, expanding their control of western Timor in the process. On the Portuguese side, after more attacks from the Topasses in Lifau, the colonial base was moved east to Dili in 1769.

The 1859 Treaty of Lisbon divided Timor, giving Portugal the eastern half, together with the north-coast pocket of Oecussi; this was formalised in 1904. Portuguese Timor was a sleepy and neglected outpost ruled through a traditional system of *liurai* (local chiefs). Control outside Dili was limited and it wasn't until the 20th century that the Portuguese intervened in a major way in the interior.

World War Two

In 1941, Australia sent a small commando force into Portuguese Timor to counter the Japanese, deliberately breaching the colony's neutral status. Although the military initiative angered neutral Portugal and dragged Portuguese Timor into the Pacific War, it slowed the Japanese expansion. Australia's success was largely due to the support it received from the locals, including young *creados* (young Timorese boys who assisted Australian servicemen during WWII). In 1942 the Portuguese handed control of Portuguese Timor to the Japanese. Japanese soldiers razed whole villages, seized food supplies and killed Timorese in areas where the Australians were operating. By the end of the war, between 40,000 and 60,000 Timorese had died.

Portugal Pulls Out, Indonesia Invades

After WWII the colony reverted to Portuguese rule. After the Carnation Revolution in Portugal on 25 April 1974, Lisbon set about discarding its colonial empire. Within a few weeks political parties had formed in East Timor, and the Timorese Democratic Union (UDT) attempted to seize power in August 1975. A brief but brutal civil war saw UDT's rival Fretilin (previously known as the Association of Timorese Social Democrats) come out on top, and it urgently declared the independent existence of the Democratic Republic of East Timor on 28 November, amidst an undeclared invasion by Indonesia. On 7 December the Indonesians finally launched their full-scale attack on Dili after months of incursions (including at Balibo, where five Australia-based journalists were killed).

Anticommunist Indonesia feared an independent East Timor governed by a left-leaning Fretilin would bring communism to its door, and commenced its invasion of East Timor just a day after Henry Kissinger and Gerald Ford departed Jakarta, having tacitly given their assent. (Indeed, the Americans urged the Indonesians to conduct a swift campaign so that the world wouldn't see them using weapons the US had provided). Australia and Britain also sided with Indonesia.

Falintil, the military wing of Fretilin, fought a guerrilla war against Indonesian troops (which numbered 35,000 by 1976) with marked success in the first few years, but weakened considerably thereafter, though the resistance continued. The cost of the takeover to the Timorese was huge; it's estimated that up to 183,000 died in the hostilities, and the ensuing disease and famine.

By 1989 Indonesia had things firmly under control and opened East Timor to limited and controlled tourism. On 12 November 1991, Indonesian troops fired on protesters who'd gathered at the Santa Cruz Cemetery in Dili to commemorate the killing of an independence activist. With the event captured on film and aired around the world, the Indonesian government admitted to 19 killings (later increased to more than 50), although it's estimated that over 280 died in the massacre.

While Indonesia introduced a civilian administration, the military remained in control. Aided by secret police and civilian pro-Indonesian militia to crush dissent, reports of arrest, torture and murder were commonplace.

MUST SEE

Visit the new **Dare Memorial & Café** (🕑 Sat & Sun) at the hairpin bend 9km south from Dili towards Maubisse. The cafe's information panels describe Australia's involvement in East Timor during WWII and beyond, and a DVD focuses on the sacrifices made by the Timorese *creados* (young Timorese boys) to help Australian soldiers in WWII.

Independence

After Indonesia's President Soeharto resigned in May 1998, his replacement BJ Habibie unexpectedly announced a referendum for East Timorese autonomy. January 1999 marked the commencement of attacks by Indonesian military-backed militias who began terrorising the population to coerce them to reject independence.

Attacks peaked in April 1999, just prior to the arrival of the UN Electoral Mission, when, according to a report commissioned by the United Nations Office of the High Commissioner for Human Rights, up to 60 people were massacred in the Liquiçá church. Other attacks occurred in Dili and Maliana while the Indonesian authorities watched on. Attacks escalated in the weeks prior to the vote, with thousands seeking refuge in the hills away from the reach of the TNI and militia.

Despite threats, intimidation and brutality, on 30 August 1999, East Timor voted overwhelmingly (78.5%) for independence from, rather than autonomy within, Indonesia. Though the Indonesian government promised to respect the results of the UN-sponsored vote, militias and Indonesian forces went on a rampage, killing people, burning and looting buildings and destroying infrastructure.

While the world watched in horror, the UN was attacked and forced to evacuate, leaving the Timorese defenceless. On 20 September, weeks after the main massacres in Suai, Dili, Maliana and Oecussi, the Australian-led International Force East Timor (INTERFET) arrived in Dili. The Indonesian forces and their militia supporters left for West Timor, leaving behind an incomprehensible scene of destruction. Half a million people had been displaced, and telecommunications, power installations, bridges, government buildings, shops and houses were destroyed. Today these physical scars remain.

The UN set up a temporary administration during the transition to independence, and aid and foreign workers flooded into the country. As well as physically rebuilding the country, East Timor has had to create a civil service, police, judiciary, education, health system and so on, with staff recruited and trained from scratch.

The UN handed over government to East Timor on 20 May 2002. Falintil leader Xanana Gusmão was elected president of the new nation, and the long-time leader of Fretilin, Mari Alkatiri, who ran the party from exile in Mozambique, was chosen as prime minister.

Birth Pangs

In December 2002, Dili was wracked by riots as years of poverty and frustration proved too much for the nascent democracy. The economy was in a shambles and people were ready for things to start improving – and fast. But without any viable industry or employment potential, East Timor was reliant almost entirely on foreign aid.

Only a small UN contingent remained in East Timor by mid-2005. As the number of outsiders shrank, the challenges of creating a new nation virtually from scratch became all too apparent. Parliamentary factions squabbled while the enormous needs of the people festered.

The Future

East Timor will continue to rely on foreign money as it struggles to establish a viable economy.

In 2006 Australia and East Timor signed an agreement that will give US$10 billion in oil revenue to both countries over the next 40 years – though Australia's Howard government was accused of using bullying tactics to deny the struggling and poor country its fair share of the money (initially offering only 20%). Only perseverance on the part of the Timorese forced the Australian government to agree on a 50/50 split.

High in the hills outside Dili is another natural resource: coffee. Some 100,000 people work seasonally to produce the country's sought-after arabica beans, noted for their cocoa and vanilla character. Shade-grown and organic, Timorese coffee is prized by companies such as Starbucks, and production is increasing.

East Timor's tourism industry has great potential, although there needs to be a perception of stability for numbers to grow beyond the 1500 or so people who visit each year.

MUST READD

Shakedown: Australia's Grab for Timor Oil, by Paul Cleary, details the efforts by Australia's Howard government to force East Timor to sign away oil and gas rights to Australia for a song.

EAST TIMOR

CAST OF CHARACTERS

Three men are important to East Timor's future.

Mari Alkatiri is the leader of Fretilin, and is uncompromising in his response to what he sees as the desertion of Fretilin by other party members who've joined the many new political parties. After being ousted as prime minister following the 2006 riots (see p143), he has staunchly defended Fretilin's role in the country; in 2007 he led protests after Fretilin won 29% of the vote but was unable to form a government. A descendent of an old Muslim trading family, Alkatiri is a bit of an anomaly in a staunchly Catholic country.

Xanana Gusmão is East Timor's most charismatic leader. Gusmão was a leader of guerrilla forces from 1978 until 1992, when he was captured and imprisoned in Jakarta. He became the first president of the country, and earned the enmity of many of his old Fretilin brethren by breaking with the party after independence. In the troubled 2007 parliamentary elections, following which he was named prime minister, he led the National Congress for the Reconstruction of East Timor (CNRT) party, which favours a pragmatic approach to relations with neighbours such as Australia and Indonesia. His wife is Australian-born Kirsty Sword Gusmão, who runs the prominent charity the Alola Foundation.

José Ramos-Horta is the charismatic Nobel Prize winner who spent 20 years in exile during the Indonesian occupation. He took over as prime minister after Alkatiri was forced from office in 2006, and was elected president in 2007 with a huge margin, despite the fact that he disassociates himself from any political party. In 2008 he was shot during an alleged assassination attempt and recovered in Darwin, Australia. Single and known for his courtly ways, Ramos-Horta has said that all the nation's women are his first ladies.

THE CULTURE

The National Psyche

East Timor's identity is firmly rooted in its survival of extreme hardship and foreign occupation. As a consequence of the long and difficult struggle for independence, the people of East Timor are profoundly politically aware – not to mention proud and loyal. While there is great respect for elders and church and community leaders, there lurks a residual suspicion surrounding foreign occupiers, most recently in the form of the UN. In a country where Catholicism cloaks animistic beliefs and practices, religious beliefs also greatly inform the national consciousness.

Lifestyle

Most East Timorese lead a subsistence lifestyle: what is farmed (or caught) is eaten. Large families are common (the birth rate is 7.7 children per woman) and infant mortality remains high. According to the World Food Program, food insecurity is widespread and 47% of children under the age of five suffer from chronic malnutrition. The infrastructure in East Timor remains limited; only a few places have 24-hour electricity and running water. Roads are particularly dismal.

Family life exists in simple thatched huts, though rising wages have meant that satellite dishes are appearing beside even the most basic huts, beaming Indonesian TV into homes. NGOs and aid projects have worked to create self-sufficiency, but the ability to rise above poverty seems to be impossible for many as civil disturbances, bad roads and drought or floods play havoc. Motorised vehicles remain rare; on weekends, buses are packed with those heading to the family events that form the backbone of Timorese life.

Population

East Timor has at least a dozen indigenous groups, the largest being the Tetun (about 25% of the total population), who live around Suai, Dili and Viqueque, as well as in West Timor. The next largest group (around 10%) is the Mambai, who live in the mountains of Maubisse, Ainaro and Same.

Other groups each account for 5% or less of the total population. The Kemak live in the Ermera and Bobonaro districts around Maliana; the Bunak also live in Bobonaro, and their territory extends into West Timor and the Suai area. The Fataluku people are famous for their high-peaked houses in the area around Lospalos. More groups are scattered among the interior mountains.

East Timor is a young country (more than 50% of the population is under 18) with a short life expectancy of 61 years.

RELIGION

Religion is an integral part of daily life for most Timorese. Recent estimates indicate 98% of East Timor's population is Catholic (underpinned by animist beliefs), 1% is Muslim and 1% Protestant.

Indigenous religions revolve around an earth mother, from whom all humans are born and shall return after death, and her male counterpart, the god of the sky or sun. These are accompanied by a complex web of spirits from ancestors and nature. The *matan d'ok* (medicine man) is the village mediator with the spirits; he can divine the future and cure illness. Many people believe in various forms of black magic and it's not uncommon for people to wish evil spells upon their rivals.

ARTS

Despite 24 years of imposed Indonesian culture, East Timor has its own music and dance, architecture and textiles.

Music & Dance

The Timorese love a party, and celebrate with *tebe* (dancing) and sometimes singing. They're serious about their dancing; weddings often involve all-night three-step sessions. Music has been passed down through the years and changed little during Indonesian times. Traditional trancelike drumming is used in ceremonies, while Timorese rock and hip-hop groups are popular. Country-and-western style is popular, too, and features plenty of guitar use and the usual lovelorn themes.

Architecture

The traditional Timorese style of housing is breathtaking, especially the tall, stilted Fataluku homes in the county's far east. There are several nautilus-draped versions of this national icon on the road to Tutuala. Spectacular *deuhoto* (conical thatched Bunak houses) appear in the west.

Textiles

Throughout the country, women weave *tais* using small back-strap looms. Each region has its own style of *tais* and they're usually used as skirts or shawls for men *(tais mane)* or sewn up to form a tube skirt/dress for women *(tais feto)*. Some are made with organic dyes. Some weavers have cottoned on that a *tais* with the words 'East Timor 2010' or similar woven into it make a good souvenir. For details on where to buy Timorese textiles, see p154.

ENVIRONMENT

The Land

With an area of 15,007 sq km, East Timor consists of the eastern half of the island of Timor, the Atauro and Jaco Islands, and the enclave of Oecussi on the north coast, 70km to the west and surrounded by Indonesian West Timor.

Once part of the Australian continental shelf, Timor fully emerged from the ocean only four million years ago, and is therefore composed mainly of marine sediment, principally limestone. Rugged mountains, a product of the collision with the Banda Trench to the north, run the length of the country, the highest of which is Mt Ramelau (2963m).

Wildlife

East Timor is squarely in the area known as Wallacea, a kind of crossover zone between Asian and Australian plants and animals, and one of the most biologically distinctive areas on earth.

East Timor's north coast has been labelled a global hot spot of whale and dolphin activity, and its coral reefs are home to a diverse range of marine life. Species spotted include dugongs, blue whales, whale sharks and dolphins.

More than 240 species of bird have been recorded in the skies over East Timor. The Lautem district was declared a national park partly because of its rich bird life: it's home to honeyeaters, critically endangered yellow-crested cockatoos and endangered *wetar* ground-doves.

The number of mammals and reptiles in the wild is limited, though crocodiles and snakes make appearances.

Environmental Issues

East Timor's first national park, the Nino Konis Santana National Park, was declared in 2008 – a 123,000-hectare parcel of land (including some tropical forest) and sea at the country's eastern tip, also incorporating Jaco Island and Tutuala. Most of the country, however, is suffering from centuries of deforestation, and erosion is a huge problem. Roads and even villages have been known to slip away. Recent droughts have exacerbated the problems.

TRANSPORT

GETTING THERE & AWAY

There are no passenger boat services to East Timor from other countries.

Air

You can fly to Dili from Denpasar (Bali), Darwin (Australia) and Singapore. Dili's Nicolau Lobato International Airport (code DIL) is a five-minute drive from town.

Air North (code TL; ☎ in Australia 1800 627 474; www.airnorth.com.au) Flies twice daily between Darwin and Dili (return fares from US$400, 1½ hours).

Austasia (code MI; ☎ 331 2700; www.austasiaairlines.com; Landmark building) Flies Singapore–Dili return on Tuesdays and Saturdays ('discount' return from US$600, four hours).

Merpati (code MZ; ☎ 332 1880; www.merpati.co.id) Flies three times per week (Tuesday, Thursdays & Saturdays) between Denpasar (Bali) and Dili (return fares from US$310, two hours).

Land

See p155 for information on leaving East Timor by land.

GETTING AROUND

Bicycle

New bikes can be purchased in Dili for around US$200. Road conditions away from the north coast can be brutal, which may appeal to mountain bikers.

Boat

Ferry transport is available between Dili and Atauro Island (p156), and Dili and Oecussi (p160) on the German-built ferry *Nakroma*. It features three classes of service: economy, business and VIP. Economy seats go quickly, so book in advance. In practice business-class tickets are for foreigners and economy tickets are for locals, but people freely mix across the ship. Secure your spot on the small top deck to avoid the many passengers who find eruptive discomfort in even the calmest of seas.

Bus

Mikrolet (small minibuses) operate around Dili and to towns like Liquiçá, but otherwise they roam expansive villages looking for passengers. Large and crowded buses do the main routes from Dili to Lospalos, Viqueque, Maliana and Suai. More rugged routes are covered by *angguna* (tray trucks where passengers, including the odd buffalo or goat, all pile into the back). If *angguna* aren't covering their usual turf you can be assured the road conditions are exceptionally dire.

Car & Motorcycle

There's nothing easy about driving in East Timor; the roads are a minefield of chickens, goats, sleepy dogs and children, and locals congregate on the side of roads in what seems to be a national pastime (moving off the road is optional). Dips, ditches and entire missing sections of road are common, as are very fast UN drivers. There are plenty of blind corners. Before heading out get updated road conditions from the **UN** (☎ 331 2210 ext 5454, 723 0635).

While conventional cars can handle Dili, a 4WD is recommended for the roads elsewhere. Better roads include those east to Com (but not to Tutuala) and west to Batugade, and the inland road to Maubisse. Bring along water and food in case you get stranded.

Rentlo (☎ 723 5089; www.rentlocarhire.com; Avenida dos Mártires de Pátria, Comoro, Dili) is the main source of rental vehicles; it's 3km from Dili airport on the main road. A compact car costs from US$40 per day, a small 4WD from US$90. Rentals include 150km free per day. Limited liability coverage is available from $15 per day (with a whopping US$6000 deductible); it's probably useful given the toll the roads take on cars.

Motorcycles are handy in East Timor, as they breeze over bumps at a respectable pace. East Timor Backpackers (p153) charges US$25 per day.

Alternatively you could make arrangements with a driver so that you can enjoy the scenery while they tackle the potholes (and use their local knowledge). Ask around and expect to negotiate; prices start from US$40 per day.

Petrol (gasoline) in Portuguese is *besin*, diesel fuel is *solar*; expect to pay around US$1 per litre.

Hitching

Locals on the long walk into towns may ask for a ride. Waiting for a lift may be the only option if you're leaving Oecussi and heading

DEPARTURE TAX

There's a departure tax of US$10 when leaving Dili airport.

EAST TIMOR

into Kefamenanu in West Timor, and it's likely your payment will be cigarettes. However, hitchhiking is never entirely safe, so it's not recommended.

DILI

pop 130,000

Dili is a city undergoing rapid changes, and while some seem at odds with common sense (oversized embassies lining prime beachfront land, for instance), most changes capture the essence of reconstruction in East Timor. Streetlights and sculptures now grace the foreshore on the popular evening-walk route to Cape Fatucama, and footpaths, shade-providing trees and parks are appearing. Burnt-out buildings still form part of the scenery, as do century-old banyan trees on the foreshore.

Dili is a good place to recharge batteries (literally) and base yourself for jaunts into the regions; it's a chance to indulge in international food, buy supplies and meet some of the locals and expats.

ORIENTATION

Dili is a mass of suburbs that spreads from the airport, along the waterfront and all the way to the Jesus statue in the east. Most of the action occurs on, or one or two blocks north of, the waterfront. The closest you'll come to a travellers' hub in this town is East Timor Backpackers (see p153) or Castaway Bar (see p153).

INFORMATION

As yet there's no tourist office. Check out the internet resources listed on p163 for tourist information.

Internet Access

Internet Café (cnr Rua Presidente Nicolau Lobato & Rua Belarmino Lobo; per hr US$6; 8.30am-8.30pm) Opposite the ANZ bank is this businesslike place to download your photos.

> **GETTING INTO TOWN**
>
> Don't pay any more than US$5 for a taxi from Nicolau Lobato International Airport, 6km west of town. If you walk the few hundred metres out to the main road you can hail a *mikrolet* (small minibus) for US$0.25.

Timor Leste Media Development Centre (TLMDC) (Rua Sebastiao da Costa; per hr US$2; 8am-10pm Mon-Sat) Near the *tais* market (p154), your support supports this local media centre.

Medical Services

Medical services in East Timor are limited; serious cases may require evacuation to Darwin. Check with your embassy for other options.

Australian Residential Compound (☎ 331 1555; Avenida de Portugal, Marconi) You don't have to be Australian to see the doctor here.

Dili Nacional Hospital (☎ 331 1008; Rua Cicade Viana do Castelo) A cadre of Western volunteers assists locals at this busy place just east of Estrada de Bidau.

Farmacia Bonita (Avenida Alves Aldeia) A 24-hour pharmacy opposite the Integration Monument.

Foho Osan Mean Farmacia (☎ 725 6978; Rua Quinze de Outubro; 8am-9pm Mon-Sat, 8am-1pm Sun) Offers consultations (from US$3 to US$10) and pharmaceuticals.

Money

Banks are generally open between 9am and 4pm Monday to Friday.

ANZ (☎ 332 4800; www.anz.com/timorleste; cnr Rua Presidente Nicolau Lobato & Rua Belarmino Lobo) The ATM dispenses US dollars but if it runs dry try the ATM at the airport, at Landmark, or at Tiger Fuel.

Western Union (☎ 332 1586; Rua José Maria Marques) Transfers funds internationally.

Post & Telephone

Post office (Rua Presidente Nicolau Lobato; 8am-5pm Mon-Fri) East of Palácio do Governo.

Timor Telecom (☎ 172; www.timortelecom.tp; cnr Rua José Maria Marques & Estrada de Balide; 8am-6.30pm Mon-Fri, 8am-5.30 Sat) Has phone and internet services.

DANGERS & ANNOYANCES

Be aware that violent outbreaks can and do occur quickly, so stay clear of simmering trouble. The city is all but deserted after dark, when you should take extra care. See p161 for general information on safety.

SIGHTS

Waterfront

From children covered in green seaweed to serious boatmen reading the weather conditions opposite the grand **Palácio do Governo** (Government Palace), Dili has a waterfront with a distinctive Timorese personality. It stretches for kilometres in a quasi-boomerang shape, with **Farol lighthouse** beaming at one end, and Lita Supermarket,

> **TRAVEL COURTESY**
>
> Smile and say *Bele?* (OK?) before taking someone's photo. You'll usually be rewarded with a *Bele!* and a smile.

opposite the **fruit & fish markets** (where prices weaken as the smells strengthen), holding up the fort at the other end. Further west is an esplanade dotted with gigantic 'look at me' embassies, which front vibrant evening **fish & chicken stalls**.

Cape Fatucama & the Jesus Statue

Around 7km east of town on Cape Fatucama is the hard-to-miss **Jesus statue**, a popular morning and evening exercise spot for locals and expats. Expect calm beaches, and bars where you sink into the sand while sipping beers and watching beach volleyball.

From the cape the views of turquoise bays backed by green-covered mountains are stunning. As you climb the well-marked path up to Jesus, look for a little path after the last of 14 grottoes. It leads down to an often-deserted beach, known as **Jesus Backside beach**, where there's decent snorkelling.

A taxi to the statue from town should cost US$3, though it can be difficult getting back.

Xanana Reading Room

Housing loads of memorabilia from its namesake, the **Xanana Reading Room** (☎ 332 2831; Rua Belarmino Lobo; admission free; 🕑 10am-6pm Mon-Fri, 10am-4pm Sat) is a small and busy library with a book-swap facility and souvenirs. The adjoining internet facility charges US$3 per hour.

Resistance Museum

Designed to commemorate the 24-year struggle against the Indonesians, the **Resistance Museum** (Rua Formosa; admission US$1; 🕑 9.30am-5pm Tue-Sat, 1.30-5pm Sun) is one of Dili's must-see attractions. The story of Falintil's resistance is brought to life with a timeline, photos, and exhibits of the weapons and tools of communication the East Timorese used in their fight for independence.

Arte Moris

There's a distinct Bob Marley/boho feel to **Arte Moris** (☎ 723 3507; Avenida dos Mártires da Pátria, Comoro; admission free; 🕑 9am-6pm Mon-Sat), a residential art gallery in what was Dili's domed Indonesian-era museum. Downstairs the collection features creative woodcarvings and paintings sprayed onto *tais*. Those with artistic bones and a yearning to hang around are welcome to impart knowledge, and you'll get to hang out with the esteemed theatrical troupe Bibi Bulak, which calls the centre home.

Travelling west from town, the compound is over the Comoro bridge, just before the airport.

Santa Cruz Cemetery

On 12 November 1991, Indonesian soldiers fired on a peaceful memorial procession at the **Santa Cruz Cemetery**. Although exact figures aren't known, it's considered by experts that at least 280 civilians died, many of them after they were rounded up and trucked away by the military. One of the people killed was Kamal Bamadhaj, a New Zealand citizen and the subject of the 1999 film *Punitive Damage*. British journalist Max Stahl filmed the bloody attack, and his footage features in the documentary *In Cold Blood*. The massacre at the Santa Cruz Cemetery is cited as a turning point in the independence struggle. The Xanana Reading Room (left) has films about the event available for viewing.

ACTIVITIES

The reef fringing the entire north coast of East Timor provides spectacular **diving** and **snorkelling** opportunities. Many sites, including the legendary K41 east of town, are easily accessed by walking in from the beach, with dramatic drop-offs just 10m offshore in parts. Two dive operators are located in Dili and both arrange trips throughout the country and to Atauro Island. Both offer trips for snorkellers.

FreeFlow (☎ 723 4614; http://freeflowdiving.blogspot.com; Avenida de Portugal) FreeFlow offers guided shore dives for US$40 per dive, including transport. Safari trips include delicious lunches. There's also a full range of PADI courses from US$350.

Dive Timor Lorosae (☎ 723 7092; www.divetimor.com; Avenida de Portugal) This place offers day-trip diving around Atauro Island, including two dives from US$165 per person (minimum four people). Shore dives around Dili (including two dives) cost from US$85. PADI courses cost from US$350.

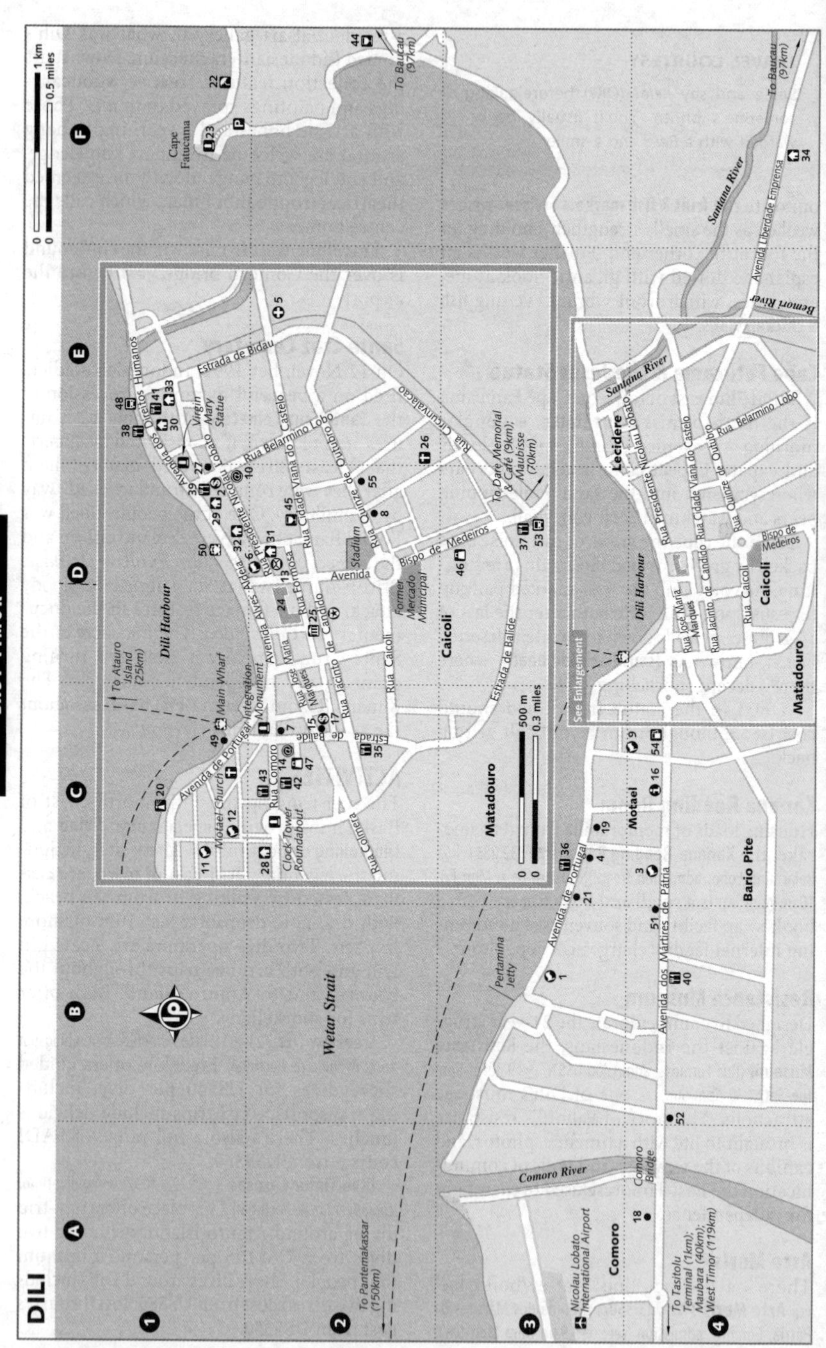

DILI
Wetar Strait
Dili Harbour
Cape Fatucama
To Pantemakassar (150km)
To Atauro Island (25km)
To Baucau (97km)
To Tasitolu Terminal (1km); Maubara (40km); West Timor (119km)
To Dare Memorial & Café (9km); Maubisse (70km)
Nicolau Lobato International Airport
Comoro
Comoro River
Comoro Bridge
Pertamina Jetty
Avenida de Portugal
Avenida dos Mártires de Pátria
Motael
Bario Pite
Matadouro
Caicoli
Lecidere
Santana River
Bemori River
Avenida Liberdade Emprensa
See Enlargement
Main Wharf
Integration Monument
Motael Church
Clock Tower Roundabout
Rua Comoro
Estrada de Balide
Rua Colmera
Rua José Maria Marques
Rua Jacinto de Candido
Rua Caicoli
Rua Formosa
Rua Cidade Viana do Castelo
Rua Quinze de Outubro
Rua Belarmino Lobo
Rua Presidente Nicolau Lobato
Avenida Alves Aldeia
Avenida dos Direitos Humanos
Estrada de Bidau
Virgin Mary Statue
Stadium
Former Mercado Municipal
Avenida Bispo de Medeiros
Rua Circunvalacao
Estrada de Balide
0 500 m
0 0.3 miles
0 1 km
0 0.5 miles

INFORMATION
American Embassy....1 B3
ANZ....2 D1
Australian Embassy....3 C4
Australian Residential Compound....4 C3
Dili Nacional Hospital....5 E2
European Commission Embassy....6 D2
Farmacia Bonita....7 C2
Foho Osan Mean Farmacia....8 D2
Indonesian Embassy....9 C4
Internet Cafe....10 D1
Irish Embassy....11 C1
New Zealand Embassy....12 C1
Post Office....13 D2
Timor Leste Media Development Centre....14 C2
Timor Telecom....15 C2
Village Hotels Timor....16 C4
Western Union....17 C2

SIGHTS & ACTIVITIES
Arte Moris....18 A4
Dive Timor Lorosae....19 C3
Eco Discovery....(see 40)
Farol Lighthouse....20 C1
Fish & Chicken Stalls....(see 36)
FreeFlow....21 C3
Fruit & Fish Market....(see 38)
Jesus Backside Beach....22 F1
Jesus Statue....23 F1
Palácio do Governo....24 D2
Resistence Museum....25 D2
Santa Cruz Cemetery....26 E2
Xanana Reading Room....27 D1

SLEEPING
East Timor Backpackers....28 C2
Hotel Dili....29 D1
Hotel Turismo....30 E1
Mega Tours....31 D2
Rocella....32 D1
Venture Hotel....33 E1
Vila Harmonia....34 F4

EATING
Bombay Kitchen....35 C2
Castaway Bar....(see 19)
Fish & Chicken Stalls....36 C3
Fresh-Food Market....37 D3
Fruit & Fish Market....38 E1
Kebab Club....39 D1
Landmark....40 B4
Lita....41 E1
Resto Manado....42 C2
Wasabe....43 C2

DRINKING
Caz Bar....44 F2
Starview Restaurant....45 D2

SHOPPING
Alola Foundation....46 D3
Noi....(see 31)
Tais Mercado....47 C2

TRANSPORT
Austasia....(see 40)
Bidau Terminal....48 E1
East Timor Backpackers....(see 28)
Nakroma Ferry Office....49 C1
Outriggers to Atauro....50 D1
Paradise Tour & Travel....51 B4
Rentlo....52 B4
Taibessi Terminal....53 D3
Tiger Fuel....54 C4
Timor Tour & Travel....55 D2

SLEEPING

Dili doesn't have many cheap beds, and until the influx of UN and NGO staff wanes, prices will remain high.

East Timor Backpackers (☎ 723 8121, 723 9821; Avenida Almirante Americo Tomas; dm US$10;) Dili's only hostel is a meeting place for backpackers, and it's located near good restaurants and 24-hour internet (at Tiger Fuel). A cheap-and-cheerful Indian restaurant fronts it, and there's a bar and kitchen out the back.

Vila Harmonia (☎ 723 8265; vilaharmonia@hotmail.com; Avenida Liberdade Emprensa 418, Becora; per person US$15) About 3km from town, this mishmash of rooms – including an *uma adat* (traditional house) – is worth staying at for the unusual sculptures that pay tribute to East Timor's long-time supporters.

Venture Hotel (☎ 331 3276; venture_hotel@hotmail.com; Rua Filomena de Camera, Lecidere; r US$23-33;) Stick a bunch of portable rooms together, insert air conditioners and this is what you get. There's nothing fancy about this place, especially the shared bathrooms, though the pool's a welcome addition and there are good views from the upstairs gym.

Hotel Turismo (☎ 331 0555; hotelturismo_04@yahoo.com; Avenida dos Direitos Humanos, Lecidere; r US$25-65;) A traditional haunt of journalists, the Turismo has survived all that Dili has had thrown at it. Its grassy courtyard is a pleasant place to relax, and some rooms have views of Atauro Island.

Rocella (☎ 723 7993; Rua Presidente Nicolau Lobato 18; r US$30;) Rooms here could do with windows that open, but they're comfortable and clean. The ostentatiously lit bar actually has a pleasant atmosphere.

Hotel Dili (☎ 331 3958; reservation@hoteldili.com; Avenida dos Direitos Humanos; r US$40-140;) Hotel Dili offers chilled, air-conditioned rooms, good tropical-fruit breakfasts and a waterfront location. The cheapest rooms share bathrooms; all rooms have high-speed internet and satellite TV.

EATING & DRINKING

Dili is the capital of the long lunch and dinner, and there are plenty of places to indulge in a variety of international flavours.

Resto Manado (☎ 744 7660; Rua Comoro, Mandarin; meals from US$2) Expect delicious fish potato cakes, spicy sauces and tasty chicken at this popular Padang-style restaurant.

Wasabe (☎ 723 3961; Rua Comoro, Mandarin; dishes US$4-8) This place does great Japanese and Indonesian mains. Stay outside for a tropical feel, or get smoked out of the air-con section (with booths) inside.

Caz Bar (☎ 723 3961; Area Branca; dishes US$4-8) Sink back in your chair on the beach at this popular place that tops the line-up of beachside joints east of town. At sunset, it's a toss-up between a beer and a US$1 fresh coconut.

Castaway Bar (☎ 723 5449; Avenida de Portugal, Marconi; mains US$4-12) Castaway is an open-air restaurant

WHY DIVE EAST TIMOR?

Expat Kym Smithies has been diving East Timor's sites since 2002:

What's so good about diving in East Timor? Only 40 minutes from Dili you can dive pristine reefs filled with small colourful marine life. While dugongs and whale sharks have been spotted, they are not a regular occurrence, but healthy, colourful coral, small shoals of fish, the occasional reef shark and turtle, and a wonderful variety of macro-life are guaranteed. Nudibranch lovers will enjoy spotting a large variety of different species (largely dependent on the season), as well as frogfish, seahorses, mimic octopus and more.

Any particular highlights? Atauro Island is spectacular and is one of the few places where you may see large pelagic creatures like turtles, hammerhead sharks, whales and dolphins (mostly from the boat). Strong currents mean that most dives are drift dives, but the company that runs the trip (Dive Timor Lorosae; see p151) is very professional and can be trusted to pick you up at the end!

that packs them in for a lunch menu that includes chilli prawns, fat sandwiches and burgers. There's a diving joint downstairs (Dive Timor Lorosae, p151) and backpackers' accommodation, complete with pool, at the rear.

Bombay Kitchen (☎ 736 5999; cnr Rua Jacinto de Candido & Estrada de Balide; meals from US$5) Head upstairs for white and bright surrounds. The blaring Bollywood movies enable you to get your fix of India even before your tasty meal arrives. Get plenty of paratha to soak up the tasty masala.

Kebab Club (☎ 729 7121; Rua Belarmino Lobo; mains US$7) This clash of decorating style (Turkey meets Timor) is expanding both its premises and menu, but felafels and chicken kebabs will still rule the roost, as will the affable owner.

If karaoke beckons, try **Starview Restaurant** (Rua Cidade Viana do Castelo; 9pm until late). For a cheap feed try the **fish & chicken stalls** opposite the Australian Residential Compound. After sunset it's a-smokin' (literally); fill up on delicious and simple chicken and fish dishes for US$0.25 to US$3.

There's a large **fresh-food market** at Taibessi and a smaller **fruit & fish market** on the waterfront near the Hotel Turismo. Vendors selling cold bottled water and beer (wipe the tops to avoid ingesting dirty water) can be found everywhere. Several supermarkets sell everything from Tim Tams to bug repellent to fishing tackle; try **Lita** (Avenida dos Direitos Humanos). **Landmark** (☎ 723 1313; Avenida dos Mártires de Pátria, Comoro) is a large complex of shops on the airport road.

SHOPPING

Alola Foundation (www.alolafoundation.org; Avenida Bispo de Medeiros) Alola sells *tais*, sculptures, soaps and other crafts from around the country to support its work with the women and children of East Timor. There's another branch in the airport departure lounge.

Tais Mercado (Rua Sebastiao da Costa) A *tais* is a piece of East Timorese woven cloth (see p148), and each region possesses its own distinctive style. This market has *tais* from all over the country. Quality varies greatly. **Noi** (☎ 724 5728; Central Hotel, Rua Presidente Nicolau Lobato) sells zip-up *tais* skirts for $25.

GETTING THERE & AWAY

Air

See p149 for details of getting in and out of Dili by air.

Boat

The **Nakroma ferry office** (☎ 728 0963; Avenida de Portugal; 9am-5pm) is in the large building at the port. Buy your tickets a few days in advance. See p160 for information on ferries for Oecussi. The Atauro Island service (business class $5, two hours) runs on Saturdays. See p149 for more details.

Bus

Dili's bus 'terminals' (which are actually more like shabby shelters) are served by taxis and *mikrolet*. Buses are more frequent in the morning.

Tasitolu Terminal, west of the airport, is the hub for destinations to the west of the country (Ermera, Maliana and Liquiçá). Buses travelling to the east (Baucau, Lospalos, Viqueque etc) leave from Bidau Terminal, on the waterfront near Hotel Turismo. The Taibessi Terminal, at the huge Taibessi market (left), is the stop for transport to Maubisse, Same and Suai.

GETTING AROUND

Bus

Mikrolet (US$0.25) buzz about on designated routes during daylight hours. They stop frequently over relatively short distances, which makes taxis way more efficient.

Car

See p149 for car-hire options. Cars are useful if you need to get around at night, but walking and using taxis should suffice otherwise.

Taxi

Smart yellow (unmetered) taxis abound in Dili, and if you negotiate before you get in, most trips cost $1. If you find, or hear of a good driver, ask for their mobile number and see if they'll be your night driver, as streets are usually taxi-free by 9pm.

ATAURO ISLAND

After busy Dili, Atauro Island seems positively deserted. Its sandy beaches are gateways to broad fringing reefs and there's great snorkelling off the pier at Beloi and in front of Tua Kóin, just minutes away from the island's accommodation. Walking trails lead through savannah and remnants of tropical forest. There's not much else to do here, other than enjoy the escapism of the two dreamy (but basic) accommodation options. The only shopping to do involves surveying the local wood carvings.

Atauro Island's location, which is 30km from Dili over a section of sea that is 3km deep in parts, made it perfect for use as a jail by both the Portuguese and Indonesian governments.

The community today comprises around 8000 people, mostly subsistence fishers and farmers, who live in a few villages spread across the island. The main centres are along the east coast: Makili (a carving centre), Vila (with leafy lanes and a few colonial vestiges) and Beloi (where the ferry docks), with Macadade in the mountains.

The Dili dive shops (p151) arrange underwater tours; you can arrange for snorkelling trips with local fishing boats from US$15, or just swim out. Ask the locals about the many hiking possibilities.

SLEEPING

Atauro Island's two unique guest houses offer thatched cabins with sea views and an almost guaranteed feeling of calm.

Booking ahead for accommodation (or even just lunch if you're on a day trip) is wise, as Atauro Island is a popular destination for expats seeking an escape from Dili. Polite folk check to see if they can bring anything from Dili's supermarkets before heading over.

Tua Kóin Eco-Village (☎ 723 6085; www.atauroisland.com; Vila; cabin per person US$15) This Timorese-owned and operated ecovillage holds true to its name. You'll pad over from your solar-powered thatched-roof cabin (one of eight, all with mosquito nets and water views) to the composting toilet and outdoor, *mandi*-style (a large tub from which you scoop water to wash yourself with) shower. Friendly staff will help you organise everything from a massage to transportation to the island and back, and the meals (US$3 to US$4) are terrific.

Nema's (☎ 723 6084; Beloi; r per person US$15) Just north of the ferry dock in Beloi, Nema's is run by an Australian named Barry and his family. There are four sun-drenched thatched cabins

EAST TIMOR

GETTING TO INDONESIA

The four-hour bus ride from Dili to the border town of Batugade costs US$5. To get to Indonesia, you have to walk 200m across the border to Motoain in West Timor, from where a *mikrolet* (small minibus) costs less than US$2 to Atambua. Buses from Atambua to Kupang (p311) cost about US$5 and take eight hours. If you're going to Oecussi, East Timor, it's one hour from Atambua to Kefamenanu then an hour to the border crossing (open 9am to 4pm, closed Sundays). You'll need an Indonesian visa before crossing the border into West Timor (see p164).

Much easier is the through bus service between Dili and Kupang offered by **Timor Tour & Travel** (Dili ☎ 333 1014; Rua Quinze de Outubro 17; Kupang ☎ 0380-881 543; Jl Timor Raya 8) and **Paradise Tour & Travel** (Dili ☎ 728 6673, 723 5678; Rua Mártires da Pátria; Kupang ☎ 0380-823 120). The two companies run services each morning (US$20, 12 hours); book in advance.

See p314 for information on crossing the border from the opposite direction.

right on the beach; the one Barry calls his writer's cabin has mesmerising views from an upper level.

GETTING THERE & AROUND

There are a couple of ways to travel from Dili to Atauro. The *Nakroma* ferry (p154) departs Dili Saturdays at 9am and returns at 4pm, taking two hours each way. Fares in business class (meaning those charged to foreigners) are US$5 each way. If you are doing a day trip on the *Nakroma*, you'll have time to ride between the two villages, do a little exploring, including the seaside market at Beloi, and possibly have a prearranged lunch at Tua Kóin (p155) or Nema's (p155).

Fishing boats and outriggers also travel the route (US$10, three hours) several days a week depending on tides (but are notably absent on Sundays). These boats leave from opposite the Palácio do Governo; you can always arrive there in the morning and see if anyone's heading over, or check details with Tua Kóin or Nema's. You're likely to get drenched on the outrigger, and it can be a hairy experience.

An outrigger can take you directly to Vila, while the ferry lands at Beloi. The road that connects the two (the only road on the island) has trucks shuttling back and forth. Flag one down; the cost is US$2. If arriving by ferry, scramble aboard the first truck you see before it fills up with chickens, kids and bags of rice.

EAST OF DILI

The east of the country is also the most tourist-ready. With your own wheels (or on painfully slow public transport) you'll stumble across wide, lime-green rice paddies, groves of mangroves, idyllic beaches where buffalos (and the occasional crocodile) roam. Some of the best diving in the country is found right off the shore along here.

Over the Laclo River is **Manatuto**, 64km east of Dili, though you can bypass this small town and the Jesus that overlooks it. After heading inland 19km you'll be at **Laleia**, the birthplace of Xanana Gusmão. Look out for the roadside monument where the land of Timor rests on skulls. A further 9km on and you'll come to **Vemasse**, which is noted for its pottery and is watched over by a fortresslike Portuguese construction on the hillside.

BAUCAU

While Baucau is best known as a beach town, it's actually a long way down (5km) to the beach from the intriguing Old Town, and even further from the bland, Indonesian-built New Town *(Kota Baru)*. Get your bearings in the Old Town from the unused, yet mightily impressive Portuguese-era **mercado municipal** (municipal market). Just west of this is the bustling roadside **town market** where pyramid-shaped piles of potatoes, neat bunches of greens and mounds of maize form a colourful patchwork on the pavement. Head down through the market and take a left to spot the pink **Pousada**. A right turn around the roundabout (past the oft-empty swimming pool) and you're at the turn-off for Lospalos, or keep travelling down the lush ravine to find the magic beach at **Osolata**. Called Wataboo, it's a series of white sand coves fringed by palms and hemmed by turquoise water. Head for the second cove.

The characterless New Town overlooks the Old Town. On the road linking the two, **Timor Telecom** (☎ 413 0017; 🕑 9am-5pm) has slow internet access (US$2 per hour), currency exchange and a neighbouring ANZ ATM.

Sleeping & Eating

Melita Guesthouse (☎ 725 0267; Rua Vao Redi Bahu, Old Town; s/d US$15/20) Ignore the Mickey Mouse sheets and enjoy clean rooms with bathrooms and fans. There is a palm-tree-and-sea view from the common area. To find it take a left at the Pousada roundabout.

Baucau Beach Bungalows (☎ 739 7467, 734 0371; Osolata; r per person US$15) Choose from a simple thatched bungalow that sleeps six, or one of three rooms in a neighbouring Indonesian-style house (with shared kitchen and lounge). Meals can be arranged for US$6 and are sourced from the fishing boats across the road.

Pousada de Baucau (☎ 724 1111; Rua de Catedral, Old Town; r from US$60; ❄ 💻) Despite its eerie history as a torture centre during the Indonesian occupation, this huge, salmon pink *pousada* (traditional Portuguese lodging) is still one of East Timor's nicest hotels, with *tais* bedheads, timber floors and air con. The restaurant has good Portuguese food (meals from US$5). Staff member Felicity offers tours to nearby attractions (hot-water springs and Japanese caves) for US$20 per person per day.

Restaurante Amalia (☎ 726 3610; Old Town; meals US$6) Take a shady spot on the outdoor terrace and enjoy the sea views, along with delicious Portuguese-style meals served with a smile.

Getting There & Away

Numerous buses each day drive the 123km between Dili and Baucau (US$4, three hours). Buses also head to Viqueque (US$4, two hours) and Lospalos (US$4, 3½ hours). Ask to be dropped off in the Old Town.

SOUTH OF BAUCAU

South of Baucau are lush hills where Fretilin members hid during the Indonesian occupation. The area remains a stronghold for the party.

After 28km of rugged road you come to the large and impressive buildings of **Venilale**, a town wedged between Mt Matebian in the east and Mt Mundo Perdido (Lost World; 1775m) in the west. The road deteriorates along the 16km to the misty village of **Ossu**. Some 9km south of here take a sharp left at the sign for **Timor Village Hotel** (Loihunu; ☎ 739 6911, 331 0616; incl breakfast tw/d US$20/35), a spotless hydropowered hotel set on a hillside near a surging river and waterfall. The meals are good and you can arrange hiking guides here.

Travel past roadside waterfalls and white cliffs to the sprawling town of **Viqueque**, 63km from Baucau. There are several guest houses on the left-hand side of the road opposite the Timor Telecom tower. **Motel Borala** (☎ 742 4953; s/d US$10/15) has seven rooms with private bathrooms, and shops and restaurants are nearby. The new town has a market and an abundance of Indonesian monuments.

Buses and *mikrolet* run daily between Viqueque and Baucau (US$4, two hours) and on to Dili (US$8, three hours).

A 45-minute drive on a half-road, half-rice paddy will get you to the outrigger-lined beach at **Beaçu**, which is watched over by a decaying Portuguese-built customs building. From here it's possible to continue east along the coast road in the dry season; plan on six or more hours to Lospalos.

AROUND BAUCAU

South of Baucau is **Mt Matebian** (2315m). Topped with a statue of Christ and known as 'Mountain of the Souls', this holy place attracts thousands of pilgrims annually for All Souls Day (2 November) to honour deceased friends and family. About 15km from Baucau is **Molia**, turn-off point for the end-of-the-road village of **Quelicai**. On the right-hand side of the road between the market and the church is the green **Matebian Guesthouse** (☎ 729 3710, 723 6039; per person incl meals US$20), a family-run guest house that offers walking tours to Matebian and the family's *uma adat* (traditional house).

One or two *mikrolet* make the 33km journey from Baucau to Quelicai in the mornings and early afternoons (US$1, 1½ hours), or you can charter one from Baucau for US$17.

Com

You're literally at the end of the road in Com, a town focused on fishing and tourism. There's excellent snorkelling and a good, long beach (although it's beaten by the one at the 171km marker to the west).

Plenty of guest houses are popping up, taking the monopoly away from the very average shell-studded **Com Beach Resort** (☎ 728 3311; r US$25-120; ⊠). The best of the bunch is the beachside, *uma adat*–styled **Kati Guesthouse** (☎ 732 4294; r US$15), which has three small rooms (with shared bathroom) and meals for US$6.

You'll be eating at the Com Beach Resort's **Ocean View Restaurant** (dishes US$6-$10) unless you book ahead at one of the guest houses.

There are regular *mikrolet* from Lospalos to Com (US$1.50, one hour).

Tutuala & Jaco Island

The 50km of road from Lautem to Tutuala ventures past the shimmering waters of Lake Ira Lalaroe, a few stilted Fataluku houses and through the newly declared Nino Konis Santana National Park (p148). The road ends on a bluff in Tutuala village, where there are sweeping views out to sea and an old, practically deserted, Portuguese *pousada* where you can rent a room; however, a better option is to push on and tackle the steep 8km track down to **Walu**, a stunning white-sand beach. Turn left after the descent and you'll find four thatched cabins at the community-run **Walu Sere** (☎ 738 2696; r US$15). Fall asleep listening to waves lapping at the shore and wake to the stunning vision of Jaco Island, just offshore, across the turquoise waters. Jaco has a sacred meaning to the Timorese, and was once the hiding place of Xanana Gusmão. No one lives there (or stays overnight), however, fisherfolk will zoom you over on their outriggers for US$7. In the two minutes the trip takes you'll be transported to an island paradise where amazing white sands circle a forested centre.

Staff at Walu Sere can organise tours of the local rock-art caves.

You can take a daily *mikrolet* to/from Lospalos (US$1.50, three hours), or you can charter one from Com for about US$15.

Lospalos

Lospalos, home to the Fataluku-language speakers, is another sprawling town about 28km south of Lautem. It's mostly of interest for its market, nearby caves and Fataluku houses. Opposite the town's central Fataluku house is **Nova Esperança** (☎ 738 0802; s/d US$15/30), which has clean rooms, a friendly atmosphere and stars carved out of the ceiling. Out of town, near the new market, **Hotel Roberto Carlos** (☎ 723 0826; s/d from US$35/45) has rooms, meals (from US$5 to US$9) and boat, motorbike and 4WD hire (US$750/25/80 per day).

Buses and *mikrolet* run between Lospalos and Baucau (US$4, 3½ hours).

WEST OF DILI

The border with Indonesian West Timor is just four hours west of Dili along a coast-gripping road punctuated by small villages selling differing wares. Look out for papaya town, pillow town, fish town, salt town and even fence-post town. Southwest of Dili (via Tibar) are the coffee regions of Ermera and Gleno (yep, coffee towns).

Black-sand beaches are a feature of the coastal route, and there are plenty of places to don a mask and wade out to reefs that teem with colourful marine life. There are also signs of development; just before **Liquiçá** (35km west of Dili), 'bubble beach' is now fenced off for gas exploration. Liquiçá itself has some grand Portuguese-era buildings, and its bustling market is a few kilometres east of the main town.

Check out the fort walls and cannons at beachside **Maubara**, 40km from Dili, before strolling around the Maubara Handicraft Market. Just off the coast here, the sandy ocean floor slopes away to a coral bed. There's a **retreat** (☎ 728 4514; per person incl meals US$25) run by Carmelite nuns 3km west of town – look for the 'Maubara–Fatubessi' sign and follow a short, steep track up. Some of the rooms have sweeping ocean views. A steady stream of *mikrolet* departs Dili and stops at both villages (US$1, one hour). Buses from Dili pass through the skimpy border town of **Batugade** (111km from Dili); see p155 for details on the border crossing into West Timor. They then head inland to the mountain town of **Balibo**, where five Australia-based journalists were killed by Indonesian soldiers in 1975. The Australian flag the journalists painted for protection is still visible on Australia Flag House, which is now a restored community centre with an excellent memorial inside.

The hills of West Timor are in plain view over the rice fields adjoining **Maliana**, 26km inland from Balibo. The place to stay here is **Tansos** (r US$20), which has clean rooms with shared bathrooms and great views of the plains. Off the road to **Bobonaro** are the rebuilt **Be Manis** (Hot Springs). The mist-covered old colonial centre of Bobonaro is 25km east of Maliana. It's a further 40km down to **Zumalai**; expect the trip to take three hours on a good day. Continue on to **Suai**, a journey totally impossible during the wet season. You can also do a round trip to **Same** and **Maubisse** from here.

SOUTH OF DILI

From bare winding passes to rainforest canopies that shade coffee beans, the area south of Dili shows how diverse this country's environment is. Coffee-country grabs you in **Aileu** before you hit the true cloud-dwelling town of Maubisse. Out of town there's a turn-off to Mt Ramelau, a popular climbing spot (and East Timor's highest peak). Past Same, the sweet fishing village of Betano beckons.

MAUBISSE

elev 1400m

Waking up in chilly Maubisse and watching clouds rising, uncovering the village below, is a highlight of any trip to East Timor. It's 70km south of Dili (a three-hour journey). The best bed in town is at its highest point: the **Pousada de Maubisse** (☎ 724 9567; r per person Mon-Thu US$17, Fri & Sat US$56, Sun US$22). Great food (US$6) and gorgeous grounds make for great-value weekdays. A cheaper weekend option is the sparkling clean **Café Maubisse** (☎ 727 4756; per person US$10) opposite Maubisse's elaborate church. There are several restaurants near the buzzing **market** on the southern side of town.

Buses depart from Dili for Maubisse (US$5, three hours) each morning.

HATUBUILICO & MT RAMELAU

Wild roses grow by the road and mountain streams trickle through the precious teeny town of **Hatubuilico**, located at the base of Mt Ramelau (2963m). Stay at the five-room **Pousada Alecrim Namrau** (☎ 724 9567; Rua Gruta Ramelau Hun 1; r per person US$10) where meals can be arranged for US$2.50. The uniquely decorated guest house is run by the village chief, who can arrange a guide (US$5) to get you up the mountain – and up at 3am in time to reach the peak for sunrise.

Hiking from the village to the Virgin Mary statue at the top of Mt Ramelau takes around three hours; with a 4WD you can drive 2.5km to a meadow from where it's two hours to the top. The trail leads steadily up, though there are plenty of slippery rocks and occasionally landslides. An open-air 'church' sits on a plateau at the 2700m mark. From the peak, mountain tops ripple out to the coast, which is visible to both the south and the north. Sunrise will give you chills, both down your spine and up your arms (temperatures average 5°C).

From Maubisse, the Hatubuilico turn-off is at the 81km post; you'll reach the village after 18km. If the road is passable, *angguna* travel from Maubisse to Hatubuilico on Wednesdays and Saturdays. The price depends on the number of passengers, but the trip should cost around US$2 and take three hours.

SAME & BETANO

Same (Sar-may), 43km south of Maubisse, is a lush town at the base of a picturesque valley. There's a great little **handicrafts market** in the centre and a couple of good places to stay.

Samata Backpackers (☎ 741 5215; per person US$10) can organise tours and a bed, or try the clean rooms at **Same Hotel & Restaurant** (☎ 731 5267; Rua Na Raran; s/d US$25/35). The restaurant does good basic meals (US$4).

If you've got this far, it is worth making the simple 45-minute journey to the quiet black-sand beach at Betano (27km). From here, in dry season, you can journey east over narrow tracks through crocodile-infested mangroves to Viqueque (this takes six or more hours).

Angguna run frequently between Maubisse and Same (US$3, two hours), and between Same and Betano (US$1, one hour).

SUAI

Suai, the south coast's main town, sprawls 5km inland and is a confusing collection of villages. The main one, Debos, is dominated by an enormous unfinished cathedral, where, in September 1999, Timorese were pushed to their deaths from the balcony. The now-demolished Our Lady of Fatima Church, also the scene of a massacre, is now the site of a memorial to 'Black September'. Sleep at the **Fronteria Guesthouse** (r US$30) and dine on garlic prawns at **Romeo's Restaurant** (meals US$10). Traverse the mangroves to see the moody black-sand beaches at the ocean.

Angguna run between Suai and Maubisse (around US$2, at least four hours), via Ainaro (with its colourful church) or Same. You can also get here via Maliana.

OECUSSI

pop 63,000

There are many reasons to feel sorry for Oecussi: it's part of East Timor yet it's surrounded on three sides by Indonesian West Timor; its only direct link with Dili is a twice-weekly ferry, and when that's being repaired Oecussi finds itself stranded; and it often seems to be forgotten by international NGOs and even, occasionally, by its own government. However, Oecussi is a Cinderella-in-waiting. It's fronted by long stretches of beach and reef, is the source of some of the most beautiful *tais* in the country and even has pools of hot mud bubbling in its southernmost region.

Oecussi is the name of one of two kingdoms that existed prior to colonisation. It was settled by descendents of Dominicans (the Topasses) in 1642, though they had been visiting Timor from nearby islands since 1551. Beachside Lifau was the Portuguese colony's capital until 1769, when Dutch-pressure made Dili look far more attractive. It was annexed by Indonesia without resistance in 1976, but it didn't escape the violence following the independence referendum in 1999; houses and businesses were burned, and members of local resistance groups were shot.

Pantemakassar, aka Oecussi town, is (literally) a one-taxi town. It's a flat, spread-out town with so little going on that any movement seems surprising. Roads are wide and empty and pass by picturesque ponds with bright lilies, monuments and palms. There are frequent sightings of dugong in the waters here, and the sheer coral drop-off about 20m offshore augurs well for **snorkelling**, though the recent resurgence of crocodiles means a 'croc watch' is essential.

The town is surrounded by red cliff mountains, and just 1.5km to its south you can climb up to the old Portuguese fort **Fatusuba**, which is a whisper of its former self. Travel 5km along the coast west of Pantemakassar and you'll find **Lifau**, the site of the original Portuguese settlement. There's a rock-studded monument commemorating the first landing, and the beach attracts local families for Sunday picnics. The best beach begins 2km east of town on **Pantai Mahata**, which ends at a stunning red-rock headland.

If you arrive overland you'll pass through the banyan-tree-shaded market at **Pasar Tono**, 12km south of Pantemakassar. Hot mud is found near the southern town of **Passabe**.

The cleanest digs are at **Rao Homestay & Restaurant** (☎ 738 9352; s/d US$15/20) though there's only one double room. Beachfront **Apartment Lifau** (☎ 728 3777; s/d US$7/10) has potential and sea views. **Restaurant Aries** does a filling *nasi rendang* for US$1.25. The internet is available at **Timor Telecom** (Rua Francisco Mousino; 🕒 8am-3pm Mon-Fri) east of the traffic circle.

The **Nakroma ferry** (☎ 728 0963; Avenida de Portugal, Dili; 🕒 9am-5pm) travels from Dili to Oecussi (economy/business class US$4/US$14, 12 hours) twice a week, departing the capital on Monday and Thursday nights. The return departure is around 5.30pm the following evening. In Pantemakassar the office is opposite the dock.

You'll need an Indonesian visa to get from Oecussi to West Timor overland (available in Dili), and if you plan to go overland to East Timor you'll need to buy a 30-day visa at the Motoain–Batugade border.

EAST TIMOR DIRECTORY

ACCOMMODATION

Simple accommodation in East Timor costs around US$10 a night, variously charged per person or per room. Facilities for travellers are improving; most towns have at least one guest house with freshly painted rooms containing decent mattresses and private bathrooms, but you'll pay from US$20 to US$50. Outside Dili the availability of rooms with fans or air-con depends on local electricity supply.

Dili's hotels have air con, sit-down loos and in-room power sockets (220V, 50Hz; there's no standard socket, so bring adaptors suitable for European and Australian wall sockets). Prices are boosted by the large UN/NGO population, so if it contracts, hotel prices will too. Most hotels are not flash, and there are still a couple that were hastily put together from shipping containers post-1999.

District guest houses are often joined to restaurants and will provide a basic room with shared *mandi* (a large concrete basin from which you scoop water to rinse your body and flush the squat toilet). Convents attached to churches often have cheap and spotless rooms. Most places provide meals; there's almost always free coffee and bread in the morning, as well as cooked meals on request. In rural areas, running water and power may only be available from 6pm to midnight, if at all, and hot water is a rarity.

In remote areas where there is little or no commercial accommodation, locals usually open their homes to travellers; etiquette would encourage payment (around US$10).

There are no formal camping options in East Timor, though it's not unknown for travellers to pitch a tent in isolated areas. In Dili, **Mega Tours** (☎ 723 5199; timormegatours@netscape.net; Rua Presidente Nicolau Lobato) rents camping equipment for US$5 per person.

ACTIVITIES

Diving the incredible coast and exploring the remote interior are two major reasons to visit East Timor.

There are tonnes of opportunities for the adventure traveller; think kayaking to Atauro Island, exploring the country's limestone caves, and really rugged mountain biking (you can purchase a new Chinese-made mountain bike in Dili for about US$200). For many activities it will be BYO equipment, or check with Dili's adventure-travel companies (p164).

Diving

The diving is sublime in East Timor, and there are two long-standing dive companies who can show you what's out there (see p151). Dive Timor Lorosae has its own boat and takes dive trips out to Atauro

EAST TIMOR

Island, while FreeFlow is best known for its experienced dive guides and delicious lunches. Conditions are best during the dry season (May to December), when visibility is at around 20m to 30m. For sample views check out **Reefscenes.net** (www.reefscenes.net) and **Underwater East Timor** (www.uwet.net).

Hiking

Serious hikers are popping up in villages around the country (and surprising the locals), and 10-day north-to-south coast hikes are not unheard of. Popular day-long hikes include those to the summit of Mt Ramelau (from where you can see the south and north coasts of East Timor) and to the sacred peak of Mt Matebian. Both mountains have accommodation nearby that can provide guides, otherwise try Dili-based tour companies (see p164). There's also hiking in Atauro Island's interior.

BOOKS

There are book exchanges at bars and hotels, so BYO to swap.

Timor-Leste Land of Discovery is a very impressive coffee-table book filled with gorgeous images of the land and people. It's widely available in Dili.

Balibo by Jill Jolliffe has been made into a movie of the same name, starring Anthony LaPaglia as one of the Australian journalists killed by the Indonesians. Jolliffe has been reporting on East Timor for over 35 years.

Dancing with the Devil by David Savage was made into the Australian miniseries *Answered by Fire* in 2006. It's based on his experiences in East Timor during the 1999 independence vote.

A Woman of Independence by Kirsty Sword Gusmão is the autobiographical account of how this Australian teacher came to be East Timor's First Lady in 2002.

BUSINESS HOURS

Public servants (including the prime minister) clean the streets on Friday mornings, so expect offices to be closed. Usually offices are open from 8am to noon and 1pm to 5pm, Monday to Friday, while shops are open from 9am to 6pm Monday to Friday and 9am to noon Saturday. Restaurants are usually open from 10am to 9pm daily.

Exceptions to these hours are noted in individual reviews.

CLIMATE

East Timor has two seasons: wet (December to April) and dry (May to November). In the dry season the north coast sees little rain (although climate change is altering this), while the cooler central mountains and south coast have an occasional shower. When the rains come, they cause floods and landslides, cutting off access to roads.

Day temperatures are around 30°C to 35°C (85°F to 95°F) year-round in the lowland areas, dropping to the low 20s overnight. In the mountain areas, warm-to-hot daytime temperatures drop to a chillier 15°C (60°F) at night, less at altitude. At the end of the dry season in parts of the north coast the mercury hovers over 35°C (95°F). See p936 for climate charts.

A good time to visit is after the wet season, from May to July.

CUSTOMS

The usual rules (1L of alcohol, 200 cigarettes) apply to arrivals in East Timor.

DANGERS & ANNOYANCES

Malaria and dengue are real concerns for those staying in East Timor; take precautions (see p960 and p958). Stick to bottled water, avoid tap water and ice, and wipe off water from the tops of beverage cans before drinking. Antibiotics and other pharmaceuticals are easily bought in Dili but are hard to find elsewhere.

East Timor has diabolical roads, and drivers should always be on the lookout for vehicles speeding around corners, roaming children and livestock, potholes, speed humps and landslides.

Cases of theft occur most frequently from cars, with mobile phones a prime target. Women should be wary of exercising in isolated spots, as there have been attacks.

Given the regular bouts of political instability in East Timor, check the current situation before you visit (although government travel advisories are usually cautious in the extreme). Outside of mass unrest, political violence is not aimed at non-Timorese. If you see stone throwing or other provocations, vamoose.

DRIVING LICENCE

Your home-country driving licence or permit is acceptable in East Timor.

LANGUAGE? WHICH LANGUAGE?

Most Timorese are multilingual and not only speak their own distinct dialect (Tetun; also known as Tetum) and their regional dialect (one of 16), but also, for the older folk, Portuguese, and, for the younger folk (those educated between 1976 and 1999), Bahasa Indonesia. There's fairly low literacy in East Timor; in 2002 just 58.6 per cent of the population over 15 could read and write. Written material usually comes in three flavours: Portuguese and Tetun (both official languages) and English. Despite the influx of English-speaking foreign workers since 1999, English is not widely spoken. A few Tetun words go a long way, and certainly any attempt to communicate in Tetun will be appreciated. Lonely Planet's *East Timor Phrasebook* is a handy (and compact) introduction, and there are Tetun courses in Dili (see p164).

EMBASSIES & CONSULATES

A number of countries have embassies in Dili. Citizens of Canada and the UK should contact their embassies in Indonesia (see p352).

Australia (☎ 332 2111; www.easttimor.embassy.gov.au; Avenida dos Mártires de Pátria)
European Commission (☎ 331 1580; ectimor@arafura.net.au; Casa Europa; Rua Presidente Nicolau Lobato)
Indonesia (☎ 331 7107; kukridil@hotmail.com; cnr Rua Maria & Rua Governador Cesar, Farol)
Ireland (☎ 332 4880; charles.lathrop@dfe.ie; Rua Alferes Duartre Arbiro 12, Farol)
New Zealand (☎ 331 0087; dili@mfat.govt.nz; Rua Geremias)
USA (☎ 332 4684; consdili@state.gov; Avenida de Portugal)

EMERGENCIES

Contact the **UN Police** (UNPOL; ☎ 112, 723 0365) for all medical, fire and policing emergencies.

FESTIVALS & EVENTS

As a staunchly Catholic country, East Timor celebrates Christian holidays with gusto; see right for dates. During any of the major holidays there will be a church celebration. Easter is particularly colourful, with parades and vigils.

FOOD & DRINK

Food

The food is not what you'll remember most about your visit to East Timor. For many locals, meat added to the staple rice-and-veg dish is a treat. That said, coastal communities do good barbecued fish, flipped straight from the sea to the grill.

The years of Indonesian and Portuguese rule have flavoured the country's palate, with Indonesian-style fried-noodle dishes and signature Portuguese items such as *bacalhau* (cod) available at many restaurants. In Dili, a number of places serve the usual melange of pizza, sandwiches and pasta as well as various Thai and Indian treats. You can join locals at modest places and eat well for under US$5.

Outside of Dili and Baucau, choices dwindle. You'll usually find a couple of simple places near the town market serving variations of chicken and beef/buffalo.

Drink

Coffee is a speciality in East Timor: it's strong, black and full-bodied – and available everywhere. Bottled drinking water is readily available as is Singapore's Tiger beer, and soft drinks. Away from Dili, beverages are usually warm. That milky liquid for sale from stalls is *sopi*, or *tua*, a home-brewed palm wine that tastes of fermenting palm fruit, which is exactly what it is. Think of it more as punch (it has one) than wine.

GAY & LESBIAN TRAVELLERS

Try gaytimor.blogspot.com for information for gay men in Timor. It's unlikely that there'll be any overt discrimination for gay men and lesbians.

HOLIDAYS

East Timor has a long list of holidays. Many special days of commemoration are declared each year – sometimes on the morning of what becomes a holiday. Particularly Timorese holidays include Independence Restoration Day, which commemorates the day in 2002 when sovereignty was transferred from the UN; Popular Consultation Day, which celebrates the start of independence in 1999; and National Youth Day, which commemorates the Santa Cruz Cemetery massacre (see p151).

East Timor also celebrates Idul Adha (the Muslim day of sacrifice) and Idul Fitri (the end of Ramadan), but dates vary each year.

New Year's Day 1 January
Good Friday March/April
Labour Day 1 May
Independence Restoration Day 20 May
Corpus Christi Day May/June
Popular Consultation Day 30 August
All Saints' Day 1 November
All Souls' Day 2 November
National Youth Day 12 November
Proclamation of Independence Day 28 November
National Heroes' Day 7 December
Immaculate Conception 8 December
Christmas Day 25 December

INTERNET ACCESS

There are plenty of internet cafes in Dili, with access averaging US$6 per hour. Also try Timor Telecom offices around the country for access.

INTERNET RESOURCES

East Timor Action Network (www.etan.org) The website of this US-based organisation has a vast and compelling array of web links, and loads of information and articles.

Lonely Planet (www.lonelyplanet.com) Has information on travel in East Timor; check out the Thorn Tree forum.

The Dili Insider (www.thediliinsider.blogspot.com) This Dili-based blog has links to the ever-changing line-up of other local blogs, some of which are excellent.

Turismo de Timor-Leste (www.turismotimorleste.com) Official Department of Tourism site, though it's infrequently updated.

UN Integrated Mission in Timor-Leste (www.unmit.org) This site has news and official information.

LEGAL MATTERS

If you are the victim of serious crime go to the nearest police station and notify your embassy. The Timorese police force is only one of a number of groups that provide security in the country. If arrested, you have the right to a phone call and legal representation, which your embassy can help to locate.

Possession and trafficking of illicit drugs carry stiff penalties.

MAPS

The Timorese government's tourism department distributes a free *Timor-Leste* country map (1:750,000), which you'll find around Dili.

MEDIA

Newspapers

The *Timor Post* and the *Suara Timor Lorosae* are among the daily local newspapers; they're mainly in Indonesian but with some news in Tetun. The *Guide Post* is aimed at English-speaking expats in Dili, and has useful service listings and maps. Don't expect to find any other newspapers or magazines in English.

Radio & TV

Radio is the most important branch of the media, particularly the national broadcaster Radio de Timor Leste (RTL) and a host of community stations. The Catholic Church's Radio Timor Kmanek (RTK) is popular. You can pick up Australian programming from the ABC in Dili on 106.5FM; the BBC is on 95.3FM.

The national public TV station is Televisao de Timor Leste (TVTL), which broadcasts for a few hours each evening. Its news program ignores no political speech, while shows featuring local concerts have the same uneven charms as videos of your cousin's recital. Most Dili hotels have satellite TV, and it's creeping into the districts, too.

MONEY

The US dollar is the official currency of East Timor. Locally minted centavos coins also circulate, which are of equal value to US cents. Make sure you arrive with at least US$30 for the visa.

In Dili and Baucau ATMs dispense US dollars but only Dili's banks change travellers cheques. A few Dili establishments accept credit cards, usually with a 5% surcharge attached.

POST

Dili's post office (p150) has poste restante. There's no actual mail-delivery service and mail out of the country is slow.

EXCHANGE RATES

Exchange rates at the time of press:

Country	Unit	US dollars (US$)
Australia	A$1	0.88
Canada	C$1	0.94
Euro zone	€1	1.47
Indonesia	10,000Rp	1.04
Japan	¥100	1.11
New Zealand	NZ$1	0.72
UK	£1	1.60

EAST TIMOR

RESPONSIBLE TRAVEL

Tourism is new to East Timor, and visitors need to be mindful of the significant impact their behaviour has on the environment and the population. Most Timorese are highly religious so will appreciate travellers dressing conservatively and eschewing public displays of affection.

Protecting the environment is not the first priority of most Timorese, but that doesn't mean you shouldn't set a good example.

STUDYING

Dili Institute of Technology (Aitumin campus) runs week-long intensive **Tetun language courses** (☎ 736 9768; tetundit@gmail.com; per week US$120) throughout the year. You'll need a Peace Corps Tetun Language Course book (US$17.50).

TELEPHONE

If you're phoning an East Timor number from overseas, the international country code is ☎ 670. When making an international call from East Timor, the access code is ☎ 0011. There are no area codes in East Timor, and few landline numbers outside Dili. Landline numbers begin with 3 or 4; mobile numbers start with 7. You can make local and international calls from any Timor Telecom office.

A mobile phone is useful in East Timor. You will need ID to purchase a SIM card from Timor Telecom for US$5, which includes US$2 of credit. In Dili, street vendors offer recharge cards of varying amounts. You'll soon need them as Timor Telecom's monopoly on phone service allows it to charge up to US$2 per minute for international calls.

TOURIST INFORMATION

East Timor doesn't have a tourist office. However, the expat community is especially generous with information. Drop by any of the popular bars, restaurants or dive shops and soon you'll be hooked into all sorts of info. Language differences aside, locals are also very happy to help.

TOURS

A tour can allow you to visit places not easily accessible by public transport, and a guide can bridge the language barrier. The following agencies are based in Dili:

Eco Discovery (☎ 332 2454; www.ecodiscovery-easttimor.com; Landmark Plaza, Avenida dos Mártires de Pátria) Manny Napoleaõ's knowledge of East Timor is encyclopedic. Custom tours plunge deep.

Mega Tours (☎ 723 5199; timormegatours@netscape.net; Rua Presidente Nicolau Lobato) Two-day trips to Mt Ramelau are popular; they cost US$280 for up to four people. Custom trips to places such as Jaco Island cost from US$150 per day for up to four people.

Village Hotels Timor (☎ 739 6911, 331 0616; www.tvh.tl; Avenida dos Mártires de Pátria) Affiliated with Ossu's Timor Village Hotel (p157), this organisation can arrange drivers and guides for a variety of destinations from US$100 per person per day.

TRAVELLERS WITH DISABILITIES

There are no provisions for travellers with disabilities in East Timor. Potholed pavements make wheelchair travel difficult.

VISAS

An entry visa (for up to 30 days) is granted to valid passport holders for US$30 on arrival in East Timor. To avoid hassles if plans change, always ask for a 30-day visa. Visas can be extended for US$35 per month if the applicant has a valid reason to do so.

Many travellers visit East Timor to renew their Indonesian visas. An Indonesian visa takes three to five working days to process. A 30-day Indonesian tourist visa costs US$45; a single-entry seven-day transit visa costs US$20 and a double-entry version costs US$40 (the latter is useful for land trips to Oecussi as you'll need a visa both to get there via Indonesia and to leave).

VOLUNTEERING

Major volunteer organisations include **Australian Volunteers International** (www.australianvolunteers.com) and **UN Volunteers** (www.unv.org).

WOMEN TRAVELLERS

Women travellers need to be aware of personal-security issues, particularly in Dili, as assaults do occur. Do not walk or take taxis after dark, unless you're in a group.

Ten years of an expat/UN presence has altered dress standards, but it still pays to dress conservatively, even if the locals seem to be wearing less than you are. At beaches it's best to swap the bikini for the one piece.

EAST TIMOR

Indonesia

HIGHLIGHTS

- **Bali** (p222) Surfing by day, partying at night and absorbing amazing culture in Ubud.
- **Gunung Bromo** (p220) Witnessing the supernatural beauty of East Java's vast cone-studded caldera at sunrise.
- **Central Java** (p210 and p208) Ascending the ancient Buddhist stupa of Borobudur, before trawling the batik markets of bustling Yogyakarta.
- **Orang-utans** (p326) Paying primate-to-primate respects to the 'man of the jungle', unique to Borneo and Sumatra.
- **Huge deadly dragons** (p285) Peeking at komodo dragons on Nusa Tenggara.
- **Togean Islands** (p336) Diving the pristine walls and coral canyons beneath seas of dimpled glass in remote Sulawesi.
- **Off the beaten track** (p346) Hiking along raging rivers and scaling exposed ridges to reach interior Papua's remote tribal villages in the Baliem Valley.

FAST FACTS

- **Budget** US$15 to US$25 a day
- **Capital** Jakarta
- **Costs** cheap room US$5 to US$8, two-hour bus ride US$2, large beer US$1.50
- **Country code** ☎ 62
- **Languages** Bahasa Indonesia and over 300 indigenous languages
- **Money** US$1 = 9645Rp (Indonesian rupiah)
- **Phrases** *salam* (hello), *sampai jumpa* (goodbye), *terima kasih* (thanks), *maaf* (sorry)
- **Population** 240 million
- **Time** Indonesia has three time zones, between seven and nine hours ahead of GMT
- **Visas** Complicated! (see p357)

TRAVEL HINT

Kaki lima (mobile food stalls) offer the cheapest grub. And learn some local lingo – Bahasa Indonesia is easy to pick up.

OVERLAND ROUTES

The Entikong border links Kalimantan with Sarawak (Malaysia), and West and East Timor connect at Motoain.

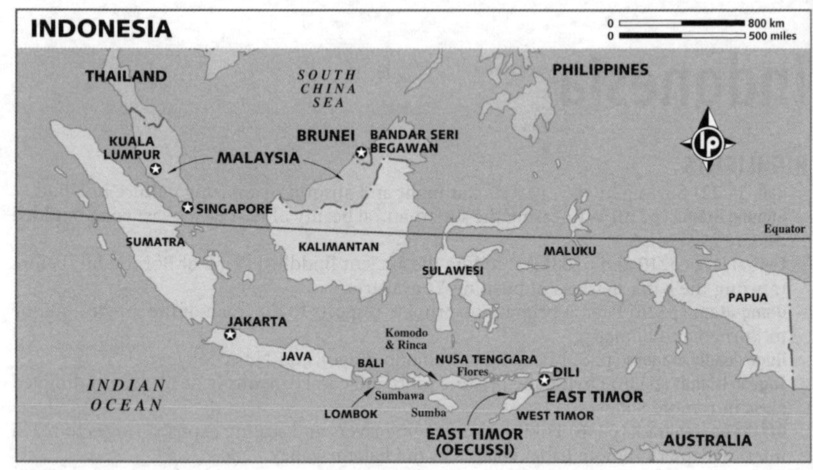

Indonesia is a trip in itself. The opportunities for exploration and adventure are only limited by how many of the 17,000 islands you can reach before your visa expires. It's one hell of a sweep. With the equator as its spine, Indonesia stretches between Malaysia and Australia. The nation's natural diversity is staggering, alluring and inspiring, from the snow-capped peaks in Papua, sandalwood forests in Sumba, primary jungle in Borneo, and impossibly green rice paddies in Bali and Java. Indonesian coral reefs are the dream of divers worldwide while the surf above is the best anywhere.

But even as the diversity on land and sea run like a traveller's fantasy playlist, it's the mash-up of people and cultures that ultimately is the most appealing. Bali justifiably leads off, but there are also the stone-age folk deep in Papua, the funeral-mad Toraja of Sulawesi, the artisans of Java, mall-rats of Jakarta and the list goes on. As different as people are, however, you won't be there for more than a day before you realise what a truly engaging and welcoming place it is. Whether blogging or tweeting, you'll be busy sharing your incredible experiences here.

CURRENT EVENTS

Indonesia needs a good press agent as it always seems to be in the headlines for the wrong reasons. The 2004 Boxing Day tsunami ravaged Aceh in northern Sumatra. Then, in 2006, a quake rocked Yogyakarta, killing 6800 people, and in 2009 a quake devastated Padang in Sumatra. Combine this with a series of ferry sinkings and plane crashes that exposed the decrepit state of Indonesia's transport network and it doesn't paint a pretty picture. Even the looting of a KFC is portrayed in the West as an example of societal breakdown.

Far less prominent have been headline-worthy events of late. Elections in 2009 went off more smoothly than many had predicted, with President Susilo Bambang Yudhoyono (SBY) cruising to re-election on a platform of continuing moderate policies that have guided the nation from the abyss. Chased off at the polls were other candidates who'd aligned themselves with figures from Indonesia's past who were often linked to extreme human-rights abuses. Also chased off in parliamentary elections earlier in the year were extremist Islamic parties who had predicted major gains but ended up with 8% of the vote. Moderates – including the party of SBY – won the day.

In September 2009 police raided a house near Solo and killed Noordin Mohamed Top, the alleged mastermind of a decade's worth of terrorism including bombings in Bali and Jakarta.

HISTORY

Beginnings

Until the last few years it was widely believed that the first humanoids *(Homo erectus)* lived in Central Java around 500,000 years ago, having reached Indonesia across land bridges from Africa, before either dying off or being wiped out by the arrival of *Homo sapiens.*

But the discovery in 2003 of the remains of a tiny islander, dubbed the 'hobbit' seems to indicate that *Homo erectus* survived much longer than was previously thought, and that previously accepted timelines of Indonesia's evolutionary history need to be re-examined (though many scientists continue to challenge the hobbit theory).

Most Indonesians are descendents of Malay people who began migrating around 4000 BC from Cambodia, Vietnam and southern China. They steadily developed small kingdoms and by 700 BC these settlers had developed skilful rice-farming techniques.

Hinduism & Buddhism

The growing prosperity of these early kingdoms soon caught the attention of Indian and Chinese merchants, and along with silks and spices came the dawn of Hinduism and Buddhism in Indonesia.

These religions quickly gained a foothold in the archipelago and soon became central to the great kingdoms of the 1st millennium AD. The Buddhist Srivijaya empire held sway over the Malay peninsula and southern Sumatra, extracting wealth from its dominion over the strategic Straits of Melaka, while the Hindu Mataram and Buddhist Sailendra kingdoms dominated Central Java, raising their grandiose monuments, Borobudur and Prambanan, over the fertile farmland that brought them their prosperity.

Indeed, when Mataram slipped into mysterious decline around the 10th century AD, it was fast replaced with an even more powerful Hindu kingdom. Founded in 1294, the Majapahit empire made extensive territorial gains under its ruler, Hayam Wuruk, and prime minister, Gajah Mada, and while claims that they controlled much of Sulawesi, Sumatra and Borneo now seem fanciful, most of Java, Madura and Bali certainly fell within their realm.

But things would soon change. Despite the Majapahit empire's massive power and influence, greater fault lines were opening up across Indonesia, and Hinduism's golden age was swiftly drawing to a close.

Rise of Islam

With the arrival of Islam came the power, the reason and the will to oppose the hegemony of the Majapahits, and satellite kingdoms soon took up arms against the Hindu kings. In the 15th century the Majapahits fled to Bali, where Hindu culture continues to flourish, leaving Java to the increasingly powerful Islamic sultanates. Meanwhile, the influential trading kingdoms of Melaka (on the Malay peninsula) and Makassar (in southern Sulawesi) were also embracing Islam, sowing the seeds that would later make modern Indonesia the most populous Muslim nation on earth.

European Expansion

Melaka fell to the Portuguese in 1511 and European eyes were soon settling on the archipelago's riches, prompting two centuries of unrest as the Portuguese, Spanish, Dutch and British wrestled for control. By 1700 the Dutch held most of the trump cards, with the Dutch East India Company (VOC) controlling the region's lucrative spice trade and becoming the world's first multinational company (see boxed text, p168). Following the VOC's bankruptcy, however, the British governed Java under Sir Stamford Raffles between 1811 and 1816, only to relinquish control again to the Dutch after the end of the Napoleonic wars, who then held control of Indonesia until its independence 129 years later.

It was not, however, a trouble-free tenancy and the Dutch had to face numerous rebellions: Javan Prince Diponegoro's five-year guerrilla war was finally put down in 1830, costing the lives of 8000 Dutch troops.

'DECENCY' LAW

As far as Islamic nations go, Indonesia has always had a reputation as being a pretty tolerant place. But in 2008 a so-called 'Decency' or anti-pornography law was enacted that potentially made many traditional forms of behaviour across the archipelago illegal – from wearing penis gourds on Papua to the modest gyrations of traditional Javanese dancers (to say nothing of the brazenly topless on Bali's beaches). With recent memories of religious and ethnic violence still sharp in many places, anything that could stoke new divisions is anathema to many, and protests have been many across the archipelago, especially on Bali where the governor has said he won't enforce it. The triumph of moderates in the 2009 elections also seems to have reduced enthusiasm for the law's enforcement.

DUTCH EAST INDIA COMPANY (VOC)

Dominating Asian trade routes for two centuries, the Dutch East India Company (VOC) was the world's first multinational corporation, monopolising the spice trade from Asia to Europe. Set up in 1602, it primarily traded pepper, nutmeg, cinnamon and sugar, and its profitability and clout were such that it minted its own currency.

By the late 17th century the VOC had established a city, Batavia, as its capital in the region, had 50,000 employees and owned over 150 merchant ships and 40 warships. It also had a private army of 10,000 soldiers, outposts from Japan to southern Africa and was the first company to pay stock dividends (which averaged an annual 18% over 200 years).

But this trading behemoth struggled in the 18th century, ultimately collapsing in 1800, being unable to compete financially with the Caribbean and Latin America, which became more productive sugar centres.

Road to Independence

By the beginning of the 20th century, the Dutch had brought most of the archipelago under their control, but the revolutionary tradition of Diponegoro was never truly quashed, bubbling beneath the surface of Dutch rule and finding a voice in the young Soekarno. The debate was sidelined as the Japanese swept through Indonesia during WWII, but with their departure came the opportunity for Soekarno to declare Indonesian independence, which he did from his Jakarta home on 17 August 1945.

The Dutch, however, were unwilling to relinquish their hold over Indonesia and – supported by the British, who had entered Indonesia to accept the Japanese surrender – moved quickly to reassert their authority over the country. Resistance was stiff and for four bitter years the Indonesian resistance fought a guerrilla war. But American and UN opposition to the reimposition of colonialism and the mounting casualty toll eventually forced the Dutch to pack it in, and the Indonesian flag – the *sang merah putih* (red and white) – was finally hoisted over Jakarta's Istana Merdeka (Freedom Palace) on 27 December 1949.

Depression, Disunity & Dictatorship

Unity in war quickly became division in peace, as religious fundamentalists and nationalist separatists challenged the fledgling central government. But after almost a decade of political impasse and economic depression, Soekarno made his move, declaring Guided Democracy (a euphemism for dictatorship) with army backing and leading Indonesia into nearly four decades of authoritarian rule.

Despite moves towards the one-party state, Indonesia's three-million-strong Communist Party (Partai Komunis Indonesia; PKI) was the biggest in the world by 1965 and Soekarno had long realised the importance of winning its backing. But as the PKI's influence in government grew, so did tensions with the armed forces. Things came to a head on the night of 30 September 1965, when elements of the palace guard launched an attempted coup. Quickly put down by General Soeharto, the coup was blamed – perhaps unfairly – on the PKI and became the pretext for an army-led purge that left as many as 500,000 communist sympathisers dead. Strong evidence later emerged that both the US (implacably opposed to communism) and the UK (seeking to protect its interests in Malaysia) aided and abetted Soeharto's purge by drawing up hit lists of communist agitators. By 1968 Soeharto had ousted Soekarno and was installed as president.

Soeharto brought unity through repression, annexing Irian Jaya (Papua) in 1969, and reacting to insurgency with an iron fist. In 1975, Portuguese Timor was invaded, leading to tens of thousands of deaths, and separatist ambitions in Aceh and Papua were also met with a ferocious military response. But despite endemic corruption, the 1980s and 1990s were Indonesia's boom years, with meteoric economic growth and a starburst of opulent building ventures transforming the face of the capital.

Soeharto's Fall

As Asia's economy went into freefall during the closing years of the 1990s, Soeharto's house of cards began to tumble. Indonesia went bankrupt overnight and the country found an obvious scapegoat in the cronyism and corruption endemic in the dictator's regime. Protests erupted across Indonesia in 1998, and the May riots in Jakarta left thousands, many of them Chinese, dead. After three decades of dictatorial rule, Soeharto resigned on 21 May 1998.

Passions cooled when Vice President BJ Habibie took power on a reform ticket, but ambitious promises were slow to materialise, and in November of the same year riots again rocked many Indonesian cities. Promises of forthcoming elections succeeded in closing the floodgates, but separatist groups took advantage of the weakened central government and violence erupted in Maluku, Irian Jaya, East Timor and Aceh. East Timor won its independence after a referendum in August 1999, but only after Indonesian-backed militias had destroyed its infrastructure and left thousands dead.

Democracy & Reform

Against this unsettled backdrop, the June 1999 legislative elections passed surprisingly smoothly, leaving Megawati Soekarnoputri (Soekarno's daughter) and her reformist Indonesian Democratic Party for Struggle (PDI-P) as the largest party with 33% of the vote. But months later the separate presidential election was narrowly won by Abdurrahman Wahid (Gus Dur), whose efforts to undo corruption met with stiff resistance. Megawati was eventually sworn in as president in 2001, but her term proved a disappointment for many Indonesians, as corrupt infrastructures were left in place, the military's power remained intact and poverty levels remained high. Nevertheless Indonesia gained from a period of economic stability and healthy growth, though much of this was at the expense of the environment through vast logging and mining concessions.

Megawati lost the 2004 presidential elections to Susilo Bambang Yudhoyono (or 'SBY'), an ex-army officer who served in East Timor but who also has an MBA. Dubbed the 'thinking general', his successes have included cracking down on Islamic militants, pumping more money into education and health, and introducing basic social-security payments. SBY's term has been rocked by a series of disasters, beginning with the 2004 tsunami and continuing with more natural disasters and an alarming number of transport disasters as planes fell from the sky and ferries went down with hundreds of casualties. However, less noticed was a steady decrease in the sectarian violence that had threatened to unravel the nation.

Economically, Indonesia has remained relatively healthy, however, with growth averaging around 5% to 6% a year. SBY has a reputation as a prudent leader, cutting the nation's huge fuel subsidies in 2005 (which forced very unpopular fuel-price rises) and even paying back an International Monetary Fund (IMF) loan four years early. A decade after the fall of Soeharto, the consensus is that Indonesia is establishing itself as a workable democracy, but a nation confronted with myriad development issues. Corruption, the destruction of the environment, poverty, fundamentalism and taxation reform are just a selection of some of these huge challenges.

THE CULTURE

The National Psyche

Soekarno, often referred to as the founder of Indonesia, must have pondered long and hard when faced with the task of welding together a nation from tens of millions of Javanese (with millennia of elaborate cultural traditions), longhouse-dwelling tribal Dayaks, Sumabanese animists and the Saudi-devout Muslims of Aceh. His solution, founded on five principles of nationhood known as the Pancasila, maintained that loyalty to the state should supersede ethnic and religious divisions, and this philosophy remains crucial to understanding what makes Indonesia tick today.

Alongside commitments to democracy and humanity, the Pancasila also enshrined the principle that all citizens must have an official state religion and that it should be 'based in the belief in one and only God'. This has meant that Indonesia's many practitioners of indigenous religions, particularly remote tribal communities, have been pressurised to adopt a state-sanctioned religion – usually Islam or Christianity. The Balinese also had to tweak their belief system, so that a supreme deity could emerge from a pantheon of gods, and Hinduism could be declared an officially recognised faith.

In recent years Indonesia's unique syncretic Islamic culture, which borrowed heavily from Hindu and animist traditions, has become much more conservative and orthodox, due to increased influence and contact with the wider Islamic world. Geopolitical factors (such as the wars in Iraq and Afghanistan) and the arrival of Saudi-sponsored mullahs have also helped radicalise many, creating tensions with those Indonesians who practise other faiths. But despite the passage of a controversial 'decency' law (boxed text, p167), the vast majority of Indonesians are fairly tolerant, as was shown in the 2009 elections.

The old Javanese saying *'bhinneka tunggal ika'* (they are many; they are one) is said to be Indonesia's national dictum, but with a population of over 240 million, 700-plus languages and 17,000 islands it's not surprising that many from the outer islands resent Java, where power is centralised. Separatist groups in Aceh, Papua and East Timor fought guerrilla wars against Jakarta for decades, with East Timor gaining independence in 2001. Indonesia is loosely bound together by a single flag and single language (Bahasa Indonesia), but in some ways can be compared to the EU – a richly diverse confederacy of peoples.

Lifestyle

The world's most populous Muslim nation is no hardline Islamic state. Indonesians have traditionally practised a very loose-fitting, relaxed form of Islam and, though there's no desire to imitate the West, most see no conflict in catching a Hollywood movie in an American-style shopping mall after prayers at the mosque. The country is becoming more cosmopolitan, as internet usage soars and chat rooms proliferate, and Indonesian hip-hop, indie, ska and reggae acts emerge. Millions of Indonesians now work overseas – mainly in the Gulf, Hong Kong and Malaysia – bringing back extraneous influences to their villages when they return. A boom in low-cost air travel has enabled a generation of Indonesians to travel internally and overseas conveniently and cheaply for the first time, while personal mobility is much easier today – it's possible to buy a motorbike on hire purchase with as little as a 500,000Rp deposit.

But not everyone has the cash or time for overseas jaunts and there remains a yawning gulf between the haves and the have-nots. Indonesia is much poorer than many of its Asian neighbours, with almost 50% surviving on US$2 a day, and in many rural areas opportunities are few and far between. Low employment is a serious issue and educational standards, despite recent improvements and extra governmental cash, are way behind countries like Malaysia or Thailand, restricting overseas investment.

Population

Indonesia's population is the fourth-biggest in the world, with over 240 million people. Over half this number live on the island of Java, one of the most crowded places on earth with a population density of 940 people per square kilometre. But while Java (and Bali and Lombok) teem with people, large parts of the archipelago are very sparsely populated, particularly Papua (under 10 per square kilometre) and Kalimantan.

Birth rates have fallen considerably in recent years (from an average of 3.4 children per woman in 1987 to 2.4 today) thanks to successful family-planning campaigns and increasing prosperity levels.

The majority of Indonesia's 100 or so ethnic groups are made up of the Javanese (42%) and their neighbours from West Java, the Sundanese (15%). Other large groups include the Madurese (3.3%), coastal Malays (3.4%) and Batak (3%).

RELIGION

If Indonesia has a soundtrack, it is the muezzin's call to prayer. Wake up to it once and it won't come as a surprise that Indonesia is the largest Islamic nation on earth, with over 220 million Muslims (88% of the total population).

But while Islam has a near monopoly on religious life, many of the country's most impressive historical monuments, such as the temples of Borobudur and Prambanan, hark back to when Hindu and Buddhist kingdoms dominated Java. These religions maintain important communities, with Hinduism (2% of the population) continuing to flourish in Bali, while Buddhists (1%) are scattered through the country. Christians make up nearly 9% of the nation, forming the majority in Papua, several islands of Nusa Tenggara and Maluku, and in parts of Sumatra. But animist traditions survive below the surface in many rural areas.

Although nominally a secular state, religious organisations (the conservative Nahdlatul Ulama has over 40 million members) still wield considerable clout in the corridors of power.

ARTS

Dance

Indonesia has a rich heritage of traditional dances. In Yogyakarta there's the Ramayana ballet, a spectacular dance drama; Lombok has a mask dance called the *kayak sando* and war dances; Malaku's *lenso* is a handkerchief dance; while Bali has a multitude of elaborate dances, including the *barong, kecak, topeng, legong* and *baris*.

Literature

Pramoedya Ananta Toer, a Javanese author, is perhaps Indonesia's best-known novelist. His famous quartet of historical realist novels set in the colonial era comprises *This Earth of Mankind, Child of All Nations, Footsteps* and *House of Glass*.

Mochtar Lubis is another well-known Indonesian writer. His most famous novel, *Twilight in Djakarta,* is a scathing attack on corruption and the plight of the poor in Jakarta in the 1950s.

Ayu Utami's *Saman* ushered in a new era of modern Indonesian writing dubbed *sastra wangi* (fragrant literature) with her taboo-breaking tale of sex, politics and religion. *The Invisible Palace* by José Manuel Tesoro recounts the murder of a journalist in Yogyakarta, plotting the intersections of hierarchy, Islam, animism and corruption in government and Javanese culture.

Music

There's much more to the Indonesian music scene than the saccharine-sweet pop and *dangdut* (Indonesian dance music with strong Arabic and Hindi influences) that dominates most airwaves. Alongside a vibrant punk scene (see below), led by bands such as Bali's Superman is Dead and Yogya's Black Boots, there's social invective from hip-hoppers Homicide and Iwa K, while house and techno DJs like Romy (see boxed text, p172) play to thousands in Jakartan clubs and around Asia.

The best-known traditional Indonesian music is *gamelan:* both Java and Bali have orchestras composed mainly of percussion instruments, including drums, gongs and *angklung* (shake-drums), along with flutes and xylophones.

Theatre

Javanese *wayang* (puppet) plays have their origins in the Hindu epics, the Ramayana and the Mahabharata. There are different forms of *wayang: wayang kulit* uses leather shadow puppets, while *wayang golek* uses wooden puppets.

ENVIRONMENT

Indonesia has lost more tropical forest than anywhere else in the world, bar Brazil, in the last few decades. That said, some incredible national parks and pristine landscapes remain virtually untouched, mainly in remote areas away from the main centres of population.

The Land

At 1.92 million sq km, Indonesia is an island colossus, incorporating 10% of the world's forest cover and 11,508 uninhabited islands (6000 more have human populations). From the low-lying coastal areas, the country rises through no fewer than 129 active volcanoes – more than any country in the world – to the snow-covered summit of Puncak Jaya (4884m) in Papua. Despite the incredible diversity of its landscapes, it is worth remembering that Indonesia is predominantly water;

INDO PUNK

Just as British bands like the Stones raided the USA for their blues-influenced tunes in the '60s, Indonesian groups have absorbed American and British musical movements, added an indigenous dimension and created a vibrant new scene. Indonesian hip hop, reggae and metal are all healthy, but today's teenagers have really identified with punk and new wave, and bands like the Ramones are massive in Indonesia, their T-shirts, stickers and garage-band style all pervasive.

Superman is Dead is one of the biggest acts, their raw social commentary and anti-establishment stance selling tens of thousands of legitimate CDs and perhaps millions of pirated copies. Their name refers to the fall of Soeharto, and SiD fills stadiums with fans who know every word of every song, the venue a maelstrom of slam-dancing mosh pits, crowd surfing and pogoing kids. Drummer Jerinx is a superstar in Indonesia.

CLUB INDONESIA

Forget Bangkok, Jakarta's clubbing scene has to be one of the world's most decadent. Centred on the Kota district, home to vast temples of trance, one club here (Stadium, capacity 4000; p188) opens on Thursday and doesn't shut till Monday morning. Clubbers get mashed-up for hours, some losing days in dark-as-sin techno clubs, where the spirit of Acid House is definitely still alive and kicking. The scene is massive, with all genres – electro, minimal, techno, tribal, progressive and House – represented.

Many young Indonesians do not drink alcohol and, perhaps consequently, ecstasy is a big part of Indonesia's club scene. It became the drug of choice for Indonesia's wealthy elite in the mid-1990s, and its popularity now transcends all social classes.

Indonesia is not only a dance-drug consumer nation but also – as Dedi Permana, a senior police commissioner, acknowledged – 'the world's biggest ecstasy producer'. One illegal factory busted in November 2005 in Serang, Banten, had a production capacity of one million ecstasy pills per week.

For the enormous risks associated with recreational drug use in Indonesia, see p937.

Indonesians refer to the country as Tanah Air Kita (literally 'Our Earth and Water'). The main islands are Kalimantan (Indonesian Borneo; 539,460 sq km), Sumatra (473,606 sq km), Papua (Indonesian New Guinea; 421,981 sq km), Sulawesi (202,000 sq km) and Java (132,107 sq km).

Wildlife

In his classic study *The Malay Archipelago*, British naturalist Alfred Russel Wallace divided Indonesia into two zones. To the west of the so-called Wallace Line (which runs between Kalimantan and Sulawesi and south through the straits between Bali and Lombok) the flora and fauna resemble that of the rest of Asia, while the species and environments to the east become increasingly like those of Australia. Scientists have since fine-tuned Wallace's findings, but while western Indonesia is known for its (increasingly rare) orang-utan, rhinos, tigers as well as spectacular *Rafflesia* flowers, eastern Indonesia boasts fauna such as the komodo dragon and marsupials, including Papuan tree kangaroos.

National Parks

There are officially 50 *taman nasional* (national parks) in Indonesia. Most are in remote areas and only have basic visitor facilities, but they are remarkable in their ecological diversity and wildlife. Some of the finest include Tanjung Puting (p326) in Kalimantan for orang-utans and wetland birds, and Komodo with its dragons and astonishing coral reefs.

Environmental Issues

From the perspective of a Jakarta-based bureaucrat, Indonesia has full environmental-responsibility credentials, with stringent land-use and environmental impact regulations, and large tracts of forest lands set aside for conservation. In the field, the picture is markedly different, as a wilful disregard of regulations, generally with the collusion of the newly empowered regional authorities, make official environmental policies mere words on paper.

However, there is an increasing political will to enforce the rules, often through innovative programs to provide economic benefit to local residents who protect forest lands.

That said, forest continues to be cleared at an horrific rate, both through illegal logging and conversion to palm-oil plantations. Greenpeace estimates that 50% of Indonesia's 150 million hectares of forests have been cleared and the government itself allows an average 1.8 million hectares a year in additional clearance. In addition upwards of 70% of Indonesia's mangrove forests have been damaged according to the US-based Mangrove Action Project. It's a double tragedy given the important role mangroves play in filtering the country's ever more polluted waters.

The side effects of deforestation are felt across the nation and beyond: floods and landslides wash away valuable topsoil, rivers become sluggish and fetid, and haze from clearing fires blankets Malaysia and Singapore every dry season. The problems flow right through to Indonesia's coastline and seas, where over 80% of reef habitat is considered to be at risk by the UN.

Of course, the people most affected are those who live closest to, or within, the forested areas. Evictions from, restricted access to and loss of land has seen many local communities lose their lifeline and spill into ever-spreading urban areas with ever-increasing populations living below the poverty line.

The rampant consumerism of the burgeoning middle class is straining the nation's wholly inadequate infrastructure: private vehicles clog urban streets creating massive air pollution, waste removal services have difficulty coping with household and industrial garbage, and a total lack of sewerage-disposal systems makes water from most sources undrinkable without boiling, putting further pressure on kerosene and firewood supplies.

TRANSPORT

GETTING THERE & AWAY

Air

Jakarta (p177) and Bali (p224) are the two main hubs, but other useful international connections include Balikpapan (Kalimantan), Mataram (Lombok), Manado (Sulawesi), Medan (Sumatra), Palembang (Sumatra), Padang (Sumatra), Solo (Java) and Surabaya (Java).

The following are some major international airlines with services to Indonesia:

Air Asia (code AK; www.airasia.com) Serves a wide range of Indonesian destinations from Kuala Lumpur, plus Bali and Jakarta from Bangkok and Singapore.

Emirates (code EK; www.emirates.com) Serves Jakarta from Dubai.

Firefly (code FY; www.fireflyz.com.my) Serves major cities on Sumatra from Kuala Lumpur and Penang in Malaysia.

Garuda Indonesia (code GA; www.garuda-indonesia.com) Indonesia's national airline serves Bali and Jakarta from Australia and points across Asia.

Japan Airlines (code JL; www.jal.co.jp) Serves Bali and Jakarta from Tokyo.

Jetstar/Qantas Airways (code QF; www.qantas.com.au) Serves Bali and Jakarta from Australia.

Lion Air (code JT; www.lionair.co.id) Fast-growing Indonesian budget airline serves airports across the country from major Asian cities.

Malaysia Airlines (code MH; ☎ 0361-764995; www.mas.com.my) Serves Bali and Jakarta from Kuala Lumpur.

Merpati Airlines (code MZ; www.merpati.co.id) Serves Dili in East Timor from Bali.

Pacific Blue (code DJ; www.flypacificblue.com) Offshoot of Australia's Virgin Blue, serves Bali from several Australian cities.

SilkAir (code MI; www.silkair.com) Serves numerous Indonesian destinations from Singapore including Balikpapan and Lombok.

Singapore Airlines (code SQ; www.singaporeair.com) Numerous flights to Bali and Jakarta daily.

Thai Airways International (code TG; www.thaiair.com) Serves Bali and Jakarta from Bangkok.

Tiger Airways (code TR; www.tigerairways.com) Fast-growing budget carrier based in Singapore, serves Jakarta, Padang etc.

Land

There are three land links between Indonesia and neighbouring countries. See p320 for information on crossing into Malaysia; p314 for information on crossing into East Timor; and p346 on information on crossing into Papua New Guinea.

INDONESIAN SUPERLATIVES

Biggest archipelago Covering an area of 1.92 million sq km, Indonesia's 17,000 (some say 20,000) islands make up the world's largest archipelago.

Biggest lizard The komodo dragon *(Varanus komodoensis)* is the biggest lizard in the world. The largest authenticated specimen was a gift from the Sultan of Bima to a US scientist and measured 3.1m.

Largest flower The world's biggest flower, *Rafflesia arnoldi,* often blooms in the thick Sumatran forests near Bukittinggi between August and November.

Longest snake The reticulated python, native to Indonesia, is the world's longest snake. A specimen killed in Sulawesi in 1912 measured 9.85m.

Most diverse Kalimantan is one of the most biologically diverse places on earth, with twice as many plant species as the whole of Africa.

Most populous Java has the largest population of any island in the world, with an estimated 140 million inhabitants.

DOMESTIC DEPARTURE TAX

Indonesian airports typically charge a departure tax to passengers flying out. This charge varies by airport – as high as 150,000Rp – and is payable in cash.

Sea

Malaysia and Singapore are linked to Sumatra by boats and ferries, and there is a link on Borneo (see boxed text, p320). There is currently no sea travel between the Philippines and Indonesia.

GETTING AROUND

Air

The domestic-flight network in Indonesia continues to grow extensively; schedules and rates are in a constant state of flux. Local carriers servicing small routes often operate cramped and dated aircrafts, whereas flights to Jakarta, Bali and other major destinations are usually on larger, newer crafts.

The larger Indonesian-based carriers have websites listing fares; however, it may be hard if not impossible to purchase tickets over the internet from outside Indonesia because of restrictive laws that limit sales to local credit cards. You may have to call the airline in Indonesia – or better, if the option exists, an office outside of Indonesia. Note that you may not reach anyone on the phone who speaks English.

Another option is to enlist the services of one of the many travel agents listed in major cities in this book. Sometimes the best way to get a ticket for travel within Indonesia is to simply go to the airport and compare prices at the various airline offices. Many airlines are strictly cash-based, and offer last-minute deals if there are empty seats.

It is *essential* to reconfirm. Overbooking is a problem and if you don't reconfirm at least a few days before departure, you may well get bumped. Expect problems in the outer islands, where flights are limited, communications poor and booking procedures haphazard – you should reconfirm and reconfirm again.

Depending on the size of the airlines and where they fly, timetables will vary from accurate, national schedules to hand-adjusted printouts of localised areas or provinces on specific islands. Website information is useful for the bigger carriers but nonexistent for the smaller ones. The best option is to check with local airline offices and travel agents (see regional transport information within this chapter for contact details) to see what's available.

Individual airlines and contacts are listed in the relevant city coverage.

Bicycle

Bicycles can be hired in all major centres for 15,000Rp to 50,000Rp per day from hotels, travel agents and shops. The tropical heat, heavy traffic and poor road conditions make long-distance travel a challenge, but some hardy souls manage it.

Boat

Sumatra, Java, Bali and Nusa Tenggara are connected by ferries. Pelni, the national passenger line, covers the archipelago, albeit infrequently.

PELNI SHIPS

Pelni (www.pelni.co.id) has a fleet of large vessels linking all of Indonesia's major ports and the majority of the archipelago's outlying areas. Pelni's website is rarely updated, so it's best to check schedules well in advance with a good travel agent or Pelni office. See also the route map, p175.

Pelni ships have four cabin classes, plus *kelas ekonomi*. Class I is luxury-plus with only two beds per cabin (and is often more expensive than using a low-cost airline); Class IV has eight beds to a cabin. *Ekonomi* is extremely basic, but is air-conditioned and mattresses can be rented.

You can book tickets up to two weeks ahead; it's best to book at least a few days in advance.

OTHER SHIPS

Sumatra, Java, Bali, Nusa Tenggara and Sulawesi are all connected by regular ferries, and you can use them to island hop all the way from Sumatra to Timor. These ferries run either daily or several times a week, so there's no need to spend days in sleepy little port towns. Check with shipping companies, the harbour office or travel agents for current schedules and fares.

However, schedules are often very vague so be prepared to hang around until something turns up. Be warned that because vessels may be ancient and routinely overcrowded, safety standards are at times poor – though most

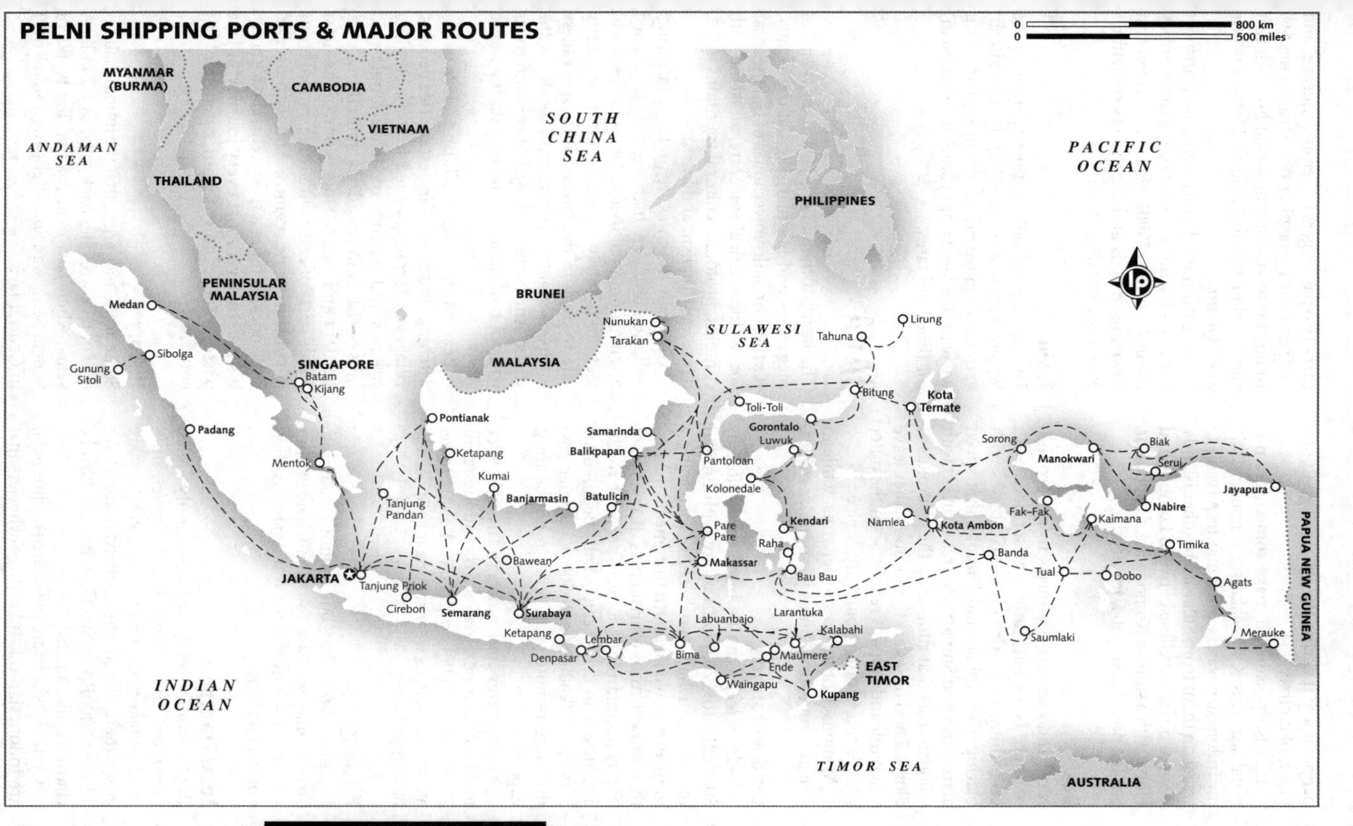
PELNI SHIPPING PORTS & MAJOR ROUTES
0 800 km
0 500 miles
MYANMAR (BURMA)
CAMBODIA
VIETNAM
ANDAMAN SEA
THAILAND
SOUTH CHINA SEA
PACIFIC OCEAN
PHILIPPINES
PENINSULAR MALAYSIA
BRUNEI
MALAYSIA
SINGAPORE
Batam
Kijang
SULAWESI SEA
Medan
Sibolga
Gunung Sitoli
Padang
Mentok
Pontianak
Ketapang
Kumai
Tanjung Pandan
Banjarmasin
Batulicin
Samarinda
Balikpapan
Nunukan
Tarakan
Toli-Toli
Pantoloan
Gorontalo
Luwuk
Kolonedale
Tahuna
Lirung
Bitung
Kota Ternate
Sorong
Manokwari
Biak
Serui
Nabire
Jayapura
Fak-Fak
Kaimana
Namlea
Kota Ambon
Kendari
Raha
Bau Bau
Pare Pare
Makassar
Bawean
JAKARTA
Tanjung Priok
Cirebon
Semarang
Surabaya
Ketapang
Lembar
Denpasar
Bima
Labuanbajo
Larantuka
Kalabahi
Maumere
Ende
Waingapu
Kupang
EAST TIMOR
Banda
Tual
Dobo
Timika
Agats
Merauke
Saumlaki
PAPUA NEW GUINEA
INDIAN OCEAN
TIMOR SEA
AUSTRALIA

INDONESIA

people make it across the archipelago in one piece, of course.

It's also possible to make some more unusual sea trips. Old Makassar schooners still ply Indonesian waters and it may be possible to travel on them from Sulawesi to other islands. Tourist boats travelling between Lombok and Flores with a stop on Komodo are also popular. See the boxed text, p304, for details.

Bus

Most Indonesians use buses to get around, so there is a huge variety of services, with everything from air-con deluxe buses with blaring TVs, toilets and karaoke that speed across Java and Sumatra, to *trek* (trucks) with wooden seats that rumble up the dirt roads of Flores. Local buses are the cheapest; they leave when full and stop on request – on the outer islands this is often your only choice.

Minibuses often do shorter runs, while in Bali air-con tourist buses ply popular routes.

Car & Motorcycle

Self-drive jeeps can be hired for as little as 80,000Rp to 120,000Rp a day with limited insurance in Bali, but become increasingly more expensive and hard to come by the further you get from tourist areas. If you're not happy negotiating Indonesia's chaotic roads, a vehicle with driver can usually be hired for between 350,000Rp and 500,000Rp per day; the more remote areas tend to be the most expensive.

Motorcycles and scooters (usually 90cc to 125cc) can be hired across Indonesia for 25,000Rp to 50,000Rp per day. Be sure to get a crash helmet, as wearing one is supposed to be compulsory.

Hitching

Hitching is possible, but cannot be advised. Drivers may well ask for as much as the bus would cost – maybe more – and safety is obviously a concern.

Local Transport

Public minibuses (most commonly called *bemo*, but also known as *colt, opelet, mikrolet, angkot, angkudes* and *pete-pete* are everywhere. Bemo run standard routes (fares average 3000Rp to 5000Rp), but can also be chartered like a taxi.

Cycle rickshaws are called *becak*, while *bajaj* are Indonesian túk-túks: three-wheelers that carry two passengers (three at a squeeze) and are powered by rasping two-stroke engines. In quieter towns, you may find horse-drawn carts, variously called *dokar, cidomo, andong* and *ben hur*.

An extremely handy form of transport is the *ojek* (motorcycle taxi); expect to pay about 2500Rp to 5000Rp for a short ride. Most towns have taxis and the drivers sometimes even use their *argo* (meters).

Train

Java has a good railway service running the length of the island (see p178). There is also an extremely limited rail service in Sumatra. Visit www.infoka.kereta-api.com (in Indonesian) for times and fares.

JAVA

The heart of the nation, Java is an island of megacities and mesmerising natural beauty. It's the economic powerhouse of Indonesia, as well as the political epicentre, an island with complex, profound cultural traditions in art, dance, spiritualism and learning.

Generally the cities are pretty uninspiring; pollution levels are high and they're plagued by environmental issues. That said, personal security is rarely an issue, and it's perfectly safe to explore the streets of most Javanese towns at night, snacking with locals on the street. And along with Bali, this island rocks with vibrant nightlife and an exciting music scene.

Leaving the cities you'll find a Java of bewitching landscapes – iridescent rice paddies, villages of terracotta-tiled houses, gurgling streams and patches of dense jungle-clad hills – the countryside is something else. Verdant and fecund, this is one of the most fertile parts of earth with three annual crops possible in some regions. And with over 40 volcanoes forming a spiky central backbone, it's safe to say almost every journey in Java passes a succession of giant, often smoking cones.

History

Some academics argue that the human habitation of Java stretches back as far as 1.7 million years, when Java man roamed the banks of Sungai Bengawan Solo (Bengawan Solo River) in Central Java.

The island's exceptional fertility allowed the development of an intensive *sawah* (wet rice) agriculture, which in turn required close cooperation between villages. Out of village alliances, kingdoms developed, most notably the Mataram rulers and Sailendra dynasties that built Borobudur (probably around AD 780) and the Hindu Prambanan complex (c AD 856).

By the year 1350 a great Majapahit kingdom had emerged, controlling Java, Madura and Bali under the leadership of Hayam Wuruk. By the 15th and 16th centuries, Islamic principalities were emerging, the greatest centred in Mataram, and holding sway over central and eastern Java. Intense regional rivalries hindered Javanese efforts to confront the invading Dutch, and the majority of the island had fallen to the colonists by the conclusion of the 18th century – although certain principalities in Solo and Yogyakarta survived until the foundation of the Indonesian republic.

After independence, Java became the centre of the new Indonesia. And that has led to resentment; to a large extent the rebellions of the Sumatrans, Minahasans and Ambonese in the 1950s and 1960s were reactions to Javanese domination of the new country. Furthermore, the abortive communist coup of 1965 started in Jakarta, and some of its most dramatic and disastrous events took place in Java as thousands of communist sympathisers were massacred. During Soeharto's rule, Java benefited as it became the most industrialised part of the nation, its businesses dominating the economy and concentrating wealth in the island (although this remained largely in the hands of a privileged few who had close links to the president).

Java continues to be the powerhouse of Indonesia, receiving the lion's share of foreign investment. Bali excepted, it's the most cosmopolitan corner of the nation. Each major city has glitzy malls that rival anything in the West, full of latte-sipping students and nightclubs where DJs spin cutting-edge electronica to designer-clad dancers.

Go across the tracks in the poor backstreets and another Java exists, where radical Islam thrives and youths taught in *madrassah* (Islamic schools) vent their fury at Western imperialism in Iraq and Afghanistan. Some have taken it far further than street protests, exporting a twisted vision of jihad to fight Christians in Sulawesi and bomb Bali and Jakarta.

But when it comes to the ballot box, the Javanese as a whole have consistently favoured secular as opposed to religious political parties: in the 2009 elections Islamist parties saw their share of the vote drop slightly.

Dangers & Annoyances

Java is not generally a dangerous or hassle-prone destination. Take extra care in Jakarta (see p183) against petty theft, as you would in any large city. It's best to avoid any large religious or political rallies, which sometimes become violent.

Occasionally, bars and clubs have been smashed up by self-appointed morality police called the Jakarta-based Front Pembela Islam (FPI or Islamic Defenders Front), especially during Ramadan.

Getting There & Away

AIR

Jakarta (p189) is Indonesia's busiest international arrival point and has numerous international connections on national and low-cost airlines to cities throughout Asia and beyond. Surabaya (p218) has a few international flights.

BOAT

Java is a major hub for shipping services. Jakarta (see p189) and Surabaya (see p219) are the main ports for Pelni ships; check www.pelni.co.id for more information.

Ferries (6000Rp, 30 minutes) shuttle between Gilimanuk in western Bali and Ketapang in Java every 30 minutes, 24 hours a day.

Between Merak in Java and Bakauheni at the southern tip of Sumatra, ferries (15,000Rp, two hours) operate every 30 minutes, 24 hours a day.

Getting Around

AIR

Domestic flight routes in Java are currently expanding rapidly and can be quite inexpensive. Surabaya to Jakarta is very popular and is covered by Air Asia and five other airlines. Flight information is listed throughout this chapter and in the Transport chapter (p945).

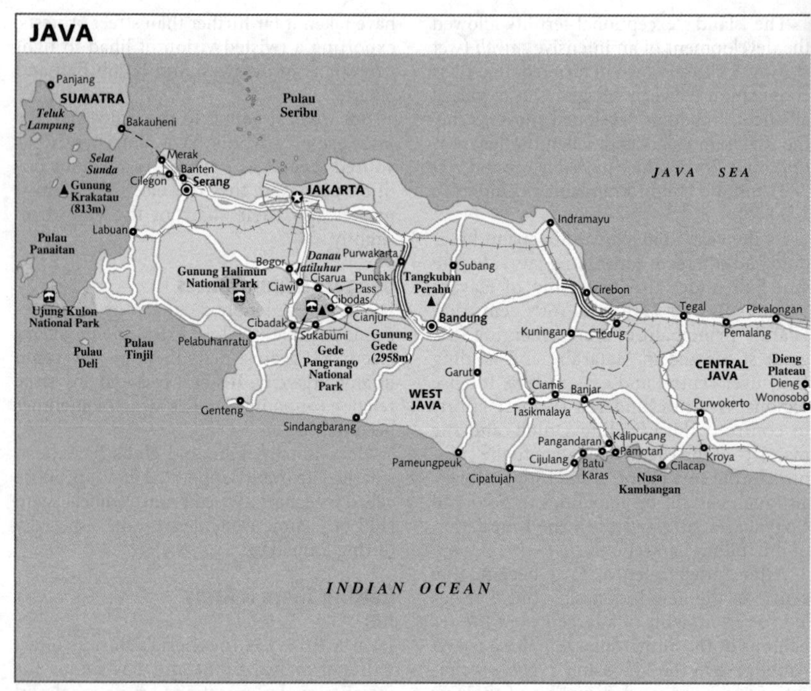

BUS

Bus travel is often slow and nerve-racking; night buses are a little faster. Trains are usually better for the long hauls, but bus departures are usually more frequent.

Public buses, 'cooled' by a flow of sooty air from an open window, are very frequent but they also stop for passengers every five minutes. Better air-con buses also run the major routes and are well worth paying the extra 25% or so they cost.

Small minibuses that cover shorter routes and back runs are commonly called *angkot* and shouldn't be confused with very useful door-to-door minibuses *(travel)*. The latter are air-con minibuses that travel all over Java and pick you up at your hotel and drop you off wherever you want to go in the destination city.

LOCAL TRANSPORT

Dream up a way of getting around and you will find it somewhere on the streets of Java; *ojek* (motorcycle taxis) are very widely available. *Dokar* – brightly coloured, horse-drawn carts, awash with jingling bells and psychedelic motifs – are a highlight.

TRAIN

Trains are usually quicker, more comfortable and more convenient than buses for getting between the main centres.

Ekonomi trains are dirt cheap, slow, crowded and often run late. Seats can be booked on the better *ekonomi plus* services. For a little extra, express trains with *bisnis* (business) and *eksekutif* (executive) sections are better and seating is guaranteed. For air-con and more comfort, go for the top-of-the-range *argo* (luxury) trains, though don't expect anything luxurious – cracked windows and semiswept aisles are the norm, but a meal is always included.

For basic *ekonomi* trains, tickets go on sale an hour before departure. *Bisnis* and *eksekutif* trains can be booked weeks ahead, and the main stations have efficient, computerised booking offices for *eksekutif* trains.

Try to book at least a day in advance, or several days beforehand, for travel on public holidays and long weekends.

The railway's **Train Information Service** (☎ 0361-227131; www.kereta-api.com) has more information (on the website, *Jadwal* means schedule).

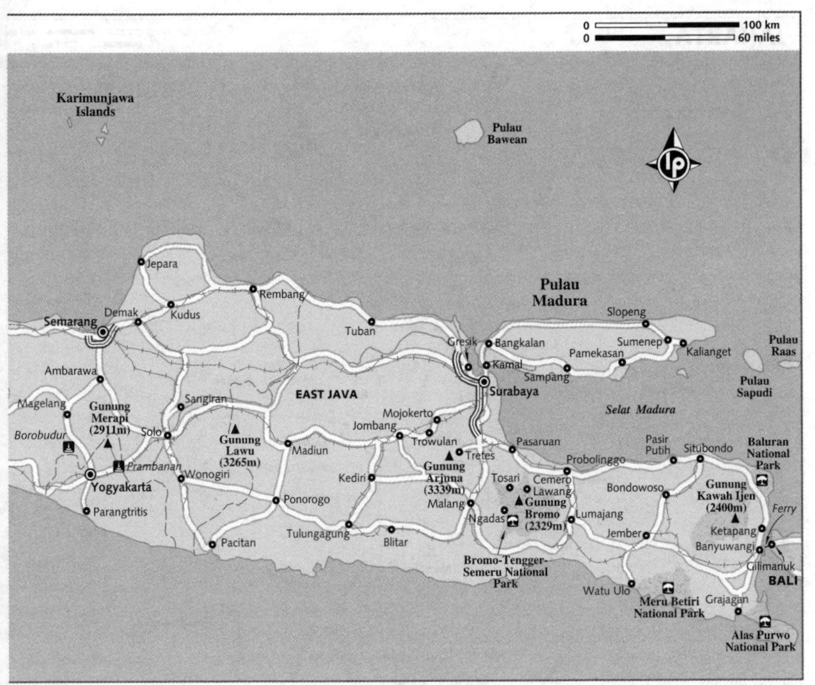

JAKARTA

☎ 021 / pop 8.9 million

Let's be honest: Jakarta is a hard city to love. One of the world's greatest megalopolises, its grey, relentlessly urban sprawl spreads for tens of kilometres across a flood-prone plain with barely a park to break the concrete monotony.

And yet beneath the unappealing facade of high-rises, slums and gridlocked streets, this is a city of surprises and many faces. The 'Big Durian' is actually a far from threatening place, and its citizens are a remarkably good-natured, optimistic and positive bunch. Compared to many of the world's capitals, crime levels are very low (as is the cost of living, with four-star hotels starting at US$50 a night).

From the steamy, richly scented streets of Chinatown to the city's riotous, decadent nightlife, Jakarta is filled with unexpected corners. Here it's possible to rub shoulders with Indonesia's future leaders, artists, thinkers, movers and shakers in a bohemian cafe or a sleek lounge bar and go clubbing till dawn (and beyond). And beyond.

Jakarta certainly isn't a primary tourist destination, but parts of the atmospheric old city (Kota) offer an interesting insight into the capital's long history, and there are a handful of good museums and dozens of swanky shopping malls. Though Jakarta's infamous *macet* (traffic jams) still choke the city, an ever-expanding modern busway network has speeded up travel considerably in recent years.

So if you really want to get under the skin of Indonesia, a visit to this mammoth city (the Greater Jakarta conurbation exceeds 20 million people) is essential.

Orientation

Metropolitan Jakarta sprawls 28km from the docks to the southern suburbs. Soekarno's national monument (Monas) in Lapangan Merdeka (Freedom Sq) is an excellent central landmark. North of the monument is the older part of Jakarta, which includes Chinatown, the former Dutch area of Kota and the old port of Sunda Kelapa. Tanjung Priok, the main harbour, is several kilometres further east. The sprawling modern suburbs of Jakarta are south of the monument.

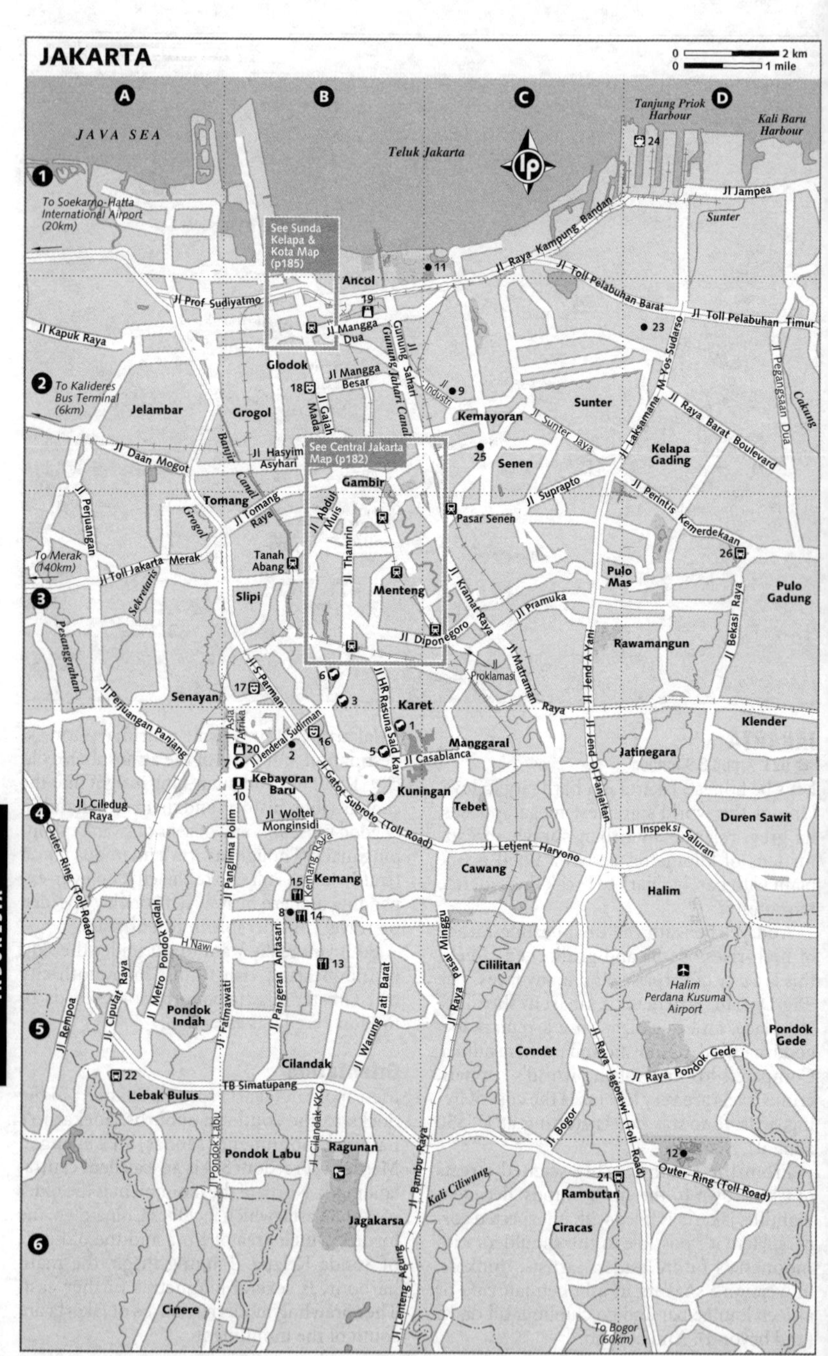
JAKARTA
0 2 km
0 1 mile
JAVA SEA
Teluk Jakarta
Tanjung Priok Harbour
Kali Baru Harbour
To Soekarno-Hatta International Airport (20km)
See Sunda Kelapa & Kota Map (p185)
Ancol
Jl Prof Sudiyatmo
Jl Kapuk Raya
Jl Mangga Dua
Jl Gunung Sahari
Gunung Jahari Canal
Jl Raya Kampung Bandan
Jl Toll Pelabuhan Barat
Jl Toll Pelabuhan Timur
Jl Jampea
Sunter
Glodok
Jl Mangga Besar
Jl Industri
Jl Gajah Mada
To Kalideres Bus Terminal (6km)
Jelambar
Grogol
Kemayoran
Jl Sunter Jaya
Jl Laksamana M Yos Sudarso
Jl Raya Barat Boulevard
Jl Pegangsaan Dua
Cakung
Kelapa Gading
Senen
Banjir Canal
Jl Hasyim Asyhari
Jl Daan Mogot
See Central Jakarta Map (p182)
Gambir
Jl Suprapto
Jl Perintis Kemerdekaan
Tomang
Jl Tomang Raya
Jl Perjuangan
Grogol
Jl Abdul Muis
Pasar Senen
To Merak (140km)
Jl Toll Jakarta Merak
Tanah Abang
Jl Thamrin
Menteng
Jl Kramat Raya
Pulo Mas
Pulo Gadung
Sekretaris
Slipi
Jl Pramuka
Jl Bekasi Raya
Pesanggrahan
Jl Diponegoro
Rawamangun
Jl Proklamasi
Jl Matraman Raya
Jl Jend A Yani
Jl S Parman
Senayan
Jl Perjuangan Panjang
Karet
Jl HR Rasuna Said Kav
Klender
Jl Asia Afrika
Jl Jenderal Sudirman
Manggarai
Jl Casablanca
Jatinegara
Jl Gatot Subroto (Toll Road)
Kebayoran Baru
Kuningan
Tebet
Jl Jend DI Panjaitan
Jl Ciledug Raya
Jl Wolter Monginsidi
Duren Sawit
Outer Ring (Toll Road)
Jl Kemang Raya
Jl Letjent Haryono
Jl Inspeksi Saluran
Cawang
Kemang
Halim
Jl Panglima Polim
H Nawi
Jl Metro Pondok Indah
Jl Pasar Minggu
Jl Raya Pasar Minggu
Cililitan
Jl Pangeran Antasari
Jl Warung Jati Barat
Halim Perdana Kusuma Airport
Jl Rempoa
Jl Cipulat Raya
Pondok Indah
Jl Fatmawati
Pondok Gede
Condet
Jl Raya Jagorawi (Toll Road)
Cilandak
Jl Raya Pondok Gede
Lebak Bulus
TB Simatupang
Jl Bogor
Jl Pondok Labu
Pondok Labu
Jl Cilandak KKO
Ragunan
Jl Bambu Raya
Outer Ring (Toll Road)
Kali Ciliwung
Rambutan
Jagakarsa
Ciracas
Jl Lenteng Agung
Cinere
To Bogor (60km)
A B C D
1 2 3 4 5 6
1 2 3 4 5 6 7 8 9 10 11 12 13 14 15 16 17 18 19 20 21 22 23 24 25 26

INFORMATION
Australian Cultural Centre........(see 1)
Australian Embassy.....................1 B4
British Council.............................2 B4
Canadian Embassy......................3 B3
Dutch Embassy.......................(see 4)
Erasmus Huis...............................4 B4
Malaysian Embassy.....................5 B4
New Zealand Embassy................6 B3
Papua New Guinean Embassy.....7 B4
Periplus..................................(see 20)
QB World Books.........................8 B4
Singaporean Embassy..............(see 4)

SIGHTS & ACTIVITIES
Jakarta Fair Grounds...................9 C2
Pizza Man Statue......................10 B4
Purna Bhakti Pertiwi Museum.............................(see 12)
Taman Impian Jaya Ancol.........11 C1
Taman Mini Indonesia Indah.... 12 D6

EATING
Kemang Food Festival............(see 15)
Kinara......................................13 B5
Payon....................................(see 15)
Place.......................................14 B4
Santong Kuo Tieh 68.............(see 11)
WWWok...................................15 B4

ENTERTAINMENT
Centro......................................16 B4
Embassy..................................17 B3
Stadium...................................18 B2

SHOPPING
Pasar Pagi Mangga Dua............19 B2
Pasar Seni..............................(see 11)
Plaza Senayan..........................20 B4

TRANSPORT
Kampung Rambutan Bus Terminal...............................21 C6
Lebak Bulus Bus Terminal.........22 A5
Merpati....................................23 D2
Pelni Passenger Terminal..........24 D1
Pelni Ticket Office....................25 C2
Pulo Gadung Bus Terminal........26 D3

Jl Thamrin is the main north–south street of the new city and has Jakarta's big hotels and banks. A couple of blocks east along Jl Kebon Sirih Raya is Jl Jaksa, the cheap accommodation centre of Jakarta.

Information

BOOKSHOPS

Periplus (Map p180; ☎ 718 7070; Level 3, Plaza Senayan, Jl Asia Afrika; 9am-7pm) Stocks a wide range of English-language titles, including Lonely Planet guidebooks and Periplus maps.
QB World Books (Map p180; ☎ 718 0818; Jl Kemang Raya 17) Offers a good selection of literature and magazines published in English.

CULTURAL CENTRES

Australian Cultural Centre (Map p180; ☎ 2550 5555; Jl Rasuna Said Kav C15-16)
British Council (Map p180; ☎ 252 4115; www.britishcouncil.org/indonesia.htm; Widjoyo Centre, Jl Jenderal Sudirman 71)
Erasmus Huis (Map p180; ☎ 524 1069; www.mfa.nl/erasmushuis; Jl Rasuna Said Kav S-3) Regularly hosts films, exhibitions and cultural events.

EMERGENCY

Fire (☎ 113)
Police (☎ 110)
Medical help (☎ 118, 119)
Tourist Police (Map p184; ☎ 566000; Jl Wahid Hasyim) On the 2nd floor of the Jakarta Theatre.

INTERNET ACCESS

Internet cafes are scattered all over Jakarta and generally charge between 4000Rp and 10,000Rp per hour. For wi-fi access, most upmarket malls have free wireless connections, as do increasing numbers of cafes, bars and restaurants.
Virtual Net (Map p184; Jl Jaksa 33)

INTERNET RESOURCES

http://metromad.blogspot.com This blogger and newspaper columnist has been a Jakarta resident for two decades and really has his finger on the pulse of the city.
www.jakarta.go.id The Jakarta City Government Tourism Office's official site; offers plenty of useful listings, though the English-language section is often down.
www.jakchat.com English-language forums where you can discuss everything from bars to politics.

MEDIA

Jakarta Globe (www.thejakartaglobe.com; 7500Rp) Excellent newspaper with stylish layout, quality reporting and illuminating features.
Jakarta Post (www.thejakartapost.com; 7500Rp) Long-running English-language daily with news, views and cultural content, though has now been eclipsed by the Jakarta Globe.
Time Out (www.timeoutjakarta.com; 33,000Rp) The best English-language listings magazine, with great cultural content and features, though tends to focus on exclusive venues.

MEDICAL SERVICES

SOS Medika (Map p180; ☎ 750 5980; www.internationalsos.com; Jl Puri Sakti 10, Kemang) Offers English-speaking GP appointments, dental care and emergency, and specialist health-care services.

MONEY

There are banks all over the city, and you're never far from an ATM in Jakarta.
BCA ATM (Map p184; Jl Haji Agus Salim) A stone's throw from the Jakarta Visitor Information office.

POST

Main post office (Map p182; Jl Gedung Kesenian 1; 8am-7pm Mon-Fri, to 1pm Sat)

TELEPHONE

Wartel Bhumi Bhakti (Map p184; Jl Wahid Hasyim; 10am-10pm)

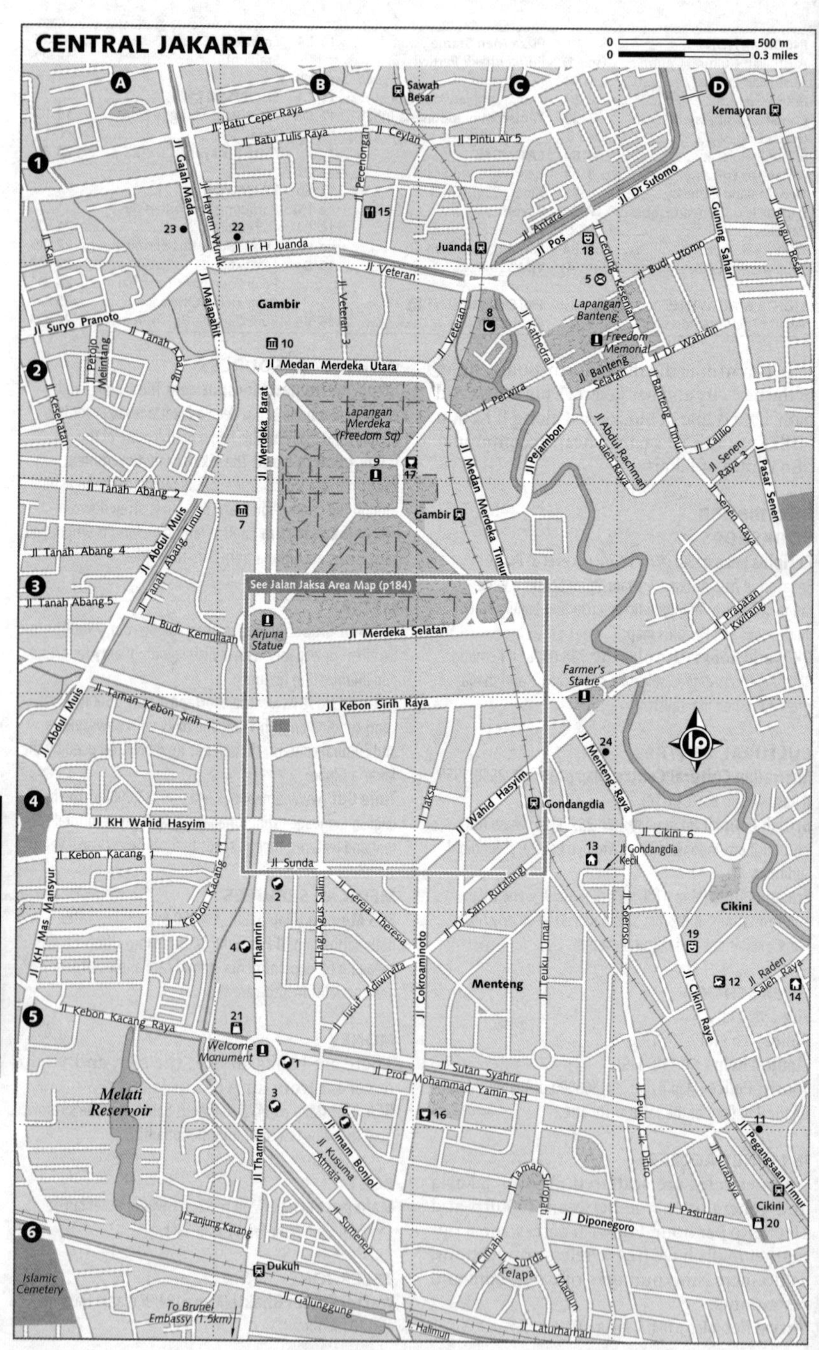
CENTRAL JAKARTA
0 500 m
0 0.3 miles
A
B
C
D
1
2
3
4
5
6
Sawah Besar
Kemayoran
Jl Batu Ceper Raya
Jl Batu Tulis Raya
Jl Ceylan
Jl Pintu Air 5
Jl Pecenongan
Jl Gajah Mada
Jl Hayam Wuruk
Jl Dr Sutomo
Jl Antara
Jl Pos
Jl Gedung Kesenian 1
Jl Gunung Sahari
Jl Bungur Besar
Jl Budi Utomo
Jl Kaji
Jl Ir H Juanda
Juanda
Jl Veteran
Jl Veteran 1
Jl Veteran 3
Jl Majapahit
Gambir
Jl Suryo Pranoto
Jl Tanah Abang 1
Jl Petojo Melintang
Jl Kesehatan
Jl Medan Merdeka Utara
Jl Katedral
Lapangan Banteng
Freedom Memorial
Jl Dr Wahidin
Jl Banteng Selatan
Jl Perwira
Jl Banteng Timur
Lapangan Merdeka (Freedom Sq)
Jl Merdeka Barat
Jl Medan Merdeka Timur
Jl Pejambon
Jl Abdul Rachman Saleh Raya
Jl Kalilio
Jl Senen Raya 3
Jl Pasar Senen
Jl Senen Raya
Jl Tanah Abang 2
Jl Abdul Muis
Jl Tanah Abang Timur
Jl Tanah Abang 4
Jl Tanah Abang 5
See Jalan Jaksa Area Map (p184)
Jl Budi Kemuliaan
Arjuna Statue
Jl Merdeka Selatan
Jl Prapatan
Jl Kwitang
Farmer's Statue
Jl Taman Kebon Sirih 1
Jl Kebon Sirih Raya
Jl Menteng Raya
Jl Wahid Hasyim
Jl Jaksa
Gondangdia
Jl KH Wahid Hasyim
Jl Cikini 6
Jl Gondangdia Kecil
Jl Kebon Kacang 1
Jl Kebon Kacang 11
Jl Sunda
Jl KH Mas Mansyur
Jl Thamrin
Jl Hagi Agus Salim
Jl Gereja Theresia
Jl Dr Sam Rutalangi
Jl Cokroaminoto
Jl Teuku Umar
Jl Soeroso
Cikini
Jl Jusuf Adiwinata
Menteng
Jl Cikini Raya
Jl Raden Saleh Raya
Jl Kebon Kacang Raya
Welcome Monument
Jl Sutan Syahrir
Jl Prof Mohammad Yamin SH
Melati Reservoir
Jl Imam Bonjol
Jl Kusuma Atmaja
Jl Teuku Cik Ditiro
Jl Pegangsaan Timur
Jl Surabaya
Jl Taman Suropati
Jl Pasuruan
Jl Diponegoro
Jl Tanjung Karang
Jl Sumenep
Jl Cimahi
Jl Sunda Kelapa
Jl Madiun
Islamic Cemetery
Dukuh
Jl Galunggung
To Brunei Embassy (1.5km)
Jl Halimun
Jl Laturharhari
1
2
3
4
5
6
7
8
9
10
11
12
13
14
15
16
17
18
19
20
21
22
23
24

INDONESIA

INFORMATION	SDN Menteng 1 School....11 D5	Eastern Promise....17 B2
British Embassy....1 B5	Swimming pool....12 D5	
French Embassy....2 B4		**ENTERTAINMENT**
German Embassy....3 B5	**SLEEPING**	Gedung Kesenian Jakarta....18 C1
Japanese Embassy....4 B5	Gondia International Guesthouse....13 C4	Taman Ismail Marzuki....19 D5
Main Post Office....5 C2	Yannie International Guesthouse....14 D5	
Thai Embassy....6 B5		**SHOPPING**
		Flea Market....20 D6
SIGHTS & ACTIVITIES		Plaza Indonesia....21 B5
Indonesian National Museum....7 B3	**EATING**	
Mesjid Istiqlal....8 C2	Night Warung....15 B1	**TRANSPORT**
National History Museum....(see 9)		Batavia Air....22 B1
National Monument....9 B2	**DRINKING**	Lion Air....23 A1
Presidental Palace....10 B2	BB's....16 C5	Menara Buana Surya....24 C4

TOURIST INFORMATION

Jakarta Visitor Information (Map p184; ☎ 315 4094, 316 1293; www.jakarta.go.id; Jl Wahid Hasyim 9; 9.30am-7pm Mon-Sat, 9am-5pm Sun) Inside the Jakarta Theatre building. A pretty helpful office; the staff here can answer many queries, though practical information is a little lacking. Has a good stock of leaflets and publications. There's also a desk at the airport.

TRAVEL AGENCIES

Crystal Tours (Map p184; ☎ 390 2929; Jl Wahid Hasyim 45) A professional new agency with helpful English-speaking staff and competitive flight prices.

Robertur (Map p184; ☎ 314 2926; Jl Jaksa 20B)

Dangers & Annoyances

Considering its size and the scale of poverty, Jakarta is generally a safe city and security incidents are rare. That said, you should be careful late at night in Glodok and Kota – muggings do occasionally occur – and only use reputable taxi companies, such as the citywide Bluebird group. Keep your eyes open on buses and trains, which are a favourite haunt of pickpockets. It's wise to steer clear of political and religious demonstrations, which may draw anti-Western militants. And note that high-profile Western hotels have been targeted by terrorists.

Dengue fever outbreaks occur in the wet season, so come armed with mosquito repellent. See p958 for more on dengue fever.

Sights & Activities

KOTA

Jakarta's crumbling historic heart is Kota, home to the remnants of the Dutch capital of Batavia. Taman Fatahillah (Map p185), the old town square, features cracked cobblestones and lonely postcard vendors as well as some fine colonial buildings and some ho-hum museums. Trains from Gondangdia, near Jl Jaksa, also run here. A taxi will cost around 30,000Rp from Jl Thamrin.

By far the finest way to relive the colonial experience is to take a drink in the magnificent Café Batavia (p188) and then explore Kota's quirkier sights on foot. The old Portuguese cannon **Si Jagur** (Mr Fertility; Map p185; Taman Fatahillah) was believed to be a cure for barrenness because of its suggestive clenched fist, and women sat astride it in the hope of bearing children.

Nearby, **Gereja Sion** (Map p185; Jl Pangeran Jayakarta 1; dawn-dusk) is the oldest remaining church in Jakarta. It was built in 1695 for the 'black Portuguese' brought to Batavia as slaves and given their freedom if they joined the Dutch Reformed Church.

More fine Dutch architecture lines the grotty Kali Besar canal, including the **Toko Merah** (Map p185; Jl Kali Besar Barat), formerly the home of Governor General van Imhoff. Further north, the last remaining Dutch drawbridge, the **Chicken Market Bridge** (Map p185), spans the canal.

The area's museums and their dusty exhibits are decidedly disappointing. Check out the **Museum Wayang** (Map p185; ☎ 692 9560; Taman Fatahillah; admission 2000Rp; 9am-1.30pm Tue-Fri & Sun, 9am-12.30pm Sat) for its shadow-puppet performances (Sundays at 10am). At the **Jakarta History Museum** (Map p185; ☎ 692 9101; Taman Fatahillah 2; admission 2000Rp; 9am-1.30pm Tue-Fri & Sun, to 12.30pm Sat), there's little but colonial bric-a-brac; the fine old (1710) City Hall building, which houses the museum, is the real star.

To the south of Kota, **Glodok** (Map p185) is a run-down Chinese district of traditional markets and infamous nightclubs that suffered very badly in the 1998 riots. These days most Jakartans favour air-conditioned shopping malls, but a stroll through Glodok's steamy, scruffy lanes past spitting street kitchens will provide plenty of colour for the day's blog entry. Avoid dark side streets at night in this zone.

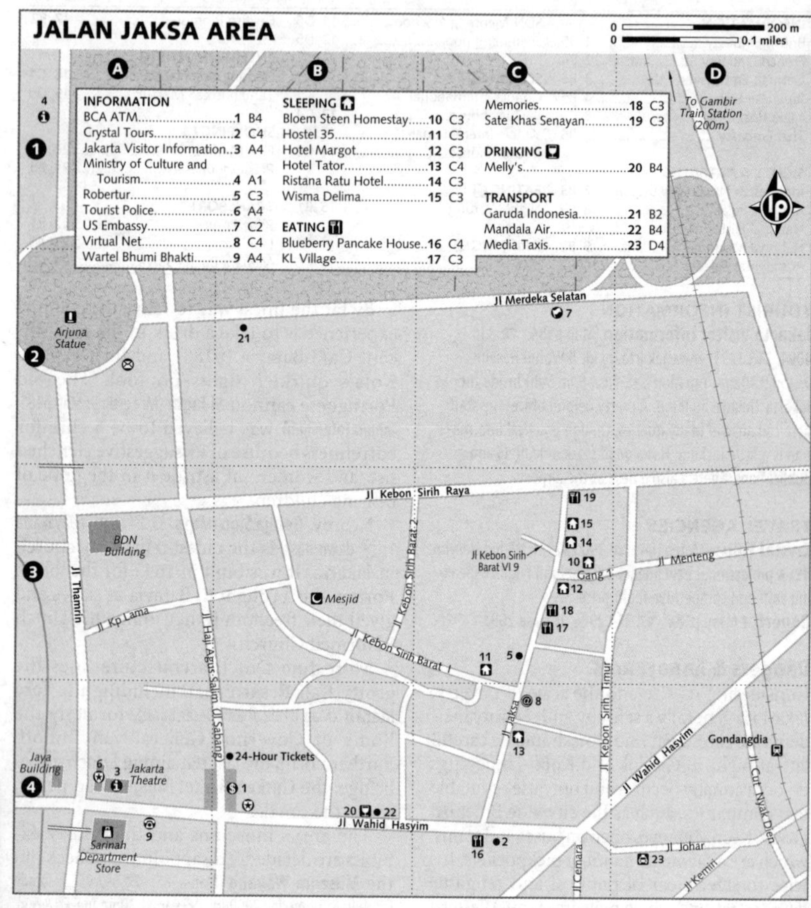

SUNDA KELAPA

Among the hubbub, floating debris and oil slicks, the old Dutch **port** (admission 2000Rp) is still used by magnificent Buginese *pinisi* (fishing boats), their cargo unloaded by teams of porters walking along wobbly gangplanks. It's a 1km walk from Taman Fatahillah, or take one of the area's unique push-bike taxis known as *ojek sepeda* (2500Rp).

Close by are the early morning **Pasar Ikan** (Fish Market; Map p185; Jl Pasar Ikan; 6am-2pm) and **Museum Bahari** (Map p185; ☎ 669 3406; www.museumbahari.org; admission 2000Rp; 9am-3pm Tue-Sun), located in one of the old Dutch East India Company warehouses (1645), which exhibits some fine photographs and sailing boats from across Indonesia.

LAPANGAN MERDEKA

Soekarno attempted to tame Jakarta by giving it a central space, Lapangan Merdeka (Freedom Sq; Map p182), and topping it with a gigantic monument to his machismo, the **National Monument** (Monas; Map p182; ☎ 384 0451; admission 6000Rp; 8.30am-5pm Mon-Fri, to 7pm Sat & Sun). The towering, 132m-high column, capped with a gilded flame, has been ungraciously dubbed 'Soekarno's last erection'; whiz up the shaft for a shot of the city. The **National History Museum** (Map p182; adult/child 1500/500Rp; 8.30am-5pm Mon-Fri, 8.30am-7pm Sat & Sun), in the base, tells the story of Indonesia's independence struggle in 48 dramatic, overstated dioramas. Admission is included in the entry fee for the monument.

Many of Soekarno's triumphalist monuments have acquired derogatory nicknames over the years: the guy at Kebayoran roundabout holding the flaming dish is now the **'Pizza Man' statue** (Map p180).

INDONESIAN NATIONAL MUSEUM

Around a 15-minute walk from Jl Jaksa, the **National Museum** (Map p182; ☎ 381 1551; Jl Merdeka Barat; adult 750Rp; ⏰ 8.30am-2.30pm Tue-Sat) is something of an oddity in Jakarta, being a museum that is genuinely worth visiting. There are some excellent displays of Han ceramics and ancient Hindu statuary, magnificent *kris* (traditional dagger) handles studded with rubies, and a huge relief map on which you can pick out all those volcanoes you plan to climb. This museum is also known as Gedung Gajah (Elephant House) on account of the bronze elephant outside, which was donated by the king of Thailand in 1871. A very impressive new wing was added onto the north side of this neoclassical colonial structure in 2007.

The **Indonesian Heritage Society** (☎ 572 5870; www.heritagejkt.org) organises free English tours of the museum at 10.30am every Tuesday and Thursday and every second Saturday and last Sunday in the month.

TAMAN MINI INDONESIA INDAH

A 100-hecatare theme park built to celebrate the nation, **Taman Mini Indonesia Indah** (Map p180; ☎ 545 4545; www.jakweb.com/tmii; TMII Pintu 1; admission 6000Rp; ⏰ 8am-5pm) includes traditional houses from (most) Indonesian provinces set around a lagoon (boats are available to hire), an Imax theatre and a bird park. There's also an assortment of museums, including an insect house full of alarming-looking specimens, and, best of all, the air-conditioned **Purna Bhakti Pertiwi Museum** (Map p180; ⏰ 8am-5pm), which houses the stupendously opulent (and downright gaudy) gifts given to Soeharto, including a 5m ship carved entirely from jade.

To get there, take Koridor 7 bus to the Kampung Rambutan terminal and then a T15 metro-mini to the park entrance. A taxi from central Jakarta costs about 70,000Rp.

OTHER ATTRACTIONS

Taman Impian Jaya Ancol (Map p180; ☎ 640 6777; www.ancol.co.id; admission 12,000Rp; ⏰ 10am-10pm) is a huge waterfront amusement complex with an oceanarium, art market and an Indonesian-style Disneyland (Dunia Fantasi, entrance an additional 80,000Rp). To get there, take bus 64, 65 or 125 or *angkot* 51 from Kota station.

To the north of Lapangan Merdeka you can stroll past the gleaming white **Presidential Palace** (Map p182; Jl Medan Merdeka Utara) – beware of the jumpy armed guards. To the northeast is the vast, modernist **Mesjid Istiqlal** (Map p182; Jl Veteran 1; ⏰ dawn-dusk), one of the grandest mosques in Southeast Asia.

Make a central splash (within walking distance of Jalan Jaksa) in the 50m **swimming pool** (Map p182; Jl Cikini Raya; admission 20,000Rp; ⏰ 7am-8pm) located behind the Formule 1 Hotel in Cikini.

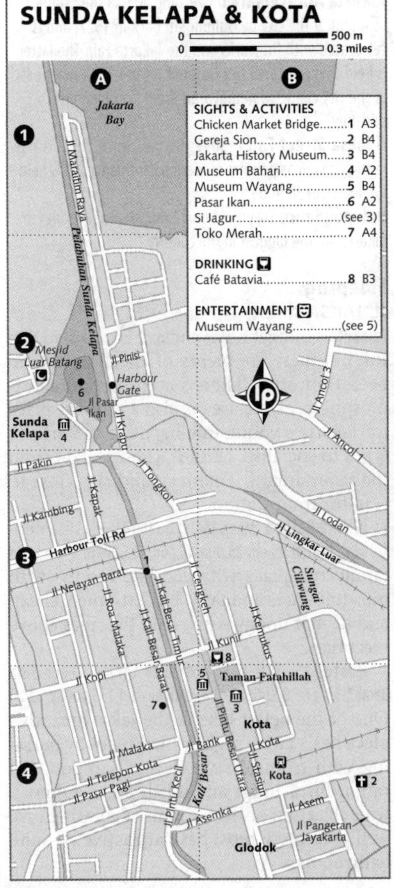

OBAMA IN JAKARTA

Barack Obama moved to Jakarta in 1967 when his mother married her second husband, Lolo Soetoro, an Indonesian whom she'd met in Hawaii. He lived for four years in the Indonesian capital, including a period in the exclusive central suburb of Menteng, where he attended the government-run **SDN Menteng 1 school** (Map p182) and studied in the Indonesian language. This school is still going strong, and there's a plaque at the front commemorating its most famous former pupil.

A popular child, he was nicknamed 'Barry' by his fellow students. It's been reported that he declared an ambition to become president while at this school. Obama lived close by on Jl Taman Amir Hamzah in a handsome terracotta-tiled Dutch villa with art deco–style windows.

When asked if he missed anything from his time in the country, Obama, who speaks Bahasa Indonesia, said he dreamt of '*bakso* (meatball soup), *nasi goreng* (fried rice) and rambutan'.

Festivals & Events

Java Jazz Festival (www.javajazzfestival.com) If you are here in early March, keep an eye out for this festival.

Jakarta Anniversary On 22 June. Marks the establishment of the city by Gunungjati back in 1527, and is celebrated with fireworks and the Jakarta Fair. The latter is held at the Jakarta Fair Grounds (Map p180), northeast of the city centre in Kemayoran, from late June until mid-July.

Jl Jaksa Street Fair Features Betawi dance, theatre and music, as well as popular modern performances. It is held for one week in August.

Independence Day Held on 17 August. The parades in Jakarta are the biggest in the country.

Sleeping

JL JAKSA AREA

Jakarta's budget hotel enclave is no Khao San Rd, but there are plenty of cheap beds (and beers) on offer. There's a cosmopolitan atmosphere, as the area is also a popular place for Jakarta's young intelligentsia and artistic types to socialise. Jaksa is a short stroll from the main drag, Jl Thamrin, and also close to Gambir train station.

Wisma Delima (Map p184; ☎ 3190 4157; Jl Jaksa 5; dm/s/d with shared mandi 25,000/45,000/60,000Rp) Ancient family-run place with cell-like rooms (with mosquito nets and fans) but extremely cheap and it's not dodgy – just read the rules above reception.

Hostel 35 (Map p184; ☎ 9824 1472; Jl Kebon Sirih Barat I 35; r 65,000-85,000Rp, with air-con 135,000Rp; ❄) One of the better bets in the Jaksa area, this place has a large, slightly bizarre lobby bursting with tropical-style decor: bamboo and rattan furnishings and a fish pond. Offers a wide selection of clean rooms, all of which are well presented; most have attractive en-suite bathrooms.

Bloem Steen Homestay (Map p184; ☎ 3192 5389; Gang I 173; r 70,000Rp; 💻) This place has its positive points, with a nice little front terrace for chilling and a quiet location down a side alley. Cleanliness is taken seriously (shoes off at the door folks!) and staff are reasonably welcoming. The 18 rooms are super-spartan but tidy, though the mattresses are ancient.

Hotel Tator (Map p184; ☎ 3192 3940; Jl Jaksa 37; r with shower & toilet 80,000Rp, r with hot water & air-con 85,000-140,000Rp) Lacks atmosphere but offers plain, functional and clean rooms (smell that bleach), and has a little cafe out the front. Breakfast is included with the more expensive rooms.

Hotel Margot (Map p184; ☎ 391 3830; margot.hotel@yahoo.com; Jl Jaksa 15; r 220,000Rp; ❄) It's not exactly homely, but this place has the appearance of a half-decent hotel. The rooms are in fair shape, all with hot-water, en-suite bathrooms, TV and weak air-con.

Ristana Ratu Hotel (Map p184; ☎ 314 2464; Jl Jaksa 7-9; r 250,000-300,000Rp; ❄) This brand-spanking-new place was just opening when we passed by and has really raised the stakes on the Jaksa strip, with large, modern, stylish rooms with contemporary decor that have great beds, bright duvets and soft pillows.

CIKINI AREA

The Cikini area is east of Jl Jaksa, and has a few good, if pricier, guest houses.

Gondia International Guesthouse (Map p182; ☎ 390 9221; gondia@rad.net.id; Jl Gondangdia Kecil 22; r incl breakfast 180,000-240,000Rp; ❄) A good alternative base to the Jaksa strip, this friendly little guest house occupies a leafy garden plot on a quiet suburban street and has quite spacious tiled rooms with bathrooms, sitting areas and a few books to browse.

Yannie International Guesthouse (Map p182; ☎ 314 0012; ygh@cbn.net.id; Jl Raden Saleh Raya 35; s/d 200,000/250,000Rp;) Two floors of plain simple rooms with the odd textile to break up the monotony. The management could be a lot more welcoming though. There's no sign, just a 'Y' out the front.

Eating

JL JAKSA AREA

Jl Jaksa's fine for no-nonsense, inexpensive Indonesian and Western fare, though many local dishes are toned down a notch to suit tourist tastes. For something more authentic, head to the night-hawker stalls grouped around the southern end of Jl Hagi Agus Salim (also known as Jl Sabang), which is famous for its street food (including satay).

KL Village (Map p184; ☎ 3192 5219; Jl Jaksa 21-23; mains from 15,000Rp; 7am-11pm Sun-Wed, 24hr Thu-Sat;) Deservedly popular new Malaysian place with pavement tables under a covered terrace. Offers great curries (try the *kambing masala*), Western food, terrific juices and fruit shakes (but no beer).

Memories (Map p184; Jl Jaksa 17; mains 20,000Rp; 24hr) A classic Jaksa haunt of fresh-in-town backpackers and seen-it-all expats. There is plenty of Chinese food, set breakfasts (starting from 19,000Rp), a book exchange and CNN round the clock. It even has a few rooms upstairs.

Blueberry Pancake House (Map p184; ☎ 390 4701; Jl Wahid Hasyim 53; mains from 20,000Rp;) Below the Cipra hotel this smart little restaurant is good for Indonesian food, pasta and snacks at moderate prices and offers a welcome air-conditioned retreat from Jaksa's steamy streets.

Sate Khas Senayan (Map p184; ☎ 3192 6238; Jl Kebon Sirih Raya 31A; mains from 25,000Rp; 11.30am-10pm) Excellent two-storey air-con restaurant at the northern end of Jl Jaksa, renowned for its superb *sate* (satay), *rawon buntut* (oxtail stew) and other classic Indonesian dishes.

OTHER AREAS

The upmarket suburb of Kemang, popular with expats, has plenty of stylish bars, clubs and restaurants, and also a couple of food courts where you can chow down on the cheap before clubbing till dawn.

Place (Map p180; Jl Kemang Raya; dinner) Highly sociable 'food bazaar' with myriad stalls, serving up everything from Indo regulars, *teppanyaki*-style steaks to Italian-style ice cream.

Kemang Food Festival (Map p180; Jl Kemang Raya; meals from 12,000Rp; 11.30am-11pm) Fifty or so stalls rustle up *roti canai* (Indian-style flaky flat bread), Japanese noodles, and Iranian, Arabic and Indonesian food here. On weekend nights there's a real buzz here and the place is rammed.

Payon (Map p180; ☎ 719 4826; Jl Kemang Raya 17; mains 40,000-110,000Rp; 11.30am-11pm) This feels a like a secret garden, as you dine under a delightful open pagoda surrounded by greenery set well off the road. Payon is a very civilised setting for authentic Javanese cuisine.

WWWok (Map p180; ☎ 719 3928; Jl Kemang Raya 9 J-K; mains 35,000-85,000Rp) Cafe-bar-restaurant with a really relaxed boho vibe that's popular with a freelance media crowd and students. There are plenty of sofas and space, pool tables, and a menu of Chinese and Indonesian faves.

Kinara (Map p180; ☎ 719 2677; Jl Kemang Raya 78B; mains 55,000-125,000Rp; 11.30am-11pm) The mock medieval doors guarding Kinara lead to an opulent interior of grand arches that's an impressive setting for some of the finest Indian dishes in Jakarta – plump samosas, sublime chicken tikka and plenty of vegetarian choices.

Santong Kuo Tieh 68 (Map p180; ☎ 692 4716; Jl Pancoran; 10 dumplings 20,000Rp; 10am-9pm) For fried or steamed Chinese pork dumplings, look no further than this humble but highly popular little Glodok place. You'll see cooks preparing them out front. The *bakso ikan isi* (fish balls) are also good.

Street food can be picked up at the **night warung** (Map p182; Jl Pecenongan), about 1km north of the National Monument.

Drinking

If you're expecting Jakarta, as the capital of the world's largest Muslim country, to be a pretty sober city with little in the way of drinking culture, think again. From expat pubs to gorgeous lounge bars with cocktail lists set at (near) London or New York prices, and far more beautiful people, Jakarta has it all. The bar zone on Jl Falatehan near Blok M (6km southwest of Jl Jaksa) is a good all-round bet, with everything from European-style pubs where you can shoot pool and sip wine, to raucous bar-clubs with heaving dance floors.

Melly's (Map p184; Jl Wahid Hasyim 84;) The best bet in the Jaksa area for a couple of drinks, this quirky little place attracts a good mix of locals and Westerners, has cheap snacks and beer (a large Bintang is 22,000Rp), and plenty of loungy sitting areas. It's open-sided (so it doesn't get too smoky) and there's a popular quiz here every Wednesday.

Café Batavia (Map p185; ☎ 691 5531; Jl Pintu Besar Utara 14; mains 50,000Rp) An essential visit if you're in Kota, this historic restaurant sits pretty overlooking Taman Fatahillah. Its teak floors and art-deco furniture make for a richly atmospheric setting, though the menu is overly grandiose and seems to be stuck in 1970s nostalgia. As it's often woefully empty you may opt to have a coffee or a cocktail instead.

BB's (Map p182; ☎ 3193 1890; Jl Cokroaminoto) Really popular with students, this scruffy multistoried bar showcases emerging acoustic, blues and reggae bands. Drinks are quite reasonable, especially if you order beer by the pitcher. Friday night is the big night here; entrance is 30,000Rp.

Eastern Promise (Map p182; ☎ 7179 0151; Jl Kemang Raya 5;) A classic British-style pub in the heart of Kemang with a pool table, a welcoming atmosphere, and filling Western and Indian grub. Service is prompt and friendly, the beer's cold and there's live music on weekends. It's a key expat hang-out.

Clubbing

Jakarta is the clubbing mecca of Southeast Asia. The city has some great venues (from dark 'n' sleazy to polished and pricey), internationally renowned DJs, world-class sound systems and some of the planet's longest party sessions (some clubs open around the clock for entire weekends). Entrance is typically 50,000Rp to 80,000Rp, but includes a free drink. Clubs open around 9pm, but don't really get going until midnight; most close around 4am.

Centro (Map p180; ☎ 7278 0818; www.centrojakarta.net; Jl Dharmawangsa IX) A huge club that attracts international DJs on a regular basis.

Embassy (Map p180; ☎ 574 3704; www.embassytheclub.com; Taman Ria Senayan, Jl Gatot Subroto) One of the most respected clubs in the city, its three levels include the main room for house and R&B, and the basement for techno and tribal sounds.

Stadium (Map p180; ☎ 626 3323; www.stadiumjakarta.com; Jl Hayum Waruk 111 FF-JJ) The big daddy of Jakarta's scene, this club has the heritage (established in 1997), the reputation (DJs including Sasha and Dave Seaman have spun here), the capacity (around 4000), the sound system and the crowd. There are four levels, but the main room is where the prime dance-floor action is – a dark, cavernous space of pounding beats full of clubbers in sunglasses. This ain't no disco – alcohol is not the drug of choice, and Stadium has a distinctly underground vibe. Its weekend session is totally hard-core – beginning on Thursday evening and running until Monday morning.

Entertainment

Check the entertainment pages of *Time Out Jakarta* or *Jakarta Kini* for films, concerts and special events.

THEATRE

Taman Ismail Marzuki (TIM; Map p182; ☎ 3193 7325; www.tamanismailmarzuki.com; Jl Cikini Raya 73) TIM is Jakarta's principal cultural centre with a cinema, theatres (performances include Javanese dance, plays and gamelan concerts), two art galleries and several restaurants in the complex. The tourist office and listings magazines have program details.

Gedung Kesenian Jakarta (Map p182; ☎ 380 8282; Jl Gedung Kesenian 1) Hosts traditional dance and theatre, as well as European classical music and dance.

Museum Wayang (Map p185; ☎ 692 9560; Taman Fatahillah) *Wayang kulit* and *golek* performances are held on Sunday between 10am and 2pm at this museum.

Shopping

Given the climate, it's not surprising that Jakartans love their air-conditioned malls – there are over 100 in the metropolitan area.

Plaza Indonesia (Map p182; www.plazaindonesia.com; Jl Thamrin;) Exclusive Plaza Indonesia tops Jakarta's A-list for shopping centres. There's a good, surprisingly inexpensive food court in the basement.

Pasar Pagi Mangga Dua (Map p180; Jl Mangga Dua) This is an enormous wholesale market with some of Jakarta's cheapest clothes, accessories and shoes, as well as a host of other goods. Quality can be a problem, though.

Plaza Senayan (Map p180; Jl Asia Afrika; 9am-9pm) One of Jakarta's glossiest malls, with a fine bookshop and a Body Shop.

For arts and crafts, also check out **Pasar Seni** (Art Market; Map p180; Jl Raya Kampung Bandan; 10am-10pm), at Taman Impian Jaya Ancol, and Jakarta's famous **flea market** (Map p182; Jl Surabaya; 9am-6pm). Bargain like crazy – prices may be up to 10 times the value of the goods.

Getting There & Away

Jakarta is the main travel hub for Indonesia, with flights and ships to destinations all over the archipelago. Buses depart for cities across Java, and Bali and Sumatra, while trains are an excellent way to get across Java.

AIR

Soekarno-Hatta International Airport (off Map p180) is 35km northwest of the city.

Domestic airline offices in Jakarta include the following:

Batavia Air (Map p182; ☎ 3899 9888; www.batavia-air.co.id; Jl Ir H Juanda 15)

Garuda Indonesia (Map p184; ☎ 231 1801, 0804-180 7807; www.garuda-indonesia.com; Garuda Bldg, Jl Merdeka Selatan 13)

Lion Air (Map p182; ☎ 632 6039; www.lionair.co.id; Jl Gajah Mada 7)

Mandala Air (Map p184; ☎ 314 4838, 0804-123 4567; www.mandalaair.com; Jl Wahid Hasyim 84-88)

Merpati (Map p180; ☎ 654 8888, 0800-101 2345; www.merpati.co.id; Jl Angkasa Blok B/15 Kav 2-3, Kemayoran)

See p173 for international airlines serving Jakarta.

BOAT

The **Pelni ticket office** (Map p180; ☎ 421 2893; www.pelni.com; Jl Angkasa 18; 8am-4pm Mon-Fri, to 1pm Sat) is 13km northeast of the city centre in Kemayoran. Tickets (plus commission) can be bought through Pelni agents, including **Menara Buana Surya** (Map p182; ☎ 314 2464; Jl Menteng Raya 29) in the Tedja Buana building, 500m east of Jl Jaksa. Routes can be found on the boat transport map (Map p175).

Pelni ships all arrive at and depart from Pelabuhan Satu (Dock No 1) at Tanjung Priok (Map p180), 13km northeast of the city centre. Busway Koridor 10 (which was slated to begin in mid-2009) should provide the fastest connection to the port, and Koridor 12 should provide an additional link some time in 2010. A taxi from Jl Jaksa costs around 70,000Rp.

BUS

So many buses leave Jakarta's bus stations that you can usually just front up at the station and join the chaos, though it pays to book ahead. Travel agencies on Jl Jaksa sell tickets and usually include transport to the terminal, which saves a lot of hassle, though they'll charge a commission for this. Jakarta has four main bus stations, all well out of the city centre. There are buses that will take you to each station from the city centre; see the boxed text, p190.

Kalideres bus terminal (off Map p180; ☎ 541 4996) is 15km northwest of the city centre and has frequent buses to destinations west of Jakarta, such as Merak (28,000Rp, two hours). Take a Koridor 3 TransJakarta bus to get here.

Kampung Rambutan bus terminal (Map p180; ☎ 840 0062) is 18km south of the city and primarily handles buses to destinations south and southeast of Jakarta, such as Bogor (normal/air-con 9000/12,000Rp, 45 minutes) and Cianjur (26,000Rp, 2½ hours). Koridor 7 TransJakarta buses serve this terminal.

Pulo Gadung bus terminal (Map p180; ☎ 489 3742), 12km east of the city centre, serves central and eastern Java, Sumatra and Bali. Destinations include Bandung, via the toll road (42,000Rp, three hours), and Yogyakarta (from 90,000Rp, 12 hours). Sumatra is a long haul from Jakarta by bus; most travellers fly these days. Services to Sumatra tend to leave between 10am and 3pm. Destinations include Bengkulu (from 210,000Rp). Koridor 4 or 2 TransJakarta buses serve here.

Lebak Bulus bus terminal (Map p180) is 16km southwest of the city and also handles some deluxe buses to Yogyakarta, Surabaya and Bali. Most departures are in the late afternoon or evening.

MINIBUS

Door-to-door *travel* minibuses are not a good option in Jakarta because it can take hours to pick up or drop off passengers in the traffic jams. Some travel agencies book them, but you may have to go to a depot on the city outskirts. **Media Taxis** (Map p184; ☎ 390 9010; Jl Johar 15) has minibuses to Bandung (75,000Rp).

TRAIN

Jakarta's four main train stations are quite central, making trains the easiest way out of the city. The most convenient and important is Gambir train station (Map p182), on the eastern side of Merdeka Sq, a 15-minute walk from Jl Jaksa. Gambir handles express trains to Bogor, Bandung, Yogyakarta, Solo, Semarang and Surabaya. Some Gambir trains also stop at Kota train station (Map p185) in the north of the city. The Pasar Senen train station (Map p180) is to the east and mostly has *ekonomi*-class trains. Tanah Abang (Map p180) train station has *ekonomi* trains to the west.

TRANSJAKARTA BUSWAY

Jakarta has a new network of clean air-conditioned buses called TransJakarta that run on busways (designated lanes that are closed to all other traffic). Journey times have been slashed, and they now represent, by far, the quickest way to get around the city.

Most busways have been constructed in the centre of existing highways, and stations have been positioned (roughly) at 1km intervals. Access is via elevated walkways and each station has a shelter. Eight busway lines (called *koridor*) were up and running at the time of research, with a total of 15 planned, which should eventually form a network from Tanjung Priok south to Kampung Rambutan.

Tickets cost 3500Rp, payable before you board, which covers you to any destination in the network (regardless of how many *koridor* you use). Buses (5am to 10pm) are well maintained and not too crowded as conductors (usually) ensure that maximum passenger numbers are not exceeded.

The busway system has been a great success, but as most middle- and upper-class Jakartans remain as addicted as ever to their cars, the city's famous *macet* (traffic jams) look set to continue for a good few years yet.

For express trains, tickets can be bought in advance at the booking offices at the northern end of Gambir train station, while the ticket windows at the southern end are only for tickets bought on the day of departure. Check timetables online at www.infoka.kereta-api.com, or consult the helpful staff at the station's **information office** (☎ 692 9194). For more information on these trains, see p178.

There's a (slightly pricey) taxi booking desk inside Gambir train station; the fare to Jl Jaksa is 35,000Rp.

Bogor

Comfortable *Pakuan Express* trains (8500Rp, one hour) leave from Juanda and Gambir train stations roughly every hour until 9pm. No-frills trains (4000Rp, 90 minutes) also run this route, about every 30 minutes, but can be horribly crowded during rush hours (watch your gear).

Bandung

There are frequent trains to Bandung along a scenic hilly track, but be sure to book in advance (especially on weekends and public holidays).

Six efficient and comfortable *Parahyangan* services depart from Gambir train station daily for Bandung (*bisnis*/*eksekutif* 45,000/65,000Rp, 3¼ hours) between 5.15am and 4.30pm. Seven more luxurious *Argo Gede* (*eksekutif* 75,000Rp, three hours) services cover the same route from 6.10am to 7.30pm.

Cirebon

Most trains that run along the north coast or to Yogyakarta go through Cirebon. Two of the best services from Gambir train station are the *Cirebon Express* (*bisnis*/*eksekutif* 60,000/75,000Rp, three hours), with five daily departures, and the *Argo Jati* (*bisnis*/*eksekutif* 70,000/85,000Rp, three hours), which runs twice daily at 9am and 5.10pm.

Surabaya

Most trains between Jakarta and Surabaya take the shorter northern route via Semarang, though a few take the longer southern route via Yogyakarta. Trains from Gambir range from the *Gumerang* (*bisnis* 140,000Rp, 13 hours), which departs at 6pm, to the smart *Argo Bromo Anggrek* (special *eksekutif* class from 260,000Rp, 9½ hours), which departs at 9.30am and 9.30pm.

Yogyakarta & Solo

The most luxurious trains are the *Argo Lawu* (220,000Rp, 8¼ hours) departing at 8pm, and the *Argo Dwipangga* (225,000Rp, 8¼ hours) departing at 8am. These trains go to Solo and stop at Yogyakarta, 45 minutes before Solo, but cost the same to either destination.

Cheaper services operating from the Pasar Senen train station to Yogyakarta are the *Fajar Yogyakarta* (*bisnis* 110,000Rp, 8½ hours), departing at 6.20am, and the *Senja Utama Yogya* (110,000Rp, nine hours) at 7.20pm. The *Senja Solo* goes to Solo (110,000Rp, 10 hours) at 8.30pm and also stops in Yogyakarta.

Getting Around

For details of Jakarta's excellent new TransJakarta busway network, see the boxed text, opposite. Other buses are not very useful for visitors as they are much slower, hotter (they have no air-conditioning) and crowded (pickpockets can be a problem). Nevertheless, you may come across regular city buses, *patas* (express) buses and orange Metro minibuses from time to time; fares generally cost between 2000Rp and 3000Rp.

LOCAL TRANSPORT

Bajaj (pronounced ba-jai) are Indonesian túk-túk. There are few about now in central Jakarta. If you hire one, it's worth remembering that they are not allowed on many major thoroughfares.

TAXI

Metered taxis cost 6000Rp for the first kilometre and 250Rp for each subsequent 100m. Make sure the *argo* (meter) is used.

Bluebird cabs (☎ 794 1234; www.bluebirdgroup.com) can be booked ahead and have the best reputation; do *not* risk travelling with the less reputable firms.

Typical taxi fares from Jl Thamrin: to Kota (20,000Rp) or Blok M (30,000Rp). Any toll road charges are extra and are paid by the passengers.

GETTING INTO TOWN

Soekarno-Hatta International Airport is 35km northwest of the city. It's about an hour away via a toll road (up to two hours during rush hour).

Damri (☎ 460 3708, 550 1290) airport buses (20,000Rp, every 30 minutes) run between 5am and 7pm between the airport and Gambir train station (near Jl Jaksa) and several other points in the city, including Blok M.

Taxis from the airport to Jl Thamrin/Jl Jaksa cost about 140,000Rp including tolls. Book via the official taxi desks to be safe, rather than using the unlicensed drivers outside.

A new train line is being constructed between Manggarai train station in central Jakarta and the airport; it's expected to be operational sometime in 2010.

BOGOR

☎ 0251 / pop 830,000

Known throughout Java as *kota hujan* (city of rain) for having over 300 storms a year, Bogor became a home from home for Sir Stamford Raffles during the British interregnum, a respite for those mad dogs and Englishmen that preferred *not* to go out in the midday sun. These days, this once-quiet town is a suburb of Jakarta, with the traffic and hubbub to match. But while Bogor itself clogs up with bemo and mopeds, the real oasis remains untouched. Planted at the very hub of the city, with *macet* to north, south, east and west, the town's world-class botanical gardens remain – in the words of one upstanding British visitor – 'a jolly fine day out'. They are a good day trip from Jakarta, one hour away.

Information

Wartels (telephone offices) can be found next to the post office and train station. There's free wi-fi available at the Botani Sq mall. ATMs abound.

BCA Bank (Jl Ir H Juanda 28) Has an ATM and changes money.

Post office (Jl Ir H Juanda; 8am-5pm Mon-Fri, to noon Sat) Has internet access.

Tourist office (☎ 081 111 0347; agus_pribadi@hotmail.com; Jl Dewi Sartika 51; 8am-4pm) The team here can help out with most queries, provide a city map and offer excellent, well-priced tours.

Sights

A veritable 'green lung' in the heart of the city, Bogor's botanical gardens, the **Kebun Raya** (Great Garden; ☎ 322187; www.bogor.indo.net.id/kri; Jl Otto Iskandardinata; admission 9500Rp; 8am-5pm), are simply outstanding. British governor Sir Stamford Raffles first laid out a garden, but this was later expanded by Dutch botanists, including Johannes Teysmann, who planted and developed the garden over a 50-year period in the 19th century. Today the garden is an important research centre, and scientists based here are investigating new medical and agricultural uses for its many rare specimens. There are more than 15,000 species of trees and plants, including 400 types of magnificent palms.

Things can get hectic on Sundays, but during the week this is one of West Java's true oases (apart from the odd mosquito – bring some repellent). Highlights include the

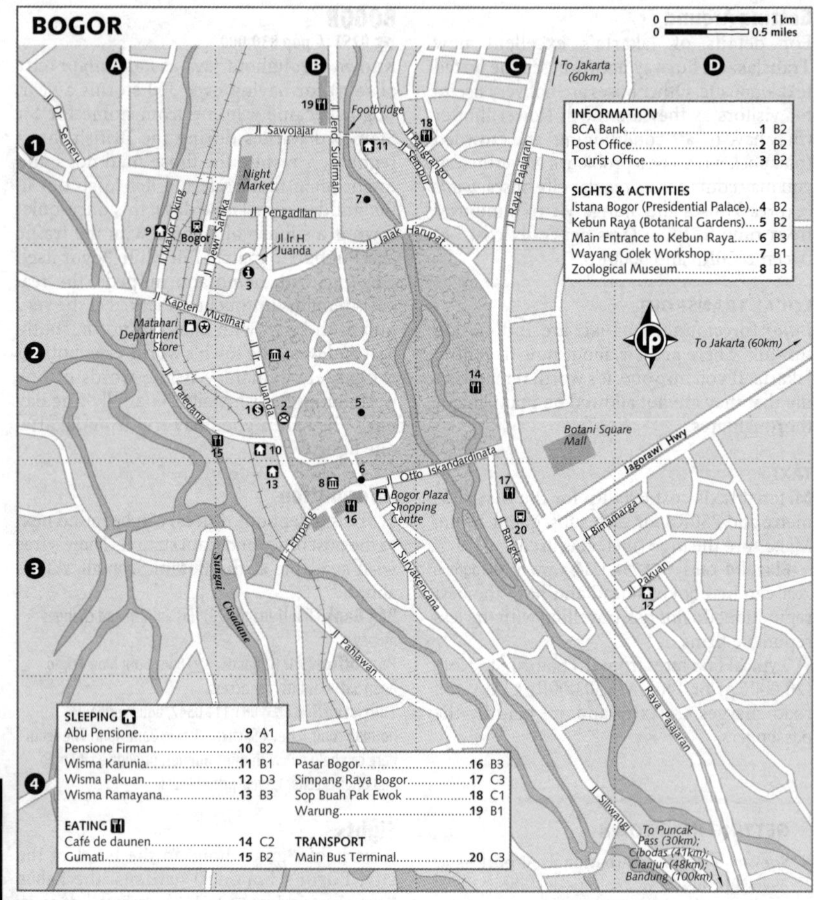

incredible collections of palms, the bizarre pandan trees with their 'spider leg' roots and the orchid house (2000Rp extra). There's a great cafe-restaurant in the grounds (Café de daunen, opposite).

The **Istana Bogor** (Presidential Palace), built by the Dutch and much favoured by Soekarno (Soeharto ignored it), stands beside the gardens, and deer graze on its lawns. Visits are by organised tour only; the tourist office may get you into one.

Near the entrance to the botanical gardens, the **Zoological Museum** (admission 2000Rp; 8am-4pm Sat-Thu, 8am-noon Fri) has a motley but interesting collection of zoological oddities, including the skeleton of a blue whale, beetles as big as tennis balls and a pooch-sized Flores rat.

If you are interested in seeing a Javanese craftsman at work, Pak Dase makes quality wooden puppets at his **wayang golek workshop** (Lebak Kantion RT 02/VI; 8am-6pm) among the labyrinthine passages on the west side of the river near Jl Jend Sudirman.

Sleeping

Bogor has some good family-run places; most include a basic breakfast in the room price.

Pensione Firman (☎ 832 3246; Jl Paledang 48; r 60,000-140,000Rp) This venerable guest house has been serving travellers for decades and though it's looking decidedly ramshackle these days, it's still a secure and friendly base – English-speaking owner Warda looks after her guests well.

INDONESIA

Abu Pensione (☎ 832 2893; Jl Mayor Oking 15; r with fan 90,000-150,000Rp, with air-con & hot water 220,000Rp; ❄) This is a good choice near the train station, with a selection of decent clean rooms set at the rear of the property around a pleasant quiet garden. There's a great little cafe, with cheap grub and views over a gurgling stream.

Wisma Pakuan (☎ 831 9430; Jl Pakuan 12; r with balcony 150,000Rp, with air-con 200,000Rp; ❄) Pakuan occupies a large, modern family home a short stroll from the bus terminal. Rooms are very generously sized, in good condition and have hot-water bathrooms, but ask for one at the rear, as it's located on a busy street.

Also recommended:

Wisma Karunia (☎ 832 3411; Jl Sempur 33-35; r 60,000Rp, s/d with private bathroom 60,000/85,000Rp) A hike from the city centre but offers a quiet base and it's run by friendly folk.

Wisma Ramayana (☎ 832 0364; Jl Ir H Juanda 54; r 80,000Rp) Worth considering as it's so close to the gardens, but some rooms are a tad damp.

Eating & Drinking

Cheap *warung* (food stalls) appear at night along Jl Dewi Sartika and Jl Jend Sudirman. During the day you'll find plenty of *warung* and good fruit at Pasar Bogor, the market close to the main Kebun Raya gates.

Sop Buah Pak Ewok (☎ 215 1369; Jl Bukittunggul 5; fruit punch 7000Rp) This is a great, very casual place popular with students for its inexpensive, delicious and refreshing bowls of fruit punch, which are tropical fruits of the season served up with ice.

Simpang Raya Bogor (☎ 420 1577; Jl Raya Pajajaran; meals from 15,000Rp) A huge Pandang restaurant serving up Sumatra's finest and spiciest. Heaves with customers by early evening; stroll on in and find a seat wherever there is room.

Gumati (☎ 832 4318; www.cafegumati.com; Jl Palendang 28; mains 15,000-59,000Rp; 🕑 10am-10pm) An imposing restaurant with wonderful vistas over Bogor's red-tiled rooftops to Gunung Salak from its two huge terraces – there's even a small pool here. You'll find an extensive menu, with tapas-style snacks and specials (try the *paket timbal komplit*); no booze though.

Café de daunen (☎ 835 0023; meals 25,000-59,000Rp) Inside the botanical gardens, this is the nicest setting in town for a meal, with sweeping views down across a meadow to the water lily ponds. It's a little pricey, but the revamped menu has tasty food, including fish 'n' chips, pasta and good Indonesian dishes.

Getting There & Away

Bogor is a good place to hire a car and driver for a trip around the countryside; ask the tourist board to recommend someone. Prices start at around 450,000Rp per day.

BUS

Every 15 minutes or so, buses depart from Jakarta's Kampung Rambutan bus terminal (normal/air-con 9000/12,000Rp, 45 minutes).

Hourly air-conditioned Damri buses head direct to Jakarta's Soekarno-Hatta International Airport (55,000Rp) from 4am to 6pm from Jl Raya Pajajaran.

Buses depart frequently to Cianjur (14,000/20,000Rp, two hours) and Bandung (30,000/42,000Rp, 3½ hours); but at weekends these buses are not allowed to go via the scenic Puncak Pass and therefore travel via Sukabumi. Other bus destinations from Bogor include Pelabuhan Ratu (27,000Rp, three hours) and Labuan (38,000Rp, four hours).

Air-con, door-to-door *travel* minibuses go to Bandung for 60,000Rp. **Dimas Dewa** (☎ 653 671) has the best buses. Phone for a pick-up.

TRAIN

Comfortable *Pakuan* express trains (8500Rp, one hour) leave Bogor for the capital roughly every hour. *Ekonomi* trains (4500Rp, 1½ hours) run even more frequently, but are usually packed.

Getting Around

Angkot (2000Rp) make slow circuits of the gardens, taking in most central locations en route.

CIBODAS & CIANJUR

☎ 0263 / pop Cibodas 20,000, Cianjur 156,000

Leaving Bogor you pass through the **Puncak Pass**, a once-lovely highland area destroyed by a rampant resort sprawl of hotels, weekend homes and factory-shopping outlets. But continuing east of here you'll travel through some of Java's finest highland scenery: a bewitching landscape of plunging valleys, tea plantations and cool, misty mornings.

Cibodas, 4km off the main road, is home to the stunning **Kebun Raya Botanical Gardens** (☎ 512233; www.bogor.indo.net.id; per person/car 6000/15,500Rp; 8am-4pm), an incredible collection of over 5000 plants and trees from over 1000 species set in impossibly lush grounds of alpine forest, waterfalls and grasslands. The gardens spread over the steep lower slopes of volcanoes Gunung Gede and Gunung Pangrango at an altitude of 1300m to 1440m, making them one of the dampest places in Java. The gardens were listed by Unesco as a World Heritage Reserve in 1977. Highlights include the cacti greenhouse, eucalyptus forests, some vertiginous Japanese bamboo and the prolific birdlife, including rare sightings of the Javan hawk eagle.

From April to October, you can also climb **Gunung Gede**, a spectacular 2958m volcanic peak with a huge crater; from its summit it's possible to see the Indian Ocean and Java Sea on clear days. Register for the climb and obtain your permit (6000Rp) from the PHKA office just outside the gardens' entrance. It's six hours to the summit so start early (usually around 2am). Guides to the summit can also be hired here for around 300,000Rp at the office, or for around 350,000Rp at Freddy's Homestay (see right).

Continuing east it's 19km to the market town of Cianjur, an important, if sprawling, rice-growing centre that makes a good base to explore the intriguing sights of the region. These include the lush hillsides and processing plants of the **Gedeh tea plantation** (admission free; 8am-4pm Mon-Sat), 15km northwest of town, and **Jangari**, a 'floating village' on a large lake with a substantial fish-farming community and a wonderful fish restaurant, 18km northeast of town. Cianjur has several banks (with ATMs) on main drag Jl Cokroaminoto, and internet cafes are grouped together on Jl Siti Jenab.

Sleeping & Eating

Accommodation tends to be expensive close to the Puncak Pass as the area is popular with wealthy weekending Jakartans. The Cianjur homestay program (see below) is a good way to interact with local people.

Freddy's Homestay (☎ 515473; r incl breakfast 150,000Rp) Located down a narrow alleyway 500m before the gardens, Freddy's is *the* base in the area for birders. Rooms here are very simple and clean but overpriced. Nevertheless this homestay does offer good information and guides can be hired.

Cibodas Guest House (☎ 512 051; r from 125,000Rp) This is an outstanding little Balinese-owned place. Very attractive and well-priced rooms are perched on a shelf overlooking a valley; all with balcony, sprung mattresses and private bathroom (and hot water on request). It's about 4km south of the entrance to the gardens. It also does meals (20,000Rp to 50,000Rp).

Cianjur's speciality is *lontong* (sticky rice with tofu in a delicious sweet coconut sauce); there are several *warung* on Jl Dewisartika that specialise in this dish.

Getting There & Away

On weekdays, buses leave Jakarta's Kampung Rambutan bus terminal every 30 minutes to Cipanas (normal/air-con 17,000/23,000Rp, two hours) and Cianjur (21,000/26,000Rp, 2½ hours). At weekends (when traffic is terrible around Puncuk Pass) buses are routed via Sukabumi (add an extra hour to your journey time, and 5000Rp). Buses to/from Bandung (14,000/20,000Rp, 1¾ hours) run every half-hour.

There are buses to Bogor from Cianjur (14,000/20,000Rp, two hours) and the highway by Cipanas every 20 minutes; *angkot* ply the route on Sundays.

INDONESIA

LIVE WITH THE LOCALS

The **Cianjur Homestay Programme** (☎ 081 7085 6691; www.cianjuradventure.com.com) is a superb initiative set up by author Yudi Sujana, who lived for years in New Zealand, that allows travellers to experience life in a nontouristy town in Java. Yudi and his team all speak fluent English, so it's a wonderful opportunity to get to understand Sundanese and Indonesian culture. School visits, sightseeing trips and hikes (and occasionally some voluntary work opportunities) are offered at backpacking rates. Guests pay US$12 per person per day, which includes family accommodation and three meals; it's best to book a place a few days in advance. Airport pick-ups and drop-offs can also be arranged at very moderate rates, allowing you to bypass Jakarta completely.

BANDUNG

☎ 022 / pop 2.7 million

Big, burly Bandung comes ball bat to the back of the head after the verdant mountains around Cibodas. Once dubbed the 'Paris of Java', this is one of Indonesia's megacities (the Bandung conurbation is over seven million) with a city centre that's prone to Jakarta-style congestion. But if you rummage through the concrete sprawl, odd pockets of interest remain, including some Dutch art-deco monuments, the quirky fibreglass statues of Jeans St, and some cool cafes popular with the thousands of students who call this city home. At an altitude of 750m, Bandung's climate is also far less oppressive than the capital's.

Orientation

The main drag, Jl Asia Afrika, runs through the heart of the city centre past the *alun alun* (main public square). Most budget accommodation is dotted around the train station, while Jl Braga has a strip of cafes, bars and restaurants.

Information

Most of the upmarket shopping malls have free wi-fi. *Wartel* aplenty can be found just south of the train station.

Adventist Hospital (☎ 203 4386; Jl Cihampelas 161) A missionary hospital with English-speaking staff.

Bandung Tourist Information Centre (☎ 420 6644; Jl Asia Afrika; 🕑 9am-5pm Mon-Sat, 9am-2pm Sun) Managed by the very helpful Ajid Suriana, this office is located in the foyer of the central mosque. There's also a desk at the train station. Offers excellent free booklets, maps and information on cultural events.

Bank Mandiri (Jl Merdeka) Has an ATM and exchanges travellers cheques and cash.

Main post office (cnr Jl Banceuy & Jl Asia Afrika; 🕑 8am-7pm Mon-Sat) Opposite the *alun alun*.

X-net (Jl Lengkong Kecil 38; per hr 5000Rp; 🕑 8am-10pm) Internet access.

Sights & Activities

CITY CENTRE

The **Museum Konperensi** (Conference Museum) in the **Gedung Merdeka** (Freedom Bldg; ☎ 423 8031; Jl Asia Afrika 65; admission free; 🕑 9am-3pm Mon-Fri) is dedicated to Bandung's 1955 Asia–Africa conference, attended by Soekarno, Ho Chi Minh, Nasser, Nehru and other leaders from the developing world. The scanty exhibits are pretty disappointing, but there are a few interesting photos.

There are some very fine Dutch art deco structures to admire on Jl Jenderal Sudirman, two of the best being the Grand Hotel Preanger and the Savoy Homann Hotel, both of which have imposing facades.

NORTH BANDUNG

Bandung Institute of Technology (ITB; Jl Ganeca) is one of the most important universities in Indonesia, with a reputation for activism – students here published corruption allegations that helped bring down Soeharto. The canteen inside the *asrama mahasiswa* (dormitory) complex is a good place to socialise with students.

About 1km west, Jl Cihampelas is known to all as **Jeans Street** on account of the profusion of cheap denim stores here, many hung with supersized promotional statues of Rambo, Superman and the like.

Museum Geologi (Geological Museum; Jl Diponegoro 57; admission free; 🕑 9am-3.30pm Mon-Thu, 9am-1.30pm Sat & Sun), northeast of the city centre, is a mecca for budding vulcanologists.

ADU DOMBA

One of Bandung's most popular pastimes is whiling away a Sunday morning watching a traditional *adu domba* (ram-butting fight). As the loser of this tête-à-tête turns and flees once the scrap is over, it's not a bloodthirsty business. Fights are usually held between 9am and 1pm but check schedules and location first with the Bandung Tourist Information Centre.

Tours

Freelance, English-speaking tour guide **Ahmadi** (☎ 0852-2106 3788; enoss_travellers@yahoo.com) runs good one-day tours (300,000Rp per person) of the sights to the north and south of the city, and can set up trips to Pangandaran (around 800,000Rp).

Sleeping

Many of Bandung's very cheapest places close to the train station on Jl Kebonjati are looking quite run down these days and the area is very dark after nightfall. Backpackers should up their budgets in this prosperous city.

Guest House Pos Cihampelas (☎ 423 5213; Jl Cihampelas 12; economy r from 50,000Rp, standard from 90,000Rp; ❄) The best bet in the city for a cheap bed, this place has a plethora of different rooms – from humble but clean economy options with shared bathroom facilities to air-con doubles. English is spoken, there's a lounge area and a very cheap in-house *warung* (meals from 10,000Rp).

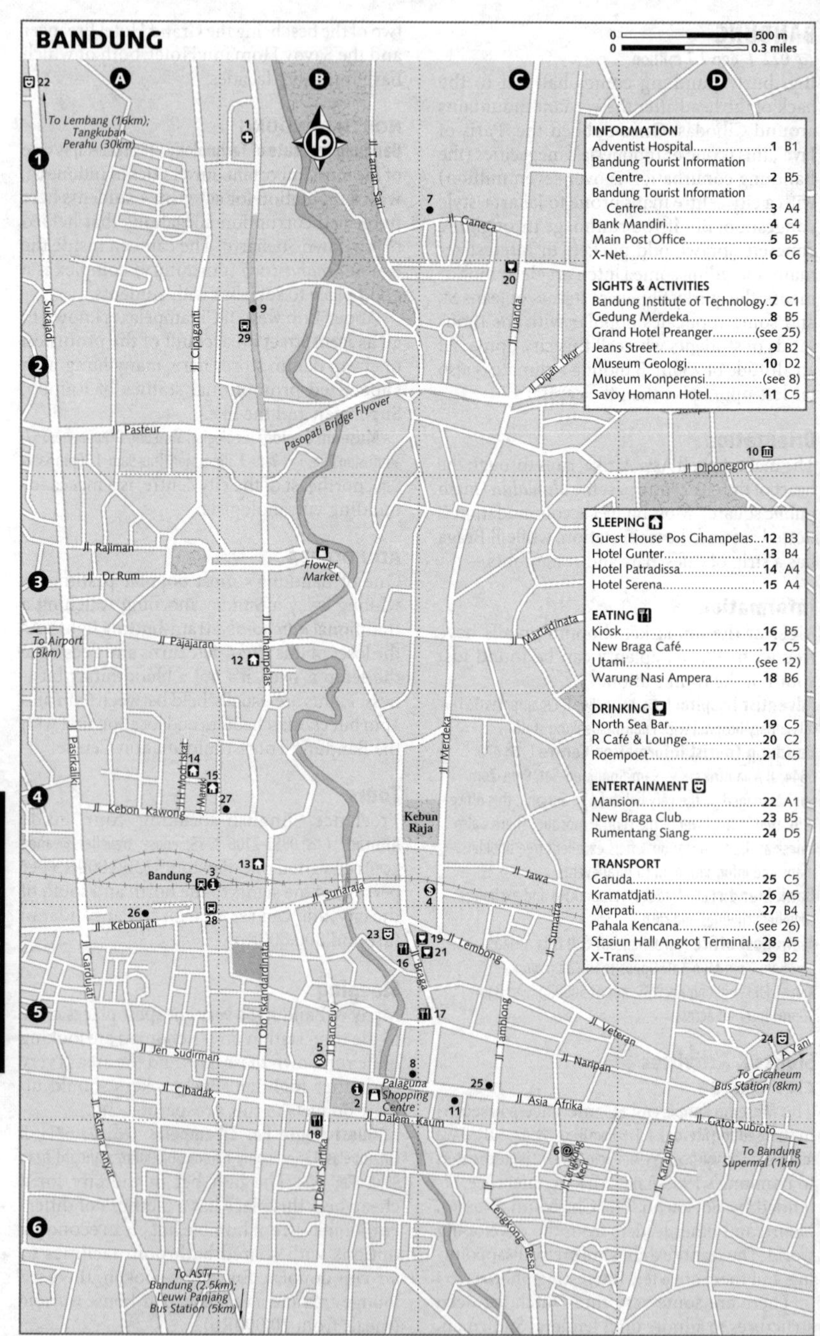
BANDUNG
0 500 m
0 0.3 miles
A
B
C
D
1
2
3
4
5
6
To Lembang (16km); Tangkuban Perahu (30km)
To Airport (3km)
To ASTI Bandung (2.5km); Leuwi Panjang Bus Station (5km)
To Cicaheum Bus Station (8km)
To Bandung Supermal (1km)
Jl Taman Sari
Jl Ganeca
Jl Juanda
Jl Sukajadi
Jl Cipaganti
Jl Dipati Ukur
Jl Pasteur
Pasopati Bridge Flyover
Jl Diponegoro
Jl Rajiman
Jl Dr Rum
Flower Market
Jl Pajajaran
Jl Cihampelas
Jl Martadinata
Jl Pasirkaliki
Jl H Moch Iskat
Jl Maruk
Jl Kebon Kawong
Kebun Raja
Jl Merdeka
Bandung
Jl Jawa
Jl Suniaraja
Jl Kebonjati
Jl Sumatra
Jl Lembong
Jl Braga
Jl Garduljati
Jl Oto Iskandardinata
Jl Banceuy
Jl Tamblong
Jl Veteran
Jl Jen Sudirman
Jl Naripan
Jl A Yani
Jl Cibadak
Palaguna Shopping Centre
Jl Asia Afrika
Jl Dalem Kaum
Jl Gatot Subroto
Jl Astana Anyar
Jl Dewi Sartika
Jl Lengkong Kecil
Jl Karapitan
Lengkong Besar
INFORMATION
Adventist Hospital 1 B1
Bandung Tourist Information Centre 2 B5
Bandung Tourist Information Centre 3 A4
Bank Mandiri 4 C4
Main Post Office 5 B5
X-Net 6 C6
SIGHTS & ACTIVITIES
Bandung Institute of Technology 7 C1
Gedung Merdeka 8 B5
Grand Hotel Preanger (see 25)
Jeans Street 9 B2
Museum Geologi 10 D2
Museum Konperensi (see 8)
Savoy Homann Hotel 11 C5
SLEEPING
Guest House Pos Cihampelas 12 B3
Hotel Gunter 13 B4
Hotel Patradissa 14 A4
Hotel Serena 15 A4
EATING
Kiosk 16 B5
New Braga Café 17 C5
Utami (see 12)
Warung Nasi Ampera 18 B6
DRINKING
North Sea Bar 19 C5
R Café & Lounge 20 C2
Roempoet 21 C5
ENTERTAINMENT
Mansion 22 A1
New Braga Club 23 B5
Rumentang Siang 24 D5
TRANSPORT
Garuda 25 C5
Kramatdjati 26 A5
Merpati 27 B4
Pahala Kencana (see 26)
Stasiun Hall Angkot Terminal 28 A5
X-Trans 29 B2
INDONESIA

Hotel Patradissa (☎ 420 6680; Jl H Moch Iskat 8; r incl breakfast 120,000-200,000Rp; ❄) This slightly quirky guest house may be old-fashioned in appearance, but it's secure, staff are friendly and helpful, and the location is quiet. There are plenty of rooms, all with a chintzy touch that granny would approve of, and some have air-con.

Hotel Gunter (☎ 420 3763; Jl Oto Iskandardinata 20; r with/without air-con 150,000/175,000Rp; ❄) Gunter vaguely resembles a motel, and has clean spacious rooms complete with 1970s style furnishings; all have a porch area with chairs that face a central garden bursting with flowering shrubs and topiary. Tours can be organised here. Prices rise a little at weekends.

our pick Hotel Serena (☎ 420 4317; Jl Maruk 4-6; http://serenabandung.multiply.com; r incl breakfast from 238,000Rp; ❄) This classy little modern hotel offers outstanding value and a good degree of minimalist style. All rooms are smart and immaculately clean, and have comfortable beds and reading lights. The hot-water bathrooms have a sparkle. Prices rise 10% at weekends.

Eating

Jl Braga has a strip of cafes, restaurants and bakeries, but the city's really swanky, hip new places are concentrated in the north of the city. For cheap food check out the night *warung* on Jl Cikapundung Barat, across from the *alun alun*.

Bandung Supermal (Jl Gatot Subroto 289; meals 10,000-45,000Rp) In the east of the city, this upmarket shopping mall has a good food court, tonnes of fast-food joints, cafes and a Bread Talk bakery.

Utami (☎ 7078 7075; Jl Cihampelas 12; meals 12,000-20,000Rp) This is a very clean, attractive little eatery where a great deal of care is taken over the food – you'll find plenty of fresh greens, tasty *ayam goreng* and two feisty sambals.

our pick New Braga Café (☎ 421 1567; Jl Braga 15; meals 12,000-21,000Rp; 🕑 11.30am-9.30pm, closed Fri) An excellent, friendly Sundansese restaurant in an elegant building that dates back to colonial days. All the food is laid out on covered plates and bowls for you to choose from; there are plenty of vegetarian dishes.

Warung Nasi Ampera (Jl Dewi Sartika 8; meals 14,000Rp; 🕑 24hr) Just south of the *alun alun*, this clean place is the best of several traditional Sundanese places on this road. Serves up delicious fresh *tempe* (tempeh) and curries around the clock.

Kiosk (Braga City Walk Mall, Jl Braga; meals 15,000-20,000Rp; 📶) This great little mini food court on the ground floor of the Braga City Walk is ideal for sampling some unusual snacks such as *pempek* (fish or egg fried with sago in a rich dark sauce) from Sumatra and noodle dishes.

Drinking

Jl Braga is the drinking hub of the city.

Roempoet (Jl Braga 80) Intimate bar with live bands (mainly playing covers) and a social vibe. Sizzling satay is also served up (mains 20,000Rp) here.

North Sea Bar (Jl Braga 82) The beer flows into the wee small hours at this pub-style expat and bar-girl hang-out. There's a popular pool table.

R Café & Lounge (Jl Juanda 97; 📶) Happening, very metropolitan bar-cafe with a terrace facing busy Juanda, stylish seating, mocktails and cocktails.

Entertainment

Bandung is a capital of Sundanese culture, particularly performing arts. Performance times are haphazard; check with the tourist information centre for the latest schedules.

Rumentang Siang (☎ 423 3562; Jl Baranangsiang 1) Bandung's premier performing arts centre, where *wayang golek*, Jaipongan (West Javanese dance), *pencak silat* (the art of self-defence), Sandiwara (traditional Javanese theatre) and *ketoprak* (popular Javanese folk theatre) performances are held.

ASTI-Bandung (☎ 731 4982; Jl Buah Batu 212) In the southern part of the city, this is a school for traditional Sundanese arts – music, dancing and *pencak silat*.

The unpretentious **New Braga Club** (☎ 423 2006; Jl Braga) is a good bet in the downtown district. Elsewhere in the city, **Mansion** (☎ 081 861 3743; Paris Van Java Mall, Jl Sukajadi 137-139) is a very popular dance club that draws a glam crowd.

Getting There & Away

AIR

Bandung airport (code BDO) is served by **Merpati** (☎ 426 0253; Jl Kebon Kawung 16; www.merpati.co.id) flying to Batam and Surabaya; **Garuda** (☎ 420 9468; Grand Hotel Preanger, Jl Asia Afrika 181), which flies to Singapore; **Air Asia** (☎ 5050 5088; www.airasia.com) connecting Bandung with Kuala Lumpur and Singapore; and **Sriwijaya Air** (☎ 640 5566; www.sriwijayaair-online.com), with planes to Surabaya and on to Denpasar.

BUS

Five kilometres south of the city centre, **Leuwi Panjang bus terminal** (Jl Sukarno Hatta) has buses west to places such as Cianjur (normal/air-con 14,000/20,000Rp, 1¾ hours), Bogor (30,000/42,000Rp, 3¼ hours) and to Jakarta's Kampung Rambutan bus terminal (36,000Rp to 45,000Rp, three hours).

Buses to the east leave from the **Cicaheum bus station** on the eastern outskirts of the city. They include Cirebon (normal/air-con 26,000/38,000Rp, four hours) and Pangandaran (52,000Rp, six hours).

X-Trans (☎ 204 2955; Jl Cihampelas 57) operates a shuttle bus every hour to various drop-off points in central Jakarta (70,000Rp, 2½ hours), and also direct hourly buses that head to Jakarta airport (90,000Rp, three hours). **Sari Harum** (☎ 607 7065) has an air-con *travel* minibus to Pangandaran (80,000Rp, five hours) at 6am. Both **Kramatdjati** (☎ 423 9860; Jl Kebonjati 96) and **Pahala Kencana** (☎ 423 2911; Jl Kebonjati 90) run luxury buses to long-distance destinations, such as Yogyakarta (85,000Rp).

TRAIN

Between them, the *Parahyangan* and *Argo Gede* (*bisnis* 45,000Rp, *eksekutif* 65,000Rp to 75,000Rp, three hours) offer hourly trains to Jakarta's Gambir train station between 4am and 7pm.

Several trains operate on the Bandung–Banjar–Yogyakarta line, most continuing on to Surabaya. The *bisnis*-class *Mutiara Selatan* passes through Bandung at 5pm on its way to Yogyakarta (110,000Rp) and Surabaya (135,000Rp). The *Lodaya* leaves Bandung at 8am for Yogyakarta and Solo (*bisnis*/*eksekutif* 100,000/165,000Rp).

Getting Around

Bandung's airport is 4km northwest of the city centre; it costs about 50,000Rp to get there by the ever-reliable **Bluebird** (☎ 756 1234) taxi.

Stasiun Hall *angkot* terminal is on the south side of the train station, with *angkots* (2000Rp to 3000Rp) to most places, such as Jl Cihampelas and Tangkuban Perahu

Abdul Muis terminal, at the Kebun Kelapa bus station, has *angkot* to Cicaheum and Luewi Panjang bus stations. Big Damri city buses 9 and 11 (2000Rp) run from west to east down Jl Asia Afrika to Cicaheum.

TANGKUBAN PERAHU AREA

Thirty kilometres to the north of Bandung, Tangkuban Perahu (literally 'Overturned Boat') is a huge active volcanic crater at 2076m. Legend tells of a god challenged to build a huge boat during a single night. His opponent, on seeing that he would probably complete this impossible task, brought the sun up early and the boat builder turned his nearly completed boat over in a fit of anger.

The huge **Kawah Ratu** (Queen Crater) at the top is impressive, but as cars can also drive right up here, it's a weekend tourist trap with the usual parade of touts offering eggs to cook in the crater's scalding surface. A park entrance fee of 20,000Rp is payable on arrival.

You can escape the crowds by walking (anticlockwise) around the main crater and along the ridge between the two craters, but parts of it are steep and slippery. Safer and more interesting is the walk to **Kawah Domas**, an active volcanic area of steaming vents and bubbling pools about 1km down from the car park. From here you can follow the trail back to the main road (ask for directions) and flag down a *colt* back to Bandung, or continue to the **Sari Ater Hot Spring Resort** (☎ 0260-471700; admission 12,000Rp, pools extra 20,000Rp; 24hr) at **Ciater**, 8km northeast of Tangkuban Perahu. Guides at Tangkuban Perahu will also offer to lead you to Ciater through the jungle.

From Bandung's minibus terminal, in front of the train station, take a Subang *angkot* (10,000Rp) via Lembang to the park entrance. Minibuses to the top officially cost 12,000Rp per person, but the drivers will probably ask for more – bargain hard.

PANGANDARAN

☎ 0265

Situated on a narrow isthmus, with a broad sweep of sand on either side and a thickly forested national park on the nearby headland, Pangandaran is Java's premier beach resort. Most of the year Pangandaran is a quiet, but the town fills up on holidays (and weekends). Swimming is dodgy but it's a great place to get out on a board, or to learn how.

Pangandaran was hit hard by a tsunami in 2006, but today the town is very much open for business again and there's little evidence of its impact. Sadly, less attention has been devoted to the beach, which is in dire need of a clean up.

Information

A 3500Rp admission charge is levied at the gates on entering Pangandaran. There's no tourist office in town.

BNI ATM (Jl Bulak Laut)

BRI bank (Jl Kidang Pananjung) Changes cash dollars and major brands of travellers cheques.

Magic Mushroom Books (Jl Pasanggrahan) Sells Western titles from a psychedelic shack and also changes money.

Post office (Jl Kidang Pananjung)

Telkom office (Jl Kidang Pananjung)

Tiara Internet (Jl Kedang Pananjung; per hour 12,000Rp)

YK (Jl Pamugaran; per hour 15,000Rp) Helpful place with modern terminals and reasonable speeds.

Sights & Activities

The **Taman Nasional Pangandaran** (Pangandaran National Park; ☎ 081 2149 0153; admission 5500Rp; 🕑 dawn-dusk), which fringes the southern end of Pangandaran, is a stretch of untouched forest populated by barking deer, hornbills and Javan gibbons, featuring some spectacular white-sand beaches. The Boundary Trail offers the best walk through the park, as it skirts the jungle. The park's other trails are somewhat vague; guides charge around 100,000Rp (for a group of four) for a two-hour walk.

Surf lessons (per half-day incl board hire 100,000Rp) are offered at the northern end of the beach. Pangandaran is a good place to learn, and local instructors have 'soft' boards ideal for beginners. You'll find instructors in the Mungil Steak House (see p201).

Tours

Popular Green Canyon tours cost 150,000Rp per person (see p202). There are also tours to **Paradise Island**, an uninhabited nearby island with good beaches and surfing. Day trips cost around 275,000Rp per person (minimum four persons). Mini Tiga Homestay (right) and Mungil Steak House (p201) are good sources for guides.

Sleeping

As Pangandaran has close to 100 hotels you should have no bother finding a bed, except during Christmas and Lebaran (the end of Ramadan) when half of Java seems to head here and prices skyrocket.

Many of Pangandaran's best homestays and *losmen* (basic accommodation) are crowded along the northern stretch of the town's western beach. None of the following have hot water.

Pondok Moris (☎ 639490; Gang Moris 3; r 60,000Rp) Close to the eastern end of the beach this friendly little place has smallish rooms with character that are surrounded by greenery. It would be a veritable oasis, if it wasn't so close to the mosque.

Losmen Mini II (☎ 639298; Jl Kalen Buhaya 14; s 60,000-80,000Rp, d 70,000-120,000Rp; ❄) An excellent choice, this efficiently managed guest house has very clean, tidy rooms and beds with good-quality mattresses; some have balconies. It's run by a friendly, house-proud lady.

our pick **Mini Tiga Homestay** (☎ 639436; katmaja95@yahoo.fr; s/d incl breakfast 65,000/80,000Rp) The most popular place in town with backpackers and rightfully so. Mini Tiga has spacious rooms (all with en-suite bathrooms and Western toilets). Catherine, the French owner, has lived in Pangandaran for years and looks after her guests really well, offering cheap tours, transport and even home-made yoghurt.

Bamboo House (☎ 639419; r with fan 70,000Rp, with air-con 90,000-100,000Rp; ❄) Another popular budget place, here there are plain, ye olde fan-powered rooms with squat toilets and outside bathrooms, or modern, air-con concrete rooms that are uber-spartan (but very clean at least).

Villa Angela (☎ 639641; Jl Pamugaran; r 100,000-150,000Rp; ❄) Offering superb value, this new guest house has spacious rooms (all with TV and bathroom) in two attractive villa-style houses. It's run by a welcoming family and has a nice little garden.

Adam's Homestay (☎ 639396; www.adamhomestay.com; Jl Pamugaran; r 160,000-440,000Rp; ❄ 🏊) A notch up in comfort, this a really relaxing, enjoyable place to stay, with a good, if slightly pricey, restaurant. Offers gorgeous, artistically presented rooms with hot water (and many with balconies, beamed ceilings and outdoor bathrooms) spread around a verdant tropical garden that's just bursting with exotic plants and ponds.

Laut Biru (☎ 639360; www.lautbiru.com; Jl E Jaga Lautan 17-18; r 400,000Rp; ❄ 📶 🏊) A new modern hotel at the southern end of the main beach that has huge rooms (each with hot water, twin beds, stylish dark-wood furniture and a balcony) that tick all the right contemporary boxes.

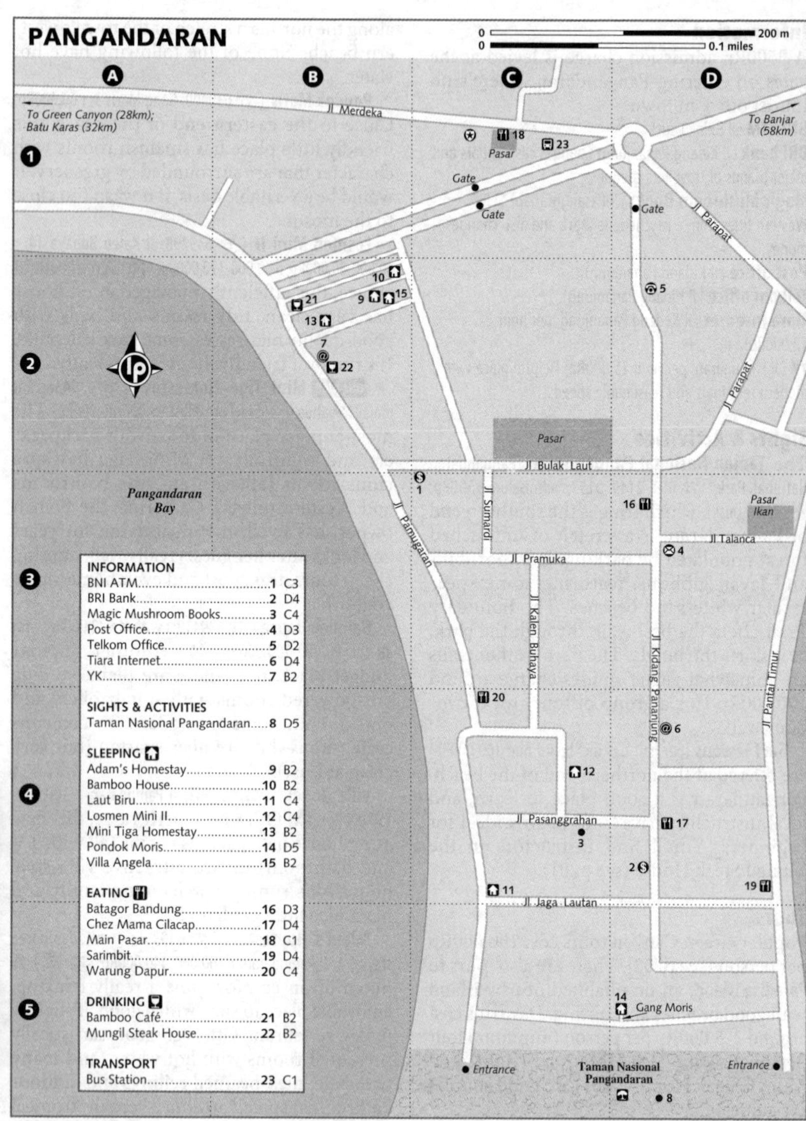

Eating

Pangandaran is famous for its excellent seafood. For cheap Indonesian nosh, the town has many *warung*.

Warung Dapur (Jl Bulak Laut 181; meals from 10,000Rp) Humble, inexpensive and friendly *warung* with bamboo walls and seats, and a street terrace where you can watch the world go by.

Batagor Bandung (☎ 630166; Jl Kidang Pananjung 116; snacks/meals 10,000/20,000Rp) Also known as the Green Garden Cafe, this excellent place has a relaxed boho vibe, with artwork on display and tables set back off the street.

Sarimbit (Jl Pantai Timor; meals around 25,000Rp) This simple place is one of several fresh fish restaurants facing east beach, and has tables looking out to the sea. Feast on red snapper or jumbo prawns cooked with a sauce of your choice.

Chez Mama Cilacap (☎ 630098; Jl Kidang Pananjung 187; mains from 28,000Rp) This large restaurant has a good reputation and specialises in seafood, especially crab, fresh from the market.

The **main pasar** (market; Jl Merdeka), near the bus terminal, is the place to stock up on fruit and groceries.

Drinking

Mungil Steak House (Jl Pamugaran) This log cabin bills itself as a 'steak house' for some bizarre reason but it works much better as a bar (the food is not great). The sea views are top-drawer.

Bamboo Café (Jl Pamugaran) Bamboo Café is fine for a cold Bintang, and though it has a great aspect over the ocean, it's looking a bit shabby these days.

Getting There & Away

Pangandaran lies roughly halfway between Bandung and Yogyakarta. Most people get here by road as there's no train station but it's perfectly possible to arrive by rail and bus. Speak to staff at the Mini Tiga Homestay (p199) for impartial transport advice and possible routes, and you can book tickets there too.

BOAT

The once-popular backwater boat trip east of Pangandaran via Majingklak harbour to Cilacap is now effectively dead in the water due to dwindling numbers and better road and rail connections.

BUS

Local buses run from Pangandaran's bus station, just north of town, to Sidareja (10,000Rp, 1¼ hours) and Cijulang (8000Rp, 40 minutes). Express buses also leave for Bandung (52,000Rp, six hours) and Jakarta's Kampung Rambutan terminal (90,000Rp, 8½ hours).

MINIBUS

The most comfortable way to travel to Bandung is aboard a **Sari Harum** (☎ 639276) door-to-door *travel* minibus for 90,000Rp. **Perkasa Jaya minibuses** (☎ 639607) pick up from hotels for the trip to Jakarta's Kampung Rambutan terminal (130,000Rp, eight hours).

TRAIN

To get to Yogyakarta by train you first need to get to Sidareja (by car costs 150,000Rp), from where there are train services to Yogya (*bisnis* class 50,000Rp); there's a fast train leaving Sidareja at noon, which takes 3½ hours.

BATU KARAS

☎ 0265 / pop 3000

The idyllic fishing village and emerging surfing hot spot of Batu Karas, 32km west of Pangandaran, is one of the most enjoyable places to kick back in Java. It's a tiny one-lane settlement, separated by a wooded promontory and has a low-key, very relaxed charm. There are two fine beaches, with sheltered sections that are usually calm enough for good swimming, but most visitors are here for the breaks, and there's a lot of surf talk. This is one of the best places in Java to learn to surf. The locally run surf co-op here charges 80,000Rp per person per day for lessons; board hire is extra (around 35,000Rp).

Sleeping & Eating

Teratai (r 90,000-135,000Rp) Budget-friendly, family-owned place with large rooms and clean *mandis* scattered around a large grassy plot.

Reef Hotel (☎ 081 3203 40193; r from 120,000Rp) Enjoys a great position right opposite one of the main surf breaks on the north side of the village, but the twin-bed rooms are overpriced and plain.

Bonsai Bungalows (☎ 709 3199; r 150,000Rp, bungalows 400,000Rp;) This is a good choice, with well-constructed, very clean and tidy thatched accommodation either in neat little fan-cooled wooden rooms with verandahs or huge air-con bungalows that can sleep six.

Java Cove (☎ 708 2020; www.javacovebeachhotel.com; economy r 120,000Rp, luxury r 420,000-620,000Rp;) Gorgeous Australian-owned beachfront hotel that offers beautiful, if a little pricey, contemporary-chic rooms as well as no-frills economy options. There's a decked, surf-facing garden.

Catch a bite to eat while watching the waves at these neighbouring places: **Kang Ayi** (☎ 708 2025; mains 10,000-20,000Rp) or **Sederhana** (mains 8000-18,000Rp).

Getting There & Away

You have to pay a toll of 3900Rp to enter the village. Batu Karas can be reached from Pangandaran by taking a bus to Cijulang (7000Rp) and then an *ojek* over the pretty bamboo bridge for 6000Rp.

AROUND BATU KARAS

About 6km inland from Batu Karas, pleasure boats run upriver to the **Green Canyon**, a lush river valley where you can swim in surging emerald currents and take a natural power shower under the streams that tumble into the gorge (don't look up!). Boats cost 75,000Rp, and run between 7.30am and 4pm. Day trips can be organised from Pangandaran (see p199) but it's easy enough to get here on a hired motorbike, as the route to the canyon is very well signposted.

WONOSOBO

☎ 0286 / pop 110,000

Wonosobo is the main gateway to the Dieng Plateau. At 900m above sea level in the central mountain range, it has a comfortable climate and is a typical country town with a busy market.

The **BNI bank** (Jl A Yani) has an ATM and exchange facilities. There's also internet access at **Bina** (Jl Veteran 36; per hr 5000Rp; 🕒 24hr), and a centrally located **tourist office** (☎ 321194; Jl Kartini 3; 🕒 8am-3pm Mon-Fri).

Citra Homestay (☎ 321880; Jl Angkatan 45; r 60,000Rp) is a simple homestay above a carpenter's with basic rooms and shared *mandis*. The mosque close by will ensure you're awake early for the ride up to Dieng.

A large concrete motel-like place, **Hotel Sri Kencono** (☎ 321522; Jl A Yani 81; economy r 60,000Rp, standard 250,000Rp, f 440,000Rp) has well-kept, spacious rooms with hot-water bathrooms and Western-style toilets. There are also a few basic economy options.

our pick **Wisma Duta Homestay** (☎ 321674; dutahomestay@yahoo.com; Jl Rumah Sakit 3; economy r 50,000Rp, standard 300,000Rp) This is one of the best homestays in the central mountains, occupying a lovely suburban house and garden. The basic rooms are a bit neglected while the sleek new rooms are exceptionally attractive.

Rumah Makan Kita (Jl Resimen 109; meals 8000-20,000Rp) is a simple clean place hits the spot for fresh inexpensive Chinese-style food, with a good selection of noodle and rice dishes.

Wonosobo's bus station is 4km out of town on the Magelang road. From Yogyakarta take a bus to Magelang (13,000Rp, 1½ hours) and then another bus to Wonosobo (15,000Rp, two hours). **Rahayu Travel** (☎ 321217; Jl A Yani 95) has door-to-door minibuses to Yogyakarta (40,000Rp, three hours).

Frequent buses to Dieng (8000Rp, one hour) leave from Jl Rumah Sakit.

DIENG PLATEAU

☎ 0286

A startling contrast from the heat and fecundity of the lowlands, the plateau of Dieng (Abode of Gods) is another world: a windswept volcanic landscape of swirling clouds, green hills, mist and damp punctuated with ancient ruins.

Information

BRI bank (🕒 8am-2pm Mon-Fri), just near Hotel Gunung Mas, changes US dollars (cash) at poor rates.

Sights & Activities

On the swampy plain in front of Dieng village are the five Hindu temples of the **Arjuna Complex** that are thought to be the oldest in Java, dating back to AD 680. Though historically important, they are small, squat and visually not that impressive. **Candi Gatutkaca**, a temple to the south, has a small **museum** (🕒 8am-4pm) containing statues and sculpture from the temples.

The plateau's natural attractions and remote allure are the main reasons to visit. From the village, you can do a two-hour loop walk that takes in the turquoise lake of **Telaga Warna** and **Kawah Sikidang**, a volcanic crater with steaming vents and frantically bubbling mud pools. You can see all the main sights, including the temples, on foot in a morning or afternoon, though to really explore the plateau and its crater lakes, allow a couple of days.

It costs 20,000Rp to visit the plateau and the main temples (Telaga Warna is an extra 7000Rp).

The walk to **Sembungan** village (2300m) to see the sunrise is heavily touted by the guest houses, though having to pay to get up at 3.30am is a dubious privilege (particularly on cloudy mornings). All the guest houses can arrange **guides** (per person 45,000Rp) and hire out warm clothing.

Sleeping & Eating

Dieng's dozen or more guest houses are notoriously poor value. Spartan conditions and draughty, semiclean rooms are the norm. Beware that hot water is not always forthcoming.

Dieng Plateau Homestay (☎ 081 3277 91565; Jl Raya Km 26; r 40,000Rp) Uber-sparse place where the very basic rooms have concrete floors, a stick or two of furniture and rough blankets.

Hotel & Restaurant Bu Jono (☎ 642046, 0813-2845 5401; Jl Raya Km 26; r 50,000-75,000Rp) This simple place does have a certain quirky, if ramshackle, charm. All rooms are small and there are three shared hot-water *mandis*. The restaurant is actually a good place to eat.

Hotel Gunung Mas (☎ 334 2017; r 100,000, with hot water 150,000Rp) This is the most 'upmarket' hotel in town, though staff are not particularly friendly at reception. Still, at least the rooms are kept clean and are in good condition.

Getting There & Away

Dieng is 26km from Wonosobo, which is the usual access point. Buses run frequently (8000Rp, one hour).

YOGYAKARTA

☎ 0274 / pop 700,000

A hotbed of Javanese intellectual and political thought, and boasting an incredibly rich artistic and cultural heritage, Yogya is now the site of an uneasy truce between the old ways of life and the onslaught of modernity. Still headed by its sultan, whose *kraton* remains the hub of traditional life, contemporary Yogya is, nevertheless, as much a city of cybercafes, lounge bars and traffic jams as batik, *gamelan* and ritual.

But while the process of modernisation homogenises many of Java's cities, Yogya continues to juggle past and present with relative ease, sustaining a slower, more conservative way of life in the quiet *kampung* that thrive only a stone's throw from the throbbing main streets.

Yogya's potency has long outweighed its size, and it remains Java's premier tourist city, with countless hotels, restaurants and attractions of its own. The city is also an ideal base for exploring Borobudur and Prambanan.

Orientation

Jl Malioboro is the main drag, running south from the train station to become Jl A Yani at its southern end (where you'll find the *kraton*). It's lined with stores, and you'll find the main budget accommodation enclave of Sosrowijayan just off it. A second hotel and restaurant district lies to the south around Jl Prawirotaman.

Information

BOOKSHOPS

Lucky Boomerang (Map p206; ☎ 895006; Gang 1-67) Has used guidebooks and fiction, Periplus maps and books, plus souvenirs.

INTERNET ACCESS

Internet cafes can be found all over Yogyakarta, although many of the cheaper cafes (which charge around 3000Rp per hour) are located north of Jl Diponegoro.

11 Net (Map p204; Jl Parangtritis; per hr 5000Rp) Equipped with modern terminals, and speeds are quite respectable.

Internet Queen (Map p206; Jl Pasar Kembang 17; per hr 7000Rp; 🕑 24hr) Pretty speedy place that also has scanning and fax facilities, and offers cheap international calls.

INTERNET RESOURCES

The website www.yogyes.com is a useful portal to the city.

MEDICAL SERVICES

Ludira Husada Tama Hospital (Map p204; ☎ 620333; Jl Wiratama 4; 🕑 24hr)

MONEY

There are numerous banks (and a few money changers) in the tourist areas. ATMs are widespread throughout the city.

Mulia (Map p206; Inna Garuda Hotel, Jl Malioboro 60) Along with Pt Barumun Abadi, this has the best exchange rates in Yogya.

Pt Barumun Abadi (Map p206; Inna Garuda Hotel, Jl Malioboro 60) Offers competitive rates.

POST

Main post office (Map p204; cnr Jl Senopati & Jl A Yani; 🕑 7am-8pm Mon-Sat)

TELEPHONE

There are *wartel* across town.

Telkom office (Map p204; Jl Yos Sudarso; 🕑 24hr)

TOURIST INFORMATION

Tourist information office (Map p204; ☎ 566000; Jl Malioboro 16; 🕑 8am-7pm Mon-Thu, 8am-6pm Fri & Sat) A very helpful office, staff here can provide excellent information and tips. Tugu train station and the airport also have desks.

Dangers & Annoyances

Yogya has more than its fair share of thieves. The Prambanan and Borobudur buses are favourites for pickpockets.

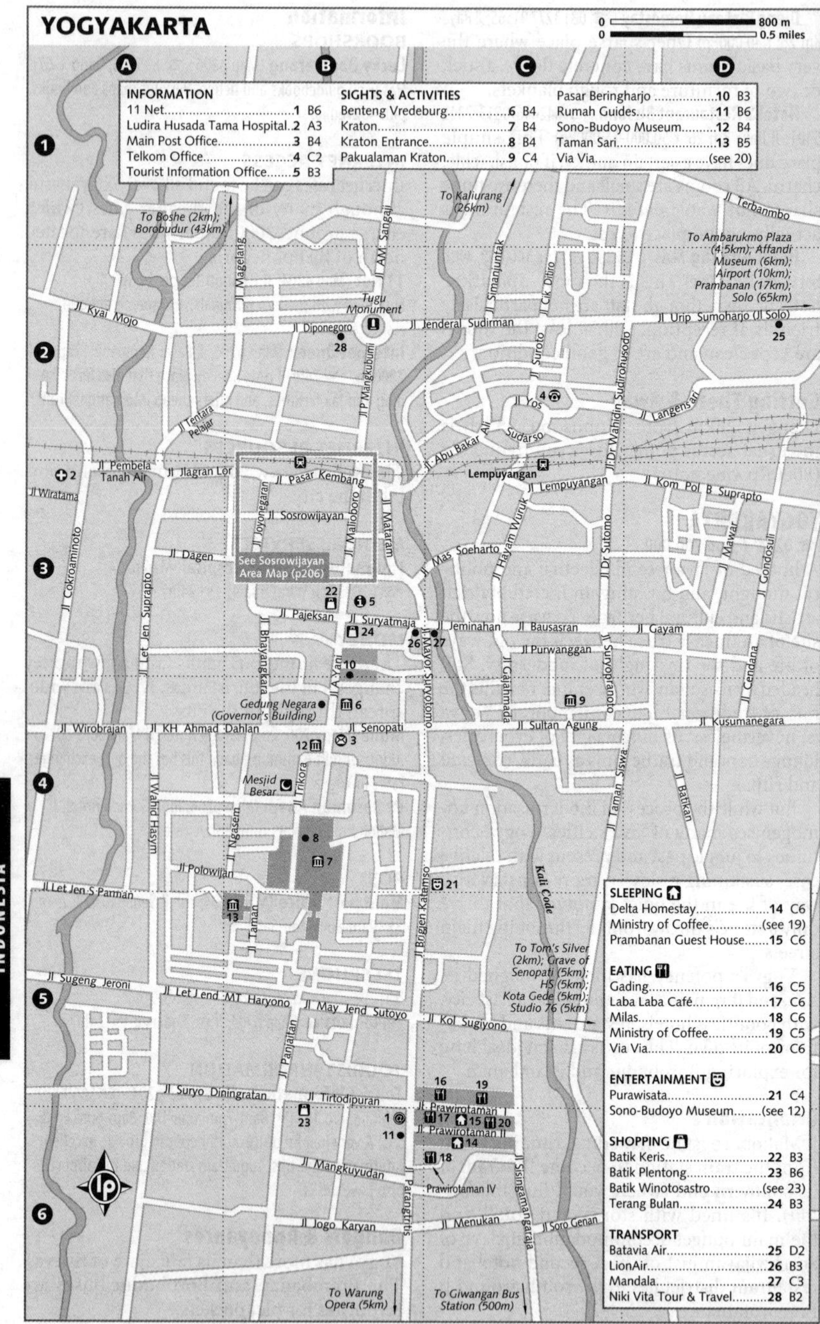

YOGYAKARTA
0 800 m
0 0.5 miles
INFORMATION
11 Net 1 B6
Ludira Husada Tama Hospital 2 A3
Main Post Office 3 B4
Telkom Office 4 C2
Tourist Information Office 5 B3
SIGHTS & ACTIVITIES
Benteng Vredeburg 6 B4
Kraton 7 B4
Kraton Entrance 8 B4
Pakualaman Kraton 9 C4
Pasar Beringharjo 10 B3
Rumah Guides 11 B6
Sono-Budoyo Museum 12 B4
Taman Sari 13 B5
Via Via (see 20)
SLEEPING
Delta Homestay 14 C6
Ministry of Coffee (see 19)
Prambanan Guest House 15 C6
EATING
Gading 16 C5
Laba Laba Café 17 C6
Milas 18 C6
Ministry of Coffee 19 C5
Via Via 20 C6
ENTERTAINMENT
Purawisata 21 C4
Sono-Budoyo Museum (see 12)
SHOPPING
Batik Keris 22 B3
Batik Plentong 23 B6
Batik Winotosastro (see 23)
Terang Bulan 24 B3
TRANSPORT
Batavia Air 25 D2
LionAir 26 B3
Mandala 27 C3
Niki Vita Tour & Travel 28 B2
To Boshe (2km); Borobudur (43km)
To Kaliurang (26km)
To Ambarukmo Plaza (4.5km); Affandi Museum (6km); Airport (10km); Prambanan (17km); Solo (65km)
Tugu Monument
Lempuyangan
See Sosrowijayan Area Map (p206)
Gedung Negara (Governor's Building)
Mesjid Besar
Kali Code
To Tom's Silver (2km); Grave of Senopati (5km); HS (5km); Kota Gede (5km); Studio 76 (5km)
To Warung Opera (5km)
To Giwangan Bus Station (500m)
Prawirotaman IV
INDONESIA

Wandering batik or art salesmen, posing as guides or instant friends, can be a pain, especially around the Taman Sari and especially around the *kraton*.

Sights & Activities

KRATON

Traditions hold firm in Yogya, and nowhere is this more evident than in the **Kraton** (Map p204; ☎ 373721; admission 12,500Rp, camera 1000Rp, guided tour by donation; 8am-2pm Sat-Thu, 8am-1pm Fri), a walled royal enclave and the cultural and political heart of the city. Effectively a city within a city, over 25,000 people live within the compound. In all honesty, information about the glittering palaces, temples and treasures is a little lacking and not that well presented to the casual visitor, but that's partly because the *kraton* primarily remains the sultan's home and a centre of political power and influence, and only secondly a tourist attraction.

The golden pavilion, the official reception hall of the sultans, boasts a marble floor and showcases a host of free cultural events; check with the tourist office for current listings. Other highlights include the souvenir house, textile room and the small museum dedicated to Hamengkubuwono IX, the current sultan's father.

Try and visit the *kraton* during the week – at weekends the compound becomes a menagerie of tour buses, screeching kids, dripping ice creams and 'hello missterrrrs!'.

TAMAN SARI & PASAR NGASEM

The **Taman Sari** (Water Castle; Map p204; ☎ 081 8027 70296; Jl Taman; admission 7000Rp; 8am-3.30pm) was a complex of canals, pools and palaces built within the *kraton* between 1758 and 1765 by a Portuguese architect who was allegedly later executed to keep the sultan's hidden 'pleasure rooms' secret. Damaged first by Diponegoro's Java War and then further by an earthquake, it is today a mass of ruins, crowded with small houses and batik galleries. The main bathing pools have been restored.

MUSEUMS

Close by the *kraton*, the **Sono-Budoyo Museum** (Map p204; ☎ 376775; admission 5000Rp; 8am-1.30pm Tue-Thu, 8-11.15am Fri, 8am-noon Sat & Sun) is the best of Yogya's museums, with an astounding assortment of stone and gold Hindu statuary, Balinese carvings, *wayang kulit* puppets, *kris* and batik. *Wayang kulit* performances are held here nightly at 8pm.

Many of Yogya's other museums are dedicated to a roll call of Indonesian national heroes and patriots. The revolution-themed dioramas at the **Benteng Vredeburg** (Map p204; Jl A Yani 6; admission 3500Rp; 8.30am-1.30pm Tue-Thu, 8.30-11am Fri, 8.30am-noon Sat & Sun) fit into this category, but the building itself, a Dutch-era fort dating back to 1765, has a brooding quality.

About 6km east of the city centre, the **Affandi Museum** (☎ 562 593; www.affandi.org; Jl Laksda Adisucipto 167; admission incl soft drink 20,000Rp, camera 10,000Rp; 9am-4pm except holidays), housed in a curious riverside tree house, exhibits the impressionist works of Affandi, Indonesia's best-known artist.

OTHER ATTRACTIONS

The smaller **Pakualaman Kraton** (Map p204; Jl Sultan Agung; admission 2000Rp; 9.30am-1.30pm Tue, Thu & Sun) has a small museum, a *pendopo* (open-sided pavilion), which can hold a full *gamelan* orchestra, and a curious colonial house.

Yogya's superb main market, **Pasar Beringharjo** (Map p204; Jl A Yani; 7.30am-4pm), is a wonderful place to spend an hour or two. Buzzing with life, here you can shop for cheap batik, clothes, bags and sandals. On the upper floors there's a spice market and an area devoted to curios and antiques.

The main street of **Kota Gede** (off Map p204), 5km southeast of Yogya, is a silverwork centre with plenty of silver jewellery on offer. The sacred **grave of Senopati**, the first king of Mataram, can also be seen here.

Tours

Rumah Guides (Map p204; ☎ 386432; www.inspirasi indonesiaholidays.com; Rumah Eyang, Gang Sartono 823, Jl Parangtritis) is an excellent new community project run by young Yogya citizens eager to show you their city and the surrounding area. Tours of the city (150,000Rp per day) and to Borobudur, Dieng and beyond can be set up in their office based in the Prawirotaman area. It's also possible to stay with local families as part of a homestay program (US$12 per day including all meals).

Courses

The **Tourist Information Centre** (p203) has a list of places offering courses.

Losmen Lucy (Map p206; ☎ 513429) Cheap batik courses, a full day costs around 110,000Rp (after bargaining!).

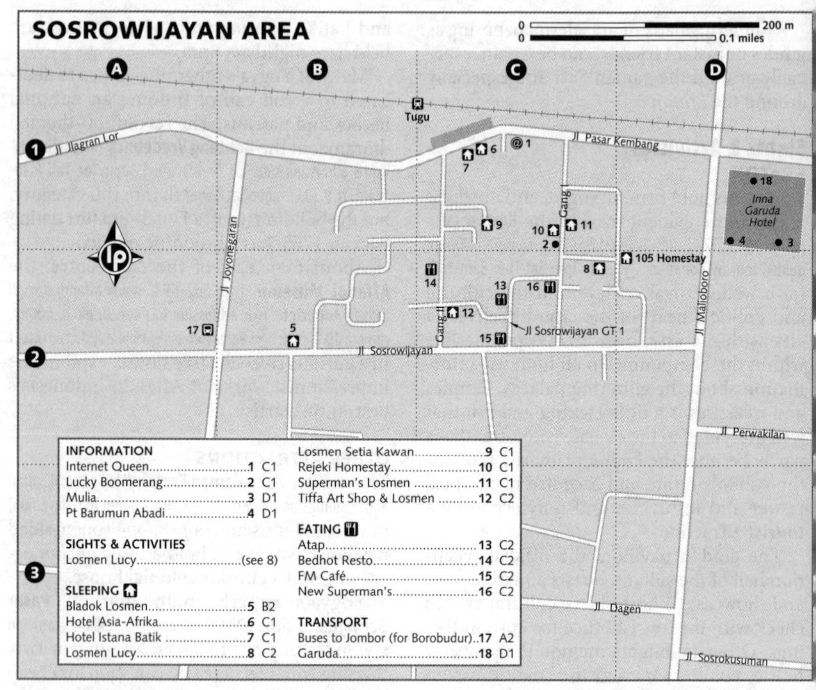

Studio 76 (off Map p204; ☎ 714 7676; Jl Purbayan, Kota Gede) Runs good full-day silversmith courses (220,000Rp per person, including lunch and 10g of silver to play around with).

Via Via (Map p204; ☎ 386557; www.viaviacafe.com; Jl Prawirotaman I 30) Has excellent half-day cooking (85,000Rp), batik- and silver jewellery-making (both 80,000Rp) courses.

Festivals & Events

The three Gerebeg festivals – held each year at the end of January and April and the beginning of November – are Java's most colourful and grand processions.

Sleeping

Yogya has dozens of good guest houses and hotels. Sosrowijayan is the main budget zone, while the Prawirotaman area, 2km south of the *kraton*, also has some cheap places as well as midrange options.

SOSROWIJAYAN AREA

Situated within a short walk of the train station, Sosrowijayan is a fascinating traditional neighbourhood of narrow *gang* (alleyways), lined with backpacker-geared accommodation, eateries, laundries and the like.

Tiffa Art Shop & Losmen (Map p206; ☎ 512 841; tiffaartshop@yahoo.com; s/d 40,000/70,000Rp) An excellent little *losmen* owned by a hospitable family with accommodation above an art shop. All the four rooms are smallish but have private *mandi*

Losmen Lucy (Map p206; ☎ 513 429; s/d 70,000/80,000Rp) One of the best *losmen* in Yogya. The 12 fan-cooled rooms here are kept really spick 'n' span and the beds still have some spring; all have en-suite *mandi* with squat toilets.

our pick **Losmen Setia Kawan** (Map p206; ☎ 512452; www.bedhots.com; economy r 70,000-100,000Rp, with air-con 125,000-200,000Rp;) First choice in Sosrowijayan, this is a superb very inviting and well-run place that occupies a fine old artistically decorated house. There is a rooftop patio and a row of computers for internet access.

Bladok Losmen (Map p206; ☎ 560452; Jl Sosrowijayan 76; r 80,000Rp, r with balcony 120,000Rp, with air-con from 195,000Rp;) A great lodge of real character and charm, Bladok caters to both budget and midrange travellers, and justifiably remains a perennial favourite.

Hotel Asia-Afrika (Map p206; ☎ 566219; Jl Pasar Kembang 21; r with fan 175,000Rp, with air-con from 210,000Rp;) This hotel's rooms are good value. The decent-sized pool and sun loungers make it a tempting choice.

Hotel Istana Batik (Map p206; ☎ 587012; www.dianagrouphotel.com; Jl Pasar Kembang 29; r 300,000-350,000Rp;) Istana Batik has real Javanese character, with elaborately carved wooden furniture in its fine lobby and spacious rooms.

Also recommended:

Superman's Losmen (Map p206; ☎ 515007; r 45,000Rp) Simple *losmen* on Gang I with very basic rooms.

Rejeki Homestay (Map p206; ☎ 516084; r 70,000Rp) Eleven neat, clean doubles and twins with a stick or two of furniture. All have fan and private *mandi*.

JL PRAWIROTAMAN AREA

This area used to be the centre for midrange hotels in Yogya, but many have slashed their prices in recent years and there are bargains to be had.

Delta Homestay (Map p204; ☎ 727 1047; www.dutagardenhotel.com; Jl Prawirotaman II 597A; s/d 75,000/85,000Rp, with mandi 105,000/115,000Rp, with air-con 140,000/150,000Rp;) An outstanding little hotel with a selection of small, but perfectly formed rooms, each with a little porch grouped around a great pool.

Prambanan Guest House (Map p204; ☎ 376167; Jl Prawirotaman I No 14; r with cold shower/air-con 90,000/160,000Rp;) A well-run place with an attractive garden and attentive staff, Prambanan is a very good option. Cheaper rooms are plain but the better doubles are comfortable.

Ministry of Coffee (Map p204; ☎ 747 3828; www.ministryofcoffee.com; Jl Prawirotaman I 15A; s/d from 300,000/330,000Rp;) This cutting-edge cafe-library not only has delectable coffee but also a few comfortable, stylish rooms, all with air-con, safety boxes and most with little balconies.

Eating & Drinking

SOSROWIJAYAN AREA

For cheap and cheerful Indonesian and Western nosh, this area fits the bill (and your pocket) nicely. It's also the place to join locals for a bite to eat; after 10pm, the souvenir vendors along the northern end of Jl Malioboro pack up and a *lesahan* area (where diners sit on straw mats) comes alive. Here you can try Yogya's famous *ayam goreng* (deep-fried chicken soaked in coconut milk) and listen to young Indonesians strumming their guitars into the wee small hours.

A whole host of good *warung* also line Jl Pasar Kembang, beside the train line.

Bedhot Resto (Map p206; Gang II; mains 10,000-22,000Rp) Bedhot means 'creative' in old Javanese and is perhaps the most stylish eatery in Sosrowijayan, with art on the walls, batik tablecloths and menus made from bark. There's tasty Indonesian and Western food, good juices and internet access upstairs.

Atap (Map p206; ☎ 085 6431 82004; www.atap.8m.com; Jl Sosrowijayan GT 1/113; dishes from 10,000Rp; 5.30-10pm) Bohemian restaurant with tables made from car tyres and a great little outdoor terrace. The menu has burgers and Indo favourites and a wicked sense of humour.

FM Café (Map p206; Jl Sosrowijayan 14; mains around 20,000Rp) FM Café has a great courtyard setting and an eclectic menu ranging from *nasi goreng* to pizza. Happy hour is gloriously lengthy, lasting from 1pm to 8pm; bands perform here on Fridays nights.

New Superman's (Map p206; meals 15,000-25,000Rp) Huge, slightly charmless place that's nevertheless a key hang-out for travellers with a long, long menu of Western food like pizzas, jaffles and pancakes, and Chinese food.

JL PRAWIROTAMAN AREA

Ministry of Coffee (Map p204; ☎ 747 3828; www.ministryofcoffee.com; Jl Prawirotaman I 15A; meals 20,000Rp) A landmark modernist structure, with a library (with English-language books and magazines) upstairs and a cafe below. It's ideal for an espresso or latte but the food (mainly snacks and cakes) is pretty average.

our pick **Via Via** (Map p204; ☎ 386557; www.viaviacafe.com; Jl Prawirotaman I 30; mains 14,000-28,000Rp;) A simply outstanding and cosmopolitan venue; a cool cafe-restaurant that gets virtually everything right. The menu is tempting with very fresh, inventive Indonesian and Western food at fair prices, a few tapas, wine by the glass and healthy juices. The decor mixes exposed concrete and bamboo screens and there's a great outdoor terrace.

Laba Laba Café (Map p204; Jl Prawirotaman I 2; mains 20,000Rp) Laba Laba (which means 'spider') has a great rear garden that's an ideal setting for some filling European or Indonesian food.

Gading (Map p204; ☎ 659 6921; Jl Prawirotaman I 9; mains 20,000-48,000Rp) A civilised restaurant with pleasant seating and lighting and a menu of Indonesian and Western food – the thin-crust pizza here is great. There's live music on Wednesdays, Fridays and Sundays.

YOGYA SPECIALITIES

Yogya has a rich culinary tradition and many dishes are unique to the region. To try many of these you'll have to head into the market areas, where some stallholders have been churning out a particular speciality for decades. *Gudeg* is young jackfruit served in a spicy coconut sauce, served with a little tempeh (or chicken), egg, and sweetened with palm sugar. Look out too for *nasi brongkos,* a dark bean and tofu stew served with small chunks of meat, rice and *krupuk* (prawn crackers).

Yogya-style espresso is *kopi jos,* a cup of potent coarsely ground Java coffee that's dunked with a few pieces of glowing charcoal – try it at the stalls around Tugu train station. *Teh poci* (traditional tea served with unprocessed sugar in a clay pot) is best sampled from the *warung* in front of the Pakualaman Kraton.

Milas (Map p204; ☎ 742 3399; Jl Prawirotaman IV 127; meals from 20,000Rp) This secret garden restaurant, located down a quiet side road, is a project centre for street youth. Offers tasty vegetarian cooking: healthy snacks, sandwiches, salads and organic coffee.

OTHER AREAS

Warung Opera (off Map p204; ☎ 718 1977; Jl Parangtritis, Km 6.3; mains 10,000-30,000Rp; ⏲ 5-10pm) Occupying a wonderful traditional Javanese house built from teak, this unusual and bohemian restaurant is an outstanding place to sample home-style Indonesian dishes. Donny, the flamboyant owner, also does fortune reading from coffee cups.

Clubbing

Boshe (off Map p204; ☎ 624 041; Jl Magelan, Km 6.5) A new club and the hottest in town with a large central dance floor, pumping sound system and karaoke rooms on lower floors. Draws a young, up-for-it crowd with trance and tribal DJs, plus less impressive boy bands and dance troupes.

Entertainment

Dance, *wayang* or *gamelan* are performed most mornings at the *kraton* (admission free). Check with the tourist office for current listings.

DANCE

Most performances are based on the Ramayana or at least billed as 'Ramayana ballet' because of the famed performances at Prambanan.

Purawisata (Map p204; ☎ 375705; Jl B Katamso) This amusement park stages Ramayana performances every day at 8pm (tickets are 120,000Rp). You can dine here and watch the show.

PUPPET PERFORMANCES

Wayang kulit performances can be seen at several places around Yogya every night of the week.

Sono-Budoyo Museum (Map p204; ☎ 376775; admission 5000Rp) Holds popular two-hour performances nightly from 8pm to 10pm (20,000Rp). The first half-hour involves the reading of the story in Javanese, so most travellers skip this and arrive later.

Shopping

Yogya is a great place to shop for crafts and artefacts; try the Beringharjo market first for bargains, or the Prawirotaman area, which has several fine antique stores.

Jl Malioboro is one great, long, throbbing bazaar of souvenir shops and stalls selling cheap cotton clothes, leatherwork, batik bags, *topeng* masks and *wayang golek* puppets.

For a regular shopping mall, **Ambarukmo Plaza** (off Map p204; Jl Laksda Adisucipto) is 5km west of the city centre on the road to Prambanan and has a great selection of boutiques, as well as a good food court, cinema and supermarket. Take bus 1A to get there.

BATIK

Most of the batik workshops and several large showrooms are along Jl Tirtodipuran, south of the *kraton*. Many, such as **Batik Plentong** (Map p204; Jl Tirtodipuran 48) and **Batik Winotosastro** (Map p204; Jl Tirtodipuran 54), give free guided tours of the batik process. These places cater to tour groups, so prices are very high – view the process here and shop elsewhere.

Batik is cheapest in the markets, especially Pasar Beringharjo, but quality is questionable. Jl Malioboro and Jl A Yani have good fixed-price places, including the following:

Batik Keris (Map p204; ☎ 557893; Jl A Yani 71) Excellent quality batik. Best for traditional shirts, don't expect fashionable styles.
Terang Bulan (Map p204; Jl A Yani 108)

SILVERWORK

Fine filigree work is a Yogya speciality, but many styles and designs are available. Kota Gede (off Map p204) has some very attractive jewellery, boxes, bowls, cutlery and miniatures, and there are dozens of smaller silver shops on Jl Kemesan and Jl Mondorakan, where you can get some good buys if you bargain.

You can get a guided tour of the process, with no obligation to buy, at the large factories: **Tom's Silver** (off Map p204; ☎ 525416; Jl Ngeski Gondo 60) has an extensive (and expensive) selection and some superb large pieces. **HS** (off Map p204; Jl Mandarokan I) is marginally cheaper; always ask for a substantial discount off the marked prices.

Getting There & Away

AIR

Yogyakarta airport (code JOG; off Map p204) has international connections to Singapore and Kuala Lumpur, plus frequent flights to Jakarta and Denpasar.

Air Asia (☎ 5050 5088; www.airasia.com) Flies to Singapore daily and KL.
Batavia Air (Map p204; ☎ 547373; www.batavia-air.co.id; Ruko Mas Plaza, Jl Urip Sumohardjo) Has flights to Balikpapan, Jakarta, Pontianak and Surabaya.
Garuda (Map p206; ☎ 551515; Inna Garuda Hotel, Jl Malioboro 60) Links Yogya with Singapore, Denpasar and Jakarta.
Mandala (Map p204; ☎ 520603; Jl Mayor Suryotomo 537A) Flies to Balikpapan, Banjarmasin, Denpasar and Jakarta.
Lion Air (Map p204; ☎ 555028; Melia Purosani Hotel, Jl Mayor Suryotomo 31) Flies to Denpasar and Jakarta.

BUS

Yogyakarta's **Giwangan bus station** (off Map p204; ☎ 410015; Jl Imogiri) is 5km southeast of the city centre, on the ring road.

Economy/air-con bus services include those to Solo (13,000/18,000Rp, two hours), Semarang (28,000/38,000Rp, four hours), Bandung (80,000/92,000Rp, 10 hours), Jakarta (90,000/120,000Rp, 12 hours) and Surabaya (58,000/76,000Rp, eight hours).

Buses also operate regularly to towns in the immediate area, including Borobudur (12,000Rp, 1½ hours) and Kaliurang (7000Rp, one hour).

For really long trips take a luxury bus. It's cheaper to buy tickets at the bus terminal, but it's less hassle to simply check fares and departures with the ticket agents along Jl Mangkubumi, Jl Sosrowijayan or Jl Prawirotaman. These agents can also arrange pick-up from your hotel. Typical fares include Denpasar (220,000Rp), Surabaya and Malang (95,000Rp), and Jakarta (135,000Rp).

Local bus 4 leaves from Jl Malioboro (2000Rp) for Giwangan.

MINIBUS

Door-to-door *travel* service all major cities from Yogyakarta, including Solo (25,000Rp, two hours), Pangandaran (95,000Rp, eight hours), Semarang (50,000Rp, four hours), Surabaya (85,000Rp), Malang (90,000Rp) and Jakarta (135,000Rp, 12 hours). Most *travel* will pick you up from your hotel. Hotels and travel agencies can arrange tickets for the minibuses, or you can book directly through **Niki Vita Tour & Travel** (Map p204; ☎ 561884; Jl Diponegoro 25).

TRAIN

Yogya's main **Tugu train station** (Map p206; ☎ 514270) is conveniently central, although some *ekonomi* trains run to/from the Lempuyangan station (Map p204) 1km further east.

The comfortable *Taksaka* (from 150,000Rp, eight hours) departs twice daily for Jakarta at 10am and 8pm. Or the best train is the *eksekutif Argo Lawu* (from 220,000Rp, seven hours), which leaves at 8.53am.

Very regular trains run to Solo, including *Prameks* (7000Rp, one hour), which depart six times daily from Tugu.

For Surabaya, the best option is the *eksekutif Argo Wilis* (from 150,000Rp, 5½ hours) which leaves at 2.22pm. Otherwise there are plenty of night trains including the *Mutiara Selatan* (*bisnis* 110,000Rp, six hours) departing at 1.13am.

Heading for Bandung, trains include the *Lodaya* (*bisnis*/*eksekutif* from 100,000/165,000Rp, 8½ hours), which passes through Yogya at 9.24pm.

From Lempuyangan train station, overnight trains run between Surabaya and Jakarta (40,000Rp, 11 hours) and Bandung (35,000Rp, 10 hours).

Getting Around

Rent motorbikes from 50,000Rp a day, bicycles 15,000Rp a day.

> **GETTING INTO TOWN**
>
> Yogya's airport is 10km east of the city centre. Buses 3A and 1A (3000Rp) serve Jl Malioboro. Taxis cost 50,000Rp to the city centre.

BUS

Yogya has a reliable new bus system called the TransJogja busway. These modern air-conditioned buses run from 6am to 10pm on six routes around the city to as far away as Prambanan. Tickets cost 3000Rp per journey, or 27,000Rp for a carnet of 10.

Bus 1A is a very useful service, running from Jl Malioboro as far as Jl Senopati then northeast past the Affandi Museum, Ambarukmo Plaza, and airport, to the ruins of Prambanan. Bus 3B connects Giwangan bus terminal with the airport and Prambanan before heading west to Jl Malioboro.

LOCAL TRANSPORT

Becaks cost around 4000Rp minimum and the asking rate is a lot more. The trip from Jl Prawirotaman to Jl Malioboro costs at least 8000Rp.

TAXI

Taxis have meters and are quite efficient, costing 5000Rp for the first kilometre, then 2500Rp for each subsequent kilometre.

PRAMBANAN

The grandest and most evocative Hindu temple complex in Java, **Prambanan** (☎ 496401; adult/student US$11/6; ⌚ 6am-6pm, last admission at 5.15pm) features some 50 temple sites. Many suffered extensive damage in the 2006 earthquake. Though the temples survived, hundreds of stone blocks collapsed to the ground or were cracked (479 in the Shiva temple alone). Parts of the complex are now fenced off and some temples are covered in scaffolding. It will take years to fully restore Prambanan. That said, Prambanan is certainly still well worth a visit, and you can get within a few metres of (if not enter) all the main monuments.

The **Shiva temple** is the largest and most lavish, towering 47 dizzy metres above the valley and decorated with an entire pantheon of carved deities. The statue of Shiva stands in the central chamber and statues of the goddess Durga, Shiva's elephant-headed son Ganesh, and Agastya the teacher stand in the other chapels of the upper part of the temple. The Shiva temple is flanked by the **Vishnu** and **Brahma temples**, the latter carrying further scenes from the Ramayana. In the small central temple, opposite the Shiva temple, stands a statue of the bull Nandi, Shiva's mount.

Built in the 9th century AD, the complex at Prambanan was mysteriously abandoned soon after its completion. Many of the temples had collapsed by the 19th century and only in 1937 was any form of reconstruction attempted.

The spectacular **Ramayana ballets** performed here have been suspended in the aftermath of the earthquake. If they've resumed they are well worth attending, with a cast of hundreds performing in front of a floodlit Shiva temple; check with the Yogya tourist information office.

The main temples face Prambanan village on the highway, while others are scattered across the surrounding fields. The site is 17km east of Yogya on the Solo road. From Yogyakarta, take TransJogja bus 1A (3000Rp, 40 minutes) from Jl Malioboro. Solo-bound buses also stop here. A motorbike or bicycle is a good way to explore all the temples in the area via the back roads.

BOROBUDUR

☎ 0293

Ranking with Bagan and Angkor Wat as one of the great Southeast Asian monuments, **Borobudur** (☎ 788266; www.borobudurpark.com; admission to temple US$12; ⌚ 6am-5.30pm) is a stunning and poignant epitaph to Java's Buddhist heyday.

The temple, 42km northwest of Yogya, consists of six square bases topped by three circular ones, and it was constructed at roughly the same time as Prambanan in the early part of the 9th century AD. With the decline of Buddhism, Borobudur was abandoned, covered in volcanic ash by an eruption in 1006, and only rediscovered in 1814 when Raffles governed Java.

Nearly 1500 narrative relief panels on the terraces illustrate Buddhist teachings and tales, while 432 Buddha images sit in chambers on the terraces. On the upper circular terraces there are latticed stupas, which contain 72 more Buddha images.

Borobudur is best witnessed at sunrise, when morning mist hangs over the lush surrounding valley and distant hills. By 7am, the tourist hordes have arrived: it is a very popular school trip for students, so expect to get requests for pictures from giggling teenagers.

Admission to the temple includes entrance to **Karmawibhangga archaeological museum**, which contains 4000 original stones and carvings. Close by the **Samudraraksa museum** is dedicated to the importance of the ocean and sea trade in Indonesia. There's an 18m wooden outrigger here, a replica of a boat depicted on one of Borobudur's panels. This boat was sailed to Africa in 2003, a voyage retracing Javanese trading links with the continent over 1000 years ago.

The **Mendut Temple** (admission 3300Rp; 🕑 8am-4pm), 3.5km east of Borobudur, has a magnificent 3m-high statue of Buddha seated with two disciples. It has been suggested that this image was originally intended to top Borobudur but proved impossible to raise to the summit. Your tour bus from Yogya will stop here if you ask, otherwise a bemo is 2000Rp.

Knowledgeable guides for Borobudur can be hired (50,000Rp) at the ticket office for a 90-minute tour. For information about the Borobudur region, its villages and culture, contact Jaker (see boxed text right).

Sleeping & Eating

There are plenty of cheap *warung* around the site's exit.

Pondok Tinggal Hotel (☎ 788 145; Jl Balaputradewa 32; dm 15,000Rp, r with fan 70,000-90,000Rp, with air-con from 120,000Rp; ❄) There's an excellent choice of inexpensive rooms around an attractive, peaceful garden, and even a couple of dorms here.

Lotus Guest House (☎ 788281; Jl Medang Kamulan 2; r incl breakfast from 60,000-200,000Rp) North of the temple, Lotus is one of the original guest houses in Borobudur and it's still run by the same super-hospitable family.

our pick **Lotus II** (☎ 788845; jackpriyana@yahoo.com.sg; Jl Balaputradewa 54; r incl breakfast 150,000Rp; ❄) Most of the artistically styled rooms here are exceptionally large, with bathrooms (with tubs) bigger than most *losmen* rooms. There's also a wonderful rear balcony with views directly onto rice fields.

Restaurant Rajasa (☎ 789690; Jl Balaputradewa; meals 20,000-30,000Rp) This is a lovely, intimate restaurant in a traditional Javanese house that has good Indonesian food: try a curry, or duck cooked in butter.

Getting There & Away

Most travellers get to Borobudur on a tour, which costs around 70,000Rp per person and includes door-to-door pick-up/drop off at about 4am/noon. To do the trip yourself from the Sosrowijayan area, flag down a northbound bus 5 on the corner of Jl Sosrowijayan and Jl Joyonegaran, which will take you to Jombor (2000Rp, 20 minutes), where you can get a Borobudur bus (12,000Rp, one hour). The last bus back from Borobudur leaves around 6pm.

KALIURANG & GUNUNG MERAPI

☎ 0274

On the flanks of Gunung Merapi, Kaliurang is a pleasant mountain resort, with crisp air and some spectacular views of one of Java's most boisterous volcanoes. It is 26km north of Yogya.

Gunung Merapi (Mountain of Fire) is Indonesia's most active volcano and has been in a near-constant state of eruption for hundreds of years. People living on its conical flanks are regularly killed by pyroclastic flows, and in 2006, 28,000 villagers had to be evacuated after intense seismic activity. It's extremely unlikely anyone will be allowed anywhere near its summit in the near future, though you get a spectacular view from the viewing point of Kali Aden.

Check the latest situation in Kaliurang, but at the time of writing the climb to the peak from Kaliurang had been strictly off limits since 1994 because of volcanic activity.

MORE THAN A MONUMENT

Jaker (☎ 0293-788 845; jackpriyana@yahoo.com.sg) is a group of guides and local activists based in the small settlement of Borobudur.

If you want to explore the region around Borobudur, Jaker can provide expert local knowledge. Many guides speak fluent English. Backpacking rates are charged for trips to Selogriyo (towering rice terraces and a small Hindu temple), Tuksongo (a centre of glass-noodle production), tofu and pottery villages, and to Mahitan hill for sunrise over the Borobudur monument.

Christian Awuy, owner of **Vogels Hostel** (☎ 895208, 081 7541 2572; Jl Astamulya 76; dm 15,000Rp, d 20,000-25,000Rp, bungalows with hot-water bathroom from 100,000Rp), has organised climbs for years and is an essential first reference point. Vogels is a travellers' institution and has been serving up the same mixture of cheap accommodation and hearty food.

Angkot from Yogyakarta's Terban station to Kaliurang cost 7000Rp; the last leaves at 4pm. A taxi from Malioboro will cost around 90,000Rp.

SOLO

☎ 0271 / pop 560,000

Arguably the epicentre of Javanese identity and tradition, Solo is one of the least Westernised cities in the island. An eternal rival to Yogyakarta, this conservative city often plays second fiddle to its more conspicuous neighbour. But with backstreet *kampung* and elegant *kraton*, traditional markets and gleaming malls, Solo has more than enough to warrant at least an overnight visit.

In many ways, Solo is also Java writ small, incorporating its vices and virtues and embodying much of its heritage. On the downside, the island's notoriously fickle temper tends to flare in Solo first – the city has been the backdrop for some of the worst riots in Java's recent history, especially in 1998. And Solo retains a reputation as a hotbed of radicalism. On the upside, most citizens are extremely hospitable and welcome visitors.

Orientation

Solo's main street is Jl Slamet Riyadi, running east–west through the centre of the city, with most budget accommodation conveniently clustered just off it around Jl Yos Sudarso and Jl Ahmad Dahlan. The oldest part of Solo is east of here around the Kraton Surakarta and Pasar Klewer.

Solo's train station is about 2km north of the city centre, the main Tirtonadi bus terminal about 1.5km north again.

Information

BCA bank (cnr Jl Dr Rajiman & Jl Gatot Subroto) Has ATM and currency-exchange facilities.
Main post office (Jl Jenderal Sudirman)
Solo Grand Mall (Jl Jenderal Sudirman; wi-fi) Free wi-fi.
Speedy Net (Jl Ronggowarsito 4; per hr 6000Rp; 24hr) Speedy connections and plenty of computers.
Telkom wartel (Jl Mayor Kusmanto) Near the post office.
Tourist office (☎ 711435; Jl Slamet Riyadi 275; 8am-4pm Mon-Sat) Most staff are helpful here, and can provide a map of Solo, and information on cultural events and places to visit. There are also desks at the bus and train stations, which can help with ticket bookings.

Sights & Activities

Once the hub of an empire, today the **Kraton Surakarta** (Kraton Kasunanan; ☎ 656432; admission 8000Rp; 9am-2pm Tue-Fri, 9am-3pm Sat & Sun) is a faded memorial of a bygone era. It's still worth a visit, but much of the *kraton* was destroyed by fire in 1985, attributed by the Solonese to the *susuhunan*'s lack of observance of tradition. Nevertheless, some fine silver and bronze Hindu-Javanese figures remain in the museum alongside dusty Javanese weapons, parasols and what must qualify as a near-definitive horse-carriage collection. Presentation could be so much better, however, and labelling is poor or nonexistent. The distinctive pagodalike tower, Panggung Songgo Buwono, built in 1782, is original and is used for meditation.

Children's **dance practise** can be seen here on Sunday from 10am to noon and adult practise from 1pm to 3pm.

Istana Mangkunegaran (☎ 644946; Jl Ronggowarsito; admission 10,000Rp; 8.30am-4pm Mon-Sat, to 1pm Sun) is a rival palace founded in 1757 by a dissident prince, Raden Mas Said. The weathered main structure itself, built in Javanese-European style with an extended front canopy, is in urgent need of restoration, but the museum rooms at the rear have some fascinating curios, including a diminutive gold genital cover, a tremendous mask collection and a wonderfully gaudy dining room complete with lashings of gild and a mirrored ceiling. One of Java's finest *gamelan* orchestras is based here.

Guided tours (a 20,000Rp donation is acceptable) are much less hurried and more informative than at Kraton Surakarta. At the pavilion, you can see excellent music, singing and dance practise sessions on Wednesday and Saturday from 10am until noon.

Solo's markets are always worth a browse, including **Pasar Gede** (Jl Urip Sumoharjo; 8am-6pm), the city's largest general market, selling all manner of produce; **Pasar Klewer** (Jl Secoyudan; 8am-6pm), the multistorey batik market; and **Pasar Triwindu** (Jl Diponegoro; 9am-4pm), the flea market.

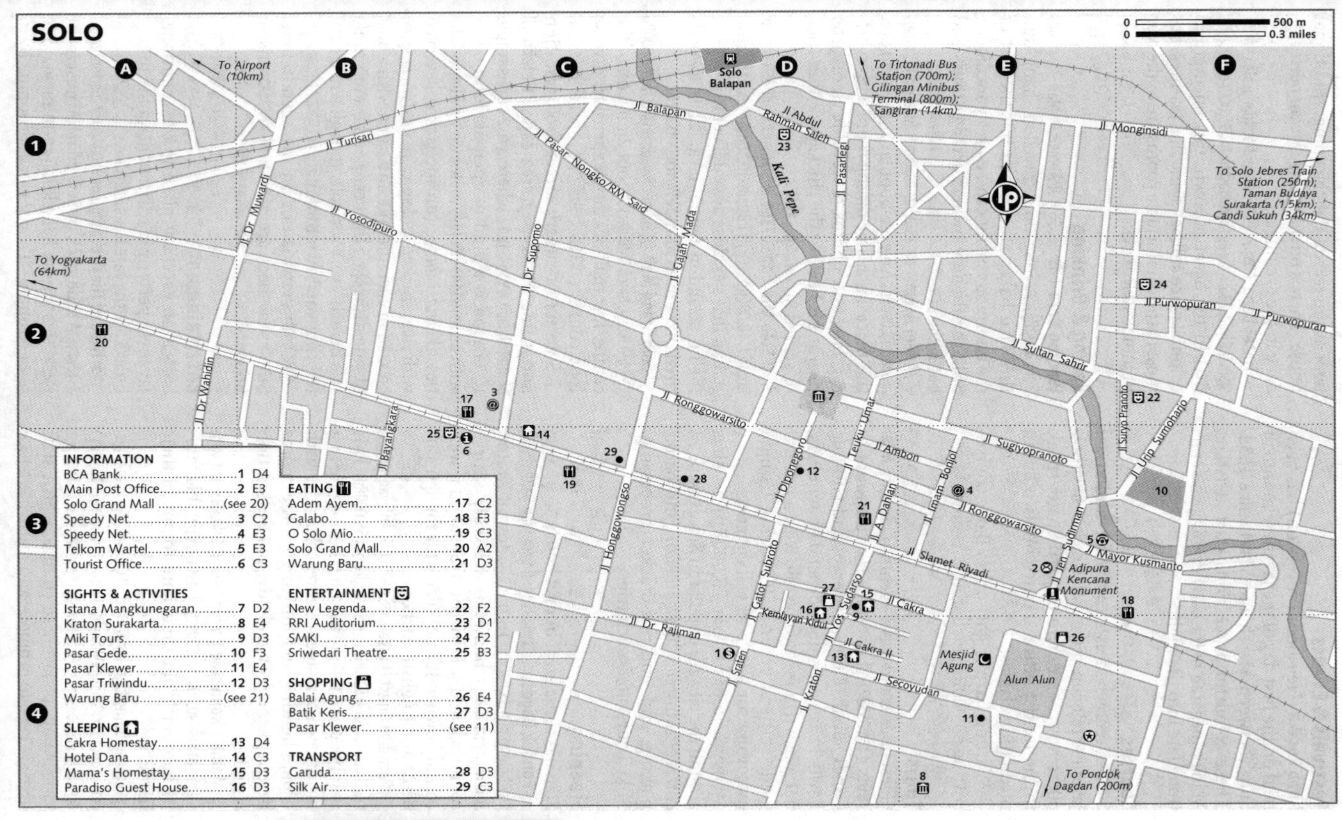
SOLO
0 500 m
0 0.3 miles
To Airport (10km)
To Yogyakarta (64km)
Solo Balapan
Kali Pepe
To Tirtonadi Bus Station (700m); Gilingan Minibus Terminal (800m); Sangiran (14km)
To Solo Jebres Train Station (250m); Taman Budaya Surakarta (1.5km); Candi Sukuh (34km)
Adipura Kencana Monument
Mesjid Agung
Alun Alun
To Pondok Dagdan (200m)
INFORMATION
BCA Bank 1 D4
Main Post Office 2 E3
Solo Grand Mall (see 20)
Speedy Net 3 C2
Speedy Net 4 E3
Telkom Wartel 5 E3
Tourist Office 6 C3
SIGHTS & ACTIVITIES
Istana Mangkunegaran 7 D2
Kraton Surakarta 8 E4
Miki Tours 9 D3
Pasar Gede 10 F3
Pasar Klewer 11 E4
Pasar Triwindu 12 D3
Warung Baru (see 21)
SLEEPING
Cakra Homestay 13 D4
Hotel Dana 14 C3
Mama's Homestay 15 D3
Paradiso Guest House 16 D3
EATING
Adem Ayem 17 C2
Galabo 18 F3
O Solo Mio 19 C3
Solo Grand Mall 20 A2
Warung Baru 21 D3
ENTERTAINMENT
New Legenda 22 F2
RRI Auditorium 23 D1
SMKI 24 F2
Sriwedari Theatre 25 B3
SHOPPING
Balai Agung 26 E4
Batik Keris 27 D3
Pasar Klewer (see 11)
TRANSPORT
Garuda 28 D3
Silk Air 29 C3

INDONESIA

Festivals & Events

Kirab Pusaka (Heirloom Procession) has been held on the first day of the Javanese month of Suro (between March and May) since 1633. These colourful processions start at Istana Mangkunegaran in the early evening and continue late into the night.

Courses

Solo is renowned as a centre for traditional Javanese religion and mysticism, but few travellers now come here to participate; speak to the tourist office about schools offering meditation classes.

Warung Baru (right) offers Batik courses costing 85,000Rp, including a T-shirt.

Tours

Guest houses and travel agents, including **Miki Tours** (☎ 653278; Jl Yos Sudarso 17), run tours to Candi Sukuh, Gunung Merapi and Gunung Lawu. Prices very much depend on numbers, but a day trip for two people with a car and guide starts at around 500,000Rp. Using a motorbike for transport will cut costs.

Bicycle tours (from 75,000Rp) to sites around the city are popular in Solo, taking in cottage industries like *gamelan*- and batik-making, *arak* and rice-cracker processing. Miki Tours offers such trips.

Sleeping

Solo has some great budget hotels.

Pondok Dagdan (☎ 669324; Jl Carangan Baluarti 42; r without mandi 35,000Rp) In the shadow of Kraton Surakarta, this homestay has very simple rooms around a leafy courtyard, and a welcoming owner. It's popular with foreign students and English teachers.

Paradiso Guest House (☎ 652960; Kemlayan Kidul 1; r without mandi 40,000Rp, with mandi from 55,000Rp) This is a fine place to stay as you'll be lodging in a historic white residence of real character with ornate lighting and mirrors. All the rooms here are kept clean and tidy, and the location is quiet.

Mama's Homestay (☎ 662466; Jl Cakra 33; s/d with shared mandi 40,000/55,000Rp) The hospitable family here rents out three bare rooms in their home.

Cakra Homestay (☎ 634743; Jl Cakra II/15; r with/without mandi 75,000/65,000Rp, with air-con 100,000Rp; ❄ 🏊) This is an excellent choice for those wanting to learn about Javanese culture, which staff here are keen to promote, and it also has a nice pool at the rear of the charming, traditional house. There's often a free *gamelan* performance in the evening.

Hotel Dana (☎ 711976; www.hoteldanasolo.com; Jl Slamet Riyadi 286; r/ste incl breakfast from 245,000/495,000Rp; ❄) In the heart of town, this once-grand colonial place still has some fine features, but most of the comfortable rooms are to the rear in motel-style blocks.

Eating & Drinking

Warung Baru (☎ 656369; Jl Ahmad Dahlan 23; mains from 8500Rp) A long-time travellers' hang-out, the Baru bakes great bread but the rest of the enormous menu can be pretty mediocre. Still, the friendly owners arrange tours and batik classes.

Adem Ayem (☎ 716992; Jl Slamet Riyadi 342; meals around 15,000Rp) An ever-popular *rumah makan*, this place has a large dining room with swirling fans and photos of ye olde Surakarta. Everone is here for the chicken – either fried or served up *gudeg*-style.

O Solo Mio (☎ 727264; Jl Slamet Riyadi 253; pizzas around 40,000Rp; 🕑 11.30am-10.30pm) Authentic Italian that's as close as you'll get to a taste of the homeland in central Java; it has a wood-fired pizza oven and delicious pasta.

Solo Grand Mall (Jl Slamet Riyadi; dishes from 8000Rp 🕑 breakfast, lunch & dinner) About 2km west of the centre, this mall has an inexpensive, diverse food court.

Solo has a superb street-food tradition and a fine traffic-free area called **Galabo** (Jl Slamet Riyadi; 🕑 5-11pm) where you can sample it. Galabo is a kind of open-air food court with around 90 stalls – tuck into local specialities like *nasi gudeg* (unripe jackfruit served with rice, chicken and spices), *nasi liwet* (rice cooked in coconut milk and eaten with a host of side dishes) or the beef noodle soup *timlo solo* here. It's very sociable, though you'll have to bring your own Bintang.

A pub crawl is not on the agenda here. Solo's few bars are attached to expensive hotels.

Entertainment

Solo is an excellent place to see traditional Javanese performing arts; contact the tourist board for the latest schedules.

Sriwedari Theatre (admission 3000Rp; 🕑 performances 8-10pm) At the back of Sriwedari Amusement Park, this theatre has a long-running *wayang orang* troupe – it's well worth dropping by to experience this masked dance-drama, and you can come and go as you please.

RRI auditorium (☎ 641178; Jl Abdul Rahman Saleh 51) RRI holds an eclectic program of cultural performances, including *wayang orang* and *ketoprak* performances.

SMKI (☎ 632225; Jl Kepatihan Wetan) The high school for the performing arts has dance practise from around 8am to noon Monday to Thursday and Saturday, and 8am to 11am Friday.

Taman Budaya Surakarta (TBS; ☎ 635414; Jl Ir Sutami 57) Cultural centre that hosts all-night *wayang kulit* performances; private dance lessons are also available.

This is not a big party town but Solo has a few clubs. All feature alternative cheesy bands with DJs playing pounding dance music. **New Legenda** (Jl Suryo Pranoto) is a popular city centre club, plays *dangdut*, techno and Indo chart hits.

Shopping

Balai Agung (🕒 8am-4pm) On the northern side of the *alun alun*, you can see high-quality *wayang kulit* puppets being made here, and *gamelan* sets are for sale.

Solo is a major batik centre. You can see the batik process on one of Warung Baru's batik tours (see opposite).

Other recommendations:

Batik Keris (☎ 643292; Jl Yos Sudarso 62; 🕒 9am-7pm) Expensive, but top quality and fixed prices.

Pasar Klewer (Jl Secoyudan; 🕒 8am-6pm) Market stuffed with cheap batik.

Getting There & Away

AIR

A new terminal is scheduled to have opened at Solo's Adi Sumarmo airport (code SOC) by the time you read this. Currently there are just two international flights.

Air Asia (☎ 5050 5088; www.airasia.com) connects Solo to Kuala Lumpur daily. On Tuesday, Thursday and Saturday, **SilkAir** (☎ 724604/5; www.silkair.com; Novotel Hotel, Jl Slamet Riyadi 272) flies to/from Singapore.

Domestic services include frequent flights to Jakarta with **Garuda** (☎ 630082; Hotel Cakra, Jl Slamet Riyadi 201) and **Sriwijaya Airlines** (☎ 723777; www.sriwijayaair-online.com; Adi Sumarmo airport).

BUS & MINIBUS

The Tirtonadi bus terminal is 3km from the centre of the city. Only economy buses leave from here to destinations such as Prambanan (13,000Rp, 1½ hours), Yogyakarta (from 13,000Rp, two hours) and Semarang (26,000Rp, 3¼ hours). Buses also travel to a number of destinations in East Java including Surabaya (52,000Rp, seven hours).

Near the bus terminal, the Gilingan minibus terminal has express air-con minibuses to almost as many destinations as the larger buses.

Travel minibus destinations include Yogyakarta (25,000Rp), Semarang (45,000Rp) and Jakarta (170,000Rp). **Citra** (☎ 713684), based at Gilingan, runs *travel* minibuses to most main cities; call if you would like a pick-up. Homestays, cafes and travel agents also sell these tickets.

TRAIN

Solo is located on the main Jakarta–Yogyakarta–Surabaya train line and most trains stop at **Balapan** (☎ 714039), the main train station.

Seventeen daily trains connect Solo with Yogyakarta so you won't have to wait long. The *pramek* (*bisnis* 7000Rp, one hour) trains are reasonably comfortable but not air-conditioned.

Express trains to Jakarta include the 8am *Argo Lawu* (*eksekutif*, 220,000Rp, eight hours), which is the most luxurious day train, and the *Senja Utama* (*bisnis*, from 100,000Rp, 10½ hours), which leaves at 6pm.

The *Lodaya* (*bisnis*/*eksekutif* 100,000/165,000Rp, nine hours) departs for Bandung at 8am and 8.30pm daily, while the *Sancaka* (*bisnis*/*eksekutif* 55,000/80,000Rp, five hours) heads for Surabaya twice daily.

Jebres train station in the northeast of Solo has a few very slow *ekonomi*-class services to Surabaya and Jakarta.

Getting Around

A taxi to/from Adi Sumarmo airport, located 10km northwest of the city centre, costs around 55,000Rp; otherwise you can take a bus to Kartosuro and then another to the airport. For a taxi, metered **Kosti Solo taxis** (☎ 856300) are reliable. Becak cost about 7000Rp from the train station or bus terminal into the centre. Public buses run up and down Riyadi and cost 2000Rp. Motorcycles and bicycles (motorcycle/bicycle per day 60,000/15,000Rp) can be hired from homestays.

AROUND SOLO

Sangiran

Prehistoric 'Java Man' fossils were discovered at Unesco-recognised Sangiran, 16km north of Solo, where a small **museum** (admission 10,000Rp; 9am-4pm Tue-Sun) has fossil exhibits of *Homo erectus*, mammoth bones and hippo teeth. To get there take a Purwodadi bus to Kalijambe (3000Rp) and it's a 4km walk from there (or 10,000Rp by *ojek*).

Candi Sukuh

This fascinating, remote **temple complex** (admission 10,000Rp; 7am-4.30pm) on the slopes of Gunung Lawu (3265m), some 36km east of Solo, is well worth a visit. Dating from the 15th century, Sukuh was one of the last temples to be built in Java by Hindus, who were on the run from Muslims and forced to isolated mountain regions (and Bali). From the site, there are sweeping views across terraced fields.

The main pyramid resembles an Incan or Mayan monument, with steep sides and a central staircase; at its base are flat-backed turtles that may have been sacrificial altars. It's clear a fertility cult built up around the temple, as there are all manner of erotic carvings, including a *yoni-lingga* (vagina-phallus) representation and a figure clasping his erect penis.

Coming by public transport is very tricky. Take a bus bound for Tawangmangu from Solo as far as Karangpandan (6000Rp), then a Kemuning minibus (3000Rp) to the turn-off to Candi Sukuh; from here it's a steep 2km walk uphill to the site or a 10,000Rp *ojek* ride. For around 35,000Rp, *ojek* will take you to both Sukuh and Cetho.

INDONESIA

SURABAYA

☎ 031 / pop 2.4 million

Surabaya is not an easy place to love. It's a big, noisy, polluted and commerce-driven city that's not well set-up for visitors or pedestrians – just crossing the eight-lane highways that rampage through the centre is a challenge in itself. But though Surabaya's sheer size seems intimidating at first, it does have the odd curious attraction, including a remarkable *Arabian Nights*–style bazaar district and a vibrant Chinatown. But one night is enough for most travellers, if that.

Orientation

There's no natural centre to this sprawling city but Jl Permuda, which runs west from Gubeng train station, is something of a main drag, with two shopping malls plus several hotels and banks.

Around 5km north of here is the Chinatown district and the Arab quarter of Qubah.

Information

Jl Pemuda has several banks with ATMs. The Tunjungan Plaza is also ATM rich.

Abacommnet (LG fl, Tunjungan Plaza, Jl Tunjungan; per hr 10,000Rp) Offers pretty speedy connections and doubles as a *wartel*.

Main post office (Jl Kebon Rojo) Inconveniently located 4km north of the city centre.

Periplus (☎ 593 7360; Galaxy Mall, Jl Dharmahusada 37) Has a great selection of English-language titles and magazines, a rarity outside Jakarta.

Tourist Information Centre (☎ 534 0444; www.sparklingsurabaya.com; Jl Pemuda; 9am-5pm Mon-Sat) Has helpful English-speaking staff, plenty of leaflets, and a good free colour map.

Sights

Surabaya may have a grand history, but she wears it lightly, for little of substance remains. The **Qubah** – the city's labyrinthine Arab quarter, centred upon the imposing **Mesjid Ampel** (Jl Ampel Suci) – is fascinating, however, and begs exploration. The mosque itself marks the burial place of Sunan Ampel, one of the *wali songo* (holy man) who brought Islam to Java; pilgrims chant and present rose-petal offerings at his grave behind the mosque. The warren of surrounding lanes are reminiscent of a Damascene souk, with stalls selling perfumes, sarongs, prayer beads, *peci* (black Muslim felt hats) and other religious paraphernalia.

Chinatown, just south of here, bursts into life at night when Jl Kembang Jepun becomes a huge street kitchen known as Kya Kya. Much of the food here is sourced from the nearby **Pasar Pabean** (Jl Panggung; 8am-6pm) and the nearby **fish market** (pasar ikan; Jl Panggung; from 8pm). Close by too is the 300-year-old Chinese temple **Kong Co Kong Tik Cun Ong** (Jl Dukuh; admission by donation; dawn-dusk).

From the old city you can head north to the **Kalimas harbour**, where brightly painted *pinisi* from Sulawesi and Kalimantan unload their wares.

Sleeping

Some of the very cheapest, and roughest, hotels can be found near Kota train station. It's best to spend a little extra.

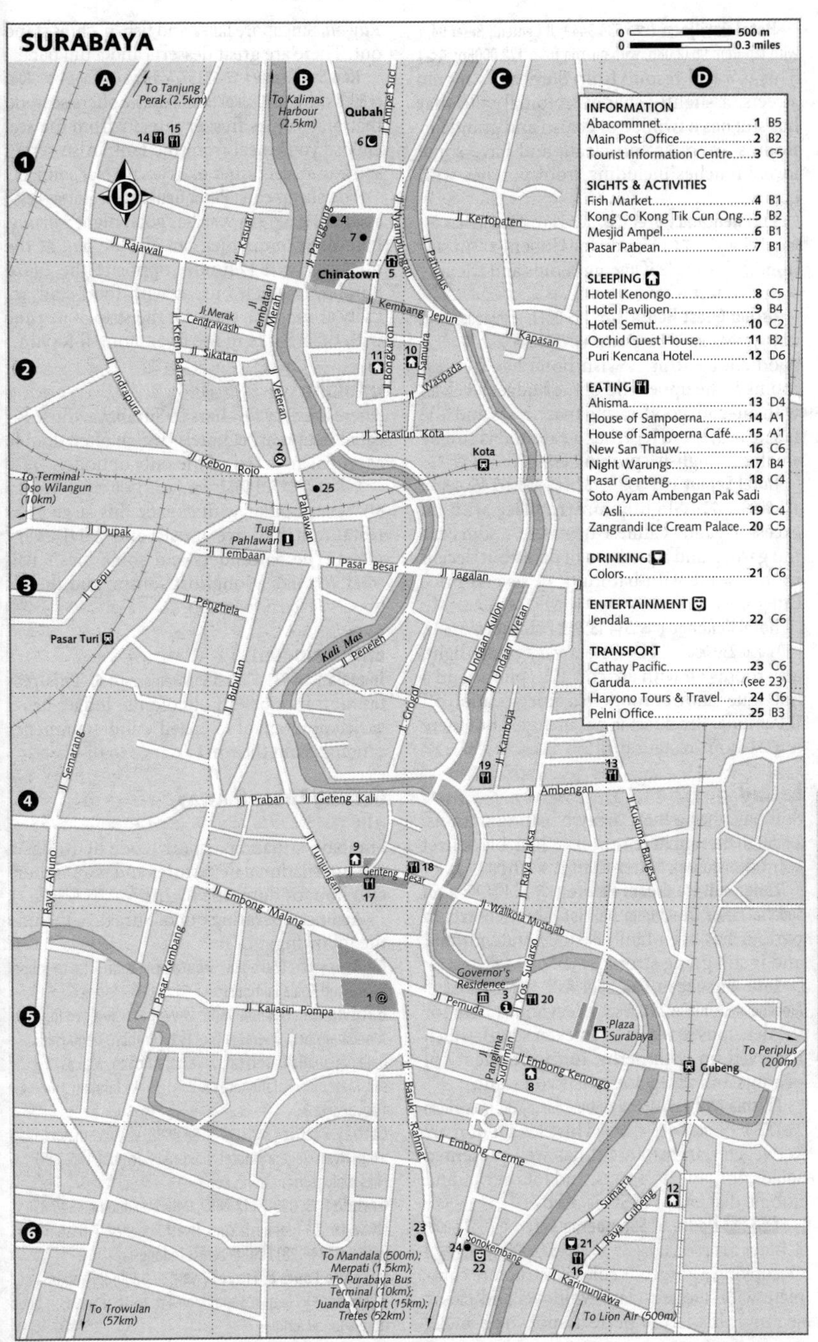
SURABAYA
0 500 m
0 0.3 miles
INFORMATION
Abacommnet....1 B5
Main Post Office....2 B2
Tourist Information Centre....3 C5
SIGHTS & ACTIVITIES
Fish Market....4 B1
Kong Co Kong Tik Cun Ong....5 B2
Mesjid Ampel....6 B1
Pasar Pabean....7 B1
SLEEPING
Hotel Kenongo....8 C5
Hotel Paviljoen....9 B4
Hotel Semut....10 C2
Orchid Guest House....11 B2
Puri Kencana Hotel....12 D6
EATING
Ahisma....13 D4
House of Sampoerna....14 A1
House of Sampoerna Café....15 A1
New San Thauw....16 C6
Night Warungs....17 B4
Pasar Genteng....18 C4
Soto Ayam Ambengan Pak Sadi Asli....19 C4
Zangrandi Ice Cream Palace....20 C5
DRINKING
Colors....21 C6
ENTERTAINMENT
Jendala....22 C6
TRANSPORT
Cathay Pacific....23 C6
Garuda....(see 23)
Haryono Tours & Travel....24 C6
Pelni Office....25 B3
To Tanjung Perak (2.5km)
To Kalimas Harbour (2.5km)
Qubah
Chinatown
Kota
Tugu Pahlawan
Pasar Turi
To Terminal Oso Wilangun (10km)
Kali Mas
Governor's Residence
Plaza Surabaya
Gubeng
To Periplus (200m)
To Mandala (500m); Merpati (1.5km); To Purabaya Bus Terminal (10km); Juanda Airport (15km); Tretes (52km)
To Trowulan (57km)
To Lion Air (500m)
Jl Rajawali
Jl Kasuari
Jl Panggung
Jl Ampel Suci
Jl Nyamplungan
Jl Kertopaten
Jl Pabean
Jl Kembang Jepun
Jl Kapasan
Jl Merak Cendrawasih
Jl Jembatan Merah
Jl Krem Barat
Jl Sikatan
Jl Bongkaron
Jl Samudra
Jl Waspada
Indrapura
Jl Veteran
Jl Setasiun Kota
Jl Kebon Rojo
Jl Pahlawan
Jl Dupak
Jl Tembaan
Jl Pasar Besar
Jl Jagalan
Jl Cepu
Jl Penghela
Jl Bubutan
Jl Peneleh
Jl Undaan Kulon
Jl Undaan Wetan
Jl Grogol
Jl Kamboja
Jl Semarang
Jl Praban
Jl Geteng Kali
Jl Ambengan
Jl Kusuma Bangsa
Jl Tunjungan
Jl Genteng Besar
Jl Raya Jaksa
Jl Embong Malang
Jl Walikota Mustajab
Jl Raya Arjuno
Jl Pasar Kembang
Jl Yos Sudarso
Jl Kaliasin Pompa
Jl Pemuda
Jl Panglima Sudirman
Jl Embong Kenongo
Jl Basuki Rahmat
Jl Embong Cerme
Jl Sumatra
Jl Raya Gubeng
Jl Sonokembang
Jl Karimunjawa
INDONESIA

Hotel Paviljoen (☎ 534 3449; Jl Genteng Besar 94; r with fan from 90,000Rp, with air-con from 128,000Rp; ❄) This is a real respite from Surabaya's manic streets, a slightly shabby colonial villa that has still has a twinkle of charm and grandeur. Rooms are plain but clean, and have some lovely touches including front porches with chairs.

Puri Kencana Hotel (☎ 503 3161; Jl Kalimantan 9; r from 115,000Rp; ❄) Handy for Gubeng train station, with simple if ageing rooms and friendly staff. No hot water.

Orchid Guest House (☎ 355 0211; orchidguesthousesby@yahoo.com; Jl Bongkaran 49; d 150,000Rp; ❄) A good choice, this newish hotel has spotless rooms at the upper end of the budget level, all with air-con, good spring mattresses and TV. It's near the Kya Kya, has a cafe and is run by a helpful English-speaking crew.

Hotel Semut (☎ 352 4578; Jl Samudra 9-15; d from 155,000Rp; ❄) Slightly bizarre place with an excess of gaudy Chinese furniture, a slim central garden and a plethora of dated but decent rooms, some with bathtubs, in several price categories.

Hotel Kenongo (☎ 534 1359; Jl Embong Kenongo 12; r 195,000-230,000Rp; ❄) Offers very clean, light, airy rooms all with air-con, TV, phone and a hot-water shower room in a quiet location off Jl Pemuda. Breakfast is not included but there is a 24-hour restaurant.

Eating

Surabaya has a huge array of eating options. Local dishes include *rawon*, a thick black beef soup that tastes better than it sounds.

Zangrandi Ice Cream Palace (☎ 534 5820; Jl Yos Sudarso 15; ice cream from 3000Rp) This ice-cream parlour has been famous since Dutch times, and is still going strong.

Soto Ambengan Pak Sadi Asli (☎ 532 3998; Jl Ambengan 3A; mains 20,000Rp) Everyone is here for the delicious *soto ayam* (chicken soup), which is served up with herbs, turmeric, plenty of peanuts and an egg or two if you want.

Ahisma (☎ 535 0466; Jl Kusuma Bangsa 80; mains from 25,000Rp; ⏲ noon-10pm; ⊠) This elegant upmarket vegetarian restaurant has well-presented salads, tofu meals, soups, and lots of rice and noodle dishes; no MSG is used.

OUR PICK **House of Sampoerna Café** (☎ 353 9000; Jl Taman Sampoerna; meals 20,000-82,000Rp; ⊠ ᯤ) Occupying a gorgeous colonial structure complete with stained-glass windows and classy seating, this is the perfect spot for a meal. *Rawon*, Singapore laksa and fish 'n' chips stand out. There are great desserts and a full bar.

New San Thauw (☎ 503 5776; Jl Raya Gubeng 64; per 100g of fish & crab from 9000Rp) San Thauw offers seafood that only comes fresher directly from the sea; choose your meal from the tank. Also serves some unusual dishes like cassava leaf soup.

For cheap eats, **Pasar Genteng** (Jl Genteng Besar; mains 8000Rp; ⏲ 9am-9pm) has good night *warung*. Late-night munchies can also be had at the offshoot of Jl Pemuda, opposite the Plaza Surabaya, which buzzes with food-stall activity around the clock, or the strip of *warung* with their backs to the river along Jl Kayun.

Drinking

There are very few bars in Surabaya, those located in upmarket hotels (which often double as clubs) are a few of the only options.

Colors (☎ 503 0562; www.colorspub.com; Jl Sumatra 81) Very popular with expats, this large pub-restaurant has live music and a DJ every night. The bartenders and some locals will treat you like a long-lost cousin, and there's good Western food too.

Entertainment

Jendala (☎ 531 4073; Jl Sonokembang 4-6) This restaurant, in a beautiful colonial lodge, has a varied program of so-called 'culturetainment', ranging from theatre to dance to disco.

Getting There & Away

AIR

Surabaya's Juanda airport (code SUB) has a few international departures and is an important hub for domestic flights.

Airlines operating out of Surabaya include the following:

Air Asia (☎ 5050 5088; www.airasia.com) Flies to Johor Bahru and Kuala Lumpur.

Batavia Air (☎ 504 9666; www.batavia-air.co.id; Juanda airport) Operates flights to Ambon, Denpasar, Balikpapan, Banjarmasin, Jakarta, Kupang, Makassar, Mataram, Palangkaraya, Pontianak, Tarakan and Yogyakarta.

Cathay Pacific (☎ 0804-188 8888; www.cathaypacific.com; Hyatt Regency Hotel, Jl Basuki Rachmat 124-128) Flies daily to/from Hong Kong.

Garuda (☎ 080-7142 7832, 24hr booking line 546 8505; www.garuda-indonesia.com; Hyatt Regency, Jl Basuki Rahmat 124-128) Flights across Indonesia.

Haryono Tours & Travel (☎ 532 5800; Jl Panglima Sudirman; ⏲ 8am-4.30pm Mon-Fri, to 1pm Sat) Can book tickets for all airlines.

Lion Air (☎ 503611; www.lionair.co.id; Jl Sulawesi 75) Flights to Ambon, Denpasar, Balikpapan, Banjarmasin, Batam, Jakarta, Makassar, Manado, Mataram, Ternate and Yogyakarta.
Mandala (☎ 561 0777; www.mandalaair.com; Jl Raya Diponegoro 91D) Flies to Denpasar, Balikpapan, Batam, Jakarta, Malang, Semarang and Solo.
Merpati (☎ 568 8111; www.merpati.co.id; Jl Darmo 109-111) Has plenty of connections across Indonesia.
SilkAir (☎ 724604/5; www.silkair.com) Flies to/from Singapore.

BOAT

Surabaya is an important port and a major transport hub for ships to the other islands. Boats depart from Tanjung Perak harbour; bus P1 from outside Tunjungan Plaza heads here.

Several Pelni ships sail to Makassar in Sulawesi (economy/1st class from 182,00/558,000Rp), and Pontianak (209,000Rp to 664,000Rp) in Kalimantan. Head to the **Pelni office** (☎ 352 1044; www.pelni.co.id; Jl Pahlawan 112) for more information.

Ferries no longer run to Madura now that the Suramadu Bridge has been completed.

BUS & MINIBUS

Most buses operate from Surabaya's main Purabaya bus terminal in Bungurasih, 10km south of the city centre. Buses along the north coast and to Semarang depart from the Terminal Oso Wilangun, 10km west of the city.

Buses from Purabaya head to Malang (economy/1st class 10,000/15,000Rp, two to three hours), Probolinggo (14,000/22,000Rp, around three hours), Banyuwangi (36,000/51,000Rp, seven hours), Solo (52,000/70,000Rp, seven hours) and Yogyakarta (58,000/76,000Rp, 8½ hours).

Luxury long-haul buses also depart from Purabaya. Most are night buses leaving in the late afternoon or early evening. Bookings can be made at the terminal, or travel agencies in the centre of town sell tickets with a mark-up.

Door-to-door *travel* operate to Solo (80,000Rp), Yogyakarta (85,000Rp) and Semarang (95,000Rp). Hotels can make bookings and arrange pick-up or you can try the agencies along Basuki Rahmat.

TRAIN

From Jakarta, trains taking the fast northern route via Semarang arrive at the Pasar Turi train station southwest of Kota train station. Trains taking the southern route via Yogyakarta, and trains from Banyuwangi and Malang, arrive at Gubeng and most carry on through to Kota. **Gubeng train station** (☎ 503 3115) is much more central and sells tickets for all trains.

Most Jakarta-bound trains leave from **Pasar Turi** (☎ 534 5014), including the luxury *Argo Bromo Anggrek* (from 260,000Rp, 10½ hours), which leaves at 8am and 8pm, and the *Gumarang* (*bisnis/eksekutif* from 140,000/240,000Rp, 12½ hours), departing at 5.30pm.

From Gubeng, the slower *Bima* (*eksekutif* 220,000Rp, 13 hours) departs at 4pm for Jakarta via Yogyakarta (*eksekutif* 140,000Rp, five hours), and the *bisnis Mutiara Selatan* (120,000Rp, 13 hours) at 4.35pm for Bandung.

The *Sancaka* leaves Gubeng at 7am and 3pm for Solo (4½ hours) and Yogyakarta (5½ hours); costing from 55,000/80,000Rp in *bisnis/eksekutif* class to either destination.

The *bisnis*-class *Malang Ekspres* is the best option for Malang (11,000Rp, two hours), leaving Gubeng at 10am daily. There are also a few very slow *ekonomi* trains, most continue on to Blitar.

Heading east, the *Mutiara Timur* goes to Banyuwangi (*bisnis/eksekutif* from 60,000/80,000Rp, six hours) via Probolinggo at 9.15am and 10.35pm.

Getting Around

Taxis from Juanda airport (17km) operate on a coupon system and cost around 85,000Rp to the city centre. Surabaya has plenty of air-con metered taxis; **Bluebird** (☎ 372 1234) is the most reliable company.

Bemo are labelled A, B, C etc and charge 2000Rp.

AROUND SURABAYA

Scattered around **Trowulan**, 60km southwest of Surabaya on the Solo road, are the ruins of the capital of the ancient Majapahit empire, Java's last great Hindu kingdom. One kilometre from the main Surabaya–Solo Hwy, the **Trowulan Museum** (admission 2500Rp; 🕑 7am-3.30pm Tue-Sun) houses superb examples of Majapahit sculpture and pottery from throughout East Java. Reconstructed temples are scattered over a large area, some within walking distance, though you need to hire a becak to see them all.

The hill resort of **Tretes**, 55km south of Surabaya, is a cool break if you have to kill time in Surabaya, with walks around town and trekking to **Gunung Welirang**.

PULAU MADURA

pop 3.7 million

The flat, rugged and deeply traditional island of Madura may now be connected to Java by Indonesia's longest bridge, but the character of the people and scenery are a world apart.

This is an island famous for its colourful **bull races**, *kerapan sapi,* which kick off in late August and September and climax with the finals held at Pamekasan. The bulls are harnessed in pairs, two teams compete at a time and they're raced along a 120m course in a special stadium – the bulls can do nine seconds over 100m. Bull races for tourists are sometimes staged at the Bangkalan Stadium, and race practise is held throughout the year in Bangkalan, Pamekasan and Sumenep, but dates are not fixed. Contact the Surabaya Tourist Information Centre (p216) for race details or the one in Sumenep (below).

Pamekasan, the capital of Madura, comes alive in the bull-racing season, but is quiet the rest of the year.

Sumenep, 53km northeast of Pamekasan, is a more refined, royal town and the most interesting on Madura. It has an excellent **tourist office** (☎ 667148; kurniadi@consultant.com; Jl Sutomo 5; 🕑 7am-3.30pm Tue-Sat), banks with ATMs, and a few internet cafes. You can see Sumenep's 18th-century mosque, and the **kraton** (admission 1000Rp; 🕑 7am-5pm) with its water palace and interesting museum. **Asta Tinggi**, the royal cemetery, is only about 3km from the town centre.

Hotel Wijaya I (☎ 662433; Jl Trunojoyo 45-47; r with/without air-con from 90,000/35,000Rp; ❄) is in the centre of town and one of the best of a bunch of bad budget places. **Hotel Garuda** (☎ 662424; Jl KH Wahid Hasyim 3; r 50,000-175,000Rp, ste 225,000Rp; ❄) is handy for the bus terminal. This new hotel is the most comfortable place in Sumenep and has a wide range of accommodation options.

Sumenep's main bus terminal is on the south side of town, a 6000Rp becak ride from the centre. Buses leave roughly hourly until 4pm for Surabaya's Purabaya bus terminal (normal/*patas* 28,000/38,000Rp, four hours), and there are also direct buses to Jakarta and Denpasar. Bus agents along Jl Trunojoyo sell tickets.

INDONESIA

GUNUNG BROMO

☎ 0335

A lunaresque landscape of epic proportions and surreal beauty, Gunung Bromo is one of Indonesia's most breathtaking sights. The smoking cone of Bromo is just one of three peaks to emerge from a vast caldera, the Tengger Massif (which stretches 10km across), its steep walls plunging down to a vast, flat sea of lava and sand. This desolate landscape has a distinctly end-of-the-world feeling, particularly at sunrise.

An even larger cone – Java's largest mountain, the fume-belching Gunung Semeru (3676m) – oversees Bromo's supernatural beauty, and the entire volcanic wonderland forms the Bromo-Tengger-Semeru National Park.

Bromo is an easy side trip from the main backpacking highway that runs between Bali and Yogyakarta, or it's about three hours from Surabaya. The usual jumping-off point is the town of Probolinggo, served by trains and buses from Surabaya and Banyuwangi.

Information

However you approach Bromo, a 25,000Rp park fee is payable at one of the many PHKA checkpoints.

The **PHKA post** (☎ 541038; 🕑 8am-3pm Tue-Sun) in Cemoro Lawang is opposite Hotel Bromo Permai, and has information about Bromo.

Sights & Activities

The best vantage point over this bewitching landscape is from the viewpoint known as Gunung Penanjakan (2770m). All the hotels, and several freelance guides, can put together 4WD trips (around 275,000Rp for four people and warm jackets), leaving around 4am to catch the sunrise from Penanjakan. It's usually well worth the early start, as the views of Bromo, the Tengger crater and towards smoking Gunung Semeru are spellbinding – this is where those postcard shots are taken. You'll then be driven back down the lip of the caldera and across the crater bed to the squat grey cone of Gunung Bromo itself, allowing you to gaze into the steaming guts of this small but highly active volcano.

Alternatively, it's a straightforward 3km hike (around an hour) from Cemoro Lawang to Bromo. Take the wide track downhill from the village and follow the white stone markers that lead the way to Bromo. In the pitch black,

JAVA'S WILDEST SURF

The 434.2-sq-km Alas Purwo National Park occupies the whole of the remote Blambangan Peninsula on the southeastern tip of Java. Facilities are limited and it is not easy to reach, but Alas Purwo has fine beaches, good opportunities for wildlife spotting and huge surf at Plengkung, on the isolated southeastern tip of the peninsula. One of the best left-handed waves in the world, it breaks over a shallow reef in a perfect tube. Surfers have dubbed it G-Land (for Grajagan, another name for the area). It's best between April and September.

The surf camps, away from the beach at Plengkung, are for tours only. Everyone comes on a surfing package that includes all transfers, usually from Bali.

Bobby's Camp (☎ in Bali 0361-755 588; www.grajagan.com;) The biggest camp, with three standards of bungalow in shady grounds with a restaurant and bar. It's run out of Kuta, Bali, and offers three-night packages from US$350.

G-Land Joyo's Surf Camp (☎ in Bali 0361-763166; www.g-land.com;) Good-quality thatched wooden bungalows with fan or air-con and most of the facilities a surfer could want: cold beer, a large screen for sports, pool tables, internet access and table tennis. Packages start at US$300 for three nights. It's open November to March only.

the route can be a little indistinct, but remember that the steaming guts of Bromo are on the left, accessed by 253 steps (the neighbouring peak is Batok). The Hindu temple at the foot of Bromo and Bator is only open for religious ceremonies.

Though Probolinggo is the usual approach, Bromo can also be reached via **Tosari** from the northwest and **Ngadas** from the southwest.

Sleeping & Eating

CEMORO LAWANG

At the lip of the Tengger crater and right at the start of the walk to Bromo, Cemoro Lawang is the most popular place to stay.

our pick **Cafe Lava Hostel** (☎ 541020; r from 100,000Rp, with breakfast & hot shower 200,000-350,000Rp) Tumbing down the side of the mountain, this is the best base in town for travellers, with a sociable vibe and English-speaking staff. Economy rooms have been renovated and are clean and neat if bare, while the smarter rooms are attractive (all have little porches with valley views). The restaurant serves up filling, inexpensive Indonesian and Western grub, and Bintang, and is the best place in town to get a group together for the jeep ride up Penanjakan.

Hotel Bromo Permai I (☎ 541049; economy r 99,000Rp, with hot shower from 240,000Rp) Ageing but reasonable cottages with porches, and a huge log cabin-style restaurant with a slightly pricey menu.

Cemara Indah Hotel (☎ 541019; old block r without/with mandi from 50,000/170,000Rp, with air-con, TV & hot water 350,000Rp;) Enjoys a great position on the edge of the crater but the staff can be a bit tour-pushy and the so-so rooms are not great value.

NGADISARI

Another 3km back towards Probolinggo is the tiny village of Ngadisari.

Yoschi's Guest House (☎ 0335-541018; yoschi_bromo@telkom.net; r without/with shower 90,000/170,000Rp, cottages with hot water from 330,000Rp;) A friendly hospitable place with loads of character, this Alpine chalet–style place has a good vibe and tasty food. Rooms are a little small but comfortable, and there's a peaceful garden. Tours and transport for the 4km to Bromo (50,000Rp per person) are offered.

PROBOLINGGO

On the highway between Surabaya and Banyuwangi, this is the jumping-off point for Gunung Bromo. Most travellers only see the bus or train station, but the town has hotels if you get stuck.

Hotel Bromo Permai (☎ 422256; Jl Panglima Sudirman 327; r 65,000Rp, with air-con 90,000-180,000Rp;) It's on a mega-busy street, but the plain, clean rooms are all situated well to the rear around a garden where noise is not an issue. There's a warnet and good travel info, and breakfast is included.

Getting There & Away

Probolinggo's bus station is 5km west of town on the road to Bromo; catch a yellow *angkot* from the main street or the train station for 2000Rp.

Shop around before you purchase a ticket. Normal/air-con buses travel to Surabaya (14,000/22,000Rp, two hours), Banyuwangi (35,000/50,000Rp, five hours), Yogyakarta (58,000/85,000Rp, nine hours) and Denpasar (78,000/115,000Rp, 11 hours).

Gunung Bromo minibuses leave from a stop just up from Probolinggo's Bayuangga bus terminal, heading for Cemoro Lawang (15,000Rp, two hours) via Ngadisari (12,000Rp, 1½ hours) until around 5pm. The late-afternoon buses charge more to Cemoro Lawang, when fewer passengers travel beyond Ngadisari. Make sure it goes all the way to Cemoro Lawang when you board.

About 2km north of town, the train station is 6km from the bus terminal. Probolinggo is on the Surabaya–Banyuwangi line. Most services are *ekonomi* class. The *Mutiara Timur* costs from 60,000/80,000Rp (*bisnis/eksekutif*) to Surabaya (two hours, departing at 1.31pm) or the same rate to Banyuwangi (five hours, departing at 11.10am). The slow *ekonomi* -class *Sri Tanjung* goes west to Solo via Surabaya at 11.36am or east to Banyuwangi at 5.08pm.

BALI

Impossibly green rice terraces, pulse-pounding surf, enchanting Hindu temple ceremonies, mesmerising dance performances, ribbons of beaches, a truly charming people: there are as many images of Bali as there are flowers on the ubiquitous frangipani trees.

This small island – you can drive the entire coast in one day – looms large for any visit to Southeast Asia. No place is more visitor friendly. Hotels range from surfer dives where the fun never stops to hidden retreats in the lush mountains. You can dine on local foods bursting with flavours fresh from the markets or snack on seafood from a beachside shack. From a cold Bintang at sunset to an epic night clubbing, your social whirl is limited only by your own fortitude. And when it comes time to relax, you can get a cheap beach massage or lose yourself in an all-day spa.

And small obviously doesn't mean homogeneous. Manic Kuta segues into luxurious Seminyak. The artistic swirl of Ubud is a counterpoint to misty treks amid the volcanoes. Mellow beach towns like Amed, Lovina and Pemuteran are found right round the coast and just offshore is the laid-back idyll of Nusa Lembongan.

As you stumble upon the exquisite little religious offerings that seem to materialise everywhere as if by magic, you'll see that their tiny tapestry of colours and textures is a metaphor for Bali itself.

History

Bali's first prehistoric tourists strolled out of the spume and onto the island's western beaches around 3000 BC. Perhaps distracted by primitive beach life, however, they got off to a relaxed start and it was only in the 9th century that an organised society began to develop around the cultivation of rice.

Hinduism followed hot on the heels of wider cultural development, and as Islam swept through neighbouring Java in the following centuries, the kings and courtiers of the embattled Hindu Majapahit kingdom began crossing the straits into Bali, making their final exodus in 1478. The priest Nirartha brought many of the complexities of the Balinese Hindu religion to the island, and established superb offshore temples, including Rambut Siwi, Tanah Lot and Ulu Watu.

In the 19th century the Dutch began to form alliances with local princes in northern Bali. A dispute over the ransacking of wrecked ships was the pretext for the 1906 Dutch invasion of the south, which climaxed in a suicidal *puputan* (fight to the death). The Denpasar nobility burnt their own palaces, dressed in their finest jewellery and, waving golden *kris*, marched straight into the Dutch guns. The rajas of Tabanan, Karangasem, Gianyar and Klungkung soon capitulated, and Bali became part of the Dutch East Indies.

In later years Balinese culture was actually encouraged by many Dutch officials. International interest was aroused and the first Western tourists arrived.

After WWII the struggle for national independence was fierce in Bali. Independence was declared on 17 August 1945 (still celebrated as Independence Day), but power wasn't officially handed over until 27 December 1949, when the Dutch finally gave up the fight. The island languished economically in the early years of Indonesian sovereignty, but Bali's greatest national resource, beauty, was subsequently marketed to great effect.

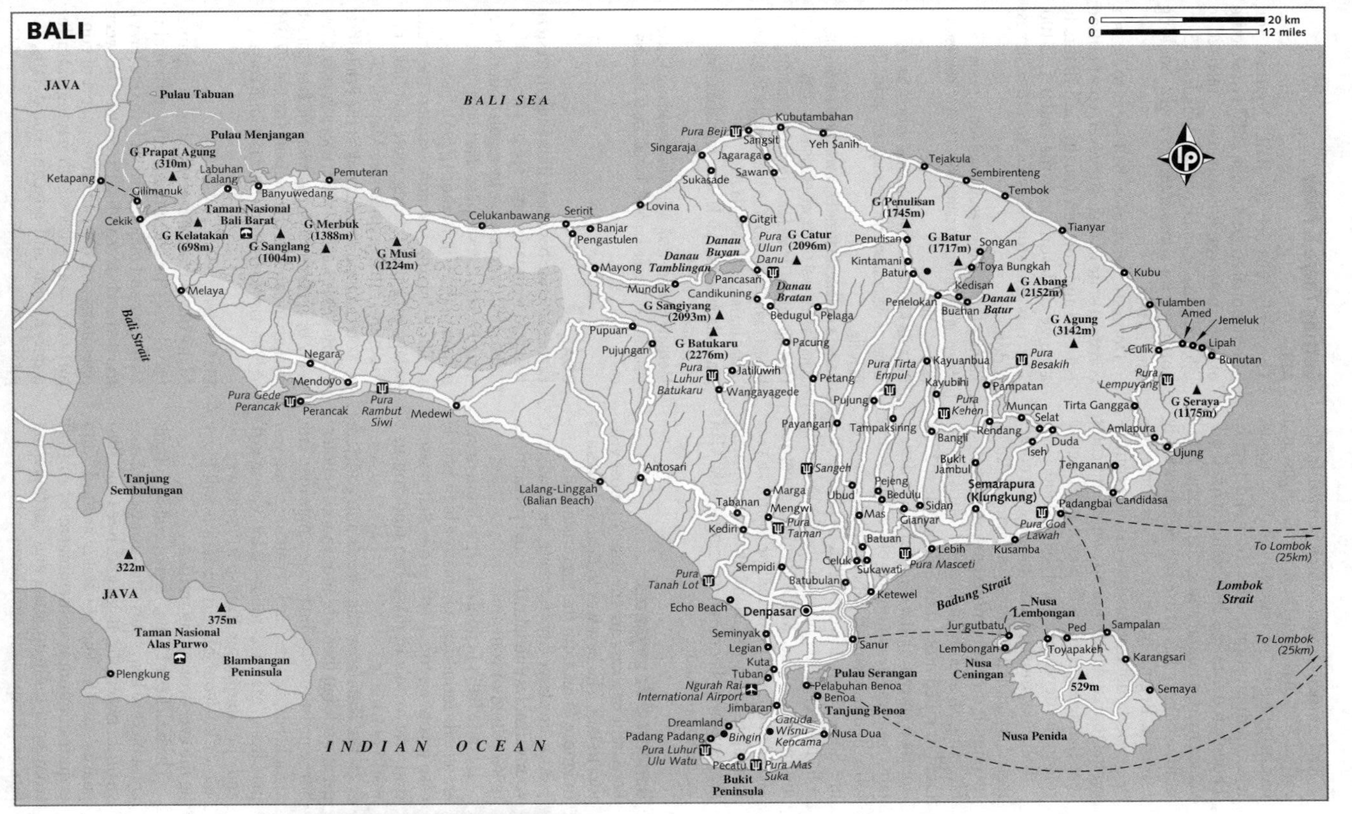
BALI
0 20 km
0 12 miles
BALI SEA
INDIAN OCEAN
Bali Strait
Badung Strait
Lombok Strait
To Lombok (25km)
To Lombok (25km)
JAVA
JAVA
Ketapang
Gilimanuk
Cekik
Pulau Tabuan
Pulau Menjangan
G Prapat Agung (310m)
Labuhan Lalang
Banyuwedang
Pemuteran
Taman Nasional Bali Barat
G Kelatakan (698m)
G Sanglang (1004m)
G Merbuk (1388m)
G Musi (1224m)
Melaya
Negara
Mendoyo
Pura Gede Perancak
Perancak
Pura Rambut Siwi
Medewi
Celukanbawang
Seririt
Banjar
Pengastulen
Lovina
Singaraja
Pura Beji
Sangsit
Kubutambahan
Yeh Sanih
Jagaraga
Sawan
Sukasade
Tejakula
Sembirenteng
Tembok
Tianyar
Kubu
Tulamben
Amed
Jemeluk
Lipah
Bunutan
Culik
Pura Lempuyang
G Seraya (1175m)
Tirta Gangga
Amlapura
Ujung
Tenganan
Candidasa
Padangbai
G Agung (3142m)
Pura Besakih
G Abang (2152m)
Danau Batur
Toya Bungkah
Songan
Kedisan
Buahan
Penelokan
G Batur (1717m)
G Penulisan (1745m)
Penulisan
Kintamani
Batur
Gitgit
Pura Ulun Danu
G Catur (2096m)
Danau Buyan
Danau Tamblingan
Danau Bratan
Pancasari
Candikuning
Bedugul
Pelaga
Mayong
Munduk
G Sangiyang (2093m)
G Batukaru (2276m)
Pura Luhur Batukaru
Jatiluwih
Wangayagede
Pacung
Petang
Pupuan
Pujungan
Antosari
Lalang-Linggah (Balian Beach)
Tabanan
Kediri
Pura Tanah Lot
Echo Beach
Marga
Mengwi
Pura Taman
Sempidi
Batubulan
Denpasar
Sangeh
Payangan
Pujung
Pura Tirta Empul
Tampaksiring
Kayuanbua
Kayubihi
Pura Kehen
Bangli
Pampatan
Muncan
Selat
Rendang
Duda
Iseh
Bukit Jambul
Semarapura (Klungkung)
Ubud
Pejeng
Bedulu
Mas
Gianyar
Sidan
Batuan
Celuk
Sukawati
Lebih
Pura Masceti
Ketewel
Pura Goa Lawah
Kusamba
Sanur
Seminyak
Legian
Kuta
Tuban
Ngurah Rai International Airport
Jimbaran
Pulau Serangan
Pelabuhan Benoa
Benoa
Tanjung Benoa
Garuda Wisnu Kencana
Nusa Dua
Dreamland
Padang Padang
Bingin
Pura Luhur Ulu Watu
Pecatu
Pura Mas Suka
Bukit Peninsula
Nusa Lembongan
Jungutbatu
Lembongan
Nusa Ceningan
Ped
Toyapakeh
Sampalan
Karangsari
Semaya
529m
Nusa Penida
Tanjung Sembulungan
322m
375m
Taman Nasional Alas Purwo
Blambangan Peninsula
Plengkung

INDONESIA

The tourism boom, which started in the early 1970s, has brought many changes, and has helped pay for improvements in roads, telecommunications, education and health. Though tourism has had some marked adverse environmental and social effects, Bali's unique culture has proved to be remarkably resilient. Beginning in the 1990s there has been vocal public opposition to some controversial tourist developments, which indicates that Balinese people will play a more active role in the development of their island.

Bali, like most places, has also been affected by global politics. In October 2002, two simultaneous bomb explosions in Kuta – targeting an area frequented by tourists – injured or killed more than 500 people (p228). Tourism (meaning the economy) was devastated and was dealt another blow 2005 when more bombs went off, albeit with less loss of life. Since then, however, Bali has been on a roll. It elected the hero of the 2002 bombing investigations, Made Pastika, governor. A record of nearly two million visitors a year turn up to enjoy the island and development is everywhere. People are starting to ask: 'Can we be too popular?'

Dangers & Annoyances

Persistent hawkers are the bane of most visitors to Bali. The best way to deal with them is to ignore them from the first instance.

As in any large city anywhere, be mindful of your valuables and take the usual precautions to keep hold of your stuff.

Despite Bali's hedonistic reputation, drugs are strictly forbidden, and many a high-profile case involving foreigners prove that possession, use or sale of drugs can land you in a world of trouble.

In the Kuta area, the streets and *gang* are usually safe but there are annoyances. Scooter-borne prostitutes (who hassle single men late at night) cruise after dark. Walking along you may hear: 'massage' followed by 'young girl' and the ubiquitous 'transport' followed by 'blow'. But your biggest irritation will likely be the ever-worsening traffic.

The beaches of Kuta, Legian and Seminyak are subject to heavy surf and strong currents – swim between the flags and heed the lifeguards' advice. The sea water around Kuta is quite commonly contaminated by run-off from both built-up areas and surrounding farmland, especially after heavy rain.

Getting There & Away

AIR

The only airport in Bali, Ngurah Rai International Airport (code DPS) is just south of Kuta, however, it is sometimes referred to internationally as Denpasar (which is 15km north) or on some internet flight-booking sites as Bali.

Domestic services in Bali seem to be in a constant state of flux. However, competition is fierce and you can usually find flights to a range of destinations for under US$100. There is nonstop service to cities across Indonesia.

Air Asia (code AK; www.airasia.com) Fast-growing Malaysian-based budget carrier with a web of Indonesian domestic flights.

Batavia Air (code 7P; www.batavia-air.co.id) Serves numerous destinations; has the enigmatic slogan: 'Trust us to fly'.

Garuda Indonesia (code GA; www.garuda-indonesia.com) The national carrier serves numerous cities.

Lion Air (code JT; www.lionair.co.id) Fast-expanding budget carrier has a web of service across the archipelago; carried the most passengers in 2008.

Mandala Airlines (code RI; www.mandalaair.com) Serves major routes.

Merpati Airlines (code MZ; www.merpati.co.id) Serves many smaller Indonesian cities, in addition to the main ones.

BOAT

Ferries operate between Gilimanuk in western Bali and Ketapang, Java; see p254.

Lombok is accessible by regular public boat from Padangbai; see p246. Fast boats for tourists serve the Gili Islands (p296).

The Pelni ship *Kelimutu* wanders the archipelago on a month-long route that links Bali to several other islands (see Map p175).

You can inquire and book at the **Pelni offices** (☎ 0361-763963, 021-7918 0606; www.pelni.co.id; Jl Raya Kuta 299; 8am-noon & 1-4pm Mon-Fri, 8am-1pm Sat) in Tuban, and at the **harbour** (☎ 0361-721377; 8am-4pm Mon-Fri, 8am-12.30pm Sat) in Benoa.

BUS

Many buses from numerous bus companies travel daily between the Ubung terminal in Denpasar and major cities in Java (via ferry); most travel overnight. Fares vary between operators, and depend on what sort of comfort you want – it's worth paying extra for a decent seat and air-con. For details, see p236.

Getting Around

Bali is a small island with good roads and regular, inexpensive public transport.

BEMO & TOURIST SHUTTLE BUS

The main bemo hub is in Denpasar (see p236).

You can flag down a bemo pretty much anywhere along its route, but Bali's bemo are notorious for overcharging tourists. Ask a local the correct fare before starting a journey, or watch what people pay and give the same when you get off. Local rides cost a minimum of 4000Rp.

It is worth noting that bemo travel is slow and inconvenient on Bali, and taxi and motorbike rental are relatively cheap. Since seemingly everyone on Bali has bought a motorbike, the bemo/bus network has suffered. Service hours are short and frequencies may be few.

Perama (www.peramatour.com) has a near monopoly on tourist shuttle-bus services in Bali. Book at least one day before you want to travel. Shuttle buses are more comfortable than bemo, but if you're with a group of three or more people (or sometimes two), it may be cheaper to charter a vehicle through your hotel.

BICYCLE

Ask at your accommodation about where you can rent a good bike; hotels often have their own. Generally, prices range from 20,000Rp to 30,000Rp per day.

BOAT

Boats of various sizes serve Nusa Lembongan (p245) and Nusa Penida from Benoa Harbour, Sanur and Padangbai.

CAR & MOTORBIKE

A small Suzuki or Toyota jeep is the usual rental vehicle in Bali. Typical costs are 150,000Rp to 180,000Rp per day, including insurance and unlimited kilometres, but not including fuel.

Motorbikes are a popular way to get around Bali, but can be dangerous. Typically you can expect to pay from around 30,000Rp to 40,000Rp a day. This includes a flimsy helmet, which is compulsory and provides protection against sunburn but not much else.

If you don't have an International Driving Permit, ask the renter to take you to the relevant police station in Denpasar, where you can buy a temporary SIM Turis licence (200,000Rp).

Hiring a car with driver will cost around 350,000Rp to 600,000Rp for an eight- to 10-hour day (includes fuel). You can arrange rentals from any place you are staying, or in tourist areas just by walking down the street. Offers will pour forth.

TAXI

Metered taxis are common in South Bali. They are essential for getting around Kuta and Seminyak, where you can easily flag one

GETTING INTO TOWN

From the official counters, just outside the airport terminals, there are supposedly fixed-price taxis. However, efforts may be made to charge you at the high end of each range and if you say you don't have a room booking, there will be heavy pressure to go to a commission-paying hotel. Approximate costs (depending on drop-off point):

Destination	Cost
Denpasar	70,000-90,000Rp
Kuta Beach	45,000-50,000Rp
Seminyak	70,000-80,000Rp
Ubud	195,000-225,000Rp

If you have a surfboard, you'll be charged at least 35,000Rp extra. Ignore any touts that aren't part of the official scheme.

The thrifty can walk from the international and domestic terminals across the airport car park to the right (northeast) and continue a couple of hundred metres through the vehicle exit to the airport road (ignoring any touts along the way), where you can hail a regular Bluebird cab for about half the above amounts.

Any taxi will take you to the airport at a metered rate that should be much less than the taxis from the airport.

down. Elsewhere, they're often a lot less hassle than haggling with bemo jockeys and charter drivers.

The usual rate for a taxi is 5000Rp flag fall and 4000Rp per kilometre, but the rate is higher in the evening. If you phone for a taxi, the minimum charge is 10,000Rp. Any driver who claims meter problems or who won't use it should be avoided.

By far the most reputable taxi agency is **Bali Taxi** (☎ 0361-701111; www.bluebirdgroup.com), which uses distinctive blue vehicles with the words 'Bluebird Group' over the windshield (watch out for fakes). Drivers speak reasonable English, won't offer you illicit opportunities and use the meter at all times.

KUTA, LEGIAN & SEMINYAK

☎ 0361

The Kuta region is overwhelmingly Bali's largest tourist beach resort. Most visitors come here sooner or later because it's close to the airport and has the greatest range of budget hotels, restaurants and tourist facilities. It is fashionable to disparage Kuta and its immediate neighbour to the north, Legian, for their rampant development, low-brow nightlife and crass commercialism, but the cosmopolitan mixture of beach-party hedonism and entrepreneurial energy can be fun. It's not always pretty, but it's not dull either, and the amazing growth is evidence that a lot of people find something to like in Kuta.

Seminyak may be immediately north of Kuta and Legian, but in many respects it feels like it's almost on another island. It's flash, brash and filled with bony models and expats. Think of it as the cool kids' section of Bali. It's beach is as deep and sandy as Kuta's, but less crowded.

INDONESIA

Orientation

The Kuta region is a disorienting place – it's flat, with few landmarks or signs, and the streets and alleys are crooked and often walled on one or both sides so it feels like a maze. The busy Jl Legian runs roughly parallel to the beach through Legian and Kuta. It's a two-way street in Legian, but in most of Kuta it's one way going south, except for an infuriating block near Jl Melasti where it's one way going north. Jl Raya Seminyak is the continuation of Jl Legian from Kuta and is lined with shops.

Between Jl Legian and the beach is a tangle of narrow side streets, with an amazing hodgepodge of tiny hotels, souvenir stalls, *warung*, bars, construction sites and even a few remaining stands of coconut palms. A small lane or alley is known as a *gang*; the best known are called Poppies Gang I and II – use these as landmarks.

Information

You'll find tourist information offices and tour-booking agencies every few metres along the main tourist streets of Kuta.

BOOKSHOPS

There are dozens of second-hand booksellers along the Poppies Gangs.

Periplus Bookshop Discovery Shopping Mall (Map p227; ☎ 769757; Jl Kartika Plaza, Tuban); Seminyak Sq (Map p229; ☎ 736851; Jl Laksmana) Has the largest selection of new books in Bali.

EMERGENCY

Police station (Map p227; ☎ 751598; Jl Raya Kuta; 24hr) Next to the tourist information centre.

Tourist police post (Map p227; ☎ 784 5988; Jl Pantai Kuta; 24hr) This is a branch of the main police station in Denpasar. Right across from the beach, the officers have a gig that is sort of like a Balinese Baywatch.

INTERNET ACCESS

There are scores of places to connect to the internet. Most have pokey connections and charge about 300Rp a minute. The following have fast broadband connections for an average 600Rp per minute.

Bali@Cyber Café (Map p227; ☎ 761326; www.balicyber.net; Jl Patih Jelantik; meals 20,000-30,000Rp; 8am-11pm) Offers snacks and tasty smoothies.

VIP Bali Internet (Map p227; ☎ 081 3371 96105; Poppies Gang I; 8.30am-midnight) Decent speed, plus wi-fi, scanning, Skype etc.

MEDICAL SERVICES

BIMC (off Map p227; ☎ 761263; www.bimcbali.com; Jl Ngurah Rai 100X; 24hr) Easily accessible from most of southern Bali. It's a modern Western-style clinic that can do tests, hotel visits and arrange medical evacuation. Basic consultations cost 600,000Rp.

Kimia Farma (off Map p227; ☎ 757483; Jl Raya Kuta 15; 24hr) Part of a local chain of pharmacies, it's well stocked and carries hard-to-find items.

Legian Medical Clinic (Map p227; ☎ 758503; Jl Benesari; on call 24hr) Has an ambulance and dental service. It's 400,000Rp for a consultation with an English-speaking Balinese doctor, or 800,000Rp for an emergency hotel visit.

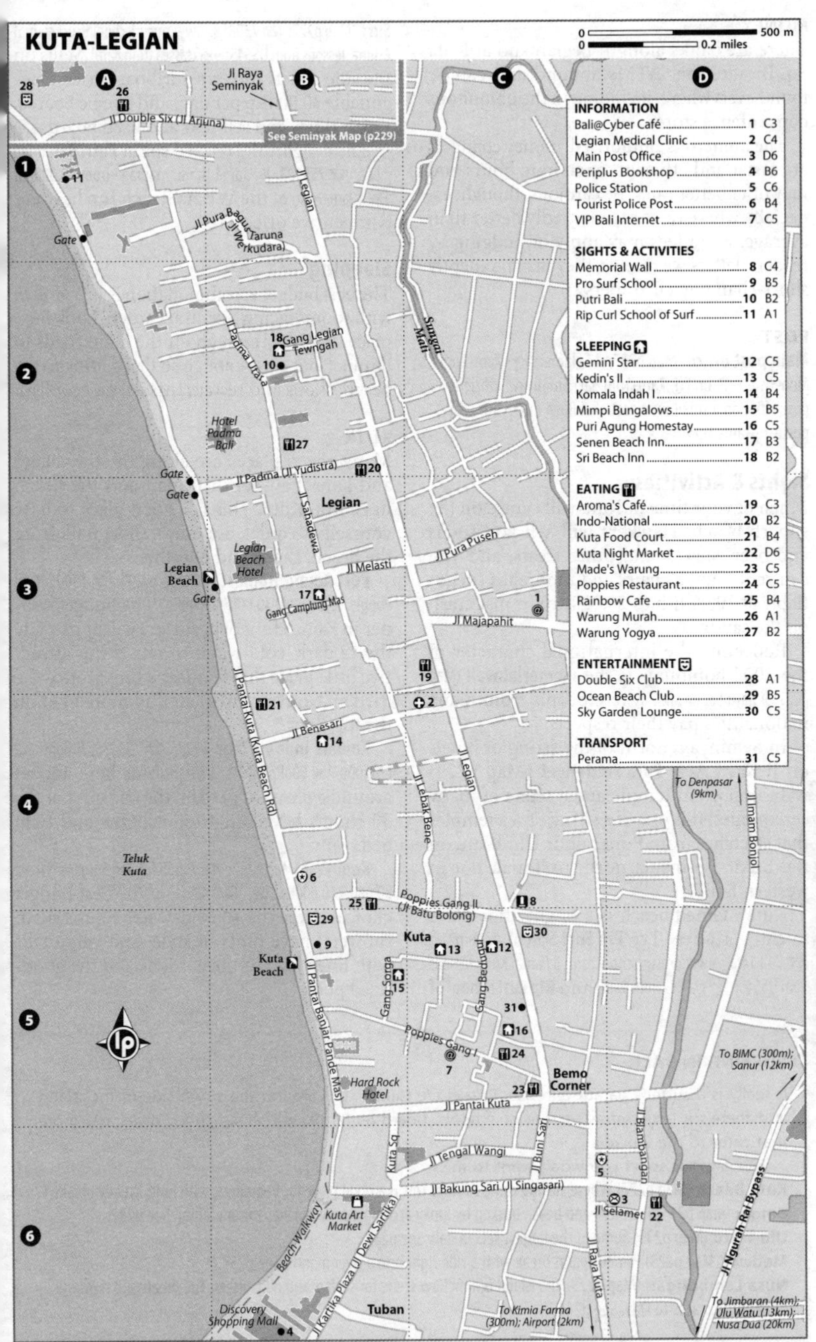
KUTA-LEGIAN
0 500 m
0 0.2 miles
INFORMATION
Bali@Cyber Café 1 C3
Legian Medical Clinic 2 C4
Main Post Office 3 D6
Periplus Bookshop 4 B6
Police Station 5 C6
Tourist Police Post 6 B4
VIP Bali Internet 7 C5
SIGHTS & ACTIVITIES
Memorial Wall 8 C4
Pro Surf School 9 B5
Putri Bali 10 B2
Rip Curl School of Surf 11 A1
SLEEPING
Gemini Star 12 C5
Kedin's II 13 C5
Komala Indah I 14 B4
Mimpi Bungalows 15 B5
Puri Agung Homestay 16 C5
Senen Beach Inn 17 B3
Sri Beach Inn 18 B2
EATING
Aroma's Café 19 C3
Indo-National 20 B2
Kuta Food Court 21 B4
Kuta Night Market 22 D6
Made's Warung 23 C5
Poppies Restaurant 24 C5
Rainbow Cafe 25 B4
Warung Murah 26 A1
Warung Yogya 27 B2
ENTERTAINMENT
Double Six Club 28 A1
Ocean Beach Club 29 B5
Sky Garden Lounge 30 C5
TRANSPORT
Perama 31 C5
Jl Raya Seminyak
Jl Double Six (Jl Arjuna)
See Seminyak Map (p229)
Jl Legian
Jl Pura Bagus Taruna (Jl Werkudara)
Gate
Jl Padma Utara
Gang Legian Tewngah
Sungai Mati
Hotel Padma Bali
Jl Padma (Jl Yudistra)
Jl Sahadewa
Legian
Jl Pura Puseh
Legian Beach Hotel
Jl Melasti
Legian Beach
Gang Camplung Mas
Jl Majapahit
Jl Pantai Kuta (Kuta Beach Rd)
Jl Benesari
Jl Lebak Bene
To Denpasar (9km)
Jl Imam Bonjol
Teluk Kuta
Poppies Gang II (Jl Batu Bolong)
Kuta
Kuta Beach
Gang Sorga
Gang Bedugul
Jl Pantai Banjar Pande Mas
Poppies Gang I
Bemo Corner
Hard Rock Hotel
Jl Pantai Kuta
To BIMC (300m); Sanur (12km)
Kuta Sq
Jl Tengal Wangi
Jl Buni Sari
Jl Blambangan
Jl Bakung Sari (Jl Singasari)
Kuta Art Market
Jl Selamet
Beach Walkway
Jl Kartika Plaza (Jl Dewi Sartika)
Jl Raya Kuta
Jl Ngurah Rai Bypass
Discovery Shopping Mall
Tuban
To Kimia Farma (300m); Airport (2km)
To Jimbaran (4km); Ulu Watu (13km); Nusa Dua (20km)

INDONESIA

MONEY

There are banks along Jl Legian and at Kuta Sq. In addition, ATMs abound and can be found everywhere, including in the ubiquitous convenience stores.

The numerous 'authorised' money changers are faster and efficient, open long hours and may offer better rates. Be cautious, though, especially where rates are markedly better than average. Extra fees may apply or, judging by readers' letters we receive, they may be adeptly short-changing customers.

POST

Main post office (Map p227; Jl Selamet; ⌚ 7am-2pm Mon-Thu, 7-11am Fri, 7am-1pm Sat) Small and efficient post office on a small road east of Jl Raya Kuta with easy poste-restante service.

Sights & Activities

Much of your time in Kuta will centre on the superb beach. Hawkers will sell you sodas and beer, snacks and other treats, and you can rent lounge chairs and umbrellas (negotiable at 10,000Rp to 20,000Rp) or just crash on the sand.

Reflecting the international character of the 2002 bombings is the **memorial wall** (Map p227; Jl Raya Seminyak), where people from many nationalities pay their respects.

In Seminyak, north of the string of hotels on Jl Kaya Aya, **Pura Petitenget** (Map p229) is an important temple and a scene of many ceremonies. It is one of a string of sea temples that stretches from Pura Luhur Ulu Watu on the Bukit Peninsula north to Tanah Lot in western Bali

Kuta's famed beach is a mighty fine place to catch a wave. Try **Pro Surf School** (Map p227; ☎ 744 1466; www.prosurfschool.com; Jl Pantai Kuta; lessons from US$45; ⌚ classes from 9am) and **Rip Curl School of Surf** (Map p227; ☎ 735858; www.ripcurlschoolofsurf.com; Jl Arjuna; lessons from US$45; ⌚ classes from 8am). Stalls on the side streets hire out surfboards (for a negotiable 30,000Rp per day) and boogie boards, repair dings and sell new and used boards.

The delightfully relaxed spa at **Putri Bali** (Map p227; ☎ 755987; Jl Padma Utara; massage from 60,000Rp; ⌚ 10am-9pm) at the Wisata Beach Inn has very competitive prices.

Sleeping

The best budget accommodation is in a *losmen* with rooms facing a central garden. Look for a place that is far enough off the main roads to be quiet, but close enough so that getting to the beach, shops and restaurants isn't a problem.

KUTA

Many cheap places are along the tiny alleys and lanes between Jl Legian and the beach in central Kuta. This is a good place to base yourself: it's quiet, but only a short walk from the beach, shops and nightlife.

Puri Agung Homestay (Map p227; ☎ 750054; off Poppies Gang I; s/d 30,000/50,000Rp) The budget winner in Kuta. Hungover surfers will appreciate the 12 dark, cold-water rooms at this attractive little place that features a tiny grotto-like garden. Nonvampires can find more light on the top floor.

Komala Indah I (Map p227; ☎ 753185; Jl Benesari; r 50,000-150,000Rp; ⛝) The rooms here are set around a pleasant garden; the cheapest of the 30 rooms have squat toilets, fans and twin beds only.

Kedin's II (Map p227; ☎ 763554; Gang Sorga; s/d from 80,000/110,000Rp; 🏊 💻) One of the best budget choices. Here the 16 cold-water rooms (with showers) have hints of style, and verandahs with fine views of the gardens and the good-sized pool.

SURFING IN BALI

It really is a surfer's paradise in Bali. Breaks are found right around the south side of the island and there's a large infrastructure of schools, board-rental places, cheap surfer dives and more that cater to the crowds.

Five famous spots you won't want to miss:

Kuta Beach (Map p227) Where surfing came to Asia. This is a good place for beginners, with long, steady breaks.

Bingin (Map p233) A white-sand beach backed by funky accommodation makes this a natural. See p232.

Ulu Watu (Map p233) Some of the largest sets in Bali. See p233.

Medewi (Map p223) Famous point break with a ride right into a river mouth. See p254.

Nusa Lembongan (Map p223) The island is a mellow scene for surfers and nonsurfers. The breaks are right in front of the places to stay. See p244.

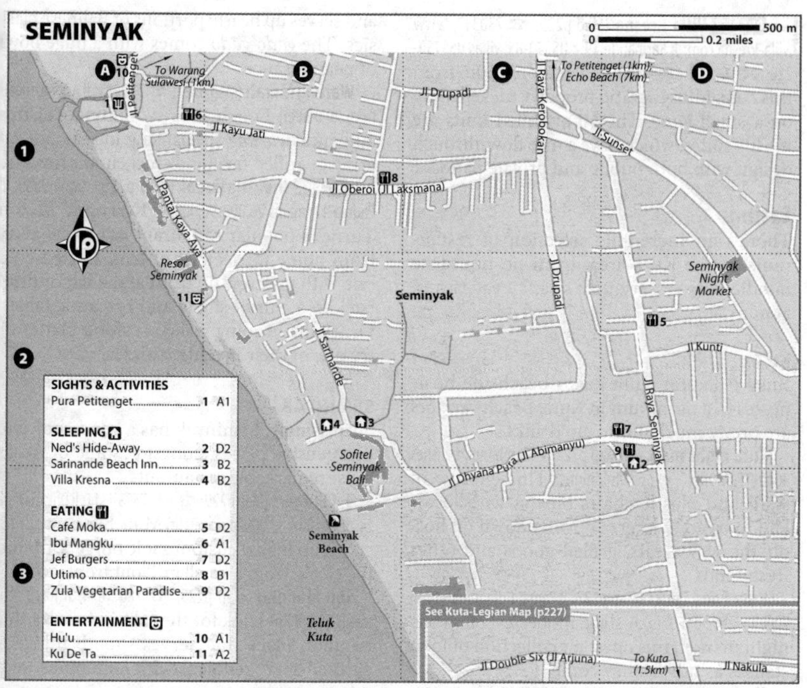

Gemini Star (Map p227; ☎ 750558; aquariushotel@yahoo.com; Poppies Gang II; r 90,000-185,000Rp;) Surfers can lounge at this small, quiet hotel on a narrow alley. Two two-storey blocks shelter the sunny and surprisingly large pool area. Cheap rooms have fans and hot water; more money adds air-con and fridges.

Mimpi Bungalows (Map p227; ☎ 751848; kumimpi@yahoo.com.sg; Gang Sorga; r 150,000R-200,000Rp;) The cheapest of the 10 bungalow-style rooms here are the best value. The private gardens boast orchids and shade, and the pool is a good size.

LEGIAN

The streets are wider here and the pace is less frenetic than just south in Kuta. Budget places tend to be larger as well.

Senen Beach Inn (Map p227; ☎ 755470; Gang Camplung Mas 25; r 50,000-70,000Rp) In a quiet little *gang* near Jl Melasti, this 18-room, cold-water place is run by friendly young guys. Rooms have outdoor bathrooms and are set around a small garden. There are several other family-run cheapies hidden back here.

Sri Beach Inn (Map p227; ☎ 755897; Gang Legian Tewngah; r 60,000Rp) Follow a series of paths into the heart of old Legian. When you hear the rustle of palms overhead, you're close to this homestay with eight simple, clean rooms.

SEMINYAK

Considering all the nightlife here, there's a dearth of cheap places to crash, but there are plenty of places to splash out.

Ned's Hide-Away (Map p229; ☎ 731270; nedshide@dps.centrim.net.id; Gang Bima 3; r from 100,000Rp) Named after Aussie icon Ned Kelly, this simple, 15-room, two-storey place is popular with those hoping to lie low between bouts of fun. Rooms have hot water and there's a character-filled bar. Look for the sign on Jl Raya Seminyak north of Bintang Supermarket.

Sarinande Beach Inn (Map p229; ☎ 730383; www.sarinandehotel.com; Jl Sarinande 15; s/d US$30/32;) An excellent-value place. The 24 rooms are in two-storey blocks around a small pool; the decor is older but everything is well maintained. Amenities include fridges, satellite TV and a cafe. The beach is three minutes by foot.

INDONESIA

our pick **Villa Kresna** (Map p229; ☎ 730317; www.villa-kresna.com; Jl Sarinande 19; r US$40-85, villas US$150-220;) The beach is only 50m from this cute, idiosyncratic property tucked away on a small *gang*. The 10 art-filled units are mostly suites, which have a nice flow-through design with both public and private patios.

Eating

There's an incredible selection of restaurants in the Kuta area, from no-nonsense noodle bars to seriously swanky eateries in Seminyak.

KUTA

Busy Jl Pantai Kuta keeps beachside businesses to a minimum in Kuta. Beach vendors are pretty much limited to drinks.

Kuta night market (Map p227; Jl Blambangan; dishes 5000-15,000Rp; 6pm-midnight) This enclave of stalls and plastic chairs bustles with locals and tourism workers chowing down on hot-off-the-wok treats, grilled goods and other fresh foods.

Kuta Food Court (Map p227; Jl Pantai Kuta; meals from 7000Rp; 5pm-3am) A slick, modern version of a night market, this open-air collection of food stalls is as tidy as they come.

Made's Warung (Map p227; ☎ 755297; Jl Pantai Kuta; dishes 15,000-90,000Rp) Made's was the original tourist *warung* in Kuta. Through the years, the Westernised Indonesian menu has been much copied. Classic dishes such as *nasi campur* (rice served with side dishes) are served with attitude and authority.

Rainbow Cafe (Map p227; ☎ 765730; Poppies Gang II; mains from 20,000Rp) Join generations of Kuta denizens quaffing the afternoon away. Deeply shaded, the vibe here is little changed in years. Many current customers are the offspring of backpackers who met at adjoining tables.

Also recommended:

Aroma's Café (Map p227; ☎ 751003; Jl Legian; dishes 20,000-45,000Rp) Great juices, breakfasts and coffee.

Poppies Restaurant (Map p227; ☎ 751059; Poppies Gang I; dishes 30,000-100,000Rp;)

LEGIAN

The clutch of places at the end of Jl Double Six afford views of sandy action by day, strolling fun-seekers by night and sunsets in between.

Warung Yogya (Map p227; ☎ 750835; Jl Padma Utara; dishes 10,000-15,000Rp) A real find in the tourist heart of Legian, this basic *warung* is spotless and serves up hearty portions of Balinese classics. The *gado gado* comes with a huge bowl of peanut sauce.

Warung Murah (Map p227; ☎ 732082; Jl Arjuna; meals from 20,000Rp) Lunch goes swimmingly at this authentic *warung* specialising in seafood. An array of grilled fish (and chicken *sate*) awaits.

our pick **Indo-National** (Map p227; ☎ 759883; Jl Padma 17; mains 20,000-90,000Rp) Kerry and Milton Turner's popular restaurant is a home away from home for legions of fans. Grab a cold one with the crew up front at the bar or head back to a pair of shady and romantic tables. Order the heaping grilled seafood platter or try one of their inventive pizzas.

SEMINYAK

Surprisingly, Seminyak has a good choice of inexpensive places alongside some of Asia's most remarkable restaurants.

Jef Burgers (Map p229; ☎ 081 7473 4311; Jl Dhyana Pura 24; dishes from 13,000Rp; 24hr) Munchies central: Jef cooks up highly customisable burgers around the clock, from a small grill out front.

Ibu Mangku (Map p229; ☎ 780 1824; Jl Kayu Jati; meals 15,000Rp) Look for the cabs in front of this bamboo place that serves superb minced-chicken satay redolent with lemongrass and other spices.

Warung Sulawesi (off Map p229; Jl Petitenget; meals 15,000Rp; 11am-4pm) Just back from the road in a family compound, fabulously fresh Balinese and Indonesian food is served in classic *warung* style (you choose white or yellow rice, then pick from a captivating array of dishes). The long beans, yum!

Zula Vegetarian Paradise (Map p229; ☎ 732723; Jl Dhyana Pura 5; dishes 15,000-40,000Rp; 8am-4am) It's all vegetarian at this newly enlarged cafe where you can get tofu cheese, a tofu spring roll and tofu cheesecake. Or go wild with a brown-rice surprise.

Café Moka (Map p229; ☎ 731424; Jl Raya Seminyak; meals 18,000-40,000Rp;) Enjoy French-style baked goods at this popular bakery and cafe. Many escape the heat and linger here for hours. The bulletin board spills over with notices.

our pick **Ultimo** (Map p229; ☎ 738720; Jl Laksmana 104; mains 30,000-100,000Rp) *Uno:* find a table overlooking the street action or out back in one of the gardens. *Due:* choose from the surprisingly authentic Italian menu. *Tre:* marvel at the efficient service from the army of servers. *Quattro:* smile at the reasonable bill.

Drinking & Clubbing

The distinction between drinking and clubbing is blurry at best, with one morphing into another as the night wears on (or the morning comes up). Most bars are free to enter, and often have special drink promotions and 'happy hours' between about 5pm and 8pm. During the low season, when tourist numbers are down, you might have to visit quite a few venues to find one with any life. A cover charge is a rarity. Ambience ranges from the laid-back vibe of the surfer dives to the high-concept nightclubs with their long drink menus and hordes of prowling servers.

You'll find many low-key boozers, amid their flashier brethren, along Jl Legian. In Seminyak, numerous scenester spots line Jl Pantai Kaya Aya.

Double Six Club (Map p227; ☎ 081 2462 7733; www.doublesixclub.com; Jl Arjuna; 🕑 11pm-6am) This legendary club (and namesake for the beach, road and more) continues reinventing itself. The swimming pool is still there and so is the bungy jump. Top international DJs play a mix of dance tunes in a sleek open-air pavilion. A cafe up front adds glitz to sunset drinks.

Ocean Beach Club (Map p227; ☎ 755423; www.escbali.com; Jl Pantai Kuta; 🕑 11am-late) This flash place occupies a swathe of prime real estate across from the beach. Lounge on vivid red pillows and watch the sunset, or plunge into the pool – before or after your stint at the pool bar.

Sky Garden Lounge (Map p227; ☎ 756362; www.escbali.com; Jl Legian 61; 🕑 24hr) Part of the ESC empire (which includes the Ocean Beach Club, above), this multilevel palace of flash flirts with height restrictions from its rooftop bar. Look for top DJs, a ground-level cafe and paparazzi-wannabes.

Hu'u (Map p229; ☎ 736443; www.huubali.com; Jl Pantai Kaya Aya; 🕑 4pm-late) There's a menu someplace, but really, this spot is all about air-kissing, seeing and making the scene in an enchanting outdoor garden and pavilion. Action peaks around midnight before people head out to the real clubs.

Ku De Ta (Map p229; ☎ 736969; www.kudeta.net; Jl Laksmana; 🕑 7am-1am) Kuh Lee Shay? Hardly an article gets written about Bali that doesn't mention this beachside lounge, heaving with Bali's beautiful and their attendant scenesters. Perfect your 'bored' look over drinks, although the gorgeous sunsets shine through many a sneer.

Entertainment

Around 6pm every day, sunset on the beach is the big attraction, perhaps while enjoying a drink at a cafe with a sea view. Later on, even as the temperature diminishes, the action heats up, especially at the raging clubs of Kuta.

Shopping

There are lots of local designers, crafts you won't find elsewhere, and more to be found just by wandering the main shopping streets to see what you can find. Kuta has a vast concentration of cheap places, as well as huge, flashy surf-gear emporiums on Kuta Sq and Jl Legian. As you head north along the latter into Legian, the quality of the shops improves and you start finding cute little boutiques, especially past Jl Melasti. Continue into Seminyak for absolutely fabulous shopping along Jl Legian and Jl Raya Seminyak. The retail strip branches off into the prime real estate of Jl Laksmana while continuing north on Jl Raya Kerobokan.

Getting There & Away

BEMO

Dark-blue public bemo regularly travel between Kuta and the Tegal terminal in Denpasar – the fare should be 8000Rp. The route goes from a bemo stop onto Jl Raya Kuta near Jl Pantai Kuta, looping past the beach and then on Jl Melasti and back past Bemo Corner (Map p227) for the trip back to Denpasar.

PUBLIC BUS

For public buses to anywhere in Bali, you'll have to go to the appropriate terminal in Denpasar first; see p236.

TOURIST SHUTTLE BUS

Perama (Map p227; ☎ 751551; www.peramatour.com; Jl Legian 39; 🕑 7am-10pm) usually has at least one bus a day to all of its destinations.

Destination	Fare	Duration
Lovina	125,000Rp	4½hr
Padangbai	60,000Rp	3hr
Sanur	25,000Rp	30 min
Ubud	50,000Rp	1½hr

Getting Around

See p225 for details on getting around. Besides the frequent taxis, you can rent a scooter – often with a surfboard rack – or a bike.

Just ask at where you are staying. Metered cabs from **Bali Taxi** (☎ 701111; www.bluebirdgroup.com) are easily hailed. A taxi to the heart of Kuta from Seminyak will be about 15,000Rp. You can beat the traffic, save the ozone and have a good stroll by walking along the beach. Legian is about 15 minutes away.

BUKIT PENINSULA

☎ 0361

Hot and arid, the southern peninsula is known as Bukit (*bukit* means 'hill' in Bahasa Indonesia). It's the centre of much tourism in Bali; backpackers will be especially interested in booming Jimbaran. The rugged west coast running down to the important temple of Ulu Watu fronts some of the best surfing in the world. Little coves anchor an increasing number of hotels at places such as Balangan and Bingin.

Jimbaran

Just south of Kuta and the airport, Teluk Jimbaran (Jimbaran Bay) is an ever-more-popular and alluring crescent of white sand and blue sea, fronted by a long string of seafood *warung* and ending at the southern end in a bushy headland, home to the Four Seasons Jimbaran Bay.

Jimbaran's seafood *warung*, in three distinct clusters on the bay, are the destination of tourists across the south. The open-sided affairs are right on the beach and perfect for enjoying sea breezes and sunsets. The usual deal is to select your seafood fresh from iced displays or tanks, and to pay according to weight.

Taxis cost about 35,000Rp between Jimbaran anad Kuta.

Balangan Beach

First of a string of small beaches backed by cliffs that run along the west coast of the Bukit Peninsula south to Ulu Watu, Balangan Beach is a real find. A long and low area at the base of the cliffs is covered with palm trees and is fronted by a ribbon of near-white sand. At the north end there is a small temple, **Pura Dalem Balangan** (Map p233); at the south end, a few surfer shacks cluster, renting out loungers and serving drinks.

Back on the bluff above the water are what are likely to be the first of many places to stay; both have cafes. The beach is a brief walk, but the road down is a labyrinth. Try **Balangan Sea View Bungalows** (Map p233; ☎ 780 0499; robbyandrosita@hotmail.com; r from 250,000Rp; 🏊), a cluster of six thatched bungalows and five rooms surrounding a small pool in an attractive compound.

Bingin

A fast-evolving scene, Bingin comprises several funky places to stay scattered across cliffs and one strip of white sand down below. A 1km dirt road turns off the paved road (look for the thicket of accommodation signs), which in turn branches off the main Ulu Watu road at the small village of Pecatu.

An elderly resident collects 3000Rp at a T-junction, which is near parking for the trail down to the **beach**. The surf is often savage but the sands are calm and the roaring breakers mesmerising. The scenery here is simply superb, with virescent cliffs dropping down to a row of houses and the foaming edge of the azure sea.

Bingin Garden (Map p233; ☎ 081 6472 2002; tommybarrell76@yahoo.com; r from 150,000Rp) has four basic, new bungalows set around tidy grounds back from the cliffs, 300m north of the toll gate. Each unit sleeps two and has cold water and a fan.

Padang Padang Beach

Small in size but not in perfection, this little cove is near the main Ulu Watu road where a stream flows into the sea. Parking is easy and it is a short walk. Experienced surfers into tubes flock here.

Thomas Homestay (Map p233; ☎ 081 2377 56030; r 100,000Rp) has stunning views up and down this spectacular coast. The seven simple rooms lie at the end of a very rough 400m track off the main road. You can easily walk down to the beach along a path through the palms.

Ulu Watu & Around

Ulu Watu has become the generic name for the southwestern tip of the Bukit Peninsula. It includes the much-revered temple and the fabled surf breaks at Padang Padang, Suluban and Ulu Watu. Surfers are most common in these parts, although a spate of villa-building is changing that. (In fact, authorities are waging war against new construction within about 2km of the temple.)

SIGHTS & ACTIVITIES

Pura Luhur Ulu Watu (Map p233; admission incl sarong & sash rental 3000Rp, parking 1000Rp; 🕒 8am-7pm) is one of several important temples to the spirits of the sea along the south coast of Bali.

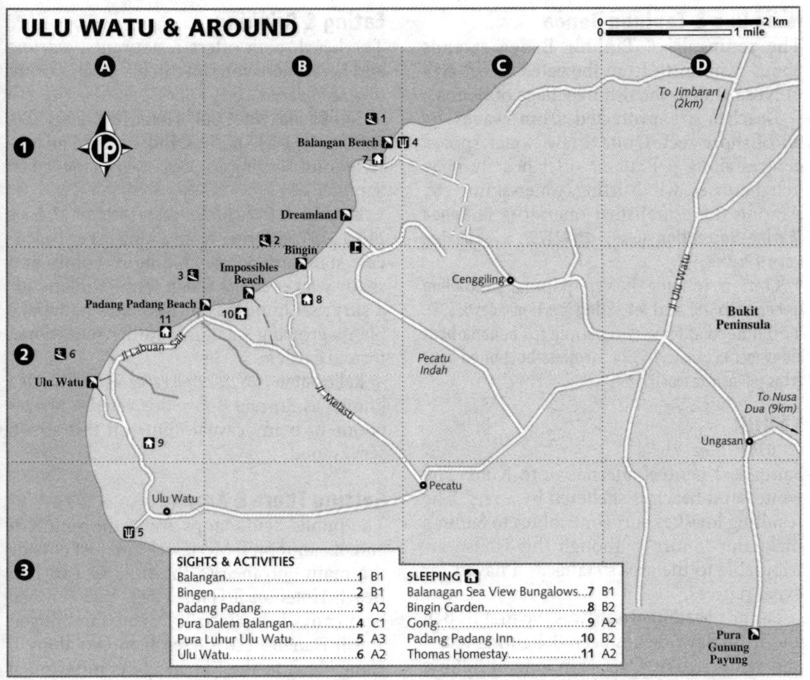

The temple is perched precipitously on the southwestern tip of the peninsula, atop sheer cliffs that drop straight into the pounding surf. You enter through an unusual arched gateway flanked by statues of Ganesha. At sunset, walk around the cliff top to the left (south) of the temple. Watch out for monkeys, who like to snatch sunglasses and anything else within reach. The views out to sea are mesmerising.

An enchanting **Kecak dance** (tickets 40,000Rp; 6-7pm) is held in the temple grounds at sunset. Although obviously set up for tourists, the gorgeous setting makes it one of the more delightful performances on the island.

Ulu Watu, or Ulu's, is a legendary surf spot – the stuff of dreams and nightmares. There are seven different breaks here, all reached through a cave where you go in the water. It's about 1km south of the fabled breaks at Padang Padang.

SLEEPING

If you're not picky you can count on being able to find accommodation of some sort near the surf break of your choice. Expect to pay at least 80,000Rp for a room with cold water, a fan and a shared bathroom. Many surfers choose to stay in Kuta and make the commute of less than an hour.

Padang Padang Inn (Map p233; ☎ 081 2391 3617; Jl Melasti 432; r from 80,000Rp) A better-than-average budget place.

Gong (Map p233; ☎ 769976; thegongacc@yahoo.com; Jl Pantai Suluban; r from US$12) Eight tidy rooms with good ventilation and hot water.

GETTING THERE & AWAY

The best way to see the region is with your own vehicle or by chartering a taxi.

Drivers' note: coming from the east to Pantai Suluban you will first encounter a gated parking area (5000Rp), about 400m from the water. Continuing over a bridge, there is an older parking area (3000Rp) that is a hilly 200m from the water. Beware 'gate-keepers' looking for bonuses.

Public bemo to Ulu Watu are infrequent and stop running by midafternoon. Some from Kuta serve Jimbaran and Ulu Watu – it's best to catch one west of Tuban (on Jl Raya Kuta, outside Supernova shopping centre) or in Jimbaran (on Jl Ulu Watu).

Nusa Dua & Tanjung Benoa

The peninsula of Tanjung Benoa extends about 4km north from the gated resort area of Nusa Dua to the fishing village of Benoa.

Beaches are protected from waves by an offshore reef. Quite a few 'water sports' centres along Jl Pratama offer heavily marketed cruises, windsurfing, water-skiing etc. Among the established operators is **Benoa Marine Recreation** (BMR; ☎ 771757; www.bmrbali.com; Jl Pratama 99).

Options include the very popular **parasailing** (per round US$25) and **jet-skiing** (per 15 minutes US$25). You'll need at least two people for **banana-boat rides** (per 15 minutes US$30), or **glass-bottomed boat trips** (60-minute tour US$25).

SANUR

☎ 0361

Sanur is a genteel alternative to Kuta. The white-sand beach is sheltered by a reef. The resulting low-key surf contributes to Sanur's nickname 'Snore', although this is also attributable to the area's status as a haven for expat retirees.

Sanur's **beachfront walk** was the first in Bali and from day one has been delighting locals and visitors alike. Over 4km long, it follows the sand south as it curves to the west. Oodles of cafes with tables in the sand give plenty of reason to pause.

Sleeping

Usually the best places to stay are right on the beach; however, beware of properties that have been coasting for decades.

Keke Homestay (☎ 287282; Jl Danau Tamblingan 96; r 60,000-135,000Rp; ❄) Set 150m down a *gang* from the noisy road, Keke welcomes backpackers into its genial family. The seven quiet, clean rooms vary from fan-only to air-con cool.

Watering Hole I (☎ 288289; www.wateringholesanurbali.com; Jl Hang Tuah 37; r 60,000-150,000Rp; ❄ 💻) In the northern part of Sanur, the Hole is a busy, friendly place close to the Nusa Lembongan boats. It has 20 pleasant, clean rooms; the cheapest having fan cooling and cold water.

Jati Homestay (☎ 281730; www.hoteljatiandhomestay.com; Jl Danau Tamblingan 168; r 200,000Rp; ♿) Jati means 'genuine' and you will feel right at home at this attractive inn. The 15 bungalow-style rooms are situated in pretty grounds; some of the units have small kitchens.

Eating & Drinking

The beach path offers restaurants, *warung* and bars where you can catch a meal, a drink or a sea breeze.

Sari Bundo (☎ 281389; Jl Danau Poso; dishes 5000-10,000Rp; ⏰ 24hr) Spotless and simple Padang-style joint serving the best curry chicken in Sanur.

Bonsai Cafe (☎ 282908; Jl Danau Tambligan 27; dishes 20,000-60,000Rp) Order from a long list of beach-cafe standards while chilling in comfy and shady wicker chairs. Then wander inland for a surprise: hundreds of the cafe's namesake plants growing small in a rather sensational formal garden.

Kalimantan (☎ 289291; Jl Pantai Sindhu 11) Also known as Borneo Bob's, this veteran boozer is one of many casual joints on this street; serves food.

Getting There & Around

The public bemo stops are at the southern end of Sanur on Jl Mertasari, and just outside the main entrance to the Inna Grand Bali Beach Hotel on Jl Hang Tuah. You can hail bemo anywhere along Jl Danau Tamblingan and Jl Danau Poso. Green bemo go along Jl Hang Tuah to the Kereneng bemo terminal in Denpasar (7000Rp).

The **Perama office** (☎ 285592; Jl Hang Tuah 39; ⏰ 7am-10pm) is at Warung Pojok at the northern end of town. Shuttle destinations include Kuta (25,000Rp, 15 minutes), Ubud (40,000Rp, one hour), Padangbai (60,000Rp, 2½ hours) and Lovina (125,000Rp, four hours).

Bemo go up and down Jl Danau Tamblingan and Jl Danau Poso for 4000Rp. Metered taxis can be flagged down in the street, or call **Bali Taxi** (☎ 701111).

DENPASAR

☎ 0361 / pop 600,000

Sprawling, hectic and ever growing, Bali's capital has been the focus of a lot of the island's growth and wealth over the last five decades. Denpasar can seem a little daunting and chaotic, but spend a some on the tree-lined streets in the relatively affluent government and business district of Renon and you will discover a more genteel side to the city. Denpasar might not be a tropical paradise, but it's as much a part of 'the real Bali' as the island's rice paddies and cliff-top temples.

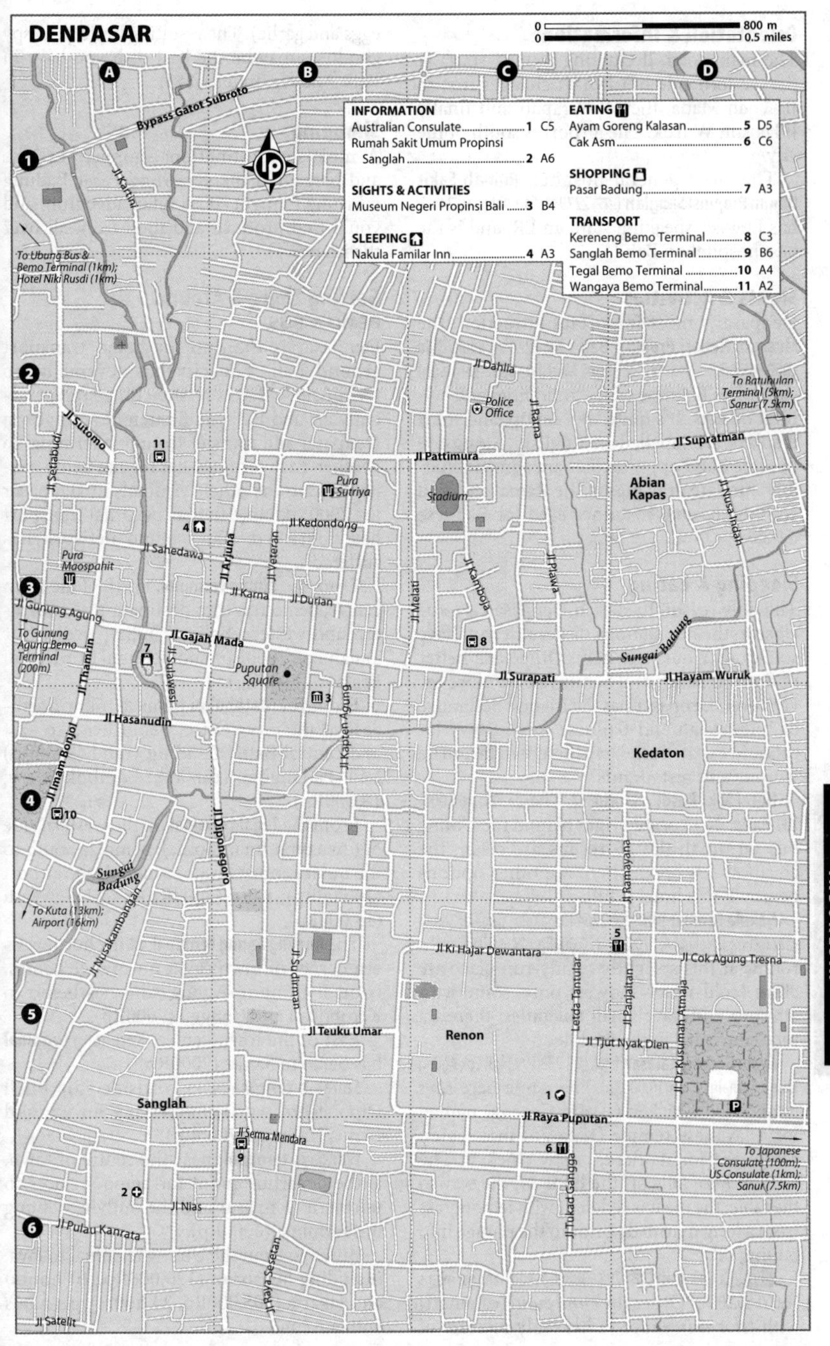
DENPASAR
0 800 m
0 0.5 miles
INFORMATION
Australian Consulate 1 C5
Rumah Sakit Umum Propinsi Sanglah 2 A6
SIGHTS & ACTIVITIES
Museum Negeri Propinsi Bali 3 B4
SLEEPING
Nakula Familar Inn 4 A3
EATING
Ayam Goreng Kalasan 5 D5
Cak Asm 6 C6
SHOPPING
Pasar Badung 7 A3
TRANSPORT
Kereneng Bemo Terminal 8 C3
Sanglah Bemo Terminal 9 B6
Tegal Bemo Terminal 10 A4
Wangaya Bemo Terminal 11 A2
Bypass Gatot Subroto
Jl Kartini
To Ubung Bus & Bemo Terminal (1km); Hotel Niki Rusdi (1km)
Jl Dahlia
Police Office
Jl Ratna
To Batubulan Terminal (5km); Sanur (7.5km)
Jl Supratman
Jl Sutomo
Jl Setiabudi
Jl Pattimura
Pura Sutriya
Stadium
Abian Kapas
Jl Nusa Indah
Jl Kedondong
Pura Maospahit
Jl Sahedawa
Jl Arjuna
Jl Veteran
Jl Kamboja
Jl Plawa
Jl Karna
Jl Durian
Jl Melati
Jl Gunung Agung
To Gunung Agung Bemo Terminal (200m)
Jl Gajah Mada
Jl Thamrin
Jl Sulawesi
Puputan Square
Jl Surapati
Sungai Badung
Jl Hayam Wuruk
Jl Kapten Agung
Jl Hasanudin
Kedaton
Jl Imam Bonjol
Jl Diponegoro
Sungai Badung
To Kuta (13km); Airport (16km)
Jl Nusakambangan
Jl Ramayana
Jl Sudirman
Jl Ki Hajar Dewantara
Jl Cok Agung Tresna
Letda Tantular
Jl Panjaitan
Jl Dr Kusumah Atmaja
Jl Teuku Umar
Renon
Jl Tjut Nyak Dien
Sanglah
Jl Raya Puputan
Jl Serma Mendara
Jl Tukad Gangga
To Japanese Consulate (100m); US Consulate (1km); Sanur (7.5km)
Jl Nias
Jl Pulau Kanrata
Jl Raya Sesetan
Jl Satelit
INDONESIA

Orientation & Information

The main road, Jl Gunung Agung, starts at the western side of town. It changes first to Jl Gajah Mada, then Jl Surapati and finally Jl Hayam Wuruk. The airport is south of the city.

The city's general hospital, **Rumah Sakit Umum Propinsi Sanglah** (☎ 227911; Sanglah; 24hr), has English-speaking staff, an ER, and is the best hospital on Bali.

Sights & Activities

Denpasar's most important attraction, the **Museum Negeri Propinsi Bali** (☎ 222680; adult/child 2000/1000Rp; 8am-12.30pm Mon-Fri, 8am-3pm Sun) showcases Balinese crafts, antiquities and cultural objects. It's quite well set up, and most displays are labelled in English. Alongside the fine hand-spun textiles are some incredibly intricate drawings of the Ramayana, and startling *barong* costumes used for Balinese dance.

Sleeping & Eating

The only reason to stay in Denpasar is to be close to the bus stations or because you have some other business here. Otherwise better options in Sanur and Seminyak are close by. However, Denpasar has the island's best range of Indonesian and Balinese food. Savvy locals and expats each have their own favourite *warung* and restaurants.

Hotel Niki Rusdi (☎ 416397; Jl Pidada XIV; r 60,000-200,000Rp;) Located right behind the Ubung bus terminal, the 26 rooms are clean; the cheapest fan only. There are other options nearby if this hotel is full.

Nakula Familar Inn (☎ 226446; nakula_familiar_inn@yahoo.com; Jl Nakula 4; r 70,000-120,000Rp;) The eight rooms at this sprightly family-run place are clean (cold-water showers only, some with air-con) and have small balconies; there's a nice courtyard in the middle.

Ayam Goreng Kalasan (☎ 081 2380 9934; Jl Cok Agung Trisna 6; mains from 10,000Rp) The name here says it all. Fried Chicken (Ayam Goreng) named for a Javanese temple (Kalasan) in a region renowned for its fiery, crispy chicken. The version here falls off the bone on the way to the table; the meat is redolent with lemongrass from a long marinade prior to the plunge into boiling oil.

our pick **Cak Asm** (☎ 798 9388; Jl Tukad Gangga; mains 10,000-30,000Rp) Order the *cumi cumi* (calamari) with *telor asin* sauce (a heavenly mixture of eggs and garlic). The resulting buttery, crispy goodness may be the best dish you have in Bali. And it's under US$1.

Shopping

A must-see destination: shoppers browse and bargain at the sprawling Pasar Badung morning to night. It's a retail adventure and you'll find produce and food from all over the island.

Getting There & Around

BEMO & BUS

Denpasar is *the* hub for bemo transport around Bali. The city has several bemo terminals – if you're travelling independently around Bali you'll often have to go via Denpasar and transfer from one terminal to another. Each terminal has regular bemo connections to the other terminals in Denpasar for 7000Rp. Note that as personal transport has flourished, Bali's bemo network has suffered.

From the **Ubung terminal**, north of the town centre, bemo travel to destinations in northern and western Bali, including Kediri (for Tanah Lot; 7000Rp) and Bedugul (for Danau Bratan; 18,000Rp).

From the **Batubulan terminal**, 6km northeast of the city centre, bemo head to east and central Bali, including Ubud (8000Rp) and Padangbai (for the Lombok ferry; 18,000Rp).

From the **Tegal terminal** on the western side of town on Jl Iman Bonjol, bemo go south to the Bukit Peninsula. Stops include the airport (10,000Rp), Kuta (8000Rp) and Ulu Watu (15,000Rp).

The **Gunung Agung terminal**, at the northwestern corner of town (look for orange bemo), is on Jl Gunung Agung, and has bemo to Kerobokan and Canggu (7000Rp).

East of the town centre, **Kereneng terminal** has bemo to Sanur (7000Rp).

Sanglah terminal is a roadside stop on Jl Diponegoro, with bemo serving Suwung and Benoa Harbour (7000Rp).

Wangaya terminal, near the centre of town, is the departure point for bemo services to northern Denpasar and the outlying Ubung bus terminal (6000Rp).

Buses go from the Ubung terminal to Java, including Surabaya (120,000Rp, 10 hours) and Jakarta (305,000Rp, 24 hours); get a bus with air-con.

TAXI

As in South Bali, taxis prowl the streets of Denpasar looking for fares. As always, the blue cabs of **Bali Taxi** (☎ 701111) are the most reliable choice.

UBUD

☎ **0361**

Perched on the gentle slopes leading up towards the central mountains, Ubud is the other half of Bali's tourism duopoly. Unlike South Bali, however, Ubud's focus remains on the remarkable Balinese culture in its myriad forms.

It's not surprising that many people come to Ubud for a day or two and end up staying longer, drawn in by the rich culture and many activities. Besides the very popular dance-and-music shows, there are numerous courses on offer that allow you to become fully immersed in Balinese culture.

Ubud is home to chilled-out restaurants and cafes, plus artful and serene places to stay. Around Ubud are temples, ancient sites and whole villages producing handicrafts (albeit mostly for visitors). Although the growth of Ubud has engulfed several neighbouring villages, leading to an urban sprawl, parts of the surrounding countryside remain unspoiled, with lush rice paddies and towering coconut trees. You'd be remiss if you didn't walk one or more of the dozens of paths during your stay.

Orientation

The centre of town is the junction of Monkey Forest Rd and Jl Raya Ubud, where the bustling market and bemo stops are found, as well as Ubud Palace and the main temple, Pura Desa Ubud. Monkey Forest Rd (officially Jl Wanara Wana, but always known by its unofficial name) runs south to Monkey Forest Sanctuary and is lined with shops, hotels and restaurants. Jl Raya Ubud ('Ubud Main Rd' – often Jl Raya for short) is the main east–west road.

Information

Along the main roads, you'll find most services you need.

BOOKSHOPS

Ubud is the best place in Bali for book shopping. Shops typically carry newspapers such as the *International Herald Tribune*.

Ganesha Bookshop (Map p238; ☎ 970320; www.ganeshabooksbali.com; Jl Raya Ubud) Bali's best bookshop has an amazing amount of stock. Excellent selection of titles on Indonesian studies, travel, arts, music and fiction (including second-hand titles).

EMERGENCY

Police station (Map p238; ☎ 975316; Jl Raya Andong; 24hr) Located east, at Andong.

INTERNET ACCESS

Many of Ubud's cafes offer wi-fi as noted in the Eating listings.

@Highway (Map p238; ☎ 972107; Jl Raya Ubud; per min 500Rp; 24hr;) Fast, full service.

MONEY

Ubud has numerous banks, ATMs and money changers along Jl Raya Ubud and Monkey Forest Rd.

POST

Main post office (Map p238; Jl Jembawan; 8am-5pm) Address poste restante to Kantor Pos, Ubud 80571, Bali, Indonesia.

TOURIST INFORMATION

Ubud Tourist Information (Yaysan Bina Wisata; Map p240; ☎ 973285; Jl Raya Ubud; 8am-8pm) The one really useful tourist office in Bali. It has a good range of information and a noticeboard listing current happenings and activities. Staff can answer most regional questions, and have up-to-date information and tickets on ceremonies and traditional dances held in the area.

Sights

MONKEY FOREST SANCTUARY

This cool and dense swathe of jungle, officially called **Mandala Wisata Wanara Wana** (Map p240; ☎ 971304; www.monkeyforestubud.com; Monkey Forest Rd; adult/child 15,000/7500Rp; 8am-6pm), houses three holy temples. The sanctuary is inhabited by a band of grey-haired, greedy long-tailed Balinese macaques who are nothing like the innocent-looking doe-eyed monkeys on the brochures.

MUSEUMS & GALLERIES

The **Museum Puri Lukisan** (Palace of Fine Arts; Map p240; ☎ 975136; www.mpl-ubud.com; off Jl Raya Ubud; admission 20,000Rp; 9am-5pm), off Jl Raya Ubud, displays excellent examples of all schools of Balinese art in a beautiful garden setting. The modern Balinese art movement started in Ubud, where

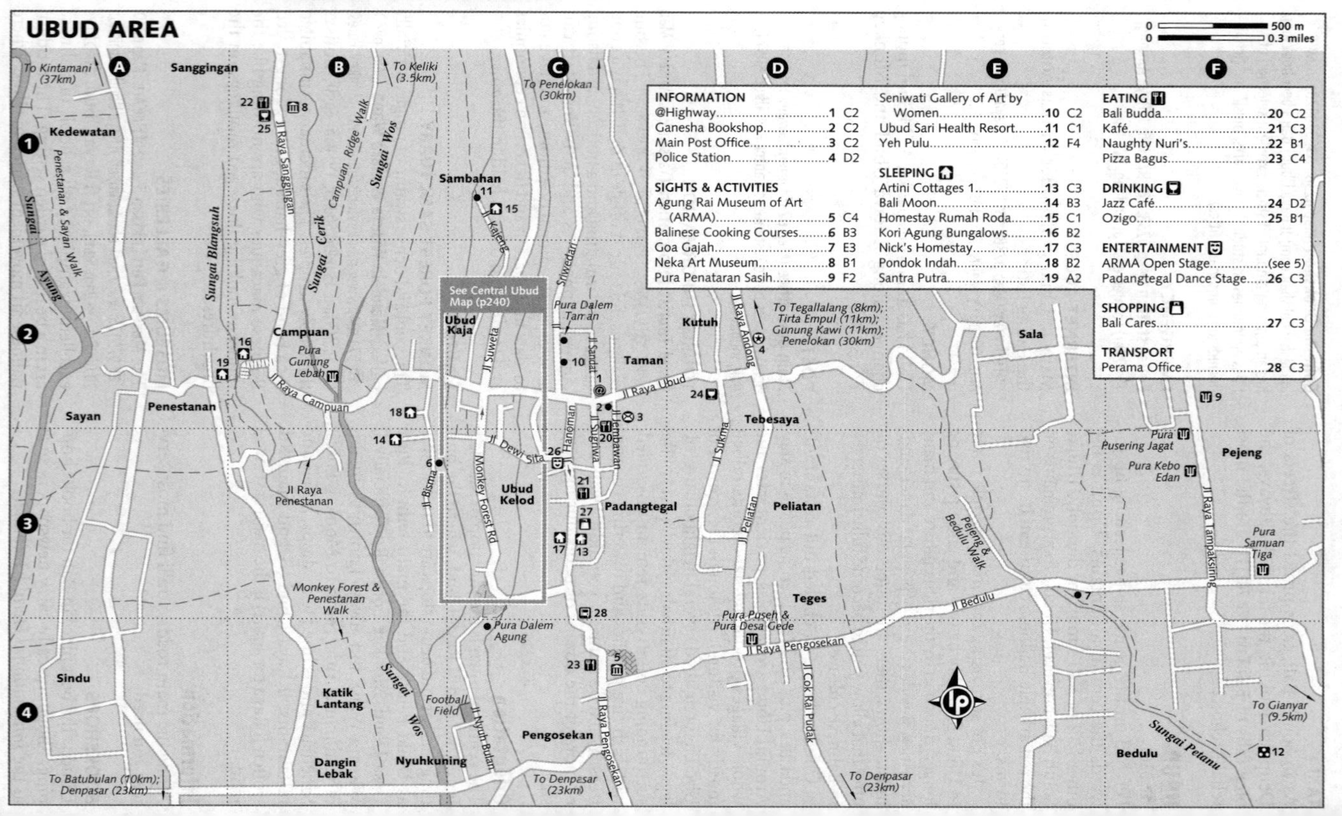
UBUD AREA
0 500 m
0 0.3 miles
INFORMATION
@Highway 1 C2
Ganesha Bookshop 2 C2
Main Post Office 3 C2
Police Station 4 D2
SIGHTS & ACTIVITIES
Agung Rai Museum of Art (ARMA) 5 C4
Balinese Cooking Courses 6 B3
Goa Gajah 7 E3
Neka Art Museum 8 B1
Pura Penataran Sasih 9 F2
Seniwati Gallery of Art by Women 10 C2
Ubud Sari Health Resort 11 C1
Yeh Pulu 12 F4
SLEEPING
Artini Cottages 1 13 C3
Bali Moon 14 B3
Homestay Rumah Roda 15 C1
Kori Agung Bungalows 16 B2
Nick's Homestay 17 C3
Pondok Indah 18 B2
Santra Putra 19 A2
EATING
Bali Budda 20 C2
Kafé 21 C3
Naughty Nuri's 22 B1
Pizza Bagus 23 C4
DRINKING
Jazz Café 24 D2
Ozigo 25 B1
ENTERTAINMENT
ARMA Open Stage (see 5)
Padangtegal Dance Stage 26 C3
SHOPPING
Bali Cares 27 C3
TRANSPORT
Perama Office 28 C3
To Kintamani (37km)
Sanggingan
To Keliki (3.5km)
To Penelokan (30km)
Kedewatan
Penestanan & Sayan Walk
Sungai Ayung
Sungai Blangsuh
Jl Raya Sanggingan
Sungai Cerik
Campuan Ridge Walk
Sungai Wos
Sambahan
Jl Kajeng
Sriwedari
See Central Ubud Map (p240)
Ubud Kaja
Jl Suweta
Pura Dalem Taman
Jl Sandat
Kutuh
Taman
Jl Raya Andong
To Tegallalang (8km); Tirta Empul (11km); Gunung Kawi (11km); Penelokan (30km)
Sala
Campuan
Pura Gunung Lebah
Jl Raya Campuan
Jl Raya Ubud
Sayan
Penestanan
Jl Jembawan
Jl Sugriwa
Hanoman
Tebesaya
Jl Dewi Sita
Jl Bisma
Monkey Forest Rd
Ubud Kelod
Jl Sukma
Jl Raya Penestanan
Padangtegal
Peliatan
Jl Peliatan
Pura Pusering Jagat
Pura Kebo Edan
Pejeng
Jl Raya Tampaksiring
Pejeng & Bedulu Walk
Pura Samuan Tiga
Monkey Forest & Penestanan Walk
Teges
Jl Bedulu
Pura Dalem Agung
Pura Puseh & Pura Desa Gede
Jl Raya Pengosekan
Jl Cok Rai Pudak
Sindu
Katik Lantang
Football Field
Jl Nyuh Bulan
To Gianyar (9.5km)
Sungai Petanu
Pengosekan
Dangin Lebak
Nyuhkuning
Bedulu
To Batubulan (10km); Denpasar (23km)
To Denpesar (23km)
To Denpasar (23km)

INDONESIA

artists first used modern materials, were influenced by foreign styles and began to depict scenes of everyday Balinese life.

Quite distinct from Neka Gallery, the **Neka Art Museum** (Map p238; ☎ 975074; www.museumneka.com; Jl Raya Sanggingan; adult/child 40,000Rp/free; 9am-5pm) is the creation of Suteja Neka, a private collector and dealer in Balinese art. It has an excellent and diverse collection and is the best place to learn about the development of painting in Bali.

Founded by Agung Rai as a museum, gallery and cultural centre, the impressive **Agung Rai Museum of Art** (ARMA; Map p238; ☎ 976659; www.armamuseum.com; Jl Raya Pengosekan; admission 25,000Rp; 9am-6pm) is the only place in Bali to see works by the influential German artist Walter Spies.

The **Seniwati Gallery of Art by Women** (Map p238; ☎ 975485; www.seniwatigallery.com; Jl Sriwedari 2B; 9am-5pm Tue-Sun) exhibits works by more than 70 Balinese, Indonesian and resident foreign women artists.

Activities

WALKING

As well as visiting the museums and galleries it is well worth exploring the natural beauty that inspires so much of it. There are wonderful walks around Ubud: east to Pejeng, across picturesque ravines south to Bedulu; north along the Campuan ridge; and west to Penestanan and Sayan, with views over the Sungai Ayung (Ayung River) gorge. There is also a loop walk to southwest Ubud via the Monkey Sanctuary.

MASSAGE

Ubud brims with salons and spas. **Eve Spa** (Map p240; ☎ 747 0910; Monkey Forest Rd; 1hr massage 75,000Rp; 9am-9pm) is straightforward and affordable.

Ubud Sari Health Resort (Map p238; ☎ 974393; Jl Kajeng; 1hr massage US$30; 8am-8pm) is a spa and hotel in one with extensive treatments that use organic and other natural materials.

Courses

Ubud is absolutely the place to spend some time developing your artistic skills or learning about Balinese culture. Most places ask that you register in advance.

Agung Rai Museum of Art (ARMA; Map p238; ☎ 976659; www.armamuseum.com; Jl Raya Pengosekan; 9am-6pm) A cultural powerhouse offering classes in painting, woodcarving and batik. Other courses include Balinese history, Hinduism and architecture. Classes cost US$25 to US$50.

Balinese Cooking Courses (Map p238; ☎ 973283; www.casalunabali.com; Honeymoon Guesthouse, Jl Bisma) Half-day courses (250,000Rp) cover ingredients, cooking techniques and the cultural background of the Balinese kitchen. Sunday tours cover sea-salt and palm-sugar production (300,000Rp).

Sleeping

There are hundreds of places to stay. Choices range from simple little *losmen* to world-class luxurious retreats. Inexpensive family lodgings are very small and tend to operate in clusters, so you can easily look at a few before choosing.

Addresses in Ubud can be imprecise – but signage at the end of a road will often list the names of all the places to stay. Away from the main roads there are no streetlights and it can be very difficult to find your way after dark. If walking, you will definitely want a torch (flashlight).

CENTRAL UBUD

Small streets east of Monkey Forest Rd, including Jl Karna and Jl Maruti, have numerous, family-style homestays, as does Jl Goutama. Don't settle for a room with road noise along Ubud's main drag.

Frog Pond Inn (Map p240; Monkey Forest Rd; r 80,000-120,000Rp) It's quiet, ultrabasic and friendly with eight cold-water rooms with open-air bathrooms. Enjoy the breakfast that has charmed generations of backpackers: banana pancakes.

Gandra House (Map p240; ☎ 976529; Jl Karna; r from 100,000Rp) Modern bathrooms and spacious gardens are the highlights of this cold-water 10-room homestay. It's one of several family-run places on this street, so compare.

Mandia Bungalows (Map p240; ☎ 970965; Monkey Forest Rd; r 100,000-130,000Rp) It's heliconia heaven in the lush gardens. The four bungalow-style rooms are shaded by coconut palms and cooled by ceiling fans

Agung Cottages (Map p240; ☎ 975414; Jl Goutama; r 150,000-250,000Rp, villas 300,000Rp;) Follow a short path to reach this slightly rural-feeling family compound. The six huge, spotless rooms (some fan only) are set in gardens tended by a lovely family.

our pick **Oka Wati Hotel** (Map p240; ☎ 973386; www.okawatihotel.com; off Monkey Forest Rd; r US$30-60;)

INDONESIA

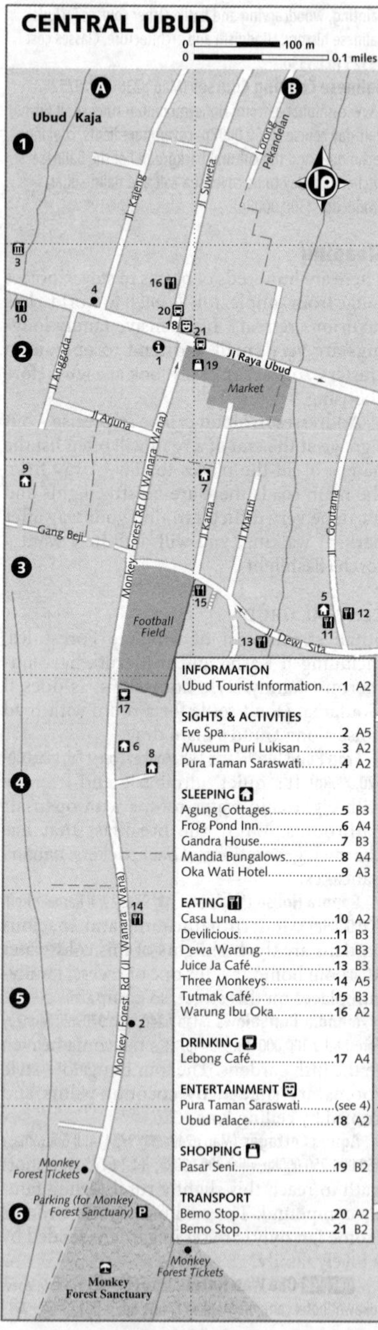

Oki Wati (the owner) is a lovely lady who grew up near the Ubud Palace. The 19 rooms have large verandahs where the delightful staff will deliver your choice of breakfast.

NORTH OF THE CENTRE

Things get quiet as you head up the gentle slope from Jl Raya Ubud; note that some places are 1km or more to the north.

Homestay Rumah Roda (Map p238; ☎ 975487; rumahroda@indo.net.id; Jl Kajeng 24; r 70,000-90,000Rp) Next door to the Threads of Life gallery on peaceful Jl Kajeng, Rumah Roda is a typically mellow homestay dedicated to sound ecological principles.

EAST OF THE CENTRE

You can get to the heart of Ubud in less than 15 minutes by foot from this low-key part of town.

Artini Cottages 1 (Map p238; ☎ 975348; www.artinicottage.com; Jl Hanoman; bungalows 150,000Rp) The Artini family runs a small empire of good-value guest houses on Jl Hanoman. This, the original, is in an ornate family compound with many flowers. The three bungalows have hot water and large bathtubs.

Nick's Homestay (Map p238; ☎ 975526; www.nickshotels-ubud.com; Jl Hanoman 57; r US$15) Nick has a minor empire of three Ubud budget hotels. This, his simplest, is the best.

WEST OF THE CENTRE

Campuan and Penestanan are west of Ubud but still within walking distance. Most places will offer discounted monthly rates (US$200 is average), and some larger bungalows are quite economical if you share with a group.

Santra Putra (Map p238; ☎ 977810; karjabali@yahoo.com; off Jl Raya Campuan; r US$12-15) Run by internationally exhibited abstract artist I Wayan Karja (whose studio/gallery is also on-site), this place has five big, open airy rooms with hot water.

Kori Agung Bungalows (Map p238; ☎ 975166; off Jl Raya Campuan; r from 150,000Rp) On the terrace with other basic inns above Campuan. Rooms are basic but the location is ideal for those looking for leafy views and solitude. The only noise at night is water coursing through the rice fields.

Pondok Indah (Map p238; ☎ 966323; off Jl Bisma; s/d 150,000/200,000Rp) Follow the swift-flowing waterways for 150m along a path hopping with frogs to this peaceful place where the top-floor terraces look over the rice fields. All five rooms have hot water.

Bali Moon (Map p238; ☎ 978293; off Jl Bisma; r from 170,000Rp) Watch the moon rise over Gunung Batukau from this simple inn set with a few others down narrow paths between the rice fields.

Eating

CENTRAL UBUD

There are busy and tasty choices on Ubud's main street, Jl Raya Ubud.

Dewa Warung (Map p240; Jl Goutama; dishes 5000-20,000Rp) A little garden surrounds tables a few steps above the road where diners tuck into plates of sizzling fresh Indo fare.

Juice Ja Café (Map p240; ☎ 971056; Jl Dewi Sita; snacks from 15,000Rp; wi-fi) Glass of spirulina? Dash of wheatgrass with your papaya juice? Organic fruits and vegetables go into the food at this funky bakery-cafe.

Warung Ibu Oka (Map p240; Jl Suweta; dishes 15,000-20,000Rp; 11am-3pm) Join the lunchtime lines opposite Ubud Palace waiting for one thing: the eponymous Balinese-style roast suckling pig. Locals and expats in the know travel far for meat they say is the most tender and tasty on the island. Order a *spesial* to get the best cut.

Tutmak Café (Map p240; ☎ 975754; Jl Dewi Sita; dishes 15,000-35,000Rp; wi-fi) The breezy multilevel location here, facing both Jl Dewi Sita and the football field, is a popular place for a refreshing drink or a meal.

Casa Luna (Map p240; ☎ 977409; Jl Raya Ubud; dishes 15,000-60,000Rp) Renaissance woman Janet de Neefe runs this ever-popular Indonesian-focused restaurant, which has recently added a wine bar.

our pick **Three Monkeys** (Map p240; ☎ 974830; Monkey Forest Rd; mains 20,000-50,000Rp) Mellow music and artworks set a cultured mood. The tables overlooking the rice field out back make it magic. By day there are sandwiches, salads and gelato. At night there's a fusion menu of Asian classics.

Devilicious (Map p240; ☎ 745972; Jl Goutama; mains from 20,000Rp) Jl Goutama is a delightful street for a stroll and this cafe is one of the reasons why. Just wandering the narrow lane is like stepping back 30 years in Ubud, and creative little places like this cafe seem to appear like mushrooms after the rain.

EAST OF THE CENTRE

Bali Buddha (Map p238; ☎ 976324; Jl Jembawan 1; dishes 15,000-40,000Rp) A local institution, Bali Buddha has a vegie cafe with a long list of tasty, healthy foods upstairs and a health-food store and bakery downstairs. Raw foodists and vegans will find much to like. The bulletin board out front is a community resource.

Kafe (Map p238; ☎ 970992; www.balispirit.com; Jl Hanoman 44; dishes 15,000-40,000Rp; wi-fi) Part of Bali Spirit, a host group for several NGOs, Kafe has an organic menu great for vegie grazing or just having a coffee, juice or house-made soda.

SOUTH OF UBUD

Many highly regarded restaurants are found along the curves of Jl Raya Pengosekan. It's always worth seeing what's new.

Pizza Bagus (Map p238; ☎ 978520; www.pizzabagus.com: Jl Raya Pengosekan; dishes 18,000-40,000Rp; wi-fi) Besides Ubud's best pizza, there's pasta and sandwiches – mostly organic.

WEST OF UBUD

The restaurants and cafes west of the centre are dotted among rice fields, lanes and roads.

Naughty Nuri's (Map p238; ☎ 977547; Jl Raya Sanggingan; dishes 15,000-60,000Rp) This legendary expat hang-out packs punters in for grilled steaks, tender ribs and burgers. This is a raw-boned joint where the stiff martinis make up for occasional lapses in the kitchen (which is mostly a barbecue out front).

Drinking & Clubbing

No one comes to Ubud for wild nightlife. A few bars get lively around sunset and later in the night, but the venues certainly don't aspire to the club partying found in Kuta and Seminyak.

Jazz Café (Map p238; ☎ 976594; www.jazzcafebali.com; Jl Sukma 2; 5pm-midnight) Always popular, Jazz Café has a relaxed vibe in a garden of coconut palms and ferns. Live music Tuesday to Saturday from 7.30pm. It provides transport around Ubud.

Lebong Café (Map p240; ☎ 971342; Monkey Forest Rd) Get up, stand up, stand up for your…reggae. Ubud's nightly sidewalk roll-up opens at least until midnight, with live reggae and rock most nights.

Ozigo (Map p238; ☎ 081 2367 9736; Jl Raya Sanggingan; 9pm-2am) Ubud's late-night action – such as it is – is right here at this small and friendly club up by Naughty Nuri's. DJs are in residence nightly, plus lots of dance competitions and prizes. Call for pick-up.

Entertainment

Few travel experiences can be more magical than experiencing a Balinese dance performance, especially in Ubud. Cultural entertainment keeps people returning and sets Bali apart from other tropical destinations. Get there a little early and buy a beer from the old women selling them out of ice-filled buckets.

In a week in Ubud, you can see Kecak, Legong and Barong dances, *wayang kulit* puppets, *gamelan* orchestras and more. Venues will usually host a variety of performances by various troupes through the week and aren't tied to a particular group:

ARMA Open Stage (Map p238; ☎ 976659; Jl Raya Pengosekan) Among the best troupes.

Padangtegal Dance Stage (Map p238; Jl Hanoman) Simple, open venue.

Pura Taman Saraswati (Water Palace; Map p240; Jl Raya Ubud) A beautiful location.

Ubud Palace (Map p240; Jl Raya Ubud) Near-nightly performances in a royal setting.

Ubud Tourist Information (p237) has performance information and sells tickets (usually 80,000Rp). For performances outside Ubud, transport is often included in the price. Tickets are also sold at many hotels, at the venues and by street vendors who hang around outside Ubud Palace – all charge the same price.

Shopping

In Ubud, Jl Raya Ubud, Monkey Forest Rd, Jl Hanoman and Jl Dewi Sita should be your starting points. Surrounding villages are also hotbeds for arts and crafts – as you'll have noticed on your drive to Ubud. Paintings are sold at many commercial galleries and museums; see p237.

TOURIST SHUTTLE BUS

Perama (Map p238; ☎ 973316; Jl Hanoman; ⌚ 9am-9pm) is the major tourist-shuttle operator in Ubud, but its terminal is inconveniently located in Padangtegal; to get to your final destination in Ubud will cost another 10,000Rp.

Destination	Fare	Duration
Kuta	50,000Rp	1¼hr
Lovina	125,000Rp	3hr
Padangbai	50,000Rp	1¼hr
Sanur	40,000Rp	1hr

The euphemistically named **Pasar Seni** (Art Market; Map p240) is a tourist-mobbed two-storey place that sells a wide range of clothing, sarongs, footwear and souvenirs of highly variable quality at highly negotiable prices.

The more inspired **Bali Cares** (Map p238; ☎ 981504; www.idepfoundation.org; Jl Hanoman 44) sells goods to benefit several local charities. Items range from woodcarvings made from sustainable woods to paintings, handicrafts and other items produced by local people.

Getting There & Around

BEMO

Ubud is on two bemo routes. Orange bemo travel from Gianyar to Ubud (8000Rp) and larger brown bemo from Batubulan terminal in Denpasar to Ubud (8000Rp), and then head to Kintamani via Payangan. Ubud doesn't have a bemo terminal; bemo stops (Map p240) are in front of the market in the centre of town. Local rides should cost 5000Rp.

BICYCLE

Shops renting bikes have their cycles on display along the main roads; your accommodation can always arrange bike rental.

CAR & MOTORBIKE

Many nearby attractions are difficult to reach by bemo, so renting a vehicle is sensible. Ask at your accommodation.

AROUND UBUD

Two kilometres east of the Central Ubud, the cavern of **Goa Gajah** (Elephant Cave; Map p238; adult/child 6000/3000Rp, parking 2000Rp; ⌚ 8am-6pm) was discovered in the 1920s; the fountains and bathing pool were not unearthed until 1954. It is believed to have been a Buddhist hermitage. Nearby is **Yeh Pulu** (Map p238; adult/child 6000/3000Rp), a 25m-long cliff face carved in bas-relief. Even if your interest in carved Hindu art is minor, this site is quite lovely and secluded. A couple of kilometres north in Pejeng, **Pura Penataran Sasih** (Map p238; Jl Raya Tampaksiring) was once the state temple of the Pejeng kingdom. In the inner courtyard, high up in a pavilion and difficult to see in any detail, is the huge bronze drum known as the **Moon of Pejeng**.

In Tampaksiring, 18km northeast of Ubud, you'll find the most impressive ancient site in Bali, **Gunung Kawi** (off Map p238; admission 4100Rp; ⌚ 8am-5pm). It is an astonishing group of stone

INDONESIA

candi (shrines) cut into cliffs on either side of the plunging Pakrisan River valley that is being considered for Unesco Heritage status. They stand in awe-inspiring, 8m-high sheltered niches cut into the sheer cliff face. From the end of the access road, a steep, stone stairway leads down to the river, at one point making a cutting through an embankment of solid rock.

A few kilometres north of Tampaksiring is the holy spring and temple of **Tirta Empul** (off Map p238; adult/child 6000/3000Rp, parking 2000Rp; 8am-6pm). There are fine carvings and *garuda* on the courtyard buildings. Come in the early morning or late afternoon to avoid the tourist buses. You can also use the clean, segregated and free public baths here.

PURA BESAKIH

Perched nearly 1000m up the side of Gunung Agung, Bali's most important temple, **Pura Besakih** (☎ 0361-222387; adult/child 10,000/7000Rp, still camera 1000Rp, video camera 2500Rp, car park 1000Rp; dawn-dusk), is an extensive complex of 23 separate but related temples, with the largest and most important being Pura Penataran Agung. Unfortunately, many people find it a deeply disappointing experience due to the avarice of numerous local characters. See the boxed text, below, for the details, which may well help you decide whether to visit.

The main entrance to the temple precinct is 2km south of the complex on the road from Menanga and the south. The fact that you may well be charged for a video camera whether you have one or not gives you a taste of the hassles ahead.

The best way to visit is with your own transportation, which allows you to explore the many gorgeous drives in the area.

You can visit by bemo from Semarapura (10,000Rp), but from other parts of Bali this can make the outing an all-day affair. Be sure to ask the driver to take you to the temple entrance, not to the village about 1km from the temple complex. Make certain you leave the temple by 3pm if you want to return to either Semarapura or Denpasar by bemo.

AN UNHOLY EXPERIENCE

Besakih's aggravations and irritations go back years and mean that many visitors now skip this important sight. Some of the ploys you should be aware of before contemplating a visit include guides who tell you you must have their services (you don't); offers to 'get in' to closed temples (you can't); and so-called guides who change their fees at the end of your tour.

GETTING INTO TOWN

Official taxis from the airport to Ubud costs 200,000Rp or more. A taxi or car with driver *to* the airport will cost about half.

GUNUNG AGUNG

Often obscured beneath a thick duvet of mist, Gunung Agung is a relatively infrequent feature of Bali's skyline. When the clouds part, however, Bali's highest and most revered mountain is an imposing sight and is visible from much of southern and eastern Bali.

Gunung Agung is a relatively moody volcano. A 700m-wide crater marks the mountain's summit and, in 1963, Gunung Agung shrank by 126m after a devastating eruption. It now stands 3142m above sea level.

A hike to the summit is best attempted in the dry season (April to September) – the route may be treacherously slippery at other times. There are several possible approaches. From the village of Besakih (about 1km south of the temple complex) it's a very demanding climb: allow at least six hours going up and four hours coming down. Start at midnight to reach the summit for sunrise, before it's enveloped in cloud. Expect to pay a negotiable 350,000Rp to 800,000Rp for one or two people for your climb. Recommended guides:

Gung Bawa Trekking (☎ 081 2387 8168; www.gb-trekking.blogspot.com) Experienced and reliable.

Ketut Uriada (☎ 081 2364 6426; Muncan) This knowledgeable guide can arrange transport for an extra fee (look for his small sign on the road east of the village).

Wayan Tegteg (☎ 081 3385 25677; Selat) Wins reader plaudits.

SEMARAPURA (KLUNGKUNG)

☎ 0366

Once the centre of an important Balinese kingdom, Semarapura (also known as Klungkung) is the capital of Klungkung regency and a great artistic and cultural focal point. Formerly the seat of the Dewa Agung dynasty, the **Semara**

DANCE TROUPES: GOOD & BAD

All dance groups on Ubud's stages are not created equal. You've got true artists with international reputations, and then you've got some that really shouldn't quit their day jobs. If you're a Balinese dance novice, you shouldn't worry too much about this; just pick a venue and go.

But after a few performances, you'll start to appreciate the differences in talent, and that's part of the enjoyment. Clue: if the costumes are dirty, the orchestra seems particularly uninterested and you find yourself watching a dancer and saying 'I could do that', then the group is B-level.

Most troupes you'll see in Ubud, however, are very good. Here's a few to watch for:

- Cak Rina – Often performs the Kecak at ARMA.
- Gunung Sari – Legong dance.
- Sadha Budaya – Legong dance.
- Sekaa Gong Wanita Mekar Sari – An all-woman Legong troupe from Peliatan.
- Semara Madya – Kekac dance.
- Tirta Sari – Legong dance.

Pura Complex (adult/child 12,000/6000Rp, parking 1000Rp; 7am-6pm) has now largely crumbled away, but history and architecture buffs will enjoy a wander past the **Kertha Gosa** (Hall of Justice) and **Bale Kambang** (Floating Pavilion). The recently renovated **Museum Semarajaya** has an interesting collection of archaeological and other pieces.

Bemo from Denpasar (Batubulan terminal) pass through Semarapura (18,000Rp) on their way to various points located further east. They can be hailed from near the Puputan Monument.

NUSA LEMBONGAN

☎ 0366

Nusa Lembongan is one of three islands (along with Nusa Penida and Nusa Ceningan) that together comprise the Nusa Penida archipelago. It's the Bali many imagine but never find: simple rooms on the beach, cheap beers with incredible sunsets, days spent surfing and diving, and nights spent riffling through a favourite book or hanging with new friends.

Information

It's vital that you bring sufficient cash for your stay, as there's no ATM. **Bank BPD** (8am-3pm Mon-Thu, 8am-1pm Fri) can exchange travellers cheques and cash but the rates are bad.

Pondok Baruna (☎ 081 2390 0686) has public internet terminals. Wi-fi is being installed at many places.

Sights

Jungutbatu beach, a lovely arc of white sand with clear blue water, has superb views across to Gunung Agung in Bali. The village itself is pleasant, with quiet lanes, no cars and a couple of temples, including **Pura Segara** and its enormous banyan tree.

Gorgeous little **Mushroom Bay,** unofficially named for the mushroom corals offshore, has a perfect crescent of white-sand beach

The most pleasant way to get here from Jungutbatu is to walk along the trail that starts from the southern end of the main beach and follows the coastline for 1km or so past a couple of little beaches.

Down a little track, on the south side of the island, **Dream Beach** is a 150m crescent of white sand that has pounding surf and a *warung* for sunset beers.

Activities

Most places will rent bicycles for 30,000Rp per day, surfboards for 50,000Rp and motorbikes for 30,000Rp per hour.

World Diving (☎ 081 2390 0686; www.world-diving.com), based at Pondok Baruna (opposite) on Jungutbatu Beach, is well regarded. It offers various courses including five-day PADI open-water courses for US$375, and dive trips from US$27 to US$40 to sites around the islands.

The dry season is surfing season in Nusa Lembongan, with winds bringing in the waves from the southeast. The Shipwreck, Lacerations and Playground surf breaks are off the island's west coast, near the little settlement of Jungutbatu.

Good snorkelling can be had just off the Mushroom Bay and Bounty pontoons off

Jungutbatu Beach, as well as in areas off the north coast of the island.

Sleeping & Eating

Unless noted otherwise, amenities in Jungutbatu are limited to cold water and fans. Leaving Jungutbatu, the island gets less tamed as you go west. With backpacks, you may want to avail yourself of the boat-greeting luggage carriers for the walk here along the hillside trail. Almost every property has a cafe serving – unless noted – basic Indonesian and Western dishes for under 25,000Rp.

Puri Nusa Bungalows (☎ 24482; r 70,000-200,000Rp; ❄) The 17 rooms here are clean and comfortable (some with hot water and air-con); the two upstairs at the front have excellent views and there's a good cafe. There are nice loungers under trees.

Pondok Baruna (☎ 081 2390 0686; www.world-diving.com; r 75,000-100,000Rp; 💻 🏊) Associated with World Diving, this simple place has eight rooms with terraces facing the ocean. The restaurant serves excellent meals. Staff, led by the manager Putu, are charmers.

Two Thousand Cafe (☎ 081 2381 2775; r 100,000-300,000Rp; ❄) Eight rooms in two-storey blocks offer decent comfort; some have hot water and air-con. There's a fun cafe-bar right on the sand.

Tamarind Beach (☎ 081 2398 4234; www.balitamarind.com; r 150,000-250,000Rp) Trance music plays in the simple common area at this wild tropical setting right on the beach. The six rooms are simple, with cold-water tubs for getting clean and cooling off. Ring ahead for a pick-up by outrigger from the boat-landing area on Jungutbatu Beach.

Getting There & Around

Getting to or from Nusa Lembongan offers numerous choices. Boats anchor offshore, so be prepared to get your feet wet. And travel light – wheeled bags are comically inappropriate in the water and on the beach and dirt tracks. Public boats to Nusa Lembongan leave from the northern end of Sanur beach at 7.45am (45,000Rp, 1¾ to two hours). The Perama tourist boat leaves Sanur at 10.15am (100,000Rp, 1¾ hours). The Lembongan office is near the Mandara Beach Bungalows.

The island is fairly small and you can easily walk most places. There are no cars. One-way rides on motorbikes or trucks cost 5000Rp.

PADANGBAI

☎ 0363

There's a real backpacker vibe about this funky little beach town that is also the port for the main public ferry connecting Bali with Lombok.

Padangbai is on the upswing. It sits on a small bay and has a nice little curve of beach. It has a whole compact seaside travellers' scene with cheap places to stay and some funky and fun cafes. The pace is slow, but should ambition strike there's good snorkelling and diving, plus some easy walks and a couple of great beaches.

Information

Bank BRI (Jl Pelabuhan) exchanges money and has an international ATM.

You can find slow internet access (300Rp per minute) at numerous places, including Kerti Beach Bungalows and Made's Homestay (see below).

Activities

There's some pretty good diving on the coral reefs around Padangbai, but the water can be a little cold and visibility is not always ideal. The most popular local dives are Blue Lagoon and Teluk Jepun (Jepun Bay), both in Teluk Amuk, the bay just east of Padangbai.

One of the best and most accessible walk-in snorkel sites is off Blue Lagoon Beach. Note that it is subject to strong currents when the tide is out.

Several good dive shops are on Jl Silayukti.

Sleeping

Accommodation in Padangbai – like the town itself – is pretty laid-back. Prices are fairly cheap and it's pleasant enough here that there's no need to hurry through to or from Lombok if you want to hang out on the beach and in cafes with other travellers.

Made's Homestay (☎ 41441; Jl Silayukti; s/d 50,000/60,000Rp; 💻) Four basic, clean and simple rooms and internet access are the draws here.

Topi Inn (☎ 41424; www.topiinn.com; Jl Silayukti; r 50,000-60,000Rp; 💻 📶) Sitting at the end of the strip in a serene location, Topi has five pleasant rooms, some of which share bathrooms. The enthusiastic owners offer courses in topics as diverse as cooking and *gamelan*, among other diversions. The cafe is excellent.

Darma Homestay (☎ 41394; Gang Segara III; r 60,000-150,000Rp; ❄) A classic Balinese family homestay. The more expensive of the 12 rooms have hot showers and air-con; choose a private room on the top floor.

Kerti Beach Bungalows (☎ 41391; Jl Silayukti; r 70,000-250,000Rp; ❄ 💻) Go for the 19 rooms in pretty bungalows built in a long narrow strip rather than the rice barns. As you move up the rate ladder here, you gain hot water and air-con.

Kembar Inn (☎ 41364; kembarinn@hotmail.com; near Ozone Café; r 100,000-250,000Rp; ❄) There are six rooms at this inn linked by a steep and narrow staircase. The best awaits at the top and has a private terrace with views.

Eating & Drinking

Beach fare and backpackers' staples are on offer in Padangbai – lots of fresh seafood, Indonesian classics, pizza and, yes, banana pancakes.

Depot Segara (☎ 41443; Jl Segara; dishes 10,000-30,000Rp) Fresh seafood such as barracuda, marlin and snapper is prepared in a variety of ways at this popular cafe. Enjoy harbour views from the slightly elevated terrace.

Ozone Café (☎ 41501; dishes 15,000-35,000Rp) This popular travellers' gathering spot has more character than every other place in East Bali combined.

Topi Inn (☎ 41424; Jl Silayukti; mains 18,000-40,000Rp) Juices, shakes and good coffees served up throughout the day. Breakfasts are big, and daily fresh fish is grilled nightly.

Getting There & Away

Padangbai is 2km south of the main Semarapura–Amlapura road. Bemo leave from the car park at the port; orange bemo go east through Candidasa to Amlapura (8000Rp); blue or white bemo go to Semarapura (8000Rp).

Perama (☎ 41419; Café Dona, Jl Pelabuhan; 🕒 7am-8pm) has a stop here for its services around the east coast; trips include Kuta (60,000Rp, three hours) and Ubud (50,000Rp, 1¼ hours).

Public ferries travel nonstop between Padangbai and Lembar on Lombok. There are also fast boats for travellers to the Gili Islands and Lombok. For details on these services, see p286.

CANDIDASA

☎ 0363

Candidasa is slouching into idle age, no longer the tourism darling it once was. The main drawback is the lack of a beach, which, except for the far eastern stretch, has eroded away as fast as hotels were built.

Activities

Diving and snorkelling are popular activities in Candidasa. Hotels and shops along the main road rent snorkel sets for about 20,000Rp per day. For the best snorkelling, take a boat to offshore sites or to Gili Mimpang (a one-hour boat trip should cost about 100,000Rp for up to three people).

Sleeping & Eating

Candidasa's main drag is well supplied with seaside accommodation. Most restaurants are dotted along Jl Raya Candidasa where traffic noise can be unpleasant, although it improves after dark.

Seaside Cottages (☎ 41629; www.balibeachfront-cottages.com; Jl Raya Candidasa; cottages 40,000-250,000Rp; ❄ 💻) Has loungers right along the breakwater.

Puri Oka Cottages (☎ 41092; puri_oka@hotmail.com; Jl Pantai Indah; r 125,000-500,000Rp; ❄ 🏊) Hidden by a banana grove east of town.

Legend Rock Café (Jl Raya Candidasa; dishes 15,000-30,000Rp) Offers food, has live music many nights.

Temple Café (☎ 41629; Seaside Cottages, Jl Raya Candidasa; dishes 15,000-35,000Rp) Popular bar with a long drinks list.

Getting There & Away

Candidasa is on the main road between Amlapura and Denpasar – there's no terminal, so hail bemo anywhere along the main road (buses probably won't stop).

Perama (☎ 41114; Jl Raya Candidasa; 🕒 7am-7pm) is at the western end of the strip. It runs tourist shuttle buses to Sanur (60,000Rp, 2¾ hours), Ubud (50,000Rp, 1¾ hours), Kuta (60,000Rp, 3½ hours), Lovina (150,000Rp, 5¼ hours).

AMLAPURA

☎ 0363

Amlapura is the capital of Karangasem district, and the main town and transport junction in eastern Bali. The smallest of Bali's district capitals, it's a multicultural place with Chinese shophouses, several mosques and confusing one-way streets (which are the tidiest in Bali). It's worth a stop to see the royal palaces, including **Puri Agung Karangasem** (Jl Teuku Umar; admission 10,000Rp; 🕒 8am-5pm), where there's an impressive three-tiered entry gate and beautiful sculpted panels. However, a lack of options means you'll want to spend the night elsewhere, such as Tirta Gangga.

Amlapura is a major transport hub. Buses and bemo regularly ply the main road to Denpasar's Batubulan terminal (20,000Rp, roughly three hours) via Candidasa, Padangbai and Gianyar. Plenty of buses also go around the north coast to Singaraja (about 16,000Rp) via Tirta Gangga, Amed and Tulamben.

TIRTA GANGGA

☎ 0363

Tirta Gangga (Water of the Ganges) is the site of a holy temple, some great water features and some of the best views of rice fields and the sea beyond in East Bali. High on a ridge, it is a relaxing place to stop for an hour or a longer period, which will allow for some treks in the surrounding terraced countryside, which ripples with coursing water.

Sights & Activities

Amlapura's water-loving rajah, the last king of Karangasem, built the palace of his dreams at **Taman Tirta Gangga** (adult/child 5000/3000Rp, parking 2000Rp; 24hr, ticket office 6am-6pm). Originally built in 1948, the water palace was damaged in the 1963 eruption of Gunung Agung. The palace has several swimming pools and ornamental ponds, which serve as a fascinating reminder of the old days of the Balinese rajahs. 'Pool A' (adult/child 6000/4000Rp) is the cleanest and is in the top part of the complex. It's a good place for a break and a stroll.

Hiking in the surrounding hills is recommended. The rice terraces around Tirta Gangga are some of the most beautiful in Bali. Back roads and walking paths take you to many picturesque traditional villages. Or you can ascend the side of Gunung Agung. Guides are a good idea. Ask at any of the accommodation we've listed, especially Homestay Rijasa where the owner I Ketut Sarjana is an experienced guide. Another local guide who comes with good marks is **Komang Gede Sutama** (☎ 081 3387 70893).

Among the possible treks is a six-hour loop to Tenganan village, plus shorter ones across the local hills, which include visits to remote temples and all the stunning vistas you can handle. Rates average about 50,000Rp per hour for one or two people.

Sleeping & Eating

Most places to stay have cafes with mains under 20,000Rp, and there's another cluster by the sedate shops near the entrance. Many places to stay are cold water only and basic.

Dhangin Taman (Friendly Hotel; ☎ 22059; r 50,000-100,000Rp) Adjacent to the water palace, this characterful place features elaborate tiled artworks in a garden. It has a range of 14 cold-water rooms – the cheapest ones facing the rice paddies are the best – and a simple cafe with tables overlooking the palace.

Homestay Rijasa (☎ 21873; r 80,000-150,000Rp) With elaborately planted grounds, this well-run place is a recommended choice opposite the water palace entrance. Better rooms have hot water, good for the large soaking tubs. The owner is an experienced trekking guide.

Good Karma (☎ 22445; r 100,000-120,000Rp) A classic homestay, Good Karma has four very clean and simple bungalows and a good vibe derived from the surrounding pastoral rice field. The good cafe is close to the parking lot.

Getting There & Away

Bemos and minibuses making the east-coast haul between Amlapura and Singaraja stop at Tirta Gangga, right outside the water palace or any hotel further north. The fare to Amlapura should be 5000Rp.

AMED & THE FAR EAST COAST

☎ 0363

Stretching from Amed to Bali's far eastern tip, this once-remote piece of semi-arid coast draws visitors to a succession of small, scalloped, black-sand beaches, a relaxed atmosphere and an excellent base for diving and snorkelling expeditions to Tulamben.

The coast here is often called simply 'Amed' but this is a misnomer, as the coast is a series of seaside *dusun* (small villages) that start with the actual Amed in the north and then run southeast to Aas. Jemeluk has cafes and a few shops; Lipah has *warung*, shops and a few services. Both have places with dial-up internet access. The closest ATM is in Amlapura.

If you're looking to get away from crowds, this is the place to come and try some yoga. Everything is spread out, so you never feel like you're in the middle of anything much except maybe one of the small fishing villages.

Diving & Snorkelling

Snorkelling is excellent along the coast. **Jemeluk** is a protected area where you can admire live coral and plentiful fish within 100m of the beach. There's a wreck of a Japanese fishing boat near **Aas**, offshore from Eka Purnama bungalows, and coral gardens and colourful marine life at **Selang**. Almost every hotel rents snorkelling equipment for about 30,000Rp per day.

Scuba diving is good and the *Liberty* wreck at Tulamben (right) is only a 20-minute drive away. Two operators with similar prices (offering local dives from about US$50, open-water dive course about US$350) are **Eco-dive** (☎ 081 658 1935; www.ecodivebali.com; Jemeluk), with a full-service shop, an ecofriendly attitude and simple accommodation for clients, and **Euro Dive** (☎ 23469; www.eurodivebali.com; Lipah), with a new facility and packages with hotels.

Sleeping & Eating

The entire area is very spread out, so take this into consideration when choosing accommodation. Most places to stay have cafes.

JEMELUK

Sama Sama Bungalows (☎ 081 3373 82945; r 70,000-150,000Rp) There are two simple cold-water rooms in bungalows here (and a good seafood cafe) across from the beach. The family that runs things is often busy making kites.

Galang Kangin Bungalows (☎ 23480; bali_amed_gk@yahoo.co.jp; r 100,000Rp-300,000Rp; ❄) Set on the hill side of the road amid a nice garden, the four rooms here mix and match fans, cold water, hot water and air-con. The beach is right over the pavement, as is the cafe.

LIPAH

Le Jardin (☎ 081 3532 15753; limamarie@yahoo.fr; r €12-25; ❄) Four rooms (some fan only) are housed in shady thatched bungalows at this French-accented B&B. Open baths have garden decor and you can avail yourself of yoga, meditation etc. The beach on the cove is just steps away.

Bayu Cottages (☎ 23495; www.bayucottages.com; r €25-50; ❄ 🏊) Bayu has six large, comfortable rooms with balconies overlooking the coast from the hillside above the road.

Wawa-Wewe I (☎ 23506; Lipah) The coast's most raucous bar – which by local standards means that sometimes it gets sorta loud. A vast CD collection is augmented by local bands on many nights. You can also eat here (mains from 15,000Rp).

AAS

our pick **Meditasi** (fax 22166; r 200,000-250,000Rp) Meditation and yoga help you relax, and the four rooms are close to good swimming and snorkelling. Open-air baths allow you to count the colours of the bougainvillea and frangipani that grow in profusion.

Getting There & Around

Most people drive here via the main highway from Amlapura to Culik. Public-transport options are limited. Infrequent public bemo go from Culik to Amed (3.5km), and some continue to Seraya until 1pm. A public bemo should cost around 8000Rp from Culik to Lipah.

Perama offers charter tourist-bus services from Candidasa (see p246); the cost is 125,000Rp each for a minimum of two people. This is similar to the cost of hiring a car and driver.

Many hotels rent bicycles for about 35,000Rp per day.

TULAMBEN

☎ 0363

The big attraction here sank over 60 years ago. The WWII wreck of the US cargo ship *Liberty* is among the best and most popular dive sites in Bali, and this has given rise to an entire town based on scuba diving. Other great dive sites are nearby, and even snorkellers can easily swim out and enjoy the wreck and the coral. These activities are the reason to come to Tulamben.

Activities

DIVING & SNORKELLING

The wreck of the *Liberty* is about 50m directly offshore from Puri Madha Bungalows (there's also a shady car park here; 2000Rp). Swim straight out and you'll see the stern rearing up from the depths, heavily encrusted with coral and swarming with dozens of species of colourful fish – and with scuba divers most of the day. Stay the night in Tulamben or – better – in nearby Amed and get an early start.

Among the many dive operators, **Tauch Terminal** is one of the longest established operators in Bali. A four-day PADI open-water certificate course costs about €350. Expect to pay about €30/50 for one/two dives at Tulamben, and a little more for a night dive or dives around Amed. For other recommended dive operators near here, see left.

Snorkelling gear is rented everywhere for 30,000Rp.

Sleeping & Eating

Look for signs along the main road for the following places; most have their own dive operations. Every place to stay has at least a cafe.

Ocean Sun (☎ 22912; www.ocean-sun.com; r 60,000-70,000Rp) The budget choice of Tulamben, Ocean Sun has four bungalow-style rooms in a small garden on the hill side of the road. Units are clean and basic.

Puri Madha Bungalows (☎ 22921; r 70,000-300,000Rp; ❄) Refurbished bungalow-style units are directly opposite the wreck on shore. Of the 12 rooms, the best have air-con and hot water. The spacious grounds feel like a public park.

Getting There & Away

Plenty of buses and bemo travel between Amlapura and Singaraja (8000Rp to either) and will stop anywhere along the Tulamben road, but they're infrequent after 2pm.

Perama offers charter tourist-bus services from Candidasa; the cost is 125,000Rp each for a minimum of two people. This is similar to the cost of hiring a car and driver.

SINGARAJA

☎ 0362 / pop 144,000

With a population of more than 100,000 people, Singaraja (which means 'Lion King' and somehow hasn't caused Disney to demand licensing fees) is Bali's second-largest city. With its tree-lined streets, surviving Dutch colonial buildings and charmingly moribund waterfront area north of Jl Erlangga, it's worth exploring for a few hours. Most people stay in nearby Lovina, however.

The regional tourist office **Diparda** (☎ 25141; cnr Jl Veteran & Jl Gajah Mada; 🕑 7.30am-3.30pm Mon-Fri) loves visitors. Ask about dance and other cultural events.

It's best to stay at Lovina, about 10km to the west, which has far better options than Singaraja. For supplies and sundries, head to **Hardy's Supermarket** (Jl Pramuka; 🕑 6am-10pm).

Singaraja has three bemo/bus terminals. From the main Sukasada terminal, about 3km south of town, minibuses go to Denpasar (Ubung terminal; 30,000Rp) via Bedugul/Pancasari (15,000Rp) sporadically through the day.

The Banyuasri terminal, on the western side of town, has buses heading to Gilimanuk (22,000Rp, two hours) and Java, and plenty of blue bemo to Lovina (7000Rp).

The Penarukan terminal, 2km east of town, has bemo to Yeh Sanih (8000Rp) and Amlapura (18,000Rp, three hours) via the coastal road; and also minibuses to Denpasar (Batubulan terminal; 30,000Rp, three hours) via Kintamani.

AROUND SINGARAJA

About 11km south of Singaraja are the pretty – and pretty touristy – waterfalls of **Air Terjun Gitgit** (adult/child 6000/3000Rp) The well-signposted path (800m) from the main road in the village is lined with souvenir stalls and *warung*. The 40m falls are a good place for a picnic when it's not too busy, but litter can be an issue. There is another small waterfall, sometimes called **Gitgit Multi-Tier Waterfall** (donation 5000Rp) about 2km further up the hill from the main falls and about 600m off the main road.

Buses and minibuses travel between the main Sukasada terminal in Singaraja and Denpasar (Ubung terminal), via Bedugul, and stop at Gitgit.

LOVINA

☎ 0362

Relaxed is how people most often describe Lovina and they are correct. This low-key, low-rise beach resort is the polar opposite of Kuta. Days are slow and so are the nights.

Almost merging into Singaraja to the west, the town is really a string of coastal villages – Pemaron, Tukad Mungga, Anturan, Kalibukbuk (the main area), Kaliasem and Temukus – that have taken on this collective name.

Lovina is a convenient base for trips around the north coast or the central mountains. The beaches are made up of washed-out grey and black volcanic sand, and they are mostly clean near the hotel areas, but generally unspectacular. Reefs protect the shore, so the water is usually calm and clear.

Information

There is a Bank BCA ATM at the corner of Jl Bina Ria and Jl Raya Lovina, plus many more in Singaraja.

Bits and Bytes (☎ 081 755 2511; Jl Raya Lovina; per hr 25,000Rp; 🕑 8am-8pm) has fast connections plus wi-fi and laptop connections.

Diving & Snorkelling

Scuba diving on the local reef is better at lower depths and night diving is popular. The island Pulau Menjangan, situated off Bali's northwestern tip, is home to reef sharks and prolific sea life, and has the best diving on the north coast. Generally, the water is clear and some parts of the reef are quite good for snorkelling.

Divers should head to **Spice Dive** (☎ 41509; www.balispicedive.com) for PADI open-water certificate courses for about US$350. It's based at the west end of the beach path.

Sleeping

Hotels are spread out along the many side roads running off Jl Raya Lovina to the beach. There are decent places to stay in every price range.

KALIBUKBUK

A little over 10km from Singaraja, this is the 'centre' of Lovina, with the biggest concentration of hotels, restaurants…and touts.

Padang Lovina (☎ 41302; Gang Binaria; r 80,000-250,000Rp;) Down a narrow lane in the very heart of Kalibukbuk. There's no pretension at all around the 12 comfortable bungalow-style rooms set around spacious grounds teeming with flowers. The best rooms have air-con and tubs.

Rini Hotel (☎ 41386; rinihotel@telkom.net; Jl Ketapang; r 120,000-250,000Rp;) This tidy 30-room place has a large saltwater pool. Cheaper rooms have fans and cold water but the more expensive ones are huge, with air-con and hot water. In fact, should you come across a keg, you could have a party.

Puri Bali Hotel (☎ 41485; www.puribalilovina.com; Jl Ketapang; r 130,000-250,000Rp;) The pool area is set deep in a lush garden – you may hang out here all day. The better of the 30 rooms, with hot water and air-con, are simple but comfortable. The cheapest, with fans and cold water, are merely simple.

INDONESIA

OUTSIDE KALIBUKBUK

A few tiny side tracks and one proper sealed road, Jl Kubu Gembong, lead to the lively little fishing village of Anturan, busy with swimming locals and moored fishing boats. It's a real travellers' hang-out though it's a long way from Lovina's evening delights.

Puspa Rama (☎ 42070; Jl Kubu Gembong; s/d incl breakfast 60,000/70,000Rp) One of several budget places on this street, Puspa Rama has grounds a few cuts above the others. The six rooms have hot water. Fruit trees abound – why not pick your own breakfast?

Gede Home Stay Bungalows (☎ 41526; Jl Kubu Gembong; r 70,000-120,000Rp;) Don't forget to shake the sand off your feet as you enter this beachside nine-room homestay. Cheap rooms have cold water while better ones have hot water and air-con.

Eating

Most hotels in Lovina serve food, and there are food carts, *warung*, cafes and quite classy restaurants – Kalibukbuk has the best choices. There's a cluster of bars at the top end of Jl Bina Ria, all of which have happy hours.

Sea Breeze Café (☎ 41138; dishes 12,000-45,000Rp) Right by the beach off Jl Bina Ria, this cafe has a range of Indonesian and Western dishes and excellent breakfasts. It's a good spot for sunset drinks and ocean views.

Pappagallo (☎ 41163; Jl Bina Ria; dishes 15,000-35,000Rp) This big, ambitious open-air restaurant brings some much-needed energy to the snoozy Kalibukbuk scene. There's all the beach standards plus good pizzas from a wood-burning oven. Opt for the wicker chairs on the breezy 2nd level.

Warung Rasta (mains 15,000-30,000Rp) In Anturan right on a strip of beach lined with fishing boats. The menu, not surprisingly, leans towards simply grilled fresh seafood; given the name, the endless loop of music shouldn't surprise either. It's run by dudes who have clearly realised that lounging around here all day beats fishing.

Mr Dolphin (☎ 081 3384 87612; Jl Pantai Banyualit; dishes 15,000-40,000Rp) Right on the beach, this cheery hang-out for dolphin-tour skippers serves a killer grilled seafood platter. There's live acoustic music most nights.

Drinking & Clubbing

Lovina's modest social scene centres on Kalibukbuk.

Kantin 21 (☎ 081 2460 7791; Jl Raya Lovina; 11am-1am) Funky open-air place where you can watch traffic by day and groove to acoustic guitar or garage-band rock by night. There's a long drinks list, fresh juices and a few local snacks.

Poco Evolution Bar (☎ 41535; Jl Bina Ria; dishes 12,000-25,000Rp; 11am-1am) Movies are shown at various times, and cover bands perform at

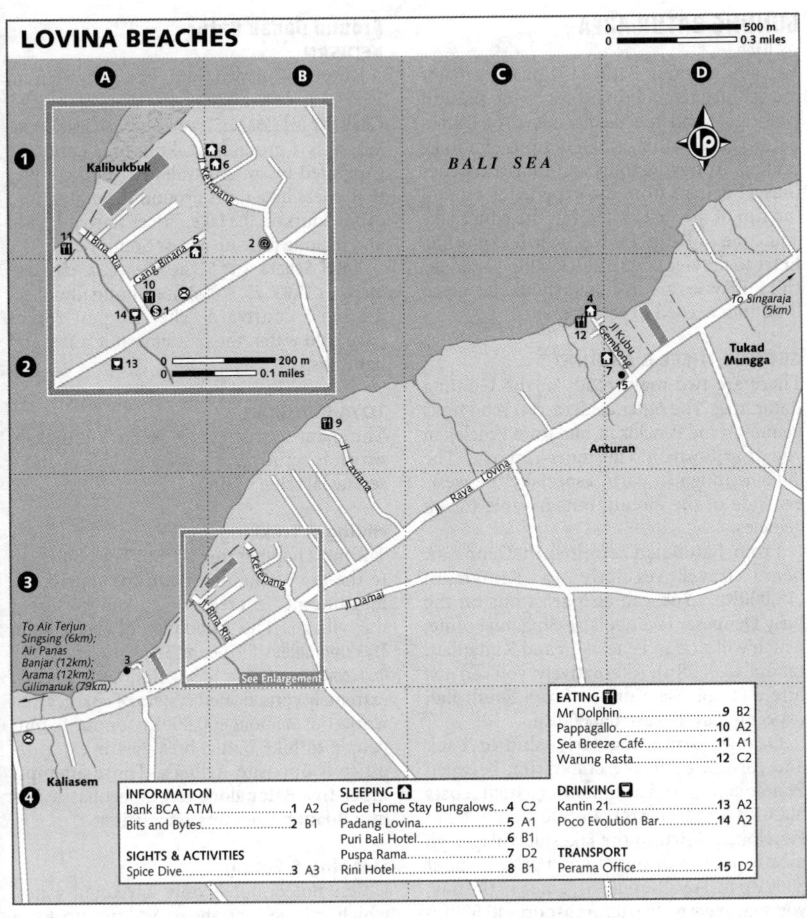

this popular bar-cafe. Classic travellers' fare is served at tables open to street life in front and the river out back.

Getting There & Around

From southern Bali by public transport, you will need a connection in Singaraja, from where there are also air-con buses to Java (see p249 for details). Regular blue bemo go from Singaraja's Banyuasri terminal to Kalibukbuk (about 7000Rp) – you can flag them down anywhere on the main road.

Perama (☎ 41161; www.peramatour.com; Jl Raya Lovina) links Lovina with Kuta and the airport (125,000Rp, four hours), Ubud (125,000Rp, 2¾ hours) and other destinations including Padangbai (150,000Rp, 4¾ hours).

The Lovina strip is *very* spread out, but you can easily travel back and forth on bemo (3000Rp). Bikes are easily rented around town for about 30,000Rp per day.

AROUND LOVINA

About 5km west of Kalibukbuk, a sign points to **Air Terjun Singsing** (Daybreak Waterfall), where you can have a refreshing swim. The falls are sometimes just a trickle in the dry season.

Air Panas Banjar (hot springs; adult/child 6000/3000Rp, parking 2000Rp; 🕒 8am-6pm) are beautifully landscaped with tropical plants. You can relax here and have lunch at the restaurant, or even stay the night. From the bemo stop on the main road to the hot springs you can take an *ojek*; going back is a 2.4km downhill stroll.

GUNUNG BATUR AREA

☎ 0366

Volcanic Gunung Batur (1717m) is a major tourist magnet, offering treks to the summit (see right) and spectacular views of Danau Batur (Lake Batur), at the bottom of a huge caldera. Annoying touts and tourist coaches (buses) detract from the experience around the rim of the vast crater, but the crater lake and cone of Batur are well worth exploring. Entry to the area costs 6000/3000Rp per adult/child. Bicycles are free (and should be, given the climb needed to get here).

GETTING THERE & AROUND

There are two main roads in the Gunung Batur area. The outer caldera-rim road links Penulisan and Penelokan, and from Penelokan you drop down onto the inner-rim road. The latter is rough in parts, especially the western side of the circuit, but drivable for all vehicles.

From Batubulan terminal in Denpasar, bemo travel regularly to Kintamani (18,000Rp). You can also get a bus on the busy Denpasar (Batubulan)–Singaraja route, which will stop in Penelokan and Kintamani (about 18,000Rp). Alternatively, you can just hire a car or use a driver. From South Bali expect to pay at least 450,000Rp.

Orange bemo regularly shuttle back and forth around the crater rim, between Penelokan and Kintamani (which costs 8000Rp for tourists). Public bemo from Penelokan down to the lakeside villages go mostly in the morning (tourist price is about 6000Rp to Toya Bungkah). Later in the day, you may have to charter transport (40,000Rp or more).

Around the Crater Rim

On a clear day, **Penelokan** has superb views across to Gunung Batur and down to the lake at the bottom of the crater. It has numerous huge places catering to busloads of tourists. Enjoy the view and leave.

The villages of Batur and Kintamani now virtually run together. Kintamani is famed for its large and colourful **market**, which is held every three days. If you don't want to go on a trek, the sunrise view from the road here is pretty good.

Continue to Penulisan, where Bali's highest temple (at 1745m), **Pura Puncak Penulisan**, has a great view to the Singaraja coast.

Around Danau Batur

KEDISAN

A hairpin-bend road winds its way down from Penelokan to Kedisan on the shore of the lake.

C.Bali (☎ 081 3532 00251; www.c-bali.com; Hotel Segara, Kedisan) is a ground-breaking tour company (operated by an Australian-Dutch couple) that offers bike tours around the craters and canoe tours on the lake. Prices start at US$40 and include pick-up across South Bali.

Hotel Segara (☎ 51136; hotelsegara@plasa.com; Kedisan; r 80,000-200,000Rp) has bungalows set around a courtyard. The cheapest rooms have cold water; the best have hot water and bathtubs.

TOYA BUNGKAH

The main tourist centre is Toya Bungkah, which is scruffy but has a cute charm and a serene lakeside setting.

Hiking & Trekking

The most popular trek is from Toya Bungkah to the top of Gunung Batur for sunrise – a magnificent sight requiring a 4am start from the village. The **Association of Mount Batur Trekking Guides** (HPPGB; ☎ 52362; volcanotrekk@hotmail.com) operates a local monopoly and an extremely complicated system of charges that works out at about 400,000Rp for one to four people to hike Batur; breakfast is extra. Its office is opposite Arlina's. Those attempting to trek Batur alone can expect hassle and intimidation from this association.

Sleeping & Eating

Unless noted, hotels only have cold water, which can be a boon for waking up for a sunset climb. Most have restaurants, some of which serve *ikan mujair*, a delicious small lake fish, which is barbecued to a crisp with onion, garlic and bamboo shoots.

Under the Volcano III (☎ 081 3386 0081; r 70,000Rp) With a lovely, quiet lakeside location opposite vegetable plots, this inn has eight clean and pretty rooms. Two other nearby inns are run by the same lovely family.

Lakeside Cottages & Restaurant (☎ 51249; www.lakesidebali.com; r US$10-35; 🏊) The lakeside pool at this option makes it a top pick. The restaurant serves home-style Japanese dishes.

Volcano Breeze (☎ 51824; dishes 15,000-25,000Rp) This sociable travellers' cafe with local art on the walls serves fresh lake fish in many forms.

INDONESIA

DANAU BRATAN AREA

☎ 0368

Approaching from the south, you gradually leave the rice terraces behind and ascend into the cool, often misty mountain country around Danau Bratan. The name Bedugul is sometimes used to refer to the whole lakeside area, but strictly speaking, Bedugul is just the first place you reach at the top of the hill when coming up from South Bali. Candikuning and Munduk hold the star attractions in this area.

Candikuning

Dotting the western side of the lake, Candikuning is a haven for plant lovers. The **Candikuning market** (parking 1000Rp) is touristy but among the eager vendors of tat you'll find locals shopping for fruit, veg, herbs, spices and potted plants. You'll find good cafes hidden in the corners.

The **Bali Botanical Gardens** (Kebun Raya Eka Karya Bali; ☎ 21273; Candikuning; walking/driving 7000/12,000Rp, parking 6000Rp; 🕑 7am-6pm) is an extensive collection of trees and flowers that covers more than 154 hectares on the lower slopes of Gunung Pohen.

The graceful, very important Hindu-Buddhist lakeside temple, **Pura Ulun Danau Bratan** (adult/child 10,000/5000Rp, parking 2000Rp; 🕑 tickets 7am-5pm, site 24hr), dates to the 17th century.

SLEEPING & EATING

In Candikuning, the best budget accommodation is along the road to the botanical gardens. Most accommodation also offers food. In the village along a lane near the road to the botanical gardens, **Pondok Wisata Dahlia Indah** (☎ 21233; Candikuning; r 80,000-125,000Rp) is a decent budget option with 17 comfortable, clean rooms with hot-water showers set in a garden of mountain flowers.

Food stalls at Candikuning market offer cheap eats from simple market snacks to meals. At the entrance to Pura Ulun Danau Bratan are several Padang *warung*, and on the grounds, a cafe with a view.

GETTING THERE & AWAY

Danau Bratan is beside the main north–south road, so it's easy to reach from South Bali or Lovina.

Although the main terminal is in Pancasari, most minibuses and bemo will stop along the road in Bedugul and Candikuning. There are frequent connections from Denpasar's Ubung terminal (18,000Rp) and Singaraja's Sukasada terminal (18,000Rp). For Gunung Batur, you have to connect through Singaraja or hire transport.

Munduk

Further west, **Munduk** is a pretty, spread-out village perched high on a ridge that's quickly growing in popularity for its very good trekking and hiking to coffee plantations, rice paddies, waterfalls and villages, or around both Danau Tamblingan and Danau Buyan. You will be able to arrange a guide through your lodgings.

On the way in, consider a stop at **Ngiring Ngewedang** (☎ 082 836 5146; dishes 15,000-40,000Rp; 🕑 10am-5pm), a coffee house 5km east of Munduk that grows its own coffee on the surrounding slopes.

SLEEPING & EATING

Perched on a precipice at the east end of Munduk, **Puri Alam Bali** (☎ 081 2465 9815; www.purialambali.com; r 200,000-250,000Rp) offers eight rooms (all with hot water), with better views the higher you go. The rooftop cafe surveys the local scene from on high. Think of the long concrete stairs down from the road as trekking practise.

North of the temple, the indoor/outdoor **Cafe Teras Lempuna** (☎ 0362-29312; dishes 15,000-40,000Rp; ⊠) is stylish and modern. The menu ranges from burgers to Japanese, and the coffees, teas and juices refresh no matter the temperature.

GETTING THERE & AWAY

Bemos leave Ubung terminal in Denpasar for Munduk frequently (22,000Rp). Morning bemo from Candikuning also stop in Munduk (13,000Rp). If you're driving to or from the north coast, a decent road west of Munduk goes through a number of picturesque villages to Mayong (where you can head south to West Bali). The road then goes down to the sea at Seririt in North Bali.

GUNUNG BATUKAU AREA

Often overlooked (probably a good thing given what the vendor hordes have done to Pura Besakih), Gunung Batukau is Bali's second-highest mountain (2276m), the third of Bali's three major mountains and the holy peak of the island's western end. Enjoy a magical visit to one of the island's holiest and most underrated temples, Pura Luhur Batukau, or just revel in the ancient rice-terrace greenery around Jatiluwih.

On the slopes of Gunung Batukau, **Pura Luhur Batukau** (donation 10,000Rp) was the state temple when Tabanan was an independent kingdom. It has a seven-roofed *meru* (multi-roofed shrine) dedicated to Maha Dewa, the mountain's guardian spirit.

At **Jatiluwih**, which means 'Truly Marvellous', you will be rewarded with vistas of centuries-old rice terraces that exhaust your ability to describe green. The locals will also be rewarded with your 'green', as there's a road toll for visitors (per person 10,000Rp, plus 5000Rp per car). The terraces have been nominated for Unesco status. You'll understand why just viewing the panorama from the narrow, twisting 18km road, but get out for a **rice-field walk**.

Getting There & Away

The only realistic way to explore the Gunung Batukau area is with your own transport.

SOUTHWEST BALI

From Denpasar's Ubung terminal, buses and bemo go west to Gilimanuk, via Tabanan and Negara. From this western road, turn north to **Mengwi**, where there's the impressive **Pura Taman Ayun** (admission 3000Rp; 8am-5pm) water palace and temple.

Down on the coast, Canggu Beach is a few kilometres along the sand northwest of Seminyak. Just 500m northwest of Canggu Beach is **Echo Beach** (Batu Mejan). It has reached critical mass in popularity and has become its own scene, with shops and cafes moving in.

A bit further west is **Pura Tanah Lot** (admission 3300Rp; dawn-dusk), south of Sangeh's main road, a reconstructed temple and major tourist trap, especially at sunset.

INDONESIA

WEST BALI

Balian Beach

Some 10km west of the junction with the road to the north at Antosari is Lalang-Linggah. Here a road (toll 2000Rp) leads 800m to the surf breaks near the mouth of Sungai Balian (Balian River) and the ever-more-popular scene at Balian Beach.

Three basic bungalow-style units at **Made's Homestay** (081 2396 3335; r 100,000Rp) are surrounded by banana trees back from the beach. The rooms are basic, clean, large enough to hold numerous surfboards and have cold-water showers.

Right down by the grey-sand beach, **Balian Segara Homestay** (081 9164 56147; r 150,000-200,000Rp) offers three simple, clean cottages, although views are a little obscured by dunes. The top unit has hot water.

Medewei

Along the main road, a large sign points down the paved road to the surfing mecca of Pantai Medewi. The beach is a stretch of huge grey rocks interspersed among black pebbles. It's a placid place where cattle graze by the beach. Medewei is noted not for its beach but for its *long* left-hand wave – there is little else here.

You'll find accommodation along the main lane to the surf break, and down other lanes about 2km east. **Mai Malu Restaurant & Guesthouse** (43897; s/d 70,000/90,000Rp), near the highway on the Medewi side road, is recommended. It's a popular (and almost the only) hang-out, serving crowd-pleasing pizza, burgers and Indonesian meals in its modern, breezy upstairs eating area. Eight cold-water rooms have the basics plus fans.

Negara

Set amid the broad and fertile flatlands between the mountains and ocean, Negara is a prosperous little town and a useful pit stop. Several banks on the main commercial road (south of the Tabanan–Gilimanuk road), Jl Ngurah Rai, change money and have international ATMs.

Gilimanuk

Gilimanuk is the terminus for the ferries to/from Java (7000Rp, one hour), which run every half-hour during the day and night. You'll find a bank (with poor exchange rates), post office, a *wartel* and a handful of gloomy hotels here.

There are frequent buses between Gilimanuk and Denpasar (Ubung terminal; 25,000Rp, three hours), or along the north coast to Singaraja (16,000Rp, two hours).

Taman Nasional Bali Barat

Visitors to Bali's only national park, Taman Nasional Bali Barat (West Bali National Park), can hike through bird-filled forests, enjoy the island's best diving at Pulau Menjangan and explore coastal mangroves.

The **park headquarters** (☎ 61060; 🕐 7am-5pm) at Cekik displays a topographic model of the park and has some information about plants and wildlife. The **Labuhan Lalang visitors centre** (🕐 7.30am-5pm) is in a hut located on the northern coast; snorkellers and dive boats launch here.

Bali's best-known dive area, **Pulau Menjangan**, has a dozen superb dive sites. The diving is excellent – iconic tropical fish, soft corals, great visibility (usually), caves and a spectacular drop-off.

The most convenient place to stay for diving Menjangana is Permuteran (below). Trips can also be organised in Lovina through Spice Dive (see p250).

Pemuteran

This oasis in the far northwest corner of Bali has a number of artful resorts set on a little bay and is the place to come for a real beach getaway. Most people dive or snorkel the underwater wonders at nearby Pulau Menjangan (above) while here.

DIVING

Reef Seen Aquatics (☎ 93001; www.reefseen.com) is the home of the nonprofit Reef Seen Turtle Project. PADI introductory dives cost US$60 and dives at Pemuteran/Pulau Menjangan cost US$60/70 for two dives.

Founder of **Easy Divers** (☎ 94736; www.easy-divers.eu), Dusan Repic, has befriended many a diver new to Bali. Prices are similar to Reef Seen.

SLEEPING & EATING

Pemuteran has many mellow midrange choices, all located on the bay, which has nice sand and is good for swimming.

Jubawa Home Stay (☎ 94745; r 180,000-270,000Rp; ❄) On the south (hill) side of the road, this clean hotel is a good budget choice. The best of the 12 rooms have hot water and air-con. The cafe serves Balinese and Thai food and there's a popular bar.

Reef Seen (☎ 93001; www.reefseen.com; r 450,000Rp; ❄) Five solid Balinese-style brick bungalows have air-con and open-air bathrooms with showers. This is a well-regarded dive centre (above).

GETTING THERE & AWAY

Pemuteran is served by any of the buses and bemo on the Gilimanuk–Lovina run. Labuhan Lalang and Taman Nasional Bali Barat are 12km west. It's a three- to four-hour drive from South Bali, either over the hills or around the west coast.

SUMATRA

Lush, enormous and intriguing, Sumatra stretches for 2000km across the equator. Happily, there is a payoff for every pothole along the Trans-Sumatran Hwy: volcanic peaks rise around tranquil crater lakes, orang-utans swing through pristine rainforests, and long white beaches offer world-class surf breaks above the surface, and stunning coral reefs below.

Besides natural beauty, the world's sixth-largest island boasts a wealth of resources, particularly oil, gas and timber. These earn Indonesia the bulk of its badly needed export dollars, even as their extraction devastates habitats.

When Mother Nature is this majestic and bountiful, there is usually a flip side, and Sumatra has seen more than its share of her fury. Eruptions, earthquakes, floods and tsunamis are regular headline grabbers, and the steep cost of living in one of the richest ecosystems in the world. Steaming volcanoes brew and bluster while standing guard over volcanic lakes that sleepily lap the edges of craters created by bursts of Jurassic-era lava.

Rugged travellers will find mind-bending beauty throughout this gorgeous, warm yet unforgiving island that's nearly four times the size of Java, but with less than a quarter of the population. At times you'll feel like a lone explorer rediscovering a magical landscape, and you will be rewarded with tranquillity, low prices and the gratitude of locals who are glad people continue to share in their lives.

History

Mounds of stone tools and shells unearthed near Medan prove that hunter-gatherers were living along the Straits of Melaka 13,000 years ago. But Sumatra had little contact with the outside world until the emergence of the kingdom of Srivijaya at the end of the 7th century. At its 11th-century peak, it controlled a great slab of Southeast Asia covering most of Sumatra, the Malay peninsula, southern

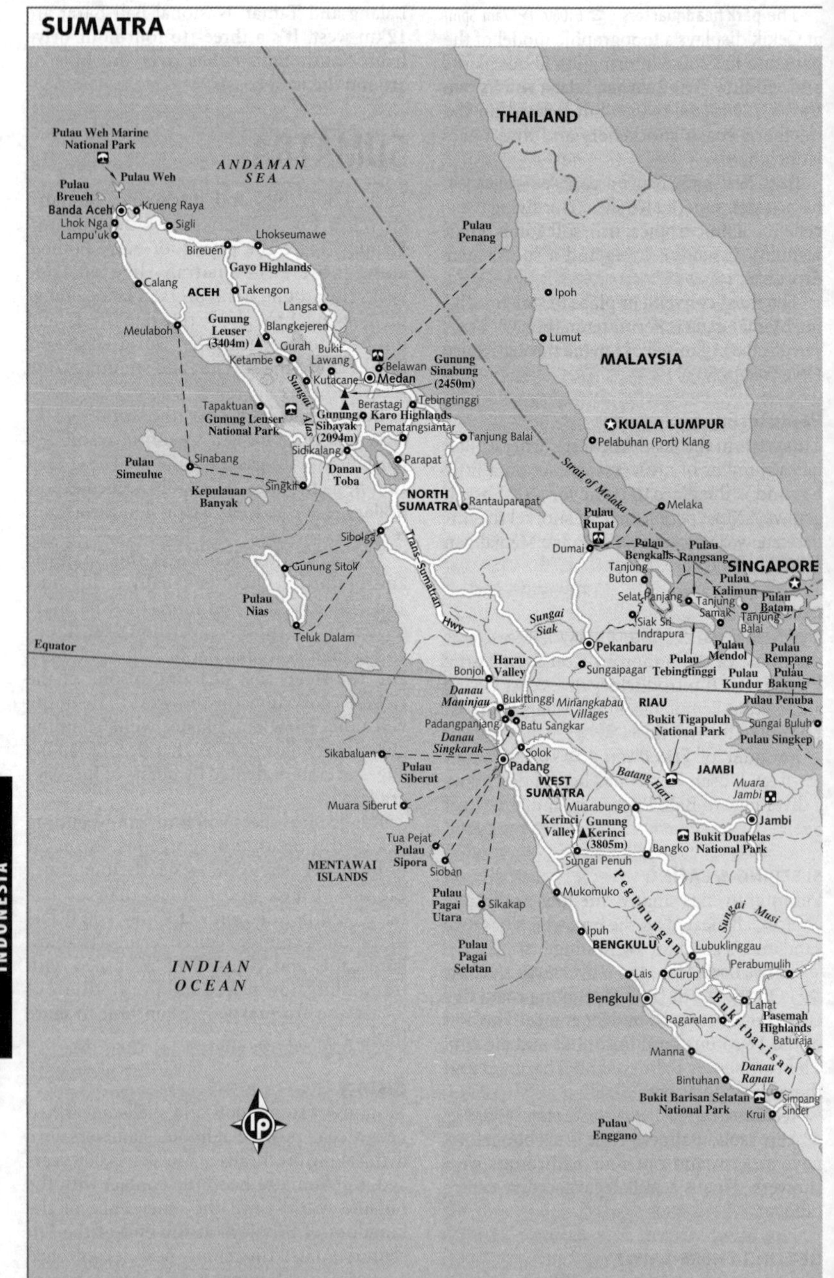
SUMATRA
THAILAND
MALAYSIA
KUALA LUMPUR
SINGAPORE
ANDAMAN SEA
INDIAN OCEAN
Strait of Melaka
Equator
Pulau Weh Marine National Park
Pulau Weh
Pulau Breueh
Banda Aceh
Krueng Raya
Lhok Nga
Lampu'uk
Sigli
Lhokseumawe
Bireuen
Gayo Highlands
Calang
ACEH
Takengon
Langsa
Meulaboh
Gunung Leuser (3404m)
Blangkejeren
Gurah
Bukit Lawang
Ketambe
Belawan
Medan
Gunung Sinabung (2450m)
Kutacane
Sungai Alas
Berastagi
Tebingtinggi
Tapaktuan
Gunung Leuser National Park
Gunung Sibayak (2094m)
Karo Highlands
Pematangsiantar
Tanjung Balai
Sidikalang
Parapat
Danau Toba
Pulau Simeulue
Sinabang
Singkil
Kepulauan Banyak
NORTH SUMATRA
Rantauparapat
Sibolga
Trans-Sumatran Hwy
Gunung Sitoli
Pulau Nias
Teluk Dalam
Pulau Penang
Ipoh
Lumut
Pelabuhan (Port) Klang
Melaka
Pulau Rupat
Dumai
Pulau Bengkalis
Pulau Rangsang
Tanjung Buton
Pulau Kalimun
Selat Panjang
Tanjung Samak
Pulau Batam
Tanjung Balai
Sungai Siak
Siak Sri Indrapura
Pekanbaru
Pulau Tebingtinggi
Pulau Mendol
Pulau Rempang
Pulau Kundur
Pulau Bakung
Harau Valley
Bonjol
Sungaipagar
Danau Maninjau
Bukittinggi
Minangkabau Villages
RIAU
Pulau Penuba
Padangpanjang
Batu Sangkar
Bukit Tigapuluh National Park
Sungai Buluh
Pulau Singkep
Danau Singkarak
Solok
Sikabaluan
Padang
Pulau Siberut
WEST SUMATRA
Batang Hari
JAMBI
Muara Jambi
Jambi
Muara Siberut
Muarabungo
Kerinci Valley
Gunung Kerinci (3805m)
Tua Pejat
Pulau Sipora
Sioban
Bangko
Bukit Duabelas National Park
MENTAWAI ISLANDS
Sungai Penuh
Mukomuko
Pulau Pagai Utara
Sikakap
Pegunungan Bukitbarisan
Sungai Musi
Ipuh
BENGKULU
Lubuklinggau
Pulau Pagai Selatan
Perabumulih
Lais
Curup
Bengkulu
Lahat
Pasemah Highlands
Pagaralam
Baturaja
Manna
Danau Ranau
Bintuhan
Bukit Barisan Selatan National Park
Simpang Sender
Krui
Pulau Enggano

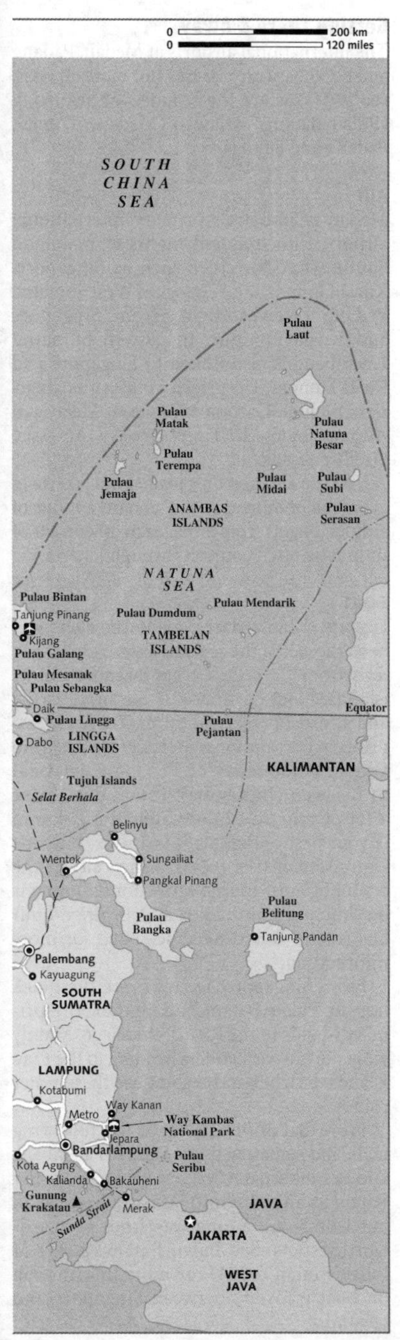

Thailand and Cambodia. Srivijayan influence collapsed after it was conquered by the south-Indian king Ravendra Choladewa in 1025, and for the next 200 years the void was partly filled by Srivijaya's main regional rival, the Jambi-based kingdom of Malayu.

After Malayu was defeated by a Javanese expedition in 1278, the focus of power moved north to a cluster of Islamic sultanates on the east coast of present-day Aceh. The sultanates had begun life as ports servicing trade through the Straits of Melaka, but many of the traders were Muslims from India, and Islam quickly gained its first foothold in the Indonesian archipelago. These traders also provided the island with its modern name, 'Sumatra', derived from Samudra, or 'ocean' in Sanskrit.

After the Portuguese occupied Melaka in 1511 and began harassing Samudra and its neighbours, Aceh took over as the main power. Based close to modern Banda Aceh, it carried the fight to the Portuguese and won substantial territory, covering much of northern Sumatra and the Malay peninsula. Acehnese power peaked with the reign of Sultan Iskandar Muda at the beginning of the 17th century.

The Dutch came next and kicked off their Sumatran campaign with the capture of Palembang in 1825, working their way north before running into trouble against Aceh. The Acehnese turned back the first Dutch attack in 1873, but succumbed two years later. The Dutch were booted out of Aceh in 1942, immediately before the Japanese WWII occupation, and did not attempt to return during their brief effort to reclaim their empire after the war.

Sumatra supplied several key figures to Indonesia's independence struggle, including future vice-president Mohammed Hatta and the first prime minister, Sutan Syahrir. It also provided some problems. First up were the staunchly Muslim Acehnese, who rebelled against being lumped together with the Christian Bataks in the newly created province of North Sumatra and declared an independent Islamic republic in 1953. Aceh didn't return to the fold until 1961, when it was given special provincial status.

The Sumatran rebellion of 1958–61 posed a greater threat, when the rebels declared their rival Revolutionary Government of the Republic of Indonesia (PRRI) in Bukittinggi on 15 February 1958. The central government showed no interest in negotiations, however, and by mid-1958 Jakarta had regained control of all the major towns. The guerrilla war continued for another three years.

Since the 1970s, Aceh has re-emerged as a trouble spot in the archipelago, with continued calls for greater autonomy and secession from the Indonesian republic. In 1989 the Free Aceh Movement (GAM) began a low-level uprising against the government, and the Indonesian armed forces were sent in to 'monitor' the situation.

Sporadic violence occurred throughout the 1990s. In 1998 the Indonesian press revealed years of army atrocities in Aceh. In July 1999 an army massacre took place, killing a religious leader and Free Aceh Movement supporters at Lhokseumawe. Over one million people rallied for independence in Banda Aceh on 8 November 1999.

In 2002 an internationally brokered peace deal was signed by both sides, but sporadic violence continued. However, no human conflict could compare to the destruction of the 2004 Boxing Day tsunami, in which a 9.0-plus-magnitude earthquake off the northwestern coast of Sumatra triggered a region-wide tsunami. In Aceh province, the landmass closest to the epicentre, waves nearly 15m high rose up like the mythical *naga* (sea serpent) and swallowed coastal development and dwellers. The Indonesian death count was estimated at more than 170,000 people, mainly in Aceh. An 8.7-magnitude aftershock that followed several months later was centred near the island of Nias, destroying the capital city and killing hundreds of inhabitants. Most of the destruction has been cleared and the area is moving on, but aid organisations have become a familiar face in both Aceh and Nias and will be in the most severely affected regions for a few more years to come.

Meanwhile the warring parties concentrated on providing emergency relief, and thousands of foreign aid workers flooded the region, acting as unofficial observers. Helsinki-brokered talks led to an agreement in August 2005 under which thousands of Indonesian security forces were withdrawn from the province and GAM gave up weapons. Although tested at times, the peace deal has so far held, bringing vital stability to this lovely island.

Getting There & Away

The international airports at Medan, Padang and Pekanbaru are visa free (for more on visas, see p357), as are the seaports of Sekupang (Pulau Batam), Belawan (Medan), Dumai, Padang and Sibolga.

AIR

Medan is Sumatra's primary international airport, with frequent flights to mainland Southeast Asian cities such as Singapore, Kuala Lumpur and Penang. In West Sumatra, Padang receives flights from Singapore and Kuala Lumpur. In eastern Sumatra, Palembang is also linked to Singapore and Kuala Lumpur. The primary international carriers include Garuda Indonesia, Malaysian Airlines, Lion Air, Tiger Airways, Air Asia, Firefly and SilkAir.

You can also hop on a plane from Jakarta to every major Sumatran city aboard a range of airlines. Flights from Sumatra to other parts of Indonesia often connect through Jakarta.

BOAT

Despite cheap airfares, many travellers still heed the call of the sea and enter Sumatra by ferry from Malaysia. Except for more remote islands, most destinations are more easily and affordably reached by air. There are two primary port options: Melaka (Malaysia) to Dumai (Indonesia) or Penang (Malaysia) to Belawan (Indonesia). If you don't have a lot of time to explore Sumatra, Belawan is your best option, as it is a short bus ride from Medan (see p278), which sits at the centre of most tourist attractions. Dumai is on Sumatra's east coast and is a five-hour bus ride to Bukittinggi; see p283 for more information.

From Singapore, ferries make the quick hop to Pulau Batam and Bintan, the primary islands in the Riau archipelago. Mainly Singaporean weekenders heading to the Riau Islands' beaches and resorts use these water routes.

From Batam, boats serve the following mainland Sumatran ports: Dumai, Palembang and Pekanbaru. Only a few backpackers use Batam as an entry into Sumatra because all but Dumai are a long way from postcard-worthy spots. See Pulau Batam (p283) or Pulau Bintan (p284) for more information on boat transfers between Singapore and beyond.

Ferries swim across the narrow Sunda Strait linking the southeastern tip of Sumatra at Bakauheni to Java's westernmost point of Merak. The sea crossing is a brief dip in a day-long voyage that requires several hours' worth of bus transport from both ports to Jakarta on the Java side and Bandarlampung on the Sumatran side. See p260 for more details.

Pelni-operated boats still paddle between Indonesia's islands, carrying freight and families. Except for more remote islands, most destinations are more easily and affordably reached by air. See p174 for details.

Getting Around

Most travellers bus around northern Sumatra and then hop on a plane to Java, largely avoiding the third-world conditions of Sumatra's highway system. Most of the island is mountainous jungle and the poorly maintained roads form a twisted pile of spaghetti on the undulating landscape. Don't count on getting anywhere very quickly on Sumatra.

AIR

An hour on a plane is an attractive alternative to what may seem like an eternity on a bone-shaking bus. For long-distance travel, airfares are competitive with bus and ferry fares. Medan to Banda Aceh and Medan to Gunung Sitoli are two popular air hops.

BOAT

Most boat travel within Sumatra connects the main island with the many satellite islands lining the coast.

BUS

If you stick to the Trans-Sumatran Hwy and other major roads, the big air-con buses can make travel fairly comfortable – which is fortunate since you'll spend a lot of time on the road in Sumatra. The best ones have reclining seats, toilets and video but run at night to avoid the traffic, so you miss out on the scenery. The non-air-con buses are sweaty, cramped, but unforgettable. Numerous bus companies cover the main routes, and prices vary greatly, depending on the comfort level. Buy tickets directly from the bus company. Agents usually charge 10% more.

Travel on the back roads is a different story. Progress can be grindingly slow and utterly exhausting.

TRAIN

Sumatra has a very limited rail network. The only useful service runs from Bandarlampung in the south to Palembang.

BANDARLAMPUNG

☎ 0721 / pop 859,000

Bandarlampung – Sumatra's fourth-largest city and an amalgam of the old coastal town of Telukbetung and Tanjungkarang further inland – is only worth visiting to experience the Krakatau volcano or Taman Nasional Way Kambas. Most visitors come on package tours arranged in Jakarta, but local guides and tour agencies can set you up nicely for less.

When Krakatau erupted in 1883, the tremors generated a 30m-high wave that devastated Telukbetung and claimed 36,000 lives. The **Krakatau Monument** is a huge steel buoy washed up on a hillside overlooking Telukbetung. Everything below this point was a wasteland.

Information

Banks and ATMs can be found all over town.

BCA bank (Jl Raden Intan 98) The branch on Jl Kartini offers the best exchange rates.

Central post office (Jl Kotaraja)

Squid Net (Jl Raden Intan 88A; per hr 5000Rp; 🕑 10am-8pm) Internet access.

Tours

Several travel agents on Jl Monginsidi offer tours to Taman Nasional Way Kambas. They can also arrange tours to Krakatau via a bus to Kalianda, followed by a boat ride to Krakatau. You may be able to get a cheaper deal from the port (see p260).

Sleeping & Eating

Budget options in Bandarlampung are seriously limited.

Hotel Purnama (☎ 261448; Jl Raden Intan 77; d incl breakfast 230,000-630,000Rp; ❄ 📶) The best option in this price range. It is well managed and maintained, with big comfortable rooms.

Kurnia Perdana Hotel (☎ 262030; Jl Raden Intan 114; d incl breakfast 150,000-250,000Rp; ❄ 📶) Clean, comfortable rooms with TV, but no charm.

Hotel Arinas (☎ 266778; Jl Raden Intan 35; d incl breakfast from 215,000-500,000Rp; ❄) Central with clean, comfortable, modern rooms, all with TV and hot water.

The market stalls around the Bambu Kuning Plaza offer a wide range of snacks.

Getting There & Away

AIR

The airport is 24km north of the city. **Arie Tour & Travel** (☎ 474675; Jl Monginsidi 143) is a helpful travel agency good for tickets on the many flights to Jakarta.

BUS

There are two bus terminals in Bandarlampung. The city's sprawling Rajabasa bus terminal is 10km north of town and serves long-distance destinations. Panjang bus terminal is 6km southeast of town along the Lampung Bay road and serves local and provincial destinations.

From Rajabasa, buses run to Palembang (90,000Rp, 10 hours) and Bengkulu (120,000Rp, 16 hours), but most people heading north go to Bukittinggi (regular/air-con 190,000/300,000Rp, 22 hours).

You've got several bus options for getting to the Bakauheni pier, where boats go to Java. The most convenient option is the Damri bus-boat combination ticket (*bisnis/eksekutif* 110,000/130,000Rp, eight to 10 hours). Buses leave from Bandarlampung's train station at 9am and 9pm, shuttling passengers to the Bakahueni pier, and then picking them up at Java's Merak pier for the final transfer to Jakarta's train station. Damri's office is in front of Bandarlampung's train station.

TRAIN

The train station is in the town centre at the northern mouth of Jl Raden Intan. Sumatra's only convenient rail service connects Bandarlampung with Palembang (*ekonomi/bisnis* 45,000/65,000, 10 hours) and then beyond to Lubuklinggau (economy/business 50,000/70,000Rp, 14 hours).

Getting Around

Taxis charge 80,000Rp to 100,000Rp for the ride from the airport to town. Take the green *opelet* from the town centre to the Rajabasa bus terminal for 2000Rp.

KRAKATAU

Krakatau's beauty masks a mean streak of apocalyptic proportions. When it combusted in 1883, the boom was heard as far away as Perth, Australia. Tens of thousands were killed by either the resulting 30m-high tsunami or the molten lava that flowed across 40km of ocean to incinerate coastal villages. The monster mountain spewed an 80km-high ash plume that turned day into night over the Sunda Strait and altered the world's climate for years. The earth kept rumbling under the remains of Krakatau. In 1927 it erupted again and this time it created an evil mini-me, the Child of Krakatau (Anak Krakatau). And it grumbles still, so make sure to seek the latest advice on seismic activity.

Most travellers head to Krakatau from Carita in West Java, but the island group actually belongs to Sumatra. Tours operate from Bandarlampung (p259) and Kalianda (below).

TAMAN NASIONAL WAY KAMBAS

The Taman Nasional Way Kambas (Way Kambas National Park), a 130,000-hectare stretch of steamy lowland rainforest and mangrove coastline, is home to dozens of tigers, some 200 wild elephants and an estimated 20 rare red Sumatran rhinoceri. With Sumatra's heavily logged, lowland rainforests on the verge of extinction, a visit here is one of the only ways to explore this stunning wild ecosystem. But get here soon because national parks in Sumatra lack the protection of those elsewhere in the world, and poaching, illegal logging and development pressure continue to threaten what's left. Simple tourist facilities include lodges, wooden pole houses, an observation centre and riverboat rides. The park and the Way Kambas elephant training centre, Pusat Latihan Gajah, are about two hours by road east of Bandarlampung, where travel agencies offer a variety of wildlife-spotting trips (these are separate from the Krakatau volcano tours). You could visit the park independently, but transport is limited and expensive. To strike out on your own, hire an *ojek* from Rajabasalama to Way Kanan, where you can hire a guide (50,000Rp to 100,000Rp) and arrange transport.

KALIANDA

☎ 0727

The small coastal port of Kalianda is the best place to arrange boat trips to Krakatau. Survey the seaworthiness of your boat and check for life jackets and a two-way radio. Kalianda is 30km north of the Bakauheni ferry terminal. Organised tours to Krakatau cost about US$90 per person, but you may have to charter a whole boat from Canti, a fishing village outside of Kalianda, if visitor numbers are low.

That will cost you 500,000Rp to 900,000Rp for up to 15 people.

Hotel Beringin (☎ 322008; Jl Kesuma Bangsa 75; d incl breakfast 55,000-75,000Rp) is an old Dutch villa with high ceilings and languid fans. The hotel has lots of information about local attractions and can arrange tours.

There are buses that go to Kalianda from Bandarlampung (20,000Rp, 1½ hours) and Bakauheni (20,000Rp, one hour), but they drop you at the highway turn-off. From there, grab an *opelet* into town (3000Rp).

BAKAUHENI

Bakauheni is the departure point for ferries to Merak, Java. Fast ferries run every 30 minutes from 7am to 5pm and cost 42,000Rp; the crossing takes 45 minutes. A slow ferry runs every 30 minutes, 24 hours a day and costs 15,000Rp for the two-hour trip.

Frequent buses depart from outside Bakauheni's ferry terminal building and travel the 90km trip to Bandarlampung (20,000Rp, two hours). If you're planning to stay the night in Bandarlampung, pay 30,000Rp for a private taxi, which will take you to the hotel of your choice.

PADANG

☎ 0751 / pop 960,000

Most backpackers fly into Padang only to catch the first bus out to Bukittinggi. Big mistake. Sumatra's largest west-coast city has gorgeous Minangkabau roofs which soar

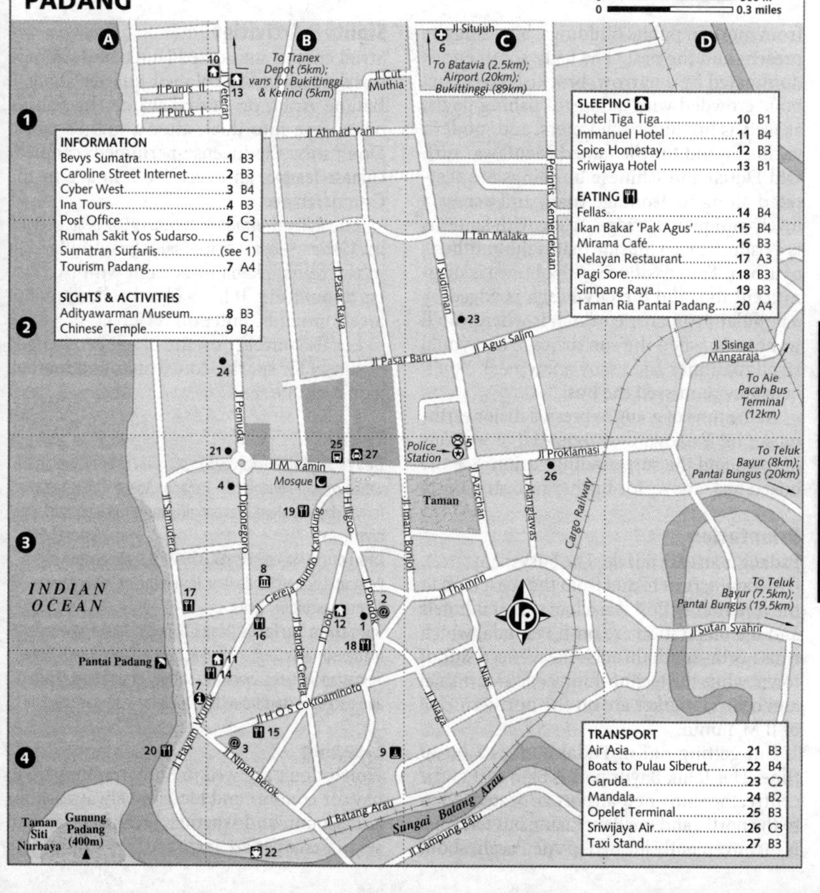

PADANG EARTHQUAKE 2009

At 5.16pm on 30 September 2009, the city of Padang was devastated by a 7.6 magnitude earthquake that struck 57km southwest of Pariaman. At the time of going to print it was estimated that as many as 5000 people had been killed. Several places reviewed in this section were destroyed, including hotels, restaurants and hospitals. Some of these places will rise again, others won't. It's strongly advised to check the situation before you arrive.

Some remote villages in the Kerinci region were wiped out completely from landslides, while Mentawai, Bungus, Bukittinggi and Danau Maninjau escaped relatively unscathed.

from modern public buildings, blending the present and the past. The leafy south end is dominated by a narrow, brackish river harbour crowded with colourful fishing boats, as well as lux Bugis schooners, and modern yachts bound for the famed Mentawai surf. Old Dutch and Chinese buildings are scattered along its frontage road, and across a lovely antiquated bridge strung with lanterns is a palm-fringed hillside that is the antithesis of urban. The coastline south of town is magnificent too, and the city beach is edged by a popular promenade, which is where you'll want to be when the sun drops. Then you'll stroll to dinner and enjoy a fab meal. You'll be glad you missed the bus.

At the time of going to press, a major earthquake hit Padang, destroying large sections of town and the surrounding region. See the boxed text, above, for further information

Orientation

Padang is an easy puzzle. The busy main street, Jl M Yamin, runs inland from the coast road to the junction with Jl Azizchan. Several hotels and the bus station are on Jl Pemuda, which runs north–south through the western side of town, while the techno-funky *opelet* terminal and central market are on the northern side of Jl M Yamin.

But getting out of Padang takes a bit of time. The Teluk Bayur port is 8km east of the centre, the shiny new airport is located 20km to the north, and the Bengkuang bus terminal is inconveniently located in Aie Pacah, about 12km from town. There are a few options for getting into Padang (see p264), and some Mentawai-bound boats leave from the old port on Batang Arau (see opposite).

Information

Padang has branches of all the major Indonesian banks. There are ATMs all over town, and a string on Jl Pondok.

Caroline Street Internet (Jl Pondok 5F; per hr 6000Rp; 9am-9pm)

Cyber West (Jl Nipa Berok 10; per hr 5000Rp 9am-late)

Post office (Jl Azizchan 7; per hr 6000Rp)

Rumah Sakit Yos Sudarso (☎ 33230; Jl Situjuh 1) Privately owned health clinic.

Tourism Padang (Dinas Kebudayaan Dan Pariwisata; ☎ 34186; www.tourism.padang.go.id; Jl Samudera 1; 8am-2.30pm Mon-Fri, 8am-1pm Sat) Its website has a handy list of events.

Sights & Activities

Stroll among antiquated Dutch and Chinese warehouses in the colonial quarter along Jl Batang Arau, or sit and watch the fishing boats ease into dock after a night's work. Don't miss the incense-perfumed, candlelit **Chinese Temple**, an evocative homage to the Confucian age.

The **Adityawarman Museum** (Jl Diponegoro; admission 1500Rp; 8am-4pm Tue-Sun) is beautifully built in the Minangkabau tradition with two rice barns out front. It has a bland collection, but lovely grounds. Enter on Jl Gereja.

Locals converge on the beach promenade at sunset for snacks, cool drinks and football games on the sand.

Tours

Bevys Sumatra (Map p261; ☎ 34878; bevyssumatra@yahoo.com; Jl Pondok 121, Padang) Agent who issues ferry tickets to Mentawai and organises trekking, surf and dive tours.

Ina Tours (Map p261; ☎ 31669; Jl Diponegoro 13, Padang) Located inside Dipo Hotel, this agent organises Mentawai cultural tours.

Sumatran Surfariis (Map p261; ☎ 34878; www.sumatransurfariis.com; Jl Pondok 121) Affiliated with Bevys, Sumatran Surfariis operates a variety of surf boat charters and packages start from USD$1600 for a 10-day tour.

Sleeping

Hotels don't age well in Sumatra. Prepare to pay for comfort and location; always ask for a 'discount' and whether breakfast, tax and service charges are included.

Most of the budget hotels are dreadful, though thankfully many midrange hotels also offer economy rooms.

Hotel Tiga Tiga (☎ 22173; Jl Veteran 33; r incl breakfast 55,000-125,000Rp, plus 10% tax; ❄) North of the centre, this old travellers' dosser has cheap, simple rooms only five minutes' walk from the sea. Grab any white *opelet* heading up Jl Permuda.

Immanuel Hotel (☎ 28560; Jl Hayam Wuruk 43; r incl breakfast 100,000-250,000Rp; ❄) Another travellers' standby, centrally located with simple rooms, helpful, cheery staff and a welcome garden.

our pick **Spice Homestay** (☎ 841388; spicehomey@yahoo.com; Jl Dobi 34; r incl breakfast 110,000-330,000Rp, plus 10% tax; ❄ 💻) Fabulous tiny Balinese-style *losmen* in the centre, with beautiful rooms, a cosy lounge and great food.

Sriwijaya Hotel (☎ 21942; http://thesriwijayahotel.com; Jl Veteran 26; r incl breakfast 250,000-325,000Rp; ❄) If the Tiga's too grungy, then try this newbie across the road. Beautiful modern rooms look onto a quiet courtyard and the ocean is (almost) close enough to smell.

Eating

Taman Ria Pantai Padang (Jl Samudera; mains 6000-8000Rp) Serves standard dishes in the evenings, with excellent sea views.

Mirama Café (☎ 23237; miramacaferst@hotmail.com; Jl Gereje 38; mains 21,000Rp) Offers pricey, blanded-down versions of Indonesian standards in a nice outdoor setting.

our pick **Ikan Bakar 'Pak Agus'** (☎ 823 1799; Jl H O S Cokroaminoto 91; set meals from 25,000Rp) Pak Agus flames his dead sea creatures to perfection. The seafood is delivered fresh every afternoon. A set meal contains a whole barbequed fish, sides, rice and a drink.

Nelayan Restaurant (Jl Samudera; mains 25,000Rp) Does great seafood the Chinese way.

Fellas (Jl Hayam Wuruk 47; 📶) A Western-style wi-fi cafe by day, the evenings see it fill with trendy young locals sucking on hookahs and tourists getting liquored.

The city is famous as the home of *nasi Padang* (Padang food), the spicy Minangkabau cooking that's found throughout Indonesia, and is served quicker than fast food. Try **Pagi Sore** (Jl Pondok 143; dishes 8000Rp) and **Simpang Raya** (Jl Bundo Kandung; dishes 8000Rp).

Jl Sumadera and Jl Batang Arau are full of cheap *wurungs* (food stalls) that spring to life at night while discerning foodies head for Jls Pondok and H O S Cokroaminoto. Juice wagons loiter near the end of Jl Hayam Wuruk. Grab a snack from the carts at the *opelet* station opposite the market.

Getting There & Away

AIR

Bandara Internasional Minangkabau airport (code BIM) is 20km north, off Jl Adinegoro. The following airlines operate international and domestic flights. There is a 100,000Rp departure tax on international flights.

Air Asia (☎ 021 5050 5088; Hotel Huangtuah, Jl Pemuda 1) Flies twice daily to Kuala Lumpur, Malaysia.

Batavia (☎ 41502; www.batavia-air.co.id; Jl Khatib Sulaiman No 63C) Flies three times daily to Jakarta.

Fireflyz (www.fireflyz.com.my) Has a daily propeller flight to Kuala Lumpur domestic airport (Subang), Malaysia.

Garuda (☎ 30737; www.garuda-indonesia.com; Jl Sudirman 2) Operates three flights daily to Jakarta.

Lion Air (☎ 7864781; www.lionair.co.id; airport) Flies to Jakarta four times daily.

Mandala (☎ 39737; www.mandalaair.com; Jl Veteran 20C) Flies daily to Jakarta, Medan and Batam.

Sriwijaya Air (☎ 811777; www.sriwijayaair-online.com; Jl Proklamasi No 39 Terandam) Daily flights to Jakarta and Medan.

SMAC (☎ 081 3635 88828; airport) Flies three times a week to Pulau Sipora in the Mentawais.

Tiger Airways (www.tigerairways.com) Flies to Singapore Tuesdays, Thursdays and Saturdays.

BOAT

Padang has three commonly used ports. Depending on the tide, boats to Siberut and other Mentawai islands will leave from either the river mouth (Sungai Muara) on Sungai Batang Arau, just south of Padang's city centre, or from Teluk Kabung port at Bungus, 20km (45 minutes) away. Check the boat's departure point with your travel agent on sailing day.

Teluk Bayur is the commercial freight port 8km from town and receives a monthly **Pelni** (☎ 61624; www.pelni.co.id) ship to/from Nias (*ekonomi*/1st class 109,000/353,000Rp, 20 hours).

BUS

The days of heading 12km out of town to the Bengkuang terminal at Aie Pacah are over. Most locals prefer to take minibuses directly from Padang.

Minibuses depart frequently for Bukittinggi (16,000Rp, two hours), from the city's northern fringes. **Tranex** (☎ 705 8577) has a depot 2km

MEET BREAKFAST, LUNCH & DINNER: PADANG CUISINE

Eating in a foreign land just got a whole lot easier thanks to Padang cuisine. Forget about pointing at a pot or snooping at your neighbour's meal. With Padang cuisine, you sit down and the whole kit and caboodle gets laid out in front of you. You decide which ones look tasty and push the others aside. You pay for what you eat.

The drawback is that you never really know what you're eating, since there's no menu. If the dish contains liquid, it is usually a coconut milk curry, a major component of Padang cuisine. The meaty dishes are most likely beef or buffalo, occasionally offal or, less likely, chicken, fish or even dog. Some of the fun of Padang-ing is identifying the mystery meat.

The most famous Padang dish is *rendang,* in which chunks of beef or buffalo are simmered slowly in coconut milk until the sauce is reduced to a rich paste and the meat becomes dark and dried. Other popular dishes include *telor balado* (egg dusted with red chilli), *ikan panggang* (fish baked in coconut and chilli) and *gulai merah kambing* (red mutton curry).

Most couples pick one or two meat dishes and a vegetable, usually *kangkong* (water spinach), and load up with a plate or two of rice. Carbs are manna in Padang cuisine. Vegetarians should ask for *tempe* or *tahu* (tofu), which comes doctored up in a spicy sambal.

Before digging into the meal – and we mean this literally, as your right hand is your utensil – wash up in the provided bowl of water. Food and sauces should be spooned onto your plate of rice, then mixed together with the fingers. The rice will be easier to handle if it is a little wet. Use your fingers to scoop up the food, and your thumb to push it into your mouth. It is messy even for people raised on it.

north of the Pangeran Beach Hotel, opposite the Indah Theatre. Catch any white *opelet* (2000Rp) heading north on Jl Permuda and ask for 'Tranex'.

Minibuses for Kerinci go to Sungai Penuh (70,000Rp, six hours) and leave from the same depot as Tranex.

For Danau Toba, take a Parapat-bound bus (350,000Rp, 17 hours), which usually leaves in the evening.

For Medan and Jakarta, it's cheaper and faster to fly.

Getting Around

Airport taxis start from 100,000Rp. White **Damri** (☎ 780 6335) buses (18,000Rp) are a cheaper alternative and loop through Padang. Tell the conductor your street and they'll drop you at the right stop. Heading to the airport, they pass by Bumiminang Hotel and Jl Pemuda/Veteran. From Bukittinggi alight at the motorway overpass and take an *ojek* to the terminal.

There are numerous *opelet* around town, operating out of the Pasar Raya terminal off Jl M Yamin. The standard fare is 2000Rp.

MENTAWAI ISLANDS

☎ 0751

Surfing put the Mentawais on the tourism radar, and dozens of wave-hunting live-aboards run from Padang harbour year-round. But more and more ecotourists are braving the rugged ocean crossing and muddy malarial jungle of this remote archipelago, 85km to 135km west of Padang, to trek, glimpse traditional tribal culture and spot endemic primates. Many consider it the highlight of their trip through Southeast Asia. Surfing is big business as the islands have consistent surf year-round at hundreds of legendary breaks. The season peaks between April and October.

The largest island, Siberut, is home to the majority of the Mentawai population – known for their tattoos and filed teeth. About 60% of Siberut is still covered with tropical rainforest and shelters a rich biological community that has earned it a designation as a Unesco biosphere reserve. The western half of the island is protected as the Siberut National Park (TNS). Sparsely populated Sipora, Pagai Utara and Pagai Selatan are seldom visited. Get here soon, though, because tourism, government-sponsored housing and *transmigrasi* (transmigration) employment projects, and continued logging, are changing the culture, environment and daily life on the Mentawais.

Tours

The economic, and culturally responsible, choice for touring is to take a public boat to Siberut and seek out a Mentawai guide. You pay less and directly benefit the community you've come to experience. Remember, more cash in hand means less poaching and illegal logging on the ground, which will help preserve the Mentawais long after you leave.

Although you can organise commercial tours in Bukittinggi, Padang offers better choices for surfers and trekkers (see p262).

Getting There & Around

Subang Merauke Airways (SMA, previously SMAC; ☎ 081 3635 88828) flies to Pulau Sipora (Rotok) on Tuesdays, Thursdays and Saturdays.

As there is no longer a speedboat, all ferries to Mentawai charge the same price (deck/cabin 105,000/125,000Rp) and usually take 10 hours. Pay the extra for the cabin, as the deck sucks. All boats run overnight, and usually return the following evening (unless continuing). The ferry schedules are changing constantly so always check what's available on arrival in Padang.

Tickets can be bought from **Bevys Sumatra** (Map p261; ☎ 34878; Jl Pondok 121). Remember to check which Padang port to leave from (see p263).

Boats to Siberut arrive at the jetty in Maileppet. It's a 10-minute *ojek* ride (15,000Rp) to the main village of **Muara Siberut**, where longboats can be hired.

BUKITTINGGI

☎ 0752 / pop 102,500

Early on a bright clear morning, the market town of Bukittinggi sits high above the valley mists as three sentinels, fire-breathing Merapi, benign Singgalang and distant Sago, all look on impassively. Modern life seems far removed until 9am. Then the traffic starts up, and soon there's a mile-long jam around the bus terminal, and the air turns the colour of diesel. The mosques counter the traffic by cranking their amps to 11.

Such is the incongruity of modern Bukittinggi, blessed by nature, choked by mortals. Lush. Fertile. Busy. And at 930m above sea level, deliciously temperate all year round.

The town (alternatively named 'Tri Arga', referring to the triumvirate of peaks) has had a chequered history, playing host at various times to Islamic reformists, Dutch colonials, Japanese invaders and Sumatran separatists.

Bukittinggi was once a mainstay of the banana-pancake trail, but regional instability, shorter visas, and the rise of lost-cost aircarriers have seen the traveller tide reduced to a low ebb.

Orientation & Information

The town centre is compact and most items of interest are easily reached on foot. By day, the *pasar* and clock tower end is bustling. In the evenings the focus shifts to the bottom of Jl Ahmad Yani where numerous *warung* open and travellers sip their drinks after a hard day's touring. Souvenir shops line Jl Minangkabau, while upper Jl Ahmad Yani is full of trendy clothes and antiques.

Banks with ATMs, and money changers are clustered along Jl Ahmad Yani, home also to dozens of travel agents and many more services.

Harau Internet (Jl Ahmad Yani; per hr 4000Rp) Internet access.

Post office (Jl Sudirman; internet per hr 6000Rp) South of town near the bus terminal.

Tourist Office (Jl Sudirman; 🕑 7.45am-3pm) Opposite the clock tower; it's got maps, tours and tickets to cultural events.

Turret Cafe (☎ 625956; Jl Ahmad Yani 140-142; per hr 6000Rp) Internet access.

Wartel (Jl Ahmad Yani, near Apache Cafe)

Sights & Activities

Taman Panorama (Jl Panorama; admission 5000Rp), on the southern edge of town, overlooks the deep Ngarai Sianok (Sianok Canyon), where fruit bats swoop at sunset. *Friendly* guides will approach visitors – settle on a price before continuing (around 20,000Rp) to avoid misunderstandings later – to lead you through **Gua Jepang** (Japanese Caves), tunnels built by Japanese slave labour.

Pasar Atas (East of Jl Minangkabau) is a large, colourful market crammed with stalls selling fruit and vegetables, second-hand clothing and crafts. It's open daily, but the serious action is on Wednesday and Saturday, when the stalls overflow down the hill and villagers from the surrounding area come to haggle and ogle.

Tours

Local tours fall into two categories: culture or nature, and can range from a half-day meander through neighbouring villages to a three-day jungle trek to Danau Maninjau, or an overnight assault on Gunung Merapi.

Half-/full-day tours start at around 100,000/175,000Rp and multiday trekking is

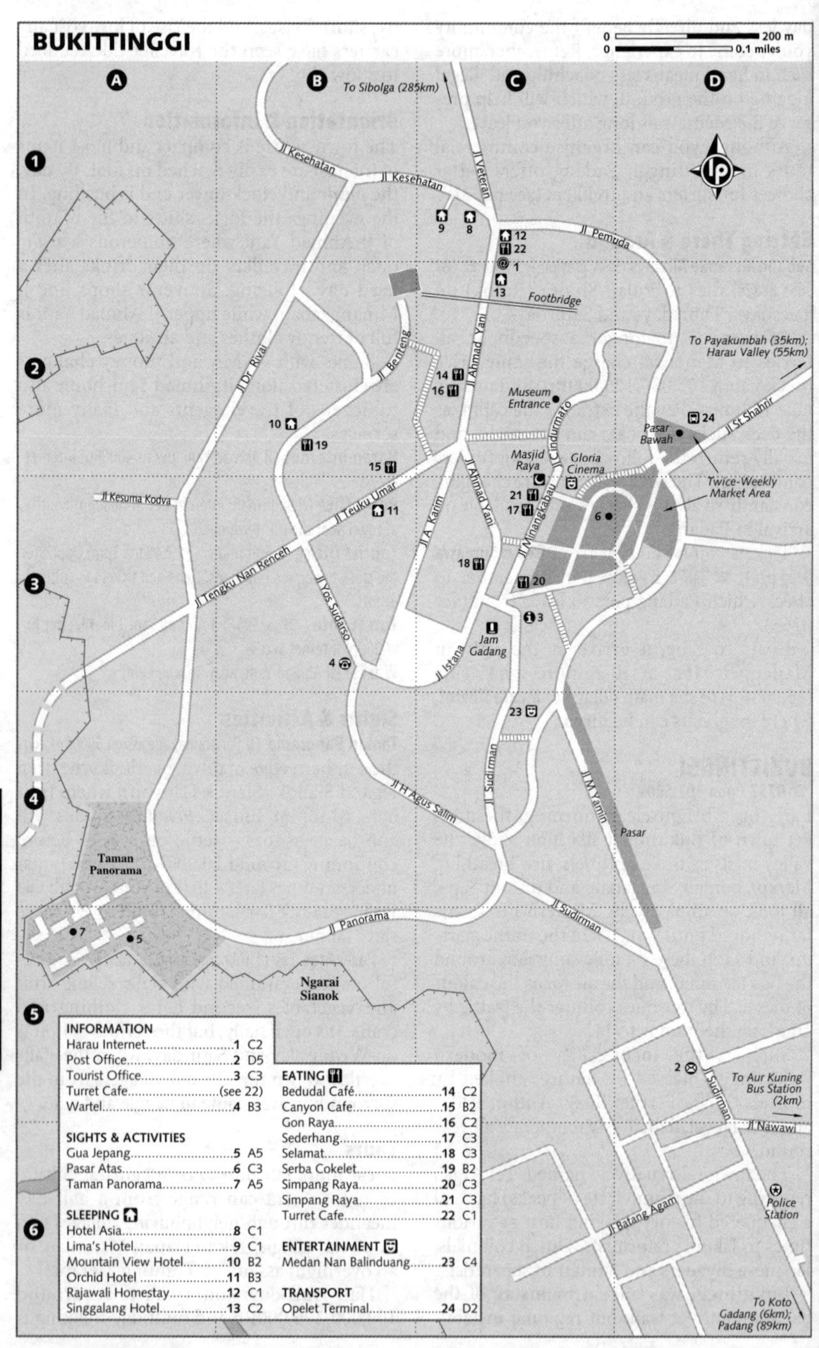
BUKITTINGGI
0 200 m
0 0.1 miles
A
B
C
D
1
2
3
4
5
6
To Sibolga (285km)
Jl Kesehatan
Jl Kesehatan
Jl Veteran
Jl Pemuda
Footbridge
To Payakumbah (35km); Harau Valley (55km)
Jl Benteng
Jl Dr Rivai
Jl Ahmad Yani
Museum Entrance
Jl Cindurmato
Jl St Shahrir
Pasar Bawah
Twice-Weekly Market Area
Masjid Raya
Gloria Cinema
Jl Kesuma Kodya
Jl Teuku Umar
Jl A Karim
Jl Ahmad Yani
Jl Minangkabau
Jl Tengku Nan Renceh
Jl Yos Sudarso
Jl Istana
Jam Gadang
Jl H Agus Salim
Jl Sudirman
Jl M Yamin
Pasar
Taman Panorama
Jl Panorama
Jl Sudirman
Ngarai Sianok
To Aur Kuning Bus Station (2km)
Jl Sudirman
Jl Nawawi
Jl Batang Agam
Police Station
To Koto Gadang (6km); Padang (89km)
INFORMATION
Harau Internet....1 C2
Post Office....2 D5
Tourist Office....3 C3
Turret Cafe....(see 22)
Wartel....4 B3
SIGHTS & ACTIVITIES
Gua Jepang....5 A5
Pasar Atas....6 C3
Taman Panorama....7 A5
SLEEPING
Hotel Asia....8 C1
Lima's Hotel....9 C1
Mountain View Hotel....10 B2
Orchid Hotel....11 B3
Rajawali Homestay....12 C1
Singgalang Hotel....13 C2
EATING
Bedudal Café....14 C2
Canyon Cafe....15 B2
Gon Raya....16 C2
Sederhang....17 C3
Selamat....18 C3
Serba Cokelet....19 B2
Simpang Raya....20 C3
Simpang Raya....21 C3
Turret Cafe....22 C1
ENTERTAINMENT
Medan Nan Balinduang....23 C4
TRANSPORT
Opelet Terminal....24 D2

INDONESIA

roughly 200,000Rp per day. Some tours have a minimum quota, though the Orchid Hotel (below) runs solo tours by motorbike.

Guides hang out in all the cafes. Be clear about what you want and what is and isn't included. If going solo, make sure somebody knows who you're going with.

There's also a healthy climbing scene and a day on the cliffs is around US$35, but if you can find some locals and avoid the entrepreneurs, it'll work out cheaper.

Sleeping

Most hotels include a simple breakfast. On holidays, rooms fill quickly with Indonesian visitors. In Bukittinggi's temperate climate, hot water is more desirable than air-con.

Rajawali Homestay (☎ 26113; Jl Ahmad Yani 152; r 50,000Rp) Basic rooms in this cosy homestay right in the centre. The irrepressible Ulrich is a font of local knowledge and has detailed maps and advice on the area's attractions.

Orchid Hotel (☎ 32634; roni_orchid@hotmail.com; Jl Teuku Umar 11; r cold/hot water 75,000/100,000Rp) Roni runs this popular backpacker inn with clean rooms and a friendly atmosphere, and he can tailor a tour to almost anywhere.

Hotel Asia (☎ 625277; Jl Kesehatan 38; r incl breakfast 100,000-250,000Rp; ❄) Centrally located, the Asia offers spotless rooms for a bargain price. The airy common balconies evoke a Himalayan vibe.

Singgalang Hotel (☎ 21576; Jl Ahmad Yani 130; r 120,000-150,000Rp) This basic cheapie is close to the action.

Mountain View Hotel (☎ 21621; Jl Yos Sodarso 31; r 150,000Rp) In a stunning location with a huge garden and plenty of room for vehicles, the simple rooms are great value.

Lima's Hotel (☎ 22641; www.limashotelbukittinggi.com; Jl Kesehatan 34; r incl breakfast 250,000-400,000Rp, plus 10% tax) Great views down the valley from the side of the hill, the economy rooms are spotless and well appointed.

Eating & Drinking

Bukittinggi has always been the one place in Sumatra that weary road-bums can give their poor chilli-nuked organs a chance to recover, with lashings of lovingly bland *makan Amerika*.

Canyon Cafe (☎ 21652; Jl Teuku Umar 8; mains from 15,000Rp) Still playing Credence and waiting for the tide to change, though the food's always good.

Turret Cafe (☎ 625956; Jl Ahmad Yani 140-142; mains from 20,000Rp; 💻) Good food, relaxed outdoor lounges, internet and the best guacamole in town.

Bedudal Café (Jl Ahmad Yani; mains from 20,000Rp) Has all the old favourites in a cosy, intimate atmosphere on the main drag.

Need a chocolate muffin fix? Try the sublime offerings at **Serba Cokelet** (Jl Yos Sudarso 6a; 🕑 8am-4pm).

If you're pizza'd out, there's plenty of *nasi padang* options. Try tiny **Sederhang** (Jl Minangkabau 63) with mouthwatering choices, **Selamat** (upper Jl Ahmad Yani), towards the clocktower, **Gon Raya** (Jl Ahmad Yani), in the middle of town, or **Simpang Raya** (Jl Minangkabau). Dishes start at 8000Rp.

Jl Ahmad Yani comes alive at night with food stalls doing excellent *sate* and *nasi/mie goreng.*

Entertainment

Medan Nan Balinduang (Jl Lenggogeni; tickets 40,000Rp; ☎ 8.30pm) Offers Minangkabau dance/theatre shows featuring graceful dancing, colourful costumes and a martial-arts demonstration. Check with the tourist office for the latest schedule.

Bloodless bullfight anyone? Known locally as *adu kerbau,* the fights – which are essentially a locked-horn wrestling match – are held irregularly and found in the nearby villages of Kota Baru and Batagak. Ask local guides about upcoming battles.

Getting There & Away

The chaos of the Aur Kuning bus terminal 2km south is easily reached by *opelet* (2000Rp). Ask for 'terminal'. Heading to town ask for 'Kampung China'.

Minibuses run regularly to Padang (16,000Rp, two hours) and Solok (16,000Rp, two hours). Decrepit buses make the Danau Maninjau run (13,000Rp, 1½ hours) while a taxi starts at 160,000Rp.

Trans-Sumatran buses also stop here, though only zombies make it to Jakarta (from 250,000Rp, 35 hours); it's quicker and cheaper to fly from Padang. Ditto for Medan (from 200,000Rp, 20 hours), though you could jump off at Parapat (from 170,000Rp, 16 hours) for Lake Toba. You'll cross the equator en-route, near Bonjol.

Minibuses head to Pekanbaru (100,000Rp, five hours) and there's a night bus direct to

Dumai (110,000Rp, 10 hours) that connects with the Melaka ferry (250,000Rp, two hours). There is a handy bus to Sibolga (90,000Rp, 12 hours) for Nias, and a few buses to Bengkulu (150,000Rp, 18 hours), Jambi (200,000Rp, 15 hours), Sungai Penuh for Kerinci (85,000Rp, 10 hours) and Palembang (140,000Rp), but most services leave from Padang.

Getting Around

Opelet cost 2000Rp. *Bendi* start from 10,000Rp. An *ojek* from the bus terminal to the hotels costs 7000Rp and a taxi costs 20,000Rp. Transfers direct to Padang airport can be arranged from any travel agent for 40,000Rp.

AROUND BUKITTINGGI

Handcrafted silver is the pride of **Koto Gadang**, a village 5km from Bukittinggi (*opelet* 2000Rp). Alternatively, it's an hour's walk from Taman Panorama. Local craftsmen display their wares in antiquated Dutch colonial homes. You can walk here through the Sianok Canyon too. Go through Taman Panorama, take the back exit down a series of overgrown steps, and the path through the forest is on the left off the first sharp bend. Of course, it's a route worked by local guides – only the truly determined will manage to avoid them.

Grab lunch in the bustling small town of **Batu Sangkar**, 41km southeast of Bukittinggi, in the heart of traditional Minangkabau country.

Five kilometres north, **Rumah Gadang Pagaruyung** (King's Palace), was a scaled-down replica of the former home of the rulers of the ancient Minangkabau kingdom of Payaruyung. Unfortunately, a fire razed it to the ground in 2007 and the reconstruction is still incomplete. Most tours now divert to **Istano Silinduang Bulan** (Silinduang Bulan; donation 2000Rp), the nearby Queen's Palace.

Or just cruise the countryside by rented motorbike or *ojek* and glimpse rice terraces that climb the base of a looming and jagged mountain range. In the villages you'll find traditional wooden Minangkabau houses with soaring, buffalo-horned roofs.

INDONESIA

DANAU MANINJAU

☎ 0752

Maninjau, 38km west of Bukittinggi, is one of Sumatra's most spectacularly peaceful crater lakes. The unforgettable final descent includes 44 hair-pin turns that offer stunning views over the shimmering sky-blue lake (17km long, 8km wide), and the 600m crater walls. Maninjau is well set up for travellers (even if low numbers mean that locals have turned to fishing), and should be considered an alternative to Bukittinggi as a place to stay. Life travels slowly here, making it the ideal place to kick back and do nothing. On the other hand, the rainforests and waterfalls of the caldera are just waiting to be explored.

Orientation & Information

The main village (and bus stop) is also called Maninjau and has one main intersection with all services nearby. Note the BRI bank changes US dollars but there is no ATM. Most people stay near Bayur, 3km north. Tell the conductor where you want to stay and he'll drop you there.

Cafe.net (Bayur; per hr 10,000Rp) Slow internet.

PT Kesuna Tour & Travel (☎ 61422; kesumatravel@yahoo.com; Jl Panurunan Air Hangat) Arranges air tickets and minibus charters to Padang (300,000Rp) and Bukittinggi (170,000Rp), and will also change money.

Rama Cafe (per hr 10,000Rp; 9am-10pm) Pokey internet.

Activities

This is an outstanding swimming lake. Though it's 480m deep in some places, the water is warmer than Danau Toba, and, outside of town, the water becomes pure as liquid crystal. Some guest houses rent dug-out canoes or truck inner tubes to float upon.

When relaxation becomes too much, many visitors tackle the 70km sealed road that circles the lake. It's about six hours by mountain bike or 2½ hours by moped.

There's a strenuous two-hour trek to Sakura Hill and the stunning lookout of **Puncak Lawang**. Catch a Bukittinggi-bound bus to Matur and climb 5km to the viewpoint; from there descend to the lake on foot.

Sleeping

Aquaculture has transformed the Maninjau foreshore. *Losmen* with sublime views now look over fishponds and jetties, although there are still beautiful spots.

Outside of Maninjau village, most *losmen* are reached by walking along rice-paddy paths, so look for the sign by the roadside. Truck tubes, canoes, bicycles and mopeds can normally be hired.

Distances indicated with listings are from the Maninjau intersection.

MANINJAU

The majority of the town options front onto aquaculture.

Riak Danau (☎ 081 2679 08153; s/d 30,000/50,000Rp; 500m N) The cheapest single in town.

Pillie Homestay (☎ 61048, 081 3633 73361; r 50,000Rp; 200m S) Simple and cheap rooms south of the intersection, with a lovely family and nice verandah.

Muaro Beach Bungalows (☎ 61189; neni967@yayoo.com; Jl Muaro Pisang 53; r 50,000Rp; 300m NW) Down a maze of footpaths on a nice stretch of private beach somehow free of fish ponds, these clean bungalows are the best value of the village group.

Beach Guest House (☎ 61082; r 50,000; 600m N; 💻) Cheap rooms on a sunny beach; it also rents bicycles and mopeds.

GASANG

Between Maninjau and Bayur, there is a sprinkling of hotels, cheap *losmen* and restaurants.

Hotel Pasir Panjang Permai (☎ 61111; Desa Gasang; r 200,000-300,000Rp; 1.2km N) Excellent rooms, with a great view from the breezy restaurant.

BAYUR

The following is beyond Bayur village.

'Arlen' Nova's Paradise (☎ 081 5352 04714; novaf@hotmail.com; Sungai-Rangeh; r 150,000Rp; 5.5km N) Walk through rice paddies to these beautiful bungalows on a private beach with nary a fishpond in sight. It's easily the nicest place on the lake.

Eating

Most of the guest houses serve standards such as *nasi/mie goreng*, some Western favourites and freshly caught fish. A few places in Maninjau village are also worth checking out.

Cafe 44 (☎ 61238; mains 12,000Rp) Down by the lakeshore, this cafe has a good selection of local food, if you can find the cook. There's also a few cheap rooms (30,000Rp).

Bagoes Cafe (☎ 61418; mains 12,000-25,000Rp) Traveller-friendly with all the usual faves and a few local dishes. It also runs movie nights and has internet access.

Rama Cafe (ramacafe@ymail.com; mains 20,000-30,000Rp) Share a *martabark* (20,000Rp) before hooking into a plate of *ikan panggang* (30,000Rp) while lazing on cushions amongst kites and drums. Look out for its excellent map.

Getting There & Around

Buses run hourly between Maninjau and Bukittinggi (13,000Rp, 1½ hours). Taxis from Bukittinggi start from 160,000Rp. There is also an economy bus to/from Dumai (50,000Rp).

Several places rent out mountain bikes (per day 15,000Rp), motorcycles (80,000Rp) and canoes (15,000Rp).

Minibuses travel the lake road during daylight hours (2000Rp). Alternatively, an *ojek* from the intersection to Bayur will cost around 7000Rp.

SIBOLGA

☎ 0631 / pop 90,000

The departure point for boats to Nias, Sibolga is a west-coast port town with a reputation for hustling tourists. As tourist numbers decline, the hassles have diminished to a fish boil of touts when you step off the bus/boat – the usual port-town bad manners. Get in and out as soon as possible, and arrive as early as possible to ensure a place on a departing boat on the same day.

The **BNI bank** (Jl Katamso) changes money and has an ATM. Get your cash here, because options on Pulau Nias are limited. **Hotel Pasar Baru** (☎ 22167; cnr Jl Imam Bonjol & Raja Junjungan; d with fan 100,000Rp, with air-con 180,000-250,000Rp; ❄) is the only budget spot worth your time. It's relatively clean and has a decent Chinese restaurant. A string of Padang diners and coffee shops can be found opposite the harbour.

Ferries to Nias leave from the harbour at the end of Jl Horas. There are two port options for Nias: the capital city of Gunung Sitoli, which is in the north of the island and a three-hour bus ride from the surf break; or Teluk Dalam, which is in the south and a 15-minute ride away.

Two ferries leave on some evenings from Sibolga's Jl Horas port for the overnight trip to Teluk Delam (economy/air-con/cabin 58,000/120,000/158,000Rp, 11 hours). Alternatively catch the boat for Gunung Sitoli for roughly the same rates. You can also take the daily fast ferry (180,000Rp, four hours) and cut your travel time in half. All ferries charge an additional cargo fee for surfboards (100,000Rp per board bag).

Trans-Sumatran Hwy express buses bypass Sibolga, but slow public buses run to Bukittinggi (80,000Rp, 12 hours), Padang (85,000Rp, 14 hours), Medan (80,000Rp, 11 hours), and Parapat (70,000Rp, six hours). Faster minibuses also run regularly to and from Medan (85,000Rp, nine hours).

PULAU NIAS

The waves deserve their legendary status, and the traditional hill villages, such as **Tundrumbaho** and famous **Bawomataluo**, captivate even casual cultural tourists and ethno-architectural buffs. But, and there is a sizeable one, Pulau Nias was hit twice by major natural disasters within three months: the tsunami and then the 2005 earthquake, which left the main town, Gunung Sitoli, in ruins. The recovery program hasn't been anywhere near as rapid as in Aceh, and the local frustration is evident and sometimes gets taken out on tourists. Patience and understanding are absolute requirements for all on Nias.

On Pantai Sorake – a surf beach located in the horseshoe bay of Teluk Lagundri, decimated by the tsunami – a string of *losmen* are open for business. From south to north you can find Morris Losmen and Eddy's Losmen, both just a few minutes' walk from the famous right break – best between June and October. Lisa's, Lili's and Peeruba Losmen are on a nice patch of sand at the other end. The going rate is between 50,000Rp and 100,000Rp per night, but you are expected to eat at your *losmen* too. And that'll cost you. A plate of chicken or fish can fetch 50,000Rp. If you do not eat where you sleep, you will hear about it. Most surfers come prepared, but you can rent gear at Key Hole Losmen, in front of the keyhole in the reef, through which you'll paddle.

If you want or need to stay in Gunung Sitoli because of transport connections, try **Miga Beach Bungalows** (☎ 21460; d incl breakfast 200,000-300,000Rp; ❄), which sits on a beach 1.5km from town. It's accessible by *opelet* (2000Rp) or becak (15,000Rp) from the bus terminal. The airport is 14km (and 50,000Rp) away. There are numerous restaurants to choose from on the main drag.

Ferries to Sibolga operate from Gunung Sitoli and Teluk Dalam; see p269 for details.

DANAU TOBA

☎ 0625 / pop 550,000

There's no denying the beauty of Danau Toba. This 1707-sq-km, 450m-deep lake, set in the collapsed caldera of an extinct volcano, is surrounded by mountains ribboned with waterfalls and terraced with rice fields. Its pale-blue magnificence hits you on the bus ride into Parapat, when you'll also spot Pulau Samosir – a Singapore-sized island where you'll make yourself at home. When there's a touch of mist in the air, and the horizon is obscured, the water seems to blend perfectly with the sky. It's a stunning place to hang out with North Sumatra's fun-loving Batak people, who once bathed in tourist dollars and now are simply happy to see anyone with a backpack and a smile. Nice hotel rooms are dirt cheap, and the food is good here. You may find it difficult to leave.

Parapat

☎ 0625

The mainland departure point for Danau Toba, Parapat has everything a transiting tourist needs: transport, lodging and supplies.

The commercial sector of the town clumps together along the Trans-Sumatran Hwy (Jl SM Raja). Branching southwest towards the pier, Jl Pulau Samosir passes most of Parapat's hotels. After 1km, a right fork (Jl Haranggaol) leads to the pier, another 1km southwest. The bus terminal is 2km east of town, but most buses pick up and drop off passengers from ticket agents along the highway or at the pier.

SLEEPING & EATING

You'll have to crash for the night if your bus gets in after the last boat to Samosir. Here are a few options:

Charlie's Guesthouse (☎ 41277; Jl Tiga Raya 7; r 50,000Rp) Beside the ferry dock, Charlie's is cheap and close; it's run by a local Toba music legend.

Hotel Singgalang (☎ 41260; Jl SM Raja 52; r without bathroom 80,000Rp) A big Chinese-run place with basic rooms and a downstairs restaurant.

The highway strip (Jl SM Raja) is well equipped to feed the passing traveller, with every variety of Indonesian cuisine.

GETTING THERE & AWAY

The **bus terminal** (Trans-Sumatran Hwy) is about 2km east of town on the way to Bukittinggi, but is not frequently used (so say the travel agents). Prices are highly negotiable, so shop around at the different ticket agents.

Buses to Medan (22,000Rp, five hours) are frequent, although services taper off in the afternoon. There are also minibuses (70,000Rp) that deliver passengers to Jl SM Raya in Medan. Other destinations include Sibolga

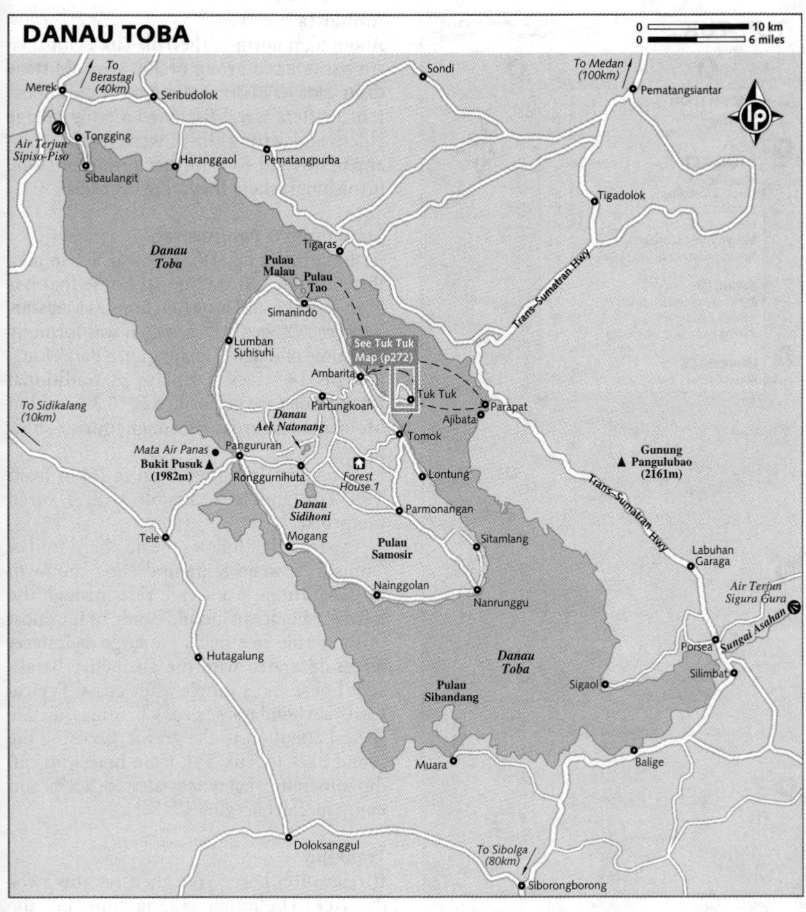

(70,000Rp, six hours), Bukittinggi (economy/super-executive 160,000/200,000Rp, 15 hours) and Padang (220,000Rp, 17 hours).

GETTING AROUND

Opelet shuttle constantly between the ferry dock and the bus terminal (2000Rp)

Pulau Samosir

☎ 0625 / pop 120,000

Trek, swim, explore traditional Batak villages, soak in hot springs, party or just chill with cool local people in Pulau Samosir. Your bus-beaten body will begin to unwind on the slow 8km ferry cruise over to this volcanic isle (it's actually connected to the mainland by a narrow isthmus, but why quibble?) 900m above sea level. **Tuk Tuk**, the island's resort town, has seen busier times, which means low prices, high value and tranquillity.

INFORMATION

The following facilities are all located in Tuk Tuk (Map p272). There is a small police station at the top of the road leading to Carolina Cottages (p273). Load up on reading material in Toba, because the rest of Sumatra is a desert for the printed word. Penny's Bookstore and Gokhan Library have both used and rental books.

Internet access (10,000Rp per hour) is available at many of the guest houses. Change your money before you get to Samosir. Exchange rates at the island's hotels and money changers

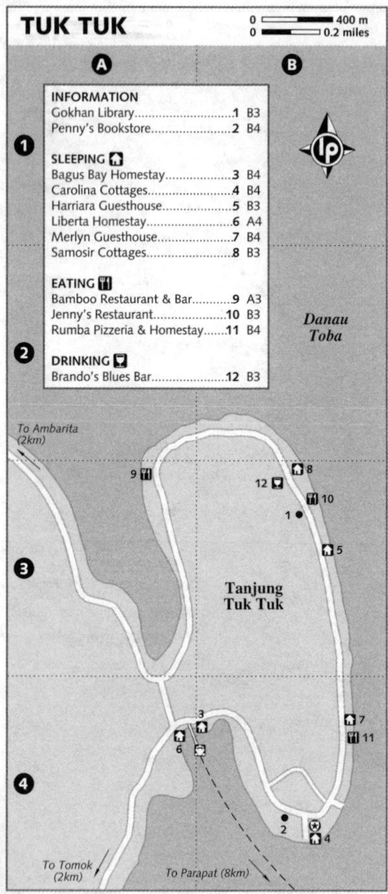

are pretty awful. The only post office is in Ambarita.

SIGHTS & ACTIVITIES

The following sights and activities are located around Danau Toba (Map p271).

Tomok

Tomok, 2km southeast of Tuk Tuk, is the main village on the east coast of Samosir and the souvenir-stall capital of the island. Tucked away among them, 500m up a path from the road, is the ancient **Tomb of King Sidabutar** (admission 5000Rp; dawn-dusk), one of the last pre-Christian animist kings. The grave's hand-carved details are intriguing, but the grounds need some love.

Ambarita

About 5km north of the Tuk Tuk Peninsula, Ambarita has a group of 300-year-old **stone chairs** (admission 2000Rp; 8am-6pm) where important matters were discussed among village elders and wrong-doers were tried – then apparently led to a further group of stone furnishings where they were beheaded.

Simanindo & Pangururan

At the northern tip of the island, in Simanindo, there's a fine old traditional house that has been restored and now functions as a **museum** (admission 30,000Rp; 10am-5pm). It was formerly the home of Rajah Simalungun, a Batak king, and his 14 wives. Displays of traditional **Batak dancing** are performed at 10.30am from Monday to Saturday if enough tourists show up.

The village of Simanindo is 15km from Tuk Tuk and is accessible with a hired motorbike.

The road that follows the northern rind of Samosir between Simanindo and the town of Pangururan is a scenic ride through the Bataks' embrace of life and death. In the midst of the fertile rice fields are large **multistorey graves** decorated with the distinctive Batak-style house and a simple white cross. Typical Christian holidays, such as Christmas, dictate special attention to the graves. Crossing the island back to Tuk Tuk from here, you can dip into hilltop **hot springs** (admission 5000Rp) and enjoy spectacular views.

Trekking

If relaxation bores you, then try this two-day trek. The jungle is long gone, but the paths are challenging and interesting as they wind past coffee and clove plantations. Get a map in Tuk Tuk because paths are not well marked.

The popular Ambarita to Pangururan trek starts opposite the bank in Ambarita. Continue along, walking straight at the escarpment and take the path to the right of the graveyard. The climb to the top is hard and steep, taking about three hours, longer in the wet season when it becomes slippery and a bit hazardous. The path then leads to the village of **Partungkoan (Dolok)**, where you can stay at **Jenny's Guest House** (r 5000Rp) or **John's Losmen** (081 3767 87733; r 5000Rp). From Partungkoan, it takes about five hours to walk to Pangururan via **Danau Sidihoni**.

SLEEPING

The best sleeping options are along the north and south coasts, where little guest houses are tucked in between village chores: washing the laundry on the rocks and collecting the news from neighbours.

Except for Thyesza, all of the places listed here are located in Tuk Tuk (Map p272).

Bagus Bay Homestay (☎ 451287; www.bagus-bay.page.tl; r without bathroom 20,000-30,000Rp, with bathroom 75,000-150,000Rp; 💻) Rooms in traditional Batak houses overlook avocado trees and a children's playground. The cheaper rooms are more like prison cells. At night its restaurant is a lively spot for young travellers to congregate.

our pick **Liberta Homestay** (☎ 451035; liberta_homestay@yahoo.com.co.id; r without bathroom 25,000Rp, with bathroom 40,000-70,000Rp; 💻) It may have only limited lake views, but a chill universe is created here by a lazy-day garden and arty versions of traditional Batak houses.The popular Mr Moon is a great source of information, including for onward travel to North Sumatra and Aceh.

Merlyn Guesthouse (☎ 451057; r 30,000-35,000Rp; 💻) Situated right on the lake, rooms in traditional Batak-style houses here are as cheap and charming as you'll find. Has hot water.

Carolina Cottages (☎ 415210; carolinacottage laketoba.blogspot.com; d 48,000-110,000Rp, f 250,000Rp; 💻 🚗 📶) Considered Tuk Tuk's swankiest (a relative term) sleep, Carolina is neat and orderly, perhaps too much so for dishevelled types. But its economy rooms are an eagle's eyrie with a hilltop perch in a polished Batak-style building.

Samosir Cottages (☎ 451170; www.samosircottages.com; r 50,000-375,000Rp; 💻) A good choice for travellers who want to hang out with young like-minded folk and boisterous young staff, plus the swimming is pretty good.

Harriara Guesthouse (☎ 451183; r 60,000-80,000Rp) A great spot on the lake, with good swimming and a pleasant flower garden. From its sparkling rooms, you'd never guess this place was 22 years old.

Thyesza (☎ 700 0443; www.flowerofsamosir.com; r 60,000Rp, with hot water & breakfast 150,000Rp) Located out of town just past Ambarita, Thyesza is a great choice for those wanting some added peace and quiet away from Tuk Tuk's backpacker scene. Rooms are immaculate, and are an opportunity to stay in a Batak house. Offers free transport from Tuk Tuk on arrival.

EATING & DRINKING

The guest houses tend to mix eating and entertainment in the evening. Most restaurants serve the Batak speciality of barbecued carp (most from fish farms).

The following restaurants are all located in Tuk Tuk (Map p272).

our pick **Jenny's Restaurant** (mains 20,000-45,000Rp) One of the busiest places on the island and with good reason. The smoky grilled fish fresh from the lake is simply the best in town. The fruit pancake is also highly recommended.

Bamboo Restaurant & Bar (mains 20,000-50,000Rp) With incredible lake views, Bamboo is a stylish place to watch the sun slink away, with cosy cushion seating, a down-tempo mood and a reliable menu. Does good cocktails too.

THE BATAKS

The Bataks are a Proto-Malay people descended from Neolithic mountain tribes from northern Thailand and Myanmar (Burma) who were driven out by migrating Mongolian and Siamese tribes. When the Bataks arrived in Sumatra they trekked inland, making their first settlements around Danau Toba, where the surrounding mountains provided a natural protective barrier. They lived in virtual isolation for centuries.

The Bataks were among the most warlike peoples in Sumatra, and villages were constantly feuding. They were so mistrustful that they did not build or maintain natural paths between villages, or construct bridges. The practice of ritual cannibalism, involving eating the flesh of a slain enemy or a person found guilty of a serious breach of *adat* (traditional law), survived among the Toba Bataks until 1816.

Today there are more than six million Bataks, most of whom are Christian, and their lands extend 200km north and 300km south of Danau Toba.

Music is a great part of Batak culture and a Batak man is never far from his guitar. The Bataks are also famous for their powerful and emotive hymn singing.

Rumba Pizzeria & Homestay (mains 20,000-70,000Rp) On Saturdays Rumba's will stay open late to show English Premiership football, served with delicious pizza where you pick your own toppings.

Brando's Blues Bar (☎ 451084) There are a handful of foreigner-oriented bars, such as this one, in between the local jungle-juice cafes. Happy hour is until 10pm.

ENTERTAINMENT

On most nights, music and spirits fill the air with the kind of camaraderie that only grows in small villages. The parties are all local – celebrating a wedding, new addition on a house or the return of a Toba expat. Invitations are gladly given and should be cordially accepted.

Bagus Bay and Samosir Cottages (see p273) both have traditional Batak music and dance performances on Wednesday and Saturday evenings at 8.15pm.

GETTING THERE & AWAY

Boat

Ferries between Parapat and Tuk Tuk (7000Rp) operate about every hour from 8.30am to 6pm. Ferries stop at Bagus Bay (35 minutes); other stops are by request. The first and last ferries from Tuk Tuk leave at about 7am and 4pm; check exact times with your hotel. When leaving for Parapat, stand on your hotel jetty and wave a ferry down.

Five ferries a day shuttle vehicles and people between Ajibata, just south of Parapat, and Tomok. There are five departures per day between 7am and 9pm. The passenger fare is 4000Rp. Cars cost 75,000Rp, and places can be booked in advance at the **Ajibata office** (☎ 41194) or **Tomok office** (☎ 451185).

Bus

See Parapat (p270), the mainland transit point, for information on bus travel to/from Danau Toba.

On Samosir, to get to Berastagi you'll have to catch a bus from Tomok to Pangururan (12,000Rp, 45 minutes), from where you take another bus to Berastagi (27,000Rp, three hours). This bus goes via Sidikalang.

GETTING AROUND

Local buses serve the whole of Samosir except Tuk Tuk. You can rent motorcycles in Tuk Tuk for 75,000Rp a day, which includes petrol and helmet. Bicycle hire costs from 25,000Rp per day.

Minibuses run between Tomok and Ambarita (3000Rp), continuing to Simanindo (6000Rp) and Pangururan (12,000Rp). The road between the neck of the peninsula is a good spot to flag down these minibuses. Services dry up after 5pm.

BERASTAGI

☎ 0628 / pop 600,000

Escaping from the infernal heat of sea-level Medan, the colonial Dutch traders climbed high into the lush, cool volcanic hills, took one look at the stunningly verdant, undulating landscape and decided to set up camp and build a rural retreat where Berastagi (also called Brastagi) now stands.

Beyond the town are the green fields of the Karo Highlands, dominated by two volcanoes: Gunung Sinabung to the west and the smoking Gunung Sibayak to the north. Each is a day hike, making them two of Sumatra's most accessible volcanoes, and the primary reason why tourists get off the bus in the first place.

Information

Berastagi is essentially a one-street town spread along Jl Veteran. Banks have ATMs.

D'Z@S Net (Jl Perwira; 7am-midnight) Decent speed internet.

Post office (Jl Veteran) Near the memorial at the northern end of the street.

Sibayak Trans Tour &Travel (☎ 91122; dicksonpelawi@yahoo.com; Jl Veteran 119) Books plane tickets and has information on local and onward travel.

Tourist Information Centre (☎ 91084; Jl Gundaling 1; 8am-5pm Mon-Sat) Has maps and can arrange guides.

Sights & Activities

Gunung Sibayak (2094m) offers summit views straight out of a tourist brochure, especially during the June to August dry season. Try to avoid weekends, when Medan day-trippers are out in force. If you're with a friend, you could probably do without a guide, but don't hike alone. Guides charge from 150,000Rp depending on the route. You'll need good walking shoes, warm clothes, food and drink.

The easiest route starts northwest of town, 10 minutes' walk past the Sibayak Multinational Guesthouse. Take the left track beside the entrance hut (2000Rp). From here it's 7km, and three hours, to the top.

INDONESIA

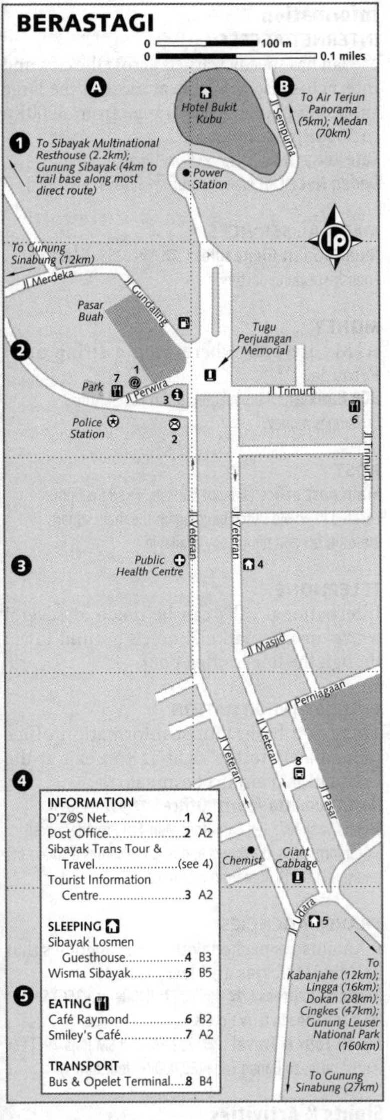

Alternatively, you can catch a local bus (5000Rp) to Semangat Gunung at the base of the volcano, from where it's a two-hour climb to the top; there are steps part of the way, but the trail is narrow and in worse condition than the one from Berastagi.

The endurance option is to trek through the jungle from the **Air Terjun Panorama**, the waterfall on the Medan road, 5km north of Berastagi. This five-hour walk demands a local guide.

On the way down, stop and soak in the **hot springs** (admission 3000-5000Rp), a short ride from Semangat Gunung on the road back to Berastagi.

Gunung Sinabung (2450m) is Sibayak's taller, better-looking (meaning the views) and far more difficult sister. It takes around 10 hours return, and should only be tackled with a guide (from 200,000Rp). Solo hikers have perished here. Sinabung is shy, often hiding behind thick cloudbanks that obscure views.

Berastagi also has plenty of guides offering treks along the well-trodden trails through **Taman Nasional Gunung Leuser** (Gunung Leuser National Park), particularly to Bukit Lawang (three days) or Kutacane (six days).

Anthro-architecture hounds will dig the traditional villages of **Lingga** and **Dokan**. Both are easily reached by *opelet*.

Sleeping

Sibayak Losmen Guesthouse (☎ 91122; dicksonpelawi@yahoo.com; Jl Veteran 119; r without/with bathroom 40,000/60,000Rp; 💻 📶) Nice cheapies with a lot of Indonesian personality make this place feel more like a homestay.

Wisma Sibayak (☎ 91104; Jl Udara 1; r without bathroom 50,000-60,000Rp, with bathroom 80,000-125,000Rp; 💻) Tidy and spacious rooms in the two-storey building have great views.

Sibayak Multinational Resthouse (☎ 91031; Jl Pendidikan 93; r 100,000-120,000Rp) Nice quiet option away from the town centre, Multinational has a manicured garden and straightforward rooms with hot shower. The hotel is a short *opelet* ride north of town on the road to Gunung Sibayak.

Eating

The rich volcanic soils of the surrounding countryside supply much of North Sumatra's produce, which passes through Berastagi's colourful produce and fruit markets.

Most of the budget hotels have restaurants, but head into town for more diversity. Along Jl Veteran there is a variety of evening food stalls, as well as simple restaurants specialising in *tionghoa* (Chinese food).

Café Raymond (Jl Trimurti 49; mains 8000-20,000Rp; 🕑 7am-midnight) Berastagi's local bohemians hang out at Café Raymond, serving fruit juices, beer and Western food.

Smiley's Café (Jl Perwira 1; mains 10,000-23,000Rp; 8am-8pm) A rickety little cafe serving steaming plates of cheesy lasagne, local food and tourist advice.

Getting There & Away

The **bus terminal** (Jl Veteran) is conveniently located near the centre of town. You can also catch buses to Padang Bulan in Medan (8000Rp, 2½ hours) anywhere along the main street.

To reach Danau Toba without backtracking through Medan, catch an *opelet* to Kabanjahe (3500Rp, 15 minutes) and change to a bus for Pematangsiantar (15,000Rp, three hours), then connect with a Parapat-bound bus (15,000Rp, 1½ hours).

MEDAN

061 / pop 2,000,000

Sumatra's major metropolis, and Indonesia's third-largest city, has a dubious legend in travellers' circles, regularly taking honours in 'What's the worst place you've ever visited?' conversations. The pollution, poverty and persistent cat calls of 'Hello Mister!' can be an unnerving jolt of dirt-under-your-fingernails Asia. However, if you've worked your way north through Sumatra and have a little more resistance to the culture shock, it's easier to see past the grime and discover an amenity-filled, leafy and modern town with more than a hint of crumbling, Dutch colonial charm.

Orientation

A taxi ride from the airport to the nearby centre should cost 30,000Rp. From the southern bus terminal, the giant Amplas, it's a 6.5km bemo ride (5000Rp) into town.

The sprawling city of Medan radiates from the confluence of the Sungai Deli and Sungai Babura. Most backpackers tend to head to the neighbourhood surrounding Mesjid Raya on Jl Sisingamangaraja (which is often abbreviated as 'SM Raja') for accommodation options. North of this area is the city centre, which is organised around Jl Pandu and Jl Pemuda. The manicured part of town is Polonia, west of Sungai Delim, which follows the spine of Jl Imam Bonjol. Little India is sandwiched in between Jl H Zainal Arifin, Jl Imam Bonjol and Jl Cik Ditiro. Just east of here are the glam shopping malls, including Sun Plaza.

Information

INTERNET ACCESS

Medan has speedy warnets across the city, and internet is also available at most of the large shopping plazas. Prices range from 3000Rp to 5000Rp per hour.

Café Zelsy (Jl SM Raja; 9am-10pm)

Dedeq Net (Jl RH Juanda Baru; 9.30am-midnight)

MEDICAL SERVICES

Rumah Sakit Gleneagles (456 6368; Jl Listrik 6) English-speaking doctors.

MONEY

ATMs are everywhere, with a string on Jl Pemuda.

BCA Bank (cnr Jl Diponegoro & Jl H Zainal Arifin) Exchanges money.

POST

Main post office (Jl Bukit Barisan; 8am-6pm) Located in an old Dutch building on the main square; internet, fax and photocopy available.

TELEPHONE

International calls can be made at several *wartel* or international hotels around town; though the line is often poor.

TOURIST INFORMATION

There is a basic tourist information office immediately to the right as you exit at the international airport terminal.

North Sumatra Tourist Office (452 8436; Jl Ahmad Yani 107; 8am-4pm Mon-Fri) Provides excellent information, brochures and maps. Also has displays of traditional North Sumatran costumes.

TRAVEL AGENCIES

Jl Katamso is packed with travel agencies that handle air tickets and ferry tickets.

Perdana Express (456 6222; Jl Katamso 35G) Sells Pelni and Penang ferry tickets.

Tobali Tour & Travel (732 4472; Jl SM Raja 79C) For tourist buses to Danau Toba (80,000Rp, four hours).

Sights & Activities

The **Istana Maimoon** (Maimoon Palace; Jl Katamso 66; admission by donation; 9am-5pm) was built by the sultan of Deli in 1888. The family still occupies one wing, but it's falling down around them.

The black-domed **Mesjid Raya** (Grand Mosque; cnr Jl Mesjid Raya & Jl SM Raja; admission by donation; 9am-5pm except prayer times) is breathtaking, especially when pilgrims stream in for Friday prayers.

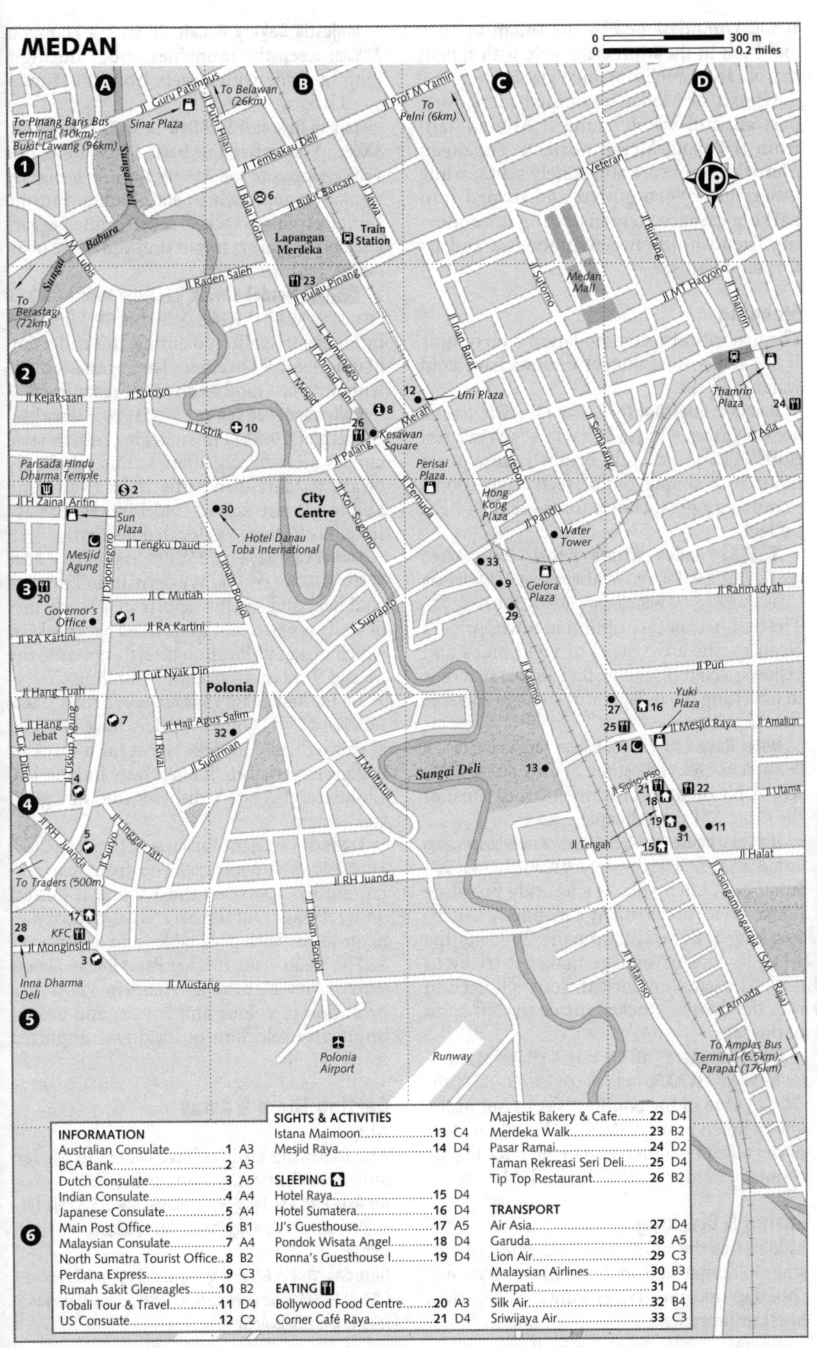
MEDAN
0 300 m
0 0.2 miles
To Pinang Baris Bus Terminal (10km); Bukit Lawang (96km)
To Belawan (26km)
To Pelni (6km)
To Berastagi (72km)
To Traders (500m)
To Amplas Bus Terminal (6.5km); Parapat (176km)
Jl Guru Patimpus
Sinar Plaza
Jl Putri Hijau
Jl Tembakau Deli
Jl Prof M Yamin
Jl Bukit Barisan
Jl Jawa
Jl Balai Kota
Sungai Deli
Sungai Babura
Jl M Lubis
Lapangan Merdeka
Train Station
Jl Veteran
Jl Bintang
Jl Raden Saleh
Jl Pulau Pinang
Jl Sutomo
Medan Mall
Jl MT Haryono
Jl Thamrin
Jl Irian Barat
Jl Kumanggo
Jl Ahmad Yani
Jl Mesjid
Jl Kejaksaan
Jl Sutoyo
Uni Plaza
Thamrin Plaza
Jl Merah
Kesawan Square
Jl Listrik
Jl Palang
Jl Semarang
Jl Asia
Jl Cirebon
Parisada Hindu Dharma Temple
Perisai Plaza
Hong Kong Plaza
Jl Pemuda
Jl H Zainal Arifin
Sun Plaza
City Centre
Jl Kol Sugiono
Jl Pandu
Water Tower
Hotel Danau Toba International
Jl Tengku Daud
Mesjid Agung
Jl Diponegoro
Gelora Plaza
Jl Rahmadyah
Jl C Mutiah
Jl Imam Bonjol
Governor's Office
Jl RA Kartini
Jl Suprapto
Jl Puri
Jl Katamso
Jl Cut Nyak Din
Polonia
Jl Hang Tuah
Yuki Plaza
Jl Haji Agus Salim
Jl Mesjid Raya
Jl Amaliun
Jl Hang Jebat
Jl Uskup Agung
Jl Rivai
Jl Sudirman
Jl Multatuli
Sungai Deli
Jl Cik Ditiro
Jl Sipiso-Piso
Jl Utama
Jl Tengah
Jl RH Juanda
Jl Suryo
Jl Linggar Jati
Jl Halat
Jl Sisingamangaraja (SM Raja)
KFC
Jl Monginsidi
Inna Dharma Deli
Jl Mustang
Jl Armada
Polonia Airport
Runway
INFORMATION
Australian Consulate 1 A3
BCA Bank 2 A3
Dutch Consulate 3 A5
Indian Consulate 4 A4
Japanese Consulate 5 A4
Main Post Office 6 B1
Malaysian Consulate 7 A4
North Sumatra Tourist Office 8 B2
Perdana Express 9 C3
Rumah Sakit Gleneagles 10 B2
Tobali Tour & Travel 11 D4
US Consuate 12 C2
SIGHTS & ACTIVITIES
Istana Maimoon 13 C4
Mesjid Raya 14 D4
SLEEPING
Hotel Raya 15 D4
Hotel Sumatera 16 D4
JJ's Guesthouse 17 A5
Pondok Wisata Angel 18 D4
Ronna's Guesthouse I 19 D4
EATING
Bollywood Food Centre 20 A3
Corner Café Raya 21 D4
Majestik Bakery & Cafe 22 D4
Merdeka Walk 23 B2
Pasar Ramai 24 D2
Taman Rekreasi Seri Deli 25 D4
Tip Top Restaurant 26 B2
TRANSPORT
Air Asia 27 D4
Garuda 28 A5
Lion Air 29 C3
Malaysian Airlines 30 B3
Merpati 31 D4
Silk Air 32 B4
Sriwijaya Air 33 C3

INDONESIA

It was commissioned by the sultan in 1906 and built in the Moroccan style with Italian marble and Chinese stained glass.

Ghosts of Medan's colonial mercantile past are still visible along Jl Ahmad Yani from Jl Palang Merah north to Lapangan Merdeka. Some are still stately relics, while others have been gutted and turned into parking garages, demonstrating the enduring friendship between Indonesia and its former coloniser.

Sleeping

The majority of accommodation is on or near Jl SM Raja. Most budget options have cold water only.

Ronna's Guesthouse I (☎ 732 4556; ronnasaloon@yahoo.com; Jl Tengah 33; r without/with bathroom 20,000/40,000Rp) Friendly bright yellow guest house with simple, but perfectly fine, rooms that make a great choice for those on a tight budget.

our pick **Pondok Wisata Angel** (Hotel Angel; ☎ 7320702; Jl SM Raja 70; s with fan without/with bathroom 50,000/70,000Rp, s/d with air-con 130,000/150,000Rp;) The best backpacker option in town, Angel's clean rooms are a swirl of vivid blues and yellows, a colour scheme that almost succeeds in offsetting the noisy traffic. It has a sociable streetfront cafe.

Hotel Raya (☎ 736 6601; hotel-raya@gmail.com; Jl RH Juanda Baru 200; r without/with air-con 65,000/85,000Rp;) A bit of an improvement from most of the other SM Raja cheapies.

JJ's Guesthouse (☎ 457 8411; www.guesthousemedan.com; Jl Suryo 18; s/d incl breakfast 100,000/180,000Rp;) In an old Dutch villa, JJ's has tidy boarding house–style rooms run by a mannerly Dutch-speaking Indonesian woman. Opposite the KFC, its lack of signage makes it tricky to find. The gates are locked, so you'll need to ring the doorbell tucked inside the left hand of the gate.

Hotel Sumatera (☎ 732 1551; Jl SM Raja 35; r without bathroom 135,000Rp, with air-con 230,000-285,000Rp;) One of the comfiest sleeps out of the glut of hotels around SM Raja. You'll find that once you add another zero to the price tag the rooms in Medan start to look a lot better.

Eating & Drinking

Medan has the most varied selection of cuisines in Sumatra, from basic Malay-style *mie* (noodle) and *nasi* (rice) joints, to top-class hotel restaurants.

Majestik Bakery & Cafe (Jl SM Raja 71; pastries 2000Rp) Keep the munchies at bay during a long bus ride with sweets from this super-sized bakery.

Taman Rekreasi Seri Deli (Jl SM Raja; dishes from 8000Rp; dinner only) For basic Malay food, this venue, opposite the Mesjid Raya, is a slightly upmarket approach to stall dining. But the *kerupuk* (prawn cracker) sellers, blind beggars and spoon players might find you more of an oddity than vice versa.

our pick **Merdeka Walk** (Lapangan Merdeka, Jl Balai Kota; dishes 10,000-15,000Rp; 5-11pm;) Inspired by Singapore's alfresco dining, this collection of outdoor cafes occupies Lapangan Merdeka with both fast food and proper restaurants.

Bollywood Food Centre (☎ 453 6494; Jl Muara Takus 7; dishes from 12,000Rp) Lip-smacking Indian-style curries are a family affair at this blindingly bright restaurant in Little India (Kampung Keling). It also serves cold Bintang. Malay-Indian roti shops are located nearby.

Corner Café Raya (cnr Jl SM Raja & Sipiso-Piso 1; dishes 15,000-40,000Rp; 24hr) Western-Indo fare plus cold beer and satellite sports in a heady mix of seedy sex-pats and fresh-faced backpackers, which makes its location directly opposite the Mesjid Raya mosque a little puzzling.

Tip Top Restaurant (Jl Ahmad Yani 92; dishes 15,000-50,000Rp;) Only the prices have changed at this old colonial relic, great for a drink of bygone imperialism. It offers tasty Indonesian, Chinese and Western dishes including a good steak menu.

Traders (Jl Kapten Pattimura 423; mains 60,000-230,000Rp; noon-midnight) The front bar-restaurant has sports on the TV and is busiest on weekends. Out the back is a swanky blue-neon-lit bar with pool tables and live music.

The main fruit market **Pasar Ramai** (Ramani Market; Jl Thamrin), next to Thamrin Plaza, is a profusion of colour and smells, and has an impressive selection of local and imported tropical fruit.

Getting There & Away

AIR

The following airlines have offices in Medan and serve the destinations as listed:

Air Asia (☎ 733 1988; www.airasia.com; Jl SM Raja 18) Inside Garuda Plaza Hotel, has flights to Jakarta and Kuala Lumpur.

Garuda (☎ 455 6777; Jl Monginsidi 340); Jl Balai Kota 2 (☎ 453 7844; Inna Dharma Deli, Jl Balai Kota 2) Flies to Jakarta and Banda Aceh.

INDONESIA

Lion Air (☎ 457 1122; Jl Katamso 41) Flies to Jakarta, Banda Aceh, Batam, Palembang and Penang.
Malaysian Airlines (☎ 451 9333; www.malaysiaairlines.com; Hotel Danau Toba International, Jl Imam Bonjol 17) Flies to Kuala Lumpur and Penang.
Merpati (☎ 736 6888; www.merpati.co.id/EN; SM Raja 92A) Flies to Pulau Simeulue, Sibolga and Gunung Sitoli.
SilkAir (☎ 453 7744; www.silkair.com; Hotel Polonia, Jl Sudirman 14) Flies to Singapore.
Sriwijaya Air (☎ 455 2111; www.sriwijayaair-online.com, in Bahasa Indonesia; Jl Katamso 29) Flies to Jakarta, Banda Aceh, Batam and Pekanbaru.

BOAT

See p320 for information on high-speed ferries to Pulau Penang in Malaysia.

Infrequent Pelni ships sail to Jakarta and Batam. The **Pelni office** (☎ 662 2526; Jl Krakatau 17A) is 8km north of the city centre, but it is much easier to buy tickets and check schedules from the agencies on Jl Katamso.

BUS

There are two main bus stations. Buses south to Parapat (22,000Rp, four hours), Bukittinggi (economy 115,000Rp, air-con 150,000Rp, 22 hours) and beyond leave from the **Amplas bus terminal** (Jl SM Raja), 6.5km south of downtown. Almost any *opelet* heading south on Jl SM Raja will get you to Amplas.

Buses to the north leave from **Pinang Baris bus terminal** (Jl Gatot Subroto), 10km west of the city centre. Get there by taxi (around 40,000Rp) or by *opelet* down Jl Gatot Subroto. There are public buses to both Bukit Lawang (15,000Rp, three hours) and Berastagi (15,000Rp, 2½ hours) every half-hour between 5.30am and 6pm.

Tobali Tour & Travel (☎ 732 4472; Jl SM Raja 79C) also runs a 'tourist' minibus to Parapat (80,000Rp, four hours).

Getting Around

Becak drivers fetch about 8000Rp for most destinations in town, and *opelets* (3000Rp) are omnipresent. The White line hits Kesawan Sq, Merdeka Walk and the train station; Yellows will take you to Little India and Sun Plaza. They cost 2500Rp per ride. Bargain hard with cab drivers, who, like shepherds, enjoy a good fleece.

BUKIT LAWANG

☎ 061 / pop 30,000

Lost in uthe depths of the Sumatran jungle is this sweet little tourist town built around an orang-utan viewing centre. But Bukit Lawang has much more to offer beyond our red-haired cousins (see p280). It's very easy to while away a few days lounging in the many riverside hammocks, listening to the mating calls over the gushing river and watching the jungle life swing and sing around you. It's also an ideal base for jungle treks into Taman Nasional Gunung Leuser, where you will see wild and semiwild orang-utans.

The town was extensively damaged by a deadly flash flood in 2003, which destroyed much of the riverfront development. The essentials of the town and tourist infrastructure have been rebuilt, but the community is still grieving for lost relatives and livelihoods.

Orientation & Information

The nearby village of Gotong Royong, 2km east of the river, is the new town centre, with *wartel* and shops, but no banks or post office. Near the radio tower, Valentine Tour and Travel changes money, cashes travellers cheques and organises bus, ferry and plane tickets. The nearest clinic and police station are 15km away in the town of Bohorok. The bus station is 1km east of the riverside tourist district. Minibuses may go a bit further to the small square at the end of the road, where a rickety hanging bridge crosses the river to the hotels.

The **Bukit Lawang Visitors Centre** (🕑 8am-3pm) has displays of flora and fauna found in Taman Nasional Gunung Leuser, plus a book of medicinal plants and their uses. Past visitors often record reviews of guides in the sign-in book.

Sights & Activities

BOHOROK ORANG-UTAN VIEWING CENTRE

Twice a day (8.30am and 3pm) visitors can watch rangers feed nearly a dozen semiwild orang-utan who are being rehabilitated from captivity or sudden habitat displacement due to logging. The bland fare of bananas and milk encourages the apes to forage on their own. So far, 200 have been successfully re-released into the jungle, mating with communities of wild apes.

The feeding platform is located on the west bank of Sungai Bohorok within the park boundaries, about a 20-minute walk up from the village. The river crossing to the park office is made by dug-out canoe. Permits are required to enter the park (20,000Rp) and are available from the **office** (🕑 8am-10am & 3-4pm) at the foot of the trail to the platform.

RED-HEADED COUSINS

Orang-utans, the world's largest arboreal mammal, once swung through the forest canopy throughout all of Southeast Asia, but are now found only in Sumatra and Borneo. Researchers fear that the few that do remain will not survive the continued loss of habitat to logging and agriculture.

While orang-utans are extremely intelligent animals, their way of life isn't compatible with a shrinking forest. Orang-utans are mostly vegetarians; they get big and strong (some males weigh up to 90kg) from a diet that would make a Californian hippie proud: fruit, shoots, leaves, nuts and tree bark, which they grind up with their powerful jaws and teeth. They occasionally also eat insects, eggs and small mammals.

The 'orang hutan' (a Malay word for 'person of the forest') has an extremely expressive face that has often suggested a very close kinship with the hairless ape (humans). But of all the great apes, the orang-utans are considered to be the most distantly related to humans.

To learn more about these animals, check out these websites: www.orangutans-sos.org and www.sumatranorangutan.com.

TREKKING

Trekking in Taman Nasional Gunung Leuser is an absolute must. Guides are mandatory in the national park and prices are fixed in euros. It's €15 for a three-hour trek; €25 for a day trek; and €50/60 without/with rafting for a two-day trek including overnight camping (gear included) in the jungle. That's the popular choice, because a night out increases your chances of spotting wild orang-utan. Most people count a Bukit Lawang trek among their favourite Sumatra memories. Remember, not all guides are sensitive to the environment. Check your guide's licence, talk to the park rangers and ask other travellers before signing up.

TUBING

A shed along the river en route to the orang-utan centre rents inflated truck inner tubes (10,000Rp per day), which can be used to ride the at-times-dangerous Sungai Bohorok rapids.

Sleeping & Eating

The further up river you go the more likely you are to ogle the swinging monkeys and apes from your porch hammock. You won't find hot water or air-con at any of the guest houses, but all serve food. The following are listed in geographic order from south to north.

Nora's Homestay (☎ 081 3620 70656; r 40,000-50,000Rp) Nora's little cluster of bamboo huts between the rice fields and the main road is an old backpacker favourite, with a reputation for being Sumatra's friendliest guest house.

Wisma Leuser Sibayak (☎ 0813 6101 0736; r 50,000-60,000Rp) A basic cheapie that's worth a stop if you've arrived at night and you don't fancy trekking up through the jungle path in the dark, though its rickety bridge across the river is rather frightening.

Green Hill (☎ 081 2636 43775; r incl breakfast 150,000Rp) For a few more rupiah you get a lot more than most of the competition. Run by an English conservation scientist, Andrea, and her Sumatran husband, Green Hill has two lovely stilt-high rooms ideal for couples, where the en-suite bamboo-shoot showers afford stunning jungle views while you wash.

Garden Inn (☎ 0812 6355 6285; fadill36@gmail.com; r 50,000-150,000Rp) A popular backpacker choice. The lovely high rooms look over the river and the jungle, plus there's a sweet little cafe to swap monkey-spotting tales in.

Tony's Restaurant (mains 25,000Rp, pizzas 40,000-63,000Rp) Relocated further up the river, Tony's fires up tasty pizzas in a riverfront shack.

Getting There & Away

There are direct buses to Medan's Pinang Baris bus terminal every half-hour between 5.30am and 5pm (10,000Rp, four hours). Minibuses (15,000Rp, three hours) also leave for Medan throughout the day.

BANDA ACEH

☎ 0651 / pop 210,000

Indonesian cities are rarely coupled with pleasant descriptions, but Banda Aceh breaks the mould. The sleepy provincial capital is a pleasant spot to spend a few days. The village-like atmosphere and dusty, unobtrusive streets make for an easy-to-explore and laid-back town filled with cheery faces. The proud folk rarely betray the tragedy experienced during the Boxing Day tsunami (which killed 61,000 here) and it's impossible to correlate the reconstructed city with the distraught images of 2004.

Banda Aceh is a fiercely religious city, and the ornate mosques are at the centre of daily life. In this devoutly Muslim city, religion and respect are everything. The hassles are few and the people are easygoing and extremely hospitable to visitors.

Orientation & Information

Airport taxis charge a set rate of 70,000Rp for the 16km ride into town. A taxi from the airport to Uleh-leh port will cost 100,000Rp.

There are plenty of ATMs around town.

Country Steakhouse (off Jl Sri Ratu Safiatuddin; noon-10pm) This restaurant has free wi-fi access for laptops.

Pante Pirak Net (Jl Dhimurthala 19; 9am-10pm) Next door to PP Café.

Post office (29487; Jl Bendahara 33; 8am-4pm Mon-Fri) A short walk from the centre; also has internet.

Sights

With its brilliant white walls and liquorice black domes, the **Mesjid Raya Baiturrahman** (Jl Mohammed Jam; admission by donation; 7-11am & 1.30-4pm) somehow survived the tsunami intact, which, despite the rampant loss of life, has been interpreted by fundamentalists as evidence of a merciful God.

The **Museum Negeri Banda Aceh** (23144; Jl Alauddin Mahmudsyah 12; admission 1000Rp; 8am-noon & 2-4pm Tue-Sun) is the site of the Rumah Aceh, a traditional stilt home built without nails.

The most famous of the tsunami sights are the **boat in the house** in Lampulo, and the 2500-tonne **power generator vessel** that was carried 4km inland by a wave. At the time of research there were plans to open a **Tsunami Museum** in 2010.

Sleeping

The influx of international aid workers jacked up the prices but not the standards of the few hotels left in town since the tsunami, and there is very little for budget travellers.

Hotel Palembang (22044; Jl Khairil Anwar 49; r with fan 70,000-100,000Rp, with air-con 120,000Rp;) A basic place with dark, uninspiring rooms.

Hotel Prapat (22159; Jl Ahmad Yani 19; d with fan/air-con 100,000/200,000Rp;) One of the more affordable spots, from the outside Prapat has the feel of a cheap rundown motel, though rooms are good value with Western toilets and clean sheets.

Eating

The square at the junction of Jl Ahmad Yani and Jl Khairil Anwar is usually the setting for the Pasar Malam Rek, Banda Aceh's lively night food market. Many night food stalls are found on JL SM Raja.

Rumah Makan Asia (Jl Cut Meutia 37/39; mains 10,000Rp) Aceh's version of *masakan Padang* (Padang dish) has an array of zesty seafood dishes that waiters plonk on to your table, such as *ikan panggang* (baked fish).

Tropicana Seafood (Jl SM Raja; mains from 20,000Rp;) Chinese restaurant serving delicious seafood dishes and cold Bintang. Vegetarians beware: even the 'mixed vegetables' contains chicken and prawns.

Getting There & Away

There are several flights a day from Banda Aceh to Medan and Jakarta on Garuda, Sriwiyaya and Lion Air. Air Asia flies daily to Kuala Lumpur, and Firefly to Penang in Malaysia. **BP Travel** (32325; Jl Panglima Polem 75) is a helpful air-ticket agent.

South of the city centre you'll find the new **Terminal Bus Bathoh** (Jl Mohammed Hasan), which has numerous buses to Medan. Economy buses (100,000Rp, 14 hours) depart at 4pm, while air-con buses leave all day (120,000Rp, 12 hours).

Getting Around

Labi labi are the main form of transport around town and cost 1500Rp. The **labi-labi terminal** (Jl Diponegoro) is that special breed of Indonesian mayhem. For Uleh-leh (5000Rp, 30 minutes), take the blue *labi labi* signed 'Uleh-leh'.

From the bus station, a becak into town will cost around 15,000Rp. A becak around town should cost between 5000Rp and 10,000Rp.

PULAU WEH

0652 / pop 25,000

A tiny tropical rock off the tip of Sumatra, Weh is a little slice of peaceful living that rewards travellers who've journeyed up through the turbulent greater mainland below. After hiking around the jungles, volcanoes and lakes of the mainland, it's time to jump into the languid waters of the Indian Ocean. Snorkellers and divers bubble through the great walls of swaying sea fans, deep canyons and rock pinnacles, while marvelling at the prehistorically gargantuan fish. This is one of the finest underwater hikes you'll find. Both figuratively and geographically, Pulah Weh is the cherry on top for many visitors' trip to Sumatra.

Orientation & Information

Most people pass through Sabang fairly quickly en route to the tourist beaches, but return to town for provisions.

You'll find internet at **2 Net Communication** (per hr 6000Rp). The **post office** (Jl Perdagangan 66) is next door to the **telephone office** (24hr).

BRI bank (Bank Rakyat Indonesia; Jl Perdagangan) changes travellers cheques and US dollars at terrible rates. It also has an unreliable ATM that's usually out of order; it's highly recommended you change money at Banda Aceh.

Sights & Activities

The castaway vibe saturates **Iboih Beach**, which attracts backpackers to pretty bungalows set on the sand and forested slopes above turquoise waters. Just offshore lies the tiny, densely forested **Pulau Rubiah**, surrounded by epic coral reefs known as the **Sea Garden**.

Around the headland from Iboih is the more social **Gapang Beach**. It's terrific for swimming, with frequent turtle sightings. Rates and visitors double on weekends. **Pantai Kasih** (Lover's Beach), about a 2km walk from town, is a palm-fringed crescent of white sand.

There are several dive operators on the island. At Iboih, **Rubiah Tirta Divers** (☎ 332 4555; www.rubiahdivers.com; 1/2/3 dives €25/45/60) is the oldest dive operation on the island. At Gapang, **Lumba Lumba Diving Centre** (☎ 332 4133; 081 168 2787; www.lumbalumba.com; 1/2/5 dives €25/45/100) is the centre of activity.

Sleeping & Eating

In Iboih, simple palm-thatch bungalows, many built on stilts and overhanging crystal-clear water, make up the majority of the accommodation. If you are staying for several days, you can negotiate 50,000Rp a night for a basic bathroom and fanless shack. **OONG's Bunglalows** (☎ 081 3607 00150; r without bathroom 50,000Rp) has the best value for money of the more comfortable huts with its two waterfront shacks. **Yulia's** (☎ 081 3772 79989; r without bathroom 70,000-80,000Rp) has the best of the basic bunch and excellent front-door snorkelling.

Occupying a sandy cove, Gapang is a lazy stretch of beach lined with shack restaurants and simple guest houses. **Ramadilla** (r 50,000-100,000Rp) has cabins that climb up the hill with big views. **Dang Dang Na** (r 100,000Rp) has basic wooden bungalows on concrete stilts with ocean views from the hillside.

Getting There & Away

Fast ferries to Pulau Weh (60,000Rp, one hour) leave from Uleh-leh, 15km northwest of Banda. Slow ferries (economy/air-con 11,500/36,500Rp, two hours) also leave daily. Check schedules at the port.

Getting Around

From the port, there are regular minibuses to Sabang (20,000Rp, 15 minutes), and Gapang and Iboih (50,000Rp, 40 minutes). You can catch a minibus from Jl Perdagangan in Sabang to Gapang and Iboih (30,000Rp).

PEKANBARU

☎ 0761 / pop 750,000

Pekanbaru was once little more than a sleepy river port on Sungai Siak. Today it is Indonesia's oil capital, with all the hustle and bustle of modern cities.

Orientation & Information

Airport taxis charge 60,000Rp for the 10km trip into town. Most banks, ATMs and hotels are on Jl Sudirman. The bus station is 7km west of town. There are plenty of travel agencies around town that can book plane and bus tickets as well as tours of the local area.

BII bank (Bank Internasional Indonesia; Jl Nangka 4) Changes US and Singapore dollars (cash and travellers cheques).

Micronet (Jl M Yamin 11; per hr 10,000Rp; 9am-10pm) Internet cafe and travel agency.

Sleeping & Eating

Poppie's Homestay (☎ 45762; Jl Cempedak III 11A; d 50,000Rp) Bunk at this budget fave located in a converted family home nestled in a residential neighbourhood. Friendly locals will point you in the right direction. It organises bus trips.

Shorea Hotel (☎ 48239; Jl Taskurun 100; d from 120,000Rp;) Clean, modern rooms in a quiet location off the main strip.

If this is your first night in Indo, take an evening food-stall crawl on Jl Sudirman, at the junction with Jl Imam Bonjol. Or bypass culinary immersion to munch burgers, cakes,

INDONESIA

pastries and ice cream in scrubbed-fresh environs at **Vanhollano Bakery** (Jl Sudirman 153; meals 15,000Rp).

Getting There & Away

Simpang Tiga airport is a visa-free entry point.

Air Asia (www.airasia.com) Flies direct to/from Kuala Lumpur, Singapore and Jakarta.
Garuda (☎ 45063; Hotel Pangeran, Jl Sudirman 371-373)
Lion Air (☎ 40670; Mutiara Merdeka Hotel, Jl Yos Sudarso 12A)
Mandala (☎ 856777; Jl Sudirman 115)
Merpati (☎ 21575; Jl Sudirman 371)

Frequent buses go to Bukittinggi (80,000Rp, five hours) from the uncharacteristically organised and modern Terminal Akap.

DUMAI

☎ 0765 / pop 154,400

Like most of Pekanbaru's oil, travellers come and go through the industrial port of Dumai. But only to use its visa-free port for ferry trips to Melaka, Malaysia. There are ATMs near the river end of Jl Sudirman.

If you get stuck here, stay at the tolerable **Hotel Tasia Ratu** (☎ 31341; Jl St Syarif Kasim 65; d 120,000Rp).

There are frequent buses from Dumai to Padang (economy/air-con 90,000/120,000Rp, 12 hours), Bukittinggi (80,000 10 hours) and Pekanbaru (50,000Rp, five hours). There are also minibus services timed with the arrivals of the boats from Batam.

PULAU BATAM

☎ 0778 / pop 440,000

Nowhere in Sumatra is the pace of development more rapid than on Batam. With the island's proximity to Singapore, Batam is the labour-intensive production leg of the Singapore–Johor Bahru industrial triangle. Features include multinational industrial plant sweatshops, low-end golf courses and sweaty, doughy business executives getting loose in girlie bars. Stay only if you miss your ferry.

Orientation & Information

Travellers usually arrive at the Sekupang port by boat from Singapore, and rush to the domestic terminal next door for Sumatran connections. Arrive with cash for immigration proceedings. Batam Centre is also a popular arrival port.

Nagoya, in the north, is the island's largest town, a cluster of hotels, necessities and diversions. Jl Imam Bonjol is the main drag, where you will find ATMs and internet cafes.

Sleeping & Eating

Many budget hotels on Pulau Batam double as brothels.

Hotel Grand Palace (☎ 432529; Komplek Nagoya Business Centre, Block 1; d from 100,000-170,000Rp; ❄) The best value around for those on a budget. The tiled-floor rooms come with air-con, hot water, cable TV and clean, sleepable beds.

Dozens of tempting outdoor food stalls gather on Pujasera Nagoya across the canal.

Getting There & Away

AIR

Hang Nadim airport (code BTH) is on the eastern side of the island. Garuda, Merpati, Mandala and Air Asia operate to/from Jakarta. Merpati destinations also include Medan, Padang, Palembang, Jambi and Pekanbaru, as well as Pontianak in Kalimantan. Jatayu also flies to Medan.

BOAT

Travellers come here from Singapore for connections to Pekanbaru on the Sumatran mainland. Boats leave from the domestic wharf next to the Sekupanng international terminal. For Pekanbaru (210,000Rp, six hours), two boats leave around 7.30am, so you'll need to catch the first ferry from Singapore to make it. Change money in Singapore to save time here.

GETTING TO SINGAPORE

From Sekupang port, 45-minute fast ferries (S$34) leave almost hourly between 7am and 9pm for Singapore's HarbourFront terminal, where visas are issued, on arrival, for many nationalities. The main operators are **Batam Fast** (www.batamfast.com) and **Penguin** (www.penguin.com.sg).

Boats from Pulau Bintan go to Singapore's Tanah Merah (one way S$28) between 7am and 6.30pm.

For details on crossing in the reverse direction, see p676.

There are also two morning boats from Sekupang to Dumai (220,000Rp, six hours).

Pelni ships pass through Batam to and from Belawan (the port for Medan) and Jakarta. The tickets can be bought at the domestic ferry terminal or at travel agencies in Nagoya.

There are also boats to Johor Bahru in Malaysia (see p320).

To get to Pulau Bintan, take a taxi (75,000Rp) to the Telaga Punggur ferry dock, 30km southeast of Nagoya. Frequent boats leave for Tanjung Pinang (45,000Rp, 45 minutes).

Getting Around

A local *ojek* ride is around 5000Rp. A taxi from Sekupang to Nagoya costs 50,000Rp.

PULAU BINTAN

Pulau Bintan is Pulau Batam's polar opposite, with the charming old harbour town of Tanjung Pinang (a visa-free entry/exit point), interesting Islamic ruins on nearby Pulau Penyengat, a population of ethnic Hakka people and Indo-Malays, and a string of beaches.

GETTING THERE & AWAY

While Pulau Batam is the main link to Sumatra proper, Tanjung Pinang is the jumping-off point to the remote islands of the Riau Islands. It also has links to Singapore and Malaysia. Most services leave from the main pier at the southern end of Jl Merdeka.

Regular speedboats leave from the main pier for Telaga Punggur on Pulau Batam (35,000Rp, 45 minutes) from 7.45am to 4.45pm daily.

There are daily ferry services to Pekanbaru (300,000Rp, two days) and Dumai (275,000Rp, two days).

Pelni (☎ 21513; Jl Ketapang 8, Tanjung Pinang) sails to Jakarta (195,000Rp, 28 hours) twice weekly from the southern port of Kijang. You can organise a trip and book with agents on Jl Merdeka.

GETTING AROUND

The bus terminal is 7km out of Tanjung Pinang. There are no regular public buses to Pantai Trikora, but you can probably flag one down on the highway and ask the driver to stop in Trikora (20,000Rp), or charter a taxi (100,000Rp). *Opelet* will shuttle you around Tanjung Pinang; most destinations cost 2000Rp, but negotiate before you climb aboard. Tanjung Pinang is also crawling with *ojek*.

Tanjung Pinang

☎ 0771 / pop 130,700

Tanjung Pinang has a busy harbour, great shopping, decent Indo-Chinese food and a smattering of traditional stilted villages on the outskirts.

INFORMATION

There are several ATMs on Jl Merdeka; bank branches are on Jl Teuku Umar.

Tanjung Pinang Tourism Office (☎ 21284; Jl Merdeka 5; 🕑 7.30am-5pm) Has English-speaking staff and maps.

SIGHTS & ACTIVITIES

The old stilted part of town around **Jl Plantar II** is worth a wander. Turn left at the col-

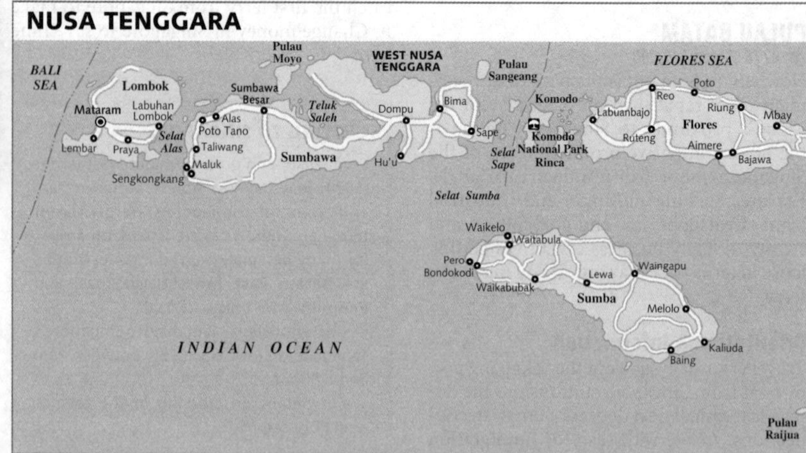

ourful **fruit market** at the northern end of Jl Merdeka.

Senggarang is a village just across the harbour from Tanjung Pinang, where the **Chinese temple** is held together by the roots of a huge banyan tree. Five hundred metres further on is the 100-year-old **Vihara Darma Sasana**. Boats (15,000Rp) leave from the end of Jl Pejantan II.

SLEEPING & EATING

Bong's Homestay (Lorong Bintan II 20; d 30,000Rp) Backpackers have been landing here since 1972. The family speaks great English and is a wealth of information.

Hotel Surya (☎ 21811; Jl Bintan 49; r 55,000-100,000Rp) Value varies here, from dank concrete boxes to sunny, freshly painted, naturally lit rooms.

Outdoor restaurants and coffee shops line the front of the volleyball stadium.

Pantai Trikora

The best beaches on Pulau Bintan, with good snorkelling and attractive offshore islands, are on the east coast at Pantai Trikora. Beach huts are just a cut above camping. At low tide the beach becomes a dull mud flat.

NUSA TENGGARA

An arc of islands extending from Bali towards northern Australia, Nusa Tenggara is lush and jungle green in the north, more arid savannah in the south, and in between has some of the worlds' best diving, almost limitless surf breaks and technicolour volcanic lakes. It's a land of pink-sand beaches, schooling sharks and rays, pods of whales, troops of monkeys, and the world's largest lizard: the swaggering, spellbinding komodo dragon.

The Gili Islands see the bulk of the tourism here, along with the rest of Lombok. But those with a hunger for adventure head further east to Flores, charter boats to the Komodo Islands and back, then keep going south and east where the *bule* crowds and creature comforts are thin on the ground and religious diversity is overlaid with exotic animism.

Note that this is adventure country: ferry, bus and flight departures are often less frequent than cancellations as you wander further east.

Getting There & Away

Most visitors use Bali as the international gateway to Nusa Tenggara. At research time, the only international flights to Nusa Tenggara were landing in Mataram, with twice-weekly connections to Singapore on SilkAir. Kupang is an international airport and rumours were swirling that the Darwin–Kupang hop once jointly operated by Air North and Merpati would resume.

Getting Around

The easiest and most popular way to explore Nusa Tenggara is to fly from Bali to Labuanbajo (Flores) or Kupang (West Timor) and island hop from there.

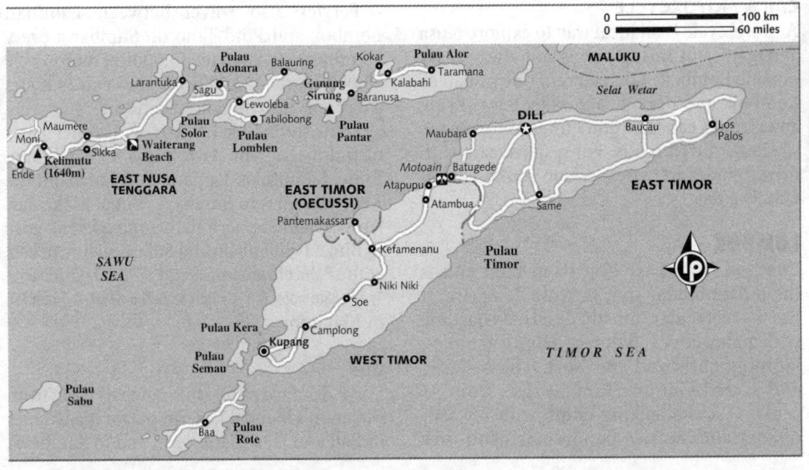

AIR

Merpati, IAT and Transnusa cover most destinations in Nusa Tenggara. Mataram gets a lot of service (p290). Kupang and Labuanbajo are hubs as well and the most reliable places to get a flight. Bima, Maumere and Ende also have flights. Overall, booking flights in Nusa Tenggara can be a nightmare. Purchase tickets from the point of departure, and reconfirm at least once or you may get bumped. Remember, schedule changes and cancellations are the norm.

BOAT

Regular vehicle/passenger ferries run Bali–Lombok, Lombok–Sumbawa, Flores–Sumbawa and Flores–Sumba. Perama makes the run from Lombok to Flores and back, taking in Komodo and Rinca. A popular way of travelling between Lombok and Flores or vice versa is on a boat tour, stopping at Komodo and other islands along the way. See boxed text, p304 for more information.

Pelni (www.pelni.com) has regular connections throughout Nusa Tenggara. See the route map (p175) for details.

BUS

Air-con coaches run across Lombok, Sumbawa, and from Kupang to Dili in Timor, but elsewhere small, slow minibuses are the only option. They constantly stop for passengers and drive around town for hours until full. A 100km ride can take up to four hours.

CAR & MOTORCYCLE

A motorcycle is an ideal way to explore Nusa Tenggara, but hiring one is not always easy outside Lombok. You can rent one in Bali or Lombok, and portage across by ferry. Bring an extra gas can, and don't underestimate the sinuous, rutted roads. For groups, cars with driver/guides are a great option and cost about US$50 a day.

LOMBOK

Lombok is an easy hop from Bali, and is the most popular spot in Nusa Tenggara. It has a spectacular, mostly deserted coastline with palm coves, Balinese Hindu temples, looming cliffs and epic surf. The majestic and sacred Gunung Rinjani rises from its centre – a challenging climb with rewards of seas and sunrise panoramas. And dive sites in the Gilis – Lombok's biggest draw, a carless collection of islands that are infused with a party vibe – are patrolled by sharks and rays. Sun-drenched and nocturnal adventures await.

GETTING THERE & AWAY

Air

Lombok's Selaparang airport (code AMI) has a fair amount of service. It is often shown as Mataram in schedules. Airlines include the following:

Garuda Indonesia (code GA; ☎ 0804-180 7807; www.garuda-indonesia.com; Hotel Lombok Raya, Mataram) Flies twice daily to Jakarta, and once daily flight to Denpasar.

IAT (☎ 639 589)

Lion Air (code JT; ☎ 629333; www.lionair.co.id; Hotel Sahid Legi, Mataram) Flies direct to Jakarta.

Merpati Airlines (code MZ; ☎ 621111; www.merpati.co.id; Jl Pejanggik 69, Mataram)

SilkAir (code MI; ☎ 628254; www.silkair.com; Hotel Lombok Raya, Mataram) Serves Singapore.

Transnusa/Trigana Airlines (code TGN; ☎ 616 2433; www.trigana-air.com)

Boat

Large car ferries travel from Bali's Padangbai port to Lombok's Lembar harbour every two hours (passenger 32,000Rp, 75,000Rp for motorcycles and 479,000Rp for cars, four hours).

Perama (☎ 0370-635928; Jl Pejanggik 66, Mataram) runs a variety of tours between Bali, Lombok and Komodo. See boxed text, p304 for more information. There is a lot of service to the Gilis; see p296 for details.

Ferries also travel between Labuhan Lombok and Poto Tano on Sumbawa every 45 minutes (passenger 15,500Rp, motorcycle 75,000Rp, car 322,000Rp). They run 24 hours a day and the trip takes 1½ hours.

Pelni ships link Lembar with other parts of Indonesia. The *Awu* heads to Waingapu, Ende, Larantuka, Kupang and Kalabahi; the *Kelimutu* goes to Surabaya, Bima, Makassar, Ambon and Papua; and the *Tilongkabila* goes to Bima, Labuanbajo and Sulawesi. Buy tickets at the **Pelni office** (Map p289; ☎ 0370-637212; Jl Industri 1; ⏲ 8am-noon & 1-3.30pm Mon-Thu & Sat, 8-11am Fri) in Mataram.

Bus

Long-distance public buses depart daily from Mataram's Mandalika terminal for major cities in Bali and Java in the west, and to Sumbawa

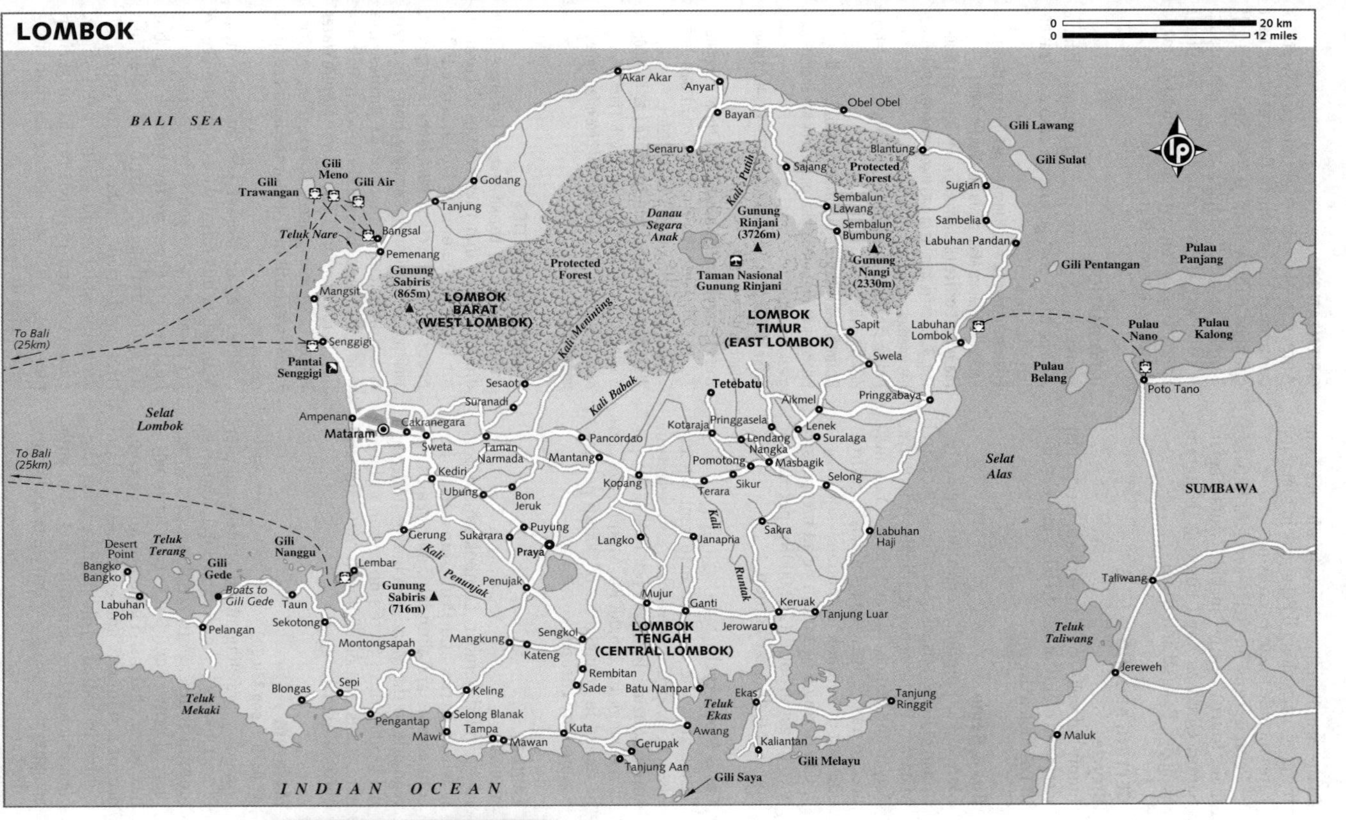
LOMBOK
0 20 km
0 12 miles
BALI SEA
Akar Akar
Anyar
Bayan
Obel Obel
Gili Lawang
Gili Sulat
Senaru
Sajang
Protected Forest
Blantung
Sugian
Sambelia
Labuhan Pandan
Gili Meno
Gili Trawangan
Gili Air
Godang
Tanjung
Bangsal
Teluk Nare
Pemenang
Danau Segara Anak
Kali Putih
Gunung Rinjani (3726m)
Sembalun Lawang
Sembalun Bumbung
Gunung Nangi (2330m)
Gili Pentangan
Pulau Panjang
Gunung Sabiris (865m)
Protected Forest
Taman Nasional Gunung Rinjani
Mangsit
LOMBOK BARAT (WEST LOMBOK)
LOMBOK TIMUR (EAST LOMBOK)
Sapit
Labuhan Lombok
Pulau Nano
Pulau Kalong
To Bali (25km)
Senggigi
Pantai Senggigi
Kali Meninting
Swela
Pulau Belang
Sesaot
Tetebatu
Poto Tano
Kali Babak
Suranadi
Aikmel
Pringgabaya
Selat Lombok
Ampenan
Cakranegara
Mataram
Sweta
Taman Narmada
Pancordao
Kotaraja
Pringgasela
Lendang Nangka
Lenek
Suralaga
To Bali (25km)
Mantang
Pomotong
Masbagik
Selat Alas
Kedin
Kopang
Terara
Sikur
Selong
SUMBAWA
Ubung
Bon Jeruk
Kali
Gerung
Sukarara
Puyung
Sakra
Labuhan Haji
Desert Point
Teluk Terang
Gili Nanggu
Kali Penunjak
Praya
Langko
Janapria
Bangko Bangko
Gili Gede
Lembar
Runtak
Taliwang
Boats to Gili Gede
Penujak
Labuhan Poh
Taun
Gunung Sabiris (716m)
Mujur
Ganti
Keruak
Tanjung Luar
Sekotong
Pelangan
LOMBOK TENGAH (CENTRAL LOMBOK)
Jerowaru
Teluk Taliwang
Montongsapah
Mangkung
Sengkol
Kateng
Rembitan
Jereweh
Blongas
Sepi
Keling
Sade
Batu Nampar
Ekas
Tanjung Ringgit
Teluk Mekaki
Selong Blanak
Teluk Ekas
Pengantap
Tampa
Kuta
Awang
Mawi
Mawan
Maluk
Gerupak
Kaliantan
Gili Melayu
Tanjung Aan
Gili Saya
INDIAN OCEAN

INDONESIA

in the east. Purchase tickets in advance from travel agencies along Jl Pejanggik in Mataram. Fares include the ferry crossings.

Perama runs bus/ferry services between main tourist centres in Bali (Kuta-Legian, Sanur, Ubud etc) and Lombok (Mataram, Senggigi, Bangsal and Kuta).

GETTING AROUND

Bicycle

Empty but well-maintained roads, spectacular vistas and plenty of flat stretches make cycling in Lombok a dream.

Bus & Bemo

Mandalika, Lombok's main bus/bemo terminal, is in Bertais, 6km southeast of central Mataram. Regional bus terminals are in Praya, Anyar and Pancor (near Selong). You may need to transfer between terminals to get from one part of Lombok to another.

Chartering a bemo can be an inexpensive way to get around (250,000Rp per day) if you're travelling in a group.

Car & Motorcycle

Senggigi is the best place to rent wheels. Elsewhere, prices skyrocket and selection suffers. Suzuki Jimmys cost 150,000Rp per day, Kijangs are 225,000Rp. Motorcycles can be rented in Senggigi for 65,000Rp per day. Scooters are cheaper.

Lembar

☎ 0370

Hassle-filled Lembar, Lombok's main port, is where ferries and Pelni ships dock. Bus connections are abundant, and bemos run regularly to the Mandalika bus/bemo terminal (3500Rp), so there's no reason to linger here. Taxis cost 60,000Rp to Mataram, and 100,000Rp to Senggigi.

Mataram

☎ 0370 / pop 330,000

Lombok's sprawling capital, actually a cluster of four towns – Ampenan (port), Mataram (administrative centre), Cakranegara (commercial centre) and Sweta (bus terminal) – has some charms. There are ample trees, decent restaurants and even a few cultural sights – including an old Balinese water temple and a bustling central market – but with Senggigi so close by few travellers spend any time here.

ORIENTATION

Ampenan-Mataram-Cakranegara-Sweta is connected by one busy thoroughfare that changes names from Jl Yos Sudarso to Jl Langko then Jl Pejanggik and Jl Selaparang. It's one way, from west to east. The parallel Jl Panca Usaha/Pancawarga/Pendidikan takes traffic back towards the coast.

INFORMATION

Banks on Jl Selaparang and Jl Penanggik have ATMs. Most change foreign cash and travellers cheques.

Elian Internet (www.elianmedia.net; 1 Panca Usaha Komplek Mataram Mall; per hr 5000Rp; 🕑 24hr)

Main post office (Jl Sriwijaya 37; 🕑 8am-5pm Mon-Thu, 8-11am Fri, 8am-1pm Sat) Inconveniently located, but has internet and poste-restante services.

Police station (☎ 631225; Jl Langko) In an emergency, dial ☎ 110.

Rumah Sakit Umum Mataram (☎ 622254; Jl Pejanggik 6) The best hospital on Lombok has English-speaking doctors.

Telkom (☎ 633333; Jl Pendidikan 23; 🕑 24hr) Offers phone and fax services.

West Lombok tourist office (☎ 621658; Jl Suprato 20; 🕑 7.30am-2pm Mon-Thu, 7.30-11am Fri, 8am-1pm Sat) Just a slim selection of maps and leaflets.

West Nusa Tenggara tourist office (☎ 634800; Jl Singosari 2; 🕑 8am-2pm Mon-Thu, 8-11am Fri, 8am-12.30pm Sat) The friendly staff here offer limited information.

SIGHTS & ACTIVITIES

Everyone loves those sweet Balinese, but did you know that they colonised Lombok for 100 years before the Dutch arrived? The proof is in the relics. **Pura Meru** (Jl Selaparang; admission by donation; 🕑 8am-5pm), built in 1720, is a Hindu temple that has 33 shrines, and wooden drums that are thumped to call believers to ceremony. The nearby **Mayura Water Palace** (Jl Selaparang; admission by donation; 🕑 7am-7.30pm) was built in 1744 for the Balinese royal court.

The **Bertais Market** (🕑 7am-5pm), near Mandalika bus terminal, is a great place to get localised after you've overdosed on the *bule* circuit. There are few tourists here, but it's got everything else: fruit and vegies, fish (fresh and dried), baskets full of colourful, aromatic spices and grains, palm sugar, enormous and pungent bricks of shrimp paste, and cheaper handicrafts than anywhere else in Lombok.

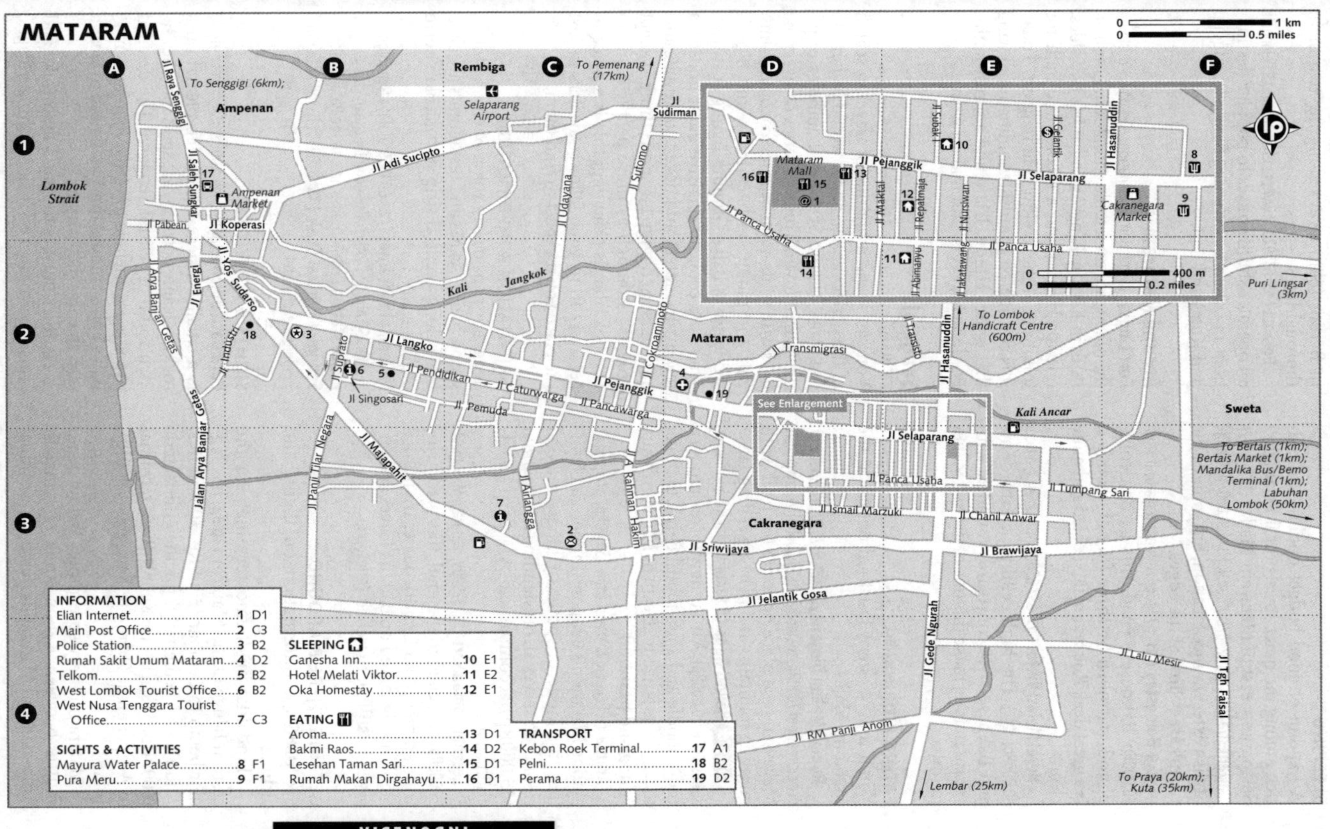
MATARAM
0 1 km
0 0.5 miles
INFORMATION
Elian Internet 1 D1
Main Post Office 2 C3
Police Station 3 B2
Rumah Sakit Umum Mataram 4 D2
Telkom 5 B2
West Lombok Tourist Office 6 B2
West Nusa Tenggara Tourist Office 7 C3
SIGHTS & ACTIVITIES
Mayura Water Palace 8 F1
Pura Meru 9 F1
SLEEPING
Ganesha Inn 10 E1
Hotel Melati Viktor 11 E2
Oka Homestay 12 E1
EATING
Aroma 13 D1
Bakmi Raos 14 D2
Lesehan Taman Sari 15 D1
Rumah Makan Dirgahayu 16 D1
TRANSPORT
Kebon Roek Terminal 17 A1
Pelni 18 B2
Perama 19 D2
Lombok Strait
Ampenan
Ampenan Market
Rembiga
Selaparang Airport
Mataram
Cakranegara
Sweta
Mataram Mall
Cakranegara Market
Kali Jangkok
Kali Ancar
See Enlargement
To Senggigi (6km);
To Pemenang (17km)
Puri Lingsar (3km)
To Lombok Handicraft Centre (600m)
To Bertais (1km); Bertais Market (1km); Mandalika Bus/Bemo Terminal (1km); Labuhan Lombok (50km)
Lembar (25km)
To Praya (20km); Kuta (35km)
Jl Raya Senggigi
Jl Saleh Sungkar
Jl Pabean
Jl Koperasi
Jl Yos Sudarso
Jl Energi
Jl Arya Banjar Getas
Jalan Arya Banjar Getas
Jl Industri
Jl Adi Sucipto
Jl Udayana
Jl Sudirman
Jl Sutomo
Jl Cokroaminoto
Jl Langko
Jl Pejanggik
Jl Pendidikan
Jl Caturwarga
Jl Pancawarga
Jl Pemuda
Jl Suprato
Jl Singosari
Jl Panji Tilar Negara
Jl Majapahit
Jl Airlangga
Jl A Rahman Hakim
Jl Sriwijaya
Jl Brawijaya
Jl Jelantik Gosa
Jl Transmigrasi
Jl Transisto
Jl Hasanuddin
Jl Selaparang
Jl Panca Usaha
Jl Ismail Marzuki
Jl Chanil Anwar
Jl Tumpang Sari
Jl Gede Ngurah
Jl Lalu Mesir
Jl Tgh Faisal
Jl RM Panji Anom
Jl Subak I
Jl Gelantik
Jl Maktal
Jl Repatmaja
Jl Nurswan
Jl Abimanyu
Jl Jakatawang
0 400 m
0 0.2 miles

INDONESIA

SLEEPING

A handful of good budget options are hidden among the quiet streets off Jl Pejanggik/Selaparang, east of Mataram Mall.

Ganesha Inn (☎ 624878; Jl Subak 1; s/d 30,000/40,000Rp) Stylish exterior, nice location, but some of the rooms are yellow at the edges.

Oka Homestay (☎ 622406; Jl Repatmaya 5; d from 40,000Rp) Balinese owned, this garden compound, patrolled by three friendly poodles, is a great deal. Rooms are fan cooled and quite clean.

Hotel Melati Viktor (☎ 633 830; Jl Abimanyu 1; d from 80,000Rp; ❄) The high ceilings, clean rooms and Balinese-style courtyard, complete with Hindu statues, make this one of the best values in town.

EATING & DRINKING

You'll find Western fast-food outlets in the Mataram Mall.

Rumah Makan Dirgahayu (☎ 637559; Jl Cilinaya 19; rice dishes from 7000Rp, seafood from 25,000Rp) A popular Makassar-style place opposite the mall, with gurgling fountains and twirling ceiling fans.

our pick Bakmi Raos (Jl Panca Usaha Karang Tapen; dishes 9000-20,000Rp) An authentic yet modern Indo noodle and soup joint behind the mall that attracts a steady stream of Mataram's hip, young and beautiful.

Aroma (Jl Pejanggik; meals from 15,000Rp) Popular among Mataram's Chinese-Indonesian families, this modern, spotless Chinese seafood restaurant serves an outstanding fried *gurami* (35,000Rp) accompanied by a fiery sweet-chilli sauce.

Lesehan Taman Sari (☎ 629909; Mataram Mall; meals 25,000Rp) Attached to the mall, this place wins with ambience and multicourse, traditional Sasak meals served on banana leaves and enjoyed in stilted, thatched *berugas*.

GETTING THERE & AROUND

See p286 for information on flights and airlines.

Mandalika bus/bemo terminal, on the eastern fringe of the Mataram area, has regular bemo to Lembar (3500Rp, 30 minutes, 22km), and Pemenang, for the Gili islands (6000Rp, 31km). The Kebon Roek terminal in Ampenan has bemo to Senggigi (4000Rp, 10km).

Mataram is *very* spread out. Yellow bemo shuttle between Kebon Roek terminal in Ampenan and Mandalika bus/bemo terminal in Bertais (6km away) along the two main thoroughfares.

Perama (☎ 635928; www.peramatour.com; Jl Pejanggik 66) operates shuttle buses to popular destinations in Lombok (including Bangsal, Senggigi and Kuta) and Bali.

Around Mataram

Puri Lingsar (admission by donation; 🕑 dawn-dusk) is the oldest, holiest temple complex in Lombok. Built in 1714 by King Agung, it has two sides, one for Hindus and a second one built for followers of the Wektu Telu religion. Today it is considered a multidenominational wing that unites Hindu, Islam and animist faiths. Feed the holy eels, and make a wish.

Senggigi

☎ 0370

You can spend a lifetime of travel in search of the perfect beach, and it would be hard to top those around Senggigi, Lombok's original tourist town. Think: a series of sweeping bays with white-sand beaches, coconut palms, cliff and mountain backdrops, and blood-red views of Bali's Gunung Agung at sunset. There are cool, inexpensive guest houses, a few luxury hotels, and dozens of restaurants and bars. Senggigi has everything, except crowds. Although as more people come to Lombok, that is changing; this is a place to get away from your fellow travellers in just the place you'd expect to find them.

ORIENTATION & INFORMATION

Senggigi spans nearly 10km of coast. Hotels, shops, banks, ATMs and restaurants are clustered along a central strip starting 6km north of Ampenan.

Millennium Internet (☎ 693860; Jl Raya Senggigi; per min 500Rp; 🕑 24hr) Also good for cheap calls.

Police station (☎ 110) Also next to the Pasar Seni.

Senggigi Medical Clinic (☎ 673210) Based at the Senggigi Beach Hotel.

SIGHTS & ACTIVITIES

Pura Batu Bolong (admission 5000Rp; 🕑 dawn-dusk) is a small Balinese-Hindu temple set on a rocky volcanic outcrop that spills into the sea, 2km south of central Senggigi. The detailed pagodas are oriented towards Gunung Agung, Bali's holiest mountain. You'll need to wear a sash to enter the temple.

Another must is to rent a motorbike and cruise the coast. You'll skirt fishing villages,

INDONESIA

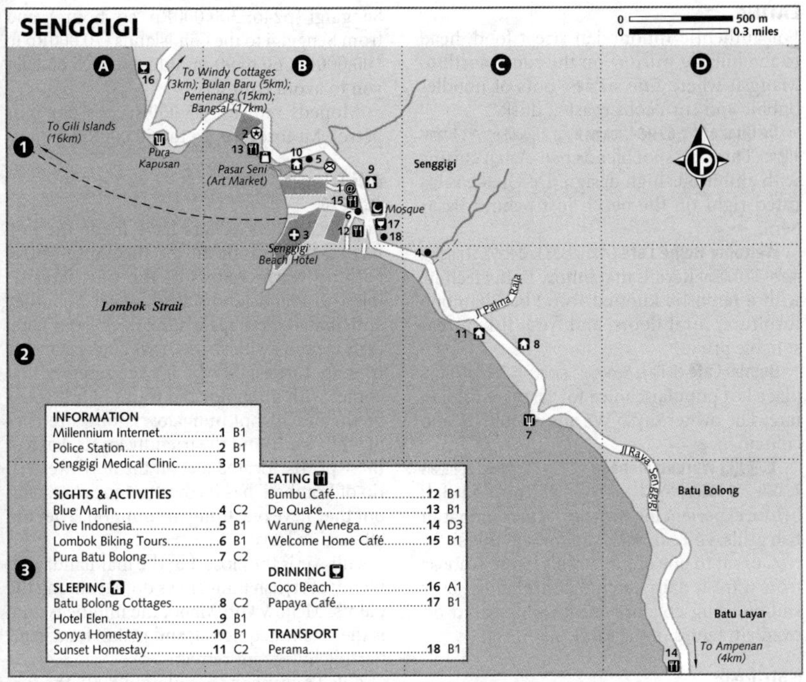

palm groves and discover wide, deserted beaches. **Lombok Biking Tours** (☎ 660 5792; Jl Raya Senggigi; day excursions per person from 200,000Rp) offer guided rides through the rural Sekotong region and the countryside around Lingsar and Suranadi.

There's decent **snorkelling** off the rocky point that bisects Senggigi's sheltered bay in front of Windy Cottages; many hotels and restaurants in central Senggigi hire out mask-snorkel-fin sets for 25,000Rp per day.

Diving trips from Senggigi normally visit the Gili Islands, so consider basing yourself there. Professional dive centres include **Blue Marlin** (☎ 081 2376 6496; www.bluemarlindive.com; Jl Raya Senggigi) and **Dream Divers** (☎ 692047; www.dreamdivers.com; Jl Raya Senggigi).

SLEEPING

Sonya Homestay (☎ 081 3398 99878; Jl Raya Senggigi; d from 50,000Rp) A shady family-run enclave of six rooms with nice patios and bright pink beds. Nathan, the owner, offers driving tours of Mataram and the surrounding area.

Hotel Elen (☎ 693077; Jl Raya Senggigi; d from 55,000Rp; ❄) Elen is the long-time backpackers' choice. Rooms are basic, but those facing the waterfall-fountain and koi pond come with spacious tiled patios that catch the ocean breeze.

Windy Cottages (☎ 693191; Mangsit; cottages with cold/hot water 110,000/150,000Rp, r 140,000Rp; ❄) These attractive thatched cottages with sea views have been popular for years. There's decent snorkelling offshore.

Batu Bolong Cottages (☎ 693065; Jl Raya Senggigi; s/d 150,000Rp/300,000Rp; ❄) Bamboo is the operative term at this charming bungalow-style hotel set on both sides of the road south of the centre. Beachfront rooms open onto a manicured lawn that fades into white sand.

Bulan Baru (☎ 693786; Mangsit; r 180,000Rp; ❄ 🏊) Set in a lovely garden and a short walk from a fine sandy beach, this welcoming hotel has spacious, well-furnished rooms, all with mini-bar, air-con and hot-water bathrooms. No children allowed.

our pick **Sunset Homestay** (☎ 692020; www.sunsethouse-lombok.com; r 275,000/400,000Rp; ❄) Its six tastefully simple bungalows on a quiet stretch of shore come with all the mod cons and homey touches.

EATING

For authentic Indonesian street food, head to the hillside *warung* on the route north to Mangsit where *sate* sizzles, pots of noodles bubble and corn cobs roast at dusk.

De Quake (☎ 693694; mains from 23,000Rp; ⏰ 10am-10pm) This new spot blends pan-Asian cuisine with ambitious high design. De Quake is located right on the beach just behind Pasar Seni.

Welcome Home Café (☎ 693833; Jl Raya Senggigi; mains 30,000Rp) Recalls that Jimmy Buffet feeling, with a fantastic knotted-wood bar, bamboo furniture, coral floors, and fresh fish at reasonable prices.

Bumbu Café (Jl Raya Senggigi; mains 35,000Rp) This place is a popular choice for tasty pan-Asian fare. The owner says, 'We always full!' It's no coincidence.

our pick **Warung Menega** (Jl Raya Senggigi 6; meals 75,000-250,000Rp; ⏰ 11am-11pm) If you fled Bali before experiencing the spectacular Jimbaran fish grills, you can make up for it at this sister restaurant to one of Jimbaran's finest. Choose from a fresh daily catch that are grilled over smouldering coconut husks and served on candlelit tables in the sand.

DRINKING

Senggigi nightlife is fairly low key. Weekends can pick up when an influx of Mataram 20-somethings hit the strip.

our pick **Coco Beach** (☎ 081 7578 0055; Pantai 2 Kerandangan, Jl Raya Senggigi; ⏰ noon-10pm) Rent comfortable beachside bamboo *berugas* for sunset drinks where the coconut groves meet the sand north of Senggigi. Sip from a bar that serves traditional Jamu tonics, fresh organic juices and tropical cocktails.

Papaya Café (☎ 693136; Jl Raya Senggigi) The decor is slick, with exposed stone walls, rattan furniture and evocative Asmat art from Papua. There's a nice selection of liquor, and it has a tight house band that rocks.

GETTING THERE & AROUND

Regular bemo travel between Senggigi and Ampenan's Kebon Roek terminal (3000Rp, 20 minutes, 10km). You can easily wave them down on the main drag. Headed to the Gilis? Organise a group and charter a bemo to Bangsal harbour (60,000Rp, one hour).

Perama (☎ 693 007; Jl Raya Senggigi) operates daily boat services from Padangbai, Bali, to Senggigi (p246; 300,000Rp, six hours), and from Senggigi to the Gili Islands (70,000Rp to 100,000Rp, 60 to 90 minutes), which enables you to avoid Bangsal.

Mopeds rent for 35,000Rp per day plus petrol. Motorcycles go for 60,000Rp.

Gili Islands

☎ 0370

For decades, travellers have made the hop from Bali for a dip in the turquoise-tinted, bathtub-warm waters of the tiny, irresistible Gili islands and stayed longer than they anticipated. Perhaps it's the deepwater coral reefs teeming with sharks, rays and reasonably friendly turtles? Maybe it's the serenity that comes with no motorised traffic? Or it could be the beachfront bungalows, long stretches of white sand, and the friendly locals. Each of these pearls, located just off the northwestern tip of Lombok, has its own unique character, but they have one thing in common. They are all hard to leave.

Gili Air is the closest to the mainland, with plenty of stylish bungalows dotted among the palms. Mellow Gili Meno, the middle island, is the smallest, quietest, and makes for a wonderful chilled-out retreat.

Gili Trawangan (population 800), the furthest out, has been tagged as the 'party island'. And with three weekly parties and a groovy collection of beach bars, you can get loose here. But Trawangan is growing up, with stylish accommodation – including a number of inland vacation villas, a fun expat community and outstanding dining.

INFORMATION

All the islands have plenty of *wartel* and internet cafes, but surfing (500Rp to 600Rp per minute) is woefully slow in most places. Trawangan offers the best connection.

At last, there's an ATM on Trawangan (Villa Ombak). Now, if only it would work all the time. For now, the old rule still applies. Bring ample rupiah with you – enough for a few extra days, at least. Though each island has shops and hotels that will change money and arrange cash advances from credit and debit cards, rates are low and commissions are high.

DANGERS & ANNOYANCES

Don't try to swim between the islands. The currents are strong, and people have died.

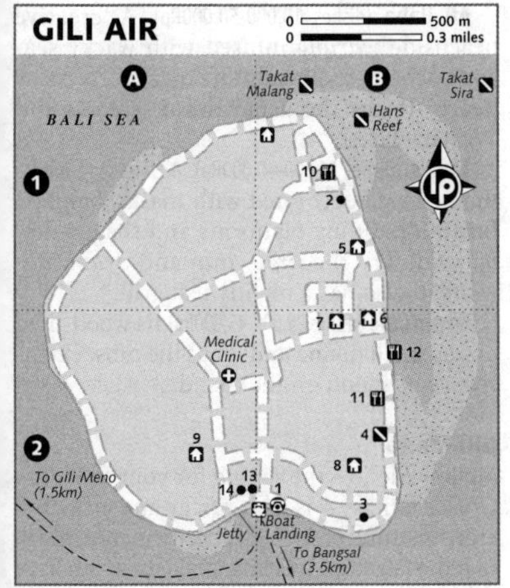

INFORMATION
Wartel 1 B2

SIGHTS & ACTIVITIES
Blue Marlin Dive Center 2 B1
Dream Divers 3 B2
Manta Dive 4 B2

SLEEPING
Abdi Fantastik 5 B1
Corner Bungalows 6 B2
Gili Air Santay 7 B2
Mawar Bungalows 8 B2
Resota Bungalows 9 A2

EATING
Ali Baba 10 B1
Tami's 11 B2
Wiwin Cafe 12 B2

TRANSPORT
Koperasi/Public Boat Office 13 A2
Perama 14 A2

When the wind gusts, watch out for jellyfish, which sting and leave a memorable rash.

There are no police on the Gilis. Report theft to the island *kepala desa* (village head) immediately. They will stop all boats out and search passengers before they can leave the island. If you need help locating them, or need someone to help you translate, the dive schools are a good point of contact. If you are on Gili Trawangan, notify Satgas, the community organisation that runs island affairs. Satgas uses its community contacts to resolve problems or track down stolen property with a minimum of fuss.

Incidents are very rare, but some foreign women have experienced sexual harassment and even assault while on the Gilis – it's best to walk home in pairs to the dark corners of the islands.

SIGHTS & ACTIVITIES

By day, you'll want to stay on land only long enough to get in the water.

Diving is the best reason to get wet. Marine life is plentiful and varied. Turtles, black- and white-tip reef sharks are common, and the macro life (small stuff) is excellent with seahorses, pipefish and lots of crustaceans. Around full moon, large schools of bumphead parrot fish appear to feast on coral spawns, while at other times of the year, manta rays soar.

Though an El Nino–inspired bleaching damaged soft corals above 18m, the reefs are now in recovery. The Gilis also have their share of virgin coral. **Hidden Reef**, a recently discovered site pops with colourful life above 20m, and there's also an abundance of deep coral shelves and walls at around 30m, where the coral is, and always has been, pristine.

Safety standards are high in the Gilis despite the modest dive costs – there are no dodgy dive schools, and instructors and training are professional. Rates are fixed (no matter who you dive with) at US$35 a dive, with discounts for packages of five dives or more. A PADI open-water course costs US$350, the advanced course is US$275. Divemaster starts at US$650.

Dive places are many.

Blue Marlin Dive Center (Map p297, Map p293, Map p295; ☎ 632 424, 081 3399 30190; www.bluemarlindive.com) On Gili Air, Meno and Gili T.

Diving Buddha (Map p297; ☎ 644179) Gili T.

Dream Divers (Map p297, Map p293; ☎ 634547; www.dreamdivers.com) Gili Air and Gili T.

Manta Dive (Map p297, Map p293; ☎ 643649; www.manta-dive.com) Gili Air and Gili T.

Trawangan Dive (Map p297; ☎ 649220, 081 3377 02332; www.trawangadive.com) Gili T.

Snorkelling is fun and the fish are plentiful on all the beach reefs. Gear can be hired for 20,000Rp to 25,000Rp per day.

Trawangan has a fast right break that can be surfed year-round and can swell overhead. It's just south of Villa Ombok. **Gili Surf Shop** (☎ 081 2372 7615) in the Pasar Seni, rents boards.

Karma Kayak (Map p297; ☎ 081 8055 93710; tours 300,000Rp), a hotel, tapas bar and kayaking school, is set on the northern end of Gili T, where Astrid, a former champion stunt kayaker (she took silver at the 1991 world championships) leads half-day kayaking trips around the Gilis when currents allow.

Walking and cycling are the best land sports. Bikes can be hired for 30,000Rp per day. On Trawangan, time your circumnavigation (2½ hours on foot) with the sunset, and watch it from the hill on the southwest corner where you'll have a tremendous view of Gunung Angung on Bali.

SLEEPING & EATING

The vibe on easygoing rural Gili Air falls somewhere between sedate Meno and social Trawangan. Air and Meno only get crowded during the high season (July, August and around Christmas), when hotels double or triple their prices. Tap water on all the islands is brackish.

Gili Air

Hotels and restaurants are scattered along the southern and eastern coasts, which have the best swimming beaches. The hotels have dining rooms, but there are a few dedicated restaurants. Walking around the island takes about 90 minutes.

Gili Air Santay (☎ 081 8037 58695, 081 9159 93782; www.giliair-santay.com; d 80,000-180,000Rp) Set back from the beach in a quiet coconut grove, these spacious bamboo-and-timber huts are a good budget choice. The shore-side restaurant serves authentic Thai Food.

Abdi Fantastik (☎ 636421; r 150,000Rp) Family-owned bungalows strung with hammocks, steps from the sea.

Mawar Bungalows (☎ 081 3622 53995; bungalow 130,000-220,000Rp) Basic, thatched bungalows set 30m from the sea in the coconut grove. The new ones have Western toilets. All have hammocks and come with breakfast in a stylish dining area. Mawar serves family dinners for guests and staff every night (50,000Rp).

Resota Bungalows (☎ 081 8057 15769, bungalow 250,000Rp) Nestled in the coconut palms near the harbour,is this charming bungalow property. Rooms feel new, and come with a stocked minibar and inviting hammocks.

Corner Bungalows (☎ 081 9172 29543; bungalow 350,000Rp) Owned by a welcoming local family, these new bamboo bungalows each have hammocks slung over a varnished deck.

Ali Baba (dishes 10,000-50,000Rp) A creative beachside *warung* infused with wacky sea- and coconut-shell sculpture on a lovely rocky beach. It has the usual Indo, seafood and Western fare.

Tami's (dishes 10,000-40,000Rp) A funky Sasak-themed cafe decorated with masks, bamboo furniture, dining platforms and shaggy new *berugas*. Try the *urap-urap* and *ayam taliwang*. It also has a nightly fish grill.

Wiwin Cafe (dishes 25,000-45,000Rp) Its wood-fired pizzas smell divine and it has the most extensive vegie menu on the island.

Gili Meno

Mellow Meno – the setting for your *Robinson Crusoe* fantasy – is a bit pricey and attracts a more 'mature' crowd. Electricity is ephemeral, so if the fan stops twirling, make sure you have a mosquito net. All guest houses serve food.

Tao Kombo (☎ 081 2372 2174; tao_kombo@yahoo.com; bungalow 100,000-300,000Rp) About 200m inland, you'll find Meno's unique bungalow property. There are open huts with bamboo screens instead of walls, and nicer, enclosed cottages.

Rawa Indah (☎ 081 9179 38813; bungalow 150,000Rp) Basic, bamboo, thatched, palm-shaded and dangling with seashell wind chimes.

Mimpi Manis (☎ 642324; s/d 200,000Rp) Basic bamboo bungalows set back from the beach.

Amber House (☎ 081 3375 69728; bungalow 250,000Rp) Attractive, circular bungalows with outdoor showers on the island's sleepy north end.

our pick Rust Warung (☎ 642324; mains 8000-75,000Rp; 🕒 7am-10am, 11am-3.30pm, 6pm-late) This restaurant has beachfront *berugas* and a terrific assortment of fresh daily catch. Fish is perfectly grilled.

Gili Trawangan

Social but not trashy, relaxed but not boring, all natural, yet updated with technology (internet and top-range sound-systems), and sprinkled with great restaurants and bars that would satisfy any devout cosmopolitan, Gili T is the road-weary backpacker's fantasy incarnate. There's over 100 places to stay and the bungalows tend to be a bit upmarket.

Sirwa Homestay (s/d 40,000/45,000Rp) Spacious rooms – some have two double beds – with prices to suit those on a strict budget.

Lisa Homestay (☎ 081 3395 23364; r 175,000Rp) Very friendly little place with airy and light tiled rooms that overlook a garden.

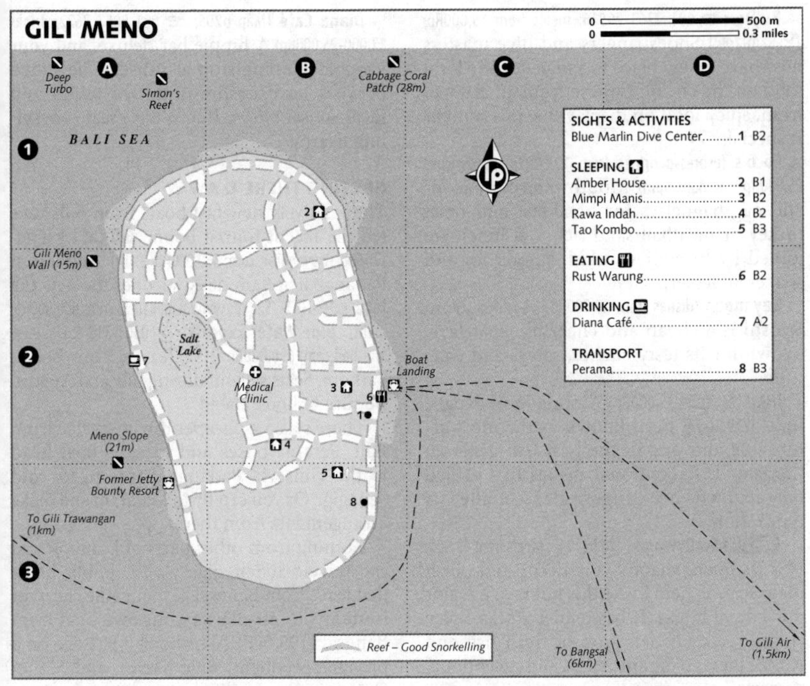

Sandy Beach Cottage (☎ 625020; d from 100,000Rp) A shady hideaway, close to the action.

Edy Homestay (d from 120,000Rp) One of the best of the village cheapies. Rooms are very clean and come with ceiling fans and a big breakfast.

Warna Homestay (☎ 623859; d from 150,000Rp) Arguably the best value on the island, Warna has five sweet tropical flower garden bungalows mere steps from the sea.

Puri Hondje (r 150,000Rp; ❄) Tucked away down a quiet village lane, these very stylish rooms overlook a small koi pond surrounded by bougainvillea and palms.

Balenta (☎ 081 8052 03464; d from 180,000Rp) Next to the upmarket Good Heart is one of Gili T's better values. It's opposite a great stretch of beach, and the rooms are large and immaculate.

Pondok Sederhana (☎ 081 3386 09964; r 200,000Rp) At the foot of the hill, and run by a house-proud, friendly Balinese lady, the spotless rooms here face a neat little garden. Low-season discounts to 80,000Rp are available.

Quiet Water (☎ 081 9175 31652; d from 250,000Rp) A plush yet affordable village choice with queen-sized beds, soft linen, air-con, hot water and in-room DVD players.

Black Sand Homestay (☎ 081 2372 0353; r from 300,000Rp) One- and two-storey wooden bungalows are nestled in a sweet garden with views of the hill. Two-storey jobs come with TV and an outdoor bath. Management is hospitable, and prices drop in the low season.

Tir na Nog (☎ 639463; tirnanog@mataram.wasantara.net.id; r from 300,000Rp; ❄) At the rear of the bar, these huge rooms with air-con have been thoughtfully designed and decorated; most have spacious private terraces and swanky modern bathrooms.

Rumah Saga (☎ 648604, 081 8057 14315; www.rumahsaga.com; cottages 350,000-500,000Rp; ❄) Clean, modern cottages with TV, air-con and hot water are set around a lovely garden area with a nice pool. The large bungalows sleep up to three people.

Anna's (dishes from 8000Rp; 🕒 24hr) Opposite the harbour is another tasty, local *warung* serving *nasi campur* for 10,000Rp. It's the cheapest meal in town, and it's damn good.

Blue Marlin (mains 9000-35,000Rp) Perhaps the best fish grill on the island. Choose your catch and enjoy it with a limitless buffet of salads and sides. It's always cooked to perfection.

Bu'De (☎ 081 2363 79516; meals from 15,000Rp; ⏰ 9am-7pm) Shoestringers and dive masters now have a new place to inhale terrific local food on the cheap. Choose from an array of fresh, spicy food on display. Its *nasi campur* is special.

Coco's (espresso drinks from 15,000Rp, sandwiches 25,000Rp; ⏰ 8am-6pm) Mouthwatering bacon-and-egg baguettes for breakfast and roast turkey or meatball sandwiches at lunch are joined by brownies, cakes, smoothies and shakes at dessert.

Kayangan (dishes from 20,000Rp) Across from Ryoshi is a cheap and cheerful expat fave, known for its tasty curries, satays and *gado gado*.

Juku (fish from 35,000Rp) Among local expats, Juku has long been known as the most affordable and one of the best fish grills on the island. Exceptional dishes like grilled barracuda with ginger glaze made its reputation.

our pick **Scallywag's** (☎ 631945; meals from 45,000; 📶) Its open, shabby-chic decor and plush patio seating help make this hot spot a major draw at all hours. It has tender steaks, spicy chorizo, a daily selection of fresh fish and Aussie pies, an organic ethos and exceptional desserts.

DRINKING

The official party nights in Gili Trawangan are on Monday, Wednesday and Friday – although given the amount of contraband on offer and the scattering of stylish bars to investigate each and every night can be a party here.

Blue Marlin (Map p297; ⏰ 8am-midnight Tue-Sun, 8am-3am Mon) Of all the party bars, this upper-level venue has the largest dance floor and the meanest sound system – which pumps out trance and tribal sounds on Monday.

Rudy's Pub (Map p297; ⏰ 8am-4am Fri, 8am-11pm Sat-Tue) Rudy's has as much to do with Gili T's party-hard reputation as all the other bars combined. Mostly due to its weekly debaucherous Friday night throw downs and a preponderance of drinks and dishes involving a certain fungus.

Sama Sama (Map p297; ⏰ 8am-late) Locally owned and easily the best reggae bar in Indonesia (and probably Southeast Asia). It has a top-end sound system, a killer live band at least six nights a week and great barmen who mix tasty mojitos.

Diana Café (Map p295; ☎ 081 8057 7622; drinks 12,000-25,000Rp) A hippie bar deluxe, and your ice-cold-Bintang stop at sunset. The stilted *berugas* have cushions, coffee tables and ideal sunset views. It also has great snorkelling nearby.

GETTING THERE & AWAY

The relatively new fast boats from Bali have fed the recent tourist boom. **Gili Cat** (⏰ 0361-271680; www.gilicat.com; 660,000Rp; 2½hr) leaves from Padangbai at 9am daily, as does the new **Eka Jaya** (⏰ 0361-752277; www.baliekajaya.com; 660,000Rp; 2½hr). **Blue Water Express** (⏰ 0361-310 4558; www.bwsbali.com; 690,000Rp; 2½hr) leaves from Benoa harbour. Seats sell out during July and August. Be sure to book ahead.

There's also a cheaper direct service from Bali. Perama buses and its slow boat head to the Gilis via Padangbai (see p246) and Senggigi. Or you can fly to Mataram and make arrangements from there.

Coming from other parts of Lombok you can travel via Senggigi; via the public boats that leave from Bangsal harbour (the cheapest route), you can charter your own boat from Bangsal (195,000Rp) or book a passage on a private speedboat. Blue Marlin and Manta Dive (p293) on Gili Trawangan can arrange transfers (600,000Rp for up to three people).

Coming by public transport, catch a bus or bemo to Pemenang, from where it's 1km by *cidomo* (3000Rp) to Bangsal harbour. Bangsal is beyond annoying (see boxed text, p298). These touts raise blood pressure for a living and you should sooner ignore than trust them. Boat tickets are sold at the Koperasi harbour office on the beach. Public boats run from roughly 8am to 5pm, but don't leave until full (about 18 people). The one-way fares at the time of research were 8000Rp to Gili Air, 9000Rp to Gili Meno and 10,000Rp to Gili Trawangan.

Boats pull up on the beach when they get to the Gilis. You'll have to wade ashore with your luggage.

GETTING AROUND

The Gilis are flat and easy enough to get around by foot or bicycle. A torch (flashlight) is useful at night. You can buy one at local shops for around 25,000Rp. Hiring a *cidomo* for a clip-clop around an island is a great way to explore; a short trip costs between 20,000Rp and 35,000Rp.

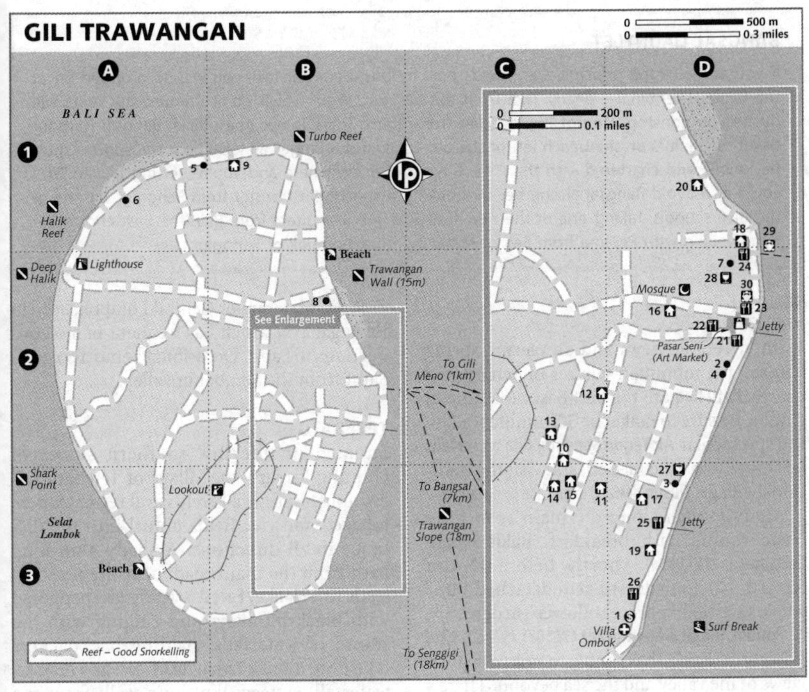

INFORMATION
Villa Ombak (ATM)....................1 D3

SIGHTS & ACTIVITIES
Blue Marlin Dive Center..............2 D2
Diving Buddha........................3 D3
Dream Divers.........................4 D2
Karma Kayak..........................5 A1
Karma Kayak..........................6 A1
Manta Dive...........................7 D2
Trawangan Dive.......................8 B2

SLEEPING
Balenta..............................9 B1
Black Sand Homestay..................10 C2
Edy Homestay.........................11 C3
Lisa Homestay........................12 C2
Pondok Sederhana.....................13 C2
Puri Hondje..........................14 C3
Quiet Water..........................15 C3
Rumah Saga...........................16 D2
Sandy Beach Cottage..................17 D3
Sirwa Homestay.......................18 D1
Tir na Nog...........................19 D3
Warna Homestay.......................20 D1

EATING
Anna's...............................21 D2
Blue Marlin..........................(see 2)
Bu'De................................22 D2
Coco's...............................23 D2
Juku.................................24 D2
Kayangan.............................25 D3
Scallywag's..........................26 D3

DRINKING
Blue Marlin..........................(see 2)
Rudy's Pub...........................27 D3
Sama Sama............................28 D2

TRANSPORT
Boat Landing & Koperasi..............29 D1
Perama...............................30 D2

There's a twice-daily island-hopping boat service that loops between all three islands (20,000Rp to 23,000Rp). Check the latest timetable at the islands' dock. You can also charter your own island-hopping boat (170,000Rp to 195,000Rp).

Gunung Rinjani

Lombok's highest peak, and the second-highest volcano in Indonesia (3726m), is home to a smattering of small villages on her slopes, and is of great climatic importance to Lombok. The Balinese call Gunung Rinjani 'the seat of the Gods' and place it alongside Gunung Agung in spiritual lore. Lombok's Sasaks also revere the volcano, and make biannual pilgrimages here to honour the mountain spirit. It sure is one hell of a climb. Reach the summit and look down upon a 6km-wide caldera with a crescent-shaped cobalt lake, hot springs and smaller volcanic cones. The stunning sunrise view from the rim also takes in north Lombok, Bali's Gunung Agung and the never-ending ocean, drenched in an unforgettable pink hue.

BANGSAL GAUNTLET

If you arrive to the principal Gili Islands port by bus, bemo or taxi, you will be dropped off at the Bangsal terminal – nearly 1km from the harbour. From which point irrepressible touts will hustle you nonstop. Do not buy a ticket from them. There is but one official Bangsal Harbour ticket office: it is on the beach left of the dirt road, and arranges all local boat transport – shuttle, public and chartered – to the Gilis. Buy a ticket elsewhere and you're getting played. You could also avoid Bangsal altogether by booking a speedboat transfer from Senggigi via one of the dive schools, taking one of the new fast-boat services direct from Bali (the best choice), or by travelling with Perama from Bali or Mataram, Kuta, Lombok or Senggigi.

SENARU

pop 1330

With sweeping views and an eternal spring climate, the mountain villages of Senaru and nearby **Batu Koq** are the best bases for Rinjani climbs. Be sure to make the 30-minute walk to the spectacular **Air Terjun Sendang Gila waterfalls** (admission 2500Rp; dawn-dusk), and visit the traditional village, **Dusun Senaru** (admission by donation).

Many *losmen* along the main road have basic rooms with breakfast. **Bukit Senaru Cottages** (r 75,000Rp), shortly before Dusun Senaru, has four decent semidetached bungalows nestled in a sweet flower garden.

Pondok Indah & Restaurant (☎ 081 7578 8018; s/d 75,000/100,000Rp;) has simple rooms with great views of the valley and the sea beyond. There's ample parking, a good restaurant (dishes 7000Rp to 18,000Rp) and free internet.

From Mandalika terminal in Mataram catch a bus to Anyar (20,000Rp, 2½ hours). Bemo leave Anyar for Senaru (7000Rp) every 20 minutes until 4.30pm.

SEMBALUN LAWANG & SEMBALUN BUMBUNG

High on the eastern side of the mountain is the remote and beautiful Sembalun valley, another Rinjani launch pad.

Lembah Rinjani (☎ 081 8036 52511; r 150,000Rp) has queen-sized beds, spotless bathrooms, and breathtaking mountain and sunrise views.

From Mandalika bus terminal take a bus to Aikmel (12,000Rp) and change there for Sembalun Lawang (12,000Rp). Hourly trucks connect Lawang and Bumbung.

SAPIT

Tiny Sapit, on Rinjani's southeastern slopes, boasts a huge panorama towards Sumbawa.

Hati Suci Homestay (☎ 081 854 5655; www.hatisuci.tk; s 40,000-45,000Rp, d 75,000-85,000Rp) has excellent bungalows in a fragrant garden.

From Mataram or Central Lombok, head to Pringgabaya, which has frequent bemo connections to Sapit. Occasional bemo also go to Sapit from the Sembalun valley.

TETEBATU

Situated on the low southern slopes of Gunung Rinjani, the village of Tetebatu (elevation 400m) is a lovely rural retreat where tobacco and rice fields unfurl into the distance in all directions. A shady 4km-long path from the main road, near the mosque, leads to a **Monkey Forest** (admission free) peppered with black monkeys and ringing with the sound of waterfalls. Balding backpackers take note: the **Air Terjun Jukut** (admission 20,000Rp) waterfall, a steep 2km-long walk from the car park at the end of the road, is said to spur hair growth. Guides are recommended for both trips. **Cendrawasih Cottages** (☎ 081 8037 26709; r 90,000Rp) is a sweet little *lumbung*-style cottages nestled in the rice fields. You'll sit on floor cushions in its stunning stilted restaurant, which has Sasak, Indonesian or Western grub (7000Rp to 22,000Rp) and 360-degree paddy views.

Kuta

☎ 0370

They may share a name, but Lombok's Kuta is no tourist ghetto like the Bali version. It's languid and stunningly gorgeous, with white-sand bays that lick chiselled cliffs and rugged hills, and world-class surf. There are some charming hotels in Kuta, but otherwise the coastline is empty, the stomping ground of seaweed collectors, fishermen and water buffalo. How long it stays this way is debatable as development may loom (see boxed text, p300). Meanwhile, the only real action Kuta sees is during the August high season and the *nyale* (seaworm) fishing festival in February or March.

INFORMATION

There's a *wartel* in town, and **Ketapang Cafe** (8am-11pm) has slow but functional internet access. The **market** fires up on Sunday and Wednesday. Virtually everything in Kuta is on a single road that parallels the beach and intersects the road from Praya.

ACTIVITIES

For surfing, stellar 'lefts' and 'rights' break on the reefs off Kuta and east of Tanjung Aan. Boatmen will take you out for around 70,000Rp. Seven kilometres east of Kuta is the fishing village of **Gerupak**, where there's a series of reef breaks, both close to the shore and further out, but they require a boat, at a negotiable 200,000Rp per day. Mawi also offers regular swells.

Drop in to the professional **Kimen Surf** (☎ 655064; www.kuta-lombok.net) just west of the junction for swell forecasts, tips and information. Boards can be rented here (50,000Rp per day), repairs undertaken, lessons booked and more.

SLEEPING & EATING

All accommodation is on or within walking distance of the beach. Breakfast is included.

our pick **Seger Reef Homestay** (☎ 655528; r 80,000-100,000Rp) Ignore the ramshackle courtyard because these bright, spotless, family-owned bungalows across the street from the beach are the sweetest deal in town.

Rinjani Bungalows (☎ 654849; s/d with fan 80,000/95,000Rp, s/d with air-con 200,000/250,000Rp;) This well-run place, 1km east of the junction,

TREKKING GUNUNG RINJANI

Agencies in Mataram and Senggigi arrange all-inclusive treks, but you can make your own, cheaper, arrangements in Senaru, Sembulan Lawang or even Sapit. Seek out the **Rinjani Trek Centre** (RTC; ☎ 086 8121 04132; www.info2lombok.com) in Senaru. Partially funded by the New Zealand government, the centre has great maps, and rotates local guides and porters for trekking tours. June to August are the best months to go. During the wet season (November to April), tracks can be slippery and very dangerous, and the view is often obscured by clouds.

The most common trek is to climb from Senaru to Pos III (2300m) on the first day (about five hours of steep walking), camp there and climb to Pelawangan I, on the crater rim (2600m), for sunrise the next morning (about two hours). From the rim, you descend into the crater and walk around to the **hot springs** (two hours) on a very exposed track. The hot springs, revered by locals for their healing properties, are a good place to relax and camp for the second night, before returning all the way to Senaru the next day.

For summit-seekers, guides and porters are mandatory. Continue east from the hot springs, and camp at Pelawangan II (about 2900m). From there a track branches off to the summit. It's a heroic climb (three or four hours) over loose footing to the top (3726m). Start at 3am so you can see the sunrise on the summit. Return to Pelawangan II (two or three hours) and go east to Sembalun Lawang (five or six hours) to complete a traverse of the mountain.

You can trek from Senaru to the hot springs and back without a guide – the trail is fairly well defined. For summit attempts, you must use guides. The most popular package is the three-day, two-night trek from Senaru to Sembalun Lawang via the summit. It includes food, equipment, guide, porters, park fee and transport back to Senaru. This costs about 1,750,000 million rupiah per person.

Two Senaru outfitters stand out. **John's Adventures** (☎ 081 7578 8018; www.lombok-rinjanitrek.com; per person 1,750,000Rp) has been leading Rinjani climbs since 1982. He has toilet tents, offers four meals a day, provides thick sleeping mats, and starts hiking from Sembalun. **Galang Jo Expedition** (☎ 081 9174 04198; per 2 people 2,300,000Rp) has competitive prices and a network of experienced guides.

Besides arranging tours, you can hire a tent, sleeping bag and stove in Senaru through the Rinjani Trek Centre. Bring several layers of clothing, solid footwear, rain gear, extra water (do not depend on your guide for your water supply, or you may suffer) and a torch (flashlight). Buy food in Mataram or Senggigi, where it's cheaper and the selection is wider.

Finally, understand that people die every year on the mountain; it shouldn't be approached lightly.

THE KUTA SITUATION

Emaar Property, a Dubai development concern, is poised to transform Kuta's pristine coast. A development could stretch from the west end of Kuta Bay to the east end of Tanjung Aan. Construction of a widened road to the site of its first new five-star hotel (possibly a Ritz Carlton) began at Tanjung Aan in January 2009.

Because developers are not required to divulge their plans, plans remain shrouded. But the Emaar Property spokesman in Jakarta did tell us that 'this project involves multiple luxury hotels and golf courses and will be rolled out over the next 10 to 15 years'. Sounds like Nusa Dua Dua to us.

offers very clean bamboo bungalows with *ikat* bedspreads. The spacious, newer concrete bungalows have two double beds, hot water, hardwood furniture and cable TV.

G'Day Inn (☎ 655342; s/d 90,000/100,000Rp) This friendly, family-run place offers clean, recently renovated rooms, some with hot water, as well as a cafe.

Melon Homestay (☎ 081 736 7892; r 100,000Rp, apt 150,000Rp) This place has two sweet apartments with a lounge and self-catering facilities, one with sea views from its balcony. There are a couple of smaller modern rooms with verandah and bathroom. It's about 400m east of the junction.

Sekar Kuning (☎ 654856; r with 150,000;) A charming beach-road inn. Top-floor rooms have ocean views.

Surfers Inn (☎ 655582; www.lombok-surfersinn.com; r 180,000-400,000Rp;) A very smart, stylish and orderly place with five classes of modern rooms, each with huge windows and large beds, and some with sofas. Book ahead as it's very popular.

Family Cafe (☎ 653748; mains 12,000-30,000Rp) You won't need that thick menu, just order the *sate pusut* (minced fish, chicken or beef mixed with fresh coconut, chilli and spices, moulded and grilled on lemongrass stalks) and *kangkung pelecing* (sautéed water spinach and bean sprouts, topped with tomato sauce and shredded coconut).

our pick Lombok Lounge (☎ 655542; chilli crab 50,000Rp) Don't search the menu because you're here for the scintillating, finger-licking, meaty chilli crab, a Chinese-Indonesian classic. It's more than just the best meal in town. It's a full body experience. Wash it down with icy Bintang.

Shore Beach Bar (10am-late) Owned by Kimen, Kuta's original surf entrepreneur, the open dance-hall interior has been recently renovated, and the sound system is fantastic. If you're in town on a Saturday night, you'll probably wind up here grooving to a live band.

GETTING THERE & AWAY

How many bemo does it take to get to Kuta? Three. Take one from Mataram's Mandalika terminal to Praya (5000Rp), another to Sengkol (3000Rp), and a third to Kuta (2000Rp).

Perama (☎ 654846), based at Segare Anak Cottages, runs tourist buses to Mataram (125,000Rp, two hours), with connections to Senggigi and elsewhere.

Labuhan Lombok

The one reason to visit this town is to catch a Sumbawa-bound ferry (see opposite).

Arrive early to avoid staying overnight. If you get mired, the only decent option is **Losmen Lima Tiga** (☎ 23316; d 55,000Rp) on the main road inland from the port.

Frequent buses and bemo travel between Labuhan Lombok and Mandalika terminal (11,000Rp, two hours).

SUMBAWA

Beautifully contorted and sprawling into the sea, Sumbawa is all volcanic ridges, terraced rice fields, jungled peninsulas and sheltered bays. The southwest coast is where Sumbawa is at its most spectacular, with layered headlands and wide, silky white beaches. The southeast is no slouch. It's also a bit more accessible, which explains why Lakey Peak has become Sumbawa's premier year-round surf magnet.

Though well connected to Bali and Lombok, Sumbawa is a very different sort of place. It's far less developed, much poorer and extremely conservative. Transport connections off the cross-island road are infrequent and uncomfortable, and most overland travellers don't even get off the bus as they roll from Lombok to Flores. For now, it's the domain of surfers, miners and mullahs.

GETTING THERE & AWAY

Air

Bima is the one and only air hub, with direct Merpati flights to Denpasar (five times per week). You can also connect to Mataram and Maumere (although flights to east Flores are forever in flux). Departure tax is 6000Rp.

Boat

Ferries run every 45 minutes, 24 hours a day, between Labuhan Lombok and Poto Tano (15,500Rp, 1½ hours). In the east, Sape is the departure point for daily ferries to Labuanbajo, Flores. Pelni ships dock at Bima.

Bus

Night buses run in a convoy from Mataram to Bima, where they hook up with smaller shuttles to the Flores ferry at Sape.

Poto Tano & Around

Poto Tano is the Lombok-bound ferry port, but there's no reason to linger. Most travellers pass straight through to Sumbawa Besar. You can also head into town, catch a bus to Taliwang and another 30km south to the superb surf at **Maluk**, a contemporary boom town thanks to a nearby copper mine. **Rantung Beach Hotel** (☎ 087 8639 35758; Rantung; s/d 50,000Rp/80,000Rp; ❄) attracts budgeteer surfers to its somewhat ramshackle rooms. Fifteen kilometres further south is another gorgeous surf beach, **Sengkongkang**, where you can find a number of beachfront *losmen*.

Ferries run regularly to/from Lombok (see above). The through buses from Mataram to Bima include the ferry fare.

Buses meet the ferry and go to Taliwang (15,000Rp, one hour) and Sumbawa Besar (12,000Rp, two hours).

Sumbawa Besar

☎ 0371 / pop 56,000

Sumbawa Besar is the provincial principality on the western half of the island. Here horse carts outnumber bemo. Aside from nearby traditional villages, the sole attraction is **Dalam Loka**, the crumbling Sultan's Palace, just off Jl Sudirman.

INFORMATION

BNI bank (Bank Negara Indonesia; Jl Kartini 10; 🕑 8am-2.30pm Mon-Fri, 8am-noon Sat) Currency exchange and an ATM.
Sejoli.Net (Jl Hasanuddin 50; per hr 5000Rp; 🕑 8am-1am) Surf well for cheap.
Sub-post office (Jl Yos Sudarso) Closer to the town centre.
Telkom office (Jl Yos Sudarso; 🕑 24hr) The cheapest place to make international calls.

SLEEPING & EATING

Hotels congregate on Jl Hasanuddin. The nearby mosque provides free wake-up calls.

Hotel Dian (☎ 21708, 22297; Jl Hasanuddin 69; s/d with fan 45,000/60,000Rp, with air-con 90,000/135,000Rp; ❄) There are a wide variety of rooms here, and the best have air-con and spring beds. The worst feel like concrete cells.

our pick **Hotel Suci** (☎ 21589; Jl Hasanuddin 57; d with fan 60,000Rp, with air-con 150,000Rp; ❄) Located right next to the mosque, this is the top of the local lodging heap. Economy rooms are not to be trusted, but the air-con rooms in the new building are large and airy with high ceilings.

Warung Kita 2 (☎ 23065; Jl Setia Budi 13; dishes 9000-17,000Rp) A bright, delicious pick-and-mix diner with trays of broiled chicken, tasty fried prawns and curried green beans.

Ikan Bakar 99 (☎ 21102; Jl Hasanuddin 15; dishes 15,000-45,000Rp) Yes, the environs are not so savoury, but it does have tasty fresh seafood, and lots of it.

Warung set up in front of the stadium on Jl Yos Sudarso.

GETTING THERE & AWAY

Transnusa (☎ 21565, 21370; Jl Hasanuddin 110) is the only active carrier, with daily flights to Denpasar via Mataram.

The long-distance bus station is Terminal Sumur Payung, 5.5km northwest of town on the highway, where seven bus lines run air-con coaches to Bima (90,000Rp, seven hours via Dompu). Routes also include Poto Tano (25,000Rp, three hours, hourly from 8am to midnight) and Mataram (65,000Rp to 70,000Rp, six hours).

Pulau Moyo

Two-thirds of Pulau Moyo, 3km off Sumbawa's north coast, is a nature reserve, and its protected reefs are teeming with marine life. There are two resorts on the island: one is basic and run by the Forest Service (PHKA), the other is expensive. Hitch a ride over on a PHKA boat from Sumbawa Besar (10,000Rp).

Hu'u & Lakey Beach

Lakey Beach, a gentle crescent of golden sand 3km south of Hu'u, is where Sumbawa's tourist pulse beats year-round, thanks to seven world-class surf breaks that curl and crash in one massive bay.

There are several attractive places to stay, from budget to midrange. This is an ideal beach retreat, even if you're not called to ride waves. **Mona Lisa Bungalows** (r with fan 50,000-75,000Rp, with air-con 100,000-150,000Rp;) has economy rooms with shared *mandi*, and comfortable bungalows in a verdant garden.

From Dompu take a bemo (2000Rp) or *benhur* to the Lepardi local terminal on the southern outskirts. There are two (slow) buses in the morning as far as Hu'u (15,000Rp, 1½ hours), where you can hire an *ojek* (10,000Rp) to Lakey Beach. Most visitors come here by chartered taxi from Bima airport (400,000Rp).

Bima & Raba

☎ 0374 / pop 100,000

These twin cities – grubby but alive Bima and orderly and dull Raba – form Sumbawa's main port and commercial hot spot. Consider it a stopover on the way through Sumbawa.

ORIENTATION & INFORMATION

BNI bank (Jl Sultan Hasanuddin) Changes currency and has an ATM.

Internet & Game Center (Jl Sumbawa; per hr 3000Rp)

Tourist office (☎ 44331; Jl Soekarno Hatta; 7am-3pm Mon-Fri, 7am-noon Sat) English-speakers staff the tourist office in Raba's Kantor Bupati.

SLEEPING & EATING

Most hotels are in central Bima, near the market.

Hotel Lila Graha (☎ 42740; Jl Lombok 6; d with fan 100,000-125,000Rp, with air-con 150,000-300,000Rp;) The labyrinthine passages access an array of rooms and a good restaurant.

Hotel La'mbitu (☎ 42222; Jl Sumbawa 4; r from 110,000Rp;) Bima's best, with several clean, bright and airy rooms to choose from.

our pick **Rumah Makan Sabar Subur** (☎ 646236; Jl Salahudin, Bandara; meals 9000Rp; 7am-6pm) These long wooden tables are always crowded with locals who come to munch *bandeng goreng*, a flash-fried freshwater fish.

GETTING THERE & AWAY

Bima's airport is 17km out of town; it's 60,000Rp by taxi. **Merpati** (☎ 44221; www.merpati.co.id) flies five times a week to Denpasar.

Pelni (☎ 42625; Jl Kesatria 2), at Bima's port, sails monthly from Bima to Maumere, Larantuka, Papua and back to Benoa in Bali. It also connects Bima with Larantuka, Benoa and Papua monthly.

Buses to points west of Bima leave from the central bus station, just south of town. Express night-bus agencies near the station sell tickets to Sumbawa Besar (70,000Rp, seven hours) and Mataram (150,000Rp, 11 hours). Most buses heading west leave around 7pm.

Buses to Sape (9000Rp, two hours) depart from Kumbe in Raba, a 20-minute bemo ride (2000Rp) east of Bima, but they can't be relied upon to meet the early morning ferry to Flores. Or charter a car (200,000Rp, 1½ hours) to Sape (about 100,000Rp, two hours) to make the 8am ferry.

Sape

☎ 0374

The only real attraction is the ferry to Labuanbajo, Flores, from Pelabuhan Sape, the small port 3km from town. Otherwise Sape's got a tumble-down port-town vibe, perfumed with the conspicuous scent of drying cuttlefish.

There's a **PHKA Komodo Information Office** (8am-2pm Mon-Sat) 500m inland from the port, with a few brochures and maps.

For a bed, **Losmen Mutiara** (☎ 71337; Jl Pelabuhan Sape; r 35,000-100,000Rp;), just outside the port entrance, is the only decent choice.

Express buses with service to Lombok and Bali meet arriving ferries.

Buses leave every half-hour for Raba (9000Rp, two hours) until around 5pm. From Raba take a bemo to Bima (1500Rp, 20 minutes). Ignore taxi touts who say the buses aren't running.

Always double-check the latest ferry schedules in Bima and Sape. **Cabang Sape** (☎ 71075; Jl Yos Sudarso, Pelabuhan Penye Berangan Sape) operates the daily ferry to Labuanbajo (60,200Rp per person, 125,000Rp per motorcycle, eight to nine hours). Do not expect comfort.

Ships leave for Waikelo, Sumba (50,000Rp, eight hours), once or twice a week. Be prepared to wait.

KOMODO & RINCA

Parched, isolated, desolate yet beautiful, Komodo and Rinca rise from waters that churn with riptides and boil with whirlpools, and they are patrolled by lizard royalty, the komodo dragon. It would be hard to create a more forbidding environment, yet a few hundred fishing families eke out a living here.

INDONESIA

DRAGON SPOTTING

Komodo's gargantuan monitor lizards *(ora)* grow up to 3m long and can weigh in at a whopping 100kg. These prehistoric beasts feed on pigs, deer and buffalo. A blood-poisoning bite from their septic jaws dooms prey within a few days. Recently the dead have included local farmers.

Banu Nggulung, a dry riverbed a half-hour walk from Loh Liang, is the most accessible place to see dragons on Komodo. It was once set up like a theatre, though the curtain has fallen on the gruesome ritual of feeding live goats to the reptiles. On Rinca, dragons will often congregate near the PHKA post when the rangers are cooking, or guides will lead hikes to their favourite lizard haunts.

Spotting dragons is not guaranteed, but a few of these royal reptiles are usually around – especially around watering holes in the June to September dry season. They rarely venture into the midday sun, so get to the islands early. A guide costs 30,000Rp per person.

The area is designated the **Komodo National Park** (www.komodonationalpark.org), the boundaries of which encompass both islands and several smaller, neighbouring isles. A three-day visitor permit includes your park entrance fee (40,000Rp) and the conservation fee (US$20 for adults), collected on arrival by rangers. There is a useful office in Labuanbajo (p304).

A short, guided dragon-spotting trek is included with your entrance fee. For a longer, hour-long trek on Rinca you'll pay an additional 50,000Rp. On Komodo, where the hiking is superb, you can pay from 50,000Rp to 250,000Rp for guided treks.

Sights & Activities

Dragons lurk year-round at the dry riverbed Banu Nggulung (see boxed text, above), but hunting (figuratively speaking) them on foot through primordial **Poreng Valley** feels wilder. **Gunung Ara** can be climbed (3½ hours) in an afternoon, and there's good snorkelling at **Pantai Merah** (Red Beach) and the small island of **Pulau Lasa**, near Kampung Komodo. The PHKA rents snorkels and masks for 50,000Rp. Guides (30,000Rp) are mandatory, and useful, for hikers.

Sleeping & Eating

Komodo's **PHKA camp** (per person per night 300,000Rp) just went through a renovation and is now an overpriced version of a basic Indonesian hotel, complete with a musty interior. Rinca's large stilted cabins, on the other hand, are riddled with mould and falling apart. New bungalow construction was underway here at the time of our research, but most folks opt to sleep on the decks of their chartered boats.

Getting There & Away

Ferries travelling between Sape and Labuanbajo have not been stopping at Komodo for several years now, so the only way here is by some sort of charter. One way to arrive is on a boat tour between Lombok and Flores – these stop at Komodo for a night or two. See the boxed text, p304, for the pros and cons of such trips.

Labuanbajo is the best jumping-off point for Komodo and Rinca. It *is* possible to charter boats from Sape in Sumbawa to Komodo, but be extremely cautious, as many boats here are barely seaworthy.

Chartering a boat to Rinca costs about 750,000Rp return from Labuanbajo. Boats usually leave at about 8am for the two-hour journey to the island and then return via snorkelling spots. You can book through your hotel, an agency or freelance agents in Labuanbajo, or speak directly to the captains at the harbour, which will allow you to size up the boat, and check that the vessel has a radio and life jackets.

Two-day Komodo trips cost a standard 1,500,000Rp from Labuanbajo for up to six people. Price includes landings on Rinca and Komodo, meals and snorkelling gear.

FLORES

Flores is the kind of gorgeous that grabs hold of you tightly. There are empty white- and black-sand beaches and bay islands; exceptional diving and snorkelling near Labuanbajo; an infinite skyline of perfectly shaped volcanoes; and a vast tapestry of hip-high, luminescent rice fields that undulate in the wind next to swaying palms in spectacular river canyons. The serpentine, potholed east–west Trans-Flores Hwy is long and slow,

BOAT TOURS BETWEEN LOMBOK & FLORES

Travelling by sea between Lombok and Labuanbajo is a popular way to get to Flores, as you get to see more of the region's spectacular coastline and dodge some painfully long bus journeys. Typical itineraries from Lombok take in snorkelling at Pulau Satonda off the coast of Sumbawa and a dragon-spotting hike on Komodo. From Labuanbajo boats usually stop at Rinca and Pulau Moyo.

Be warned, this is no luxury cruise – a lot depends on the boat, the crew and your fellow travellers. Some shifty operators have reneged on 'all-inclusive' deals en route, and others operate decrepit old tugs without life jackets or radio. And this crossing can be extremely hazardous during the rainy season, when the seas are rough.

The well-organised tours on decent boats run by Perama from Lombok (see Mataram or Senggigi for contact details) are safe, however. Current charges for cabin/deck are 2,600,000/2,000,000Rp for the three-day trip.

but never boring. It skirts waterfalls, conquers mountains, brushes by traditional villages in Bajawa, leads to the incredible multicoloured volcanic lakes of Kelimutu and connects both coasts. The Portuguese named it 'Flowers' when they colonised Flores in the 16th century. The name stuck (so did Catholicism) because of its sheer, wild beauty.

GETTING THERE & AWAY

Air

Labuanbajo has become Flores' primary gateway because scores of tourists funnel in to see the dragons and dive the reefs of Komodo National Park. Maumere, Ende and Ruteng are also serviced by flights that are often cancelled. Purchase your ticket at an airline office at the point of departure only, and always reconfirm.

Boat

Daily ferries connect Labuanbajo with Sape, Sumbawa. From Larantuka, ferries go to Kupang (West Timor) and Pulau Solor and Pulau Alor. From Ende and Aimere, boats will take you to Waingapu on Sumba.

The **Pelni agent** (☎ 41106) in Labuanbajo is easy to miss, tucked away in a side street in the northeast of town. The monthly Pelni ship, *Tilongkabila,* heads to Makassar and the east coast of Sulawesi; or to Bima, Lembar and Benoa.

See the boxed text, above, for details on tourist boat trips from Lombok to Flores.

GETTING AROUND

The Trans-Flores Hwy twists and tumbles for 700 (often) paved, tremendously scenic kilometres from Labuanbajo to Larantuka. Luxury buses don't exist on Flores, but cheap, cramped public buses run when full, which means packed! Many tourists hire a car and driver. Trans-Flores trips run from 500,000Rp to 550,000Rp a day, including petrol. You can arrange trips with hotels and agents in Labuanbajo or Maumere.

The flat, coastal 'Trans-Northern Hwy' runs from Maumere to Riung.

Labuanbajo

☎ 0385 / pop 7500

Welcome to Indonesia's 'Next Big Thing' in tourism. At least it feels that way, with a steady stream of Komodo-bound package tourists and younger backpackers descending on this gorgeous ramshackle harbour. It's freckled with bay islands, blessed with surrealist sunsets and surrounded by rugged, undeveloped coastline. Dive boats leave day and night for world-class reefs in the nearby national park, there are sweet beach bungalows on empty islands closer to shore and there's an ever-expanding collection of restaurants with a view.

INFORMATION

The Telkom office is near the tourist office.

BNI bank (Jl Yos Sudarso) Changes money, and has an ATM.

PHKA information booth (☎ 41005; tnkomodo@indosat.net.id; Jl Yos Sudarso; 🕑 8am-2.30pm Mon-Thu, to 11am Fri) PHKA administers the Komodo National Park, and provides practical information for Komodo and Rinca islands.

Post office (Jl Yos Sudarso)

Tourist Office (Dinas Pariwisata; ☎ 41170; 🕑 7am-2pm Mon-Thu & Sat, to 11am Fri) About 1km out of town on the road to the airport.

INDONESIA

SIGHTS & ACTIVITIES

Diving Komodo National Park is one of the big draws to Labuanbajo. Currents are strong and unpredictable with cold up-swellings and dangerous down currents thanks to the convergence of the warm Flores Sea and the cooler Selat Sumba (Sumba Strait). These conditions also nourish a rich plankton soup that attracts whales, mantas, dolphins, turtles and sharks. Factor in pristine coral and clouds of colourful fish, and the diving is nothing short of exhilarating. But it isn't easy, so it's best to tune into local conditions on shallower dives before you endeavour to venture into the depths.

Local dive operators share uniform prices. At research time the price was 800,000Rp for two dives around Rinca, plus a 200,000Rp surcharge to stop and see the dragons. Dive offices are strung along or just off the seafront road:

Dive Komodo (☎ 41862; www.divekomodo.com)
Divine Diving (☎ 41948; www.divinediving.info; Jl Soekarno Pelabuhan 1)
Reefseekers (☎ 41443; www.reefseekers.net)

TOURS

Labuanbajo is the main jumping-off point for tours to Komodo and Rinca; see p303 for details.

SLEEPING

Gardena Hotel (☎ 41258; Jl Yos Sudarso; bungalows 85,000-100,000Rp) A collection of basic bamboo huts on a rambling hillside, overlooking the gorgeous bay harbour and distant islands. The restaurant is solid, and this is easily the most popular spot in town.

Chez Felix (☎ 41032; Jl Bidaderi; r 150,000-200,000Rp) Set in a quiet location above the bay and run by a friendly family who all speak good English, this is a fine option, with cute, clean, tiled rooms.

Golo Hilltop (☎ 41337; www.golohilltop.com; d with fan 175,000, d with air-con 325,000-450,000Rp) Modern, super-clean concrete bungalows in a hilltop garden setting with magnificent views of Labuanbajo Bay (but not the harbour).

Bajo Komodo Eco Lodge (☎ 41362; www.ecolodgesindonesia.com; s/d 660,000/720,000Rp; 🏊) Down on the beach where there's much new upscale development, this imposing neo-colonial house has six bright and spacious rooms and two detached bungalows, each with stylish pebble-floored bathrooms.

EATING

Matahari (☎ 41083; Jl Yos Sudarso; dishes 10,000-23,000Rp) Terrific views from the deck, particularly at sunset, and a tasty menu recommended by locals that includes sandwiches, soups and hot plates.

Porto Moro (Jl Yos Sudarso; fried chicken & squid 10,000Rp) This funky two-storey place with warped floors and harbour views serves the cheapest food in town. It's always packed with locals, and not just because of the price.

our pick **Lounge** (☎ 41962; Jl Yos Sudarso; tapas from 20,000Rp, mains 22,000-60,000Rp) Across from Arto Moro is a sleek dining room with red lounges, Balinese art and (of course) amazing views. Tapas are exceptional, so are the pizzas and home-made ravioli.

Pesona (☎ 41950; Jl Soekarno Hatta; meals 26,000Rp) Cute, ramshackle wooden restaurant perched above the harbour, specialising in fresh seafood.

GETTING THERE & AWAY

Air

Labuanbajo's Bandar Udara Komodo has regional service, including the following:

IAT Flies to Denpasar.
Merpati (☎ 41177) Flies to Denpasar.
Transnusa (☎ 41800, 41955; Jl Yos Sudarso) Flies to Denpasar and Kupang.

Boat

The ferry from Labuanbajo to Sape (27,000Rp, eight to nine hours) leaves at 8am daily. Tickets can be purchased at the harbour master's office (in front of the pier) one hour before the vessel's departure.

For Pelni ship details, see opposite.

Bus

Buses leave for Ruteng (40,000Rp, four hours), Bajawa (100,000Rp, 10 hours) and even Ende (150,000Rp, 15 hours) from the Garantolo bus terminal 10km outside of town. Buy your tickets in advance and buses will stop in town.

Bajo Express (☎ 42068) runs regular minibus routes to Bajawa, Ruteng, Maumere and Ende, and they leave on time, without looping around town in search of passengers.

Ruteng

☎ 0385 / pop 37,000

Cool, refreshing, and nestled among lush volcanos and rice fields in the heart of Manggarai country, Ruteng is a good place to stretch your legs between bus trips. Compang Ruteng, 3km southwest, is a semitraditional village, home to the local Manggarai people, and nearby Gunung Ranaka is an active volcano.

INFORMATION

BNI bank (Jl Kartini) Currency exchange, and an ATM.
Post office (Jl Dewi Sartika 6; 7am-2pm Mon-Sat)
Z-Net (21347; Jl Adisucipto 8; per hr 10,000Rp; 9am-6pm) Ruteng's only connection.

SLEEPING & EATING

Hotel Rima (22196; Jl A Yani 14; r 75,000-175,000Rp) A kitschy Swiss Alpine knockoff with clean, comfy rooms. Has a sweet patio garden and a street side terrace.

Rumah Makan Surya (Jl Bhayangkara; dishes 3000-10,000Rp) Heaping portions of tasty, spicy Padang food.

GETTING THERE & AWAY

The airport is 2km southeast of town, but at research time it was still under renovation with no flights available.

Buses to Labuanbajo leave at 7am, 1pm and 3pm (40,000Rp, four hours), while those to Bajawa (60,000Rp, five hours) and Ende (120,000Rp, nine hours) leave around 7am. Take a bemo to the terminal (2000Rp), located 3.5km out of town. Tickets can be booked through hotels

Bajawa

0384

With a pleasant climate, and surrounded by forested volcanoes, Bajawa is a great base from which to explore dozens of traditional villages that are home to the Ngada people. Their fascinating architecture features *ngadhu* (carved poles supporting a conical thatched roof).

INFORMATION

BNI bank (Jl Pierre Tendean) Has an ATM.
Telkom office (21218; Jl Soekarno Hatta)

SIGHTS & ACTIVITIES

Bena, 19km south of Bajawa on the flank of Gunung Inerie, is one of the most spectacular traditional villages in the area. **Nage** and **Wogo** are also interesting. Guides linger around hotels and can arrange day trips for 250,000Rp per person with transport, village entry fees and lunch.

SLEEPING & EATING

There once was a good choice of budget digs in Bajawa, but virtually all the cheap rooms have suffered from neglect.

Hotel Korina (21162; Jl Ahmad Yani 81; s/d 50,000/60,000Rp) The bottom of the Bajawa barrel in terms of room size, frills and cleanliness, but the staff is friendly and it will do for a night.

our pick **Villa Silverin** (222 3865; www.villasilverinhotel.com; Jl Bajawa; r 75,000-275,000Rp) Set just outside of town on the road to Ende, with beckoning verandahs and jaw-dropping valley views. VIP rooms are the cleanest in Bajawa.

Edelweis (21345; Jl Ahmad Yani 76; r 90,000-120,000Rp;) Great volcano views, reasonably clean VIP rooms and friendly ownership, which may boil water for a very welcome hot-water morning *mandi*, make this an appealing choice.

Lucas (21340; Ahmad Yani 6; mains 10,000-15,000Rp) Set in a cute cabin, it serves fine pork *sate* and other local faves, including a fearsome, yet quaffable, *arak*.

Camellia (21458; Jl Ahmad Yani 74; mains 15,000Rp) It has Western dishes, but try the chicken *sate*. It comes with a unique sweet, smoky pepper sauce.

GETTING THERE & AWAY

Merpati has resumed Bajawa–Kupang flights. Contact its office in Kupang (see p313).

The Watujaji bus station is 3km south of town, but hotels arrange tickets and pick-ups. Buses to to Labuanbajo (100,000Rp, 10 hours) leave at 6am; buses to Ruteng (60,000Rp, five hours) are at 7am; and buses to Ende (35,000Rp, five hours) go at 7am and 11am. There are also buses to Riung (20,000Rp, three hours), along a tough, winding road, at 8am and noon.

Bemo and trucks to surrounding villages depart from the Jl Basuki Rahmat terminal.

Riung

Fans of laid-back coastal mangrove villages will love Riung, but the 21 offshore islands of the **Seventeen Islands Marine Park** (named in honour of Indonesia's 17 August Independence Day), with luscious white-sand beaches and excellent snorkelling, are the real attraction. The park entrance fee is 15,000Rp per person plus 20,000Rp per boat. Day trips (250,000Rp for up to six people) are easily arranged in Riung.

INDONESIA

THE NGADA

Over 60,000 Ngada people inhabit the upland Bajawa plateau and the slopes around Gunung Inerie. Older animistic beliefs remain strong, and most Ngada practise a fusion of animism and Christianity. They worship Gae Dewa, a god who unites Dewa Zeta (the heavens) and Nitu Sale (the earth).

The most evident symbols of continuing Ngada tradition are pairs of *ngadhu* and *bhaga*. The *ngadhu* is a parasol-like structure about 3m high, consisting of a carved wooden pole and thatched 'roof', and the *bhaga* is a miniature thatched-roof house.

The *ngadhu* is 'male' and the *bhaga* is 'female', and each pair is associated with a particular family group within a village. Some were built over 100 years ago to commemorate ancestors killed in long-past battles.

In addition to *ngadhu, bhaga* and the ancestor worship that goes with them, agricultural fertility rites continue (sometimes involving gory buffalo sacrifices), as well as ceremonies marking birth, marriage, death and house building.

Pondok SVD (☎ 081 3393 41572; r 110,000-300,000Rp), a missionary-run place, has absolutely spotless rooms with desks, reading lights and Western toilets.

Rumah Makan Murah Muriah (mains 15,000-30,000Rp, large beer 15,000Rp) serves delicious, fresh grilled fish and icy Bintang.

From Ndao terminal in Ende (40,000Rp, four hours), a bus leaves every afternoon at 1pm. Two buses from Bajawa (20,000Rp, three hours) leave at 1pm. This road is a mess and is 4WD only. Buses to Bajawa depart at 6am.

Ende

☎ 0381 / pop 81,600

Muggy, dusty and crowded, this south-coast port's ultimate saving grace is its spectacular setting. The eye-catching cones of Gunung Meja and Gunung Iya loom over the city, while barrels roll in continuously from the Sawu Sea and crash over a coastline of black sand and blue stones.

Soekarno was exiled here during the 1930s, where he reinvented himself as a truly horrid playwright. Fortunately the whole national revolutionary-hero thing worked out.

INFORMATION

BNI bank (Bank Negara Indonesia; Jl Gatot Subroto) Near the airport, this bank offers the best exchange rates and has an ATM.

Tourism office (☎ 21303; Jl Soekarno 4; 8am-1pm Mon-Sat) Enthusiastic staff.

Zyma Internet (☎ 24697; Jl Sudarso 3; per hr 5000Rp; 11am-10pm) Good connection in the cathedral's shadow.

SIGHTS

Meander through the aromatic **waterfront market** (Jl Pasar), with the requisite fruit pyramids and an astonishing fish section, including giant tuna and sharks. The adjacent **ikat market** (cnr Jl Pabean & Jl Pasar) sells hand-woven tapestries from across Flores and Sumba.

History buffs can visit Soekarno's house of exile, now **Musium Bung Karno** (Jl Perwira; admission by donation; 7am-noon Mon-Sat); most of the original period furnishings remain. This is where he penned the epic Frankenstein-inspired *Doctor Satan*.

SLEEPING & EATING

Accommodation is spread all over town, but frequent bemo make it easy to get around.

Hotel Ikhlas (☎ 21695; Jl Ahmad Yani 69; r 50,000-90,000Rp) This well-run place has plenty of basic but neat little rooms at good prices. Those at the rear, around a sunny courtyard, are the most desirable.

Hotel Safari (☎ 21997; Jl Ahmad Yani 65; economy s/d 100,000/125,000Rp, with air-con s/d 200,000/250,000Rp;) Right next door to Hotel Ikhlas, this is a step up. Rooms are large, clean and open onto a courtyard garden. Air-con rooms should be booked in advance. Breakfast is included.

Rumah Makan Tiana (Jl Pahlawan 31; dishes 6000-15,000Rp) A fun hole-in-the-wall with terrific Indonesian soul food, including a gingery *soto ayam*, a chilli-fired *rendeng*, and *ayam sate* drenched in ginger sauce.

GETTING THERE & AWAY

Air

At the time of research, **Transnusa** (☎ 24333, 085 2392 58392; Jl Kelimutu 37) offered daily flights to

Denpasar. **Merpati** (☎ 21355; Jl Nangka) offered four flights a week to Denpasar and Kupang (Monday, Wednesday, Thursday, Saturday).

Boat

ASDP (☎ 22007) operates weekly ferries to Waingapu (71,000Rp, six hours) and Kupang (125,000Rp, seven hours).

Pelni's *Awu* stops in Ende every two weeks. It sails west to Waingapu, Benoa and Surabaya, then east to Kupang, Kalabahi and Larantuka. Visit the helpful **Pelni office** (☎ 21043; Jl Kathedral 2; 8am-noon & 2-4pm Mon-Sat).

Bus

It's about 5km from town to Wolowana terminal, where you catch buses for eastern Flores. Buses to Moni (15,000Rp, two hours) operate from 6am to 2pm. Buses to Maumere (40,000Rp, five hours) leave at 7am, 9am and 4pm.

Buses heading west leave from the Ndao terminal, 2km north of town, on the beach road to Ruteng (120,000Rp, nine hours) at 7.30am; Labuanbajo (150,000Rp, 15 hours) at 7am; and Bajawa (35,000Rp, five hours) at 7am and 11am.

Kelimutu

There aren't many better ways to wake up than to sip ginger coffee as the sun crests Mt Kelimutu's western rim, filtering mist into the sky and revealing three deep, volcanic lakes – each one a different striking shade. Minerals in the water account for the chameleonic colour scheme – although the turquoise lake never changes, the other lakes can fluctuate to yellow, orange and red.

Most visitors glimpse them at dawn, leaving nearby Moni at 4am. But afternoons are usually empty and peaceful at the top, and when the sun is high the colours sparkle. Clouds are your only obstacle, and they can drift in at anytime.

To get there, hire an *ojek* (one way/return 35,000/60,000Rp), bemo (one way/return 150,000/250,000Rp, maximum four people) or car (400,000Rp return, maximum five people) from Moni. Negotiate! The park entry post, halfway up the road, charges a 20,000Rp entry fee.

You can walk the 13.5km down through the forest and back to Moni in about 2½ hours. There's a short cut from just beside the entry post, which comes out by the hot springs and waterfall.

Moni

Moni is a picturesque village sprinkled with rice fields, ringed by soaring volcanic peaks, with distant sea views. It's a slow-paced, easygoing town that serves as a gateway to Kelimutu. The cool, comfortable climate invites long walks, and a few extra days, but there are no banks and only one telephone. About 2km west of Moni is the turn-off to Kelimutu. The Monday market, on the soccer pitch, is a major local draw and a good place to snare *ikat*.

SLEEPING & EATING

Moni has a cluster of cheapies to choose from.

Bintang Guest House (☎ 085 2379 06259; s/d 60,000/75,000Rp) Just four tidy rooms with little garden patios out front and great views of the valley below. You'll be hanging with Mr Tobias and his brood. They rent motorbikes for 75,000Rp per day.

Watugana Bungalow (s/d/tr 75,000/90,000/125,000Rp) Reasonably priced older tiled rooms with a shady porch, set downhill from the main road. Management is very friendly and informative.

our pick **Hidayah** (☎ 085 3390 11310; d 200,000Rp) Four huge, super-clean rooms with outstanding mountain and valley views from the common porch. Without question, this is the most comfortable choice in town.

Restaurant Nusa Bunga (dishes 8000-27,000Rp) The funkiest grub shack in town belongs to this long-time standby across from the market. It has chicken club sandwiches, *gado gado*, omelettes and all the Indo basics.

Chenty Restaurant & Café (☎ 085 23924 30080; dishes 12,000-40,000Rp) Long-running, popular place with a nice porch overlooking the rice fields. The special here is the Moni cake (25,000Rp), a vegetable and mashed-potato pie topped with cheese.

our pick **Flores Sare Restaurant** (☎ 085 2390 29357; dishes 15,000-45,000Rp) Attached to the perpetually incomplete hotel of the same name, this is Moni's best kitchen, with a wide array of fresh fish, squid, chicken and pork dishes to choose from. Hire an *ojek* to get here, then burn off the meal and stroll the 1.5km back to town.

GETTING THERE & AWAY

For Ende (15,000Rp, two hours), buses start around 7am. Other buses come from Ende through to Maumere (35,000Rp, four hours) at about 9am or 10am, then later at around

7pm. Additional buses and trucks leave on Monday (market day). Travel in the morning, when buses are often half empty.

Maumere

☎ 0382 / pop 51,000

Compared to Ende and Labuanbajo, Maumere is a dump. But it has the second-most connected airport on the island and unless you are doubling back west by car, you're likely to do some time here. Fortunately you can escape to beach bungalows lining the coast. And some of Flores' best *ikat* weavers live in traditional villages outside of town.

ORIENTATION & INFORMATION

BNI bank (Jl Soekarno Hatta 4) Best rates in town; ATM.
Comtel (☎ 22132; Jl Bandeng 1; per hr 12,000Rp; 9am-9pm) High-speed internet access.
Post office (Jl Pos; 8am-2pm Mon-Sat)
Telkom office (Jl Soekarno Hatta 5)
Tourist office (☎ 21652; cnr Jl Melati & Jl Wairklau; 8am-1pm Mon-Sat) Not a great resource.

SLEEPING & EATING

The harbour doubles as restaurant row, with a string of inexpensive seafood and Indonesian kitchens.

Hotel Wini Rai (☎ 21388; Jl Gajah Mada 50; r 50,000-350,000Rp;) About 1km west of the centre, this sprawling courtyard hotel has five classes of rooms. The best deal here is on the spotless, air-con rooms out back.

Gardena Hotel (☎ 22644; Jl Patirangga 28; s/d with fan 60,000/80,000Rp, with air-con 100,000/120,000Rp;) A terrific budget spot on a quiet residential street east of the harbour crush.

Gading Beach Hotel (☎ 085 2390 04490; Jl Raya Don Siripe; r with fan 90,000Rp, with air-con 130,000Rp;) A new beach property, right on the sea, 8.5km west of town. This one is a collection of very clean bamboo bungalows with imaginative paint jobs. There's free transport to the airport and bus stations.

our pick **Rumah Makan Jakarta** (☎ 081 2379 5559; most dishes 6000-30,000Rp) The popular choice among seamen for the fish – fresh and perfectly prepared and served almost instantly with a sensational roasted chilli sambal that will make you sweat.

Restaurant Bamboo (☎ 085 7375 59981; dishes 10,000-32,500Rp) Bringing a little design panache to Maumere's funky harbour is this newish spot, dressed tastefully in black bamboo with floor and table seating.

GETTING THERE & AROUND

Maumere has good air connections. **Merpati** (☎ 21393; Jl Raya Don Tomas) has daily flights to/from Kupang and Denpasar. The airport is 3km away, and a taxi there costs 10,000Rp.

Pelni (☎ 21013; Jl M Sugiyo Pranoto 4) sails the *Wilis* fortnightly to Kupang, Larantuka, Kalimantan and Makassar. *Siguntang* sails to Lewoleba and Kupang every two weeks.

Buses to Larantuka (32,000Rp, four hours), and buses and bemo to Geliting, Waiara, Ipir and Wodong leave from the Lokaria (or Timur) terminal, 3km east of town, at 7.30am and 3pm. The Ende (or Barat) terminal 1.5km southwest of town is the place for buses west to Moni (35,000Rp, three hours) and Ende (40,000Rp, five hours), leaving at 7am and 3pm.

Buses often endlessly cruise town searching for passengers. Hotels can arrange pick-up. Bemo around town cost 2000Rp.

Around Maumere

A small army of expert artisans lays in wait in the weaving village of **Sikka**, 26km south of Maumere. Along the north coast, east of Maumere, is where you'll find the best beaches and healthiest reefs.

Waiara, 9km east of Maumere, was once considered the gateway to the Maumere 'sea gardens' before the 1992 tsunami wreaked havoc on the reefs. They are now well into recovery mode, and it's a nice spot to linger in or out of the water. **Sea World Club** (Pondok Dunia Laut; ☎ 21570; www.sea-world-club.com; bungalows US$25-60) is worth a splurge. It charges US$60 for two dives. To get there, catch any Talibura- or Larantuka-bound bus from Maumere (3000Rp).

The beaches of **Ahuwair** and **Waiterang**, 24km and 26km east of Maumere, ooze tranquillity. **Sunset Cottages** (☎ 085 2530 99597; sunsetcottages@yahoo.co.uk; s/d bungalows with mandi 60,000/100,000Rp) has coconut wood and bamboo beachside bungalows, snorkelling trips to nearby islands and fantastic fish dinners.

our pick **Ankermi** (☎ 081 2466 9667; www.ankermi-happydive.com; bungalows per person 165,000Rp, mini villa 210,000Rp) has cute, thatched concrete and bamboo bungalows with squat toilets and showers, and front decks with ocean views. Meals are included in the price. The dive shop, Happy Dive, is the best in the Maumere area and the Javanese meals are spectacular.

Come via a Larantuka-bound bus or bemo from Maumere's Lokaria terminal (3000Rp, 35 minutes).

Larantuka

☎ 0383

This busy little port, and former Portuguese enclave, nestles at the base of Gunung Ili Mandiri on the eastern tip of Flores, separated from the Solor and Alor archipelagos by a narrow strait. Most people come simply to hop on a ferry.

Telkom Warnet (per hour 10,000Rp; 24hr;) has solid internet access. **BNI** (Jl Fernandez 93) and **BRI** (Jl Udayana) have ATMs and change dollars and travellers cheques.

SLEEPING & EATING

our pick **Hotel Rulies** (☎ 21198; Jl Yos Sudarso 40; r 50,000-90,000Rp) This funky spot near the harbour has clean rooms with shared *mandi*.

Hotel Fortuna I (☎ 21140; Jl Basuki Rahmat 170; s/d with mandi 60,000/90,000Rp, r with air-con 175,000-200,000Rp;) Best of the three Fortunas in town. Rooms are a bit scruffy, but have queen-sized beds and air-con.

Rumah Makan Nirwana (Jl Yos Sudarso; dishes 5000-14,000Rp) Larantuka's first choice. The Chinese and Indonesian dishes come in filling portions.

Or stop by the **night market** (Jl Yos Sudarso; dishes 8000-27,000Rp) opposite Hotel Tresna.

GETTING THERE & AWAY

All boats depart from the main pier in the centre of town. Double-check departure times.

Wooden boats to Lewoleba on Lembata (30,000Rp, four hours), all via Waiwerang (Adonara, 12,000Rp) and Solor (Lamalera, 16,000Rp), depart from the pier in the centre of town at 8am and 1pm.

Infrequent Pelni ships serve Lewoleba, Kalimantan, Semarang, Maumere, Kupang and Makassar.

Regular buses run between Maumere and Larantuka (32,000Rp, five hours). The main bus station is 5km west of town (3000Rp by bemo), but you can pick buses up in the town centre.

Solor & Alor Archipelagos

If you're hoping to trek to authentic head-hunting villages or shove off with indigenous whalers in rowboats, armed with nothing but bamboo harpoons, or otherwise have an *adventure*, come here. This remote, mountainous chain of volcanic islands, separated by swift, narrow straits from the eastern end of Flores, is reached by ferry from Larantuka. Lembata, in the Solor chain, is home to the traditional whaling village of Lamalera. Alor is protected by rich coral reefs that attract divers.

LEMBATA

The sleepy commercial centre of Lewoleba is overshadowed by the smoking cone, **Gunung Ili Api**. Lewoleba has banks with ATMs. Stay at the slick and central **Hotel Lewoleba** (☎ 41012; Jl Awololong 15; s/d with fan 45,000/60,000Rp, s/d with air-con 90,000/110,000Rp;), or the long-running Dutch-Indo-owned **Lile Ile homestay** (☎ 41250; s/d 25,000/40,000Rp), with overgrown volcano views.

On the south coast, **Lamalera** is an isolated whaling village, where locals hunt whales with spears, rowboats and prayer. Being a small-scale subsistence activity, the hunting is considered legal. Villagers take occasional visitors out on a hunt during the May to October whaling season. It's as harrowing as it sounds.

Merpati operates three flights a week to Kupang from the Lamahora airstrip 4km west of Lewoleba.

Daily ferries to Larantuka (30,000Rp), via Pulau Adonara, depart at 8am and 1pm. At research time there was also one ferry a week to Kalabahi (59,000Rp) on Alor leaving on Monday night at 9pm. Pelni's *Siguntang* offers an almost weekly service to Kupang (economy/private cabin 120,000Rp/270,000Rp), leaving at 11pm and arriving the next morning.

ALOR

☎ 0386 / pop 170,000

Alor, the final link in an island chain that extends east of Java, is as remote, rugged and beautiful as it gets. Thanks to impenetrable terrain, the 170,000 inhabitants are fractured into 50 tribes with 14 languages, and they were still taking heads into the 1950s. Alor is also famous for its strange, bronze *moko* drums.

Superb diving can be arranged through **La Petite Kepa** (☎ 081 3382 00479; www.la-petite-kepa.com; bungalows incl meals per person 150,000-200,000Rp) on Pulau Kepa. **Alor Dive** (☎ 222 2663, 081 3396 48148; www.alor-dive.com; Jl Gatot Subroto 33, Kalahabi) also arranges trips.

Kalabahi, located on a sweeping, palm-fringed bay, is the main port. There are banks and ATMs. **Hotel Pelangi Indah** (☎ 21251; Jl Diponegoro 100; r 50,000-200,000Rp; ❄), on the main drag, has reasonably clean rooms flanking a flower garden.

The airport is 9km from town, and offers one of the most dramatic approaches in the country. **Transnusa** (☎ 21039; Jl Sudirman 100) flies to and from Kupang.

To Kupang, ferries leave on Tuesday and Sunday (70,000Rp, around 18 hours). Ferries depart from Kalabahi for Larantuka (75,000Rp, around 24 hours) on Sunday and Thursday, passing through Baranusa, Balauring and Lewoleba.

Pelni (☎ 21195) ships leave from the main pier in the centre of town. For details, see p175.

WEST TIMOR

With rugged countryside, empty beaches and scores of traditional villages, West Timor is an undiscovered, if at times drought-prone, gem. Deep within its lontar palm-studded interior, animist traditions persist alongside tribal dialects and *ikat*-clad, betel-nut chawing chiefs govern beehive-shaped hut villages. Kupang, its coastal capital and East Nusa Tenggara's top metropolis and transport hub, buzzes to a typical Indonesian beat. Expect to hear several of the 14 tongues spoken on the island.

GETTING THERE & AWAY

Air

A good way to explore eastern Nusa Tenggara is to fly directly from Bali to Kupang and island hop from there. For details on flights, see p313.

Boat

ASDP (☎ 0380-890420; Bolok) has regular car-and-passenger ferries in east Nusa Tenggara but routes and schedules are prone to change. Check with the office in Kupang. Ferries typically run from Kupang to Larantuka (Flores) and Ende among other destinations.

Pelni passenger ships serve a wide number of places infrequently; see p175 for details plus p313 for Kupang departures.

GETTING AROUND

The good main highway is surfaced all the way from Kupang to East Timor, though the buses are of the cramped, crowded, thumping-disco variety. Away from the highway, roads are improving but can be impassable in the wet season.

Kupang

☎ 0380 / pop 340,000

Kupang, the capital of Nusa Tenggara Timur (NTT), is noisy, energetic, scruffy, bustling with commerce, and a fun place to hang around for a few days. Captain Bligh did, after his mutiny problem in 1789.

ORIENTATION

Kupang sprawls, and you'll need to take bemo or *ojek* to get around. You will likely land in one of two main areas. The waterfront district, which stretches along Jl Sumba and rambles inland with Jl Ahmad Yani, has the bulk of the budget lodging options. Jl Mohammad Hatta/Sudirman, to the south, is the new commercial centre.

INFORMATION

The NTT Tourist Office is out in the sticks near the bus station – it's not worth the trip. Kupang has scores of banks and ample ATMs in both ends of town.

Lavalon (www.lavalontouristinfo.com; Jl Sumatera 44) The best internet access.

Main post office (Jl Palapa 1) Take bemo 5.

Plasa Telkom (Jl Urip Sumohardjo 11; ⏲ 8am-4pm Mon-Fri, 8am-noon Sat) Offers international calls and wi-fi.

SIGHTS

East Nusa Tenggara Museum (admission 2000Rp; ⏲ 8am-noon & 1-4pm Mon-Sat) is worth a look for its dusty collection of crafts and artefacts. But the rambling **Pasar Inpres**, the main market, is more energising. It's southeast of the centre. Take bemo 1 or 2.

TOURS

Kupang is a gateway to West Timor's fascinating, and welcoming, traditional villages. Bahasa Indonesia – let alone English – is often not spoken, so a local guide is advisable. **Oney Meda** (☎ 081 3394 04204) organises tours and treks for 300,000Rp to 600,000Rp per day depending upon the itinerary.

Dive Alor (☎ 821154; www.divealor.com; Jl Raya El Tari 19), run by the Australian father-son team of Graeme and Donovan Whitford, is an experienced scuba outfit that arranges trips to the island.

INDONESIA

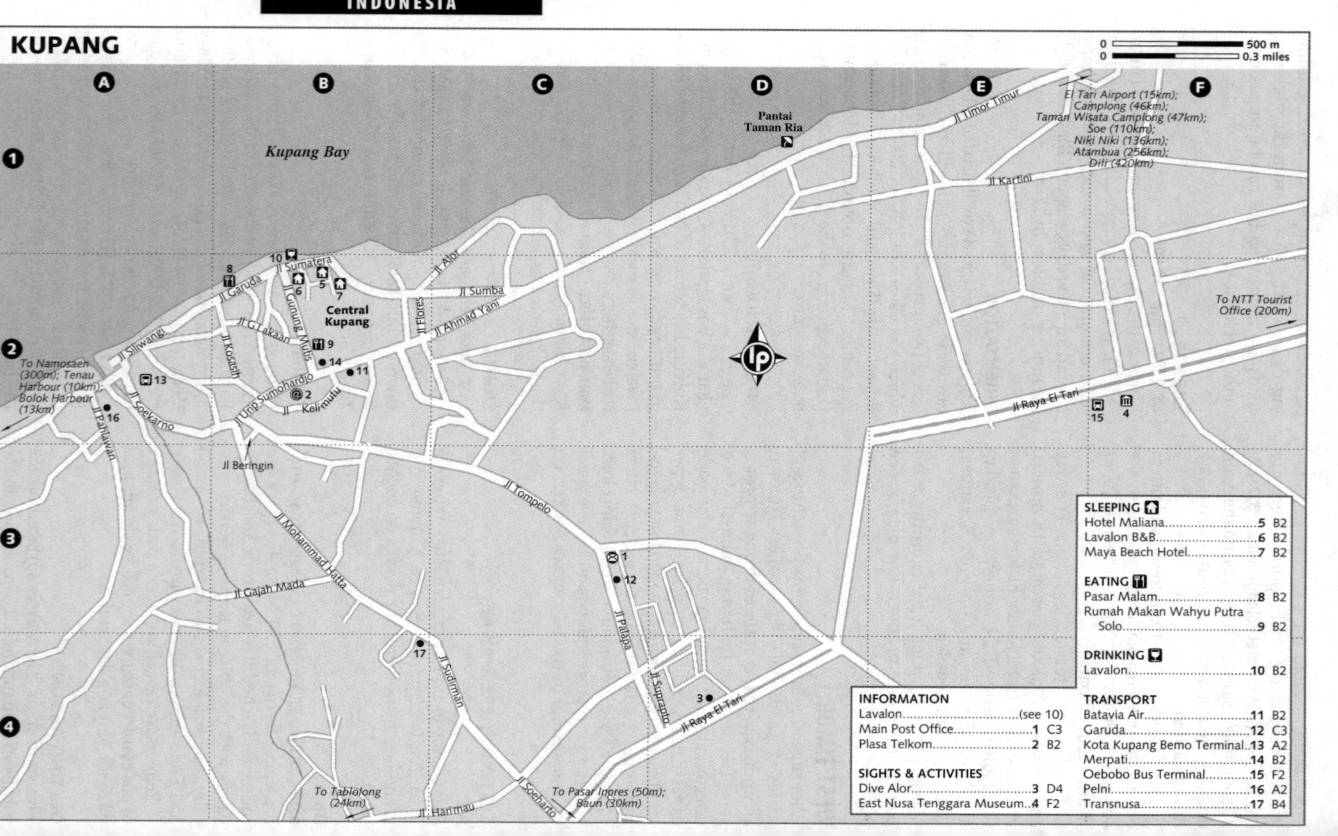
KUPANG
0 500 m
0 0.3 miles
Kupang Bay
Pantai Taman Ria
Central Kupang
El Tari Airport (15km); Camplong (46km); Taman Wisata Camplong (47km); Soe (110km); Niki Niki (136km); Atambua (256km); Dili (420km)
To NTT Tourist Office (200m)
To Namosaen (300m); Tenau Harbour (10km); Bolok Harbour (13km)
To Tablolong (24km)
To Pasar Inpres (50m); Baun (30km)
Jl Timor Timur
Jl Kartini
Jl Raya El Tari
Jl Alor
Jl Sumba
Jl Flores
Jl Ahmad Yani
Jl Sumatera
Jl Garuda
Jl Gunung Mutis
Jl G Lakaan
Jl Kosasih
Jl Siliwangi
Jl Soekarno
Jl Pahlawan
Jl Urip Sumohardjo
Jl Kelimutu
Jl Beringin
Jl Tompelo
Jl Mohammad Hatta
Jl Gajah Mada
Jl Sudirman
Jl Palapa
Jl Suprapto
Jl Harimau
Jl Soeharto
SLEEPING
Hotel Maliana 5 B2
Lavalon B&B 6 B2
Maya Beach Hotel 7 B2
EATING
Pasar Malam 8 B2
Rumah Makan Wahyu Putra Solo 9 B2
DRINKING
Lavalon 10 B2
TRANSPORT
Batavia Air 11 B2
Garuda 12 C3
Kota Kupang Bemo Terminal 13 A2
Merpati 14 B2
Oebobo Bus Terminal 15 F2
Pelni 16 A2
Transnusa 17 B4
INFORMATION
Lavalon (see 10)
Main Post Office 1 C3
Plasa Telkom 2 B2
SIGHTS & ACTIVITIES
Dive Alor 3 D4
East Nusa Tenggara Museum 4 F2

SLEEPING

Lavalon B&B (☎ 832236; Jl Sumatera I 8; r with shared bathrooms 40,000Rp, r with fan 55,000Rp) The best value in town, with clean, ceramic-tiled rooms. Guide Oney Meda owns this place.

our pick **Hotel Maliana** (☎ 821879; Jl Sumatera 35; r with fan 100,000Rp, with air-con 160,000Rp;) These basic yet comfy motel rooms are a popular budget choice. Rooms are clean and have ocean views from the front porch.

Maya Beach Hotel (☎ 832169; Jl Sumatera 31; r 115,000-135,000Rp;) A decent choice, this large concrete hotel has plenty of clean-ish rooms just a cut above basic. Some have sea views.

EATING & DRINKING

Jl Garuda has become the domain of streetside grill and wok chefs that expertly prepare inexpensive dishes. *RW* is dog meat, a Kupang speciality.

Pasar Malam (Jl Garuda; dishes from 6000Rp; 6-10pm) Kupang was never considered a good eating town until this wonderful, lamp-lit place was launched.

Rumah Makan Wahyu Putra Solo (☎ 821552; Jl Gunung Mutis 31; meals 10,000-25,000Rp) Kupang's best pick-and-mix *warung* offers beef, chicken, fish, potatoes and greens deep- and stir-fried, stewed in coconut sauce, and chilli-rubbed and roasted.

Lavalon (☎ 832256, 081 2377 0533; www.lavalontouristinfo.com; Jl Sumatera 44;) This open-air, tin-roof watering hole with spectacular sea views is a must for any new traveller in town. Edwin and his crew will give you the NTT lowdown.

GETTING THERE & AROUND

Air

Kupang's El Tari airport (code KOE) is 15km east of town. Taxi fare into town is fixed at 50,000Rp. It's the most important hub for air travel in Nusa Tenggara. Services include:

Batavia Air (☎ 830555; Jl Ahmad Yani 73) Flies to Surabaya.
Garuda (☎ 827333; Jl Palapa 7) Flies to Denpasar.
Lion Air (☎ 882119; El Tari airport) Flies to Surabaya.
Merpati (☎ 833833; Jl Timor Timur km 5) Flies to Denpasar, Mataram, Waingapu, Waikkabubak, Maumere, Ende, Lewoleba and Atambua.
Transnusa (☎ 822555; Jl Sudirman 68) Flies to Kalabahi, Ende, Maumere and Rote.

Boat

Pelni (☎ 824 357; Jl Pahlawan 3; 8.30am-3pm Mon-Sat, 9-11am Sun) is near the waterfront. Pelni's *Dobonsolo* runs every two weeks from Bali to Kupang, and on to Kota Ambon and Papua. The fortnightly *Awu* sails from Kupang to Ende, Waingapu, Lombok and Bali, or Kalabahi, Larantuka and Sulawesi. *Sirimau* sails between Kupang, Alor and Makassar every two weeks. The fortnightly *Pangrango* sails from Kupang to Surabaya, Waingapu and Bima. The *Tatamailau* connects Kupang with Maumere, Bima and Benoa, and on the return trip heads to Saumlake and Tual. Finally, the *Siguntang* links Kupang with Lewoleba and Maumere.

Ferries leave from Bolok, 13km southwest of Kupang. **ASDP** (☎ 890420) has ferries to Larantuka (Sunday and Thursday), and Ende on Friday. The Ende ferry continues on to Waingapu.

Bus

Long-distance buses depart from Oebobo terminal on the eastern side of town – catch bemo 10. Daily departures include Soe (45,000Rp to 60,000Rp, three hours) and Niki Niki (45,000Rp to 60,000Rp, 3½ hours) every hour from 5am to 6pm; Kefamenanu (50,000Rp to 70,000Rp, 5½ hours) and Atambua (75,000Rp, eight hours) at 7am, 9am, noon and 5pm.

See boxed text, p314, for information on getting to East Timor.

Around Kupang

Head to the great **Tablolong** beaches, 27km southwest of Kupang. The small islands of **Pulau Semau** and **Pulau Kera**, just off the coast, are also interesting. Grab a local boat from Namosaen, west of the city.

Baun, a tiny village in the hills 30km southeast of Kupang, is an *ikat*-weaving hot spot with a few colonial edifices. Visit the *rumah raja*, the last raja's house, occupied by his widow.

Camplong, a mellow foothill town 46km from Kupang, is home to the **Taman Wisata Camplong**, a forest reserve that has caves and a spring-fed swimming pool.

Soe

☎ 0368

The traditional, beehive-like *lopo* (hut) villages and the indigenous Dawan people who live in them are the attraction of this modernising market town 800m above sea level. On the outskirts, ubiquitous *lopo* rise from bush reminiscent of Australia. Government has deemed

GETTING TO EAST TIMOR

From Kupang, direct minibuses (175,000Rp one way, 11 hours) to Dili are operated by **Timor Tour and Travel** (☎ 881543), **Paradise Tours and Travel** (☎ 823120) and **Livau** (☎ 821892). Call for a hotel pick-up. This is the easiest and most cost-effective way to cross the border.

This route is the cheapest way to renew your Indonesian visa from Nusa Tenggara; once in East Timor, you can get another 30-day visa at the Indonesian embassy. It costs a lot less than getting back to Bali and flying to Singapore or Kuala Lumpur.

See boxed text, p155, for information on doing the trip in the reverse direction.

the *lopo* a health hazard (they're smoky and lack much ventilation) and is in the process of replacing them with modern homes. Once received, the Dawan simply build new *lopo* behind them. It's a great system. Village tours are easily arranged in Soe.

The **tourist information centre** (☎ 21149; Jl Diponegoro) can arrange guides. **BNI** (Jl Diponegoro) and **BRI** (Jl Hatta) branches have ATMs, which is good because currency exchange rates are low.

Nope's Royal Homestay (☎ 21711; Jl Merpati 8; bungalows incl breakfast 100,000Rp) has one ageing little bungalow. Pae Nope is Soe's best guide.

Hotel Bahagia II (☎ 21095; Jl Gajah Mada 55; d 145,000Rp, cottages 225,000-495,000Rp; 💻) has plenty of spacious rooms, queen-sized beds and a few cottages that make sense for families.

The Haumeni bus terminal is 4km west of town (2000Rp by bemo). Regular buses go to Kupang (45,000Rp to 60,000Rp, three hours), Kefamenanu (25,000Rp, 2½ hours) and Oinlasi (10,000Rp to 15,000Rp, 1½ hours), while bemo cover Niki Niki (5000Rp) and Kapan (5000Rp).

Around Soe

Market days attract villagers from miles in every direction, who arrive wearing traditional dress and sell exquisite hand-woven *ikat*, carvings and masks. This is why you travel. The Tuesday market at **Oinlasi**, 51km from Soe, is one of the biggest and best in West Timor, and the Wednesday market at **Niki Niki**, 34km east of Soe, is a lively, more accessible, second choice.

The main attraction around Soe is **Boti**, a traditional village presided over by a self-styled raja who is something of a fundamentalist animist. Traditional dress code and hairstyle is enforced, and locals maintain strict adherence to *adat* (customary law), a devotion that has proven almost completely immune to Christian missionaries.

It's possible to stay with the raja in his house with all meals provided for 75,000Rp per person. Day-trippers are expected to contribute a donation (25,000Rp should work); bring a guide from Soe conversant with local *adat*.

From Niki Niki, there is a new turn-off to Boti. It's a 20km trip on a rocky, hilly road that's passable by motorcycle or 4WD.

Kefamenanu

☎ 0388 / pop 32,000

Kefamenanu (Kefa) is another cool, quiet town with a few colonial buildings, and a passionate weaving tradition. Prepare to haggle with the *ikat* cartel. They will find you. **Temkessi**, 50km northeast of Kefa, is a spectacular traditional village. The only way in is a small passage between two huge rocks. Bahasa Indonesia won't get you far, so bring a guide. Kefa is also the gateway to the poor and isolated East Timorese enclave of Oecussi. The best overnight option is the new, posh and central **Hotel Livero** (☎ 233 2222; Jl El Tari; standard/deluxe 250,000/300,000Rp; ❄).

There are regular buses that travel to Kupang (50,000Rp to 70,000Rp, 5½ hours) and Soe (25,000Rp, 2½ hours).

Atambua

☎ 0389 / pop 38,000

Atambua is a scruffy border town close to East Timor. Large numbers of pro-Jakarta refugees and militias settled here after East Timor's independence – a period when pro-Jakarta forces went on a rampage in East Timor. Three UN workers were murdered here in 2000; it is best avoided. Fortunately direct Dili–Kupang minibuses mean you won't need to stop.

SUMBA

According to local legend, humankind first made landfall on earth by climbing down a huge celestial ladder from heaven to Sumba – a dry, lowland isle made of limestone and covered in grasslands. Broken off the archipelago's southeastern arc, in the Sawu Sea, Sumba has kept to itself ever since, and although

INDONESIA

Christianity has seeped in, tribal traditions – such as *marapu*, a religious belief system that revolves around ancestral spirits, bloody sacrificial funeral rites, hand-carved tombs, divine *ikat* weaving, and the use of horses for status, wealth and to score a hot wife – remain strong and pure. Generational tribal tensions also simmer beneath the surface, and are recalled every year during western Sumba's Pasola festivals (see boxed text, p316), when mock battles between mounted warriors often descend into actual violence.

Most of the 540,000 residents live in comparatively moist and fertile West Sumba, and though some Bahasa Indonesia is spoken throughout the island, six tribal languages are more prevalent. Note that as international aid has poured in, remote villagers expect larger and larger donations from visitors – whether they be government officials, NGO staff or tourists.

GETTING THERE & AWAY

Air

Waingapu is the main airport. See right for its limited service.

Boat

Waingapu has weekly ASDP ferries to Ende (and on to Kupang) and Aimere on Flores. Pelni has useful services from Waingapu to Ende, and on to several more points. See right for details of sea services.

Waingapu

☎ 0387 / pop 53,000

Sumba's gateway town has grown up from a dusty trading post to an urbanising commercial centre. But just like in the old days, business revolves around dyewoods, timber and the island's prized horses. You're here to explore the surrounding villages.

ORIENTATION & INFORMATION

Waingapu spreads from the harbour in the north, 1.5km southeast to the main market and bus station.

BNI bank (Bank Negara Indonesia; Jl Ampera) ATM accepts Visa/plus cards. It usually has the best exchange rates.

Post office (Jl Hasanuddin; 8am-4pm Mon-Fri) Close to the harbour.

Telkom office (Jl Tjut Nya Dien; 24hr)

Warnet Green Corner (Jl El Tari 4; per hr 5000Rp; 11am-10pm) Internet access.

SLEEPING & EATING

Most hotels are in the new part of Waingapur, near the bus station. Cheap rooms are rare. The best dinner option is the *pasar malam* at the old wharf.

Hotel Sandle Wood (☎ 61887; Jl Panjaitan 23; r 77,000-209,000Rp;) Decent-value rooms set around a bright courtyard on a quiet street. Management is top notch and can hook you up with cars (with drivers) and motorbikes.

our pick **Hotel Merlin** (☎ 61300; Jl Panjaitan 25; r 110,000-200,000Rp;) The longstanding travellers' favourite has a decent assortment of rooms on three floors, with Flores views from the rooftop restaurant. Top-floor fan rooms are nicer and cleaner than the VIP rooms on the 1st floor. The rooftop dining room is one of the best choices in town.

Rumah Makan Swandayani (☎ 256 4145; Komplek Ruko; dishes 7000-25,000Rp) The biggest deal in the slowly sputtering Komplek Ruko, it has a substantial menu of Indo and Chinese cuisine featuring seafood, chicken and vegie dishes.

GETTING THERE & AROUND

Air

The airport is 6km south on the Melolo road. A taxi into town costs about 20,000Rp, but most hotels offer a free pick-up and drop-off service for guests. **Merpati** (☎ 61323; Jl Soekarno 4) serves Kupang and Denpasar.

Boat

Waingapu is well serviced by weekly **ASDP ferries** (☎ 61533; Jl Wanggameti 3), all departing from the old pier in the centre of town. One ferry departs from Ende for Waingapu and on to Kupang. There's also a connection to Aimere in Flores and a regular service to Pulau Sabu.

Pelni (☎ 61665; Jl Hasanuddin) ships leave from the newer Darmaga dock to the west of town. Don't try and walk. It's further than it looks; bemo charge 5000Rp per person. The *Awu* sails for Ende and on to Larantuka, Kalabahi, Benoa in Bali, Surabaya and Kalimantan.

Bus

Eastbound buses to Meolo, Rende and Baing leave from the bus station near the market. The West Sumba terminal is 5km west of town. Buses to Waikabubak (30,000Rp, five hours) leave here at 7am, 8am, noon and 3pm. Book at the hotels or the agencies opposite the bus station.

Around Waingapu

Several traditional villages in the southeast can be visited from Waingapu by bus and bemo. The stone tombs are impressive and the area produces some of Sumba's best *ikat*. Almost every village gatekeeper will produce a visitor book to sign. Small donations are expected.

Just 3km southeast of town, **Prailiu** is a busy *ikat*-weaving centre that's worth a peek. There are also some interesting traditional thatched huts and carved concrete tombs.

Located about 7km away from unspectacular **Melolo** – accessible by bus from Waingapu (20,000Rp, 1½ hours) – is **Praiyawang**, the ceremonial centre of **Rende** village, with its traditional Sumbanese compound and stone-slab tombs. The massive one belongs to a former raja. **Umabara** and **Pau**, 4km from Melolo, are other places to snap traditional Sumba architecture and tombs, and witness the weaving process. These villages are a 20-minute, 1.5km walk from the main road; the turn-off is 2km northeast of Melolo.

Some 70km from Waingapu, **Kaliuda** has Sumba's best *ikat*. Seven buses a day make the trip from Waingapu (30,000Rp, four hours).

There's epic surf at **Kalala**, about 2km from Baing, off the main road from Melolo. The well-respected namesake of the worn **Mr David's** (☎ 081 3378 73589; all-inclusive bungalows 250,000Rp) has lived and surfed here for 30 years. Four buses a day depart Waingapu for Baing (30,000Rp, four hours), but they'll gladly drop you off at the beach.

An even more rustic and life-altering beautiful beach is at **Tarimbang**, a palm-draped cove south of Lewa. The reef break is superb, the snorkelling decent and either of the two homestays will do just fine. Both charge 50,000Rp, all inclusive. Daily trucks to Tarimbang leave Waingapu in the morning (35,000Rp, five hours).

INDONESIA

Waikabubak

☎ 0387 / pop 19,000

At the greener end of Sumba, Waikabubak, a conglomeration of thatched clan houses, ancient tombs, concrete office buildings and satellite dishes, is strange but appealing. Interesting traditional villages such as **Kampung Tarung**, up a path next to Tarung Wisata Hotel, are right within the town. One of the spectacular attractions of West Sumba is the **Pasola**, the mock battle held near Waikabubak each February or March (see boxed text, right).

INFORMATION

BNI bank (Bank Negara Indonesia; Jl Ahmad Yani; 8am-3.30pm Mon-Fri) Has an ATM and offers fair exchange rates.

Tourist office (☎ 21240; Jl Teratai 1; 8am-3pm Mon-Sat) On the outskirts of town. Staff are well informed about forthcoming funerals and cultural events in the area.

SLEEPING & EATING

Karanu Hotel (☎ 21645; Jl Sudirman 43; r 85,000-110,000Rp) A bright garden hotel east of the downtown swirl within view of nearby rice fields. Rooms are clean, with new tiles and crisp sheets.

Aloha Hotel (☎ 21245; Jl Sudirman 26; r 100,000-225,000Rp;) Bright, clean-ish, basic fan rooms are set around a plot of grass and a fledgling garden.

Hotel Manandang (☎ 21197; Jl Pemuda 4; 2nd-class r 185,000Rp, 1st-class r 285,000Rp;) Tidy, good-value rooms, and management works hard to keep it that way.

our pick **Rumah Makan Gloria** (☎ 21389; Jl Bhayangkara 46; dishes 10,000-25,000Rp) Cute and cheerful, it rolls out all the Indo-Chinese hits, including a mean *ifu mie* with seafood.

Warung congregate opposite the mosque on the main strip.

GETTING THERE & AWAY

The airport is at Tambolaka, 42km north. Taxis to the airport cost 100,000Rp. **Merpati** (☎ 21051; Jl Bhayangkara 20) serves Kupang and Denpasar.

PASOLA FESTIVAL – SUMBA AT WAR

The thrilling, often gruesome mock battles between spear-hurling horsemen during Sumba's Pasola festival are a must for travellers passing through Nusa Tenggara in February or March. The high-energy pageant aims to placate the spirits and restore harmony with the spilling of blood. Happily, though, blunt spears have been used in recent decades to make the affair less lethal. The ritualistic war kicks off when a sea worm called *nyale* washes up on shore, a phenomenon that also starts the planting season. Call Waingapu or Waikabubak hotels to find out the latest schedules. The festival is generally held in the Lamboya and Kodi districts in February, and at Wanokaka and Gaura in March.

The bus station is central. Buses run to Waingapu (30,000Rp, five hours) throughout the day, and to Waitabula (12,000Rp, one hour). Frequent bemo rattle to Anakalang, Wanokaka and Lamboya.

Around Waikabubak

Set in a fertile valley carpeted in rice fields and 22km east of Waikabubak, **Anakalang** sports some of Sumba's most captivating megalith tombs (right beside the highway). More interesting villages are south of town past the market. **Kabonduk** has Sumba's heaviest tomb. It took 2000 workers over three years to carve it. A pleasant 15-minute walk from there is the hillside village of **Matakakeri** and the original settlement in the area, **Lai Tarung**, which has more tombs and breathtaking views. A festival honouring the ancestors is held every odd year in July.

Located directly south of Waikabubak is the Wanokaka district, which is a centre for the Pasola festival (see boxed text, opposite). **Praigoli** is a somewhat isolated, and therefore deeply traditional, village. The south coast has some blissfully desolate fishing beaches that immediately silence brain chatter. Head to **Pantai Rua**, with basic accommodation, or the white sands of **Pantai Morosi**.

On the west coast, **Pero** is a charming village with a couple of decent surf breaks. If you sail due west from here, the first land you hit would be Africa. **Homestay Stori** (per person incl all meals 100,000Rp) is comfortable and the food is fantastic. From Waikabubak, take a bus to Waitabula and one of many bemo from there to Pero.

KALIMANTAN

Indonesia's portion of Borneo is famous for orang-utans – Malay for forest person – and Dayaks, forest people who resist modern intrusions on their traditions. Here in one of the earth's great rainforest lungs and last frontiers, visitors can still find wonders that captivated naturalist Alfred Russel Wallace and novelist Joseph Conrad.

Kalimantan's natural attractions also draw miners, loggers and oil-palm planters, legal and otherwise. Their exploitation of resources means travellers need more time, energy and money to reach unspoiled nature. But issues here come as thickly layered as the jungle: logging and mining roads are now principal paths to reach the green heart of Kalimantan.

Still, when you are visiting longhouses on Sungai Mahakam, spotting orang-utans in Tanjung Putting National Park or traversing the jungle gorges of Pengunungan Maeratus, the rest of the world will seem like a distant place indeed.

Getting There & Away

AIR

At least eight different airlines have flights to Kalimantan destinations. These destinations include otherwise isolated interior communities from major cities elsewhere in Indonesia such as Jakarta. Main air hubs are Pontianak (p326), Balikpapan (p322) and Banjarmasin (p325). Bookings often require cash payment for confirmation, and schedules change without notice.

BOAT

Ferries to Tawau in Sabah, Malaysia, depart daily except Sunday from Tarakan. Speedboats run daily between Nunukan and Tawau.

State shipping line **Pelni** (www.pelni.co.id) and other carriers link most coastal cities to Java and Sulawesi; see p175 for Pelni routes. Cargo ships offer rides in many ports.

BUS

Air-con buses connect downtown Pontianak with Kuching. Economy buses to the Entikong border crossing leave from Batu Layang outside Pontianak (see boxed text, p320), and from Singkawang and Sintang. At the time of research, immigration officials allowed foreingers to exit at Entikong, immediately obtain a new visa and re-enter Indonesia.

Getting Around

Vast distances, dense jungle and mountain ranges make travel difficult, especially by land. Where available, *kapal biasa* (river ferries) or *long bots* (narrow wooden boats with covered passenger cabins) are the best ways into the jungle. Expensive speedboats also ply the Barito, Kapuas, Pinoh, Kahayan and Kayan Rivers.

Flying can save days of travel time and is reasonably priced. **KalStar** (☎ 021 5315 3456; www.kalstaronline.com) gets high marks for variety of destinations and reliability.

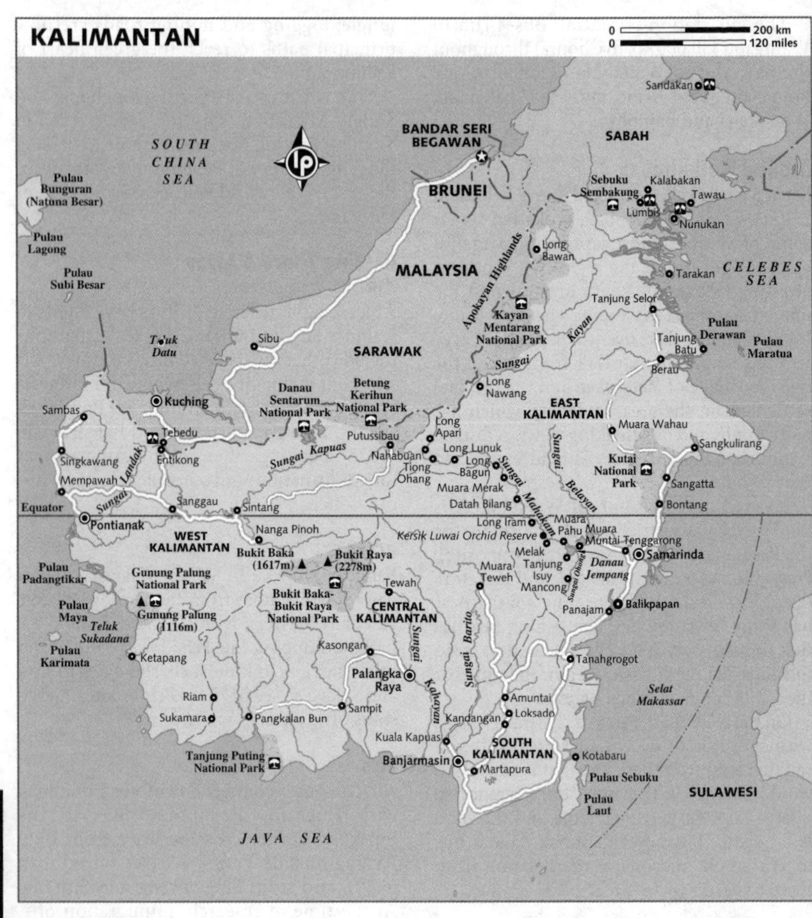

TARAKAN

☎ 0551 / pop 103,000

The usual reason to visit Tarakan is border crossing, to or from Tawau in Malaysia. Combat buffs may inspect memorials to bloody WWII battles between Australian and Japanese troops. A joint WWF-government project recently created a **mangrove forest** (Jl Gadjah Mada; admission 5000Rp; 8am-5pm), 300m from the town centre. From the wooden walkway, see proboscis monkeys, macaques and *ikan tempakul*, a fish exclusive to Kalimantan that crawls over mudflats on its fins.

Orientation & Information

Banks changing dollars are along Jl Yos Sudarso, with more ATMs along Jl Sudirman and at Gusher. Karisma at THM Plaza and Granmedia at Grand Tarakan Mall sell maps of Tarakan and beyond. Many businesses close Sundays.

Angkasa Express (☎ 30288; aex_trk@yahoo.com; Hotel Tarakan Plaza, Jl Yos Sudarso) Air and Pelni tickets with free delivery.

HappyCom (3rd fl; Grand Tarakan Mall; per hr 6000Rp; 10am-9.30pm) Internet.

Immigration office (☎ 21242; Jl Sumatra) Information on visas and crossings to/from Malaysia.

Post office (Jl Yos Sudarso)

Tourism office (☎ 32100; 4th fl, Jl Sudirman 76) Good maps.

Warnet Kopegtel (☎ 35000; kopegeteltravel@yahoo.com; Jl Sudirman 19; per hr 4000Rp; 8am-10.30pm;) Internet access with wi-fi, attached to a travel agency.

Sleeping & Eating

Hotel Bunga Muda (☎ 21349; Jl Yos Sudarso 7; r 66,000-150,000Rp; ❄) Clean, friendly, basic accommodation between the harbours. Economy rooms have shared bathrooms. Only VIP rooms have air-con and sleep up to four.

Hotel Bahagia (☎ 37141; fax 24778; Jl Gajah Mada; r incl breakfast 80,000-200,000Rp; ❄) Big, bright economy digs at 'Hotel Happiness' opposite Gusher Plaza have shared Asian and Western bathrooms. Higher-priced rooms include private Western bathrooms and air-con, but some lack windows.

Hotel Gemilang (☎ 21521; fax 35588; Jl Diponegoro 4; r 90,000-160,000Rp; ❄) Miles ahead of typical budget haunts, all rooms are meticulously kept and boast fabulous wood furniture.

Food stalls are banned from most streets. **Turi Ikan Bakar** (☎ 21153; Jl Yos Sudarso 32; per person 50,000-70,000Rp; 🕑 10am-3pm & 6-10pm; ⊠) and **Bagi Alam I** (☎ 22371; Jl Yos Sudarso 17; per person 40,000-60,000Rp; 🕑 10am-10pm) offer restaurant fish feasts. For economical eats, the best bets are THM Plaza and Jl Seroja off Jl Sudirman.

Getting There & Around

Taxis to/from Juwata airport (6km away) cost 50,000Rp. Alternatively, walk 200m to the street for an *angkot* (3000Rp). *Angkot* routes follow Jl Yos Sudarso, Jl Sudirman and Jl Gajah Mada. *Ojek* drivers gather on Jl Sudirman above THM Plaza and across from Gusher.

AIR

Batavia Air (☎ 32262; Jl Yos Sudarso 11), **KalStar** (☎ 25840; Jl Sudirman 9), **Lion Air** (☎ 202 6009), **Mandala Airlines** (☎ 22929; Jl Yos Sudarso 10) and **Sriwijaya Air** (☎ 33777; Jl Sudirman 21) fly to Balikpapan, connecting to Jakarta and beyond. KalStar and **Trigana Air** (☎ 31800; Hotel Tarakan Plaza, Jl Yos Sudarso) serve Samarinda. Check with **Mission Aviation Fellowship** (MAF; ☎ 34348) for scheduled and charter flights into the interior.

BOAT

Pelni (☎ 51169; Jl Yos Sudarso) ships steam weekly to Pantaloan (261,000Rp), Pare Pare (377,000Rp), Makassar (379,000Rp) and Surabaya (561,000Rp), and biweekly to Nunukan (75,000Rp), Maumere (409,000Rp), Kupang (587,000Rp), Jakarta (687,000Rp) and Kijang (841,000Rp), all from Pelabuhan Malundung, the main harbour at the south end of Jl Yos Sudarso. Travel agents are generally more helpful than Pelni's office.

SAMARINDA

☎ 0541 / pop 356,000

At the mouth of Sungai Mahakam, this trading port is the customary launch point for exploring the natural and cultural treasures of East Kalimantan's mightiest river. But Samarinda is overrated as a backpacker haven, while nearby Balikpapan is underrated. Either way, head upriver ASAP.

Orientation & Information

Banks along Jl Sudirman, including several just west of Pasar Pagi, exchange currency and have ATMs.

Borneo Warnet (Jl Abul Hassan; per hr 5000Rp; 🕑 9am-midnight) Internet.

Cendana Travel (☎ 739791; Jl Cendana 7) Delivers tickets.

East Kalimantan Tourism office (☎ 736850; cnr Jl Sudirman & Jl Awang Long)

Prima Tour & Travel (☎ 737777; www.travelprima.com; Hotel MJ, Jl Khalid 1)

RS Bhakti Nguraha (☎ 741363; Jl Basuki Rahmat 150) Clinic.

RS Haji Darjad (☎ 732698; Jl Dahlia) Large, modern hospital.

Sumangkat Internet (Jl Agus Salim 35; per hr 6000Rp; 🕑 8am-midnight) Postal services and *wartel*, too.

Sleeping & Eating

For cheap Indonesian food and local specialities, such as *udang galah*, try Jl Nilam, Jl Khalid or Citra Niaga market.

our pick **Hotel Gelora** (☎ 742024; gelora@smd.mega.net.id; Jl Niaga Selatan 62; r incl breakfast 100,000-225,000Rp; ❄) Samarinda's best budget choice, Gelora overlooks Citra Niaga market and is routinely overlooked by foreigners. Immaculate rooms include private *mandi*, with air-con.

Hotel Gading Kencana (☎ 731512; fax 731 954; Jl Sulawesi 4; r incl breakfast 135,000-235,000Rp; ❄) Even fan-cooled economy rooms are spacious and have private *mandi* or Western bathroom. The 2nd-floor restaurant has a bright, breezy terrace.

Hotel Andika (☎ 742358; fax 747389; Jl Agus Salim 7; r incl breakfast 160,000-400,000Rp; ❄ 📶) Bridging budget and midrange, Andika rooms all include air-con, TV and telephone. Economy rooms have shared bathrooms.

Syari 2 (Jl Sudirman; mains 10,000-15,000Rp) A busy, bright, family-run *warung* that dishes up home-cooked, Banjar-style grilled fish and chicken, vegetarian choices, *nasi campur* and soups.

INDONESIA

GETTING TO MALAYSIA

See p467, p455 and p472 for details of crossing from Malaysia to Indonesia.

Tarakan to Tawau

Morning ferries to Tawau in Sabah, Malaysia (300,000Rp, 3½ hours), depart daily except Sunday from Pelabuhan Malundung in Tarakan. *Indomaya* and *Tawindo Express* run on alternate days and are very similar; choose the day, not the boat. Immigration formalities are at the ferry terminal. Officials take your passport and return it, stamped for Malaysian entry, upon arrival in Tawau.

Nunukan to Tawau

It's also possible to cross from closs to the border at Nunukan (170,000Rp, 2½ hours), where boats to Tawau (90,000Rp, 1¼ hours) run daily. But the direct boats from Tarakan are the easiest and most cost efficient.

Entikong to Tebedu

In Pontianak, along Jl Sisingamangaraja, several companies run air-con express buses to Kuching (economy/executive 165,000/230,000Rp, 11 hours) via the border crossing at Entikong (Indonesia) and Tebedu (Malaysia). **SJS** (☎ 734626; Jl Sisingamangaraja 155) has the most choices. This is the easiest most cost-efficient way to cross.

Private vehicles and hikers can also cross. The border is open 7.30am to 5pm. Malaysia grants 90-day visas to tourists at the border.

Belawan to Penang

High-speed ferries (one way/return RM140/210, five hours, from 12pm Tuesday, Thursday and Saturday) depart from the port of Belawan, 26km from Medan, to the Malaysian city of Penang.

There is a 35,000Rp surcharge for harbour tax and a complimentary bus transfer to Belawan from Medan. Tickets can be bought from agents on Jl Katamso or Jl SM Raja (see p276). Arriving in Belawan from Penang, the bus transfer to Medan is *not* included in the price. You can take the green *opelet* 81 between Belawan and Medan (8000Rp).

Dumai to Melaka

Melaka-bound ferries depart from the Yos Sudarso port of Dumai three times a day at 8am, 10.30am and 1pm (one way/return 260,000/470,000Rp, two hours). You must check-in at the port two hours before departure in order to clear immigration. The port tax is 3500Rp.

Pekanbaru to Melaka

There are also boats between Pekanbaru (Sumatra) and Melaka, which take around eight hours.

Bengkalis to Melaka

Melaka-bound ferries depart from Bengkalis at least three times a week. Tickets are available from RM50/80 one way/return. Going to Indonesia, confirm whether the visa-on-arrival scheme is in effect.

Riau Islands (Pulau Batam & Pulau Bintan) to Johor Bahru

At Sekupang port on Pulau Batam don't buy a ticket from the many touts and refuse any offers of 'assistance' to see you through immigration.

From Batam Centre ferry terminal there are (almost) hourly morning departures to Johor Bahru in Malaysia (www.zon.com.my/ferry.html; 200,000Rp, six hours) from 7.30am to 12.30pm. Numerous taxis and public minibuses make the run between Sekupang port, Nagoya and the Batam Centre ferry terminal. Malaysian visas are available upon arrival in Johor Bahru.

From Pulau Bintan, there are four boats a day to Johor Bahru (www.zon.com.my/ferry.html; 250,000Rp, eight hours).

our pick **Rumah Makan Darmo** (☎ 737287; Jl Abul Hassan 38; mains 15,000-30,000Rp; 11am-2.30pm & 6-10pm;) Rare Chinese restaurant attuned to individual diners and couples, specialises in fresh seafood, with smoke-free air-con upstairs.

Getting There & Around

Airport taxis cost 35,000Rp, or walk 100m down Jl Gatot Subroto to catch a route B *angkot* (3000Rp). *Angkot* (also called taxis) routes cover main streets.

AIR

KalStar (☎ 742110; Jl Gatot Subroto 80) and **Trigana Air** (☎ 746 721) fly to Berau, Tarakan and Nunukan. Trigana also flies to Balikpapan. **Bintang Sendawar** (☎ 707 0045) flies to Balikpapan and Melak.

Susi Air (☎ 7913282/3) flies to Balikpapan and Long Ampung four times weekly, and Data Dawai three times weekly. Balikpapan has a bigger airport and better connections.

BOAT

Mahakam river boats – called *kapal biasa* or *kapal taxi* – leave by 7am (sometimes 6.30am) from Sungai Kunjang terminal (3km via *angkot* C) for Tenggarong (25,000Rp, two hours), Melak (124,000Rp, 16 hours), Long Iram (155,000Rp, 21 hours) and – sometimes – Long Bagun (250,000Rp, 36 hours).

Pelni (☎ 741402; Jl Yos Sudarso 76) serves Pare Pare (170,000Rp, 24 hours), Surabaya (383,000Rp, three days) and Batu Licin (287,000Rp, two days) in South Kalimantan from the main harbour on Jl Yos Sudarso.

After an early-2009 sinking, private ferry service to/from Pare Pare was suspended. Ask the **harbour master** (☎ 741046; Jl Yos Sudarso 2) for updates and for ships in port that may accept passengers.

BUS

Samarinda has multiple bus terminals. The Sungai Kunjang terminal serves Kota Bangun (23,000Rp, three hours), a short cut to upper Mahakam destinations, and Balikpapan (27,000Rp, 2½ hours). Use the Lempake terminal on *angkot* route B at the north end of town for Bontang (25,000Rp, three hours), Sangatta (30,000Rp, four hours) and Berau (135,000Rp, 20 hours, but takes days during rainy season). Buses leave when full from 6am until early afternoon. Minibuses heading for Sunday afternoon Dayak rituals at Pampang (15,000Rp, one hour) leave from the Segiri terminal at the north end of Jl Pahlawan.

SUNGAI MAHAKAM

Combining cultural and natural wonders, 920km-long Sungai Mahakam is rightly renowned and richly rewarding. Public ferries provide economical access to Dayak tribes of East Kalimantan's interior and to jungle treks. These *kapal biasa* have dormitory-style sleeping decks upstairs. Samarinda is the usual starting point since boats originate there, and independent guides frequent budget hotels. Balikpapan also has good guides; if that's your point of entry, try making arrangements there.

One usual travellers' route is to take a ferry to **Muara Muntai** (100,000Rp, 10 hours from Samarinda), stay overnight, then travel via a smaller boat to **Tanjung Isuy** on the south shore of Danau Jempang. **Louu Taman Jamrot** (Jl Indonesia Australia; r per person 60,000Rp), a longhouse, arts centre and *losmen*, stages dancing in the Kenyah, Kayan and Banuaq Dayak styles – it's touristy but worthwhile. Nearby scenic **Mancong** offers a more authentic longhouse experience; you'll need to bring your own bedding, candles and food.

The critically endangered **Irawaddy dolphin** (*orcaella bervirostris;* known locally as *pesut Mahakam*) with its rounded snout is best spotted around **Muara Pahu** (13 to 14 hours from Samarinda). **Yayasan Konservasi RASI Information Centre** (Foundation for Conservation of Rare Aquatic Species of Indonesia; ☎ 081 253 729 933; www.geocities.com/yayasan_konservasi_rasi) organises dolphin-spotting trips. Fewer than 100 dolphins may remain in the Mahakam.

For a more uncommon adventure, continue to **Melak** (16 hours from Samarinda), the upper Mahakam's biggest town, famous for what remains of **Kersik Luwai Orchid Reserve**, a 20-sq-km black-orchid habitat devastated by fire in 1997–98. From there, ride a minibus to **Eheng**, with a traditional longhouse busiest on Monday nights before the festive Tuesday market. Overnight at the longhouse or in Melak at **Penginapan Rahmat Abadi** (☎ 0545-41007; Jl Tendean; s 30,000Rp, d 55,000-65,000Rp) or **Hotel Flamboyant** (☎ 081 2532 31994; Jl A Yani; r 80,000-130,000Rp;). Nearby **Mencimai** has an excellent museum detailing Banuaq Dayak traditions.

Long Iram, 409km and 21 hours from Samarinda (155,000Rp), is where ferries terminate if the river is low. It's a pleasant 1½-hour walk or 40-minute *ces* (outboard boat) ride (60,000Rp) to Tering, three villages straddling the Mahakam where inhabitants sport elongated earlobes and traditional tattoos. Stay at **Penginapan Wahyu** (Jl Soewondo 57; per person incl breakfast 40,000Rp).

Further upriver find Bahau, Kenyah and Punan longhouses between **Datah Bilang** and **Muara Merak**. **Long Bagun** (1½ days from Samarinda) is the end of the line for river ferries in high water. Continue upriver by motorised canoe or trek to **Long Lunuk**, **Tiong Ohang** and **Long Apari**, the uppermost longhouse settlement on the Mahakam. From there, cross-Borneo trekkers head for West Kalimantan.

TOURS & GUIDES

De'gigant Tours Borneo (☎ 081 2584 6578; www.borneotourgigant.com; Jl Martadinata Rauda 1 No 21) is a tour organiser in Samarinda.

These travel agencies in Balikpapan offer tours:

Puri Tours & Travel (☎ 749540; puri_bpn@indo.net.id; Jl Sutoyo 88)
River Tours (☎ 081 2533 12333; www.borneokalimantan.com)
Transborneo Adventure (☎ 762671; tborneo@indo.net.id; Jl Sudirman 21)

Reliable independent guides in Samarinda:

Jailani (☎ 081 3463 38343; jailani.borneo_tours@yahoo.com; Hotel MJ)
Junaid Nawawi (☎ 081 25363 00057; junaid.nawawi56@yahoo.com; Hotel Pirus; 2-5pm)
Rustam (☎ 735641; 081 2585 4915; rustam_kalimantan@yahoo.co.id)
Suryadi (☎ 081 6459 8263; Hotel Hadiyah I)

BALIKPAPAN

☎ 0542 / pop 450,000

An oil town gushing with some of Kalimantan's best food, nightlife and other expensive treats, Balikpapan bursts with energy. Sungai Mahakam journeys can originate here via Loajanan, and many find Balikpapan more pleasant than Samarinda.

Orientation & Information

The shopping mall, Balikpapan Plaza (corner of Jl Sudirman and Jl Ahmad Yani), is the centre of town. There are plenty of banks that change currencies and have ATMs. Cruise Jl Sudirman for internet places open until at least 10pm.

Agung Sedayu (☎ 420601; agung_sedayu_trv@yahoo.com.sg; Jl Sudirman 28; 7am-9pm) Tops for Pelni info and all boat bookings. Also handles domestic flights.
Gelora Equatorial Travel (GET; ☎ 423251; getbpp@yahoo.com; Jl ARS Muhammad 7) Foreigner-friendly travel and tour agency. Fluent English, Dutch and more.
Global Net (RT2 No 35 Klandasan; per hr 6000Rp; 9am-11pm) Has wi-fi.
Gramedia (2nd fl, Balikpapan Plaza) Maps.

Sleeping

Most hotels are clustered north and west of Balikpapan Plaza, with a clutch of budget places in Gunung Kawi, 2km up Jl Ahmad Yani on *angkot* routes 3 and 5.

Hotel Sinar Lumaian (☎ 736092; Jl Ahmad Yani 5/49; r 75,000-230,000Rp;) Range of well-kept, mainly fan-cooled rooms.

Hotel Aida (☎ 421006; fax 733 940; Jl Ahmad Yani 1/12; r incl breakfast 105,000-275,000Rp;) Long red staircase leads to basic digs popular with students.

Hotel Ayu (☎ 425290; Jl P Antasari 18; r 120,000-180,000Rp;) Cosy hidden gem with a variety of homely layouts, including triples.

our pick **Hotel Gajah Mada** (☎ 734634; fax 734636; Jl Sudirman 328; r 125,000-325,000Rp;) Comfortable, spotless rooms off breezy corridors leading to waterfront terraces and prime location make Gajah Mada a favourite with local travellers. Reservations a must.

Eating

Cheap *warung* abound near the water, particularly around Pasar Klandasan, 500m west of Balikpapan Plaza.

our pick **Warung Mubarokah** (Jl ARS Muhammad; mains 10,000-15,000Rp) Versatile, friendly *warung* on a breezy ridge, with precooked *nasi campur*, fresh grilled fish and chicken, and beef soup bubbling on the cooker.

Wisma Ikan Bakar (Jl Sudirman 16; mains 20,000-45,000Rp; 11am-9.30pm) At 'Grilled Fish Inn' pick fish or seafood from the cooler and enjoy it *lalapan* style with hot sambal and fragrant *kemangi* leaves.

Getting There & Around

Taxis from Sepinggan airport (7km away) cost 35,000Rp.

AIR

Air Asia (☎ 021 5050 5088) Flies to Jakarta.
Batavia Air (☎ 760655, 887 0808; Jl Haryono) Flies to Banjarmasin, Jakarta, Manado, Surabaya, Tarakan and Yogyakarta.

Garuda (☎ 422301; Adika Hotel Bahtera, Jl Sudirman 2) Flies to Jakarta and Makassar.
KalStar (☎ 737473; Jl Sudirman 86) Flies to Samarinda and Tarakan.
Lion Air (☎ 7073761) Flies to Jakarta and Surabaya.
Mandala Air (☎ 410708; Blk H1/04, Jl Sudirman) Flies to Jakarta, Surabaya and Tarakan.
Merpati (☎ 424452; B3-2, Komplek Pantai Mas Permai, Jl Sudirman) Flies to Makassar.
SilkAir (☎ 730800; Hotel Gran Senyiur, Jl ARS Muhammad 7) Flies daily to Singapore.
Sriwijaya Air (☎ 749777; H2/4 Komplek Balikpapan Permai) Flies to Jakarta, Makassar, Palu, Surabaya and Tarakan.
Trigana Air (☎ 762298) Flies to Banjarmasin and Kota Baru.

BOAT

Agung Sedayu (opposite) is the best source for all nautical transport information and tickets.

Dharma Lautan (☎ 423292; Ruko Tanah Citra Rapat, Jl Sukarno-Hatta) runs ferries twice weekly to Surabaya (275,000Rp, 36 hours) and weekly to Makassar (175,000Rp, 24 hours). **Prima Vista** (☎ 732607; Jl Sudirman 138) serves Pare Pare (190,000Rp), Makassar and Surabaya. **Pelni** (☎ 424171; Jl Yos Sudarso 76) sails to Makassar, Pare Pare (14 hours), Tarakan (195,000Rp, 24 hours), Pantoloan (115,000, 12 hours), Surabaya, and beyond.

BUS

Buses to Samarinda (economy/air-con 22,000/27,000Rp, 2½ hours) leave from Batu Ampar bus terminal at the north end of town. Buses to Banjarmasin (economy/air-con 130,000/150,000Rp, 12 hours) leave from a terminal on Jl Sukarno-Hatta. Use *angkot* route 3 for both.

BANJARMASIN

☎ 0511 / pop 607,000

Beyond its space-age mosque, office towers and extensive air links. Banjarmasin's back streets still teem with old-time charm. The city is also known as the Venice of Asia for its network of canals featuring stilt houses teetering over the water. This heartland of Banjar culture is also the gateway to scenic trekking in the Dayak villages of Pegunungan Meratus (Meratus Mountains).

Orientation & Information

Banks exchanging money and ATMs cluster along Jl Lambung Mangkurat.

Adi Angkasa Travel (☎ 436 6100; fax 436 6200; Jl Hasanudin 27) Flight bookings and contact for independent guide Tailah.
Apotek Piala (☎ 436 7500; Jl Haryono 3A) Top chemist.
Family Tour & Travel (☎ 326 8923; www.bestborneotour.com; Komp Aspol Bina Brata 1E, Jl A Yani) Flights and tours throughout Kalimantan. Helpful owner Syamsuddinnor speaks English.
Gramedia (Jl Veteran 55-61 & Duta Mall) Maps.
Rumah Sakit Ulin (☎ 325 2180; www.rsudulin.com; Jl A Yani Km 2 No 43) Clinic.
Tekat Aneng Samudera (☎ 327 2330; Jl Pramuka 21) At the Km 6 bus terminal, Ibu Yuni and her team sort air, sea and ground transport.
Warnet Kyagi (Jl Pangeran Samudera 94-96; per hr 3000Rp; 🕒 8am-midnight Sun-Fri & 8am-2am Sat) Internet access.

Sights & Activities

Banjarmasin's top attractions are **Pasar Kuin** and **Pasar Lokbaintan floating markets** (🕒 5-9am), as well as **canal tours** to observe residents of the stilt homes that line the waterways washing dishes, clothing and themselves in a joyful festival of smiles, splashes and high fives.

Pasar Baru, a market and harbour area, is a hub of daytime activity, seguing from late afternoon into **Belauran Niaga** (Niaga Night Market; Jl Niaga & Jl Katamso). Guided canal tours at early-morning or late-afternoon washing time run about two hours and start at 75,000Rp per person. Floating market tours cost around 100,000Rp and usually offer a stop at **Pulau Kembang**, home to an aggressive troop of long-tailed macaques.

Sleeping

Cheap sleeps are clustered around Belaruan Niaga or Pasar Pagi off Jl Pangeran Antasari.

Hotel Perdana (☎ 335 2376; perdanahotel@plasa.com; Jl Katamso 8; r incl breakfast 70,000-325,000Rp; ❄) Best of the *belaruan* budget bunch, spotless Perdana is a sweet deal with free afternoon cake, TV and private bathroom for all; economy rooms have fan only.

Hotel Asia Baru (☎ 325 3260; asiabaru_hotel@yahoo.co.id; Jl Sugiono 48; r 85,000-155,000Rp; ❄) Sleek new place near Pasar Pagi has Western bathroom and 42 TV channels in every room.

More choices:

Hotel Niaga (☎ 335 2595; Jl Niaga 14; s/d/tr 35,000-40,000/60,000/75,000Rp) Clean and basic.
Hotel Niagara (☎ 335 6355; Jl Katamso 1; s 35,000-60,000Rp, d 60,000-80,000Rp; ❄) The upmarket cousin has some air-con rooms.

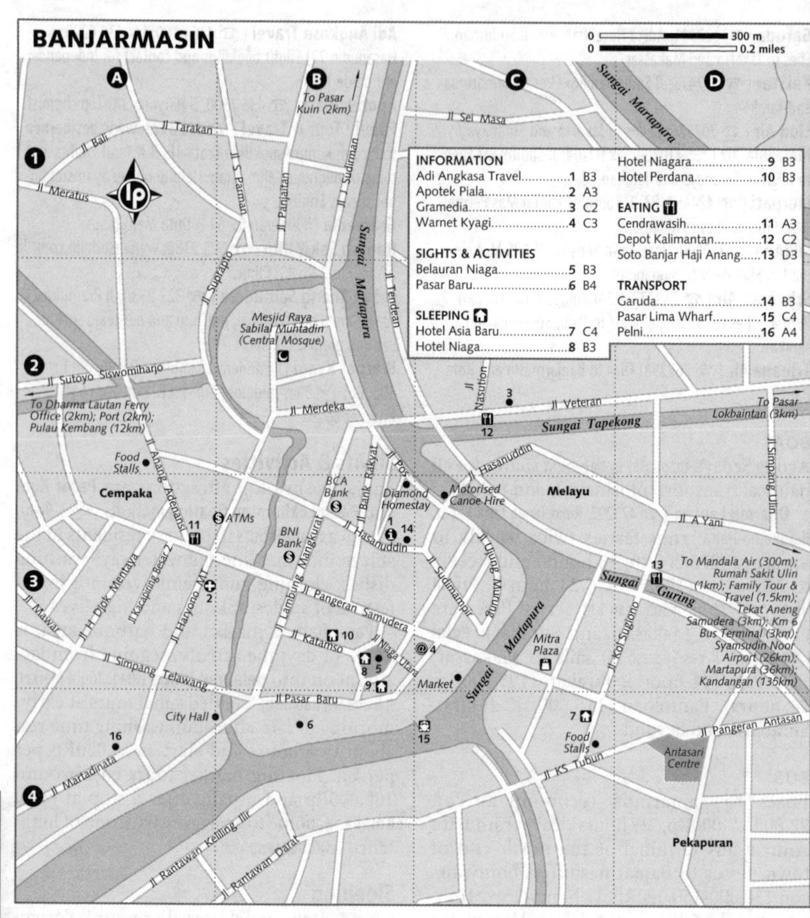

Eating & Drinking

Banjar cuisine combines unique dishes, such as *bingka barandum* (boiled pancakes), and twists on Indonesian standards like grilled fish and fried chicken. Pasar Wadai, the cake market outside the main mosque during Ramadan, is famous throughout Indonesia. Sample these sweets year-round at Jl Niaga *belauran,* or nail some at a floating market.

Depot Kalimantan (☎ 325 8286; Jl Veteran 19; mains 8000-15,000Rp; ☒) Bright, air-con, nonsmoking refuge for Banjar and Chinese dishes plus fruit juices. Popular with families and couples.

our pick **Soto Banjar Haji Anang** (Jl Pekapuran; mains 15,000-20,000Rp; 🕓 6am-5.30pm Sat-Thu) Riverside *warung* renowned for *soto banjar* with a full chicken piece, not a few shavings. Broth here is savoury, *lontong* lush, home-made sambal scorching.

Cendrawasih (Jl Pangeran Samudera; mains 15,000-30,000Rp) Delve deeper into Banjar cuisine at this renowned spot. Pick fish, seafood or chicken for grilling, served with an array of Banjar sauces.

Getting There & Around

Taxis cost 70,000Rp to or from the airport, located 26km from the centre of town. Alternatively, take an *angkot* from Jl Pasar Baru to Km 6 bus terminal, then a Martapura-bound *colt* to the branch road leading to the airport and walk (1.5km).

AIR

Garuda (☎ 335 9065; Jl Hasanudin 13) Flies to Jakarta.
KalStar (☎ 436 4465) Flies to Ketapang, Pangkalan Bun and Pontianak.
Lion Air (☎ 470 5277) Flies to Jakarta.
Mandala Air (☎ 326 6737; Jl A Yani Km 3) Flies to Surabaya, Yogyakarta.
Susi Air (☎ 081 1211 3080; info@susiair.com) Flies to Muara Teweh continuing to Palangka Raya.
Trigana Air (☎ 757 6249) Flies to Balikpapan, Kota Baru.

BOAT

Pelni (☎ 335 3077; Jl Martadinata 10) sails weekly to Semarang (333,000Rp, 24 hours) from Trisakti Harbour (3km away) on Sungai Barito. **Dharma Lautan Utama** (☎ 442 0547; Jl Yos Sudarso 8) and **Prima Vista** (☎ 335 9487; Jl Sutoyo 1) ferries depart for Surabaya (235,000Rp, 18 hours) on alternate days.

Longboats from Sudi Mampir wharf leave for Marabahan (15,000Rp, six hours) Monday and Tuesday at 9am, and from Pasar Lima wharf to Negara (20,000Rp, 18 hours) Tuesday and Saturday at 1pm.

BUS

The main bus terminal is at Jl A Yani Km 6, southeast of downtown. *Colts* (minibuses) depart frequently for Banjarbaru (16,000Rp, 25 minutes), Martapura (16,000Rp, 35 minutes), Kandangan (30,000Rp, four hours), Negara (35,000Rp, five hours) and other Pegunungan Meratus destinations.

Buses depart from here for Balikpapan (economy/air-con 110,000/165,000Rp, 10 hours), Samarinda (135,000/180,000Rp, 13 hours), Muara Teweh (125,000/150,000Rp, 12 hours), Palangka Raya (60,000/75,000Rp, five hours) and Pangkalan Bun (125,000/165,000Rp, 17 hours).

AROUND BANJARMASIN

Three sights near Banjarmasin can be combined into a day trip by *colt*. Banjarbaru's **Museum Lambung Mangkurat** (Jl Ahmad Yani 36; admission 5000Rp; ⌚ 9.30am-2.30pm Tue-Thu, Sat & Sun, 9.30-11am Fri, closed Mon), on the road to Martapura, features Banjar and Dayak artefacts, plus statues excavated from pre-Islamic Hindu temples. **Cempaka mines** (⌚ closed Fri), 43km south of Banjarmasin, show the dark side of diamonds. Miners labour in muddy water – often up to their necks – sifting for gold, agates and gems. Stone shops at **Martapura market** sell local finds. This Friday market also sees brightly dressed Banjar women amid a cornucopia of exotic fruit.

For nature enthusiasts, Banjarmasin is the launch point for treks into **Pegunungan Meratus**, a 2500-sq-km mountain range. Tailah at Adi Angkasa Travel (p323) in Banjarmasin can arrange treks.

To go independently, take a *colt* to Kandangan, then a pick-up (15,000Rp, 1½ hours) to Loksado, a small village that's literally the end of the road. **Amat** (☎ 081 3487 66573) assists tourists in Loksado. He can point you in the right direction for treks through breathtaking primary forest, overnighting in village homestays. Many trips end with bamboo rafting down Sungai Amandit to Muara Tanuhi and a dip in the hot-spring pool there.

PONTIANAK

☎ 0561 / pop 520,000

Situated bang on the equator, Pontianak is a gateway to Dayak settlements in wild Kapuas Hulu (Upper Kapuas River) and South China Sea beaches. But KalBar's capital is also Kalimantan's most ardently urban destination and has a vibrant, compact city centre. Pontianak buzzes with commerce driven by produce from the interior, displayed at fruit stalls peddling whatever has made its way downriver on that particular morning, and fabulous food in *warung* and street stalls, mixing Dayak, Malay and Chinese cooking, all washed down with coffee and conversation at kerbside tables.

Orientation & Information

Pontianak's inner core is centred along Jl Gajah Mada. Main streets have banks and ATMs aplenty, while various newsstands and bookstores stock city and regional maps.

Aria Tour (☎ 577868; Jl Gaja Mada 3) Local jetsetters' pick for flights.
Centrine Online (off Jl Nusa Indah III; per hr 3500Rp; ⌚ 7.30am-10pm; ⊠) Signposted in a short alley.
Kalimantan Barat tourist office (☎ 736172; Jl Sutoyo 17) English-speaking staffer Pak Iwan presses pamphlets and ambitious itineraries.
Klinik Kharitas Bhakti (☎ 734373; Jl Siam 153) Clinic.
Spectra Gaming & Internet (Jl Jendral Urip; per hr 3000Rp; ⌚ 24hr; ⊠)
Times Tours & Travel (☎ 770259; www.timestravelpnk.com) Delivers air tickets, organises tours to Kapuas Hulu and beyond.

OUR ORANGE COUSINS AT TANJUNG PUTING

Once ranging across Southeast Asia, orang-utans survive only on Sumatra and Borneo, threatened by destruction of their rainforest habitat. Borneo has several spots for seeing orang-utans, but the best place here and on earth is Tanjung Puting National Park.

An oasis amid mining, logging and oil-palm plantations, Tanjung Puting harbours gibbons, macaques, sun bears, clouded leopards, proboscis monkeys, crocodiles, hundreds of bird species and brilliant butterflies. The park's three research camps attract orang-utans with daily handouts of bananas, cassava and milk. Guided jungle treks reveal more wildlife and, especially in February and March, wild orchids.

Visiting Tanjung Puting begins with registration at Pangkalan Bun's police station. Bring photocopies of your passport and visa. (Airport taxi drivers know the steps.) Next stop, the **PHKA office** (national parks office; ☎ 61500; Jl HM Idris, Kumai; 🕑 7am-2pm Mon-Thu, 7am-11am Fri, call ahead for weekend arrivals). Park registration costs 65,000Rp per person per day, 35,000Rp for cameras and 5000Rp per day for a *klotok* (15,000Rp for a speedboat).

Bali-based **Friends of the National Parks Foundation** (☎ 29953, 0361-977978; www.fnpf.org; Jl Malijo) supports **Tegari Lestari** (☎ 081 2516 4727; tegari_lestari@yahoo.co.id) in Tajung Harapan, a village across from the orang-utan camp. It runs ecotourism programs.

The best way to appreciate Tanjung Puting is staying aboard a *klotok*. These 8m wooden boats offer basic comforts for up to four adults and a put-putting motor straight out of *African Queen*. Sleep on deck, with mattresses under mosquito nets, jungle sounds your lullaby and morning alarm.

Rent a *klotok* in Kumai, near Pangkalan Bun. Budget 725,000Rp daily, including boat, captain, park fees and options such as food, cook and English-speaking guide. Booking gets more difficult May to August and during Indonesian school holidays.

Kumai is easily reached from Pangkalan Bun by minibus (10,000Rp, 35 minutes). Taxis from Pangkalan Bun airport cost 150,000Rp, including all stops for visiting Tanjung Punting National Park. You can get to Pangkalan Bun from Banjarmasin by bus (125,000Rp, 17 to 19 hours). You can fly from Banjarmasin (p325) or Pontianak (below) for about 600,000Rp.

Travel and tour companies offer bookings and packages that make visits fairly easy:

Borneo Holidays (☎ 29673, 081 2500 0508; harnovia@yahoo.com) In Pangkalan Bun.
Family Tour & Travel (p323) In Banjarmasin.
Rivertours (p322) In Balikpapan.
Times Tours and Travel (p325) In Pontianak.

INDONESIA

Sleeping & Eating

Warung and stalls abound along major streets and surrounds, with Jl Diponegoro/H Agus Salim, Jl Pattimura, Jl Hijas and Jl Setia Budi.

Hotel Patrisia (☎ 736063; Jl Cokroaminoto 497; r 50,000-85,000Rp; ❄) Clean, sparse rooms, all with private (some Western) bathrooms and two beds. Higher rate buys air-con and TV.

Mess Hijas (☎ 744068, 081 2569 6003; Jl Hijas 106; r 75,000-135,000Rp; ❄) Every room at this business-traveller favourite includes air-con, TV and Western bathroom, many with hot water, plus a friendly, efficient vibe throughout.

Hotel Merpati (☎ 745481; Jl Imam Bonjol 111; r 84,000-156,000Rp; ❄ 📶) Budget rooms include air-con and private *mandi*. More expensive rooms are good value.

our pick Oukie (Jl Nusah Indah I; mains 10,000-16,000Rp; 🕑 6am-5pm, closed Mon) Third-generation local institution serving noodles at the intersection of Indonesian and Chinese cooking.

Getting There & Around

Airport taxis cost 70,000Rp to town (15km). *Opelet* (2500Rp) routes converge around Jl Sisingamangaraja.

AIR

Batavia (☎ 734488; Jl Cokroaminoto 278A) Flies to Jakarta, Kuching and Yogyakarta.
Garuda (☎ 734986; Jl Tanjungpura) Flies to Jakarta.
IAT (☎ 762247; Jl Juanda 40) To Ketapang, Pangkalan Bun.
KalStar (☎ 739090; Jl Tanjungpura 429) Flies to Banjarmasin, Ketapang and Pangkalan Bun.
Lion Air (☎ 7066111) Flies to Jakarta.

BOAT

Boats to Java leave from the main harbour on Jl Pak Kasih, north of the Kartika Hotel. **Prima**

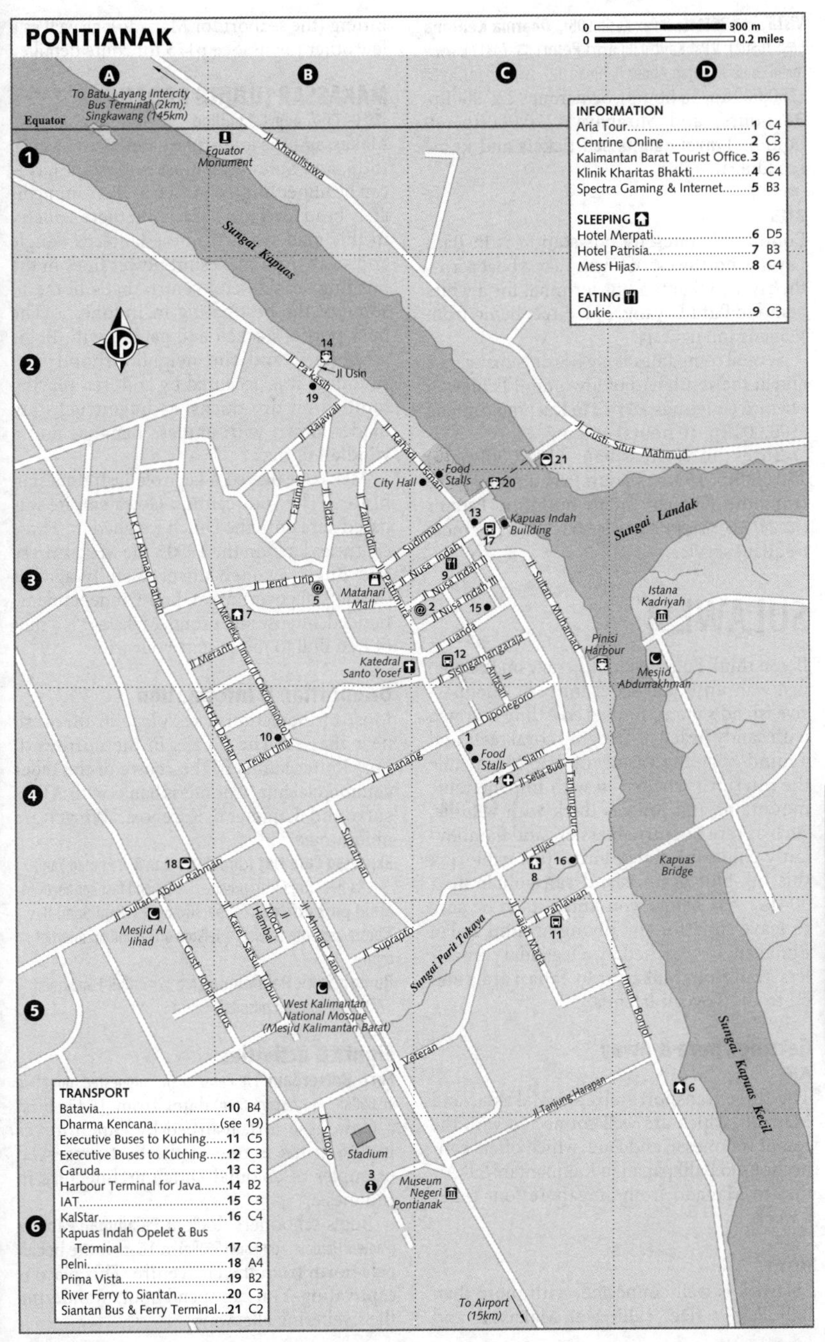
PONTIANAK
0 300 m
0 0.2 miles
INFORMATION
Aria Tour....1 C4
Centrine Online....2 C3
Kalimantan Barat Tourist Office.3 B6
Klinik Kharitas Bhakti....4 C4
Spectra Gaming & Internet....5 B3
SLEEPING
Hotel Merpati....6 D5
Hotel Patrisia....7 B3
Mess Hijas....8 C4
EATING
Oukie....9 C3
TRANSPORT
Batavia....10 B4
Dharma Kencana....(see 19)
Executive Buses to Kuching....11 C5
Executive Buses to Kuching....12 C3
Garuda....13 C3
Harbour Terminal for Java....14 B2
IAT....15 C3
KalStar....16 C4
Kapuas Indah Opelet & Bus Terminal....17 C3
Pelni....18 A4
Prima Vista....19 B2
River Ferry to Siantan....20 C3
Siantan Bus & Ferry Terminal....21 C2
To Batu Layang Intercity Bus Terminal (2km); Singkawang (145km)
Equator
Equator Monument
Sungai Kapuas
Jl Khatulistiwa
Jl Usin
Jl Pa'kasih
Jl Rajawali
Jl Fatimah
Jl Sidas
Jl Zainuddin
Jl Rahadi Usman
City Hall
Food Stalls
Jl Gusti Situt Mahmud
Sungai Landak
Kapuas Indah Building
Jl Sudirman
Jl Nusa Indah I
Jl Nusa Indah II
Jl Nusa Indah III
Jl Jend Urip
Matahari Mall
Jl Pattimura
Jl KH Ahmad Dahlan
Jl Merdeka Timur (Jl Cokroaminoto)
Jl Meranti
Jl Juanda
Jl Sisingamangaraja
Jl Antasari
Katedral Santo Yosef
Jl Sultan Muhamad
Pinisi Harbour
Istana Kadriyah
Mesjid Abdurrakhman
Jl KHA Dahlan
Jl Teuku Umar
Jl Diponegoro
Jl Lelanang
Food Stalls
Jl Siam
Jl Setia Budi
Jl Tanjungpura
Jl Suprapman
Jl Hijas
Kapuas Bridge
Jl Sultan Abdur Rahman
Mesjid Al Jihad
Jl Moch Hambal
Jl Karel Satsui Tubun
Jl Ahmad Yani
Jl Suprapto
Sungai Parit Tokaya
Jl Gajah Mada
Jl Pahlawan
Jl Gusti Johan Idrus
West Kalimantan National Mosque (Mesjid Kalimantan Barat)
Jl Imam Bonjol
Sungai Kapuas Kecil
Jl Veteran
Jl Tanjung Harapan
Jl Sutoyo
Stadium
Museum Negeri Pontianak
To Airport (15km)

INDONESIA

Vista (☎ 761145; Jl Pak Kasih 90B), **Dharma Kencana** (☎ 765021; Jl Pak Kasih 42F) and **Pelni** (☎ 748124; www.pelni.co.id; Jl Sultan Abdur Rahman 12) serve Jakarta (250,000Rp, 36 hours), Semarang (225,000Rp, 34 hours) and Surabaya (270,000Rp, 40 hours). Travel agents sell tickets and know schedule details.

BUS

Pontianak's intercity bus station is in Batu Layang, northwest of town. Take a boat across the river to Siantan bus terminal for a white bemo to Batu Layang, or a direct bemo from Jl Sisingamangaraja.

Several companies along Jl Sisingamangaraja and at the south end of town on Jl Pahlawan offer executive bus service to Kuching, Sintang (100,000Rp, 10 hours) and more.

Buses to Putussibau (175,000Rp to 270,000Rp, 16 to 18 hours) via Sintang leave from the Kapuas Indah building. **Perintis** (☎ 767 886; Komplek Kapuas Indah 1-2) has the most frequent service.

SULAWESI

If you think Sulawesi looks crazy on the map just wait until you see it for real. The massive island's many-limbed coastline is drawn with sandy beaches, fringing coral reefs and a mind-boggling variety of fish. Meanwhile the interior is shaded in with impenetrable mountains and jungles thick with wildlife, such as rare nocturnal tarsiers and flamboyantly colourful maleo birds. Just exploring this ink-blot of an island can gobble up a 30-day visa before you know it, so be sure to leave time for the diving around Pulau Bunaken; it's reached by a legendary travellers' trail from Makassar to Tana Toraja and on to the Togean Islands.

Getting There & Away

AIR

The three transport hubs are Makassar and Manado, which are well connected with the rest of Indonesia, and Palu, which offers connections to Balikpapan in Kalimantan. SilkAir flies to Manado from Singapore four times a week.

BOAT

Sulawesi is well connected, with more than half Pelni's fleet calling at Makassar and Bitung (the seaport for Manado), as well as a few other towns. See p175 for route details.

MAKASSAR (UJUNG PADANG)

☎ 0411 / pop 1.6 million

Makassar – the long-time gateway to Eastern Indo, and Sulawesi's most important city – can be unnerving, so most travellers immediately head for Tana Toraja. But there's poetry in this mad swirl. Chinese lanterns dangle and sway from makeshift power lines in the bustling seaside city centre that's home to some of the best eating in Indonesia. The busy port is stacked and packed with Bugis schooners, and the neighbourhood surrounding it is accented by children playing football on dry docks, as huge trucks are loaded down with endless bananas and a windfall of rice.

Makassar played a key role in Indonesian history. The 16th-century Gowa empire was based here until the Dutch weighed in. Three centuries later, in the 1950s, the Makassarese and Bugis revolted unsuccessfully against the central government. Loud, independent-minded, intense and proud, Makassar is a shot of Red Bull to jump-start your trip.

Orientation & Information

Most of the action takes place in the west, near the sea. The port is in the northwest; Fort Rotterdam is in the centre of the older commercial hub. Countless banks with ATMs surround Lapangan Karebosi. *Wartel* are ubiquitous.

Expresso Cafe Net (cnr Jl Pasar Ikan & Jl Ahmad Yani; 8am-12am) Clean private booths and fast connections.

Main post office (Jl Slamet Riyadi; 8am-9pm) Has a poste-restante service, a Telkom office and an internet centre.

Rumah Sakit Pelamonia (☎ 324710; Jl J Sudirman 27) Well-equipped hospital.

Sights & Activities

Fort Rotterdam (Jl Pasar Ikan; suggested donation 10,000Rp; 7.30am-6pm) dates from 1545. First a Gowanese fort, usurped by Dutch forces in 1667, this is one of the best-preserved examples of colonial Dutch architecture in Indonesia.

Bugis schooners dock at **Pelabuhan Paotere** (Paotere Harbour; admission 500Rp), a 15-minute becak ride north from the city centre. This place is captivating. You can spend hours wandering the sweltering alleyways.

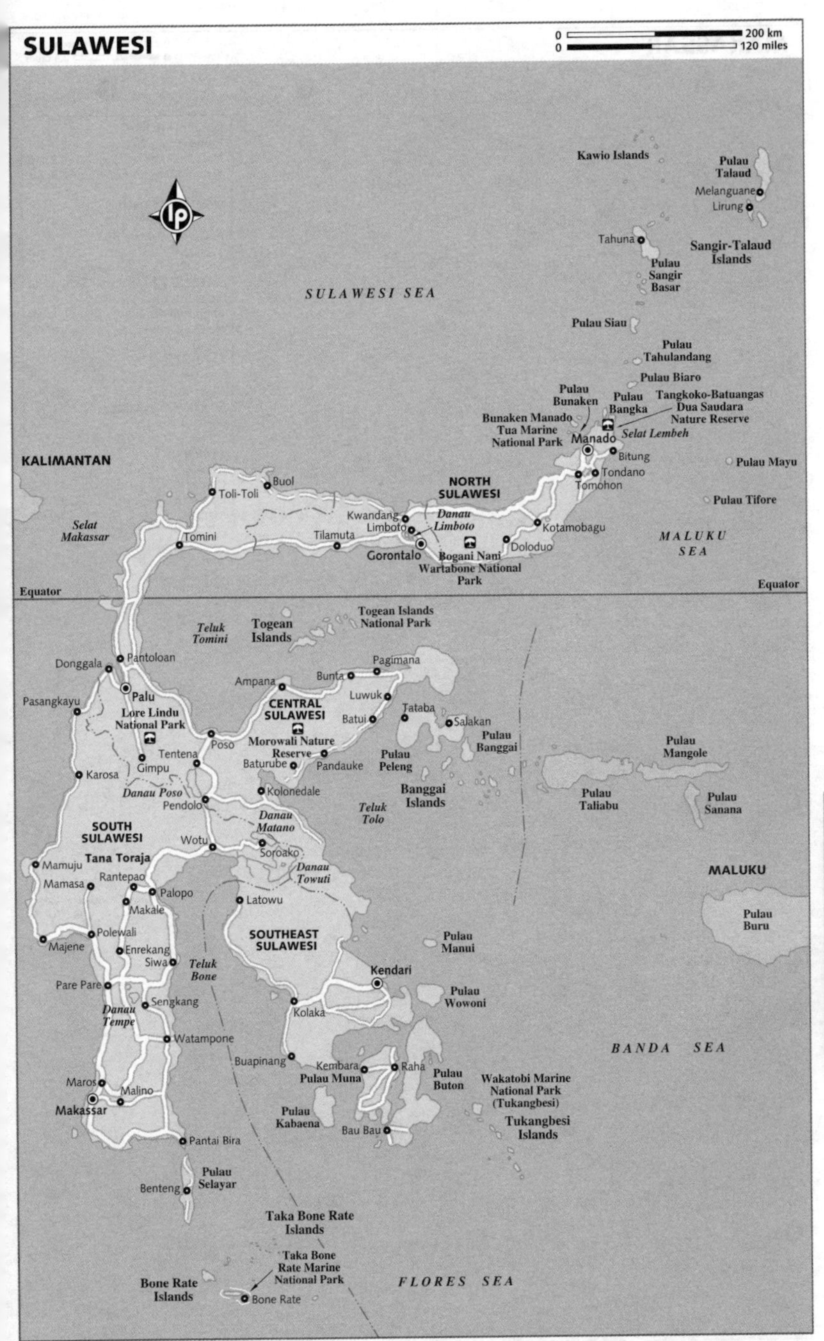
SULAWESI
0 200 km
0 120 miles
SULAWESI SEA
Kawio Islands
Pulau Talaud
Melanguane
Lirung
Tahuna
Sangir-Talaud Islands
Pulau Sangir Basar
Pulau Siau
Pulau Tahulandang
Pulau Biaro
Pulau Bunaken
Pulau Bangka
Tangkoko-Batuangas Dua Saudara Nature Reserve
Bunaken Manado Tua Marine National Park
Manado
Selat Lembeh
Bitung
Tondano
Tomohon
Pulau Mayu
Pulau Tifore
KALIMANTAN
NORTH SULAWESI
Buol
Toli-Toli
Kwandang
Limboto
Danau Limboto
Kotamobagu
Doloduo
Tilamuta
Gorontalo
Bogani Nani Wartabone National Park
Tomini
Selat Makassar
MALUKU SEA
Equator
Equator
Togean Islands
Togean Islands National Park
Teluk Tomini
Pagimana
Bunta
Ampana
Luwuk
Donggala
Pantoloan
Palu
CENTRAL SULAWESI
Tataba
Salakan
Batui
Pasangkayu
Lore Lindu National Park
Poso
Morowali Nature Reserve
Pulau Banggai
Pulau Mangole
Tentena
Baturube
Pandauke
Pulau Peleng
Gimpu
Karosa
Kolonedale
Banggai Islands
Pulau Taliabu
Pulau Sanana
Danau Poso
Pendolo
Danau Matano
Teluk Tolo
SOUTH SULAWESI
Wotu
Soroako
Mamuju
Tana Toraja
Danau Towuti
MALUKU
Rantepao
Mamasa
Palopo
Makale
Latowu
Pulau Buru
Polewali
SOUTHEAST SULAWESI
Majene
Enrekang
Pulau Manui
Siwa
Teluk Bone
Kendari
Pare Pare
Sengkang
Pulau Wowoni
Kolaka
Danau Tempe
Watampone
BANDA SEA
Buapinang
Kembara
Raha
Pulau Muna
Pulau Buton
Wakatobi Marine National Park (Tukangbesi)
Maros
Malino
Makassar
Pulau Kabaena
Bau Bau
Tukangbesi Islands
Pantai Bira
Pulau Selayar
Benteng
Taka Bone Rate Islands
Taka Bone Rate Marine National Park
Bone Rate Islands
Bone Rate
FLORES SEA
INDONESIA

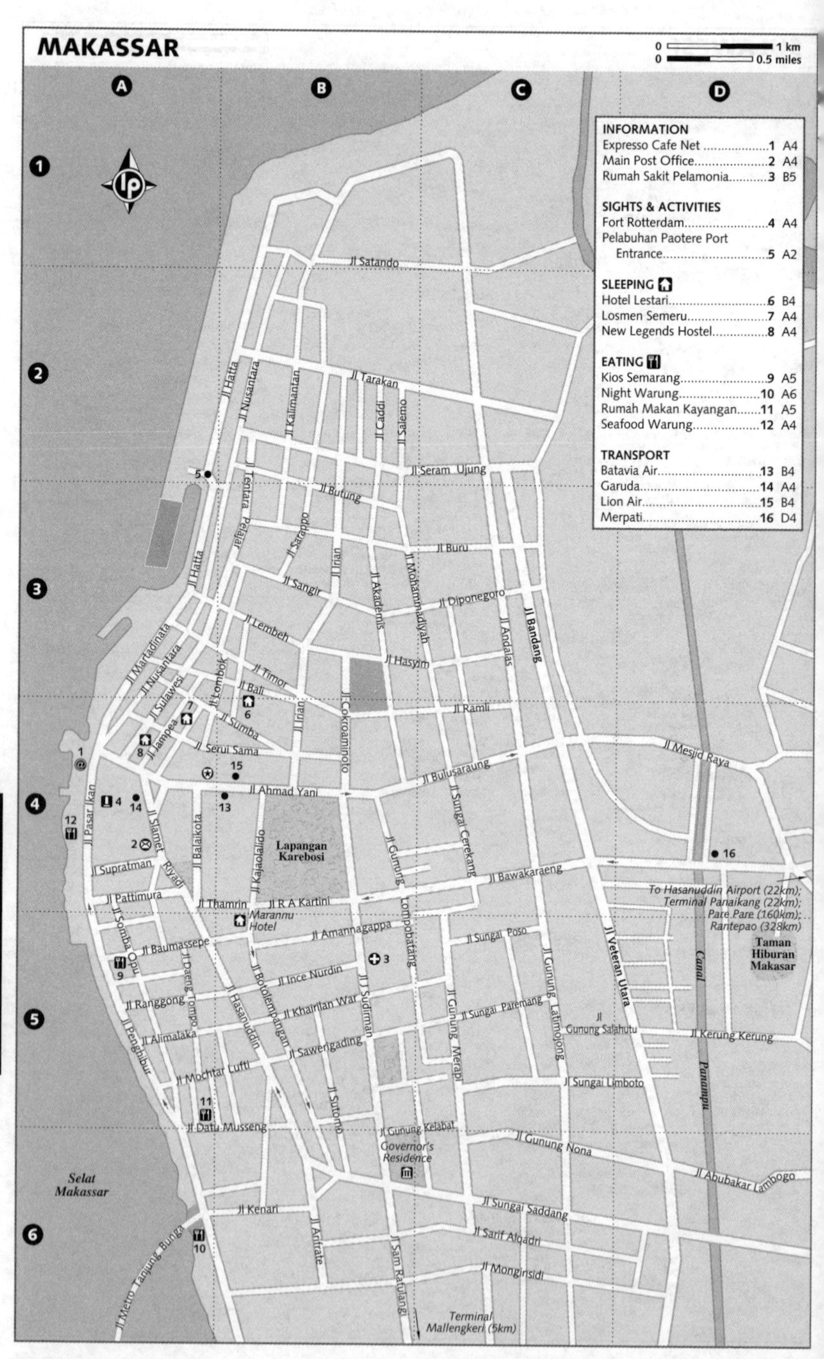
MAKASSAR
0 1 km
0 0.5 miles
INFORMATION
Expresso Cafe Net 1 A4
Main Post Office 2 A4
Rumah Sakit Pelamonia 3 B5
SIGHTS & ACTIVITIES
Fort Rotterdam 4 A4
Pelabuhan Paotere Port Entrance 5 A2
SLEEPING
Hotel Lestari 6 B4
Losmen Semeru 7 A4
New Legends Hostel 8 A4
EATING
Kios Semarang 9 A5
Night Warung 10 A6
Rumah Makan Kayangan 11 A5
Seafood Warung 12 A4
TRANSPORT
Batavia Air 13 B4
Garuda 14 A4
Lion Air 15 B4
Merpati 16 D4
Jl Satando
Jl Tarakan
Jl Hatta
Jl Nusantara
Jl Kalimantan
Jl Caddi
Jl Salemo
Jl Seram Ujung
Jl Butung
Jl Tentara Pelajar
Jl Sarappo
Jl Buru
Jl Irian
Jl Akademis
Jl Mohammadiyah
Jl Sangir
Jl Diponegoro
Jl Bandang
Jl Andalas
Jl Lembeh
Jl Martadinata
Jl Hasyim
Jl Timor
Jl Lombok
Jl Sulawesi
Jl Bali
Jl Ramli
Jl Cokroaminoto
Jl Sumba
Jl Jampea
Jl Serui Sama
Jl Mesjid Raya
Jl Bulusaraung
Jl Ahmad Yani
Jl Pasar Ikan
Jl Slamet Riyadi
Jl Balaikota
Jl Kajaolalido
Lapangan Karebosi
Jl Gunung Lompobatang
Jl Sungai Cerekang
Jl Supratman
Jl Bawakaraeng
To Hasanuddin Airport (22km); Terminal Panaikang (22km); Pare Pare (160km); Rantepao (328km)
Jl Pattimura
Jl Thamrin
Jl R A Kartini
Marannu Hotel
Jl Somba Opu
Jl Amannagappa
Jl Sungai Poso
Taman Hiburan Makasar
Jl Baumassepe
Jl Veteran Utara
Canal
Jl Daeng Tompo
Jl Ince Nurdin
Jl Hasanuddin
Jl Botolempangan
Jl Ranggong
Jl Khairilan War
Jl Sudirman
Jl Gunung Merapi
Jl Sungai Paremang
Jl Gunung Latimojong
Jl Gunung Salahutu
Jl Kerung Kerung
Panampu
Jl Alimalaka
Jl Penghibur
Jl Sawerigading
Jl Mochtar Lufti
Jl Sutomo
Jl Sungai Limboto
Jl Datu Musseng
Jl Gunung Kelabat
Governor's Residence
Jl Gunung Nona
Selat Makassar
Jl Abubakar Lambogo
Jl Kenari
Jl Sungai Saddang
Jl Metro Tanjung Bunga
Jl Arifrate
Jl Sam Ratulangi
Jl Sarif Alqadri
Jl Monginsidi
Terminal Mallengkeri (5km)

INDONESIA

Sleeping

New Legends Hostel (☎ 313777; Jl Jampea 5G; dm 65,000, r 90,000-125,000Rp; ❄) Catering to backpackers, this clean and very helpful place has rooms and dorms, but they are small, windowless and boxlike.

Losmen Semeru (☎ 318113; Jl Jampea 28; r 70,000Rp; ❄) This long-running budget stalwart still offers some of the best basic crash pads in town. Rooms are miniscule but have TV, attached Indonesian-style bathroom and air-con.

Hotel Lestari (☎ 327337; Jl Savu 16; r 145,000-200,000Rp; ❄) Freshly painted rooms all with satellite TV, minibar, hot water and air-con are among the best deals in Makassar.

Eating & Drinking

For many it's the food that makes Makassar a great destination. There's an abundance of seafood, Chinese dishes and local 'specialities' such as *coto makassar* (soup made from buffalo innards).

Hundreds of night *warung* just off Jl Metro Tanjung Bunga serve up fresh and cheap Indonesian and Chinese meals. Just as good is the string of makeshift seafood *warung* set up every night on the foreshore opposite Fort Rotterdam.

Kios Semarang (Jl Penghibur; mains 15,000-35,000Rp; 🕑 lunch & dinner) The closest thing to a Makassar institution, climb the stairs to the 3rd floor where you will be rewarded with a rowdy crowd, good seafood and cheap beer. Start with a sunset and a Bintang or two before trying the fresh squid or prawns.

Rumah Makan Kayangan (☎ 325273; Jl Datu Musseng 20; fish from 20,000Rp; 🕑 lunch & dinner) Kayangan is a slightly more upmarket affair, with tablecloths and air-con. The fish is fresh, the service swift and the Bintangs are ice cold.

Getting There & Away

AIR

Makassar is well connected to the rest of Indonesia. Airlines include:

Batavia Air (☎ 365 5255; Jl Ahmad Yani 35) Flies to Gorontalo, Luwuk and Jayapura.

Garuda (☎ 365 4747; Jl Slamet Riyadi 6) Flies to Manado, Denpasar, Jakarta, Jayapura and Biak.

Lion Air (☎ 327038; Jl Ahmad Yani 22) Flies to Manado, Kendari, Gorontalo, Palu, Jakarta, Surabaya and Denpasar.

Merpati (☎ 442892; Jl Bawakaraeng) Flies to Jakarta, Balikpapan, Kendari, Surabaya, Luwuk, Palu and Yogyakarta.

Sriwijaya Air (☎ 424800; Jl Blvd Raya 23) Flies to Surabaya, Palu, Gorontalo, Kendari and Ambon.

BOAT

Pelni (☎ 331401; Jl Sam Ratulangi; 🕑 8am-2pm Mon-Sat) has connections to countless destinations across Indonesia, including Surabaya, Jakarta, East Kalimantan, Ambon and Papua. See p175 for details.

BUS

Buses heading north leave from Terminal Panaikang, aka Terminal Daya, in the eastern suburbs, to Pare Pare (24,300Rp, three hours), Sengkang (38,000Rp, four hours) and Rantepao (51,600Rp, eight hours). **Bintang Prima** (☎ 47728) buses are the most comfortable choice in which to make the 330km journey to Rantepao. Get here by grabbing a blue *pete-pete* from Makassar Mall (2000Rp, 30 minutes).

Southbound buses leave from Terminal Mallengkeri, 10km southeast of the centre, a 3000Rp bemo ride.

Getting Around

Hasanuddin airport is 22km east of the city centre, 80,000Rp by taxi or 5000Rp by *pete-pete*. The main *pete-pete* station is at Makassar Mall, and the standard fare is 2000Rp. Becak drivers/hawkers can be charming and exhausting all at once. Their shortest fare is 3000Rp. Taxis are metered.

TANA TORAJA

Get ready for a dizzying cocktail of stunning serene beauty, elaborate, brutal and captivating funeral rites, exquisite traditional architecture and a profoundly peculiar fascination with the dead. It comes garnished with a pinch of Indiana Jones intrigue, and is served by some of the warmest and toughest people you'll ever meet: the Torajans. Life for the Torajans revolves around death and their days are spent earning the money to send away their dead properly. During funeral season, in July and August, the tourist numbers swell to uncomfortable proportions and prices soar, but the rest of the year it's empty and starved for visitors, which means grateful hosts, good deals and a frontierlike appeal.

The capital, Makale, and Rantepao, the largest town and tourist magnet, are the main centres. Bemo link them to surrounding villages, where you'll find cultural hot spots tucked into spectacular countryside (see boxed text, p333).

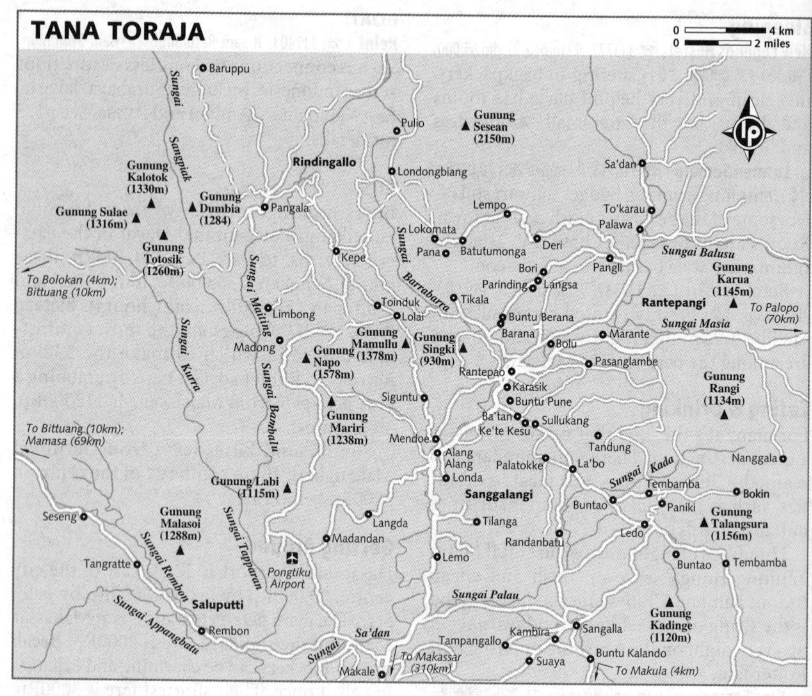

Rantepao

☎ 0423 / pop 45,000

With a variety of budget lodging and solid public transport, Rantepao is the best base for exploring Tana Toraja. There is one unforgettable sight: **Pasar Bolu**, the market 2km northeast of town. It peaks every six days, with an overflowing livestock market. The main market is a very big, social occasion that draws crowds from all over Tana Toraja.

INFORMATION

Jl Diponegoro has banks and ATMs. There are internet cafes all over town and the cheaper ones charge 5000Rp per hour.

Government Tourist Office (☎ 21277; Jl Ahmad Yani 62A) Provides accurate information about local ceremonies, festivals and other activities, as well as arranging guides. Just south of the hospital.

Post office (Jl Ahmad Yani; 8am-4pm Mon-Sat)

Rumah Sakit Elim (☎ 21258; Jl Ahmad Yani) The main hospital in town. If anything serious should befall you in Toraja, make for Makassar, as facilities here are basic.

Telkom office (Jl Ahmad Yani; 24hr) Next door to the post office.

ACTIVITIES

Guides charge 200,000Rp for an all-day circuit by motorbike, including a funeral if there's one on. You can also hire a guide with a car for 275,000Rp, but much of the Toraja region is only accessible on foot or by motorbike.

To truly immerse yourself in Toraja land, you've got to trek off the main roads. Good footwear is vital, and so is ample food, water, a torch (flashlight; some villages lack electricity) and rain gear. If you desire a professional trekking outfitter, contact **Indosella** (☎ 0423-25210; www.sellatours.com; Jl Andi Mappanyukki 111), which also organises white-water rafting trips.

For a brilliant day trek, take a morning bemo to Deri, then veer off-road and traverse the incredible cascading rice fields all the way to Tikala. Farmers and villagers will help point the way, but a guide would be a wise decision for this trek. Popular multiday treks include the following:

Batumonga–Lokomata–Pangala–Baruppu–Pulu Pulu–Sapan Three days.

Bittuang–Mamasa Three days.

Pangala–Bolokan–Bittuang Two days on a well-marked trail.

SLEEPING

Wisma Maria I (☎ 21165; adespasakal@yahoo.com; Jl Sam Ratulangi 23; r 50,000-150,000Rp) Our favourite rock-bottom cheapie in the town centre; rooms are plain but good sized.

Wisma Tanabua (☎ 21072; Jl Diponegoro 43; r without/with bathroom 60,000/80,000Rp) A friendly, family-run central spot that has basic rooms, and doubles as a beauty salon.

our pick Pia's Poppies Hotel (☎ 21121; s/d 66,000/88,000Rp) Rooms have some quirky details like stone bathrooms, and each terrace overlooks a languorous garden. There's hot water and you're even served a welcome fruit juice on arrival.

Wisma Imanuel (☎ 21416; Jl W Monginsidi 16; r 80,000-100,000Rp) Set in a large house backed by the river, the rooms here are a generous size and the more expensive include hot-water showers. Big balconies out front offer views over the garden.

Hotel Pison (☎ 21344; s/d 85,000/100,000Rp) Opposite Pia's, the bland but good-value Pison has 32 rooms, each with a clean bathroom and mini-balcony with mountain views. All the rooms come with hot water.

EATING & DRINKING

The best-known dish is *pa'piong* (meat stuffed into bamboo tubes along with vegetables and coconut). Order in advance and enjoy it with black rice.

Rumah Makan Saruran (Jl Diponogoro 19; mains around 15,000Rp) Indonesian-style Chinese food is served at this hopping restaurant that's popular with young travelling Indonesians.

Mart's Café (Jl Sam Ratulangi 44; dishes 15,000-45,000Rp) The best tourist trap in town, Mart's gets lively in the evenings when the resident guides start crooning and strumming their guitars. The Bintang flows…

Rimiko Restoran (Jl Andi Mappanyukki; dishes from 20,000Rp) This place serves the best food of the tourist-oriented restaurants and has a few Torajan specialities on the menu that don't require ordering in advance.

GETTING THERE & AROUND

Bus companies are clustered in the town centre around Jl Andi Mappanyukki. Many buses head south to Pare Pare (35,000Rp, five hours).

TORAJA CULTURE

Architecture

Traditional *tongkonan* houses – shaped like boats or buffalo horns, with the roof rearing up at the front and back – are the enduring image of Tana Toraja. They are similar to the Batak houses of Sumatra's Danau Toba and are always aligned north–south, with small rice barns facing them.

A number of villages are still composed entirely of these traditional houses, but most now have corrugated-iron roofs. The houses are painted and carved with animal motifs, and buffalo skulls often decorate the front, symbolising wealth and prestige.

Burial Customs

The Toraja generally have two funerals, one immediately after the death, and a second, more elaborate, four-day ceremony after enough cash has been raised. Between the two ceremonies, the dead will live at home in the best room of the house and visitors will be obliged to sit, chat and have coffee with them. Regularly. This all ends once buffalo are sacrificed (one for a commoner, as many as 24 for a high-ranking figure, and these animals aren't cheap: a medium-sized buffalo costs several million rupiah) and the spirit soars to the afterlife.

To deter the plundering of generous burial offerings, the Toraja started to hide their dead in caves or on rocky cliff faces. You can often see *tau tau* – life-size, carved wooden effigies of the dead – sitting in balconies on rock faces, guarding the coffins. Descendents are obliged to change and update their fake deceased relatives clothing. Also regularly.

Funeral ceremonies are the region's main tourist attraction.

Ceremonies & Festivals

The end of the rice harvest, from around May onwards, is ceremony time in Tana Toraja. These festivities involve feasting and dancing, buffalo fights and *sisemba* kick-boxing. Guides around Rantepao will take you to ceremonies for a negotiable price.

Northbound buses travel to Pendolo (80,000Rp, eight hours), Tentena (110,000Rp, 10 hours), Poso (120,000Rp, 12 hours) and Palu (150,000Rp, 20 hours)

Kijangs leave for Makale (5000Rp, 20 minutes) constantly, and will drop you at the signs for Londa, Tilanga or Lemo, to walk to the villages.

From Terminal Bolu, 2km northeast of Rantepao, frequent vehicles go east to Palopo, and regular bemo and Kijangs go to all the major villages, such as Lempo (near Batutumonga).

Motorbikes can be rented from hotels and tour agencies for 70,000Rp per day.

Around Rantepao

On day trips from Rantepao there's the beautiful: stunning panoramas, magical bamboo forests and rice terraces, shaped by natural boulders and fed by waterfalls, that drop for 2000m. There's the strange: *tau tau* (wooden effigies) of long-lost relatives guarding graves carved out of vertical limestone rock faces or hung from the roof of deep caves. And there's the intermingling of the two: incredibly festive and colourful four-day funerals where buffalo are slaughtered and stewed, palm wine is swilled from bamboo carafes and a spirit soars to the afterlife.

SOUTH OF RANTEPAO

Karasik (1km from Rantepao) is on the outskirts of town, just off the road leading to Makale. The traditional houses were erected years ago for a funeral.

Just off the main road, southeast of Rantepao, **Ke'te Kesu** (6km) is famed for its woodcarving. On the cliff face behind the village are cave graves and some very old hanging graves – the rotting coffins are suspended from an overhang.

Located about 2km off the Rantepao–Makale road, **Londa** (6km) is an extensive burial cave, one of the most interesting in the area. Above the cave is a line-up of *tau tau* that peer down, in fresh clothes, from their cliffside perch. Inside the dank darkness, coffins hang above dripping stalagmites. Others lie rotting on the stone floor, exposing skulls and bones. Very Indiana Jones. Hire a guide with an oil lamp from the village gate (20,000Rp).

Lemo (11km) is among the largest burial areas in Tana Toraja. The sheer rock face has dozens of balconies for *tau tau*. There would be even more *tau tau* if they weren't in such demand by unscrupulous antique dealers who deal in bad karma. A bemo from Rantepao will drop you off at the road leading up to the burial site, from where it's a 15-minute walk.

EAST OF RANTEPAO

Marante (6km) is a traditional village right by the road east to Palopo, near rice fields and stone and hanging graves guarded by *tau tau*. Further off the Palopo road, **Nanggala** (16km) has a grandiose traditional house with 14 rice barns. Charter a bemo from Rantepao, and you can be taken straight there, or take a public one, and walk 7km from the Palopo road.

NORTH & WEST OF RANTEPAO

This is where you'll find the finest scenery in Tana Toraja. **Batutumonga** (20km) has an ideal panoramic perch, sensational sunrise views and a few homestays. The best is **Mentirotiku** (☎ 081 142 2260; r 75,000-220,000Rp). The views are even more stunning from the summit of **Gunung Sesean**, a 2150m peak towering above the village. Most bemo stop at **Lempo**, an easy walk from Batutumonga.

There are more cave graves and beautiful scenery at **Lokomata** (26km), just a few kilometres west past Batutumonga.

The return to Rantepao is an interesting and easy trek down the slopes through tiny villages to **Pana**, with its ancient hanging graves, and baby graves in the trees. The path ends at **Tikala**, where regular bemo go to Rantepao.

The three-day, 59km trek from **Mamasa** in the west to Bittuang is popular, and there are plenty of villages en route with food and accommodation (remember to bring gifts). There's no direct transport from Rantepao to Mamasa because the roads are appalling. Currently, jeeps are running from Mamasa to Ponding for 80,000Rp every day, where you can hook up with a horse on to Bittuang for about 150,000Rp.

PENDOLO

Pendolo is a quiet village with lonely swimming beaches on the south shore of enormous **Danau Poso** in Central Sulawesi.

Pendolo Cottages (Jl Ahmad Yani 441; r 60,000Rp, bungalow s/d 55,000/80,000Rp), right next to the boat

INDONESIA

landing, about 1km east of the village centre, gets good traveller reviews on service and ambience.

Pendolo is on the main Palopo–Poso highway, but there is no bus terminal. To go north the best option is to catch a bemo to Tentena (45,000Rp) then transfer there.

TENTENA

☎ 0458

This lakeside town of white picket fences and churches lacks Pendolo's fine beaches, but is larger and has better accommodation. Surrounded by clove-covered hills, it's a peaceful and very easy to manage town.

Hotel Pamona Indah (☎ 21245; Jl Yos Sudarso 25; d from 110,000Rp) is grand, with large columns and peach trim, the 20 rooms are spotless and comfortable, and the restaurant, serving the town's famous *sugili* (giant eels), is the best in town.

Buses make the run to Poso (20,000Rp, 1½ hours) throughout the day.

POSO

☎ 0452 / pop 47,000

Poso is the main town, port and terminal for road transport on the northern coast of Central Sulawesi. It's a spread out, noisy place and there's little reason to stay besides to hit up an ATM, check your email or change buses.

Poso is the last chance for Togean- and Tentena-bound travellers to change money; the best option is BNI bank, with an ATM, near the port about 2km from town centre – take an *ojek*.

Losmen Alugoro (☎ 21336; Jl Sumatera 20; d 40,000-175,000Rp;) is a reliably decent but characterless place that's central to the bus offices and restaurants.

Losmen Lalanga Jaya (☎ 22326; Jl Yos Sudarso; d 75,000Rp) has creaky rooms with a view, and is conveniently located next to the port.

Buses leave the terminal, 800m north of the post office, for Palu (35,000Rp, six hours), Tentena (20,000Rp, two hours), Ampana (35,000Rp, five hours) and Rantepao (115,000Rp, 13 hours).

PALU

☎ 0451 / pop 307,500

Set in a rain shadow, Central Sulawesi's characterless capital is one of the driest places in Indonesia. The main reason to visit Palu is to arrange the 100km trip to trek the remote 2290-sq-km **Taman Nasional Lore Lindu**, where you can glimpse ancient stone megaliths, and explore lowland and montane rainforest, home to 227 bird species (including 77 varieties endemic to Sulawesi).

Orientation & Information

Warnets are everywhere in Palu and generally charge 4000Rp per hour. Palu has banks and ATMs at every corner.

Balai Taman Nasional Lore Lindu office (☎ 457623; Jl Prof Mohammad Yamin SH) Issues licenses; can set you up with Indonesian-speaking guides.

Sleeping & Eating

Purnama Raya Hotel (☎ 423646; Jl Wahidin 4; s/d 30,000/40,000Rp) The brightest of Palu's subpar cheapies. The knowledgeable English-speaking manager moonlights as a local guide.

Rama Garden Hotel (☎ 429500; Jl Monginsidi 81; r 165,000-440,000Rp;) The rooms border on plush, making this a worthy step up. The outdoor lounge is lovely.

Restoran Marannu (Jl Setia Budi; mains 20,000-40,000Rp; breakfast, lunch & dinner) One of the smarter spots in town, the menu here includes tasty seafood and Chinese cuisine.

Getting There & Around

Palu's airport is 7km east of town, 45,000Rp by taxi.

CENTRAL CONCERNS

It's been pretty quiet around Central Sulawesi since late 2006, but for eight years prior the region was torn apart by secular violence. Christians grouped in predominantly Christian Tentena while Muslims stood their ground in Poso and Palu. Over 1000 people had been killed, houses had been burned and markets bombed. Tourists were never targets but the region was, for obvious reasons, best avoided.

It's still debated what caused these communities to start to fight each other after generations of living peacefully together. The common belief is that the influx of Muslim immigrants from Java under President Suharto's *transmigrasi* (transmigration program) abruptly shifted the Christian majority and power in the region. Today locals chat easily about this dark time and about how happy they are it's over.

There are flights to Makassar with **Merpati** (☎ 423341; Jl Monginsidi), **Sriwijaya Air** (☎ 428777; 37 Jl Monginsidi) and **Lion Air** (☎ 428777; Jl Raden Saleh 1). Merpati also flies from Palu to Kendari, Sriwijaya has services to Balikpapan, while Lion Air flies to Manado.

Pelni (☎ 421696; Jl Kartini 96) is well connected to East Kalimantan and other Sulawesi ports. Ships dock at Pantoloan, 22km north of Palu, where there is another Pelni office.

Buses to Poso (75,000Rp, six hours), Ampana (125,000Rp, 11 hours), Rantepao (165,000Rp, 19 hours) and Manado (24 hours) all leave from inconvenient bus-company offices dotted around the suburbs of Palu.

DONGGALA

☎ 0457

Donggala's main attractions are the reefs at **Tanjung Karang** (Coral peninsula), north of town. Prince John Dive Resort is the only scuba shack. Its house reef suits snorkellers and beginner divers.

Travellers buzz about this slice of white sand at **Kaluku Cottages** (bungalows all-inclusive 75,000Rp), 15km from Donggala. The nearby coral reef is ideal for snorkellers. Get here by *ojek*.

Prince John Dive Resort (☎ 71104; www.prince-john-diveresort.de; bungalows for 2 people incl meals from 380,000Rp) has comfortable varnished wood bungalows with large bathrooms and a seaview.

Take an *ojek* direct from Palu to Tanjung Karang (30,000Rp).

AMPANA

☎ 0464

Ampana is the gateway to the Togeans. Given bus and ferry schedules, you will likely spend a night here. The lone ATM only takes MasterCard.

Oasis Hotel (☎ 21058; Jl Kartini; dm 60,000Rp, r from 90,000Rp; ❄) has clean rooms and dorms but don't expect to sleep till the karaoke shuts down at 11pm. The most expensive rooms include air-con and hot water.

Several minibuses travel each day to Luwuk (100,000Rp, six hours), Poso (60,000Rp, five hours) and Palu (125,000Rp, 11 hours).

Ferries depart everyday but Thursday and Sunday to Wakai (40,000Rp, three hours), then to Katupat, Malenge and Kalia before returning to Ampana. Boats to Bomba on Pulau Batu Daka leave from a jetty in Labuhan village (25,000Rp).

TOGEAN ISLANDS

Yes, it does take some determination to get to the Togean Islands, but believe us, it takes much more determination to leave. Island hop from one forested golden-beach beauty to the next where hammocks are plentiful, the fish is fresh and the welcome is homey. There are lost lagoons and forgotten coves, and arguably the best diving in Sulawesi (which ranks it near the top worldwide). Disregard those outdated dynamite-fishing whispers and plunge into crystal-clear, bottomless seas to explore all three major reef systems – atoll, barrier and fringing. Colours absolutely pop. Fish are everywhere.

GETTING THERE & AROUND

The quickest way to get to the Togeans is to fly from Manado to Luwuk and travel by road from there to Ampana (six hours). Overland travellers often make their way up from Tana Toraja to Ampana. See left for ferry details.

Charters around the Togeans are easily arranged in Wakai, Bomba and Kadidiri (250,000Rp).

Pulau Kadidiri

This is definitely the island to go to if you're feeling social, but during the low season you could still potentially wind up on your own here. Just a short boat trip from Wakai, the three lodging options (all right next to each other) are on a perfect strip of sand with OK snorkelling and swimming, and superb diving beyond.

SLEEPING & EATING

Hotels usually provide transport from Wakai.

Pondok Lestari (cottages 75,000Rp) Stay with a charming Bajo family who take their guests on daily free snorkelling trips. The older bamboo bungalows are very rustic and share a rudimentary bathroom.

Black Marlin Cottages (☎ Gorontalo 0435-831869; www.blackmarlindive.com; cottages from 145,000Rp) This is arguably the most lively place on Kadidiri and is home to British-run Black Marlin Dive. Cottages are large, wooden, well decorated and have good bathrooms. Travellers amass on the pontoon here for sunsets.

Kadidiri Paradise Resort (☎ in Ampana 0464-21058; www.visitkadidiriparadise.com; r per person €16-27) This resort on stunning planted grounds, nearly

INDONESIA

surrounded by water, is Kadidiri's poshest option. Rooms are huge and all have generous decks and big stone bathrooms. The dive centre here is well run.

Togean Island & Around

The main settlement on this island is the very relaxed Katupat village, which has a small market and a couple of shops. Around the island there are magical **beaches**, and some decent **hikes** for anyone sick of swimming, snorkelling and diving.

Losmen Melati (r 90,000Rp), near the boat jetty in Katupat, offers the traveller simple accommodation. **Fadhila Cottages** (cottages from 125,000Rp), opposite the village on private Pagempa Island, offers wooden cottages with superb beaches and snorkelling.

Pulau Malenge

Remote Pulau Malenge has great snorkelling near the village.

The best place to stay is **Lestari Cottages** (r 80,000Rp, cottages 100,000Rp) run by friendly Rudy, who offers rooms in Malenge village and cottages on a secluded beach.

Pulau Batu Daka

BOMBA

This tiny outpost at the southeastern end of Pulau Batu Daka has nearby reefs and exquisite beaches.

Island Retreat (www.togian-island-retreat.com; r per person US$15-28) is run by an expat Californian woman and her band of friendly dogs. Set on the beautiful beach at Pasir Putih, the 20 cottages are very well cared for and the food is great. There's a dive centre here, plus snorkelling gear.

WAKAI

The Togeans' largest settlement is a departure point for ferries to Ampana and Gorontalo and for charters to Pulau Kadidiri and beyond. There are a few general stores, if you need supplies, but there's no reason to stay the night.

MANADO

☎ 0431 / pop 479,700

Once described by anthropologist Alfred Russel Wallace as 'one of the prettiest [cities] in the East', Manado has sold its soul to commerce. However, it remains a necessary base for exploring North Sulawesi.

Orientation

Along Jl Sam Ratulangi, the main north-south artery, you'll find restaurants, hotels and supermarkets. The shopping-mall blitz dominates parallel Jl Piere Tendean, closer to the sea.

Information

You're never far from a bank, ATM or *wartel* in Manado. The best internet places in town can be found at the IT Center mall across from the Mega Mall.

Main post office (Jl Sam Ratulangi 23; 8am-7.30pm Mon-Fri, 8am-6pm Sat & Sun)

Rumah Sakit Umum (☎ 853191; Jl Monginsidi; Malalayang) The general hospital is about 4.5km from town and includes a decompression chamber.

Telkom office (Jl Sam Ratulangi; 24hr)

Sleeping

Rex Hotel (☎ 851136; Jl Sugiono 3; r 35,000-90,000Rp;) These are the best budget rooms in town: all are clean and have windows letting in natural light.

New Angkasa Hotel (☎ 864062; Jl Sugiono 10; r with fan from 60,000Rp, with air-con from 85,000Rp;) This place is always full because of its good value though basic rooms.

Hotel Regina (☎ 8550091; Jl Sugiono 1; r from 190,000Rp;) Bland but big rooms here are spotless and very plush for the price. The hearty Indonesian breakfasts are another perk.

Eating & Drinking

Adventurous diners migrate to the night *warung* along Jl Piere Tendean. Regional delights include *kawaok* (fried 'forest rat') and *rintek wuuk* (spicy dog meat).

Hidden behind the massive Mega Mall on Jl Piere Tendean is an excellent stretch of surprisingly chic seafood *warung* open every night. The price, variety and sunsets are unbeatable. **Blue Terrace** (sheesha pipe 35,000Rp) is the most hip and doubles as a candlelit *sheesha* bar.

There is another stretch of *warung* behind the Bahu Mall, Jl Walter Monginsidi, just south of the town centre. Live bands sometimes play on a stage here.

Singapura Bakery (Jl Sam Ratulangi 22; pastries from 5000Rp) Has a mind-boggling array of baked goods, fresh juices and shakes, plus a popular cheap cafe next door serving yummy Javanese fare.

Rumah Makan Green Garden (Jl Sam Ratulangi; lunch 19,000Rp) Looks a bit funky but the food here is really good. Try the tofu dishes and fresh juices.

Clubbing

Ha Ha Café (entry incl 1 drink 50,000Rp) The leading club in town, this place is on the top floor of the Mega Mall. It only really fills up on Wednesdays (ladies' night), Fridays and Saturdays.

Getting There & Around

AIR

Mikrolet from Sam Ratulangi International Airport go to Terminal Paal 2 (3500Rp), where you can change to a *mikrolet* heading to Pasar 45 or elsewhere in the city for a flat fee of 2300Rp. Fixed-price taxis cost 85,000Rp for the trip from the airport to the city (13km).

Manado is well connected by air.

Air Asia (☎ 215 050 5088; Airport) Flies to Kuala Lumpur.
Batavia Air (☎ 386 4338; Mega Mall) Flies to Balikpapan, Gorontalo, Surabaya and Jakarta.
Garuda (☎ 877737; Jl Sam Ratulangni) Flies to Makassar, Balikpapan and Denpasar.
Lion Air (☎ 847000; Mega Mall) Flies to Makassar, Jakarta, Denpasar, Ternate, Sorong, and Singapore and Kuala Lumpur.
Merpati (☎ 842000; Jl Sudirman 111) Flies to Jakarta and Makassar.
SilkAir (☎ 863744; Jl Sarapung) Flies to Singapore.
Wings Air (☎ 847000; airport) Weekly flights to/from Davao, Philippines.

BOAT

All Pelni boats use the deep-water port of Bitung, 55km from Manado. Pelni liners call by once or twice every week: the *Sangiang* goes to Ternate (economy/1st class 436,000/1,473,000Rp); the *Lambelu* goes to Namlea (111,000/317,000Rp) and Ambon (233,000/617,000Rp); the *Dorolonda* to Sorong (228,000/695,000Rp) and Fak Fak; and the *Tilongkabila* to Luwuk (168,000/442,000Rp) and other ports along the southeastern coast.

PT Virgo Ekspres (☎ 858610; Jl Sam Ratulangi 5) is a reliable Pelni agent for checking information and purchasing tickets.

Small, slow, uncomfortable boats from Manado sail north to Tahuna (Pulau Sangihe) and Lirung (Talaud Islands), or east to Ternate and Ambon.

BUS

From Karombasan terminal, 5km south of the city, buses go to Tomohon (6000Rp, 40 minutes) and destinations south; from Malalayang terminal they go to Gorontalo (70,000Rp, eight hours); and from Paal 2 terminal, at the eastern end of Jl Martadinata, public transport runs to Bitung (6500Rp, one hour).

PUBLIC TRANSPORT

There's no *mikrolet* shortage in Manado. Destinations are shown on a card in the front windscreen. There are various bus stations around town for destinations outside Manado; get to any of them from Pasar 45. Private, inexpensive metered taxis are usually within shouting distance.

PULAU BUNAKEN

Pulau Bunaken is Sulawesi's top destination: 300 varieties of pristine coral and 3000 species of fish in Bunaken Manado Tua Marine National Park draw acolytes from around the globe. Tourist accommodation is spread out along two beaches and, other than that, the island belongs to the islanders; these friendly folk have a seemingly endless reserve of authentically warm smiles.

Activities

The Bunaken park fee is 50,000Rp per day or 150,000Rp for an annual pass. Trips around Bunaken and nearby islands will cost from €45 for two dives. Whole schools of dive operators are at the resorts, including these:

Bunaken Divers (☎ 3306034; www.bunakendivers.com; Seabreeze Resort) Friendly Australian-run outfit that has been around a while.
Froggies Dive Centre (☎ 850210; www.divefroggies.com; Froggies) Pioneers of the famed lazy dive where the current does the work.
Living Colours (☎ 081 2430 6063; www.livingcoloursdiving.com; Living Colours) Has some of the best equipment on the island and is very professionally run.

Sleeping & Eating

Pantai Liang, to the west, has a beautiful stretch of sand that doubles as Manado's de-facto refuse dump when tides turn. Pantai Pangalisang, near Bunaken village, is the eco-choice. There's no beach to lie on, but it overlooks an armada of stately mangrove trees closer to Bunaken village, and the nearby reef is ideal for snorkelling. Most hotels quote rates per person for full board.

PANTAI LIANG

Panorama (☎ 013 4083 0872; ester_kasehung@hotmail.com; cottages from 125,000Rp) Tucked up in a corner on a hillside, the basic wood bungalows here with terraces and comanding views are the best budget deal on the island.

Nelson's Homestay (☎ 043 185 6288; cottages 175,000Rp) These huts are built on cliffs and have bay views and an OK stretch of beach below.

Froggies (☎ 812 430 1356; www.divefroggies.com; cottages €25-35) Good beachfront location, rooms are well decorated and spotless, and the interesting restaurant area feels a bit like the bat cave. Nondivers not welcome.

PANTAI PANGALISANG

Daniel's Homestay (☎ 813143; daniels@indostat.net.id; bungalows from 150,000Rp) Wood cottages are very basic but spacious. Pay a little more for a seafront cottage.

Novita Homestay (r 125,000Rp) Right in Bunaken village (at the northern end), these spotless rooms with shared bathroom in a charming family home are the place to stay for an authentic local experience.

Seabreeze Resort (☎ 811 439 558; www.bunakendivers.com; cottages €13-25) A large, sprawling resort, there are quite a few different types of bungalows here; beers are very cold thanks to the Aussie owner.

Getting There & Away

Every day at about 3pm, except Sunday, a public boat leaves the harbour, near Pasar Jengki fish market in Manado, for Bunaken village and Pulau Siladen (50,000Rp, one hour). The return from Pulau Bunaken is at 8am. A charter costs at least 200,000Rp one way. If you're staying and/or diving with one of the upmarket resorts, call ahead for a shuttle.

TOMOHON

Pleasantly cool and lush, this popular weekend escape from Manado rests at the foot of Gunung Lokon in the Minahasa Highlands.

Volcano Resort (☎ 352988; cottages 100,000-150,000Rp) is spread out around a grassy garden. Wooden bungalows are a great deal, plus the staff are helpful and speak English. There are also some budget rooms with shared bathroom for 80,000Rp.

Frequent *mikrolet* travel to Tomohon (6000Rp, 40 minutes) from Manado's Karombasan terminal.

BITUNG

☎ **0438 / pop 137,000**

Bitung, the chief port of Minahasa, is 55km east of Manado. The **Pelni office** (☎ 35818) is in the port complex.

Mikrolet depart regularly from Manado's Paal 2 terminal. They drop you at the Mapalus terminal, outside Bitung, where you catch another *mikrolet* for the short trip into town.

MALUKU (MOLUCCAS)

Welcome to the original 'spice islands'. Back in the 16th century when nutmeg, cloves and mace were global commodities that grew nowhere else, Maluku was a place where money really did grow on trees. Today the spices have minimal economic clout and Maluku (formerly known as 'the Moluccas') has dropped out of global consciousness. The region is protected from mass tourism by distance, unpredictable transport and memories of a brief if tragically destructive period of intercommunal conflict between 1999 and 2002.

While transport can prove infuriatingly inconvenient, given flexibility and patience you can snorkel the brilliant Bandas, explore the beach-strewn Kei Islands, survey North Maluku's mesmerising volcano islands and explore ruined Dutch fortresses. And it's cheap.

Getting There & Around

Ambon and Ternate are the region's air hubs. Both have several connections daily to Jakarta, mostly via Makassar or Manado (Sulawesi). There are several connections from Ambon to Papua but only one weekly flight to Nusa Tenggara, Merpati's heavily booked Ambon–Kisar–Kupang run.

Four Pelni liners visit Ambon on biweekly cycles from Bau Bau (southeast Sulawesi, 12 hours), Makassar (31 to 36 hours), Surabaya (60 to 68 hours) and/or Jakarta/Tanjung Priok (four days).

PULAU AMBON

Pulau Ambon is ribboned with villages, dressed in shimmering foliage, defined by two great bays. This is your launch pad to the Bandas, but also a charming retreat and diving base in its own right.

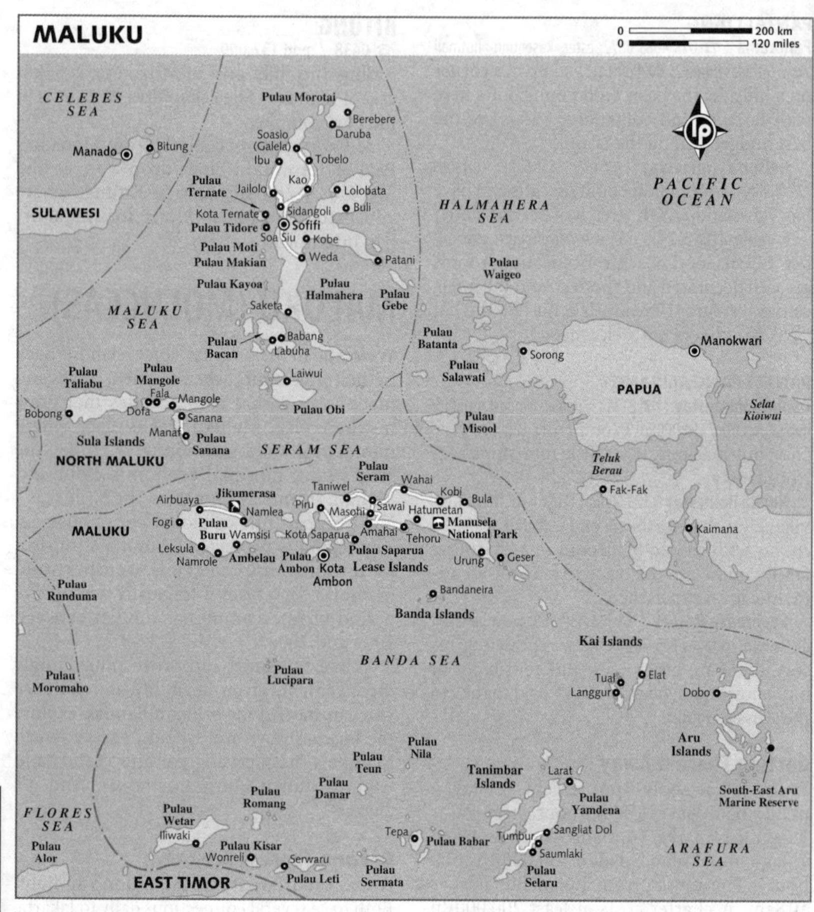

Kota Ambon

☎0911 / pop 380,000

By the region's dreamy tropical standards, Maluku's capital, commercial centre and transport hub is a busy, throbbing metropolis. Sights are minimal and architecture wins no prizes, but compared to cities elsewhere, Kota Ambon retains a languid charm.

INFORMATION

Change or withdraw enough money in Ambon for trips to outlying islands where there are no exchange facilities whatsoever.

Tourist office (☎312300; Jl Jenderal Sudirman, Tantui; 8am-4pm Mon-Fri) Offers fistfuls of colourful free brochures.

www.virtualtourist.com For an expat's view.

SLEEPING & EATING

For cheap eats, there are *warung* near the Batu Merah market and on Jl Ahmad Yani.

Hotel Jamilah (☎353626; Jl Soabali; d 125,000Rp;) Behind a grotto of fake golden rocks, this 15-room family hotel has a peaceful, homely charm.

Pondok Wisata 'Avema' Lestari (☎355596, 081 3430 33842; Jl WR Supratman 18; s/d/tr 150,000/165,000/220,000Rp;) This welcoming family homestay has neat, clean rooms and airy communal spaces. Helpful owner speaks fluent Dutch and English.

GETTING THERE & AWAY

Pattimura airport is 30km round the bay from central Kota Ambon. **Batavia** (☎346380; Jl Ay Patty 31), **Lion Air/Wings Air** (☎351532; airport) and

Sriwijaya (☎ 354498; Jl AM Sangaji 79) operate daily Jakarta–Ambon flights. Lion Air/Wings Air serves Makassar, while **Merpati** (☎ 352481; Jl Ahmad Yani) flies Ambon–Kisar–Kupang weekly.

Pelni (☎ 342328) has an office opposite the Pattimura Memorial. Boats leave from Yos Sudarso harbour.

Smaller boats from Slamat Riyadi Harbour serve north, east and remote southeast islands in Maluku.

BANDA ISLANDS

☎ 0910 / pop 15,000

This tiny yet historically fascinating cluster of 10 picturesque islands is Maluku's most inviting travel destination: a gathering of epic tropical gems, with deserted stretches of white sand and crescent bays. In the 1990s they briefly blipped onto the backpacker radar and have now faded back into glorious anonymity. Which means you'll have the beaches and those stark undersea drop-offs draped in technicolour coral gardens to yourself.

Bandaneira

The main port of the Banda islands, situated on Pulau Neira, is a friendly, pleasantly sleepy town of colonial villas and blooming flowers.

Stop by the impressive **Benteng Belgica** (admission 20,000Rp; sporadic), built on the hill above Bandaneira in 1611. The fort's upper reaches have incredible views of **Gunung Api**. Several historic Dutch houses have been restored.

our pick Vita Guesthouse (Fita; ☎ 21332; allandarman@gmail.com; Jl Pasar; d with fan/air-con from 80,000/100,000Rp) Has comfortable rooms. Allan and family are endlessly helpful.

Mutiara Guesthouse (☎ 21344, 081 3303 43377; banda_mutiara@yahoo.com; r 80,000-125,000) has superb-value new rooms and sturdy, classically styled furniture. Guests meet up for the generous, convivial dinner (50,000Rp).

Merpati (☎ 21060; Jl Pelabuhan) flies both ways Ambon–Bandaneira–Amahai on Sundays; cancellations happen. Biweekly Pelni ships sail from Ambon to Bandaneira. To tour the reef and explore other islands, charter a longboat at the fish market.

Other Islands

Pulau Banda Besar is the largest of the Banda islands, and the most important historical source of nutmeg. You can still visit nutmeg groves at the **Kelly Plantation** or explore the ruins of fort **Benteng Hollandia** (c 1624).

Pulau Hatta has crystal waters and a mind-expanding, coral-encrusted vertical drop-off near Lama village. **Pulau Ai** is more accessible and is also blessed with rich coral walls and postcard beaches. On Ai, **Green Coconut** (Jl Patalima; r per person 100,000Rp) has the best seafront location with wonderful views.

Passenger longboats buzz between Bandaneira and Pulau Banda Besar (4000Rp) and Pulau Ai (20,000Rp). To land on Pulau Hatta, you'll have to leave early and charter a sturdy covered boat for a day trip (one way from 300,000Rp, three hours).

PULAU TERNATE & TIDORE

The perfect volcanic cone of Ternate highlights north Maluku's gateway and transport hub. Pulau Tidore, Ternate's age-old, next-door rival, is a laid-back island of charming villages and empty beaches.

Kota Ternate

☎ 0921 / pop 106,000

With frequent air connections, the town of Kota Ternate on Pulau Ternate is a logical first stop, and a good base for exploring north Maluku.

ORIENTATION & INFORMATION

The city centre is compact and walkable. Several banks on Jl Pahlawan Revolusi have ATMs but only **BNI** (8am-3pm Mon-Thu, 8am-noon Fri) changes money, and then only US dollars in new unfolded $100 bills.

D@gimoi (Jl Sultan Khairun; internet/wi-fi per hr 8000/13,000Rp; 8am-midnight) Internet and an attractive outdoor garden.

North Maluku Tourist Office (☎ 312 7396; www.malukuutaraprov.go.id; Jl Kamboja 14; 8am-4pm Mon-Fri) Helpful English-speaking staff can organise guides.

SIGHTS

Built in 1796, **Keraton Sultan** (Sultan's Palace; ☎ 21166; admission by donation; 6am-6pm) is 2km north of town. It has an interesting collection of colonial swords and armour, and the current Sultan's sister loves telling tales of the Ternetean royal family, a history that dates back to 1257.

SLEEPING & EATING

Hotel Indah (☎ 312 1334; Jl Bosoiri 3; r 66,000-154,000) Modest old-style *penginapan* (simple lodging house) with a little garden area and quaintly dated sitting room.

Taman Ria (☎ 322 2124; r with fan/air-con 125,000/165,000Rp) Set back behind an under-construction, waterfront zoo 700m beyond Benteng Kalamata, most rooms are new and well appointed, but fan rooms overheat and a handful of older cheapies (doubles for 75,000Rp) are sad.

Rumah Makan Jailolo (Jl Pahlawan Revolusi 7; meals from 13,000Rp; 7am-9.30pm) Bright, reliable place for inexpensive point-and-pick meals.

GETTING THERE & AROUND

For the 6km from Babullah airport to central Ternate, taxis want 50,000Rp; walk 10 minutes south, where bemo from outside Hairun University cost only 3000Rp.

Batavia (☎ 312 2799; Jl Pattimura) Flies to Jakarta via Makassar.
Lion Air/Wings Air (Almas Mega Travel; ☎ 311 1555; Jl Pattimura) Flies to Manado.
Merpati (☎ 312 1651; Jl Bosoiri) Flies to Makassar, Galela and other regional cities.

Pelni (☎ 312 1434; 8am-4pm Mon-Sat) liners link Ternate, Ambon and Bitung and other ports.

Around Kota Ternate

On the southern outskirts, the 1540 Portuguese **Benteng Kalamata** proves too much restoration can ruin ruins, but the setting, with waves licking its angled walls, is sensational.

Not far from Takome, in the west, is **Danau Tolire Besar**, a deep-green volcanic lake crawling with crocs. A trail from the main road leads to the lake.

The island's dominant force is 1721m **Gunung Api Gamalama**. It exhaled fire and ash most recently in 1994. With a guide and five hours of masochism, you'll reach the summit.

Pulau Tidore

☎ 0921 / pop 47,300

Pulau Tidore, Ternate's better-looking rural reflection, lacks its rival's infrastructure, but therein lies its charm.

In and around **Soasio**, the capital, are hot springs, beaches, the photogenic village of **Lada-Ake** and the looming **Gunung Kiematubu**. Between Rum and Soasio are the splintering remnants of **Benteng Tohula** and the **Sultan's Memorial Museum**, where you can glimpse the magical sultan's crown, if you can find the absentee curator. **Penginapan Seroja** (☎ 316 1456; Jl Sultan Hassanuddin; r 75,000-150,000Rp;), an attractive waterside family house-hotel, lies 50m south of the museum in old Soasio.

Frequent speedboats (8000Rp) rocket over from Bastiong port in Ternate.

PAPUA (IRIAN JAYA)

Even a country as full of travel adventure as Indonesia has to have its final frontier, and here it is – Papua, half of the world's second-biggest island, New Guinea. A land where numberless rivers rush down from 5km mountains to snake across sweating jungles populated by rainbow-hued birds of paradise and kangaroos that climb trees. Peaks are frosted with glaciers and snowfields, and slopes and valleys are home to an array of exotic cultures (250 and counting), like the gourd-wearing Dani, woodcarving Asmat warriors and tree-house-dwelling Korowai. The coast is more modern, and more Indonesian feeling, unless you venture to the Raja Ampats, a remote archipelago where you can find empty beaches and, according to experts, the world's richest reefs.

Papua's history is no slouch either. The battle for the Pacific was decided here – with memorials and WWII wrecks to prove it. Indonesia didn't inherit Papua until 1963, when they named it Irian Jaya, and immediately began liquidating its abundant resources with the giddy complicity of multinational corporations and paltry reinvestment into Papua. This did not sit well with the proud Papuans, whose Free Papua Organisation (OPM) remains active. Most Papuans want to be free of Indonesian rule, but their chances of that seem as slim as ever, now that Papua is home to over a million non-Papuans.

Getting There & Around

AIR

Papua is well connected with the rest of Indonesia, and with so few viable roads, flying is the only way to travel once you're here. The transport centres are Sorong (the biggest city on the bird's-head-shaped island), Biak and Jayapura

Merpati, Garuda and Lion Air are the main carriers to, from and within Papua, but seats can be double booked, airports run out of fuel, and flights are regularly cancelled. Wings Air flies to Sorong from Manado daily.

INDONESIA

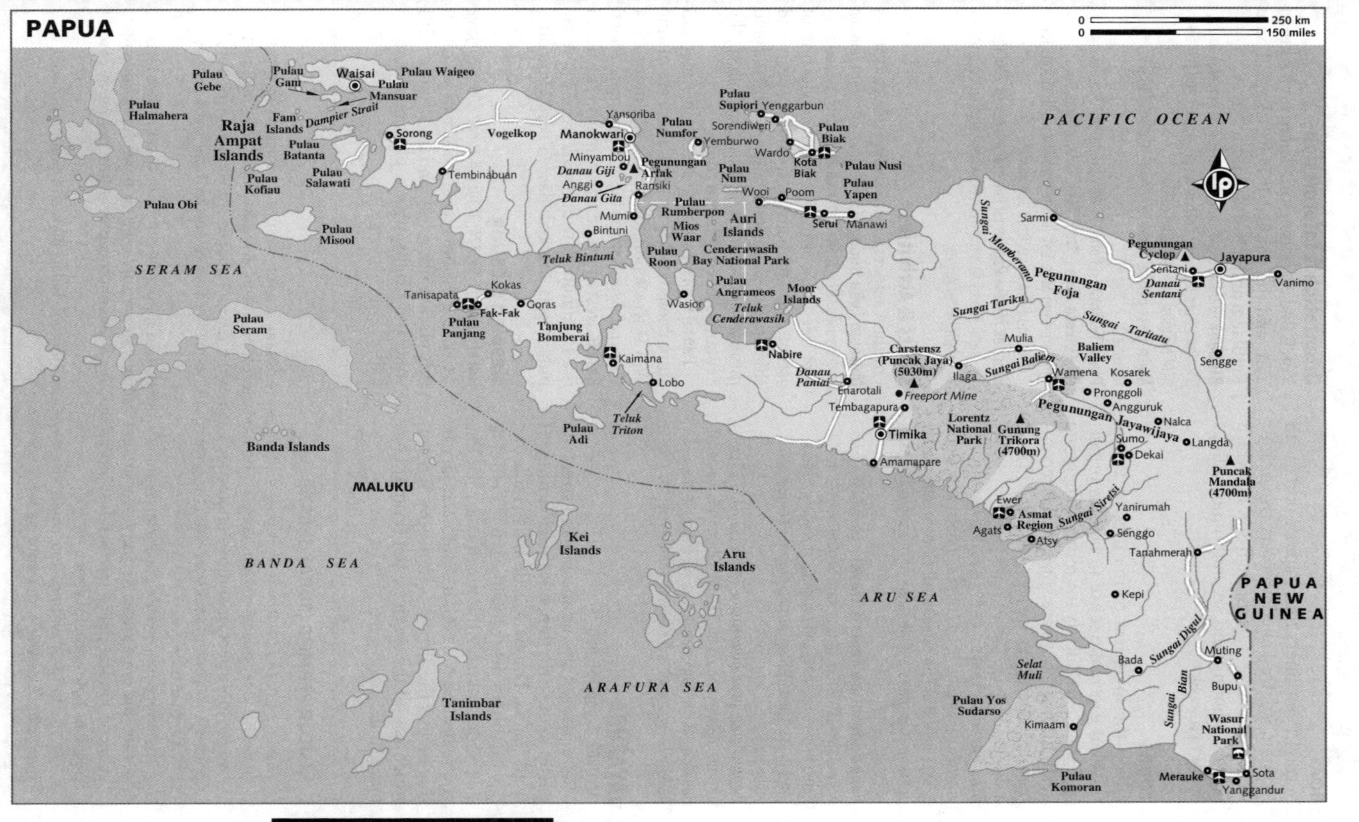
PAPUA
0 250 km
0 150 miles
PACIFIC OCEAN
Pulau Gebe
Pulau Halmahera
Pulau Gam
Waisai
Pulau Waigeo
Pulau Mansuar
Dampier Strait
Fam Islands
Raja Ampat Islands
Pulau Batanta
Pulau Salawati
Pulau Kofiau
Pulau Obi
Pulau Misool
Sorong
Vogelkop
Tembinabuan
Yansoriba
Manokwari
Minyambou
Pegunungan Arfak
Danau Giji
Anggi
Ransiki
Danau Gita
Mumi
Bintuni
Teluk Bintuni
Pulau Numfor
Yemburwo
Pulau Supiori
Yenggarbun
Sorendiweri
Wardo
Pulau Biak
Kota Biak
Pulau Nusi
Pulau Num
Wooi
Poom
Pulau Yapen
Serui
Manawi
Pulau Rumberpon
Mios Waar
Auri Islands
Pulau Roon
Cenderawasih Bay National Park
Pulau Angrameos
Wasior
Moor Islands
Teluk Cenderawasih
SERAM SEA
Tanisapata
Kokas
Fak-Fak
Goras
Pulau Panjang
Tanjung Bomberai
Pulau Seram
Kaimana
Lobo
Pulau Adi
Teluk Triton
Nabire
Danau Paniai
Enarotali
Carstensz (Puncak Jaya) (5030m)
Freeport Mine
Tembagapura
Timika
Amamapare
Ilaga
Mulia
Sungai Baliem
Lorentz National Park
Gunung Trikora (4700m)
Sarmi
Sungai Mamberamo
Pegunungan Foja
Sungai Tariku
Sungai Taritatu
Pegunungan Cyclop
Sentani
Jayapura
Danau Sentani
Vanimo
Sengge
Baliem Valley
Wamena
Kosarek
Pronggoli
Angguruk
Pegunungan Jayawijaya
Nalca
Sumo
Langda
Dekai
Puncak Mandala (4700m)
Ewer
Asmat Region
Agats
Atsy
Sungai Siretsi
Yanirumah
Senggo
Tanahmerah
Kepi
PAPUA NEW GUINEA
Banda Islands
MALUKU
BANDA SEA
Kei Islands
Aru Islands
ARU SEA
ARAFURA SEA
Tanimbar Islands
Selat Muli
Pulau Yos Sudarso
Kimaam
Pulau Komoran
Bada
Sungai Digul
Muting
Bupu
Sungai Bian
Wasur National Park
Merauke
Sota
Yanggandur

INDONESIA

BOAT

Several Pelni liners link Papuan ports with Maluku, Sulawesi and Java every two or four weeks. Almost all pass through Sorong, which has six inbound and six outbound sailings every two weeks.

TOURS

Given the logistical difficulties of Papua travel, it can make sense to take an organised tour, particularly for more challenging destinations. These are some of the recommended operators (prices start at US$100 a day):

Biak Paradise Tours (☎ 0981-23196; www.discoverpapua.com; Hotel Arumbai, Jl Selat Makassar 3, Kota Biak, Biak) An established, efficient, Biak-based operator that offers a wide range of tours in many parts of Papua.

Papua Adventure Tours & Travel (☎ 0967-572622; www.papuaadventure.com; Jl Raya Sentani 20, Waena) Based between Sentani and Jayapura, this agency offers tours in the Baliem Valley, Asmat, Korowai/Kombai and other areas.

Papua/Irian Jaya Adventure (☎ 0852-4413 1512; justinus_daby@yahoo.com; Jl Gatot Subroto 15, Wamena) Run by a Baliem Valley native who offers trips in the Baliem Valley, Asmat and Korowai/Kombai regions.

JAYAPURA

☎ 0967 / pop 150,000

Most residents are Indonesian and street life pulses to their rhythm, but the environment is all Papua. Dramatic jade hills cradle the city on three sides, while the gorgeous Teluk Yos Sudarso kisses the north coast. Unless you're headed to PNG, it's not necessary to stay here as the airport is in nearby Sentani, which has all the services. But Jayapura has more soul.

Orientation & Information

You'll find everything you'll need on Jl Ahmad Yani and the parallel Jl Percetakan. Jl Sam Ratulangi and Jl Koti front the bay.

BII bank (Bank Internasional Indonesia; Jl Percetakan 22; 8am-3pm Mon-Fri) Exchanges US dollars and has an ATM for most international cards.

Main post office (Jl Koti 3; 7.30am-6.30pm Mon-Sat)

Plasa Telkom (Jl Koti; 8am-midnight) Phones.

PT Kuwera Jaya (☎ 533333; Jl Percetakan 96; 8am-9pm Mon-Sat, 10am-9pm Sun) Sells tickets for flights and Pelni boats from Jayapura.

Warnet Media Papua (Jl Percetakan; per hr 7000Rp; 9am-10pm) As slow as everywhere else, but bigger and with better prices.

Sights & Activities

On the Cenderawasih University campus is **Museum Loka Budaya** (Jl Abepura, Abepura; admission by donation; 8.30am-4pm Mon-Fri). The curator offers free tours of his incredible collection of sculptures, bark paintings, canoes, spears and shields. The small, authentic art shop is a gold mine for collectors. The museum is along the Sentani–Abepura bemo route.

Pantai Hamadi was the site of an American amphibious landing in 1944. There are rusting WWII wrecks on the beach. A famous 1944 General MacArthur photo op made **Pantai Base G**, west of the centre, famous. The beach is a 10-minute downhill walk from where the public taxis, marked 'Base G', drop you off.

Sleeping & Eating

Hotel Ayu (☎ 532174; Jl Tugu II 1; r 82,500-198,000Rp;) Being the best cheap choice in Jayapura, this place is often full, and no wonder – it's snug and bright, with a pleasant common hall.

VISITOR PERMITS (SURAT JALAN)

Within 24 hours of arrival in Papua, visitors must obtain a *surat jalan*, a permission to travel, from the local police station *(polres)*. They are easiest to get in Jayapura. Take your passport, two passport photos, and one photocopy each of the passport pages showing your personal details and your Indonesian visa. The procedure normally takes about an hour with no payment requested.

List every conceivable place you might want to visit, as it might be difficult to add them later, outside the large cities. As you travel around Papua, you are supposed to have the document stamped in local police stations. It is worth keeping a few photocopies of the permit in case police or hotels ask for them.

At the time of writing, you could visit Jayapura, Sentani, Pulau Biak and Sorong without a *surat jalan*. Elsewhere, get your papers in order.

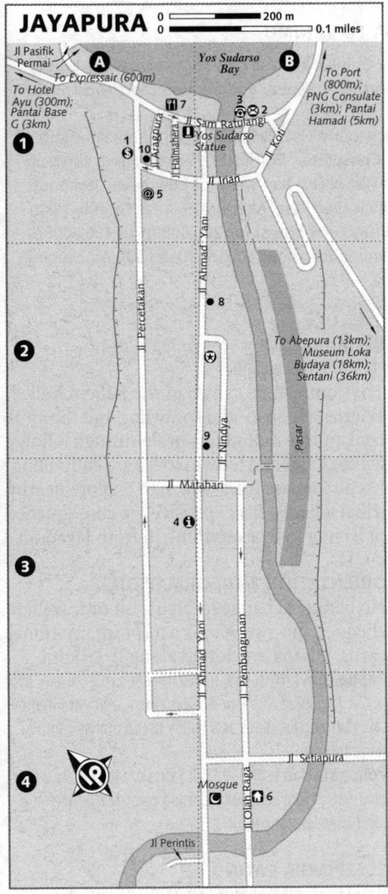

INFORMATION
- BII Bank......1 A1
- Main Post Office......2 B1
- Plasa Telkom......3 B1
- PT Kuwera Jaya......4 A3
- Warnet Media Papua......5 A1

SLEEPING
- Permata Hotel......6 B4

EATING
- Duta Café......(see 7)
- Seafood Warung......7 A1

TRANSPORT
- Garuda......8 B2
- Merpati......9 B2
- Pelni......10 A1

OUR PICK Permata Hotel (☎ 531333; hotelpermata@yahoo.co.id; Jl Olah Raga 3; s 195,000-430,000Rp; ❄) This new hotel on the edge of the market zone provides good, modern rooms with hot showers. Staff are welcoming and the restaurant is open 24 hours.

Seafood *warung* line the bay along Jl Pasifik Permai. Try **Duta Café** (meals 45,000Rp; 🕑 dinner), where the Makassar-style dishes come with four types of *sambal*. Only major hotels have bars.

Getting There & Away

Jayapura's airport is actually located in Sentani 36km west; see right.

Pelni (☎ 533270; Jl Argapura 15) liners leave Jayapura every two weeks bound for Sorong (1st/economy class 950,000/315,000Rp, two days) via selections of the intermediate ports – including Biak, Serui and Manokwari – and then on to Maluku and/or Sulawesi.

SENTANI

☎ 0967

Sentani, the growing airport town 36km west of Jayapura, is set between the forested Pegunungan Cyclop and beautiful Danau Sentani. It's quieter, cooler and more convenient than Jayapura. Don't miss the soul-soothing views of Danau Sentani from **Tugu MacArthur**. Most facilities are on Jl Kemiri Sentani Kota.

SLEEPING & EATING

Hotel Semeru Anaron (☎ 591447; Jl Yabaso 10; r 150,000-250,000Rp; ❄) This is the best-value cheapie, as well as very convenient to the airport. Rooms are slightly worn, but clean and comfortable.

OUR PICK Hotel Ratna (Hotel Ratna Keyko; ☎ 591119; fax 594449; Jl PLN 1; s/d incl breakfast 250,000/280,000Rp; ❄) The Ratna's rooms are very clean and comfortable and mostly good sized. Staff speak English, though the showers aren't heated. Dinners are available, and airport drop-offs are free.

GETTING THERE & AWAY

Jayapura airport (☎ 591809) is actually at Sentani. Airlines, most with Jayapura offices, include the following:

Expressair (☎ 550444; Blok G 10/2, Jl Pasifik Permai, Jayapura) Flies to Sorong, Makassar and Jakarta.

Garuda (☎ 522221/2; Jl Yani 5-7, Jayapura) Flies to Biak, Timika, Denpasar, Makassar and Jakarta.

Lion Air (☎ 594042/3; airport) To Makassar and Jakarta.

Merpati (☎ 533111; Jl Yani 15, Jayapura) Flies to Biak, Timika, Merauke, Makassar, Jakarta and Manado.

GETTING TO PAPUA NEW GUINEA: JAYAPURA TO VANIMO

There are no flights between Papua and Papua New Guinea, and the only route across the border that is open to foreigners is between Jayapura (northeast Papua) and Vanimo (northwest PNG, about 65km from Jayapura).

Most visitors to PNG need a visa; the standard 60-day tourist visa (225,000Rp) can be obtained (after a two- to five-day wait) at the **Papua New Guinea Consulate** (☎ 0967-531250; congenpng_id@yahoo.com; Jl Raya Argapura; ⏰ 9am-noon & 1-3pm Mon-Thu, variable hr Fri), 3km south of downtown Jayapura.

You can charter a *taksi* from the market at Abepura (called Pasar Abepura or Pasar Yotefa), 13km south of downtown Jayapura, to the border at Wutung (1½ hours) for 200,000Rp to 400,000Rp. Cross the border itself on foot then hire a car to Vanimo for about 10 kina (US$3.50). Air Niugini links Vanimo with Port Moresby three times weekly.

Getting to Sentani from Jayapura via public transport demands three different bemo, and 90 minutes. Taxis are pricey (200,000Rp, half-price outside the airport).

PULAU BIAK

☎ 0981 / pop 41,600

Pulau Biak has an impressive line-up of WWII sights, but with the emergence of the Raja Ampats as Papua's top beach and dive destination, Biak has been eclipsed.

Kota Biak is compact and easy to manage. Services are strung along Jl Ahmad Yani, Jl Sudriman and Jl Imam Bonjol. **Erick Farwas** (☎ 0813-4436 6385; laurenslexy@yahoo.co.id) offers dive outings.

Small, basic, yet clean, **Hotel Maju** (☎ 21841; Jl Imam Bonjol 45; s/d 85,000/115,000Rp; ❄) remains the best budget choice on Pulau Biak.

The Frans Kaisiepo airport is a short bemo ride away. **Merpati** (☎ 21213) and **Garuda** (☎ 25737) fly to Jayapura and beyond.

BALIEM VALLEY

The Baliem Valley is the most accessible gateway to tribal Papua. It's a place where *koteka* (penis gourds) are not yet out of fashion, pigs can buy love, sex or both, and the hills bloom with flowers and deep-purple sweet-potato fields. Unless you land here during the August high season, when Wamena and nearby villages host a festival with pig feasts, mock wars and traditional dancing to attract the tourism buck, you will be outnumbered by Christian missionaries (a constant presence since the valley's 'discovery' in 1938) and Javanese *transmigrasi*. You may also be startled by blatant evidence of Indonesia's neocolonisation of Papua, but mostly you will marvel at the mountain views, roaring rivers, tribal villages and at the tough but sweet spirit of the warm Dani people.

Wamena

☎ 0969 / pop 8500

The commercial centre in the Baliem Valley, Wamena is dusty and sprawling, but the air is cool, purple mountains peak through billowy white clouds and local markets are enthralling. It's also a base from which to explore nearby tribal villages. It's expensive – a consequence of having to fly everything in from Jayapura.

ORIENTATION & INFORMATION

No banks exchange foreign cash or travellers cheques, but two ATMs accept international cards. *Wartel* are dotted along Jl Trikora.

Papua.com (☎ 34488; fuj0627@yahoo.co.jp; Jl Yani 49; per hr 15,000Rp; ⏰ 9am-8.30pm) Busy, efficient internet cafe that also functions as a highly useful tourist information centre.

Police Station (☎ 31972; Jl Safri Darwin; ⏰ 9am-3pm Mon-Sat, 3-5pm Sun) For reporting on arrival or issuing a *surat jalan* (visitor permit).

SLEEPING & EATING

Hotel Syahrial Makmur (☎ 31306; Jl Gatot Subroto 51; r 150,000Rp) Each room is different at this cheapest place in town, but most are simple, with squat toilet and no hot water. The management speaks some English.

Hotel Mas Budi (☎ 31214; Jl Patimura 32; s 240,000-360,000Rp, d 290,000-410,000Rp) A very well-run place with 12 clean, good-sized rooms. All except the cheapest have hot showers in ample bathrooms; the hotel's restaurant is good.

our pick **Putri Dani Inn** (☎ 31685; Jl Irian 40; s 280,000Rp, d 300,000-350,000Rp) About 600m west of Jl Trikora, this family-run place offers spotless rooms with hot showers. Book ahead.

Restoran Blambangan (☎ 32444; Jl Trikora 99; mains 25,000-150,000Rp) Has a pleasant ambience and a typical Indonesian/Chinese menu. It serves beer.

SHOPPING

Possible souvenirs include *noken* (string bags; 25,000Rp to 100,000Rp); *suale* (head decorations made from cassowary feathers); the inevitable *koteka* (5000Rp to 60,000Rp, depending on size but no one ever asks for small); *mikak* (necklaces made of cowrie shells, feathers and bone); and *kapak* (black- or blue-stone axe blades; upward from 100,000Rp). Prepare to bargain.

GETTING THERE & AROUND

The main carriers between Jayapura (Sentani) and Wamena are **Trigana Air** (☎ 31611; airport) and **Aviastar** (☎ 34872; airport). Both normally fly four or more times daily each way, charging 825,000Rp. Book well ahead!

Around Wamena

Trekking is the best way to taste traditional life, and considering lodging prices in Wamena, the cost isn't prohibitive, but you can also see traditional people and customs, mummies, markets and terrific scenery during day trips from Wamena, Jiwika and Kurima.

Getting Around

From Wamena, hopelessly overcrowded bemo go as far south as Sugokmo (15,000Rp, 30 minutes); as far north, on the western side of the valley, as Pyramid (20,000Rp, one hour); and as far north on the eastern side as Tagime. They gather at the **'Misi' taksi terminal** (Jl Ahmad Yani).

CENTRAL & SOUTH BALIEM VALLEY

Wesaput is just across the airport, and home to the valley's only museum, the **Palimo Adat Museum** (admission by donation; noonish), with its limited collection of Dani artefacts.

Behind the museum, a swinging bridge leads to **Pugima**, a flat 4km walk on a trail that skirts charming Dani villages. At the end of Jl Yos Sudarso is **Sinatma**, where you'll find a bustling market and trails that lead to the thundering Sungai Wamena.

The road south through Baliem Valley stops a few kilometres short of **Kurima**, a village bursting with flowers, divided by the river and fed by cascading streams. This is the land of eternal spring. The walk here and around will take you through sweet-potato terraces to the best panoramas in the valley. You can rent a room in Kurima at the missionary house, but the best plan is to keep walking up the ridge to **Kilise**, where you can bed down at Alberth Elopore's **Kilise Guest House** (per person 50,000Rp, bring your own food) on clean bamboo mats in a traditional Dani grass hut with sweeping views that will simply immobilise you. Guides are a good idea for this trek, but they're not essential if you don't mind cooking. A popular three-day trek to the best southern villages is **Wamena–Kurima–Syoma–Wamena**.

EAST BALIEM VALLEY

Near **Pikhe**, the northern road crosses mighty Sungai Baliem and passes **Aikima**, the resting place of a 270-year-old **Werapak Elosak mummy** (admission 30,000Rp; daylight hr). **Jiwika** is the best base to explore the east. **Sumpaima**, 300m north of Jiwika, is home to the 280-year-old **Wimontok Mabel mummy** (admission 30,000Rp; daylight hr), the best of its kind near Wamena.

TREKKING THE BALIEM VALLEY

This is outstanding trekking country. Trails skirt and traverse rivers and sweet-potato fields, scale steep mountains, wind through remote mountain villages and lead you to magnificent panoramas. The hiking isn't easy, but you will come across old local women carrying bulging *noken* (string bags) strapped to their foreheads like saddlebags, so quit whining. It's normally cold at night, and it often rains, so bring appropriate gear. Your guide will arrange meals, but you should bring your own water, and plenty of it

Staying in village huts is an unforgettable experience. They should cost about 60,000Rp per person per night.

In Wamena, guides greet you at the airport and can be tough to shake. But if you plan on trekking, you should hire one. They may ask for some money upfront for supplies. That's standard, so don't stress.

English-speaking guides should cost around 300,000Rp per day, and a porter around 100,000Rp. Papua/Irian Jaya Adventure (p344) is run by Justinus Daby, an English-speaking Dani.

At the turn-off to Iluwe in Jiwika, you'll find **Lauk Inn** (r 80,000Rp), a pleasant spot with basic but clean rooms.

In **Wosilimo**, the incredible **Gua Wikuda** (admission 10,000Rp; 8am-4pm Mon-Sat) cave is 900m long and has stalagmites that are 1000 years old. Stay in a hut and fish well at **Danau Anegerak**, an hour's walk west of Wosilimo. From Wosilimo, a trekking trail continues beyond Pass Valley. A popular three-day trek will also take you from Jiwika, off the main road, to Pass Valley.

Public transport continues north to **Manda**, where there is more pretty countryside and hut-style sleeps. From Manda, trek to the Protestant, nonsmoking village of **Wolo**.

WEST BALIEM VALLEY

Pyramid is a graceful missionary village with churches, a theological college and a bustling market. You may be able to stay at **Kimbim**, a pleasant administrative centre with a few shops and a busy market.

SORONG

☎0951 / pop 140,000

Papua's second-biggest city, Sorong sits at the northwest tip of the Vogelkop. It's a busy port and base for oil and logging operations in the region. Few travellers stay longer than it takes to get on a boat to the absolutely fabulous Raja Ampat islands.

INFORMATION

Raja Ampat Tourism Office (☎/fax 326576; JE Meridien Hotel, Jl Basuki Rahmat Km 7; www.gorajaampat.com, www.diverajaampat.org; 9am-4pm Mon-Fri) Helpful office has maps and printed information sheets in English. It also runs a booth in the airport arrivals hall, open when flights arrive. Pay your 500,000Rp fee to visit the islands at one of these places.

SLEEPING & EATING

Most hotels are on Jl Yos Sudarso.

Hotel Tanjung (☎323782; Jl Yos Sudarso; s 126,000-225,000Rp, d 136,000-255,000Rp;) Situated on the Pantai Lido waterfront, popular Hotel Tanjung has a range of acceptable rooms, though the cheapest ones share bathrooms and lack air-con.

our pick **Rumah Makan Ratu Sayang** (☎321184; Jl Yos Sudarso; mains from 20,000Rp; noon-3pm & 6-10pm) Pick up the scent of fish on the grill and head inside this popular spot, 200m from Hotel Tanjung.

GETTING THERE & AROUND

The town sprawls, so taxis, *ojek* and chartered *angkot* are the best way to visit banks, airline offices, the main port or government offices. Official airport taxis charge 70,000Rp to hotels in town; out on the street you can charter a public *taksi* for half that.

Airlines flying here:

Expressair (☎328200; JE Meridien Hotel, Jl Basuki Rahmat Km 7) Flies to Jakarta, Jayapura and Makassar.

Lion Air (☎321444; Jl Basuki Rahmat Km 7) Flies to Ambon, Jakarta, Makassar and Manado.

Merpati (☎327000; Jl Sam Ratulangi 50, Kampung Baru) Flies to Jakarta and Makassar.

Pelni (☎321716; Jl Yani 13), near the west end of Jl Yani, has five ships sailing every two weeks east to Jayapura (via various combinations of intermediate ports, including Manokwari, Biak and Serui) and west to ports in Maluku, Sulawesi and Java.

RAJA AMPAT ISLANDS

pop 40,000

This group of 610 mostly uninhabited islands off the coast of Sorong offers some of the best – if not *the* best – diving in Indonesia. Raja Ampat's sheer numbers and variety of fish and its huge reef systems have divers in raptures. It's like swimming in a tropical aquarium.

Little known until the last few years, Raja Athe now sees a steady increase in visitors. The sparsely populated islands – though not geared to travellers on tight budgets – are also great for exploring jungle-covered islands, pristine white-sand beaches and hidden lagoons.

The four biggest islands are Waigeo in the north, with the fast-growing new regional capital, Waisai; Salawati, just southwest of Sorong; Batanta, off northern Salawati; and Misool to the southwest. The Dampier Strait between Waigeo and Batanta has many of the best dive sites, so most accommodation options are on Waigeo, Batanta or two smaller islands between them, Mansuar and Kri.

Visitors to the islands must pay a fee at the Raja Ampat Tourism Office in Sorong (left).

Diving

You can get up close and personal with huge manta rays and giant clams and gape

INDONESIA

at schools of barracuda, fusiliers or parrotfish. The reefs have hundreds of different brilliantly coloured soft and hard corals, and the marine topography varies from vertical walls and pinnacles to reef flats and underwater ridges.

Most dives are drift dives due to the currents washing over the reefs. The dive resorts offer packages but also provide diving services to people visiting independently, normally for €30 to €40 per dive, with equipment rental at around €30 per day.

Sleeping & Eating

The number of dive resorts is growing fast.

Kobe Oser Resort (☎ 081 3443 73398; mariarumbiak@yahoo.com; Yenwaupnor, Pulau Gam; full board per person 350,000Rp) Also known as Ibu Maria's, Kobe Oser has two rustic stilt bungalows set over the water at Yenwaupnor on the south coast of Pulau Gam. Meals are basic.

our pick **Kri Eco Resort** (☎ 0951-328038; www.papua-diving.com; Pulau Kri; 7-night dive package per person €998-1295) In operation since 1994, this is the original Raja Ampat dive lodge It has a gorgeous setting on little Pulau Kri, just off the eastern tip of Mansuar, and six of the spacious, airy, wooden guest bungalows have been built over crystal-clear waters along the jetty.

If you just turn up at a village you can usually sleep in someone's house. You should pay anything from 10,000/20,000Rp for a mat/bed, and another 10,000Rp if a meal is provided. A few villages have constructed basic tourist accommodation where you can sleep on mats for around 150,000Rp per person (take a mosquito net and some food with you; the villagers will usually cook for you):

Yenbuba East end of Pulau Mansuar: contact English-speaking Pak Dedy (☎ 081 2485 57279).

Yensawai North coast of Batanta: the 'homestay' is on Pulau Dayan, a few kilometres away. Contact Pak Leo (☎ 081 3447 54379).

Getting There & Around

Mega Express operates fast passenger boats with airline-style seating (economy/VIP 105,000/125,000Rp, two hours) to Waisai from Sorong's Usaha Mina harbour. The main dive resorts include boat transfers from and back to Sorong in their dive packages. Smaller places will usually collect you at Waisai if you contact them ahead.

INDONESIA DIRECTORY

ACCOMMODATION

Hotel, *losmen, penginapan, wisma:* there are several words for somewhere to lay a weary head, and options to suit every budget in most Indonesian towns.

Cheap hotels are usually pretty basic, but a simple breakfast is often included. Traditional washing facilities consist of a *mandi,* a large water tank from which you scoop cool water with a dipper. Climbing into the tank is very bad form! Rooms are assumed to come with a private *mandi* in this chapter, unless otherwise specified, although Western-style toilets are fairly common in tourist areas. The air-con symbol (❄) denotes whether air-con rooms are available, otherwise rooms are assumed to come with a fan.

Accommodation prices in tourist areas peak in July and August, and also during Easter and the Christmas period, though at the budget end of the market, price hikes are marginal. Elsewhere in the country, rates increase during Idul Fitri (the period following Ramadan).

Finding a room for 50,000Rp to 100,000Rp a night is possible wherever you are. In the large cities and provincial towns, expect a very plain, purely functional room for this. But along the main travelling trail, in Yogyakarta and in parts of Lombok and Sumatra, many budget places can be very attractive and decorated with artistic touches, and often come with a verandah. Bali is in a league of its own in terms of value for money, and for 100,000Rp a night there are some wonderful places, many with pools.

ACTIVITIES

Indonesia has world-class surfing, diving and snorkelling, trekking and rafting, and operators' prices are very competitive.

Diving & Snorkelling

Indonesian waters are some of the world's richest, its coral reefs incredibly diverse. But damage by destructive fishing practices has damaged and destroyed many once-pristine areas. Visibility can be limited during the wet season (roughly October to April).

Diving highlights include western Flores and Komodo, the Gili islands, Pulau Menjangan in Bali, Pulau Bunaken and the

PRACTICALITIES

- Videos you buy or watch are based on the PAL system, also used in Australia, New Zealand, the UK and most of Europe. Pirated DVDs are abundant and you usually get what you pay for.
- Electricity supply is 220V AC, 50Hz. The sockets accommodate two round prongs, the same as in most of Europe.

Togean Islands in Sulawesi, Pulau Weh in Sumatra, the Banda Islands in Maluku and the incredible Raja Ampat Islands in Papua.

PADI-linked schools are by far the most common. You'll need to bring your certification card if you are already qualified. If you want to get qualified, the Gili islands, Pulau Bunaken and Labuanbajo in Flores have the best choice of dive schools.

For information on responsible diving, see boxed text, p934.

All the above dive sites also offer excellent snorkelling, but if you're looking for a beach somewhere where you can just roll out of your bungalow in the morning, don a mask and fins and explore a wonderful reef, the Gilis and Pulau Bunaken fit the bill perfectly. Snorkelling gear costs about 20,000Rp a day to hire.

Spas & Treatments

If you fancy a pamper, Indonesia has some excellent-value options. From a humble massage on the beach (about 40,000Rp) through to facials and beauty treatments (starting at 60,000Rp) in salons to luxe spa sessions (from around 100,000Rp), you'll find plenty of opportunity to indulge.

Bali leads the way, with a multitude of beauty salons and spas in all the main travellers' centres. You'll also find a fair selection of spas in Yogyakarta (Java) and Senggigi (Lombok).

Surfing

Indonesia has waves that will send most surfers weak at the knees. With waves building momentum across the expanse of the Indian Ocean, all the islands on the southern side of the Indonesian archipelago – from Sumatra to Timor – get reliable, often exceptional, and sometimes downright frightening surf. The dry season, May to September, offers the most consistent waves, but is also the busiest time of year. During the wet season, the easterly beaches come into their own.

If you are just starting out, courses are run in Bali (see boxed text, p228). Surf stores in Bali stock most surfing accessories, including a wide range of boards, but come fully equipped if you're planning on surfing off the beaten track.

Trekking

Despite massive potential, trekking is far less established in Indonesia than it is in, say, Thailand. Local guide services are developing where demand exists, however, and the national parks offer some wonderful terrain to explore.

In Java, organised trekking is largely confined to some spectacular volcano hikes. There's more variety in Bali, the location of the wonderful Gunung Batur region, and the region around Munduk, which offers walks amid cool hillside forests, spice plantations and waterfalls.

Gunung Rinjani on Lombok is one of Indonesia's most dramatic and rewarding treks (from two to five days).

The Baliem Valley in Papua is also one of Indonesia's better-known walking destinations, and Tana Toraja has plenty of fabulous trekking opportunities through Sulawesi's spectacular traditional villages.

BOOKS

Lonely Planet's *Bali & Lombok*, *Borneo* and *Indonesia* guides explore the country in more detail, while Lonely Planet's *Indonesian Phrasebook* is the perfect guide to the language. Read *Healthy Travel: Asia* for the lowdown on keeping healthy during your travels.

Lyall Watson's *Gifts of Unknown Things* observes the symbiotic relationship of a community and its environment on an unnamed Indonesian island. The value of the natural world features highly in the book, and fans describe it as life affirming.

Tim Flannery's *Throwim Way Leg* is a must for Papuan inspiration. The author recounts his scientific expeditions to the province, where he discovered new species in Indiana Jones–style adventures.

Simon Winchester's highly readable *Krakatoa – The Day the World Exploded* melds history, geology and politics, all centred on the 1888 eruption of Krakatau – the world's biggest bang.

In Search of Moby Dick, by Tim Severin, is an engagingly written search for the globe's last whale-hunters that includes an extended stay in the remote whaling village of Lamalera, Nusa Tenggara.

The Year of Living Dangerously by Christopher J Koch is the harrowing tale of a journalist in Soekarno's Indonesia of 1965. Many have seen the movie with a young Mel Gibson and Linda Hunt. The book is more harrowing.

Eat, Pray, Love by Elizabeth Gilbert is a publishing sensation. Fans of the lurid, self-absorbed prose flock to Ubud looking for love. The movie version will only add to the onslaught.

BUSINESS HOURS

Government offices are *generally* open Monday to Friday from 8am to 4pm – with a break for Friday prayers from 11.30am to 1.30pm – and Saturday until noon. Go early if you want to get anything done.

Banks are open Monday to Friday, usually from 8am to 4pm. In some places banks open on Saturday until around noon. Foreign exchange hours may be more limited and some banks close their foreign exchange counter at 1pm. Money changers are open longer hours.

Restaurants are generally open daily from around 7am until 9pm, though many large cities have 24-hour places and late-night stalls.

Most shops are open daily between 8am and 6pm; in tourist areas, they'll often open as late as 9pm.

Listings in this chapter don't indicate hours unless they vary from those above.

CLIMATE

Indonesia is hot and humid all year round, with wet and dry seasons. In coastal areas the heat is usually less oppressive, and it can get downright chilly in the high mountains at dawn.

Generally, the wet season starts later the further southeast you go. In North Sumatra, the rain begins to fall in September, but in Timor it doesn't fall until November. In January and February it rains most days. The dry season is basically from May to September. The odd islands out are those of Maluku, where the wet season is the reverse, running from May to September.

See the regional climate charts (p936).

CUSTOMS

Customs regulations allow you to bring in 1L of alcohol and 200 cigarettes (or 50 cigars).

Any material containing partial nudity will be deemed pornographic and may be confiscated.

WHERE TO SURF

New surf spots are being discovered all the time in Indonesia, the choices simply never end.

Java

Batu Karas (p201), with fine breaks, is one of the most enjoyable places to kick back in Java.

Grajagan (G-Land) at Alas Purwo National Park (see boxed text, p221) on Java's southeastern tip is home to a world-famous and world-class surfing break.

Bali

Bali is touted as a surfing mecca. Though getting to the breaks can be an adventure in itself, the rewards at the end of the road can be well worth it. See boxed text, p228 for details.

Nusa Tenggara

Lombok's Kuta (p298) has world-class waves and turquoise water.

Sumbawa has superb surf at isolated Maluk (p301).

Sumatra

Northern Sumatra's Pulau Nias (p270) is the most-visited surfing destination in the province.

The Mentawai Islands have good surf camps and draw charters (p264).

DANGERS & ANNOYANCES

If you've never been before, Indonesia might seem like one of the world's most dodgy nations: accident-prone, and cursed by natural disasters and terrorist outrages.

But while transport safety standards are dodgy, earthquakes are frequent and there has been a number of highly publicised incidents of terrorism and sectarian violence, Indonesia is actually a very safe nation for travellers, unless you're very unlucky.

Personal safety, even in the big cities, is not usually a major concern. Keep your wits about you, yes, but violent crime (and even petty theft) is very rare in Indonesia. Be mindful of your valuables and take the usual precautions and the chances of getting into trouble are tiny.

It *is* important to keep abreast of current political developments, however, and maybe give political or religious demos a wide berth. At the time of writing, most of the country was peaceful. The internet should keep you in touch with developments, or consult your embassy.

See also p937 for information on the risks associated with recreational drug use. As they say in Singapore, the penalties if caught can be severe. And beware of noncommercial arak, the potent rice or palm hootch. There have been incidents of poisoning.

But most importantly, go and enjoy yourself.

DRIVING LICENCE

If you plan to drive a car or motorbike in Indonesia it's useful to have an International Driving Permit. There can be nettlesome 'fines' for unlicensed driving, particularly in Bali, where some policeman regularly target drivers.

EMBASSIES & CONSULATES

Consult p357 for details of visa and entry requirements.

BALI

All telephone numbers take the area code ☎0361:

Australia (Map p235; ☎241118; www.dfat.gov.au/bali; Jl Tantular 32, Denpasar; ⏰8am-noon & 12.30-4pm Mon-Fri) The Australian consulate has a consular sharing agreement with Canada, and may also be able to help citizens of New Zealand and Ireland.

Japan (off Map p235; ☎227628; konjpdps@indo.net.id; Jl Raya Puputan 170, Renon, Denpasar)

USA (off Map p235; ☎233605; amcobali@indosat.net.id; Jl Hayam Wuruk 188, Renon, Denpasar; ⏰8am-4.30pm) A consular agent.

JAKARTA

All phone numbers take area code ☎021:

Australia (Map p180; ☎2550 5555; www.indonesia.embassy.gov.au; Jl HR Rasuna Said Kav 15-16)

Brunei (off Map p182; ☎3190 6080; Jalan Teuku Umar 9, Menteng)

Canada (Map p180; ☎2550 7800; www.geo.international.gc.ca/asia/jakarta/; World Trade Centre, 6th fl, Jl Jenderal Sudirman Kav 29-31)

France (Map p182; ☎2355 7600; www.ambafrance-id.org/; Jl Thamrin 20)

Germany (Map p182; ☎3985 5000; www.jakarta.diplo.de; Jl Thamrin 1)

Japan (Map p182; ☎3192 4308; www.id.emb-japan.go.jp/; Jl Thamrin 24)

Malaysia (Map p180; ☎522 4947; www.kln.gov.my/perwakilan/Jakarta; Jl HR Rasuna Said Kav X/6 No 1)

Netherlands (Map p180; ☎524 8200; www.indonesia.nlembassy.org; Jl HR Rasuna Said Kav S-3)

New Zealand (Map p180; ☎2995 5800; www.nzembassy.com; 10th fl, Sentral Senayan 2, Jl Asia Afrika No 8)

Papua New Guinea (Map p180; ☎725 1218; 6th fl, Panin Bank Centre, Jl Jenderal Sudirman 1)

Singapore (Map p180; ☎2995 0400; www.mfa.gov.sg/jkt/; Jl HR Rasuna Said, Block X/4 Kav 2)

Thailand (Map p182; ☎390 4052; www.thaiembassy.org/Jakarta/; Jl Imam Bonjol 74)

UK (Map p182; ☎2356 5226; www.ukinindonesia.fco.gov.uk; Jl Thamrin 75)

USA (Map p184; ☎3435 9000; www.usembassyjakarta.org; Jl Merdeka Selatan 4-5)

MEDAN

All phone numbers listed for Medan take area code ☎061:

Australia (Map p277; ☎415 7810; Australia Centre, Jl RA Kartini 32)

Germany (☎456 8006; Jl Samanhudi 16)

India (Map p277; ☎453 1308; Jl Uskup Agung)

Japan (Map p277; ☎457 5193; Wisma BII 5, Jl Diponegoro 18)

Malaysia (Map p277; ☎453 1342; Jl Diponegoro 43)

Netherlands (Map p277; ☎456 9853; Jl Monginsidi 45T)

UK (☎821 0559; J1 Kapt Pattimura 459B)

USA (Map p277; ☎451 9000; Jl MT Haryono A-1, Uni Plaza)

FESTIVALS & EVENTS

Although some public holidays have a fixed date, the dates for many events vary each year depending on Muslim, Buddhist or Hindu calendars.

January/February

New Year's Day Celebrated on 1 January.
Imlek (Chinese New Year) Special food is prepared, decorations adorn stores and homes, and *barongasai* (lion dances) are performed; held in January/February.
Muharram (Islamic New Year) The date varies each year, but is usually in late January.

March/April

Mohammed's Birthday Celebrated in February in 2010; prayers are held in mosques throughout the country, and there are street parades in Solo and Yogyakarta.
Hindu New Year (Nyepi) Held in March/April; in Bali and other Hindu communities, villagers make as much noise as possible to scare away devils. Virtually all of Bali closes.
Good Friday Occurs in March or April.

April/May

Waisak (Buddha's Birthday) Mass prayers are said at the main Buddhist temples, including Borobudur.

May/June

Ascension of Christ Occurs in May/June.

August

Independence Day Celebrated on 17 August with plenty of pomp and circumstance; government buildings are draped in huge red-and-white flags and banners, and there are endless marches.

September/October

Ascension of Mohammed Special prayers are held in mosques; it occurs in July 2010.
Lebaran (Idul Fitri) Celebrated in September in 2010; everyone returns to their home villages for special prayers and gift giving, and it's a time for charity donations.

November/December

Idul Adha The end of the Haj is celebrated with animal sacrifices, the meat of which is given to the poor; occurs in November in 2010.
Christmas Day Marked by gift giving and special church services in Christian areas; the celebration falls on 25 December.

The Muslim fasting month of Ramadan requires that Muslims abstain from food, drink, cigarettes and sex between sunrise and sunset. Many bars and restaurants close and it is important to avoid eating or drinking publicly in Muslim areas during this time. For the week before and after Lebaran (Idul Fitri), the festival to mark the end of the fast, transport is often fully booked and travelling becomes a nightmare – plan to stay put at this time. Ramadan, Idul Fitri and Idul Adha (Muslim day of sacrifice) move back 10 days or so every year, according to the Muslim calendar.

With such a diversity of people in the archipelago there are many other local holidays, festivals and cultural events.

The *Indonesia Calendar of Events* covers holidays and festivals throughout the archipelago; some tourist offices stock it.

FOOD & DRINK

Food

A *rumah makan* (literally 'eating house') is the cheaper equivalent of a *restoran*, but the dividing line is often hazy. The cheapest option of all is the *warung*, a makeshift or permanent food stall, but again the food may be the same as in a *rumah makan*. With any roadside food it pays to be careful about the hygiene. The *pasar* (market) is a good food source, especially the *pasar malam* (night market). Mobile *kaki lima* (food stalls) serve cheap snack foods and meals.

As with food in the rest of Southeast Asia, Indonesian cuisine is heavily based on rice. *Nasi goreng* is the national dish: it's basically fried rice, with an egg on top in *istimewa* (deluxe) versions. *Nasi campur*, rice with a little meat, fish or vegetables (whatever is available), is a *warung* favourite and is often served cold. The two other typical Indonesian dishes are *gado gado* and satay (*sate* in Bahasa Indonesia). *Gado gado* is a fresh salad with prawn crackers, boiled egg and peanut sauce. It tends to vary a lot, so if your first one isn't so special try again somewhere else. Satay are tiny kebabs served with a spicy peanut sauce.

Padang food, from the Padang region in Sumatra, is famed for its rich, chilli-heavy sauces, and is popular throughout Indonesia. It's usually delicious, though not cooked fresh – dishes are displayed for hours (days even) in the restaurant window. Padang restaurant *(masakan Padang)* food is served one of two ways. Usually a bowl of rice is plonked in front of you, followed by a whole collection of small bowls of vegetables, meat and fish. Or you approach the window display and pick a few dishes yourself. Either way you pay for what you eat (typically 8000Rp to 15,000Rp).

Drink

Bottled water and soft drinks are available everywhere, and many hotels and restaurants provide *air putih* (boiled water) for guests. The iced juice drinks can be good, but take care that the water/ice has been purified or is bottled. (Ice in Jakarta and Bali is usually fine.)

Indonesian tea is fine and coffee can be excellent; for a strong local brew ask for *kopi java* or *kopi flores*, depending where you are of course. Beer is quite superb: Bintang is one of Asia's finest and costs 12,000Rp to 20,000Rp for a large bottle in most places. Bali Brem rice wine is really potent, and the more you drink the nicer it tastes. *Es buah*, or *es campur*, is a strange concoction of fruit salad, jelly cubes, syrup, crushed rice and condensed milk. And it tastes absolutely *enak* (delicious).

GAY & LESBIAN TRAVELLERS

Gay travellers in Indonesia will experience few problems, especially in Bali. Physical contact between same-sex couples is acceptable (Indonesian boys and girls often hold hands or link arms in public). Homosexual behaviour is not illegal – the age of consent is 16. Immigration officials may restrict entry to people who reveal HIV-positive status. Gay men in Indonesia are referred to as *homo* or *gay;* lesbians are *lesbi.*

Indonesia's transvestite/transsexual *waria* – from *wanita* (woman) and *pria* (man) – community has always had a public profile.

Indonesia has a number of gay and lesbian organisations. The coordinating body is **GAYa Nusantara** (www.gayanusantara.or.id), which publishes the monthly magazine *GAYa Nusantara*. **Utopia Asia** (www.utopia-asia.com) also has an extensive list of gay and lesbian venues throughout Indonesia and the rest of Asia.

HOLIDAYS

See p353 for a list of public holidays, which are often religious days or festivals.

INTERNET ACCESS

Internet places are common in most towns and tourist centres. Speeds are usually very pedestrian though, and broadband access is less common outside Bali and larger cities (where you will also find hotels, cafes and shops with wi-fi). Expect to pay between 5000Rp and 12,000Rp per hour.

INTERNET RESOURCES

The following sites are all good for giving you a feel for current events in Indonesia; some go further and explore the ever-evolving culture of the country.

Antara (www.antara.co.id/en) This is the site for the official Indonesian news agency; it has a searchable database.

Inside Indonesia (www.insideindonesia.org) News and thoughtful features; excellent.

Indonesia Traveling (www.indonesiatraveling.com) Fantastic site with detailed information about Indonesia's parks, nature reserves and the critters you might encounter. Also links to charter sailing boats and much more.

Jakarta Globe (www.thejakartaglobe.com) The top-notch new national English-language newspaper.

Jakarta Post (www.thejakartapost.com) Indonesia's original English-language daily; good cultural coverage.

LonelyPlanet.com (www.lonelyplanet.com) Share knowledge and experiences with other travellers about islands that have been Lonely Planet favourites from the start.

LEGAL MATTERS

Drugs, gambling and pornography are illegal, and it is an offence to engage in paid work, or stay in the country for more than 60 days, on a tourist pass.

Despite claims of reform, corruption is still widespread. Police often stop motorists on minor or dubious traffic infringements in the hope of obtaining bribes. The best advice is to remain calm, keep your money in your pocket until it is asked for and sit through the lecture – it is unlikely more than 50,000Rp will be demanded.

In case of an accident involving serious injury or death, the best advice is to drive straight to the nearest police station, as an angry mob may soon gather.

MAPS

Many locally produced maps are pretty inaccurate. Periplus produces good maps of many Indonesian cities and regions.

MEDIA

Newspapers & Magazines

English-language press includes the *Jakarta Post* and the impressive new *Jakarta Globe*. The *International Herald-Tribune* is sold in Jakarta and Bali. In Bali, European and Australian newspapers are sold by street hawkers; elsewhere you can find the odd one in the major bookshops.

Radio & TV

You can pick up BBC World Service, Voice of America, Radio Australia and many more stations with a short-wave radio, though reception quality varies a lot.

Many hotel rooms have TVs – a box is almost standard in midrange places. Thanks to satellite broadcasting, most major sporting events can be seen (often on ESPN) and you'll have no problem seeing English Premier League football games; Australian and American sports are far less popular, although bars with expats anywhere will show sports.

MONEY

The unit of currency in Indonesia is the rupiah (Rp). Coins of 50, 100, 200 and 500 rupiah are in circulation in both the old silver-coloured coins and the newer bronze-coloured coins. Both 1000Rp and 25Rp coins exist but are very rarely seen. Notes come in 1000, 5000, 10,000, 20,000, 50,000 and 100,000 rupiah denominations. The largest can be hard to break.

ATMs

ATMs are common on the main islands of Indonesia – indeed, it's possible to travel through most of the nation with just a card or two without ever setting foot inside a bank (although a good rule is if the place isn't served by good, paved roads you may not find ATMs). But ATMs fail regularly, and some only dispense pitifully small amounts (500,000Rp) in one transaction. Others will only accept certain cards.

It's wise to carry a stash of cash in rupiah for emergencies.

Bargaining & Tipping

Bargaining is generally required in markets and for transport (particularly taxis) in places where prices are not fixed. Tipping is not a normal practice in Indonesia but is appreciated and often expected for special service.

Credit Cards

MasterCard and Visa are by far the most widely accepted plastic cards.

Don't expect to pay for a meal in a *warung* with plastic; generally it's only top-end places that accept credit cards (and they're virtually useless in places like Papua and Maluku).

Getting a cash advance on your card is a particularly useful way to obtain a large chunk of money in one transaction, though it's often only the major bank branches in larger towns that will give you this facility in Indonesia; you should expect a charge of around 15,000Rp to 30,000Rp for the privilege.

Exchanging Money

After years of turmoil the rupiah has been relatively stable for several years; check out the latest rates on www.xe.com.

US dollars are the most widely accepted foreign currency and have the best exchange rates; euros are a distant second.

Money changers are open longer hours and change money (cash or cheques) much faster than the banks. Be careful in Kuta, Bali, where money changers are notorious for short-changing.

POST

The postal service in Indonesia is generally good and the poste-restante service at *kantor pos* (post offices) is reasonably efficient in the main tourist centres. Expected mail always seems to arrive, eventually.

RESPONSIBLE TRAVEL

You have to haggle in Indonesia, but it's important to do so respectfully and learn when to draw the line. It's very bad form to shout or lose your temper. Remember that a few extra rupiah may make a great deal of difference to the other party.

Indonesia is a conservative, largely Muslim country, and while bikinis and Speedos are tolerated in the beach resorts of Bali, try to respect local clothing traditions wherever possible. This is particularly true if you are near a mosque.

EXCHANGE RATES

Exchange rates at the time of press:

Country	Unit	Rupiah (Rp)
Australia	A$1	8532
Canada	C$1	9026
Euro zone	€1	14,136
Japan	¥100	10,756
Malaysia	RM10	27,926
New Zealand	NZ$1	6976
Singapore	S$1	6852
Thailand	10B	2887
UK	UK£1	15,415
USA	US$1	9648

Couples should avoid canoodling or kissing in public.

A little Bahasa Indonesia, which is very easy to pick up, will get you a long way. Not only will you delight the locals, but it'll save you cash when it comes to dealing with stall owners, hoteliers and becak drivers.

But the best way to responsibly visit Indonesia is to try to be as less invasive as possible. Resources are often scarce and serving travellers can have a huge impact on local ecology through water use, refuse etc. Travelling green is easier than it sounds, especially in a country where environmental awareness is nascent at best, but consider the following tips:

- Watch your use of water. Demand often outstrips supply. Take up your hotel on its offer to save lots of water by not washing your sheets and towels every day. Don't stay at a place with a pool, especially if the ocean is next door.
- Don't hit the bottle. Those bottles of water are convenient but they add up. The zillions of such bottles tossed away each year are a major blight. Still, you're wise not to refill from the tap, so what do you do? Ask your hotel or eatery if you can refill from their huge containers of drinking water if they have them. Look for bottle refilling stations.
- Conserve power. Open the windows at night for often cooler breezes if the room has air-con. Don't cheat, turn it off when you go out.
- Don't drive yourself crazy. Can you take a bus or bemo instead of a chartered or rental car? Would a walk, trek or hike be more enjoyable than a road journey to an overvisited tourist spot? You can hire a bike for US$3 per day or less.
- Slow down. If you have the time, enjoy a ferry, don't fly. The train service in Java is a democratic experience.

STUDYING

Many cultural and language courses are available, particularly in the main tourist areas. Bali takes the lead, offering a little something for just about everyone. Ubud is Bali's culinary capital and there are courses to teach the inquisitive gastronome a thing or two. Look for advertisements at your hotel, enquire at local restaurants and bars, ask fellow travellers and hotel staff, and check out the tourist newspapers and magazines.

Culture junkies and art addicts are also looked after with a host of courses in Ubud (see p239 for more information). Short batik courses are popular in Yogyakarta (see p205) and in Solo (p214).

TELEPHONE

The country code for Indonesia is ☎ 62; the international access code is usually ☎ 001, but it varies from *wartel* to *wartel*.

International calls are usually cheap from the state-run Telkom offices found in every town. Privately run *wartel* offer the same services. You can also call home using phonecards *(kartu chip)* for similar rates to a *wartel*.

Internet connections fast enough to support Voice Over Internet (VOI) services like Skype are now common in the most popular parts of Bali, Jakarta and other modern areas. Some internet centres are hip to this and some allow it, while others add a surcharge for the call to your connection time (perhaps 3000Rp per minute). If you're staying at a place with fast wi-fi in your room, you're really set.

Indonesia has an extensive and reliable mobile network. SIM cards (around 30,000Rp) are sold everywhere and call rates are very cheap. At phone kiosks used by foreigners, such as those on South Bali, staff can sell you a SIM card that offers the cheapest rates to your home country (as low as US$0.25 per minute).

TIME

Indonesia has three time zones. Western Indonesia time (Sumatra, Java, West and Central Kalimantan) is seven hours ahead of GMT, central Indonesia time (Bali, South and East Kalimantan, Sulawesi and Nusa Tenggara) is eight hours ahead, and east Indonesia time (Maluku and Irian Jaya) is nine hours ahead.

TOILETS

Public toilets are extremely rare except in bus and train stations. Expect to have to dive into restaurants and hotels frequently.

Indonesian toilets are holes in the ground with footrests on either side, although Western toilets are becoming more common in tourist areas. To flush, reach for that plastic scooper, take water from the tank and flush it away.

TOURIST INFORMATION

The usefulness of tourist offices varies greatly from place to place. Some provide good maps and information, while others may have nothing to offer at all. Wherever you are, signs are not always in English; look for *dinas pariwisata* (tourist office).

Indonesia's national tourist organisation, the **Ministry of Culture and Tourism** (Map p184; ☎ 021-383 8167; www.budpar.go.id; Jl Merdeka Barat 17, Jakarta), maintains a head office in Jakarta as well as offices in each province. Its website is a good source of links; otherwise you won't find it overly useful.

Often a guest-house owner or travel agent is the best source of tourist information.

TRAVELLERS WITH DISABILITIES

Laws covering the disabled date back to 1989, but Indonesia has very few dedicated programs and is a difficult destination for those with limited mobility. Bali, with its wide range of tourist facilities, and Jakarta are the easiest destinations to navigate.

VISAS

Depending on your nationality you may be able to obtain a visa on arrival (VOA) at recognised entry points in Indonesia, which comprise 15 airports and 21 sea ports. These include ferry ports to/from Sumatra: Penang–Medan, Penang–Belawan, Melaka–Dumai and Singapore–Batam/Bintan. All major international airports are covered.

There are two types of VOA; a seven day (US$10) and a 30 day (US$25). Both visas are nonextendable.

At the time of writing, citizens of 63 countries were eligible for a VOA, including those from Australia, Canada, France, Germany, Ireland, Japan, the Netherlands, New Zealand, the UK and the USA.

To get a much-prized 60-day visa you have to apply through an embassy or consulate before you arrive in Indonesia.

Indonesia requires that your passport is valid for six months following your date of arrival.

Travel Permits

Technically, if you're heading to Papua you should obtain a *surat jalan* (visitor permit; see boxed text, p344).

VOLUNTEERING

There are excellent opportunities for aspiring volunteers in Indonesia. For additional info, see p943.

Bali is a hub for many charitable groups and NGOs, including the following:

Friends of the National Parks Foundation (☎ 0361-977 978; www.fnpf.org; Jl Bisma 3, Ubud) Its main office is in Bali. It has volunteer programs in and around Tanjung Puting National Park in central Kalimantan.

ProFauna (☎ 0361-424731; www.profauna.or.id) Large animal-protection organisation operating across Indonesia; the Bali office has been aggressive in protecting sea turtles.

SOS (Sumatran Orangutan Society; www.orangutans-sos.org) An Ubud-based group that works to save endangered species throughout Indonesia.

Papua has **Peace Brigades International** (www.peacebrigades.org) for people committed to working for human rights and 'positive peacebuilding'. It is also active in Jakarta.

On Sulawesi, the following are always looking for support:

Borneo Orangutan Survival Foundation (BOS; www.orangutan.or.id) Accepts volunteers for its orang-utan and sun bear rehabilitation and reforestation programs at Samboja Lestari between Balikpapan and Samarinda.

Kalaweit Care Centre (☎/fax 0536-322 6388; www.kalaweit.org) Accepts volunteers (not visitors) for rehabilitating ex-captive gibbons.

WOMEN TRAVELLERS

Plenty of Western women travel in Indonesia, and most seem to get through the country without major problems. However, women travelling solo will receive extra attention, and some of it will be unwanted. To avoid this, some women invent a boyfriend or a husband, who they are 'meeting soon'. A wedding ring can also be a good idea, while a photo of you and your 'partner' also works well. Sunglasses and a hat are a good way to avoid eye contact.

While Indonesian men are generally very courteous, there is a macho element that indulges in puerile behaviour – horn honking, lewd comments etc. Ignore them, as Indonesian women do; they are unsavoury but generally harmless. There are some things you can do to minimise harassment – the most important is dressing appropriately. Dressing modestly won't stop the attention but it will lessen its severity. In fundamentalist regions such as Aceh in northern Sumatra, it is essential that women cover up (including the arms, although a loose-fitting T-shirt that covers the tops of your arms will do). Walk around in shorts and a singlet and you'll be touched, grabbed and leered at by men in the street; cover up and they'll just call out as you walk past.

Many women travel alone on Bali, especially in Ubud.

Laos

HIGHLIGHTS

- **Luang Prabang** (p383) The pearl of the Orient and arguably Southeast Asia's most romantic city: mystical temples, tasty cuisine and Indochinese architecture. Prepare to stay a while.
- **Luang Nam Tha and Muang Sing** (p399) The heart of responsible trekking in the ethnically diverse wilderness of Nam Ha National Park Area.
- **Si Phan Don** (p417) A series of lazy islands kissed by the turquoise waters of the Mekong. Get thee to a hammock – between tubing, cycling and spotting the rare Irrawaddy dolphin.
- **Wat Phu Champasak** (p416) These serenely positioned Khmer-era ruins lie beside the sleepy, riverside village of Champasak and may have been the blueprint for Angkor Wat.
- **Kong Lo cave** (p407) Enter this creepy underworld: bats, stalactites, cathedral-high darkness and the sound of your heartbeat echoing along the 7.5km tunnel.
- **Off the beaten track** (p397) Visit the atmospheric Vieng Xai caves, HQ of the Pathet Lao resistance during Laos' fight for independence, and prison of its last king.

FAST FACTS

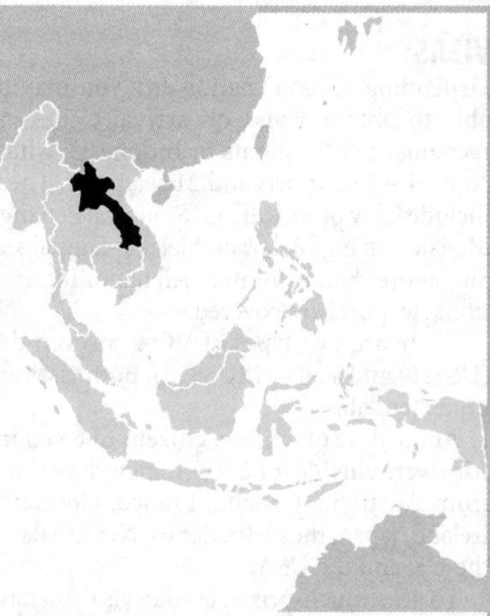

- **Budget** US$15 to US$20 a day
- **Capital** Vientiane
- **Costs** city guest house 50,000 to 100,000 kip (US$6 to US$12), four-hour bus ride 40,000 kip (US$4.70), Beer Lao 7500 kip (US$0.90)
- **Country code** ☎ 856
- **Languages** Lao, ethnic dialects
- **Money** US$1 = 8513 kip
- **Phrases** *sábąai-dii* (hello), *sábąai-dii* (goodbye), *khàwp jąi* (thank you)
- **Population** 6.8 million
- **Time** GMT + seven hours
- **Visas** Thirty-day tourist visas are available in advance in Thailand, China, Vietnam or Cambodia. On-the-spot 30-day visas are available for US$30 to US$40 (depending on nationality) with two passport photos on arrival in Vientiane, Luang Prabang and Pakse international airports, and when crossing the border from Thailand, China and Vietnam.

TRAVEL HINT

Despite newly sealed roads making life easier on long journeys, Laos' buses are still ancient and seemingly made of wet cardboard (watch the sides folding in on tight corners!). Factor in plenty of spare time for your journey to account for punctures and breakdowns, and arm yourself with fluids, fruit and plenty of patience.

OVERLAND ROUTES

Landlocked Laos has multiple entry points from Thailand and Vietnam, one from China and one from Cambodia.

This sleepy country of gilded temples, tangerine-robed monks, emerald rice padi and impossibly friendly people is unlike any other. Whether it's ecotrekking in pristine jungles, romantically meandering down the Mekong River or living it up in the old Indochinese capital of Luang Prabang, the choices are myriad. As a developing nation Laos is balancing the preservation of its rich natural resources with its hungry ambition to escape its status as one of the poorest nations on earth (logging is still a major issue); however, responsible, low-impact trips into its many protected areas allow you authentic adventures and sometimes very close encounters with the wild things that dwell in them!

Laos has recently become the darling of glossy editorials, with the emergence of boutique-style digs, but at its heart it's still very much a shoestringer's gem, where rugged travel off the package circuit reaps the greatest rewards. The Land of a Million Elephants is only just stirring and the typical rustic scene of thatched houses, colourful ethnic tribes and unbroken forests is much the same as that which greeted French colonials over a century ago, but with recently improved highways you can expect easier journeys than they did, not to mention a considerably revamped national airline. Now really is the best time to visit, before mystical Laos inevitably slips into the 21st century.

CURRENT EVENTS

Since the 1980s, socialism, following its unsuccessful attempt to flourish, has been softened to allow for private enterprise and foreign investment. Recently Laos has reinvented itself as the crossroads state between China, Thailand and Vietnam; its economy is growing with an annual GDP of 8%, which sees its ambition – of escaping its current status as one of the world's 20 poorest nations by 2020 – as fast becoming a reality. Interestingly, of the major nations, only Japan and China have remained stronger than Laos' fledgling currency in the 2008–2009 global recession.

China has become Laos' *new best friend* as it muscles in on the country's rich timber resources (see the boxed text, p363). In return for its building stadiums and improved sealed highways, Laos allows the red giant an apparent carte blanche to take what it needs. A huge area of land in Vientiane has just been leased to the Chinese to allow 50,000 migrant workers to come and settle a satellite town.

The world's environmentalists are more anxious as to what's happening to the country's unique diversity of wildlife, disrupted by the building of lucrative hydroelectric dams and the continued logging of huge swathes of forest. It's a difficult balance – the preservation of one of the world's richest ecosystems versus Laos' need to financially support itself and keep up with other members of Asean (Association of South-East Asian Nations).

Rural poverty – and the skyrocketing scrap-metal trade in China – has also seen a rise in unexploded ordnance (UXO) fatalities. A lasting legacy of the US-led Secret War, UXOs are another factor in Laos' slow development as land is virtually unusable until it's cleared – an expensive and time-consuming process. You can do your bit by not buying war relics.

On the plus side, education has improved in recent years with school enrolment rates at 85%, though many drop out by the time of their secondary education; the planting and harvesting of crops, especially among the highlands, is seen as more important than education.

In May 2009 a British national brought Laos to the world media when she was sentenced to death for trafficking heroin. She later had her sentence commuted to life when she succeeded in inseminating herself while incarcerated (under Lao law a pregnant woman cannot be executed).

HISTORY

The Kingdom of Lan Xang

Before the French, British, Chinese and Siamese drew a line around it, Laos was a collection of disparate principalities subject to an ever-revolving cycle of war, invasion, prosperity and decay. Laos' earliest brush with nationhood was in the 14th century, when Khmer-backed Lao warlord Fa Ngum conquered Wieng Chan (Vientiane). It was Fa Ngum who gave his kingdom the title still favoured by travel romantics and businesses – Lan Xang, or (Land of a) Million Elephants. He also made Theravada Buddhism the state religion and adopted the symbol of Lao sovereignty that remains in use today, the Pha Bang Buddha image, after which Luang Prabang is named. Lan Xang reached its peak in the 17th century, when it was the dominant force in Southeast Asia.

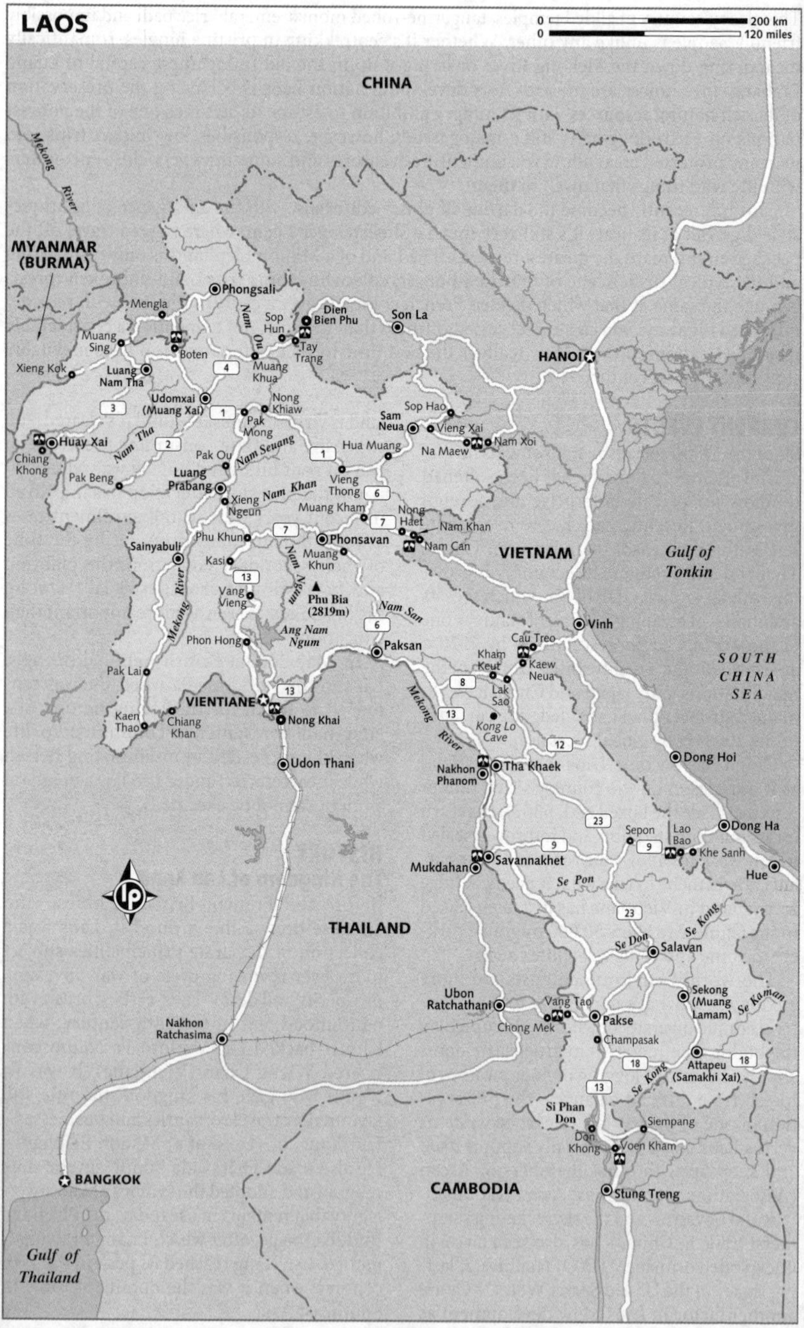

LAOS

0 200 km
0 120 miles

CHINA
Mekong River
MYANMAR (BURMA)
Phongsali
Mengla
Nam Ou
Sop Hun
Dien Bien Phu
Son La
Muang Sing
Boten
Tay Trang
Xieng Kok
Luang Nam Tha
4
Muang Khua
HANOI
Udomxai (Muang Xai)
Nong Khiaw
3
1
Pak Mong
Sop Hao
Sam Neua
Vieng Xai
Huay Xai
Nam Tha
2
Nam Seuang
Hua Muang
Na Maew
Nam Xoi
Chiang Khong
Pak Ou
1
Pak Beng
Luang Prabang
Vieng Thong
6
Xieng Ngeun
Nam Khan
Muang Kham
Nong Haet
7
7
Nam Khan
Phu Khun
Phonsavan
Nam Can
Sainyabuli
Muang Khun
VIETNAM
Gulf of Tonkin
Kasi
Nam Ngum
13
Phu Bia (2819m)
Mekong River
Vang Vieng
Nam San
Vinh
6
Ang Nam Ngum
Phon Hong
Paksan
Cau Treo
Kham Keut
Kaew Neua
SOUTH CHINA SEA
Pak Lai
8
Lak Sao
13
VIENTIANE
Kaen Thao
Chiang Khan
Nong Khai
13
Mekong River
Kong Lo Cave
12
Udon Thani
Dong Hoi
Nakhon Phanom
Tha Khaek
23
Sepon
Lao Bao
Dong Ha
9
9
Khe Sanh
Mukdahan
Savannakhet
Hue
Se Pon
23
THAILAND
Se Kong
Se Don
Salavan
Ubon Ratchathani
Sekong (Muang Lamam)
Se Kaman
Vang Tao
Chong Mek
Pakse
Nakhon Ratchasima
Champasak
18
Attapeu (Samakhi Xai)
18
13
Se Kong
Si Phan Don
Siempang
Don Khong
Voen Kham
BANGKOK
CAMBODIA
Stung Treng
Gulf of Thailand

LAOS

French Rule

By the 18th century the nation had crumbled, falling under the control of the Siamese, who coveted much of modern-day Laos as a buffer zone against the expansionist French. It was to no effect. Soon after taking over Annam and Tonkin (modern-day Vietnam), the French negotiated with Siam into relinquishing her territory east of the Mekong, and Laos was born.

The country's diverse ethnic make-up and short history as a nation-state meant nationalism was slow to form. The first nationalist movement, the Lao Issara (Free Lao), was created to prevent the country's return to French rule after the invading Japanese left at the end of WWII. In 1953, without any regard for the Lao Issara, sovereignty was granted Laos by the French. Internecine struggles followed with the Pathet Lao (country of the Lao) Army forming an alliance with the Vietnamese Viet Minh (also opposing French rule in their own country). Laos was set to become a chessboard on which the clash of communist ambition and US anxiety over the perceived Southeast Asian 'domino effect' played itself out.

The Secret War

In 1954 at the Geneva Conference, Laos was declared a neutral nation – as such neither Vietnamese nor US forces could cross its borders. Thus began a game of cat and mouse as a multitude of CIA operatives secretly entered the country to train anticommunist Hmong fighters in the jungle. From 1965 to 1973, the US, in response to the Viet Minh funnelling massive amounts of war munitions down the Ho Chi Minh Trail, devastated eastern and northeastern Laos with nonstop carpet-bombing (a reported plane-load of ordnance dropped every eight minutes). The intensive campaign exacerbated the war between the Pathet Lao and the Royal Lao armies and, if anything, increased domestic support for the communists.

The US withdrawal in 1973 saw Laos divided up between Pathet Lao and non-Pathet Lao, but within two years the communists had taken over completely and the Lao People's Democratic Republic (PDR) was created under the leadership of Kaysone Phomvihane. Around 10% of Laos' population fled, mostly into Thailand. The remaining opponents of the government – notably tribes of Hmong (highland dwellers) who had fought with and been funded by the Central Intelligence Agency – were suppressed, often brutally, or sent to re-education camps for indeterminate periods.

A New Beginning

Laos entered the political family of Southeast Asian countries known as Asean in 1997, two years after Vietnam. In 2004 the USA promoted Laos to Normal Trade Relations, cementing the end to a trade embargo in place since the communists took power in 1975. Politically, the Party remains firmly in control. And with patrons like one-party China and Vietnam, there seems little incentive for Laos to move towards any meaningful form of democracy. While still heavily reliant on foreign aid, Laos has committed to income-generating projects in recent years in a bid to increase its prosperity. Ecotourism is flourishing and the country is enjoying more Western visitors every year.

THE CULTURE

National Psyche

Trying to homogenise the people and psyche of Laos is precarious, for the country is really a patchwork of different beliefs, ranging from animism to the prevailing presence of Thervada Bhuddism – and often both combined. But certainly there's a commonality in the laid-back attitude you'll encounter. Some of this can be ascribed to Buddhism and its emphasis on controlling extreme emotions by keeping *jai yen* (cool heart) and making merit; doing good in order to receive good. But the rest is a Lao phenomenon. Thus you'll rarely hear a heated argument, and can expect a level of kindness unpractised to such a national degree in other neighbouring countries.

Lifestyle

Laos' strongest cultural and linguistic links are with Thailand, with Thai music and TV an almost ubiquitous presence in the country. Similarly, touching another person's head is taboo, as is pointing your feet at another person or at a Buddha image. Strong displays of emotion are also discouraged. The traditional greeting gesture is the *nop* or *wâi,* a prayerlike placing together of the palms in front of the face or chest, although in urban areas the handshake is becoming more commonplace.

For all temple visits, dress neatly. In general you won't see many shirtless Lao; to their credit, *falang* (foreigners) are generally respectful of this rule.

Population

The government has been at pains to encourage national pride and a unifying 'Lao' identity, despite the fact that 132 ethnic groups comprise the people of Laos. Sixty per cent of this is Lao Loum (lowland Lao), who have the most in common with their Thai neighbours, and it's their cultural beliefs and way of life that are known as 'Lao culture'. The remainder is labelled according to the altitude the groups live at: Lao Theung (midlevel mountain group including Khmu, Lamet and Alak) Lao Thai (upland valleys), Lao Theung (upland Lao) and Lao Soung (1000m or above sea level, including Hmong, Mien and Akha).

RELIGION

Most lowland Lao are Theravada Buddhists and many Lao males choose to be ordained temporarily as monks, typically spending anywhere from a month to three years at a wat (temple). Indeed, a young man is not considered 'ripe' until he has completed his spiritual term. After the 1975 communist victory, Buddhism was suppressed, but by 1992 the government had relented and it was back in full swing, with a few alterations. Monks are still forbidden to promote *phî* (spirit) worship, which has been officially banned in Laos along with *sâiyasaat* (folk magic).

Despite the ban, *phî* worship remains the dominant non-Buddhist belief system. Even in Vientiane, Lao citizens openly perform the ceremony called *sukhwăn* or *bạsî,* in which the 32 *khwăn* (guardian spirits of the body) are bound to the guest of honour by white strings tied around the wrists (you'll see many Lao people wearing these).

Outside the Mekong River valley, the *phî* cult is particularly strong among tribal Thai, especially among the Thai Dam. *Mâw* (priests), who are trained to appease and exorcise troublesome spirits, preside over important Thai Dam festivals and other ceremonies. The Khamu and Hmong-Mien tribes also practise animism; the latter group also adds ancestral worship (see the boxed text, p388).

DOS & DON'TS IN LAOS

- Always ask permission before taking photos.
- Don't prop your feet on chairs or tables while sitting.
- Never touch any part of someone else's body with your foot.
- Refrain from touching people on the head.
- Remove your shoes before entering homes or temple buildings.

ARTS

Lao art and architecture are mostly religious in nature. Distinctively Lao is the Calling for Rain Buddha, a standing image with a rocket-like shape, while wat in Luang Prabang feature *sĭm* (chapels), with steep, low roofs.

Traditional Lao art has a more limited range than its Southeast Asian neighbours, partly because Laos has a more modest history as a nation-state and because successive colonists from China, Vietnam, Thailand, Myanmar and France have run off with it.

Crafts include gold- and silversmithing among the Hmong and Mien tribes, and tribal Thai weaving (especially among the Thai Dam and Thai Lü peoples). Classical music and dance have been all but lost, although performances are occasionally held in Luang Prabang at the Royal Palace (p390) and in Vientiane.

Foot-tapping traditional folk music, usually featuring the *khaen* (Lao panpipe), is still quite popular and inspires many modern Lao tunes. Increasingly, though, soppy heartbreak Thai pop and its Lao imitations are the music of choice.

ENVIRONMENT

The Land

With a landmass of 236,800 sq km, Laos is a little larger than the UK and, thanks to its relatively small population and mountainous terrain, one of the least altered environments in Southeast Asia. Unmanaged vegetation covers an estimated 85% of the country, and 10% of Laos is original-growth forest. A hundred years ago this statistic was nearer 75%, which provides a clear idea of the detrimental effects of relentless logging and slash-and-burn farming.

Nonetheless, most Lao still live at or just above subsistence level, consuming far fewer of their own natural resources than the people of any developed country.

Wildlife

Laos' forest cover means it has a much greater concentration of wild animals than neighbouring Thailand. Its pristine forests, mountains and rivers harbour a rich variety of creatures, including an estimated 437 kinds of bird (in southern Laos alone) and an incredible 320 different fish species.

There are also wild elephants, jackals, bears, leopards, tigers and the rare Irrawaddy dolphin. Its habitat is concentrated in the southern Mekong, particularly around Si Phan Don, where you have the best chance of sighting it in the dry season (we saw three of the 10-strong pod within minutes of waiting, so it's worth the journey).

National Parks

In 1993 the government set up 18 National Protected Areas (NPAs), comprising a total of 24,600 sq km, just over 10% of the land. An additional two were added in 1995 (taking the total coverage to 14% of Laos). International consulting agencies have also recommended another nine sites, but these have yet to materialise. Despite these conservation efforts, illegal timber felling and the smuggling of exotic wildlife are still significant threats to Laos's natural resources.

Most conservation areas are in southern Laos. However, for the majority of foreign travellers Nam Ha NPA in the northern province of Luang Nam Tha is the most accessible and popular wilderness to visit (see p399).

TRANSPORT

GETTING THERE & AWAY

Air

There are no intercontinental flights operating to Laos. You can fly into or out of Laos at Vientiane (from or to Cambodia, China, Thailand and Vietnam), Luang Prabang (Cambodia, Thailand and Vietnam) or Pakse (Cambodia and Thailand).

Lao Airlines, Thai Airways International (THAI), Bangkok Airways and Vietnam Airlines all operate flights into the country. Note that all fares listed in this chapter are one-way.

Bangkok Airways (Map p384; ☎ 071-253334; www.bangkokair.com; 57/6 Th Sisavangvong, Ban Xiengmuan, Luang Prabang)
Lao Airlines (Map p370; ☎ 021-212051; www.laoairlines.com; Th Pangkham, Vientiane)
Thai Airways International (Map pp368-9; ☎ 021-222527; www.thaiair.com; Th Luang Prabang, Vientiane)
Vietnam Airlines (Map p370; ☎ 021-217562; www.vietnamairlines.com; 1st fl, Lao Plaza Hotel, Th Samsenthai, Vientiane)

CAMBODIA

Between Phnom Penh and Vientiane (1,400,000 kip, 1½ hours) there are two flights per week with Lao Airlines (stopping in Pakse) and a daily direct flight with Vietnam Airlines. Lao Airlines also flies between Siem Reap and Vientiane (1,667,000 kip, 2½ hours) five times a week, stopping at Pakse (1,310,000 kip, 50 minutes), and from November to March offers two more flights between Siem Reap and Pakse that continue to Luang Prabang (1,785,000 kip).

TIMBER!

According to the Earth Policy Institute – an independent environmental-research agency – a major shortfall exists in the amount of timber China consumes each year and the amount it produces domestically. Increasingly it's turning to imports and illegal logging to make up the shortage and Laos, hungry for the income, is often willing to oblige. Added to this the Environmental Investigation Agency (EIA) claims the furniture industry in Vietnam has grown tenfold since 2000, with Laos facilitating the flow of its timber to enable this. While an outwardly hardline approach has been taken against mass logging by the Lao government, it's the corrupt military and local officials in remote areas who fall prey to bribes.

Aside from the obvious impact on endangered mammals and thousands of amphibians, insects and plants endemic to the same forests, deforestation accounts for an estimated 15% to 20% of the world's annual carbon emission.

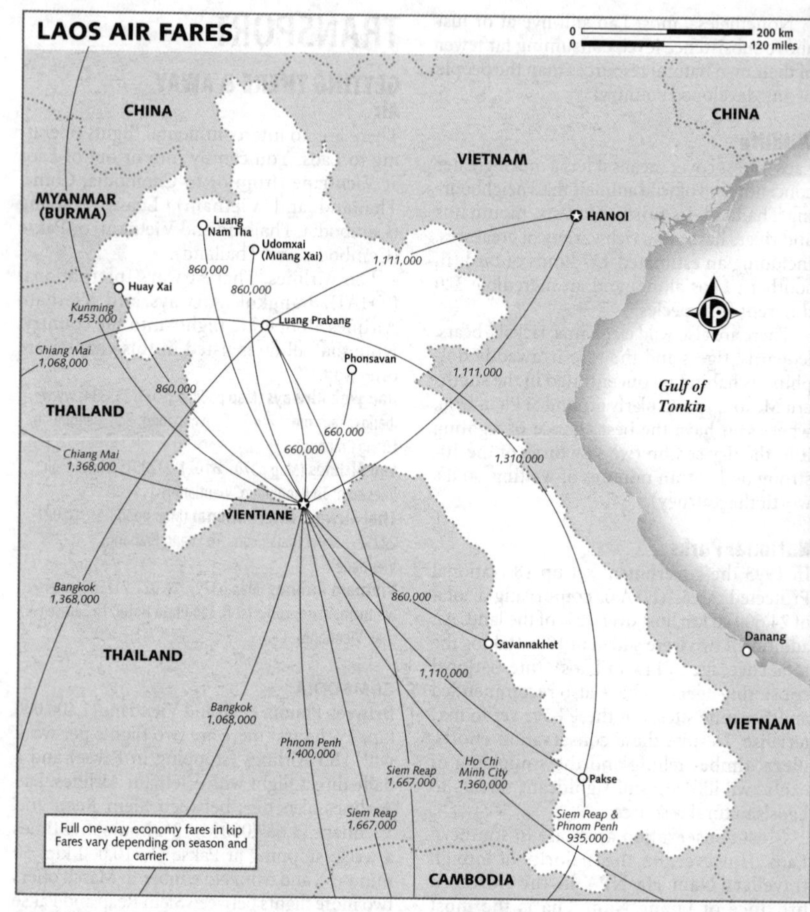

CHINA

Lao Airlines has three services a week between Kunming and Vientiane (1,453,000 kip, three hours).

THAILAND

Lao Airlines and THAI (Thai International Airways) have regular flights between Bangkok and Vientiane (starting from US$168). Bangkok Airways flies daily between Bangkok and Luang Prabang (starting from US$240, two hours), and Lao Airlines has three flights a week for around 2,108,000 kip. Lao Airlines operates five flights a week between Vientiane and Chiang Mai (1,368,000 kip, 2½ hours), via Luang Prabang (660,000 kip, one hour).

Some people save money by flying from Bangkok to Udon Thani in Thailand, then carrying on by road to Vientiane. Udon Thani is 55km south of Nong Khai and Bangkok–Udon tickets on **Thai Air Asia** (www.airasia.com) start at about 1500B/362,000 kip.

VIETNAM

Lao Airlines fly between Vientiane and Hanoi (1,111,000 kip, one hour, 10 times a week), and Ho Chi Minh City (1,360,000 kip, three hours) daily; and between Luang Prabang and Hanoi (1,111,000 kip).

Land

Laos has open land borders with Cambodia, China, Thailand and Vietnam, but the situation at all of them is prone to change without warning. Under current rules, a 30-day tourist visa is available on arrival at all international checkpoints (except at the Cambodian border), but this can change rapidly, so check the situation before leaving. See p952 for a list of border crossings.

GETTING AROUND

Air

Lao Airlines (www.laoairlines.com) handles all domestic flights in Laos. Fortunately, the days of radar-bereft M12 prop planes descending blindly through the mist-laced karst (and broken air-con units spewing dry ice into the gangway) are over. The new fleet has slick MA60s, with the airline rapidly improving its safety record. Check the Lao calendar for public festivals before you fly, as it can be difficult getting a seat. In provincial Lao Airlines offices you'll be expected to pay in cash.

Always reconfirm your flights a day or two before departing as undersubscribed flights may be cancelled, or you could get bumped off the passenger list.

Bicycle

The light and relatively slow traffic in most Lao towns makes for great cycling conditions and you'll see many a hardy cyclist scaling mountains. Bicycles are available for rent in major tourist destinations, costing around 10,000 kip per day for a cheap Thai or Chinese model. For long-distance cyclists, bicycles can be brought into the country usually without any hassle.

Boat

With the main highway upgrading process complete in Laos, the days of mass river transport are over. The most popular river trip in Laos – the slow boat between Huay Xai and Luang Prabang – remains a daily event. From Huay Xai (p404) boats are often packed, while from Luang Prabang (p390) there's usually a bit of legroom. Other popular journeys – between Pakse and Si Phan Don, or between Nong Khiaw and Luang Prabang – are no longer regular, so you'll have to charter a boat.

> **DEPARTURE TAX**
>
> Departure tax is 85,000 kip (cash only), paid at the airport. Domestic airport tax is 8500 kip.

River-ferry facilities are quite basic and passengers sit, eat and sleep on the wooden decks. It's a good idea to bring something soft to sit on. The toilet (if there is one) is an enclosed hole in the deck at the back of the boat.

For shorter river trips, such as Luang Prabang to the Pak Ou caves, you can easily hire a river taxi. Along the upper Mekong River, between Luang Prabang and Huay Xai and between Xieng Kok and Huay Xai, Thai-built *héua wái* (speedboats) – shallow, 5m-long skiffs with 40HP outboard engines – are common. These are able to cover a distance in six hours that might take a river ferry two days or more. They're not cheap but some ply regular routes, so the cost can be shared among several passengers. For some people, a ride on these boats is a major thrill. For others, it is like riding on a giant runaway chainsaw, a nightmare that cannot end soon enough. Remember that speedboats, as well as being deafeningly loud, kill and injure people every year. They tend to flip and disintegrate upon contact with any solid floating debris, which is in plentiful supply in Laos during the wet season. Is it really worth the risk?

Bus & Săwngthăew

Long-distance public transport in Laos is either by bus or săwngthăew (literally 'two rows'; converted pick-ups or trucks with two wooden benches down either side). Most decent-sized villages have at least one săwngthăew, which will run to the provincial capital daily except Sunday, stopping wherever you want. Buses are more frequent and travel further. Privately run VIP buses operate on some busier routes throughout the country, but slow, simple standard buses (occasionally with air-con) remain the norm.

The majority of main highways in Laos are now in a decent condition, but despite improvements road trips in Laos can still be a test of endurance, especially in the northeast where there is barely a straight stretch of road to be found (you'll soon find out why they hand out those little plastic bags on local buses!).

Car & Motorcycle

Second-rate Chinese and sturdier Japanese-built 100cc scooters can be rented for 70,000–80,000 kip a day in Vientiane, Tha Khaek,

Savannakhet, Pakse and Luang Nam Tha. Try to get a Japanese bike if you're travelling any distance out of town (or across mountains). In Vientiane, Pakse and Vang Vieng it's also possible to rent dirt bikes for around 85,000–170,000 kip per day. Motorcycle tours of Laos are offered by **Asian Motorcycling Adventures** (www.asianbiketour.com). **Jules' Classic Rental** (Map p370; ☎ 020 7600813; www.bike-rental-laos.com; Th Setthathirat; per day 85,000-255,000 kip) is a great new company with a range of performance bikes and the option to rent in Vientiane and drop off in Luang Prabang.

Car rental in Laos is expensive, but nevertheless it is a great way of reaching out-of-the-way places. In Vientiane, **Asia Vehicle Rental** (AVR; Map p370; ☎ 021-17493; avr@loxinfo.co.th; Th Samsenthai) has sedans, minibuses, 4WDs and station wagons, with or without drivers, from around 600,000 kip per day, not including fuel. If you have your own car or motorcycle, you are allowed to import it for the length of your visa after filling in a few forms at the border. Temporary import extensions are possible for up to two weeks, sometimes more.

Hitching

Hitching is certainly possible in Laos, but it is never entirely safe and we definitely don't recommend it, particularly for women, as the act of standing beside a road and waving at cars might be misinterpreted. In any case, public transport is inexpensive and will pick you up almost anywhere. Otherwise, long-distance cargo trucks or cars with red-on-yellow number plates (private vehicles) are also a good bet.

VIENTIANE

☎ 021 / pop 203,000

With its sunbaked boulevards, locals playing pétanque and orange-hued monks whispering through its many temples, the city's easy ambience is more akin to that of a town. Settled by the French as an important hub of Indochina, the architectural refinement and culinary stamp of those former colonists lingers mercifully on in Vientiane; many of their old villas have been restored and there are Gallic restaurants at every turn piping out the scent of fresh baguettes.

Every year the place feels more sophisticated, with high-lux bars and achingly lovely boutique hotels opening up, but there are still plenty of bargains to be had. Visit the labyrinthine Morning Market or eccentric Buddha Park, followed by a little shopping down Th Setthathirat. And having wandered through the Soviet-, Sino-and Franco-styled architecture your tastebuds will be scrambling to make a decision on the equally eclectic spectrum of cuisine. Capital cities aren't supposed to be this friendly.

HISTORY

Vientiane was first settled as an early Lao fiefdom. Its name translates as Sandalwood City and is pronounced Wieng Chan. Through a millennium of history it was variously controlled, ravaged and looted by the Vietnamese, Burmese, Siamese and Khmers.

In 1828 it was razed to the ground by the Siamese after the overarching ambitions of Lao king Anouvong (Chao Anou). When Laos became a French protectorate at the end of the 19th century, it was renamed as

LPDR (LAO PLEASE DON'T RUSH)

One of the first things you'll notice entering Laos is the sudden slow of pace; both in its people, its traffic and its general approach to life. We met Peter, a Dutchman, who'd been seriously ill in Berlin. A week after his arrival in Laos he found that his constitution became stronger; a month later he'd dispensed with his medication. 'There's something about this place,' he said, 'it just slows my heartbeat.' And it does, but sometimes your Western sense of urgency may get the better of you.

Bus journeys in particular, can be protracted, uncomfortable affairs, with your space invaded by an old-timer being sick into a plastic bag, while a cage of chickens are squawking in your ear. Your bus will most probably break down and you'll be forced to sit in the skirts of the forest near a sign that reads 'We Welcome Tigers Here', while a broken axle is bound together with rope and ingenuity; but take a breath, smile, and remember you'll get to where you're going…in Lao time.

the capital, rebuilt and became one of the classic Indochinese cities along with Phnom Penh and then Saigon (Ho Chi Minh City). By the early 1960s and onset of the Vietnam War, the city was teeming with CIA agents, madcap Ravens (maverick plain-clothes US pilots) and Russian spies.

Post-1975 saw the puritanical Pathet Lao carting off dissenters to re-education camps and exfoliating the city of its colourful elements. These days prostitution flourishes, police corruption is a norm, and 21st-century architecture comes in the form of Lego monstrosities like Don Chan Palace. In 2009 the city hosted the SEA Games, a major coup, but a symbiotic dilemma as 50,000 Chinese workers moved to the city to further assist Vientiane with its 'development'.

ORIENTATION

The three main streets parallel to the Mekong – Th Fa Ngum, Th Setthathirat and Th Samsenthai – form the central inner city of Vientiane and are where most of the budget guest houses, bars and restaurants are located. Nam Phu is the best central landmark if you're catching a taxi or túk-túk into town. Heading northeast at a 90-degree angle to Th Setthathirat is the wide tree-lined boulevard of Th Lan Xang, where you'll find the Talat Sao, Patuxai monument and Pha That Luang, Laos' most distinctive structure.

INFORMATION

Bookshops

Kosila Bookshop 1 (Map p370; ☎ 241352; Th Chanta Khumman; 9am-5pm Mon-Fri) Shelves are stocked with second-hand fiction and old travel guides selling for around 80,000 kip.

Monument Books (Map p370; ☎ 243708; Th Nokeo Khumman; 9am-5pm Mon-Fri) A great range of English, French and German books on offer, ranging from thrillers and nonfiction to coffee-table pictorials. The kids' section out the back has an upstairs gallery exhibiting local artists.

Vientiane Book Centre (Map p370; ☎ 213031; Th Pangkham; 8.30am-5.30pm Mon-Fri, to 4pm Sat) As well as second-hand and antique books, it sells international news magazines, academic texts and old NGO reports.

Cultural Centres

Centre Culturel et de Coopération Linguistique (Map p370; ☎ 215764; www.ambafrance-laos.org/centre; Th Lan Xang; 9.30am-6.30pm Mon-Fri, to noon Sat) Exhibitions, French films (see p376), a useful library and regular program of visiting virtuosos; the 'French Centre' also has Lao language classes and a terrific cafe. A real oasis!

Emergency

Ambulance (☎ 195)
Fire (☎ 190)
Police (☎ 191)
Tourist Police (Map p370; ☎ 251128; Th Lan Xang)

Internet Access

There are several internet cafes located on Th Samsenthai and Th Setthathirat. Rates around 6000 kip per hour with a decent speed of broadband. Most have international telephone facilities.

A1 Internet (Map p370; Th Setthathirat; broadband per hr 6000 kip; 9am-9pm) Broadband, plus Skype.

Apollo Net (formerly PlaNet) (Map p370; Th Setthathirat; per hr 6000 kip; 8.30am-11pm) Broadband.

Fastnet Internet (Map p370; Th Samsenthai; broadband per hr 8000 kip; 7.30am-11pm) International calls and Skype too.

Laundry

Most guest houses offer same-day laundry service for 10,000 kip per kilo.

House of Fruit Shakes (Map p370; Th Samsenthai; per item 500-4000 kip; 7am-9pm) Do your laundry at this delightful family-run fruit-drink bar that delivers a vitamin punch.

Media

The government-run *Vientiane Times* is a bland sketch of improving Sino-Lao relations, however, the excellent *Paisai? What's On* is much better, offering daily breakdowns of events in the capital as well as sports and embassy listings. French speakers should look for the weekly *Le Rénovateur*. The *Bangkok Post, Economist, Newsweek* and *Time* can also be found in minimarts and bookshops.

Medical Services

Vientiane's medical facilities will do for broken bones, diagnosis of dengue fever and malaria, but for anything more serious cross to Thailand for **Aek Udon International Hospital** (☎ 0066-42-342555; www.aekudon.com; Amphur Muang, Udon Thani), which can dispatch an ambulance or – in critical situations – an airlift. Friendship Bridge closes 10pm to 6am; however, Thai-Lao immigration will open for ambulances.

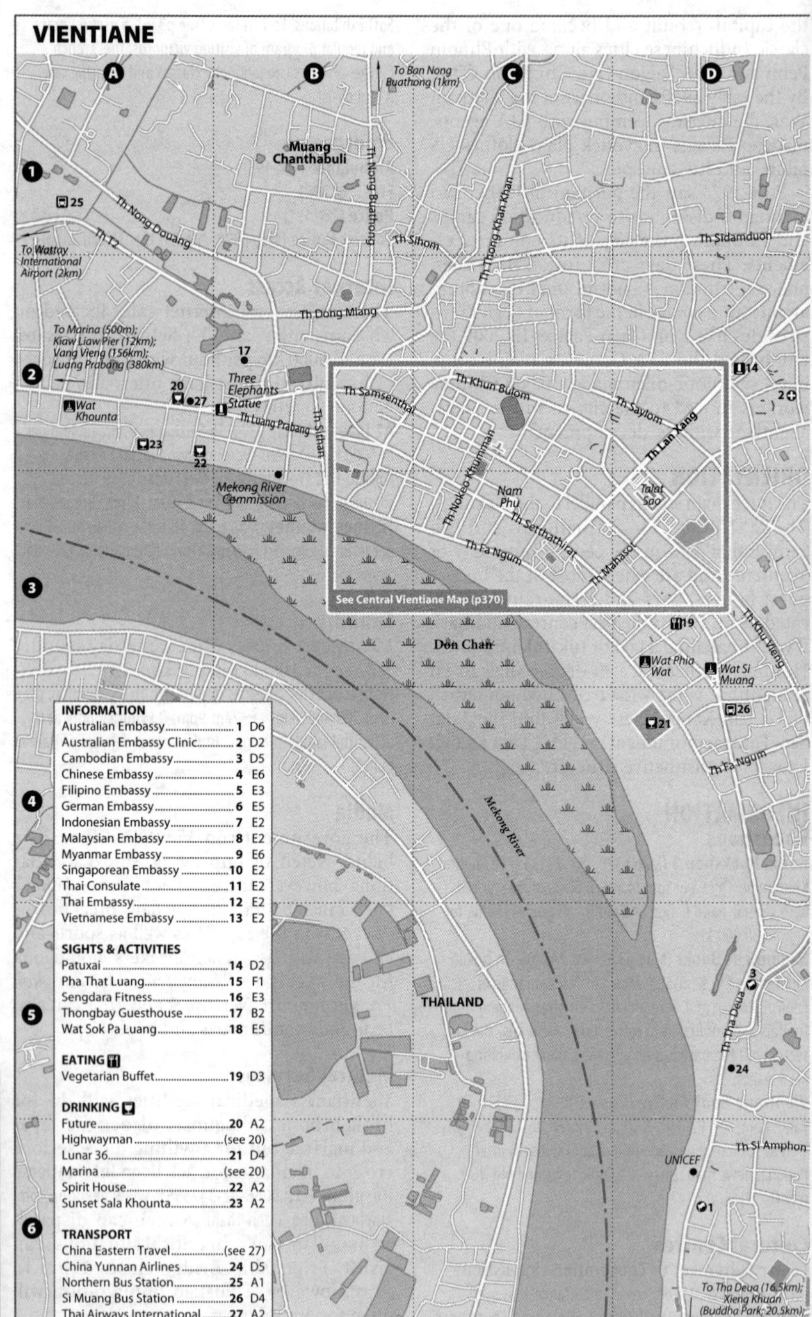
VIENTIANE
A
B
C
D
1
2
3
4
5
6
To Ban Nong Buathong (1km)
Muang Chanthabuli
Th Nong Buathong
Th Thong Khan Khan
Th Nong Douang
Th T2
To Wattay International Airport (2km)
Th Sihom
Th Sidamduon
Th Dong Miang
To Marina (500m); Kiaw Liaw Pier (12km); Vang Vieng (156km); Luang Prabang (380km)
17
20
27
Three Elephants Statue
Wat Khounta
Th Luang Prabang
Th Sithan
23
22
Mekong River Commission
Th Samsenthai
Th Khun Bulom
Th Saylom
Th Lan Xang
14
2
Th Nokeo Khumman
Nam Phu
Talat Sao
Th Setthathirat
Th Fa Ngum
Th Mahasot
See Central Vientiane Map (p370)
19
Th Khu Vieng
Don Chan
Wat Phia Wat
Wat Si Muang
26
21
Th Fa Ngum
Mekong River
THAILAND
3
Th Tha Deua
24
Th Si Amphon
UNICEF
1
To Tha Deua (16.5km); Xieng Khuan (Buddha Park; 20.5km); Friendship Bridge (22km)
INFORMATION
Australian Embassy 1 D6
Australian Embassy Clinic 2 D2
Cambodian Embassy 3 D5
Chinese Embassy 4 E6
Filipino Embassy 5 E3
German Embassy 6 E5
Indonesian Embassy 7 E2
Malaysian Embassy 8 E2
Myanmar Embassy 9 E6
Singaporean Embassy 10 E2
Thai Consulate 11 E2
Thai Embassy 12 E2
Vietnamese Embassy 13 E2
SIGHTS & ACTIVITIES
Patuxai 14 D2
Pha That Luang 15 F1
Sengdara Fitness 16 E3
Thongbay Guesthouse 17 B2
Wat Sok Pa Luang 18 E5
EATING
Vegetarian Buffet 19 D3
DRINKING
Future 20 A2
Highwayman (see 20)
Lunar 36 21 D4
Marina (see 20)
Spirit House 22 A2
Sunset Sala Khounta 23 A2
TRANSPORT
China Eastern Travel (see 27)
China Yunnan Airlines 24 D5
Northern Bus Station 25 A1
Si Muang Bus Station 26 D4
Thai Airways International 27 A2

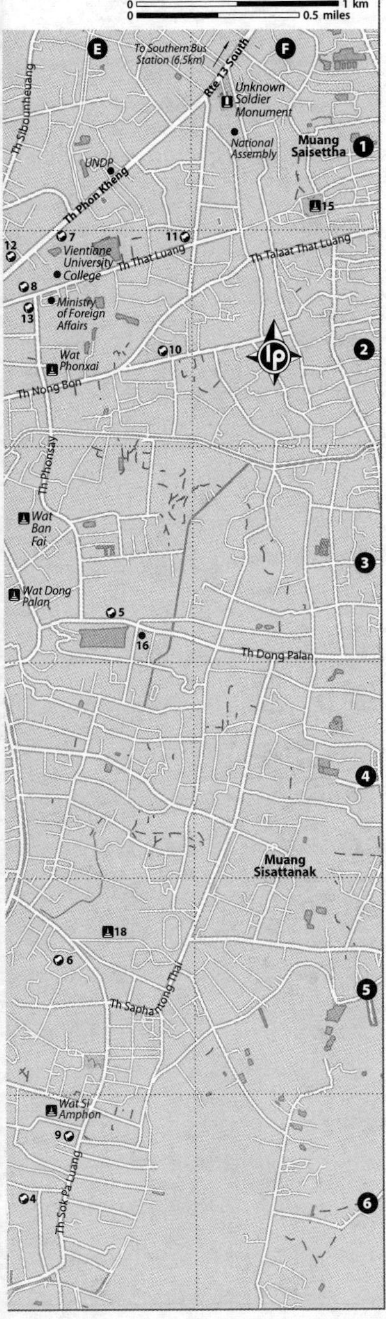

In Vientiane try the following:

Australian Embassy Clinic (Map pp368-9; ☎ 353840; 8.30am-5pm Mon-Fri) For nationals of Australia, Britain, Canada, PNG and NZ only. This clinic's Australian doctor treats minor problems by appointment; it doesn't have emergency facilities. Accepts cash or credit cards.

International Clinic (Map pp368-9; ☎ 214021/2; Mahasot Hospital, Th Fa Ngum; 24hr) Part of the Mahasot Hospital; probably the best place for not-too-complex emergencies. Some English-speaking doctors. Take ID and cash.

Money

There are now at least five ATMs in central Vientiane and counting. Several banks change cash and travellers cheques and will do cash advances against credit cards for a commission.

Given you can only withdraw about 700,000 kip (US$80) at a time, it's often cheaper to get a cash advance manually. Alternatively, the unofficial money changers near Talat Sao have good rates and keep longish hours.

BCL (Map p370; ☎ 213200; cnr Th Pangkham & Th Fa Ngum; 8.30am-7pm Mon-Fri, to 3pm Sat & Sun) Best rates. Longest hours. Exchange booth on Th Fa Ngum and ATM attached to the main building.

Joint Development Bank (Map p370; ☎ 213535; 75/1-5 Th Lan Xang) Usually charges the lowest commission on cash advances. Also has an ATM.

Lao Development Bank (Map p370; ☎ 213300; Th Setthathirat; 8.30-11.30am & 2-4pm Mon-Fri).

Siam Commercial Bank (Map p370; ☎ 227306; 117 Th Lan Xang) ATM.

Post

Post, Telephone & Telegraph (PTT; Map p370; cnr Th Lan Xang & Th Khu Vieng; 8am-noon & 1-5pm Mon-Fri, 8am-noon Sat) Stamps, poste restante and (slow) internet services available here.

Telephone

International call phonecards can be purchased from the PTT (above) and minimarts. Cheaper internet calls can be made at internet shops (p367). For inexpensive local calls have your mobile unlocked and buy a pay-as-you-go SIM. M Phone top-up cards are widely available.

Tourist Information

Lao National Tourism Authority (NTAL; Map p370; ☎ 212251; www.tourismlaos.com, www.ecotourismlaos.com; Th Lan Xang; 8.30am-4.30pm) Well worth a visit for its descriptions of provincial attractions, helpful English-speaking staff, brochures and regional maps. Staff can arrange trips to nearby Phu Khao Khuay NPA for no charge.

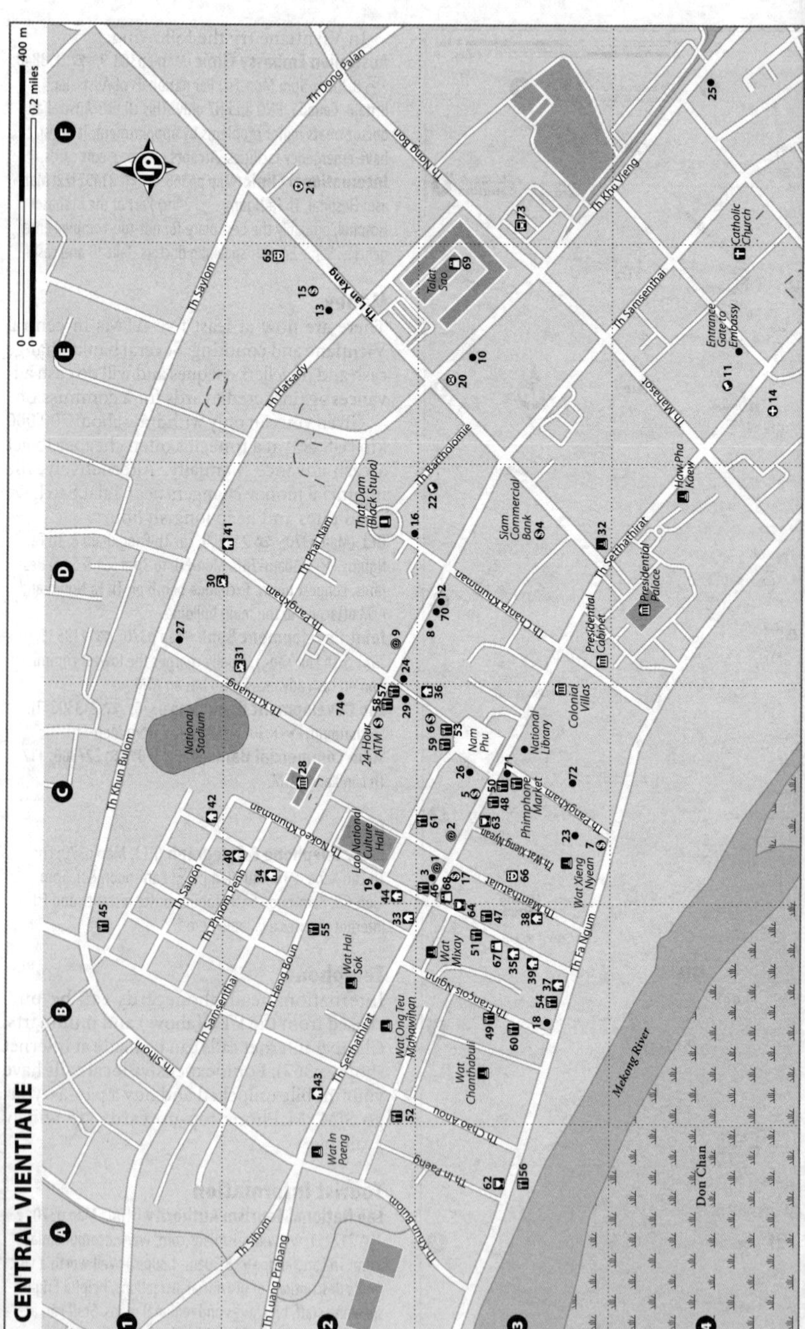

CENTRAL VIENTIANE
0
0
400 m
0.2 miles
A
B
C
D
E
F
1
2
3
4
Th Dong Palan
Th Nong Bon
Th Khu Vieng
Th Saylom
Th Lan Xang
Th Hatsady
Talat Sao
Catholic Church
Th Samsenthai
Entrance Gate to Embassy
Th Mahasot
Th Bartholomie
That Dam (Black Stupa)
Th Phai Nam
Th Pangkham
Siam Commercial Bank
Haw Pha Kaew
Th Chanta Khumman
Th Setthathirat
Presidential Palace
Presidential Cabinet
Colonial Villas
National Library
Phimphone Market
Nam Phu
24-Hour ATM
Th Khun Bulom
National Stadium
Th Ki Huang
Lao National Culture Hall
Th Nokeo Khumman
Th Saigon
Th Phnom Penh
Th Heng Boun
Wat Hai Sok
Th Wat Xieng Nyean
Th Manthatulat
Wat Xieng Nyean
Wat Mixay
Th François Ngin
Th Fa Ngum
Wat Ong Teu Mahawihan
Th Sihom
Wat Chanthabuli
Th Chao Anou
Wat In Paeng
Th In Paeng
Th Luang Prabang
Mekong River
Don Chan

LAOS

INFORMATION

- A1 Internet ... 1 C3
- Apollo Net ... 2 C3
- A-Rasa Tours ... 3 C3
- ATM ... 4 D3
- ATM ... 5 C3
- ATM ... 6 C3
- BCL ... 7 C3
- Boualian Travel 1 ... 8 D3
- Centre Culturel et de Coopération Linguistique ... (see 65)
- Fastnet Internet ... 9 D2
- Federal Express ... 10 E3
- French Embassy ... 11 E4
- Green Discovery ... (see 26)
- House of Fruit Shakes ... 12 D3
- Immigration Office ... 13 E2
- International Clinic ... 14 E4
- Joint Development Bank ... 15 E2
- Kosila Bookshop 1 ... 16 D2
- Lao Development Bank ... 17 C3
- Lao National Tourism Authority ... (see 21)
- Lao Youth Travel ... 18 B3
- Monument Books ... 19 C2
- Post, Telephone & Telegraph ... 20 E3
- Tourist Police ... 21 F2
- US Embassy ... 22 D3
- Vientiane Book Centre ... 23 C3

SIGHTS & ACTIVITIES

- Champa Health Spa ... 24 D2
- Cope Centre ... 25 F4
- Green Discovery ... 26 C3
- Lao Bowling Centre ... 27 D1
- Lao National History Museum ... 28 C2
- Mandarina Massage ... 29 C2
- Settha Palace Hotel ... 30 D1
- Vientiane Swimming Pool ... 31 D2
- Wat Si Saket ... 32 D3

SLEEPING

- Chantha Guesthouse ... 33 B2
- Dragon Lodge ... 34 C2
- Mixay Guest House ... 35 B3
- Nali Namphu Guest House ... 36 C3
- Orchid Guest House ... 37 B3
- Phatoumphone Guest House ... 38 B3
- RD Guest House ... 39 B3
- Saysouly Guesthouse ... 40 C2
- Soukxana Guest House ... 41 D2
- Syri 1 Guest House ... 42 C1
- Syri 2 Guest House ... 43 B2
- Vayakorn Guest House ... 44 C2

EATING

- Ban Anou Night Market ... 45 B1
- Café Indochine ... 46 C3
- Croissant D'Or ... 47 B3
- Dao Fa Bistro ... 48 C3
- Full Moon Café ... 49 B3
- JoMa Bakery Café ... 50 C3
- Khop Chai Deu ... (see 26)
- La Terrasse ... 51 B3
- La Vendome ... 52 B2
- Le Provencal ... 53 C3
- Nazim ... 54 B3
- Noy's Fruit Heaven ... 55 B2
- Open-air Riverside Food Vendors ... 56 A3
- Rashmi's Indian Fusion ... 57 C2
- Restaurant Nam Phu ... 58 C2
- Scandinavian Bakery ... 59 C3
- Sticky Fingers Café & Bar ... 60 B3
- Taj Mahal Restaurant ... 61 C3

DRINKING

- Bor Pen Nyang ... 62 A3
- Jazzy Brick ... 63 C3
- Martini Bar ... 64 B3
- Sticky Fingers Café & Bar ... (see 60)

ENTERTAINMENT

- Centre Culturel et de Coopération Linguistique ... 65 E2
- Laos Traditional Show ... 66 C3

SHOPPING

- Camacrafts ... 67 B3
- Satri Lao ... 68 C3
- Talat Sao ... 69 E3

TRANSPORT

- Asia Vehicle Rental ... 70 D3
- Jules' Classic Rental ... 71 C3
- Lao Airlines ... 72 C3
- Talat Sao Bus Station ... 73 F3
- Vietnam Airlines ... 74 C2

Travel Agencies

Boualian Travel 1 (Map p370 ☎ 263772, 020 551 1646; Th Samsenthai) Books bus and sleeper train tickets to Bangkok and Vietnam. Mrs Boualian also organises visas for Vietnam and Cambodia, plus extensions, charging 5% commission.

A-Rasa Tours (Map p370; ☎ 213634; www.laos-info.com; Th Setthathirat; 8.30am-5pm Mon-Sat) Now working with the excellent X-Plore Asia, providing adventure trips across the country as well as booking VIP bus tickets.

Green Discovery (Map p370; ☎ 251564, 223022; www.greendiscoverylaos.com; Th Setthathirat) As well as city temple tours, also offers bicycle, kayaking, rafting and trekking trips to Ban Pako NPA and Khao Khuay NPA.

Lao Youth Travel (Map p370 ☎ 216314; Th Fa Gnum) Organises onward bus tickets to Laos, Vietnam and Thailand; also books train tickets from Nong Khai to Bangkok; arranges visas and Laos visa extensions.

SIGHTS

Pha That Luang

The beautiful golden **Pha That Luang** (Great Sacred Stupa; Map pp368-9; Th That Luang; admission 2000 kip; 8am-4pm Tue-Sun) is the most important national monument in Laos, a symbol of both the Buddhist religion and Lao sovereignty. An image of the main stupa appears on the national seal. Legend has it that Ashokan missionaries from India erected a *thâat* (Buddhist stupa) here to enclose a piece of Buddha's breastbone as early as the 3rd century BC. Construction began again in 1566 and, over time, four wat were built around the stupa. Only two remain, Wat That Luang Tai to the south and Wat That Luang Neua to the north. The latter is the monastic residence of the Supreme Patriarch of Lao Buddhism.

The temple is the site of a major festival held in early November (see p373). Pha That Luang is about 4km northeast of the city centre at the end of Th That Luang. It's a decent walk but shared túk-túks go this way, or you can hire a bike. The best time to visit is late afternoon to catch the reflected setting sun.

Wat Si Saket

Built in 1818 by King Anouvong (Chao Anou), **Wat Si Saket** (Map p370; cnr Th Lan Xang & Th Setthathirat; admission 2000 kip; 8am-noon & 1-4pm, closed public holidays) is the oldest temple in Vientiane and well worth a visit even if you've overdosed on temples. Wat Si Saket has several unique features. The interior walls of the cloister are riddled with small niches that contain more than 2000 silver and ceramic Buddha images. More than 300 seated and standing Buddhas of varying age (15th–19th century), size and material rest on long shelves below the niches.

Patuxai

Vientiane's haughty **Arc de Triomphe replica** is an imposing if slightly incongruous sight, dominating the commercial district around Th Lan Xang. The **Patuxai** (Victory Monument; Map pp368-9 Th Lan Xang; admission 3000 kip; 8am-5pm) commemorates Lao who died in prerevolutionary wars and was built in 1969 with cement donated by the USA for the construction of a new airport; hence expats refer to it as 'the vertical runway'. The entrance fee allows you to climb the stairway interior to the top of the monument, with striking views over Vientiane.

Lao National History Museum

Housed in a well-worn French administrative building built in the 1920s, the **Lao National Museum** (Map p370; ☎ 212461; Th Samsenthai; admission 10,000 kip; 8am-noon & 1-4pm) was formerly known as the Lao Revolutionary Museum and much of the collection retains an unmistakable revolutionary zeal. Artefacts and photos document the Pathet Lao's lengthy struggle for power, and there's enough historic weaponry to arm all the extras in a Rambo film. Most exhibits are labelled with at least some English. If you get museum-fatigue, you can keep your ticket and come back later the same day.

Xieng Khuan (Buddha Park)

In a grassy field by the Mekong River, 25km southeast of Vientiane, **Xieng Khuan** (Buddha Park; off Map pp368-9; off Th Tha Deua; admission 5000 kip, camera 2000 kip; 8am-sunset) is a park full of Buddhist and Hindu sculptures, a monument to one eccentric man's bizarre ambition. Xieng Khuan was designed and built in 1958 by Luang Pu (Venerable Grandfather) Bunleua Sulilat, a yogi/priest/shaman who merged Hindu and Buddhist philosophy, mythology and iconography into a cryptic whole. The concrete sculptures at Xieng Khuan (which means Spirit City) include statues of Shiva, Vishnu, Arjuna, Avalokiteshvara, Buddha and just about every other Hindu or Buddhist deity imaginable.

Bus 14 (8000 kip, one hour, 24km) leaves the Talat Sao bus station every 15 or 20 minutes throughout the day and goes all the way to Xieng Khuan. Alternatively, charter a túk-túk (about 85,000–100,000 kip return, depending on your bargaining skills) or take a shared jumbo (big túk-túk, 8000 kip) to Tha Deua and walk the final 4km to the park. Going by rented motorbike is also popular.

ACTIVITIES

Bowling

Bright lights and the high-pitched clatter of wooden pins await you at the **Lao Bowling Centre** (Map p370; ☎ 218661; Th Khun Bulom; per game incl shoe hire 20,000 kip; 9am-midnight). Even before its 'official' closing time, it may look deserted, but entry is on the right side of the building. As well as good old-fashioned bowling, you'll find pool tables, beer and refreshments available.

Gym & Aerobics

Sengdara Fitness (Map pp368-9; ☎ 414061; 5/77 Th Dong Palan; 6am-10pm) Top-notch facilities with contemporary equipment, sauna, pool, massage, aerobics and yoga classes. Visitors can buy a 32,000 kip day-pass, which includes use of everything. Also evening Taekwondo classes.

Massage & Herbal Saunas

Wat Sok Pa Luang (Map pp368-9; Th Sok Pa Luang; 1-7pm) For a traditional massage, head here. Located in a semirural setting (*wat pàa* means 'forest temple') 3km from the city centre, the wat is famous for herbal saunas (10,000 kip) and massages (25,000 kip).

Th Pangkham was once known for its tailors; these days it's home to a clutch of chichi massage spas. **Mandarina Massage** (Map p370; ☎ 218703; Th Pangkham; per hr 50-300,000 kip; 10am-10pm) offers a range of foot, herbal and oil massages in tasteful, eucalyptus-scented surroundings. At **Champa Health Spa** (Map p370; ☎ 215203; Th Pangkham; per hr 60-85,000 kip; 10am-10pm), relax with a full-body massage in fresh new premises piping birdsong.

Meditation

Foreigners are welcome at a regular Saturday-afternoon sitting at Wat Sok Pa Luang (see above). The session runs from 4pm until 5.30pm with an opportunity to ask questions afterwards.

Rafting

Green Discovery (Map p370; ☎ 251564; www.greendiscoverylaos.com; Th Setthathirat) has reliable, well-trained guides with Laos' most widespread low-impact ecotourism specialists.

COPE CENTRE

An estimated 260 million submunition 'bombies' were dropped on Laos between 1964 and 1973; sadly, 78 million of them failed to explode. On the outskirts of Vientiane, **COPE** (Map p370; ☎ 218427; www.copelaos.org; Th Khou Vieng; admission free; 🕑 9am-4pm Mon-Fri) is an inspiring organisation dedicated to supporting the victims of UXO (unexploded ordnance), providing clinical mentoring and training programs for local staff in the manufacture of high-tech but low-cost artificial limbs and related rehabilitation activities. Since the end of the war over 12,000 people have fallen prey to UXO (many of them children), rendering the work that takes place here among the most vital in the country.

Despite the dark subject matter COPE has a very sunny atmosphere, understandable when you consider people are being given their lives and pride back. The permanent UXO exhibition is fascinating with photographs portraying the salvaged lives of victims, as well as a bunker-style cinema showing an educational documentary.

Swimming

Vientiane Swimming Pool (Map p370; ☎ 020-552 1002; Th Ki Huang; admission 10,000 kip; 🕑 8am-7pm) is a 25m alfresco delight, but hire some goggles – there's enough chlorine in there to strip the barnacles off Davy Jones' locker. For Hollywood glamour try the kidney-shaped pool at the **Settha Palace Hotel** (Map p370; ☎ 217581; Th Pangkham; admission 50,000 kip) and don't forget to order a Bloody Mary!

COURSES

Lao-language courses are held at the Centre Culturel et de Coopération Linguistique. See p367.

Cooking

Courses at the beautiful **Thongbay Guesthouse** (Map pp368-9; ☎ 242292; www.thongbay-guesthouses.com; Ban Nong Douange; courses 125,000 kip) are organised on demand (maximum 10 people) and start at 10am. A half-day class includes a trip to the market, cooking and feasting on your culinary creations.

Yoga

To regain your balance look for signposted information on yoga classes in shop windows around Nam Phu or in *Paisai? What's On*.

FESTIVALS & EVENTS

Vietnamese Tet/Chinese New Year Usually in February.

Pii Mai (Lao New Year) New Year is celebrated once more in mid-April for this mass water-fight. Be warned – drunk driving and theft go through the roof at these times so remain vigilant of your driver and wallet!

Awk Phansa In October, celebrating the end of Buddhist Lent and rain's retreat is this magical festival. Monks are busy making *heua fai* (little bamboo boats) in which candles are lit then floated downstream. Thousands flock to river cities to launch their own *heua fai*, believing their bad luck will float away (hopefully to Thailand!).

Bun Nam (River Festival) Following directly after, this is when boat races are held on the Mekong River. Rowing teams from across the country compete, and for three nights the riverbank is lined with food stalls, temporary discos and carnival games.

That Luang Festival (Bun Pha That Luang) Held in early November is the largest temple fair in Laos, incandescent with fireworks and a colourful procession between Pha That Luang (p371) and Wat Si Muang.

International New Year Also celebrated here.

SLEEPING

Change has come to Vientiane's sleeping horizon in a big way – edging out the rickety flophouse accommodation with quality guest houses, while also increasing the tariff. Maybe it's a good thing, for what remains on the cheaper scale is invariably fresh and keen to keep up with the competition. Don't worry – there are still plenty of decent shoestring options that won't crucify your wallet.

Mixay Guesthouse (Map p370; ☎ 262210; 39 Th Nokeo Khumman; dm/r 35,000/70,000 kip) With the smell of fresh paint in the air, this atmospheric travellers haunt has shed its spooky skin to represent real value for money. Some rooms have hot-water bathrooms, while others are bereft of windows.

Syri 2 Guest House (Map p370; Th Setthathirat; r with/without bathroom 100,000/50,000 kip; ❄) A good place to meet travellers; rooms are basic, clean and have a choice of attached and outside toilets, air-con and cable TV as optional extras. Syri also offers a laundry service and bicycles for rent.

Syri 1 Guest House (Map p370; ☎ 212682; Th Saigon; r with/without bathroom 80,000/50,000 kip;) In a quiet location, this charming old villa welcomes travellers with its array of individual, colourful rooms. There are quiet areas to read in, with old '70s sofas and a flame-illuminated lounge where you can lose yourself in a library of countless films. The owner, Air, also offers special bike rides promising another side of Vientiane. Atmospheric.

our pick **Chantha Guest House** (Map p370; ☎ 243204; Th Setthathirat; standard/deluxe 60,000/120,000 kip;) A recent addition, Japanese-owned Chantha has scrupulously clean rooms with wood-varnished floors and minimal furnishings. Its attractive restaurant next door serves authentic Japanese grub.

Saysouly Guest House (Map p370; Th Manthatulat; ☎ 218383; r with/without bathroom & air-con 120,000/70,000 kip;) Spacious, clean rooms with en suites and cable TV. This oldie is keeping up with neophyte competition thanks to its warm service.

Phatoumphone Guest House (Map p370; ☎ 212318; Th Manthatulat; r with/without bathroom 80,000/65,000 kip) Long a *falang* fave, this wilting accommodation urgently needs a facelift – the couches in the lobby scream '70s porno, the freaky mural Frank Zappa '60s. Make sense of it over a Beer Lao.

Orchid Guest House (Map p370; ☎ 252825; Th Fa Ngum; r 90,000-160,000 kip;) Surging into the Vientiane sky with 20 new generously sized rooms enjoying bathrooms and cable TV. Its tiled rooftop has great views to watch the sunset over the Mekong. Bikes available to hire.

RD Guest House (Map p370; Th Nokeo Khumman; ☎ 262112; r 100,000-120,000 kip;) RD has clean rooms but could do with a visit from the Dulux dog. Rooms have fans and en suites, with air-con extra. Laundry service.

Vayakorn Guest House (Map p370; ☎ 241911; 91 Th Nokeo Khumman; s/d 100,000-130,000 kip;) Beside Monument Bookstore, Vayakorn has cool, crisp rooms with fresh linen daily and TV. Welcoming staff and stylish downstairs cafe and lounge.

Soukxana Guesthouse (Map p370; ☎ 264114; soukxana_guest_house@yahoo.com; 13 Th Pangkham; r 130,000-150,000 kip;) Mint-fresh, family-run Soukxana has quiet, basic rooms (all with TV) opposite Settha Palace. Prices depend on the number of people in the room and whether it's air-con or overhead fan.

Mali Namphu Guest House (Map p370; Th Pangkham; ☎ 263298; www.malinamphu.com; s/d incl breakfast 150,000/200,000 kip;) In its third year now, central Mali Namphu has lovely white rooms with bamboo furnishings, all huddled round a lush courtyard. Ask for a room out the back.

Dragon Lodge (Map p370; ☎ 250112; dragonlodge2002@yahoo.com; Th Samsenthai; r 150,000-230,000 kip;) Small but nicely finished modern rooms with fresh bathrooms and verandahs. The bar's colourful too, packing in a lively crowd come evening. Its information boards are full of useful tips if you've just arrived.

EATING

The word myriad hardly describes the international spectrum of eating options on offer; in short, Vientiane is a gastronome's dream. Noodle houses and street vendors bubble and boil at every turn (if you're monitoring your kip these are a great bet). Alternatively, head down Th Heng Boun for Chinese fare, or wander the maze of sidestreets from Nam Phu to Setthathirat for some affordable French and Italian restaurants.

Breakfast

Scandinavian Bakery (Map p370; ☎ 215199; Nam Phu; meals 10,000-30,000 kip; 7am-7pm;) When travellers remember Vientiane they recall this oasis with a smile. Ever-evolving Scandinavian has fresh subs, salads, gateaux, brownies and a useful noticeboard outside.

Croissant D'Or (Map p370; ☎ 223741; Th Nokeo Khumman; meals 10,000-30,000 kip; 7am-9pm;) Cool enough to ice the Savannakhet plain and more tranquil than Scandinavian and JoMa bakeries, this is a great place to read and take coffee and Danish.

Noy's Fruit Heaven (Map p370; ☎ 030 5262369; Th Heng Boun; 7am-9pm) Delicious fruit shakes (6000 kip) in flavours ranging from dragon fruit to papaya. A welcoming little joint run by cheeky Noy.

JoMa Bakery Café (Map p370; ☎ 215265; Th Setthathirat; meals 10,000-30,000 kip; 7am-9pm Mon-Sat;) The choice of cookies, brownies, subs and salads in the city's favourite oasis is almost overwhelming. Wi-fi costs 25,000 kip an hour.

French

Indochina is evoked in a clutch of stylish restaurants dishing up delicious grub at unbeatable prices.

La Terrasse (Map p370; ☎ 218550; Th Nokeo Koumane; meals 40,000-100,000 kip; ⏰ lunch & dinner Mon-Sat) This brasserie-cum-gelaterie is patronised by expats who appreciate its old-world service, elegant ambience and some of the best Gallic cuisine in the city.

our pick **Le Provencal** (Map p370; ☎ 216248; Nam Phu; meals 40,000 kip; ⏰ lunch Mon-Sat, dinner daily; ❄) A long-time resident of Nam Phu circle, Le Provencal is never empty, with tender wood-fired steaks and delicious pizzas dished up in rustic Breton-style ambience. All accompanied by husky jazz. *Parfait*.

La Vendome (Map p370; ☎ 216402; 39 Th Inpeng; meals 50,000 kip; ⏰ 5-10pm Tue-Sun) Dripping in ivy and candlelit atmosphere, this hidden gem played host to journalists during the Secret War. Soufflés, pâtés, salads and wood-fired pizzas, plus a good wine selection. Timeless.

Vegetarian

Vegetarian food is widely available in noodle houses and Indian restaurants, and features on many menus. Only the following is solely marketing itself to vegetarians.

Vegetarian Buffet (Map pp368-9; ☎ 020-566 6488; Th Saysetha; lunch buffet 12,500 kip, meals 5000-12,000 kip; ⏰ lunch & dinner Mon-Sat) This place has an excellent, all-you-can-eat vegetarian buffet and an à la carte menu for dinner. Head east along Th Setthathirat to Th Saysetha (a Honda store on the left side marks the street). Turn left and the restaurant is a few doors along with a wooden front.

Lao & Asian

Ban Anou night market (Map p370; meals 8000-15,000 kip; ⏰ 5-10pm) On a street off the north end of Th Chao Anou every afternoon, this market is an encyclopedia of street food, selling *ping kai* (barbecue chicken on a stick), *làap* (spicy salad), curries, noodles and other delights.

Open-air riverside food vendors (Map p370; Th Fa Ngum; meals 10,000-30,000 kip; ⏰ 5-11pm) Numerous stands serve up fresh Lao- and Chinese-influenced dishes. If it's popular with locals, it's probably good.

Restaurant Nam Phu (Map p370; Th Pangkham; meals 5000-15,000 kip; ⏰ 11am-10pm) On the corner of Th Pangkham and Samsenthai, you'll see a few discerning expats among the locals, hunkered down over a bowl of noodles and pork. Authentic.

Café Indochine (Map p370; ☎ 262978; Th Setthathirat; meals 30,000-38,000 kip; ⏰ 11am-10pm) This recently opened restaurant serves exclusively Vietnamese food. The ambience is upscale with modern furnishings and walls hung with old B&W photographs.

Indian

Nazim (Map p370; ☎ 223480; Th Fa Ngum; meals 10,000-30,000 kip; ⏰ lunch & dinner) Great riverside location, dining alfresco with excellent breakfast and lunchtime options. Consistent as ever.

Rashmi's Indian Fusion (Map p370; ☎ 251513; Th Samsenthai; meals 40,000 kip; ⏰ 5-11pm) Swanky Rasmi's is all chrome and ambient lighting; good portions, impeccable service and a cool escape from the heat.

Taj Mahal Restaurant (Map p370; ☎ 020-561 1003; Th Setthathirat; meals 11,000-20,000 kip; ⏰ 10am-10.30pm Mon-Sat, 4-10.30pm Sun; ❄) Flavoursome Indian fare in this no-frills cafe; portions are generous and you can sit semi-alfresco. Good vegie selection too (20 dishes). Watch out, Nazim.

International

Dao Fa Bistro (Map p370; Th Setthathirat; meals 40,000-65,000 kip; ⏰ 7am-9pm) Dao Fa delivers with its pop art–adorned walls, friendly service and heavily French–Italian menu. The Greek salad is to die for.

Full Moon Café (Map p370; ☎ 243373; Th François Nginn; meals 30,000-40,000 kip; ⏰ 5-11pm) Mellow tunes and style converge in this sumptuously comfy haunt, with an upstairs bar and quiet verandah to read. Asian-fusion menu, featuring a combo of Lao–Thai and Vietnamese dishes.

Khop Chai Deu (Map p370; ☎ 223022; Th Setthathirat; meals 30,000-50,000 kip; ⏰ lunch & dinner; ❄) An old stalwart of Vientiane's nightlife, this handsomely restored French villa offers a range of Western and Asian fare and a lively atmosphere to go with your beer.

Sticky Fingers Café & Bar (Map p370; ☎ 215972; 10/3 Th François Nginn; meals 40,000-65,000 kip; ⏰ 10am-11pm Tue-Sun; ❄) Superfriendly Western joint with a *falang*-heavy menu ranging from fried chicken to sausage-and-mash. Good place to catch live bands and meet expats. The noticeboard is useful too: secondhand mopeds, cars and rooms to rent.

DRINKING

Choose between uberstylish bars or basic riverfront vendors to watch the sun sink into the Mekong.

Sunset Sala Khounta (Map pp368-9; ☎ 251079; 11am-11pm) Adding to its mythic status as the best sundown escape, Khounta was (literally) shipwrecked by the 2008 September rains and collapsed. It's now back on its sea legs.

Bor Pen Nyang (Map p370; ☎ 020-787 3965; Th Fa Ngum; 10am-midnight) This is a kicking rooftop bar with a great view of the Mekong, widescreen TV (generally showing sports) pool tables and an 'up for it' crowd.

Jazzy Brick (Map p370; ☎ 212489; Th Setthathirat; lunch & dinner) With its exposed brick walls peppered with antique jazz posters, this boutique bar is full of downlit atmosphere and does a mean turn in cocktails (50,000 kip). If the spirits inspire you, reach for the old Royal typewriter on the bartop.

Martini Bar (Map p370; ☎ 020-771 1138; Th Nokeo Khumman; 7pm-late;) As if transplanted from London's Soho, this ubersleek watering hole has cocktails with names like Crouching Tiger. The walls are ochre, the vibe as chilled as the resident fish tank.

Spirit House (Map pp368-9; ☎ 243795; 1-11pm) By far the most modish joint on the river, this is a place to drink and betray your Shoestringer genes for a few hours. Dim-lit Manhattan ambience and a list of cocktails that would make your liver glow.

Sticky Fingers Café & Bar (Map p370; ☎ 215972; Th François Nginn; 9am-11pm Sun-Sat) During happy hour, on Wednesday and Friday nights, 'Stickies' heaves with NGO workers letting off steam.

Clubbing

Conveniently, three of Vientiane's better nightclubs – **Future** (Map pp368-9; Th Luang Prabang; 8pm-1am), **Highwayman** (Map pp368-9; Th Luang Prabang; 8pm-midnight) and **Marina** (Map pp368-9; ☎ 216978; Th Luang Prabang; 8pm-1am) – are all situated near each other on the road to the airport. Elsewhere, **Lunar 36** (Map pp368-9; Don Chan Palace Hotel; 6pm-3am Wed, Fri & Sat), off Th Fa Ngum, is Vientiane's official late-night altar to hedonism, with a decent disco and outside verandah.

ENTERTAINMENT

Check *Paisai? What's On* for info on book festivals, photo expos, Lao boxing, European cinema and public events.

Laos Traditional Show (Map p370; ☎ 242978; Th Manthatulat; child/adult 35,000/60,000 kip, still/video camera charge 8500/25,000 kip) This performance of traditional music and dancing, aimed directly at tourists, plays nightly from about November to March.

Centre Culturel et de Coopération Linguistique (French Cultural Centre; Map p370; ☎ 215764; www.ambafrance-laos.org/centre; Th Lan Xang; 9.30am-6.30pm Mon-Fri, to noon Sat) Library, French cinema (Tuesday, Thursday and Saturday, 6.30pm), art exhibitions and live music. Check *Paisai? What's On* to see listings of its nightly subtitled screenings.

SHOPPING

Numerous handicraft and souvenir boutiques are dotted around the streets radiating from Nam Phu, particularly on Th Pangkham and Th Setthathirat.

Talat Sao (Morning Market; Map p370; Th Lan Xang; 7am-5pm) The new, facelifted Talat Sao is packed to the gills with electronics, cheap jewellery and white goods. It's a good place to buy a cheap phone or stock up on pay-as-you-go cards. Beside it, the remaining original market is much more fun; the labyrinthine aisles spil with silk scarves, cheap T-shirts and tapestries.

GETTING INTO THAILAND: VIENTIANE TO NONG KHAI

The Thai–Lao Friendship Bridge is 22km southeast of Vientiane. The border is open between 6am and 10pm, and the easiest way to cross is on the comfortable Thai–Lao International Bus (12,000 kip, 90 minutes), which leaves Vientiane's Talat Sao bus station at 7.30am, 9.30am, 12.40pm, 2.30pm, 3.30pm and 6pm. From Nong Khai in Thailand, it leaves at the same times for 55B. Similar buses run to Udon Thani (20,000 kip, two hours) six times a day. Visas are issued on arrival in both countries. Alternative means of transport between Vientiane and the bridge include taxi or jumbo (60,000–70,000 kip – bargain hard) or regular public buses from Talat Sao (13,000 kip) between 6.30am and 5pm. At the bridge, regular shuttle buses ferry passengers between immigration posts. For information on crossing this border in the other direction, see p781.

LEAVING VIENTIANE BY BUS

All services depart daily except where noted. For buses to China, contact the **Tong Li Bus Company** (☎ 242657). For Vietnam, buses leave daily for Hanoi (200,000 kip, 24 hours) via Vinh (160,000 kip, 16 hours); and less often for Hue (170,000 kip), Danang (200,000 kip) and even Ho Chi Minh City (450,000 kip, up to 48 hours).

Destination	Fare normal/ air-con/VIP (kip)	Distance (km)	Duration (hr)	Departures
Talat Sao Bus Station				
Vang Vieng	40,000	153	4	7am, 9.30am, 10.30am, 11.30am, 1.30pm, 2pm
Northern Bus Station				
Huay Xai	230,000	869	30-35	5.30pm
Southern Bus Station				
Kunming	610,000	781	30	2pm
Luang Nam Tha	170,000	676	18	8.30am
Luang Prabang	120,000-130,000	384	11/9-10 (VIP)	6.30am, 7.30am, 8am (VIP), 9am (air-con), 11am, 1.30pm, 4pm, 6pm, 8pm (air-con)
Udomxai	130,000-180,000	578	13-15	6.45am, 1.45pm (local), 5pm (express)
Phongsali	185,000	811	26	7.15am (doesn't leave every day)
Phonsavan	100,000-120,000	374	9-11	6.30am, 7.30am (air-con), 3.30pm, 7pm, 8pm (air-con)
Sainyabuli	120,000-135,000	485	14-16	4.30pm, 6.30pm
Sam Neua	180,000-220,000	612	15-17	12.30am (VIP), 7am (via Luang Prabang, taking up to 30hr), 9.30am, 12.30pm (via Phonsavan)
Attapeu	185,000	812	22-24	7.30am, 8.30am, 5pm
Lak Sao	35,000	334	7-9	5am, 6am, 7am
Paksan	21,500	143	3-4	take any bus going south, roughly every 30min from 4.30am to 5pm
Pakse	130,000-180,000	677	14-16/9½ (VIP)	every 30min from 9.30am to 5pm (normal), 7pm & 8pm (air-con), 8.30pm (VIP)
Salavan	100,000-200,000	774	15-20	4.30pm (VIP), 7.30pm
Savannakhet	130,000-180,000	457	8-10	every 30min from 6am to 9am (normal), 8.30pm (air-con), or any normal or air-con bus to Pakse
Tha Khaek	75,000/ 95,000 (air-con)	337	6/4½	4am, 5am, 6am, noon, or any bus to Savannakhet or Pakse, 1pm (VIP)
Voen Kham	185,000	818	17-20	11am

Camacrafts (Mulberries; Map p370; ☎ 241217; www.mulberries.org; Th Nokeo Khumman; ⌚ 10am-6pm Mon-Sat) Nonprofit organisation engendering sustainability for Hmong women through the sale of their beautiful handicrafts. Also fine silk scarves sold in the same shop by sister co Mulberries. Members of the International Fair Trade Organization.

Satri Lao (Map p370; ☎ 216592; Th Setthatharit; ⌚ 9am-8pm) This is a byword for quality: silk garments, scarves, hand-made soaps, bespoke jewellery and oil paintings. This three-storey emporium is definitely the most eclectic in town.

GETTING THERE & AWAY

Air

Wattay International Airport (off Map pp368–9) is the hub for flights to the rest of the country and Cambodia and Thailand (see p363).

Boat

Rare, no-frills cargo boats head upstream to Luang Prabang (four days to one week) from Kiaw Liaw Pier (off Map pp368–9), 3.5km west of the fork in the road where Rte 13 heads north in Ban Kao Liaw. Go there and speak with the boatmen in advance to see if, when and how far they're running. During dry season, November to May, it's out of the question.

Bus & Săwngthăew

Buses use three different stations in Vientiane, all with some English-speaking staff. The **Northern Bus Station** (Map pp368-9; ☎ 260255; Th T2), about 2km northwest of the centre, serves all points north of Vang Vieng, including China, and has some buses to Vietnam.

The **Southern Bus Station** (off Map pp368-9; ☎ 740521; Rte 13 South), commonly known as Dong Dok Bus Station or just *khíw lot lák kāo* (Km 9 Bus Station), is 9km out of town and serves everywhere south. Buses to Vietnam will usually stop here.

The **Talat Sao Bus Station** (Map p370; ☎ 216507) is where desperately slow local buses depart for destinations within Vientiane Province, including Vang Vieng, and some more distant destinations, though for these you're better going to the northern or southern stations. It's also home to the Thai-Lao International Bus (see p376).

See p377 for timetable info.

GETTING AROUND

Central Vientiane is entirely accessible on foot.

Bicycle & Motorcycle

Bicycles can be rented for 8000 kip per day from tour agencies and guest houses. Scooters are also a great way to get about town, but remember to keep your helmet on (the police fine is a movable feast). The excellent **Jules' Classic Rental** (Map p370; ☎ 020 7600813; www.bike-rental-laos.com; Th Setthathirat; per day 85,000-255,000 kip) outside Phimphone Market has new bikes ranging from classic Vespas to heavy-duty 450cc motocross giants. Another major plus is you can drop your bike off in Vang Vieng or Luang Prabang. Comprehensive insurance is standard.

Túk-Túk

Many túk-túk have a laminated list of vastly inflated tourist prices and won't budge for less than the price already agreed upon with the other drivers (starting at 10,000 kip). You're better off trying a free-roaming túk-túk (one driving along the street), where negotiation is possible. You can also flag down a shared túk-túk (with passengers already in it); shared túk-túk ply fixed routes and cost about 2000–5000 kip depending on your destination.

NORTHERN LAOS

To many the mountainous north with its mystical forests, enchanting karst topography and rich ethnicity crystallises exactly what we imagine as Laos. Over the last few years, from Luang Prabang to far-flung Muang Sing, trekking opportunities have improved, with ecologically minded tour companies running one-to-three-day treks and homestays in some of Southeast Asia's most pristine forests. With dramatically improved roads the north is no longer such a struggle, though until they invent crow-flying buses you'll still have serpentine roads and interminable journeys.

VIENTIANE PROVINCE

Heading north through Vientiane province (a different area from Vientiane Prefecture, which holds the capital) you may wish to take in the serenity of the Ang Nam Ngum Reservoir or, if it's safe, the spectacular and mountainous Saisombun Special Zone. The roads are poor but navigable by motocross bike, the landscape pristine and rarely seen due to the government's historical problems in the area with Hmong guerrillas.

Vang Vieng

☎ 023 / pop 25,000

If you're returning after a long spell you may bemoan the peaceful riverside village it once was, backdropped by mist-laced karsts, the Nam Song river puttering with fishermen. But despite the long-ranging debate as to whether Vang Vieng is a 'paradise lost' beyond redemption, these rural ingredients still exist. Walking down newly christened Khao San Rd you can see how keenly the town tries to secure the *falang* dollar, with multiple video bars looping *Friends* episodes, plus an occasionally diffident attitude to service brought on by Westerners' drunken antics. But with a rich selection of caving, trekking, mountain-biking and climbing opportunities, there's plenty to counterbalance horizontal slacking. The real

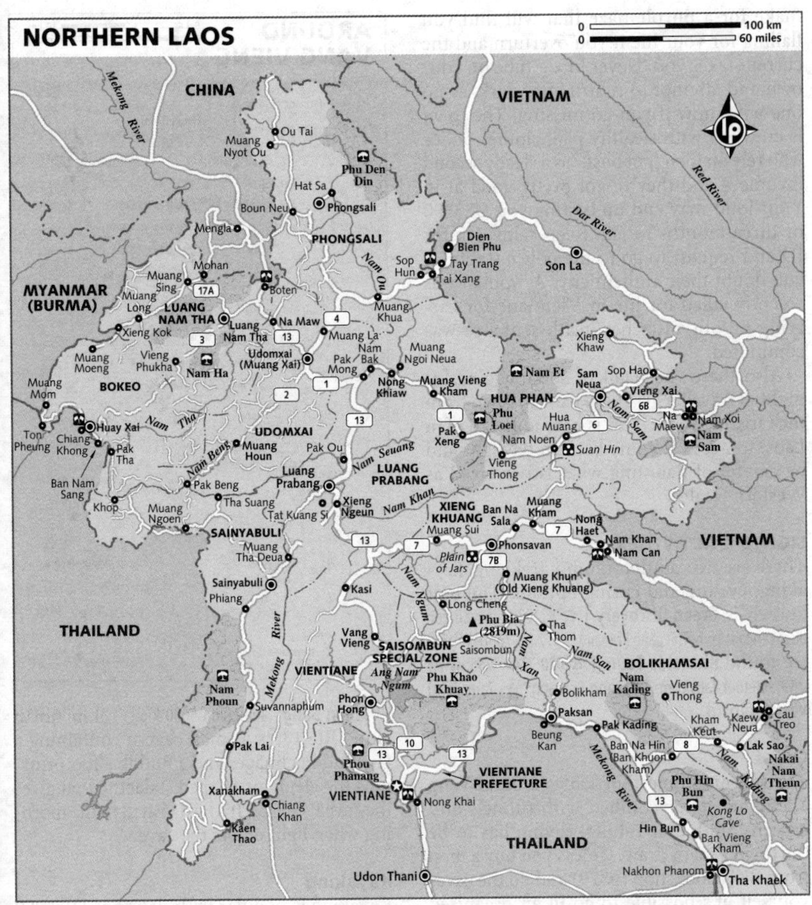

draw is the tubing, allowing you to cool off in the Nam Song, stop for a beer en route, and take in the enchanting river life.

ORIENTATION & INFORMATION

Buses now stop at the new bus station, 2km north of the main town. Guest houses, bars and restaurants radiate west from Khao San Rd all the way to the river. Parallel to the main street are a basic provincial hospital, several restaurants, plus a few stylish guest houses along the river. Internet cafes in Vang Vieng charge around 6000 kip per hour.

Banque pour le Commerce Extérieur Lao (☎ 5114480; 8.30am-3.30pm Mon-Sun) Just west of Xayoh Café, does exchanges and cash advances and has a 24-hour ATM.

BKC Bookshop (☎ 511303; Market St; 7am-7pm) Sells a small selection of secondhand novels, old guidebooks and hand-drawn tourist maps.

PlaNet Online (☎ 511209; per hr 6000 kip; 8am-11pm) Internet access, CD burning, international internet phone calls. Organises onward visas.

Post office (☎ 511009; 8.30am-3.30pm Mon-Fri) Beside the old market.

Provincial Hospital (☎ 511604)) This flash new hospital has X-ray facilities and is fine for broken bones, cuts and malaria.

DANGERS & ANNOYANCES

The two *bêtes noires* of VV are drugs and drowning. The Nam Song is potentially lethal when it runs high – while it might be *de rigueur* here to imbibe, pot and beer combined make for a purple haze that will find you flailing for your life if you overturn and the current takes you. Never hire a tube on your own and attempt to return after dark, as no one will know if you go missing. The town is crawling with stealthy plainclothes police who rely on their 'pot busts' as a steady second income – and they've got pretty good at it. Your joint may end up costing you US$500 or three months in jail. Keep calm, ask for ID and request to go to the police station if you doubt their authenticity. A woman was recently jailed for life in Vientiane for carrying heroin, after her death sentence was commuted.

Also, there's been talk of 'soft muggings' at night of travellers walking back to town from the Organic Farm. This is near unheard of in Laos; to avoid it come back in daylight and be careful of flaunting what is perceived as Western wealth.

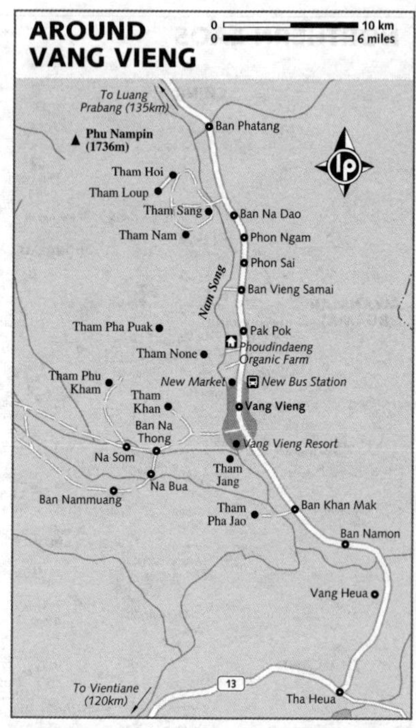

SIGHTS & ACTIVITIES

There are two outfits running trekking, kayaking, cycling and caving options. The best known is **Green Discovery** (☎ 511230; www.greendiscoverylaos.com; Th Luang Prabang; 7am-7pm), while we found **Riverside Tours** (☎ 020 2244 7755; www.riversidetourslaos.com; Th Luang Prabang; 7am-7pm) very helpful.

Caves

The stunning limestone karsts around Vang Vieng are honeycombed with tunnels and caverns, and after tubing, caving has to be the town's main draw. Unless you buy a map from BKC bookshop (p379) and do the caves yourself, it's possible to go in an organised group. Check your guest house for info.

The most famous cave, **Tham Jang** (admission 9000 kip), 1km south of town, was used as a hideout from marauding Yunnanese Chinese in the early 19th century. A set of stairs leads up to the main cavern entrance. There's also a cool spring at the foot of the cave.

Another popular cave is **Tham Phu Kham** (Blue Lagoon; admission 5000 kip). To reach it, cross the **bamboo footbridge** (toll walking/cycling 4000/6000 kip) then walk or pedal 7km along a scenic, unsealed road to Ban Na Thong, from where you have to walk 1km to a hill on the northern side of the village. It's a tough final 200m climb but worth it for a dip in the blue stream afterwards.

Tham Sang (admission 5000 kip), 13km north along Rte 13, is a small cavern containing a few Buddha images and a Buddha 'footprint', plus the elephant-shaped stalactite that gives the cave its name. It's best visited in the morning when light enters the cave.

Kayaking

Kayaking is popular with day trips (100,000 kip per person) typically taking you down a few rapids and stopping at caves and villages. Before using a cheap operator, check guides' credentials and the quality of their kit; for example is there a briefing beforehand? Do they have medical kits and life jackets? We recommend Riverside Tours and Green Discovery.

Rafting is less popular but more adventurous, with trips down the Nam Ngum being the pick. The operators below ordinarily charge between 100,000 and 127,000 kip depending on the size of the group and duration of the trip.

Rock Climbing

Green Discovery (☎ 511230; www.greendiscoverylaos.com) and **Riverside Tours** (☎ 511500; www.riverside

toursl aos.com; cycling tours incl lunch 127,000 kip; 7am-7pm) operate guided rock-climbing courses for novices (around 170,000 kip per day) and can lead more experienced climbers up Vang Vieng's dramatic limestone cliffs.

Tubing

Vang Vieng's biggest attraction involves hiring an inner tube from the cartel by the old market, who will take you 3km upriver and leave you to drift back in your own time. Prices are fixed at 55,000 kip (make sure you are back before 6pm), which includes the túk-túk ride to the launch point. The trip can take two or more hours depending on river conditions (it's quicker during the wet season) and how many of the makeshift bars you stop at en route! At least one person a year loses their life to the river – usually because of too many 'happy shakes', reefer and beer. Make sure it's not you.

SLEEPING

Cricket song is in symphony with tapping hammers as new guest houses spring up at an alarming rate – Vang Vieng had 1300 rooms at the last count! If you're in search of tranquillity, head to the river but away from newly named 'Party Island' where the beat never sleeps.

Sunset Home (511439; r 30,000-40,000 kip;) Just north of Champa Lao GH, Sunset gives new meaning to 'basic' with spartan cells furnished with a mattress and gossamer-thin walls. That said, it has great river views and Jaidee 2 is throbbing just yards away.

our pick **Nam Song Garden** (511544; Khao San Rd; r 30,000-50,000 kip;) Set in a peaceful garden with bungalows or rooms in an adjoining house, this is clean and simple accommodation with en suites, showers and fans. Run by a friedly Norwegian, Nam Song makes its own ice cream and can organise rock-climbing excursions. Tempted?

Champa Lao Guest House (511124; r 30,000-80,000 kip) Opposite the Provincial Hospital, with sweeping vistas of the river and mountains beyond, Champa has tasteful bungalows beside the river with fans and en suites as well as rooms in the main building. Soporific reclining area and lush gardens combined with friendly owners make this one of the best Shoestring options.

Phoubane Guest House (511306; r 35,000-200,000 kip;) Just west of the post office, Phoubane has cool, river-facing bungalows with tiled floors, fresh walls and clean bathrooms with hot water. Its original wooden bungalows are fan-cooled, well maintained and a tenth of the price of the new ones.

Paradise Island Bungalows (s/d 40,000/50,000 kip) West of the bamboo footbridge, Paradise has uberbasic, stilted cabanas with balconies, bathrooms and great river views. Also a decent alfresco bar.

Maylyn Guest House (020-5604095; jophus_foley@hotmail.com; r 40,000-60,000 kip) On the far side of the Nam Song with terrific views of the karsts, Maylyn's beautiful garden alone should win an award. If the blue tiger butterflies don't delight, the 15 pristine cabanas and homely cafe will.

THE WEREWOLF WARRIOR TRIBE

One of the best-known tribes in Laos, the Hmong playfully propogate the myth they were werewolves who flew into Laos on magic carpets. In the late 19th century thousands of Chinese opium farmers drove them into high-altitude regions of Laos where they've practised opium cultivation (until recently) and slash-and-burn farming ever since. Their mistrust of lowland Lao has not endeared them to the present administration. Because of their political sympathies with the US (during the Secret War), which provided them with guns, dollars and penicillin in return for their expertise in jungle warfare and copious amounts of opium, the Hmong have been persecuted more than any other ethnic tribe in Laos. An estimated 10% of their population lost their lives in this conflict, after which 3000 per month poured across the Mekong to Thailand, some to refugee camps, others to the US (where approximately 100,000 now live) and France. Their old resistance leader, the charismatic General Vang Pao, is still alive in San Francisco, allegedly masterminding the few continuing guerrilla attacks executed by the geriatric freedom fighters.

The Hmong are devout animists (believing everything has a spirit) – every powder-blue homestead has an altar, and every village enjoys the guidance of a shaman.

Pan's Place (☎ 511484; neilenolix@hotmail.com; r 50,000 kip) Beside the old CIA runway, expat-run Pan's has basic rooms with fan and bathroom, plus an internet cafe and tasty restaurant with a Western-leaning menu. Upstairs there's a TV room with a choice of 300 films, and at the time of research five new cabanas were being built out the back.

Organic Mulberry Farm (☎ 511220; www.laofarm.org; r 50,000-90,000 kip) Known locally as Phoudindaeng Mulberry Farm, this organic farm a few kilometres out of town has simple accommodation and a great restaurant – try the mulberry pancakes or mulberry mojitos! If you're looking to do something useful after a few days chilling, see Mr Thi, Ward or Rachel about volunteering. Tranquil.

Dok Khoun 1 Guest House (☎ 511032; r 50,000-100,000 kip;) Right in the centre of town between the old market and Th Luang Prabang, Dok Khoun has what might generously be described as 'functional' accommodation. The management could use a wave of the happy wand. Fan and en suite are standard.

EATING

If you're after more something more authentic than Western comfort fare, here are a few joints that serve consistently good food at reasonable prices.

Nokeo (meals 6000-20,000 kip; lunch & dinner) Located on a corner opposite the old market, Nokeo offers a wide range of Lao dishes plus alfresco lounging cushions to eat beneath the stars. Vang Vieng young-bamboo soup recommended.

Restaurant Luang Prabang Bakery (☎ 511145; meals 7000-30,000 kip; breakfast, lunch & dinner) Hansel and Gretel sanctuary of fruit shakes, brownies, cakes, juicy subs and nightly films on demand. Munchies heaven.

Organic Mulberry Farm Café (☎ 511174; meals 20,000-30,000 kip) Peacefully parked down the end of the main strip, the wide range of shakes on offer is worth the walk, as are the mulberry pancakes confected with fruit from the idyllic farm out of town. A great selection for vegetarians and friendly staff make this one of the best places in town.

Erawan Restaurant (☎ 511093; Th Luang Prabang; meals 40,000-65,000 kip) A little more upmarket than its counterparts, Erawan has tasteful furnishings, wall-mounted animal heads and an authentic Lao menu. The steamed whole fish and lemon sauce is mouth-watering.

Xayoh Café (☎ 511403; meals 20,000-40,000 kip; breakfast, lunch & dinner) This attractive Khao San favourite features a menu of pizzas, Thai food and light snacks. Dimly lit, with a pool table, it's a worthy start to a night's hedonism.

Khun Kham Restaurant (☎ 511369; meals 16,000-30,000 kip) Featuring Lao, Thai and Western fare, this recently opened, peaceful joint is much more appropriate for a quiet evening meal. A spit north of the Provincial Hospital.

Nazim Indian Restaurant (☎ 511214; Khao San Rd; meals 30,000 kip; breakfast, lunch & dinner) Still a decent option, this Nazim is spacious and clean with generic Indian fare such as chicken masala and korma. There's also a fruit-juice kiosk.

DRINKING

Babylon Bar (Khao San Rd; 5-11.30pm) Comfortably numb with reclining cushions, nightly films and a stylish ambience, Babylon's a tranquil option – everything further south of Khao San tends to be.

Jaidee's Bar (☎ 606339; Khao San Rd; 5-11.30pm) Graffiti walls, scatter cushions and moody lighting make this an obvious haunt to equalise if that 'happy' pizza is dragging you down, man. Music glides from Latin to Linkin Park in the blink of an eyelid.

Sakura (5-11.30pm) is a lively joint for après-tubing, with its freaky murals, hanging lanterns, lounging area and cinema at the back.

GETTING THERE & AWAY

From the **bus station** (☎ 511341; Rte 13) 2km north of town, buses leave for Luang Prabang (85,000 kip, seven to 11 hours, 168km, several daily), Vientiane (35,000 kip, 3½ to 4½ hours, 156km, four times daily) and Phonsavan (85,000 kip, six to seven hours, 219km, daily at about 9am). For Vientiane, pick-ups (30,000 kip, 3½ to 4½ hours) leave every 20 minutes from 5am until 4pm.

Tickets for minibuses and VIP buses with air-con travelling direct to Vientiane (60,000 kip, three hours) or Luang Prabang (105,000 kip, six to eight hours) are sold at guest houses, tour agencies and internet cafes in town. There is no VIP bus to Phonsavan.

GETTING AROUND

The township is small enough to walk around with ease. Bicycles can be rented for around 10,000 kip a day. Motorcycles are sadly off limits due to drunken accidents. A túk-túk up to the Organic Farm or Tham Sang Triangle costs around 10,000 kip per person.

LUANG PRABANG PROVINCE

Luang Prabang

☎ 071 / pop 52,466

There are places that linger in the imagination long after you visit them; Mekong-bordered Luang Prabang, with its Unesco-protected peninsula of gleaming wat and crumbling French villas, is such a place. Timeless, and reinvigorated by a new airport, this once-inaccessible Shangri La is an absolute must for its Buddhist architecture, the tangerine stream of monks taking alms at 6am and its vast array of shopping and cuisine. In short, Luang Prabang is a sensual cocktail with a heavy measure of history to match.

With pashmina-draped A-listers descending quietly, the town has reinvented itself as an affordably upscale city of taste. Between eating your way through a global smorgasbord of Scandinavian cafes, French cuisine and authentic Lao, you can elephant ride, take a cooking course, visit waterfalls or just hire a bicycle and pedal your way around what may be the most beguiling ancient city in Southeast Asia.

ORIENTATION

Most of the tourist sights are in the old quarter, on the peninsula bounded by the Mekong and Nam Khan rivers. Dominating the centre of town, Wat Tham Phu Si is an unmissable landmark. The majority of restaurants, accommodation, tour companies and internet cafes line and radiate from Th Sisavangvong, while additional bars are blossoming on Th Kingkitsarat, also known as 'Entertainment Village'. The old quarter is easily covered on foot, but hiring a bicycle is an excellent way to explore the city and its attractions.

INFORMATION

Bookshops

L'Etranger Books & Tea (booksinlaos@yahoo.com; Th Kingkitsarat; 8am-10pm Mon-Sat, 10am-10pm Sun) Secondhand books, plus travel guides, as well as book exchange. Upstairs there's a comfy lizard-lounge whose walls are plastered with *National Geographic* covers. Films shown nightly at 7pm.

Monument Books (www.monument-books.com; Ban Wat Nong; 9am-8pm Mon-Fri, to 6pm Sat & Sun) Next to Ock Pop Tock, selling new novels and magazines.

Internet Access

For wi-fi try Le Café Ban Vat Sene, Morning Glory Café or JoMa Bakery Café (p389). Internet cafes along Th Sisavangvong charge 1000 kip per hour, including the following:

All Lao Travel Co (Th Sisavangvong; 7.30am-10pm)

Thanaboun Guest House (Th Sisavangvong; 8am-11pm)

Medical Services

Serious cases need to be flown to Bangkok or **Aek Udon International** (☎ 0066-4234 2255; www.aekudon.com; Amphur Muang, Udon Thani, Thailand).

Lao-China Friendship Hospital (☎ 252049; Th Setthathirat) All-new and eerily deserted. About 3km south off Th Naviengkham, after the stadium (10,000 kip by túk-túk). A large white tower signals the spot.

Pharmacie (Th Sakkarin; 8.30am-8pm) Stocks basic medicines. Open daily, although closes sometimes for a few hours on weekends.

Money

Banque pour le Commerce Extérieur Lao (☎ 252983; Th Sisavangvong; 8.30am-5pm Mon-Fri, 8.30am-3.30pm Sat & Sun) Changes major currencies in cash or travellers cheques, has a 24hr ATM & allows you to make cash advances against Visa and MasterCard.

Lao Development Bank (65 Th Sisavangvong; 8.30am-3.30pm Mon-Sat) Has a 24hr ATM.

Post

Post office (Th Chao Fa Ngum; 8.30am-3.30pm Mon-Fri, to noon Sat) Phone calls and Western Union facilities too.

Telephone

Most internet cafes in Luang Prabang have Skype and also offer international/mobile calls for 3000/4000 kip per minute.

Tourist Information

Provincial Tourism Department (☎ 212487; Th Wisunalat) This office, opposite Wat Wisunalat, stocks a few brochures but is largely useless. Opening hours are erratic.

Unesco World Heritage Information (www.unesco.org; Villa Xiengmouane, Th Sakkarin; 9am-6pm Mon-Fri) Situated in an anteroom of an old French customs house, this office contains information on the Unesco World Heritage project operating in Luang Prabang.

Travel Agencies

There's a number of tour companies down Th Sisavangvong, but we recommend the following:

All Lao Travel Co (☎ 253522; Th Sisavangvong; 8am-6pm) A one-stop shop for flights, boat and bus tickets.

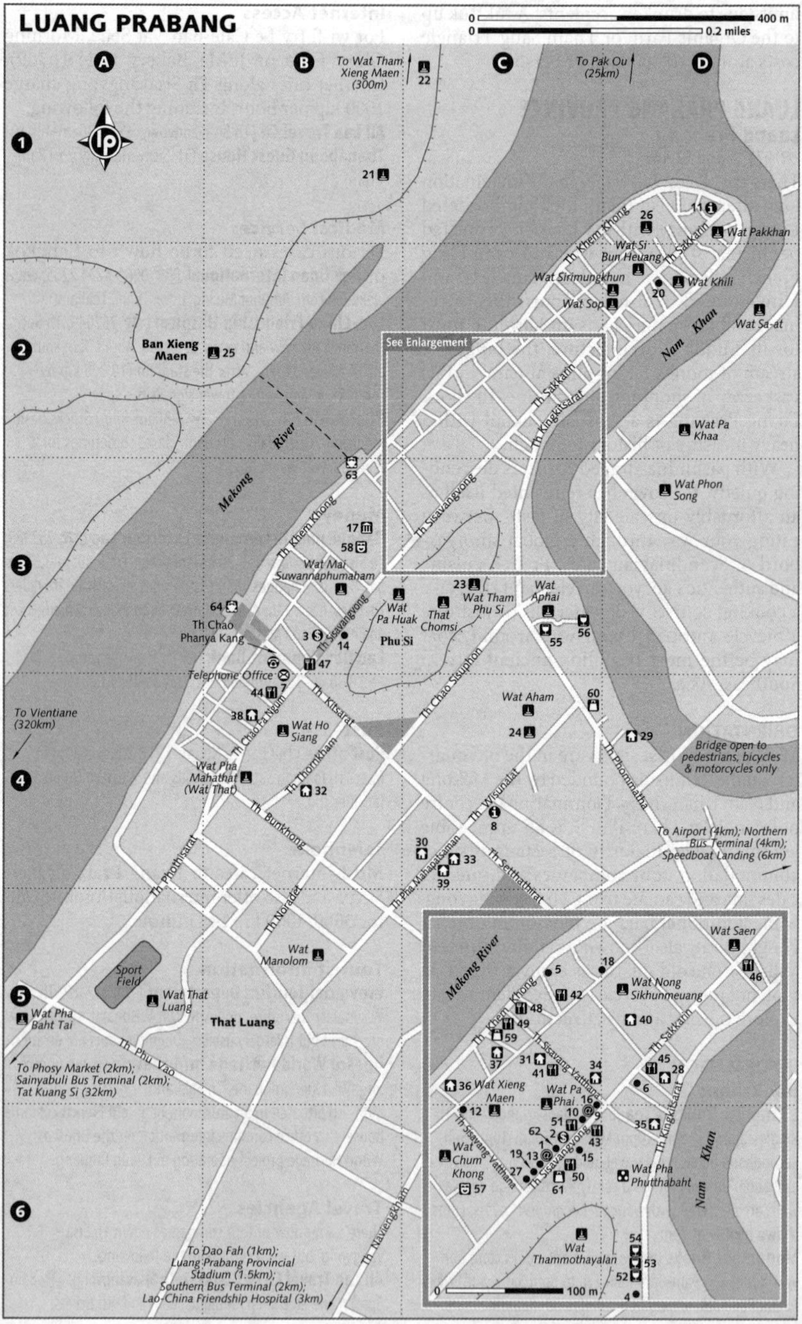

LUANG PRABANG

0 400 m
0 0.2 miles

A B C D
1 2 3 4 5 6

To Wat Tham Xieng Maen (300m)
To Pak Ou (25km)
22
21
Ban Xieng Maen 25
Mekong River
63
Th Khem Khong
17
58
Wat Mai Suwannaphumaham
64
Th Chao Phanya Kang
3
14
Th Sisavangvong
Wat Pa Huak
That Chomsi
Phu Si
23
Wat Tham Phu Si
Wat Aphai
55
56
Telephone Office
7
47
44
38
Th Chao Fa Ngum
Th Kitsarat
Wat Ho Siang
Th Thomkham
To Vientiane (320km)
Wat Pha Mahathat (Wat That)
32
Th Bunkhong
Th Phothisarat
Th Noradet
Wat Manolom
Sport Field
Wat That Luang
That Luang
Wat Pha Baht Tai
Th Phu Vao
To Phosy Market (2km); Sainyabuli Bus Terminal (2km); Tat Kuang Si (32km)
To Dao Fah (1km); Luang Prabang Provincial Stadium (1.5km); Southern Bus Terminal (2km); Lao-China Friendship Hospital (3km)
Th Naviengkham
Th Pha Mahapatsaman
30
33
39
Th Setthathirat
Th Wisunarat
8
Th Chao Sisuphon
Wat Aham
24
60
Th Phommatha
29
Bridge open to pedestrians, bicycles & motorcycles only
To Airport (4km); Northern Bus Terminal (4km); Speedboat Landing (6km)
See Enlargement
Th Sakkarin
Th Kingkitsarat
Nam Khan
Wat Pa Khaa
Wat Phon Song
Wat Sa-at
Th Khem Khong
26
11
Wat Pakkhan
Wat Si Bun Heuang
Th Sakkarin
Wat Sirimungkhun
Wat Khili
20
Wat Sop

Mekong River
5
18
Wat Saen
46
Wat Nong Sikhunmeuang
42
48
49
40
59
37
31
41
34
Th Sisavang Vatthana
Th Sakkarin
45
28
36
Wat Xieng Maen
6
Wat Pa Phai
16
12
10
9
51
35
Th Kingkitsarat
62
2
43
Th Sisavang Vatthana
1
15
Wat Chum Khong
19
13
Th Sisavangvong
27
50
61
Wat Pha Phutthabaht
Nam Khan
57
Wat Thammothayalan
54
53
52
4
0 100 m

INFORMATION
All Lao Travel Co....1 C6
Banque pour le Commerce Extérieur Lao....2 C6
Lao Development Bank....3 B3
L'Étranger Books & Tea....4 D6
Monument Books....5 C5
Pharmacie....6 D5
Post Office....7 B4
Provincial Tourism Department....8 C4
Thanaboun Guest House....9 C6
Treasure Travel....10 C6
Unesco World Heritage Office....11 D1

SIGHTS & ACTIVITIES
Elephant XL....12 C6
Green Discovery....13 C6
Hmong Night Market....14 B3
Khmu Spa....15 C6
Lotus Du Lao Massage....16 C5
Royal Palace Museum....17 B3
Tamarind....18 C5
Tiger Trails....19 C6
Tum Tum Cheng Cooking School....20 D2
Wat Chom Phet....21 B1
Wat Long Khun....22 C1
Wat Tham Phu Si....23 C3
Wat Wisunalat....24 C4
Wat Xieng Maen....25 B2
Wat Xieng Thong....26 D1
White Elephant....27 C6

SLEEPING
Chittana Guest House....28 D5
Cold River....29 D4
Jaliya Guest House....30 C4
Kinnaly Guest House....31 C5
Koun Savan Guest House....32 B4
Mano Guest House & Restaurant....33 C4
Paphai Guest House....34 C5
Pathoumphone Guest House....35 D6
Phousi Guest House II....36 C5
Silichit Guest House....37 C5
Suankeo Guest House No 2....38 B4
Thavisouk Guest House....39 C4
Vatthanaluck Guest House....40 D5

EATING
Café Toui....41 C5
Couleur Café....42 C5
Dao Fa Bistro....43 C6
JoMa Bakery Café....44 B4
Le Café Ban Vat Sene....45 D5
Morning Glory Café....46 D5
Night Food Market....47 B3
Riverfront Restaurants....48 C5
Saffron Café....49 C5
Scandinavian Bakery....50 C6
Tamarind....(see 18)
Tum Tum Cheng Restaurant....51 C6

DRINKING
Hive Bar....52 D6
House Bar....53 D6
Lao Lao Garden....54 D6
Martin's Pub....55 C3
Utopia....56 C3

ENTERTAINMENT
Le Cinema....57 C6
L'Étranger Books & Tea....(see 4)
Royal Ballet Theatre....58 B3

SHOPPING
Hmong Night Market....(see 14)
Orange Tree....59 C5
Pathana Boupha Antique House....60 C4
Samsara....61 C6

TRANSPORT
Bangkok Airways....62 C6
Boats to Pak Ou....(see 63)
Ferry Boat Pier....63 B3
Long-Distance Ferries....64 B3

Treasure Travel (☎ 254682; www.treasuretravellaos.com; Th Sisavangvong; 8am-6pm)Can organise trips to Pak Ou caves (80,000 kip per person) & Kuang Si waterfalls (300,000 kip).

SIGHTS

Royal Palace Museum

Known to locals as Haw Kham (Golden Hall), the **Royal Palace Museum** (☎ 212470; Th Sisavangvong; admission 20,000 kip; 8.30-10.30am & 2-4pm, closed Tue) was constructed in 1904 for King Sisavangvong and his family. Its design reflects two very different architectural styles – European and traditional Lao. When the king died in 1959 his son, Savang Vattana, briefly inherited the throne, but after the 1975 revolution he and his family were exiled to the caves of Vieng Xai in northern Laos, following which the palace was converted into a museum.

Various royal religious objects are on display in the large entry hall, as well as rare Buddhist sculptures from India, Cambodia and Laos. The museum's most prized art is the Pha Bang, the gold standing Buddha after which the town is named.

Take a look at the King's fleet of vehicles in a new exhibition, including a Lincoln Continental, dilapidated Citroen DS and old wooden speedboat used to visit Vattana's vegetable allotment. Footwear can't be worn inside the museum, no photography is permitted and you must leave bags with the attendants. A dress code declares that foreigners must not wear shorts, T-shirts or sundresses, though recent feedback suggests it's a fairly loose arrangement. Last entry 3.30pm.

Markets

Luang Prabang's main market, the newly built **Phosy Market** (Th Phothisarat; 6am-5pm), which is located just a few kilometres south of the town centre, is heaving with vendors selling hardware, cookware and mountains of fresh produce. To get there follow Th Chao Fa Ngum south towards Tat Kuang Si. You'll see the market on the left at a major intersection.

At sundown, Th Sisavangvong is closed to traffic between the Royal Palace and Th Kitsalat for the candlelit necklace of the **Hmong Night Market** (5.30-10pm) selling lanterns, T-shirts and colourful woven textiles.

Phu Si

The temples on the slopes of 100m-high **Phu Si** (admission 20,000 kip; 8am-6pm) are a favourite haunt for sunset junkies; it's also an opportune place to chat to novice monks. At the summit is That Chomsi, the starting point for a colourful Pii Mai (Lao New Year) procession. Behind this is a small cave-shrine sometimes referred to as **Wat Tham Phu Si**. Around the northeast flank is a Buddha footprint.

Wat Xieng Thong

Near the northern tip of the peninsula formed by the Mekong and Nam Khan rivers, **Wat Xieng Thong** (off Th Sakkarin; admission 20,000 kip; 8am-5pm) is Luang Prabang's most magnificent temple. Built by King Setthathirat in 1560, it remained under royal patronage until 1975. Like the royal palace, Wat Xieng Thong was placed within easy reach of the Mekong River. The *sĭm* (main sanctuary) represents classic Luang Prabang temple architecture, and its rear wall features an impressive tree-of-life mosaic. Inside, richly decorated wooden columns support a ceiling that's vested with *dhammacakka* (dharma wheels). Near the compound's eastern gate stands the royal funeral chapel. Inside are an impressive 12m-high funeral chariot and various funeral urns for each member of the royal family. The exterior of the chapel features gilt panels depicting erotic episodes from the Ramayana.

Wat Wisunalat (Wat Visoun)

To the east of the town centre and originally constructed in 1513 (which makes it the oldest continually operating temple of Luang Prabang) is **Wat Wisunalat** (Th Wisunalat; admission 5000 kip; 8am-5pm). It was rebuilt in 1898 following an 1887 fire started by a marauding gang of Yunnanese robbers known as the Black Flag Haw. Inside the high-ceilinged *sĭm* is a collection of wooden 'calling for rain' Buddhas and 15th- to 16th-century Luang Prabang *sima* (ordination stones). In front of the *sĭm* is That Pathum (Lotus Stupa), which was built in 1514.

Other Temples

In the old quarter, the ceiling of **Wat Xieng Maen** (admission free; 8am-5pm) is painted with gold *naga* (mythical dragons) and the elaborate *háang thíen* (candle rail) has *naga* at either end. With backing from Unesco and New Zealand, young novices and monks have been trained in the artistic skills needed to maintain and preserve Luang Prabang's temples.

Across the Mekong from central Luang Prabang are several notable temples, including **Wat Long Khun** (admission 5000 kip; 8am-5pm). **Wat Tham Xieng Maen** (admission 5000 kip; 8am-5pm) is in a 100m-deep limestone cave where decayed Buddha statues come to rest. At the top of the hill peaceful **Wat Chom Phet** (admission free; 8am-5pm) offers undisturbed views of the Mekong.

ACTIVITIES

Cycling

An enjoyable way to really explore the city and its environs is by bike, meandering through the peninsula's backstreets past somnolent monasteries, hidden galleries and paper-makers. Once you've got your bearings head out beyond Talat Phosy to the nearby countryside. The road to Kuang Si Waterfalls is a gently undulating 35km through rice paddy. Basic/mountain bikes cost 40,000/80,000 kip per day and can be hired on Th Sisavangvong.

Massage

As if to complement the city's sybaritic past is a delightful new wave of pampering spas. After a day's trekking or arduous cafe lounging, indulge in a Swedish, Thai or Lao massage. Prices are reasonable at 50,000 kip for an hour-long body or foot massage, 40,000 kip for an oil massage, and 10,000 kip for a sauna. Quality varies, so shop around till you find manual nirvana. At the following, prices start at 50,000 kip.

Khmu Spa (☎ 212092; Th Sakkarin; 10am-10pm) Irresistible oeuvre of herbal steams, foot, body and neck massages brought to you with flair and style. Prices similar to above.

Lotus du Lao Massage (☎ 253448; Th Sisavangvong; 9am-10.30pm) Traditional surroundings of wood rafters, cool fans and stone floors, sample a range of head and body massage, steams, reflexology and aromatherapy.

COURSES

Luang Prabang is well known for its quality cooking courses.

Tamarind (☎ 770484; www.tamarindlaos.com; Ban Wat Nong; 1-day course 210,000 kip) Distinguishes itself by offering Lao sampling platters (30,000 kip and a great intro to the country's cuisine) and cooking courses, including buying trips to the market. See p389.

Tum Tum Cheng Restaurant & Cooking School (☎ 252019; 29/2 Th Sakkarin; 1-day course 250,000 kip) Celebrated chef Chandra teaches you the secrets of his alchemy. Includes a visit to the market. See p389.

TOURS

The following are recommended for trekking, rafting, elephant-riding and cycling excursions:

Elephant XL (☎ 252417; www.laos-adventures.com; cnr Th Ounheuan & Th Khem Khong) An affiliate of Tiger Trails, environmentally conscious XL offers treks with ex-logging elephants. Prices per day/two days incl overnight accommodation at the elephant sanctuary 250,000/850,000 kip.

Tiger Trails (☎ 252655; www.laos-adventures.com; Th Sisavangvong) Associated with Fair Trek community-based tourism – 10% of its profits are ploughed back into improving the lives of the villagers visited. Single-day and multiday trips involving trekking, rafting, cycling and homestays. Prices range from 350,000 to 470,000 kip per day.

White Elephant (☎ 254481; www.white-elephant-adventures-laos.com; Th Sisavangvong) Seemingly less money-hungry and more keen to match you with the right trek. Feedback from travellers suggests it's one of the most ethical outfits – with solid Hmong guides and interesting, bespoke packages. Also kayaking, rafting and mountain biking. Look for the old BMW and communist flag.

FESTIVALS & EVENTS

The two most important annual events in Luang Prabang are **Pii Mai** (Lao or Lunar New Year) in April, when Luang Prabang is packed to the gills with locals armed with water pistols (book accommodation well in advance), and boat races during **Bun Awk Phansa** (End of the Rains Retreat) in October. See p424 for more.

SLEEPING

The most memorable area to stay is on the historic peninsula, where accommodation veers from affordable to world-class expensive. Here are also decent budget guest houses near the Mekong, a few blocks southwest of the Hmong night market and 10 minutes walk from the centre.

Try and book ahead if you're here in high season. During low season, some accommodation has a reduced tariff.

Luang Prabang

Thavisouk Guest House (☎ 252022; Th Pha Mahapatsaman; r 70,000-150,000 kip; ❄ 💻) Located down a quiet street, this guest house has recently freshened rooms with comfy beds and communal areas to read and meet other travellers. Some rooms enjoy air-con and en suites.

Koun Savan Guest House (☎ 212297; Th Thornkham; r 70,000-150,000 kip; ❄) Secluded in its own grounds, peaceful Koun Savan has fine views of Mt Phu Si. Rooms have private bathrooms, air-con and comfy, blanket-laden beds. Equally warm management.

Mano Guest House & Restaurant (☎ 253112; manosotsay@hotmail.com; Th Pha Mahapatsaman; r 80,000-120,000 kip; ❄) Parked down a quiet street, this fresh accommodation is favoured by Lao Airlines pilots, and has a restaurant serving Lao food and tasty Western breakfasts. Rooms have TVs and couches. Why not move in permanently!

Suankeo Guest House No 2 (☎ 254740; Ban Ho Xiang; r 80,000-120,000 kip; ❄) Ever clean and friendly, Suankeo has milk-fresh rooms (especially the ones up top) with nice some homely details and immaculate bed linen. You're pretty close to the Mekong and right near the Hmong Night Market. Fan and air con optional. The kindly owner can organise trips to Pak Ou caves (70,000 kip).

Jaliya Guest House (☎ 252154; Th Pha Mahapatsaman; r with/without bathroom 90,000/60,000 kip; ❄) Superior minimalist accommodation, a lobby full of chocolate plus an orchid-blooming garden out the back make this option a winner. Rooms have fans and en suites. A bit of a walk out of town, but a nice, quiet street.

Old Quarter

In and around the old quarter budget options are also limited, but at the following you will get what you pay for.

Paphai Guest House (☎ 212752; Th Sisavang Vatthana; r without bathroom 30,000-60,000 kip) Opposite a crumbling wat near the hub of Th Sisavangvong,

HOMESTAYS

Beyond the cities 80% of Laos lives in a *ban* (village), and the most authentic way to experience this way of life is a 'homestay'. Usually just a mattress on a floor, dip-and-pour shower and tasty simple fare, it's the company that really brings it to life. Not only do you eat and wash with the family, you also sleep with them. Obviously language is a barrier, so take family photos, a phrasebook and a dose of curiosity with you.

Whatever the ethnicity of the tribe they'll be keen to make sure you have a decent time. A few things you can do to assist this: if offered food or drink (with exception to water) taste a bit – however toxic it might seem – otherwise your host will lose face. Take off your shoes before entering a house. Don't expose your body overly while bathing in the river/tub (for ladies a sarong is a vital accessory). Finally, take a torch, flip-flops, toilet paper and spare soap, plus Big Brother books (see the boxed text, p399) and ballpoints to give to the kids.

SPIRITS, ARE YOU THERE?

The life of a Lao person involves a complex appeasement of spirits through a carousel of sacrifices and rituals designed to protect the supplicant and engender health and fortune. The *phii heuan* (good spirits) represent both the guardian spirits of the house and ancestral spirits; come crisis-time it's their job to recalibrate a troubled household.

In the backyard you'll often see miniature ornamental temples in which live the *pha phum* (spirits of the land). Before anything is built within their grounds, offerings must be made and permission granted. The same is to be said for a tree that must be knocked down to make way for a bridge, a field before a harvest – an endless animistic communion between the seen and unseen.

The Lao soul is composed of 32 components, each protecting various body organs and mental faculties. In order to prevent a weak link straying, propelling the person's body into chaos, the *su khwăn* ('calling of the soul') ritual is practised. It involves binding the *khwăn* by tying little threads to a person's wrist.

this is great-value accommodation in a traditional wooden house. Bags of atmosphere with a funky garden, friendly management and superior rooms upstairs.

Chittana Guest House (☎ 020 567 2243; off Th Sakkarin; r without bathroom 40,000-80,000 kip) Sneaked under the nose of the peninsula's costliest real estate, Chittana is great value and a slice of old Luang Prabang before the lucre arrived. Basic and low key, its rooms – some with bathroom – are faded but very clean. Atmospheric.

Pathoumphone Guest House (☎ 212946; Th Kingkitsarat; r 50,000-80,000 kip) Basic, superfriendly guest house on the old peninsula. Wooden rooms enjoy serene views of the nearby Nam Khan River and you're a two-minute walk from the main street, Th Sisavangvong.

Vatthanaluck Guest House (☎ 212838; off Th Sakkarin; r 60,000-80,000 kip) Down a sleepy, palm-studded street in the old peninsula opposite the gardens of Villa Santi, this is a real shoestring gem. Its immaculate rooms – with optional fan and bathroom – are a little cramped admittedly but the management is lovely and you can haggle the price down off-season.

Kinnaly Guest House (☎ 212416; Th Sisavang Vatthana; r 70,000 kip; ❄) Terrific value, sparkling-white rooms – all with fan and bathroom – in this lovely old building next to Café Toui.

Silichit Guest House (☎ 212758; Th Sisavang Vatthana; r 70,000-95,000 kip; ❄) You'll find this homely guest house on a quiet sidestreet choking with flowers. Rooms, though immaculate and spacious, can be a little shadowy – opt for rooms 4 and 6 upstairs. There's also a nice cafe and handicraft shop attached.

Phousi Guest House II (☎ 253717; Th Khem Khong; r with/without bathroom 100,000/80,000 kip; ❄ 💻) This Mekong-facing guest house has OK rooms (clean if a little paint-thirsty); however, the place is redeemed by a great alfresco restaurant and internet cafe in its lobby.

East of Phu Si

More budget options are found 300m east of Phu Si down a rocky lane running to the Nam Khan. Recommended:

our pick **Cold River** (☎ 252810; off Th Phommatha; r 70,000-80,000 kip) Charming family-run establishment with an informal, friendly atmosphere. The best rooms, all cosy with fan and bathroom, have their own balconies with Edenic views of the Nam Khan River, bridge and temple to the east. Authentic.

EATING

Munching your way through a spectrum of Gallic, international and Lao cuisine is part of the Luang Prabang experience. If you're hankering for a snack of local noodles or fire-grilled meat, head for the night food stalls that crackle to life down Th Kitsarat. Th Sisavangvong is peppered with pizza and comfort food joints. For fresh Mekong fish and delicious local fare at reasonable rates, head for one of the many riverfront restaurants on Th Khem Khong.

Cafes

Stylish cafes are a Luang Prabang mainstay, with the scent of ground coffee and hot baked bread at every turn.

our pick **Saffron Café** (☎ 020-539 9557; Th Khem Khong; meals 40,000 kip; 🕑 breakfast, lunch & dinner) Riverfront Saffron has an alfresco cafe, and another set back from the road decorated with old sepia photos. Its arabica coffee, cultivated by local hill tribes, accompanies delicious Western breakfasts and sandwiches. Could this be the best new cafe in town?

JoMa Bakery Café (☎ 252292; Th Chao Fa Ngum; meals 10,000-30,000 kip; 🕑 breakfast, lunch & dinner) A sanctuary of air-con cool, JoMa delivers with cakes, sandwiches, coffee and goodies. Loads of room upstairs with great lounging sofas, and views of the distant mountains through a tangle of frangipani.

Also recommended:

Scandinavian Bakery (☎ 252223; Th Sisavangvong; meals 25,000 kip; 🕑 breakfast, lunch & dinner) Comfort food made with panache: ham and egg sandwiches on sugar buns, wafer-thin pizzas, brownies, cookies and flavoursome coffee.

Restaurants

There are scores of *falang*-friendly restaurants on Th Sisavangvong, but for somewhere more authentic head down the peninsula.

Café Toui (☎ 253397; Th Sisavang Vatthana; meals 30,000-40,000 kip; 🕑 breakfast, lunch & dinner) Chichi eatery with ox-blood walls illustrated in gold leaf. The menu is Asian fusion, the main winner being the *làap*.

Tamarind (☎ 770484; www.tamarindlaos.com; Ban Wat Nong; meals 30,000 kip; 🕑 breakfast & lunch) Chic little Tamarind has invented its very own make of 'Mod-Lao' cuisine. The à la carte menu boasts delicious sampling platters with bamboo dip, stuffed lemongrass and *meuyang* (DIY parcels of noodles, herbs, fish and chilli pastes, and vegetables).

our pick **Tum Tum Cheng Restaurant** (☎ 254725; Th Siasavangvong; meals 10,000-30,000 kip; 🕑 lunch & dinner) Renowned for its excellent cooking classes (p386), this lovely new restaurant has defiantly Lao food, based on the traditional recipes of the former royal chef. Its fish *làap* makes your taste buds sing with the music of spice. Recommended.

Le Café Ban Vat Sene (Th Sakkarin; meals 30,000 kip; 🕑 breakfast, lunch & dinner; wi-fi) This stylish restaurant set in an old villa retains a sense of period chic with classical music and flower-shaded lights. The menu features meatballs, brochettes, *tom yum* soup and croque monsieur. With wi-fi, it's a relaxing place to work.

Dao Fa Bistro (☎ 020-562 1064; Th Sisavang Vatthana; meals 50,000 kip; 🕑 lunch & dinner) Stylish French restaurant serving delectable Gallic dishes with panache, not forgetting its homemade ice cream; one of the best restaurants on the strip, this place should be busier.

Couleur Café (☎ 252656; Th Sisavangvong; meals 60,000-90,000 kip; 🕑 breakfast, lunch & dinner) Run by a French expat, Couleur offers cool tunes and a Franco-Italian menu. Carbonara recommended.

Morning Glory Café (☎ 020-777 4122; Th Sakkarin; meals 30,000 kip; 🕑 breakfast & lunch, closed Tue; wi-fi) Amalgamated with Fruit Shake cafe, this funky eatery is housed in a distinctive Unesco-protected building. Wood floors, chilled vibe and alfresco dining make this well worth a visit. Oh, and the food – vegie, Lao curry and stir-fries – is pretty special too.

DRINKING

There's a collection of sophisticated bars on Th Kingkitsarat (loosely known as the Entertainment Village), with plenty of happy hours and liquid incentives, but you'll have to be quick – it's pumpkin time by 11.30pm, and the curfew's a strict one.

Lao Lao Garden (Th Kingkitsarat; 🕑 5pm-late) One of the most popular beer gardens in town, Lao Lao packs them in with colourful cocktails, decent snacks, an alluring garden and nightly bonfire. Plenty of 'buy-one-get-one-free' incentives.

Martin's Pub (Th Phommatha; 🕑 8.30 am-11.30pm) Unpretentious, no-frills bar with a low-key ambience and healthy wine and spirit selection. Also stocks Guinness (canned) plus (oddly) a raft of used sci-fi novels. Golden oldie movies like *The Killing Fields* show nightly at 6pm.

House (Th Kingkitsarat; 🕑 5pm-late) Great new venue near Hive Bar. With an interior decked in fairylights, House is a friendly alternative to its moody neighbour. Belgian-owned, it has a wide range of European beers. Should become a favourite.

Hive Bar (Th Kingkitsarat; 🕑 5pm-late) Oozing cool, this downlit haunt lives up to its name with plenty of niches and darkened corridors. Its outside garden, chill-some tunes and happy hour (5pm to 9pm) make it one of the best spots in town. Also serves tapas.

Utopia (☎ 254482; 🕑 5-11pm) Zen-style garden bar. Drink Bloody Marys under the stars in this riverside addition to the Entertainment Village. Chilled ambience and a nightly 'open musicians' mic. Promises to be a new favourite. Take the turn off Th Phommatha just before Martin's Pub.

Dao Fah (9-11.30pm) A young Lao crowd packs this cavernous club. Live bands playing Lao and Thai pop alternate with DJs who spin rap and hip-hop.

ENTERTAINMENT

Royal Ballet Theatre (Th Sisavangvong; admission 50,000-125,000 kip; shows 6pm) Inside the Royal Palace Museum compound, local performers put on a show that includes a *bąasii* (sacred string-tying ritual to bring the guardian spirits of the body back down to earth) ceremony, traditional dance and folk music. There are traditional dances of Lao ethnic minorities such as the Phoo Noi and Hmong people.

There are several minicinemas where you can catch a flick, including the following:

Le Cinema (Ban Xieng Mouane; tickets 20,000 kip; 6pm-midnight) On a laneway opposite the eastern wing of the Royal Palace, this ingenious spot enables you to hire a room and recent-release DVD for the night. It's fun and cosy.

L'Etranger Books & Tea (booksinlaos@yahoo.com; Th Kingkitsarat; screenings 7pm) Screens free films nightly (but you must drink its tea).

SHOPPING

Hmong Night Market (Th Sisavangvong; 5.30-10pm) Your first visit to this night market will be a magical experience: a seemingly endless candlelit ribbon of colourful woven textiles, paper lanterns and T-shirts. Vendors are low-pressure and, most satisfyingly of all, the money you pay them goes straight into their pockets.

Be it locally designed jewellery, the finest silk scarves or paintings by local artists, you're sure to find something in Luang Prabang to remember your trip.

Pathana Boupha Antique House (☎ 212262; 29/4 Ban Visoun) Follow the sweeping stairs in the garden to this Aladdin's cave of antique Buddhas, golden *naga* (mythical serpent being), silver betel-nut pots and ethnic jewellery. Also sells Belle Epoque busts and Bakelite radios.

Orange Tree (☎ 020-657 5494; Th Khem Khong) Hugely eclectic emporium of antiques ranging from colonial vanity cases and Art Deco clocks to revolutionary Chairman Mao plates; all collected with a tasteful magpie's eye.

Samsara (☎ 254678; Th Sisavangvong) Specialising in lacquer prints (Tintin book covers) and quirky figurative statuary, Samsara also sell papyrus paintings, antique opium pipes and quality glass Buddhas.

GETTING THERE & AWAY

Air

Luang Prabang International Airport (☎ 212173) is 4km from the city centre. **Lao Airlines** (☎ 212172; www.laoairlines.com; Th Pha Mahapatsaman) flies from Luang Prabang to Vientiane (660,000 kip, one-way, daily) and Pakse (1,310,000 kip, every day in high season). Internationally, flights go to Chiang Mai in Thailand (1,068,000 kip, one-way, daily), Bangkok (1,368,000 kip, one-way, daily), Hanoi (1,111,000 kip one-way, daily except Friday), Siem Reap (1,667,000 kip one-way, daily) and Udon Thani (897,000 kip, one-way, daily).

Bangkok Airways (☎ 253334; www.bangkokair.com; Th Sisavangvong) flies from Luang Prabang to Bangkok (1,428,000 kip, one-way, daily).

Boat

Despite rumblings and threats due to mortalities, the ludicrously dangerous but undeniably expedient speedboat service is still running.

Slow boats motor northwest daily to **Huay Xai** (220,000 kip), departing at 8am. These boats stand by the Mekong and you can buy tickets direct from them or from a travel agent. The trip takes two days with an overnight stop in **Pak Beng** (110,000 kip, nine hours). From Pak Beng it's also possible to take the bus northeast to Udomxai.

White-knuckle speedboats up the Mekong leave 8.30am daily from Ban Don pier, a 7km, 10,000 kip shared túk-túk ride from the centre. They race to Pak Beng (200,000 kip, three hours) and Huay Xai (350,000 kip, six hours) in half the time…but 10 times the danger. Avoid sitting at the front, pad your back and bring some earplugs!

Although it's quicker by road, many travellers charter a boat for the beautiful trip up the Nam Ou to **Nong Khiaw** (850,000 kip per boat, seven hours). Inquire at the Navigation Office in Luang Prabang or with travel agents in town, where you can add your name to the passenger list of impending departures. With enough passengers, speedboats travel

PAK BENG BLUES

Stories have circulated about rucksacks occasionally disappearing from rooms in Pak Beng. If you do decide to stay here make sure you opt for digs with a sturdy lock on the window and door.

from Luang Prabang to Nong Khiaw (170,000 kip, two hours), usually from June to January only.

Bus

Several local buses leave the southern bus terminal (3km south of town) headed south for Vientiane (120,000 kip, 10 to 14 hours) between about 6.30am and 9.30am, sometimes later. Express buses en route for Vientiane (120,000 kip, about 10 hours, 9am) stop in Vang Vieng (100,000 kip, six to nine hours). Travel agents also sell tickets to Vientiane on 'VIP' buses (135,000 kip, about 10 hours, one at 9am). Neither is much more comfortable, but they are faster. Local buses also leave daily from here to Phonsavan (115,000 kip, eight hours, 8.30am), Sainyabouli (60,000 kip, five hours, 7.30am and 8am) and Huay Xai (150,000 kip, 12 hours, 5pm), although in the rainy season the Huay Xai bus might not run.

From the northern bus terminal (on Rte 13 about 4km north of town) daily săwngthăew and local buses go north to Udomxai (60,000 kip, four hours, four daily), Luang Nam Tha (105,000 kip, nine hours, 9am), Nong Khiaw (50,000 kip, four hours, two to five daily), and Sam Neua (105,000 kip, 16 hours, 9am and 5pm).

GETTING AROUND

Most of the town is accessible on foot. Jumbos usually ask foreigners for 10,000 kip a ride. Motorcycles can no longer be hired due to frequent accidents; however, mountain/ordinary bikes will cost 80,000/40,000 kip per day.

> **GETTING INTO TOWN**
>
> From the airport a túk-túk ride will cost around 50,000 kip per vehicle, though túk-túk drivers have become accustomed to charging foreigners 'special' tourist prices. In the reverse direction you can usually charter an entire jumbo for 20,000 to 40,000 kip.

Around Luang Prabang

PAK OU

About 25km up the Mekong River from Luang Prabang, and at the mouth of the Nam Ou River, are the famous **caves** at Pak Ou. The two caves in the lower part of a limestone cliff are crammed with a variety of Buddha images, a kind of graveyard where unwanted images are placed. If you go by boat, most trips will involve a stop at Ban Xang Hai, or what boatmen call the 'Whisky Village', a now-tourist-dominated village that specialises in producing large jars of *lào-láo* (rice whisky).

You can hire longtail boats to Pak Ou from Luang Prabang's charter-boat landing at 130,000 kip for one to three people or 170,000 kip for four to five people, including petrol. The trip takes two hours upriver and downstream, plus stops. Túk-túks make the trip for about half the price. Trips can also be arranged through guest houses and tour operators.

TAT KUANG SI

At 32km from the city, Kuang Si has a whimsical beauty that sets a smile on your face; with its multitiered cascade tumbling over limestone formations into menthol green pools, it's a great place to wash off the leeches and heat. The falls themselves are set in a spotlessly clean **public park** (admission 16,000 kip) with a slippery path that leads to their vertiginous summit. Near the entrance are enclosures housing cuddly sun bears rescued from poachers. For lunch there's a little market outside the park gates where you can pick up some barbecued chicken and rice.

Some come by hired bicycle (for the fit only) or motorcycle, stopping in villages along the way. Freelance guides proliferate down Th Sisavangvong and offer trips by jumbo, or boat and jumbo (both for about 60,000 kip per person).

Nong Khiaw

☎ 071

Often overlooked by travellers in favour of the now-mythic Muang Ngoi Neua, this pretty little riverside village is a destination in itself and in many ways just as appealing. For sheer drama its view is one of the most picturesque in Laos; Nong Khiaw is set between colossal green-blue karsts and joined by a handsome bridge to the miniature village of Ban Hop Soun (where most of the – limited – action is). With its friendly locals, nearby caves and slowly improving outward-bound infrastructure, Nong Khiaw definitely merits a night or two.

SIGHTS & ACTIVITIES

You can **trek** by yourself to **Tham Pha Tok**, an enormous multilevel cave where villagers hid out during the Second Indochina War.

Careful descending the rickety ladder and keep an eye out for the Buddhist graffiti! To get there, walk 2.5km east of the bridge then look for a clearly visible cave mouth in the limestone cliff on the right (it's about 100m from the road). And remember to tip the little lad who may accompany you.

When we visited Nong Khiaw, **Tiger Trail** was setting up, offering trekking, tubing and kayaking; meanwhile **Lao Youth Travel** (laoyouthtravel.com) had just opened at the boat landing. Also, the town's only **cinema**, run by Mr Tir, can sometimes be found open. You'll find it opposite Delilah's Place.

SLEEPING & EATING

There are a number of reasonably priced guest houses on both sides of the Nam Ou but you'll find the best selection over in Ban Sop Houn.

Sunrise Guest House (Ban Sop Houn; r 40,000 kip) Opposite Phanoy, Sunrise has basic cabanas perched on the riverbank. Hot showers, mosquito nets and – depending on availability – your own lurking giant moth! Informal tours offered with the owner's son, Mong.

Sengdao Guest House (Nong Khiaw; r 30,000-150,000 kip) Eight quiet bungalows in a riverside garden bursting with cherry blossom. The rooms, all with river-facing balconies, are capacious with basic bathrooms, 24-hour electricity and fans. Asleep by day, Sengdao's restaurant lights up at night with its locally patronised restaurant.

Sunset Guest House & Restaurant (Ban Sop Houn; ☎ 253933; sunsetgh@hotmail.com; s/d 100,000/150,000 kip) First on your right after Phanoy Guest House, Sunset's hidden down a U-bend lane. There are some new cabanas here with beautiful views over the Nam Ou – though sadly the sundeck has had to be constricted to accommodate them. Good food, pleasant management. Cheaper rooms in the house, bikes also for hire.

our pick **Nong Kiau Riverside Restaurant** (Ban Sop Houn; ☎ 254770; www.nongkiau.com; meals 20,000 kip) Considering the wondrous view and tasteful setting, this is an affordably romantic place to eat. An eclectic menu ranges from pancakes to salads plus a spectrum of Lao fare. We tried the chicken *làap* (20,000 kip) – scrumptious!

Phanoy Guest House (Ban Sop Houn; meals 20,000-30,000 kip) A longtime favourite with travellers, this place oozes atmosphere and its Lao food is terrific. Ponder the river or recruit others to share the boat to Luang Prabang (the owners don't mind you putting up a sign to that effect).

Delilah's Place (Nong Khiaw; meals 30,000 kip) This tasteful eatery offers plenty; from delicious pancakes, spring rolls and crispy fried chicken, to excellent bacon and eggs.

GETTING THERE & AWAY

Boat

Heading upriver to Muang Ngoi Neua (70,000 kip, one hour), boats leave regularly till about 3pm, stopping frequently en route. In low season they can leave only at 11am and 2pm. Tickets are bought at an office at the bus station. Boats sometimes continue to Muang Khua from Muang Ngoi Neua (88,000 kip, seven hours). The journey by boat to Luang Prabang is one of the most dramatic in Laos; that said you need a few of you to cut the cost as the boatman charges 850,000 kip per boat (up to 10 people).

Bus & Săwngthăew

Săwngthăew going to Udomxai (45,000 kip) leave thrice daily from the west end of the bridge. You can also take one of the more frequent săwngthăew southwest to Pak Mong (20,000 kip, two hours), then change to another săwngthăew to Udomxai (17,000 kip, two to three hours from Pak Mong) and anywhere further west. Săwngthăew and local buses to Luang Prabang (50,000 kip, three hours) depart 9am, 11am and 12pm; usually the earliest is the public bus.

If you're heading east towards Hua Phan or Xieng Khuang, you can get a bus to Sam Neua (120,000 kip, 13 hours, one daily at 1pm), or start a săwngthăew hop by heading to Muang Vieng Kham and changing there. Note: buses now depart from the bus station at the Nong Khiaw side of the bridge – not the boat landing.

Muang Ngoi Neua

In recent years this remote village, sitting beneath a jagged backdrop of saw-toothed karsts, has enjoyed a heavy influx of travellers. There's something delightful in its seclusion – no real roads, and only accessible by boat. Given it was heavily bombed during the Secret War for its proximity to the Ho Chi Minh Trail, Muang Ngoi Neua deserves all the praise and trade now justly lavished upon it.

GETTING INTO VIETNAM: SOP HUN TO TAY TRANG

The border at Sop Hun in Phongsali Province, just across from Tay Trang (32km west of Dien Bien Phu), has now opened as an international border. If you're headed into Vietnam there are three buses a week bound for Dien Bien Phu, leaving from the Lao village of Muang Khua (50,000 kip, leaves 6.30am). The same applies from the other side – catch a return bus to Laos from Dien Bien Phu. However, while you can get a visa on arrival in Laos you'll need to organise one in Vientiane to cross into Vietnam. The road is unsealed and sometimes impassable during the rainy season. A 40,000 kip 'processing' fee is demanded by Lao immigration. If leaving from Nong Khiaw ask around the boatmen to take you upriver to Muang Khua. Border is open 8am to 5pm). For information on crossing this border in the other direction, see p856.

Take a trek to the nearby caves, kayak on the peaceful river or lie back in your hammock taking in what may be the most serene spot in the north.

INFORMATION

Generators provide electricity from 6pm to 10pm. The only place with internet connection is **Lao Youth Travel** (2000 kip per minute!) at the top of the boat-landing steps. There are no banks here so bring sufficient cash to get back. A couple of pharmacies sell basic medicines; for anything serious get yourself back to Luang Prabang.

SIGHTS & ACTIVITIES

Fishing, **tubing**, **kayaking** and **trekking** are all on offer. Treks cost 80,000 kip per day and tubing costs around 13,000 kip per day.

Recommended English-speaking guides include **Sang Tours** (8am-9pm), not far from the boat landing on the main 'street', and **Lao Youth Travel** (www.laoyouthtravel.com; 7.30-10.30am & 1.30-6pm) to the left of the boat landing. **Muang Ngoi Tour Office** (7-8am & 6-7pm), located behind the main street 300m south of the boat landing, organises small-group treks to Hmong and Khamu villages for around 68,000 kip per day including food, and **fishing trips**.

SLEEPING & EATING

If you fancy a village stay, try the **Konsavan Guest House** (8500 kip) in Huay Bo.

With 'budget' tattooed over its dip-and-pour, hammock-slung cabanas, you're in traveller territory. The more basic, rattan-constructed bungalows change name and go out of business with saddening regularity. Most have attached family-run restaurants.

Phetdavanh Guest House (☎ 030-514 1599; r 20,000 kip) This old-fashioned comfortable guest house has clean rooms with attached bathrooms. There's a communal verandah to read on, plus Penny's Bar and Restaurant. In high season they have a Lao buffet every night (8000 kip).

Banana Café & Restaurant (r 20,000 kip; breakfast, lunch & dinner) Simple balconied bungalows with outside toilet and pour-and-scrub showers. Ideal for pondering the river. The family-run restaurant is nondescript but fresh.

Saylom Guest House (r without bathroom 50,000 kip) This welcoming place to the right of the boat ramp has clean bungalows with decent beds. The restaurant has delightful river views.

Lattanavongsa Guest House (☎ 030-514 0770; r 100,000-150,000 kip) Found to the left of the boat landing, this house-proud guest house has immaculate gardens and rooms in a handsome wooden house. En suites, verandahs and an alfresco restaurant add a touch of style above the competition. Try the hearty noodle soup.

Ning Ning Restaurant (meals 20-30,000 kip) Ning Ning has gone a little upscale with improved, more permanent accommodation, but its delicious Asian-fusion menu remains much the same.

Aloune Mai Restaurant (meals 35,000 kip) A little more upmarket than its competitors; the Lao food here is excellent, the atmosphere romantic.

Sengala Bakery (meals 25,000 kip; breakfast, lunch & dinner) Mouth-watering noodles, pancakes and delectable buffalo-steak baguettes. Water-bottle refills cost 1000 kip per litre.

GETTING THERE & AWAY

Boats to Nong Khiaw leave at 9am and cost 20,000 kip. Heading north, the very occasional public boat (88,000 kip, seven hours) goes to Muang Khua for the recently opened Sop Hun to Tray Hung border (see p391), or you can hire one for about 420,000 kip. It's a stunning trip. From Muang Khua, take a boat to Hat Sa (another five hours, 85,000 kip or charter 680,000-850,000 kip) or a bus back to Udomxai (50,000 kip, eight to 12 hours, 8am). From Hat Sa sǎwngthǎew take the rough road to Phongsali (12,000 kip per person, 127,000 kip charter). There's a basic guest house in Hat Sa.

XIENG KHUANG PROVINCE

One of Laos' worst-hit provinces during the nine-year US air assault, with its wooded alpine hills and chilly climate Xieng Khouang has a melancholy beauty of its own. Since most buildings were razed to the ground during the Secret War the province isn't winning any architecture awards; rapidly erected Soviet ugliness is the rule of thumb. But look beyond the initially depressing facade and you'll find, like its cratered hillsides cloaked in poppies, an area aglow with contemporary and ancient history. Xieng Khuang is also home to the mysterious Plain of Jars.

Phonsavan

☎ 061 / pop 57,000

Illustrating the former point, Phonsavan is a sprawl of flat-topped, Soviet-style shopfronts, its streets haunted by careworn faces. The town may have missed the queue when they were handing out beauty awards but is notable for its pivotal role in the Secret War and the more ancient, nearby Plain of Jars – an eerie conundrum of randomly placed stone urns. Travellers here tend to be scant and as such it feels more authentic. Learn more about the Secret War at a number of fascinating sites via Kong Keo Guest House (right) or pop into **Mines Advisory Group** (MAG; www.maginternational.org; Rte 7; ⏲ 4pm-8pm) to see its harrowing nightly documentary, *Harvest* (starts 7pm). There was an outbreak of E coli in 2008 here, so check the ice in your drink originated from a bottle.

INFORMATION

Medical emergencies will need to be taken to Thailand – **Aek Udon International Hospital** (☎ 0066-42-342555; www.aekudon.com) via Vientiane.

BCL (☎ 213291; Rte 7) Located past the dry goods market. Has a 24-hour ATM.

Khonsavanh Net (Rte 7; per hr 12,000 kip; ⏲ 8am-10pm) Slow connections.

Lao Development Bank (☎ 312188) Currency exchange.

Lao-Mongolian Friendship Hospital (☎ 312166) Good for minor needs.

Post office (⏲ 8am-4pm Mon-Fri, 8am-noon Sat) Domestic phone service.

Provincial tourist office (☎ 312217) Useful for simple information.

Sousath Travel (☎ 312031; www.malyht.laotel.com; Maly Hotel) Trips further afield include Tham Piu, Muang Sui, Sam Neua and Long Cheng (former CIA site during the Secret War). A group of five can expect to pay 200,000 kip per person.

SLEEPING

Decent accommodation here is slim pickings but there are a couple of cosy hobbit holes.

Phoukham Guest House (☎ 020 640 5505; r with/without hot water 40,000/30,000 kip) Opposite the old bus station, this modern, two-storey guest house has functional rooms with low-slung beds and cold water showers as standard. It's redeemed a little by its cleanliness and resident internet cafe (a steep 12,000 kip per hour).

Vanearoun Guest House (☎ 312070; Rte 7; r 30,000-50,000 kip) Definitely a dingy option, Vanearoun has a creepy atmosphere, with wall-mounted skulls in the lobby and the odd furry animal watching you. Rooms cramped and faded. Doors close at 11pm. Boo!

UXO – AN ENDURING LEGACY

Between 1964 and '73, the USA conducted one of the largest sustained aerial bombardments in history, flying 580,344 missions over Laos and dropping two million tons of bombs, costing US$2.2 million a day. Around 30% of the bombs dropped on Laos failed to detonate, leaving the country littered with unexploded ordnance (UXO).

For people all over eastern Laos, living with this constant threat has become an intrinsic part of daily life. Since the British Mines Advisory Group (MAG) began clearance work in 1994, only a tiny percentage of the quarter of a million pieces in Xieng Khuang and Salavan has been removed. At the current rate of clearance it may take more than 100 years to make the country safe. The **Mines Advisory Group** (www.magclearsmines.org) has information on UXO-clearing projects in Laos, while **COPE** (www.copelaos.org) valiantly rehabilitates the human victims of the UXO legacy.

JARS OF THE STONE AGE

The purpose of these possibly 2000-year-old jars remains a mystery, and without any organic material such as bones or food remains surviving, there is no reliable way to date them. Archaeological theories and local myth suggest the enigmatic jars were used for burial purposes – as stone coffins or urns – or maybe for storing *lào-láo* (rice whisky) or rice.

In the 1930s, pioneering French archaeologist Madeleine Colani documented the jars in a 600-page monograph, *Mégalithes du Haut Laos (Megaliths of Highland Laos)*, concluding that they were funerary urns carved by a vanished people.

our pick Kong Keo Guest House (☎ 211354; www.kongkeojar.com; r 50,000-100,000 kip) Kongkeo has a new block of luxurious, mint-fresh rooms as well as decent wooden cabanas in the garden. The likeable owner runs tours to the Jars as well as specialised trips to a bombed-out village. Its restaurant hosts nightly bonfires and it cooks up tasty barbecued fare. Atmospheric.

Nice Guest House (☎ 020-248 0804; s/d 60,000/80,000 kip) Festooned in red Chinese lanterns throwing off an inviting glow into the chilly night, rooms are fresh and roomy, and manager Moa is helpful. Our bed was a little itchy.

Thiengchaleun Guest House (☎ 211774; r 80,000 kip) Threadbare, adequate digs if a little out of the way. Rooms are clean and functional, ones upstairs with TV and hot water.

Banna Plain of Jars House (☎ 212484; www.bannagroup.com; r 100,000 kip) Simple accommodation with bathroom, fan and TV, plus an uninterrupted view of the paddy fields out the back.

EATING

Not exactly brimming with Michelin stars, there are, however, a couple of eateries with simple, flavoursome grub. The food market (6am to 5pm) sells anything from fruit to Korean, Indian and Lao fare at its many stalls.

Kong Keo Guest House (☎ 211354; www.kongkeojar.com; dishes 8000-20,000 kip) Even if you're not staying, this is a great place to eat and sip a beer by the fire. Try the excellent rice-paper rolls.

Phonekeo Restaurant (meals 8500 kip; breakfast, lunch & dinner) This friendly noodle shop serves the best *fŏe* (noodle broth, usually with chicken or beef) in town.

Nisha Restaurant (meals 12,000 kip; breakfast, lunch & dinner) Tasty and great value for money, Nisha has a wide range of vegetarian options, makes lovely *dosa* (flat bread), tikka masalas and rogan josh, as well as great lassis.

Sanga Restaurant (Sa-Nga; ☎ 312318; meals 15,000 kip; lunch & dinner) Popular local and NGO hang-out Sanga has a varied Lao menu with a few Western dishes and by night looks more atmospheric and inviting. Travellers recommended the fried Morning Glory to us.

Craters Bar & Restaurant (☎ 020-780 5775; meals 25,000 kip; breakfast, lunch & dinner) With its chilled Western vibe, Craters is a good place to gravitate to. The sweet-and-sour chicken is delicious. Check out the bottled witch's broth on the counter – ear of traveller, wing of bat! Western-style coffee here too.

ENTERTAINMENT

Besides taking in the documentary at MAG, or going over to Kong Keo Guest House, there's not much to do here by night. The Maniyore Pub on the main street serves as a dimly lit nightclub.

GETTING THERE & AWAY

Lao Airlines (☎ 212027) flies to/from Vientiane (one-way 660,000 kip, daily except Tuesday and Thursday). Jumbos to the airport cost around 8500 kip per person.

Buses now leave from the new bus station 4km west of town. Most long-distance buses depart between 7am and 8am – check times the day before. Buses run to Sam Neua (120,000 kip, eight hours, two daily), Vientiane (local/minibus/VIP 120,000/130,000/140,000 kip, 11 hours, several daily commencing 7am), Vang Vieng (ordinary 100,000 kip, six hours once daily at 7am) and Luang Prabang (ordinary bus 110,000 kip, 10 hours, leaves 8.30am – some VIP buses occasionally run). For Paksan catch a bus to Vientiane and change there.

There are public buses and săwngthăew to Muang Kham (30,000 kip, two hours, four daily), Muang Sui (30,000 kip, one hour, three daily) and Nong Haet (40,000 kip, four hours, four daily).

Other destinations include Lat Khai (Plain of Jars Site 3; 20,000 kip, 30 minutes, one daily) and Muang Khoun (20,000 kip, 30 minutes, six daily). Buses also go all the way through to Vinh in Vietnam (138,000 kip, 11 hours, 6.30am Tuesday, Thursday and Sunday).

GETTING INTO VIETNAM: NONG HAET TO NAM CAN

The Nong Haet–Nam Can crossing is little used by travellers because it's difficult, potentially expensive if you get ripped off, and not really convenient if you're heading north in Vietnam (you have to go 200km south to grim Vinh first). On the Laos side, Nam Khan is 13km east of Nong Haet via Rte 7. You can get between Nong Haet and Phonsavan by bus (20,000 kip, three to four hours, four daily) or chartered car for about 250,000 kip or 340,000 kip. There is also a direct bus between Phonsavan and Vinh (90,000 kip, 11 hours, Tuesday, Thursday and Sunday). A Lao visa is granted on arrival; however, this is not possible when entering Vietnam. Open 8am to 3pm. For information on crossing this border in the other direction, see p856.

Plain of Jars

The Plain of Jars extends around Phonsavan in three principal sites, all of which have been largely cleared of UXO.

The largest is **Site 1**, 10km southwest of Phonsavan, featuring 250 jars mostly between 1m and 3m tall and weighing between 600kg and one tonne. There's an undercover rest area at this site, where you can buy snacks and drinks.

Two other jar sites are accessible by an unsealed road from Phonsavan and have fewer jars, but much better views. **Site 2**, about 25km south of town, features 90 jars spread across two adjacent hillsides. Vehicles can reach the base of the hills, then it's a short, steep walk to the jars.

More impressive is 150-jar **Site 3**, which is also known as Hai Hin Lat Khai, located about 10km south of Site 2. This site is on a scenic hilltop near the charming village of Ban Sieng Di, where there's also a small monastery containing the remains of Buddha images damaged in the war. The site is a stiff 2km walk across rice paddies and up a hill.

GETTING THERE & AWAY

It's possible to charter a săwngthăew to Site 1 for about 85,000 kip return, including waiting time, for up to six people. All three sites are reachable by bike or motorcycle (per day 160,000 kip through guest houses), and Craters Bar & Restaurant (p395) has two bicycles for rent (25,000 kip per day).

Otherwise, you're on a tour. Guest houses and a number of travel agents offer tours for 150,000 to 200,000 kip per person in a minivan of around five passengers. **Sousath Travel** (☎ 312031; sousathp@laotel.com), **Phou Kham** (☎ 312121) and **Kong Keo Guest House** (☎ 211354; www.kongkeojar.com; off Rte 7) have all received good reports.

Tours are often extended to include other interesting sites, including a crashed US F-105 Thunderchief, a Russian tank, Viet Cong bunkers, the US Lima Site 108 airstrip supposedly used for drug running, and hot springs.

HUA PHAN PROVINCE

Situated in the northeast of Laos, Hua Phanh's rugged isolation led the Lao People's Army to use it as a base during the struggle of the Secret War. A landscape of many faces – one moment thick jungle, gothic karst scenery, then gleaming paddies – Hua Phanh feels unlike any other province; something to do perhaps with its 22 ethnic groups, or its cool, altitude-driven climate. The mountain road to Sam Neua surges through silkscreen vistas of green, misty peaks, past powder-blue Hmong houses and excited roadside children. Now that the nearby border here to Vietnam is open to foreigners, you no longer have to turn around and go all the way back. A blessing indeed!

Sam Neua

☎ 064 / pop 46,800

It's worth the discomfort getting here by local bus, for this buzzing little border town oozes frontier authenticity, with passing trade lorries from nearby Vietnam, cool alpine air, rugged-faced locals and visible traces of Soviet influence. Wander the wet- and dry-goods market by the peaceful river. A short cycle away, past cottages neatly stacked with harvested pumpkins and firewood, are picture-postcard karst and stunning rice paddies. It gets cold here too, so bring a sweater.

INFORMATION

Lao Development Bank (☎ 312171; ⌚ 8am-4pm Mon-Fri) On the main road 400m north of the bus station on the left; exchanges cash and travellers cheques.

Post office (⌚ 8am-4pm Mon-Fri) In a large building directly opposite the bus station. A telephone office at its rear offers international calls.

LAOS

Provincial tourist office (☎ 312567; ⏲ 8am-noon & 1.30-4pm Mon-Fri) An excellent tourist office with English-speaking staff eager to help.

SLEEPING & EATING

In general Sam Neua's digs are clean if a little nondescript. Most guest houses and restaurants are located between the Nam Sam River and dry-goods market.

Phootong Guest House (☎ 312271; r 40,000 kip) Despite the flophouse entrance down an alley – like something out of an old Bruce Lee flick – this place has spacious rooms with hot water and bathroom, plus a verandah from which to take in the mountains.

Kheamxam Guest House (☎ 312111; r 40,000-70,000 kip) No-nonsense accommodation with comfy rooms, freshly painted walls and showers powerful enough to jet you over the Vietnam border. Rooms vary from basic to larger rooms with immaculate bathroom and TV. Friendly owner.

Dan Nao Restaurant (☎ 314126; meals 15,000 kip; ⏲ breakfast, lunch & dinner) The best of a limited bunch, this restaurant is peppered with posters of Beer Lao girls to dispel the drizzle. The food is basic – tender beef salad, egg fried rice – but tasty enough. At the end of the bridge round the corner from Kheamxam GH.

For cheap *fŏe*, samosas, spring rolls and fried sweet potato, the **market** (⏲ 6am-6pm) is the place to go.

GETTING THERE & AWAY

Lao Airlines (www.laoairlines.com) has suspended flights to Sam Neua for the foreseeable future. Keep an eye on the website for changes.

Sam Neua bus station has relocated to the top of a hill overlooking the town, roughly 2km away (8500 kip by săwngthăew). There's two buses a day to Phonsavan (80,000 kip, eight to 10 hours, 9am and noon). It's a beautifully sinuous hike through the mountains, passing powder-blue Hmong cottages and villagers farming on the vertiginous slopes. The bus then continues on to Vientiane (from Sam Neua 150,000 kip, 20 to 24 hours), on a winding sealed road. A VIP bus runs to Vientiane (200,000 kip, 18 hours, 2pm).

A daily bus leaves Sam Neua, heading southeast to Nong Khiaw (120,000 kip, 12 hours, 8am) en route to Luang Prabang (from Sam Neua 150,000 kip, 16 hours, 7.30am). If you're heading for Udomxai, take this bus and change at Pak Mong (120,000 kip).

Vieng Xai (Pathet Lao Caves)

The idyllic village of Vieng Xai seems an unlikely recipient for one of the greatest poundings of the American conflict, but the reason is simple; selected as the HQ of the Pathet Lao war effort, it was honeycombed with over a hundred sizeable caverns – almost unassailable from the air. As the bombs fell, entire sheltered communities were catered for with bakeries, schools, politburo offices, a hospital and barracks; not forgetting the humble grotto of the soon-to-be president and cultural hero, Kayson Phomvihane. A visit to these dank, candlelit caves is an unforgettable experience and just reward for having ventured this far.

Kaysone Phomvihane Memorial Tour Cave Office (☎ 314321; ⏲ 8am-11.30am & 1-4.30pm) is a gentle downhill 2km walk from the bus station. Admission to the caves costs 30,000 kip and includes a mandatory guide. Bicycles are available per tour/day 10,000/20,000 kip. It's another 40,000 kip for a camera. Two-hour tours leave the office at 9am and 1pm and take in three or four caves. At other times you'll need to pay an additional fee of 40,000 kip per tour to cover staff costs.

Fringed in frangipani trees, the beautiful gardens that adorn the caves can easily make you forget what their inhabitants had to endure. Perhaps the most atmospheric, as it also housed his politburo meetings and the long-reigning president himself, is Phomvihane's eponymously named **Tham Than Kaysone**. The electricity is often out and like us you may be exploring by candlelight, your flame falling on his meagre library, a Russian oxygen machine poised for a chemical attack, a bust of Lenin…

Tham Than Souphanouvong, named after the communist-leaning Red Prince, has a crater from a 230kg bomb near the entrance, while **Tham Than Khamtay**, where up to 3000 Pathet Lao would hide out, is the most spectacular of the caves.

SLEEPING & EATING

Naxay Guest House (☎ 314336; r 17,000 kip) Simple accommodation in a rattan hut, Naxay have five clean rooms with comfy blanketed beds and communal squat toilets. Food can be ordered in advance; if it gets too cold there's a badminton court to warm up on!

Thavisay Hotel (☎ 020-571 2392; r 34,000 kip) Currently being renovated, this two-storey hotel in a lovely setting promises to be the

GETTING INTO VIETNAM: NA MAEW TO NAM XOI

The remote, seldom-used and often difficult border (open 7.30am to 11.30am and 1.30pm to 4.30pm) at Na Maew in Laos and Nam Xoi in Vietnam is an adventurer's delight and the nearest crossing to Hanoi. There's a daily săwngthăew from Sam Neua (20,000 kip, four hours, 6.30am), or several from Vieng Xai (13,000 kip, two hours, 8am to 11am). Visas are not available on arrival. In Vietnam you can negotiate a motorbike to Thanh Hoa or to Ba Thuoc. Both options can be pricey and drivers may rip you off. There are a couple of guest houses on the Vietnamese side. For information on crossing this border in the other direction, see p856.

best in town, with attached hot-water bathrooms and two double beds with mosquito nets. There's also a restaurant (meals 20,000 kip) overlooking an artificial lake.

GETTING THERE & AWAY

Săwngthăew run regularly between Sam Neua's Nathong Bus Station and Vieng Xai (10,000 kip, 50 minutes, 29km, 6.20am to 5.20pm). The last scheduled bus from Vieng Xai to Sam Neua is 3pm – if you miss this, one *sometimes* leaves at 4pm.

UDOMXAI PROVINCE

Home to some of northern Laos' thickest forests, this rugged province is a great place to visit Hmong and Khamu villages. Close to China's Yúnnán province, it's home to 23 ethnic minorities, but the dominant group is increasingly the Yunnanese working in construction and plantation operations. While Udomxai town is undesirable, the surrounding hills make for excellent trekking. See below.

Udomxai

☎ 081 / pop 80,000

An important staging post for Chinese troops supporting the Pathet Lao during the Secret War, modern Udomxai has lost none of its Sino-Lao bonds, with Chinese truckers and workers overseeing the construction of superhighways. As such there is little here that is Lao.

INFORMATION

BCL (☎ 211260; Rte 1) Changes foreign currency into kip; 24-hour ATM.

Udomxai Internet (Rte 1; per hr 10,000 kip; 🕑 8am-7pm) Speedy and reliable.

Udomxai provincial tourism office (☎ 211797; Rte 1; 🕑 8am-noon & 1.30-4pm Oct-Mar, 7.30-11.30am & 1.30-6pm Apr-Sep) West of the bridge; has information about accommodation, ecotourism tours and transport. Five tour packages on offer including the recently discovered Chom Ong cave.

Udomxai Travel (☎ 212020; travel_kenchan@yahoo.com; Rte 1) For tours to local attractions such as the Houay Nam Kat Reserve, find Mr Kenchan O'Phetsan at this travel agency, located next to the bus station.

SIGHTS & ACTIVITES

OK, so your connecting bus to Luang Nam Tha or Nong Khiaw has already gone – take a wander to the **Chinese market**, a vast sprawl of stalls beside the **Kaysone Monument**, or treat yourself to a Swedish-style massage at the **Lao Red Cross** (☎ 312269; massage per hr 15,000 kip). Alternatively you can take a sunset trip up to **Wat Santiphap** to chat with the monks.

SLEEPING & EATING

Most places are along Rte 1. The **Vivanh Guest House** (☎ 212219; r 60,000-100,000 kip) is hands-down winner with sparkling rooms, bathrooms, TV and hot water, while the welcoming **Lithavixay Guest House** (☎/fax 212175; Rte 1; r 60,000-80,000 kip; ❄ 💻), east of the bridge, is one of the better options with internet facilities (10,000 kip per hour) plus a variety of decent rooms with bathrooms and satellite TV.

Vivanh Guest House (☎ 212219; Rte 1; r 50,000 kip; ❄) This still-fresh accommodation by the bridge has sparkling rooms with TV, fan and en suites as standard. Recommended.

The **Sinphet Restaurant** (meals 20,000 kip; 🕑 breakfast, lunch & dinner), near the bridge, has a heavily Lao menu with tasty, clean fare and a pleasant atmosphere. The chicken soup is delicious.

GETTING THERE & AWAY

Lao Airlines (☎ 312047; airport) flies to/from Vientiane (one-way 860,000 kip) every Tuesday, Thursday and Saturday. The bitumen roads that radiate from Udomxai are in fair condition (except for the road to Pak Beng). The **bus terminal** (☎ 212218) at the southwestern edge of town has buses to Luang Prabang (ordinary 60,000 kip, five hours, three daily), Nong Khiaw (40,000 kip, four hours, four daily), Pak Beng (45,000 kip, five hours, two daily), Luang Nam Tha (40,000 kip, four hours, three daily), Muang Khua (65,000 kip, four hours, three daily), Boten (38,000 kip, four hours, two daily), Phongsali (60,000 kip, eight to 12 hours, daily) and Vientiane (ordinary 100,000 kip, 16 hours, two daily; VIP 140,000 kip, 11 hours, leaves 11am and 2pm).

LUANG NAM THA PROVINCE

Luang Nam Tha

☎ 086 / pop 35,400

Located near China and Myanmar, the original town was razed in an all-too-familiar story of US carpet-bombing. Nowadays the remnants of old Luang Nam Tha can be found near the Boat Landing while the new town has sprung up some 7km north. Ecosustainable tourism in Laos was pioneered here in the early 1990s, and as such Luang Nam Tha has become a 'trekker's Mecca' offering trips into neighbouring **Nam Ha NPA**, as well as kayaking and homestays. There are plenty of great spots to stay, decent cafes and local waterfalls to give you reason to stay an extra few days.

INFORMATION

BCL (8.30am-3.30pm Mon-Fri) Changes US-dollar travellers cheques and cash; gives cash advances on credit cards. ATM.

KNT Internet (per hr 9000 kip; 8am-10pm) Quick connection with Skype.

Lao Development Bank (8.30am-noon & 2-3.30pm Mon-Fri) Exchanges US-dollar travellers cheques and cash.

Lao Telecom Long-distance phone calls.

Luang Nam Tha provincial tourism office (☎ 211534, 312047; 8am-noon & 2-5pm) Excellent tourist office with English-speaking staff.

Post office (8am-noon & 1-4pm Mon-Fri)

Smile Internet Cafe (per hr 9000 kip)

SIGHTS & ACTIVITIES

Most people visit Luang Nam Tha for its amazing **trekking** opportunities in the nearby **Nam Ha NPA** (see the boxed text, p402), a vast citadel of dense jungle, home to clouded leopard, gaur, monkey, tiger and elephant. The guide services here are the country's pioneers of ecotourism and also offer **mountain biking**, **canoeing** and **rafting** on the Nam Ha River, as well as **homestays**. Group sizes are usually limited to a maximum of eight to minimise your eco-footprint, and 32% of your money is returned to the villages you visit.

The competitively priced **Jungle Eco-Guide Services** (☎ 212025; 8am-9pm) is run by two ex–Green Discovery employees and specialises in three-day treks into Nam Ha, giving you a little more scope to penetrate its Eden-like interior as well as kayaking and rafting. Speak to tiger-resistant Khet. The office is home to **Big Brother Mouse** (www.bigbrothermouse.com).

Well-honed **Green Discovery** (☎ 211484; www.greendiscoverylaos.com; 8am-9pm) offers a range of trekking, mountain biking and rafting options of varying difficulty and duration. Larger group numbers keep the prices down. For **mountain biking** tours contact the **Boat Landing Guest House** (☎ 312398; www.theboatlanding.com), which runs one- to four-day tours of the dramatic Nam Tha valley for around 250,000 kip a day.

The provincial tourism office has information on trips as well as excellent photocopied brochures on responsible tourism, local flora and fauna, local ethnic minorities, customs and etiquette, and maps. Places of interest within easy cycling or motorcycling distance include two 50-year-old wat, **Wat Ban Vieng Tai** and **Wat Ban Luang Khon**, near the airfield; a hilltop stupa, **That Phum Phuk**, about 4km west of the airfield; a small **waterfall** about 6km northeast of town past **Ban Nam Dee**, a Lenten tribe paper-making village; plus a host of Khamu, Thai Dam and Thai Lü villages dotted along dirt roads through rice fields. Pick up a map and brochures at the provincial tourist office before setting off.

MIGHTY MOUSE

If you want to get involved in improving local literacy, seek out **Big Brother Mouse** (www.bigbrothermouse.com), a homegrown initiative that aims to bring the written word to infants who, for lack of materials, rarely get the chance to read. Buy a few books and carry them with you to donate to children. BB employees set out on difficult trips by boat, pedi power and truck to deliver books to distant villages; if you're particularly keen you might offer to go with them. Look out for Big Brother in Luang Nam Tha, Luang Prabang and Vientiane.

ARE YOU REALLY GREEN?

Ecotourism in Laos is big business, with an estimated half of the annual US$150 million generated by tourism in some way eco-related. Increasingly, new trekking companies are setting up shop, which arguably increases quality; however, the words 'green' and 'ecotourism' are often used with little substance to back them up. Ensure authentic operators aren't neglected by using these criteria drawn up by **Ecotourism Laos** (www.ecotourismlaos.com) to decide on your tour company.

- Does my trip financially benefit local people, help to protect biodiversity and support the continuation of traditional culture? Is my guide local?
- What will I learn on this trip, and what opportunities will local people have to learn from me?
- Is there a permit, entrance fee or other fee included in the price that is directed towards conservation activities?
- Are there sensible limits in place concerning group size and the frequency of departures to minimise negative impacts?

SLEEPING

The quality of accommodation on offer is pretty good, and if you travel on to Muang Sing (opposite) you'll lament the cosy guest houses and cafes here. Rooms are reasonably priced with hoteliers working hard to grab your trade.

Sinsavanh Guest House (r without bathroom 30,000 kip) Basic, clean rooms with fans and mosquito nets. It's a bit of a walk out of town and despite its proximity to the main road leading to Muang Sing, it's peaceful and atmospheric. Pleasant management.

Bounthavong Guest House (☎ 312256; r 40,000 kip) Secluded down a quiet street, this is clean and simple accommodation and great value. Rooms have fans, cool tiled floors and attached squat toilets and hot-water showers. Family run.

Vienghkam Guest House (☎ 211090 r 40,000-50,000 kip) Previously called Bus Station Guest House, this recently refreshed place is located in a flowery courtyard. Basic, clean cells plus delightful new rooms right at the back, with TV and en suite.

Adounsiri Guest House (☎ 312257; r 50,000-70,000 kip) Sitting on the road directly behind Zuela Guesthouse, this new establishment has pristine rooms with comfy beds, a nice lobby and very relaxing atmosphere. Amazing value.

Khamking Guest House (r 60,000 kip) Immaculate refurbished rooms with TV, bathroom and free coffee facilities, in these tidy lodgings beside Manychan. Opt for a room out the back.

Manychan Guest House-Restaurant (☎ 312209; r 60,000-80,000 kip) A long-time favourite among trekkers, the paint-thirsty rooms are tidy with en suite, cable TV and fan as standard (air-con an extra 20,000 kip). The restaurant shows no signs of wear, with decent steaks and warm service (meals 20,000 kip).

Thavyxai Guest House (r 70,000 kip) Judging by the posters of communist heroes, this is a favourite place for visiting party officials. Rooms are spotless with fan, bathroom, cable TV and hot water, but perhaps a little too much Soviet austerity in the air.

our pick **Zuela Guest House-Restaurant** (☎ 020-578 5978; r 80,000 kip) The premier option in the new town for taste and tranquillity. Set in a blooming courtyard, this traditional-style house has glazed-brick rooms with bathrooms and wood floors. It also rents Honda scooters (70,000 kip). Its peaceful cafe features a heavily Lao menu with soup, noodle and rice dishes; also Western-style coffees, pancakes and fruitshakes. Bring your earplugs to deflect the town's 7am public-service announcements!

EATING

Cuisine here is equally diverse, ranging from Indian food to Western-style menus and Lao fare. The candlelit ambience of the night market is a great place to grab a banana crepe or stick of barbecued chicken and bowl of sticky rice while taking in the Akha handicrafts.

Panda Restaurant (☎ 606549; meals 15,000 kip; breakfast, lunch & dinner) In a much-improved spot on stilts near the river, the new Panda is spacious and cool with a vaulted ceiling ornamented by bees' nests and buffalo horns. Its heavily Western menu has dishes like *carbonara* and even bacon sandwiches!

Coffee House (meals 10,000-20,000 kip) With its Western and Thai menu, this earthy cafe has a friendly atmosphere. Owner Nithat is an ecologist and invaluable if you're interested in finding out more about environmental matters.

Yamuna Indian Restaurant (meals 20,000 kip; ⏰ breakfast, lunch & dinner) Delicious Yamuna serves a mean curry under Chinese lanterns at the end of the main street. The chicken masala is recommended and they may even let you play Playstation 2 if you're nice to them.

Banana Restaurant (meals 20,000 kip) Cosy joint offering equal measures of Western comfort food and tasty Lao fare. The yoghurts and fruit shakes make a healthy preface to a long day's trekking.

GETTING THERE & AWAY

Air

The little building at the side of the airstrip doesn't exactly scream 'International' at you, but there are intentions to extend the runway for larger planes. For now **Lao Airlines** (☎ 312180; www.laoairlines.com) has regular flights to/from Vientiane (one-way 860,000 kip). See the website for updates on new routes.

Boat

Charter boats make the wonderful trip along the Nam Tha River through truly remote country, to Pak Tha on the Mekong, or all the way to Huay Xai. They leave from the boat landing 7km south of town on the Nam Ha, and cost 1,800,000 kip to Pak Tha, or 1,900,000 kip to Huay Xai. Sign up here before your departure to share the charter costs for this two-day trip in an open longtail boat. In the high season a boat leaves almost every day, depending on passenger numbers. An additional 50,000 kip covers food and lodgings with the boatman's family. Bring sun protection, plus plenty of water and snacks.

Bus

The **bus terminal** (☎ 312164) has relocated 11km south, beyond the airport. A sǎwngthǎew should cost 20,000 kip to/from Luang Nam Tha new town. Buses run to Udomxai (40,000 kip, three to five hours, three daily) and Boten (45,000 kip, two hours, one daily, 8am) on the Laos–China border. One bus runs to Vientiane (170,000 kip, 19 hours) via Luang Prabang (90,000 kip, eight hours, 9am); two buses run to Huay Xai (65,000 kip, 9am and 1.30pm). Arrive in good time to buy your ticket and get a decent seat – advance purchase is not possible.

The local bus station has also moved; on the same route south as the bus station you'll find it on your left about 500m from the outskirts of town. Sǎwngthǎew travel daily to Vieng Phoukha (25,000 kip, four hours, 9am and noon) About six sǎwngthǎew run to Muang Sing daily (22,000 kip, two hours) and one bus goes to Muang Long (44,000 kip, five hours, 8.30am). Zuela Guesthouse also offer minibuses and drivers to Muang Sing (500,000 kip, incl tour of Muang Sing market and Akha villages).

GETTING AROUND

Jumbos from the main street to the airport, 7km away, cost 10,000 kip. To the Nam Tha boat landing, or the nearby Boat Landing Guest House, figure on 20,000 kip per person on a shared jumbo.

Mountain/one-speed bikes cost 15,000 /10,000 kip per day from the **bicycle shop** (⏰ 9am-6pm) on the main street, which also rents motorcycles for 70,000 kip for a decent Honda – for longer trips avoid the cheap Chinese models built with less-durable components. Luang Nam Tha to Muang Sing by scooter is an exhilarating experience and gives you a chance to pass through Nam Ha NPA and visit waterfalls en route. It should take about two to three hours.

Muang Sing

☎ 081

Tantalisingly close to China and Myanmar, picturesque Muang Sing sits in a lush valley bookended by green mountains and forests. With its listing Thai Lu wooden houses it feels as if you've stepped back into the early 20th century. Head to the **morning market** at dawn to witness a rush of vivid colour as Hmong, Thai

BAD TRIPS

Muang Sing was once at the heart of the infamous Golden Triangle, and though Lao government programs to eradicate poppy fields have been largely successful, opium is still grown here and you may well be offered some. Not long ago a *falang* imbibed more than he could handle and ran naked and screaming into a *ban* (village) in the middle of the night – he was badly beaten by villagers who presumed he was an evil spirit!

Lü, Akha and Thai Dam women descend from the mountains to sell their handicrafts.

Muang Sing is more off the beaten track than Luang Nam Tha (60km away) and in many ways it's more authentic, with a wealth of homestays and treks into the Nam NPA.

INFORMATION

Muang Sing has a **Lao Development Bank** (8am-noon & 2-3.30pm Mon-Fri), which changes cash only, and a **post office** (8am-4pm Mon-Fri) opposite the market.

The **Visitor Information & Trekking Guide Services** (020 570 80318; 8-11.30am & 2-5.30pm) is just north of the post office. Bicycles are available for rent around town for between 5000 and 10,000 kip per day.

SIGHTS & ACTIVITIES

Most people come to Muang Sing to trek in the pristine, triple-canopied **Nam Ha NPA**, a vast fortress of wildlife and steamy jungle. Treks can only be organised through the **Muang Sing Tourism Information & Trekking Guide Service Center** (020 239 3534; 8-11am & 1.30-5pm Mon-Fri, 8-10am & 3-5pm Sat & Sun), which has seven different treks to remote hill-tribe villages, ranging from one to three days with homestays. Prices are 298,000 kip per person per day for one person, but drop significantly the more people there are (as little as 85,000 kip with seven people). Unlike Thailand, Laos has gone to considerable trouble to ensure its ethnic culture is viewed by outsiders without the 'human zoo' syndrome, developing a blueprint that ensures your brief stay with villagers has a positive impact.

Set in a delightful old wooden building, the **Muang Sing Exhibitions Museum** (Tribal Museum; admission 5000 kip; 8.30am-4pm Mon-Fri, 8-11am Sat) has an interesting display of traditional textiles, woven baskets, handicrafts, amulets and cymbals, as well as photographic exhibitions. Saturday opening hours vary.

SLEEPING & EATING

Muang Sing gives fresh definition to the word 'sleepy' and such is its charm. The same can be said of its sleeping and culinary options – neither of which is too bothered about excelling itself. Rooms are like dishes here, basic but clean and very appealing after a long day's trek!

Thai Lü Guest House & Restaurant (212375; r 30,000-40,000 kip; meals 8000-12,000 kip; breakfast, lunch & dinner) This wilting building has bags of atmosphere. Verandahs, spacious rooms, squat toilets and dip-and-pour showers. The open restaurant downstairs is a trekker's magnet and serves Thai, Lao and Western dishes. *Khao soy* soup is a local speciality.

Muang Sing Guest House (r 20,000-30,000 kip) Flophouse digs opposite Thai Lü Guest House are run by a charming multilingual lady. Rooms are spartan with mosquito nets and fan. The ones out the back are preferable. There's also a rooftop overlooking the local wat and distant mountains – perfect for sundowners.

Adima Guest House (212372; r 40,000-50,000 kip) A bit of a hike from town (8km) but well worth it for its cosy wooden bungalows 3km from the Chinese border and near Mien and Akha tribe villages (self-guide tour info in Adima's restaurant).

Stupa Mountain Lodge & Restaurant (020 568 6555; stupamtn@laotel.com; r 50,000 kip) Five kilometres out of town with bewitching views of the rice paddies and distant China, this hillside perch has comfy bungalows secluded in lush gardens. Also has hot showers and en suites.

WHERE THE WILD THINGS ARE

Nam Ha NPA was the first of its kind, set up in 1993 as part of a government initiative that aimed to protect swathes of its natural heritage from slash-and-burn farmers, poaching and logging. The key species in this 2224 sq km wilderness of secondary deciduous forest are tiger, clouded leopard, gaur, Asian elephant, black-crested gibbon and muntjac, plus an estimated 280 species of birds. A number of ethnic peoples live within its perimeter including Thai Dam, Hmong, Lao Theung, Ikor and Kui. These tribes depend on the forest for their food, fires and building materials. Of poaching rare animals (which are then sold abroad), 40% is conducted by the inhabitants of Nam Ha, the remaining 60% by outsiders. Further threats facing this evergreen paradise are illegal logging – rare hardwood timber such as rosewood, teak and mahogany fetch great prices – as well as the free-roaming of domestic animals that spread diseases and compete for habitat.

Sangduane Guest House (☎ 212376; r 50,000 kip) Sengduane, 100m north of the main street, has a couple of Lao-style cabanas in a quiet garden as well as a clutch of forgettable rooms. Clean and simple, the cabanas catch the afternoon light on their sundecks. The restaurant also has a Korean-style barbecue garden by night.

Chanthimeng Guest House (☎ 212351; r 60,000 kip) Lovely rooms in a large modern house, overlooking the mountains and rice paddies. Great for afternoon sun with verandahs, en suites and hot showers.

our pick Phoui 2 Guest House (☎ 030 5110316; r 80,000-250,000 kip) Set off the south end of the main drag, Phoui boasts lovingly crafted rattan cabanas in a landscaped garden. With spotlessly clean rooms and hot water and fan as standard, this accommodation is ahead of the sloppy competition. Massage and sauna available.

Many of the guest houses double as restaurants. Beyond the reasonably comprehensive menu at Thai Lu, there's only the **Hasina Indian Restaurant** (meals 7000-25,000 kip) worth a visit. You'll find it at the northern end of town after the bridge.

Fresh fruit and vegetables as well as local delicacies can be bought at the **morning market** (⏰ 6-8am). To get here, turn left (west) at the exhibitions building and then right (north) two blocks up. *Fŏe* (rice noodle) stands are bustling early in the morning, and Laos' ubiquitous roaming baguette vendors sell fresh rolls with condensed milk for breakfast.

GETTING THERE & AROUND

Săwngthăew ply back and forth between Muang Sing and Luang Nam Tha (22,000 kip, two hours, 8am, 9.30am and 11am) and the Chinese border (15,000 kip, 8am). There are also about four săwngthăew a day to Xieng Kok (30,000 kip, three to four hours) on the Burmese border, from where speedboats race down to Huay Xai. Most passenger vehicles depart from the bus station opposite the market on the northwest of town. Rent bikes from shops and guest houses.

BOKEO PROVINCE

Most travellers visiting Laos' smallest province do so en route from Thailand, journeying down the Mekong River to Luang Prabang. Bokeo is home to the rugged Bokeo Nature Reserve and a rich biodiversity of large mammals; 34 different ethnic groups also live here.

> **GETTING INTO CHINA: BOTEN TO MÓHĀN**
>
> The only crossing between China and Laos that is open to foreigners is between Móhān, in Yúnnán province, and Boten, in the Luang Nam Tha Province. Laos issues 30-day visas on arrival; China does not. The crossing is open from 8am to 4pm on the Lao side and 8am to 5pm in China. In both directions, onward transport is most frequent in the mornings, soon after 8am. In Laos, transport runs to Luang Nam Tha and Udomxai. Buses from Muang Sing to Boten run every morning from 8am. If you get stuck in Boten there are a couple of cheap guest houses.

Huay Xai

☎ 084 / pop 15,500

Back in the days of Golden Triangle infamy when this corner of Southeast Asia provided much of the world's heroin, Huay Xai was a sleazy trafficking mule. Fortunately its new identity is that of a busy border town overlooking Thai neighbour Chiang Khong. It's an okay place to spend the evening with a cool Beer Lao before catching a boat down the Mekong to Luang Prabang, but by no means the shape of Laos to come. There's a couple of decent cafes and guest houses; however, the real jewel is the **Gibbon Experience** (☎ 212021; Th Saykhong; www.gibbonx.org), which takes you to Peter Pan–style treehouses in the truly beautiful Bokeo Nature Reserve (see the boxed text, p405).

INFORMATION

There's a glut of outfits offering different prices for the same trip; avoid mental meltdown and go to **Luang Prabang Travel** (☎ 211095; Th Saykhong), a government-sanctioned tour company offering homestays, rafting, kayaking and treks. Speak to Mr Loon.

BCL (⏰ 8.30am-3.30pm Mon-Fri) Opposite BAP Guest House; 24-hour ATM. Stock up on plenty of cash if you're going on the Gibbon Experience.

Internet Café (Th Saykhong) Decent connection with Skype, 15,000 kip per hour.

Post office (⏰ 8am-10pm Th Saykhong) Contains a telephone office.

SLEEPING & EATING

Budget traveller haunts are going strong here with a wealth of choice.

Friendship Guest House (☎ 211219; Th Saykhong; r 50,000 kip) Beside Deen's restaurant, this clean guest house has spacious rooms plus a verandah with unbeatable views of the Mekong. By night it becomes a bar and is the best place to take in the sunset. TVs in rooms are an extra 15,000 kip.

BAP Guest House (☎ 211083; bapbiz@live.com; Th Saykhong; s/d 80,000-150,000 kip;) This travellers' favourite has rooms with en suites and hot water (air-con and TV come as extra). Owner Mrs Changpeng can organise bus and boat tickets and has information on boats to Luang Nam Tha via Pak Tha or Xieng Kok. Good restaurant too (meals 14,000 kip).

Sabaydee Guest House (☎ 020 6929 458; Th Saykhong; r incl breakfast 80,000 kip;) Sparkling rooms in this fresh and comfortable guest house give a much-needed shot in the arm to downtown accommodation. All rooms have hot showers and fan.

Arimid Guest House (Alimit; ☎ 211040; Ban Huay Xai Neua; r 800,000-150,000 kip;) Despite the sometimes tetchy owner, Armid's flower-fringed, wood cabanas are something of an oasis, with a peaceful courtyard and nice cafe; 200m from the slow boat pier.

Oudomphone 2 Guest House (☎ 211308; r 70,000 kip) Fresh accommodation with cool en suite rooms, tiled floors and hot water. Oudomphone is fairly recent so the paint is still bright. There's an OK adjoining restaurant doing a fair trade in breakfasts and fried-rice dishes.

Thanormsub Guest House (☎ 211095; Th Saykhong; r 65,000 kip;) Pristine rooms in a large, cool house at the north end of town with fans, desk, bathroom and hot water. Bargain. Air-con an additional 55,000 kip.

Riverview Restaurant (Th Saykhong; meals 30,000 kip; 6.30am-10pm) Ageing like a fine wine, candle-lit, reindeer-horned Riverview has decent wood-fired pizzas and bespoke sandwiches – an infusion of carbs before the Gibbon Experience? Great place to swap tales with other travellers.

Deen Restaurant (Th Saykhong; meals 30,000 kip; 9am-10pm) At the south end of the main drag, Deen's is as tasty as it is inviting. Half a dozen vegie dishes. The chicken tikka masala is still the best dish.

Bar How (Th Saykhong; noon-11pm) The only cool haunt in town, How plays decent indie tunes, is festooned with lanterns and lounging cushions and dripping shadowy ambience. Cocktails a dizzying 50,000 kip, but the rest of the drinks are business as usual. Oasis.

GETTING INTO THAILAND: HUAY XAI TO CHIANG KHONG

Longtail boats (one-way 10,000 kip, five minutes, 8am to 6pm) run across the Mekong between Huay Xai in Laos and Chiang Khong in Thailand. A huge vehicle ferry (42,000 kip) also does the trip. On the Huay Xai side, the Lao immigration post is alongside the pedestrian ferry landing and issues 30-day visas on arrival. Boats from Pak Beng and buses from Luang Nam Tha always seem to arrive just after the border shuts. Available on arrival in Chiang Khong are 15-day Thai visas. For information on crossing this border in the other direction, see p772.

GETTING THERE & AWAY

Air

Huay Xai's airport lies a few kilometres south of town. **Lao Airlines** (☎ 211026; www.laoairlines.com) flies to/from Vientiane (one-way 860,000 kip, three times a week).

Boat

The slow boat down this scenic stretch of the Mekong River to Luang Prabang (280,000 kip per person, two days) is hugely popular among travellers. However, your experience will depend largely on the condition of the boat and how many people are on it. Boats should hold about 70 people, but captains try to cram in more than 100. If this happens, passengers can refuse en masse and a second boat might be drafted in. Even better, you can get a group together and charter your own boat and captain for 4,250,000 kip and enjoy the trip with plenty of space.

Boats leave from the boat landing at the north end of town at 10.30am and stop for one night in Pak Beng (75,000 kip, six to eight hours). Tickets are available from the boat landing the afternoon before you travel, or from guest houses. It is wise to see the boat in person (not just the photo) before you buy. Some boats are enclosed, with no view out and 80 or more people plus their cargo packed inside, which makes it a cramped, disappointing experience.

ZIPPING IN NEVERLAND

Adrenaline meets conservation in this ecofriendly adventure in the 106,000-hectare wilderness of Bokeo Nature Reserve. The **Gibbon Experience** (☎ 212021; Th Saykhong; www.gibbonx.org; 3-day trek 1,600,000 kip) is essentially a series of navigable 'ziplines' criss-crossing the canopy of some of Laos' most pristine forest, home to tiger, clouded leopard, black bear, macaque, migrating wild elephant and the eponymous black crested gibbon.

Five years ago poaching was threatening the extinction of the black crested gibbon, but thanks to Animo – a conservation-based tour group – the hunters of Bokeo were persuaded to become the forest's guardians. As guides and zip instructors they now make more for their families than in their old predatory days.

Guests stay for two nights in fantastical tree houses that are perched 200ft up in the triple canopy. The communal lodges, admitting a maximum of eight, come complete with cooking facilities and running rainwater showers! In between spotting the wildlife, the zipping is life-affirming – essentially, your safety harness, with a wheel on the end of a cable, is attached to a cable; all you require then is just a little faith and some adventurism. It's a heart-stopping, superhero experience.

Your day will also involve a serious amount of trekking. Bring a pair of hiking boots and long socks to deter the ever-persistent leeches, plus torches and earplugs – the sound of a million crickets in song may just keep you awake! The guides here are helpful (but make sure you're personally vigilant with the knots in your harness), but should it rain remember you need more time to slow down with your humble brake. This is definitely one funky gibbon you will never forget.

Two trips: Classic or Waterfall (1,660,000 kip, includes transport to and from the park, food and refreshment). Both options are for two nights; however, the Waterfall involves considerably more trekking.

Six-passenger speedboats to Pak Beng (110,000 kip, three hours) and Luang Prabang (416,000 kip, six hours) leave from a landing about 2km south of the town centre, at 9.30am – though only when full. If there are few takers and you're in a hurry you'll have to pay extra. Buy your ticket at any one of the guest houses or on arrival at the kiosk above the boat landing. Deaths are not uncommon; given the recklessness of the drivers this is no great surprise. Bring some earplugs and sit at the stern (what you can't see will scare you less!).

Slow boats also run to Luang Nam Tha (1,530,000 kip to 1,700,000 kip per boat split between passengers, plus 40,000 kip each for food and accommodation) via Ban Na Lae. However, in the dry season this small river can be so shallow you'll need to wade some of the way. These boats are uncovered, so bring sun protection. Ask at BAP Guest House for more information.

For any journey take plenty of water, food supplies and padding for your back.

Bus

Buses and large săwngthăew ply the road northeast to Vieng Phoukha (50,000 kip, five hours, three to four daily), Luang Nam Tha (60,000 kip, four hours, daily, 9.30am and noon) and Udomxai (100,000 kip, six hours, one daily, noon). There are also daily buses that operate to Luang Prabang (130,000 kip, eight hours) and Vientiane (170,000 kip, 18 hours).

CENTRAL & SOUTHERN LAOS

Those who step off the northern circuit to weave their way down to the Four Thousand Islands in the extreme south are rewarded by a very different view of Laos: steamy rice plains, gothic limestone karst, lazy riverine life and vast swathes of forest and coffee-growing plantations. With Kong Lo (a 7.5km subterranean cave navigated only by longtail) now on the map, untrodden central Laos will steadily develop over the coming years. Further south, Savannakhet and Pakse are well geared to the traveller, and are authentic places to spend a few days, with decent trekking and kayaking options.

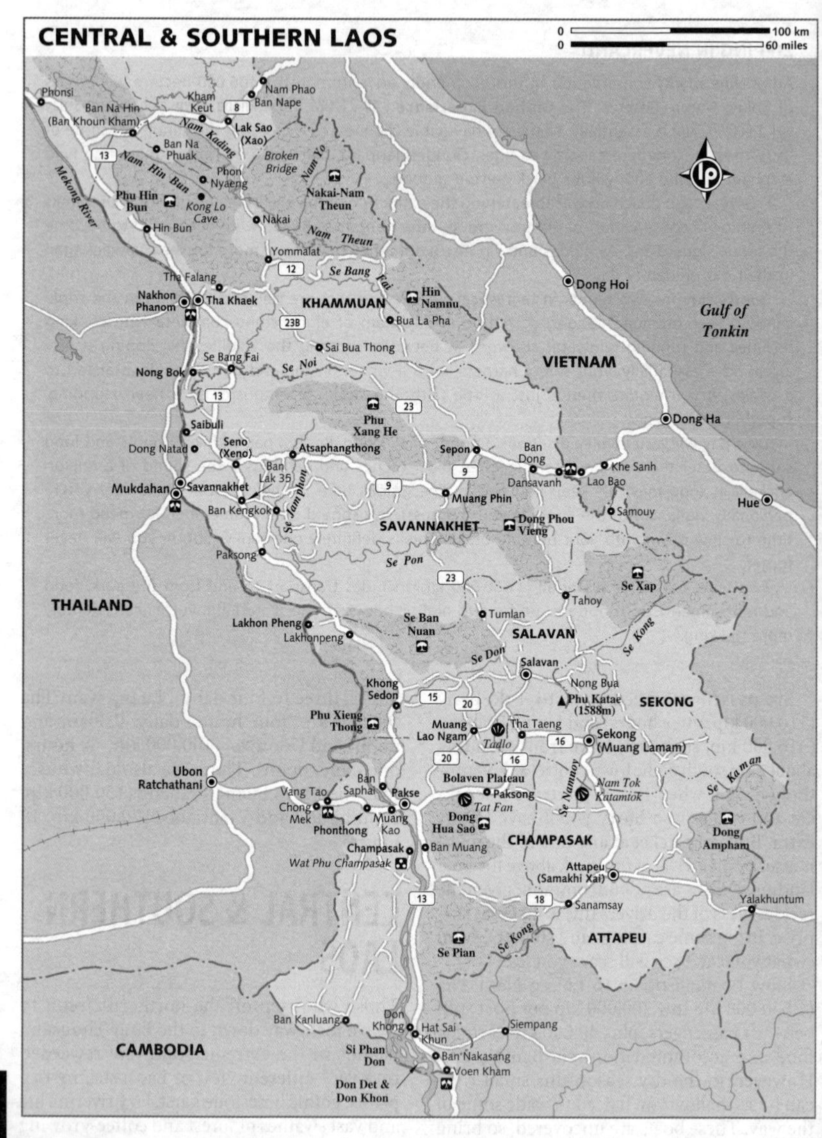

BOLIKHAMSAI & KHAMMUAN PROVINCES

Bolikhamsai and Khammuan, both heavily bombed during the Secret War (and still polluted with UXO), straddle the narrow waistline of the country, bookended by the Mekong River and Thailand to the west and the Annamite Mountains headed east to Vietnam. If you're passing this way to see Tham Kong Lo (Kong Lo Cave), languid Tha Khaek (opposite) is a pleasant base.

Route 8 to Lak Sao

Described by some as 'the trippiest bit of Laos', the route from Tha Khaek to the infamous Kong Lo cave is a many-levelled video game of serpentine roads heading through cathedralesque karst buttressed by forests. The first major stop on your odyssey to the cave is **Ban Khoun Kham** (also known as Ban Na Hin, 41km east of Rte 13) located in the lush Hin Bun valley. From here, it's an easy bus journey on recently sealed roads to Tham Kong Lo. **Inthapanya Guesthouse** (☎ 020 561 6054; Rte 8; r 60,000 kip; ❄) on the west side of town offers minty new digs in Ban Khoun Kham, with air-con, en suites, plus a very nice cafe with Lao and Western food. For 100,000 kip per person (cheaper in a larger group) English-speaking manager Jimmy can organise a minibus directly to Kong Lo village (one hour) and back.

THAM KONG LO

Situated in the 1580 sq km wilderness of **Phu Hin Bun NPA**, this 7.5km tunnel running beneath an immense limestone mountain is unlike anything you can imagine, and in the words of an Aussie traveller: 'I've done loads of caves, but this is the creepiest and the best I've ever seen.'

Puttering upriver past frolicking kids you suddenly witness the gaping mouth of the cave, your breath stolen before you've even entered the eerie, black cavern. Passing into the church-high darkness (100m in some places), watching the light of the cave mouth recede, is an uncomfortably spooky experience. As you moor up to the riverbank, wandering through a stalactite wood, you feel like you've wandered into an old *Star Trek* set, your water bottle spiked with LSD.

Remember to bring a decent flashlight, plus rubber sandals. You can make a long day trip to Tham Kong Lo from Ban Khoun Kham, but it's more fun to to make an overnight **homestay** (per person incl dinner & breakfast 50,000 kip) in Ban Kong Lo (the nearest village), about 1km downstream from the cave mouth. For more on homestays, see p387.

Getting There & Away

With the 50km road from Ban Khoun Kham (Ban Na Hin) to Ban Kong Lo now finished, it's an easy and picturesque journey here by scooter or sǎwngthǎew (25,000 kip).

In Ban Kong Lo boatmen charge 50,000 kip per person – including entrance fee – for the return trip (about 2½ hours, maximum four people) through the cave. Ask at Inthapanya GH for more information or, if you are doing 'the loop' and returning to Tha Khaek, ask Mr Somkiad for more details at the tourist information centre, see p408.

Tha Khaek

☎ 051 / pop 70,000

Languid, Mekong-hugging Tha Khaek, with its tree-shaded boulevard, scattering of cafes and sleepy square with a dried-out fountain, looks a little like Vientiane before the fashion police arrived. There's little to do here but wander cracked streets aglow with braziers, the air rich with the scent of bougainvillea, stopping off at a riverfront noodle house or taking in the sunset over nearby Thailand.

INFORMATION

BCL (☎ 212686; Th Vientiane) Changes major currencies and travellers cheques, and makes cash advances on Visa.

Lao Development Bank (☎ 212089; Th Kuvoravong) Cash only.

Post office (Th Kuvoravong) Also offers expensive international phone calls.

Tha Khaek Hospital (cnr Th Chao Anou & Th Champasak) Fine for minor ailments or commonly seen problems such as malaria or dengue.

Tha Khek Travel Lodge (☎ 030 \530 0145; travell@laotel.com; per hr 25,000 kip) Tha Khaek's only internet when we passed.

GETTING INTO VIETNAM: NAM PHAO TO CAU TREO

The border at Nam Phao (Laos) and Cau Treo (Vietnam) through the Kaew Neua Pass is 32km from Lak Sao and is open from 7am to 6pm. Sǎwngthǎew (12,750 kip, 45 minutes) leave every hour or so from Lak Sao market. Alternatively, direct buses from Lak Sao to Vinh (48,000 kip, three to four hours) leave several times between about noon and 2pm; you might need to change conveyance at the border. You'll need your Vietnamese visa in advance. Laos issues 30-day visas on arrival.

From the border to Lak Sao, jumbos and sǎwngthǎew leave when full or cost about 170,000 kip to charter. There's a good chance you'll get ripped off crossing here, particularly on the Vietnamese side. For info on crossing this border the other way, see p856.

GETTING INTO THAILAND: THA KHAEK TO NAKHON PHANOM

Boats cross the Mekong from Tha Khaek to Nakhon Phanom in Thailand about every hour from the boat landing and **immigration office** (8am-6pm) about 400m north of Fountain Sq. The ferry costs about 13,000 kip or 60B. On weekends boats might be less frequent and you'll be asked for an extra 8500 kip on the Lao side, and an extra 10B in Thailand.

In Tha Khaek, Lao immigration *usually* issues 30-day tourist visas on arrival and there is a **money exchange service** (8.30am-3pm) at the immigration office. A free 15-day Thai visa is granted on arrival in Nakon Phanom. For info on crossing this border in the other direction, see p779.

Tourist information centre (212512; Th Vientiane; 8am-4pm) Get information on community-based treks and meet the English-speaking guides here. As trek prices vary depending on group size, it's worth calling Mr Somkiad (020 571 1797) to see when other travellers are booked in.

Tourist police (250610; Fountain Sq)

SLEEPING

Tha Khaek's accommodation is limited to a few Soviet-style hotels on the riverfront and a few other moth-eaten digs. However, we consider Tha Khaek Travel Lodge to be one of the best travellers' oases in Laos.

Phoukkana Guest House (2163579; r 65,000-80,000 kip;) There's something a little David Lynchy about this place – or is it just us!? The musty rooms could use a lick of paint, its garden is eerily quiet and the staff is unnervingly giggly. Last option if you can't get a place at the Travel Lodge.

our pick **Tha Khaek Travel Lodge** (030-530 0145; travell@laotel.com; dm 25,000 kip, r 90,000-100,000 kip;) Located near the main bus terminal, this traveller's dream exudes summer-camp ruggedness (with its nightly alfresco fire) and has individually finished rooms with four-poster beds, framed around a leafy courtyard. Scooters for hire (85,000 kip per day). Great place to meet others who want to head to Kong Lo cave by scooter.

Mekong Khammouane Hotel (250778; Th Setthathirat; r 120,000 kip;) Large functional rooms in this pastel-blue colossus presiding over the waterfront. Beds are springy, rooms a little nondescript with Soviet fixtures, but for the price it's not bad if you like faded grandeur.

EATING & DRINKING

Smile Barge Restaurant (212150; meals 25,000 kip; noon-1am) Perched on/by the Mekong, Smile lives up to its moniker with a fairylit area full of atmosphere and perfect for languid sundowners. The menu covers fried food as if it was desperate to put kilos on you. Try the local squid.

Inthira Hotel (251237; www.inthirahotel.com; Th Annou; meals 70,000 kip; 8.30-midnight;) With its ox-blood walls, open-range kitchen and enticingly lit bar, this place could have leapt from the pages of *Wallpaper*. Asian-fusion menu.

Several *khào jįi* (baguette) vendors can be found on or near Fountain Sq in the morning, and the riverfront near here is good for a cheap meal any time. **Duc Restaurant** (meals 10,000 kip; 6am-10pm) serves delicious *fŏe hàeng* (dry rice noodles served in a bowl with herbs and seasonings but no broth).

GETTING THERE & AWAY

Tha Khaek's **bus station** (Rte 13) is about 3.5km from the centre of town and has a sizeable market. For Vientiane (75,000 kip, six hours, 332km), buses leave every hour or so between 4.30am and midnight, stopping at Vieng Kham (Thang Beng; 40,000 kip, 90 minutes, 102km) and Paksan (55,000 kip, three to four hours, 193km).

Southward buses to Savannakhet (30,000 kip, two to three hours, 125km) and Pakse (95,000 kip, six to seven hours, 368km) are reasonably frequent between 10.30am and midnight. For Vietnam, buses leave at 8am for Hue (150,000 kip) and 8pm for Danang (150,000 kip) and Hanoi (300,000 kip, 17 hours).

Săwngthăew heading east along Rte 12 depart every hour or so from the Talat Lak Sam Bus Terminal (Sooksomboon Bus Terminal) between 7am and 3pm for Mahaxai (20,000 kip, 1½ to 2½ hours, 50km), Nyommalat (25,000 kip, two to three hours, 63km), Nakai (35,000 kip, 2½ to 3½ hours, 80km) and Na Phao for the Vietnam border (45,000 kip, five to seven hours, 142km).

GETTING AROUND

Chartered jumbos cost about 15,000 kip to the bus terminal. The Tha Khek Travel

Lodge (opposite) rents Chinese 110cc bikes for 85,000 kip a day. The tourist information centre can arrange bicycle hire.

Around Tha Khaek

Travellers are hiring motorbikes and taking on the **Loop**, a three- or four-day motorbike trip through the province via Nakai, Lak Sao, Khoun Kham (Na Hin) and Tham Kong Lo; for details look at the travellers' log at Tha Khek Travel Lodge (opposite).

SAVANNAKHET PROVINCE

Savannakhet

☎ 041 / pop 120,000

This tropical backwater of faded temples and crumbling stucco mansions listing in amber light is magically unpretentious. While many of its walls could use some refreshment, a number of the city's older buildings are being restored to their former colonial glory. Hire a bike and cycle down the tree-shaded riverfront before eating dinner at one of a clutch of authentic Lao and Parisian-style restaurants. Take a trek with the local tourist organisation into two untrodden NPAs, or simply grab a Beer Lao and soak up the romantic riverside atmosphere.

ORIENTATION

Savannakhet is a sprawl of boulevards and narrow streets, and the best way to meander through its sleepy midst is on a bicycle. Most of the town's (charmingly) limited activity is near the river.

From the bus station on the north side of town, you should be paying around 10,000 kip to travel the 2km into the centre.

INFORMATION

Internet Access

Nang Internet (☎ 252066; Th Ratsavongseuk; per hr 4000 kip; 9am-10pm) Broadband connection in a cool room on the cnr of Th Sutthanu.

SPS Computer Shop (Th Khanthabuli; per hr 6000 kip; 10am-10pm) The pick of several internet places.

Money

The following two banks, located in close proximity to each other, have exchange counters. You can also exchange money next to the immigration office.

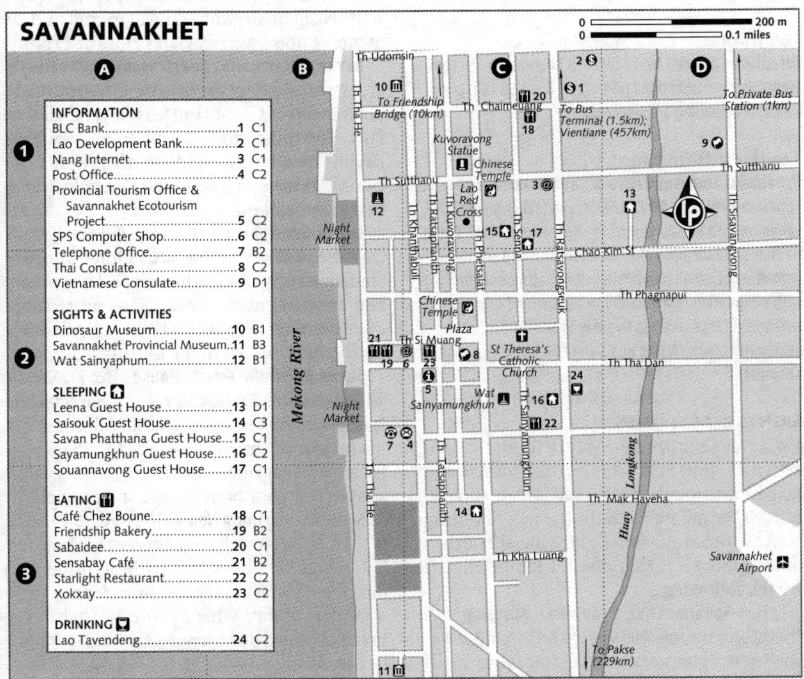

LAOS

GETTING INTO VIETNAM: NA PHAO TO CHA LO

Rarely used by Westerners, this border is so out of the way it might be easier to opt for a more popular crossing. No visas are issued here and transport on either side is infrequent. The best way to get here is by catching a săwngthăew from Thah Khaek (30,000 kip, six hours, 142km). Over in Vietnam the nearest town is Dong Hoi. For a direct bus here from Thah Khaek (980,000 kip, 10 to 14 hours) one leaves at 7am on Wednesday and Sunday and returns from Dong Hoi at 6am Monday and Friday. Open: 7am to 5pm. See p856 for information on crossing this border in the other direction.

BCL Bank (☎ 212226; Th Ratsavongseuk; 🕒 8.30am-4pm) Cash exchange and credit-card advances. ATM.
Lao Development Bank (☎ 212272; Th Udomsin; 🕒 8.30-11.30am & 1.30-3.30pm) Same services as BCL.

Post

Post office (☎ 212205; Th Khantabuli; 🕒 8am-noon & 1-5pm) This is situated a couple of blocks south of the plaza.

Telephone

Telephone office (☎ 212047; Th Khantabuli; 🕒 8am-10pm) Located behind the post office. Overseas calls are available here using a phonecard.

Tourist Information

Provincial Tourism Office & Savannakhet Eco-tourism Project (☎ 214203; savannakhet guides2@yahoo.com; Th Ratsaphanith; 🕒 8am-noon & 1.30-4pm) Has hand-drawn maps of town, brochures and photos with descriptions of nearby sites. It can also can help with information from laundry to car hire and organise well-run ecotrips (one- to five-day excursions) into two nearby NPAs: Dong Natad and Dong Phu Vieng. Speak to Khampat.

SIGHTS & ACTIVITIES

Since there's little in the way of tourist-geared activities, your best bet is hiring a bicycle and pedalling through the cracked streets and riverfront, or taking a trek in the neighbouring NPAs with Savannakhet's Provincial Tourism office (above). If that doesn't tempt, maybe try the following.

The **Savannakhet Provincial Museum** (Th Khantabuli; admission 5000 kip; 🕒 8-11.30am & 1-4pm Mon-Sat) is a good place to see war relics, artillery pieces and inactive examples of the deadly UXO that has claimed the lives of over 12,000 Lao since the end of the Secret War.

In 1930 a major dig in a nearby village unearthed a palaeontologist's dream when the 200-million-year-old fossils of dinosaurs were recovered. The enthusiastically run, if undervisited **Dinosaur Museum** (☎ 212597; Th Khanthabuli; admission 5000 kip; 🕒 8am-noon & 1-4pm) is an interesting place to divert yourself for an hour so. Savannakhet Province is home to five dinosaur sites.

The oldest and largest monastery in southern Laos, **Wat Sainyaphum** (Th Tha He) was originally built in 1542. The large grounds include some centuries-old trees and a workshop near the river entrance that's a veritable golden-Buddha production line.

SLEEPING

Savannakhet has some atmospheric digs that are both clean and hospitable. The following were our favourites.

Saisouk Guesthouse (☎ 212207; Th Phetsalat; r 40,000-60,000 kip; ❄) One of the best midrange options, this old villa has well-sized rooms with bathroom, optional air-con, plus an upstairs cushion-strewn verandah to chill in. The owner is noise-averse. Gates close at 11pm.

Savan Phatthana Guest House (☎ 214242; Th Saenna; r 40,000-60,000 kip) An OK option if Souannavong Guest House is full and all else fails. The musty rooms – in an austere East Berlin–style block – radiate off a wide corridor. All have fan and attached cold-water bathroom without sink. Creepy.

Leena Guesthouse (☎ 212404, 020 564 0697; Th Chaokeen; r 40,000-80,000 kip; ❄) Quiet and secluded, rooms have bathroom and hot water, and are particularly clean. You can rent bicycles/scooters (15,000/70,000 kip per day). Fresh coffee served in the morning.

Sayamungkhun Guest House (☎ 212426; Th Ratsavongseuk; r 50,000-80,000 kip; ❄) Characterful, spotless rooms in a faded colonial house on the main road (try for a room out the back); its friendly management makes this a memorable spot to rest your bones. Air-con optional.

Souannavong Guest House (Th Saenna; ☎ 212600; r 60,000-80,000 kip) A welcoming place to hang your hat; rooms have hot water, bathroom and TV, plus there's a pleasant communal lounge with a modest library where you can catch your breath. Located down a peaceful bougainvillea-bordered street.

EATING & DRINKING

For cheap *páa-tê* (meat paste) baguettes head to the vendors on the corners of Th Ratsavongseuk and Th Phagnapui. There are also plenty of street vendors (especially by the river in the evening) serving up barbecued food and atmosphere to go with it. For more upscale dining – evoking the city's heady colonial days (Savannakhet translates as the 'golden place') – there are a couple of refined restaurants serving up excellent French fare.

Sensabay Café (Th Tha Dan; meals 15,000 kip; 7am-10pm) With its high-back chairs and rattan lanterns, this is a nice spot to take in the crumbling backstreets over a decent coffee and Western breakfast.

Starlight Restaurant (☎ 213026; Th Sainyamungkhun; meals 20,000 kip; breakfast, lunch & dinner) Situated in an attractive colonial building, Starlight has a dazzlingly comprehensive menu ranging from steamboat barbecue to Western, noodles and a handsome selection of Mekong seafood. Try the fried squid…umm!

Sabaidee (☎ 253336; Dao Heuang Market, Th Ratsavongseuk; meals 50,000-100,000 kip; 7am-10pm) Revisit the '70s in this alfresco fondue restaurant. A favourite with locals, the menu is heavily Vietnamese with plenty of seafood dishes.

Café Chez Boune (☎ 215190; Th Ratsavongseuk; meals 50,000-100,000 kip; 7am-11pm) Tasteful new haunt decked in aquariums, water features and lanterns. A great spot to cool down and stock up on the carbs – the heavily French menu offers great steaks. Its Lao owner hails from Paris.

Friendship Bakery (Th Tha Dan; ☎ 213026; meals 10,000-20,000 kip; breakfast & lunch) Next to Sensabay Café, Friendship has a decent selection of chocolate fudge brownies, cakes and pastries.

Xokxay (☎ 213122; Th Si Muang; meals 25,000 kip; breakfast, lunch & dinner) This old favourite in the church square does a fine turn in Lao food, ice cream and shakes. The sour fish soup is worth a try.

You can also try **Lao Tavendeng** (Th Ratsavongseuk; 6-11pm), for live music. Watch out for over-friendly ladies!

GETTING THERE & AWAY

Lao Airlines (☎ 212140; www.laos-airlines.com) flies from Savannakhet Airport to Vientiane (860,000 kip) three times a week. Savannakhet's **bus terminal** (☎ 212143), 2km out of town on Th Makkasavan, is near the Talat Savan Xai at the northern edge of town. Buses leave here for Vientiane (55,000 kip, nine hours, 470km) hourly from 6am to 10pm, stopping at Tha Khaek (20,000 kip, 2½ to four hours, 125km). A VIP bus (70,000 kip, six to seven hours) to Vientiane leaves at 9.30pm. For Salavan catch the 12.30pm bus (45,000 kip, 190km, 7hours)

Heading south, loads of buses either start here or pass through from Vientiane for Pakse (45,000 kip, five to six hours, 230km). Buses for Lao Bao (30,000 kip, five to seven hours) leave at 6.30am, 9.30am and noon, stopping at Sepon (45,000 kip, four to six hours). Săwngthăew leave more frequently.

GETTING AROUND

A túk-túk to the bus terminal costs about 10,000 kip; prices double at night. The town is fairly sprawling so it can be a good idea to rent a bicycle/scooter for 15,000/70,000 kip per day, from Sayamungkhun or Leena guest houses.

Pakse

☎ 031 / pop 70,000

At first glimpse it might not be the best-looking town around, but Pakse's sultry charms unravel as lazily as the Se Don and Mekong rivers whose confluence it sits on. There are some lovely faded French villas evoking the town's once-august status as the colonial trading capital of southern Laos, and great trekking and kayaking opportunities courtesy of Xplore-Asia and Green Discovery opening up offices. The locals here have a practised sense of calm and given the baking temperatures you'll soon see why. Between visiting the nearby Khmer ruins of Wat Phu, sleepy island of Don Kho, and waterfalls Tad Lo and Tad Fan, high up in the coffee-growing

GETTING INTO THAILAND: SAVANNAKHET TO MUKDAHAN

The new Friendship Bridge that links Savannakhet and Mukdahan in Thailand means the days of regular ferries might be numbered. A Thai–Lao International Bus connects the town's bus stations 12 times a day; check the tourism office for details. Ferries should continue from the boat pier, crossing (13,000 kip or 50B, 30 minutes) the Mekong six times between 9.10am and 4pm on weekdays, less often on weekends. Visas are usually available on arrival in Laos (see p428). For information on crossing this border in the other direction, see p778.

region of the Bolaven Plateau, take time to wander the riverbank, perhaps having a massage.

ORIENTATION

Central Pakse is bound by the Mekong to the south and by the Se Don to the north and west. Rte 13 cuts through the northern edge of town. On and below Rte 13 towards the Mekong are most of Pakse's guest houses, shops and restaurants. Heading west across Se Don takes you to the northern bus terminal. The southern bus station and market are 8km in the opposite direction.

INFORMATION

Emergency

Hospital (☎ 212018; cnr Th 10 & Th 46)
Police (☎ 212145; Th 10)

Internet Access

@d@m's Internet (☎ 251445; Rte 13; per hr 5000 kip) Also does faxing and scanning.
Lankham Internet (☎ 213314; Rte 13; per hr 6000 kip) Broadband connection in a cool room annexed to the Lankham Hotel, drinks available.
SK Internet (Rte 13; per hr 5000 kip; ⌚ 7am-8pm).

Money

There are two ATMs in town: one at the **Banque pour le Commerce Exterieur Lao** (☎ 212770; Th 11; ⌚ 8.30am-3.30pm Mon-Fri) south of Wat Luang, which has the best rates for cash and travellers cheques and offers cash advances against Visa and MasterCard; and the **Lao Development Bank** (☎ 212168; Rte 13; ⌚ 8am-4pm Mon-Fri, to 3pm Sat & Sun), which changes cash and travellers cheques in the smaller exchange office – cash advances are available (Monday to Friday only) in the main building. The latter also houses Western Union (money transfers available on weekdays).

Post

Post office (☎ 212293; cnr Th 1 & Th 8; ⌚ 8am-noon & 1-5pm)

Travel Agencies

Most hotels and guest houses can arrange day trips to the Bolaven Plateau, Wat Phu Champasak and Si Phan Don.
Green Discovery (☎ 252908; www.greendiscoverylaos.com; Rte 13) operates rafting and kayaking (270,000 kip) trips to Si Phan Don. They should be running excursions on Baja motorbikes by the time you read this.

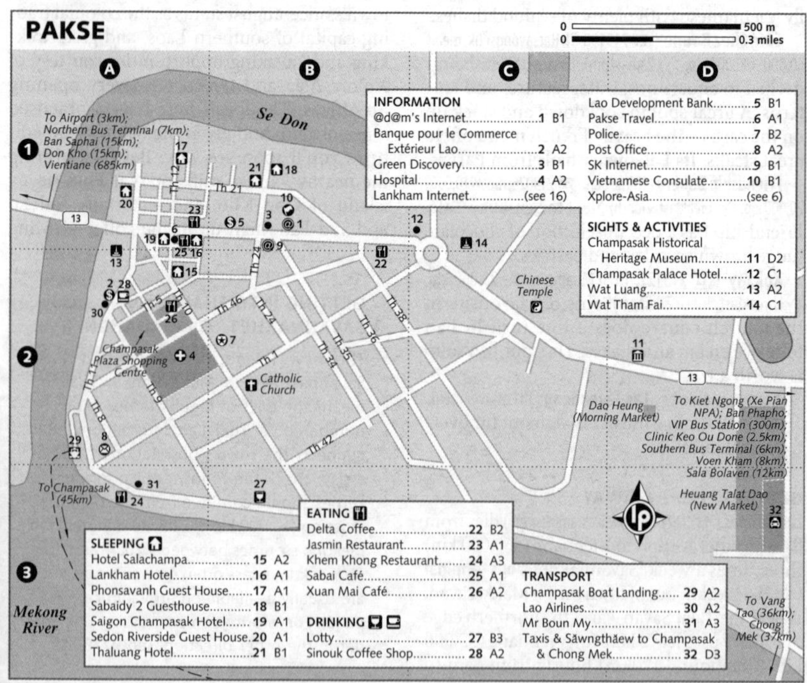

GETTING INTO VIETNAM: DANSAVANH TO LAO BAO

The busy border (open 7am to to 6pm) at Dansavanh (Laos) and Lao Bao (Vietnam) is regularly used by travellers and is a good road. Buses leave from Savannakhet (25,500 kip, five to seven hours) at 6.30am, 9.30am and noon, and regularly from Sepon (12,000 kip, one hour, 45km). It's a walk between the border posts, but formalities don't take long if you have your Vietnam visa. Vietnam issues 30-day visas on arrival at Lao Bao. Laos also issues 30-day visas on arrival. Entering Laos, săwngthăew to Sepon leave fairly regularly. There is simple accommodation on both sides of the border. Alternatively, a daily 10pm bus runs from Savannakhet to Dong Ha (100,000 kip, about eight hours, 329km), Hue (110,000 kip, about 12 hours, 409km) or Danang (140,000 kip, about 14 hours, 508km). No matter what you are told, you *will* have to change buses at the border. For information on crossing this border in the other direction, see p877.

Pakse Travel (☎ 277277; Rte 13) Next to the Lankham Hotel, this little outfit can organise visas, forward travel tickets north and south and a range of treks.

Xplore-Asia (212893; www.xplore-asia.com; Rte 13) Runs treks in Xe Pian NPA as well as kayaking trips to Don Dhet. It can also oganise air-con tranport to Si Phan Don (50,000 kip, leaves 8am). Speak to Hom.

SIGHTS & ACTIVITIES

There are 20 wat in town; the largest are **Wat Luang**, featuring ornate concrete pillars and carved wooden doors and murals, and **Wat Tham Fai**, which has a small Buddha footprint shrine in its grounds.

Champasak Historical Heritage Museum (Rte 13; admission 5000 kip; 8-11.30am & 1-4pm) documents the history of the province, with historical photos and ethnological displays.

A massage and sauna at the **Clinic Keo Ou Done** (Traditional Medicine Hospice; ☎ 251895, 020 543 1115; 1hr massage 20,000 kip; 4-9pm Mon-Fri & 10am-9pm Sat & Sun) is a real Lao experience. Go east on Rte 13, turn right about 100m before the Km 3 marker, and follow the 'Massage Sauna' signs another 800m. The **Champasak Palace Hotel** (gym visitors 8000 kip; 2-10pm) has a decent gym, massages, sauna and Jacuzzi.

SLEEPING

Despite the arrival of expensive hotels in Pakse, the affordable guest house is still very much a fixture with plenty of decent choices to be had. The winner, though, for the umpteenth year running, is Sabaidy 2.

our pick Sabaidy 2 Guesthouse (☎/fax 212992; www.sabaidy2laos.com; Th 24; dm 25,000 kip, s/d 40,000/58,000 kip;) Run by charismatic Mr Vong and his friendly team, Sabaidy has traditional, airy rooms bedecked in Lao textiles in an atmospheric, old townhouse. The best place to meet other travellers; homestays and elephant treks can be arranged here as well as enjoyable two-day trips to the Bolaven Plateau. Scooter hire, plus minibuses to Si Phan Don (one-way/return 60/110,000 kip). Memorable.

Saigon Champasak Hotel (☎ 254181; Th 14; s/d 100,000/150,000 kip;) Seven large, mint-fresh rooms in a new family-run hotel opposite Jasmin Restaurant, each with bathroom, air-con and TV. At the current rate it's great value and should become a favourite.

Sedon Riverside Guest House (☎ 212735; Th 10; r 50,000-60,000 kip) With new management this sleepy set of bungalows has changed very little. Languidly perched by the Se Don River, it also has a pleasant arbour to watch river-life drift by. Rooms are basic though functional with attached bathrooms.

Phonsavanh Guest House (☎ 212482; Th 12; r without/with air-con 50,000/80,000 kip; a) Sixteen rooms in a quiet house down a dirt track set back from the road. While the rooms are without character, the management seems friendly.

Lankham Hotel (☎ 213314; latchan@laotel.com; Rte 13; r 50,000-80,000 kip;) Looking increasingly like an aged Soviet exoskeleton, the Lankham has a great lobby and useful adjoining internet cafe. The rooms out the back have better views. Lankham also rents bikes (25,000 kip per day) and Baja motorbikes (150,000 kip per day).

Thalaung Hotel (☎ 251399; Th 21; r 60,000 kip;) Opposite Sabaidy 2, this is an adequate spot to crash, and has friendly staff and a resident myna bird who'll make you feel welcome. Somewhat spartan, air-con rooms with bathrooms, the bungalows out the back remind us of Robben Island. Also offers minibus service to Wat Phu and Bolaven Plateau.

Hotel Salachampa (☎ 212273; fax 212646; Th 14; r 120,000-150,000 kip;) Beautiful courtyard accommodation in an old French mansion.

The two rooms in the house itself are wood-floored, with huge beds and sizeable bathrooms – some with great views. It's so tasteful, even the air is fragrant. Bungalows are more generic, but still great value with air-con and TV.

EATING & DRINKING

Street-side noodle vendors are great for a cheap and tasty snack. Alternatively, there are baguette vendors near Jasmin's, and by night braziers crackle to life on Rte 13 selling barbecued chicken and pork.

our pick **Delta Coffee** (☎ 030-534 5895; Rte 13; meals 20,000 kip; 🕑 7am-10pm) Delta dishes up great coffee from its own plantation in Paksong. Its vast menu ranges from Italian with plenty of pasta dishes, to Thai. The Western breakfasts are a treat – definitely worth the walk from town.

Jasmin Restaurant (☎ 251002; Rte 13; meals 20,000-30,000 kip; 🕑 8am-10pm) Consistently offers mouth-watering food and laid-back ambience. The owner has an old-world touch that should be exported – globally. The chicken tikka masala is full of vim – you'll be wiping your plate with a pillow-soft naan.

Xuan Mai Café (☎ 213245; Th 4; meals 20,000 kip; 🕑 6am-midnight) On the corner opposite the Pakse Hotel, Xuan Mai serves top-notch *fŏe* (8000 kip), *khào pûn* (white-flour noodles with sweet-spicy sauce), fruit shakes and even garlic bread. It's the best place for a late feed.

Khem Khong Restaurant (☎ 213240; Th 11; meals 24,000 kip; 🕑 11am-10pm) Set upon pontoons on the Mekong River and flanked by fishing boats, this is a romantic sunset spot to sample some decent seafood. The *pîing pąa* (grilled fish) is delicious.

Sabai Café (☎ 212893; Rte 13; meals 20,000 kip; 🕑 6.30am-10pm) Cosy and clean, this central, new coffee joint is a welcome travellers' addition with its second-hand book section (heavy on thrillers) and comfort fare. Grab a toastie while using the free internet.

Sinouk Coffee Shop (☎ 212552; cnr Th 9 & Th 11; coffee 70,000 kip; 🕑 7am-8pm) has great Bolaven arabica coffee in a cosmopolitan cafe near the Mekong. To get down and dirty with the locals try riverside **Lotty** (Th 11; 🕑 6-11pm). With its downstairs dungeon daubed in fluorescent demons and dragons, Hendrix might have felt at home here were it not for the cacophonic karaoke.

> **DELTA COFFEE: MAKING YOUR CUPPA WORK HARDER**
>
> As well as its tasty fare, Delta is known for serving up excellent coffee harvested from its plantation in Paksong. It uses the proceeds from its Thai and French arabica coffee sales to generate a better level of schooling for local kids around the plantation. Three primary schools have been established on the Bolaven Plateau following Delta's efforts and your vital donations, which pay for schoolbooks. If you're a carpenter and want to get involved in building a new school, speak to manager Alan in the restaurant.

GETTING THERE & AWAY

Air

Lao Airlines (☎ 212252; Th 11; www.laoairlines.com; Th 11; 🕑 8-11.30am & 1.30-4.30pm Mon-Fri) flies between Pakse and Vientiane daily (one-way 1,010,000 kip, 70 minutes), and usually twice a week to Luang Prabang (1,310,000 kip, one hour 40 minutes). International flights go to Siem Reap (935,000 kip, 45 minutes) two or three times a week, and Bangkok daily (1,827,000 kip, one-way, two hours 30 minutes)

The airport is 3km northwest of town (10,000 kip in a jumbo) and has a BCL exchange office. Note: make sure you purchase tickets in advance from one of the tour companies opposite Jasmine's Restaurant, or the Lao Airlines office.

Boat

A boat for Champasak (160,000 kip, three hours) leaves daily at 8am from the Boat Landing taking a minimum of four people. Alternatively, get a group together and find **Mr Boun My** (☎ 020-563 1008; Th 11) at the first barbecue pork stall opposite the Mekong as the road bends left. He rents boats to Champasak (from 424,000 kip, one hour) and Don Khong (from 1,187,000 kip, four to five hours).

Bus & Săwngthăew

Pakse has several bus and săwngthăew terminals. VIP buses leave the **VIP Bus Station** (Km 2 Bus Station; ☎ 212228), off Rte 13, for Vientiane (180,000 kip, eight to 10 hours, 677km) every evening, though they usually also stop in town. The handy Thai-Lao International Bus also leaves from here; see opposite for details.

At the **northern bus terminal** (☎ 251508; Rte 13), usually called *khíw lot lák jét* (Km 7 bus terminal), agonisingly slow normal buses (without air-con) rattle north every hour or so between 6.30am and 4.30pm for Savannakhet (50,000 kip, four to five hours, 277km), Tha Khaek (65,000 kip, eight to nine hours) and, for those with a masochistic streak, Vientiane (100,000 kip, 16 to 18 hours).

For buses or săwngthăew anywhere south or east, head to the **southern terminal** (Rte 13), which is usually called *khíw lot lák pąet* (Km 8 bus terminal). The terminal is 8km south of town and costs 10,000 kip on a túk-túk. For Si Phan Don, transport departs for Muang Khong (40,000 kip, including ferry, three hours, 120km) between 10am and 3pm; and to Ban Nakasang (for Don Det and Don Khon; 40,000 kip, three to four hours) between 7.30am and 3pm. A săwngthăew runs to Kiet Ngong (Xe Pian NPA) and Ban Phapho (20,000 kip, two to three hours) at 1pm.

To the Bolaven Plateau, transport leaves for Paksong (15,000 kip, 90 minutes) hourly between 9am and 1pm, stopping at Tat Fan if you ask. Transport leaves for Salavan (20,000 kip, three to four hours, 115km) five times between 7.30am and 2pm, most going via Tat Lo (35,000 kip). Transport also leaves for Sekong (25,000 kip, 3½ to 4½ hours, 135km) at 7.30am, 9.30am, 11.30am and 12.30pm; and for Attapeu (35,000 kip, 4½ to six hours, 212km) at 6.30am, 8am and 10.30am.

Regular buses and săwngthăew leave the Dao Heung Market for Champasak (15,000 kip, one to two hours) and Ban Saphai (for Don Kho; 8000 kip, about 40 minutes).

GETTING AROUND

Pakse's main attractions are accessible on foot. Bicycles/scooters (10,000/85,000 kip per day) can be hired from **Sabaidy 2 Guesthouse** (☎ 212992; Th 24) and **Lankham Hotel** (☎ 213314; latchan@laotel.com; Rte 13), which also has some decent Honda Bajas for 170,000 kip a day.

Bolaven Plateau

Laos' principal coffee-growing region, the Bolaven Plateau (Phu Phieng Bolaven in Lao) is home to dense jungles and celebrated by travellers for its handful of refreshing waterfalls and cooler climate. Surging 1500m above the Mekong valley, the claw-shaped plateau is home to several Mon-Khomer ethnic groups, including the Alak, Laven (Bolaven means 'land of the Laven'), Ta-oy, Suay and Katu. The Alak and Katu are known for a water-buffalo sacrifice they perform yearly, usually on a full moon in March. You're probably here for the rustic serenity of Tat Lo, which is an excellent place to hire a bike, take an elephant trek or explore the nearby waterfalls.

TAT LO

Around 90km from Pakse on the Salavan road (Rte 20), Tat Lo is a broad, 10m-high **waterfall** boasting mint-green pools by the peaceful Seset River. For those with sufficient time it's a rewarding, chillsome place to head to; there aren't too many other *falang* and you may well stay longer than planned.

Activities

Most travellers spend their time **swimming** around waterfalls Tat Lo, Tat Hang and Tat Suong (10km away – get directions from Soilideth at Tim's Guest House), reading, walking in the surrounding forest, and generally relaxing with the soporific thrum of tumbling cascades.

Other activities include **trekking** in the forest either on your own (stick to the track) or with a guide from Tim's Guest House to surrounding villages and waterfalls. Guided

GETTING INTO THAILAND: VANG TAO TO CHONG MEK

The crossing at Vang Tao (Laos) and Chong Mek (Thailand) is the busiest in southern Laos and is open from 5am to 6pm. From Pakse, săwngthăew (8500 kip, 75 minutes, 44km) and taxis (20,000 kip per person or 100,000 kip for whole vehicle, 45 minutes) run between Talat Dao Heung (New Market) and Vang Tao. Easier is the Thai–Lao International Bus (60,000 kip, 2½ to 3 hours, 126km) direct from the VIP Bus Station to Ubon at 7am, 8.30am, 2.30pm and 3.30pm, returning at 7.30am, 9.30am, 2.30pm and 3.30pm. For details on crossing the border in the other direction, see p777.

At the border you have to walk a bit but formalities are straightforward. Laos issues visas on arrival, as do the Thais.

treks start at 35,000 kip per person. For more information and maps ask at Tim's, which also organises **elephant rides** through the forest and streams, costing 50,000 kip for 1½ hours, as well as rent bikes (8000 kip per hour).

Sleeping & Eating

Tim Guesthouse & Restaurant (☎ 211885; 020 564 8820; soulidet@gmail.com; r 40,000-60,000 kip; 💻) is a travellers' haven. While the wooden bungalows do not exactly spell luxury, the sheer wealth of information at reception on things to see in the area, plus the English- and French-speaking manager, Soulideth, and his natty restaurant (open from 6.30am to 10pm) support all the good press Tim's receives from our readers.

our pick **Siphaseth Guest House & Restaurant** (☎ 211890; r 30,000-60,000 kip) The pick of the bunch with newish fan-rooms with bathroom (60,000 kip) and more traditional bamboo rooms (30,000 kip) without bathroom. The restaurant (meals 15,000 to 25,000 kip) is ideal for sundowners.

Saylomyen Guest House (r 25,000 kip) next door to Siphaseth has rustic cabanas with fans, porches and hammocks right beside the river. All without bathroom.

Getting There & Away

Just say 'Tat Lo' at Pakse's southern bus station and you'll be pointed to one of the several morning buses to Salavan that stop at Ban Khoua Set (two hours, 20,000 kip). It's 1.8km to Tat Lo from here. To Paksong (1½ hours, 15,000 kip), get yourself up to Ban Beng, at the junction, and jump on a bus coming through from Salavan.

Champasak

☎ 031 / pop 12,900

Champasak's lazy one-street town may belie its history as an ex-capital of a Lao kingdom, but continue on to the dramatic mountainside location of Wat Phu Champasak and it soon becomes clear. Activity centres around the town's ferry wharf and the cultural traffic to Wat Phu. Guest houses are mainly found near the fountain. Pilgrims from near and far amass annually for **Bun Wat Phu Champasak**, a three-day Buddhist festival (usually held in February); worshippers wind their way up to Wat Phu Champasak, along with traditional live music, Thai boxing, comedy shows and cockfights.

If you've got time, visit the nearby fishing island of **Don Daeng**, secluded, sleepy and utterly unblemished by the tourist trail. You can stay in a basic community guest house (20,000 kip) or try a homestay – ask at the new **Champasak District visitor information centre** (☎ 020 220 6215; 🕑 8am-4.30pm Mon-Fri) for details. It's a short ferry trip (3000 kip return) but make sure you agree a time for your boatman to pick you up.

SIGHTS

Overlooking the Mekong valley, **Wat Phu Champasak** (admission 30,000 kip; 🕑 8am-4.30pm), while not being in the same league as Angkor Wat, is one of the most impressive archaeological sites in Laos and well worth visiting. It's divided into lower and upper parts and joined by a steep, flower-bordered stone stairway.

The lower part consists of two ruined palace buildings at the edge of a large square pond, itself split in two by a causeway, used for ritual ablutions. The upper section is the temple sanctuary itself, which once enclosed a large Shiva phallus. Some time later the sanctuary was converted into a Buddhist temple, but original Hindu sculpture remains in the lintels. Just north of the Shiva-lingam sanctuary you'll find the elephant stone and the enigmatic crocodile stone (if you can locate it!). The *naga* stairway leading to the sanctu-

GETTING INTO VIETNAM: PHOU KEAU TO BO Y

In far southeastern Attapeu Province a new border to Vietnam links Phou Keua to Bo Y. It's 113km southeast of attractive Attapeu town, where there are several guest houses. Visas are not issued here (yet). Transport is sketchy, but at least three Vietnamese-run buses are operating each week from Attapeu to Pleiku via Kon Tum (160,000 kip, 12 hours). Buses depart Attapeu at 9am Monday, Wednesday and Friday, and come the other way on Tuesday, Thursday and Saturday. Tickets are sold at the Thi Thi Restaurant just west of the bridge. Lao visas are granted on arrival; however, you'll need to obtain your Vietnamese visa in advance. Open: 8am to 5pm. For information on crossing this border in the other direction, see p899.

ary is lined with *dok jampa* (frangipani) trees. The upper platform affords spectacular views of the Mekong valley below.

As well as Bun Wat Phu Chamapasak, in February each year a ritual water-buffalo sacrifice to the ruling earth spirit for Champasak, Chao Tengkham, is performed each year. The blood of the buffalo is offered to a local shaman who serves as a medium for the appearance of this spirit.

SLEEPING & EATING

There are a couple of good sleeping options: most rooms are in atmospheric old houses, with fan and bathrooms. Eat in the guesthouse restaurant or walk to the south of the roundabout for cheap noodle stalls.

Khamphoui Guest House (☎ 252700; r 30,000 kip) Has spotless wooden bungalows south of the roundabout. All rooms have hot-water showers, and the staff here is welcoming.

Souchitra Guesthouse (☎ 920059; r 25,000-50,000 kip; ❄) The best of the bunch, riverside Souchitra has a communal verandah and hammocks that are great for chilling on steamy afternoons. Generous rooms with fans, bathrooms and optional air-con. As well as a nice little restaurant there are scooters for hire (40,000/80,000 kip per half-/full day).

Vong Phaseud Guest House (☎ 920038; r 30,000 kip) A popular and friendly place on the river with plain rooms and a small but social restaurant area serving up good Lao food with fantastic views over the Mekong. Crack a Beer Lao and watch the river slide through a dozen colour changes before nightfall.

GETTING THERE & AROUND

Regular buses and săwngthăew run between Champasak and Pakse from about 6.30am until 3pm (15,000 kip, one to two hours); early morning is busiest.

If you're heading south to Ban Nakasang (for Don Det) or Muang Khong (on Don Khong), take a ferry from Ban Phaphin (1.8km north of Champasak) over the Mekong to Ban Muang (3000 kip), then a săwngthăew or motorcycle taxi to Ban Lak 30 (on Rte 13), where you can flag down anything going south.

Bicycles (8000 to 15,000 kip per day) and scooters (40,000/80,000 kip per half-/full day) can be hired from guest houses. A túk-túk to Wat Phu costs about 50,000 to 65,000 kip, including waiting time.

Si Phan Don (Four Thousand Islands)

☎ 031

This beguiling archipelago of islets and palm-studded sandbars is the sapphire near the end of the Mekong's 4350km necklace, when the 'mother of all rivers' is at her widest. It's best to visit these tropical islands in the dry season, when the water iridesces from teal blue to turquoise and is perfect for tubing (on Don Det this has become a rite of passage). Between kayaking and cycling around the three main islands – Don Khong, and sister islands Don Det and Don Khon – spotting the rare Irrawaddy dolphin or visiting waterfalls, there's little to do but hammock-dwell, listening to chirruping kids and the putter of fishermen's longtails.

DON KHONG

Don Khong is the biggest of the three islands (18km long, 8km wide) and the most developed with 24-hour electricity. On arrival in its main settlement, Muang Khong – a one-street affair with a couple of guest houses, massage parlour and some decent restaurants – you'll be struck by the friendliness of the locals. Perhaps that's something to do with the fact most *falang* give Khong a miss in favour of the other two islands where there's more to do, so in many ways Don Khong is *still* itself. The skies seem wider and less claustrophobic here, the green mountains of Cambodia within view.

Information

One road back from the river, 400m south of the distinctive *naga*-protected Buddha at Wat Phuang Kaew, the **Agricultural Promotion Bank** (🕑 8.30am-3.30pm Mon-Fri) exchanges travellers cheques and cash (but no sterling) at poor rates. For any medical complaints, the hospital is a 200m south of the bank; ask for English- and French-speaking Doctor Souban.

Alpha Internet (☎ 214117; per min 1000 kip; 🕑 8am-9pm) Has slow internet and international calls at high prices; 100m north of Pon's River Guest House.

Don Khong Massage (per 1/2 hr 30,000/75,000 kip) Offers traditional Lao and Swedish massage. Beside Alpha Internet.

Khong Island Travel (☎ 213011; www.khongisland travel.com; Villa Muong Khong) Can organise boat trips to Don Dhet and Don Khon and forward travel and visas to Cambodia.

Post office (🕑 8am-noon & 2-4pm Mon-Fri) Just south of the bridge.

Telephone office (🕑 8am-noon & 2-4pm Mon-Fri) West of the boat landing.

SI PHAN DON

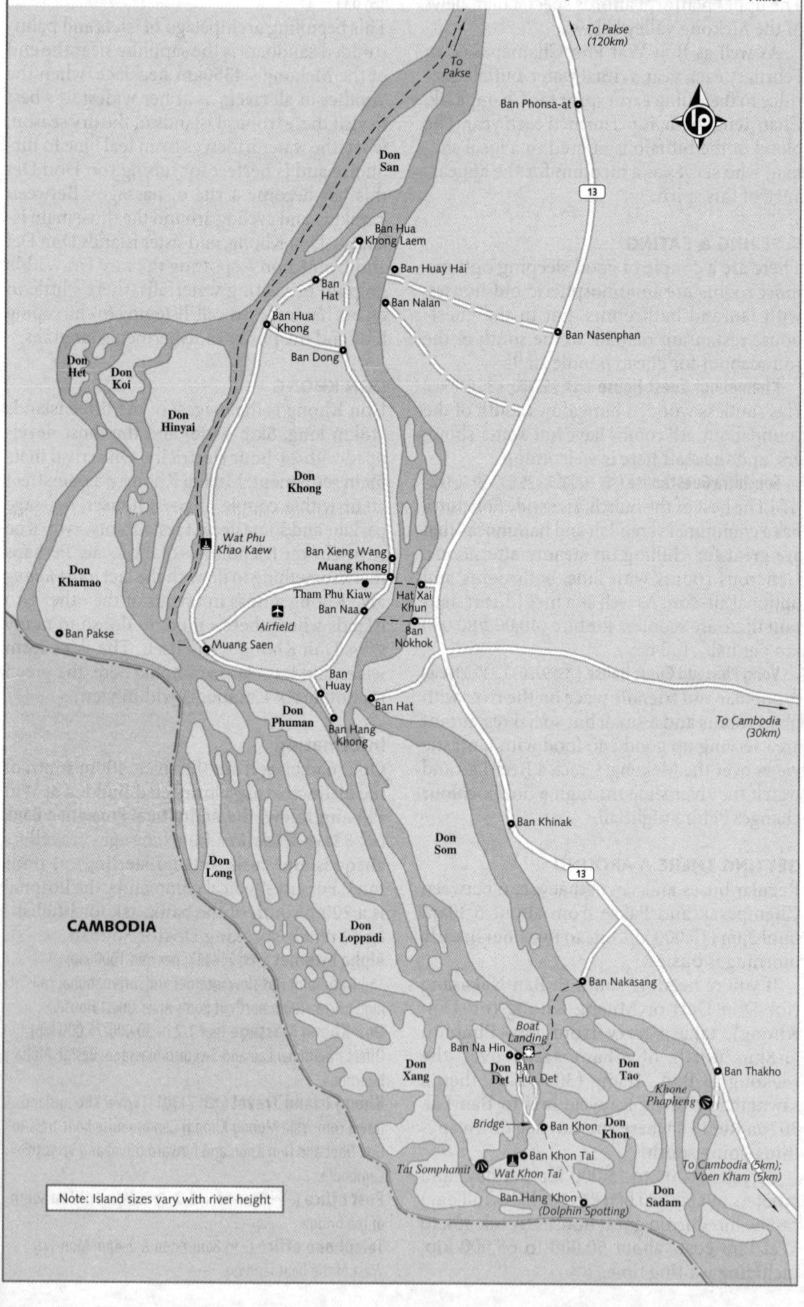

0 6 km
0 4 miles
To Pakse (120km)
To Pakse
Ban Phonsa-at
Don San
13
Ban Hua Khong Laem
Ban Huay Hai
Ban Hat
Ban Nalan
Ban Hua Khong
Ban Nasenphan
Ban Dong
Don Het
Don Koi
Don Hinyai
Don Khong
Wat Phu Khao Kaew
Ban Xieng Wang
Muang Khong
Don Khamao
Tham Phu Kiaw
Hat Xai Khun
Ban Naa
Airfield
Ban Nokhok
Ban Pakse
Muang Saen
Ban Huay
Ban Hat
Don Phuman
Ban Hang Khong
To Cambodia (30km)
Ban Khinak
Don Som
Don Long
13
CAMBODIA
Don Loppadi
Ban Nakasang
Boat Landing
Ban Na Hin
Ban Hua Det
Don Xang
Don Det
Don Tao
Ban Thakho
Khone Phapheng
Bridge
Ban Khon
Don Khon
Ban Khon Tai
Tat Somphamit
Wat Khon Tai
To Cambodia (5km); Voen Kham (5km)
Don Sadam
Ban Hang Khon (Dolphin Spotting)
Note: Island sizes vary with river height

LAOS

Sleeping & Eating

Fewer shoestring options are found on Don Khong, however, there are a couple of great-value, enticing oases at which to rest your bones. Conveniently, all the guest houses are in diminutive Muang Khong.

Mekong Guesthouse (☎ 213668; r 30,000 kip; ❄) By the time you read this, Mekong's new air-con rooms should be complete (price not yet available). The original rooms out the back are spacious, teak-decked affairs with verandahs and without bathroom. There's also an attached restaurant that serves up Lao and Western food (meals 20,000 kip). Located about 500m south of the boat landing.

Phoukhong Guesthouse & Restaurant (☎ 213673; r 40,000 kip) Next door to Pon's with outdoor decking overlooking the Mekong, offering a mixed Asian menu. It's open for breakfast, lunch and dinner, and meals cost from 7000 to 15,000 kip. Phoukhong's paint-parched, small rooms come with cold-water bathrooms.

Done Khong Guest House & Restaurant (☎ 214010; r 50,000-150,000 kip; ❄) Facing the river and village green, Done Khong is both relaxing and fastidiously clean. There's plenty of shaded areas on the balcony for keeping cool, and owner Madame Khampiew's simple restaurant has a range of Western dishes (meals 20,000 kip) and Lao food.

Souk Sabay Guest House (☎ 214122; r with/without air-con 100,000/60,000 kip) Set back from the road down a little alley, this place has lush gardens and immaculate though occasionally musty rooms in a handsome old house. The atmosphere is languid and friendly. Laundry service available.

Souksan Guesthouse & Restaurant (☎ 212071; r with/without air-con 150,000/80,000 kip) This affluent looking Thai-Roman–style guest house may look a little nondescript but its rooms – all with bathroom – are palatially large and incredibly cold (a virtue!). Its restaurant (meals 20,000 to 40,000 kip) sits by the river and has some tasty dishes. We tried the delicious sizzling pork.

our pick Villa Kang Khong (☎ 213539; r 70,000-150,000 kip; ❄) So full of old-world style it should be arrested. With its cosy rooms, stripped-wood floors and cool lobby, Kang Khong pulls off being fresh yet antiquated with *élan*. Minimart, bikes for hire, optional air-con and laundry services – all at an affordable price.

Pon's River Guest House & Restaurant (☎ 214037, 020-227 0037; r 60,000-100,000 kip; ❄) Mr Pon's elegant guest house has 18 fresh rooms with optional air-con, cable TV and bathroom. The restaurant, which serves breakfast, lunch and dinner (meals 15,000 kip), is on decking overlooking the Mekong – the fish specialities are a highlight.

Getting There & Away

From Don Khong to Pakse, buses (40,000 kip, 2½ to 3 hours, 128km) and sǎwngthǎew leave from outside Wat Phuang Kaew between 6am and 8am. After that, head over to Rte 13 and wait for anything going north. Guest houses also run daily minibuses to Pakse (40,000 kip).

If you're heading south to Cambodia, guest houses arrange transport to the border, which links with minibuses from the border to Stung Treng, so this is recommended. Otherwise, cross the river to Hat Xai Khun, get to Rte 13 and wait for the Pakse–Voen Kham bus, which usually passes about 8.30am or 9am. There are regular boats between Hat Xai Khun and Don Khong; it's 27,000 kip per boat for one to three people, or 14,000 kip per person for more. Bargaining is futile.

Boats for Don Det and Don Khon (40,000 kip, 1½ hours) leave whenever you stump up the cash – boatmen hang out under the tree near the bridge. Alternatively, ask your guest house to arrange it for you. Mr Pon's boat leaves daily at 8.30am.

Getting Around

Bicycles can be rented for 8500 kip per day from guest houses along the river road or from Alpha Internet. Villa Khan Khong has motorcycles for 85,000 kip per day. Buses, motorcycle taxis or túk-túk run irregularly from Ban Hua Khong to Muang Khong and Ban Huay, from where the car ferry departs.

DON DET & DON KHON

These two islands are a tropical *yin* and *yang*, for while Don Det is somewhat overcrowded in its *falang*-concentrated areas, losing a certain element of its Lao-ness, sultry Don Khon couldn't be more authentic. If you're looking for an 'up for it' traveller crowd then Don Det is where you should head, particularly 'sunrise' side (eastern tip) where you'll find the ferry point of **Ban Hua Det** and a few bars and restaurants. If, on the other hand, you want to experience a near-flat line of calm, then head over the old French bridge to Don Khon and pay a little more to immerse yourself in village life; you'll also be nearer the dolphins and two very impressive waterfalls.

Either way your time on these two firefly-flickering islands is likely to be a highlight; 24-hour electricity has finally arrived and is gradually working its way through guest houses. Hire a bike and thread your way past gleaming rice paddies and islanders taking ablutions in the blue water; cycle on to the southern tip of Don Khon to see the rare Irrawaddy dolphin, or hire a tube and float downstream past fishermen and doe-eyed buffalo.

Information

You'll find internet services by the Ban Hua Det boat landing as well as along 'sunrise' side. There's no bank here so stock up on funds before you leave Pakse. Nor is there a post office. **Xplore-Asia** (☎ 212893; www.xplore-asia.com; Ban Hua Det) offers kayaking, rafting and forward travel to Pakse as well as Cambodian destinations: Kratie, Stung Treng, Phnom Penh and Siem Reap. Speak to Noi.

Sights & Activities

With gill-net fishermen now playing a hand in the conservation of the rare **Irrawaddy dolphin**, the cetacean's numbers have increased to around 20 in this area. You can sometimes see them – early evening and first thing in the morning are the best times – off the southern tip of Don Khon right beside Cambodia, where they congregate in a 50m-deep pool. Boats are chartered (42,500 kip, maximum three people) from the old French pier. Sightings are regular, but the boat journey through the unearthly, rocky waterways is worth the money alone. Alternatively, walk or ride to the beach at Ban Hang Khon and ask the boatman to take you from there.

Alternatively, **walk** or hire a **bike** (13,000 kip) for the day and explore the dirt pathways criss-crossing Don Det and Don Khon. The defunct **railway line** takes you to a French loading pier at the southern end of Don Khon. You can also visit the French-built **concrete channels** on the eastern edge of the Don Khon (head northwest from the railway bridge then turn south about 1km along), or the dramatic **Tat Somphamit** waterfalls (go under the railway bridge then follow the road southwest for around 2km). There's a charge of 19,000 kip per day to cross the bridge.

Admirers of thundering waterfalls will like **Khone Phapheng**, considered the largest (by volume) in Southeast Asia. Entry is 9000 kip and the falls are often included on the itinerary of dolphin-viewing day trips.

Tubing, **kayaking** and **rafting** are also possible – speak to Xplore-Asia for the best-organised options. Note that post-monsoon the Mekong is churned a dirty brown for a few months – at least from September till December – and swimming in a sewer would probably be more fun.

Sleeping & Eating

Accommodation on the two islands varies in quality and price. Near the boat landing on Don Det, there's an alley with an overcrowded spawn of cabana guest houses and self-styled restaurants. Head further south along Don Det and you'll find superior places. Over the bridge on Don Khon, fresh, affordable accommodation with fans and en suites is the norm.

If opting for a thatched, nonelectric bungalow, pick a sturdy-looking one as some stilt huts have recently collapsed into the river! Also, make sure yours has a mosquito net and hammock plus two windows so you can rely on natural ventilation to keep cool. On Don Det:

River Garden (☎ 020-527 4785; near old bridge, Don Det; r with/without bathroom 50,000/20,000 kip) Barely two years old, gay-friendly River Garden has great value, pristine cabanas. There's also a cosy decked restaurant offering a Western and Lao menu. Quality.

Santiphab Guesthouse (☎ 030-534 6233; near old bridge, Don Det; bungalow with/without bathroom 40,000/20,000 kip) Run by a mischievous old lady, Santiphab has some recently built cabanas (rooms 3 and 4 are the best) with bathroom as well as a lovely garden and view of the nearby bridge. Its cafe offers everything from fried Western breakfast to excellent *làap*.

Mama Leuah's Guest House (☎ 020-656 9651; Don Det; r 20,000 kip) Just south of Mr Phao's place (following), Mama has pastel-blue cabanas with simple, two-window rooms enjoying private balconies and stunning river views.

Mr Phao's Riverview Guesthouse (Near old bridge, Don Det; r 20,000-40,000 kip) Colourful cabanas with immaculate basic rooms, a lovely manicured garden and, as the name suggests, great views. The restaurant is decent with Lao and Western fare. Friendly management.

GETTING INTO CAMBODIA: DONG KALAW TO DONG KRALOR

This remote but popular border actually has two different crossings, but when we passed only one was really being used. That was the road via Dom Kralor that continues on smooth tar to Stung Treng. Cambodia issues 30-day visas on arrival at Dong Kralor for US$20 (not kip) plus 'processing fee' – have small notes ready as well as two passport photos; Laos does not issue visas. From the islands, most travellers are taking a traveller minibus at least as far as Stung Treng (110,000 kip, two hours) and, given there is barely any other transport on the Cambodian side, this makes sense despite the cost. Minibuses leave in the morning and tickets are available all over the islands. For information on crossing this border in the other direction, see p128.

The second crossing is by boat from Voen Kham, but given Cambodia has closed its border post here and speedboats are hugely expensive and hard to find, it's not recommended.

Souksan Guest House (Sunrise Blvd, Ban Hua Det, Don Det; bungalow 50,000-100,000 kip;) Upmarket Souksan has stylish bungalows with comfy beds, natural ventilation and beautiful gardens. The restaurant is quality and you can also hire bikes here. It may now have air-con in every room.

Pool Bar (Ban Hua Det, Don Det) Near the boat landing and Souksan Guesthouse, this lively joint is about as kicking as it gets, with *falang* congregating here for retro tunes (or to put their own iPods on); convivial ambience, pool table and decent library.

Jasmin's Restaurant (Sunrise Blvd, Don Det; meals 25,000 kip) Following its success in Pakse, delectable Jasmin's has spawned a newborn on sunrise. The dimly lit atmosphere and slow service are offset by the delicious Malaysian and Indian fare. Friendly atmosphere.

On Don Khon:

Boun's Guesthouse & Café (Don Khon; r 25,000-50,000 kip) Still going strong, Boun's 10 cabanas (six with bathroom) are set back in a garden crowded with hibiscus. A lovely cafe (meals 30,000 kip) over the road enjoys great sunset views over the river.

Pan's Guesthouse & Restaurant (☎ 020-534 6939; pkounnavong@yahoo.co.uk; Don Khon; r 70,000-100,000 kip;) Set in pleasant riverside gardens, Pan's upscale cabanas have nicely finished rooms with bathroom, fan and balcony. Try the excellent restaurant too (meals 12,000 to 15,000 kip). Can also organise forward travel to Vietnam, Bangkok and Cambodia.

Seng Ahloune Guest House (☎ 030-534 5807; Don Khon; r 80,000-110,000 kip) Newly constructed wood and rattan cabanas with bathroom set in a serene location beside the old bridge. The courtyard garden is crowded with banana plants while the restaurant does a fine turn in comfort food (meals 10,000 to 30,000 kip).

Chanthounma's Restaurant (Don Khon; mains 15,000 kip) A shaded little cafe north of the bridge, Chathounma's dishes up a combo of Western and traditional Lao food. The steamed local fish in banana leaves with coconut was tasty.

Bamboo Restaurant (Don Khon; meals 20,000-30,000 kip) One of the most romantic dining spots on the river, this fairylit option manages elegance and simplicity with aplomb. Offering European, Thai and Lao food.

Getting There & Around

Boats regularly leave Don Det for Ban Nakasan (15,000 kip per person). Boats for Don Khon leave according to demand though you're looking at an extortionate price of 200,000 kip per boat. For the same price Little Eden will *also* bring you back. Boats can be hired to go anywhere in the islands for about 85,000 kip an hour.

For Pakse (40,000 kip, 2½ to 3 hours, 148km), buses or săwngthăew leave Ban Nakasang at 6am, 8am, 9am and 10am. See p415 for buses from Pakse. **Mr Chong's Travel** (☎ 030-526 3083; Don Det) at Ban Hua Det boat landing organises one VIP bus daily (110,000 kip, leaves Ban Nakasan 8.30am) to Stung Treng, Cambodia.

LAOS DIRECTORY

ACCOMMODATION

Accommodation in Laos has been improving in tandem with rising tariffs. In remote villages you'll find fewer options, and you might consider trying a homestay rather than a regular guest house. The money goes directly to the family and benefits both your trip and their coffers. Guest houses increasingly charge kip as part of a national initiative to oust the dollar and baht, but given this is a trading nation you can usually get away with paying in baht.

Accommodation is cheapest in the rural north and far south, where it's still possible to find a bungalow for 20,000 kip in backpacker spots like Muang Ngoi Neua and Si Phan Don. In larger towns like Vientiane, Luang Prabang, Savannakhet, Pakse and Luang Nam Tha, expect to pay 50,000 kip for a budget room with shared bathroom and around 130,000 kip for a room with a bathroom or air-con. Unless otherwise noted, prices are for rooms with private bathroom.

ACTIVITIES

Cycling

Laos' small population and relatively peaceful roads are a haven for cyclists with a head for heights and decent set of gears. Many of the roads are now sealed, though if you're visiting straight after the monsoon you'll find them dotted with potholes or, in the case of the Bolaven Plateau, completely mired in mud. Some of the mountains in the north are back-breakers; if you're dead beat just hitch a ride on a passing sǎwngthǎew. Remember to stock up on fluids and spare inner tubes before a big trip. Riding through Vientiane can be a little precarious during festivals when drivers are drunk at the wheel and petty crime goes through the roof (motorbike bag theft, particularly). Laos' main towns all have bicycle-rental shops. Several companies offer mountain-bike tours, particularly from Luang Nam Tha and Luang Prabang (see White Elephant Tours, p387).

Kayaking & Rafting

Kayaking and white-water rafting have taken off and Laos has several world-class rapids, as well as lots of beautiful, although less challenging, waterways. Unfortunately, the industry remains dangerously unregulated and you should not go out on rapids during the wet season unless you are completely confident of your guides and equipment. Vang Vieng has the most options. **Green Discovery** (☎ 023 511230; www.greendiscoverylaos.com) has a good reputation, as does **Xplore-Asia** (☎ 031 212893; www.xplore-asia.com; Don Det).

Rock Climbing

Organised rock-climbing operations are run by safety-conscious **Green Discovery** (☎ 023 511230; www.greendiscoverylaos.com) in the karst cliffs around Vang Vieng and, on a smaller scale, near Luang Prabang. Vang Vieng has the most established scene, with dozens of climbs ranging from beginner to expert. Climbers have compared the routes and guides here favourably to the climbing at Krabi in Thailand.

Trekking

Where else can you wander through forests past ethnic hill tribes and rare wildlife, the triple canopy towering above you? Several environmentally and culturally sustainable tours allow you to enter these pristine areas and experience the lives of the indigenous people without exploiting them. These treks are available in several provinces and are detailed on www.ecotourismlaos.com. You can trek from Luang Nam Tha, Muang Sing, Udomxai, Luang Prabang, Vientiane, Tha Khaek, Savannakhet and Pakse. Treks organised through the provincial tourism offices are the cheapest, while companies such as **Green Discovery** (☎ 023 511230; www.greendiscoverylaos.com) offer more expensive and professional operations.

Tubing

'Tubing' involves inserting yourself into an enormous tractor inner tube and floating down a river. Vang Vieng, Muang Ngoi Neua and Si Phan Don are all hot spots to do this. Just keep an eye on reefer intake and how much you drink; the two combined can be lethal, especially in the dark if you take a tumble in a rogue current.

BOOKS

Lonely Planet's *Laos* has all the information you'll need for extended travel in Laos. Lonely Planet also publishes the *Lao Phrasebook*, an introduction to the Lao language. Here are a few titles you might read to give you a taste of Laos' past and present history:

A Dragon Apparent (1951) This sees Norman Lewis travelling through the twilight of French Indochina, animating his subjects with atmosphere and pathos, as the colonies are about to be lost.

Another Quiet American (2003) Brett Dakin's account of two years working at the National Tourism Authority of Laos reveals a lot about what drives – or does not drive – people working in Laos, both local and *falang* (Western).

Stalking the Elephant Kings: In Search of Laos (1998) Christopher Kremmer's thoroughly researched book

LAOS

details his pursuit of the truth behind the final demise of the Lao monarchy in the late 1970s; great for history fans.
The Lao (2008) Robert Cooper's locally published book (available in Vientiane) is a pithy yet penetrating insight into Lao culture and its psyche.
The Ravens: Pilots of the Secret War of Laos (1987) Christopher Robbins' page-turning account of the Secret War and the role of American pilots and the Hmong is an excellent read.

BUSINESS HOURS

Government offices are typically open from 8am to noon and 1pm to 4pm, Monday to Friday. Banking hours are generally 8.30am to 4pm Monday to Friday. Shops have longer hours and are often open on weekends. Restaurants typically close by 10pm and bars stay open until around 11.30pm, sometimes later.

CLIMATE

Laos has two distinct seasons: May to October is wet and November to April is dry. The coolest time of year is November to January and the hottest is March to May, when southern Laos becomes almost too hot for the locals. The lowlands of the Mekong River valley are the hottest, peaking at around 38°C in March and April and dropping to a minimum of around 15°C in the cool season. Up in the mountains of Xieng Khuang and Sam Neua, cool-season night-time temperatures can drop to freezing and even in the hot season it can be pleasant.

The wettest area of the country is southern Laos, where the Annamite mountain peaks get more than 3000mm of rain a year. Luang Prabang and Xieng Khuang receive less than half that amount of rain and Vientiane and Savannakhet get from 1500mm to 2000mm.

See the climate charts, p936.

CUSTOMS

Customs inspections at ports of entry are very lax as long as you're not bringing in more than a moderate amount of luggage. You're not supposed to enter the country with more than 500 cigarettes or 1L of distilled spirits. Of course, all the usual prohibitions on drugs, weapons and pornography apply.

DANGERS & ANNOYANCES

Urban Laos is generally safe. You should still exercise vigilance at night, but thanks to the country's comparatively gentle psyche the likelihood of your being robbed, mugged, harassed or assaulted are much lower than in most Western countries. Since the 1975 revolution, there have been occasional shootings by Hmong guerrillas on Rte 13 between Vang Vieng and Luang Prabang, though it seems quiet at the moment with barely any trace of resistance.

While there have been no recent incidents of civil unrest (since the Vientiane bombings in 2003) that have affected tourists, the population of Laos is not entirely peacefully governed by the current administration, so be sure to stay abreast of the political situation before – and while – travelling in Laos.

In the eastern provinces, particularly Xieng Khuang, Salavan and Savannakhet, UXO is a hazard. Never walk off well-used paths.

EMBASSIES & CONSULATES

Australia (Map pp368-9; ☎ 021 413600; www.laos.embassy.gov.au; Th Tha Deua, Ban Phonxai) Also represents nationals of Britain, Canada and New Zealand.
Cambodia (Map pp368-9; ☎ 021 314952; fax 021 314951; Km 3, Th Tha Deua, Ban That Khao) Issues visas for 170,000 kip.
China (Map pp368-9; ☎ 021 315105; fax 021 315104; Th Wat Nak Nyai, Ban Wat Nak) Issues visas in four working days.
France (Map p370; ☎ 021 215258, 215259; www.ambafrance-laos.org; Th Setthathirat, Ban Si Saket)
Germany (Map pp368-9; ☎ 021 312111, 312110; Th Sok Pa Luang)
Myanmar (Burma; pp368-9; ☎ 021 314910; Th Sok Pa Luang) Issues tourist visas in three days for 170,000 kip.
Singapore (Map pp368-9; ☎ (021 416860; Nongbone Rd, Ban Naxay, Unit 12, Saysettha, Vientiane)
Thailand Savannakhet (Map p409; ☎ 041 212373; Th Kuvoravong); Vientiane (Map pp368-9; Th That Luang; 🕑 8am-noon & 1-4.30pm); Vientiane (Map pp368-9; ☎ 021 900238; www.thaiembassy.org/vientiane; Th Phonkheng; 🕑 8.30am-noon & 1-3.30pm Mon-Fri)
USA (Map p370; ☎ 021 267000; http://laos.usembassy.gov; Th That Dam)
Vietnam Savannakhet (Map p409; ☎ 041 212418; Th Sisavangvong); Vientiane (Map pp368-9; ☎ 021 413400; Th That Luang) The embassy in Vientiane issues tourist visas in three working days for 425,000 kip, or in one day for 467,000 kip. The consulate in Savannakhet issues a one-month tourist visa for 382,000 kip, one photo, three working days.

FESTIVALS & EVENTS

Festivals are mostly linked to agricultural seasons or historic Buddhist holidays. Dates change with the lunar calendar and even from village to village, but www.tourismlaos.gov.la has more accurate dates for some major festivals, known as *bun* in Lao.

February

Magha Puja (Makkha Busaa; Full Moon) This is held on the full moon of the third lunar month. It commemorates a speech given by Buddha to 1250 enlightened monks who came to hear him without prior summons. Chanting and offerings mark the festival, culminating in the candlelit circumambulation of wat throughout the country.

Vietnamese Tet-Chinese New Year This is celebrated in Vientiane, Pakse and Savannakhet with parties, deafening nonstop fireworks and visits to Vietnamese and Chinese temples. Chinese- and Vietnamese-run businesses usually close for three days.

April

Pii Mai (Lunar New Year) This festival begins in mid-April (the 15th, 16th and 17th are official public holidays) and practically the entire country comes to a halt and celebrates. Houses are cleaned, people put on new clothes and Buddha images are washed with specially purified water. Later the citizens, their hair dyed red, their faces whitened with talcum powder, take to the streets, drink lots of beer and dowse one another with water. Expect to get very, very wet.

May

Visakha Puja (Visakha Busaa; Full Moon) Falling on the 15th day of the sixth lunar month (usually in May), this is considered the day of the Buddha's birth, enlightenment and *parinibbana* (passing into nirvana).

Bun Bang Fai (Rocket Festival) One of the wildest festivals in Laos, a pre-Buddhist rain ceremony celebrated alongside Visakha Puja, involving huge homemade rockets, music, dance, drunkenness, cross-dressing, large wooden penises and sometimes a few incinerated houses.

July

Khao Phansaa (Khao Watsa; Full Moon) Late July is the beginning of the traditional three-month rains retreat, when Buddhist monks are expected to station themselves in a single monastery.

September/October

Awk Phansaa (Awk Watsa; Full Moon) Celebrating the end of the three-month rains retreat.

Bun Nam (Water Festival) Held in association with Awk Phansaa. Boat races are commonly held in towns on the Mekong, such as Vientiane, Luang Prabang and Savannakhet.

November

That Luang Festival (Bun That Luang; Full Moon) Takes place at Pha That Luang in Vientiane in early November. Hundreds of monks assemble to receive alms and floral votives early in the morning on the first day of the festival. There is a colourful procession between Pha That Luang and Wat Si Muang.

December

Lao National Day Held on 2 December, this public holiday celebrates the 1975 victory of the proletariat over the Royal Lao with parades and speeches.

FOOD & DRINK

Food

Lao cuisine lacks the variety of Thai food and foreigners often limit themselves to a diet of noodles, fried rice and the ubiquitous 'travellers' fare' that has swept Southeast Asia (fruit pancakes, muesli, fruit shakes…) But there are some excellent Lao dishes to try.

The standard Lao breakfast is *fõe* (rice noodles), which are usually served floating in a bland broth with some vegetables and a meat of your choice. The trick is in the seasoning, and Lao people will stir in some fish sauce, lime juice, dried chillies, mint leaves, basil, or one of the wonderful speciality hot chilli sauces that many noodle shops make, testing it along the way, before slurping it down with chopsticks in one hand and a spoon in the other.

Làap is the most distinctively Lao dish, a delicious spicy salad made from minced beef, pork, duck, fish or chicken, mixed with fish sauce, small shallots, mint leaves, lime juice, roasted ground rice and lots of chillies. Another famous Lao speciality is *tạm màak hung* (known as *som tam* in Thailand), a salad of shredded green papaya mixed with garlic, lime juice, fish sauce, sometimes tomatoes, palm sugar, land crab or dried shrimp and, of course, chillies by the handful.

Most Lao food is eaten with *khào níօ* (sticky rice), which is served up in a small wicker container. Take a small amount of rice and, using one hand, work it into a walnut-sized ball before dipping it into the food. When you've finished eating, replace the lid on the container. Less often, food is eaten with *khào jâo* (plain white rice), which is eaten with a fork and spoon.

In rural areas, where hunting is more common than raising animals for food, you're likely to encounter some exotic meat. Apparently these are delicious: wild boar, wild fowl, wild dog and wild squirrel. Monitor lizard and bush rat might take some getting used to.

In main centres, French baguettes are a popular breakfast food. Sometimes they're eaten with condensed milk or with *khai* (eggs) in a sandwich that contains Lao-style pâté and vegetables. When they're fresh, they're superb.

Drink

The Lao Brewery Co produces the ubiquitous and excellent Beer Lao. Despite Tiger Beer's attempts to subtly muscle in, Beer Lao remains a firm favourite with 90% of the nation's beer drinkers, and a source of national pride. Imported beers are also available in cans. Lao Bia – a dark, sweetish palm beer made in Savannakhet – is an interesting brew and is sold mostly around southern and central Laos in small bottles with a distinctly antique-looking label.

Lào-láo (Lao liquor, or rice whisky) is a popular drink among lowland Lao. Strictly speaking, *lào-láo* is not legal but no one seems to care. The government distils its own brand, Sticky Rice, which is of course legal. *Lào-láo* is usually taken neat, sometimes with a plain water chaser.

In a Lao home the pouring and drinking of *lào-láo* takes on ritual characteristics – it is first offered to the house spirits, and guests must take at least one offered drink or risk offending the spirits.

In rural provinces, a weaker version of *lào-láo* known as *lào hái* (jar liquor) is fermented by households or villages. *Lào hái* is usually drunk from a communal jar using long reed straws. It's not always safe to drink, however, since unboiled water is often added to it during and after fermentation.

Water purified for drinking purposes is simply called *nâam deum* (drinking water), whether it's boiled or filtered. All water offered to customers in restaurants or hotels will be purified and bottles of purified water are sold everywhere.

Lao coffee is usually served very strong and sweet enough to make your teeth clench. If you don't want sugar or sweetened condensed milk, ask for *kąa-fáe dąm* (black coffee).

Chinese-style green or semicured tea is the usual ingredient in *nâam sáa* or *sáa láo* – the weak, refreshing tea traditionally served free in restaurants. The black tea familiar to Westerners is usually found in the same places as Lao coffee and is usually referred to as *sáa hâwn* (hot tea).

GAY & LESBIAN TRAVELLERS

Like Thailand, Laos has a very liberal attitude towards homosexuality, but a very conservative attitude to public displays of affection. Gay couples are unlikely to be given frosty treatment anywhere. Unlike Thailand, Laos does not have an obvious gay scene, but in Vientiane's late-night clubs you'll see plenty of young gay Lao whooping it up with everyone else. Luang Prabang boasts Laos' first openly gay bar, Khob Chai, with the rainbow-coloured gay pride flag flying in a few places around town. See p426 for information on relations with Lao nationals.

HOLIDAYS

Aside from government offices, banks and post offices, many Lao businesses do not trouble themselves with weekends and public holidays. Most Chinese- and Vietnamese-run businesses close for three days during Vietnamese Tet and Chinese New Year in February. International Women's Day is a holiday for women only.

International New Year 1 January
Army Day 20 January
International Women's Day 8 March
Lao New Year 14–16 April
International Labour Day 1 May
International Children's Day 1 June
Lao National Day 2 December

INTERNET ACCESS

In Vientiane, Luang Prabang and in most major towns there are plenty of high-speed internet places with rates at a standard 5000 kip per hour. Many internet cafes have Skype (some with cameras) and air-con. In towns where there are only one or two places, or where they need to call long-distance to reach the server, rates will be higher. For wi-fi there are a few places, including JoMa Bakery in Vientiane and Thanaboun Guesthouse in Luang Prabang.

INTERNET RESOURCES

Ecotourism Laos (www.ecotourismlaos.com) Excellent site focusing on trekking and other ecotourism activities. Recommended.

Lao National Tourism Authority (www.tourismlaos.gov.la) Mostly up-to-date travel information from the government.

Stay Another Day (www.stay-another-day.org) Listings of the best things to do in the country, from wildlife to food, shopping and current exhibitions.

Travelfish (www.travelfish.org) The most consistently updated website for independent travellers in Southeast Asia, including excellent coverage of Lao border crossings.
Vientiane Times (www.vientianetimes.org.la) Website of the country's only English-language newspaper. Operated by the government.

LEGAL MATTERS

There is virtually nothing in the way of legal services in Laos. If you get yourself in legal strife, contact your embassy in Vientiane, though the assistance it can provide may be limited. For Brits, contact your embassy in Bangkok or the Australian Embassy.

It's against the law for foreigners and Lao to have sexual relations unless they're married. Be aware that a holiday romance could result in being arrested and deported.

MAPS

An excellent road map of Laos, with city maps of Vientiane, Luang Prabang, Vang Vieng, Muang Sing and Luang Nam Tha, is produced by motorcycle-tour company **Golden Triangle Rider Ltd** (www.gt-rider.com).

MEDIA

The government-run *Vientiane Times* is a bland, censored sketch of improving Sino-Lao relations and reveals very little. The excellent *Paisai? What's On* is much better, offering daily breakdowns of events in the capital as well as sports and embassy listings. French speakers should look for the weekly *Le Rénovateur*. The *Bangkok Post, Economist, Newsweek* and *Time* can also be found in minimarts and bookshops. BBC and CNN are widely available on satellite TV.

MONEY

Increasingly the government is imposing sole use of the national currency and the rejection of the dollar. The same may happen eventually to Thai baht, though given Laos' proximity to and trade with its neighbour this seems unlikely. As such all prices (but for some of the flights) in this chapter have been quoted in kip to make your life a little more straightforward. At the time of research the American dollar was in freefall and yielding only 8500 kip.

ATMs

ATMs are now proliferating (phew) in the main cities: with half a dozen spread around Vientiane, three in Luang Prabang, one in Vang Vieng, one in Luang Nam Tha, one in Phonsavan, one in Udomxai, one in Houay Xai, two in Pakse and one in Savannakhet. You can only withdraw 700,000 kip at a time (about US$80).

EXCHANGE RATES

Exchange rates at the time of press:

Country	Unit	Kip
Australia	A$1	7526
Cambodia	1000r	2038
Canada	C$1	7962
Euro zone	€1	12,469
Japan	¥100	9489
New Zealand	NZ$1	6158
Thailand	10B	2545
UK	UK£1	13,595
USA	US$1	8513
Vietnam	10,000d	4770

Bargaining

With the exception of túk-túk drivers in Vientiane (who are a law to themselves), most Lao are not looking to rip you off – it's not worth losing all that merit they've accrued. Take your time when haggling, smile throughout, start lower and gradually meet in the middle. But keep things in perspective – in remote places where villagers are particularly poor, do you really need to waste half an hour bargaining your room or purchase down that extra 8500 kip?

Credit Cards

A number of hotels, upmarket restaurants and gift shops in Vientiane and Luang Prabang accept Visa and MasterCard and, to a much lesser extent, Amex and JCB. Visa is best. Banque pour le Commerce Extérieur Lao (BCL) branches in Vientiane, Luang Prabang, Vang Vieng, Savannakhet and Pakse offer cash advances/withdrawals on Visa credit/debit cards for a 3% transaction fee.

Exchanging Money

US dollars and Thai baht can be exchanged all over the country. US-dollar travellers cheques can be exchanged in most provincial capitals and attract a better rate than cash. Banks in Vientiane and Luang Prabang change UK pounds, euro, Thai baht, Japanese yen, and Canadian, US and Australian dollars.

The best overall exchange rate is usually offered by BCL. In rural areas exchange rates can be significantly lower. For the latest rates check www.bcel laos.com.

Travellers Cheques

Banks in all provincial centres will exchange US-dollar travellers cheques. If you are changing cheques into kip there is usually no commission, but changing into dollars attracts a minimum 2% charge.

POST

Postal services from Vientiane are painfully slow but generally reliable, the provinces less so. If you have valuable items or presents to post home, there is a **Federal Express** (Map p370; ☎ 021-223278; ⏲ 8am-noon & 1-5pm Mon-Fri, 9am-noon Sat) office inside the main post office compound in Vientiane.

RESPONSIBLE TRAVEL

On the environmental front, rapid economic growth has seen traditional packaging, such as banana leaves, replaced by millions of plastic bags. Try to set a positive example by either not accepting a plastic bag in the first place, or at the least demonstratively putting any bags or other rubbish in a bin. This is one way we can really help the Lao to protect their environment at a grassroots level.

Begging children seldom keep the money they are given and kids grow up with an expectation that survival depends upon handouts; if you want to give something to a child give food or a Big Brother book. On the other hand, the legless beggars you'll see, mostly victims of the Second Indochina War, have mostly fallen through the sizeable gaps in the Lao system and, unable to work, rely almost completely on handouts.

One of the most appealing aspects of Laos has always been the friendly, open nature of the Lao people. However, many of those who work in the tourism business have become jaded in recent years by what they see as unreasonably aggressive bargaining, usually by travellers who lose a little perspective in their pursuit of the cheapest stay possible. By all means try to get the best rate you can – that's part of travelling – but don't stretch your dollar to the point the Lao begin to regard Westerners as hostile and greedy.

Finally, sex tourism is driving a thorn into the country's villages with many young girls being sold into the flesh trade. While Thailand may have lost control of this, Laos hasn't and we should endeavour to help it by not supporting prostitution.

STUDYING

There are no formal opportunities to study in Laos, but if you are passionately keen to learn more about this country, consider setting up your own study exchange, or develop a research topic, through your home university. Short courses in cooking are available in the capital and Luang Prabang (p386) and informal Lao-language lessons are advertised in Vientiane.

TELEPHONE

Laos' country code is ☎ 856. To dial out of the country press ☎ 00 first. As a guide, all mobile phone numbers have the prefix ☎ 020 followed by seven digits, while the newer WIN Phones (fixed phones without a landline) begin with ☎ 030.

Mobile Phones & Phonecards

With recently improved signals, you can use your own GSM mobile phone in Laos, either on roaming (expensive) or by buying a local SIM card for about 45,000 kip, then purchasing prepaid minutes. Domestic calls are reasonably cheap. In our experience, Telecom Lao and ETL have the widest network coverage. Phonecards for domestic calls can be bought at telephone offices and minimarts for use at the increasing number of public phones in provincial towns. The cheapest international calls can be made in internet cafes using a Skype account (www.skype.com).

TOILETS

Unlike Thailand, the hole-in-the-floor toilet is not common. The exception is if you're visiting destinations such as hill-tribe villages.

TOURIST INFORMATION

The Lao National Tourism Authority (NTAL) maintains offices throughout Laos, some better than others. Travel agencies and tour companies like Green Discovery, Diethelm and Lane Xang Travel are also excellent sources of information. Here are three websites useful for information on ecotourism and trekking:

Central Laos Trekking www.trekkingcentrallaos.com
Lao Ecotourism www.ecotourismlaos.com
Lao National Tourism Administration www.tourismlaos.gov.la

TRAVELLERS WITH DISABILITIES

Laos is woefully unprepared for people with physical special needs; however, its main cities such as Vientiane, Savannakhet and Luang Prabang have decent pavements (generally) and disabled toilets in most international hotels. Transport is a no-no with cramped conditions on most buses. If you're planning on a trip to Laos it's worth contacting the hotels in advance to see how well prepared they are.

VISAS

On-the-spot 30-day tourist visas – from US$30 (255,000 kip) to US$42 (360,000 kip) – are available at Vientiane, Luang Prabang and Pakse Airports, as well as at the Thai–Lao Friendship Bridge at Nong Khai, the Thai border at Huay Xai, Savannakhet, Pakse and the Boten border with China in Luang Nam Tha. Bring two passport photos.

Once in Laos it is easy to obtain a visa extension costing 17,000 kip per day from the **Immigration Office** (Map p370; ☎ 021-212250; Th Hatsady; ⏰ 8am-4.30pm Mon-Fri) in Vientiane, up to a maximum of 30 days. Outside Vientiane, travel agents and guest houses can usually arrange extensions for 25,500 kip per day. Your passport will be sent to Vientiane, so it can take a few days. If you overstay your visa, you'll have to pay a fine on departure of 85,000 kip for each day over.

VOLUNTEERING

It's not easy to find short-term volunteer work in Laos. The Organic Mulberry Farm in Vang Vieng (p382) needs volunteers occasionally. If you're professionally skilled as an orthotist, physio or surgeon you may be able to work with the excellent Cope Project in Vientiane (see p373). Finally, if you're in Pakse and have carpentry skills, drop in to Delta Coffee to speak to Alan about building schools in the Bolaven Plateau (see p414).

WOMEN TRAVELLERS

Stories of women being hassled are few – Lao men are more likely to be a little intimidated by you than anything else, as Western women are so physically different from Lao women. Some women have been hassled on overnight bus trips, particularly the bus to Vietnam from Vientiane; the best way to combat this threat is to travel in a group and stay alert.

Remember, you're in a strictly Buddhist country and the revealing of flesh, despite the heat, is seen as cheap, disrespectful and possibly asking for trouble. Sarongs and long-sleeve T-shirts are a good idea, though we realise some places – like the open-air sauna that is Si Phan Don – inhibit this. To Lao people, wearing bikinis is no different than wandering around in your underwear.

WORKING

Compared to other countries in the region, finding work in Laos is relatively simple. There are an inordinate number of development organisations in Laos (160 at last count), where foreigners with skills can find employment; see www.directoryofngos.org for info. The old standby of teaching English is always an option and schools in Vientiane are often hiring. Ask around.

Malaysia

HIGHLIGHTS

- **Pulau Perhentian** (p481) Wake up; swim; lie on beach; nap; snorkel; eat; wander; snooze.
- **Mt Kinabalu** (p497) Hoofing it over pitcher plants and moonscapes for the sunrise atop a looming granite spire.
- **Semporna Archipelago** (p505) Smiling in your scuba mask while backstroking past peaceful turtles, aloof sharks and technicolour coral.
- **Pulau Tioman** (p473) Hopping from one perfect beach village to the next, diving reefs and wrecks and spotting monkeys in the jungle.
- **Taman Negara** (p487) Getting wet, muddy and covered in leeches but loving every swash-buckling minute of it.
- **Pulau Penang** (p461) Gorging on the country's best hawker food, breathing in sinus-tingling incense and exploring Georgetown's rickety alleyways.
- **Off the beaten track** (p523 & p523) Sipping wild teas and crunching pineapple at a wobbly longhouse in Bario and the Kelabit Highlands, then climbing the limestone crags at Gunung Mulu's Pinnacles.

FAST FACTS

- **Budget** US$18 a day
- **Capital** Kuala Lumpur (KL)
- **Costs** dorm bed RM12, two beers RM18, four-hour bus ride RM26
- **Country code** ☎ 60
- **Languages** Bahasa Malaysia (official), Chinese (Hakka and Hokkien dialects), Tamil, English
- **Money** US$1 = RM3.46 (ringgit)
- **Phrases** *selamat pagi* (good morning), *terima kasih* (thank you)
- **Population** 25 million
- **Time** GMT + eight hours
- **Visas** people of most nationalities visiting Malaysia are presented with a 30- to 90-day visa on arrival

TRAVEL HINTS

Malaysia is a Muslim country so dress appropriately by covering everything to the knees and over the shoulders. Airfares can be so cheap around Borneo that flying is sometimes cheaper than bussing.

OVERLAND ROUTES

From Peninsular Malaysia, you can head into Thailand and Singapore. From Sarawak, you can enter Indonesia (Kalimantan) and Brunei. Brunei can also be entered from Sabah.

Malaysia is really like two countries in one, cleaved in half by the South China Sea. The peninsula is a multicultural buffet of Malay, Chinese and Indian flavours while Borneo hosts a wild jungle smorgasbord of orang-utans, granite peaks and remote tribes. Within and throughout these two very different regions are an impressive variety of microcosms ranging from the space-age high-rises of Kuala Lumpur to smiling longhouse villages of Sarawak and the calm, powdery beaches of the Perhentian Islands. And did we mention the food? Malaysia (particularly along the peninsular west coast) has one of the best assortments of delicious cuisines in the world. Start with Chinese–Malay 'Nonya' fare, move on to Indian banana leaf curries, Chinese buffets, spicy Malay food stalls and even some impressive Western food. Yet despite all the pockets of ethnicities, religions, landscapes and the sometimes-great distances between them, the beauty of Malaysia lies in the fusion of it all, into a country that is one of the safest, most stable and easiest to manage in Southeast Asia.

CURRENT EVENTS

In 1970 a 'New Economic Policy' set a target whereby 30% of Malaysia's corporate wealth had to be in the hands of indigenous Malays *(bumiputra)* – as opposed to ethnic Indian and Chinese – within 20 years. Malay companies were heavily favoured for government contracts; low-interest *bumiputra* loans were made easily available; and thousands of Malays were sent abroad on government scholarships. A coalition of the major political parties that backed the *bumiputra* was renamed the Barisan Nasional (BN; National Front), and this party continues to rule Malaysia to this day.

As of 2009 the *bumiputra* laws still stand but many Malaysians argue that they are unfair and racist. Early this year Datuk Nik Aziz Nik Mat, the Chief Minister of Kelantan and an Islamic scholar, was quoted as comparing *bumiputra* to apartheid. Meanwhile, members of the Indian community have been increasingly vocal in demonstrating for Hindu rights and made headlines throughout 2009.

In reality, the position of ethnic Malays in the economy remains more or less the same even after more than 30 years of *bumiputra* and the majority remain poor. After the BN was defeated in Penang in 2008, the state announced that it will no longer favour *bumiputra* in state sector employment. Anwar Ibrahim, leader of the Pakatan Rakyat (PR; People's Alliance) opposition coalition that made sweeping gains against the BN in March 2008, is one of the few big-time politicians who openly advocates scrapping *bumiputra* altogether.

HISTORY

Early Influences

The earliest evidence of human life in the region is a 40,000-year-old skull found in Sarawak's Niah Caves. But it was only around 10,000 years ago that the aboriginal Malays, the Orang Asli (see p432), began moving down the peninsula from a probable starting point in southwestern China.

By the 2nd century AD, Europeans were familiar with Malaya, and Indian traders had made regular visits in their search for gold, tin and jungle woods. Within the next century Malaya was ruled by the Funan empire, centred in what's now Cambodia, but more significant was the domination of the Sumatra-based Srivijayan empire between the 7th and 13th centuries.

In 1405 Chinese admiral Cheng Ho arrived in Melaka with promises to the locals of protection from the Siamese encroaching from the north. With Chinese support, the power of Melaka extended to include most of the Malay Peninsula. Islam arrived in Melaka around this time and soon spread through Malaya.

European Influence

Melaka's wealth and prosperity attracted European interest and it was taken over by the Portuguese in 1511, then the Dutch in 1641 and the British in 1795.

In 1838 James Brooke, a British adventurer, arrived to find the Brunei sultanate fending off rebellion from inland tribes. Brooke quashed the rebellion and in reward was granted power over part of Sarawak. Appointing himself Raja Brooke, he founded a dynasty that lasted 100 years. By 1881 Sabah was controlled by the British government, which eventually acquired Sarawak after WWII when the third Raja Brooke realised he couldn't afford the area's upkeep. In the early 20th century the British brought in Chinese and Indians, which radically changed the country's racial make-up.

Independence to the Current Day

Malaya achieved *merdeka* (independence) in 1957, but it was followed by a period of

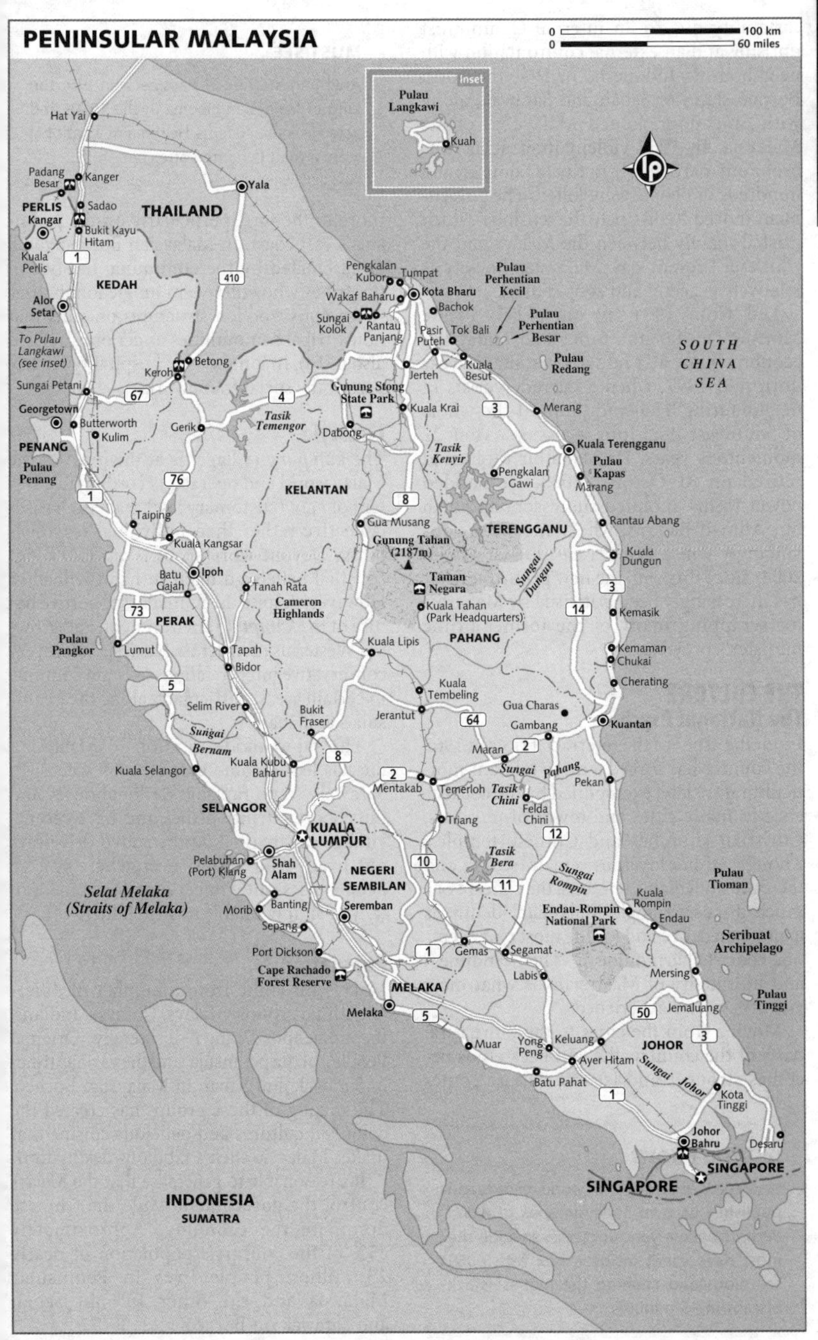
PENINSULAR MALAYSIA
0 100 km
0 60 miles
Inset
Pulau Langkawi
Kuah
THAILAND
Hat Yai
Yala
Padang Besar
Kanger
Sadao
PERLIS
Kangar
Bukit Kayu Hitam
Kuala Perlis
KEDAH
Alor Setar
To Pulau Langkawi (see inset)
Betong
Keroh
Sungai Petani
Georgetown
Butterworth
Kulim
PENANG
Pulau Penang
Gerik
Tasik Temengor
Taiping
Kuala Kangsar
Ipoh
Batu Gajah
PERAK
Pulau Pangkor
Lumut
Tapah
Bidor
Tanah Rata
Cameron Highlands
Selim River
Sungai Bernam
Kuala Selangor
Kuala Kubu Baharu
Bukit Fraser
SELANGOR
KUALA LUMPUR
Pelabuhan (Port) Klang
Shah Alam
Banting
Morib
Sepang
Seremban
NEGERI SEMBILAN
Port Dickson
Cape Rachado Forest Reserve
MELAKA
Melaka
Selat Melaka (Straits of Melaka)
INDONESIA
SUMATRA
Pengkalan Kubor
Tumpat
Kota Bharu
Wakaf Baharu
Bachok
Sungai Kolok
Rantau Panjang
Pasir Puteh
Tok Bali
Jerteh
Kuala Besut
Gunung Stong State Park
Dabong
Kuala Krai
KELANTAN
Gua Musang
Gunung Tahan (2187m)
Taman Negara
Kuala Tahan (Park Headquarters)
Kuala Lipis
Kuala Tembeling
Jerantut
Mentakab
Temerloh
Triang
PAHANG
Pulau Perhentian Kecil
Pulau Perhentian Besar
Pulau Redang
SOUTH CHINA SEA
Merang
Kuala Terengganu
Tasik Kenyir
Pengkalan Gawi
Pulau Kapas
Marang
Rantau Abang
TERENGGANU
Kuala Dungun
Sungai Dungun
Kemasik
Kemaman
Chukai
Cherating
Gua Charas
Kuantan
Gambang
Maran
Sungai Pahang
Pekan
Tasik Chini
Felda Chini
Tasik Bera
Sungai Rompin
Kuala Rompin
Endau
Endau-Rompin National Park
Pulau Tioman
Seribuat Archipelago
Gemas
Segamat
Labis
Mersing
Jemaluang
Pulau Tinggi
Muar
Yong Peng
Keluang
Ayer Hitam
Batu Pahat
JOHOR
Sungai Johor
Kota Tinggi
Johor Bahru
Desaru
SINGAPORE
1
410
67
4
76
73
5
8
3
14
64
2
10
11
12
50

instability due to an internal Communist uprising and an external confrontation with neighbouring Indonesia. In 1963 the north Borneo states of Sabah and Sarawak, along with Singapore, joined Malaya to create Malaysia. In 1969 violent interracial riots broke out, particularly in Kuala Lumpur, and hundreds of people were killed. The government moved to dissipate the tensions, which existed mainly between the Malays and the Chinese. Present-day Malaysian society is relatively peaceful and cooperative.

Led from 1981 by outspoken Prime Minister Dr Mahathir Mohamad, Malaysia's economy grew at a rate of over 8% per year until mid-1997, when a currency crisis in neighbouring Thailand plunged the whole of Southeast Asia into recession. After 22 momentous years, Dr Mahathir Mohamad retired on 31 October 2003. He handed power to his anointed successor, Abdullah bin Ahmad Badawi, who went on to convincingly win a general election in March 2004. Since this win, the new prime minister has increasingly been criticised by Mahathir for scrapping many of the former prime minister's projects.

THE CULTURE

The National Psyche

From the ashes of the interracial riots of 1969 the country has forged a more tolerant multicultural society, exemplified by the coexistence in many cities and towns of mosques, Christian churches and Chinese temples. Though ethnic loyalties remain strong and there are undeniable tensions, the concept of a much-discussed single 'Malaysian' identity is gaining credence and for the most part everyone coexists harmoniously. The friendliness and hospitality of Malaysians is what most visitors see and experience.

Moving from the cities to the more rural parts of the country, the laid-back ethos becomes stronger and Islamic culture comes more to the fore, particularly on the peninsula's east coast. In Malaysian Borneo you'll be fascinated by the communal lifestyle of the tribes who still live in jungle longhouses (enormous wooden structures on stilts that house tribal communities under one roof; see also p518). In longhouses, hospitality is a key part of the social framework.

DID YOU KNOW?

Malaysia is obsessed with world records and publishes its own *Malaysia Book of World Records* once a year. Successes include the most days spent inside a box with 6069 scorpions and creating the highest stack of cans in 15 minutes.

MUST SEE

Anything starring P Ramlee who was the king of Malaysian cinema in the 1950s and acted in some 70 films. He remains a national icon; a road is named after him in KL.

Lifestyle

The *kampung* (village) is at the heart of the Malay world and operates according to a system of *adat* (customary law) that emphasises collective rather than individual responsibility. Devout worship of Islam and older spiritual beliefs go hand in hand with this. However, despite the mutually supportive nature of the *kampung* environment, and growing Westernisation across Malaysia, some very conservative interpretations of Islam continue in certain areas, particularly along the peninsula's east coast.

The rapid modernisation of Malaysian life has led to some incongruous scenes. In Sarawak, some ramshackle longhouses and huts sport satellite dishes and have recent-vintage cars parked on the rutted driveways out front. And almost everywhere you go people incessantly finger mobile phones as if they're simply unable to switch them off.

Population

Malaysians come from a number of different ethnic groups: Malays, Chinese, Indians, the indigenous Orang Asli (literally, 'Original People') of the peninsula, and the various tribes of Sarawak and Sabah in Malaysian Borneo. The mixing of these groups has created the colourful cultures and delicious cuisine that makes Malaysia such a fabulous destination.

It's reasonable to generalise that the Malays control the government while the Chinese dominate the economy. Approximately 85% of the country's population of nearly 25 million people lives in Peninsular Malaysia and the other 15% in Sabah and Sarawak on Borneo.

THE PERANAKANS

One of Peninsular Malaysia's most celebrated cultures is that of the Peranakans, descendants of Chinese immigrants who, from the 16th century onwards, settled in Singapore, Melaka and Penang. While these arrivals often married Malay women others imported their wives from China; all of them like to refer to themselves as Straits-born or Straits Chinese to distinguish themselves from later arrivals from China. Another name you may hear for these people is Baba-Nonyas, after the Peranakan words for males *(baba)* and females *(nonya)*.

The Peranakans took the religion of the Chinese, but the customs, language and dress of the Malays. The Peranakans were often wealthy traders who could afford to indulge their passion for sumptuous furnishings, jewellery and brocades. Today they are most famous for their delicious fusion cooking that's best experienced in Melaka (see p453).

There are still small, scattered groups of Orang Asli in Peninsular Malaysia. Although most of these people have given up their nomadic or shifting-agriculture techniques and have been absorbed into modern Malay society, a few such groups still live in the forests.

Dayak is the term used for the non-Muslim people of Borneo. It is estimated there are morc than 200 Dayak tribes in Borneo, including the Iban and Bidayuh in Sarawak and the Kadazan in Sabah. Smaller groups include the Kenyah, Kayan and Penan, whose way of life and traditional lands are rapidly disappearing.

RELIGION

The Malays are almost all Muslims. But despite Islam being the state religion, freedom of religion is guaranteed. The Chinese are predominantly followers of Taoism and Buddhism, though some are Christians. The majority of the region's Indian population comes from the south of India and are Hindu and Christian, although a sizeable percentage are Muslim.

While Christianity has made no great inroads into Peninsular Malaysia, it has had a much greater impact in Malaysian Borneo, where many indigenous people have been converted and carry Christian as well as traditional names. Others still follow animist traditions.

MUST READ

The Harmony Silk Factory, by Malaysian author Tash Aw, is set deep in the heart of Peninsular Malaysia partly during WWII and won the 2005 Whitbread First Novel award.

ARTS

It's along the predominantly Malay east coast of Peninsular Malaysia that you'll find Malay arts and crafts, culture and games at their liveliest. Malaysian Borneo is replete with the arts and crafts of the country's indigenous peoples.

Arts & Crafts

A famous Malaysian Bornean art is *pua kumbu*, a colourful weaving technique used to produce both everyday and ceremonial items.

The most skilled woodcarvers are generally held to be the Kenyah and Kayan peoples, who used to carve enormous, finely detailed *kelirieng* (burial columns) from tree trunks.

Originally an Indonesian craft, the production of batik cloth is popular in Malaysia and has its home in Kelantan. A speciality of Kelantan and Terengganu, *kain songket* is a handwoven fabric with gold and silver threads through the material. *Mengkuang* is a far more prosaic form of weaving using pandanus leaves and strips of bamboo to make baskets, bags and mats.

Dance

Menora is a dance-drama of Thai origin performed by an all-male cast dressed in grotesque masks; *mak yong* is the female version. The upbeat *joget* (better known around Melaka as *chakuncha*) is Malaysia's most popular traditional dance, often performed at Malay weddings by professional dancers.

Rebana kercing is a dance performed by young men to the accompaniment of tambourines. The *rodat* is a dance from Terengganu and is accompanied by the *tar* drum.

Music

Traditional Malay music is based largely on the *gendang* (drum), of which there are more

ARTS WEB TIP

The best source of information on what's currently going on in the Malaysian arts scene is www.kakiseni.com.

than a dozen types. Other percussion instruments include the gong, *cerucap* (made of shells), *raurau* (coconut shells), *kertuk* and *pertuang* (both made from bamboo), and the wooden *celampang*.

Wind instruments include a number of types of flute (such as the *seruling* and *serunai*) and the trumpet-like *nafiri*, while stringed instruments include the *biola*, *gambus* and *sundatang*.

The *gamelan*, a traditional Indonesian gong-orchestra, is also found in the state of Kelantan, where a typical ensemble will comprise four different gongs, two xylophones and a large drum.

ENVIRONMENT

The Land

Malaysia covers 329,758 sq km and consists of two distinct regions. Peninsular Malaysia is the long finger of land extending south from Asia and though the mountainous northern half has some dense jungle coverage, unprotected forests are getting cut down at an alarming rate, mostly to create palm oil plantations. The peninsula's western side has a large fertile plain running to the sea, while the eastern side is fringed with sandy beaches. Malaysian Borneo consists of Sarawak and Sabah; both states are covered in thick jungle and have extensive river systems. Sabah is crowned by Mt Kinabalu (4095m), the highest mountain between the Himalayas and New Guinea.

Wildlife

Malaysia's ancient rainforests are endowed with a cornucopia of life forms. In Peninsular Malaysia alone there are over 8000 species of flowering plants, including the world's tallest tropical tree species, the *tualang*. In Malaysian Borneo, where hundreds of new species have been discovered since the 1990s, you'll find the world's largest flower, the rafflesia, measuring up to 1m across, as well as the world's biggest cockroach. Mammals include elephants, rhinos (extremely rare), tapirs, tigers, leopards, honey bears, *tempadau* (forest cattle), gibbons and monkeys (including, in Borneo, the bizarre proboscis monkey), orang-utans and *pangolins* (scaly anteaters). Bird species include spectacular pheasants, sacred hornbills and many groups of colourful birds such as kingfishers, sunbirds, woodpeckers and barbets. Snakes include cobras, vipers and pythons. Once a favourite nesting ground for leatherback turtles, recorded landings now hover around 10 per year.

National Parks

Malaysia's 19 national parks cover barely 5% of the country's landmass. The country's major national park is Taman Negara, on the peninsula, while Gunung Mulu and Kinabalu are the two main parks in Sarawak and Sabah respectively. Especially on Borneo, the rarity and uniqueness of local flora and fauna is such that scientists – from dragonfly experts to palm-tree specialists – are regular visitors and vocal proponents of new parks and reserves both on land and in the surrounding waters. There are also 13 marine parks in Malaysia, notably around Pulau Perhentian, Tioman and Sipadan, although enforcement of protection measures is very loose.

Environmental Issues

When it comes to environmental faux pas, Malaysia has done it all. Logging is believed to have destroyed more than 60% of the country's rainforests and generates some US$4.5 billion per year for big business. Another growing phenomenon is palm-tree plantations, where vast swathes of land are razed and planted with trees that yield lucrative palm oil. But the crown of eco and social irresponsibility goes to the construction of the controversial Bakun Dam in Sarawak, scheduled to become Southeast Asia's biggest dam, at the time of writing expected to be completed by 2010. The dam will drown approximately 700 sq km of virgin rainforest and will have forced up to 10,000 indigenous people from their homes. In equally bad environmental news, much of the power generated at Bakun looks likely to go to a giant aluminium smelter in Sarawak.

Responsible ecotourism is the traveller's best weapon in a country where cold cash is fiercer than tigers; see p530 for more information.

TRANSPORT

GETTING THERE & AWAY

Air

The gateway to Peninsular Malaysia is the city of Kuala Lumpur, although Pulau Penang and Johor Bahru (JB) also have international connections. Singapore is a handy arrival/departure point, since it's just a short trip across the Causeway from JB. Malaysia Airlines is the country's main airline carrier although Air Asia and Firefly flights are much cheaper. Air Asia connects KL to Europe, Australia, India, Indonesia, Thailand and China.

The following are some airlines servicing Malaysia; numbers beginning with ☎ 03 are for Kuala Lumpur.

Air Asia (code AK; ☎ 03-8775 4000; www.airasia.com)
Air India (code AI; ☎ 03-2142 0166; www.airindia.com)
British Airways (code BA; ☎ 1800 881 260; www.britishairways.com)
Cathay Pacific Airways (code CX; ☎ 03-2035 2788; www.cathaypacific.com)
China Airlines (code CI; ☎ 03-2142 7344; www.china-airlines.com)
Garuda Indonesian Airlines (code GA; ☎ 03-2162 2811; www.garuda-indonesia.com)
Japan Airlines (code JL; ☎ 03-2161 1722; www.jal.com)
Lufthansa (code LH; ☎ 03-2161 4666; www.lufthansa.com)
Malaysia Airlines (code MH; ☎ 1300 883 000, 03-2161 0555; www.malaysiaairlines.com)
Qantas (code QF; ☎ 1800 881 260; www.qantas.com)
Royal Brunei Airlines (code BI; ☎ 03-2070 7166; www.bruneiair.com)
Singapore Airlines (code SQ; ☎ 03-2692 3122; www.singaporeair.com)
Thai Airways International (code TG; ☎ 03-2031 2900; www.thaiairways.com)
Vietnam Airlines (code VN; www.vietnamairlines.com)

BRUNEI

Malaysia Airlines and Air Asia have direct flights between Bandar Seri Begawan and KL.

CAMBODIA

Flights between KL and Phnom Penh are available with Malaysia Airlines, Air Asia and Royal Khmer Airways. Air Asia also flies from KL to Siem Reap.

> **DEPARTURE TAX**
>
> The RM40 airport departure tax is always included in the ticket price.

INDONESIA

Air Asia and Firefly have connections between KL and 15 destinations in Indonesia between them. **Kartika Airlines** (www.kartika-airlines.com) flies between Medan in Sumatra and Penang.

From Kuching **Batavia Air** (www.batavia-air.co.id) flies to Pontianak.

PHILIPPINES

You can fly with Malaysia Airlines, Philippine Airlines or Air Asia from KL to Cebu/Manila. Air Asia also has flights to Manila from Kota Kinabalu.

SINGAPORE

Air Asia, Firefly, Malaysia Airlines and Singapore Airlines operate frequent flights between Singapore and KL as well as several other destinations in Malaysia.

THAILAND

Air Asia has flights from Bangkok and 11 other Thai cities to KL. Firefly connects KL (Subang) with Koh Samui and Phuket as well as Penang with Phuket.

VIETNAM

Malaysia Airlines and Vietnam Airlines operate flights from KL to Ho Chi Minh City and Hanoi. Air Asia runs flights from KL to Hanoi.

Land

BRUNEI

You can catch buses from Miri in Sarawak and Kota Kinabalu in Sabah to Brunei. You can also cross from Lawas to Bangar (in Brunei), and then head on to Limbang. See p508 for more details on both crossings.

INDONESIA

Buses run between Pontianak in Kalimantan and Kuching and Miri in Sarawak, and Kota Kinabulu in Sabah. The buses cross at the Tebedu/Entikong border (see p511)

SINGAPORE

At the southern tip of Peninsular Malaysia you can cross into Singapore via Johor Bahru by bus (see p472). Taking the train from JB is less convenient.

THAILAND

From western Peninsular Malaysia, you can travel by bus from Alor Setar to the border crossing at Bukit Kayu Hitam (p469) and on to the transit town of Hat Yai in Thailand, via Sadao. There are trains passing through Alor Setar to Padang Besar and then continuing north into Thailand (see p469).

Though there is a border crossing at Rantau Panjang on the eastern peninsula that is geographically convenient to Kota Bharu, all travel through this section of southern Thailand should be avoided until the security situation vastly improves; see p485 for border-crossing information.

There is also a border crossing between Keroh (Malaysia) and Betong (Thailand), but at the time of writing it was inadvisable to travel here due to the violence in Yala Province, Thailand (see p805).

Sea

There are no services connecting the peninsula with Malaysian Borneo.

BRUNEI

Boats connect Brunei to Lawas and Limbang in Sarawak, and to Pulau Labuan, from where boats go to Sabah. With the exception of speedboats for Limbang, all international boats depart from Muara, 25km northeast of Bandar Seri Begawan.

See p53 for more information and details on boat services.

INDONESIA

The following are the main ferry routes between Indonesia and Malaysia:

- Pulau Bengkalis, Sumatra to Melaka (see p455)
- Dumai, Sumatra to Melaka (see p455)
- Medan, Sumatra to Pulau Penang (see p467)
- Pekanbaru, Sumatra to Melaka (see p455)
- Tanjung Pinang on Pulau Bintan (Riau Islands) to JB (p472)
- Pulau Batam (Riau Islands) to JB (p472)
- Tarakan, Kalimantan to Tawau (see p320).

THAILAND

Regular ferries run between Pulau Langkawi and Satun in Thailand and to Ko Lipe in Thailand with onward service as far as Ko Lanta (see p471).

GETTING AROUND

Air

The main domestic operators are **Malaysia Airlines** (code MAS; ☎ 1300 883 000, outside Malaysia 03-2161 0555; www.malaysia-airlines.com.my), MAS subsidiary **Firefly** (☎ 03-7845 4543; www.fireflyz.com.my) and **Air Asia** (☎ 1300 889 933, outside Malaysia 603 8660 4343; www.aira sia.com).

Berjaya Air (☎ 03-7847 8228; www.berjaya-air.com) flies between KL (Subang), Pulau Tioman, Pulau Pangkor and Pulau Redang, as well as Singapore and Koh Samui in Thailand.

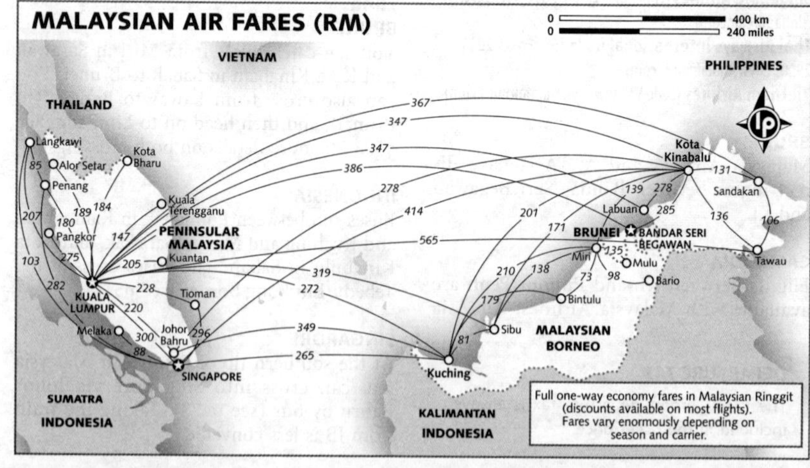

In Malaysian Borneo, **MASwings** (☎ 1300 883 000, outside Malaysia 03-7843 3000; www.maswings.com.my) offers local flights within and between Sarawak and Sabah. These services are very much reliant on the vagaries of the weather and book up during school holidays.

Bicycle

The main road system in Malaysia has good surfaces, making the country good for bike touring, but the secondary road system is limited. Mountain bikes are recommended for forays off the beaten track.

KL Bike Hash (www.bikehash.freeservers.com) has a whole load of useful information and links to other cycling-connected sites in Malaysia. Also see **David's Cycling Adventure** (www.bicycletouringmalaysia.com).

Boat

There are no ferry services between Malaysian Borneo and the peninsula. On a local level, there are boats and ferries between the peninsula and offshore islands, and along the rivers of Sabah and Sarawak – see the relevant sections for details. If a boat looks overloaded or otherwise unsafe, do not board it.

Bus

Peninsular Malaysia has an excellent bus system. Public buses do local runs and a variety of privately operated buses generally handle the longer trips. In larger towns there may be several bus stations. Local and regional buses often operate from one station and long-distance buses from another; in other cases, KL for example, bus stations are differentiated by the destinations they serve.

Buses are economical and comfortable, and on major runs you can usually just turn up and get on the next bus. On many routes there are air-conditioned buses, which usually cost just a few ringgit more than regular buses – but take your arctic gear, the air-con is usually pumped up to the max! *Ekspres,* in the Malaysian context, often means indeterminate stops.

In Sabah, daily express buses follow the paved arc from Kota Kinabalu to Tawau, passing most of the tourism hotspots. Circling back to Kota Kinabalu through the south is a more difficult task, as there's no public bus. It's important to note that many of Sabah's natural gems are managed by private organisations, so you may find yourself on a tour more times than not.

Travel by road in Sarawak is generally good, and the road from Kuching to the Brunei border is surfaced all the way. Express buses ply the Kuching–Brunei route all the time, although it should be noted that the boat ride from Kuching to Sibu is significantly faster than the bus route (see p513 for details).

Car & Motorcycle

Roads in Malaysia are generally high quality and driving standards aren't too hair-raising. Road rules are basically the same as in Britain and Australia. Driving in KL and some of the bigger cities can be a nightmare, however, and you'll always have to keep an eye out for motorcyclists and animals. Cars are right-hand drive and you drive on the left side of the road. The speed limit is officially 110km per hour.

Unlimited-distance car-rental rates cost from around RM176/1155per day/week, including insurance and collision-damage waiver.

Be aware that insurance companies will most likely wash their hands of you if you injure yourself driving a motorcycle without a licence.

Hitching

Malaysia has long had a reputation for being an excellent place to hitchhike but, with the ease of bus travel, most travellers don't bother. On the west coast hitching is quite easy but it's not possible on the main *lebuhraya* (highway). On the east coast traffic is lighter and there may be long waits between rides. Of course hitching is never entirely safe and you do so at your own risk.

Local Transport

Local transport varies but almost always includes local buses and taxis. In a few Peninsular Malaysian towns there are also bicycle rickshaws but in general these are dying out. The best towns for rickshaws are Georgetown and Melaka.

In the bigger cities across Malaysian Borneo you'll find taxis, buses and minibuses. Once you're out of the big cities, though, you're basically on your own and must either walk or hitch. If you're really in the bush your alternatives are riverboats, aeroplanes or lengthy jungle treks.

Taxi

For metered taxis rates are as follows: flagfall (first 2km) is RM2; 10 sen for each 200m or 45 seconds thereafter; 20 sen for each additional passenger over two passengers; RM1 for each piece of luggage in the boot (trunk); plus 50% of everything between midnight and 6am. Drivers are legally required to use meters if they exist – you can try insisting that they do so, but more often than not you'll just have to negotiate the fare before you get in.

Compared to buses, long-distance (or share) taxis are expensive. The taxis work on fixed fares for the entire car and will only head off when a full complement of passengers (usually four people) turns up. Between major towns you'll have a reasonable chance of finding other passengers without having to wait around too long; otherwise, you'll probably have to charter a whole taxi.

Train

Malaysia's privatised national railway company is **Keretapi Tanah Melayu** (KTM; ☎ 03-2267 1200; www.ktmb.com.my). It runs a modern, comfortable and economical railway service, although there are basically only two lines and for the most part services are slow.

One line runs up the west coast from Singapore, through KL, Butterworth and on into Thailand. The other branches off from this line at Gemas and runs through Kuala Lipis up to the northeastern corner of the country near Kota Bharu in Kelantan. Often referred to as the 'Jungle Railway', this line is properly known as the 'East Coast Railway'.

In Sabah on Borneo there is the **North Borneo Railway** (www.northborneorailway.com.my), a narrow-gauge railway line that runs from Kota Kinabalu south to Beaufort and then through Sungai Pegas gorge to Tenom. This line is closed.

There are two main types of rail services: express and local trains. Express trains are air-conditioned and have 'premier' (1st class), 'superior' (2nd class) and sometimes 'economy' seats (3rd class). Similarly on overnight trains you'll find 'premier night deluxe' cabins (upper/lower berth RM50/70 extra), 'premier night standard' cabins (RM18/26), and 'standard night' cabins (RM12/17). Local trains are usually economy class only, but some have superior seats. Express trains stop only at main stations, while local services stop everywhere, including the middle of the jungle.

KTM offers a Tourist Railpass for five days (adult/child US$35/18), 10 days (US$55/28) and 15 days (US$70/35). This pass entitles the holder to unlimited travel on any class of train but does not include sleeping-berth charges on night express services. Railpasses are available only to foreigners and can be purchased at Sentral KL, JB, Butterworth, Port Klang, Padang Besar, Wakaf Baharu and Penang train stations, as well as at Singapore station.

KUALA LUMPUR

☎ 03 / pop 1.5 million

Kuala Lumpur's metamorphosis from a jungle hovel of tin prospectors to a gleaming 21st-century city of high-rises and highways seems like a triumph of man over nature. However, peer down on KL (as it's commonly known) from the bird's-eye height of Menara KL and it's clear that nature continues to fight back: this remains one of the greenest cities in Southeast Asia and is all the better for it.

The cream of Malaysian creativity can be experienced here in the traditional crafts and cutting-edge art, design and fashion that can be found in the city's abundant malls and markets. Each ethnic community brings something to the table – most importantly in the form of cuisine – making eating the standout experience in this urban star.

ORIENTATION

Merdeka Sq is the traditional heart of KL. Southeast across the river, the banking district merges into Chinatown, popular with travellers for its budget accommodation and lively night market.

East of Merdeka Sq is Masjid Jamek, at the intersection of the Star and Putra Light Rail

KL SCAMS

Like any big city Kuala Lumpur has its share of rip-off artists. A popular con is some friendly person asking you where you come from, then going on to lament that a relative studying abroad needs money to continue their studies. Even more creative is a clutch of Buddhist monk impersonators who hang out around Jln Sultan Ismail in the Golden Triangle – they'll offer you a 'free' good luck charm, then expect you to pay a big donation.

GETTING INTO TOWN

The efficient KLIA Ekspres (adult one way/return RM35/70, 28 minutes, every 15 to 20 minutes from 5am to 1am) spirits you to/from the international airport (KLIA) to the KL City Air Terminal, located in KL Sentral train station. This is without doubt the easiest way to travel to/from the airport.

If you have more time than money, catch the **Airport Coach** (☎ 8787 3894; www.airportcoach.com.my; one way/return RM10/18) to KL Sentral (one hour); it can also take you onwards to any central KL hotel from KLIA and pick up for the return journey for a total of round-trip RM25. The bus stand is clearly signposted inside the terminal.

Taxis from KLIA operate on a fixed-fare coupon system. Purchase a coupon from a counter at the arrival hall and use it to pay the driver. Standard taxis cost RM67.

Transit (LRT) lines. Jln Tun Perak, a major trunk road, leads east to the long-distance transport hub of the country, the Puduraya bus station.

To the east of Puduraya bus station, around Jln Sultan Ismail, the Golden Triangle is the modern, upmarket heart of the new KL.

The transport hub KL Sentral station (which holds the KL City Air Terminal, from where you catch the KLIA Ekspres to the international airport) is in the Brickfields area, southwest of the centre.

INFORMATION

Bookshops

Kinokuniya (Map pp440-1; ☎ 2164 8133; 4th fl, Suria KLCC Shopping Complex)

MPH Bookstores (Map p444; ☎ 2142 8231; ground fl, BB Plaza, Jln Bukit Bintang) Also a branch at Mid Valley Megamall (off Map pp440-1).

Emergency

Fire (☎ 994)

Police & ambulance (☎ 999)

Immigration Offices

Immigration Office (off Map pp440-1; ☎ 2095 5077; Block I, Pusat Bandar Damansara) It's 2km west of the Lake Gardens; handles visa extensions.

Internet Access

Internet cafes are everywhere; the going rate per hour is RM3. Hundreds of cafes, restaurants, bars and several hotels have free wi-fi; sign up for an account with **Wireless@KL** (www.wirelesskl.com), which has 1500 hot spots around the city.

Media

KLue (www.klue.com.my; RM5) is an excellent local-listings magazine, with features about what's going on in and around the city.

Medical Services

Hospital Kuala Lumpur (Map pp440-1; ☎ 2615 5555; www.hkl.gov.my; Jln Pahang)

Twin Towers Medical Centre (Map pp440-1; ☎ 2382 3500; Lot 401 F&G, 4th fl, Suria KLCC Shopping Complex)

Money

You'll seldom be far from a bank or ATM. Money changers offer better rates than banks for changing cash and (at times) travellers cheques; they are usually open later hours and on weekends and are found in shopping malls.

Post

Main post office (Map p442; Jln Raja Laut; ⏲ 8.30am-6pm Mon-Sat) The office is closed on the first Saturday of the month.

Telephone

Many internet cafes offer competitive Net-phone and fax services.

Telekom Malaysia (Map p442; Jln Raja Chulan; ⏲ 8.30am-4.30pm Mon-Fri, to 12.30pm Sat) You can make international calls and send faxes.

Tourist Information

Malaysian Tourist Centre (MaTiC; Map pp440-1; ☎ 9235 4900; www.mtc.gov.my; 109 Jln Ampang; ⏲ 8am-10pm) Almost a tourist attraction in its own right, this is Kuala Lumpur's most useful tourist information office. It also hosts good cultural performances (see p448).

Tourism Malaysia (www.tourismmalaysia.gov.my) KL Sentral (Map pp440-1; ☎ 2274 5823; ⏲ 9am-6pm); Kuala Lumpur International Airport (KLIA; ☎ 8776 5651; International Arrival Hall, Sepang); Putra World Trade Centre (Map pp440-1; ☎ 2615 8188; Level 17, 45 Jln Tun Ismail; ⏲ 9am-6pm Mon-Sat)

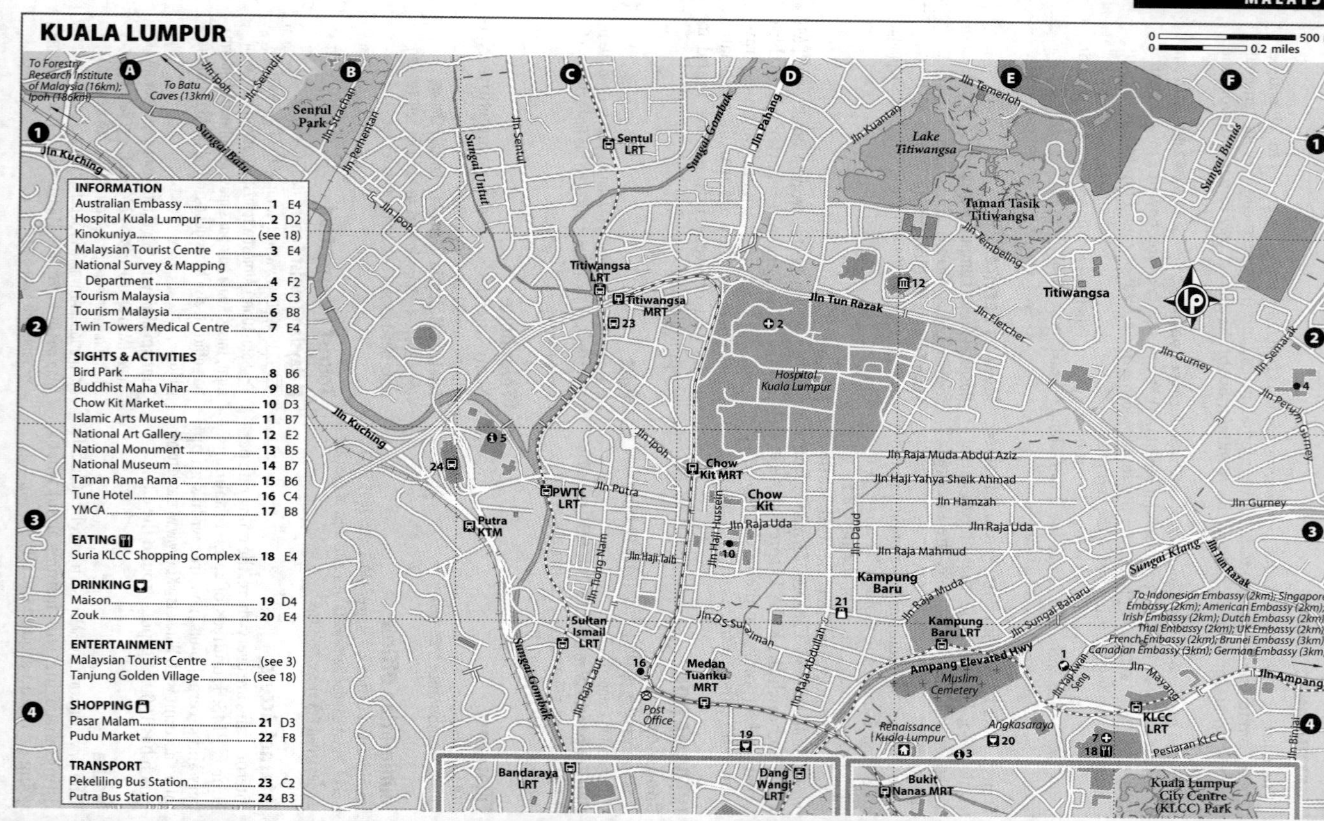
KUALA LUMPUR
0 500 m
0 0.2 miles
INFORMATION
Australian Embassy 1 E4
Hospital Kuala Lumpur 2 D2
Kinokuniya (see 18)
Malaysian Tourist Centre 3 E4
National Survey & Mapping Department 4 F2
Tourism Malaysia 5 C3
Tourism Malaysia 6 B8
Twin Towers Medical Centre 7 E4
SIGHTS & ACTIVITIES
Bird Park 8 B6
Buddhist Maha Vihar 9 B8
Chow Kit Market 10 D3
Islamic Arts Museum 11 B7
National Art Gallery 12 E2
National Monument 13 B5
National Museum 14 B7
Taman Rama Rama 15 B6
Tune Hotel 16 C4
YMCA 17 B8
EATING
Suria KLCC Shopping Complex 18 E4
DRINKING
Maison 19 D4
Zouk 20 E4
ENTERTAINMENT
Malaysian Tourist Centre (see 3)
Tanjung Golden Village (see 18)
SHOPPING
Pasar Malam 21 D3
Pudu Market 22 F8
TRANSPORT
Pekeliling Bus Station 23 C2
Putra Bus Station 24 B3
To Forestry Research Institute of Malaysia (16km); Ipoh (186km)
To Batu Caves (13km)
Sentul Park
Lake Titiwangsa
Taman Tasik Titiwangsa
Titiwangsa
Sentul LRT
Titiwangsa LRT
Titiwangsa MRT
Chow Kit MRT
Chow Kit
Hospital Kuala Lumpur
Kampung Baru
Kampung Baru LRT
PWTC LRT
Putra KTM
Sultan Ismail LRT
Medan Tuanku MRT
Post Office
Dang Wangi LRT
Bandaraya LRT
Bukit Nanas MRT
KLCC LRT
Kuala Lumpur City Centre (KLCC) Park
Muslim Cemetery
Renaissance Kuala Lumpur
Ampang Elevated Hwy
To Indonesian Embassy (2km); Singapore Embassy (2km); American Embassy (2km); Irish Embassy (2km); Dutch Embassy (2km); Thai Embassy (2km); UK Embassy (2km); French Embassy (2km); Brunei Embassy (3km); Canadian Embassy (3km); German Embassy (3km)
Jln Tun Razak
Jln Pahang
Jln Ipoh
Jln Kuching
Jln Sentul
Jln Putra
Jln Raja Laut
Jln Tiong Nam
Jln Haji Taib
Jln Haji Hussein
Jln Raja Uda
Jln Raja Muda Abdul Aziz
Jln Haji Yahya Sheik Ahmad
Jln Hamzah
Jln Raja Mahmud
Jln Raja Muda
Jln Daud
Jln Raja Abdullah
Jln DS Sulaiman
Jln Gurney
Jln Perumahan Gurney
Jln Semarak
Jln Fletcher
Jln Tembeling
Jln Temerloh
Jln Kuantan
Jln Perhentian
Jln Strachan
Jln Sungai Baharu
Jln Yap Kwan Seng
Jln Ampang
Jln Mayang
Jln Binjai
Pesiaran KLCC
Angkasaraya
Sungai Gombak
Sungai Klang
Sungai Bunus
Sungai Untut
Sungai Batu

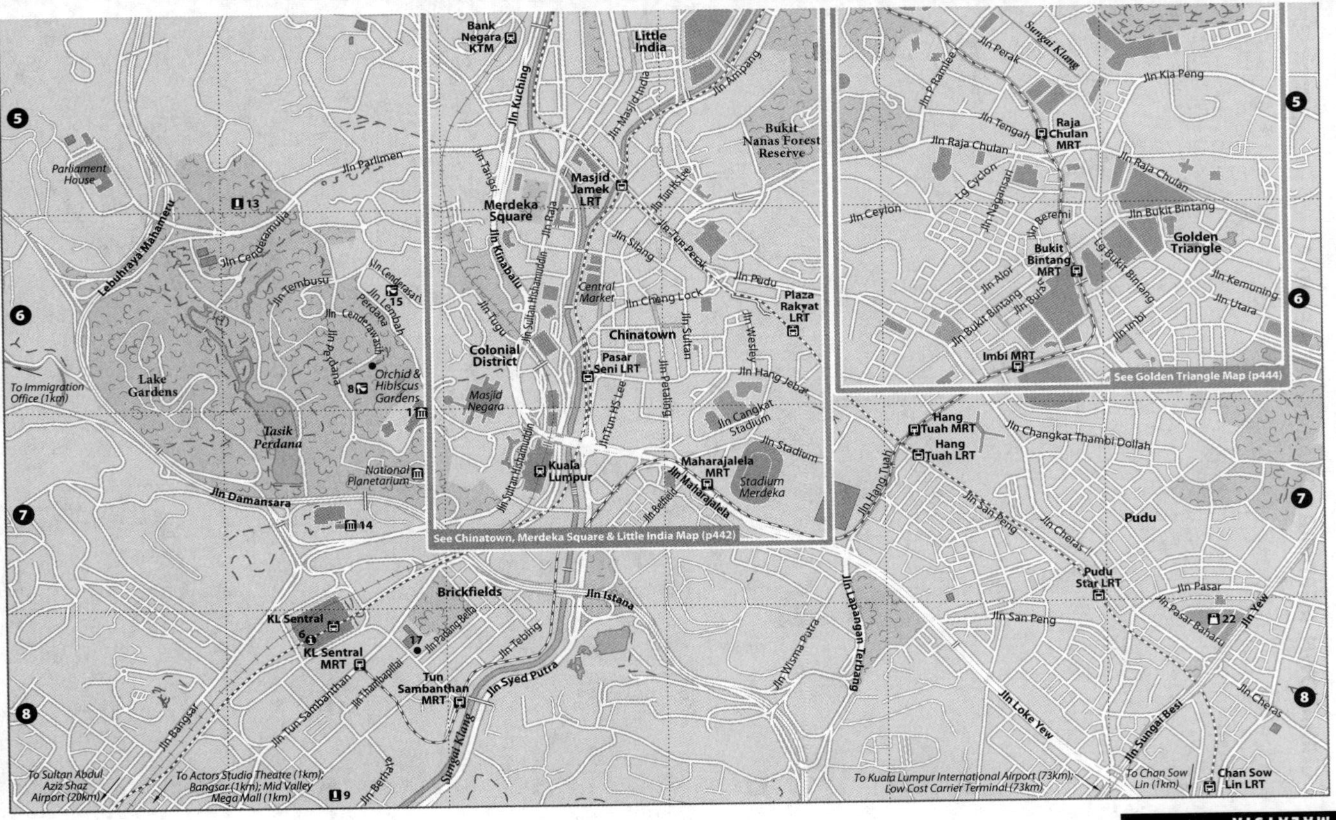
Bank Negara KTM
Little India
Jln Kuching
Jln Masjid India
Jln Ampang
Bukit Nanas Forest Reserve
Jln Parlimen
Parliament House
Lebuhraya Mahameru
Jln Cenderamulia
Jln Tangsi
Masjid Jamek LRT
Jln Tun HS Lee
Merdeka Square
Jln Raja
Jln Kinabalu
Jln Sultan Hishamuddin
Jln Silang
Jln Tun Perak
Jln Pudu
Plaza Rakyat LRT
Central Market
Jln Cheng Lock
Jln Tembusu
Jln Cenderasari
Jln Lembah Perdana
Jln Cenderawasih
Jln Perdana
Orchid & Hibiscus Gardens
Lake Gardens
To Immigration Office (1km)
Jln Tugu
Colonial District
Chinatown
Jln Sultan
Jln Wesley
Pasar Seni LRT
Jln Petaling
Jln Hang Jebat
Masjid Negara
Jln Tun HS Lee
Jln Cangkat Stadium
Jln Stadium
Tasik Perdana
Kuala Lumpur
Maharajalela MRT
Jln Maharajalela
Stadium Merdeka
Jln Belfield
National Planetarium
Jln Damansara
See Chinatown, Merdeka Square & Little India Map (p442)
Jln Perak
Sungai Klang
Jln P Ramlee
Jln Kia Peng
Jln Tengah
Raja Chulan MRT
Jln Raja Chulan
Lg Cyclon
Jln Nagasari
Jln Ceylon
Jln Beremi
Jln Bukit Bintang
Golden Triangle
Bukit Bintang MRT
Lg Bukit Bintang
Jln Alor
Jln Bulan
Jln Kemuning
Jln Utara
Jln Imbi
Imbi MRT
See Golden Triangle Map (p444)
Hang Tuah MRT
Hang Tuah LRT
Jln Changkat Thambi Dollah
Jln Hang Tuah
Jln San Peng
Jln Cheras
Pudu
Pudu Star LRT
Jln Pasar
Jln Pasar Baharu
Jln Yew
Brickfields
Jln Istana
Jln San Peng
KL Sentral
KL Sentral MRT
Jln Padang Belia
Jln Thambapillai
Jln Tebing
Tun Sambanthan MRT
Jln Syed Putra
Jln Wisma Putra
Jln Lapangan Terbang
Jln Loke Yew
Jln Sungai Besi
Jln Cheras
Jln Bangsar
Jln Tun Sambanthan
Sungai Klang
Jln Berhala
To Sultan Abdul Aziz Shaz Airport (20km)
To Actors Studio Theatre (1km); Bangsar (1km); Mid Valley Mega Mall (1km)
To Kuala Lumpur International Airport (73km); Low Cost Carrier Terminal (73km)
To Chan Sow Lin (1km)
Chan Sow Lin LRT

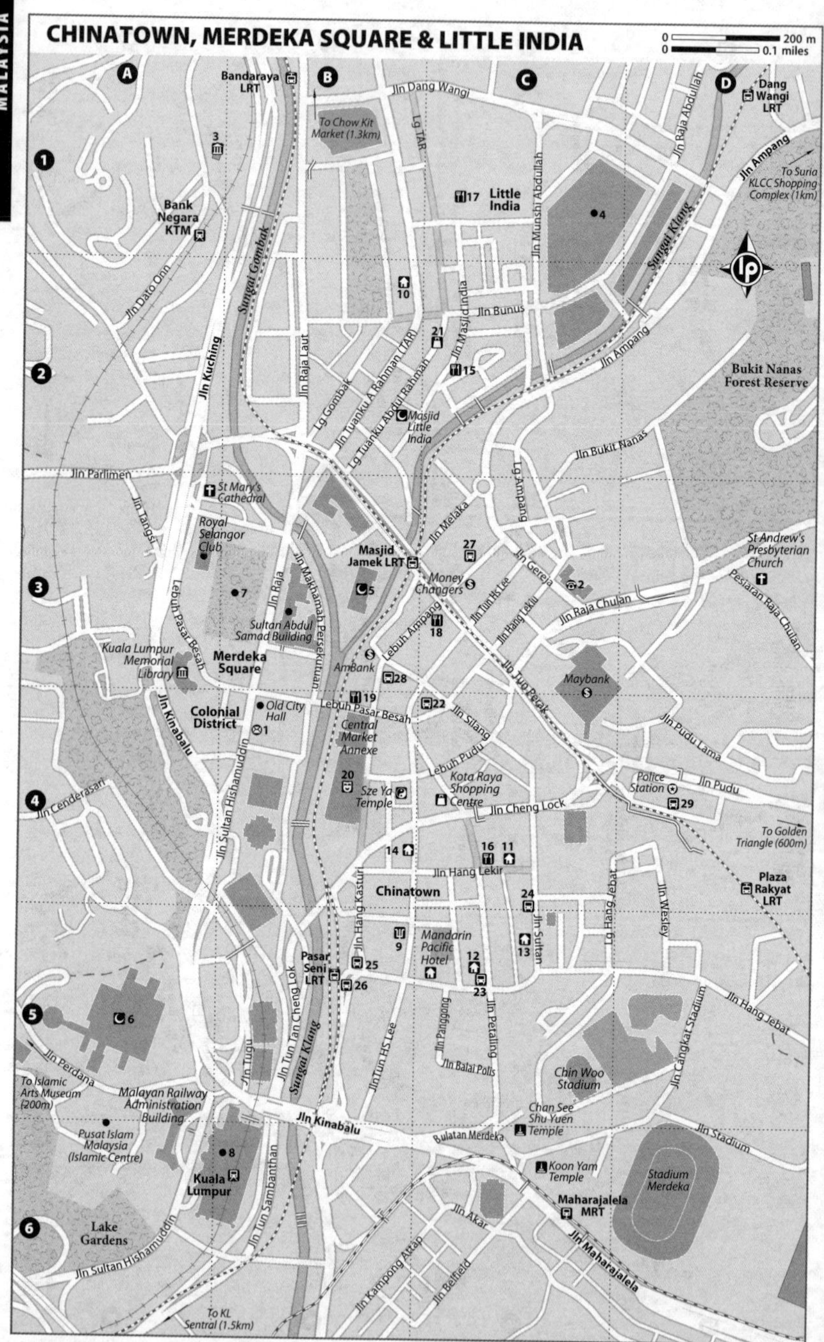
CHINATOWN, MERDEKA SQUARE & LITTLE INDIA
0 200 m
0 0.1 miles
Bandaraya LRT
To Chow Kit Market (1.3km)
Jln Dang Wangi
Lg TAR
Jln Raja Abdullah
Dang Wangi LRT
Jln Ampang
To Suria KLCC Shopping Complex (1km)
Little India
Jln Munshi Abdullah
Sungai Klang
Bank Negara KTM
Jln Dato Onn
Sungai Gombak
Jln Bunus
Jln Masjid India
Jln Tuanku A Rahman (TAR)
Jln Kuching
Jln Raja Laut
Lg Gombak
Lg Tuanku Abdul Rahman
Masjid Little India
Bukit Nanas Forest Reserve
Jln Bukit Nanas
Jln Parlimen
St Mary's Cathedral
Jln Tangsi
Lg Ampang
Royal Selangor Club
Jln Metaka
Masjid Jamek LRT
Money Changers
Jln Gereja
St Andrew's Presbyterian Church
Persiaran Raja Chulan
Jln Raja
Jln Makhamah Persekutuan
Lebuh Pasar Besah
Sultan Abdul Samad Building
Jln Tun HS Lee
Jln Hang Lekiu
Jln Raja Chulan
Lebuh Ampang
Kuala Lumpur Memorial Library
Merdeka Square
AmBank
Jln Tun Perak
Maybank
Colonial District
Old City Hall
Lebuh Pasar Besah
Central Market Annexe
Jln Silang
Jln Kinabalu
Jln Pudu Lama
Lebuh Pudu
Kota Raya Shopping Centre
Police Station
Jln Pudu
Jln Cenderasari
Sze Ya Temple
Jln Cheng Lock
To Golden Triangle (600m)
Jln Sultan Hishamuddin
Jln Hang Lekir
Chinatown
Jln Hang Kasturi
Lg Hang Jebat
Jln Wesley
Plaza Rakyat LRT
Jln Sultan
Mandarin Pacific Hotel
Pasar Seni LRT
Jln Hang Jebat
Jln Panggong
Jln Petaling
Jln Cangkat Stadium
Jln Tun Tan Cheng Lok
Sungai Klang
JlnTun HS Lee
Jln Balai Polis
Jln Tugu
Jln Perdana
Chin Woo Stadium
To Islamic Arts Museum (200m)
Malayan Railway Administration Building
Chan See Shu Yuen Temple
Jln Kinabalu
Bulatan Merdeka
Jln Stadium
Pusat Islam Malaysia (Islamic Centre)
Koon Yam Temple
Stadium Merdeka
Kuala Lumpur
Jln Tun Sambanthan
Maharajalela MRT
Jln Akar
Lake Gardens
Jln Maharajalela
Jln Sultan Hishamuddin
Jln Kampong Attap
Jln Belfield
To KL Sentral (1.5km)

INFORMATION		
Main Post Office	**1**	B4
Telekom Malaysia	**2**	C3
SIGHTS & ACTIVITIES		
Bank Negara Malaysia Museum & Art Gallery	**3**	A1
CapSquare	**4**	C1
Masjid Jamek	**5**	B3
Masjid Negara	**6**	A5
Merdeka Square	**7**	B3
Old Railway Station	**8**	B6
Sri Mahamariamman Temple	**9**	B5
SLEEPING		
Coliseum Hotel	**10**	B2
Grocer's Inn	**11**	C4
Lee Mun Guest House	**12**	C5
Original Backpackers Travellers Inn	**13**	C5
Wheelers Guest House	**14**	B4
EATING		
Food Court	**15**	C2
Ikan panggang stall	**16**	C4
Sagar	**17**	C1
Sangeetha	**18**	C3
Sing Seng Nam	**19**	B4
ENTERTAINMENT		
Central Market	**20**	B4
SHOPPING		
Pasar Malam	**21**	C2
TRANSPORT		
Buses for Batu Caves	**22**	C4
Buses to Kuala Tembeling (Hotel Mandarin Pacific)	**23**	C5
Buses to Kuala Tembeling (Swiss Inn)	**24**	C4
Jl Sultan Mohammed Bus Stop	**25**	B5
Klang Bus Station	**26**	B5
Lebuh Ampang Bus Stop	**27**	C3
Long-distance taxis	(see 29)	
Medan Pasar Bus Stop	**28**	B3
Puduraya Bus Station	**29**	D4

SIGHTS

Six-lane highways and flyovers may slice up the city but the best way to get a feel for KL's atmosphere is to walk.

Chinatown & Merdeka Square

Circuitous streets and cramped chaos create a pressure-cooker of sights and sounds in Chinatown. **Jln Petaling** is a bustling street market selling souvenirs, such as 'authentic' Levis and cheap Crocs; it opens around 10am and shuts late at night.

Chinese **coffee shops** are along Jln Panggong and Jln Balai Polis (Map p442). You'll spot temples and shophouses in the side streets –check out KL's principal Hindu temple, **Sri Mahamariamman Temple** (Map p442; Jln Tun HS Lee).

Heading north you'll find the one-time cricket field formerly known as the Padang, **Merdeka Square** (Map p442; Jln Raja Laut), where Malaysia's independence (Merdeka) was proclaimed in 1957. Today it's a choice spot to see some fetching colonial architecture. South is the **old railway station** (Map p442; Jln Hishamuddin), a fanciful castle of Islamic arches and spires.

Masjid Negara (National Mosque; Map p442; Jln Perdana; 9am-12.30pm, 2-3.30pm & 5-6.30pm) is one of Southeast Asia's largest mosques. The main dome is an 18-point star, that symbolises the 13 states of Malaysia and the five pillars of Islam.

Chinatown is reached on the Putra LRT to Pasar Seni station or on the KL Monorail to Maharajalela station.

Little India & Around

Little India has all the feel of a bazaar. The sari shops and the women shopping along **Jln Masjid India**, the district's main street, are swathed in vibrant sherbets, turquoise and vermilions. Meanwhile Indian pop blasts through tinny speakers, and musky incense and delicious spices flavour the air. The district swings into a full spectacle during the Saturday *pasar malam* (night market). On the 1st and 3rd weekends of every month **CapSquare** (Map p442; www.capsquare.com.my) also hosts a bazaar that features food and fashion as well as some interesting knick-knacks.

Masjid Jamek (Friday Mosque; Map p442; off Jln Tun Perak; 8.30am-12.30pm & 2.30-4pm, closed Fri 11am-2.30pm), set in a grove of palm trees, is KL's most delightful mosque. Built in 1907, the mosque is a creation of onion domes and minarets of layered pink and cream bricks.

Yet to open at the time of research is the **Bank Negara Malaysia Museum & Art Gallery** (Map p442; http://museum.bnm.gov.my) in a futuristic, metal-clad complex west of Jln Kuching.

Little India is best reached on the Star or Putra LRT to Masjid Jamek station.

Golden Triangle

A forest of high-rises, the Golden Triangle is central KL's business, shopping and entertainment district.

Sitting on a forested hill, **Menara Kuala Lumpur** (KL Tower; Map p444; ☎ 2020 5448; www.menarakl.com.my; 2 Jln Punchak; adult/child RM38/28; 9am-10pm; last tickets up 9.30pm) easily trumps the Petronas Towers when it comes to the view. The tower's bulbous pinnacle is inspired by a Malaysian spinning top and the 276m-high **viewing**

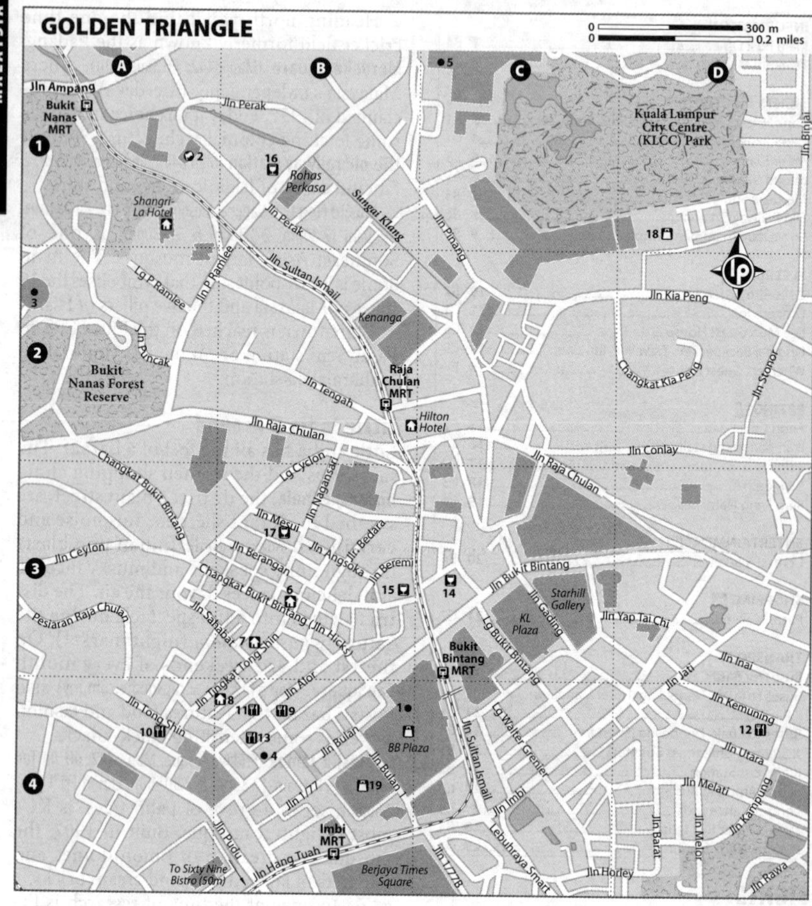

deck is over 100m higher than the Petronas Towers' skybridge.

A free **shuttle bus** (every 15 min; 9am-9.30pm) runs to the tower from the gate on Jln Punchak opposite the PanGlobal building. Alternatively, get a workout climbing the short nature trails that run through the forest reserve, which you can explore alone or on a free guided tour starting from the entrance to the tower at 11am, 12.30pm, 2.30pm and 4.30pm daily and lasting about 45 minutes.

Formerly the world's tallest skyscrapers (until Taipei 101 took the title in 2004), the twin **Petronas Towers** (Map p444; www.petronas.com.my/petronas; Jln Ampang; admission free; 9am-1pm & 2.30-7pm Tue-Sun) serve as the elegant headquarters of the national petroleum company. This steel-and-glass monument weaves together traditional Islamic symbolism with modern sophistication. First-come, first-serve tickets are available for visiting the 41st-floor Skybridge that connects the two towers; tickets are issued from 8.30am and 15-minute visits start at 10am. Arrive around 8am to start queuing if you're particular about the time you want to go up, but tickets are often available until around 11am.

To get here, take the Putra LRT to KLCC station.

Lake Gardens & Around

Escape from the heat and concrete to this inner-city garden district at the western edge

INFORMATION
MPH Bookstores 1 B4
New Zealand Embassy 2 A1

SIGHTS & ACTIVITIES
Menara Kuala Lumpur 3 A2
Old Asia 4 B4
Petronas Towers 5 C1

SLEEPING
Bedz KL 6 B3
Green Hut Lodge 7 B3
Red Palm 8 B4

EATING
1+1 9 B4
Blue Boy Vegetarian Food Centre 10 A4
Frog Porridge Stall 11 B4
Imbi Market 12 D4
Wong Ah Wah 13 B4

DRINKING
Blue Boy 14 C3
Finnegan's Irish Pub & Restaurant 15 B3
Oblique 16 B1
Palate Palette 17 B3

SHOPPING
Kompleks Budaya Kraf 18 D1
Low Yat Plaza 19 B4

of central KL. From Chinatown, Intrakota Bus 21C from the Jln Sultan Mohammed bus stop, or buses 21B, 22, 48C and F3, will take you there. It is also a 20-minute walk from Masjid Jamek.

The gardens contain a host of attractions such as the **Bird Park** (Map pp440-1; ☎ 2272 1010; www.klbirdpark.com; adult/child RM39/29; 9am-6pm) and **Taman Rama Rama** (Butterfly Park; Map pp440-1; ☎ 2693 4799; Jln Cendarasari; adult/child RM15/8; 9am-6pm). You can take a leisurely stroll around them, or catch the shuttle bus that does a loop of the area.

At the edge of the Lake Gardens, the recently renovated **National Museum** (Muzium Negara; Map pp440-1; ☎ 2282 6255; www.muziumnegara.gov.my; Jln Damansara; adult/child RM2/free; 9am-6pm) boasts colourful displays on Malaysia's history, economy, arts, crafts and culture. Free guided tours in English are held at 11am Tuesday, Thursday and Saturday and in French at 9am and noon Thursday.

Near Lake Gardens, the **Islamic Arts Museum** (Muzium Kesenian Islam Malaysia; Map pp440-1; ☎ 2274 2020; www.iamm.org.my; Jln Lembah Perdana; adult/child RM12/6; 10am-6pm) has exquisite displays of textiles, carpets, jewellery, calligraphy-inscribed pottery and a reconstruction of an ornate Ottoman room. The building itself is also a stunner, with decorated domes and glazed tilework.

Northern KL

It's sensory overload at the **Chow Kit Market** (Map pp440-1; 469-473 Jln TAR; 6am-8pm), where tightly jammed stalls sell clothes; toys; spices; meat; live, flapping fish; and weird and wonderful tropical fruit.

Further north near Lake Titiwangsa, the **National Art Gallery** (Balai Seni Lukis Negara; Map pp440-1; ☎ 4026 7000; www.artgallery.org.my; 2 Jln Temerloh, off Jln Tun Razak; admission free; 10am-6pm) displays works by contemporary Malaysian and international artists. Take any Len Seng bus from Lebuh Ampang (north of Central Market) in Chinatown or from along Jln Raja Laut; get off at the hospital stop.

ACTIVITIES

There's a concentration of **Chinese massage** and reflexology places along Jln Bukit Bintang, south of BB Plaza. The going price is usually RM65 for a one-hour full-body massage, but try bargaining for RM50. Expect to pay about RM30 for 30 minutes of foot reflexology. **Old Asia** (Map p444; ☎ 2143 9888; 14 Jln Bukit Bintang; 10am-10pm) is one of the more reliable and pleasantly designed places.

If you'd rather be the one pounding your hands, you can join the **Tugu Drum Circle** at

BATU CAVES

Get closer to KL's Indian culture by visiting the **Batu Caves** (off Map pp440-1; admission free; 8am-8pm), a system of three caves 13km northwest of the capital. The most famous is Temple Cave, because it contains a Hindu shrine reached by a straight flight of 272 steps, guarded by a 43m-high Murga statue, the highest in the world. About a million pilgrims come here every year during Thaipusam (January/February) to engage in or watch the spectacularly masochistic feats of the devotees.

To get there take Bus 11 (RM2, 45 minutes) from where Jln Tun HS Lee meets Jln Petaling, just south of Medan Pasar in KL. The bus also stops along Jln Raja Laut in the Chow Kit area. A taxi shouldn't cost more than RM20.

FORESTRY RESEARCH INSTITUTE OF MALAYSIA (FRIM)

Birdsong and wall-to-wall greenery replaces the drone of traffic and air-conditioning at the **Forestry Research Institute of Malaysia** (FRIM; ☎ 6279 7525; www.frim.gov.my; admission RM1, cars RM5; 🕑 8am-6.30pm), 16km northwest of KL. The highlight of this 600-hectare jungle park is its 200m-long, 30m-high **Canopy Walkway** (adult/child RM5/1; 🕑 9.30am-2.30pm Tue-Thu, Sat & Sun).

The walkway is reached by a steep trail from FRIM's **information centre** (🕑 8am-5pm Mon-Fri, 9am-4pm Sat & Sun). Heading down from the walkway the trail picks its way through the jungle to a shady picnic area where you can cool off in a series of shallow waterfalls. The return hike incorporating the walkway takes around two hours.

Take a KTM Komuter train to Kepong (RM1.30) and then a taxi (RM5); arrange for the taxi to pick you up again later.

the National Monument (Map pp440–1) in the Lake Gardens from 5.30pm to 8.30pm every Sunday.

COURSES

Buddhist Maha Vihar (Map pp440-1; ☎ 2274 1141; www.buddhistmahavihara.com; 123 Jln Berhala) This Brickfields landmark offers a variety of courses. Meditation and chanting classes are held daily.

Kompleks Budaya Kraf (see p448) Try your hand at traditional Malay crafts such as batik or pottery at the craft village in the grounds of this one-stop crafts complex.

YMCA (Map pp440-1; ☎ 2274 1439; www.ymcakl.com; 95 Jln Padang Belia, Brickfields) Offers Bahasa Malaysia classes as well as Thai, Mandarin/Cantonese and Japanese. You can also study martial arts and different types of dancing.

SLEEPING

Vibrant Chinatown is your best hunting ground for rock-bottom crash pads and is an easy walk from the Puduraya bus station. The Golden Triangle area's budget options are pricier but cleaner and in a more low-key (and arguably less exciting) neighbourhood. Unless otherwise noted, all the options listed share bathrooms.

Chinatown & Little India

If you're arriving from the airport or a long-distance bus station other than Puduraya, these guest houses can be reached via the Star LRT to Plaza Rakyat, Putra LRT to Pasar Seni or the KL Monorail to Maharajalela station.

Lee Mun Guesthouse (Map p442; ☎ 2078 0639; 5th fl, 109 Jln Petaling; dm/s/d RM10/25/35; ❄) A skeletal 'authentic Chinatown' cheapie where the cardboard partition walls are covered with a collage of magazine clippings.

Wheelers Guest House (Map p442; ☎ 2070 1386; www.backpackerskl.com/wheelers.htm; level 2, 131-133 Jln Tun HS Lee; dm/r R10/25, r with private bathroom RM50; ❄ 💻) With its mini-aquarium, potted plants and murals, Wheelers is one of KL's quirkier hostels. Yummy home-made yoghurt and muesli is served for breakfast and free Friday night dinners are held on the rooftop terrace.

Original Backpackers Travellers Inn (Map p442; ☎ 2078 2473; www.backpackerskl.com; 60B Jln Sultan; dm/s/d RM11/28/30, r with private bathroom from RM54; ❄ 💻) The highlight of this long-running hostel is its rooftop bar where you can get breakfast and meet fellow travellers.

Grocer's Inn (Map p442; ☎ 2078 7906; www.grocersinn.com.my; 78 Jln Sultan; dm/s/d from RM13/35/45; ❄ 💻) In a century-old building that was once home to the grocers' association this backpackers has good fan and air-con rooms as well as rooftop dorm and balconies overlooking Chinatown. The entrance is in an alley, just off Jln Sultan.

Coliseum Hotel (Map p442; ☎ 2692 6270; 98-100 Jln TAR; s/d RM38/45; ❄) If high-ceilinged rooms with ancient electric switches and furnishings are your thing, you'll love this place. All bathrooms are shared. Book well in advance, as it's often full.

Tune Hotel (Map pp440-1; ☎ 7962 5888; www.tunehotels.com; 316 Jln TAR; r from RM50; ❄ 💻) It's just like a budget airline: book online in advance and snag a room with bathroom for under RM50. The basic rate just gets you the room – air-con, toiletries and wi-fi access are extra. There's also a branch next to the Low Cost Airport Terminal (LCCT) if you arrive on a late-night flight.

Golden Triangle

These guest houses can be reached via the KL Monorail to Bukit Bintang station.

Red Palm (Map p444; ☎ 2143 1279; www.redpalm-kl.com; 5 Jln Tingkat Tong Shin; dm/s/d/tr incl breakfast RM25/50/70/105; 💻) Its rooms are tiny and separated by thin walls and all bathrooms are shared, but with its friendly management and comfy communal areas Red Palm feels like home.

Green Hut Lodge (Map p444; ☎ 2142 3339; www.thegreenhut.com; 48 Jln Tingkat Tong Shin; dm/s/d incl breakfast RM25/50/65, d with private bathroom RM90; ❄ 💻) A classic travellers' choice, complete with towel-draped 12-bed dorm, noticeboards and staff who speak Bahasa Backpacker.

Bedz KL (Map p444; ☎ 2144 2339; www.bedzkl.com; 58 Changkat Bukit Bintang; dm RM30; ❄ 💻) There are only dorms at this new choice, shielded from busy Changkat Bukit Bintang by a grove of bamboo. Rain showers, foosball, plenty of internet terminals and souvenir T-shirts are all part of the package.

EATING

All the food groups – including Indian, Chinese, Malay and Western fast food – abound in the Malaysian capital.

Chinatown & Little India

In the morning, grab a marble-topped table in one of the neighbourhood's *kedai kopi* (coffee shops) for a jolt of coffee spiked with condensed milk. The midday meal can be slurped down at the stalls that line Jln Sultan serving all the you-name-it noodles, from prawn or *won ton mee* (Chinese-style egg noodles served with stuffed wontons) to *laksa lemak* (white rounded noodles served with coconut milk, also called curry laksa). Jln Petaling market is closed to traffic in the evenings and Chinese restaurants set up tables beside all the action.

Little India is your best hunting ground for a slap-up Indian curry sopped up with flaky *roti canai* (Indian-style flaky flat bread, also known as 'flying dough').

Ikan panggang stall (Map p442; ☎ 019 315 9448; 🕒 5-11pm Tue-Sun) Outside Hong Leong Bank, unsigned and tucked behind the stalls on the corner of Jln Petaling and Jln Hang Lekir. Order ahead – it takes about 20 minutes for your foil-wrapped pouch of seafood to cook.

Sing Seng Nam (Map p442; Medan Pasar; 🕒 7am-5pm Mon-Sat) A genuine *kopitam* (coffee shop), busy with lawyers from the nearby courts who come to enjoy a breakfast of *kaya* toast and runny boiled egg or a *kopi peng* (iced coffee with milk).

Sagar (Map p442; ☎ 2691 3088; Semua House, Jln Masjid India; meals RM10; 🕒 8am-8pm) Enjoy *thali* meals (rice or bread served with assorted vegetables and curries) at this sidewalk cafe, and soak up the street life of Little India.

Sangeetha (Map p442; ☎ 2032 3333; 65 Lebuh Ampang; meals RM10; 🕒 8am-11pm) A vegetarian restaurant serving South Indian delights such as *idli* (savoury, soft, fermented-rice-and-lentil cakes) and *masala dosa* (rice-and-lentil crepes stuffed with spiced potatoes).

A busy **food court** (Jln Masjid India) gobbles up a big block. Little India's Saturday night market, at the north end of Lorong TAR, has sensational tucker and a great atmosphere.

Golden Triangle & KLCC

Jln Nagansari, off Changkat Bukit Bintang, is lined with Malay food stalls and open-air restaurants. Jln Alor, two streets northwest of Jln Bukit Bintang, has a carnival-like night market of Chinese hawker stalls. When it's hot outside, head to central KL's air-con shopping centres for international and local food. Take the KL Monorail to Bukit Bintang to reach the following listings.

Blue Boy Vegetarian Food Centre (Map p444; ☎ 2144 9011; Jln Tong Shin; meals RM5-10; 🕒 7.30am-9.30pm) Get all your meat and fish substitutes prepared local style at this spotless, back-street eatery. The *char kway teow* (broad noodles fried in chilli and black-bean sauce) is highly recommended.

our pick **Imbi Market** (Map p444; Jln Kampung; meals RM10; 🕒 7am-11am) The official name is Pasar Baru Bukit Bintang, but everyone knows it simply as Imbi Market. Breakfast is almost like a party here with all the friendly and curious locals happily recommending their favourite stalls. We like Sisters Popiah; Teluk Intan Chee Cheung Fun, which serves oyster and peanut congee (rice porridge); and Bunn Choon for the creamy mini egg tarts.

1 + 1 (Map p444; 21A Jln Alor; meals R10-15; 🕒 24hr) One of the few round-the-clock operations on this eats street that does good dim sum for breakfast and lunch.

Frog porridge stall (per bowl RM7; 🕒 5pm-2am) Opposite 1 + 1; you can choose to have 'spicy', where the frogs legs are served separately, or 'non-spicy', where they're mixed in with the tasty rice gruel.

Suria KLCC Shopping Complex (Map pp440-1; ☎ 2382 2828; Jln Ampang; meals RM10-20; 🕒 lunch & dinner) This upscale shopping centre has a modern 2nd-floor food court with everything from sushi and pizza to Malaysian cuisine.

our pick Wong Ah Wah (Map p444; Jln Alor; meals RM15-20; 4pm-4am) At the southern end of the street, and justly famous for its seriously addictive chicken wings, an ideal late-night snack with a beer.

DRINKING

Drinking in Malaysia is definitely no budget activity and drinks at 'proper' bars are nearly double in price. The cheapest places to imbibe are Chinese eateries or open-air hawker stalls.

Meat-market bars congregate along Jln P Ramlee while sophisticates and the indie-inclined heat up at nearby CapSquare. Head to Bangsar for classy expat bars and cafes.

Check out the latest club news in **KLue** (www.klue.com.my; RM5). Clubs are typically open Wednesday to Sunday and usually charge a cover (including one drink) of RM20 to RM40 Thursday to Saturday.

Finnegan's Irish Pub & Restaurant (Map p444; ☎ 2284 9024; 6 Jln Telawi Lima) This is a first-rate place for a knees-up with live ESPN sports coverage, enthusiastic staff, stout and a decent menu.

our pick Palate Palette (Map p444; ☎ 2142 2148; www.palatepalette.com; 21 Jln Mesui; noon-midnight Tue-Thu, noon-2am Fri & Sat) Gotta love a place that offers a drink called Kick in the Nuts. Colourful, creative and quirky, this cafe-bar is a great place to eat (mains RM10 to RM30), drink, play board games, and check out KL's boho crowd.

Sixty Nine Bistro (off Map p444; ☎ 2144 3369; 14 Jln Kampung Dollah; noon-midnight) Worth checking out for its eclectic junk-shop-chic furnishings, milk and fruit shakes and resident fortune tellers and tarot card readers.

Zouk (Map pp440-1; ☎ 2171 1997; www.zoukclub.com.my; 113 Jln Ampang) There's a theme for everyone here from the small and edgy Loft Bar to a plastic palm-fringed main venue and sophisticated Velvet Underground (RM45 including entry to Zouk).

Maison (Map pp440-1; ☎ 2381 2088; www.maison.com.my; 8 Jln Yap Ah Shak) Five shophouses have been knocked together to form a great space for this club where house music, in all its forms, rules.

GAY & LESBIAN KUALA LUMPUR

Check out www.utopia-asia.com and www.fridae.com for the latest on KL's small but friendly gay scene. **Prince World KL** (www.princeworldkl.com) organises big gay dance parties several times a year.

Oblique (Map p444; www.princeworldkl.com; Jln P Ramlee; cover RM25; 10-3am Sat) Non-straight club that sees a twinky crowd feverishly juggling its stuff to hard house and techno. You'll find it beneath Modestos.

Blue Boy (Map p444; ☎ 2142 1067; 54 Jln Sultan Ismail; 5pm-3am) Malaysia's oldest gay club is a gritty pick-up joint with karaoke-singing lady boys.

ENTERTAINMENT

Tanjung Golden Village (Map pp440-1; ☎ 7492 2929; www.tgv.com.my; 3rd fl, Suria KLCC Shopping Complex) The latest Bollywood and Hollywood blockbusters are shown at this arctic multiscreen cinema.

Regular cultural performances and shows are held at the **Malaysian Tourist Centre** (MaTiC; Map pp440-1; ☎ 2164 3929, 2163 3667; 109 Jln Ampang; adult RM5; 2-2.30pm Tue, Thu, Sat & Sun) and the **Central Market** (Map p442; ☎ 2274 6542; admission free; available from information desk).

SHOPPING

Jln Petaling in the heart of Chinatown is a noisy, writhing mass of people and outdoor stalls selling cheap clothes, fruit, pirated DVDs and a smattering of crafts; bargain very, very hard. More everyday items can be found at the tightly jammed **Chow Kit Market** (see p445 for details). For produce and weird meats – from stingray to pig's penises – go to KL's largest wet market, the frenetic **Pudu Market** (Map pp440-1; 6am-2pm). The best *pasar malam* are on Saturday nights along Lorong TAR in Little India (Map p442) and Jln Raja Muda in Kampung Baru (Map pp440–1), southeast of Chow Kit. Jln Masjid India in Little India is the place to shop for saris, Indian silks, carpets and other textiles.

Low Yat Plaza (Map p444; ☎ 2148 3651; 7 Jln 1/77 off Bukit Bintang) Go here for all your digital and electronic needs.

Kompleks Budaya Kraf (Map p444; ☎ 2162 7459; Jln Conlay; 9am-8pm Mon-Fri, to 7pm Sat & Sun) This place has a large selection of handicrafts.

GETTING THERE & AWAY

Kuala Lumpur is Malaysia's principal international arrival gateway and it forms the crossroads for domestic bus, train and taxi travel.

Air

For details of international airlines, see p435.

Kuala Lumpur International Airport (KLIA; off Map pp440-1; ☎ 8777 8888; www.klia.com.my; Pengrus Besar) is a flamboyant structure, located 75km south of the city centre at Sepang. Many airlines service this airport, but the country's international airline, **Malaysia Airlines** (☎ 1300 883 000; www.malaysiaairlines.com.my), is the major carrier. **Air Asia** (☎ 8775 4000; www.airasia.com) flights arrive and depart from the nearby **Low Cost Carrier Terminal** (LCCT; off Map pp440-1; ☎ 8777 8888; www.lcct.com.my), while **Firefly** (☎ 03-7845 4543; www.fireflyz.com.my) and **Berjaya Air** (☎ 2145 2828; www.berjaya-air.com) flights use **Sultan Abdul Aziz Shah Airport** (off Map pp440-1; ☎ 7845 8382) in Subang, about 20km west of the city centre. See p436 for information on domestic routes and costs.

Bus

Most long-distance buses operate from the **Puduraya bus station** (Map p442; Jln Pudu), situated just east of Chinatown. A few travellers have reported being robbed late at night, so stay alert while in the area. The tourist police and information counters are right inside the main entrance. The left-luggage office is at the back. From Puduraya, buses go all over Peninsular Malaysia, Singapore and Thailand. The only long-distance destinations that Puduraya doesn't handle are Kuala Lipis and Jerantut, which leave only from Pekeliling bus station.

Pekeliling (Map pp440-1; ☎ 4042 7256; Jln Tun Razak) and **Putra** (Map pp440-1; ☎ 4042 9530; Jln Putra) bus stations in the north of the city handle a greater number of services to the east coast than Puduraya. Buses at these stations often have seats available when Puduraya buses are fully booked.

TYPICAL BUS FARES AND JOURNEY TIMES FROM KL

Destination	Fare (RM)	Duration (hr)
Cameron Highlands	30	4
Georgetown (Penang)	32	5
Ipoh	17	3
Johor Bahru	31.30	4
Kota Bharu	42.90	8
Kuala Terengganu	39	7
Kuantan	22	4½
Lumut	24.50	4
Melaka	12.40	2½
Mersing	29.90	5½
Singapore	39.10	5½

Taxi

The long-distance taxi stand is on the 2nd floor of the **Puduraya bus station** (Map p442; Jln Pudu). Fixed whole-taxi fares include Cameron Highlands (RM350), Melaka (RM300) and Penang (RM600). Do your homework on prices before dealing with taxi drivers who can sometimes be unscrupulous about ripping off tourists.

Train

KL is the hub of the **KTM** (☎ 2267 1200; www.ktmb.com.my) national railway system. The long-distance trains depart from KL Sentral (Map pp440–1). The **KTM information office** (⏲ 10am-7pm) in the main hall can advise on schedules. There are departures for Butterworth (RM19, seven hours), Alor Setar (RM22, 12 hours), Wakaf Baharu (RM30, 14 hours), Johor Bahru (RM18, six hours), Singapore (RM19, 7½ hours) and Hat Yai, Thailand (RM48, 15 hours). Express-train seats can be booked up to 60 days in advance.

Not to be confused with the intercity long-distance line is the KTM Komuter, which runs from KL Sentral, linking central KL with the Klang Valley and Seremban.

GETTING AROUND

KL has an extensive public transport system. See p439 for details of getting to the city centre from KLIA airport. The only transport option to Sultan Abdul Aziz Shah Airport is a taxi; expect to pay RM50 to RM80.

Bus

Most buses in KL are provided by either **Rapid KL** (☎ 1800 388 228; www.rapidkl.com.my) or **Metrobus** (☎ 5635 3070). There's an **information booth** (Map p442; ⏲ 7am-9pm) at the Jln Sultan Mohammed bus stop in Chinatown. Local buses leave from many of the bus terminals around the city, including **Puduraya bus station** (Map p442; Jln Pudu), near Plaza Rakyat LRT station, and Klang bus station (Map p442), near Pasar Seni LRT station. The maximum fare is usually RM1 for destinations within the city limits; try to have the correct change ready when you board.

Taxi

KL's taxis are cheap, starting at RM2 for the first kilometre, with an additional 10 sen for each 200m. Although required to use the meter by law, taxi drivers often need coercing to do so, and tend to overcharge tourists. It should cost no more than RM10 to go right across the central city area, even in moderate traffic. Note that taxis will often only stop at the numerous officially signposted taxi stands.

Train

KL's pride and joy is the user-friendly **Light Rail Transit** (LRT; ☎ 1800 388 288; www.rapidkl.com.my) system, which is composed of the Ampang/Sentul Timur, Sri Petaling/Sentul Timur and Kelana Jaya/Terminal Putra lines. Fares range from RM1 to RM2.80 and trains run every six to 10 minutes from 6am to 11.50pm (11.30pm Sunday and holidays).

KL's zippy **monorail** (☎ 2273 1888; www.klmonorail.com.my; RM1.20-2.50; 🕑 6am-midnight) runs between KL Sentral in the south to Titiwangsa in the north. It's a very handy service linking up many of the city's sightseeing areas and providing a cheap air-con tour as you go.

KTM Komuter (☎ 2272 2828; tickets from RM1), not to be confused with the long-distance KTM service (see p449), links Kuala Lumpur with outlying suburbs and the historic railway station.

KL Sentral station, in the Brickfields area, is the central transit station for all train travel in KL. Other interchange stations include Masjid Jamek (Map p442), for transfer between Star and Putra LRT; Hang Tuah (Map pp440–1) and Titiwangsa (Map pp440–1), for transfer between KL Monorail and Star LRT; Bukit Nanas (Map p444), for transfer between KL Monorail and Putra LRT; and Tasik Selatan, for transfer between KTM Komuter and Star LRT.

PENINSULAR MALAYSIA – WEST COAST

Malaysia's multiculturalism is best viewed along the west coast. Nestled against the Straits of Melaka, the convenient shipping route has, over the centuries, created a cosmopolitan populace, well schooled in English. Besides Pulau Langkawi, the islands of this coast don't compare to those in the east or in Thailand, but they are always host to great seafood and an array of cultural adventures.

MELAKA

☎ 06 / pop 648,500

Melaka has all the advantages of a metropolis: seemingly hundreds of cheap fantastic places to eat and stay, artistic and tolerant locals, diverse entertainment and nightlife and a colourful history that you can nearly touch. Yet it's a small, manageable place that exudes a calm that's only a notch more stressful than a tropical beach. Melt into the daily grind of dim sum breakfasts, the call to prayer followed by church bells down the road, laksa lunches, rides in crazy and gaudy trishaws, tandoori dinners and late-night drinks at balmy bars. It's hard not to like this town.

Melaka was founded in the 14th century by Parameswara, a Hindu prince from Sumatra, became protected by the Chinese in 1405, then dominated by the Portuguese in 1511, then the Dutch in 1641 and then finally ceded to the British in 1795. The intermingling of peoples created the Peranakan people (also called Baba Nonya) who are descended from Chinese settlers (see p433), the Chitties, who are of mixed Indian and Malay heritage, and Eurasians born of Malay and Portuguese love affairs.

Orientation

Chinatown is Melaka's most interesting and scenic area. Town Sq, also known as Dutch Sq, is the centre of a well-preserved museum district. Further to the northeast is Melaka's tiny Little India. Backpacker guest houses are found in Chinatown and around the nearby and less scenic Jln Melaka Raya.

Information

BOOKSHOPS

MPH (Ground fl, Mahkota Parade Shopping Complex, Jln Merdeka)

EMERGENCY

Tourist Police (☎ 285 4114; Jln Kota)

IMMIGRATION OFFICES

Immigration office (☎ 282 4958; 2nd fl, Wisma Persekutuan, Jln Hang Tuah)

INTERNET ACCESS

Fenix Internet Centre (Fenix Hotel, 156 Jln Taman Melaka Raya; per hr RM3) Also has fax and full business services.

MEDICAL SERVICES

Mahkota Medical Centre (☎ 281 4426/442; www.mahkotamedical.com; No 3, Mahkota Melaka, Jln Merdeka)

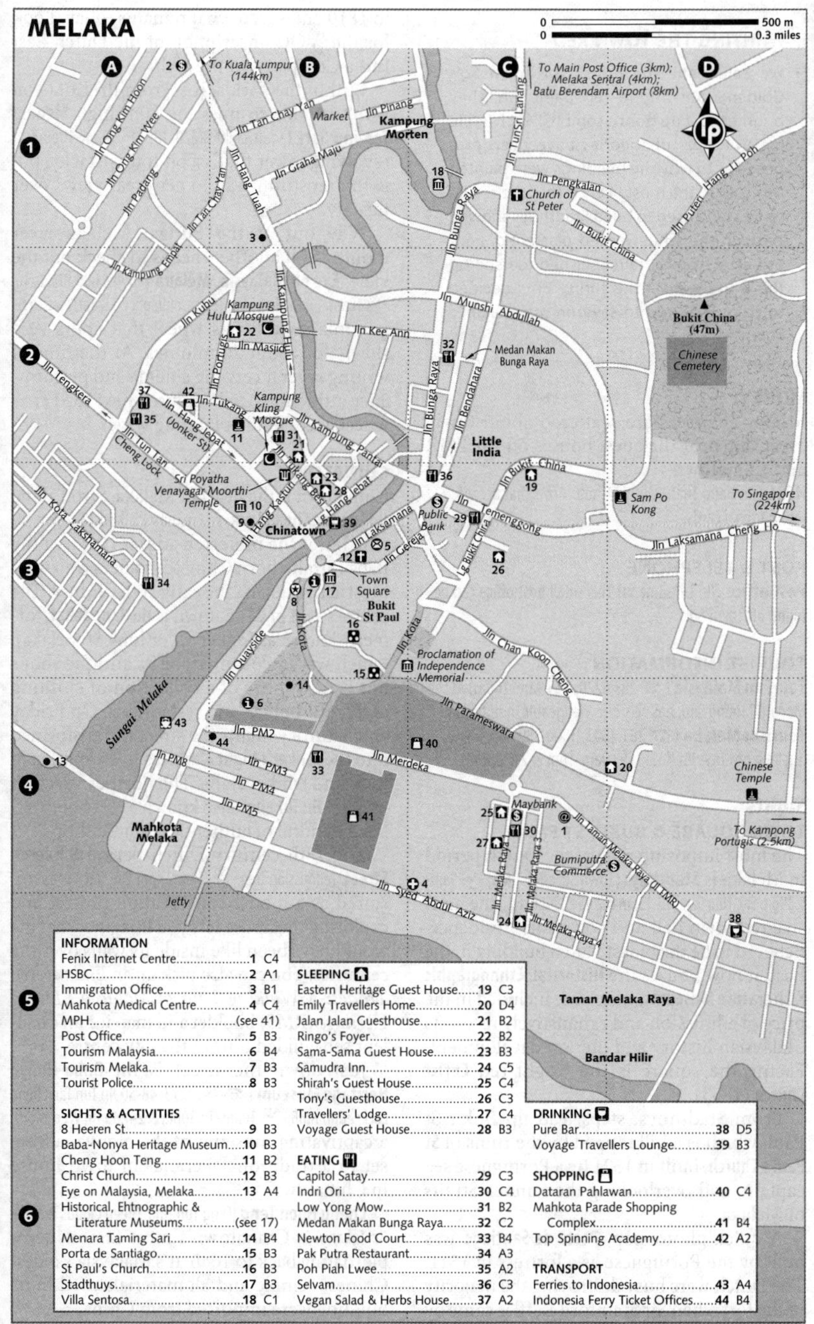

MELAKA
0 500 m
0 0.3 miles
To Kuala Lumpur (144km)
To Main Post Office (3km); Melaka Sentral (4km); Batu Berendam Airport (8km)
To Singapore (224km)
To Kampong Portugis (2.5km)
Kampung Morten
Market
Kampung Hulu Mosque
Kampung Kling Mosque
Sri Poyatha Venayagar Moorthi Temple
Chinatown
Little India
Medan Makan Bunga Raya
Church of St Peter
Bukit China (47m)
Chinese Cemetery
Sam Po Kong
Public Bank
Town Square
Bukit St Paul
Proclamation of Independence Memorial
Sungai Melaka
Mahkota Melaka
Jetty
Maybank
Bumiputra Commerce
Chinese Temple
Taman Melaka Raya
Bandar Hilir
Jln Tengkera
Jln Kubu
Jln Hang Tuah
Jln Kampung Hulu
Jln Bunga Raya
Jln Munshi Abdullah
Jln Laksamana Cheng Ho
Jln Temenggong
Jln Chan Koon Cheng
Jln Parameswara
Jln Merdeka
Jln Syed Abdul Aziz
Jln Taman Melaka Raya (TMR)
Jln Kota
Jln Quayside
Jln Hang Jebat (Jonker St)
Jln Tun Tan Cheng Lock
Jln Kota Laksamana

INFORMATION
Fenix Internet Centre....1 C4
HSBC....2 A1
Immigration Office....3 B1
Mahkota Medical Centre....4 C4
MPH....(see 41)
Post Office....5 B3
Tourism Malaysia....6 B4
Tourism Melaka....7 B3
Tourist Police....8 B3

SIGHTS & ACTIVITIES
8 Heeren St....9 B3
Baba-Nonya Heritage Museum....10 B3
Cheng Hoon Teng....11 B2
Christ Church....12 B3
Eye on Malaysia, Melaka....13 A4
Historical, Ehtnographic & Literature Museums....(see 17)
Menara Taming Sari....14 B4
Porta de Santiago....15 B3
St Paul's Church....16 B3
Stadthuys....17 B3
Villa Sentosa....18 C1

SLEEPING
Eastern Heritage Guest House....19 C3
Emily Travellers Home....20 D4
Jalan Jalan Guesthouse....21 B2
Ringo's Foyer....22 B2
Sama-Sama Guest House....23 B3
Samudra Inn....24 C5
Shirah's Guest House....25 C4
Tony's Guesthouse....26 C3
Travellers' Lodge....27 C4
Voyage Guest House....28 B3

EATING
Capitol Satay....29 C3
Indri Ori....30 C4
Low Yong Mow....31 B2
Medan Makan Bunga Raya....32 C2
Newton Food Court....33 B4
Pak Putra Restaurant....34 A3
Poh Piah Lwee....35 A2
Selvam....36 C3
Vegan Salad & Herbs House....37 A2

DRINKING
Pure Bar....38 D5
Voyage Travellers Lounge....39 B3

SHOPPING
Dataran Pahlawan....40 C4
Mahkota Parade Shopping Complex....41 B4
Top Spinning Academy....42 A2

TRANSPORT
Ferries to Indonesia....43 A4
Indonesia Ferry Ticket Offices....44 B4

PAINTING THE TOWN RED

We can thank the British for Town Sq's Golden Gate Bridge–red paint job; they brightened it up from a sombre Dutch white in 1911. Lots of theories have been proposed as to why the buildings were painted this colour; the most likely is that the red laterite stone used to build Stadthuys showed through the whitewashed plastering, and/or heavy tropical rain splashed red soil up the white walls – the thrifty Brits decided to paint it all red to save on maintenance costs.

MONEY

Money changers are scattered about town, especially near the guest houses off Jln TMR and Chinatown.

HSBC (Jln Hang Tuah) With 24-hour ATMs that accept international cards.

POST & TELEPHONE

Post office (Jln Laksamana) This small post office can be found off Town Sq.

TOURIST INFORMATION

Tourism Malaysia (☎ 283 6220; ⏰ 9am-10pm) At the Menara Taming Sari; has very knowledgeable, helpful staff.

Tourism Melaka (☎ 281 4803, 1800 889 483; www.melaka.gov.my; Jln Kota; ⏰ 9am-1pm & 2-5.30pm)

Sights

TOWN SQUARE & BUKIT ST PAUL

The most imposing relic of the Dutch period in Melaka is **Stadthuys** (Town Sq; adult RM5; ⏰ 9am-5.30pm Sat-Thu, 9am-12.15pm & 2.45-5.30pm Fri), the massive red town hall and governors' residence. Believed to be the oldest Dutch building in the East, it now houses the **Historical, Ethnographic & Literature Museums**, which are included in the price of admission and exhaustively recounts Malaysian history and literary development. Facing the square is the bright-red **Christ Church** (1753).

From Stadthuys, steps lead up Bukit St Paul, which is a hill topped by the ruins of **St Paul's Church**, built in 1521 by a Portuguese sea captain, and overlooking the famous Straits of Melaka.

A quick photo stop, **Porta de Santiago** was built by the Portuguese as a fortress in 1511. The Dutch were busy destroying the majority of the fort when Sir Stamford Raffles came by in 1810 and saved what remains today. Look for the 'VOC' inscription of the Dutch East India Company on the arch.

Within the park across from Jln Kota you won't be able to miss the 80m-high **Menara Taming Sari** (adult/child RM20/10; ⏰ 10am-10pm), a revolving tower that's a bit tourist-tacky, but is the most fun way to get great views over the city.

Way out at the Sungai Melaka river mouth is yet another means to check out the view, **Eye on Malaysia, Melaka** (adult/child RM20/10; ⏰ 10am-11pm Mon-Thu, 10am-midnight Fri & Sat), a giant gondola-style Ferris wheel that spins very slowly for about 20 minutes. At the time of writing several very big cinema and performance attractions, to be housed next the Ferris wheel, were in the planning stages.

CHINATOWN

Chinatown is the heart of Melaka. Stroll along **Jln Tun Tan Cheng Lock**, formerly called Heeren St, which was the preferred address for wealthy Baba (Straits-born Chinese) traders who were most active during the early 20th century. The centre street of Chinatown is **Jln Hang Jebat**, formerly known as Jonker St (or Junk St Melaka), which was once famed for its antique shops but is now more of a collection of clothing and crafts outlets and restaurants. On Friday and Saturday nights the street is transformed into the **Jonker's Night Market**, a lively market of food and trinket stalls. The northern section of quiet **Jln Tukang** (also known as Harmony St) has a handful of authentic Chinese shops.

The 18th-century Dutch-period **8 Heeren Street** (admission free; ⏰ 11am-4pm Tue-Sat) was restored as a model conservation project and exploring the house lets you imagine what life would have been like inside its walls over the centuries. You can also pick up an *Endangered Trades: A Walking Tour of Malacca's Living Heritage* (RM5) booklet and map for an excellent self-guided tour of the city centre.

Just down the street is the **Baba-Nonya Heritage Museum** (☎ 283 1273; 48-50 Jln Tun Tan Cheng Lock; adult RM8; ⏰ 10am-12.30pm & 2-4.30pm Wed-Mon), a captivating museum of the Nonya culture set in a traditional Peranakan town house in Chinatown.

Cheng Hoon Teng (Qing Yun Ting, Green Clouds Temple; Jln Tukang) is Chinatown's most famous temple, dating back to 1646. It's Malaysia's oldest Chinese temple and all materials used in its building were imported from China.

VILLA SENTOSA

After sampling Melaka's Chinese and European heritage, don't overlook the city's Malay family tree. **Villa Sentosa** (☎ 282 3988; www.travel.to/villasentosa; 138 Kampong Morten; admission by donation; ⏲ 9am-1pm & 2-5pm Sat-Thu, 2.45-5pm Fri) is a private museum on the Melaka River in Kampung Morten. Tours led by family members include a visit to the ancestral *kampung* home, dating from the 1920s, filled with Malay handicrafts and architecture.

Sleeping

JLN TAMAN MELAKA RAYA (JLN TMR)

A clutch of guest houses congregate at the western end of Jln Taman Melaka Raya (Jln TMR), a charmless complex of shophouses about five- to 10-minutes' walk from Chinatown. From Melaka Sentral, take town Bus 17 (RM1) or the Panorama Melaka bus (RM2 to RM5). Most places have a choice of shared or private bathrooms.

Shirah's Guest House (☎ 286 1041; shirahgh@tm.ent.my; 207-209, 2nd fl, Jln Melaka Raya 1; fan dm/d RM12/30, air-con d RM45; ❄ 💻) Lots of Mediterranean colours and a gentle Malay vibe make Shirah's a particularly cosy backpackers'. The three-bed dorms and doubles are excellent value.

Samudra Inn (☎ 282 7441; samudrainn@hotmail.com; 348B Jln Melaka Raya 3; dm/d from RM12/30; ❄) The owners at the very quiet Samudra run a tight ship and go above and beyond standard service to make sure guests are comfortable. It's a homestay atmosphere with chirping birds and satellite telly at night.

our pick **Emily Travellers Home** (☎ 012 301 8524; 71 Jln Parameswara; dm/s RM16/24, d RM32-48) A humble entrance off the busy road brings you to another dimension of plants, koi ponds, a bunny hopping around and happy, mingling people. Sleeping options range from funky cottages with semi-outdoor 'jungle showers', to simple wooden rooms in the house – the dorm rooms have two beds apiece.

Travellers' Lodge (☎ 226 5709; 214B Jln Melaka Raya 1; fan d from RM30; ❄) With an enticing elevated sitting area that has mats on the floors, a plant-filled rooftop terrace and good rooms – some of which have lofts – this is a great place to meet other travellers.

CHINATOWN & AROUND

Melaka's most scenic section of town is a really fun place to stay. Because of preservation restrictions, however, most places only have shared bathrooms. Take town Bus 17 (RM1) or the Panorama Melaka bus (RM2 to RM5) from Melaka Sentral to Town Sq.

Eastern Heritage Guest House (☎ 283 3026; 8 Jln Bukit China; dm/s/d RM10/28/30) In a 1918 building, Eastern Heritage has polished wood floors, ancient tiles and an antique style from lots of eroding paint. The dorm is airless but the rooms are brightened up with murals.

Voyage Guest House (☎ 281 5216; Jln Tukang Besi; dm RM12) Clean, industrial-sized dorm rooms and common areas are decorated with a nouveau-heritage lounge look.

Sama-Sama Guest House (☎ 305 1980; 26 Jln Tukang Besi; dm RM12, d RM20-40) Big creaky rooms are arranged around an interior courtyard of water lilies and cool breezes. Downstairs lazy cats and the odd human snooze to a soundtrack of reggae.

Jalan Jalan Guesthouse (☎ 283 3937; www.jalanjalanguesthouse.com; 8 Jln Tukang Emas; dm/s/d RM12/23/34; 💻 📶) In a restored periwinkle-blue shophouse, fan-cooled rooms with one shared bathroom are spread out over a tranquil inner courtyard garden.

Ringo's Foyer (☎ 016 354 2223; www.ringosfoyer.com; 46-A Jln Portugis; dm/s/d/tr RM12/25/30/40; 📶) Just far enough out of central Chinatown to be quiet, but close enough to be convenient, Ringo's is plain and clean, has friendly staff and a relaxing rooftop chill-out area.

Tony's Guesthouse (☎ 688 0119; 24 Lg Banda Kaba; r RM24-28; 📶) A scatter-brained, old-school hippy backpacker's place, this is a great spot to meet other budget road warriors over tea.

Eating

Melaka's most famous cuisine is Nonya food (see the boxed text, p433). In Melaka the Portuguese might have wreaked havoc on civic order, but they built up a tradition for cakes and seafood, which is most obvious in the Eurasian dish of devil's curry. Then there are the immigrant contributions of Indian curries and the ever-versatile Chinese noodle dishes.

Low Yong Mow (32 Jln Tukang Emas; dim sum RM1-3; ⏲ 5am-noon Wed-Mon) A bustling Chinese favourite for a traditional dim sum breakfast and famed for its giant *pao* (pork buns).

Poh Piah Lwee (Jln Kubu; ⏲ 9am-5pm) An authentic and lively hole in the wall with one specialist cook preparing delicious Hokkein-style *popiah* (RM2), another making near-perfect *rojak* (a fruit-and-vegie salad topped with a

DON'T LEAVE MELAKA WITHOUT TRYING...

- **Cendol** Shaved-ice treat with jellies, coconut milk and Melaka's famous cane syrup
- **Laksa** The regional version is distinguished by its coconut milk and lemongrass-infused broth
- **Nonya pineapple tarts** Buttery pastries with a chewy pineapple-jam filling
- **Popiah** An uber–spring roll stuffed with shredded carrots, prawns, chilli, garlic, palm sugar and much, much more
- **Satay celup** Like fondue but better; dunk tofu, prawns and more into bubbling soup to cook it to your liking

sweet-and-spicy gravy; RM3) while the third whips up a fantastic laksa (RM3).

Indi Ori (☎ 282 4777; 236 & 237 Jln Melaka Raya 1; dishes RM1-15; ⏰ breakfast, lunch & dinner) Mmm, Indonesian Padang food: just like the real thing but without the flies. Favourites include avocado juice with chocolate sauce (RM4.50), and Sekotang (hot ginger with egg yolk, sweet cream and peanut dumplings; RM6).

Medan Makan Bunga Raya (btwn Jln Bunga Raya & Jln Bendahara; dishes RM2-6; ⏰ breakfast, lunch & dinner) When you hear the sound of the meat cleaver, you've reached 'Hungry Lane', known for Indian-style curry-pork rice and *gula melaka* (palm sugar) during the day.

Newton Food Court (Jln Merdeka; meals RM3-15; ⏰ lunch & dinner) Get Chinese in the main hall and halal food at the back of this clean food court under an elegant Malay-style roof.

our pick **Pak Putra Restaurant** (56 Jln Taman Kota Laksamana; tandoori from RM5; ⏰ dinner, closed every other Mon) This Pakistani place cooks up a variety of meats and seafood in clay tandoori ovens perched on the sidewalk. Side dishes of veg are around RM5 and a mango lassi costs RM4.

Capitol Satay (☎ 283 5508; 41 Lg Bukit China; meals RM5-10; ⏰ Tue-Sun) Capitol is famous for satay *celup* (a Melaka adaptation of satay steamboat). Stainless-steel tables have a bubbling vat of satay sauce in the middle and you dunk skewers of okra (ladies' finger) stuffed with fish, tofu, Chinese sausage, chicken, pork, prawns and bok choy, and side dishes of pickled egg with pickled ginger.

Selvam (☎ 281 9223; 3 Jln Temenggong; meals RM7; ⏰ breakfast, lunch & dinner) Melakans love this Little India banana-leaf smorgasbord. There's a choice range of tasty and cheap curries and roti, plus a Friday afternoon vegetarian special with 10 tasty dishes for only RM6.

Vegan Salad & Herbs House (☎ 282 9466; 22 Jln Kubu; meals RM10; ⏰ 8.30am-4pm Fri-Wed) This spot offers healthy uncooked, crisp vegetables, brown rice set lunches and wholemeal bread buns.

Kampong Portugis (⏰ dinner) In the eastern part of the city, 3km from Town Sq, is a small community that claims mixed Portuguese–Indian ancestry. This otherwise nondescript neighbourhood caters to the curious tourists with food stalls and a number of clunky Eurasian restaurants. At weekend evenings, Restoran de Lisbon (meals RM30) is known for its chilli crabs and devil curry. At any other time of the week, Medan Portugis has a variety of food stalls, serving many of the same dishes at seaside tables. Take town Bus 17 or the Panorama Melaka tourist bus to Kampong Portugis and walk towards the sea.

Drinking

During the weekend night market on Jonker St, the happening bar strip on Jln Hang Lekir turns into a street party closed off to traffic. Medan Portugis, in Kampong Portugis (see above), has cheap beers and sunset views. The alleys in the backpacker ghetto off Jln TMR have lots of watering troughs.

Voyage Travellers Lounge (40 Lg Hang Jebat; 💻) Melt into a wicker chair with a snack and a beer and chat with the friendly regulars. Patrons can use the internet for half an hour for free.

Pure Bar (591-A Jln Taman Melaka Rayal; ⏰ 5pm-2am) This has become Melaka's most fun bar–nightclub, popular with locals.

Shopping

A wander through Chinatown, with its quality assortment of clothing, trinket and antique shops, will have you wishing for more room in your pack. **Dataran Pahlawan** (Jln Merdeka) and **Mahkota Parade Shopping Complex** (Jln Merdeka) are Melaka's two megamalls, the former being the larger and more fashion-conscious and the latter being better for practical needs such as a pharmacy or camera shop.

If you stop by the **Top Spinning Academy** (79 Jln Tokong; ⏰ 10am-4pm), be prepared for a very enthusiastic traditional top-spinning lesson by *gasing* extraordinaire Simpson Wong. You aren't expected to purchase anything although you probably will if you get the hang of the spin – a top is only RM2.

Getting There & Away

Melaka is 144km southeast of KL.

Melaka's local bus station, express bus station and taxi station are all combined into the massive **Melaka Sentral** (Jln Panglima Awang), roughly 5km north of Town Sq. Because Melaka is a popular weekend destination, make advance bus reservations for Singapore and Kuala Lumpur.

You can get to nearly every major city in Malaysia from Melaka. Some long-distance destinations include: KL (RM12, two hours, hourly departures), Jerantut (RM23, five hours, one daily), Johor Bahru (RM19, three hours, hourly departures), Kota Bharu (RM51, 10 hours, five daily), Kuala Terengganu (RM43, nine hours, five daily), Mersing (RM23, 4½ hours, two daily) and Singapore (RM22, 4½ hours, hourly departures).

You can take the **A-Bus Express** (☎ 281 7669; RM36) to KL International Airport (two hours, seven daily departures). Book tickets at the tourist offices or your guest house.

Firefly (☎ 03-7845 4543) flies to/from Singapore three days a week. Melaka's airport is at Batu Berendam, 9km north of the town centre.

Getting Around

Bus 17 runs frequently from the Melaka Sentral bus station to Town Sq, Mahkota Parade Shopping Complex, Taman Melaka Raya (RM1) and Medan Portugis (RM1.20).

GETTING TO INDONESIA: MELAKA TO DUMAI, PEKANBARU & PULAU BENGKALIS

High-speed ferries make the trip from Melaka to Dumai, Indonesia, daily at around 10am (one way/return RM119/170, 1¾ hours), from Melaka to Pekanbaru (one way/return RM159/269, six hours), Indonesia, at 9.30am on Tuesday, Thursday and Sunday, and to Pulau Bengkalis in Indonesia four days per week. Tickets are available at offices near the wharf.

See p320 for information on doing the trip in reverse.

Panorama Melaka tourist bus offers hop-on, hop-off services (RM2 to RM5, 9am to 8.30pm, every 30 to 45 minutes). Buy your ticket (good all day) on the bus. Stops include the Hang Tua Mall, Melaka Sentral, Jln Hang Jebat (Jonker Walk), the Stadthuys and Kampung Portugis. Route maps and more information are available at the Tourism Malaysia office (p452).

Melaka is a walking city. Bicycles can be hired at some guest houses for around RM10 per day; there are also a few bike-hire outfits around town.

A trishaw should cost around RM15 for any one-way trip within town, but you'll have to bargain. Taxis charge around RM10 within a 5km radius.

PORT DICKSON

☎ 06

The pretty strip of white sand at Port Dickson lazily meanders for some 16km. Although it's a cheesy resort area and the water is fairly polluted, it's one of the few places on this coast where you can have a real beach holiday without going to an island. Beach aside, the real highlight of this area is the 80-hectare **Cape Rachado Forest Reserve** (also called the Tanjung Tuan Forest Reserve), the only patch of coastal forest left on the west coast of Peninsular Malaysia. This lowland jungle has secluded beaches and is also a stopover for over 300,000 migratory birds every year.

The turn-off to the reserve is near the Km 16 marker (take the local bus); head down the road for 2km to the Ilham Resort and then through the forest reserve for another kilometre to the **Tanjung Tuan lighthouse**, which isn't open to the public. From here the views are stunning and on a clear day you can see Sumatra, 38km away across Selat Melaka. A network of trails leads into the forest and to some beaches (bring lots of water – it's a steep climb).

Beachside food is limited to a few mediocre food courts and restaurants selling crab by the kilo. To stay at the beach, head to the **Rotary Sunshine Camp Holiday Hostel** (☎ 647 3798; Km 5 Jln Pantai; dm/r RM7/25), a well-tended barracks-like place. Shower and cooking facilities are shared and it's a short walk to a good beach and cheap food. Near the forest reserve entrance is the Caribbean-themed **Casa Rachado** (☎ 662 5177; casaranchado@maa.com.my; Tanjung Biru, Km 16 Jln Pantai; camp sites for 2/4 people RM30/50, r from RM99;).

Rooms are musty but there's a nice mangrove-fringed beach and a pool. Camping gets you access to the amenities and includes a tent, floor mat and kerosene lantern.

Getting There & Around

Hourly buses depart for Seremban (RM4, one hour), from where you can get connections to KL, Melaka and beyond.

All buses arrive in Port Dickson town from where local buses (RM1) run about every hour and will drop you off anywhere along the beach. Ubiquitous share taxis are more reliable and cost RM2 for the first few kilometres – expect to pay RM5 to RM15 to get from Port Dickson Town to your hotel.

CAMERON HIGHLANDS

☎ 05

If you've been sweating through jungles and beaches for weeks and another sticky day will make your clothes unwearable, we grant you a reprieve: the Cameron Highlands. This alpine-scape of blue peaks, green humps, fuzzy tea plantations and white waterfalls has a temperature that rarely drops below 10°C or climbs above 21°C. Trekking, tea tasting and visiting local agro-tourism sites are all on the to-do list; you can also meet other backpackers, as this is one of the major nodes on the banana-pancake trail.

Unfortunately, development, erosion and poorly planned agriculture have taken their toll on the highlands, and landslips and floods have been the environmental by-product. Tourists are the backbone of the economy in this part of the country, and their purchasing power will have a huge impact on what the Cameron Highlands eventually becomes: blighted blockhouses scarring the hills, or the cultivated, beautiful heart of the upland Malaysian peninsula.

Orientation & Information

The Cameron Highlands stretches along the road from the town of Ringlet, through to the main highland towns of Tanah Rata, Brinchang and beyond to smaller villages in the northeast.

Tanah Rata is the main highland town for budget accommodation and other essentials. Most guest houses offer internet access for around RM5 an hour. See p532 for volunteer opportunities.

Maybank (Pesiaran Camellia 4)

Tourist Information Centre (☎ 519 7246; mctic@tm.net.my; off Jln Dayang Endah; 8.30am-12.30pm & 1.30-5pm Mon-Fri, 8.30am-2pm Sat) Very helpful with maps and trail information.

Sights & Activities

Taking in a jungle stroll is often the best way to reach some of the area's other tourist attractions. Most walks and sights can be accessed by the local bus, a rattler that chugs up and down the main highway.

Visiting one of the tea plantations is a must. The rolling hills are carpeted with hectares of green and occasionally speckled with tea pickers wading between the rows, snipping the tender green tips. **Sungai Palas Boh Tea Estate** (Gunung Brinchang Rd, Brinchang; admission free; 9am-4.30pm Tue-Sun) is the easiest plantation to visit on your own. Tours are free and the tea rooms out the back offer grand vistas. Take the local bus north from the main (Tanah Rata) bus station, past Brinchang towards Kampung Raja. In between is a tourist strip of strawberry and butterfly farms; hop off the bus at the roadside vegetable stalls and follow the intersecting road.

Boh Tea Estate (Boh Rd Habu, Ringlet; admission free; tours hourly 10am-3.30pm) below Tanah Rata, 8km from the main road, is also open to the public. It's only a 45-minute walk from the end of jungle Trail 9A, which you can pick up outside Tanah Rata.

Sam Poh Temple (Brinchang; admission by donation) is a typically Chinese kaleidoscope of Buddha statues, stone lions and incense burners. It's accessible from Tanah Rata – take Trail 3, near the golf course, and then connect to Trail 2.

When you head out on a trail, go in pairs and take lots of drinking water and rain gear. Check with the Tourist Information Centre about the state of the trails and recommended walks. Guest houses in Tanah Rata often employ informal guides who lead daily walks. Inexperienced walkers are advised to employ a guide on the longer trails; in recent years, several people have become lost. Single women have also been attacked in remote areas.

Tour operators in Tanah Rata offer a variety of day trips that include visits to a tea plantation, strawberry farm, flower and cactus nursery, honey farm and butterfly farm for around RM25 per person. Tours operating out of Father's Guest House include a good jungle-flora trip perfect for plant nerds.

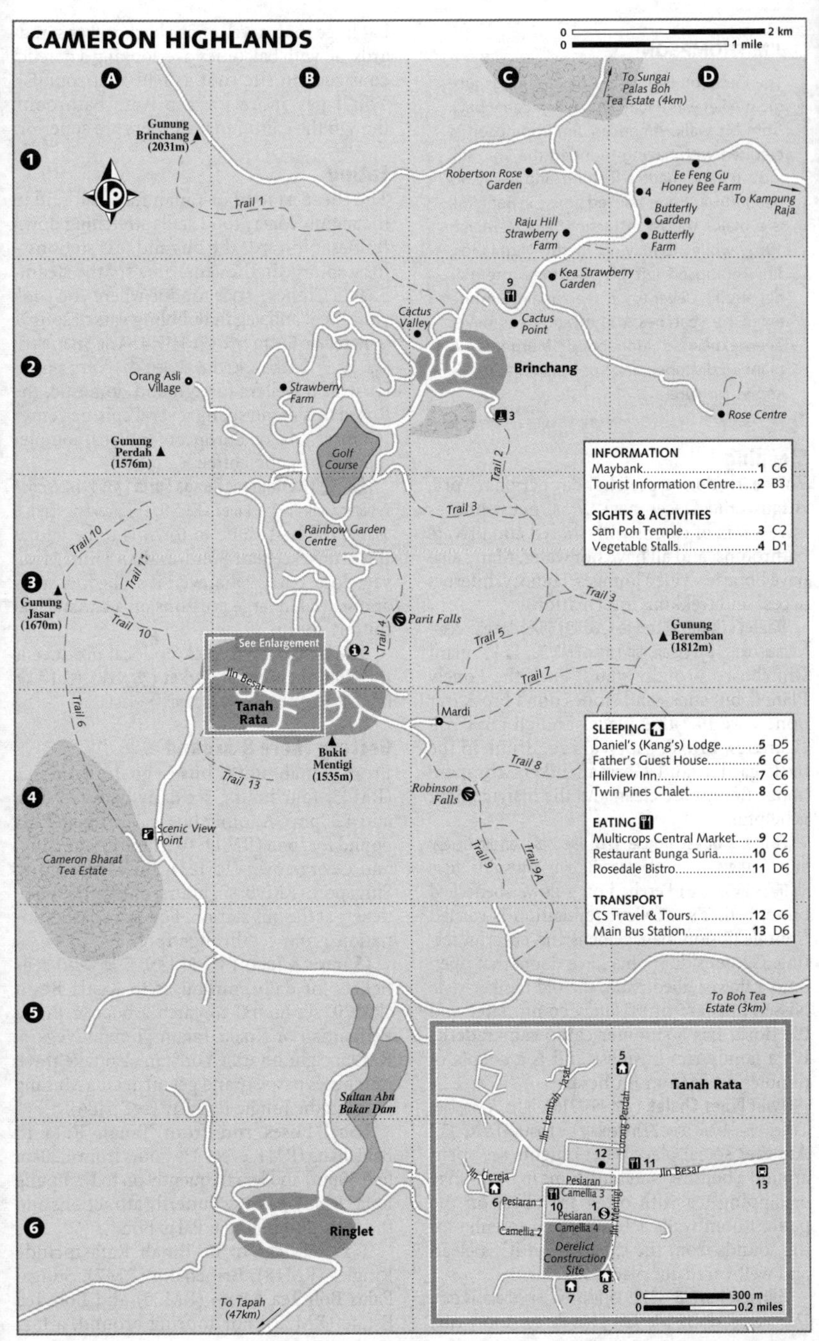

INFORMATION

Maybank.......1 C6
Tourist Information Centre.......2 B3

SIGHTS & ACTIVITIES

Sam Poh Temple.......3 C2
Vegetable Stalls.......4 D1

SLEEPING

Daniel's (Kang's) Lodge.......5 D5
Father's Guest House.......6 C6
Hillview Inn.......7 C6
Twin Pines Chalet.......8 C6

EATING

Multicrops Central Market.......9 C2
Restaurant Bunga Suria.......10 C6
Rosedale Bistro.......11 D6

TRANSPORT

CS Travel & Tours.......12 C6
Main Bus Station.......13 D6

JIM THOMPSON

The Cameron Highlands' most famous jungle trekker was a man who never came back from his walk. American Jim Thompson is credited with having founded the Thai silk industry and made a fortune, and today his beautiful, antique-packed house in Bangkok is a major tourist attraction. On 26 March 1967, while holidaying in the Highlands, Jim Thompson left his villa for a pre-dinner stroll – never to be seen again. Despite extensive searches, the mystery has never been explained. Kidnapped? Murdered? A planned disappearance or suicide? Nobody knows for sure.

Sleeping

Book early during peak holiday periods (April, August and December). Most guest houses have a mix of rooms with shared and private bathrooms, and all have hot water. Many also have libraries, video lounges, laundry, internet access and trekking information.

Daniel's (Kang's) Lodge (☎ 491 5823; danielslodge@hotmail.com; 9 Lg Perdah; dm/r from RM8/20; 💻) A giant whiteboard proudly states 'Fuck the Lonely Planet', but sticks and stones don't break our bones, we like this place! French guys roll cigarettes, British gap-years get drunk in the back garden and German hikers compare boots. Rooms are clean and the management is helpful.

Father's Guest House (☎ 491 2484; off Jln Gereja; http://fathers.cameronhighlands.com; dm/s/d/tr from RM10/25/30/50; 💻) Perched on a flower-bedecked butte, Father's excellent reputation is earned from its tip-top management and cheerful setting. Gardenside rooms have doors that open onto a flower-filled patio, the old bunker-style Nissen huts are surprisingly comfortable and the dorm has a summer-camp camaraderie. It's a family-run business and is a couple of minutes' walk from Jln Besar.

Twin Pines Chalet (☎ 491 2169; http://twinpines.cameronhighlands.com; 2 Jln Mentigi; s/d from RM12/20; 💻) Another social place where nights are spent around a bonfire, watching films in the lounge or sipping tea with other travellers on the patio. Room walls actually seem to enhance the sounds from the exterior but it's a clean and well-cared-for place.

Hillview Inn (☎ 491 2915; hillview_inn@hotmail.com; 17 Jln Mentigi; r RM55-140; 💻) This three-storey villa has large rooms well above backpacker standards, all with balconies overlooking a derelict construction site (not as bad as it sounds). You'll pay more for a private bathroom, though the communal showers are superior.

Eating

The cheapest food in Tanah Rata is found in the mainly Malay food stalls stretching down Jln Besar towards the bus and taxi stations – for a splurge in the same area try the steamboat (a Chinese-style fondue where you cook your meat and veg in bubbling vats of soup).

Rosedale Bistro (☎ 491 1419; 42-A Jln Besar; mains RM5-18; 🕑 breakfast, lunch & dinner; 📶) Very popular with travellers foreign and domestic, the Rosedale's menu spans several cuisine genres (Chinese, Malay, European, Indian), complemented by good coffee.

our pick **Restaurant Bunga Suria** (☎ 491 4666; 66A Pesiaran Camellia 3; set meals RM5-9; 🕑 breakfast, lunch & dinner) The best value in town is to be had at this truly excellent South Indian joint. Meat, veg, dosa, curry, whatever: it's all good, spicy and served in large portions on a banana leaf for dirt cheap.

The best place to pick up local produce is the **Multicrops Central Market** (☎ 491 5188; 1 Arkid Peladang Sungai Burung, Brinchang; 🕑 9am-6pm).

Getting There & Around

From Tanah Rata, buses go to/from KL (RM23, four hours, six daily between 8am and 4.30pm). Another bus leaves Tanah Rata bound for Ipoh (RM11, two hours, four daily) and Georgetown (RM23). Buses also go to Singapore (RM90, six hours, one daily). Book tickets at the bus station. For east coast destinations, connect through Ipoh.

CS Travel & Tours (☎ 491 1200; 47 Jln Besar) sells tickets for daily minibuses to Kuala Besut (RM70, six hours) to catch a boat to Pulau Perhentian or Kuala Tahan (Taman Negara; RM95, eight hours). You can also take these minibuses partway and get off at Gua Musang to catch the Jungle Railway (see p486).

Local buses run from Tanah Rata to Brinchang (RM1, every 1½ hours from 6.30am to 6.30pm) and less frequently on to Kampung Raja (RM3), passing butterfly attractions and the turn-off to Sungai Palas Boh.

Taxi services from Tanah Rata include Ringlet (RM18), Brinchang (RM7), Sungai Palas Boh Tea Estate (RM20) and Boh Tea Estate (RM25). For touring around, a taxi

CAVE TEMPLES

Ipoh's jungle-clad limestone hills are riddled with caves that locals believe to be a great source of spiritual power. There are Buddhist cave-temples on the outskirts of town, including the beautiful mural-heavy **Perak Tong** (8am-5pm), 6km north on the road to Kuala Kangsar, and **Sam Poh Tong** (8am-5pm), a few kilometres to the south, which is the largest cave temple in Malaysia and has an ornamental garden in front. Both are easily accessible by local bus.

costs RM25 per hour, or you can go up to Gunung Brinchang and back for RM80.

While we never recommend hitch-hiking, many travellers do so here to get between Tanah Rata and Brinchang and the tea plantations beyond.

IPOH

05 / pop 710,800

Ipoh (ee-po) is chock full of faded tropical mansions and a few green lungs. The **Old Town** showcases elegant colonial architecture and the magnificent **train station** (known locally as the 'Taj Mahal'), but it's also where you'll find the local bus stations. The elegant layout and design of the town comes from the prosperity once generated from tin mining; this was once one of the wealthiest cities in Southeast Asia. Traffic-clogged New Town east of the river is home to most of the hotels and restaurants.

For most, the town is a transit link to the Cameron Highlands, Pulau Pangkor and beyond but it merits a day if you have the time. The **tourist information centre** (241 2959, 529 0894; Jln Tun Sambathan; 8am-5pm Mon-Fri) is near the *padang* and **HSBC** (Jln Tun Sambathan) bank is near the clocktower.

Sleeping & Eating

Ipoh's culinary specialities include *kway teow* (rice-noodle soup) and Ipoh white coffee, made with palm-oil margarine and served with condensed milk.

Steer clear of some of the city's cheap dingy 'hotels' that are actually brothels. The following are respectable:

Embassy (254 9496; 19 Jln CM Yusuf; r from 25) This is as cheap and cheerful as Ipoh gets (it does get cheaper, but definitely not more cheery). Not a lot of character, but rooms are clean.

Sun Golden Inn (243 6255; 17 Jln Che Tak; r RM40-80) One of Ipoh's better budget choices, the Sun Golden Inn is a clean and friendly Chinese hotel, with good management who is used to dealing with Westerners.

MBI Terrace (off Jln Sultan Abdul Jalil; 7pm-midnight) Essentially attached to the city's municipal sports complex, many Ipoh residents will tell you the best *kway teow* in town is served here.

Medan Selera Dato Tawhil Azar (Jln Raja Musa Aziz; dinner) This large open-air food stall around a small square is a good spot for a Malay meal.

Getting There & Away

The **long-distance bus station** (Medan Gopeng) is south of the train station and the city centre; frequent shuttle buses to the city bus station cost RM1.30.

Destinations include: Alor Setar (RM17, four hours, two daily), Butterworth (RM15, three hours, five daily), Hat Yai in Thailand (RM65, nine hours, one daily), Johor Bahru (RM37, eight hours, two daily), Kota Bharu (RM25, seven hours, one daily), KL (RM14, three hours, hourly), Lumut (RM7, two hours, frequent) and Melaka (RM23, five hours, three daily).

The local bus station is northwest of the long-distance station on the other side of the roundabout. Local buses depart from here for outlying regions close to Ipoh, such as Kuala Kangsar (RM6) and Tanah Rata in the Cameron Highlands (RM10).

Ipoh's **train station** (254 0481; Jln Panglima Bukit Gantang Wahab) is on the main Singapore–Butterworth line. There are daily trains to both KL (RM12, 4½ hours) and Butterworth (RM17, five hours), the latter continuing to Hat Yai in Thailand (RM30, 10 hours).

LUMUT

05

Lumut is the departure point for Pulau Pangkor. **Tourism Malaysia** (683 4057; Jln Sultan Idris Shah; 9am-5pm Mon-Fri, 9am-1.45pm Sat) is midway between the jetty and the bus station. Next door you'll find a money changer offering better rates than on Pulau Pangkor, and Maybank further down the street.

If you get marooned in town, head straight to **Era Backpackers Hotel** (☎ 013 598 3005, 683 8910; 7-9 Jln Raja Muda Musa; dm/r from RM15/25; ❄), directly across from the bus station, which has a helpful and knowledgeable owner. Some rooms have private bathrooms.

Direct buses run to/from KL (RM19, four hours, eight daily), Butterworth (RM13, five hours, three daily) and Johor Bahru (RM40, 10 hours, two daily). There are no direct buses from Lumut to the Cameron Highlands; take a bus to Ipoh (RM6, two hours, hourly), then transfer to Tanah Rata.

The Pulau Pangkor pier is an easy walk from the bus station. Boats run every 30 to 45 minutes and cost RM10.

PULAU PANGKOR

☎ 05 / pop 25,000

Pulau Pangkor is more of a girl-next-door island as opposed to the supermodels of the east coast and Langkawi. That said, it feels good to get away from the glitz and settle into an honest *kampung* with a lazy island atmosphere. The jungle is swarming with monkeys and hornbills and you can dine nightly on fresh fish while watching the sunset.

Pangkor's piece of history, the foundations of a **Dutch fort** dating from 1670, is 3km south of Pangkor Town at Teluk Gedong.

Ferries from Lumut first stop on the eastern side of the island at Sungai Pinang Kecil (SPK) and then go to Pangkor Town, where you'll find banks, restaurants and shops.

Sights & Activities

Snorkel gear and boats can be hired at hotels or on the beach. The main beaches are on the west coast. Travellers, especially women, should take care on empty stretches at the island's northeastern side and south of Pangkor Town. There's also good **walking** here, arguably better than on any other Malaysian island; most guest houses have lots of information and can organise a guide.

Five minutes' walk north of Teluk Nipah, **Coral Bay** is the best beach on this side of the island, with clear, emerald-green water, due to the presence of limestone.

Pasir Bogak is a swimming beach favoured by holidaying Malaysians, and gets crowded during holidays when it also gets trashed. A popular backpacker haven, **Teluk Nipah** is north of Pasir Bogak. This is a scenic beach with a variety of budget accommodation and a lively atmosphere.

Sleeping, Eating & Drinking

Most accommodation is set on access roads between the beachfront road and the jungle. Options are pricey and we found that anything costing under RM30 was pretty dire. Several of Teluk Nipah's guest houses have restaurants, though outside the high season (November to March) these often close down. Most restaurants serve alcohol. There are also some basic food stalls at the beach.

Nazri Nipah Camp (☎ 685 2014, 012-576 0267; rozie1982@hotmail.com; dm/r from RM10/40) Located at the edge of the jungle, there's (surprise) a chilled-out reggae theme going on here. Accommodation ranges from simple A-frames to more comfortable chalets with bathrooms. There's also a secluded beer garden and TV lounge.

Purnama Beach Resort (☎ 685 3530; www.purnama.com.my; r RM30-80; ❄ 💻 🏊) This spiffy complex of chalets includes some fairly simple (and lovely) fan huts and neat, motel-style doubles. There's a good restaurant and a very small pool and breakfast is included.

Olala Chalet (☎ 685 5112; s/d RM50/70; ❄) For chalets with AC and TV these are pretty good deals, but some cabins are in better shape than others, so ask to see a few. Attracts a lot of domestic tourists.

Takana Juo (TJ's) Restoran (mains from RM6; 🕑 breakfast, lunch & dinner) A family-run Indonesian restaurant at the bungalows of the same name. TJ's serves delicious, cheap food. It's regularly full, so you'll need to get there early.

Getting There & Away

Berjaya Air (☎ 685 5828; www.berjaya-air.com) flies to/from KL's Sultan Abdul Aziz Shah Airport (RM275) daily except on Tuesday and Thursday.

In the high season, ferries (return RM10, 45 minutes, every 30 to 45 minutes from 7am to 8.30pm) run to and from Lumut and Pangkor Town.

Getting Around

There are no public buses but pink minibus taxis operate between 6.30am and 9pm. Fares are set for the entire vehicle to/from the jetty in Pangkor Town and go to Teluk Nipah (RM10) and around the island (RM40).

Motorcycles (RM35) and bicycles (RM15) can be rented in Pangkor Town and at main beaches.

BUTTERWORTH

This mainland town is the jumping-off point for Pulau Penang. The Butterworth–Penang ferry jetty (RM1.20, every 20 minutes from 5.30am to 12.30am) is conveniently located next to the train and bus stations. Fares for the ferry are charged only for the journey from Butterworth to Georgetown (on Penang); returning to Butterworth is free.

Buses depart from Butterworth to the following destinations: Johor Bahru (RM49, 12 hours, six daily), KL (RM26, five hours, hourly), Kota Bharu (RM28, seven hours, two daily), Kuala Terengganu (RM40, 10 hours, two daily), Kuantan (RM43, 12 hours, six daily), Melaka (RM36, 12 hours, two daily) and Singapore (RM53, nine hours, two daily).

There are four daily trains to KL (from RM19) from the **train station** (☎ 323 7962). Heading north, there are two daily trains to Hat Yai, Thailand (economy/berth RM19/68); the afternoon service continues to Bangkok, arriving at around noon the next day.

PULAU PENANG

Penang, along with Singapore, Hong Kong and Macau, is arguably one of the most fascinating islands in Asia. No joke; this is the oldest of the British Straits settlements, predating both Singapore and Melaka. Look at the Straits on a map and the geographical importance of Penang is obvious: this was a prime stop on the watery road between Asia and the markets of Europe and the Middle East. As such, Penang straddles the juncture of both Asia's great kingdoms and the colonial empires that conquered them.

The island's mixed population, dominated by the business-savvy Chinese, is the byproduct of Penang's strategic location. Beyond Georgetown's heat and decay are mediocre beach resorts, such as Batu Ferringhi, and the sleepy Malay fishing village of Teluk Bahang, but Penang is more a place for food and culture than for beaches.

Georgetown

☎ 04 / pop 178,304

Georgetown is a mainstay on the Southeast Asian backpacker trail, and you'll have no problems finding friends here. We highly recommend leaving the hostel ghettoes and wandering through the sensory playground of Georgetown's backstreets where you'll pass fortune tellers, joss smoke, chicken rice, Chinese opera, coffee roasting over a fire and the tingly scent of roasting chillies. Blocks away the serious white buildings of the Colonial District sit mutely along the waterfront. Be sure to eat up – the food here is arguably the best in Malaysia.

ORIENTATION

Georgetown is at the northeastern corner of Pulau Penang. Central Georgetown is compact and easily navigated on foot. Many of the town's oldest mosques, temples and churches can be found at, and around, Lebuh Pitt (also called Jln Masjid Kapitan Keling). Following Jln Penang southwest, you'll reach Kompleks Komtar (Kompleks Tun Abdul Razak), the island's transport hub and shopping centre.

INFORMATION

Branches of major banks and 24-hour ATMs are concentrated around Kompleks Komtar and around Lebuh Pantai and Lebuh Downing. Almost every guest house has internet access, and it's easy to pick up on a wi-fi signal around town. You can stock up on reading supplies at the host of second-hand bookshops.

The monthly *Penang Tourist Newspaper* (RM3) has comprehensive listings of shops, tourist attractions and hotel promotions, as well as detailed pull-out maps. It's usually available free from tourist offices and some hotels.

General Hospital (☎ 229 3333; Jln Residensi) About 2km west of Kompleks Komtar.

Immigration Office (☎ 261 5122; 29A Lebuh Pantai)

Tourism Malaysia (☎ 262 0066; 10 Jln Tun Syed Sheh Barakbah; 8am-5pm Mon-Fri)

DANGERS & ANNOYANCES

While generally a safe place to wander around, Georgetown has its seamy side. Travellers have been mugged at Love Lane and other dimly lit side streets, so take care around this area if you're out late. Motorcycle snatch thieves are also a problem so keep bags and purses strapped across your chest. Women get hassled a lot here, mostly by silent leerers or locals looking for an easy date; dressing conservatively eases, but doesn't erase, the problem.

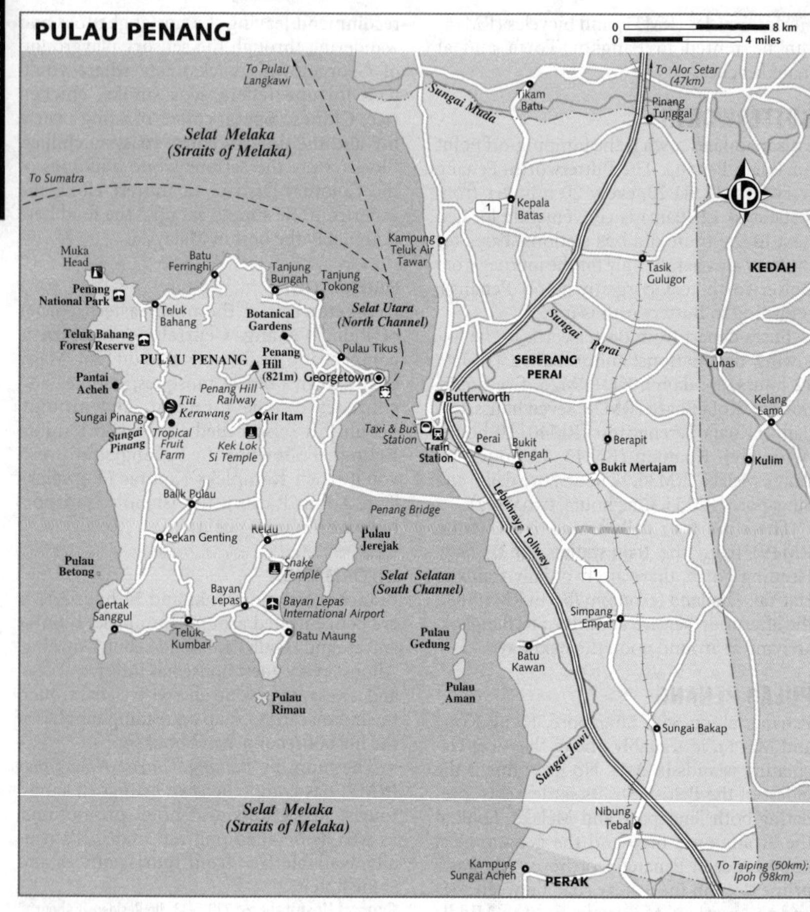

SIGHTS & ACTIVITIES

Temples & Mosques

In honour of the goddess of mercy, good fortune, peace and fertility, the **Kuan Yin Teng** (Lebuh Pitt; admission by donation; 9am-5pm) was built in the early 19th century by the first Hokkien and Cantonese settlers in Penang. It's usually buzzing with worshippers burning paper money.

Built by Penang's first Indian-Muslim settlers, the yellow **Kapitan Keling Mosque** (Lebuh Pitt) has a single minaret in an Indian-influenced Islamic style. This building is best appreciated from the street.

Don't miss **Khoo Kongsi** (Lebuh Cannon; adult RM5; 9am-5pm), Penang's finest *kongsi* (clan house), decorated with a colourful mix of dragons, other statues, paintings, lamps, coloured tiles and carvings. A *kongsi* is a building that's used partly as a temple and partly as a meeting hall for Chinese people of the same clan or surname. This stunning building dates from 1906.

Sri Mariamman Temple (Lebuh Pitt; 8am-noon & 4-9pm) is where local Tamils pay homage to Tamil Nadu by worshipping Mariamman, a mother goddess popular with diaspora Indians. This temple was built in 1883 and is Georgetown's oldest Hindu house of worship.

Other Sights

A magnificent periwinkle-blue mansion, **Cheong Fatt Tze Mansion** (262 5289; www.cheong

fatttzemansion.com; Lebuh Leith; adult RM12; tours 11am & 3pm Mon-Fri, 11am Sat & Sun) was built in the 1880s by Cheong Fatt Tze, a local Hakka merchant-trader who left China penniless and eventually established a financial empire, earning himself the sobriquet 'Rockefeller of the East'. The mansion doubles as a luxurious bed and breakfast (rooms from RM250).

Fort Cornwallis (Lebuh Light; adult RM3; 9am-7pm) was built on Georgetown's cape, the historic landing of the city's founder Captain Francis Light in 1786. A visit involves lots of panel reading.

Penang Museum (261 3144; Lebuh Farquhar; adult RM1; 9am-5pm Sat-Thu) is one of the best-presented museums in Malaysia. Excellent exhibits on the ground floor illustrate the customs and traditions of Penang's various ethnic groups with impressive appreciation for diversity. Upstairs is the history gallery.

European art and Chinese opulence crash together beautifully in the restored **Pinang Peranakan Mansion** (264 2929; www.pinangperanakanmansion.com.my; 29 Lebuh Gereja; adult/child RM10/free; 9.30am-5pm Mon-Sat), former home of Chung Keng Quee, 19th-century merchant, secret-society leader and all-round community pillar. His ornate home is full of antiques. There's also an exhibition on Nonya customs, and guided tours are at 11.30am and 3.30pm.

SLEEPING

Georgetown has plenty of cheap accommodation, mainly clustered in Chinatown along bustling Lebuh Chulia and quieter Love Lane. During holidays, most notably Chinese New Year (January/February), hotels fill up very quickly and prices soar. Cheaper rooms have shared bathrooms.

Blue Diamond Hotel (261 1089; 422 Lebuh Chulia; dm/s/d from RM8/20/28;) Barflies apply here; even staff have stiff drinks in hand by 11am and the place is dominated by its sidewalk-side beer garden. The Chinese clunker of a building is graced with natural light, some lovely old carvings and high ceilings but the rust-stained tubs and grotty staircase take away from the charm. Still, the large rooms are enticingly old world.

100 Cintra Street (264 3581; 100 Lebuh Cintra; dm/s/d RM10/25/38) Housed in a sometimes-operating museum in an atmospheric, semirestored Peranakan mansion, you get a (very thin) mattress on a wooden platform with a fan and a mosquito net for that Eastern colonial experience – some might think it's too authentic. Dorm beds are on an open landing and have zero privacy but are social.

Old Penang Guest House (263 8805; 53 Love Lane; dm/s/d RM15/26/32.50) Hardwood floors, white walls, high ceilings and splashes of red paint add a solid-coloured hip vibe to this hostel set in a restored pre-WWII house. Air-con rooms run to RM50.

Banana Guest House (262 6171; www.bananannewguesthouse.com; 355 Lebuh Chulia; s/d from RM18/25;) The backpacker route lands very firmly at the friendly Banana Guest House, one of those all-purpose hostels-bars–travel agencies you encounter from Bangkok to Bali. Rooms are OK, although some are sectioned off by the thinnest of walls. Pricier air-con digs come with or without toilet (RM50/60).

PENANG MUST EATS

Penang is known as the hawker capital of Malaysia and most of the city's specialities – claiming mixed Malay and Chinese extraction – are best fetched from a portable cart or food centre. Don't leave without trying:

- **Cendol** Garishly coloured green strands (made from sweetened pea flour) are layered with crushed ice, coconut milk and brown-sugar syrup.
- **Char kway teow** Medium-width rice noodles are stir-fried with egg, vegetables, shrimp and Chinese sausage in a dark soy sauce.
- **Laksa asam** Also known as Penang laksa, this is a fish-broth soup spiked with a sour tang from tamarind paste *(asam)* and a mint garnish; it's served with thick, white rice noodles (laksa).
- **Rojak** A fruit-and-vegetable salad tossed in a sweet-tamarind-and-palm-sugar sauce and garnished with crushed peanuts, sesame seeds and chillies.

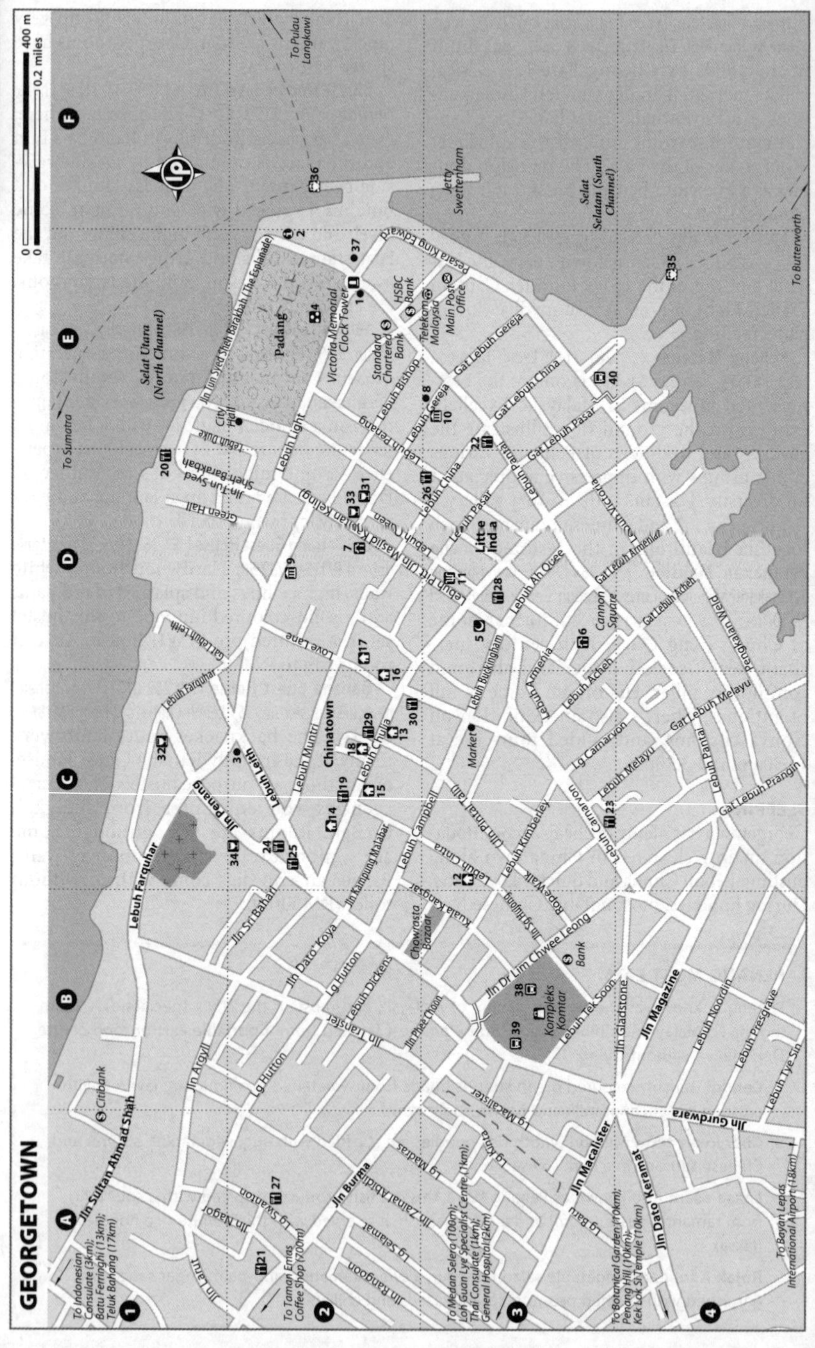
GEORGETOWN
A
B
C
D
E
F
1
2
3
4
0 400 m
0 0.2 miles
To Indonesian Consulate (3km); Batu Ferringhi (13km); Teluk Bahang (17km)
To Taman Emas Coffee Shop (700m)
To Medan Selera (100m); Loh Guan Lye Specialist Centre (1km); Thai Consulate (1km); General Hospital (2km)
To Botanical Garden (10km); Penang Hill (10km); Kek Lok Si Temple (10km)
To Bayan Lepas International Airport (18km)
To Butterworth
To Sumatra
To Pulau Langkawi
Selat Utara (North Channel)
Selat Selatan (South Channel)
Jetty Swettenham
Padang
City Hall
Victoria Memorial Clock Tower
Standard Chartered Bank
HSBC Bank
Telekom Malaysia
Main Post Office
Chinatown
Little India
Cannon Square
Market
Chowrasta Bazaar
Kompleks Komtar
Bank
Citibank
Jln Sultan Ahmad Shah
Lebuh Farquhar
Jln Penang
Lebuh Leith
Lebuh Muntri
Lebuh Chulia
Love Lane
Lebuh Light
Lebuh Penang
Lebuh Bishop
Lebuh Gereja
Lebuh China
Lebuh Pasar
Lebuh Pantai
Gat Lebuh Gereja
Gat Lebuh China
Gat Lebuh Pasar
Gat Lebuh Armenian
Gat Lebuh Acheh
Gat Lebuh Melayu
Gat Lebuh Prangin
Gat Lebuh Leith
Pengkalan Weld
Pesara King Edward
Jln Tun Syed Sheh Barakbah (The Esplanade)
Jln Tun Syed Sheh Barakbah
Lebuh Duke
Green Hall
Lebuh Queen
Jln Masjid Kapitan Keling
Lebuh Pitt
Lebuh Ah Quee
Lebuh Buckingham
Lebuh Armenia
Lebuh Acheh
Lebuh Carnarvon
Lg Carnarvon
Lebuh Melayu
Lebuh Kimberley
Lebuh Cintra
Jln Pinang Tali
Lebuh Campbell
Jln Kampung Malabar
Kuala Kangsar
Jln Sg Ujong
Rope Walk
Jln Dr Lim Chwee Leong
Lebuh Tek Soon
Jln Sri Bahari
Jln Dato' Koya
Lg Hutton
Lebuh Dickens
Jln Transfer
Jln Phee Choon
Jln Argyll
Jln Gladstone
Jln Magazine
Lebuh Noordin
Lebuh Presgrave
Lebuh Tye Sin
Jln Gurdwara
Lg Macalister
Jln Macalister
Lg Kinta
Lg Baru
Jln Dato' Keramat
Jln Burma
Lg Madras
Jln Zainal Abidin
Lg Selamat
Jln Rangoon
Lg Swatow
Jln Nagor
Jln Larut
Lebuh Victoria
Lebuh Farquhar

SD Guesthouse (☎ 264 3743; 15 Love Lane; s/d/t from RM18/25/35;) Creaky floors and cubicle walls but a social vibe; the ups and downs must balance out, because SD is very popular with Georgetown backpackers.

Jim's Place (☎ 16-653 6963, 261 8731; 431 Lebuh Chulia; r RM20-30;) The handful of fan and air-con rooms are above a popular travellers' cafe. It's the usual backpacker-basic arrangement, with shared bathrooms.

Stardust (☎ 263 5723; 370 Lebuh Chulia; s/d from RM25/35;) Despite the name that sounds like an ABBA album, Stardust is several cuts above the average Chulia hotel or Love Lane flophouse. Rooms are spotless and airy.

EATING

Penang cuisine is legendary: Indian, Chinese and Malay purveyors jostle with one another for affection from a constantly snacking populace. Along with Melaka, Penang boasts the indigenous fusion of Baba Nonya cuisine (see p433). If you want something Western, the best choice is **Ecco Cafe** (☎ 262 3178; 402 Lebuh Chulia; meals from RM15; lunch & dinner Mon-Sat), which serves European-style pizza in a cosy, contemporary space.

Chinese

Lebuh Cintra is lined with bustling Chinese noodle and dim sum joints.

Jit Seng Duck Rice (☎ 262 2172; 246 Lebuh Carnarvon (Jln Cheong Fatt Tze); RM3-6; noon-3pm) This hawker stall has a reputation as serving the best duck rice (seasoned and roasted duck with a crisp, sweet skin) in town. The roast pork is great too. Located by the Star Hotel.

Hui Sin Vegetarian Restaurant (11 Lebuh China; meals RM3-6; breakfast & lunch Mon-Sat) Pick from an excellent buffet of vegie and tofu dishes at great prices.

Kheng Pin (80 Jln Penang; mains from RM4; 7am-3pm Tue-Sun) Locals swear by the *lorbak* (spiced ground pork wrapped in bean curd dipped in black gravy) and Hainan chicken rice served at this stall.

Sky Hotel (☎ 262 2322; 348 Lebuh Chulia; around RM6; 11.30am-2.30pm) This place lies in the heart of backpacker central (yet patronised mostly by locals). Don't miss trying the pork dishes and roast duck here. Order your pork '*pun fei sau*' (half-fat, half-lean) to get that proper combination of slightly wet and firm roasted goodness.

our pick **Teik Sen** (Lebuh Carnavon; meals RM8-24; lunch & dinner Wed-Mon) Try the crispy chicken with plum sauce (RM12) or curry prawns (RM6) and show up early if you don't want to wrestle the locals for a table.

> **WALK ABOUT**
>
> The best way to see Penang is on a DIY walking tour. Head to **Penang Heritage Trust** (☎ 264 2631; www.pht.org.my; 26 Lebuh Gereja; 9.30am-12.30pm & 2.30-4.30pm Mon-Fri) for free brochures with details of self-guided walks, such as the Endangered Trades Walk and Historic Georgetown Trails. Another highly recommended walk is Global Ethic Penang's World Religions Walk, which takes you past the iconography and houses of worship of Christians, Muslims, Hindus, Sikhs, Buddhists and Confucians and even to a Jewish cemetery. Details and a map are available at www.globalethicpenang.net/webpages/act_02b.htm.

INFORMATION

Immigration Office	1	E2
Tourism Malaysia	2	E2

SIGHTS & ACTIVITIES

Cheong Fatt Tze Mansion	3	C2
Fort Cornwallis	4	E2
Kapitan Keling Mosque	5	D3
Khoo Kongsi	6	D3
Kuan Yin Teng	7	D2
Penang Heritage Trust	8	E3
Penang Museum	9	D2
Pinang Peranakan Mansion	10	E3
Sri Mariamman Temple	11	D3

SLEEPING

100 Cintra Street	12	C3
Banana Guest House	13	C2
Blue Diamond Hotel	14	C2
Jim's Place	15	C2
Old Penang Guest House	16	C2
SD Guesthouse	17	D2
Stardust	18	C2

EATING

Ecco Cafe	19	C2
Esplanade Food Centre	20	D1
Hot Wok	21	A2
Hui Sin Vegetarian Restaurant	22	E3
Jit Seng Duck Rice	23	C3
Khaleel Restaurant	24	C2
Kheng Pin	25	C2
Madras New Woodlands Restaurant	26	D3
New World Park	27	A2
Restoran Kapitan	28	D3
Sky Hotel	29	C2
Tiek Sen	30	C2

DRINKING

B@92	31	D2
Coco's	32	C1
Glo	(see 32)	
Pitt Street Corner	33	D2
Soho Free House	34	C2

TRANSPORT

Ferries to Butterworth	35	E4
Ferries to Pulau Langkawi	36	F2
Ferry Ticket Offices	37	E2
Kompleks Komtar Bus Stop	38	B3
Long-Distance Bus Offices	39	B3
Pengkalan Weld Bus Stop	40	E3

Malay & Nonya

Lg Baru, just off Jln Macalister, has a row of food stalls whipping up satay; however, things don't start sizzling until nightfall.

New World Park (102 Jln Burma; meals RM3-6 lunch & dinner) Laughing families and friends all line up for curry *mee* (noodles in a curry-like soup), fishball soup and other specialities, served under indisputably clean and safe conditions.

Esplanade Food Centre (Jln Tun Syed Sheh Barakbah; meals RM3-6; dinner) A great hawker centre for delightful sea breezes and Malay stalls serving *laksa asam, rojak* and radioactive-coloured bowls of ABC and *cendol*. The restaurant-like Chinese section features seafood and icy-cold cheap beer.

Hot Wok (227 3368; 124 Jln Burma; mains from RM9; lunch & dinner Wed-Mon) Located in a grand Nonya mansion, this restaurant feels slightly upscale but is pretty reasonably priced. Try the *otak otak* (fish wrapped in banana leaves) and *sambal sotong* (chilli squid).

Indian

Little India is replete with cheap eating places, especially along Lebuh Pasar and Lebuh Penang, serving up curries, roti, tandoori and biryani.

Restoran Kapitan (264 1191; 93 Lebuh Chulia; mains from RM3; breakfast, lunch & dinner) A very busy restaurant that specialises in tandoori chicken and biryani, along with fish and mutton curries. It does an excellent masala tea, too.

Madras New Woodlands Restaurant (263 9764; 60 Lebuh Penang; mains from RM3; breakfast, lunch & dinner) One of the best bets for vegetarians offers tasty banana-leaf meals and North Indian specialities, including lots of traditional sweets.

Khaleel Restaurant (885 1469; 48 Jln Penang; mains from RM4; 24hr) When you've hit the sauce too hard, there's always Khaleel, a 24-hour curry house that is consistently packed with masticating, happy Tamil customers. The chow is just as good sober as sloshed.

DRINKING

Most of the backpacker hostels serve beer, but it's not cheap and places tend to shut by 11pm. We found Blue Diamond to be the exception: it seemed to close whenever the last person passed out.

Pitt Street Corner (94 Lebuh Pitt) Sit back with a beer to the sounds of Bollywood at this very friendly Wild West–style saloon in Little India.

Soho Free House (50A Jln Penang) This place starts rocking out early ('80s music anyone?) with a mostly Chinese clientele who nosh bangers and mash (RM14) and swill pints like good Brits.

B@92 (92 Lebuh Gereja) Hip bar that features some live acts and hosts a large expat and well-to-do locals crowd.

Coco's (263 8003; cnr Lebuh Farquhar & Jln Penang) This popular expat beer garden is open till late. There are dance shows on Wednesday and live acts other times.

Glo (261 1066; the Garage, 2 Jln Penang) If you've been longing for superclubs/meat markets while travelling in Malaysia, here's a taste of what you've been missing. There's ear-splitting bass, lots of smoke, guys with slicked back hair and ladies in little dresses.

GETTING THERE & AWAY

See p461 for information about reaching Pulau Penang from the mainland, and for long-distance train and bus travel from the mainland.

Air

Airlines with services to Pulau Penang:

Air Asia (code AK; 261 5642; www.airasia.com)
Cathay Pacific Airways (code CX; 226 0411; www.cathaypacific.com)
Firefly (250 2000; www.fireflyz.com.my)
Malaysia Airlines (code MH; 217 6321/3/6; www.malaysiaairlines.com)
Singapore Airlines (code SQ; 226 3201; www.singaporeair.com)
Thai Airways International (code TG; 226 6000; www.thaiairways.com)

Boat

All the offices for the ferry service between Pulau Langkawi or Belawan (Sumatra, Indonesia) and Penang are clustered together on Pesara King Edward, and all put you on the same boats.

For info on ferries to Belawan, see opposite. There are daily ferries from Georgetown to Langkawi (one way/return RM60/115, 2½ hours). Boats leave at 8.30am (direct) and 8.45am (one stop at Pulau Payar), returning from Langkawi at 2.30pm and 5.30pm. Check the times the day before, as schedules vary.

GETTING TO INDONESIA: PULAU PENANG TO BELAWAN

Travellers can skip over to the Indonesian island of Sumatra from Pulau Penang via ferry. There are several ferries each way generally departing Georgetown at 8.30am and returning at 10.30am (one way/return RM110/180); the trip takes 4½ to five hours. The boats land in Belawan where the remaining journey to Medan is completed by bus (included in the price). Buy tickets the day before to verify departure times. Upon arriving at Belawan port, most nationalities will need to pay a US$25 per person fee for a 30-day Indonesian visa.

See p320 for information on doing the trip in reverse.

Note that Langkawi ferries depart the jetty off Pesara King Edward near the clock tower.

Bus

Buses to all major towns on the peninsula leave from both Georgetown and Butterworth. Several long-distance bus services leave from Kompleks Komtar; some leave from the long-distance bus offices, while others leave from the local bus stop. Buy tickets direct from the bus companies, because we've both received letters and talked to travellers whose agent-bought tickets from Georgetown only got them part way to where they wanted to go.

There are daily buses to Ipoh (RM11, three hours, hourly), Tanah Rata in the Cameron Highlands (RM25, six hours, five daily), KL (RM28, five hours, hourly), Kuantan (RM43, eight hours, one daily), Melaka (RM36, seven hours, two daily), and Singapore (RM53, nine hours, two daily).

There are also bus and minibus services to Thailand: Hat Yai (RM35), Phuket (RM61 to RM70), Ko Samui (RM80) and Bangkok (RM105 to RM120). The minibuses usually don't go directly to some destinations so there are significant waiting times. The train from Butterworth is usually quicker and more comfortable.

GETTING AROUND

Penang has a good public transport system that connects Georgetown with the rest of the island.

Bus

There are several local bus stops in Georgetown. Kompleks Komtar and Pengkalan Weld, in front of the Butterworth–Penang jetty, are two of the largest stops. Most of the buses also have stops along Lebuh Chulia. Fares within Georgetown are RM1.50 to RM3; points beyond are RM1 to RM3 depending on the destination (exact change required).

For around RM6 you can do a circuit of the island by public transport.

Motorcycle & Bicycle

You can hire bicycles from shops at Lebuh Chulia, Batu Ferringhi (13km northwest of Georgetown) and some guest houses. Bicycles cost RM10, and motorcycles start at RM30 per day. Remember that if you don't have a motorcycle licence, your travel insurance probably won't cover you in the case of an accident.

Taxi

You'll need to bargain for a reasonable fare. Typical taxi rates around town are RM6 to RM12. Other fares include Batu Ferringhi (RM45), Penang Hill/Kek Lok Si Temple (RM30) and Bayan Lepas airport (RM38).

Trishaw

Bicycle rickshaws are an ideal way to negotiate Georgetown's backstreets and cost around RM30 per hour but, as with taxis, agree on the fare before departure. From the ferry terminals, a trishaw to the hotel area around Lebuh Chulia should cost RM10.

Penang Hill

Once a fashionable retreat for the city's elite, Penang Hill (821m) provides cool temperatures and spectacular views. There are pretty

GETTING INTO TOWN

Penang's Bayan Lepas International Airport is 18km south of Georgetown. The 307 and 401 buses run to/from the airport (RM3, one hour) every half-hour from 6am to 11pm. Buses stop at Komtar and terminate at Weld Quay.

If arriving via the Butterworth–Penang ferry, exit towards Pengkalan Weld and catch any Kompleks Komtar–bound bus (RM1.50, 15 minutes) to reach accommodation in Chinatown.

gardens, an old-fashioned kiosk, a restaurant and a hotel, as well as a lavishly decorated Hindu temple and a mosque at the top.

From Kompleks Komtar or at Lebuh Chulia in Georgetown, you can catch one of the frequent local buses (201, 202 or 203) to Air Itam. From Air Itam, walk five minutes to the funicular railway (adult/child RM4/3 one way, 30 minutes, every 15 to 30 minutes from 6.30am to 9.30pm), where long queues may await. Those who feel energetic can get to the top by an interesting three-hour trek, starting from the Moon Gate at the Botanical Gardens, or, if you're really fit, hike through the forest from the upper funicular station to Teluk Bahang, 6.6km away (around five hours).

Kek Lok Si Temple (9am-6pm), the largest Buddhist temple in Malaysia, stands on a hilltop at Air Itam. Construction started in 1890, took more than 20 years and was largely funded by donations. To reach the entrance, walk through the souvenir stalls until you reach the seven-tier, 30m-high **Ban Po Thar** (Ten Thousand Buddhas Pagoda; admission RM2). There are several other temples here, as well as shops and an excellent **vegetarian restaurant** (828 8142; mains from RM5; lunch & dinner Tue-Sun), while a **cable-car** (one way/return RM4/2) whisks you to the highest level, presided over by an awesome 36.5m-high bronze statue of **Kuan Yin**, goddess of mercy.

Botanical Gardens

The lush, 30-hectare **Botanical Gardens** (227 0328; www.jkb.penang.gov.my; Waterfall Rd; admission free; 5am-8pm) has an orchid house, palm house, bromeliad house, cactus garden and numerous tropical trees, all labelled in English. The most famous tree is the cannonball tree, which produces large pink flowers that eventually form stinking fruits about the size and shape of a human head. You can get all your kooky horticultural questions answered at the **Plant Information Kiosk** (8am-4.30pm Mon-Fri).

To get here, take Bus 102. There's also a path that leads to/from the top of Penang Hill.

Batu Ferringhi

04

Following the coastal road east will lead you to Batu Ferringhi, Penang's best beach area, which is lined with resorts at one end and guest houses at the other. While it doesn't compare with Malaysia's east coast beaches or those on Langkawi, the sleepy village ambience at the eastern end of the beach is a lovely respite. An increasing amount of folks from the Gulf States stay at the resorts – you're likely see men walking shirtless next to women in full *chador* and veil on the beach.

Low-key guest houses are clustered together opposite the beach, and most will give discounts for multiday stays. **ET Budget Guest House** (881 1553; 47 Batu Ferringhi; r RM25-60;) is a laid-back double-storey Chinese house with basic rooms, most with a shared bathroom. The pricier rooms come with air-con, TV and shower. Livelier is **Baba Guest House** (881 1686; babaguesthouse2000@yahoo.com; 52 Batu Ferringhi; r RM30-60;), a big Chinese family home with plain rooms (most with shared bathrooms) that's a hive of activity with sister at reception, grandma doing laundry, dad fixing the plumbing and so on.

Bus 101 or 105 from Kompleks Komtar takes around 40 minutes to reach Batu Ferringhi and costs RM3.

Teluk Bahang

04

There's not enough beach at the sleepy fishing village of Teluk Bahang for any resorts to crop up, so the main thing to do is tool around the 2300-hectare **Penang National Park** (Taman Negara Pulau Pinang). The area encompasses white, sparkling beaches that are devoid of humans but popular with monkeys, and has some challenging trails through the jungle. Start at the **Penang National Park Office** (881 3500; end of Jln Hassan Abbas; 8am-4.30pm Mon-Fri, 8am-noon & 2-4pm Sat & Sun) for maps and suggestions.

If you want to stay the night, stop at **Miss Loh's Guest House** (885 1227; off Jln Teluk Bahang; dm/s/d from RM8/15/30;), a ramshackle throwback to the good ol' days of long-term backpacking. To find the guest house, look for a store on Teluk Bahang's main street that says 'GH Information.'

Fisherman Village Guest House (885 2936; 60 Jln Hassan Abbas, Kampong Nelayan; dm/d from RM7/18;) isn't quite as laid-back as Miss Loh's, but is still just the sort of garden spot to fully immerse yourself in some indolent idleness.

Bus 101 runs from Georgetown every half-hour all the way along the north coast of the island to just beyond the roundabout in Teluk Bahang.

GETTING TO THAILAND

There are several options for crossing the Malay–Thai border on the west coast; see also p471.

Bukit Kayu Hitam to Sadao

Frequent buses go from Alor Setar to the Bukit Kayu Hitam–Sadao border crossing (RM4), which is open from 7am to 7pm daily. You'll have to take a minibus on the Thai side of the border to the transport hub of Hat Yai.

Padang Besar to Kanger

Trains travelling south and north pass through the border towns of Padang Besar and Kanger, linking the towns along the train line (including Penang–Butterworth) to the border. Trains leave Alor Setar and arrive at the currently dodgy transport hub town of Hat Yai (2nd class/berth RM27/45) three hours later; travellers can also catch an international express that leaves Alor Setar for Bangkok, also via Hat Yai. The border is open 7am to 10pm daily.

See p804 for details on travelling from Thailand to Malaysia.

ALOR SETAR

☎ 04

Most travellers use strongly Islamic Alor Setar as a hopping-off point to Thailand, Langkawi or southern Malaysia, but there's enough of interest here to keep you exploring for a few hours. The city's long association with Thailand is evident in Thai temples scattered around town, while its small Chinese population lives in an atmospheric, compact Chinatown.

Flora Inn (☎ 732 2375; http://florainn.tripod.com; 8 Kompleks Medan Raja, Jln Pengkalan Kapal; s/d RM13/65; ❄) overlooks the Sungai Kedah river, which is little more than algal green gloop. Rooms are clean and cheap, and the management is bend-over-backwards friendly.

To reach Langkawi from Alor Setar, take one of the frequent local Kuala Kedah buses (RM1, 15 minutes) to the ferry jetty. A shuttle bus (90 sen) connects the town centre with the bus station, 3.5km away; a taxi will cost RM8. Between April and October, from about 7am to 7pm, ferries operate roughly every half-hour in either direction between Kuala Kedah and Kuah on Langkawi (RM23, 1½ hours).

Buses from Alor Setar serve the following destinations: Ipoh (RM20, four hours, three daily), Johor Bahru (RM55, 10 hours, one daily), Kota Bharu (RM29, two daily, six hours), Kuala Lumpur (RM30, hourly, six hours), Kuala Terengganu (RM38, 10 hours, one daily), Kuantan (RM42, 10 hours, one daily) and Melaka (RM39, eight hours, two daily).

The **train station** (☎ 731 4045; Jln Stesyen) is a 15-minute walk southeast of town. There is one daily northbound train to Hat Yai, Thailand (from RM12, three hours), and one southbound to KL (from RM35, 11½ hours).

KUALA PERLIS

☎ 04

This small port town in the extreme northwest of the peninsula is a departure point for ferries to Pulau Langkawi. Your least-grotty sleeping option if you stop to sample the region's special laksa is **Pens Hotel** (☎ 985 4122; Jln Kuala Perlis; r from RM50; ❄).

Ferries (RM15) depart for Kuah, on Pulau Langkawi, every hour between the hours of 8am and 6pm.

The bus and taxi stations are behind the row of shophouses across from the jetty. From here infrequent buses go to Butterworth, Alor Setar and KL and Padang. A greater selection of bus services can be found at Kangar; the frequent Bus 56 to/from Kangar (RM1.20) swings by the jetty before terminating at the station.

PULAU LANGKAWI

☎ 04

You'd think these 99 islands, dominated by 478.5 sq km Pulau Langkawi, would have been overdeveloped past recognition by now – the district's been duty-free since 1986 and was roping in tourists long before that. Yet the knife-edged peaks floating in dark vegetation and the colour contrast of the ocean blues make this island an undisputed tropical paradise despite the resort buildup. Just a little way off the main (quite lovely) beaches is idyllic rural Malaysia, all *kampungs* and oil lamps.

Plus Langkawi is fun. You'll see all sorts of wholesome Malaysian revelry going on (hundreds of Malays line dancing on a beach is unforgettable), but come night, there's plenty of Western-style booze-fuelled fun about – and the beer is cheaper here than nearly anywhere else in Malaysia.

Orientation

The Langkawi archipelago sits 30km off the coast from Kuala Perlis and 45km from the border town of Satun – Langkawi is the biggest and most-visited island. In the southeast corner of Langkawi is Kuah, the major town and the arrival point for ferries. On the west coast are Pantai Cenang (cha-*nang*), a lively beach strip with shops and restaurants, and adjacent Pantai Tengah, which is a bit quieter and a short walk to Pantai Cenang. During the monsoons (May to October) and sometimes beyond, jellyfish make swimming a problem.

Information

The only banks are at Kuah, although there are ATMs at the airport and Telaga Harbour Park and money changers tucked into and around duty-free shops and at Pantai Cenang.

Tourism Malaysia (☎ 966 7789; Jln Persiaran Putra, Kuah; 9am-1pm & 2-6pm) offers comprehensive information and advice about the island.

Sleeping

During peak tourist times (November to February) Langkawi's rooms fill quickly but at other times of the year supply far outstrips demand.

PANTAI CENANG

The gorgeous 2km-long strip of sand at Pantai Cenang has the biggest concentration of hotels, and is popular with everyone from 20-something backpackers to package tourists. The water is good for swimming, but jellyfish are common, so you might feel a bit tingly when you go for a dip.

our pick **Gecko Guesthouse** (☎ 019 428 3801; rebeccafiott@hotmail.com; dm RM10, r RM25-70;) 'How long you been here?' 'Two weeks.' 'How long were you going to stay originally?' 'Three days.' Yep – that's the vibe in this most backpacker of backpacker joints. There's a jungly collection of bungalows, chalets and dorms, lots of dreadlocked folk in the common area and very good chocolate milkshakes behind the bar – book early.

Rainbow Lodge (☎ 955 8103; dm RM15, r from RM40) Set a little ways back from the beach, this is a cheap place to rest in between eating, drinking, hangover and more drinking. The dorm looks like a barracks, but it's a good spot for meeting folks.

Sweet Inn (☎ 955 8864; r RM50-70;) A cute yellow building dotted with umbrella-ed tables, rooms that keep cool and a common area where meeting fellow travellers is easy and breezy. Just behind and almost sharing the same grounds is **Daddy's Guest House** (r RM40), where rooms are a bit cheaper. It looks a little like an apartment block, but rooms are nice and top-floor ones have sea views.

Palms Guest House (☎ 017 631 0121; r from RM65;) Run by a friendly English couple, rooms here feel like the guest suite in a family cottage by the sea. They're clean and centred around a gravel-strewn courtyard shaded by palms, and there's free wi-fi.

PANTAI TENGAH

Pantai Tengah is less built-up and is popular with Malay families. **Zackry Guest House** (www.zackryguesthouse.langkawinetworks.com; dm/s/d RM20/30/40;) is a friendly, sprawling guest house inhabited by happy travellers boozing it up in the common area, Irish owner Neve and her Malaysian boyfriend Chaz and several large, friendly dogs. Rooms are clean and cosy, and there are no phone bookings.

Eating

Langkawi's proximity to Thailand means that the Thai penchant for fiery chillies has found its way into local dishes. There's a *pasar malam* north of Pantai Cenang held once or twice a week; it's a good place to get authentic Malay food on the cheap.

Tomato (☎ 955 5853; mains from RM4; 24hr) Not red but still good, this branch serves excellent rotis and a standard curry-rice Indian/Malay menu at all hours.

Red Tomato (☎ 955 9118; mains from RM18; 8am-3pm & 6-11pm Sat-Thu) Run by expats, this place cranks out some of the best pizza and pasta on the island.

our pick **Champor-Champor** (☎ 955 1449; mains from RM18; 7-10.30pm) Dine on imaginative regional cuisine such as pan-fried *bamakoise* (a local fish) with banana, tofu satay and coconut-crusted calamari. The tranquil, open-air garden filled with sweet incense and surrounded with plants and native carvings provides a romantic setting to while away a tropical evening.

At Pantai Tengah try **Boom Boom Corner** (☎ 012 473 7167; mains from RM4; ⌚ 5pm-late), a bustling Malay and Pakistani food court at the northern end of the strip.

Drinking

Langkawi is arguably the best (and cheapest) spot for a drink in Malaysia. Most bars open around 5pm and close late.

You can start at Bob Marley Bar, which usually opens around lunchtime. There are beach mats, posters of the great dreaded one, a predictable soundtrack and very good vibe. If you head south along Pantai Cenang, you'll hit the 1812 Bar, which is run by a slightly mad but friendly northern Englishman who is one of the best barmen on the island.

As the evening wears on lots of folks end up in Pantai Tengah at **Reggae Bar** (⌚ noon-2am Sat-Thu), a beachside affair, and Sunba Retro Bar, which turns into a dancey mega-club and is open till about 3am. If you're still ready to party after that, Little Lylia's Chill Out Bar is, as the name suggests, a laid-back spot that stays open till – wow, is that sunrise?

Getting There & Away

AIR

Malaysia Airlines (☎ 955 6322; www.malaysiaairlines.com), **Air Asia** (☎ 32-171 9333; www.airasia.com) and **Firefly** (☎ 37-845 4543; www.fireflyz.com.my) all have two or three flights daily between Langkawi and KL. Malaysia Airlines and Firefly fly to Penang and **Tiger Airways** (www.tigerairways.com) and **SilkAir** (☎ 955 9771; www.silkair.com) fly to Singapore.

BOAT

All passenger ferries to/from Langkawi operate out of Kuah. From about 8am to 6.30pm, ferries operate roughly every hour to/from the mainland port of Kuala Perlis (RM18, one hour) and every 30 minutes to/from Kuala Kedah (RM23, 1½ hours).

Langkawi Ferry Services (LFS; ☎ 966 9439) and **Ekspres Bahagia** (☎ 966 5784) operate two daily ferries between Kuah and Georgetown on Penang (RM60/115 one way/return, 2½ hours). Boats depart from Georgetown at 8.30am and 8.45am and leave Kuah at 2.30pm and 5.30pm.

> **GETTING TO THAILAND: PULAU LANGKAWI TO SATUN OR KO LIPE**
>
> There are three daily ferries from Kuah on Pulau Langkawi to Satun (one way RM60, 1¼ hours). From 1 November to 15 May **Tigerline** (www.tigerlinetravel.com) runs two daily ferries each way between Langkawi and Ko Lipe (one way RM115, 1½ hours) in Thailand (during high season) with onward service available to as far as Ko Lanta.
>
> See p804 for information on doing the border crossing in the opposite direction.

Getting Around

There is no public transport. Car hire is excellent value starting at RM60 per day for a Kancil or RM35 for a motorbike. A few places also rent mountain bikes for RM15 per day.

Otherwise, taxis are the main way of getting around. Fixed fares for the entire vehicle (which can be split between passengers) include the following from the Kuah jetty: Kuah town (RM6), Pantai Cenang (RM24) and Pantai Tengah (RM24).

PENINSULAR MALAYSIA – EAST COAST

Refreshingly Malay, the peninsula's east coast is an entirely different experience from the mobile-phone-obsessed, traffic-clogged west coast. Headscarves, skullcaps and the hauntingly melodious call to prayer are as ubiquitous here as the white-sand beaches that fringe the sunrise-drenched coasts and jewel-like islands.

JOHOR BAHRU

☎ 07

You'll pass through the state capital of Johor Bahru (known as JB) if you're travelling to/from peninsular Malaysia and Singapore. The city is connected to Singapore by the 1038m-long Causeway bridge.

JB has never been a travellers' favourite but it's been cleaned up over the years and isn't a bad place to grab some hawker food and explore the colourful culture-packed streets of the walkable downtown area west of the Customs, Immigration and

GETTING TO SINGAPORE & INDONESIA

Johor Bahru to Singapore

There are frequent buses between JB's Larkin bus station, 5km north of the city, and Singapore's Queen St bus station. Most convenient is the Singapore–Johor Bahru Express (RM2.40, one hour, every 10 minutes from 6.30am to midnight). Alternatively, there's the slower city Bus 170 (RM1.70). Both buses stop at the Malaysian and Singapore immigration checkpoints; disembark from the bus with your luggage, go through immigration and reboard on the other side (keep your ticket). From central JB, board any bus after clearing Malaysian immigration just before the Causeway – you can buy a ticket on the bus.

There are also trains to Singapore, but it's more convenient to take a bus or taxi. Walking across the Causeway was technically forbidden at the time of research but plenty of Singaporeans do it anyway and there are plans to open a legal pedestrian route; the trip takes 25 minutes.

See p674 for details on doing the trip in the opposite direction.

Johor Bahru to Pulau Batam & Pulau Bintan (Riau Islands)

There are several daily departures to Batam (one way RM69, 1½ hours) and Tanjung Pinang on Bintan (one way RM86, 2½ hours), both islands (part of Indonesia's Riau Islands) with connections to Sumatra in Indonesia. Additional boats depart from Kukup, southwest of JB, to Tanjung Balai, also in Indonesia. See p320 for information on doing the trip in reverse.

Quarantine complex (which is linked to the train station). That said, this is one of the edgiest towns in Malaysia and you'll need to keep alert for motorcycle snatch thieves.

There's a **Tourism Malaysia** (8am-4.30pm Mon-Thu, 8am-12.15pm & 2.45-4.30pm Fri, 8am-12.45pm Sat) in the Customs, Immigration and Quarantine complex just as you clear Singapore immigration that have some handy maps and pamphlets, but the staff are pretty useless.

The finest museum of its kind in Malaysia, **Muzium Diraja Abu Bakar** (☎ 223 0555; adult US$7; 9am-5pm Sat-Thu) conveys the wealth and privilege of the sultans. Tickets are payable in ringgit at a bad exchange rate; the ticket counter closes at 4pm.

Sleeping & Eating

If you're on a tight budget hop on any bus and leave town – JB has some of the priciest rooms in Malaysia. Most budget hotels ask for a room deposit of around RM30 that's returned to you when you check out.

Meldrum Hotel (☎ 227 8988; www.meldrumhotel.com; 1 Jln Siu Nam; dm/s/d RM32/64/76) Air-conditioned, clean, spacious and freshly painted with TVs, free drinking water and kettles, the rooms here are downright plush.

JB Hotel (☎ 223 4989; 80-A Jln Wong Ah Fook; r RM70;) Small air-con rooms come with TV, tiled floor and sinks but bathrooms are shared. It's family-run, helpful and very clean.

Make the best of your time in JB by eating at the excellent hawker venues, including the **Medan Selera Meldrum Walk** (meals from RM3; dinner), crammed along the alley that runs parallel to Jln Meldrum, and the **Tepian Tebrau food centre** (Jln Abu Bakar), which is famous for its *ikan bakar* (grilled fish).

Getting There & Away

AIR

JB is served by **Malaysia Airlines** (☎ 334 1011; www.malaysiaairlines.com.my), **Firefly** (☎ 603 7845 4543; www.fireflyz.com.my) and **Air Asia** (☎ 1300 889 933; www.airasia.com). Most domestic flights connect through KL, a four-hour bus ride away. Larkin bus station is 2.5km north of the city centre.

JB's airport is 32km northwest of town at Senai.

BOAT

Ferries leave Johor Bahru for islands in Indonesia; see above for details.

BUS & TAXI

Most people travel from Johor Bahru to Singapore by bus; see above for information.

Johor Bahru's long-distance bus station is Larkin station, located 5km north of the centre. Buses run to and from Larkin to all parts of the country, including Melaka (RM19, three hours, hourly), KL (RM31, four hours, hourly), Ipoh (RM49, seven hours, one daily),

Butterworth (RM53, 12 hours, one daily), Mersing (RM12, three hours, four daily), Kuantan (RM20, five hours, four daily), Kuala Terengganu (RM27, nine hours, two daily) and Kota Bharu (RM49, 10 hours, two daily). Long-distance taxis also leave from Larkin (there's a price list at the stand).

A taxi from central JB to the bus station should cost RM8.

TRAIN

Daily express trains depart Johor Bahru (RM33 to RM64) three times per day for Kuala Lumpur. It is also possible to change at Gemas (RM21 to RM38) and hop aboard the Jungle Railway for connections to Jerantut (if you're headed for Taman Negara) and Kota Bharu. See p486 for further information on the Jungle Railway.

MERSING

☎ 07

The jumping-off point for Pulau Tioman, Mersing is busy and compact, and has everything that travellers might need: cheap internet, good sleeping options, grocery stores, cold beer and a pharmacy. The river is clogged with colourful fishing boats but beyond the riverfront there's not much to explore.

Sleeping & Eating

Omar's Backpackers' Hostel (☎ 799 5096, 019-774 4268; Jln Abu Bakar; dm/d RM10/25) A tiny, clean and social backpackers' pad very near the jetty, Omar's is just as well known for the owner's tours to some of the lesser-visited islands around Tioman. Reservations are recommended during the peak season.

Hotel Golden City (☎ 799 5028; 23 Jln Abu Bakar; s RM15, d RM35-45; ❄) Rudimentary rooms have cement floors and saggy mattresses but it's passably clean. Singles have shared bathrooms and only the most expensive options have air-conditioning.

Hotel Embassy (☎ 799 3545; 2 Jln Ismail; d/tr/q with private bathroom RM45/55/65; ❄) This is a fabulously posh-feeling choice compared to the other cheapies in town: all rooms are huge, and have cable TV, air-con and private bathrooms.

Port Café & Bistro (Jln Abu Bakar; mains RM8-25; 🕒 lunch & dinner) A surprisingly hip bar and eatery right at the jetty, serving Western grub like pizzas (from RM22) and Malay specialities like a dolled-up *nasi lemak* (RM9). The bar serves beer, wine and cocktails and there's live music some nights.

There are several places around town for *roti canai* and *kopi* (coffee) and seafood stalls open up nightly near the bus station along the river.

Getting There & Away

Buses depart from the station near the bridge on the river. Destinations include Kuala Lumpur (RM38, six hours, five daily), Johor Bahru (RM12, three hours, two daily), Kuantan (RM16, five hours, two daily), Kuala Terengganu (RM34, nine hours, two daily) and Singapore (RM14, three hours, twice daily).

See p475 for information on ferries to/from Pulau Tioman.

PULAU TIOMAN

☎ 09

From late nights at Salang bars to days of trekking through the wild jungles, surfing the beaches at Juara or diving the reefs and wrecks off the coast, Tioman has as much action or non-action as anyone could hope for. The beaches aren't as voluptuous as those on Langkawi or the Perhentians, but it's not a hardship to saunter past crystalline rivers and rows of hibiscus to find a patch of sand. The proximity to Singapore and the availability of upscale digs has made Tioman relatively touristy but the island is so big and the locals are so mellow that most people forget to be bothered by this.

During the east coast monsoon, from about November to March, boat services to the island are infrequent or suspended. If you plan to visit Tioman during this time be prepared to get stuck in Mersing overnight or longer.

Orientation & Information

Most budget accommodation is clustered in Air Batang (ABC) and Salang on the

TIOMAN SCAMS

Several agents around Mersing might try to sell you accommodation on Tioman. Rates from these agencies are sometimes doubled, turning what would otherwise be a great budget hut into an overpriced disappointment. If you're worried about finding accommodation, call the guest house yourself to reserve a room.

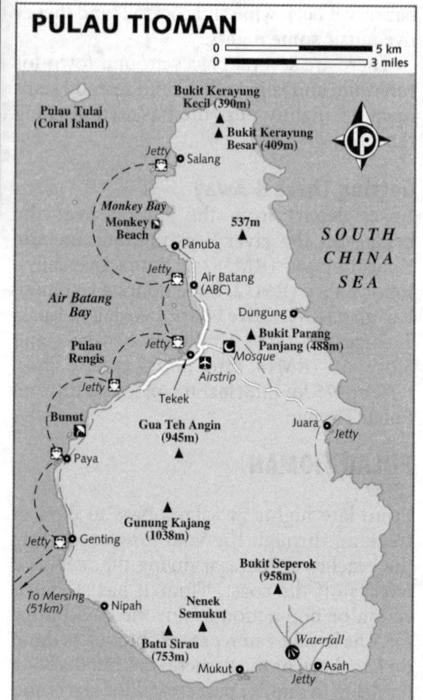

northern end of the west coast. Salang has wider stretches of sand and the mood is decidedly 'spring break', while ABC has a more Malay, chummy camaraderie vibe. Other small beaches reachable only by boat (such as Nipah) run south along the west coast.

Connected to ABC by a footpath over a rocky headland, Tekek is the island's main village, where you'll find a bank, telephones and a post office. The duty-free shop at the airport in town sells beer cheaper than water.

On the east coast of the island, Juara has a stunning beach, surfing during the monsoon and affordable accommodation, but lifts over the hill from Tekek can be pricey. A great option is to hike – leave as much as your stuff in Salang and ABC as you can to lighten your load. See right for more information.

Sights & Activities

According to one guest house operator, you come to Tioman for what's under the water, not above – since the land is jaw-droppingly gorgeous, this says a lot for the diving. Most places rent snorkelling gear and you can join day trips to Pulau Tulai, better known as Coral Island, where you can swim with fish and sometimes sharks.

Open-water dive courses cost around RM1000, and fun dives are around RM100. There are nearly more dive shops than accommodation options so shop around for the best deal.

There's a fantastic 7km hike that crosses the island's waist from Tekek to Juara (carry plenty of water). It takes around 2½ hours, is steep in parts and starts about 1km north of the jetty in Tekek. Near the top of the hill you pass a small waterfall, and the jungle is awesome.

Sleeping & Eating

From June to August, when the island swarms with visitors, accommodation becomes tight. Either side of these months it's a buyer's market. Budget digs around the island are nearly identical and are of low standard – think old mattresses and saggy floors – but most do have private bathrooms, fans and mosquito nets.

Restaurants, with similar menus, are usually attached to chalet operations. ABC, Tekek and Salang all have small convenience stores.

AIR BATANG (ABC)

The far northern and southern ends of the beach here have the best sand while some in-between areas are rocky and marshy. Places here are listed from north to south.

Johan's Resort (☎ 419 1359; dm/chalets/f RM15/30/130) The good, clean two four-bed dorms here are up on the hillside and some of the chalets face the sea.

South Pacific (☎ 419 1176; chalets RM30) Just north of the jetty, this simple, family-run and clean place offers laundry, shows films in the evening, and has a small library of second-hand books. The pricier chalets are by the sea.

My Friend's Place (☎ 419 1150; r RM25) Busy, social and priced a hair lower than the competition, this is a clean place with all rooms facing the garden.

Mokhtar's Place (d RM30-45, tr RM55; ❄ 💻) There's a very mellow family vibe going on at this quiet spot. Cheaper bungalows are set back from the beach under pleasant shady trees and all rooms are spacious and clean though ageing. Internet is available (when it's working) for RM10 per hour.

SALANG

The small bay at the south of Salang has a beautiful beach and swimming area backed by a murky river that's teeming with giant monitor lizards. At night everyone who slept on the beach all day is keen to indulge in duty-free beer till the wee hours of the morn. Accommodation is listed here from north to south.

our pick **Ella's Place** (☎ 419 5004; chalets RM40-100;) There's usually a loungeable patch of sand here at this cute-as-a-button family-run place at the quiet northern end of the beach. There are 10 clean chalets (some with air-con) but you'll have to reserve in advance to nab one.

Salang Indah Resort (☎ 419 5015; www.salangindah.com; d/longhouse tw RM30/60, chalets hillside-/sea-view RM80/90, q RM120;) The expanse of chalets sprawl on seemingly forever and if you look at several you'll probably find one to your liking. The mosque-looking restaurant serves everything from cheeseburgers to cheap local-style seafood (dishes around RM8). There's also a bar, a shop and internet access (per hour RM10).

Pak Long Island Chalet (☎ 419 5000; enquiry@paklongislandchalet.com.my; chalets with fan/air-con RM50/60;) Has wooden chalets with peeling plastic flooring and OK verandahs, the more expensive of which face the sea. What sets this place apart is the family-run atmosphere that makes it feel like it's a mini-village.

JUARA

There's little to do in Juara except swim, surf (between November and April), snooze under the swaying palms or take a gander into the jungle. It's actually two connected beaches and both are wide and white.

our pick **Beach Hut** (☎ 012 696 1093; camp sites with tent for 2 people RM15, dm/chalets RM20/40) A super-social, bona fide surf shack, chalets here (on the southern beach) are decorated with shell mobiles, driftwood and some fake flowers. Budget warriors can get a tent (which come with sleeping bags) next to the beach, and at the time of writing dorms were due to be completed by 2010. Take a surf lesson (RM60) or body surf out front.

Paradise Point (☎ 419 3145; r incl breakfast RM35) North of the jetty and with a homey vibe, this place offers simple, un-noteworthy rooms in a longhouse.

Bushman (☎ 419 3109; matbushman@hotmail.com; chalets RM50) Nabbing one of Bushman's three new varnished wood chalets is like winning the Juara lottery – reserve in advance! It's right up against the boulder outcrop and a flat knuckle of white sand.

Rainbow Chalets (☎ 419 3140; d RM50, t RM60-70) These fittingly colourful beachfront chalets have an excellent reputation and so are always full. It's right before Bushman at the southern end of the northern bay and its Sunrise Café serves some of the best grub on the beach.

NIPAH

Isolated Nipah Beach is a long jungle-clad strip of sand with plenty of surrounding walking opportunities to more empty beaches and a jungle waterfall.

You can stay at either the **Nipah Beach Tioman** (☎ 019 735 7853; chalets from RM70), which offers some rustic chalets, or at **Bersatu Nipah Chalets** (☎ 07-797 0091; bersatunipah_tioman@yahoo.com; r with fan/air-con RM60/90;), which has clean beachfront longhouse rooms and a riverside restaurant.

Both places can arrange pick up from the ferry stop in Genting for RM20 each way.

Getting There & Away

Berjaya Air (code J8; ☎ 419 1303; www.berjaya-air.com), with offices at Berjaya Tioman Beach Resort (about halfway up the west cost) and at the airstrip, has daily flights to/from KL and Singapore.

Mersing is the ferry port for Tioman. Several companies run boat services to the island; tickets can be bought around Mersing town or at the jetty. There are usually four to six departures throughout the day between 7am and 5pm, but specific departure times vary with the tides. Ferries (RM35, two to three hours) leave from the Mersing jetty and drop off passengers in south to north order on the island.

Getting Around

Getting around the island is, for the moment, problematic. You can walk from ABC to Tekek in about 20 minutes. But you'll need to charter a boat through a guest house or restaurant to travel between ABC and Salang (RM25).

Boats from Mersing will sometimes stop in Juara if there are four or more people who want to stop; otherwise you'll have to get off at Tekek and then hire a 4WD (RM90 for four people). Alternatively, you can walk through the jungle to Juara from Tekek (7km).

KUANTAN

☎ 09

Many travellers find themselves on an overnight stopover in Kuantan, the pious and functional state capital, as it's the main transit point between Taman Negara and Pulau Tioman. Kuantan's star attraction is **Masjid Negeri**, the east coast's most impressive mosque. At night it's a magical sight with its spires and lit turrets.

Information

Banks are clustered at Jln Bank and there are plenty of ATMs around Jln Haji Abdul Aziz (the continuation of Jln Mahkota).

Main post office (Jln Haji Abdul Aziz) Near the soaring Masjid Negeri.

Mega Tech (2nd fl, cnr of Lg Pasar Baru 3 & Jln Stadium; per hr RM2; 9am-midnight) Internet access next to the long-distance bus station (Terminal Makmur).

Tourist information centre (☎ 516 1007; Jln Mahkota; 9am-10pm Mon-Thu, 2.45-5pm Fri, 9am-1pm & 2-5pm Sat) One of Malaysia's most helpful.

Sleeping & Eating

Kuantan has some seriously dismal budget options and the following are the only ones we found worth mentioning.

Sungai Wang Utama Hotel (☎ 514 8273; 16 Jln Penjara; r RM15-35;) The vibe is a little sleazy but it's cleanish and cheap.

Hotel Makmur (☎ 514 1363; 1st & 2nd fl, B 14 & 16 Lg Pasar Baru 1; r RM30-70;) Totally boring and functional but it's clean, reception is friendly and it's an easy pack haul to the long-distance bus station.

Classic Hotel (☎ 516 4599; chotel@tm.net.my; 7 Jln Besar; d incl breakfast RM90;) All rooms here are spacious and clean and have free filtered water, tea-making facilities, TVs and air-con. Add the central location and Malay-style breakfast and it's worth the splurge.

our pick **Akob Patin House** (☎ 013 931 2709; lunch) This riverfront place serves wild-caught (RM20) and farmed (RM8) *patin* (silver catfish – the local delicacy) in a *tempoyak* (fermented durian sambal) sauce served buffet-style with other Malay-style meat and vegetable dishes – the price is per fish.

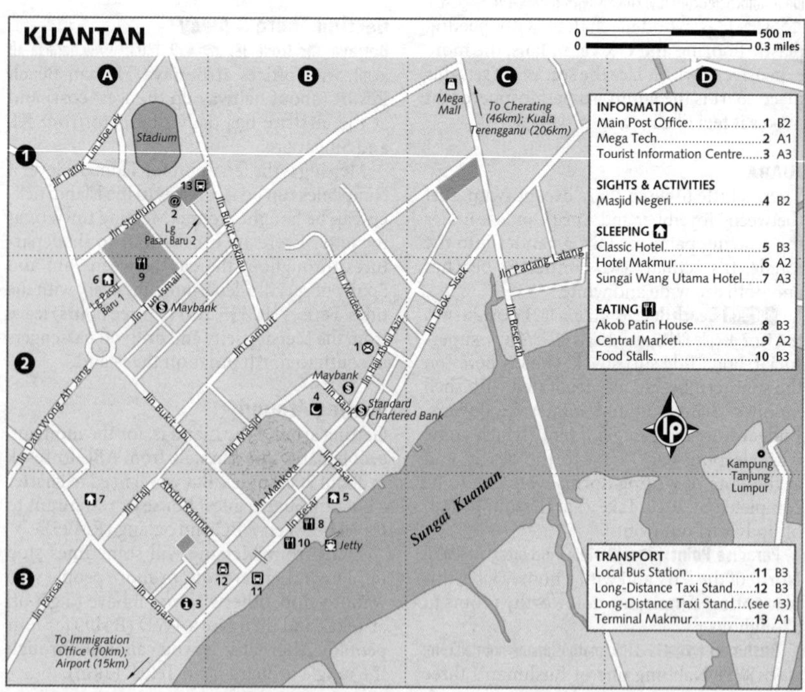

Food stalls can be found along the riverbank across from Hotel Baru Raya, and at the **central market** (Jln Bukit Ubi).

Getting There & Away

AIR

Malaysia Airlines (☎ 531 2123; www.malaysiaairlines.com.my) has direct flights to KL (three daily), and **Firefly** (☎ 03-7845 4543; www.fireflyz.com.my) also has two daily flights to/from KL's Subang Airport. **Kuantan airport** (Lapangan Terbang Sultan Ahmad Shah; ☎ 538 2923) is 15km from the city centre; take a taxi (RM25).

BUS & TAXI

Long-distance buses operate from **Terminal Makmur** (Jln Stadium). Services include KL (RM22, 4½ hours, hourly), Mersing (RM14, 3½ hours, three daily), Kuala Terengganu (RM15, three hours, frequent), Kota Bharu (RM29, seven hours, frequent), Jerantut (RM16, 3½ hours, five daily) and Butterworth (RM48, eight hours, four daily).

Northbound local buses operate out of a **local bus station** (Jln Besar) near the river, including services between Cherating (RM4) and Marang (RM9).

There are two long-distance taxi stands in town – one on Jln Stadium in front of the long-distance bus station, and the other on Jln Mahkota, just near the local bus station. Destinations and costs (per car) include Mersing (RM180), Cherating (RM50) and Jerantut (RM190).

TASIK CHINI

☎ 09

So hard to get to and yet so worth it, Tasik Chini (Lake Chini) is a series of 12 lakes linked by vegetation-clogged channels, its shores inhabited by the Jakun people, an Orang Asli tribe of Melayu Asli origin. The surrounding waves of jungle hills are some of the least visited trekking areas in the country and still hide tigers and elephants in its tangle as well as glorious waterfalls and caves. Locals believe the lake is home to a serpent known as Naga Seri Gumum, sometimes translated in tourist literature as a 'Loch Ness Monster'. The best time to visit the lakes is from June to September when the lotuses are in bloom. You can also visit the lakes as part of a group tour from Cherating for around RM70 per person.

At Kampung Gumum, **Rajan Jones Guest House** (☎ 017 913 5089; r per person incl breakfast & dinner RM25) offers extremely basic accommodation. Rajan speaks excellent English, is knowledgeable about the Orang Asli and can arrange a spectrum of activities from day treks (RM50 per person) to lake trips (RM50 to RM100 per person).

Buses run to Kampung Chini four times per day from Kuantan's local bus station (RM5, two hours). To get to Kampung Gumum ask to be let off at the Chini 2 bus stop. From here you'll have to ask around for a private car to take you the remaining 7.5km – this should cost about RM20. You can also call Rajan Jones and ask him to help arrange a private car. A taxi all the way to Kampung Gumum from Kunatan should cost around RM80.

CHERATING

☎ 09

Back when there were no direct transport links between Taman Negara and the Perhentian Islands, Cherating was a major backpacker stop (breaking up the trip between the two major destinations). Nowadays only dedicated wanderers, surfers and a few intrepid backpackers make it out this way but most who do find that there's something special about this place.

The village itself is just a half-dead strip of guest houses and shops with more monkeys, monitor lizards and cats walking around than humans, but between the cracks are a resident band of hipster Malay surfers, artists and *kampung* folk who genuinely want to hang out over a beer and share in the holiday spirit. Get in with these characters and you'll understand why so many people end up staying here much longer than expected.

There's an exceptional amount to do in Cherating. During the monsoon season (November to March) storms kick up surfable waves, especially good for beginners. Several places in town rent out surfboards for around RM20 per hour and you can get surf lessons at **Satu Saku** (Main Rd; 🕑 Nov-Mar). **Balzaction** (🕑 9.30am-11pm), right on the beach, rents out windsurfing and kitesurfing equipment from around RM50 per hour and offers classes.

Batik-making is another speciality. Matahari Chalets (p478) and Limbong Art (a shop on the Main Rd) both offer courses (from RM25) where you can make your own batik handkerchief or sarong.

Myriad adventures are available on the river – firefly-spotting, kayaking, fishing trips etc.

Information

There are no banks in Cherating.

Tourist Information Centre (hwy at Cherating turn-off) Rarely open.

Travelpost (☎ 581 9796; 9am-11pm) Organises bus tickets to just about anywhere (takes a commission), has bike hire (per hr RM3), internet access (per hr RM4) and tourist information, and exchanges money at a poor rate.

Sleeping, Eating & Drinking

Cherating has a 'strip' where most of the restaurants and guest houses congregate. Book in advance during the monsoon surf season from November through January.

Maznah's Guest House (☎ 581 9072; chalets incl breakfast RM20-35) Half-naked kids happily chase chickens around the collection of sturdy wooden bungalows here. The owners speak little English and *nasi lemak* is served for breakfast, making this a great, friendly place to go local.

Matahari Chalets (☎ 581 9835; small/large chalets RM25/35) Chalets have shared showers but are clean and equipped with a fridge, windows, mosquito nets and spacious verandahs. The atmosphere is relaxed with a TV common room, and a kitchen for guests.

Payung Guesthouse (☎ 581 9658; chalets s/d RM30/35, f with kitchen RM50) Backs onto the river, with neat rows of ordinary chalets in the garden. The attached tour office offers everything from bike and surfboard rentals to mangrove or snorkelling tours.

Coconut Inn (☎ 581 9299; chalets RM30-80) This place has an eclectic ensemble of wooden chalets (priced by size) in a garden of tall trees and hanging potted plants.

Mimi's Guest House (☎ 012 939 7309; chalets RM40-60;) A surfer favourite with some long-term residents clinging onto a bungalow or two, Mimi's has a charming selection of small wood bungalows all with TVs and fridges.

our pick **Don't Tell Mama** (till late) The hippest bar in town is right on the beach and is a great place to stop by day or night to make friends over a cold beer. Impromptu barbeques and parties are the norm.

Most guest houses run their own restaurants, the best being **Matahari Restaurant** (seafood barbeque from RM10; breakfast, lunch & dinner) at the west end of town.

Getting There & Away

Cherating doesn't have a bus station, but any Kuantan–Terengganu bus will drop off passengers at the turn-off to the village road, which will involve a short stroll. To go south from Cherating you'll need to wave down the local bus bound for Kuantan that runs every 30 minutes (RM4.50, 1¼ hours); for Kuala Terengganu book long-distance bus tickets (RM16, three hours, frequent) through **Travelpost** (☎ 581 9796; 9am-11pm).

MARANG

☎ 09

Marang is the jump-off point for ferries to Pulau Kapas and a quiet fishing town, a little overbuilt by the highway but still pleasant in a rural way. If you're around on Sunday, check out the excellent **Sunday Market**, which starts at 3pm near the town's jetties.

There are regular local buses to/from Kuala Terengganu (RM2). For long-distance buses there's a **ticket office** (☎ 618 2799; Jln Tanjung Sulong Musa) near the town's main intersection. There are buses to/from Kuala Lumpur (RM30, two daily), Johor Bahru (RM35, two daily), and Kuantan (RM15, two daily) via Cherating.

PULAU KAPAS

☎ 09

Kapas is the kind of place you could melt into and forget to leave. Not that there's much going on, but that's the beauty of the place. Outside July, August and a few holiday weekends expect to have the scorching white beaches and aquamarine waters to yourself. All accommodation and the few restaurants are clustered together on two small beaches on the west coast, but you can walk around the headlands to quieter beaches.

Note that accommodation on the island shuts down during monsoon season (November to March).

The most budget-oriented option on Kapas is **Lighthouse** (☎ 019 215 3558; dm/d RM20/50), an elevated jungle longhouse with Che posters, hammocks and Nora Jones tunes. Otherwise **Kapas Island Resort** (☎ 631 6468; www.kapasisland resort.com; dm RM20, r RM90-200;), set among pretty landscaped gardens, is a good choice. Choose from timber chalets or a longhouse dorm sleeping up to 30 people.

Six kilometres offshore from Marang, Kapas is reached by boats in mere minutes from Marang's main jetty. Tickets (RM40 return) can be purchased from any of the agents nearby and boats depart when four or more people show up. Be sure to arrange a pick-up time when you purchase your ticket. You can usually count on morning departures from 8.30am.

KUALA TERENGGANU

☎ 09

Kuala Terengganu has a made-for-the-movies Southeast Asian success story: fishing village finds oil, money flows in, modernity ensues. Here and there you'll find an old *kampung* house seemingly hiding among the high-rises, and these glimpses, plus a seafood-heavy local cuisine, make Kuala Terengganu worth a day or two of exploration.

Note that Kuala Terengganu is very, very Islamic and official business is closed on Friday and Saturday.

Information

Jln Sultan Ismail is the commercial hub and home to most banks, which are open 9.30am to 3.30pm, except Friday.

Golden Wood Internet (☎ 631 0128; 59 Jln Tok Lam; per hr RM5)

Tourism Malaysia Office (☎ 630 9087; 11 Tingkat Bawah; 9am-5pm Sat-Thu) General information on Malaysia.

Tourist Information Office (☎ 617 1553; Jln Sultan Zainal Abidin; 9am-5pm Sat-Thu) Brochures on Terengganu.

Sights

Kuala Terengganu's compact **Chinatown** is situated along Jln Kampung Cina (also called Jln Bandar). It's a colourful array of hole-in-the-wall Chinese shops, hairdressing salons and restaurants, as well as a sleepy **Chinese temple** and some narrow alleys leading to jetties on the waterfront.

The **central market** (cnr Jln Kampung Cina & Jln Banggol; 8am-5pm Sat-Thu) is a lively place to graze on exotic snacks, and the floor above the fish section has a wide collection of batik and *kain songket* (handwoven fabric). Across from the market is a flight of stairs leading up to **Bukit Puteri** (Princess Hill), a 200m hill with city vistas and the remains of a fort. **Istana Maziah** (Sultan's Palace; Jln Masjid Abidin) and **Zainal Abidin Mosque** (Jln Masjid Abidin) are not camera shy.

Kompleks Muzium Negeri Terengganu (Terengganu State Museum; ☎ 622 1444; adult RM5; 9am-5pm) claims to be the largest museum in the

region, and it attractively sprawls over landscaped gardens along the banks of the Sungai Terengganu. Traditional architecture, fishing boats and textiles comprise the bulk of the collection. The museum is 5km south of Terengganu; to get there take minibus 10 (RM1).

In the middle of Sungai Terengganu, **Pulau Duyung Besar** carries on the ancient boatbuilding tradition handed down for generations; the village is good for a day of wandering and snacking. Take the local ferry (60 sen) from the jetty near the Immigration Office across Bukit Puteri.

Sleeping & Eating

Ping Anchorage Travellers' Inn (☎ 626 2020; www.pinganchorage.com.my; 77A Jln Sultan Sulaiman; dm/r from RM10/26; ❄) Spread over two floors above the travel agency of the same name, Ping's rooms are reasonably clean, but it doesn't have much going for it besides a vaguely social vibe and a central location.

Awi's Yellow House (☎ 624 7363, 622 2080; r RM18-25) Built over the Sungai Terengganu river on Pulau Duyung, Awi's welcomes you with the smell of fish paste, salt and chilli, no air-con and nights that stick to you like a wet kiss. Don't come here if you don't like roughing it a little, but do if you want a taste of *kampung* life.

Restoran Golden Dragon (☎ 622 3034; 198 Jln Kampung Cina; mains from RM5; 🕑 lunch & dinner) The Golden Dragon is constantly packed, serves beer and has one of the finest menus of Chinese seafood in town – anything steamed and off the fish list should serve you right.

Terapung Puteri (☎ 631 8946; Jln Sultan Zainal Abidin; mains from RM5; 🕑 lunch & dinner) This busy Malay restaurant is perched on stilts, *kampung*-style, on the seafront next to the jetty. There's a huge menu, with fish, prawns and crab featuring heavily, as well as local items such as *kerepok* (prawn crackers) and a few 'Western' dishes.

There are cheap food stalls inside the main bus station and a night market along the beachfront every Friday evening; the latter is a great place to sample *kerepok*, satay and sweets. Chinatown's outdoor **hawker centre** (off Jln Kampung Cina) is divided into Chinese and Malay sections and sizzles with cooking and socialising at night.

Getting There & Away

AIR

Malaysia Airlines (☎ 662 6600; Airport) and **Air Asia** (☎ 32-171 9333; Airport) have direct flights to KL, and **Firefly** (☎ 03-7845 4543) has flights to/from Singapore four times per week. A taxi to/from the **airport** (☎ 666 3666), located 13km northeast of the town centre, costs around RM30.

BUS & TAXI

The **main bus station** (Jln Masjid Abidin) serves as a terminus for all local buses. Some long-distance buses depart from here as well, but most use the **express bus station** (Jln Sultan Zainal Abidin), in the north of town.

At the main bus station, there are services to/from Marang (RM3, 30 minutes, every half-hour from 6.30am to 6.30pm).

From the express bus station, there are regular services running to and from Kuala Besut (RM10), Johor Bahru (RM37, nine hours, two daily), Ipoh (RM40, 10 hours, two daily), Kuala Lumpur (RM35, seven hours, frequent), Melaka (RM37, nine hours, one daily), Mersing (RM29, seven hours, two daily) and Kota Bharu (RM13, three hours, seven daily).

The main taxi stand is at Jln Masjid Abidin across from the main bus station.

KUALA BESUT

The primary jetty town for boats to Pulau Perhentian is Kuala Besut (bee-su), south of Kota Bharu. It is a sleepy fishing village with a handful of collaborating boat companies and a small bus station.

Some taxi drivers get paid commission to take travellers to the jetty of **Tok Bali**, just across the river. Ferries here are nearly as frequent as Kuala Besut–based boats so this shouldn't pose a problem for you. For details of ferries between Kuala Besut and Pulau Perhentian see p482.

There is no direct bus running from Kota Bharu – you'll have to travel via Jerteh or Pasir Puteh for an onward connection. The total fare ends up being between RM5 and RM10. A taxi to/from Kota Bharu costs RM65 per car (to Tok Bali it's about RM60); most people choose this easier option. From the south, you can go to/from Kuala Terengganu by bus (RM8) or taxi (RM80 per car). There are also two daily buses to/from KL (RM34, nine hours).

The agent at Kuala Besut's jetty also sells minibus tickets to the Cameron Highlands (RM85, six hours) and Taman Negara (RM110, eight hours), which leave at 10am daily.

PULAU PERHENTIAN

☎ 09

Long Beach on Pulau Kecil of the Perhentian Islands is one of Malaysia's most popular backpacker congregation spots. The near-perfect crescent of white sand is clogged with guest houses (but no cars!) but the jungle setting and chummy vibe are hypnotic, the turquoise water utterly sublime. Some travellers show up here expecting a big party but be warned, these are quiet islands and those looking for a full-moon fiesta atmosphere are very much in the wrong place. Coral Beach, also on Kecil, is a touch classier than Long Beach, while the digs on Pulau Besar verge on the resortlike.

The best time to visit is from March to mid-November. The Perhentians close for the monsoon season – some places don't bother opening till April or later – although some hotels remain open for hardier tourists.

There are no banks on the Perhentians. Generators are the source of power and are run during limited hours. There are no public phones but mobile phones work. Internet is scarce and costs around RM20 per hour.

Also please, please note: this is still Malaysia, and topless sunbathing is rude. Locals are too polite to tell people to their face, but baring your breasts insults their sense of modesty.

Activities

Dive operators on the island contend that the Perhentians offer all the underwater delights of the east coast of Thailand without the 'dive-factory' feel. A four-day open-water course costs RM850 to RM1100. For the surface skimmers, guest houses arrange snorkelling trips around the island (around RM40).

Sleeping & Eating

On Pulau Kecil (Small Island), Long Beach has the biggest range of budget chalets and 'nightlife' (that means two beachfront bars). In the high season (usually from late May to early September), finding accommodation here can be tough, so book ahead or arrive early. Accommodation on Pulau Besar (Big Island) is more upmarket and usually includes air-con and a private bathroom.

Alcohol is available in a few bars and hotel restaurants on both islands. The best hunting grounds for a beer are the more popular Long Beach cafes and Watercolours Resort on Pulau Perhentian Besar.

PULAU PERHENTIAN KECIL

A trail over the narrow waist of the island leads from Long Beach to smaller Coral Bay (sometimes known as Aur Bay) on the western side of the island. It's a 15-minute walk along a footpath through the jungle interior.

Long Beach

The surf can get rather big on Long Beach and several places along the beach rent bogie boards and old clunky surfboards. Take care when swimming here as there have been several near tragedies.

Chempaka Chalets (☎ 010 985 7329; r RM20-70) A group of bungalows in a bland but tidy garden, Chempaka gets extra points for cleanliness and its beach-bum vibe.

Matahari Chalets (☎ 019 956 5756; chalets RM25-120) The spacious longhouse rooms and A-frame huts are in much better condition than those of the competition. They ramble around a well-kept but shadeless garden off the beach.

Mohsin Chalet (☎ 961 1580; r from RM30) Mohsin has some wonderful chalets sprawling into the sand and up a hill. The receptionist is surreally friendly, and the ambience is tropically languid.

Lemon Grass (☎ 012 956 2393; r RM35) At the southern tip of Long Beach, Lemon Grass has no-frills huts. There are great views from the verandah at reception and some nice secluded spots to sit and gaze out to sea.

Rock Garden (r RM40) On the rocky cliff behind Lemon Grass, this place has new owners and might not be called Rock Garden by the time you read this. The view from the huts overlooking Long Beach is fabulous.

Coral Bay & Other Beaches

Coral Bay has a more chilled ambience than Long Beach and faces the west for brilliant sunsets and calm swimming. There are also a number of small bays around the island, each with one set of chalets, and often only accessible by boat.

D' Lagoon Chalets (☎ 019 985 7089; r RM25-60) This place fronts a gorgeous but often agitated bay on the northeastern side of the island. There are longhouse rooms and chalets, as well as a more unusual tree house (RM25) for a more Tarzan experience.

Aur Bay Chalets (☎ 010 985 8584; r RM30-40) This well-groomed but fading place at Coral Bay feels like a mini *kampong* with its sweet Malay owners and kids skipping in the sand.

our pick **Petani Beach House** (r RM30-65) On a secluded south coast beach, the driftwood naturalistic decor here is set off by bows of magenta bougainvillea. We've had very enthusiastic traveller recommendations for the quality of the bungalows, the service and the food.

Mira Chalets (☎ 010 964 0582; r RM30-70) Mira, on the west coast, has sea-weathered, rustic huts with mosquito nets perched over a beach so deserted and perfect you'll think you're hallucinating. There's one rather adventurous jungle toilet for everyone to share.

Maya Beach Resort (☎ 019 937 9136; r RM35-45) British-run Maya on Coral Bay is neat and trim and a good place for friendly advice.

Butterfly Chalets (r RM45-60) Ageing huts look out over Coral Bay and are tucked in by hibiscus flowers.

PULAU PERHENTIAN BESAR

Of the three main beaches, the sand surrounding the Perhentian Island Resort is the rockiest, heading south the sand is less cluttered, and finally Teluk Dalam, a secluded bay with a long stretch of shallow beach, is just silken. An easily missed track leads from behind the second jetty over the hill to Teluk Dalam.

It is possible to camp on the beach south of the Government Resthouse ('Love Beach'), although this area is far from quiet on long weekends. You'll need a permit (RM5 per night), available at a little cafe here, if it's open. The beach and bays down this way are spectacular.

The options here are listed from north to south.

Watercolours Resort (☎ 691 1111; www.watercolоursworld.com; r RM70-130;) This friendly resort has clean chalets and a dive centre; both are about the best value on Besar.

Mama's Place (☎ 019 985 3359; www.mamaschalet.com; r RM60-100) The southernmost place on this section of beach has a choice of reasonably comfortable chalets that come with or without bathrooms.

Abdul's (☎ 010 983 7303; r RM40-80) Clambering over the next headland brings you to a quiet beach where you'll find this popular place with fan chalets and attached bathrooms.

Everfresh Beach Resort (☎ 697 7620; Teluk Dalam; r RM30-80) Rooms here are tatty and dark but who cares when you've got a beach like this one out front.

Getting There & Around

Speedboats (RM70 return, 35 minutes) run several times a day from Kuala Besut to the Perhentians from 8.30am to 5.30pm. There used to be cheaper (and safer) slow boats plying this route, but this wasn't the case during our research. The boats will drop you off at any of the beaches.

In the other direction, speedboats depart from the islands daily at around 8am, noon and 4pm. It's a good idea to let the owner of your guest house know a day before you leave so they can arrange a pick-up.

When the waves are high on Long Beach, you'll be dropped off or picked up on the other side of the island at Coral Bay. Also, guest house operators on Kecil charge RM3 per person for ferry pick-ups and drop-offs.

The easiest way to island (or beach) hop is by boat. Posted fares and boat operators usually camp out under a shady coconut tree. From island to island, the trip costs RM20 per boat.

KOTA BHARU

☎ 09

Kota Bharu is supremely pleasant; it has the energy of a mid-sized city, the compact feel and friendly vibe of a small town, superb food and a good spread of accommodation. It's the logical overnight stop between Thailand and the Perhentians, but you'd be wise to give Kota Bharu more time than a pit stop.

Information

Banks and ATMs are scattered around town; **Maybank** (Jln Pintu Pong), near the night market, is usually open till 7pm. Internet shops can be found in the alleys around Jln Doktor and Jln Kebun Sultan.

Immigration office (☎ 748 212; Jln Temenggong)
Tourist Information Centre (☎ 748 5534; Jln Sultan Ibrahim; 8am-1pm & 2-4.30pm Sun-Wed)

Sights & Activities

Kota Bharu's **Central Market** (Pasar Besar Siti Khadijah; Jln Hulu; 6am-6pm) is one of the most colourful and active in Malaysia and is at its busiest first thing in the morning – it's usually packed up by early afternoon. Downstairs is the produce section, while upstairs stalls sell spices, brassware and batik.

For a dose of Malay tradition, don't miss the cultural centre, **Gelanggang Seni** (☎ 744 3124; Jln Mahmud; admission free; 3.30-5.30pm & 9-

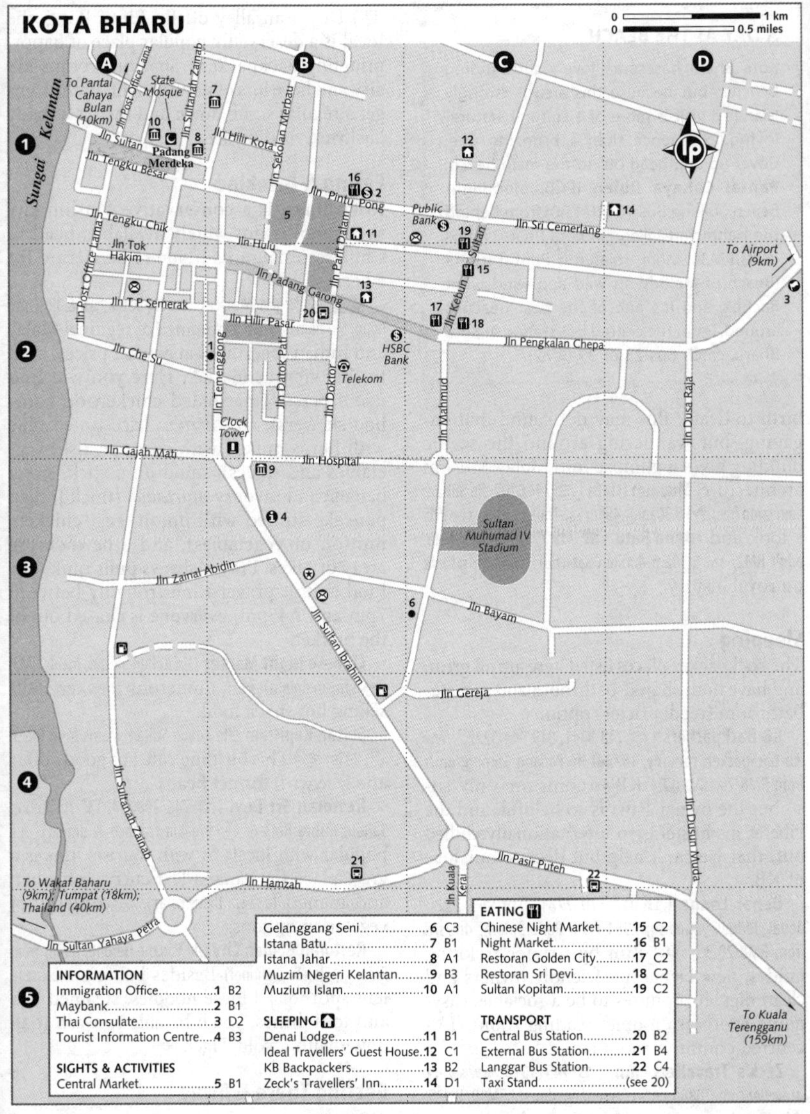

11pm Mon, Wed & Sat Feb-Sep), for top-spinning, *seni silat* (martial arts), shadow puppetry, kite-making etc. Check with the tourist information centre, as opening and performance times vary.

The **Muzium Negeri Kelantan** (State Museum; ☎ 748 2266; Jln Hospital; adult RM2; 🕒 8.30am-4.45pm Sat-Thu) has interesting exhibits about the state's history and culture, but the accompanying signage is poor.

Other museums are clustered around Padang Merdeka (Independence Sq). **Istana Jahar** (Royal Customs Museum; ☎ 748 2266; Jln Hilir Kota; adult RM3; 🕒 8.30am-4.45pm Sat-Thu) exhibits royal rites of passage and traditional ceremonies, such as circumcision and engagement, from

A DAY AT THE BEACH

Kota Bharu has some lovely surrounding beaches but because this area is strongly Islamic a visit is more of a cultural, nature-loving experience than a bronzing one. Cover up and head out to the main beach, **Pantai Cahaya Bulan** (PCB; Moonlight Beach), taking Bus 10 (RM1.30) from behind the Handicraft Village in Kota Bharu. A taxi costs RM30. More isolated is **Pantai Irama** (Beach of Melody) in wild and windswept Bachok, and it's one of the best beaches around. From the central bus station in Kota Bharu, catch Bus 23 or 39 (RM2).

birth to death; this may not sound that engaging, but wandering around the scenic building gives a glimpse into Malay Muslim architecture. **Muzium Islam** (☎ 744 0102; Jln Sultan; admission free; 🕑 8.30am-4.45pm Sat-Thu) is also worth a look and **Istana Batu** (☎ 748 7737; Jln Hilir Kota; adult RM2; 🕑 8.30am-4.45pm Sat-Thu) has displays on royal history.

Sleeping

The backpacker places listed here are all great, and have both shared-bathroom and private-bathroom (read: pricier) options.

KB Backpackers (☎ 748 8841, 019 944 5222; www.kb-backpackers.com.my; 1872-D Jln Padang Garong; dm/r from RM8/20; ❄ 💻) KB's rooms are only so-so but the owner Pawi is so helpful, and the vibe at his hostel is so internationally chilled out, that we can't help but declare our love of KB.

Denai Lodge (☎ 017 370 7781, 019 963 2324; denai_lodge@yahoo.sg; 2984-F Jln Parit Dalam; dm/s/d from RM8/20/35; 💻) Run by former trekking guides, new Denai has friendly owners and clean digs. It promises to be a sociable, easy-going spot with a quiet reading room, TV-centred common room etc.

Zeck's Travellers' Inn (☎ 743 1613; www.zeck-traveller.com; 7088G Jln Sri Cemerlang; dm/s/d RM10/18/25; ❄ 💻) An oasis just 10 minutes' walk from the city, Zeck's is relaxed, clean and over-the-top hospitable. Many travellers on a short stop stay on longer just because of this place. The turn-off from Jln Sri Cemerlang is easy to miss; keep an eye out for the roadside shack selling fresh fritters.

Ideal Travellers' Guest House (☎ 744 2246; www.ugoideal.com; 3954F Jln Kebun Sultan; s/d from RM10/25; 💻) Down an alley off Jln Pintu Pong, the Ideal is a deservedly popular place of happy, mingling backpackers. Spacious rooms are airy and have lots of natural light. Bathrooms get a regular scrub down and there's a shady backyard reading area.

Eating & Drinking

Kota Bharu is a conservative Muslim city so alcohol is not widely available; head to Chinese restaurants if you're hankering for a beer.

our pick **Night Market** (cnr Jln Datok Pati & Jln Pintu Pong; 🕑 dinner) For a bonanza of regional Malay and Indian specialities at hawker prices, head to this vibrant market. Here you will find *ayam percik* (marinated chicken on bamboo skewers), *nasi kerabu* (rice tinted blue with herbs, mixed with coconut, fish, vegetables and spices), squid-on-a-stick, sweet banana and savoury *murtabak* (thick Indian pancake stuffed with onion, egg, chicken, mutton or vegetables), and a bewildering array of cakes. Prayer always pulls rank over food and at prayer time (roughly between 7pm and 7.45pm) everyone is chased out of the market.

Chinese Night Market (Jln Kebun Sultan; meals RM3; 🕑 6pm-midnight) Has numerous hawker stalls selling hot snack food.

Sultan Kopitiam (Jln Kebun Sultan; mains from RM 3; 🕑 24hr; 📶) This bustling cafe has good coffee and free wi-fi for net heads.

Restoran Sri Devi (☎ 746 2980; 4213F Jln Kebun Sultan; dishes RM3-6; 🕑 breakfast, lunch & dinner) As popular with locals as with tourists, this is a great place for banana-leaf curry, *roti canai* and mango lassi. There are also plenty of vegetarian options.

Restoran Golden City (Jln Padang Garong; mains from RM5; 🕑 lunch & dinner) Besides being an excellent spot for Chinese noodles, steamed fish and tofu dishes, you'll be able to wash it all down with a cold Tiger.

Getting There & Away

AIR

Air Asia (☎ 746 1671) and **Firefly** (☎ 037-845 4543) have direct daily flights to KL.

BUS

There are three bus stations in Kota Bharu. Local buses depart from the **central bus station** (Jln Padang Garong), also known as the state-run SKMK bus station. Most long-distance buses

GETTING TO THAILAND: RANTAU PANJANG TO SUNGAI KOLOK

It's not advised to cross the border here due to violence and instability on this coast of southern Thailand. If you must risk it, buses depart on the hour from the central bus station (RM3.80, 1½ hours) to Rantau Panjang where you can walk across the border; it's about a kilometre from here to the Sungai Kolok train station. Share taxis from Kota Bharu to Rantau Panjang cost RM30 per car and take 45 minutes.

An alternative (and some say safer) route into Thailand is to take a regular bus to Pengkalan Kubor, on the coast, cross the border to Ban Ta Ba, then get a *songthaew* to Tak Bai, Sungai Kolok from there. Do know, however, that this entire area is considered unsafe and crossing here is a risky endeavour.

For information about getting to Malaysia from Thailand see p804.

will drop off passengers near here, but do not depart from here. All long-distance companies serving Kota Bharu have ticket agents nearby. When buying your ticket, verify which long-distance terminal the bus departs from. Most Transnacional long-distance buses depart from **Langgar bus station** (☎ 748 3807; Jln Pasir Puteh), in the south of the city. All the other long-distance bus companies operate from the **external bus station** (Jln Hamzah).

A few handy local buses include the ones to Pasir Puteh (RM5) and Jerteh (RM7) – for connections to Kuala Besut and the Perhentians – Kota Bharu airport (RM1.20, every 20 minutes), and Wakaf Baharu (RM1.20).

Long-distance destinations from here include Butterworth (RM29, seven hours, one daily), Ipoh (RM25, eight hours, five daily), Johor Bahru (RM49, 10 hours, five daily), Kuala Lumpur (RM31, 10 hours, hourly), Kuala Terengganu (RM11, three hours, two daily) and Kuantan (RM24, seven hours, five daily).

TAXI

The taxi stand is on the southern side of the central bus station. Destinations and costs per car (which can be split between four passengers) include Wakaf Baharu (RM25), Kota Besut (RM65) and Tok Bali (RM60). Taxi drivers in Kota Bharu are uncharacteristically aggressive; do your homework on fares. Most guest houses arrange shared taxis, especially for early morning departures.

TRAIN

The nearest **train station** (☎ 719 6986) to Kota Bharu is at Wakaf Baharu, on the Jungle Railway line (see p486). There is also a train to Bangkok, although services have sometimes been suspended due to violence in southern Thailand.

PENINSULAR INTERIOR

A thick band of jungle buffers the two coasts from one another. Within the middle is Taman Negara, the peninsula's most famous national park, and the Jungle Railway, an engineering feat.

JERANTUT

☎ 09

Jerantut is the first of several stepping stones to Taman Negara. It's a dingy yet easy town, where you can pick up supplies, change money or stay overnight to break up your trip.

There are two ATMs, both near the bus station, where you can cash up before heading to the jungle.

Sleeping & Eating

A food court specialising in *tom yam* (spicy Thai-style) seafood is on Jln Pasar Besar. Chinese liquor stores line up along Jln Diwangsa hoping you'll want to stock up on booze before heading to dry Kuala Tahan.

Hotel Sri Emas (☎ 266 4499; tamannegara@hotmail.com; 46 Jln Besar; dm RM8, d with shower RM38, d without shower RM15-35, tr RM21, f RM64; ❄ 💻) Many people get herded here by the handy NKS minivan that picks up at the bus and train station and it's not a bad place to end up. Fan doubles with shared hot-water bathrooms have saggy mattresses but are clean and excellent value (RM15).

Hotel Chet Fatt (☎ 266 5805; 177 Jln Diwangsa; dm/d RM10/20; 💻) Stumble across the street from the bus station if you arrive late at night to this place with window-lit rooms, internet terminals and free filtered water.

Greenleaf Traveller's Inn (☎ 267 2131; 3 Jln Diwangsa; dm RM10, d RM20-30; ❄) Run by a sweet

JUNGLE RAILWAY

This line trundles into the mountainous, jungle-clad interior, stopping at every ramshackle *kampung,* packing in chattering school children and headscarfed women lugging oversized bundles. Travellers' reports range from awe of the natural splendour and amusement with the local camaraderie to boredom and irritation with the rickety carriages and dirty windows. If you're in good company and have a lot of time, then there are worse ways to travel between Pulau Perhentian and Taman Negara.

The northern terminus is Tumpat, but most travellers start/end at Wakaf Baharu, the closest station to the transport hub of Kota Bharu. The train departs from Wakaf Baharu on its southbound journey around (ouch!) 4am (to get the children to school on time) and it reaches Jerantut, the jumping-off point for Taman Negara, anywhere from eight to 11 hours later (RM13). Trains invariably run late. The journey continues south to Gemas (RM19), meeting the Singapore–KL train line. By far the most interesting leg of the ride is between Wakaf Bahru and Gua Musang – south of Jeruntut the forest becomes a stretch of palm oil and rubber plantations that gives you an idea of how vast deforestation is on the peninsula.

There are also express trains that travel at night, but that would defeat the purpose of seeing the jungle. Note that information on these local services aren't available on the KTM railway website and you cannot book tickets online. The train's schedule changes every six months, so it pays to double-check departure times locally.

lady and her family, this is a quiet choice with simple, clean rooms and dorms.

NKS Hostel (21-22 Jln Besar; d incl breakfast with/without shower RM50/35) Run by the same folks as Sri Emas, NKS has clean, tiled rooms, and all the NKS buses to Kuala Tahan and Kuala Tembeling (for the boat) stop right outside the restaurant and internet cafe on the ground floor.

Getting There & Away

BOAT

Motor-run canoes make the scenic journey between Kuala Tembeling and Kuala Tahan. Travel agents sell combination tickets that include transfer from Jerantut to the jetty and ferry to Kuala Tahan.

For more information on boats to Kuala Tahan, see p489.

BUS & TAXI

The bus station and taxi stand are in the centre of town.

Most people arriving in Jerantut want to head directly to the Kuala Tembeling jetty (where boats leave for Taman Negara). To do this, follow the NKS representative, who meets arriving buses and trains and organises minibus transfers (RM5) from Jerantut to Kuala Tembeling.

You can also skip the boat journey and hop on a Kuala Tahan–bound bus (signed as 'Latif'; RM7, one to two hours, four daily); Kuala Tahan is the base-camp village for Taman Negara. You save money by doing this, although many travellers cite the voyage upriver from Kuala Tembeling as a highlight of visiting Taman Negara.

Alternatively, you can hire a taxi to Kuala Tembeling (RM20 for the entire car) or to Kuala Tahan (RM65).

When you are ready to get the hell out of Jerantut, there are several daily buses to/from KL's Pekeliling bus station (RM17, 3 hours) via Temerloh (last bus to/from Jerantut 5/4pm). If you miss the bus to KL, buses go every hour to Temerloh (RM5, one hour, last bus 6.30pm), from where there are more connections to KL and other destinations. Three daily buses run to/from Kuantan (RM16, 3½ hours). One bus runs daily to Johor Bahru (RM38).

NKS arranges minibuses and buses to a variety of destinations, including KL (RM40), Perhentian Island Jetty (RM65), Kota Bharu (RM65) and Cameron Highlands (RM65), all of which leave from the NKS cafe.

Long-distance taxis go to Temerloh (RM50), KL (RM200) and Kuantan (RM180).

TRAIN

Jerantut is on the Jungle Railway (Tumpat-Gemas line; see above). The train station is off Jln Besar, just behind Hotel Sri Emas. For the famed jungle view, catch the northbound local train at around 8.30am to Wakaf Bahru (RM13). If you opt to skip the view, a daily northbound express train leaves Jerantut at 1.45am (seat/berth RM17/31, four hours).

Two express trains run daily to Singapore (2am and 12.30pm), via Johor Bahru. For KL Sentral, take the 12.30am express. For an up-to-date timetable and list of fares, consult **KTM** (www.ktmb .com.my).

TAMAN NEGARA

☎ 09

Taman Negara blankets 4343 sq km in shadowy, damp, impenetrable jungle. Inside this tangle, trees with gargantuan buttressed root systems dwarf luminescent fungi, orchids and even the giant rafflesia (which is the world's largest flower). Trudge along muggy trails in search of elusive wildlife (tigers, elephants and rhinos can hide much better than you'd think), explore bat caves, balance on the creaky canopy walk or spend the night in a 'hide' where jungle sounds make you feel like you've gone back to the caveman days.

The best time to visit the park is in the dry season between February and September. During the wet season, or even after one good rainfall, leeches come out in force.

Orientation & Information

Kuala Tahan is the base camp for Taman Negara and has accommodation, minimarkets and floating-barge restaurants. It's a scruffy place and standards are low but it's pleasant enough. Directly opposite Kuala Tahan, across Sungai Tembeling, is the entrance to the national park, Mutiara Taman Negara Resort and the park headquarters located at the Wildlife Department.

Most people purchase permits (park entrance/camera RM1/5) when they buy their bus and/or boat tickets to Kuala Tahan in Jerantut. Otherwise you'll need to get your permits at the **Wildlife Department** (☎ 266 1122; 🕑 8am-10pm Sat-Thu, 8am-noon & 3-10pm Fri). The reception desk also provides basic maps, guide services and advice.

Internet access is expensive (per hour RM5 to RM6). There are a handful of terminals at Agoh Chalets and a few more at an unnamed shop across from Teresek View Motel. There are no banks in Taman Negara.

Activities

HIDES & SALT LICKS

Animal-observation hides *(bumbun)* are built overlooking salt licks and grassy clearings, which attract feeding nocturnal animals. You'll need to spend the night in order to see any real action. There are several hides close to Kuala Tahan (Tabing and Kumbang hides being the most popular) and Kuala Trenggan that are a little too close to human habitation to attract the shy animals. Even if you don't see any wildlife, the jungle sounds are well worth it – the 'symphony' is best at dusk and dawn.

Hides (per person per night RM5) need to be reserved at the Wildlife Department and they are very rustic with pit toilets. Some travellers hike independently in the day to the hides, then camp overnight and return the next day, while others go to more far-flung hides that require some form of transport and a guide; the Wildlife Department can steer you in the right direction. For overnight trips you'll need food, water and a sleeping bag. Rats on the hunt for tucker are problematic, so hang food high out of reach.

Some of the following hides can be reached by popular treks (see p488):

PLANNING FOR TAMAN NEGARA

Stock up on essentials in Jerantut. If it's been raining, leeches will be unavoidable. Tobacco, salt, toothpaste and soap can be used to deter them, with varying degrees of success. A liberal coating of insect spray over shoes and socks works best. Tuck pant legs into socks; long sleeves and long pants will protect you from insects and brambles. Even on short walks, take more water than you think you'll ever need, and on longer walks take water-purifying tablets.

Camping, hiking and fishing gear can be hired at the Mutiara Taman Negara Resort shop or at several shops and guest houses on the Kampung Kuala Tahan side. Asking prices per day are around RM8 for a sleeping bag, RM10 for a rucksack, RM25 for a tent, RM20 for a fishing rod, RM5 for a sleeping pad, RM8 for a stove and RM8 for boots. Prices can be negotiated and it's good to shop around for bargains as well as quality.

Bumbun Blau & Bumbun Yong On Sungai Yong. From the park headquarters it's roughly 1½ hours' walk to Bumbun Blau (3.1km), which sleeps 12 people and has water nearby, and two hours to Bumbun Yong (4km). You can visit Gua Telinga along the way. Both hides can also be reached by the riverbus service (see p490).
Bumbun Cegar Anjing Once an airstrip, this is now an artificial salt lick, established to attract wild cattle and deer. A clear river runs a few metres from the hide. It's 1½ hours' walk from Kuala Tahan; after rain Bumbun Cegar Anjing may only be accessible by boat (RM40 per four-person boat). The hide sleeps eight people.
Bumbun Kumbang From the park headquarters it's roughly five hours' walk to Bumbun Kumbang. Alternatively, take the riverbus service from Kuala Tahan up Sungai Tembeling to Kuala Trenggan (RM90 per four-person boat, 35 minutes), then walk 45 minutes to the hide. Tapirs, monkeys and gibbons are rarely seen here and elephant sightings are even rarer. The hide has bunks for 12 people.
Bumbun Tahan Roughly five minutes' walk from the park headquarters. There's little chance of seeing any animals apart from monkeys and deer at this artificial salt lick.
Tabing Hide About 1½ hours' walk (3.1km) from park headquarters, this hide is near the river so it's also accessible by the riverbus service. The best animal-watching (mostly tapir and squirrels) here is at nightfall and daybreak.

TREKKING

There are treks to suit all levels of motivation, from a half-hour jaunt to a steep nine-day tussle up and down Gunung Tahan (2187m). It's unanimous that the guides are excellent.

Popular do-it-yourself treks, from one to five hours, include the following:

Bukit Teresik From behind the Canopy Walkway a trail leads to the top of this hill, from which there are fine views across the forest. It's steep and slippery in parts. The return trip is about one hour.
Canopy Walkway (admission RM5; ⌚ 10am-3.30pm Sat-Thu, 9am-noon Fri) Anyone who says walking isn't an adrenalin sport has never been suspended on a hanging rope bridge constructed of wooden planks and ladders elevated 45m above the ground; come early to avoid long waits in line.
Gua Telinga From the park headquarters it's roughly a 1½-hour walk (2.6km). Think wet: a stream runs through this cave (with sleeping bats) and a rope guides you for the strenuous 80m half-hour trek – and crawl – through the cave. Return to the main path through the cave or take the path round the rocky outcrop at its far end. From the main path it's 15 minutes' walk to Bumbun Blau hide or you can walk directly back to Kuala Tahan.
Kuala Trenggan The well-marked main trail along the bank of Sungai Tembeling leads 9km to Kuala Trenggan. This is a popular trail for those heading to Bumbun Kumbang.
Lubok Simpon This is a popular swimming hole. Near the Canopy Walkway, take the branch trail that leads across to a swimming area on Sungai Tahan.

Longer treks, which require a guide, include the following:

Gunung Tahan For the gung-ho, Gunung Tahan, 55km from the park headquarters, is Peninsular Malaysia's highest peak (2187m). The return trek takes nine days at a steady pace, although it can be done in seven. Guides are compulsory (RM550 per person for nine days if there are four people; prices vary depending on how many are in the group). Try to organise this trek in advance through the Wildlife Department (p487).
Rentis Tenor (Tenor Trail) From Kuala Tahan, this trek takes roughly three days. Day one: take the trail to Gua Telinga, and beyond, for about seven hours, to Yong camping ground. Day two: a six-hour walk to the Rentis camping ground. Day three: cross Sungai Tahan (up to waist deep) to get back to Kuala Tahan, roughly six hours' walk, or you can stop over at the Lameh camping ground, about halfway.

OTHER ACTIVITIES

The sport fish known locally as *ikan kelah* (Malaysian mahseer) is a cousin of India's king of the Himalayan rivers and is a prized catch. You'll need a fishing licence, transport and a guide to fish along the river; head to the **Wildlife Department** (☎ 266 1122; ⌚ 8am-10pm Sat-Thu, 8am-noon & 3pm-10pm Fri) for more information. If that sounds too hard, you can fish along Sungai Tembeling without a permit.

Tours

Everyone in Kuala Tahan wants to take you on a tour. There are popular night tours (RM35) on foot or by 4WD. You're more likely to see animals (such as slow loris, snakes, civets and flying squirrels) on the drives, which go through palm-oil plantations outside the park, but even these don't guarantee sightings.

Many travellers sign up for tours to an Orang Asli settlement where you'll be shown how to use a long blowpipe and start a fire. While local guides insist that these tours provide essential income for the Orang Asli, most of your tour money will go to the tour company. A small handicraft purchase in the village will help spread the wealth.

You really don't need a guide or tour for day trips – or even overnight trips – to the hides if you're prepared to organise your own gear, food and water. You'll need one for longer treks, however, and the going rate is RM150 per day (one guide can lead up to

12 people), plus a RM100 fee for each night spent out on the trail. Guides who are licensed by the Wildlife Department have completed coursework in forest flora, fauna and safety and are registered with the department. Often the Kuala Tahan tour operators offer cheaper prices than the Wildlife Department, although there is no guarantee that the guide is licensed.

Sleeping & Eating

Guest houses are listed here in south-to-north order. Arrive early in the day or book in advance since the better places fill up quickly and there's invariably a nightly collection of lost souls searching for rooms in the rain.

For details on staying at a hide, see p487.

Yellow Guesthouse (☎ 266 4243; dm/d RM10/80;) Up and over the top of the hill from the NKS floating restaurant, this quiet new place is cleaner and in better shape than most of the others. The big rooms and dorms have brightly painted walls and new mattresses and the owner is super friendly and helpful.

Tembeling Riverview Hostel (☎ 266 6766; rosnahtrv@hotmail.com; dm RM10, r RM35-50) Straddling the thoroughfare footpath, folks stay here to be close to the action, not for privacy. There are some pleasant communal areas overlooking the river. Rooms are lodge-basic.

Liana Hostel (☎ 266 9322; dm RM10) Has barrackslike, 4-bed dorm rooms and nonexistent service.

Agoh Chalets (☎ 266 9570; d/f RM50/80;) Chalets here are made from concrete modelled to look like logs and all surround a shady garden in the middle of the village. The interiors are ageing but are in better shape than many other places.

our pick Tahan Guesthouse (☎ 266 7752; dm/d RM10/50) Far enough from 'town' to feel away from it all but close enough to be convenient, Tahan Guesthouse has excellent four-bed dorms and colourfully painted bright rooms upstairs. The whole place feels like a happy preschool with giant murals of insects and flowers all over the place.

our pick Durian Chalet (☎ 266 8940; dm/d/f RM10/40/50, A-frames RM25) About 800m outside the village between rubber and durian plantations, this forest hideaway has a 6-bed dorm, microscopic, rustic twin-sized A-frame huts with bathrooms and large doubles and family rooms. All options have fans and mosquito nets, there's a simple restaurant and you can pitch a tent for RM2.

Mat Leon Village (☎ 013 998 9517; dm/chalets RM15/60) Supreme forest location with a view over the river (swimming possible) from its restaurant, clean four-bed dorms and ageing chalets (with shower). Has free boat pick-up from the Mat Leon floating desk at the Kampung Kuala Tahan jetty. Walking, it's about 500m onwards along the road and a forest trail from Durian Chalet.

Malay food (dishes around RM3 to RM10) is available from barge restaurants and at a couple of places attached to guest houses. These restaurants tend to come and go but at the time of research the best was **Mama Chop** (meals around RM7; breakfast, lunch & dinner) at the far northern end of the strip, which serves Indian vegetarian banana-leaf meals at lunchtime. Kuala Tahan is dry, so if you're after a beer you'll have to cross over to **Mutiara Taman Negara Resort** (☎ 266 3500; beers RM8), where you can also dine on overpriced Western food (RM17 to RM55).

Getting There & Away

Most people reach Taman Negara by taking a bus from Jenatut to the jetty at Kuala Tembeling then a river boat from there to the park, but there are also popular private minibus services that go directly to/from several tourist destinations around Malaysia directly to/from Kampung Kuala Tahan. You can also take a bus from Jerantut direct to Kampung Kuala Tahan (see p486 for details), but by doing this you miss the scenic boat trip.

BOAT

The river jetty for Taman Negara-bound boats is in Kuala Tembeling, 18km north of Jerantut.

Boats (one way RM35) depart Kuala Tembeling daily at 9am and 2pm (9am and 2.30pm on Friday). On the return journey, boats leave Kuala Tahan at 9am and 2pm (and 2.30pm on Friday). The journey takes three hours upstream and two hours downstream. Note that the boat service is irregular during the November-to-February wet season.

BUS & TAXI

For details on buses and taxis from Jerantut to Kuala Tembeling, see p486. A public bus from Kampung Kuala Tahan goes to KL (RM26) every day at 8am via Jerantut. **NKS** (☎ 03-2072

0336; www.taman-negara.com) and **Banana Travel & Tours** (☎ 017 902 5952; Information Centre, Kampung Kuala Tahan) run several useful private services including daily buses to KL (RM35) and minibuses to Penang (RM120), the Perhentian Islands (RM165 including boat) and the Cameron Highlands (RM95). These minibuses can also drop you off en route anywhere in between.

Getting Around

There is a frequent cross-river ferry (RM1) that shuttles passengers across the river from Kuala Tahan to the park entrance and Mutiara Taman Negara Resort.

Nusa Camp's floating information centre in Kuala Tahan runs scheduled riverboat (also called riverbus) services along the river to Bumbun Blau/Bumbun Yong (RM15 one way, three daily), the Canopy Walkway (RM10 one way, two daily), Gua Telinga (RM10 one way, four daily), Kuala Tembeling (RM25 one way, one daily) and Kuala Trenggan (RM30 one way, two daily). Check with the information desk for times and prices, as these services may be dropped entirely during the wet season. You can arrange for the boats to pick you up again for the return trip on their schedule, and there's a slight discount for a round-trip fare.

In addition to the riverbus, you can also charter a boat for considerably more – Bumbun Blau (RM75) and Kuala Trenggan (RM110). You can arrange private boat trips at the Wildlife Department, at the resort or at the restaurants in Kuala Tahan (the latter are usually 10% cheaper).

GUNUNG STONG STATE PARK

Once known as the 'Jelawang Jungle', Gunung Stong State Park consists of 21,962 hectares of remote, hardly inhabited green: sharp mountain peaks, thickly matted vegetation and Stong Waterfalls, reputed to be the highest in Southeast Asia.

Due to infrequent transport links it can be frustrating to visit this area without your own wheels or on an organised tour from Kota Bharu. The main base for exploring is Dabong *kampung*, located on the Jungle Railway. There are several caves in the limestone outcrops a few kilometres southeast of town; **Gua Ikan** (Fish Cave) is the most accessible, but the most impressive is **Stepping Stone Cave**. A narrow corridor leads to a hidden grotto and on to **Kris Cave**.

From Dabong, cross over Sungai Galas for 80 sen and take a minivan (RM3) out to the **falls** on 1422m-high Gunung Stong. The main falls are a 20-minute climb past the Perdana Stong Resort; a further 45 minutes of climbing brings you to the top of the falls and a camping ground. From the base of **Baha's Camp** you can make longer excursions to the summit of **Gunung Stong** and the upper falls.

Rumah Rehat Dabong (☎ 09-744 0725; r from RM25; ❄) is a 1980s longhouse and the only decent place to stay in Dabong; ask at the district office opposite the resthouse. There's the usual collection of food stalls near Dabong station.

MALAYSIAN BORNEO – SABAH

Malaysia's state of Sabah proves that there is a God, and we're pretty sure that he's some sort of mad scientist. Sabah was his giant test tube – the product of a harebrained hypothesis. You see, on the seventh day, God wasn't taking his infamous rest, he was pondering the following: 'What would happen if I took an island, covered it with impenetrable jungle, tossed in an ark's worth of animals, and turned up the temperature to a sweltering 40°C?'

The result? A tropical Eden with prancing mega-fauna and plenty of fruit-bearing trees. This 'land below the wind', as it's known, is home to great ginger apes that swing from vine-draped trees, blue-hued elephants that stamp along marshy river deltas, and sun-kissed wanderers who slide along the silver sea in bamboo boats. Oh but there's more: mighty Mt Kinabalu rises to the heavens, governing the steamy wonderland below with its imposing stone turrets. The muddy Sungai Kinabatangan roars through the jungle – a haven for fluorescent birds and cheeky macaques. And finally there's Sipadan's seductive coral reef that lures large pelagics with a languid, come-hither wave.

In order to make the most of *your* days of rest, we strongly encourage you to plan ahead. Sabah's jungles may be wild and untamed, but they're covered in streamers of red tape. With a bit of patience and a lot of preplanning, you'll breeze by the permit restrictions and

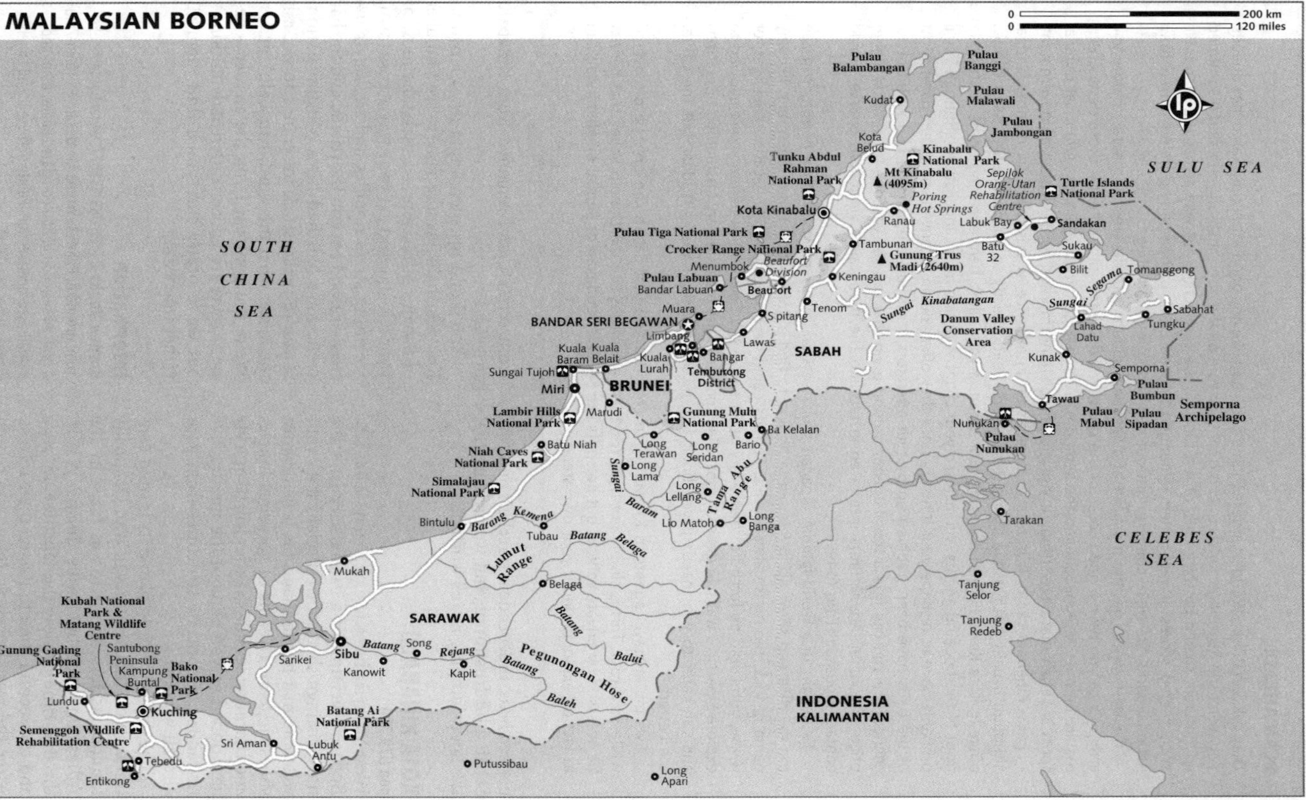
MALAYSIAN BORNEO
0 200 km
0 120 miles
SOUTH CHINA SEA
SULU SEA
CELEBES SEA
SABAH
SARAWAK
BRUNEI
INDONESIA
KALIMANTAN
Pulau Balambangan
Pulau Banggi
Pulau Malawali
Pulau Jambongan
Kudat
Kota Belud
Kinabalu National Park
Mt Kinabalu (4095m)
Poring Hot Springs
Ranau
Sepilok Orang-Utan Rehabilitation Centre
Turtle Islands National Park
Sandakan
Labuk Bay
Batu 32
Sukau
Bilit
Sungai Segama
Tomanggong
Sabahat
Tungku
Lahad Datu
Semporna
Pulau Bumbun
Pulau Sipadan
Pulau Mabul
Semporna Archipelago
Kunak
Tawau
Pulau Nunukan
Nunukan
Tarakan
Tanjung Selor
Tanjung Redeb
Danum Valley Conservation Area
Sungai Kinabatangan
Gunung Trus Madi (2640m)
Tambunan
Keningau
Tenom
Tunku Abdul Rahman National Park
Kota Kinabalu
Crocker Range National Park
Beaufort Division
Beaufort
Pulau Tiga National Park
Menumbok
Pulau Labuan
Bandar Labuan
Sipitang
Lawas
Ba Kelalan
Bario
Bangar
Temburong District
Gunung Mulu National Park
Long Seridan
Tama Abu Range
Long Banga
Lio Matoh
Long Lellang
Muara
BANDAR SERI BEGAWAN
Limbang
Kuala Lurah
Long Terawan
Long Lama
Sungai Baram
Batang Belaga
Kuala Belait
Kuala Baram
Marudi
Miri
Sungai Tujoh
Lambir Hills National Park
Batu Niah
Niah Caves National Park
Simalajau National Park
Bintulu
Batang Kemena
Tubau
Lumut Range
Belaga
Batang Balui
Pegunongan Hose
Batang Baleh
Long Apari
Putussibau
Kapit
Batang Rejang
Song
Kanowit
Mukah
Sibu
Sarikei
Batang Ai National Park
Lubuk Antu
Sri Aman
Bako National Park
Kampung Buntal
Santubong Peninsula
Kuching
Kubah National Park & Matang Wildlife Centre
Gunung Gading National Park
Lundu
Semenggoh Wildlife Rehabilitation Centre
Tebedu
Entikong

PLAN AHEAD!

They call Sabah 'the World's Largest Theme Park', and like any good attraction, Sabah has queues. You won't see frowning tourists queuing for their turn on the ride – instead you'll find disgruntled adventurers snared by thick coils of red tape. As we researched our way across the island, we encountered scores of vacationers lamenting booked beds, or bemoaning being barred from national parks. So, we're coming right out and saying it – plan ahead!

The best way to get the most out of a Sabahan sojourn is to develop an itinerary before you arrive. Once you have a good sense of the sights you'd like to visit, find out if those destinations require permits. Mt Kinabalu and the Semporna Archipelago (Sipadan) are the two most popular spots in Sabah that have stringent visitation regulations imposed by the Malaysian government.

For a Kinabalu climb, it is best to book as far in advance as possible – six months is ideal although usually not feasible for most travellers. Head directly to the Sutera Sanctuary Lodges office in Kota Kinabalu (KK) if you did not organise your climb before leaving home – sitting in front of the booking agents will increase your chances of finding a cancellation (although you'll probably have to reshape your itinerary once they offer you an inconvenient ascent date). Most of the beds have been gobbled up by tour operators, so if you can't snag a bed with Sutera, chances are you can find a travel agency around town that can sell you one (at a much higher price of course). Adventurers interested in tackling the mountain's *via ferrata* course should contact Mountain Torq (p499).

To delight in a world-famous Sipadan scuba session, divers must obtain a permit. You can roll the dice and show up in Semporna hoping to find a golden ticket, but remember, like any game of luck, the house always wins. Permits could be cloaked in frilly vacation packages, or worse, you could be forced to dive every other site in the Celebes Sea before you're allowed to explore Sipadan's walls. In general, most dive centres in the area are very upstanding operations and can cater to your needs if you book well in advance (four weeks is ideal, but the earlier the better).

Swarms of travel agents in KK will try to convince you that Sabah can only be discovered while on a tour. This is simply not true. Yes, there are places like the Danum Valley that cannot be accessed by private vehicle, but hotspots like Sepilok, Sandakan or Sungai Kinabatangan can in fact be explored under your own steam!

booked beds. Independent travellers may find Sabah a bit frustrating, but we promise that the hoop-jumping is well worth it.

KOTA KINABALU

pop 579,300

West Malaysia has KL; East Malaysia has KK. Borneo's version of a capital city isn't the most distinguished spot, especially if it's your welcome mat to the island (as it is for most shoestringers). Dreams of gorgeous jungles and charming seaside shanties will be quickly abandoned as you glimpse the unattractive tic-tac-toe of concrete structures from your aircraft window.

The city is quick to blame its insipid central core on the atrocities of war. Originally founded as Jesselton, KK was razed by the Allies not once but twice during WWII, the first time to slow the Japanese advance and the second time to hasten their retreat. After the war the whole thing was rebuilt from scratch, and renamed Kota Kinabalu in 1963.

You'll end up spending a day or two in Kota Kinabalu if you're game to see a number of Sabah's attractions, so make the most of your KK stay and eat your way across town. Steaming street noodles and fresher-than-fresh seafood beckon the palate, and the bar scene ain't half bad for a Muslim nation. If you're really stuck for things to do, ask the locals what the word 'Kinabalu' means. We're not gonna tell you the answer – because there are a dozen different definitions – but we're pretty sure you'll find them all rather interesting…

Information

Borneo Books 2 (☎ 088-538077; www.borneobooks.com; ground fl, Phase 1, Wisma Merdeka; ⌚ 10am-7pm) A brilliant selection of Borneo-related books, maps and a small used-book section. Plenty of those useful Lonely Planet guides too. Wink.

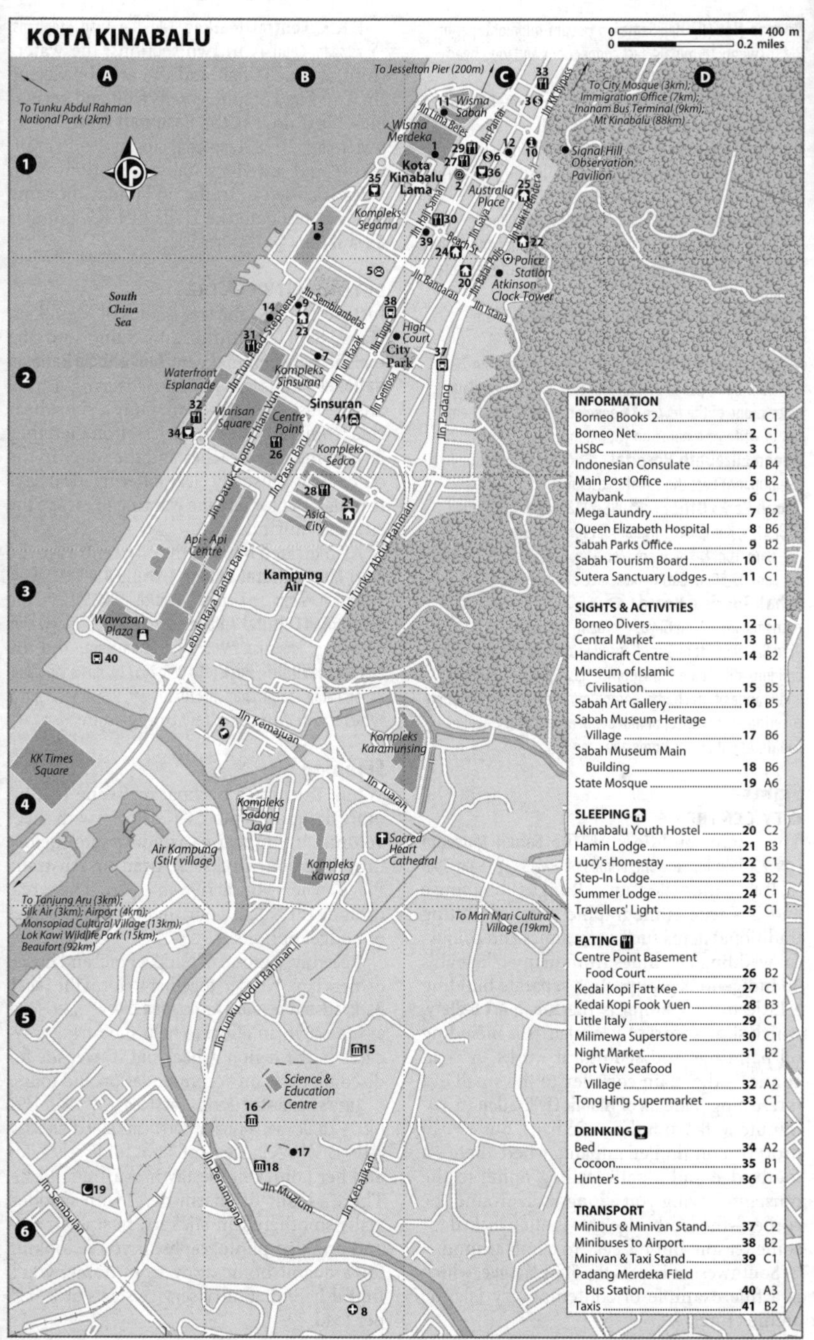
KOTA KINABALU
0 400 m
0 0.2 miles
To Jesselton Pier (200m)
To City Mosque (3km); Immigration Office (7km); Inanam Bus Terminal (9km); Mt Kinabalu (88km)
To Tunku Abdul Rahman National Park (2km)
Signal Hill Observation Pavilion
Wisma Sabah
Wisma Merdeka
Kota Kinabalu Lama
Australia Place
Kompleks Segama
Police Station
Atkinson Clock Tower
South China Sea
High Court
City Park
Waterfront Esplanade
Kompleks Sinsuran
Sinsuran
Warisan Square
Centre Point
Kompleks Sedco
Asia City
Api - Api Centre
Kampung Air
Wawasan Plaza
KK Times Square
Kompleks Karamunsing
Kompleks Sadong Jaya
Sacred Heart Cathedral
Kompleks Kawasa
Air Kampung (Stilt village)
To Tanjung Aru (3km); Silk Air (3km); Airport (4km); Monsopiad Cultural Village (13km); Lok Kawi Wildlife Park (15km); Beaufort (92km)
To Mari Mari Cultural Village (19km)
Science & Education Centre
Jln Lima Belas
Jln Pantai
Jln KK Bypass
Jln Haji Saman
Jln Gaya
Beach St
Jln Bukit Bendera
Jln Balai Polis
Jln Bandaran
Jln Istana
Jln Sembilanbelas
Jln Tun Fuad Stephens
Jln Tun Razak
Jln Tugu
Jln Sentosa
Jln Padang
Jln Datuk Chong Thian Vun
Jln Pasar Baru
Lebuh Raya Pantai Baru
Jln Tunku Abdul Rahman
Jln Kemajuan
Jln Tuaran
Jln Tunku Abdul Rahman
Jln Penampang
Jln Muzium
Jln Kebajikan
Jln Sembulan
INFORMATION
Borneo Books 2 ... 1 C1
Borneo Net ... 2 C1
HSBC ... 3 C1
Indonesian Consulate ... 4 B4
Main Post Office ... 5 B2
Maybank ... 6 C1
Mega Laundry ... 7 B2
Queen Elizabeth Hospital ... 8 B6
Sabah Parks Office ... 9 B2
Sabah Tourism Board ... 10 C1
Sutera Sanctuary Lodges ... 11 C1
SIGHTS & ACTIVITIES
Borneo Divers ... 12 C1
Central Market ... 13 B1
Handicraft Centre ... 14 B2
Museum of Islamic Civilisation ... 15 B5
Sabah Art Gallery ... 16 B5
Sabah Museum Heritage Village ... 17 B6
Sabah Museum Main Building ... 18 B6
State Mosque ... 19 A6
SLEEPING
Akinabalu Youth Hostel ... 20 C2
Hamin Lodge ... 21 B3
Lucy's Homestay ... 22 C1
Step-In Lodge ... 23 B2
Summer Lodge ... 24 C1
Travellers' Light ... 25 C1
EATING
Centre Point Basement Food Court ... 26 B2
Kedai Kopi Fatt Kee ... 27 C1
Kedai Kopi Fook Yuen ... 28 B3
Little Italy ... 29 C1
Milimewa Superstore ... 30 C1
Night Market ... 31 B2
Port View Seafood Village ... 32 A2
Tong Hing Supermarket ... 33 C1
DRINKING
Bed ... 34 A2
Cocoon ... 35 B1
Hunter's ... 36 C1
TRANSPORT
Minibus & Minivan Stand ... 37 C2
Minibuses to Airport ... 38 B2
Minivan & Taxi Stand ... 39 C1
Padang Merdeka Field Bus Station ... 40 A3
Taxis ... 41 B2

Borneo Net (Jln Haji Saman; 9am-midnight; per hr RM3) Twenty terminals, fast connections and loud head-banger music wafting through the air.

HSBC (088-212622; 56 Jln Gaya; 9am-4.30pm Mon-Thu, to 4pm Fri) Has a 24-hour ATM.

Immigration office (088-488700; Kompleks Persekutuan Pentadbiran Kerajaan, Jln UMS; 8am-1pm & 2-5pm Mon-Thu, 8-11.30am & 2-5pm Fri)

Main post office (088-210855; Jln Tun Razak; 8am-5pm Mon-Fri) Western Union cheques and money orders can be cashed here. Has an efficient poste restante counter.

Maybank (088-254295; 9 Jln Pantai; 9am-4.30pm Mon-Thu, to 4pm Fri) Has a 24-hour ATM.

Mega Laundry (088-238970; Ruang Sinsuran 2; 8am-8pm; per kilo RM6) This fast and efficient laundry place is one of the few in KK open on Sunday. Ask them not to write your name on your laundry.

Queen Elizabeth Hospital (088-218166; Jln Penampang) Past the Sabah Museum.

Sabah Parks Office (088-211881; Lot 1-3, ground fl, Block K, Kompleks Sinsuran, Jln Tun Fuad Stephens; 8am-1pm & 2-4.30pm Mon-Thu, 8-11.30am & 2-4.30pm Fri, 8am-12.50pm Sat) Good source of information.

Sabah Tourism Board (088-212121; www.sabahtourism.com; 51 Jln Gaya; 8am-5pm Mon-Fri, 8am-4pm Sat, 9am-4pm Sun) Housed in the historic post office building, KK's main tourist office has helpful staff and a wide range of brochures, pamphlets and other information covering every aspect of independent and tour travel in Sabah. Ask about its homestay program.

Sights

CITY CENTRE

The main building of the **Sabah Museum** (253199; Jln Muzium; admission RM15; 9am-5pm Sat-Thu) is modelled on a Rungus longhouse and is a true ethnographic treat, exhibiting traditional items such as ceramics and colourful wedding costumes from many of Sabah's 30 indigenous groups. In a separate building a little further along is the **Sabah Art Gallery**, which shows works by local artists, including oil paintings and sculptural works. A road connects the main complex to the small but interesting **Museum of Islamic Civilisation** (a 10-minute walk from the main hall). Bus 13 can drop you on Jln Penampang, where there's a footbridge and a path leading uphill to the museum, saving you a long walk around the corner – the footbridge gate is often locked for some reason, but it's easy to climb around.

Southwest of here is the **State Mosque**, which is a fine example of contemporary Islamic architecture.

KK's **Central Market** (Jln Tun Fuad Stephens; 8.30am-6pm) is in two sections: the waterfront area sells fish and the area bordering Jln Tun Fuad Stephens sells fruit and vegetables. Next door is the **Handicraft Centre** (Jln Tun Fuad Stephens; 8.30am-6pm), jammed with craft, textile and jewellery stalls. A section of Jln Gaya is closed to traffic on Sunday morning to accommodate the stalls of KK's popular **Gaya St Fair** (7am-1pm Sun).

BEYOND CITY CENTRE

Just west of KK, the five islands of Manukan, Gaya, Sapi, Mamutik and Sulug and the reefs in between make up **Tunku Abdul Rahman National Park** (admission RM10), covering a total area of just over 49 sq km. Only a short boat ride from the city centre's Jesselton Pier, they have some nice beaches and the water in the outer areas is usually clear, offering ideal day-trip material for anyone wanting to escape the city and unwind.

Also located beyond the city centre are the **Mari Mari Cultural Village** (019 820 4921; www.traversetours.com, Jln Kiansom; adult/child RM150/130), the **Monsopiad Cultural Village** (088-761336; www.monsopiad.com; admission RM65; 8.30am-5pm), and the **Lok Kawi Wildlife Park** (088-765710; Jln Penampang, Papar Lama; adult/child RM20/10; 9.30am-5.30pm), where you can see a few orang-utans.

Sleeping

While Kuching's backpacker scene is a bit more design-oriented, KK delivers with sheer volume. If you wanna window-shop before dropping your rucksack, head to 'Australia Place' when you arrive in town. This area, orbiting the Sabah Tourism Board, has tonnes of budget options.

Recently, a group of budget hotel and hostel owners have banded together to form the **Sabah Backpackers Operators Association** (SBA; www.sabahbackpackers.com) in an effort to help shoestring travellers in the region. Check out its website for discount deals on accommodation and tours.

Lucy's Homestay (Backpacker's Lodge; 088-261495; Lot 25 Lg Dewan, Australia Place; dm/s/d incl breakfast RM18/45/50) We have a soft spot for lovely Lucy and her homey homestay in Australia Place. There's loads of charm here, with wooden walls smothered in stickers, business cards and crinkled photographs. If you're looking for a quaint home away from home, you'll find it here. Laundry service starts at RM15 per load.

Akinabalu Youth Hostel (☎ 088-272188; akinabaluyh@yahoo.com; Lot 133 Jln Gaya; dm/r incl breakfast from RM20/50) Friendly staff, fuchsia-accent walls and trickling Zen fountains make this a solid option among KK's hostels, particularly if you find a quiet time to take advantage of the gratis internet and pirated DVDs. Accommodation is mostly in basic four-bed rooms, with windows facing an interior hallway.

Summer Lodge (☎ 088-244499; www.summerlodge.com.my; Lot 120 Jln Gaya; dm/d RM28/65;) Summer Lodge feels a bit like a bed factory, with mattresses indiscriminately stuffed behind every door. Quality varies so you'll probably have to check out a few rooms before you find a comfy one. The friendly owners also run a hostel (dorm/double from RM25/60) near the base of Mt Kinabalu.

Step-In Lodge (☎ 088-233519; Block L, Kompleks Sinsuran; www.stepinlodge.com; dm with fan/air-con RM28/38, d with fan/air-con RM70/90;) This popular spot wins the award for KK's smartest hostel with larger-than-normal bunk beds, comfy mattresses, *real* coffee at breakfast, and an excellent (not to mention knowledgeable) staff. These clever touches make Step-In feel much more homey than some of the factory-style operations nearby.

Other backpacker options:

Travellers' Light (☎ 088-238877; Lot 19 Lg Dewan, Australia Place; www.travellerslight.com; dm/d incl breakfast from RM25/65;) Only a few rooms here, but they're spick and span.

Hamin Lodge (☎ 088-272008; Lot 19 Block C, Kompleks Sedco; www.haminlodge.com; dm/tw from RM28/62;) A great find. Ten-bed dorms are cramped, but basic private rooms are good value.

Eating

KK is one of the few cities in Borneo with an eating scene diverse enough to refresh the noodle-jaded palate. Besides the ubiquitous Chinese *kedai kopi* and Malay halal restaurants, you'll find plenty of interesting options around the city centre – head to the suburbs if you're looking for some truly unique local fare.

Kedai Kopi Fook Yuen (G33 Ground fl, No 4 Asia City; kaya RM2.60; 6.30am-1am;) Cheap and quick, a snack of sweet *kaya* is the perfect energy booster after a morning of sightseeing. And this isn't your standard Singaporean coconut-egg-jam: Sabahans have developed their own version of this tasty confection.

Night Market (off Jln Tun Fuad Stephens; meals from RM2; dinner) The night market is the best, cheapest and most interesting place in KK for dinner.

Centre Point Basement Food Court (Basement, Centre Point Shopping Centre, Jln Pasar Baru; mains RM3-10; lunch & dinner) Your ringgit will go a long way at this popular and varied basement food-court in the Centre Point mall. There are Malay, Chinese and Indian options, as well as drink and dessert specialists.

Kedai Kopi Fatt Kee (28 Jln Bakau; mains from RM5; lunch & dinner Mon-Sat) The woks are always sizzlin' at this popular Chinese place next to Ang's Hotel. Long queues are guaranteed, but it's always worth the wait. Its *sayur manis* cooked in *belacan* (shrimp paste) is a classic, and salt-and-pepper prawns are great.

Little Italy (☎ 088-232231; Jln Haji Saman; mains from RM23; lunch & dinner) Dear homesick holidaymaker: this is your place. Create your own carbo-load with a variety of saucey tributes to the Bootland. All things considered, it's a rather pricey endeavour, but it's definitely worth stopping by if you're in desperate need of a rice respite.

Port View Seafood Village (☎ 088-221753; Lot 18 Waterfront Esplanade; dinner from RM50; lunch & dinner) This cavernous Chinese seafood specialist feels like an aquarium where you can eat the displays – we've never seen such an extravagant array of live fish. Even if you don't eat here, it's worth walking into the foyer to check out the veritable cascade of turquoise tanks.

In the early evening, head to Tanjung Aru at the south end of town near the airport for sunset cocktails and light snacks along the ocean. A taxi to Tanjung Aru costs RM20, or you can take public transportation (RM1.80) – try Bus 16, 16a or City Bus 2.

Self-catering choices in KK include the following:

Milimewa Superstore (Jln Haji Saman)
Tong Hing Supermarket (Jln Gaya)

Drinking & Entertainment

Averaging 12 cans of beer a month per capita (not including smuggled goods), Sabahans are big drinkers by Malaysian standards, and KK's nightlife allows plenty of scope for visitors to join the party. The **Waterfront Esplanade** (Jln Tun Fuad Stephens) houses a good number of upscale 'resto-bars', while Beach St, in the centre of town, is a semi-pedestrian street cluttered with bars and eateries.

Bed (☎ 088-251901; Waterfront Esplanade) Get those bedpuns ready: the space that launched a thousand quips is arguably the fulcrum of KK nightlife, and it's a rare night out that won't see you ending up in Bed at some point. Bands play from 9pm, followed by DJs til closing; it's best with a crowd, so, as in life, the more people you can get into Bed the more fun you'll have…

Cocoon (☎ 088-211252; Jln Tun Razak Segama) In the busy corner of town opposite the Hyatt, Cocoon is a smart bar–restaurant that goes all bar in the evening when the live bands emerge. The post-gig DJs have a tendency to talk over the records, but at least their R&B-leaning tunes are danceable.

Hunter's (☎ 016 825 7085; Kinabalu Daya Hotel) A favourite for local guides and expats, Hunter's offers up karaoke, sports on the plasma TV and balmy outdoor seating in the heart of the action.

Getting There & Away

AIR

In March 2009 **Jetstar** (www.jetstar.com) and **Tiger Airways** (www.tigerairways.com) announced a bevy of new flights from Singapore, giving Air Asia some serious competition when it came to Borneo-bound flights. These days, flying through Borneo can actually be cheaper than taking a bus (and obviously much less of a time suck). **Malaysia Airlines** (code MAS; ☎ 1300 883 000, 088-515555; www.malaysiaairlines.com) connects KK to Singapore, South Korea, Japan, Brunei, Hong Kong, KL, Pulau Labuan, Sandakan and Miri, although it is usually much more expensive than the budget carriers. **MASwings** (www.maswings.com.my) services domestic destinations like Mulu, Miri, Sandakan and Lahad Datu.

BOAT

Passenger boats connect KK to Pulau Labuan twice daily (RM30, with onward service to Brunei), to Tunku Abdul Rahman National Park, and a schedule is in the works to link the state capital to Pulau Tiga. The Tunku Abdul Rahman Marine Park is linked to KK's Jesselton Pier by a 20-minute speedboat ride. Boats run from 7.30am to 5pm and cost RM23/13 for adults/children. A two-island ticket is an extra RM10.

BUS & MINIVAN

You need to know ahead of time where you want to travel to because there are several different stations around KK serving a variety of out-of-town destinations. In general, buses heading east depart from Inanam (Utara Terminal; 9km north of the city) and buses heading south leave from Padang Merdeka Field Bus Station (also called Wawasan or 'old bus station'; at the south end of town). Ask the staff at your ho(s)tel to call ahead to the bus station to book your seat in advance.

TAXI

Share taxis operate from the Padang Merdeka Field Bus Station. Several share taxis do a daily run between KK and Ranau, passing the entrance road to the Kinabalu National Park office. The fare to Ranau or Kinabalu National Park is RM20 or you can charter a taxi for RM80 per car (note that a normal city taxi will charge RM150 to RM200 for a charter).

TRAIN

At the time of research, the North Borneo rail line was closed and a reopening date was yet to be confirmed.

MAIN DESTINATIONS & FARES FROM KOTA KINABALU

The following bus and minivan transportation information was provided to us by the Sabah Tourism Board and should be used as an estimate only as transportation times can fluctuate due to weather, prices may change, and the transportation authority has been known to alter departure points.

Destination	Time (hr)	Cost	Terminal	Departure Time
Beaufort	2	RM10	Padang Merdeka	7am-5pm (frequent)
Lahad Datu	8	RM40	Inanam	7am, 8.30am, 9am, 8pm
Mt Kinabalu NP	2	RM15	Inanam & Padang Merdeka	7am-8pm (very frequent)
Sandakan	6	RM33	Inanam	7.30am-2pm & 8pm (frequent)
Semporna	9	RM50	Inanam	7am, 8.30am, 9am, 8pm
Tawau	9	RM55	Inanam	7.30am, 2pm, 8pm

GETTING INTO TOWN

Kota Kinabalu International Airport (KKIA) is 7km southwest of the centre. Minivans leaving from the main terminal charge RM2, while minivans or local buses that pass the airport bus stop (turn right as you leave the terminal and walk for 10 minutes) charge RM1. Taxis heading from the terminal into town operate on a system of vouchers (RM20), sold at a taxi desk on the terminal's ground floor. In practice, you can usually just board a taxi and pay RM20 in cash.

Getting Around

Minivans operate from several stops in KK, including the Padang Merdeka Field Bus Station and the parking lot outside Milimewa Superstore. They also circulate the town looking for passengers. Since most destinations within the city are within walking distance, it's unlikely that you'll need to catch a minivan. If you do catch one, most destinations within the city cost RM1.

Most of KK's taxis have meters, but few drivers will agree to use them. Set prices rule the roost, but you should always negotiate a fare before heading off. There are several hubs where taxis congregate, including the Milimewa Superstore in the centre of town. Figure around RM7 to RM10 for a ride in the city centre.

MT KINABALU & KINABALU NATIONAL PARK

Towering above the island with its haunting husk of granite and halo of cotton-puff clouds, 'Borneo's roof' majestically rises over Sabah's swatch book of rainforest greens as if it were shouting 'Climb me!' to wandering travellers. And climb it they do. Mt Kinabalu, or Gunung Kinabalu in Bahasa Malaysia, is the region's biggest tourist attraction.

As far as mountains go, the 4095m peak of Mt Kinabalu may not be as wow-inducing as, say, a Himalayan sky-poker, but Malaysia's first Unesco World Heritage Site is by no means an easy climb. Around 60,000 visitors of every ilk make the gruelling trek up Borneo's ultimate Thighmaster each year, returning to the bottom with stories of triumph, pictures of sun-lit moonscapes, and *really* sore legs.

Information

A park fee, climbing permit, insurance and a guide fee are mandatory if you intend to climb Mt Kinabalu. All permits and guides must be arranged at the **Sabah Parks office** (7am-7pm), which is directly next door to the Sutera Sanctuary Lodges office, immediately on your right after you pass through the main gate of the park. Pay all fees at park HQ before you climb and don't ponder an 'unofficial' climb as permits are scrupulously checked.

All visitors entering the park are required to pay a park entrance fee (adult/child RM15/RM10). A climbing permit costs RM100/RM40. Climbing insurance costs a flat rate of RM7 per person. Guide fees for the summit trek are the following: RM85 per small group (one to three climbers) or RM100 per large group (four to six climbers). If you ask, the park staff will try to attach individual travellers to a group so that guide fees can be shared. The total minimum price for a couple climbing the mountain is (drum roll please) RM164.50 per person, and that does not include the RM360 for room and board atop the mountain at Laban Rata (that's a grand total of RM524.50 for all of you maths whizzes out there).

EQUIPMENT & CLOTHING

No special equipment is required to successfully summit the mountain; however, a headlamp is strongly advised for the predawn jaunt to the top – you'll need your hands free to climb the ropes on the summit massif. Expect freezing temperatures near the summit, not to mention strong winds and the occasional rainstorm.

The Climb to the Summit

Climbing the great Mt Kinabalu is a heart-pounding two-day adventure that you won't soon forget. You'll want to check in at park headquarters around 9am to pay your park fees, grab your guide, and start the ascent (four to seven hours) to Laban Rata (3273m) where you will spend the night before finishing the climb. On the following day you'll finish scrambling to the top around 2.30am in order to reach the summit for a breathtaking sunrise over Borneo.

The trek is tough, and the ascent is unrelenting as almost every step you take will be uphill. You will negotiate several obstacles along the way, including slippery stones, blinding humidity, frigid winds, and slow-paced Japanese 50-somethings donning Chanel tracksuits.

There are two trail options leading up the mountain – the Timpohon Trail and the Mesilau Trail. If this is your first time climbing Kinabalu, we strongly advise taking the Timpohon Trail – it's shorter, easier (but by no means easy!), and convenient to the park headquarters by a long walk (one hour) or short park shuttle ride (RM17 per vehicle one way, four persons max). The Mesilau Trail offers second-time climbers (or uber-fit hikers) the opportunity to really enjoy some of the park's natural wonders. This trail is less trodden so the chance of seeing unique flora and fauna is higher.

Track down a copy of our *Malaysia, Singapore & Brunei* guide for a play-by-play of the trek to the summit.

Sleeping

LABAN RATA (ON THE MOUNTAIN)

Organising your accommodation on the mountain can be the most difficult part of your Kinabalu adventure. Access to the summit is essentially rationed by access to the huts on the mountain at Laban Rata (3273m) and this *must* be booked in advance (the earlier the better!).

Sutera Sanctuary Lodges (Map p493; ☎ 088-243629; www.suterasanctuarylodges.com; Lot G15, Wisma Sabah, Jln Haji Saman, Kota Kinabalu; 🕑 8.30am-4.30pm Mon-Sat, to 12.30pm Sun) operates almost all of the accommodation here, but space is very limited, so plan ahead (see also p492). The most common sleeping option is the heated dormitory (bedding included) in the Laban Rata building, which sells for RM360 per person. Three meals (dinner, breakfast and lunch)

TOP FIVE BORNEO TREKS

Borneo is like a steaming equatorial cauldron bubbling over with a veritable encyclopaedia of flora and fauna, and the best way to discover this fascinating world is by trekking straight through it. We've assembled a list with our five favourite treks – if you can check off three of these, consider yourself an accomplished adventurer. Those who tick off all five are Borneo superstars.

- **Mt Kinabalu** (p497) Yes Kinabalu, we all know that you're the big cheese. And, yes, the reputation is well deserved. In addition to the summit's granite spires offering awe-inducing views, there are several pleasant jaunts around the mountain's base, including the 6km Liwagu Trail, which would be swarming with people if it weren't for the fact that it's located below the island's most celebrated climb.
- **Kelabit Highlands** (p523) Borneo's real trekking hotspot is Sarawak's stunning Kelabit Highlands spiking up along the Indonesian border like the spine of a sleeping dinosaur. This is the closest it gets to Himalayan teahouse treks as visitors pass between hidden runes and lonely longhouse communities peppered throughout the region.
- **Temburong** (p59) Due to the surplus of oil and gas, Brunei never had to log their pristine rainforest to earn a few extra bucks. Thus the jungle in Temburong (the smaller of the sultanate's two jigsaw-puzzle-like land holdings) is a stunning realm of sweltering primary forest. All-inclusive adventures through this emerald expanse can be organised through one of several tour operators based in Bandar Seri Begawan (p63; self-planned excursions are currently impossible due to national park regulations and transport restrictions).
- **Headhunters Trail** (p523) According to legend, the Headhunters Trail was an ancient tribal warpath (it was actually a docile trading route) – today it's a fantastic two-day jungle trek connecting the island's green interior to the crystal coastal waters. Fit trekkers can include a side trip to the Pinnacles – an expanse of jagged stone that looks like a collection of granite toothpicks. But be warned: if the Kinabalu Climb is, say, a '7' on the difficulty scale, then the Pinnacles add-on is about a '10'.
- **Bako National Park** (p514) Bako is one of the most rewarding 'do it yourself' destinations in all of Borneo and it proves that you don't have to travel deep into the jungle to mingle with island's infamous wildlife. Try the Telok Limau Trail (10km), ending at a stunning deserted beach, or the Lintang Trail (5.25km), boasting samples of the park's diverse vegetation. Proboscis monkeys and sneaky macaques abound.

VIA FERRATA

In 2007 the good folks at Mountain Torq dramatically changed the Kinabalu climbing experience by creating an intricate system of rungs and rails crowning the mountain's summit. Known as *via ferrata* (literally 'iron road' in Italian), this alternative style of mountaineering has been a big hit in Europe for the last century and is just starting to take Asia by storm. In fact, Mountain Torq is Asia's first *via ferrata* system, and, according to the Guinness Book of World Records, it's the highest 'iron road' in the world!

After ascending Kinabalu in the traditional fashion (p497), participants use the network of levers to return to the Laban Rata rest camp along the mountain's dramatic granite walls. *Via ferrata* may be an Italian import, but Mountain Torq is pure Bornean fun.

For more information about Mountain Torq (including a YouTube video documenting the experience) check out www.mountaintorq.com or the 'Via Ferrata Asia' group on facebook (where you'll find photos of our climb!). Prices start at RM300.

are included in the price, although guests can bring their own food up the mountain and negotiate with Sutera for a price reduction (boiling water can be purchased for RM1 if you bring dried noodles). Non-heated facilities surrounding the Laban Rata building are also available for RM320 per person (meals included). Yes, the inflated prices feel monopolistic, and to make matters worse, Sutera is trying to force climbers to stay in the park for two nights – one night at Laban Rata and one night at the base.

The other option at Laban Rata is to stay at Pendant Hut, which is owned and operated by Mountain Torq (above; pricing is on par with Sutera). Pendant Hut is slightly more basic (no heat – although climbers sleep in uber-warm sleeping bags); however, there's a bit of a summer-camp vibe here while Laban Rata feels more like a Himalayan orphanage.

PARK HEADQUARTERS (AT THE BASE)

The following sleeping options are located at the base of the mountain and are all operated by Sutera Sanctuary Lodges. As per Sutera's monopolistic reputation, these options are overpriced when compared to the non-affiliated sleeping spots outside the park (p500).

Grace Hostel (dm RM120) Clean, comfortable 20-bed dorm with fireplace and drink-making area.

Rock Hostel (dm RM120) Somewhat institutional 20-bed hostel with similar facilities to Grace Hostel. Twin-share rooms are available here as well (RM350 per room).

Getting There & Away

It is strongly advised that summit-seekers check in at the park headquarters by 9am, which means that if you are coming from KK, you should plan to leave by 7am, or consider spending the night somewhere near the base of the mountain.

A shuttle bus runs from the Pacific Sutera (9am), the Magellan Sutera (9.10am), and Wisma Sabah (9.20am) to Kinabalu Park HQ, arriving at 11.30am (RM40). In the reverse direction it leaves Kinabalu Park HQ at 3.30pm. Express buses and minivans travelling between KK and Ranau (and Sandakan) pass the park turn-off, 100m uphill from the park entrance. Air-con express buses (RM15, three hours) and taxis leave from both Inaman and Wawasan (see p496). A share-taxi from one of these transport junctions is significantly cheaper than hailing a cab in the city centre (which will cost you RM150).

AROUND KINABALU

Kinabalu National Park is home to Borneo's highest mountain and some of the island's best-preserved forest. Most travellers make a beeline for the mountain and the main park headquarters area, but the following spots are also worth exploring.

The junction for the Mesilau Nature Resort on the KK–Ranau highway is the site of the **Kundasang War Memorial** (Kundasang; admission RM10; 8am-5.30pm). There are English and Anzac gardens here, commemorating the prisoners from these countries who died on the infamous Sandakan Death March.

One of the few positive contributions the Japanese made to Borneo during WWII, **Poring Hot Springs** (adult/child RM15/10) has become a popular weekend retreat for locals. The complex is actually part of the Kinabalu National Park, but it's 43km away from the park headquarters, on the other side of Ranau. If you're expecting some kind of natural paradise with rock pools and the like, think again: the setting's real forest but the facilities themselves are quite patently artificial. For some, wading in a cauldron of floating skin flakes is a huge anticlimax, for others a perfect playground worth far more than the customary quick stop.

Sleeping & Eating

It's worth spending a night around the base of Kinabalu before your ascent, and there are plenty of accommodation options suiting everyone's budget.

Puncak Borneo Resort (☎ 012 828 0866; Kundasang; dm/s/d incl breakfast from RM40/168/188;) A respectable choice, Puncak (pronounced 'poon-chak') makes a few worthy attempts at style with lipstick-red accent walls and animal-print rugs. The stairs up to the reception can feel like an impossible obstacle if you've just climbed the mountain.

Kinabalu Rose Cabin (☎ 088-889233; krc145@yahoo.com; Km 18, Jln Ranau-Tuaran; r RM130-250) Look for the shiny blue-roofed pagoda and you've found Rose Cabin. Rooms are as kitschy as their shimmery brochures, but frequent midweek discounts sweeten the deal. A minivan from there to nearby attractions will cost RM5.

Kinabalu Pine Resort (☎ 088-889388; Kundasang–Ranau Hwy; r from RM150) A paradigm of country-club landscaping, this welcoming camp-style resort is extremely popular with Sabahans, who sit on the wooden balconies while enjoying the breezy sunsets. Ask for a room with hardwood floors – the carpeting here is a bit tattered.

Getting There & Around

The area around Mt Kinabalu is easily accessible from KK, with buses running at a high frequency throughout the day (7am to 8pm). Transport stops in front of park headquarters and in Ranau (RM15, two hours).

Shuttle buses and minivans are constantly moving tourists around the base of the mountain and taxis can be hired if you don't have time to wait for public transport. Minivans operate from a blue-roofed shelter in Ranau servicing the nearby attractions (park HQ, Poring etc) for RM5. Opting for a taxi will set you back RM30 (if you negotiate).

SANDAKAN

pop 453,750

With a colourful history of slow boats and fast women, Sandakan has been a dot on a trader's map for centuries. After the nearby natural wonders – Sepilok and an archipelago of idyllic islands – the city's biggest draw is its turbulent history retold through religious relics, haunting cemeteries and stunning colonial mansions. Although Sandakan is far less exciting than it used to be, the city has plenty of character and even a certain down-market charm, though once the shop shutters come down in the evening the centre can feel a bit deserted and creepy. Nights are best spent singing karaoke, clinking cocktails at sunset, and devouring an aquarium's worth of seafood.

Information

Cyber Café (3rd fl, Wisma Sandakan, Lebuh Empat; per hr RM3; 9am-9pm)
Duchess of Kent Hospital (☎ 089-219460; Mile 2, Jln Utara)
Forestry Department (☎ 089-213966; 2nd fl, Jln Leila) Get permits for the mangrove forest walk to Sepilok Bay. Located next to UMW Toyota, 2km west of the main post office.
MayBank (Lebuh Tiga) In addition to full-service bank and ATM, a sidewalk currency-exchange window is open 9am to 5pm daily, changing cash and travellers cheques.
Main post office (☎ 089-210594; Jln Leila)
Standard Chartered Bank (Lebuh Tiga)
Tourist Information Centre (☎ 089-229751; pempt.j.mps@sabah.gov.my; Wisma Warisan; 8am-12.30pm & 1.30-4.30pm Mon-Thu, 8-11.30am & 2-4.30pm Fri) Located opposite the municipal offices (known as MPS) and up the stairs from Lebuh Tiga.

Sights

Central Sandakan is light on 'must-see' attractions, although history buffs will appreciate the *Sandakan Heritage Trail* brochure available at the tourist office.

On the hill above town overlooking Sandakan Bay, **Agnes Keith House** (Jln Istana; admission RM15; 9am-5pm) is a trip back to Sandakan's colonial heyday. Keith was an American who came to Sandakan in the 1930s and wrote several books about her experiences, most famously *The Land Below the Wind*. The two-storey wooden villa was destroyed during WWII and rebuilt identically when the Keiths returned. To reach the museum, follow Jln Singapura and turn right up the hill, or head up the shady Tangga Seribu to Jln Residensi Dr and turn left.

Now just a quiet patch of woods, **Sandakan Memorial Park** (Taman Peringatan; admission free;

9am-5pm) was the site of a Japanese POW camp and starting point for the infamous Death Marches to Ranau. Of the 1800 Australian and 600 British troops imprisoned here, the only survivors by July 1945 were six Australian escapees. To reach the park, take any Batu 8 or higher bus (RM1.80); get off at the Taman Rimba signpost and walk down Jln Rimba.

Sleeping

Over the last two years, the number of hotel rooms has doubled in Sandakan despite the decrease in tourists; spontaneous travellers won't be too hard-pressed to find an available room. If you're only passing through Sandakan to see the orang-utans, it's better to stay at Sepilok itself, since the rehabilitation centre is about 25km from town.

Sunset Harbour Botik Hostel (089-229875; www.sunsethostels.com; 1E, HS14, Harbour Sq; dm/d incl breakfast from RM20/60;) The dorm rooms are bit too 'little orphan Annie', but there are excellent kitchen facilities here, and a large market around the corner to buy your meal-to-be.

Sandakan Backpackers (089-221104; www.sandakanbackpackers.com; Lot 108 Block SH-11, Sandakan Harbour Sq; dm/s/d RM25/40/60;) Cheap sleeps is the name of the game – the young backpacker crowd seems to congregate here (maybe 'cause they're on a package tour?).

Nak Hotel (089-272988; www.nakhotel.com; Jln Pelabuhan Lama; dm/r incl breakfast from RM30/88;) If you're into architectural anomalies (or Soviet-style riffs) then this concrete behemoth might be the place for you. Picky travellers fear not – the owners have a real *nak* for chic interior decor, outfitting the oddly shaped rooms with clever design details. Don't miss the hotel's kick-arse roof lounge (right).

Eating & Drinking

The city's large Chinese population means that there are excellent homages to the motherland, and the region's port history equals fresher-than-fresh seafood. For an authentic Malay meal, head to the KFC in the new development on the sea – but don't eat there! The restaurants surrounding it are cheap and flavourful. If you're wondering where everyone goes when Sandakan shuts down in the evening, just hop in a taxi to Bandar Indah, commonly known as Mile 4. This buzzing grid of two-storey shophouses is the playground of choice for locals and expats alike. It's packed with restaurants, bars, karaoke lounges and nightclubs.

our pick **English Tea House & Restaurant** (089-222544; www.englishteahouse.org; 2002 Jln Istana; mains RM24-40, cocktails RM27; breakfast, lunch & dinner) Soak up the recherché colonial atmosphere and elegant food at this exquisitely restored restaurant on the grounds of the historic Agnes Keith House. The manicured gardens are a particular joy, with wicker furniture and a small croquet lawn overlooking the bay, perfect for afternoon tea (RM17), a round of sunset Pimms, or perhaps some snobbish guffawing.

our pick **Balin** (089-272988; www.nakhotel.com; Jln Pelabuhan Lama; mains from RM15, drinks from RM7; lunch & dinner) Bringing a certain LA rooftop sexiness to drab Sandakan, Balin is your best bet for nightlife in the city centre. The three tiers of uber-chill lounge space are accented by a factory's worth of pillows.

Getting There & Away

AIR

Malaysia Airlines (089-273966; www.malaysiaairlines.com) has daily flights to/from KK and KL. **Air Asia** (089-222737; www.airasia.com) operates two daily direct flights to/from KL and KK. **MASwings** (1300 883 000; www.maswings.com.my) offers one daily flight to/from Tawau and two to/from KK.

BUS

Buses from Sandakan to KK, Lahad Datu, Semporna and Tawau depart from the long-distance bus station in a large parking lot at Batu 2.5, 4km north of town – not a particularly convenient location. Most buses, and all minivans, leave in the morning. To reach the bus station, you can catch a local bus (RM1) from the stand at the waterfront. A taxi from the station to town will cost you around RM10.

Bus companies have booths at the station and touts abound. Most express buses to KK (RM40, six hours) leave between 7.30am and 2pm, with a couple of evening departures. All pass the turn-off to Kinabalu National Park headquarters (RM30).

Buses depart regularly for Lahad Datu (RM20, 2½ hours) and Tawau (RM30, 5½ hours). There's also a bus to Semporna (RM30, 5½ hours) at 8am. If you miss it, head to Lahad Datu, then catch a frequent minivan to Semporna.

Getting Around

The airport is about 11km from downtown. The Batu 7 Airport bus (RM1.80) stops on the main road about 500m from the terminal. A coupon taxi from the airport to the town centre costs RM24; going the other way, a taxi should cost around RM20.

The local bus terminal is on Jln Pryer, in front of Gentingmas Mall. Buses run from 6am to about 6pm on the main road to the north, Jln Utara, and are designated by how far from town they go, ie Batu 8. Fares range from RM1 to RM4.

Local minivans wait behind Centre Point Mall; fares are from RM2. Use them for Pasir Putih seafood restaurants and the harbour area.

Taxis cruise the town centre, and park near main hotels. Many hotels will steer you toward a preferred driver – not a bad thing. Short journeys around the town centre should cost RM5; it's RM12 to Bandar Indah, and RM40 for a lift to Sepilok.

SEPILOK

The little hamlet of Sepilok sees almost as many visitors as the granite spires of Mt Kinabalu. With up to 800 visitors daily, the Sepilok Orang-Utan Rehabilitation Centre is the most popular place on earth to see Asia's great ginger ape in its native habitat. Those who have time to stick around will also undercover several scenic nature walks, a sanctuary for the elusive proboscis monkey, and a couple of great places to call home for a night or two.

Orientation & Information

Sepilok's main attraction, the Sepilok Orang-utan Rehabilitation Centre, is located at Batu 14 – 14 miles (23km) from Sandakan. The street connecting the highway to the rehab centre is lined with a variety of accommodation suiting all budget types. Banks and medical services are located in Sandakan. Money can be changed at the upmarket sleeping spots (for a hefty change fee).

Sights & Activities

SEPILOK ORANG-UTAN REHABILITATION CENTRE (SORC)

One of only four orang-utan sanctuaries in the world, the Sepilok Orang-Utan Rehabilitation Centre (SORC) occupies a corner of the Kabili-Sepilok rainforest reserve about 25km west of Sandakan. The centre was established in 1964; it now covers 40 sq km and has become one of Sabah's top tourist attractions, second only to Mt Kinabalu.

Orphaned and injured orang-utans are brought to Sepilok to be rehabilitated to return to forest life. When we visited there were only seven primates on campus. It's unlikely you'll see this many at feeding time – three or four is more likely, or maybe none at all.

Feedings are at 10am and 3pm and last for around 30 to 50 minutes. Schedules are posted at the **visitor reception centre** (☎ 089-531180; soutan@po.jaring.my; admission RM30, camera fee RM10; 🕑 9-11am & 2-3.30pm).

A worthwhile 20-minute video about Sepilok's work is shown five times daily (9am, 11am, noon, 2.10pm and 3.30pm) opposite reception in the **Nature Education Centre** auditorium.

RAINFOREST DISCOVERY CENTRE (RDC)

The **Rainforest Discovery Centre** (RDC; ☎ 089-533780; adult/child RM10/5; 🕑 8am-5pm), about 1.5km from SORC, offers an engaging graduate-level education in tropical flora and fauna. Outside the exhibit hall, a botanical garden presents varying samples of tropical plant life with the accompanying descriptions every bit as vibrant as the foliage. There's a 1km lakeside walking trail here as well. A series of eight canopy towers are being built – three have been completed.

LABUK BAY PROBOSCIS MONKEY SANCTUARY

Proboscis monkeys *(Nasalis larvatus)* are an even more exclusive attraction than orang-utans. After all, you can see orang-utans in Sumatra but the proboscis is found only on Borneo. An ecofriendly plantation owner has created a private **proboscis monkey sanctuary** (☎ 089-672133; www.proboscis.cc; admission RM60, camera/video fee RM10/20), attracting the floppy-conked locals with sugar-free pancakes at 11.40am and 4.30pm feedings. An estimated 300 wild monkeys live in the 600-hectare reserve. The sanctuary offers package trips. A half-day visit costs RM160, including transfers from Sandakan (RM150 from Sepilok). Overnight trips with meals and a night walk start at RM250.

Sleeping & Eating

Although most tourists rush in and out of Sepilok faster than the flash of a camera, it's well worth spending the night in this sleepy township. Most accommodation options are scattered along Jln Sepilok, the 2.5km-long access road to the rehabilitation centre.

Sepilok B&B (☎ 089-534050, 089-532288; www.sepilokbednbreakfast.com; Jln Arboretum; dm/s/d RM23/40/60) The former head of Sabah's reforestation division manages this unpretentious option, which has a palpable summer-camp vibe. It's popular with large groups, who pile into the simple dorm rooms accented with pale-pastel curtains. The B&B is opposite the forest research centre, about 250m off Jln Sepilok and 1km short of the SORC entrance.

our pick **Paganakan Dii** (☎ 089-532005; www.paganakandii.com; dm/d RM28/98;) Hands down the best budget place to stay in Sepilok (if not all of Sabah), this welcoming and quiet retreat sits deep within a deer preserve on the far side of the highway. Chic design details (made from recycled materials), crisp white linen and friendly staff will have you thinking that the owners surely left a zero off the price tag. Transfers to the Sepilok Rehabilitation Centre are included in the price.

Sepilok Forest Reserve & Labuk B&B (☎ 089-533190, 089-223100; labukbb@yahoo.com; dm/d/chalets from RM28/65/180;) Dorm and double rooms (located in the Labuk B&B portion of the property) are fine – it's the chalets that are property's pièce de résistance.

Uncle Tan's (☎ 089-531639; www.uncletan.com; dm/tw incl all meals RM38/100;) Uncle Tan built a reputation among backpackers for providing great river tours along the Kinabatangan. Now he's set up shop right in the heart of Sepilok with a couple of thatch-roofed gazebos and a stack of backpacker shacks – they're pretty dank but unbeatably cheap.

Most accommodation in the Sepilok area serves breakfast – some offer guests three-meal packages. The **rehabilitation centre cafeteria** (meals from RM5; 7am-4pm) vends sandwiches, noodle bowls, rice plates, snacks and beverages.

Getting There & Away

If you are coming directly from Sandakan, a taxi should cost no more than RM35 (either from the airport or the city centre). Bus 14 from Sandakan (RM3) departs hourly from the city centre and stops at the RDC. If you are coming from KK, board a Sandakan-bound bus and ask the driver to let you off at Batu 14 (RM30).

Taxi 'pirates', as they're known, wait at Batu 14 to give tourists a ride into Sepilok. It's RM3 per person for a lift. Travellers spending the night can arrange a lift with their accommodation if they booked in ahead of time. Walking to the rehab centre is also an option – it's only 2.5km down the road.

To reach the Labuk Bay Proboscis Monkey Sanctuary, have the bus drop you off at Batu 19 (Mile 19; 32km from Sandakan), but note that it's too far from the highway to walk, so you will have to arrange transportation from the junction (it's a 15-minute drive). If you're coming from KK it is the same price as being dropped off at Batu 14 (Sepilok); if you're coming from Sandakan the driver may ask for an additional RM5. Transport from Sepilok/Sandakan to Labuk Bay costs RM110/RM130 per person for a share van.

SUNGAI KINABATANGAN

If an artist were to paint a portrait of the mighty Sungai Kinabatangan, they'd need a palette of green, blue, and brown…lots and lots of brown… This mighty muddy river is Sabah's longest, measuring a lengthy 560km from its headwaters deep in the southwest jungle to the marshy delta on the turquoise Sulu Sea.

The Kinabatangan's great menagerie of jungle creatures is an ironic by-product of the rampant logging and oil-palm industries. As plantations and camps continue to gobble up virgin rainforest, the area of unruffled jungle becomes thinner, forcing the animals to seek refuge along the river's flood plains. Dozens of tin boats on 'wildlife river cruises' putter along the shores offering tourists the opportunity to have a close encounter with a rhinoceros, hornbill or perhaps a doughy-eyed orang-utan. Even if you went ape over Sepilok's crew of ginger beasts, seeing an orang-utan in the *wild* is a truly magical experience (we saw three!).

Sleeping & Eating

In Kinabatangan lingo, a 'three-day/two-night' stint usually involves the following: arrive in the afternoon on day one for a cruise at dusk, two boat rides (or a boat/hike combo) on day two, and an early morning departure on day three after breakfast and a sunrise cruise. When booking a trip, ask about pick-up and drop-off prices – this is usually extra. The 'B&Bs' along the Kinabatangan – like the B&Bs elsewhere in Sabah – do not fit the Western definition of a traditional bed and breakfast. No dainty grey-haired dames serving milk and cookies by the roaring fire – these are basic, budget-friendly sleep spots, many of which don't even include breakfast in the price.

SUKAU

If you are planning to visit Sungai Kinabatangan on your own, then Sukau is your best option for lodging and river tours. A paved road connects Sukau to the highway.

Sukau B&B (☎ 019 583 5580, 089-565269; www.sukaubnb.com; dm/s/tw incl breakfast RM20/40/40) The road leading into Sukau ends here: a grassy knoll with longhouse-style accommodation and a small cottage in the back. It's a good spot for backpackers, sporting clean (and cheap!) bedrooms and a passable shared bathroom that doesn't feel as cringe-worthy as a lot of backwater backpacker places in Borneo. Two-hour cruises cost RM80 per boat (six persons maximum), night cruises are RM100.

Sukau Greenview B&B (☎ 013 869 6922, 089-565266; sukau_greenview@yahoo.com; s/tw RM45/60, meals RM10) Another cheapie in central Sukau, this pleasant option offers nine rooms (all with twin-size beds) in a small Cape Cod–style lodge. It's basic (the floors are made from particle board) but comfy enough for the price. River cruises cost RM35, night rides are RM45 and trips to Oxbow Lake are RM45 (prices are per person). The friendly owners can organise a Sandakan-bound van (RM30 per person) when you depart – it leaves at 6.30am.

Barefoot Sukau Lodge (☎ 089-235525; www.barefootsukau.com; r per person RM80, meals RM25) Barefoot's best features are the scenic eating area yawning over the river and the super-smiley staff (the English is a bit thin, but they get an 'A' for effort). The rooms are small but covered with thick coats of white paint. A two-day/one-night package costs RM200 and includes accommodation, three meals and one cruise.

BILIT

Bilit is the new Sukau, with its own collection of jungle lodges and homestays. All of the accommodation here is located at the end of a *very* rutty road (4WD needed!) or on the far side of the river, which means that independent travel here is not as simple as in Sukau.

our pick **Nature Lodge Kinabatangan** (☎ 013 863 6263, 088-230534; www.naturelodgekinabatangan.com) Located just around the river bend from Bilit, this charming jungle retreat is an excellent choice for backpacker budgets. The campus of prim bungalows is divided into two sections: the Civet Wing caters to penny-pinchers with dorm-style huts, while the spiffed-up Agamid Wing offers higher-end twin-bed chalets. A three-day/two-night package (includes three boat tours, three guided hikes *and* all meals!) is RM300 for a dorm and RM335 for a chalet.

Kinabatangan Jungle Camp (☎ 089-533190; www.kinabatangan-jungle-camp.com) This earth-friendly retreat caters to a niche market of birders and serious nature junkies. A two-day/one-night package (including three meals, two boat rides, guiding and transfers) will set you back RM400. The owners, Robert and Annie, also run the Labuk B&B in Sepilok, and four out of five travellers opt for a Kinabatangan–Sepilok combo tour.

Getting There & Away

Taking a bus instead of tour-operated transport to – or at least near – Sungai Kinabatangan can save quite a bit of cash. To reach Sungai Kinabatangan by bus from KK, board a Tawau- or Lahad Datu–bound bus and ask the driver to let you off at Meeting Point (sometimes called Sukau Junction) – the turn-off road to reach Sukau. If you are on a Sandakan-bound bus, make sure your driver remembers to stop at the Tawau-Sandakan junction – it's called Batu 32 or Checkpoint (sometimes it's known as Sandakan Mile 32). It should cost no more than RM30 to reach Meeting Point from KK. From Sepilok or Sandakan, expect to pay around RM15 to reach Batu 32, and around RM20 if you're on a Sandakan–Tawau bus and want to alight at Meeting Point. You can arrange transport from these drop-off points with your tour operator or with a local minivan.

DANUM VALLEY CONSERVATION AREA

They say that at any given time, there are over a hundred scientists doing research in the Danum Valley. And we aren't surprised – this steaming primary forest overflows with colourful wildlife. It's like owning one of those relaxation machines that coos and caws when you're trying to fall asleep, except that at Danum, you get to see the animals too.

An outpost for scientists and researchers, the **Danum Valley Field Centre** (☎ 089-880441, 088-326318) also welcomes tourists. Accommodation at the centre is organised into three categories: hostel, rest house and VIP. We recommend the rest house rooms, which are located at arm's length from the canteen (the only place to eat). These rooms are basic but clean, sporting ceiling fans and twin beds. Towels are provided for the cold-water showers. The simple hostel is about a seven-minute walk from the canteen, and the barrack-style rooms are separated by gender. All buildings at the field centre run on generated power, which shuts off between midnight and 7am. There are no professionally trained guides at the centre – only rangers who can show you the trails. Tourists take their meals in the cafeteria-style canteen (vegie friendly). Room and board deals start at around RM155 per night (for a room in the rest house). Transportation is RM60 per person each way – ask about all-inclusive packages for discounts.

Tourists must board one of the two jungle-bound vans that leave the booking office in Lahad Datu at 3.30pm on Mondays, Wednesdays and Fridays. The vans return to Lahad Datu from the field centre at 8.30am on the same days. There are 12 seats in each van and this is the only way to reach the centre unless you charter a pricey private vehicle.

SEMPORNA

pop 133,000

Semporna is the kind of town that makes tourists want to swear – especially if they're travelling on a tight schedule. As your bumpy ride trundles into this sleepy burg, you'll quickly realise that you haven't reached your oceanic Eden just yet. Semporna is one of those necessary evils – a lacklustre layover that'll snag you for a night on your way to the Semporna Archipelago.

'Diving' is the answer tourists provide when someone asks them why they're in Semporna, and 'Sipadan' is the answer to 'where do you want to dive?' Scuba is the town's lifeline, and there's no shortage of places to sign up for some serious bubble blowing. Operators (p506) are clustered around the Semporna Seafront, a newer neighbourhood near the Dragon Inn, while other companies have offices in KK.

Sleeping

Semporna is no great shakes, but the town offers a lot of passable options at the low end of the budget spectrum. If you've already signed up with a scuba operator ask them about sleeping discounts (and don't be shy about trying to finagle a good deal, especially if you're sticking around for a while).

Try one of the following options:

Dragon Inn (Rumah Rehat Naga; ☎ 089-781088; www.dragoninnfloating.com.my; 1 Jln Kastam; dm RM15-20, r incl breakfast RM66-88; ❄ 💻) Long rows of dark rooms sit on stilts above the greenish tidewater at the far corner of the town's dive-centric district. The tiki-chic vibe kind of falls flat…

Borneo Global Sipadan BackPackers (☎ 089-785088; borneogb@gmail.com; Jln Causeway; dm/tr incl breakfast RM22/90; ❄) Dozens of dorm beds.

Scuba Junkie Backpackers (☎ 089-785372; www.scuba-junkie.com; Block B, Lot 36, Semporna Seafront; dm/r incl breakfast RM30/80; ❄) Sociable spot offering 50% discounts for divers.

Sipadan Inn (☎ 089-782766; www.sipadan-inn.com; Block D, Semporna Seafront; r incl breakfast RM84; ❄) Spotless rooms are light on decor. A better deal than Dragon Inn's RM88 rooms.

Getting There & Away

The advent of uber-cheap airfares has made Semporna easily accessible from both KK and KL. Planes land at Tawau Airport, roughly an hour's drive from town. Tawau–Semporna buses (RM15) will stop at the airport if you ask the driver. Buses that do not stop at the airport will let you off at Mile 28, where you will have to walk a few kilometres to the terminal. Note that flying less than 24 hours after diving can cause serious health issues, even death.

The bus 'terminal' hovers around the Milimewa supermarket not too far from the mosque's looming minaret. Morning and night buses to Kota Kinabalu (RM50, nine hours) leave around 7am or 7pm. Minivans to/from Tawau (RM10 to RM15, 1½ hours), Lahad Datu (RM20 to RM25, 2½ hours) and Sandakan (RM35 to RM40, 5½ hours) arrive and depart around the grocery store area as well. All run from early morning until 4pm.

SEMPORNA ARCHIPELAGO

The stunning islets of the Semporna Archipelago freckle the cerulean sea like a shattered earthen pot – each sandy chunk a lonely spot on the ocean's mirrorlike surface. Bands of sun-kissed sea gypsies patrol the waters scooping up snapping crabs and ethereal shells. But another world exists below – a silent realm inspiring even more wonder and awe. **Sipadan**'s technicolour sea walls reach deep down – 2000m to the distant ocean floor – and act like an underwater beacon luring docile turtles, slippery sharks and waving mantas.

Although Sipadan outshines the neighbouring sites, there are other reefs in the marine park that are well worth exploring. The macro-diving around **Mabul** (or Pulau Mabul to some) is world-famous. In fact, the term 'muck diving' was invented here. The submerged sites around **Kapalai**, **Mataking** and **Sibuan** are also of note.

The following dive operators are among the growing laundry list of companies in the area. It is *highly* recommended that you book in advance (see p492).

Billabong Scuba (☎ 089-781866; www.billabongscuba.com; Lot 28, Block E, Semporna Seafront) Semporna-based outfitted with reasonable prices. Accommodation can be arranged at a rickety homestay on Mabul.

Blue Sea Divers (☎ 089-781322; www.thereefdivers.com; Semporna Seafront) Reputable day-trip operator in Semporna.

Borneo Divers (Map p493; ☎ 088-222226; www.borneodivers.info; 9th fl, Menara Jubili, 53 Jalan Gaya, Kota Kinabalu) The original operators in the area, Borneo Divers were the good folks who unveiled Sipadan to an awestruck Jacques Cousteau. Recommended.

Scuba Junkie (☎ 089-784788; www.scuba-junkie.com; Lot 36, Block B, Semporna Seafront) Popular with the young backpacker crowd, Scuba Junkie invented the hard sell in Semporna. Prices are kept low and diving gear is well maintained.

Sipadan Scuba (☎ 089-784788, 919128; www.sipadanscuba.com; Lot 23, Block D, Semporna Seafront) Twenty years of Borneo experience and an international staff makes Sipadan Scuba a reliable choice. This is the only PADI 5 Star Instructor Development Centre in Semporna.

Uncle Chang (Borneo Jungle River Island Tours; ☎ 089-785372; www.scuba-junkie.com; 36 Semporna Seafront) Offers diving and snorkelling day trips, plus stays at its lodge on Mabul.

Sleeping

Sleeping spots are sprinkled across the archipelago, with the majority of options clustered on the peach-fringed island of Mabul (Sipadan's closest neighbour). All options include three meals per day in the price. Divers and snorkellers can also opt to stay in the town of Semporna, which offers a slightly better bang for your buck, but you'll miss out on post-dive chill sessions along flaxen strips of sand.

Mabul Beach Resort (☎ 089-784788, 089-919128; www.sipadanscuba.com; r per person RM80-120) Owned and operated by Scuba Junkie, this brand-new spot on Mabul is shaking things up for shoestringers. No more are the days of dingy 'longhouse' accommodation. Most of the resort was still under construction when we visited, but we think it looks very promising!

The following options are located within Mabul's 'town' (and we use that term lightly) of sea shanties. The quality is fairly similar at all four places: in need of an upgrade. At the time of research we noticed a couple of renovation attempts underway, but guests should still expect uber-basic digs in wobbly shacks, flimsy mattresses, grim toilet stalls, cold showers, floating pieces of rubbish, and roosters crowing in the early morning.

Arung Hayat Resort (☎ 089-782526; r/ste per person RM50/80) An autonomous homestay with low-slung beds, baby-blue walls and plenty of smiles. Also caters to nondivers.

Billabong (☎ 089-781866; r per person RM50) Six basic rooms hovering on stilts above the ebbing tide. Associated accommodation for Billabong Scuba.

Uncle Chang's (☎ 089-781002; www.sipadanbackpackers.com; dm/s/d per person RM50/120/60, d with aircon & private bathroom per person RM90; ☒) A Sipadan backpacking stalwart catering to the like-named dive operator. We've received reports from several travellers that a charming family of rats also calls this place home.

Lai's Homestay (r per person RM60) Features a large, wood-planked verandah stretching over the sea. Slightly newer, but still shanty-esque.

Getting There & Around

All transportation to the marine park is funnelled through the town of Semporna. Tourists who are staying on one of the many offshore islets must book ahead as space is quite limited and there is no public transportation to any of the archipelago's islands. Your accommodation will arrange any transportation needs (usualy for an extra fee), which will most likely depart in the morning (meaning that if you arrive in Semporna in the afternoon, you will be required to spend the night in town before setting off into the park).

BEAUFORT DIVISION

With Borneo's clutch of unpronounceable tribal names (try saying 'Balambangan' three times fast!), it's a pleasure asking for a bus to Beaufort. This shield-shaped peninsula, popping out from Sabah's southwestern coast, is a marshy plain marked with curling rivers and fringed by golden dunes. Tourists with tight travel schedules should consider doing a wildlife river cruise here if they don't have time to reach Sungai Kinabatangan.

The tea-brown **Sungai Klias** harkens the mighty Kinabatangan, offering short-stay visitors a chance to spend an evening in the jungle cavorting with saucy primates. There are several companies offering two-hour river cruises. We recommend **Borneo Authentic** (☎ 088-773066; www.borneo-authentic.com; package trip RM150). Trips include a large buffet dinner and a short night walk to view the swarms of fireflies that light up the evening sky like Christmas lights. Cruises start at dusk (around 5pm), when the sweltering heat starts to burn off and animals emerge for some post-siesta prowling.

Narrower than the river Klias, the **Sungai Garama** is another popular spot for the popular day-trip river cruises from KK. Like Klias, the tours here start around 5pm (with KK departures at 2pm), and include a buffet dinner before returning to KK. Try **Only In Borneo** (☎ 088-260506; www.oibtours.com; package tour RM190), an offshoot of Traverse Tours. It has a well-maintained facility along the shores of Sungai Garama and offers an overnight option in prim dorms or double rooms.

PULAU LABUAN

pop 85,000

Pulau Labuan is Sabah's version of Vegas, but if you're expecting shmancy hotels and prostitutes you're only half-right... The island doesn't feel seedy though; in fact, think of Labuan as a giant airport terminal – everything here is duty free, because politically it's part of a federal territory governed directly from KL. The island's main town, Bander Labuan, is the transit point for ferries linking Kota Kinabalu and Brunei. WWII buffs will find several sights of interest, but for most travellers the **Labuan Homestay Program** (☎ 087-422622; www.labuantourism.com; r RM65, 2 days incl full board RM140) is the only draw. This excellent service matches visitors with a friendly local in one of three villages around the island: Patau Patau 2, Kampong Sungai Labu and Kampong Bukit Kuda. Some of the homes are just as grand as one of the international-class hotels on the waterfront! If you want to be near Bandar Labuan, ask for accommodation at Patau Patau 2 – it's a charming stilt village out on the bay. Stay a bit longer and learn how to make *ambuyat,* a Bruneian favourite (see p61).

Passenger ferries (first class/economy class RM39/31, 3¼ hours) depart KK for Labuan Monday to Saturday at 8am and 1.30pm. On Sunday they sail at 8am and 3pm. In the opposite direction they depart Labuan for KK Monday to Saturday 8am and 1pm, while on Sunday they depart at 10.30am and 3pm. Note that the air-con on these ferries is always turned up to 'arctic' – bring a fleece. There are also daily speedboats from Labuan to Limbang in Sarawak (RM28, two hours, 2.30pm) and Lawas, also in Sarawak (RM33, two hours, 12.30pm). There are also daily speedboats to Sipitang, which cost RM25 and take 40 minutes.

MALAYSIAN BORNEO – SARAWAK

While Sabah sees itself as 'nature', Sarawak plays up its cultural counterpoint. With a thriving indigenous population featuring dozens of dialects and tribes, Sarawak's local people are the keepers of Borneo – the ancient storytellers and guardians of lost traditions. Many communities still cling to the longhouse lifestyle – a coveted way of communal life steeped in hundreds of years of myth, legend and lore.

But make no mistake, Sarawak offers oh so much more than blowpipes, rice wine and sacred dances. The state has its fair share of natural wonders as well. The yawning Niah Caves reveal the island's 40,000 years of human history through haunting burials and cryptic cavern drawings. Caves are super-sized at Gunung Mulu National Park – home to more bats than there are people in the entirety of Sarawak. Don't miss the trek up to the Pinnacles, a curious formation

GETTING TO BRUNEI

Travelling by boat from Pulau Labuan to the Serasa Port in the Muara region of Brunei is much less of a red-tape nightmare than travelling overland. The journey by boat will save plenty of time as you will only cross the border once (overland adventurers will rack up a handful of stamps while weaving between Brunei and Malaysia before reaching Bandar Seri Begawan or the Sarawak border). See p53 for everything you need to know about getting to/from Brunei.

of limestone spikes shooting straight up into the balmy jungle air. Then it's on to the Kelabit Highlands, an earthen kingdom tucked high in the clouds along the dark green borders of Kalimantan. Wild macaques and prowling proboscis monkeys patrol the southern shores as they swing past trekking tourists in Bako National Park.

Ultimately, Sarawak is a land of dreaming – a place where fantasies are fulfilled. If you're imagining a world of steaming jungles, secreted villages, curious beasts and muddy treks into the unknown, then you've come to the right place. Sarawak promises to deliver on all of those magical Bornean stereotypes, and it'll keep you coming back for more.

KUCHING

pop 632,500

A capital, a kingdom, a cat, a colonial relic – Kuching wears many hats. Sarawak's main point of entry plays its romantic Indochine card quite well, yet manages to be Borneo's most trendy, forward-thinking destination. There's a certain cosmopolitan *je ne sais quoi* that floats through the air, especially in the evenings as hookah smoke fills the streets amid the clinking of designer cocktails – shaken not stirred, of course. In the daytime the colourful shophouses in Chinatown are abuzz as sweaty tinsmiths hawk their wares and smartly dressed businessmen line up for steamy meat buns on their lunch break.

Kuching means 'cat' in Malay, a mascot exploited at every souvenir stall and highway roundabout. The city was so named by Charles Brooke, one of the white rajas, who must have sensed his capital's feline fierceness. Kuching embodies the spirit of a lion, sitting regally in its wild surrounds as it guards the roaring Sungai Sarawak from other prowlers.

Information

BOOKSHOPS

Mohamed Yahia & Sons (☎ 082-416928; Basement, Sarawak Plaza, Jln Tunku Abdul Rahman; 🕑 9am-5pm) Has English-language fiction and books on Borneo, plus Sarawak maps.

Popular Book Co (☎ 082-411378; Level 3, Tun Jugah Shopping Centre, 18 Jln Tunku Abdul Rahman; 🕑 9am-7pm) This is a more modern and spacious bookshop with a good selection of international titles but fewer local-interest books, however.

IMMIGRATION

Immigration office (☎ 082-245661; 2nd fl, Sultan Iskandar Bldg, Jln Simpang Tiga; 🕑 8am-noon & 2-4.30pm Mon-Fri) Visa extensions 3km south of town centre. From in front of the mosque, take CLL Bus 11 or 14A/B/C. Get off at Simpang Tiga.

INTERNET ACCESS

The Coffee Bean & Tea Leaf in Sarawak Plaza offers free wi-fi to its customers.

Cyber City (☎ 082-243680; www.cybercity.com.my; Taman Sri Sarawak Mall; per hr RM4; 🕑 10am-11pm Mon-Sat, 11am-11pm Sun) A clean, friendly place with printing and scanning services.

LAUNDRY

Mr Clean (Jln Green Hill; per kg RM6; 🕑 8am-6pm Mon-Sat, to 4pm Sun) Reliable and economical; in the popular Green Hill area of town.

MEDICAL SERVICES

Normah Medical Specialist Centre (☎ 082-440055; www.normah.com.my; Jln Tun Abdul Rahman) A private hospital with good facilities and staff. It's favoured by many residents and expats.

Sarawak General Hospital (☎ 082-257555; Jln Ong Kee) For emergencies and major ailments only.

Timberland Medical Centre (☎ 082-234991; Mile 3, Jln Rock) Private hospital with highly qualified staff.

MONEY

There is an exchange counter at the airport. Expect money changers in town to only take large bills (B$50, S$50 etc.)

Everrise Money Changer (☎ 082-233200; 199 Jln Padungan; 🕑 9am-5pm) Cash only. Ever rise? Seriously?

Majid & Sons (☎ 082-422402; 45 Jln India) A licensed money changer dealing in cash only.

Maybank (☎ 082-416889; Jln Tunku Abdul Rahman; 🕑 9.15am-4.30pm Mon-Thu, 9.15am-4pm Fri, ATM 6am-midnight daily)

POST

Main post office (Jln Tun Abang Haji Openg; 🕑 8am-4.30pm Mon-Sat)

TOURIST INFORMATION

The excellent **Visitors Information Centre** (☎ 082-410944; www.sarawaktourism.com; Sarawak Tourism Complex, Jln Abang Tun Haji Openg; 🕑 8am-6pm Mon-Fri, 9am-3pm Sat & Sun) is in the old courthouse. The centre's staff can tell you just about everything you need to know about travelling in Sarawak, and there are enough brochures to paper your living room. Maps abound and transportation schedules are also readily available if you're unsure about which buses go where. Ask about the invaluable *Official Kuching Guide.*

The **National Parks & Wildlife Booking Office** (☎ 082-248088; 🕑 8am-5pm Mon-Fri) is next door to the visitors centre (with the same hours of operation) and arranges accommodation at national parks (most people swing by to arrange an overnight stay at Bako; p514).

Sights

Like many cities, Kuching is a whole lot greater than the sum of its parts. There are a few interesting museums and historical attractions to keep you occupied, but the main attraction is the city itself. Note that the **Astana** and **Fort**

OFF WITH THEIR HEADS!

Borneo has often been dubbed 'the Land of the Headhunters' – a catchphrase popularised by the Sarawak Tourism Board when they chose it as their promotional slogan (then they promptly abandoned the motto after realising that travellers weren't particularly psyched about the threat of decapitation). Headhunting has been a key facet of Borneo's indigenous culture for over 500 years, yet many of the rites, rituals and beliefs surrounding the gruesome tradition remain shrouded in mystery.

The act of taking heads was treated with the utmost seriousness; warriors practised two types of premeditated expeditions. The first was known as the *kayo bala* – a group raid involving several warriors – and the second, *kayo anak,* was performed by a lone brave, or a *bujang berani.* In the upper regions of the Batang Rejang, the *kayo anak* was a common method of wooing a prospective bride. Believe it or not, the most valuable heads were those belonging to women and children, who were usually hidden away from marauders near the longhouse hearth. Only the savviest and sneakiest warrior could ambush a child or woman as they bathed or picked berries unattended.

After a successful hunt, the warrior would wander the jungle, wrestling with the taken spirit rather than letting down his guard for a nap. In the morning he would return to his longhouse where the head would be smoked and strung up for the others to see and honour. Heads were worshipped and revered, and food offerings were not uncommon. A longhouse with many heads was feared and respected by the neighbouring clans.

The fascinating tradition began its gradual decline in 1841 when James Brooke, at the behest of Brunei's sultan, started quashing the hunt for heads in order to attract foreign traders. No one wanted to trade in Borneo due to the island's nasty reputation for harbouring ferocious noggin-grabbing warriors. However, the sultan wasn't interested in importing goods – he wanted to charge traders hefty port taxes (you see, Brunei's cache of black gold hadn't yet been discovered). A nasty skirmish involving a knife-wielding pirate and a Chinese merchant's noodle gave Brooke the opportunity to show the Dayaks that he meant business – he promptly executed the criminal.

Headhunting flew under the radar until WWII, when British troops encouraged the locals to start swinging machetes at Japanese soldiers (many of their heads still hang as longhouse cranium ornaments). Today, murmurs about headhunting are usually sensationalised to drum up foreign intrigue – the last '*tête* offensive' was during the ethnic struggles in the late 1990s (in Indonesian Kalimantan). As Borneo's indigenous people continue to embrace Christianity over animistic superstition, many longhouses have dismantled their dangling dead, although, if you ask around, you'll quickly learn that the heads haven't actually been tossed away – that would just be bad luck!

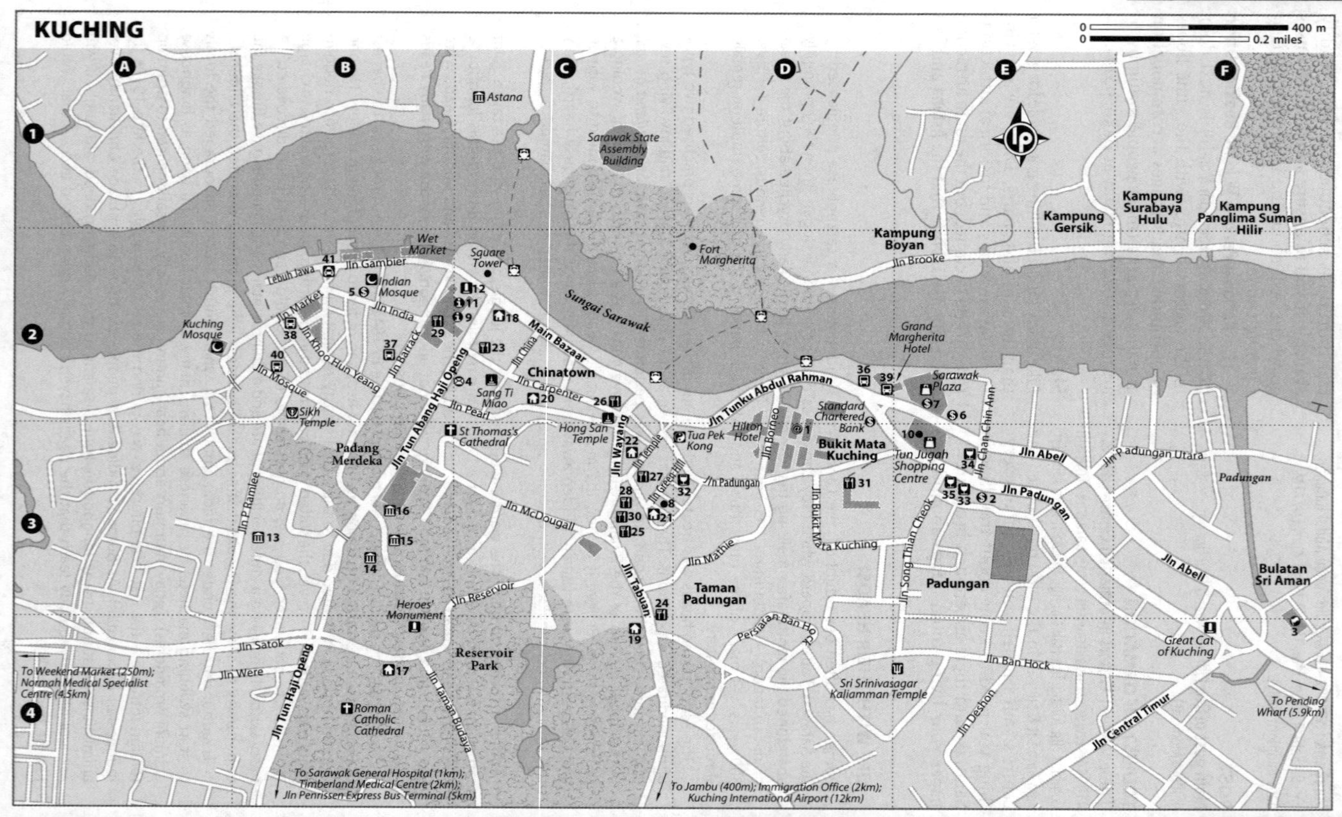
KUCHING
0 400 m
0 0.2 miles
Astana
Sarawak State Assembly Building
Fort Margherita
Sungai Sarawak
Kampung Boyan
Kampung Gersik
Kampung Surabaya Hulu
Kampung Panglima Suman Hilir
Jln Brooke
Wet Market
Square Tower
Jln Gambier
Lebuh Jawa
Indian Mosque
Jln India
Jln Market
Kuching Mosque
Jln Khoo Hun Yeang
Jln Mosque
Jln Barrack
Main Bazaar
Chinatown
Jln China
Jln Carpenter
Sang Ti Miao
Jln Pearl
Sikh Temple
St Thomas's Cathedral
Hong San Temple
Padang Merdeka
Jln Tun Abang Haji Openg
Jln Tunku Abdul Rahman
Tua Pek Kong
Hilton Hotel
Jln Borneo
Standard Chartered Bank
Bukit Mata Kuching
Grand Margherita Hotel
Sarawak Plaza
Tun Jugah Shopping Centre
Jln Chan Chin Ann
Jln Abell
Jln Padungan Utara
Padungan
Jln Wayang
Jln Temple
Jln Green Hill
Jln Padungan
Jln Bukit Mata Kuching
Jln Song Thian Cheok
Jln McDougall
Jln P Ramlee
Jln Mathie
Taman Padungan
Jln Tabuan
Persiaran Ban Hock
Bulatan Sri Aman
Great Cat of Kuching
Jln Ban Hock
Sri Srinivasagar Kaliamman Temple
Jln Deshon
Jln Central Timur
To Pending Wharf (5.9km)
Heroes' Monument
Jln Reservoir
Jln Satok
Reservoir Park
Jln Were
Jln Tun Haji Openg
Roman Catholic Cathedral
Jln Taman Budaya
To Weekend Market (250m); Normah Medical Specialist Centre (4.5km)
To Sarawak General Hospital (1km); Timberland Medical Centre (2km); Jln Penrissen Express Bus Terminal (5km)
To Jambu (400m); Immigration Office (2km); Kuching International Airport (12km)

INFORMATION

Cyber City	1	D3
Everrise Money Changer	2	E3
Indonesian Consulate	3	F4
Main Post Office	4	C2
Majid & Sons	5	B2
Maybank	6	E2
Mohamed Yahia & Sons	7	E2
Mr Clean	8	C3
National Parks & Wildlife Booking Office	9	C2
Popular Book Co	10	E3
Visitors Information Centre	11	C2

SIGHTS & ACTIVITIES

Brooke Memorial	12	C2
Islamic Museum	13	B3
Sarawak Museum	14	B3
Sarawak Museum Art Museum	15	B3
Sarawak Museum Natural Science Museum	16	B3

SLEEPING

Fairview	17	B4
Kuching Waterfront Lodge	18	C2
Lodge 121	19	C4
Mr D's B&B	20	C2
Nomad	21	C3
Singgahsana Lodge	22	C3

EATING

43 Jalan Carpenter Chinese Food Stalls	23	C2
a-ha Café	24	C3
Bla Bla Bla	25	C3
Black Bean Coffee & Tea Company	26	C2
Green Hill Corner	27	C3
Junk	28	C3
Little Lebanon	29	B2
Living Room	30	C3
Top Spot Food Court	31	D3

DRINKING

99	32	D3
Ipanema	33	E3
Mojo	34	E3
Ruai	(see 21)	
Soho	35	E3

TRANSPORT

Bus Stop for Pending Wharf	36	D2
Bus Stop for STC Bus to Express Bus Terminal	37	B2
Petra Jaya Bus Station	38	B2
Shuttle buses to Sarawak Cultural Village	39	D2
STC–CLL Bus Stand	40	B2
Taxi Stand	41	B2

Margherita, both on the northern banks of the Sungai Sarawak, are not currently open to the public.

The south bank of the Sungai Sarawak has been tastefully developed with a paved walkway, lawns and flowerbeds, a children's playground, cafes and food stalls. It's a quiet, pleasant place to walk or sit and watch the *tambang* glide past with their glowing lanterns. In the evening it's full of couples and families strolling by or eating snacks. While you're strolling, be sure to have a look at the **Brooke Memorial**, in front of the Visitors Information Centre.

Kuching's **Chinatown** is centred on Jln Carpenter and runs roughly from Jln Wayang to Jln Tun Abang Haji Openg. It's a collection of beautiful colonial-era shophouses and Chinese temples that is conducive to strolling (if you can take the heat).

Established in 1891, the **Sarawak Museum** (☎ 082-244232; www.museum.sarawak.gov.my; Jln Tun Abang Haji Openg; admission free; 9am-6pm) has a fascinating collection of cultural artefacts and is a must-visit for anyone who wants to learn more about the region's indigenous peoples and natural environment. It consists of two wings connected by an ornate footbridge. While you're at the Sarawak Museum, be sure to have a look at its **Art Museum** and **Natural Science Museum**, both of which are just down the hill from the museum's Old Wing. Over the hill from the Sarawak Museum, the **Islamic Museum** (Muzium Islam Sarawak; ☎ 082-244232; Jln P Ramlee; admission free; 9am-6pm) is well worth the walk.

Kuching's best and busiest market, the **weekend market** (known locally as Pasar Minggu) sits along Jln Satok. The market begins late on Saturday afternoon, when villagers bring in their produce and livestock and start trading. They sleep at their stalls and resume trading at around 5am on Sunday.

GETTING TO INDONESIA: TEBEDU TO ENTIKONG

There is only one official land border crossing between Sarawak and Kalimantan, at Tededu (M) and Entikong (I). Located close to Kuching, this crossing point is used on the tourist trail as the gateway between nations for the Miri–Pontianak and KK–Pontianak buses. A series of unofficial crossings line the border throughout the Kelabit Highlands; a vestige of blurred tribal grounds.

Festivals & Events

The three-day **Rainforest World Music Festival** (www.rainforestmusic-borneo.com) unites Borneo's indigenous tribes with international artists for a musical extravaganza in the Sarawak Cultural Village outside Kuching. It's held annually in the middle of July. Check out our website (lonelyplanet.com) for an informative podcast about the festival.

Sleeping

Mr D's B&B (☎ 082-248852; www.misterdbnb.com; 26 Jln Carpenter; dm/s/tw/d from RM20/55/65/75;) 'Tribal chic' is the name of the game here – the hang-out room at the entrance is stuffed with leopard-skin pillows and there are arty black-and-white prints of tribal warriors on the wall.

Rooms are quite standard though – they're very clean, but most don't have windows. Thoughtful perks include wi-fi throughout and power points beside everyone's pillow.

Fairview (☎ 082-240017; http://thefairview.com.my; 6 Jln Taman Budaya; dm/s/d RM25/50/70; ❄) An oldie but a goodie, Fairview scores big points for its unpretentious atmosphere and friendly owners who dispense oodles of information about hidden Kuching gems.

Nomad (☎ 082-237831; www.borneobnb.com; 3 Jln Green Hill; dm/s/tw/d from RM26/55/65/75; ❄ 💻) There is a buzzing backpacker vibe at this Iban-run favourite. Bright patches of paint liven the rooms, and guests congregate in the common area to hang out with the friendly management or watch the latest episode of Malaysian reality TV. Our favourite thing was the all-day breakfast – swing by the kitchen for toast, fruit and sugary snacks any time you want. If Nomad is full, try Tracks next door – it's owned by the same people (and looks exactly the same, except slightly smaller).

Lodge 121 (☎ 082-428121; www.lodge121.com; 121 Jln Tabuan; dm/s/d/tr RM30/59/79/99; ❄ 💻) Polished concrete abounds at this mod charmer. The owners have transformed a commercial space into a multilevelled hang-out for flashpackers. The dorm room is in the attic, and although the lack of bunks is welcoming, the mattresses are on the floor.

our pick Singgahsana Lodge (082-429277; www.singgahsana.com; 1 Jln Temple; dm RM30, r RM88-138; ☎ ❄ 💻) Tourists can thank Singgahsana for upping the ante in Kuching's budget-bed game. The trendsetting owners out-swanked the competition early on with an effective use of colourful accent walls and tribal knick-knacks – now everyone's playing catch-up, though no one has completely caught up just yet. Don't miss the hunting lodge–style bar at the top of the stairwell – it's only open to guests.

Kuching Waterfront Lodge (☎ 082-231111; www.kuchingwaterfronlodge.com; 15 Main Bazaar; dm/d RM30/110; ❄ 💻) The only spot right in the heart of Main Bazaar, this up-and-comer has a large welcoming lobby stacked with lacquered furnishings. Rooms are light on designer details, but they're comfortable enough (ask to see a few options before dropping your bags). The best deal here is the dorm rooms – they're slightly pricier than most of the competition so you'll usually find yourself with a suite to yourself!

Eating

RESTAURANTS & CAFES

Pick up the *Guide to Kuching* for a veritable laundry list of top eats.

Black Bean Coffee & Tea Company (☎ 082-420290; 87 Jln Carpenter; drinks from RM3.90; 🕑 9am-6.30pm Mon-Sat) Serving fresh, fairtrade coffee, this quaint cafe, housed in a converted Chinese shophouse, strikes the guiltless balance between Starbucks and Sarawak.

Little Lebanon (☎ 082-247523; Japanese Bldg; mains from RM6, sheesha RM11; 🕑 breakfast, lunch & dinner) Borneo's only Arabic restaurant sits in an elegant breezeway overlooking colourful Jalan India. Belly dancing music wafts through the air as contented customers slurp some muddy Turkish coffee and dip their pita pillows into freshly mashed hummus. Swing by in the evenings for flavourful puffs on a *sheesha* pipe.

a-ha Café (☎ 016 889 3622; 38 Jln Tabuan; mains RM6-28; 🕑 breakfast, lunch & dinner; 📶) The emphasis here is firmly focused on healthy eating, with organic produce, all-natural ingredients and no MSG or artificial additives. Whether you treat yourself to Norwegian salmon, ostrich steak or deer kebabs, or just pop in for a fruit-'n'-vegetable smoothie, a-ha is a rare treat with virtually zero guilt factor. Wi-fi available.

Bla Bla Bla (☎ 082-233944; 27 Jln Tabuan; mains from RM15; 🕑 dinner Wed-Mon) Spiffier than a pimp's outfit, Bla Bla Bla brings a splash of Hollywood to Kuching. The tasty fusion food is anything but blah, and patrons will adore the coy pond and golden Buddhas.

our pick Junk (☎ 082-259450; 80 Jln Wayang; mains from RM15; 🕑 dinner Wed-Mon) The coolest *vide-grenier* you'll ever see, Junk is filled to the brim with…well…junk. But it's all so very chic – when you walk in you'll think, 'Did Amelie explode in here?' A favourite among Malaysian celebs, Bla Bla Bla's sister restaurant offers superb sophisticated Western food with an Italian bias. A word to the wise: don't set your watch by any of the wall clocks…

Living Room (☎ 082-233944; Jln Wayang; mains from RM25; 🕑 dinner) Living Room completes Kuching's trendy triumvirate of fusion eats. The menu mixes the top noshes at Junk and Bla Bla Bla and guests dine in breezy open-air *salas*. You will no doubt find yourself wondering where you are: is this Borneo, Bali or Barcelona?

HAWKER CENTRES & FOOD STALLS

43 Jalan Carpenter Chinese Food Stalls (43 Jln Carpenter; meals from RM3; 🕑 breakfast, lunch & dinner) Start your day with a brilliant, old-school Kuching breakfast. Note that Chinese locals refer to this hawker centre as Lau Ya Keng in Hokkien.

Green Hill Corner (Jln Temple; meals RM3-4; breakfast, lunch & dinner) Several stalls here crank out a variety of noodle and rice dishes, including a brilliant plate of *kway teow goreng* (fried rice noodles). Problem is, the chef who makes this dish only shows up when he damn well feels like it.

Top Spot Food Court (Jln Padungan; meals RM4-35; lunch & dinner) The double entendre definitely holds true. This excellent rooftop plaza has acres of tables and a good variety of stalls. Order anything from abalone to banana prawns or numerous varieties of fish, and chase it down with a cold bottle of Tiger. To get here, climb the stairs leading from Jln Padungan to Tapanga restaurant, and keep heading upstairs from there.

Drinking

Like most places in Borneo, a lively night scene usually focuses around an evening meal, but cosmopolitan Kuching has a clutch of spirited drinking spots as well (pun intended). Bars and other entertainment venues stay open until around 1am, although live music can blare on until later (especially on weekends). The *Official Kuching Guide* has a lengthier list for those who plan on sticking around for a while. Several of our eating options double as swank bar spots.

Jambu (32 Jln Crookshank) Jambu? Crookshank? The names in Kuching are pretty weird, but this local fave, in a blazing pink bungalow just outside the city centre, is a hip spot to sling back a few designer cocktails with friends. Closed on Mondays.

Soho (64 Jln Padungan) This is arguably the hippest bar in the centre – even the name oozes London cool. Local Gossip Girl–esque youngsters hobnob to grind-worthy play lists of jazz, dance and Latin beats. The atmosphere starts out relaxed but can definitely build up some heat under the red lights as the night draws on!

Mojo (Jln Chan Chin Ann) Wander through to the back of the Denise wine shop and you may think you've entered another world – this is a cocktail lounge every bit as fashionable as you might find in KL or Singapore, with a giggly young crowd trying to live up to the style.

Also worth a look:

99 (98-99 Jln Green Hill) Football on the big screen, thumping tracks on the weekend.

Ipanema (66 Jln Padungan) 'Minimal-chic' theme, with trendy tapas snacks.

Ruai (3 Jln Green Hill) Iban-themed pub below Nomad hostel.

Shopping

If it's traditional Borneo arts and crafts you're after then you've come to the right place. Kuching is undoubtedly the best spot in Borneo for collectors and cultural enthusiasts. Traditional handicrafts on Borneo include Orang Ulu beadwork, Bidayuh basket-weaving, traditional wooden carvings and hand-woven rugs, just to name a few. Also, Sarawak pepper can be a unique and inexpensive gift for friends back home. Check out www.mpb.gov.my for more info about this aromatic spice.

Don't expect many bargains, but don't be afraid to negotiate either – there's plenty to choose from, and the quality varies as much as the price. Start on the aptly named Main Bazaar – a seemingly unending promenade of souvenir shops, some outfitted like art galleries, others with more of a 'garage sale' appeal.

Getting There & Away

AIR

Air Asia (☎ 03-8775 4000; www.airasia.com) has numerous daily flights to/from Kuala Lumpur at bargain-basement prices. It also flies to/from Penang and Johor Bahru. Within Borneo, it flies to/from Bintulu, Kota Kinabalu, Miri and Sibu. Check for prices as they constantly change.

Batavia Air (☎ 082-626299; www.batavia-air.co.id) has flights to/from Jakarta (Java) and Pontianak (Kalimantan)

Malaysia Airlines (code MAS; ☎ anywhere in Malaysia 1300 883 000, 03-7843 3000, in Kuching 220618; www.malaysiaairlines.com) offers flights between Kuching and Kuala Lumpur and Johor Bahru. It also flies between Kuching and Hong Kong and Guangzhou. Within Borneo, MAS flies to/from Bintulu, Kota Kinabalu, Miri and Sibu.

BOAT

Express Bahagia (☎ 082-410076) has boats running to and from Sibu (RM35 to RM45, 4½ hours), departing from the express boat wharf in Pending at 8.30am daily. Note that this is an easier and faster trip to Sibu than the bus, which takes eight hours.

GETTING INTO TOWN

Kuching International Airport (KCH) is 12km south of the city centre. At the time of research there were no public buses connecting the airport and the city centre. If you don't want to take a cab, head left when exiting the airport (which will feel counterintuitive as taxis head right) and walk for 500m until you hit the main route. Venture across the road to the bus shelter and flag a bus down (all buses in this direction are heading downtown). It may require a bit of patience, but the ride will only cost RM1. Taxis will cost around RM24; buy a coupon before you leave the airport at the counter outside the terminal entrance.

The express-boat wharf is 6.5km east of town in the suburb of Pending. Chin Lian Leong (CLL) Bus 1 (RM1.50, 40 minutes) connects the wharf with Kuching. It operates from the STC-CLL bus stand near Kuching Mosque and stops on Jln Tunku Abdul Rahman just west of the Hotel Grand Margherita Kuching. Taxis from town cost RM20.

The express bus terminal is 5km southeast of the city centre. Numerous STC buses run between the terminal and city for 90 sen. A taxi costs RM20.

BUS

Long-distance buses depart from the **Express Bus Terminal** (Jln Penrissen), 5km southeast of the centre. There are regular services to Sibu (RM45, eight hours, 10 departures daily between 6.30am and 10pm), Bintulu (RM60, 10 hours, nine departures daily between 6.30am and 10pm), and Miri (RM80, 14 hours, eight departures daily between 6.30am and 10pm).

Getting Around

For information on travelling into Kuching from the airport, express boat wharf or express bus station, see boxed text, above.

There are taxi ranks at the market and at the Express Bus Terminal. Most short trips around town cost between RM6 and RM10. Taxis in Kuching do not have meters, so be sure to settle on the fare before setting out.

SOUTHERN SARAWAK

Kuching's biggest asset is its proximity to a dozen natural wonders. The city is a great base for day trips to the coast and into the jungle. Almost all of the destinations in this section are within arm's reach of Kuching.

Bako National Park

Sarawak's oldest national park proves that you don't have go too far to find Borneo's signature jungles stuffed to the treetops with wildlife. **Bako National Park** (☎ 082-478011; admission RM10; ⌚ park office 8am-5pm) is a 27-sq-km natural sanctuary located on a jagged jade peninsula jutting out into the South China Sea. Although it's only a stone's throw from the capital, it's well worth spending the night here.

Bako is a storehouse of incredible natural diversity: biologists estimate that the park is home to 37 species of mammals, 24 reptile species and 184 bird species (some of which are migrant species). The park has a total of 17 trails ranging from short walks around park headquarters to strenuous day treks to the end of the peninsula. Guides are available (RM20 per hour), but it's easy to find your way around because all trails are colour-coded and clearly marked with splashes of paint.

Register for the park (adult/child RM10/5) upon arrival at the boat dock in Bako Bazaar. From here it's a choppy 20-minute boat ride to **park headquarters** (Telok Assam), where you'll find accommodation, a cafeteria and the park office. Staff will show you to your quarters and can answer any questions you have about trails. At the time of research, some of the chalets were getting a much-needed renovation. Accommodation bookings can be made at the National Parks & Wildlife Centre (p509) in Kuching.

GETTING THERE & AWAY

Arriving and departing Bako is dependent on the tides. Call ☎ 082-431336 for daily tide information.

To get to Bako from Kuching, first take a bus to Bako Bazaar in Kampung Bako, then charter a boat to the park. Petra Jaya Bus 6 leaves from near the hawker centre (open-air market) near Kuching Mosque in Kuching every hour (approximately) from 7.20am to 6pm (RM2.50, 45 minutes). The last bus back to Kuching leaves Kampung Bako at 5pm. You can also go by taxi all the way from Kuching (RM35, 30 minutes).

A boat from Bako Bazaar to the park headquarters takes 20 minutes and costs RM45 each way for up to five people. The chances are high that someone on the bus or at the pier will be looking to share a boat too. Boats generally operate between 8am and 5pm, though this is generally weather and tide dependent.

Take note of the boat's number (or ask for the driver's mobile phone number) and be sincere when you agree to a pick-up time. If you do want to share a different boat back, tell park headquarters your boat number – staff will be happy to call and cancel your original boat.

Santubong Peninsula (Damai)

The Santubong Peninsula is like Kuching's Malibu – a stunning seaside strip home to high-end resorts and the private villas of the elite. The main drawcards are the beaches, a golf course, modest jungle trekking and a clutch of seafood restaurants in the small fishing village of Kampung Buntal, at the base of the peninsula.

Surrounding an artificial lake at the foot of Gunung Santubong, the **Sarawak Cultural Village** (☎ 846411; www.scv.com.my; adult/child RM60/30; 🕑 9am-5pm) is an excellent living museum. It has examples of traditional dwellings built by different peoples of Sarawak – Orang Ulu, Bidayuh, Iban and Melanau – as well as Malay and Chinese houses. Hotels and travel agencies in Kuching have packages that include admission, lunch and transport ranging in price from RM90 to RM150. There's no public transport to the village, but a shuttle bus leaves from the riverfront and from the Hotel Grand Margherita Kuching at 9am and 12.30pm, returning at 1.45pm and 5.30pm (RM10 each way).

If you want to spend the night on the serene peninsula, try the **Village House** (☎ 082-846166; www.villagehouse.com.my; Santubong; dm/d RM88/220;) The owners of Singgahsana (p512) have done it again: lipstick-red walls, double-stuffed mattresses, dreamy white linen and fusion cuisine – this is boutique elegance par excellence.

At the time of research Petra Jaya buses were no longer running between Kuching and Kampung Buntal, although a van service (RM3–4) departing from Jln India had been shuttling passengers. Ask at the tourist information centre for the last transportation update. For Santubong, take a taxi from Kampung Buntal (around RM10, 15 minutes). If you want to stay for a meal the only option is to take a taxi back to Kuching (around RM25, 45 minutes). There's also a shuttle to Damai that stops in front of Singgahsana Lodge in central Kuching.

Semenggoh Wildlife Rehabilitation Centre

Semenggoh Wildlife Rehabilitation Centre (☎ 082-442180; adult/child RM3/1.50; 🕑 8am-12.45pm & 2-4.15pm) is a great place to sneak a peek at our ginger-haired cousins (no, not the Irish). Over 25 of Borneo's great orang-utans live in the centre, and although there isn't sufficient natural forest in the surrounding area to make actual reintroduction into the wild possible, it's still a good opportunity for a photo shoot. Semenggoh is noticeably less touristy (and much, much cheaper) than the widely publicised Sepilok in Sabah. Note that you're not guaranteed any orang-utan sightings, because the apes are free to come and go as they please. Feeding times are at 9am and 3pm.

Semenggoh is 24km south of Kuching. Take STC Bus 6 from Kuching (RM4, 40 minutes). Get off at the Forest Department Nursery, and walk 1.3km down the paved road to the centre. The last return bus passes Semenggoh at 1.30pm, but you should be able to flag down a private van (RM3) or a bus from the main road. At the time of research there were only two bus services per day – at 7.30am and 1.30pm. Ask the bus driver for details on his desired return time. A taxi from Kuching to the centre costs around RM40 to RM45. Tour companies also operate guided day trips out to the centre for RM60 per person. Note that some tours don't leave sufficient time to explore the gardens and arboretum at the centre (ask before you sign up).

Kubah National Park & Matang Wildlife Centre

Only 15km from downtown Kuching, **Kubah National Park** (☎ 011 225 003; RM10/5 adult/child) is yet another good natural retreat within easy striking distance of the city. While Bako has the edge for wildlife, Kubah offers good trekking and the trails are more shaded and twist past 22 sq km of lush rainforest. The park has also played host to two Hollywood productions, *Farewell to the King*, starring Nick Nolte, and the more recent *The Sleeping Dictionary*, with Jessica Alba.

A short drive beyond Kubah National Park, the **Matang Wildlife Centre** (☎ 082-22012; admission RM10; ⏰ 8am-5.30pm) was set up as a rehabilitation centre for endangered species released from captivity, particularly Borneo's larger mammals.

Matang Transport Bus 11 leaves Kuching (from the stand near Kuching Mosque) for Red Bridge, near the turn-off for Kubah, at regular intervals (RM2, 40 minutes); there's no set timetable, but services run roughly every 90 minutes in the morning. The bus will drop you off at Red Bridge, near the Jublee Mas Recreation Park, from where it's a 4km walk to the park entrance, quite a lot of it uphill. Note that at the time of research this bus was not operating and may not be operating during your visit. A taxi from town will cost at least RM75 return; arrange with the driver a time to be picked up.

Gunung Gading National Park

There is some good walking in this pleasant little **park** (☎ 082-735714; adult/child RM10/5; ⏰ 8am-12.30pm & 2-5pm), but most visitors come to see the rare *Rafflesia tuanmudae*. These massive flowers, blessed with a spectacular bouquet of rotting flesh, appear year-round, but at unpredictable times and in varying locations. Check whether any are in bloom by ringing the park headquarters before heading to the park.

To get to Gunung Gading, first take STC Bus EP07 from the Jln Penrissen Express Bus Terminal to Lundu (RM10, 1¼ hours, four daily). The park entrance is 2km north of Lundu, on the road to Pantai Pandan; you can either walk there or take a taxi (RM15) from the Lundu bus station. Vans also operate on this route (RM2), but they only leave when full.

BATANG REJANG

Carrying the mystic resonance of the exotic interior, the mighty Batang Rejang is Borneo's jugular, the main trade artery for all of central and southern Sarawak. But if it's an Amazonian tangle of jungle vines you're after, you'll be sorely disappointed. These days, the Rejang feels like a wide, muddy conveyor belt for the insatiable logging industry. Topsoil and logging detritus have been clogging the waters for years, and it's not a pretty sight. And let's not forget the bungled Bakun Dam hydroelectric plant, which has yet to be completed thanks to mismanagement, financial problems and the overambitious scale of the project.

It's not all bad, though – the serpentine tributaries splintering off the main river hide dozens upon dozens of remote longhouse communities. Visiting a longhouse offers travellers the unique opportunity to interact with the island's indigenous people, and it's an experience you won't soon forget (see p518).

Sibu

pop 255,000

While Kuching takes the cat as its mascot, it comes as no surprise that Sibu aspires to be a swan – the city is, after all, quite the ugly duckling. If you are from your nation's (or region's) second city, then you might have a soft spot for Sibu as you wander through the town's bustling markets. Locals are staunchly proud of their roaring burg despite the noticeable lack of attractions. Sibu is the gateway to the Rejang, and is home to a large Chinese population as evidenced by **Tua Pek Kong Temple** (Jln Temple; admission free; ⏰ dawn-dusk).

INFORMATION

Greatown Travel (☎ 084-211243, 0198565041; www.greatown.com; No 6, 1st Floor, Lorong Chew Siik Hiong 1A) Reliable inbound tour operator.

ibrowse Netcafé (☎ 084-310717; 4th fl, Wisma Sanyan, 1 Jln Sukan; per hr RM3; ⏰ 8am-10pm) Internet access.

Main post office (☎ 084-332312; Jln Kampung Nyabor; ⏰ 8am-4.30pm Mon-Fri, to 3pm Sat)

Rejang Medical Centre (☎ 084-330733; www.rejang.com.my; 29 Jln Pedada) A group of private specialist clinics with 24-hour emergency services.

Sibu General Hospital (☎ 084-343333; Jln Abdul Tunk Rahman)

Standard Chartered Bank (Jln Tukang Besi) Opposite the visitors information centre; changes travellers cheques and has an ATM. Be prepared to wait for the cheques to go through.

Visitors Information Centre (☎ 084-340980; 32 Jln Tukang Besi; ⏰ 8am-5pm Mon-Fri) Has friendly and informative staff (ask for Jessie) who can help with information about upriver trips out of Song, Kapit and Belaga. Has plenty of materials, including maps, bus schedules, and brochures on sights and travel to other destinations in Sarawak.

SLEEPING

Most of the budget lodging in Sibu is of a very low standard and this is a city where even budget travellers should opt for a midrange option if at all possible.

Li Hua Hotel (☎ 084-324000; Lg Lanang 1; r RM45-80; ❄) On the riverfront, about 100m south (upriver) of the Swan Statue, you will find Sibu's best-value hotel, with spotless tile-floor rooms and good views from the upper floors.

Victoria Inn (☎ 084-320099; 80 Jln Market; r RM50-85; ❄) If the Li Hua is full, this centrally located budget hotel is a good choice. It's a tightly packed warren of rooms about a block away from the high-rise Tanahmas Hotel.

Medan Hotel (☎ 084-216161; Jln Pahlawan, Jaya Li Hua; s/d RM65/75) For those needing to stay near the Sibu bus terminal, prim and proper Medan will do the trick.

EATING

Sibu is a great spot for local eats. Try *kam pua mee,* the city's signature dish, which is thin noodle strands soaked in pork fat and served with a side of roast pork. Check out www.sibu.sarawakfoodguide.com for the most up-to-date info on where to eat in town.

Café Café (☎ 084-328101; 10 Jln Chiew Geok Lin; mains from RM3; 🕑 10am-10pm) Tucked down the street in the shadow of the towering pagoda, this local hotspot puts a modern spin on the traditional *kedai kopi*. Excellent local fare (and a smattering of designer coffee beverages) is served up amid bodacious decor and flickering candles.

Le Ark Café (☎ 084-321813; Rejang Esplande; mains from RM8; 🕑 lunch & dinner daily, breakfast Sat-Sun) Undoubtedly the trendiest spot in town, Le Ark sits along the waterfront like a beached boat, serving up a variety of cocktails to trendier types who laze on the comfy patio seating. A selection of local and international eats is available as well.

New Capital Restaurant (☎ 084-326066; Jln Kampong Nyabor; meals per person around RM25; 🕑 lunch & dinner) If you feel like a splurge, this brilliant Chinese eatery is sure to satisfy, with excellent fresh fish, meat and vegetable dishes. We recommend the butter prawns and stir-fried *midin* washed down with a fresh fruit juice.

For Chinese and Malay snacks, try the evening food stalls that set up in the late afternoon along Jln Market. You'll also find several stalls on the 1st floor of PSS (Pasar Sentral Sibu).

GETTING THERE & AROUND

Air

Malaysia Airlines (☎ 1300 883 000; www.malaysiaairlines.com.my) has several flights daily from Sibu to Kuching, Miri, Kota Kinabalu and Kuala Lumpur. **Air Asia** (☎ 1300 889 933; www.airasia.com) has dirt-cheap flights to/from Kuala Lumpur, Johor Bahru and Kuching.

Boat

If you are heading to Sibu from Kuching, check the local newspaper for the most up-to-date speedboat departure times (times to Kapit are published as well). Boats leave from the River Express Terminal at the western end of Jln Bengkel (which is at the southwestern end of town). There is one boat per day at around 11.30am (RM35).

Getting to Kapit is the first leg of the journey up Batang Rejang. Several boats motor the 140km from Sibu to Kapit (RM17 to RM30, three hours, departures between 5.30am and 1pm).

Bus

Bus companies have ticket stalls at the long-distance bus station (Sungai Antu) and around the local bus station on the waterfront. Buses run between the long-distance bus station and Sibu's downtown all day for RM1. A taxi to/from town will cost RM10.

Buses run between Sibu and Kuching (RM40, eight hours, regular departures between 6.30am and 10pm), Miri (RM40, 7½ hours, roughly hourly from 6am to 10pm) and Bintulu (RM20, 3½ hours, roughly hourly from 5.30am to 6pm).

Kapit

pop 19,500

After a three-hour journey in what feels like a cramped space shuttle, you'll arrive in the *kapit*al of the mighty, murky Batang Rejang. It's not much to look at, but after a few hours you'll quickly discover that this far-flung trading centre is an important commerce hub for the smattering of longhouses hidden in the nearby jungle. Have a wander through the lively fresh markets and sample savoury jungle ferns. We recommend organising your longhouse visits from Kapit rather than Belaga as there is a wider variety of river systems from which to choose. Ask at the visitor information centres in either Sibu or Kuching for an updated list of authorised tour providers in the area.

It's important to take note that there's an antiquated permit system in place for those wishing to travel from Kapit and Belaga. However, we've never heard of any authority

THE BORNEO LONGHOUSE

Longhouses are the traditional dwellings of the indigenous people of Borneo and the island's most distinctive feature of tribal life. These large communal dwellings, raised on stilts above the forest floor, can contain over a hundred individual family 'apartments' beneath one long, long roof. The most important part of a longhouse is the covered common verandah, which serves as a social area, 'town hall' and sleeping space.

The longhouse lifestyle is by no means a forgotten tradition in Borneo, even in the face of globalisation. Community living is a very sustainable way of life – most youngsters that leave for greener pastures (read: more money) usually keep close ties to their village and return home later on in life. Over time, some longhouse communities have upgraded their building materials from thatch and bamboo to wood and linoleum. But don't let the errant satellite antenna betray your wild Kipling-esque fantasies; a trip to a longhouse is a must for anyone who wants to know the real Borneo.

Planning a Visit

You may be initially surprised to discover that longhouse visits can be a pricey venture. Tours are not cheap, and if you go on your own you'll need to pay for a boat and/or 4WD (figure RM300 to RM800), a guide (RM80 per day, plus RM35 per night), and lodging (usually RM10 per night).

There are two essential ingredients in organising a memorable longhouse visit: finding an excellent guide and choosing the right longhouse (the latter is always a function of the former). A great guide or tour company has a clutch of longhouse options and will always be receptive to the type of experience you desire. When searching for a tour operator or freelance guide, it is best to keep an open mind – after all, they are the experts – but do not hesitate to be upfront about your desires and concerns.

Scouting a tour locally is significantly cheaper than any pre-departure booking on the internet, and it's well worth spending a day checking out your options. If you want to assemble your own trip, the Sarawak Tourism Board publishes a yearly 'Members Directory' listing all registered freelance guides and their contact information. Membership can be expensive and some of the best guides opt to work for tour operators rather than renewing their freelancer's licence. Unregistered freelance guides may be friendly and knowledgeable, but they cannot be held accountable if something goes wrong during your trip.

We cannot overstress the importance of doing your research and finding a great guide. Yes, you could potentially head upriver on your own, but you'll still need to find someone to take you to a longhouse. An invitation is essential, and turning up unannounced is not only bad manners, it can also be a major cultural faux pas. Even if you make your way into a longhouse without a guide, you will find major communication and cultural barriers. Interacting spontaneously with locals isn't always easy as the elders usually don't speak English, and the younger people are often out working the fields or have moved to the big city to earn more money. A great guide usually knows several people at the longhouse (including the chief) and can act as a translator while you try to strike up a conversation. Your guide will always keep you abreast of any cultural differences – like when and where to take off your shoes – so you needn't worry too much about saying or doing the wrong thing.

actually checking these permits, especially since, strangely, a permit is not required for travel in the other direction. The permit office is located in an ultra-modern building called **Resident's Office** (8am-5pm Mon-Fri, closed for lunch) on Jln Airport, past the old airport on the west side of town. It takes about 15 minutes walking in each direction. There are plenty of banks and ATMs around town; if you're looking for wireless internet, ask around for 'wi-five'.

SLEEPING & EATING

For accommodation, try **Kapit River View Inn** (084-796310; krvinn@tm.net.my; 10 Jln Tan Sit Leong; s & d RM55-60;) or **Greenland Inn** (084-796388; 463-464 Jln Teo Chow Beng; s/d RM80/90;). Kapit is packed with small restaurants and *kedai kopi*, but the best place to eat in the evening has to be the busy **Taman Selera Empura** (dishes RM0.50-3.50), which is near the centre of town, roughly behind Ing Hing Cold Storage. In contrast

Visiting the Longhouse

When you arrive at a longhouse, you may be surprised to find that it's quite modernised, with satellite TV, electric lighting, corrugated iron and other upgrades – after all, even if their manner of living is old-fashioned, the people here are living in the 21st century. A longhouse is a way of life, not just a building. It embodies a communal lifestyle and a very real sense of mutual reliance and responsibility, and it is this spirit rather than the physical building that makes a visit special. Do your best to engage with the inhabitants of any community you are allowed to enter, rather than just wandering around snapping photographs.

Depending on the various goings-on at the longhouse, you may or may not spend time with the *tuai rumah* (chief) – although he (it's always a he) will usually 'show face' as it is impolite for him not to do so. Your guide will usually be the one showing you where to sleep – either on the verandah, in a specially built hut next door, or in a resident's living room within the longhouse itself.

If you are travelling with your own guide, he or she will be in charge of organising your meals – whether it's a separately prepared repast, or a feast with some of the longhouse residents. The Iban in particular like to honour their guests by offering meat on special occasions. Vegetarians and vegans should be adamant about their dietary restrictions as vegetable dishes are often served in a chicken sauce. Meals will be plentiful no matter what, and it is not considered rude or disrespectful to bring your own food. Two important things to remember when eating with longhouse residents: don't put your feet near the food (which is always served in a family-style communal fashion) and don't step over anyone's plate if you need to excuse yourself from the eating area.

After dinner, when the generators start clicking off, it's time hunker down with the evening's bottle of milky white broth: rice wine, or *tuak*. You'll be a big hit if you bring a bottle of brand-name liquor – 'Johnny Walker' and 'Southern Comfort' are oftentimes the extent of the locals' English vocabulary. The ceremonial shot glass will be passed from person to person amid chitchat and belly laughter. Drink the shot when it's your turn (you won't really have a choice – those Iban women can be pretty forceful!) and pass the glass along. *Tuak* may taste mild but it is pretty potent stuff, and you can expect a stunning hangover the next day. When you reach your limit, simply press the rim of the glass with your finger like you're pushing an eject button. If that doesn't work then feign a sudden medical condition. Smiles, big hand gestures and dirty jokes go a long way, even in your native language (and it'll all be second nature when you're nice and lubricated!).

Gifts

Gift giving has become rather controversial over the last few years, with locals, tourists and tour operators offering a wide variety of advice on the subject. Longhouse communities do not traditionally require gifts from guests; in fact, some say that the tradition of gift giving actually began when travellers started visiting. Your best bet to avoid any awkward cultural miscommunications is to ask your guide for their opinion. Some travellers bring an item that can be shared over glasses of rice wine. Any way you do it, gifts are never a must, nor are they expected. Many tourists prefer contributing to the longhouse economy by taking a local longboat trip or buying one of the handicrafts for sale.

to the rest of Kapit's dining scene, which is overwhelmingly Chinese, this market is almost exclusively Malay-Muslim. As such the emphasis is on satay and other halal dishes.

GETTING THERE & AWAY

Express boats leave for Sibu between 6.30am and 2.30pm (for information on boats from Sibu, see p517). The trip takes three hours and tickets are RM20 for economy, or RM25 to RM30 for 1st class. Boats depart for Belaga (RM30, five to six hours) at 9am. When the river is low, express boats can't get past the Pelagus Rapids, and smaller speedboats are used instead. Fares start at RM50. Express boats bound for the Batang Baleh depart before noon and go as far as Rumah Penghilu Jambi (RM30, four to five hours), an Iban longhouse. The last boat back to Kapit departs Rumah Penghilu Jambi at 12.30pm.

Belaga

pop 2500

By the time you pull into Belaga after the long journey up the Rejang, you may feel like you've arrived at the very heart of Borneo – in reality you're only about 100km from the coastal city of Bintulu (as the crow flies). Despite this, Belaga certainly feels remote. It's the main bazaar and administrative centre along the upper Rejang.

The main reason that tourists visit Belaga is to venture deep into the jungle in search of hidden longhouses and secreted waterfalls. But before you can share shots of rice wine with smiling locals, you have to find a tour guide. Unfortunately, we have received a lot of reports from unhappy travellers stating that there are several fraudulent operations in town. The Sarawak Tourism Board encourages tourists to use licensed guides, as only a licensed operator can be accountable for any wrongdoings. In Belaga, the most common form of fraud is overcharging. Try tracking down **Hamdani** (☎ 019 886 5770) or **Hasbie** (☎ 084-461240) to organise your tours.

SLEEPING & EATING

Belaga's accommodation is of the cheap and cheerful variety, but if you're doing the longhouse circuit you shouldn't really need to sleep here for more than a night or two. Try **Belaga B&B** (☎ 086-461512; Lot 168, No. 2b, Jln Penghulu Hang Nypia; r RM22-28), affiliated with Sarawak Tourism, or **Hotel Belaga** (☎ 084-461244; 14 Main Bazaar; r RM30-60; ❄), whose convenient location makes up for less than perfect standards.

GETTING THERE & AWAY

Returning to Kapit from Belaga, express boats leave Belaga early (between 6am and 6.30am), from where you can catch onward boats downriver to Sibu. Boats go upriver from Belaga as far as the Bakun Dam area near Rumah Apan (RM10, one hour), from where you can explore the resettled river country north of the Rejang. It's possible to do a loop back to Bintulu this way along a recently paved road (around RM60, 4½ hours in a 4WD van).

BINTULU

pop 180,000

The name Bintulu means 'place of gathered heads' in an ancient local dialect – the area was prime noggin-nabbing territory until the Brooke era. In 1861 James Brooke set up shop and stamped out the gruesome tradition in order to encourage foreign trade (see p509 for a brief history of headhunting in Borneo). Today, Bintulu is an undistinguished commercial centre servicing offshore oil and gas installations and upriver logging.

For tourists, Bintulu is nothing more than a transfer hub. If you need to spend the night, try **Kintown Inn** (☎ 086-333666; 93 Jln Keppel; r from RM70; ❄) – if you can spare a little bit of extra cash, it is a great choice.

Malaysia Airlines (☎ 1300 883 000, 331554; www.malaysiaairlines.com.my; Jln Masjid) flies between Bintulu and Kota Kinabalu, Kuching, Miri, Sibu and KL. **Air Asia** (☎ 1300 889 933; www.airasia.com) connects to Kuching. Bintulu airport is 24km west of the centre. A taxi there costs RM25. The long-distance bus station is 5km north of town. Travel between the two by local bus or taxi (RM8). There are frequent daily services between Bintulu and Kuching (RM60, 10 hours), Miri (RM20, 4½ hours) and Sibu (RM20, 3½ hours).

NIAH CAVES NATIONAL PARK

Near the coast about 115km south of Miri, this small national park (32 sq km) protects one of Borneo's gems, the **Niah Caves** (☎ 085-737454; adult/child RM10/5; ⌚ 8am-5pm). Alongside Gunung Mulu National Park, these caves must be the most famous natural attraction in Sarawak – not bad for a bunch of hollowed-out hills. The caves contain some of the oldest evidence of human habitation in Southeast Asia: rock art and small canoe-like coffins (death ships) within the greenish walls of the **Painted Cave** indicate that it was once a burial ground, and carbon dating places the oldest relics back 40,000 years.

A lovely Malay-style building, the **Niah Archaeology Museum** (admission free; ⌚ 9am-5pm) houses interesting displays on the geology, archaeology and ecology of the caves. It's in the park, just across the river from the park headquarters.

From the museum, a plank leads through the forest to the caves. It's 3.1km to the Great Cave (which lies beyond a limestone overhang called the **Traders' Cave**) and another 1.4km to the Painted Cave. The impressive **Great Cave** measures 250m across at the mouth and 60m at its greatest height. Since you approach the cave from an angle, its enormous size probably won't strike you straight away. It's usually only after descending the steep stairs into the bowels of the cavern for half an hour or so that visitors pause to look back at where they've come from. At any given time some 470,000 bats and four million swiftlets called the cave home. After following the walkway through the Great Cave, a short forest path emerges and leads to the Painted Cave. It's easy to miss the small fenced-off area by the cave entrance that protects the (now empty) death ships and the ancient paintings. A set of small travel binoculars are useful to make out the red hematite figures, as many have faded beyond recognition.

If you would like to stay at or near the caves, the best choice is the park accommodation.

Getting There & Away

Access to Batu Niah, the town nearest the caves, is by road only. At time of research, bus services to Batu Niah itself were suspended, with no indication of when they might reume Express buses on the coastal highway make a brief stop at the Batu Niah turn-off (RM10, two hours), 102km south of Miri, but you'll have to make your own way to the town itself, 13km west of the main road, and then get to the park headquarters.

Private cars often hang around the junction offering transport to Batu Niah and the park gate; the going rate is RM10, though it can be harder finding a lift on the way out. For convenience, though, you may be better off organising return-trip transport from Miri, especially if you're only coming for the day. At RM20 each way, unless you're on your own it should be no more expensive and much quicker than doing the journey in stages. Ask at **Highlands** (☎ 085-422327; 1271 Jln Dagang) or the **visitors information centre** (☎ 085-434181; vic-miri@sarawaktourism.com; 452 Jln Melayu; ⏲ 8am-6pm Mon-Fri, 9am-3pm Sat & Sun), both in Miri. Coming from Bintulu, you can also charter a minivan or private vehicle, but this could cost around RM100 per car each way, which is hardly viable without a group.

Getting Around

Transport to the park headquarters from Batu Niah is usually by taxi or boat. A short but exhilarating journey past jungle-clad limestone cliffs, the boat trip costs RM10, plus RM2 per person for more than five people. Taxis also cost RM10. Boats do most of their business in the morning; in the afternoon it's usually quicker to get a taxi, a few of which are always waiting next to the bus stand.

MIRI

pop 269,380

It's funny, the closer one gets to the Bruneian border, the more one notices shady characters coming out of the woodwork. Is it the repressed Bruneians stepping over the border for some afternoon delight, or is it the oil-loving expats who fill up suburban communities with their country club accommodation? (We're pretty sure it's the latter…) Either way, Miri's memorable cast of characters gives the city an interesting border-town vibe, despite its size and population. Perhaps it's because Miri is the gateway to a variety of Borneo's oft-travelled destinations. Tourists pass through here in order to reach Gunung Mulu National Park, the Kelabit Highlands and, for some, the Niah Caves. If you're hanging around for a couple of days, check out the Central Market, the **Tamu Muhibbah**, where local Dayak come to sell their vegetables, **San Ching Tian temple**, the largest Taoist temple in Southeast Asia, and **Lambir Hills National Park** (☎ 085-491030; admission RM10; ⏲ park office 8am-5pm, last entry 4pm), a slice of primary rainforest 30km south of town.

Information

Cyber Corner (1st fl, Wisma Pelita, Jln Padang; per hr RM3)
Main post office (☎ 085-441222; Jln Post)
Maybank Bureau de Change (☎ 085-438467; 1271 Centre Point Commercial Centre; ⏲ 9am-5pm) Dedicated exchange and cash-advance facilities.
Miri City Medical Centre (☎ 085-426622; 918 Jln Hokkien) Private medical centre.
Miri General Hospital (☎ 085-420033; Jln Cayaha) South of town, off the Miri bypass.
Popular Book Store (☎ 085-439052; 2nd fl, Bintang Plaza, 1264 Jln Miri Pujut)
Tally Laundry Services (☎ 085-430322; Jln Merbau; ⏲ 8am-6pm)

TOURIST INFORMATION

The **visitors information centre** (☎ 085-434181; 452 Jln Melayu; ⏲ 8am-6pm Mon-Fri, 9am-3pm Sat & Sun) is at the southern end of the town centre. The helpful staff can provide city maps, transport schedules and information on accommodation and tours, and the centre also produces the useful free *Visitors' Guide to Miri*. You can book accommodation with the **National Parks & Wildlife office** (Sarawak Forestry Corporation;

(☎ 085-436637, 085-434184) here for Niah Caves, Lambir Hills and Similajau National Parks.

Sleeping & Eating

Minda Guesthouse (☎ 085-411422; www.mindaguesthouse.com; 1st/2nd fl Lot 637 Jln North Yu Seng; dm/tw RM20/RM25 per person) New to the budget scene, Minda is great value for money. The sundeck and bright common space sweeten the deal.

Highlands (☎ 085-422327, 016 809 0328; www.borneojungles.com; 1271 Jln Sri Dagang; dm/r RM25/50;) Highlands styles itself a 'budget tourist and travel information centre', and scores a bull's-eye on all counts. Look out for the affable owner, a Twin Otter pilot from New Zealand. If you're allergic to cats you might have to give this place a miss.

Dillenia (☎ 085-434204; dillenia.guesthouse@gmail.com; 846 Jln Sida; dm/s/d RM30/50/80;) Dillenia is a new backpacker option with eager-beaver management and fresh coats of paint on the walls.

our pick Summit Café (☎ 019 354 7306; Jln Melayu; mains from RM2; breakfast & lunch) Not to be confused with the Summit Café across from the Apollo, this spot, specialising in traditional Kelabit cuisine, is a 10-minute walk southwest of Mega Hotel in the Waterfront Area. If Bario isn't on your travel itinerary, then a meal here is a must. Try the colourful array of 'jungle food' – *canko manis* (forest ferns), minced tapioca and wild boar – served on leaves instead of plates. It's best to come for an early lunch, 'cause once the food runs out it closes!

Ming Café (cnr Jln North Yu Seng & Jln Merbau; dishes from RM3; lunch & dinner) Take your pick of Malay, Chinese, Indian and Western food at this ever-busy corner eating emporium. There's a good drink counter here serving fresh juices and signature tapioca teas.

Khan's Islamic Restaurant (229 Jln Maju; mains from RM4; breakfast, lunch & dinner) This simple canteen is one of Miri's best Indian eateries, whipping up tasty treats like mouth-watering tandoori chicken and *aloo gobi* (Indian potato-and-cauliflower dish), as well as the usual *roti canai*. It's opposite Mega Hotel.

Getting There & Away

AIR

Miri is the hub for flights to Gunung Mulu National Park and the Kelabit Highlands. **MASwings** (☎ 1300 883 000; www.maswings.com.my) has flights to both – see the respective destination coverage for more information. **Malaysia Airways** (www.malaysiaairlines.com.my), the umbrella company of MASwings, also flies to Bintulu, Kota Kinabalu, Kuching, Lawas, Limbang, Pulau Labuan and Sibu. Book flights to/from Bario and Mulu as far in advance as possible.

Air Asia (☎ 1300 889 933; www.airasia.com) has cheap flights between Miri and KL, Kuching, Kota Kinabalu and Johor Bahru.

BUS

Most buses operate from the long-distance bus terminal (also called local bus terminal) outside of town. Miri Transport Company Bus 33A runs there from the downtown bus terminal on Jln Melayu (RM1, 15 minutes). A taxi to the long-distance bus terminal costs around RM20. For travel information to Brunei, see p508. Buses go to Bintulu (RM20, 4½ hours), Sibu (RM40, 7½ hours) and Kuching (RM80, 15½ hours).

GUNUNG MULU NATIONAL PARK

Hey, remember on BBC's *Planet Earth* documentary when that poor cameraman had to wade through thick steaming mounds of bat shit? Well, they filmed that here in Mulu! The park's intricate systems of underground haunted houses are stuffed to the brim with braids of stalactites, armies of alien insects, and over two million bats plus their noxious piles of roach-ridden excrement. Even if you haven't seen the show, we're pretty sure you can imagine that seething mountain of bat dung – you'll love it, we promise.

It comes as no surprise that the park's yawning caverns had a cameo in this documentary of superlatives – these caves are some of the biggest on earth. In fact, several years ago a team of local explorers discovered the world's largest visitable chamber, the Sarawak Chamber, reputed to be the size of 16 football fields. If you want to score some cave action but don't want to do the dirty work, there are five 'show caves' featuring plankwalks and dim lighting. The star of the lot is **Deer Cave**, which contains one of the world's largest cave passages – over 2km in length and 174m in height. **Lang Cave** has countless jagged stalagmites and stalactites and some other strange formations. After visiting these caves your guide will take you to the 'bat observatory' viewing area with informal, amphitheatre-like seating facing the gaping mouth of Deer Cave. Between 5pm and 6.30pm an endless stream of bats (which kind of looks like a cartoon swarm of bees) emerges from the cave to search the jungle for tasty insects. A second tour features the not-to-be-missed **Cave of the Winds** and **Clearwater Cave**. The newly opened **Lagang Cave** rounds out the list. In between visits to the show caves, try the **Mulu Canopy Skywalk** (RM30), easily one of Borneo's best.

If you thought the caves were amazing, wait until you hit the trails! Mulu offers some of the best and most accessible jungle trekking in all of Borneo. The three main treks in the park are the **Headhunters Trail**, the routes to the **Pinnacles**, and the hike to the **Gunung Mulu** summit. An attempt at any of them will involve some expense (around RM610/RM470 per person for Headhunters/Pinnacles when travelling in twos), so it's best to form a group with other travellers to reduce the cost of both transport and guide. All three trips are multiday affairs. Although only a fraction of visitors attempt these trails, it's best to book in advance as the park officials cap the number of daily hikers for conservation purposes.

Sleeping & Eating

Given Mulu's popularity and penchant for tour groups, you must book your accommodation in advance with **Mulu Park** (☎ 085-792300; www.mulupark.com). Park accommodation takes the form of a 21-bed **hostel** (dm RM40), which is a clean, spacious room sleeping both men and women. Hot showers and lockers are available. Comfortable private rooms are available as well, including simple Rainforest rooms (from RM110) and the charming Deluxe Longhouse rooms (from RM170). Camping is permitted at the park HQ for RM7.50 per night. See the website for images and additional info.

There are no cooking facilities in park accommodation. Simple but tasty meals are served at **Café Mulu** (the Canteen; meals RM10-15; breakfast, lunch & dinner) – try the Mulu laksa, it's a staff favourite. There are also a couple of low-key eating spots peppered around the main road back to the airport.

Getting There & Away

The most practical way to reach Gunung Mulu is by direct flight from Miri. **MASwings** (☎ 1300 883 000; www.maswings.com.my), a branch of Malaysia Airlines, operates two flights per day (usually in the morning) on either their Fokker 50- or 68-seater ATR aircraft. The flight takes approximately 30 minutes. It's possible to travel to Mulu from Miri by river, but it's a long, long journey and it actually costs more than flying.

BARIO & THE KELABIT HIGHLANDS

A land of sacred stones, of muddy longhouse pilgrimages, of wispy clouds thumbing thick greens like lazy fingers – the Kelabit Highlands is a faraway land indeed. Snuggled up against the Indonesian border like a sleeping leviathan, this kingdom of earth and sticks rests quietly under the rain as time tiptoes by oh-so slowly.

Bario, a gathering of wooden cabins and quaking rice paddies, is the region's largest community and the best place to base oneself for a visit to the region. Short day trips from Bario include **fishing**, **bird watching**, trekking to **Prayer Mountain** (two hours return), and visits to the nearby villages of **Pa' Umor** and **Pa' Ukat**. You can also hike up to **Bario Gap** (half-day return), a visible notch that was cut in the rainforest on a ridge above town to celebrate the millennium and 2000 years of Christianity. A variety of intriguing tribal **megaliths** are strewn throughout the quiet landscape – many are within a day's reach. Multiday treks are quite popular and can be tailored to one's interests and time constraints. A popular option is the three- to five-day trek known as the **Kelapang Loop** (the trail is actually more of an oar shape), which takes in three of the main longhouses south of Bario: Pa' Dalih, Ramadu and Pa' Mada. The three-day hike from Bario to Ba Kelalan is a good route for those who don't want to cover the same ground twice (you can arrange to fly out of Ba Kelalan).

There are no bank, ATM or credit-card facilities in the whole Kelabit Highlands. Travellers should bring plenty of small-denomination cash for accommodation, food and guides, plus some extra ringgit in case you get stranded.

Sleeping & Eating

Little Bario is a great place to base yourself during a visit to the highlands. There are several cosy options – most offering bed-and-board services for a flat per-person rate. You don't need to book ahead in Bario – internet connections are limited and tourist traffic isn't exactly bustling. Check out www.ebario.com for more information about accommodation.

Labang's Longhouse (ncbario@yahoo.com; r per person RM20, with 2/3 meals RM43/58) A friendly place owned by a retired Sarawak Forestry employee, this longhouse-style establishment offers prim twin-bed rooms and plenty of comfy common space decked with posters, world flags and cowboy hats. It's a great place for large groups.

Bariew Backpackers Lodge (☎ 014 892 3431, 019 859 0937; bariewlodge@yahoo.com; r RM20, full-board packages RM65-70) The quietly affable Raddish runs this excellent family-run guest house near the centre of Bario. He knows everyone in town and has an intimate knowledge of the trails and longhouses scattered throughout the highlands – his large collection of hand-drawn maps are regularly updated to reflect the region's changing geography. Rooms are simple but well kept – no need for fans as it is pleasantly cool in the evenings.

Jungle Blues Dream (☎ 019 884 9892; jungleblues dream@gmail.com; r & board per person RM60) Owned by local artist Stephen Baya and his lovely Danish wife, this lodge-cum-gallery is a fantastic place to call home during your Highlands visit. Rooms are lofted above the gallery and have subtle touches of Western comfort. Stephen's art hangs on all of the walls and guests are encouraged to leave an artistic message on a wooden plaque before departing.

Getting There & Away

The most practical way to reach the Kelabit Highlands is by direct flight between Miri and Bario. **MASwings** (☎ 1300 883 000; www.maswings .com.my) operates at least one flight per day (always in the morning) on its Twin Otter aircraft. Two weekly flights connect Miri to Ba Kelalan and Long Lellang. All flights take approximately one hour. Online bookings at the MASwings website can be temperamental (the site may incorrectly announce that a flight is full) so it is best to swing by its office in Miri. Planes are small and demand is high, so it's best to book as far in advance as possible.

Once in Bario, it's roughly a 30-minute walk into the central part of the village (turn left at the T-junction), although the chances are high that you'll be greeted like a celeb when you get off the plane. Local lodging operators often swing by to scoop up trekkers when the planes land.

It is also possible to reach Bario overland. The trip between Miri and Bario (RM900 per vehicle, four person maximum) takes more than a day, and passes several remote longhouses along the snaking network of logging roads.

LIMBANG DIVISION

Limbang

If you've only seen Limbang on the map, you may be in for a surprise when you rock up expecting a backwoods outpost and find a prosperous, bustling river town. Tourism is pretty much an irrelevance in these parts, so there are few reasons to stay over, but trekkers coming from the Headhunters' Trail might well appreciate an evening here to relax before hitting the road again.

Much better value than the budget fleapits in the centre of town, **Royal Park Hotel** (☎ 212155; Lot 1089 Jln Buagsiol; r from RM60; ❄) is worth the walk. From the town centre, walk north (downstream) 400m along the river. There are food stalls on the 1st floor of the waterfront market, at the bus station and along the river. Basic Malay food, roti and *murtabak* are served in halal cafes around the centre.

MASwings (☎ 1300 883 000; www.maswings.com.my) has flights to Miri. The airport is 4km south of the town centre, a RM10 taxi ride.

The express boat to Pulau Labuan in Sabah leaves at 8.30am daily (RM25, two hours). When sufficient passengers turn up (you may find yourself waiting quite a while) speedboats go to Lawas in Sarawak (RM25, one hour) and to Brunei; see p508 for more details. Boats leave from the jetty outside the immigration hall on the river, just upstream from the large pink building housing the market (Bengunan Tamu Limbang).

Lawas

Lawas is a transit point in the sliver of Sarawak pinched between Sabah and the Temburong district of Brunei. There is little of interest to travellers. **Hotel Perdana** (☎ 085-285888; Lot 365 Jln Punang; r from 46; ❄) is the best economy hotel in town, although it's a little frayed round the edges. **Malaysia Airlines** (☎ 1300 883 000; www.malay siaairlines.com.my) flies to/from Miri several times a week. The airport is 2km from town. A boat to Limbang (from RM28, one hour) leaves at 9am every day but Thursday. A boat to Labuan (from RM33, two hours) leaves at 7.30am every day except Tuesday and Thursday. Boats leave from the jetty on the west side of town, just downstream from the Shell petrol station. Buses head to Kota Kinabalu in Sabah (RM20) at 7am and 1pm daily.

MALAYSIA DIRECTORY

ACCOMMODATION

Accommodation in Malaysia costs slightly more than elsewhere in Southeast Asia. You'll pay more for a place to stay in Malaysian Borneo than in Peninsular Malaysia, and beach and island accommodation is generally more expensive than mainland digs. Note also that bed bug infestations are common in Malaysia.

The cheapest accommodation is found at hostels and guest houses (or backpackers) that cluster around tourist hot spots. These places often book tours and offer laundry services and transport.

A dorm bed costs anywhere from RM7 to RM35, fan-only rooms with a shared bathroom RM17 to RM50, and rooms with air-con and private bathroom RM40 to RM70. Bathrooms are often a hand-held shower with cold water above a toilet. Prices quoted throughout this chapter are for rooms with shared bathrooms unless otherwise stated.

In big cities most backpackers are in multistorey buildings, while at beaches and smaller towns accommodation ranges from A-frame chalets with a fan and private bathroom to rooms in a private house.

The cheapest hotels are Chinese-run and usually offer little more than simple rooms with a bed, a table and chair and a sink. The showers and toilets (which will sometimes be Asian squat-style) may be down the corridor. Note that couples can sometimes economise by asking for a single, since in Chinese-hotel language 'single' means one double bed, and 'double' means two beds. Don't think of this as being tight; in Chinese hotels you can pack as many into the room as you wish.

Budget hotels can sometimes be noisy as they're often on main streets and the walls rarely reach the ceiling – the top is simply meshed or barred in, which is great for ventilation but terrible for privacy.

Check-out times are usually 11am or noon for hostels and guest houses and from around noon until 3pm for hotels. Cheap Malaysian hotels generally quote a net price inclusive of the government tax (5%), but double-check before checking in.

Many of Malaysia's national parks have camping grounds, and permit camping at nondesignated sites once you are into the back country. There are also many lonely stretches of beach through Malaysia, particularly on the peninsula's east coast, which are ideal for camping. Likewise, it is possible to camp on uninhabited bays on many of Malaysia's islands.

Tourism Malaysia (www.tourismmalaysia.gov.my) and each of the state tourism bodies offer information about homestay programs operating throughout the country in off-the-beaten-track *kampung* (villages). Staying with a Malaysian family will give you a unique experience many times removed from the fast-paced life of the cities and towns.

In Borneo you can stay in longhouses, communal homes that are the traditional dwellings of the indigenous peoples of Borneo; these may contain up to 100 individual family 'apartments' under one long roof. These days there are two main types of longhouse: tourist longhouses and authentic longhouses. While a visit (or stay overnight) to a tourist longhouse is easy enough, it's unlikely to be of much interest. A visit to an authentic longhouse can be a magical experience, but is tricky to arrange and there's a very specific etiquette; see p518 for details.

ACTIVITIES

Caving

Malaysia's limestone hills are riddled with caves. Some are easily accessible and can be visited without any special equipment or preparation, while others are strictly for experienced spelunkers. There are caves on the peninsula and dotted around Malaysian Borneo, including one of the world's premier caving destinations: Gunung Mulu.

Climbing

Sabah's Mt Kinabalu is an obvious choice for those interested in mountain climbing, but it isn't the only Malaysian mountain worth climbing. Sarawak's Gunung Mulu is a challenging four-day climb, and on the peninsula there are overnight climbs in Taman Negara National Park.

Cycling

Malaysia's excellent roads make it one of the best places in Southeast Asia for bike touring. The most popular route heads up the east coast via relatively quiet, flat roads – Malaysian Borneo and the peninsular interior are more hilly while the west coast of the peninsula has more traffic. Rental bikes aren't usually of a high standard so it's best to bring your own. **MTB Asia** (www.mtbasia.com/Links/links1.htm) is a portal with links to several mountain-biking-related sites covering both Peninsular Malaysia and Borneo.

Diving & Snorkelling

Malaysia has many beautiful dive sites, decorated with shipwrecks, intricate coral formations and gloriously colourful marine life. Most dive centres charge around RM180 to RM250 for two dives, including equipment rental, and PADI open-water courses cost from RM800 to RM1000. Prime spots include Pulau Perhentian, Pulau Redang and Pulau Tioman, but the best site of all is the spectacular limestone abyss off Pulau Sipadan.

Surfing

Seasoned and wannabe surfers should head to Cherating (p477) and Juara on Pulau Tioman (p473). The main wave season is during the monsoon from November to February and the beach and point breaks are excellent for learning on.

Trekking

Mt Kinabalu (p497) is an obvious choice – and it's recently got a tad more challenging thanks to the addition of a *via ferrata* descent; see p499 for details.

Borneo's blockbuster is not the only mountain worth climbing in Malaysia. Sarawak's Gunung Mulu (p523) is a challenging four-day climb, while on the peninsula there are several good climbs in Taman Negara, including Gunung Tahan (p488), which stands at 2187m. There are also a few lesser peaks scattered around that make pleasant day outings.

BOOKS

Lonely Planet's *Malaysia, Singapore & Brunei* has all the information you'll need for extended travel to these countries while *Kuala Lumpur, Melaka & Penang* focuses on those three cities. Lonely Planet also publishes the *Malay Phrasebook*, an introduction to the Malay language.

Budding explorers should read *Stranger in the Forest*, Eric Hansen's account of a remarkable half-year journey across Borneo on foot, and Redmond O'Hanlon's marvellous *Into the Heart of Borneo*. Essential reading for anyone intending to do a lot of local mountain walking is *Mountains of Malaysia – A Practical Guide and Manual*, by John Briggs.

Ghost Train to the Eastern Star by the forever opinionated Paul Theroux sees the writer get laid low by a tummy bug in Penang. For an inside, modern view of the country read *Urban Odysseys*, edited by Janet Tay and Eric Forbes, which is a mixed bag of short stories set in Kuala Lumpur that capture the city's flavour.

BUSINESS HOURS

Banks are open from 10am to 3pm Monday to Friday, and 9.30am to 11.30am Saturday. Department stores open from 10am to 8pm. Government offices open 8am to 12.45pm and 2pm to 4.15pm Monday to Thursday, and 8am to 12.15pm and 2.45pm to 4.15pm Friday. Shopping malls are open from 10am to 9pm, while shops open 9am to 6pm Monday to Saturday.

In the more Islamic-minded states of Kedah, Perlis, Kelantan and Terengganu, government offices, banks and many shops close on Friday and on Saturday afternoon.

Exceptions to these hours are noted in individual reviews.

CLIMATE

Malaysia is hot and humid year-round. The temperature rarely drops below 20°C, even at night, and usually climbs to 30°C or higher during the day.

It rains throughout the year. Peninsular Malaysia gets heavier rainfall from September to March, with the east coast bearing the full brunt of the monsoon rains from November to February. Rainfall on the west coast peaks slightly during the May to October monsoon. Malaysian Borneo also gets the northeast and southwest monsoons, but they are less pronounced and rain tends to be variable.

See p936 for more information on Southeast Asia's climate.

CUSTOMS

When arriving in Malaysia, note that you are legally entitled to carry 1L of alcohol and 200 cigarettes. Cameras, portable radios, perfume, cosmetics and watches do not incur duty. Trafficking of illegal substances can result in the death penalty – don't do it.

DANGERS & ANNOYANCES

In general Malaysia is very safe, with violent attacks being uncommon. However, the usual travel precautions apply, such as restraining your urge to go wandering around seedy areas alone late at night. Credit-card fraud is a growing problem so only use your cards at established businesses and guard your credit-card numbers. The snatching of bags by thieves on motorcycles is a recurring crime in KL, Johor Bahru and Penang's Georgetown, so keep bags away from the roadside in these areas. In seedy areas such as Ipoh and KL's Golden Triangle, male travellers may be harassed to buy pirated porn DVDs, drugs or the services of prostitutes.

A disturbingly high incidence of theft occurs in guest house dorms. Sometimes this involves an outsider sneaking in and other times it involves fellow travellers. Don't leave valuables or important documents unattended, and carry a small padlock.

See p532 for issues specific to women travellers.

Rabies is an ever-present problem in Malaysia – you should treat any animal bite very seriously. Leeches can be a nuisance after heavy rain on jungle walks; see p487 for tips on discouraging them.

DRIVING LICENCE

A valid overseas driving licence is required for vehicle rental.

EMBASSIES & CONSULATES

Unless otherwise specified, all the following foreign embassies are in Kuala Lumpur and are generally open 8am to 12.30pm and 1.30pm to 4.30pm Monday to Friday.

Australia (Map pp440-1; ☎ 03-2146 5555; www.australia.org.my; 6 Jln Yap Kwan Seng)
Brunei (off Map pp440-1; ☎ 03-2161 2800; Level 19, Menara Tan & Tan, 207 Jln Tun Razak)
Canada (off Map pp440-1; ☎ 03-2718 3333; Level 18, Menara Tan & Tan, 207 Jln Tun Razak)
France (off Map pp440-1; ☎ 03-2053 5500; 196 Jln Ampang)
Germany (off Map pp440-1; ☎ 03-2142 9666; www.kuala-lumpur.diplo.de; Level 26, Menara Tan & Tan, 207 Jln Tun Razak)
Indonesia Georgetown (off Map p464; ☎ 04-227 5141; 467 Jln Burma, Georgetown, Penang); Kota Kinabalu (Map p493; ☎ 088-219110; Jln Kemajuan; 🕒 8am-1pm Mon-Fri); Kuala Lumpur (off Map pp440-1; ☎ 03-2116 4100; 233 Jln Tun Razak; visa R170, ready in one day); Kuching (Map p510; ☎ 082-241734; 111 Jln Tun Haji Openg, Kuching, Sarawak; 🕒 8.30am-noon & 2-4pm Mon-Fri); Tawau (☎ 089-772052; Jln Apas, Tawau, Sabah)
Ireland (off Map pp440-1; ☎ 03-2161 2963; Ireland House, the Amp Walk, 218 Jln Ampang)
Netherlands (off Map pp440-1; ☎ 03-2168 6200; www.netherlands.org.my; 7th fl, the Amp Walk, 218 Jln Ampang)
New Zealand (Map p444; ☎ 03-2078 2533; Level 21, Menara IMC, 8 Jln Sultan Ismail)
Singapore (off Map pp440-1; ☎ 03-2161 6277; 209 Jln Tun Razak)
Thailand Georgetown (off Map p464; ☎ 04-226 8029; 1 Jln Tunku Abdul Rahman, Georgetown, Penang); Kota Bharu (☎ 09-744 0867; 4426 Jln Pengkalan Chepa, Kota Bharu, Kelantan); Kuala Lumpur (off Map pp440-1; ☎ 03-2148 8222; 206 Jln Ampang)
UK (off Map pp440-1; ☎ 03-2148 2122; www.britain.org.my; 185 Jln Ampang)
US (off Map pp440-1; ☎ 03-2168 5000; http://malaysia.usembassy.gov; 376 Jln Tun Razak)

EMERGENCIES

Ambulance (☎ 999)
Fire (☎ 994)
Police (☎ 999)

FESTIVALS & EVENTS

There are many cultures and religions co-existing in Malaysia, which means there are many occasions for celebration throughout the year.

Ramadan is the major annual Muslim event, connected with the 30 days during which Muslims cannot eat, drink, smoke or have sex from sunrise to sunset. The dates of Ramadan change every year; in 2010 it begins on 11 August, and in 2011 it begins on 1 August.

January–February

Thaipusam (January/February) One of the most dramatic Hindu festivals, in which devotees honour Lord Subramaniam with acts of amazing physical resilience. Self-mutilating worshippers make the procession to the Batu Caves outside KL.

March–April

Malaysian Grand Prix Formula One's big outing in Southeast Asia is held at the Sepang International Circuit in Selangor either at the end of March or early April

May–June

Gawai Dayak (late May/early June) Festival of the Dayaks in Sarawak, marking the end of the rice season. War dances, cock fights and blowpipe events take place.

Festa de San Pedro Christian celebration on 29 June in honour of the patron saint of the fishing community; notably celebrated by the Eurasian-Portuguese community of Melaka.

July–August

Dragon Boat Festival (June to August) Celebrated in Penang.
Rainforest World Music Festival Held either in July or August for three days at the Sarawak Cultural Village (p515), this music and arts festival features musicians from around the world and highlights indigenous music from Borneo.
National Day (Hari Kebangsaan) Malaysia celebrates its independence on 31 August with events all over the country, but particularly in KL where there are parades and a variety of performances in the Lake Gardens.

September–October

Moon Cake Festival (September) Chinese festival celebrating the overthrow of Mongol warlords in ancient China with the eating of moon cakes and the lighting of colourful paper lanterns.
Festival of the Nine Emperor Gods (October) Involves nine days of Chinese operas, processions and other events honouring the nine emperor gods.

November

Deepavali (November) The Festival of Lights, in which tiny oil lamps are lit outside Hindu homes, celebrates Rama's victory over the demon King Ravana.

FOOD & DRINK

Food

Mealtime in Malaysia is a highly social event and the food strongly reflects the country's Malay, Chinese and Indian influences. You can feast at hawker stalls for RM1 to RM5. A meal in a low-end restaurant costs around RM4 to RM20.

There are fewer culinary choices outside the cities, where staple meals of *mee goreng* (fried noodles) and *nasi goreng* (fried rice) predominate. Vegetarian dishes are usually available at both Malay and Indian cafes, but are hardly sighted at *kedai kopi* (coffee shops). You can also find an excellent selection of fruits and vegetables at markets.

Roti canai (flaky flat bread dipped in a small amount of dhal and potato curry) is probably the cheapest meal (around RM1) in Malaysia. But really everything, from seafood laksa to the freshly caught and cooked wild cat or mouse deer you may be offered at a longhouse, is good and often cheap.

Halfway between a drink and a dessert is *ais kacang*, something similar to an old-fashioned snow-cone, except that the shaved ice is topped with syrups and condensed milk, and it's all piled on top of a foundation of beans and jellies (sometimes corn kernels). It sounds and looks gross but tastes terrific.

Drink

Tap water is safe to drink in many cities but check with locals if you're unsure.

With the aid of a blender and crushed ice, simple and delicious juice concoctions are whipped up in seconds. Lurid soybean drinks are sold at street stalls and soybean milk is also available in soft-drink bottles. Medicinal teas are a big hit with the health-conscious Chinese.

Alcohol isn't popular with the Muslim population and incurs incredibly high taxes. A mug of beer at a *kedai kopi* will cost around RM6, and around RM12 to RM15 at bars and clubs. Anchor and Tiger beers are popular, as are locally brewed Carlsberg and Guinness. Indigenous people have a soft spot for *tuak* (rice wine), which tends to revolt first-timers but is apparently an acquired taste. Another rural favourite is the dark-coloured spirit *arak*, which is smooth and potent.

GAY & LESBIAN TRAVELLERS

Conservative political parties and religious groups make a regular habit of denouncing gays and lesbians in Malaysia, a country where Muslim homosexuality is punishable by imprisonment and caning. Fortunately, these groups remain on the fringe and outright persecution of gays and lesbians in the country is rare. Nonetheless, while in Malaysia, gay and lesbian travellers (particularly the former) should avoid any behaviour that attracts unwanted attention. Visit www.utopia-asia.com or www.fridae.com, both of which provide good coverage of gay and lesbian events and activities right across Southeast Asia.

HOLIDAYS

Although some public holidays have a fixed annual date, Hindus, Muslims and Chinese follow a lunar calendar, which means the dates for many events vary each year.

Chinese New Year is the most important celebration for the Chinese community and is marked with dragon dances and street parades. The major holiday of the Muslim calendar, Hari Raya Puasa marks the end of the month-long fast of Ramadan with three days of joyful celebration. During Hari Raya Puasa and Chinese New Year, accommodation may be difficult to obtain. At these times, many businesses may also be closed and transport can be fully booked.

In addition to national public holidays, each state has its own holidays, usually associated with the sultan's birthday or a Muslim celebration.

National holidays:

New Year's Day 1 January
Chinese New Year January/February
Birth of the Prophet March
Wesak Day April/May
Labour Day 1 May
Agong's (King's) Birthday 1st Saturday in June
National Day 31 August
Hari Raya Puasa September/October
Deepavali November
Hari Raya Haji December
Awal Muharam December
Christmas Day 25 December

INTERNET ACCESS

Internet access is widespread and available at numerous internet cafes, backpacker hangouts and shopping malls, generally on fast broadband connections. In cities, rates range from RM2 to RM4 per hour; on islands and in remote areas, rates skyrocket (and speed plummets) to around RM6 to RM10 per hour. Wi-fi is easily found in cities, sparingly in medium-sized towns and often not at all in the countryside.

INTERNET RESOURCES

Lonely Planet (lonelyplanet.com) Succinct summaries on travelling to Southeast Asia, and the Thorn Tree bulletin board; plus the Travel Links site for other useful travel resources.
Malaysiakini (www.malaysiakini.com) Find out what's really going on in the country at Malaysia's best online news site.
Tourism Malaysia (www.tourismmalaysia.gov.my) The official government site for tourist information has events calendars, regional links, background information and listings of domestic and international tourist offices.

LEGAL MATTERS

In any of your dealings with the local police it pays to be deferential. Minor misdemeanours may be overlooked, but don't count on it and don't offer anyone a bribe.

It's simply not worth having anything to do with drugs in Malaysia: drug trafficking carries a mandatory death penalty, and even the possession of tiny amounts of drugs for personal use can bring about a lengthy jail sentence and a beating with the *rotan* (cane).

MAPS

Periplus (https://periplusPublishinggroup.com) has maps covering Malaysia, Peninsular Malaysia and KL. Tourism Malaysia's free *Map of Malaysia* has useful distance charts, facts about the country and inset maps of many of the major cities.

For accurate maps of rural areas contact the **National Survey & Mapping Department** (Map pp440-1; Ibu Pejabat Ukur & Pemetaan Malaysia; ☎ 03-2617 0800; www.jupem.gov.my; Jln Semarak, Kuala Lumpur; 🕑 7.30am-5.30pm Mon-Fri).

MEDIA

The government tightly controls the main media outlets, and will often pursue its critics through the courts. The main newspapers tend to parrot the official line and the less said about news on Malaysian TV channels, the better.

Newspapers

Malaysia has newspapers in English, Malay, Chinese and Tamil. The *New Straits Times* is the main English-language publication, while *Borneo Post* focuses more on issues relevant to Sabah and Sarawak. Foreign magazines are widely available.

Radio

There's a variety of radio stations in Malaysia broadcasting in Bahasa Malaysia, English and various Chinese and Indian languages and dialects. The number of English stations is highest around KL, while radio-wave pickings are scarce in Malaysian Borneo.

TV

Malaysia has two government TV channels (RTM 1 and 2) and two commercial stations. Programs range from local productions in various languages to Western imports.

MONEY

For information on basic costs, see Fast Facts (p429).

The Malaysian ringgit (RM) consists of 100 sen. Coins in use are one, five, 10, 20 and 50 sen, and RM1; notes come in RM1, RM2, RM5, RM10, RM50 and RM100. Locals sometimes refer to the ringgit as a 'dollar'.

Bargaining & Tipping

Bargaining is not usually required for everyday goods in Malaysia, but feel free to bargain when purchasing souvenirs, antiques and other tourist items, even when the prices are displayed. Transport prices are generally fixed, but negotiation is required for trishaws and taxis around town or for charter.

Tipping is not common in Malaysia.

Exchanging Money

The US dollar is the most convenient currency to take to Malaysia, but you'll have no problems changing other major currencies either.

Banks are efficient and there are plenty of money changers in the main centres. Credit cards are accepted at midrange to high-end restaurants and lodgings, and many ATMs accept international key cards, Visa and MasterCard. Some banks are also connected to networks such as Cirrus, Maestro and Plus.

EXCHANGE RATES

Exchange rates at the time of press:

Country	Unit	Ringgit (RM)
Australia	A$1	3.06
Brunei	B$1	2.46
Canada	C$1	3.23
Euro zone	€1	5.06
Indonesia	10,000Rp	3.51
Japan	¥100	3.85
New Zealand	NZ$1	2.50
Philippines	P100	7.33
Singapore	S$1	2.46
Thailand	10B	1.03
UK	UK£1	5.52
USA	US$1	3.46

POST

There are poste restante services at all major post offices, which are open from 8am to 5pm daily except Sundays and public holidays (also closed on Fridays in Kedah, Kelantan and Terengganu districts).

Aerograms and postcards cost 50 sen to send to any destination. Letters weighing 20g or less cost 90 sen to Asia, RM1.40 to Australia or New Zealand, RM1.50 to the UK and Europe, and RM1.80 to North America.

You can send parcels from any major post office, although the rates are fairly high (from RM20 to RM60 for a 1kg parcel, depending on the destination).

RESPONSIBLE TRAVEL

Malaysia has a serious rubbish problem, so try to create as little waste as possible by avoiding packaged drinks and eating locally grown food; if possible, bring your own water filter to avoid buying water in plastic bottles. When diving and snorkelling never touch or walk on coral and avoid tour operators who practise poor ecological habits such as dropping anchor on coral. Try to buy local handicrafts and souvenirs in preference to mass-produced items, so that the money goes back to local communities. It might seem obvious, but never buy butterflies or any products made from endangered species.

STUDYING

Kota Bharu and Cherating are the best places to get a hands-on feel for batik, while Kuala Lumpur is the place to study Bahasa Malaysia. Cooking courses are occasionally offered in Kuala Lumpur and Penang.

Ask at local tourist offices to see what's on offer when you're in town.

TELEPHONE

If you have your mobile phone with you, once you've sorted out a local SIM you should have no problem dialling overseas. Otherwise our advice is to buy a cheap local mobile phone to avoid the frustration of having to deal with the neglected and run-down public phone system.

If you're sticking to Peninsula Malaysia any of the major mobile phone service providers are fine, but if you're heading into the remoter parts of Malaysian Borneo then get **Celcom** (www.celcom.com.my), which has the largest coverage; numbers begin with 013 or 019. Rates for a local call are around 40 sen per minute and an SMS is 10 to 15 sen. Top-up cards for prepaid SIM cards are available at all 7-Elevens and, if you're planning on calling overseas a lot, it's probably worthwhile getting a calling card too; a good one is TM's **iTalk** (www.i-tal k.com.my).

International direct dial (IDD) phone calls and operator-assisted calls can be made from any private phone. The access code for making international calls to most countries is ☎ 00. For information on international calls, dial ☎ 103.

To make an IDD call from a pay phone, look for a Telekom pay phone marked 'international' (with which you can use coins or Telekom phonecards; dial the international access code and then the number). However, these phones are often in disrepair and frustratingly difficult to find.

The third option is to go to a TM office, where you can make IDD or operator-assisted international calls.

To call Malaysia from outside the country, dial ☎ 60, drop the 0 before the Malaysian area code, then dial the number you want.

TOILETS

Although there are still some places with Asian squat-style toilets in Malaysia, you'll most often find Western-style ones these days. At public facilities toilet paper is not usually provided. Instead, you will find a hose which you are supposed to use as a bidet or, in cheaper places, a bucket of water and a tap.

Public toilets in shopping malls and at transport depots are usually staffed by attendants and cost 10 sen to 30 sen to use; an extra 10 sen often gets you a dozen sheets of toilet paper.

TOURIST INFORMATION

Tourism Malaysia (www.tourismmalaysia.gov.my) has a network of overseas offices, which are useful for predeparture planning. Its domestic offices range from extremely helpful to hardly ever open, depending on the region. All stock some decent brochures as well as the excellent *Map of Malaysia*.

TRAVELLERS WITH DISABILITIES

For the mobility impaired, Malaysia can be a nightmare. In most cities and towns there are often no footpaths, kerbs are very high and pedestrian crossings are few and far between. Budget hotels almost never have lifts. On the upside, KL's modern urban railway lines are reasonably wheelchair-accessible.

Malaysia Airlines and Keretapi Tanah Melayu (the national railway service) offer 50% discounts for disabled travellers.

VISAS

Visitors must have a passport valid for at least six months beyond the date of entry into Malaysia. Nationals of most countries are given a 30- to 60-day visa on arrival. The following gives a brief overview of other requirements – full details of visa regulations are available on the website www.kln.gov.my.

Commonwealth citizens (except those from India, Bangladesh, Sri Lanka and Pakistan) and citizens of the Republic of Ireland, Switzerland, the Netherlands, San Marino and Liechtenstein do not require a visa to visit Malaysia.

Citizens of Austria, Belgium, the Czech Republic, Denmark, Finland, France, Germany, Hungary, Iceland, Italy, Japan, Luxembourg, Norway, Slovak Republic, South Korea, Sweden, the United States and most Arab countries do not require a visa for a visit not exceeding three months.

Citizens of Greece, South Africa and many South American and African countries do not require a visa for a visit not exceeding one month. Most other nationalities are given a shorter stay-period or require a visa.

Citizens of Israel cannot enter Malaysia.

Sarawak is semi-autonomous. If you travel from Peninsular Malaysia or Sabah into Sarawak, your passport will be checked on arrival and a new stay-permit issued, usually for 30 days. Travelling from either Sabah or Sarawak back to Peninsular Malaysia there are no formalities and you do not start a new entry

NOT STAMPED?

Some travellers report having problems when they leave Malaysia after having entered the country by train from Singapore – this is because the Malaysian immigration officials at Singapore's railway station, at the southern terminus of Malaysia's Keretapi Tanah Melayu (KTM), do not stamp your passport. This shouldn't be a problem as long as you keep your immigration card and your train ticket to show how you entered the country. Your information should be in the computer records.

period, so your 30-day permit from Sabah or Sarawak remains valid. You can then extend your initial 30-day permit, though it can be difficult to get an extension in Sarawak.

VOLUNTEERING

Opportunities include the following:

LASSie (www.langkawilassie.org.my) Dog and cat lovers may want to help out at the Langkawi Animal Shelter & Sanctuary Foundation, next to Bon Ton Resort.

Ma Daerah turtle sanctuary (http://madaerah.org) About 70km south of Terengganu, you can help work to protect turtle populations along the east coast.

Malaysian AIDS Council (www.mac.org.my) Assist in its campaigning work.

Miso Walai homestay program (http://misowalaihomestay.com) Gets travellers involved with local wetlands restoration projects.

Regional Environmental Awareness Cameron Highlands (Reach; www.reach.org.my) Take part in reforestation and recycling programs in the Cameron Highlands.

Sepilok Orang-utan Centre (p502) Has one of the best established volunteer centres.

Wild Asia (www.wildasia.net) Options are generally connected with the environment and sustainable tourism in the region.

WOMEN TRAVELLERS

Foreign women travelling in Malaysia can expect some attention, though most of it will just involve stares from locals unfamiliar with (or curious about) Westerners. It helps, and is much more respectful of the culture, if you dress conservatively by wearing long pants or skirts and loose tops that cover the shoulders. Western women are not expected to cover their heads with scarves (outside mosques, that is). In resort areas you can wear shorts, sleeveless tops and swimwear, but it isn't appropriate anywhere in the country to sunbathe topless. On more remote beaches you're better off doing like the locals do and swimming fully clothed. Keep a watch out for sleazy local beach boys in Langkawi, Cherating and the Perhentians.

Tampons and pads are widely available, especially in big cities, and over-the-counter medications are also fairly easy to find.

Myanmar (Burma)

HIGHLIGHTS

- **Bagan** (p581) Climb a quiet temple and witness the beauty of a misty dawn breaking over 4000 Buddhist temples on the plains of Bagan.
- **Inle Lake** (p565) Spend longer than you planned at this pristine lake, a mythical landscape of floating villages, stilted monasteries and aquatic gardens.
- **Around Mandalay** (p578) Burma's former capital is the gateway to the intriguing old cities of Amarapura, with its famed teak bridge, and some stupa-pendous views from Sagaing.
- **Yangon** (p544)The social, economic and cultural capital of the country, if no longer the political capital, Yangon is home to the dazzling Shwedagon Paya, where all that glitters is gold.
- **Kalaw** (p568) This is Myanmar's trekking HQ and the place to begin a walk through forested hills and fascinating, friendly minority villages to Inle Lake.
- **Kyaiktiyo** (p562) Test your mettle by making the full 11km uphill pilgrimage to this sacred and gravity-defying Golden Rock.
- **(Way) off the beaten track** (p588) Embrace the concept of journey as destination by taking a series of boats along the Ayeyarwady from Myitkyina to Mandalay.

FAST FACTS

- **Budget** US$15 to US$30 a day
- **Capital** officially Nay Pyi Taw, but to most people it's still Yangon
- **Costs** guest house US$4 to US$15, four-hour bus ride US$4 to US$6, big bottle of beer US$1.50
- **Country code** ☎ 95
- **Languages** Burmese, English
- **Money** US$1 = about K1050 (kyat)
- **Phrases** *min gala ba* (hello), *thwa-ba-oun-meh* (goodbye), *chè zù bèh* (thanks)
- **Population** about 55 million
- **Time** GMT + 6½ hours
- **Visas** around US$20 for 28 days, issued by Myanmar embassies and consulates abroad

TRAVEL HINT

Plastic doesn't work here so bring plenty of crisp, clean US dollar bills (see p597 for details). Bring books about Burma which, when they're read, become priceless gifts in a country so starved of intellectual perspective.

OVERLAND ROUTES

It is *possible* to enter Myanmar from Ruili in China, and from Mae Sai and Ranong in Thailand, but onward travel requires expensive permits that can be difficult or time-consuming to get. Few bother.

'This is Burma', wrote Rudyard Kipling. 'It is quite unlike any place you know about.' How right he was, and more than a century later Myanmar remains a world apart. To travel here is to encounter men wearing skirt-like *longyi,* women smothered in *thanaka* (traditional make-up) and betel-chewing grannies with blood-red juices dripping from their mouths – and that's just the airport! Contemplate 4000 sacred stupas scattered across the plains of Bagan. Stare in disbelief at the Golden Rock teetering impossibly on the edge of a chasm. Ride a Wild West stagecoach past grand British mansions. Meet the multitalented monks who have taught their cats to jump. Trade jokes about the rulers who move capitals on the whim of a fortune teller. Indeed, this is Burma.

Turn back the clock with a trip to this time-warped country where there's no such thing as 7-Eleven and the journey is often as interesting as the destination. Liberate yourself from your phone and connect instead with a culture where holy men are more revered than rock stars. Drift down the Ayeyarwady in an old river steamer, stake out a slice of beach on the blissful Bay of Bengal, trek through pine forests to minority villages around Kalaw, then start planning your next trip.

Isolated and ostracised by the international community, the country is in the grip of a repressive regime. Many travellers avoid a visit, backing the boycott. But the long-suffering people are everything the regime is not. Gentle, humorous, engaging, considerate, inquisitive and passionate, they want to play a part in the world, and to know what you make of their world. Yes, this is Burma – come with your mind open and you'll leave with your heart full.

CURRENT EVENTS

You wouldn't call it a standout couple of years for Myanmar. Things kicked off after the military regime suspended fuel subsidies in August 2007, sending the price of petrol skyrocketing. Monks took to the streets in an outpouring of popular protest and for a moment it looked like Myanmar might enjoy its own saffron revolution. But a brutal army crackdown and mass arrests ended all that. The international reaction was swift and strong, with the US applying even heavier economic sanctions. But its impact was muted by the silence of China and India, two of the regime's biggest backers, and the dollars that continue to flow from sales of gas to Thailand.

In the following year the generals paid lip service to the idea of political compromise. They posed for smiling photos with UN envoy Ibrahim Gambari and secretary general Ban Ki Moon, but still sent protest organisers away for 65-year stretches. In May 2008 things got much worse when Cyclone Nargis decimated the Ayeyarwady Delta and battered Yangon, leaving more than 138,000 dead (see p557 for details). It was one of the deadliest storms in history and was followed by months of misery for millions of people. Just a week after the cyclone hit, the generals stuck rigidly to their 'seven-step political roadmap to democracy' by conducting a referendum on a new constitution most people had never heard of, let alone seen. It was passed in a landslide; national elections were announced for 2010.

Details, however, were sketchy. At the time of research the elections were the subject of much (hushed) discussion. People wanted to know who would be allowed to run? How the 'parliament' would work? And what would happen to the generals? The answers were pure speculation, but the gist of opinion could be summed up by the man who told us 'Same rulers, different uniforms'.

Aung San Suu Kyi, the woman who won the last elections in 1990 but has spent most of the time since imprisoned in her Yangon home, was thrust back into the headlines when American John Yettaw swam across Inya Lake to see her. After spending a night he was arrested as he swam back, and Suu Kyi was charged with illegally having a foreigner stay overnight in her home. For her crimes she was handed a three-year prison sentence, which was then commuted to another 18 months of house arrest by regime leader Than Shwe. Any hopes she had of participating in some way in the 2010 elections were killed.

HISTORY

Myanmar was ruled with an iron fist long before the current regime came to power. From the early 19th century until WWII, the British Empire held sway over Burma. Before the British, there were the kings of old, who rose to power by eliminating rivals with claims to the throne. Tracing the conflicts back to the 9th century, we find the Himalayan Bamar people, who comprise two-thirds of the population,

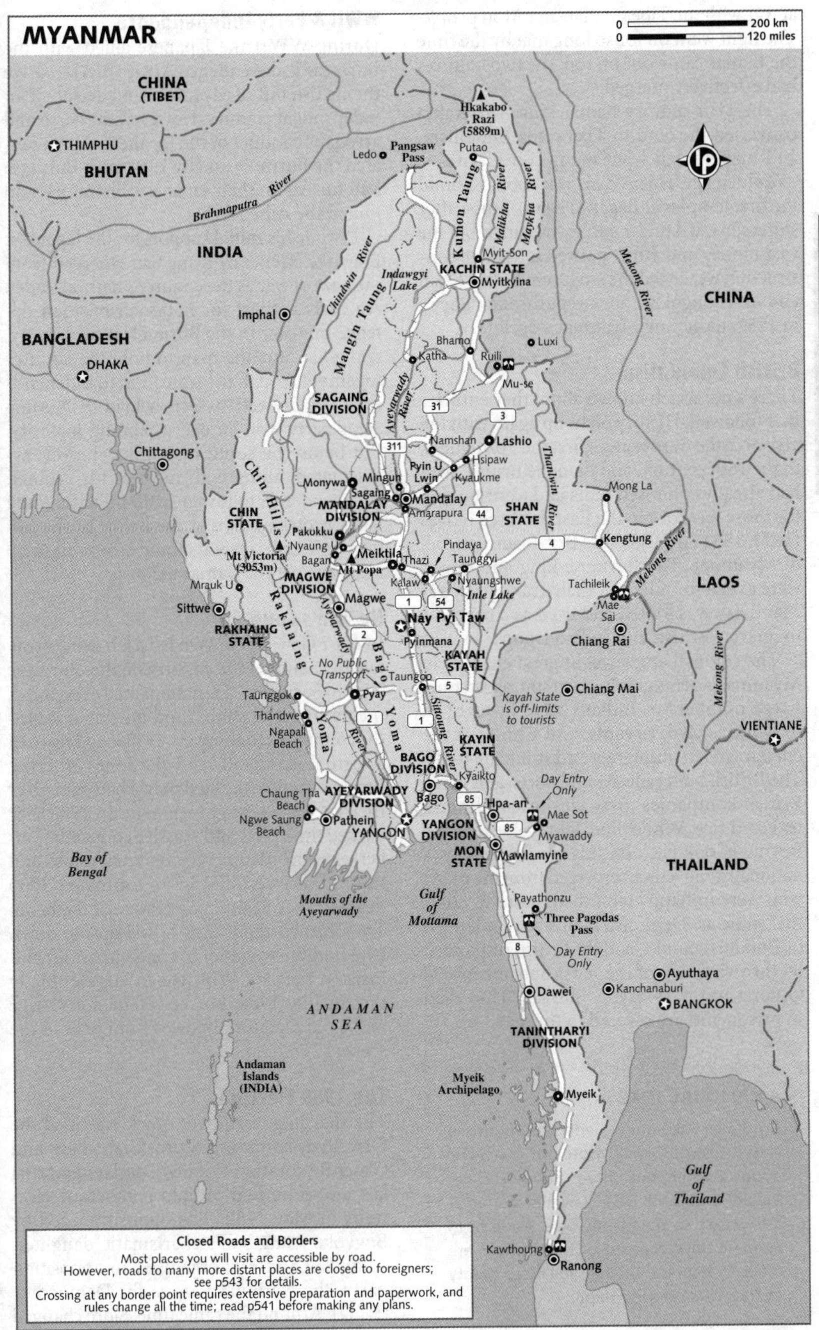
MYANMAR
CHINA (TIBET)
THIMPHU
BHUTAN
INDIA
BANGLADESH
DHAKA
Chittagong
Imphal
Ledo
Pangsaw Pass
Hkakabo Razi (5889m)
Putao
KACHIN STATE
Myitkyina
Myit-Son
CHINA
Luxi
Bhamo
Katha
Ruili
Mu-se
SAGAING DIVISION
Namshan
Lashio
Hsipaw
Kyaukme
Pyin U Lwin
Monywa
Mingun
Sagaing
Mandalay
Amarapura
MANDALAY DIVISION
CHIN STATE
SHAN STATE
Mong La
Kengtung
Tachileik
Mae Sai
Chiang Rai
LAOS
Pakokku
Nyaung U
Bagan
Mt Victoria (3053m)
Meiktila
Mt Popa
Thazi
Pindaya
Taunggyi
Kalaw
Nyaungshwe
Inle Lake
MAGWE DIVISION
Magwe
Mrauk U
Sittwe
RAKHAING STATE
Nay Pyi Taw
Pyinmana
KAYAH STATE
Kayah State is off-limits to tourists
Chiang Mai
VIENTIANE
No Public Transport
Taungoo
Taunggok
Pyay
Thandwe
Ngapali Beach
KAYIN STATE
BAGO DIVISION
Kyaikto
Bago
Day Entry Only
AYEYARWADY DIVISION
Chaung Tha Beach
Ngwe Saung Beach
Pathein
YANGON
YANGON DIVISION
Hpa-an
Mae Sot
Myawaddy
MON STATE
Mawlamyine
THAILAND
Bay of Bengal
Mouths of the Ayeyarwady
Gulf of Mottama
Payathonzu
Three Pagodas Pass
Day Entry Only
Ayuthaya
Kanchanaburi
BANGKOK
Dawei
ANDAMAN SEA
TANINTHARYI DIVISION
Andaman Islands (INDIA)
Myeik Archipelago
Myeik
Gulf of Thailand
Kawthoung
Ranong
Closed Roads and Borders
Most places you will visit are accessible by road.
However, roads to many more distant places are closed to foreigners; see p543 for details.
Crossing at any border point requires extensive preparation and paperwork, and rules change all the time; read p541 before making any plans.

at war with the Tibetan Plateau's Mon people. The fight went on for so long that by the time the Bamar came out on top, the two cultures had effectively merged.

The 11th-century Bamar king Anawrahta converted the land to Theravada Buddhism, and inaugurated what many consider to be its golden age. He used his war spoils to build the first temples at Bagan (Pagan). Stupa after stupa sprouted under successive kings, but the vast money and effort poured into their construction weakened the kingdom. Kublai Khan and his Mongol hordes swept through Bagan in 1287, hastening Myanmar's decline.

British Colonialism

There's not much known about the centuries that followed. History picks up again with the arrival of the Europeans – first the Portuguese, in the 16th century, and then the British, who had already colonised India and were looking for more territory in the East. In three moves (1824, 1852 and 1885) the British annexed all of Myanmar. The Burmese king and queen were exiled to India and their grand palace at Mandalay was looted and used as a barracks to quarter British and Indian troops.

The colonial era wrought great changes in Myanmar's demographics and infrastructure. Large numbers of Indians were brought in to work as civil servants, and Chinese were encouraged to immigrate and stimulate trade. The British built railways and ports, and many British companies grew wealthy trading in teak and rice. While hindsight has seen some Burmese look back on this era favourably, a nationalist movement emerged from the many who were unhappy with their status as colonial subjects. Demonstrations were often led by Buddhist monks, and the British responded by throwing two of the most outspoken – U Ottama and U Wizaya – into jail. They died in prison and are revered to this day.

A NATIONAL JOKE

A popular joke among educated Burmese is that George Orwell wrote not one novel about Burma, but three: *Burmese Days, Animal Farm* and *1984*. It would be funny if it wasn't so poignantly true. Aside from *Burmese Days,* the rest of these books are officially banned, though you'll see plenty of travellers carrying them.

WWII & Early Independence

During WWII the Japanese allied with the Burmese Independence Army (BIA) to drive the British out of Myanmar and declare it an independent country. However, the harsh and arrogant conduct of the Japanese soon alienated the Burmese and by 1944 most Burmese had turned on their Japanese 'liberators' and joined the Allied fight.

Despite his initial support for the Japanese, Bogyoke (General) Aung San emerged from the haze of war as the country's natural leader. An early activist for nationalism, then defence minister in the Burma National Army, Aung San was the man to hold the country together through the transition to independence. When elections were held in 1947, Aung San's party won an overwhelming majority. But before he could take office, he was assassinated, along with most of his cabinet. Independence followed in 1948, with Aung San's protégé U Nu at the helm. In the following decade several ethnic groups took up arms against the Bamar majority.

Ne Win's Coup

In 1962 General Ne Win led a left-wing army takeover and set the country on the 'Burmese Way to Socialism'. He nationalised everything, including retail shops, and quickly crippled the country's economy. By 1987 it had reached a virtual standstill, and the long-suffering Burmese people decided they'd had enough of their incompetent government. In 1988 they packed the streets and massive confrontations between pro-democracy demonstrators and the military resulted in an estimated 3000 deaths. Once again, monks were at the helm. They turned their alms bowls upside down (the Buddhist symbol of condemnation) and insisted that Ne Win had to go. He finally did, in July 1988, but he retained a vestige of his old dictatorial power from behind the scenes.

The 1989 Election

The shaken government quickly formed the Orwellian-sounding Slorc (State Law and Order Restoration Council), declared martial law and promised to hold democratic elections in May 1989. The opposition, led by Bogyoke Aung San's charismatic daughter, Aung San Suu Kyi, organised an opposition party, the National League for Democracy (NLD). Around the same time, Slorc changed

SHOULD YOU GO?

Lonely Planet believes anyone thinking of going to Myanmar must consider this complicated question before undertaking a trip.

Myanmar is ruled by an oppressive military regime. Some refugee and human-rights groups urge foreigners not to visit Myanmar, believing that tourism legitimises the government and contributes to its coffers. Others have reversed their stance in recent years. National League for Democracy (NLD) general secretary Aung San Suu Kyi urged outsiders to boycott Myanmar during the government's 'Visit Myanmar Year 1996' campaign, in which the forced labour of tens of thousands (maybe more) of Burmese was used to rebuild infrastructure and some sites such as Mandalay Palace. Suu Kyi asked visitors to 'visit us later', saying that visiting at the time was 'tantamount to condoning the regime'. The boycott worked; fewer than 200,000 tourists visited.

Much of the international criticism is directed towards package tourists, who spend the most money and stay in expensive joint-venture hotels that are often in cahoots with the government. Thai, Chinese and Japanese tourists are the main visitors, with Americans, Germans and French leading the way in the West. Tourism in all its forms brought in about US$100 million in 2007–08, possibly 12% of which went to the government. (This compares with more than US$2 billion in natural-gas exports to Thailand in 2007.) Obviously the less you spend, the less that 12% figure will be. A pro-NLD, pro-tourism Yangon resident told us, 'Don't come in with your camera and only take pictures. We don't need that kind of tourist. Talk to those who want to talk. Let them know of the conditions of your life.'

Tourism remains one of the few industries to which ordinary locals have access in terms of income and communication; the vast majority of locals seem to want you here. And there are plenty of other reasons to consider visiting. Human-rights abuses are less likely to occur in areas where the international community is present; keeping the people isolated from international witnesses to internal oppression may only cement the government's ability to rule. The government has stopped forcing foreigners to change US$200 into government notes upon arrival.

The boycott debate will rumble on, but right now, with oil and gas, minerals, heroin, timber and other resources to draw on, and with sanctions-busters such as China, India, Thailand and Singapore (which the locals describe as 'the generals' Switzerland') as close allies, tourism is pretty much loose change to the generals, but not to the people trying their hardest to survive.

If You Go

Here are a few ways to minimise the money that goes to the government:

- Avoid government-run hotels (often named after the city, eg Mrauk U Hotel) and stay instead in family-run guest houses. See p593 for more.
- Try to avoid government-run services: Myanmar Travel & Tours (MTT) is the government-operated travel agency and Myanma Airways is the government airline. Most buses are independent, while IWT ferries and trains are government-controlled. See p544 for more.
- Spread the wealth – don't take care of all your needs (food, beer, guides, taxi, toilet paper) at one source (eg a guest house).
- Buy handicrafts directly from artisans.
- Try to get off the beaten track a bit, including towns not covered in this book.
- Read about Myanmar – see p593 for some book suggestions. It's important to know about Ne Win's coup, the events of 1988 and Aung San Suu Kyi before coming.

About this Chapter

We believe travellers to Myanmar should support private tourist facilities wherever possible. We've not reviewed any restaurants, hotels or shops known to be government-run. We flag any government-run services.

Read Lonely Planet's expanded 'Should You Go?' coverage in the *Myanmar* guidebook or get the free download at www.lonelyplanet.com/worldguide/destinations/asia/myanmar (click on 'Show Full Overview').

the country's official name from the Union of Burma to the Union of Myanmar, claiming 'Burma' was a vestige of European colonialism.

While the Burmese people rallied around the NLD, the Slorc grew increasingly nervous. It placed Aung San Suu Kyi under house arrest and postponed the election. In spite of this and other dirty tactics, the NLD won more than 85% of the vote. Sore losers, Slorc refused to allow the NLD to assume its parliamentary seats and arrested most of the party leadership.

The Plight of Aung San Suu Kyi

Aung San Suu Kyi was awarded the Nobel Peace Prize in 1991 and was finally released from house arrest in July 1995. She was arrested again in 2000 and held in her home until the UN brokered her unconditional release in May 2002. She was rearrested in May 2003 and held under house arrest for almost six years, contravening Myanmar's own law that says no one can be held without trial for longer than five years. In May 2009, less than two weeks before her (latest) official release date, she was sent to the notorious Insein Prison after an uninvited American man stayed overnight in her home (see p534). The resulting international pressure was not enough to prevent her being locked up again. She is now due to be released in February 2011.

As we write, Aung San Suu Kyi has spent more than 14 of the past 20 years under arrest on dubious charges and convictions, if she was charged at all. Despite this, and the fact she could not be with her husband when he died of cancer and has not seen her children for years, she has repeatedly refused the regime's offers of freedom in exchange for exile. Not everyone in Myanmar and not even everyone within her party agrees completely with Suu Kyi, and you will rarely hear people speaking about her openly. But 'the Lady' remains an inspiration to many. For more on recent developments in Myanmar, see p534.

MUST READ

From the Land of Green Ghosts: A Burmese Odyssey (2002), by Pascal Khoo Thwe, is the tragic-yet-uplifting literary memoir of a Paduang tribesman escaping the post-1988 chaos to study literature at Cambridge.

THE CULTURE

The National Psyche

Although isolated, subjugated and poor, the Myanmar people are as proud of their country and culture as any nationality on earth. Locals gush over ancient kings, *pwe* (festivals), *mohinga* (noodles with chicken or fish) breakfasts, great temples and their religion. A typical Burmese Buddhist values meditation, gives alms freely and sees his or her lot as the consequence of sin or merit in a past life. The social ideal for most Burmese is a standard of behaviour commonly termed *bamahsan chin* (or 'Burmese-ness'). The hallmarks of *bamahsan chin* include showing respect for elders, acquaintance with Buddhist scriptures and discretion in behaviour towards the opposite sex. Most importantly, *bamahsan chin* values the quiet, subtle and indirect over the loud, obvious and direct.

Lifestyle

Outside the cities, families are generally big and several generations may share one roof. Electricity remains in short supply and even running water is uncommon in the countryside, where farming is the backbone of life. Visitors find it easy to engage with city folk, particularly the older generation, who often speak English well.

Beneath the smiles, life is one long struggle for survival for many in Myanmar, thanks in no small part to a government that governs in the interests of a small military elite and not the wider nation. Higher education is disrupted every time there's a hint of unrest, as the government shuts the universities. The banks are under government control, so savings can be (and have been – see the boxed text, p540) wiped out at the whim of the rulers. Nominally, Burmese people have relative economic freedom, but just about any business opportunity requires bribes or connections. The small elite has modern conveniences, good medical treatment, fancy, well-fortified homes and speedy cars. Peaceful political assembly is banned and citizens are forbidden to discuss politics with foreigners, although many relish doing so as long as they're sure potential informers aren't listening.

Population

Exactly how many people live in Myanmar is a mystery, given the last census was in 1983. All population numbers in this chapter are

> **DOS & DON'TS**
>
> - Don't touch anyone's head, as it's considered the spiritual pinnacle of the body.
> - Don't point feet at people if you can help it, and avoid stepping over people.
> - Burmese women don't ride atop pick-ups as it can be insulting to men beneath them.
> - Hand things – food, gifts, money – with your right hand, tucking your left under your right elbow.
> - Dress modestly when visiting religious sites – avoid above-the-knee shorts, tight clothes or sleeveless shirts.
> - Take off your shoes when entering temple precincts, usually including the long steps up to a hilltop pagoda.

guesstimates. There are 135 indigenous ethnic groups, of which the Bamar (or Burman, 68%) is the biggest and most dominant. Seven other groups – the Shan (9%), Kayin (or Karen, 7%), Rakhaing (4%), Mon (less than 3%), Kachin (less than 3%), Chin (less than 3%) and Kayah (1%) – each have their own state, private army (some groups have several of these) and means of raising cash, like opium production. The states get little money for infrastructure, and have been subject to years of heavy-handed policing and military offensives. The result is a population significantly poorer than your average Bamar (himself not exactly a millionaire, even in kyat).

There are large numbers of Indians and Chinese in Myanmar, but only a sprinkling of other foreigners and immigrants.

RELIGION

About 87% of Myanmar's citizens are Theravada Buddhists, but this is blended with a strong belief in *nat* (guardian spirit beings). Many hill tribes are Christian, and smaller Hindu and Muslim communities are dotted throughout the country.

For the average Burmese Buddhist much of life revolves around the merit (*kutho*, from the Pali *kusala*, meaning 'wholesome') one is able to accumulate through rituals and good deeds. One of the more common rituals performed by individuals visiting a stupa is to pour water over the Buddha image at their astrological post (determined by the day of the week they were born) – one glassful for every year of their current age plus one extra to ensure a long life.

Every Burmese male is expected to take up temporary monastic residence twice in his life: once as a *samanera* (novice monk), between the ages of five and 15, and again as a *pongyi* (fully ordained monk), some time after the age of 20. Almost all men or boys under 20 years of age participate in the *shinpyu* (initiation ceremony), through which their family earns great merit.

While there is little social expectation that they should do so, a number of women live monastic lives as *dasasila* ('ten-precept' nuns). Burmese nuns shave their heads, wear pink robes and take vows in an ordination procedure similar to that undertaken by monks.

Buddhism in Myanmar has overtaken, but never entirely replaced, the pre-Buddhist practice of *nat* worship. The 37 *nat* figures are often found side by side with Buddhist images. The Burmese *nats* are spirits that can inhabit natural features, trees or even people. They can be mischievous or beneficent.

The *nat* cult is strong. Mt Popa (p588) is an important centre. The Burmese divide their devotions and offerings according to the sphere of influence: Buddha for future lives, and the *nat* – both Hindu and Bamar – for problems in this life. A misdeed might be redressed with offerings to the *nat* Thagyamin, who annually records the names of those who perform good deeds in a book made of gold leaves. Those who commit evil are recorded in a book made of dog skin.

ARTS

Burmese fine art, at the court level, has not had an easy time since the forced exile of the last king, Thibaw Min. Architecture and art were both royal activities and they have floundered without royal support. On the other

> **MUST READ**
>
> *The River of Lost Footsteps: Histories of Burma* (2006), by UN diplomat Thant Myint U, is a beautifully crafted assessment of the country's current plight in the context of its long and complex history.

MYANMAR (BURMA)

YOU CALL THAT A FINANCIAL CRISIS?

As the world watched its savings whittle away by the international financial meltdown in 2008 and 2009, many Burmese rolled their eyes as if to say 'at least your money is still worth something'. In 1985 the government of deeply superstitious ruler Ne Win announced that 25, 50 and 100 kyat notes (the largest then available) were no longer legal tender. They were soon replaced with 15, 35 and 75 kyat notes; it was ruler Ne Win's 75th birthday. So far, so odd, but the real problem was that only small amounts of the old notes could be exchanged for new currency, leaving millions of people nearly destitute.

Despite this, Ne Win was still not happy and in 1987 he did what most Burmese thought impossible, he demonetised the currency again. Out went the 35 and 75 kyat notes and in came 45s and 90s, reflecting Ne Win's reported obsession with the number nine. This time no exchanges were allowed at all and cash savings became little more than toilet paper overnight. The people, however, would have the last laugh. The demonetisation sparked protests which led to the 1988 uprising and Ne Win's ousting.

Today the odd-numbered notes are sold as souvenirs, while any real wealth is stored not in banks, but in gold.

hand, Burmese culture at the street level thrives as one of the few means of relatively free expression.

Marionette Theatre

Yok-thei pwe, or Burmese marionette theatre, was the forerunner of Burmese classical dance. Marionette theatre declined following WWII and is now mostly confined to tourist venues in Mandalay and Bagan.

Music

Traditional Burmese music relies heavily on rhythm and is short on harmony, at least to the Western ear. Younger Burmese listen to heavily Western-influenced sounds – you will often hear Burmese-language covers of classic oldies, usually sappy love or pop tunes. A number of Burmese rock musicians, such as Lay Phyu of the band Iron Cross, produce serious songs of their own, but the country's censors keep a lid on anything remotely rebellious.

Pwe

The *pwe* (show) is everyday Burmese theatre. A religious festival, wedding, funeral, celebration, fair, sporting event – almost any gathering is a good excuse for a *pwe*. Once under way, a *pwe* traditionally goes on all night. If an audience member is flaking at some point during the performance, they simply fall asleep. Ask a trishaw driver if one is on nearby.

Myanmar's truly indigenous dance forms are those that pay homage to the *nat*. In a special *nat pwe*, one or more *nat* are invited to possess the body and mind of a medium. Sometimes members of the audience seem to be possessed instead, an event greatly feared by most Burmese.

ENVIRONMENT

Myanmar covers an area of 671,000 sq km, which is roughly the size of Texas or France. From the snow-capped Himalaya in the north to the coral-fringed Myeik (Mergui) Archipelago in the south, Myanmar's 2000km length crosses three distinct ecological regions, producing what is likely the richest biodiversity in Southeast Asia.

Unfortunately, that wildlife – which includes a third of the world's Asiatic elephants, more venomous snakes than any other country, and the largest tiger reserve on the planet – is threatened by habitat loss. Rampant deforestation by the timber industry, which occurs in order to feed demand in Thailand and China, is a primary cause, as is destructive slash and burn agriculture. Optimistically, about 7% of the country is protected in national parks and other protected areas, but most of these are just lines on maps. Wildlife laws in Myanmar are seldom enforced, due to a desperate lack of funding, and in recent years some wildlife reserves that date back to the colonial era have been un-reserved to allow logging.

For travellers, seeing wildlife will be more a matter of luck than design. And without some serious cash, forget about visiting national parks.

TRANSPORT

GETTING THERE & AWAY

Air

Aside from occasional, unpredictable services to Mandalay (MDL), all international flights arrive at Yangon's shiny new airport (RGN). Most budgeteers come from Bangkok on Air Asia's daily flight, which has one-way/return tickets from US$70/120 depending on season. At the time of writing tourists were staying away and so too were airlines, meaning direct flights to/from Yangon were limited to Bangkok, Kolkata, Kuala Lumpur, Kunming and Singapore. Flights to Dhaka, Delhi and Hong Kong had been discontinued.

Airlines with offices in Yangon and regular flights to Myanmar:

Air Asia (code FD; ☎ 01-251885; www.airasia.com) Cheapest flights from Bangkok.

Air China (code CA; ☎ 01-505024; www.airchina.com) Three a week from Kunming.

Bangkok Airways (code PG; ☎ 01-255265; www.bangkokair.com) Most days from Bangkok.

Indian Airlines (code IC; ☎ 01-253598; http://indian-airlines.nic.in) Twice weekly from Kolkata.

Malaysia Airlines (code MH; ☎ 01-241007; www.malaysiaairlines.com) Connects Yangon and Kuala Lumpur.

Myanmar Airways International (MAI; code 8M; ☎ 01-255260; www.maiair.com) National carrier connects to Bangkok, Kuala Lumpur and Singapore.

SilkAir (code MI; ☎ 01-255287; www.silkair.com) Twice- or thrice-daily from Singapore.

Thai Airways International (code TG; ☎ 01-255499; www.thaiair.com) Daily from Bangkok.

> **BURMA OR MYANMAR?**
>
> The government changed many geographical names after the 1988 uprising in an attempt to purge the country of the vestiges of colonialism, and to avoid exclusive identification with the Bamar ethnic majority ('Burma' is actually an English corruption of 'Bamar', and was never used locally to describe the country prior to the British arrival). So Rangoon switched to Yangon, Pagan to Bagan, Irrawaddy River to Ayeyarwady River and so on.
>
> In this book, 'Myanmar' is used in text to describe the country's history and people. 'Burmese' refers to the language, the food and the Bamar people.

Land

Most of Myanmar's borders are closed or entry is severely restricted, with regular rule changes making it tough to keep on top of the options. Foreigners cannot enter Myanmar overland from Bangladesh or India, but at significant cost and hassle you can from China, Thailand and (maybe) Laos. Check the Thorn Tree (www.lonelyplanet.com/thorntree) for the latest, or call MTT in Yangon (p546).

CHINA

You can enter Myanmar from China, but you'll pay dearly for the privilege. You'll require a 28-day tourist visa – get one at Kunming's **Myanmar consulate** (☎ 0871-360 3477; Room A504, 5th fl, Longyuan Haozhai, 166 Weiyuan Jie; 🕑 8.30am-noon & 1-4.30pm Mon-Fri). You must then find a travel agency (those at the Kunming Camelia Hotel are recommended) to organise paperwork and book a mandatory multiday 'package trip' to go first to Ruili, 20 hours from Kunming, and then by taxi from Mu-se, Myanmar (at the border) to Lashio (northeast of Hsipaw). At about US$200, arriving this way could blow a nasty hole in your budget. It is theoretically possible to exit at Mu-Se, but in practice it is often closed. Check with MTT and guest houses in Kengtung before planning on leaving this way.

LAOS

MTT assured us crossing from Myanmar to Laos was possible (see p570), but seemed much less certain about the reverse journey. It *might* be possible to exit at Xieng Kok and cross there, with a Myanmar visa and prearranged permission, but we haven't heard of anyone doing it.

THAILAND

It's possible to cross from the northern Thai town of Mae Sai to dreary Tachileik (see p767), then either fly on to Mandalay or take a bus to Kengtung (and then fly to Mandalay). Either way, it's expensive and you must arrange a permission in advance. To exit Myanmar at Tachileik, see p570.

Similar costs and paperwork mean crossing from the Thai town of Ranong to the southern tip of Myanmar at Kawthoung (see p807) isn't really feasible either. From Kawthoung you need to wait for an irregular, expensive flight north to Yangon, as further travel overland is banned and boat journeys are uncertain.

DEPARTURE TAX

Departure tax on international flights is US$10, payable in US dollars only.

Exiting at Kawthoung isn't much fun either, see p564.

Some travellers do single-day 'visa runs' from Thailand to Myanmar, leaving their passports at the border. Aside from the crossings mentioned above, it's also (usually) possible to do this at the Mae Sot–Myawaddy border, where full crossings are not allowed. See p752 for more information.

GETTING AROUND

Unless you fly, all travel in Myanmar takes time. Lots of time. Much of the country remains off limits to travellers, including places not covered in this chapter, such as Chin State and much of Shan State. However, there is no law against stopping in villages between places listed in this chapter and having a look around.

Air

Four airlines, including three private companies and the government-run Myanma Airways, ply Myanmar's skyways (and 66 airstrips). Schedules are approximate at best, and can change right up to the departure time; recheck all bookings. Bear in mind that two out of three private airlines are pretty close to the government.

Myanmar's domestic airlines:

Air Bagan (code W9; ☎ 01-513322; www.airbagan.com) Sanctions have stopped all international flights.

Air Mandalay (code 6T; ☎ 01-525488; www.airmandalay.com) Myanmar-Singapore-Malaysia joint venture. Look mum, no sanctions!

Myanma Airways (MA, code UB; ☎ 01-374874; www.mot.gov.mm/ma/index.html) The government's airline. Fleet includes old-as-your-parents Fokkers. Also has a super-dodgy safety record.

Yangon Airways (code HK; ☎ 01-383106; www.yangonair.com) Sanctions have been imposed by the US government because of links to 'drug kingpins'.

One-way tickets are half the return fare and should be bought at least a day ahead. You'll need your passport and US dollars. Travel agencies sell air tickets for slightly less than airline offices. There's no domestic departure tax.

Boat

There is 8000km of navigable river in Myanmar and, unlike elsewhere in Asia, slow boats remain a vital transport link here. Even in the dry season, boats can travel on the Ayeyarwady (Irrawaddy) from the delta to Bhamo, with small boats continuing to Myitkyina. Other important rivers include the Twante Canal, which links the Ayeyarwady to Yangon, and the Chindwin, which joins the Ayeyarwady a little north of Bagan. Most ferries are operated by the government's Inland Water Transport (IWT).

The Mandalay–Bagan service is popular among travellers. A government ferry runs at least twice a week, and in season there are two faster, more comfortable private services; **Malikha** (www.malikha-rivercruises.com) and Shwe Keinnery; buy tickets from travel agencies. Some slower local boats continue to Pyay (Prome) and even Yangon. The best long-haul river trip – in season – is drifting south from Myitkyina or Bhamo. For something shorter, take the boat from Mawlamyine (Moulmein) to Hpa-an.

The government's Myanma Five Star Line (MFSL) travels infrequently and irregularly from Yangon's MFSL Passenger Jetty (south of Strand Rd) to Sittwe (Akyab) and Kawthoung. Ask at Myanmar Travel & Tours (MTT; Map p550) or call the **MFSL office** (Map p548; ☎ 01-295279; 132-136 Thein Byu Rd) in Yangon.

Bus

A few long-distance buses are new and comfortable. More common are the ancient beasts packed with people and produce and often running hours late. Breakdowns are frequent and roads are so bad in most places that two vehicles travelling in opposite directions can't pass without pulling off the road. On the other hand, bus travel is cheap and reasonably frequent, and it's easy to meet local people during the regular food stops.

Buying tickets in advance is recommended, lest you get stuck sitting on a sack in the aisle. On minibuses, beware of the back seat – on Myanmar's rough roads you'll be bouncing around like popcorn. Keep something warm handy for air-con or trips through mountains.

Bus tickets are priced in kyat and foreigners usually pay more, particularly on popular tourist routes. This money doesn't go to the government, so feel free to argue about it.

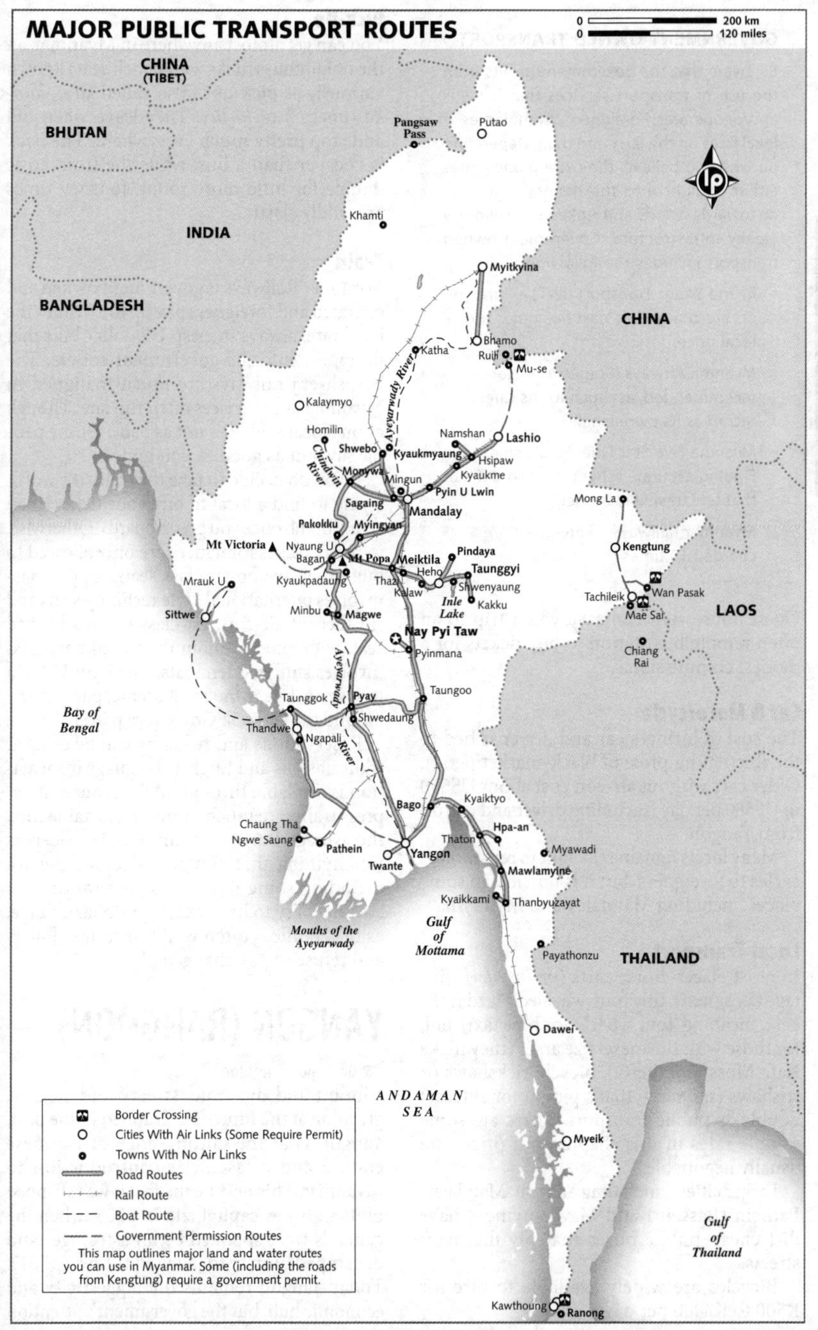
MAJOR PUBLIC TRANSPORT ROUTES
0 200 km
0 120 miles
CHINA (TIBET)
BHUTAN
INDIA
BANGLADESH
CHINA
LAOS
THAILAND
Bay of Bengal
Mouths of the Ayeyarwady
Gulf of Mottama
ANDAMAN SEA
Gulf of Thailand
Pangsaw Pass
Putao
Khamti
Myitkyina
Bhamo
Ruili
Mu-se
Katha
Ayeyarwady River
Kalaymyo
Homilin
Chindwin River
Namshan
Lashio
Shwebo
Kyaukmyaung
Hsipaw
Kyaukme
Monywa
Mingun
Pyin U Lwin
Sagaing
Mandalay
Mong La
Pakokku
Myingyan
Mt Victoria
Nyaung U
Bagan
Mt Popa
Meiktila
Pindaya
Heho
Taunggyi
Kyaukpadaung
Thazi
Kalaw
Shwenyaung
Kengtung
Wan Pasak
Tachileik
Mae Sai
Inle Lake
Kakku
Mrauk U
Sittwe
Minbu
Magwe
Nay Pyi Taw
Pyinmana
Chiang Rai
Taungoo
Taunggok
Pyay
Shwedaung
Thandwe
Ngapali
Ayeyarwady River
Bago
Kyaiktyo
Chaung Tha
Ngwe Saung
Pathein
Thaton
Hpa-an
Yangon
Twante
Myawadi
Mawlamyine
Kyaikkami
Thanbyuzayat
Payathonzu
Dawei
Myeik
Kawthoung
Ranong
Border Crossing
Cities With Air Links (Some Require Permit)
Towns With No Air Links
Road Routes
Rail Route
Boat Route
Government Permission Routes
This map outlines major land and water routes you can use in Myanmar. Some (including the roads from Kengtung) require a government permit.
MYANMAR (BURMA)

GOVERNMENT-OWNED TRANSPORT

Be aware that the government profits from the use of transport services that it owns and/or operates. Foreigners pay multiples of local fares on the ferry and train. Depending on who you believe, the extra money goes either straight into the general's pockets or towards wages and upkeep of seriously creaky infrastructure. Government-owned transport includes the following:

- Inland Water Transport (IWT) – Foreigners are charged at least five times the local price.
- Myanma Airways (domestic) – Not recommended, as much for its safety record as its ownership.
- Myanma Five Star Line (MFSL; ships) – Finding accurate schedules is so difficult that few travellers bother.
- Myanmar Railways – Foreigners are charged 10 times the local fare.

Guest house staff can save you a trip to an often remote bus station to buy tickets for a modest commission.

Car & Motorcycle

The cost of hiring a car and driver is tied to the fluctuating price of black-market petrol. Older cars without air-con cost about US$50 to US$80 per day (including driver and petrol) from Yangon.

Many locals remain reluctant to rent motorcycles to foreigners, but it is possible in some places, including Mandalay and Myitkyina.

Local Transport

In most places, horse carts *(myint hlei)*, vintage taxis *(taxi)*, tiny four-wheeled Mazdas (*lei bein*, meaning 'four wheels', or blue taxi) and, for those with Burmese-size arses (they make Kate Moss look hefty), bicycle rickshaws or trishaws (*sai-kaa* – that's pidgin for sidecar) double as public transport. There are some sample rates in this chapter, but prices are usually negotiable.

Larger cities – including Yangon, Mandalay, Pathein (Bassein) and Mawlamyine – have dirt-cheap public buses that ply the main streets.

Bicycles are widely available to hire for K500 to K3000 per day.

Pick-Up

You can get almost anywhere in Myanmar on the ubiquitous trucks with bench seats known variously as pick-ups (also called *kaa*), *lain-ka* (linecar) or *hi-lux*. They leave when full and stop pretty much everywhere. The back is cheaper than a bus, while the front costs double for little more room. Journey times are wildly elastic.

Train

Myanmar Railways is government owned and operated and foreigners pay up to 10 times the local rate, always in crisp US dollar bills that disappear into the government coffers. The British-era railways are much-maligned in Myanmar, and services often run late. Though as one local said: 'It's not as bad as some people say, not as good as you hope.'

If you do decide to take the train, it's worth trying to find a local to buy your ticket (then acting dumb once you get on board). Otherwise, in many places foreigners are only allowed to buy expensive upper-class seats. Upper class involves international-style reclining seats and (in theory) air-con, 1st class is hard-backed seats with some cushioning and ordinary class involves stiff wooden seats. The Pyin U Lwin to Hsipaw line is the most scenic, particularly around the Gokteik Gorge (see p581).

Reservations and ticketing can be done at train stations and English-language information is available through MTT. Note that express trains are much more comfortable than the average Burmese train. Reserve sleepers (ie anything that contains sleeping berths, including some day trains) several days in advance. Try to have exact US dollar change, as ticket offices often won't have any dollars and refuse to pay change in kyat.

YANGON (RANGOON)

☎ 01 / pop 5 million

Vibrant and dynamic, sweaty and steamy, grasping at the future but trapped in the past, Yangon is at the cutting edge of Burmese culture and a fascinating introduction to Myanmar. This despite the fact it was stripped of its status as capital city in 2005, when the generals were spooked by an astrologer and decamped north to Nay Pyi Taw (p561). Today Yangon remains the biggest city and economic hub, but the government's attention (and money) is elsewhere and infrastructure is really starting to creak.

Despite this, Yangon remains a hive of underground intellectual debate and the gateway for most international visitors. The stunning Shwedagon Paya is the centrepiece, a gleaming golden stupa visible from all over town. Closer to the waterfront, downtown Yangon is a warren of historic streets concealing some of the best British colonial-era architecture in the region. A walk along the Strand or Pansodan St is like strolling down Pall Mall – sans paint. It's diverse, too – home to Burmese, Shan, Mon, Chinese, Indians and Western expats. So spend a couple of days soaking up the chaos, it will grow on you.

ORIENTATION

The city is bounded to the south and west by the Yangon River (also known as the Hlaing River) and to the east by Pazundaung Creek, which flows into the Yangon River. The whole city is divided into townships, and street addresses are often suffixed with these (eg 52nd St, Botataung Township).

Most travellers choose to walk around downtown Yangon, which has an easily navigable grid-style layout, and take taxis to places further afield, like the Shwedagon Paya.

INFORMATION

Bookshops

There are lots of bookstalls (Map p550) across from Bogyoke Aung San Market and along 37th St near the corner of Merchant St, selling pulpy Buddhist comics, maps and old books, some in English.

Bagan Bookshop (Map p550; ☎ 377227; 100 37th St) The friendly owner has a complete selection of titles on Myanmar, including old reprints.

Inwa Bookstore (Map p550; ☎ 243216; 232 Sule Paya Rd) Stocks some maps, coffee-table books, general English titles and news magazines.

Cultural Centres

Alliance Francaise (Map p548; ☎ 536900; Pyay Rd; 🕑 Tue & Fri) Check the *Myanmar Times* for film and concert listings.

American Center (Map p548; ☎ 223140; 14 Taw Win Rd; 🕑 8am-4.30pm Mon-Fri) English-language magazines and books. Behind the Ministry of Foreign Affairs.

British Council Library (Map p550; ☎ 254658; Strand Rd; 🕑 9am-6pm Mon-Sat, to 1pm Sun) Excellent collection of English-language Burmese-history books adjoining the UK embassy.

Emergency

Your embassy may also be able to assist in an emergency.

Ambulance (☎ 192)

Fire (☎ 191)

Police (☎ 199)

Red Cross (☎ 383680)

Internet Access

At the time of research there were plenty of internet cafes scattered around central Yangon, charging about K600 an hour, including the following:

Mother Home Internet (Map p550; 119A Sule Paya Rd; per hr K600) Central location, nice guys, fast machines.

Medical Services

Any local clinic can conduct blood tests for malaria and other tropical ailments.

City Mart Supermarket (Map p548; cnr Anawrahta Rd & 47th St) Well-stocked place (tampons available) that includes a pharmacy.

International SOS Clinic (off Map p546; ☎ 24hr alarm centre 667879; 37 Kaba Aye Pagoda Rd) In the Dusit Inya Lake Hotel; expensive but fairly reliable and has Western doctors.

Money

Yangon offers the best exchange rates in the country. Touts around Sule Paya and Mahabandoola Garden will set upon you, but make sure you count all the kyat carefully. More reputable dealers loiter in the main aisle of Bogyoke Aung San Market, or try your hotel or guest house. Don't change money at the airport.

At a pinch, a couple of top-end hotels accept credit cards.

GETTING INTO TOWN

Walk past the taxi stands in the airport terminal (about 15km north of the centre) and negotiate with the drivers outside. It will cost you about US$6 to the centre of Yangon; make sure you have small bills handy. All airport taxi drivers can arrange money exchanges at reasonable (if not great) rates (see p598). Most buses arrive at the Aung Mingalar Bus Terminal (Highway Bus Centre), a few kilometres northeast of the airport; a taxi to town will cost about the same as the airport run, or follow the locals to a city bus.

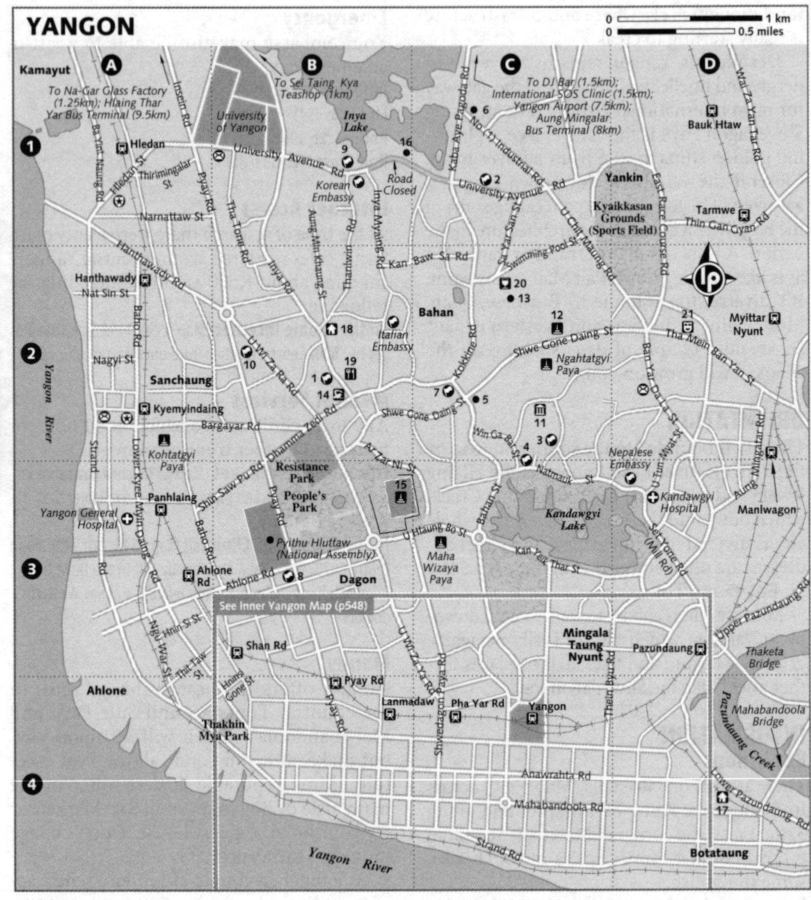

Post

DHL (Map p548; ☎ 664423; Park Royal Hotel, 33 Ah Lan Paya Pagoda Rd; 🕑 8am-6pm Mon-Fri)

Main post office (Map p550; Strand Rd; 🕑 7.30am-6pm Mon-Fri) Grand old building for all postal services, but not phone calls.

Telephone

Internet cafes throughout Yangon are increasingly offering international calls at mercifully cheap rates, though they are subject to Myanmar's dire internet connection. If all other options are exhausted, head to **Central Telephone & Telegraph office** (CTT; Map p550; cnr Pansodan St & Mahabandoola Rd), a government-run place where overseas calls cost between US$2 and US$6 per minute.

Tourist Information

Myanmar Travel & Tours (MTT; Map p550; ☎ 252859; Mahabandoola Garden Rd; 🕑 8.30am-5pm) Government-run travel agency. Partake of its free maps and very useful advice on border crossings and permissions, but not its paid services.

Travel Agencies

Yangon's privately run travel agencies are the best place in the country for hiring a car or guide, booking an air ticket and checking on the latest travel restrictions.

Columbus Travel & Tours (Map p550; ☎ 255123; www.travelmyanmar.com; 3rd fl, Sakura Tower, 339 Bogyoke Aung San Rd) Convenient location.

Good News Travel (Map p550; ☎ 09 511 6256; www.myanmargoodnewstravel.com; 4th fl, FMI Centre, 380 Bo-

INFORMATION	
Bangladesh Embassy	1 B2
Cambodian Embassy	2 C1
German Embassy	3 C2
Japanese Embassy	4 C2
New Horizons Travels & Tours	5 C2
Sedona Hotel	6 C1
Singapore Embassy	7 C2
Thai Embassy	8 B3
US Embassy	9 B1
Vietnamese Embassy	10 B2
SIGHTS & ACTIVITIES	
Bogyoke Aung San Museum	11 C2
Chaukhtatgyi Paya	12 C2
Mahasi Meditation Centre	13 C2
Savoy Hotel	14 B2
Shwedagon Paya	15 B3
Suu Kyi's Home	16 B1
SLEEPING	
Motherland Inn 2	17 D4
Winner Inn	18 B2
EATING	
Café Dibar	19 B2
DRINKING	
Mr Guitar Café	20 C2
ENTERTAINMENT	
San Francisco DJ Club	21 D2

gyoke Aung San Rd) Very helpful, professionally run agency; not the cheapest in town, but possibly the most reliable.

DANGERS & ANNOYANCES

Yangon holds few dangers, but some annoyances. Money changers on the street will often try to short-change you, and sometimes just bolt with your cash; see p598. Buying bus tickets around Aung San Stadium can sometimes lead to slight overcharging.

SIGHTS

Shwedagon Paya

If you only see one *zedi* (stupa) on your whole trip through Southeast Asia, make sure it's the glorious gilded spire of **Shwedagon Paya** (Map p546; admission US$5; 5am-10pm). Located a couple of kilometres north of the centre, Shwedagon is the defining image of Yangon and a symbol of Burmese identity for 2500 years. Burmese revere it, but Rudyard Kipling is responsible for some of the most evocative descriptions:

> 'A beautiful winking wonder that blazed in the sun, of a shape that was neither Muslim dome nor Hindu temple spire… The Golden dome said, 'This is Burma, and it will be quite unlike any land that one knows about.'

In truth this 2500-year-old testament to religious faith, this gold-draped symbol of exotica, is the very heart and soul of this country. Every good Buddhist in Myanmar tries to make at least one pilgrimage here in their lifetime; many come for the **Shwedagon festival**, held on the last full moon before Myanmar New Year (normally late February/early March). The compound, with its main *zedi* and 82 other buildings, is astounding any time of day, but evening and sunrise – when slanting light illuminates the gilding – are the most magical times to visit.

The *paya* ('holy one', a religious monument) is said to be built upon a hill where Buddha relics have been enshrined, including eight hairs of the Buddha. In the 15th century Queen Shinsawbu gilded it with her own weight in gold, beaten to gold leaf. Her son-in-law offered four times his own weight and that of his wife's. Over the years the *zedi* has grown to 98m tall and reportedly accumulated more than 53 metric tonnes of gold leaf. The top of the spire is encrusted with more than 5000 diamonds and 2000 other stones.

In the compound's northwestern corner is a huge bell that the British managed to drop into the Yangon River while trying to carry it off. Unable to recover it, they gave the bell back to the Burmese, who refloated it using low-tech lengths of bamboo.

The entrance fee supposedly goes to pagoda upkeep. There is a lift large enough to accommodate a wheelchair, an impressive rarity when it comes to ancient sites in Southeast Asia. To get here, either take bus 37 from the east side of Mahabandoola Park, or grab a taxi (about K2000 one way).

Other Attractions

One of Yangon's top *paya*, the slightly kitsch riverside **Botataung Paya** (Map p548; Strand Rd; admission US$2; 6am-9.30pm) is named for the 1000 military leaders who escorted Buddha relics from India 2000 years ago. Its *zedi* is, unusually, hollow, so you can walk through it. There are good river views nearby.

If you don't make it to Bago (Pegu), the reclining Buddha at **Chaukhtatgyi Paya** (Map p546; Shwe Gone Daing St) is nearly as impressive.

It's not possible to visit Aung San Suu Kyi's lakeside home (unless you fancy a swim and a stay at the junta's pleasure), and since the 2007 protests the **Bogyoke Aung San Museum**

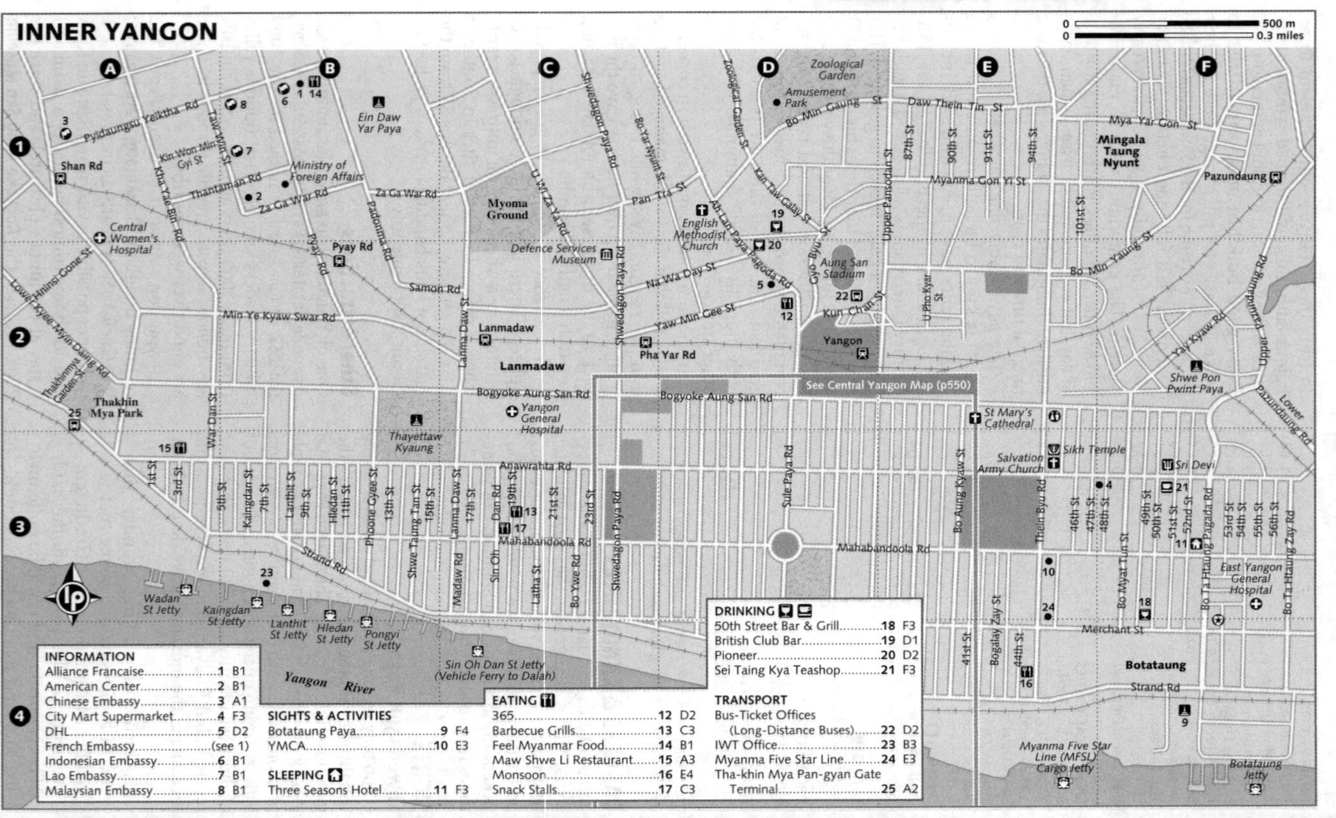

INNER YANGON
0 500 m
0 0.3 miles
A
B
C
D
E
F
1
2
3
4
Zoological Garden
Amusement Park
Mingala Taung Nyunt
Pazundaung
Ein Daw Yar Paya
Ministry of Foreign Affairs
Myoma Ground
Defence Services Museum
English Methodist Church
Aung San Stadium
Central Women's Hospital
Shan Rd
Pyay Rd
Lanmadaw
Pha Yar Rd
Yangon
Shwe Pon Pwint Paya
See Central Yangon Map (p550)
Thakhin Mya Park
Thayettaw Kyaung
Yangon General Hospital
St Mary's Cathedral
Sikh Temple
Salvation Army Church
Sri Devi
East Yangon General Hospital
Botataung
Wadan St Jetty
Kaingdan St Jetty
Lanthit St Jetty
Hledan St Jetty
Pongyi St Jetty
Sin Oh Dan St Jetty (Vehicle Ferry to Dalah)
Yangon River
Myanma Five Star Line (MFSL) Cargo Jetty
Botataung Jetty
Pyidaungsu Yeiktha Rd
Taw Win St
Kin Won Min Gyi St
Thantaman Rd
Za Ga War Rd
Kha Yae Bin Rd
Padonma Rd
Samon Rd
Min Ye Kyaw Swar Rd
Lower Hninsi Gone St
Lower Kyee Myin Daing Rd
Thakhinmya Garden St
U Wi Za Ya Rd
Shwedagon Paya Rd
Bo Yar Nyunt St
Pan Tra St
Na Wa Day St
Yaw Min Gee St
Ah Lan Paya Pagoda Rd
Kan Taw Galay St
Zoological Garden St
Gyo Byu St
Kun Chan St
Bo Min Gaung St
Daw Thein Tin St
Upper Pansodan St
U Pho Kyar St
Myanma Gon Yi St
Mya Yar Gon St
Bo Min Yaung St
Yay Kyaw Rd
Upper Pazundaung Rd
Lower Pazundaung Rd
Lanma Daw St
Bogyoke Aung San Rd
Anawrahta Rd
Mahabandoola Rd
Sule Paya Rd
Strand Rd
Merchant St
Bo Aung Kyaw St
Thein Byu Rd
Bo Myat Tun St
Bo Ta Htaung Pagada Rd
Bo Ta Htaung Zay Rd
Bogalay Zay St
War Dan St
1st St
3rd St
5th St
Kaingdan St
7th St
Lanthit St
9th St
Hledan St
11th St
Phoone Gyee St
13th St
Shwe Taung Tan St
15th St
Madaw Rd
17th St
Sin Oh Dan Rd
19th St
21st St
Latha St
Bo Ywe Rd
23rd St
41st St
44th St
46th St
47th St
48th St
49th St
50th St
51st St
52nd St
53rd St
54th St
55th St
56th St
87th St
90th St
91st St
94th St
101st St
INFORMATION
Alliance Francaise 1 B1
American Center 2 B1
Chinese Embassy 3 A1
City Mart Supermarket 4 F3
DHL 5 D2
French Embassy (see 1)
Indonesian Embassy 6 B1
Lao Embassy 7 B1
Malaysian Embassy 8 B1
SIGHTS & ACTIVITIES
Botataung Paya 9 F4
YMCA 10 E3
SLEEPING
Three Seasons Hotel 11 F3
EATING
365 12 D2
Barbecue Grills 13 C3
Feel Myanmar Food 14 B1
Maw Shwe Li Restaurant 15 A3
Monsoon 16 E4
Snack Stalls 17 C3
DRINKING
50th Street Bar & Grill 18 F3
British Club Bar 19 D1
Pioneer 20 D2
Sei Taing Kya Teashop 21 F3
TRANSPORT
Bus-Ticket Offices (Long-Distance Buses) 22 D2
IWT Office 23 B3
Myanma Five Star Line 24 E3
Tha-khin Mya Pan-gyan Gate Terminal 25 A2

(Map p546; Bogyoke Aung San Museum St, Bahan Township), where she spent some of her childhood, has been closed as well. When open (usually just Martyr's Day, 19 July) it memorialises her father, an independence leader who was assassinated in 1947. The museum is just north of Kandawgyi Lake.

For the best 360-degree views of Yangon take the (free) lift to the top of the **Sakura Tower** (Map p550; cnr Bogyoke Aung San & Sule Paya Rds).

For more Yangon sights, see the walking tour (below).

ACTIVITIES

Good strolling grounds can be found at **Kandawgyi Lake** (Map p546), north of the city centre. About 3km north, **Inya Lake** (Map p546) offers little chance for shade, but is five times larger, and not far from **Suu Kyi's home** (Map p546; 54 University Ave).

Get a taste of how people live by taking the **Yangon Circle Line** (US$2), a slow-moving two-hour trip around Yangon and the neighbouring countryside. Hop off wherever you like, though if you choose Insein don't try taking pictures of the infamous Insein Prison. Trains run every 30 minutes from 6am to 5pm, from platform 6/7 at the **Yangon Train Station** (Map p548; ☎ 274 027; Bogyoke Aung San Rd). Not everyone does the full circuit.

The **YMCA** (Map p548; ☎ 294128; Mahabandoola Rd) offers first-rate kickboxing instruction; enquire about class times.

If you fancy taking the plunge, the best place for **swimming** is the **Savoy Hotel** (Map p546; ☎ 526289; 129 Dhamma Zedi Rd; wi-fi), where admission, wi-fi and a towel are free as long as you buy some food or drink.

COURSES

Yangon is a popular centre for *satipatthana vipassana* (insight-awareness meditation). Centres include the following:

Chanmyay Yeiktha Meditation Centre (☎ 661479; www.chanmyay.org; 55A Kaba Aye Rd) There's a second centre north of Yangon.

Mahasi Meditation Centre (Map p546; ☎ 541971; http://web.ukonline.co.uk/buddhism/mahasi.htm; 16 Thathana Yeiktha Rd, Bahan Township) Myanmar's most famous meditation centre.

Panditarama Meditation Centre (☎ 535448; http://web.ukonline.co.uk/buddhism/pandita.htm; 80A Thanlwin Rd, Bahan Township) Also has several other centres around Myanmar.

FESTIVALS & EVENTS

Several festivals and events centre on Yangon, although some of the more political ones may shift to Nay Pyi Taw in time. **Independence Day** on 4 January includes a seven-day fair at

DOWNTOWN WALKING TOUR

Central Yangon (Map p550) is like a time capsule of grand colonial architecture, full of imposing government buildings and faded old apartment blocks. This tour looks at these and flirts with Indian flamboyance, gets serene in Buddhist temples, lightens your wallet in the markets and throws in some pickled serpents and crystal ball gazing for good measure.

Start at the 2200-year-old **Sule Paya** (admission US$2), the geographic and commercial heart of Yangon. Head east past huge, yellow **City Hall**, with its attractive Moorish flourishes. On the next corner further east is the **Immigration Office**, once one of Asia's largest department stores. Opposite is the **Immanuel Baptist Church**, dating from 1885. Continuing east on Mahabandoola Rd you'll pass a couple of alleyways crammed with **food stalls** and **markets**. Take the next major right onto Pansodan St. About halfway down on the right is the **High Court Building**, and a block further south is the grand **Inland Water Transport** offices and, on the corner of Strand Rd, the even grander **Myanma Port Authority** building.

Turn left onto Strand Rd for the posh, steamship-era **Strand Hotel**, whose air-conditioned lobby and cafe make a good, if pricey, rest stop. Turn back to the west and walk a block past Pansodan St to **Customs House**, built in 1915, on one corner and the imposing, colonnaded **Law Court** on the other, though police will likely prevent you approaching. Turn north up Mahabandoola Garden St to scruffy **Mahabandoola Garden** (admission K500), perhaps stopping at a **fortune teller** en route. You're now back at Sule Paya. Turn west on Mahabandoola Rd and wander through the chaotic **Indian and Chinese quarters**, pause at **Sri Siva temple**, and continue to the bustling **Theingyi Zei** market to see if you can find the pickled snakes. Exit onto Anawrahta Rd, turn east and then north to finish in **Bogyoke Aung San Market**.

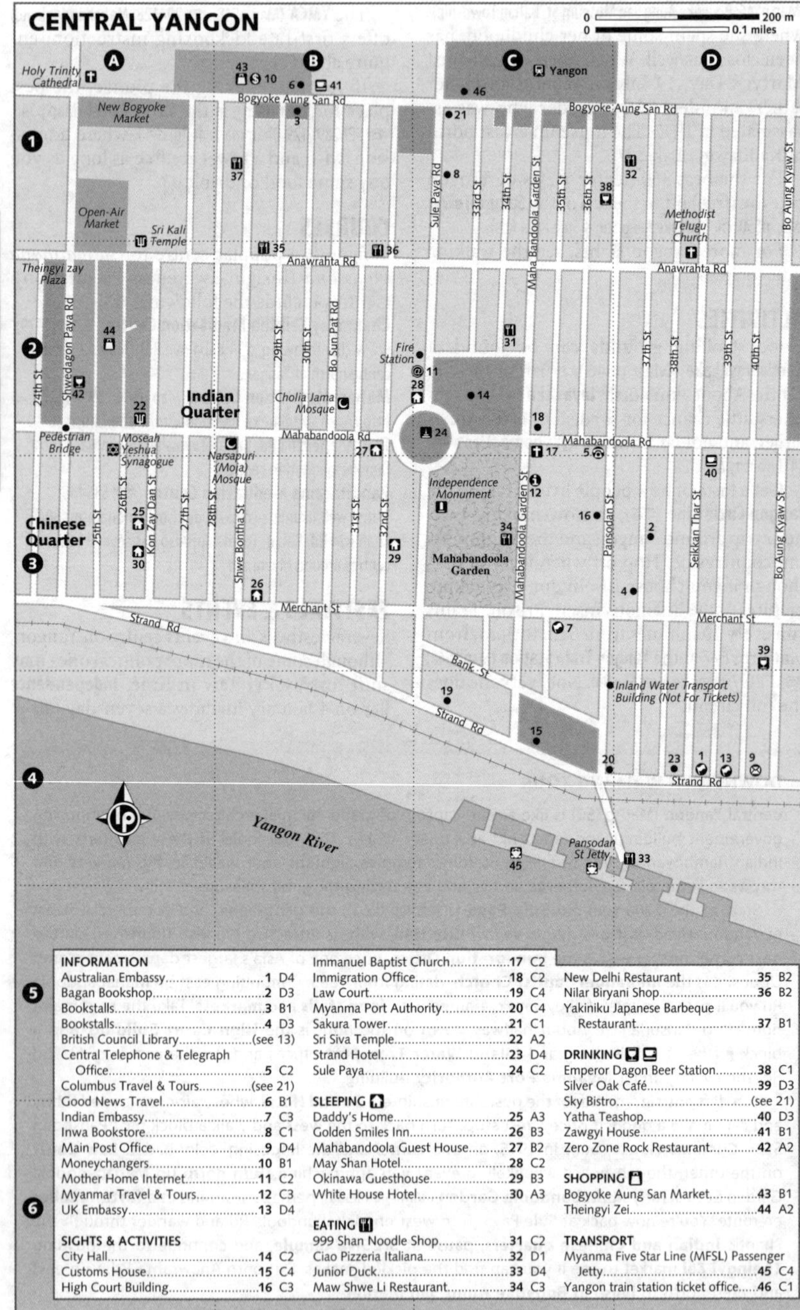

INFORMATION
Australian Embassy....1 D4
Bagan Bookshop....2 D3
Bookstalls....3 B1
Bookstalls....4 D3
British Council Library....(see 13)
Central Telephone & Telegraph Office....5 C2
Columbus Travel & Tours....(see 21)
Good News Travel....6 B1
Indian Embassy....7 C3
Inwa Bookstore....8 C1
Main Post Office....9 D4
Moneychangers....10 B1
Mother Home Internet....11 C2
Myanmar Travel & Tours....12 C3
UK Embassy....13 D4

SIGHTS & ACTIVITIES
City Hall....14 C2
Customs House....15 C4
High Court Building....16 C3
Immanuel Baptist Church....17 C2
Immigration Office....18 C2
Law Court....19 C4
Myanma Port Authority....20 C4
Sakura Tower....21 C1
Sri Siva Temple....22 A2
Strand Hotel....23 D4
Sule Paya....24 C2

SLEEPING
Daddy's Home....25 A3
Golden Smiles Inn....26 B3
Mahabandoola Guest House....27 B2
May Shan Hotel....28 C2
Okinawa Guesthouse....29 B3
White House Hotel....30 A3

EATING
999 Shan Noodle Shop....31 C2
Ciao Pizzeria Italiana....32 D1
Junior Duck....33 D4
Maw Shwe Li Restaurant....34 C3
New Delhi Restaurant....35 B2
Nilar Biryani Shop....36 B2
Yakiniku Japanese Barbeque Restaurant....37 B1

DRINKING
Emperor Dagon Beer Station....38 C1
Silver Oak Café....39 D3
Sky Bistro....(see 21)
Yatha Teashop....40 D3
Zawgyi House....41 B1
Zero Zone Rock Restaurant....42 A2

SHOPPING
Bogyoke Aung San Market....43 B1
Theingyi Zei....44 A2

TRANSPORT
Myanma Five Star Line (MFSL) Passenger Jetty....45 C4
Yangon train station ticket office....46 C1

Kandawgyi Lake; **Buddha's birthday** in April or May is a big event at Shwedagon Paya; **Thingyan**, the New Year water festival, is complete madness in mid-April; and **Martyr's Day** commemorates the assassination of Bogyoke Aung San on 19 July, when his home-cum-museum is open to the public. For more details, see p595.

SLEEPING

The best bargains are found in the downtown area, by far the liveliest part of the city. Not only is this the heart of Yangon, but staying here will save you a small fortune in taxi fares. All prices include a free breakfast.

Okinawa Guesthouse (Map p550; ☎ 374318; 64 32nd St; dm US$5, s US$9-14, d US$13-17;) Down a potholed street a minute from Sule Paya, this bougainvillea-fronted old A-frame houses a hotchpotch of rooms in wood, bamboo and faux-brick. The atmosphere is invariably relaxed; the attic dorm has character.

Golden Smiles Inn (Map p550; ☎ 373589; myathiri@mptmail.net.mm; 644 Merchant St; s US$5-8, d US$8-12;) The cheaper, bathroom-less rooms in this bare-bones place are cleaner than those with bathrooms and, strangely, the better deal. There's a nice breakfast/hang-out balcony.

White House Hotel (Map p550; ☎ 240780; whitehouse@mptmail.net.mm; 69/71 Kon Zay Dan St; s US$6-15, d US$10-18;) The positives in this long-running backpacker joint are the rooftop hammocks, cold beer, expansive views and useful travel desk. The negatives are a thigh-burning number of stairs, small and sometimes windowless rooms and basic bathrooms (both shared and private).

our pick **Motherland Inn 2** (Map p546; ☎ 291343; www.myanmarmotherlandinn.com; 433 Lower Pazundaung Rd; s US$7-10, d US$10-15;) It's a little way from the action, but the Motherland is the first choice of most travellers, and not only because of the free airport shuttle. Staff are almost unfeasibly good-humoured and the clean rooms come in several combinations involving bathrooms, fans or air-con. Recommended.

Three Seasons Hotel (Map p548; ☎ 293304; phyuaung@mptmail.net.mm; 83/85 52nd St; s/d US$15/20;) From the people who created the popular Haven Inn (which is being rebuilt but may reopen during the life of this book), the welcoming Three Seasons offers sparkling polished wood floors and eight rooms in an old two-storey building.

May Shan Hotel (Map p550; ☎ 252986; www.mayshan.com; 115 Sule Paya Rd; s/d from US$15/25;) The unbeatable location, overlooking Sule Paya in the very centre of town, is compromised by the fact most rooms are windowless, a word that doesn't sit well with 'view'. Still, the welcome is warm and, window or no, the rooms are comfortable, with satellite TV and hot-water bathtubs. The lift is a bonus.

Winner Inn (Map p546; ☎ 535205; www.winnerinnmyanmar.com; 42 Thanlwin Rd; r US$20-30;) Up near the Shwedagon Paya, the Winner is one of those small, personal hotels that you buy books like this to find. The good-value rooms come in a variety of shapes (see a few) but all are crystal clean and fitted with fridge, satellite TV and 24-hour power.

Other central cheapies:

Mahabandoola Guest House (Map p550; ☎ 248104; 93 32nd St; s/d US$4/6) This decaying colonial relic has seen better days…a loooong time ago. It's cheap, that's it.

Daddy's Home (Map p550; ☎ 252169; 107 Kon Zay Dan St; r per person US$6;) Clean but cell-like rooms *sans* bathroom near the White House.

EATING

Yangon has Myanmar's best range of restaurants. Downtown is packed with streetside stalls selling a dizzying array of cheap snacks, and many inexpensive Bamar, Shan, Chinese and Indian restaurants. Smarter places are found in the more affluent, expat-occupied north. Remember that while most restaurants are open from about 7am until 9pm daily, it can be hard to find a meal anywhere after 9pm.

Bamar & Shan

999 Shan Noodle Shop (Map p550; 130B 34th St; noodles from K800) This blink-and-you'll-miss-it place behind City Hall has an English-language menu for sampling Shan meals such as *hkauq sweh* (thin rice noodles in spiced chicken broth).

Maw Shwe Li Restaurant (Map p548; ☎ 221103; 316 Anawrahta Rd, Lanmadaw Township; mains K2000) One of the more popular Shan restaurants is this one west of the centre, where the usual range of rich curries is spiced up with specialities such as the tasty fried dried eel with chilli. There is a second branch on Mahabandoola Garden St (Map p550).

Feel Myanmar Food (Map p548; ☎ 725736; 124 Pyidaungsu Yeiktha Rd; meals from K3500) Want to get a feel for Myanmar cuisine? This is the place

'MOUTH-WATERING SNACKS'

Fancy yourself as an adventurous eater? Seek out *tha yei za* (literally 'mouth-watering snack' in Burmese) at 'night markets' in Yangon and street stalls around the country. Desserts are common, and come in the form of multicoloured sticky-rice sweets, poppy-seed cakes, banana puddings and the like. Others test local claims that 'anything that walks on the ground can be eaten' – not to mention any claims you might have to 'hardcore traveller' status – and are definitely in the unidentified frying object category:

- *wek thaa douk htoe* (barbecue stands) – footpath stools selling graphic, sliced-up pig parts
- *pa-yit kyaw* (fried cricket) – sold on skewers or in a 10-pack for about K500
- *bi-laar* (beetle) – prepared like crickets; locals suggest 'suck the stomach out, then chew the head part'
- *thin baun poe* (larva) – insect larva, culled from bamboo, are lightly grilled and served still wriggling

to do it, with dozens of traditional dishes to assess, point at and eat. Staff speak enough English to help with selections.

For a lively local night out, head to the open-air **barbecue grills** (Map p548; 19th St; after 5pm) in Chinatown, located between Mahabandoola and Anawrahta Rds. The area is wall to wall with smoking grills. Pick some skewers from the meat, fish and vegetable selection (from K200 each) and down a chilled Myanmar Beer while your dinner's cooking. If you're game, pick up some 'mouth-watering snacks' (crickets and the like; see above) at the snack stalls (Mahabandoola Rd) around the corner to accompany the beer.

Other Asian

There are loads of Indian restaurants in Yangon. Along Anawrahta Rd, west of Sule Paya Rd, there are many super-cheap Indian biryani shops (*keyettha dan bauk* in Burmese) and roti- and dosa-makers set up at night. All-you-can-eat thali meals or biryani cost from about K800. Nilar Biryani Shop (Map p550) on Anawrahta Rd will leave your mouth watering.

New Delhi Restaurant (Map p550; Anawrahta Rd; meals from K800) This tiny, hard to find hole-in-the-wall between 29th and Shwe Bontha Sts doesn't look much but serves superb South Indian dishes. These include *puris* (puffy breads), *idli* (rice ball in broth), breathtaking masala dosa, banana-leaf thalis and curries. And just look at the price!

Yakiniku Japanese Barbeque Restaurant (Map p550; ☎ 274738; 357 Shwe Bontha St; barbecue dishes from K1500; 9am-10pm) Unashamed good fun, Yakiniku has anything you can think of to barbecue plus some you can't. Go for the DIY cooking on your own gas-fired grill, or go wild and sample the sushi.

our pick Junior Duck (Map p550; ☎ 249421; Nan Thida Bldg, Pansodan Rd; mains from K2000; lunch & dinner) Overlooking the Yangon River from a British-era ferry pier that reminds of Hong Kong, this place is equally good for a delicious, good-value, slap-up Chinese meal or as the beer station of choice at sunset.

365 (Map p548; ☎ 243047; 5 Ah Lan Paya Pagoda Rd; meals from K4000; 24hr) Yangon's cool set can be found here – at any hour – chilling with a drink in the lounge-style setting or tucking into the wide range of well-prepared Asian dishes. It's under the Thamada Hotel.

International

Monsoon (Map p548; ☎ 295224; 85 Thein Byu Rd; mains K2500-8000; 10am-11pm) An expat favourite and with good reason. Monsoon has an eclectic menu of regional favourites from Myanmar, Cambodia, Laos and beyond, plus plenty of comfort food from home. Set in a grand old colonial-era building, the menu is very reasonably priced given the elegant surrounds.

Café Dibar (Map p546; ☎ 09 500 6143; 14 Thanlwin Rd; mains from K3000; 10am-10pm) A little way out, but in striking distance of Shwedagon Paya, Café Dibar is a homely Italian bistro with authentic pizzas and pastas and delicious risotto.

Ciao Pizzeria Italiana (Map p550; ☎ 249992; 262 Pansodan St; mains K5000) After a month upcountry this no-frills pizza joint is a welcome sight indeed. It's often frequented by Italian aid workers, who insist the pizzas and pastas are the best available at this price. The coffee's pretty good, too.

DRINKING

After one night in Bangkok, you would be forgiven for thinking Yangon is a sleepy backwater. However, dig a little deeper and there is some action. For those on a strict budget, the cheapest options are downtown beer gardens serving Dagon or Myanmar draught beer. Expat-oriented places – mostly north of the centre – are comparatively pricey. Check out the *Myanmar Times* for more extensive listings.

Pubs & Bars

Emperor Dagon Beer Station (Map p550; Pansodan St; 10am-11pm) The Emperor is one of the largest of the genre and its grungy beer hall is as good as anywhere for a Burmese-style night out with countless draft beer glasses for company.

Sky Bistro (Map p550; 255277; 20th fl, Sakura Tower, 339 Bogyoke Aung San Rd; 9am-10.30pm) *The* place to come for big views of Yangon. Drinks are pricey (draft beer K2500), but the god's-eye views of Shwedagon Pagoda make it worth one or two.

50th Street Bar & Grill (Map p548; 298287; 9-13 50th St; 11am-10.30pm) This place feels a little lost and lonely in the backstreets, but it's worth a drink or two during the extensive happy hours. Wednesdays, with its US$5 pizzas, are popular with expats.

Mr Guitar Café (Map p546; 550105; 22 Sa Yar San St; 6pm-midnight) Burmese music legends sometimes swing by this dark cafe-bar, founded by popular singer Nay Myo Say. There is live music here every night between 7pm and 11pm and musos are welcome to jam with the band, though it's pretty soft stuff. Drinks are expensive compared with downtown bars.

> **GAY & LESBIAN YANGON**
>
> After Bangkok, expect a subdued scene here in conservative Yangon. **Silver Oak Café** (Map p550; 299993; 83/91 Bo Aung Kyaw St; 10am-11pm) has live music nightly (except football-season weekends) and is known for its gay-friendly vibe. But the main draw is **San Francisco DJ Club** (Map p546; Tarmway Plaza; admission usually K5000; 8pm-late), a popular club that has regular events and gay nights but is also more-than-welcoming of straights.

British Club Bar (Map p548; off Gyo Byu St; 1st Fri evening of the month until midnight) Once a month the ever-so-prim British Club throws open its doors and kicks up its heels. For expats of all nationalities it's the social event of the month. It's informal, but it's worth digging through your backpack in pursuit of a clean pair of pants. Bring your passport.

Clubs

Yangon nightclubs can be an interesting cultural experience for the uninitiated. Most seem to include lots of competitive fashion shows, beer-drinking blokes and little dancing. To see what it's all about, head to Theingyi Zay Plaza, on Shwedagon Paya Rd in Chinatown, where several rooftop clubs are open from early evening until late. Most clubs have a nominal cover charge that includes the first drink. The beach-club-style **Zero Zone Rock Restaurant** (Map p550; 4th fl, 2 Thaingyi Zay) is one such institution. Women (at least respectable women!) might want to stay clear.

More conventional places include **Pioneer** (Map p548; Yuzuna Garden Hotel, 44 Ah Lan Paya Pagoda Rd; admission K5000), which is close to town, and **DJ Bar** (off Map p546; Dusit Inya Lake Hotel, 37 Kaba Aye Paya Rd; no cover), *the* in place where people actually dance until 4am on weekends. It's fun, but way out on Inya Lake and pricey (drinks from K4000), so hit the beer station first.

Cafes & Teashops

Teashops in Myanmar are the social equivalent of pubs in the West, and you won't need a map to find one in Yangon. They can loosely be categorised as 'Chinese' or 'Indian' in style.

Zawgyi House (Map p550; 380398; 372 Bogyoke Aung San Rd; breakfast, lunch & dinner) Take a pew on the porch for some top people-watching in front of this grand old wooden house. Teas, coffees, shakes and snacks, plus a pricey menu.

Sei Taing Kya Teashop (off Map p546; 7am-5pm) This is the Burmese teashop answer to Starbucks, with several branches serving tea by the gallon with plenty of snacks, including *mohinga* and *palata* (flat breads). This is the liveliest, but the 103 Anawrahta Rd branch (Map p548) is easier to get to.

Yatha Teashop (Map p550; 352 Mahabandoola Rd; 7am-5pm) A traditional Indian-style teashop – serving teas with samosas and *palata* – between Seikkan Thar and 39th Sts.

SHOPPING

Theingyi Zei (Map p550) is the local market for everyday homewares and textiles. It extends four blocks east to west from Kon Zay Dan St to 24th St, and north to south from Anawrahta Rd to Mahabandoola Rd. Theingyi Zei is also renowned for its traditional Burmese herbs and medicines.

Bogyoke Aung San Market (Scott Market; Map p550; Bogyoke Aung San Rd; ⌚ 8am-6pm Tue-Sun) This grand old labyrinthine market has the largest selection of Burmese handicrafts in Yangon, as well as jewellery, *longyi* (wraparound garment worn by women and men), shoes, bags and pretty much anything else. Money changers will find you on the main aisle and are relatively reliable.

GETTING THERE & AWAY

Air

See p541 for information on international air services. Domestic flights leave from the same airport and include daily services to Nyaung U (for Bagan, around US$80), Mandalay (from US$75) and Heho (for Inle Lake and Kalaw, about US$70).

Boat

There are four main passenger jetties on the Yangon River waterfront, which wraps itself around southern Yangon. Long-distance ferries head up the delta towards Pathein (deck/cabin US$6/40, 18 hours) or crawl north along the none-too-scenic lower Ayeyarwady River to Pyay, Bagan and Mandalay.

When purchasing a ticket for a particular ferry from the government-run **IWT** (Map p548; ☎ 381912) at the back of Lanthit St jetty, be sure to check from which jetty the boat departs.

Bus

Yangon has two main bus stations. The Aung Mingalar Bus Terminal (Highway Bus Centre; off Map p546) serves the most destinations, while the **Hlaing Thar Yar Bus Terminal** (off Map p546; Hwy No 5, Yangon-Pathein Rd) serves the Delta. The Highway Bus Centre is a confusing array of competing bus companies in a dusty lot southwest of Yangon airport. The Hlaing Thar Yar Bus Terminal is west of the centre on the other side of the Hlaing River. Give yourself at least 45 minutes in a taxi (at least K4000) to either station. A third, smaller station is Tha-khin Mya Pan-gyan Gate Terminal (Map p548), which has buses to Bago from the city centre.

Guest houses can assist with purchasing tickets, which will certainly save time, if not money. Several larger companies have convenient bus-ticket offices (Map p548) opposite the Yangon train station.

Several buses to Pathein (K5000, four to five hours), and both Chaung Tha and Ngwe Saung beaches (both about K7000 to K10,000, five to seven hours), leave from the Hlaing Thar Yar Terminal from early morning until about 3pm; the fastest, comfiest ones leave early.

Train

If you choose to take the train (see p544) there are several options from Yangon. The 716km-long trip to Mandalay (ordinary class US$15, upper class US$30 to US$35, sleeper class US$40 to US$50, 14 hours) is the most popular, with four trains a day. Three of these depart between 4am and 5.30am, while the fourth pulls out at 12.45pm – timed for a convenient evening arrival in Pyinmana (for Nay Pyi Taw), but a rather less convenient 3am in Mandalay.

Other useful services are Kyaikto (for Golden Rock, ordinary/upper class US$4/10, four to six hours) and Mawlamyine (ordinary/upper class US$7/18, nine hours). There are no longer any trains direct to Bagan.

Advance tickets are available from the ticket office on the south side of **Yangon train station** (Map p548; ☎ 202178; Bogyoke Aung San Rd; ⌚ 6am-4pm), which often refuses to sell ordinary class seats to foreigners.

GETTING AROUND

Bus

More than 40 numbered city bus routes, often on WWII-era antiques or pick-ups, connect the townships of Yangon. They're usually slow and packed like sardine tins, but midday hops across the centre (for example) beat a taxi. Tickets cost from K100.

Useful routes:

- Bogyoke Aung San Market to Mingala Zei (near Kandawgyi Lake) – Pick-up 1
- Sule Paya to Pyay Rd (University of Yangon; near Inya Lake) to airport – blue buses 51, 53 and air-con bus 51
- Sule Paya to Aung Mingalar Bus Terminal – bus 43, 45, 51
- Sule Paya to Hlaing Thar Yar Bus Station – bus 54, 59, 96
- Sule Paya to Shwedagon Paya – bus 37, 43, 46

BUSES FROM YANGON

The following are some sample fares, trip durations and departure times (double-check these) for buses leaving the Highway Bus Centre.

Destination	Fare	Duration	Departure
Bagan	K17,000	14hr	3-4pm
Bago	K1500	2hr	9am-5pm
Hpa-an	K9500	8hr	7am, 7pm
Kyaiktiyo	K7000	5hr	6.30am-5pm
Mandalay	K11,000	12hr	5-6pm
Mawlamyine	K10,500	7-8hr	7am, 9pm
Taunggyi (for Kalaw & Inle Lake)	K18,000	15hr	12.30pm
Thandwe (for Ngapali)	K10,000	16hr	3pm

Taxi

Licensed taxis carry red licence plates, though there is often little else to distinguish a taxi from any other vehicle in Yangon. The most expensive are the *car-taxis,* beaten-up old Japanese cars. Breakdowns are not exactly unknown. Fares are highly negotiable; trips around the central area cost about K1000 to K1500. Sule Paya to Shwedagon Paya runs to about K2000. Late at night, expect to pay more. A taxi for the day is US$20 to US$30.

Trishaw

Due to a government ban on city-centre traffic there are fewer trishaws, bicycles or motorcycles in Yangon than elsewhere in Myanmar. Trishaws are useful for getting around downtown, but Yangon is too hilly and spread out to use them for sightseeing. Trishaws aren't allowed near Sule Paya and, in theory, can't take passengers from midnight to 10am. Rides cost about K300 to K1000.

WEST COAST BEACHES & THE DELTA

Myanmar's curvaceous coastline has some tasty slices of sand and, unlike the teeming beaches in neighbouring Thailand, they are virtually empty except on weekends. Remote Ngapali Beach is the finest, but the long and/or expensive trip and the flashpacker prices mean most shoestringers skip it. Instead, head from Yangon through the Ayeyarwady Delta to sleepy Pathein and on to serendipitous Ngwe Saung or scruffy Chuang Tha. During the monsoon season (mid-May to mid-September) some resorts shut up shop.

Since Cyclone Nargis (see p557) struck in May 2008, any trip into the Delta (including trips to Chaung Tha and Ngwe Saung) requires a free permit from the MTT in Yangon (p546); take three photos and your passport. For us, it took about 20 minutes.

PATHEIN (BASSEIN)

☎ 042 / pop 300,000

A good staging post on the way to Chaung Tha or Ngwe Saung beaches, Pathein is, believe it or not, Myanmar's fourth-largest city. Despite being the commercial and administrative heart of the Ayeyarwady delta, Pathein has a languid, easygoing ambience and it doesn't take long to feel comfortable. It's known primarily for its parasol industry and fragrant rice, but much of the appeal comes from the wide, scenic Pathein River flowing through town.

Sights

Pathein is famous for its 'umbrella' industry – actually parasols for the sun, not rain. Parasols are made in workshops scattered across the northern part of the city, particularly around the Twenty-Eight Paya, off Mahabandoola Rd. It's fun to just wander the area, sticking your head into a workshop here and there to see how they're made. They're cheap, and the saffron-coloured ones, made for monks, actually are waterproof. **Shwe Sar Umbrella Workshop** (☎ 25127; 653 Tawya Kyaung Rd; 🕑 8am-5pm) is particularly welcoming.

Shwemokhtaw Paya, in the centre of Pathein near the riverfront, is a huge, golden, bell-shaped *zedi*. The *hti* (decorated top of a pagoda) consists of a top tier made from 6.3kg of solid gold, a middle tier of pure silver and a bottom tier of bronze – the Olympic pagoda, perhaps? The seated Buddha in the southern shrine apparently floated here on a raft from Sri Lanka.

Settayaw Paya is the most charming of the several lesser-known *paya* in Pathein.

Sleeping & Eating

Electricity ebbs and flows in Pathein, but mostly ebbs.

Taan Taan Ta Guest House (☎ 22290; 7 Merchant St; s/d US$6/10;) The traveller's choice and a great place to meet the locals. Top-floor rooms here are brighter (and colourful!); all are clean and include a bathroom.

Paradise Hotel (☎ 25055; 14 Zegyaung Rd; r US$10;) 'Paradise' is overstating it, but this welcoming place delivers the best bang for your buck. Fronting a canal, a short walk from the central market, the clean rooms include satellite TV.

Shwe Zin Yaw Restaurant (24/25 Shwezedi Rd; mains K1400) This unassuming place near where the buses depart throws up some refreshingly different Bamar options, including a delicious sardine salad.

Night market (Strand Rd) After dark, this riverside market draws the young-uns for a spot of flirting. It offers a veritable smorgasbord of treats, including coconut crêpes with syrup, fritters, fresh fruit and peanuts steamed in bamboo.

Getting There & Away

Pathein is about 120km west of Yangon.

BOAT

Chinese triple-deckers sail between Yangon and Pathein (ordinary class/cabin US$6/40, 18 hours), leaving at 5pm in either direction. In Yangon, boats depart from the Lanthit St jetty.

BUS

Eight buses run between Pathein and Yangon's Hlaing Thar Yar Bus Terminal, departing between 3.30am and 2pm. Tickets range from K3500 to K5000 for the three- to five-hour trip.

Overloaded minibuses leave for Chaung Tha (K4000, 2½ hours) every two hours from 7am to 3pm from Pathein's **bus station** (Yadayagone St). Direct buses from Yangon are more comfortable.

Buses and pick-ups leave for Ngwe Saung (K4000, 1½ hours) every other hour from 7am to 3pm. Motorbike taxis cost K8000 to Ngwe Saung and K10,000 to Chaung Tha.

NGWE SAUNG BEACH

☎ 042

Can't face the bus-ride-from-hell to Ngapali? Don't worry. If you're looking for 13km of wide, white-sand beach that seldom gets busy, with a chilled, almost meditative vibe, then Ngwe Saung will be a revelation. The water here is deeper and clearer than that at Chuang Tha, and a small forested island off the southern end of the beach is perfect for some leisurely snorkelling and fishing. It's good, laid-back fun with a big dollop of discovery.

Sleeping & Eating

The following two places are about 3km south of the village – get there by foot (1L of sweat), motorbike taxi (K1000) or trishaw (K800).

Golden Sea Resort (☎ in Yangon 01-241747; bungalows US$10-20) Beach-shack-basic bamboo and concrete bungalows with private bathroom aren't exactly 'resort' material, but are appropriate to the setting. English is spoken and, unusually, there are hammocks!

Shwe Hin Tha Hotel (☎ 40640, 09 520 0618; bungalows US$15-25) Clean, palm-shaded bungalows in bamboo or concrete, plus surprisingly good service (breakfast brought to your balcony) and delicious food make this the backpacker favourite. Prepare to stay longer than you planned.

Most people eat freshly caught seafood at their hotel, but if you make the trek cheaper options can be found in the village.

Getting There & Away

Buses take the once-forested road to/from Pathein (K4000, two hours) every hour or so from 7am to 3pm. A bus that travels directly to Yangon (K7000 to K9000, seven hours) leaves at 6.30am. To get to Chaung Tha by four wheels is a painful six-hour trip via Pathein. Go by motorbike instead, via shaded paths, quiet villages and three river crossings. Either pay one bike guy US$15 for the whole 2½-hour trip, or do it yourself for about 6000K, taking the public boats (100K each) and a different bike for each leg (they'll be waiting).

CHAUNG THA BEACH

☎ 042

A bumpy, barren 45km west of Pathein, Myanmar's original beach resort is overdeveloped and, let's be honest, a bit ordinary. But it remains incredibly popular on weekends and holidays, with locals having fun in the sun and sea – fully clothed. The best stretches of sand are north of town, though development is fast-eroding their charm, too. For us, Ngwe Saung is a better bet.

CYCLONE NARGIS

On 2 and 3 May 2008, Cyclone Nargis tore its way northeast across the Ayeyarwady Delta and Yangon. Yangon was badly damaged, with thousands of huge old trees blown over like matchsticks and parts of the city left without electricity for weeks. But it was the fishing and rice-farming villages of the Delta that were hardest hit. Many of the wood-and-thatch homes survived the 215km/h winds, only to be literally overwhelmed by the storm surge that followed.

Hundreds of thousands of people were left without food or shelter, but the military government was nowhere to be seen. And with the UN, international relief agencies and foreign governments denied access, in typical fashion local people decided to DIY disaster relief. They used small boats to deliver food and water to the Delta and handsaws to clear away fallen trees. In spite of their efforts, a staggering 138,000 people (many local and international organisations put the figure much higher) died during or after Cyclone Nargis – one of the most deadly natural disasters in history. Foreign agencies were eventually allowed in, and it's their work that has been responsible for much of the reconstruction.

For travellers, the areas most affected – around the cities of Labutta and Bogale – were still no-go zones at the time of research. Several foreign NGO workers told us that the reconstruction effort was proceeding as well as could be expected, though the government had already started clamping down on aid visas so their days were numbered. If you want to enter the area it's best to get a permit from MTT to visit Pathein and the coastal beaches; see p546 for details.

Boats head out to aptly-named **Whitesand Island** (one way K3000, 30 minutes) every hour or so from 8am; the last returns at 5pm. It's a good place for swimming and snorkelling, although there are only three trees for shade. The village **market** (⌚ 6-9am) is a lively vestige of a time before tourism; it comes to life when the catch comes in.

Sleeping & Eating

Of Myanmar's beach towns, Chaung Tha has the cheapest places to stay, if not the most inviting. The **Top Chaung Tha 2 Guesthouse** (☎ 42127; s/d US$5/10; ❄) is the pick of the cheaper options; BYO mosquito net. **Shwe Hin Tha Hotel** (☎ 42118; r US$10-30; ❄) is the only affordable hotel on the beach, and its cheaper rooms facing a courtyard are popular, despite the annoying hard-sell. At night, check out rustic **Rhythm Food House** (mains from K2000; ⌚ 9am-10pm), near Shwe Hin Tha Hotel, for delicious seafood and tasty open-to-everyone jam sessions.

Getting There & Away

Seriously overcrowded minibuses leave for Pathein (K4000, 2½ hours) every two hours from 7am to 3pm. Direct buses leave for Yangon at 6.30am (K7000) and 10.30am (K10,000, with air-con); both take six to seven hours. Alternatively, motorbike taxis go to Pathein (K10,000, two hours) and Ngwe Saung (see opposite).

NGAPALI BEACH

☎ 043

Myanmar's premier beach destination is easily reached by air but one hell of a ride for those travelling overland. Given its name, some say, by a homesick Italian, Ngapali boasts 3km of glorious palm-fringed sands on the Bay of Bengal. The turquoise waters deliver a bounty from the sea and this town serves up some mouth-watering, dirt-cheap seafood. It has moved steadily upmarket in recent years, so there are slim pickings for budget travellers. As such, it's only really worth the trip for those planning to continue on to Sittwe and the temples of Mrauk U.

Sights & Activities

Half-day **snorkel trips** (per person incl boat, mask & snorkel, for up to 5 people, K15,000) are widely promoted. There are towering cones to chase colourful fish around but the coral's not spectacular when compared with Thailand.

Jade Taw is a fishing village south of the beach, easily reached on foot, where fish lie drying in the sun on bamboo mats. Further south by road is **Lontha**, home to a hilltop stupa with superb views. Turn left at the market crossroads and follow the water.

A thoroughly enjoyable local 'activity' is taking a pick-up north to Thandwe, getting off at the crossroads and walking right off the tourist trail to the beach. Here, nestled on the beach beneath tall trees, you'll find the **Golden**

Sea Beer Station (⌚ 9am-9pm), waiting for you to partake of its primary activity – downing draft beer (K700).

Sleeping & Eating

Try booking ahead through an agency for discounts, or bargain your arse off when you arrive.

Linn Thar Oo Lodge (☎ 42322, in Yangon 01-547216; s US$25-40, d US$30-45) These 42 bungalows at the Thandwe end of the beach are pretty comfortable and the staff are helpful. Most have sea views from the balcony but only the expensive rooms have hot water and satellite TV.

Royal Beach Hotel (☎ 42411, in Yangon 01-544484; www.royalbeachngapali.com; r US$25-55) This atmospheric little hotel, hidden away amid a small forest of palms at the south end of the beach, has several categories of wood-trimmed room, with mosquito nets and private bathrooms.

Loads of open-air, family-run restaurants line the street running parallel to the beach. Squid with garlic and ginger sauce is a local speciality, though you can order just about any seafood (from K2000). A few hundred metres north of Linn Thar Oo, march straight past Excellence to **Brilliance** (⌚ breakfast, lunch & dinner) for cheap and, yes, brilliant seafood. Ask about guided forest walks.

Getting There & Around

Most people reach Ngapali via **Thandwe airport** (☎ 42722), 5km north of the beach, or Thandwe bus station, 9.5km northeast. Flights go to Yangon (around US$75, one hour, at least daily), Heho (one hour, seasonal), and Sittwe (30 minutes, your guess is as good as ours).

Long-distance bus services to Yangon (K11,000, 18 hours) leave Ngapali around 11am. **Ye Aung Lan** (☎ 65160) sends buses via Gwa and the Delta. **Aung Thit Sar** (☎ 65363) goes via Pyay on a stomach-churning trip over the mountains, the bus stuffed with bags of dried fish. Buses pick you up from your guest house. Alternatively, a local bus/truck from Ngapali heads to Thandwe (K400, 30 minutes), from where it's a trishaw ride to the bus station.

Overland travel is not allowed to or from Sittwe but boats run from Taunggok; see p590 for details. Line cars (aka truck/crappy bus, K3000, four hours), buses (K5000, two to three hours) and motorcycles (K17,000, two to three hours) link Thandwe and Taunggok.

Hotels at Ngapali rent bicycles for about K2000 per day.

CENTRAL MYANMAR

The central plains of Myanmar may lack the iconic sights of places such as Bagan and Inle Lake, but the towns in this area are definitely a rewarding way to escape the tourist trail. The region is primarily an agricultural heartland, but there are some historic towns as well as Nay Pyi Taw – the secret, surreal new capital city where, if you're up for it and you get a bit lucky, you can sneak in to see first-hand the full weirdness of the ruling regime.

BAGO (PEGU)

☎ 052 / pop 220,000

Welcome to Buddha World! Bago has carved a niche for itself – and many thousands of niches for its sacred Buddhas – as home to some monumental religious sites. The town lies 80km north of Yangon (en route to Inle Lake or Mandalay), but sees just a handful of travellers, most of whom are on day trips or on their way to the Golden Rock. Founded in AD 573 by the Mon, Bago's days as a major river-port town declined as the river changed course, and the final nail in the coffin came when marauding Burmese king Alaungpaya destroyed it in 1757.

Sights

A US$10 ticket covers your entrance to Shwethalyaung, Shwemawdaw Paya, Mahazedi Paya, Kyaik Pun Paya and the Kanbawzathadi Palace. Some of this money may go to site maintenance, but the bulk goes to the government. A common way of avoiding the fee is to pay it to your motorbike taxi driver instead: for K10,000 he will get you around and dodge the ticket.

SHWETHALYAUNG & AROUND

The Shwethalyaung is a 55m reclining Buddha image, which extends 9m longer than the famous one at Wat Pho in Bangkok and has a sweet, lifelike face. A mural tells the temple's melodramatic story, which began in 994.

Just before the Shwethalyaung is the reconstructed **Maha Kalyani Sima** (Hall of Ordination) and another, hastily reconstructed, reclining Buddha image.

Carry on beyond the Shwethalyaung and you reach the **Mahazedi Paya**, where men (only) can climb to the top for fine views. Just be-

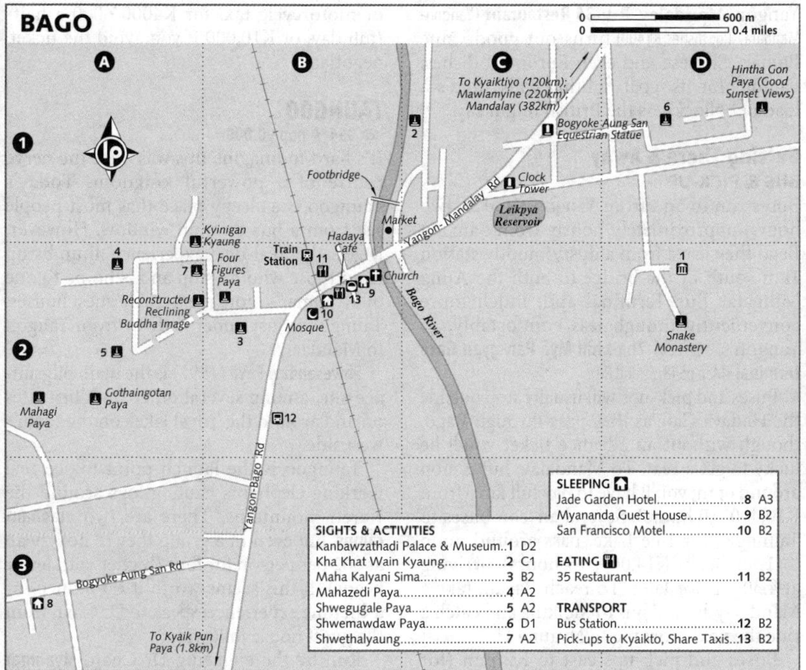

yond is **Shwegugale Paya**, including a tunnel lined with 64 seated Buddha images.

SHWEMAWDAW PAYA & AROUND

Rebuilt after an earthquake in 1930, the Shwemawdaw Paya is 14m higher than Shwedagon Paya in Yangon. Look out for the large chunk of the *zedi*'s spire, toppled by an earthquake in 1917, resting at the northeastern corner of the *paya*. The busy stupa draws plenty of pilgrims during the **full-moon festival** at Tagu (March/April).

KHA KHAT WAIN KYAUNG

One of the three biggest *kyaung* (Buddhist monasteries) in Myanmar, this is a bustling hive of several hundred monks – a welcoming place. Tourists come to watch the 10.30am lunch, but it's more relaxed at other times.

KANBAWZATHADI PALACE & MUSEUM

This Mon-style palace, which lies just south of Shwemawdaw Paya, was the home of a 16th-century Taungoo king. The excavated walls are the only authentic 16th-century artefacts. Everything else is a reproduction.

Sleeping & Eating

Bago has some good-value rooms, but few travellers spend the night. The first two listed here are right in town, on the deafeningly noisy main road – ask for a room at the back.

San Francisco Motel (☎ 22265; 14 Yangon-Mandalay Rd; s/d from US$5/8; ❄) The SF's small rooms won't have you writing home, but the people running it are cool. If there are backpackers staying in Bago, they'll probably be here.

Myananda Guest House (☎ 22275; 10 Yangon-Mandalay Rd; s US$5-8, tw US$8-10; ❄) This sleepy place has better rooms than the San Fran with rates depending on whether you have air-con and private bathroom, or not. Recommended local guide Mr Han hangs out here.

Jade Garden Hotel (☎ 30570; 364 Bogyoke Aung San Rd; r US$10; ❄) If comfort is more important than character, this place in a quiet (boring) location 2km south of town has clean, spacious rooms.

A number of food stalls, including some good Indian biryani sellers, are in the centre of town near the market. As usual, brightly lit beer stations are liberally scattered along

Yangon-Mandalay Rd. **35 Restaurant** (Yangon-Mandalay Rd; dishes K1400) turns out good-value Bamar, Chinese and even European dishes. Famous for its 'goat fighting balls', that's a load of bollocks, as the British might say.

Getting There & Away

BUS & PICK-UP

Buses run to and from Yangon (K3000, two hours) approximately hourly from 5am. In Bago they leave from a dusty/muddy station 1km south of the bridge to both the Aung Mingalar Bus Terminal and, much more conveniently though less comfortably, to Yangon's central **Tha-khin Mya Pan-gyan Gate terminal** (Map p548; Strand Rd).

Buses and pick-ups will usually stop outside the Hadaya Cafe as they pass through Bago, though without an advance ticket you'll be lucky to get a seat. To Mandalay, buses stop around 6pm; you'll have to pay full fare (from K10,400, 10 hours). Several air-con buses to Taunggyi, for Inle Lake, pass around noon to 1pm (from K14,000, 15 hours), arriving at 4.30am…or later. To reach Bagan, take a Mandalay-bound bus to Meiktila and catch a ride the next morning to Nyaung U.

Buses and pick-ups east to Kinpun (for Golden Rock, K4000, three hours) leave every hour or so, while Mawlamyine buses (from K10,000, six to seven hours) leave at 8am and about 9pm.

TAXI

Some travellers make a day trip out of Bago with a hired car from Yangon, starting from about US$35. A seat in a share taxi is very good value at K5000 one way (especially if your bus stops at Aung Mingalar, from where you'll need to spend K6000 on a taxi); ask your guest house to arrange it a few hours in advance.

TRAIN

Four trains from Yangon stop in Bago en route to Taungoo (ordinary/upper class US$4/8, four hours) and Mandalay (US$11/29, 14 hours) between 6.50am and 2pm, though it can be tricky getting a seat. There are also trains for Mawlamyine (US$5/13, five hours) at 9.15am and 11.45am, and several to Yangon (US$2/5, two hours).

Getting Around

You can get around the sights by trishaw or horse cart (both K4000 to K5000 a day), or motorcycle taxi for K4000/6000 a half-/full day, or K10,000 if you avoid the ticket; negotiate.

TAUNGOO

☎ 054 / pop 90,000

It's hard to imagine this was once the nerve centre of a powerful kingdom. Today's Taungoo is a sleepy place that most people see from a bus or train window. However, it gets the 'real-deal experience' thumbs up from those who do stop and is home to one of Myanmar's more memorable guest houses. Taungoo is just under halfway from Yangon to Mandalay.

Shwesandaw Paya (1597) is the main pilgrimage site, among several other Buddhist sites on and around the 'royal lake', on the town's west side.

Taungoo is the launch point to see real working elephants hauling logs around the Karen mountains. There are two **elephant camps**, but even in a group they're not cheap at $62 per person for four (higher with fewer heads). If this seems worth it for a once-in-a-lifetime experience, speak to Dr Chan from the guest house following.

Run by the engaging Dr Chan, **Myanmar Beauty Guest House II, III & IV** (☎ 23270; chan_aye@yangon.net.mm; Pauk Hla Gyi St; r US$10-30; ☒) consists of three teak houses with poster beds, hot showers and wide-open views of the rice paddies and hills that loom beyond. Rates include a large local breakfast. It's located just to the north of the bridge, in the south of town.

Heading north or south on air-con buses you'll pay the full fare. Most stop near the hospital, in the centre. Local buses to Yangon (K4000, six hours) leave at 6am, 9am, noon and 8pm. Mandalay buses (K11,000) pass about 6pm.

PYAY (PROME)

☎ 053 / pop 95,000

All roads lead to Pyay, at least some important ones from Yangon, Bagan and Ngapali Beach do, not forgetting the mighty Ayeyarwady River. Most visitors just steam on through, which is a pity because it's a laid-back place with river views and nearby ruins older than Bagan's. The central statue of Aung San on horseback is 2km west of the bus station, just south of the main market, and a block east of the Ayeyarwady.

THROUGH THE LOOKING GLASS TO NAY PYI TAW

Myanmar can be a pretty weird place, and nowhere so much as Nay Pyi Taw. Meaning 'Royal Capital' or 'Abode of the Kings' (delusions, anyone?), Nay Pyi Taw became the capital in 2005 after these scrubby low hills between Yangon and Mandalay were chosen, it is widely speculated, by superstitious leader Than Shwe's astrologer.

There is no reason to stay, and we're not encouraging it. But given the place is such a mystery to the international media, and you'll definitely be the first of your friends to get there, it's worth breaking your trip for a look around. That's what we thought, anyway. After arriving in Pyinmana, 5km away, we hired a motorcycle taxi (K9000 for four hours) and set off. The smooth, six-lane roads were largely deserted except for some bedraggled pedestrians and air-con Japanese buses ferrying bureaucrats around. The ministry buildings, the enormous three kings statue and, no surprise here, the generals' mansions are off-limits to foreigners.

So instead we went to the expensive hotel zone, the market and nearby 'beer-station hill', past hundreds of empty-looking modern apartments and endless construction to the first 'tourist attraction', the 200-acre National Herbal Park (about 750m or so west of the roundabout). The whole place was surreal, like a model city built to impress some VIP visitor, but totally without a population.

But the best was saved for last. Uppasanti Pagoda, aka the 'Generals' Shwedagon', is a nearly life-size replica of the Shwedagon Paya that the generals hope will buy legitimacy for their new capital. We were met by members of the Nay Pyi Taw police special branch and the welcome wasn't exactly warm. But after five looks at our passports and much chatter on their walkie talkies, they decided it was OK to take a look around. The complex is huge, with two lifts leading up and a dozen other buildings surrounding the central, hollowed out stupa. 'Work started in November 2006 and it will be finished very soon', one of my 'guides' proudly explained as grim-faced women polished the tiled floors nearby. By comparison the real Shwedagon took almost 2500 years to reach its current height. As we left we couldn't help wondering how much money had been spent on Myanmar's second Shwedagon, and whether one wasn't enough.

Sights

Perched atop a central hill, the attractive **Shwesandaw Paya** is actually 1m taller than Shwedagon Paya in Yangon, and apparently dates from 589 BC. The double golden *hti* atop the *zedi* represent peace between the Mon and Burmese; the second was put up when Burmese leader Alaungpaya captured the city in 1755. Facing the *paya* from the east is **Sehtatgyi Paya** (Big Ten Storey), a giant seated Buddha.

Sleeping & Eating

Myat Lodging House (☎ 21361; 222 Bazaar St; s US$6-12, d US$10-14; ❄) Two blocks north of Aung San, and two in from the river, this family-run guest house has simple, well-loved rooms. Share bathrooms are clean, but only the top-priced rooms have private bathrooms. Pyay maps are available.

Lucky Dragon (☎ 24222; luckydragon@mail4u.com.mm; Strand Rd; r US$20-25; ❄ 💻 🚗) If you're after more luxury, these modern, bungalow-style rooms, situated across from the river, should satisfy.

Hline Ayar (Strand Rd; dishes K1200-6500; 🕑 9am-9pm) The tables overlooking the river, the big menu and the regular 7pm pop-singing thing make this live-house spot an entertaining after-hours choice.

Getting There & Away

Ferries run along the Ayeyarwady from Pyay, but schedules are notoriously variable. Most weeks there is at least one ferry each to Yangon (deck/cabin US$8/18, three days) and Mandalay (US$12/25, five days). The **IWT office** (☎ 24503; Strand Rd; 🕑 9am-5pm Mon-Fri) has details.

The highway bus station, 2km east of the centre, sends frequent buses to Yangon (K4500, six hours). No direct buses go to Bagan; either jump on a Yangon–Bagan bus (for full fare) or take the 8am bus to Magwe and pick-ups to Nyaung U via Kyaukpadaung. To reach Thandwe (near Ngapali Beach), catch a bus to Taunggok (K14,500, nine hours) at 6pm, from where you can catch a bus or pick-up to Thandwe (four hours).

A lone daily train to Yangon (ordinary/upper class US$6/15, eight hours) leaves at 8pm.

AROUND PYAY

About 8km east of Pyay, **Thayekhittaya** (Sri Ksetra; admission US$5, plus for the (unworthy) museum another US$5; 8am-5pm) is a sprawling oval-shaped walled city of the enigmatic Pyu, who ruled here as far back as 1500 years ago. The only real way around the site is by ox cart (K4000), which makes a 12km loop in about three hours. Most sites are at least partly ruined, but you'll likely have the place to yourself. The 46m-high cylindrical Bawbawgyi Paya is the finest of the temples. There are no direct pick-ups, so most people take a return blue taxi for about K6000. It is possible to cycle to the site, but not around it.

West of the road to Yangon, about 14km south of Pyay, **Shwemyetman Paya** (Paya of the Golden Spectacles) is home to a large, white-faced, seated Buddha – sporting a pair of giant gold-plated glasses! Hop on a local Yangon-bound bus or south-bound pick-up, and get off in Shwedaung town.

SOUTHEASTERN MYANMAR

Teetering on the brink, the Golden Rock of Kyaiktiyo draws a few visitors off the main trail for a tough-but-rewarding pilgrimage. There is, however, more to the southeast than this surreal sacred stone. Mawlamyine offers glimpses of old Burma and is the launching pad for the scenic boat ride upriver to Hpa-an, the way-off-the-beaten-track, way welcoming capital of Kayin (Karen) State.

KYAIKTIYO (GOLDEN ROCK)

☎ 057

The gravity-defying golden rock Kyaiktiyo is one of the most enigmatic and intriguing sights in Myanmar. Perched on the very edge of a cliff on Mt Kyaiktiyo, this giant, gold-leaf-covered boulder is topped by a stupa containing a Buddha hair donated by a hermit in the 11th century. Apparently, the hair was salvaged from the bottom of the sea and brought here by boat. The boat subsequently turned to stone and is visible a few hundred metres away.

Kyaiktiyo has a mystical aura; it's a place of miracles, not least of which is how the boulder has managed to hang on, withstanding several earthquakes, for all these years. Pilgrims come in their thousands and the experience is more interesting because of them. That said, on weekends especially the mountaintop can feel like a theme park.

Some travellers make a gruelling day trip from Yangon. This is madness, as it warrants more time and is especially beautiful illuminated at night. Plan on spending a night in nearby Kinpun.

Orientation

It's a bit confusing. The town of Kyaikto is about 24km from the Golden Rock and there's no reason to stop here. Instead, go direct to **Kinpun**, 13km from Kyaikto town and often referred to as 'base camp'. Kinpun is a collection of restaurants and guest houses 11km from the summit of Mt Kyaiktiyo. There's no internet.

Sights

There are two ways to see the rock: hiking 11km uphill from Kinpun (four to six hours one way), or trucking and then walking. On this trip we wanted to see the sunrise, but didn't want to pay for the top-of-the-hill hotels, so set off at 2am and arrived – thighs freakin' burning – for a 6.30am 'sunrise' sans soleil. Was it worth it? Kind of…. Most sane people take the packed trucks from Kinpun (K1500, front seat K3000) that ply upwards from 6am to 5.30pm, stopping for a 45-minute walk to the rock along a steep, paved path thronging with pilgrims.

If you want to feel like an extra in *Burmese Days,* four sweating men can carry you up in a bamboo sedan-chair for about K10,000. Only men are permitted to walk along a short chasm-spanning bridge to the boulder itself.

There is a US$6 government fee collected from foreigners at an **office** (6am-6pm), just beyond the Mountain Top Inn; some travellers report dodging this by immersing themselves in a gaggle of pilgrims.

Sleeping & Eating

These three Kinpun places are the only ones that accept foreigners; the first two are metres from where the transport stops. All include breakfast.

Pann Myo Thu Inn (☎ 60285; s US$5-10, d US$10-12;) This plant-filled, family-run place is more personal than the Sea Sar, and the cheaper rooms are good value.

Sea Sar Guest House (☎ 60367; s US$5-15, d US$8-25; ❄) Another popular choice with a wide variety of rooms, in varying states of repair; ask to see several.

Golden Sunrise Hotel (☎ in Yangon 01-701027; gsunrise@myanmar.com.mm; s/d U$17/20; ❄) A few minutes' walk outside Kinpun in the direction of the highway, these eight clean, spacious, bamboo-heavy bungalows are the pick for anyone seeking comfort.

To see the sunset and/or sunrise over the Golden Rock without walking in the dark you need to stay up top. Rooms at **Mountain Top Inn & Restaurant** (☎ in Yangon 01-502479; grtt@goldenrock.com.mm; s/d US$45/60) are pretty basic for your buck, but then you're paying for the location, five minutes' walk to the rock.

Several Chinese and Bamar restaurants line the main street of Kinpun. All are decent, though none outstanding, so just look for somewhere with a crowd. There's plenty of food up top, too.

Getting There & Away

Buses en route from Yangon to points further south stop in Kyaikto, but often arrive at inconvenient late-night times. Direct services run between Yangon's Aung Mingalar Bus Terminal and Kinpun (K7000, 4½ hours), leaving Yangon several times between 7am and 1pm. From Kinpun you can take a bus/pick-up (K3000/2500, two/three hours) to Bago.

Pick-ups travel south to Hpa-an and Mawlamyine (K3500, front seat K5000, five hours) from 6am to 1pm.

Three trains a day stop at Kyaikto en route to/from Yangon (ordinary/1st/upper class US$4/7/10, five hours) and Mawlamyine (US$3/6/8, four hours). Trains depart both Yangon and Mawlamyine between 7am and 9.45am.

MAWLAMYINE (MOULMEIN)

☎ 057/pop 300,000

Known as Moulmein to George Orwell during his time as a policeman here, and also to Rudyard Kipling who wrote about it after spending just three days, Myanmar's third-largest city feels more like an overgrown provincial town. Much of the colonial architecture has been replaced by bland Chinese blocks overlooking the Thanlwin (Salween) River, though there is enough character to keep you amused for a day or two. A 3km-long bridge, which was opened in 2005, has reduced to a trickle the traditional river traffic. Which is a pity, because it means the best reason to visit Mawlamyine – the ferry ride to Hpa-an through jungle and sheer limestone karsts – is on borrowed time. Mawlamyine has all the traveller life-support systems, including several internet places on the main street.

The **Mon Cultural Museum** (cnr Baho & Dawei Jetty Rds; admission US$2) has a modest selection of Mon pieces. For a cityscape and peaceful ramble, climb the tallest stupa, **Kyaikthanlan Paya**, or other nearby pagodas. The sprawling *zeigyo* (market), between the river and South Bogyoke Rd, was being rebuilt when we passed so will probably reopen cleaner but less photogenic sometime in 2010.

Pa-Auk-Taw-Ya Kyaung (☎ 032-22132; www.paauk.org) is one of the largest meditation centres in Myanmar, and indeed the world, about 14km south of town.

Picturesque **Shampoo Island** (Guangse Kyun) is a pleasant diversion for an hour or two. It's reached by boat (1500K return) from near the Mawlamyine Hotel, at the north end of town.

The best budget lodging is **Breeze Rest House** (Lay Hnyin Tha; ☎ 09 870 1180; 6 Strand Rd; s US$5-15, d US$8-15; ❄). Set in an old, blue-painted villa on the riverfront, rooms range from bed-sized cells downstairs to enormous rooms with bathroom upstairs; see a few. The friendly owner is a wealth of information on the area, and will probably offer an impromptu meditation lesson.

Sandalwood Hotel (☎ 27253; Myoma Tadar St; s/d US$8/15; ❄), a centrally located newbie, has a bit more comfort (think air-con, hot water and satellite TV) and cleanliness, but less character.

Ferries to Hpa-an (US$2, five hours) leave from the Hpa-an jetty about noon Mondays and Fridays.

Buses to Yangon (K10,000, seven or eight hours) leave the bus station on the far side of town between 6pm and 7pm. Buses and pick-ups to Hpa-an (K1500, two hours) leave hourly from 8am to 3pm from the bus station, less often from the *zeigyo*.

The train station is on the east side of Mawlamyine (about 800K by moto taxi). Three daily express trains run to Yangon (ordinary/1st/upper class US$7/13/18, nine hours), stopping in Kyaiktiyo and Bago.

GETTING TO THAILAND: KAWTHOUNG TO RANONG

It is possible to enter Thailand at Kawthoung, but given you need to fly here or – if you're very lucky – arrive by several boats from the north, most shoestringers don't bother. If the trip is more important than the money to you, then you'll need to visit MTT in Yangon (p546) at least 10 days before you intend to cross so they can organise a permit for you. That permit (US$15) can be picked up from the **Kawthoung MTT office** (☎ 059-51578; Bosunphet Rd). MTT in Yangon can also advise on whether you still need a permit just to fly to Kawthoung.

Right, so assuming (and that's always dangerous when it comes to Myanmar border crossings) that you get the above all sorted, boats shuttle between Kawthoung and Ranong (Thailand), 10km away, regularly from about 7.30am to 5.30pm (250B, 40 minutes). The **immigration office** (🕑 8am-5.30pm) in Kawthoung is at the jetty, while the Thai **immigration office** (Th Ruangrat; 🕑 8.30am-6pm) is 700m north of Saphan Pla (Pla Bridge) pier, where the boats dock; it issues 15-day entry permits on arrival (see p831). The pier is 4.5km from the centre of Ranong, but you should be able to catch a *săwngthăew* (small pick-up truck with two benches in the back) into town (7B). Myanmar is half an hour behind Thailand.

See p807 for information on doing the trip in the opposite direction.

HPA-AN

☎ 058

Verdant, village-like Hpa-an is hemmed in by higgledy-piggledy hills rising abruptly from fields of rice and sugarcane. There are the inevitable golden stupas, but the best activities are outside town. Climb the steps up **Mt Zwegabin** (722m), 11km south of town, for gods'-eye views, an 11am monkey-feeding session and free monastery lunch at noon. Vast **Saddar Cave**, aka the Gates of Hell, is full of Buddhist iconography and stalagmites. Bring a torch and clamber 15 minutes through the darkness to a clear lake. Public transport is possible, but slow; Soe Brothers offers an all-day motorbike tour to these plus other sights (30,000K), or take a map and bike and DIY.

Accommodation pickings are slim, but all have helpful managers. **Soe Brothers Guest House** (☎ 21372; 46 Thitsa Rd; s US$4-7, d US$8-10), near the market, is the backpacker fave due mainly to the owners, who have handy maps of town and can arrange tours. Rooms range from tiny wooden cells to slightly larger spaces with modest private bathrooms; either way, you can forget about swinging cats. Rooms with private bathroom and air-con can be found at the **Golden Sky** (s/d US$10-15/15-20; ❄), nearer the river.

The boat to Mawlamyine (US$2, four hours) leaves Hpa-An on Mondays and Fridays around 5.45am, meaning you pass the best scenery in the dark. Buses run to Yangon (K8000, eight hours) at 6.30am and 5pm (yes, rubbish timing); buy tickets at the highway bus station, 2km from town, or ticket offices beside the clock tower. Alternatively, you could take a pick-up to Tha Tein (K1500, two hours) from outside the central maroon-painted mosque, then another to Kyaiktiyo (K1000).

KAWTHOUNG

Crossing the Pagyan River from Ranong, Thailand to Myanmar's southernmost tip is like stepping back in time. The waterfront is lined with teashops and money changers, plus touts offering to take visa-running tourists back to Thailand. The offshore **Myeik (Mergui) Archipelago** is one of the most beautiful, unexplored parts of Southeast Asia. Unfortunately, however, if you want to venture into these drop-dead gorgeous seas then you're better off in Phuket, with pockets full of cash.

For other reasons why you probably won't come to Kawthoung, read the Getting to Thailand boxed text (above). If you do happen to wind up here, you'll find accommodation options are limited and bad value. **Kawthoung Motel** (Bogyoke Rd; r 800B; ❄), 400m uphill from the jetty, has simple rooms with cold-water private bathrooms.

In theory, Kawthoung is connected to Myeik (US$26, 6½ hours) and Dawei (another US$20, 6½ hours) to the north by 'daily' fast boats, but in reality you might wait days for a departure. Flying is little better, with both Air Bagan and Yangon Airways flights to Yangon often cancelled. Foreigners cannot travel north by road.

INLE LAKE & SHAN STATE

Shan State is vast, untamed and – with rebel groups, warlords and drug dealers living in its mysterious mountains – largely unexplored by and off-limits to foreigners. Of the places you can go Inle Lake is the main attraction, a beautiful body of water hemmed in by mountains and populated by floating communities and endless tomato farms. Trekking is hugely popular here and Kalaw is the affordable base for adventure. This is one of the few parts of Myanmar where homestays are possible and the Shan are some of the friendliest folk in the country.

INLE LAKE

☎ 081 / pop 150,000

A wonderful watery world of floating gardens, stilted villages and crumbling stupas, Inle Lake is one of those few places that are a tonic for the soul. Mountains tumble down towards the lakeshore, blurring the distinction between heaven and earth. And for many travellers, Inle is heaven on earth, a place to while away the days canoeing, cycling and walking through the lush countryside. The Intha people are famous for their leg rowing, although these days many just turn it on for the tourists. There is even a monastery where meditating monks have taught the (enlightened?) cats to jump. Inle deserves to be savoured, not rushed, and many travellers end up staying longer than they expected.

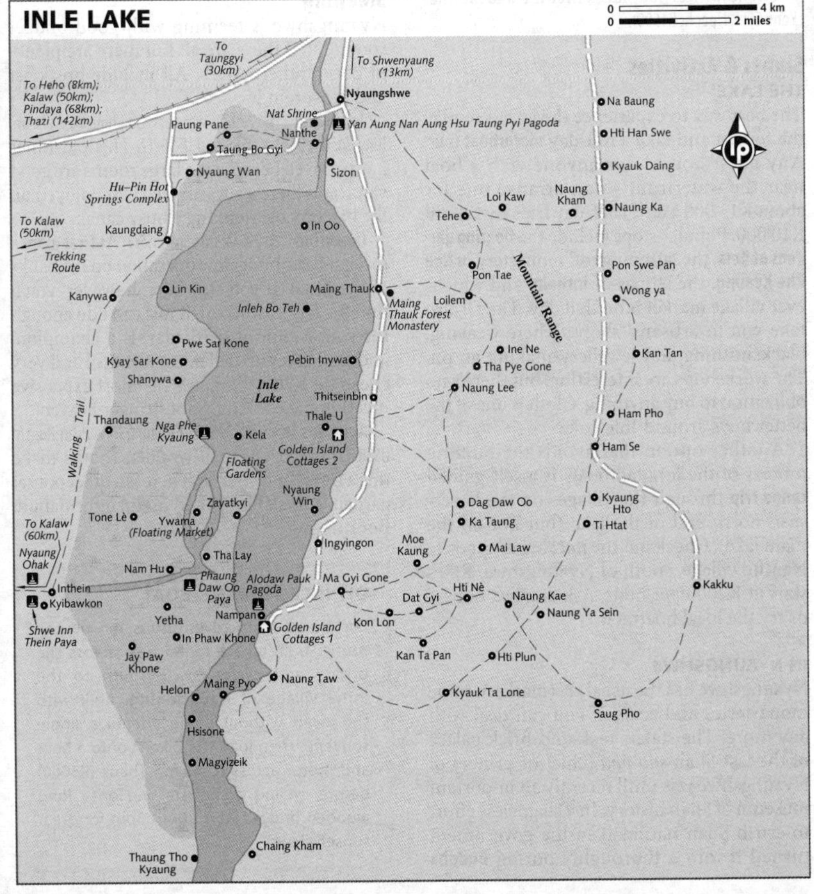

In September and October the **Phaung Daw U festival** runs for nearly three weeks, and is followed by the **Thadingyut festival**, one of Myanmar's best-known events (see p595). Always cooler than the rest of the country, Inle gets downright chilly at night in January and February.

Orientation & Information

The village of Nyaungshwe (Yaunghwe), at the north end of Inle Lake, is home to all the budget accommodation and traveller services and is easily navigated by foot or bicycle. Most transport will drop you at Shwenyaung, the transport hub 13km north, en route to the Shan State capital of Taunggyi. From here you'll take a taxi or pick-up to Nyaungshwe, stopping to pay a US$3 fee to enter the Inle Lake zone.

The few internet places include **KKO Internet** (Yone Gyi Rd; per hr K1500).

Sights & Activities

THE LAKE

The best way to experience the lake is to play the tourist and take a full-day **motorboat tour**. Any guest house – or anyone with a boat near the waterfront – can arrange one for about K15,000 a day. Half-day trips cost about K10,000. Popular stops include the **floating gardens of Kela**, the 'jumping cat' monastery of **Nga Phe Kyaung**, the stupas of **Inthein**, and whichever village market is on that day. They'll also take you to artisans' shops, where weaving, blacksmithing and jewellery-making go on. The workshops are interesting, but there's no obligation to buy anything. Cloth is one of the better buys around Inle Lake.

Another option that avoids the buzzing motors of the longtail boats is a self-guided **canoe trip** through the villages on the lesser-seen north end of the lake (but not on the main lake). Check out the *nat* shrine opposite Nanthe village, south of Nyaungshwe. Rates start at K2000 per hour. Ask at guest houses or try the local boatmen.

IN NYAUNGSHWE

Nyaungshwe has the usual *zei* (market), some monasteries and *zedis*, if you can deal with any more. The stately teak-and-brick palace of the last Shan *sao pha* (chief or prince) of Nyaungshwe was until recently an important museum of Shan history. In a shameless effort to crush Shan nationalism the government turned it into a thoroughly boring **Buddha Museum** (Museum St [Third St]; admission US$2; ⏲ 9.30am-3.30pm Tue-Sun); take a look from outside, but save your money.

OTHER ACTIVITIES

Turn up the heat at the **hot spring** (public/private bathing US$4/8, mixed sex US$5; ⏲ 5am-6pm), 1.5km north of Kaungdaing. Rent a *longyi* for bathing for K500. A boat comes here from Nyaungshwe (K2000 each way), or cycle on a bumpy, hour-long ride.

Guided **day treks** can usually be arranged through guest houses for approximately US$8 per person. There is a good, but fairly rugged, all-day trip that leads to the monastery of **Koun Soun Taungbo** and a nearby cave, via two Pa-O villages.

Sleeping

Nyaungshwe is teeming with good budget rooms, so if these are all full there are plenty of decent alternatives. All include breakfast and most rent bicycles.

Joy Hotel (☎ 29083; warwarkhamkhine@gmail.com; Jetty Rd; dm US$4, s US$5-9, d US$6-12) This old-timer has survived because the large rooms are good value and there's a warm feel, best enjoyed on the balcony overlooking a busy canal.

Queen Inn (☎ 29544; s/d from US$5/7) At first glance this is a basic bungalow operation on the banks of the canal. If you stay here, however, you'll find the family who run it just can't do enough for you. Mum, in particular, is a champion, and she serves up delicious, plentiful and very cheap (at K2000 dinner is the most expensive meal) home cooking. Shoestringer heaven.

Aquarius Inn (☎ 29615; 2 Phaung Daw Pyan Rd; s/d US$6/12) Large, cosy, all-wooden rooms make this a traveller favourite. There is a quiet bonsai garden, a small library and useful information. Book ahead.

DIY INLE BY BIKE & BOAT

For cheap, semi-adventurous fun off the tourist trail, take a rental bike across the bridge and cycle slowly south to the Intha village of **Kaungdaing**. Chill with the locals without being offered a single souvenir, then load the bike(s) onto a boat and motor across to Maing Thauk (K5000) before cycling home, starting on a long wooden bridge. Start about 3pm for great sunset views.

Teakwood Hotel (☎ 29250; teakwood.htl@gmail.com; s US$15-20, d US$20-30) This old teakwood home has been expanded and renovated and the smart rooms are excellent value if you're seeking more comfort. The family is very welcoming, including matriarch Mrs Tin, who looks exactly how you'd imagine a Shan princess. Ask about its guided canoe tours (US$15).

Golden Island Cottages 1 & 2 (☎ 29389, in Yangon 01-549019; www.gicmyanmar.com; s US$40, d US$70) Fancy a dash more romance than bare guest house walls and squeaky beds? These two hotels sit on Inle Lake, with a main lodge connected to smart, stilted cottages via elevated walkways. Thale U (no 2), which backs onto a bird-filled wetland, is the pick, especially in low season (single/double US$30/50). Both places are run by a Pa-O collective.

Other budget options:

Nawng Kham (Little Inn; ☎ 29195; Phaung Daw Pyan Rd; s/d US$5/10) Seven simple-but-clean rooms set around a garden; good if the Aquarius is full.

Min Ga Lar (☎ 29198; Phaung Daw Pyan Rd; s US$7-10, d US$10-15) Crisp sheets, communal space, fair value.

Four Sisters Inn (☎ 29190; 105 Nan Pan Qtr; s/d US$7/12) Only two sisters left, but they're plenty nice.

Eating & Drinking

Lotus Restaurant (Museum St [Third St]; dishes K1000-2500) One of several small, open-fronted places in town serving Intha and Shan dishes, such as a mild fish curry with plenty of tomato and onion (K2000). Owner U Pyone Cho doubles as a trekking guide.

Smiling Moon Restaurant (Yone Gyi Rd; dishes from K1000) A laid-back terrace restaurant serving hill tribe food and the traveller holy trinity of Chinese, pasta and pancakes.

Shanland Restaurant (Jetty Rd; meals from K1500) Go native and enjoy it at this rustic, Shan-style place serving cheap local dishes; the fish cooked in banana leaf is particularly good.

View Point (☎ 29062; Talk Nan Bridge; mains K2500-5000) Where are we again? Looking more like a Mediterranean villa and feeling like a European lounge bar, this Swiss-Intha venture is well worth a splurge. The 'Shan nouvelle cuisine' is delicious, blending European presentation with local flavours. It's not cheap, but doable if you stop in a beer station first (View Point's beer is K4000).

If you are no longer egg-cited by the hotel breakfast, head to Nyaungshwe's **Mingala market**

(Main Rd) for a Shan *hkauq-sweh* (noodle soup) in the morning. Later in the day there is a range of exotic-looking snacks available, plus luscious fresh fruits.

Entertainment

Aung Traditional Puppet Show (off Yone Gyi Rd; admission K3000; ⏰ 7pm & 8.30pm) This local puppet troupe performs a 30-minute show nightly. It's a good deal compared with US$8 in Mandalay.

Getting There & Away

AIR

Yangon Airways, Air Mandalay and Air Bagan all fly between Heho, 41km northwest, and Yangon (about US$70), Mandalay (about US$30) and Nyaung U (for Bagan, US$50); the Mandalay flight is particularly popular as it saves you a 10-hour bus trip. Local travel agents can issue tickets. A taxi from Heho will cost at least K18,000; less going to the airport.

BUS & PICK-UP

Road transport to anywhere takes the Union Hwy, aka Shan Hwy, a national disgrace that just keeps getting worse; expect delays. All buses start or finish at Taunggyi and stop at the Shwenyaung junction: the bus to Bagan (K13,000, 10 hours) passes by about 7.30am; the bus to Mandalay (K10,000, 10 hours) from 7.30pm to 9pm; and night buses to Yangon (K18,000, 16 to 20 hours) stop around 2.30pm.

Pick-ups ply these routes but take much more time. Be prepared for cold if you are travelling in January.

Getting Around

Bicycles are available for about K1000 per day. Pick-ups from Shwenyaung, 13km away, to Nyaungshwe (K500) run from 6am to 6pm. Buses also come and go.

PINDAYA

☎ 081 / pop 20,000

The **Pindaya Caves** (admission US$3) are a popular stop on the Shan State circuit. Here 8090 Buddha images form a labyrinth throughout the chambers of the caves. The condensation on the 'perspiring Buddhas' is rubbed on the face for good luck.

Golden Cave Hotel (☎ 40227; 106 Zaytan Quarter; r from US$20) is worth the money for its warm location on the steps of the Shwe Oo Min cave, and helpful staff.

From Kalaw, take a bus or pick-up to Aungban and change for Pindaya (K1500, two hours); be at Aungban by 8am and allow a full day. Easier is hiring a taxi from Kalaw for K35,000 return.

KALAW

☎ 081 / pop about 25,000

Kalaw is Myanmar's trekking heartland, combining cool mountain climbs and a chilled vibe to become, for budgeteers, the most-visited destination in the country outside the 'Big Four'. Located at 1320m on the rolling, pine-clad hills of the Shan Plateau, Kalaw is the beginning point for hikes heading west to Inle Lake (about 45km), over mountains dotted with Palaung, Pa-O, Intha and Shan villages.

Kalaw is easy to navigate on foot. An **internet cafe** (Aung Chantha Rd; per hr 1500; ⏰ 8am-10pm) is just uphill from the mirror-mosaics of **Aung Chan Tha Zedi** (Aung Chantha Rd).

Activities

Exploring the pretty countryside on foot is the main reason to stop in Kalaw; colourful minority villages and striking scenery are the main rewards. An array of local guides can tailor individual itineraries. During high season (November to February) it can get pretty busy on the more popular routes, while in the wet season paths get miserably muddy and few tourists head this way. Every man and his dog in Kalaw is a potential guide, but the better ones are licensed. Prices vary, starting at about US$8 for a day trek for one person, US$10 for two. Overnight treks are more, as are longer routes.

The Singh brothers from Golden Lily Guest House and guides from **Sam's Family Trekking** (☎ 50237; samtrekking@gmail.com; Union Hwy) are consistently good. Shop around before agreeing on a price.

Treks to Inle Lake take two or three days and include nights in a village or a monastery. It's worth requesting a route via the villages of several different ethnic groups. Have good shoes and warm clothing for the cool evenings. Guest houses can transport your unneeded bags for a small charge.

When visiting villages, it's better to contribute cash to the monastery's *sayadaw* (head teacher) than hand out gifts of any kind.

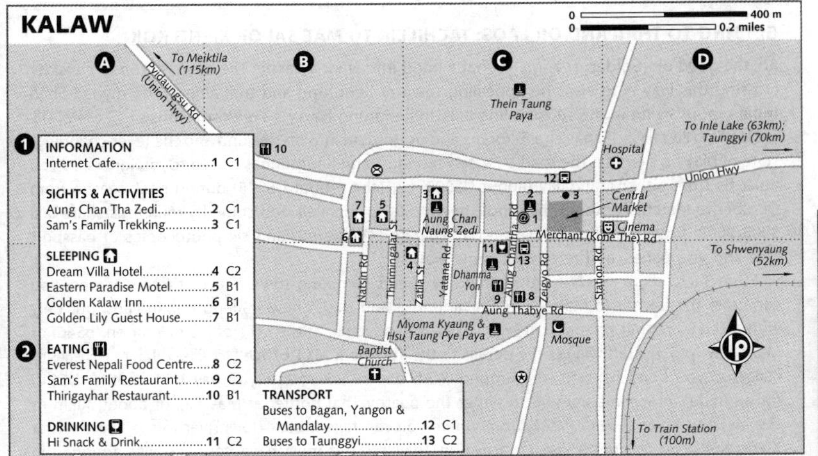

Sleeping

Electricity is especially temperamental here, but you won't need air-con (or even a fan) to sleep. All rates include breakfast.

Golden Kalaw Inn (☎ 50311; 5/92 Natsin Rd; s US$3-5, d US$6-8) Right next door to Lily, this simple place in a rambling old house has large rooms, a communal hanging area downstairs and views across town from the balcony.

Golden Lily Guest House (☎ 50108; goldenlily@myanmar.com.mm; 5/88 Natsin Rd; s/d US$5/10; 💻) A popular family-run place, the Golden Lily has large, bare-but-clean rooms with private bathroom, most opening onto a wide deck overlooking town. Reliable guides Harri and Robin Singh are based here. Some family members, however, take selling treks too seriously. But they serve tasty Indian breakfasts.

Eastern Paradise Motel (☎ 50315; 5 Thirimingalar St; s/d from US$6/12) A cheerful, chintzy place where the upstairs rooms are better than those off the lobby. Gets regular good reports.

Dream Villa Hotel (☎ 50144; dreamvilla@myanmar.com.mm; Zatila St; s US$18-25, d US$22-35) Dream Villa's clean, bright, wood-panelled rooms and easy-going family atmosphere make it a top choice in this range. More expensive rooms are bigger, with bathtubs and satellite TV.

Eating & Drinking

Sam's Family Restaurant (☎ 50377; Aung Chantha Rd; dishes from K1000) Candlelit tables are nicely complemented by a big menu of cheap-but-delicious Shan dishes, plus helpful trekking advice from Sam.

Everest Nepali Food Centre (Aung Chantha Rd; dishes from K1500; 🕑 7.30am-9pm) This old favourite, recently made over in bold orange, serves lassis, chapatis and curries with Indian movies or (just shoot me!) back-to-back Mr Bean cartoons.

Thirigayha Restaurant (Seven Sisters; ☎ 50216; Union Hwy; meals from K5000; 🕑 till 10pm) For romance, there's really only one choice. The menu runs from well-prepared Shan traditional meals to beef stroganoff, noodle soups and Indian curries and there's often a guitarist serenading diners.

Hi Snack & Drink (Merchant Rd) For a dose of local nightlife, this hole-in-the-wall wooden bar churns out beer and hosts occasional impromptu guitar concerts.

Getting There & Away

Many buses pass through Kalaw en route from Bagan, Yangon and Mandalay (usually arriving late at night) to Taunggyi. Despite the timing, many travellers get off here to walk to Inle Lake. Guest houses can help with tickets, as can the general store near the bus stop in town.

From Taunggyi, buses pass en route to Yangon (K18,000, about 18 hours) at about 2.30pm, to Bagan (K12,000, nine hours) about 7.30am, and to Mandalay (K12,000, nine hours) from 7.30pm to 9pm. For Shwenyaung (the Inle Lake junction), occasional minibuses (K2500, three hours) and more frequent pick-ups (K3000, three hours) leave at least every hour from 6am to 4pm. You can charter taxis to Pindaya or Nyaungshwe (both US$30, two hours).

GETTING TO THAILAND OR LAOS: TACHILEIK TO MAE SAI OR XIENG KOK

Ah, the good old Golden Triangle – what a hoot! And what a hassle! The main reason to consider crossing this way is to visit the appealing town of Kengtung and trek among the myriad Shan tribal groups living in the surrounding hills. In Kengtung **Harry's Trekking House** (☎ 084-21418; 132 Mai Yang Rd; r US$6-15) has cheap rooms and up-to-date info on trekking and the (ever-changing) state of play on permits. The road between Taunggyi and Kengtung is closed to foreigners, so you must fly from either Mandalay (about US$90) or Heho (about US$75) during peak season from October to March. At other times you'll need to fly to Tachileik and come by road (bus/share taxi 300B/900B, four/three hours), packing a separate MTT permit and six photocopies of passport face and visa pages, and return the same way.

From Tachileik, a seedy frontier smuggling and gambling town if ever there was one, you can cross the border to Mae Sai in Thailand or – and this is new – Xieng Kok in Laos, but only with a US$50 permit arranged at least 10 days in advance at the MTT office in Yangon (p546) or Mandalay (p573). Staff will fax the details to the **Tachileik MTT office** (☎ 084-51023; near Friendship Bridge) so you don't have to wait around. With paperwork sorted, you pay MTT another US$15 for a 'guide' to accompany you to either the nearby Thai border at Mae Sai, or about 30km to the Mekong River at Wan Pasak, from where you can take a boat downriver to the Lao town of Xieng Kok. You can get a visa on arrival in Thailand, but must have your Lao visa arranged in advance (or continue to Huay Xai and get one there).

In Thailand, buses connect Mae Sai with Bangkok, Chiang Mai and Chiang Rai. In Laos, you can go by road to Maung Sing or take a fast boat downriver to Huay Xai. See p767 for information on doing the trip in reverse, from Mae Sai to Tachileik. MTT says crossing from Laos to Myanmar is possible, but the Lao might not agree and we haven't heard of anyone doing it.

Just to reiterate – the above was correct at the time of research, but double-check everything before setting off. Good luck!

Slow but scenic trains run to Thazi (ordinary/upper class US$3/5, six hours), Heho (US$1/3) and Shwenyaung (US$1/3, four hours) three times daily. Expect delays.

Kalaw is about 45km from Heho airport and a taxi costs K20,000 (see p568 for more on flights.) Coming from Heho it's hard to find people to share with, as most passengers head to Inle Lake. Consider negotiating to Heho village and boarding a pick-up (K3000) from there.

MANDALAY & AROUND

Booming Mandalay may not live up to the mental scenes evoked by Kipling, but the city and its surrounding royal cities are worth a stop. That said, many travellers find the hills of Shan State more memorable. A short drive east of Mandalay are the Shan Hills and an area in stark contrast to the sweltering flatlands. Surreal Pyin U Lwin is worth a visit for nothing more than seeing the country's future military leaders riding in Old West–style stage coaches. And trekking from Hsipaw has become a backpacker favourite.

MANDALAY

☎ 02 / pop 950,000

Thanks to poet Rudyard Kipling – a man who never actually made it here – the name Mandalay evokes images of a timeless, peaceful and alluring Asia unsullied by modern life. But when your road does eventually make it to Mandalay you'll need some imagination to use any of those adjectives to describe the country's second-largest city.

Modern Mandalay is a sprawling, booming place where dusty streets teem with traffic and there's a construction project on every block. In spite of this, it's impossible not to be impressed by the golden Buddha of Mahamuni Paya, or the sunset views across the flat landscape from stupa-studded Mandalay Hill. Mandalay became the capital of the Burmese empire in 1861, an entity that by 1885 had been exiled into history by the British. Prior to Mandalay, several other places within a short distance also served as capitals, and it's these ancient cities that are the real attractions.

Unlike Yangon, Mandalay is booming thanks largely to Chinese investment and, according to the locals, from the red, green and white trades – rubies, jade and heroin.

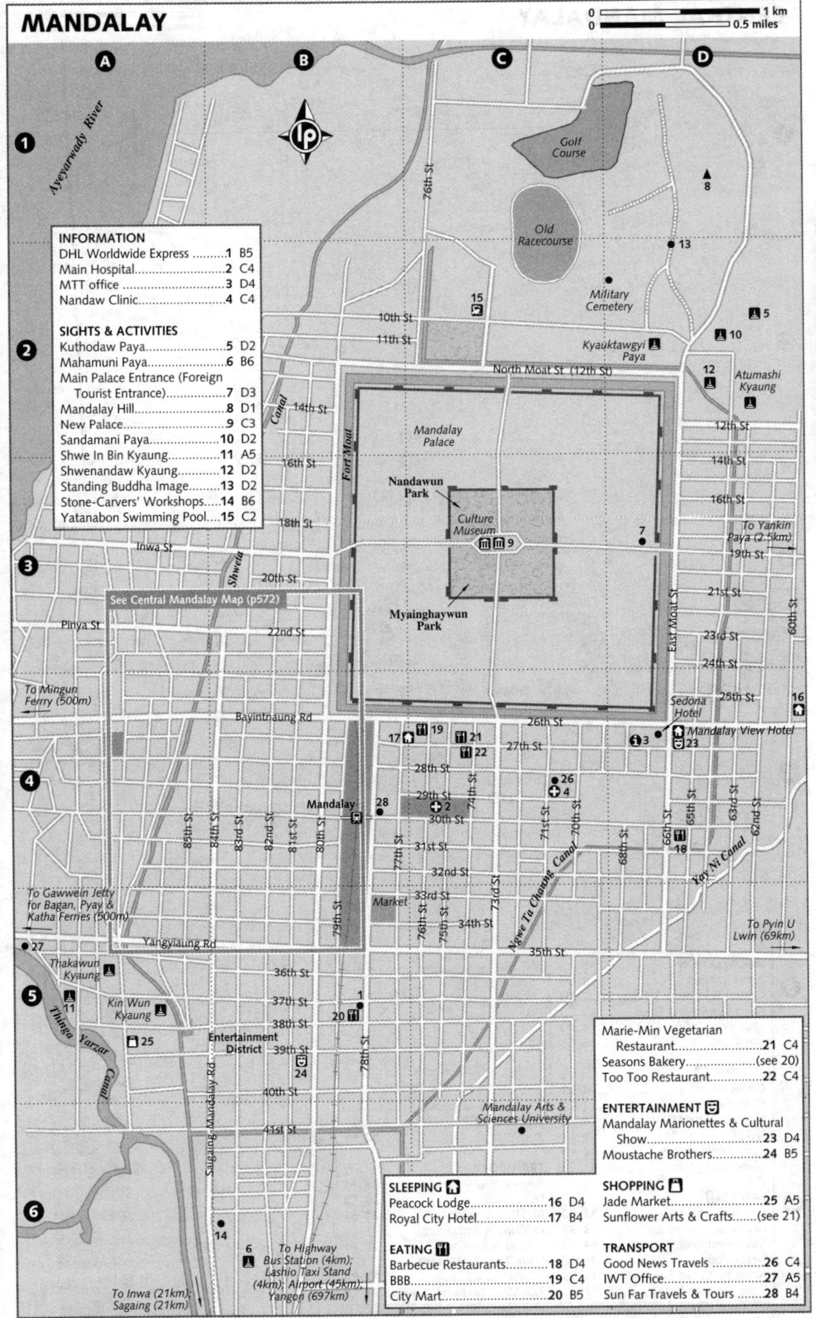
MANDALAY
INFORMATION
DHL Worldwide Express..........1 B5
Main Hospital..........2 C4
MTT office..........3 D4
Nandaw Clinic..........4 C4
SIGHTS & ACTIVITIES
Kuthodaw Paya..........5 D2
Mahamuni Paya..........6 B6
Main Palace Entrance (Foreign Tourist Entrance)..........7 D3
Mandalay Hill..........8 D1
New Palace..........9 C3
Sandamani Paya..........10 D2
Shwe In Bin Kyaung..........11 A5
Shwenandaw Kyaung..........12 D2
Standing Buddha Image..........13 D2
Stone-Carvers' Workshops..........14 B6
Yatanabon Swimming Pool..........15 C2
SLEEPING
Peacock Lodge..........16 D4
Royal City Hotel..........17 B4
EATING
Barbecue Restaurants..........18 D4
BBB..........19 C4
City Mart..........20 B5
Marie-Min Vegetarian Restaurant..........21 C4
Seasons Bakery..........(see 20)
Too Too Restaurant..........22 C4
ENTERTAINMENT
Mandalay Marionettes & Cultural Show..........23 D4
Moustache Brothers..........24 B5
SHOPPING
Jade Market..........25 A5
Sunflower Arts & Crafts..........(see 21)
TRANSPORT
Good News Travels..........26 C4
IWT Office..........27 A5
Sun Far Travels & Tours..........28 B4
Ayeyarwady River
Golf Course
Old Racecourse
Military Cemetery
Kyauktawgyi Paya
Atumashi Kyaung
Mandalay Palace
Nandawun Park
Culture Museum
Myainghaywun Park
North Moat St (12th St)
East Moat St
Fort Moat
Canal
Shweta
See Central Mandalay Map (p572)
To Yankin Paya (2.5km)
To Mingun Ferry (500m)
Sedona Hotel
Mandalay View Hotel
Mandalay
Market
To Gawwein Jetty for Bagan, Pyay & Katha Ferries (500m)
Thakawun Kyaung
Kin Wun Kyaung
Thinga Yarzar Canal
Entertainment District
Ngwe Ta Chaung Canal
Yay Ni Canal
To Pyin U Lwin (69km)
Mandalay Arts & Sciences University
To Highway Bus Station (4km); Lashio Taxi Stand (4km); Airport (45km); Yangon (697km)
To Inwa (21km); Sagaing (21km)
Inwa St
Pinya St
Bayintnaung Rd
Yangyiaung Rd
Sagaing-Mandalay Rd
10th St
11th St
14th St
16th St
18th St
20th St
22nd St
26th St
27th St
28th St
29th St
30th St
31st St
32nd St
33rd St
34th St
35th St
36th St
37th St
38th St
39th St
40th St
41st St
76th St
85th St
84th St
83rd St
82nd St
81st St
80th St
79th St
78th St
77th St
75th St
74th St
73rd St
71st St
70th St
68th St
66th St
65th St
63rd St
62nd St
60th St
12th St
19th St
21st St
23rd St
24th St
25th St
MYANMAR (BURMA)

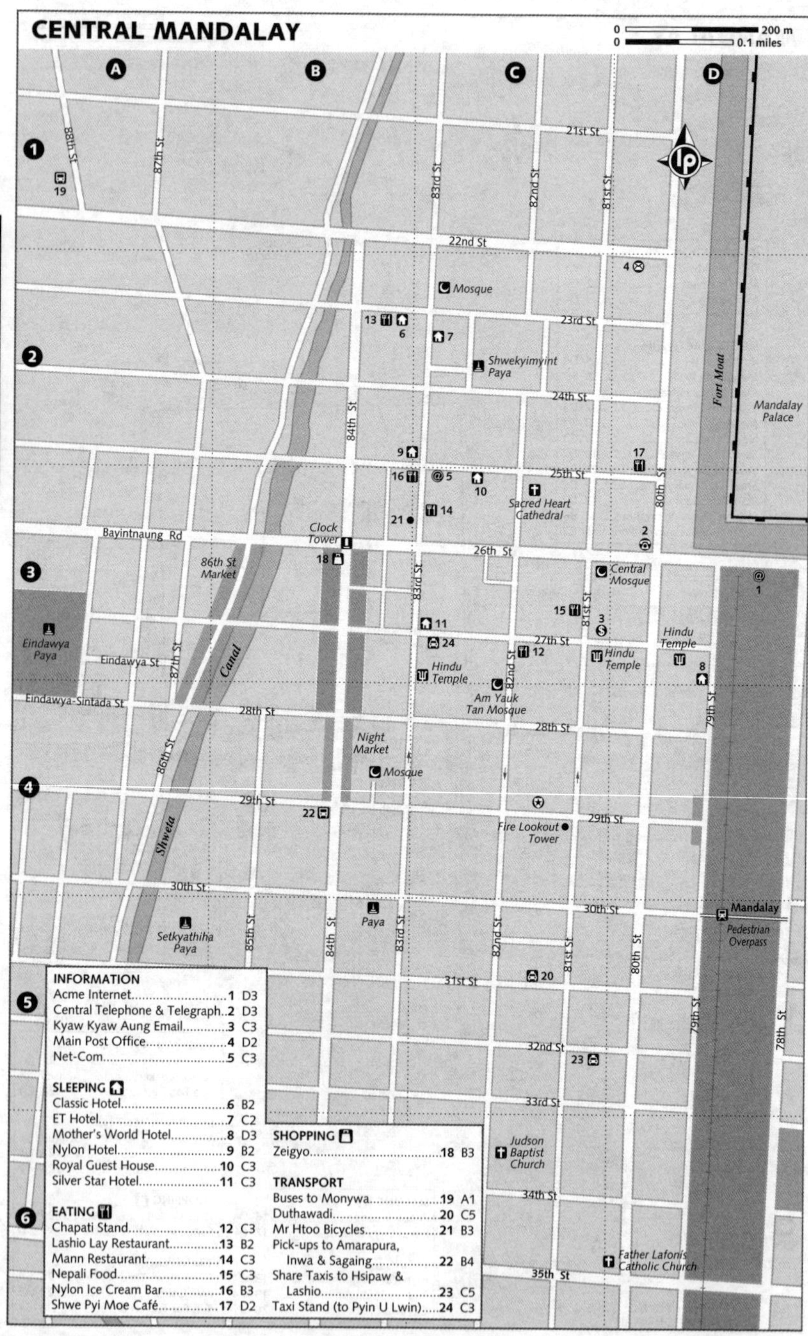
CENTRAL MANDALAY
0 200 m
0 0.1 miles
21st St
22nd St
23rd St
24th St
25th St
26th St
27th St
28th St
29th St
30th St
31st St
32nd St
33rd St
34th St
35th St
88th St
87th St
86th St
85th St
84th St
83rd St
82nd St
81st St
80th St
79th St
78th St
Bayintnaung Rd
Eindawya St
Eindawya-Sintada St
Mosque
Shwekyimyint Paya
Fort Moat
Mandalay Palace
Sacred Heart Cathedral
Clock Tower
86th St Market
Central Mosque
Eindawya Paya
Canal
Hindu Temple
Am Yauk Tan Mosque
Night Market
Shweta
Fire Lookout Tower
Setkyathiha Paya
Paya
Mandalay
Pedestrian Overpass
Judson Baptist Church
Father Lafon's Catholic Church
INFORMATION
Acme Internet 1 D3
Central Telephone & Telegraph 2 D3
Kyaw Kyaw Aung Email 3 C3
Main Post Office 4 D2
Net-Com 5 C3
SLEEPING
Classic Hotel 6 B2
ET Hotel 7 C2
Mother's World Hotel 8 D3
Nylon Hotel 9 B2
Royal Guest House 10 C3
Silver Star Hotel 11 C3
EATING
Chapati Stand 12 C3
Lashio Lay Restaurant 13 B2
Mann Restaurant 14 C3
Nepali Food 15 C3
Nylon Ice Cream Bar 16 B3
Shwe Pyi Moe Café 17 D2
SHOPPING
Zeigyo 18 B3
TRANSPORT
Buses to Monywa 19 A1
Duthawadi 20 C5
Mr Htoo Bicycles 21 B3
Pick-ups to Amarapura, Inwa & Sagaing 22 B4
Share Taxis to Hsipaw & Lashio 23 C5
Taxi Stand (to Pyin U Lwin) 24 C3

Beneath the bustling bravado and low-slung Chinese jeeps, Mandalay's more meditative side is reflected in the fact that it's home to at least 200,000 monks.

Orientation

Mandalay's grid has streets numbered 1 to 59 running east–west, while north–south streets are numbered 60 and above, higher streets to the west. The main arteries include 35th and 80th Sts. The city centre, or 'downtown', runs roughly from 21st to 35th Sts, and 80th to 88th Sts. Street addresses usually include cross streets; '66th St, 26/27' means '66th St between 26th and 27th Sts'.

Information

INTERNET ACCESS

Many guest houses have a lone computer offering internet access for about K1000 per hour. Elsewhere there are plenty of internet cafes, particularly along 27th St. Others include the following:

Acme Internet (Map p572; 26th St, 78/79; per hr 1000K; 9am-10.30pm)
Net-Com (Map p572; 25th St, 82/83; per hr 1000K; 8am-10pm)

MEDICAL SERVICES

Main Hospital (Map p571; 30th St, 74/77)
Nandaw Clinic (Palace Clinic; Map p571; ☎ 36128, 60443; cnr 29th & 71st Sts) This private clinic is a better bet.

MONEY

Exchange rates in Mandalay are slightly lower than in Yangon, but better than elsewhere. You can use credit cards at the Mandalay View Hotel (for 10% commission) and Sedona Hotel (for 4.5%).

Kyaw Kyaw Aung Email (Map p572; 27th St, 80/81; 9am-6pm) No internet, but can cash travellers cheques, change money and arrange credit card cash advances at, steady yourself, a 27% commission.

POST

Main post office (Map p572; 22nd St, 80/81; 10.30am-4pm)

TELEPHONE

Domestic calls can be made cheaply from street stands. Some internet cafes offer VoIP calls for about K500 a minute.

Central Telephone & Telegraph (CTT; Map p572; cnr 80th & 26th Sts; 7am-8.30pm) Absurdly expensive international calls.

TOURIST INFORMATION

Guest houses and hotels are usually reliable sources of local information. For details on boat departures and permissions for travel further upcountry, the women at the government-run **MTT office** (Map p571; ☎ 60356; cnr 68th & 27th Sts; 9am-5pm) are helpful.

Sights

The government collects a flat US$10 fee for a ticket that covers the main sights in Mandalay. Tickets are checked at the palace, Kuthodaw Paya, Shwenandaw Kyaung and Shwe Ta Bin Kyaung. The same ticket is also valid for Amarapura (p578) and Inwa (Ava; p578). Sometimes collection desks don't operate before 8am or after 4.30pm, and alternative entrances bypass ticket checkers. Hint hint.

MAHAMUNI PAYA

If you only see one sight in Mandalay, go for Mahamuni (Map p571), a couple of kilometres south of downtown. Its central Buddha image – the nation's most famous – was brought from Rakhaing State in 1784, and is so highly venerated that it's covered in 6in of gold leaf. It may have been cast as early as the 1st century AD. Every morning at 4am a team of monks lovingly washes the image's face and the soupy run-off is bottled as holy water. Women are not permitted to approach the central altar. In the northwest corner of the surrounding pavilion are six intricate bronze **Khmer figures**, war booty that's been dragged, carted and floated from Angkor Wat via Thailand. It's worth having small notes ready for would-be guides and palm-readers.

There are lots of new Buddha images being hewn from stone at workshops just to the west of the *paya*.

SHWE IN BIN KYAUNG

This elegant **monastery** (Teak Monastery; Map p571; cnr 89th & 38th Sts) located between downtown and Mahamuni Paya dates from 1895, when wealthy Chinese jade merchants funded its construction. It's lovely, off the tourist trail, entry is free, and toothless monks might invite you to watch their prayers. Shwe In Bin Kyaung is at the heart of the city's 'monks' district', so come early and just wander from monastery to monastery, among hundreds of monks walking to and fro along the leafy lanes.

GETTING INTO TOWN

Most visitors arrive at the dusty Highway Bus Station, 7km south of the centre. A taxi to town is about K3000, or take a pick-up. The train station is downtown, south of Mandalay Palace; walk or take a trishaw to most accommodation (trishaws loiter outside). The airport is a staggering 45km southwest of the centre. Taxis are the only option, and depending on your negotiating skills will cost about 15,000K into town and K11,000 going *to* the airport.

MANDALAY HILL

It's a long, hot barefoot climb to the top of Mandalay Hill (Map p571), but what a view. Two hundred and thirty metres above the plain, you can rest your eyes on the Shan hills, the Ayeyarwady and the vast palace grounds, and imagine that they might one day be to Mandalay what Central Park is to New York.

The path is lined with souvenir-sellers, cold-drink hawkers and astrologers. Near the top, a **standing Buddha image** (Map p571) points down at Mandalay, to where, legend has it, Buddha once stood and prophesied a great city would be built in the Buddhist year 2400 (the Roman equivalent of 1857), the year Mindon Min decided to move the capital here.

Most people leave their shoes at the bottom and walk up via the lion-guarded south gate. Alternatively, an elevator/escalator combo leads up from a halfway point reached by switchback road allegedly built by forced labour in the mid-'90s.

A number of pagodas draw visitors and worshippers to the south and southeast of Mandalay Hill. **Kuthodaw Paya** (Map p571), aka the 'world's biggest book', draws tour buses for its 729 slabs that retell the Tripitaka canon. It's included in the US$10 ticket (see p573). Nearby, the more haggard **Sandamani Paya** (Map p571) has more such slabs and is free to get in.

A couple of hundred metres south, the intricately carved wooden **Shwenandaw Kyaung** (Map p571), the only surviving part of the original Mandalay Palace, is worth seeing. It was moved outside the palace walls following King Mindon's death. It's also included in the US$10 ticket.

MANDALAY PALACE & FORT

On the advice of their celestial advisors, the kings of old moved their palaces every generation or two. Mindon Min, one of the last kings of Myanmar, ordered the old palace in Amarapura dismantled in 1861 and relocated to this sprawling, moated complex. Thibaw Min occupied it until the Brits drove him out.

During WWII, fierce fighting between occupying Japanese forces and advancing British and Indian troops resulted in fires that burned the original to the ground.

The **new palace** (Map p571; 7.30am-5pm) was built using concrete, aluminium and, allegedly, forced labour. It's not exactly authentic and, to be frank, isn't worth the unavoidable US$10 ticket imposed at the east entrance, the only one open to foreigners. The rest of the interior – restricted to visitors – is a leafy army barracks. Most visitors, and locals remembering the work it took to rebuild it, avoid visiting the palace at all.

You can walk along a shady **promenade** on the south wall, near downtown, to admire the original walls close up for free.

Activities

Yatanabon Swimming Pool (Map p571; admission K1000; 6am-6pm), located north of the palace, is an Olympic-sized outdoor pool that's the best cheap dip in town.

Sleeping

For a city this size, character and value can be hard to find. Most budget options are concentrated in the downtown area. Many fill up by afternoon in the high season from October to March. Breakfast is included at all places.

our pick **Royal Guest House** (Map p572; ☎ 65697; 41 25th St, 82/83; s US$4-8, d US$8-12;) The long-running Royal squeezes a lot into a rabbit-warren of a space. Rooms are, erm, compact, though consistently clean and comfortable enough. But it's the company, of both friendly and informed staff and fellow travellers, that makes this the most popular backpacker joint in town. Book ahead in high season.

Nylon Hotel (Map p572; ☎ 66550; nylon@mandalay.net.mm; cnr 25th & 83rd Sts; s US$6-8, d US$8-12;) Incongruously housed above a generator shop (no excuse for power cuts!), this place has small clean rooms, all with private bathroom (and some with tubs). Light sleepers beware!

ET Hotel (Map p572; ☎ 65006; 129 83rd St, 23/24; s/d from US$8/10; ❄) Moving towards the Shan district, the ET has functional rooms with private bathrooms that are bigger than the Royal, but there's less atmosphere. That said, the welcome is warm and advice generous.

Peacock Lodge (Map p571; ☎ 61429, 09 204 2059; http://peacocklodge.com; No 5 60th St, 25/26; s/d US$16/20; ❄) There may be better-value rooms elsewhere, but only in this homestay-style lodge do the engaging owners treat you like part of the family. Expect lively conversation over breakfast, and chilled hours reading in the quiet garden. The seven rooms are hidden a fair way out, but it's easy enough to cycle into town. Bamar dinners by request.

Royal City Hotel (Map p571; ☎ 31805; 130 27th St, 76/77; s/d US$17/22; ❄) This smart, central hotel is for those wanting creature comforts without breaking the bank. The large rooms include air-con, TV, private bathroom and worthy views from the upper floors.

Silver Star Hotel (Map p572; ☎ 33394; silverstar@mandalay.net.mm; cnr 27th & 83rd Sts; s US$20-25, d US$25-28; ❄ 💻) This modern, midtown high-rise is the pick of several soulless midrange places. Shock! Horror! It actually feels like a real hotel, with real cleaners, efficient reception staff and facilities that work. The corner rooms, with two windows, are higher priced.

Downtown back-up options:

Classic Hotel (Map p572; ☎ 32841; 59 23rd St, 83/84; s/d US$12/18; ❄) 'Classic' as in 'aging' rooms with private bathrooms.

Mother's World Hotel (Map p572; ☎ 33627; 58 79th St, 27/28; s/d US$15/22; ❄) There be dragons…green Chinese dragons. No lift, so ask for a lower floor.

Eating & Drinking

There is a lively little dining scene in Mandalay, with plenty of inexpensive Asian restaurants. However, there is definitely not a lively little night scene, particularly when you consider this is a city of almost one million inhabitants. Leave your dancing shoes in Yangon.

Shwe Pyi Moe Café (Map p572; 25th St, 80/81; 🕑 breakfast & lunch) This traditional teashop is always packed with locals mulling over life, the universe and, well, something. It serves good tea, a mix of cheap Bamar lunches and cooks up *ei-kyar-kwe* (long, deep-fried pastries) and even banana pancakes.

our pick **Chapati Stand** (Map p572; cnr 27th & 82nd Sts; meals from K300; 🕑 dinner) We've been eating at this bustling streetside stall for years, and every time we're left shaking our head at how good the chapatis and vegie and meat curries are, and how embarrassingly cheap (this time the bill came to K300 for potato curry, two chapatis and tea). Love it!

Marie-Min Vegetarian Restaurant (Map p571; 27th St, 74/75; dishes K600-1400; 🕑 closed May) Long a budget favourite, this Indian-run place offers a wholesome range of vegetarian dishes served with chapatis or rice, and lassis made with purified water. It also rents motorbikes.

our pick **Lashio Lay Restaurant** (Map p572; 65 23rd St, 83/84; dishes around K1000; 🕑 lunch & dinner) This no-frills Shan restaurant has some of the best food in town. If you don't believe us, just look at the queue of locals coming for lunchtime takeaway. Choose from about 25 or more dishes daily, all with soup, salad and rice.

THE MOUSTACHE BROTHERS: STILL LAUGHING DESPITE THE RISKS

The **Moustache Brothers** (Map p571; 39th St, 80/81; donation US$5; 🕑 8.30pm) have earned their reputation as Myanmar's best-known dissident comedy troupe the hard way. Two members of the comedy trio, Par Par Lay and Lu Zaw, served six years hard labour after joking about the government during a performance at Aung San Suu Kyi's house in 1996; English-speaking Lu Maw had been 'holding the fort' back home at the time. Their detention became a cause célèbre among foreign comedians and Par Par Lay was mentioned in the Hugh Grant film *About a Boy* (ask to see the clip).

They were eventually released in 2002. Before long, however, they were banned from performing their *a-nyeint pwes* (traditional folk operas), a blend of in-yer-face slapstick, dancing and painted signs, by a government fearful of their influence. But they refused to be silenced. The shows went on as 'demonstrations' in their tiny home theatre in the Mandalay backstreets. Despite a further arrest in 2007, they continue to take the mickey out of the government, so long as they only perform at home and, most depressing for the two non-English-speakers, not in Burmese.

As one of the few dissenting voices in a nation silenced by oppression, it's well worth supporting their performance.

Too Too Restaurant (Map p571; 27th St, 74/75; curries from K1500; ⏲ lunch & dinner) Burma's greatest culinary hits are all available here, bubbling away in pans and best at lunch. Curries include fish, prawn, chicken and vegie, and with all the extras one is more than enough.

Mann Restaurant (Map p572; 83rd St, 25/26; dishes K1500-2000) This crusty Chinese place is a Mandalay institution, with locals tucking into decent middle kingdom meals and, perhaps more importantly, washing them down with amber offerings from Ms Dagon Beer reps.

BBB (Map p571; ☎ 25623; No 292 76th St, 26/27; dishes K1800-5000; ⏲ 8.30am-11pm) Can't face another oily Bamar curry? BBB (Barman Beer Bar) serves up a few Western classics (think pasta, pizza, chips) and a couple of tasty variations, like the fried prawn burger (K2000).

Nepali Food (Map p572; 81st St, 26/27; meals K2000) This place serves no meat, no alcohol and no eggs, just bargain thalis with three curries, chapati, rice and dhal.

Nylon Ice Cream Bar (Map p572; 173 83rd St, 25/26) This timeless ice-cream parlour–cum–beer station is a popular afternoon meeting place to sample durian in non-confronting ice-cream form.

Barbecue Restaurants (Map p571; 30th St, 65/66; ⏲ lunch & dinner) In Myanmar's appetite-sapping heat, when all you want is a few snacks and some cold beer, there's nowhere better than a barbecue joint. At this strip of open-air restaurants along 30th St, you can order skewers of pork, chicken, fish, vegies, spiced bean curd and lady fingers, among other items. A full meal with a drink costs about K4000.

If you're heading up country, or just fancy a comfort Mars Bar, head for **City Mart** (Map p571; 78 Shopping Centre, 78th St, 37/38), with its imported temptations, and while you're there, **Seasons Bakery** (Map p571; 78 Shopping Centre, 78th St, 37/38) for fresh breads, cakes and savouries. Purchase fresh fruit, curries and rice from locals along the way.

Entertainment

Mandalay Marionettes & Cultural Show (Map p571; ☎ 34446; 66th St, 26/27; admission US$8; ⏲ 8.30pm) This one-hour traditional puppet show, with live musical accompaniment, includes episodes of *zat pwe* (re-creation of Buddhist tales) and *yama pwe* (tales from the Indian epic Ramayana). Cheaper shows (some free) are available in Bagan and Inle Lake.

Shopping

If Bagan is the worldwide hub for lacquerware and sand paintings, the same can be said of Mandalay and marionettes (new and old), which make exotic, good-value gifts. Also look for *kalaga* (a traditional tapestry). Drivers on the ancient cities tour invariably stop in interesting workshops that double as shops.

Sunflower Arts & Crafts (Map p571; 27th St, 74/75) Opposite Marie-Min Vegetarian Restaurant, there's a huge range of old wood and bronze pieces, plus some anatomically correct (read dangling genitalia) puppets.

Zeigyo (Central Market; Map p572; 84th St, 26/28) Spread over two large modern buildings, this market is packed with plenty of Myanmar-made items (including handicrafts) that spill onto the surrounding footpaths.

Jade market (Map p571; ⏲ 7am-5pm) Amid the 'monk district', this market features dozens of stalls and tables where locals get serious – and sketchy – about green rocks. Beware of fakes.

Getting There & Away

See p578 for details on pick-ups and other transport to Amarapura, Inwa, Sagaing and Mingun.

AIR

Mandalay sees daily services to and from Yangon (prices starting from US$75), Nyaung U (for Bagan; from US$32) and Heho (for Inle Lake; from US$35), as well as flights to Myitkyina, Tachileik and, seasonally, Kengtung

MANDALAY BUSES & FARES

Destination	Fare	Duration	Departures	Type of Bus
Bagan	K10,000	8hr	9am, 2pm	local
Hsipaw	K4000	6-7hr	6am	local
Taunggyi (to Inle Lake)	K11,000	10-12hr	5.30am, 6pm	air-con
Yangon	K11,000	12-15hr	5pm-6pm	air-con

MANDALAY TRAINS

Sample fares (ordinary/upper class/sleeper) and schedules:

Destination	Price (US$)	Duration	Departure
Hsipaw	US$4/7/-	10hr	4.35am
Myitkyina	US$11/36/40	20-22hr	noon, 1.30pm, 4pm
Naba (near Katha)	US$7/20/23	12-14hr	noon, 1.30pm, 4pm, 8pm
Nyaung U (Bagan)	US$4/10/-	8hr	9pm
Pyin U Lwin	US$3/5/-	4hr	4.35am
Yangon	US$15/35/40	14-16hr	4am, 5am, 5.30am & 8am

and Bhamo. Domestic fares are slightly cheaper at travel agents; **Sun Far Travels & Tours** (Map p571; ☎ 69712; No H, 30th St, 77/78) and **Good News Travels** (Map p571; ☎ 02-73571; No B6 71st St, 28/29) are reliable.

BOAT

The **IWT office** (Map p571; ☎ 36035; 35th St; 9am-4pm Mon-Fri) has information on boats on the Ayeyarwady, including government-owned 'slow boat' trips to Bagan (US$10, 15 to 18 hours, 5.30am Wednesday and Sunday), and Bhamo (deck/cabin US$9/54, two to three days, 6am Monday, Thursday and Sunday… probably). Gawwein Jetty is a little further to the west and is the place to buy tickets (US dollars only).

From about September to January two private 'express' boats run to Bagan (US$27, about nine hours) several times a week. The two-deck *Shwe Keinnery*, with outside decks, is better than the *Malikha*. Your hotel or travel agent can arrange tickets.

BUS

Mandalay's dusty Highway Bus Station (off Map p571), 7km south of town, farewells buses to destinations across the country. Common routes are in the table, opposite, but schedules are flexible and expect fewer services to places like Bagan in low season. You can buy tickets at the station, but most travellers save the trip and get them through their guest house.

Buses for Monywa (K2000, three hours) leave at least hourly from a small downtown station (Map p572) off 88th St. Some Monywa-bound drivers refuse to take foreigners; there are loads, so try another.

TAXI

The easiest way to Pyin U Lwin (Maymyo) is via share taxi (back/front seat K5000/6000, 1½ hours). They depart a taxi stand (Map p572) at the corner of 27th and 83rd Sts, but your guest house can usually arrange to have you picked up.

Duthawadi (Map p572; ☎ 61938; 31st St, 81/82) arranges share taxis to Hsipaw (K12,000, six hours); a full car is K50,000. Share taxis also leave from 32nd St (80/81) for Hsipaw (per person K11,000 to K13,000) and Lashio (per person K15,000, eight hours).

TRAIN

Mandalay's gargantuan, butt-ugly **train station** (Map p571; 30th St, 78/79) dominates the centre of town and disgorges trains around the country.

Getting Around

Try not to shop with a driver, as you'll end up paying over the odds thanks to commission deals drivers work out with shop owners.

BICYCLE & MOTORCYCLE

There are several central places to rent bicycles, including **Mr Htoo Bicycles** (Map p572; 83rd St, 25/26; per day K2000; 8am-6pm). Marie-Min Vegetarian Restaurant (p575) can help arrange a motorbike.

TAXI

White taxis and 'blue taxis' – ancient Mazda 600cc pick-ups – whisk folks around Mandalay most hours. They'll find you; prices are negotiable. A ride from downtown to the Bagan jetty is about K2000 or so.

TRISHAW

There are more than 13,000 trishaws plying Mandalay's streets. Short rides cost about K500, and upwards of K1000 to destinations like Mandalay Hill. Negotiate. Prices rise at night.

AROUND MANDALAY

For most visitors, the real draw of Mandalay is day-tripping to the four old cities nearby. It's possible to get there and around by cheap pick-ups, but it's a hassle and most shoestringers team up and pay for a blue taxi (about 15,000K per day) for Amarapura, Inwa and Sagaing. Monywa is on an interesting, less-travelled route from Mandalay to Bagan via Pakokku.

Amarapura

The 'City of Immortality', a short-lived capital 11km south of Mandalay, is famed for **U Bein's Bridge**, the world's longest teak bridge at 1.2km. At 200 years old, the bridge sees lots of life along its 1060 teak posts, with monks and fishers commuting to and fro. It leads to **Kyauktawgyi Paya** and small **Taungthaman** village, with tea and toddy shops. A popular sunset activity is renting a **boat** (about K2500) to drift by as the skies turn orange, or watching life go by from a waterside beer station.

Just west is the **Ganayon Kyaung**, where hundreds of monks breakfast at 10.30am. Resist the temptation to thrust a camera in their faces, as some travellers do.

The highway is about 1km west of the bridge; ask the pick-up driver for directions. Otherwise you can cycle from Mandalay in about 45 minutes.

Amarapura is included in the Mandalay US$10 ticket (see p573) but checks are lax.

Inwa (Ava)

Cut off by rivers and canals, Inwa (called Ava by the British) served as the Burmese capital for nearly four centuries. **Horse carts** (K4000) lead a three-hour loop around Inwa's beaten track, but you can insist on stopping at other crumbling sights sans vendors, or getting out to rest your butt and chat with villagers tilling soil or bathing in ponds among the abandoned temples.

The finest sight is the atmospheric and unrenovated **Bagaya Kyaung**, a teak monastery supported by 267 posts. You'll need a US$10 Mandalay ticket (see p573) to get in here, but not elsewhere. The 27m **Nanmyin** watchtower leans precariously. Look for the breast-shaped Kaunghmudaw Paya in the distance, across the river about 10km west of Sagaing. **Maha Aungmye Bonzan** (aka Ok Kyaung) is a brick-and-stucco monastery dating from 1822.

By pick-up, head to Inwa junction and walk 1km south to the water for boats to Inwa.

Sagaing

Across the Ava Bridge from the Inwa junction and 18km from Mandalay, the stupa-studded hilltops of Sagaing loom over the Ayeyarwady. With 500 stupas and monasteries galore, Sagaing is where Burmese Buddhists come to relax and meditate. Sagaing is also known for **silver shops** and **guitars**.

Sagaing Hill (Sagaing/Mingun ticket US$3) is the big attraction. Trees hang over stone steps leading past monasteries to the top. **Tilawkaguru**, near the southwest base, is a mural-filled cave temple dating from 1672. There are great views above, and pathways lead all the way to the water for the adventurer. The hill is 1km north of the market. Some locals know free ways up.

Sagaing is spread out. A trishaw driver can take the strain for about K4000 for half a day.

Mingun

Up and across the Ayeyarwady from Mandalay, **Mingun** (Sagaing/Mingun ticket US$3) is a more adventurous trip. The peaceful 11km boat ride arrives at half a dozen sights facing the water, all peppered with peddlers of noodles, art and postcards. The **Mingun Paya** is actually the remains of a planned 150m stupa, surely a candidate for the world's largest pile of bricks. It

SEEING THE ANCIENT CITIES 101

Frequent **pick-ups** (Map p572; cnr 29th & 84th Sts) leave when full from Mandalay, stopping at Amarapura (30 minutes) and the Inwa junction (40 minutes) before reaching Sagaing (45 minutes). It's K200 during the day, K400 after dark. However, pick-ups can be a hassle so many shoestringers scrape together their tatty kyat notes for a 'blue taxi', which costs K15,000 to K20,000 per day for four people (real taxis are more). This is the only reasonable way of seeing all three in one day, and as a bonus you can have a 50-year-old, bright blue buzz box in any picture you like. If you're fit and sun-proof, see Mr Htoo (p577) about a bike. Mingun is only accessible by boat.

is still possible to climb up. Just to the north is the **Mingun Bell**, which holds the record for the world's largest uncracked bell. It's worth pressing on 200m north to the white, wavy-terraced **Hsinbyume Paya**.

There is also a government-run boat (K1500, 1½ hours) that departs daily at 9am and returns at 1pm. Alternatively, negotiate with private boats for a return ride for about K13,000, including stops; head there in the afternoon for sunset atop Mingun Paya.

Monywa

☎ 071 / pop 140,000

This scrappy trade town, 136km to the west of Mandalay, is missed by most visitors, but has some superb sights nearby. About 20km south, **Thanboddhay Paya** (admission US$3; 6am-5pm) bursts with carnival shades of pink, orange, yellow and blue. Inside are over half a million Buddhas filling nooks and crannies. About 4km east of the *paya* is a Buddha frenzy in the foothills, including a 90m **reclining Buddha** and the world's second-tallest standing Buddha. The easiest way to visit is by taxi.

Across the Chindwin River and 25km west, the 492 **Hpo Win Daung Caves** (admission US$2) occupy a mountain shaped like a reclining Buddha. There are many carved Buddhas, with streams of light beaming through holes in the walls, plus whole temples carved into the rock, giving the feeling of a mini Petra. It's best to go with a guide. To get here, catch a boat from the Monywa jetty (each way K3000), then a jeep (five people one way K12,000).

The rooms at the rear of **Shwe Taung Tarn Hotel & Restaurant** (☎ 21478; 70 Station Rd; r/bungalows per person US$5/8;) are a pretty good deal, with wooden floors, air-con and TV. There is also a good range of Burmese food available in the restaurant.

Hourly buses leave for Mandalay (K2000, four hours) from 3km south of the clock tower. For information on going the other way, see p577. Six daily buses go to Pakokku (K1500, 4½ hours) from 6.30am to 3pm, to catch the ferries to Bagan (leaving between 1pm and 4pm). There are no passenger ferries from Monywa.

Pyin U Lwin (Maymyo)

☎ 085 / pop 80,000

This is little Britain, colonial style, with cooler weather than in Mandalay and wide boulevards lined with stately homes from a bygone era. Set in the foothills of northern Shan State, this hill station was established by British Captain May as a retreat from the stifling heat of Mandalay, and was subsequently named for him (*myo* means town). Under the British it served as a summer capital and domestic tourists still flock here during the hottest months (March to May).

The main activity is cycling through history, passing dozens of English country mansions and cute pony-led miniature wagons, straight out of the Wells Fargo days of the American West (actually India, 1914, as one driver told us), that serve as local transport. You will no doubt also notice a lot of green uniforms around here as Pyin U Lwin is home to the Defence Services Academy, the alma mater of Than Shwe and his fellow rulers.

ORIENTATION & INFORMATION

For a small town, Pyin U Lwin is very spread out. The Mandalay to Lashio highway doubles as the main road. Bicycle is the best way to get around.

There are several internet options, including **AnT** (Bogyoke St; 8am-9pm), near Purcell Tower. Check out the excellent www.pyinoolwin.info for local information.

SIGHTS

Modelled on the famous Kew Gardens of London and boasting 480 plant species, the **National Kandawgyi Gardens** (☎ 22130; admission US$5, camera/video K1000/K3000; 8am-6pm) is a 176-hectare little Eden, with an inviting pool facing a small lake. It's a scenic cycle south of town, via a series of big, old and sometimes abandoned British-era mansions.

In town, the **Purcell Tower** still chimes to the tune of Big Ben, while other colonial relics are all around, and particularly along Multi-Office Rd. The **market** is filled with local strawberry jam and wine, plus tailors stitching together bespoke military uniforms over old sewing machines.

The most enjoyable day trip is to the attractive **Anisakan Falls** (Dat Taw Gyaik Falls; admission free), a 45-minute hilly trek from the village of Anisakan, itself 9km south of Pyin U Lwin. Pick-ups run to Anisakan (around K500) from the main road in Pyin U Lwin, or take a motorcycle taxi for K5000 including waiting time.

SLEEPING & EATING

Pyin U Lwin has loads of accommodation, but most is either closed to foreigners or owned by men in green. Those listed here are all in or within walking distance of the centre and include breakfast. Decent Shan, Burmese, Chinese and Indian food is available on or just off the main road; eat early or miss out.

Golden Dream Hotel (☎ 21302; 42/43 Main Rd; s US$3-5, d US$6-10) Neither golden nor a particularly pleasant dream, this place is cheap but needs love (and brooms). Cheaper rooms have no bathroom.

Grace Hotel 1 (☎ 21230; 114A Nann Myaing Rd; s & d per person US$10) The Grace is set in spacious gardens a stroll south from the town centre. Rooms are basic but include (leaky) bathrooms and TV.

Bravo Hotel (☎ 21223; Main Rd; s/d US$12/20) This new, mauve, faux-colonial place near Purcell Tower is the cleanest and most professionally run of the bunch. All rooms have private bathrooms and satellite TV.

Golden Triangle Café & Bakery (Main Rd; sandwiches & pizzas K2000-4000) Housed in a grand old building, this is a good bet for a pastry, sandwich, pizza, shake or freshly brewed local coffee.

GETTING THERE & AWAY

Offices along the Mandalay–Lashio Rd sell tickets on the limited bus services to Yangon (K11,000, 14 hours) via Mandalay (K3000, two hours), departing about 2pm, and to Hsipaw and Lashio (both K4000, 7am). Much easier are the shared taxis. They leave from the main road, 200m east of Purcell Tower, for Mandalay (K6000, two hours), Hsipaw and Lashio (both K8000, three hours). Most go from 7am to 2pm or 3pm.

Pick-up trucks, lingering near Purcell Tower, head to Mandalay (K2000) and, less frequently, Hsipaw (K3500).

The train station is north of the main road, 1km east of the taxi stand.

Hsipaw

☎ 082 / pop 15,000

In the Shan Hills beyond Pyin U Lwin, Hsipaw has its own time zone where the clocks tick more slowly. Travellers come to this laid-back highland town for a couple of days and before they know it a week has passed. Trekking is the main draw, but Hsipaw is not without charms, including a bustling riverside market, good food and, in season, lively guest houses.

> **DIY KYAUKME**
>
> To get far off the beaten track, get off the bus or train in Kyaukme (pronounced 'Chao May'). This rural town between Pyin U Lwin and Hsipaw had, when we passed, only one guest house licensed to take foreigners – locals will point the way. From here you can set off by foot or motorbike, or a combination of the two, into minority villages that rarely, if ever, see tourists. The guest house can help with guides, or ask for highly recommended Thura (check out his homemade website www.thuratrips.page.tl).

The famous Bawgyo Paya Pwe is held at the monastery of the same name near Hsipaw every February or March.

Hsipaw has one glacially slow internet cafe opposite the Baptist Church.

SIGHTS & ACTIVITIES

Hsipaw's large **central market** (⏲ 5am-5pm) is best visited early in the morning, when Shan and other tribal people come from nearby villages to trade. There's an interesting **produce market** (⏲ 5am-noon) further south on the riverbank.

A collection of crumbling Shan-style brick-and-stucco stupas, which is known as **Little Bagan**, sprawls just north of town. Nearby is the **Bamboo Buddha Monastery** (Maha Nanda Kantha), which contains a 150-year-old lacquered Buddha made from bamboo strips.

For a great sunset, walk to either **Five Buddha Hill** or **Nine Buddha Hill**. Cross the bridge on the Lashio road, walk 200m and look for a path leading to both hills.

The **haw sao pha** (Shan Palace), built in 1924, has been closed to visitors since Mr Donald, the nephew of the last *sawbwa* (sky lord) of Hsipaw, was jailed for 13 years for acting as an unlicensed tour guide (the real reason is related to Burmese attempts to neuter Shan nationalism).

Both guest houses listed under Sleeping can arrange **trekking** to surrounding villages, or a three-day, two-night hike to Namshan. Prices are negotiable depending on numbers, but start at US$10 per day for one person, or US$15 for overnight trips. Those with delicate thighs can add a motorbike for K10,000 a day.

Mr Book, who runs a bookshop on the main road, has hand-drawn maps of outlying-area treks. Mr Charles has maps of town and the surrounds.

SLEEPING & EATING

Nam Khae Mao Guest House (☎ 80088; nkmao@myanmar.com.mm; 134 Bogyoke Rd; s/d with shared bathroom US$4/6, with private bathroom US$10/12) Next to the green clock tower, this is a perfectly good, clean and friendly alternative to Mr C. Rooms with air-con are more.

Mr Charles Guest House (☎ 80105; 105 Auba St; s US$4-15, d US$8-20) Mr Charles is known throughout Myanmar for its service, wide range of rooms (in a wooden house or concrete annexe) and all-round traveller vibe, that tends to coalesce around beer bottles on the verandah. Recommended.

The market stalls offer Hsipaw's best cheap eats. **Mr Food** (Law Chun; Namtu Rd; meals from K1000), on the main road, pulls the travellers thanks to its English-language menu of Chinese standards. Opposite is **Burmese Cuisine** (Namtu Rd; meals from K1000), where a row of pots are filled with tasty curries.

GETTING THERE & AWAY

Bus services often involve unscheduled stops, known as breakdowns. Buses leave Hsipaw at 5.30am for Mandalay via Pyin U Lwin (K4000 to either). Buses also head to Lashio (K2000, two hours), 72km northeast.

Share taxis run to and from Mandalay (per person K12,000, five hours), leaving about 7am, and to Lashio (K5000). Pick-ups are also an option.

The train to Pyin U Lwin (ordinary/upper class US$2/6, six hours) and Mandalay (US$3/7, 11 hours) crosses the breathtaking Gokteik Gorge and is revered as one of Myanmar's most beautiful, if somewhat slow, rail journeys. It's supposed to leave Hsipaw at 9.30am daily but is often late.

BAGAN (PAGAN) REGION

Known as 'the heart of Myanmar', the central plain is littered with the history of dynasties past. The greatest of these is at Bagan, which is quite simply breathtaking in its scale. Further afield Mount Popa is living proof of the Burmese obsession with *nats*, and is one very few parts of the region that aren't pancake flat.

BAGAN

☎ 02 & 061

Gather all of Europe's medieval cathedrals onto Manhattan island and throw in a whole lot more for good measure, and you'll start to get a sense of the ambition of the temple-filled plains of Bagan. Rivalling the temples of Angkor for the crown of Southeast Asia's most memorable ancient site, the 4400 temples here date from around the same period, more than 800 years ago. Angkor's individual temples may be more spectacular, but Bagan's brilliance is in the wonderful collective views of stupa upon stupa dotting the plain; dawns here are simply unforgettable.

While high season gets relatively busy (but nothing like Angkor), in low season you'll have the place to yourself…and a sand-painting seller or 10.

History

Bagan was born when King Anawrahta took the throne in 1044. He unified the country, embraced Theravada Buddhism and began building Bagan's first temple, the grand Shwezigon. The hubristic Anawrahta coveted the sacred Buddhist scriptures (the Tripitaka) held by the very Mons who enlightened him. When they refused, he sent an army and took them by force. Anawrahta was eventually killed by, of all things, a wild buffalo, but his dynasty ruled for 200 years. This was Bagan's golden age, a period of manic temple building. Things began to go bad under the decadent King Narathihapati, who built the gorgeous Mingalazedi pagoda but bankrupted the city, leaving it vulnerable to attack by Kublai Khan in 1287.

The city was crushed again in 1975, when an earthquake measuring 6.5 on the Richter scale damaged many of its principal structures.

Bagan's most recent upheaval happened in 1990, when the government forcibly relocated the residents of Old Bagan, planting them in undeveloped land 4km to the south (now known as New Bagan).

Orientation

The vast Bagan Archaeological Zone stretches 42 sq km and is home to the 'towns' of Nyaung U, Old Bagan, Myinkaba, New Bagan and a

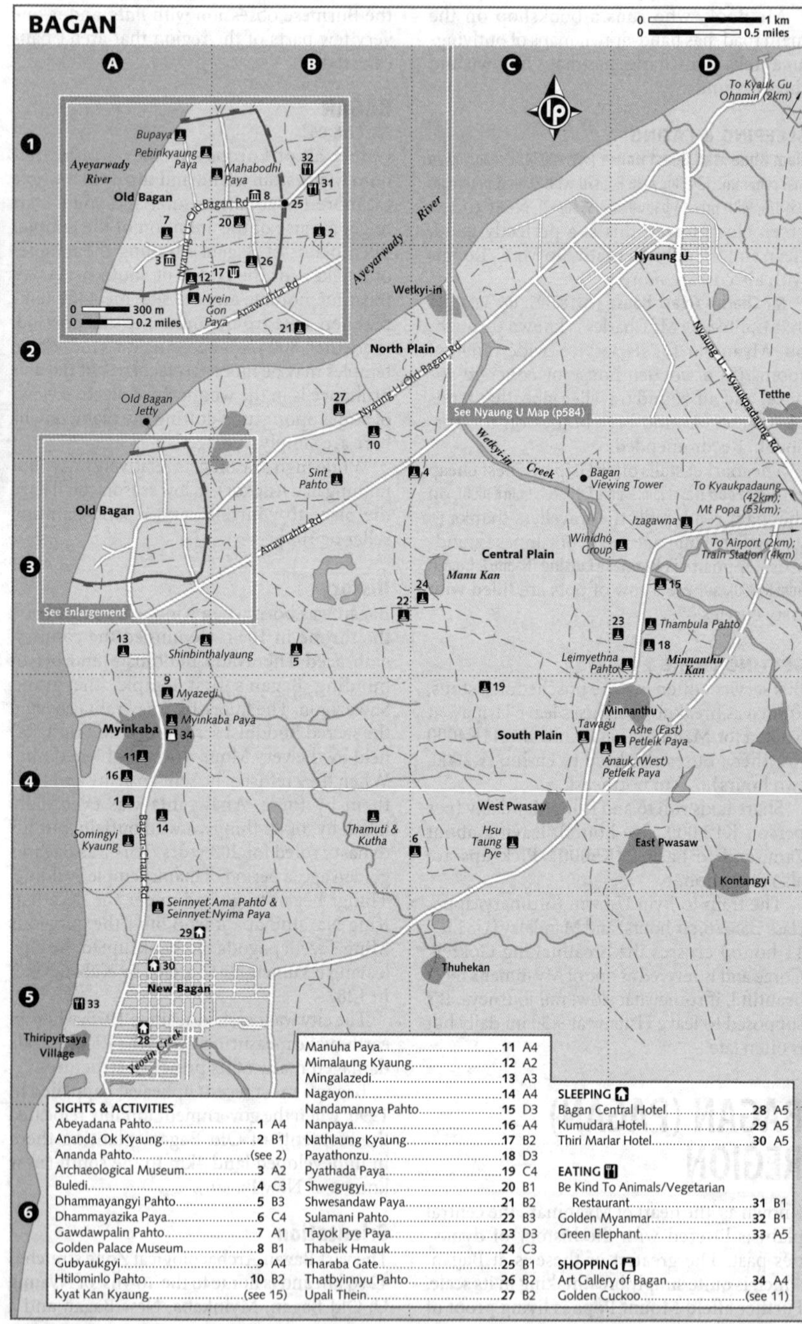
BAGAN
0 1 km
0 0.5 miles
A
B
C
D
1
2
3
4
5
6
Bupaya
Pebinkyaung Paya
Ayeyarwady River
Mahabodhi Paya
Old Bagan
Bagan Rd
8
25
32
31
7
20
2
3
Nyaung U-Old Bagan
17
26
12
Nyein Gon Paya
Anawrahta Rd
21
0 300 m
0 0.2 miles
Ayeyarwady River
Wetkyi-in
North Plain
Nyaung U-Old Bagan Rd
To Kyauk Gu Ohnmin (2km)
Nyaung U
Nyaung U - Kyaukpadaung Rd
Tetthe
See Nyaung U Map (p584)
Old Bagan Jetty
27
10
Sint Pahto
4
Wetkyi-in Creek
Bagan Viewing Tower
To Kyaukpadaung (42km); Mt Popa (53km);
Izagawna
Old Bagan
Anawrahta Rd
Winidho Group
To Airport (2km); Train Station (4km)
Central Plain
Manu Kan
24
22
15
See Enlargement
23
Thambula Pahto
18
13
Shinbinthalyaung
5
Leimyethna Pahto
Minnanthu Kan
9
Myazedi
19
Minnanthu
Myinkaba Paya
Myinkaba
34
Tawagu
South Plain
Ashe (East) Petleik Paya
11
Anauk (West) Petleik Paya
16
1
14
West Pwasaw
Bagan-Chauk Rd
Somingyi Kyaung
Thamuti & Kutha
Hsu Taung Pye
6
East Pwasaw
Kontangyi
Seinnyet Ama Pahto & Seinnyet Nyima Paya
29
30
Thuhekan
New Bagan
33
28
Thiripyitsaya Village
Yeosin Creek
SIGHTS & ACTIVITIES
Abeyadana Pahto 1 A4
Ananda Ok Kyaung 2 B1
Ananda Pahto (see 2)
Archaeological Museum 3 A2
Buledi 4 C3
Dhammayangyi Pahto 5 B3
Dhammayazika Paya 6 C4
Gawdawpalin Pahto 7 A1
Golden Palace Museum 8 B1
Gubyaukgyi 9 A4
Htilominlo Pahto 10 B2
Kyat Kan Kyaung (see 15)
Manuha Paya 11 A4
Mimalaung Kyaung 12 A2
Mingalazedi 13 A3
Nagayon 14 A4
Nandamannya Pahto 15 D3
Nanpaya 16 A4
Nathlaung Kyaung 17 B2
Payathonzu 18 D3
Pyathada Paya 19 C4
Shwegugyi 20 B1
Shwesandaw Paya 21 B2
Sulamani Pahto 22 B3
Tayok Pye Paya 23 D3
Thabeik Hmauk 24 C3
Tharaba Gate 25 B1
Thatbyinnyu Pahto 26 B2
Upali Thein 27 B2
SLEEPING
Bagan Central Hotel 28 A5
Kumudara Hotel 29 A5
Thiri Marlar Hotel 30 A5
EATING
Be Kind To Animals/Vegetarian Restaurant 31 B1
Golden Myanmar 32 B1
Green Elephant 33 A5
SHOPPING
Art Gallery of Bagan 34 A4
Golden Cuckoo (see 11)

few others. Most independent travellers stay in Nyaung U. In the northeast corner of the zone, this town is home to the bus station, and is about 5km northwest of the airport and train station. Old Bagan is about 4km southwest, atmospherically located amid the bulk of the temples. Expensive hotels here cater to tour groups. New Bagan is about 4km further south and has some good-value midrange options. Well-paved roads connect these centres, crisscrossed by dirt trails venturing to the temples.

In Nyaung U, 'Main Rd' is used (locally and in text) to refer to the main strip, which runs along the north–south Bagan–Nyaung U Rd, and along the Anawrahta Rd from the market to the Sapada Paya. Just east of the bus station is an unnamed street known variously as 'restaurant row' or 'FIT road', with lots of eating options.

The Map of Bagan, found at most guest houses, is very useful. It should be free, but sometimes costs K500 to K1000.

Information

All foreign visitors to the Bagan Archaeological Zone must pay a US$10 entrance fee, technically lasting as long as you'd like to stay. Half of this fee is supposed to go to the Bagan Archaeology Department, but whether this actually happens or not is open to debate.

Nyaung U is home to most traveller life-support systems, including a post office, several internet cafes and pricey international calls.

Ever Sky Information Service (Map p584; ☎ 061-60146; Restaurant Row, Nyaung U; 🕒 7am-9.30pm) Conveniently located in restaurant row, Ever Sky can arrange cars, trips and guides, and has a small bookstore.

Shwe Pyi Nann Thanakha Gallery (Map p584; cnr Main Rd & Restaurant Row, Nyaung U; per hr K1000; 🕒 9am-10pm) 'The only one *thanakha* gallery in the world' also offers spa services and Bagan's best internet cafe.

Sleeping

Bagan accommodation can be loosely categorised as: Nyaung U for budget travellers, New Bagan for good-value midrange rooms, and Old Bagan's mostly joint-venture hotels for bigger wallets. The latter are not covered here, so sneak a look at someone's Lonely Planet *Myanmar* guide if you feel like indulging. Bagan might be tourist central, but electricity supply is still rubbish.

NYAUNG U

our pick New Heaven (Map p584; ☎ 061-60921; s US$5-8 d US$8-12; ❄) The price is way right for these clean, compact rooms on a quiet street off 'Restaurant Row'. The vibe isn't bad, either, making this a traveller favourite.

Eden Motel (Map p584; ☎ 061-60639; Main Rd; s US$5-10, d US$8-12; ❄) The original Eden is a shoestringer favourite thanks to its fair-value cane-themed rooms with private bathroom, no-hassle staff and rooftop chill-out zone. This is a better bet, and cheaper, than the newer annexe across the road.

May Kha Lar Guest House (Map p584; ☎ 061-60304; Main Rd; s US$5-14, d US$8-15; ❄) This deceptively large guest house with a no-stress vibe has a mind-boggling selection of rooms (and tiles!), which are all well tended by a hospitable family. The upstairs rooms are larger, have TVs and are worth the extra couple of bills.

Inn Wa Guest House (Map p584; ☎ 061-60902; Main Rd; s/d from US$6/10; ❄) A stone's throw from the market, this clean-if-uninspiring place has decent air-con rooms with bathrooms, some brighter than others.

New Park Hotel (Map p584; ☎ 061-60322; www.newparkmyanmar.com; 4 Thiripyitsaya; s US$10-18, d US$16-25; ❄) For a little more comfort near 'Restaurant Row', these motel-style rooms with wooden floors, private bathrooms and porches are fair value. Higher-priced rooms have TVs.

Golden Express Hotel (Map p584; ☎ 02-60034; www.goldenexpresstours.com; Main Rd; s US$15-24, d US$18-30; ❄ 🏊) Go for the comfortable 'superior' rooms here for the chance to watch satellite TV, hang out with package tourists and – the real draw – swim (US$3 for nonguests). It is close to the temples, but a couple of kilometres southwest of town.

Also in Nyaung U:

Pann Cherry Guest House (Map p584; ☎ 061-60075; Main Rd; s/d from US$3/6) Rooms in this colourful place are pretty simple but the price is right. Close to the bus station.

Thante Hotel (Map p584; ☎ 02-60315; nyaungu thante@mptmail.net.mm; Main Rd; s/d US$30/35; ❄ 🏊) For a pool right in Nyaung U town, the Thante's comfy bungalows are the only option. Or just visit for a swim (US$3).

NEW BAGAN

Some travellers spend a couple of days in Nyaung U, then opt for some luxury in the good-value midrange hotels here.

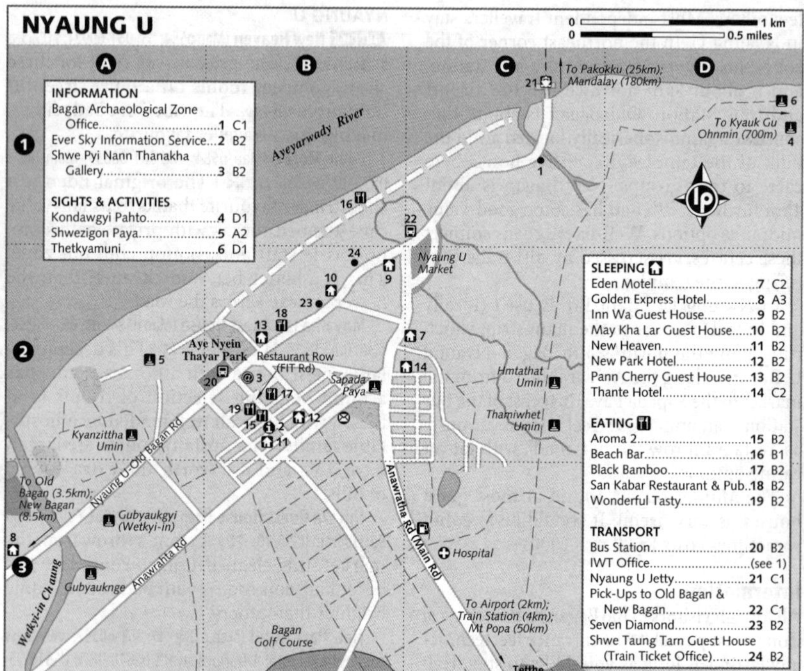

Bagan Central Hotel (Map p582; ☎ 02-65057; Main Rd; s US$15-20, d US$20-25; ❄) These large, modern-if-dark rooms with satellite TV, hot water and wooden floors are set around a leafy courtyard with tables for open-air breakfast. Discounts are given to those who stayed at Okinawa in Yangon.

our pick **Kumudara Hotel** (Map p582; ☎ 061-65142; www.kumudara-bagan.com; s US$18-30, d US$22-30; ❄ 💻 🏊) Sick of sweating your arse off in powerless guest houses? The new, Zen-styled junior suites (single/double US$26/30, $5 less in low season) here are possibly the best-value accommodation in Myanmar. All rooms have balconies offering an unobscured panorama across the temple-strewn plain, as do the sun-lounges around the pool. But wait, there's more…good service, 24-hour power, satellite TV, bathrooms with tubs, massage, free internet and delicious food at cheap prices.

Thiri Marlar Hotel (Map p582; ☎ 061-65229; thirimarlar@mptmail.net.mm; s/d US$20/25; ❄) Service matters at this quiet retreat with 21 clean, compact rooms (request a room with a view). Breakfast or prearranged dinner is taken on the rooftop overlooking the Bagan plain.

Eating

NYAUNG U

This is the dining capital of Bagan, with cuisines including Burmese, Chinese, Thai, Indian and Italianesque, often on the same menu. The first three places listed following are among many on or near relatively quiet 'Restaurant Row'.

Wonderful Tasty (Map p584; Restaurant Row; mains from K1200) Dishes up some wonderfully tasty vegetarian dishes. The Nepali and Burmese options are better than the Tibetan dishes we tried.

Black Bamboo (Map p584; off Restaurant Row; meals from K2000) This chilled new garden cafe has that all-too-rare treat in Myanmar – real coffee. It also serves decent Chinese food.

Aroma 2 (Map p584; Restaurant Row; dishes K2000-7000; 🕑 lunch & dinner) The spicy selection of classics here will keep even curry-craving Brits happy. The garden overflows with candlelit tables in the dry season.

Beach Bar (Map p584; 12 Youne Tan Yat; dishes K3000-8000) The Beach is a thoroughly unexpected pavilion overlooking the Ayeyarwady's dry season 'beach'. The menu includes flavours from Europe and the East, though many just come for a sundowner. Alas, when we visited happy hour had turned sad and a Myanmar Beer was K3500.

San Kabar Restaurant & Pub (Map p584; Main Rd; pizzas K4000-6000) The birthplace of Bagan pizza, the San Kabar remains a popular stop for its Italian-inspired creations and tasty salads. Pastas are not as good.

OLD BAGAN

Save yourself the schlep back to Nyaung U by having lunch in Old Bagan.

Be Kind To Animals/Vegetarian Restaurant (Map p582; dishes from K1000). Near the Ananda Pahto, this is one of several popular little lunch joints.

Golden Myanmar (Map p582; buffet K3000; lunch & dinner) Come here hungry, as the 'personal buffet', delivered to your table, is enough to feed a family. Your choice of chicken, pork, mutton or fish curry comes with a table full of condiments. Invite your horse cart driver along to help.

NEW BAGAN

The cheapest eats in New Bagan are the teashops and hole-in-the-wall Burmese places either along, or just off, the main drag. There are several large riverside restaurants in New Bagan, with fine views, nightly puppet shows and busloads of tourists in peak season. Among the best is the **Green Elephant** (Map p582; mains K3000-6000; lunch & dinner), which serves top-notch Burmese cuisine in a romantic garden setting.

Shopping

Bagan is the lacquerware capital of Myanmar (if not the entire universe) and, given the prices, is probably the best place to pick some up. Head to Myinkaba, a village between Old Bagan and New Bagan where several family-run workshops produce high-quality traditional pieces – look for earthy colours. Reliable places include the **Art Gallery of Bagan** (Map p582; ☎ 061-60307) and **Golden Cuckoo** (Map p582; ☎ 061-60428).

Getting There & Away

Most travel services operate out of Nyaung U. Ask at Ever Sky (p583) or your guest house about air tickets or hiring a share taxi. A charter to Inle is about US$90, Mandalay US$60.

AIR

Air Bagan, Yangon Airways and Air Mandalay have regular services connecting Bagan with Yangon (from US$82), Mandalay (from US$32) and Heho (from US$50). **Seven Diamond** (Map p584; ☎ 061-60883; Main Rd; 8am-5.30pm Mon-Sat, 8am-4pm Sun) can arrange tickets.

BOAT

Boats to/from Mandalay go from either Nyaung U or Old Bagan, depending on water levels. The Nyaung U jetty (Map p584) is about 1km northeast of Nyaung U market. The IWT office (Map p584), about 300m inland from the jetty, sells tickets on the government-owned slow boat to Mandalay (US$10, 15 to 24 hours), which departs on Monday and Thursday at 4.30am. There are also services to Pyay (US$9, two to three days).

Despite the billboards all around town, the private boats run only during the tourist season (approximately September to February). Of these, the Shwe Keinnery Express ferry is most popular. It leaves Bagan for Mandalay at 5.30am (US$16, 12 hours, five times weekly), but it wasn't operating at the time of writing. **Malikha Express** (www.malikha-rivercruises.com; US$12) is the other option (the trip takes seven hours), with rates discounted due to weaker demand. Schedules vary from twice a month to several times a week – any travel agency in Myanmar can find out the latest.

From the Nyaung U jetty local boats go to Pakokku (K3000, 2½ hours) a few times between 6am and noon, from where there are buses to Monywa.

BUS

Local buses to Mandalay (K6500, eight hours), via Meiktila, leave at 7am and 9am from the bus station in Nyaung U (Map p584). Here you can catch a 3pm air-con bus to Yangon (K15,000, 12 to 15 hours) via Pyay (nine hours), or a 4am bus (or minibus) to Taunggyi (K10,500, about 12 to 14 hours) via Kalaw (nine to 10 hours). Book tickets well in advance in peak season.

TRAIN

The Bagan train station (off Map p582) is about 4km southeast of Nyaung U. **Shwe Taung Tarn Guest House** (Map p584; ☎ 60949; Main Rd) sells tickets. Presently a 7am train leaves for Mandalay (ordinary/upper class US$4/9, nine hours). There are no longer direct trains to Yangon. You

THE TEMPLES OF BAGAN

Ancient Bagan is one of the most spectacular sights in Southeast Asia, but with more than 4000 temples to choose from it is easy to find a solitary stupa or decaying mural to take in alone. This section groups some of the more popular (and impressive) temples in Bagan (all on Map p582, unless otherwise noted). But remember to use it as a guide only. The real fun in Bagan is in 'discovering' a temple as you cycle around, climbing up and just taking it all in with nary a sand-painting vendor in sight. And here's the tip: look for anything with a doorway, which usually means there is a narrow, dark stairway leading up to a viewing platform. Bring a torch (flashlight), and try to park your bike away out of sight of the road if you don't want company.

Top Temples

It pays to target a few big-name temples and stop at any that take your fancy in between.

- Ananda Pahto – one of the finest, best-preserved and most revered of all the Bagan temples.
- Dhammayangyi Pahto – an absolute colossus, this red-brick temple is visible from all over Bagan.
- Sulamani Pahto – this late-period beauty is known as Crowning Jewel, and with good reason.
- Pyathada Paya – super sunset (or sunrise) spot, with a fun trip and few touts.
- Thatbyinnyu Pahto – the tallest temple at Bagan, topped with a golden spire.

Old Bagan

This 2km anticlockwise circuit takes in sites within the old city walls. It's manageable on foot or by bicycle.

North of the unsubtle **Archaeological Museum** (Nyaung U-Old Bagan Rd), the 60m-high **Gawdawpalin Pahto**, one of the finest late-period temples, was rocked by the 1975 earthquake but has been restored.

About 200m south of here, a dirt road leads past **Mimalaung Kyaung** (note the *chinthe*, a half-lion, half-guardian deity) and **Nathlaung Kyaung** (the only remaining Hindu temple at Bagan) to **Thatbyinnyu Pahto** (Omniscience Shrine). Bagan's highest temple, which was built in 1144, it has a square base, surrounded by diminishing terraces and rimmed with spires, but you can't climb it.

Another 200m north of Thatbyinnyu is **Shwegugyi**, a temple dating from 1131 with lotus *sikhara* (Indian-style temple finial) atop and stucco carvings inside. Back on the main Nyaung U–Old Bagan Rd you'll pass the ostentatious **Golden Palace Museum** (admission US$5; 9am-4.30pm), a recreation that's worth skipping as the money goes to the government. Continue to the 9th-century **Tharaba Gate**, the former eastern entry to the walled city.

The Northern Plain

Much of 'Bagan' fills the broad space between Nyaung U and Old Bagan. These sites are (roughly) west to east between the two paved roads linking the two.

About half a kilometre east of Thatbyinnyu, the 52m-high **Ananda Pahto**, with its golden *sikhara* top and gilded spires, is probably Bagan's top draw. Finished in 1105, the temple has giant teak Buddha images facing each of the four entranceways. On the full moon of the month of Pyatho (between mid-December and mid-January), a three-day *paya* festival attracts thousands of pilgrims.

Just northwest is **Ananda Ok Kyaung**, with colourful murals detailing 18th-century life, some showing Portuguese traders; no photos allowed.

Midway between Old Bagan and Nyaung U, **Upali Thein** features large, brightly painted murals from the early 18th century. Across the road, the location for the terraced 46m-high **Htilominlo Pahto** was picked in 1218 by King Nantaungmya, using a 'leaning umbrella'.

The Central Plain

This rural area to the south of Anawrahta Rd has a stunning congregation of impressive temples.

Buledi is good for sunrise and to get your bearings. South of Thatbyinnyu, the 11th-century five-terraced **Shwesandaw Paya** is a graceful white pyramid-style pagoda with 360-degree views of Bagan's temples. It is packed for sunset, but pretty empty during the day. Note the original *hti* lying to the south – it was toppled by the quake. Half a kilometre south, the ever-visible, walled **Dhammayangyi Pahto** has two encircling passageways, the inner one of which has been intentionally filled. It's said that King Narathu was such a bastard that the workers ruined it after his assassination in 1170.

One kilometre to the east, the broad two-storeyed **Sulamani Pahto** (1181) is one of the Bagan region's prettiest temples, with lush grounds and carved stucco. Just 150m east, **Thabeik Hmauk** looks like a mini Sulamani, but without the hawkers – *and* you can climb to the top. And at sunset, don't miss the broad viewing platform at **Pyathada Paya**, 750m south.

Around Myinkaba

The area around Myinkaba village, located between Old Bagan and New Bagan, is brimming with sites. One of the most popular is **Mingalazedi** (1274), with three receding terraces lined with 561 glazed tiles and tasty views of the nearby river and temples.

Just north of town, **Gubyaukgyi** (1113) sees a lot of visitors thanks to its richly coloured interior paintings; bring a torch. In the village, the modern-looking **Manuha Paya** (1059) was named for the Mon king who was held captive here. Note the four giant Buddha images that are seemingly too large for the enclosure, symbolic of Manuha's discontent with his prison life. Stairs at the rear lead above the reclining Buddha. Just south, **Nanpaya**, from the same era, is a cave-style shrine; Nanpaya was possibly once Hindu, as suggested by the three-faced Brahma situated on the pillars.

About 400m south of town, the Singhalese-style stupa of the 11th century, **Abeyadana Pahto**, was likely built by King Kyanzittha's Bengali wife and features original frescoes. Across the road, **Nagayon** has some tight stairs leading up to the roof. Its lotus-shaped *sikhara* was possibly a prototype for Ananda.

South Plain

This rural stretch is accessed via the road from New Bagan to the airport, or by dirt roads from the Central Plain. About 3.5km east of New Bagan, **Dhammayazika Paya** (1196) is unusual for its five-sided design. It's very well tended with lush grounds and lavish attention from worshippers. A dirt road leads 2km to Dhammayangyi.

An excellent cluster of sites is about 3km east. North of the road, **Tayok Pye Paya** has good westward views of Bagan. To the south, 13th-century **Payathonzu**, a small complex of three interconnected shrines, draws visitors to its murals.

About 200m north, **Nandamannya Pahto**, from the same period, features the 'temptation of Mura' murals – in the form of topless women reaping no response from a meditating Buddha. It's often locked; ask at Payathonzu for the 'key master'. Just behind, **Kyat Kan Kyaung** has been a cave-style monastery for nearly 1000 years.

Around Nyaung U

In town, the gilded bell of **Shwezigon Paya** (1102; Map p584) is considered by many to be the prototype for many Burmese pagodas. A yellow compound located on the east side (called '37 Nats' in English) features figures of each.

From the Nyaung U jetty, it is possible to arrange a fun boat trip (about K5000 or so) to see temples just off the Ayeyarwady: **Thetkyamuni** (Map p584) and **Kondawgyi Pahto** (Map p584) are about 1km east. **Kyauk Gu Ohnmin** cave temple (off Map p584), dating back 1000 years, was supposedly the start of a tunnel intended to go 18km – only 50m is accessible nowadays.

can, in theory, take the daily 8.45am train to Pyinmana (ordinary US$5, 10 hours) and continue from there to Yangon. In practice, however, you are not allowed to stay in Pyinmana and connections don't really work.

Getting Around

Bicycles are a leisurely way to see Bagan. The going rate is K1000 per day in Nyaung U, double that in New Bagan. Carry water, though, as some temples don't have vendors.

A horse cart isn't a bad way to get to grips with Bagan on day one. It's K10,000 for the whole day, but there is only really sufficient space for two people. Try and arrange one with a foam cushion, as it can get pretty uncomfortable after a few hours.

Pick-ups between Nyaung U, Old Bagan and New Bagan run along the main street, starting from the roundabout outside the Nyaung U market. A ride costs K400.

A taxi for the day costs about US$20 to US$25. A taxi from the airport costs K5000/6000/7000 to Nyaung U/Old Bagan/New Bagan.

AROUND BAGAN

Mt Popa

The Mt Olympus of Myanmar, Mt Popa is the stupa-studded centre of *nat* worship in the country. This 737m-high monastery-topped hill is visible from Bagan on a clear day – look to the right end of the mountains to the west – and offers breathtaking views of the plain. The 20-minute climb up goes past devout pilgrims, cheeky monkeys and, occasionally, slow-stepping hermit monks called *yeti*. The **Mahagiri shrine**, at the foot of the mountain, features a display of the 37 *nat*. Festivals include the full moon of **Nayon** (May/June) and **Nadaw** (November/December).

The Popa trip is only worth it if you have at least two full days for Bagan itself. A pick-up (K3000 each way,) leaves Nyaung U bus station at 8.30am, often with a change in Kyaukpadaung. Far easier is a slot in a share taxi for about K7000 per person. Ask the driver to point out remnants of the petrified forest.

Meiktila & Thazi

If you find yourself in Meiktila while travelling the Bagan-to-Inle corridor, the **Honey Hotel** (☎ 064-25755; Pan Chan St; s US$8-10, d US$10-20; ❄) is a converted mansion on the shores of Lake Meiktila.

Thazi, a rail junction, is home to the basic **Moon-Light Rest House** (☎ 064-69056; r US$3-10; ❄).

Pakokku

An alternative route between Bagan and Monywa goes by this slow-paced, authentic town on the west bank of the Ayeyarwady. Staying isn't as appealing since the priceless old couple who ran the unique Mya Yatanar Inn (75 Lanmataw St) lost their licence, though they're still happy for a chat. Instead, the **Tha Pye No Guest House** (☎ 21166; Myoma Rd; s/d K10,000/20,000; ❄) has half-decent rooms.

Buses run to Monywa (K1500, 4½ hours), and ferries to Nyaung U (K3000, two to three hours).

UPPER AYEYARWADY

Drifting down the Ayeyarwady, through jungle-clad gorges and past friendly villagers for whom the river and its traffic are a lifeline to the outside world, is one of the most memorable experiences in Myanmar. The best of the action is way north of Mandalay in Kachin State. Most travellers fly north or take the train to Myitkyina or Bhamo before enjoying life in the slow lane on the return journey. Which, in this case, is as much the destination as towns along the way.

Much of the area away from the river is closed to foreigners.

MYITKYINA

☎ 074 / pop about 170,000

This is the end of the line as far as overland travel in the north goes. The Kachin capital of Myitkyina is a popular embarkation point for a river trip south. It is also a low-key trekking centre for visits to nearby Kachin villages.

Khin Thu Maung from **Snowland Tours** (☎ 23499; snowland@mptmail.net.mm), southwest of the market, can help with trekking tours to Kachin villages. The Y has maps of town and can arrange motorbikes (K10,000 to K15,000) for the scenic 90-minute ride north to **Myit-son**, where the Ayeyarwady begins at the confluence of the Malikha and Maykha Rivers. Several Buddhist sites are in the area, though many locals are Christian. Internet is available.

The **YMCA** (☎ 23010; mka-ymca@myanmar.com.mm; 12 Myothit Rd; s US$6-10, d US$10-14; ❄) is where most travellers stay. The Y has basic, clean rooms and staff can help with transport details and local attractions.

Air Bagan (☎ 01-513322; www.airbagan.com) connects Myitkyina and Mandalay (US$75) two to four times a week.

For Bhamo, boats depart Myitkyina for Sinbu (K6000, four to six hours) at 8.30am. You must stay in the no-frills government guest house (K4000) in Sinbu, then continue to Bhamo (K4000, five to seven hours) about 9am. Buses (K12,000, six hours) and pick-ups take the 188km cobblestone road to Bhamo; get to the dusty bus station by 7am to guarantee a seat. Have five passport and visa copies ready for checkpoints.

A blanket is mandatory for nights on the train to and from Mandalay (ordinary/1st-class/sleeper from US$11/35/40, 20 to 25 hours).

BHAMO

☎ 074 / pop 20,000

More of a charmer than Myitkyina, the riverside town of Bhamo has a bustling daily market, drawing Lisu, Kachin and Shan folk from surrounding villages. The ruinous old Shan city walls of **Sampanago** are located 5km north of town. Interesting **Kachin villages** lie within reach; local guide and helicopter improviser (he'll tell you) Sein Win is your man.

Ask for him at the **Friendship Hotel** (☎ 50095; yonekyi@baganmail.net.mm; per person with shared bathroom US$7, s/d with private bathroom US$20/25; ❄), one of the better provincial pads, with good-value rooms, luxury and otherwise, useful transport information and a handy map.

By road, your only option is Myitkyina. By the Ayeyarwady River, boats leave for Sinbu (for Myitkyina) about 9am; government-run IWT ferries putter along to Mandalay (deck/cabin US$9/54, at least 1½ days) on Monday, Wednesday and Friday mornings; and private Shwe Keinnery has a seasonal boat to Mandalay (US$60, 18 to 24 hours) via Katha (US$30, seven to nine hours) three days a week. Daily 'express boats' to Katha (K15,000, six hours) leave at 9am.

KATHA

Fans of George Orwell's *Burmese Days* will enjoy foraging around this sleepy town on the Ayeyarwady. Eric Blair (Orwell's real name) was stationed here in 1926–27 and based his novel on this setting. The old **British Club**, around which much of the novel revolves, is now an agricultural co-op, and the nearby tennis court mentioned in the novel is still used.

The basic **Ayeyarwady Guest House** (Strand Rd; s K5000-6000, d K10,000), with rooms overlooking the river near the ferry landing, is the place to stay.

Foreigners are not allowed to take buses from Katha to anywhere except the rail junction 25km west at Naba (K800, one hour), where trains between Mandalay (ordinary/upper class US$7/20) and Myitkyina stop between 4pm and midnight (the 8pm 'express' is best). The IWT ferry and the Shwe Keinnery boat pass three times weekly en route to Mandalay and Bhamo.

WESTERN MYANMAR

Western Myanmar, home to the proud Rakhaing people, is a land unto itself. Isolated and inaccessible from the rest of the country, this enigmatic region is in many ways closer to Bangladesh than Burma. For travellers Sittwe is only accessible by air or water and 'baby Bagan', the atmospheric temple city of Mrauk U, is reached by a further boat ride inland. If you're here, you're really travelling.

The Rakhaing people are dubbed 'Burmese' by the government but are passionate about their distinct language and culture. The Mahumuni Buddha remains a sensitive subject and locals love telling the story of how it was stolen by the Burmese and moved to Mandalay in 1784.

A large Muslim population, known as Rohingya, live in and around Sittwe. However, they are routinely discriminated against by the government, which doesn't recognise them as citizens and insists that travel even to the next village requires them to hold a permit. The Rohingya made international headlines in early 2009 after the Thai navy was accused of disabling, then abandoning, their refugee boats.

See p557 for information on Ngapali Beach, which is in southern Rakhaing State.

SITTWE (AYKAB)

☎ 043 / pop 200,000

For most people, a trip to Mrauk U will include a stay in Sittwe, a port town where the wide Kaladan River meets the Bay of Bengal. The British moved the regional capital here from Mrauk U in the 1820s and there's no denying Sittwe has seen better days. Still, it retains a lively yet laid-back atmosphere; think of Sittwe as a place to experience Rakhaing culture, not as a sightseeing centre, and you'll probably have a good time. The population is about 30% Muslim, with the central Jama Mosque the most historic and impressive religious site in town.

Information

Kiss Internet (Main Rd; per hr K1000; 7.30am-10.30pm) ADSL connection, Skype and helpful staff.

Sights

Sittwe's main attractions relate to its soul as a maritime and trading centre. The clear pick is the morning **fish market**, which kicks off at 6am when fishermen haul thousands of fish out of their wooden boats and they're sold in the grubby old market. Explore the greater market to find a banana market (who knew there were this many varieties of banana?) north off the main lane leading to the fish market, and a rice market that's more interesting than it sounds. About 2km south, via the Strand, is the **Point**, a peninsula boasting big sunset views.

Back in the centre, the **Rakhaing State Cultural Museum** (Main Rd; admission US$2; 10am-4pm Tue-Sat) features a Mrauk U model, many artefacts of the era, and watercolours of traditional wrestling moves, all presented in typically uninspired Myanmar style.

A few hundred metres north of the centre, the **Maka Kuthala Kyaungdawgyi** (Large Monastery of Great Merit; Main Rd; admission free, donation encouraged) is more interesting for the colonial-era mansion than the dusty array of old coins, banknotes and Buddha images.

Sleeping & Eating

Electricity is consistently erratic. Try some Rakhaing specialities, which involve seafood and spice, for the best dining. Main Rd has food to cater to those looking to go native as well as those after something more familiar, like a menu.

Sittwe Prince Hotel (☎ 22539; www.mraukuprincehotel.com; 27 Main Rd; s US$5-15, d US$10-20;) The most traveller-friendly hotel, cheaper rooms here are small and have shared bathrooms. Air-con is available in the more expensive rooms, but they all need some lovin'.

Noble Hotel (☎ 23558; 45 Main Rd; noble@myanmar.com.mm; s/d with breakfast US$20/30;) The compact-but-comfy rooms are fair value, with 24-hour power, air-con and satellite TV.

Mondi stand (bowls K300; breakfast & lunch) *Mondi* is the tasty local variant of Burmese *mohinga,* with chillies instead of peanuts. Locals swear this place has the best in town. It's opposite City Hall on the airport road.

City Point Music Restaurant (The Strand; dishes K2000-4000; breakfast, lunch & dinner) Live music every night makes the popular City Point good for drinks at sunset and later. Eat elsewhere.

Getting There & Away

Foreigners cannot travel by road to Sittwe. It seems all other transport to Sittwe is notoriously prone to schedule changes (if you're lucky) or cancellation (if you're not).

AIR

All three private airlines fly to Yangon (from US$88), often via Thandwe (from US$49), though frequency can range from daily to twice a week. The airport is 2.5km southwest of the centre; head outside the gate to get a cheap ride.

BOAT

Malikha Express (☎ 24248; www.malikha-rivercruises.com; Main Rd; 9am-5pm) operates fast boats between Sittwe and Taunggok (US$40, eight hours) three or four times a week between October and March, but from April to September only on Mondays to Taunggok, and Saturdays return. It also has fast boats to/from Mrauk U (see p592).

A government slow ferry runs to Taunggok (deck/cabin US$9/54, 36 hours) at least once a week – usually on Friday but for us a Saturday, once the monks had turned up. Expect delays. From Taunggok, buses or pick-ups go to Pyay or Thandwe (Ngapali).

MRAUK U (MYOHAUNG)

☎ 043 / pop 25,000

Like Bagan to the east, the ancient Rakhaing kings of Mrauk U decided no amount of temples was too many, and more than 150 remain today. Accessible via a 65km boat ride northeast from Sittwe, Mrauk U is smaller than Bagan but much more alive. The temples are dotted across a series of low hills, but the town they emerge from is as much of an attraction – think laid-back smiles, no hassle, almost no motorised transport and few foreign tourists. A huge **pagoda festival** is held in May.

Mrauk U served as the Rakhaing capital from 1430 to 1784, when the Brits relocated

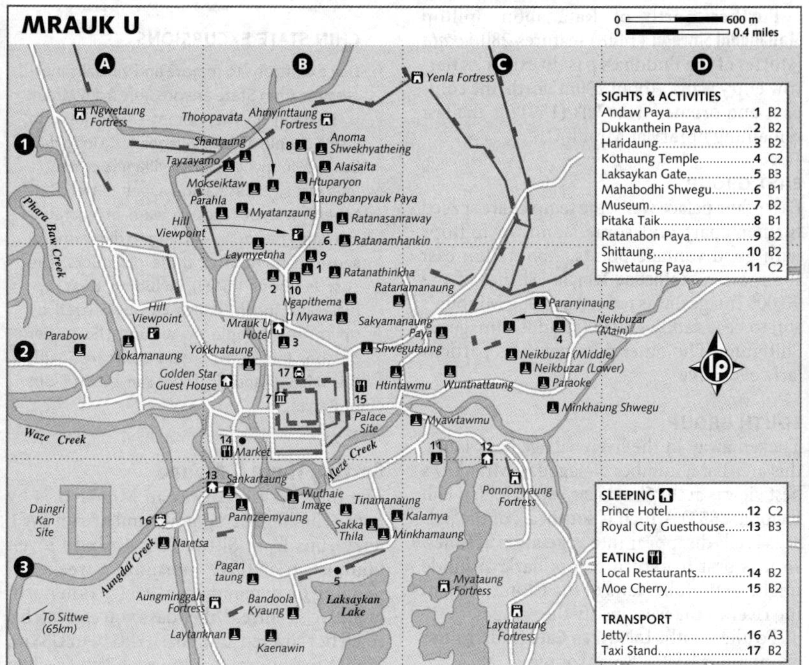

it to Sittwe. It was a fine time, with the kings hiring Japanese samurais as bodyguards and a naval fleet of 10,000 boats terrorising neighbouring countries from the Bay of Bengal. It's worth reading up: U Shwe Zan's *The Golden Mrauk U: An Ancient Capital of Rakhine* is available only in Yangon.

Sights

More than 150 temples blend into the small town over a 7-sq-km area. Foreigners pay US$5 to visit, plus an optional K3000 'light fee' to have tacky fluoros turned on in some temples. Payments are made at Shittaung temple.

PALACE SITE & AROUND

Apart from crumbling walls, little is left of the central palace, located just east of the market. Apparently astrologers advised King Minbun to move his home here in 1429 to shun 'evil birds' at his Launggret palace. Inside the western walls, the Department of Archaeology's **museum** (admission US$5; ⌚ 11am-3pm Mon-Fri) has prerestoration photos, a site model and a replica of the Shittaung pillar. You can see most of it from the door.

On a hill just to the north, the 18th-century **Haridaung** pagoda has nice westward views.

NORTH GROUP

The main sites of Mrauk U are clustered beyond the **Shittaung** (Shrine of the 80,000 Images), the most intricate of the surviving temples. Built in 1535, the pagoda has a mazelike floor plan. An outer passage, accessible via two doors from the entry hall to the east side, passes 1000 sculptures; the inner chamber coils to a dead end via a 'Buddha footprint'. Young monks will likely point you to the (now fenced off) relief of a frisky couple with their, erm, hands full.

Just north is the sublime 16th-century **Andaw Paya**, and beyond is the **Ratanabon Paya**, a stupa dating from 1612 that survived a WWII bomb.

Across the road west from Shittaung, the bunkerlike **Dukkanthein Paya** (1571), set amid a green field, is the most impressive of the batch: look for Mrauk U's 64 traditional hairstyles on sculptures on the coiling path leading to a sun-drenched Buddha in the inner chamber.

Further north of Ratanabon, hilltop **Mahabodhi Shwegu** (1448) features 280 *jakata* (stories of the Buddha's past lives) on its narrow entry walls. About 200m north, the compact and ornate **Pitaka Taik** (1591) is the last remaining library at Mrauk U.

EAST GROUP

East of the palace walls, the temples are spaced further apart and some stand on hilltops with good vantage points. About 2km east the massive **Kothaung Temple** (Shrine of the 90,000 Images) was named by King Minbun's son to beat daddy's 80,000 Buddha images at Shittaung. The outer passageway is particularly evocative.

SOUTH GROUP

Tucked away in the lively village back lanes, this area has a number of pagodas. Mrauk U's best view is at the **Shwetaung Paya** (Golden Hill Pagoda; 1553), which is southeast of the palace. Trails disappear into vegetation at times, so it is best to return before dark. A guide might be useful. Views of the Chin Hills and the river to the west justify the scrapes.

To the south, **Laksaykan Gate** leads to the eponymous lake, a water source.

Sleeping & Eating

Due to a prolonged lull in tourism, Mrauk U's cheapest guest houses no longer had licences to accommodate foreigners when we passed.

Royal City Guesthouse (☎ 24200-05; s US$10-15, d US$15-20; ❄) The closest accommodation to the jetty, this amiable orange guest house has a mix of older rooms with fresh paint and newer bungalows, all very clean. Share bathrooms are open air – that's basic not Balinese style.

Prince Hotel (☎ 24200; www.mraukuprincehotel.com; s US$10-25, d US$15-30) It's looking a little creaky, but the large, comfortable rooms at the Prince have private bathrooms and hot water on request. Staff give away free maps of the temples.

Moe Cherry (dishes K1500-3000; 🕑 lunch & dinner) The traveller favourite, Moe Cherry has a range of Rakhaing-style curries, a couple of vegie options, an airy balcony setting and a larger-than-life woman owner. It can also arrange car and boat rental.

Three cheaper places can be found opposite the west side of the market.

> **CHIN STATE EXCURSIONS**
>
> Day excursions to remote and virtually inaccessible Chin State are possible from Mrauk U, heading up the vibrant Lamro River to visit a couple of local villages. It's a long day, but we found the Chin villagers a hoot – let's just say that having a web pattern tattooed on their faces to ward off marauding kings has done nothing to diminish the sense of humour of these old ducks. The cost is about US$80 including boat, vehicle and lunch, which can be shared by up to four people. At around US$20 per person, this is a bargain compared with the US$550-and-up tours run by MTT out of Bagan.

Getting There & Around

The only permitted way to Mrauk U is by boat. The lumbering government-run IWT ferry runs from Sittwe (US$4, six to seven hours) two or three mornings a week, depending on demand, from a jetty 1km north of Sittwe's centre. Other days you can catch a small but covered 'line boat' (US$10 to US$15, four to five hours) that leaves at 7am or when full. Private boat charter is possible for between US$80 and US$100 return per boat, including up to four nights waiting (get that clear up front). **Malikha** (☎ 24248; www.malikha-rivercruises.com) runs enclosed 'fast boats' (US$40, three hours) one to three days a week, leaving at 7am. Going back, boats leave Mrauk U at 7am or 8am. Most boats arrive and depart from the 'jetty' south of the market.

A horse cart around the temples is K8000 to K12,000 per day. Bicycle rental is about K2500 per day. The taxi stand (for jeeps, from US$20 a day) is on the north side of the palace.

MYANMAR DIRECTORY

ACCOMMODATION

Hotels and guest houses are a touch more expensive in Myanmar than in neighbouring countries. In places with choice, it is possible to find a plain room for US$4 to US$6 per person. And we do mean plain; think concrete floors, squashed mosquitoes on the walls, a fan (usually) and a shared bathroom down the hall, with a basic breakfast if you're lucky.

For a few dollars more, you get air-con, hot water and even TV. These, however, will be of limited value unless your lodging has a generator, because electricity supplies are sketchy right across Myanmar. Unless stated otherwise, prices include private bathroom.

Nearly all hotels and guest houses quote prices in US dollars. Most accept kyat at a slightly disadvantageous rate. Prices listed in this chapter are for peak season, roughly October to March. Small discounts may be available in the low season; don't be afraid to haggle gently if planning a longer stay. Passport and visa details are required at check-in, but hotels don't need to hold your passport.

All accommodation supposedly must be licensed to accept foreign guests, meaning the cheapest places are usually off-limits. Sometimes unlicensed guest houses will say they're 'full' rather than explain the full story. In out-of-the-way towns, some local guest houses will accept weary travellers.

ACTIVITIES

Barefoot pilgrimages up pagoda-topped hills (such as Mandalay Hill) or biking around town are the most common activities, but there are more adventurous options.

Cycling

With your own bike and spare parts, Myanmar's highways are there to be conquered. Popular stretches include Mandalay to Bagan, via Myingyan, or the hilly terrain between Mandalay and Hsipaw. Roads range from poor to diabolical, but are still easily passable by bicycle. That said, the brutally hot season may deflate even the most committed pedal-pusher.

> **GOVERNMENT HOTELS**
>
> In Myanmar, many travellers ask themselves how to avoid government-run hotels. Government officials have their fingers in the pockets of top-end and joint-venture hotels, but rarely bother with small-time guest houses. Full-on government hotels are often named after the destination (eg Mrauk U Hotel in Mrauk U) and fly the national flag outside. Generally 10% of what you spend at any guest house goes to the government. The less your room costs, the less the government gets its hands on.

Diving & Snorkelling

Unfortunately, there's not much underwater action available in Myanmar for the budget traveller. You can snorkel past colourful fish and some coral off Ngapali or Ngwe Saung beaches. The more spectacular Myeik Archipelago, near Kawthoung, is generally only accessible via expensive live-aboard cruises operating out of Thailand.

Trekking

There are two main options: two- or three-day treks between Kalaw and Inle Lake (see p568), staying in local villages; or hikes along the less-touristed trails around Hsipaw (p580). Winter nights can get chilly so pack some warm clothes. Not surprisingly, the wet season makes for slippery trails.

BOOKS

Even more than with most countries, it's worth reading up before arriving in Myanmar. Pick up Lonely Planet's *Myanmar* for more comprehensive coverage, and the helpful *Burmese Phrasebook*. Other top books:

- *Trouser People* (2002) by Andrew Marshall. The author follows the footsteps of a colonial-era Scot who introduced football to hill tribes in the late 19th century. A great read.
- *Burmese Days* (1934) by George Orwell. The definitive novel of the last lonely days of Britain's colonial experience, this is a must on any trip to old Burma.
- *The Glass Palace* (2001) by Amitav Ghosh. This modern classic interweaves a motley crew of locals (Indians, Chinese, Burmese) amid lushly recounted historical events.
- *Freedom from Fear & Other Writings* (1995) by Aung San Suu Kyi. A collection of essays from The Lady herself.
- *Finding George Orwell in Burma* (2006) by Emma Larkin. US journalist Larkin follows in the footsteps of the famous novelist and discovers more Animal Farm than Burmese Days.

BUSINESS HOURS

Business hours tend to be flexible, especially for restaurants and drinking establishments, which might close early when it's raining, and stay open late for a big football match. Government offices open from 9.30am to 4.30pm, Monday to Friday, while private offices, such as travel agencies, are usually open from about 9am to 6pm Monday to Saturday. Post offices open 9.30am to 3.30pm Monday to Friday. Restaurants generally open 7am to 9pm, but often earlier or later depending on demand. Unless otherwise stated, restaurants are open for breakfast, lunch and dinner. Shops open 9.30am to 6pm or later.

CLIMATE

November through to February is the best time to visit. Temperatures can get quite cold in the hills, and close to freezing in places such as Kalaw. From mid-February it gets increasingly hot – April being the 'cruellest month', to quote TS Eliot, until monsoonal rains bless the land from (approximately) mid-May through to mid-October. See the climate charts (p936) for average temperatures and rainfall.

CUSTOMS

Officially, visitors must declare foreign currency in excess of US$2000, as well as electronic goods such as laptops, iPods, radios, cameras and especially mobile phones. In reality, checks usually range from lax to non-existent. Genuine antiques cannot be taken out of the country.

DANGERS & ANNOYANCES

Usually the only time a local will be running with your money or belongings is if they're chasing you down the road with something you've dropped. For now theft remains quite rare, but don't tempt fate in this poor country by flashing valuables or leaving them unguarded. The only real scams are dodgy money changers shortchanging you, and drivers or guides getting a commission for purchases at any shops you visit.

Areas around the Myanmar–Thai border, home to the country's notorious drug trade, can be dangerous (and off limits) to explore.

Power outages are highly annoying and commonplace everywhere except the surreal capital, Nay Pyi Taw. Many businesses have their own generators, but check with your guest house whether the power will be on all night, especially in the hot season.

EMBASSIES & CONSULATES

For visa information, see p600.

The capital was moved to Nay Pyi Taw in 2005, but foreign embassies and consulates stayed behind in Yangon. Check the **Ministry of Foreign Affairs** (www.mofa.gov.mm) for more information.

Australia (Map p550; ☎ 01-251810; www.burma.embassy.gov.au; 88 Strand Rd)
Bangladesh (Map p546; ☎ 01-515275; 11B Thanlwin Rd, Kamayut Township)
Cambodia (Map p546; ☎ 01-549609; 25 New University Ave, B3/4B)
Canada Represented by the Australian embassy.
China (Map p548; ☎ 01-221281; 1 Pyidaungsu Yeiktha Rd, Dagon)
France (Map p548; ☎ 01-212520; www.ambafrance-mm.org; 102 Pyidaungsu Yeiktha Rd, Dagon)
Germany (Map p546; ☎ 01-548951; 9 Bogyoke Aung San Museum Rd)
India (Map p550; ☎ 01-243972; 545-547 Merchant St)
Indonesia (Map p548; ☎ 01-254465; 100 Pyidaungsu Yeiktha Rd)
Japan (Map p546; ☎ 01-549644; 100 Nat Mauk Rd)
Laos (Map p548; ☎ 01-222482; A1 Diplomatic Quarters, Taw Win St)
Malaysia (Map p548; ☎ 01-220249; 82 Pyidaungsu Yeiktha Rd)
New Zealand Represented by the UK embassy.

TALKING POLITICS

The people of Myanmar take heart from knowing the rest of the world is aware of their plight, so it's important to let them know. However, talking politics with locals can potentially endanger them, so be discreet. A good time to broach the subject subtly is when someone asks you what you think of Myanmar. After telling them (as you likely will) how much you like the country and particularly the people, you could mention that, however, you understand their situation is difficult.

From here it will be up to the individual. In private places, and some teashops, some will be quite frank. Others, however, will avoid the conversation entirely. During research, I was chatting with a well-educated hotel manager in a private place when I asked what he thought about elections scheduled for 2010. He replied: 'You know, the easiest way to meditate is to concentrate on the cold air coming in and hot air going out.' I thought he'd misheard me, but he hadn't. He just didn't want to have that conversation.

Singapore (Map p546; ☎ 01-559001; www.mfa.gov.sg/yangon; 238 Dhamma Zedi Rd, Bahan)
Thailand (Map p546; ☎ 01-226721; 94 Pyay Rd, Dagon)
UK (Map p550; ☎ 01-370863; http://ukinburma.fco.gov.uk; 80 Strand Rd)
USA (Map p546; ☎ 01-536509; http://burma.usembassy.gov; 110 University Ave, Kamayut)
Vietnam (Map p546; ☎ 01-511305; www.vietnamembassy-myanmar.org; 72 Thanlwin Rd, Bahan)

FESTIVALS & EVENTS

Traditionally, Myanmar follows a 12-month lunar calendar, so most festival dates cannot be fixed on the Gregorian calendar. Most festivals in Myanmar are on the full moon of the Burmese month in which they occur, but the build-up can go for days. Besides Buddhist holy days, some Hindu, Muslim and Christian holidays and festivals are also observed. For much more detail see http://myanmartravelinformation.co m/mti-myanmar-festivals/index.htm.

February/March

Union Day 12 February. Marks Bogyoke Aung San's (short-lived) achievement of unifying Myanmar's disparate ethnic groups.
Shwedagon Festival This is the largest *paya* festival in Myanmar and takes place on the full moon (usually in March).
Armed Forces Day 27 March. Military parades and fireworks. Since 1989 the government has pardoned prisoners on this day.

March/April

Full-Moon Festival The Tagu full moon is the biggest event of the year at Shwemawdaw Paya in Bago.

April/May

Buddha's Birthday The full moon also marks the day of the Buddha's enlightenment and his entry to nirvana. One of the best places to observe this ceremony is at Yangon's Shwedagon Paya.
Thingyan (Water Festival) The Burmese New Year is the biggest holiday of the year, celebrated with a raucous nationwide water fight. Traditional Burmese restraint goes out the window and you'll see people expressing themselves (often drunkenly) in a rash of denim, leather and mohawk haircuts. It is impossible to go outside without getting drenched so just join the fun. The water cleanliness is, however, questionable, so remember to 'close all orifices' as you're getting drenched. Businesses close and some transport – especially buses – stop running.
Workers' Day 1 May.

June/July

Buddhist Lent Start of the Buddhist Rains Retreat (aka 'Buddhist Lent'). Laypeople present monasteries with new robes, because during the three-month Lent period monks are restricted to their monasteries.

July/August

Martyr's Day 19 July. Commemorates the assassination of Bogyoke Aung San and his comrades on 19 July 1947. Wreaths are laid at his mausoleum, north of Shwedagon Paya in Yangon.
Wagaung Festival Nationwide exercise in alms-giving.

September/October

Boat Races This is the height of the wet season, so boat races are held in rivers, lakes and even ponds all over Myanmar. Inle Lake is best.
Thadingyut Celebrates Buddha's return from a period of preaching.

October/November

Tazaungdaing The biggest 'festival of lights' sees all Myanmar lit by oil lamps, fire balloons, candles and even mundane electric lamps. In Taunggyi, Shan State, there are fire-balloon competitions.
Kathein A one-month period at the end of Buddhist Lent during which new monastic robes and requisites are offered to the monastic community.

December/January

Christmas 25 December. A surprisingly popular public holiday in deference to the many Christian Kayin (Karen) and Chin.
Independence Day 4 January. A major public holiday with countrywide celebrations.
Kayin New Year Considered a national holiday, when Karen communities throughout Myanmar celebrate by wearing their traditional dress and by hosting folk-dancing and singing performances. The largest celebrations are held in the Karen suburb of Insein, just north of Yangon, and in Hpa-an.
Ananda Festival Held at the Ananda Pahto in Bagan at the full moon.

FOOD & DRINK

Food

Mainstream Burmese cuisine represents a blend of Bamar, Mon, Indian and Chinese influences. If you're arriving from Thailand, Vietnam or Malaysia, it may not instantly inspire, but there are some cracking dishes out there.

A typical meal has *htamin* (rice) as its core, eaten with a choice of *hin* (curry dishes), most commonly fish, chicken, pork, prawns or

MYANMAR (BURMA)

mutton. Soup is always served, along with a table full of condiments (including pickled vegies as spicy dipping sauces). Most meals include free refills, so come hungry.

Outside of Rakhaing State (near Bangladesh), most Burmese food is pretty mild on the chilli front. Most cooks opt for a simple masala of turmeric, ginger, garlic, salt and onions, plus plenty (and we mean loads!) of peanut oil and shrimp paste. *Balachaung* (chillies, tamarind and dried shrimp pounded together) or the pungent *ngapi kyaw* (spicy shrimp paste with garlic) is always nearby to add some kick. Almost everything in Burmese cooking is flavoured with *ngapi* (a salty paste concocted from dried and fermented shrimp or fish).

Noodle dishes are often eaten for breakfast or as light snacks between meals. By far the most popular is *mohinga* ('moun-hinga'), rice noodles served with fish soup and as many other ingredients as there are cooks.

Shan khauk-swe (Shan-style noodle soup; thin wheat noodles in a light broth with meat or tofu) is a favourite all over Myanmar, but is most common in Mandalay and the Shan State. Another Shan dish worth seeking out is *htamin chin*, literally sour rice, a turmeric-coloured rice salad. See p552 for examples of snacks found in street markets around Myanmar.

The seafood served along the coasts, particularly on Ngapali and Ngwe Saung beaches, is some of the best and cheapest you'll find in the entire region.

Drink

Only drink purified water. Be wary of ice in remote areas, but it is usually factory produced in towns and cities. Bottled water costs from K300 a litre and is widely available. Consider sterilising your own water, and saving dozens of PET bottles, using a UV sterilising wand.

Burmese tea, brewed Indian-style with lots of condensed milk and sugar, is the national drink. Most restaurants will provide as much free Chinese tea as you can handle. Teashops, a national institution, are good places to meet people over a drink and inexpensive snacks such as *nam-bya* and *palata* (flat breads) or Chinese fried pastries. Ask for *lahpeq ye* (tea with a dollop of condensed milk); *cho bouk* is less sweet, and *kyauk padaung* is very sweet.

Locally produced soft drinks (such as Fantasy, Crusher and Star) are just K300 per bottle, compared with the (rare) can of Coke for nearer K1000. Sugarcane juice is a very popular streetside drink.

Let's not forget the beer, which is almost as popular as tea. Myanmar Beer (about K1500 for a 640ml bottle) is the best local brew. It's available in draught, as is Dagon Beer. Mandalay Beer is horrible piss, especially the 7% 'red label'. Yangon is one of the only places to find out-and-out bars. Elsewhere open-air barbecue restaurants and 'beer stations' embrace a steady crew of red-faced local drinkers. It's fine to buy a bottle or two to take to your guest house, and many people do just this, or to sit at a restaurant and get plastered.

Local wine, Aythaya, is now produced near Inle Lake and is very palatable. Local firewaters are not, but sampling them is a great way to earn your stripes with the local boozers.

GAY & LESBIAN TRAVELLERS

Lesbians and gays are generally accepted in Burmese culture. In fact local women walking with foreign men raise more eyebrows. Yangon has the most active gay 'scene', if you can call it that. It's OK to share rooms, but public displays of affection – for anyone – are frowned upon.

HOLIDAYS

Apart from the big festivals such as Thingyan (New Year), other public holidays include the following:

Independence Day 4 January
Union Day February 12
Peasants Day 2 March
Armed Forces Day 27 March
Workers' Day 1 May
National Day late November/early December
Christmas Day 25 December

Government offices take any excuse for a day off, but many private businesses remain open.

INTERNET ACCESS

Internet access in Myanmar depends on how the government is feeling. If there's nothing bugging them, you'll find plenty of well-equipped internet cafes in major cities charging about K1000 per hour. Smaller towns usually have at least one public access centre. Service is slow, especially between 5pm and 8pm. The government tries to restrict Hotmail and Yahoo mail, but Gmail is usually accessible; always use https://when logging in to Gmail. Lots of places advertise Skype and other VoIP services, but don't get your hopes up.

Bear in mind that all local email ending in '.mm' is subject to government censorship in both directions. This can result in emails being delayed by hours, days or, when a backlog develops, being summarily deleted! If trying to book a room via email, resend if you don't hear anything after a few days.

INTERNET RESOURCES

Burma Today (www.burmatoday.com) Posts recent Myanmar articles.
Irrawaddy (www.irrawaddy.org) Chiang Mai–based publication run by exiles and focusing on political issues, but also covering cultural news.
Mizzima (www.mizzima.com) A nonprofit news service organised by Burmese journalists in exile.
Myanmar Home Page (www.myanmar.com) Government site with funny government dictum, and the latest propaganda from the New Light of Myanmar.
Myanmar Times (www.mmtimes.com) English-language newspaper.
Myanmar Travel Information (www.myanmartravelinformation.com) Includes train and airline schedules (though these date quickly).
Online Burma/Myanmar Library (www.burmalibrary.org) Comprehensive database of books on Myanmar.

LEGAL MATTERS

As Aung San Suu Kyi could tell you, Myanmar does not have an independent judiciary. If you engage in political activism (eg handing out pro-democracy leaflets as some Westerners have), illegally cross the border into the country, or get caught with drugs, you have no legal recourse. Drug trafficking crimes are punishable by death. Political activists, or those entering illegally from Thailand (unless you're Rambo, of course), are more likely to be locked up then deported.

MAPS

Periplus Editions (scale 1:2,000,000), ITMB (1:1,350,0000) and Nelles (1:1,500,000) all make dedicated maps of Myanmar. Design Printing Services' (DPS) *Myanmar Guide Map* is free at the MTT office, travel agents and (sometimes) the airport in Yangon. DPS also makes maps of Yangon, Mandalay and Bagan.

MEDIA

Reporters Without Borders (ww.rsf.org) reports that in 2008 the all-powerful military censorship bureau told Burmese media that 'the publication of any photo, sketch, painting, article, novel or poem without being sent [in advance to the censor] will be punished'. And they often are, with many journalists, bloggers and writers currently behind bars.

Newspapers

For the official line, the *New Light of Myanmar* is hilarious, overflowing with Orwellian propaganda and clunky English. Look out for the anti-Western poems. Far more useful is the *Myanmar Times*, with a flight schedule and entertainment listings. Both are scarce beyond Yangon.

Radio

All legal radio and TV broadcasts are state controlled. Radio Myanmar broadcasts news in Burmese, English (8.30am, 1pm and 9pm) and eight other national languages three times a day. Many Burmese listen to Burmese-language broadcasts from the Voice of America, BBC and Radio Free Asia – described by the junta as 'killers in the airwaves' – for news from the outside world.

TV

TV Myanmar (MRTV) operates from 5pm to midnight, although it's at the mercy of the local power supply. Check out the 9.15pm national news, when a conservatively dressed newscaster coldly reads the censored news before a mural of a power plant. Military-owned Myawaddy, being in effect above the law, gets away with more outlandish attire (like jeans) and shows English Premiership football, during which the power usually stays on.

Satellite TV is illegal but you'll find it in many hotels. Al Jazeera and, of course, the Fashion Channel are common.

MONEY

Kyat, dollars, even the dreaded FECs (see p599): money comes in many shapes and sizes here. Kyat covers the little things (bottles of water, renting a bike, rice), while dollars (or vanishing FEC notes) are usually requested for ferries, air tickets, hotels and museums. While inflation has skyrocketed in recent years, costs in US dollars usually don't rise much.

What money doesn't come in is plastic – that's right, forget Visa, MasterCard, Amex, Cirrus and Plus which, since foreign banks decamped in 2003, are as good as merkins – ornamental but basically useless. Be sure to carry all the US dollars you need and more (see Bring New Bills, below). Hundreds get the best exchange rate, while small bills are useful for guest houses, most of which price rooms in dollars rather than kyat. The euro can be changed in a few places in Yangon, but not spent.

ATMs
Dream on…

Bargaining, Bribes & Tipping
Essentially almost any price is open to negotiation, an art best performed with a smile on your face. Exceptions are transport (other than taxis) and entrance fees. Handicrafts can often be purchased for half the first offer. Guest houses and hotels may drop prices during quiet periods, or if you're planning a longer stay.

Minor bribes – called 'presents' or 'tea money' in Burmese English – are part of everyday life in Myanmar. Extra compensation is expected for the efficient completion of many standard bureaucratic services, such as a visa extension.

Tipping, as it is known in the West, is not the rule in any but the fanciest hotels and restaurants. Rounding up a restaurant bill is certainly appreciated.

Cash
Myanmar's everyday currency, the kyat (pronounced chat, and abbreviated K), is divided into the following banknotes: K1, K5, K10, K20, K50, K100, K200, K500 and K1000. In practice, the smallest notes you'll likely see are filthy K50s and K100s. Myanmar's divisible-by-nine funny money (K45 and K90 notes) has been phased out.

DOLLARS VS KYAT

Prices in this book follow local usage: dollars when locals ask for them, kyat otherwise. Note some strict museum staff and boat operators will insist on dollars.

Credit Cards & Travellers Cheques (are useless)
Need a credit card bailout? Fly to Bangkok! Very, very few upmarket hotels in Yangon and Mandalay accept credit cards (and usually don't advance money) or change travellers cheques. When they do a hefty commission is added. They're pretty much useless elsewhere.

Exchanging Money
Essentially the only sensible way to get kyat is via the 'black market', meaning guest houses, shops (look for suits and jewels), travel agencies or, less reliably, blokes on the street. Despite the 'official' listed exchange rate being a hilarious K6.55 to US$1, and the airport exchange counter offering a seemingly generous K450 to the dollar, the real rate (the one everyone, including the government, uses in everyday life) is *much* higher – at research time about K1050.

US dollars are – by some distance – the easiest currency to exchange. Euros are possible in major centres, and while it's *possible* to change other currencies in, say, Aung San market in Yangon, rates will be very poor.

Many travellers do the bulk of their changing in Yangon, where rates are a little better

BRING NEW BILLS!

Don't expect to change any rumpled, torn, worn, sweaty or dirty US dollar bills, which are welcomed with less enthusiasm than a bed bug convention in a guest house. Money changers, hotels, taxi drivers – almost everyone – will insist on crisp, clean (and mostly uncreased) bills, and only take post-1996 US dollar 'big head' bills or more recent. On this research trip we were quoted a range of rates for a range of bills (by the same money changer), found that bills with even the most microscopic tear (we couldn't even see it) were handed back, and tested the rumour that US$100 bills with the serial number starting 'CB' are rejected outright (it's true).

We also found that businesses routinely try to offload their unwanted US cash to unsuspecting tourists. The best reply is to smilingly imitate the locals: 'I'm sorry, do you have another one.' If that fails, a hot iron might make your cash more appealing.

EXCHANGE RATES

For the latest rates ignore online currency converters and look at www.irrawaddy.org.

These are exchange rates we were quoted during research:

Country	Unit	Kyat (K)
Australia	A$1	740
Euro zone	€1	1370
New Zealand	NZ$1	580
Thailand	B100	2900
UK	UK£1	1450
USA	US$1	K1050

than elsewhere. Count the cash before handing over dollars, and expect to be short-changed by guys in the street. Honest exchangers won't mind you counting. Generally kyat are banded in stacks of 100 K1000 bills.

Foreign Exchange Certificates (FECs)

In 2003 the government stopped requiring visitors to buy US$200 worth of Foreign Exchange Certificates (FEC) upon arrival. The FEC, pegged at 1:1 to the US dollar, is still accepted at hotels and for tourism-related services such as ferries or air tickets, but why would you bother?

PHOTOGRAPHY & VIDEO

Most internet cafes can burn digital photos onto a CD for about K1000. Some sights, including some pagodas, charge small camera fees. Avoid taking photos of military facilities, uniformed individuals, road blocks, bridges, NLD offices and Aung San Suu Kyi's house.

POST

Myanmar is the place to get retro with postcards at just K30 to anywhere in the world. That's US$0.03! And it's likely to get there. The government has to be losing money on this, so send as many as you can – it's not like they're hard to find. For more valuable packages, DHL Worldwide Express has offices in Yangon (p546) and Mandalay (Map p572; ☎ 02-39274; Hotel Mandalay, 652 78th St, 37/38) and sends packages to anywhere but the US (restricted due to sanctions). A 0.5kg package starts at about US$80 to Europe.

RESPONSIBLE TRAVEL

More so than anywhere else in Southeast Asia, using your head is important when travelling in Myanmar and can make a vital difference. See 'Should You Go?' (p537) for the pros and cons of visiting Myanmar and suggestions on keeping your money out of the generals' pockets. See Responsible Travel (p4) for more general ways of spreading your money where it does the most good, and the least harm.

STUDYING

Most foreign students in Myanmar are getting busy with *satipatthana vipassana,* or insight-awareness meditation. Yangon (p549) is meditation HQ, with several centres. Often food and lodging are provided at no charge, but meditators must follow eight precepts, including no food after noon, as well as no music, dancing, jewellery or perfume. Daily schedules are rigorous – sometimes nonstop practice from 3am to 11pm. It's for the experienced only. Note that 'meditation visas' are now much harder to get than before. For more information see http://web.ukonline.co.u k/buddhism/meditate.htm.

TELEPHONE

Local calls can be made cheaply or for free from guest houses. Domestic long distance is cheap from phone stalls on the street. Bear in mind, however, that actually getting through can take forever – patience and perseverance are required. International calls – made at a CTT office or from hotels – cost a whopping US$4 or US$5 per minute to Australia or Europe, an extra dollar to North America; much of this goes directly to the government. Some smaller towns still use manual switchboards, which can be a hoot to see in action.

Look out for (the few) internet cafes that have cheaper internet telephone services using MediaRing Talk or other software that isn't blocked; these usually cost about 500K or 1000K a minute.

Mobile Phones

Most mobile phone numbers in Myanmar cost a staggering US$1000 to US$2500 (depending on how close to the military you are) before you even think about handsets. For visitors, roaming is impossible, making Myanmar a rare opportunity to unplug your life. However, if you're twitching at the thought of it, don't despair. A pre-paid SIM is now available from mobile-phone stores for K20,000 (more outside Yangon). The number lasts until the money runs out or 30 days pass, and calls cost about K1500 a minute international. If you're carrying a mobile, it is supposed to be declared on arrival, though few people bother.

Phone Codes

To call Myanmar from abroad, dial your country's international access code, then ☎95 (Myanmar's country code), the area code (less the 0) and the five- or six-digit number. To dial long distance within Myanmar, dial the area code (including 0) and then the number.

TOILETS

In many out-of-the-way places, Burmese toilets are often squat jobs, generally in a cobweb-filled outhouse that is reached by a dirt path behind a restaurant. In guest houses and hotels you will usually find Western-style thrones. Toilet paper is widely available but as Confucius might have said: 'The wise traveller carries an emergency TP stash, the unwise traveller uses this page'. Either way, don't flush it.

TOURIST INFORMATION

Myanmar Travel & Tours (MTT; http://myanmartravelsandtours.com) is part of the Ministry of Hotels & Tourism (MHT). Its main office is in Yangon (p546) and there are also offices in Mandalay and Bagan. We don't recommend using its services, but it does have brochures and maps, arranges permits to travel in restricted areas (such as through the Delta to Ngwe Saung beach), and knows the latest news on border crossings.

TRAVELLERS WITH DISABILITIES

Myanmar is a tricky country for mobility-impaired travellers. Wheelchair ramps are virtually unheard of and public transport is crowded and can be difficult even for the fully ambulatory.

VISAS

Passport holders from Asean countries, China, Bangladesh and Russia do not need to apply for visas to visit Myanmar. All other nationalities do. A tourist visa's validity expires 90 days after issue (except those issued in Kuala Lumpur and Bangkok, where you must enter within 30 days) and only allows a 28-day, single-entry visit. It costs US$20, or thereabouts. You'll need two or three passport-sized photos.

Business visas are available, but meditation visas (US$30) are much harder to get than before; your chosen meditation centre can help.

Most budget travellers get their visa in Bangkok, either through a travel agency (which adds several hundred baht to the cost) or by going direct to the embassy. For the DIY option you need two mug shots, a photocopy of your passport's photo page and 810B (for 'two- or three-day' turnaround) or 1265B (for same-day service). It's often easier and cheaper, if not quicker, to arrange the visa in a 'quieter' capital, such as Phnom Penh or Vientiane.

Visitors from Thailand can get very short-term entry permits allowing minimal travel in border regions of Myanmar.

Applications

Myanmar's embassies and consulates can be scrupulous in checking the backgrounds of visa applicants; they told us 'Google finds everything, you know…' If you're a journalist, photographer, editor, publisher, motion-picture director or producer, cameraperson or writer, consider becoming something else for your trip to Myanmar or you'll likely be rejected.

Extensions & Overstaying Your Visa

Tourist visa extensions are no longer possible. You can, however, overstay if you're flying out of Yangon. Yangon airport's immigration allows visitors to overstay their visa for a charge of US$3 per day, plus a US$3 'registration fee'; try to have exact change and give yourself 30 minutes for form filling. No one seems to know exactly how long you can overstay. Some reports say '90 days', others say that any overstay will make it very tough to get another visa (with the same passport). We've not heard of anyone having problems for short overstays, but it's wise to not push it more than 14 days.

Note, however, that once you've overstayed your visa, you may have difficulties with airport immigration if you're planning domestic flights, particularly in far-flung airports (like Sittwe or Mytkyina). Try to stick with land routes.

VOLUNTEERING

Labour is cheap in Myanmar so offering to, for example, paint a school isn't really helping. For most travellers, volunteering to help locals speak better English will be appreciated. That could be in a teashop, on a bus, or in a more organised environment such as a monastery or school English course. In Yangon, the **Eden Centre for Disabled Children** (☎ 640399; www.edencentre.org) is the first Myanmar-run NGO that is working to better the lives of disabled children in the city. The organisation welcomes volunteers, particularly those with experience in special education.

WOMEN TRAVELLERS

Women travelling alone are more likely to be helped than harassed. In some areas you'll be regarded with friendly curiosity – and asked, with sad-eyed sympathy, 'Are you only one?' – because Burmese women tend to prefer to travel en masse. At more remote religious sites, a single foreign woman may be 'adopted' by a Burmese woman, who will take you and show you the highlights. At some, such as Mandalay's Mahamuni Paya and Golden Rock, 'ladies' are not permitted to the central shrine; signs will indicate if this is the case.

Tampons are available only at upmarket shops in Yangon and Mandalay.

Philippines

HIGHLIGHTS

- **El Nido** (p659) Drifting among the limestone cathedrals and azure lagoons of the Bacuit Archipelago.
- **Rice terraces** (p625) Trekking through immense rice terraces around Banaue and Bontoc in North Luzon's Cordillera Mountains.
- **Boracay** (p637) Chilling on the Philippines' trophy beach between kitesurf or dive sessions.
- **Whale sharks** (p632 and p653) Snorkelling with the gentle *butanding* of Donsol and the *tiki-tiki* of Southern Leyte.
- **Cebu** (p644) Partying hard in Cebu City then taking off for a few days' detox on idyllic Malapascua Island.
- **Southern Negros** (p641) Leaving the world behind in isolated hideaways like Apo Island, Sipalay and Danjugan Island.
- **Off the beaten track** (p660) Exploring sunken WWII wrecks and kayaking amid the myriad islands around Coron, Palawan.

FAST FACTS

- **Budget** US$20 to US$25 a day
- **Capital** Manila
- **Costs** island cottage US$7 to US$15, four-hour bus ride US$4 to US$5, beer US$0.50 to US$0.70
- **Country code** ☎ 63
- **Languages** Filipino (Tagalog), English, 11 more major languages and some 170 dialects
- **Money** US$1 = P47 (peso)
- **Phrases** *paalam* (goodbye), *salámat* (thanks), *kumusta* (hello/how's it going), *magkano* (how much is it?), *iskyus* (sorry/excuse me)
- **Population** 93 million
- **Time** GMT + eight hours
- **Visas** free 21-day visa given on arrival; extensions for up to 59 days are US$61, and are available in major cities

TRAVEL HINTS

Don't lose your temper – Filipinos will think you're *loco loco* (crazy). Bring zip-lock bags to protect valuables on splashy *bangka* (outrigger boat) rides.

WARNING

Travel in the Sulu Archipelago and parts of Mindanao should be considered dangerous and only undertaken with careful, independent research.

Just when you thought you had Asia figured out you get to the Philippines. Instead of monks you have priests; instead of túk-túk you have tricycles; instead of *pho* you have *adobo*. At first glance the Philippines will disarm you more than charm you, but peel back the country's skin and there are treasures to be found – aplenty. Just for starters, you can swim with whale sharks, scale volcanoes, explore desert islands, gawk at ancient rice terraces, submerge at world-class dive sites and venture into rainforests to visit remote hill tribes.

Beyond its obvious physical assets, the Philippines possesses a quirky streak that takes a bit longer to appreciate. There are secret potions and healing lotions, guys named Bong and girls named Bing, grinning hustlers, deafening cock farms, wheezing bangkas (outrigger boats), crooked politicians, fuzzy carabao (water buffalo), graffiti-splashed jeepneys and – best of all – cheap beer to enjoy as you take it all in.

Transport connections are extensive, but in remote areas you may require intestinal fortitude and affinity for the Filipino maxim *bahala na:* go with the flow. Gregarious locals everywhere dispense smiles like they're going out of style. Be sure not to leave before seeing one of the country's spirited festivals and sampling the Filipino zeal for living *la vida loca*.

CURRENT EVENTS

All eyes are on the presidential election of May 2010, which will bring an end to the nine-year reign of President Gloria Macapagal-Arroyo ('GMA'), who took over from disgraced ex-actor Joseph Estrada in 2001 before winning a disputed vote for re-election in 2004. GMA's second term has been dogged by one scandal after another, many brought about by her husband, 'First Gentleman' Mike Arroyo, whom she banished from the country for a spell in 2005 as allegations swirled that he was involved in an illegal gambling ring. At every scandal Arroyo's opponents tried to raise public ire, but the populace mostly stayed off the streets.

Arroyo staked much of her presidency on eradicating the communist New People's Army (NPA), but the group continues to fight the government from remote bases in Luzon, Mindanao, Samar and elsewhere. A more tangible threat, especially as far as tourists are concerned, are two Muslim separatist groups, the Moro Islamic Liberation Front (MILF) and Abu Sayyaf, which occasionally kidnaps foreigners from bases in Mindanao. See p606 for more on these groups.

As the unpopular Arroyo's term draws to a close, even critics acknowledge that GMA has given the country a semblance of stability – something it has lacked since the pre-Marcos era. Whether that stability will continue under a new leader remains unclear.

HISTORY

First Filipinos

Negrito tribes may have started migrating here over land bridges up to 30,000 years ago. Later migrants arrived by boat, first from China and Vietnam and then from Malaysia and Indonesia. Outrigger canoes safely carried new crops and animals such as pigs, and you can bet that a proto-cockfighting fanatic on board was tenderly holding his prize rooster.

Spanish Colonialists

In the early 16th century all signs pointed to the archipelago universally adopting Islam, but in 1521 Portuguese explorer Ferdinand Magellan changed the course of Filipino history by landing at Samar and claiming the islands for Spain. Magellan set about converting the islanders to Catholicism and winning over various tribal chiefs before he was killed by Chief Lapu-Lapu on Mactan Island near Cebu City.

In 1565 Miguel de Legazpi returned to the Philippines and, after conquering the local tribes one by one, declared Manila the capital of the new Spanish colony. But outside of Manila real power rested with the Catholic friars – the notoriously unenlightened *friarocracia* (friarocracy), who acted as sole rulers over what were essentially rural fiefdoms.

The Philippine Revolution

At the end of the 18th century, Spain was weakened by the Seven Years War, which briefly saw Great Britain take over Manila.

DID YOU KNOW?

One of the first major email viruses was invented and unleashed by a Filipino IT student in 1999. It seems very Filipino that it was called the 'I love you' virus.

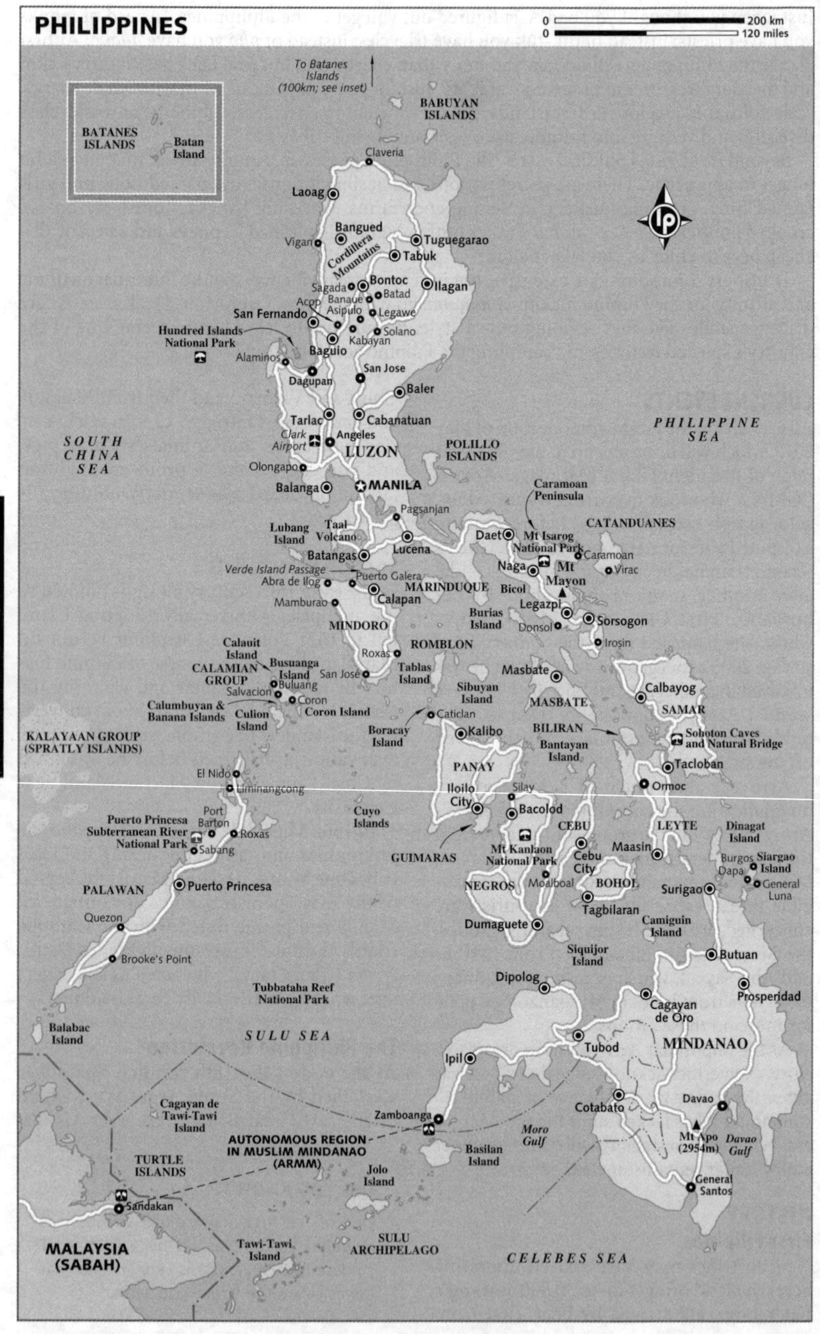

PHILIPPINES

GEMS OF THE PHILIPPINES

These are our completely subjective lists of the best and strangest in this incredible country.

Favourite Small Mercies

- The widespread distribution of what is probably the cheapest beer in the world
- The availability of tricycles to take you anywhere, any time, for less than US$5
- All-you-can-eat buffets after all-day bus or boat journeys

Most Tragically Popular Karaoke Songs

- 'Glory of Love', Peter Cetera
- 'Even the Nights Are Better', Air Supply
- 'My Heart Will Go On', Celine Dion

Most Challenging Moments

- Finding out the hard way – at 5am – that your hotel is next to a cock farm
- It's 6pm and you've got two motorcycles, one friend with broken ribs and 75km of rough road between you and your home base
- Being stuck on the tarmac with a Tanduay hangover in a sweltering plane running on 'Filipino time'

As Spain grew weaker, and as the friars grew ever more repressive, the indigenous people started to resist. The Spanish sealed their fate in 1896 by executing the writer José Rizal for inciting revolution. A brilliant scholar and poet, Rizal had worked for independence by peaceful means. His death galvanised the revolutionary movement.

With aid from the USA, already at war with Spain over Cuba, General Emilio Aguinaldo's revolutionary army drove the Spanish back to Manila. American warships defeated the Spanish fleet in Manila Bay in May 1898, and independence was declared on 12 June 1898.

American Rule

Alas, the Americans had other ideas. They acquired the islands from Spain and decided to make the Philippines an American colony. War inevitably broke out in February 1899. But the expected swift American victory didn't materialise, and as the Philippine-American war dragged on, public opposition mounted in the US. The themes of the American home-front debate, and the ensuing drawn-out guerrilla war, would have eerie parallels to the Vietnam and Iraq wars many decades later. It was only on July 4 1902, that the US finally declared victory in the campaign.

The Americans quickly set about healing the significant wounds their victory had wrought, instituting reforms aimed at improving Filipinos' lot and promising eventual independence. The first Philippine national government was formed in 1935 with full independence pencilled in for 10 years later.

This schedule was set aside when Japan invaded the islands in WWII. For three years the country endured a brutal Japanese military regime before the Americans defeated the Japanese in the Battle for Manila in February 1945. The battle destroyed a city that had been one of the finest in Asia and resulted in the deaths of at over 100,000 civilians.

Independence

During the early years of independence the Philippines bounced from one ineffectual leader to another until Ferdinand Marcos was elected in 1965. With a nod and wink from the US he took a *datu*-style (local chief) approach to government and marched the Philippines towards dictatorship, declaring martial law in 1972. Violence, previously widespread, was curtailed, but the Philippines suffered from stifling corruption and the economy became one of the weakest in an otherwise-booming region.

The 1983 assassination of Marcos' opponent Benigno 'Ninoy' Aquino pushed opposition to Marcos to new heights. Marcos called elections for early 1986 and the opposition united to support Aquino's widow, Corazon 'Cory' Aquino. Both Marcos and Aquino claimed to have won the election, but 'people power' rallied behind Cory Aquino, and within days Ferdinand and his profligate wife, Imelda, were packed off by the Americans to Hawaii, where the former dictator later died.

Cory Aquino failed to win the backing of the army but managed to hang on through numerous coup attempts. She was followed by Fidel Ramos, Imelda's cousin. In 1998 Ramos was replaced by B-grade movie actor Joseph 'Erap' Estrada, who promised to redirect government funding towards rural and poor Filipinos. Unfortunately, Erap spent much of his time redirecting government funding towards his own coffers and was impeached and overthrown in a second 'people power' revolt 2½ years later. Replacing Estrada was his diminutive vice-president, Arroyo.

The Moro Problem

Muslim dissent emanating out of Mindanao has been the one constant in the Philippines' roughly 450 years of history as a loosely united territory. In the 16th century, Legazpi managed to dislodge Muslim chiefs from Maynilad (now Manila) and other central settlements with relative ease, but the southern territories would prove more difficult to conquer, and over the next 400 years a religious war would smoulder in Mindanao.

The country's largest Muslim rebel group is the 12,500-strong MILF, but the group that grabs all the headlines is Abu Sayyaf, which was responsible for a highly publicised kidnapping in 2001 that became the basis of the 2009 movie *Jihadists in Paradise*. More recently, Abu Sayyaf kidnapped three aid workers on the southern island of Jolo in January 2009. The last of the abductees, an Italian, was released in July 2009.

Meanwhile, the MILF signed a ceasefire with the government in 2001, but periodic violence and bombings continued to occur in Mindanao's predominantly Muslim Autonomous Region in Muslim Mindanao (ARMM), with violence occasionally spilling into other parts of Mindanao.

Then in August 2008 the ceasefire collapsed. A series of violent incidents rocked the ARMM, with MILF rebels fighting openly against government troops in parts of Mindanao. At press time the security situation in Mindanao remained tenuous, although the areas of northern Mindanao covered in this book are considered safe.

THE CULTURE

The National Psyche

It's impossible to deny it: Filipinos have a zest for life that may be unrivalled on our planet. The national symbol, the jeepney, is an apt metaphor for the nation. Splashed with colour, laden with religious icons and festooned with sanguine scribblings, the jeepney flaunts the fact that, at heart, it's a dilapidated, smoke-belching pile of scrap metal. Like the jeepney, Filipinos face their often dim prospects in life with a laugh and a wink. Whatever happens…'so be it'.

This fatalism has a name: *bahala na,* a phrase that expresses the idea that all things shall pass and in the meantime life is to be lived. It influences much about Filipino society – both good and bad. *Bahala na* helps shape the carefree, welcoming, tolerant nature of the Filipino people. But it also contributed to the country's reputation as the 'Sick Man of Asia' – a reference to its steady economic fall from grace over the last 40 years or so.

Another force that shapes the Filipino psyche is *hiya,* which means, roughly, 'sense of shame'. Showing a lack of *hiya* in front of others is similar to 'losing face' and for the Filipino there are few worse fates. Expressing strong or negative emotions in public are sure ways to show you are *walang-hiya* – without shame. When travelling in the Philippines, treat problems with the same graciousness as the average Filipino. A smile and a joke go a long way, while anger just makes things worse.

RIZAL'S TOWER OF BABEL

The Philippines' answer to Gandhi, writer and gentle revolutionary Dr José Rizal, could read and write at the age of two. He grew up to speak more than 20 languages, 18 of them fluently, including English, Sanskrit, Latin, French, German, Greek, Hebrew, Russian, Japanese, Chinese and Arabic. His last words were *consummatum est!* (it is done!).

MUST READ

Playing with Water – Passion and Solitude on a Philippine Island, James Hamilton-Paterson's account of life on a remote islet, sheds light on many aspects of Philippine culture.

Lifestyle

An ample supply of shopping malls and US fast-food chains in Manila often lulls first-time visitors into thinking the Philippines is Americanised. They soon realise that it's all a big, giant facade disguising a unique Asian culture.

For centuries the two most important influences on the lives of Filipinos have been family and religion. The Filipino family unit extends to distant cousins, multiple godparents and one's *barkada* (gang of friends). Filipino families, especially poor ones, tend to be large. It's not uncommon for a dozen family members to live together in a tiny apartment, shanty or *nipa* hut (traditional hut made of palm leaves).

The Philippines is the only predominantly Christian country in Asia – almost 90% of the population claims to be Christian and over 80% are Roman Catholic. Besides affecting everyday life this also affects politics. A subtle hint from the church can swing a mayoral race and mean millions of votes for presidential or senatorial candidates.

Filipinos are a superstitious lot. In the hinterland, a villager might be possessed by a wandering spirit, causing them to commit strange acts. In urban areas, faith healers, psychics, fortune-tellers, tribal shamans, self-help books and evangelical crusaders can all help cast away ill-fortune.

Another vital thread in the fabric of Filipino society is the overseas worker. At any given time well more than 1 million Filipinos are working abroad. Combined they sent a record US$16 billion back home in 2008, according to official figures. The Overseas Filipino Worker (OFW) – the nurse in Canada, the construction worker in Qatar, the entertainer in Japan, the cleaner in Singapore – has become a national hero.

Population

A journey from the northern tip of Luzon to the southern tip of the Sulu islands reveals a range of ethnic groups speaking some 170 different dialects. Filipinos are mainly of the Malay race, although there's a sizeable and economically dominant Chinese minority and a fair number of *mestizos* (Filipinos of mixed descent).

The country's population is thought to be upwards of 90 million and expanding at a rapid clip of about 2% per year – one of the fastest growth rates in Asia. As the population grows it's becoming younger and more urban: the median age is only 22.5 and almost a quarter of the population lives in or around metro Manila.

ARTS

Cinema

The Philippines has historically been Southeast Asia's most prolific film-making nation. The movie industry's 'golden age' was the 1950s, when Filipino films won countless awards. In the 1980s and '90s the industry surged again thanks to a genre called 'bold' – think sex, violence and dudes with great hair in romantic roles. Today the mainstream studios are in decline, but the quality of films is improving with the proliferation of independent films such as *Kubrador* (see the boxed text, p608) and the international success of indy directors like Brillante Mendoza, who won Best Director at the 2009 Cannes Film Festival for his graphic, controversial film *Kinatay* (Slaughtered).

Music

Filipinos are best-known for their ubiquitous cover bands and their love of karaoke (see the boxed text, p605), but they need not be in imitation mode to show off their innate musical talent. 'OPM' (Original Pinoy Music – 'Pinoy' is what Filipinos call themselves) encompasses a wide spectrum of rock, folk and new age genres – plus a subset that includes all three.

Embodying the latter subset is the band Pinikpikan, which performs a sometimes frantic fusion of tribal styles and modern jam-band

DID YOU KNOW?

Apocalypse Now, Platoon and *Born on the 4th of July* are among the many films that were shot fully or partially in the Philippines.

VIEWING LIST

- *Imelda* (2004) – Filipina American Ramona Diaz directs this fascinating look into the psyche of Imelda Marcos.
- *Kubrador* (2006) – Top actress Gina Pareño stars in this superb film about the illegal numbers game jueteng.
- *Serbis* (2008) – Pareño also stars in Brillante Mendoza's film about life in a family-run porn-movie house in the Philippines' prostitution capital, Angeles.
- *Manila 1945: The Forgotten Atrocities* (2007) – Damning documentary about the Japanese role in the destruction of Manila, available at Manila's Solidaridad bookshop (p614).
- *Paper Dolls* (2006) – Interesting film about the lives of transvestite Filipino OFWs in Tel Aviv.

rock. The 11-piece band uses bamboo-reed pipes, flutes and percussion instruments and sings in languages as diverse as Visayan, French and Bicol.

The big three of Pinoy rock are slightly grungy eponymous band Bamboo, agreeable trio Rivermaya (formerly fronted by Bamboo), and sometimes sweet, sometimes surly diva Kitchie Nadal, who regularly tours internationally. All of the above sing in both Filipino and English.

ENVIRONMENT

The Land

An assemblage of 7107 tropical isles scattered about like pieces of a giant jigsaw puzzle, the Philippines stubbornly defies geographic generalisation. The typical island boasts a jungle-clad, critter-infested interior and a sandy coastline flanked by aquamarine waters and the requisite coral reef. More-populated islands have less jungle and more farmland.

Wildlife

The Philippines' flora includes well over 10,000 species of trees, bushes and ferns, including 900 types of orchid. About 25% of the Philippines is forested, but only a small percentage of that is primary tropical rainforest.

Endangered animal species include the mouse deer (see the boxed text, p650), the tamaráw (a species of dwarf buffalo) of Mindoro, the Philippine crocodile of Northeast Luzon, the Palawan bearcat and the flying lemur. As for the country's national bird, there are thought to be about 500 pairs of *haribon,* or Philippine eagles, remaining in the rainforests of Mindanao, Luzon, Samar and Leyte.

There's an unbelievable array of fish, seashells and corals, as well as dwindling numbers of the *duyong* (dugong, or sea cow). If your timing's just right you can spot *butanding* (whale sharks) in Donsol and Southern Leyte.

National Parks

The Philippines' numerous national parks, natural parks and other protected areas comprise about 10% of the country's total area, but most lack services such as park offices, huts, trail maps and sometimes even trails. The most popular national park is surely Palawan's Subterranean River National Park (p658).

Environmental Issues

As with many of the government departments, the budget of the Department of Environment & Natural Resources (DENR) is never quite what it seems. The Philippines has strict environmental laws on its books, but they just aren't enforced. Only 1% of the reefs are in a pristine state, according to the World Bank, while more than 50% are unhealthy.

The biggest culprit of reef damage is silt, which is washed down from hills and valleys indiscriminately – and often illegally – cleared of their original forest cover. Illegal logging also exacerbates flooding and is the cause of landslides, such as the one in February 2006 that killed more than 1000 people in St Bernard, Southern Leyte. Some lip service is given to the issue by the government, but little is done to combat illegal logging.

Incredibly short-sighted techniques for making a few extra bucks include dynamite and cyanide fishing. The uncontrolled harvesting of seashells for export, particularly in the Visayas, is another problem. Souvenirs made from shell or coral are probably not good buys.

TRANSPORT

GETTING THERE & AWAY

Air

The three main points of entry are Manila, Cebu and Clark Special Economic Zone. In addition, Cebu Pacific has a few international flights into Davao (Mindanao).

MANILA

The recently upgraded **Ninoy Aquino International Airport** (NAIA; Map pp612-13; ☎ 02-877 1109) is currently in flux – see the boxed text, p610. The Philippines' primary low-cost carrier, Cebu Pacific, serves an ever-growing list of Asian cities, including Bangkok, Jakarta, Kota Kinabalu, Kuala Lumpur, Saigon and Singapore. The other low-cost airline flying to/from NAIA is Singapore's Jetstar. The country's flagship carrier, Philippine Airlines (PAL), also serves many Southeast Asian destinations.

The following are the main airlines serving Manila nonstop from Southeast Asia:

Cathay Pacific (code CX; ☎ 02-757 0888; www.cathaypacific.com)
Cebu Pacific (code 5J; ☎ 02-702 0888; www.cebupacificair.com)
Jetstar (code 3K; ☎ 1-800 1611 0280; www.jetstar.com)
Malaysia Airlines (code MH; ☎ 02-887 3215; www.malaysiaairlines.com)
Philippine Airlines (code PR; ☎ 02-855 8888; www.philippineairlines.com)
Thai Airways International (code TG; ☎ 02-812 4744; www.thaiairways.com)
Singapore Airlines (code SQ; ☎ 02-756 8888; www.singaporeairlines.com)

> **MOVING ON FROM CLARK**
>
> Several bus companies run trips directly from Clark to Manila (see p622 for a list of companies).
>
> For points northwest of Clark, make your way by jeepney or taxi (P215, 15 minutes) to Angeles' Dau bus terminal, where you'll find plenty of buses going to Baguio, Vigan and elsewhere.
>
> Getting to Banaue from Clark airport is trickier. The least complicated way is to backtrack to Manila and get a bus there. If you're comfortable changing buses, the recommended route is Clark–Dau–Tarlac–San Jose (or Cabanatuan)–Solano–Lagawe–Banaue.

> **DEPARTURE TAX**
>
> International departure tax is P750 at NAIA, and P550 at Cebu and Clark.

CEBU

If you're heading to the Visayas, a much better option is to fly into Cebu City's **Mactan International Airport** (☎ 032-340 2486; www.mactan-cebuairport.com.ph). Cebu Pacific flies direct to Cebu from Guangzhou, Hong Kong, Jakarta, Kuala Lumpur and Singapore. Cathay Pacific has direct flights to/from Hong Kong, and **SilkAir** (www.silkair.com) services Singapore. PAL and Malaysia Airlines fly direct to Kuala Lumpur, and PAL also services Kota Kinabalu.

CLARK SPECIAL ECONOMIC ZONE

Macapagal International Airport (DMIA, Clark Airport; www.clarkairport.com) in the Clark Special Economic Zone (near Angeles, about a two-hour bus ride north of Manila) is a hot destination for Asian low-cost airlines. **Tiger Airways** (code TGW; ☎ 02-884 1524; www.tigerairways.com) flies from Singapore and Macau, while **Air Asia** (code AXM; www.airasia.com) serves Kuala Lumpur and Kota Kinabalu.

Sea

Although there are plenty of shipping routes within the Philippines, international services are scarce. The only route open to foreigners, as of this writing, was Zamboanga to Sandakan in the Malaysian state of Sabah. See p655 for further details.

GETTING AROUND

Air

The main domestic carriers are PAL and low-cost carrier Cebu Pacific. Together they serve most main cities out of Manila and/or Cebu.

PAL has two subsidiaries, PAL Express and Air Philippines, to compete with the rapidly expanding Cebu Pacific in the low-cost domestic market. PAL's other domestic affiliate, Air Philippines, is gradually being phased out. Smaller carriers include ITI, Seair and Zest Air. The latter two both fly from Manila to Caticlan (Boracay) and a few other cities. ITI flies exclusively from Manila to El Nido, Palawan.

One-way flights on Cebu Pacific, PAL Express and Zest Air usually only cost P1000 to P2000 (including taxes) on most routes provided you book in advance. PAL domestic

TERMINAL CHAOS

Plans are in place at Ninoy Aquino International Airport (NAIA) to shift all international flights from dismal, antiquated Terminal 1 (NAIA 1) to newly opened Terminal 3 (NAIA 3).

However, as of this writing PAL Express and Cebu Pacific were the only airlines using NAIA 3. All Philippine Airlines (PAL) flights continued to use yet another terminal, the relatively modern Centennial Terminal 2 (NAIA 2). All international carriers continued to use NAIA 1, while domestic carriers Zest Air and Seair continued to use the old Manila Domestic Airport, located about 2km from NAIA 1.

Once NAIA 3 becomes fully operational, domestic flights will presumably shift to NAIA 1 (or possibly NAIA 2), and the domestic airport will be mothballed.

The four NAIA terminals share runways, but they are not particularly close to each other. A free shuttle bus links the four terminals.

flights are typically only slightly more expensive. Seair and ITI are pricier 'boutique' airlines.

Flight times range from 45 minutes for short hops such as Manila–Caticlan to 1½ hours for flights from Manila to southern Mindanao.

Airline details:

Air Philippines (code 2P; ☎ 02-855 9000; www.airphils.com; NAIA Terminal 3)
Cebu Pacific (code 5J; Map pp612-13; ☎ 02-702 0888; www.cebupacificair.com; NAIA Terminal 3)
ITI (Map pp612-13; ☎ 815 5674; www.islandtransvoyager.com; Andrews Ave, Pasay City)
PAL Express (code PR; Map pp612-13; ☎ 02-855 8888; www.palexpressair.com; NAIA Terminal 3)
Philippine Airlines (code PR; Map pp612-13; ☎ 02-855 8888; www.philippineairlines.com; NAIA Terminal 2)
Seair (code DG; Map pp612-13; ☎ 02-849 0100; www.flyseair.com; 2nd fl Doña Concepcion Bldg, A Arnaiz Ave, Makati)
Zest Air (code 6K; Map pp612-13; ☎ 02-855 3333; www.zestair.com.ph; Domestic Rd cnr Andrews Ave, Pasay City)

Boat

If boats are your thing, this is the place for you. The islands of the Philippines are linked by an incredible network of ferry routes and prices are generally affordable. The vessels used range from tiny, narrow outrigger canoes (known locally as *bangka,* also called pumpboats) to speedy 'fastcraft' vessels and, for long-haul journeys, vast multidecked ships.

The jeepney of the sea, the *bangka,* comes with or without a roof. *Bangkas* ply routes between islands and are also available for hire for diving, sightseeing or getting around. The engines on these boats can be deafeningly loud, and they aren't the most stable in rough seas, but on rugged islands the *bangka* can be preferable to travelling overland.

'Fastcraft' services are popular on shorter routes. They can cut travel times by half but usually cost twice as much as slower 'roll-on, roll-off' (RORO) car ferries. Some shipping lines give 20% to 30% off for students.

Booking ahead is essential for long-haul liners and can be done at ticket offices or travel agents in most cities. For fastcraft and *bangka* ferries, tickets can usually be bought at the pier before departure.

For the most part, ferries are an easy, enjoyable way to hop between islands, but accidents are not unknown. In May 2008 a Sulpicio Lines ferry went down off Romblon in Typhoon Frank; less than 60 passengers survived and more than 800 perished. Sulpicio's passenger services remained suspended as of this writing. In May 2009 an overloaded *bangka* ferry sank en route to Puerto Galera from Batangas. Twelve of the 60 passengers drowned. A large SuperFerry vessel went down off Mindanao in September 2009. Miraculously all but nine of the 900 passengers were rescued.

Bus & Van

Philippine buses come in all shapes and sizes, from rusty boxes on wheels to luxury air-con coaches. Bus depots are dotted throughout towns and the countryside, and most buses will stop if you wave them down. Terminals are usually on the outskirts of town, but tricycle drivers should know where they are.

Generally, more services run in the morning – buses on unsealed roads may run only in the morning, especially in remote areas. Most buses follow a fixed schedule but may leave early if they're full. Night services are common between Manila and major provincial hubs in Luzon.

Air-con minivans shadow bus routes in many parts of the Philippines and in some cases have replaced buses altogether (such as on the Legazpi–Donsol route). However, you may have to play a waiting game until the vehicles are full. Minivans are a lot quicker than buses, but they are also more expensive and more cramped.

Local Transport

HABAL-HABAL

Common in many Visayan islands and northern Mindanao, these are simply motorcycle taxis with extended seats (literally translated as 'pigs copulating', after the level of intimacy attained when sharing a seat with four people). *Habal-habal* function like tricycles, only they are a little bit cheaper. Outside of the Visayas they're known as 'motorcycle taxis'.

JEEPNEY

The first jeepneys were modified army jeeps left behind by the Americans after WWII. They have been customised with Filipino touches such as chrome horses, banks of coloured headlights, radio antennae, paintings of the Virgin Mary and neon-coloured scenes from action comic books. Modern jeepneys are built locally from durable aluminium and stainless steel but are faithful to the original design.

Jeepneys form the main urban transport in most cities and complement the bus services between regional centres. Within towns, the starting fare is usually P6 to P7, rising modestly for trips outside of town. Routes are clearly written on the side of the jeepney.

KALESA

Kalesa are two-wheeled horse carriages found in parts of Manila, Vigan (North Luzon) and Cebu City (where they're known as *tartanillas*). In Manila they seem to exist solely to help tourists part with large sums of money, so be careful to agree on a fare before clambering aboard. You shouldn't pay more than P200 for a 20-minute ride.

DID YOU KNOW?

The Philippine eagle was known as the 'monkey-eating eagle' until the government officially changed the name in 1978.

TAXI

Taxis are common in Manila and most major provincial hubs. Flag fall is a mere P30, and a 20-minute trip rarely costs more than P150.

Most taxi drivers will turn on the meter; if they don't, politely request that they do. If the meter is 'broken' or your taxi driver says the fare is 'up to you', the best strategy is to get out and find another cab.

Taxi drivers at many regional airports charge a fixed price – usually P150 to P250 – to get into the town centre. An exception is Manila's airport, where metered cabs are readily available at all four terminals.

TRICYCLE

Found in most cities and towns, the tricycle is the Philippine rickshaw – a little, roofed sidecar bolted to a motorcycle. The standard fare for local trips in most provincial towns is P6. Tricycles that wait around in front of malls, restaurants and hotels will attempt to charge five to 10 times that for a 'special trip'. Avoid these by standing roadside and flagging down a passing P6 tricycle. You can also charter tricycles for about P200 per hour or P120 per 10km if you're heading out of town.

Many towns also have nonmotorised push tricycles, alternately known as pedicabs, *put-put* or *podyak*, for shorter trips.

MANILA

☎ 02 / pop 11.5 million

Manila's moniker, the 'Pearl of the Orient', couldn't be more apt – its cantankerous shell reveals its jewel only to those resolute enough to pry. No stranger to hardship, the city has endured every disaster both man and nature could throw at it, and yet today the chaotic 600-sq-km metropolis thrives as a true Asian megacity. Gleaming skyscrapers pierce the hazy sky, mushrooming from the grinding poverty of expansive shantytowns. The congested roads snarl with traffic, but like the overworked arteries of a sweating giant, they are what keep this modern metropolis alive. The tourist belt of Ermita and Malate flaunts an uninhibited nightlife that would make Bangkok's go-go bars blush, and the gleaming malls of Makati foreshadow Manila's brave new air-conditioned world. The determined will discover Manila's tender soul, perhaps among the leafy courtyards and cobbled streets of serene Intramuros, where little has

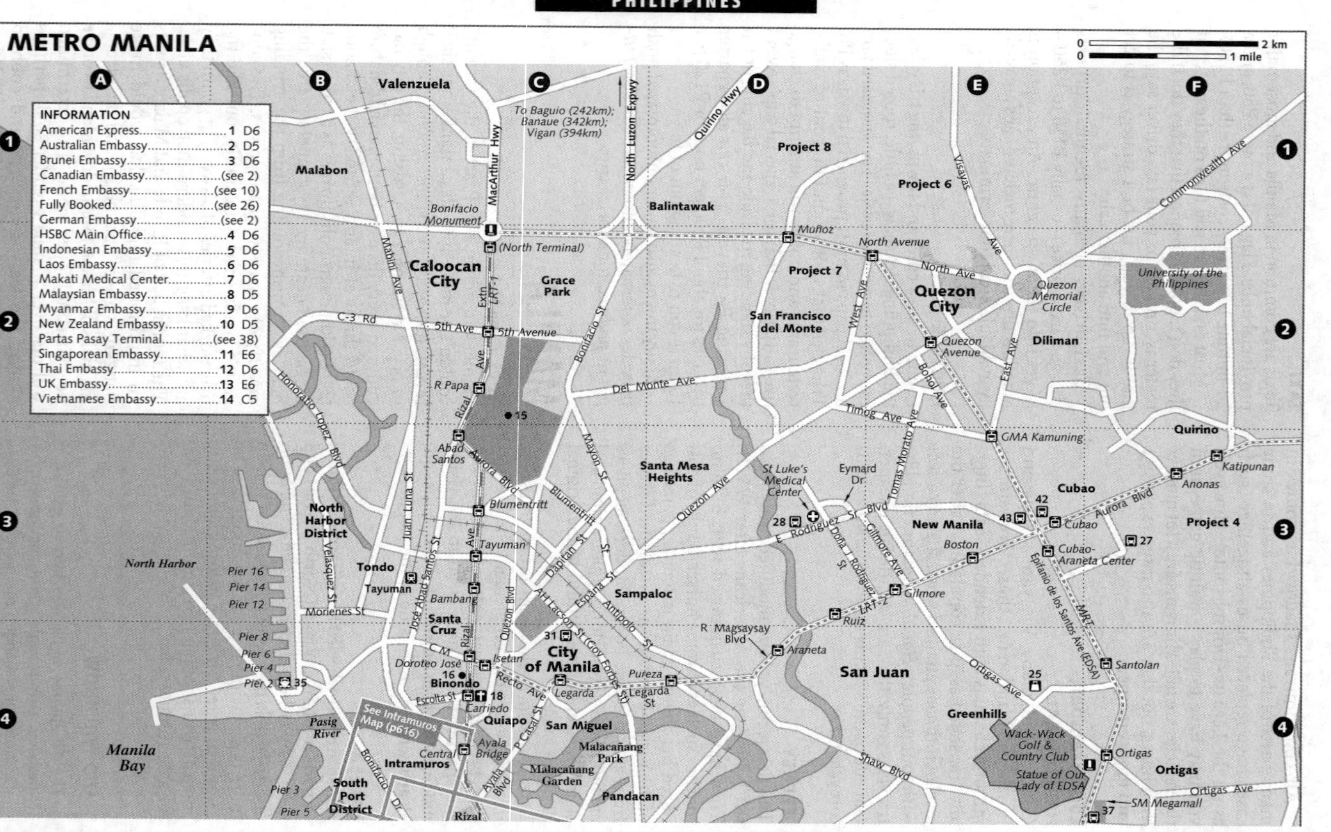
METRO MANILA
INFORMATION
American Express 1 D6
Australian Embassy 2 D5
Brunei Embassy 3 D6
Canadian Embassy (see 2)
French Embassy (see 10)
Fully Booked (see 26)
German Embassy (see 2)
HSBC Main Office 4 D6
Indonesian Embassy 5 D6
Laos Embassy 6 D6
Makati Medical Center 7 D6
Malaysian Embassy 8 D5
Myanmar Embassy 9 D6
New Zealand Embassy 10 D5
Partas Pasay Terminal (see 38)
Singaporean Embassy 11 E6
Thai Embassy 12 D6
UK Embassy 13 E6
Vietnamese Embassy 14 C5
0 2 km
0 1 mile
To Baguio (242km); Banaue (342km); Vigan (394km)
North Luzon Expwy
Valenzuela
Malabon
Caloocan City
Bonifacio Monument
(North Terminal)
Grace Park
Balintawak
Project 8
Project 7
Project 6
San Francisco del Monte
Quezon City
Quezon Memorial Circle
University of the Philippines
Diliman
Quirino
Project 4
Cubao
Cubao-Araneta Center
New Manila
Santa Mesa Heights
St Luke's Medical Center
San Juan
Greenhills
Wack-Wack Golf & Country Club
Statue of Our Lady of EDSA
Ortigas
SM Megamall
Sampaloc
City of Manila
San Miguel
Malacañang Park
Malacañang Garden
Pandacan
Quiapo
Binondo
Santa Cruz
Tondo
Tayuman
North Harbor District
North Harbor
Manila Bay
Intramuros
See Intramuros Map (p616)
South Port District
Pasig River
Pier 16
Pier 14
Pier 12
Pier 8
Pier 6
Pier 4
Pier 2
Pier 3
Pier 5
Epifanio de los Santos Ave (EDSA)
MRT
LRT-1
LRT-2
Commonwealth Ave
Quirino Hwy
MacArthur Hwy
Mabini Ave
Honoratio Lopez Blvd
Velasquez St
Juan Luna St
José Abad Santos St
Rizal Ave
Bonifacio St
Mayon St
Del Monte Ave
West Ave
North Avenue
North Ave
Visayas Ave
East Ave
Quezon Avenue
Quezon Ave
Timog Ave
Tomas Morato Ave
Bohol Ave
Aurora Blvd
E Rodriguez Sr Blvd
Doña J Rodriguez St
Eymard Dr
Gilmore Ave
Ortigas Ave
Shaw Blvd
R Magsaysay Blvd
España St
Dapitan St
Antipolo St
Blumentritt
AH Lacson St (Gov Forbes St)
Legarda St
Quezon Blvd
Recto Ave
P Casal St
Ayala Blvd
Ayala Bridge
Bonifacio Dr
C-3 Rd
5th Ave
Katipunan
Anonas
Santolan
GMA Kamuning
Boston
Araneta
Ruiz
Gilmore
Pureza
Legarda
Abad Santos
R Papa
5th Avenue
Muñoz
Bambang
Carriedo
Doroteo José
Isetan
Central
Escolta St
Moriones St
Rizal

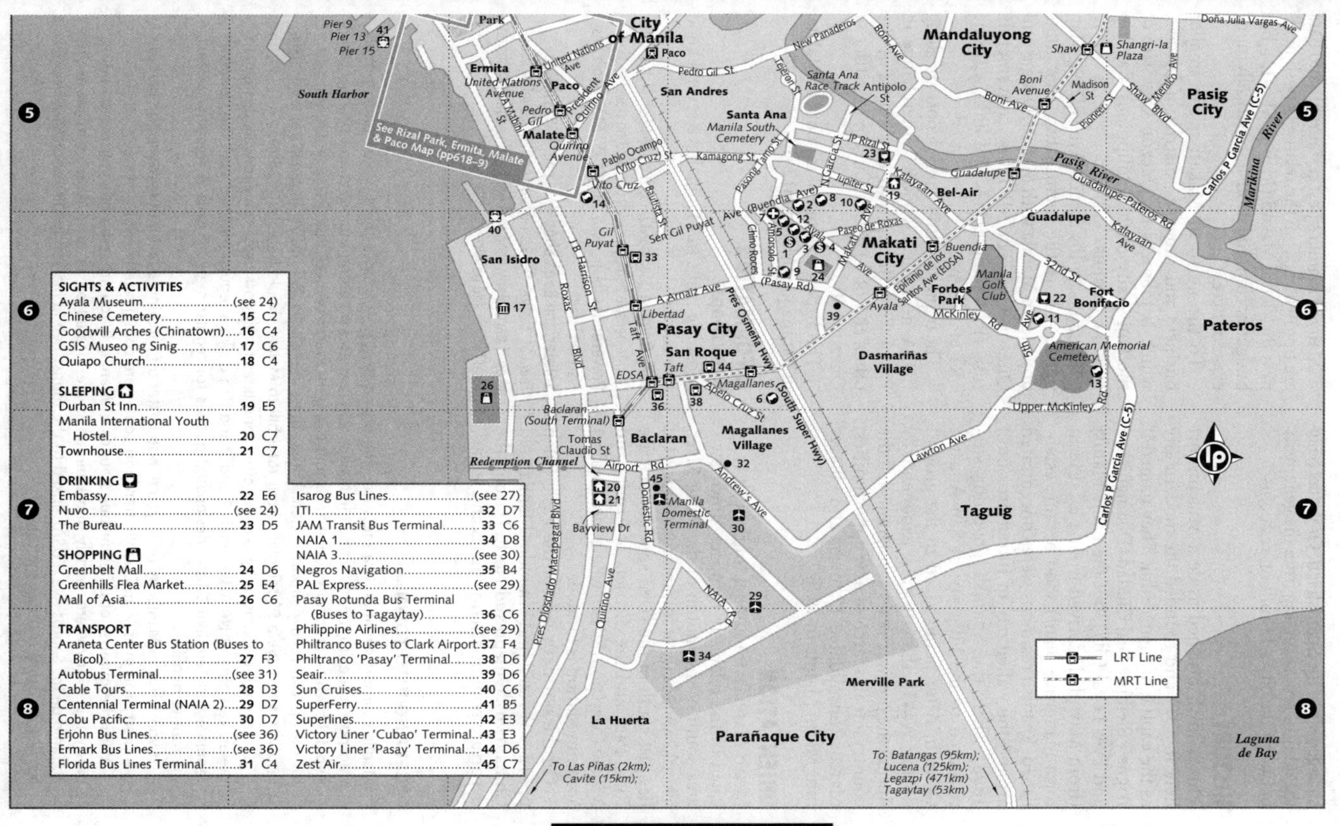

SIGHTS & ACTIVITIES
Ayala Museum (see 24)
Chinese Cemetery 15 C2
Goodwill Arches (Chinatown) 16 C4
GSIS Museo ng Sinig 17 C6
Quiapo Church 18 C4
SLEEPING
Durban St Inn 19 E5
Manila International Youth Hostel 20 C7
Townhouse 21 C7
DRINKING
Embassy 22 E6
Nuvo (see 24)
The Bureau 23 D5
SHOPPING
Greenbelt Mall 24 D6
Greenhills Flea Market 25 E4
Mall of Asia 26 C6
TRANSPORT
Araneta Center Bus Station (Buses to Bicol) 27 F3
Autobus Terminal (see 31)
Cable Tours 28 D3
Centennial Terminal (NAIA 2) 29 D7
Cobu Pacific 30 D7
Erjohn Bus Lines (see 36)
Ermark Bus Lines (see 36)
Florida Bus Lines Terminal 31 C4
Isarog Bus Lines (see 27)
ITI 32 D7
JAM Transit Bus Terminal 33 C6
NAIA 1 34 D8
NAIA 3 (see 30)
Negros Navigation 35 B4
PAL Express (see 29)
Pasay Rotunda Bus Terminal (Buses to Tagaytay) 36 C6
Philippine Airlines (see 29)
Philtranco Buses to Clark Airport 37 F4
Philtranco 'Pasay' Terminal 38 D6
Seair 39 D6
Sun Cruises 40 C6
SuperFerry 41 B5
Superlines 42 E3
Victory Liner 'Cubao' Terminal 43 E3
Victory Liner 'Pasay' Terminal 44 D6
Zest Air 45 C7
LRT Line
MRT Line
See Rizal Park, Ermita, Malate & Paco Map (pp618–9)
City of Manila
Mandaluyong City
Pasig City
Pateros
Makati City
Pasay City
Taguig
Parañaque City
La Huerta
Merville Park
Laguna de Bay
South Harbor
To Las Piñas (2km); Cavite (15km);
To: Batangas (95km); Lucena (125km); Legazpi (471km) Tagaytay (53km)
PHILIPPINES

changed since the Spanish left. Or it may be in the eddy of repose arising from the generosity of one of the city's 11 million residents.

HISTORY

The Spanish brushed aside a Muslim fort here in 1571 and founded the modern city as the capital of their realm. They named it Isigne y Siempre Leal Ciudad (Distinguished and Ever Loyal City), but the name Manila (from Maynilad, derived from a local term for a mangrove plant) soon became established. Spanish residents were concentrated around the walled city of Intramuros until 1898, when the Spanish governor surrendered to the Filipinos at San Agustin Church. After being razed to the ground during WWII, the city grew exponentially during the postwar years as migrants left the countryside in search of new opportunities. Marcos consolidated 17 towns and villages into Metro Manila in 1976.

ORIENTATION

Metro Manila's traditional tourist belt is located in the relatively compact 'downtown' area south of the mouth of the Pasig River. The old walled city of Intramuros (Map p616) lies just south of the river; south of that are Rizal Park and the districts of Ermita and Malate (Map pp618–19), where most budget accommodation is located.

On the northern side of the Pasig (Map pp612–13) you'll find Binondo (Manila's old Chinatown), Quiapo and North Harbor, the departure point for many interisland ferries.

Many of Manila's best restaurants and bars are uptown (east) in the relatively posh business district of Makati (Map pp612–13), but budget accommodation is practically nonexistent here.

To the north of Makati is the smaller business and shopping district of Ortigas, which is followed by Quezon City, site of the University of the Philippines' flagship Diliman campus.

Epifanio de los Santos Ave (EDSA; Map pp612–13) is the main artery that links downtown Manila with Makati, Ortigas and Quezon City. The MRT line conveniently runs right along EDSA, and links with the LRT at Taft Ave.

The main downtown bus depots are along EDSA near the LRT-MRT interchange in Pasay City; the uptown bus hub is at the other end of EDSA in Cubao, a district of Quezon City.

The airport is about 6km south of Malate, in Parañaque (Map pp612–13).

INFORMATION

Bookshops

Most big malls in Manila have several good bookshops.

Fully Booked (Map pp612-13; ☎ 556 0264; Mall of Asia) Comprehensive bookstore with outstanding travel section.

Powerbooks (Map pp618-19; ☎ 757 6428; Robinsons Place) In Ermita.

Solidaridad Book Shop (Map pp618-19; 531 Padre Faura St, Ermita; 9am-6pm) This famous leftie bookshop is particularly good for books and documentaries on local history and politics.

GETTING INTO TOWN

Manila's airport situation is a mess (see the boxed text, p610). Since there are no direct public transport routes to the tourist belt in Malate, you're better off biting the bullet and taking a taxi. Avoid the white, prepaid 'coupon' taxis that charge set rates of more than P400, and look instead for the special yellow airport metered taxis. These have a flagfall of P70 (regular metered taxis on the street have a P30 flagfall). Your total bill to Malate should be about P150.

To save a few pesos or bypass the often long lines for airport taxis, you can walk upstairs to the arrivals area of NAIA Terminals 1 and 2 and flag down a regular metered taxi. The domestic terminal and Terminal 3 have designated queues for regular metered taxis. A free shuttle links the four terminals.

If you arrive in Manila by boat, you're also better off catching a taxi into town, as the harbour is a pretty rough area and public transport routes are complicated.

With the number of different bus stations in Manila, if you arrive by bus you could end up pretty much anywhere. Luckily, most terminals are located on or near Manila's major artery, Epifanio de los Santos Ave (EDSA), linked to the tourist belt in Malate by MRT and LRT (see p622 for tips on using Manila's metro).

Emergency

Ambulance (☎ 911 1121)
Fire brigade (☎ 522 2222)
Police (☎ 117)
Tourist Security Division (Map pp618-19; ☎ 524 1728/1660; 24hr) Based at the Department of Tourism, this unit is more reliable than regular police.

Internet Access

There are internet cafes all over the place; malls such as Robinsons Place (Map pp618–19) often have several. Rates vary from P30 to P60 per hour.

Medical Services

Makati Medical Center (Map pp612-13; ☎ 888 8999; 2 Amorsolo St, Makati)
Manila Doctors Hospital (Map pp618-19; ☎ 524 3011; 677 United Nations Ave, Ermita)

Money

Malate, Ermita and Makati are littered with ATM machines. For cash transactions, there are numerous money changers along Mabini and Adriatico Sts but, as always, be careful when using these services. Cashing travellers cheques is difficult (see p666) and is best done through the office of the issuing company.

The following places are particularly useful:

American Express (Map pp612-13; ☎ 524 8681; Ground fl Eurovilla 1, Rufino St cnr Legazpi St, Makati; 9.30am-4.30pm Mon-Fri, 9am-noon Sat)
HSBC main office (Map pp612-13; 6766 Ayala Avenue, Makati) Allows P40,000 withdrawals.

Post

Ermita Post Office (Map pp618-19; Pilar Hidalgo Lim St) Contrary to what the name implies, it's actually in Malate.
Manila Central Post Office (Map p616; ☎ 527 1018; 8am-noon & 1-5pm Mon-Fri, 8am-noon Sat) A landmark, offers full services.

Tourist Information

Department of Tourism Information Centre (DOT; Map pp618-19; ☎ 524 2384; www.wowphilippines.ph; TM Kalaw St; 7am-6pm) This large, friendly office is in a beautiful pre-WWII building at the Taft Ave end of Rizal Park. There are also smaller DOT offices at the various NAIA terminals.

Travel Agencies

Malate and Ermita are filled with travel agencies that can help with domestic air and bus tickets (for a fee). Shop around for international air tickets, as prices vary. The following cater specifically to foreign tourists:

Filipino Travel Center (Map pp618-19; ☎ 528 4504; www.filipinotravel.com.ph; 1555 Adriatico St, Ermita) Organises a wide variety of tours.
Swagman Travel (Map pp618-19; ☎ 523 8541; www.swaggy.com; 411 A Flores St, Ermita)

DANGERS & ANNOYANCES

Manila is probably no more dangerous than the next city, but it can still be dodgy, particularly after dark. The district of Tondo, particularly around the north ports, is one area to avoid walking around solo after dark. The tourist areas of Ermita, Malate and Makati are considered some of the safer areas, but even here it pays to be careful late at night.

Traffic is the big annoyance in Manila; you'll probably spend half your time either stuck in it or talking about it. Leave extra time to get to airports, bus stations and dinner dates.

Scams

Manila is notorious for scams that target tourists. The most common scam involves gangs befriending, drugging and robbing tourists (see the boxed text, p663). Be wary of any overly friendly stranger offering to buy you a drink.

Some money changers, especially on Mabini St, can nail you with amateur-magician card tricks – turning P1000 into P100 with sleight of hand. If an exchange kiosk asks to recount the wad of pesos they've just handed you, don't let them.

Several of the *kalesa* (two-wheeled horse-drawn cart) drivers around Ermita and Intramuros can be dishonest – prices can change suddenly. Agree on the price before setting off.

SIGHTS

Intramuros

A spacious borough of wide streets, leafy plazas and lovely colonial houses, the old walled city of Intramuros (Map p616) was the centrepiece of Spanish Manila. At least it was until WWII, when the Americans and Japanese levelled the whole lot. Only a handful of buildings survived the firestorm; over 100,000 Filipino civilians were not so lucky.

The Spanish replaced the original wooden fort with stone in 1590, and these walls stand much as they were 400 years ago. They're still

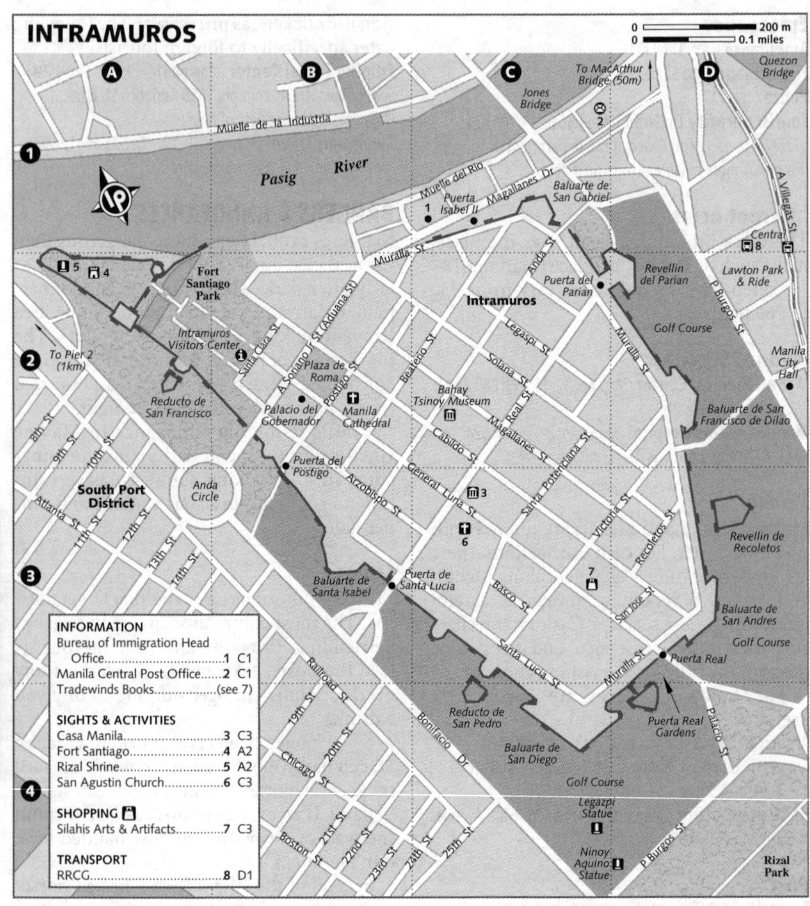

studded with bastions and pierced with gates *(puertas)*. At the mouth of the Pasig River you'll find Manila's premier tourist attraction, **Fort Santiago** (Map p616; adult/child P75/50; 8am-6pm), fronted by a pretty lily pond and the Intramuros Visitors Center. During WWII the fort was used as a prisoner-of-war camp by the Japanese. Within the fort grounds you'll find the **Rizal Shrine** in the building where national hero José Rizal was incarcerated as he awaited execution. It contains Rizal's personal effects and an original copy of his last poem, 'Mi Ultimo Adios' (My Last Farewell).

The most interesting building to survive the Battle of Manila is the church and monastery of **San Agustin** (Map p616; General Luna St). The interior is truly opulent and the ceiling, painted in 3-D relief, will make you question your vision. **Casa Manila** (Map p616; ☎ 527 4088; cnr Real & General Luna Sts; adult/child P75/50; 9am-6pm Tue-Sun) is a beautifully restored, three-storey Spanish colonial mansion filled with priceless antiques.

Rizal Park

One of the precious few bits of green in Manila, the 60-hectare Rizal Park (also known as Luneta; Map pp618–19) offers urbanites a place to decelerate among ornamental gardens and a whole pantheon of Filipino heroes. Located at the bay end of the park are the **Rizal Monument** (Map pp618–19) and the moving **site of Rizal's execution** (Map pp618-19; admission P10; 7am-8.30pm Wed-Sun).

The splendid **National Museum of the Filipino People** (Map pp618-19; T Valencia Circle, Rizal Park; adult/student P100/70, Sun free; 10am-4.30pm Wed-Sun) has interesting displays on the wreck of the *San Diego*, a Spanish galleon from 1600, plus plenty of artefacts and comprehensive exhibits on the various Filipino ethnic groups. It's kitty-corner to the **National Art Gallery** (Map pp618-19; adult/student P100/70, Sun free; 10am-4.30pm Wed-Sun), which contains many works of Filipino masters, including Juan Luna's impressive signature work, *Spoliarium*.

Quiapo & Binondo

These are some of the oldest parts of Manila, but sadly the few pieces of Spanish colonial architecture remaining are being rapidly torn down. Quiapo is a must-visit if only to witness the incredible mass of humanity that packs its streets and outdoor markets, especially on weekends. The centre of the action is **Quiapo Church** (Map pp612-13; Quezon Blvd), where the hordes line up to view the **Black Nazarene**, a life-size image of Christ believed to be miraculous. Around Quiapo Church are dozens of dubious apothecary vendors selling all manner of herbal and folk medicines and amulets that are said to ward off evil spirits. The markets south of here, around Quezon Bridge, are worth a look, as are the lively stalls along Carriedo St. From here you're just a short walk to the **Goodwill Arches** (Map pp612-13; Ongpin St) that demarcate **Chinatown** in Binondo.

Chinese Cemetery

Boldly challenging the idea that you can't take it with you, the mausoleums of wealthy Chinese in the **Chinese Cemetery** (Map pp612-13; Rizal Ave Extension or Aurora Blvd; admission free; 7.30am-7pm), north of Binondo, are fitted with flushing toilets and crystal chandeliers. Hire a bicycle (per hour P100) to get around the sprawling grounds, and considering hiring a guide (P350) for access to the best tombs. To get here take the LRT to Abad Santos then walk or take a tricycle (P25) to the South entrance.

Museums

As well as the offerings in Intramuros and Rizal Park, Manila has plenty of other interesting museums. The best is probably the **Ayala Museum** (Map pp612-13; Greenbelt 4, foreigner/resident P425/225; 9am-6pm Tue-Fri, 10am-7pm Sat & Sun), where dioramas tell the story of the Filipino quest for independence. It also houses the Philippines' best contemporary art collection. More contemporary art is on display at the decidedly more affordable **GSIS Museo ng Sining** (Museum of Art; Map pp612-13; GSIS Bldg; admission free; 9am-noon & 1-4pm Tue-Sat).

TOURS

If you're in Manila over a weekend don't miss out on the flamboyant tours of Intramuros and other destinations by **Carlos Celdran** (0920 909 2021; www.carlosceldran.com; tours P600-1000). Carlos' 'Living La Vida Imelda!' tour is fast attaining legend status.

SLEEPING

Manila's budget accommodation centres around Ermita and Malate, with a couple of good deals near the airport as well.

Townhouse (Map pp612-13; 854 3826; bill_lorna@yahoo.com; 31 Bayview Dr, Parañaque; dm P180, r P300-950;) The creaky but homey Townhouse is conveniently close to the airport and boasts a motley assortment of rooms, including an annexe with dorm beds haphazardly strewn about.

Stone House (Map pp618-19; 524 0302; stonehouse_apt@yahoo.com; 1529 Mabini St; s/d from P300/550;) This chic place is a contemporary habitat for style-savvy backpackers. While the budget singles are shoeboxes, the better doubles are great value. There's also a Quezon City location.

our pick **Malate Pensionne** (Map pp618-19; 523 8304; www.mpensionne.com.ph; 1771 Adriatico St, Malate; dm P350, d P750-P1400;) This homey, woodsy old mansion shares a quiet courtyard with Starbucks and has a useful traveller message board. The rooms, while small, are much better appointed than anything else in this price range. The dorms are simple three-bed affairs so you won't have to arm-wrestle 10 neighbours for fan rights.

Friendly's Guesthouse (Map pp618-19; 0917 333 1418; www.friendlysguesthouse.com; 1750 Adriatico St, Malate; dm with/without air-con P375/325, d P560-1010;) Captained by the suitably friendly Benjie, this is backpacker HQ, with an air-con dorm, wi-fi, a great balcony-lounge area and free coffee. Evidently familiar with Keynesian economics, Benjie recently supplied a second hostel to meet the considerable demand for cheap beds in Manila – the nearby Manila Backpacker's Guesthouse (corner J Bacobo and Alonzo Sts). Contact details and price structure are the same.

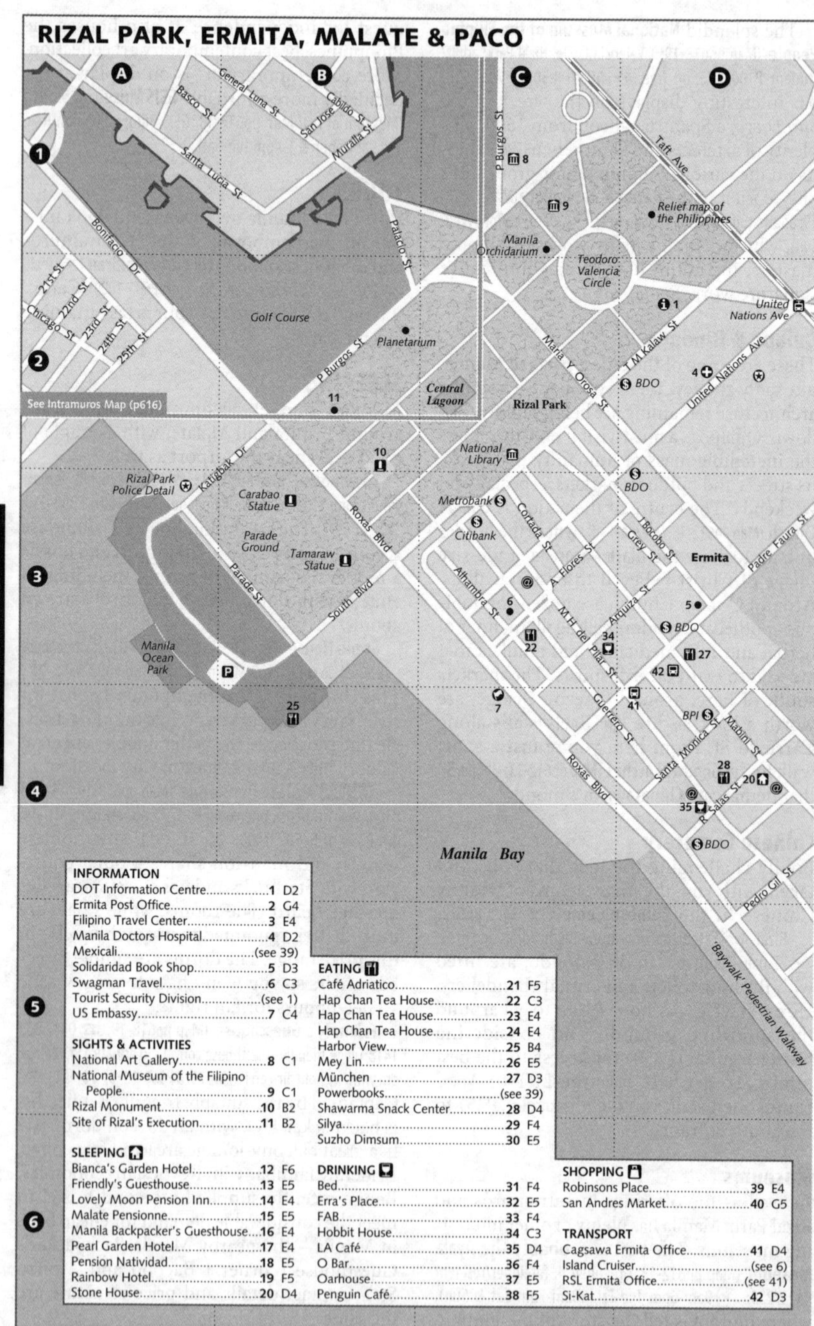
RIZAL PARK, ERMITA, MALATE & PACO
A
B
C
D
1
2
3
4
5
6
General Luna St
Basco St
Cabildo St
San Jose St
Muralla St
Santa Lucia St
Bonifacio Dr
Palacio St
21st St
22nd St
Chicago St
23rd St
24th St
25th St
Golf Course
Planetarium
P Burgos St
Central Lagoon
See Intramuros Map (p616)
P Burgos St
8
9
Taft Ave
Relief map of the Philippines
Manila Orchidarium
Teodoro Valencia Circle
United Nations Ave
T M Kalaw St
Maria Y Orosa St
BDO
United Nations Ave
Rizal Park
National Library
BDO
Metrobank
Citibank
Cortada St
J Bocobo St
Grey St
Ermita
Padre Faura St
A Flores St
Alhambra St
M H del Pilar St
Arquiza St
BDO
Guerrero St
BPI
Mabini St
Santa Monica St
R Salas St
BDO
Pedro Gil St
Roxas Blvd
Rizal Park Police Detail
Katigbak Dr
Carabao Statue
Parade Ground
Tamaraw Statue
Roxas Blvd
South Blvd
Parade St
Manila Ocean Park
P
Manila Bay
'Baywalk' Pedestrian Walkway
INFORMATION
DOT Information Centre....1 D2
Ermita Post Office....2 G4
Filipino Travel Center....3 E4
Manila Doctors Hospital....4 D2
Mexicali....(see 39)
Solidaridad Book Shop....5 D3
Swagman Travel....6 C3
Tourist Security Division....(see 1)
US Embassy....7 C4
SIGHTS & ACTIVITIES
National Art Gallery....8 C1
National Museum of the Filipino People....9 C1
Rizal Monument....10 B2
Site of Rizal's Execution....11 B2
SLEEPING
Bianca's Garden Hotel....12 F6
Friendly's Guesthouse....13 E5
Lovely Moon Pension Inn....14 E4
Malate Pensionne....15 E5
Manila Backpacker's Guesthouse....16 E4
Pearl Garden Hotel....17 E4
Pension Natividad....18 E5
Rainbow Hotel....19 F5
Stone House....20 D4
EATING
Café Adriatico....21 F5
Hap Chan Tea House....22 C3
Hap Chan Tea House....23 E4
Hap Chan Tea House....24 E4
Harbor View....25 B4
Mey Lin....26 E5
München....27 D3
Powerbooks....(see 39)
Shawarma Snack Center....28 D4
Silya....29 F4
Suzho Dimsum....30 E5
DRINKING
Bed....31 F4
Erra's Place....32 E5
FAB....33 F4
Hobbit House....34 C3
LA Café....35 D4
O Bar....36 F4
Oarhouse....37 E5
Penguin Café....38 F5
SHOPPING
Robinsons Place....39 E4
San Andres Market....40 G5
TRANSPORT
Cagsawa Ermita Office....41 D4
Island Cruiser....(see 6)
RSL Ermita Office....(see 41)
Si-Kat....42 D3

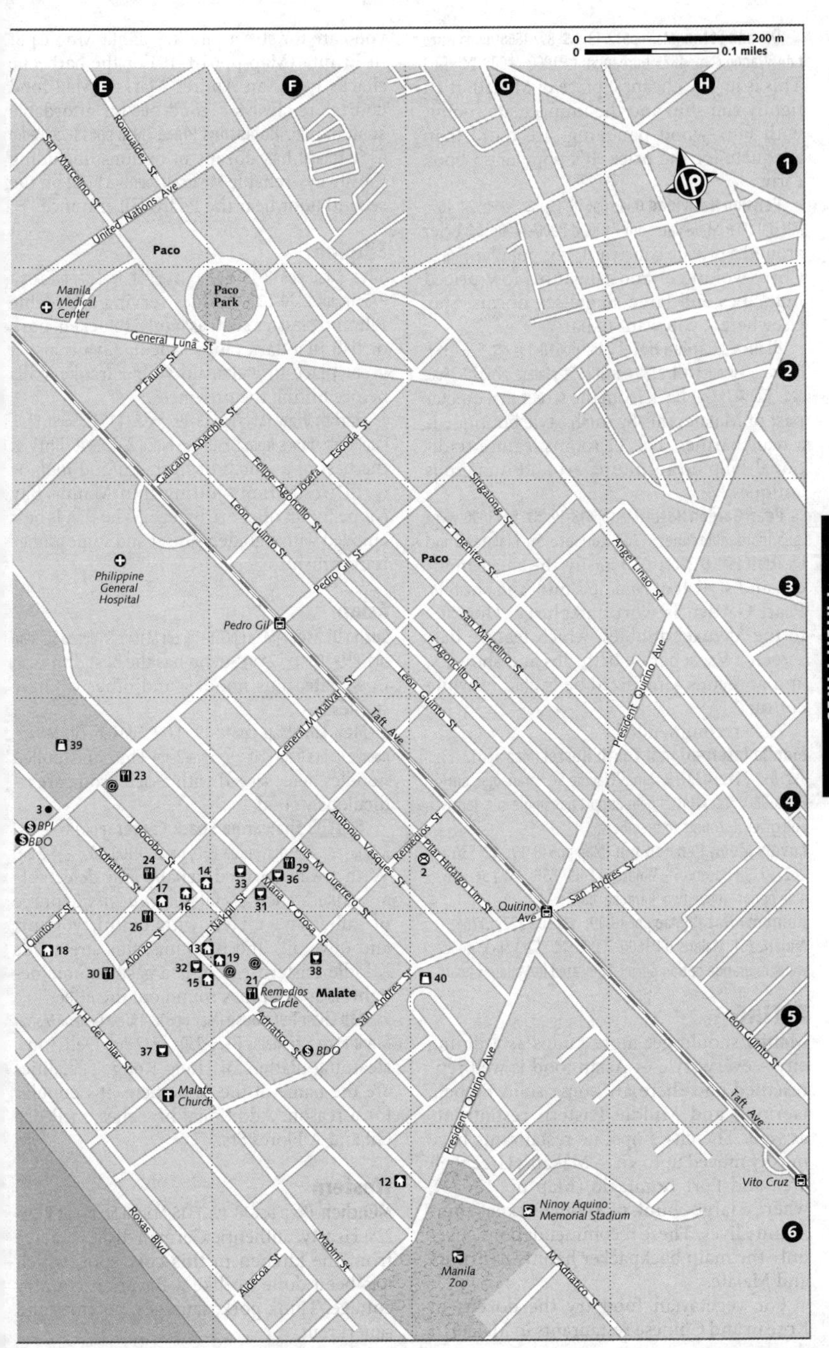

0 200 m
0 0.1 miles
Romualdez St
San Marcelino St
United Nations Ave
Paco
Paco Park
Manila Medical Center
General Luna St
P Faura St
Galicano Apacible St
Felipe Agoncillo St
Josefa L Escoda St
Leon Guinto St
Pedro Gil St
Philippine General Hospital
Pedro Gil
Singalong St
F T Benitez St
Paco
Angel Linao St
San Marcelino St
F Agoncillo St
Leon Guinto St
President Quirino Ave
General M Malvar St
Taft Ave
Antonio Vasques St
Remedios St
Pilar Hidalgo Lim St
San Andres St
Quirino Ave
Luis M Guerrero St
Maria y Orosa St
J Nakpil St
J Bocobo St
Adriatico St
J Quintos Jr St
Alonzo St
BPI
BDO
Remedios Circle
Malate
San Andres St
Adriatico St
BDO
M H del Pilar St
Malate Church
President Quirino Ave
Leon Guinto St
Taft Ave
Vito Cruz
Ninoy Aquino Memorial Stadium
Roxas Blvd
Aldecoa St
Mabini St
Manila Zoo
M Adriatico St
PHILIPPINES

Durban St Inn (Map pp612-13; ☎ 897 1866; durbanstreetinn@yahoo.com; 4875 Durban St; r P1000-1400;) This is it: The cheapest place in Makati. It's a tightly run ship and the immaculate rooms, with faux-wood panelling, are more than adequate for the price. It's popular so book early.

Pension Natividad (Map pp618-19; ☎ 521 0524; 1690 MH del Pilar St, Malate; dm P400, d P900-1400;) Set around a private courtyard, this popular Peace Corps volunteer roost features low-priced munchies and large single-sex dorms. Stay elsewhere if you want to party.

Bianca's Garden Hotel (Map pp618-19; ☎ 526 0351; biancasg@skyinet.net; 2139 Adriatico St, Malate; r P1120-2800;) Set back from the street in a quieter part of Malate, this Spanish-style boutique is a real charmer. The 11 rooms feature traditional Filipino furniture, art and numerous antiques.

Pearl Garden Hotel (Map pp618-19; ☎ 525 1000; www.pearlgardenhotel.net; 1700 Adriatico St, Malate; d incl breakfast P2400-3100;) Easily the most modern and stylish of Malate's midrange hotels, Pearl Garden is worth a splurge. Upgrade to the 'deluxe' doubles, which feature flat-screen TVs, separate bathtubs and showers, and gorgeous king-sized beds clad in white cotton.

Also recommended:

Manila International Youth Hostel (Map pp612-13; ☎ 832 2112; 4227-9 Tomas Claudio St, Parañaque; dm/d P250/900;) Hostel near airport has single-sex dorms and gives discounts to members.

Lovely Moon Pension Inn (Map pp618-19; ☎ 536 2627; 1718 Bocobo St, Malate; d P400-850;) Serviceable option above two 'karaoke' bars.

Rainbow Hotel (Map pp618-19; ☎ 302 2222; 1766 Adriatico St, Malate; d P1600-2000;) Slick, good-value midrange option perfectly located in Malate's heart.

EATING

Manila should get more kudos as a dining city – every style of Asian food is well represented and there are some solid French, German and Middle Eastern restaurants as well. The city's upscale restaurants have mostly moved uptown to Makati's Greenbelt area and Fort Bonifacio (Map pp612–13), where a large chunk of Manila's expat community lives. These recommendations cover only the main backpacker haunts of Ermita and Malate.

For vegetarian food try the dozens of Korean and Chinese restaurants in Malate. If you care for street fare, try Santa Monica St in Ermita (Map pp618–19) or the barbecue shacks near San Andres Market. Mall food courts are always a good bet for affordable sustenance. **Robinsons Place** (Map pp618-19; Pedro Gil St, Ermita) has dozens of options, including the always-reliable **Mexicali** (burritos P125) on the second floor near the Pedro Gil entrance.

Filipino

Silya (Map pp618-19; 642 J Nakpil St, Malate; breakfast P75, mains P110-160) Besides serving affordable Filipino classics such as *adobo* (chicken, pork or fish in a dark tangy sauce), Silya is also a great place to warm up your karaoke skills before hitting the provinces.

Harbor View (Map pp618-19; ☎ 524 1532; South Blvd, Rizal Park; dishes from P150; lunch & dinner) This is the best of a clutch of fresh seafood *inahaw* (grill) restaurants jutting into Manila Bay (hope for an offshore breeze). The fish is best enjoyed with a golden sunset and some amber refreshments.

Asian

Suzho Dimsum (Map pp618-19; cnr Mabini & Alonzo Sts; dim sum P50-100; 24hr) Suzho has the best dim sum in Malate, plus noodles and other Chinese staples.

Mey Lin (Map pp618-19; 1717 Adriatico St, Malate; noodle dishes from P80; 5pm-2am) The hand-pulled noodles here, served with a rich broth, are ridiculously good.

our pick **Shawarma Snack Center** (pp618-19; 485 R Salas St; pita shawarma P50, meals P100-200; 24hr) With freshly grilled kebabs and delectable appetisers such as falafel, *muttabal* (purée of aubergine mixed with tahini, yoghurt and olive oil) and hummus, this street-side Middle Eastern eatery is a gastronomic delight. Hookah pipes round out the effect.

Hap Chan Tea House (Map pp618-19; cnr General Malvar & Adriatico Sts; mains P120-250; 24hr) Delicious, steaming platters of Hong Kong specialities are the name of the game here. It's popular for a reason. Additional branches on Pedro Gil and A Flores Sts.

Western

München (Map pp618-19; 1316 Mabini St; mains P125-225) Hearty, authentic German dishes emerge from the kitchen in this cosy spot, which has been done up like a Bavarian country cottage. Think pork, sausages, potatoes and sauerkraut.

Café Adriatico (Map pp618-19; 1790 Adriatico St, Malate; meals P200-400; 24hr) Longtime Malate residents call this their 'Cheers'. The menu is Spanish with English, American and Italian effects, but you come here for the people-watching as much as the food.

DRINKING

You're rarely far from a drinking opportunity in Malate. There are three areas to look out for. You'll find the college crowd chugging cheap suds curbside just west of Remedios Circle on Remedios St – dubbed the 'Monoblock Republic' because of the preponderance of brittle plastic furniture. There are some trendy clubs and lounges here too. The stretch of Adriatico St between Remedios Circle and J Nakpil St is lined with more-touristy watering holes and live-music bars. Lastly, the corner of J Nakpil and M Orosa streets is ground zero for the gay-entertainment scene. Scattered liberally among it all are various karaoke bars offering the chance to sing and/or meet girls euphemistically called GROs – 'guest relations officers'.

our pick **Penguin Café** (Map pp618-19; ☎ 710 8056; 604 Remedios St; from 6pm Tue-Sat) This tiny bar-cum-gallery is a magnet for bohemian types and on Fridays and Saturdays squeezes in some of the finest musical talent in the Philippines, including, on occasion, Pinikpikan (see p607).

Erra's Place (Map pp618-19; Adriatico St) Cheap snacks and P27(!!) San Miguel in an perfectly located open-air setting make Erra's and neighbouring Ice Bar a logical warm-up – or warm-down – spot.

Oarhouse (Map pp618-19; 1803 Mabini St) This snug little haunt, a favourite among Peace Corps volunteers, is one oar house you won't mind getting caught in late at night – or early-morning, as is often the case.

Hobbit House (Map pp618-19; ☎ 521 7604; 1212 MH del Pilar St; admission P125-150; 5pm-2am) Often forgotten amid the vertically challenged waiters is that Hobbit House consistently draws Manila's best live blues acts.

LA Café (Map pp618-19; 1429 MH del Pilar St; 24hr) A notorious dive, this place features live music, billiards, fairly priced food and drinks, a rowdy expat crowd and round-the-clock GROs. If you want to get a glimpse of the raunchy side of Manila, look no further.

The gay bars and clubs at the corner of J Nakpil and M Orosa Sts spill out into the streets until the wee hours on weekends and sometimes on weekdays. Popular places include tiny **O Bar** (Map pp618-19; nightly), the infamous **Bed** (Map pp618-19; Thu-Sat) and **FAB** (Map pp618-19; nightly), where there's acoustic music on weekdays and wild weekend foam parties on weekends.

The trendy clubs are all up in Makati, where you'll find the likes of **Bureau** (Map pp612-13; A. Venue mall, Makati Ave), **Nuvo** (Map pp612-13; Greenbelt 2; nightly) and **Embassy** (Map pp612-13; The Fort Entertainment Centre, Fort Bonifacio; cover incl 3 drinks P500; Wed-Sat), although the latter was closed indefinitely as we went to press due to a stabbing incident.

Entertainment

Manila's 200 movie screens are dominated by imported blockbusters. All the big malls have multiscreen, air-con cinemas, including Robinsons Place Ermita. Admission is P75 to P150.

Manila sadly lacks a *Time Out*–style weekly entertainment guide, but the website www.clickthecity.com fills the gap, with extensive movie and entertainment listings, as well as shopping and eating listings.

SHOPPING

With a hulking shopping centre seemingly around every corner, Manila is a mall rat's fantasy. The closest to the tourist belt is Robinsons Place (Map pp618–19). With its green, pleasant outdoor shopping and eating courtyard, **Greenbelt Mall** (Map pp612-13; Makati Ave) is an oasis of calm in the centre of Makati. The newish **Mall of Asia** (Map pp612-13; Pasay City) is the third-largest mall in the world. It has an Olympic-sized ice rink and an Imax theatre.

KARAOKE & COVERS

You haven't *really* travelled in the Philippines until you've spent an inebriated evening around a karaoke machine paying homage to Celine Dion and Chicago. Filipinos pursue karaoke without a hint of irony, so whatever you do don't insult the guy who sounds like a chicken getting strangled. Live music is also popular; most towns have live-music bars with local talent belting out flawless cover versions of classic rock and recent hits. Adriatico St in Malate has several such venues.

Away from these air-conditioned temples, the masses shop in vast flea markets like **Greenhills** (Map pp612–13) in Ortigas, or on the frenzied streets of Quiapo (see p617).

Worthy souvenir items include woodcarved Ifugao *bulol* (rice guards), *barong* (traditional Filipino shirts), lacquered coconut-shell trinkets and textiles from North Luzon and Mindanao. **Silahis Arts & Artifacts** (Map p616; 744 General Luna St, Intramuros; 10am-7pm) carries all of the above and more, and has a textile museum on the top floor.

GETTING THERE & AWAY

Air

Most international airlines have offices at the NAIA 1 terminal, as well as satellite offices in Makati. PAL is based at Centennial Terminal II. Other domestic airlines have offices at NAIA and booking agents dotted around town. See p609 for details on airlines and domestic flights, and the boxed text 'Terminal Chaos' on p610 for information on which terminal to use.

Boat

Manila's port is divided into two sections, South Harbor and the hardscrabble, hard-to-reach North Harbor. The following are the two main lines operating long-haul ferries out of Manila to most major cities in the Visayas, Mindanao and Palawan. Full schedules are on their websites.

Negros Navigation (Map pp612-13; ☎ 554 8777; www.negrosnavigation.ph; Pier 2, North Harbor)

SuperFerry (Map pp612-13; ☎ 528 7000; www.superferry.com.ph; Pier 15, South Harbor) Also has a ticket office on Level 1 of Robinsons Place in Ermita.

Bus

Confusingly there's no single long-distance bus station in Manila. The terminals are mainly strung along EDSA, with a cluster near the intersection of Taft Ave in Pasay City to the south, and in Cubao (part of Quezon City) to the north. Another cluster is north of Quiapo in Sampaloc. If you're confused just tell a taxi driver which station you want in which city (eg 'the Victory Liner terminal in Cubao'), and they should know where it is. Buses heading into Manila will usually just have 'Cubao', 'Pasay' or 'Sampaloc' on the signboard.

Comfortable 27-seat 'deluxe' express buses – usually overnight – are available to Legazpi via Naga in Southeast Luzon, and to Vigan and Baguio in North Luzon. It's recommended to book these several days ahead. Advance reservations are also highly recommended for the few direct buses to Banaue.

GETTING AROUND

Bus

Buses that run along EDSA are a decent alternative to the packed MRT at rush hour. There are also buses to Makati from Malate via Sen Gil Puyat Ave (Buendia). Destinations are displayed in the bus window. Fares are from P8 on regular buses, and P10 on aircon services.

Jeepney

Heading south from Ermita/Malate along M H del Pilar St, 'Baclaran' jeepneys end up on EDSA just west of the Pasay bus terminals and just east of the Mall of Asia. Going north from Ermita/Malate along Mabini St, jeepneys go to Rizal Park before heading off in various directions: 'Santa Cruz' and 'Monumento' jeepneys take the MacArthur Bridge, passing the main post office, while 'Cubao' and 'Espana' jeepneys traverse the Quezon Bridge to Quiapo church before peeling off to, respectively, the Cubao and Sampaloc bus terminals.

Taxi

Metered taxis, a few of which even have working air conditioners, are the easiest way to get anywhere and are dirt cheap by world standards. Short trips cost only about P50, and even the longest hauls rarely cost more than P200.

Train

There are three elevated railway lines in Manila. The most useful, if you are staying in the Malate/Ermita tourist belt, is the LRT-1, which runs south along Taft Ave to the MRT interchange at EDSA near the Pasay bus terminals, and north to Quiapo. From the EDSA interchange, the MRT runs north to Makati and Cubao. The Metro Manila map on pp612–13 shows all metro routes. During rush hour these trains can get mosh-pit crowded, but for the rest of the day they are a great way to avoid traffic. Rides start from P11, and stored-value tickets do exist but can be hard to find. Trains run between 4am and midnight.

AROUND MANILA

Several worthy excursions offer opportunities to escape the oppressive heat and traffic of Manila. Aside from the following, there's good wreck diving and hiking north of Manila at Subic Bay, or you can climb Mt Pinatubo, site of a cataclysmic volcanic eruption in 1991. The latter is doable as a day trip from Angeles – make your way to Capas, 20km north of Angeles, and take a long tricycle ride or jeepney to Sta Juliana, where you'll find guides.

CORREGIDOR

Jealously guarding the mouth of Manila Bay, this tiny island is where General MacArthur is said to have uttered 'I shall return' as he fled the invading Japanese. He was eventually true to his word, and day-tripping Filipinos have also been heeding his call: Corregidor's rusty WWII relics are now a big tourist draw. The **Malinta tunnels**, which once housed an arsenal and a hospital, penetrate the island's rocky heart and there's a small museum displaying leftover uniforms and weapons.

Sun Cruises (Map pp612-13; ☎ 02-831 8140; www.corregidorphilippines.com; CCP Complex jetty, Pasay; excursions adult/child P2000/1120) has the market cornered for trips to Corregidor. It loads up 100 to 150 passengers every morning at 7.30am; you shall return to Manila by 3.45pm. The price includes two meals and a comprehensive tour of the island.

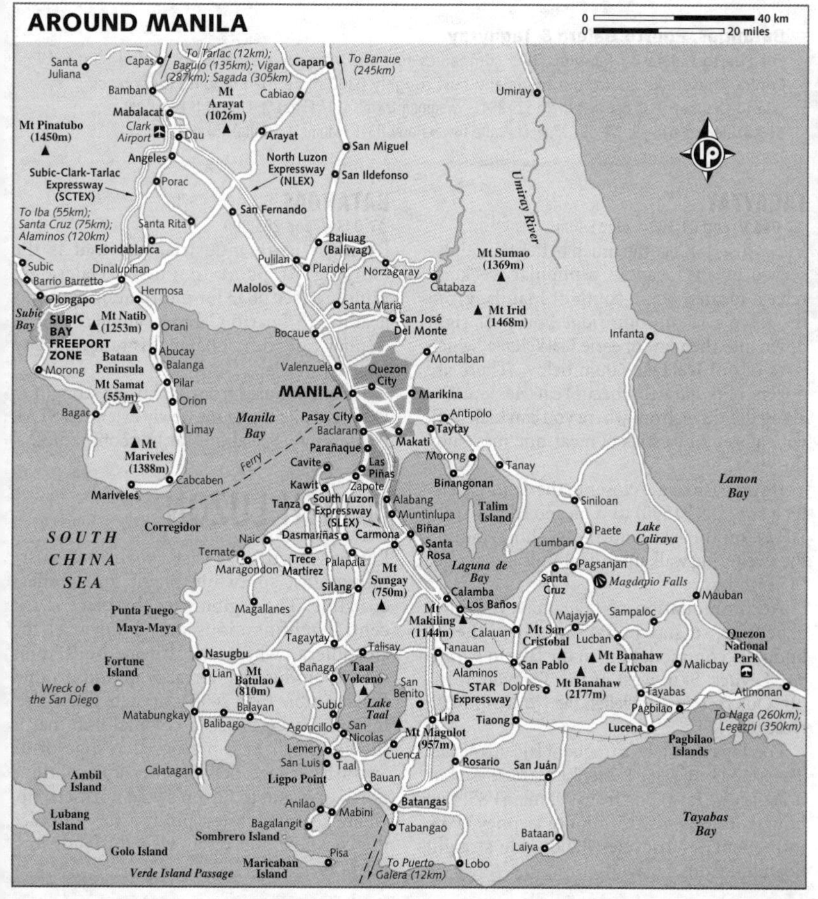

USEFUL BUS COMPANIES

North Luzon

Autobus (Map pp612-13; ☎ 493 4111; Loyola St cnr Cayco St, Sampaloc) Nightly bus to Banaue (P425, eight hours).
Cable Tours (Map pp612-13; ☎ 0908 207 8465; 269 E. Rodriguez St, Quezon City) Nightly bus to Bontoc (P650, 12 hours).
Florida Bus Line (Map pp612-13; ☎ 749 4862; cnr Extremadura & Earnshaw Sts, Sampaloc) Buses to Banaue (P450, eight hours) and Solano (hourly).
Partas Pasay Terminal (Map pp612-13; ☎ 851 4025; EDSA cnr Tramu St) Hourly buses to Vigan (air-con/deluxe P560/702, 8½ hours).
Victory Liner (Map pp612-13); Cubao (☎ 727 4688; cnr EDSA & New York Ave); Pasay (☎ 833 5020; cnr EDSA & Taft Ave) Hourly buses to Baguio (air-con/deluxe P445/700 4½/six hours) and Solano (frequent).

Clark Airport

Philtranco runs a convenient shuttle service to Clark airport, with five trips daily from its Pasay station (P350, two hours), stopping to pick up passengers at Megamall in Ortigas (Map pp612–13; P300, 1¾ hours). Partas runs two daily trips to Clark from its Pasay terminal and two trips from its Cubao terminal (see above). Another option is to take any northbound bus north to Dau (near Angles), a short taxi ride from Clark.

Batangas, Puerto Galera & Tagaytay

For Puerto Galera on Mindoro, two companies run bus/boat services, leaving around 8am from Ermita. These take about four hours and cost roughly P300 more than fending for yourself:
Island Cruiser (Map pp618-19; ☎ 523 8541; Swagman Travel, 411A Flores St, Ermita) Tickets P700.
Si-Kat (Map pp618-19; ☎ 521 3344; Citystate Tower Hotel, 1315 Mabini St, Ermita) Tickets P700.

TAGAYTAY

☎ 046 / pop 61,500 / elev 640m

Views just don't come much better than those served up in Tagaytay, a popular weekend retreat located 60km south of Manila. From the town's 15km-long ridge you peer right down into the maw of eerie **Taal Volcano**, which rises out of **Taal Lake** 600m below. There are dozens of *inahaw* (barbecue) eateries situated along the ridge, from where you can kick back with a beer and a stick of meat, and just enjoy the vista.

If you wish to get closer to the action, charter a *bangka* (P1500) to 'Volcano Island' from **Talisay**, on the lake's northeast shore, and do the sweltering walk up to Taal Volcano's crater (45 minutes).

Accommodation in Tagaytay is rather expensive, so stay in Talisay, where there's budget accommodation on the lake in *barangay* Leynes, 5km west of the Tagaytay turn-off. Our fave was **Travellers Inn** (☎ 043-723 6021; r P600-800; ❄).

For Tagaytay, take a frequent **Erjohn & Almark** (Map pp612-13; ☎ 529 6148; Pasay Rotunda Bus Terminal, cnr EDSA & Taft Ave, Pasay) bus from Manila (P85, two hours). Talisay is a 25-minute jeepney (P35, infrequent) or tricycle (P200) ride straight downhill from Tagaytay.

BATANGAS

☎ 043 / pop 295,000

Batangas is an industrial city that is the jumping-off point to Puerto Galera on Mindoro (see p633 for information on boats heading to Puerto Galera). Situated a short jeepney ride west of Batangas are several **dive resorts** at Anilao.

Frequent buses from Manila go straight to Batangas pier along the newly extended STAR Expressway. See above for bus companies.

NORTH LUZON

Luzon's north is a vast expanse of misty mountains, sprawling plains and endless coastline. The region's trophy piece is the central mountainous area known as the Cordillera, where the Ifugao built their world-famous rice terraces in and around Banaue more than 2000 years ago. Elsewhere, historic Vigan boasts a colonial hub that is the country's best-preserved vestige of its Spanish heritage. Self-explorers can continue north of Vigan to Luzon's wild northern tip, where remote white-sand beaches embrace the coastline and rarely visited islands lurk offshore.

Air-con buses to Batangas pier cost P170 and take about two hours. Companies leaving roughly every 20 minutes throughout the day:

JAM Transit (Map pp612-13; ☎ 831 0465; cnr Taft Ave & Sen Gil Puyat Ave, Pasay)

RRCG (Map p616; Lawton Park 'n' Ride, A Villegas St, Intramuros)

For Tagaytay take a Nasugbu- or Matabungkay-bound bus from the 'Pasay Rotunda' terminal at the corner of Taft Ave and EDSA in Pasay (Map pp612–13). Erjohn & Almark and Kirby Bus Lines have frequent trips.

Southeast Luzon

The hub for Bicol-bound buses is the Araneta Center bus station opposite Ali Mall in Cubao (Map pp612–13). RSL and Cagsawa have overnight buses straight from the tourist belt in Ermita (Map pp618–19). Expect to about pay about P650 for air-con buses to Naga (nine hours) and P800 to Legazpi (11 hours). 'Deluxe' services are quicker and cost more.

Cagsawa (Map pp618-19; ☎ 524 8704; Padre Faura Centre, Ermita) Has two nightly trips to Legazpi.

Isarog Bus Lines (Map pp612-13; ☎ 913 3551; Araneta Center bus station) Runs deluxe and air-con buses to Naga (six daily) and Legaspi (six daily).

Philtranco Pasay Terminal (Map pp612-13; ☎ 851 5420; cnr EDSA & Apelo Cruz St) Buses head to Naga (twice daily) and Legaspi (twice daily).

RSL (Map pp618-19; ☎ 525 7077; Padre Faura Center, Ermita) Has a nightly bus to Legazpi via Naga.

Superlines (Map pp612-13; ☎ 912 3449; cnr EDSA & Aurora Blvd, Cubao) Runs cheaper ordinary buses to Legaspi (P450) via Naga.

THE CORDILLERA

Most venturers into North Luzon set their sights squarely on the Cordillera, a river-sliced hinterland of lush green forests covering hectare after hectare of jagged earth. The amazing rice terraces near Banaue are perhaps the Philippines' most iconic site, yet they receive relatively few tourists. Lesser known but no less spectacular terraces exist throughout the Cordillera, most notably around Bontoc. Hippy-esque Sagada has a few terraces of its own, although the main attractions there are caving, hiking and the laid-back ambience.

The tribespeople of the Cordillera, collectively known as the Igorot, are as compelling as the landscape, and it's worth studying their culture if you're heading up this way. In remote areas you may observe *cañao* (sacrificial ceremonies) and see elders wearing indigenous garb such as G-strings (loin cloths).

The weather is more volatile in the Cordillera than in the lowlands. The driest time to visit is February to April, but heavy rain can fall any time of year. The rains are particularly intense from May to October, when the normal pattern is a clear morning quickly giving way to intense afternoon thunderstorms. Throw a poncho in your bag, as the Cordillera can get chilly at night. There are no functioning ATMs outside of Baguio so bring cash, but not too much because you'll only need about P1000 a day.

GETTING THERE & AROUND

The usual way into the Cordillera is via Baguio or Banaue, although more obscure routes exist. Rainy season landslides often close the Cordillera's twisting roads, so pack patience. The Halsema 'highway' linking Banaue with Bontoc is mostly sealed. A real engineering feat when it was built in the 1920s, the Halsema snakes along a narrow ridge at altitudes up to 2255m, offering great views of precipitous valleys, green rice terraces and the Philippines' third-highest peak, Mt Pulag (2922m).

Baguio

☎ 074 / pop 302,000 / elev 1450m

Vibrant, woodsy and cool by Philippine standards, Baguio (*bah*-gee-oh) is the Cordillera's nerve centre. The Philippines' 'summer capital' was founded as a hill station for the US military in the early 1900s. Today Baguio's character is shaped by the quarter of a million college students who double the city's population for much of the year. The city is known for live-music bars, artist colonies, faith healers, and funky restaurants.

PHILIPPINES

Unfortunately, even without tricycles (which can't make it up the hills), Baguio has major air- and noise-pollution problems. The city's charm lies well outside the centre, in pine-forested parks such as Camp John Hay.

INFORMATION

Session Rd hosts a number of internet cafes, banks and telephone offices. **Cordillera Regional Tourist Office** (☎ 442 8848; Governor Pack Rd) has information on tours throughout the Cordillera.

SIGHTS

Baguio is a shopping mecca where you can find all manner of handicrafts, including basketwork, textiles, Ifugao woodcarvings and jewellery (silver is a local speciality). Bargain hunters might check out the lively **city market** near the west end of Session Rd – it's an infinite warren of stalls selling everything from knock-off handicrafts to fresh-grilled chicken foetus.

Eight traditional Ifugao homes and two rare Kalinga huts were taken apart and then reassembled on the side of a hill at the artists colony **Tam-awan Village** (☎ 446 2949; www.tam-awanvillage.com; Long-Long Rd, Pinsao; s/d P500/900). Spending the night in one of these huts is a rare treat. You can participate in art workshops, learn dream-catcher making and see indigenous music and dance demonstrations. On clear days there are wonderful views of the South China Sea. To get here, take a Quezon Hill–Tam-awan or Tam-awan–Long-Long jeepney from the corner of Kayang and Shagem Sts.

SLEEPING

The most unique choice is Tam-awan Village, but note it's at least a 15-minute ride from the centre.

Baguio Village Inn (☎ 442 3901; 355 Magsaysay Ave; s P300, d P600-1500) This warm and inviting backpacker special is reminiscent of the cosy pinewood guest houses in Sagada. Only the noisy location, beyond the Slaughterhouse Bus Terminal, spoils the illusion.

our pick Burnham Hotel (☎ 442 2331; 21 Calderon St; d from P985; wi-fi) This graceful place off Session Rd is beautifully adorned with local handicrafts and staffed by a lively, informative family. Request a room away from the noisy street.

Villa Cordillera (☎ 442 6036; villa.cordillera@gmail.com; 6 Outlook Dr; d/tr/q P1400/2100/3000) This woodsy lodge overlooking Baguio Country Club on the city outskirts is so quiet you'll hardly realise you're in Baguio. Rooms are spiffy with wood floors and tightly made single beds. Wi-fi available.

Also recommended:

Baguio Harrison Inn (☎ 442 7803; 37 Harrison Rd; d P400-700) Boxlike rooms, some without windows, in the centre.

Mile Hi-Inn (☎ 446 6141; Mile Hi Center; dm/d P500/1700) Immaculate four-bed dorms within peaceful Camp John Hay, a 10-minute FX van ride from Session Rd.

Red Lion Pub/Inn (☎ 304 3078; 92 Upper General Luna Rd; d P800) Has a few basement rooms if you don't mind the noise overhead.

EATING

Baguio has some truly unique eateries that are worthy of a few extra pesos – think funky, earthy and often vegetarian.

our pick Cafe by the Ruins (25 Chuntug St; mains P150-275) The 'ruins' in this case are merely the former residence of an ex-governor, but the effect is still sublime, and the organic, Cordillera-inspired Filipino food as original as the ambience.

Bliss Cafe (Elizabeth Hotel lobby, 1 J Felipe St; www.blissnbaguio.multiply.com; mains P150-250; 🕐 11am-9pm) Owner-chef Shanti home-cooks delectable vegetarian pasta and a few Indian dishes. Art-house flicks are shown every Sunday evening.

Oh My Gulay (La Azotea Bldg, Session Rd; mains P150-250; 🕐 11am-8.30pm) Baguio's most creative interior is five stories up under a vast atrium. The mercifully compact all-vegetarian menu is equally creative.

Don Henrico's (Session Rd btwn Carlo & Assumption Sts) Don Henrico's sturdy pizza wraps (P120) have no rival when it comes to slaying the late-night munchies.

DRINKING

Worthy watering holes include expat fave **Red Lion Pub/Inn** (92 Upper General Luna Rd) and Peace Corps Volunteer hang-out **Rumours** (56 Session Rd). **City Tavern** (cnr Abanao & Chuntug Sts; 🕐 8am-3am) and **18 BC** (16 Legarda Rd; 🕐 6.30pm-late) are the best of Baguio's many live-music establishments. For a raucous, fraternity-party atmosphere take your act to the collection of bars and clubs at **Nevada Square** (Loakan Rd off Military Circle).

PHILIPPINES

GETTING THERE & AWAY

Victory Liner (☎ 619 0000; Upper Session Rd) has express buses to/from Manila along the newly opened Subic–Clark–Tarlac Expressway (P700, 4½ hours, five daily). Otherwise you are looking at a six-hour trip with Victory Liner or one of several bus companies that operate from Governor Pack Rd.

GL Lizardo has hourly buses until 1pm to Sagada (P220, seven hours) from the **Dangwa Terminal** (Magsaysay Ave), a five-minute walk north of Session Rd. D'Rising Sun buses to Bontoc (P212, six hours) leave hourly until 4pm from the **Slaughterhouse Terminal** (Magsaysay Ave), five minutes by jeepney beyond the Dangwa Terminal. Both routes follow the Halsema Hwy.

KMS and Ohayami have several buses to Banaue (P465, 8½ hours) each day along the sealed, southern route via Solano. Their terminals are near each other on Shanum St, west of Burnham Park.

Sagada

pop 1550 / elev 1547m

The epitome of mountain cool, Sagada (1477m) is where you go if you want to escape from civilisation for a few days – or months. **Caves**, **peaks**, **waterfalls** and **hanging coffins** beckon the active traveller, while more sedate types can just kick back with a hot drink and a book and revel in Sagada's delightfully earthy ambience. Try to time your visit for a *begnas* (traditional community celebration), when the hearty Kankanay locals gather in *dap-ay* (meeting places) to bang gongs, smoke pipes, swill brandy and sacrifice chickens.

Take a guide for any trekking or caving you do around here or you'll almost surely get lost; grab one (per day P600 to P800) at the tourist information centre, where you can also snag a map (P10) and hire a private jeepney if need be. Our favourite excursion is the thrilling half-day **cave connection**.

Golinsan Internet Café (per hr P40; ⏰ 8am-8.30pm) is below Alfredo's Cabin.

SLEEPING

Sagada's basic but charming guest houses, featuring cosy linen and buckets of hot water (P50), are a delight.

Sagada Guesthouse (☎ 0918 938 5601; edaoas@yahoo.com; s/d P200/400) The rustic, cheerful doubles here, overlooking the central square, are perhaps the town's best value.

Sagada Homestay (☎ 0919 702 8380; s/d P250/500; 💻 📶) It's not really a homestay (it's a guest house), but it's nonetheless friendly, eminently affordable, and loaded with character born of polished pine. It also boasts righteous views.

Alfredo's Cabin (☎ 0918 588 3535; s/d P350/500) The simple doubles are a step up from most in town, and the restaurant has immense charm – woody and fragrant, with a big fireplace.

EATING & DRINKING

Sagada has a few surprisingly good eating options.

Yoghurt House (breakfasts P60-140, mains P85-160) Fuel up here with mountain coffee and the trademark yoghurt muesli breakfasts before a long day of hiking or caving. Also has a book exchange.

our pick **Log Cabin** (☎ 0920 520 0463; mains P175-225; ⏰ dinner) The fireplace dining here hits the spot on those chilly Sagada evenings. On Saturdays there's a wonderful buffet (P350; prepaid reservations only) prepared by a French chef.

Persimoon Café (⏰ till last customer) Sagada's only watering hole draws a good mix of local guides and out-of-towners, who discuss the day's events over a San Miguel or 12.

GETTING THERE & AWAY

There are jeepneys to Bontoc every hour until noon (P40, one hour). The last bus to Baguio leaves at 1pm (see left for details). For Manila, you must transfer in Baguio, Bontoc or Banaue.

> **OFF THE BEATEN TRACK**
>
> A road heading north out of Baguio for 50 winding kilometres leads to picturesque **Kabayan**, the site of several caves containing eerie mummies entombed centuries ago by the Ibaloi people. Some of these caves can be visited, while others are known only to Ibaloi elders. After exploring Kabayan for a day or two you can walk back to the Halsema Hwy (about five hours, straight uphill) via the **Timbac Caves**, the spot where the best-preserved mummies lurk. The keys are with a caretaker who lives up the hill from the caves. From the caves it's about a 45-minute walk out to the Halsema Hwy.

Bontoc

☎ 074 / pop 3300

This Wild West frontier town is the central Cordillera's transport and market hub. You can still see tribal elders with full body tattoos and G-strings strolling the streets, especially on Sunday when people descend from the surrounding villages to sell their wares at Bontoc's bustling market. Make a point to visit the **Bontoc Museum** (admission P50; 8am-noon & 1-5pm), which has fascinating exhibits on each of the region's main tribes. Check out the grisly photos of head-hunters and their booty.

There's some mint trekking to be done around Bontoc, most notably to the stone-walled **rice terraces of Maligcong**, which rival those in Batad. To really get off the beaten track, head even further north into Kalinga Province, where you can hike to remote villages and meet aged former head-hunters. Ask around the hotels for **Kinad** (☎ 0929 384 1745) for treks around Bontoc, or Francis Pa-In for Kalinga treks. Guides cost about P1000 per day.

If you are staying a night, **Churya-a Hotel & Restaurant** (☎ 0906 430 0853; darwin_churyaa@yahoo.com; s/d/tr P150/400/700) has clean if unspectacular rooms, and a pleasant balcony over Bontoc's main street.

Cable Tours has the only direct bus to/from Manila, leaving Bontoc daily at 3pm (P650, 12 hours) and leaving Manila nightly at 8.30pm. It goes via Banaue (P150, two hours). Also to Banaue there is a jeepney around noon and four morning buses. Jeepneys to Sagada (P40, one hour) leave hourly until 5.30pm. For buses to Baguio, see p627.

Banaue & the Rice Terraces

☎ 074 / pop 2600

Banaue is synonymous with the Unesco World Heritage–listed Ifugao rice terraces, hewn out of the hillsides using primitive tools and an ingenious irrigation system some 2000 years ago. Legend has it that the god Kabunyan used the steps to visit his people on earth.

The Ifugao by no means had a monopoly on rice terraces in the Cordillera, but they were arguably the best sculptors, as the mesmerising display above Banaue suggests. Banaue itself – a ragged collection of tin-roofed edifices along a ridge – often spoils things for those looking for a perfect first ooh-and-aah moment. But you can't argue with the setting. Meanwhile, that perfect ooh-and-aah moment is not too far away, in Batad.

Two kilometres north of town you can ogle rice terraces to your heart's content at the **viewpoint**; a tricycle there and back costs P200. If your heart's still not content, there are similarly impressive specimens lurking in nearby Bangaan, Hapao, Kiangan and of course Batad.

The weather tends to be a bit more volatile in Banaue than in more western parts of the Cordillera. Incessant fog and rain can ruin the view for weeks. Call the Tourism Information Centre (below) to get a weather update before setting out.

INFORMATION

The **Tourist Information Centre** (☎ 386 4010; 6am-7pm) adjacent to the plaza arranges accredited guides (full day P1200) and private transport according to a remarkably transparent list of prices. Good little maps of the main hiking routes are widely available for P15. You can change dollars at poor rates at Uyami's or People's Lodge.

SLEEPING & EATING

People's Lodge (☎ 386 4014; s/d from P200/400) Service couldn't be friendlier at this sweet-value spot, with fine views and one a popular if ugly restaurant.

Uyami's Greenview Lodge (☎ 386 4021; www.ugreenview.wordpress.com; s P250, d P500-1500) It's the busiest place in town so they must be doing something right. The rooms are cosy and clean, with shiny parquet floors, and there's a rustic restaurant downstairs.

Family Inn (huts P300-600) Accommodation here is in transplanted Ifugao huts. It's in a gorgeous spot overlooking scenic Bangaan, 14km east of Banaue on the road to Batad.

A little past Greenview are two neighbouring cheapies: **Halfway Lodge & Restaurant** (☎ 386 4082; s/d from P200/300) and **Stairway Lodge & Restaurant** (r P200 per person).

GETTING THERE & AWAY

For bus companies making the overnight trip from Manila, see p624. If you prefer daytime travel, take a bus to Solano (P375, seven hours) and continue by jeepney to Banaue (P110, 2¼ hours with a change in Lagawe).

For bus companies serving Baguio, see p627. Buses to Baguio ply the lowland route via Solano. To take the scenic highland route (ie via Bontoc and the Halsema Hwy), you must transfer in Bontoc. There's an early-morning jeepney to Bontoc, and a handful of Bontoc-bound buses pass through Banaue throughout the day (about P150, two hours).

Batad

pop 1100

To really see the **Ifugao rice terraces** in all their glory, you'll need to trek to Batad (900m), which sits at the foot of a truly mesmerising amphitheatre of rice fields. Most of the inhabitants still practise traditional tribal customs in what must be one of the most serene, picture-perfect villages to grace the earth.

A slippery 40-minute walk beyond the village itself is the gorgeous 30m-high **Tappiya Waterfall** and swimming hole. To escape tourists altogether, hike 1½ hours to the remote village of **Cambulo**, which has several simple guest houses.

SLEEPING

Most guest houses are in *sitio* (small village) Chung Chung, perched on a spectacular hill facing Batad village and the amphitheatre. Hillside Inn, Batad Pension, Rita's and Simon's Inn all have restaurants and rooms for P150 per head. They're all simple, clean and rustic, but Rita's wins our hearts with its all-round charm.

GETTING THERE & AWAY

From Banaue, it's 12km over a rocky road to Batad Junction, where a 4WD track leads three bone-jarring kilometres up to the 'saddle' high above Batad. From the saddle it's a 45-minute hike to Batad.

From Banaue, a few (mostly afternoon) jeepneys/buses pass by Batad junction (P50, one hour). From there you'll have to walk to the saddle. Alternatively, you can team up with other travellers and hire a private jeepney to the saddle (return P2500). Tricycles can get you to the junction (return P650). Motorcycle taxis can go all the way to the saddle (return P800).

If you are overnighting in Batad, get out to the junction early the next morning to catch jeepneys heading to Banaue.

VIGAN

☎ 077 / pop 47,246

Spanish-era mansions, cobblestone streets and *kalesa* are the hallmarks of Unesco World Heritage Site Vigan. Miraculously spared bombing in WWII, the city is considered the finest surviving example of a Spanish colonial town. Two of Vigan's finer mansions are now the **Crisologo Museum** (Liberation Blvd; admission free; 🕑 8.30-11.30am & 1.30-4.30pm Tue-Sat) and the **Syquia Mansion Museum** (Quirino Blvd; admission P20; 🕑 9am-noon &1.30-5pm).

The **Vigan Town Fiesta** is in the third week of January, while the **Viva Vigan Festival of the Arts** takes place in early May.

WILD ABOUT WWOOFING

You can do more than just eat the many wonderful vegetables plucked from the earth in the Cordillera Mountains. Fulfil your farming fantasies as a volunteer on one of two organic farms certified by **Willing Workers on Organic Farms** (WWOOF; www.wwoof.org).

In Pula, a *barangay* of Asipulo in Ifugao Province, there's a WWOOF project run out of the **Julia Campbell Agroforest Memorial Park** (☎ 0905 732 2942; juliacampbellampark.org, jcamgerald@yahoo.com). Julia Campbell was a US Peace Corps volunteer whose murder at the hands of a local man on the main trail to Batad in April 2007 shocked the country. The park dedicated to her is a working organic coffee farm that produces a rare type of coffee derived from the excrement of the coffee bean–eating **civet**. The park accepts both volunteers and regular tourists to enjoy electricity-free life in a small Ifugao village surrounded by natural forest. Accommodation is in basic Ifugao huts. The cost is P150 per night, or free if you're volunteering.

Closer to Baguio, the Cosalan family's organic **Enca Farm** (☎ 0919 834 4542; encaorganicfarm@yahoo.com.ph) is in Acop, Benguet, an hour north of Baguio on the Halsema Hwy. Their farm grows beans, lettuces, broccoli, carrots, radishes and coffee. Volunteers usually do about eight hours of farm work per day and sleep in tents. There's hiking to be done and caves to explore on off days. Contact the farm or the **Benguet Provincial Tourism Office** (☎ 422 1116) in La Trinidad for help getting to the farm.

Sleeping & Eating

It's worth paying a little extra to stay in one of Vigan's charismatic colonial homes. Prices drop from June to October.

Vigan Hotel (☎ 722 1906; Burgos St; s/d from P395/495; ❄) The once-popular Vigan Hotel today suffers from a decided lack of TLC. It's still cheap though.

Grandpa's Inn (☎ 722 2118; 1 Bonifacio St; d incl breakfast from P650; ❄ wi-fi) With a great restaurant, top-notch service and an impressive array of rooms in a rustic old house, this is Vigan's best value.

our pick **Villa Angela** (☎ 722 2914; www.villangela.com; 26 Quirino Blvd; d/q incl breakfast from P1400/2800; ❄) This magnificent 130-year-old mansion has a giant *sala* (living room) festooned with fabulous antique furniture and four huge bedrooms looking much as they would have in the 18th century. One of the Philippines' true gems.

Evening **street stalls** (Plaza Burgos) peddle local snacks such as *empanadas* (deep-fried tortillas with shrimp, cabbage and egg) and *okoy* (shrimp omelettes). **Uno Grille** (Bonifacio St; mains P100-180) and **Cafe Uno** (1 Bonifacio St; cakes P60) are sister restaurants run by neighbouring Grandpa's Inn. **Cafe Leona** (Crisologo St; meals P100-300) serves terrific Ilocano food and passable Japanese specials on the cobbled street.

PHILIPPINES

Getting There & Away

There are many companies serving Manila (see p624). The three nightly 'deluxe' buses run by **Partas** (☎ 722 3369; Alcantara St) are the most comfortable. Partas also has 10 daily trips to Baguio (P350, five hours).

SOUTHEAST LUZON

Fiery food, fierce typhoons and furious volcanoes characterise the adventure wonderland known as Bicol. The region's most famous peak, Mt Mayon, may just be the world's most perfect volcano. And it's no sleeping beauty, either. A steady stream of noxious fumes leaks out of its maw, and minor eruptions are frequent. You can climb most of the way up Mayon, but there is better hiking to be had in Mt Isarog National Park near Naga. Underwater, Bicol is home to one of the Philippines' top attractions: the gentle, graceful *butanding* (whale sharks) of Donsol.

You'll want to pay extra attention to the news before heading to Bicol, lest you waltz into one of the region's patented typhoons. The Pan-Philippine or Maharlika Hwy runs right through Bicol down to Matnog, where ferries cross to Samar.

NAGA

☎ **054** / **pop 160,516**

Naga, the capital of Camarines Sur ('CamSur'), is relatively cosmopolitan by Philippine standards, with a vibrant student population and a burgeoning reputation as an adventure-sports mecca. The city centres on a pleasant double plaza that often hosts large concerts or festivals after sundown. In September the immensely popular **Peñafrancia Festival** kicks off, packing hotels to the gills. Be sure to sample the spicy local Bicol cuisine, as well as *pili* nuts (a local favourite).

Activities

The **CamSur Watersports Complex** (☎ 475 0689; www.cwcwake.com, wakeboarding per hr/day P165/590, ⏰ 8.30am-7pm Mon-Thu, to 9pm Fri & Sat Mar-May; wi-fi), 12km south of Naga in the town of Pili, is an impressively modern cable wakeboarding centre, complete with surfer-dude music, restaurants, wi-fi and a range of accommodation. It's heaps of fun for experienced riders and beginners alike. The ever-growing list of activities on offer includes a waterpark, a go-cart track and a downhill mountain-bike facility on nearby Mt Isarog (1966m).

Superb hiking is available in **Mt Isarog National Park**, 20km east of Naga. You can launch an assault on the summit or there are several shorter hikes through the jungle lower down. Access to the national park is from the town of Panicuason, where you can find guides.

The **Kadlagan Outdoor Shop & Climbing Wall** (☎ 472 3305; kadlagan@yahoo.com; 16 Dimasalang St, Naga) hires out tents and other camping gear, and guides day and overnight excursions on Mt Isarog. Jojo Villareal knows all the local rocks and routes and is usually here in the evenings. Guides cost P550 to P800 per day, excluding meals and equipment.

Sleeping

Book way ahead if you plan on coming to Naga during the Magayon Festival.

Sampaguita Tourist Inn (Panganiban Dr) main wing (☎ 473 8896; s/d from P150/350; ❄ wi-fi); annexe (☎ 473 2158; s P300-600, d P400-750; ❄) You want the gleaming new annexe (with wi-fi) which flanks the river in the back as opposed to the tattier original on noisy Panganiban Dr – although the cheaper rooms are in the latter.

The Ecovillage (☎ 477 5636; d/q from P350/850,) The cheapest accommodation option at the Camsur Watersports Complex. The 14 basic tin shacks are set in a quiet garden and share a large, clean, locker room–style bathroom.

Moraville Hotel (☎ 473 1247; www.moraville.com.ph; Caceres St; d P500-2800;) This friendly, centrally located old standby has a wide range of rooms. The cheaper rooms are slightly faded but plenty sizeable.

Eating & Drinking

Mama Eñga (Peñafrancia Ave cnr Burgos St; portions P15-35; 8am-8pm) and **Geewan** (Burgos St; mains P25-75) are great places to sample fiery Bicol dishes such as *pinangat* (taro leaves wrapped around minced fish or pork), 'Bicol *exprés*' (spicy minced pork dish) and *ginataang pusit* (squid cooked in coconut milk). Both are *turo-turo* (point-point) style.

'Magsaysay' jeepneys along Peñafrancia Ave lead to a new food mall, **Avenue Square** (Magsaysay Ave). Beyond this mall you'll find popular restobar **Molino Bar & Grill** (Magsaysay Ave) in a huddle of slightly upscale restaurants and bars. Next door, nightclub **Club M8** (Magsaysay Ave; admission P100-200; 8pm-4am Thu-Sat) gets going on weekends. No shorts or sandals.

Getting There & Away

Air Philippines, Cebu Pacific and Zest Air have regular flights to/from Manila.

The bus station is over Panganiban Bridge next to brand-new SM Mall. **RSL** (☎ 472 6885) and **Philtranco** (☎ 811 2541) go directly to Ermita in Manila, while several others go to Cubao (see p625). The deluxe night buses to/from Manila fill up fast so book a few days ahead.

The fastest way to Legazpi is by minivan (P150, two hours) from the van terminal, opposite SM Mall. They leave when full, usually every 30 minutes, until 7pm. Air-con buses to Legazpi take much longer and cost P120, while ordinary (nonair-con) buses sometimes take six hours!

Infrequent jeepneys to Panicuason depart from just off Caceres St, near the Naga City Market (P25, 30 minutes). Alternatively, take a frequent jeepney to nearby Carolina and transfer to a tricycle.

LEGAZPI

☎ 052 / pop 179,481

Charm is in short supply in the city of Legazpi, but with the towering cone of Mt Mayon hogging the horizon no one seems to really notice. The city is divided into Albay District, where the provincial government offices and airport are located, and commercial Legazpi City. A steady stream of jeepneys connects the two districts along the National Hwy (Rizal St). The **Provincial Tourism Office** (☎ 481 0250; http://tourism.albay.gov.ph; Astrodome Complex, Aquende Dr, Albay District) hands out the excellent *EZ Map* of the city for free.

Make the vigorous 30-minute climb up **Liñgon Hill**, north of the city near the airport, for the best views of Mt Mayon. The **Magayon Festival** in Albay District lasts the entire month of April, packing all hotels to the gills.

Sleeping

Rooms are tough to come by during the month-long Magayon Festival in April so book way ahead.

Sampaguita Tourist Inn (☎ 480 6258; Rizal St, Legazpi City; s/d from P150/300;) There are a ton of rooms here in case everything else is booked out. Even the simplest rooms are clean and bright, if nothing else.

Catalina's Lodging House (☎ 481 1634; 96 Peñaranda St, Legazpi City; s P180-250, d P240-600;) The small rooms here have fragrant old wooden floors and range from very cheap and basic to less cheap and basic.

Legazpi Tourist Inn (☎ 480 6147; V&O Bldg, Quezon Ave, Legazpi City; s/d from P600/700;) The best midrange option is this modern place, with clean and well-kept rooms, quality TVs and lots of mirrors.

Eating & Drinking

Try the nightly street stalls along Quezon Ave near the Trylon Monument in Legazpi City for budget Bicol fare.

Waway's Restaurant (Peñaranda St, Legazpi City; dishes P60-100) Just north of Legazpi City, this is a great place to try Bicol food. A surprisingly palatable choice for the adventurous eater is *candingga* (diced pig liver and carrots sweetened and cooked in vinegar).

our pick **Small Talk** (Doña Aurora St & National Hwy, Albay District; mains P75-155; lunch & dinner) This delightful little eatery adds Bicol touches to its Italian fare. Try the pasta *pinangat* or 'Bicol express' pasta.

Getting There & Away

Cebu Pacific and PAL each fly at least twice daily to/from Manila. Zest Air has a cheap thrice-weekly flight.

The main bus terminal is at the Satellite Market, just west of Pacific Mall in Legazpi City. Cagsawa and RSL bus lines have popular deluxe night buses that go directly to Ermita in Manila, while several others go to Cubao (see p625).

For options to Naga, see p631. Air-con minivans zip to Donsol roughly hourly until 5pm or so (P60, 1¼ hours) and to Sorsogon (P60, one hour, frequent), where you can pick up a jeepney to Matnog, gateway to Samar.

AROUND LEGAZPI

Mt Mayon

Bicolanos sure hit the nail on the head when they named this monolith – *magayon* is the local word for 'beautiful'. The impossibly perfect slopes of the volcano's cone rise to a height of 2462m above sea level, and emit a constant plume of smoke across the flat plains and over the surrounding coconut plantations.

The spirit of the mountain is an old king whose beloved niece ran away with a young buck. The grumpy old man's pride still erupts frequently. In February 1993, an eruption killed 77 people. Shortly after lava flows subsided in 2006, a biblical typhoon triggered mudslides on Mt Mayon that killed more than 1000 people.

The mountain's 'knife edge' – the highest point to which you can climb, at about 2200m – closes from time to time but was open as of this writing. For most people it's a 1½-day climb with an overnight at 'Camp 2' (1600m), but fit climbers can do it in a day. Guides are mandatory. The 1½-day trek costs about US$125/150/175 for one/two/three persons and includes transport from Legazpi, camping equipment, porters, food etc.

The best time of year to climb Mt Mayon is February to April. From May to August it's unbearably hot; from September to January it's wet. The following organise Mt Mayon climbs:

Bicol Adventure (☎ 480 2266; www.bicoladventure.com; V&O Bldg, Quezon Ave, Legazpi City)

Mayon Outdoor Guides Association (☎ 0915 422 4508; pinangat2001@yahoo.com)

Donsol

pop 4200

Every year, between December and early June, large numbers of whale sharks, or *butanding*, frolic in the waters off this sleepy fishing village about 50km from Legazpi. It's truly an exhilarating experience swimming along with these silver-spotted marine leviathans, which can reach 14m in length. In the peak months of February to May sightings are virtually guaranteed, although bad weather can make sightings more difficult. Check the forecast and contact the **Donsol Visitors Center** (☎ 0919 707 0394, 0921 969 9544; nenitapedragosa@yahoo.com; 🕑 7.30am-5pm) before you visit.

When you arrive in town head to the Visitors Center to pay your registration fee (P300) and arrange a boat (P3500, good for seven people) for your three-hour tour. The Visitors Center does its best to ensure each boat is full. Each boat has a spotter and a *Butanding* Interaction Officer on board – tip them a couple hundred pesos, especially if you've had a good day. Snorkelling equipment is available for hire (P300). Scuba diving is prohibited.

SLEEPING

Shoreline (☎ 0917-861 0231; hut P500, d incl breakfast P1500-1700; ❄) The open-air huts with mosquito nets and shared bathrooms are as basic as it gets. Location near the Visitors Center a plus.

Amor Farm Beach Resort (☎ 0909 518 1150; rasyl_r_amor@yahoo.com; r with fan/air-con from P800/1500; ❄) A peaceful resort with cottages scattered around a garden. The fan rooms are the best value in the Visitors Center area.

The cheapest lodging is in Donsol proper, 2km south of the Visitors Center. **Santiago Lodging House** (r P400) is basically a homestay with three good, clean rooms in a beat-up wooden house. Right across the street is **Hernandez Guest House** (☎ 0906 431 4173; r P500-1200; ❄), which has a few simple fan rooms.

GETTING THERE & AWAY

Air-con minivans leave to Legazpi every hour until about 3pm (P60, 1¼ hours).

DID YOU KNOW?

Many *Butanding* Interaction Officers, boatmen and spotters are former fishermen who once hunted whale sharks and dynamite-fished on the local reefs.

PHILIPPINES

MINDORO

There are two sides to this large island just south of Luzon: Puerto Galera, and the rest of Mindoro. The thriving dive centre of Puerto Galera is in the heart of the Verde Island Passage – one of the world's most biologically diverse underwater environments. It's essentially an extension of Luzon.

Then there's the rest of Mindoro – an untamed hinterland of virtually impenetrable mountains populated by one of one of Asia's most primitive tribes, the Mangyan. Those who like to get *way* off the beaten track need look no further. Off the west coast, accessible from the small island of **North Pandan**, dive wonderland **Apo Reef** is populated by sharks and sting rays.

Getting There & Away

The way to Puerto Galera is by boat from Batangas (see below).

Frequent fastcraft ferries zip from Batangas to Calapan in northern Mindoro (P255, one hour). Slower car ferries (P160, 2½ hours) also ply this route. From Batangas you'll also find frequent ferries to Abra de Ilog (P208, 2½ hours), gateway to North Pandan Island.

Regular ferries to Boracay depart from Roxas (see p635).

PUERTO GALERA

☎ 043 / pop 28,035

It lacks the beautiful beach, classy resorts and hip nightlife of Boracay, but this diving hot spot on the northern tip of Mindoro is conveniently located just a hop, skip and a *bangka* ride from Manila. That alone qualifies it as the country's second-most popular tourist destination after Boracay.

The name Puerto Galera typically refers to the town of Puerto Galera and the resort areas surrounding it – namely Sabang, 7km, and White Beach, 7km to the west. The town proper has a breathtakingly beautiful harbour, but otherwise is of little interest.

There are no ATMs in the area, so bring cash. The privately owned **Tourist Center** (☎ 287 3108; 9am-9pm Mon-Sat), on the main road in Sabang, has information on transport and hotels and also exchanges travellers cheques.

GETTING THERE & AROUND

Speedy *bangka* ferries to Puerto Galera town, Sabang Beach and White Beach leave regularly throughout the day from Batangas pier until about 4.30pm (P230, one hour). The last trip back to Batangas from Sabang leaves at 1.45pm (on Sundays and in peak periods there's a later boat). From Puerto Galera it's the 5.30pm car ferry (P182, 2½ hours) from Balatero Pier, 2.5km west of Puerto Galera town. Be prepared for a rough crossing.

To reach Roxas, where ferries depart for Caticlan (Boracay), first take a jeepney to Calapan from the Petron station in Puerto Galera proper (P80, two hours, frequent), then transfer to a Roxas-bound van (P180, three hours). First trip to Calapan is 5am – take that to reach Roxas in time for the 11am ferry to Caticlan.

Regular jeepneys connect Sabang and Puerto Galera town (P15, 20 minutes). A tricycle from Sabang to Puerto Galera costs P150; from Sabang to Talipanan it's P300. You can also save some money by taking a motorcycle taxi.

Motorbike rentals start at P800 per day but that's *very* negotiable.

Sabang Beach

Drinking and underwater pursuits are the activities of choice in Sabang, with plenty of establishments offering variations on these themes. Dive prices vary wildly so shop around. Capt'n Gregg's and Dive VIP charge about $25 per dive, including equipment. An open-water course will set you back US$330 to US$450. By night Sabang serves up plenty of action, much of it less than wholesome.

Just around the headland from Sabang, the cleaner and more laid-back **Small La Laguna Beach** has several resorts fronting a brown strip of sand. Beyond that is **Big La Laguna Beach**.

SLEEPING

Expect big discounts off these prices in the June to October low season.

At-Can's Inn (☎ 0920 857 0756; r P600-1400; ❄) Flash they ain't, but the rooms here are huge and boast kitchens, seafront balconies and a prime central location in Sabang.

Capt'n Gregg's Divers Lodge (☎ 287 3070; www.captngreggs.com; d P700-1400; ❄ 💻) This Sabang institution is great value. The compact but cosy wood-lined rooms, right over the water, earn the best-view plaudit. Wi-fi available.

El Galleon Beach Resort (☎ 0917 814 5170; www.elgalleon.com; Small La Laguna Beach; d from US$51; ❄ 💻 📶 🏊) Elegant hut-style rooms with

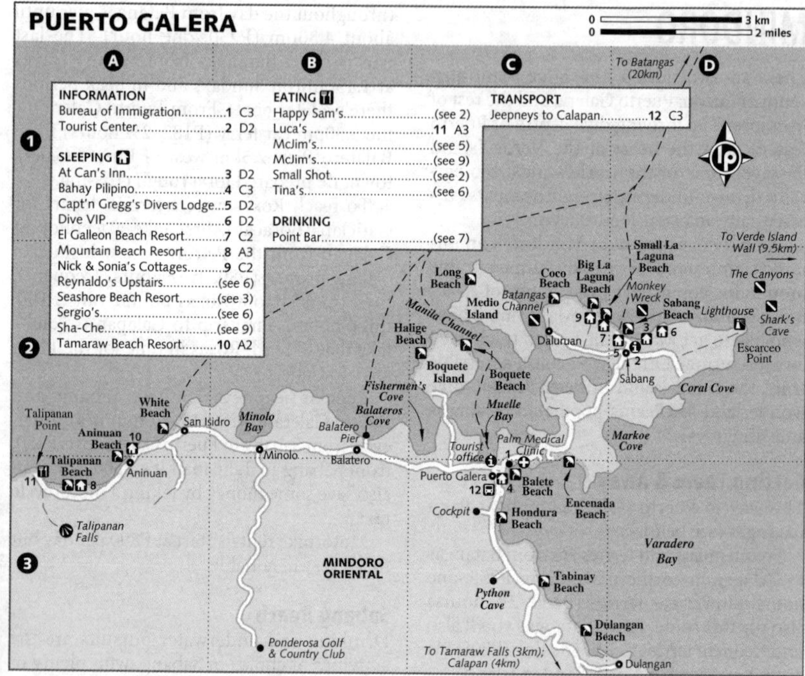

wicker furniture and verandahs creep up a beachfront cliff and slink around a pool. There's a fine restaurant and one of Asia's top technical dive schools on premises. It's definitely worth a splurge, especially if you want to distance yourself from somewhat seedy Sabang. For a super-splurge, ask about the incredible villas, starting at US$105.

Right next to each other on Small La Laguna Beach are two good-value places: **Nick & Sonia's Cottages** (☎ 0917 803 8156; r P600-1500) and **Sha-Che** (☎ 0917 641 0112; shacheinn@yahoo.com.ph; r from P600).

You'll find some great-value places down at the far eastern end of Sabang Beach, including the following:

Reynaldo's Upstairs (☎ 0917 489 5609; r with fan/air-con P450/700) Sabang's cheapest rooms are found here; most even have kitchens and balconies.

Dive VIP (☎ 287 3140; r P500) Rooms are worn but have verandahs, hot water and small kitchens.

Sergio's (☎ 0919 159 9147; r with fan/air-con P500/1000) Five simple rooms on a hill behind Tina's.

Seashore Beach Resort (☎ 287 2031; r with fan/air-con P700/1200; wi-fi) Big concrete rooms with big balconies staring at the sea, near At-Can's.

EATING & DRINKING

You'll find that restaurants in Sabang are, in a word, expensive.

McJim's (sandwiches P25, breakfasts P70, fried rice P60; 24hr) This basic fast-food shack next to Big Apple Dive Resort is a hit with peso pinchers. There's a second branch next to Action Divers on Small La Laguna Beach.

Tina's (mains P175-350) Way down at the east end of Sabang Beach, Tina's has some of the best food on the beachfront, although prices have gone up recently. Do try Tina's schnitzel.

Point Bar (10am-midnight) El Galleon's well-placed bar is the best spot for a sundowner, with a CD collection as colourful as the cocktails.

There are a few *turo-turo* and fast-food restaurants down the main road leading away from the Sabang beachfront. Try **Small Shot** (noodle dishes from P50) or **Happy Sam's** (burgers P99; 7am-3am) above the Tourist Center.

Puerto Galera Town

The town proper boasts a row of restaurants by Muelle Pier and some seriously cheap lodging in the noisy town centre. **Bahay Pilipino**

(☎ 422 0266; s/d P290/390) near the public market has simple clapboard rooms and a German restaurant on premises.

West Beaches

About 7km west of Puerto Galera are three neighbouring beaches. First up is overpriced, dirty **White Beach**. It's popular with Manila weekend warriors.

If you want to escape the girlie bars of Sabang, a much better option is the mellower, cleaner **Aninuan Beach**. It's almost entirely occupied by **Tamaraw Beach Resort** (☎ 0927 597 5588; www.tamarawbeachresort.com; r P800-2000;), a sprawling, full-service hotel with a few cosy cottages facing the beach. The cheaper rooms are in a large, concrete edifice.

At the end of the road is quiet, attractive **Talipanan Beach**, in the shadow of Mt Malasimbo (860m). It's worth the trip down here just to eat at **Luca's** (mains from P220; 7am-9pm). The Italian owner was a chef in his homeland before migrating to Puerto Galera, and the delicious food reflects that.

There are a few places to stay in Talipanan, the best of which is **Mountain Beach Resort** (☎ 0906 362 5406; mbeachresort@yahoo.com.ph; r P800-1500;) where the cottages have bamboo porches and partial sea views.

ROXAS

☎ 043 / pop 10,000

Roxas is a dusty little spot with ferry connections to Caticlan. The **Roxas Villa Hotel & Restaurant** (☎ 289 2026; roxasvillahotel@yahoo.com; Administration St; s/d from P350/450;) has basic rooms in the town centre.

Montenegro Shipping (☎ in Batangas 043-723 8294; 5 daily) and **Starlite** (☎ 289 2886; twice daily) sail to Catilcan (P330, four hours) from **Dangay Pier** (☎ 289 2813), about 3km from town. Crucially, there are seldom ferries between 11am and 4pm.

Vans to Calapan (P100, three hours) leave from Dangay pier and from Morente St near the town plaza.

THE VISAYAS

If it's white sand, rum and coconuts you're after, look no further than the jigsaw puzzle of central islands known as the Visayas. From party-mad Boracay and Cebu, to mountainous Leyte and Negros, to dreamy Siquijor and Malapascua, the Visayas has about everything an island nut could ask for. Hopping among paradisiacal, palm-fringed isles, you'll inevitably wonder why you can't go on doing this forever. Indeed, many foreigners *do* give it all up, take a local partner and live out their years managing this resort or that dive centre on some exquisite patch of white sand. Others end up simply extending their trip for months – or years. This is one area of the country where you can dispense with advance planning. Just board that first ferry and follow your nose.

Getting There & Around

All the major cities in the Visayas are well connected to Manila by both air and sea. Cebu City and ports in the southern Visayas have good ferry connections to Mindanao, including Surigao and Cagayan de Oro.

To travel to the Visayas overland from Luzon, head to Matnog on the southern tip of southeast Luzon, which is just a short ferry hop to Allen in northern Samar. From Allen, buses head south into Leyte, which is well connected by boat to Cebu and the rest of the central Visayas. Otherwise, you could enter the region via Roxas on Mindoro, a town that is connected by boat to Caticlan (see p639).

The six main islands of the Visayas – Panay, Negros, Cebu, Bohol, Leyte and Samar – are all linked to each other by a veritable armada of so-called 'fastcraft' ferries, with plenty of 'roll-on, roll-off' car ferries (ROROs), which follow in their wake. Cebu City is the Visayas' main hub, and has frequent ferry connections to all major and minor Visayan ports.

PANAY

The large, triangular island of Panay is where you'll enter the Visayas if taking the ferry from Mindoro. To most travellers, mainland Panay is just a large planet around which orbits diminutive party satellite Boracay island. Yet Panay has plenty to offer plucky independent travellers willing to part with their guidebooks for a few days, including decaying forts, Spanish churches, remote thatch-hut fishing villages and the mother of all Philippine fiestas, Kalibo's Mardi Gras–like **Ati-Atihan**, which peaks in the third week of January. Panay's capital and gateway to the rest of the Visayas is Iloilo, a five-hour bus ride south of Boracay.

THE VISAYAS

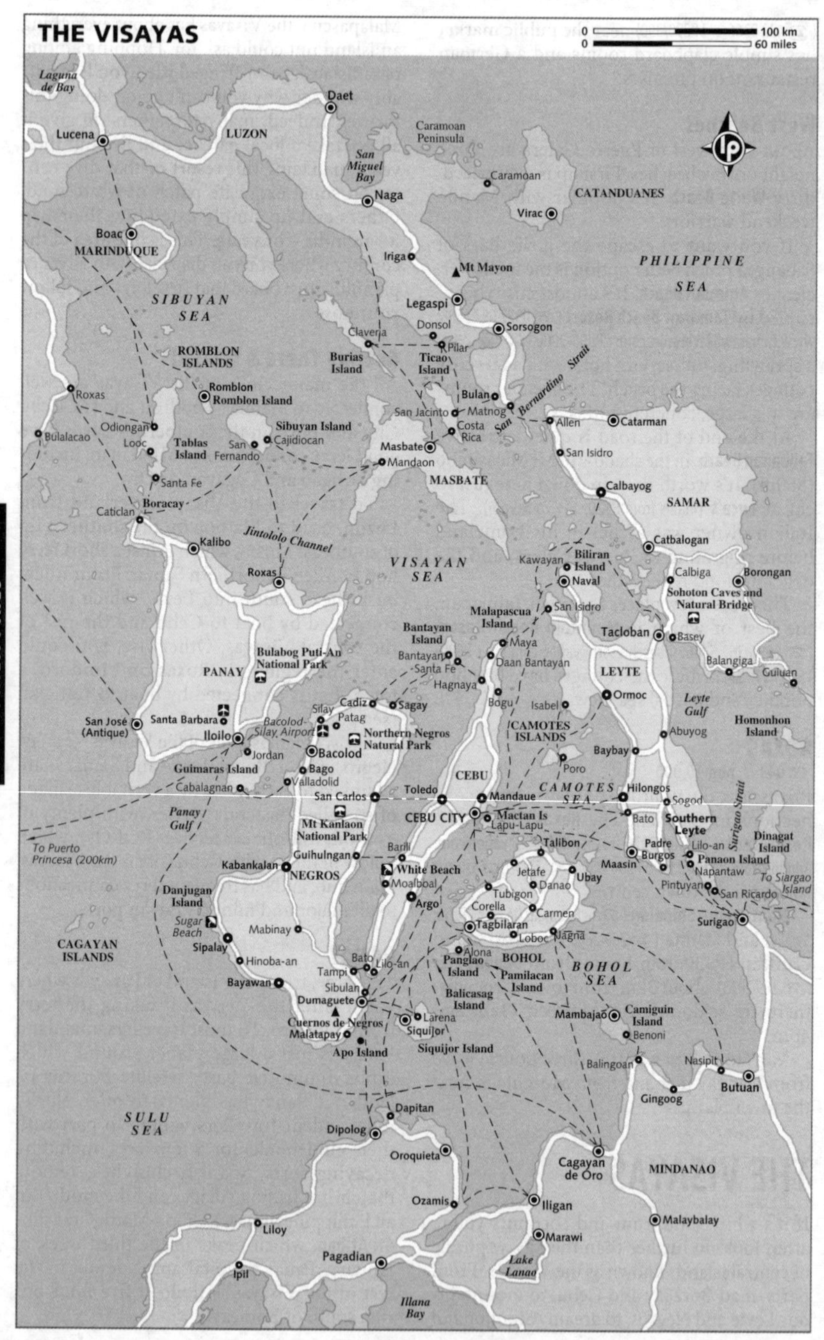
0 100 km
0 60 miles
Laguna de Bay
Daet
Lucena
LUZON
Caramoan Peninsula
San Miguel Bay
Caramoan
CATANDUANES
Naga
Virac
Boac
MARINDUQUE
Iriga
Mt Mayon
PHILIPPINE SEA
SIBUYAN SEA
Legaspi
Sorsogon
Donsol
Claveria
Pilar
ROMBLON ISLANDS
Burias Island
Ticao Island
San Bernardino Strait
Romblon
Romblon Island
Roxas
Bulan
Matnog
San Jacinto
Allen
Catarman
Odiongan
Sibuyan Island
Costa Rica
Bulalacao
Tablas Island
San Fernando
Cajidiocan
Looc
Masbate
San Isidro
Mandaon
Santa Fe
MASBATE
Calbayog
Boracay
SAMAR
Caticlan
Kalibo
Jintotolo Channel
Catbalogan
VISAYAN SEA
Kawayan
Biliran Island
Borongan
Roxas
Naval
Calbiga
Sohoton Caves and Natural Bridge
Malapascua Island
San Isidro
Bantayan Island
Maya
Tacloban
Basey
Bulabog Puti-An National Park
Bantayan
Santa Fe
Daan Bantayan
Balangiga
PANAY
Hagnaya
LEYTE
Guiuan
Bogu
Ormoc
Cadiz
Sagay
Isabel
Leyte Gulf
San José (Antique)
Santa Barbara
Silay
Patag
CAMOTES ISLANDS
Homonhon Island
Bacolod-Silay Airport
Northern Negros Natural Park
Abuyog
Iloilo
Jordan
Bacolod
Baybay
Guimaras Island
Bago
CEBU
Poro
Cabalagnan
Valladolid
Toledo
CAMOTES SEA
Hilongos
San Carlos
Mandaue
Sogod
Panay Gulf
CEBU CITY
Mactan Is
Lapu-Lapu
Bato
Southern Leyte
Surigao Strait
Mt Kanlaon National Park
To Puerto Princesa (200km)
Barili
Talibon
Padre Burgos
Lilo-an
Dinagat Island
Guihulngan
Maasin
Panaon Island
Kabankalan
White Beach
Jetafe
Ubay
Napantaw
NEGROS
Moalboal
Danao
To Siargao Island
Tubigon
Pintuyan
San Ricardo
Danjugan Island
Argo
Corella
Carmen
Surigao
Sugar Beach
Tagbilaran
Mabinay
Loboc
Jagna
Sipalay
CAGAYAN ISLANDS
Alona
Hinoba-an
Panglao Island
BOHOL
BOHOL SEA
Bato
Tampi
Lilo-an
Pamilacan Island
Bayawan
Sibulan
Balicasag Island
Dumaguete
Mambajao
Camiguin Island
Larena
Cuernos de Negros
Siquijor
Benoni
Malatapay
Apo Island
Siquijor Island
Balingoan
Nasipit
Butuan
Gingoog
Dapitan
SULU SEA
Dipolog
Oroquieta
Cagayan de Oro
MINDANAO
Ozamis
Iligan
Malaybalay
Liloy
Marawi
Lake Lanao
Pagadian
Ipil
Illana Bay

Boracay

☎ 036 / pop 9800

With a postcard-perfect, 3km-long white beach on its résumé and the country's best island nightlife, it's not hard to figure out why Boracay is the country's top tourist draw. Overdevelopment has made some old-timers long for the halcyon days of no electricity, but the debate about whether it's better now or was better then won't worry you too much when you're digging your feet into the sand on White Beach and taking in the Philippines' most famous sunset. Parasails, seabirds, Frisbees and *paraw* (small *bangka* sailboats) cut across the technicolour horizon, while palm trees whisper in the breeze and reggae wafts through the air. Oh yeah, and you're in a beachfront bar that's generously serving you two-for-one cocktails. Yes, even 'developed' Boracay remains a master mixologist of that mellow island vibe.

ORIENTATION

Most of the action is on White Beach, where three out-of-service 'boat stations' orient visitors. The area south of Station 3 most resembles the less-developed 'old Boracay' and is where most of the budget accommodation is located. The stretch between Station 1 and Station 3 is busy and commercial. Most top-end accommodation is on an incredible stretch of beach north of Station 3.

INFORMATION

BPI (D'mall) and **Metrobank** (D'mall) have the only viable ATM machines on Boracay. Both have additional ATMs on the main road.

Boracay Island Municipal Hospital (☎ 288 3041; 24hr) Off the main road, behind Boat Station 2.

Tourist Center (9am-11pm; Station 3) Private company offering a range of services, including internet access, postal services and money-changing facilities (including Amex travellers cheques). Also sells plane tickets and posts ferry schedules.

ACTIVITIES

On Boracay you can try your hand at a stupendous array of sporting pursuits, including **paraw rides** (per hr P500), **diving**, **windsurfing** and **parasailing**. From December to March, consistent winds, shallow water and good prices (about US$350 for a 12-hour certification course) make Bulabog Beach on the east side of the island the perfect place to learn kitesurfing. The action shifts to White Beach during the less consistent May-to-October SW monsoon season. Operators include **Hangin** (www.kite-asia.com), **Islakite** (www.islakite.com) and **Habagat** (www.kitebo racay.com).

Daily games of **football**, **volleyball** and **ultimate Frisbee** kick off in the late afternoon on White Beach.

SLEEPING

Head south of Station 3 for the lower prices and mellow island vibe of yesteryear. Rates drop about 20% in the low season (November to May). Bargaining might bear fruit at any time of year.

South of Station 3

Tree House (☎ 288 4386; treehouse_damario@yahoo.com.ph; dm P200, d P1200-3500; air-con) Proprietor Mario offers a wide variety of rooms spread across two complexes. The four-bed dorm rooms, behind Da Mario's tasty Italian restaurant, are the island's cheapest crash pads.

LM Beach Resort (☎ 288 3537; coffe_827@yahoo.com; r P800-1500) Spick-and-span bathrooms, TVs and comfortable porches add value to the rooms here. It's close to a particularly mellow stretch of White Beach.

Walk-in guests are advised to walk beyond Station 3 to a cluster of about 10 resorts located up a path behind Arwana. Cheapest (and furthest from the beach) is **Bora Bora Inn** (☎ 288 3186; r P700-1500; air-con), while co-managed **Dave's Straw Hat Inn** (☎ 288 5465; www.davesstrawhatinn.com; r P1000-2000; air-con internet wi-fi) and **Arwana Hotel** (☎ 288 1530, 0917-716 8647; www.arwanabeachresort.com; r from P1400; air-con wi-fi) are cosiest and most stylish. Other good options here are **The Orchids** (☎ 288 3313; www.orchidsboracay.com; r P915-2350; air-con wi-fi), also with wi-fi, and **Escurel** (☎ 288 3611, 0928-341 1911; r P1000-1500; air-con). Haggle hard at all of the above.

Blue Mango Inn (☎ 288 6954; www.bluemangoinn.com; d incl breakfast from P3000; air-con internet wi-fi) The attractive, recently renovated rooms (some with ocean views) are worth a splurge. Divers doing courses net huge discounts on rooms, and rates drop big-time for all comers in the low season.

North of Station 3

Frendz Resort (☎ 288 3803, 0928-728 7436; frendzresort@hotmail.com; Station 1; dm P500, r P1800-2500; internet wi-fi) Frendz has tidy, although somewhat overpriced, dorm rooms.

our pick **Villa Lourdes** (☎ 288 3448; www.villalourdesboracay.com; D'Mall; r P700-1700; air-con) Incongruously

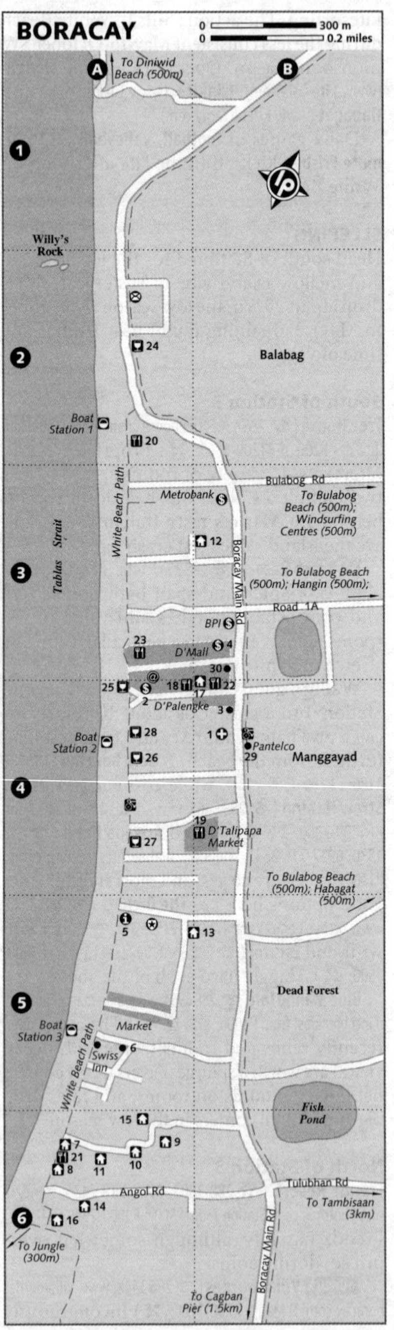

INFORMATION
Boracay Island Municipal Hospital....1 B4
BPI....2 A4
Bureau of Immigration....3 B4
Metrobank....4 B3
Tourist Center....5 A5

SIGHTS & ACTIVITIES
Boracay Nutria Water....6 A5

SLEEPING
Arwana Hotel....7 A6
Blue Mango Inn....8 A6
Bora Bora Inn....9 A6
Dave's Straw Hat Inn....10 A6
Escurel....11 A6
Frendz Resort....12 B3
Jung's House Resort....13 B5
LM Beach Resort....14 A6
Orchids....15 A6
Tree House....16 A6
Villa Lourdes....17 B4

EATING
Cyma....18 A4
Plato D'Boracay....19 B4
Real Coffee & Tea Café....20 A2
RNRC....21 A6
Smoke....22 B4
Smoke....23 A3

DRINKING
Arwana Hotel....(see 7)
Cocamangas....24 A2
Hey Jude....25 A4
Juice....26 A4
Nigi Nigi Nu Noos....27 A4
Summer Place....28 A4

TRANSPORT
PAL Express....29 B4
Seair....(see 23)
Zest Air....30 B3

tucked away in D'Mall is this shoestringer delight, with seven simple but spacious *nipa* huts. P1000 nets you a kitchen on your private balcony.

Jung's House Resort (☎ 288 5420; Station 2; r with fan/air-con P700/1000;) The Korean owner offers up the island's cheapest air-con rooms in a concrete edifice about 150m in from the beach.

EATING

You'll find the best deals on Filipino food near two wet markets: D'Palengke in the southeast corner of D'Mall, and D'Talipapa near Station 2. Of course, it's worth paying a bit more for the ambience of White Beach – just stroll along until you see something that takes your fancy.

RNRC (meals P75-110) The cheapest food on the beach is served on the sand in front of this fast-food and barbecue shack.

our pick **Smoke** (mains P85-110; 9am-6am) Now with two branches on opposite ends of D'Mall, Smoke is Boracay's best value, with freshly cooked Filipino food, appetising coconut-milk curries and a P70 Filipino breakfast.

Real Coffee & Tea Cafe (Station 1; breakfasts P100-200) This cafe has, believe it or not, real coffee and tea as well as yummy sandwiches, fresh fruit shakes and baked goods.

Plato D'Boracay (D'Talipapa; seafood per kg P100-150) The lobster, prawns and other shellfish at this family-style seafood grill come straight from the adjoining market; prices reflect the reduced transport costs.

Cyma (288 4283; D'Mall; mains P150-300) This Greek restaurant is known for grilled meat, appetisers such as flaming *saganaki* (fried salty cheese) and outstanding salads. Affordable gyros are available for thriftier diners.

DRINKING

Bars range from peaceful, beachfront cocktail affairs where you can sip a mai tai while you watch the sunset, to throbbing discos on the sand.

our pick **Jungle** (happy hr 5-7pm) With a relatively isolated location at the south end of White Beach, funky wooden bar and furniture, hammocks, daily sunset bongo jam sessions, full-moon parties and the legendary 'F*** you Archie' cocktail, this new bar best captures the spirit of the 'old Boracay'.

Nigi Nigi Nu Noos (Station 2; happy hr 5-7pm) The legendary mason jars of Long Island iced tea – they're two-for-one during happy hour – more than capably kick-start any evening.

Arwana (beer P30) It's happy hour all day here, and that means Boracay's cheapest San Miguel on demand.

Three open-air bars near Station 2 dominate the late-night scene: **Hey Jude** (9am-late) is the swankiest of the lot and has the best DJs; **Summer Place** (11am-late) begins the evening as a Mongolian barbecue and ends it as White Beach's rowdiest disco; and relative newbie **Juice** (11am-late) is the most reliable late-night option.

If those are dead you can usually count on notorious **Cocamangas** (11am-late; Main Rd) to have a mixed crowd.

GETTING THERE & AWAY

To get to Boracay you must first travel to Caticlan. From Caticlan small *bangka* ferries shuttle you to Boracay's Cagban pier (P125 including terminal and environmental fee, 15 minutes). Tricycles from Cagban pier cost P100 per tricycle, or P20 per person, regardless of your destination.

Air

Cebu Pacific, **PAL Express** (Pantelco Bldg, Main Rd), **Seair** (D'Mall) and **Zest Air** (D'Mall) have flights from Manila to Caticlan at least every hour until late afternoon, while Cebu Pacific (two daily) and PAL Express (one daily) ply the Cebu–Caticlan route. However, in July 2009 all flights to Caticlan except those of Seair (which uses smaller planes) were suspended indefinitely and rerouted to nearby Kalibo due to safety concerns. Regular flights to Caticlan should be restored by early 2010, but nothing's certain.

Regardless of what happens in Caticlan, flights to Kalibo will remain a cheaper alternative to flying to Caticlan. Air-con vans meet flights in Kalibo and run to Caticlan pier (P100, one hour).

From Caticlan airport to Caticlan pier is a five-minute walk or a one-minute tricycle ride (P40).

Boat

Caticlan is well connected by ferry to Roxas, Mindoro (see p635).

Bus

Ceres Lines has hourly buses to Iloilo from Caticlan, the last one departing at 5pm (ordinary/air-con P280/330, 5½ hours). Save time by taking a speedier, more frequent van to Kalibo and grabbing a bus from there to Iloilo.

GETTING AROUND

To get from one end of White Beach to the other, either walk or flag down a tricycle along the main road. These cost only P7 provided you steer clear of the disingenuously named 'special' trips offered by stationary tricycles, which cost a not-so-special P40 to P60.

> **THRIFT TIP**
>
> Save the environment – and plenty of money – by refilling plastic water bottles at filling stations dotted along Boracay's main road. Closer to the beach, near Station 3, is **Boracay Nutria Water** (1L refill P7).

Iloilo

☎ 033 / pop 419,000

Panay's bustling capital is a pleasant enough stopover on the Boracay–Negros route. **Museo Iloilo** (Bonifacio Dr; admission P15; 9am-5pm Mon-Sat) has a worthwhile display on Panay's indigenous *ati* (negrito) people and a collection of old *piña* (pineapple fibre) weavings, for which the area is famous. Next door is the **tourist office** (☎ 337 5411; Bonifacio Dr). Adventure lovers should talk to anthropologist Daisy at **Panay Adventures** (☎ 0918 778 4364; panay_adventures@yahoo.com.ph), which organises mountain bike trips on nearby Guimaras Island, climbing and caving in Bulabog Puti-An National Park, and ecocultural tours to visit tribal groups around Panay.

SLEEPING & EATING

Family Pension House (☎ 335 0070; familypension@yahoo.com; General Luna St; s P275, d P350-575;) Backpackers love this homey riverside neoclassical building with polished floorboards and clean, bargain-basement rooms. It's popular so book ahead.

If that's booked out there's bare-bones **Eros Travellers Pensionne** (☎ 337 1359; Gen Luna St; s/d from P370/445) or classy **Highway 21** (☎ 335 1839; General Luna St; s/d from P725/850;).

Iloilo's vibrant restaurant and entertainment scene is centred just north of the centre in the **Smallville Complex** (Diversion Rd). Try the superb **Bluejay Coffee & Delicatessen** (sandwiches P100-150; 8am-midnight;), with free wi-fi and imported-meat sandwiches. There's another branch at the corner of Gen Luna St and Jalandoni St. **SM City Mall** (Diversion Rd) and **Atrium Shopping Mall** (Gen Luna St) have food courts.

GETTING THERE & AROUND

There are many daily flights to and from Manila with Zest Air, Cebu Pacific and PAL. The latter two also have daily flights to/from Cebu. The brand-new **airport** is 15km north of town in Santa Barbara. Take a jeepney or van from the Travellers Lounge at SM City Mall.

Fastcraft operators Sea Jet, Oceanjet and Weesam Express, based at Iloilo's central Muelle Pier, take on the rough crossing between Iloilo and Bacolod (P290, one hour, 20 daily).

Milagrosa Shipping (☎ 335 0955; La Puz Norte Pier) and **Montenegro Shipping** (☎ in Puerto Princesa 048-434 9344; www.montenegrolines.com.ph) sail weekly between Iloilo and Puerto Princesa (P1220, 30 hours).

From the Fort San Pedro Pier, Negros Navigation (five weekly) and SuperFerry (two weekly) have ferries to Manila (from P1600, 21 hours). For boats to Cebu see p647. SuperFerry has weekly services to Cagayan de Oro (14 hours, P2000).

Ceres buses to Caticlan leave every hour until 3pm from the **Tagbac Bus Terminal** (☎ 320 3163), about 7km north of the centre. Alternatively, take a bus to Kalibo (P224, four hours, every 30 minutes until 5pm) and grab an air-con van there.

NEGROS

If any Visayan island can boast to have it all it is surely Negros. Here you'll find one of the country's top dive spots (Apo Island), one of the top remote beaches (Sipalay) and one of the top treks (volcanic Mt Kanlaon). The heavily forested interior, besides being a major biodiversity hotbed, provides a stunning backdrop for drives around the island. Along the west coast, sprawling, bright green sugarcane fields abut the shimmering waters of the Sulu Sea. Lovely, laid-back Dumaguete makes a fine base for exploring it all.

Bacolod

☎ 034 / pop 500,000

Bacolod is a little too large and intractable to be of much appeal. The city boomed in the 19th century when Iloilo's clothing industry collapsed and the textile barons migrated across the Panay Gulf to try their luck at sugar. Locals masquerade in grinning masks for October's **MassKara Festival**.

ACTIVITIES

The main reason to stay in Bacolod is to get permits for protected areas scattered around Negros. The main attraction is **Mt Kanlaon National Park** where the Visayas' highest peak (2645m) lurks. Permits (P300) can be obtained at the **Protected Area Superintendent Office** (☎ weekdays 433 3813, weekends 0917 301 1410; eioibibar@yahoo.com; DENR-PENRO compound, off South Capitol Rd). Access to the mountain is tightly controlled and guides (P500 per day) are mandatory, so reserve ahead. There are three routes to the top, one of which can be done by fit climbers in a day. The climbing seasons are March to May and October to November.

PHILIPPINES

The trekking is at least as good in bird-infested **Northern Negros Natural Park**, accessible from Patag, a small town 32km east of Silay. The **Silay Tourism Office** (☎ 495 5553) can help you get a guide, or just ask around in Patag. The **Biodiversity Conservation Center** (☎ 433 9234; South Capitol Rd; 9am-5pm Mon-Sat) has information on the natural park and also runs a small zoo. It shares an office with the **Philippine Reef & Rainforest Resource Conservation Foundation** (PRRCF; ☎ 432 1260, 0909 207 3865; www.prrcf.org), which manages Danjugan Island (see below).

SLEEPING & EATING

Pension Bacolod (☎ 433 3377; 27 11th St; s P185-490, d P245-600;) Look no further than this professionally run bargain, with a diverse array of rooms on a quiet side street near the Ceres north bus terminal. Mice reportedly like this place too.

Café Bob's (cnr Lacson Ave & 21st St; sandwiches P75-175; 8am-midnight;) In a cluster of hip restaurants north of the city is this clean, bright, coffee shop/deli/pizzeria/ice cream parlour with free wi-fi.

About 3km south of the centre, the city's nightlife centres around the once-blighted, now-flashy **Goldenfield's Commercial Complex**, where you'll find a gaggle of bars, restaurants, nightclubs and a casino.

GETTING THERE & AWAY

Cebu Pacific and PAL each have a couple flights per day to/from Manila and Cebu. PAL Express serves Cebu twice daily. Zest Air flies daily to Manila.

For info on fastcraft ferries to Iloilo see opposite. Iloilo-bound ferries call in at the Bredco Port, near SM Mall about 1km west of the centre.

From the **Ceres north bus terminal** (☎ 433 4993; cnr Lopez Jaena St & IV Ferrer Ave) there are frequent buses to San Carlos (P160, 3½ hours), where four daily ferries depart for Toledo, Cebu. Morning buses to Cebu (P650, seven hours) also take this ferry.

From the **Ceres south bus terminal** (☎ 434 2386; cnr Lopez Jaena & San Sebastian Sts), buses run regularly until 7pm to Dumaguete (P255, 5½ hours) via Kabankalan, and until mid-evening to Sipalay (P170, five hours).

Danjugan Island

Off-limits for years, this wonderful, wildlife-rich **island** (admission incl transport & lunch P1500, overnight incl admission, transport & full board for 1st/subsequent nights P2500/2000) reopened to the public in 2009. It's a truly special spot, with seven lagoons to be explored, hiking trails, isolated beaches, bats, sea eagles and a host of more exotic creatures. There's sea kayaking, exceptional snorkelling and a dive centre on premises.

Danjugan makes a wonderful day trip from Sipalay, or you can spend one or several nights on mattresses in a big open-air cabana near the ranger base station. Call Ramie of the PRRCF in Bacolod (opposite) to arrange a *bangka* pick-up in Bulata, about 15km north of Sipalay. Any Sipalay-Bacolod bus can drop you off in Bulata.

Sipalay

☎ 034 / pop 11,275

You could get stuck for days – make that months – in this remote fishing town on Negros' southwest edge. At delicious Sugar Beach a small outcrop of resorts caters to those looking to achieve the full Robinson Crusoe effect. The town proper has an endless beach where every morning fishermen unload their catches, which can include several-hundred-pound tuna. Divers should head 6km south of Sipalay to the pricier resorts of *barangay* (village) Punta Ballo.

SLEEPING

The following are all on Sugar Beach.

our pick **Driftwood Village** (☎ 920 900 3663; www.driftwood-village.com; cottages P400-1100;) Hosts Daisy and Peter (he's Swiss) are a lot of fun, and so is their resort, which features a dozen cosy *nipa* huts, good Thai food and a range of bar sports, including table football.

Sulu Sunset (☎ 0919 716 7182; www.sulusunset.com; r P400-950) The cheapest rooms here are open-air 'tree-houses' – lofts actually – accessible by ladder. The bigger cottages are great value. It's at the less-appealing far end of the beach.

Takatuka Lodge & Dive Resort (☎ 0920 230 9174; www.takatuka-lodge.com; cottages P850-1550;) Awash in funky furniture, psychedelic colours and kitsch, this eclectic boutique offers five rooms done up in different themes.

GETTING THERE & AWAY

Ceres buses to/from Bacolod leave every half-hour until evening (P170, 4½ hours). For Dumaguete, see p642.

Sugar Beach is about 5km north of Sipalay proper, across two rivers. Arrange a boat transfer from your resort from Sipalay proper (per boat P300 to P400, 15 minutes), or disembark from the Bacolod–Sipalay bus in *barangay* Montilla and take a tricycle to *barangay* Nauhang (P100, 15 minutes), where small paddleboats bring you across the river to Sugar Beach for P10.

Dumaguete

☎035 / pop 116,000

There are only a few Philippine provincial cities worth more than a day of your time, and Dumaguete (doo-ma-*get*-ay) is one of them. A huge college campus engulfs much of its centre, saturating the city with youthful energy and attitude. The location – in the shadow of twin-peaked Cuernos de Negros (1903m) and just a few clicks from some marvellous hiking, beaches and diving – takes care of the rest.

Perdices St is the main commercial drag, but most dining, drinking and strolling happens on and around the attractive waterfront promenade flanking Rizal Blvd. The **Anthropology Museum** (Hibbard Ave; admission free; 8am-noon & 2-5pm Mon-Fri) on the campus of Siliman University is worth a look on a rainy day.

ACTIVITIES

The Dumaguete area boasts top-notch diving, hiking, caving and many other adventures.

Apo Island (opposite) is the big draw for underwater breathers. For your diving needs try **Scuba Ventures** (☎225 7716; www.divedumaguete.com; Hibbard Ave) under Harold's Mansion. Open-water dive certification courses cost a very reasonable US$300.

> **COCKSURE GAMBLERS**
>
> Heavy male drinking and bonding occur over gambling – on anything from *sabong* (cockfights) to horse racing. But *sabong* are what Filipino men get most excited about. All over the country, every Sunday and public holiday, irritable and expensive fighting birds are let loose on one another. The cockpits are full to bursting and the audience is high with excitement – as much as P100,000 may be wagered on a big fight. All this plus cheap booze, lots of guns, pimps, players and prostitutes make for an interesting life for police.

Back on terra firma you'll find caving, rock climbing and trekking on Cuernos de Negros and around the **Twin Lakes**, north of Dumaguete near Bais. Michelle and Chad at **Dumaguete Outdoors** (☎226 2110; www.dumaguete outdoors.com; 3 Noblefranca St) arrange tours and dispense advice.

SLEEPING

Vintage Inn (☎225 1076; Surban St; s/d from P242/352;) Cheap is the name of the game at this centrally located option opposite the market. Rooms are simple, clean and mostly windowless, which tempers the noise outside.

Harold's Mansion (☎225 8000; www.haroldsmansion.com; 205 Hibbard Ave; dm/s/d from P280/330/415;) With free coffee, wi-fi, a roomy six-bed dorm room and a down-to-earth owner who runs cool tours, Harold's deserves its immense popularity among independent travellers.

Bethel Guest House (☎225 2000; www.bethelguesthouse.com; Rizal Blvd; s/d from P850/1000;) This big, bright, sea-facing property with spacious rooms, giant TVs, wi-fi and all the mod-cons is a worthwhile splurge.

EATING & DRINKING

Qyosko (cnr Santa Rosa & Perdices Sts; mains P50-85; 24hr;) A budget traveller's dream, this spot serves up hot Filipino dishes, free wi-fi, and delicious shakes and coffee from its adjoining coffee shop.

Hayahay (Flores St; mains P100-250; lunch & dinner) In a cluster of bars and restaurants on the waterfront 2km north of Why Not, Hayahay is known for delicious fresh seafood and rockin' reggae Wednesdays.

Why Not (☎225 4488; Rizal Blvd; mains P150-200) The continental and Thai food here is wildly popular among foreigners, but Why Not is most famous for its always-happening nightclub.

There's a pair of noteworthy eateries just west of Rizal Blvd on San Juan St. **Persian Palate** (dishes P95-175; lunch & dinner) has plenty of vegetarian options among its line-up of Middle Eastern staples. Alcohol-free **Café Antonio** (mains P50-100) is a student favourite upstairs in an exquisite Spanish-era building.

GETTING THERE & AWAY

Cebu Pacific and PAL fly several times daily to/from Manila. Cebu Pacific has a daily flight to Cebu.

OceanJet fastcraft go to/from Cebu (P900, four hours, twice daily) via Tagbilaran (P650, two hours) on Bohol. There are also RORO ferries to Cebu (see p647). For Siquijor, see right. SuperFerry has a Sunday ferry to Cagayan de Oro and a Wednesday ferry to Manila via Cebu.

From the nearby port of Sibulan, frequent fastcraft (P60) and *bangkas* (P47) alternate trips to Lilo-an on Cebu island (25 minutes), from where there are buses to Cebu City and Moalboal.

Ceres Bus Lines (Perdices St) connects Dumaguete and Bacolod (P255, 5½ hours, hourly).

Getting to Sipalay requires three separate Ceres buses: Dumaguete–Bayawan (two hours), Bayawan–Hinoba-an (1½ hours) and Hinoba-an–Sipalay (45 minutes). Connections are easy. The entire trip costs P200 and takes 4½ to 5½ hours.

Apo Island

☎ 035 / pop 745

For a taste of small-village life on an isolated island, it's hard to beat this coral-fringed charmer off the coast of southern Negros. It's also one of the Philippines' best snorkelling spots.

Most people visit on day trips from Dauin or Dumaguete (diving/snorkelling trips about P2900/1600 per person including two dives), but thrifty souls will fare better staying in one of the island's two resorts. **Liberty's Community Lodge** (☎ 424 0888, 0920 238 5704; liberty_apoisland@yahoo.com; dm/s/d from P300/900/1150) in the village proper has a dormitory and transfers guests to the island for P300 per person. Around the point from Liberty's, the more stylish **Apo Island Beach Resort** (☎ 225 5490, 0910 219 3359; www.apoislandresort.com; dm P350-600, r P1800-2500) has a lovely secret cove all to itself. You'll really feel like you're away from it all here. Both resorts offer diving. There are also homestays available on the island for P500.

Getting to Apo cheaply is somewhat problematic. A couple of *bangka*s depart the island for Malatapay, 18km south of Dumaguete, around 7am and return around 3pm (P250, 45 minutes), but they are not all licensed to take tourists. Chartering a five-passenger *bangka* costs P1700.

SIQUIJOR

☎ 035 / pop 87,700

Spooky Siquijor is renowned for its witches and healers, but don't be scared away. This is backpacker paradise, with breathtaking scenery and some of the best-value accommodation in the Philippines. With your own transport you can travel around the island in a day and explore beaches, colonial relics, waterfalls, caves and charming villages.

A good strategy is to arrange for motorbike hire (per day P350) at the pier in Siquijor town when you arrive and investigate accommodation options on your own. The best budget places are in **Sandugan**, 15km northeast of Siquijor town. The best beaches and a few good midrange lodging options are along the west coast at **Solangon**, 9km southwest of Siquijor town.

Sleeping

Guiwanon Spring Park Resort (☎ 0905 390 8516; cottages P250-350) The three cottages here are essentially stilted, overwater tree houses in the middle of a mangrove reserve. They are very basic, but two of them directly face the ocean. This is certainly one of the quirkiest lodging experiences you'll ever have. Look for the hard-to-spot sign on the left about 5km east of Siquijor town.

Just east of Siquijor town are two excellent budget options if you don't mind being off the beach: **Swiss Stars Guest House** (☎ 480 5583; National Hwy; r P350-850; 💻), which also has an incredibly affordable restaurant; and **Das Traum** (☎ 480 9117; r P250-700; ❄), with homey digs boasting plenty of space and blond-wood floors. Das Traum has a cafe at the pier offering motorbike rental and other useful services.

Coral Cay Resort (☎ 0919 269 1269; www.coralcayresort.com; d P750-2700; ❄ 🏊) This fine resort has lavish rooms on a perfect stretch of white-sand beach at Solangon. The beachfront cottage suites are practically lapped by waves and at P1700 are a steal. There's a sweet pool, mountain-bike rental, sea kayaks and a thatch-hut gym.

In Sandugan the two best options are beachfront **Kiwi Dive Resort** (☎ 424 0534; www.kiwidiveresort.com; r P450-990; ❄ 💻 📶), which has wi-fi, and **Hard Rock Cottages** (☎ 0926 278 6070; www.hardrockcottages.com; cottages P600-700), with wonderful hillside cottages staring at the sea.

Getting There & Around

The vast majority of visitors arrive at the pier in Siquijor town via diminutive fastcraft from Dumaguete. Delta and OceanJet ply the route (P160, one hour, five total trips daily). GL

Shipping and Montenegro Lines follow with slower RORO ferries (P100); Montenegro adds a daily trip to Larena, 9km northeast of Siquijor town. Palacio Shipping services Tagbilaran from Larena (P180 to P280, 3½ hours, three weekly), while Cokaliong has a Monday night ferry from Larena to Cebu via Tagbilaran.

Jeepneys meet ferries at the pier and run to all points on the perimeter of the island.

CEBU

Surrounded on all sides by the Philippine isles and dotted with tranquil fishing villages, Cebu is the island heart of the Visayas. Cebuanos are proud of their heritage – it is here that Magellan sowed the seed of Christianity and was pruned for his efforts at the hands of the mighty chief Lapu-Lapu. The island's booming metropolis, Cebu City, is a transport hub to pretty much anywhere you may wish to go. Pescador Island, near the laid-back town of Moalboal, placed Philippine diving on the world map, while the Malapascua marine scene boasts close encounters of the thresher-shark kind.

Cebu City

☎ 032 / pop 799,000

The island capital is much more laid-back than Manila as a place to arrive in or leave the Philippines. One of the first stops on Spain's conquest agenda, Cebu lays claim to everything old – including the oldest street (Colon St), the oldest university and the oldest fort. By night Cebu turns decidedly hedonistic. However, the excellent transport links to the rest of the Philippines are the city's biggest attraction.

Cebu's downtown district (Map p645) is its mercantile nucleus. Most of the sights are here, but you must wade through exhaust fumes, beggars, prostitutes and block after block of downmarket retail madness to get to them. Uptown (Map p646) is much more pleasant and has better accommodation, mostly near the central Fuente Osmeña roundabout. **Mactan Island**, where Magellan came a distant second in a fight with Chief Lapu-Lapu, is now the site of Cebu's airport and is joined to the city by a bridge.

INFORMATION

There are plenty of internet cafes and ATMs around Fuente Osmeña.

Cebu Doctors Hospital (Map p646; ☎ 253 7511; Pres Osmeña Blvd)
Central post office (Map p645; Quezon Blvd)
Department of Tourism Region VII Office (Map p645; ☎ 254 2811; LDM Bldg, Legazpi St; 🕑 7.30am-5.30pm Mon-Fri) Informative office has great maps of Cebu City and other Visayan locales.
Fully Booked (off Map p646; The Terraces, Ayala Center) Manila's best bookstore is now in Cebu.
HSBC Bank (off Map p646; Cardinal Rosales Ave) Allows P40,000 ATM withdrawals and cashes travellers cheques; opposite Ayala Center.

SIGHTS

Most sights worth seeing are downtown within walking distance of **Fort San Pedro** (Map p645; Legazpi St; adult/child P21/13; 🕑 8am-7pm). This gently crumbling ruin, built by Miguel Legazpi in 1565, is the oldest Spanish fort in the country. West of here, the sprawling **Carbon Market** (Map p645) is a boisterous, cacophonous frenzy that seemingly never sleeps. It's a must for market lovers. Nearby, the **Basilica Minore del Santo Niño** (Map p645; Juan Luna St), built in 1740, houses a revered statuette of the Christ child (Santo Niño). People line up for hours to pray in front of the icon, which dates to Magellan's time.

A bit north of the church, the **Casa Gorordo Museum** (Map p645; ☎ 255 5630; 35 L Jaena St; adult/student P70/50; 🕑 10am-6pm Tue-Sun), in an astonishingly beautiful ancestral house, offers a glimpse into upper-class life in Cebu in the 19th century.

For a more adrenaline-fuelled experience, ascend the 40-storey Crown Regency Hotel and take a spin on the **Edge Coaster** (Map p646; www.skyexperienceadventure.com; Osmeña Blvd; admission for 2 before/after 6pm P500/250; 🕑 2pm-midnight Mon-Fri, 10am-midnight Sat & Sun), which gradually circles

GETTING INTO TOWN

Airport taxis from Mactan International Airport to Cebu City cost a flat P295, or you can cross the street outside the arrivals area, climb the stairs and look for a rank of metered taxis. Taking public transport is complicated but possible; ask the tourist desk in the arrival hall for directions.

To get uptown from the ports, catch one of the jeepneys that pass by the piers to Pres Osmeña Blvd, then transfer to a jeepney going uptown.

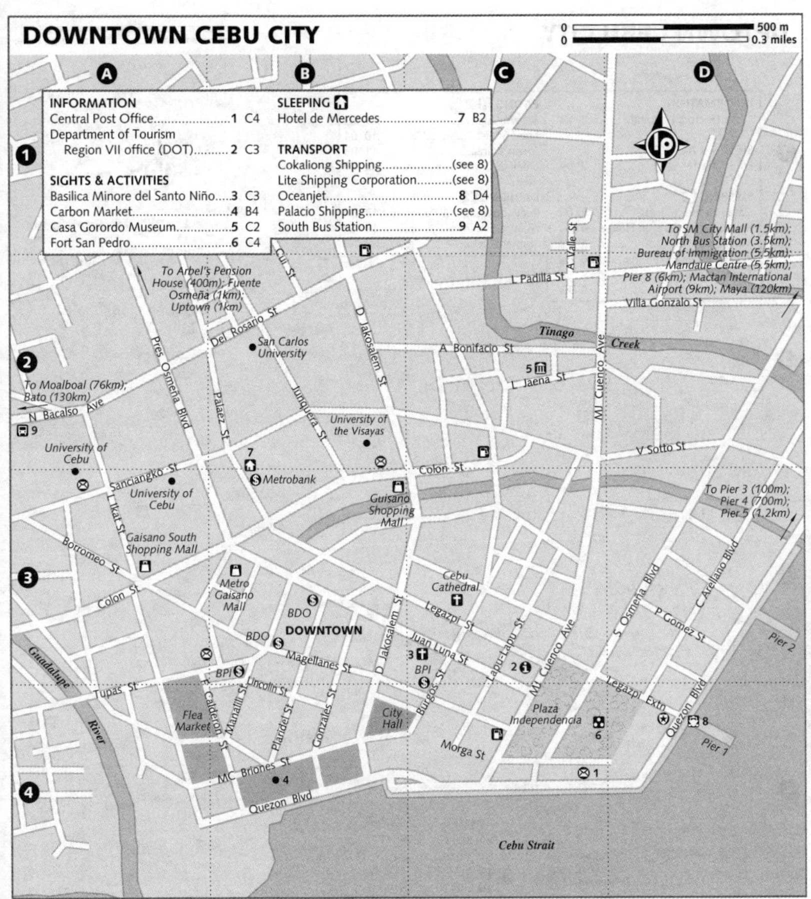

the hotel's roof in carts tilted forward over the edge of the building. Or make your way to JY Square Mall (off Map p646), where motorcycle taxis depart for the thrilling 30-minute ride (round trip P300) to the **Tops lookout point** (off Map p646; admission P100) 600m above Cebu.

SLEEPING

Passable super-budget rooms are practically non-existent in Cebu. Snoot around downtown in the commercial district and you might turn up a double for P200 to P300, but it won't be pretty. It's worth spending a couple of hundred extra pesos to be uptown.

Arbel's Pension House (off Map p646; ☎ 253 5303; 57 Pres Osmeña Blvd; s/d/tr from P300/400/500; ❄) This is about as cheap as it gets in Cebu without venturing into 'disgusting' territory. Rooms are predictably basic but at least they have windows and the location is relatively quiet.

our pick **Kukuk's Nest Pension House** (Map p646; ☎ 231 5180; www.geocities.com/kukuksnestcebu; 157 Gorordo Ave; s P330, d P430-730; ❄ 💻 📶) This colourful old house defines 'quirky', with contemporary art hanging about, a resident armless charcoal sketcher and a 24-hour resto-bar that draws all types. Booking ahead is essential.

Villa de Mercedes (Map p646; ☎ 253 3320; villademercedescebu@yahoo.com; 366 Orchid St; d P610-1300, tr P745-960; ❄) This is a no-nonsense option near the Capitol Compound. For well less than P1000 you get two or three beds in a clean, simple, generously sized room. Breakfast costs P85.

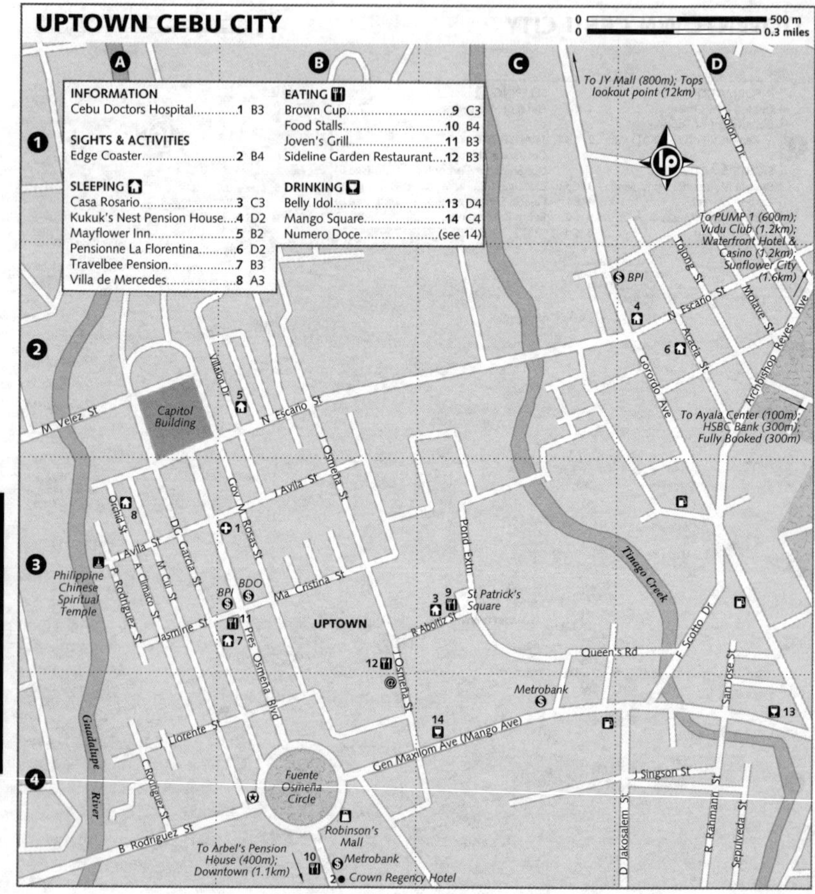

Mayflower Inn (Map p646; ☎ 255 2800; http://mayflowerinn.multiply.com; Villalon Dr; s/d/tr P900/1250/1700;) The rooms are spacious, the soundproofing is tight and the earthy-toned paint is meticulously applied at this clean and modern gem.

Also recommended:

Travelbee Pension (Map p646; ☎ 253 1005; travelbeepension@yahoo.com; d P400-900;) No-frills option with mostly windowless rooms.

Hotel de Mercedes (Map p645; ☎ 253 1105; 7 Pelaez St; s/d from P634/860;) Good downtown choice with wide range of rooms.

Pensionne La Florentina (Map p646; ☎ 232 6738; 18 Acacia St; r P800;) Quiet digs in a stately wooden house.

Casa Rosario (Map p646; ☎ 253 5134; R Aboitiz St; r P1100-1400;) Cebu's best midrange option.

EATING

Sideline Garden Restaurant (Map p646; J Osmeña St; mains P75-175) The smell of fresh seafood being grilled under a large pagoda heralds the presence of this charming streetside eatery. Equally pleasant for eating or drinking.

Joven's Grill (Map p646; cnr Pres Osmeña Blvd & Jasmine St; all-you-can-eat buffet P165; lunch & dinner) The best place to gorge after an extended boat journey.

As is the case in Manila, many of the best restaurants are in the malls, particularly the **Ayala Center** (off Map p646; Lahug district). There is a food court on the 3rd floor for budget meals, or for finer dining you should consider one of the eateries at 'The Terraces' on the north side of the mall.

St Patrick's Sq (Map p646) near Casa Rosario has a great little coffee shop, **Brown Cup** (breakfast P110), and some cheap restaurants.

Opposite the Crown Regency Hotel on Pres Osmeña Blvd you'll find outdoor **food stalls** (dishes P30-50) that serve exotic dishes like *sinagang bakasi* (sea-snake soup) and more familiar Filipino dishes.

DRINKING

Belly Idol (Map p646; Gen Maxilom Ave) How can you not love a place called Belly Idol? There's occasional live music, P40 San Miguel and a simple menu of Filipino bar food, including 'The pork belly that rock' (sic).

Cebu has no shortage of nightclubs. Near the Waterfront Hotel & Casino in Lahug you'll find **Sunflower City** (off Map p646; Salinas Dr; weekend/weekday P150/100) and **PUMP 1** (off Map p646; Majesty Grand Convention Centre; men/women P50/free). The former features DJs and live music performing on a giant stage; the latter is a DJ-powered club popular with college kids. Both go off nearly every night of the week. Serious clubbers can try to breach the velvet rope at chic **Vudu Club** (off Map p646; Crossroads Mall, Lahug; admission P200-300; ⌚ Tue-Sat). All three are about a five-minute cab ride (P50) northeast of the Ayala Center.

Closer to Fuente Osmeña, Mango Square has a clutch of rowdy bars and clubs, including gay-friendly **Numero Doce** (Map p646; cnr Gen Maxilom Ave & J Osmeña St).

GETTING THERE & AWAY

Air

For international flights into Cebu's Mactan International Airport, see p609. Cebu Pacific and PAL have regular connections to Manila and a number of regional destinations. Zest Air has a daily flight to Manila.

Boat

SuperCat, Oceanjet and Weesam Express have speedy 'fastcraft' boats to Tagbilaran (Bohol), Ormoc (Leyte) and Dumaguete. The *Sun Star* daily newspaper runs up-to-date schedules. Useful shipping companies in Cebu City include the following:

Cokaliong Shipping (Map p645; ☎ 232 7211-18; www.cokaliongshipping.com; Pier 1) Boats to Surigao (P537, 13 hours, daily except Sunday); Maasin, Leyte (P280, five hours, five weekly); Dumaguete (P300, six hours, daily); Tagbilaran (P190, four hours, weekly); and Iloilo (P650, 12 hours, three weekly).

Kinswell (off Map p645; ☎ 416 6516; Pier 3) Boats to Hilongos, Leyte (P250, three hours, daily); and Tubigon, Bohol (P180, 1½ hours, two daily).

Lite Shipping Corporation (☎ 255 1721; http://lite-shipping.com; Pier 1) Ferries to Tagbilaran (P265, four hours, three daily), Tubigon (P150, two hours, three daily) and Ormoc (P350, four hours, six weekly).

Oceanjet (Map p645; ☎ 255 7560; www.oceanjet.net; Pier 1) Oceanjet has fastcraft to Tagbilaran (P500, two hours, five daily) and Dumaguete (P900, four hours, two daily).

Negros Navigation (off Map p645; ☎ 231 1004; Pier 5) Serves Manila (P1300, 23 hours, weekly).

Palacio Shipping (Map p645; ☎ 254 6629; Pier 1) Serves Tagbilaran (P170, four hours, three weekly) and Calbayog, Samar (P595, 12 hours, three weekly).

Roble Shipping Lines (Map p645; ☎ 232 2236; Pier 3) Daily ROROs to Ormoc (P350, 4½ hours) and Hilongos (P200, 4½ hours).

SuperCat (off Map p645; ☎ 233 7000; www.supercat.com.ph; Pier 4) Supercat has fastcraft to Ormoc (P625, 2¾ hours, three daily) and Tagbilaran (P525, 1¾ hours, three daily).

SuperFerry (off Map p645; ☎ 233 7000; www.superferry.com.ph; Pier 4) Four boats weekly to Manila (P1320, 23 hours) and five weekly to Cagayan de Oro (P980, eight hours).

Super Shuttle Ferry (off Map p645; ☎ 233 5733; Pier 8) Ferries to Ormoc (P350, 6½ hours, three weekly) and Camiguin (P880, 11 hours, weekly).

Trans Asia Shipping Lines (off Map p645; ☎ 254 6491; www.transasiashipping.com; Pier 5) Serves Cagayan de Oro (P615, 12½ hours, daily) and Iloilo (P650, 12 hours, daily).

Weesam Express (off Map p645; ☎ 412 9562; www.weesamexpress.com; Pier 4) Fastcraft to Tagbilaran (P500, 1¾ hours, three daily) and Ormoc (P550, 2¼ hours, twice daily).

You can buy ferry tickets for many ferries at the handy **Travellers Lounge** (off Map p645; ☎ 232 0291; ⌚ 8am-8pm) just outside SM City Mall. You can also buy tickets at the piers.

Bus

There are two bus stations in Cebu. **Ceres Bus Lines** (☎ 345 8650) services southern and central destinations, such as Bato (P120, four hours, frequent) via Moalboal (P80, three hours), from the **South bus station** (Map p645; Bacalso Ave). Quicker air-con vans ('V-hires') leave for Moalboal/Bato (P100/150) from the Citilink station near the South bus station.

The **North bus station** (Wireless St) is beyond SM City Mall. From here Ceres has frequent buses to Hagnaya (P90, 3½ hours, hourly) for Bantayan Island, and Maya (P100, four hours, hourly) for Malapascua Island.

Moalboal

☎032 / pop 27,400

The Philippines' original diving hotbed, Moalboal remains a throwback to the days when diving came cheap and minus the attitude. **Panagsama Beach**, where the resorts are, meanders lazily along a sea wall within rock-skipping distance of a stunning diving wall (which can also be snorkelled). While the beach itself is hardly worthy of the name, Moalboal's mellow vibe and mischievous weekend nightlife attract divers and nondivers alike.

ACTIVITIES

Divers can paddle out to the coral-studded wall or take a 10-minute *bangka* ride to **Pescador Island**, which swarms with marine life. A single-tank dive shouldn't exceed US$25. Beach lovers can take a tricycle (P150) 5km north to lovely **White Beach**. For adrenaline junkies, **Planet Action** (☎474 3016; www.action-philippines.com), which is run by the wry and affable Jochen, runs mountain biking, canyoning and other mountain tours, including a trip across the Tañon Strait to climb Mt Kanlaon on Negros (2½ days, per person P9000).

SLEEPING & EATING

Moalboal Backpacker Lodge (☎474 3053; www.moalboal-backpackerlodge.com; dm with/without linens P229/199) This new hostel is Moalboal's first experiment with backpacker-style lodging. It has an airy dorm and a couple of semiprivate rooms over a coffee shop.

Sumisid Lodge (☎346 9629; d P550-1500;) The tidy budget rooms at this gem in central Panagsama share clean bathrooms over an attractive, immaculately kept restaurant-lounge area. Out front, wicker *chaises longues* are perched on a stone wall over Panagsama's lone strip of white sand.

Quo Vadis (☎474 0018; www.visayadivers.info; d P750-1700;) Moalboal's best all-round resort has something to suit every taste, from tidy 'economy' rooms to tasteful deluxe digs facing the sea.

EATING & DRINKING

Drinking is the national sport of the Moalboal Republic, and there are dozens of eateries where you can secure food to soak up the deluge of beer. Our faves are Planet Action's **Last Filling Station** (meals P100-250) for its protein-heavy breakfasts and **Sunset View & Restaurant** (mains P100-200) for its views, affordable dinners and P25 San Miguel. Lloyd's Music Lounge takes over when others shut down, while the Saturday-night discos at Pacita's Resort are famous – or infamous, depending on your point of view.

GETTING THERE & AROUND

Frequent Ceres buses pass through town heading south to Bato (P60, two hours) and north to Cebu's South bus terminal (75, three hours). To Cebu, there are also air-con vans driven by notoriously sadistic drivers (P100, two hours).

Motorbikes to Panagsama Beach from Moalboal cost about P20, tricycles up to five times that.

Malapascua Island

pop 3500

Blessed with a long ribbon of pearly white sand, this sleepy little dive mecca off the northern tip of Cebu has long been touted as the 'next Boracay'. With a walking path set back from the beach and a few restaurants offering seaside seating in the sand, signature **Bounty Beach** does resemble Boracay in parts, but Boracay-like crowds are probably a long way off.

ACTIVITIES

Thresher sharks are the big attraction here. Divers head out at 5.30am to **Monad Shoal**, where they park on the seabed at 35m hoping to catch a glimpse of these critters. The chances are pretty good – about 70%. By day Monad Shoal attracts manta rays. More terrestrial sorts can hike the walking path leading up to a **lighthouse** on the northern tip.

SLEEPING

Malapascua's electricity grid functions only from 6pm to midnight, so make sure your resort has a generator to avoid sweltering to death. Rates decrease significantly in the low season.

BB's (☎0906 547 5454; r from P400) The fan rooms here are serviceable and friendly on the wallet but get hot when the power cuts out at midnight. It's off the beach, next to Ging-Ging's restaurant.

PHILIPPINES

Mike & Josie's Beach Cottages (☎ 0905 263 2914; r from P500) This backpacker special at the far east end of Bounty Beach has a few basic cottages facing the beach – and is building some more.

The best two resorts in Malapascua are neighbouring, co-managed **Logon Beach Resort** (☎ 0920 472 1451; r P1200; ❄) and **Tepanee Beach Resort** (☎ 0917 435 1122; www.tepanee.com; r from P2000; ❄). They occupy the rocky outcrop separating Bounty Beach from Logan Beach and share a small private cove. Logon has five coveted *nipa* huts with balconies overlooking the cove. Newcomer Tepanee's cottages have great sunset views and ooze Italian style.

EATING & DRINKING

Expect anything on Bounty Beach to cost more than you want to pay.

Ging-Ging's Flower Garden (mains P40-100) Inland from the beach, Ging-Ging's serves tasty, cheap filling vegetarian food and curries.

La Isla Bonita Restaurant (mains P170-255) Hidden off the beach near Ging-Ging's, this was the best restaurant on the island until Angelina opened in 2009. It's still recommended for its range of lovingly cooked Continental and Thai offerings.

Angelina (mains P290-400) The eponymous chef at this *ristorante* under Tepanee Beach Resort cooks up heavenly creations that will have you craving Italian food for weeks. The homemade *tagliatelle asparagi* is *al dente* bliss. Looks pricey but for food this good it's a stunning value.

GETTING THERE & AWAY

Scheduled *bangkas* from Maya (P50, 30 minutes) to Malapascua leave when full, roughly every hour until 4pm or 5pm. If you miss the last boat you'll have to charter a *bangka* for P500 to P800. At low tide you must pay a barge operator P20 to shuttle you to/from the *bangka*.

For information on getting to Maya from Cebu City see p647.

BOHOL

Bohol is a short hop from Cebu. It's difficult to reconcile its bloody history with the relaxed isle of today. It's here that Francisco Dagohoy led the longest revolt in the country against the Spaniards, from 1744 to 1829. The Chocolate Hills, rounded mounds resembling chocolate drops, are the big tourist magnet. Bohol also has endearing little primates, coral cathedrals off Panglao Island and lush jungle, ripe for exploration, around the town of Loboc.

GETTING THERE & AWAY

Tagbilaran is the main gateway, but there are also ferries between Cebu and Tubigon in northwest Bohol; between Bato, Leyte, and Ubay in northeast Bohol; and from Jagna in southeast Bohol to Cagayan de Oro and Camiguin (Mindanao).

Tagbilaran

☎ 038 / pop 92,000

There's no reason to waste much time in traffic-snarled Tagbilaran. Your first port of call should be the **tourist office** (🕑 8am-6pm) at the ferry dock, which can help with transport arrangements.

If you do need to stay the night, your best bets are **Charisma Lodge** (☎ 412 3094; CPG Ave; s/d from P135/275; ❄) and across the street at the homier **Nisa Travelers Inn** (☎ 411 3731; CPG Ave; s/d incl breakfast from P350/450; ❄). Both are susceptible to street noise so request rooms at the back. Eat, cool off and escape the tricycle madness in the food court in BQ Mall opposite Nisa Travellers Inn.

Cebu Pacific and PAL each have several daily flights from Tagbilaran to Manila.

There are various fastcraft and slow craft heading to Cebu (see Boat, p647). OceanJet operates two daily fastcraft to/from Dumaguete (P650, two hours). SuperFerry and Negros Navigation have weekly trips to/from Manila (P1300, 30 hours). Trans Asia has three trips weekly to/from Cagayan de Oro (P625, 11 hours).

The main bus terminal is next to Island City Mall in Dao, 3km north of the centre.

To avoid expensive van rides and slow public transport, consider hiring your own motorbike in Tagbilaran (P500 to P600 per day) to explore the rest of Bohol.

Around Tagbilaran

It's just a short drive north of Tagbilaran to two of the Philippines' signature attractions – the **Chocolate Hills** and that lovable palm-sized primate, the **tarsier**.

You can visit both in a single day on an excursion from Tagbilaran, but you're much better off basing yourself in Loboc at **Nuts Huts** (☎ 0920 846 1559; www.nutshuts.com; s P250-350, d P350-800), a backpacker Shangri-la in the middle of the jungle. With a sublime location overlooking the emerald-tinged Loboc River, Nuts Huts provides at least as much reason to visit inland Bohol as brown loam lumps or miniature monkeys. The Belgian hosts can tell you everything you need to know about exploring the area, and you can hike and mountain bike on a network of trails in the immediate vicinity.

To get to Nuts Huts from Tagbilaran, catch a Carmen-bound bus and get off at the Nuts Huts sign. It's a 15-minute walk from the road. Alternatively, take a bus to Loboc and then a *habal-habal* (P50) or shuttle boat up the river from the Sarimanok landing (per person P150).

You are unlikely to spot the nocturnal tarsier in the wild, so head to the **Tarsier Visitors Center** (www.philippinetarsier.org; admission P20; 9am-4pm) in *barangay* Canapnapan, between the towns of Corella and Sikatuna. About 10 saucer-eyed tarsiers hang out in the immediate vicinity of the centre – the guides will bring you right to them. This is a much more humane and ecofriendly way to appreciate the tarsier than visiting the animals kept in cages by tourist operators in Loboc.

From Nuts Huts the Tarsier Center is a 30- to 45-minute motorbike ride, or take a jeepney from Loboc (P25, 45 minutes). From Tagbilaran catch a bus to Sikatuna (P25, one hour) from the Dao terminal and ask to be dropped off at the centre.

An interesting quirk of nature, the **Chocolate Hills** consist of over 1200 conical hills, up to 120m high. They were supposedly formed over time by the uplift of coral deposits and the effects of rainwater and erosion. Since this explanation cannot be confirmed, the local belief that they are the tears of a heartbroken giant may one day prove to be correct. In the dry season, when the vegetation turns brown, the hills are at their most chocolate-y.

From Nuts Huts, the Chocolate Hills are a 45-minute motorbike ride; alternatively, flag down a bus bound for Carmen (4km north of the Chocolate Hills) and hop off at the Chocolate Hills viewpoint turn-off. *Habal-habal* whisk tourists up to the **viewpoint** (admission P50) from the **turn-off** (P20). A more fun method is to take a *habal-habal* in and around the hills; a one-hour ride costs P250.

From Tagbilaran there are regular buses from the Dao terminal to Carmen (P50, two hours).

Danao

☎ 038 / pop 3000

This unassuming town 20km north of Carmen is home to the new **Eco/Extreme/Educational Adventure Tour Danao** (EAT Danao; ☎ 507 3106 loc 187, 0917 302 1701; www.eatdanao.multiply.com; park admission P25 plus per activity P100-400). The main attraction here is the thrilling 500m 'Suislide', akin to a zipline only instead of instead of sitting upright you soar horizontally like a flying squirrel over a gorge 200m below. Adrenaline junkies have a range of other action-packed pursuits to choose from, including rappelling, kayaking and rock climbing.

With a motorbike it's easy to combine EAT Danao with the Chocolate Hills as a day trip from Nuts Huts, or you can spend the night (basic fan cottages cost P600). The park is about 7km west of Danao, which is about 22km north of Carmen. Buses to Danao from Tagbilaran's Dao terminal leave hourly until late afternoon (P75, three hours).

Panglao Island

☎ 038

Linked by two bridges to Bohol, Panglao is where divers head to take advantage of the spectacular coral formations and teeming marine life on the nearby islands of Balicasag and Pamilacan. Ground zero for divers is **Alona Beach**, which is sort of like a mini Boracay minus the stunning beach and nightlife. Alona Beach has gone upscale in recent years, but determined deal-hunters can still find bargains on diving and accommodation.

ACTIVITIES

Balicasag Island is the area's trophy piece for **diving**. In June 2009 dive shops were asking

> **ALL CREATURES SMALL & GREAT**
>
> Contrary to popular belief, the lovable tarsier is *not* the world's smallest primate. That distinction belongs to the pygmy mouse lemur of Madagascar. However, the Philippines can still proudly lay claim to the world's smallest hoofed mammal – the rare Philippine mouse deer of Palawan. Meanwhile, the Philippines' 24mm *Hippocampus bargibanti* recently lost the title of world's smallest seahorse to a newly discovered rival in Indonesia: the 16mm *Hippocampus denise*.

PHILIPPINES

P1200 per dive on average, not including equipment. Rates vary wildly so shop around. Expect those rates to rise once the global recession ends, as diving in Alona is traditionally expensive. There's good **snorkelling** about 100m offshore from Alona Beach.

You can arrange early-morning **dolphin-watching tours** near Pamilacan Island through most resorts and dive centres. Figure on paying P1500 for a four-person boat. You might get lucky and spot a whale, but don't count on it.

SLEEPING & EATING

Casa-Nova Garden (☎ 502 9101; s/d from P300/500; ❄ 🅡) True shoestring accommodation survives in Alona thanks to this cosy oasis. It's a bit out of the way, however. The turn-off is 700m beyond (west of) Helmut's Place.

Bohol Divers Resort (☎ 502 9047; s P500, d P800-4000; ❄ 💻 🅡) This sprawling complex is one of the few places on the beach still offering budget rooms. Accommodation runs the gamut from basic fan rooms to upscale villas.

Citadel Alona Inn (☎ 502 9424; www.citadelalona.com; d P570-1000; ❄) Inland from the beach is this appealing, artsy house where all rooms share squeaky-clean bathrooms. There's a big kitchen for self-caterers.

Beachfront dining opportunities on Alona Beach are ample but come at a price. The exception is **Trudi's Place** (mains P85-205). Other affordable eateries and bars are located north of the beach, towards Citadel Alona, including **Helmut's Place** (🕐 3pm-2am), the watering hole of choice for crusty expats living in the area.

GETTING THERE & AROUND

From Tagbilaran, buses with 'Tawala Alona' signboards head to Alona Beach roughly hourly until 3pm from the corner of Dagahoy and F Rocha Sts (P25, 45 minutes). An easier option is to hire a *habal-habal* (P200) or tricycle (P250).

SAMAR & LEYTE

'Rugged' is usually the word you hear associated with these two eastern Visayan provinces, separated from each other by the narrowest of straits near Leyte's capital, Tacloban. It's an apt tag. The interior of both islands is consumed by virtually impenetrable forest. This naturally creates opportunities for adventure, although you either have to learn advanced backcountry navigation or scrounge up one of the region's few qualified guides to take advantage of it.

The coastlines of both islands serve up a few gems of their own, most notably tourist-free whale shark viewing in Southern Leyte. There's history here too – in 1521 Magellan first stepped ashore on what would become Philippine soil on the island of Homonhon, off Samar. In October 1944, General MacArthur fulfilled his pledge to return to the Philippines on Red Beach south of Tacloban.

Catbalogan

☎ 055 / pop 92,454

Catbalogan is the preferred base for exploring the interior of Samar. A ban on motorised tricycles in the city centre also makes it a pleasant stopover on the road from Allen to Tacloban. From the pier you can spot about 30 different islands offshore, plus some giant peaks on Biliran Island off Leyte.

Spelunking, climbing, scrambling, birdwatching, mountain biking – you name it, Samar's got it. **Trexplore** (☎ 251 2301; www.bonifaciojoni.blogspot.com; Allen Ave), run by North Face–clad Joni Bonifacio, is the only one doing tours around here, and yes, you will need a guide. Check out his website for some ideas for adventure. Joni's tour of the **Jiabong Caves**, close to Catbalogan, is one of the Visayas' top one-day adventures. One-third of the six-hour tour, which ends with a pleasant 45-minute paddle downriver in a dugout canoe, is spent swimming underground in full spelunking kit. Joni's tours of the huge **Langub-Gobingob Cave** near Calbiga, 50km south of Catbalogan, involve a night camping underground.

SLEEPING & EATING

Your best budget options are the bare-bones but homey **San Roque** (☎ 0908 408 1716; s/d P100/200), with bucket showers in the common bathrooms, and **Fortune Hotel** (555 Del Rosario St; s/d from P290/390), where even the budget rooms are fastidiously cared for.

Rolet Hotel (☎ 251 5512; s/d P750/950; ❄) The well-kept rooms here (some windowless) are somewhat small, but you could bounce a 25-centavo coin on the expertly made beds. Unbelievable value.

For American-style snacks and pizza try **Ernie's Pizza** (pizzas P75-150) by the town square. **Tower Grill** (Callejon St; meals P50-200) is the place for sizzling Filipino fare washed down with San Miguel (P27).

GETTING THERE & AWAY

Cebu Pacific, PAL Express and Zest Air fly from Manila to Calbayog, 72km north of Catbalogan.

To get to Allen (P180, four hours), departure point for ferries to Matnog in southeast Luzon, hail a Manila-bound bus on the National Hwy, or take a more regular bus (P80) or van (P100) to Calbayog (two hours) and transfer to a van, bus or jeepney there. Matnog-bound ferries (P120, one hour) depart at least every couple of hours.

Heading south to Tacloban there are buses (P80, 2¾ hours) and air-con vans (P100, 2¼ hours).

Tacloban

☎053 / pop 217,199

The birthplace of Imelda Marcos – the 'Rose of Tacloban' – is a busy commercial centre and transport hub. It's hardly chic, but it does have a strip of decent restaurants where you can escape the rat race and cool off with an iced latte and air-con.

The **regional tourism office** (☎321 2048; F Mendoza Commercial Complex, 141 Santo Niño St) has maps, brochures and information about both Leyte and Samar.

There's a unique **memorial** of Macarthur's Red Beach landing in Palo, 6km south of Tacloban. Take a 'Tacloban–Gov't Center–Baras' jeepney from the plaza next to McDonald's on Trece Martirez St to get there (P12, 15 minutes). Northwest of Tacloban, volcanic **Biliran Island** has some splendid beaches and waterfalls.

SLEEPING & EATING

Steer clear of the noisy, congested city centre and stay closer to the internet cafes, restaurants and bars around Burgos and MH del Pilar Sts.

Welcome Home Pension (☎321 2739; 161 Santo Niño St; r from P350;) This quiet place set off the street has a mix of simple rooms with shared bathrooms (some windowless) and bigger, brighter digs that are a great deal for groups of three or four.

Rosvenil Pensione (☎321 2676; Burgos St; s/d from P520/550;) Located in a great rambling house, Rosvenil offers an enticing mix of rooms, including some truly swanky digs in its new wing.

Restaurant row is Veteranos Ave near the corner of MH del Pilar St. **Bo's Coffee** (Veteranos Ave; breakfasts P125-175; 7am-midnight;) has heavenly air-con, filling breakfasts and free wi-fi. The breezy, waterfront **San Pedro Bay Seafood Restaurant** (mains P100-200; 10am-11pm) on the grounds of the Leyte Park Hotel, is justifiably popular among expats.

THE BALANGIGA MASSACRE

On 28 September 1901, Filipino guerrillas masquerading as women massacred 59 members of the US garrison stationed at Balangiga in Eastern Samar. For the Americans it was the bloodiest day of the Filipino-American War, and the massacre triggered a massive retribution campaign which was led by General Jacob 'Howling Mad' Smith, who killed scores of innocent civilians while fulfilling his vow to turn Samar into a 'howling wilderness'. There is an annual re-enactment and commemoration on that date.

GETTING THERE & AWAY

PAL Express, Zest Air, Cebu Pacific and PAL fly at least daily to Tacloban from Manila. The latter two also have a daily flight to Cebu.

Duptours (cnr Ave Veteranos & Santo Niño St) runs speedy vans to Ormoc (P120, two hours), Naval on Biliran Island (P140, 2½ hours) and Catbalogan (P100, 2¼ hours). At the New Bus Terminal, about 3km west of the centre, you'll find more buses and vans to these and many other destinations, including Sogod (bus/van P120/150, 3½/2½ hours), where there are connections to Padre Burgos and Pintuyan.

Ormoc

☎053 / pop 177,524

Ormoc is mainly a springboard for boats to Cebu. If you arrive late, stay in the hulking **Don Felipe Hotel** (☎255 2460; I Larrazabal St; s/d from P360/420;) on the waterfront opposite the pier. Pricier rooms have wonderful views.

SuperCat and Weesam Express have several fastcraft per day to Cebu (P550 to P625, 2¼ hours). For slower, cheaper options see Boat on p647. Conveniently, the bus terminal is opposite the port, with connections to Tacloban and all points south.

PAL Express has four weekly flights to Manila.

PHILIPPINES

Southern Leyte

☎ 053

Leyte's bowlegged rump straddles Sogod Bay, where **whale sharks** frolic from about mid-November to late April. The sharks here are fewer and more elusive than their more famous cousins in Donsol (see p632), but this just makes the thrill of spotting one that much greater. For now the village of Pintuyan, where the whale sharks (*tiki-tiki* in the local dialect) tend to congregate, is a far cry from the *butanding*-chasing frenzy of Donsol. The hope is that Pintuyan is too remote to draw Donsol's hordes. If you go, tread softly around these beasts and go only with sanctioned operators, who are collectively working to control the number of visitors.

PADRE BURGOS

pop 1300

If you have the money, an organised boat trip from this friendly little dive colony (simply called 'Burgos') is the easiest way to see the *tiki-tiki*. The dive resorts listed here run two or three excursions per week (in season) across Sogod Bay to snorkel with the whale sharks near Pintuyan. Excursions take most of the day and cost roughly P3000 per person. Scuba diving with the sharks is prohibited at the main site in Pintuyan, but the local population is a mobile bunch and sightings are common on dives in Sogod Bay.

Whale sharks aside, the reef diving on both sides of Sogod Bay is first-rate all year. One of the best sites is 20km north of Pintuyan at Napantaw, a protected reef where **Coral Cay Conservation** (www.coralcay.org) accepts volunteers to help survey the local marine environment, with the goal of establishing more protected reserves. Apply through Coral Caye's UK office.

Sleeping

Peter's Dive Resort (☎ 573 0015; www.whaleofadive.com; s P600-700, d P800-1900;) Peter's has a colourful, turtle-laden reef just offshore, and rooms that cater to all budgets. The rooms have verandahs with superb sea views. A few cottages are practically lapped by waves.

Southern Leyte Dive Resort (☎ 572 4011; www.leyte-divers.com; r P850-1450;) This charming resort sports imaginative 'roundalows' (circular duplex bungalows). It's 1km northeast of Burgos, which makes whale shark excursions a bit longer. On the other hand, there's an actual beach and sunset views here.

Getting There & Away

From Cebu you can take a ferry to Ormoc, Bato, Hilongos or Maasin (see p647) and continue to Burgos by frequent bus or multicab. There are also boats between Ubay, on Bohol, and Bato (P180, 2½ hours, two daily).

From Tacloban, head to Sogod (bus/van P120/150, 3½/2½ hours) and transfer to Burgos (P60, one hour). From Lilo-an, bus it to Sogod (P60, one hour) and transfer.

LILO-AN

pop 3500

This scenic town is where the ferries from Surigao disembark (although the port will soon move to San Ricardo, 10km south of Pintuyan). **Ofelia's Lodge** (☎ 0910 342 7773; s/d P150/250) pretty much lives up to its slogan: 'Safe, Cheap, Clean & Windy'.

Five ferries per day ply the route between Surigao and Lilo-an (P266, four hours). Occasional vans make the trip to/from Tacloban (P300, three hours), or take a frequent bus to Sogod and transfer.

PINTUYAN

pop 1000

Few tourists make the incredibly scenic overland journey down to Pintuyan, where the local tourist office organises community-based snorkelling trips to see the whale sharks in three-passenger *bangka* owned by the local fishermen's association. Tours are run out of *barangay* Sonok, about 3km north of Pintuyan, and cost P1800/2050/2300 for one/two/three people, including boat, guide and spotters. Snorkelling equipment costs P100.

Pintuyan's *tiki-tiki* are more fickle than their friends in Donsol – 2007 and 2009 were banner years. In 2008 they showed up only briefly. Before setting out, call local tourism chief **Moncher Bardos** (☎ 0916 952 3354) or head guide **Karl Mosot** (☎ 0909 995 2548) to make sure they are around.

There are homestays (P200) available in Sonok, or you can stay in Pintuyan proper at motel-style **La Guerta** (☎ 0926 142 6986; s/d from P150/250;).

Regular buses to Pintuyan from Sogod (P100) take 2½ hours over a smooth sealed road and go via Lilo-an. A *habal-habal* to/from Lilo-an costs P250. There's one morning *bangka* ferry from Pintuyan to Surigao (P120, two hours).

MINDANAO

Sprawling Mindanao, the world's 19th-largest island, is known for dazzling scenery, primitive hill tribes and an almost complete lack of tourists because of political unrest and occasional fighting between the government and Muslim separatists. What most tourists don't realise is that the lovely coastal stretch of northern Mindanao between Cagayan de Oro and Siargao Island is Catholic, Cebuano (Visayan) speaking – and quite safe. The area is known for first-rate surfing on Siargao and a peaceful island-life existence on Camiguin. Elsewhere, Mindanao offers up plenty of cherries for the intrepid traveller, including the Philippines' highest mountain, Mt Apo (2954m), accessible from Davao in southern Mindanao. Exercise caution if you are heading south or west of Cagayan de Oro (see the boxed text, below).

Getting There & Away

The four Philippine domestic airlines together service most major cities in Mindanao. Popular jumping off points for ferries from the Visayas include Cebu City, Lilo-an (Leyte) and Jagna (Bohol). There are also plenty of ferries from Manila.

SURIGAO

☎ 086 / pop 132,000

Congested Surigao is a key transport hub and the gateway to Siargao Island. If you need to stay the night, **Dexter Pension House** (☎ 232 7526; cnr San Nicolas & Magallanes Sts; s P180, d P350-650; ❄) has a central location and small but passable rooms – many windowless – in an antique house. Next door, the **Garcia Hotel** (s/d from P180/230) is just a minor downgrade.

> **WARNING**
>
> Most embassies strongly warn tourists against travelling to potential conflict zones such as Maguindanao province (and its notoriously violent capital, Cotabato), Zamboanga and the entire Sulu Archipelago. While embassies tend to be a bit alarmist, it pays to exercise considerable caution when travelling to these areas. Check local news sources to make sure your destination and travel route are safe. See p606 for more on the conflict in Mindanao.

Speedy, super-sized *bangka* ferries head to Dapa on Siargao (P200, 2¼ hours, four daily, last trip at 1pm). In bad weather, opt for the twice-daily RORO (P144, 3¼ hours). Dapa-bound *bangka* dock in front of the Tavern Hotel. ROROs use the **main pier** (Borromeo St). If your destination on Siargao is Burgos instead of Cloud Nine, take the noon *bangka* to Santa Monica from Bilang Bilang Point, a short walk southwest from the main pier.

For ferries to Lilo-an see p653; these call in at the port of Lipata, 10km northwest of Surigao, accessible by tricycle (P200).

SuperFerry has a weekly trip to Manila (from P1900, 32 hours) via Bacolod. For services to Cebu, see p647.

PAL Express flies daily to/from Manila. Cebu Pacific has three flights per week to Cebu.

Bachelor buses run regularly from Surigao to Butuan (P155, 2½ hours). Change in Butuan for Cagayan de Oro. Buses depart from the Integrated Bus & Jeepney Terminal near the airport, 5km west of the city centre.

SIARGAO

☎ 086 / pop 70,000

It's best known for having one of the world's great surf breaks, but Siargao is no one-trick pony. Surrounded by idyllic islands and sprinkled with coves and quaint fishing villages, it has plenty on offer for nonsurfers too.

GETTING THERE & AROUND

Cebu Pacific has three weekly flights from Cebu to Siargao's small airport in Del Carmen. Otherwise you'll need to arrive by boat from Surigao – see left.

From the pier in Dapa, a *habal-habal* should cost P200 to General Luna ('GL') (20 minutes), P250 to Cloud Nine (30 minutes) or P500 to Burgos (1¼ hours). Tricycles cost the same but are much slower.

Sporadic jeepneys run from Dapa to GL and points north. To explore the island you're better off hiring a motorcycle (per day P500).

Cloud Nine & General Luna

The legendary **Cloud Nine break** off Tuazon Point is what put Siargao on the map. While it's now dubbed 'Crowd Nine' by locals, that's probably an exaggeration – although the sleepy village of Cloud Nine does get overrun in October for the **Siargao International Surfing Cup**. The breaks around here are reef

> **GETTING TO MALAYSIA BY SEA**
>
> At the time of writing, the only sea route to Malaysia was Zamboanga to Sandakan, Sabah. **Weesam Express** (www.zimnet.com/weesam/php/booking.php) has a fast ferry that covers this route twice a week (P2800, 13 hours) and there are slower ferries that make this trip too. However, travel in the Zamboanga region is considered risky (see opposite).

breaks, but it's a soft, spongy reef and there are some moderate swells around for beginners, especially in the flat season (May to July). Lessons cost about P500 per hour including board rental – inquire at Ocean 101 or Sagana Beach Resort. Peak season for waves is late August to November.

Most of the resorts are in Cloud Nine, a bumpy 10-minute *habal-habal* ride north of GL. All resorts can organise island-hopping trips. In GL you'll find cheap eateries and a couple of bars frequented by local surfer dudes and chicks.

SLEEPING & EATING

Prices mushroom and rooms fill up fast from August to October. Some resorts shut down during the rainy low season (December to March).

Ocean 101 Beach Resort (☎ 0919 826 8837; www.ocean101coud9.com; r P450-2000; ❄ 💻 📶) This is surfing HQ, with a great common area and a mix of well-maintained budget rooms and pricier beachfront quarters distributed among two ugly blue concrete edifices. Pay for your wi-fi.

Neighbouring **Cloud Nine** (☎ 0920 231 0044; r from P600; ❄) and **Kesa Cloud Nine** (☎ 0921 281 2960; r P700-2500; ❄) stare straight at the Cloud Nine break and offer a mix of basic fan rooms and downright elegant cottages.

Jadestar Lodge (☎ 0919 234 4367; cottages from P350) is a budget option just south of GL centre.

In Cloud Nine, try the chicken mango curry at **Catangnan Seaside Restaurant** (mains P100), in an unsigned shack 150m beyond Ocean 101.

Around the Island

An altogether different experience awaits travellers who venture up to the sparsely populated northern tip of the island, where the sleepy township of **Burgos** awaits its destiny as the next big thing on the Philippines' surfing circuit (you heard it here first). Burgos' broad, blond beach envelops a yawning bay with about a dozen breaks peeling off in every direction – and nary a soul in site. The villages of **Alegria** to the north, and **Pacifico** to the south, feature a similarly enviable mix of white sand, tasty waves and good old-fashioned isolation.

Tasteful **Bohemia Bungalows** (☎ 0916 391 0195; www.bohemiabungalows.com; r P700-2000) is right on the beach in Burgos. Owner Graham rents boards and is planning to open a surf school. There are also simple resorts in Pacifico and Alegria.

CAGAYAN DE ORO

☎ 088 / pop 554,000

It may not be the world's most cosmopolitan city, but every Friday and Saturday night the good people of this city descend on the central thoroughfare and engage in a giant, boozy street party. Take that, Rio! 'CDO' also has some kickin' nightclubs.

The **tourist office** (☎ 856 4048; Velez St) is south of the city centre.

Situated on the banks of the Cagayan River, CDO is the one place in the Philippines that features year-round **white-water rafting**. Of the several rafting companies in town, **Rafting Adventure Philippines** (☎ 857 1270, 0917 707 3583; raftingadventurephilippines.com; cnr Tiano Brothers & Hayes Sts; per person P700-1200) has been around the longest.

Sleeping

Park View Hotel (☎ 857 1197; cnr T Neri & General Capistrano Sts; d P325-725; ❄) An organised place that has economical rooms – check out a few, as many are windowless.

Ramon's Hotel (☎ 857 4804; cnr Burgos & Tirso Neri Sts; r P550-950; ❄) Rooms here are nothing special, but the quiet, riverside location is. Alas, river-view rooms lack balconies, although the restaurant has one.

Nature's Pensionne (☎ 857 2274; T Chavez St; r P680-1380; ❄) This hotel, located in the concrete jungle of downtown CDO, is the best midrange option. Its clean, tastefully decorated rooms have cable TV and hot water.

Eating & Drinking

The weekend street party on the central boulevard known as Divisoria – dubbed 'Night Café' – is a wallet-friendly culinary fiesta. There's a buzzing restaurant and bar scene northeast of the centre at flashy Rosario Arcade, next to Limketkai Mall.

Butcher's Best Barbeque (cnr Corrales & Hayes Sts; skewer of meat P15) CDO is awash in cheap barbecue places. This one's the preferred pick among CDO's expats.

our pick **Karachi** (Hayes St; mains P50-120; 9am-10pm) Feels like a hole in the wall, but has absolutely fabulous curries, kebabs and other Pakistani food. Top it off with a flavoured hookah (P100). Get here early before the evening karaoke begins.

The club action is centred on Tiano Brothers St between Hayes and Gaerlan Sts. **Pulse** (Tiano Brothers St) and **Club Mojo** (Tiano Brothers St) are live-music clubs, while DJs hold court at swanky **Eleven Fifty** (Gaerlan St; admission P100). Shorts and flip-flops are frowned upon.

Getting There & Around

Between Cebu Pacific, PAL and PAL Express there are many daily flights to both Manila and Cebu. The airport is about 10km west of town. From Divisoria take a Carmen jeepney, then transfer to a Lumbia jeepney. Taxis cost an inflated P250.

At Macabalan Pier, 5km north of the city centre, various ferry companies serve Cebu (see p647), Tagbilaran (P625, 11 hours), and Jagna, Bohol (P600, six hours). SuperFerry sails to/from Manila (from P1920, 36 hours, four weekly), Dumaguete (P1000, seven hours, Saturdays) and Iloilo P1995, 14 hours, Sundays).

Bachelor Tours buses head up the coast to Butuan (air-con P360, 4½ hours) via Balingoan (P160, two hours). Change buses in Butuan for Surigao. The main bus terminal is located on the edge of town, just beside the Agora Market.

CAMIGUIN

☎ 088 / pop 81,000

With seven volcanoes, various waterfalls, hot springs, cold springs, deserted islands offshore and underwater diversions aplenty, Camiguin is developing a reputation as a top adventure-tourism destination. The dramatic landscape makes it a great place to strike out on your own and explore, preferably by motorbike (per day P400 to P500), mountain bike (per day P250) or on foot.

Adventure lovers should seek out Barbie at Camiguin Action Geckos (see opposite) or Johnny at **Johnny's Fun N' Dive** (☎ 387 9588; www.johnnysdive.com; Secret Cove Beach Resort). They both offer a range of trekking, rappelling, mountain biking and diving tours, and are happy to dispense advice to do-it-yourselfers.

GETTING THERE & AROUND

The most reliable way to Camiguin is to catch a ferry from Balingoan on mainland Mindanao to Benoni, 17km southeast of Mambajao (P135, one hour, roughly hourly until 4pm). The on-again, off-again **Paras Sea Cat** (☎ 856 4112) fastcraft direct from CDO was on again when we visited (P400, 2½ hours, daily).

From the Balbagon pier near Mambajao, Super Shuttle Ferry has a daily 8am boat to Jagna on Bohol (P380, four hours), and a Sunday boat to Cebu (P880, 11 hours).

Multicabs circle the island mostly counter-clockwise, passing any given point roughly every hour until about 5pm. A special trip from Benoni to Mambajao/Bug-Ong costs P350/400.

Mambajao

In this shady capital of Camiguin, life rarely gets out of first gear. Mambajao is a good place to observe ornate *okkil* architecture. The best example is the Landbank building along the National Hwy in the town centre. Notice the intricate patterns cut into the wooden awning.

our pick **Enigmata Treehouse Ecolodge** (☎ 0918 230 4184; http://camiguinecolodge.com; dm P200-250, ste from P950;) This hippyesque artist hang-out in the woods is more a way of life than a resort. Most rooms are in a fantastic house built around a towering hardwood tree and swathed in wooden furniture, murals and artwork. Head honcho Ros does much to promote Camiguin arts and is a fine artist in her own right. The dirt road here turns off the highway at the Tarzan statue about 2km east of Mambajao.

There are a couple of Filipino eateries on the waterfront in Mambajao, or try **Green Tropical Pub** (meals P100-250; 11am-midnight Tue-Sun), an open-air German-Filipino restaurant just west of Mambajao. It has various bar sports and a local-centric Saturday night disco.

Around Mambajao

Most of Camiguin's resorts are on the black-sand beaches in *barangay* Bug-Ong, about

4km west of Mambajao. A tricycle to Bug-Ong costs P75 to P100 from Mambajao.

The big bungalows at **Seascape** (☎ 387 9534; Bug-Ong; r P500-800), all bamboo and native materials, are barren inside but have big balconies boasting hammocks and prime views of the ocean. Cheaper rooms are concrete with inlaid bamboo. **Camiguin Action Geckos** (☎ 387 9146; www.camiguinactiongeckos.com; Bug-Ong; r/cottages P700/1800; wi-fi) has cosy budget rooms flanking an exquisite chill-out deck above the restaurant, as well as some truly exceptional beachfront cottages. **Secret Cove Beach Resort** (☎ 387 9084; www.secretcovecamiguiin.net; r P850-1600; air-con wi-fi) is a compact, friendly resort with great food, wi-fi, inoffensive rooms and a warm ambience. It's a couple kilometres beyond Bug-Ong in the village of Yumbing.

PALAWAN

Palawan is fast becoming a haven for nature buffs and intrepid adventurers. Drifting on the Philippines' western edge, this long sliver of jungle is one of the country's last ecological frontiers. The Amazonian interior is barely connected by a few snaking roads that will make your fillings jingle, and the convoluted coast is comprised of one breathtaking bay after another. Puerto Princesa is the energetic capital of the island, from where you can explore nearby Sabang, with its sublime beach and famous Subterranean River, and laid-back Port Barton. Towering limestone cliffs shelter the northern community of El Nido, while the Calamian group of islands offers beaches, unbeatable wreck diving and a number of El Nido–esque cliffs of their own.

Getting There & Around

Cebu Pacific has daily flights to Puerto Princesa from both Manila and Cebu, while PAL and Zest Air serve Manila only. Cebu Pacific and PAL Express have several flights daily between Manila and Coron. Seair has on-again, off-again flights to El Nido (they were off again as of this writing). The other option to El Nido from Manila is with pricey **ITI** (☎ in Manila 02-851 5674; www.islandtransvoyager.com; tickets P6750); three daily.

SuperFerry (☎ 048-434 5736; Rizal Ave, Puerto Princesa) has a weekly vessel to Puerto Princesa from Manila (from P1450, 27 hours) via Coron (P1250, 13 hours). **Milagrosa Shipping** (☎ 048-433 4806; Rizal Ave) and **Montenegro Shipping** (☎ 048-434 9344; www.montenegrolines.com.ph; Puerto Princesa Pier) sail weekly between Puerto Princesa and Iloilo (P1220, 30 hours) via the Cuyo Islands.

PUERTO PRINCESA

☎ 048 / pop 210,000

If only all Philippine cities could be a little more like earthy Puerto Princesa. Strictly enforced fines for littering (P200) keep the streets clean (we're not kidding!), while the municipal government actively promotes the city as an eco- and adventure-tourism hub. Scattered around town is a handful of funky restaurants and guest houses, where the design motif is part ethnic Filipino, part tripped-out '60s hippy. Yes, there's the usual stream of tricycles down the main commercial drag, Rizal Ave. But even the tricycles seem a bit quieter and less dense than in most other provincial centres. In short, 'Puerto' makes a great launching pad for checking out the myriad natural attractions in the surrounding area. The big one is the Subterranean River, while overnight hikes to tribal villages in the south are also gaining traction. If you're in town, give the small **Palawan Museum** (Mendoza Park, Rizal Ave; admission P10; 8am-noon & 1-5pm Mon-Sat) a gander.

Information

Internet cafes line busy Rizal Ave. Metrobank, BDO and BPI, all on Rizal Ave, have Palawan's only working ATMs.

Pasyar: Developmental Tourism (☎ 723 1075; www.pasyarpalawan.tripod.com; Rizal Ave) Genuinely dedicated to conservation and community-based tourism, it's a great choice for local tours like Honda Bay and dolphin watching.

Tourist Information & Assistance Counter (☎ 434 4211; airport arrivals hall; 8am-5pm) Run by City Tourism Office, which has an office next door, it distributes a city map and can help with hotel bookings.

WARNING

Malaria is an issue in rural areas. Use the mosquito nets provided by most guest houses and coat yourself with insect repellent at dusk. Minuscule, stinging sandflies (aptly named *nik-niks*) delight in biting exposed skin and can be a curse on some western beaches.

Underground River Booking Office (☎ 433 2409; 7 Plates Bldg, National Hwy, north of Rizal Ave; 8am-5pm) Issues Subterranean River permits (see right).

Sleeping

Ancieto's Pension (☎ 434 6667; arc_tess@yahoo.com.ph; cnr Mabini & Roxas Sts; s/d/tr from P200/300/400;) Another good choice near Banwa is this family-run bargain. Rooms are basic and susceptible to some street noise, but there's a cosy sitting area with a TV.

our pick **Banwa Art House** (☎ 434 8963; www.banwa.com; Liwanag St; dm P250, s/d from P350/450;) This backpacker oasis oozes charm from every artisan craft adorning its walls. There's a groovy lounge, surrounded by a waterfall of vines, that has cool tunes wafting from the house CD player.

Manny's Guesthouse (☎ 725 1938; emmanuellucena@yahoo.com; 2B Mendoza St; r P400-600;) An appealing newcomer near Banwa, Manny's has four spacious rooms in an attractive house with sweeping views of Puerto Bay.

Badjao Inn (☎ 433 2761; badjao_inn@yahoo.com; 350 Rizal Ave; s/d from P422/522;) To be closer to the airport and the bars, Badjao isn't a bad choice. It has a wide variety of rooms in an ugly edifice surrounding a pleasant interior garden courtyard and restaurant.

Eating & Drinking

Ima's Vegetarian (Fernandez St; dishes P50-70) A decidedly healthy – and delicious, and remarkably cheap – option run by a warm husband-and-wife team. Try the spicy black-bean burger or tofu burger for *merienda* (daytime snack).

Neva's Place (Taft St; mains P50-150) Great budget Filipino and Thai food, as well as pizzas, all served in a blissful garden.

Kinabuch Grill & Bar (Rizal Ave; mains P100-150) Sprawling 'KGB' has two pool tables and is the watering hole of choice for the thirsty masses.

our pick **Ka Lui Restaurant** (369 Rizal Ave; mains P135-200; lunch & dinner Mon-Sat) This seafood specialist in a funky *nipa* complex thoroughly deserves its reputation as one of the finest restaurants in the country. It's a splurge only by the standards of Puerto, where delicious food at low prices is the norm.

Also recommended:

Vegetarian House (cnr Burgos & Manalo Sts; dishes P35-100) More tasty vegetarian chow in decidedly austere surroundings.

OFF THE BEATEN TRACK

To really see Palawan in all her jungle-clad glory, tackle the so-called 'Ultimate Adventure' – the coast-to-coast walk from Tanabag, an hour's drive north of Puerto Princesa, to Sabang. The three-day trek brings you up close and personal with Batak tribespeople, tropical birds, monkeys and possibly snakes. Local guides for this trek cost P1000 per day; inquire at Pasyar: Developmental Tourism (see p657).

Café Itoy's (Rizal Ave;) 'Bo's'-style coffee shop with free wi-fi.

Getting There & Around

The main bus terminal is at the San Jose market 6km north of town; to get there grab a multicab (mini-jeepney) from anywhere along Rizal Ave (P15). Buses and/or vans serve El Nido, Port Barton and Sabang – see those sections for details.

SABANG

☎ 048

Tiny Sabang has a heavenly expanse of beach and is famed for the navigable **Puerto Princesa Subterranean River National Park** (park/cave admission P75/200), which winds through a spectacular cave before emptying into the sea. Tourist paddleboats are allowed to go 1.5km upstream into the cave (45 minutes return). At certain times of the year it's possible to proceed further upstream with a permit (P400) from the Underground River Booking Office in Puerto Princesa (see left). From the beach in Sabang it's a thrilling 5km walk through the jungle to the mouth of the river, or you can book a boat (P600 for up to six people, 15 minutes) through the Sabang Information Office at the pier.

South of Sabang, in Cabayugan, a jungle trail leads two hours to the origin of the Subterranean River. Secure a guide (P500) at the **Ethnographic Museum** (admission free) in Cabayugan.

Sleeping & Eating

Most places run their generators from 6pm to 10pm or 11pm.

Blue Bamboo Cottages (cottages P300-800) Walk past Dab Dab, through a small village and find Sabang's cheapest quarters in an eclectic

PHILIPPINES

compound. The simple raised cottages have private porches and shaggy thatched roofs.

Dab Dab Resort (☎ 0910 924 1673; cottages P400-800) The most appealing budget option in Sabang, Dab Dab has tasteful dark-wood and bamboo cottages, great food and a glorious common area under a soaring octagonal canopy. Unfortunately, it lacks a good beach. It's 200m south of the pier.

Mary's Cottages (☎ 0919 757 7582; cottages P400-700) Mary's occupies the peaceful north end of Sabang Beach, a 10-minute walk from the pier. Expect simplicity and you will not be let down.

Getting There & Away

Three jumbo jeepneys and one bus ply the sealed road between Sabang and Puerto Princesa every day. Departures are at 7am, 10am, noon and 2pm in either direction (P200, 2½ hours). If you're heading to Port Barton or El Nido backtrack by road to Salvacion and flag down a northbound bus from the highway.

High-season *bangkas* chug up to El Nido (P2000, seven hours) almost daily, with drop-offs, but not pick-ups, in Port Barton (P1200, 3½ hours).

PORT BARTON

☎ 048 / pop 4425

People find themselves unable to leave Port Barton, and only partly because of the town's poor transport links. Set on a small, attractive cove, the area has some fine islands in the bay and good snorkelling. **Island-hopping excursions** (for up to 4 people P1500) can be easily arranged.

Sleeping & Eating

El Dorado Sunset Cottages (☎ 0920 329 9049; d P400-800) Just short of Greenviews at the northern end of town, El Dorado has nine clean cottages set amid gardens behind a beachfront bar.

our pick Greenviews Resort (☎ 0929 268 5333; www.palawandg.clara.net; s/d from P450/600) The last place on the north end of the beach is probably the best all-round choice. It certainly has the finest restaurant – try the shrimp omelette (P150). The cheaper rooms are more than acceptable, and the more luxurious cottages are set around a garden.

Summer Homes Beach Resort (☎ 0928 594 4484; www.portbarton.info/summerhomes; d P550-1200;) Summer Homes spurns the native look with well-kept concrete cottages set on a manicured lawn. Rates go down to P350 in the low season.

Getting There & Away

There's one morning jeepney to Roxas (P100, 1½ hours) and another one to Puerto Princesa (P250, four hours). To get to El Nido, make your way to Roxas and flag down a northbound jeepney.

From Puerto, you can take a more frequent Roxas-bound jeepney as far as San Jose, 2km south of Roxas, and transfer to a motorcycle taxi (P400, one hour). Heavy rains occasionally close this road.

The notorious Port Barton boatman's association bans the high-season Sabang–El Nido *bangkas* from picking up passengers in Port Barton. Hiring a private three-passenger boat costs P6000 to El Nido, P4000 to Sabang.

EL NIDO

☎ 048 / pop 5600

El Nido is the primary base for exploring Palawan's star attraction, the stunning **Bacuit Bay Archipelago**. Tiny swiftlets build edible nests out of saliva in the immense limestone cliffs that surround the ramshackle town – hence the name, El Nido (nest in Spanish). The town feels touristy by Philippine standards, but sporadic electricity (it cuts off from 6am to 2pm each day), rugged access roads and adventure opportunities galore are firm reminders that you are still in Palawan.

Information

Run like clockwork by the Swiss owner, the **El Nido Boutique & Art Café** (☎ 0920 902 6317), near the wharf, is a repository for all things informative about El Nido. You can buy plane tickets here, check boat and bus schedules, get cash advances on credit cards (with an 8% surcharge), browse the library, buy art,

> **THE PERFECT BEACH**
>
> There's a rumour that the island described in Alex Garland's backpacker classic *The Beach* was somewhere in the Calamian Group. Garland set the book in Thailand, but admits that the real island was somewhere in the Philippines. He lived in the Philippines for a spell and set his second novel, *The Tesseract*, in Manila.

eat good food and drink real coffee. It's also as good a place as any to arrange boat or sea kayaking excursions into stunning Bacuit Bay.

Activities

All-day island-hopping trips cost about P500 to P800 per person, including lunch. Miniloc Island's **Big Lagoon** and **Small Lagoon** are not to be missed; for full effect get there at dawn when you'll have them to yourself. There are several dive operators in town. Art Café has a list of short hiking expeditions you can do on your own.

Sleeping

There's remarkably little to differentiate the resorts lining El Nido's beach in terms of price (P500 to P800 for a fan room) or quality (mediocre), so consider strolling the beach until you find something you like. Prices drop substantially in the low season – negotiate hard.

OG's Pensionne (☎ 0916 707 0393; ogspensionne@yahoo.com; s/d from P500/600) Has enough rooms (15) that there's a good chance of something being available. The rooms are good value to boot – especially the luscious triples.

our pick **Alternative Centre** (☎ 0917 896 3506; d P650; 💻 📶) The beach-facing rooms here are beyond creative. Enter through the garage-style front doors into a tangle of intricately carved wooden furniture, cascading streamers and vinelike plants. The cheaper rooms upstairs have octagonal mattresses among other design liberties, adjoin an equally funky, vegetarian-friendly restaurant which features banana heart curry (P190) alongside other original dishes.

The two cheapest options when we visited were **Bayview Inn** (☎ 0917 273 3153; betcha_delatorre@yahoo.com; r P400), with dark but passable rooms in a creaky wooden house on the beach near the pier, and **El Nido Plaza Inn** (☎ 0926 254 6342; d/cottage from P300/600), with a few rote basic rooms on the wrong side of the beach road. Save additional dosh at the latter by utilising the guest kitchen.

Eating & Drinking

Balay Tubay (Real St; mains P120) Tribal-infused live music sets a perfect vibe at this welcome addition to the El Nido nightlife scene, and the food isn't half bad either.

For fans of grilled seafood and suds in the sand there are three or four establishments near OG's that set up tables on the beach, including **Seaslug's** (Hama St; mains P100-220).

On the other side of the road, **Barracks** (Hama St, frappes P85) has fresh sashimi, reggae, internet browsing and insanely good cookies 'n' cream frappes.

Getting There & Around

Seair and ITI fly from El Nido to Manila (see p657). The only way to the airport is by tricycle for P150.

For boats to Coron, see above. **Atienza Shipping Lines** (☎ 0919 566 6786) has a trip to Manila via Coron every Friday.

High-season *bangkas* wade down to Sabang (P2000 seven hours) roughly every other day, stopping in Port Barton (P1500, four hours) by request.

Two or three morning vans (P600, about 6½ hours) and four morning buses (P350, about eight hours) make the journey to Puerto Princesa.

CORON

pop 10,000

Divers know it as a wreck-diving hot spot, but the area known as Coron also has untouched beaches, crystal-clear lagoons and brooding limestone cliffs to tempt nondivers. Coron itself is actually just the sleepy main town of Busuanga Island – not to be confused with Coron Island to the south. Both Busuanga Island and Coron Island are part of the Calamian Group, located about halfway between Mindoro and Palawan.

Activities

Fifteen Japanese ships sunk by US fighter planes roost on the floor of Coron Bay just south of Busuanga. Getting to the wrecks from Coron involves a 1½- to four-hour boat ride, but diving is still affordable, averaging about US$40 for a two-tank dive. Most of the wrecks are for advanced divers, although there are a few in less than 25m that are suitable for beginners.

DID YOU KNOW?

In the early 1900s, the Americans turned the Calamian Group island of Culion into what would eventually become the world's largest leper colony.

OFF THE BEATEN TRACK IN CORON

Looking to get off the beaten track? Hire a boat or sea kayak and wade around the untouched beaches and islands off the west coast of Busuanga. Or tackle the rough coastal road to Busuanga's northwest tip by motorbike (P500), taking pit stops at beaches along the way.

Highlights of the area include **Calumbuyan Island** and **Banana Island**, both of which have world-class snorkelling. Off the northwest tip is **Calauit Island**, home to the **Calauit Safari Park** (admission P350), where the ancestors of giraffes, zebras and gazelles brought over from Kenya by Marcos in the 1970s roam. Boats to Calauit leave from Macalachao, 7km north of Buluang (P350, 10 minutes).

Some off-road experience is advised if you go the motorcycle route (the author's riding partner suffered two broken ribs in a fall near Buluang).

Coron town lacks a beach, but you can hire a boat (four-/eight-person boat per day about P1500/2500) to explore the seemingly infinite supply of islands nearby. **Coron Island**, with its towering spires of stratified limestone, is the star attraction. You can paddle around on a bamboo raft and swim in Coron Island's unspoiled **Lake Cayangan** (admission P200), or go diving in **Barracuda Lake** (admission P100), where the clear water gets scorching hot as you descend.

Sleeping & Eating

The following are in Coron town and hire out boats for island hopping.

Sea Dive Resort (☎ 0918 400 0448; www.seadiveresort.com.ph; d P300-1100;) A three-storey monolith on the sea accessed by a long walkway, this place has it all – decent rooms, restaurant, bar, internet and a busy dive shop.

Crystal Lodge (☎ 0928 410 8074; d P300-600, cottages P800-1100) Like much of Coron, this bamboo complex is built on stilts over the water. It's a maze of shady walkways ending in rooms that range from passable boxes to utterly unique overwater 'apartments'.

Sangat Island Reserve (☎ 0920 954 4328; www.sangat.com.ph; cottages per person from US$63) If you really want to treat yourself – and be much closer to the wrecks – this jewel of a resort is on its own island, about a one-hour boat ride from Coron (free transfer for guests). Prices include all meals.

our pick **Bistro Coron** (meals P150-500) A mouth-watering French bistro on one of the Philippines' most isolated islands? It works for us. Consider splurging for the tiger prawns, one of the best meals we've had in the Philippines. Proprietor-chef Bruno plans to move back to his former home in southern Palawan soon, but vows to keep Bistro running.

Getting There & Away

For air connections, see p657. Coron's YKR airport is a smooth 35-minute ride north of Coron town; vans (P150) meet the flights.

The weekly SuperFerry vessel between Manila and Puerto Princesa passes through Coron town (see p657). To/from Manila takes about 14 hours and costs from P1100; Puerto Princesa takes 13 hours and costs from P800.

San Nicolas Shipping (☎ 0928 744 5944, in Manila 02-243 4595) and Atienza Shipping Lines run weekly cargo boats from Manila with space for 80 to 100 passengers (P850, 22 hours). Atienza's boat continues to El Nido (P950, 10 hours) every Wednesday evening. The pricier option to El Nido are 15-passenger *bangka* that depart most mornings (P2200, eight hours).

PHILIPPINES DIRECTORY

ACCOMMODATION

Accommodation in the Philippines ranges from plush beachside bungalows to stuffy hotel shoeboxes, and everything in between. Many budget hotels offer a mix of fan-cooled and air-con rooms. In this book, unless otherwise noted, rooms in the P150 to P350 range are generally fan-cooled with a shared bathroom, and rooms in the P400 to P550 range usually have fan and private bathroom. Anything higher should have air-conditioning. Prices are approximately double in Manila and in trendy resort areas such as Boracay and Alona Beach, although reasonable dorm beds can be had in Manila for about P350.

As the Philippines becomes more popular, it's becoming more difficult to just walk in and find a room in smaller resort areas and touristy towns such as El Nido. Booking ahead is a good idea, at least in the high season (roughly December to May, with some regional variations).

Prices listed in this chapter are high-season rates. Room rates in tourist hot spots go down by up to 50% in the low season, but may triple or even quadruple during Holy Week (Easter) and around New Year's.

ACTIVITIES

Scuba diving is the most popular adventure activity in the Philippines, but there is also a small surf scene, kitesurfing and windsurfing on Boracay, and trekking just about everywhere. Other popular adventure sports covered in less detail in this book include cycling and mountain biking (see www.bugoybikers.com), birdwatching (see www.birdwatch.ph) and rock climbing (see www.geocities.com/powerupgyms).

Diving

Despite the destruction wrought by widespread dynamite fishing, the Philippines still boasts some top-notch dive sites. The WWII shipwrecks at Coron (Busuanga Island) offer outstanding wreck dives, while the impressive reefs around Puerto Galera (Mindoro), Apo Island (Negros), Panglao Island (Bohol), Padre Burgos (Leyte), and Moalboal and Malapascua Island (Cebu) offer a more traditional fish-and-coral environment. Generally, it costs certified divers about US$25 to US$30 for a single-tank dive with all equipment. PADI open-water certification courses vary widely from resort to resort and can cost anywhere from US$300 to US$450.

Kitesurfing & Windsurfing

The island of Boracay is the Philippine mecca for windsurfers and kitesurfers. The east side of Boracay has a huge, shallow lagoon that gets steady onshore winds from November to March. That and cheap prices (US$350 for a 12-hour certification course, equipment included) make Boracay one of the best places in the world to learn kitesurfing.

Surfing

The top surfing destination in the Philippines is Siargao Island, off the northeast coast of Mindanao. In the right weather conditions, the waves here can be Hawaiian in scale. The island's best surfing spot, Cloud Nine, is considered one of the top waves in the world. Other good breaks can be found all along the Philippines' eastern border, although many of the best breaks are virtually inaccessible and must be reached by boat. The season on the east coast generally coincides with typhoon season, roughly August to November. There is smaller but more consistent surf to be had from November to early March in San Juan, near San Fernando (La Union) on the west coast of Luzon. See www.surfpinoy.com for a rundown of surf spots in the Philippines.

Trekking

The entire archipelago is criss-crossed with paths and trails. They are not always clearly marked, so bring a guide unless you have extensive experience in backcountry navigation. Some of the best trekking areas are in the Cordillera Mountains of North Luzon, the rainforests of Palawan and the rugged interior of Samar and Leyte. Volcano climbing is a Philippine speciality – the big names are Mt Mayon in southeast Luzon and Mt Kanlaon on Negros. Check out www.pinoymountaineer.com for a comprehensive run-down of Philippine peaks.

BOOKS

Alongside this book, Lonely Planet also publishes a *Philippines* guide as well as the pint-sized *Filipino (Tagalog) Phrasebook*. Stanley Karnow's Pulitzer Prize–winning effort *In Our Image* is the definitive work on America's role in the Philippines over the years. Also a good read is *Invented Eden: the Elusive, Disputed History of the Tasaday,* in which Robin Hemley investigates the 1971 'discovery' of a primitive tribe in Mindanao, shedding light on Filipino society and (recent) history in the process.

BUSINESS HOURS

In the Philippines, banks open between 9am and 3pm, and government and tourist offices from 8am to noon and 1pm to 5pm Monday to Friday. Bars open from 6pm to late, and restaurants for breakfast, lunch and dinner. Shopping malls are open from 10am to around 9.30pm. Any exceptions to these hours are noted in individual reviews.

CLIMATE

The Philippines is hot throughout the year, with brief respites possible from December to February. For most of the country, the dry season is roughly November to May. Rains start in June, peak in August, and start tapering off in October. Typhoons are common from June to early December.

But in parts of the country the seasons are flipped. Eastern Mindanao, Southern Leyte, Samar and Southeast Luzon are rainy from December to March and relatively dry when the rest of the country is sopping.

The central Visayas are sheltered from the monsoon rains and thus have less pronounced seasons. These areas are liable to have rain at any time of the year, but it usually won't be too serious unless there's a typhoon stirring up trouble.

Use the website of **PAGASA** (www.pagasa.dost.gov.ph) to avoid meteorological trouble spots. See p936 for climate charts.

CUSTOMS

You can bring up to 2L of alcohol and 400 cigarettes into the country without paying duty.

DANGERS & ANNOYANCES

The Philippines certainly has more than its share of dangers. Typhoons, earthquakes, volcano eruptions, landslides and other natural disasters can wreak havoc with your travel plans – or worse if you happen to be in the wrong place at the wrong time. The 2009 typhoon season was particularly hellacious, as tropical storms Ketsana and Parma slammed the country days apart, killing hundreds and causing some of the worst flooding in recent memory in Manila and parts of North Luzon. Keep an eye on the news and be prepared to alter travel plans to avoid weather trouble spots.

Mindanao (the central and southwest regions in particular) and the Sulu Archipelago are the scenes of clashes between the army on one side and Muslim separatist groups on the other (see p606 and p654).

As for annoyances, you'll probably find you don't share the Filipino enthusiasm for roosters, particularly when the little beasts wake you for the 15th time in one night. Just as inescapable are the wails of karaoke.

Public transport presents its own set of annoyances. In addition to having poor safety records, buses and boats are notoriously loose with their schedules. Drivers often won't leave until they have a full bus – even if that means waiting overnight. Almost as often, they'll leave early. Patience and flexibility are key.

SCAMS

The most common scam in the Philippines involves confidence tricksters posing as a group of friends or a family and befriending (usually solo) travellers. They eventually invite them home or on a short excursion. The situation ends with the traveller being drugged and robbed. If you feel that a stranger is acting overly friendly to you, walk away. Beware as well of people who claim to have met you before or claim to be staying in your hotel.

This and most other scams are most common in Manila – see p615 for more on Manila scams.

DRIVING LICENCE

Tourists can use their home-country driving licence in the Philippines.

EMBASSIES & CONSULATES

The **Philippines Department of Foreign Affairs** (DFA; www.dfa.gov.ph) website lists all Philippine embassies and consulates abroad.

The following are located in Manila:

Australia (Map pp612-13; ☎ 02-757 8100/8102; www.australia.com.ph; 23rd fl, Tower 2, RCBC Plaza, 6819 Ayala Ave, Makati)

Brunei (Map pp612-13; ☎ 02-816 2836; 11th fl, BPI Bldg, cnr Ayala Ave & Paseo de Roxas, Makati)

Canada (Map pp612-13; ☎ 02-857 9000; www.dfait-maeci.gc.ca/manila; Levels 6-8, Tower 2, RCBC Plaza, 6819 Ayala Ave, Makati)

France (Map pp612-13; ☎ 02-857 6900; www.ambafrance-ph.org; 16th fl, Pacific Star Bldg, cnr Gil Puyat Ave & Makati Ave, Makati)

Germany (Map pp612-13; ☎ 02-702 3000; www.manila.diplo.de; 25/F Tower 2, RCBC Plaza, 6819 Ayala Ave, Makati)

Indonesia (Map pp612-13; ☎ 02-892 5061; 185 Salcedo St, Makati)

Laos (Map pp612-13; ☎ 02-852 5759; 34 Lapu-Lapu Ave, Magallanes, Makati)

Malaysia (Map pp612-13; ☎ 02-864 0761-68; www.kln.gov.my/perwakilan/manila; 330 Sen Gil Puyat Ave, Makati)

Myanmar (Map pp612-13; ☎ 02-893 1944; Gervasia Bldg, 152 Amorsolo St, Makati)

New Zealand (Map pp612-13; ☎ 02-891 5358-67; www.nzembassy.com; 23rd fl, BPI Buendia Centre, Gil Puyat Ave, Makati)

Singapore (Map pp612-13; ☎ 02-856 9922; 505 Rizal Drive, Fort Bonifacio)
Thailand (Map pp612-13; ☎ 02-815 4220; 107 Rada St, Makati)
UK (Map pp612-13; ☎ 02-858 2200; http://ukinthephilippines.fco.gov.uk; 120 Upper McKinley Rd, McKinley Hill, Taguig City)
USA (Map pp618-19; ☎ 02-301 2000; http://manila.usembassy.gov; 1201 Roxas Blvd, Ermita)
Vietnam (Map pp612-13; ☎ 02-524 0364; www.vietnamembassy-philippines.org; 670 Pablo Ocampo St, Malate)

FESTIVALS & EVENTS

Every Filipino town manages to squeeze in at least one fiesta a year, accompanied by frenzied eating, drinking and merry-making. These are our top five festivals:

Ati-Atihan (p635) Kalibo, Panay; mid-January.
Moriones Festival (Marinduque; Holy Week) Easter; Island south of Luzon is overrun by masked locals engaging in mock sword fights and playing pranks on bystanders.
Peñafrancia Festival (p630) Naga, southeast Luzon; third week of September.
MassKara (p640) Bacolod, Negros; around October 19
Crucifixion Ceremony Many locations, but the most famous, in San Fernando, Pampanga, sees Catholic devotees actually nailed to crosses every Good Friday.

FOOD & DRINK

Food

The indigenous cuisine blends a number of influences, particularly from China and Spain, with the main flavours being ginger, tamarind, onion, vinegar, soy sauce and herbs such as bay leaves rather than Asian spices. *Turo-turo* (literally 'point-point') restaurants are everywhere – they display their food in cafeteria-style glass cases and you simply point-point to your order.

Favourite Filipino snacks and dishes:

Adobo Chicken, pork or fish in a dark tangy sauce.
Balut Half-developed duck embryo, boiled in the shell.
Bibingka Fluffy rice-flour cakes topped with cheese.
Crispy pata Deep-fried pork hock or knuckles.
Halo-halo A tall, cold glass of milky crushed ice with fresh fruit and ice cream.
Kare-kare Meat (usually oxtail) cooked in peanut sauce.
Kinilaw Delicious Filipino-style *ceviche.*
Lechon Spit-roast suckling pig.
Lumpia Spring rolls filled with meat or vegetables.
Mami Noodle soup, like *mee* soup in Malaysia or Indonesia.
Pancit Stir-fried *bihon* (white) or *canton* (yellow) noodles with meat and vegetables.
Pinakbet Vegetables with shrimp paste, garlic, onions and ginger.
Sisig Crispy fried pork ears and jowl.

Drink

The national brew, San Miguel, is very palatable and despite being a monopolist is eminently affordable at around P20 (P25 to P50 in bars). San Miguel also brews a beer called Red Horse; it's ludicrously strong so make sure you are close to home when you order your 1L bottle. Tanduay rum is the national drink, and amazingly cheap at around P75 per litre. It's usually served with coke. Popular non-alcoholic drinks include *buko* juice (young coconut juice with floating pieces of jelly-like flesh) and sweetened *calamansi* juice (*calamansi* are small local limes).

GAY & LESBIAN TRAVELLERS

Bakla (gay men) and *binalaki* or *tomboy* (lesbians) are almost universally accepted in the Philippines. There are well-established gay centres in major cities, but foreigners should be wary of hustlers and police harassment. Remedios Circle in Malate, Manila, is the site of a June gay-pride parade and the centre for nightlife.

Online gay and lesbian resources for the Philippines include **Utopia Asian Gay & Lesbian Resources** (www.utopia-asia.com), and there's a useful link on www.filipin olinks.com.

HOLIDAYS

Offices and banks are closed on public holidays, although shops and department stores stay open. Maundy Thursday and Good Friday are the only days when the entire country closes down – even most public transport and some airlines stop running. Public holidays:

New Year's Day 1 January
People Power Day 25 February
Maundy Thursday, Good Friday & Easter Sunday March/April
Araw ng Kagitingan (Bataan Day) 9 April
Labour Day 1 May
Independence Day 12 June
Ninoy Aquino Day 21 August
National Heroes Day Last Sunday in August
All Saints' Day 1 November
End of Ramadan Varies; depends on Islamic calendar
Bonifacio Day (National Heroes Day) 30 November
Christmas Day 25 December
Rizal Day 30 December
New Year's Eve 31 December

INTERNET ACCESS

Internet cafes are all over the Philippines. Speedy connections are readily available in all cities for P15 to P25 per hour. Figure on double or triple that in very remote or particularly touristy areas. Wi-fi is now the rule rather than the exception in hotels and coffee shops in large cities and touristy areas. With an internet-enabled mobile phone you can access the internet through the Philippines' primary mobile-phone providers, Globe Telecom and Smart. Both also have internet cards you can plug into your laptop. Get set up at any Smart or Globe wireless centre; most malls in Manila and elsewhere have them.

INTERNET RESOURCES

ClickTheCity.Com (www.clickthecity.com) A great listings site for happenings in Manila and around the country, with a decent travel section to boot.
National Commission for Culture & the Arts (www.ncca.gov.ph) This outstanding website contains primers on the arts and background on the Philippines' various ethnic groups and tribes.
Philippine Newslink (www.philnews.com) This has a fantastically thorough pile of local news and views, and includes links to all the main daily newspapers.
PinoyPress (www.pinoypress.net) Hard-hitting webzine with insightful analysis of the Mindanao conflict and other key national issues.
US Department of State (www.travel.state.gov) Mildly paranoid but useful travel information and advisories. The US is said to have the best Western intelligence-gathering network in the Philippines.

LEGAL MATTERS

Drugs are risky; even being caught with marijuana for personal use can mean jail, while traffickers could face life in prison. Should you find yourself in trouble, your first recourse is your embassy, so make a point of writing down the phone number. If you are arrested your embassy may not be able to do anything more than provide you with a list of local lawyers and keep an eye on how you're being treated. Another good number to know is the Department of Tourism's **Tourist Security Division** (☎ in Manila 02-524 1728/1660; 24 hr).

MAPS

The Nelles Verlag *Philippines* map is a good map of the islands at a scale of 1:1,500,000. More useful to the traveller are the excellent locally produced *E-Z* maps of each region, which are widely available at P99 per map.

LEGAL AGE

- you can begin driving at 16
- voting age is 18
- drinking is allowed from 18
- sex is legal at 18

MEDIA

Magazines & Newspapers

There are about 20 major national and regional English-language newspapers, ranging from the staid *Manila Bulletin* to the critical *Philippine Daily Inquirer* and the feel-good *Philippine Star*. Two of the better newspapers are *Business World* and *Business Mirror*, which contain national news and good-weekend guides in addition to business news. These national papers can be found in newspaper stands all over the country, although they have a heavily Manila-centric world view. The formerly weekly, now quarterly *Newsbreak* is the best news magazine of the lot. It's connected to the Philippine Centre for Investigative Journalism (www.pcij.org).

TV

There are about seven major channels broadcast from Manila, sometimes in English, sometimes in Tagalog. Most midrange hotels have cable TV with access to between 20 and 120 channels, including some obscure regional channels, a couple of Filipino and international movie channels, the big global news and sports channels such as BBC and ESPN, and the country's own 24-hour English-language news channel, ANC. The latter is owned by ABS-CBN, which competes with the GMA network for national supremacy, providing Tagalog-language programming aimed at the lowest common denominator. Think racy Latin American–style variety shows, cheap local soaps and Filipino action movies.

MONEY

The unit of currency is the peso, divided into 100 centavos. Banknotes come in denominations of 20, 50, 100, 200, 500 and 1000 pesos. The most common coins are one, five and 10 pesos.

ATMs

ATMs are located in all major cities and towns throughout the country. Where a region covered in this chapter does not have ATMs (such as most of Palawan), it is noted in that section. The Maestro-Cirrus network is most readily accepted, followed by Visa/Plus cards, then by American Express (Amex). The most prevalent ATMs that accept most Western bank cards belong to Banco de Oro (BDO), Bank of the Philippine Islands (BPI) and Metrobank. Most ATMs have a P10,000-per-transaction withdrawal limit; the HSBC and Citibank ATMs in Manila and Cebu let you take out P25,000 to P40,000 per transaction.

Cash

Emergency cash in US dollars is a good thing to have in case you get stuck in an area with no working ATM. Other currencies, such as the euro or UK pound, are more difficult to change outside of the bigger cities.

'Sorry, no change' becomes a very familiar line. Stock up on notes smaller than P500 at every opportunity.

Credit Cards

Major credit cards are accepted by many hotels, restaurants and businesses. Outside of Manila, businesses sometimes charge a bit extra (about 4%) for credit-card transactions. Most Philippine banks will let you take a cash advance on your card.

Exchanging Money

Money changers are much faster than the banks and give a better rate for cash, but can be dodgy, particularly in Manila. They prefer US dollars. Ask your hotel front desk to recommend a local money changer. In the provinces, hotels will often change money for you.

Travellers Cheques

We don't recommend bringing travellers cheques as banks in the Philippines seem to have a vendetta against them. Without exception you will need your passport and the original receipts. You stand the best chance with Amex US-dollar cheques – other companies and denominations may not be changeable. The best place to cash Amex travellers cheques is at its branch in Makati (see p615).

POST

The postal system is generally quite efficient, but mail from the provinces can take weeks to reach Manila, let alone the outside world. Wait until you get back to the capital if you're sending anything internationally.

EXCHANGE RATES

Exchange rates at the time of going to press:

Country	Unit	Pesos (P)
Australia	A$1	41.68
Canada	C$1	44.08
Euro zone	€1	69.06
Indonesia	10,000Rp	48.87
Japan	¥100	52.45
Malaysia	RM1	13.66
New Zealand	NZ$1	34.17
UK	UK£1	75.35
US	US$1	47.17

RESPONSIBLE TRAVEL

As in other Asian countries, always allow locals a way of extracting themselves from an awkward situation. Publicly dressing down a Filipino is a surefire way to stir up trouble. Most Filipinos love having their photo taken, but tribespeople in rural areas in particular might resent it if you snap away without asking.

The Philippines is home to 100 or so cultural groups, and while it is rather adventurous to trek to a tribal village, you have to be a little more cautious. It might just be a fleeting visit for you, but the impression you make could be long remembered. Obvious displays of wealth are a no-no. Gifts are warmly received but should be kept modest; matches and small bottles of *ginebra* (local gin) work well. Ask to meet the village headman before staying overnight, and always respect the wishes of the locals.

The Philippines has a pretty abominable environmental record, and visitors are often put off by the way Filipinos throw their garbage everywhere and urinate in public. This is certainly one situation where the 'When in Rome…' maxim does not apply. Set an example by using garbage bins (when you can find them) and politely refusing the 7-Eleven clerk's offer to put your minute packet of chewing gum in a plastic bag. As with anywhere, tread particularly softly in environmentally sensitive areas such as coral reefs, rice terraces, rainforests and whale shark zones.

TELEPHONE

The Philippine Long Distance Telephone Company (PLDT) operates the Philippines' fixed-line network. Local calls cost almost nothing; long-distance domestic calls are also very reasonable. PLDT 'Pwede' and 'Touch' prepaid cards allow dirt-cheap domestic calls from any PLDT landline or payphone. Use the PLDT 'Budget' card to call the US for only P3 per minute (other international destinations cost slightly more). These cards are available at phone kiosks in malls and elsewhere.

Mobile phones are huge here, and half the country spends much of the time furiously texting the other half. For travellers, a cellphone can be a good thing to have in the event of an emergency. They are also useful for booking rooms (often accomplished by text message) and texting newly made Filipino friends.

The best strategy is to bring your own GSM phone and purchase a local prepaid SIM card (P100) to avoid hefty overseas roaming charges. Globe Telecom and Smart are the main mobile companies. Text messages cost P1 to P2 per message, while local calls cost P7.50 per minute (less if calling within a mobile network). International text messages cost P15, and international calls cost US$0.40 per minute. Philippine mobile-phone numbers begin with 09.

The country code for the Philippines is ☎ 63. The international dialling code is ☎ 00. For local area codes, dial the first zero when calling from within the Philippines. For the PLDT directory, call ☎ 187 nationwide. For the international operator, dial ☎ 108.

TOILETS

Toilets are commonly called a 'CR', an abbreviation of the delightfully euphemistic 'comfort room'. Public toilets are virtually nonexistent, so aim for one of the ubiquitous fast-food restaurants should you need a room of comfort.

TOURIST INFORMATION

The Philippines' tourism authority is run out of the **Department of Tourism Information Centre** (DOT; Map pp618-19; ☎ 02-524 2384; www.wowphilippines.ph; TM Kalaw St; 🕒 7am-6pm) in Manila. The DOT's website has contact information for DOT representatives in the US, UK, Australia and other countries.

TRAVELLERS WITH DISABILITIES

Steps up to hotels, tiny cramped toilets and narrow doors are the norm outside of four-star hotels in Manila, Cebu and a handful of larger provincial cities. Lifts are often out of order, and boarding any form of rural transport is likely to be fraught with difficulty. On the other hand, most Filipinos are more than willing to lend a helping hand, and the cost of hiring a taxi for a day and possibly an assistant as well is not excessive.

VISAS

Citizens of nearly all countries do not need a visa to enter the Philippines for stays of less than 22 days. When you arrive you'll receive a 21-day visa free of charge. If you overstay your visa you face fines and airport immigration officials may not let you pass through immigration.

Avoid this inconvenience by extending your 21-day visa to 59 days before it expires. Extensions cost P3030 and are a breeze at most provincial BOI offices (see following). The process is infinitely more painful at the **BOI head office** (Map p616; ☎ 02-527 3248; Magallanes Dr, Intramuros, Manila; 🕒 8am-noon & 1-5pm Mon-Fri).

PROSTITUTION IN THE PHILIPPINES

One social issue related to travel in the Philippines is prostitution and its most insidious form, child prostitution. In some European and Japanese magazines, the Philippines is actively promoted as a prime sex-tourism destination. Among the major sex-tour operators is the Japanese organised-crime group Yakuza.

Although prostitution is officially illegal in the Philippines, the 'red light' districts of most big cities operate openly and freely, with karaoke bars, 'discos', go-go bars and strip clubs all acting as fronts. The call girls are euphemistically called 'GROs' – guest relations officers.

The Asia-Pacific office of the **Coalition Against Trafficking in Women** (☎ 02-426 9873; www.catw-ap.org) is based in Quezon City. Its website has information about prostitution in the Philippines and several useful links.

Another option is to secure a three-month visa before you arrive in the Philippines. These cost US$30 to US$45 depending on where you apply.

For a full list of provincial immigration offices, hit the 'BI-Subport' link at http://immigration.gov.ph. The site also has updated visa regulations and fees. Useful provincial offices include the following:

Baguio (☎ 074-447 0800; cnr Yandoc St & Abanao Rd)

Boracay (Map p638; ☎ 036-288 5267; Nirvana Resort, Main Rd; 🕒 8am-5.30pm Mon & Tue, 3-6pm Wed)

Cebu City (off Map p645; ☎ 032-345 6442; cnr Burgos St & Mandaue Ave) Relatively hassle-free visa extensions. It's behind the Mandaue Fire Station, opposite the Mandaue Sports Complex, 6.5km northeast of town.

Puerto Galera (Map p634; ☎ 043-288 2245; Puerto Galera municipal compound; 🕒 Mon-Wed)

Puerto Princesa (☎ 048-433 2248; 2nd fl, Servando Bldg, Rizal Ave)

Onward Tickets

Be prepared to show your airline a ticket for onward travel within three weeks of your arrival date if you want a 21-day visa on arrival. If you don't have one, the airline will more often than not make you buy one on the spot. BOI offices also sometimes ask to see onward tickets before they process visa extensions.

VOLUNTEERING

Hands On Manila (☎ 02-386 6521; www.handsonmanila.org) is a wonderful organisation that is always looking for eager volunteers to help with disaster assistance and other projects. The **Center for Education, Research & Volunteering Philippines** (CERV; ☎ 703 2227; www.volunteerphilippines.com) offers volunteer opportunities in metro Manila and Romblon, while **Volunteer for the Visayas** (☎ 053-325 2462; www.visayans.org) runs various volunteer programs around Tacloban, Leyte. **Habitat for Humanity** (☎ 897 3069; www.habitat.org.ph) builds houses for the poor all over the country, concentrating on disaster-affected areas.

WOMEN TRAVELLERS

Many male Filipinos think of themselves as irresistible macho types, but by the same token can also be surprisingly considerate, and they are especially keen to show their best side to foreign women. They will address you as 'Ma'am', shower you with compliments and engage you in polite conversation. Do note that in Filipino dating culture, striking up a private conversation may be seen as first step towards something more intimate.

Filipinas rarely miss the chance to ask personal questions simply out of curiosity – about your home country, family, marital status and so on. It is worth packing a few stock answers to these questions in your luggage for cheerful distribution.

Tampons are fairly widely available but it's a good idea to stock up.

Singapore

HIGHLIGHTS

- **Little India** (p680) A jumble of gold, textiles, temples and cheap eats minutes from Orchard Rd, this could be another country entirely.
- **Singapore Zoo** and **Night Safari** (p684) Tucked into the forest, these outstanding open-concept zoos are notable for housing over 2000 species.
- **Baba House** (p680) Book the detailed tour through this gorgeous restored Peranakan house.
- **Southern Ridges** (p684) Pack lots of water and spend the day walking along Singapore's best urban trail.
- **Colonial architecture** (p677) Hark back to the days of the empire as you take a stroll through the Colonial District.
- **Off the beaten track** (p685) Take a hike through one of the world's only patches of urban primary rainforest at Bukit Timah, or over a treetop walk at MacRitchie Reservoir.

FAST FACTS

- **Budget** US$40 a day
- **Costs** hostel dorm bed S$18 to S$20, average bus ride S$2, beer S$7 to S$8
- **Country code** ☎ 65
- **Languages** English, Mandarin, Malay, Tamil
- **Money** US$1 = S$1.41 (Singaporean dollar)
- **Phrases** *ni hao ma?* (how are you?), *zai jian* (goodbye), *xie xie* (thanks), *dui bu qi* (sorry)
- **Population** 4.8 million
- **Time** GMT + eight hours
- **Visas** most travellers get a 30-day tourist visa on arrival

TRAVEL HINTS

Some museums are free after 6pm (National Museum of Singapore) or after 7pm (Asian Civilisations Museum, on Fridays). The Singapore Art Museum is also free from 12pm to 2pm daily. Also, each neighbourhood in Singapore tends to radiate out from a mall and a food centre or two – great places to people watch, have cheap meals and order large S$7 bottles of Tiger beer.

OVERLAND ROUTES

Take the Causeway bridge across to Johor Bahru in Malaysia, or cross the Second Links bridge at Tuas to Tanjung Kupang in Malaysia. Weekends are crazy.

Let's clear up a misconception: Singapore isn't the police state that some media has made it out to be. Sure, there are signs indicating fines for a variety of misdemeanours, but who needs litter or chaos on the streets anyway? Singapore is a 'fine' city in more of a metaphorical sense.

One of Asia's success stories, tiny little Singapore's GDP consistently ranks it as one of the wealthiest countries in the world. Along with that attendant wealth comes a rich culture borne of a multiracial population. Get lost in the mad swirl of skyscrapers in the central business district (CBD), be transfixed by the Bolly beats in the streets of ramshackle Little India, hike a dense patch of rainforest in Bukit Timah or just give yourself up to the retail mayhem of Orchard Rd.

It's affluent, hi-tech and occasionally a little snobbish, but Singapore's great leveller is the hawker centre, the ubiquitous and raucous food markets where everyone mucks in together to indulge the local mania for cheap eating. Singapore makes for a perfect pit stop to recover from the rough-and-tumble of the rest of Southeast Asia.

CURRENT EVENTS

Singapore is undergoing a development boom, gearing up to boost its population to 6.5 million and reposition itself as a centre for everything from biomedical research to tourism. Two huge casino resorts are being built on Sentosa Island (due for completion in 2010) and at Marina South (due for completion in 2009), while the entire Marina Bay area around the futuristic Esplanade theatre (p680) is being turned into an upmarket commercial, residential, leisure and water-sports centre.

The economic downturn hit Singapore in early 2009, affecting much of its export business. However, despite this, the two casinos were still proceeding with their planned 2010 opening dates. There was election buzz in mid-2009 though at the time of writing, nothing had yet been formally announced.

What we do know is that the government dug S$4.9 billion deep into reserves (now standing at S$170 billion) for a S$20 billion 'resilience' package to combat the financial crisis. It seems to be working, as life in Singapore ticks on.

HISTORY

Lion City

Records of Singapore's early history are patchy; originally it was a tiny sea town squeezed between powerful neighbours Sumatra and Melaka. According to Malay legend, a Sumatran prince spotted a lion while visiting the island of Temasek, and on the basis of this good omen he founded a city there called Singapura (Lion City).

Raffles

Sir Thomas Stamford Raffles arrived in 1819 on a mission to secure a strategic base for the British Empire in the Strait of Melaka. He decided to transform the sparsely populated, swampy island into a free-trade port. The layout of central Singapore is still as Raffles drew it.

World War II

The glory days of the empire came to an abrupt end on 15 February 1942, when the Japanese invaded Singapore. For the rest of WWII the Japanese ruled the island harshly, jailing Allied prisoners of war (POWs) at Changi Prison and killing thousands of locals. Although the British were welcomed back after the war, the empire's days in the region were numbered.

Foundation for the Future

The socialist People's Action Party (PAP) was founded in 1954, with Lee Kuan Yew as its secretary general. Lee led the PAP to victory in elections held in 1959, and hung onto power for over 30 years. Singapore was kicked out of the Malay Federation in 1965, but Lee made the most of one-party rule and pushed through an ambitious industrialisation program and a strict regulation of social behaviour.

His successor in 1990 was Goh Chok Tong, who loosened things up a little, but maintained Singapore on the path Lee had forged. In 2004 Goh stepped down to make way for Lee's son, Lee Hsien Loong.

Lee the Younger faces the huge challenge of positioning Singapore to succeed in the modern, globalised economy. As manufacturing bleeds away to cheaper competitors, the government knows it must boost its population, attract more so-called 'foreign talent' and develop industries like tourism, financial services, digital media and biomedical research if its success story is to continue into the future.

THE CULTURE

The National Psyche

Affluent Singaporeans live in an apparently constant state of transition, continuously urged by their ever-present government to upgrade, improve and reinvent.

On the surface, these are thoroughly modernised people, but many lives are still ruled by old beliefs and customs. There is also a sharp divide between the older generation, who experienced the huge upheavals and relentless graft that built modern Singapore, and the pampered younger generation, who enjoy the fruits of that labour.

Lifestyle

While family and tradition are important, many young people live their lives outside of home, either working long hours or visiting bars, hawker stalls and shopping malls after work. Intergenerational families (where several generations live together) are not uncommon, and some Singaporeans live at home well into their 30s.

The majority of the population lives in Housing Development Board flats (you can't miss them). These flats are heavily subsidised by the government (which even dictates the ratio of races living in each block). These subsidies favour married couples, while singles and gay and lesbian couples have to tough it out on the open real-estate market.

Although the three main cultures in Singapore are still very boy-child focused, women have more or less equal access to education and employment. Likewise, despite the oft-touted antihomosexual stance of the government, gay men and lesbians are a highly visible part of everyday life in Singapore.

With Singapore being so small, most activities are of sedentary nature. Aside from shopping, Singaporeans love eating and watching movies. There are still pockets of space for sporting activities and outdoor walks.

MUST READ

Former local expat (a rather apt misnomer) Neil Humphreys fully embraced living local in Singapore. The journalist wrote three very tongue-in-cheek books about the ten years he spent here, now collected in one volume, *Complete Notes from Singapore*. Neil's books were best sellers in Singapore and he continues writing columns for the *Straits Times*. The book can be found in most local bookstores.

Population

The majority of the country is Chinese (75.2% of the population). Next come the Malays at 13.6%. Singaporean Indians (8.8%) mostly come from south India and speak Tamil. The rest of the population is a mixture of races conveniently lumped under the heading of 'others'. Western expats are a very visible group. Not so visible is the large population of domestic maids and foreign labourers. Note that contrary to popular belief, English is the first language of Singapore. Many Singaporeans speak a second language or dialect (usually Mandarin, Malay or Tamil).

Religion

The Chinese majority are usually Buddhists or Taoists, and Chinese customs, superstitions and festivals dominate social life. It's not uncommon for many Chinese homes to have an altar where daily offerings of prayers and joss sticks are made.

The Malays embrace Islam as a religion and a way of life. *Adat* (customary law) guides important ceremonies and events, including birth, circumcision and marriage.

Over half the Indians are Hindus and worship the pantheon of gods in various temples across Singapore.

Christianity, including Catholicism, is also popular in Singapore with both Chinese and Indians pledging their faith to this religion.

ARTS

Singapore's arts scene has blossomed in recent years. The number of art galleries has grown and there is a small but significant theatre scene with groups such as the **Singapore Repertory Theatre** (www.srt.com.sg), **Wild Rice** (www.wildrice.com.sg) and the **Necessary Stage** (www.necessary.org). The **MICA building** (Map pp678-9) contains a few worthy art galleries.

The construction of the Esplanade theatre (p680) has helped place Singapore on the world arts map and has drawn more international performers – from Western classical to Chinese opera, Asian dance troupes to American jazz quartets. The best time to catch the cream of Singapore's performing arts is during the annual **Arts Festival** (www.singaporeartsfest.com), held in June.

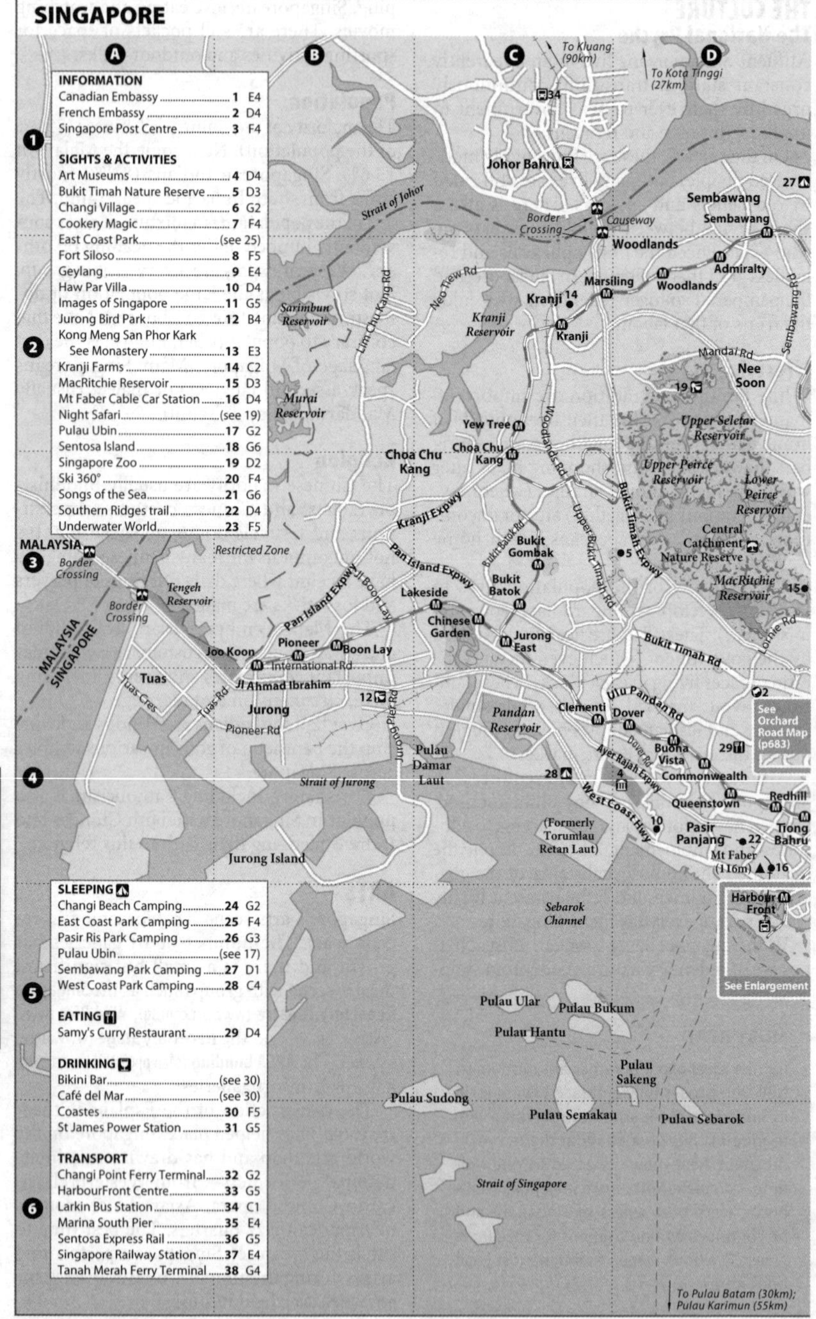
SINGAPORE
INFORMATION
Canadian Embassy 1 E4
French Embassy 2 D4
Singapore Post Centre 3 F4
SIGHTS & ACTIVITIES
Art Museums 4 D4
Bukit Timah Nature Reserve 5 D3
Changi Village 6 G2
Cookery Magic 7 F4
East Coast Park (see 25)
Fort Siloso 8 F5
Geylang 9 E4
Haw Par Villa 10 D4
Images of Singapore 11 G5
Jurong Bird Park 12 B4
Kong Meng San Phor Kark See Monastery 13 E3
Kranji Farms 14 C2
MacRitchie Reservoir 15 D3
Mt Faber Cable Car Station 16 D4
Night Safari (see 19)
Pulau Ubin 17 G2
Sentosa Island 18 G6
Singapore Zoo 19 D2
Ski 360° 20 F4
Songs of the Sea 21 G6
Southern Ridges trail 22 D4
Underwater World 23 F5
SLEEPING
Changi Beach Camping 24 G2
East Coast Park Camping 25 F4
Pasir Ris Park Camping 26 G3
Pulau Ubin (see 17)
Sembawang Park Camping 27 D1
West Coast Park Camping 28 C4
EATING
Samy's Curry Restaurant 29 D4
DRINKING
Bikini Bar (see 30)
Café del Mar (see 30)
Coastes 30 F5
St James Power Station 31 G5
TRANSPORT
Changi Point Ferry Terminal 32 G2
HarbourFront Centre 33 G5
Larkin Bus Station 34 C1
Marina South Pier 35 E4
Sentosa Express Rail 36 G5
Singapore Railway Station 37 E4
Tanah Merah Ferry Terminal 38 G4
To Kluang (90km)
To Kota Tinggi (27km)
Johor Bahru
Strait of Johor
Border Crossing
Causeway
Woodlands
Sembawang
Admiralty
Marsiling
Kranji
Kranji Reservoir
Sarimbun Reservoir
Murai Reservoir
Lim Chu Kang Rd
Neo Tiew Rd
Mandai Rd
Nee Soon
Sembawang Rd
Upper Seletar Reservoir
Upper Peirce Reservoir
Lower Peirce Reservoir
Central Catchment Nature Reserve
MacRitchie Reservoir
Lornie Rd
Yew Tree
Choa Chu Kang
Woodlands Rd
Upper Bukit Timah Rd
Bukit Timah Expwy
Kranji Expwy
Bukit Batok Rd
Bukit Gombak
Bukit Batok
Pan Island Expwy
Jl Boon Lay
Restricted Zone
MALAYSIA
Border Crossing
Tengeh Reservoir
MALAYSIA SINGAPORE
Lakeside
Chinese Garden
Jurong East
Bukit Timah Rd
Joo Koon
Pioneer
Boon Lay
International Rd
Tuas
Jl Ahmad Ibrahim
Tuas Cres
Tuas Rd
Jurong
Pioneer Rd
Jurong Pier Rd
Pandan Reservoir
Clementi
Ulu Pandan Rd
Dover
Dover Rd
Ayer Rajah Expwy
Buona Vista
Commonwealth
Queenstown
Redhill
Tiong Bahru
See Orchard Road Map (p683)
Pulau Damar Laut
Strait of Jurong
West Coast Hwy
(Formerly Torumlau Retan Laut)
Pasir Panjang
Mt Faber (116m)
Jurong Island
Harbour Front
See Enlargement
Sebarok Channel
Pulau Ular
Pulau Bukum
Pulau Hantu
Pulau Sakeng
Pulau Sudong
Pulau Semakau
Pulau Sebarok
Strait of Singapore
To Pulau Batam (30km); Pulau Karimun (55km)

SINGAPORE

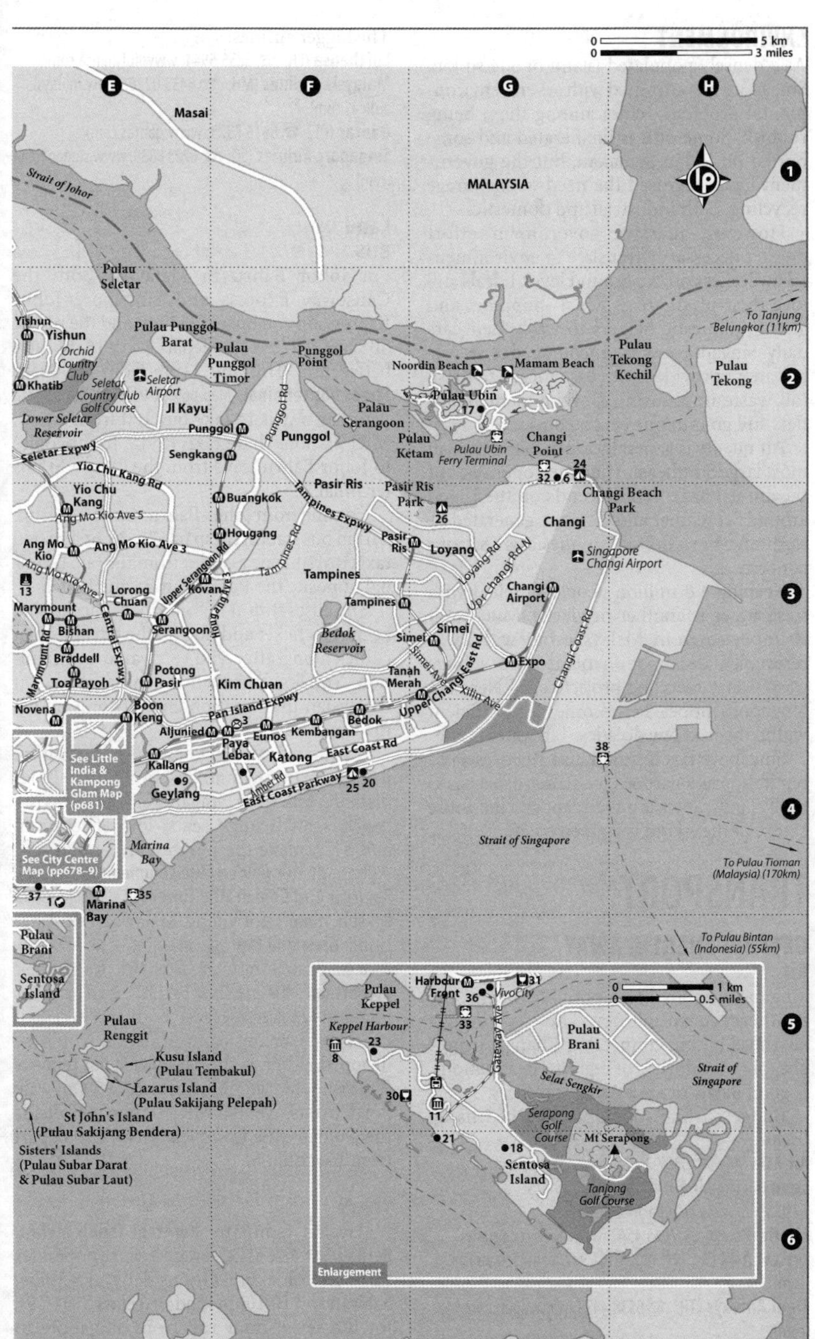
MALAYSIA
Masai
Strait of Johor
Pulau Seletar
Yishun
Orchid Country Club
Khatib
Seletar Country Club Golf Course
Seletar Airport
Lower Seletar Reservoir
Pulau Punggol Barat
Pulau Punggol Timor
Jl Kayu
Punggol Point
Punggol Rd
Punggol
Sengkang
Seletar Expwy
Yio Chu Kang Rd
Yio Chu Kang
Ang Mo Kio Ave 5
Ang Mo Kio
Ang Mo Kio Ave 3
Ang Mo Kio Ave 1
Buangkok
Hougang
Upper Serangoon Rd
Kovan
Hougang Ave 3
Lorong Chuan
Marymount
Bishan
Central Expwy
Serangoon
Braddell
Marymount Rd
Toa Payoh
Potong Pasir
Novena
Boon Keng
Kim Chuan
Pan Island Expwy
Aljunied
Paya Lebar
Eunos
Kembangan
Bedok
Kallang
Geylang
Katong
East Coast Rd
Amber Rd
East Coast Parkway
See Little India & Kampong Glam Map (p681)
See City Centre Map (pp678–9)
Marina Bay
Pulau Brani
Sentosa Island
Pulau Renggit
Kusu Island (Pulau Tembakul)
Lazarus Island (Pulau Sakijang Pelepah)
St John's Island (Pulau Sakijang Bendera)
Sisters' Islands (Pulau Subar Darat & Pulau Subar Laut)
Tampines Expwy
Tampines Rd
Pasir Ris
Pasir Ris Park
Tampines
Bedok Reservoir
Simei
Simei Ave
Tanah Merah
Upper Changi East Rd
Upper Changi Rd
Xilin Ave
Expo
Loyang
Loyang Rd
Upr Changi Rd N
Changi Airport
Changi Coast Rd
Singapore Changi Airport
Changi
Changi Point
Changi Beach Park
Palau Serangoon
Pulau Ketam
Pulau Ubin
Pulau Ubin Ferry Terminal
Noordin Beach
Mamam Beach
Pulau Tekong Kechil
Pulau Tekong
To Tanjung Belungkor (11km)
Strait of Singapore
To Pulau Tioman (Malaysia) (170km)
To Pulau Bintan (Indonesia) (55km)
Harbour Front
VivoCity
Pulau Keppel
Keppel Harbour
Gateway Ave
Selat Sengkir
Serapong Golf Course
Mt Serapong
Tanjong Golf Course
Strait of Singapore
Enlargement
0 5 km
0 3 miles
0 1 km
0 0.5 miles

SINGAPORE

ENVIRONMENT

As a densely populated island of 604 sq km, Singapore is confronted with several environmental problems, chief among them being rubbish. Some of it is incinerated and some buried on Pulau Semakau, but the government has recognised the need to encourage recycling, both industrial and domestic.

However, massive government effort doesn't necessarily translate to environmental awareness on the ground level. Locals still love their plastic bags when shopping, and getting domestic helpers to wash their cars daily. Singaporeans are encouraged to recycle but aren't provided with easy means to do so (all waste in Housing Development Board flats still go into one central bin).

Air quality is generally much better than in most large Southeast Asian metropolises, but the annual haze that descends on the island around September and October, generated by slash-and-burn fires in Indonesia, is a serious concern.

Keeping 4.8 million people supplied with fresh water is another headache. Much of it is imported from Malaysia, but with large reservoirs, desalination plants and a huge waste-water recycling project called Newater, Singapore hopes to become self-sufficient within the next few decades. Tap water is safe.

Singapore has a proud and well-deserved reputation as a garden city. Parks, often beautifully landscaped, are abundant and the entire centre of the island is a green oasis.

TRANSPORT

GETTING THERE & AWAY

Air

Singapore is an ideal point to begin any Southeast Asian journey. The city's budget air-travel boom, connecting Changi Airport cheaply with dozens of regional destinations, is good news for shoestring travellers.

Budget airlines operating out of Changi include:

Air Asia (AK; ☎ 6307 7688; www.airasia.com)
Cebu Pacific Air (5J; ☎ agents 6735 7155, 6737 9231, 6220 5966; www.cebupacificair.com)
Firefly (FY; ☎ 03-7845 4543; www.fireflyz.com.my)
Jetstar Asia (3K; ☎ 1800 6161 977; www.jetstarasia.com)
Tiger Airways (TR; ☎ 6538 4437; www.tigerairways.com)

The bigger airlines:

Lufthansa (LH; ☎ 6835 5944; www.lufthansa.com)
Malaysia Airlines (MH; ☎ 6433 0220; www.malaysiaairlines.com)
Qantas (QF; ☎ 6415 7373; www.qantas.com)
Singapore Airlines (SQ; ☎ 6223 8888; www.singaporeair.com)

Land

BUS

For Johor Bahru in Malaysia, both the Causeway Express and Singapore–Johor Express air-con buses (S$2.40) and the public SBS bus 170 (S$1.70) depart every 15 minutes between 6.30am and 11pm from the **Queen Street bus terminal** (Map p681; cnr Queen & Arab Sts). Another way is to take bus 160 from Kranji MRT station. Share taxis (S$10, four people) to Johor Bahru leave from the Queen St bus terminal.

Coming from Johor Bahru, take a bus from Larkin bus station (Map pp672–3), or a shared taxi (RM10, four people) from the taxi terminal opposite the Puteri Pan Pacific Hotel.

The buses stop at the Singapore checkpoint; keep your ticket and hop on the next bus that comes along after you've cleared immigration. You'll go through the same process at Malaysian immigration and customs across the Causeway.

If you are travelling beyond Johor Bahru, it is easier to catch an air-conditioned long-distance bus from Singapore. Cheap luxury coaches, with huge seats, lots of legroom and TVs, make the journey pretty pleasant. Agents at the **Golden Mile Complex** (off Map p681; Beach Rd) and **Golden Mile Tower** (off Map p681; Beach Rd) sell tickets for many Malaysian destinations. **Grassland Express** (off Map p681; ☎ 6293 1166; www.grassland.com.sg; 01-26 Golden Mile Complex) and **Konsortium** (off Map p681; ☎ 6392 3911; www.konsortium.com.sg; 01-52 Golden Mile Tower) both run excellent coaches. Arriving from Malaysia, you'll be dropped either at the **Lavender St bus terminal** (Map p681; cnr Lavender St & Kallang Bahru), a 500m walk north from Lavender MRT station, or outside the Golden Mile Complex. Buses also depart from Lavender St.

TRAIN

Malaysian company **Keretapi Tanah Melayu Berhad** (☎ 6222 5165; www.ktmb.com.my) operates three air-con express trains daily, at 8.10am, 3.05pm and 10.10pm (2nd/3rd class S$34/19), for the seven-hour run from Singapore to

> **GETTING TO MALAYSIA**
>
> The 1km-long Causeway bridge in the north, at Woodlands, connects Singapore with Johor Bahru in Malaysia. To the west a bridge connects the suburb of Tuas with Tanjung Kupang, also in Malaysia. Immigration procedures on both sides of the bridges are straightforward. See opposite for details of buses and trains heading across the border.

Kuala Lumpur, with connections on to Thailand. Trains depart from the **Singapore Railway Station** (Map pp672-3; ☎ 6222 5165; Keppel Rd; ticket office 8.30am-2pm, 3pm-7pm).

When travelling into Malaysia by train, passports are checked by Malaysian immigration at the Singapore train station (officially part of Malaysia) but not stamped. This should not be a problem when you leave Malaysia if you keep your train ticket and immigration card.

Sea

Ferries connect Singapore to Indonesia's Riau archipelago (including Pulau Batam, Pulau Bintan, Tanjung Balai and Tanjung Batu). There are two departure points: the **HarbourFront Centre** (Map pp672-3; ☎ 6513 2200), next to HarbourFront MRT station, and **Tanah Merah ferry terminal** (Map pp672-3; ☎ 6542 7102). To get to Tanah Merah ferry terminal, take the MRT to Bedok and then bus 35. A taxi from the city is around S$15.

From HarbourFront, boats leave for Pulau Batam, Tanjung Balai and Tanjung Batu, all about 20km away. The Tanah Merah terminal handles boats to/from Desaru in Malaysia, and to Pulau Bintan and Nongsapara on Batam. Ferries dock at Sekupang, where you can take a boat to Tanjung Buton on the Sumatran mainland. From there it's a three-hour bus ride to Palembang.

Ferry operators are **Penguin** (☎ 6377 6335; www.penguin.com.sg), for Batam, Bintan and Tanjung Balai; **Dino/Batam Fast** (☎ 6270 0311; www.batamfast.com), **Berlian** (☎ 6546 8830); **Indo Falcon** (☎ 6275 7393; www.indofalcon.com.sg) for all four Riau destinations, plus Malaysia; and **Bintan Resort Ferries** (☎ 6542 4369; www.brf.com.sg). Expect to pay around S$16 for a one-way ticket to Batam, S$24 to S$36 to Bintan, Balai or Batu.

Ferries depart the **Changi Point Ferry Terminal** (Map pp672-3; ☎ 6546 8518) for Tanjung Belungkor, east of Johor Bahru. The 11km journey takes 45 minutes and costs S$18/22 one way/return. From the Tanjung Belungkor jetty, buses operate to Desaru and Kota Tinggi. Ferries also sail from for Pengerang (one way S$6), across the Straits of Johor in Malaysia. There's no fixed schedule; ferries leave between 7am and 4pm when full (12 people). The best time to catch one is before 8am. Clear Singapore immigration at the small post in the terminal. To get to Changi Ferry Terminal, take the MRT to Tanah Merah, then bus 2 to Changi Village (or just a taxi!).

GETTING AROUND

Bicycle

There is an ever-expanding network of bike paths connecting Singapore's many parks, and the paths will eventually stretch 300km around the island. The 12km bike path along East Coast Park (Map pp672–3) makes a decent ride, but avoid weekends when it's extremely crowded. Search for 'Park Connectors' on the website of the **National Parks Board** (www.nparks.gov.sg) for a map of the bike paths.

Hire a decent mountain bike from S$6 at one of the numerous booths at East Coast Park. You can also get in-line skates here.

Boat

Bumboat cruises depart from various jetties along the Singapore River, including Clarke Quay, Raffles Landing and Boat Quay, as well as Merlion Park and the Esplanade Jetty on Marina Bay, generally between 9am and 11pm. Bumboats also leave the Changi Point ferry terminal (Map pp672–3) for Pulau Ubin.

Hippo River Cruise (Map pp678-9; ☎ 6338 6877; www.ducktours.com.sg) Thirty-minute open-top boat rides (adult/child S$13/9) departing from Clark Quay every 25 minutes. You can opt for a day pass (adult/child S$23/13), which allows ticket holders to hop on/off at nine stops along the Singapore River.

Singapore Explorer (Map pp678-9; ☎ 6339 6833; www.singaporeexplorer.com.sg) Offers trips up and down the river in a glass-top boat (adult/child S$15/6, 45 minutes) or traditional bumboat (adult/child S$12/6, 30 minutes). Commentary ensures that you know what you're looking at.

Bus

Public buses run between 6am and midnight. Each bus stop has information on bus numbers and routes. Fares start from S$0.90 and rise to a

GETTING TO INDONESIA

Ferries and speedboats run between Singapore and the Riau archipelago (Pulau Bintan and Pulau Batam) in Indonesia; see p675 for details. Immigration in Singapore is straightforward, though you should expect to pay for an Indonesian visa (US$20 for three days) when doing the trip in reverse. See p283 for details.

maximum of S$1.80. When you board the bus, tell the driver where you're going, drop the exact money into the fare box (no change is given) and collect your ticket from the machine.

Ez-Link cards (see below) can be used on all buses and trains. You'll need to tap the card on the card reader when boarding the bus and again when leaving.

Nutty and garish, the **City Hippo** (☎ 6228 6877; www.ducktours.com.sg) offers a confusing array of tour options round all the major sites. Two-day tickets including a river cruise (see p675) costs adult/child S$33/17. There's live commentary and an open-top deck.

Car

Hiring a car in Singapore is easy, but with efficient public transport, and parking a nightmare, it's pointless unless you plan to explore the outer reaches of the island.

Mass Rapid Transit

The ultramodern MRT subway system is the easiest, quickest and most comfortable way to get around. The system operates from 6am to midnight, with trains at peak times running every three minutes, and off-peak every six minutes.

Single-trip tickets cost from S$0.90 to S$2.70, but you have to pay a S$1 deposit for every ticket, then redeem it at the end of the trip. If you're going to be using the MRT a lot, it's cheaper and more convenient to buy a S$15 Ez-Link card from any MRT station (which includes a S$5 deposit and S$10 credit). This electronic card can be used on all public buses and trains. Fares using an Ez-Link card are 20% cheaper than cash fares.

Taxi

The major cab companies are **City Cab** and **Comfort** (☎ 6552 1111) and **SMRT** (☎ 6555 8888).

Fares for most companies start from S$2.80 to S$3.20 for the first kilometre, then 20c for each additional 385m. There are a raft of surcharges, eg for late-night services, peak-hour charges, restricted-zone charges, airport pickups and bookings, but they are still pretty cheap. All taxis are metered. Extra charges are always shown on the meter except for that of going into a restricted zone during peak hours. You can flag down a taxi any time or use a taxi rank outside hotels and malls.

TRISHAW

Bicycle trishaws congregate at popular tourist places, such as Raffles Hotel, the pedestrian mall at Waterloo and Albert Sts, and outside Chinatown Complex. Always agree on the fare beforehand, and expect to pay around S$40 for half an hour.

SINGAPORE

Let's face it, Singapore is the nicest place you'll find in Southeast Asia. After dealing with the in-your-faceness of Ho Chi Minh City and slumming it with the masses in polluted Bangkok, you'll find sweet blessed (and often air-conditioned) relief in Singapore. It's modern, efficient and not that expensive at all. There's a dense variety of sights and cultures jam-packed into little clusters of neighbourhoods and the city never seems to sleep!

ORIENTATION

The Singapore River cuts the city in two: south is the CBD and Chinatown, and to the north is the Colonial District. The trendy Clarke and Robertson Quays, and the popular Boat Quay dining areas, hug the riverbanks.

Further north from the Colonial District is Little India and Kampong Glam, the Muslim quarter. Northwest of the Colonial District is Orchard Rd, Singapore's premier shopping strip.

To the west of the island, the predominantly industrial area of Jurong contains a number of tourist attractions. Heading south you'll find the recreational islands of Sentosa, Kusu and St John's.

Eastern Singapore has some historical (and sleazy) suburbs such as Geylang and Katong, and East Coast Park and Changi Airport. The central north of the island has much of Singapore's remaining forest and the zoo.

INFORMATION

Bookshops

Kinokuniya (Map p683; ☎ 6737 5021; 03-09/15 Ngee Ann City, 391 Orchard Rd; 10.30am-9.30pm Sun-Fri, 10am-10pm Sat) Singapore's best bookstore.

Sunny Books (Map p683; ☎ 6733 1583; 03-58/59 Far East Plaza, 14 Scotts Rd; 10am-8pm Mon-Sat, 11.30am-7pm Sun) Also stocks second-hand books.

Internet Access

Every backpacker hostel now offers internet – the majority of them for free, some for a nominal charge. Travellers with laptops or phones with wi-fi should sign up for free wireless internet, Wireless@SG. Wireless@SG hotspots are located in most malls and many public buildings in Singapore. All you need is a mobile phone with a working SIM (local or global roaming) and a wi-fi enabled device.

Medical Services

Raffles Hospital (Map p681; ☎ 6311 1111; www.raffleshospital.com; 585 North Bridge Rd; 24hr)

Singapore General Hospital (Map pp678-9; ☎ 6222 3322; www.sgh.com.sg; Level 2, Block 1, Outram Rd; 24hr)

Money

Money changers can be found in every shopping centre and most do not charge fees on foreign money or travellers cheques. Many shops accept foreign cash and travellers cheques at lower rates than you'd get from a money changer.

Post

Most tourist-information centres sell stamps and post letters. Large post offices can be found at:

Lucky Plaza (Map p683; 02-09 Lucky Plaza, Orchard Rd)

Ngee Ann City (Map p683; 04-15 Takashimaya, 391 Orchard Rd)

There's also a post office in Terminal 2 at Changi Airport.

Tourist Information

Singapore Tourism Board (STB; www.visitsingapore.com) Singapore Tourism Board Head Office (Map p683; ☎ 1800-736 2000; 1 Orchard Spring Lane; 8.30am-5pm Mon-Fri, to 1pm Sat); Singapore Visitors Centre@Liang Court (Map pp678-9; 1st fl, Liang Court Shopping Centre, 177 River Valley Rd; 10am-10pm); Singapore Visitors Centre@Little India (Map p681; ☎ 6296 9169; Inn Crowd, 73 Dunlop St; 10am-10pm); Singapore Visitors Centre@Orchard (Map p683; ☎ 6336 7184; cnr Orchard & Cairnhill Rds; 9.30am-10.30pm); Singapore Visitors Centre@Suntec (Map pp678-9; Suntec City Mall; 10am-6pm) Most STB offices provide a wide range of services, including tour bookings and event ticketing.

SIGHTS

Colonial District

To the north of Singapore River is the Colonial District (Map pp678–9), where you'll find many imposing remnants of British rule, including **Victoria Concert Hall & Theatre**, **Old Parliament House** (now an arts centre), **St Andrew's Cathedral**, **City Hall** and the **Old Supreme Court**, which are arranged around the **Padang**, a cricket pitch. Rising above them is the spaceship of the Norman Foster–designed **Supreme Court** building.

Nearby, the classy **Asian Civilisations Museum** (Map pp678-9; ☎ 6332 7798; www.acm.org.sg; 1 Empress Pl; adult/child S$8/4, free after 7pm Fri; 1-7pm Mon, 9am-7pm Tue-Thu, Sat & Sun, Fri 9am-9pm) has 10 thematic galleries that explore different aspects of Asian culture, from the Islamic world to Japanese anime. The **Peranakan Museum** (Map pp678-9; ☎ 6332 7591; 39 Armenian St; adult/child $6/3; 1-7pm Mon, 9.30am-7pm Tue-Sun, till 9pm Fri) stands as a testament to the Peranakan (Straits-born Chinese) cultural revival in the Lion City and is a must-visit for anyone who wants to understand local culture. A combined ticket for both museums costs S$10/$5 per adult/child.

The sparkling white Victorian splendour of the **National Museum of Singapore** (Map pp678-9; ☎ 6332 5642; www.nationalmuseum.sg; 93 Stamford Rd; adult/child Singapore History Gallery S$10/5, Living Galleries free 6-9pm; Singapore History Gallery 10am-6pm, Living Galleries 10am-9pm), with its architecturally brilliant modern annex, is well worth a look.

GETTING INTO TOWN

Changi Airport, about 20km from the city centre, is served by the Mass Rapid Transit (MRT). From Changi to City Hall is only S$2.70 (28 minutes, every seven minutes, change train at Tanah Merah).

Public bus 36 leaves for the city approximately every 10 minutes between 6am and midnight, and takes about an hour. Make sure you have the right change (S$2) when you board.

Taxis from the airport charge a supplementary charge (S$3 to S$5 depending on time) on top of the metered fare, which is around S$20 to most places in the city centre.

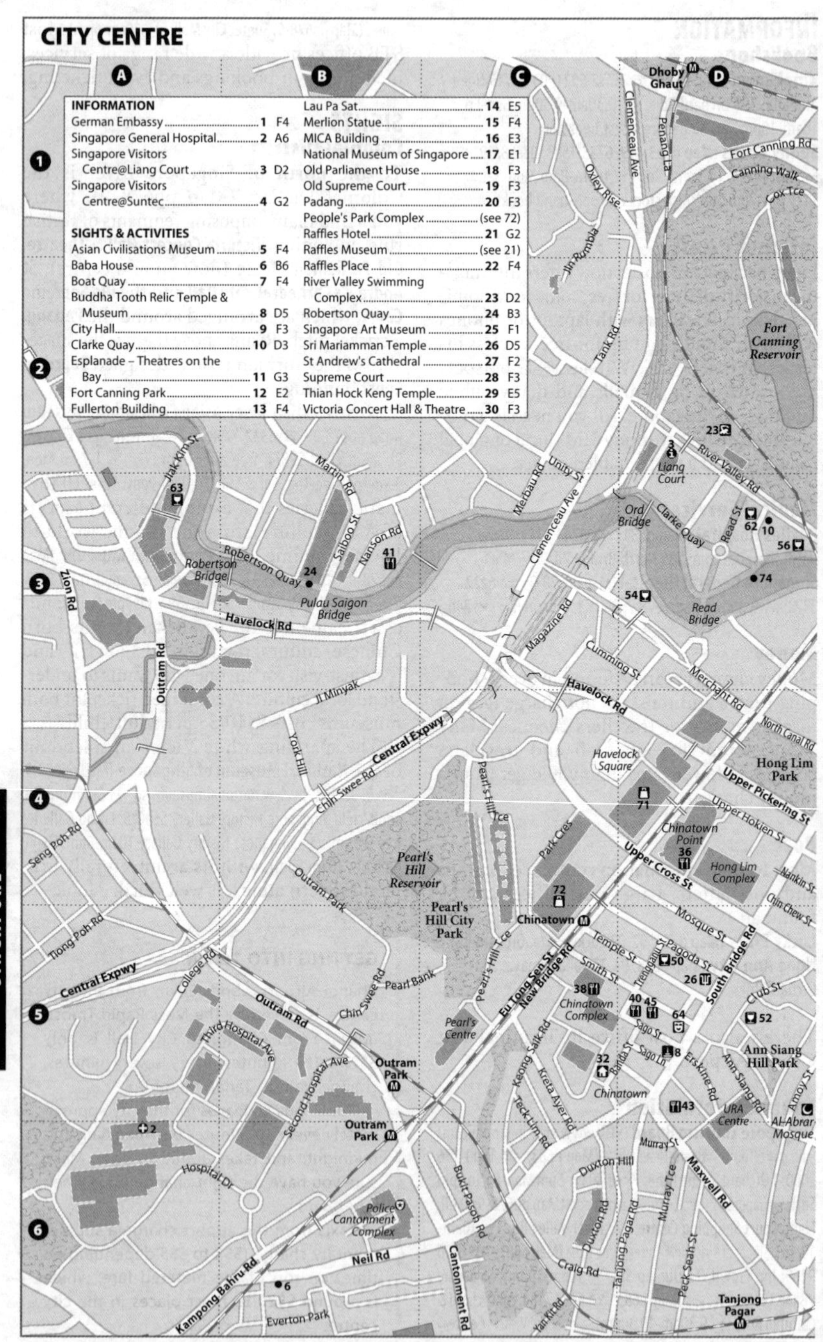
CITY CENTRE
A
B
C
D
1
2
3
4
5
6
INFORMATION
German Embassy 1 F4
Singapore General Hospital 2 A6
Singapore Visitors Centre@Liang Court 3 D2
Singapore Visitors Centre@Suntec 4 G2
SIGHTS & ACTIVITIES
Asian Civilisations Museum 5 F4
Baba House 6 B6
Boat Quay 7 F4
Buddha Tooth Relic Temple & Museum 8 D5
City Hall 9 F3
Clarke Quay 10 D3
Esplanade – Theatres on the Bay 11 G3
Fort Canning Park 12 E2
Fullerton Building 13 F4
Lau Pa Sat 14 E5
Merlion Statue 15 F4
MICA Building 16 E3
National Museum of Singapore 17 E1
Old Parliament House 18 F3
Old Supreme Court 19 F3
Padang 20 F3
People's Park Complex (see 72)
Raffles Hotel 21 G2
Raffles Museum (see 21)
Raffles Place 22 F4
River Valley Swimming Complex 23 D2
Robertson Quay 24 B3
Singapore Art Museum 25 F1
Sri Mariamman Temple 26 D5
St Andrew's Cathedral 27 F2
Supreme Court 28 F3
Thian Hock Keng Temple 29 E5
Victoria Concert Hall & Theatre 30 F3
Dhoby Ghaut
Clemenceau Ave
Penang La
Fort Canning Rd
Canning Walk
Cox Tce
Oxley Rise
Jln Rumbia
Tank Rd
Fort Canning Reservoir
23
3
Liang Court
River Valley Rd
Unity St
Merbau Rd
Martin Rd
Jiak Kim St
63
Ord Bridge
Clarke Quay
Read St
62
10
56
Saiboo St
Nanson Rd
41
Robertson Quay
24
Robertson Bridge
Zion Rd
Pulau Saigon Bridge
Havelock Rd
74
54
Read Bridge
Magazine Rd
Cumming St
Merchant Rd
Outram Rd
Jl Minyak
Havelock Rd
North Canal Rd
York Hill
Central Expwy
Chin Swee Rd
Havelock Square
Hong Lim Park
Upper Pickering St
Pearl's Hill Tce
71
Upper Hokien St
Chinatown Point
36
Seng Poh Rd
Park Cres
Upper Cross St
Hong Lim Complex
Nankin St
Pearl's Hill Reservoir
Outram Park
72
Chin Chew St
Pearl's Hill City Park
Chinatown
Mosque St
Tiong Poh Rd
Pearl's Hill Tce
Temple St
Pagoda St
South Bridge Rd
Trengganu St
50
College Rd
Eu Tong Sen St
New Bridge Rd
Smith St
26
Central Expwy
Pearl Bank
Chin Swee Rd
38
Chinatown Complex
40
45
64
Club St
52
Outram Rd
Third Hospital Ave
Pearl's Centre
Sago St
Sago Ln
8
Erskine Rd
Ann Siang Hill Park
Keong Saik Rd
32
Banda St
Ann Siang Rd
Amoy St
Second Hospital Ave
Outram Park
Chinatown
43
URA Centre
Al-Abrar Mosque
Kreta Ayer Rd
Teck Lim Rd
2
Outram Park
Murray St
Hospital Dr
Duxton Hill
Maxwell Rd
Bukit Pasoh Rd
Police Cantonment Complex
Duxton Rd
Tanjong Pagar Rd
Murray Tce
Peck Seah St
Neil Rd
Cantonment Rd
Craig Rd
Kampong Bahru Rd
6
Everton Park
Yan Kit Rd
Tanjong Pagar
SINGAPORE

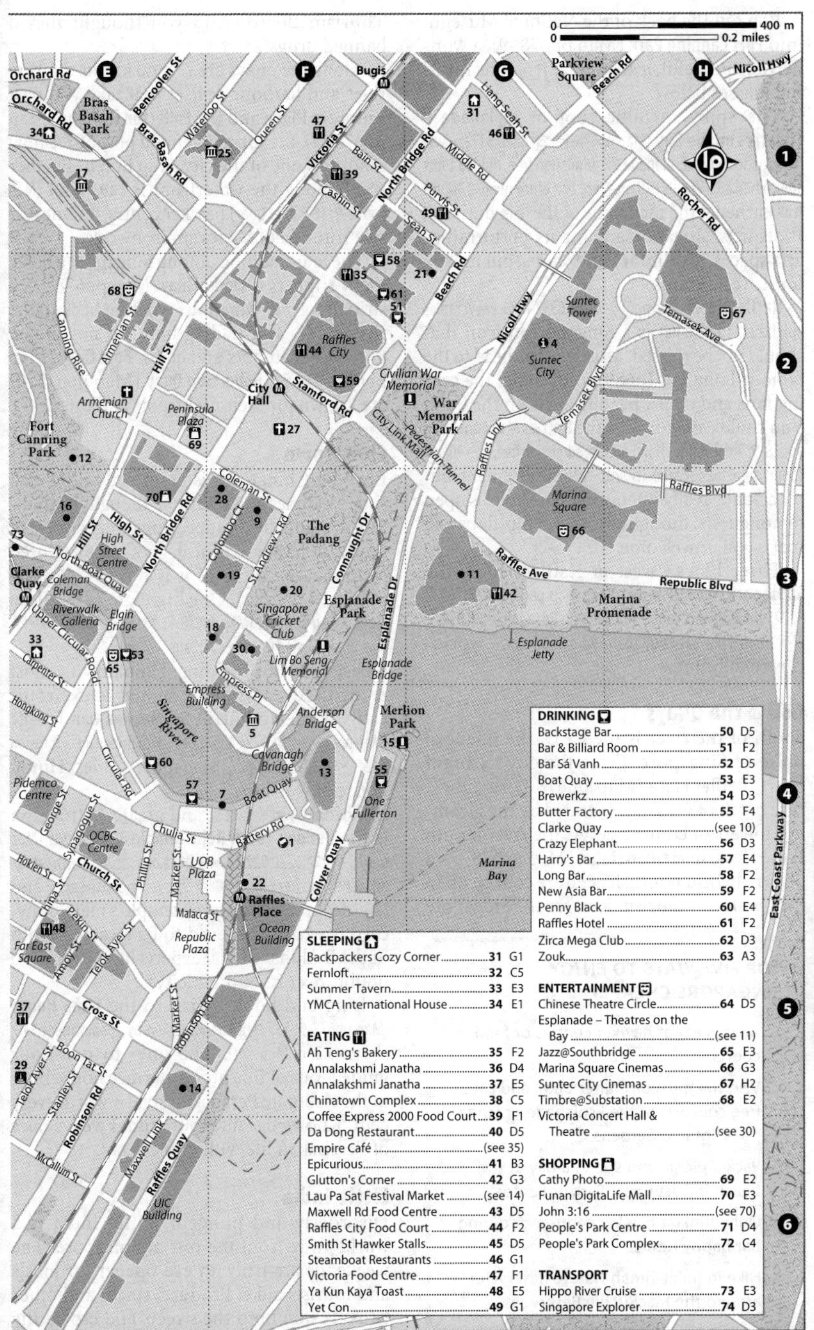
0 400 m
0 0.2 miles
E
F
G
H
1
2
3
4
5
6
Orchard Rd
Bras Basah Park
Bencoolen St
Waterloo St
Queen St
Bugis
Victoria St
Parkview Square
Beach Rd
Nicoll Hwy
Liang Seah St
Bras Basah Rd
Bain St
North Bridge Rd
Middle Rd
Cashin St
Purvis St
Seah St
Rocher Rd
Canning Rise
Armenian St
Hill St
Raffles City
Suntec Tower
Temasek Ave
Suntec City
Armenian Church
City Hall
Stamford Rd
Civilian War Memorial
War Memorial Park
Temasek Blvd
Peninsula Plaza
City Link Mall
Pedestrian Tunnel
Raffles Link
Fort Canning Park
Coleman St
Raffles Blvd
Marina Square
Colombo Ct
St Andrew's Rd
The Padang
Connaught Dr
High St
High Street Centre
North Boat Quay
Clarke Quay
Coleman Bridge
Raffles Ave
Republic Blvd
Riverwalk Galleria
Elgin Bridge
Singapore Cricket Club
Esplanade Park
Esplanade Dr
Marina Promenade
Upper Circular Road
Esplanade Jetty
Carpenter St
Lim Bo Seng Memorial
Esplanade Bridge
Empress Building
Empress Pl
Hongkong St
Singapore River
Anderson Bridge
Merlion Park
Circular Rd
Cavanagh Bridge
Pidemco Centre
Boat Quay
One Fullerton
George St
Synagogue St
OCBC Centre
Chulia St
Battery Rd
Phillip St
Hokien St
Church St
Market St
UOB Plaza
Collyer Quay
Marina Bay
East Coast Parkway
China St
Malacca St
Raffles Place
Pekin St
Ocean Building
Far East Square
Amoy St
Telok Ayer St
Republic Plaza
Cross St
Robinson Rd
Boon Tat St
Stanley St
McCallum St
Maxwell Link
Raffles Quay
UIC Building
SINGAPORE
DRINKING
Backstage Bar 50 D5
Bar & Billiard Room 51 F2
Bar Sá Vanh 52 D5
Boat Quay 53 E3
Brewerkz 54 D3
Butter Factory 55 F4
Clarke Quay (see 10)
Crazy Elephant 56 D3
Harry's Bar 57 E4
Long Bar 58 F2
New Asia Bar 59 F2
Penny Black 60 E4
Raffles Hotel 61 F2
Zirca Mega Club 62 D3
Zouk 63 A3
ENTERTAINMENT
Chinese Theatre Circle 64 D5
Esplanade – Theatres on the Bay (see 11)
Jazz@Southbridge 65 E3
Marina Square Cinemas 66 G3
Suntec City Cinemas 67 H2
Timbre@Substation 68 E2
Victoria Concert Hall & Theatre (see 30)
SHOPPING
Cathy Photo 69 E2
Funan DigitaLife Mall 70 E3
John 3:16 (see 70)
People's Park Centre 71 D4
People's Park Complex 72 C4
TRANSPORT
Hippo River Cruise 73 E3
Singapore Explorer 74 D3
SLEEPING
Backpackers Cozy Corner 31 G1
Fernloft 32 C5
Summer Tavern 33 E3
YMCA International House 34 E1
EATING
Ah Teng's Bakery 35 F2
Annalakshmi Janatha 36 D4
Annalakshmi Janatha 37 E5
Chinatown Complex 38 C5
Coffee Express 2000 Food Court 39 F1
Da Dong Restaurant 40 D5
Empire Café (see 35)
Epicurious 41 B3
Glutton's Corner 42 G3
Lau Pa Sat Festival Market (see 14)
Maxwell Rd Food Centre 43 D5
Raffles City Food Court 44 F2
Smith St Hawker Stalls 45 D5
Steamboat Restaurants 46 G1
Victoria Food Centre 47 F1
Ya Kun Kaya Toast 48 E5
Yet Con 49 G1

Pop out the back of the National Museum into **Fort Canning Park** (Map pp678–9), a wonderfully peaceful, leafy retreat from the broiling masses below.

The spiky metallic roof of **Esplanade – Theatres on the Bay** (Map pp678-9; ☎ 6828 8377; www.esplanade.com; 1 Esplanade Dr; admission free, guided tours adult/child S$10/8; 🕑 10am-6pm, box office noon-8.30pm) has earned it the nickname of the 'big durians'. It attracts Singaporeans for its performing-arts spaces, arts library and shops, but mostly for its restaurants.

Raffles Hotel (Map pp678-9; ☎ 6337 1886; www.raffleshotel.com; 1 Beach Rd) is a Singaporean icon that should not be missed. Most tourists head to the famous Long Bar (p689) to sit under the ceiling fans and chuck peanut shells on the floor. You could easily dismiss the **Raffles Museum** (Map pp678-9; 3rd fl, Raffles Hotel Arcade; admission free; 🕑 10am-10pm) as an exercise in self-aggrandisement, but it's actually really interesting. The hotel is open to nonguests, though shorts and flip-flops will make you unwelcome.

Three blocks west of Raffles Hotel, the **Singapore Art Museum** (SAM; Map pp678-9; ☎ 6332 3222; www.singart.com; 71 Bras Basah Rd; adult/child S$8/5; 🕑 10am-7pm Sat-Thu, 10am-9pm Fri) hosts world-class exhibitions.

CBD & the Quays

South of the river is the CBD, the financial pulse of Singapore. Once the city's vibrant heart, **Raffles Place** (Map pp678–9) is now a rare patch of grass surrounded by the gleaming towers of commerce. At the river mouth is the freakish **Merlion statue** (Map pp678–9), a bizarre hybrid lion/fish creature cooked up in the 1960s as a tourism icon for the Singapore Tourism Board. And you thought they'd banned drugs.

Along the quays are several kiosks offering river and harbour cruises that take you past Empress Place and the **Fullerton Building** (Map pp678–9), the former general post office now reborn as one of the city's top hotels. Further south along the waterfront is **Lau Pa Sat** (Map pp678-9; 18 Raffles Quay) hawker centre, an impressive rotunda of Victorian ironwork.

The latest darling among Singapore's fickle night-trippers is **Clarke Quay** (Map pp678–9), a strip of former warehouses dating back to the river's days as a trading hub and now home to bars, restaurants and clubs. **Boat Quay** (Map pp678–9) and **Robertson Quay** (Map pp678–9) are known for their nightspots and eateries.

TOP FIVE WAYS TO ENJOY SINGAPORE CHEAPLY

- Always eat at hawker centres or food courts.
- Visit the museums after 6pm, and catch free concerts at the Esplanade or Singapore Botanic Gardens.
- Pack a picnic and spend a day at the beach in East Coast Park or Sentosa.
- Only drink at hawker centres, or during bar happy hours.
- Hike in Bukit Timah Nature Reserve or around the MacRitchie Reservoir.

Chinatown

Bustling Chinatown is crammed with small shops, eateries and tradition, though the tradition is gradually disappearing under a wave of renovation. Some of it is good (the restored shophouses), some of it is not (the Pagoda St tourist market). One highlight is the **Thian Hock Keng Temple** (Map pp678-9; ☎ 6423 4616; 158 Telok Ayer St; admission free; 🕑 7.30am-5.30pm), Singapore's oldest Hokkien building. Chinatown's most recognised and photographed icon, ironically, is the colourful **Sri Mariamman Temple** (Map pp678-9; ☎ 6223 4064; 244 South Bridge Rd; admission free; 🕑 7.30am-8.30pm), Singapore's oldest Hindu house of worship.

Chinatown's latest and greatest attraction is the **Buddha Tooth Relic Temple & Museum** (Map pp678-9; ☎ 6220 0220; www.btrts.org.sg; 288 South Bridge Rd; admission free; 🕑 4.30am-9pm). The massive and jaw-dropping five-storey temple's main drawcard is what is believed to be a sacred tooth of the Buddha (dental experts have expressed doubts over its authenticity).

Ring and book a visit to the **Baba House** (Map pp678-9; 157 Neil Rd; admission by appointment $10; 🕑 tours 2pm Mon-Sat). The one- to two-hour guided tour of this prewar terrace house built in the elaborate Peranakan style is worth every cent. Knowledgeable tour guides weave tales of Peranakan life with every detail.

Little India

Disorderly and pungent, Little India is a world away from the rest of Singapore. The weekends are truly an eye-opener for locals and tourists alike. Produce, spices and other trinkets spill onto the streets and crowd the

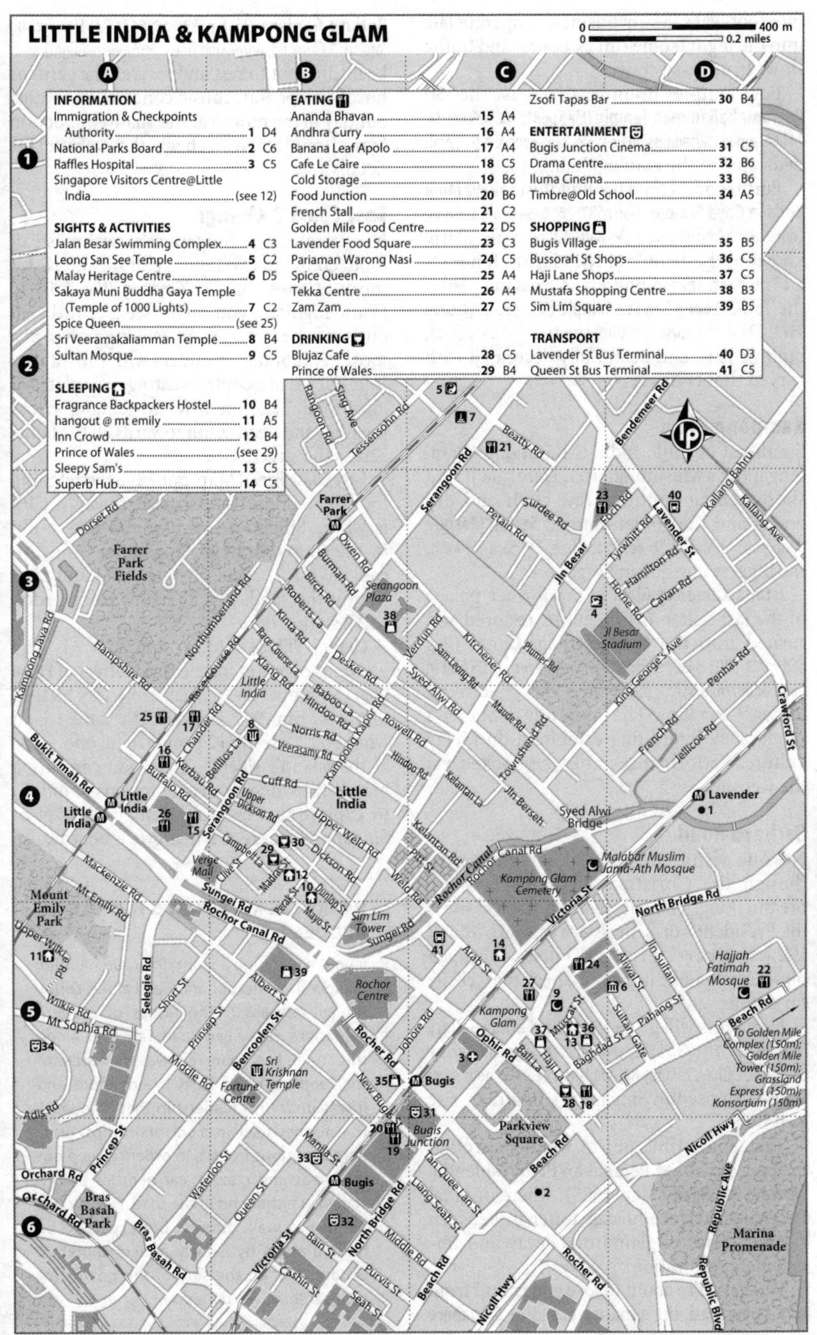
LITTLE INDIA & KAMPONG GLAM
0 400 m
0 0.2 miles
INFORMATION
Immigration & Checkpoints Authority 1 D4
National Parks Board 2 C6
Raffles Hospital 3 C5
Singapore Visitors Centre@Little India (see 12)
SIGHTS & ACTIVITIES
Jalan Besar Swimming Complex 4 C3
Leong San See Temple 5 C2
Malay Heritage Centre 6 D5
Sakaya Muni Buddha Gaya Temple (Temple of 1000 Lights) 7 C2
Spice Queen (see 25)
Sri Veeramakaliamman Temple 8 B4
Sultan Mosque 9 C5
SLEEPING
Fragrance Backpackers Hostel 10 B4
hangout @ mt emily 11 A5
Inn Crowd 12 B4
Prince of Wales (see 29)
Sleepy Sam's 13 C5
Superb Hub 14 C5
EATING
Ananda Bhavan 15 A4
Andhra Curry 16 A4
Banana Leaf Apolo 17 A4
Cafe Le Caire 18 C5
Cold Storage 19 B6
Food Junction 20 B6
French Stall 21 C2
Golden Mile Food Centre 22 D5
Lavender Food Square 23 C3
Pariaman Warong Nasi 24 C5
Spice Queen 25 A4
Tekka Centre 26 A4
Zam Zam 27 C5
DRINKING
Blujaz Cafe 28 C5
Prince of Wales 29 B4
Zsofi Tapas Bar 30 B4
ENTERTAINMENT
Bugis Junction Cinema 31 C5
Drama Centre 32 B6
Iluma Cinema 33 B6
Timbre@Old School 34 A5
SHOPPING
Bugis Village 35 B5
Bussorah St Shops 36 C5
Haji Lane Shops 37 C5
Mustafa Shopping Centre 38 B3
Sim Lim Square 39 B5
TRANSPORT
Lavender St Bus Terminal 40 D3
Queen St Bus Terminal 41 C5
To Golden Mile Complex (150m); Golden Mile Tower (150m); Grassland Express (150m); Konsortium (150m)

five-foot ways. Many businesses operate late into the night (some run 24 hours) and traffic slows to a messy crawl.

For temple hounds there is the **Sri Veeramakaliamman Temple** (Map p681; ☎ 6293 4634; 141 Serangoon Rd; admission free; 8am-noon & 4-8.30pm), dedicated to the goddess Kali.

Further out is the Thai Buddhist **Sakaya Muni Buddha Gaya Temple** (Map p681; ☎ 6294 0714; 366 Race Course Rd; admission free; 8am-4.30pm), popularly known as the Temple of 1000 Lights. It houses a 15m-high seated Buddha. Across the road is the Taoist **Leong San See Temple** (Map p681; ☎ 6298 9371; 371 Race Course Rd; admission free; 6am-6pm), built in 1917 and beautifully decorated with carved timber beams.

Kampong Glam

Southeast of Little India is Kampong Glam, Singapore's Muslim quarter. Here you'll find shops selling clothing, raw cloth and dry goods and the golden-domed **Sultan Mosque** (Map p681; 3 Muscat St; admission free; 5am-8.30pm), the biggest mosque in Singapore.

Istana Kampong Glam is the former palace of the last Sultan of Singapore, restored and turned into the **Malay Heritage Centre** (Map p681; ☎ 6391 0450; www.malayheritage.org.sg; 85 Sultan Gate; adult/child S$4/3, performances S$11; 10am-6pm Tue-Sun, 1-6pm Mon). The museum contains a moderately interesting exhibition on Malay culture. Performances must be booked via the website.

Orchard Road

No one visits Orchard Rd for the sights, though the Christmas light displays are breathtaking. The only major historical site is the President's digs, the **Istana** (Map p683; ☎ 6737 5522; www.istana.gov.sg; Orchard Rd) but it's only open on selected public holidays. Check the website for details.

Film buffs will go ga-ga at the **Cathay Gallery** (Map p683; ☎ 6737 5522; www.thecathaygallery.com.sg; 02-16 The Cathay, 2 Handy Rd; admission free; noon-8pm Mon-Sat), housed in Singapore's first high-rise building.

Take some time out to wander through the pedestrianised Peranakan Pl to residential **Emerald Hill Road** (Map p683), where original Peranakan terrace houses totter in between various states of glamorous decay and immaculate restoration.

When you're about to lose your mind from retail overload, the expansive, serene **Singapore Botanic Gardens** (Map p683; ☎ 6471 7361; www.sbg.org.sg; 1 Cluny Rd; admission free; 5am-midnight) is a beautiful spot to rest and revive. The gardens host free open-air music concerts on the last Sunday of the month at the Shaw Foundation Symphony Stage – check the website for details.

East Coast & Changi

Nowhere else is Singapore's mishmash of food, commerce, religion, culture and sleaze more at ease than at **Geylang** (Map pp672-3). Come nightfall, you might see a crowd spill out onto the streets from evening prayer at a mosque, rubbing shoulders with prostitutes. Join hordes of people sweating over plates of local food. Take the MRT to Kallang. Cross the road and head south towards all the lights across the street.

East Coast Park (Map pp672–3), stretching for 10km along East Coast Parkway (ECP), is where Singaporeans come to take a dip in the soupy Strait of Singapore, windsurf, cable-ski, eat, cycle, in-line skate and chill out on the sand. Bus 401 runs from Bedok MRT station here.

Changi Village (Map pp672–3) is the jumping-off point for the rural retreat of **Pulau Ubin** (Map pp672–3). Boats (one way S$2, 15 minutes) run 24/7 and depart for the island whenever there are 12 people to fill one. Once at the island's sleepy village you can hire a bicycle (S$5 to S$10, depending on condition) to explore this last undeveloped pocket of Singapore. There are mangrove boardwalks

HARRY LEE KUAN YEW'S HUMBLE ABODE

If you're planning a jaunt down Orchard Rd, make a short detour and head along **Oxley Rd** (off Map p683). The father of modern Singapore, Harry Lee Kuan Yew lives along this street. Lee Kuan Yew was the leader of the People's Action Party in Singapore, and it was under his leadership that Singapore transformed itself into one of the most prosperous nations in Asia. In order to keep out the plebs and crazies, car gantries are installed at either end of the road. Pedestrians are free to walk through but expect to be hurried along by heavily armed Ghurkhas. Go on, walk on the side of the guards for a closer look, we dare you.

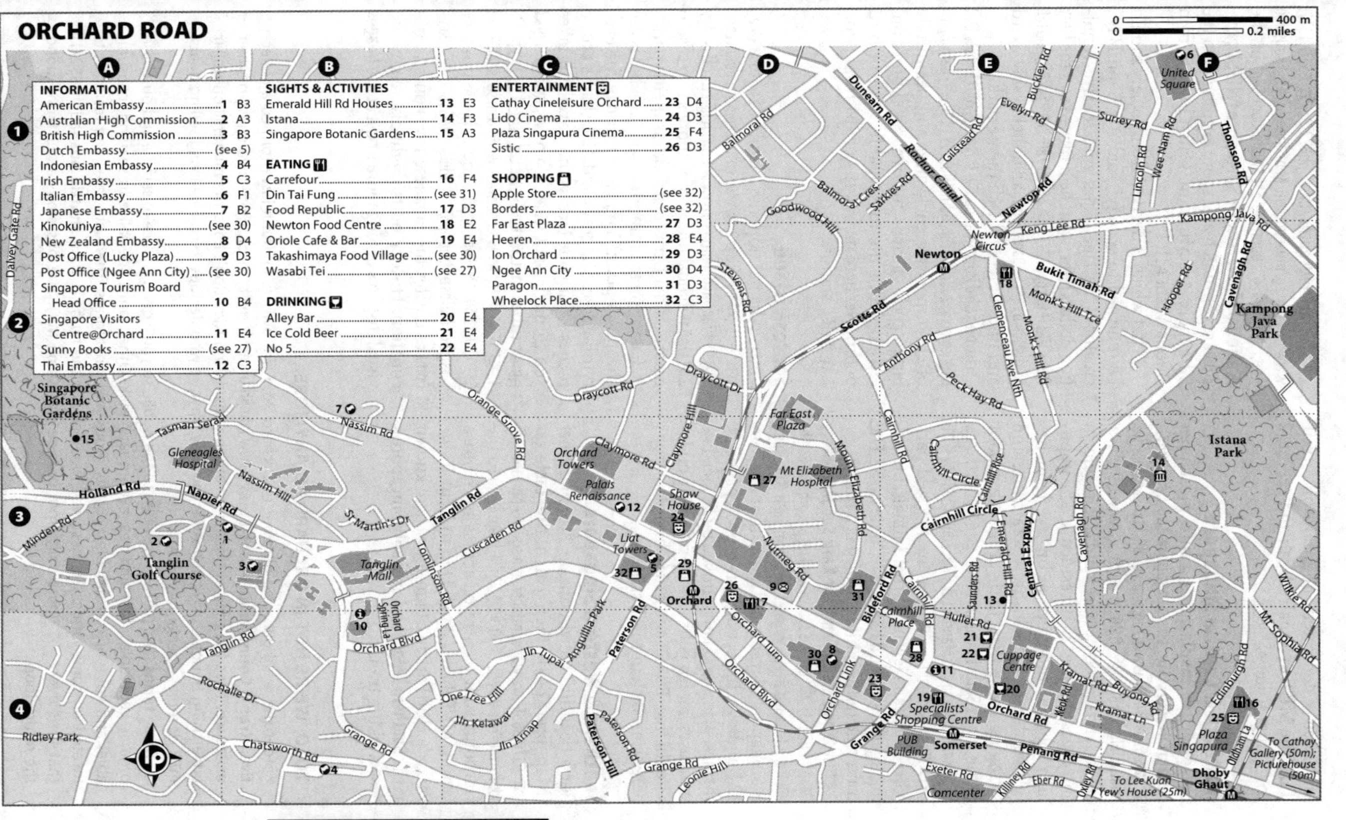
ORCHARD ROAD
0 400 m
0 0.2 miles
A
B
C
D
E
F
1
2
3
4
INFORMATION
American Embassy 1 B3
Australian High Commission 2 A3
British High Commission 3 B3
Dutch Embassy (see 5)
Indonesian Embassy 4 B4
Irish Embassy 5 C3
Italian Embassy 6 F1
Japanese Embassy 7 B2
Kinokuniya (see 30)
New Zealand Embassy 8 D4
Post Office (Lucky Plaza) 9 D3
Post Office (Ngee Ann City) (see 30)
Singapore Tourism Board Head Office 10 B4
Singapore Visitors Centre@Orchard 11 E4
Sunny Books (see 27)
Thai Embassy 12 C3
SIGHTS & ACTIVITIES
Emerald Hill Rd Houses 13 E3
Istana 14 F3
Singapore Botanic Gardens 15 A3
EATING
Carrefour 16 F4
Din Tai Fung (see 31)
Food Republic 17 D3
Newton Food Centre 18 E2
Oriole Cafe & Bar 19 E4
Takashimaya Food Village (see 30)
Wasabi Tei (see 27)
DRINKING
Alley Bar 20 E4
Ice Cold Beer 21 E4
No 5 22 E4
ENTERTAINMENT
Cathay Cineleisure Orchard 23 D4
Lido Cinema 24 D3
Plaza Singapura Cinema 25 F4
Sistic 26 D3
SHOPPING
Apple Store (see 32)
Borders (see 32)
Far East Plaza 27 D3
Heeren 28 E4
Ion Orchard 29 D3
Ngee Ann City 30 D4
Paragon 31 D3
Wheelock Place 32 C3
Dalvey Gate Rd
Singapore Botanic Gardens
Tasman Serasi
Gleneagles Hospital
Holland Rd
Napier Rd
Minden Rd
Tanglin Golf Course
Nassim Rd
Nassim Hill
St Martin's Dr
Tanglin Rd
Tanglin Mall
Orchard Spring La
Orchard Blvd
Tomlinson Rd
Cuscaden Rd
Orange Grove Rd
Draycott Rd
Draycott Dr
Claymore Rd
Claymore Hill
Orchard Towers
Palais Renaissance
Shaw House
Liat Towers
Orchard
Paterson Rd
Anguilla Park
Jln Tupai
One Tree Hill
Jln Kelawar
Jln Arnap
Paterson Hill
Grange Rd
Leonie Hill
Chatsworth Rd
Rochalie Dr
Ridley Park
Balmoral Rd
Balmoral Cres
Goodwood Hill
Sarkies Rd
Stevens Rd
Scotts Rd
Newton
Newton Circus
Dunearn Rd
Rochor Canal
Newton Rd
Gilstead Rd
Evelyn Rd
Buckley Rd
Surrey Rd
Lincoln Rd
Wee Nam Rd
United Square
Thomson Rd
Keng Lee Rd
Kampong Java Rd
Bukit Timah Rd
Monk's Hill Tce
Monk's Hill Rd
Clemenceau Ave Nth
Hooper Rd
Cavenagh Rd
Kampong Java Park
Istana Park
Anthony Rd
Peck Hay Rd
Far East Plaza
Mt Elizabeth Hospital
Mount Elizabeth Rd
Cairnhill Rd
Cairnhill Circle
Cairnhill Rise
Nutmeg Rd
Bideford Rd
Cairnhill Place
Emerald Hill Rd
Saunders Rd
Central Expwy
Hullet Rd
Cuppage Centre
Orchard Turn
Orchard Link
Specialists' Shopping Centre
Somerset
PUB Building
Penang Rd
Orchard Rd
Kramat Rd
Kramat Ln
Keok Rd
Buyong Rd
Edinburgh Rd
Wilkie Rd
Mt Sophia Rd
Plaza Singapura
Oldham La
Exeter Rd
Comcenter
Killiney Rd
Eber Rd
Oxley Rd
To Lee Kuan Yew's House (25m)
Dhoby Ghaut
To Cathay Gallery (50m); Picturehouse (50m)

SINGAPORE

and even a dedicated mountain bike trail. Take the MRT to Tanah Merah and get bus 2 to Changi Village.

Northern & Central Singapore

Set on a peninsula jutting into the Upper Seletar Reservoir, the **Singapore Zoo** (Map pp672-3; ☎ 6269 3411; www.zoo.com.sg; 80 Mandai Lake Rd; adult/child S$18/9; 8.30am-6pm) is world class. Its 28 landscaped hectares and open concept (no cages) houses 2530 residents. The popular proboscis monkeys sit on tree branches in two different enclosures, scratching and swinging more than their arms. Next door is the **Night Safari** (Map pp672-3; ☎ 6269 3411; www.nightsafari.com.sg; 80 Mandai Lake Rd; adult/child S$21/11; 7.30pm-midnight), a 40-hectare forested park where you can view nocturnal animals, including tigers, lions and leopards. Come early. The train ride (adult/child S$10/5) is a must.

The **Kong Meng San Phor Kark See Monastery** (Map pp672-3; ☎ 6453 5300; www.kmspks.org; 88 Bright Hill Rd; admission free; gates 6am-9pm, halls 8am-4pm) is Singapore's largest and most stunning with 12 buildings. Expect dragon-topped pagodas, shrines, plazas and lawns linked by Escher-like staircases. Finish your visit by reflecting under a bodhi tree. Bus 52 and 410 (white plate) runs here from Bishan MRT station.

Southern & Western Singapore

For a beautiful view, walk up 116m **Mt Faber** (Map pp672–3), then catch the **cable car** (☎ 6270 8855; www.mountfaber.com.sg; 109 Mt Faber Rd; adult/child one way S$18.90/9.50; 8.30am-9pm) to the HarbourFront Centre or across to Sentosa Island. Mt Faber is connected to Kent Ridge Park via HortPark in a 9km-long chain known as the **Southern Ridges** and arguably Singapore's best walking trail.

The **art museums** (Map pp672-3; ☎ 6516 4617; www.nus.edu.sg/museum; 50 Kent Ridge Cres; admission free; 10am-7.30pm Tue-Sat, 10am-6pm Sun) in the National University of Singapore (NUS) campus are top-notch and more exciting than the Singapore Art Museum. Catch bus 95 from Buona Vista MRT.

'That which is derived from society should be returned to society', said Aw Boon Haw, creator of the Tiger Balm miracle salve. A million dollars later, what he returned was the **Haw Par Villa** (Map pp672-3; ☎ 6872 2780; 262 Pasir Panjang Rd; admission free; 9am-7pm), an unbelievably weird and undoubtedly kitsch theme park.

Jurong Bird Park (Map pp672-3; ☎ 6265 0022; www.birdpark.com.sg; 2 Jurong Hill; adult/child S$18/9, 8am-6pm) offers impressive enclosures and beautifully landscaped gardens for over 8000 birds (all enveloped in the inescapable scent of bird poop). Get here on bus 194 or 251 from Boon Lay MRT station.

Sentosa Island

Once a dismal flop, the island of **Sentosa** (Map pp672-3; ☎ 6736 8672; www.sentosa.com.sg; adult/child S$2; 7am-midnight) is now a roaring success. By 2010 it will host one of Singapore's two casino resorts and a Universal Studios theme park.

Lazing on the imported-sand beaches is the cheapest option. You've got to pay for everything else. Stingrays and 10ft sharks cruise inches from your face as the travellator takes you through the Ocean Colony's submerged glass tubes in the **Underwater World** (Map pp672-3; ☎ 6275 0030; www.underwaterworld.com.sg; adult/child S$19.50/12.50; 9am-9pm). The former military base **Fort Siloso** (Map pp672-3; adult/child S$8/5; 10am-6pm) re-creates the Japanese invasion and occupation. History buffs might also enjoy the visual displays of Singapore's past at the **Images**

TOTO, WE'RE NOT IN ORCHARD RD ANYMORE...

Forget the retail glitz and glamour of Orchard Rd. Farm owners in Kranji have formed a collective, **Kranji Countryside Association** (www.kranjicountryside.com), to promote awareness of their existence. Thus far, they've done a great job considering they don't have the multimillion-dollar advertising budgets of retail heavies, but hey, anyone who decides to make a living selling goats' milk deserves special mention.

These **farms** (Map pp672-3) are open to the public so you'll get a chance to sample and purchase organic vegetables, fruit and yes, even goats' milk. Other farms specialise in seafood (consumable) and koi (not consumable), pottery, frogs and wheatgrass. There are cafes and restaurants located on some farms. The best way to check out the farms is via a **shuttle bus** (adult S$2/1) that runs every 1½ hours daily from outside the Kranji MRT. The bus stops at 12 farms along the return loop.

of Singapore (Map pp672-3; adult/child S$10/7; 9am-7pm). The **Songs of the Sea show** (Map pp672-3; admission S$10 7.40 & 8.40pm) is set out on *kelongs* (offshore fishing huts) and combines musical gushings with a spectacular S$4 million sound, light and laser nightly extravaganza.

The easiest way to get to Sentosa is via shuttle bus (S$3) from HarbourFront Bus Interchange, which runs every 15 minutes from 7am to 11pm Sunday to Thursday, and until 12.30am on Fridays and Saturdays. You can also catch the **Sentosa Express rail** (Map pp672-3; return ticket S$3; 7am-midnight) link from the 3rd floor of the mammoth mall, VivoCity, next to HarbourFront MRT. For a more spectacular ride, take the cable car (adult/child one way S$18.90/9.50) from the HarbourFront centre, also signposted from the MRT station.

Southern Islands

Three other **islands** (Map pp672–3) popular with castaway-fantasising locals are **St John's**, **Lazarus** and **Kusu**. They're usually quiet and are great for fishing, swimming, a picnic and guzzling BYO six packs. Islands have changing rooms and toilets. You can camp here for free. Kusu Island is culturally interesting; devotees come to pray for health, wealth and fertility at its Taoist temple and Malay *kramat* (shrine).

Catch a ferry from the **Marina South Pier** (Map pp672-3; 6275 03888; www.islandcruise.com.sg; 31 Marina Coastal Drive; adult/child return S$15/12; 10am & 2pm Mon-Fri, 9am, 12pm & 3pm Sat, every 2hr 9am-5pm Sun). To get to Marina South Pier, take bus 402 from outside the Marina Bay MRT station.

ACTIVITIES

Though the national pastimes are probably shopping and eating, there are opportunities for athletic, outdoorsy types. To find out more about sports and activities in Singapore check out www.ssc.gov.sg.

Trekking & Cycling

There are good trails in **Bukit Timah Nature Reserve** (Map pp672-3; 1800-468 5736; www.nparks.gov.sg; 8.30am-6pm), the only large area of primary rainforest left in Singapore. Pulau Ubin also has dedicated mountain-biking trails. Or try **MacRitchie Reservoir** (Map pp672-3; 6256 4248; www.nparks.gov.sg; Lornie Rd; admission free; 8.30am-6pm) with its fantastic treetop walk. The best spot for cycling is definitely East Coast Park (p682).

Water Sports

Wakeboarders and water-skiers should check out the **Ski360°** (Map pp672-3; 6442 7318; www.ski360degree.com; per hr Mon-Fri S$32, per hr Sat & Sun S$42; 10am-10pm Mon-Fri, 9am-10pm Sat & Sun) circuit at East Coast Park Lagoon.

For **swimming** there are reasonable beaches on Sentosa, the Southern Islands and East Coast Park. The latter holds regular **triathlons** (www.triathlons ingapore.org).

Or you can do a few laps at the public pools:

Jalan Besar Swimming Complex (Map p681; 6293 9058; 100 Tyrwhitt Rd; per adult S$1-1.30, child $0.50-0.70; 8am-9.30pm)

River Valley Swimming Complex (Map pp678-9; 6337 6275; 1 River Valley Rd; per adult S$1-1.30, child $0.50-0.70; 8am-9.30pm)

Spas & Massages

Spas in Singapore tend to be of the upmarket variety. Massages, however, are cheap and readily available. Foot reflexology is a major trade. For a good foot rub, look out for places with wizened old men. Check out **People Park Complex** (Map pp678–9) for foot reflexology. Most malls have at least one reflexology place. For Thai massage, try Golden Mile Complex (off Map p681). Prices should be displayed on the doors and if you aren't sure, shop around. Expect to pay roughly S$28 for a 45-minute massage.

COURSES

There are a few short-term options for the casual cooking enthusiast:

Cookery Magic (Map pp672-3; 6348 9667; www.cookerymagic.com; Haig Rd, Katong; classes S$65-130) Ruqxana conducts standout Asian-cooking classes in her own home. Paya Lebar is the closest MRT station. She also conducts classes on an eco farm (harvest your own vegies before cooking!) and on Pulau Ubin (in an old kampong home). Splash out for the hands-on classes.

Spice Queen (Map p681; 6255 2440; www.spice-queen.com; 24 Race Course Rd; classes from S$40) Local celebrity chef Devagi Sanmugam conducts Indian cooking demos in a kitchen above her restaurant. Shopping trips are a highlight.

TOURS

Original Singapore Walks (6325 1631; www.singaporewalks.com; half-day adult/child from S$25/15) offers insightful tours of Chinatown, Little India, Kampong Glam, the Colonial District and Singapore's battlefields.

SLEEPING

Once, budget-room hunters in Singapore were limited to flea-bitten flophouses (they still exist!), but thankfully these days there are excellent hostels and guest houses even in the more expensive parts of the city. Unless otherwise stated, prices are for shared bathrooms.

Colonial District

Backpackers Cozy Corner (Map pp678-9; ☎ 6339 6128; www.cozycornerguest.com; 490 North Bridge Rd; dm S$12-17, d incl breakfast S$36-60;) Yes, we'll say it – this place can get a li'l *too* cosy when it's busy (and it usually is). The location is a huge plus, though rooms are dark and a little cramped. Ask for a dorm facing away from North Bridge Rd unless you like the noise of heavy traffic and merrymakers from the street. Expect to wait for internet access.

Summer Tavern (Map pp678-9; ☎ 6535 6601; 31 Carpenter St; dm/d incl breakfast S$25/60;) Summer Tavern offers fine dorm beds, medium-sized rooms good for one or two, and a rooftop beer lounge. A recent expansion includes a second building across the street, in which you'll find deluxe rooms with queen-sized beds and attached bathrooms. Rooms can be booked online.

YMCA International House (Map pp678-9; ☎ 6336 6000; www.ymcaih.com.sg; 1 Orchard Rd; dm/d/f incl breakfast S$35/180/215;) Even after you add on the S$3 temporary membership, the Y's roomy four-bed dorms (attached bath) are a steal. There's a pool and it's centrally located, and hotel-quality rooms can be had for cheap online. Staff attitudes have improved markedly since we last visited.

Chinatown

Fernloft (Map pp678-9; ☎ 6225 6696, www.fernloft.com; 02-82, 5 Banda St; dm/d incl breakfast S$20/60;) Fernloft is set in a traditional Singapore housing-development block and offers visitors a chance to live like a local. Its location is fantastic: Chinatown, with all its food and sights, opens up down a flight of stairs. There are limited beds and only two large (windowless) private air-con rooms so book in advance. There's only one shower.

Little India & Kampong Glam

Inn Crowd (Map p681; ☎ 6296 9169; www.the-inncrowd.com; 73 Dunlop St; dm/d/tr incl breakfast S$20/59/79;) As close to a typical backpackers hostel as you'd find in Singapore. Clean accommodation, living areas where travellers like to hang and saccharine-sweet staff. The atmosphere's decidedly convivial, with free lockers and internet, discounted tickets to sights and cheap Tiger draft beer on tap.

Prince of Wales (Map p681; ☎ 6299 0130; www.pow.com.sg; 101 Dunlop St; dm/d S$20/60;) This Australian-style pub and hostel has a raucous beer-and-sawdust rock bar downstairs and clean, high-ceilinged dorms upstairs. The two private rooms share a bathroom. Not everyone wants to rock out, but it's a lively place in an ace location.

Fragrance Backpackers Hostel (Map p681; ☎ 6295 6888; www.fragrancebackpackers.com.sg; 63 Dunlop St; dm S$22-25;) The ever-growing midrange Fragrance chain (18 branches at last count) has sniffed out a sweet-smelling niche in the budget market. Its Little India outfit is sparklingly clean, with leather couches strewn through the (small) TV lounge, great security, chunky mattresses and backpack-sized lockers. Avoid the basement dorms, which are sans windows.

hangout @ mt emily (Map p681; ☎ 6438 5588; www.hangouthotels.com; 10A Upper Wilkie Rd, dm/d/tr incl breakfast $40/100/200;) Prices for the comfy seven-bed (not bunk) dorms are a relative bargain considering the location; walking distance to Orchard Rd, the Colonial District and Little India (though it's quite a hike up to the hotel itself). There's a lovely rooftop terrace with a 'standing pool', a library, a cafe, free internet and cosy lounge areas with a large plasma TV.

Kampong Glam

Sleepy Sam's (Map p681; ☎ 9277 4988; www.sleepysams.com; 55 Bussorah St; dm/s/d incl breakfast S$29/59/89;) Prices at this main-staying budget hostel (if we could call it that) have gone steadily upwards over the years. But the ambience is more boutique hotel than hostel. Expect lots of woody, earthy tones, little nooks, and chairs and cushions in the common areas. The location, on a pedestrianised street, is right in the middle of a bohemian district and steps away from the imposing Sultan Mosque (p682).

Superb Hub (Map p681; ☎ 6299 0993; superbhub@yahoo.com.sg; 1148 Arab St; s & d from S$50-70;) Positioning itself in between a fully fledged hostel and a motel, Superb Hub offers smallish one-, two- or three-bed windowless rooms with ample privacy but lacking in congenial

SINGAPORE

CAMPING IT UP

The **National Parks Board** (Map p681; ☎ 6391 4488; www.nparks.gov.sg; 18-01/08 Gateway West, 150 Beach Rd) maintains five camp sites around Singapore: **Changi Beach** (Map pp672–3), **East Coast Park** (Map pp672–3), **Sembawang Park** (Map pp672–3), **West Coast Park** (Map pp672–3), and the east end of **Pasir Ris Park** (Map pp672–3). You need a S$1 permit to camp during the week, obtainable online (www.axs.com.sg) or from several AXS (ATM-like) machines in most malls. You can camp a maximum of eight days per month. There's a small fee to use the barbecue pits and shower facilities. On **Pulau Ubin** (Map pp672–3) you can camp at Noordin or Maman Beach on the north coast. The sites are free, but very basic. There's no drinking water, so bring your own. You can also camp on the **Southern Islands** (Kusu, Lazarus and St John's; Map pp672–3) for free. BYO drinking water too.

atmosphere. Where are the people lounging on common couches, watching bad cable TV? Owner Ronnie is extremely helpful and is ready to dispense bottled water and tourist information.

EATING

Singaporean life, in a microcosm, is best epitomised by the ubiquitous (but wholly unique) hawker centre. Grab a seat, order a supersweet coffee or a Tiger beer, join the queue for a local meal and listen to people talk about the weather, English Premier League, Hollywood diets and maids. Dishes rarely cost more than S$5 (unless you're eating seafood) and each centre has a huge variety of cuisines, including Malay, South Indian, Cantonese, Hokkien, Teochew and Indonesian. There are also countless excellent restaurants, though costs are going to spiral up to at least S$12 per plate.

Colonial District

Ah Teng's Bakery (Map pp678-9; ☎ 6337 1886; Raffles Hotel, 2 Stamford Rd; tea & pastries S$12; ⌚ 7.30am-6.30pm) One of the Raffles Hotel eateries, this splendid genteel cafe, serving up scones, pasties and even dim sum, looks like the sort of place your grandmother used to frequent before the war. For shoestringers, it's about the only opportunity to experience Raffles without busting your wallet. The attached Empire Cafe also serves up upmarket local hawker fare.

Yet Con (Map pp678-9; ☎ 6337 6819; 25 Purvis St; mains S$8-24; ⌚ lunch & dinner) We doubt that much has changed in the 50-odd years that Yet Con has been in business. The chicken rice and steamboat are popular dishes at this retro eatery…just look around. The air-con is the only modern (and welcome) addition to this joint.

Also try the following food centres:

Coffee Express 2000 Food Court (Map pp678-9; 01-79 Brash Basah Complex, 232 Victoria St; ⌚ 24 hr)
Glutton's Corner (Map pp678-9; beside the Esplanade Mall; ⌚ lunch & dinner)
Raffles City (Map pp678-9; 3rd fl, 252 North Bridge Rd; ⌚ breakfast, lunch & dinner)
Victoria St Food Centre (Map pp678-9; 143 Victoria St; ⌚ 10am-3am)

For an ultracheap feed, pull up a table at one of several **steamboat restaurants** (Map pp678-9; cnr Beach Rd & Liang Seah St; ⌚ dinner) where S$15.50 to S$19 will buy you an 'all you can eat' spread of meats, seafood and vegies.

The supermarket **Cold Storage** (Map p681; www.coldstorage.com.sg; B1-16, Bugis Junction, 200 Victoria St) has several branches across the city.

CBD & the Quays

Ya Kun Kaya Toast (Map pp678-9; 01-01 Far East Sq, 18 China St; ⌚ 7.30am-7am Mon-Fri, 9am-5pm Sat & Sun) Though a chain of outlets have mushroomed across Singapore, this outlet most closely matches the original 1940s stall selling strong coffee, the runny eggs and the *kaya* toast that so many Singaporeans love.

Epicurious (Map pp678-9; ☎ 6734 7720; 01-02 The Quayside, 60 Robertson Quay; mains S$4-20; ⌚ lunch & dinner Tue-Fri, 9am-10pm Sat & Sun) The worn coffeeshop tables and breakfast bench here are a direct result of diners frantically shovelling down walnut-bread french toast with orange butter, laksa pesto and numerous other delights. The weekend breakfast menu singlehandedly breathes life to this largely ignored quay.

Famous for its renovated Victorian market building, **Lau Pa Sat festival market** (pp678-9; 18 Raffles Quay; ⌚ 24hr) hawker centre can be so bewildering it even has street numbers.

Chinatown

Da Dong Restaurant (Map pp678-9; ☎ 6221 3822; 39 Smith St; yum cha S$2.80-4.80; mains S$12-20; 11am-10.45pm Mon-Fri, 9am-10.45pm Sat & Sun) One of Chinatown's longest-lasting restaurants first opened doors in 1928. These days, it still serves up some of the best dim sum in town. Longevity hasn't equated with great service but with *char siew* (BBQ pork) buns this good, who cares?

Annalakshmi Janatha (Map pp678-9; ☎ 6223 0809; 104 Amoy St; meals S$5-10; 11am-3pm Mon-Sat) A real gem, serving up Indian vegetarian buffets on an 'eat as you like, pay as you feel' basis (S$5 per head is acceptable). It's run by volunteers and profits help support various charities. There's another branch in **Chinatown Point** (Map pp678-9; B1-02 Chinatown Point, 133 New Bridge Rd).

Explore the overwhelming options at the following food centres:

Chinatown Complex (Map pp678-9; cnr Sago & Trengganu Sts; 9am-11pm)

Maxwell Rd Food Centre (Map pp678-9; cnr Maxwell & Neil Rds; 24hr) Generally esteemed as one of Singapore's best hawker centres, this is in an open-sided food barn with over 100 stalls under the roof.

Smith St Hawker Stalls (Map pp678-9; Smith St; 4pm-11pm)

Little India & Kampong Glam

Ananda Bhavan (Map p681; ☎ 6297 9522; 58 Serangoon Rd; mains from S$4; 7.30am-10pm) There are several branches of this superlative South Indian vegetarian eatery, which serves up excellent *idli* (rice dumplings), *thali* (traditional 'all-you-can-eat' meals) and *dosa* (paper-thin lentil-flour pancakes) and lots of Indian sweets.

Andhra Curry (Map p681; ☎ 6293 3935; 41 Kerbau Rd; meals from S$7; lunch & dinner) No-frills restaurant that prides itself on fiery recipes from the Indian state of Andhra Pradesh. Order up some Hyderabadi biryani (oven-baked rice with vegetables and meat), or absorb a flavoursome punch from the lamb dry curry. Masala tea helps quell the fire in your belly.

Spice Queen (Map p681; ☎ 6255 2240; 24/26 Race Course Rd; mains S$8-20; lunch & dinner) Self-taught celebrity chef Devagi Sanmugam serves Indian dishes with a distinctly Singaporean twist in the heart of Little India. The staff are ultrafriendly and happy to make recommendations. Take home recipe books or sign up for a cooking class (p685).

Banana Leaf Apolo (Map p681; ☎ 6293 8682; 54 Race Course Rd; mains S$10-20; lunch & dinner) Supremely tourist-friendly restaurant famed for its fish-head curry (S$20; dig into the delish meat on those fishy cheeks!) Can't face a fish face? Standards like rogan josh and lamb vindaloo are less confronting.

French Stall (Map p681; ☎ 6299 3544; 544 Serangoon Rd; mains S$10-22; drinks & dessert 3-6pm Tue-Sun, dinner Tue-Sun) French chef Xavier Le Henaff married a Singaporean and set up this place for regular folks – the best of France (good wine, great food, better desserts and lilting accordion music) merged with Singaporean affordability and no-frills outdoor dining. No reservations; cash only.

Food centres:

Lavender Food Square (Map p681; cnr Jln Besar & Foch Rd; 24hr) People queue ages for the wonton noodles.

Tekka Centre (Map p681; cnr Serangoon & Buffalo Rds; 10am-10pm) Under renovation at time of research but usually has plenty of atmosphere and food.

Kampong Glam

Zam Zam (Map p681; ☎ 6298 7011; 699 North Bridge Rd; meals S$4-8; breakfast, lunch & dinner) These guys have been here since 1908, so we figure they know what they're doing. Tenure hasn't bred complacency – the touts try to herd passers-by through the door as frenetic chefs whip up *murtabaks* (mutton-, chicken- or vegetable-filled flaky, flat bread).

Pariaman Warong Nasi (Map p681; ☎ 6292 2374; 738 North Bridge Rd; meals S$6-10; 7.30am-3.30pm) Cars roll up for quick takeaways at lunchtime and you'll smell the food before you see the crowd waiting to order the Malay dishes at this corner coffee shop. The *beef rendang* (dry beef curry) and *sambal goreng* (long beans, tempeh and fried bean curd) are dishes to try.

Cafe Le Caire (Map p681; ☎ 6292 0979; 39 Arab St; mains S$8-17, shisha S$15; lunch & dinner) This casual Egyptian hole-in-the-wall comes to life at night and attracts a multinational crowd. For a filling budget meal, you can't go past the mezze platter, washed down with an iced mint tea and a relaxing puff on a water pipe.

The **Golden Mile Food Centre** (Map p681; 505 Beach Rd; 10am-10pm) offers a wide range of local specialities, while across the road in the **Golden Mile Complex** (off Map p681; 10am-10pm) you'll find many Thai food stalls.

Orchard Road Area

Samy's Curry Restaurant (Map pp672-3; ☎ 6472 2080; Civil Service Clubhouse, Dempsey Rd; dishes from S$3; noon-10pm) A Singaporean institution and well worth the effort to get here. Housed in an old wooden army mess hall, this banana-leaf curry joint is magnificent. Grab a table and the waiters will come round with silver buckets of curry (they always bring the most expensive stuff first). A vegie meal will cost around S$4, meat a fair bit more.

Wasabi Tei (Map p683; 05-70 Far East Plaza, 14 Scotts Rd; dishes $5-15; noon-3pm & 5.30-9.30pm Mon-Fri, noon-4.30pm & 5.30-9.30pm Sat) Join the queue snaking out of this 20-seat mom-and-pop sushi bar. The chef is Chinese but he sure can slice raw fish. You'd better make your choices before you sit because seconds and postorder amendments are strictly not allowed. Soup Nazi–like you say? Nineteen other people will gladly take your place.

Din Tai Fung (Map p683; 6836 8336; B1-03 Paragon, 290 Orchard Rd; mains $6-17; lunch & dinner) The queues at this Taiwanese restaurant are testament to its excellent food. While waiting, watch chefs at work through 'fishbowl' windows; they painstakingly make 18 folds in the dough used for the *xiao long pao* (steamed pork dumplings). Delicate dumplings are served steaming fresh in bamboo baskets and literally burst with an explosion of flavour in your mouth.

Oriole Cafe & Bar (Map p683; 6238 8348; 01-01 Pan Pacific Serviced Suites, 96 Somerset Rd; mains S$10-18; lunch & dinner) Oriole's modern bistro sensibilities are reflected in a wide-ranging menu guaranteed to induce dining indecision. Do you go with the beef-cheek tagliatelle, good old fish and chips or a Philly steak and cheese? Singapore's barista champion, John Ting, pulls perfect espressos behind the impressive La Marzocco machine.

Most malls have food courts, usually in the basement:

Food Republic (Map p683; Wisma Atria; 435 Orchard Rd; 10am-10pm) Slightly upmarket food court, with views along Orchard Rd.

Newton Food Centre (Map p683; Newtown Circus; 24hr) Outdoor dining and excellent chilli stingray.

Takashimaya Food Village (Map p683; Takashimaya, Ngee Ann City, 391 Orchard Rd; 10am-10pm)

Carrefour (Map p683; Plaza Singapura, 68 Orchard Rd) is a outlet of the French hypermarket chain.

DRINKING

Drinking in Singapore is an expensive pastime. The cheapest way to drink is to park yourself in a hawker centre, where beers cost S$7 to $8 for a large bottle. If you're hitting the bars and clubs, start early: happy hours generally finish at 9pm. The main drinking places include Clarke and Boat Quays, and Emerald Hill Rd off Orchard Rd. Most bars open from 5pm daily until at least midnight Sunday to Thursday, and until 2am on Fridays and Saturdays.

Colonial District

Raffles Hotel (Map pp678-9; 6337 1886; raffles@raffles.com; 1 Beach Rd) It's a compulsory and costly cliché to sink a Singapore Sling (S$25, or S$32 with a souvenir glass) in the Long Bar (open 11am to 12.30am), but for a less touristy experience head for the century-old snooker tables at the Bar & Billiard Room (open 11.30am to 12.30am), where you can almost hear Somerset Maugham clacking away on his typewriter in the courtyard.

New Asia Bar (Map pp678-9; 6831 5681; cover Fri & Sat incl 1 drink S$25; 3pm-late) Save the S$30 you would have spent on the Singapore Flyer and spend it on drinks here instead! The panoramic views from the 70th floor help your drinks go down a little easier. Come early for S$12 sundowners and once you tire of the views, shake it on the dance floor. There are strict dress codes.

CBD & the Quays

Falling into disrepair a few years ago, Clarke Quay has been breathtakingly revamped, and is now far and away the most popular (though very gaudy) nightspot in Singapore.

Brewerkz (Map pp678-9; 6438 7438; www.brewerkz.com; 01-05 Riverside Point Centre, 30 Merchant Rd; Mon-Thu noon-midnight, Fri & Sat noon-1am, Sun 11am-midnight) Across the river from Clarke Quay, this large microbrewery (the irony doesn't escape us) brews eight beers on site. Happy hours run from opening to 9pm, with prices escalating throughout the day (pints S$4 to S$15, jugs S$10 to S$37).

Crazy Elephant (Map pp678-9; 6337 7859; www.crazyelephant.com; 01-03/04 Clarke Quay; 5pm-2am Sun-Thu, till 3am Fri & Sat) Anywhere that bills itself as 'crazy' should set the alarm bells ringing, but you won't hear them once you're inside. This touristy rock bar is beery, blokey, loud, graffiti-covered and testosterone-heavy – rock on!

Boat Quay is a popular haunt for expat city workers. The British-style **Penny Black** (Map pp678-9; 6538 2300; 26/27 Boat Quay) gets very busy, as does **Harry's Bar** (Map pp678-9; 6538 3029; 28 Boat Quay) next door, a relaxed jazz pub that has been a long-time favourite and now has branches all over the city.

Chinatown

Tanjong Pagar Rd has an active gay and lesbian bar scene but welcomes drinkers regardless of their sexuality. The sophisticated bars of Club St are housed in attractive, restored shophouses (many are closed Sunday).

Backstage Bar (Map pp678-9; ☎ 6227 1712; 13A Trengganu St; 🕑 7pm-2am Sun-Thu, to 3am Fri & Sat) This gay and lesbian hang-out has a breezy balcony with great views of the street below.

Bar Sá Vanh (Map pp678-9; ☎ 6323 0503; 49A Club St) Ultratrendy, dim-lit bar with a water wall, koi pond and lots of Buddhas.

Little India & Kampong Glam

Prince of Wales (Map p681; ☎ 6299 0130; www.pow.com.sg; cnr Dunlop & Madras Sts) The drinking scene in Little India is quiet, but the Australian-style Prince of Wales has drink specials and regular live bands. Also has accommodation (p686).

Zsofi Tapas Bar (Map p681; ☎ 6297 5875; 68 Dunlop St; 🕑 4pm-1am Mon-Thu, 4pm-2am Fri & Sat) Inspired by their travels through Spain, two mates decided to open a tapas bar named after a travelling companion. All drinks come with a tapas dish of your choice. Now that's choice!

Blujaz Cafe (Map p681; ☎ 6292 3800; 1 Bali Lane) One of the few places to get alcohol in Kampong Glam – a relaxed, friendly bar right next door to an artists' commune, with occasional live jazz.

Orchard Road Area

Emerald Hill has a collection of bars in the renovated shophouses just off Orchard Rd, including the cool **Alley Bar** (Map p683; ☎ 6738 8818; 2 Emerald Hill Rd) and even cooler **No 5** (Map p683; ☎ 6732 0818; 5 Emerald Hill Rd). At the end of the strip, **Ice Cold Beer** (Map p683; ☎ 6735 9929; 9 Emerald Hill Rd) is a raucous spot with indie/rock music at high decibels and a range of chilled brews.

Sentosa Island

Sentosa has recently shaken off its tacky image and become something of a fashionable hang-out, especially at weekends, when its beach bars are busy day and night with the tanned and scantily clad. Beach parties are held here reasonably regularly. **Coastes** (Map pp672-3; ☎ 6274 9668; Siloso Beach), **Bikini Bar** (Map pp672-3; ☎ 6274 9668; Siloso Beach), and **Café del Mar** (Map pp672-3; ☎ 6235 1296; Siloso Beach) are all Ibiza-inspired restaurant–bars.

CLUBBING

Singapore is party central and though many clubs come and go, there are several mainstayers worth visiting.

Zouk (Map pp678-9; ☎ 6738 2988; www.zoukclub.com.sg; 17 Jiak Kim St; men/women incl 2 drinks S$45/38, before 10pm S$25) This stayer of the Singaporean club scene still nabs top-name DJs. It's actually three clubs in one, plus a wine bar, so go the whole hog and pay the full entrance.

Butter Factory (Map pp678-9; ☎ 6333 8243; www.thebutterfactory.com; 02-02 One Fullerton, 1 Fullerton Rd; admission incl 2 drinks from S$21; 🕑 7pm-1am Tue, 7pm-3am Thu, 8pm-3am Wed & Fri, Sat 8pm-4am) At 8000 sq ft, Butter Factory digs is also slick as hell. Street art on the walls of Bump, their hip-hop and R&B room, appeals to the younger crowds.

Zirca Mega Club (Map pp678-9; ☎ 6235 2292; www.zirca.sg; 01-02 Block 3C River Valley Rd, The Cannery, Clarke Quay; admission incl two drinks men S$25-28, women S$20-25; 🕑 9.30pm till late Wed-Sat) Located in the premises of the former Ministry of Sound. Mash with the mainly 20-somethings in Zirca (dance club), Rebel (hip-hop arena) or Yellow Jello (retro disco).

St James Power Station (Map pp672-3; ☎ 6270 7676; www.stjamespowerstation.com; 3 Sentosa Gateway; admission men/women $12/10, men Wed S$30) An entertainment complex housed in a 1920s coal-fired power station. Pure genius. All the bars and clubs are interconnected, so one cover charge gets access to all of them. Some bars have no cover charge at all. Minimum age is 18 for women and 23 for men at all except Powerhouse, where the age is 18 for both. The bars include **Dragonfly** (🕑 6pm-6am), a Mando- and Canto-pop club, Latin live-band dance club **Movida** (🕑 6pm-3am), **Powerhouse** (🕑 8pm-4am Wed, Fri & Sat), a large dance club aimed at the younger crowd, and the **Boiler Room** (🕑 8.45pm-3am Mon-Sat), a mainstream rock club featuring live bands.

ENTERTAINMENT

The *Straits Times*, *I-S Magazine* and *Time Out* have listings for movies, theatre and music. Tickets for most events are available through **Sistic** (Map p683; ☎ 6348 5555; www.sistic.com.sg; Wisma Atria, 435 Orchard Rd) or **Tickets.com** (☎ 6296 2929; www.tdc.com.sg). Sistic also has agencies at Bugis Junction, Raffles City, the Singapore Visitors Centre located on Orchard Rd, Suntec City, and Esplanade – Theatres on the Bay.

Chinese Opera, Comedy & Theatre

Chinese Theatre Circle (Map pp678-9; ☎ 6323 4862; www.ctcopera.com.sg; 5 Smith St; 1-/2-hr show S$20/35, tickets through Sistic) Get into Chinese opera at a teahouse session organised by this nonprofit company. Friday and Saturday shows start at 7pm and 8pm with a brief talk (in English) on Chinese opera, followed by an excerpt from a Cantonese opera.

Other big venues that feature various comedy, theatre and musical acts:

Drama Centre (Map p681; ☎ 6837 8400; Level 3, National Library, 100 Victoria St)

Esplanade – Theatres on the Bay (Map pp678-9; ☎ 6828 8222; www.esplanade.com; 1 Esplanade Dr)

Victoria Concert Hall & Theatre(Map pp678-9; ☎ 6338 8283; 9 Empress Pl)

Cinema

Movie-going is huge in Singapore, and at around S$9 per ticket it's pretty good value too. Films are mainly Hollywood blockbusters and Chinese, Korean and Japanese crowd-pleasers, plus a few art-house hits from around the world. Non-English films are subtitled. Singaporean cinemas are notoriously chilly.

There are multiplex cinemas around the Colonial District at **Bugis Junction** (Map p681) and **Iluma** (Map p681), **Suntec City** (Map pp678–9) and **Marina Square** (Map pp678–9). Around Orchard Rd you'll find cinemas at **Cathay Cineleisure Orchard** (Map p683) and **Plaza Singapura** (Map p683), **Lido cinema** (Map p683) at Shaw House and the **Picturehouse** at the Cathay (off Map p683).

Live Music

Jazz@Southbridge (Map pp678-9; ☎ 6327 4671; www.southbridgejazz.com.sg; 82B Boat Quay; admission free, touring acts from S$20; 🕑 5pm-1am Tue-Thu, till 2am Fri & Sat) This intimate jazz bar sets plush sofas in front of a small stage. Inhouse croooner Alemay Fernandez ably entertains, and famous internationals often take to the stage (Pat Metheny did an impromptu jam once). Sets kick off around 9.30pm.

Timbre@Old School (Map p681; ☎ 6338 0800; 11 Mt Sophia Rd; 🕑 6pm-midnight) At night, groups of art-school types hang out and bob heads to live acoustic sets while downing pints of Erdinger, their hands oily from one too many buffalo wings. There's a branch featuring alt-rockers on weekends at **Substation** (Map pp678-9; ☎ 6337 7800; 45 Armenian St; 🕑 6pm-midnight).

Local bands play every night at the knockabout Prince of Wales (opposite). The Esplanade – Theatres on the Bay (left) has free outdoor gigs on Fridays, Saturdays and Sundays that kick off around 7pm; check the website for details.

SHOPPING

Once renowned as a bargain paradise, Singapore has been overtaken by other cities in the region, but there are still bargains to be had on items such as clothing, electronics, IT gear and books. Prices are usually fixed except at markets and in smaller nonchain stores (don't start bargaining if you don't have any real interest in purchasing). Most shops open at 10am or 11am and close around 9pm or 10pm.

Orchard Road

Orchard Rd (Map p683) is so overwhelming it would take a week to explore thoroughly. Starting at the Scotts Rd end, there is **Wheelock Place** (☎ 6738 8660; 501 Orchard Rd) for the Apple store and a huge Borders bookshop. Up Scotts Rd is **Far East Plaza** (☎ 6235 2411; 14 Scotts Rd), great for cheap books, clothes and shoes, including funky Japanese street fashions. Next to Orchard MRT is the new **Ion Orchard** (430 Orchard Rd) with a shimmery 21st-century media wall, an art space and a wide range of stores. **Ngee Ann City** (☎ 6733 0337; 391 Orchard Rd) is packed with high-end brands and Kinokuniya (p677), the best bookshop in the city. **Paragon** (☎ 6738 5535; 290 Orchard Rd) is only for those who enjoy receiving red-coloured credit-card bills. Then comes **Heeren** (☎ 6733 4725; www.heeren.com.sg; 260 Orchard Rd), which specialises in hip clothing and accessories for the young, and also has a large HMV outlet. There's a lot more, so explore away.

Colonial District

IT greenhorns should try **Funan DigitaLife Mall** (Map pp678-9; ☎ 6337 4235; 109 North Bridge Rd), where computers, software, camera gear and MP3 players are priced and labelled.

For cameras, try the extensively stocked **Cathy Photo** (Map pp678-9; ☎ 6337 4274; 01-11 Peninsula Plaza, 111 North Bridge Rd) or the family-run **John 3:16** (Map pp678-9; ☎ 6337 2877; 05-46 Funan DigitaLife Mall, 109 North Bridge Rd).

Chinatown

Chinatown's Pagoda, Smith and Temple Sts are full of the usual shops selling touristy trinkets, and several touts keen to tailor you a suit (see boxed text, p692).

People's Park Complex (Map pp678-9; 1 Park Cres) and **People's Park Centre** (Map pp678-9; 110 Upper Cross St) sell almost everything (watch out for tourist prices), and house lots of travel agents. **Bugis Village** (Map p681; Victoria St, opposite Bugis Junction), not far from Raffles Hotel, is a good hunting ground for cheap clothes and is one of the few places you'll encounter knock-offs of famous brands.

Little India & Kampong Glam

Little India bursts with handicrafts, gold, saris, incense, Bollywood music and DVDs. In Kampong Glam, for handicrafts, raw cloth and tourists trinkets, wander along **Bussorah St** (Map p681). **Haji Lane** (Map p681) has a series of stores selling up-to-the-minute fashion…assuming they haven't shut down because of soaring rents.

Sim Lim Square (Map p681; ☎ 6332 5839; 1 Rochor Canal Rd) is geek paradise, overflowing with cheap IT gear and electronics. It's a cut-throat world in there and we'd only advise going if you know your stuff, because novices will be fleeced.

Mustafa Shopping Centre (Map p681; ☎ 6294 7742; www.mustafa.com.sg; 145 Syed Alwi Rd; 24hr) has all manner of goods (electronics, jewellery, household items, toys, shoes etc). A new (and less fire hazardous) extension has a supermarket with a wide range of Indian foodstuff.

SINGAPORE DIRECTORY

ACCOMMODATION

Hostels are booming in Singapore, so expect competitive prices (S$18 to S$20 for a dorm bed) and facilities like free internet, breakfast and laundry use. Cheaper hotel rooms (S$50 to S$100) are cramped, often windowless, with shared facilities. Most places offer air-con rooms, with cheaper fan rooms. Most establishments will quote net prices, which include all taxes. If you see +++ after a price it means you'll need to add on 10% service charge, 7% GST and 1% government tax. Room prices quoted in this chapter include all taxes.

BUSINESS HOURS

Government offices are usually open from Monday to Friday and on Saturday morning. Hours vary, starting at around 7.30am to 9.30am and closing between 4pm and 6pm. On Saturday, closing time is between 11.30am and 1pm.

TOP FIVE TOUTS' CALLS

Sure they may be annoying, but touts can also be very witty in their attempts to lure you. The five best we've heard:

- 'I'll make you long pants for short price.'
- 'Here's my business card so you can send me Christmas cards.'
- 'You have beautiful English skin, like fish and chips.'
- 'Why pay so much, lah? My brand also the same for less!'
- 'Would you like a ride in my air-conditioned helicopter?' (from a rickshaw driver).

Shopping malls are open from around 10am to 10pm daily; and though many small shops in Chinatown close Sundays, it is the busiest shopping day in Little India. Banks are open from 9.30am to 3pm weekdays (and until 1pm on Saturday).

Singapore's food centres and hawker stalls open various hours (some 24 hours), but regular restaurants open for lunch from 11.30am to 2.30pm and then for dinner from 6pm to 10.30pm.

Most bars are open from 5pm until at least midnight Sunday to Thursday, and from 5pm to 2am on Friday and Saturday.

CLIMATE

There are virtually no seasons in Singapore – the weather is uniformly hot, humid and wet all year round. November to January are considered slightly wetter months, though you should always be prepared for a soaking, no matter how clear the skies appear when you go out. See p936 for climate charts.

CUSTOMS

You can bring in 1L each of wine, beer and spirits duty free, but no unopened packets of cigarettes. Electronic goods, cosmetics, watches, cameras, jewellery (but not imitation jewellery), footwear, toys, arts and crafts are not dutiable; the usual duty-free concession for personal effects, such as clothes, applies. Duty-free concessions are not available if you are arriving from Malaysia or if you leave Singapore for less than 48 hours.

Toy currency and coins, obscene or seditious material, gun-shaped cigarette lighters, pirated recordings and publications, and retail quantities of chewing gum are prohibited.

DANGERS & ANNOYANCES

Short-term visitors are unlikely to be troubled by Singapore's notoriously tough laws, which have turned the city into one of the safest in Asia. Street crime is minimal, though pickpockets have been known to operate in Chinatown, Little India and other tourist areas. See also Legal Matters, p694.

DRIVING LICENCE

To drive in Singapore you'll need your home driver's licence and an international permit from a motoring association in your country.

EMBASSIES & CONSULATES

Embassies, consulates and high commissions in Singapore:

Australia (Map p683; ☎ 6836 4100; www.australia.org.sg; 25 Napier Rd)
Canada (Map pp672-3; ☎ 6854 5900; www.dfait-maeci.gc.ca/asia/singapore; 11-01 One George St)
France (Map pp672-3; ☎ 6880 7800; www.ambafrance-sg.org; 101-103 Cluny Park Rd)
Germany (Map pp678-9; ☎ 6533 6002; www.singapur.diplo.de; 12-00 Singapore Land Tower, 50 Raffles Pl)
Indonesia (Map p683; ☎ 6737 7422; www.kbrisingapura.com; 7 Chatsworth Rd)
Ireland (Map p683; ☎ 6238 7616; www.embassyofireland.sg; 08-00 Liat Towers, 541 Orchard Rd)
Italy (Map p683; ☎ 6250 6022; www.ambsingapore.esteri.it; 27-02 United Square, 101 Thomson Rd)
Japan (Map p683; ☎ 6235 8855; www.sg.emb-japan.go.jp; 16 Nassim Rd)
Netherlands (Map p683; ☎ 6737 1155; www.mfa.nl/sin; 13-01 Liat Towers, 541 Orchard Rd)
New Zealand (Map p683; ☎ 6235 9966; www.nzembassy.com/singapore; 15-06/10 Ngee Ann City, 391A Orchard Rd)
Thailand (Map p683; ☎ 6737 2475; www.thaiembassy.sg; 370 Orchard Rd)
UK (Map p683; ☎ 6424 4200; www.britishhighcommission.gov.uk; 100 Tanglin Rd)
USA (Map p683; ☎ 6476 9100; http://singapore.usembassy.gov; 27 Napier Rd)

For information on visas, see p695.

EMERGENCIES

Ambulance (☎ 995)
Fire (☎ 995)
Police (☎ 999)

FESTIVALS & EVENTS

Singapore's multicultural population celebrates an amazing number of festivals and events. For details on public holidays in Singapore, see below.

Chinese New Year The major festival, held in January/February. Look out for parades throughout Chinatown and festive foods in shops.
Singapore Food Festival (www.singaporefoodfestival.com) This month-long festival in March and April celebrates eating, and is held at hawker centres and gourmet restaurants.
Great Singapore Sale During this sale, in June and July, merchants drop prices to boost Singapore's image as a shopping destination.

FOOD & DRINK

Singapore's rich cultural brew has spawned one of Asia's great eating cities. Food is often cheap and since English is nearly universal you'll rarely have trouble ordering. There is not really such a thing as Singaporean cuisine, though. Most of the island's specialities are imported: Hainanese chicken rice, Chinese *char kway teow* (stir-fried flat noodles with soy sauce, prawns, cockles, egg and Chinese sausage), the Indo-Malay breakfast favourite *roti pratha* (flaky flat bread served with curry sauce) and the famous laksa (noodles served in a rich, spicy coconut broth with prawns, cockles, fried bean curd and bean sprouts). Unmissable local innovations include chilli crab and fish-head curry, which is far tastier than it sounds.

GAY & LESBIAN TRAVELLERS

Male homosexuality is still technically illegal, but the city is slowly opening up and the laws have not prevented the emergence of a thriving gay scene. In 2007, former prime minister Lee Kuan Yew made a public statement opposing the repression of homosexuals – and when Mr Lee speaks, government policy is never far behind. However, ministers are still reluctant to endorse what they see as a promiscuous, antifamily lifestyle.

Check out www.utopia-asia.com and www.fridae.com for coverage of venues and events.

HOLIDAYS

The following days are public holidays. Many are based on the lunar calendar, and their dates are variable.

New Year's Day 1 January
Chinese New Year January/February (three days)

Good Friday March/April
Vesak Day May
Labour Day 1 May
Vesak Day May (variable)
National Day 9 August
Deepavali October
Hari Raya Puasa October/November
Christmas Day 25 December
Hari Raya Haji December/January

INTERNET ACCESS

You'll have no problem finding places to get online, and many hostels offer free internet – some even have zippy broadband connections – and much of the city is covered by a free wireless access zone. Expect to pay S$5 per hour in internet cafes.

INTERNET RESOURCES

SINGOV Government Information (www.gov.sg) With seemingly endless information and services.
Singapore Tourism Board (www.visitsingapore.com) Singapore Tourism's site, with plenty of links to things to see and do.
TalkingCock.com (www.talkingcock.com) Singapore's favourite satirical website, offering a biting but affectionate look at the city's life, politics and people.

LEGAL MATTERS

The law is extremely tough in Singapore, but also relatively free from corruption. Possession and trafficking of drugs is punishable by death. Smoking in all public places, including bars, restaurants and hawker centres, is banned.

MAPS

The Official Map of Singapore, available free from the STB and hotels, is excellent.

MEDIA

Magazines

Free publications with events information, such as *Where Singapore* and *I-S Magazine* are available at tourist offices, most major hotels and several restaurants, cafes and bars. The international listings magazine *Time Out* now has a Singapore edition, too.

Newspapers

English dailies include the parochial progovernment spin sheet *Straits Times* (which includes the *Sunday Times*), the *Business Times* and the tabloid-style *New Paper*. *Straits Times* has decent coverage of Asia, if you want to get the latest on your future destinations. *New Paper* is best for a flavour of 'real life' Singapore. Many Singaporeans and foreigners prefer the more free-speaking *Today* newspaper, a freebie tabloid that you can pick up at MRT stations in the mornings and afternoons.

MONEY

The unit of currency is the Singaporean dollar, which is made up of 100 cents. Singapore uses 5c, 10c, 20c, 50c and S$1 coins, while notes come in denominations of S$2, S$5, S$10, S$50, S$100, S$500 and S$1000.

Banks and ATMs are everywhere. Exchange rates vary from bank to bank and some charge a service fee on each exchange transaction – usually S$2 to S$3, but it can be more, so ask first. Money changers are easily found in most malls and busy locations. You don't get charged any fees and you can haggle a little if you're changing a largeish quantity.

Contact details for credit-card companies in Singapore:

American Express (☎ 6396 6000)
Diners Club (☎ 6571 0128)
MasterCard (☎ 1800 1100 113)
Visa (☎ 6437 5800; 1800 1100 344)

POST

Post in Singapore is among the most reliable in Southeast Asia. Postcards cost S$0.50 to anywhere in the world, but letters cost from S$1.50 to S$2.50 depending on where it's going. Post offices (see p677) are open from 8am to 6pm Monday to Friday, and 8am to 2pm Saturday. Call ☎ 1605 to find the nearest post office branch, or check www.singpost.com.sg. Letters

EXCHANGE RATES

Exchange rates at time of press:

Country	Unit	Singapore dollars (S$)
Australia	A$1	1.24
Canada	C$1	1.32
Euro zone	€1	2.06
Indonesia	10,000Rp	1.46
Japan	¥100	1.57
Malaysia	RM10	4.07
New Zealand	NZ$1	1.02
Philippines	100P	2.98
Thailand	100B	4.21
UK	UK£1	2.25
USA	US$1	1.41

addressed to 'Poste Restante' are held at the **Singapore Post Centre** (Map pp672-3; ☎ 6841 2000; 10 Eunos Rd), next to the Paya Lebar MRT.

RESPONSIBLE TRAVEL

Modern and cosmopolitan though it appears, Singapore is a little sensitive when it comes to any brash behaviour by foreigners – quiet, polite behaviour will win you more respect. Public transport is efficient and you can even call hybrid-fuel taxis.

TELEPHONE

Mobile Phones

Mobile-phone numbers in Singapore start with 8 or 9. If you have global roaming, your GSM digital phone will tune into one of Singapore's three networks, MI-GSM, ST-GSM or Starhub.

You can buy a SIM card (usually S$10) or a 'disposable' mobile from most post offices and 7-Eleven stores, though you need to show your passport.

Phonecards

Local phonecards are widely available from 7-Eleven stores, post offices, Telecom centres, stationers and bookshops. Most phone booths take phonecards, and some take credit cards, with a few booths that still take coins. From public phones, local calls cost S$0.10 for three minutes.

Phone Codes

To call Singapore from overseas, dial your country's international access number and then dial ☎ 65 (Singapore's country code), before entering the eight-digit telephone number.

Calls to Malaysia are considered to be STD (trunk or long-distance) calls. Dial the access code 020, followed by the area code of the town in Malaysia that you wish to call (minus the leading zero) and then the number.

There are no area codes in Singapore; telephone numbers are eight digits unless you are calling toll free (☎ 1800).

TOILETS

Generally toilets in Singapore are clean and well maintained, though they might vary between the sit-down and rarer squatting types. In some hawker centres you may have to pay a small fee of S$0.10. You can usually find a toilet in malls, fast-food outlets and large hotels.

TOURIST INFORMATION

See p677 for branches of the Singapore Tourist Board (STB).

TRAVELLERS WITH DISABILITIES

Travellers using wheelchairs can find Singapore difficult, though a massive accessibility project to improve life for the elderly and those with disabilities has seen things improve. Check out *Access Singapore*, a useful guidebook for people with disabilities, which is available from STB offices (see p677), or contact the **National Council of Social Services** (☎ 6336 1544; www.ncss.org.sg).

The **Disabled People's Association** (☎ 6899 1220; www.dpa.org.sg) has an online accessibility guide to the country.

VISAS

Citizens of most countries are granted 30-day visas upon arrival in Singapore whether by air or overland (though the latter may be granted 14-day visas). The exceptions are citizens of the Commonwealth of Independent States, India, Myanmar, China and most Middle Eastern countries. Visitors must have a valid passport or internationally recognised travel document valid for at least six months beyond the date of entry into Singapore. Extensions can be applied for at the **Immigration & Checkpoints Authority** (Map p681; ☎ 6391 6100; www.ica.gov.sg; 10 Kallang Rd). This can also be done online. Applications take at least a day to process.

For details of embassies and consulates, see p693.

VOLUNTEERING

Singapore serves as a base for many NGOs, but most recruit skilled volunteers from their home countries. In Singapore itself the **National Volunteer & Philanthropy Centre** (www.nvpc.org.sg) coordinates a number of community groups, including grassroots projects in areas such as education, the environment and multiculturalism.

WOMEN TRAVELLERS

There are few problems for women travelling in Singapore. In Kampong Glam and Little India skimpy clothing may attract unwanted stares, so consider wearing long pants or skirts and loose tops. Tampons and pads are widely available across the island, as are over-the-counter medications.

Thailand

HIGHLIGHTS

- **Bangkok** (p710) Join the urban orbit in this rowdy metropolis that never sleeps, always eats and specialises in a good time.
- **Ko Phi Phi** (p817) Ogle the perfect proportions of this beach paradise.
- **Chiang Mai** (p749) Soak up the university-town atmosphere of this northern city where you can *finally* become Thai through cooking, massage or meditation courses.
- **Ko Tao** (p799) Learn to swim like a fish at this world-class dive spot.
- **Ko Pha-Ngan** (p795) Laze your way through the day on this popular, laid-back isle.
- **Off the beaten track** (p774 and p737) Track down the old Khmer ruins of Phanom Rung Historical Park or follow the road all the way to the end for sleepy but scenic Sangkhlaburi.

FAST FACTS

- **Budget** US$16 to US$20 a day
- **Capital** Bangkok
- **Costs** guest house in Bangkok US$11 to US$14, four-hour bus ride US$4, a plate of rice and curry US$1, big bottle of Beer Chang US$2.50
- **Country code** ☎ 66
- **Language** Thai
- **Money** US$1 = 33B *(baht)*
- **Phrases** *sà wàt dii* (hello), *khàwp khun* (thank you), *a·ròy* (delicious)
- **Population** 65 million
- **Time** GMT + seven hours
- **Visas** 30-day visa-free entry for most nationalities at airports, 15-day visas at land borders

TRAVEL HINTS

Skip the bus services that originate out of Bangkok's Th Khao San; these often have hidden costs and hassles.

OVERLAND ROUTES

Enter via Laos from Vientiane to Nong Khai or from Luang Prabang to Chiang Mai (via Huay Xai-Chiang Khong crossing); via Cambodia from Siem Reap to Bangkok (via Poipet–Aranya Prathet).

Lustrous Thailand radiates a hospitality that makes it one of the most accessibly exotic destinations on earth. Its natural landscape is part of the allure: the blonde beaches are lapped at by cerulean seas sheltering vibrant schools of fish and magical underwater gardens; and the northern mountains cascade into the misty horizon. In between are emerald-coloured rice fields and busy, prosperous cities. It is a bountiful land where food is practically worshipped, the markets are piled high with pyramids of colourful tropical fruits and vegetables and the *rót khēn* (vendor cart) is an integral piece of a city's infrastructure.

The new millennium has brought Thailand into a new era of prosperity, with a widening middle class that is one more generation removed from subsistence farming. This means that Bangkok is a tried-and-true international city on par with Singapore for affluence and sophistication and that the young urban generation only knows about village life through TV and story books. With the old ways becoming ancient history, the country is stepping into unchartered territory and the ongoing political stand-off has provided a dramatic and unresolved domestic cliffhanger. Though the global economic downturn and internal political strife has hurt the once raging tourist industry, now is a historic time to observe the kingdom at a crossroads. Plus there will be fewer backpackers to share the trail with.

You'll suffer few travelling hardships in Thailand and be rewarded with tales of island paradises, elephant encounters, renowned cuisine and a deeply spiritual culture where saffron-robed monks walk barefoot through city streets and riotous temples reflect the harsh midday sun. Just prepare your friends for potential boredom from too many 'in-Thailand' stories.

CURRENT EVENTS

Thailand has been garnering unfavourable headlines since its most recent coup in 2006, which ousted the popular but controversial prime minister, Thaksin Shinawatra. The military spent the next year attempting to 'clean house' of Thaksin's political party (Thai Rak Thai) only to have the regenerated (and re-christened) party win the 2007 reinstatement of democratic elections. In response, the aristocrats, organised under the group calling itself the People's Alliance for Democracy (PAD) but often dubbed 'Yellow Shirts' because they wear the colour associated with the monarchy, were unhappy with the return of Thaksin's political friends and staged massive protests in Bangkok that took over the parliament building and closed down the city's two airports for a week in November 2008. This dealt a deep blow to Thailand's economy and tourist industry just as the US financial crisis was morphing into a global recession.

The Constitutional Court got involved to satisfy PAD's demands to dissolve the ruling (and popularly elected) party. A new coalition was formed in December 2008, led by Oxford-educated Abhisit Vejjajiva, leader of the Democrat party and Thailand's fourth prime minister of the year. He has no popular mandate, is facing mounting unemployment and economic problems, and has fumbled with a human-rights scandal in which Rohingya refugees from Myanmar were abandoned at sea by the Thai navy.

In April 2009, coinciding with the Songkran festival, the Thaksin-supporters, calling themselves the United Front for Democracy Against Dictatorship (UDD) but better known as the 'Red Shirts', staged violent street protests in an outer district of Bangkok and stormed a hotel in Pattaya where the Asean summit was being held. Their demands were the removal of the prime minister and the return of elections, neither of which were met but their actions proved that the Abhiset government could not mend the political divide. Though many of the key UDD leaders have been arrested, the movement remains popular with rural and working-class people. And so the story shall continue…

HISTORY

Rise of Thai Kingdoms

It is believed that the first Thais migrated southwest from modern-day Yúnnán and Guangxi, China, to what is today known as Thailand. They settled along river valleys and formed small farming communities that eventually fell under the dominion of the expansionist Khmer empire of present-day Cambodia. What is now southern Thailand, along the Malay peninsula, was under the sway of the Srivijaya empire based in Sumatra.

By the 13th and 14th centuries, what is considered to be the first Thai kingdom – Sukhothai (meaning 'Rising Happiness') – emerged and began to chip away at the crumbling Angkor empire. The third Sukhothai

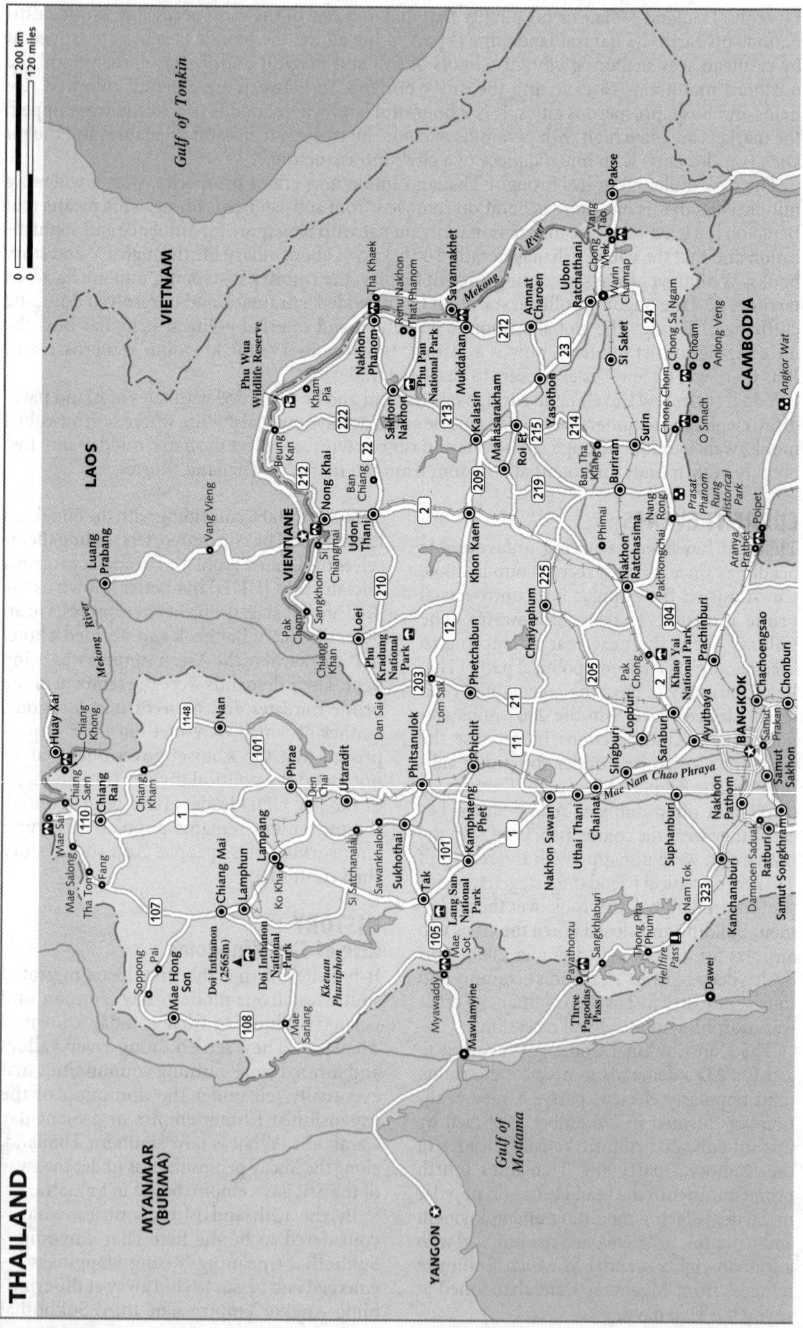

THAILAND

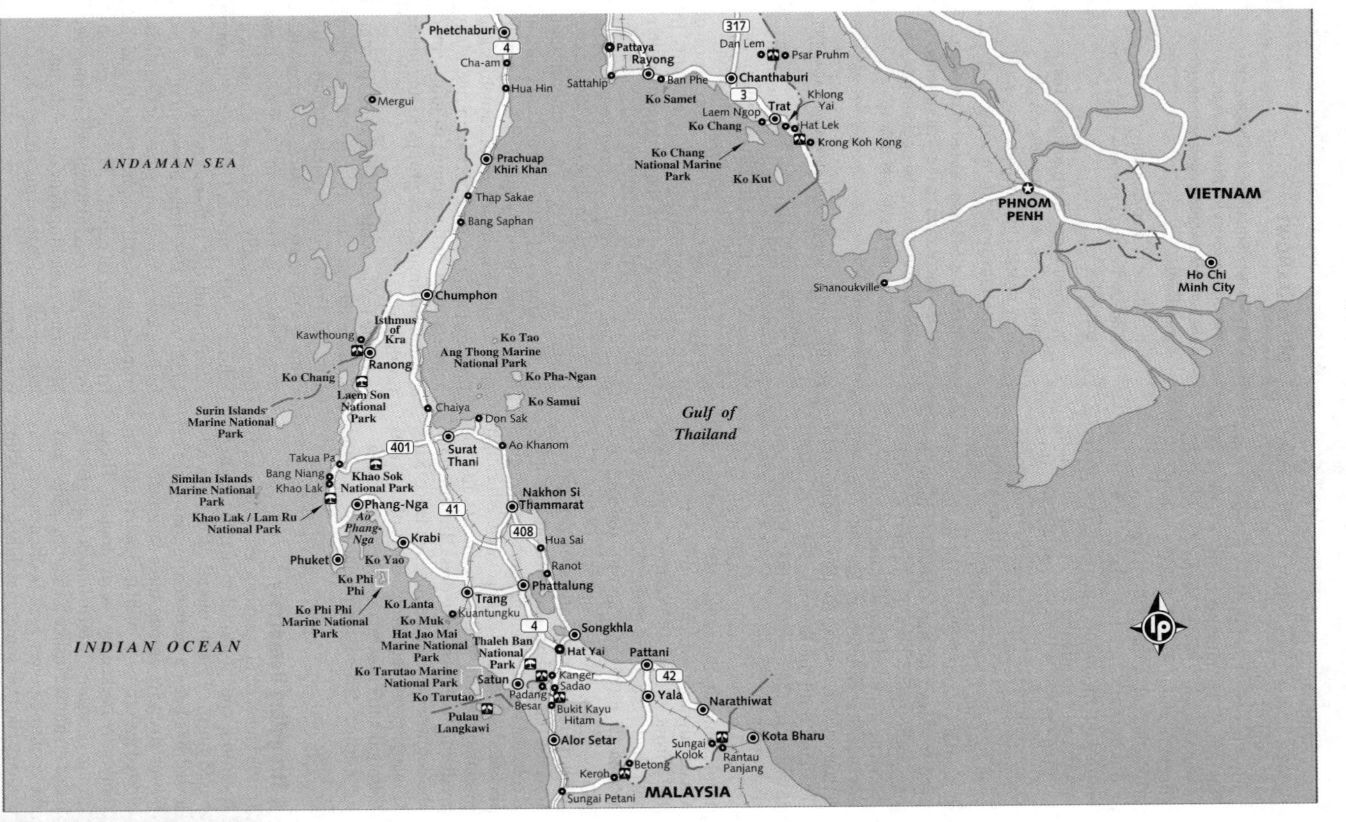
Phetchaburi
4
Cha-am
Hua Hin
Mergui
ANDAMAN SEA
Pattaya
Rayong
Sattahip
Ban Phe
317
Dan Lem
Psar Pruhm
Chanthaburi
3
Ko Samet
Laem Ngop
Trat
Khlong Yai
Hat Lek
Ko Chang
Krong Koh Kong
Ko Chang National Marine Park
Ko Kut
PHNOM PENH
VIETNAM
Ho Chi Minh City
Sihanoukville
Prachuap Khiri Khan
Thap Sakae
Bang Saphan
Chumphon
Isthmus of Kra
Kawthoung
Ranong
Ko Tao
Ang Thong Marine National Park
Ko Pha-Ngan
Ko Samui
Ko Chang
Laem Son National Park
Surin Islands Marine National Park
Chaiya
Don Sak
Gulf of Thailand
401
Surat Thani
Ao Khanom
Takua Pa
Bang Niang
Khao Lak
Khao Sok National Park
Similan Islands Marine National Park
Nakhon Si Thammarat
Phang-Nga
Khao Lak / Lam Ru National Park
41
Ao Phang-Nga
408
Hua Sai
Krabi
Phuket
Ko Yao
Ranot
Ko Phi Phi
Phattalung
Trang
Ko Phi Phi Marine National Park
Ko Lanta
Kuantungku
Ko Muk
4
Songkhla
Hat Jao Mai Marine National Park
INDIAN OCEAN
Thaleh Ban National Park
Hat Yai
Pattani
Ko Tarutao Marine National Park
Kanger
Sadao
42
Satun
Padang Besar
Yala
Narathiwat
Ko Tarutao
Bukit Kayu Hitam
Pulau Langkawi
Alor Setar
Kota Bharu
Sungai Kolok
Rantau Panjang
Betong
Keroh
MALAYSIA
Sungai Petani

king, Ramkhamhaeng, is credited for developing a Thai writing system as well as building Angkor-inspired temples that defined early Thai art. The kingdom sprawled from Nakhon Si Thammarat in the south to the upper Mekong River and even into Myanmar (Burma), and is regarded as the cultural and artistic kernel of the modern state.

Sukhothai's intense flame was soon snuffed out by another emerging Thai power, Ayuthaya, established by Prince U Thong in 1350. This new centre developed into a cosmopolitan port on the Asian trade route, courted by various European nations attracted to the region by plenty of commodities and potential colonies. The small nation managed to thwart foreign takeovers, including one orchestrated by a Thai court official, a Greek man named Constantine Phaulkon, to advance French interests. For 400 years and 34 successive reigns, Ayuthaya dominated Thailand until the Burmese led a successful invasion in 1765, ousting the monarch and destroying the capital.

The Thais eventually rebuilt their capital in present-day Bangkok, established by the Chakri dynasty, which continues to occupy the throne today. As Western imperialism marched across the globe, King Mongkut (Rama IV, r 1851–68) and his son and successor, King Chulalongkorn (Rama V, r 1868–1910), successfully steered the country into the modern age without becoming a colonial vassal. Their progressive measures included adopting Western-style education systems, forging trade agreements and introducing Western-style dress. In return for the country's continued independence, King Chulalongkorn ceded huge tracts of Laos and Cambodia to French-controlled Indochina – an unprecedented territorial loss in Thai history.

A Struggling Democracy

In 1932 a peaceful coup converted the country into a constitutional monarchy, loosely based on the British model. What has followed has been a near-continuous cycle of power struggles among three factions – the elected government, military leaders and the monarchy backed by the aristocrats. These groups occasionally form tenuous allegiances based on mutual dislike for the opposition and the resulting power grab is often a peaceful military takeover sometimes dubbed 'smooth as silk' coups, a political paradigm that persists today.

During the mid-20th century, the military dominated the political sphere with an anticommunist tenure that is widely regarded as being ineffectual except in the suppression of democratic representation and civil rights. In 1973, student activists staged demonstrations calling for a real constitution and the release of political dissidents. A brief respite came, with reinstated voting rights and relaxed censorship. But in October 1976, a demonstration on the campus of Thammasat University in Bangkok was brutally quashed by the military, resulting in hundreds of casualties and the reinstatement of authoritarian rule. Many activists went underground to join armed communist insurgency groups hiding in the northeast.

In the 1980s, as the regional threat of communism subsided, the military-backed Prime Minister Prem Tinsulanonda stabilised the country and moved towards a representative democracy. But the military overthrew the democratically elected government in February 1991. This was Thailand's 19th coup attempt and the 10th successful one since 1932. In May 1992 huge demonstrations led by Bangkok's charismatic governor Chamlong Srimuang erupted throughout the city and the larger provincial capitals. The bloodiest confrontation occurred at Bangkok's Democracy Monument, resulting in nearly 50 deaths, but it eventually led to the reinstatement of a civilian government.

DID YOU KNOW?

- His Majesty Bhumibol Adulyadej, on the throne for more than 60 years, is the longest-reigning current monarch worldwide.
- It is illegal to step on money in Thailand, as the king's image is on all coins and notes.
- In ancient times, the traditional Thai tattoos were worn by soldiers and were mystical incantations that would protect the wearer from bodily injury.
- Thailand is 543 years ahead of the West, at least according to the Thai calendar that measures from the beginning of the Buddhist Era (in 543 BC).

Still a Struggling Democracy

Through the turn of this century, Thailand's era of coups seemed to have ended. Democratically elected governments oversaw the 1997 enactment of Thailand's 16th constitution, commonly called the 'people's constitution' because it was the first charter in the nation's history not written under military order. The country pulled through the 1997 Asian currency crisis and entered a more stable period of prosperity in the early 2000s. Telecommunications tycoon Thaksin Shinawatra and his populist Thai Rak Thai party were elected into power in 2001 and over the next five years effectively engineered one-party rule. As Thaksin consolidated power in all ranks of government and stifled press criticism and scrutiny of his administration, the urban elite and the urban middle class began to turn against him and staged large protests in Bangkok calling for his resignation in 2005 over corruption and conflict-of-interest charges. Meanwhile Thaksin's working-class and rural base rallied behind him, spotlighting longstanding class divides within Thai society.

Behind the scenes the military and the aristocrats forged an allegiance that resulted in the 2006 coup of the Thaksin government, forcing the charismatic prime minister into exile. At first the military takeover was heralded as a necessary step in ridding the country of an elected dictator. But three years and one election later the country is still in a political stalemate that has clearly outlined irreconcilable class divisions, injured the economy and portends continued political instability.

Further complicating matters is the ailing health of the revered King Bhumibol Adulyadej (Rama IX, r 1946–), who defined a new political role for the monarchy as a paternal figure who restrained excesses in the interests of all Thais and acted with wisdom in times of crisis. The most recent political crisis, however, has revealed the importance the king plays in securing power for the aristocrats, an arrangement that was threatened by the mounting strength of the now-deposed Thaksin government and the perceived weakness of the heir apparent who does not enjoy as much popular support as his father. What happens next is uncertain, but it is possible that as long as the aristocrats have handpicked the government, Thailand will move smoothly through the impending transfer of the crown.

THE CULTURE

Thais are master chatters and for a Westerner they have a shopping list of questions: Where are you from? How old are you? Are you married? Do you have children? Occasionally they get more curious and want to know how much you weigh or how much money you make; these questions to a Thai are matters of public record and aren't considered impolite. They also love to dole out compliments. Foreigners who can speak even the most basic Thai are lauded for being linguistic geniuses. And the most reluctant smile garners heaps of flattery about your ravishing looks. Why do some foreigners come to Thailand and never leave? Because Thais know how to make visitors feel like superstars.

The National Psyche

Thais are laid-back, good-natured people whose legendary hospitality has earned their country a permanent place on the global travel map. Paramount to the Thai philosophy of life is *sànùk* (fun) – each day is celebrated with

TRAVEL HINT: NO REFUNDS

Refunds and returns are not common commercial practices in Thailand and are often sources of unpleasant culture clashes. While a business owner in the West might appease a dissatisfied customer with some type of gift like a partial refund, Thais do not operate under the same principle and presume that foreigners are trying to cheat them when demands for a refund are made. In the Thai view, the customer has already used the service and now wants it retroactively rendered for free. This means that you aren't entitled to your money back if a huge cockroach scurries across your guest-room floor or if you get sick on your hill-tribe trek. Returning merchandise to stores is also met with resistance and confusion. To avoid hassles, carefully scrutinise any potential purchase since refunds and returns are cultural peculiarities to the West, not universal consumer rights.

food and conversation, foreign festivals are readily adopted as an excuse for a party and every task is measured on the *sànùk* meter.

The social dynamics of Thai culture can be perplexing. Whole books are dedicated to the subject and expats spend hours in speculation. The ideals of the culture are based on Buddhist principles, called 'blessings', and include humility, gratitude and filial piety. These golden rules are translated into such social conventions as saving face *(nâa)* – a unifying element in many Asian cultures in which confrontation is avoided and people endeavour not to embarrass themselves or other people.

An important component of saving face is knowing one's place in society: all relationships in Thai society are governed by conventions of social rank defined by age, wealth, status and personal and political power. For example, the elder of the table always picks up the tab, while the junior employee does the elder's menial chores and is not encouraged to participate in meetings or decision making.

The first entry point into the culture's hierarchical ladder is the family, a fundamental building block. Take all the pressures your parents put on you about a career, education, a future spouse and multiply that by 10 – now you are approaching the environment of your Thai peer. Young Thais from poor families are expected to support the family financially. Many do so with side jobs; they sell sweets from their front porch, run small internet cafes or sell orange juice to tourists. For a culture that values having a good time, they work unimaginably long hours.

BEING WISE ABOUT THE WÂI

Traditionally, Thais greet each other not with a handshake but with a *wâi,* a prayerlike palms-together gesture that Hollywood actors have recently and inexplicably adopted. It is an elegant gesture but a tad confusing for foreigners to figure out when and how high to *wâi*. In general, if someone *wâi*s you, you should *wâi* back (unless *wâi*-ed by a child or a service person). The placement of the fingertips in relation to the facial features varies with the recipient's social rank and age. The safest, least offensive spot is to place the tips of your fingers to nose level and slightly bow your head.

Religion and the monarchy, which is still regarded by many as divine, are the culture's sacred cows. You can turn your nose up at fish sauce or dress like a retro hippy, but don't insult the king and always behave respectfully in the temples. One of Thailand's leading intellectuals, Sulak Sivarak, was once arrested for describing the king as 'the skipper' – a passing reference to his fondness for sailing. Pictures of the king, including Thai currency and stamps, are treated with deference as well.

Lifestyle

Thailand has a split personality – the highly Westernised urban Thais in major cities and the rural farming communities more in tune with the ancient rhythms of life. But regardless of this divide, several persisting customs offer a rough snapshot of daily life. Thais wake up early, thanks in part to the roosters that start crowing sometime after sunset. The first events of the day are to make rice and to sweep the floor – very distinct smells and sounds that will linger with your travelling memories. In the grey stillness of early morning, barefoot monks carrying large round bowls travel through the town to collect their daily meals from the faithful. Several hours later, business is in full swing: the vendors have arrived at their favourite corner to sell everything imaginable, and some things that are not, and the civil servants and students clad in their respective uniforms swoop in and out of the stalls like birds of prey.

A neat and clean appearance complements Thais' persistent regard for beauty. Despite the hot and humid weather, Thais rarely seem to sweat and never stink. Soap-shy backpackers take note: if you don't honour the weather with regular bathing you will be the sole source of stench on the bus. Thais bathe three or four times a day, more as a natural air-conditioner than as compulsive cleaning. They also use talcum powder throughout the day to absorb sweat and, as one Thai explained, 'for freshy'.

Superficially, eating makes up the rest of the day. Notice the shop girls, ticket vendors or even the office workers: they can be found in a tight circle swapping gossip and snacking (or *gin lên,* literally 'eat for fun'). Then there is dinner and after-dinner and the whole seemingly chaotic, yet highly ordered, affair starts over again.

DON'T GET TIED-UP BY THAI ETIQUETTE

Steer clear of the typical etiquette foibles that earn foreigners visiting Thailand an unfavourable reputation. Master this simple list of dos and don'ts (mainly don'ts) and you'll be a celebrated companion.

- The king's anthem is played before every movie in a theatre and the national anthem is played twice a day (in the morning and evening) in public places like bus and train stations. You are expected to stand respectfully during both.
- Thailand is a nonconfrontational culture. Don't get angry, yell or get physically violent; keep your cool and things will usually work out in your favour.
- Feet are the lowest and 'dirtiest' part of the body. Keep your feet on the floor, not on a chair; never touch anyone or point with your foot; never step over someone (or something) sitting on the ground; and take your shoes off when you enter a home or temple.
- Dress modestly and don't sunbathe topless.
- Woman aren't allowed to touch or sit next to a monk or his belongings. The very back seat of the bus and the last row on public boats are reserved for monks.

Population

About 75% of citizens are ethnic Thais, further divided by geography (north, central, south and northeast). Each group speaks its own Thai dialect and to a certain extent practises customs unique to its region or influenced by neighbouring countries. Politically and economically the central Thais are the dominant group. People of Chinese ancestry make up roughly 14% of the population, many of whom have been in Thailand for generations. Ethnic Chinese probably enjoy better relations with the majority population here than in any other country in Southeast Asia. Other large minority groups include the Malays in the far south, the Khmers in the northeast and the Lao, spread throughout the north and east. Smaller non–Thai-speaking groups include the hill tribes living in the northern mountains.

SPORT

Thailand is obsessed with football, like the rest of the world, but there are some home-grown sports worth watching.

Muay Thai (Thai Boxing)

Enjoying a global appreciation, *muay thai* is a martial sport akin to boxing but all surfaces of the body are fair targets and everything but the head can deliver a blow. Many foreigners come to Thailand to study the sport or to watch the skilled boxers in their home setting where matches are accompanied by wild musical orchestration and frenzied betting. You'll know when a match is on because all the taxi and motorcycle drivers will be huddled around a communal TV, cheering in unison.

Bouts are limited to five three-minute rounds separated by two-minute breaks. Contestants wear international-style gloves and trunks (always either red or blue) and their feet are taped. Unlike boxing, punching in a *muay thai* match is considered the weakest of all blows and kicking merely a way to 'soften up' one's opponent; knee and elbow strikes are decisive in most matches. Other common blows include elbow thrusts to the face and head, knee hooks to the ribs and low crescent kicks to the calf. A contestant may even grasp an opponent's head between his hands and pull it down to meet an upward knee thrust.

The most famous matches are at the major stadiums in Bangkok (see p727). There are also 'tourist' matches held at stadiums throughout the country.

Tàkrâw

Sometimes called Siamese football, *tàkrâw* is best described as volleyball for the feet. This sport does not enjoy much commercial success but it is a popular pastime often played in school yards or as informal pick-up games in empty lots. In its most formal variation, players assemble on either side of a net and volley a *lûuk tàkrâw* (rattan ball) using their feet or head to touch the ball. Like gymnasts, the players perform aerial pirouettes to spike the ball. Another variation has players kicking the ball into a hoop 4.5m above the ground – basketball with feet, but without a backboard! But the most common variation is for players to stand in a circle and simply try to keep the ball airborne by kicking it, like hacky sack. Points are scored for style, difficulty and variety of kicking manoeuvres.

RELIGION

Alongside the Thai national flag flies the yellow flag of Buddhism – Theravada Buddhism (as opposed to the Mahayana schools found in East Asia and the Himalayas). Country, family and daily life are all married to religion. Every Thai male is expected to become a monk for a short period in his life, since a family earns great merit when a son 'takes robe and bowl'. Traditionally, the length of time spent in a wat is three months, during the Buddhist lent *(phansăa),* which begins around July and coincides with the wet season.

More evident than the philosophical aspects of Buddhism is the everyday fusion with animist rituals. Monks are consulted to determine an auspicious date for a wedding or the likelihood of success for a business. Spirit houses *(phrá phuum)* are constructed outside buildings and homes to encourage the spirits to live independently from the family but to remain comfortable so as to bring good fortune to the site. The spirit houses are typically ornate watlike structures set on a pedestal in a prominent section of the yard. Food, drink and furniture are all offered to the spirits to smooth daily life. Even in commerce-crazy Bangkok, ornate spirit houses eat up valuable real estate and become revered shrines to local people.

Roughly 95% of the population practises Buddhism, but in southern Thailand there is a significant Muslim minority community.

ARTS

Music

TRADITIONAL

Classical Thai music was developed for the royal court as an accompaniment to classical dance-drama and shadow theatre. Many of the traditional orchestras' most common instruments have more pedestrian applications and can often be heard at temple fairs or provincial festivals. Whether used in the high or low arts, traditional Thai music has an incredible array of textures and subtleties, hair-raising tempos and pastoral melodies. Among the more common instruments is the *pìi,* a woodwind instrument with a reed mouthpiece; it is heard prominently at Thai boxing matches. A bowed instrument, similar to examples played in China and Japan, is aptly called the *saw.* The *ránâat èhk* is a bamboo-keyed percussion instrument resembling the Western xylophone, while the *khlùi* is a wooden flute.

In the north and northeast there are several popular wind instruments with multiple reed pipes, which function basically like a mouth organ. Chief among these is the *khaen,* which originated in Laos; when played by an adept musician it sounds like a rhythmic, churning calliope organ. It is used chiefly in *măw lam* music, a rural folk musical tradition often likened to the American blues. A near cousin to *măw lam* is *lûuk thûng* (literally, 'children of the fields'), which enjoys a working-class fan base much like country music does in the US.

MODERN

Popular Thai music has borrowed rock-and-roll's instruments to create a distinct flavour that ranges from perky teeny-bop hits to hippy protest ballads and even urban indie anthems. It is an easy courtship with Thai classic rock, like the decades-old group Carabao and the folk style known as *phleng phêua chiiwít* (songs for life), which features political and environmental topics. More recently, indie groups like Modern Dog have defined Thailand's new millennial sound.

Sculpture & Architecture

On an international scale, Thailand has probably distinguished itself more in traditional religious sculpture than in any other art form. Thailand's most famous sculptural output has been its bronze Buddha images, coveted the world over for their originality and grace.

Architecture, however, is considered the highest art form in traditional Thai society. Ancient Thai homes consist of a single-room teak structure raised on stilts, since most Thais once lived along river banks or canals. The space underneath also served as the living room, kitchen, garage and barn. Rooflines in Thailand are steeply pitched and often decorated at the corners or along the gables with motifs related to the *naga* (mythical sea serpent), long believed to be a spiritual protector.

> **BUDDHA IMAGES**
>
> Elongated earlobes, no evidence of bone or muscle, arms that reach to the knees, a third eye: these are some of the 32 rules, originating from 3rd-century India, that govern the depiction of Buddha in sculpture. With such rules in place, why are some Buddhas sitting and others walking? Known as 'postures', the pose of the image depicts periods in the life of Buddha:
>
> - **reclining** – exact moment of Buddha's enlightenment and death
> - **sitting** – Buddha teaching or meditating; if the right hand is pointed towards the earth, Buddha is shown subduing the demons of desire; if the hands are folded in the lap, Buddha is turning the wheel of law
> - **standing** – Buddha bestowing blessings or taming evil forces
> - **walking** – Buddha after his return to earth from heaven

Theatre & Dance

Traditional Thai theatre consists of six dramatic forms, including *khŏhn*, a formal masked dance-drama depicting scenes from the Ramakian (the Thai version of India's Ramayana) that were originally performed only for the royal court. Popular in rural villages, *lí-keh* is a partly improvised, often bawdy folk play featuring dancing, comedy, melodrama and music. The southern Thai equivalent is *mánohraa*, which is based on a 2000-year-old Indian story. Nearly a dying art is *năng*, or shadow puppet plays, which once proliferated in southern Thailand. Other types of puppet theatre include *hùn lŭang* or *lákhon lék*, which describes the different types of puppets used to enact such stories as the Ramakian.

ENVIRONMENT

Thailand's shape on the map has been likened to the head of an elephant, with its trunk extending down the Malay peninsula. The country covers 517,000 sq km, which is slightly smaller than the US state of Texas. The centre of the country, Bangkok, sits at about 14° north latitude – level with Madras, Manila, Guatemala and Khartoum. Because the north–south reach spans roughly 16 latitudinal degrees, Thailand has perhaps the most diverse climate in Southeast Asia.

The Land

The country stretches from dense mountain jungles in the north to the flat central plains to the southern tropical rainforests. Covering the majority of the country, monsoon forests are filled with a sparse canopy of deciduous trees that shed their leaves during the dry season to conserve water. The landscape becomes dusty and brown until the rains (from July to November) transform everything into a fecund green. Typically, monsoon rains are brief afternoon thunderstorms that wet the parched earth and add more steam to a humid day. As the rains cease, Thailand enters its 'winter', a period of cooler temperatures, virtually unnoticeable to a recent arrival except in the north where night-time temperatures can drop to 13°C. By March, the hot season begins and the mercury climbs to 40°C or more at its highest, plus humidity.

In the south, the wet season lasts until January, with months of unrelenting showers and floods. Thanks to the rains, the south supports the dense rainforests more indicative of a 'tropical' region. Along the coastline, mangrove forests anchor themselves wherever water dominates.

Thailand's national flower, the orchid, is one of the world's most beloved parasites, producing such exotic flowers that even its host is charmed.

Wildlife

Thailand is particularly rich in bird life: more than 1000 resident and migrating species have been recorded and approximately 10% of all world bird species dwell here. Thailand's most revered indigenous mammal, the elephant, once ran wild in the country's dense virgin forests. Since ancient times, annual parties led by the king would round up young elephants from the wild to train them as workers and fighters. Integral to Thai culture, the elephant symbolises wisdom, strength and good fortune. White elephants are even more auspicious and by tradition are donated to the king. Sadly, elephants are now endangered, having lost their traditional role in society and much of their habitat.

National Parks

Thailand designated its first national park (Khao Yai) in the 1960s and has added over 100 parks, including marine environments, to the list since. Together these cover 15% of the country's land and sea area, one of the highest ratios of protected to unprotected areas of any nation in the world.

Though the conservation efforts are laudable, Thailand's national parks are poorly funded and poorly protected from commercial development, illegal hunting and logging, or swidden agriculture. Visitors to such tourist destinations as Ko Phi Phi, Ko Samet and Ko Chang will be surprised to learn that such intensive development has occurred on protected land.

Environmental Issues

Like all countries with a high population density, there is enormous pressure on Thailand's ecosystems: in the middle of last century about 70% of the countryside was forest; by 2000 an estimated 20% of the natural forest cover remained. In response to environmental degradation, the Thai government created protected natural areas and outlawed logging. The stated goal is to raise forest cover to 40% by the middle of this century, and forest loss has slowed since the turn of the millennium to about 0.2% per year according to statistics published by the World Bank in 2008.

Air and water pollution are problems in urban areas. The passing of the 1992 Environmental Act was an encouraging move by the government, but standards still lag centuries behind Western nations.

Thailand is a signatory to the UN Convention on International Trade in Endangered Species (CITES). Forty of Thailand's 300 mammal species are on the International Union for Conservation of Nature (IUCN) list of endangered species. As elsewhere in the region, the tiger is one of the most endangered of large mammals. Tiger hunting or trapping is illegal, but poachers continue to kill the cats for the lucrative overseas Chinese pharmaceutical market. Around 200 wild tigers are thought to be hanging on in the national parks of Khao Yai, Kaeng Krachan, Thap Lan, Mae Wong and Khao Sok.

Corruption continues to impede the government's attempts to shelter species coveted by the illicit global wildlife trade. The Royal Forest Department is currently under pressure to take immediate action in those areas where preservation laws have not been enforced, including coastal zones where illegal tourist accommodation has flourished.

TRANSPORT

GETTING THERE & AWAY

Air

Thailand has one primary international airport in Bangkok, while Chiang Mai, Phuket and Ko Samui receive some international flights from East Asia.

The following airlines operate out of Thailand:

Air Asia (code AK; ☎ 0 2515 9999; www.airasia.com)
Bangkok Airways (code PG; ☎ 0 2265 6699; www.bangkokair.com)
China Airlines (code CI; ☎ 0 2250 9898; www.china-airlines.com)
Cathay Pacific Airways (code CX; ☎ 0 2263 0606; www.cathaypacific.com)
Garuda Indonesia (code GA; ☎ 0 2679 7699; www.garuda-indonesia.com)
Lao Airlines (code QV; ☎ 0 2236 9822; www.laoairlines.com)
Malaysia Airlines (code MH; ☎ 0 2263 0565; www.malaysiaairlines.com)
Myanmar Airways International (code 8M; ☎ 0 2261 5060; www.maiair.com)
Orient Thai (code OX; ☎ 0 2269 4260; www.orient-thai.com)
Singapore Airlines (code SQ; ☎ 0 2353 6000; www.singaporeair.com)
Thai Airways International (THAI; code TG; ☎ 0 2356 1111; www.thaiair.com)
Vietnam Airlines (code VN; ☎ 0 2655 4137; www.vietnamairlines.com)

Land

Thailand enjoys open and safe border relations with Cambodia, Laos and Malaysia. Myanmar's internal conflicts require a restricted border that is subject to frequent closings and shifting regulations.

DEPARTURE TAX

Thailand's departure tax has been folded into the ticket price and is no longer a separate fee paid upon leaving the country. There is, however, an international departure fee still in effect at Ko Samui's airport.

CAMBODIA

Most visitors cross at Poipet (Cambodia) to Aranya Prathet (Thailand; p731). This is the most direct land route between Bangkok and Angkor Wat. If you're travelling along the southeastern coast of Thailand, you can cross into Cambodia from Hat Lek to Koh Kong (p785), which has boat access to Sihanoukville.

Several more remote crossings exist between southeastern Thailand and southwestern Cambodia, including: O Smach–Chong Chom, Chong Sa Ngam–Choam; and Dan Lem–Psar Pruhm. Private or hired transport is required to access most of these crossings; Dan Lem (p785) is an exception as minibuses connect this border crossing to Chanthaburi, making it an underutilised crossing point to Battambang.

LAOS

Nong Khai to Vientiane (p781) is one of the most popular land border crossings between Thailand and Laos, followed closely by Chiang Khong–Huay Xai (p772). Other crossings include Chong Mek–Vang Tao (p777), Mukdahan–Savannakhet (p778) and Nakhon Phanom–Tha Khaek (p779).

MALAYSIA

The train heading into Malaysia from Bangkok splits at Hat Yai with one spur heading west through Padang Besar (p804) to Butterworth, the transfer point to Penang or other destinations along the west coast of Malaysia. Another spur heads east to the border town of Sungai Kolok (p805), which was once a popular migration route through Malaysia's Kota Bharu and on to the Perhentian Islands. Due to the unrest in the far southern provinces of Thailand, it is not advisable to take the train east to Sungai Kolok; stick to the western side of the peninsula instead.

Buses and minibuses also cross the border into the Malaysian towns of Padang Besar and Dan Nawk (south of Thailand's Sadao). By boat you can cross to several points along the Malaysian west coast, including Pulau Langkawi, from the mainland town of Satun or from Ko Lipe. See p804 for more details.

MYANMAR

Most of the land crossings into Myanmar have peculiar restrictions that don't allow full access to the country. These border points are also subject to unannounced closures, lasting anywhere from a day to years. Most foreigners use these border crossings as exit points to renew a Thai visa rather than transit routes.

The most reliable crossing with the greatest access is at Mae Sai (p767) into Tachileik. A day-trip visa into Myanmar is available from Mae Sot (p752) into Myawaddy. The Three Pagodas Pass (p737) used to be another day-trip crossing but it has been closed to foreigners since 2006. In southern Thailand, you can legally enter Myanmar by boat from Ranong (p807) to the island of Kawthoung, but you can't travel onward from here into mainland Myanmar.

GETTING AROUND

Air

Thailand's major domestic carrier is Thai Airways International (THAI), with Bangkok Airways running a close second. But there are several budget airlines serving popular routes that make air travel a price-competitive option over long-distance buses. The most useful routes for shoestringers are Bangkok to Chiang Mai, Ko Samui or Phuket. Book your tickets several days in advance for all domestic air travel. When researching domestic flights, compare fares on www.domesticflightsthailand.com.

Leading airlines for domestic routes:

Air Asia (code AK; ☎ 0 2515 9999; www.airasia.com)
Bangkok Airways (code PG; ☎ 0 2270 6699; www.bangkokair.com)
Nok Air (code DD; ☎ 1318; www.nokair.com)
One-Two-Go (code OX; ☎ 1126; www.fly12go.com)
Thai Airways International (THAI; code TG; ☎ 0 2356 1111; www.thaiair.com)

Bicycle

Bicycles are available for visitors to rent in most towns with a backpacker scene: guest houses often have a few for rent for about 50B per day. Just about anywhere outside Bangkok, bikes are the ideal form of local transport because they're cheap, nonpolluting and keep you moving slowly enough to see everything. Carefully note the condition of the bike before hiring; if it breaks down, you are responsible and parts can be expensive.

See p821 for information on bicycle touring in Thailand.

Boat

Being a riverine people, Thais have colourful boats of traditional design. With a long graceful breast that barely skims the water and an elongated propeller, longtail boats are used as island-hoppers, canal coasters and river ferries. Small wooden fishing boats, brilliantly painted, sometimes shuttle tourists out to nearby islands. Longer trips to the islands of Ko Pha-Ngan and Ko Tao are undertaken by slow yet determined cargo boats through the dark of night. Boat schedules are subject to change depending on weather conditions and demand.

Bus

The Thai bus service is widespread, convenient and phenomenally fast – nail-bitingly so. While private companies working in Bangkok's Th Khao San usually bag unsuspecting travellers, you're better off with companies operating out of the government bus station. These buses cater to the Thai community, making them more culturally engaging and safer for your belongings. Starting at the top, VIP buses are the closest you will come to a rock star's tour bus. The seats recline, the air-con is frosty and an 'air hostess' dispenses refreshments and snacks. Various diminishing classes of air-con buses begin to strip away the extras until you're left with a fairly beat-up bus with an asthmatic cooling system.

Incredibly punishing but undeniably entertaining are the 'ordinary' buses. These rattletraps have fans that don't work when the bus has come to a stop, school-bus sized seats and a tinny sound system that blares the driver's favourite music. The trip is sweaty, loud and usually involves as many animals and babies as adult passengers. At stops along the way, vendors walk the aisles selling food, everyone throws their rubbish out the window and the driver honks at every passer-by hoping to pick up another fare. In the past five years, the ordinary buses have been phased out of most long-distance routes and now mainly serve local or intraprovincial destinations.

For long-distance trips, check out schedules and/or purchase tickets the day before.

Car & Motorcycle

Cars, 4WDs or vans can be rented in Bangkok and large provincial capitals. Check with travel agencies or hotels for rental locations. Always verify that the vehicle is insured for liability before signing a rental contract, and ask to see the dated insurance documents. If you have an accident while driving an uninsured vehicle, you're in for some major hassles.

Motorcycle travel is a popular way to get around Thailand. Dozens of places along the guest-house circuit rent motorbikes for 150B to 300B a day. It is also possible to buy a new or used motorbike and sell it before you leave the country – a good used 125cc bike costs around 40,000B. If you've never ridden a motorcycle before, stick to the smaller 100cc step-through bikes with automatic clutches. Motorcycle rental usually requires that you leave your passport. Be sure to wear a helmet, especially on the islands where this law is enforced with zeal on perceived wealthy tourists.

Thais drive on the left-hand side of the road – most of the time. Like many places in Asia, every two-lane road has an invisible third lane in the middle that all drivers feel free to use at any time. Passing on hills and curves is common – as long as you've got the proper Buddhist altar on the dashboard, what could happen? The main rule to be aware of is that 'might makes right' and smaller vehicles always yield to bigger ones. Drivers usually use their horns to indicate that they are passing.

YOUR FUTURE'S SO BRIGHT

If you get on board a bus and everyone has clustered to one side, don't celebrate that you've scored a whole row to yourself. Thais usually figure out which side of the bus the sun will glare down on and sit on the opposite side to avoid getting cooked through the journey. It usually isn't until there are no seats left on the 'dark' side that an unsuspecting traveller realises the mistake.

Hitching

It is uncommon to see people hitching alongside the highway, since bus travel between towns is fairly inexpensive and reliable. Hitching becomes a better option in the country where public transport isn't available. If you get dropped off by a bus outside a national park or historical site, you can catch a ride along the remainder of the road with an incoming vehicle. Just remember to use the Asian style of beckoning: hold your arm out towards the road, palm-side down and wave towards the ground.

That said, hitching is never entirely safe, and travellers who do so should understand that they are taking a small but potentially serious risk.

Local Transport

Though car ownership has increased in the last decade, many Thais still rely on public or chartered transportation.

SĂAMLÁW & TÚK-TÚK

Săamláw (also written 'samlor'), meaning 'three wheels', are pedal rickshaws, and they are a dying breed of transport found mainly in small towns. These are good for relatively short distances, but expect to pay a little more if you take one further afield, as they are all human powered. Their modern replacements are the motorised túk-túk, named for the throaty cough of their two-stroke engines. In Bangkok especially, túk-túk drivers give all local transport a bad name. The worst are unscrupulously greedy – inflating the fares or diverting passengers to places that pay commissions. In other towns they tend to be more reliable.

You must bargain and agree on a fare before accepting a ride, but in many towns there is a more-or-less fixed fare anywhere in town.

SĂWNGTHĂEW

Săwngthăew (literally, 'two benches') are small pick-ups with a row of seats down each side. In some towns, săwngthăew serve as public buses running regular routes for fixed fares. But in tourist towns, you'll also find săwngthăew performing the same function as túk-túk, transporting people to and from the bus station or to popular attractions for a bargained fare.

> **GOING BONKERS**
>
> Sometimes you don't know where you're going and you don't care. But a leisurely stroll is not an acceptable deterrent to aggressive drivers hoping to turn you into a fare. Especially in touristed areas, túk-túk drivers have concocted one of the most irritating phrases in the English language: 'Hey you, where you go?', which is a literal translation from the typical Thai beseechment for customers. The question is not intended to drive you bonkers but is asked only because they'd like to make a living. Likewise you can reply like a Thai, which is to give no response whatsoever.

Train

All rail travel originates in Bangkok and radiates out, forming the following four spurs: Ayuthaya–Phitsanulok–Chiang Mai; Nakhon Ratchasima (Khorat)–Surin–Ubon Ratchathani; Nakhon Ratchasima–Khon Kaen–Nong Khai; and Hua Hin–Surat Thani–Hat Yai. The **government-operated trains** (www.railway.co.th) in Thailand are comfortable and moderately priced, but rather slow. On comparable routes, buses can often be twice as fast, but the relatively low speed of the train means you can often leave at a convenient hour in the evening and arrive at your destination at a pleasant hour in the morning. Very useful condensed railway timetables are available in English at the Hualamphong train station in Bangkok. These contain schedules and fares for all rapid and express trains, as well as a few ordinary trains.

First-, 2nd- and 3rd-class cabins are available on most trains, but each class may vary considerably depending on the type of train (rapid, express or ordinary). First class is typically a private cabin. Second class has individually reclining seats or padded bench seating; depending on the train some cabins have air-con. Non–air-conditioned, 3rd class is spartan and cheap with shared bench seating.

Ordinary trains only have the most basic version of 3rd class and stop at every itsy bitsy station. Express and rapid are, well, faster and make fewer stops, but there is a 150B surcharge for express trains and 110B for rapid trains. Some 2nd- and 3rd-class services have air-con, in which case there is a 60B to 110B surcharge. For the special-express trains that run between Bangkok and Padang Besar (Malaysia) and between Bangkok and Chiang Mai, there is a 100B to 170B surcharge.

Overnight trains have sleeping berths in 1st and 2nd class. The charge for 2nd-class sleeping berths is 120B for an upper berth and 170B for a lower berth. For 2nd-class sleepers with air-con add 250/320B for upper/lower berth. No sleepers are available in 3rd class.

All 1st-class cabins come with individually controlled air-con. For a two-bed cabin the surcharge is 500B per person.

Trains are often heavily booked, especially during holidays, so it's wise to reserve ahead of time, especially for long-distance trips. You can purchase advance tickets in person at all principal train stations up to 60 days prior to your travel date. Tickets are not available for purchase over the phone or online. If you are planning long-distance train travel from outside the country, you can email the **State Railway of Thailand** (passenger-ser@railway.co.th) at least two weeks before your journey. You will receive an email confirming the booking. Pick up and pay for tickets an hour before leaving at the scheduled departure train station. Bangkok's **Hualamphong station** (☎ 0 2220 4334) is the railway's primary station and offers advance booking services as well as timetables in English. For more information visit www.railw ay.co.th.

BANGKOK

pop 7.7 million

Bored in Bangkok? You've got to be kidding. This high-energy city loves neon and noise, chaos and concrete, fashion and the future. Although it's constantly on the move, everyone is stuck in a traffic jam somewhere within a mountain range of skyscrapers and soot-stained apartment towers. And past the ringing mobile phones and blaring pop music is an old-fashioned village napping in the shade of a narrow *soi* (lane). It's an urban connoisseur's dream come true with the past, present and future jammed into a humid pressure cooker. Because it's a revolving door for travel throughout the region, you'll be confused and challenged when you first arrive, relieved and pampered when you return, and slightly sentimental when you depart for the last time.

ORIENTATION

Bangkok can be roughly divided into two parts: the old and new city. The older parts of town stretch east from the banks of the Mae Nam Chao Phraya (Chao Phraya River) to the main railway line, which terminates at Hualamphong station. Sandwiched between is the main sightseeing district of Ko Ratanakosin, the backpacker ghetto in Banglamphu and bustling Chinatown. This section of town is less urban, relatively speaking, with temples claiming the highest strata of skyline.

East of the railway line is the new city, which is mind-blowingly modern. Skyscrapers, shopping centres, traffic jams, slick elevated trams and mammoth construction sites. The Siam Square area defines the shopping mall corridor. Th Sukhumvit is a busy international residential and commercial centre where the rich and famous (as well as the average and ho-hum) live in terraced condo towers. South of these districts is Th Silom, considered to be Bangkok's financial district. This new part of town is fused together mostly by the fast and efficient Skytrain and less so by the underground Metro.

On the west bank of the Mae Nam Chao Phraya is the suburb of Thonburi, where the Southern bus terminal and the Bangkok Noi commuter train station are located.

In short, you will need a good map and a lot of patience. If you plan to use Bangkok's economical bus system, purchase Roadway's *Bangkok Bus Map*. Check out *Nancy Chandler's Map of Bangkok*, a schematic map of attractions, popular restaurants and other tips compiled by mother-daughter mapping team Nancy and Nima Chandler. Another contender on the market, *Groovy Map's Bangkok by Day Map 'n' Guide*, features a selection of restaurant and bar reviews.

INFORMATION

Bookshops

The bookshops in Bangkok are among the best in Southeast Asia. Options include the following places:

Asia Books (www.asiabooks.com) Th Sukhumvit (Map pp716-17; Soi 15, 221 Th Sukhumvit); Siam Discovery Center (Map pp716-17; 4th fl, Th Phra Ram I) Books on anything and everything.

Dasa Book Café (Map pp712-13; ☎ 0 2661 2993; 710/4 Th Sukhumvit, btwn Soi 26 & 28; Skytrain Phrom Phong) Multilingual, used books.

Kinokuniya Siam Paragon (Map pp716-17; ☎ 0 2610 9500; www.kinokuniya.com; 3rd fl, Th Phra Ram I); Emporium (Map pp716-17; ☎ 0 2664 8554; 3rd fl, Th Sukhumvit) Another well-rounded contender.

Shaman Books (Map p720; ☎ 0 2629 0418; D&D Plaza, 71 Th Khao San, Banglamphu) Two locations in the backpacker ghetto boasting a huge selection of used books.

Emergency

If you have a medical emergency and need an ambulance, contact the hospitals with English-speaking staff (listed under Medical Services, opposite).

Fire (☎ 199)
Police/Emergency (☎ 191)
Tourist police (☎ 1155; 24hr) An English-speaking unit that investigates criminal activity involving tourists, including gem scams. It can also act as a bilingual liaison with the regular police.

Internet Access

Internet cafes are ubiquitous and most are equipped with Skype and headsets for inexpensive overseas calls. The cheapest access is found around Th Khao San, where it starts at around 20B an hour. Siam Square is the next best bet, while the Th Sukhumvit and Silom areas are more expensive.

Wi-fi is mostly free of charge and is becoming increasingly available at businesses and public hotspots.

Internet Resources

Absolutely Bangkok (www.absolutelybangkok.com) Peep over the whitewashed fence into a land of snarky opinions about Bangkok's current events.
Gnarly Kitty (www.gnarlykitty.org) Follow along with this Bangkok-ista as she shops and eats her way through life.
Khao San Road (www.khaosanroad.com) News, reviews and profiles of Bangkok's famous tourist ghetto.

Media

The two English-language dailies, the *Bangkok Post* and the *Nation*, are available at streetside newsagents near hotels or tourist areas. Monthly magazines are available in bookstores.
Bangkok 101 (www.bangkok101.com) A monthly city primer with photo essays and reviews of sights, restaurants and entertainment.
Bangkok Post (www.bangkokpost.net) The main English-language daily with Friday and weekend supplements covering city events.
BK Magazine (www.bkmagazine.com) Free weekly listings mag for the young and hip.
The Nation (www.nationmultimedia.com) English-language daily with a focus on business and culture.

THÀNŎN & SOI

Throughout this book, *Thànŏn* (meaning 'street') is abbreviated as 'Th'. A *soi* is a small street or lane that runs off a larger street. The address of a site located on a *soi* will be written as 48/3-5 Soi 1, Th Sukhumvit, meaning off Th Sukhumvit on Soi 1.

Medical Services

There are several outstanding hospitals in Bangkok with English-speaking staff.
Bangkok Christian Hospital (Map pp716-17; ☎ 0 2235 1000-07; 124 Th Silom)
BNH (Map pp716-17; ☎ 0 2686 2700; 9 Th Convent)
Bumrungrad Hospital (Map pp716-17; ☎ 0 2667 1000; 33 Soi 3, Th Sukhumvit)

Money

Thai banks have currency exchange kiosks that have extended hours (usually 8am to 8pm) in many parts of Bangkok, especially tourist areas. ATMs are also widely distributed throughout the city. Regular bank hours in Bangkok are 10am to 4pm. Go to 7-Eleven shops or other reputable places to break 1000B bills; don't expect a vendor or taxi to able to make change on a note 500B or larger.

Post

Main post office (Map pp716-17; Th Charoen Krung; 8am-8pm Mon-Fri, 8am-1pm Sat & Sun) Poste restante and a packing service for parcels. Branch post offices also offer poste restante and parcel services.

Telephone

CAT (Map pp716-17; ☎ 0 2573 0099; Th Charoen Krung; 24hr) Next to the main post office, with Home Country Direct, fax and phone-card services.
TOT (Map pp716-17; ☎ 0 2251 1111; Th Ploenchit) International faxes and calls.

Tourist Information

Bangkok Information Center (Map p720; ☎ 0 2225 7612-5; www.bangkoktourist.com; 17/1 Th Phra Athit; 9am-7pm)
Tourism Authority of Thailand (TAT; www.tourismthailand.org) Main office (Map pp716-17; ☎ 0 2250 5500; 4th fl, 1606 Th Phetburi Tat Mai; 8.30am-4.30pm); Banglamphu (Map pp716-17; ☎ 0 2283 1555; Th Ratchadamnoen Nok; 8.30am-4.30pm); Suvarnabhumi International Airport (☎ 0 2134 4077; 2nd fl, btwn Gate 2 & 5; 8am-4pm).

Travel Agencies

There is no shortage of travel agents in Bangkok, but not all of them are trustworthy. Commissions can sometimes be absurdly inflated so shop around and make bus ticket arrangements yourself at the bus station to avoid hassles. These are established agencies:
Diethelm Travel (Map pp716-17; ☎ 0 2660 7000; www.diethelmtravel.com; 12th fl, Kian Gwan Bldg II, 140/1 Th Withayu)

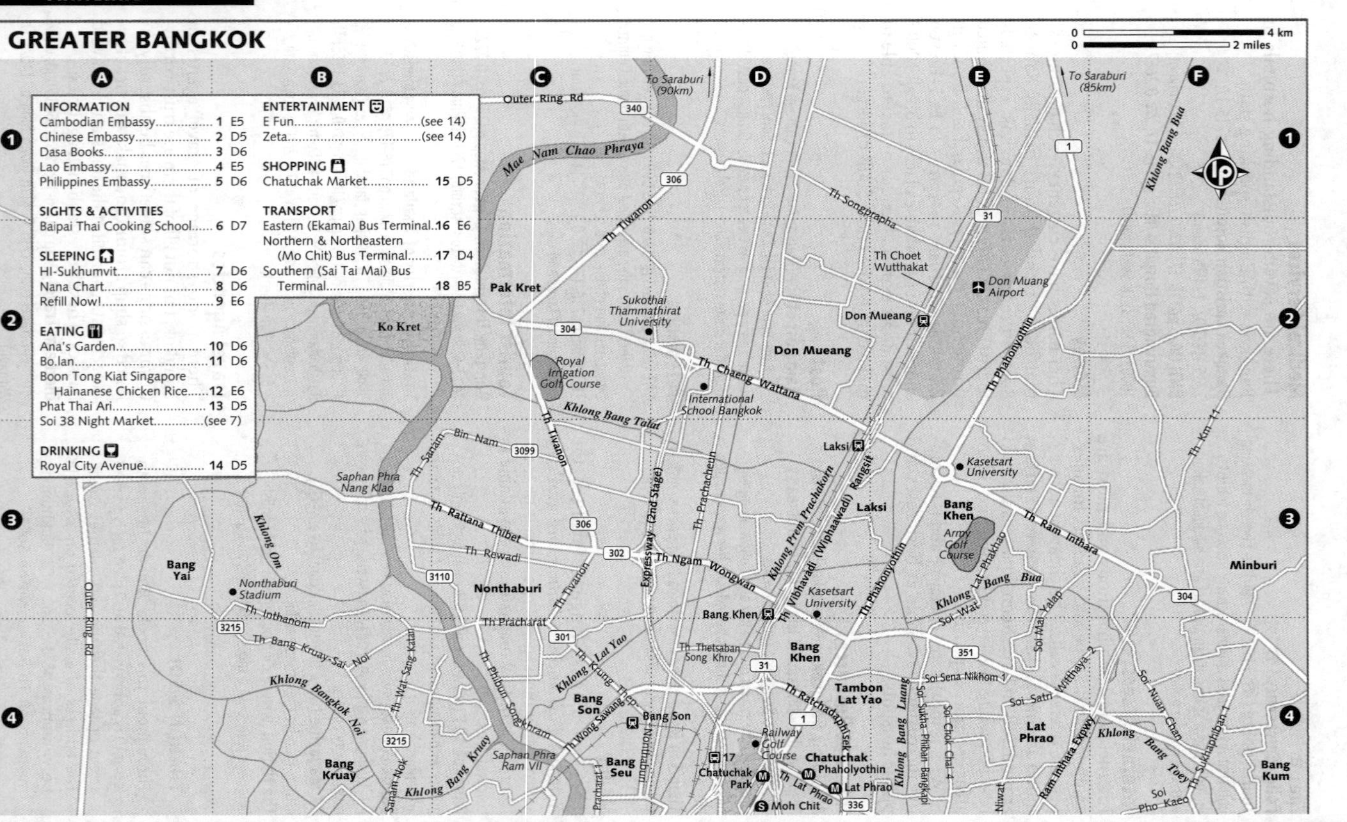
GREATER BANGKOK
INFORMATION
Cambodian Embassy 1 E5
Chinese Embassy 2 D5
Dasa Books 3 D6
Lao Embassy 4 E5
Philippines Embassy 5 D6
SIGHTS & ACTIVITIES
Baipai Thai Cooking School 6 D7
SLEEPING
HI-Sukhumvit 7 D6
Nana Chart 8 D6
Refill Now! 9 E6
EATING
Ana's Garden 10 D6
Bo.lan 11 D6
Boon Tong Kiat Singapore Hainanese Chicken Rice 12 E6
Phat Thai Ari 13 D5
Soi 38 Night Market (see 7)
DRINKING
Royal City Avenue 14 D5
ENTERTAINMENT
E Fun (see 14)
Zeta (see 14)
SHOPPING
Chatuchak Market 15 D5
TRANSPORT
Eastern (Ekamai) Bus Terminal 16 E6
Northern & Northeastern (Mo Chit) Bus Terminal 17 D4
Southern (Sai Tai Mai) Bus Terminal 18 B5
0 4 km
0 2 miles
To Saraburi (90km)
To Saraburi (85km)
Outer Ring Rd
Mae Nam Chao Phraya
Pak Kret
Ko Kret
Sukothai Thammathirat University
Royal Irrigation Golf Course
International School Bangkok
Don Mueang
Don Muang Airport
Th Choet Wutthakat
Th Songprapha
Th Tiwanon
Th Chaeng Wattana
Khlong Bang Talat
Th Phahonyothin
Khlong Bang Bua
Th Km 11
Laksi
Kasetsart University
Bang Khen
Army Golf Course
Th Ram Inthara
Minburi
Saphan Phra Nang Klao
Th Rattana Thibet
Th Rewadi
Nonthaburi
Bin Nam
Th Sanam
Khlong Om
Bang Yai
Nonthaburi Stadium
Th Inthanom
Th Bang Kruay-Sai Noi
Khlong Bangkok Noi
Bang Kruay
Th Wat Sang Katan
Sanam Nok
Khlong Bang Kruay
Th Phibun Songkhram
Saphan Phra Ram VII
Th Pracharat
Khlong Lat Yao
Th Krung Thep
Th Wong Sawang
Bang Son
Bang Seu
Nonthaburi
Pracharat 1
Expressway (2nd Stage)
Th Prachacheun
Th Ngam Wongwan
Khlong Prem Prachakorn
Th Vibhavadi (Wiphaawadi) Rangsit
Th Thetsaban Song Khro
Railway Golf Course
Chatuchak Park
Chatuchak
Phaholyothin
Lat Phrao
Moh Chit
Th Lat Phrao
Th Ratchadaphisek
Tambon Lat Yao
Khlong Bang Luang
Soi Sukha Phiban Bangkapi
Soi Chok Chai 4
Soi Sena Nikhom 1
Soi Satri
Lat Phrao
Niwat
Ram Inthara Expwy
Khlong Bang Toey
Soi Nuan Chan
Th Sukhaphiban 1
Soi Pho Kaeo
Bang Kum
Soi Wat
Khlong Lat Phakhao
Soi Mai Yalap
Witthaya 2

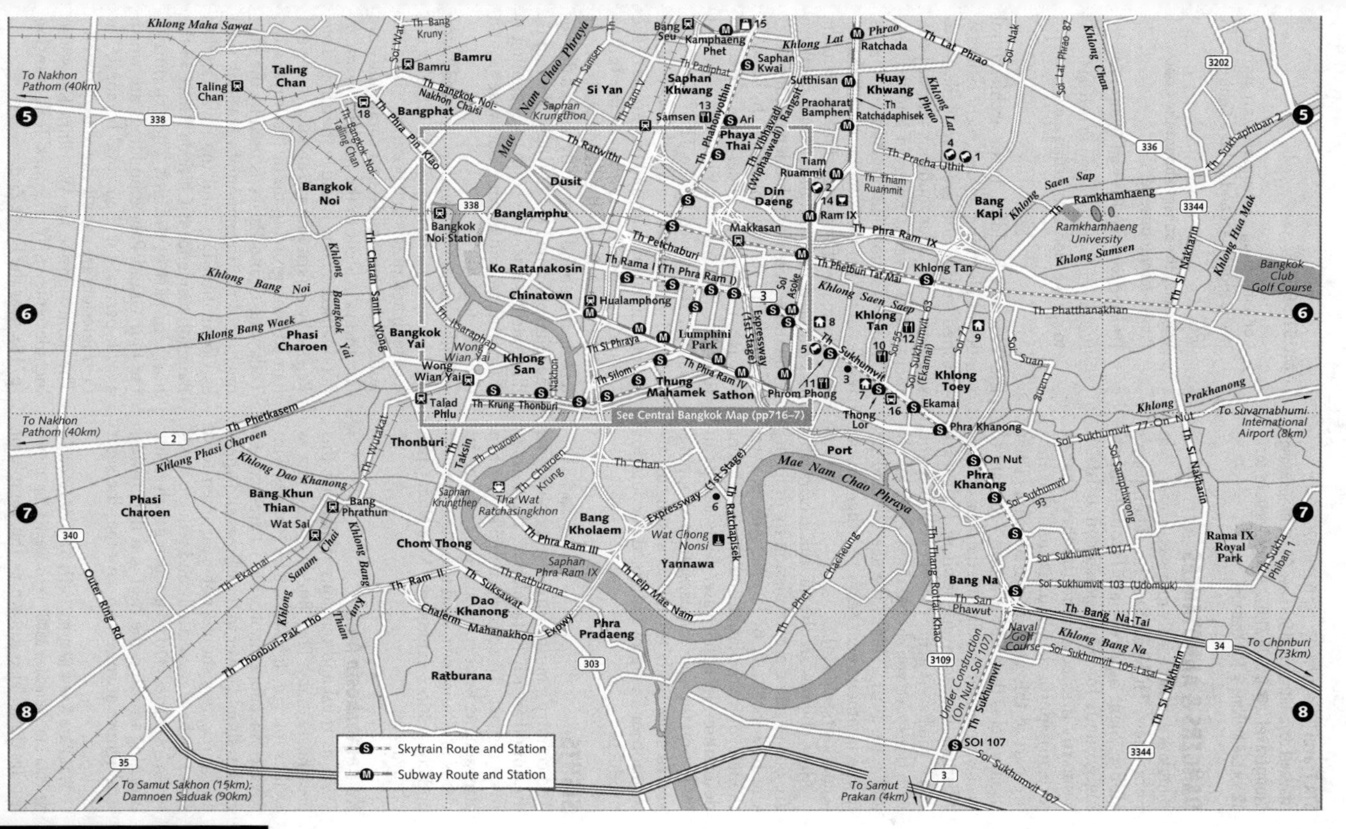
See Central Bangkok Map (pp716–7)
Skytrain Route and Station
Subway Route and Station
Bamru
Taling Chan
Bangphat
Bangkok Noi
Phasi Charoen
Bangkok Yai
Wong Wian Yai
Talad Phlu
Thonburi
Chom Thong
Dao Khanong
Ratburana
Bang Khun Thian
Wat Sai
Bang Phrathun
Khlong San
Chinatown
Hualamphong
Ko Ratanakosin
Banglamphu
Bangkok Noi Station
Dusit
Si Yan
Saphan Khwang
Samsen
Bang Seu
Kamphaeng Phet
Saphan Kwai
Ari
Phaya Thai
Din Daeng
Tiam Ruammit
Ram IX
Makkasan
Sutthisan
Praoharat Bamphen
Ratchada
Huay Khwang
Bang Kapi
Khlong Tan
Khlong Toey
Ekamai
Thong Lor
Phra Khanong
On Nut
Bang Na
SOI 107
Port
Yannawa
Wat Chong Nonsi
Bang Kholaem
Phra Pradaeng
Thung Mahamek
Sathon
Phrom Phong
Lumphini Park
Mae Nam Chao Phraya
Khlong Saen Saep
Khlong Bangkok Yai
Khlong Bang Noi
Khlong Bang Waek
Khlong Maha Sawat
Khlong Phasi Charoen
Khlong Dao Khanong
Khlong Bang Kun Thian
Khlong Sanam Chai
Khlong Lat Phrao
Khlong Chan
Khlong Samsen
Khlong Hua Mak
Khlong Prakhanong
Khlong Bang Na
Th Phra Pin Klao
Th Charan Sanit Wong
Th Phetkasem
Outer Ring Rd
Th Thonburi-Pak Tho
Th Sukhumvit
Th Si Nakharin
Th Phra Ram IX
Th Petchaburi
Th Rama I (Th Phra Ram I)
Th Phra Ram IV
Th Ratwithi
Th Lat Phrao
Th Ratchapisek
Th Thang Rotfai Khao
Th Bang Na-Tai
Expressway (1st Stage)
Under Construction (On Nut - Soi 107)
Rama IX Royal Park
Bangkok Club Golf Course
Naval Golf Course
Ramkhamhaeng University
To Nakhon Pathom (40km)
To Suvarnabhumi International Airport (8km)
To Chonburi (73km)
To Samut Prakan (4km)
To Samut Sakhon (15km); Damnoen Saduak (90km)

THAILAND

STA Travel (Map pp716-17; ☎ 0 2236 0262; www.statravel.com; 14th fl, Wall St Tower, 33/70 Th Surawong)
Viengtravel (☎ 0 2326 7191/2; www.viengtravel.com; 12 Soi Lad Krabang 9, Lad Krabang).

DANGERS & ANNOYANCES

Bangkok's most heavily touristed areas – Wat Phra Kaew, Th Khao San, Jim Thompson's House, Siam Square – are favourite hunting grounds for professional con artists. If a smartly dressed person (be they Thai or foreign) approaches you, assume that they are part of this well-rehearsed scam. Their usual spiel is that the attraction you want to visit is closed for the day and they can arrange a bargain tour for you elsewhere. If they ask you if you have a map or say they can help you with transport, you should thank them kindly and walk away. This is the age-old lead-up to the infamous gem scam or other rip-off scenarios (see p824).

More obvious are the túk-túk drivers who are out to make a commission by dragging you to a local silk or jewellery shop, even though you've requested an entirely different destination. In either case, if you accept an invitation for 'free' sightseeing or shopping, you're quite likely to end up wasting an afternoon or being overcharged for inferior products.

SIGHTS

The country's most historic and holy sights are found in Ko Ratanakosin, the former royal district. To soak up Bangkok's urban atmosphere, wander around the commercial chaos of Chinatown. And to escape the heat and congestion, explore the Mae Nam Chao Phraya.

Ko Ratanakosin Area

With its royal and religious affiliations, this area hosts many Thai Buddhist pilgrims as well as foreign sightseers. The temples with royal connections enforce a strict dress code – clothes should cover to the elbows and knees and foreigners should not wear open-toed shoes. Behave respectfully and remove shoes when instructed. Do your touring early in the morning to avoid the heat and the crowds. And ignore anyone who says that the sight is closed.

Wat Phra Kaew (Map pp716-17; ☎ 0 2623 5500; Th Na Phra Lan; admission 350B; 8.30am-3.30pm; river ferry Tha Chang), also known as the Temple of the Emerald Buddha, is an architectural wonder of gleaming, gilded *chedi* (stupas), polished orange and green roof tiles, mosaic-encrusted pillars and rich marble pediments. The revered Emerald Buddha, one of Thailand's most famous Buddha images, resides in the temple complex's main chapel. Actually made of jasper, the Emerald Buddha has endured an epic journey from northern Thailand, where it was hidden inside a layer of stucco, to its present home. In between it was seized by Lao forces and carried off to Luang Prabang and Vientiane, where it was later recaptured by the Thais. Recently restored murals line the interior walls of the *bòht* (ordination hall), and the murals of the Ramakian (the Thai version of the Indian epic Ramayana) line the inside walls of the temple compound. Originally painted during the reign of Rama I (1782–1809), the murals illustrate the epic in its entirety, beginning at the north gate and moving clockwise around the compound.

Within the same grounds is the **Grand Palace**, the former royal residence. The intrigue and regerminated rituals that occurred within the walls of this once-cloistered community are not always evident to the modern visitor. A fictionalised version is told in the trilogy *Four Reigns*, by Kukrit Pramoj, about a young girl named Ploi, growing up in the Royal City. Today the Grand Palace is used by the king only for certain ceremonial occasions such as Coronation Day, and the royal family's Bangkok residence is Chitlada Palace in the northern part of the city. The exteriors of the four Grand Palace buildings are worth a swift perusal for their royal bombast, but their interiors are usually closed to the public. The admission fee for Wat Phra Kaew also includes entry to Vimanmek Teak Mansion (p718), near the Dusit Zoo.

MUST SEE

- Contemplating contemporary art at the new Bangkok Art and Culture Centre (p719)
- Watching the sunset aboard the Chao Phraya ferry (opposite)
- Hanging with hip Thais on Th Khao San
- Waking up early (or going to bed late) to see the monks collecting alms

Nearby **Wat Pho** (Map pp716-17; ☎ 0 2221 9911; admission 50B; 🕑 8am-5pm; river ferry Tha Tien) sweeps the awards for superlatives: it's the oldest and largest temple in Bangkok, dating from the 16th century; it houses the country's largest reclining Buddha; and it has the biggest collection of Buddha images in the country. The *big* attraction is the stunning reclining Buddha, 46m long and 15m high, illustrating the passing of the Buddha into final nirvana. The figure is modelled out of plaster around a brick core and finished in gold leaf. Mother-of-pearl inlay ornaments the eyes and feet, and the feet display 108 different auspicious *láksànà* (characteristics of a Buddha).

Wat Pho is also the national headquarters for the teaching and preservation of traditional Thai medicine, including Thai massage. The temple's famous massage school has two massage pavilions within the temple grounds as well as air-con facilities within the training school (see p719).

The **National Museum** (Map p720; ☎ 0 2224 1370; Th Na Phra That; admission 200B; 🕑 9am-3.30pm Wed-Sun; river ferry Tha Maharat) is reportedly the largest in Southeast Asia and offers visitors an overview of Thai art and culture, a useful stepping stone to exploring the ancient capitals of Ayuthaya and Sukhothai. On the downside, the labelling isn't exactly illuminating so try one of the free guided tours (9.30am Wednesday and Thursday in English, French and German).

Wat Arun (Map pp716-17; ☎ 0 2891 1149; Th Arun Amarin; admission 20B; 🕑 9am-5pm; cross-river ferry from Tha Tien) is a striking temple, named after the Indian god of dawn, Aruna. It looms large on the Thonburi side of the Mae Nam Chao Phraya, looking as if it were carved from granite; a closer inspection reveals a mosaic of porcelain tiles covering the imposing 82m Khmer-style *praang* (spire). The tiles were left behind by Chinese merchant ships no longer needing them as ballast.

Chinatown & Phahurat

Cramped and crowded Chinatown is a beehive of commercial activity. The main thoroughfare is lined with gleaming gold shops, towering neon signs bearing Chinese characters and serpentine lanes with shopfronts spilling out onto the footpath. The neighbourhood's energy is at once exhilarating and exhausting. Slicing through the centre of the district, the wholesale market of **Sampeng Lane** (Map pp716-17; Soi Wanit; river ferry Tha Ratchawong) runs roughly parallel to Th Yaowarat and is jam-packed with the useful and the useless, all in bulk. The market terminates on the western side of Chinatown in a small Indian district known as Phahurat. Th Chakraphet is popular for its Indian restaurants and shops selling Indian sweets.

Slicing another commercial byway through the concrete is **Talat Mai** (Map pp716-17; Soi 6, Th Yaowarat; river ferry Tha Ratchawong, Metro Hualamphong, bus 73), a nearly three block–long market selling exotic food stuff and Chinese Buddhist religious paraphernalia. Th Yaowarat is fun to explore at night when it is lit up like a Christmas tree.

Wat Traimit (Golden Buddha; Map pp716-17; ☎ 0 2225 9775; cnr Th Yaowarat & Th Charoen Krung; admission 20B; 🕑 9am-5pm) shelters a 3m-tall, 5.5-tonne, solid-gold Buddha image – an impressive sight, even in the land of a million Buddhas. Like many treasured Buddhas, this figure was once covered in stucco, a common measure to deter looters during periods of unrest.

Mae Nam Chao Phraya

Once upon a time, Bangkok was called the 'Venice of the East'. Canals, not roads, transported goods and people, and the mighty Mae Nam Chao Phraya (Chao Phraya River) was the superhighway leading from the Gulf of Thailand to the interior of the country. All life centred on the river and its related canal networks and Thais considered themselves *jâo náam* (water lords).

Times have changed, but you can observe remnants of urban river life – slow barges being pulled by determined tug boats, kids splashing around the river banks, majestic Wat Arun rising in the distance – by boarding a Chao Phraya River Express boat at any riverside *thâa* (pier). The river ferry is also one of the more pleasant commuting options in Bangkok and is used by a cross-section of the populace, from uniformed schoolchildren to saffron-robed monks. Women should take care not to accidentally bump into a monk and should not sit next to them or stand in the same area of the boat. For more information about the river ferry, see p730.

You can also charter a longtail boat to explore the Khlong Bangkok Noi and other scenic canals in Thonburi for a quick escape from Bangkok's modern madness. Longtail boats can be arranged from any river pier, including Tha Chang. Just remember to negotiate a price before departure.

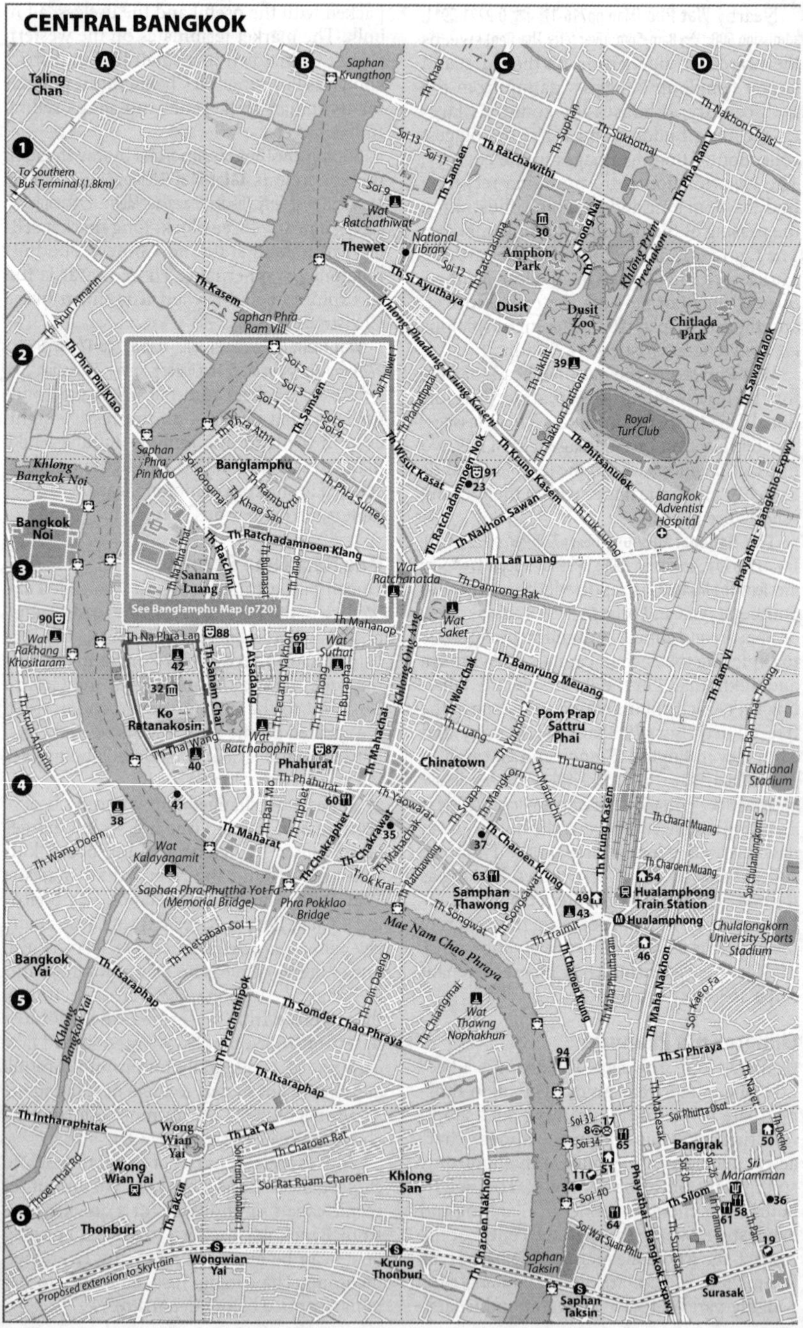

CENTRAL BANGKOK

A B C D
1 2 3 4 5 6

Taling Chan
Saphan Krungthon
Th Khao
Th Nakhon Chaisi
Th Sukhothai
Th Suphan
Soi 13
Soi 11
Th Samsen
Th Ratchawithi
Th Phra Ram V
To Southern Bus Terminal (1.8km)
Soi 9
Wat Ratchathiwat
30
Th U Thong Nai
Khlong Prem Prachakon
Th Ratchasima
National Library
Thewet
Soi 12
Amphon Park
Th Si Ayuthaya
Th Kasem
Th Arun Amarin
Dusit
Dusit Zoo
Chitlada Park
Saphan Phra Ram VIII
Khlong Phadung Krung Kasem
Th Phra Pin Klao
Soi 5
Soi 3
Soi 1
Th Samsen
Soi 6
Soi 4
Soi Thewet 1
Th Prachathipatai
Th Likhit
39
Th Nakhon Pathom
Th Sawankalok
Royal Turf Club
Th Phra Athit
Saphan Phra Pin Klao
Soi Rongmai
Banglamphu
Th Phra Sumen
Th Wisut Kasat
Th Ratchadamnoen Nok
91
23
Th Krung Kasem
Th Phitsanulok
Phayathai - Bangkhlo Expwy
Khlong Bangkok Noi
Th Rambutri
Th Khao San
Th Nakhon Sawan
Bangkok Adventist Hospital
Bangkok Noi
Th Na Phra That
Th Ratchini
Th Ratchadamnoen Klang
Th Luk Luang
Th Buranasat
Th Tanao
Th Lan Luang
Wat Ratchanatda
Th Damrong Rak
Sanam Luang
See Banglamphu Map (p720)
90
Wat Rakhang Khositaram
Th Na Phra Lan
88
Th Atsadang
69
Wat Suthat
Th Mahanop
Wat Saket
Th Saham Chai
42
32
Ko Ratanakosin
Th Feuang Nakhon
Th Ti Thong
Th Burapha
Khlong Ong Ang
Th Bamrung Meuang
Th Ram VI
Th Ban That Thong
Th Arun Amarin
Th Thai Wang
Wat Ratchabophit
87
Th Mahachai
Th Wora Chak
Th Luang
Th Yukhon 2
Pom Prap Sattru Phai
40
Phahurat
Chinatown
Th Luang
National Stadium
Th Phahurat
Th Mangkorn
Th Maitrichit
41
38
Th Ban Mo
Th Triphet
60
Th Yaowarat
Th Suapa
Th Charat Muang
Soi Chulalongkorn 5
Th Wang Doem
Th Maharat
Th Chakraphet
Th Chakrawat
35
37
Th Charoen Krung
Th Krung Kasem
Wat Kalayanamit
Th Mahachak
Th Ratchawong
Trok Krai
63
Th Charoen Muang
54
Saphan Phra Phuttha Yot Fa (Memorial Bridge)
Phra Pokklao Bridge
Samphan Thawong
Th Songwat
Th Songsawat
49
43
Hualamphong Train Station
Hualamphong
Th Traimit
Chulalongkorn University Sports Stadium
Mae Nam Chao Phraya
Th Thetsaban Soi 1
Bangkok Yai
Th Itsaraphap
Th Din Daeng
Th Charoen Krung
Th Maha Phruttharam
46
Th Maha Nakhon
Soi Kaeo Fa
Khlong Bangkok Yai
Th Prachathipok
Th Somdet Chao Phraya
Th Chiangmai
Wat Thawng Nophakhun
94
Th Si Phraya
Th Itsaraphap
Th Mahesak
Th Naret
Th Intharaphitak
Wong Wian Yai
Th Lat Ya
Soi 32
8
17
65
Soi Phutta Osot
50
Th Decho
Soi 34
Bangrak
Th Charoen Rat
Soi Krung Thonburi 1
51
Soi 30
Soi 26
Sri Mariamman
Thoet Thai Rd
Wong Wian Yai
Soi Rat Ruam Charoen
Khlong San
11
34
Soi 40
Phayathai - Bangkok Expwy
Th Silom
Th Pramuan
36
Th Taksin
Th Charoen Nakhon
64
61
58
Thonburi
Th Surasak
Th Pan
19
Soi Wat Suan Phlu
Wongwian Yai
Krung Thonburi
Saphan Taksin
Proposed extension to Skytrain
Saphan Taksin
Surasak

THAILAND

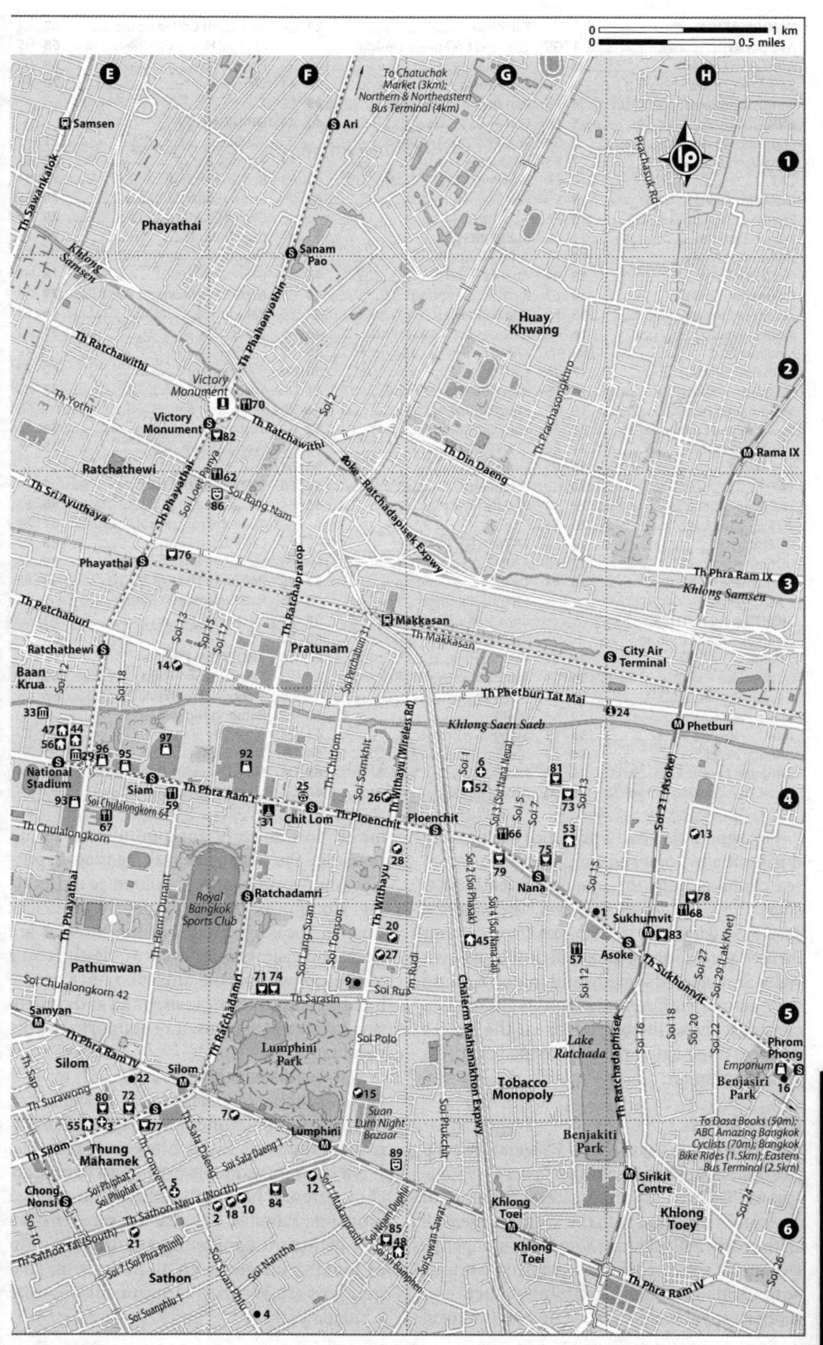

To Chatuchak Market (3km); Northern & Northeastern Bus Terminal (4km)
Samsen
Ari
Th Sawankalok
Phayathai
Khlong Samsen
Sanam Pao
Prachasuk Rd
Huay Khwang
Th Ratchawithi
Th Phahonyothin
Victory Monument
Th Yothi
Soi 2
Th Prachasongkhro
Ratchathewi
Th Din Daeng
Rama IX
Th Sri Ayuthaya
Th Phayathai
Soi Loet Panya
Soi Rang Nam
Ratchadapisek Expwy
Phayathai
Th Ratchaprarop
Th Phra Ram IX
Khlong Samsen
Th Petchaburi
Makkasan
Th Makkasan
Ratchathewi
Pratunam
City Air Terminal
Baan Krua
Soi 12
Soi 18
Soi 13
Soi 15
Soi 17
Soi Petchaburi 31
Th Phetburi Tat Mai
Khlong Saen Saeb
Phetburi
National Stadium
Siam
Th Phra Ram I
Soi Chulalongkorn 64
Th Chulalongkorn
Chit Lom
Th Ploenchit
Ploenchit
Th Chitlom
Soi Somkhit
Th Withayu (Wireless Rd)
Soi 1
Soi 3 (Soi Nana Neua)
Soi 5
Soi 7
Soi 13
Soi 21 (Asoke)
Th Withayu
Soi 2 (Soi Phasak)
Soi 4 (Soi Nana Tai)
Nana
Soi 15
Royal Bangkok Sports Club
Ratchadamri
Th Henri Dunant
Th Phayathai
Soi Lang Suan
Soi Tonson
Sukhumvit
Asoke
Th Sukhumvit
Soi 29 (Lak Khet)
Soi 27
Pathumwan
Soi Chulalongkorn 42
Th Sarasin
Soi Ruam Rudi
Soi 12
Samyan
Th Ratchadamri
Chalerm Mahanakhon Expwy
Lake Ratchada
Th Ratchadaphisek
Soi 16
Soi 18
Soi 20
Soi 22
Phrom Phong
Th Phra Ram IV
Silom
Th Sap
Lumphini Park
Soi Polo
Emporium
Benjasiri Park
Th Surawong
Th Sala Daeng
Suan Lum Night Bazaar
Tobacco Monopoly
Soi Ptukchit
To Dasa Books (50m); ABC Amazing Bangkok Cyclists (70m); Bangkok Bike Rides (1.5km); Eastern Bus Terminal (2.5km)
Th Silom
Thung Mahamek
Th Convent
Soi Sala Daeng 1
Lumphini
Benjakiti Park
Chong Nonsi
Soi Phiphat 2
Soi Phiphat 1
Th Sathon Neua (North)
Soi 1 (Atakanprasit)
Sirikit Centre
Khlong Toei
Khlong Toey
Soi 24
Soi 10
Th Sathon Tai (South)
Soi Ngam Duphli
Soi Sri Bamphen
Soi Suwan Sawat
Khlong Toei
Soi 7 (Soi Phra Phinij)
Sathon
Soi Suan Phlu
Soi Nantha
Soi Suanphlu 1
Th Phra Ram IV
Soi 26
0 1 km
0 0.5 miles
E F G H
1 2 3 4 5 6

THAILAND

INFORMATION
Asia Books 1 G5
Australian Embassy 2 F6
Bangkok Christian Hospital 3 E6
Bangkok Immigration Office 4 F6
BNH 5 E6
Bumrungrad Hospital 6 G4
Canadian Embassy 7 F5
CAT 8 C6
Diethelm Travel 9 F5
French Consulate 10 F6
French Embassy 11 C6
German Embassy 12 F6
Indian Embassy 13 H4
Indonesian Embassy 14 E3
Japanese Embassy 15 F5
Kinokuniya 16 H5
Kinokuniya (see 97)
Main Post Office 17 D6
Malaysian Embassy 18 F6
Myanmar Embassy 19 D6
New Zealand Embassy 20 F5
Singapore Embassy 21 E6
STA Travel 22 E5
TAT 23 C3
TAT Main Office 24 H4
TOT 25 F4
UK Embassy 26 F4
US Embassy 27 F5
Vietnamese Embassy 28 F4

SIGHTS & ACTIVITIES
Bangkok Art and Culture Centre 29 E4
Dusit Palace Park 30 C1
Erawan Shrine 31 F4
Grand Palace 32 A4
Jim Thompson's House 33 E4
Oriental Hotel 34 C6
Sampeng Lane 35 B4
Silom Thai Cooking School 36 D6
Talat Mai 37 C4
Thailand Creative & Design Center (see 16)
Wat Arun 38 A4
Wat Benchamabophit 39 C2
Wat Pho 40 A4
Wat Pho Thai Traditional Massage School 41 A4
Wat Phra Kaew 42 A3
Wat Traimit 43 C5

SLEEPING
A-One Inn 44 E4
Atlanta Hotel 45 G5
Baan Hualampong 46 D5
Bed & Breakfast Inn 47 E4
Café des Arts Guest House 48 F6
Krung Kasem Srikung Hotel 49 C5
Lub*d 50 D6
New Road Guesthouse 51 D6
Pranee Building (see 56)
Soi 1 Guesthouse 52 G4
Suk 11 53 G4
Train Inn 54 D4
Urban Age 55 E6
Wendy House 56 E4

EATING
AH! (see 45)
Cabbages & Condoms 57 G5
Chennai Kitchen 58 D6
Coca Suki 59 E4
India Emporium Food Centre 60 B4
Kalapapruek 61 D6
Mahboonkrong (MBK) Food Centre (see 93)
Mallika 62 F3
Mangkorn Khâo 63 C4
Muslim Restaurant 64 D6
Naaz 65 D6
Nasser Elmassry Restaurant 66 G4
New Light Coffee House 67 E4
Pharani Home Cuisine 68 H5
Poj Spa Kar 69 B3
Victory Point 70 F2

DRINKING
70s Bar 71 F5
Balcony Bar 72 E5
Bed Supperclub 73 G4
Brown Sugar 74 F5
Cheap Charlie's 75 G4
Club Culture 76 E3
Coyote on Convent 77 E6
Glow 78 H4
Nana Entertainment Plaza 79 G4
Patpong 80 E5
Q Bar 81 G4
Saxophone Pub & Restaurant 82 F2
Soi Cowboy 83 H5
Telephone Bar (see 72)
Vertigo 84 F6
Wong's Place 85 F6

ENTERTAINMENT
Aksra Theatre 86 F3
Chalermkrung Royal Theatre 87 B4
Lak Muang Shrine 88 B3
Lumphini Boxing Stadium 89 F6
Patravadi Theatre 90 A3
Ratchadamnoen Boxing Stadium 91 C3

SHOPPING
Central World Plaza 92 F4
Mahboonkrong (MBK) 93 E4
Patpong Night Market (see 80)
River City Shopping Center 94 C5
Siam Center 95 E4
Siam Discovery Center 96 E4
Siam Paragon 97 E4

Foreigners also had a presence on the river during the bygone shipping era. Two Dutch sea captains built the majestic **Oriental Hotel** (Map pp716-17; ☎ 0 2659 9000; www.mandarinoriental.com; 48 Soi Oriental/Soi 38, Th Charoen Krung; river ferry Tha Oriental or Tha Sathon), an attraction in its own right. Somerset Maugham and Joseph Conrad were among the Oriental's famous guests. You can toast those literary giants in the hotel's Author Wing cafe or the riverside bar; dress smartly, though.

Other Areas

Dusit Palace Park (Map pp716-17; ☎ 0 2628 6300; adult/child 100/50B, free with Grand Palace ticket; 9.30am-4pm; bus 70, 510) is an atmospheric example of Thailand's flirtation with the Victorian period. In the early 20th century King Chulalongkorn (Rama V) returned from his European tour with exotic ideas for establishing a new and modern royal residence. He moved the royal family to this leafy compound and set up house in the **Vimanmek Teak Mansion**, reputedly the world's largest golden teak building. Compulsory tours by poorly proficient English-speaking guides of the interior are given and visitors must dress modestly (cover to the elbows and the ankles). Other ornate buildings decorate the compound and contain small craft and art museums supported by the royal family.

Wat Benchamabophit (Map pp716-17; cnr Th Si Ayuthaya & Th Phra Ram V; admission 20B; 8am-5.30pm; bus 72, 503) was built under the reign of Rama V in 1899 and is made of white Carrara marble. It is a stunning example of modern temple architecture and houses the ashes of the revered monarch, Rama V. The real treasure here is a rear courtyard containing a large collection of Buddha images from all periods of Thai Buddhist art. Wat Ben is diagonally opposite Chitlada Park.

Jim Thompson's House (Map pp716-17; ☎ 0 2216 7368; Soi Kasem San 2, Th Phra Ram I; adult/child 100/50B; 🕐 9am-5pm; Skytrain National Stadium) is a beautifully maintained example of traditional Thai architecture. The house was the residence of American entrepreneur Jim Thompson, who successfully promoted Thai silk to Western markets. After a long career in Thailand, Thompson mysteriously disappeared in 1967 in Malaysia's Cameron Highlands; to this day the reason remains unknown and some suspect foul play, though an auto accident seems more likely. Atmospherically sited on a small *khlong*, his house was built from salvaged components of traditional Thai houses. In addition to remarkable architecture, his collection of Thai art and furnishings is superb.

Bangkok Art and Culture Centre (BACC; Map pp716-17; ☎ 0 2214 6630; www.bacc.or.th; cnr Th Phaya Thai & Th Phra Ram 1; Skytrain National Stadium) is a brand new showcase for Thailand's burgeoning contemporary artists. The building is a bit of a rip on New York's Guggenheim Museum but the collections inside are a phenomenal introduction to the country's vibrant contemporary arts scene.

COURSES

Cooking

One of the best ways to crack Thailand's lengthy menu is to take a cooking course.

Silom Thai Cooking School (Map pp716-17; ☎ 0 84726 5669; www.bangkokthaicooking.com; 68 Soi 13, Th Silom; 🕐 lessons 9.30am-1pm) Although the facilities are basic, Silom crams in a visit to a local market and instruction of six dishes into 3½ hours (1000B).

Baipai Thai Cooking School (Map pp712-13; ☎ 0 2294 9029; www.baipai.com; 150/12 Soi Naksuwan, Th Nonsee; 🕐 lessons 9.30am-1.30pm & 1.30-5.30pm Tue-Sun) Housed in an attractive suburban villa, Baipai offers two daily lessons of four dishes each (1800B). Transportation is available.

Massage

Wat Pho Thai Massage School (Map pp716-17; ☎ 0 2622 3533; www.watpomassage.com; 392/25-28 Soi Phenphat, Th Maharat; course from 6500B) Affiliated with Wat Pho, this respected massage school offers courses in both general Thai massage and foot massage.

Muay Thai (Thai Boxing)

Sor Vorapin Gym (Map p720; ☎ 0 2282 3551; www.thaiboxings.com; 13 Trok Krasab, Th Chakraphong; tuition per day/month 500/9000B) Specialises in training foreign students of both genders. The gym is sweating distance from Th Khao San, but more serious training is held outside the city.

TOURS

ABC Amazing Bangkok Cyclists (off Map pp716-17; ☎ 0 2665 6364; www.realasia.net; tour from 1000B; 🕐 10am & 1pm) Discover the rural aspects of the city on a cycling tour.

Bangkok Bike Rides (off Map pp716-17; ☎ 0 2712 5305; www.bangkokbikerides.com; tours from 1000B) This division of Spice Roads tour company offers a variety of pedal-powered tours, both urban and rural.

WEIRD & WONDERFUL BANGKOK

Bangkok worships at many altars: from colourful religious shrines to gleaming shopping malls. Whether it's a sanctioned space or a commercial enclave, the city's fascination with fashion and beauty are foremost rituals.

To drink from the fountain of youth, hang out at **Siam Sq** (Map pp716–17), a series of interconnected streets sheltering small boutiques and fast-food restaurants. Hipsters and wannabes flock here to show off fashion experiments big and small, from the modest retrofit of the Thai school uniform to the pop-rocker wolf hairdo. The serious students of couture and design visit the rotating exhibits at **Thailand Creative & Design Center** (TCDC; Map pp716-17; ☎ 0 2664 8448; www.tcdc.or.th; 6th fl, Emporium Shopping Center, Th Sukhumvit; admission free; 🕐 10.30am-10pm Tue-Sun).

Nothing provides a better window into the average person's practise of Thai Buddhism than the extraordinary **Erawan shrine** (San Phra Phrom; Map pp716-17; cnr Th Ratchadamri & Th Ploenchit), which sits outside the Grand Hyatt Erawan hotel and is dedicated to the four-headed deity Brahma (Phra Phrom), Hindu god of creation. The faithful bustle in and out at all hours due to the fact that the shrine is so well known among Thais for answering prayers and bestowing good fortune. If a wish is granted, the favour is repaid by hiring musicians and dancers to perform in front of the shrine.

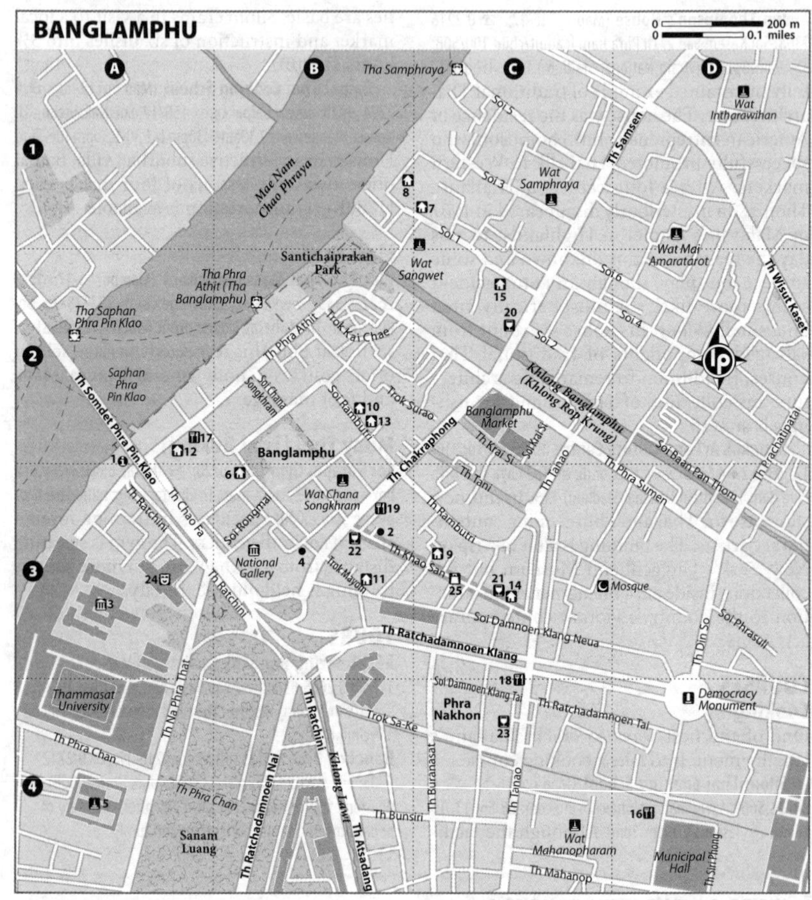

FESTIVALS & EVENTS

Chinese New Year (February/March) Thai-Chinese celebrate the lunar new year with a week of house-cleaning, lion dances and fireworks. Festivities centre on Chinatown.

Kite-Flying Season (March) During the windy season, colourful kites battle it out over the skies of Sanam Luang.

Songkran (mid April) Bangkok's celebration of the Thai New Year has morphed into water warfare centred around Th Khao San. Prepare to be soaked.

Royal Ploughing Ceremony (early May) The Crown Prince commences rice-planting season with a royal-religious ceremony at Sanam Luang.

Queen's Birthday (12 August) The queen's birthday is recognised as the national Mother's Day and celebrated in Bangkok with festivities centreD around Th Ratchadamnoen and the Grand Palace.

Vegetarian Festival (September/October) A 10-day Chinese-Buddhist festival strives for religious perfection by consuming meatless meals. Look for yellow-flagged vegetarian vendors in Chinatown.

King Chulalongkorn Day (23 October) Rama V is honoured on the anniversary of his death in front of his statue in Dusit.

Loi Krathong (early November) The Mae Nam Chao Phraya receives huge devotional crowds who float small lotus-shaped boats throughout this river-honouring festival.

King's Birthday (5 December) Locals celebrate their monarch's birthday with lots of parades and festivities on the royal avenue of Th Ratchadamnoen.

Bangkok International Film Festival (www.bangkokfilm.org; date varies) A showcase for Thai and Southeast Asian filmmakers.

INFORMATION

Bangkok Information Center	1	A2
Shaman Books	2	B3

SIGHTS & ACTIVITIES

National Museum	3	A3
Sor Vorapin Gym	4	B3
Wat Mahathat	5	A4

SLEEPING

Baan Sabai	6	B3
Bamboo Guest House	7	C1
Bella Bella Riverview	8	B1
Khao San Palace Inn	9	C3
Lamphu House	10	B2
New Joe Guesthouse	11	B3
New Merry V Guest House	12	A2
Rambuttri Village Inn	13	B2
Rikka Inn	14	C3
Villa Guest House	15	C2

EATING

Arawy	16	D4
Hemlock	17	A2
Kim Leng	18	C4
Shoshana	19	B3

DRINKING

Ad Here the 13th	20	C2
Brick Bar	21	C3
Hippie de Bar	22	B3
Taksura	23	C4

ENTERTAINMENT

National Theatre	24	A3

SHOPPING

Th Khao San Market	25	C3

SLEEPING

Bangkok possesses arguably the best variety and quality of budget places in any Asian capital city. Because the city has legendary traffic jams, narrow your search first by the geographic area that best suits your needs. If you're in the city for a layover, stay as close to your mode of transport as possible. If you're returning to 'civilisation' and need to do souvenir shopping and other traveller errands, then the backpacker ghetto on Th Khao San and around are super convenient. The drawback is that Banglamphu is far from central Bangkok and transport to the more modern parts of town can take a *long* time.

If you need to be centrally located, then opt for Siam Square, which is on both Skytrain lines. Accommodation in Siam Square is more expensive and not necessarily better value than Banglamphu.

The closest option to the airport is Th Sukhumvit, a high-end and modern area that now has a few budget options. It is also nearby the Eastern (Ekamai) bus station and on the Skytrain and Metro lines. Be warned that the lowered numbered *sois* attract sex tourists visiting the nearby go-go bars. The financial district around Th Silom also has a handful of new budget hostels, though the neighbourhood is mainly for bigger budgets. The bonus of both of these neighbourhoods is that the Metro now links them to the Hualamphong train station. Alternatively you could stay in Chinatown if you want to be as close to the train station as possible.

In Bangkok, budget accommodation ranges from about 200B to 750B per night.

Th Khao San & Banglamphu

The backpacker's ghetto of Th Khao San (Khao San Rd) is packed tight with guest houses, flashpacker hotels and even a few boutiques. For the real cheapies (sweaty boxes with a bed), just show up and start searching along the main strip or on the small *soi* across Th Tanao. Quieter and more charming enclaves are on Th Rambutri and on the numbered *soi* off Th Samsen.

New Merry V Guest House (Map p720; ☎ 0 2280 3315; 18-20 Th Phra Athit; r 150-700B; bus 53, 506, river ferry Tha Phra Athit;) The cheapest rooms here are as bare as it gets but are spotless with ample natural light and a bit of a view. Skip the more expensive rooms, though; you can do better elsewhere.

Lamphu House (Map p720; ☎ 0 2629 5861; www.lamphuhouse.com; 75-77 Soi Rambutri; r 200-920B; bus 53, 506, river ferry Tha Phra Athit;) A budget friend indeed, with clean, quiet rooms around a friendly and serene courtyard. The cheapest rooms are a tad tiny by Khao San standards, but climbing up the price point delivers more modern, boutique decor.

Rambuttri Village Inn (Map p720; ☎ 0 2282 9162; www.khaosan-hotels.com; 95 Soi Rambutri; r 290-950B; bus 53, 506, river ferry Tha Phra Athit;) Adopt the unflappable Buddhist composure to survive the gauntlet of tailors ('Excuse me, suit?') that line the entrance to this high-rise budget hotel. The rooms are good value surrounded by a courtyard of restaurants and shops.

Bella Bella Riverview (Map p720; ☎ 0 2628 8077; 6 Soi 3, Th Samsen; r 300-570B; bus 53, 506, river ferry Tha Phra Athit;) River views are slim and the rooms are largely bare and lean on amenities, but it's a good choice for those who want to stay near Th Khao San, but not *too* close.

MINDFULNESS: MEDITATION COURSES & RETREATS

The seekers and the curious often come to Thailand to explore the spiritual discipline of meditation. Bangkok, an otherwise demanding urban experience, offers several easy-to-access introductions to the practice at **Wat Mahathat** (Map p720; ☎ 0 2222 6011; Th Maharat), where daily instruction is held every three hours starting at 7am and ending at 9pm.

Other 'lite' introductions are available in Chiang Mai at **Wat Suan Dok** (see p753), which conducts two-day meditation retreats (Tuesday to Wednesday) and thrice-weekly '**monk chats**' (5pm to 7pm Monday, Wednesday and Friday).

For the more serious student, **Wat Pa Nanachat**, in the northeastern town Ubon Ratchathani, was opened specifically for non-Thai Buddhists. English is the primary language and those with previous meditation experience should write to the Guest Monk at this address: Wat Pa Nanachat, Ban Bung Wai, Amphoe Warin, Ubon Ratchathani 34310.

Slightly radical in temple circles is the **Daen Maha Mongkol Meditation Centre** (Hwy 323, Sai Yok district, Kanchanaburi), which is a forest mediation retreat catering mainly to female nuns and meditators. Meditation classes are available and English-speaking nuns can usually help with translations. The centre is not well known in international circles but ask around in Kanchanaburi to arrange transport.

Perhaps Thailand's most famous and strenuous meditation retreat is **Wat Suanmok** (Wat Suan Mokkhaphalaram; www.suanmokkh.org), near the southern town of Chaiya. It is a forest temple founded by Ajahn Buddhadasa Bhikkhu, one of Thailand's most famous monks. At the hermitage, resident monks hold English-language guided meditation retreats on the first 10 days of every month. Check the website for program details and fees. To get to Wat Suanmok, catch a sǎwngthǎew (60B, 45 minutes) from Surat Thani's Talat Kaset 2 bus station to Chaiya or take the train to Chaiya's train station. Sǎwngthǎew from Chaiya's train station travel the 7km to Wat Suanmok (20B, until 3pm) or hire a motorcycle taxi for 75B.

You can merge your beach needs with your spiritual needs at Ko Pha-Ngan's **Wat Khao Tham** (www.watkowtahm.org; PO Box 18, Ko Pha-Ngan, Surat Thani 84280), on a hilltop on the southwestern side of the island. Periodic meditation retreats are held by an American-Australian couple. The website provides details on retreat schedules and registration procedures.

Villa Guest House (Map p720; ☎ 0 2281 7009; 230 Soi 1, Th Samsen; s/d 300/600B; bus 53, 506, river ferry Tha Phra Athit) Satisfy your urge to spend the night in a traditional teak house at this old-fashioned and beloved place. Rustic but atmospheric rooms are furnished with aged antiques and bathrooms are shared.

New Joe Guesthouse (Map p720; ☎ 0 2281 2948; www.newjoeguesthouse.com; 81 Trok Mayom; r 300-700B; bus 53, 506, river ferry Tha Phra Athit;) Tucked away in an alley that runs parallel to Th Khao San, New Joe Guesthouse has the usual assortment of high-rise rooms that are a bit sweaty, but there's a garden restaurant, a large lobby complete with pool table, and young and friendly staff.

Khao San Palace Inn (Map p720; ☎ 0 2282 0578; 139 Th Khao San; r 400-1000B; bus 53, 506, river ferry Tha Phra Athit;) Right on the Khao San strip, with a variety of old and newish rooms that are mostly clean. Ascend to the top floor for a swimming pool and a knockout city view. The cheapest rooms are fan only.

Rikka Inn (Map p720; ☎ 0 2282 7511; www.rikkainn.com; 259 Th Khao San; r 600-950B; bus 53, 506, river ferry Tha Phra Athit;) Splurge on affordable luxury at Rikka, boasting tight but attractive rooms, a rooftop pool and a central location.

Other places worth considering:

Baan Sabai (Map p720; ☎ 0 2629 1599; 12 Soi Rongmai; r 190-600B; bus 53, 506, river ferry Tha Phra Athit;) Quiet and relaxing with a range of basic rooms and a shaded sitting garden.

Bamboo Guest House (Map p720; ☎ 0 2282 3412; bamboo-guesthouse.com; 67 Soi 1, Th Samsen; s/d 220/280B; bus 53, 506, river ferry Tha Phra Athit;) Advertising itself as a return to the backpacker heyday of the 1990s, Bamboo, a converted wooden house has quiet and basic rooms in a charming residential neighbourhood.

Hualamphong & Chinatown

Hotels near the Hualamphong train station are cheap but not especially interesting and the traffic along Th Phra Ram IV has to be heard to be believed. The surrounding neighbourhood of Chinatown makes for interesting walks but is not especially geared for tourists.

Baan Hualampong (Map pp716-17; ☎ 0 2639 8054; www.baanhualampong.com; 336/20 Soi 21, Th Charoen Krung; dm 220B, s 290B, d 520-700B; Metro Hualamphong;) The homey setting and personal service draws many repeats to this rather hard-to-find guest house. Kitchen and laundry facilities are also available, and there are lots of chill-out areas and computers.

Train Inn (Map pp716-17; ☎ 0 2215 3055; www.thetraininn.com; 428 Th Rong Meuang; r 450-900B;) Located directly behind Hualamphong, this tidy guest house is a good place to base yourself if you've got an early or late date with a train.

Krung Kasem Srikung Hotel (Map pp716-17; ☎ 0 2225 0132; fax 0 2225 4705; 1860 Th Krung Kasem; d 650-700B; Metro Hualamphong;) Despite the sooty exterior, the rooms here are tidy and have balconies and views of Chinatown. It is located across the *khlong* from Hualamphong train station.

Siam Square

Siam Square is a microcosm of this megacity: supermodern shopping centres, nonstop traffic jams and simple villages squatting in the small lanes. Unofficially known as the 'secret *soi*', San Kasem San 1 has a low-key personality and traveller-friendly facilities. You can also bypass rush hour traffic between here and Th Khao San by hopping on the *khlong* ferry at Tha Ratchethewi.

Pranee Building (Map pp716-17; ☎ 0 2215 3053; Soi Kasem San 1; d 500B; Skytrain National Stadium;) Cheapest spot on the *soi*, Pranee has large but outdated rooms and slightly mouldy bathrooms.

Bed & Breakfast Inn (Map pp716-17; ☎ 0 2215 3004; Soi Kasem San 1; s/d 600/700B; Skytrain National Stadium;) Standard guest house–style rooms come with air-con and – surprise! – breakfast included.

A-One Inn (Map pp716-17; ☎ 0 2215 3029; www.aoneinn.com; 25/13-15 Soi Kasem San 1; d from 650B; Skytrain National Stadium;) The lobby is a tad messy but the rooms are A+ value.

Wendy House (Map pp716-17; ☎ 0 2216 2436; www.wendyguesthouse.com; Soi Kasem San 1; s/d from 800/900B; Skytrain National Stadium;) Easily the most modern digs on the street, Wendy has cheery if small rooms. The staff is especially sweet.

Sukhumvit

Th Sukhumvit is a major commercial artery through the modern and most international part of town. Although it has mainly high-end condos and international chain hotels, more budget spots have been popping up.

HI-Sukhumvit (Map pp712-13; ☎ 0 2391 9338; www.Hlsukhvmit.com; 23 Soi 38, Th Sukhumvit; dm 300B, s 550-600B, d 800-850B; Skytrain Thong Lor;) Located in a quiet residential street, this multistorey hostel is a brief walk from Thong Lor Skytrain station and is one of the closest budget options to the Eastern (Ekamai) bus station. The dorms are tidy, bathrooms immense and there's loads of tourist information, as well as a rooftop deck, laundry and kitchen.

Soi 1 Guesthouse (Map pp716-17; ☎ 0 2655 0604; www.soi1guesthouse.com; 220/7 Soi 1, Th Sukhumvit; dm 350B; Skytrain Nana;) This narrow converted shophouse holds four cluttered dorm rooms and a chummy communal area with pool table, TV and computers.

Nana Chart (Map pp712-13; ☎ 0 2259 4900; www.thailandhostel.com; cnr Soi 25, Th Sukhumvit; dm 390, r 1200-1800B; Skytrain Asoke, Metro Sukhumvit;) This tidy, newish backpacker hostel packs in plain but adequate budget rooms and better-than-average dorms, all of which feature en suite bathrooms.

Suk 11 (Map pp716-17; ☎ 0 2253 5927; www.suk11.com; 1/33 Soi 11, Th Sukhumvit; r 500-2000B; Skytrain Nana;) An otherwise boring concrete shophouse has been given an artsy makeover with salvaged wood, hanging vines and other Robinson Crusoe accents to create one of Bangkok's funkiest guest houses. This place is extremely popular and requires advance reservations.

Atlanta Hotel (Map pp716-17; ☎ 0 2252 1650, 0 2252 6069; fax 0 2656 8123; 78 Soi 2, Th Sukhumvit; r 535-650B; Skytrain Ploenchit;) A Bangkok institution, the Atlanta maintains its mid-century time-capsuled lobby, filled with writing desks and shadow-casting ceiling fans. The rooms are more skeletal than stylish. But the Atlanta has a devout following for its tropically landscaped pool, retro coffeeshop and its slightly rabid policy against sex tourists (a discriminating but necessary one in this neighbourhood).

Refill Now! (Map pp712-13; ☎ 0 2713 2044; www.refillnow.co.th; 191 Soi Pridi Banhom Yong 42, Soi 71, Th Sukhumvit; dm 560B, s/d 1085/1470B;) This is about as close as it gets for budget accommodation near Bangkok's new airport.

The hostel-hotel sports a chic look with a chill-out area and massage centre as well as a túk-túk service (30B per passenger) to nearby Skytrain stations.

Silom

For backpackers, Silom doesn't have the strongest résumé, but some recent additions have been improving the neighbourhood's budget appeal.

New Road Guesthouse (Map pp716-17; ☎ 0 2630 6994; fax 0 2237 1102; 1216/1 Th Charoen Krung; dm 130-220B, d 280-1500B; river ferry Tha Si Phraya;) This chipper Danish-run hostel offers a wide variety of plain but clean rooms and dorms (the fan ones rank among the city's cheapest).

Urban Age (Map pp716-17; ☎ 0 2634 2680; theurbanage@hotmail.com; 130/6 Soi 8, Th Silom; dm 230B, s/d 600/800B; Skytrain Chong Nonsi;) Smack dab in the middle of Silom, this hostel features private rooms and dorms, all with shared bathrooms. Advance booking is a must.

Café des Arts Guest House (Map pp716-17; ☎ 0 2679 8438; 27/39 Soi Sri Bamphen; r 350-450B; Metro Lumphini;) Run by a French-Thai couple, there's no cafe (or art), but rather a Korean barbecue restaurant and eight simple rooms upstairs.

Lub*d (Map pp716-17; ☎ 0 2634 7999; www.lubd.com; 4 Th Decho; dm 520B, s/d 1280/1800B; Skytrain Chong Nonsi;) The four-storey building has dorms (including a ladies-only wing) and a few private rooms, both with and without bathrooms. The communal area has traveller information, free internet, games and a bar.

EATING

No matter where you go in Bangkok, food is never far away. Surfing the street stalls is the cheapest and tastiest culinary pursuit, but don't neglect the city's mall food courts that combine the variety of an outdoor market without the noise and heat.

Bangkok also offers an international menu thanks to its many immigrant communities. Chinatown is naturally good for Chinese food; Middle Eastern fare can be found in Little Arabia, off Th Sukhumvit; Indian hangs out near the Hindu temple on Th Silom; and Western cuisine dominates Th Sukhumvit.

Vegetarians are onto a good thing in Bangkok where they'll find meatless meals aplenty. During the vegetarian festival in October, the whole city goes mad for tofu, and stalls and restaurants indicate their vegie status with yellow flags.

Th Khao San & Banglamphu

Th Khao San is lined with restaurants, but the prices tend to be higher and the quality incredibly inauthentic. Serial snackers can survive by venturing off Khao San and into the *sois* around Th Samsen or the old district of Phra Nakhon.

Arawy (Map p720; 152 Th Din So; dishes 20-40B; breakfast, lunch & dinner; bus 15, khlong taxi Tha Phan Fah) The greasy spoon of authentic Thai vegetarian, Arawy's idea of decor is old boxes piled up beside a TV set. But the pre-made point-and-eat dishes are delicious and authentic. The restaurant was inspired by ex-Bangkok governor Chamlong Srimuang's strict vegetarianism. The roman-script sign reads 'Alloy' and it is opposite the Municipal Hall.

Shoshana (Map p720; ☎ 0 2282 9948; 88 Th Chakraphong; dishes 30-150B; lunch & dinner; bus 30, 53, 506, river ferry Tha Phra Athit) One of Khao San's original Israeli restaurants, Shoshana is still a favourite for its secret-like location, garlicky baba ganoush and anything deep fried.

Kim Leng (Map p720; ☎ 0 2622 2062; 158-160 Th Tanao; dishes 40-100B; lunch & dinner Mon-Sat; bus 15, khlong taxi Tha Phan Fah) This tiny family-run restaurant specialises in central Thai dishes. Simply point at whatever looks good from the well-stocked glass case, or refer to the English-language menu. Note that there is no roman-script sign.

Hemlock (Map p720; ☎ 0 2282 7507; 56 Th Phra Athit, Banglamphu; dishes 60-220B; dinner; bus 30, 53, 506, river ferry Tha Phra Athit) With a menu ranging from the usual suspects to relatively obscure regional dishes, this longstanding local is an excellent intro to Thai food and a stylish date as well.

Poj Spa Kar (Map pp716-17; ☎ 0 2222 2686; 443 Th Tanao; dishes 80-200B; lunch & dinner; bus 15, khlong taxi Tha Phan Fah) This is the oldest restaurant (the name is pronounced '*pôht sà·pah kahn*') in Bangkok, and continues to maintain recipes handed down from a former palace cook. Savour history in the simple lemongrass omelette or the deliciously sweet and sour *kaeng sôm*, a traditional central Thai curry.

Hualamphong & Chinatown

India Emporium Food Centre (Map pp716-17; Th Chakraphet, Phahurat; dishes 20-100B; lunch & dinner; bus 73, river ferry Tha Saphan Phut) In the Indian fabric district of Phahurat, the resuscitated ATM building now has a few Indian food stalls on the top floor. Poke around the nearby alleys for more ethnic stalls.

Mangkorn Khao (Map pp716-17; ☎ 0 2682 2352; cnr Th Yaowarat & Th Yaowaphanit; dishes 30B; 🕑 7-11pm; bus 73, river ferry Tha Ratchawong) This streetside stall is a lauded vendor of *bà·mèe* (Chinese-style wheat noodles) and delicious wontons. Note that there is no roman-script sign.

Siam Square

Food vendors on Soi Kasem San 1 do a brisk business of feeding hungry clockwatchers and lounging *faràng* (foreigners); they are masters at communicating with hand gestures.

Mahboonkrong Food Centre (MBK; Map pp716-17; cnr Th Phra Ram I & Th Phayathai; 🕑 lunch & dinner; Skytrain National Stadium) The 6th-floor food court in this shopping centre is one of the busiest in the city, thanks to an assortment of tasty dishes, including a popular vegetarian stall. The English menus help new arrivals identify common street stall masterpieces.

Coca Suki (Map pp716-17; ☎ 0 2251 6337; 416/3-8 Th Henri Dunant; dishes 60-200B; 🕑 lunch & dinner; Skytrain Siam) When in Thailand we prefer to have others do our chores, but this cook-it-yourself restaurant is a popular outing for Thai friends who masterfully manage dipping the raw ingredients into the bubbling hotpot of broth and gossiping without interruption.

New Light Coffee House (Map pp716-17; ☎ 0 2251 9592; 426/1-4 Siam Sq; dishes 60-200B; 🕑 breakfast, lunch & dinner; Skytrain Siam) Travel back to the near past at this vintage diner popular with Chulalongkorn University students. Try old-school Western dishes, accompanied by a roll and green salad, or choose from the extensive Thai menu.

Sukhumvit

Fine dining is Sukhumvit's strong suit but you can find a few modest mom-and-pops too.

Soi 38 Night Market (Map pp712-13; Soi 38, Th Sukhumvit; dishes 30-60B; 🕑 8pm-3am; Skytrain Thong Lor) For budget noshing in an expensive part of town, this nightly collection of Thai-Chinese stalls is something of an oasis.

Pharani Home Cuisine (Saen Saeb Boat Noodle; Map pp716-17; ☎ 0 2664 4454; Soi 23, Th Sukhumvit; dishes 35-200B; 🕑 lunch & dinner; Skytrain Asoke, Metro Sukhumvit) This longstanding place originally gained its reputation from its meaty 'boat noodles' but now dabbles in a bit of everything, from ox tongue stew to fried rice with shrimp paste.

AH! (Map pp716-17; ☎ 0 2252 6069; Atlanta Hotel, 78 Soi 2, Th Sukhumvit; dishes 60-150B; 🕑 breakfast, lunch & dinner; Skytrain Ploenchit) The Atlanta Hotel's delightful vintage diner is the rare place that excels both in atmosphere and cuisine. Delve back into 1950's era 'Continental' dishes, such as Hungarian goulash or Wiener schnitzel, or acclaimed vegetarian Thai.

Boon Tong Kiat Singapore Hainanese Chicken Rice (Map pp712-13; ☎ 0 2390 2508; 440/5 & 396 Soi 55/Thong Lo, Th Sukhumvit; dishes 60-150B; 🕑 lunch & dinner; Skytrain Thong Lor) That long text on the wall is this restaurant's chicken rice manifesto and is proof that you don't need exotic ingredients or four-star cooks to make a profoundly delicious dish.

Nasser Elmassry Restaurant (Map pp716-17; ☎ 0 2253 5582; 4/6 Soi 3/1, Th Sukhumvit; dishes 80-350B; 🕑 8am-5am; Skytrain Nana) Step into the bazaar atmosphere of Little Arabia and claim a seat at this all-metallic restaurant and shisha cafe.

Cabbages & Condoms (Map pp716-17; ☎ 0 2229 4610; Soi 12, Th Sukhumvit; dishes 100-200B; 🕑 lunch & dinner; Skytrain Asoke) A Thai nongovernmental organisation established this chain of restaurants as a part of its public outreach for family planning, safe sex and AIDS prevention. Marrying a meal with copulation is a novel concept that elevates the otherwise unspectacular Thai dishes to a beloved institution. Even more entertaining, diners are offered complimentary condoms instead of after-meal mints.

Ana's Garden (Map pp712-13; ☎ 0 2391 1762; 67 Soi 55/Thong Lo, Th Sukhumvit; dishes 150-250B; 🕑 dinner; Skytrain Thong Lor) For a date-worthy, full-flavoured Thai meal that won't blow the budget, try this place. The *yam tòoa ploo* (wing bean salad) and the house speciality grilled chicken are musts.

Bo.lan (Map pp712-13; ☎ 0 2260 2962; www.bolan.co.th; 42 Soi 26/Rongnarong Phichai Songkhram, Th Sukhumvit; set meal 1500B; 🕑 lunch & dinner) If you're going to do one upscale Thai meal in Bangkok, do it here. Started up by two former chefs of London's Michelin-starred Nahm, the emphasis is on set meals featuring full-flavoured regional Thai dishes.

Silom

The small *soi* on the western end of Th Silom and parallel Th Surawong are home to active Muslim and Indian communities, which provide visiting import-exporters with a taste of home. Check out the food vendors on Soi 20 (Soi Pradit), off Th Silom near the mosque.

Muslim Restaurant (Map pp716-17; 1356 Th Charoen Krung; dishes 30-90B; 🕑 breakfast & lunch; river ferry Tha Oriental) This faded old restaurant may not look all that great, but it has been feeding various Lonely Planet authors for decades.

Naaz (Map pp716-17; ☎ 0 2234 4537; 24/9 Soi 45, Th Charoen Krung; dishes 40-90B; ⏰ breakfast, lunch & dinner Mon-Sat; river ferry Tha Oriental) Pronounced 'Nat' in Thai, this neighbourhood cafe has long cooked up rich *khâo mòk kài* (chicken biryani).

Chennai Kitchen (Map pp716-17; ☎ 0 2234 1266; 10 Th Pan; dishes 50-150B; ⏰ lunch; Skytrain Surasak) Located next door to a Hindu temple, this tiny restaurant puts out some of the most authentic southern Indian vegetarian in town. If you're feeling indecisive go for the *thali* set.

Kalapapruek (Map pp716-17; ☎ 0 2236 4335; 27 Th Pramuan; dishes 60-120B; ⏰ breakfast, lunch & dinner; Skytrain Surasak) The menu of this venerable Thai eatery spans regional Thai specialities from just about every region, daily specials and, occasionally, seasonal treats as well.

Greater Bangkok

Both of the following places are easily accessible by Victory Monument Skytrain station.

Victory Point (Map pp716-17; cnr Th Phayathai & Th Ratwithi; dishes 25-50B; ⏰ dinner; Skytrain Victory Monument) Lining the busy roundabout is a squatters' village of stalls known collectively as 'Victory Point'.

Phat Thai Ari (Map pp712-13; ☎ 0 2270 1654; 2/1-2 Soi 7/Ari, Th Phahonyothin; dishes 40-95B; ⏰ lunch & dinner; Skytrain Ari) Forget the stuff sold from street stalls along Th Khao San; real *phàt thai* as the locals eat it is available at the original branch of this popular franchise.

Mallika (Map pp716-17; ☎ 0 248 0287; 21/36 Th Rang Nam; dishes 70-180B; ⏰ lunch & dinner Mon-Sat; Skytrain Ari) Mallika does authentic southern Thai with a legible English menu, good service and a tidy setting. Be forewarned that in this case, authentic equals spicy.

DRINKING

Bangkok's curfew is quite strictly enforced (though this does vary with the ever-changing government). The Th Khao San area tends to be the exception through various illogical loopholes. Smoking has been banned and successfully enforced from all indoor bars and clubs and some open-air places as well.

Bars

Most backpackers are pleased to find that the party finds them on Th Khao San, where nighttime equals the right time for a drink. Beer and cocktails are sold from every corner and a tonne of hip Thais have carved out a local's scene among the foreigners.

Hippie de Bar (Map p720; ☎ 0 2629 3508; 46 Th Khao San; river ferry Tha Phra Athit) Despite the name, you'll be hard-pressed to find dreadlocks or a yoga mat at this boozer shack, popular with local university students. Regardless, everybody's welcome, and there's food, pool tables and a rockin' soundtrack.

Taksura (Map p720; ☎ 0 2622 0708; 156/1 Th TanaoTanao; khlong taxi to Tha Phan Fah) Part of the adventure is actually locating this seemingly abandoned, nearly century-old house. Reward your discovery with some spicy nibbles and a bottle of Saeng Som.

Coyote on Convent (Map pp716-17; ☎ 0 2631 2325; 1/2 Convent Rd, Th Silom; Skytrain Sala Daeng, Metro Silom) Howl with the Coyote thanks to its 75-plus varieties of margaritas. Keep an ear out for its weekly ladies-night specials.

Cheap Charlie's (Map pp716-17; Soi 11, Th Sukhumvit; ⏰ closed Sun; Skytrain Nana) Owned and operated for over 25 years by a legendary Bangkok character, this outdoor beer stall is decorated with hundreds of novelty trinkets and other curiousities. As the name suggests, drinks are easy on the wallet, so it figures that expats flock here in big numbers. It is located on a sub-*soi* off Soi 11, look for the 'Sabai Sabai Massage' sign.

Moon Bar at Vertigo (Map pp716-17; ☎ 0 2679 1200; Banyan Tree Hotel, 21/100 Th Sathon Tai; Metro Lumphini) If you've packed for high-end, put on your best duds and climb into the heavens at this sky-high, open-air bar that will quite literally take your breath away. From ground level, the elevator delivers you to the 59th floor where you emerge above the roar of Bangkok traffic.

Wong's Place (Map pp716-17; 27/3 Soi Sri Bumphen, off Soi Ngam Duphli, Th Phra Ram IV; ⏰ 8pm until late; Metro Lumphini) This is an after-hours' joint beloved by backpackers who stayed so long they're now expats; don't show up until after midnight.

Live Music

Brick Bar (Map p720; ☎ 0 2629 4477; basement, Buddy Lodge, 265 Th Khao San; river ferry Tha Phra Athit) This underground pub hosts a revolving cast of live Thai bands slotted for an almost exclusively domestic crowd. If this all sounds a bit too foreign, come just before midnight and rock to Teddy Ska, one of the city's best ska/reggae bands.

Saxophone Pub & Restaurant (Map pp716-17; ☎ 0 2246 5472; 3/8 Th Phayathai; Skytrain Victory Monument) A Bangkok live-music legend, Saxophone fills its beer-cellar-style bar with jazz, blues, reggae and rock.

Ad Here the 13th (Map p720; 13 Th Samsen; river ferry Tha Phra Athit) Just over the Khlong Banglamphu bridge, elbow space is at a premium in this lively hole-in-the-wall bar. A blues band bangs out crowd favourites almost nightly.

Brown Sugar (Map pp716-17; ☎ 0 2250 0103; 231/20 Th Sarasin; Skytrain Ratchadamri)) Jazz it up with a visit to this intimate club dedicated to brass and occasionally the blues. Accessible by a bit of a walk from Ratchadamri Skytrain station.

Clubbing

High-powered cocktails and high heels are the name of the game in the dance and lounge clubs in the City of Angels. Cover charges start at 500B and usually include a drink or two. Don't even think about showing up before 11pm.

There are a few club 'zones' throughout town: Soi 11, Th Sukhumvit; Soi 2 and Soi 4, Th Silom; and Royal City Ave (RCA), Th Phra Ram IX.

Royal City Avenue (RCA; Map pp712-13; Royal City Avenue, Th Phra Ram IX) This suburban strip of megaclubs packs in barely legal Thais, professional drunks of every nationality (including a few dirty old 'uncles') and enthusiastic backpackers. The club venues change but at the moment you'll find the crowds at 808 Club, Flix/Slim and Route 66.

Bed Supperclub (Map pp716-17; ☎ 0 2651 3537; 26 Soi 11, Th Sukhumvit; Skytrain Nana) One of Bangkok's terminally trendy spots, VIP clubbers lounge about on reserved mattresses while the walk-ins down overpriced cocktails. We've always scratched our heads about this one but always relent. Soi 11 is one of the closest in-town club zones.

Q Bar (Map pp716-17; ☎ 0 2252 3274; 34 Soi 11, Th Sukhumvit; Skytrain Nana) The original importer of lounge chic, the Q Bar still excels with its DJ selection, but has become something of a working girl (local euphemism for 'prostitute') HQ.

Club Culture (Map pp716-17; ☎ 08 9497 8422; Th Sri Ayuthaya; 🕑 7pm-late Wed, Fri & Sat; Skytrain Phayathai) Housed in a unique 40-year-old Thai-style building, Culture is the biggest and quirkiest recent arrival on Bangkok's club scene. Come to shake to internationally recognised DJs and the most-touted system in town.

Glow (Map pp716-17; ☎ 0 2261 3007; 96/4-5 Soi 23, Th Sukhumvit; Skytrain Asoke, Metro Sukhumvit) This tiny club packs 'em in with a menu of music ranging from hip-hop to electronica, and just about everything in between.

ENTERTAINMENT

Muay Thai (Thai Boxing)

The country's best fighters bubble up from the rice paddy rings to the city's most famous stadiums: **Lumphini Boxing Stadium** (Map pp716-17; Th Phra Ram IV; 🕑 bouts 6pm Tue, Fri, Sat; Metro Lumphini), near Lumphini Park, and **Ratchadamnoen Boxing Stadium** (Map pp716-17; Th Ratchadamnoen Nok; 🕑 bouts 6pm Mon, Wed & Thu, 5pm Sun; bus 503 & 70). The cheapest seats are 1000/1500/2000B for 3rd/2nd/1st class. Matches usually include eight to 10 fights of five rounds each; the last three are the headliner events when the stadiums fill up.

BAWDY BANGKOK

Many Western men descend on Thailand to dole out their pensions on a hormone-fuelled life they'd only dreamed about back home. The industry that caters to these men-acting-like-boys is a diverse social phenomenon that consumes a whole subset of Bangkok's nightlife, from massage parlours and go-go clubs to hostess bars. For the puritanicals we list these establishments only as a deterrence guide.

Patpong (Map pp716-17; Soi Patpong 1 & 2, Th Silom; Skytrain Sala Daeng, Metro Silom) was once Bangkok's most famous red light but has since been tamed into a bustling night market and risqué circus sideshow. There are still a handful of go-go bars that specialise in ping-pong shows for tourists. The gay men's equivalent can be found on nearby Soi Pratuchai.

Soi Cowboy (Map pp716-17; btwn Soi 21 & Soi 23, Th Sukhumvit; Skytrain Asoke, Metro Sukhumvit) is a single-lane strip of 25 to 30 bars that claims direct lineage to the post–Vietnam War era, when an American ex-GI nicknamed 'Cowboy' was among the first to open a self-named go-go bar off Th Sukhumvit.

Nana Entertainment Plaza (Map pp716-17; Soi 4/Soi Nana Tai, Th Sukhumvit; Skytrain Nana) is a self-enclosed 'strip' mall surrounded by a throng of hostess bars and loads of pot-bellied men. Among the real ladies are a few ladyboys (pre- and post-op).

GAY & LESBIAN BANGKOK

Bangkok's gay community is loud, proud and knows how to party. A newcomer might want to visit the websites **Utopia** (www.utopia-asia.com), **Dreaded Ned** (www.dreadedned.com) and **Fridae** (www.fridae.com) for updated nightlife info. The **Lesbian Guide to Bangkok** (www.bangkoklesbian.com) is the only English-language tracker of the lesbian scene.

Soi 4 forms one portion of Bangkok's so-called pink triangle of gay nightlife spots. The old-timers on the block are **Balcony Bar** (Map pp716-17; ☎ 0 2235 5891; 86-88 Soi 4, Th Silom; Skytrain Sala Daeng, Metro Silom) and **Telephone Bar** (Map pp716-17; ☎ 0 2234 3279; 114/11-13 Soi 4, Th Silom; Skytrain Sala Daeng, Metro Silom). Th Sarasin, behind Lumphini Park, is lined with more loungey options, such as **70s Bar** (Map pp716-17; ☎ 0 2253 4433; 231/16 Th Sarasin, Lumphini; 🕑 6pm-1am; Skytrain Rachadamri).

After all these years, Bangkok finally has something of a lesbian scene: **E Fun** (Map pp712-13; Royal City Avenue/RCA, Th Phra Ram IX; 🕑 10pm-2am; Metro Rama 9) and **Zeta** (Map pp712-13; ☎ 0 2203 0994; 29 Royal City Avenue/RCA, Phra Ram IX; 🕑 10pm-2am; Metro Rama 9).

Aficionados say the best-matched bouts are reserved for Tuesday nights at Lumphini and Thursday nights at Ratchadamnoen. Always buy tickets from the ticket window, not from a hawker hanging around outside the stadium.

Traditional Arts Performances

Chalermkrung Royal Theatre (Sala Chaloem Krung; Map pp716-17; ☎ 0 2222 0434; cnr Th Charoen Krung & Th Triphet; tickets 1000-2000B; river ferry Tha Saphan Phut) In this Thai art deco building, Chalermkrung provides a striking venue for *khŏhn* performances (see p705). When it opened in 1933, the royally funded Chalermkrung was the largest and most modern theatre in Asia, with film-projection technology and the first chilled-water air-con system in the region. The theatre requests that patrons dress respectfully, which means no shorts, tank tops or sandals. Bring along a wrap or long-sleeved shirt in case the air-con is running full blast.

Aksra Theatre (Map pp716-17; ☎ 0 2677 8888 ext 5604; www.aksratheatre.com; King Power Complex, 8/1 Soi Rang Nam, Th Phayathai; tickets 800B; 🕑 show 7pm Tue-Fri, 1pm & 7pm Sat & Sun; Skytrain Victory Monument) The former Joe Louis Puppet Theatre has changed its location and its name. A variety of performances are now held at this modern theatre, but the highlight is the Ramakian performances by the traditional knee-high puppets requiring three puppeteers to strike humanlike poses.

National Theatre (Map p720; ☎ 0 2224 1352; Th Na Phra That; admission 50-100B; river ferry Tha Phra Chan) Near Saphan Phra Pin Klao, the National Theatre hosts performances of the traditional *khŏhn,* but its performance schedule is poorly publicised in English; have a Thai speaker call about its monthly schedule.

Patravadi Theatre (Map pp716-17; ☎ 0 2412 7287; www.patravaditheatre.com; 69/1 Soi Tambon Wenglang 1; tickets from 500B; cross-river ferry from Tha Maharat) This open-air theatre is Bangkok's leading promoter of avant-garde dance and drama. A free river shuttle picks up patrons at Tha Mahathat, near Silpakorn University.

To see Thai classical dancing for free, stop by Lak Muang Shrine (Map pp716–17), near Sanam Luang, or Erawan Shrine (p719), next to Grand Hyatt Erawan hotel; shrine dancers are often hired in thanks for granted wishes. Dusit Palace Park (p718) also hosts daily classical dance performances at 10am and 2pm.

SHOPPING

Bangkok is not the place for recovering shopaholics as the temptations – from packed markets to glitzy shopping centres – are just too powerful.

Markets

Chatuchak Market (Map pp712-13; Th Phahonyothin; 🕑 9am-6pm Sat & Sun; Skytrain Mo Chit, Metro Chatuchak Park) Chatuchak is the mother of all markets. It sprawls over a huge area with tens of thousands of stalls and hundreds of thousands of visitors a day. Everything is sold here, from live chickens and snakes to handicrafts and antiques as well as huge piles of clothes. Everyone leaves thoroughly exhausted, totally dehydrated and overloaded with armfuls of plastic bags – it's great fun. To navigate the market like a pro, pick up a copy of *Nancy Chandler's Map of Bangkok,* which comes with a detailed Chatuchak section. The market is north of central Bangkok.

Tap into the Thai psyche at the many street markets. Most sell an odd assortment of plastic toys, household goods, braziers and cheap clothes. At the tourist markets such as **Th Khao San Market** (Map p720; Th Khao San; 🕑 11am-11pm; river ferry Tha Phra Athit) you'll meet for the first time all of the factory souvenirs you'll soon grow tired of seeing. But for now the hippie gear and clever T-shirts are novel. Knock-off designer bags and watches are the speciality at **Patpong Night Market** (Map pp716-17; Patpong Soi 2, Th Silom; 🕑 7pm-1am; Skytrain Sala Daeng, Metro Silom).

The food markets are a spectacle in their own right and where home cooks forage for brightly coloured tapioca desserts, spicy curries and fruits that look like medieval torture devices.

Shopping Centres

Mahboonkrong (MBK; Map pp716-17; cnr Th Phayathai & Th Phra Ram I; Skytrain National Stadium) Bangkok's most hyperactive mall, MBK is an air-conditioned playground for average folks, from trendy Thai teenagers to escalator-shy grannies. Small, inexpensive stalls and shops sell mobile-phone accessories, cheap T-shirts, wallets and handbags, plus there is the mid-range Tokyu department store.

Siam Center & Siam Discovery Center (Map pp716-17; cnr Th Phayathai & Th Phra Ram I; Skytrain National Stadium) Thailand's first shopping centre, Siam Center opened its doors in 1976 and has tried to keep up with the times by repurposing itself for the fashion-conscious teens. The attached Siam Discovery Center is the leading lady of home decor. Peruse the 3rd-floor stores for an idea of what a Bangkok socialite's sky-high apartment might look like.

Siam Paragon (Map pp716-17; ☎ 0 2610 8000; Th Phra Ram I; Skytrain Siam) The Paragon tries to live up to its name: the world's luxury brands have branches in what is touted as Southeast Asia's biggest mall – it is exhausting to explore beyond the main lobby. Locals don't come here to shop; they use the common spaces like an urban park. And often the attached courtyard hosts popular Thai bands, fashion shows and other excessively amplified events.

WARNING: THE GEM SCAM

Unless you really know your stones, Bangkok is no place to seek out the 'big score'. Never accept an invitation from a friendly stranger to visit a gem shop, as you will end up with an empty wallet and a nice collection of coloured glass.

Central World Plaza (Map pp716-17; cnr Th Ploenchit & Th Ratchadamri; Skytrain Chit Lom) Central World has been retrofitted into a lifestyle mall, just what Bangkok needed.

River City Shopping Centre (Map pp716-17; Th Charoen Krung; river ferry Tha Si Phraya) For those without the funds, this antiques mall is a de facto museum. Most antique stores occupy the 3rd and 4th floors, while a small print at **Old Maps & Prints** (☎ 0 2237 0077, ext 432; shop 432) might fit in a globetrotters backpack.

GETTING THERE & AWAY

Air

Bangkok is the air-travel hub for Thailand and mainland Southeast Asia. The **Suvarnabhumi International Airport** (off Map pp712-13; ☎ 0 2723 0000; www.airportsuvarnabhumi.com), 30km east of Bangkok, handles all international air traffic and most domestic routes. The airport name is pronounced '*sù·wan·ná·poom,*' and its airport code is BKK.

Don Muang airport (Map pp712-13; ☎ 0 2535 1111; www.airportthai.co.th), 25km north of central Bangkok, was retired from commercial service in 2006 but partially reopened to handle overflow from Suvarnabhumi. At the beginning of 2009, it was announced that *all* domestic routes would operate out of Suvarnabhumi but a final move-out date from Don Muang has not been set. In the meantime, verify which Bangkok airport you're using for domestic flights on the following airlines: Nok Air and One-Two-Go.

For a list of international and domestic airlines in Bangkok, see p706.

Bus

Buses departing from the government bus station are recommended over those departing from Th Khao San and other tourist areas, due to a lower incidence of theft and greater reliability. The Bangkok bus terminals (all with left-luggage facilities) are as follows:

Eastern bus terminal (Ekamai; Map pp712-13; ☎ 0 2391 2504; Soi 40/Soi Ekamai, Th Sukhumvit; Skytrain Ekamai) Serves southeastern cities such as Pattaya, Rayong, Chanthaburi and Trat.

Northern & Northeastern bus terminal (Mo Chit; Map pp712-13; ☎ northern routes 0 2936 2852, ext 311/442, northeastern routes 0 2936 2852, ext 611/448; Th Kamphaeng Phet) Serves all northern and northeastern cities, including Chiang Mai, Nakhon Ratchasima (Khorat), Ayuthaya, Lopburi and Aranya Prathet (near the Cambodian border). From the Mo Chit Skytrain station take bus 3.

GETTING INTO TOWN

Airport Express Bus

These buses (150B, 5am to midnight) run four routes between Suvarnabhumi airport and central Bangkok. The Airport Express counter is near entrance 8 on level 1. Routes stop at Skytrain stations, major hotels and other landmarks.

- **AE-1 to Silom** (by expressway) Via Pratunam, Central World Plaza, Ratchadamri Skytrain, Lumphini Park, Th Saladaeng, Patpong, finishing at Saladaeng Skytrain station.
- **AE-2 to Banglamphu** (by expressway) Via Democracy Monument, Royal Hotel, Th Phra Athit, Th Phra Sumen, Th Khao San.
- **AE-3 to Sukhumvit** Along Th Sukhumvit starting at Soi 52, Eastern bus terminal, Soi 34, 24, 20, 18, 10, 6, Central Chit Lom shopping centre, Central World Plaza.
- **AE-4 To Hualamphong train station** Via Victory Monument, Phayathai Skytrain, Siam Square, MBK, Chulalongkorn University.

Suvarnabhumi Airport Link (SARL)

A new rail line linking Suvarnabhumi airport to central Bangkok should be ready for public use by spring 2010. Trains will arrive in central Bangkok at the newly constructed City Air terminal (Map pp716–17) at Makkasan, near the corner of Th Phetburi Tat Mai and Soi Asoke. There will be interchange access to Skytrain and Metro.

Taxi

Public meter taxis (not the 'official airport taxis') queue outside of baggage claim. Depending on traffic, meter rates should cost 200B to 250B to Th Sukhumvit, 300B to 350B to Th Silom and 350B to 425B to Banglamphu; you must also pay a 50B airport surcharge to the driver and toll charges (usually about 60B). Try to get a 100B note (or the equivalent in smaller notes) before you leave the airport so you'll be able to pay the tolls.

Taxi lines tend to be long and touts will approach you with inflated flat fares (some meter taxis will try the same shenanigans). If you want to ditch the line, feel free to bargain hard for a rate closer to the meter fare. You can also dodge the line by catching a cab in front of the arrivals hall.

Southern bus terminal (Sai Tai Mai; Map pp712-13; ☎ 0 2435 1200; cnr Th Bromaratchachonanee & Th Phuttamonthon 1, Thonburi) Serves southern and western cities like Nakhon Pathom, Kanchanaburi, Hua Hin, Surat Thani, Phuket and Hat Yai. Accessible via bus 503 from Th Phra Athit in Banglamphu.

Train

Bangkok's central train station is **Hualamphong station** (Map pp716-17; ☎ 0 2220 4334, general information & advance booking 1690; Th Phra Ram IV). See p709 for information on train travel to/from Bangkok. To get to the station from Sukhumvit and Silom, take the Metro to the Hualamphong stop; from Banglamphu take bus No 53.

A minor commuter line operates across the river out of the **Bangkok Noi station** (Map pp712–13), with service to Nakhon Phanom and Kanchanaburi; though an exorbitant 'tourist fare' has made this option significantly less attractive. The station can be reached by river ferry to Tha Rot Fai. In Thonburi there is also the Mahachai Shortline, which departs from Wong Wian Yai station to Samut Sakhon and Samut Songkhram.

GETTING AROUND

Bangkok is nearly always choked with traffic, but it can be especially impossible to travel down Th Sukhumvit or Th Ratchadamoen during rush hour.

Boat

Chao Phraya River Express (☎ 0 2623 6001) is a scenic and efficient way of exploring the sights in Ko Ratanakosin, Banglamphu and parts of Silom. The boats ply a regular route along the Mae Nam Chao Phraya between Tha Wat Ratchasingkhon in the south to Nonthaburi in the north and overlaps with the Saphan Taksin Skytrain station at Tha Sathon.

The company operates express (indicated by an orange, yellow or yellow-and-green flag; 11B to 32B, morning and evening rush hour till 7pm), local (without a flag; 9B to 13B, morning and evening rush hour till 7pm) and tourist (larger boat; 19B, one-day pass 150B;,9.30am to 4pm) services. During rush hour pay close attention to the flags to avoid being hijacked beyond your stop.

Bangkok Metropolitan Authority operates a khlong taxi (tickets 7B to 20B, 6am to 7pm) route along the canals: Khlong Saen Saep (Banglamphu to Bang Kapi). The Khlong Saen Saep canal service is the most useful for a traffic-free trip between Siam Square (Tha Hua Chang) and Banglamphu (Tha Phan Fah). The canals are something akin to an open sewer so try not to get splashed.

Bus

The Bangkok bus service is frequent and frantic and is operated by **Bangkok Mass Transit Authority** (☎ 0 2246 4262; www.bmta.co.th). Fares for ordinary buses start at 7.50B and air-con buses at 12B. Most buses operate between 5am and 10pm or 11pm; a few run all night.

Metro

Bangkok's subway or underground (depending on your nationality) is operated by the **Metropolitan Rapid Transit Authority** (MRTA; www.mrta.co.th). Thais call it the Metro, which no doubt pleases the French. The line connects the train station of Bang Sue with Chatuchak (which has a Skytrain interchange at Mo Chit station), Sukhumvit (Skytrain interchange to Asoke), Lumphini Park and Silom (Skytrain interchange to Sala Daeng) and terminates at Hualamphong station. For visitors the Metro is most useful if travelling from Silom or Sukhumvit to the Hualamphong train station.

Trains operate from 5am to midnight and cost 15B to 39B, depending on distance. Planned extensions will eventually extend the system deeper into the suburbs.

Skytrain

The elevated **Bangkok Mass Transit System Skytrain** (BTS; ☎ 0 2617 7300; www.bts.co.th) is a slick ride through the modern parts of town. There are two lines: the Sukhumvit line and Silom line.

The Sukhumvit line starts at Mo Chit station, near Chatuchak Market and swings east along Th Sukhumvit. The Silom line runs from the National Stadium station, near Siam Square, through Th Silom area and a recent expansion has extended the line across the banks of the Mae Nam Chao Phraya to Thonburi's Wong Wian Yai. The two lines share an interchange at Siam station and there are interchanges with the Metro at the Sala Daeng Skytrain station (to Silom Metro) and Asoke Skytrain station (to Sukhumvit Metro).

GETTING TO CAMBODIA: ARANYA PRATHET TO POIPET

Anyone undertaking the Angkor pilgrimage will want to cross over the border at Aranya Prathet–Poipet. Most people start this epic journey from Bangkok and finish up in Siem Reap, Cambodia.

Air-con buses leave from Bangkok's Northern and Northeastern (Mo Chit) bus terminal to Aranya Prathet (215B, four hours, hourly). There's also a direct bus from Bangkok's Suvarnabhumi airport to the border (190B, four hours). Resist the urge to book this trip through guest houses and travel agencies as the bus scams to Angkor are numerous, annoying and time-consuming.

Two daily trains depart Bangkok's Hualamphong station for Aranya Prathet (3rd-class only, 48B, six hours, 5.55am & 1.05pm).

From Aranya Prathet hire a túk-túk to the border (open 7am to 8pm). Poipet's casinos are a popular weekend outing for Thais and the immigration lines can be quite long; arrive early to avoid delays. Cambodia visas are available on arrival and a free shuttle bus outside the immigration office delivers passengers to Poipet's taxi stand, where onward transport can be arranged. The road from Poipet to Siem Reap has been improved greatly and travel time is down to a reasonable two hours.

If you get delayed in Aranya Prathet, there are a string of guest houses along the road to the border that are happy to have guests.

See p109 for information on crossing from Cambodia into Thailand.

Trains run frequently from 6am to midnight along the two lines and fares vary from 10B to 40B. Ticket machines only accept coins (get change from the ticket windows). There is a variety of stored-value tickets for one-day and multiday unlimited trips; inquire at the agent booth. Trains are labelled with their terminal destinations and there are in-station maps to help you figure out which direction you're going.

Taxi

Most taxis in Bangkok are meter taxis, though some drivers 'forget' to use their meters or prefer to quote a flat (and grossly inflated) fare to tourists. Many of the taxis that park near tourist haunts operate under an informal no-meter policy. We suggest skipping these cabs and instead flagging down a roving cab on one of the main streets who will happily use the meter. Unless it is a rainy rush hour, there is usually no problem finding an available cab. Fares should generally run from 60B to 100B.

In most large cities, the taxi drivers are seasoned navigators familiar with every nook and cranny, but this is not the case in Bangkok where many an upcountry farmer moonlights while his fields rest. To ensure that you'll be able to return home, grab your hotel's business card, which will have directions in Thai.

Motorcycle taxis will camp out at the mouth of a *soi* to shuttle people from the main road to their destinations done the lane. *Soi* trips cost 10B; don't ask, just pay them as you disembark

Túk-Túk

The Thai version of a go-kart is Bangkok's most iconic vehicle and its most enduring hassle. They chatter like a chainsaw, take corners at an angle and are relentless in drumming up business. There are so many túk-túk scams that you really need at least a one-month tenure in the city to know how much your trip should cost before bargaining for a ride and when a túk-túk is handier and cheaper than a cab. If you climb aboard just for the fun of it, you might end up being taken for a ride, literally. Beware of túk-túk drivers who offer to take you on a sightseeing tour for 10B or 20B – it's a touting scheme designed to pressure you into purchasing overpriced goods. You must fix fares in advance for all túk-túk rides.

AROUND BANGKOK

If you're tied to Bangkok for several days but feel the urge for some fresh air, take a day trip to some of the nearby attractions.

NAKHON PATHOM

Not a lot goes on in sleepy Nakhon Pathom, 64km west of Bangkok, and that is precisely its draw. It's an easy day trip from the capital but is as provincial as the furthest flung hamlet with wide-eyed schoolchildren tickled by the sight of a foreigner and easy-going food stalls that serve as informal community centres.

Though thoroughly unpretentious, Nakhon Pathom ranks in the Thai history books as the country's oldest city. The only clue to its longevity is the **Phra Pathom Chedi** that sits in the centre of town and attracts a steady crowd of wat-tripping Thais. The *chedi* was originally erected in the early 6th century by the Theravada Buddhists of Dvaravati kingdom, but a bell-shaped structure was built over the original in the early 11th century by the Khmer king Suryavarman I of Angkor. This alteration created the world's tallest Buddhist monument, 127m high. In November, there's the **Phra Pathom Chedi Fair**, which packs in everyone from fruit vendors to fortune-tellers.

Air-con buses leave from Bangkok's Southern bus terminal to Nakhon Pathom (39B, one hour, frequent). You can also catch a shared minivan from Bangkok's Victory Monument to Nakhon Pathom (60B, frequently). To return to Bangkok, catch one of the idling buses from Th Phayaphan on the canal side of the road, a block from the train station. Bus 78 to Damnoen Saduak leaves from the same stop.

Nakhon Pathom is connected to Bangkok by two train lines: Hualamphong (3rd/2nd/1st class 14/31/60B, one hour) and Bangkok Noi in Thonburi, but the latter charges a flat 'tourist' fare that makes it an uncompetitive option.

SAMUT PRAKAN'S ANCIENT CITY

The industrial town Samut Prakan is an unlikely place for an open-air architectural museum that replicates Thailand's famous monuments and preserves old building techniques. Located 12km south of Samut Prakan (also known as Pak Nam), the **Ancient**

City (Meuang Boran; ☎ 0 2709 1644; www.ancientcity.com; 296/1 Th Sukhumvit; adult/child 300/150B; ⌚ 8am-5pm) is home to more than 100 scaled-down replicas of Thailand's most famous historic sites, including some that no longer exist. For students of Thai architecture or even for those who want an introduction to the subject, it is definitely worth the trip. It is also a good place for leisurely bicycle rides (available for rent from the ticket office), as it's rarely crowded.

From Bangkok take air-con bus No 511 from the eastern side of Th Sukhumvit to Samut Prakan's bus station. From there board a No 36 minibus (25B), which will pass the entrance of the Ancient City.

SAMUT SONGKHRAM

The riverine character of central Thailand is still alive and well in the quaint canalside villages in Samut Songkhram province, less than 100km from Bangkok. City slickers often make the weekend journey to the **Amphawa Floating Market** (⌚ 4-9pm Fri-Sun) to explore the canals and enjoy the slow pace of life outside of the big city. Though this isn't the closest or the most photographed floating market in Thailand, it is an adventure to reach, especially if you take the **Mahachai short-line train** from Bangkok's Wong Wian Yai station now accessible via Skytrain. Hourly trains depart for Samut Sakhon (12B), from where you'll transfer to another nearby line to Samut Songkhram; in order to catch the connecting train you'll need to start by 8.30am. The ride is a scenic trip through the back lots of Bangkok's urban grid and the marshy landscape along the Gulf of Thailand. At Samut Sakhon, work your way through the fresh market to the river pier and across by ferry to Ban Laem (3B), where you'll find the train station for the second leg of the train journey. From the sleepy station of Tha Chalong trains depart for Samut Songkhram (10B, 1.30pm and 4.40pm). Arriving at yet another busy market, you can take a săwngthăew (9B) for the 10-minute ride to Amphawa. Since the floating market is an evening affair, many Thai tourists overnight in the village at one of the simple homestays. Contact **Baan Song Thai Plai Pong Pang** (☎ 0 3475 7333) for lodging and information about visiting the floating market or touring the canals. Amphawa is also accessible by bus from Bangkok's Southern bus terminal (72B, hourly) in Thonburi.

CENTRAL THAILAND

Thailand's heartland, the central region is a fertile river plain that birthed the country's history-shaping kingdoms of Ayuthaya and Sukhothai and crafted the culture and language that defines the mainstream Thai identity. The nationally revered river of the Mae Nam Chao Phraya is the lifeblood of the region and connects the country's interior with the Gulf of Thailand. Geographically, central Thailand is a necessary thoroughfare for any Chiang Mai–bound traveller, but culturally it is a worthwhile stop.

KANCHANABURI

pop 63,100

If you don't have time for Chiang Mai and its surrounding mountain scenery, head to Kanchanaburi, west of Bangkok, nestled in between rugged limestone peaks and the pretty Mae Nam Khwae (Kwai River). The town has a healthy soft adventure scene – elephant rides and bamboo rafting – and is a peaceful place to relax if Bangkok made you dizzy. It also has an unlikely claim on WWII history as the site of a Japanese-operated WWII prisoner-of-war camp made famous by the book and movie *The Bridge Over the River Kwai*. Today visitors come to pay their respects to fallen Allied soldiers or to learn more about this chapter of the war.

Information

Several major Thai banks can be found along Th Saengchuto near the market and bus terminal. Internet cafes can be found along Th Mae Nam Khwae. Check out www.kanchanaburi-info.com for general information.

Post office (Th Saengchuto)

TAT office (☎ 0 3451 1200; Th Saengchuto; ⌚ 8.30am-4.30pm) Near the bus terminal, it provides information on trips beyond Kanchanaburi.

Thanakarn Hospital (☎ 0 3462 2366) Best-equipped place for foreigners.

Tourist police (☎ 0 3451 2668; Th Saengchuto)

Sights

THAILAND-BURMA RAILWAY CENTRE

So you know that there was a bridge, a war and a catchy movie song but that's all you know about Kanchanaburi's minor role in WWII. Before you head out to see the Kwai River Bridge, get a little history at this **museum** (☎ 0 3451 0067; www.tbrconline.com; 73 Th Chaokanen; adult/child 60/30B; ⌚ 9am-5pm). Professional exhibits outline

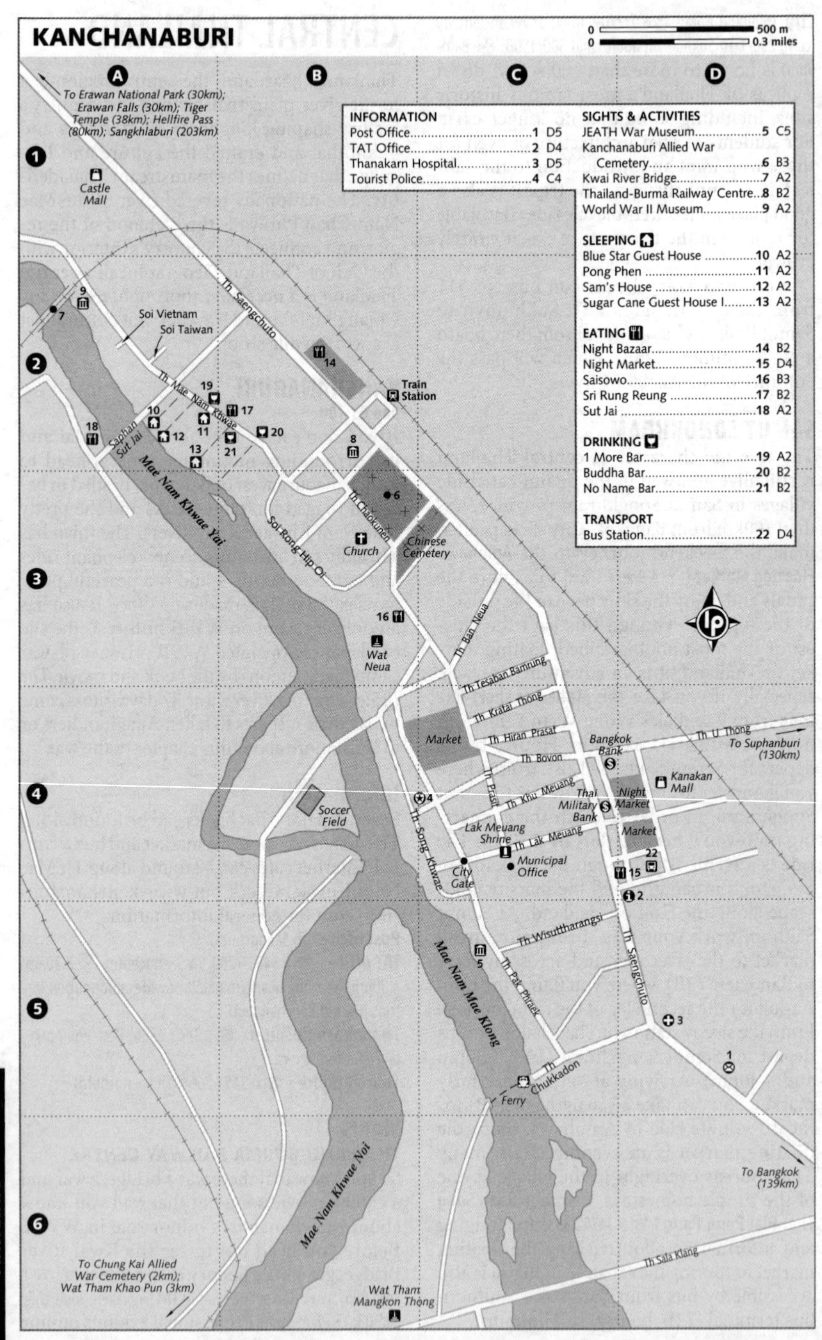
KANCHANABURI
0 500 m
0 0.3 miles
INFORMATION
Post Office 1 D5
TAT Office 2 D4
Thanakarn Hospital 3 D5
Tourist Police 4 C4
SIGHTS & ACTIVITIES
JEATH War Museum 5 C5
Kanchanaburi Allied War Cemetery 6 B3
Kwai River Bridge 7 A2
Thailand-Burma Railway Centre 8 B2
World War II Museum 9 A2
SLEEPING
Blue Star Guest House 10 A2
Pong Phen 11 A2
Sam's House 12 A2
Sugar Cane Guest House I 13 A2
EATING
Night Bazaar 14 B2
Night Market 15 D4
Saisowo 16 B3
Sri Rung Reung 17 B2
Sut Jai 18 A2
DRINKING
1 More Bar 19 A2
Buddha Bar 20 B2
No Name Bar 21 B2
TRANSPORT
Bus Station 22 D4
To Erawan National Park (30km); Erawan Falls (30km); Tiger Temple (38km); Hellfire Pass (80km); Sangkhlaburi (203km)
Castle Mall
Soi Vietnam
Soi Taiwan
Th Saengchuto
Th Mae Nam Khwae
Saphan Sut Jai
Mae Nam Khwae Yai
Train Station
Th Chaokunen
Soi Rong Hip Oi
Church
Chinese Cemetery
Wat Neua
Th Ban Neua
Th Tesaban Bamrung
Th Kratai Thong
Th Hiran Prasat
Th Bovon
Th U Thong
To Suphanburi (130km)
Market
Bangkok Bank
Kanakan Mall
Th Prasit
Th Khu Meuang
Thai Military Bank
Night Market
Market
Soccer Field
Th Song Khwae
Lak Meuang Shrine
Th Lak Meuang
Municipal Office
City Gate
Th Wisuttharangsi
Mae Nam Mae Klong
Th Pak Phraek
Th Saengchuto
Th Chukkadon
Ferry
To Bangkok (139km)
Mae Nam Khwae Noi
Th Sala Klang
To Chung Kai Allied War Cemetery (2km); Wat Tham Khao Pun (3km)
Wat Tham Mangkon Thong
THAILAND

Japan's military endeavours in Southeast Asia during WWII and its plan to connect Yangon (in Burma) with Bangkok via rail for transport of military supplies.

KANCHANABURI ALLIED WAR CEMETERY

Across the street from the Thailand-Burma Railway Centre, this **war cemetery** (Th Saengchuto; admission free; 7am-6pm) is a touching gift from the Thai people to remember the POWs, mainly from Britain and Holland, who died on their soil.

KWAI RIVER BRIDGE (DEATH RAILWAY BRIDGE)

This ordinary-looking bridge has become a tourist attraction not because of its remarkable construction or appearance but because it is a visible piece of an intangible part of history. A bit of imagination and some historical context will greatly augment a visit.

Starting in 1942 during the Japanese occupation of Thailand, captured Allied soldiers and Burmese and Malay conscripts were transported to the jungles of Kanchanaburi to build 415km of rail – known today as the Death Railway because of the many lives (more than 100,000 men) lost. The railway was intended to link Thailand and Burma (Myanmar) in order to secure an alternative supply route for future Japanese conquests in Southeast Asia. The Japanese completed the rail line in Thailand in an astonishing 16 months considering the rough terrain and rudimentary equipment. The rails were joined 37km south of Three Pagodas Pass and in use for 20 months before Allied planes destroyed the bridge in 1945. Bomb damage on the now-reconstructed span is still apparent on the pylons closest to the riverbank. Hellfire Pass (Konyu Cutting), one of the most demanding construction points, can be seen today at the Hellfire Pass Memorial (p737).

During the first week of December there's a sound-and-light show put on at the bridge. The town gets a lot of tourists during this week, so book early.

The bridge is roughly 3km from the town centre and is best reached via rented bicycle. There are also three daily departures across the bridge on the Kanchanaburi–Nam Tok train; see Getting There & Away (p736) for information about riding this historic route.

WORLD WAR II MUSEUM

Just south of the bridge is a privately owned **museum** (Th Mae Nam Khwae; admission 40B; 8am-6.30pm), sometimes also called the JEATH War Museum to capitalise on the popularity of another museum by the same name in town. The collection might be the oddest assortment of memorabilia under one roof, but the building does afford picture-postcard views of the bridge.

JEATH WAR MUSEUM

This outdoor **museum** (Th Wisuttharangsi; admission 30B; 8.30am-6pm) is hosted by Wat Chaichumphon (Wat Tai) and is built to resemble the simple bamboo shelters where the POWs were kept. More a photo gallery than museum, it isn't very informative, but it is heartfelt, especially the fading pictures of surviving POWs who returned to Thailand for a memorial service.

CHUNG KAI ALLIED WAR CEMETERY

Chung Kai was the site of a major prisoner camp during WWII, and Allied prisoners built their own hospital and church close to here. Today relatively few people come to see this remote cemetery, which is the final resting place of 1700 soldiers. Most graves have short, touching epitaphs for the Dutch, British, French and Australian soldiers.

The cemetery is 4km south of central Kanchanaburi across the Mae Nam Khwae Noi and can be easily reached by bicycle or motorcycle.

WAT THAM KHAO PUN

Continue past the Chung Kai Allied War Cemetery and go over a railway crossing to find this **temple** (20B; 6am-6.30pm), which has a collection of nine different caves. The first and biggest cave is home to a reclining Buddha. The others have some particularly unusual features, including a fig tree's roots that hang all the way down into the cave, a crystallised column and a rock formation said to resemble a mermaid from the literature of Thai poet Sunthorn Phu. Cave shrines are a common feature of Thai Buddhism because of their mystical connection to nature and as meditation aids.

Sleeping

The most atmospheric places to stay are built along the river. Everything is conducive to a day of chilling out until floating karaoke bars and discos fire up. The noise polluters are supposed to be in bed by 10pm but Thai time, in this case, runs behind.

Blue Star Guest House (☎ 0 3451 2161; 241 Th Mae Nam Khwae; r 150-650B;) Set in leafy surroundings, it's one laid-back pad with great staff and cheap fan rooms.

Pong Phen (☎ 0 3451 2981; www.pongphen.com; Th Mae Nam Khwae; r 150-900B;) If you're quick you can snap up one of the few 150B rooms. All rooms are centred around the swimming pool rather than the river.

Sugar Cane Guest House I (☎ 0 3462 4520; 22 Soi Pakistan, Th Mae Nam Khwae; r 250-550B;) Most rooms come with great river views, although some could do with a clean. There is a sister guest house closer to the bridge.

Sam's House (☎ 0 3451 5956; www.samsguesthouse.com; Th Mae Nam Khwae; d 450-600B;) Bright and airy from reception to terrace, rooms are basic but come with fine views of the lotus-covered water. Fan rooms are particularly good value.

Eating

Saisowo (no roman-script sign; Th Chaokunen; dishes 20-30B; 8am-4pm) This long-running noodle emporium has some of the finest *kŭaytĭaw mŭu* (pork noodles) and fish balls for miles around.

Sri Rung Reung (Th Mae Nam Khwae; dishes 40-120B) Has the largest vegetarian menu in town. The food is reasonably authentic but you'd best ask if you want some kick to your *sôm-tam* (papaya salad).

Sut Jai (dishes 60-120B) Cross the Sut Jai Bridge to find this relaxed riverfront restaurant, which serves a good selection of full-flavour Thai dishes.

The cheap and cheerful **night market** (Th Saengchuto) sets up near the bus station and prepares some of the best *hăwy thâwt* (fried mussels in an egg batter) in town. There's also a small **night bazaar** (Th Saengchuto; closed Wed) near the train station that sells mainly clothes and a few takeaway meals.

Drinking

The main nightlife in town is centred around Th Mae Nam Khwae, where there are several expat bars. Here you'll find 1 More Bar, a cosy lounge bar where a Nintendo Wii console is in constant demand. No Name Bar sports the slogan: 'Get shitfaced on a shoestring.' There's a good selection of snacks and vegie food to wash down the beers. With its dreadlocked-manager, reggae soundtrack and scrawls on the wall, every self-respecting backpacker finds refuge in the Buddha Bar.

Getting There & Away

Kanchanaburi's **bus station** (Th Saengchuto) is near Th Lak Meuang and the TAT office. The following destinations are served: Bangkok's Southern bus terminal (112B, three hours, every 20 minutes until 8pm), Nakhon Pathom (50B, two hours, frequent), Sangkhlaburi (174B to 273B, five hours, frequent) and Suphanburi (50B, 2½ hours, frequent). Connect through Suphanburi if you're headed to Ayuthaya. If you're going south, head to Ratchaburi (50B, 2½ hours) with connections to Hua Hin or Phetchaburi.

Kanchanaburi's **train station** (Th Saengchuto) is 500m from the river, near the guest-house area. This train line goes to Bangkok Noi station in Thonburi, which is across the river from Bangkok. The northwestern terminus is at Nam Tok and includes a portion of the historic Death Railway. The State Railway of Thailand (SRT) promotes the line as a tourist attraction and charges a flat 100B fare for any one-way journey regardless of distance. The most historic part of rail line begins north of Kanchanaburi as the train crosses the Death Railway Bridge and terminates at Nam Tok station. Ordinary trains leave Thonburi's Bangkok Noi station at 7.44am and 1.55pm for Kanchanaburi. Trains do the return trip leaving Kanchanaburi at 7.19am and 2.44pm. The journey takes three hours.

Trains along the historic section of the rail line leave Kanchanaburi heading north to Nam Tok at 5.57am, 10.50am and 4.19pm. Return trains depart from Nam Tok at 5.20am, 12.50pm and 3.15pm. The trip takes about two hours. From Nam Tok train station it's possible to walk to Sai Yok Noi waterfall, or you can flag down one of the frequent Sangkhlaburi–Kanchanaburi buses.

The SRT runs a daily **tourist train** (☎ 0 3451 1285) from Kanchanaburi to Nam Tok (one way 300B). This is the same train that carries the 100B passengers, but if you want to pay the extra you'll be rewarded with a certificate and a snack.

Getting Around

Săamláw within the city cost 50B a trip. Regular săwngthăew ply Th Saengchuto for

10B, but be careful you don't accidentally 'charter' one. There are plenty of places hiring motorbikes along Th Mae Nam Khwae. The going rate is 150B to 250B per day and it's a good way of getting to the rather scattered attractions around Kanchanaburi. Bicycles can be hired from most guest houses for around 50B a day.

AROUND KANCHANABURI

Head out of town to explore Kanchanaburi's forests and rivers. Most of the guest houses will book minivan tours that do a little bit of everything in a hurry.

Erawan National Park (☎ 0 3457 4222; admission 200B; ⏰ 8am-4pm) is the home of the seven-tiered **Erawan Falls**, which makes for a refreshing day swimming in pools and climbing around the trails. Go early as this is a popular tour spot. Buses from Kanchanaburi stop at the entrance to the falls (55B, 1½ hours, hourly from 8am to 5.20pm) The last bus back to Kanchanaburi leaves at 4pm.

Carved out of unforgiving mountain terrain, the section of the Death Railway called **Hellfire Pass** (suggested donation 30-100B; ⏰ 9am-4pm) was so named for the unearthly apparitions cast by the nightly fires of the labouring POWs. Today a 4km-long trail follows the old route with some remnants of the rail line still intact. Located near the Km 66 marker on the Sai Yok–Thong Pha Phum road, Hellfire Pass can be reached by a Sangkhlaburi-bound or Thong Pha Phum–bound bus (27B, 1½ hours, last bus back at 4pm); use the Thai script for 'Hellfire Pass' that is printed on the TAT-distributed map to inform the attendant of your destination.

Kanchanaburi's most expensive and controversial attraction is the **Tiger Temple** (Wat Luang Ta Bua Yanna Sampanno; ☎ 0 3453 1557; admission 500B; ⏰ noon-3.30pm), which according to the temple's abbot cares for orphaned tigers as a part of its Buddhist mission to provide refuge to all living creatures. To subsidise this expensive work the temple allows visitors to pose for pictures with the big cats during their daily walks in an enclosed canyon. Such an up-close experience is justifiably amazing but critics maintain that the temple is operating an illegal breeding program and selling the cats into the wildlife trade. The evidence is not conclusive but it has cultivated a fairly outspoken protest movement. We suggest that potential visitors research this issue and decide if it is a reputable attraction on their own. The temple is 38km from Kanchanaburi on Hwy 323 and most visitors arrive via an afternoon tour.

SANGKHLABURI & AROUND

The western frontier of Thailand bumps up against a dramatic landscape of limestone mountains sheltering an ethnically diverse population that has spilled over from Myanmar's ongoing internal conflicts. Few tourists know the scenic but small town of Sangkhlaburi, but for international aid workers this is one of various remote outposts for refugee relief work. Many displaced people, whether they be Mon, Karen or Burmese, arrive in Thailand with few belongings and fewer rights. The town itself consists of just a few paved roads overlooking the enormous Kheuan Khao Laem (Khao Laem Dam). Guest houses in town can arrange outdoor outings upon request.

Further on down the road is the actual border crossing, known as **Three Pagodas Pass**. At the time of writing the border had been closed to foreigners, but should this change, foreigners can usually obtain a day pass into the neighbouring Myanmarese market; border formalities can be arranged at the checkpoint.

Sleeping & Eating

Burmese Inn (☎ 0 3459 5146; www.sangkhlaburi.com; 52/3 Mu 3; r 120-800B; ❄) The one true budget place in town. The single, flimsy, room could have been imported straight from Th Khao San in Bangkok.

P Guest House (☎ 0 3459 5061; www.pguesthouse.com; 8/1 Mu 1; r 250-900B; ❄) With English-speaking staff and rooms with lake views, P Guest House is another favourite. Fan rooms are plain and have shared bathrooms.

Travellers tend to eat at the main guest houses, which all have restaurants with great views of the waterfront. The day market is across from the bus stop and is good for sampling Mon-style curries (look for the large metal pots). **Baan Unrak Bakery** (snacks 25-90B) is a meat-less café with excellent pastries and Thai dishes and is run by a local charitable organisation.

Getting There & Away

Ordinary bus 8203 trundles between Kanchanaburi and Sangkhlaburi (130B, five hours, four daily departures). There's also an air-con bus (195B, four hours, four daily departures) that continues to Bangkok (259B to 333B). A minivan service to Kanchanaburi (180B, three daily departures) leaves Sangkhlaburi from near the market.

From Sangkhlaburi, there are hourly sǎwngthǎew (40B, 40 minutes, frequent) to Three Pagodas Pass.

AYUTHAYA

pop 137,553

The fabled city, the fallen city: Ayuthaya crowned the pinnacle of ancient Thai history and defined the country's ascendance to regional domination. It was built at the confluence of three rivers (Mae Nam Lopburi, Chao Phraya and Pa Sak) on a unique island of land and was auspiciously named after the home of Rama in the Indian epic Ramayana.

The rivers formed both a natural barrier to invasion and an invitation to trade allowing the city state to flourish into a full-fledged nation from 1350 to 1767. Though the Thai kings outmanoeuvred Western power plays, it was the repeated attempts by the Burmese that eventually sacked the city and ended Ayuthaya's reign. After two years of war the capital fell in 1767; the Burmese looted the city and the Thais re-established their power centre near present-day Bangkok.

Today ruins of the old city have resisted gravity and looters while a modern city has sprung up around them. Life revolves around the river, which acts as transport, bath and kitchen sink for its residents.

The holiday of **Loi Krathong**, when tiny votive boats are floated on rivers as a tribute to the River Goddess, is celebrated with great fanfare in Ayuthaya.

Information

ATMs are abundant throughout Ayuthaya, especially along Th Naresuan near Amporn Shopping Centre. The internet shops on and around Soi 1, Th Naresuan, offer the cheapest deals.

Main post office (Th U Thong)

Nakorn Sri Ayutthaya Hospital (☎ 1669, 0 3532 2555; cnr Th U Thong & Th Si Sanphet)

TAT office (☎ 0 3524 6076; 108/22 Th Si Sanphet; 🕑 8.30am-4.30pm) Distributes tourist information and maps; also has an interactive historical display.

Tourist police (☎ 0 3524 1446, emergency 1155; Th Si Sanphet)

Sights

A Unesco World Heritage Site, Ayuthaya's historic temples are scattered throughout the city and along the encircling rivers. The ruins are divided into two geographical areas: ruins 'on the island', in the central part of town between Th Chee Kun and the western end of Th U Thong, which are best visited by bicycle; and those 'off the island' on the other side of the river, which are best visited on an evening boat tour or by bicycle. Most temple ruins are open from 8am to 4pm; the more famous sites charge an entrance fee. A one-day pass for most sites on the island is available for 220B and can be bought at the museums or ruins.

ON THE ISLAND

The most distinctive example of Ayuthaya architecture is **Wat Phra Si Sanphet** (admission 50B) thanks to its three bell-shaped *chedi* that taper off into descending rings. This site served as the royal palace from the city's founding until the mid-15th century, when it was converted into a temple. Although the grounds are now well tended, these efforts cannot hide the ravages of war and time. The surrounding buildings are worn through to their orange bricks, leaning to one side as gravity takes its toll. The complex once contained a 16m-high standing Buddha covered with 250kg of gold, which was melted down by the Burmese conquerors.

The adjacent **Wihaan Phra Mongkhon Bophit** houses a huge bronze seated Buddha, the largest in Thailand.

Wat Phra Mahathat (admission 50B) has one of the first Khmer-style *praang* built in the capital. One of the most iconic images in Ayuthaya is the Buddha head engulfed by tentacle-like tree roots.

Getting a handle on the religious and historical importance of the temples is difficult to do without some preliminary tutoring. **Ayuthaya Historical Study Centre** (☎ 0 3524 5124; Th Rotchana; adult/student 100/50B; 🕑 9am-4.30pm Mon-Fri, to 5pm Sat & Sun) has informative, professional displays about the ancient city. Also purchase the *Ayuthaya* pamphlet (15B) for sale at Wat Phra Si Sanphet's admission kiosk.

There are also two national museums in town. The building that houses the **Chantharakasem National Museum** (Th U Thong; admission 100B; 🕑 9am-4pm Wed-Sun) is a museum in itself. The less charming but larger **Chao**

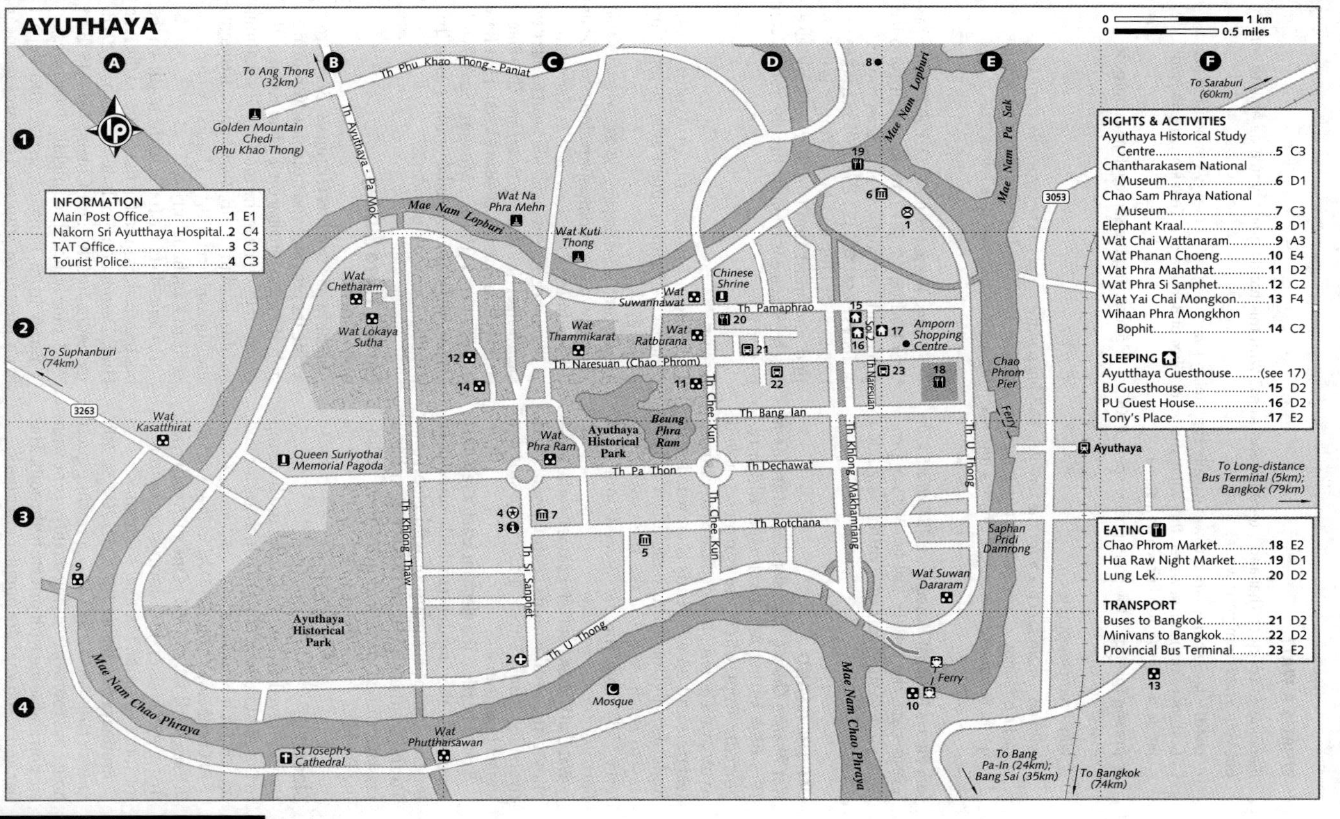
AYUTHAYA
0 1 km
0 0.5 miles
INFORMATION
Main Post Office.....1 E1
Nakorn Sri Ayutthaya Hospital..2 C4
TAT Office.....3 C3
Tourist Police.....4 C3
SIGHTS & ACTIVITIES
Ayutthaya Historical Study Centre.....5 C3
Chantharakasem National Museum.....6 D1
Chao Sam Phraya National Museum.....7 C3
Elephant Kraal.....8 D1
Wat Chai Wattanaram.....9 A3
Wat Phanan Choeng.....10 E4
Wat Phra Mahathat.....11 D2
Wat Phra Si Sanphet.....12 C2
Wat Yai Chai Mongkon.....13 F4
Wihaan Phra Mongkhon Bophit.....14 C2
SLEEPING
Ayutthaya Guesthouse.....(see 17)
BJ Guesthouse.....15 D2
PU Guest House.....16 D2
Tony's Place.....17 E2
EATING
Chao Phrom Market.....18 E2
Hua Raw Night Market.....19 D1
Lung Lek.....20 D2
TRANSPORT
Buses to Bangkok.....21 D2
Minivans to Bangkok.....22 D2
Provincial Bus Terminal.....23 E2
To Ang Thong (32km)
Th Phu Khao Thong - Paniat
Th Ayuthaya - Pa Mok
Golden Mountain Chedi (Phu Khao Thong)
To Saraburi (60km)
Mae Nam Lopburi
Mae Nam Pa Sak
Mae Nam Chao Phraya
Wat Na Phra Mehn
Wat Kuti Thong
Chinese Shrine
Wat Suwannawat
Th Pamaphrao
Soi 2
Amporn Shopping Centre
Wat Chetharam
Wat Lokaya Sutha
Wat Thammikarat
Wat Ratburana
Th Naresuan (Chao Phrom)
Th Naresuan
Chao Phrom Pier
Ferry
To Suphanburi (74km)
3263
3053
Wat Kasatthirat
Th Bang Ian
Th Chee Kun
Beung Phra Ram
Ayuthaya Historical Park
Wat Phra Ram
Queen Suriyothai Memorial Pagoda
Th Pa Thon
Th Dechawat
Th Khlong Makhamriang
Th U Thong
Ayuthaya
To Long-distance Bus Terminal (5km); Bangkok (79km)
Th Khlong Thaw
Th Si Sanphet
Th Rotchana
Saphan Pridi Damrong
Wat Suwan Dararam
Mosque
St Joseph's Cathedral
Wat Phutthaisawan
To Bang Pa-In (24km); Bang Sai (35km)
To Bangkok (74km)
THAILAND

WHAT'S A WAT?

Planning to conquer Thailand's temples and ruins? With this handy guide, you'll be able to sort out your wats from your what's that:

- **chedi** – large bell-shaped tower usually containing five structural elements symbolising (from bottom to top) earth, water, fire, wind and void; relics of Buddha or a Thai king are housed inside the *chedi;* also known as a stupa.
- **praang (prang)** – towering phallic spire of Khmer origin serving the same religious purpose as a *chedi.*
- **wat** – temple complex.
- **wíhaan** – main sanctuary for the temple's Buddha sculpture and where laypeople come to make offerings; classic architecture typically has a three-tiered roofline representing the triple gems: Buddha (the teacher), Dharma (the teaching) and Brotherhood (the followers).

Sam Phraya National Museum (cnr Th Rotchana & Th Si Sanphet; admission 150B; 9am-4pm Wed-Sun) protects the few survivors of Ayuthaya's golden period.

OFF THE ISLAND

Wat Phanan Choeng (admission 20B) contains a 19m-high sitting Buddha image, which reportedly wept when the Burmese sacked Ayuthaya. The temple is dedicated to Chinese seafarers and on weekends is crowded with Buddhist pilgrims from Bangkok. The best way to get here is to take the cross-river ferry (5B) from the pier near Phom Phet Fortress.

Wat Chai Wattanaram (admission 50B) is the most photogenic of all with its central *praang* and riverside setting. This is a favourite stop for sunset boat tours.

To the north is the **elephant kraal**, a restored version of the wooden stockade once used for the annual roundup of wild elephants. To the southeast, **Wat Yai Chai Mongkon** has a massive ruined *chedi* and a 7m-long reclining Buddha.

Sleeping

Budget travellers can walk from the bus stop to the guest houses, most of which are located on Soi 2, Th Naresuan.

BJ Guesthouse (0 3525 1526; Soi Thaw Kaw Saw, Th Naresuan; s/d 100/160B;) One of Ayuthaya's first guest houses, this dorm-style option is for those who don't hanker for luxury.

Ayutthaya Guesthouse (0 3523 2658; Soi 2, Th Naresuan; r 160-400B;) This sprawling guest house has rooms of varying quality, some with air-con and some with private bathroom. The bar and restaurant are popular after dark.

PU Guest House (0 3525 1213; 20/1 Soi Thaw Kaw Saw; r 180-550B;) Low-key, well-rounded place with comfortable and clean rooms.

Tony's Place (0 3525 2578; 12/18 Soi 2, Th Naresuan; r 200-500B;) Big and busy, Tony's is easy to find and most don't bother looking elsewhere. Service is friendly but the rooms can be noisy.

Eating

The range of restaurants in Ayuthaya can come as a disappointment after living it up in Bangkok.

Lung Lek (Th Chee Kun; dishes 30-40B; 8.30am-4pm) Slurp down the noodle soup alongside locals while admiring the view of Wat Ratburana.

For a slice of provincial life head to **Hua Raw Night Market** (Th U Thong; dinner) and **Chao Phrom Market** (Th Naresuan; breakfast & lunch). Hua Raw showcases Ayuthaya's Muslim legacy with several roti stalls and halal vendors as well as popular Thai wok-wonders.

Getting There & Away

BUS

Ayuthaya has two bus terminals. Buses from within the province and from nearby provinces stop at the **bus terminal** on Th Naresuan in the centre of town near the market. Destinations include Lopburi (40B, two hours, frequent) and Suphanburi (60B, two hours), which connects to Kanchanaburi.

For long-distance travel to the north, go the bus terminal, 5km east of the centre on the Asia Hwy. Destinations include Sukhothai (291B, six hours, hourly) and Chiang Mai (463B to 596B, nine hours, three nightly departures).

Buses from Bangkok arrive and depart from their own stop on Th Naresuan near the provincial terminal. Frequent buses run to Bangkok's Don Muang airport (56B, 1½ hours) and Bangkok's Northern and Northeastern (Mo Chit) bus terminal (59B, two hours). Minivans to Bangkok's Victory Monument (65B, two hours) leave from the same general area on Th Naresuan.

TRAIN

Ayuthaya's train station is on the eastern banks of the Mae Nam Pa Sak and is an easy walk from the centre city via a short ferry ride (5B).

Trains to Ayuthaya leave Bangkok's Hualamphong station (ordinary 15B to 20B, 1½ hours) almost hourly between 6am and 10pm, usually stopping at Don Muang airport. From Ayuthaya, the train continues north to Chiang Mai (ordinary/rapid/express 586/856/1198B, six departures a day) or northeast to Pak Chong (ordinary/rapid/express 23/73/130B, frequent), the nearest station to Khao Yai National Park. If heading to Bangkok, save time by disembarking at Bangkok's Bang Sue station and taking the nearby subway to the city centre.

Getting Around

Bikes can be rented at most guest houses (50B). Túk-túk can be hired for the day to tour the sites (200B per hour); a trip within the city should be about 30B or 40B to the train station.

LOPBURI

pop 57,600

This small, low-key town is a delightful respite from the rigours of the pancake trail. No aggressive túk-túk drivers, no grumpy guesthouse staff and few foreigners making you feel that you flew a long way to be with familiar faces. Lopburi is an ancient town with plenty of old ruins to prove its former occupation by almost every Southeast Asian kingdom: Dvaravati, Angkor and Ayuthaya. The old city is brought to life by ordinary Thai life: noodle stands, motorcycle stores and, most importantly, a gang of monkeys. The city celebrates its monkey invasion with an annual festival during the last week of November.

Information

Hospital (☎ 0 3662 1537; Th Ramdecho)
Post office (Th Phra Narai Maharat)
TAT office (☎ 0 3642 2768; Th Phraya Kamjat; 8.30am-4.30pm)

Sights

Lopburi's old ruins are easy to walk to from the town centre and a 150B day pass allows entry to all sights. **Phra Narai Ratchaniwet** (Th Sorasak; admission 150B; museum 8.30am-4pm, grounds 7am-5.30pm) is a good place to begin a tour of Lopburi. Built between 1665 and 1677, this former royal palace was designed by French and Khmer architects, creating an unusual blend of styles. Inside the grounds is the **Lopburi National Museum**, which contains an excellent collection of Lopburi period sculpture, as well as an assortment of Khmer, Dvaravati, U Thong and Ayuthaya art, plus traditional farm implements.

The most distinctive of Lopburi's ruins is **Prang Sam Yot** (Sacred Three Spires; Th Wichayen; admission 50B; 8am-6pm), which comprises three linked towers symbolising the Hindu Trimurti of Shiva, Vishnu and Brahma. Like any good Hindu shrine in this region, it was successfully converted to Buddhism with the addition of a few Lopburi-style Buddha images. This is also the resident monkeys' favourite hang-out place.

Directly across from the train station, **Wat Phra Si Ratana Mahathat** (Th Na Phra Kan; admission 50B; 7am-5pm) is a large 12th-century Khmer temple that's worth a look.

Sleeping

Budget guest houses are about all there is in Lopburi. In the old town most are old and basic, but they are within walking distance of the ruins.

Muang Thong Hotel (☎ 0 3641 1036; 1/1-11 Th Prang Sam Yot; r 160B) Be sure to get one of the rooms with a view of Prang Sam Yot. It will compensate for the grubby bed and squat toilet.

Supornpong Hotel (☎ 0 3641 2178; 30-31 Th Na Phra Kan; r 160B) A bed, fan, squat toilet and not much else, although its location close to the train station and the temple ruins is a plus.

Rama Plaza Hotel (☎ 0 3641 1663; 4 Th Banpom; r 200-250B;) The rooms may be simple but they do come with hot water and a TV. It is a five-minute walk from the town centre.

Nett Hotel (☎ 0 3641 1738; 17/1-2 Th Ratchadamnoen; r 300-500B;) In the heart of the old town, the Nett's renovated rooms offer the best value in town.

Eating

Chok Dee Dimsum Restaurant (Th Ratchadamnoen; dishes 16-22B; 8.30am-10pm) Meat dumplings and steamed pork balls are among the tiny but tempting dishes here. The waiters herald the arrival of every dish with a little cry.

Som Tam Lek Lek (Th Phraya Kamjat; dishes 20-60B; 6am-5am) Get in tune with the eponymous papaya salad; there are also more substantial options for vegetarians.

Zon (Th Naresuan; dishes 30-120B; 7am-11pm;) Zon is very Zen, with its funky furniture, hand-written menu and collection of board games. There's a Thai/Western menu but it's the coffees and smoothies and the free wi-fi that are the main attractions.

Good View Restaurant (Th Naresuan; dishes 80-150B, 5pm-1am) A three-storey, country-style bar in the new part of town, specialising in *tôm yam kûng* (spicy prawn soup) and fried fish.

Just north of the palace, the **central market** (cnr Th Ratchadamnoen & Surasongkhram) is a great place to pick up *kài thâwt* or *kài yâang* (fried or grilled chicken) with sticky rice for a long trip. A **night market** sets up along Th Na Phra Kan.

Drinking

Tahwahw (Th Naresuan; cover 400B) When it comes to clubs Lopburi is thin on the ground, but this hip-hop venue is popular with the foreign troops who come to train in this garrison town. The cover charge includes a bottle of whisky.

Bank (Th Naresuan) This is where young Thais head for a night out. An enormous stage dominates, with the live music covering Thai pop favourites such as Big Ass and Da Endorphine.

Getting There & Away

Lopburi's **bus station** (Th Naresuan) is nearly 2km outside of the old town. Ordinary buses leave from Ayuthaya (32B, two hours, frequent) or from Bangkok's Northern & Northeastern bus terminal (120B, three hours, frequent). For Kanchanaburi, take a bus to Suphanburi (65B, three hours, every 1½ hours) and change.

Lopburi's **train station** (Th Na Phra Kan) is in the old town and an easy walk to accommodation. Trains heading south to Ayuthaya (ordinary/rapid/express 13/20/310B) and Bangkok's Hualamphong station (ordinary/rapid/express 28/50/344B) leave roughly every hour up until 2.50pm, followed by a handful of early evening departures. Express trains take about three hours, ordinary trains 4½ hours. The train station has a left-luggage facility and some savvy travellers arrive early from Ayuthaya, stow their luggage for a few hour's visit and then hop on the train northward.

Getting Around

Săamláw go anywhere in old Lopburi for 30B. Săwngthăew run a regular route between the old and new towns for 10B per person and can be used between the bus station and the old town.

PHITSANULOK

pop 80,300

Because of its convenient location on an important train route, many travellers use Phitsanulok as a base for visiting the ancient city of Sukhothai as well as other parts of the lower north. As an attraction in itself, Phitsanulok (often abbreviated as 'Philok') boasts a famous Buddha and a few minor curiosities.

Information

Internet shops dot the streets around the railway station and on the western bank of the river.

Bangkok Bank (35 Th Naresuan) ATM, plus after-hours money exchange window.

Post office (Th Phuttha Bucha)

Pra Buddha Chinnaraj Hospital (0 5371 1303)

TAT office (0 5525 2742; 209/7-8 Th Borom Trailokanat; 8.30am-4.30pm)

Sights

Wat Phra Si Ratana Mahathat (known locally as Wat Yai) contains Phra Phuttha Chinnarat, regarded as one of the most beautiful and revered Buddha images in all of Thailand.

The **Sergeant Major Thawee Folk Museum** (26/43 Th Wisut Kasat; adult/child 50/20B; 8.30am-4.30pm Tue-Sun) displays a remarkable collection of tools, textiles and photographs from the province. It is spread throughout five traditional-style buildings with well-groomed gardens. Nearby is the founder's other hobbies: a small Buddha-casting foundry and an aviary.

Sleeping

Phitsanulok Youth Hostel (0 5524 2060; www.tyha.org; 38 Th Sanam Bin; dm 120B, r 200-400B;) A classic collection of weathered wooden buildings, this camaraderie-building hostel has several rustic rooms, a leafy compound and a large '38' sign out front to identify the building number.

Lithai Guest House (☎ 0 5521 9626; 73 Th Phayalithai; r incl breakfast 220-460B;) These airy rooms don't have much character but they don't cost much either. Most have large en suite bathrooms with hot water, cable TV, plentiful furniture and a fridge. As well as breakfast, rates include free bottled water.

Bon Bon Guest House (☎ 0 5521 9058; 77 Th Phayalithai; r 350-450B;) Peek in beyond the ho-hum exterior to find cute and quiet rooms with hot-water showers and cable TV.

Eating

By day you might sojourn elsewhere but return to Phitsanulok for dinner. At any of the nondescript restaurants in town you can savour the pick of the country's vegetable harvest, since Phitsanulok sits at an important shipping crossroads. A good sampler is *phàt phàk ruam mit* (stir-fried vegetables).

Fah-Kerah (786 Th Phra Ong Dam; dishes 5-20B; 6am-2pm) For honest food without a gimmick, stop by this Thai-Muslim cafe near the mosque. Here you'll find thick roti served with *kaeng mátsàmàn* (Muslim curry) and fresh yoghurt.

Rim Nan (☎ 08 1379 3172; 5/4 Th Phaya Sua; dishes 20-35B; 9am-4pm) North of Wat Phra Si Ratana Mahathat, Rim Nan does another Phitsanulok speciality: '*kŭaytĭaw hâwy khàa*' (literally, 'legs-hanging' noodles). The name comes from the way customers sit on a raised platform facing the river, with their legs dangling below deck. Thais regard this novel dining method as a great treat and a required stop after visiting the temple.

A **night market** (dishes 20-40B; 5pm-midnight) lines either side of Th Phra Ong Dam north of Th U Thong and boasts a famous vendor known for deep-fried insects. Near the night bazaar along the river, **riverfront restaurants** (dishes 40-80B; dinner) specialise in *phàk bûng lawy fáa* (literally 'flying water spinach'), a fairly standard dish that is given an acrobatic name because of the cook's flourish of tossing the dish about the wok. The spectacle usually requires an audience larger than one order.

Drinking

Wood Stock (☎ 08 1785 1958; 148/22-23 Th Wisut Kasat; dishes 35-70B; 5pm-midnight) Combines funky '60s- and '70s-era furniture, live music, and a cheap menu of *gàp glâam* (Thai-style nibbles).

A couple of floating pubs can be found along the strip of Th Wangchan, directly in front of the Grand Riverside Hotel, including **Sabai Boat** (Th Wangchan; dishes 40-140B; 11am-11pm) and **Wow!** (Th Wangchan; dishes 50-150B; 5pm-midnight).

Getting There & Away

Phitsanulok's **airport** (☎ 0 5530 1002) is 5km south of town. **Thai Airways International** (THAI; code TG; ☎ 0 5524 2971; www.thaiair.com; 209/26-28 Th Borom Trailokanat) offers daily connections to/from Bangkok (3185B, 55 minutes, twice daily).

Phitsanulok is a major junction between the north and northeast so you can get almost anywhere. The bus terminal is 2km east of town on Hwy 12. Destinations include Sukhothai (ordinary 45B, one hour, frequent), Lampang (air-con 176B to 227B, VIP 265B, four hours), Nan (air-con 197B to 254B, two hours), Kamphaeng Phet (air-con 60B to 81B, three hours, hourly) and Chiang Mai (air-con 241B to 310B, VIP 361B, six hours, hourly). There are also buses to Tak (air-con 101B, three hours) and minivans for Mae Sot (176B, four hours). To the northeast there are buses to Nakhon Ratchasima (air-con 280B to 360B, VIP 420B, six hours) and Khon Kaen (air-con 231B to 297B, seven hours).

There's no lack of buses heading to Bangkok (air-con 246B to 317B, VIP 490B, six hours, hourly).

The train station is in the centre of town on Th Ekathotsarot and Th Naresuan. There are 10 trains to Bangkok (3rd class 219B, 2nd class 449B to 309B, 2nd-class sleeper 409B to 699B, 1st-class sleeper 1064B; six hours) departing at virtually all times of day and night. Trains north to Chiang Mai usually depart in the afternoon.

Getting Around

Ordinary city buses cost 8B to 11B. The main bus stop is next to the Asia Hotel on Th Ekathotsarot, and there is a chart describing the various bus routes in English.

Run by the TAT, the **Phitsanulok Tour Tramway** (PTT; adult/child 30/20B) is a quick way to see Wat Yai and other sights. The ride takes around 45 minutes, with the first departing at 9am and the last at 3pm.

Săamláw start at 60B.

SUKHOTHAI

pop 39,800

The Cambodians get irritated by such claims, but the ruins of Sukhothai are a miniversion of the architectural styles found in Angkor. Considered the first independent Thai kingdom, Sukhothai emerged as the Khmer empire was crumbling in the 13th century and subsequently ruled over parts of the empire's western frontier for 150 years. The new Thai kingdom took artistic inspiration from its former overseers and the resulting city of temples is now a compact and pleasant collection of gravity-warped columns, serene Buddha figures and weed-sprouting towers.

Though Ayuthaya has a more interesting historical narrative, Sukhothai's ancient city is better preserved and architecturally more engaging. No surprise since Sukhothai (meaning 'Rising Happiness') is regarded as the blossoming of a Thai artistic sensibility.

The modern town of Sukhothai (often referred to as New Sukhothai; 12km from the ruins) is a standard, somewhat bland, provincial town, and many travellers opt for Sukhothai as a day trip from nearby Phitsanulok.

Information

There are banks with ATMs in New Sukhothai, plus one in Old Sukhothai. Internet is common in New Sukhothai. The tourist police maintain an office in the Sukhothai Historical Park, opposite the Ramkhamhaeng National Museum.

Post office (☎ 0 5561 1010; Th Nikhon Kasem; 🕒 8.30am-noon Mon-Fri, 1-4.30pm Sat & Sun) Has an attached international phone office.

TAT office (Th Prawet Nakhon; 🕒 9am-5pm Mon-Fri) North of the River View Hotel in New Sukhothai.

Tourist police (Map p745; ☎ 1155; Sukhothai Historical Park)

Sights & Activities

SUKHOTHAI HISTORICAL PARK

Ranked as a World Heritage Site, the **Sukhothai Historical Park** (admission 100-350B, plus bicycles/motorcycles/cars 10/20/50B; 🕒 6am-6pm) comprises most of the ancient kingdom, which was surrounded by three concentric ramparts and two moats bridged by four gateways – important celestial geometry. Inside the old walls are the remains of 21 historical sites; there are an additional 70 sites within a 5km radius. The ruins are divided into five geographic zones, each of which charges a 100B admission fee. A combination ticket for 350B allows entry to all zones plus several museums as well as nearby Si Satchanalai and Chaliang Historical Park. The historical park also hosts a beautiful version of Thailand's popular **Loi Krathong** festival in November.

The historical park (known in Thai as '*meuang kào*' or 'old city') is best reached from town by săwngthăew. Once at the park, renting a bicycle is ideal; shops nearby rent bikes for 30B per day.

Ramkhamhaeng National Museum (☎ 0 5561 2167; admission 150B; 🕒 9am-4pm) is a good place to start an exploration of Sukhothai history and culture. The most impressive display is a replica of the famous Ramkhamhaeng inscription, said to be the earliest example of Thai writing.

Wat Mahathat is the crown jewel of the old city and is one of the best examples of Sukhothai architecture, typified by the classic lotus-bud stupa that features a conical spire topping a square-sided structure on a three-tiered base. This vast assemblage, the largest in the city, once contained 198 *chedi*, as well as various chapels and sanctuaries. Some of the original Buddha images remain, including a 9m standing Buddha among the broken columns.

Wat Si Sawai, just south of Wat Mahathat, has three Khmer-style *praang* and a moat. From images found in the *chedi*, this was originally a Hindu temple, later retrofitted for Buddhism.

Wat Sa Si is a classically simple Sukhothai-style temple set on an island. **Wat Trapang Thong**, next to the museum, is reached by the footbridge crossing the large, lotus-filled pond that surrounds it. It remains in use today.

You'll need your own transport to reach these sites outside of the old city walls. Northwest of the old city, **Wat Si Chum** contains a massive seated Buddha with long tapered fingers that are famously photographed. Somewhat isolated to the north of the old city, **Wat Phra Pai Luang** is similar in style to Wat Si Sawai. **Wat Chang Lom**, 1km to the east, is surrounded by 36 elephant sculptures. **Wat Saphaan Hin** is 4km west of the old city walls on a hillside and features a large Buddha looking back to Sukhothai.

Guided bike tours (☎ 0 5561 2519; www.geocities.com/cycling_sukhothai; half/full day 550/650B, sunset tour

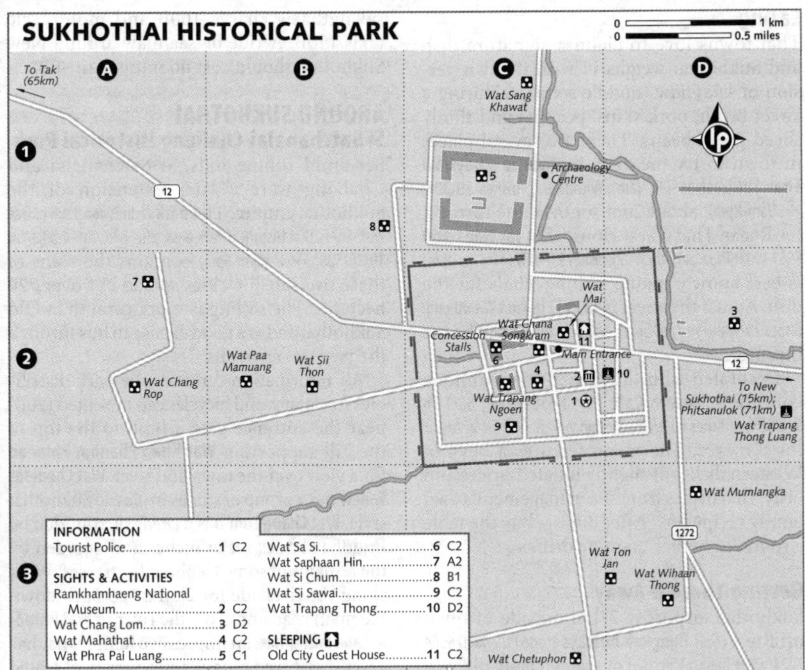

250B), led by a Belgian expat, visit lesser known temples in the historical park and do village pit stops.

Sleeping

Garden House (☎ 0 5561 1395; 11/1 Th Prawet Nakhon, New Sukhothai; r 150-350B;) Popular and a tad chaotic, retreat from the scene to the quieter bungalows out back. The restaurant screens movies nightly.

River House (☎ 0 5562 0396; riverhouse_7@hotmail.com; 7 Soi Watkuhasuwan, New Sukhothai; r 150-350B) This Thai-style wooden home exudes a relaxed feel and is one of the few guest houses to take advantage of the cool breezes from the Mae Nam Yom.

Old City Guest House (Map p745; ☎ 0 5569 7515; 28/7 Mu 3, Sukhothai Historical Park; r 150-400B;) This is the best budget choice if you want to stay near the historical park. The vast compound features a variety of rooms for all budgets and styles; ask to see a few before you make a decision.

Ban Thai (☎ 0 5561 0163; 38 Th Prawet Nakhon, New Sukhothai; r 200B, bungalows 300-500B;) With its welcoming staff and wealth of travellers information, Ban Thai might be a hard place to leave. Rooms are large and clean, though the shared bathrooms need an upgrade. The pretty garden rooms include private bathroom.

J&J Guest House (☎ 0 5562 0095; www.jj-guesthouse.com; 122 Soi Mae Ramphan, New Sukhothai; r 300-500B, bungalows 700-800B;) This tidy compound is more resort than guest house. The bungalows and spacious rooms span just about every budget category. Plus the restaurant makes homemade bread and there's a swimming pool.

Sukhothai Guest House (☎ 0 5561 0453; www.sukhothaiguesthouse.net; 68 Th Vichien Chamnong, New Sukhothai; r 350-750B;) This long-running guest house has 12 bungalows with terraces packed into a shaded garden. The communal area is filled with an eclectic mix of bric-a-brac and the owners are friendly and helpful.

No 4 Guest House (☎ 0 5561 0165; 140/4 Soi Khlong Mae Ramphan, New Sukhothai; s/d 200/300B) and **Ninety-Nine Guest House** (☎ 0 5561 1315; 234/6 Soi Panitsan, New Sukhothai; s/d 120/150B) are two sister properties under the same management. No 4 features several rustic, slightly worn bungalows. Ninety-nine's rooms are in a two-storey teak house surrounded by a garden.

Eating

Thai towns love to claim a signature dish and Sukhothai weighs in with its own version of *kŭaytĭaw* (noodle soup), featuring a sweet broth, pork skins, peanuts and thinly sliced green beans. There are several places in town to try the dish, including **Kuaytiaw Thai Sukhothai** (Th Jarot Withithong; dishes 20-30B; 9am-8pm), about 20m south of the turn-off for Ruean Thai Guest House. But **Jay Hae** (0 5561 1901; Th Jarot Withithong; dishes 25-40B; 7am-4pm) is best known among visiting Thais for the dish. Across the street is **Ta Pui** (Th Jarot Withithong; dishes 20-30B; 7am-3pm), which claims to be the inventor.

Decorated with the owner's own antique collection, **Dream Cafe** (0 5561 2081; 86/1 Th Singhawat; dishes 80-150B; lunch & dinner) is a feast for the eyes. The menu features a bevy of Western dishes at slightly inflated prices and tasty Thai dishes from the management's own family recipe box. After dining, buy the table a round of herbal 'stamina drinks'.

Getting There & Away

Sukhothai airport is 27km outside of town off Rte 1195. **Bangkok Airways** (code PG; 0 5564 7224; www.bangkokair.com) operates a daily flight to Bangkok (2870B).

The bus station is 4km northwest of the town centre on Hwy 101. Destinations include Bangkok (2nd/1st class 267/344B, seven hours, hourly), Chiang Mai (2nd/1st class 167/234B, six hours, frequent), Phitsanulok (ordinary 32B, air-con 42B to 58B, one hour, frequent), Sawankhalok (ordinary/2nd class air-con/1st class 21/29/38B, 45 minutes, hourly), Si Satchanalai (ordinary 37B, air-con 52B to 67B, one hour, hourly). There are also minivans to Mae Sot (136B, three hours, eight departures).

Getting Around

Săwngthăew run between New Sukhothai and Sukhothai Historical Park (20B, 30 minutes, frequently from 6.30am to 6pm), leaving from Th Jarot Withithong near Poo Restaurant. The sign is on the north side of the street, but săwngthăew actually leave from the south side. Bicycles can be rented from shops near the historical park entrance for 30B per day.

Transport from the bus terminal into New Sukhothai costs 60B by charter or 10B per person in a shared săwngthăew. Motorbike taxis charge 40B. If going directly to Old Sukhothai, săwngthăew charge 100B and motorcycle taxis 120B. A ride by săamláw around New Sukhothai should cost no more than 40B.

AROUND SUKHOTHAI

Si Satchanalai-Chaliang Historical Park

Set amid rolling hills, Si Satchanalai and Chaliang were a later extension of the Sukhothai empire. The **park** (admission 220B or free with Sukhothai Historical Park pass, plus bike/motorbike/car 10/30/50B; 8.30am-5pm) contains the ruins of these two satellite cities spread out over 720 hectares. The setting is more rural than Old Sukhothai and is a good excuse to bus through the pastoral environs.

An information centre at the park distributes free maps, and bicycles can be rented (20B) near the entrance gate. Climb to the top of the hill supporting **Wat Khao Phanom Phloeng** for a view over the town and river. **Wat Chedi Jet Thaew** has a group of stupas in classic Sukhothai style. **Wat Chang Lom** has a *chedi* surrounded by Buddha statues set in niches and guarded by the remains of some elephant buttresses. Walk along the riverside for 2km or go back down the main road and cross the river to **Wat Phra Si Ratana Mahathat**, an impressive temple that has a well-preserved *praang* and a variety of seated and standing Buddhas.

The Si Satchanalai-Chaliang area was famous for its beautiful **pottery**, much of which was exported. The Indonesians were once keen collectors, and some fine specimens can still be seen in the National Museum in Jakarta, Indonesia. Rejects, buried in the fields, are still being discovered. Several of the old kilns have been carefully excavated and can be viewed along with original pottery samples at the **Si Satchanalai Centre for Study & Preservation of Sangkhalok Kilns** (admission 100B). Two groups of kilns are open to the public: one in Chaliang with excavated pottery samples, and a larger outdoor site called Sawankhalok Kilns, 5km northwest of the Si Satchanalai ruins. The exhibits are interesting despite the lack of English labels. Admission is included in the 220B park ticket.

Si Satchanalai-Chaliang Historical Park is off Rte 101 between Sawankhalok and new Si Satchanalai. From Sukhothai, take a Si Satchanalai bus (38B, two hours) and ask to get off at *'meuang kào'* (old city). Alternatively, catch the 9am bus to Chiang Rai, which costs the same but makes fewer stops. The last bus back to New Sukhothai leaves at 4.30pm.

KAMPHAENG PHET

pop 30,114

An easy detour from the tourist trail en route to Chiang Mai, Kamphaeng Phet (Diamond Wall) is a peaceful provincial town known for its whitewashed city walls. Historically it played a protective role on the front lines of defence for the Sukhothai kingdom. It's a nice place to spend a day or so wandering around the ruins and experiencing daily Thai life.

Kamphaeng Phet Historical Park (☎ 0 5571 1921; admission 100-150B, plus bicycle/motorbike/car 10/20/50B; 8am-5pm) contains a number of temple ruins dating back to the 14th century, as well as remains of a long city wall. Wat Phra Sri Iriyabot features the shattered remains of standing, sitting, walking and reclining Buddha images. Wat Chang Rawp (Temple Surrounded by Elephants) is just that – a temple that has an elephant-buttressed wall.

Sleeping & Eating

Gor Choke Chai (☎ 0 5571 1247; 19-43 Soi 8, Th Ratchadamnoen 1; r 260-320B;) The small and tidy rooms here are popular with Thai businessmen. It's conveniently located near the centre of the new town.

Three J Guest House (☎ 0 5571 3129; threejguest@hotmail.com; 79 Th Rachavitee; r 300-600B;) Mr Charin is the congenial host of this backpackers' centre and he is happy to pick up guests from the bus terminal. Each of the bungalows is different, and the cheaper ones share a clean bathroom. Bicycles and motorbikes are available for rent.

Navarat (☎ 0 5571 1211; 2 Soi Prapan; r 400-500, ste 950B;) The Navarat has changed little, if at all, since its apparent construction in the early '70s. Despite this, it's a clean, cosy place and some rooms have nice views.

Bamee Chakangrao (no roman-script sign; ☎ 0 5571 2446; Th Ratchadamnoen; dishes 25-30B 8.30am-3pm) This restaurant is famous for its freshly made *bàmèe* (wheat-and-egg noodles), a speciality of Kamphaeng Phet.

A busy night market sets up every evening near the river, just north of the Navarat Hotel, and there are some cheap restaurants near the roundabout.

Getting There & Away

The bus station is 1km west of town and serves the following destinations: Bangkok (air-con 244B to 308B, five hours), Sukhothai (săwngthăew 50B, air-con 62B, 1½ hours), Phitsanulok (ordinary/air-con 60/84B, 2½ hours) and Tak (air-con 48B, 1½ hours). If coming from Sukhothai or Phitsanulok ask to be let off in the old city or at the roundabout on Th Tesa to save a săwngthăew back to town.

A shared săwngthăew (15B per person) goes from the bus station to the roundabout across the river. From there take a săamláw anywhere in town for 20B to 30B. Motorcycle taxis from the bus station to most hotels downtown cost 40B.

MAE SOT

Mae Sot is a scruffy border town preoccupied with trading and cross-border traffic. But it's the population's diversity that is most striking – Indo-Burmese, Chinese, Karen, Hmong and Thai – an ethnic mix typically found only in a big metropolis. The town also hosts a relatively large population of foreign doctors and NGO aid workers, whose presence attests to the human cost of an unstable border.

There aren't a lot of official sites to lure tourists this far west, but a few come for a visa run and stay longer, realising that they can tap into the charitable spirit through a variety of volunteer organisations or escape the tourist crowds of northern Thailand with visits to the nearby underdeveloped nature preserves and hill-tribe communities.

Information

There are several banks with ATMs in the town centre.

Se Southeast Express Tours (Th Intharakhiri; per hr 20B) Internet and international phones.

Tourist police (☎ 1155; 738/1 Th Intharakhiri) Has an office east of the centre of town and at the market by the Friendship Bridge.

Sights & Activities

There is an expansive **border market** alongside the Mae Nam Moei on the Thai side that legally sells workaday Burmese goods and cheap Chinese electronics. On the other side of the border in Myanmar is the town of **Myawaddy**, where you can poke around for the day (see the boxed text, p752).

Borderline Shop (☎ 0 5554 6584; borderlinecollective.org; 674/14 Th Intharakhiri; 10am-6pm Tue-Sun) Has a bit of everything: cafe, tea garden, gallery and handicrafts shop. It was started by a Burmese refugee women's group. The shop offers cooking courses focusing on Shan, Burmese and Karen dishes and includes a trip to the market. It also offers weaving courses (2000B)

OF MIGRANTS AND MISFORTUNE

Burmese refugees first crossed into Thailand in 1984, when the Myanmarese army penetrated the ethnic Karen state and began a campaign of forced relocation of the indigenous populations. Today there are three refugee camps around Mae Sot, and the UN High Commissioner for Refugees (UNHCR) estimates that 121,383 Burmese live in nine camps that line the border between Thailand and Myanmar. Within the camps, the refugees are assured of protection from the military, but have little opportunities to gain an education, employment or an independent life because the Thai government does not recognise them as citizens or residents. Some live in this limbo state for decades.

More recently the Burmese have come to Thailand as economic migrants escaping destitute poverty in their homeland. These newcomers do not qualify to live in the camps because they aren't escaping active fighting and they enter into the workforce illegally earning sub par wages and are subject to exploitation.

To tend to this geopolitical crisis, many international or grassroots organisations work with volunteers to address the various challenges of the Burmese situation. Contact the following for more information (and see also Volunteering in the Directory, p831):

Mae Tao Clinic (☎ 0 5556 3644; Mae Sot; www.maetaoclinic.org) Established in 1989 by Dr Cynthia Maung, a Karen refugee, this clinic provides free medical treatment to around 80,000 Burmese migrants a year and helps pay for medical care at one of Mae Sot's hospitals if the treatment is beyond their capabilities. If you have medical training, the clinic offers volunteer positions for a minimum of six months. There are also administrative and English-teaching opportunities with three-month commitments.

Ban Thai Guest House (below) Can help visitors find informal volunteer spots in schools, childcare and at HIV centres. The minimum commitment is usually one month.

The surrounding mountain landscape, especially closer to Um Phang, is beginning to develop as a trekking destination. Some guest houses and tour operators in Mae Sot organise white-water rafting, hiking and hill-tribe tours (starting at 1500B for a one-day trip). Contact **Max One Tour** (☎ 0 5554 2942; www.maxonetour.com; Mae Sot Sq, Th Intharakhiri) or **Mae Sot Conservation Tour** (☎ 0 5553 2818; maesotco@hotmail.com; 415/17 Th Tang Kim Chiang).

Sleeping

Smile Guest House (☎ 08 5129 9293; smilemaesot@gmail.com; 738 Th Intarahakhiri; r 100-300B; ❄ 💻) This large wooden home is steps from Mae Sot's main strip of restaurants and bars. The cheaper rooms share bathrooms and long-term stays can be arranged.

Green Guest House (☎ 0 5553 3207; krit.sana@hotmail.com; 406/8 Th Intarahakhiri; dm 100B, r 150-250B) Run by a teacher and her husband, this peaceful guest house offers a variety of good-sized rooms with TV and decent furniture. It's great value, centrally located and has a pretty garden.

DK Mae Sot Square Hotel (Duang Kamol Hotel; ☎ 0 5554 2648; 298/2 Th Intharakhiri; r with fan or air-con 250-450B; ❄ 💻) If the beds, towels and sheets here were upgraded, it would be a fantastic budget deal. Until then the large rooms in this three-storey hotel are average but conveniently located.

our pick **Ban Thai Guest House** (☎ 0 5553 1590; banthai_mth@hotmail.com; 740 Th Intharakhiri; r 250-950B; ❄ 💻 📶) Mae Sot's best budget spot is also a favourite among visiting volunteers. Five converted Thai houses sit atop a well-manicured lawn, and the common area is conducive to meeting someone doing something interesting.

Eating

Mae Sot is a culinary crossroads with a diversity of food not seen in most other Thai towns. For breakfast head to the area south of the mosque where several Muslim restaurants serve sweet tea, roti and *nanbya* (a tandoori-style bread). The town's vibrant day market is the place to try Burmese dishes such as *mohinga*, a popular noodle dish. And Mae Sot's night market, at the eastern end of Th Prasat Withi, features mostly Thai-Chinese dishes.

Khrua Canadian (☎ 0 5553 4659; 3 Th Sri Phanit; dishes 40-280B; 🕐 breakfast, lunch & dinner) This is the place to go if you want to forget you're in Asia for a meal. The servings are large, the menu is varied and when you finally remember that you're in Thailand, local information is also available.

Aiya (☎ 0 5553 0102; 533 Th Intharakhiri; dishes 45-80B; ⏰ lunch & dinner) Opposite Bai Fern Guest House, Aiya is a simple place that serves good Burmese food and vegetarian options. There's live music some nights.

Drinking

For a night on the town Mae Sot style, head to the bars at the western end of Th Intharakhiri. Current faves include **Kung's Bar** (Th Intharakhiri) and **Thaime's** (Th Intharakhiri), both featuring an extensive selection of mixed drinks, live music and many drunken travellers and volunteers.

Getting There & Around

There are frequent minivans to Sukhothai (140B, six departures from 7am to 2.30pm) and Phitsanulok (176B, six departures from 7am to 2.30pm). There are several daily departures to Bangkok (air-con 328B to 421B, VIP 655B, eight hours, hourly).

The **Green Bus** (☎ 114, ext 8000; www.greenbusthailand.com) goes to Chiang Mai (air-con 237B to 304B, six hours, two departures). Orange săwngthăew to Mae Sariang (200B, six hours, five departures from 6am to noon) depart from the old bus station near the centre of town.

NORTHERN THAILAND

Sitting upon the crown of the country is a mountainous region beloved for its misty mornings, lush forest cover, and unique cultural and natural attractions. This cascade of peaks and valleys unites northern Thailand with the peoples and the cultures of neighbouring Myanmar, Laos and southwestern China. The fertile river valleys were populated by traders and migrants from the Yúnnán province of China and their cultural legacy survives today in traditional food, architecture and customs. Eventually the independent state known as Lanna Thai (Million Thai Rice Fields) emerged and established its capital in Chiang Mai, a charming northern city filled with beautiful temples. Other wanderers, such as the autonomous hill-tribe peoples, traversed the range, limited only by altitude rather than political boundaries.

Northern Thailand is a well-established stop on the tourist trail. Bangkok Thais make weekend trips here to relish the sensation of cool temperatures. Backpackers have long come to tromp through the woods and camp out alongside hill-tribe villages. Along twisting mountain roads, small towns awaken to a thick morning fog, offering the simple pleasures of reflective walks and breathtaking vistas.

CHIANG MAI

pop 174,000

Chiang Mai is a cultural darling: it is a cool place to kick back and relax, the streets are alive with monks and motorcycle-driving housewives, bookshops outnumber glitzy shopping centres and the region's Lanna heritage is worn with pride. For culture vultures, Chiang Mai is a vibrant classroom to study Thai language, cooking, meditation and massage.

The old city of Chiang Mai is a neat square bounded by a moat and remnants of a medieval-style wall built 700 years ago to defend against Burmese invaders. A furious stream of traffic flows around the old city, but inside the old district narrow *soi* lead to a quiet world of family-run guest houses, leafy gardens and friendly smiles.

Orientation

Th Moon Muang, along the east moat, is the main traveller centre. Intersecting with Th Moon Muang, Th Tha Phae runs east from the exterior of the moat towards the Mae Nam Ping. Once it crosses the river, the road is renamed Th Charoen Muang and eventually arrives at the main post office and train station.

Finding your way around Chiang Mai is fairly simple. A copy of Nancy Chandler's *Map Guide to Chiang Mai* is a good investment if you plan extensive exploration of the city. Pick up a copy at bookshops or guest houses.

Information

BOOKSHOPS

Backstreet Books (☎ 0 5387 4143; 2/8 Th Chang Moi Kao) A local chain for used books.

Gecko Books (☎ 0 5387 4066; Th Chiang Moi Kao) Local chain for used books.

Lost Book Shop (☎ 0 5320 6656; 34/3 Th Ratchamankha) Second-hand books free of plastic wrap for easy browsing; same owner as Backstreet Books.

On the Road Books (☎ 05341 8169; 38/1 Th Ratwithi) Small selection of good quality reads.

Suriwong Book Centre (☎ 0 5328 1052; 54 Th Si Donchai) A Chiang Mai institution for new books.

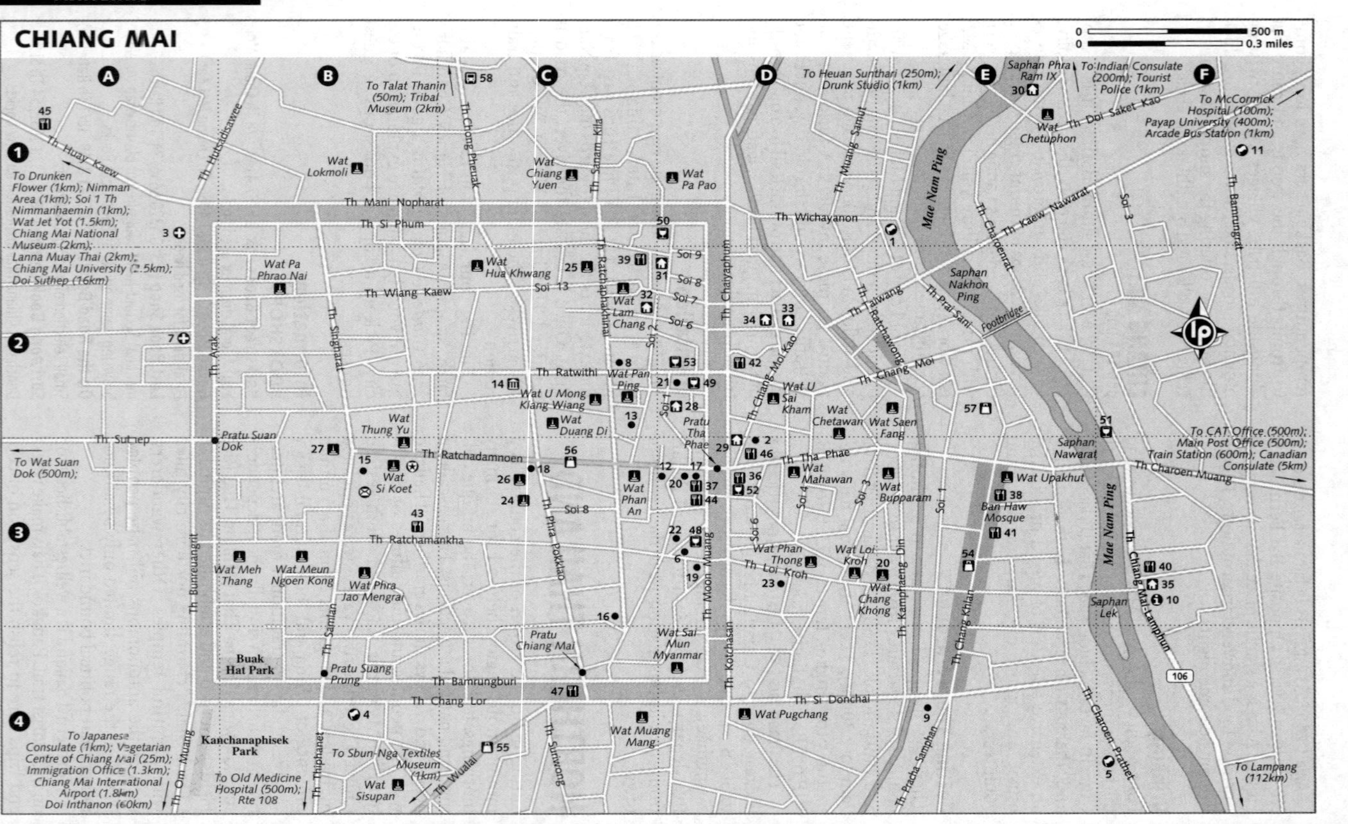
THAILAND
CHIANG MAI
0 500 m
0 0.3 miles
To Drunken Flower (1km); Nimman Area (1km); Soi 1 Th Nimmanhaemin (1km); Wat Jet Yot (1.5km); Chiang Mai National Museum (2km); Lanna Muay Thai (2km); Chiang Mai University (2.5km); Doi Suthep (16km)
To Talat Thanin (50m); Tribal Museum (2km)
To Heuan Sunthari (250m); Drunk Studio (1km)
Saphan Phra Ram IX
To Indian Consulate (200m); Tourist Police (1km)
To McCormick Hospital (100m); Payap University (400m); Arcade Bus Station (1km)
To Wat Suan Dok (500m);
To CAT Office (500m); Main Post Office (500m); Train Station (600m); Canadian Consulate (5km)
To Japanese Consulate (1km); Vegetarian Centre of Chiang Mai (25m); Immigration Office (1.3km); Chiang Mai International Airport (1.8km) Doi Inthanon (60km)
To Old Medicine Hospital (500m); Rte 108
To Sbun-Nga Textiles Museum (1km)
To Lampang (112km)
Mae Nam Ping
Saphan Nakhon Ping
Saphan Nawarat
Saphan Lek
Footbridge
Th Huay Kaew
Th Hutsadisawee
Th Chong Pheuak
Th Sanam Kila
Th Mani Nopharat
Th Si Phum
Th Wiang Kaew
Th Arak
Th Singharat
Th Ratchaphakhinai
Th Chaiyaphum
Th Ratwithi
Th Suthep
Th Ratchadamnoen
Th Ratchamankha
Th Phra Pokklao
Th Bunreuangrit
Th Samlan
Th Moon Muang
Th Kotchasan
Th Bamrungburi
Th Chang Lor
Th Si Donchai
Th Om Muang
Th Thiphanet
Th Wualai
Th Suriwong
Th Wichayanon
Th Muang Samut
Th Taiwang
Th Ratchawong
Th Chiang Moi Kao
Th Chang Moi
Th Tha Phae
Th Loi Kroh
Th Kamphaeng Din
Th Chang Khlan
Th Pracha Samphan
Th Charoen Prathet
Th Charoenrat
Th Prai Sani
Th Kaew Nawarat
Th Doi Saket Kao
Th Bamrungrat
Th Charoen Muang
Th Chiang Mai-Lamphun
Soi 1
Soi 3
Soi 4
Soi 6
Soi 7
Soi 8
Soi 9
Soi 13
Pratu Suan Dok
Pratu Tha Phae
Pratu Chiang Mai
Pratu Suang Prung
Buak Hat Park
Kanchanaphisek Park
Wat Lokmoli
Wat Chiang Yuen
Wat Pa Pao
Wat Pa Phrao Nai
Wat Hua Khwang
Wat Lam Chang
Wat Pan Ping
Wat U Mong Klang Wiang
Wat Duang Di
Wat Thung Yu
Wat Si Koet
Wat Phan An
Wat Meh Thang
Wat Meun Ngoen Kong
Wat Phra Jao Mengrai
Wat Sai Mun Myanmar
Wat Muang Mang
Wat Sisupan
Wat Pugchang
Wat U Sai Kham
Wat Chetawan
Wat Saen Fang
Wat Mahawan
Wat Bupparam
Wat Phan Thong
Wat Loi Kroh
Wat Chang Khong
Wat Upakhut
Ban Haw Mosque
Wat Chetuphon
106
A B C D E F
1 2 3 4

INFORMATION
American Consulate....1 E1
Backstreet Books....2 D3
Chiang Mai Ram Hospital....3 A1
Chinese Consulate....4 B4
French Consulate....5 F4
Gecko Books....(see 2)
Lost Book Shop....6 D3
Malaria Centre....7 A2
On the Road Books....8 C2
Suriwong Book Centre....9 E4
TAT Office....10 F3
UK Consulate....11 F1

SIGHTS & ACTIVITIES
American University Alumni....12 D3
Baan Thai....13 C2
Chiang Mai City Arts & Cultural Centre....14 C2
Chiang Mai Mountain Biking....15 B3
Chiang Mai Rock Climbing Adventures....16 C3
Chiang Mai Thai Cookery School....17 D3
Chiang Mai Thai Language Center....18 C3
Elephant Nature Park....19 D3
Lek Chaiya....20 D3
Siam River Adventures....21 D2
Smile House Cookery School....22 D3
Thai Kitchen Cookery School....23 D3
Wat Chedi Luang....24 C3
Wat Chiang Man....25 C2
Wat Phan Tao'....26 C3
Wat Phra Singh....27 B3

SLEEPING
Ban Wiang....28 D2
Daret's House....29 D3
Hollanda Montri Guesthouse....30 E1
Kham Kaew House....31 D2
Malak House....32 C2
Pagoda Inn....33 D2
Pao Come Inn....34 D2
Riverside House....35 F3

EATING
Art Cafe....36 D3
AUM Vegetarian Restaurant....37 D3
Ban Haw Mosque....38 E3
Blue Diamond....39 C2
Duke's....40 F3
Duke's....(see 54)
Galare Food Centre....41 E3
Gigantea Restaurant....42 D2
Heuan Phen....43 B3
Jerusalem Falafel....44 D3
Lemon Tree....45 A1
Pulcinella da Stefano....46 D3
Talat Pratu Chiang Mai....47 C4

DRINKING
John's Place....48 D3
Kafé....49 D2
Rasta Art Bar & Restaurant....50 D1
Riverside Bar & Restaurant....51 F2
THC....52 D3
UN Irish Pub....53 D2

SHOPPING
Chiang Mai Night Bazaar....54 E3
Saturday Walking Street....55 C4
Sunday Walking Street....56 C3
Talat Warorot....57 E2

TRANSPORT
Chang Pheuak Bus Station....58 C1

EMERGENCY

Tourist police (☎ 0 5324 7318, 24hr emergency 1155; Th Faham; 6am-midnight) New location northeast of the centre.

INTERNET ACCESS

Internet cafes are everywhere and most guest houses include the service for free.

INTERNET RESOURCES

1 Stop Chiang Mai (www.1stopchiangmai.com) City attractions with an emphasis on day trips and outdoor activities.
City Life (www.chiangmainews.com) Online content from City Life magazine.

MEDIA

Chiangmai Mail Weekly English-language newspaper.
City Life Monthly lifestyle magazine.
Chiang Mai 101 Quarterly tourist magazine.

MEDICAL SERVICES

Chiang Mai Ram Hospital (☎ 0 5322 4861; Th Bunreuangrit) Most internationally savvy hospital in town.
Malaria Centre (☎ 0 5322 1529; 18 Th Bunreuangrit) Does blood checks for malaria.
McCormick Hospital (☎ 0 5324 2200; Th Kaew Nawarat) Best-value place for minor treatments.

MONEY

All major Thai banks have bank branches and ATMs throughout Chiang Mai; many of them along Th Tha Phae and Th Moon Muang.

POST

Main post office (Th Charoen Muang) Inconveniently east of town with handy branches on Th Singarat/Samlan, Th Praisani and the airport.

TELEPHONE

Many internet cafes have headsets so that users can use Skype. Overseas calls can also be made from one of the private offices along Th Moon Muang.
CAT office (Th Charoen Muang; 7am-10pm) Behind the main post office.

TOURIST INFORMATION

TAT office (☎ 0 5324 8604; 105/1 Th Chiang Mai-Lamphun; 8.30am-4.30pm) Provides maps and brochures and answers basic tourist questions; does not make travel or accommodation bookings.

Dangers & Annoyances

Most hassles you'll encounter in Chiang Mai involve trekking, the local tourism industry's cash cow. The majority of guest houses in town subsidise their cheap room rates through commissions on booking trekking tours, in turn making nontrekkers unwelcome guests. Most guest houses are upfront about their policies and limit nontrekkers to three days, stay, but ask about this at check-in. Years ago, travellers used to report that their belongings (particularly credit cards) stored at Chiang Mai guest houses went on walkabout while they were trekking, but we haven't heard news of this for several years. To be on the safe side,

GETTING TO MYANMAR: MAE SOT TO MYAWADDY

Mae Sot is a legal crossing point into the Myanmarese town of Myawaddy for a one-day stay. Immigration exit procedures are taken care of at the **Thai immigration booth** (☎ 0 5556 3000; Friendship Bridge; 🕑 6.30am-6.30pm) and entry procedures are handled on the other side of the bridge at the Myanmar immigration booth, where you'll pay US$10 (or 500B) for a day pass and leave your passport as a deposit. Then you're free to wander around Myawaddy as long as you're back at the bridge by 5.30pm Myanmar time (which is a half-hour behind Thai time). On your return to Thailand, the Thai immigration office at the bridge will give you a new 15-day visa.

Before going to the border, ask around town to confirm that the border is open as it is periodically closed with little warning.

The border is 6km west of Mae Sot and accessible via a Rim Moei–bound săwngthăew (15B, frequent departures from 6.30am to 5.30pm).

Once in Myawaddy, you can do some temple spotting. The most important temple is **Shwe Muay Wan**, a traditional bell-shaped *chedi* gilded with many kilos of gold and topped by more than 1600 gemstones. Another noted Buddhist temple is **Myikyaungon,** called Wat Don Jarakhe in Thai for its crocodile-shaped sanctuary. A hollow *chedi* at Myikyaungon contains four marble Mandalay-style Buddhas around a central pillar. Myawaddy's 1000-year-old earthen city walls, probably erected by the area's original Mon inhabitants, can be seen along the southern side of town.

keep valuables with you as most routes are no longer prone to banditry.

Bus or minivan services from Th Khao San in Bangkok often advertise a free night's accommodation in Chiang Mai if you buy a Bangkok–Chiang Mai ticket. What usually happens on arrival is that the 'free' guest house demands you sign up for a trek immediately; if you don't, the guest house is suddenly 'full'. The better guest houses don't play this game.

Sights

TEMPLES

Chiang Mai's primary attractions are the old city's historic and holy temples that show off distinctive northern Thai architecture, a blend of Thai, Burmese and Yunnanese influences. A few stand-out features include intricate carved gables, colourful exterior mosaics, Singha lions guarding the entrances and octagonal high-based *chedi*.

Wat Phra Singh (☎ 0 5381 4164; Th Singharat; donations appreciated; 🕑 6am-6pm) is the star amid the old city's famous temples and is a perfect example of Lanna architecture. Established in 1345, it houses the city's revered Buddha image, Phra Singh, which is the focal point for the religious festivities of Songkran (Thai New Year) in mid-April.

Wat Chiang Man (☎ 0 5337 5368; Th Ratchaphakhinai; donations appreciated; 🕑 6am-6pm) is considered to be the oldest wat within the city walls and was erected by King Mengrai, Chiang Mai's founder, in 1296. Two famous Buddha images (Phra Sila and Phra Satang Kamanee, or the Crystal Buddha) are kept here in the *wíhăan* (sanctuary) to the right of the main *bòht*. The Crystal Buddha is believed to have the power to bring seasonal rains.

Wat Chedi Luang (☎ 0 5327 8595; Th Phra Pokklao; donations appreciated; 🕑 6am-6pm) contains the ruins of a huge *chedi* dating from 1441 that was destroyed either by an earthquake or cannon fire in either the 16th or 18th century. A partial restoration has preserved the 'ruined' look. The venerable Emerald Buddha, now housed in Bangkok's Wat Phra Kaew, occupied the eastern niche here in 1475. The temple's other attraction is the *làk meuang* (city pillar, believed to house the city's guardian deity) enshrined in a small building to the left of the compound's main entrance. In May, the building is opened to the public for merit-making.

Wat Phan Tao (☎ 0 5381 4689; Th Phra Pokklao; donations appreciated) Near Wat Chedi Luang, this small temple is hardly historic but immensely pretty with its old teak *wíhăan* constructed entirely of moulded teak panels fitted together and supported by 28 gargantuan teak pillars. The *wíhăan* also features *naga* bargeboards inset with coloured mirror mosaic.

Wat Jet Yot (☎ 0 5321 1947; Rte 11/Th Superhighway; donations appreciated; 🕑 6am-6pm) is modelled somewhat imperfectly on the Mahabodhi Temple in Bodhgaya, India. The seven spires represent the seven weeks Buddha was supposed to have spent in Bodhgaya after his enlightenment. It is 1.5km northwest of town and 500m from the National Museum.

Wat Suan Dok (☎ 0 5327 8967; www.monkchat.net; Th Suthep; donations appreciated; 6am-6pm) is not as beautiful as the old city's temples but its collection of whitewashed *chedi* framed by the nearby mountains of Doi Suthep and Doi Pui is a favourite photographic subject. The temple also hosts a Buddhist university and conducts religious outreach programs for laity (see the boxed text Mindfulness: Meditation Courses & Retreats, p722). It's 1km west of town.

MUSEUMS

Conveniently located in the old city, the **Chiang Mai City Arts & Cultural Centre** (☎ 0 5321 7793; www.chiangmaicitymuseum.org; Th Phra Pokklao; adult/child 90/40B; 8.30am-5.30pm Tue-Sun) is a municipally funded introduction to the city's history with surprisingly engaging displays.

Less modern but more academically important is the **Chiang Mai National Museum** ☎ 0 5322 1308; www.thailandmuseum.com; off Rte 11/Th Superhighway; admission 100B; 9am-4pm Wed-Sun), northwest of the old city. The best curated exhibits are the Lanna art sections, which display Buddha images in all styles and periods.

North of the old city, the **Tribal Museum** (☎ 0 5321 0872; Suan Ratchamangkhla, Th Chotana; admission free; 9am-4pm Mon-Fri) houses a large collection of artefacts and ethnographic information about the hill tribes in Thailand; video shows run from 10am to 2pm (20B to 50B).

A delightful museum, **Sbun-Nga Textile Museum** (☎ 0 5320 0655; www.sbunnga.com; Old Chiang Mai Cultural Centre, 185/20 Th Wualai; admission 100B; 10.30am-6.30pm Thu-Tue) displays northern Thai textiles along with ethno-cultural information about the different Lanna tribes.

DOI SUTHEP

Perched on a hilltop, **Wat Phra That Doi Suthep** (admission 30B) is one of the north's most sacred temples. The site was 'chosen' by an honoured Buddha relic mounted on the back of a white elephant; the animal wandered until it stopped (and died) on Doi Suthep, making this the relic's new home. A snaking road ascends the hill to a long flight of steps, lined by ceramic-tailed *naga*, that leads up to the temple and the expansive views of the valley below.

About 4km beyond Wat Phra That Doi Suthep are the palace gardens of **Phra Tamnak Phu Phing** (Phu Phing Palace; admission 50B; 8.30-11.30am & 1-3.30pm), a winter residence for the royal family.

The road that passes the palace splits off to the left, stopping at the peak of Doi Pui. From there, a dirt road proceeds for a couple of kilometres to a nearby **Hmong village**, which is well touristed and sells handicrafts. A more interesting Hmong village is **Ban Kun Chang Kian**. Instead of going left on the road past the palace head right. The road is paved just past the camping ground and then for the last 500m or so it is a bumpy dirt track. You'll find an open-air, village-run coffee house surrounded by coffee plants that are harvested in January. Nearby is basic **accommodation** (from 600B) with fantastic views.

Doi Suthep is 16km northwest of Chiang Mai and is accessible via shared sǎwngthǎew that leave from the main entrance of Chiang Mai University on Th Huay Kaew. One-way fares start at 40B and increase from there depending on the destination within the park and the number of passengers. You can also charter a sǎwngthǎew for about 600B or rent a motorcycle for much less. Sǎwngthǎew also depart from Pratu Chang Pheuak and the Chiang Mai Zoo. Cyclists also make the 13km ascent to the temple either early in the morning or in the late evening when traffic is diminished.

Activities

TREKKING

Chiang Mai is one of the easiest and most popular places in Thailand to arrange a hill-tribe trek so competition for business is fierce. It is difficult for Lonely Planet to recommend a specific company because guides often float between companies and the standards fluctuate. Relying on the travellers grapevine is a good start though the drawback here is that opinions often diverge wildly: some might think a particular company offered a brilliant trek, while others will complain about the same company's wretchedness. The difference in opinion often comes down to the trek's social dynamic. Although it is a tour of the outdoors, the social camaraderie often becomes the highlight. For this reason, try to team up with travellers you enjoy hanging out with as you'll spend more time with them than the elephants or the hill-tribe villagers.

Most companies offer the same itinerary: about an hour trekking, another hour riding an elephant, some waterfall spotting then spending the night in a hill-tribe village. Repeat if it is a multiday tour. Some trekkers have complained that the hike was too short, others report that it was too strenuous. Keep in mind that the humidity makes physical exertion feel more demanding.

Don't expect to have any meaningful connections with the hill-tribe villagers; in most cases, the trekking tours stay in rudimentary lodging outside of the village and travellers have reported that the village hosts were most unwelcoming. Instead a trek is a good time to get to know Thailand better through the Thai guide, who is usually young and charismatic. If you want meaningful interaction with hill-tribe villagers, donate your time to one of the nonprofits working with these communities; see Volunteering (p831) for more information.

We don't advise prebooking in Bangkok as the potential for rip-off is too great. Instead shop around locally to find the lowest commission rates, which tend to vary greatly.

It is also possible to go trekking in Mae Hong Son and Chiang Rai, the latter has trekking companies with an economic and educational development component.

OTHER ACTIVITIES

Chiang Mai has developed a fairly sophisticated soft-adventure scene for travellers looking for more of a workout than the hill-tribe treks.

Chiang Mai Mountain Biking (☎ 08 1024 7046; www.mountainbikingchiangmai.com; 1 Th Samlan; tours 1450-1550B) Guided mountain-biking tours through Doi Suthep.

Chiang Mai Rock Climbing Adventures (☎ 0 6911 1470; www.thailandclimbing.com; 55/3 Th Ratchaphakhinai; climbing course 1800-6600B) Teaches and leads rock-climbing tours on Crazy Horse Buttress, about 20km east of Chiang Mai.

Click & Travel (☎ 0 5328 1553; www.clickandtravelonline.com; tours 950-1300B) Bicycles tours of cultural sights in Chiang Mai.

Elephant Nature Park (☎ booking office 0 5320 8246; www.elephantnaturepark.org; 1 Soi 1, Th Ratchamankha; full-day tour 2500B) Semiwild sanctuary for abused or retired elephants; tours include watching the herd and bathing the animals.

Flight of the Gibbon (☎ 08 9970 5511; www.treetopasia.com; tours from 2000B) Whiz through the forest canopy on a 2km-long zipline. You can also tack on a waterfall hike or an overnight at a village homestay.

Peak (☎ 0 5380 0567; www.thepeakadventure.com; climbing course 1500-2500B) Variety of soft adventure outings, from white-water rafting and trekking to rock climbing and abseiling.

Siam River Adventures (☎ 0 895151917; www.siamrivers.com; Kona Café, 17 Th Ratwithi; tours from 1800B) White-water rafting and kayaking on Mae Nam Taeng.

Courses

COOKING

Cooking classes are a big hit in Chiang Mai and typically include a tour of a local market, hands-on cooking instructions and a recipe booklet. Classes usually cost 900B a day and are held at either an in-town location for those with limited time or at an out-of-town garden setting for more ambiance. There are dozens of schools; here are a few:

Baan Thai (☎ 0 5335 7339; www.baanthaicookery.com; 11 Soi 5, Th Ratchadamnoen)

Chiang Mai Thai Cookery School (☎ 0 5320 6388; www.thaicookeryschool.com; booking office 47/2 Th Moon Muang) Owned by a famous Thai TV chef.

Smile House Cookery School (☎ 0 5320 8661-2; www.smilehousechiangmai.com; Smile House, 5 Soi 2, Th Ratchamankha) Also offers jungle survival cooking course.

Thai Kitchen Cookery School (☎ 0 5327 6886; 32 Th Loi Kroh)

LANGUAGE

American University Alumni (AUA; ☎ 0 5327 8407; www.learnthaiinchiangmai.com; 73 Th Ratchadamnoen; course 4200B) Six weeks of structured Thai-language coursework at different fluency levels.

Chiang Mai Thai Language Center (☎ 0 5327 7810; www.thaicultureholidays.com; 131 Th Ratchadamnoen; course 3000B) Flexible class schedule for all Thai language levels.

Payap University (http://ic.payap.ac.th; Th Kaew Nawarat) Intensive Thai language courses through the languages department (☎ 0 5324 1255, ext 7220; course from 7500B) as well as a Southeast Asian Studies certificate program (☎ 0 5385148, ext 7227; http://thaistudies.payap.ac.th).

MUAY THAI (THAI BOXING)

Lanna Muay Thai (Kiatbusaba; ☎ 0 5389 2102; www.lannamuaythai.com; 64/1 Soi Chiang Khlan; day/month courses 400/8000B) A boxing camp northwest of town that offers authentic *muay thai* instruction to foreigners as well as Thais. Lanna-trained *kàthoey* (transvestite) boxer Parinya Kiatbusaba triumphed at Lumphini stadium in Bangkok in 1998.

TRADITIONAL MASSAGE

Lek Chaiya (☎ 0 5327 8325; www.nervetouch.com; 25 Th Ratchadamnoen; course from 5200B) Specialises in *jàp sên* (similar to acupressure) and the use of medicinal herbs, a technique perfected by Khun Lek and passed on to her son.

Old Medicine Hospital (OMH; ☎ 0 5327 5085; www.thaimassageschool.ac.th; 78/1 Soi Siwaka Komarat, Th Wualai; courses 2500-5000B) A traditional northern Thai program with two 10-day courses a month. Classes tend to be large during the months of December to February.

Festivals & Events

Flower Festival (early February) The mother of Chiang Mai festivals, including parades, the Queen of the Flower Festival beauty contest and plenty of flower-draped floats.

Songkran (mid-April) Celebrate the Thai New Year in wet and wild Chiang Mai.

Loi Krathong (late October to early November) In Chiang Mai this national festival is known as Yi Peng and is celebrated by launching cylindrical hot-air balloons as well as candle-lit miniature boats.

Sleeping

A concentration of guest houses can be found in the northeastern corner of the old city on Soi 7 and Soi 9 off Th Moon Muang. Most guest houses make their 'rice and curry' from booking trekking tours and reserve rooms for those customers; see Dangers & Annoyances, p751. Some guest houses will arrange free transport from the bus/train station with advance warning and most have free wi-fi.

Daret's House (☎ 0 5323 5440; darets-house@yahoo.com; 7/1 Soi 5, Th Chaiyaphum; r 100-350B) One of CM's old-school backpacker spots with basic cell-house rooms and a dash of northern Thai hospitality to save it from feeling like just another Khao San flophouse. Meals are cheap too.

Kham Kaew House (☎ 0 5328 7549; 29 Soi 9, Th Moon Muang; s 150-190B, d 250B) An old Thai house with old Thai furnishings, rambling stairs and a garden so quiet that even the manager whispers.

Malak House (☎ 0 5322 7257; 23/5 Soi 7, Th Moon Muang; s 180B, d 300-400B; ❄ 💻) A new arrival that has introduced itself with outrageously cheap rates for four square-walled rooms with en suite bathrooms and a rooftop garden terrace.

Pao Come Inn (☎ 0 5325 2377; 3 Soi 3, Th Chang Moi Kao; d 250-450B; ❄) Just a handful of rooms occupy this old-fashioned guest house in a converted Thai house tucked deep into a residential *soi*.

Pagoda Inn (☎ 0 5323 3290; 49 Th Chang Moi; r 250-450B; ❄) Flashpacker style at backpacker prices, this funky place is dolled up like a Chinese concubine and rooms occupy a maze-like corner property.

Ban Wiang (☎ 0 5321 0542; www.banwiang-guesthouse.com; 38/1 Soi 1, Th Ratchadamnoen; d 250-500B; ❄ 💻) A converted apartment building with rooms covering every price and amenities combo. It is quiet and nondescript, and has a free coffee corner and sitting area.

Hollanda Montri Guesthouse (☎ 0 5324 2450; www.hollandamontri.com; 365 Th Charoenrat; d 450-550B; ❄ 💻) The air-con rooms are the better bargain at this riverside guest house, with ample garden space but a bit outside the centre.

Riverside House (☎ 0 5324 1860; www.riversidehousechiangmai.com; 101 Th Chiang Mai-Lamphun; r 500-900B; ❄ 💻) Be an adventurer on the east bank of the river at this modest abode. Reception is via the attached travel agency and the quietest rooms are deeper into the property.

Eating

Unlike Bangkok, restaurants in Chiang Mai tend to be low-key and unpretentious. Vegetarian fare excels in a proliferation of religious society restaurants. For a date night, try the riverside restaurants north of Nawarat Bridge. Cafes abound serving locally grown coffee.

THAI

The weekend walking streets (see Shopping) have great eats, especially when it comes to northern Thai specialities like *khâo sawy* (a mild chicken curry with flat egg noodles). More northern Thai specialities can be found near the Night Bazaar at the string of restaurants around **Ban Haw Mosque** (Soi 1, Th Charoen Prathet), the anchor for Chiang Mai's Yunnanese Muslim community. But honestly, the atmosphere is way better than the food.

Vegetarian Centre of Chiang Mai (☎ 0 5327 1262; 14 Th Mahidon; dishes 10-15B; 🕒 breakfast, lunch & dinner) Sponsored by the Asoke Foundation, an ascetic Buddhist society, this cafeteria specialises in wholesome Thai vegetarian fare at a pauper's price.

Galare Food Centre (Th Chang Khlan; dishes 50-80B; 🕒 6pm-midnight) This classic food court offers a stress-free version of a night market, easy access to the Chiang Mai Night Bazaar and nightly entertainment like Thai classical dancing.

NORTHERN CUISINE

Thanks to northern Thailand's cooler climate, familiar vegetables such as broccoli and cauliflower might make an appearance in a stir-fry or bowl of noodles. Untranslatable herbs and leaves from the dense forests are also incorporated into regional dishes, imparting a distinct flavour of mist-shrouded hills. Even coffee grows here and chewy cups of Arabica abound. Day-market vendors sell blue sticky rice, which is dyed by a morning glory–like flower and topped with a sweetened egg custard that will make your teeth itch.

Showing its Burmese, Chinese and Shan influences, the north prefers curries that are milder and more stewlike than the coconut milk–based curries of southern and central Thailand. Sour notes are enhanced with the addition of pickled cabbage and lime, rather than the tear-inducing spiciness favoured in most Thai dishes. The most famous example of northern cuisine is *khâo sawy,* a mild chicken curry with flat egg noodles. A Burmese expat, *kaeng hang-leh* is another example of a northern-style curry. Like the Chinese, northern Thais love pork and vendors everywhere sell *kâap mŭu* (deep-fried pork crackling) as a snack and side dish.

Northern Thais prefer sticky rice with their meals.

AUM Vegetarian Restaurant (☎ 0 5327 8315; 66 Th Moon Muang; dishes 50-140B; 🕑 8am-5pm) An easy-going place filled with used paperbacks and newspaper-thumbing expats, AUM does respectable vegetarian Thai food, healthy juices and organic coffee.

Heuan Phen (☎ 0 5327 7103; 112 Th Ratchamankha; dishes 60-150B; 🕑 8am-3pm & 5-10pm) One of Chiang Mai's most famous purveyors of northern Thai cuisine, this restaurant serves dinner in an antique-cluttered room that attracts visiting appetites. The food is a tad lacklustre but the ambiance is a treat. Daytime meals are served in a large canteen.

Lemon Tree (☎ 0 5322 2009; 26/1-2 Th Huay Kaew; dishes 65-150B) Near Kad Suan Kaew shopping mall, this cheery place does an exhaustive list of authentic Thai dishes, like *kaeng paa lûuk thûng kài* (spicy jungle curry with free-range chicken).

Chiang Mai is well known for its covered markets. **Talat Pratu Chiang Mai** (Th Bamrungburi) is a busy morning market selling fresh fruit, piles of fried food and fistfuls of sticky rice. After its midday siesta, the market caters to the dinner crowd around plastic tables and steaming woks. **Talat Thanin** (off Th Chang Pheauk) is the market lovers' market. It is clean and bountiful.

INTERNATIONAL

Blue Diamond (☎ 0 5321 7120; 35/1 Soi 9, Th Moon Muang; dishes 50-100B; 🕑 Mon-Sat 8am-8pm) A relaxed garden cafe where you can catch up on your journal and enjoy a healthy breakfast of fresh baked goods, wake-me-up coffee and mainly vegie fare.

Art Cafe (☎ 0 5320 6365; cnr Th Tha Phae & Th Kotchasarn; dishes 60-150B; 🕑 breakfast, lunch & dinner) It would be too easy for this centrally located diner to be too lazy, but the breakfasts stand up to scrutiny, the coffee is thick and the menu is massive enough to please the persistently picky.

Pulcinella da Stefano (☎ 0 5387 4189; 2/1-2 Th Chang Moi Kao; dishes 100-200B; 🕑 lunch & dinner) This romantic trattoria is the perfect place to bring a date without maxing out the credit card. Great seafood pastas, antipasto and northern Italian fare.

Jerusalem Falafel (☎ 0 5327 0208; 35/3 Th Moon Muang; dishes 100-280B; 🕑 breakfast, lunch & dinner) A well-travelled friend when you need a break from rice, this Middle Eastern restaurant is a fun outing with friends.

Gigantea Restaurant (☎ 0 5323 3464; Th Chang Moi; dishes 100-350B; 🕑 lunch & dinner Tue-Sun) Considering its proximity from the sea, Chiang Mai has a respectable crop of Japanese restaurants, including this cafe run by a husband and wife team and much loved by locals.

Duke's (☎ 0 5324 9231; 49/4-5 Th Chiang Mai-Lamphun; dishes 150-300B; 🕑 lunch & dinner) A homage to the American cowboy, the Duke's feeds frontier-sized appetites, mainly expat NGOs and missionaries as well as special-occasion Thais. There's a second branch at the night market.

Drinking & Entertainment

The ale flows fast and furious at the bars along Th Moon Muang near Pratu Tha Phae, such as Kafé and John's Place. Another backpacker watering hole is the cluster of outdoor bars on the corner of Th Ratwithi and Th Ratchaphakinai often referred to as Little Jamaica.

Riverside Bar & Restaurant (☎ 0 5321 1035; Th Charoenrat) Chiang Mai's version of the Hard Rock Café, Riverside has been serving meals and music on the banks of the Mae Nam Ping for more than two decades. On weekends, the Riverside knits together *faràng* and Thais into sing-along parties.

THC (19/4-5 Th Kotchasan) The marijuana motif says it all. This place is so chilled out it's horizontal. Occupying a rooftop overlooking the old city, there are music and beers nightly.

Rasta Art Bar & Restaurant (☎ 0 1690 1577; Th Si Phum) The newish location of Chiang Mai's most famous Jamaican-inspired club introduces visitors to dreadlocked Thais and reliable reggae covers.

Drunken Flower (☎ 0 5389 4210; 28/3 Soi 17, Th Nimmanhaemin) A bohemian mix of Chiang Mai University (CMU) students and NGO expats gather at this cosy bar in the trendy Nimman area to fill the marble tables with empty beer bottles.

UN Irish Pub (☎ 0 5321 4554; 24/1 Th Ratwithi) Show off your knowledge with the popular Thursday-night quiz.

Shopping

Chiang Mai has long been an important centre for handicrafts. Th Tha Phae is filled with interesting antique and textile stores. Soi 1, Th Nimmanhaemin is Chiang Mai's nascent boutique scene with arts and decor suited to handsome budgets.

Chiang Mai Night Bazaar (Th Chang Khlan; 🕒 7pm-midnight) The leading night-time tourist attraction is a direct descendant of the original Yunnanese trading caravans that stopped here along the ancient trade route between China and Myanmar. Today commerce sprawls over several blocks on Th Chang Khlan from Th Tha Phae to Th Si Donchai towards the river and includes itinerant vendor carts and covered buildings. The market offers a huge variety of ordinary souvenirs, some northern Thai handicrafts, and lots of people-watching and people-dodging as the footpaths are often congested.

Talat Warorot (Th Chang Moi near Th Praisani) is the city's oldest market and sells cheap but colourful fabrics and clothes. The **Saturday Walking Street** (Th Wualai; 🕒 4pm-midnight Sat) and the **Sunday Walking Street** (Th Ratchadamnoen; 🕒 4pm-midnight Sun) close off the respective streets to vehicles for a festive shopping bazaar known for crafts and souvenirs.

Getting There & Away

AIR

Regularly scheduled international and domestic flights arrive at **Chiang Mai International Airport** (☎ 0 5327 0222). Airlines operating out of Chiang Mai include:

Air Asia (code AK; ☎ 0 2515 9999; www.airasia.com) Flies to Bangkok and Kuala Lumpur.

Bangkok Airways (code PG; ☎ 0 2265 5556; www.bangkokair.com) Flies to Bangkok and on to Ko Samui.

China Airlines (☎ 0 5320 1268; www.china-airlines.com) Flies to Taipei.

Lao Airlines (code QV; ☎ 0 5322 3401; www.laoairlines.com) Flies to Vientiane and Luang Prabang.

Nok Air (code DD; ☎ 1318; www.nokair.com) Flies to Bangkok, Pai and Mae Hong Son.

One-Two-Go (code OX; ☎ 1126; www.fly12go.com) Flies to Bangkok.

Siam GA (SGA; ☎ 0 5328 0444; www.sga.co.th) Code-share flight with Nok Air to Pai and Mae Hong Son.

SilkAir (code MI; ☎ 0 5390 4985; www.silkair.com) Flies to Singapore.

Thai Airways International (THAI, code TG; ☎ 0 5321 1044; www.thaiair.com) Flies to Bangkok and Mae Hong Son.

BUS

There are two bus stations in Chiang Mai: the long-distance **Arcade bus station** (Th Kaew Nawarat), northeast of town, handles Bangkok and most other major cities; and **Chang Pheuak bus station** (Th Chang Pheuak), north of the old city, handles buses to provincial towns, such as Fang and Tha Ton, as well as Lamphun. From the town centre, a túk-túk or chartered sǎwngthǎew to the Arcade bus station should cost about 40B to 60B; to the Chang Pheuak bus station get a sǎwngthǎew at the normal 20B rate.

TRAIN

The **train station** (☎ 0 5324 5364; Th Charoen Muang) is 2.5km east of the old city. There are six daily departures between Chiang Mai and Bangkok and the journey takes 12 to 15 hours. Fares on rapid trains are 231/391B for 3rd-/2nd-class seats and 491/541B for upper/lower sleeping berths in the 2nd-class cars. Fares on express trains are 271/431B for 3rd-/2nd-class seats, 541B for 2nd-class air-con seats, 531/581B for upper/lower sleeping berths in 2nd-class cars and 751/821B for upper/lower sleeping berths for 2nd-class air-con cars. Sprinter (special express diesel) fares are 611B for 2nd-class air-con seats, and special express trains are 1253B for 1st-class air-con sleeper or 791/881B for upper/lower 2nd-class air-con sleeper.

BUSES FROM CHIANG MAI

Destination	Class	Fare (B)	Duration (hr)	Frequency
Bangkok	VIP	695	10	several evening departures
Chiang Rai	ordinary	110	3	hourly
	air-con	150-295		
Khon Kaen	air-con	578	12	one evening departure
Mae Hong Son	ordinary	150	8	three departures
	air-con	210		
Mae Sai	ordinary	188	5	frequent
	air-con	241		
Mae Sariang	ordinary	106	5	three departures
	air-con	191		
Mae Sot	ordinary	253	6	two departures
	air-con	280-347		
Nan	air-con	235-302	6	hourly
	VIP	578		
Pai	ordinary	84	4	three departures
	air-con	118		
Phitsanulok	air-con	306	6	four departures

Advance bookings, especially for air-con sleepers, are advised, particularly around public holidays. Transport to the station via săwngthăew should cost 40B.

Getting Around

Airport taxis cost a flat 150B. If you aren't in a hurry, you can also walk out to the main road and flag down a túk-túk or red săwngthăew, which should cost 60B or 70B to your hotel.

Plenty of red săwngthăew circulate around the city operating as shared taxis. Flag one down and tell them your destination; if they are going that way, they'll nod and maybe pick up other passengers along the way. The starting fare is 20B, with longer trips 40B. Túk-túk are about 20B more expensive than săwngthăew and only operate as charters; most trips around town should cost 40B to 60B.

You can rent bicycles (50B a day) or 100cc motorcycles (from 150B to 200B) to explore Chiang Mai. Bicycles are a great way to get around the city.

AROUND CHIANG MAI

Doi Inthanon

The highest peak in the country, Doi Inthanon (2565m), and the surrounding **national park** (admission 200B) have hiking trails, waterfalls and two monumental stupas erected in honour of the king and queen. It's a popular day trip from Chiang Mai for tourists and locals, especially during the New Year's holiday when there's the rarely seen phenomenon of frost.

Most visitors come on a tour from Chiang Mai but the park is accessible via public transport. Buses leave from Chang Pheuak terminal and yellow săwngthăew leave from Pratu Chiang Mai for Chom Thong (61B), 58km from Chiang Mai and the closest town to the park. Some buses go directly to the park's entrance gate near Nam Tok Mae Klang, and some are bound for Hot and will drop you off in Chom Thong.

From Chom Thong there are regular săwngthăew to the park's entrance gate at Nam Tok Mae Klang (30B), about 8km north. Săwngthăew from Mae Klang to the summit of Doi Inthanon (80B) leave almost hourly until late afternoon.

Lampang

Lampang is a mini Chiang Mai: it was constructed as a walled city and boasts magnificent teak temples built by Burmese and Shan artisans. Adding to its Old World charm are the horse-drawn carriages that are a colourful alternative to the túk-túk commute.

Wat Phra Kaew Don Tao (admission 20B) is one of the many former homes of the exalted Emerald Buddha, now residing in Bangkok's Wat Phra Kaew. Other noteworthy temples include **Wat Si Rong Meuang** and **Wat Si Chum**, both fine examples of Burmese woodworking and artisanship.

Th Talat Kao hosts a **walking street market** (Kat Korng Ta; ⏰ 4-10pm Sat & Sun), when vehicle traffic is blocked off and vendors set up stalls selling souvenirs, snack and handicrafts. The street is dotted with old shophouses showcasing the international styles associated with the timber trade: English, Chinese and Burmese.

Rustic herbal saunas are a hallmark of northern Thailand and can be found at **Samakhom Samunphrai Phak Neua** (☎ 08 9758 2396; 149 Th Pratuma; massage per hr 200B, sauna 100B; ⏰ 8am-7.30pm), next to Wat Hua Khuang in the Wiang Neua area.

Tip Inn Guest House (☎ 0 5422 1821; 143 Th Talat Kao; r 150-350B; ❄) is a homey alternative to Lampang's characterless cheapies. It's also the only accommodation to be located in the middle of historic Th Talat Kao. The newer building in the back of **TT&T Back Packer Guesthouse** (☎ 0 5422 1303; 82 Th Pa Mai; r 200-350B; ❄) offers intermittent glances of the Mae Nam Wang. The attractive and comfortable chill-out area makes up for lean amenities elsewhere.

Lampang's **night market** (Th Ratsada; ⏰ 4-8pm), across the river, and **lunch stalls** (Th Phahonyothin; dishes 20-30B; ⏰ 10am-2pm), directly opposite Khelangnakorn Hospital, have cheap Thai food. Lampang is known for *khâo taan*, tasty deep-fried rice cakes drizzled with palm sugar, the making of which can be observed at **Khun Manee** (☎ 0 5431 2272; 35 Th Ratsada).

The Chinese-Thai fare at **Aroy One Baht** (☎ 0 8970 0944; cnr Th Suan Dok & Th Talat Kao; dishes 20-90B; ⏰ dinner) is both delicious and cheap, the service lightening fast and the setting in a wooden house-cum-balcony-cum-garden heaps of fun.

GETTING THERE & AWAY

Lampang's bus terminal is outside of town (accessible via 15B shared sǎwngthǎew). Destinations include Chiang Mai's Arcade bus station (ordinary 25B, air-con 50B to 65B, two hours, frequent), Chiang Rai (162B, four hours, three departures), Phitsanulok (air-con 176B to 265B, four hours) and Bangkok (air-con/VIP 513/710B, eight to nine hours, evening departures). Lampang-bound sǎwngthǎew also leave from near Chiang Mai's TAT office in the direction of Lamphun.

Lampang's historic **train station** (☎ 0 5421 7024; Th Phahonyothin) is a slow but comfortable ride from Chiang Mai (3rd/2nd class 23/50B, two to three hours, six times daily) or Bangkok (3rd class 256B, 2nd class air-con/fan 574/394B, sleeper from 494B, 12 hours, six times daily).

PAI

pop 3500

This cool corner of the northern mountains started out as a hippie enclave for Chiang Mai bohos who would come here to hang out beside the rambling river and strum out blues tunes at night. Word spread and the dusty little town now does a thriving trade in

ELEPHANT WELFARE

At one time in Thai society, elephants were war machines, logging trucks and work companions. But Thailand's logging ban and modern machines have rendered the elephant jobless and orphaned in the modern world. Recently, enterprising activists have figured out how to help: they've brought mistreated or retired elephants back to nature and turned their eco-retirement homes into tourist attractions.

Thai Elephant Conservation Center (☎ 0 5424 7875; www.changthai.com; Lampang; adult/child 70/30B) promotes elephant ecotourism through educational shows (10am, 11am and 1.30pm), rides, bathing (9.45am and 1.15pm) and a gift centre selling pachyderm-produced art. The centre also provides medical care for injured elephants, mahout training courses and homestay programs. To reach the centre, take a Lampang-bound bus or sǎwngthǎew (25B) from Chiang Mai and get off at the Km 37 marker. Free vans shuttle visitors the 1.5km distance between the highway and the centre.

Elephant Nature Park (☎ booking office 0 5320 8246; www.elephantnaturepark.org; 1 Soi 1, Th Ratchamankha, Chiang Mai; full-day tour 2500B) is run by Khun Lek (Sangduan Chailert), who has won numerous awards for her elephant sanctuary, 60km from Chiang Mai. The retired or rescued elephants live in a semiwild environment. Visitors can help wash the elephants and watch the herd, but there is no show or riding. Khun Lek also operates a pachyderm medical program and invites volunteers to help her with her work. See p754 for more.

THAILAND'S HILL-TRIBE COMMUNITIES

The term 'hill tribe' refers to ethnic minorities living in mountainous northern and western Thailand. The Thais refer to them as *chao khao,* literally 'mountain people'. Each hill tribe has its own language, customs, mode of dress and spiritual beliefs. Most are of seminomadic origin, having migrated to Thailand from Tibet, Myanmar, China and Laos during the past 200 years or so, although some groups may have been in Thailand for much longer. The Tribal Research Institute in Chiang Mai recognises 10 different hill tribes, but there may be up to 20 in Thailand. Lonely Planet's *Hill Tribes Phrasebook* gives a handy, basic introduction to the culture and languages of a number of the tribes.

The **Karen** are the largest hill-tribe group in Thailand and number about 47% of the total tribal population. They tend to live in lowland valleys and practise crop rotation rather than swidden agriculture. Their numbers and proximity to the mainstream society has made them the most integrated and financially successful of the hill-tribe groups. Thickly woven V-neck tunics of various colours (unmarried women wear white) are typically worn. There are four distinct Karen groups – the Skaw (White) Karen, Pwo Karen, Pa-O (Black) Karen and Kayah (Red) Karen.

The **Hmong** are Thailand's second-largest hill-tribe group and are especially numerous in Chiang Mai province, with smaller enclaves in the other northern Thai provinces. They usually live on mountain peaks or plateaus above 1000m. Tribespeople wear simple black jackets and indigo or black baggy trousers (White Hmong) with striped borders or indigo skirts (Blue Hmong) and silver jewellery. Sashes may be worn around the waist, and embroidered aprons draped front and back. Most women wear their hair in a large bun.

The **Akha** are among the poorest of Thailand's ethnic minorities and live mainly in Chiang Mai and Chiang Rai provinces, along mountain ridges or steep slopes 1000m to 1400m in altitude. They are regarded as skilled farmers but are often displaced from arable land by government intervention. Their traditional garb is a headdress of beads, feathers and dangling silver ornaments.

Other minority groups include the Lisu, Lahu and Mien.

Village Etiquette

The minority tribes of Thailand living in the northern mountains have managed to maintain their own distinct cultural identity despite increased interaction with the majority culture and even forced relocation over the last 30 years. Even with the adoption of outside influences – like Christianity or Buddhism or wearing donated Western-style clothes instead of traditional garb – many hill-tribe villages continue their animistic traditions, which define social taboos and

everything *faràngs* do when they cross long distances to be with each other – from fruit shakes to altered states. Urban Thais have joined the Pai altar for its stress-reducing setting within a picturesque valley. The town itself – a modest mixture of Shan, Thai and Muslim Chinese residents – can be explored in a matter of minutes, but the real adventure lies along the paths in the hills beyond. Some might sniff that Pai is played out, but remember folks this isn't a race.

Information

Several places around town offer internet services and they all charge round 20B to 30B per hour. Banks and ATMs can be found along Pai's two main streets, Th Rangsiyanon and Th Chaisongkhram.

Siam Books (☎ 0 5369 9075; Th Chaisongkhram) Boasts the town's largest selection of new and used books.

Tourist information booth (☎ 0 5369 9935; 🕑 8.30am-4.30pm) Small booth near the District Office staffed with officials who speak basic English and who can provide a simple map of the area.

Sights & Activities

Since Pai is more of a 'state of mind', it is lean on full-fledged tourist attractions. If you need an outing, head to **Wat Phra That Mae Yen** (1km east of town) for its hilltop vista. The other main contender is **Tha Pai Hot Springs** (admission 200B; 🕑 7am-6pm), a well-kept park featuring a scenic stream and pleasant hot-spring bathing pools. The park is 7km southeast of town across Mae Nam Pai.

The rest of your time will be spent on various wanderings or pamperings.

All the guest houses in town can provide information on **trekking** (starting at 700B per day). We've heard complaints that trekking conventions. If you're planning on visiting hill-tribe villages on an organised trek, talk to your guide about dos and don'ts. Here is a general prescription to get you started:

- Always ask permission before taking any photos of tribespeople, especially at private moments inside dwellings. Many traditional belief systems view photography with suspicion.
- Show respect for religious symbols and rituals. Don't touch totems at village entrances or sacred items hanging from trees. Don't participate in ceremonies unless invited to join.
- Avoid cultivating a tradition of begging, especially among children. Don't hand out candy unless you can also arrange for modern dentistry. Talk to your guide about donating to a local school instead.
- Avoid public nudity and be careful not to undress near an open window where village children might be able to peep in.
- Don't flirt with members of the opposite sex unless you plan to marry them. Don't drink or do drugs with the villagers; altered states sometimes lead to culture clashes.
- Smile at villagers even if they stare at you. And ask your guide how to say 'hello' in the tribal language.
- Avoid public displays of affection, which in some traditional systems is viewed as offensive to the spirit world.
- Don't interact with the villagers' livestock, even the free-roaming pigs; these creatures are valuable possessions not entertainment oddities. Also avoid interacting with jungle animals, which in some belief systems are viewed as visiting spirits.
- Don't litter.
- Adhere to the same feet taboos of Thai culture (see the boxed text on p703). Plus don't step on the threshold of a house, don't prop your feet up against the fire and don't wear your shoes inside.

See Volunteering, p831, in the Directory for information on organisations working with hill-tribe communities.

groups can be too big; a good size is fewer than 10 people.

Folks rave about rafting on the Mae Nam Pai, available during the wet season only (July to December). **Thai Adventure Rafting** (☎ 0 5369 9111; www.activethailand.com; Th Rangsiyanon; per person 2500B) has two-day, white-water rafting trips from Pai to Mae Hong Son.

Thom's Pai Elephant Camp Tours (☎ 0 5369 9286; www.thomelephant.com; 4 Th Rangsiyanon; rides 500-700B) offers jungle elephant rides year-round; trips include a soak in the camp's hot spring–fed tubs afterwards.

Perfect the art of relaxation at **Pai Traditional Massage** (☎ 0 5369 9121; 68/3 Soi 1, Th Wiang Tai; massage per one/two hr 180/350B, sauna 80B; 9am-9pm), which offers northern Thai massage, *sàmùn phrai* (medicinal herbs) sauna and even massage courses. A remnant from Pai's earlier era, **Mr Jan's Massage** (Mr Jan's Bungalows; Soi Wanchaloem 18; per hr 150B) employs a more forceful Shan-Burmese massage technique.

No hippie haven would be complete without yoga, available at **Mam Yoga House** (☎ 0 89954 4981; Th Rangsiyanon; one-day course 200-550B) and **Fluid** (Ban Mae Yen; admission fee 60B; 9am-6pm), outside of town across from Sun Hut.

Sleeping

Pai used to be an inexpensive place to stay, but the 2005 flood demolished most of the cheapies which have since been replaced by more expensive choices. The most atmospheric guest houses are spread along the banks of the Mae Nam Pai and they number in the dozens. During the cool season (November to April) it can be difficult to find a room; accommodation gets tighter during late December to early January (the Thai tourist season), when tents are available for about 100B.

Duang Guest House (☎ 0 5369 9101; 8 Th Rangsiyanon; r 150-500B) One of the first guest houses in Pai, Duang has bare and aged rooms, but there's a reliable trekking agency, a decent restaurant and it has a convenient central location.

Charlie's House (☎ 0 5369 9039; Th Rangsiyanon; r 200-600B; ❄) This longstanding and locally run place offers a range of apartment-like options located steps from all the action.

Unicorn's House (☎ 0 5369 8068; Wiang Tai; bungalows 250-350B) This is one of the few remaining places still offering dirt-cheap bamboo huts. Unicorn is located just across the permanent bridge east of town.

Sun Hut (☎ 0 5369 9730; www.thesunhut.com; 28/1 Ban Mae Yen; r 350-1350B) This psychedelic collection of zodiac-inspired bungalows upholds Pai's countercultural personality. You'll need a motorcycle to come and go. The turn-off is signposted about 1km from town on the road to the hot springs.

Golden Hut (☎ 0 5369 9949; 107 Moo 3; r 400-600B) A long-running backpacker favourite, Golden Hut has modest bungalows encircling a decent-sized lawn, and the main common area looks directly out over the Mae Nam Pai. If it's empty (and if you're a steady climber), give the tree house a try.

Eating & Drinking

During the day there's takeaway food at **Saengthongaram Market** (Th Khetkelang). For tasty local eats, try the **Evening Market** (gàht láang; Th Ratchadamnoen) that unfolds every afternoon from about 3pm to sunset. And every night vendors turn Th Chaisongkhram and Th Rangsiyanon into an open-air buffet, hawking all manner of food and drink from stalls and refurbished VW vans.

Baan Phleng (cnr Th Khetkalang & Th Chaisongkhram; dishes 30-60B; 🕑 10am-10pm) This popular place does a mix of northern Thai and Mae Hong Son–specific dishes. The English-language sign reads 'Local Northern Thai food' and an English-language menu with photos helps the decision-making process.

All About Coffee (☎ 0 5369 9429; Th Chaisongkhram; dishes 45-75B; 🕑 8.30am-6.30pm) A powerful hangover antidote, the espresso here will help you bound through town. Like most everything in Pai, the decor is creative and inviting. The sandwiches are fantastic here too.

Bebop (Th Rangsiyanon; 🕑 6pm-1am) If you want to become a card-carrying member of the Pai night-crawlers, simply show up at Bebop around midnight, when half the town seems to arrive. Live rock and cover bands perform nightly.

Phu Pai Art Café (Th Rangsiyanon; 🕑 5pm-midnight) This attractive, wooden house is a highlight of Pai's live music scene. The amps turn on at 8pm and impress the crowds by 8.01pm.

Getting There & Around

The **bus stop** (Th Chaisongkhram) is in a dirt lot in the centre of town. All buses that stop here follow the Chiang Mai–Pai–Mae Hong Son–Mae Sariang loop in either direction. As well as buses to Chiang Mai (ordinary 112B, four hours, two morning departures) and Mae Hong Son (80B, four hours), there are also more frequent minivans (150B). The road is savagely steep and snaking; grab a window seat and ride on an empty stomach if prone to motion sickness.

Most of Pai is accessible by foot but you'll need to rent a bicycle or motorcycle for trips to the hot springs or further-flung guest houses.

MAE HONG SON

pop 8300

Northern Thai aficionados prefer the far-flung border feel of Mae Hong Son to that of Pai. Mae Hong Son is a quiet provincial capital that practically peers into Myanmar and is skirted by forested mountains. The local trekking scene in Mae Hong Son is the primary draw but the daily market and local eats further impress its fan base.

Information

Most of the banks on Th Khunlum Praphat have ATMs. A few internet shops can be found around the southern end of Th Khunlum Praphat.

Post office (Th Khunlum Praphat)

Srisangwarn Hospital (☎ 0 5361 1378; Th Singhanat Bamrung)

TAT office (☎ 0 5361 2982; Th Khunlum Praphat; 🕑 8.30am-4.30pm Mon-Fri) Across from the post office.

Tourist police (☎ 0 5361 1812, emergencies 1155; Th Singhanat Bamrung; 🕑 8.30am-4.30pm) Report thefts or lodge complaints against trekking companies or guest houses here.

Sights & Activities

Mae Hong Son's temples are surviving monuments to their Burmese and Shan artisans and benefactors and hint at the town's past as a

HILL-TRIBE HOMESTAYS

It is hard to appreciate some of Thailand's minority cultures from the bus window or the comfort of a guest house. Homestays offer insight into a people's hearth and home.

Lisu Hill Tribe Homestay (☎ 08 9998 4886, 08 5721 1575; www.lisuhilltribe.com; Nong Thong; r incl meals 300B) is in a Lisu village in the northern mountains near Soppong. Run by an American and his Lisu wife, guests can participate in craft and culture classes. Visit the website for booking and transport information.

Akha Association for Education and Culture in Thailand (Afect; ☎ 0 5371 4250, 08 1952 2179; www.akhaasia.multiply.com; 468 Th Rimkok, Chiang Rai) runs a Life Stay program in which volunteers live and work in an Akha village with a local family. Depending on the agricultural season, the days can be quite physical: working in the fields, helping build a house or gathering food in the forest. Proceeds from the Life Stay are put back into the community for health and education programs.

logging and elephant training centre. **Wat Jong Klang** and **Wat Jong Kham** boast whitewashed stupas and glittering zinc fretwork.

The town's signature feature is **Nong Jong Kham**, a well-photographed lake that often awakens to a thick blanket of fog. Another fog-spotting sight is **Wat Phra That Doi Kong Mu**, which sits on a hilltop west of town.

The **Poi Sang Long Festival** in March takes place at Wat Jong Klang and Wat Jong Kham and is a surviving Shan custom in which young boys entering the monastery as novice monks are dressed in ornate costumes and paraded around the temple under festive parasols.

Guest houses in town arrange **treks** to nearby hill-tribe villages, as well as **white-water rafting** and **longtail boat trips** on the Mae Nam Pai. Reliable operators:

Friend Tour (☎ 0 5361 1647; 21 Th Pradit Jong Kham; 1-day trek 700-900B) With nearly 20 years experience, this recommended outfit offers trekking, elephant riding and rafting, as well as day tours.

Nature Walks (☎ 0 5361 1040, 08 9552 6899; natural_walks@yahoo.com) Treks range from one-day nature walks (1000B) to multiday journeys across the province (2500B).

Sleeping

Friend House (☎ 0 5362 0119; 20 Th Pradit Jong Kham; r 150-400B) Clean, efficient and deservedly popular, this guest-house complex covers all the bases and a few rooms overlook the lake.

Home For Relaxing (☎ 0 5362 0313; 26/1 Th Chamnan Sathit; r 200B) Run by a friendly young couple from Chiang Mai, the handful of rooms here are in a cosy wooden house near Nong Jong Kham.

Palm House Guest House (☎ 0 5361 4022; 22/1 Th Chamnansthit; r 300-600B; ❄) Slightly sterile, Palm House is clean and predictable with a few flourishes: the fan rooms have satellite TV and little balconies.

Romtai (☎ 0 5361 2437; Th Chumnanatit; r 500-1200B; ❄) Behind the lakeside temples, Romtai has a variety of sleeps in a garden setting.

Eating

Mae Sri Bua (☎ 0 5361 2471; 51 Th Singhanatbamrung; dishes 20-30B ⏰ lunch) For authentic local eats, try this restaurant specialising in Shan curries, soups and dips. Auntie Bua doesn't speak English, but the universal language of pointing should work.

Salween River Restaurant (☎ 0 5361 2050; Th Singhanat Bamrung; dishes 50-160B; ⏰ breakfast, lunch & dinner) Salween is the place to come for hill-tribe coffee and hearty Western breakfasts. The owners are a source of information and it's a popular hang-out for volunteers. Thai, Shan and Burmese food is available.

Sunflower Café (☎ 0 5362 0549; Th Pradit Jong Kham; ⏰ 7am-midnight) This open-air place combines draught beer, live lounge music and views of the lake. Sunflower also does meals (35B to 180B) and runs tours.

Mae Hong Son's morning market is a cultural and culinary adventure. Several vendors at the north end of the market sell local dishes such as *tòoa òon*, a Burmese noodle dish with thick gram porridge. Others sell a local version of *kà·nŏm jeen nám ngéeo*, a thin noodle soup topped with deep-fried vegetables.

There are two night markets: the one near the airport is mostly takeaway northern Thai food, while the market near Nong Jong Kham has more generic Thai food and a few tables and chairs.

Getting There & Away

Mae Hong Son is 368km from Chiang Mai, but the terrain is so rugged that the trip takes at least eight long, but scenic, hours. For this reason, many people opt to fly, a journey of 35 minutes. The airport is near the centre of town.

Flights to/from Chiang Mai are available on **Thai Airways International** (code TG; ☎ 0 5361 2220; www.thaiair.com) and **Nok Air** (code DD; ☎ 1318; www.nokair.co.th) via its subsidiary **SGA Airlines** (☎ 0 5379 8244; www.sga.co.th). Thai also flies to Bangkok.

The bus station has moved 1km outside of town. Destinations include Pai (ordinary/air-con 80/100B, three hours) and Chiang Mai (ordinary/air-con 143/210B, eight hours). Minivans also go to Pai (150B, two hours) and Chiang Mai (250B, six hours).

AROUND MAE HONG SON

Tham Lot

The insides of northern Thailand's vast limestone mountains have been tunnelled and carved for millennia by the sculpting powers of subterranean water. One of the most dramatic underground landscapes is Tham Lot (pronounced *tâm lôrt* and also known as *tâm nám lôrt*), a large limestone cave about 70km from Mae Hong Son outside of the town of Soppong. It is one of the largest known caves in Thailand, stretching 1600m. There are impressive stalagmites, 'coffin caves' (an ancient and little-understood burial ritual) and a stream that runs through it. The tourism infrastructure is also applauded as a local ecotourism model. Local guides from nearby Shan villages must be hired to tour the caverns. You can base your stay at nearby **Cave Lodge** (☎ 0 5361 7203; www.cavelodge.com; dm 90-120B, r 250-2000B), which is run by an unofficial spelunking expert.

Tham Lot can be reached by motorcycle taxis (70B) from Soppong, which is accessible by bus from Pai (ordinary/air-con/minivan 40/80/100B, two hours) or Mae Hong Son (ordinary/air-con 60/80B, two hours).

CHIANG RAI

pop 61,200

Leafy and well groomed, Chiang Rai is more liveable than visitable. The town itself is a convenient base for touring the Golden Triangle and an alternative to Chiang Mai for arranging hill-tribe treks. Don't assume you'll be the only foreigner in town, Chiang Rai is well-loved by well-heeled package tourists.

Information

Banks can be found along Th Thanalai and along Th Utarakit. Internet access is readily available.

CAT office (cnr Th Ratchadat Damrong & Th Ngam Meuang; ⏰ 7am-11pm Mon-Fri)

Garé Garon (869/18 Th Phahonyothin; ⏰ 10am-10pm) New and used English books, plus coffee, tea and handicrafts in an artsy environment.

Orn's Bookshop (1051/61 Soi 1, Th Jet Yot; ⏰ 8am-8pm) Great store of used books.

Overbrook Hospital (☎ 0 5371 1366; www.overbrookhospital.com; Th Singkhlai) Modern, English-speaking hospital.

Post office (Th Utarakit) South of Wat Phra Singh.

TAT office (☎ 0 5374 4674; 448/16 Th Singkhlai; ⏰ 8.30am-4.30pm)

Tourist police (☎ 0 5371 1779; Th Ratanaket)

Sights & Activities

In the mid-14th century, lightning struck open the *chedi* at **Wat Phra Kaew** (cnr Th Trairat & Th Reuang Nakhon), thus revealing the much honoured Emerald Buddha now residing in Bangkok.

The **Oub Kham Museum** (☎ 0 5371 3349; www.oubkhammuseum.com; 81/1 Military Front Rd; adult/child 300/100B; ⏰ 8am-5pm) houses an impressive collection of Lanna-era paraphernalia along with an odd assortment of Thai kitsch. Guided tours are obligatory.

Hilltribe Museum & Education Center (☎ 0 5374 0088; www.pda.or.th/chiangrai; 3rd fl, 620/1 Th Thanalai; admission 50B; ⏰ 8.30am-6pm Mon-Fri, 10am-6pm Sat & Sun) is run by the nonprofit Population & Community Development Association (PDA) and displays clothing and the history of major hill tribes. PDA also organises hill-tribe treks.

Trekking is big business in Chiang Rai. Most tours (starting at 950B) typically cover the areas of Doi Tung, Doi Mae Salong or Chiang Khong areas. The following are primarily nonprofit community development organisations working in hill-tribe communities that use trekking as an awareness campaign and fundraiser.

Mirror Art Group (☎ 0 5373 7412-3; www.mirrorartgroup.org; 106 Moo 1, Ban Huay Khom, Tambon Mae Yao) An NGO sponsoring educational workshops and Thai citizenship advocacy, it offers trekking with meaningful interaction with the villagers; see also p831.

Natural Focus (☎ 08 5888 6869; Soi 4, 129/1 Mu 4, Th Pa-Ngiw, Rop Wiang) Specialises in nature tours and hill-tribe culture.

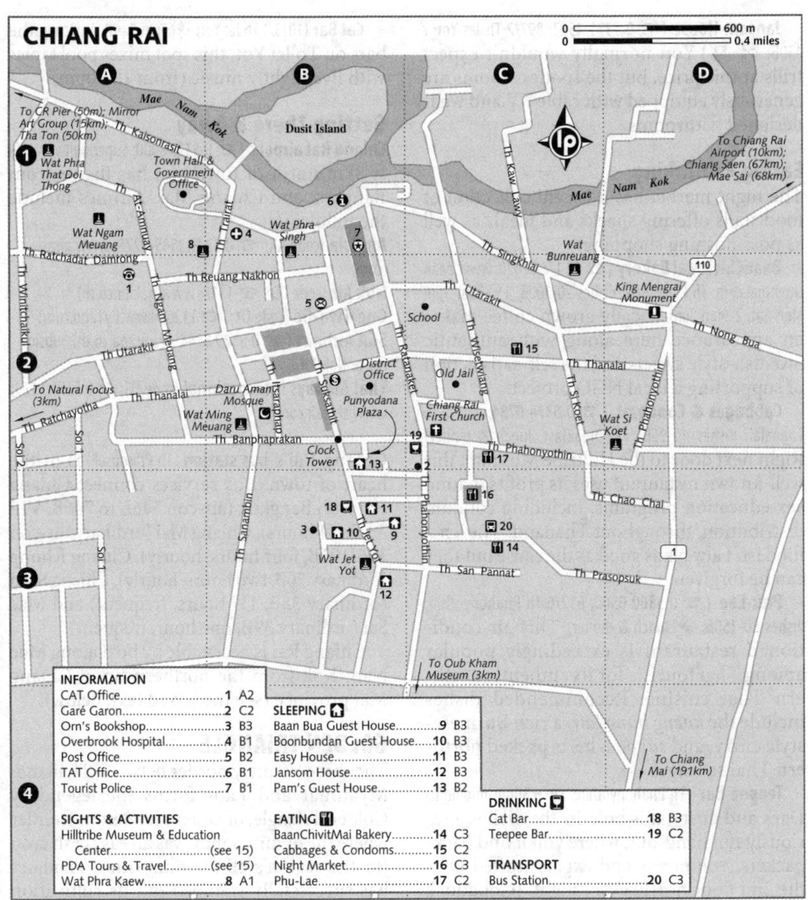

PDA Tours & Travel (☎ 0 5374 0088; www.pda.or.th/chiangrai; Hilltribe Museum & Education Center, 620/1 Th Thanalai) Culturally sensitive tours led by PDA-trained hill-tribe members. Profits are recycled back into the community.

Sleeping

Easy House (☎ 0 5360 0963; 869/163-4 Th Premaviphat; r 170B) The simple but clean rooms at Easy House are irresistible for budget hawks. The shared bathrooms are spotless, staff friendly and helpful, and there's a convivial restaurant-pub.

Boonbundan Guest House (☎ 0 5375 2413-4; 1005/13 Th Jet Yot; r 170-500B; ❄) This large compound has something to suit every budget, although the older rooms could do with a lick of paint. The newer rooms are great value and come with cable TV, fridge and a kitchenette.

Pam's Guest House (☎ 08 9433 5134; Th Jet Yot; r 180-250B) The rooms here are basic indeed, but are nicer than the dark hallways suggest. The communal area has a small bar and pool table, plus lounge with cable TV and DVDs. The cheaper rooms have shared hot-water bathrooms.

Baan Bua Guest House (☎ 0 5371 8880; www.baanbuaguesthouse.com; 879/2 Th Jet Yot; r 200-350B; ❄) A little luxury for a little more *baht*, this guest house boasts a large garden area perfect for lazy breakfasts. All rooms have private bathrooms with hot showers. Advanced booking is advised.

Jansom House (☎ 0 5371 4552; 897/2 Th Jet Yot; r 450B;) You normally wouldn't expect frills at this price, but the spotless rooms are generously equipped with cable TV and well-designed bathrooms.

Eating & Drinking

The night market has a decent collection of food stalls offering snacks and meals as well as post-noshing shopping.

BaanChivitMai Bakery (☎ 08 1764 7020; www.baanchivitmai.com; Th Prasopsuk; dishes 20-100B; 7am-9pm Mon-Sat, 2-9pm Sun) Locally grown coffee makes an appearance here along with authentic Swedish-style sweets and the self-satisfaction of supporting a local NGO project.

Cabbages & Condoms (☎ 0 5374 0784; 620/1 Th Thanalai; dishes 40-95B; breakfast, lunch & dinner) Right next door to the Hilltribe Museum, this well-known restaurant uses its profits to fund sex-education programs, including condom distribution, throughout Thailand. The Thai food isn't always as good as the cause but they can be forgiven.

Phu-Lae (☎ 0 5360 0500; 612/6 Th Phahonyothin; dishes 60-150B; lunch & dinner) This air-conditioned restaurant is exceedingly popular among Thai tourists for its authentic northern Thai cuisine. Recommended dishes include the *kaeng hang·lair,* a rich Burmese-style curry, and *sâi òoa,* herb-packed northern Thai sausages.

Teepee Bar (Th Phahonyothin; 6.30pm-midnight) Dark and dusty, this hole-in-the-wall is a seriously fun hang-out, where you'll find backpackers, volunteers and expats stuffed onto the 2nd floor nearly every night. (Good luck finding the staircase.)

Cat Bar (1013/1 Th Jet Yot; 5pm-1am) Among the bars on Th Jet Yot, this spot mixes pool tables with live nightly music (from 10.30pm).

Getting There & Away

Chiang Rai airport (☎ 0 5379 8000; Superhighway 110) is 8km north of town and has flights from Bangkok and Chiang Mai. Airlines include the following:

Air Asia (code AK; ☎ 0 5379 3545-8275; www.airasia.com)
Nok Air (code DD; ☎ 1318; www.nokair.co.th)
One-Two-Go (code OX; ☎ 1126; www.fly12go.com)
SGA Airlines (☎ 0 5379 8244; www.sga.co.th) Subsidiary of Nok Air.
Thai Airways International (code TG; ☎ 0 5371 1179; www.thaiair.com)

Chiang Rai's **bus station** (Th Prasopsuk) is in the heart of town. Bus services connect Chiang Rai with Bangkok (air-con 546B to 706B, VIP 733B, 11 hours), Chiang Mai (ordinary/air-con 106/191B, four hours, hourly), Chiang Khong (ordinary 70B, two hours, hourly), Chiang Saen (ordinary 38B, 1½ hours, frequent) and Mae Sai (ordinary 39B, one hour, frequent).

Chiang Rai is accessible by boat along Mae Nam Kok from the northern tip of Chiang Mai province (see the boxed text, below).

GOLDEN TRIANGLE

The three-country border between Thailand, Myanmar and Laos forms the legendary Golden Triangle, once a mountainous frontier where the opium poppy was an easy cash crop for the region's ethnic minorities. Thailand has successfully stamped out its cultivation through crop-substitution programs and

SLOW BOATS TO CHIANG RAI

Escape the daredevil highway antics of Thailand's bus drivers with a slow ride on the Mae Nam Kok. The river ride is a big hit with tourists and includes stops at hill-tribe villages that specialise in Coca-Colas and souvenirs. This isn't unchartered territory but it is relaxing.

Chiang Rai–bound boats (☎ 0 5345 9427; 350B; departs 12.30pm), carrying 12 passengers, leave from Tha Ton, a small town in northern Chiang Mai province. The trip takes three to five hours depending on river conditions.

If you catch the earliest bus leaving Chiang Mai you'll arrive in Tha Ton in time for the 12.30pm boat departure. From Chiang Mai's Chang Pheuak bus terminal, buses go to Tha Ton (105B, three hours, every 30 minutes); sometimes they'll only go as far as Fang, from where it's another 45 minutes by yellow săwngthăew to Tha Ton (25B).

You can also do the trip in reverse (from Chiang Rai to Tha Ton), a less popular direction affording you more leg room, but it also takes longer. Go to **CR Pier** (☎ 0 5375 0009) in the northwest corner of Chiang Rai. Passenger boats embark daily at 10.30am.

GETTING TO MYANMAR: MAE SAI TO TACHILEIK

In peaceful times, foreigners may cross from Mae Sai into Tachileik, Myanmar. On occasion and without notice, the border may close temporarily. Ask about current conditions before making the trip to Mae Sai.

The **Thai immigration office** (6.30am-6.30pm) is just before the bridge over the Mae Nam Sai. On the other side is the Myanmarese immigration office, which charges US$10 (or 500B) for a temporary ID card allowing you 14 days in the country; your passport is held for this period at the office.

The border town of Tachileik looks a lot like Mae Sai, with except more teashops and Burmese restaurants. Via this entry point, you're allowed to venture as far into Myanmar as Kengtung (p570; the capital of the Shan state) and Mong La (near the Chinese border), but you'll need certain permits and permissions. Contact Myanmar Travel & Tours, next to the immigration booth for immigration procedures and additional fees.

On your return to Thailand, the Thai immigration office will give you a new 15-day visa. For information on this border crossing in the other direction, see the boxed text, p570.

aggressive law enforcement, but the porous border and lawless areas of the neighbouring countries has switched production to the next generation's drug of choice: methamphetamine and, to a lesser extent, heroin. Much of this illicit activity is invisible to the average visitor and the region's heyday as the leading opium producer is now marketed as a tourist attraction.

Mae Salong

pop 25,400

Built along the spine of a mountain, Mae Salong is more like a remote Chinese village in Yúnnán than a Thai town. It was originally settled by the 93rd Regiment of the Kuomintang Nationalist Party (KMT), which fled from China after the 1949 revolution. The ex-soldiers and political exiles initially settled in Myanmar but later were forced to Thailand, where they supported themselves as middlemen between the opium growers and the opium warlords. The modern-day descendants still carry on the language and traditions (minus the profession) of their forefathers: Chinese is more frequently spoken here than Thai and the land's severe incline boasts tidy terraces of tea and coffee plantations.

An interesting **morning market** (6-8am) convenes at the T-junction near Shin Sane Guest House. The market attracts town residents and tribespeople from the surrounding districts. Most of the guest houses in town can arrange **treks** to nearby hill-tribe villages, though the surrounding area has been significantly denuded over the years.

Shin Sane Guest House (0 5376 5026; 32/3 Th Mae Salong; s/d from 50/100B, bungalow 300B;) is Mae Salong's original guest house boasting the standards and prices of decades past. **Little Home Guesthouse** (0 5376 5389; www.maesalonglittlehome.com; 31 Moo 1, Th Mae Salong; s/d from 50/100B, bungalow 600B;), next door to Shin Sane, is a delightful wooden house with basic rooms and spiffy bungalows. The friendly owner has produced an accurate map of the area.

Getting to Mae Salong is an adventure in transport: take a Chiang Rai–Mae Sai bus and get off at Ban Basang (ordinary 20B, 30 minutes, frequent). From there, săwngthăew climb the mountain to Mae Salong (500B per vehicle split between passengers, one hour). You can also approach Mae Salong from the scenic western road via Fang or Tha Ton (50B).

Mae Sai

pop 21,800

Thailand's northernmost town is a busy trading post for gems, jewellery, cashews and lacquerware, and is also a legal border crossing into Myanmar. Many travellers make the trek here to extend their Thai visa or to dip their toes into Myanmar. For information on crossing into Myanmar, see the boxed text, above.

Most guest houses line the street along the Mae Nam Sai to the left of the border checkpoint. **Bamboo Guesthouse** (08 6916 1895; 135/3 Th Sailomjoi; r 150-200B) has bare-bones shelters. **Top North Hotel** (0 5373 1955; 306 Th Phahonyothin; d 400-600B, tr 900B;) located along the main strip, is a short walk to the border bridge; it is an older hotel with spacious rooms. Mae Sai has a **night market** (Th Phahonyothin) with an excellent mix of Thai and Chinese dishes. **Khrua Bismillah** (no roman-script sign; ☎ 08 1530 8198; Soi 4, Th Phahonyothin; dishes 25-40B; 6am-6pm) is run by Burmese Muslims and does an excellent biryani; look for the green halal sign.

The **bus station** (☎ 0 5364 6437) is 4km from the immigration office. Destinations include Bangkok (air-con 582B to 749B, VIP 874B, 15 hours, six departures), Chiang Mai (air-con/VIP 241/375B, four to five hours, five departures) and Chiang Rai (ordinary 38B, 1½ hours, frequent). The bus to Tha Ton (51B) and Fang (71B) leaves at 7am and takes two hours.

On Th Phahonyothin by Soi 8 there's a 'bus stop' sign, from which săwngthăew run to Sop Ruak (45B, frequent) and terminate in Chiang Saen (50B).

Chiang Saen

pop 10,800

A sedate river town, **Chiang Saen** is famous in the Thai history books as the 7th-cenutry birthplace of the Lanna kingdom, later centred in Chiang Mai. You can wander around the kingdoms' ruins at **Wat Pa Sak** (admission 50B), about 200m from Pratu Chiang Saen, or survey the artefacts at **Chiang Saen National Museum** (☎ 0 5377 7102; 702 Th Phahonyothin; admission 100B; 8.30am-4.30pm Wed-Sun). Today huge river barges from China moor in town, heralding the expanding and sanctioned interior Asian trade.

An easy day trip from Chiang Saen is the so-called 'official' centre of the Golden Triangle, **Sop Ruak**, an odd souvenir and museum stop for package tourists. The **House of Opium** (Baan Phin; ☎ 0 5378 4060; www.houseofopium.com; admission 50B; 7am-8pm), across from Phra Chiang Saen Si Phaendin, has historical displays pertaining to opium culture. Another drug-themed museum is **Hall of Opium** (☎ 0 5378 4444; www.goldentrianglepark.com; admission 300B; 10am-3.30pm), 1km south of town opposite the Anantara Resort & Spa. Run by royally sponsored Mah Fah Luang Foundation, the facility includes a fascinating history of opium and examines the effects of abuse on individuals and society.

Sleeping options in Chiang Saen include **Chiang Saen Guest House** (☎ 0 5365 0196; 45/2 Th Rimkhong; r 150-300B), opposite the river and night

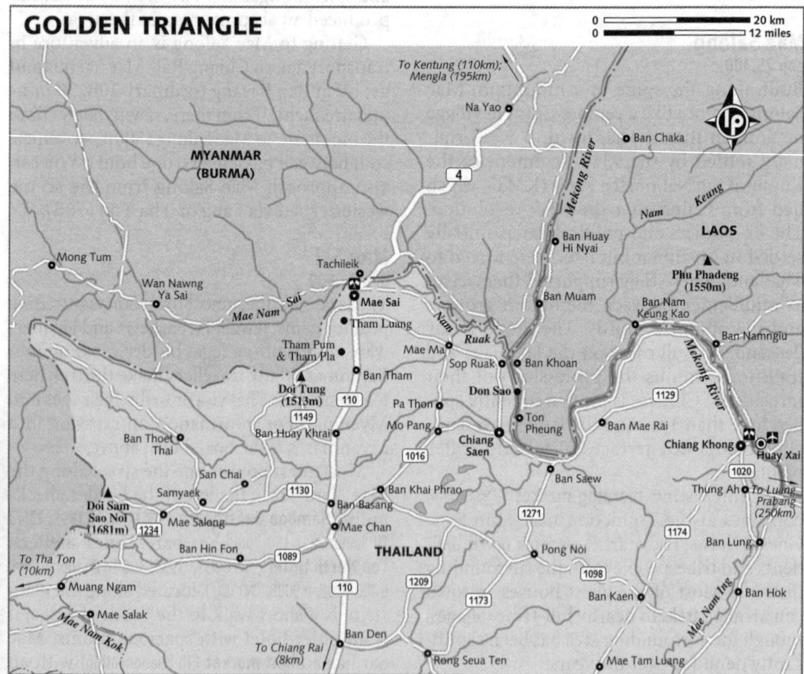

GETTING TO CHINA: CHIANG SAEN TO JINGHONG

Passenger boats operated by **Maekhong Delta Travel** (☎ 0 5364 2517; 230/5-6 Th Phaholyothin, Mae Sai; www.maekhongtravel.com; one way 4000B; ⏲ departs 5am Mon & Wed) do the 15-hour journey to Jinghong in Yúnnán province. You must already have your visa for China arranged before departure.

stalls, and **Gin's Guest House** (☎ 0 5365 0847; 71 Mu 8; r 300-700B, bungalows 200B), on the north side of town (about 1.5km north of the bus terminal) with views of the Mekong River. A night market sets up each along the bank of the Mekong River.

Chiang Saen has an informal bus terminal at the eastern end of Th Phahonyothin. Destinations include Chiang Rai (ordinary 70B, two hours, frequent), Chiang Saen (ordinary 35B, 1½ hours, frequent) and Chiang Mai (ordinary/air-con 126/227B, five hours, two departures). To Chiang Mai be sure to take the *săi mài* (new route), which is more direct. There are frequent săwngthăew between Chiang Saen and Sop Ruak (20B, every 20 minutes from 7am to 5pm). Six-passenger speedboats also shuttle between the two towns (one way/return 500/600B, 35 minutes).

NORTHEASTERN THAILAND

Thailand's other regions have natural beauty, but the northeast has all of the personality. The main event in this undervisited region are the people, plain and simple folks who might invite you over to share their picnic under a shade tree or wake up their sleeping kid to spot a foreigner, a sight as exotic as an elephant in the middle of Times Square.

That's not to say that there isn't beauty in the flat, sun-beaten landscape of rice fields punctuated by shade trees and lonely water buffaloes. Indeed you've never seen such a vivid green until you've trundled through in the wet season when rice shoots are newly born. And there's a dramatic element to the dry season when the fields wither and crack and wait thirstily for the next life-giving rain.

Also referred to as Isan, the northeast is one of Thailand's most rural and agricultural regions. It is a rich tapestry of Lao, Thai and Khmer traditional cultures, which meandered across the shifting borders much like the mighty Mekong River. The Mekong defines a wide arc across the northern reaches of the region, and along the way are small riverfront towns. Their local festivals display the region's unique fusion of cultures. Elsewhere lie magnificent mini-Angkor Wats, left behind by the ancient Angkor kings who claimed this land as their western frontier.

There's little in the way of guest-house culture here and few English speakers. Indeed this is the end of the tourist trail and the beginning of the Thailand trail.

NAKHON RATCHASIMA (KHORAT)

pop 2 million

To most shoestringers, Nakhon Ratchasima (or 'Khorat') is just a useful transit hub with little else to waylay them. Bland concrete development has buried much of its history, and its status as Thailand's second-largest city makes Bangkok look exponentially more interesting. But if you're calibrated to this region, then Khorat is a part of the urban Isan puzzle, where village kids grew up to be educated bureaucrats living comfortable middle-class lives. Access into the tidy housing developments will yield a personal perspective on a society's migration from the field to the office. But without this, feel free to use Khorat as a base for a visit to Phimai or pass on through without guilt.

Information

There are banks galore in central Nakhon Ratchasima, all with ATMs and some with exchange services.

Post office (Th Jomsurangyat; ⏲ 8.30am-4.30pm Mon-Fri, 8.30am-noon Sat)

Bangkok Hospital (☎ 0 4426 2000; Th Mittaphap)

TAT office (☎ 0 4421 3666; 2102-2104 Th Mittaphap; ⏲ 8.30am-4.30pm) On the western edge of the city, beyond the train station.

Tourist police (☎ 0 4434 1777, ☎ 1155) Opposite Bus Station 2, north of the city centre.

Sights

In the city centre is the defiant statue of **Thao Suranari Memorial** (Khun Ying Mo Memorial; Th Ratchadamnoen), a local heroine who led the inhabitants against Lao invaders during the

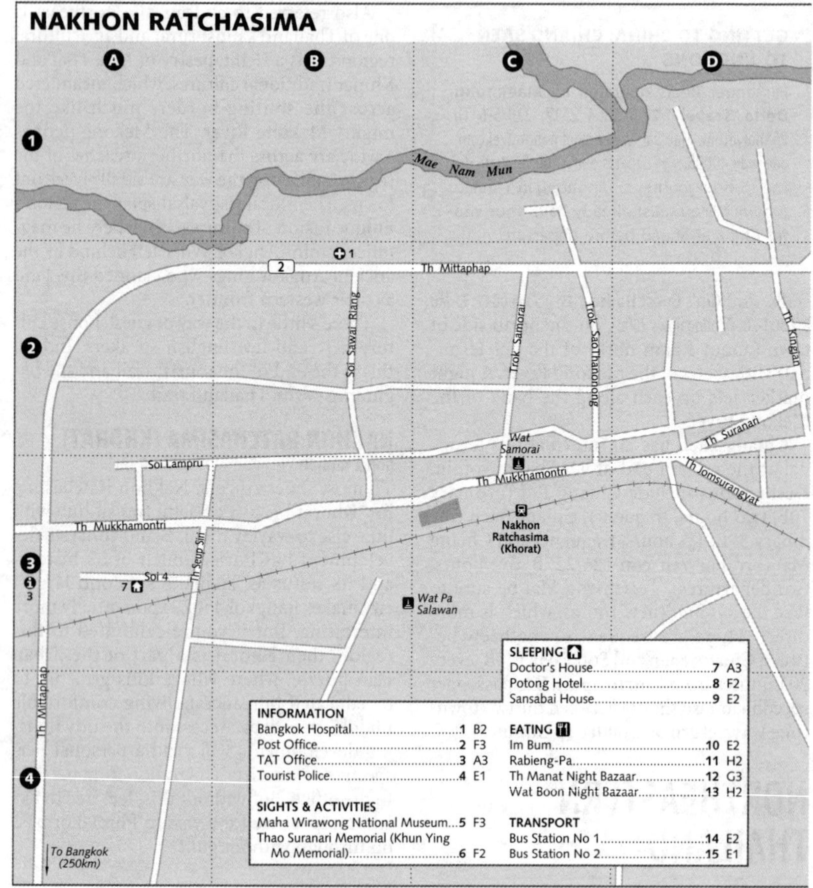

reign of Rama III (r 1824–51). A holy shrine, the statue receives visitors offering gifts and prayers or hired singers to perform Khorat folk songs. The steady activities of the devotees make for a lively cultural display.

For a dose of Khmer and Ayuthaya art, visit **Maha Wirawong National Museum** (☎ 0 4424 2958; Th Ratchadamnoen; admission 50B; 9am-4.30pm Wed-Sun), housed in the grounds of Wat Sutchinda.

Just a quick trip out of town, **Dan Kwian** has been producing pottery for hundreds of years and is something of a magnet for Thailand's artistic hippies. The ceramic creations are famous for their rough texture and rustlike hue derived from local kaolin sources. The village is essentially a row of art-gallery shops lining the highway. To get here, hop on a bus (14B, 30 minutes) from Khorat's southern city gate, the eastern gate or Bus Station 2.

Sleeping

Potong Hotel (☎ 0 4425 1962; 652 Th Ratchadamnoen; s 190, d 240-350B;) This old-timer by the Thao Suranari Memorial has some of the cheapest rooms in the city, for good reason. They barely pass the steeply graded curve.

Doctor's House (☎ 08 5632 3396; 78 Soi 4, Th Seup Siri; r 200-350B;) One of the few backpack joints in town, this guest house has simple but clean rooms with shared bathroom in an old wooden house. It's not for party animals as the gate is locked at 10pm. Bikes (50B) and motorcycles (200B) are available for hire.

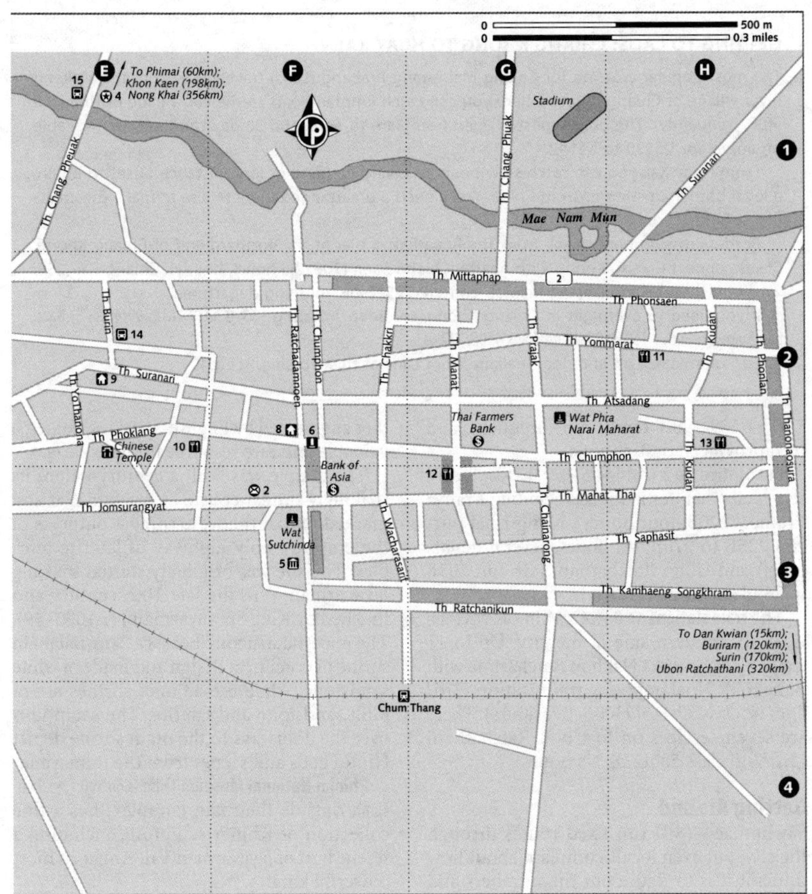

Sansabai House (☎ 0 4425 5144; 335 Th Suranari; r 270-500B; ❄) Though the lobby might dampen your spirits, even the cheapest rooms are bright and spotless and come with minifridge and little balconies.

Eating & Drinking

Khorat is famous for *pàt mèe khorâht*, a local twist on the ubiquitous *phàt thai*.

Im Bum (☎ 08 1725 6008; Th Buarong; dishes 25-130B; ⏰ breakfast & lunch) Vegetarians who are adept at communicating with non-English speakers will be delighted to sample these mock-meat versions of Thai-Chinese standards.

Rabieng-Pa (☎ 0 4424 3137; 284 Th Yommarat; dishes 45-220B; ⏰ dinner) The leafiest and loveliest restaurant on this busy stretch of Th Yommarat has a massive picture menu so ordering Thai food is risk free. There are several more energetic restaurants-bars nearby for post-dinner destinations.

You can eat and drink on the fringes of the popular **Th Manat Night Bazaar** (Th Manat; ⏰ 6-10pm) but this is mostly a fashion zone. Or head east to the **Wat Boon Night Bazaar** (Th Chumphon; ⏰ 6-10pm) where you can sample deep-fried crickets, pork sausages and other Isan specialities along with more standard Thai stir-fries.

Getting There & Away

Nakhon Ratchasima has two bus stations: **Bus Station No 1** (☎ 0 4424 2899; Th Burin) serves Bangkok's Northern & Northeastern bus terminal (ordinary/2nd class/1st class/VIP

GETTING TO LAOS: CHIANG KHONG TO HUAY XAI

The most popular crossing for Chiang Mai–Luang Prabang (Laos) travellers is from the Mekong River village of Chiang Khong where you can catch longtail boats to the Lao village of Huay Xai (40B, frequently). The border post is open from 8am to 6pm, and 30-day Lao visas are available on arrival for US$30 to US$42.

From Huay Xai, you can catch slow boats to Luang Prabang or long-distance buses to Boten, a legal border crossing to/from China. You'll need a prearranged Chinese visa to make the crossing at Boten.

Border-crossing boats leave from Tha Reua Bak, a pier at the northern end of Chiang Khong. Buses connect Chiang Khong with nearby Chiang Saen (70B, 2½ hours, hourly), Chiang Rai (75B, 2½ hours, hourly) and Chiang Mai (air-con/VIP 225/290B, morning departures).

If you need to overnight in Chiang Khong, try **Baanrimtaling** (☎ 0 5379 1613; 99/4 Mu 3, Baan Sop Som; dm 80B, r 160-350B, bungalows 450B; 💻).

For information on entering Thailand from Laos at this crossing, see p404.

75/154/189/198B, three hours, frequent) and intraprovincial destinations.

Bus Station No 2 (☎ 0 4425 6006; Th Chang Pheuak) serves all other destinations, including Aranya Prathet (220B, four hours), Nong Khai (air-con 225B to 270B, six hours, several departures) and Ubon Ratchathani (air-con 203B to 269B, six hours, hourly).

The **train station** (☎ 0 4424 2044; Th Mukkhamontri) is on the western side of the city. Up to 11 trains a day connect Nakhon Ratchasima with Bangkok's Hualamphong train station (3rd/2nd/1st class 50/115/2300B, five hours). There are seven services on to Ubon Ratchathani (3rd/2nd class 58/423B, six hours).

Getting Around

Săwngthăew (8B) run fixed routes through the city, but even locals complain about how difficult it is to figure out the numbers and colours assigned to the routes. Most pass down Th Suranari near the market, which is a good place to start. The green-and-white No 5 will take you from downtown to Bus Station 2. The white with green-and-yellow stripes No 1 goes near Doctor's House and the yellow with white-and-green stripes No 1 goes to the TAT office.

Túk-túk and motorcycle taxis cost between 30B to 70B around town and there are metered taxis at Bus Station No 2.

PHIMAI

Of the many Khmer temples that pepper Isan, **Prasat Phimai** (☎ 0 4447 1568; Th Anantajinda; admission 100B; ⏰ 7.30am-6pm) is an easy day trip from Khorat, making it an ideal ruin for those pressed for time. Tourist infrastructure is further augmented by English-speaking guides, a valuable and rare resource in these parts.

The temple was built a century before its strikingly similar cousin of Angkor Wat and marked one of the westernmost outposts of the empire's holy highway of laterite temples. The site was originally started by King Jayavarman V in the late 10th century and finished by King Suryavarman I (r 1002–49). The majestic structure boasts a 28m-tall main shrine of cruciform design and made of white sandstone, while the adjunct shrines are of pink sandstone and laterite. The sculptures over the doorways to the main shrine depict Hindu gods and scenes from the Ramayana.

Phimai National Museum (admission 30B; ⏰ 9am-4pm), outside the main complex, has a fine collection of Khmer sculpture, including a serene bust of Jayavarman VII, Angkor's most powerful king.

If Khorat is too busy for you, consider overnighting in the town of Phimai. Options include **Old Phimai Guesthouse** (☎ 0 4447 1918; www.phimaigh.com; 214/14 Th Chomsudasadet; dm 90B, s 150-350, d 180-450B; ❄ 💻), a historic wooden house tucked away down a quiet *soi*. The friendly hosts are a great source of information.

Sai Ngam (Beautiful Banyan; admission free; ⏰ daylight hr) is a tree 350-plus years old that blankets an island east of town where food vendors serve *pàt phimai*, which is basically *pàt mèe khorâht*, which is basically *phàt thai*.

All buses to Phimai leave from Khorat's Bus Station 2 (ordinary/2nd class 45/50B, 1¼ hours, half-hourly departures until 7pm). Catching the 8am bus to Phimai leaves ample time to explore the ruins; the last bus back to Nakhon Ratchasima is at 6pm.

KHAO YAI NATIONAL PARK

Thailand's oldest and most remarkable national park, **Khao Yai** (☎ 08 1877 3127; admission 400B) is a vast wilderness astonishingly close to the country's major population centres. This is one of the largest intact monsoon forests in mainland Asia and, along with neighbouring forest complexes, it was named a Unesco World Heritage Site.

The park is centred around a 1351m-high mountain on the western edge of the Dangrek range, which forms a natural boundary between Thailand and Cambodia. There are more than 50km of trekking trails (many of them formed by the movement of wildlife), some wild elephant herds, majestic waterfalls (for part of the year) and impressive bird life.

The most beautiful time to visit is just after the monsoon rains in November through to the start of the hot season (around April) when the landscape is green and the waterfalls are full. But this is also when leeches are at their fiercest: mosquito repellent and leech-proof socks help keep them at bay.

The park headquarters has some general trail information but doesn't have an accurate trail map. For the major highlights it is easy enough to visit on your own but you'll need a guide for minor trails. Getting around the park is a further complication: the nearby guest houses can arrange transport and tours. Another option is **Wildlife Safari** (☎ 0 4431 2922; www.khaoyaiwildlife.com), 2km north of Pak Chong, which leads jungle and birdwatching tours.

Sleeping & Eating

Within the park there is **camping** (camp sites per person 30B) and the park headquarters rents tents and other gear. There are also **park accommodation bungalows** (800-3500B), which are popular for Thai family outings. To make reservations contact the national park's **accommodation system**: (☎ 0 2562 0760; www.dnp.go.th/parkreserve). The park has restaurants at the visitor centre, camping grounds and some waterfalls. All restaurants here close around 7pm, so plan ahead.

Most backpackers base themselves in the nearby town of Pak Chong where you'll find these options:

our pick **Greenleaf Guesthouse** (☎ 0 4436 5024; www.greenleaftour.com; Th Thanarat, Km 7.5; r 200-300B) Midway between the park gate and the town, this guest house has 14 concrete rooms that come with the added perks of being good value and providing a warm welcome.

Khao Yai Garden Lodge (☎ 0 4436 5178; www.khaoyai-gardenlodge.com; Th Thanarat, Km 7; r 350-6800B;) This lodge is mainly an upscale resort but there are a few shared-bath cheapies for the hoi polloi. There's free wi-fi in the lounge.

Getting There & Away

Most Bangkok–Khorat bound buses stop in Pak Chong (from Bangkok 108B to 139B, two hours; from Khorat 59B to 74B, one hour), so you can reach the town in either direction. From Bangkok, use the Northern & Northeastern bus terminal.

ISAN CUISINE: PUTTING THE FIRE IN SPICY

Isan cuisine is true grit and demands a flame-retardant capacity for spiciness. The holy trinity – *kài yâang* (grilled chicken), *sôm-tam* (papaya salad) and *khâo niaw* (sticky rice) – are integral to the culture and the identity of hard-working farmers who have honed their tolerance for chilli peppers, droughts and physical exhaustion. Wherever Isan-ers go as economic migrants – be it to Bangkok to drive a taxi in between rice harvests or to Ko Samui to construct a new hotel – they smuggle with them these edible reminders of home. And their diaspora has been so widespread that Isan cuisine has now been adopted as mainstream and appears with fashionable flair at upscale Bangkok restaurants.

But to truly appreciate their adoration, these meals must be experienced in their birthplace. Early in the morning a veritable chicken massacre is laid out on an open grill, sending wafts of smoke into the dry air as advertising. Beside the grill is a huge earthenware *khrók* (mortar) and wooden *sàak* (pestle) beating out the ancient rhythm of *sôm-tam* preparation: in go grated papaya, sliced limes, a fistful of peppers, sugar and a host of preferential ingredients. People taste the contents and call out adjustments: more *náam plaa* (fish sauce) or *plaa ráa* (fermented fish sauce, which looks like rotten mud). Everything is eaten with the hands, using sticky rice and a plate of fresh, chalky-tasting vegetables to help offset the chilli burn.

Săwngthăew travel the 30km from Pak Chong to the park's northern gate (40B, 45 minutes, every half-hour from 6am to 5pm); hop aboard on Th Thanarat in front of the 7-Eleven store and hop off at the ticket gate. From here it is another 14km to the visitor centre; hitchhiking this stretch is quite common. There are also motorcycle rentals at the gate and in Pak Chong town (300B to 500B).

Pak Chong is also on the rail line, but this is a good option only if you're coming from Ayuthaya (3rd class 173B, 2nd-class 203B to 333B, two hours, 11 daily), which saves you from backtracking into Bangkok.

If you're headed to Phanom Rung, you can catch a Nang Rong–bound bus (1st class 140B, 2½ hours, hourly), which departs from the Shell petrol station on the east side of town and is the closest town to the temple.

PHANOM RUNG HISTORICAL PARK

Spectacularly located atop an extinct volcano, **Prasat Phanom Rung** (☎ 0 4463 1746; admission 100B; 🕑 6am-6pm) is the largest and best restored of the ancient Khmer sanctuaries in Thailand. Dating from the 10th to 13th centuries, the complex faces east towards the sacred capital of Angkor in Cambodia. It was first built as a Hindu monument and features sculpture relating to Vishnu and Shiva. Later the Thais converted it into a Buddhist temple.

The craftsmanship at Phanom Rung represents the pinnacle of Khmer artistic achievement, on a par with the bas-reliefs at Angkor Wat in Cambodia. One of the most striking design features at Phanom Rung is the promenade, an avenue sealed with laterite and sandstone blocks and flanked by sandstone pillars with lotus-bud tops. It leads to the first and largest of three *naga* bridges, which are the only surviving architectural features of their kind in Thailand.

The central *prasat* (tower) has a gallery on each of its four sides, and the entrance to each gallery is itself a smaller incarnation of the main tower. The galleries have curvilinear roofs and windows with false balustrades. Once inside the temple walls, check out the galleries and the *gopura* (entrance pavilion), paying particular attention to the lintels over the doors.

If you can, plan your visit for one of the four times of the year when the sun shines through all 15 sanctuary doorways. This solar alignment happens during sunrise on 3 to 5 April and 8 to 10 September and sunset on 5 to 7 March and 5 to 7 October (one day earlier in leap years).

Several English-speaking guides (fees are negotiable) are available at the information centre.

Sleeping

Phanom Rung is a day trip from Nakhon Ratchasima (Khorat) and Surin, but some people pass a night in Nang Rong, the nearest town to the temple.

Honey Inn (☎ 0 4462 2825; www.honeyinn.com; 8/1 Soi Si Kun; r 200-400B; ❄ 💻), 1km from the bus station, has simple but bright rooms. Further away, on the east side of town, **P California Inter Hostel** (☎ 0 4462 2214; www.nangronghomestay.com; 59/9 Th Sangkakrit; r 250-700B; ❄ 💻) is somewhat shinier though some of the rooms are a little more cramped. The friendly, English-speaking owners of both places are full of advice about the area and arrange bike and motorcycle hire and tours at reasonable prices.

Getting There & Away

Despite its attractiveness, Phanom Rung is not the easiest place to get to by public transport. For day-trippers from Nakhon Ratchasima or Surin, take a bus to Ban Ta-Ko (60B to 85B, two hours, hourly), a well-marked turnoff. From here the easiest option is to hire a motorcycle taxi (300B to 400B) for a round trip visit to the site. Alternatively you can wait for a passing săwngthăew that will take you to the foot of Phanom Rung (20B, 45 minutes), though they are not frequent and you'd need to hire additional transport (from 40B to 100B) up the mountain.

If you're overnighting in Nang Rong, buses pass through from Khorat (70B to 80B, two hours, hourly) and Pak Chong (1st class 140B, 2½ hours, hourly). From Nang Rong there's a săwngthăew that leaves from the old market on the east end of town to the parking lot at the foot of Phanom Rung. You'll need to hire transport up the mountain.

SURIN

pop 41,200

There's not a lot to see in sleepy Surin until the annual **Elephant Roundup** comes to town in November. The festival showcases the elephants in mock battles and various feats of strength and dexterity, and all of the hotels fill up with foreigners, an astonishing feat in itself.

The rest of the year, a few travellers trickle into Surin in order to visit the Khmer temples, such as **Phanom Rung** and other minor ones that line the Cambodian border. The province is also renowned for its silk-weaving, best observed at nearby **craft villages**. Pirom at Pirom-Aree's House can help arrange tours of these attractions.

Lately Surin has evolved into a volunteering centre thanks to groups like **Starfish Ventures** (☎ 08 1723 1403; www.starfishvolunteers.com) and **LemonGrass Volunteering** (☎ 08 1977 5300; www.lemongrass-volunteering.com), which arrange English-teaching opportunities in rural schools.

Culturally, Surin has a strong Khmer influence, which is best observed at the **day market** where the vegetable vendors squawk at each other in what is often called *phasaa Isan* (a mix of Thai, Khmer and to a lesser extent Lao). Everybody in town turns up for the pedestrian-only **night bazaar** (Th Krung Si Nai; 5-10pm) to shop, eat dinner and watch each other.

To see Surin's elephants on their home turf, head to the **Elephant Study Centre** (☎ 0 4414 5050; admission free; 9.30am-4.30pm), in Ban Tha Klang, about 50km north of Surin. This is the village of the Suay people, a minority group who have traditionally herded elephants. Many of the tusker performers at the annual festival are trained here and there are daily **shows** (donations expected; 10am & 2pm) and **mahout-training programs** (from 1000B). The village also runs a **homestay** (☎ 08 1879 5026; per person 350B) that includes meals and some elephant time. Săwngthăew run here from Surin's bus terminal (45B, two hours, hourly), with the last one returning at 4pm.

Surin is also a launching point for a little-used border-crossing point for Siem Reap–bound travellers; see p776.

Sleeping & Eating

During the elephant roundup, every hotel in town is booked and rates can triple; reserve well in advance.

Pirom-Aree's House (☎ 0 4451 5140; Soi Arunee, Th Thungpo; s/d 120/200B) Surin's only guest house is 1km west of the city; a peaceful but somewhat far-flung location from town. Still, Pirom is a wonderful asset for tourism in Isan. The wooden, shared bathrooms back onto a shady garden.

New Hotel (☎ 0 4451 1341; 6-8 Th Tanasan; s 160-330, d 180-440B;) This place is steps from the train station and is so old the name's almost ironic. Rooms are clean, though; those in the front of the building have sit-down toilets.

Petmanee 2 (no roman-script sign; ☎ 08 4451 6024; Th Murasart; dishes 20-60B; lunch) Surin's most famous purveyor of *sôm-tam* and *kài yâang* is down a small *soi* south of Ruampaet Hospital and next to Wat Salaloi. There's no English spoken or written here, but the food is so good it's worth the hassle.

Surin Chai Kit (no roman-script sign; 297-299 Th Tanasan; dishes 25-60B; breakfast & lunch) This no-frills spot is popular for breakfast (try a plate of pan eggs and Isan sausages). The food is good and the owner is friendly and speaks English.

Getting There & Away

The **bus terminal** (Th Jit Bamrung) is one block from the train station. Destinations include Bangkok (2nd/1st class 345/399B, seven hours, frequent), Ubon Ratchathani (2nd/1st class 144/212B, three hours, hourly) and Nakhon Ratchasima (2nd/1st class 120/178B, four hours, every half-hour).

These destinations, however, are more convenient by train and fares are as follows: Ubon Ratchathani (3rd/2nd class 81/150B, three hours), and Bangkok (3rd/2nd class 183/389B, 1st-class sleeper 1149B, seven to nine hours). The train station is centrally located at the intersection of Th Nong Toom and Th Thawasan.

UBON RATCHATHANI

pop 115,000

Although it is one of the bigger cities in the region, Ubon still retains a small-town feel thanks to the relaxing nature of the Mae Nam Mun, Thailand's second-longest river, and its palpable Lao heritage. It is easily traversed by foot and easily appreciated by aimless wandering.

Ubon doesn't see a lot of foreign visitors because it is in an odd corner of the country, but there is a nearby Thai–Lao border crossing that provides an alternative route into southern Laos; see the boxed text, p777.

Information

Blink Internet Cafe (105-107 Th Yutthaphan; per hr 15B; 9am-10pm) Around the corner from TAT.

Krung Thai Bank (Th Ratchathani; 10am-7pm) Inside Ying Charoen Park shopping centre.

Main post office (Th Luang; 8.30am-4.30pm Mon-Fri, 9am-noon Sat, Sun & holidays)

GETTING TO CAMBODIA

Chong Chom to O Smach

Foreigners are able to cross the border from Chong Chom in Thailand to O Smach in Cambodia. Because of the Cambodian casino, there's a lot of minibuses (65B, 1½ hours, every half-hour) from Surin to the **Cambodian border** (7am-8pm), where visas are available on the spot. Once on the Cambodian side, a shared taxi will cost 500B for the four-hour drive to Siem Reap, but if you arrive late you may have to pay 2500B for the whole vehicle.

See p110 for information on doing the trip in the opposite direction.

Chong Sa Ngam to Choam

There is also a more remote crossing through Choam Srawngam with Choam, in the former Khmer Rouge stronghold of Anlong Veng, but transport access is tough on both sides of the border (see p112).

See p707 for general information on travelling from Cambodia to Thailand.

Ubonrak Thonburi Hospital (0 4526 0285; Th Phalorangrit)
TAT Office (0 4524 3770; www.tatubon.org; 264/1 Th Kheuan Thani; 8.30am-4.30pm)
Tourist police (0 4524 5505, emergency 1155; Th Suriyat)

Sights & Activities

Housed in a former palace of the Rama VI era, **Ubon National Museum** (0 4525 5071; Th Kheuan Thani; admission 100B; 9am-4pm Wed-Sun) is a good place to delve into local history and culture.

To get your requisite amount of temple-spotting, check out **Wat Thung Si Meuang** (Th Luang; daylight hr), which was built during the reign of Rama III (1824–51) and has a classic *hŏr đrai* (Tripitaka hall) and a small *bòht* painted with 200-year-old murals depicting ordinary life. **Wat Si Ubon Rattanaram** (Th Uparat; daylight hr) houses the 7cm-tall Topaz Buddha (Phra Kaew Butsarakham), which was reportedly brought here from Vientiane at Ubon's founding and is the city's holiest possession.

Ubon is most famous for its **Candle Parade** (Hae Tian), when huge wax sculptures are paraded to the temples. It marks the beginning of the Buddhist rains retreat in July.

Sleeping

Rates shoot up and availability goes down during the Candle Festival.

River Moon Guesthouse (0 4528 6093; 21 Th Sisaket 2; s 120, d 150-180B) It's a crumbling old place with rustic but cheap rooms, 300m from the train station.

our pick Aree Mansion (0 4526 5518; 208-212 Th Pha Daeng; r 250-350B) This ageing but earnest budget spot has big, clean rooms; even the cheap fan versions come with hot water, minifridge and free wi-fi.

Eating & Drinking

Boon Ni Yon Uthayan (0 4524 0950; Th Si Narong; per plate 10-15B; breakfast & lunch Tue-Sun) Run by the ascetic Sisa Asoka group, this restaurant has an impressive vegetarian buffet. Most of the food is grown organically just outside the city.

Porntip (08 9720 8101; Th Saphasit; dishes 30-100B; 9am-6pm) Ubon's premier purveyor of *kài yâang, sôm tam,* sausages and other Isan food. It's just east of Wat Jaeng.

Pakse (no roman-script sign; Th Uparat; 6pm-12.30am) This cool pub has oodles of character, a pool table and a full menu.

The city's new-and-improved **night market** (4pm-1am) sits at the southeast corner of Thung Si Meuang Park. Also fun are the floating restaurants on the Mun River.

Shopping

The speciality of Ubon Province is natural-dyed, hand-woven cotton, and you'll find a fantastic assortment of clothing, bags and fabric here. First stop should be **Camp Fai Ubon** (0 4524 1821; 189 Th Thepyothi; 8am-5pm), which is signed as Peaceland. Smaller, but also good, is **Grass-Root** (0 4524 1272; 87 Th Yutthaphan; 9am-5pm).

Getting There & Around

Thai Airways International (THAI; code TG; www.thaiairways.com) has two daily flights to/from Bangkok, while **Air Asia** (code AK; www.airasia.com) has one.

Ubon's **bus terminal** (☎ 0 4531 6085; Th Chayangkun) is located at the far northern end of town, 3km from the centre, accessible via săwngthăew No 2, 3 or 10. Buses link Ubon with Bangkok's Northern & Northeastern bus terminal (2nd/1st class 396/473B, eight hours), Nakhon Ratchasima (203/269B, seven hours), Mukdahan (ordinary/air-con 85/144B, 3½ hours) and Surin (ordinary/air-con 144/212B, three hours).

The **train station** (☎ 0 4532 1588; Th Sathani) is located in Warin Chamrap, south of central Ubon, accessible via săwngthăew No 2. There are a couple of night trains in either direction connecting Ubon and Bangkok (express 3rd class 245B, 2nd-class fan/air-con sleeper 471/551B, 1st class 1180B). Six other trains run throughout the day and also stop in Surin and Nakhon Ratchasima.

Numbered săwngthăew (10B) run throughout town. A túk-túk trip will cost at least 40B.

MUKDAHAN

pop 34,300

Mukdahan is a well-oiled revolving door between Thailand and Savannakhet, Laos, thanks to the Thai–Lao Friendship Bridge 2, an infrastructure link brought about by the ambitious Trans-Asia Highway project that continues by road all the way to the Vietnamese port town of Danang. Though the world has arrived at Mukdahan's doorstep, the town provides little distraction between arrival and departure.

A popular **Talat Indojin** (Indochina Market) sets up along the river near the border checkpoint. Outside of town, **Phu Pha Thoep National Park** (☎ 0 4260 1753; Rte 2034; admission 100B) has some beautiful clifftop views and unusual mushroom-shaped rocks. The park is 15km south of Mukdahan and is accessible via săwngthăew headed to Amphoe Don Tan (20B, 30 minutes, frequent). Ask to be let off at the park entrance and hitchhike the last 1.3km to the visitor centre.

If you need to overnight, there are a few cheap if cheerless sleeping options near the pier. **Bantomkasen Hotel** (no roman-script sign; ☎ 0 4261 1235; 25/2 Th Samut Sakdarak; r 150-300B;) has some back-in-the-day charm, plus little extras like hot-water showers and Western-style toilets. A moderate walk to the south, **Ban Rim Suan** (☎ 0 4263 2980; Th Samut Sakdarak; r 330B;) is the best budget deal in the city. The owners put in extra effort and there's free wi-fi.

Wine Wild Why? (☎ 0 4263 3122; 11 Th Samron Chaikhongthi; dishes 40-150B; lunch & dinner) is an atmospheric eatery for Thai and Isan food with a riverside setting. **Goodmook** (☎ 0 4261 2091; 414/1 Th Song Nang Sathit; dishes 70-380B; breakfast, lunch & dinner;) has all the ingredients of a travellers cafe: an international menu, free wi-fi and actual decor. The **night market** (Th Song Nang Sathit; 4-10pm) provides plenty of Vietnamese food along with the usual suspects.

Mukdahan's bus terminal is on Rte 212, west of town. Take a yellow săwngthăew (10B) from Th Phitak Phanomkhet near the fountain.

There are frequent buses to Nakhon Phanom (ordinary/air-con 52/92B, two hours, hourly), That Phanom (ordinary/air-con 28/50B, one hour), Khon Kaen (2nd class 155B, 4½ hours, frequent), Ubon Ratchathani (ordinary/air-con 80/144B, 3½ hours, hourly) and Bangkok's Northern & Northeastern bus terminal (air-con 390B to 502B, 10 hours, morning and evening departures).

THAT PHANOM

This drowsy hamlet is a little piece of Laos on the wrong side of the Mekong River. It is no place you'd chart a course to on purpose but if you're headed to Nong Khai from the

GETTING TO LAOS: CHONG MEK TO VANG TEO

Chong Mek is the only place in Thailand where you don't have to cross the Mekong to get into Laos. The southern Lao city of Pakse is about 45 minutes away by road via Vang Tao, the Lao border village, where you can now buy a 30-day visa on the spot. The crossing is largely hassle-free save for the continued practice of a 50B 'stamping' levy by Lao officials.

Ubon–Pakse buses (200B, three hours, 9.30am and 2pm departures) stop at the border for immigration formalities. If you need more transport options, Phibun Mangsahan has frequent bus connections to Ubon Ratchathani (35B, 1½ hours) and săwngthăew to Chong Mek (35B, one hour).

For information on crossing this border in the opposite direction, see p415.

GETTING TO LAOS: MUKDAHAN TO SAVANNAKHET

With the second Thai–Lao Friendship Bridge now linking Mukdahan and Savannakhet, travellers cross the Mekong by bus (weekday/weekend 45/50B, 45 minutes, hourly from 7.30am to 7pm). Though the river ferry is still used by locals, border formalities for foreign nationals are handled on the bridge. Lao visas are available on arrival.

For information on crossing from Laos into Thailand, see p411.

Mukdahan border crossing, That Phanom is a lovely detour. The highlight in town is **Wat Phra That Phanom** (Th Chayangkun; 5am-8pm), crowned by an iconic *tâht,* a needle-like Lao-style *chedi.* A lively **market** (8.30am-noon Mon & Thu) gathers by the river north of the pier where Lao merchants sell herbal medicines, forest roots and river crabs. During the **That Phanom Festival** (late January or early February) visitors come for a boisterous temple fair including *mŏr lam* (Isan-style roots music often compared to American blues).

The original backpacker pad, **Niyana Guesthouse** (0 4254 0880; 65 Soi 33; r 120-160B), northeast of the Lao Arch of Victory, is a tad chaotic, but smiles and advice flow freely from the friendly owner. There's a small **night market** (4-10pm) and **riverside eateries** (Th Rimkhong) for dinner.

That Phanom's new bus station is west of town with services to Ubon Ratchathani (ordinary/air-con 102/184B, 4½ hours, hourly), Mukdahan (ordinary/1st class 28/50B, one hour), Udon Thani (ordinary/air-con 109/196B, four hours, five daily) and Nakhon Phanom (ordinary/air-con 27/49B, one hour, five daily). You can also catch the Nakhon Phanom buses in front of the school on Hwy 212 or instead take one of the frequent săwngthăew (35B, 90 minutes) that park a bit further north.

NAKHON PHANOM

pop 31,700

This tidy provincial capital has a picturesque setting beside the Mekong River overlooking the asymmetrical peaks of Laos. With its French colonial buildings and Vietnamese influences, this is a little piece of Indochina on the far northeastern fringes of Siam. There's also a legal border crossing into Laos should you be looking for an escape hatch.

The **TAT Office** (4251 3490; Th Sunthon Wijit; 8.30am-4.30pm) has a map pointing out several heritage buildings.

Wat Okat Si Bua Ban (Th Sunthon Wijit; daylight hr) has an amazing mural depicting the temple's famous Buddhas floating across the Mekong.

The neighbouring village of **Ban Na Chok,** 3km west of town, gave refuge to Vietnamese liberator Ho Chi Minh. He planned the resistance movement in what is now called **Uncle Ho's House** (donations appreciated; daylight hr), which served as his residence from 1928–29. More Uncle Ho memories are kept at the **Friendship Village** (donations appreciated; 8am-5pm), a community centre a bit northwest.

The city runs an hour-long **sunset cruise** (08 6230 5560; 50B) along the Mekong on *Thesaban 1,* which docks across from the Indochina Market and departs at 5pm.

Nakhon Phanom is famous for its October **Illuminated Boat Procession**, a modern twist on the ancient tradition of floating offerings to the Mekong *naga,* a mythical serpent that appears in Buddhist art and iconography.

Sleeping & Eating

First Hotel (0 4251 1253; 16 Th Si Thep; r 160-300B;), near the pier, has the cheapest beds in town, for good reason. **Grand Hotel** (0 4251 1281; 210 Th Si Thep; r 190-320B;) is hardly grand but it's better than average for the price.

The outdoor terrace at the **Indochina Market** (Th Sunthon Wijit; breakfast, lunch & dinner) has choice seats that frame the mountain views. The **night market** (Th Fuang Nakhon; 4-9pm) rocks out a great variety of take-away food. **Luk Tan** (0 4251 1456; 83 Th Bamrung Meuang; buffet 89B; dinner), in the centre of town, is a quirky spot featuring an American home-style buffet, pizza and tonnes of local advice.

Getting There & Away

The **bus terminal** (Th Fuang Nakhon) is east of the town centre. Destinations include Nong Khai (ordinary/air-con 175/220B, six hours, hourly morning departures); Udon Thani (air-con 165B to 211B, five hours, frequent morning and afternoon departures), Mukdahan (air-con 52B to 92B, two hours, hourly), That Phanom (ordinary/air-con 27B/49B, one hour, five daily) and Bangkok (air-con 442B to 569B, 12 hours, morning and evening departures).

NONG KHAI

pop 61,500

Adorable Nong Khai has a winning recipe: a sleepy setting beside the Mekong River, enough tourist amenities to dispel isolation and enough local attractions to fill a day with sightseeing, snacking and wandering. It's an easy overnight train ride from Bangkok and sits right on a convenient border crossing into Vientiane, Laos. What more could you ask for?

Information

There is no shortage of banks with ATMs in town. For a wealth of information on Nong Khai and the surrounding area, visit www.mut mee.net.

Hornbill Bookshop (☎ 0 4246 0272; off Th Kaew Worawut; ⏰ 10am-7pm Mon-Sat) Best used English-language bookstore in Isan.

Nong Khai Hospital (☎ 0 4241 1504; Th Meechai) For medical emergencies.

Post office (Th Meechai; ⏰ 8.30am-4.30pm Mon-Fri, 9am-noon Sat & Sun)

TAT office (☎ 0 4242 1326; Hwy 2; ⏰ 8.30am-4.30pm Mon-Fri)

Tourist police (☎ 0 4246 0186; Th Prajak)

Sights

A curious and must-see attraction, **Sala Kaew Ku** (Wat Khaek; admission 20B; ⏰ 8am-6pm) is a sculpture park that was born from a spiritual vision by a Brahmanic yogi-priest-shaman who emigrated from Laos. The statues are a potpourri of the Hindu and Buddhist pantheon, and the immense statues offer some freaky photo opportunities. While the motivations for its 20-year construction were undoubtedly spiritual, the end result is a masterpiece of modern religious art. The sculpture park is 5km southeast of town. It is easily reached by bicycle from Nong Khai; Mut Mee Guest House distributes maps.

Talat Tha Sadet (Th Rimkhong) follows the river, obscuring the view with stalls selling crusty French baguettes, salted and grilled river fish, silks, souvenirs, and, if you look really hard, possibly the kitchen sink.

Like Surin, Nong Khai has sprouted a volunteer 'scene'. **Sarnelli House** (www.sarnelli orphanage.org) cares for HIV-positive orphans and can use a hand playing with the children on weekend mornings. **Open Mind Projects** (☎ 0 4241 3578; www.openmindprojects.org; 856/9 Mu 15, Th Prachak, Nong Khai) and **Travel to Teach** (☎ 08 4246 0351; www.travel-to-teach.org; 1161/2 Soi Chitta Panya, Th Nong Khai-Phon Phisai, Nong Khai) place English speakers in teaching jobs in and around Nong Khai. Open Mind Projects also has IT and ecotourism projects.

The river-based festivals marking the end of Buddhist Lent in October have become national celebrities in Nong Khai thanks to the unexplained natural phenomenon of the so-called '**Naga Fireballs**', small bursts of light emitted from the river and said to be greetings from the resident *naga*.

GETTING TO LAOS: NAKHON PHANOM TO THA KHAEK

Though not the most convenient crossing, Nakhon Phanom is a border crossing that feeds into the Lao town of Tha Khaek, which is a two-hour bus ride from Savannakhet. Ferries (60B, every half-hour from 8.30am to 6pm) leave from Nakhon Phanom's terminal on Th Sunthon Wijit to cross the Mekong River. Lao visas are available at the border.

See p408 for information on doing the trip in the reverse direction.

Sleeping

Nong Khai is the only Isan town with a full-fledged backpacker scene so enjoy it while you can.

Mut Mee Garden Guesthouse (☎ 0 4246 0717; www.mutmee.com; off Th Kaew Worawut; dm 100B, r 140-750B; ❄) Overlooking the mighty Mekong, the Mut Mee is a destination in itself. The rooms are good value, the garden is *soooo* relaxing and the friendly English owner is a great storyteller.

E-San Guesthouse (☎ 08 6242 1860; 538 Th Khun Muang; r 150-450B; ❄) This quiet place east of Talat Tha Sadet has simple rooms in a restored wooden house. There's also a modern air-con wing as well.

Ruan Thai Guesthouse (☎ 0 4241 2519; 1126/2 Th Rimkhong; r 200-400B, f 1000B; ❄ 💻 📶) Many people end up here after finding Mut Mee full. It boasts a good variety of rooms, many snagging the free wi-fi, behind a flower-filled garden.

Jumemalee Guesthouse (☎ 08 5010 2540; 419/1 Th Khun Muang; r 250B) Another converted wooden house, Jumemalee has rooms with private baths.

VILLAGE HOMESTAY

Thailand's rural northeast is flush with village homestay programs, mainly aimed at tour groups of Thais who didn't grow up beside a rice paddy. Of the few that can accommodate English-speaking visitors is **Kham Pia Homestay** (☎ 0 4241 3578/08 7861 0601; www.thailandwildelephanttrekking.com; per person 200B, meals 50-90B), which is located within walking distance of the 186-sq-km Phu Wua Wildlife Reserve. The reserve has nature treks and a resident herd of elephants. Kham Pia is 190km east of Nong Khai, just 3km off Hwy 212. Buses from Nong Khai (180B, 3½ hours) will drop you at Ban Don Chik, 3km away.

Eating

Darika Bakery (☎ 0 4242 0079; 668-669 Th Meechai; dishes 30-60B; breakfast & lunch) A backpacker favourite, with delicious breakfasts and an English menu.

Daeng Namnuang (☎ 0 4241 1961; 526 Th Rimkhong; dishes 35-180B; breakfast, lunch & dinner) Vietnamese spring rolls are the speciality at this local institution known as far away as Bangkok.

Nung-Len Coffee Bar (☎ 08 3662 7686; 1801/2 Th Kaew Worawut; dishes 35-180B; breakfast, lunch & dinner) Superfriendly place west of Mut Mee, with good coffee and juice and an eclectic menu of Thai and *faràng* food.

Mut Mee Garden Guesthouse (dishes 40-130B; breakfast, lunch & dinner) Best guest-house food in town, including a healthy vegetarian selection.

Rom Luang (☎ 08 7853 7136; 45/10 Th Prajak; dishes 40-150B; dinner) The Yellow Umbrella's best known dishes are Isan specialities such as sausages and *kor mŏo yâhng* ('grilled pork neck').

For quick, colourful eats swing by the **Hospital Food Court** (no roman-script sign; Th Meechai; breakfast, lunch & dinner) or the **night market** (Th Prajak; 4-11pm).

Drinking

There are several pubs along Th Rimkhong, the riverfront road. Two standouts are **Gaia** (☎ 0 4246 0717; 7pm-late Wed-Mon), floating on a raft below Mut Mee Garden Guesthouse, and **Warm Up** (☎ 08 1965 7565; 476/4 Th Rimkhong; 7pm-2am), which has a free pool table and is popular with both Thais and travellers.

For something a lot more Thai, follow the road east past Talat Tha Sadet (keep going, don't give up) until you hit the neon-lit restaurant-bars churning out dinner and drinks.

Getting There & Away

Nong Khai's main **bus terminal** (☎ 0 4241 1612) is just off Th Prajak, by the Pho Chai market, about 1.5km from the riverfront guest houses. Destinations include Udon Thani (ordinary/1st class 25/47B, one hour, frequent), Khon Kaen (2nd/1st class 120/157B, 3½ hours, hourly), Nakhon Phanom (ordinary/2nd class 175/220B, six hours, six daily) and Bangkok (2nd/1st class/VIP 350/450/700B, 11 hours, afternoon and evening departures). For more options, go to Udon Thani, which is a major transport bus hub.

The **train station** (☎ 0 4241 1592; Hwy 212) is 2km west of town. Overnight express trains leave Bangkok at 6.30pm and 8pm. Going the other way, the express train departs from Nong Khai at 6am and 6.20pm. The fares range from 1317B for a 1st-class sleeper to 253/388B for a 3rd-/2nd-class seat. There's also one rapid train (3rd/2nd class 213/348B) leaving Bangkok at 6.40pm and returning to Bangkok at 7.15pm.

UDON THANI

pop 227,200

Sprawling Udon Thani is too big to be charming and too conservative to be cultured. It boomed on the back of the Vietnam War when it hosted a US air base. Udon sees relatively few foreign travellers other than a large number of sex tourists.

The rest of us might roll through for a bus connection or to visit **Ban Chiang**, one of the earliest prehistoric cultures known in Southeast Asia. The affiliated **museum** (☎ 0 4220 8340; admission 150B; 8.30am-4.30pm) displays pottery and tools from the civilisation and includes an excavation pit used as a burial ground dating to 300 BC. Ban Chiang is 50km from Udon Thani and accessible from bus terminal 1 via Sakhon Nakhon– or Nakhon Phanom–bound buses; get off at Ban Nong Mek (35B, one hour) and hire a túk-túk or motorcycle taxi (60B) for the remainder.

If you need to overnight, **Puttarag Hotel** (☎ 0 4224 7032; 380/15 Th Prajak Silpakorn; r 160B) is a shared-bath, cold-water flophouse near the train station and right in the thick of Udon's *faràng* nightlife district. The nearby

Top Mansion (☎ 0 4234 5015; topmansion@yahoo.com; 35/3 Th Sampanthamit; r 350-490B;) is a huge leap up in quality; it even has wi-fi in the rooms.

Udon's trio of **night markets** (Th Prajak Silpakorn; 4-11pm) is in front of the train station.

Thai Airways International (THAI; code TG; www.thaiair.com), **Nok Air** (code DD; www.nokair.co.th) and **Air Asia** (code AK; ☎ 0 2515 9999; www.airasia.com) fly to Bangkok.

Udon has two bus stations. Bus Terminal No 1, near the Charoen Hotel in the southeastern part of town, serves Bangkok (2nd/1st class/VIP 321/412/641B, eight hours, every half-hour), Khorat (2nd/1st class 207/248B, 4½ hours, every half-hour), Khon Kaen (2nd/1st class 83/104B, 2½ hours, frequent) and Suvarnabhumi airport (418B, eight hours, 9pm). If you already have a Lao visa, there's a bus to Vientiane (80B, two hours, six daily).

Bus Terminal No 2 is on the Ring Rd west of the city (take sǎwngthǎew No 6, 7 or 15 or the yellow bus). Destinations include Loei (ordinary/1st class 70/113B, three hours, frequent) and Chiang Mai (2nd class/VIP 438/657B, 12 hours, five daily). For Nong Khai (ordinary/1st class 25/47B, one hour, frequent) you can use either terminal, but the most frequent departures are from Rangsina Market, reached by the white bus or sǎwngthǎew No 6.

Udon Thani is on the Bangkok–Nong Khai line. Express trains leave Bangkok at 8.20am, 6.30pm and 8pm. In the reverse direction, departures are at 6.54am, 6.40pm and 7.20pm.

GETTING TO LAOS: NONG KHAI TO VIENTIANE

Nong Khai is the most popular Lao–Thai border crossing. Take a túk-túk (50B) from central Nong Khai to the Thai–Lao Friendship Bridge where you get stamped out of Thailand. From there regular minibuses (15–20B) carry passengers across the bridge to the Lao immigration checkpoint, where 30-day visas are available. From there it's 22km to Vientiane, accessible via buses, túk-túk and taxis. If you already have a Lao visa, there are also six direct buses to Vientiane from Nong Khai's bus terminal (60B, one hour).

For information on making this crossing in the opposite direction, see p376.

The fares to Bangkok are 245/369/1277B for a 3rd-class seat/2nd-class seat/1st-class sleeper.

LOEI & AROUND

The city of **Loei** is a necessary and uninspiring transport hub for accessing the province's remote and mountainous countryside. If you need to spend the night, try **Sugar Guest House** (☎ 0 4281 2982; 4/1 Th Wisut Titep Soi 2; r 180-380B;), the cheapest and friendliest place in town.

What most people are looking for is the slow-going Mekong town of **Chiang Khan**, which is full of traditional timber shophouses and sarong-clad grannies. Rest and relax at **Chiang Khan Guesthouse** (☎ 0 4282 1691; www.thailandunplugged.com; 282 Th Chai Khong; r 300-400B;), run by a Dutch tour guide and his affable Thai wife, or **Rimkong Pub & Guesthouse** (☎ 08 7951 3172; http://rimkhong.free.fr; 294 Th Chai Khong; r 200-500B), a polished teak house run by a French expat.

Phu Kradung National Park (☎ 0 4287 1333; admission 200B), about 75km to the south of Loei, includes a bell-shaped mountain with unhindered sunrise and sunset views. The climb to the summit takes about four hours if you're in shape. Being the northeast's version of a 'spring break' destination, the park fills up with guitar-toting college students during school holidays and weekends. Atop the mountain there are **camp sites** (☎ bookings 0 2562 0760; www.dnp.go.th/parkreserve; per person 30B, 3-/6-person tent hire 225/450B) and **bungalows** (r 900-3600B). It gets cold up here so a sleeping bag is a must. There are also several small open-air eateries serving the usual stir-fry dishes.

The raucous **Phi Ta Khon Festival** (Spirit Festival) is held in the innocuous town of Dan Sai usually in June and is a cross between the drunken revelry of Carnival and the ghoulishness of Halloween. The festival coincides with the more subdued Buddhist holy day of Bun Phra Wet (Phra Wet Festival), honouring the penultimate life of the Buddha, Phra Wessandara (often shortened in Thai to Phra Wet). But in Dan Sai the main event is an elaborate and rice-whisky-fuelled parade in which villagers don masks to transform themselves into the spirits who welcomed Phra Wet's return. **Kawinthip Hattakham** (☎ 08 9077 2080; phitakhon@yahoo.com; 70/1 Th Kaew Asa; 6.30am-8pm) is a shop selling Phi Ta Khon masks and other festival-related souvenirs and can arrange basic **homestay accommodation** (per person 150B).

Getting There & Around

From Loei's **bus terminal** (☎ 0 4283 3586) destinations include Udon Thani (ordinary/1st class 70/113B, three hours, frequent), Phitsanulok (2nd/1st class 139/178B, four hours, hourly) and Bangkok (2nd class/32-seat VIP 321/481B, 11 hours), among others. There's only one bus to Nong Khai (130B, seven hours, 6am) and it's worth catching because it follows the scenic Mekong River. It's faster, however, to go via Udon Thani.

In Chiang Khan, sǎwngthǎew to Loei (35B, 1¼ hours, frequent) depart from a stop on Rte 201, while eight buses (45B, 45 minutes) leave from Nakhonchai Air's bus terminal, 250m further south.

Buses from Loei go to the town of Phu Kradung (50B, 1½ hours, frequent). From Phu Kradung town, hop on a sǎwngthǎew (20B) to the park's visitor centre at the base of the mountain, 10km away. The last sǎwngthǎew leaves the mountain around 8pm.

To get to Dan Sai, buses leave from Loei (2nd class 60B, 1½ hours) and from Phitsanulok (ordinary/2nd class 67/94B, three hours).

KHON KAEN

pop 145,300

It's not the big cities that draw visitors to Isan, but Khon Kaen might just be the exception. Home to the northeast's largest university, the city is youthful, educated and on the move. It also makes a sensible base for exploring nearby silk-weaving villages and is a gateway to the northeast from Phitsanulok and Sukhothai.

Information

It's hard to walk around Khon Kaen without bumping into an ATM or bank. Internet shops can be found on Th Glang Meuang.

Khon Kaen Ram Hospital (☎ 0 4333 3900; Th Si Chan)

Post office (cnr Th Si Chan & Th Glang Meuang)

TAT office (☎ 0 4324 4498; 15/5 Th Prachasamoson; 8.30am-4.30pm)

Tourist police (☎ 0 4323 6937, emergency 1155; Th Mittaphap) Next to HomePro.

Sights

The well-curated **Khon Kaen National Museum** (☎ 0 4324 6170; Th Lang Sunratchakan; admission 100B; 9am-4pm Wed-Sun) features ancient art and artefacts as well as agricultural displays that explain what's going on in the countryside.

For more Isan explanations head to **Khon Kaen City Museum** (Hong Moon Mung; ☎ 0 4327 1173; Th Robbung; admission 90B; 9am-5pm Mon-Sat).

Sleeping & Eating

First Choice (☎ 08 1546 2085; firstchoicekhonkaen@lycos.com; 18/8 Th Phimphaseut; r 150-200B) This close approximation of a backpacker hostel has no-frills quarters upstairs and a traveller-friendly eatery below.

Saen Samran Hotel (☎ 0 4323 9611; 55-59 Th Glang Meuang; s 170-200B, d 250B) The city's oldest hotel has spic and span rooms and wi-fi.

Roma Hotel (☎ 0 4333 4444; 50/2 Th Glang Meuang; s 230-500B, d 250-500B, ste 800B) Roma's air-con rooms are good value, spotless and comfy, and the fan rooms are…well, good value and comfy.

our pick **Dee Dee** (☎ 08 5006 3922; 348/25 Soi Ruenrom 1; dishes 30-60B; breakfast, lunch & dinner) A humble made-to-order shop that does a phenomenal plate of *pàt tim* (egg noodles stir-fried with red curry paste).

Hom Krun (☎ 0 4327 0547; Th Ruenrom; dishes 35-129B; 9am-midnight, no coffee after 7pm) With its shady patio, kitchen and free wi-fi, this is a favourite coffee shop. It's at the foot of Th Prachasumran and anchors the city's nightlife district.

Turm-Rom (☎ 0 4322 1752; 4/5 Th Chetakhon; dishes 35-129B; dinner) Great kitchen, great garden, great pub. You'll be a fan too.

The **lakeside market** (dinner) at the north end of Beung Kaen Nakhon is a fun place to dine, but the food is better at the city-centre **night market** (Th Reunrom; 5pm-midnight), the heart and soul of the budget dining scene.

Shopping

Khon Kaen is a good place to buy Isan handicrafts, like *mát-mìi* (cloth made of tie-dyed silk or cotton thread), silk, silverwork and basketry.

Prathamakhan (☎ 0 4322 4080; 79/2-3 Th Reunrom; 9am-8pm) Stocks the largest textile selection in town.

Phrae Phan (☎ 0 4333 7216; 131/193 Th Chatapadung; 8am-6pm) Run by the Handicraft Centre for Northeastern Women's Development; it is out of the way but has a superb selection of natural dyed, hand-woven silk and cotton produced in nearby villages.

Sueb San (no roman-script sign; ☎ 0 4334 4072; 16 Th Glang Meuang; 8am-6.30pm) Easier to get to and stocking natural-dyed fabrics, plus some atypical souvenirs.

Getting There & Away

The **airport** (☎ 0 4324 6345) is a few kilometres west of the city centre. **Thai Airways International** (THAI; code TG; ☎ 0 4322 7701; www.thaiair.com) flies to Bangkok.

Khon Kaen is a major transit hub for the region and beyond. It has two bus stations: the **ordinary bus terminal** (☎ 0 4333 3388; Th Prachasamoson) is a five-minute walk northwest of Th Glang Meuang; and the **air-con bus terminal** (☎ 0 4323 9910; Th Glang Meuang) is in the town centre near the night market. A simple enough distinction that is complicated by the fact that 2nd-class air-con buses leave from the ordinary bus terminal.

Buses travel to and from Bangkok (air-con 383B, VIP 414B to 585B, 6½ hours, hourly), Khorat (air-con 129B to 187B, three hours, frequent), Loei (air-con 141B, 2½ hours, frequent), Mukdahan (air-con 155B, 4½ hours, frequent), Nong Khai (air-con 120B, 3½ hours, hourly) and nearly every other Isan town. There's also service to Phitsanulok (air-con 223/280B, five hours, hourly) and Chiang Mai (570B, 12 hours, 8pm and 9pm). If you already have your Lao visa, you can catch a bus to Vientiane (180B, four hours, 7.45am, 1.30pm and 3.15pm).

Khon Kaen is on the Bangkok–Nong Khai railway line, but buses are much faster. Bangkok-bound express trains leave Khon Kaen at 8.39am, 8.11pm and 9.05pm. The fares to Bangkok are 227/399B for a 3rd-/2nd-class seat and 1168B for 1st-class sleeper.

EASTERN GULF COAST

Thailand's east coast isn't as stunning as the postcard-famous southern coast, but it is an ideal beach jaunt (only a half-day's bus ride) from jostling Bangkok. While your friends are still packed into buses en route to Ko Pha-Ngan, you'll be sun-kissed and sandy-toed. This is also the main gateway to Cambodia's coastal town of Sihanoukville. During the rainy season, the eastern gulf gets less deluge than the south, though every time we've tested this theory we've met days of rain.

KO SAMET

Bangkok's beachy backyard, Ko Samet is close enough for a weekend escape, yet worlds away from the urban hustle and bustle. Traffic-weary Thais, foreign expats and beach-hopping backpackers are Samet's steady clientele – and everyone squeezes into the petite east-coast beaches. It's been a **national park** (admission 200B) since 1981 and it is still surprisingly rustic considering Thailand's penchant for urban makeovers for its seaside parks. Walking trails connect the beaches and the rocky headlands, traffic is insignificant and the coconut trees tower over the buildings.

The northeast part of the island has the most popular and populated areas. **Hat Sai Kaew** is the widest swathe of sand and thus the busiest with jet skis, karaoke and nightly discos. **Ao Hin Khok** has an unshaven ambiance; its beach is smaller but backpackers don't seem to mind. **Ao Phai** is another perfectly relaxing bay around the next headland. Further south is **Ao Wong Deuan**, a wide arc of sand filled with bars and mayhem. The further south you go, the more Thai and isolated it becomes.

Bring along mosquito spray as the forested island is home to everyone's favourite blood suckers.

Information

Internet access is available at some of the guest houses on Ao Hin Khok.

Ko Samet Health Centre (☎ 0 3861 1123; 🕑 8.30am-9pm Mon-Fri, to 4.30pm Sat & Sun) For minor medical problems; on the main road between Na Dan pier and Hat Sai Kaew.

Siam City Bank (Th Nadaan) There are no banks on Ko Samet, but this ATM is located at the 7-Eleven near the national-park entrance. There's another ATM near the pier.

Sleeping & Eating

Naga Bungalows (☎ 0 3864 4035; Ao Hin Khok; r 350-700B; 💻) Simple fan bungalows climb up the forested hillside; the common area is a common place to meet travellers.

PJ House (☎ 0 3864 4182; Ao Wong Deuan; r 500B; ❄) Next to Baywatch Bar, this small place delivers air-con for the price of a fan. There's a pool table downstairs dominated by the local 10-year-old sharks.

Blue Sky (☎ 08 1509 0547; Ao Wong Deuan; r 600-800B; ❄) One of the last budget spots on Ao Wong Deuan, Blue Sky has simple bungalows set on a rocky headland. The restaurant does tasty things with seafood.

Tub Tim Resort (☎ 0 3864 4025; www.tubtimresort.com; Ao Phutsa; r 600-1500B; ❄) Just over the rocks from Ao Phai, Tub Tim has a range of bungalows, from fan to fab and a garden that may

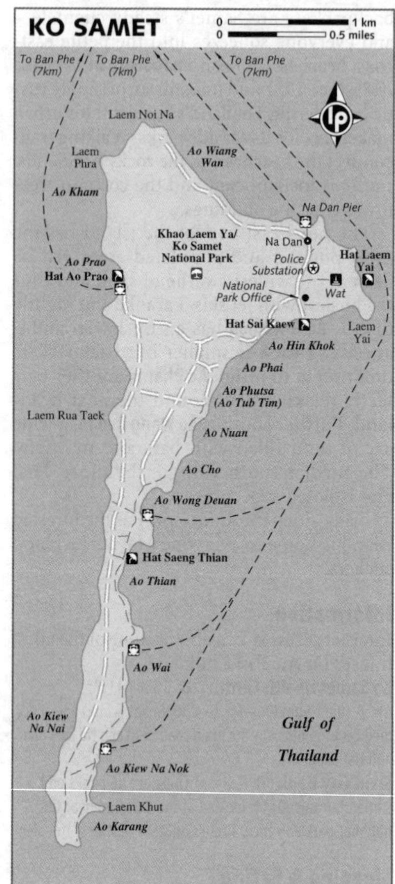

soon be a jungle. Ao Phutsa is sometimes called Ao Tub Tim.

Jep's Bungalows (☎ 0 3864 4112; www.jepbungalow.com; Ao Hin Khok; r 600-2600B;) Spearheading the upscale evolution of Ao Hin Khok, Jep's has diversified from dingy fan bungalows to air-con rooms with satellite TV. But there are still the backpacker favourites: nightly movies and beachside barbecues.

Ao Nuan (Ao Nuan; r 700-1500B) The best place for chillaxin', this basic bungalow is hidden amid the vegetation on a tiny, quiet curve of sand. The funky cafe has books, beats and conversation: like hanging out at a friend's house. Space is limited and reservations aren't taken. Just walk on over from Ao Phutsa and hope for the best.

Most bungalows have restaurants offering mixed menus of Thai and traveller food. Eat locally at the cheap noodle bars and seafood joints in Na Dan, the small village next to the pier.

Getting There & Around

Ko Samet is reached by boat from the mainland town of Ban Phe (one way/return 50/100B, 45 minutes, 7am to 5pm). On the island, the main pier is at Na Dan in the north, but services also run to other beaches during peak tourist times.

There are two air-con bus stations in Ban Phe that have buses to Bangkok's Eastern (Ekamai) bus terminal. The faster but less frequent service leaves from the station 50m west of Ban Phe pier; buses depart four times a day in the afternoon starting at 12.30pm and leave Bangkok as many times in the mornings beginning at 7am (138B, 2½ hours).

Much slower but more frequent buses depart across from Nuan Tip pier, 100m east of Ban Phe pier. But it is faster to transit through Rayong. From Bangkok's Eastern bus terminal, take a bus to Rayong (145B) and then transfer to a blue sǎwngthǎew to Ban Phe (25B, frequent).

Sǎwngthǎew on the island cost from 20B to 50B, depending on your destination and the number of passengers. From the pier, some southerly locations can cost as much as 300B to 500B for one or two passengers.

CHANTHABURI & TRAT

Surrounded by palm trees and plantations, Chanthaburi and Trat are mainly transit transfers for travellers headed to Ko Chang or the Cambodian border. If you stop to catch your breath, you'll find that Chanthaburi dazzles with its weekend **gem market**, and sleepy Trat is filled with old teak shophouses and genuine small-town living.

Information

Om.com (134 Th Si Chan, Chanthaburi; per hr 10B; 9am-10pm) Darn cheap internet connection.

Sawadee@Café Net (☎ 0 3952 0075; Th Lak Meuang, Trat; per min 1B; 10am-10pm) Internet and Skype are both available.

Tratosphere Bookshop (23 Rimklong Soi, Trat; 8am-10pm) Load up on beach reading or get travel tips on the area.

Sleeping & Eating

CHANTHABURI

You're unlikely to need a bed in Chantaburi, but just in case…

River Guest House (☎ 0 3932 8211; 3/5-8 Th Si Chan; r 150-350B;) Chanthaburi's real gems are the clean rooms and relaxed sitting area by the river at this friendly place. There's a fair bit of highway noise, but air-con can drown it out.

Chanthorn Phochana (☎ 0 3931 2339; Th Benchamarachutit 102/5-8; dishes 30-120B; breakfast, lunch & dinner) Stock up on some bus snacks, such as Vietnamese spring rolls or a bag of durian chips (tastier than you think), or sit down to a Thai-Chinese meal and some house oddities like stir-fried papaya and local mangosteen wine.

TRAT

You're more likely to need to overnight in Trat and the town has a small but friendly guest-house scene.

Sawadee (☎ 0 3951 2392; 90 Th Lak Meuang; r 100-300B) Simple but fastidiously clean fan rooms.

Ban Jaidee Guest House (☎ 0 3952 0678; 6 Th Chaimongkol; r 150-200B) This relaxed Thai-style home decorated with artistic flourishes has simple rooms. It's very popular, so book ahead.

Residang House (☎ 0 3953 0103; www.trat-guesthouse.com; 87/1-2 Th Thana Charoen; r 260-500B;) Big beds with thick mattresses, good bathrooms with hot showers – what more do you need? Fan rooms come with breezes and balconies; some overlook the river.

our pick **Cool Corner** (☎ 08 4159 2030; 49-51 Th Thana Charoen; dishes 50-150; breakfast, lunch & dinner) Though it's no longer on the corner since the original building burned down in 2008, the hip artist/owner still serves up great vibes, good beats, heaping portions and darn good mango lassies.

In the evenings, visit Trat's night market (advertised confidently as 'Food Safety Street') or a **vegetarian restaurant** (dishes 20B; 6am-11am) down a nearby lane, offering tasty vegie food at knockdown prices from the crack of dawn. It usually closes at midday.

Getting There & Away

Trat airport is 40km from town and a taxi to or from the airport will cost around 300B (depending on the number of passengers). **Bangkok Airways** (☎ in Bangkok 0 2265 5555; www.bangkokair.com) has two daily flights to Trat.

Chanthaburi has the larger **bus station** (Th Saritidet) with connections to Bangkok's Eastern bus terminal (200B, 4½ hours, frequent), Trat (55B to 70B, 1½ hours) and some northeastern towns.

Ko Chang–bound travellers should take a bus from Bangkok's Eastern bus terminal to Trat (223B to 260B, 5½ hours, hourly). From Trat take a săwngthăew to Laem Ngop's Centrepoint pier (40B to 60B); skip the săwngthăew that want you to charter the entire vehicle. At Laem Ngop's pier, ferries make the crossing to the island for 80B to 100B; see p786 for more information.

GETTING TO CAMBODIA

Hat Lek to Cham Yeam

This is the most convenient border crossing for Sihanoukville. Take an air-con minibus from Trat's bus station to the border at Hat Lek (120B, one hour, departures every 45 minutes from 6am to 6pm). Motorcycles and taxis carry passengers across the border to Krong Koh Kong (50B to 80B). From Krong Koh Kong, there is only one boat per day to Sihanoukville (US$15, four to five hours, departing at 8am). There are also minibuses that go to Sihanoukville (550B) that depart at 9am. If you want to get from Trat to Sihanoukville in one day, you should be on the 6am minibus and at the border as soon as it opens at 7am. Hold on to your Thai baht for the Cambodian visa fee (1200B) as this border does not accept payment in US currency.

For information on making this crossing in the other direction, see p114.

Dan Lem to Psar Pruhm

Foreigners can cross the border from Ban Pakard in Thailand to Psar Pruhm in Cambodia, and then on to Pailin. Take a minibus from Chanthaburi to Ban Pakard (125B, one to two hours). Cross the border to Psar Pruhm and then arrange a share taxi into Pailin. From Pailin it is possible to connect with Battambang.

See p108 for information on crossing in the other direction.

Also note that there are hourly buses leaving Trat for Bangkok's Northern and Northeastern (Mo Chit) bus terminal that stop at Suvarnabhumi airport, which might spare you a trip back into the city if you're catching a flight.

See p785 for info on crossing over the border into Cambodia.

KO CHANG

Jungle-clad Ko Chang used to sit on the forgotten eastern frontier but these days it has been lassoed into Bangkok's gravitational pull, with an assortment of sophisticated resorts, tonnes of bars and daily flights from the capital to nearby Trat. So why travel the extra kilometres to Ko Chang instead of Ko Samet? Ko Chang appeals to hyperactive visitors: the beaches are bigger, diving and snorkelling spots are offshore, and the forested interior can be explored by foot or by elephant. If you wanted cosmo amenities within reach of the beach, then Ko Chang strikes a good balance. Ko Chang is part of a larger **national park** (admission 200B) that includes neighbouring islands.

Mainly the western coast has been developed for tourism. In the northwest is Hat Sai Khao, by far the biggest, busiest and brashest beach. Further south is Ao Khlong Phrao, an upmarket outpost. The backpacker fave is Lonely Beach (Hat Tha Nam), which is lonely no more, especially at night. An old-fashioned fishing community is settled around Bang Bao. The east coast is largely undeveloped with only a few low-key spots, like Hat Yao (Long Beach).

Information

Internet cafes and banks with ATMs are plentiful on the island, especially in Hat Sai Khao.

Ko Chang Hospital (☎ 0 3952 1657; Ban Dan Mai) Near the police headquarters.

Police (☎ 0 3958 6191; Ban Dan Mai)

Post office (☎ 0 3955 1240; Hat Sai Khao)

Sleeping & Eating

Independent Bo's (☎ 0 3955 1165; Hat Sai Khao; r 250-500B) A colourful place that clambers up the jungle hillside, Bo's is a psychedelic version of the Swiss Family Robinson's wooden chalet. The cheapest rooms are 'way, way' up in the jungle.

Treehouse Lodge (www.treehouse-kohchang.de; Hat Yao; r 300B) The original Treehouse Lodge moved here from Hat Tha Nam and handed over management to new owners. Nevertheless, the backpacker vibe is the same and basic huts (which share superbasic bathrooms) chill along a hillside gazing at a slice of beach.

Bang Bao Cliff Cottage (☎ 08 5904 6706; www.cliff-cottage.com; Bang Bao; r 300B) Partially hidden on a forested hillside are a few dozen thatch huts. Most have good views of the small cove below, where there's snorkelling.

Magic Garden (☎ 08 3756 8827; www.magicgardenresort.com; Hat Tha Nam; r 500-750B; 💻) Perfect for the sociable 21st-century neohippies, the Magic Garden's two-storey bungalows resemble tree houses, while the smaller huts are standard backpacker shelter. All have private bathrooms with hot showers.

our pick **Blue Lagoon Resort** (☎ 08 1940 0649; Ao Khlong Prao; r 600-1000B; ❄) White-washed bungalows with private decks and striped curtains sit right above a calm lagoon, and further back are two-storey air-con bungalows in a shady grove. A wooden walkway leads to the beach and there's even a hand-pulled raft across the water. The exceeding friendly resort runs a Thai cooking class.

Menus at all the bungalows on Ko Chang are pretty similar. There are several small eateries (dishes 40B) along the eastern side of the main road in Hat Sai Khao.

Also worth trying out are the seafood restaurants located on the pier at Ban Bang Bao, including **Ruan Thai** (☎ 08 7000 162; Bang Bao; dishes 80-300B; 🕑 lunch & dinner). Across the road from Blue Lagoon Resort is **KaTi** (☎ 08 1903 0408; Ao Khlong Prao; dishes 60-120B; 🕑 lunch & dinner), another Thai cooking school and another safe bet.

Getting There & Around

Ko Chang is accessible from the mainland port of Laem Ngop, where there are three piers that go to different points on the island. From the mainland, Tha Ko Chang Centrepoint (one way/return 80/160B, 45 minutes, hourly from 6am to 7pm) goes to Tha Dan Kao on the northeast coast. Tha Thammachat has a car ferry (per person/car 60/120B, 30 minutes, hourly) that docks at Ao Sapparot on the north coast. Tha Laem Ngop is serviced by a rusty fishing boat (100B, one hour, hourly) that goes to the southern coast

Săwngthăew on the island will shuttle you from the pier to the various beaches (50B to 200B).

SOUTHERN GULF COAST

Palm-fringed beaches, warm lazy days, jewel-toned seas: the southern gulf coast pours an intoxicating draught of paradise that attracts a steady crowd of sun worshippers. Most are bound for one or more of the offshore islands: resorty Ko Samui, hippie Ko Pha-Ngan and dive-centric Ko Tao.

If the Vitamin D treatments have you recharged, stop off en route at a few of the mild-mannered provincial capitals that live and work by the sea, for a glimpse at the rhythms of coastal Thailand. Even further south, Thailand starts to merge with Malaysia: onion-domed mosques peep over the treeline; the diction is fast and furious as southern Thais are legendary speed talkers; and a roti seller can be found on every corner.

The best time to visit Thailand's southern reaches is from March to May, when the rest of the country is practically melting from the angry sun. If the earth is burning in the city, in other words, it might be time to sample the many surprises of the gulf.

CHA-AM

pop 46,000

A mainly Thai affair, this seaside town provides a cultural perspective on how the locals frolic along their coast. Food is a top priority – ranging from dilapidated seafood shacks to homemade picnics under the casuarina trees and vendors selling plumb grilled squid. Provincial Thai fun also means jet skis and banana boats, fully clothed swimmers in inner tubes (most Thais don't know how to swim) and families scooting around on tricycles. Weekends go crazy with students and busloads of holidaymakers, while weekdays are sleepy and charming.

Sleeping & Eating

Cha-am has two types of accommodation: low-grade apartment-style hotels along the beach road (Th Ruamjit) and more expensive 'condotels'. Expect a 20% to 40% rata increase on weekends.

At the far northern end of the beach are seafood restaurants along the fishing pier. Along the beach road are simple Thai restaurants, all similar in ambience and price.

Cha-Am Villa Beach (☎ 0 3247 1241; www.chaamvillahotel.com; 241/2 Th Ruamjit; r from 500B;) Though it's far from charming, the 500B fan rooms are bargains and grant access to a swimming pool and wi-fi.

Nirundorn 3 (☎ 0 3247 0300; 26/171 Th Ruamjit; r 600, bungalow 1000B;) One of several 'Nirundorn' properties, No 3 wins with the hotel rooms that have pillow-top mattresses and verandahs with a slice of a sea view.

German Food House (☎ 08 7082 6252; 234/28-30 Soi Bus Station; dishes 90-375B; breakfast, lunch & dinner) Run by a butcher and baker (no candlestick maker, though), this sausage-and-bread joint is deservedly popular with expats.

Poom Restaurant (☎ 0 3247 1036; 274/1 Th Ruamjit; dishes 120-250B; lunch & dinner) Slightly more expensive than others but is worth it for the fresh seafood served under tall sugar palms.

Getting There & Away

Most ordinary and air-con buses stop in the town centre on Phetkasem Hwy. Some Bangkok air-con buses conveniently go all the way to the beach, stopping at a small bus station a few hundred metres south of the Th Narathip intersection.

Destinations include Bangkok (ordinary/air-con 130/150B, three hours, frequent), Phetchaburi (air-con 100B, 40 minutes, frequent) and Hua Hin (ordinary 30B, 30 minutes, frequent).

SOUTHERN CUISINE: THE SHOWGIRL OF THAI FOOD

The bounty of the sea mixed with the exotic seasonings of various seafaring cultures (Indian, Malay and Chinese) has endowed southern cuisine with a flamboyant regional character. The curries are technicoloured thanks to turmeric; the average Thai dipping sauce made from chillies and fish sauce is concentrated into a tastebud-punching paste; and the humble coconut is grated and milked into all manner of meals. Dishes such as *khâo mòk kài* (chicken biryani) and *khanŏm jiin náam yaa* (thin rice noodles doused in a fish-curry sauce and served with a plate of fresh and pickled vegetables) are offspring from Malay and Chinese culinary parents. Malay-style *roti kaeng* is a fluffy flat bread served with a curry dip; order another if you like to watch the headscarved Muslim women slap the dough into a gossamer circle, then fry it into a spitting wok.

The **train station** (Th Narathip) is west of Phetkasem Hwy and a 30B motorcycle ride from the beach. There are daily services to Cha-am from Bangkok: Hualamphong station (9.20am and 3.35pm). Tickets cost from 60B to 150B. Cha-am isn't listed on the English-language train schedule.

HUA HIN

pop 42,000

Within reach of Bangkok, Hua Hin is considered the elegant alternative to seedy Pattaya. Older Europeans agree and have long made the pilgrimage or even retirement here. Though Hua Hin has the pedigree of being the beach for the Bangkok elite (including the royal family), the colossal hotel towers have the prettiest beaches in a tight bear hug that leaves little space for everything else. For budget-conscious travellers there are cheaper, more tantalising beaches elsewhere, but if you feel the urge you'll find pockets of Hua Hin's old fishing port character and a lively seafood night market.

Sleeping

All Nations Guest House (☎ 0 3251 2747; www.geocities.com/allnationsguesthouse; 10-10/1 Th Dechanuchit; r 200-550B; ❄) This place is often packed with backpackers as Hua Hin is lean on cheapies.

Euro-Hua Hin City Hotel YHA (☎ 0 3251 3130; 15/15 Th Sasong; r incl breakfast 250-1000B; ❄) Institutional and predictable, this hostel has cramped six-person dorms and single rooms for snorers.

our pick Pattana Guest House (☎ 0 3251 3393; 52 Th Naresdamri; r 350-550B; ❄) Affordability and serenity under one roof, this restored fisherman's house has small but whimsically decorated rooms and a plant-filled lobby.

Tong Mee House (☎ 0 3253 0725; tongmeehuahin@hotmail.com; 1 Soi Raumpown; r 450-550B; ❄ 💻) Built out on a fishing pier, the tide migrates just under foot. Hidden away in a residential *soi*, this boutique-ish hotel is the best value in town.

Eating & Drinking

Hua Hin's major attraction is the inexpensive **Chatchai Market** (Th Phetkasem & Th Dechanuchit) in the centre of town, where vendors gather nightly to cook fresh seafood, like *plaa sǎmlii* (cotton fish or kingfish), *plaa kràphong* (perch), *plaa mèuk* (squid), *hǎwy málaeng phûu* (mussels) and *puu* (crab). Fresh seafood can also be found in the seafood restaurants on Th Naresdamri, at the intersection with Th Dechanuchit. On the beach you can order a cold Singha and cracked crab without leaving your deckchair.

Sidewalk Café (☎ 0 8438 55187; Soi Selakam; dishes 70-130B; 🕑 8.30am-1am) Tasty coffee, fluffy scrambled eggs and fresh-squeezed juice provides a mellow morning meal.

Hua Hin Brewing Company (☎ 0 3251 2888; 33 Th Naresdamri; 🕑 open 5pm) Though there's no longer any beer brewed here, most nights there's a live band followed by a relatively clued-up DJ.

Getting There & Around

Buses to Bangkok's Southern bus station (air-con 140B to 165B, three hours, hourly) leave from a stop 70m north of Rajana Garden House on Th Sasong (outside the Siripetchkasem Hotel). Minivans run regularly from Bangkok's Victory Monument to Th Phetkasem (200B).

The new **main bus station** (Th Phetkasem) is south of town and serves Phetchaburi (85B, 1½ hours), Cha-am (45B, 30 minutes), Prachuap Khiri Khan (60B to 80B, 1½ hours), Chumphon (160B, four hours) and Surat Thani (270B, seven hours). Frequent ordinary buses leave from near the intersection of Th Chomsin and Th Phetkasem for Phetchaburi (50B, 1½ hours) and Cha-am (25B, 30 minutes).

The train station, at the end of Th Damnoen Kasem, has trains to/from Bangkok's Hualamphong station (3rd class 100B to 234B, 2nd class 292B to 382B, four hours).

You'll need to bargain hard for sǎamláw fares. Here are some sample fares: train station to the beach 50B; main bus terminal to Th Naresdamri 40B to 50B (depending on size of your bags).

PRACHUAP KHIRI KHAN

pop 27,700

A prettier-than-average seaside town, Prachuap Khiri Khan is relaxed and untouristed with only a few minor attractions, a draw in itself if you're looking to escape 'Khao San' culture.

The bus dumps you off in the centre of town – not a pushy motorcycle taxi or foreigner in sight. At the base of town is a sparkling blue bay sprinkled with brightly coloured fishing boats. To the north is **Khao Chong Krajok** (Mirror Tunnel Mountain), topped by a wat with spectacular views; the hill is claimed by a clan of monkeys who supposedly hitched a ride into town on a bus from Bangkok to pick up some mangoes. There isn't much else to do except walk along the waterfront promenade or explore the boat-building village of **Ao Bang Nang Lom**, 4km north, or the fishing village at **Ao Noi**, a couple of kilometres beyond. You'll find a clean white-sand beach at **Ao Manao**, 6km south of the city within the ground of a Thai air-force base.

Sleeping & Eating

Yuttichai Hotel (☎ 0 3261 1055; 115 Th Kong Kiat; r 150-200B) Run by a friendly family, this place is close to the bus station and night market and has a collection of basic rooms.

Happy Inn (☎ 0 3260 2082; 149-151 Th Suanson; bungalows 500B) North of town on a small beach, Happy Inn has simple bungalows (no hot showers) that face each other along a brick drive. The sitting area overlooks a mangrove-lined canal.

Sun Beach Guesthouse (☎ 0 3260 4770; www.sunbeach-guesthouse.com; 160 Th Chai Thaleh; r 800-1000B;) A pricier option in Prachuap? Guess this sleepy town has been 'discovered'. Neoclassical styling and bright yellow paint liven things up, while the rooms are clean and have verandahs.

Ma Prow (☎ 08 5293 7278; 48 Th Chai Thaleh; dishes 80-160B; lunch & dinner) An airy wooden pavilion across from the beach that cooks up excellent *Ɓlah plaa sămlii dàet diaw* (sun-baked cottonfish), a Prachuap speciality.

Krua Chaiwat (☎ 0 3260 4534; 143/1 Th Sarachip; meals 80-220B; breakfast, lunch & dinner) High ceilings and tiered floors appeal to those looking for a little ambience with their Thai food.

At the foot of Th Thetsaban Bamrung is a small **night market** (Th Chai Thaleh) that's good for seafood.

Getting There & Away

There are frequent air-con buses to Bangkok (190B to 256B, five hours), Hua Hin (80B, 1½ hours), Cha-am (90B, 2½ hours) and Phetchaburi (95B to 105B, three hours) leaving from Th Phitak Chat near the centre of town. Ordinary buses to Hua Hin (60B) and Chumphon (155B, 3½ hours) leave from the southeast corner of Th Thetsaban Bamrung and Th Phitak Chat.

For southern destinations such as Phuket or Krabi, go 2km northwest to the police station on the highway to catch passing buses (motorcycle taxis will take you for 40B to 50B).

The train station is at the end of Th Kong Kiat, a block from Th Phitak Chat. There are frequent train services to/from Bangkok (3rd class 168B, 2nd class 210B to 357B, six hours). A 1st-class express departs Hualamphong at 7.30pm (1100B, 5¼ hours). Trains also run to Chumphon, a transfer point for Samui island–bound boats.

CHUMPHON

pop 480,000

Southern Thailand unofficially 'begins' at Chumphon, roughly 500km from Bangkok. This is where you'll start to hear the southern dialect and begin to spot Islamic mosques. Chumphon is a jumping-off point for boats to Ko Tao. The transition from bus to boat is painless. Travel agencies are within spitting distance of the bus station and provide all sorts of free amenities (such as luggage storage, shower and toilet).

Suda Guest House (☎ 0 7750 4366; 8 Soi Bangkok Bank; r 200-500B;) keeps prices low but standards high. The management can help with Ko Tao travel arrangements. If Suda is full, try **Sanatavee New Rest House** (☎ 0 7750 2147; 4 Soi Bangkok Bank; r 150-250B) two doors down. The four rooms are small but clean and have fans and shared bathroom.

You can stock up on food supplies for the slow boat at the small **night market** (Th Krom Luang Chumphon). **Yota Vegetarian** (Th Sala Daeng; 7am-5pm) is located beside Fame and has delicious self-serve vegetarian dishes. **Montana** (☎ 7750 2864; 116 Th Suksamoe; 6pm-1am), a Western-themed bar, isn't a bad way to kill some time before a boat departure. There are nightly music gigs and a zingy Thai menu.

Getting There & Away

Chumphon has several piers with service to Ko Tao.

Tha Yang is 7km away and is where the slow night boat (200B, six hours, midnight) departs from. One of Thailand's most memorable rides, this is a converted fishing boat with seating/sleeping on the mat-covered floor of the upper deck. A car ferry (with cabin 300B, six hours, 11pm) has more comfort if the seas are rough. A shared taxi/săwngthăew to Tha Yang costs 50/30B.

Faster options include *Songsrem Express* (450B, 2½ hours, 7am), which leaves from Tha Talaysub, 1km from the centre, and continues on to Ko Pha-Ngan before returning to the mainland. The **Lomprayah express catamaran** (www.lomprayah.com) leaves from Tha Tummakam, 25km from town (550B, 1½ hours, 7am and 1pm). Seatran Discovery (550B, two hours, 7am) runs a catamaran out of Tha Pak Nam (or Seatran Jetty), 7km from Chumphon, that continues on to Ko Pha-Ngan and Ko Samui. Tha Pak Nam is a 30B shared sǎwngthǎew ride.

The main bus terminal is on the highway, 16km from Chumphon. Local bus or sǎwngthǎew (30B) go there from Th Nawaminruamjai. There's also a small bus stop in town near the train station where most Bangkok buses will disembark island-bound passengers. Destinations served from Chumphon include Bangkok (air-con 375B, VIP 419B to 550B), Hua Hin (165B to 230B, five hours), Prachuap Khiri Khan (120B to 160B, 3½ hours), Ranong (100B to 110B, three hours), Surat Thani (170B, 3½ hours), Krabi (270B, eight hours), Phuket (320B, seven hours) and Hat Yai (310B to 350B, seven hours).

The **train station** (Th Krom Luang Chumphon) is within walking distance of the centre of town. Destinations include Bangkok (3rd class 202B to 252B, 2nd class 310B to 390B, 7½ to nine hours, 11 daily), Surat Thani (35B, two to 3½ hours, 11 daily) and Hat Yai (80B, six to 8½ hours, five daily). Northern- and southern-bound trains have several afternoon departures.

SURAT THANI

pop 111,900

This busy port is another of the primary jumping-off points for Ko Samui, and to a lesser extent for Ko Pha-Ngan and Ko Tao. If you arrive in Surat by train or bus in the morning you'll have no problem making a connection with one of the daily ferries.

Surat's revolving door position to the islands is being eclipsed as air fares from Bangkok to Ko Samui are becoming more competitive. Some travellers are doing the air hop to Samui and then transferring directly to boats bound for Ko Pha-Ngan or Ko Tao. Another alternative for beach-bound travellers from Bangkok is the mainland port of Chumphon (see p789), which provides a geographically closer train–boat connection than Surat Thani. But if you're hopping across the peninsula to the Andaman coast, Surat's got all the transport options you'll need.

Sleeping & Eating

The centre city has a few grimy options that will make you wish you could sleep on the boat instead.

Ban Don Hotel (☎ 0 7727 2167; 268/2 Th Na Meuang; d from 220B; ❄) The best of a questionable bunch in the city centre.

100 Islands Resort & Spa (☎ 0 7720 1150; www.roikoh.com; 19/6 Moo 3, Bypass Rd; r 590-1200B; ❄ 💻 🏊) Out of town and across the street from the suburban Tesco-Lotus shopping centre is this spacious teak place with immaculate rooms and a lagoonlike swimming pool.

The **night market** (Th Ton Pho) is the place for fried, steamed, grilled or sautéed delicacies. If you're overnighting in Tesco-Lotus land, **Crossroads Restaurant** (☎ 0 7722 1525; Bypass Rd; dishes 50-200B; 🕐 11am-1am) does gulf oysters, a Surat Thani speciality.

Getting There & Away

Be wary of dirt-cheap combo tickets to the islands that are sold on Th Khao San in Bangkok – they often have extra surcharges, invalid legs or dubious security. For the Bangkok–Surat Thani trip, it is recommended that you use buses departing from government bus stations or ask an island survivor to advise of a reliable travel agent.

AIR

Thai Airways International (THAI; code TG; ☎ 0 7727 2610; www.thaiair.com) and **Air Asia** (www.airasia.com) both fly two daily services to Bangkok.

BOAT

The primary piers are Ban Don, which is in the centre of town and receives the night ferries and Seatran Express service, and Don Sak, 60km away, which receives Samui-bound car ferries. Many of the companies offer combo tickets that will provide transfer from the airport and train or bus stations for an extra 100B or so; it is probably money well spent if you're heading to the pier at Don Sak. In general, the travel agents in town will put you on the next available ferry and charge you extra to get there. Considering how tired you'll be upon your arrival it will be tough to make any shrewd financial decisions, so just go with it.

For travellers heading to Ko Samui, there are various ferry companies, boat types and island piers to consider. Seatran car ferry (150B, 1½ hours, hourly between 6am and 7pm) departs from Surat's Don Sak pier and arrives at Samui's Thong Yang pier in the Lipa Noi area. Raja Ferry also leaves as frequently from Don Sak (120B, 1½ hours, hourly between 6am and 6pm). A night ferry (150B, six hours, departing at 11pm) leaves from Ban Don pier and arrives at Samui's main Na Thon pier. The Seatran Express ferry leaves from Ban Don pier (200B, 1½ hours, three departures) to Samui's Na Thon pier.

To get to Ko Pha-Ngan, Raja Ferry (220B, 2½ hours, every two hours 6am to 6pm) does a direct sail from Don Sak. The night ferries (200B, seven hours, departing at 11pm) leave from Ban Don pier. To Ko Tao, night ferries (500B, seven to eight hours, departing at 11pm) leave from Ban Don pier.

Some of the Surat–Samui ferries continue on to Ko Pha-Ngan and Ko Tao. There are also numerous interisland ferries.

BUS & MINIVAN

There are three bus stations in Surat Thani: **Talat Kaset 1** (cnr Th Talat Mai & Th Na Meuang), for local and provincial destinations, including Chumphon and the Surat Thani train station; **Talat Kaset 2** (btwn Th Talat Mai & Th That Thong) for air-con minivans and destinations outside the province. There's also a station outside town for Bangkok-bound buses. The travel agencies run cramped minivan services to popular Andaman beach destinations; these are usually faster but have unreliable departure times and tickets tend to be more expensive.

Buses travel to and from Bangkok (air-con/VIP 525/780B, 10 to 11 hours), Chumphon (170B, 3½ hours), Hat Yai (air-con 350B, four to five hours), Krabi (270B to 366B, three to four hours, hourly) and Phuket (air-con 280B, seven hours). Minivans also run to all the tourist spots on the Andaman coast.

TRAIN

The train station is in Phun Phin, 14km from Surat Thani. Fares from Bangkok are 3rd class 297B, 2nd-class seat fan/air-con 438/578B, 2nd-class sleeper fan/air-con 548/848B and 1st class 1279B. If you take an early evening train from Bangkok, you'll arrive in the morning.

Getting Around

Local orange buses chug between the train station in Phun Phin and Surat (15B, 30 minutes, every 10 minutes). Air-con vans to/from the Surat Thani airport cost around 70B per person and they'll drop you off at your hotel. To travel around town, sǎwngthǎew cost 10B to 30B, while sǎamláw charge 30B to 40B.

KO SAMUI

pop 45,800

One of the original islands that started the backpacker migration to Thailand, Ko Samui has matured into an all-purpose beach resort. The hotels have international standards, the guests are mainly package tourists and the transition from home to deck chair involves little culture shock. Families and honeymooners put Ko Samui at the top of their lists for its conveniences and impressive stoles of sand.

But for all the 'too-touristy' talk, Samui is underappreciated for its size and variety of beaches: with one cab ride you can travel from brash and beautiful to sleepy and rustic. Plus there is a thriving Thai community on the island where you can nosh at roadside curry shacks or grab a cup of thick coffee at the morning market with the gossiping vendors. Samui is a unique hybrid for beach people who also want to see Thailand.

Information

Banks and internet access abound in the commercial areas of the popular beaches and the main town of Na Thon.

Bangkok Samui Hospital (☎ 0 7742 9500, emergency 0 7742 9555; Chaweng)

Post office (Th Chenwithee, Na Thon; ⏲ 8.30am-4.30pm Mon-Fri, 9am-noon Sat & Sun)

Samui International Hospital (☎ 0 7742 2272; Chaweng) For medical or dental needs.

TAT Office (☎ 0 7742 0504; Th Malitra Vanitchroen, Na Thon; ⏲ 8.30am-noon & 1-4.30pm)

Tourist police (☎ 0 7742 1281, emergency 1155) Based at the south of Na Thon.

Sights & Activities

Samui has perhaps the best variety of beach 'personalities' of any Thai island. **Hat Chaweng** is famous for a reason – it is a pin-up model of curvaceous blonde sand (stretching for 6km) and clear water that arcs gracefully ashore thanks to a steady surf. It is also packed with bodies, which can be fun for sunbathing and socialising. Chaweng Central is the centre of it all while the extremities (referred to as Chaweng North and Chaweng Noi) are quieter.

A close runner-up is **Hat Lamai**, which is punctuated by picturesque boulders in

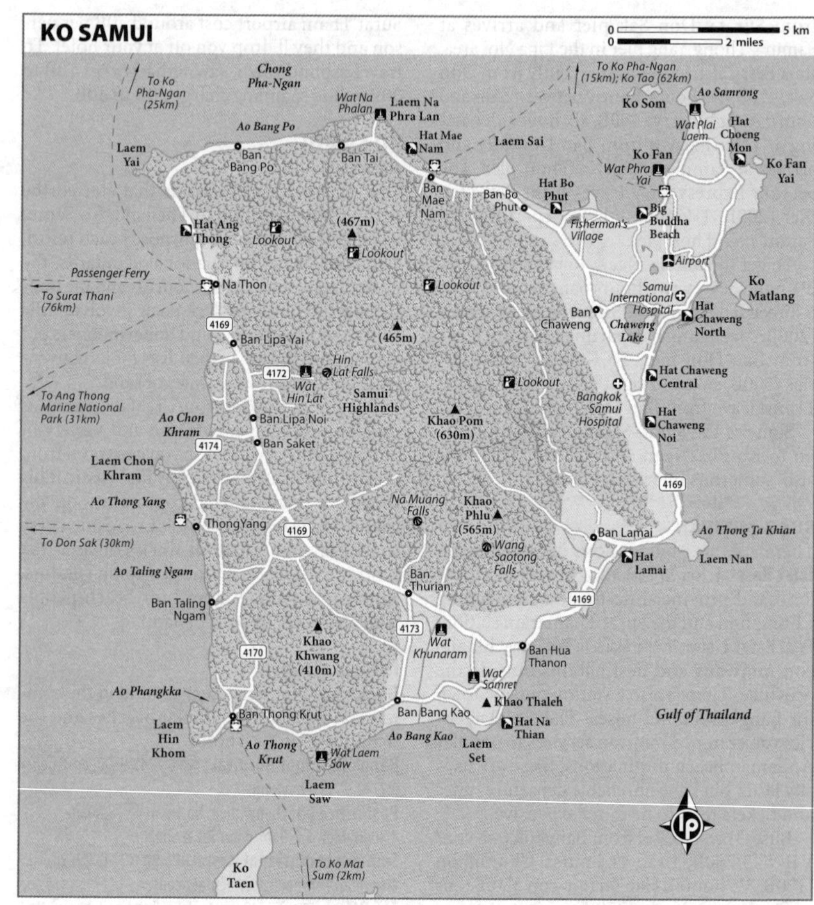

the southern stretches near the famous Grandparent Rocks; the drawback to Lamai is its honky-tonk village, a favourite of biker-gang types. **Hat Bo Phut** has the best village ambience with its old wooden shophouses and funky seaside shops and restaurants. The beach, however, is a bummer: rough sand, murky water and a steep pitch.

A little further west is our favourite, **Hat Mae Nam**. The beach is soft and wide, though not as spectacular as Chaweng or Lamai, while the village is almost 100% Thai so there's good food and a strong sense of place.

Wat Phra Yai (Big Buddha Temple), with its 12m-high Buddha image, is located at the northeastern end of the island, on a small rocky islet joined to the main island by a causeway. **Wat Khunaram**, which is south of Rte 4169 between Th Ban Thurian and Th Ban Hua, features the mummified corpse of Luang Phaw Daeng, a monk famous for his meditation skills.

Snorkelling and diving are not Samui's strong suits though some companies do shuttle people over to the dive spots between Ko Pha-Ngan and Ko Tao; factoring in the price and the time to commute, you should base yourself on either of these islands if you want to strap on a mask. If you can't resist a tour, head to **Ang Thong Marine National Park**, a scenic collection of limestone mountain islands explored above and below the water. Several guide companies arrange kayaking and snorkelling tours to the park.

Sleeping & Eating

NA THON

The only reason to stay in Na Thon is for an early morning boat departure. Several restaurants face Na Thon's harbour and offer a combination of Western food and Thai seafood.

Jinta Hotel (☎ 0 7742 0630, 0 7723 6369; www.jintasamui.com; r 500-650B;) Jinta's white walls and linoleum floors feel a bit institutional, but it gets the job done. All rooms have satellite TV.

About Art & Craft Cafe (☎ 08 9724 9673; 90/3 Th Chonwithi; dishes 80-180B) We're devoted fans of this arty and healthful cafe that stands testament to Samui's now forgotten bohemian era.

Many travellers fill up on *kŭaytĭaw* and beer at the **night market** (Th Chonwithi; 5pm-midnight) near the pier before catching the slow boat back to the mainland. The **day market** (Th Thawee Ratpakdee) is brimming with fresh fruit and southern-style fried chicken.

CHAWENG

With its rocking discos and deluxe hotels, Chaweng offers more amusement than relaxation. Fittingly, the accommodation scene in Chaweng is boom or bust. There are very few cheapies left these days and even the bare-bones joints start at 400B.

Wave Samui (☎ 0 7723 0803; www.thewavesamui.com; r from 400B;) The Wave is still holding on to the good old backpacker vibe with a convivial restaurant and library and charismatic expat owners. The rooms are good enough considering the price and proximity to the beach.

Green Guest House (☎ 0 7742 2611; d 450-1000B) If penny-pinching is your game, you won't find much cheaper than Green in Chaweng, although there isn't much in the way of atmosphere.

Queen Boutique Resort (☎ 0 7741 3148; queen-samui@yahoo.com; Soi Colibri; s/d from 600/800B;) Pray that these promo rates are still around so that you can pay homage to this new boutique-y arrival on an oh-so-charming side street.

Jungle Club (☎ 0 1894 2327; bungalows 600-2900B, villas 3500B;) You can certainly see the beach from this mountainside hideaway, though it's a journey to go for an ocean. Regardless, you'll find a groovy back-to-nature vibe, good food and likeminded friends. Call ahead for a pick-up.

P Chaweng (☎ 0 7723 0684; r 700B;) Hardly a beach pad, but the pink-tiled rooms are spacious and clean (minus a couple of furniture knicks). Pick a room facing away from the street – it seems a tad too easy for someone to slip through an open window.

Akwa (☎ 08 4660 0551; www.akwaguesthouse.com; r 999-2599B;) A charming B&B-style spot, Akwa has a few funky rooms decorated with bright colours, but it doesn't have a beachfront location.

At night, beachfront restaurants set up romantic candle-lit tables and fire up the seafood barbecues. Salty folklore says to pick a fish with unclouded eyes (a sign of freshness). **Laem Din Market & Night Market** (dishes from 30B; market 4am-6pm, night market 6pm-2am) is by day a busy fresh market and by the end of the day it becomes a busy dinner spot for workaday Thais.

LAMAI

Samui's second-most popular beach is just as busy as Chaweng but the crowd is more haggard. Steer clear of the centre of the village and head to the northern or southern fringes for a more peaceful and natural setting.

New Hut (☎ 0 7723 0437; newhut@hotmail.com; Lamai North; r 200-500B) New Hut is a rare beachfront cheapie with tiny but charming A-frames.

Sunrise Bungalow (☎ 0 7742 4433; www.sunrisebungalow.com; Lamai South; r 400-1300B;) Steps away from the Grandparent Rocks (Hin Ta Hin Yai, the island's infamous genital-shaped rocks), Sunrise offers budget travellers a relaxing place to hang their backpack. The owner is a sixth-generation Samui native.

Beer's House Beach Bungalows (☎ 0 7723 0467, 0 1958 4494; Lamai North d 450-500B) Run by a pleasant Thai couple, the bungalows here are small but clean. Best feature? They all come with front decks large enough to daydream the day away in front of the sea.

Spa Samui Resort (☎ 0 7723 0855; www.spasamui.com; Lamai North; r 900-3500B;) The spa that put Samui on the health-tourism map is an unassuming collection of beachfront bungalows. Residents come for a detox program – fasts, colonics, meditation, yoga, massage, raw-food classes and more. The basic bungalows are perfectly well manicured and the vegetarian food and the affiliated restaurant is top notch. There's another Spa Samui location in the jungle that's quieter but more of a workout to get around the grounds.

Lamai Night Food Centre (☎ 0 7742 4630; Central Lamai; dishes from 30B; dinner) This outdoor food centre, next door to a 7-Eleven, is an easy place to eat all the Thai standards and be entertained by the nearby hostess bars.

Hua Thanon Market (☎ 0 7742 4630; Ban Hua Thanon; dishes from 30B; 6am-6pm) Sample southern Thailand's Muslim heritage at this day market, south of Lamai, in the island's Muslim village. Follow the market road to the food shops specialising in chicken biryani or fiery curries.

BO PHUT & MAE NAM

Many backpackers to Ko Samui are prepared to sacrifice the picture-perfect contours of crowded Chaweng for the slower pace of Bo Phut (and its atmospheric Fisherman's Village) and nearby Mae Nam. Plus the food is better in these parts.

Shangrilah (☎ 0 7742 5189; Mae Nam; r 300-2000B;) A backpacker's Shangri-La indeed – these are some of the cheapest huts around and they're in decent condition.

Khuntai (☎ 0 7724 5118, 08 6686 2960; Bo Phut; r 600-850B;) This clunky orange guest house is a block away from the beach, on the outskirts of Fisherman's Village. Khuntai's 2nd-floor rooms are drenched in afternoon sunshine and feature outdoor lounging spots.

Ko-Seng (☎ 0 7742 5365; Mae Nam; dishes 100-300B; dinner) Hidden down a narrow side street near Mae Nam's Chinese temple, this local haunt dishes out top-notch soft-shell crab and plump, flash-fried prawns in a peppery sauce.

Drinking

Ko Samui's nightlife can be summed up with one word: Chaweng. You can party with the surf and the stars on the beach or blow out your eardrums at the discos along Soi Green Mango.

Green Mango (☎ 0 7742 2148; Soi Green Mango, Chaweng; admission free; from 10pm) This huge open-air dance club has been blasting bass on Samui for 20-plus years straight. Hard house on the hi-fi gets the place popping around midnight.

Reggae Pub (☎ 0 7742 2331; Chaweng; 6pm-2am) An open-air warehouse on Chaweng Lake is the resident altar to Bob Marley and the gang.

Frog & Gecko Pub (☎ 0 7742 5248; Bo Phut) This British watering hole is famous for its noodle-bending 'Wednesday Night Pub Quiz' competitions.

Getting There & Away

AIR

Samui's airport is in the northeast corner of the island and is now serviced by multiple carriers making plane tickets more competitive. **Bangkok Airways** (code PG; ☎ in Chaweng 0 7742 2512-9) and **Thai Airways International** (THAI; code TG; ☎ in Bangkok 0 2134 5403; www.thaiair.com) fly frequently between Ko Samui and Bangkok (1½ hours). Bangkok Air also flies from Samui to Phuket (one hour, three daily), Pattaya (one hour, three daily), Krabi (one hour, three times a week) and Chiang Mai (2½ hours, twice a week).

International flights go directly from Samui to Singapore (three hours, daily) and Hong Kong (four hours, five days a week). There's an international departure tax of 400B.

BOAT

Na Thon is Ko Samui's main pier for overnight ferries to Surat Thani and passenger ferries to Ko Pha-Ngan (180B to 250B), continuing on to Ko Tao (see p801).

The slow night boat (150B) leaves Na Thon at 9pm, arriving at the mainland around 3am. Seatran Express (200B, 1½ hours, three departures) goes to Surat's central Ban Don pier. The car ferries to/from Surat (110B to 150B, 1½ hours, hourly from 5am to 7pm) dock at Thong Yang, 10km south of Na Thon.

Most people staying in Chaweng go to the pier at Big Buddha Beach (Bang Rak) to hop over to Ko Pha-Ngan. Hat Rin Queen runs to Ko Pha-Ngan's popular Hat Rin (200B, one hour, four departures), while Seatran Discovery runs a faster service to the main port of Thong Sala (250B, 30 minutes, two departures). There's a very fast daily service on Lomprayah's catamaran leaving from Mae Nam pier to Ko Pha-Ngan (250B to 300B, 20 minutes, three departures) continuing on to Ko Tao and Chumphon. There are also special shuttle boats for Samui-based visitors during the Full Moon parties.

Ferry schedules are subject to change and services decrease during the low season.

Getting Around

Ko Samui's roads need an upgrade, especially around the congested areas of Chaweng and Lamai. Outside of these areas, the main roads are well sealed and easy to travel, though the terrain can be a challenge and local driving habits can be erratic. Red sǎwngthǎew do an around-the-island loop and are convenient for jumping between the beaches or the port town of Na Thon (20B to 80B, depending on distance); at night these shared rides turn into chartered vehicles. Taxis are widespread but expensive; they operate on a charter basis, so establish the price beforehand. Most taxi trips cost around 200B to 300B.

You can rent motorcycles for about 200B a day; but be aware that serious or even fatal motorcycle accidents are common, especially for drivers' without Third World driving experience. Wear your helmet to protect your noggin and avoid a ticket. To deter snatch thieves, don't put valuables in the bike's basket.

KO PHA-NGAN

pop 10,300

Swaying coconut trees, brooding mountains, ribbons of turquoise water: Ko Pha-Ngan has held fast to its title as favourite backpacker idyll. Despite some modernisation during the upscale push of the early 2000s, Ko Pha-Ngan is still rustic and remote, it doesn't have an airport and there are still some cheap beachfront bungalows intended for hammock hanging and simple living.

Every sunburnt face you meet in Khao San's bars will tell you all about the most brilliant beaches on Ko Pha-Ngan, which means you won't be alone in paradise, but nobody really wants a lonely planet.

Information

Banks are located in the port town of Thong Sala and ATMs can be found at most of the beaches. Internet is widespread and reasonably priced.

Backpacker's Thailand (www.backpackersthailand.com; Hat Rin) Online and on-site travellers' information.

Ko Pha-Ngan Hospital (☎ 0 7737 7034; Thong Sala) Twenty-four-hour emergency service.

Police (☎ 0 7737 7114)

Sights & Activities

Most boats arrive in the southwestern corner of the island at **Thong Sala**, a dusty port town of shops and tourist services. In the far southeastern corner is the famed party beach quarter of **Hat Rin**, divided into Hat Rin Nai (or Sunset Beach, to the west), a pretty stretch of sand where everyone is comparing tans, and Hat Rin Nok (or Sunrise Beach, to the east), which is a little less spectacular and a little less rowdy.

The east coast is the island's most rugged stretch and an ideal outpost for leaving behind civilisation (except the essentials of course). **Than Sadet Falls** (Nam Tok Than Sadet) has attracted three generations of Thai kings as well as countless *faràng*. Take a longtail boat from Hat Rin to Hat Than Sadet and walk into the island along the river for 2.5km.

The west coast is the most developed side with a paved road that extends from the main pier all the way to the fishing village of Ao Chalok Lam on the northern coast. The island's best swimming spot is the wide bay of **Hat Yao** (Long Beach). The northern coast is more wild and dramatic, capturing the castaway essence at **Hat Khuat** (Bottle Beach), reachable only by boat.

Snorkellers usually head to **Ko Ma** (Horse Island), a small island in the northwest connected to Ko Pha-Ngan by a sandbar. There are also some rock reefs on the eastern side of the island around **Hat Thian** and **Ao Thong Nai Pan**. The island is close to **Sail Rock** (Hin Bai), considered one of the gulf's best dive sites. Ko Pha-Ngan's dive scene is more relaxed and more experienced than Ko Tao, where newbies get cycled through certification programs.

Sleeping

As you get off the ferry in Ko Pha-Ngan, consider this question: do you want to party like a rock star or sleep like a baby? If your answer is the former, head straight to Hat Rin; if it's the latter, pick any beach *except* Hat Rin.

HAT RIN & AROUND

Accommodation tends to be expensive most of the time and exponentially expensive for Full Mooning. The budget huts have nearly all upgraded to upper budget standards.

Chill House (☎ 08 4689 2056; Hat Rin Nok; dm 100B, bungalows 350B) Occupying an enviable slice of land overlooking Hat Rin Nok, Chill House features cheap, ramshackle accommodation

Seaside Bungalow (☎ 08 6940 3410, 08 7266 7567; Hat Rin Nai; bungalows 300-600B; ❄) Seaside sees loads of loyal customers returning for the mellow atmosphere, cheap drinks, free pool table and comfy wooden bungalows. At 500B, we're pretty sure that these huts are the cheapest air-con rooms on the island.

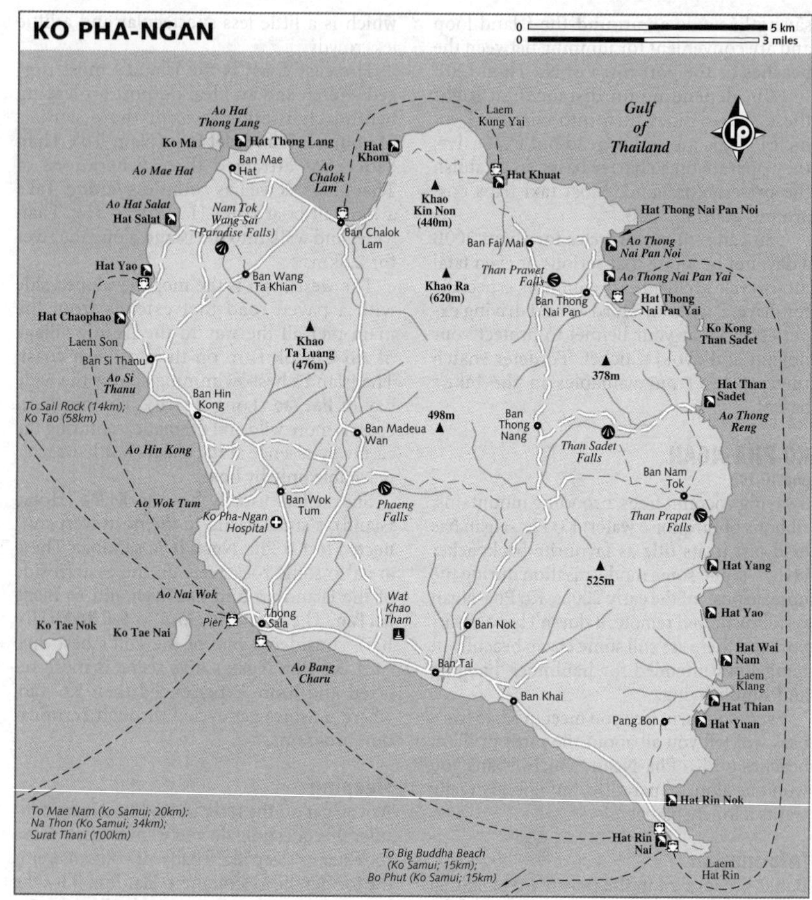

Paradise Bungalows (☎ 07737 5242; Hat Rin Nok; d & tw from 350B;) According to backpacker legend, the Full Moon party was launched at this scruffy batch of bungalows, and the place has been living on that fame ever since. It is indisputably a piece of backpacker 'history', though the grounds are collecting junk instead of customers.

Same Same Lodge & Restaurant (☎ 0 7904 3923; www.same-same.com; 139/19 Th Ban Tai, Hat Rin Nok; r 400-700B) Targeted toward the Scandinavian travellers, Same Same has a party-prone restaurant and an affable staff working on drinks and smiles. Upstairs, the no-frills rooms get plenty of sunlight, but they need to be renovated.

our pick **Coral Bungalows** (☎ 07737 5023; www.coralhaadrin.com; Hat Rin Nai; bungalows 500-800B;) This party-centric paradise has firmly planted its flag in 'Backpackerland'. By day, sun worshippers straddle beachside chaises or jet skis. Then, by night, Coral transforms into its alter ego; a pool-party machine fuelled by gregarious employees and vodka–Red Bull cocktails.

SOUTHERN COAST

If Hat Rin is a flashy pair of trainers, then the southern coast (4km west of Hat Rin between Ban Khai and Ban Tai) is a happily weathered sandal. Although the area isn't ideal for swimming, it is within attack-and-retreat range of Hat Rin and you have a better chance of securing beachfront real estate.

Lifestyle Bungalows (☎ 08 5916 3852; Ban Tai; bungalows 250-600B;) A skin artist by trade, the owner has tattooed each fan bungalow with an assortment of designs and colours. The cluster of sandy huts embodies the true essence of Ko Pha-Ngan, summed up by the on-site sign: 'eat, drink and chill'.

Lee's Garden (☎ 08 5916 3852; Ban Khai; bungalows 250-600B) This clump of comfy wooden huts is a wonderful throwback to a time when Pha-Ngan attracted a grittier backpacker who wasn't fussed about hot showers or air-con.

Boom's Cafe Bungalows (☎ 0 7723 8318; Ban Khai; www.boomscafe.com; bungalows 300-1000B;) Staying at Boom's is like visiting the Thai family you never knew you had. The friendly owners dote on their sandy acreage and the contented clientele. Boom's is located at the far eastern corner of Ban Kai, near Hat Rin.

Chokana (☎ 0 7723 8085; Ao Bang Charu; bungalows 400-1200B;) Chokana is the Jabba the Hut of huts: enormous beachside bungalows. The bubbly owner genuinely cares about her clientele – the cabins have loads of personal touches like wooden carvings and mosaics, and it feels as though all of the guests are repeat customers.

Coco Garden (☎ 0 7737 7721, 08 6073 1147; Ban Tai; www.cocogardens.com; bungalows 500-1000B;) The best budget spot along the southern coast, Coco Garden one-ups the nearby resorts with well-manicured grounds and bungalows.

Mac Bay (☎ 0 7723 8443; Ban Khai bungalows 500-1500B;) Home to the Black Moon Party (another lunar party), Mac Bay occupies a sandy slice of Ban Khai where the bungalows are cheap and clean.

WESTERN COAST

Too old or cynical to do Hat Rin but still celebrate happy hour? Check out the slightly more sober but sociable beaches, such as Hat Yao, on the west coast. Further north, Ao Mae Hat has a small fishing community whose colourful longtail boats break up the monotony of sun, sand and sea. A sandbar connects the beach to Ko Ma, a nearby island during low tide.

Ibiza (☎ 0 7734 9121; Hat Yao; bungalows 150-1300B;) Ibiza brings Hat Rin's youthful backpacker vibe to the pretty bay of Hat Yao. The no-frills bungalows are run of the mill, but the friendly staff, appealing central garden and cheap rates keep budget travellers coming back for more.

Royal Orchid (☎ 0 7737 4182; Ao Mae Hat; royal_orchid_maehaad@hotmail.com; bungalows 300-800B;) Handsome backpacker bungalows are arranged like a zipper along quiet Ao Mae Hat. Most have fleeting views of the serene beach and sandbar that extends to offshore Ko Ma.

Tantawan Bungalows (☎ 0 7734 9108; www.tantawanbungalow.com; Hat Yao; bungalows 450-550B;) Little Tantawan sits high up in the jungle like a tree house with a sprinkling of rustic bungalows boasting sea views. Don't forget to try the tasty French and Thai dishes at the on-site restaurant.

MOON MANIA

Ko Pha-Ngan's monthly Full Moon parties are so well known these days that they have become more like a spring break boozefest than a Southeast Asian Burning Man. During the high season, it is estimated that tens of thousands of revellers descend upon the white sand beaches at Hat Rin to slather themselves in day-glo paint and swallow their weight in whisky buckets and other substances. Such fun comes with a crate of caveats, so let us list them here.

The buying, selling and taking of drugs introduces a host of pitfalls. Firstly, the drug dealers have been known to work with the police in so-called 'sting' operations. They sell you a product then the police show up and bust you, asking for a huge fine/bribe in return. This happens all the time and those who can't pay it end up in jail. If you do manage to alter your state, don't be so crazy that you lose all your money, get beat up and wake up in the gutter. Don't go swimming in the ocean at night; Hat Rin has dangerous riptides and Full Moon drownings are common. Keep track of your belongings as pickpockets and thieves meticulously work the parties. Women should be extra keen about their safety, especially when returning home alone; we routinely receive reports of rapes and assaults.

If you plan on sleeping off your Full Moon hangover, arrive a few days before the party to score a room since accommodation gets slim.

Now be safe and have a good time.

NORTHERN COAST

Travelling the winding road towards Ao Chalok Lam you descend into a verdant valley shadowed by mountains the colour of bruised storm clouds. Camped out by the water is the small fishing village of Ban Chalok Lam, where residents have seen their island change like a growing child. The road officially stops at Ban Chalok Lam, and to continue on to remote Hat Khuat, you have to catch a longtail boat (50B to 120B, depending on the number of passengers).

Sarisa Place (Ao Chalok Lam; bungalows from 250B) Trippy seashells dangle on the porches at Sarisa, which offers cheap (but lacklustre) semidetached bungalows. Guests get a free motorbike rental to tool around the island (petrol not included).

Fanta (☎ 0 7737 4132; fantaphangan@yahoo.com; Ao Chalok Lam; bungalows 300-700B) Not to be confused with Fantasea next door, Fanta sits at the far eastern end and boasts rows of old-school Pha-Ngan bungalows (think lots of worn wood and thatch) on a sizeable chunk of sand.

Bottle Beach II (☎ 0 7744 5156; Hat Khuat; bungalows 350-400B) This is the spot where penny pinchers can live out their castaway fantasies.

Smile (☎ 08 1956 3133; smilebeach@hotmail.com; Hat Khuat; bungalows 400-700B) At the far west corner of Bottle Beach, Smile features an assortment of wooden huts that climb up a forested hill. The two-storey bungalows (700B) are our favourite.

EASTERN COAST

Cut off from 'civilisation', the east coast is where you come for scenery and seclusion. The twin bays of Ao Thong Nai Pan Yai and Ao Thong Nai Pan Noi have well-regarded swimming beaches and are separated by a steep 20-minute walk over a headland. Quiet Ao Thong Reng, Hat Thian and Hat Yuan are other reclusive contenders. All of these beaches can be reached via longtail boats from Thong Sala and Hat Rin.

Treehouse (Ao Thong Reng; bungalows from 200B) The ultimate in serene beach scene, the Treehouse made its name on the gulf coast's Ko Chang but has packed up and moved to more remote waters. Follow the cheery plastic flowers over the hill from Hat Than Sadet to find uberbasic digs drenched in bright shades of paint.

Barcelona (☎ 0 7737 5113; Hat Yuan; bungalows 200-600B) Solid wood huts come in two shades: natural wood or creamy white. They climb up the hill on stilts behind a palm garden and have good vistas and jovial staff.

Beam Bungalows (☎ 0 7927 2854, 08 6947 3205; Hat Thian; bungalows 300-500B) Though geographically close to Hat Rin, Beam Bungalows sits on Hat Thian, a beach that is buffeted from commercial assault thanks to a lack of sealed roads. The charming wooden huts have hammocks and big windows that face the ocean through the swaying palms. Water taxis are available from Hat Rin for around 150B.

Sanctuary (☎ 08 1271 3614; www.thesanctuary-kpg.com; Hat Thian; dm 120B, bungalows 400-3800B) A long-running health retreat, the Sanctuary combines beach laziness with holistic hard work, with everything from yoga classes to detox sessions. Accommodation, in various manifestations of twigs, is scattered around the resort, married to the natural surroundings.

our pick **Dolphin** (Ao Thong Nai Pan; bungalows 500-1300B, ❄) Sorry to blow your cover but this hidden retreat gives yuppie travellers a chance to rough it in style, while granola-types won't feel guilty. Quiet afternoons are spent lounging on the comfy cushions in one of the small pavilions hidden throughout the jungle. Lodging is only available on a first-come basis.

Plaa's (☎ 0 7744 5191; Hat Than Sadet; bungalows 600B; 💻) Plaa's colourful village of bungalows sits on the northern headland of Hat Than Sadet overlooking the bay below.

Mai Pen Rai (☎ 0 7744 5090; www.thansadet.com; Hat Than Sadet; bungalows 600B; 💻) 'Don't worry, be happy' at this easygoing spot boasting bungalows planted on the hilly headland.

Eating & Drinking

Ko Pha-Ngan is no culinary capital, especially since most visitors quickly absorb the lazy lifestyle and wind up eating at their guest house. Those with an adventurous appetite should check out Thong Sala and the island's southern coast.

Thong Sala Night Market (Thong Sala; dishes 25-180B; 🕑 6.30pm-10.30pm) Nosh and nibble with the locals for a mix of basic noodles, fish platters and, of course, banana pancakes.

our pick **Boat Ahoy** (☎ 0 7723 8759, 0 7737 7334; dishes 100-180B 🕑 breakfast, lunch & dinner) A compound of open-air pavilions, Boat Ahoy offers a night's worth of fun. Feast on a variety of Asian victuals (the beef salad and cashew chicken are especially delish), grab a drink at the boat-shaped bar or make-out with the microphone in a private karaoke suite.

Hat Rin's beachside bars are cocktail-in-a-bucket heaven for ragers, regardless of the phases of the moon. **Coral Bungalows Bar** (Hat Rin Nai) hosts pool-centric powwows and **Backyard Club** (Hat Rin Nok) goes for full daylight after the Full Moon parties go to sleep.

Getting There & Around

The island of Ko Pha-Ngan is 100km from Surat Thani and 15km north of Ko Samui. Ferries make the journey from the mainland port towns of Surat Thani and Chumphon as well as from the neighbouring islands of Ko Samui and Ko Tao. Schedules and frequency vary according to the season. Beware of travel agencies in Bangkok selling fake combinations tickets; stick to the bus-boat tickets from the reputable ferry companies of Lomprayah and Seatran Discovery.

There are approximately six daily departures from the mainland to Ko Pha-Ngan's Thong Sala pier (220B to 350B, 2½ hours, from 7am to 8pm), with stops in Ko Samui (250B) or Ko Tao (350B) depending on the direction of the journey. There's also a night ferry from Surat Thani (250B, 11pm). Boats in the opposite direction leave Ko Pha-Ngan at 10pm.

During the high season there are also direct links between Ko Samui's north coast (Mae Nam and Big Buddha Beach) to Ko Pha-Ngan's Hat Rin or Thong Sala.

Săwngthăew do daytime routes from Thong Sala to Hat Yao, Ban Chalok Lam or Hat Rin for 50B to 100B. At night these vehicles operate on a charter basis. Longtail boats depart from Thong Sala, Ao Chalok Lam and Hat Rin to Hat Khuat and Ao Thong Nai Pan. Expect to pay anywhere from 50B for a short trip to 300B for a lengthier journey.

KO TAO

pop 5000

Little Ko Tao perches on a ledge of coral reefs like a sunbathing turtle (*tao* means 'turtle'), earning it worldwide fame as a diving and snorkelling mecca. The water has a high visibility, there are abundant coral formations and diverse marine life, and the diving certification courses are amazingly cheap. Nondivers will find a few day's diversion exploring the remote and rocky coves but will have to migrate elsewhere for leggy beaches.

Information

The port 'town' of Mae Hat has a small collection of travel services, internet cafes and post and money-exchange facilities. There are no hospitals on the island, but the storefront clinic of **Bangkok Samui Hospital** (☎ 0 7742 9500; Hat Sai Ri; ⏰ 24hr) offers competent medical service.

Sights & Activities

The island's dive scene is headquartered around **Hat Sai Ri**, a long but unimpressive beach. A sealed road leads to Hat Sai Ri from Mae Hat, which is lined with commercial amenities.

Ko Tao's best **diving and snorkelling** sites are offshore islands or pinnacles, including White Rock, Shark Island, Chumphon Pinnacle, Green Rock, Sail Rock and Southwest Pinnacles. Dozens of diver operators eagerly offer their services to travellers. The larger dive operators aren't necessarily better than the smaller ones. For the most part, diving prices are standardised across the island, so there's no need to hunt for the best price, especially since safety measures might get slashed as superfluous in order to reduce prices. Open Water Certification courses range from 9000B to 9800B, depending on the licensing organisation. Most dive shops can offer free or reduced lodging packages at nearby guest houses.

Any bungalow or dive shop can arrange snorkelling day trips around the island for 500B. If you just want to rent a snorkel, mask and fins, it will cost you about 100B to 200B for the day.

The **Secret Garden** (www.secretgarden-kohtao.com) offers volunteer opportunities for those who are interested in conservation and educational programs, including beach clean ups, erosion prevention and marine protection. Native English speakers can help out in the classroom offering English lessons to the local Thai children.

Sleeping & Eating

HAT SAI RI

The island's most populous beach (also known as Sairee Beach) is best suited for divers looking for accommodation packages with a dive company.

Big Blue Resort (☎ 0 7745 6050; www.bigbluediving.com; r 200-1000B; ❄ 💻) This scuba-centric resort – with basic fan bungalows and motel-style aircon rooms – has a summer-camp vibe.

Blue Wind (☎ 0 7745 6116, 0 7745 6015; bluewind_wa@yahoo.com; bungalows 300-900B;) Hidden within a clump of bodacious lodging options, Blue Wind offers a breath of fresh air from the high-intensity dive resorts. Sturdy bamboo huts are peppered along a dirt trail behind the beachside bakery.

Sairee Cottage (☎ 0 7745 6126, 0 7745 6374; saireecottage@hotmail.com; bungalows 400-1500B;) The air-con bungalows are hard to miss since they've been painted fuchsia. The low prices mean low vacancy – so arrive early to score one of the brick huts facing a grassy knoll.

Ban's Diving Resort (☎ 0 7745 6466, 0 7745 6061; www.amazingkohtao.com; r 400-3000;) This divers party palace offers a wide range of quality accommodation from basic digs to sleek hillside villas.

'White House' Food Stalls (dishes 30-70B; lunch & dinner) Plonked in front of a humble white house amid the bustling Sairee, these metal food stalls sling *sôm-đam* (spicy papaya salad) and barbecue treats to hungry locals.

Café Corner (dishes 30-100B; breakfast & lunch) The flaky *pain au chocolat* can easily be mistaken for a Parisian patisserie. Customers enjoy their desserts while watching movies on a swank plasma TV. Swing by at 5pm to stock up on the scrumptious baked breads that are buy-one-get-one-free before being tossed at sunset.

Blue Wind Bakery (☎ 0 7745 6116; dishes 50-120; breakfast, lunch & dinner) This beachside shanty dishes out Thai favourites, Eastern confections and blended fruit juices.

MAE HAT

On either side of the pier, small bungalow operations fall in between categorisation.

Mr J Bungalow (☎ 0 7745 6066, 0 7745 6349; bungalows 250-1000B) Rooms here are plain but the owner is wildly eccentric.

Sai Thong Resort (☎ 0 7745 6868; www.saithong-resort.com; bungalows 300-2500B;) Sai Thong emerges along sandy Hat Sai Nuan. Bungalows, in various incarnations of weaving and wood, have hammocks and palm-filled vistas. Guests frequent the restaurant's relaxing sun deck – a favourite spot for locals too.

Tao Thong Villa (☎ 0 7745 6078; bungalows from 500B) Very popular with long-termers, these funky, no-frills bungalows have killer views. Tao Thong actually straddles two tiny beaches on a craggy cape about halfway between Mae Hat and Chalok Ban Kao.

Crystal (☎ 0 7745 6107; www.crystaldive.com; bungalows 800-1500B;) This dive company's lodging operation has bungalows and motel-style rooms. Guests can take a dip in the refreshing pool when it isn't overflowing with bubble-blowing newbie divers.

our pick **Whitening** (☎ 0 7745 6199; dishes 90-160B; dinner) Foodies will appreciate the modern twists on indigenous dishes while beer toters will love the beachy atmosphere, which hums with lounge music. Although the menu is multicultural, diners should stick to the assortment of Thai dishes, like the garlic prawns or the slow-stewed red curry with duck.

AO CHALOK BAAN KAO

A crowded but good-looking bay favoured by the young and carefree, Chalok Bay is a tad muddy for good swimming.

Freedom Beach (☎ 0 7745 6539; bungalows 100-250B) On its own secluded beach at the eastern end of Ao Chalok, Freedom is a classic backpacker haunt with a string of bungalows (from wooden shacks to sturdier air-con huts) that link to a breezy cliffside bar.

JP Resort (☎ 0 7745 6099; bungalows 400-700B) This little cheapie has prim motel-style rooms stacked on a small scrap of jungle across the street from the sea. Sun-soaked rooms have polished, pastel-coloured linoleum floors and refurbished bathrooms.

EAST COAST

Through the dense jungle canopy along roads better suited for water drainage, you'll reach the northeast cape of Laem Thian and its small rocky cove. Further south, Ao Tanot is a pretty cove surrounded by huge limestone rock formations and a sandy beach. Here you have a handful of guest houses making an amenable compromise between isolation and socialisation.

Hin Wong Bungalows (☎ 0 7745 6006, 08 1229 4810; Hin Wong; bungalows from 300B) Pleasant wooden huts are scattered across vast expanses of untamed tropical terrain. A rickety dock, jutting out just beyond the breezy restaurant, is the perfect place to watch schools of sardines slide through the cerulean water

Bamboo Hut (☎ 0 7745 6531; Ao Tanot; bungalows 300-500B) Surrounded by trees, there are 20 decked bungalows here, but the older they are, the smaller they are.

Diamond Beach (☎ 0 7745 6591; Ao Tanot; bungalows 300-1100B) Diamond's beachy batch of huts sits directly on Tanot's sand. There's also a mix of bungalows, including A-frames for tinier wallets.

Laem Thian Bungalows (☎ 0 7745 6477; Laem Thian; r 400-1500B) The lone occupier of this cove has ultrabasic huts and dim shared bathrooms. Ring ahead for pick-up from Mae Hat pier.

Drinking

After diving, Ko Tao's favourite pastime is drinking, and there's no shortage of places to get tanked. Keep an eye out for various theme and jungle parties. In Hat Sai Ri check out mellow Fizz, late-night Lotus Bar and sundowner fave Vibe.

Getting There & Away

Ko Tao lies 45km north of Ko Pha-Ngan and is most easily accessible from the mainland town of Chumphon. Songserm and Seatran Discovery make the daily crossing (350B, 2½ hours, two departures). There's also a midnight ferry to Ko Tao (150B) that returns to Chumphon at 11pm. There are various bus/train-to-boat transfers from Bangkok and Hua Hin through the ferry companies. Ferries also make the island stops: Ko Pha-Ngan, Ko Samui and to the mainland town of Surat Thani.

Săwngthăew crowd around the pier in Mae Hat and take passengers to guest houses; prices range from 100B to 300B, depending on the number of passengers. Prices double for trips to the east coast. If you know where you intend to stay, you can call ahead for a pick-up. Only 21 sq km in area, you can also walk around most of Ko Tao if you're not in a hurry.

NAKHON SI THAMMARAT

pop 118,100

Off the tourist trail, Nakhon Si Thammarat is a quintessential southern town. During early Thai history, it functioned as a major hub for the Asia sea trade. Clergy from Hindu, Islamic, Christian and Buddhist denominations established missions here over the centuries, and many of their houses of worship are still active today.

Information

Bovorn Bazaar (Th Ratchadamnoen) A small *faràng*-oriented mall with a few restaurants and internet cafes.

Post office (Th Ratchadamnoen; 🕒 8.30am-4.30pm Mon-Fri)

TAT office (☎ 0 7534 6515; tatnakon@nrt.cscoms.com; Th Ratchadamnoen; 🕒 8.30am-4.30pm)

Sights

The city boasts the oldest and biggest temple in southern Thailand: **Wat Phra Mahathat** (Th Ratchadamnoen). It's reputed to be over 1500 years old and comparable in size to Wat Pho in Bangkok. It's is also known for a famous amulet that draws customers from around the country. It is 2km south of town and accessible via any south-bound săwngthăew (10B).

To atone for all that mindless island sunbathing, pay a visit to the **National Museum** (☎ 0 7534 1075, 0 7534 0419; Th Ratchadamnoen; admission 30B; 🕒 9am-4pm Wed-Sun), 1km south of Wat Phra Mahathat, for its collection of southern art.

Thai *năng tàlung* (shadow theatre) was developed in Nakhon Si Thammarat, but the craft is slowly disappearing and viewing a performance is increasingly difficult.

Little **Ao Khanom** sits halfway between Surat Thani and Nakhon Si Thammarat along the blue gulf waters and is a worthy stop for adventurous beach hunters. You can get a share taxi from Nakhon Si Thammarat to Khanom town for 85B, where you can arrange another taxi to the beach.

Sleeping

You're not going to fall in love with the city's budget hotels, but at least you're out of the gutter.

Thai Hotel (☎ 0 7534 1509; fax 0 7534 4858; 1375 Th Ratchadamnoen; r 220-450B, ste 750B; ❄) Thai Hotel is the most central sleeping spot in town. The walls are thin, but the air-con options are a good deal. Each room has a TV and the higher floors have views of the urban bustle.

Nakorn Garden Inn (☎ 0 7532 3777; 1/4 Th Pak Nakhon; r 445B; ❄) The motel-style Nakorn Garden Inn offers a pleasant alternative to the usual cement cube.

Eating

At night the entire block running south of Th Neramit is lined with cheap food vendors preparing *roti klûay* (banana pancakes), *khâo mòk kài* (chicken biryani) and *mátàbà* (pancakes stuffed with chicken or vegetables).

Hao Coffee (☎ 0 7531 7999; 1180/807, Bavorn Bazaar; dishes 40-100B; 🕒 breakfast & lunch) Select one of international or southern Thai–style coffees and sit at a table encasing old collectables.

Khrua Nakhon (☎ 0 7531 7197; Bovorn Bazaar; dishes 60-200B 🕒 breakfast & lunch) This joint, next to Hao Coffee, has a great selection of traditional Nakhon cuisine.

Getting There & Away

Thai Airways International (THAI; code TG; www.thaiair.com) flies to/from Bangkok and Nakhon (3500B, one hour, six daily).

Many bus companies have in-town offices on Th Jamroenwithi, Th Wakhit and Th Yommarat with services to Bangkok (2nd/1st class 600/700B, 12 to 13 hours, morning and evening departures). There are also frequent minivans to Krabi (180B to 240B, 2½ hours), Phuket (175B to 275B, five hours), Surat Thani (100B, one hour), Khanom (85B, one hour) and Hat Yai (around 120B, three hours).

HAT YAI

pop 193,700

The south's commercial and transport hub, Hat Yai provides a boisterous welcome to new arrivals from Malaysia – be it prostitutes for Malaysian businessmen or rail and bus connections for Bangkok-bound tourists. The peninsula's ethnic diversity (Chinese, Muslim and Thai) is on full display in all of its provincial glory, from the sweaty street markets to the ho-hum shopping malls. You might not purposefully disembark here, but if you're passing through you'll find an energetic border town.

Information

Bangkok Bank (cnr Th Prachathipat & Th Niphat Uthit 3) Currency exchange between 8.30am and 5pm, plus ATM.

Bangkok Hat Yai Hospital (☎ 0 7436 5780-9; 75 Soi, 15 Th Pechkasam)

Immigration office (☎ 0 7425 7079; Th Phetkasem) Near the railway bridge; handles visa extensions.

TAT office (☎ 0 7424 3747; 1/1 Soi 2, Th Niphat Uthit 3; 🕑 8.30am-4.30pm)

Tourist police (☎ 0 7424 6733, emergency 1155) Near the TAT office.

Sleeping

Hat Yai has dozens of hotels within walking distance of the train station.

Cathay Guest House (☎ 0 7424 3815; 93/1 Th Niphat Uthit 2; r 160-250B) Super-helpful staff and plentiful information about onward travel make up for the not-so-super rooms at this popular cheapie.

Kings Hotel (☎ 0 7422 0966; 126-134 Th Niphat Uthit; s/d 450/50B; ❄) It's no royal palace, but Kings offers prim rooms stocked with TV, minifridge, and dated decorations (c 1983). It is two blocks from the train station.

Eating & Drinking

You can eat your way through three superb ethnic cuisines in Hat Yai. Start by nibbling at a string of casual Muslim restaurants. The extensive **night market** (Th Montri 1), across from the Songkhla bus station, specialises in fresh seafood and southern-style fried chicken. After gorging on street-stall food, try hitting up one of Hat Yai's upmarket hotels, like the **Novotel** (Th Pratchathipat), which features an all-you-can-eat sushi dinner (450B; Saturday evenings).

Kai Tod Daycha (☎ 08 1098 3751; Th Chi-Uthit; dishes 30-50B; 🕑 lunch & dinner) Hat Yai–style fried chicken is a dish known across Thailand, and locals claim that Daycha does it best. Enjoy it over fragrant yellow rice.

Sor Hueng 3 (☎ 08 1896 3455; 79/16 Th Thamnoonvithi; dishes 30-120B; 🕑 4pm-3am) This popular legend with multiple branches prepares heaps of delicious Thai-Chinese and southern Thai faves. Simply point to whatever looks good.

Post Laserdisc (☎ 0 7423 2027; 82/83 Th Thamnoonvithi; 🕑 9am-1am) A great joint to watch the latest pirated blockbuster after dark. Rockers replace movies on some nights, and the bands tend to be relatively good. Quash the booze with cheap pub grub from the East and West.

Getting There & Around

For information on travelling to Malaysia from Hat Yai, see p804.

There are flights to Bangkok with **Thai Airways International** (THAI; code TG; ☎ 0 7423 3433; www.thaiair.com), **One-Two-Go** (code OX; www.fly12go.com), **Nok Air** (code DD; ☎ 1318; www.nokair.com) and **Air Asia** (code AK; www.airasia.com). Nok Air and One-Two-Go both use Bangkok's Don Muang airport. The Hat Yai airport is 13km west of town and has flights to Phuket and Singapore.

The bus station is off Th Siphunawat, roughly 2km east of the town centre. Destinations include Bangkok (740B to 1075B, 14 hours), Krabi (235B, five hours), Kuala Lumpur (350B to 450B, nine hours) and Phuket (370B, eight hours). There are also minivan services to Satun (83B, 1½ hours) and Songkhla (25B, one hour).

The **train station** (Th Rotfai) is an easy stroll from the centre of town. Destinations include Bangkok (1st-class air-con/2nd class 1394/558B) and Butterworth, Malaysia (180B to 322B).

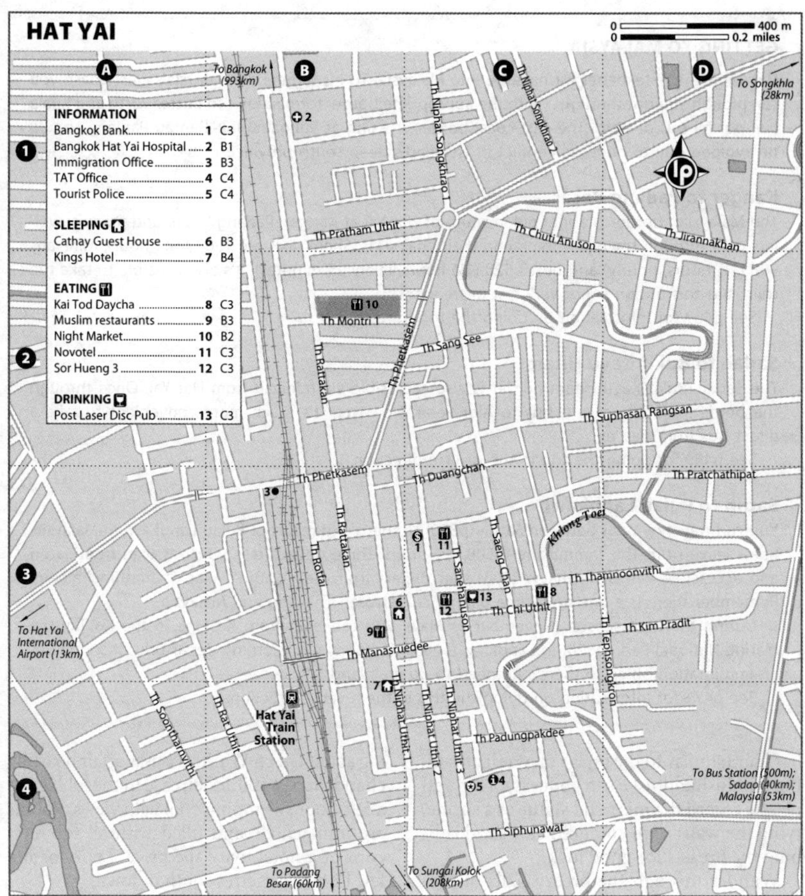

Săwngthăew run along Th Phetkasem and charge 5B per person. A túk-túk around town should cost 10B per person, though they more likely to charge foreigners 20B to 30B instead.

SONGKHLA

pop 87,800

Once upon a time, visitors breaking up an overland journey would pass over chaotic Hat Yai to slow-paced Songkhla. The coastal town is filled with charming colonial architecture, generous front-yard gardens and wooded twin hills. But those were the days before the troubles in the deep south spooked away all the foreigners except those married to southern Thais. It is a pity that the provincial capital has been grouped in the violence triangle, as the populous is peaceful and ethnically mixed and is rarely targeted by the troublemakers. See the boxed text, p805, for details on the southern unrest.

Information

Police station (☎ 0 7431 2133) Corner of Hat Samila.

Post office (Th Wichianchom; 🕒 8.30am-4.30pm Mon-Fri, 9am-noon Sat, Sun & holidays)

Sights

The biggest draw in town is the municipal beach of **Hat Samila** in the northeast corner. It is an average sandy pitch lined with leafy trees and open-air seafood restaurants. At one end is a sculptured mermaid squeezing water from

GETTING TO MALAYSIA

Hat Yai is the gatekeeper for passage into Malaysia. To hit targets on Malaysia's west coast, you can plough straight through – with the appropriate border formalities – to Butterworth and Kuala Lumpur by bus or train. The east-coast border crossing at Sungai Kolok–Rantau Panjang should be avoided due to ongoing conflict in Thailand's deep south provinces.

Kanger to Padang Besar

The Malaysian border is about 60km south of Hat Yai at Kanger–Padang Besar, and many travellers pass through town just to extend their Thai visas. Share taxis are 180B (one hour), minivans 90B (1½ hours, hourly) and buses 52B (1½ hours, every 25 minutes). It's also possible to take the train, but this option is not very fast or frequent.

See p469 for information on doing the trip in reverse.

Sadao to Bukit Kayu Hitam

The Sadao–Bukit Kayu Hitam border is also accessible via minivan from Hat Yai. Once through the border, you can take a bus to Alor Setar. However, it's much more convenient to take a direct bus from Hat Yai.

See p469 for doing the trip in the reverse direction.

Satun to Pulau Langkawi

You can travel by boat between Satun (p820) to the island resort of Pulau Langkawi in Malaysia. Boats leave from Tha Tammalang (250B, 1½ hours, three departures), which is 9km from Satun and accessible via săwngthăew (50B) that depart from near Satun's Wat Chanathipchaloem. Remember there is a one-hour time difference between Thailand and Malaysia.

During the high season (November to May), you can boat from Ko Lipe in the Ko Tarutao Marine National Park (p820) to Langkawi (600B, 1½ hours, two morning departures). Ko Lipe has an immigration office so there's no need to go mainland.

See p471 for information on doing the trip in the reverse direction.

her hair (similar to the image of Mae Thorani, the Hindu-Buddhist earth goddess). The local people regard the mermaid statue as a shrine, tying the waist with coloured cloth and rubbing the breasts for good luck.

Wander through the breezy halls of polished teak at the **National Museum** (☎ 0 7431 1728; cnr Th Rong Meuang & Th Saiburi; admission 100B; 9am-4pm Wed-Sun), housed in a 100-year-old Sino-Portuguese palace.

Sleeping

Yoma Guest House (☎ 0 7432 6433; Th Rong Meuang; r 250-350B) Like staying at the house of your Thai grandmother you never knew you had, this homey option offers a batch of cute, brightly coloured rooms.

Romantic Guest House (☎ 0 7430 7170; 10/1-3 Th Platha; r 250-380B) Substantial, airy abodes come with TVs and charming bamboo beds. The cheapest rooms have shared toilets.

Green World Palace Hotel (☎ 0 7443 7900-8; 99 Th Samakisukson; r 750-900B) When expats say that sleeping in Songkhla is a steal, they're talking about Green World, a classy affair boasting chandeliers, a spiral staircase in the lobby and a 5th-floor swimming pool with views. Rooms are immaculate and filled with all the mod cons of a hotel twice the price. Look for it a few hundred metres south of town.

Eating & Drinking

For cheap food, try the seafood places on Th Ratchadamnoen. Curried crab claws or fried squid are always a hit. At the tip of Songkhla's northern finger are food carts that set out mats in the waterfront park.

Khao Nawy (☎ 0 7431 1805; 14/22 Th Wichianchom; dishes 30-50B; breakfast & lunch) Songkhla's most lauded curry shop serves up an amazing variety of authentic southern-style curries, soups, stir-fries and salads. Look for the glass case holding several stainless-steel trays of food, just south of the sky-blue Chokdee Inn.

J Glass (☎ 0 7444 0888; Th Nakronnai; dishes 50-420B; lunch & dinner) J Glass is one of the top *farăng* hang-outs in town where you can enjoy (slightly adulterated) Thai faves.

Near the Pavilion Songkhla Hotel, on Th Platha, are a few other casual bars worth checking out. As the sun begins to set, **Corner Bier** (Th Sisuda) swells with the town's expat community.

Getting There & Away

The bus station is located a few hundred metres south of the Viva Hotel. Destinations include Bangkok (2nd class/VIP 650/1125B), stopping in Surat Thani (289B) and Chumphon (350B), among other places. To Hat Yai, buses (20B) and minivans (25B) take around 40 minutes and leave from Th Ramwithi.

Motorcycle taxis around town cost around 20B during the day; rates double at night. There's a taxi and motorcycle taxi stand beside Corner Bier.

SUNGAI KOLOK

This used to be a convenient eastern gateway for train travellers heading to/from Malaysia's Pulau Perhentians, but since the start of the violence in Thailand's southernmost provinces, we no longer recommend using this border crossing. Travellers should instead pass through the western border crossings accessible via Hat Yai.

ANDAMAN COAST

The better coast, Thailand's west coast abuts the Andaman Sea and is its most dramatic thanks to the missile-shaped limestone cliffs and mountains that punctuate the tropical seas. Images of these curious rock formations framed

SOUTHERN UNREST

Relations between the central Thai government and the southernmost and predominantly Muslim provinces (Yala, Pattani, Narathiwat and parts of Songkhla) have never been harmonious. Culturally foreign, geographically isolated and economically depressed, these provinces were the battle grounds for a communist insurgency in the late 20th century that was successfully suppressed by Thai military operations.

Today violence has emerged again but the conflict is less cohesive or articulated than years past. Most analysts believe it to be an ethno-nationalistic struggle that began around the start of the new millennium with attacks on symbols of the national government: military and police posts, soldiers and police officers. Then the targets widened to attacks on monks and teachers, a series of school arsons and sophisticated coordinated bombings aimed at civilians

The 2004 Tak Bai incident, in which 78 arrested demonstrators died from suffocation inside military transport trucks, and the Krue Se Mosque massacre, in which 108 assailants armed with machetes were killed by overreaching military force, became symbols of the government's failed handling of the early insurgency and recruitment tools for discontented citizens. By 2006–07, the trouble exploded into terror throughout Yala, Pattani and Narathiwat, and mixed villages of Buddhist and Muslim residents began to be forcibly segregated. From 2004 to 2007 there was an average of 160 violent occurrences per month and by 2008 the death toll had climbed above 3000. Attacks varied from insurgent-style coordinated bombings to ganglike shootings to terror-inducing beheadings further complicating attempts to clearly define the groups and their intentions.

Most violence is confined to the three provinces known collectively as the deep south and primarily to more rural districts within these provinces, though bombings have occurred in downtown sections of Yale's and Pattani's provincial capitals. Periodic bombings have also occurred in Hat Yai, Songkhla town and in border districts of Songkhla province.

As of writing, no foreign tourists have been directly targeted, though a Canadian schoolteacher was killed in a 2006 bomb attack in Hat Yai and bombs have been detonated at the Hat Yai airport. As the south's largest city, Hat Yai is still a functioning and necessary transit link for overland travel into Malaysia. Songkhla town is also operating normally. Violent episodes wax and wane and it is impossible to predict when and where a bombing might occur next. For now, if you need to pass through Hat Yai and/or Songkhla, monitor the situation carefully. It is not advisable to travel between Hat Yai and Songkhla after dark. We would discourage any travel into the three southernmost provinces and avoid the border crossing of Sungai Kolok.

by sky and sea have long defined 'exotic' Asia and a personal investigation of the landscape will reveal that complimentary camera angles and tricks of light are not responsible for its stunning beauty.

Many come only for Phuket, the country's largest and most visited island, where both amusements and package tourists abound. Phuket certainly has wide sandy beaches that are somewhat rare among the Thai beaches. But it is the smaller islands with thinner inheritances of sand where the limestone monoliths crowd in for a souvenir picture. Ko Phi Phi could sweep all the global beach 'best' categories and everyone knows it. Krabi isn't too far behind looks-wise and its topographical charms are appreciated many metres up along one of the many famous rock-climbing routes. The diving is also better on this coast with live-aboards sailing out of the mainland resort town of Khao Lak to reefs that Cousteau allegedly discovered. In between the big names are Muslim fishing-village islands or stopovers for itinerant sea gypsies. And just before Thailand cedes the peninsula to Malaysia is the Ko Tarutao Marine National Park where you can gulp down some much needed coastal wilderness.

RANONG

pop 24,500

If time is ticking away on your visa, chart a course to Ranong for an overland visa-renewal trip before or after visiting either coast. If you linger for awhile, you'll find a small and friendly provincial capital with a bustling fishing port and a distinctly southern Burmese influence.

Information

Most of Ranong's banks are on Th Tha Meuang (the road to the fishing pier), near the intersection with Th Ruangrat. Many have ATMs.

J Net (☎ 0 7882 2877; Th Ruangrat; per hr 40B; 🕑 9am-9pm)

Post Office (Th Chonrau; 🕑 9am-4pm Mon-Fri, 9am-noon Sat)

Sights & Activities

Ranong is one of the mainland bases for **dive trips** to the Burma Banks, within the Mergui (Myeik) Archipelago, as well as the world-class Surin and Similan Islands. Because of the distances involved, dive trips are mostly live-aboard and not cheap. Prices start at around 16,000B for a four-day package. Try **A-One-Diving** (☎ 0 7783 2984; www.a-one-diving.com; 77 Saphan Plaa).

Sleeping & Eating

Suta (☎ 0 7783 2707; Th Ruangrat; r 350B; ❄) For overnighters Suta is one of the comfier choices and popular with repeat visa-running expats; it is an off-the-road place with a clump of simple bungalows overlooking a small garden/car park.

Sophon's Hideaway (☎ 0 7783 2730; Th Ruangrat; dishes 60-200B; 🕑 lunch & dinner) An expat fave with all the bells and whistles: internet access, pool table, pizza and cocktails.

For inexpensive Thai and Burmese breakfasts, try the **morning market** (Th Ruangrat) or nearby traditional Hokkien coffee shops with marble-topped tables.

Getting There & Away

The airport is 20km south of town; **Air Asia** (code AK; www.airasia.com) has three or four flights per week to Bangkok.

The Ranong **bus station** (Th Phetkasem) is towards the southern end of town, although some buses stop in town beforehand. Destinations include Bangkok (220B to 700B, 10 hours), Chumphon (120B to 150B, three hours), Hat Yai (410B to 430B, five hours), Krabi (190B to 220B, six hours), Phuket (180B to 250B, 5½ hours) and Surat Thani (100B to 200B, 4½ hours).

From town, blue sǎwngthǎew 2 passes the bus station.

SURIN ISLANDS MARINE NATIONAL PARK

The five gorgeous islands that make up **Surin Islands Marine National Park** (www.dnp.go.th; admission 400B; 🕑 mid-Nov–mid-May) nearly straddle the Thailand–Myanmar marine border. The granite-outcrop islands boast healthy rainforests, pockets of white-sand beaches in sheltered bays and rocky headlands that jut out into the ocean. The underwater spectacle is an equal attraction: marine life is robust and underwater visibility often measures up to 20m in distance.

Park headquarters and all visitor facilities including accommodation are at Ao Chong Khad on Ko Surin Nuea, near the jetty. The town of Khuraburi is the jumping-off point

GETTING TO MYANMAR: RANONG TO KAWTHOUNG

Foreigners can travel from Ranong, Thailand, into the southernmost tip of Myanmar at Kawthoung (Victoria Point). Most visitors use this as a visa-renewal day trip. Boats to Kawthoung leave the pier at Ranong's Saphan Pla (Pla Bridge), which is about 4.5km from the centre of Ranong. Departures are frequent from around 8.30am until 6pm, and cost around 300B. To reach the pier, take săwngthăew 2 from Ranong (10B) and get off at the immigration office, 700m north of the pier, to get your passport stamped.

Upon arrival at the Kawthoung jetty, there's a stop at Myanmar immigration. At this point you must inform the authorities if you're a day visitor – in which case you must pay a fee of US$10 for a day permit (technically it is a three-day, two-night entry pass). Bear in mind when you are returning to Thailand that Myanmar time is half an hour behind Thailand's. Various travel agencies in Phuket and Ranong organise visa trips if you'd rather just look out a bus window. Though it is fraught with bureaucracy, it is possible to enter Myanmar for a longer trip through this border; contact a travel agent for details on arranging the necessary visa and any other travelling restrictions.

See p564 for making this crossing in the opposite direction.

for the park. The pier and the mainland **national park office** (☎ 0 7649 1378; ⏲ 8am-5pm) are about 9km north of town.

Sights & Activities

There are plenty of **dive sites** in and around the park but there are no dive companies based on the islands. For dive trips to the area, join a multiday live-aboard out of Khao Lak (p808). **Snorkelling** is excellent due to relatively shallow reef depths of 5m to 6m. Snorkelling trips (250B, two hours, 9am and 2pm) leave from island headquarters daily.

Around the park headquarters you can **trek** the forest fringes, looking out for the crab-eating macaques and some of the 57 resident bird species, which include the fabulous Nicobar pigeon, endemic to the islands of the Andaman Sea. Along the coast you're likely to see the chestnut Brahminy kite and reef herons. Twelve species of bat live here, most noticeably tree-dwelling fruit bats, also known as flying foxes.

A rough-and-ready **walking trail** winds 2km along the coast and through forest to the beach at Ao Mai Ngam, where there's good snorkelling. At low tide it's easy to walk between the bays near the headquarters.

The islands' sheltered waters are also home to a **chao náam village**. Also known as 'sea gypsies', this ethnic minority migrates by boat along the northwestern Andaman coast and they wait out the May to November monsoon season on Ko Surin Tai, one of the two largest islands in the park. They are known locally as Moken, from the word *oken* meaning 'salt water'. The village welcomes visitors and is accessible via a longtail boat from park headquarters (100B). Around the sheltered bay there is a major ancestral worship ceremony (Loi Reua) in April.

Sleeping & Eating

Accommodation is simple but *very* tightly packed because the beaches are narrow. It can feel crowded when at capacity of 300 people. A power generator turns off at around 10pm. To book park accommodation, use the **online reservation system** (www.dnp.go.th) or contact the **mainland park office** (☎ 0 7649 1378) in Khuraburi.

Bungalows (from 2000B) and **camp sites** (from 80B) are available at Ao Chong Khad; tents can be rented for about 350B per night. There's a nearby restaurant but provisions should be acquired for the off-duty hours.

If you need to stay overnight in Khuraburi, try **Boon Piya Resort** (☎ 08 1752 5457; bungalows 600B; ❄), beside Tom & Am Tour, or the more basic accommodation at **Tararin Resort** (☎ 0 7649 1789; r from 300-500B; ❄).

Getting There & Away

Many tour companies organise tours and transport to the park from Khao Lak (see p808). Alternatively you can reach the mainland town of Khuraburi by bus from Phuket (190B, 3½ hours, three daily), from where boats depart for the islands (1500B, 2½ hours, once daily), 60km offshore. You can also arrange a tour from Khuraburi; try the affable **Tom & Am Tour** (☎ 08 6272 0588).

KHAO LAK

Khao Lak is the official gateway to the renowned underwater reefs of the northwestern Andaman. Companies offering some diving and snorkelling day trips, but mainly live-aboard excursions, operate out of Khao Lak, which is itself a pretty coastal patch of beaches and mangrove forests.

Sights & Activities

Khao Lak was one of the worst affected areas during the 2004 Boxing Day tsunami. Still standing testament to the surging waves is a police boat that was deposited about 2km inland slightly south of central Khao Lak.

The area immediately south of Hat Khao Lak has been incorporated into the 125-sq-km **Khao Lak/Lam Ru National Park** (☎ 0 7642 0243; www.dnp.go.th; adult/child 200/100B; ⏰ 8am-4.30pm), a beautiful collection of sea cliffs, hills, beaches, estuaries, forested valleys and mangroves. The visitors centre, just off Hwy 4 between the Km 56 and Km 57 markers, has little in the way of maps or printed information, but there's a nice open-air restaurant overlooking the sea. Guided treks can be arranged through Poseidon Bungalows.

Depending on the duration, **live-aboard dive trips** go to some combination of the following dive sites: the Similan and Surin marine parks; the horseshoe-shaped Richelieu Rock, where whale sharks are often spotted during March and April; the Burma Banks, a system of submerged seamounts covered in coral gardens; and other sites where sharks, rays and barracuda hang out.

Trips range in length from three to five days and are priced accordingly from 12,000B up. When shopping for a live-aboard, determine what the fee includes and if you must pay extra for national park permits, equipment rental etc. The diving season starts in late October and runs to May, but varies with park restrictions and the monsoons. Check out www.backpackersthailand.com for information about several live-aboard options. Here are a few starter options:

IQ Dive (☎ 0 7648 5614; www.iq-dive.com) A quality operation that focuses on diving and snorkelling day trips.

Sea Dragon Diver Center (☎ 0 7648 5420; www.seadragondivecenter.com; Th Phetkasem) One of the older operations in Khao Lak, Sea Dragon has maintained high standards.

Wicked Diving (☎ 0 7648 5868; www.wickeddiving.com) Relatively new to the Khao Diving scene, Wicked is already garnering oohs and aahs for its seriously awesome staff, well-run excursions and eco-friendly approach to tourism. Ask about the whale-shark exploration project.

Sleeping & Eating

Poseidon Bungalows (☎ 0 7644 3258; www.similantour.com; bungalows from 900B) On the other side of the headland near Khao Lak/Lam Ru National Park, about 5km south of Hat Khao Lak, this quiet spot features a gaggle of huts scattered throughout coastal forest.

Khao Lak has recently acquired a selection of backpacker digs, like **Fasai** (☎ 0 7648 5867; r 500-700B; ❄), which has immaculate motel-style rooms, **Khao Lak Seafood** (☎ 0 7642 0318; r 600B), a restaurant that also rents bungalows, and **Khao Lak Banana** (☎ 0 7648 5889; www.khaolakbanana.com; r 500-1200B; 🏊).

Eating options are pretty touristy so fill up on Western grub while you can at **Stempfer Café** (Th Phetkasem; dishes 90-150B; ⏰ 9am-10pm) or **Pizzeria** (☎ 0 7648 5271; dishes 200-300B; ⏰ lunch & dinner).

Getting There & Away

Buses following Hwy 4 between Takua Pa (50B, 45 minutes) and Phuket (80B, two hours) will stop at Hat Khao Lak if you ask the driver. Don't accidentally disembark at Kokloi (about 40km south of Khao Lak). VIP buses in either direction breeze through town in the early morning (6am to 8am), while regular buses pass by every hour. Buses will also stop near the Merlin Resort and the Khao Lak/Lam Ru National Park headquarters.

SIMILAN ISLANDS MARINE NATIONAL PARK

Renowned by divers the world over, the beautiful **Similan Islands Marine National Park** (www.dnp.go.th; admission 400B; ⏰ Nov-May) is located 70km offshore. Its smooth granite islands are as impressive above water as below, topped with rainforest, edged with white-sand beaches and fringed with coral reef.

Two of the nine islands, Ko Miang (Island Four) and Ko Similan (Island Eight), have ranger stations and accommodation; park headquarters and most visitor activity centres on Ko Miang. 'Similan' comes from the Malay word *sembilan*, meaning 'nine', and while each island is named they're just as commonly known by their numbers.

Khao Lak is the jumping-off point for the park. The pier is at Thap Lamu, 10km south of town. The **mainland park office** (☎ 0 7659 5045;

(8am-4pm) is about 500m before the pier, but there's no information in English available.

Sights & Activities

The Similans offer exceptional **diving** for all levels of experience, at depths from 2m to 30m. There are seamounts (at Fantasy Rocks), rock reefs (at Ko Payu) and dive-throughs (at Hin Pousar or 'Elephant-head'), with marine life ranging from tiny plume worms and soft corals to schooling fish and whale sharks. No facilities for divers exist in the national park itself, so you'll need to take a dive tour departing from Khao Lak or Phuket.

Snorkelling is good at several points around Ko Miang, especially in the main channel; you can hire snorkel gear from the park (per day 100B). Day-tour operators out of Khao Lak usually visit three or four different snorkelling sites.

The forest around the park headquarters on Ko Miang has a couple of **walking trails** and some great wildlife. The fabulous Nicobar pigeon, with its wild mane of grey-green feathers, is common here. Hairy-legged land crabs and flying foxes (or fruit bats) are relatively easily seen in the forest.

On Ko Similan there's a 2.5km **forest hike** to a viewpoint, and a shorter, steep scramble off the main beach to the top of Sail Rock.

Sleeping & Eating

Accommodation in the national park can be booked online at www.dnp.go.th or with the mainland park office at Khao Lak.

On Ko Miang there are sea-view **bungalows** (r 2000B;), **longhouses** (r 1000B) and crowded **camp sites** (80B, tent rental from 270B). There's electricity from 6pm to 6am. A **restaurant** (dishes 100B) near the park headquarters serves simple Thai food.

Getting There & Away

There's no public transport to the park. Agencies in Khao Lak and Phuket book day/overnight tours (from around 2500/3500B) and dive trips (three-day live-aboards from around 15,000B) – this is about how much you would pay if you tried to get to the islands on your own steam.

KHAO SOK NATIONAL PARK

Take a breather from the beaches with a trip through the ancient jungles of this national park. It's littered with clear streams and swimming holes and jagged limestone peaks. Adding to its credentials, the Khao Sok rainforest is a remnant of a 160-million-year-old forest ecosystem that is believed to be much older and richer than the forests of the Amazon and central Africa – at least according to Thom Henley, author of *Waterfalls and Gibbon Calls*.

The best time of year to visit Khao Sok is during the dry season (December to May), when there are fewer blood-sucking leeches. In January and February, a wild lotus *(Rafflesia kerri meyer)*, the largest flower in the world, bursts into bloom emitting a rotten-meat stench that attracts pollinating insects.

The **park headquarters** (0 7739 5025; www.dnp.go.th; admission 400B) is 1.8km off Rte 401, near the Km 109 marker.

Sleeping & Eating

The road leading into the park is lined with privately run guest houses.

Art's Riverview Jungle Lodge (0 7739 5009; r 350-550B) Art's has a pleasant range of simple, solid and airy rooms with mosquito nets that are all in a beautiful, tranquil and lush setting. You can watch wild macaques from the riverside restaurant.

Khao Sok Rainforest Resort (0 7739 5006; www.krabidir.com/khaosokrainforest; r 400-600B) This place has huts perched high on stilts along the snaking river. In-house conservation programs target both low-impact hiking and forest restoration.

Morning Mist Resort (0 7885 6185; bungalows 600B) Plenty of twigs and thatch with views of the jagged rock formations. Bookings should be made through the National Park Services.

Near the park headquarters you can pitch your own **tent** (2-person camp site 80B, tent hire from 225-405B) or rent **bungalows** (800-1000B). At picturesque Chiaw Lan Lake, park-managed substations have **floating raft houses** (0 7739 5139; 2/4/6 people 400/800/1200B).

Getting There & Away

The park is conveniently wedged between Surat Thani to the east and Takua Pa to the west and can be reached by bus travelling between the two cities. Khao Sok is 40km from Takua Pa (25B, one hour, nine daily) and almost 100km from Surat Thani (80B, one hour, twice daily).

PHUKET

pop 83,800

Phuket (pronounced 'poo-get') flexes serious muscle in the world's best beach category. The beaches are wide and luxurious with silken sand and jade-coloured water. The resorts are oh-so fabulous and package tourists can descend on to the teardrop-shaped island with an orchid lei and a fruit shake as the nearest interactions with local culture and then spend the rest of their time toddling around the nearly private beach. A new crop of boutique hotels gives urbanites from Bangkok enough city amenities not to feel itchy in the provinces.

Despite the accommodation diversity, the beachfront price tag is high and most backpackers hunker down in Phuket Town, a near cousin to Penang in Malaysia and filled with old Sino-Portuguese architecture, a vestige from the era of sea shipping between India and China. Staying away from the beach isn't as bad as it sounds, since the beach communities are way overpriced and look like a version of Bangkok's Th Sukhumvit by the sea. From Phuket town, public transport radiates out to a buffet of silky sand beaches.

Information

Banks and ATMs are widespread through Phuket Town and the beach areas. Wi-fi access is widely available and mostly free. Internet cafes are also common.

Phuket International Hospital (Map p811; ☎ 0 7624 9400, emergency 0 7621 0935; Th Charlerm Pra Kiat)

Post office (Map p813; ☎ 0 7621 1020; Th Montri; 🕑 8.30am-4.30pm Mon-Fri, 9am-noon Sat)

TAT office (Map p813; ☎ 0 7621 2213; 73-75 Th Phuket; 🕑 8.30am-4.30pm) Distributes a handy guide to local transport fares.

Sights & Activities

BEACHES & PARKS

Phuket is the largest island in Thailand; in fact it's so large that it doesn't feel like an island at all until you trundle through the average sights of any Thai town to the stunning west coast, which is scalloped by long sandy beaches and forested coves.

Set along the jagged western coast of this 810-sq-km island are the beach communities of Patong, Karon and Kata. One of the widest and most popular stretches is **Hat Patong**, which is reminiscent of honky-tonk beach towns in the US; there's a lot of neon and souvenir shops, plus Thailand's special knack for seediness with a thriving ladyboy cabaret district and a rowdy nightlife scene. The beaches are packed during the day and beach chairs are rented for 300B a day.

South of Patong is a string of three beaches: the long golden sweep of **Hat Karon**, the smaller but equally beautiful **Hat Kata** (divided by a headland into Kata Yai and Kata Noi) and southern **Hat Nai Han**.

Hat Kata is younger and less seedy than Patong, though still a comrade-in-arms. The beach is particularly gorgeous and the crowd tends to be a little more sophisticated due to the boutique hotels in the area. You'll find good snorkelling here and it's also a great

FRAGILE PARADISE

If you hear travellers complain about rubbish on the islands then there is an environmental message buried underneath. Many of the Thai islands develop on a piecemeal basis: landowners rip out the mangroves and throw up bungalows, but the island infrastructure, which is usually governed by a distant mainland office, is never augmented to accommodate an increase in the population. So a small city develops on an island equipped for a village-sized population: basic septic systems, no formal rubbish removal and, in some cases, individual resort generators. It is a perfect convergence of bureaucratic ineffectiveness and capitalistic opportunism that undermines the islands' primary draw: its natural beauty.

The average visitor can't build a waste-water treatment plant or construct alternative energy generators, though the Thai beaches are in dire need of this kind of know-how. The rest of us can do a little bit by using biodegradable soap, since waste water goes straight to sea. Or trying to reduce our consumption of water and energy by shortening showers, opting for fan instead air-con and hanging out instead of zipping around the island on a motorcycle. You can also try to reduce your plastic waste and dispose of cigarette butts in a rubbish bin instead of the beach. All are small but considerate gestures.

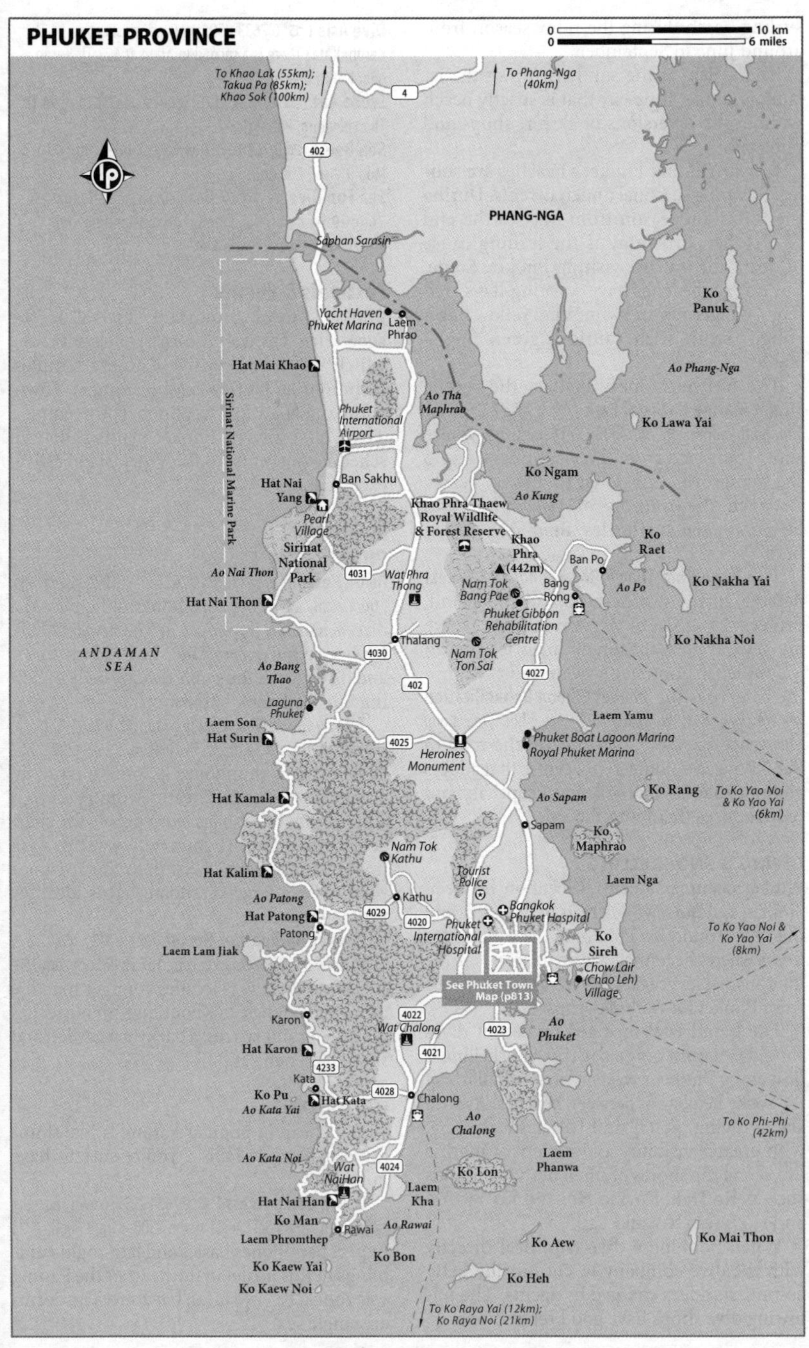
PHUKET PROVINCE
0 10 km
0 6 miles
To Khao Lak (55km); Takua Pa (85km); Khao Sok (100km)
To Phang-Nga (40km)
PHANG-NGA
Saphan Sarasin
Yacht Haven Phuket Marina
Laem Phrao
Ko Panuk
Ao Phang-Nga
Hat Mai Khao
Sirinat National Marine Park
Ao Tha Maphrao
Phuket International Airport
Ko Lawa Yai
Ko Ngam
Ao Kung
Ban Sakhu
Hat Nai Yang
Pearl Village
Khao Phra Thaew Royal Wildlife & Forest Reserve
Khao Phra (442m)
Ko Raet
Sirinat National Park
Ban Po
Ko Nakha Yai
Ao Nai Thon
Wat Phra Thong
Nam Tok Bang Pae
Bang Rong
Ao Po
Hat Nai Thon
Phuket Gibbon Rehabilitation Centre
Ko Nakha Noi
ANDAMAN SEA
Thalang
Nam Tok Ton Sai
Ao Bang Thao
Laguna Phuket
Laem Son
Hat Surin
Laem Yamu
Phuket Boat Lagoon Marina
Royal Phuket Marina
Heroines Monument
Hat Kamala
Ao Sapam
Ko Rang
To Ko Yao Noi & Ko Yao Yai (6km)
Sapam
Ko Maphrao
Nam Tok Kathu
Hat Kalim
Tourist Police
Laem Nga
Ao Patong
Kathu
Hat Patong
Bangkok Phuket Hospital
Patong
Phuket International Hospital
Ko Sireh
To Ko Yao Noi & Ko Yao Yai (8km)
Laem Lam Jiak
Chow Lair (Chao Leh) Village
See Phuket Town Map (p813)
Karon
Wat Chalong
Ao Phuket
Hat Karon
Kata
Ko Pu
Hat Kata
Ao Kata Yai
Chalong
Ao Chalong
To Ko Phi-Phi (42km)
Ao Kata Noi
Wat NaiHan
Laem Kha
Ko Lon
Laem Phanwa
Hat Nai Han
Ko Man
Rawai
Ao Rawai
Laem Phromthep
Ko Aew
Ko Mai Thon
Ko Bon
Ko Kaew Yai
Ko Heh
Ko Kaew Noi
To Ko Raya Yai (12km); Ko Raya Noi (21km)
4
402
4031
4030
4027
4025
4029
4020
4022
4023
4021
4233
4028
4024

THAILAND

surfing beach during the rainy season from around June to September.

Hat Nai Han, at the southern tip of the island, is a quiet little bay that is strictly beach without the diversions of T-shirt shops and pub grub.

Be warned that Phuket's beaches are subject to strong seasonal undercurrents. During the monsoon season from May to the end of October, drowning is the leading cause of death for tourists visiting Phuket. Some, but not all, beaches have warning flags (red flag – dangerous for swimming; yellow flag – rough, swim with caution; green flag – stable).

The northern coast shelters the serene **Sirinat Marine National Park** (☎ 0 7632 8226; www.dnp.go.th; admission 200-400B; 8am-5pm), where short trails lead from the visitor centre into the mangroves and down to a steep beach. Between the months of November and February, sea turtles lay their eggs along here.

The **Khao Phra Thaew Royal Wildlife & Forest Reserve**, in the northern part of the island, protects 23 sq km of virgin rainforest. There are several pleasant jungle hikes leading to a couple of photogenic waterfalls. Within the reserve is the **Phuket Gibbon Rehabilitation Centre** (Map p811; ☎ 0 7626 0492; www.gibbonproject.org; admission by donation; 9am-4pm), on the road to Bang Rong, a volunteer-run centre that adopts gibbons that have been kept in captivity and reintroduces them into the wild.

DIVING & SNORKELLING

Phuket occupies a central location between Similan and Burma Bank reefs to the north and the sites around Ko Phi Phi to the south. Plus this is where the tourists are, so this is where the dive businesses are based. Live-aboards depart from Phuket for multiday trips.

The island is also ringed by decent dives should you want only a day trip. Snorkelling is best along Phuket's west coast, particularly at the rocky headlands between beaches. As with scuba diving, you'll find better snorkelling, with greater visibility and variety of marine life, along the shores of small outlying islands such as Ko Hah, Ko Yao Noi and Ko Yao Yai and Ko Raya (Noi and Yai).

When booking a dive trip, deal directly with the dive company to cut out the hefty commission fees charged by agents. The following dive shops have good reputations:

Dive Asia (☎ 0 7633 0598; www.diveasia.com; 24 Th Karon, Kata) There is a second location at 623 Th Karon near Karon Beach.

Scuba Cat (☎ 0 7629 3120; www.scubacat.com; 94 Th Thaweewong, Patong)

Sea Bees (☎ 0 7638 1765; www.sea-bees.com; 69 1/3 Moo 9 Viset, Chalong)

Sea Fun Divers (☎ 0 7634 0480; www.seafundivers.com; 29 Soi Karon Nui, Patong) An outstanding and professional dive operation.

Festivals & Events

Phuket's most important festival is the **Vegetarian Festival** (www.phuketvegetarian.com), which is centred on five Chinese temples, including **Jui Tui** (Th Ranong) in Phuket Town, and Bang Niaw and Sui Boon Tong temples. The TAT office in Phuket prints a helpful schedule of events for the Vegetarian Festival each year.

Sleeping

PHUKET TOWN

On On Hotel (Map p813; ☎ 0 7621 1154; 19 Th Phang-Nga; r from 200B;) This bare-bones oldie played a dirty Khao San flophouse in *The Beach* (2000). It's been a full decade since Leo's sandy foray, and it still looks the same: droopy beds, creaking fans and dank bathrooms.

Talang Guest House (Map p813; ☎ 0 7621 4225; talanggh@phuket.ksc.co.th; 37 Th Thalang; r 250-420B;) This decrepit shophouse is something of an architectural classic. Creature comforts are at a premium, but it bags extra points for character and charm. If you really want to soak up the atmosphere, check in to the 3rd-floor room with a large verandah that is ideal for nostalgia junkies.

Phuket Backpacker Hostel (Map p813; ☎ 0 7625 6680; www.phuketbackpacker.com; 167 Th Ranong; dm 350-500B, d from 1000B;) Decades younger than the other budget digs, this boutique-ish hostel has great hang-out spaces, a backyard garden and shared kitchen.

HAT PATONG

Going cheap in popular Patong is like slumming in Beverly Hills – you're sure to have hotel envy.

Crown Backpackers (☎ 0 7634 2297; crown_hostel@yahoo.com; 169/3 Soi Sansabai; dm 250B, r from 500B;) Expect bare-bones basics and late-night rumblings in this hostel in the heart of the Patong war zone…er…we mean bar zone. The dorms are single sex.

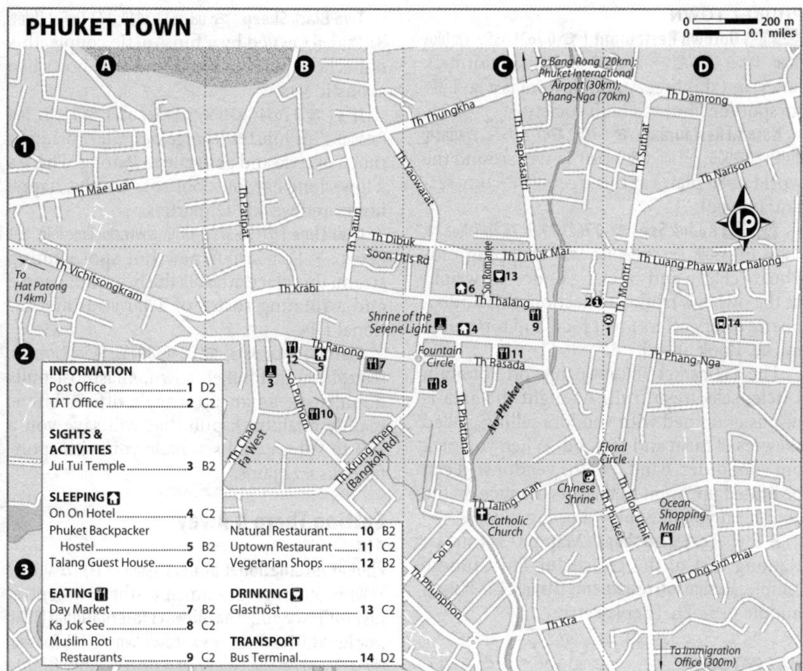

Capricorn Village (0 7634 0390; 2/29 Th Rat Uthit; r from 700B) Capricorn is a rare cheapie in Patong's inflated sleeping scene. Bright little bungalows with terraces wind back into a quiet garden. Guests can take a dip in the pool at K's Hotel next door.

Casa Jip (0 7634 3019; www.casajip.com; 207/10 Th Rat Uthit; r 1000B) Italian run and great value, this place has big rooms (for the price bracket) with comfy beds and some Thai style.

Swarms of low-priced accommodation hovers around Th Nanai. The following are recommended:

Khun Vito Guest House (0 7629 7061; 74/7 Soi Nanai; s/d from 600/1000B) Friendly Vito offers a dozen spic-and-span rooms.

Chalermporn (0 7629 6994; chalermporn9@hotmail.com; 74/32 Soi Nanai; r 1000B) Standard-issue rooms are spotless.

HAT KARON & HAT KATA

Lucky Guest House (0 7633 0572; 110/44-45 Th Thai Na, Hat Kata Yai; d from 450B) Phuket penny-pinchers usually wind up at Lucky, which offers the basic necessities: a bed and a bathroom. The extra-friendly staff can offer insider tips about the island.

Kata on Sea (0 7633 0594; 96/6 Th Thai Na, Hat Kata Yai; d 450-1000B) Hardly on the sea. This collection of modest bungalows is a steep 100m climb to a quiet green hilltop, but for the price, it's well worth the effort. Spacious bungalows have massive picture windows that maximise views.

Karon Living Room (0 7628 6618; www.karonlivingroom.com; 481 Th Patak; r incl breakfast 900-2000B) Karon Living Room provides sparkling clean rooms with air-con set to cryogenic levels. The rooms don't have oodles of personality, but it's a solid pick in the upper budget range.

Brazil (0 7639 6317; www.phukethomestay.com; 9 Th Luang Pho Chuan; r 1100-1600B) Simple rooms have Carnival styling, which makes this friendly spot a standout operation. There's a convivial cafe on the ground level. It's a short walk to both Kata and Karon beaches.

Eating

Phuket cuisine is a mix of Thai, Malay and Chinese, with some exceptional twists on the country's standard dishes.

PHUKET TOWN

our pick Uptown Restaurant (☎ 0 7621 5359; Th Tilok Uthit; dishes 30-60B; 10am-9pm) It may not look fancy, but this breezy noodle joint is a favourite spot for Phuket's high society.

Natural Restaurant (☎ 0 7622 4287; 62/5 Soi Phuthon; dishes 80-200B; lunch & dinner) Travel around the world in 80 plates at this treehouse-cum-restaurant spot.

our pick Ka Jok See (☎ 0 7621 7903; 26 Th Takua Pa; dishes 180-480B; dinner Tue-Sun) Dripping old-Phuket charm and creaking under the weight of the owner's trinket collection, this atmospheric eatery offers great food and top-notch music. Book ahead.

The **day market** (Th Ranong), just off Fountain Circle, sells fresh fruit. At night the area is just as crammed with vendors selling grilled skewers of meat and seafood. When you pick out your order, hand it to the vendor so it can be heated up; point to the vats of sauce on the counter if you like spicy dipping sauces.

A few **vegetarian shops** (Map p813) line Th Ranong east of the garish Jui Tui Chinese temple. **Muslim roti restaurants** (Map p813; Th Thalang) huddle near Th Thepkasatri.

HAT PATONG

our pick Fried Chicken (63/5 Th Phra Barami; dishes from 45B; 10am-7pm) Three huge fryers are bubbling and splattering with juicy, crispy 'yard bird'. It's Muslim owned, so Halal doctrine dictates that this joint is clean. The chicken is served with a tangy hot sauce and sticky rice.

Got a hankering for some seafood but are intimidated by the restaurants packed with platinum-card users? Head on down to Soi Eric, a claustrophobic alley just off Th Bang-La. With barely space to loiter, the cheap **seafood stalls** (dishes 80-100B) feed a rotating crowd of expectant diners, who are rarely disappointed.

Drinking & Entertainment

Patong is the indisputable nightlife champion on the island and Th Bang-La is a neon-lit zoo after dark where throngs of people graze at open-air bars, hostess pubs and cheesy ladyboy cabarets.

Molly Malone's (☎ 0 7629 2771; Th Thawiwong, Hat Patong) This pub rocks with Irish gigs every night at 9.45pm. There's a good atmosphere, pub grub and a front-row view of the ocean and the herds of tourists.

Two Black Sheep (☎ 08 9872 2645; 172 Th Rat Uthit; Hat Patong) Owned by a fun Aussie couple, this old-school pub is a great find that hosts live acoustic sets.

JP's (☎ 0 7634 3024; 5/28 Th Rat Uthit, BYD Lofts, Hat Patong) This hipster lounge definitely brings a touch of style and panache to Patong. There's a low-slung bar, outdoor sofa booths, happy hours and weekly DJ parties.

Club Lime (☎ 08 5798 1850; www.clublime.info; Hat Patong; 10pm-2am) A new hot spot gaining steam, this place attracts the beautiful people and a rotating roster of Thai and international DJs.

Glastnöst (Map p813; ☎ 08 4058 0288; 14 Soi Rommani, Phuket Town) In Phuket Town, Glastnöst pulls doubletime as an attorney's office, but is mainly a laidback pub that will save you a trip to Patong and serenade you with spontaneous jazz jams.

Getting There & Away

AIR

Phuket international airport (Map p811; ☎ 0 7632 7230) is 30km to the north of the city centre, just off Hwy 402. **Thai Airways International** (THAI; code TG; ☎ 0 7621 1195; www.thaiair.com; 78/1 Th Ranong, Phuket Town) operates about a dozen daily flights to Bangkok.

Bangkok Airways (code PG; ☎ 0 7622 5033; www.bangkokair.com) has daily flights to Ko Samui, Bangkok and Pattaya.

Nok Air (code DD; ☎ 1318; www.nokair.co.th), **One-Two-Go** (code OX; ☎ 1141, ext 1126; www.fly12go.com) and **Air Asia** (code AK; www.airasia.com) all fly to/from Bangkok. Air Asia also flies to Kuala Lumpur and Singapore.

Other airlines:

Dragonair (☎ 076 215734; Th Phang-Nga) Flights to Hong Kong.

Malaysia Airlines (☎ 076 216675; 1/8-9 Th Thungkha) Flights to Kuala Lumpur.

SilkAir (☎ 076 213891; www.silkair.com; 183/103 Th Phang-Nga) Flights to Singapore.

To reach the airport, you'll need to hire a taxi (500B to 800B). From the airport you can catch the airport shuttle (to Phuket Town 120B; to Patong, Karon or Kata 180B).

BOAT

Ferries link Phuket to Ko Phi Phi (400B, 8.30am, 1.30pm and 2.30pm). Boats depart in the opposite direction at 9am, 2.30pm and 3pm.

BUS

Phuket's bus terminal (Map p813) is off Th Phang-Nga, right in the centre of Phuket Town and walking distance from the nearby guest houses. Destinations include Bangkok (air-con/VIP 630/970B, 12 to 15 hours, morning and evening departures), Hat Yai (air-con 370B, six to eight hours, morning departures), Krabi (air-con 165B, three to four hours, frequent), Phang-Nga (air-con 100B, 2½ hours, five departures from 10am to 4.30pm), Surat Thani (air-con 205B, five to six hours, several daily) and Ko Samui (bus-boat combo 500B).

Getting Around

When you first arrive in Phuket, do beware of the rip-off artists who claim that the tourist information office is 5km away, that the only way to get to the beaches is to take a taxi or that a săwngthăew from the bus station to Phuket's town centre will cost you a small fortune.

Săwngthăew depart from Phuket Town's Th Ranong, near the market, to different spots on the island for 40B to 70B from 7am and 5pm. Túk-túk to the beaches from Phuket Town will set you back 250B to Patong, 280B to Kata and Karon, and 340B for beaches beyond. Between the beaches should cost 300B to 500B.

You can also hire motorcycles almost anywhere for 250B to 500B. Exercise extreme caution as Phuket's roads are winding and accidents claim hundreds of lives every year on Phuket alone.

AROUND PHUKET

Ao Phang-Nga

Fringed by limestone cliffs and the dazzling Andaman Sea, Phang-Nga is a scenic day trip from Phuket. The biggest attraction is a longtail boat tour through **Ao Phang-Nga**, a bay of mangrove forests, jagged mountainous islands and caves looking like unkempt candelabras. The exotic landscape appeared in the James Bond movie *The Man with the Golden Gun* and tours make a stop at the island rock now dubbed the **James Bond Island**. Tours can be arranged with agencies at the Phang-Nga bus station.

Frequent Phuket-bound buses (75B) run until 8pm and take 1½ to 2½ hours depending on who's at the wheel. Buses depart from the **bus station** (Th Phetkasem) in Phang-Nga.

Ko Yao

These two Muslim fishing villages provide a dose of sleepy island culture within reach of Phuket. **Ko Yao Noi** is more populated than its sister **Ko Yao Yai**. Neither has particularly good swimming beaches but the rock-strewn bay, part of the Ao Phang-Nga Marine National Park, provides solo sojourns with the scenery. **Koh Yao Noi Eco-Tourism Club** (☎ 0 7659 7409, 0 1089 5413; www.koh-yao-noi-eco-tourism-club.com; r incl meals 400B), works with a Bangkok-based NGO to provide homestays within the Muslim fishing community as well as educational programs about the local ecology and resident's livelihoods.

Make sure to bring enough cash when visiting Ko Yao, as there is only one ATM and it's often empty.

To get to the islands from Phuket Town, catch a săwngthăew from in front of the day market to Bang Rong (on Ao Po) for 50B. From the public pier there are up to six daily boats (50B, one hour, departures between 8am and 5pm). Once you arrive on the islands, it costs an additional 70B to 100B to get to your resort.

KRABI & AROUND

pop 90,000

Krabi (gra-*bee*) is part of a well-balanced beach diet following a rendezvous on the Gulf of Thailand coast or vice versa. In fact, the path between is so well oiled that you will no doubt find yourself being herded off the ferry into cramped bicoastal minivans before you can even deliberate. Krabi Town is the gateway to a peninsula of mainland beaches – Ao Nang, Hat Ton Sai and Hat Rai Leh – that are often referred to generally by the same name outside of the area. Once you arrive in Krabi Town, you'll have to be more precise.

Whichever beach you choose, the Krabi peninsula is a dramatic collection of karst formations soaring forth from emerald waters, creating the illusion of being farflung islands. These beaches attract an energetic crowd of rockclimbers, kayakers and snorkellers who scramble over every nook of this surreal landscape. Dedicated sunbathers will be disappointed to find that Krabi's beaches are small rocky coves instead of long voluptuous stoles – for blonde sand ambition you'll have to go to Ko Phi Phi or Ko Samui.

Krabi Town

This is the jumping-off point for the mainland beaches of Ao Nang, Ton Sai and Rai Leh and the islands of Ko Phi Phi and Ko Lanta. It is a good place to take care of all the modern necessities – internet, bank and shopping chores – before going off the grid again.

INFORMATION

Immigration office (☎ 0 7561 1350; Th Chamai Anuson; ⏲ 8.30am-4pm Mon-Fri) Handles visa extensions.

Krabi Hospital (☎ 0 7561 1210; Th Utarakit) One kilometre north of town.

SLEEPING & EATING

Good Dream Guesthouse (☎ 0 7562 2993; 83 Th Utarakit; r 250-550B; ❄ 💻) It isn't as slick as the nearby Chan-Cha-Lay, but it does have some of the cheapest rooms in Krabi Town, with a helpful manager, free internet and other guest-house goods.

KR Mansion (☎ 0 7561 2761; krmansion@yahoo.com; 52/1 Th Chao Fah; r 300-600B; ❄ 💻) There's a fun rooftop beer garden with panoramic views and the rooms in this bright-pink building are quite comfortable.

Chan-Ch-Lay (☎ 0 7562 0952; www.geocities.com/chan_cha_lay; 55 Th Utarakit; r 300-650B; ❄ 💻) The tiled rooms are immaculate and the cafe has dainty trimmings, artistic photos and other bits of art on the walls.

Ruan Pae (☎ 0 7561 1956; Th Utarakit; dishes 60-150B; ⏲ lunch & dinner) This old-fashioned floating restaurant is a fine place to watch the evening mist gather around the mangroves, though the atmosphere is better than the food. Wear your mozzie spray in lieu of cologne.

Near the Khong Kha pier, the **night market** (Th Khong Kha; meals 20-50B; ⏲ dinner) presents edible Southern culture right at your feet. For takeaway food, check out the **morning market** (Th Si Sawat & Th Pruksauthit), near the Vieng Thong Hotel in the centre of town.

GETTING THERE & AROUND

Krabi's airport is 17km northeast of town on Hwy 4. **Thai Airways International** (THAI; code TG; ☎ 0 7562 2439; www.thaiair.com) has three daily flights to/from Bangkok. **Bangkok Air** (code PG; www.bangkokair.com) has a daily service to Ko Samui.

The bus station is 4km north of Krabi town at Talat Kao. Destinations include Bangkok's Southern bus terminal (air-con/VIP 700/1100B, 12 hours, three departures), Hat Yai (air-con 173B to 210B, four hours, hourly), Phuket (air-con 120B to 140B, three to four hours, hourly) and Surat Thani (130B to 150B, two to three hours, frequent). But most tourists arrive and depart on the minivans that maniacally drive between the coasts.

Boats to Ko Lanta and Ko Phi Phi leave from the new passenger pier at Khlong Chilat, about 3km southwest of Krabi. Travel agencies will arrange free transfers with a ticket purchase. In the high season, there are boats to Ko Phi Phi (450B to 490B, 1½ hours, 9am, 10.30am and 2.30pm). From September to May, there are boats to Ko Lanta (450B, 1½ hours, 10.30am and 1.30pm).

For travel around Krabi, sǎwngthǎew deliver passengers to/from Krabi Town and the bus station (20B) and Ao Nang (40B, 45 minutes), the only beach accessible by road. Longtail boats bounce between Krabi's central Khong Kha pier and Hat Rai Leh (200B, 45 minutes) and Hat Ton Sai (210B), when enough passengers have accumulated.

> **ROCKIN' KRABI'S CLIFFS**
>
> If you think that Krabi is beautiful from sea level, check out the view from atop those craggy cliffs. For the past decade, rock-climbers have answered that scenery call by scrambling up the pock-marked cliffs to reward their aching muscles with 100m-high views of sea, jungle and sky, earning these hills legendary status among global climbers. Hat Rai Leh is climbing central where you can sign up for a beginner's course, rent gear or get the lowdown on more advanced routes. There are also several rockclimbing guidebooks to the area available at climbing schools. The going rate for courses is 800B to 1200B for a half-day and 1500B to 2200B for a full day.

Ao Nang

Of Krabi's peninsular beaches, Ao Nang is leashed to the mainland by Hwy 4203 and provides 'civilisation' instead of scenery. The paved road separates the hotels from the beach and is lined with the typical beach-town tourist shops. It is convenient for a 'night out' but not the tropical hideaway that most people are looking for.

There's a cluster of guest houses along the main road, including **Bernie's Place** (☎ 0 7563 7093; r 200-600B), which stays cheap even in high season; and **Panan** (☎ 0 7563 8105; r 400-500B), with crisp, white rooms, TV and some ocean views. **J Mansion** (☎ 0 7563 7876, 0 7569 5128; j_mansion10@hotmail.com; r 800-1000B; ❄ 💻) is the most popular place on the strip, so book in advance.

our pick **Sala Bua & Lo Spuntino** (☎ 0 7563 7110; dishes 80-520B; 🕑 10am-11pm) is within the bustle of 'Seafood Street' and serves an excellent selection of East and West cuisines with sunset views.

Hat Ton Sai

The next beach over from Ao Nang is a short longtail boat ride but feels worlds away. Footpaths lead from the barely there spit of sand through coastal woods to the cheap guest-house shanties for rockclimbers and professional beach bums. The scenery isn't as spectacular as neighbouring Hat Rai Leh, but it remains the cheapest and least-developed of Krabi's beaches, has easy access to popular climbing routes and is undeniably relaxed.

Tucked in the woods away from the fray and dangling climbers, **Forest Resort** (☎ 08 9290 0262; bungalows 300-500B) is a friendly resort that has a cluster of basic bungalows scattered on a small hill. The on-site Indian restaurant is an added bonus.

Paasook (☎ 08 9645 3013; bungalows 500B), at the far west end of the beach, has basic bungalows with large picture windows.

Hat Rai Leh

Hemmed in by towering limestone mountains anchored in the shimmering sea, Hat Rai Leh is a stunning spit of land from which to launch jungle and sea forays. The front-row view of this picture-postcard landscape is from West Rai Leh, monopolised by expensive resorts. A small dirt path leads to the mangrove beach of East Rai Leh, where the cheaper hotels can be found. It is a minor commute between the two. There's also a path leading to Tham Phra Nang (south of East Rai Leh), another sandy altar beside these limestone monoliths.

Plenty of outfitters run kayaking and snorkelling trips and rock-climbing courses. There are plenty of jungle walks in Rai Leh if you want to sweat more than usual.

SLEEPING & EATING

Rapala Cabana (☎ 08 6957 8096; East Rai Leh; bungalows 200B) Superbly located deep in the jungle and high in the hills, this uber-rustic, Rasta-run place is the cheapest place to crash in Rai Leh.

Anyavee (☎ 08 1537 5517; www.anyavee.com; r 1500-3000B) Not really shoestring prices, but you're a captive audience. Anyavee sports modern, comfortable rooms.

Restaurants and bars are limited to the resort's on-site options. If you get bored of these, hop on a longtail to Ao Nang.

GETTING THERE & AWAY

Hat Rai Leh is accessible via longtail boat from Krabi Town (200B). You can also hop over to the neighbouring beaches of Ton Sai (80B, 15 minutes) and Ao Nang (100B, 20 minutes) via a longtail boat. After dark you'll pay around 120B.

KO PHI PHI

A truly jaw-dropping beauty, Ko Phi Phi is blessed with phenomenal curves, from the altitude of the limestone cliffs to fine arcs of white sand and bejewelled tropical waters. Backpackers might have discovered it first but Speedo-wearing jetsetters have it firmly under their control now. Despite Phi Phi's tony abodes, backpackers can still wiggle in and enjoy one of the world's most impressive beaches without blowing the budget.

The crowds and development belie the fact that Ko Phi Phi (officially named Ko Phi Phi Don) is part of a marine national park. Ko Phi Phi Leh, a satellite island, remains uninhabited thanks in part to a more profitable business than tourism – harvesting nests of swiftlets for medicinal purposes. Visiting the island is expensive, but just to behold it for a day is worthwhile.

Ko Phi Phi was hit particularly hard by the tsunami – virtually every standing structure on the twin bays of Ao Ton Sai and Ao Lo Dalam was destroyed, although much has been rebuilt.

Activities

The **diving** on Ko Phi Phi is superb. The best months for visibility are December to April. Where there is diving, there is **snorkelling** too. Recommended dive operators include **Adventure Club** (☎ 08 1970 0314, 08 1895 1334; www.divingphi.com), which has educational, eco-focused diving, hiking and snorkelling tours. **Rock climbing** has caught on; talk to **Cat's Climbing Shop** (☎ 08 1787 5101), in Tonsai Village, for more information.

Sleeping

Budget accommodation on Ko Phi Phi? Don't kid yourself: there isn't any, although there are a few pockets of relative affordability, especially in the interior of the island. Things get tight during the high season from December to March.

Rock Backpacker (☎ 0 7561 2402; therockbackpacker@hotmail.com; dm 350B, r 800B) Solo penny-pinchers will thrive in the 16-bed dorm room, a real rarity on Ko Phi Phi, though the digs are cramped. Rock Backpacker is inland, but close to Ao Lo Dalam, and the funky restaurant, on a dry-docked boat, is conducive to mingling.

Phi Phi Long Beach (☎ 08 6281 4349; r 500-1000B) Standard-issue bungalows are nothing to write home about, but the price is right (cheap!) and there's a chill backpacker vibe along the sand.

Tropical Garden Bungalows (☎ 08 9729 1436; r from 800B;) If you don't mind walking 10 minutes to eat, drink or sunbathe, then you'll love Tropical Garden. At the far end of the main path from Ao Ton Sai, it feels pretty isolated in its fragment of hillside jungle. The cabins are frontier-style log affairs.

Viking Resort (☎ 0 7581 9399; tak_blobk@hotmail.com; r 800-2000B;) Viking Resort has oodles of tiki-chic charm on a great beach for swimming and tanning.

White (☎ 0 7560 1300; www.whitephiphi.com; r 1600-1900B;) Geared towards the flashpacker crowd, the White has two locations in Tonsai Village, with squeaky-clean rooms and everything's white (duh).

Phi Phi Casita (☎ 0 7560 1214; r 2000-3000B;) A step back from Ao Lo Dalam, this place looks like a classy fishermen's village: tiny wooden bungalows hover over weathered planks and flower-planted mud flats. There's not much privacy but the infinity pool and proximity to the beach are major draws.

Eating & Drinking

Most of the hotels and bungalows around the island have their own restaurants. Cheaper and often better food can be found in the restaurants and cafes in Tonsai Village. Some of the most popular eateries are relative newcomers, having been built – along with the rest of the village – after the tsunami. Others are old favourites that were lovingly reconstructed.

D's Books (☎ 08 4667 7730; coffee 50-110B; breakfast, lunch & dinner;) In the beating heart of Tonsai Village, this classy cafe has amazing coffee drinks and stacks of cheap reading. Good luck finding a seat – the free wi-fi attracts email-aholics from all over the island.

Papaya (meals 80-180B; lunch & dinner) The closest you'll come to an authentic Thai restaurant on the island.

Getting There & Away

Ko Phi Phi is equidistant from Phuket (400B, 1½ to two hours, three daily) and Krabi (350B, 1½ hours, three daily). Boats run regularly from November to May, but schedules depend on the weather during the monsoon.

KO LANTA

pop 20,000

Ko Lanta enjoys cult status among backpackers, partly because it is has a Ko Pha-Ngan hippie vibe, an unusual find on the otherwise upscale Andaman coast. But Lanta is a mixed bag: the beaches where you can afford to be poor are sub par and the flat island doesn't enjoy the dramatic limestone peaks that make the Andaman such a tourist draw. Nonetheless the easy-going Muslim and Thai community is friendly enough to make you feel like you've been born an island child and the lazy days act like goo on otherwise well-planned itineraries.

Sleeping & Eating

our pick **Bee Bee Bungalows** (☎ 08 1537 9932; www.diigii.de; Hat Khlong Khong; r 300-700B;) A great budget pick, Bee Bee's super-friendly staff cares for a dozen Bali-inspired cabins perched high in the trees. The on-site restaurant has a library to keep you busy while you wait for your meal.

Sanctuary (☎ 0 1891 3055; Hat Phrae Ae; r 400-800B) A delightful place to stay, these artistically designed wood-and-thatch bungalows have lots of grass and a hippyish atmosphere. The restaurant offers Indian and vegetarian eats among the Thai usuals, and holds yoga classes.

Kantiang Bay View Resort (☎ 0 1787 5192; Ao Kantiang; r 400-1500B;) The staff can be dreadfully rude and the food is mediocre, but Kantiang Bay View remains a popular spot for backpackers, probably because the bungalows are decent and they sit right in the centre of the stunning beach.

Lanta Emerald (☎ 7566 7037; www.lantaemeraldresort.com; Hat Khlong Khong; r from 500B;) Lanta Emerald has all the trappings of a resort, but it's tailored to smaller budgets. Concrete air-con bungalows mix with a handful of comfy bamboo huts on the well-manicured grounds.

Where Else? (☎ 0 1536 4870; Hat Khlong Khong; r 500-1500B) Make your way here for a slice of bohemia. The bungalows are a bit rickety but the place buzzes with backpackers. The restaurant is a growing piece of art in itself.

our pick **Sang Kha Ou Resort & Spa** (☎ 08 1443 3232; Ban Sang Ga U; r 500-3500B;) It's like you stumbled into 'Alice in Jungleland' – the rooms are in the trees, the trees are in the rooms. The smiley owner chortles as wide-eyed backpackers stumble through the twilight zone of classical statues, terracotta warriors and papier mâché projects.

Bamboo Bay Resort (☎ 0 7561 8240; www.bamboobay.net; Ao Mai Pai; r 700-1700B) Clinging to the hillside above a lovely isolated beach, this place has a variety of brick and concrete bungalows and a fine restaurant down on the sand.

Drunken Sailors (☎ 0 7566 5076; Ao Kantiang; dishes 100-200B; breakfast, lunch & dinner) This hip, ultrarelaxed, octagonal pad is smothered with beanbags. The coffee drinks are top-notch and go well with interesting bites like the chicken green curry sandwich.

Getting There & Away

There are two piers at Ban Sala Dan. The passenger jetty is about 300m from the main strip of shops, while vehicle ferries leave from a second jetty several kilometres further east.

Passenger boats run between Krabi's Khlong Chilat pier and Ko Lanta from November through May (450B, 1½ hours). Boats depart from Ko Lanta at 8am and 1pm. In the reverse direction boats leave at 10.30am and 1.30pm.

Boats between Ko Lanta and Ko Phi Phi (400B, 1½ hours) run mainly in the high season and usually leave Ko Lanta at 8am and 1pm; in the opposite direction boats leave Ko Phi Phi at 11.30am and 2pm.

Two high-speed ferries connect Ko Lanta and Ko Lipe (1800B) with variable seasonal schedules.

Most visitors use the minivan/car ferry services from Krabi (350B, 1½ hours) or Trang (250B, two hours).

Pick-up share taxis (80B to 180B) shuttle people to/from the pier to the beaches; some guest houses provide free transfer. Motorcycles can be rented for 250B and because the island is flat it is an easier drive.

TRANG TOWN & THE TRANG ISLANDS

pop 70,000

Back on the mainland, bustling Trang is a cheekrful and pleasant Thai town midway between Krabi and Hat Yai. It is a convenient spot to soak up some of the Malay peninsula's Chinese heritage at marble-topped table coffeeshops or enjoy the roar of the lolly-coloured Vespas and vintage túk-túk. But most travellers whiz through Trang town themselves en route to the nearby Trang Islands, where the Andaman's iconic limestone peaks make one last southern spectacle just offshore. Ko Muk boasts a golden beach and is one of the few Trang Islands with budget options.

Sleeping & Eating

TRANG TOWN

Ko Teng Hotel (☎ 0 7521 8148; 77-79 Th Praram VI; r 180-300B;) The undisputed king of backpacker lodgings. Don't forget to pack your adventurous spirit, 'cause if you left it on the bus, these slightly grungy rooms will get you down.

Look for Trang's speciality, *khànŏm jiin* (rice noodles doused with a soupy spicy curry), at the night market, just east of the provincial offices. Trang is also famous for its **Hokkien-style coffeeshops** (*ráan kaa-fae* or *ráan ko-píi*) that serve real filtered coffee. **Sin Ocha Bakery** (Th Sathani; dishes 25-50B; breakfast, lunch & dinner) is the most convenient *ráan ko-píi* around.

KO MUK

The following places are a short walk north from the pier on a shallow beach.

Charlie Beach Resort (☎ 0 7520 3281-3; www.kohmook.com; bungalows 1000-4000B;) Basic shacks and swish air-con deals.

Ko Mook Resort (☎ in Trang 0 7520 3303; 45 Th Praram VI; bungalows 500-1000B) Comfortable huts concealed in a thick garden.

Mookies (tents 200B) Open year-round and is a fun place to grab a drink even if you don't pitch a tent.

Getting There & Away

Trang Town has an airport served by **Thai Airways International** (THAI; code TG; www.thaiair.com) and **Air Asia** (code AK; www.airasia.com) that fly to/from Bangkok.

The **bus station** (Th Huay Yot) is 400m from the town centre. Destinations include Bangkok (air-con/VIP 850/1050B, 12 to 13 hours, morning and evening departures), Hat Yai (air-con 110B to 135B), Satun (air-con 130B, two hours), Krabi (air-con 180B, three hours) and Phuket (air-con 240B to 265B, five hours).

Share taxis and minibuses also service many of the popular destinations. Local transport is by minibus.

The **train station** (Th Phra Ram VI) serves only two trains travelling all the way from Trang to Bangkok (2nd-class fan/air-con sleeper/1st class 531/731B/1240B, 16 hours, evening departures).

To get to Ko Muk from Trang Town, take an air-con minivan to Kuantungku (100B), where you can catch a ferry to the island (55B, 30 minutes). The ferry schedule varies with the seasons. You can also charter a longtail for 700B. Contact your resort ahead of time and ask about transport updates. From November to May, Ko Muk is a stop on the speedboats between Ko Lanta and Ko Lipe.

SATUN

pop 33,400

Travelling to the deepest western corner of Thailand, you pass woven bamboo huts and harvested fields where villagers stage football games. Along the highways saunter men dressed in the traditional Muslim garb and headscarved women. Satun is barely Thailand, with a majority of the population speaking the Malay Yawi dialect, and it didn't join the country as a province until 1932. It is a small town doing small-town things that few shoestringers pay much attention to. Satun is en route to Malaysia's Pulau Langkawi, though these days it is not a necessary transit link since the expansion of interisland ferries and share taxis that operate directly from the pier.

Sleeping & Eating

There is just a handful of large rundown hotels in Satun, including **Sinkiat Thani Hotel** (☎ 0 7473 0255; 50 Th Buriwanit; r 663B; ❄), right in the centre of town.

Near the gold-domed Bambang Mosque in the centre of town there are several inexpensive Muslim food shops. Morning coffee can be shared with chatty vegetable sellers at the **day market** (Khlong Bambang), south of town. The **night market** (btwn Th Buriwanit & Th Satun Thani), north of the mosque, provides the pleasurable evening entertainment of eating fluffy roti and watching the communal TV.

Getting There & Away

Buses to Bangkok (air-con/VIP 820/1030B, 14 hours, three departures) leave from a small depot on Th Hatthakham Seuksa, east of the centre. Buses to Hat Yai (80B, two hours) and Trang (100B, 1½ hours) leave regularly from in front of the 7-Eleven on Th Satun Thanee.

To get to Ko Tarutao Marine National Park, you must take a shared taxi to Pak Bara pier (400B, 1½ hours), from where ferries and speedboats depart for the marine park (from 350B to 650B, twice a day).

See the boxed text, p804, for information on ferries to Pulau Langkawi.

KO TARUTAO MARINE NATIONAL PARK

Wonderfully wild and remote, Ko Tarutao Marine National Park is a little-known archipelago of 51 islands in the furthest southwestern reaches of Thai territory. Admission to the park is 400B for foreigners and it is only 'officially' open from around November to May, depending on the weather patterns during the monsoon period.

Of the five accessible islands, park accommodation is available on mountainous **Ko Tarutao** and **Ko Adang**. Accommodation can be booked at the **park office** (☎ 0 7478 3485; cabins 600-1200B) in Pak Bara or through the **online reservation system** (www.dnp.go.th). Before leaving the mainland, load up on food, water and cash as the park shop and canteen is limited.

But it is **Ko Lipe** that boasts the park's largest concentration of private accommodation and traveller amenities. In fact it is in the midst of 'being discovered' by folks who like to find other folks like themselves. Making the journey easier, a ferry service now links Lipe to Ko Lanta and Ko Phi Phi should you develop a phobia of the mainland. In the high season you can also bypass the mainland and ferry straight into Malaysia's Pulau Langkawi (see p804).

There are no ATMs or 7-Elevens (gasp!) and the island has limited capacity to generate power, dispose of litter, properly treat sewer and other big infrastructure projects that typically lag behind the building of hotels and guest houses. But if you're in the neighbourhood, you might as well stop by, everyone else is. Budget options include **Porn Resort** (☎ 08 9464 5765; Sunset Beach; r 700-800B) and **Forra Bamboo** (☎ 08 4407 5691; www.forradiving.com; Sunrise Beach; r 700-1200B).

Getting There & Away

From the mainland, boats disembark from Pak Bara pier to Ko Tarutao (350B, one hour), Ko Adang (5500B, 1½ hours) and Ko Lipe (650B, 2½ hours). The schedule varies with the seasons but there are multiple departures throughout the day during the high season (November to May).

Speedboats also travel from Ko Phi Phi through Ko Lanta to Ko Lipe (from 1800B) about once a day. To travel between the islands of the marine park hire a longtail boat for about 600B.

To travel onward from Pak Bara pier in Satun, you can catch a minibus from Hat Yai (150B, two hours) or hire a share taxi to popular beach destinations, like Krabi (600B).

THAILAND DIRECTORY

ACCOMMODATION

There is a healthy range of budget accommodation in Thailand, kicking off at around 100B to 250B for a dorm bed, or 250B to 300B for a bed-in-a-box single with fan and share dbathroom. Depending on the town, 400B and higher should get you a private bathroom and air-con.

Guest houses are the primary budget options. Many of these establishments started out as family-run businesses and converted homes, though these days the family has moved elsewhere and, in some cases, the old house has been torn down and replaced with an apartment-like tower. Regardless of the structure, guest houses make a community of strangers. There's usually an on-site restaurant that helps subsidise the cheap room rates and where travellers swap advice, and the desk clerks can help you find your way around town.

More impersonal but sometimes the only choice in nontouristed places are the Thai-Chinese hotels that cater to a local clientele. The rates run a little higher (usually around the 500B-plus range) and include a private bathroom, TV and sometimes a view. However, communication with the staff will require a lot of hand gestures.

During Thailand's peak season (December to February), prices increase and availability decreases especially on the islands and other beach resorts.

Unless otherwise noted, reservations at the guest houses are not recommended as standards vary from room to room and year to year, and it's imperative for a traveller to inspect the room beforehand since refunds are not a common practice in Thailand. Advance payment to secure a reservation is also discouraged.

In this chapter, high-season prices have been quoted. Enquiries for discounts can be made during off-tourist seasons.

ACTIVITIES

Despite the hot and humid weather, Thailand offers all sorts of athletic escapes. The most popular pursuits include diving, snorkelling and jungle trekking, but cycling, kayaking and rock climbing aren't far behind.

Cycling

Long-distance cycling is becoming a popular touring option. There are also countrywide cycling and mountain-biking tour programs available through **SpiceRoads** (spiceroads.com) as well as tour operators out of Bangkok and Chiang Mai. Cycling around certain cities in Thailand is a great way to see the sites.

Diving & Snorkelling

Thailand's two coastlines and countless islands are popular among divers for warm, clear waters, abundant marine life and dramatic underwater landscapes. The gulf-coast island of Ko Tao is the country's leading centre for dive certification. Ko Tao is also an easy spot for snorkellers who might be intimidated by the open ocean.

The dive sites in the Gulf of Thailand are nearly as stunning as the dive spots around the northwestern Andaman Sea. Khao Lak has become the Andaman's dive base for liveaboard trips that go out to the Burma Banks (in the Mergui Archipelago) and sites within the Surin and Similan Marine National Parks. There is also some diving around Ko Lanta and plenty of snorkelling around Krabi and Ko Phi Phi.

Most islands have some snorkelling amid offshore reefs that are covered by water no deeper than 2m. Local fisherman will also take out groups for day-long snorkelling tours to various sites around the islands. Masks, fins and snorkels are readily available for rent at dive centres and guest houses in beach areas. If you're particular about the quality and condition of the equipment you use, however, you might be better off bringing your own mask and snorkel – some of the stuff for rent is second rate.

Kayaking & Other Water Sports

The most dramatic scenery for kayaking is along the Andaman coast. It's littered with bearded limestone mountains and semi-submerged caves. Many sea-kayaking tours are available in Krabi and Ao Phang-Nga. Kayaking trips through the Ang Thong Marine Park, off the coast of Ko Samui, is the gulf's premier paddling spot.

Most tour operators use open-deck kayaks since water and air temperatures in Thailand are warm. When signing up for a tour, find out if you or a guide is the primary paddler; some are more sightseeing than exercise.

The rivers of northern Thailand offer white-knuckle, white-water trips during and after the monsoon season. Trips are organised out of Pai and Chiang Mai.

There's some seasonal surfing in Phuket.

Rock Climbing

Krabi's Hat Rai Leh is a world-famous climbing mecca. The huge headland and tiny islands nearby offer high-quality limestone with steep, pocketed walls, overhangs and the occasional hanging stalactite. But what makes climbing here so popular are the views. Your reward for a vertical assault on a cliff isn't just the challenge to gravity but also a bird's eye perspective of a sparkling blue bay and humpbacked mountains. To a lesser extent there is rock climbing outside of Chiang Mai and Lopburi.

Trekking

Trekking is one of northern Thailand's biggest attractions. Typical trekking programs run from one to five days and feature daily walks through forested mountain areas, coupled with overnight stays in hill-tribe villages to satisfy both ethnotourism and ecotourism urges. Chiang Mai is the most popular base for trekking. If you don't have time to do the north, Kanchanaburi has a soft-outdoor-adventure scene and it is a half-day's bus ride from Bangkok.

Other trekking opportunities are available in Thailand's larger national parks, including Khao Sok and Khao Yai, where guest houses can arrange guides.

BOOKS

If you need more guidebook coverage, Lonely Planet titles include *Thailand, Thailand's Islands & Beaches* and *Bangkok*. *Diving & Snorkelling Thailand* is chock-a-block full of colour photos and essential diving information, while *Bangkok Encounter* is a compact guide that's ideal for short-stay visitors.

For pretrip armchair travel, check out James Eckardt's *Bangkok People,* which profiles motorcycle drivers, noodle vendors, go-go dancers and captains of industry. *Fieldwork* (2008), by Mischa Berlinski, is set in a fictional hill-tribe village in northern Thailand with a complicated cast of anthropologists, missionaries and an aimless journalist all pursuing their own version of the title. *Sightseeing* (2005) is a debut collection of short stories by Rattawut Lapcharoensap that gives readers a 'sightseeing' tour into Thai households and coming-of-age moments. On the surface, *Bangkok 8* (2004), by John Burdett, is a hard-boiled whodunit, but the lead character, a Thai-Westerner cop, provides an excellent conduit towards understanding Thai Buddhism. *Touch the Dragon* (1992) is the diary of Karen Connelly, a Canadian who worked as a volunteer in a northern Thai village at the age of 17. Her book about culture and culture shock is well circulated among the paperback-swapping expats posted in rural areas.

The Beach (1998), by Alex Garland, is the ultimate beach read about a backpacker who finds a secluded island utopia off the coast of Ko Samui.

Celebrated writer Pira Sudham was born into a poor family in northeastern Thailand and brilliantly captures the region's struggles against nature and nurture. *Monsoon Country* is one of several titles Sudham wrote originally in English.

BUSINESS HOURS

Most government offices are open from 8.30am to 4.30pm weekdays. Some close from noon to 1pm for lunch, while others might have limited Saturday hours. Banking hours are typically 9.30am to 3.30pm Monday to Friday, though ATMs are accessible 24 hours a day. Private businesses usually operate between 10am to 5pm or 6pm every day; some shops will close on Sunday but it isn't a widespread practice. Shopping malls open from 10am or 11am to 8pm or 9pm.

Most local restaurants are open from 10am until 10pm, with an hour's variation on either side. Some restaurants, specialising in morning meals, close by 3pm.

Any exceptions to these hours are noted in specific listings. Note that all government offices and banks are closed on public holidays.

CLIMATE

Tropical Thailand is warm year-round. The three seasons are hot (from March to May), wet (from June to October) and cool (from November to February). These seasons are variable by about a month on either side. Each region has its extreme season. During the hot season, the northeast is the hottest and most parched. This is also called 'fire season' in the north, especially around Chiang Mai, when farmers burn off debris from their fields. Northern Thailand, especially in the mountains, gets chilly and even cold during the cool season; night-time temperatures in the north can drop as low as 4°C. And during the rainy season, southern Thailand sees days and days of rain, rough seas and even occasional flooding.

See the climate charts on p936 for more.

CUSTOMS

Thailand prohibits the import of firearms and ammunition (unless registered in advance with the police department), illegal drugs and pornographic media. A reasonable amount of clothing for personal use, toiletries and professional instruments are allowed in duty free. Up to 200 cigarettes and 1L of wine or spirits can be brought into the country duty free. The **customs department** (www.customs.go.th) maintains a helpful website with more specific information.

When leaving Thailand, you must obtain an export licence for any antiques or objects of art, including newly cast Buddha images. Export licence applications can be made by submitting two front-view photos of the object(s), a photocopy of your passport, along with the purchase receipt and the object(s) in question, to the **Department of Fine Arts** (DFA; ☎ 0 2628 5032). Allow three to five days for the application and inspection process to be completed.

DANGERS & ANNOYANCES

Although Thailand is not a dangerous country, it's wise to be cautious, particularly if travelling alone. Most tourist-oriented towns will have a **tourist police office** (☎ 1155), with officers who can speak English and liaise with the Thai police. The tourist police can also issue official documentation for insurance purposes if valuables are stolen. It is also not recommended to travel into Thailand's southernmost provinces of Yala, Narathiwat, Pattani and remote corners of Songkhla. See p805 for more information.

Assault

Assault of travellers is rare in Thailand, but it does happen. We've received letters detailing fights between travellers and Thai guest-house workers or other Thai youths. While both parties are probably to blame (and alcohol is often a factor), do be aware that causing a Thai to 'lose face' (feel public embarrassment or humiliation) might elicit an inexplicably strong and violent reaction. While a good tongue-lashing might be an acceptable way to vent anger in the West, it is an invitation for a sneak attack or worse by a Thai. Gun violence is almost unheard of in Thailand, but there have been a few instances of foreigners getting into fights with off-duty police officers who have used their weapons in retaliation.

There are a surprising amount of assaults on Ko Samui and Ko Pha-Ngan considering their idyllic settings. Oftentimes alcohol is the number-one contributor to bad choices and worse outcomes. Ko Pha-Ngan's Full Moon party is becoming increasingly more violent and dangerous. There are often reports of fights, rapes and robbings.

Women, especially solo travellers on Ko Samui or Ko Pha-Ngan, need to be smart and somewhat sober when interacting with the opposite sex, be they Thai or *faràng*. Opportunists pounce when too many whisky buckets are involved. Also be aware that an innocent flirtation might convey firmer intentions to a recipient who does not share your culture's sexual norms.

Drugs

It is illegal to buy, sell or possess opium, heroin, amphetamines, hallucinogenic mushrooms and marijuana in Thailand. A new era of vigilance against drug use and possession was ushered in by former prime minister

Thaksin's 2003 war on drugs; during the height of the campaign police searched partygoers in Bangkok nightclubs and effectively scared many of the recreational drug users into abstinence for a time. Things have relaxed somewhat since the 2006 coup but the country is no longer a chemical free-for-all.

There are severely strict punishments for drug possession and trafficking that are not relaxed for foreigners. Possession of drugs can result in at least one year of prison time. Drug smuggling – defined as attempting to cross a border with drugs in your possession – carries considerably higher penalties, including execution.

In some cases, enforcement of the drug laws is merely leverage for exacting massive bribes. Ko Pha-Ngan's police are notorious for bribable 'sting' operations in which a drug dealer makes an exchange with a customer, followed shortly by a police bust and an onsite demand of 70,000B to avoid arrest.

Another party town, Pai has seen a recent revival of the Thaksin-era urine drug tests on bar patrons by police. As of writing, the strong-arm gift of freedom in such cases is 10,000B. The Pai police have been following a policy of intimidation towards foreign revellers, often fining bars for creative applications of the entertainment prohibitions and entering establishments visibly carrying weapons.

Scams

Thais can be so friendly and laid-back that some visitors are lulled into a false sense of security making them vulnerable to scams of all kinds. Bangkok is especially good at long-involved frauds that dupe travellers into thinking that they've made a friend and are getting a bargain.

Most scams begin in the same way: a friendly and well-dressed Thai, or sometimes even a foreigner, approaches you and strikes up a conversation. Invariably your destination is closed or being cleaned, but your new friend offers several alternative activities, such as sightseeing at smaller temples or shopping at authentic markets. After you've come to trust the person, you are next invited to a gem and jewellery shop because your new-found friend is picking up some merchandise for himself. Somewhere along the way he usually claims to have a connection, often a relative, in your home country (what a coincidence!) with whom he has a regular gem export-import business. One way or another, you are convinced that you can turn a profit by arranging a gem purchase and reselling the merchandise at home. After all, the jewellery shop just happens to be offering a generous discount today – it's a government or religious holiday, or perhaps it's the shop's 10th anniversary, or maybe they've just taken a liking to you!

There are seemingly infinite numbers of variations on the scam described above, almost all of which end up with you making a purchase of small, low-quality gems and posting them to your home country. Once you return home, of course, the cheap jewels turn out to be worth much less than you paid for them (perhaps one-tenth to one-half).

Touts

Touting is a long-time tradition in Asia, and while Thailand doesn't have as many touts as, say, India, it has its share.

In the popular tourist spots you'll be approached, sometimes surrounded, by touts who get a commission for bringing in potential guests. While it is annoying for the traveller, it is an acceptable form of advertising among small-scale businesses. Take anything a tout says with scepticism. Some places refuse to pay commissions so in return the touts will steer customers to places that do pay. This type of commission work is not limited to low-budget guest houses. Travel agencies are notorious for talking newly arrived tourists into staying at badly located, overpriced hotels.

Travel agencies often masquerade as Tourism Authority of Thailand (TAT), the government-funded tourist information office. They might put up agents wearing fake TAT badges or have signs that read TAT in big letters to entice travellers into their offices where they can sell them overpriced bus and train tickets. The official TAT offices do not make hotel or transport bookings. If such a place offers to do this for you, then they are a travel agent not offering tourist information.

When making transportation arrangements, talk to several travel agencies to look for the best price as the commission percentage varies greatly between agents. Also resist any high-sales tactics from an agent trying to sign you up for everything: plane tickets, hotel, tours etc. The most honest Thais are typically very low-key and often sub-par salespeople.

Theft & Fraud

Exercise diligence when it comes to your personal belongings. Ensure that your room is securely locked and carry your most important effects (passport, money, credit cards) on your person. Take care when leaving valuables in hotel safes.

Follow the same practice when you're travelling. A locked bag will not prevent theft on a long-haul bus when you're snoozing and the practised thief has hours alone with your luggage. This is a common occurrence on the tourist buses from Th Khao San to the southern beaches or north to Chiang Mai.

When using a credit card, don't let vendors take your credit card out of your sight to run it through the machine. Unscrupulous merchants have been known to rub off three or four or more receipts with one purchase. Sometimes they wait several weeks – even months – between submitting each charge receipt to the bank, so that you can't remember whether you'd been billed by the same vendor more than once.

To avoid losing all of your travel money in an instant, always use a non-ATM credit card (like MasterCard or Visa that doesn't automatically draw funds directly from a bank account) so that the operator doesn't have access to immediate funds.

DRIVING LICENCE

An International Driving Permit is necessary to drive vehicles in Thailand, but this is rarely enforced for motorcycle hire.

EMBASSIES & CONSULATES

For information on Thai visas, see p831.

Most foreign embassies are located in Bangkok; a few have consulates in Chiang Mai or Phuket.

Australia (Map pp716-17; ☎ 0 2344 6300; www.austembassy.or.th; 37 Th Sathon Tai, Bangkok)
Cambodia (Map pp712-13; ☎ 0 2957 5851/2; Soi Pracha Uthit/Soi 39, Th Ramakamhaeng)
Canada Embassy Bangkok (Map pp716-17; ☎ 0 2636 0540; www.dfait-maeci.gc.ca/bangkok; 15th fl, Abdulrahim Bldg, 990 Th Phra Ram IV); Consulate Chiang Mai (off Map p750; ☎ 0 5385 0147; 151 Superhighway, Tambon Tahsala)
China Embassy Bangkok (Map pp712-13; ☎ 0 2245 7044; www.chinaembassy.or.th; 57 Th Ratchadaphisek); Consulate Chiang Mai (Map p750; ☎ 0 5327 6125; 111 Th Chang Lor)
France Embassy Bangkok (Map pp716-17; ☎ 0 2657 5100; www.ambafrance-th.org; 35 Soi 36, Th Charoen Krung); Consulate Bangkok (Map pp716-17; ☎ 0 2627 2150; 29 Th Sathon Tai); Consulate Chiang Mai (Map p750; ☎ 0 5328 1466; 138 Th Charoen Prathet)
Germany (Map pp716-17; ☎ 0 2287 9000; 9 Th Sathon Tai, Bangkok)
India Embassy Bangkok (Map pp716-17; ☎ 0 2258 03006; 46 Soi Prasanmit/Soi 23, Th Sukhumvit); Consulate Chiang Mai (off Map p750; ☎ 0 5324 3066; 344 Th Charoenrat)
Indonesia (Map pp716-17; ☎ 0 2252 3135; www.kbri-bangkok.com; 600-602 Th Petchaburi, Bangkok)
Japan Embassy Bangkok (Map pp716-17; ☎ 0 2207 8500; 177 Th Withayu); Consulate Chiang Mai (off Map p750; ☎ 0 5320 3367; 104-107 Airport Business Park, Th Mahidol)
Laos (Map pp712-13; ☎ 0 2539 6678; www.bkklaoembassy.com; 502/1-3 Soi Sahakarnpramoon, Pracha Uthit/Soi 39, Th Ramakamhaeng, Bangkok)
Malaysia (Map pp716-17; ☎ 0 2679 2190-9; 35 Th Sathon Tai, Bangkok)
Myanmar (Map pp716-17; ☎ 0 2233 2237, 0 2234 4698; www.mofa.gov.mm; 132 Th Sathon Neua, Bangkok)
New Zealand (Map pp716-17; ☎ 0 2254 2530; www.nzembassy.com; 14th fl, M Thai Tower, All Seasons Pl, 87 Th Withayu, Bangkok)
Philippines (Map pp712-13; ☎ 0 2259 0139; www.philembassy-bangkok.net; 760 Th Sukhumvit, Bangkok)
Singapore (Map pp716-17; ☎ 0 2286 2111; www.mfa.gov.sg/bangkok; 129 Th Sathon Tai, Bangkok)
UK Embassy Bangkok (Map pp716-17; ☎ 0 2305 8333; www.britishembassy.gov.uk; 14 Th Withayu); Consulate Chiang Mai (Map p750; ☎ 0 5326 2015; 198 Th Bamrungrat)
USA Embassy Bangkok (Map pp716-17; ☎ 0 2205 4000; bangkok.usembassy.gov; 95 Th Withayu, Bangkok); Consulate Chiang Mai (Map p750; ☎ 0 5310 7700; 387 Th Wichayanon)
Vietnam (Map pp716-17; ☎ 0 2251 5836-8; www.vietnamembassy-thailand.org; 83/1 Th Withayu, Bangkok)

EMERGENCIES

Fire (☎ 199)
Police/Emergency (☎ 191)
Tourist police (☎ 1155; 24hr)

FESTIVALS & EVENTS

Many Thai festivals are linked to Buddhist holy days and follow the lunar calendar. Thus they fall on different dates each year, depending on the phases of the moon. Many provinces hold annual festivals or fairs to promote their agricultural specialities. A complete, up-to-date schedule of events around the country is available from TAT offices in each region. Businesses typically close and transport becomes difficult preceding any public holiday or national festivals. See opposite for public holiday listings. The following are national festivals or Buddhist holy days:

Songkran Festival From 12 to 14 April, Buddha images are 'bathed', monks and elders have their hands respectfully sprinkled with water by younger Thais and a lot of water is wildly tossed about on everyone else for fun. Songkran generally gives everyone a chance to release their frustrations and literally cool off during the peak of the hot season. Bangkok and Chiang Mai are major water battlegrounds.

Magha Puja (Maakhá Buuchaa) Held on the full moon of the third lunar month to commemorate Buddha preaching to 1250 enlightened monks who came to hear him 'without prior summons'. It culminates with a candlelit walk around the main chapel at every wat.

Visakha Puja (Wísǎakhà Buuchaa) This event falls on the 15th day of the waxing moon in the sixth lunar month and commemorates the date of the Buddha's birth, enlightenment and passing away. Activities are centred on the wat.

Loi Krathong On the night of the full moon, small lotus-shaped baskets or boats made of banana leaves containing flowers, incense, candles and a coin are floated on Thai rivers, lakes and canals.

FOOD & DRINK

Food

Thai food is a complex balance of spicy, salty, sweet and sour. The ingredients are fresh and light with lots of lemongrass, basil, coriander and mint. The chilli peppers pack a slow, nose-running, tongue-searing burn. And pungent *náam plaa* (fish sauce; generally made from anchovies) adds a touch of the salty sea. Throw in a little zest of lime and a pinch of sugar and the ingredients make a symphony of flavours that becomes more interesting with each bite. A relationship with Thai food has a long courtship phase – at first the flavours are too assertive and foreign, the hot too hot, the fish sauce too fishy. But with practise you'll smell rice cooking in the morning and crave a fiery curry instead of dull toast and jam. Now you are 'eating', which in Thai literally means to 'eat rice', or *kin khâo*.

Thailand is a country where it is cheaper and tastier to eat out than to cook at home. Day and night markets, pushcart vendors, makeshift stalls, open-air restaurants – prices stay low because of few or no overheads, and cooks become famous in all walks of life for a particular dish. No self-respecting shoestringer would shy away from the pushcarts in Thailand for fear of stomach troubles. The hygiene standards are some of the best in the region, and sitting next to the wok you can see all the action, unlike some of the guest houses where food is assembled in a darkened hovel.

Take a walk through the day markets and you will see mounds of clay-coloured pastes all lined up like art supplies. These are the finely ground herbs and seasonings that create the backbone for Thai *kaeng* (curries). The paste is thinned with coconut milk and decorated with vegetables and meat. Although it is the consistency of a watery soup, *kaeng* is not eaten like Western-style soup, but is ladled onto a plate of rice.

For breakfast and late-night snacks, Thais nosh on *kǔaytǐaw*, a noodle soup with chicken or pork and vegetables. There are two major types of noodles you can choose from: *sên lek* (thin) and *sên yài* (wide and flat). Before you dig into your steaming bowl, first use the chopsticks (or a spoon) to cut the noodles into smaller segments so they are easier to pick up. Then add to taste a few teaspoonfuls of the provided spices: dried red chilli, sugar, fish sauce and vinegar. Now you have the true taste of Thailand in front of you. The weapons of choice when eating noodles (either *kǔaytǐaw* or *phàt thai*) are chopsticks, a rounded soup spoon or a fork.

Not sure what to order at some of the popular dinner restaurants? These are the greatest hits of the culinary menu:

- *kài phàt bai kà-phrao* – fiery stir-fry of chopped chicken, chillies, garlic and fresh basil
- *khâo phàt* – fried rice
- *phàt phrík thai krà-thiam* – stir-fried chicken or pork with black pepper and garlic
- *phàt thai* – fried rice noodles, bean sprouts, peanuts, eggs, chillies and often prawns
- *phàt phàk khanáa* – stir-fried Chinese greens, simple but delicious

Thais are social eaters: meals are rarely taken alone and dishes are meant to be shared. Usually a small army of plates will be placed in the centre of the table, with individual servings of rice in front of each diner. The protocol goes like this – ladle a spoonful of food at a time on to your plate of rice. Dishes aren't passed in Thailand; instead you reach across the table to the different items. Using the spoon like a fork and your fork like a knife, steer the food (with the fork) onto your spoon, which enters your mouth. To the Thais placing a fork in the mouth is just plain weird. When you are full, leave a little rice on your plate (an empty plate is a silent request for more rice) and place your fork so that it is cradled by the spoon in the centre of the plate.

Even when eating with a gang of *faràng*, it is still wise to order 'family style', as dishes are rarely synchronised. Ordering individually will leave one person staring politely at a piping hot plate and another staring wistfully at the kitchen.

Drink

Water purified for drinking is simply called *náam dèum* (drinking water), whether boiled or filtered. All water offered in restaurants, offices or homes will be purified. Ice is generally safe in Thailand. *Chaa* (tea) and *kaa-fae* (coffee) are prepared strong, milky and sweet – an instant morning buzz.

Thanks to the tropical bounty, exotic fruit juices are sold on every corner. Thais prefer a little salt to cut the sweetness of the juice; the salt also has some mystical power to make a hot day tolerable. Most drinks are available in a clear plastic bag designed especially for takeaway customers; in time you'll come to prefer the bag to a conventional glass.

Cheap beer appears hand-in-hand with backpacker ghettos. Beer Chang and Beer Singha (pronounced 'sing', not 'sing-ha') are a couple of local brands you'll learn to love, although they pack a punch. Thais have created yet another innovative method for beating the heat; they drink their beer with ice to keep the beverage cool and crisp.

More of a ritual than a beverage, Thai whisky usually runs with a distinct crowd – soda water, Coke and ice. Fill the short glass with ice cubes, two-thirds whisky, one-third soda and a splash of Coke. Thai tradition dictates the youngest in the crowd is responsible for filling the other drinkers' glasses. Many travellers prefer to go straight to the ice bucket with shared straws, not forgetting a dash of Red Bull for a cocktail to keep them going.

GAY & LESBIAN TRAVELLERS

Gays and lesbians won't have a problem travelling through Thailand as the country has a long history of homosexuality. Prominent gay communities exist in large cities such as Bangkok and Chiang Mai, and gay-pride events are celebrated in Bangkok, Pattaya and Phuket. Although public displays of affection are common (and are usually platonic) between members of the same sex, you should refrain from anything beyond friendly hand-holding, for the sake of social etiquette.

Gay, lesbian and transsexual Thais are generally tolerated, living peaceably in even the most conservative Thai towns. All is not love and understanding, though. Labelled 'sexual deviants', suspected gays are barred from studying to become teachers or from joining the military.

Utopia (www.utopia-asia.com) is a good starting point for more information on Thailand for gay or lesbian travellers.

HOLIDAYS

Government offices and banks close on the following days:

New Year's Day 1 January
Chakri Day 6 April; commemorating the founder of the Chakri dynasty, Rama I.
Coronation Day 5 May; commemorating the 1946 coronation of HM the King and HM the Queen.
Khao Phansaa July (date varies); the beginning of Buddhist 'lent'.
Queen's Birthday 12 August
Chulalongkorn Day 23 October
Ork Phansaa October/November (date varies); the end of Buddhist 'lent'.
King's Birthday 5 December
Constitution Day 10 December

Also see p825 for details on national festivals and Buddhist holy days.

INTERNET ACCESS

You'll find plenty of internet cafes in most towns and cities, and in many guest houses and hotels as well. The going rate is anywhere from 40B to 120B an hour, depending on how much competition there is. Connections tend to be pretty fast and have been speeded up with the proliferation of wi-fi access, which is fairly widespread throughout the country, including the rural northeast. Only Bangkok has been slow to make wi-fi affordably accessible. Most guest houses will offer wi-fi for free, while high-end hotels offer it only in lobbies for a usage fee.

INTERNET RESOURCES

Bangkok Post (www.bangkokpost.com) This English-language newspaper posts its newspaper content online.
Nation (www.nationmultimedia.com) Another English-language newspaper that also posts content on the web.
One Stop Thailand (www.onestopthailand.com) Comprehensive tourism site to popular Thai destinations.
Thailand Daily (www.thailanddaily.com) Part of World News Network, offering a thorough digest of Thailand-related news from English news sources.
ThaiVisa.com (www.thaivisa.com) Extensive info on visas, user forums and news alerts.
Tourism Authority of Thailand (www.tourismthailand.org) Thailand's official tourism website covers major tourist spots and lists operators.

LEGAL MATTERS

In general, Thai police don't hassle foreigners, especially tourists. One major exception is in regard to drugs (see p823).

If you are arrested for any offence, the police will allow you the opportunity to make a phone call to your embassy or consulate in Thailand, if you have one, or to a friend or relative if not. Thai law does not presume an indicted detainee to be either 'guilty' or 'innocent' but rather a 'suspect', whose guilt or innocence will be decided in court. Trials are usually speedy.

MAPS

ThinkNet (www.thinknet.co.th) produces high-quality city and country map series, including interactive map CDs to Bangkok. For GPS users in Thailand, most prefer the Garmin units and the associated map products that are accurate and fully routed. An online world map showing adequate street detail for Thailand can be found at **Multimap** (www.multimap.com).

MEDIA

Newspapers

Thailand is considered to have the freest print media in Southeast Asia, though it is currently undergoing a period of political censorship and retaliation during the ongoing political crisis. During quieter times, all papers exercise self-censorship in matters relating to the monarchy, and the Royal Police Department reserves the power to suspend publishing licences for national security reasons. The *Bangkok Post* and the *Nation* are the country's two English-language newspapers.

> **LEGAL AGE**
> - voting starts at 18
> - you can begin driving at 18
> - sex is legal at 15

Radio

Thailand has more than 400 radio stations, most of them government owned. There are many more community-based pirate stations operating with low frequencies. English-language broadcasts of the international news services can be picked up over short-wave radio. The frequencies and schedules appear in the *Bangkok Post* and *Nation*.

TV

Thailand possesses six VHF TV networks based in Bangkok that are all owned by the government. There is also TrueVision UBC cable with international programming.

MONEY

The *baht* (B) is divided into 100 *satang*, although 25 and 50 *satang* are the smallest coins that you're likely to see. Coins come in 1B, 2B, 5B and 10B denominations. Notes are in 20B (green), 50B (blue), 100B (red), 500B (purple) and 1000B (beige) denominations of varying shades and sizes. Note that the newly introduced 2B coin is similar in size to the 1B coin.

ATMs

All major Thai banks, which are well distributed throughout the country, offer ATM services; most of the machines will accept international credit and debit cards. ATMs typically dispense 1000B notes that should be broken at 7-Elevens or guest houses rather than in the market.

Bargaining

Bargaining is mandatory in markets and small family-run stores that do not have posted prices. If there is a price written on or near the product then it is non-negotiable. Fares must also be negotiated with túk-túk and taxi drivers (unless the cab is metered). By and large bargaining is not appropriate in hotels or guest houses, but you can ask politely if there's anything cheaper. Always smile and never become frustrated.

Credit Cards

Credit cards are widely accepted at hotels, high-end restaurants and other upscale business establishments. Visa and MasterCard are the most commonly accepted. American Express (Amex) is accepted rarely and usually only at international chain hotels. Cash advances are available on Visa and MasterCard at many banks and exchange booths.

Exchanging Money

Banks give the best exchange rates and hotels give the worst. In the larger towns and tourist destinations, there are also foreign-exchange kiosks that open longer hours, usually from 8am to 8pm. Since banks charge commission and duty for each travellers cheque cashed, use larger cheque denominations to save on commission. British pounds and euros are second to the US dollar in general acceptability.

POST

The Thai postal system is relatively efficient and few travellers complain about undelivered mail or lost parcels. Never send cash or small valuable objects through the postal system, even if the items are insured. Poste restante can be received at any town that has a post office.

RESPONSIBLE TRAVEL

Be aware about having a negative impact on the environment or the local culture. Read the Culture, p701, for guidance on observing social mores. See the boxed text Thailand's Hill-tribe Communities, p760, for etiquette considerations in tribal peoples' villages. Also see the boxed text Fragile Paradise, p810, for environmental considerations on the Thai islands.

Despite Thailand's reputation among sex tourists, prostitution was declared illegal in the 1950s, though this is not enforced and the industry offers a living for uneducated women. The Thai police, however, do enforce the age restrictions for prostitutes and often work with foreign governments to apprehend foreign nationals coming to Thailand in search of child prostitutes. If you suspect such behaviour, you can contact **End Child Prostitution & Traffic International** (Ecpat; ☎ 0 2215 3388; www.ecpat.org; 328 Th Phayathai, Bangkok 10400).

EXCHANGE RATES

Exchange rates at the time of going to press:

Country	Unit	Baht (B)
Australia	A$1	29.54
Cambodia	1000r	8.05
Canada	C$1	31.28
Euro zone	€1	48.99
Japan	¥100	37.23
Laos	1000 kip	3.92
Malaysia	RM1	9.66
New Zealand	NZ$1	24.17
Singapore	S$1	23.75
UK	£1	53.36
USA	US$1	33.41

STUDYING

Thai cooking, traditional medicine, language, *muay thai* (Thai boxing): the possibilities of studying in Thailand are endless and range from formal lectures to week-long retreats.

Unique to Buddhism is the system of meditation known as *vipassana*, a Pali word that roughly translates as 'insight'. Foreigners who come to study *vipassana* can choose from dozens of temples and meditation centres. Thai language is usually the medium of instruction but several places provide instruction in English. See the boxed text Mindfulness: Meditation Courses & Retreats (p722) for more information.

Described by some as a 'brutally pleasant experience', Thai massage uses the hands, thumbs, fingers, elbows, forearms, knees and feet to work the traditional pressure points. The objective is to distribute energies evenly throughout the nervous system to create a harmony of physical energy flows. Thailand offers ample opportunities to study its unique tradition of massage therapy. Wat Pho (p719) in Bangkok is considered the master source for all Thai massage pedagogy, although Chiang Mai (p755) boasts a 'softer' version.

Training in *muay thai* takes place at dozens of boxing camps around the country. Be forewarned, however: training is gruelling and features full-contact sparring. The website www.muaythai.com contains loads of information including the addresses of training camps. Also see the Bangkok (p703) and Chiang Mai (p754) sections for information on *muay thai* training programs in these two cities.

It is most affordable for shoestringers to study Thai language in Chiang Mai. See p754 for further detail.

TELEPHONE

The telephone system in Thailand has been deregulated and the once state-owned entities have been privatised. The telecommunications sector is dominated by the now-private TOT Public Company Limited (formerly Telephone Organisation of Thailand, or TOT) and CAT Telecom Public Company Limited (formerly Communications Authority of Thailand, or CAT). For domestic service, TOT and its subsidiary TT&T are the primary service providers, while CAT and TOT compete for international service.

The telephone country code for Thailand is ☎ 66 and is used when calling the country from abroad. You must also dial an international exchange prefix (for the US it is ☎ 001, for the UK ☎ 00) before the country code.

Thailand no longer uses separate area codes for the provinces, so all phone numbers in the country use eight digits (preceded by a ☎ 0 if you're dialling domestically). To accommodate the growth in mobile phone usage, Thailand has introduced an '8' prefix to all mobile numbers; ie ☎ 0 1234 5678 is now ☎ 08 1234 5678. If you're calling a mobile phone from overseas you would omit the initial '0' for both mobile and land-line numbers.

If you want to call an international number from a telephone in Thailand, you must first dial an international access code before dialling the country code followed by the subscriber number. In Thailand, there are varying international access codes charging different rates per minute. The standard direct-dial prefix is ☎ 001; it is operated by CAT and is considered to have the best sound quality and connects to the largest number of countries, but it is the most expensive. The next best is ☎ 007, a prefix operated by TOT with reliable quality and slightly cheaper rates. Economy rates are available with ☎ 008 and ☎ 009; both of which use voice-over internet protocol (VoIP), with varying but adequate sound quality.

Many expats are now using **DeeDial** (www.deedial.com), a direct-dial service that requires a prepaid account managed through the internet. The cheapest service it offers is the 'ring-back' feature, which circumvents local charges on your mobile phone.

There are also a variety of international phonecards available through **CAT** (www.cthai.com) offering promotional rates as low as 1B per minute.

Dial ☎ 100 for operator-assisted international calls. To make a collect (or reverse charges) call, use this prefix. Alternatively contact your long-distance carrier for their overseas operator number, a toll-free call, or try ☎ 001 9991 2001 from a CAT phone and ☎ 1 800 000 120 from a TOT phone.

TOILETS

As in many other Asian countries, the 'squat toilet' is the norm in Thailand except in hotels and guest houses that are geared towards tourists and international business travellers. These sit more-or-less flush with the surface of the floor, with two footpads on either side. You flush by filling the plastic bowl beside the toilet with water and pouring it into the toilet.

Even in places where sit-down toilets are installed, the plumbing may not be designed to take toilet paper. In such cases the usual washing bucket will be standing nearby or there will be a waste basket where you're supposed to place used toilet paper.

TOURIST INFORMATION

The **Tourist Authority of Thailand** (TAT; www.tourismthailand.org) has offices throughout the country that are helpful for local maps and sightseeing advice. Do note that these offices do not book accommodation, transport or tours. Contact information for regional offices is listed under each town.

TRAVELLERS WITH DISABILITIES

Thailand presents one large, ongoing obstacle course for the mobility-impaired. With its high kerbs, uneven pavements and nonstop traffic, Bangkok can be particularly difficult. Rarely are there ramps or other access points for wheelchairs.

For wheelchair travellers, any trip to Thailand will require advance planning. The book *Exotic Destinations for Wheelchair Travelers* by Ed Hansen and Bruce Gordon contains a useful chapter on seven locations in Thailand. See p943 for organisations that promote travel for special-needs individuals.

VISAS

The **Ministry of Foreign Affairs** (www.mfa.go.th) oversees immigration and visas issues. Check the website or the nearest Thai embassy or consulate for application procedures and costs. In the past five years there have been some shifting rules on visas and visa extensions; **Thaivisa** (www.thaivisa.com) stays abreast of any changes and developments.

Visa Exemptions & Tourist Visas

The Thai government allows tourist visa exemptions for 41 different nationalities, including those from most of Europe, Australia, New Zealand and the USA, to enter the country without a prearranged visa. Note that in 2008, the length of stay for citizens of exempted countries was slightly altered from years past. It's now a 30-day visa if arriving by air and a 15-day visa if arriving by land (no fee is charged in either case).

Without proof of an onward ticket and sufficient funds for one's projected stay any visitor can be denied entry, but in practice your ticket and funds are rarely checked if you're dressed neatly for the immigration check.

If you plan to stay in Thailand longer than 30 days (or 15 days for land arrivals), you should apply for the 60-day Tourist Visa from a Thai consulate or embassy abroad before you enter the country.

Visa Extensions

You can extend your visa in Thailand by crossing a land border (which will give you another 15 days) or applying for a visa extension at the nearest immigration office. The usual fee for a visa extension is 1900B and the stay is usually extended for seven to 10 days (depending on the immigration office); this should be handled before the visa expires. For all visa extensions, bring along two passport-sized photos and one copy each of the photo and visa pages of your passport. Remember to dress neatly and visit the immigration office yourself, rather than hiring a third party to do it as proxy.

If you overstay your visa, the usual penalty is a fine of 500B per day, with a 20,000B limit. Fines can be paid at the airport or in advance at an immigration office. If you've overstayed only one day, you don't have to pay. Children under 14 travelling with a parent do not have to pay the penalty.

The following are immigration offices where visa extensions can be handled:

Bangkok (Map pp716-17; ☎ 0 2287 3101; Soi Suan Phlu, Th Sathon Tai; ⏲ 9am-noon & 1-4.30pm Mon-Fri, 9am-noon Sat)

Chiang Mai (off Map p750; ☎ 0 5320 1755-6; Th Mahidon; ⏲ 8.30am-4.30pm Mon-Fri)

Krabi (☎ 0 7561 1350; Th Chamai Anuson, Krabi Town)

Phuket (off Map p813; ☎ 0 7622 1905; Th Phuket, Phuket Town)

VOLUNTEERING

Voluntary and paid positions with charitable organisations can be found in the education, development or public-health sectors. In recent years Thailand has had a growing informal voluntourism industry that places short-term visitors in do-good positions.

One particularly vulnerable group in Thailand are the refugees from Myanmar. See the boxed text Of Migrants and Misfortune, p748 for information about the humanitarian crisis and groups working to aid those in need.

Other organisations working with displaced people from Myanmar are based in Chiang Mai and include **Cultural Canvas Thailand** (☎ 08 6920 2451; www.culturalcanvas.com; Chiang Mai), which unites volunteers with positions in a variety of Chiang Mai–based social-justice organisations, such as migrant learning centres and hill-tribe schools. Time commitments vary from one-day art workshops to month-long stints teaching English.

The minority hill-tribe communities often struggle with fitting into the mainstream society due to a lack of access to education and full citizenship rights and displacement from arable land. Many groups in Chiang Rai work with ethnic villagers in the areas of education and skills building. **Mirror Art Group** (☎ 0 5373 7412-3; www.mirrorartgroup.org; 106 Moo 1, Ban Huay Khom, Tambon Mae Yao, Chiang Rai) operates volunteer teaching programs that need English speakers and IT specialists for a minimum of five days. Donations of books, toys and clothes are also appreciated. **Hill Area and Community Development Foundation** (☎ 0 5371 5696; Soi 4, 129/1 Mu 4, Th Pa-Ngiw, Rop Wiang, Chiang Rai) has volunteering opportunities for teaching English in the Mae Chan/Mae Salong area for six months, but shorter stays may be possible.

Two towns in the northeast have developed as voluntourism bases: see Surin (p774) and

Nong Khai (p779) for profiles of organisations that place volunteers in the community.

WOMEN TRAVELLERS

By and large women are safe travelling in groups or solo through Thailand. Extra caution needs to be exercised at night, especially when returning home from a bar or arriving in a new town late at night. Thais, both men and women, are chatty and will extend the hand of friendship, give you a ride or take you to the disco. Often accepting these invitations is a fun experience, but women should be aware that Thai men don't adhere to their own culture's rules when dealing with foreign women. While hand-holding, hugging or any other public contact between members of the opposite sex is a huge no-no in Thai society, Thai men think it is appropriate to touch (however innocently) foreign women even if the advances aren't encouraged.

Despite Thailand's peaceful nature, rape is a concern. Over the past decade, several foreign women have been attacked while travelling alone in remote areas and there have been several high-profile murders. Still, given the huge tourist numbers visiting Thailand, there is no need to be paranoid.

WORKING

Teaching English is one of the easiest ways to immerse yourself into a Thai community. Those with academic credentials, such as teaching certificates or degrees in English as a second language (ESL) or English as a foreign language (EFL), get first crack at the better-paying jobs at universities and international schools. But there are hundreds of language schools for every variety of native English speaker.

Maintained by an EFL teacher in Bangkok, **Ajarn.com** (www.ajarn.com) has job listings and tips on where to find teaching jobs and how to deal with Thai classrooms.

Rajabhat University has English-teaching positions available in 41 schools across the country. These positions pay well by Thai standards, and most students are preparing to be the country's next generation of primary- and secondary-school English teachers.

Vietnam

HIGHLIGHTS

- **Hanoi** (p842) Explore the captivating capital, a city steeped in history, pulsating with life, bubbling with commerce and buzzing with motorbikes.
- **Halong Bay** (p861) Experience nature at its most expressive, where hundreds, nay thousands, of limestone peaks soar above the shimmering seas.
- **Hoi An** (p881) Fall for the old-world atmosphere of the town, score some new threads and flop on the blissful beaches.
- **Nha Trang** (p886) Welcome to party central, a place where even the boat trips involve drinking and dancing, plus striking beaches and great diving.
- **Mekong Delta** (p916) Enter a world of water, a bountiful land carpeted in dazzling greens, a place of slow boating, markets floating and fresh fish.
- **Off the beaten track** (p868) Head to the northern mountains, home to traditional hill tribes, stunning scenery and remote tribal villages set in lush terraced valleys.

FAST FACTS

- **Budget** US$20 to US$35 a day
- **Capital** Hanoi
- **Costs** guest house in Hanoi US$8 to US$15, four-hour bus ride US$5 to US$8, beer US$1
- **Country code** ☎ 84
- **Languages** Vietnamese, ethnic dialects
- **Money** US$1 = approx 17,725d (dong)
- **Phrases** *xin chao* (hello), *tam biet* (goodbye), *cam on* (thanks), *xin loi* (sorry), *khong cam on, di bo* (no thanks, I'll walk)
- **Population** 86 million
- **Time** GMT + seven hours
- **Visas** arrange in advance via a Vietnamese embassy; US$30 to US$60 for 30 days

TRAVEL HINT

To avoid unwanted attention from persistent touts, say no politely and keep walking; escape the big cities to enjoy the country's natural beauty and warm people.

OVERLAND ROUTES

Take a boat to Phnom Penh in Cambodia from Chau Doc, or a high-speed hydrofoil to the Chinese border from Halong City. Those who prefer terra firma can travel via road to Cambodia and Laos, or by bus or rail to China.

Welcome to a world where the colours are more vivid, where the landscapes are bolder, the coastline more dramatic, where the history is more compelling, where the tastes are more divine, where life is lived in the fast lane. This world is Vietnam, the latest Asian dragon to awake from its slumber.

Nature has blessed Vietnam with a bountiful harvest of soaring mountains, a killer coastline and radiant rice fields, Vietnam is a cracker. Inland, peasant women in conical hats still tend to their fields, children ride buffalos along country paths and minority people scratch out a living from impossible gradients.

Vietnam is a nation of determined optimists who have weathered war after war, survived colonialism *and* communism, and are now getting to grips with the wheeler-dealer world of capitalism. Fiercely protective of their independence and sovereignty, the Vietnamese are graciously welcoming of foreigners who come as guests not conquerors.

Don't believe the hype. Or the propagandist party billboards that are as common as statues of 'Uncle Ho'. Believe your senses, as you discover one of the most enriching, enlivening and exotic countries on earth.

CURRENT EVENTS

Politically, Vietnam remains a perplexing place. Apparently, so we're told, it's a communist country, but it's hard to believe. Capitalism is no longer a four-letter word. It's full steam ahead, China style, with Vietnam consistently one of the world's fastest-growing economies for more than a decade now. Ho Chi Minh may be a hero, but it is Deng Xiaoping's school of economics that has prevailed, not the austere collectivism once espoused by Ho.

The cities are awash with money, but not everyone is getting a share. Transparency International rated Vietnam 121st out of 179 countries surveyed for their corruption index, on a par with Nigeria. Although the authorities have embarked on several campaigns to stamp out corruption, there was a severe setback in the summer of 2008 when two journalists were jailed for exposing a major scandal where public officials were using state money to bet on major football matches in Europe.

Some observers argue this is why Vietnam needs to embrace democracy, to hold the politicians accountable for their actions; others argue that a firm hand drives the country forward economically, creating a stable environment for investors. Either way, like the rest of the world, Vietnam has had some tough times as the global downturn has spread.

The Central Highlands continues to be an Achilles heel for the Hanoi government. As more and more highland areas were settled by ethnic Vietnamese, the ethnic minorities protested against this Vietnamisation of their traditional land and culture. The Vietnamese government cracked down hard, sending hundreds of political refugees fleeing to Cambodia where they have been sent back by an unsympathetic government in Phnom Penh. Today there is a tense stalemate in the region and there are still some sensitive areas for foreigners.

The future is bright, but ultimate success depends on how well the Vietnamese can follow the Chinese road to development: economic liberty without political liberties. With only two million paid-up members of the Communist Party and 86 million Vietnamese, it is a road they must tread carefully.

HISTORY

Early Vietnam

The sophisticated Indian-influenced kingdom of Funan flourished from the 1st to the 6th centuries AD in the Mekong Delta area. Archaeological evidence reveals that Funan's busy trading port of Oc-Eo in the Mekong area had contact with China, India, Persia and even the Mediterranean.

Around the late 2nd century AD when the Cham empire was putting down roots in the Danang area, the Chinese conquered the Red River Delta near Hanoi. So began a 1000-year cycle of Vietnamese resistance against Chinese rule, while simultaneously adopting many Chinese innovations. The most famous uprising during this period (ending in AD 938) was the rebellion of the two Trung sisters (Hai Ba Trung), who drowned themselves rather than surrender to the Chinese.

By the 10th century, Vietnam declared independence from China and so began almost 1000 years of Vietnamese independence. During this era, the Vietnamese successfully repulsed attacks by the Khmers, Chams, Mongols and Chinese, eventually assimilating the Cham empire into an expanding Vietnam.

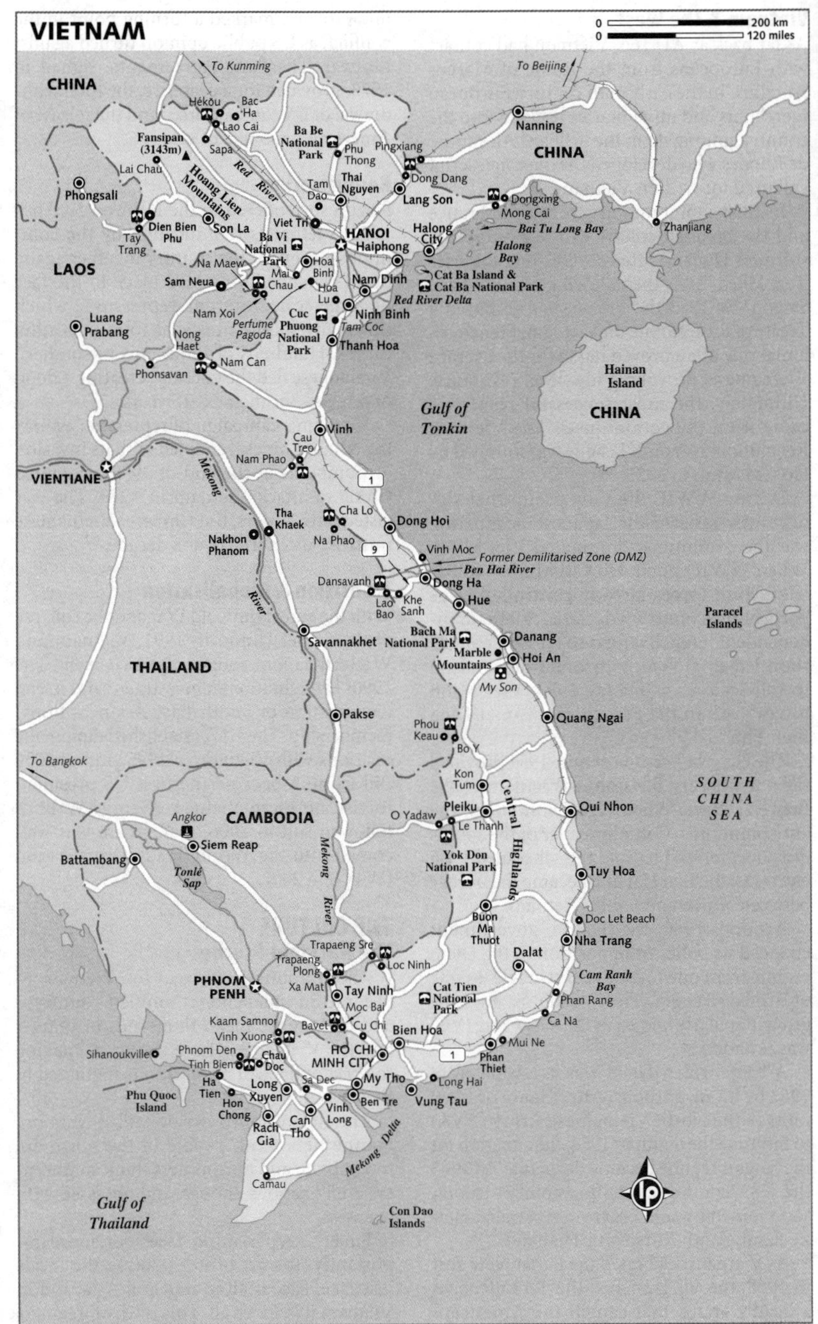
VIETNAM
0 200 km
0 120 miles
To Kunming
To Beijing
CHINA
Hékou
Bac Ha
Lao Cai
Sapa
Fansipan (3143m)
Lai Chau
Phongsali
Hoang Lien Mountains
Red River
Ba Be National Park
Phu Thong
Pingxiang
Dong Dang
Nanning
CHINA
Tam Dao
Thai Nguyen
Lang Son
Dongxing
Mong Cai
Bai Tu Long Bay
Zhanjiang
Dien Bien Phu
Tay Trang
Son La
Viet Tri
HANOI
Haiphong
Halong City
Halong Bay
Ba Vi National Park
LAOS
Na Maew
Mai Chau
Hoa Binh
Hoa Lu
Nam Dinh
Cat Ba Island &
Cat Ba National Park
Sam Neua
Red River Delta
Nam Xoi
Perfume Pagoda
Cuc Phuong National Park
Ninh Binh
Tam Coc
Luang Prabang
Nong Haet
Nam Can
Thanh Hoa
Phonsavan
Hainan Island
CHINA
Gulf of Tonkin
Vinh
Cau Treo
Nam Phao
VIENTIANE
Mekong
1
Tha Khaek
Nakhon Phanom
Cha Lo
Na Phao
Dong Hoi
9
Vinh Moc
Former Demilitarised Zone (DMZ)
Ben Hai River
Dansavanh
Lao Bao
Khe Sanh
Dong Ha
Hue
River
Paracel Islands
Savannakhet
Bach Ma National Park
Danang
Marble Mountains
Hoi An
My Son
THAILAND
Quang Ngai
Pakse
Phou Keau
Bo Y
To Bangkok
Kon Tum
SOUTH CHINA SEA
Pleiku
Qui Nhon
CAMBODIA
O Yadaw
Le Thanh
Central Highlands
Angkor
Siem Reap
Yok Don National Park
Battambang
Tonlé Sap
Mekong River
Tuy Hoa
Buon Ma Thuot
Doc Let Beach
Nha Trang
Trapaeng Sre
Loc Ninh
Dalat
Trapaeng Plong
Cam Ranh Bay
PHNOM PENH
Xa Mat
Tay Ninh
Cat Tien National Park
Phan Rang
Moc Bai
Kaam Samnor
Bavet
Cu Chi
Ca Na
Vinh Xuong
Bien Hoa
Mui Ne
Sihanoukville
Phnom Den
Chau Doc
HO CHI MINH CITY
1
Phan Thiet
Tinh Bien
Long Xuyen
Sa Dec
My Tho
Long Hai
Ha Tien
Ben Tre
Vung Tau
Phu Quoc Island
Hon Chong
Rach Gia
Can Tho
Vinh Long
Mekong Delta
Camau
Gulf of Thailand
Con Dao Islands

Vietnam & the West

As far back as AD 166, Vietnam had contact with Europeans from the Rome of Marcus Aurelius. In the early 16th century European merchants and missionaries trickled into the country, among them the brilliant Alexandre de Rhodes who developed the *quoc ngu* script still used for written Vietnamese.

In 1858 a joint military force from France and the Spanish colony of the Philippines stormed Danang after several missionaries were killed. Early the following year, it seized Saigon. By 1883 the French had imposed a Treaty of Protectorate on Vietnam; French colonial rule often proved harsh for the average Vietnamese, provoking low-level resistance. Ultimately, the most successful resistance came from the communists. The Vietnam Revolutionary Youth League was founded by Ho Chi Minh in 1925.

During WWII, the only group that significantly resisted the Japanese occupation was the communist-dominated Viet Minh. When WWII ended, Ho Chi Minh – whose Viet Minh forces already controlled large parts of the country – declared Vietnam independent. French efforts to reassert control soon led to violent confrontations and on to full-scale war. In May 1954, Viet Minh forces overran the French garrison at Dien Bien Phu.

The Geneva Accords of mid-1954 provided for a temporary division of Vietnam at the Ben Hai River. When Ngo Dinh Diem, the anticommunist, Catholic leader of the southern zone, refused to hold the scheduled 1956 elections, the Ben Hai line became the border between North and South Vietnam.

Around 1960 the Hanoi government changed its policy of opposition to the Diem regime from one of 'political struggle' to one of 'armed struggle'. The communist guerrilla group popularly known as the Viet Cong (VC) was founded.

A brutal ruler, Diem was assassinated in 1963 by his own troops. After Hanoi ordered units of the North Vietnamese Army (NVA) to infiltrate the South in 1964, the situation for the Saigon regime became desperate. In 1965 the USA committed its first combat troops, soon joined by soldiers from Australia, New Zealand, South Korea and Thailand.

As Vietnam celebrated the Lunar New Year in 1968, the VC launched the Tet Offensive, a deadly attack that caught the Americans unaware and marked a turning point in the conflict, as US public opinion turned against the war. The Paris Agreements, signed in 1973, provided for a ceasefire, the total withdrawal of US combat forces and the release of American prisoners of war.

Reunification

Saigon surrendered to the NVA on 30 April 1975. Vietnam's reunification by the communists brought the country together again, but it remained a divided place in the face of large-scale internal repression, which saw many southerners sent to re-education camps. Hundreds of thousands of southern Vietnamese fled the country, creating a flood of refugees for the next 15 years.

Vietnam's campaign of repression against the ethnic Chinese, coupled with its invasion of Cambodia at the end of 1978, prompted China to attack Vietnam in 1979. The war lasted only 17 days, but Chinese–Vietnamese mistrust lasted well over a decade.

Transition & Globalisation

With the end of the Cold War and the collapse of the Soviet Union in 1991, Vietnam and Western nations sought *rapprochement*. The 1990s brought foreign investment and Asean (Association of South-East Asian Nations) membership. The USA established diplomatic relations with Vietnam in 1995, and in 2000 Bill Clinton became the first US president to visit northern Vietnam. George W Bush followed suit in 2006, as Vietnam was welcomed into the World Trade Organisation (WTO) in 2007.

THE CULTURE

The National Psyche

It's been a long hard road for Vietnam to become an independent, unified country – and by long we mean thousands of years – and the Vietnamese have the art of making the best of the worst conditions ingrained in their DNA.

The north–south divide still lingers on. Southerners think people in the north are too uptight, and northerners think southerners aren't serious enough and obsessed with business.

Finally, keep in mind 'face' – or, more importantly, the art of not making the locals lose face. Face is all in much of Asia, and in Vietnam it is above all. This is why foreigners

COPY CULTURE

Even people who understand that pirating hurts legitimate businesses will have a hard time finding the real thing in Vietnam. A US-based software group estimates that 90% of the software for the Windows operating systems in Vietnam is pirated. The country's recent admission into the World Trade Organization (WTO), though, means that the pirating party may slowly be winding down.

Vietnam has had antipiracy laws on the books for some time, but one of the conditions of WTO membership – and, by extension, the international business ties needed to grow the economy – is that officials have to start cracking down on counterfeiting. Local newspapers have been reporting more police visits to the fake-DVD shops in Hanoi, and international companies have been hosting seminars galore for customs officials on how to stop counterfeit goods from leaving the country.

The Vietnamese people have said they're afraid they won't be able to afford the technological basics, such as computer software, that they need to run a business or go to school. Nevertheless, some business people are accepting of the change, and in a few years there just might be one less hassle for travellers; the heads of reputable tour companies say they're looking forward to a future where it won't be so easy for others to steal their good name.

should never lose their tempers with the Vietnamese; this will bring unacceptable 'loss of face' to the individual involved and end any chance of a sensible solution to the dispute.

Lifestyle

Family, work, working with family, then more work. It's no surprise that the country has an almost nonexistent unemployment rate (guys lounging on their motorbikes calling out to tourists are considered to be on the job), as people of all ages work from sunrise to late at night, seven days per week on a regular basis.

Between working, people socialise over small meals throughout the day with friends and family and then return to back-breaking labour without a moment's hesitation.

Population

Vietnam's population hovers at around 86 million, making it the 13th most populous country in the world, and with its population growth rate it might soon make the top 10. Vietnam is a young country, with an incredible 65% of the people under the age of 30. Traditionally a rural agrarian society, the race is on to migrate to the cities for a share of the economic boom.

RELIGION

Over the centuries, Confucianism, Taoism and Buddhism have fused with popular Chinese beliefs and ancient Vietnamese animism to form what's collectively known as the Triple Religion (Tam Giao). Most Vietnamese people identify with this belief system, but if asked, they'll usually say they're Buddhist. Vietnam also has a significant percentage of Catholics (7% of the population).

The unique and colourful Vietnamese sect called Cao Daism was founded in the 1920s. It combines secular and religious philosophies of the East and West, and was based on seance messages revealed to the group's founder.

ARTS

Water Puppetry

Vietnam's ancient art of *roi nuoc* (water puppetry) originated in northern Vietnam at least 1000 years ago. Developed by rice farmers, the wooden puppets were manipulated by puppeteers using water-flooded rice paddies as their stage. Hanoi is the best place to see water-puppetry performances, which are accompanied by traditional music.

Architecture

Most early Vietnamese buildings were made of wood and other materials that proved ephemeral in the tropical climate. The grand exception is the architecture of Vietnam's ancient Cham culture. These are most numerous in central Vietnam. The Cham ruins at My Son (p886) are a major draw.

Plenty of pagodas and temples founded hundreds of years ago are still functioning, but they have usually been rebuilt many times with little concern for the original.

Sculpture

Vietnamese sculpture has traditionally centred on religious themes and has functioned as an adjunct to architecture, especially that of pagodas, temples and tombs.

The Cham civilisation produced exquisite carved sandstone figures for its Hindu and Buddhist sanctuaries. Cham sculpture was influenced by Indian art, but over the centuries it managed to also incorporate Indonesian and Vietnamese elements. The largest single collection of Cham sculpture is at the Museum of Cham Sculpture (p878) in Danang.

Cinema

Vietnamese cinema is the most exported of the contemporary arts. Tran Anh Hung, who fled to France, is the most famous Vietnam-born *auteur;* he wrote and directed *The Scent of Green Papaya, Cyclo* and *Vertical Rays of the Sun.* The lyrical, sombre *Buffalo Boy,* by Minh Nguyen-Vo, was Vietnam's submission to the Academy Awards in 2005.

Music

Like the rest of Southeast Asia, Vietnam has a thriving domestic pop scene. The most celebrated artist is Khanh Ly, who left Vietnam in 1975 for the USA. Other celebrated local pop singers include sex symbol Phuong Thanh, Vietnam's answer to Madonna or Britney Spears, only with more clothes. Vietnamese girls are seriously into heart-throb Lam Truong, a Robbie Williams–style performer who woos the crowd.

Painting & Photography

The work of contemporary painters and photographers covers a wide swathe of styles and gives a glimpse into the modern Vietnamese psyche. The work of one of the country's most acclaimed photographers, Long Thanh, is on display in Nha Trang (see p887).

Theatre & Dance

It's sometimes possible to catch modern dance, classical ballet and stage plays in Hanoi and Ho Chi Minh City (HCMC; Saigon). Check the *Guide* or the *Word* for current theatre or dance listings in Hanoi and HCMC.

> **MUST SEE**
>
> *The Daughter from Danang* (2002) is a gut-wrenching documentary about a woman sent to the US for adoption as a child and her return to Vietnam.

ENVIRONMENT

The Land

Vietnam stretches more than 1600km along the eastern coast of the Indochinese peninsula. The country's area is 326,797 sq km, making it a bit bigger than Italy and slightly smaller than Japan. Vietnam has 3451km of mostly gorgeous coastline and 3818km of land borders.

As the Vietnamese are quick to point out, the country resembles a *don ganh,* or the ubiquitous bamboo pole with a basket of rice slung from each end. The baskets represent the main rice-growing regions of the Red River Delta in the north, and the Mekong Delta in the south.

The most striking geological features are the karst formations (limestone with caves and underground streams), particularly in the north around Halong Bay and Tam Coc.

Wildlife

With a wide range of habitats – from equatorial lowlands to high, temperate plateaus and even alpine peaks – the wildlife of Vietnam is enormously diverse. It is home to 275 species of mammal, more than 800 species of bird, 180 species of reptile, 80 species of amphibian, hundreds of species of fish and thousands of species of invertebrates.

Officially, the government has recognised 54 species of mammal and 60 species of bird as endangered. In a positive sign, some wildlife populations are re-establishing themselves in reforested areas. Birds, fish and crustaceans have reappeared in replanted mangrove forests.

National Parks

The number of national parks in the country has been rapidly expanding and there are now 30, covering about 3% of Vietnam's total territory. The most interesting and accessible are: Cat Ba (p863), Ba Be (p866) and Cuc Phuong (p860) National Parks in the north; Bach Ma National Park (p877) in the centre; and Yok Don National Park (p899) and Cat Tien National Park in the south.

Flora and Fauna International produces the excellent *Nature Tourism Map of Vietnam,* which includes detailed coverage of all the national parks in Vietnam.

MUST READ

The Girl in the Picture by Denise Chong (2000) tells the fascinating story of how one picture – of a terrified, naked child running from a bombing attack – changed many lives.

Environmental Issues

The country is facing a slew of environmental problems. Logging and slash-and-burn agricultural practices contribute to deforestation and soil degradation; pollution and overfishing threaten marine life; groundwater contamination limits potable water supply; and growing urban industrialisation and population migration are rapidly degrading the environment.

The government passed environmental protection laws in 1993 but changing the decades-long habits of farmers and loggers is easier said than done and even industrial-waste enforcement has been patchy. The exhaust fumes from motorbikes are so bad in the cities that a face mask is standard motorbike apparel.

To its credit, the government has been proactive about expanding the boundaries of national parks and adding new protected areas, and has made the planting and taking care of trees part of the school curriculum.

TRANSPORT

GETTING THERE & AWAY

Air

Hanoi has fewer international flights than HCMC, but with a change of aircraft in Hong Kong or Bangkok you can get to either city. Danang international airport offers minimal international connections. Maximise your time and minimise cost and hassle by booking an open-jaw ticket – then you can fly into HCMC and out of Hanoi (or vice versa). These tickets save you from backtracking and are easily arranged in hubs such as Bangkok and Hong Kong.

Keep in mind that international flights purchased in Vietnam are more expensive than the same tickets purchased outside. For more information about flights from outside Southeast Asia, see p945; from within the region, see p947.

Airlines flying to and from Vietnam within the region often operate code-share flights with Vietnam Airlines. The following phone numbers are for Hanoi.

Air Asia (code AK; ☎ 04-3928 8282; www.airasia.com) Daily budget flights connecting Hanoi and HCMC to Kuala Lumpur and Bangkok.

Air France (code AF; ☎ 04-3825 3484; www.airfrance.fr) Regular connections from Hanoi and HCMC to Paris via Bangkok.

Cathay Pacific (code CX; ☎ 04-3826 7298; www.cathaypacific.com) Has daily connections from both Hanoi and HCMC to Hong Kong.

Jetstar Pacific (code 3K; ☎ 04-3955 0550; www.jetstar.com) Daily budget flights from Hanoi and HCMC to Australia's major cities.

Lao Airlines (code QV; ☎ 04-3822 9951; www.laoairlines.com) Regular flights from Hanoi and HCMC to Vientiane and Luang Prabang.

Malaysia Airlines (code MY; ☎ 04-3826 8820; www.malaysiaairlines.com) Daily connections from Hanoi and HCMC to Kuala Lumpur.

Philippine Airlines (code PR; ☎ in HCMC 08-3822 2241; www.philippineair.com) Regular flights from HCMC to Manila.

Singapore Airlines (code SQ; ☎ 04-3826 8888; www.singaporeair.com) Daily flights linking Hanoi and HCMC with Singapore. Regional wing SilkAir also connects Danang and Siem Reap.

Thai Airways (code TG; ☎ 04-3826 6893; www.thaiair.com) Daily flights connecting Bangkok to Hanoi and HCMC, plus regular services to Danang.

Tiger Airways (code TR; ☎ 08-3824 5868; www.tigerairways.com) Budget flights connecting both Hanoi and HCMC to Singapore.

Vietnam Airlines (code VN; ☎ 04-3943 9660, in HCMC 08-3832 0320; www.vietnamair.com.vn) Global reach including the rest of Asia, Australia, Europe and the US.

Land

Vietnam shares land border crossings with Cambodia, China and Laos. See p953 for a full list of the crossings. Vietnam visas are not currently available at any land borders.

When it comes to Cambodia, most people exit Vietnam via Moc Bai or Vinh Xuong, taking the road from HCMC to Phnom Penh or the boat from Chau Doc to the Cambodian capital. However, the new crossing via Xa Xia near Ha Tien is proving a great way to link the Mekong Delta and Phu Quoc with Cambodia's south coast. There are a cluster of border crossings in the southwest of Vietnam that connect with obscure towns in Cambodia and are not really on the radar. The Xa Mat–Trapaeng Plong and Loc Ninh–Trapaeng Sre

DEPARTURE TAX

There is an international departure tax of US$14 from the main airports at Hanoi, HCMC and Danang. Dollars or dong will do, but take small change if paying in dollars.

crossings are both off NH7 in Cambodia and the Xa Mat crossing could be useful for those planning to visit the Cao Dai temple when travelling to or from Ho Chi Minh City.

There are also three crossings into China in the north, all of which are relatively straightforward to use as there are major towns on both sides of the border.

Looking at Laos, it is these border crossings that cause travellers the most headaches, with poor transport links, bad roads, petty corruption and rampant overcharging. The easiest way to exit is via Lao Bao, the most established crossing. Many use Cau Treo when travelling between Hanoi and Vientiane, but it's no picnic: in fact it's a set menu from hell. The other crossings are in remote areas and rarely used by travellers. Only use these crossings if you are willing to expect the unexpected and are prepared to pay over the odds to do so. Lao visas are not currently available at some of the more remote borders.

GETTING AROUND

Air

Air travel within Vietnam is dominated by **Vietnam Airlines** (www.vietnamairlines.com), although budget newcomer **Jetstar Pacific** (www.jetstar.com/vn/en/index.html) offers an improving selection of routes connecting HCMC with Danang, Hue and Haiphong, plus Hanoi with Danang, Nha Trang and Can Tho. Reasonably priced domestic flights can trim precious travel time off a busy itinerary.

A domestic departure tax of 25,000d is included in the ticket price.

Bicycle

Long-distance cycling is becoming a popular way to tour Vietnam, most of which is flat or moderately hilly. With the loosening of borders in Southeast Asia, more and more people are planning overland trips by bicycle. All you need to know about bicycle travel in Vietnam, Laos and Cambodia is contained in Lonely planet's *Cycling Vietnam, Laos & Cambodia*.

The main hazard for bicycle riders is the traffic, and it's wise to avoid certain areas (notably National Hwy 1). The best cycling is in the northern mountains and the Central Highlands, though you'll have to cope with some big climbs. The Mekong Delta is a picturesque option for those with an aversion to hills.

Purchasing a good bicycle in Vietnam is hit or miss. It's recommended that you bring one from abroad, along with a good helmet and spare parts.

Hotels and some travel agencies rent bicycles for about US$2 to US$3 per day and it is a great way to explore some of the smaller cities. Be sure to check the condition of the bicycle before pedalling into the sunset.

Boat

The extensive network of canals in the Mekong Delta makes getting around by boat feasible in the far south. Travellers to Phu Quoc Island can catch hydrofoils from Ha Tien (p921) or Rach Gia (p923). There are also hydrofoils to Vung Tau.

In the country's northeast, hydrofoils connect Haiphong with Cat Ba Island (near Halong Bay), and cruises on Halong Bay are extremely popular. In the south, a trip to the islands off the coast of Nha Trang is popular.

Bus

Vietnam has an extensive network of bargain buses that reach the far-flung corners of the country. Until recently, few foreign travellers used them because of safety concerns and overcharging, but the situation has improved dramatically with modern buses and fixed-price ticket offices at all major bus stations.

Bus drivers rely on the horn as a defensive driving technique. Motorists use the highway like a speedway; accidents, unsurprisingly, are common. On bus journeys, keep a close eye on your bags, never accept drinks from strangers, and consider bringing earplugs.

Travelling on the backloads, you'll see local buses of every vintage, packed to the gills. You can travel on these rattletraps, but expect breakdowns, lots of stops and overcrowded conditions. You'll rub shoulders with everyday people, giving you a slice of life many foreigners don't experience.

Most buses pick up passengers along the way until full. It's a good idea to try buying tickets at the station the day before. Avoid these buses (and the public ones) around Tet when drivers are working overtime and routes are dangerously overcrowded.

Generally, buses of all types leave early in the morning, but shorter, more popular routes will often leave at intervals throughout the day.

Costs are negligible, though on rural runs foreigners are typically charged anywhere from twice to 10 times the going rate. As a benchmark, a typical 100km ride is between US$2 and US$3.

There are also now private companies offering smart minibuses with allocated seats on short and medium-distance routes, such as **Mai Linh Express** (www.mail inh.vn).

OPEN-TOUR BUS

For the cost of around US$25 to US$40 (depending on fuel prices), the ubiquitous open ticket can get you from HCMC to Hanoi at your own pace, in air-con comfort. Open-tour tickets entitle you to exit or board the bus at any city along its route, without holding you to a fixed schedule. Confirm your seat the day before departure.

These tickets are inexpensive because they're subsidised by an extensive commission culture. All of the lunch stops and hotel drop-offs give monetary kickbacks to the bus companies. But you're never obligated to stay at the hotel you've been dropped at; if you don't like it, find another.

More Vietnamese travellers are now using these buses, particularly in the major cities, as the buses depart from central places, such as the Pham Ngu Lao area in HCMC, thus avoiding an extra journey to the bus station.

An alternative to the open-tour ticket is to buy individual, point-to-point tickets along the way; although this will cost a bit more, there is the flexibility to take local buses, trains or flights, or to switch open-tour companies.

All companies offering open-tour tickets have received both glowing commendations and bitter complaints from travellers. As a general guide, the original Sinh Café still has some of the best buses, but it pays to browse the various options the day before departure to see what is on offer.

Car & Motorcycle

Self-drive rental cars have yet to make their debut in Vietnam, which is a blessing in disguise given traffic conditions, but cars with drivers are popular and plentiful.

For sightseeing trips around HCMC or Hanoi, a car with driver can be rented by the day. It costs about US$25 to US$50 per day, depending on the car.

For the rough roads of northwestern Vietnam, the only sensible vehicle is a 4WD. The cheapest (and least comfortable) are Russian made, while more cushy Japanese vehicles are about twice the price. Expect to pay about US$80 to US$100 a day for a decent 4WD in the far north of Vietnam.

Motorbikes can be hired for US$5 to US$10 per day, depending on the make and what region you're in. Prices with a driver start at about US$8 for day tours around town. In smaller towns and cities, observe how people drive and go with the flow. In HCMC or Hanoi, consider hiring a driver unless you're used to driving in Asian cities. Fifteen minutes on a bus travelling Hwy 1A should convince you to leave the long-distance driving to a local, unless in off-the-beaten-track destinations like the far north or the Mekong Delta.

Hiring a motorbike guide leaves you free to observe the kaleidoscope of daily life and scenery, and guides are experts on their own turf. Many travellers hit it off so well with their guides that they hire them for the long haul. It's a wonderful way to travel, and you'll get an insider's perspective on the country.

Except for legal foreign residents, buying a motorbike for touring Vietnam is technically illegal. However, so far the authorities seem to be turning a blind eye to the practice. The big issue is what to do with the motorbike at trip's end. Some sell it back to the shop they bought it from (for less than they paid, of course). Others sell it to another shop or to a foreigner travelling in the opposite direction.

The road rule to remember: small yields to big (always). Traffic cops may (or may not) be looking for a pay-off. Vehicles drive on the right-hand side of the road (usually). Spectacular accidents are frequent. There were almost 13,000 traffic fatalities in 2006, a 10% increase from the year before.

When driving on Vietnam's highways, helmets are required by law only for motorbikes (but are a necessary accessory if you're fond of your skull).

Hitching

As in any country, hitching is never entirely safe in Vietnam, and it is not recommended. If you do decide to hitch, keep in mind that drivers will usually expect to be paid for picking you up, so negotiate the fare before getting in. Never hitch alone, especially if you're female.

Local Transport

You'll never have to walk in Vietnam if you don't want to; drivers will practically chase you down the street.

At least once during your visit, take a whirl on a *xich lo (cyclo)*, a bicycle rickshaw with the seat at the front, and the bicycle at the back. They're a pleasant, nonpolluting way to see a city but are being phased out by authorities. Generally, short *cyclo* rides should cost 15,000d, and an hourly rate equivalent to US$2 is the norm. Be sure to negotiate up front and make sure the final price is crystal clear; bring a map if possible and stick to bargaining in dong. Don't take *cyclo*s at night; travellers have been mugged by their drivers.

Xe om or *Honda om* (literally, 'Honda hug'; motorcycle taxi) are faster – made up of a motorbike, a driver and you. Prices are roughly the same as with *cyclo*s.

Metered taxis are abundant, but check the meter before you get in and make sure the driver uses it. Some Hanoi taxis operate dodgy meters.

Hiring a bicycle is arguably the most fun way to see any city, and an adventure in itself. Hotels and traveller cafes usually hire them out for US$2 per day.

Train

Vietnam Railways (Duong Sat Viet Nam; ☎ 04-3747 0308; www.vr.com.vn) operates the 2600km-long Vietnamese train system that runs along the coast between HCMC and Hanoi, and links the capital with Haiphong and northerly points to China. Odd-numbered trains travel south; even-numbered trains go north.

The *Reunification Express* chugs along the 1726km journey between Hanoi and HCMC at an average speed of 50km per hour, and takes from 29 to 41 hours. There are several classes of train travel in Vietnam, including hard seat, soft seat, hard sleeper and soft sleeper. All now come with the option of air-con for an extra fee. Conditions in hard seat and soft seat have improved greatly on the main coastal routes and are a leisurely alternative to the bus.

Theft can be a problem. In sleeper cars, the bottom bunk is best because you can stow your pack underneath the berth; otherwise, secure it to something for the duration of the trip. Though trains are sometimes slower than the bus, they are more comfortable and a terrific way to meet local people.

STAYING ALIVE ON THE STREETS

If you don't want to wind up like a bug on a windshield, pay close attention to a few pedestrian survival rules when crossing the street, especially in motorbike-crazed HCMC and Hanoi. Foreigners frequently make the mistake of thinking that the best way to cross a busy street in Vietnam is to run quickly across it. This does not always work in practice, and could get you creamed. Most Vietnamese cross the street slowly – very slowly – giving the motorbike drivers sufficient time to judge their position so they can pass on either side. They won't stop or even slow down, but they will try to avoid hitting you. Just don't make any sudden moves. Good luck!

HANOI

☎ 04 / pop 3.7 million

Imagine a city where the exotic chic of old Asia blends seamlessly with the dynamic face of new Asia. Where the medieval and modern coexist. A city with a quixotic blend of Parisian grace and Asian pace, an architectural museum piece that is evolving in harmony with its history, rather than bulldozing through it like so many of the region's other capitals. Hanoi is where imagination becomes reality.

A mass of motorbikes swarms through the tangled web of streets that is the Old Quarter, which has been a cauldron of commerce for almost 1000 years and still the best place to check the pulse of this resurgent city. Hawkers in conical hats ply their wares, locals sip coffee and *bia hoi* watching life, and plenty of tourists, pass them by. Hanoi has it all, the ancient history, a colonial legacy and a modern outlook. There is no better place to untangle the paradox that is contemporary Vietnam.

Known by many names down the centuries, Thanh Long (City of the Soaring Dragon) is the most evocative, and let there be no doubt that this dragon is on the up once more.

ORIENTATION

Rambling along the banks of the Red River (Song Hong), Hanoi's centre extends out from the edges of Hoan Kiem Lake. Just to the north of this lake is the Old Quarter, with narrow streets whose names change every block or two. Travellers usually base themselves in this part of town.

About 1.5km west of the Old Quarter is Ho Chi Minh's mausoleum, in the neighbourhood where most foreign embassies are found, many housed in classical architectural masterpieces from the French colonial era. Hanoi's largest lake, Ho Tay (West Lake), lies north of the mausoleum.

Street designations in Hanoi are shortened to P for *Pho* or Đ for *duong* (both meaning street).

There are decent city maps for sale at bookshops in Hanoi, plus a helpful bus map (*Xe Buyt Ha Noi;* 5000d).

INFORMATION

Bookshops

Bookworm (Map pp844-5; ☎ 3747 8778; bookworm@fpt.vn; 4B P Yen The; ⏲ 10am-7pm Tue-Sun) Hanoi's best selection of new and used English-language books. Ten minutes east of the Temple of Literature.

Love Planet (Map p850; ☎ 3828 4864; 25 P Hang Bac) Trade in used books for other second-hand reads.

Thang Long Bookshop (Map p850; ☎ 3825 7043; 53-55 P Trang Tien) One of the biggest bookshops in town, with English and French titles.

Cultural Centres

American Club (Map p850; ☎ 3824 1850; 19-21 P Hai Ba Trung) Regular sports and events.

British Council (Map pp844-5; ☎ 3728 1922; 20 Thuy Khue, Tay Ho). Hosts cultural events, exhibitions, workshops and fashion shows.

Centre Culturel Française de Hanoi (Map p850; ☎ 3936 2164; 24 P Trang Tien) In the L'Espace building, a modernist venue near the Opera House.

Emergency

Ambulance (☎ 115)

Fire (☎ 114)

Police (☎ 113)

Internet Access

There are countless internet cafes in Hanoi, notably along P Hang Bac in the Old Quarter. Rates start as low as 3000d, but overcharging isn't unheard of in some places. Most budget and midrange hotels offer free internet access as standard.

Wi-fi has come to Hanoi with a vengeance, and lots of hotels, cafes and bars offer free access. In the claustrophobic Old Quarter, it's not uncommon to have a choice of several networks. Try to sign into a secure network.

Internet Resources

There are several good websites to help you get the most out of Hanoi.

Hanoi Grapevine (www.hanoigrapevine.com) A culture vulture's paradise, this site has a useful events calendar.

New Hanoian (www.newhanoian.com) This is *the* place to get the rub on what Hanoi expats get up to in the city.

Sticky Rice (http://stickyrice.typepad.com) The website for foodies in Hanoi, this has the lowdown on wining and dining in the city.

GETTING INTO TOWN

From Noi Bai airport, Vietnam Airlines' airport minibus (US$2, 45 minutes, 35km) is cheap and easy. It terminates at P Quang Trung in the Old Quarter.

Official airport taxis charge US$12 for a ride door-to-door to or from Noi Bai airport. Drivers do *not* require that you pay the toll for the bridge you cross en route. Some other taxi drivers require that you pay the toll, so check first.

The cheapest option is the public bus (5000d). Lines 7 and 17 go to Kim Ma bus station and Long Bien bus station (Map pp844–5) respectively, every 15 minutes from 5am to 9pm.

From the city's three central train stations, you can walk the 15 to 20 minutes to the Old Quarter to find budget accommodation. However, it's worth the 15,000d for a *xe om* (motorcycle taxi) if you have a big pack to haul around. The same goes for Long Bien bus station (Map pp844–5), which is across the street from Long Bien train station.

From other bus stations, a motorbike taxi to the Old Quarter should cost 15,000d to 30,000d, depending on the distance involved.

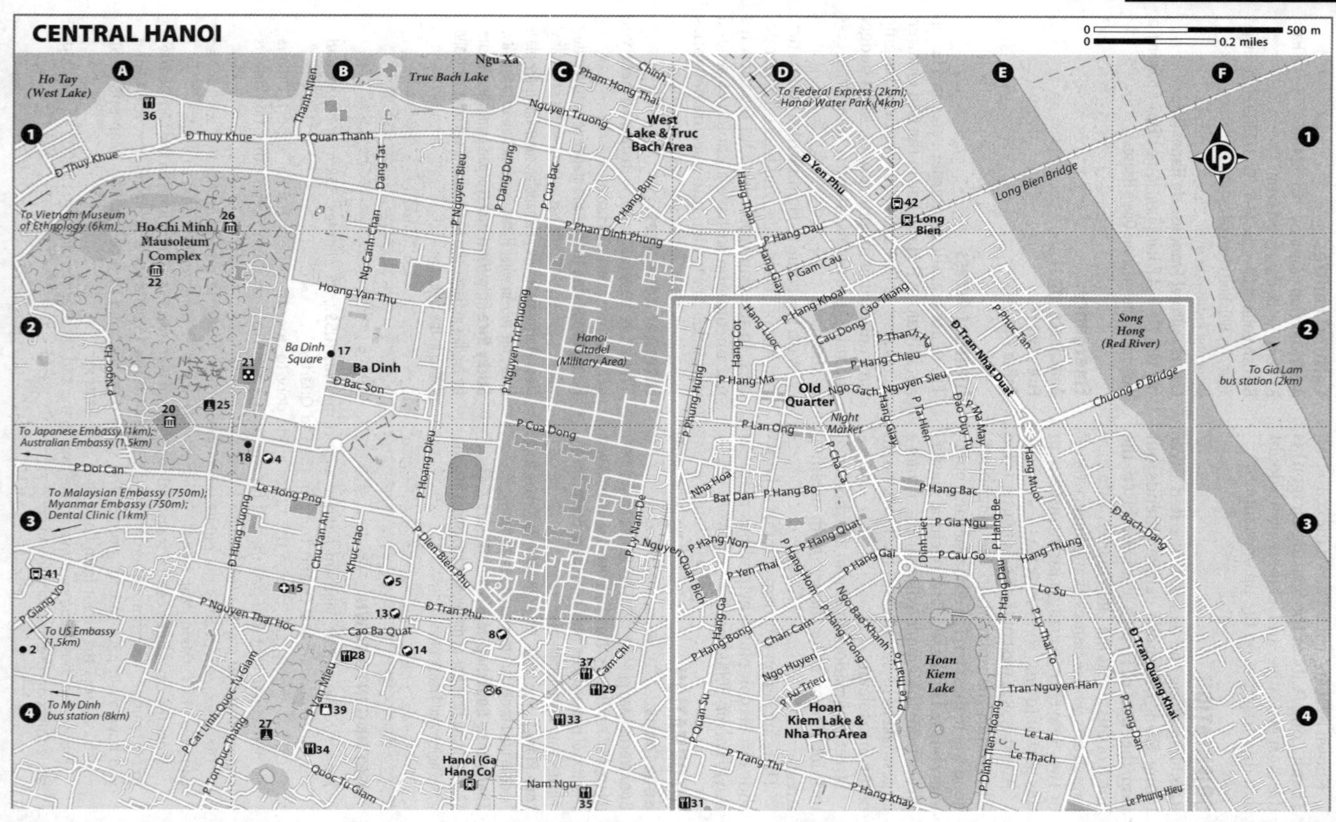
CENTRAL HANOI
0 500 m
0 0.2 miles
A
B
C
D
E
F
1
2
3
4
Ho Tay (West Lake)
Truc Bach Lake
Ngu Xa
Song Hong (Red River)
Long Bien Bridge
Chuong Đ Bridge
To Gia Lam bus station (2km)
To Federal Express (2km); Hanoi Water Park (4km)
Long Bien
Đ Yen Phu
West Lake & Truc Bach Area
Old Quarter
Night Market
Hoan Kiem Lake
Hoan Kiem Lake & Nha Tho Area
Hanoi Citadel (Military Area)
Ba Dinh
Ba Dinh Square
Ho Chi Minh Mausoleum Complex
Hanoi (Ga Hang Co)
To Vietnam Museum of Ethnology (6km)
To Japanese Embassy (1km); Australian Embassy (1.5km)
To Malaysian Embassy (750m); Myanmar Embassy (750m); Dental Clinic (1km)
To US Embassy (1.5km)
To My Dinh bus station (8km)
Đ Thuy Khue
P Quan Thanh
Thanh Nien
Dang Tat
P Nguyen Bieu
P Dang Dung
P Cua Bac
Pham Hong Thai
Chinh
Nguyen Truong
P Hang Bun
Hang Than
P Hang Dau
Hang Giay
P Gam Cau
P Phan Dinh Phung
Ng Canh Chan
Hoang Van Thu
Đ Bac Son
P Ngoc Ha
P Doi Can
Le Hong Png
Đ Hung Vuong
Chu Van An
Khuc Hao
P Hoang Dieu
P Nguyen Tri Phuong
P Cua Dong
P Dien Bien Phu
Đ Tran Phu
P Ly Nam De
Nguyen Quan Bich
P Giang Vo
P Nguyen Thai Hoc
Cao Ba Quat
P Cat Linh Quoc Tu Giam
P Ton Duc Thang
P Van Mieu
Quoc Tu Giam
Cam Chi
Nam Ngu
P Hang Khoai
Cao Thang
Hang Luoc
Hang Cot
Cau Dong
P Thanh Ha
P Hang Chieu
Đ Tran Nhat Duat
P Phuc Tan
P Phung Hung
P Hang Ma
Ngo Gach
Nguyen Sieu
P Ta Hien
Dao Duy Tu
P Ma May
P Lan Ong
P Cha Ca
Hang Muoi
Nha Hoa
Bat Dan
P Hang Bo
P Hang Bac
P Gia Ngu
P Hang Be
Dinh Liet
Đ Bach Dang
P Hang Non
P Hang Quat
P Hang Gai
P Cau Go
Hang Thung
P Yen Thai
P Hang Hom
Ngo Bao Khanh
P Hang Dau
Lo Su
P Hang Ga
P Hang Bong
Chan Cam
P Hang Trong
P Ly Thai To
Đ Tran Quang Khai
Ngo Huyen
P Au Trieu
P Le Thai To
Tran Nguyen Han
P Quan Su
P Tong Dan
Le Lai
Le Thach
P Dinh Tien Hoang
P Trang Thi
P Hang Khay
Le Phung Hieu
2
4
5
6
8
13
14
15
17
18
20
21
22
25
26
27
28
29
31
33
34
35
36
37
39
41
42

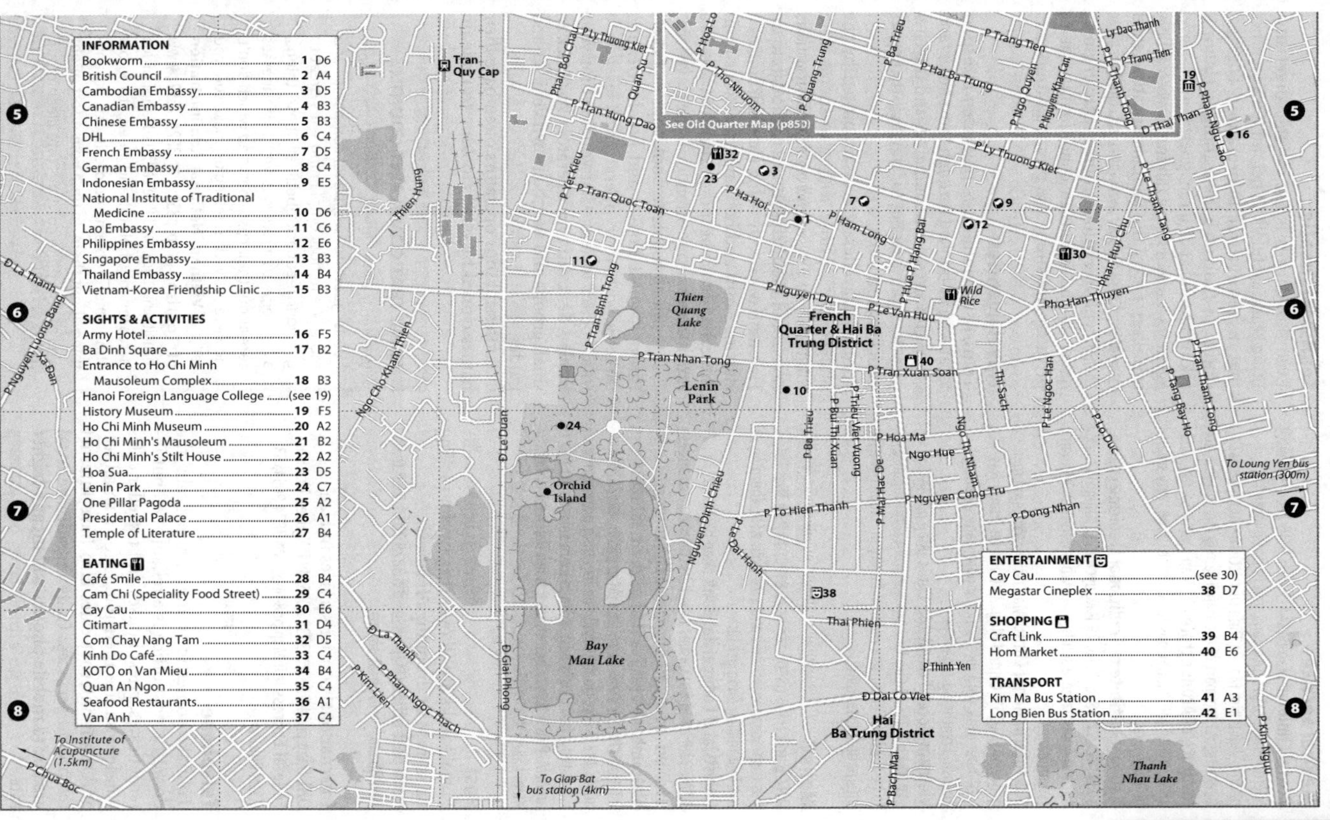
INFORMATION
Bookworm 1 D6
British Council 2 A4
Cambodian Embassy 3 D5
Canadian Embassy 4 B3
Chinese Embassy 5 B3
DHL 6 C4
French Embassy 7 D5
German Embassy 8 C4
Indonesian Embassy 9 E5
National Institute of Traditional Medicine 10 D6
Lao Embassy 11 C6
Philippines Embassy 12 E6
Singapore Embassy 13 B3
Thailand Embassy 14 B4
Vietnam-Korea Friendship Clinic 15 B3
SIGHTS & ACTIVITIES
Army Hotel 16 F5
Ba Dinh Square 17 B2
Entrance to Ho Chi Minh Mausoleum Complex 18 B3
Hanoi Foreign Language College (see 19)
History Museum 19 F5
Ho Chi Minh Museum 20 A2
Ho Chi Minh's Mausoleum 21 B2
Ho Chi Minh's Stilt House 22 A2
Hoa Sua 23 D5
Lenin Park 24 C7
One Pillar Pagoda 25 A2
Presidential Palace 26 A1
Temple of Literature 27 B4
EATING
Café Smile 28 B4
Cam Chi (Speciality Food Street) 29 C4
Cay Cau 30 E6
Citimart 31 D4
Com Chay Nang Tam 32 D5
Kinh Do Café 33 C4
KOTO on Van Mieu 34 B4
Quan An Ngon 35 C4
Seafood Restaurants 36 A1
Van Anh 37 C4
ENTERTAINMENT
Cay Cau (see 30)
Megastar Cineplex 38 D7
SHOPPING
Craft Link 39 B4
Hom Market 40 E6
TRANSPORT
Kim Ma Bus Station 41 A3
Long Bien Bus Station 42 E1
See Old Quarter Map (p850)
French Quarter & Hai Ba Trung District
Hai Ba Trung District
Thien Quang Lake
Lenin Park
Bay Mau Lake
Orchid Island
Thanh Nhau Lake
Tran Quy Cap
Wild Rice
To Loung Yen bus station (300m)
To Giap Bat bus station (4km)
To Institute of Acupuncture (1.5km)
Đ Le Duan
Đ Giai Phong
Đ Dai Co Viet
Đ La Thanh
P Tran Hung Dao
P Tran Quoc Toan
P Nguyen Du
P Le Van Huu
P Tran Nhan Tong
P Tran Xuan Soan
P Ly Thuong Kiet
P Hai Ba Trung
P Trang Tien
P Ham Long
P Ha Hoi
P Hue
P Hang Bai
Ngo Thi Nham
P Nguyen Cong Tru
P To Hien Thanh
Nguyen Dinh Chieu
P Le Dai Hanh
Thai Phien
P Tran Binh Trong
P Yet Kieu
Quan Su
Phan Boi Chau
Ngo Cho Kham Thien
P Kim Lien
P Pham Ngoc Thach
P Chua Boc
P Nguyen Luong Bang
Xa Đan
Thien Hung
Pho Han Thuyen
Phan Huy Chu
P Le Thanh Tong
P Le Thanh Tang
P Tran Thanh Tong
P Tang Bay Ho
P Lo Duc
P Le Ngoc Han
Thi Sach
P Dong Nhan
P Pham Ngu Lao
Đ Thai Than
P Ngo Quyen
P Bach Mai
P Kim Nguu
P Thinh Yen
P Mai Hac De
P Hoa Ma
Ngo Hue
P Trieu Viet Vuong
P Bui Thi Xuan
P Ba Trieu
P Quang Trung
P Tho Nhuom
P Hoa Lo
P Nguyen Khac Can
Ly Dao Thanh

Medical Services

Dental Clinic (off Map pp844-5; ☎ 3846 2864; www.vietnammedicalpractice.com; Van Phuc Diplomatic Compound, 298 P Kim Ma, Ba Dinh District) The tooth hurts? Deal with it here, part of the Hanoi Family Medical Practice.
Institute of Acupuncture (off Map pp844-5; ☎ 3853 3881; 49 P Thai Thinh) Holistic medicine? Well, very small holes anyway.
National Institute of Traditional Medicine (Map pp844-5; ☎ 3826 3616; 29 P Nguyen Binh Khiem) Check out some Vietnamese solutions to what might be Vietnamese problems.
SOS International Clinic (Map p850; ☎ 24hr emergency 3934 0555; Central Bldg, 31 P Hai Ba Trung) Has a 24-hour clinic with international physicians speaking English, French and Japanese.
Vietnam-Korea Friendship Clinic (Map pp844-5; ☎ 3843 7231; 12 Chu Van An) Nonprofit clinic reputed to be the least expensive medical facility in Hanoi; good international standard.

Money

ANZ Bank (Map p850; ☎ 3825 8190; 14 P Le Thai To) Has cash-advance facilities and a 24-hour ATM, churning out four million dong per hit.
Industrial & Commercial Bank (Map p850; ☎ 3825 4276; 37 P Hang Bo) Cashes travellers cheques, exchanges US dollars and also gives credit-card cash advances.
Vietcombank P Hang Bai (Map p850; ☎ 3826 8031; 2 P Hang Bai); P Tran Quang Khai (Map p850; ☎ 3826 8045; 198 P Tran Quang Khai) The towering headquarters is located a few blocks east of Hoan Kiem Lake and it has an ATM. Plus a handy branch on P Hang Bai, near Hoan Kiem Lake.

Post

Postal kiosks are all over the city, for picking up stamps or dropping off letters.
Main post office (Map p850; ☎ 3825 7036; 75 P Dinh Tien Hoang; ⏲ 7am-8.30pm)

International courier services in Hanoi:
DHL (Map pp844-5; ☎ 3733 2086; 49 P Nguyen Thai Hoc)
Federal Express (off Map pp844-5; ☎ 3824 9054; 63 P Yen Phu)

Telephone

To make domestic or international calls, the domestic post office is a reliable bet, but internet cafes, guest houses and traveller cafes will let you use their phone for a small fee, and many internet cafes also have internet telephone services. Calls outside the local area or to mobile phones will incur a higher rate.

Tourist Information

Even though this is the capital, forget anything really useful like a helpful tourism office that dishes out free information. The best source of tourism information in Hanoi is asking around at different guest houses, travel agencies and bars, and talking to your fellow travellers. Or try the **Tourist Information Center** (Map p850; ☎ 3926 3366; www.vntourists.com; P Dinh Tien Hoang), with free information, plenty of glossy handouts and serious air-conditioning, but it's privately run and it also promotes tours.

Travel Agencies

Tourist-style minibuses that often transport locals can be booked through most hotels and cafes. However, tour companies and traveller cafes are your best bet for buying other types of tickets and tours.

Many travellers are disappointed by the budget tours. Those willing to spend extra for quality or get around on their own usually rave about their trips. It's easy enough to do Halong Bay solo, by using Cat Ba Island as a starting point and booking excursions from there, but it may be more expensive. Sapa is a much easier proposition for indie travellers.

It is not advisable to book trips or tickets through guest houses and hotels. Dealing directly with tour operators gives you a much better idea of what you'll get for your money. Seek out tour operators that stick to small groups and use their own vehicles and guides.

Successful tour operators often have their names cloned by others looking to trade on

MAKE THAT COMPLAINT COUNT...

We get a lot of letters complaining about hotels, guest houses, travel companies and more. We're not complaining – it's great to get your feedback about all these things, as it helps us work out which businesses care about their customers and which don't. However, as well as telling us, make sure you tell the **Vietnam National Administration of Tourism** (Map p850; ☎ 3824 7652; www.hanoitourism.gov.vn; 3 P Le Lai); its Hanoi office is reasonably helpful and needs to know about the problems before it can do anything about them. In time your effort might well pressure the cowboys into cleaning up their act.

their reputations, so check addresses and websites carefully. Consider the following places:

ET Pumpkin (Map p850; ☎ 3926 0739; www.et-pumpkin.com; 89 P Ma May) Tours throughout the north, and it operates its own private carriage on the night train to Sapa.

Ethnic Travel (Map p850; ☎ 3926 1951; www.ethnictravel.com.vn; 35 P Hang Giay) Offers an innovative selection of low-impact adventures that ensures you meet the real Vietnamese.

Handspan Adventure Travel (Map p850; ☎ 3926 0581; www.handspan.com; 80 P Ma May) A popular company offering Halong Bay, Bai Tu Long Bay and jeep tours in the far north. The walk-in office is in the Tamarind Café.

Ocean Tours (Map p850; ☎ 3926 1294; www.oceantoursvietnam.com; 7 P Dinh Liet) This operator has been earning a good name for itself by specialising in Halong Bay.

Onbike Tour (☎ 3732 4788; www.onbikevietnam.com) Specialises in cycling tours to undiscovered villages around Hanoi and avoids city pedalling.

DANGERS & ANNOYANCES

One of the most scenic cities in Vietnam is unfortunately also the most prone to scams. Taxis and motorbikes have the annoying habit of taking travellers to hotels that give a commission. We've even heard stories of travellers who took a legitimate Vietnam Airlines bus from the airport into the Old Quarter only to see a fake representative of Vietnam Airlines board the bus and try to tout people into hotels. There are several substantiated reports of verbal aggression and physical violence towards tourists when deciding against a hotel room or tour. Stay calm and back away slowly or things could quickly flare up.

If coming in from the airport, it's a good idea to call your hotel and ask for an airport pick-up. If arriving by train or bus, get to the hotel where you have 'reservations' and if that fails, pick a good neighbourhood with lots of hotels where you are supposedly meeting friends.

Some Western women have been hassled by young men around town who follow them home, so it pays to hit the town in larger numbers. Walking alone in well-lit areas of the Old Quarter is usually safe, but stay alert in the darker streets, particularly in the early hours of the morning. When getting from one part of town to the other at night, particularly from late-night spots, it is more sensible for solo women, and even men, to take a metered taxi.

Be wary of friendly strangers who want to take you out somewhere. All too often, travellers face an outrageous bill or downright extortion at the end of the night. This has happened to a number of gay men approached near Hoan Kiem Lake and kind-hearted people taken to restaurants by 'English students' supposedly looking for conversation practice. Whether travelling solo or with a local, always ask for prices beforehand, check the bill, and politely but firmly point out any discrepancies.

SIGHTS

Old Quarter

This is the Asia we dreamed of from afar. Steeped in history, pulsating with life, bubbling with commerce, buzzing with motorbikes and rich in exotic scents, the Old Quarter is Hanoi's modern yet medieval historic heart. Hawkers pound the streets, sizzling and smoking baskets hiding a cheap meal for the locals. *Pho* (noodle soup) stalls and *bia hoi* (draught beer) dens hug every corner, resonant with the sound of gossip and laughter. There is no better way to spend some time in Hanoi than walking the streets, simply soaking up the sights, sounds and smells. The following are all on the Old Quarter map (p850).

Hoan Kiem Lake is the liquid heart of the Old Quarter and a good orientation landmark. Legend has it that, in the mid-15th century, Heaven sent Emperor Ly Thai To a magical sword, which he used to drive the Chinese out of Vietnam. One day after the war he happened upon a giant golden tortoise swimming on the surface of the water; the creature grabbed the sword and disappeared into the depths of the lake. Since that time, the lake has been known as Ho Hoan Kiem (Lake of the Restored Sword) because the tortoise restored the sword to its divine owners. A respected Vietnamese scientist has been crusading since 1991 for the protection of the very few real giant turtles that live in the lake. Tiny **Thap Rua** (Tortoise Tower), on an islet in the southern part of the lake, is often used as an emblem of Hanoi.

Ngoc Son Temple (Jade Mountain Temple; admission 3000d; 🕐 8am-5pm), which was founded in the 18th century, is on an island in the northern part of Hoan Kiem Lake. It's a meditative spot to relax, but also worth checking out for the embalmed remains of a gigantic tortoise supposedly from the lake itself.

Memorial House (87 P Ma May; admission 5000d; ⌚ 9-11.30am & 1-5pm) is worth a visit. Thoughtfully restored, this traditional Chinese-style dwelling gives you an excellent idea of how local merchants used to live in the Old Quarter.

Bach Ma Temple (cnr P Hang Buom & P Hang Giay; ⌚ 8-11.30am & 2.30-5.30pm) is the oldest temple in Hanoi. Legend has it that Emperor Ly Thai To prayed at this temple for assistance in building the city walls because they continually collapsed, no matter how many times he rebuilt them. His prayers were finally answered when a white horse appeared from the temple and guided him to the site where he eventually built his walls.

Stepping inside **St Joseph Cathedral** (P Nha Tho; ⌚ 5-7am & 5-7pm) is like being transported to medieval Europe. The cathedral (inaugurated in 1886) is noteworthy for its square towers, elaborate altar and stained-glass windows. The main gate is open when Mass is held.

Ho Chi Minh Mausoleum Complex

This is the holiest of holies for many Vietnamese. In the tradition of Lenin, Stalin and Mao, the final resting place of Ho Chi Minh is a glass sarcophagus set deep within a monumental edifice. As interesting as the man himself are the crowds coming to pay their respects.

Built despite his dying wishes to be cremated, **Ho Chi Minh's Mausoleum** (Map pp844-5; cnr P Ngoc Ha & P Doi Can; admission free; ⌚ 8-11am Sat-Thu) was constructed between 1973 and 1975, using native materials gathered from all over Vietnam. Ho Chi Minh's embalmed corpse gets a three-month holiday to Russia for yearly maintenance, so the mausoleum is closed from September to early December. Some sceptics have suggested Madame Tussaud's has the contract these days.

All visitors must register and leave their bags and cameras at a reception hall (a free service). You'll be refused admission to the mausoleum if you're wearing shorts, tank tops or other 'indecent' clothing. Hats must be taken off inside the mausoleum building, and a respectful demeanour should be maintained at all times. Photography is absolutely prohibited inside the building and this includes mobile phones with cameras.

After exiting the mausoleum, check out the following sights in the complex.

Ho Chi Minh Museum (Map pp844-5; ☎ 3846 3757; admission 10,000d; ⌚ 8-11.30am & 2-4.30pm Tue-Thu, Sat & Sun) Displays each have a message, such as 'peace', 'happiness' or 'freedom'. Find an English-speaking guide, as some of the symbolism is hard to interpret on your own.

Ho Chi Minh's Stilt House (Map pp844-5; admission 5000d; ⌚ 8-11am & 2-4pm) Supposedly Ho's official residence, on and off, between 1958 and 1969.

One Pillar Pagoda (Map pp844-5; admission free) Built by Emperor Ly Thai Tong (r 1028–54) and designed to represent a lotus blossom, a symbol of purity, rising out of a sea of sorrow.

Presidential Palace (Map pp844-5; admission 5000d; ⌚ 8-11am & 2-4pm Sat-Thu) In stark contrast to Ho's stilt house, this imposing building was constructed in 1906 as the palace of the governor general of Indochina.

A DAY IN HANOI

Travellers with one day in Hanoi can spend the morning paying homage to Uncle Ho at the **Ho Chi Minh Mausoleum Complex** (left). Stroll by French colonial embassy buildings on P Hoang Dieu before grabbing lunch at **KOTO** (p852), opposite the striking **Temple of Literature** (below). Later, browse the **Vietnam Museum of Ethnology** (below) before finishing up with some *bia hoi* (draught beer) in the Old Quarter. Simple, cheap, satisfying.

Temple of Literature

Hanoi's peaceful **Temple of Literature** (Van Mieu; Map pp844-5; P Quoc Tu Giam; admission 5000d; ⌚ 8am-5pm) is a well-preserved jewel of traditional Vietnamese architecture in 11th-century style. The site of the country's first national university, the temple is a must-visit.

Five courtyards are enclosed within the grounds. The front gate is inscribed with a request that visitors dismount from their horses before entering. Please do. There's a peaceful reflecting pool in the front courtyard and the Khue Van pavilion at the back of the second courtyard.

Vietnam Museum of Ethnology

The wonderful **Vietnam Museum of Ethnology** (off Map pp844-5; ☎ 3756 2193; www.vme.org.vn; Đ Nguyen Van Huyen; admission 25,000d; ⌚ 8.30am-5.30pm Tue-Sun) should not be missed. It features a fascinating collection of art and everyday objects gathered from Vietnam and its diverse tribal people. From the making of conical hats to the ritual of a Tay shamanic ceremony, the museum explores Vietnam's cultural diversity.

Displays are labelled in Vietnamese, French and English.

The museum is in the Cau Giay district, about 7km from the city centre. The trip is 30 minutes by bicycle; a *xe om* ride costs around 30,000d, or you can catch local bus 14 from Hoan Kiem Lake (3000d) and get off at the junction between Đ Hoang Quoc Viet and Đ Nguyen Van Huyen.

Other Attractions

The terrific **Women's Museum** (Bao Tang Phu Nu; Map p850; 36 P Ly Thuong Kiet; admission 20,000d; 9am-4.30pm) includes a rousing tribute to women soldiers, balanced by some wonderful exhibits from the international women's movement protesting the American War. The 4th floor of the museum displays costumes worn by ethnic-minority groups in Vietnam. Exhibits have Vietnamese, French and English explanations.

Hoa Lo Prison Museum (Map p850; 3824 6358; 1 P Hoa Lo; admission 5000d; 8-11.30am & 1.30-4.30pm Tue-Sun) is all that remains of the former Hoa Lo Prison, ironically nicknamed the 'Hanoi Hilton' by US POWs during the American War. The bulk of the exhibits focus on the Vietnamese struggle for independence from France.

One block east of the Opera House, the **History Museum** (Map pp844-5; 1 P Pham Ngu Lao; admission 20,000d; 8-11.30am & 1.30-4.30pm Tue-Sun) is one of Hanoi's most stunning structures, incorporating design elements from Chinese and French styles in the architecture.

ACTIVITIES

Feel like a dip? There are several places for swimming in Hanoi. Some of the nicer hotels charge a US$10 or more day-use fee.

Army Hotel (Khach San Quan Doi; Map pp844-5; 3825 2896; 33C P Pham Ngu Lao; day use US$3) Big enough to do laps, the pool is open all year.

Hanoi Water Park (off Map pp844-5; 3753 2757; admission 30,000-50,000d; 9am-9pm Wed-Mon Apr-Nov) About 5km from the city centre, this complex features a variety of pools and slides.

COURSES

Cooking

Hoi An (p881) offers some cheaper options to learn the culinary arts of Vietnam.

Highway 4 (Map p850; 3926 0639; 5 P Hang Tre) This popular restaurant-bar also offers cooking classes. Prices range from US$26 to US$51 depending on numbers.

Hoa Sua (Map pp844-5; 3824 0448; www.hoasuaschool.com; 28A P Ha Hoi) Offers classes for a cause to raise funds for its training program for disadvantaged youth. Costs vary (US$32 to US$47) depending on the dishes cooked.

Language

Hanoi Foreign Language College (Map pp844-5; 3826 2468; 1 P Pham Ngu Lao), housed in the History Museum compound, is a branch of Hanoi National University where foreigners can study Vietnamese for around US$7 per lesson.

TOURS

For more information on tours around and beyond Hanoi, see p846.

FESTIVALS & EVENTS

Hanoi will celebrate its 1000th birthday in 2010. Expect a series of celebratory events throughout the year.

Tet (Tet Nguyen Dan/Vietnamese Lunar New Year) A flower market is held on P Hang Luoc during the week preceding Tet, in late January or early February. In addition, there's a colourful two-week flower exhibition and competition, which takes place in Lenin park (Cong Vien Le Nin; Map pp844–5).

Vietnam's National Day Celebrated at Ba Dinh Square (Map pp844-5) – in front of the Ho Chi Minh Mausoleum Complex – with a rally and fireworks on 2 September; boat races are also held on Hoan Kiem Lake in the Old Quarter.

SLEEPING

Head to the Old Quarter once you land in Hanoi; the majority of Hanoi's budget accommodation lies within 1km of Hoan Kiem Lake. Most of the budget hotels are near P Hang Bac or St Joseph Cathedral.

Dong A Hotel (Map p850; 3926 2353; www.dongahotels.com; 50 P Ma May; dm/r US$3/15;) A good-value place in a central location, and rooms here are spacious and have bathtubs and TV. The no-frills dorm has 14 beds, with slim-line mattresses, fans and lockers.

Youth Hotel (Map p850; 3828 5822; www.hanoiyouthhotel.com; 33 P Luong Van Can; dm US$5, r US$15-30;) A popular choice that offers hot-water bathrooms, and a backpacker-friendly dorm (with four beds).

Hanoi Backpackers Hostel (Map p850; 3828 5372; www.hanoibackpackershostel.com; 48 P Ngo Huyen; dm US$7.50, r US$30-36;) An efficiently run, perennially popular hostel that now occupies two buildings on a quiet lane. It has custom-built bunk beds with lockers, and the dorms all have en-suite bathrooms. There's a bar downstairs.

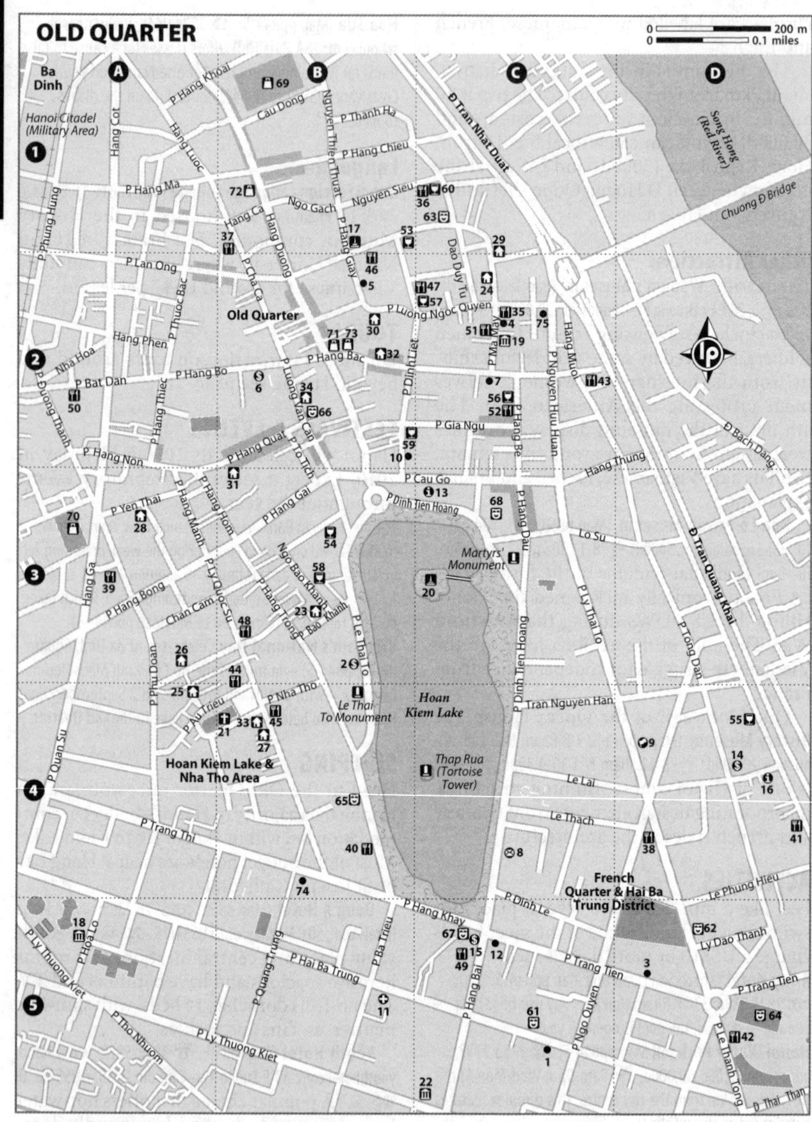

our pick Especen Hotel (Map p850; ☎ 3824 4401; www.especen.vn; 41 P Ngo Huyen; s/d US$14/17;) Trying harder than most bog-standard budget places, this hotel has a great location. The big, airy and light rooms – most with balcony and all with wi-fi – are in good shape.

Hotel Thien Trang (Map p850; ☎ 3826 9823; thientranghotel24@hotmail.com; 24 P Nha Chung; r US$15-20;) Boasting a terrific, quiet location in the stylish Nha Tho area, this hotel's spacious rooms retain a degree of character.

Sports Hotel (Map p850; ☎ 3926 0154; www.hanoistays.com; 96 P Hang Bac; r US$15-28;) Located on busy P Hang Bac, Sports Hotel has smart, well-presented and well-equipped rooms. Also has wi-fi.

INFORMATION
American Club ... 1 C5
ANZ Bank ... 2 B3
Centre Culturel Française de Hanoi ... 3 D5
ET Pumpkin ... 4 C2
Ethnic Travel ... 5 B2
Handspan Adventure Travel ... (see 51)
Industrial & Commercial Bank ... 6 B2
Love Planet ... 7 C2
Main Post Office ... 8 C4
New Zealand Embassy ... 9 D4
Ocean Tours ... 10 B2
SOS International Clinic ... 11 B5
Thang Long Bookshop ... 12 C5
Tourist Information Center ... 13 C3
UK Embassy ... (see 11)
Vietcombank ... 14 D4
Vietcombank ... 15 C5
Vietnam National Administration of Tourism ... 16 D4

SIGHTS & ACTIVITIES
Bach Ma Temple ... 17 B1
Highway 4 ... (see 43)
Hoa Lo Prison Museum ... 18 A5
Memorial House ... 19 C2
Ngoc Son Temple ... 20 C3
St Joseph Cathedral ... 21 B4
Women's Museum ... 22 C5

SLEEPING
Bamboo Hotel ... 23 B3
Dong A Hotel ... 24 C2
Especen Hotel ... 25 A4
Hanoi Backpackers Hostel ... 26 A3
Hotel Thien Trang ... 27 B4
Manh Dung Guesthouse ... 28 A3
Old Street Hotel ... 29 C1
Prince 1 Hotel ... 30 B2
Real Darling Café ... 31 B3
Sports Hotel ... 32 B2
Spring Hotel ... 33 B4
Youth Hotel ... 34 B2

EATING
69 Bar-Restaurant ... 35 C2
Café Ket Noi ... 36 C1
Cha Ca La Vong ... 37 B1
Club 51 Ly Thai To ... 38 D4
Cyclo ... 39 A3
Dong Xuan Market ... (see 69)
Fanny Ice Cream ... 40 B4
Fivimart ... 41 D4
Highlands Opera ... 42 D5
Highway 4 ... 43 C2
La Place ... 44 B3
La Salsa ... 45 B4
Ladybird Restaurant ... 46 B2
Little Hanoi 1 ... 47 C2
Pepperoni's Pizza & Cafe ... 48 B3
Pho 24 ... 49 C5
Pho Gia Truyen ... 50 A2
Tamarind Café ... 51 C2
Tandoor ... 52 C2

DRINKING
Cheeky Quarter ... 53 B1
Funky Monkey ... 54 B3
Gambrinus ... 55 D4
Le Pub ... 56 C2
Mao's Red Lounge ... 57 C2
Polite Pub ... 58 B3
Quan Bia Minh ... 59 B2
Roots ... 60 C1

ENTERTAINMENT
Centre Culturel Française de Hanoi ... (see 3)
Cinematheque ... 61 C5
Club Opera ... 62 D5
Egypt Club ... 63 C1
Hanoi Opera House ... 64 D5
I-Box ... 65 B4
Jazz Club By Quyen Van Minh ... 66 B2
Loop ... 67 C5
Municipal Water Puppet Theatre ... 68 C3

SHOPPING
Dong Xuan Market ... 69 B1
Hang Da Market ... 70 A3
Hanoi Gallery ... 71 B2
Night Market ... 72 B1
Old Propaganda Posters ... 73 B2

TRANSPORT
Airport Minibus ... 74 B4
Cuong's Motorbike Adventure ... 75 C2
Vietnam Airlines ... (see 74)

Bamboo Hotel (Map p850; ☎ 3926 2378; www.tnktravel.com; 32 P Hang Be; r US$15-35;) This new place has been tastefully designed, and the rooms have an understated elegance. Complimentary breakfast is served in the cafe.

Spring Hotel (Map p850; ☎ 3826 8500; spring.hotel@fpt.vn; 8A P Nha Chung; r US$16-30;) This hotel, in a classy historic building with high ceilings, is run by a friendly family. Bathrooms are tiny.

Prince 1 Hotel (Map p850; ☎ 3828 0155; www.hanoiprincehotel.com; 51 P Luong Ngoc Quyen; r US$18-28;) The original Prince hotel has a grand-looking lobby, helpful staff and large rooms with all the trimmings (including TV and minibar).

Also worth a peek:

Real Darling Café (Map p850; ☎ 3826 9386; darling_cafe@hotmail.com; 33 P Hang Quat; r US$5-12;) Almost as old as the Old Quarter, it's still one of the cheapest in town.

Old Street Hotel (Map p850; ☎ 3828 0195; www.oldstreethotel.com; 23 P Ma May; r US$10-15;) Clean rooms, smart touches and a good location make this worth the walk.

Manh Dung Guesthouse (Map p850; ☎ 3826 7201; tranmanhdungvn@yahoo.com; 2 P Tam Thuong; r US$12-18;) A popular budget place run by a friendly family, but some rooms are on the small side.

EATING

What's on the menu in Hanoi? Everything, ranging from the famous local speciality of *cha ca* (filleted fish slices grilled over charcoal) to the less appealing option of Fido over an open fire. In between, if it comes from a Vietnamese kitchen, it's here. There's also a wide choice of international cuisine.

Finding good budget eats at a sit-down restaurant can be a tad more challenging here than in other cities, but street vendors and tiny sidewalk eateries are cheaper than cheap.

A number of speciality food streets dot the city. P Cam Chi (see Map pp844–5), 500m northeast of Hanoi train station, is an alley crammed full of street stalls serving delicious budget-priced food. P Mai Hac De, in the south-central area east of Bay Mau Lake, has several blocks of restaurants running south from the northern terminus at P Tran Nhan Tong. Đ Thuy Khue, on the south bank of West Lake, features a strip of 30-odd outdoor seafood restaurants (see Map pp844–5) with pleasant lakeside seating. P To Hien Thanh, east of Bay Mau Lake, also specialises in small seafood restaurants. P Nghi Tam, 10km north of central Hanoi, has a 1km-strip of dog-meat restaurants.

GOOD CAUSE DINING

Combine food for the body with food for the soul at restaurants and cafes that run vocational training programs for street kids. Good cause, good food, good idea.

- **Café Ket Noi** (Map p850; ☎ 3926 2743; 28 P Dao Duy Tu; snacks & meals from 25,000d; 🕒 8.30am-midnight; 💻) Another branch of the Hoa Sua family, this place employs staff from ethnic minority groups. Head here for a bite to eat, coffee or beer.
- **Café Smile** (Map pp844-5; ☎ 3843 8850; 5 P Van Mieu; meals 50,000-120,000d 🕒 breakfast, lunch & dinner; 💻) This relaxed cafe–restaurant is renowned for its cakes and pastries, but also serves delicious Vietnamese and European dishes. The Hoa Sua organisation trains a steady stream of disadvantaged kids for culinary careers.
- **KOTO on Van Mieu** (Map pp844-5; ☎ 3747 0338; www.streetvoices.com.au; 59 P Van Mieu; meals 55,000-79,000d; 🕒 breakfast, lunch & dinner, except Mon dinner; 💻 📶) A stunning four-storey cafe–restaurant overlooking the Temple of Literature, KOTO offers local specialities, home comforts, real coffees and fruit shakes. KOTO ('Know One, Teach One') is a not-for-profit grassroots project providing opportunities for former street kids.

It's also easy to self-cater thanks to the supermarkets and outdoor markets around the usual backpacker neighbourhoods.

Vietnamese

Pho Gia Truyen (Map p850; 49 P Bat Dan; meals from 15,000d; 🕒 breakfast, lunch & dinner) Squat down with the locals at this famous *pho bo* joint where the soup is said to gain its special flavour from the home-brewed fish sauce and field-fresh herbs used.

Little Hanoi 1 (Map p850; ☎ 3926 0168; 9 P Ta Hien; meals from 20,000d; 🕒 breakfast, lunch & dinner) Venerable travellers' hang-out that's popular for its do-it-yourself fish spring rolls, a delicious dish.

Pho 24 (Map p850; ☎ 3747 4840; www.pho24.com.vn; 1 P Hang Khay; meals from 25,000d) Fast *pho*. This place offers exquisite noodle soups without the plastic chairs and street chaos. Choose by the cut.

our pick Quan An Ngon (Map pp844-5; ☎ 3942 8162; 15 P Phan Boi Chau; dishes 35,000-70,000d; 🕒 11.30am-10.30pm) Street food in style, this incredibly popular place brings mini-kitchens to the middle-class masses. It's rammed with locals and foreigners, so you might have to wait for a table.

69 Bar-Restaurant (Map p850; ☎ 3926 0452; 69 P Ma May; www.69mamay.com; mains 35,000-90,000d) A highly atmospheric restaurant, 69 occupies a historic house, and the creative menu is predominantly Vietnamese.

our pick Highway 4 (Map p850; ☎ 3926 0639; www.highway4.com; 5 P Hang Tre; meals 50,000-120,000d; 🕒 lunch & dinner) A memorable dining experience, this place specialises in Vietnamese cuisine from the northern mountains. The menu includes true exotica like *cha de men* (meat patties with crickets…crunch!). Wash it all down with a bottle or two of delicious Son Tinh rice wine, which comes in flavours including 'five times a night'.

Cyclo (Map p850; ☎ 3828 6844; 38 P Duong Thanh; mains from 70,000d; 🕒 lunch & dinner) Very memorable thanks to the Indochine atmosphere and the converted *cyclos* that have been creatively transformed into tables. Set lunch is a worthy indulgence at 90,000d.

Cha Ca La Vong (Map p850; ☎ 3825 3929; 14 P Cha Ca; cha ca 80,000d; 🕒 lunch & dinner) Family-run for five generations, this is the *cha ca* capital of the Old Quarter. It's DIY: grill your own succulent fish with a little shrimp paste and plenty of herbs.

Other Asian

Asian cuisine, especially Japanese, can be pricey in Hanoi but the following offer some decent deals.

Van Anh (Map pp844-5; ☎ 3928 5163; 5A P Tong Duy Tan; meals 30,000-100,000d; 🕒 lunch & dinner) This was the first 'foreign' place to take on the Vietnamese eateries in speciality food street P Cam Chi. The taste of Thailand.

Tandoor (Map p850; ☎ 3824 5359; 24 P Hang Be; mains 45,000-95,000d, sets 90,000d; 🕒 lunch & dinner) Right in the heart of the Old Quarter, this is an ideal place to spice up your life with a tandoori chicken, good-value *thali* or the Goan-style fish curry. Good vegetarian selection, plus halal.

International

Ladybird Restaurant (Map p850; ☎ 3926 1863; 57 P Hang Buom; meals 25,000-45,000d; ⏲ breakfast, lunch & dinner) Inexpensive place serving hearty Vietnamese food like stir-fried rice noodles and filling Western grub including pasta and burgers.

La Salsa (Map p850; ☎ 3828 9052; 25 P Nha Tho; meals 50,000-180,000d; ⏲ 10.30am-midnight) On the hip strip opposite St Joseph Cathedral, this relaxing place is good for a tapa or two, or something more substantial like paella or cassoulet.

Pepperoni's Pizza & Cafe (Map p850; ☎ 3928 5246; 29 P Ly Quoc Su; pizzas from 60,000d; ⏲ lunch & dinner) A US$2 or so all-you-can-eat weekday lunchtime pasta and salad bar – that's *amore*. It also has authentic pizza and takeaway.

La Place (Map p850; ☎ 3928 5859; 4 P Au Trieu; meals from 60,000d; ⏲ 7.30am-10.30pm) Popular little cafe opposite St Joseph Cathedral with walls covered in propaganda art and an East–West menu, including iced shakes and savoury crepes.

Vegetarian

Com Chay Nang Tam (Map pp844-5; ☎ 3826 6140; 79A P Tran Hung Dao; meals from 40,000d; ⏲ lunch & dinner) The illusionist chefs here make vegetables and pulses that look and taste like meat, reflecting an ancient Buddhist tradition designed to make carnivores feel at home.

Tamarind Café (Map p850; ☎ 3926 0580; 80 P Ma May; meals US$3-7; ⏲ 6am-midnight; 💻 📶) A relaxed cafe–restaurant with wi-fi. Its eclectic menu is best for tabouleh, eggplant claypot and salads. Plus heavenly lassis and zesty juices.

Cafes

Check out the slightly manic, fun Vietnamese coffee shops along P Hang Hanh, and watch the motorbikes come and go from the balconies upstairs.

Fanny Ice Cream (Map p850; ☎ 3828 5656; www.glacefanny.com; 48 P Le Thai To; ice cream from 10,000d) The place for French-style ice cream and sorbets, including *com* (young sticky rice) or *mang cau* (custard apple).

Kinh Do Café (Map pp844-5; ☎ 3825 0216; 252 P Hang Bong; light meals from 40,000d; ⏲ 7am-10pm) Fans of Catherine Deneuve will want to make a pilgrimage here, the setting for her morning cuppa during the making of the film *Indochine*.

Highlands Opera (Map p850; ☎ 3933 4947; 1A P Trang Tien; sandwiches from 49,000d; ⏲ breakfast & lunch) The most elegant of the classy Highlands cafes, this branch is situated right next to the stunning Opera House.

Self-Catering

Citimart (Map pp844-5; Hanoi Towers, 49 Hai Ba Trung) Supermarket that's full of deli-style treats.

Dong Xuan Market (Map p850; P Dong Xuan) Swing by for fresh fruits and vegies and baguettes.

Fivimart (Map p850; 210 Đ Tran Quang Khai) One of the best-stocked supermarkets in the centre.

DRINKING

There is something for everyone in Hanoi, with sophisticated bars, congenial pubs and grungy clubs. Don't forget to warm up with some quality time drinking *bia hoi*, the world's cheapest beer. One of the best places to sample this is '*bia hoi* junction' (Map p850) in the heart of the Old Quarter where P Ta Hien meets P Luong Ngoc Quyen. Thirsty travellers will find the following drinking places within stumbling distance of each other in the Old Quarter.

Cheeky Quarter (Map p850; 1 P Ta Hien). At the top end of the Ta Hien strip, this quirky, sociable little bar has table *footie* (foosball) and drum 'n' bass or house music.

Mao's Red Lounge (Map p850; 5 P Ta Hien) The most popular place on Ta Hien, it is rammed with a sociable crowd on weekend nights. It's a classic dive bar with dim lighting and swirling smoke.

Le Pub (Map p850; ☎ 3926 2104; 25 P Hang Be). The name is spot on: the attitude of a British pub with the atmosphere of a Continental bar. It's a friendly place and draws a good mix of travellers and foreign residents. Good grub.

Roots (Map p850; 2 P Luong Ngoc Quyen; ⏲ 8pm-late) Primarily a reggae bar, this is *the* place for some serious bass-line pressure and can be a riot on the right night. Lock-ins have been known.

Funky Monkey (Map p850; ☎ 3928 6113; 31 P Hang Thung) Very popular with local movers and shakers, this place keeps shifting location (probably in a bid to dodge the fun police). Hanoi's party people groove to pumping beats at the weekend.

Other places include the following:

Gambrinus (Map p850; ☎ 3935 1114; 198 Đ Tran Quang Khai) Czech this place out. For a Prague-style brew head to this vast, impressive *brauhaus* with shiny vats of freshly brewed beer.

Polite Pub (Map p850; ☎ 3825 0959; 5 P Bao Khanh) Pulls a crowd for big sporting events, and drinks are affordable.

Quan Bia Minh (Map p850; ☎ 3934 5233; 7A P Dinh Liet) An old backpacker fave, this no-frills bar has an upper terrace and cheap beer.

ENTERTAINMENT

Clubbing

Hanoi's nightspots seem to have the lifespan of a butterfly, so ask around about what's hot or not during your visit.

Egypt Club (Map p850; ☎ 3926 4185; 8 P Hang Buom; 9am-midnight) The Egyptian theme includes hubbly bubbly pipes to puff on, while DJs spin club anthems.

Loop (Map p850; ☎ 6270 0595; 6 P Hang Bai; 8pm-late) Opened in late 2008, this hip new place has a top sound system and attracts a good mix of foreigners and locals.

Water Puppetry

Municipal Water Puppet Theatre (Roi Nuoc Thang Long; Map p850; ☎ 3824 9494; 57B P Dinh Tien Hoang; www.thanglongwaterpuppet.org; admission 25,000-50,000d, camera fee 15,000d, video fee 50,000d; performances 4pm, 5.15pm, 6.30pm, 8pm & 9.15pm) This fascinating art form originated in northern Vietnam, and Hanoi is the best place to catch a show. The higher admission buys better seats.

Live Music

Jazz Club By Quyen Van Minh (Map p850; ☎ 3825 7655; 31-33 P Luong Van Can; performances 9-11.30pm) *The* place in Hanoi to catch some live jazz. Jams feature father–son team Minh and Dac, plus other local and international jazz acts.

I-Box (Map p850; ☎ 3828 8820; 32 P Le Thai Tho) Stylish cafe–bar that resembles a private members' club with luxurious drapes and elegant seating. There's live music most nights, including jazz and cover bands.

There is traditional live music performed daily at the Temple of Literature (p848). Upmarket Vietnamese restaurants in central Hanoi are also good places to catch traditional Vietnamese music. **Cay Cau** (Map pp844-5; ☎ 3824 5346; De Syloia Hotel, 17A P Tran Hung Dao) in De Syloia Hotel and **Club Opera** (Map p850; ☎ 3824 6950; 59 P Ly Thai To) are reliable, if expensive, options.

Hanoi Opera House (Nha Hat Lon; Map p850; ☎ 3993 0113; Pho Trang Tien) This magnificent 900-seat venue, built in 1911, hosts occasional classical music performances and the atmosphere is incredible. The theatre's Vietnamese name appropriately translates to 'House Sing Big'.

Cinemas

Megastar Cineplex (Map pp844-5; ☎ 3974 3333; www.megastarmedia.net/en; 6th fl, Vincom Tower, 191 P Ba Trieu) Multiplex cinema with tickets from just US$2.

GAY & LESBIAN HANOI

There's a thriving gay scene in Hanoi, with cruising areas such as the cafes on P Bao Khanh and around Hoan Kiem Lake. Gay guys should take care not to fall victim to the organised extortion scam going on around the lake (see p847).

Gay and lesbian venues tend to maintain a low profile; Funky Monkey (p853) is a gay-friendly place with good Friday and Saturday night parties. Ditto for Mao's Red Lounge (p853).

Cinematheque (Map p850; 22A Hai Ba Trung; ☎ 3936 2648) A mecca for art-house film lovers, this is a Hanoi institution.

Centre Culturel Française de Hanoi (Map p850; ☎ 3936 2164; 24 P Trang Tien) Set in L'Espace building near the Opera House, it offers French flicks.

SHOPPING

Your first shopping encounter will likely be with the kids selling postcards and books on the streets. They're notorious overchargers (asking about triple the going price), so a reasonable amount of bargaining is called for. The Old Quarter (Map p850) is crammed with appealing loot; price tags usually indicate fixed prices.

Handicrafts & Souvenirs

If you don't make it up to Sapa, you can find a wide selection of ethnic-minority garb and handicrafts in Hanoi; a stroll along P Hang Bac or P To Tich will turn up around a dozen places.

Local artists display their paintings at private art galleries, the highest concentration of which is on P Trang Tien, between Hoan Kiem Lake and the Opera House. The galleries are worth a browse even if you're not buying. If you're after communist propaganda art posters there are several good places on P Hang Bac in the Old Quarter including **Hanoi Gallery** (Map p850; 110 P Hang Bac) and **Old Propaganda Posters** (Map p850; ☎ 3926 2493; 122 P Hang Bac).

Make socially conscious purchases at **Craft Link** (Map pp844-5; ☎ 3843 7710; www.craftlink-vietnam.com; 43 P Van Mieu), near the Temple of Literature. It is a nonprofit organisation that buys tribal handicrafts at fair-trade prices.

Markets

Dong Xuan Market (Map p850; P Dong Xuan) With hundreds of stalls that sell everything under the sun, this three-storey market is 600m north of Hoan Kiem Lake.

Hom Market (Map pp844-5; P Hue) On the northeastern corner of P Hue and P Tran Xuan Soan, this is a good general-purpose market with lots of imported food items.

Hang Da Market (Map p850; P Yen Thai) West of Hoan Kiem Lake, Hang Da is relatively small, but good for imported food and drink. The 2nd floor has fabric and ready-made clothing.

There's also a **night market** (Map p850; 7pm-midnight) running north to south through the heart of the Old Quarter, starting on P Hang Giay and heading down to P Hang Dao. Watch out for pickpockets.

Silk Products & Clothing

P Hang Gai, about 100m northwest of Hoan Kiem Lake, and its continuation, P Hang Bong, is a good place to look for embroidery such as tablecloths, T-shirts and wall hangings. This is also the modern-day silk strip, with pricey boutiques offering tailoring services and selling ready-to-wear clothing. Other fashionable streets include P Nha Tho, near St Joseph Cathedral, west of the lake.

GETTING THERE & AWAY

Air

For details of international flights to Hanoi, see p839. For domestic flights, see p840.

Bus

Hanoi has several bus stations, each with services to a particular area. It's a good idea to arrange travel a day or two before you want to leave. The stations are well organised with ticket offices, printed schedules and prices.

Gia Lam bus station (off Map pp844-5; ☎ 3827 1569; Đ Ngoc Lam) is the place for buses northeast of Hanoi, including Halong Bay (66,000d, 3½ hours), Haiphong (50,000d, two hours), Lao Cai (155,000d, nine hours) and Lang Son (60,000d to 80,000d, three hours). It's about 3km northeast of the centre on the bank of the Song Hong, so take a taxi or motorbike.

Loung Yen bus station (off Map pp844-5; ☎ 3942 0477; Tran Quang Khai & Nguyen Khoai), 3km southeast of the Old Quarter, serves the same places as Gia Lam, plus Cao Bang (110,000d, eight hours), Mong Cai (110,000d to 150,000d, eight hours) and Ha Giang (110,000d, eight hours). Hoang Long Buses also offers a through service to Cat Ba (170,000d, 4½ hours).

Kim Ma bus station (Map pp844-5; cnr P Nguyen Thai Hoc & Pho Giang Vo) is for buses to the northwest regions, including Dien Bien Phu (from 235,000d, 14 hours).

Giap Bat bus station (off Map pp844-5; ☎ 3864 1467; Đ Giai Phong) serves points south of Hanoi, including Ninh Binh (50,000d, two hours) and Hue (185,000d, 12 hours). It is 7km south of the Hanoi train station.

My Dinh bus station (off Map pp844-5; ☎ 3768 5549, Đ Pham Hung) is an option in the west of town, which serves a range of destinations, including Halong City, Lang Son, Cao Bang, Ha Giang and Dien Bien Phu.

Tourist-style minibuses can be booked through most hotels and cafes. Popular destinations include Halong Bay and Sapa.

Car & Motorcycle

To hire a car or minibus with driver, contact a traveller cafe or travel agency (see p846). The main roads in the northeast are generally OK, but in parts of the northwest they're beautiful but bumpy, requiring a high-clearance vehicle or 4WD.

A six-day trip in a 4WD can cost US$200 to US$400 (including 4WD, driver and petrol). You should inquire about who is responsible for the driver's room and board – most hotels have a room set aside for drivers, but work out ahead of time what costs are included.

CROSSING INTO CHINA: DONG DANG TO PINGXIANG

This is the most popular border crossing. The border post itself is at Huu Nghi Quan (Friendship Gate), 3km north of Dong Dang. Catch a bus from Hanoi to Dong Dang (80,000d, three hours) and a *xe om* (20,000d) to the border. On the Chinese side, it's a 20-minute drive from the border to Pingxiang by bus or a shared taxi. Pingxiang is connected by train and bus to Nanning.

Trains from Hanoi to Běijīng via the Friendship Pass depart the capital on Tuesday and Friday at 6.30pm, a 48-hour journey that involves a three-hour stop for border formalities. It's not possible to board this train in Lang Son or Dong Dang.

GETTING INTO LAOS: THE ROADS LESS TRAVELLED

All of the border crossings between north and central Vietnam and Laos have a degree of difficulty. Be aware that unscrupulous travel agencies sell bus tickets purportedly going to various destinations in Laos, when in fact they drop travellers at the Lao border without onward transport. Talk to other travellers before booking through an agency.

If you've got the time, it is easier to head south and cross at Lao Bao.

Tay Trang to Sop Hun

The Lao border at Tay Trang is 34km from Dien Bien Phu and is finally open (7am to 5pm) after years of rumours. Buses from Dien Bien Phu to Muang Khua (80,000d, seven hours) leave at 5.30am on Mondays, Wednesdays, Fridays and Sundays. This bus passes the border crossing and terminates in Muang Khua, Laos. It is possible to hire a motorbike taxi from DBP to the border for around 120,000d, but you'll probably have to walk 5km to the nearest Laos village for transport to Muang May. Muang May has basic guest houses (both 45,000 kip) and a daily 9am bus to Muang Khua.

Nam Xoi to Na Maew

This is the most remote border in a mountainous area 175km northwest of Thanh Hoa city and 70km east of Sam Neua (Laos). Try to find a bus or take a motorbike from Thanh Hoa. All in all, expect a 15-hour ordeal if you take this route and the possibility of an overnight near the border. There is a bus from Thanh Hoa to Sam Neua, scheduled to leave every Friday at 8am (160,000d). Onward transport into Laos is extremely irregular; expect to hitch a ride on a truck to Sam Neua or Vieng Xai for US$5 to US$10.

Nam Can to Nong Haet

This crossing links Vinh with Phonsavan. Catch a morning bus from Vinh to Muong Xen (90,000d, eight hours) and grab a motorbike for the spectacular 25km uphill run to the border (aim to pay US$5). Local transport on to Nong Haet is about 30,000 kip if anything shows up. From Nong Haet, there are several buses a day on to Phonsavan (30,000 kip, four hours, 119km). On Wednesdays, Fridays, Saturdays and Sundays it's possible to catch a 6am bus from Vinh to Phonsavan (235,000d, 11 hours).

Cau Treo to Nam Phao

This border is 96km west of Vinh and about 30km east of Lak Sao in Laos. There are still lots of horror stories from travellers on this route. Catch a bus from Vinh to Tay Son (formerly Trung Tam; 70,000d, three hours). Chronic overcharging and being kicked off in the middle of nowhere are common. From Tay Son, it's 26km to the border. Take a minibus or hire a motorbike (aim to pay US$5) to cover the last stretch.

The Vietnamese border guards have been known to close the country for lunch – any time from 11.30am to 1.30pm. From the Vietnamese side it's a short walk to the Laos border. Once in Laos, *jumbo* (three-wheeled taxis) and *sawngthaew* (pick-up trucks) to Lak Sao (35,000k) leave the border when full or cost about US$20 to charter.

One way to avoid the circus altogether is to book a direct bus to Vientiane (360,000d, departs 8am daily) or Phonsavan (300,000d, departs 7am daily) through **Hai Café** (☎ 090-927 5992) at Vinh bus station. It's located immediately to the left of the station gate and Mr Hai speaks English.

Cha Lo to Na Phao

Bus services link Dong Hoi and Tha Khaek (200,000d, 11 hours) on Monday, Wednesday and Friday, returning from Tha Khaek the next morning.

For reliable motorbike rental, make for **Cuong's Motorbike Adventure** (Map p850; ☎ 3926 1534; cuongminsk@yahoo.com; 1 P Luong Ngoc Quyen), which offers Minsks or Honda Futures with spare parts and tools.

Train

Hanoi train station (Gad Hang Co; Map pp844-5; ☎ 3825 3949; 120 Đ Le Duan; ticket office 7.30-11.30am & 1.30-7.30pm) is the terminus for most trains and is at the western end of P Tran Hung Dao. Trains from here go to destinations south. It's best to buy tickets at least one day before departure to ensure a seat or sleeper. Look for the sign for foreign travellers – this agent, and the person at the information booth in the next room, usually speak some English.

For trains to Lao Cai, gateway to Sapa, buy tickets as early as possible, especially if travelling over the weekend or if you're set on a soft sleeper. For local trains, it's often only possible to purchase tickets 30 minutes to one hour before departure, but room for baggage is limited. The place you purchase your ticket is not necessarily where the train departs, so be sure to ask exactly *where* you need to catch your train.

Tran Quy Cap station (B station; Map pp844-5; ☎ 3825 2628; P Tran Qui Cap) is just two blocks south of the main station on Đ Le Duan. Northbound trains leave from here.

Gia Lam station (Nguyen Van Cu, Gia Lam District), east of the Red River, has some northbound (Yen Bai, Lao Cai, Lang Son) and eastbound (Haiphong) trains.

To make things complicated, some of the same destinations served by Gia Lam can also be reached from **Long Bien bus station** (Map pp844-5; ☎ 3826 8280).

Check with **Vietnam Rail** (www.vr.com.vn) for current timetables and prices.

GETTING AROUND

Bicycle

Pedalling around the city is invigorating, to say the least. Some hotels and cafes offer cycles to rent for about US$2 per day.

If you want to purchase your own set of wheels for a big trip, P Ba Trieu and P Hue are the best places to look for bicycle shops.

Bus

Public buses are clean and comfortable, and the fare is just 3000d. Pick up a copy of the *Xe Buyt Hanoi* (Hanoi Bus Map; 5000d) from almost any bookshop with a decent map selection.

Cyclo

Cyclos in Hanoi are wider than the HCMC breed, making them big enough for two to share the fare. Around the city centre, most *cyclo* rides should cost around 10,000d to 20,000d. Longer rides – from the Old Quarter to the Ho Chi Minh Mausoleum Complex, for example – would cost double or more again.

The *cyclo* drivers in Hanoi are even less likely to speak English than in HCMC, so take a map of the city with you.

Motorcycle

Walk 5m down any major street and you'll be bombarded by offers for *xe om*. They should cost about the same as a *cyclo* and are infinitely quicker. Insist on getting to your final destination, as occasionally to save time drivers like to drop people off a few blocks early.

For travellers well versed in the ways of Asian cities, Hanoi is a lot of fun to explore by motorbike. Most guest houses and hotels can arrange motorbikes for around US$5 to US$10 a day. However, for the uninitiated, it is *not* the easiest place to learn.

Taxi

There are several companies in Hanoi offering metered taxi services. Flag fall is around 10,000d to 15,000d, which takes you 1km or 2km; every kilometre thereafter costs about 10,000d. Bear in mind that there are lots of dodgy operators with high-speed meters. Try and use the more reliable companies:

Airport Taxi (☎ 3873 3333)
Hanoi Taxi (☎ 3853 5353)
Mai Linh Taxi (☎ 3822 2666)

AROUND HANOI

Rural Vietnam, a land of scenic countryside filled with handicraft villages and ancient pagodas, is only a short hop from Hanoi. The area includes two standout national parks – one of them a personal favourite of Ho Chi Minh – and incredible karst formations that seemingly dropped from the sky into the Tam Coc area around Ninh Binh.

HANDICRAFT VILLAGES

There are numerous villages surrounding Hanoi that specialise in particular cottage industries. Visiting these villages can make a rewarding day trip, though you'll need a good guide to make the journey worthwhile. Travel agencies in Hanoi (p846) offer day excursions covering several handicraft villages.

Bat Trang is known as the ceramic village. Watch artisans create superb ceramic vases and other masterpieces in their kilns. Bat Trang is located 13km southeast of Hanoi.

See silk cloth being produced on a loom in **Van Phuc**, a silk village that is 8km southwest of Hanoi in Ha Tay province. There's also a small produce market every morning.

So, known for its delicate noodles, is where the yam and cassava flour for noodles are milled. It is in Ha Tay province, about 25km southwest of Hanoi.

The locals in **Le Mat** raise snakes for the upmarket restaurants in Hanoi and for producing medicinal spirits. Le Mat is 7km northeast of central Hanoi.

Dong Ky survives by producing beautiful, traditional furniture inlaid with mother-of-pearl. It is 15km northeast of Hanoi.

Other handicraft villages in the region produce conical hats, delicate wooden bird cages and herbs.

PERFUME PAGODA

The **Perfume Pagoda** (Chua Huong; boat journey & admission 40,000d), about 60km southwest of Hanoi by road, is a complex of pagodas and Buddhist shrines built into the limestone cliffs of **Huong Tich Mountain** (Mountain of the Fragrant Traces). The pagoda is a highlight of the area. The scenery resembles that of Halong Bay, though you're on a river rather than by the sea.

Vast numbers of Buddhist pilgrims come here during a festival that begins in the middle of the second lunar month and lasts until the last week of the third lunar month. These dates usually end up corresponding to March and April. Also keep in mind that weekends tend to draw large crowds, with the attendant litter, vendors and noise.

If you want to do the highly recommended scenic river trip, you need to travel from Hanoi by tour or car to My Duc (two hours), then take a small boat rowed by two women to the foot of the mountain (1½ hours).

The main pagoda area is about a 4km walk uphill from where the boat disembarks. Two bits of advice: be in decent shape, and bring good walking shoes. Shorts are considered disrespectful at the pagoda; wear long trousers.

The good news is that there is now a cable car to the summit, costing 30,000d one way. A smart combination is to use the cable car to go up and then walk down.

Hanoi's travel agencies (see p846) offer day tours to the pagoda from US$10, inclusive of transport, guide and lunch (drinks excluded). If you're going with a small-group tour, expect to spend around US$25. You can also rent a motorbike to get here on your own.

BA VI NATIONAL PARK

☎ 034 / elev 1276m

Centred on scenic Ba Vi Mountain (Nui Ba Vi), **Ba Vi National Park** (☎ 388 1205; per person/motorbike 10,000/5000d) boasts more than 2000 flowering plants. There are trekking opportunities through the forested slopes of the mountain, and those who climb up to the summit will be rewarded with a spectacular view of the Red River valley – at least between April and December, when the mist doesn't hide the landscape.

Ba Vi Guesthouse (☎ 388 1197; r weekdays 130,000-190,000d, weekends 180,000-240,000d) spreads over several blocks in the heart of the park and has a big swimming pool and a moderately priced restaurant (meals 50,000d). Go for one of the less-noisy rooms away from the pool and restaurant area if you're here on a weekend. You need your passport to check in. The park restaurant serves good, cheap, fresh-cooked food.

Ba Vi National Park is about 65km west of Hanoi, and is not served by public transport. Make sure your driver knows you want to go to the park rather than Ba Vi town.

NINH BINH

☎ 030 / pop 130,000

Ninh Binh is increasingly popular with overland travellers looking to discover the 'real' Vietnam. Although it started as a travel hub due to its proximity to Tam Coc (9km away; opposite), Hoa Lu (12km; p860) and Cuc Phuong National Park (45km; p860), it has evolved into a slow-paced destination in its own right – a welcome respite if you've just escaped the bustle of Hanoi.

The surrounding countryside is gorgeous, with water buffalos, golden-green rice paddies, majestic limestone formations and more. While not a difficult place to visit, Ninh Binh seems to attract interesting travellers with a zest for new experiences.

Information

Internet cafes are spread around town, with a cluster on Đ Luong Van Tuy.

BIDV (☎ 387 1082; Đ Le Hong Phong) Exchange services and an ATM.

Main post office (Đ Tran Hung Dao)

Sleeping

Ninh Binh has some of the best-value accommodation and delightful hoteliers in Vietnam. Most can make tour arrangements or advise on cycling and motorbiking routes for travellers who'd rather go it alone. Many hotel staff and guides also speak English, and some speak French and German.

Queen Mini Hotel (☎ 387 1874; luongvn2001@yahoo.com; 21 Đ Hoang Hoa Tham; dm US$2, r US$5-7;) Located right by the train station, this small hotel has simple rooms, including dorms. It runs popular tour services and has a big book of travellers' comments to prove it.

Thanh Binh Hotel (☎ 387 2439; www.thanhbinhhotelnb.com.vn; 31 Đ Luong Van Tuy; r US$5-25;) Tucked away in a quiet street off the main highway, this hotel has a mixture of older, still-serviceable rooms and more modern accommodation on the new upper floors. The latter have decent views too.

Ngoc Anh Hotel (☎ 388 3768; ngocanhhotel@gmail.com; 30 Đ Luong Van Tuy; r US$8;) Directly opposite Thanh Binh Hotel is this smaller outfit. Rooms are tight but clean; just be prepared to make your way up a narrow but navigable staircase.

Bao Ngoc Hotel (☎ 388 9186; baongochotel@yahoo.com; 50A Pho Nam Thanh; s/d US$8/10;) This newish operation has 20 gleaming rooms in a quiet residential lane off Hwy 1A.

our pick **Thanhthuy's Guest House & New Hotel** (☎ 387 1811; www.hotelthanhthuy.com; 128 Đ Le Hong Phong; r guest house US$6-10, hotel s/d US$10/12;) Comfortable, clean, well run and friendly, with a crew of tour guides who really know the ins and outs of the area. The restaurant doubles up as a place to plan trips and meet travellers.

Xuan Hoa Hotel (☎ 388 0970; www.xuanhoahotel.com; 31D Pho Minh Kai; r US$8-30;) A friendly place with airy, light-filled rooms, spread across two buildings. The old building is still in good shape while the new one has a lift, and rooms at the rear have a balcony overlooking the quiet neighbourhood. The hotel offers little extras like a luggage storage room or a free shower after checkout.

Hoang Hai Hotel (☎ 387 5177; hoanghaihotel@gmail.com; 36 Đ Truong Han Sieu; r US$10;) Not much English is spoken at this gleaming peach establishment, but rooms are clean and spacious. The cheapest rooms are on the top (5th) floor – no lift, though.

Eating & Drinking

Although Ninh Binh is popular with backpackers, the town doesn't have much in the way of restaurants. The local speciality is *de* (goat meat), which is usually served with fresh herbs and rice paper to wrap it in. A good place to try this is the blue-walled **Huong Mai Restaurant** (☎ 387 1351; 12 Đ Tran Hung Dao; dishes 10,000d-80,000d; lunch & dinner). There is a menu in English, although the staff don't speak English. Try the fried goat with chilli and citronella, and don't let the oversized goat's head mounted over the counter intimidate you.

There are casual eateries near Thanhthuy's and Xuan Hoa Hotel, including delicious **pho ngan** (duck noodle soup; Đ Tran Hung Dao) round the corner from Thanhthuy's. Otherwise, most travellers eat at their hotel (dishes 20,000d to 60,000d). Mrs Xuan's cooking at Xuan Hoa Hotel is legendary.

For *bia hoi*, try the sidewalk setups directly opposite Thanhthuy's or the equally casual riverside places near Ximang Bridge beside the local brewery.

Getting There & Away

Regular public buses leave almost hourly from the Giap Bat bus terminal in Hanoi (45,000d, 2½ hours, 93km). The bus station in Ninh Binh is across the Van River from the post office. Ninh Binh is also a hub on the north–south open-tour bus route.

Ninh Binh is a scheduled stop for some *Reunification Express* trains travelling between Hanoi and HCMC, but travelling by road is faster.

AROUND NINH BINH

Tam Coc

Known as 'Halong Bay on the Rice Paddies' for its huge rock formations jutting out of vibrant green rice paddies, Tam Coc gives Halong Bay a run for its money.

Tam Coc (admission 30,000d, boat 60,000d) is named after the low caves through which the Ngo Dong River flows. The essential Tam Coc experience is to sit back and be rowed through the caves – a serene and scenic trip, which turns into a surreal sales experience towards the end.

The boat trip through the caves takes about two hours and tickets are sold at the small booking office by the car park. Even on cloudy days, bring sunscreen and a hat or umbrella, as there's no shade in the boats. It pays to arrive early in the morning or around mid-afternoon to avoid the day-tripping crowds from Hanoi.

Restaurants are plentiful at Tam Coc, and if you want to see where all the embroidery on sale comes from, you can visit **Van Lan village**. Here local artisans make napkins, tablecloths, pillowcases and T-shirts.

About 2km past Tam Coc is **Bich Dong**, a cave with a built-in temple. Getting there is easy enough by river or road.

Tam Coc is 9km southwest of Ninh Binh. Follow Hwy 1A south and turn west at the Tam Coc turn-off. Ninh Binh hotels run day tours, but it is more fun to make your own way by bicycle or motorbike. Hotel staff can also advise you on some beautiful back roads that link Tam Coc with Hoa Lu. Travel agencies in Hanoi book day trips to Tam Coc and Hoa Lu; the fast-food version goes for about US$20, but it's closer to US$30 with a smaller group, comfortable vehicle and professional guide.

Hoa Lu

The scenery here resembles nearby Tam Coc, though Hoa Lu has an interesting historical twist. Hoa Lu was the capital of Vietnam under the Dinh dynasty (968–80) and the Le dynasties (980–1009). The site was a suitable choice for a capital city due to its proximity to China and the natural protection afforded by the region's bizarre landscape.

The **ancient citadel** (admission 10,000d) of Hoa Lu, most of which, regrettably, has been destroyed, once covered an area of around 3 sq km. The outer ramparts encompassed temples, shrines and the palace where the king held court. The royal family of the time lived in the inner citadel.

There is no public transport to Hoa Lu, which is 12km northwest of Ninh Binh. Most travellers get here by bicycle, motorbike or car; guest houses in Ninh Binh can provide basic maps for guidance. Travel agencies in Hanoi organise day tours combining visits to Hoa Lu and Tam Coc.

CUC PHUONG NATIONAL PARK

Ho Chi Minh personally took time off from the war in 1963 to dedicate **Cuc Phuong National Park** (☎ 030-384 8006; www.cucphuongtourism.com; adult/child 20,000/10,000d), one of Vietnam's first and most important reserves. The hills are laced with grottos and the climate is subtropical at the park's lower elevations.

Excellent trekking opportunities abound in the park, including a hike (8km return) to an enormous **1000-year-old tree** (*Tetrameles nudiflora*, for botany geeks), and to a **Muong village** where you can also go rafting. A guide is not essential for short walks, but is recommended for longer trips and mandatory for the longest treks.

During the wet season (July to September) leeches are common in the park; the best time to visit is between December and April. Try to visit during the week, as weekends and Vietnamese school holidays get hectic.

One marvellous organisation based in the park is the **Endangered Primate Rescue Center** (☎ 030-384 8002; www.primatecenter.org; 9-11am & 1-4pm), run by German biologists. The centre is home to around 140 rare primates bred in captivity or confiscated from illegal traders. These gibbons, langurs and lorises are rehabilitated, studied and, whenever possible, released back into their native environments or into semiwild protected areas. Seeing them in full swing (quite literally) is certainly a sight.

Guided tours of the primate centre are free, but must be arranged from the main park office. Consider making a donation or buying some postcards to support this critical conservation project.

Sleeping & Eating

There are three accommodation areas in the park, with a complicated range of prices and options.

The centre of the park, 18km from the gate, is the best place to be for an early-morning walk or birdwatching. Here there are forlorn rooms in a **stilt house** (per person US$6), or there's a couple of self-contained **bungalows** (US$25). There's also an enormous river-fed swimming pool.

At the park entrance, there are **guest-house rooms** (US$20) and **self-contained bungalows** (US$25) as well as rooms in a **stilt house** (per person US$5). Nicer are the **bungalows** (r US$20) around the artificial Mac Lake, 2km inside the park.

WHERE TO VISIT THE HILL TRIBES

The hill tribes of Vietnam are spread throughout the highland areas in the north and centre of the country. The old French hill station of Sapa (p868) is the gateway to the northwest and the most popular place in the country to encounter the Montagnards. Most famous for Black Hmong and Red Dzao villages, it is also within striking distance of the colourful Flower Hmong markets around Bac Ha (p870).

Homestays with minority families are a rewarding experience and Mai Chau (p867) is famous for the warm welcome of the White Thai people. Down in the central highlands, Buon Ma Thuot (p899), Dalat (p894), Kon Tum (p900) and Pleiku (p900) are useful bases to meet the Bahnar, Jarai and Sedang. However, most families here have forsaken their traditional costume, so hill-tribe tourism has less pulling power than in the north.

You can camp (per person US$2) at any location, but need to bring your own gear. Meals (20,000d to 50,000d) are available from reception, including a vegetarian option.

Homestays with Muong families are available at Kanh village (per person US$5).

Getting There & Away

Cuc Phuong National park is 45km from Ninh Binh. The turn-off from Hwy 1A is north of Ninh Binh and follows the road that goes to Kenh Ga and Van Long Nature Reserve. There is no public transport all the way to the park so it's best to arrange a motorbike or car in Ninh Binh.

NORTHERN VIETNAM

This is where the magic happens. Here in the head of this dragon-shaped country are many of Vietnam's best sights; limestone cliffs looming in Halong Bay like stone sentinels, rice paddies carved from impossible mountain gradients and colourful gangs of hill-tribe women surrounding you with warm hellos.

A highly recommended adventure from Hanoi is the 'northwest loop'. Head first for Mai Chau, followed by Son La and Dien Bien Phu, then on to Sapa, Lao Cai, Bac Ha and back to Hanoi. This loop route requires a 4WD or motorbike on many sections, and you should allow at least a week for the trip.

HALONG BAY

Majestic and mysterious, inspiring and imperious, words alone cannot do justice to the natural marvel that is Halong Bay, a Unesco World Heritage Site where 3000 or more incredible islands rise from the emerald waters of the Gulf of Tonkin. The vegetation-covered islands are dotted with innumerable grottos created by the wind and the waves, and it is possible to kayak into hidden lagoons.

From February to April, the weather is often cold and rainy, and the ensuing fog can cause low visibility, although the temperature rarely falls below 10°C. Tropical storms are frequent during the summer months.

Halong City is the gateway to Halong Bay, but not the ideal introduction to the site. Developers have not been kind to the city and most visitors sensibly opt for tours that include sleeping on a boat in the bay. In short, Halong Bay is the attraction, Halong City is not.

Travellers can either book a two- or three-day Halong Bay tour through a budget travel agency in Hanoi (p846), or can head to Halong City themselves and book a day tour, or travel to Cat Ba Island (p864) and explore at their leisure.

Organised trips are reasonably priced, starting as low as US$20 per person for a standard hit-and-run day trip and rising to US$150 or more for small-group tours with two nights on a junk, and kayaking. Most tours include transport, meals, accommodation and boat tours.

Visitors must purchase a 30,000d ticket that covers all sights in the bay. Tickets are available at the tourist boat dock in Bai Chay, but are usually included for those on a tour.

If you book a tour package, there is always a small chance that the boat trip may be cancelled due to bad weather. This may entitle you to a partial refund, but remember that the boat trip is only a small portion of the cost of the journey.

It's hard to do it any cheaper on your own, but if you prefer travelling independently, it's simple enough to do so. Take a bus to Halong City from Hanoi (65,000d, 3½ hours) and book a passage on a Cat Ba tourist boat (140,000d including entry ticket, six hours). Chill out on Cat Ba before taking a hydrofoil to Haiphong.

Halong Bay Management Department (☎ 033-384 6592; http://halong.org.vn/; 166 Đ Le Thanh Tong), about 1.5km west of Halong City, regulates pricing for independent cruises on the bay. There is no need to rent a whole boat for yourself as there are plenty of other travellers, Vietnamese and foreign, to share with. The official prices are reasonable, starting at about 50,000d an hour.

Halong City

☎ 033 / pop 195,000

Halong City is the main gateway to Halong Bay. Overdeveloped but underloved, the seafront has been blighted by high-rise hotels, and the artificial beaches are definitely not the region's best. It is also sin city, with 'massage' promoted at many hotels.

ORIENTATION & INFORMATION

Halong is a tale of two cities. The western side is called Bai Chay, where all the tourist life-support systems are found. Across the bay on the eastern side is Hon Gai, a much more Vietnamese entity, connected to Bai Chay by an impressive new suspension bridge.

Post office (☎ 840 000; Đ Halong; 7.30am-5pm) Internet access available.

Vietcombank (Đ Halong) Exchange services and an ATM.

SLEEPING & EATING

The heaviest concentration of hotels is in the aptly named 'hotel alley' of Đ Vuon Dao. There are more than 50 minihotels, most of them almost identical (a guidebook-author's nightmare).

Tung Lam Hotel (☎ 364 0743; 29 Đ Vuon Dao; r US$8-12;) A good bet, as the rooms have been recently renovated. Those at the front are really spacious and have a balcony.

Hoang Lan Hotel (☎ 846 504; 17 Đ Vuon Dao; r US$9-15;) One of the first places that you come to on hotel alley, this place offers clean, well-presented rooms and rates that include a free breakfast in the cafe downstairs.

Unsurprisingly, seafood is a serious feature of most menus in the area. There are a couple of seafood strips in the centre of town, just south of the post office along Đ Halong. Aim for the places with fresh seafood in tanks out the front, or gravitate to where the locals are dining.

GETTING THERE & AWAY

All buses leave from the new bus station, which is 6km south of central Bai Chay, just off Hwy 18. Destinations include Hanoi (65,000d, 3½ hours), Haiphong (35,000d, 1½ hours), Mong Cai (65,000d, 4½ hours), and Cai Rong (35,000d, 1½ hours) for Van Don Island and Bai Tu Long Bay.

The best way to get to Cat Ba Island is to hop onto the regular tourist boats (one way 140,000d, six hours) from Bai Chay tourist-boat dock, including a leisurely cruise through the most beautiful parts of the bay.

> **CROSSING TO CHINA: MONG CAI TO DONGXING**
>
> In the far northeast, the Mong Cai border crossing (open 7.30am to 4.30pm) is just opposite the Chinese city of Dongxing. To use this border, rarely done by foreigners, your Chinese visa *must* be issued in Hanoi. **Mui Ngoc** (☎ 384 7888; Đ Halong) operates hydrofoils (US$20, three hours) to Mong Cai, leaving Halong City at 8am and 1pm.

Cat Ba Island

☎ 031 / pop 13,500

Rugged, craggy and jungle-clad Cat Ba feels like something straight out of *Jurassic Park*. Laid-back and oddly endearing, the only populated island in Halong Bay is a fine destination on its own, but the location makes it a must-visit. Half the island was declared a national park in 1986 in order to protect the diverse ecosystems and wildlife here. There are long beaches, lakes, waterfalls and grottos set in the spectacular limestone hills.

Cat Ba is emerging as northern Vietnam's adventure-sport and ecotourism mecca. There's a terrific roll-call of activities here – sailing trips, birdwatching, biking, hiking and rock-climbing – and some fine tour operators organising them.

The most famous native here is the endangered Cat Ba langur, a golden-haired little monkey that has a punk-rock hairdo.

INFORMATION

Agribank has an ATM on the harbourfront and a **branch** (☎ 388 8227) 1km north of town for changing dollars. **Vu Binh Jewellers** (☎ 388 8641) cashes travellers cheques at 3% commission and does credit-card cash advances at 5%.

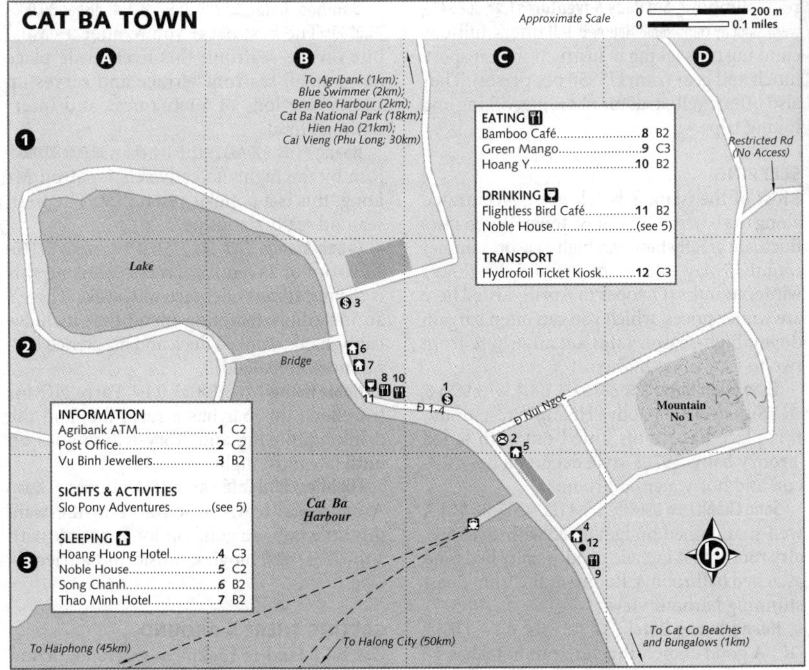

There are now several internet cafes in Cat Ba. Prices are higher than the mainland, at 15,000d an hour or more. The **post office** (Đ 1-4) is on the waterfront.

SIGHTS & ACTIVITIES

Home to various species of monkey, wild boar and hedgehog, **Cat Ba National Park** (☎ 321 6350; admission up to 2hr 15,000d, 4-7hr 35,000d; guide 50,000-150,000d; ⏲ dawn-dusk) has plenty of trekking opportunities. Although a guide is not mandatory, it's definitely recommended.

There's a very challenging 18km trek (five to six hours) through the park that many enjoy. You need a guide, transport to the trailhead and a boat to return, all of which can be arranged in Cat Ba town. If you're planning on doing this trek, equip yourself with proper trekking shoes, rainwear, a generous supply of water, and some food.

To reach the national-park headquarters at Trung Trang, take a minibus (12,000d, 30 minutes, 17km) from Cat Ba town. All restaurants and hotels should be able to sell you minibus tickets. Another option is to hire a motorbike (one way 40,000d).

Hospital Cave (☎ 368 8215; admission 15,000d; ⏲ 7am-4.30pm) is the intriguing site that was used as a secret hospital during the American War – another amazing example of Vietnamese engineering born of necessity.

The white-sand Cat Co beaches (called simply Cat Co 1, Cat Co 2 and Cat Co 3) are perfect places to lounge around for the day; however, Cat Co 1 and 3 have been taken over by big resorts. Luckily, Cat Co 2 is the most attractive beach, also offering simple accommodation and camping. The beaches are about 1km from Cat Ba town and can be reached on foot or by motorbike (15,000d).

You certainly shouldn't miss the spectacular islands and beaches of Lan Ha Bay, a short trip away from Cat Ba town. Environmentally conscious **Blue Swimmer** (☎ 368 8237; www.blueswimmersailing.com; Ben Beo Harbour) offers wonderful sailing excursions at reasonable rates to the myriad islands around Cat Ba. They also have kayaks (US$12), which you can use to explore the Cat Ba coast or mountain bikes (US$12) to explore the interior.

Cat Ba island and Lan Ha Bay's spectacular limestone cliffs make for world-class rock climbing. **Slo Pony Adventures** (☎ 368 8450; www.slopony.com; Noble House, Đ 1-4) offers full-day climbing trips taking in instruction, transport, lunch and gear from US$50 per person. They also offers well-structured sailing, biking and hiking trips.

SLEEPING

Most of the island's hotels are concentrated along the bayfront in Cat Ba town. Room rates fluctuate greatly between high-season summer months (May to September) and the slower winter months (October to April). Listed here are winter prices, which you can often bargain down; high-season rates are anywhere from two to four times higher.

Thao Minh Hotel (☎ 388 8408; D 1-4 197; r US$6-8; ❄) Situated right above Hoang Y restaurant, this place has rooms kitted out with faded 'groovy baby' 1970s-style decor; all have air-con and hot-water bathrooms.

Song Chanh (☎ 388 8402; Đ 1-4 178; r US$7-10; ❄) A well-maintained budget place with spacious, airy rooms that include good-quality beds and attached bathrooms. Rooms at the front boast stunning harbour views.

Hoang Huong Hotel (☎ 388 8274; Đ 1-4, r US$8; ❄) A good choice, this seafront hotel has 12 clean, spacious rooms with TV and hot-water bathrooms.

Noble House (☎ 388 8363; thenoblehousevn@yahoo.com; Đ 1-4; r US$8-17; ❄) A cut above the competition, this excellent place includes the town's best bar, a good cafe and Slo Pony Adventures on-site. Prices double between June and August though. Book ahead.

If the town gets too busy, try one of the thatched wooden **bungalows** (☎ 350 8408; 250,000d) over on Cat Co 2. This is a really peaceful place to stay on a beautiful sandy cove beach.

Alternatively, the small village of Hien Hao offers homestays in local houses. For more details contact **Mr Tuan** (☎ 388 8737). Hien Hao is about 20km from Cat Ba town or just 12km from the ferry landing at Phu Long.

EATING & DRINKING

For a memorable dining experience in Cat Ba, try the floating seafood restaurants, where you choose your own seafood from pens under the restaurant. A rowing boat there and back should cost about 60,000d with waiting time; a feast for two should cost around 100,000d or so. Overcharging is a possibility, so work out meal prices beforehand.

Bamboo Café (☎ 388 7552; Đ 1-4; dishes 30,000-75,000d) The best bet if you're after a casual bite on the seafront, this lively little place has a small seafront terrace and serves up hearty portions of Vietnamese and international food.

Hoang Y (☎ 090 403 7902; Đ 1-4; dishes 30,000-90,000d) Run by the highly talkative chef–patron Mr Long, this is a popular restaurant. The fresh seafood really stands out.

Green Mango (☎ 388 7151; Đ 1-4; mains 80,000-220,000d) For inventive, creative cuisine this is *the* restaurant of choice in Cat Ba. There's an incredibly tempting menu that includes lamb shank, smoked duck and blackened barramundi (160,000d).

Noble House (☎ 388 8363; Đ 1-4) Party HQ for travellers, this bar has a real vibe, and the drinking, flirting and story-telling goes on until late most nights.

Flightless Bird Café (☎ 388 8517; 🕑 from 6.30pm) A congenial Kiwi-owned hole-in-the-wall, this little pub is a good option for those with a thirst. Darts, movies, music and a friendly vibe.

GETTING THERE & AROUND

Cat Ba Island is 133km from Hanoi, 45km east of Haiphong, and 20km south of Halong City. Hydrofoils link Cat Ba and Haiphong (one hour). There are three departures a day in the high summer season and just one a day the rest of the year. **Transtour** (☎ 388 8314) runs the *Mekong Express* (120,000d, 2.45pm departure), which is the safest and most comfortable option.

If you're heading for Hanoi, it is best to buy a combined bus–boat–bus ticket (160,000d, 4½ hours) from **Hoang Long** (☎ 268 8008) or **Hoang Yen** (☎ 098 294 1285). Both offer through tickets, including the boat. The same deal is possible to Haiphong (120,000d, 2½ hours).

Government-operated boats run trips between Cat Ba and Halong Bay (140,000d, five hours); make inquiries at the pier at either end.

Rented bicycles are a good way to explore the island. Most hotels can provide a cheap Chinese bicycle.

Motorbike rentals (with or without driver) are available from most of the hotels. If you're heading to the beaches or national park, pay the parking fee to ensure the bike isn't stolen.

OFF THE BEATEN TRACK: BAI TU LONG BAY

There's more to northeastern Vietnam than Halong Bay. The sinking limestone plateau, which gave birth to the bay's spectacular islands, continues for some 100km to the Chinese border. The area immediately northeast of Halong Bay is part of **Bai Tu Long National Park** (☎ 033-379 3365).

Bai Tu Long Bay is every bit as beautiful as its famous neighbour. Indeed, in some ways it's more beautiful, since it has scarcely seen any tourist development. This is good news and bad news. The bay is unpolluted and undeveloped, but there's little tourism infrastructure. Highlights include amazing karst formations, hidden beaches and a few surf breaks off **Quan Lan Island**.

Charter boats can be arranged to Bai Tu Long Bay from Halong Bay (five hours); boats start at 200,000d per hour. A cheaper alternative is to travel overland to Cai Rong and visit the remote outlying islands by boat from there.

Haiphong

☎ 031 / pop 1.67 million

Haiphong is a graceful city that has the flavour of Hanoi in the days before tourism. Vietnam's third-most populous city retains a relaxed feel with its tall colonial-style buildings and tree-lined avenues. An important seaport and a major industrial centre, Haiphong is mostly used as a stepping-stone by travellers on their way to Cat Ba Island and Halong Bay.

INFORMATION

There are a couple of internet cafes on P Le Dai Hanh near P Dien Bien Phu.

Main post office (3 P Nguyen Tri Phuong) A grand old yellow dame on the corner of P Hoang Van Thu.

Vietcombank (11 P Hoang Dieu; closed Sat) Cashes travellers cheques, does cash advances and has an ATM.

Vietnam-Czech Friendship Hospital (☎ 370 0514; Benh Vien Viet-Tiep; P Nha Thuong) In emergencies, seek help here; otherwise, head back to Hanoi.

SIGHTS & ACTIVITIES

Though there is not a whole lot to see in Haiphong, its slow-paced appeal is enhanced by the French-colonial architecture lining the streets.

Du Hang Pagoda (Chua Du Hang; 121 P Chua Hang; 7-11am & 1.30-5.50pm), founded three centuries ago and rebuilt several times since, has architectural elements that look Khmer. Equally enjoyable is wandering along the narrow alley to get here, **P Chua Hang**, which is buzzing with Haiphong street life.

SLEEPING & EATING

Hotel du Commerce (☎ 384 2706; 62 P Dien Bien Phu; r US$10-18;) Housed in a fine historic building, the gently decaying rooms have high ceilings and gigantic bathrooms. Think atmosphere above amenities.

Kim Thanh Hotel (☎ 374 5264; 67 P Dien Bien Phu; r US$17-21;) Nothing fancy, but probably the best bet for a reasonably priced hotel in Haiphong. The rooms are old-fashioned but clean, and have TV.

Com Vietnam (☎ 384 1698; 4A P Hoang Van Thu; mains 30,000-80,000d) Diminutive, unpretentious restaurant with a small patio that hits the spot for its affordable local seafood and Vietnamese specialities.

BKK (☎ 382 1018; 22 P Minh Khai; mains 35,000-90,000d) The card proclaims 'trendy Thai restaurant' and it's absolutely true. All the Thai tastes, plus a serious amount of seafood.

P Minh Khai offers a good selection of cheap eateries, and most hotel restaurants dish up variations on the fresh seafood available in Haiphong. Also check out P Quang Trung with its many cafes and *bia hoi*.

GETTING THERE & AWAY

Vietnam Airlines (☎ 381 0890; www.vietnamair.com.vn; 30 Pho Hoang Van Thu) has flights to HCMC and Danang. **Jetstar Pacific** (☎ 04-3955 0550; www.jetstar.com) has cheaper flights to HCMC.

Transtour (☎ 384 1009) runs the *Mekong Express* (120,000d), which is the safest and most comfortable boat to Cat Ba. There are no longer hydrofoils operating to Halong City, as the road journey is faster. All boats leave from the **ferry pier** (Đ Ben Binh), 10 minutes' walk from the centre of town.

Minibuses bound for Hanoi (50,000d, 103km, two hours) depart from the **Tam Bac bus station** (P Tam Bac), 4km from the waterfront. Buses heading south leave from **Niem Nghia bus station** (Đ Tran Nguyen Han). **Lac Long bus station** (Pho Cu Chinh Lan) has buses to Halong City (35,000d, 1½ hours), as well as Hanoi, which is convenient for those connecting with the Cat Ba hydrofoil.

There are four trains per day to Hanoi (33,000d, two hours) from **Haiphong train station** (Đ Luong Khanh Thien & Đ Pham Ngu Lao).

BA BE NATIONAL PARK

☎ 0281 / elev 145m

Boasting mountains high, rivers deep, as well as waterfalls, lakes and caves, **Ba Be National Park** (☎ 389 4014; www.babenationalpark.org; per person/car 3000/20,000d) has it all. This region is surrounded by steep mountains up to 1554m high, home to members of the Tay minority, who live in stilt houses. The park is a tropical rainforest area with more than 400 named plant species. The 300 wildlife species in the forest include bears, monkeys, bats and butterflies.

Ba Be (Three Bays) is in fact three linked lakes, the largest freshwater-lake system in the country. The Nang River is navigable for 23km between a point 4km above Cho Ra and the **Dau Dang Waterfall** (Thac Dau Dang), which is a series of spectacular cascades between sheer walls of rock. The interesting **Puong Cave** (Hang Puong) is about 30m high and 300m long, and passes completely through a mountain. A navigable river flows through the cave.

Park staff can organise several **tours**. Costs depend on the number of people; think about US$22 per day for solo travellers, less if there's a group of you. The most popular excursion is a **boat trip** (boat hire 300,000-550,000d). The boats can carry about 12 people and you should allow at least seven hours to take in most sights. The boat dock is about 2km from park headquarters.

Sleeping & Eating

Not far from the park headquarters are two accommodation options.

Park Guesthouse (☎ 389 4026; r 200,000d) is a newer place with rooms that are fine, if a bit pricey. Choose from semi-detached bungalows (300,000d), each with two double beds, and chalets (200,000d) that are small and fairly basic. The complex has two restaurants (meals from 50,000d), though you should order early.

It is also possible to arrange to stay in one of a dozen stilt houses (per person 60,000d) at Pac Ngoi village on the lakeshore. The park office can help organise this. Meals (20,000d to 60,000d) are available, and can include fresh fish from the lake.

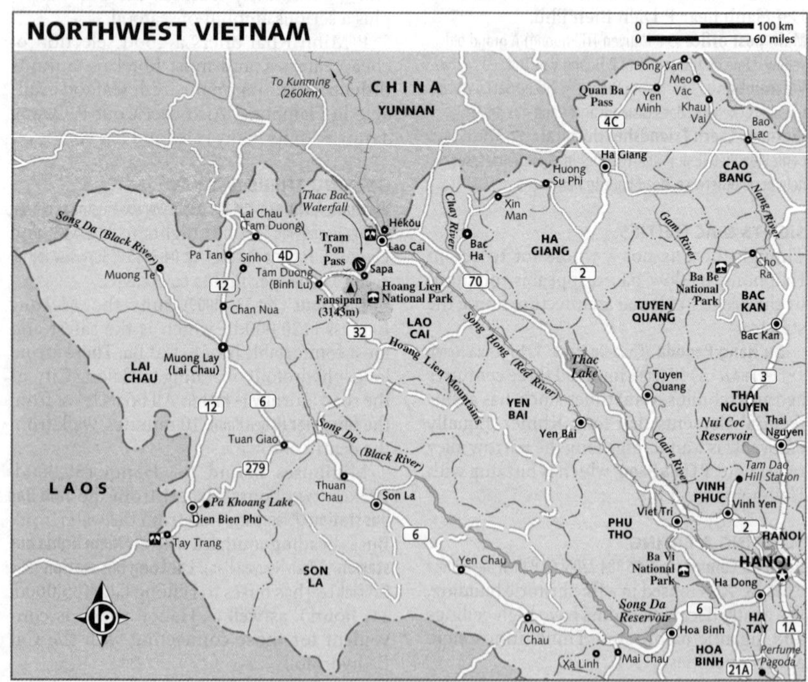

EXPLORING THE FAR NORTH

Motorcycling in Vietnam's wild northern territory is unforgettable. If you're not confident riding a motorbike yourself, it's possible to hire someone to drive you. Four-wheel-drive trips in the north are also highly recommended, though the mobility of travelling on two wheels is unrivalled.

One of the most popular routes is the 'Northwest Loop', which follows Hwy 6 through the heart of the Tonkinese Alps. There are many variations, but the standard route takes in a homestay in the **White Thai villages** (below) around Mai Chau, a stop in **Son La**, a visit to the historic battlefield of **Dien Bien Phu**, before finishing up at **Sapa** (p868), the queen of the mountains. However, some companies also specialise in taking bikers right off the trail into the lakes of **Ba Be National Park** (opposite).

While it's possible to organise a motorcycling trip on your own, hiring a guide will certainly make the trip run smoothly and get you to places you'd never discover from a cursory scan of a map.

Minsks used to be the bike of choice, but many companies are switching to more reliable Japanese bikes. Daily hire rates start from US$5 to US$10, depending on the bike. Foreign guides usually charge more than local Vietnamese guides. Check out these outfits in Hanoi:

- **Explore Indochina** (☎ 0913-524 658; www.exploreindochina.com) Run by back road-explorer Digby and Minsk master mechanic Cuong, these guys have biked all over the country and can take you to the parts others cannot reach. Prices from US$150 per day.
- **Free Wheelin Tours** (☎ 04-3747 0545; www.freewheelin-tours.com) Run by Fredo (Binh in Vietnamese), this company has its own homestays in the northeast, as well as 4WD trips. Prices start from US$100 per day with a group of four.
- **Offroad Vietnam** (☎ 04-3904 5049; www.offroadvietnam.com) A Vietnamese-run company, these guys generate really good feedback from their guests. Tours from US$100 per day.
- **Voyage Vietnam** (☎ 04-3926 2373; www.voyagevietnam.net) Another locally run outfit, this company has earned itself a good reputation. Prices from US$100 per day.

Take enough cash for your visit – there are no money-exchange facilities, although there are banks in Bac Kan, the provincial capital en route from Hanoi.

Getting There & Away

Ba Be National Park is 240km from Hanoi, 61km from Bac Kan and 18km from Cho Ra. Most visitors get here by chartered vehicle from Hanoi (six hours) and most allow three days and two nights for the trip. Budget travel agencies in Hanoi (p846) offer trips here.

Reaching the park by public transport is possible, but not easy. Take a bus from Hanoi to Phu Thong (90,000d, five hours) via Thai Nguyen and/or Bac Kan, and from there take another bus to Cho Ra (25,000d, one hour). In Cho Ra arrange a motorbike (about 50,000d or so) to cover the last 18km.

MAI CHAU

Mai Chau is the closest place to Hanoi in which you can experience a hill-tribe village. The modern village is an unappealing sprawl, but as you emerge on the rice fields and scenes of rural life it is transformed into a real paradise. Most people here are ethnic White Thai, distantly related to tribes in Thailand, Laos and China. Traditional weaving is practised here and the beautiful results can be purchased directly from the weaver. Be aware that Mai Chau sees a lot of tourists and has all the modern, Western comforts: TVs, toilets and all.

Sights

Guides can be hired for around US$5 for a 7km to 8km walk. There is a popular 18km trek from **Lac village** (Ban Lac) in Mai Chau to **Xa Linh village**, near a mountain pass (elevation 1000m) on Hwy 6. Lac village is home to the White Thai people, while the inhabitants of Xa Linh are Hmong. The trek is quite strenuous to undertake in a day, so most people spend the night in a village along the way. Arrange a local guide and a car to meet you at the mountain pass for the journey back to Mai Chau.

Sleeping & Eating

Most backpackers prefer to stay a few hundred metres back from the main road in **White Thai stilt houses** (per person 80,000-150,000d) in Lac or Pom Coong villages. Double-check the meal prices before committing to a spread. Villagers will sometimes organise traditional song-and-dance performances in the evenings. Reservations are not necessary, but it's advisable to arrive before dark. The bathroom doors may have fairly large gaps between the walls, so use your towel to good effect.

Getting There & Away

Mai Chau is 135km from Hanoi and just 5km south of Tong Dau junction on Hwy 6. There's no direct public transport to Mai Chau from Hanoi; catch a Son La–bound bus as far as Tong Dau (45,000d, 3½ hours) and a *xe om* from there to Mai Chau for around 25,000d.

Many budget travel agencies in Hanoi (p846) run inexpensive trips to Mai Chau.

Officially, there is a 5000d entry fee to Mai Chau, but the toll booth is usually out of action.

LAO CAI

☎ 020 / pop 100,000

One of the gateways to China, Lao Cai lies at the end of the train line on the Chinese border. The border crossing slammed shut during the 1979 war between China and Vietnam and remained closed until 1993. Lao Cai is now a major hub for travellers journeying between Hanoi, Sapa (38km away) and Kūnmíng.

There is a post office next door to the train station, plus an internet cafe close by. **BIDV bank** (Đ Thuy Hoa) offers currency exchange and an ATM.

There is no need to stay the night with Sapa just up the mountain, but most of the guest houses opposite the station on P Moi offers showers (20,000d with towel and soap) to freshen up before the night train.

Getting There & Away

Minibuses to Sapa (28,000d, 1½ hours) leave regularly until late afternoon. Minibuses to Bac Ha (50,000d, two hours) leave several times daily, the last at 1pm.

Lao Cai is 340km from Hanoi (155,000d, nine hours by bus), but most travellers sensibly prefer the train.

When it comes to life on the rails, tickets to Hanoi (10 hours) start at 98,000d for a hard seat (bad choice) to 300,000d for an air-conditioned soft sleeper, and rise by about 10% at weekends. There are also several companies operating special private carriages with comfortable sleepers, including the affordable **ET Pumpkin** (www.et-pumpkin.com). There are two night trains and one day train in either direction.

SAPA

☎ 020 / pop 36,200

Clinging to the hillside, Sapa overlooks a plunging valley of cascading rice terraces, with mountains towering above the town on all sides. Founded as a French hill station in 1909, Sapa is the premier destination of northwestern Vietnam. The whole area is spectacular and frequently shrouded in mist.

Hill-tribe women with colourful headgear, and some with retro-looking leggings, dye and sell their fabrics on the sidewalk while their children chase tourists. Hill-tribe men have an out-of-this-world look as they run errands on motorbikes wearing black petticoats with high collars, leather tunics, silver chain-link necklaces and modern helmets. This city in the clouds is nestled in spectacular scenery and

CROSSING TO CHINA: LAO CAI TO HÉKŎU

The Lao Cai–Hékǒu crossing (open 7am to 7pm) is popular with travellers making their way between northern Vietnam and Yúnnán. China is separated from Vietnam by a bridge over the Red River that pedestrians pay a 3000d toll to cross. The border is about 3km from Lao Cai train station, costing about 20,000d by *xe om*.

The train service running directly from Hanoi to Kūnmíng in China has been suspended indefinitely since 2002. However, it's possible to take a train to Lao Cai, cross the border into China, and catch a midmorning or overnight sleeper bus (87Y, 12 hours) from the Chinese border town of Hékǒu to Kūnmíng.

Note that travellers have reported Chinese officials confiscating Lonely Planet *China* at this border, so you may want to conceal the cover.

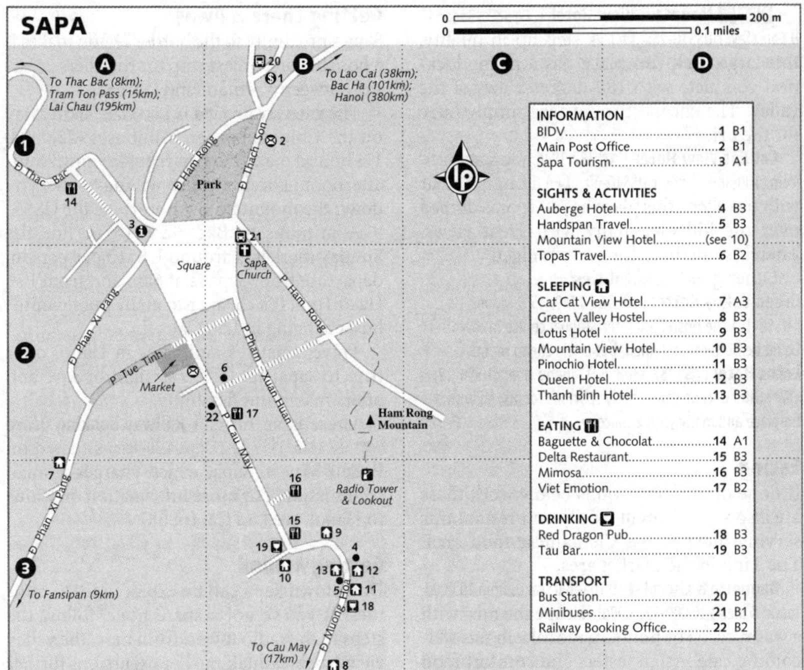

makes a great base for day trips or overnights in the many hill-tribe villages nearby. Don't forget your warm clothes – Sapa is known for its cold, foggy winters.

Information

Internet access is available in countless hotels and travel offices around town, usually at 5000d per hour.

BIDV (☎ 872 569; Đ Ngu Chi Son; ⏲ 7-11.30am & 1.30-4.30pm) Offers an ATM, plus exchanges travellers cheques and cash.

Main post office (Đ Ham Rong) Post things from Hanoi, as it is much faster.

Sapa Tourism (☎ 387 3239; www.sapa-tourism.com; 103 Đ Xuan Vien; ⏲ 7.30-11.30am & 1.30-5pm) This is a rarity: a well-run and informative tourism office with helpful staff.

Sights & Activities

Surrounding Sapa are the Hoang Lien Mountains, including **Fansipan**, which at 3143m is Vietnam's highest peak. The trek from Sapa to the summit and back can take several days. Treks can be arranged at guest houses and travel agencies around town, including **Mountain View Hotel** (☎ 387 1334; 54A P Cau May) and **Auberge Hotel** (☎ 387 1243; P Cau May).

Topas Travel (☎ 387 1331; www.topas-adventure-vietnam.com; 24 Muong Hoa) is a reliable ecotourism operator that employs many guides from the local area. **Handspan Travel** (☎ 387 2110; www.handspan.com; 8 P Cau May) is a popular place to arrange treks with homestays and mountain biking in the area.

Some of the better-known sights around Sapa include the epic **Tram Ton Pass**; the pretty **Thac Bac** (Silver Falls); and **Cau May** (Cloud Bridge), which spans the Muong Hoa River.

Sleeping

Queen Hotel (☎ 387 1301; www.sapaqueenhotel.com; Đ Muong Hoa; r US$5-12) This place has been hosting backpackers for years and remains a solid choice. Size matters when it comes to price, but all rooms have hot water and TV.

Pinochio Hotel (☎ 387 1876; quysapa1978@yahoo.com; 15 Đ Muong Hoa; r US$6-9; 💻) The young, lively staff who run this excellent guest house really make the place. The rooms, all with simple but attractive decor, creep up the hillside. Plus there's a rooftop restaurant.

ourpick Mountain View Hotel (☎ 387 1334; 54A Đ Cau May; r US$10-25; 💻) A step up in quality, this large, well-run place has a prime location complete with 180-degree views of the valley. The cheapest rooms are simply huge for the price.

Cat Cat View Hotel (☎ 387 1946; www.catcathotel.com; 1 Phan Xi Pang; r US$10-60; 💻) Long popular with travellers, this place has 40 rooms draped over the hillside, many with great views. There's something for every budget.

Other good possibilities:

Green Valley Hostel (☎ 387 1449; 45 Đ Muong Hoa; r US$6-10) The Hostelling International choice in town. Could be better maintained, but offers cheap rooms.

Lotus Hotel (☎ 387 1308; 5 Đ Muong Hoa; r US$6-12; 💻) Offer decent-value, fairly spacious rooms, all with a fireplace and many with a balcony.

Eating

If none of the suggestions below work there are also several small family-run restaurants serving inexpensive Vietnamese food on P Tue Tinh in the market area.

Baguette & Chocolat (Đ Thac Bac; cakes from 10,000d, snacks & meals 40,000-120,000d) Escape the mist with a warm cocoa or home-made cake in this welcoming cafe. Asian tasters and comfort food complete the menu, all helping disadvantaged teenagers.

Mimosa (☎ 387 1377; meals from 14,000d) A few steps off the main drag, this atmospheric old place scores for inexpensive Vietnamese and Western food.

Viet Emotion (☎ 387 2559; 27 P Cau May; meals 40,000-120,000d) This stylish, intimate little place has a bistro feel about it, with an original tapas menu.

Delta Restaurant (☎ 387 1799; P Cau May; mains US$5; 🕑 lunch & dinner) Delta Restaurant is renowned for its pizzas, which are the most authentic in town, though the pasta is pretty reliable as well.

Drinking & Entertainment

Red Dragon Pub (☎ 872 085; 21 Đ Muong Hoa) Don't be put off by the genteel tearoom below, as hiding upstairs is a cosy little pub that is a friendly place to booze.

Tau Bar (☎ 871 322; 42 P Cau May) Aiming to be 'slightly lounge', Tau brings a different kind of cool to the mountains of the north. There is a DIY jukebox on the computer, the cocktails are mixed by a pro and there is a good pool table.

Getting There & Away

Sapa's proximity to the border region makes it a possible first or last stop for travellers crossing between Vietnam and China.

The gateway to Sapa is Lao Cai, 38km away on the Chinese border. Minibuses (26,000d, 1½ hours) make the trip regularly until mid-afternoon. Locals are also willing to take you down the mountain by motorbike for US$5.

A minibus to Bac Ha (110km) for the Sunday market is around US$12 per person; departure from Sapa is at 6am and from Bac Ha at 1pm. It's cheaper to go by public minibus, changing in Lao Cai.

Travel agencies and cafes in Hanoi offer trips to Sapa, but DIY is straightforward and offers maximum flexibility.

There is an official **Railway Booking Office** (☎ 387 1480; 🕑 7.30-11am & 1.30-4pm) situated on P Cau May in Sapa, which charges a small commission. For more information on trains to Hanoi, see Lao Cai (p868).

Getting Around

Downtown Sapa can be explored in 20 minutes. If you've got a spare hour, follow the steps to the radio tower; from here, the valley views are breathtaking. For excursions further out, hire a self-drive motorbike from US$5 per day, or take one with a driver from US$10.

BAC HA

☎ 020 / pop 70,200

A quieter and slightly less scenic alternative to Sapa, Bac Ha is a small highland town that becomes downright hectic during the Sunday market. Unless travellers are looking for a souvenir water buffalo or horse, the most interesting thing for sale here is moonshine – rice wine, cassava wine and corn liquor. There's an entire area devoted to Bac Ha's famous hooch at the Sunday market.

Arriving midweek makes for a relaxing visit and it's a good base from which to explore the surrounding highlands. Around 900m above sea level, it is noticeably warmer than Sapa. There are 10 Montagnard ethnic groups that live around Bac Ha, with the colourful Flower Hmong being the most visible. Many groups sell their handicraft wares.

Sights & Activities

BAN PHO VILLAGE

The Hmong villagers in Ban Pho are some of the kindest people you'll meet in Vietnam. Ban

Pho is a 7km return trip from Bac Ha. You can take a loop route to get there and back.

Other nearby villages include **Trieu Cai** (8km return), **Na Ang** (6km return) and **Na Hoi** (4km return). Ask at your hotel for directions.

MONTAGNARD MARKETS

Other than the colourful Sunday **Bac Ha market** in town, there are several interesting markets nearby, all within about 20km of each other.

Can Cau market One of Vietnam's most exotic open-air markets, it is 20km north of Bac Ha and just 9km south of the Chinese border. The market is held on Saturday.

Coc Ly market Takes place on Tuesday, about 35km from Bac Ha. There's a pretty good road, or you can go by road and river; ask at hotels in Bac Ha.

Lung Phin market Between Can Cau market and Bac Ha, about 12km from the town. It's less busy, and is open on Sunday.

Sleeping & Eating

Room rates tend to increase on weekends, when tourists arrive for a piece of the Sunday-market action.

Hoang Vu Hotel (☎ 388 0264; r from US$6) It's nothing fancy, but the large spacious rooms are good value, with TV and fan. Bac Ha's best tour operator is here.

Quynh Trang Hotel (☎ 388 0450; r from 150,000d) A well-run place with spotless rooms that have wood-panelled walls, solid furniture, fans and TV.

Congfu Hotel (☎ 388 0254; congfuhotel@gmail.com; r from 260,000d; ❄ 💻 📶). This new place has very attractive rooms, almost minimalist in design. There's wi-fi, internet in the lobby, helpful staff and a good restaurant (meals from 30,000d).

Hoang Yen Restaurant (mains 15,000-40,000d) Arguably the best eatery in town, it has a great front terrace and a well-priced menu, including noodle dishes and cheap beer.

Getting There & Around

Buses make the 63km trip from Lao Cai to Bac Ha (50,000d, two hours) about five times daily.

Sunday minibus tours from Sapa to Bac Ha cost around US$12, including transport, guide and trekking to a minority village. On the way back to Sapa, hop off in Lao Cai and catch the night train to Hanoi.

Bac Ha is about 330km (10 hours) from Hanoi. Travel agencies in Hanoi (see p846) offer four-day bus trips to Sapa, with a visit to Bac Ha included.

CENTRAL COAST

Ancient history, compelling culture, fantastic food and iconic beaches – central Vietnam is one of the must-see regions of the country. The coast has the country's third-largest city, its former imperial capital and its bloodiest modern battle sites – but also an architectural gem that time forgot, an ancient religious capital and nature reserves so dense that scientists discover new creatures every few years. Danang's airport is the perfect gateway for visitors who want to avoid long overland journeys.

HUE

☎ 054 / pop 335,000

Hue is the intellectual, cultural and spiritual heart of Vietnam. Palaces and pagodas, tombs and temples, culture and cuisine, history and heartbreak – there's no shortage of poetic pairings to describe Hue. It served as the political capital from 1802 to 1945 under the 13 emperors of the Nguyen dynasty. Today, Hue's decaying, opulent tombs of the Nguyen emperors and grand, crumbling Citadel comprise a Unesco World Heritage Site. Most of these architectural attractions lie along the northern side of the Song Huong (Perfume River), but for rest, refreshment and recreation, the south side is on the pulse.

Information

INTERNET ACCESS

There are lots of internet cafes on the tourist strips of Đ Hung Vuong and Đ Le Loi.

MEDICAL SERVICES

Hue Central Hospital (Benh Vien Trung Uong Hue; ☎ 382 2325; 16 Đ Le Loi)

MONEY

Vietcombank (30 Đ Le Loi; 🕑 7am-10pm Mon-Sat) Located at the Hotel Saigon Morin.

Vietinbank (☎ 383 0212; 12 Đ Hung Vuong; 🕑 7.30am-6pm Tue-Sat, 8-11.30am Sun) An ATM plus exchange services.

POST

Main post office (14 Đ Ly Thuong Kiet) Postal and telephone services.

TRAVEL AGENCIES

Café on Thu Wheels (☎ 383 2241; minhthuhue@yahoo.com; 3/34 Đ Nguyen Tri Phuong) Cycling and motorcycling tours around Hue, overseen by the gregarious and inimitable Mrs Thu.

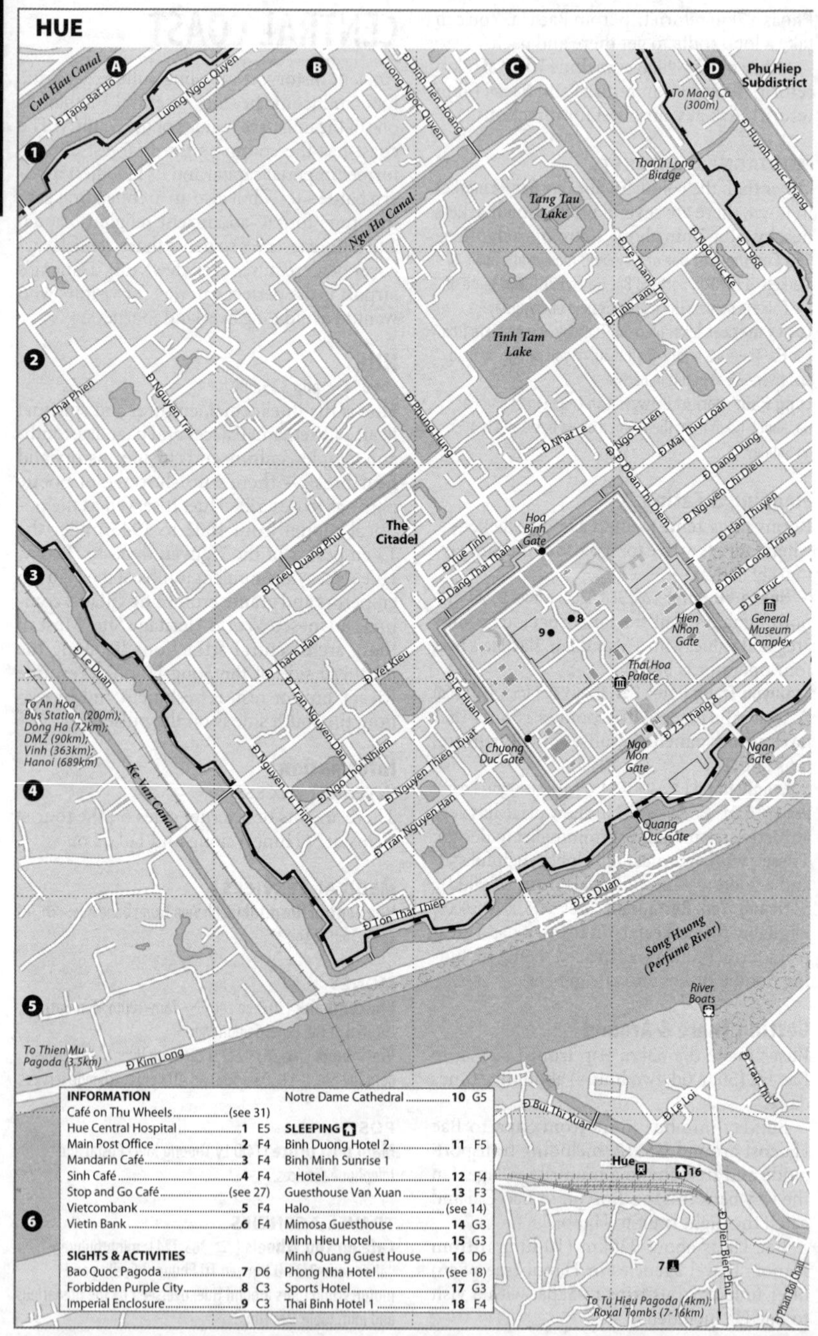
HUE
Cua Hau Canal
Đ Tang Bat Ho
Luong Ngoc Quyen
Đ Dinh Tien Hoang
Luong Ngoc Quyen
Phu Hiep Subdistrict
To Mang Ca (300m)
Đ Huynh Thuc Khang
Thanh Long Birdge
Tang Tau Lake
Ngu Ha Canal
Đ Le Thanh Ton
Đ Ngo Duc Ke
Đ 1968
Đ Tinh Tam Ton
Tinh Tam Lake
Đ Thai Phien
Đ Nguyen Trai
Đ Phung Hung
Đ Nhat Le
Ngo Si Lien
Đ Mai Thuc Loan
Đ Doan Thi Diem
Đ Dang Dung
Đ Nguyen Chi Dieu
Đ Han Thuyen
Đ Dinh Cong Trang
Đ Le Truc
General Museum Complex
The Citadel
Hoa Binh Gate
Đ Tue Tinh
Đ Dang Thai Than
Đ Trieu Quang Phuc
Hien Nhon Gate
Thai Hoa Palace
Đ Le Duan
To An Hoa Bus Station (200m); Dong Ha (72km); DMZ (90km); Vinh (363km); Hanoi (689km)
Đ Thach Han
Đ Tran Nguyen Dan
Đ Yet Kieu
Đ Le Huan
Chuong Duc Gate
Ngo Mon Gate
Đ 23 Thang 8
Ngan Gate
Ke Van Canal
Đ Nguyen Cu Trinh
Đ Ngo Thoi Nhiem
Đ Nguyen Thien Thuat
Đ Tran Nguyen Han
Quang Duc Gate
Đ Ton That Thiep
Đ Le Duan
Song Huong (Perfume River)
River Boats
To Thien Mu Pagoda (3.5km)
Đ Kim Long
Đ Tran Thu
Đ Bui Thi Xuan
Đ Le Loi
Hue
Đ Dien Bien Phu
To Tu Hieu Pagoda (4km); Royal Tombs (7-16km)
Đ Phan Boi Chau
INFORMATION
Café on Thu Wheels ....(see 31)
Hue Central Hospital 1 E5
Main Post Office 2 F4
Mandarin Café 3 F4
Sinh Café 4 F4
Stop and Go Café ....(see 27)
Vietcombank 5 F4
Vietin Bank 6 F4
SIGHTS & ACTIVITIES
Bao Quoc Pagoda 7 D6
Forbidden Purple City 8 C3
Imperial Enclosure 9 C3
Notre Dame Cathedral 10 G5
SLEEPING
Binh Duong Hotel 2 ....11 F5
Binh Minh Sunrise 1 Hotel 12 F4
Guesthouse Van Xuan 13 F3
Halo ....(see 14)
Mimosa Guesthouse 14 G3
Minh Hieu Hotel 15 G3
Minh Quang Guest House 16 D6
Phong Nha Hotel ....(see 18)
Sports Hotel 17 G3
Thai Binh Hotel 1 ....18 F4

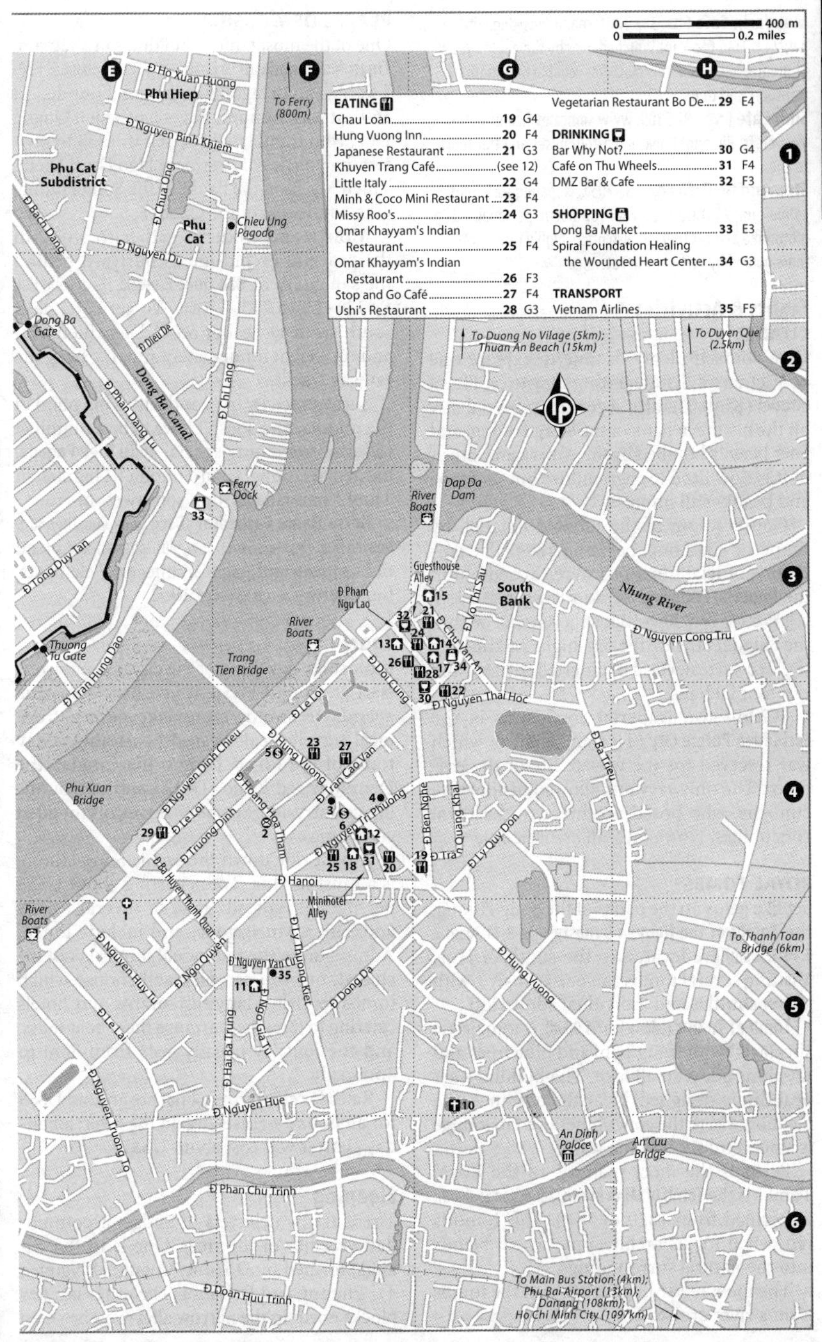

0 400 m
0 0.2 miles
EATING
Chau Loan....19 G4
Hung Vuong Inn....20 F4
Japanese Restaurant....21 G3
Khuyen Trang Café....(see 12)
Little Italy....22 G4
Minh & Coco Mini Restaurant....23 F4
Missy Roo's....24 G3
Omar Khayyam's Indian Restaurant....25 F4
Omar Khayyam's Indian Restaurant....26 F3
Stop and Go Café....27 F4
Ushi's Restaurant....28 G3
Vegetarian Restaurant Bo De....29 E4
DRINKING
Bar Why Not?....30 G4
Café on Thu Wheels....31 F4
DMZ Bar & Cafe....32 F3
SHOPPING
Dong Ba Market....33 E3
Spiral Foundation Healing the Wounded Heart Center....34 G3
TRANSPORT
Vietnam Airlines....35 F5
Đ Ho Xuan Huong
Phu Hiep
To Ferry (800m)
Đ Nguyen Binh Khiem
Phu Cat Subdistrict
Đ Chua Ong
Phu Cat
Chieu Ung Pagoda
Đ Bach Dang
Đ Nguyen Du
Dong Ba Gate
Đ Dieu De
Dong Ba Canal
Đ Phan Dang Luu
Đ Chi Lang
To Duong No Vilage (5km); Thuan An Beach (15km)
To Duyen Que (2.5km)
Ferry Dock
Dap Da Dam
River Boats
Đ Tong Duy Tan
Guesthouse Alley
Đ Pham Ngu Lao
South Bank
Đ Vo Thi Sau
Nhung River
Đ Chu Van An
Đ Nguyen Cong Tru
Thuong Tu Gate
Trang Tien Bridge
Đ Tran Hung Dao
Đ Doi Cung
Đ Le Loi
Đ Nguyen Thai Hoc
Đ Ba Trieu
Đ Hung Vuong
Đ Nguyen Dinh Chieu
Đ Tran Cao Van
Phu Xuan Bridge
Đ Hoang Hoa Tham
Đ Nguyen Tri Phuong
Đ Ben Nghe
Đ Quang Khai
Đ Ly Quy Don
Đ Truong Dinh
Đ Tra
Đ Ba Huyen Thanh Quan
Đ Hanoi
Minihotel Alley
Đ Ly Thuong Kiet
Đ Nguyen Huy Tu
Đ Ngo Quyen
Đ Nguyen Van Cu
Đ Ngo Gia Tu
Đ Dong Da
To Thanh Toan Bridge (6km)
Đ Le Lai
Đ Hai Ba Trung
Đ Nguyen Truong To
Đ Nguyen Hue
An Dinh Palace
An Cuu Bridge
Đ Phan Chu Trinh
Đ Doan Huu Trinh
To Main Bus Station (4km); Phu Bai Airport (13km); Danang (108km); Ho Chi Minh City (1097km)

Mandarin Café (☎ 382 1281; mandarin@dng.vnn.vn; 24 Đ Tran Cao Van) Watched over by the eagle eyes of photographer Mr Cu, this place has reliable information, transport and tours.

Sinh Café (☎ 382 3309; www.sinhcafevn.com; 7 Đ Nguyen Tri Phuong) Books open-tour buses and transport to Laos.

Stop and Go Café (☎ 382 7051; stopandgocafetours@yahoo.com; 25 Đ Tran Cao Van) Top-notch, personalised motorbike and car tours. It also offers highly rated DMZ tours guided by Vietnamese veterans.

Sights & Activities

CITADEL

Give yourself plenty of time to explore one of Vietnam's disintegrating treasures, Hue's **Citadel** (Kinh Thanh). A former imperial city on the northern bank of the Song Huong, and later heavily bombed by the Americans, much of it is now used for agriculture but its scope and beauty still impress.

Construction of the moated Citadel, by Emperor Gia Long, began in 1804. The emperor's official functions were carried out in the **Imperial Enclosure** (Dai Noi or Hoang Thanh; admission 55,000d; 6.30am-5.30pm), a 'citadel within the Citadel'. Inside the 6m-high, 2.5km-long wall is a surreal world of deserted gardens and ceremonial halls.

Within the Imperial Enclosure is the **Forbidden Purple City** (Tu Cam Thanh), which was reserved for the private life of the emperor. The only servants allowed inside were eunuchs, who posed no threat to the royal concubines. Nowadays, all are welcome.

ROYAL TOMBS

Set like gems on the banks of the Song Huong, the **Tombs of the Nguyen Dynasty** (8-11.30am & 1.30-5.30pm) are located to the south of Hue. Visiting several tombs can be expensive, with *xe om* shuttles and individual admission.

Tomb of Tu Duc (admission 55,000d) is a majestic site, laced with frangipani and pine trees and set alongside a small lake. The buildings are beautifully designed. Near the entrance, the pavilion where the concubines used to lounge is a peaceful spot on the water.

Perhaps the most majestic of the Royal Tombs is the **Tomb of Minh Mang** (admission 55,000d), who ruled from 1820 to 1840. This tomb is renowned for its architecture, which blends into the natural surroundings.

The most rewarding way to visit the tombs is on a river cruise.

PLACES OF WORSHIP

One of the most famous buildings in Vietnam, **Thien Mu Pagoda** (Đ Le Duan; 7.30-11.30am & 1.30-5.30pm) is an octagonal structure. Founded in 1601, it was the home pagoda of Thich Quang Duc, who immolated himself in 1963 to protest the policies of President Ngo Dinh Diem. Thien Mu is on the banks of the Song Huong, 4km southwest of the Citadel.

Monks and students gather to study in the peaceful orchid-lined courtyard behind the sanctuary of **Bao Quoc Pagoda** (Ham Long Hill; 7.30-11.30am & 1.30-4.30pm). To get here, head south from Đ Le Loi on Đ Dien Bien Phu and turn right immediately after crossing the railway tracks.

Surrounded by trees and with a big pond in the middle, one doesn't have to be a Buddhist to sense something special at **Tu Hieu Pagoda**, located at Duong Xuan Thuong III hamlet, in Thuy Xuan village, 4km southwest of Hue.

Notre Dame Cathedral (Dong Chua Cuu The; 80 Đ Nguyen Hue; Mass 5am & 5pm, plus 7pm Sun) is a blend of European and Asian architectural elements, built between 1959 and 1962.

Tours

Motorbike day tours of the city and environs start at around US$6. If you have a specific agenda in mind, motorbike guides from local traveller cafes can do customised day tours of the Royal Tombs, the Citadel, the Demilitarised Zone (DMZ) and surrounding countryside. See p877 for recommended companies.

A boat ride down the scenic Song Huong is a must in Hue. Tours costing about US$3 per person typically take in several tombs and Thien Mu Pagoda, and include lunch. Admission to the individual tombs is not included, but you can pick and choose which tombs to visit. Many restaurants and hotels catering to foreigners arrange these boat tours, and the journey usually lasts from 8am to 4pm daily.

Rates for chartering a boat are around US$8 for an hour's sightseeing on the river; a half-day charter will cost about US$15.

Sleeping

There are two clusters of budget accommodation south of the river. One is in the triangle formed by Đ Hung Vuong, Đ Nguyen Tri Phuong and Đ Hanoi. The other is a few blocks north in the narrow alleyways between

Đ Le Loi and Đ Vo Thi Sau. It's worth comparing prices to get a better bargain.

Guesthouse Van Xuan (☎ 382 6567; 10 Đ Pham Ngu Lao; r US$5-6; ❄) Though it's run down and has tatty bathrooms, this place has the cheapest rooms on the main drag. It's run by an elderly couple who speak hardly any English.

Mimosa Guesthouse (☎ 382 8068; tvhoang4@hotmail.com; 66/10 Đ Le Loi; r US$7-8; ❄) Not for the claustrophobic, this cheapie has narrow staircases and spartan rooms. It's run by an affable former French teacher who also speaks good English.

Phong Nha Hotel (☎ 382 7729; phongnha_hotel@yahoo.com; 10/10 Đ Nguyen Tri Phuong; r incl breakfast US$8-15; ❄ 💻) Strategically located opposite Café on Thu Wheels, this newish minihotel has friendly staff and rooms that are good value for money.

Thai Binh Hotel 1 (☎ 382 8058; www.thaibinhhotel-hue.com; 6/34 Đ Nguyen Tri Phuong; r US$8-15; ❄ 💻) With only four spacious rooms on each floor, this hotel is a peaceful oasis amid the buzz of the backpacker alley.

Halo (☎ 382 9371; huehalo@yahoo.com; 10A/66 Đ Le Loi; r US$8-15; ❄ 💻) Gleaming, immaculate rooms right in backpacker central. Rooms at the front have a large balcony, good for hanging out in the evening.

Binh Duong Hotel 2 (☎ 384 6466; binhduong2@dng.vnn.vn; 8 Đ Ngo Gia Tu; r US$8-15; ❄ 💻) A short walk from the tourist thicket, this friendly outfit in a residential neighbourhood has everything from cheapies to spacious rooms with modern bathrooms.

Minh Hieu Hotel (☎ 382 8725; minhhieu008@gmail.com; 3Đ Chu Van An; r US$10; ❄ 💻) Simple, neat rooms that do the trick in a family-run establishment.

Minh Quang Guest House (☎ 382 4152; 16 Đ Phan Chu Trinh; r US$12; ❄) Spotless accommodation near the railway station. Little English is spoken, but rooms are surprisingly nice, with modern appliances and bathroom fixtures.

our pick Binh Minh Sunrise I Hotel (☎ 382 5526; www.binhminhhue.com; 36 (12) Đ Nguyen Tri Phuong; s US$12, d US$15-20; ❄ 💻) This hotel has all the ingredients for a pleasant stay: a central location, effortlessly pleasant staff and clean, fair-sized rooms. To sweeten the deal, there's complimentary in-room coffee and tea. Staff are helpful but not pushy about tours.

Sports Hotel (☎ 382 8096; www.huestays.com; 15 Đ Pham Ngu Lao; r US$15-25; ❄ 💻) Despite the fact that it's a chain hotel, this place has is redeemed by cheerful staff and tasteful contemporary decor. Prices includes breakfast and every room has a minifridge.

Eating

There's plenty of inexpensive street food to try in Hue, particularly around Dong Ba Market (Đ Tran Hung Dao). Look out also for the noodle stalls set up around the Citadel at night and the *com pho* places along Đ Tran Cao Van.

Minh & Coco Mini Restaurant (☎ 382 1822; 1 Đ Hung Vuong; mains 10,000-35,000d; 🕑 breakfast, lunch & dinner) Run by two lively (some say feisty) sisters, this neighbourhood dive has the usual range of inexpensive traveller eats. Locals come in at night to shoot the breeze over beer.

Vegetarian Restaurant Bo De (☎ 382 5959; 11 Đ Le Loi; dishes 10,000-50,000d; 🕑 lunch & dinner) A pleasant nook where you can fill up on inexpensive Vietnamese vegetarian fare (and we don't mean mock meat). Tucked away on a deserted stretch by the river, it's good for avoiding the tourist ruckus. Menus are in English and French, and patio seating is available.

Omar Khayyam's Indian Restaurant (☎ 381 0310; 22 Đ Pham Ngu Lao; dishes 10,000-89,000d; 🕑 lunch & dinner) Successful enough to spawn a second joint, this is a good place to fill up on staples from the subcontinent. The new space at Đ Pham Ngu Lao is dressed up in traditional style, while the original renovated location at 34 Đ Nguyen Tri Phuong is more modern, with a rooftop terrace. The latter also has some Vietnamese menu items.

Chau Loan (☎ 382 2777; 78 Đ Ben Nghe; meals 15,000-50,000d; 🕑 breakfast, lunch & dinner) Grab some tasty rice or noodle dishes with the locals at this neighbourhood eatery. The food is Chinese-influenced and an English menu is available. Just don't inspect the grubby walls and floor too closely.

Khuyen Trang Café (☎ 384 9793; 40 Đ Nguyen Tri Phuong; meals 15,000-50,000d; 🕑 breakfast, lunch & dinner) A friendly no-frills place that offers simple Vietnamese and backpacker fare – great for unwinding over a cold beer at the end of the day.

Stop and Go Café (☎ 382 7051; 25 Đ Tran Cao Van; meals 20,000-60,000d; 🕑 breakfast, lunch & dinner) This mellow indoor-outdoor cafe has airy seating around a pleasant little fish pond. There's good Vietnamese and backpacker fare on the menu, including home-made tacos.

Hung Vuong Inn (☎ 382 1068; 20 Đ Hung Vuong; pastries 15,000d, meals 30,000-60,000d; ⌚ breakfast, lunch & dinner) The kind of casual, clean eatery where everyone knows your name – or tries to, anyway, despite the constant stream of travellers passing through. There's a decent wine list and French-style pastries and bread. Rooms are available upstairs.

Ushi's Restaurant (☎ 382 1143; ushivietnam@yahoo.com.vn; 42 Đ Pham Ngu Lao; dishes 15,000-110,000d; ⌚ breakfast, lunch & dinner) Don't mind the odd decor, with bright orange walls and oversized pictures of the owner. The menu here is predominantly Vietnamese, with some pizzas to keep the homesick happy, and there's an extensive vegetarian selection. A pool table is also available.

Missy Roo's (☎ 383 1923; 11 Đ Pham Ngu Lao; mains 20,000-70,000d; ⌚ breakfast, lunch & dinner) Besides the usual backpacker fare, this laid-back cafe serves good salads and barbecue, including 'Vietnamese barbecue' – kebabs with a local twist.

Little Italy (☎ 382 6928; www.littleitalyhue.com; 2A Đ Vo Thi Sau; dishes 20,000-100,000d; ⌚ breakfast, lunch & dinner) Despite the bamboo decor and *ao dai*–wearing waitresses, this casual trattoria is as Italian as it gets in Hue. The menu is pretty extensive, with a wide range of reasonable pasta and pizzas.

Japanese Restaurant (☎ 382 5146; 12 Đ Chu Van An; dishes US$1.50-9.00; ⌚ dinner) If you're after a pleasant change of pace, this restaurant has sushi and other Japanese standards. It also employs and supports a home for street children, so your meal dollars are also going to a good cause.

Drinking

Café on Thu Wheels (☎ 383 2241; minhthuhue@yahoo.com; 10/2 Đ Nguyen Tri Phuong) It's small but packs a powerful punch, with the gregarious owner Ms Thu keeping the scene lively every night (and all day too). A great place for making new travel buddies, swapping on-the-road tales and, of course, kicking back with Hue beer.

DMZ Bar & Cafe (☎ 382 3414; www.dmz-bar.com; 60 Đ Le Loi) A long-running hot spot on the backpacker trail, this energetic bar has rock(ing) music, free pool and a steady circulation of expats and travellers. Things get predictably more boisterous as the night wears on. Food is served till midnight, including the entire menu from Little Italy.

Bar Why Not? (☎ 382 4793; www.whynotbarhue.com; 21 Đ Vo Thi Sau) At the other end of Đ Pham Ngu Lao is this less raucous hang-out, good for people-watching and pool. There's a sensational list of cocktails.

Shopping

Hue produces the finest conical hats in Vietnam. The city's speciality is 'poem hats', which, when held up to the light, reveal shadowy scenes of daily life. It's also home to one of the largest and most beautiful selections of rice-paper and silk paintings available in Vietnam, but the prices quoted are usually sensationally inflated.

Dong Ba Market (Đ Tran Hung Dao; ⌚ 6.30am-8pm) On the north bank of the Song Huong a few hundred metres north of Trang Tien Bridge, this is Hue's largest market, where anything and everything can be bought.

Spiral Foundation Healing the Wounded Heart Center (☎ 383 3694; 69 Đ Ba Trieu) This social enterprise sells a wide array of handicrafts made by 40 disabled artisans.

Getting There & Away

AIR

Vietnam Airlines (☎ 382 4709; 23 Đ Nguyen Van Cu; ⌚ closed Sun) offers several flights a day connecting Hue to both Hanoi and HCMC.

Phu Bai airport is 13km south of the centre and takes about 25 minutes by car. Taxi fares are around US$10, although share taxis cost as little as US$3 – ask at hotels. Vietnam Airlines runs a connecting shuttle (45,000d) from its office to the airport.

BUS

The Au Cuu bus station is 4km to the southeast on the continuation of Đ Hung Vuong (it becomes Đ An Duong Vuong and Đ An Thuy Vuong). The first main stop south is Danang (40,000d, three hours). **An Hoa bus station** (Hwy 1A), northwest of the Citadel, serves northern destinations, including Dong Ha (30,000d, 1½ hours).

Hue is a stop on the open-tour bus routes. Mandarin and Stop and Go Cafés (p871) can arrange bookings for the bus to Savannakhet, Laos (see the boxed text, opposite).

TRAIN

Hue train station (Ga Hue; ☎ 382 2175; 2 Đ Bui Thi Xuan; ⌚ ticket office 7.30am-5pm) is on the south bank of the river, at the southwestern end of Đ Le Loi.

CROSSING INTO LAOS: LAO BAO TO DANSAVANH

The **Lao Bao border** (🕑 7am-6pm) is the most popular and least problematic land crossing between Laos and Vietnam. You can get a 30-day Lao visa (US$30) on arrival in Dansavanh, but Vietnamese visas still need to be arranged in advance; drop in on the Vietnamese consulate in Savannakhet.

Sepon Travel (☎ 385 5289; www.sepon.com.vn; 189 Đ Le Duan) in Dong Ha has buses to Savannakhet (180,000d, 7½ hours), leaving Dong Ha at 8am every second day and returning the next day. These buses also come through Hue (US$20, add 1½ hours).

If you're travelling across the border by tourist bus, expect a wait while documents are checked. When booking a tourist bus, be sure to confirm (preferably in writing) that the same bus carries on through the border. We've heard plenty of stories of tourists on this route being bundled off nice buses on the Vietnamese side and on to overcrowded local buses once they reach Laos.

Travelling independently is possible but hefty overcharging is likely to make it more expensive in the long run. Catch a bus from Dong Ha to Lao Bao (50,000d, two hours, 85km) and then a *xe om* (motorbike taxi) to the border (10,000d). Once in Laos, there is only one public bus a day direct to Savannakhet (60,000 kip, five hours, 250km), which leaves when full. *Sawngthaew* (pick-up trucks) leave fairly regularly to Sepon with connections to Savannakhet. For information on crossing this border in the other direction, see p413.

Getting Around

Bicycles (US$2), motorbikes (from US$5) and cars (US$30 per day) can be hired through hotels all over town. **Gili** (☎ 382 8282) and **Mai Linh** (☎ 389 8989) both have air-con taxis with meters. *Cyclos* and *xe om* will find you when you need them, and when you don't.

AROUND HUE

Demilitarised Zone (DMZ) Tours

From 1954 until 1975, the Ben Hai River served as the dividing line between South Vietnam and North Vietnam. The DMZ, 90km northwest of Hue, consisted of the area 5km on either side of the line and saw some of the fiercest fighting in the American War.

Many of the 'sights' around here are places where historical events occurred, and may not be worthwhile unless you're into war history. To make sense of it, and to avoid areas where there is unexploded ordnance, take a guide. Day tours from Hue are around US$25.

Significant sites:

Khe Sanh Combat Base (admission 20,000d; 🕑 7am-5pm) The site of the American War's most famous siege, on a barren plateau about 130km from Hue.

Truong Son National Cemetery (Nghia Trang Liet Si Truong Son) A memorial to the tens of thousands of North Vietnamese soldiers killed along the Ho Chi Minh Trail. Row after row of tombstones stretch across the hillsides, about 105km from Hue.

Vinh Moc Tunnels (admission 20,000d; 🕑 7am-4.30pm) Similar to the tunnels at Cu Chi (p914), but less adulterated for tourists; 110km from Hue.

BACH MA NATIONAL PARK

☎ 054 / elev 1450m

A French-era hill station known for its cool weather, **Bach Ma National Park** (Vuon Quoc Gia Bach Ma; ☎ 387 1330; www.bachma.vnn.vn; admission 20,000d) is 45km southeast of Hue. Although quite close to a major city, the steep road up to the park entrance feels like it is heading to a different world. Sometimes the mist is so thick it's hard to see more than 10m ahead, and on the many trekking trails scenes of raging waterfalls or lazy brooks suddenly materialise from nowhere. From the peak of the summit trail there are sweeping views across the stone remains of villas dotted around the nearby hills.

The national park is rich in flora and fauna and is a birdwatcher's paradise. The best time to visit is between March and June. It's a good idea to bring decent rain gear as they only sell very thin ponchos at the snack shop. Guides (200,000d per day) can point out the many medicinal plants in the park. Leeches are common so take precautions.

Trails are marked on the national-park map, which you receive with your ticket. Further information is found in the *Bach Ma National Park* booklet, available for 12,000d at the park entrance.

Sleeping & Eating

National Park Guesthouse (☎ 387 1330; camp sites per person 10,000d, entrance r 150,000d, summit r 150,000-300,000d) The park authority has a small camping ground, two guest houses near the entrance and four guest houses near the summit. One of the summit guest houses has a 12-person dorm with a shared bathroom. The more expensive twin-bed rooms are a better bet for views and facilities. Give at least four hours' notice for meal requirements, as fresh food is brought up to the park on demand.

Getting There & Around

The entrance and visitors centre is at Km 3 on the summit road, which starts at the town of Cau Hai on National Hwy 1. It's another meandering 16km from the gate to the summit, and unless you are willing to walk it (three to four hours; bring lots of water and wear a hat), you'll need to hire private transport from the park. Eight-seater passenger vans are available to hire (350,000d to 500,000d) from the park entrance for same-day return. Motorbikes and private cars are strictly forbidden.

There are buses to the park from Danang (35,000d, two hours) and Hue (20,000d, one hour) that will drop travellers on the main road near the entrance of the park. Numerous local buses stop at Cau Hai town, where *xe om* drivers can ferry you to the entrance.

DANANG

☎0511 / pop 1.1 million

One of Vietnam's largest cities, Danang is where the first US Marines waded ashore to join the war effort. The economic powerhouse of central Vietnam, it combines the buzz of a bigger city with beautiful beaches and fine dining. For most travellers this is not enough and it remains primarily a transit stop to visit the Museum of Cham Sculpture.

Information

INTERNET ACCESS

There are internet cafes scattered all over Danang, including several by the river on Đ Bach Dang.

MEDICAL SERVICES

Danang Family Medical Practice (☎ 358 2700; www.vietnammedicalpractice.com; 50-52 Đ Nguyen Van Linh) One of Vietnam's most trusted foreign-owned clinics operates in Danang.

Hospital C (Benh Vien C; ☎ 382 2480; 35 Đ Hai Phong) The most advanced hospital in Danang.

MONEY

Vietcombank (140 Đ Le Loi) Full exchange services plus an ATM.

POST

Main post office (☎ 383 7407; 64 Đ Bach Dang) Near the Song Han Bridge.

TRAVEL AGENCIES

Dana Tours (☎ 382 5653; 76 Đ Hung Vuong; Mon-Sat) Offers car hire, boat trips, visa extensions and treks in nearby Ba Na or Bach Ma.

Trong's Real Easy Riders (☎ 090-359 7971; trongn59@yahoo.com) A group of about 30 Easy Riders (see p896) who operate out of Danang.

Sights & Activities

Danang's jewel is the famed **Museum of Cham Sculpture** (Bao Tang Dieu Khac Cham; 1 Đ Trung Nu Vuong; admission 30,000d; 7am-5pm). This classic, colonial-era building houses the finest collection of Cham sculpture to be found anywhere on earth. These intricately carved sandstone pieces come from Cham sites all over Vietnam, and it's worth the detour to Danang just for this.

Guides hang out at the museum's entrance; should you hire one, agree on a fee beforehand.

Sleeping

Budget options aren't easy to scare up in Danang, as most hotels cater to business types. The better deals are generally slightly further from the centre of town.

Hoa's Place (☎ 396 9216; hoasplace@hotmail.com; 215/14 Đ Huyen Tran Cong Chua, My An Beach; r US$9) Blessed with laid-back charm, this is the kind of classic backpacker joint where you might drop in for a night, only to find yourself making buddies and staying a week. Rooms are unabashedly basic, but the point of staying here is to be a short walk away from the beach and get chummy with fellow travellers and the gregarious Mr Hoa himself.

Hai Van Hotel (☎ 382 3750; kshaivan.dng@vnn.vn; 2 Đ Nguyen Thi Minh Khai; s/d US$12/19;) It's more old-fashioned than retro, and in need of a paint job, but it has cheap digs (for Danang). Some rooms are more run down than others, so choose carefully and inspect the bathrooms.

Minh Travel Hotel (☎ 381 2661; minhtraveldn@gmail.com; 105 Đ Tran Phu; r US$15;) This minihotel has the cheapest rooms in the city centre, and they look it too. Expect a very spartan set-up and shabby paintwork. Fan rooms are available for US$10.

Phu An Hotel (☎ 382 5708; phuanhoteldng@gmail.com; 29 Đ Nguyen Van Linh; s 220,000d, d 250,000-270,000d;) Don't be put off by the gloomy lobby.

DANANG
0 400 m
0 0.2 miles
A
B
C
D
1
2
3
4
5
6
Bay of Danang
Thanh Binh Beach
Nguyen Tat Thanh
Ong Ich Khiem
Cao Thang
Dinh Tien Hoang
Tran Cao Van
Danang
Hai Phong
Le Duan
Hoang Hoa Tham
Dong Da
Tran Qui Cap
Ly Thuong Kiet
Bach Dang
Nguyen Du
Ly Tu Trong
Le Loi
Tran Phu
Nguyen Chi Thanh
Quang Trung
Nguyen Thi Minh Khai
Caodai Temple
Ngo Gia Tu
Danang Stadium
Pasteur
Phan Dinh Phung
Hung Vuong
Nguyen Thai Hoc
Pham Hong Thai
Phan Chu Trinh
Yen Bai
Pham Phu Thu
Tran Quoc Toan
To China Beach (2km); Hoa's Place (9km)
Song Han Bridge
Han River
To Danang Intercity Bus Station (2km); Local Bus Station (2km); National Highway 1A (4km); Hai Van Pass (29km); My Son (31km); Hue (109km)
Nguyen Hien Dinh Theatre
Thai Phien
Le Hong Phong
Hoang Van Thu
Co Giang
Le Dinh Duong
Pham Ngu Lao
Trieu Nu Vuong
Hoang Dieu
Phap Lam Pagoda
Nguyen Van Linh
To Danang International Airport (2km)
Huynh Thuc Khang
Trung Nu Vuong
To My Khe Beach (5km); China Beach (10km); Non Nuoc Beach (10km); Marble Mountains (10km); Hoi An (29km)
INFORMATION
Dana Tours....1 D4
Danang Family Medical Practice....2 B5
Hospital C....3 B3
Lao Consulate....4 C1
Main Post Office....5 D3
Vietcombank....6 C3
SIGHTS & ACTIVITIES
Museum of Cham Sculpture....7 D5
SLEEPING
Hai Van Hotel....8 B2
Minh Travel Hotel....9 D3
Phu An Hotel....10 B5
Prince Hotel....11 D3
EATING
Bread of Life....12 D4
Café Truc Lam Vien....13 C5
Com Nieu....14 D3
Com Tay Cam Cung Dinh....15 B5
DRINKING
Bamboo 2 Bar....16 D4
Christie's Cool Spot....17 D4
Nep Café....18 D4
TRANSPORT
Jetstar Pacific....19 C5
Vietnam Airlines....20 D3

There are big rooms with modern bathrooms upstairs, and pleasant staff. Rooms at the front suffer from street noise, so try to get one at the back.

ourpick Prince Hotel (☎ 381 7929; tranthai2003@dng.vnn.vn; 60 Đ Tran Phu; s/d US$17/22;) If you can spare a few extra bucks, this boutique hotel offers the best value for money in downtown Danang. The location is great, rooms are very nice and staff are helpful and earnest.

Eating

Com Nieu (☎ 386 7026; 25 Đ Yen Bai; dishes 14,000-120,000d; lunch & dinner) Very popular with locals, this contemporary restaurant has hearty meals and affable staff. Besides its namesake dish, there's a full spread of Vietnamese fare. Try the savoury grilled beef wrapped in seaweed, or ask about the seafood of the day.

Com Tay Cam Cung Dinh (☎ 389 7638; K254/2 Đ Hoang Dieu; dishes 15,000-75,000d; lunch & dinner) This brightly painted restaurant is a surprising find, tucked away down a dingy alley. It serves local specialities like *com nieu* (rice cooked in a claypot) and *hoanh thanh* – a wonton-like combination of minced pork and shrimp served fried or steamed.

ourpick Café Truc Lam Vien (☎ 358 2428; www.truclamvien.com.vn; 37 Đ Le Dinh Duong; meals 35,000-80,000d; lunch & dinner) A delightful oasis not far from the Museum of Cham Sculpture. Dine alfresco in a pretty garden courtyard or, if it's too hot, duck into one of the sleek wooden pavilions. Service is efficient and the menu, including local favourites like *mi quang*, is available in English.

Bread of Life (☎ 356 5185; breadoflife@pobox.com; 12 Đ Le Hong Phong; meals 40,000-100,000d; breakfast, lunch & dinner Mon-Sat) Load up on all your favourites from home here: pancakes, pizzas and specials like biscuits, and gravy or sloppy Joes. All baked goods are made fresh in the bakery behind. The restaurant is almost entirely run by deaf staff and proceeds go towards training activities for the deaf in Danang.

Drinking

Bamboo 2 Bar (☎ 090-554 4769; 230 Đ Bach Dang) Your typical backpacker hang-out, with a pool table and drunken messages scrawled on the wall. This place also attracts lots of expats. A Western food menu is available.

Christie's Cool Spot (☎ 382 4040; ccdng@dng.vnn.vn; 112 Đ Tran Phu) US war veterans tend to hold court here, though you can sit by and quietly nurse an ice-cold beer if you want to. There's also a decent restaurant upstairs with American and Vietnamese fare.

Nep Café (☎ 091-344 1234; 115 Đ Tran Phu) An old trombone, a Che poster and a bicycle poking out of an exposed brick wall are just some of the oddments decorating this indie hang-out right across from Christie's. Live bands play upstairs three times a week.

Getting There & Away

Danang international airport has connections to Bangkok, Hong Kong, Siem Reap and Singapore. **Vietnam Airlines** (☎ 382 1130; www.vietnamairlines.com; 35 Đ Tran Phu) has an extensive domestic schedule connecting Danang with the rest of Vietnam. **Jetstar Pacific** (☎ 358 3538; 307 Đ Phan Chu Trinh) has flights to HCMC and Hanoi. Both **Mai Linh** (☎ 356 5656) and **Taxi Xanh** (☎ 368 6868) operate in Danang and serve the airport (50,000d).

The **Danang intercity bus station** (☎ 382 1265; 33 Đ Dien Bien Phu; 7-11am & 1-5pm) is 3km west of the city centre. Buses run to Hue (25,000d, three hours) and Hoi An (10,000d, one hour).

To get to Hoi An, you can rent a car (around US$15) or a friendly neighbourhood *xe om* (around US$6). A stop at the Marble Mountains will cost a little extra. Travel agencies can also arrange passage on open-tour minibuses running between Danang and both Hoi An and Hue. Regular buses to Hoi An (10,000d, one hour) depart from a **local bus station** directly opposite the ticket office in the intercity bus station, but foreigners tend to be overcharged.

Danang train station (Ga Da Nang) is about 1.5km from the city centre on Đ Hai Phong at Đ Hoang Hoa Tham. Danang is served by all *Reunification Express* trains. The train ride to Hue is one of the most beautiful stretches in the country.

AROUND DANANG

About 10km south of Danang are the immense **Marble Mountains** (admission 15,000d; 7am-5pm) consisting of five marble outcrops that were once islands. With natural caves sheltering small Hindu and Buddhist sanctuaries, a picturesque pagoda and scenic landings with stunning views of the ocean and surrounding countryside, it's well worth the climb.

China Beach (Bai Non Nuoc), once an R&R hang-out for US soldiers during the American War, is actually a series of beaches stretching

30km between Hoi An and Danang. Nearest to central Danang, **My Khe Beach** is well touristed and has beachside restaurants and roving vendors. Opposite the Marble Mountains is **Non Nuoc Beach**, and in between the two are countless spots to spread your beach towel.

For surfers, China Beach's break gets a decent swell from mid-September to December. The best time for swimming is from May to July, when the sea is at its calmest. There's a mean undertow at China Beach, worst in the winter, so take care.

Buses and minibuses running between Danang and Hoi An can drop you off at the entrance to the Marble Mountains and China Beach, and it's easy to find a *xe om* for onward travel. From Danang, it's also possible to reach this area by bicycle.

HOI AN

☎ 0510 / pop 122,000

For the flavour of old Vietnam, Hoi An is a glorious place to soak up for a few days. Set on the Thu Bon River, Hoi An – or Faifo, as early Western traders knew it – was an international trading port as far back as the 17th century. Influences from Chinese, Japanese and European cultures are well preserved in local architecture and art. Roaming the narrow lanes, weaving between the cafes, restaurants and shops, it's easy to imagine how it might have looked 150 years ago.

Hoi An's charms aren't limited to its exquisite architecture, though; it's the best place in the country to get affordable custom-made clothing, and the nearby beach and Cham ruins make excellent expeditions out of town, and it's a gastronomic delight.

Information

Hoi An Hospital (☎ 386 1364; 4 Đ Tran Hung Dao) Serious problems should be addressed in Danang.

Hoi An police station (☎ 386 1204; 84 Đ Hoang Dieu)

INTERNET ACCESS

Internet cafes are hard to miss in Hoi An. Popular places to check email over a cool drink include the following:

Banana Split Café (☎ 386 1136; 53 Đ Hoang Dieu)

Hai Scout Café (☎ 386 3210; 98 Đ Nguyen Thai Hoc)

MONEY

Vietcombank (☎ 391 6374; 642 Đ Hai Ba Trung) and **Vietinbank** (☎ 386 1340; 4 Đ Hoang Dieu) have full exchange services, plus ATMs.

POST

Main post office (☎ 386 1480; 48 Đ Tran Hung Dao) At the corner of Đ Ngo Gia Tu.

TRAVEL AGENCIES

Travel agencies are scattered throughout town with a concentration of places along Đ Tran Hung Dao. Since most agencies offer the same services and tours for similar costs, one cannot be recommended over another. Competition is fierce, so if you want to book something expensive or complicated, check out a few options and then negotiate. One popular tour is to My Son (p886).

Dangers & Annoyances

For the most part, Hoi An is very safe at any hour. However, late-night bag-snatchings in the isolated, unlit market are on the rise. There have also been (extremely rare) reports of women being followed to their hotels and assaulted. Lone women should have a friend walk home with them at night (and don't underestimate the results of yelling your lungs out).

At the My Son ruins, there's a running scam involving motorbike vandalism and extortionist 'repairs' made by the vandals themselves. It's recommended that you hire a driver if you visit independently.

Sights

HOI AN OLD TOWN

As a Unesco World Heritage Site, **Hoi An Old Town** (admission 75,000d) ostensibly charges an admission fee, which goes towards funding the preservation of the town's historic architecture, but this fee is not always enforced. Buying the ticket gives you a choice of heritage sites to visit, including an 'intangible culture' option, like a traditional musical concert or stage play.

This list of sites is by no means comprehensive; buying a ticket at the Hoi An Old Town ticket booths will also get you a local guide at all the sites.

Tan Ky House (☎ 861 474; 101 Đ Nguyen Thai Hoc; 🕓 8am-noon & 2-4.30pm) is a lovingly preserved 19th-century house that once belonged to a Vietnamese merchant. Japanese and Chinese influences are visible throughout the architecture. The house is a private home, and the owner – whose family has lived here for seven generations – speaks French and English.

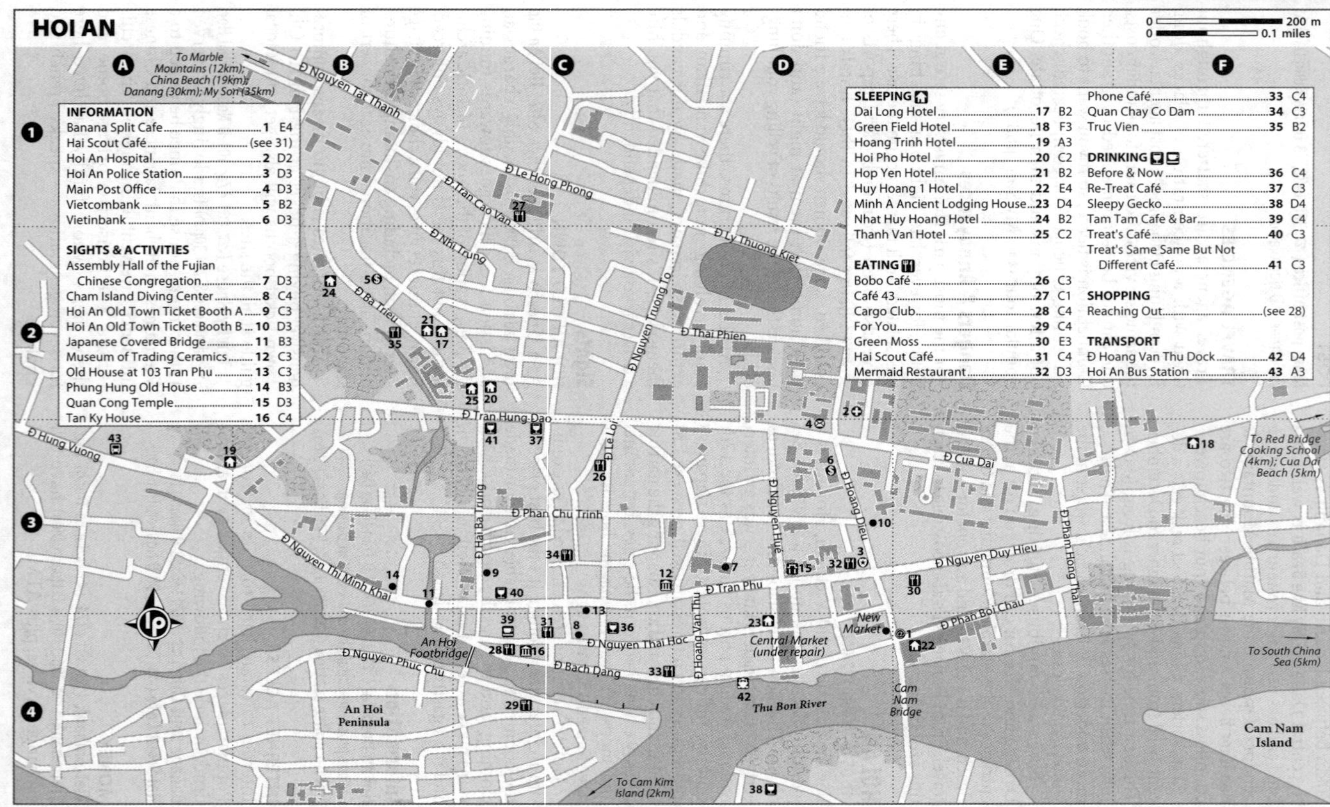
HOI AN
0 200 m
0 0.1 miles
A B C D E F
1 2 3 4
To Marble Mountains (12km); China Beach (19km); Danang (30km); My Son (35km)
INFORMATION
Banana Split Cafe 1 E4
Hai Scout Café (see 31)
Hoi An Hospital 2 D2
Hoi An Police Station 3 D3
Main Post Office 4 D3
Vietcombank 5 B2
Vietinbank 6 D3
SIGHTS & ACTIVITIES
Assembly Hall of the Fujian Chinese Congregation 7 D3
Cham Island Diving Center 8 C4
Hoi An Old Town Ticket Booth A 9 C3
Hoi An Old Town Ticket Booth B 10 D3
Japanese Covered Bridge 11 B3
Museum of Trading Ceramics 12 C3
Old House at 103 Tran Phu 13 C3
Phung Hung Old House 14 B3
Quan Cong Temple 15 D3
Tan Ky House 16 C4
SLEEPING
Dai Long Hotel 17 B2
Green Field Hotel 18 F3
Hoang Trinh Hotel 19 A3
Hoi Pho Hotel 20 C2
Hop Yen Hotel 21 B2
Huy Hoang 1 Hotel 22 E4
Minh A Ancient Lodging House 23 D4
Nhat Huy Hoang Hotel 24 B2
Thanh Van Hotel 25 C2
EATING
Bobo Café 26 C3
Café 43 27 C1
Cargo Club 28 C4
For You 29 C4
Green Moss 30 E3
Hai Scout Café 31 C4
Mermaid Restaurant 32 D3
Phone Café 33 C4
Quan Chay Co Dam 34 C3
Truc Vien 35 B2
DRINKING
Before & Now 36 C4
Re-Treat Café 37 C3
Sleepy Gecko 38 D4
Tam Tam Cafe & Bar 39 C4
Treat's Café 40 C3
Treat's Same Same But Not Different Café 41 C3
SHOPPING
Reaching Out (see 28)
TRANSPORT
Đ Hoang Van Thu Dock 42 D4
Hoi An Bus Station 43 A3
Đ Nguyen Tat Thanh
Đ Le Hong Phong
Đ Tran Cao Van
Đ Nhi Trung
Đ Ly Thuong Kiet
Đ Ba Trieu
Đ Nguyen Truong To
Đ Thai Phien
Đ Tran Hung Dao
Đ Hung Vuong
Đ Le Loi
Đ Cua Dai
Đ Hai Ba Trung
Đ Phan Chu Trinh
Đ Nguyen Hue
Đ Hoang Dieu
Đ Pham Hong Thai
Đ Nguyen Duy Hieu
Đ Nguyen Thi Minh Khai
Đ Tran Phu
Đ Hoang Van Thu
Đ Phan Boi Chau
Đ Nguyen Thai Hoc
Đ Bach Dang
Đ Nguyen Phuc Chu
An Hoi Footbridge
Central Market (under repair)
New Market
Cam Nam Bridge
Thu Bon River
An Hoi Peninsula
Cam Nam Island
To Red Bridge Cooking School (4km); Cua Dai Beach (5km)
To South China Sea (5km)
To Cam Kim Island (2km)

The **Japanese Covered Bridge** (Cau Nhat Ban/Lai Vien Kieu; Đ Tran Phu & Đ Nguyen Thi Minh Khai) was constructed in 1593. The bridge has a roof for shelter and a small temple built into its northern side. According to one story, the bridge's construction began in the year of the monkey and finished in the year of the dog; thus one entrance is guarded by monkeys, the other by dogs (however neither side is willing to confirm this).

Just a few steps down from the Japanese Covered Bridge, **Phung Hung Old House** (4 Đ Nguyen Thi Minh Khai; 8am-7pm) has a wide, welcoming entrance hall decorated with exquisite lanterns, wall hangings and embroidery.

Showcasing a collection of blue-and-white pottery of the Dai Viet period, the **Museum of Trading Ceramics** (80 Đ Tran Phu; 8am-noon & 2-4.30pm) is in a simply restored house. It's delightful. Look out for the great ceramic mosaic that's set above the pond in the inner courtyard.

The **Old House at 103 Tran Phu** (103 Đ Tran Phu; 8am-noon & 2-4.30pm) is picturesque with its wooden front and shutters; inside is an eclectic shop where women make silk lanterns. There are also ornamental aquarium fish for sale, *and* you can buy shampoo.

The **Assembly Hall of the Fujian Chinese Congregation** (opposite 35 Đ Tran Phu; 7.30am-noon & 2-5.30pm) was founded for community meetings; the hall later became a temple to worship Thien Hau, a deity born in Fujian Province in China. Check out the elaborate mural and the replica of a Chinese boat.

Quan Cong Temple (24 Đ Tran Phu) is dedicated to Quan Cong and has some wonderful papier-mâché and gilt statues, as well as carp-shaped rain spouts on the roof surrounding the courtyard. Shoes should be removed before mounting the platform in front of Quan Cong.

ARTS & CRAFTS VILLAGES

All those neat fake antiques sold in Hoi An's shops are manufactured in nearby villages. Cross the An Hoi footbridge to reach the **An Hoi Peninsula**, noted for its boat factory and mat-weaving factories. South of the Peninsula is **Cam Kim Island**, where you see many people engaged in the woodcarving and boat-building industries (take a boat from the Đ Hoang Van Thu dock). Back in town, cross the Cam Nam bridge to **Cam Nam village**, a lovely spot also noted for arts and crafts.

Activities

Rainbow Divers (www.divevietnam.com) can book dives at Cu Lao Cham Marine Park.

Courses

Hoi An is foodie heaven, and budding gourmands who want to take a step further into Vietnamese cuisine will find ample opportunity here. Many of the popular eateries offer cooking classes.

Red Bridge Cooking School (☎ 393 3222; www.visithoian.com) runs a course that starts with a trip to the market, and is followed by a cruise down the river to its relaxing retreat about 4km from Hoi An. Half-/full day costs US$23/39 per person.

More informal classes can be found at Green Moss (choose off the menu and pay a US$2 supplement).

Festivals & Events

The **Hoi An Legendary Night** takes place on the 14th day (full moon) of every lunar month from 5.30pm to 10pm. These festive evenings feature traditional food, song and dance, and games along the lantern-lit streets in the town centre.

Sleeping

There are heaps of hotels in Hoi An, but many are gunning for that growing midrange market, and true budget options are getting harder to find. During low season you'll have a better chance of haggling a good price. Most budget accommodation is spread out to the northwest around Đ Hai Ba Trung and Đ Ba Trieu. For starters, skip the hotels with swimming pools (there are more of them than you'd think).

Hop Yen Hotel (☎ 386 3153; hopyenhotel@yahoo.com; 694 Đ Hai Ba Trung; dm US$5, r US$8-15;) Nothing fancy here, but rooms are cheery and good-sized, and the staff are helpful.

Green Field Hotel (Dong Xanh Hotel; ☎ 386 3484; www.greenfieldhotel.com; 423 Đ Cua Dai; dm US$5, r US$20-45;) This midrange hotel has US$5-a-bed dorms – basically a shared triple room. The price includes the hour of free-flow cocktails by the pool every evening.

Minh A Ancient Lodging House (☎ 386 1368; 2 Đ Nguyen Thai Hoc; r US$15) The cheapest option for staying overnight in an Old Town traditional house. This snug guest house occupies a well-maintained 180-year-old building near the central market and is chock-full of antique furniture for that added old-world charm. As is to be expected, rooms are basic and there's no air-con.

Hoi Pho Hotel (☎ 391 6382; hoiphohotel@yahoo.com; 627 Đ Hai Ba Trung; r US$15; ❄) Yet another family-run minihotel, this one is distinguished for providing good and hassle-free service. Rooms are plain but large, and have lots of windows. There's a Techcombank ATM on the premises.

Huy Hoang I Hotel (☎ 386 1453; kshuyhoang@dng.vnn.vn; 73 Đ Phan Boi Chau; r US$15-18; ❄ 💻) Although it's not ageing well at all, its location is pretty unbeatable – right beside the market and Cam Nam Bridge. Be warned that rooms are pretty shabby and service can be curt.

Thanh Van Hotel (☎ 391 6916; www.thanhvanhotel.com; 78 Đ Tran Hung Dao; r US$15-20; ❄ 💻 🏊) One of the best-value places in town, this hotel has comfortable rooms in a good location near the livelier section of the Old Town. Prices include breakfast, served beside the pool, and the staff are forthcoming with information.

Dai Long Hotel (☎ 391 6232; dailonghotel@vnn.vn; 680 Đ Hai Ba Trung; r US$15-20; ❄ 💻) Popular with backpackers, and for good reason – this hotel has 12 large and clean rooms, and very friendly staff. Many open-tour buses stop right out front.

Hoang Trinh Hotel (☎ 391 6579; www.hoianhoangtrinhhotel.com; 45 Đ Le Quy Don; r US$15-20; ❄ 💻) A short stroll from the Old Town is this clean, modern hotel overlooking a Confucian temple in a quiet neighbourhood. Rooms are nice and smart, with high ceilings, and service is tip-top.

Nhat Huy Hoang Hotel (☎ 386 1665; nhathuyhoang.coltd@vnn.vn; 58 Đ Ba Trieu; r US$15-30; ❄) This new hotel is earning a reputation for clean rooms at good prices. The only caveat is that rooms on the ground floors are windowless, although one is large enough to sleep six.

Eating

There are several local specialities that you'll find on almost every menu in town: *cao lau*, doughy flat noodles combined with croutons, bean sprouts and greens and topped off with pork slices in a savoury broth; fried *hoanh thanh* (wonton); *banh xeo* (crispy savoury pancakes rolled with herbs in fresh rice paper); and 'white rose' (shrimp encased in rice paper and steamed). Most restaurants serve these items but the quality varies widely.

Truc Vien (☎ 391 7301; 88 Đ Ba Trieu; dishes 15,000-50,000d; 🕑 breakfast, lunch & dinner) This cosy cafe in the backpacker district serves good Vietnamese fare such as *pho* or *cao lau*. Pizzas cost a little more.

Bobo Café (☎ 386 1939; thuyph.ha@dng.vnn.v; 18 Đ Le Loi; dishes 15,000-50,000d; 🕑 breakfast, lunch & dinner) It's not much to look at, but this family-run eatery has all the usual backpacker fare and local specialities. The courtyard seating is pleasant at night.

For You (☎ 391 0295; 33 Đ Nguyen Phu Chu; dishes 15,000-100,000d; 🕑 lunch & dinner) The decor's a little beat up but the river view from the balcony seating area is worth lingering for, particularly during happy hour (cocktails 20,000d). Besides the usual Hoi An specialities, there's an extensive menu of Vietnamese fare to choose from.

Mermaid Restaurant (☎ 386 1527; www.hoianhospitality.com/mermaid.htm; 2 Đ Tran Phu; dishes 18,000-68,000d; 🕑 lunch & dinner) One of the original Hoi An eateries (since 1991), this place is still going strong with its menu of Hoi An specialities and family recipes. Try the fried spring rolls and the excellent 'white rose'.

Quan Chay Co Dam (☎ 386 3733; 71/20 Đ Phan Chu Trinh; meals 20,000d-30,000d; 🕑 breakfast, lunch & dinner) It's worth hunting down this hole-in-the-wall joint for flavourful vegetarian meals that are easy on the wallet. Lots of locals eat here and it's easy to order – just point at what you want from the spread on the counter.

Café 43 (☎ 386 2587; 43 Đ Tran Cao Van; dishes 20,000-50,000d; 🕑 lunch & dinner) With good food and a friendly family running this place, no wonder it's popular with travellers on a budget. As the cafe sign proudly states, there's also fresh beer available, on tap from a big ol' keg.

Phone Café (☎ 324 1988; thanhphone72@yahoo.com; 80B Đ Bach Dang; dishes 20,000d-60,000d; 🕑 lunch & dinner) Don't be fooled by the dingy appearance – this modest operation has excellent food that tastes just like Mum's cooking (assuming your mother cooks Vietnamese). The *cao lau*'s not bad and the claypot specialities quite delectable.

Green Moss (☎ 386 3728; 341 Đ Nguyen Duy Hieu; dishes 20,000-80,000d; 🕑 lunch & dinner) Duck into this pretty French-colonial building for an inexpensive meal of Vietnamese or Thai food in a casual chic setting. Cosy enough for lounging away an entire afternoon. Cooking classes cost US$2 plus the menu price of the dish.

Hai Scout Café (☎ 386 3210; www.visithoian.com/haicafe.html; 98 Đ Nguyen Thai Hoc; dishes 30,000-110,000d; ⏰ breakfast, lunch & dinner) If you're missing food from home and having chairs large enough to sprawl comfortably in, pop into this stylish cafe, ensconced in a charming Old Town building. The menu is extensive, with sandwiches, Western breakfasts, Vietnamese dishes and some European mains. There's a pleasant garden courtyard for lounging around in, and if you hang around till late, the place takes on more of a bar vibe. There's a display on WWF projects and some minority craftwork for sale.

Cargo Club (☎ 391 0489; 107 Đ Nguyen Thai Hoc; dishes 35,000-105,000d; ⏰ breakfast, lunch & dinner) Another Hoi An institution, this cheery cafe–restaurant has a full spread of hearty international cuisine. The freshly baked patisserie and boulangerie selections are 'to die for', in the words of a Hoi An expat. It's always abuzz with expats and travellers, and at night it turns into a groovy bar.

Drinking

For a little place, Hoi An has quite the selection of bars, many with helpfully hedonistic happy hours and extensive food menus. It's entirely possible to party till dawn if you want to, but beware of *xe om* drivers offering to take you to out-of-the-way venues at night. We've had reports of extortionate prices being demanded for the return trip, occasionally accompanied by physical threats.

Before & Now (☎ 391 0599; www.beforennow.com; 51 Đ Le Loi) This all-too-modern bar is nothing like the old houses around it, with local artist Tran Trung Linh's pop-art portraits on the walls (check out Bono-as-Superman) and an energetic pop-rock-funk playlist. The pool table is always busy and if you get hungry, there's a Milan-trained chef at your service.

Tam Tam Cafe & Bar (☎ 386 2212; 110 Đ Nguyen Thai Hoc) Set in a lovingly restored tea warehouse, this cool hang-out indulges in comfortable tropical decor and plenty of lounge space upstairs. The sidewalk seating is good for people-watching, while the scene is livelier around the pool table and the balcony.

Sleepy Gecko (☎ 090-842 6349; sleepygecko@gmail.com; To 5 Khoi Xuyen Trung, Cam Nam Island) It looks like a beach bar but it's nestled in a blissfully quiet lane on Cam Nam Island, away from the tourist ruckus. Enjoy an ice-cold beer and pub grub with your views of the river. Owner Steve can be counted on for witticisms and scads of local information – ask about his very good 'byke tours'.

Treat's Café (☎ 386 1125; 158 Đ Tran Phu) is the classic backpacker bar of Hoi An, no doubt thanks to its generous 4pm to 9pm happy hour. It's spawned two virtually identical joints on the same formula: **Re-Treat Café** (☎ 391 0527; 69 Đ Tran Hung Dao) and **Treat's Same Same But Not Different Café** (☎ 386 2278; 93 Đ Tran Hung Dao).

Shopping

Tailor-made clothing is one of Hoi An's best trades, and there are more than 200 tailor shops in town that can whip up a custom-tailored *ao dai* (traditional Vietnamese tunic and trousers) or formal wear for the weddings and graduation ceremonies waiting back home. Custom shoes are also popular, and those who want ready-to-wear duds will find a huge selection.

Bargaining is possible, but basically you get what you pay for. The better tailors and better fabrics are more expensive. One of the hundreds of tailors will probably knock out a men's suit for US$20, but a good quality suit is more likely to cost US$50 and up. Shirts, skirts and casual trousers hover around the US$10 mark.

Hoi An also boasts a growing array of interesting art galleries, especially on the west side of the Japanese Covered Bridge, and does a thriving business in wood carvings, fake antiques, and reproductions of famous paintings.

Reaching Out (☎ 386 2460; www.reachingoutvietnam.com; 103 Đ Nguyen Thai Hoc; ⏰ 7.30am-9.30pm) A great place to spend your dong, this is a fair-trade gift shop with profits going towards assisting disabled artisans.

Getting There & Away

The main **Hoi An bus station** (☎ 386 1284; 96 Đ Hung Vuong) is 1km west of the centre of town. Buses from here go to Danang (10,000d, one hour) and other points north.

A regular stop on the open-bus route, it's easy to pick up a service to or from Hue or Nha Trang.

The nearest airport and train station are both in Danang.

Getting Around

It's extremely easy to get around on foot here but motorbike drivers wait to solicit business outside all the tourist hotels. Prices without/with a driver are around US$6/10 per day.

Metered taxis are available to get to the beach. Many hotels also offer bicycles for hire for around 20,000d per day.

AROUND HOI AN

Cua Dai Beach

This beautiful stretch of sand runs all the way to Danang where it's marketed as the legendary China Beach. Palm-thatch huts give shelter and roaming vendors sell drinks and fresh seafood. Swimming is best between April and October. Weekends can get a little crowded. There are now wall-to-wall resorts along some stretches.

To get here, take Đ Cua Dai east out of Hoi An for about 5km; cycling is a wholesome option.

My Son

Set under the shadow of Cat's Tooth Mountain are the enigmatic ruins of **My Son** (☎ 373 1309; admission 60,000d; 6.30am-4pm), the most important remains of the ancient Cham empire and a Unesco World Heritage Site. Although Vietnam has better preserved Cham sites, none are as extensive and few have such beautiful surroundings as this, with brooding mountains and clear streams running between the temples.

Day tours to My Son can be arranged in Hoi An for between US$5 and US$7, not including admission, and some trips return to Hoi An by boat. Independent travellers can hire a motorbike, *xe om* or car. Get here early in order to beat the tour groups, or later in the afternoon.

SOUTH-CENTRAL COAST

The south-central coast is Vietnam at its most extroverted, a place for parties, adrenalin-junkies and sun-worshippers. The country has an incredibly curvaceous coastline and it is in this region that it is at its most alluring. Nha Trang and Mui Ne attract the headlines here: if your idea of paradise is reclining in front of turquoise waters, weighing up the merits of a massage or a mojito, then you have come to the right place.

With most visitors not venturing outside these two main enclaves, the rest of the beautiful coast is wonderfully overlooked, leaving empty beaches to be explored by the more independently minded.

NHA TRANG

☎ 058 / pop 315,200

Welcome to the beach capital of Vietnam. It may not be a charmer like Mui Ne or a historic jewel like Hoi An, but there is a certain something about Nha Trang that just keeps them coming back. For most it is the best municipal stretch of sand in the country, while the offshore islands add to the appeal, offering decadent boat trips on the water and some of Vietnam's best diving under it.

The setting is stunning, with towering mountains looming up behind the city and the sweeping beach stretching into the distance, the turquoise waters dotted with little islands.

Information

Nha Trang has dozens of designated internet cafes all over town, and you can also get online in many hotels and travellers cafes, including with wi-fi access.

Highland Tours (☎ 352 4477; www.highlandtourstravel.com; 54G Đ Nguyen Thien Thuat) Fun boat trips off the coast, plus affordable tours in the Central Highlands.

Main post office (☎ 382 1271; 4 Đ Le Loi)

Mama Linh's Boat Tours (☎ 352 2844; 23C Đ Biet Thu) Famed for its raucous boat tours, Mama Linh can also arrange trips around the province and the highlands.

Vietcombank Đ Hung Vuong (☎ 352 4500; 5 Đ Hung Vuong; Mon-Fri); Đ Quang Trung (☎ 382 2720; 17 Đ Quang Trung; Mon-Fri) Both branches exchange travellers cheques and have ATMs.

Dangers & Annoyances

Though Nha Trang is generally a safe place, be very careful on the beach at night. The best advice is to stay away completely after dark. We've heard countless reports of rip-offs, mostly instigated by kamikaze hookers who cruise the coast.

Though not all the rip-offs here are alcohol-related, most are. Getting too drunk, especially by yourself, at a bar or club late at night is like spraying on 'rob me' perfume. Consider leaving surplus cash at the hotel reception; count it in front of the clerk and put it in an envelope that you both sign.

Sights

Built between the 7th and 12th centuries on a site used by Hindus for worship, the **Po Nagar Cham Towers** (Đ 2 Thang 4; admission 10,500d; 6am-6pm) are 2km north of central Nha Trang on the left bank of the Cai River. From the hill are blue views of the harbour below.

The impressively adorned **Long Son Pagoda** (Chua Tinh Hoi Khanh Hoa; Đ 23 Thang 10; 7.30-11.30am & 1.30-8pm) is decorated with mosaic dragons covered with glass and ceramic tile. Founded in the late 19th century, the pagoda still has resident monks. At the top of the hill, behind the pagoda, is the **Giant Seated Buddha** visible from town. From where the Buddha sits, you too can contemplate the view of Nha Trang. A number of little extortionists are at work around this pagoda. If anyone approaches you claiming to work for the monks, tell them your contribution will go in the donation box. The pagoda is about 500m west of the train station.

The work of Nha Trang's most acclaimed photographer, Long Thanh, is shown at **Long Thanh Gallery** (3824 4875; lvntrang50@hotmail.com; 126 Đ Hoang Van Thu; 8.30-11.30am & 1-6pm Mon-Sat). Even if it looks closed the staff will usually turn on the lights for visitors.

Swimming around in the **National Oceanographic Museum** (Vien Nghiem Cuu Bien; 359 0037; 1 Cau Da; adult/child 15,000/7000d; 6am-6pm), a French colonial building 6km south of the town centre, are colourful representatives of squirming sea life. There are thousands of pickled specimens of marine life, and sunlight passing through the jars gives the place an eerie beauty.

Nha Trang's answer to Disneyland (well, sort of), the island resort of **Vinpearl Land** (359 0111; www.vinpearlland.com; Hon Tre Island; adult 250,000, child 175,000; 9am-10pm) has funfair rides, a water park, arcade games and more. The water park is great; everything else is decidedly average. The 15-minute, 3320m-long cable-car ride is a great way to see Nha Trang and the surrounding islands from a bird's-eye view.

BEACHES

Coconut palms provide shelter for sunbathers and strollers along most of Nha Trang's 6km of beachfront; beach chairs are available for hire.

Hon Chong promontory, 1.8km north of central Nha Trang, is a scenic collection of granite rocks jutting into the South China Sea. The beach here has a more local flavour than Nha Trang Beach, but the accompanying rubbish makes it a less attractive option for swimming or sunbathing.

ISLANDS

The outlying islands of Nha Trang beckon offshore. Hop on one of the boat tours sold all over town. For as little as US$8, you can join a day tour visiting four islands. Or you could cobble together your own trips to various islands.

There's a working fish farm on **Hon Mieu** (Mieu Island) that's also a beautiful outdoor **aquarium** (Ho Ca Tri Nguyen). From there, you can rent canoes, or hire someone to paddle you out to **Hon Mun** (Ebony Island) or **Hon Yen** (Swallow Island). Rustic bungalows on the island rent for about 90,000d. Ferries to Hon Mieu (5000d) leave regularly throughout the day from Cau Da dock at the southern end of Nha Trang. Catch ferries back to Nha Trang at Tri Nguyen village on Hon Mieu.

Idyllic **Hon Tre** (Bamboo Island) is the largest island in the area. You can get boats to **Bai Tru** (Tru Beach) at the northern end of the island, but it's also recommended to take the day trips or overnight trips here offered by **Con Se Tre** (381 1163; www.consetre.com.vn; 100/16 Đ Tran Phu). There's great snorkelling and diving off **Hon Mun**, **Hon Tam** and **Hon Mot**.

Mama Linh's Boat Tours (352 2844; 23C Đ Biet Thu) have the hottest ticket for island-hopping, guzzling fruit wine at the impromptu 'floating bar', and deck-side dancing.

The cheapest way to get out on the water is to take the regular local ferry to Vinpearl on Hon Tre (adult/child 40,000/15,000d one way), leaving from Phu Quy harbour. Or, more expensive but more scenic, take the cable car across.

Activities

DIVING

Nha Trang is Vietnam's premier diving destination, with around 25 dive sites in the area. Visibility averages 15m, but can be as much as 30m, depending on the season (late October to early January is the worst time of year). There are some good drop-offs and small underwater caves to explore and an amazing variety of corals. Among the colourful reef fish, stingrays are occasionally spotted.

A full-day outing, including two dives and lunch, costs between US$45 and US$75. Dive operators also offer a range of courses. Consider the following outfits, but shop around:

CENTRAL NHA TRANG

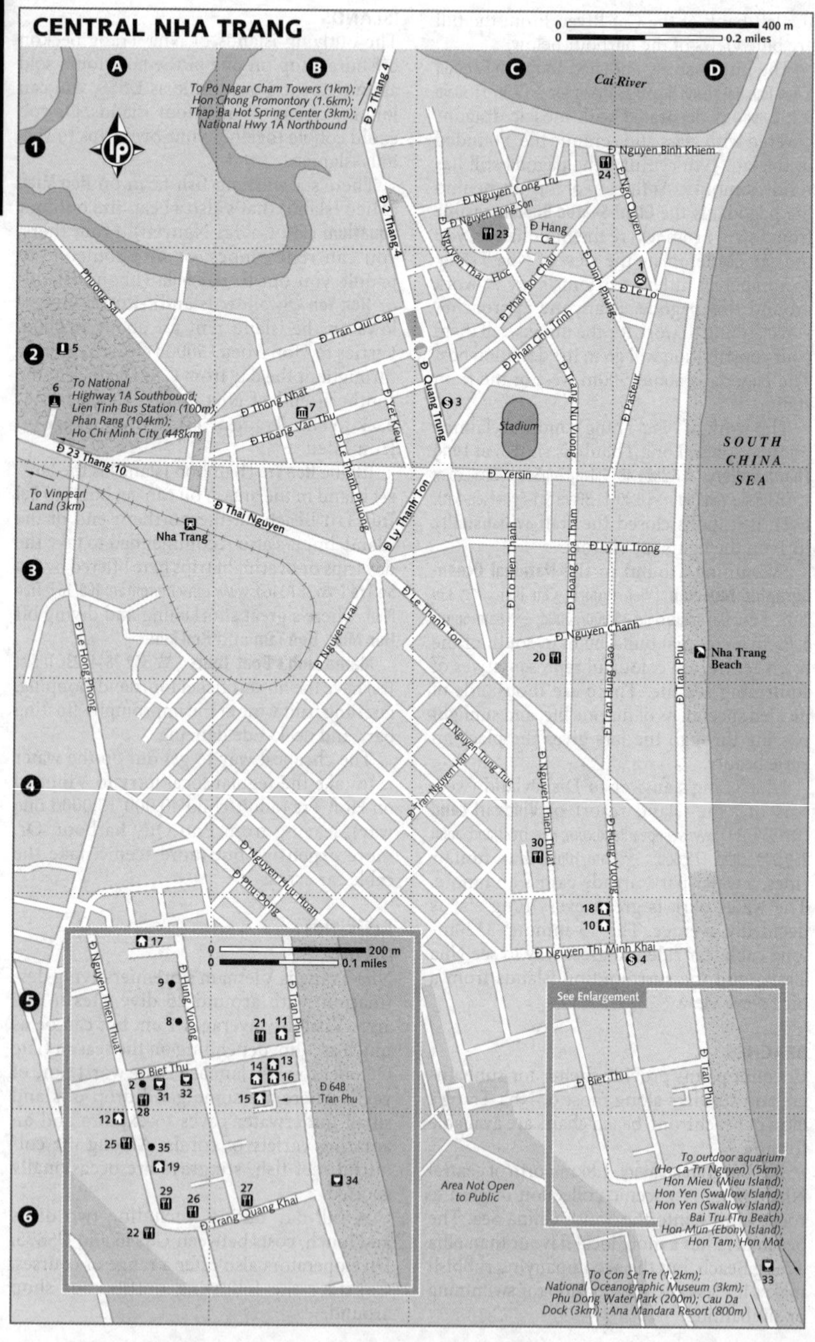

INFORMATION		
Highlands Tours	(see 12)	
Main Post Office	1	D2
Mama Linh's Boat Tours	2	A5
Vietcombank	3	C2
Vietcombank	4	D5
SIGHTS & ACTIVITIES		
Giant Seated Buddha	5	A2
Long Son Pagoda	6	A2
Long Thanh Gallery	7	B2
Rainbow Divers	8	A5
Sailing Club Diving	(see 34)	
Vietnam Explorer	9	A5
Waves Watersports	(see 33)	
SLEEPING		
56 Hung Vuong Hotel	10	C5
62 Tran Phu Hotel	11	B5
Backpacker's House	12	A6
Blue Star Hotel	13	B5
Hotel An Hoa	14	B5
Hotel Nhi Hang	15	B5
Pho Bien	16	B5
Phong Lan Hotel	17	A5
Phu Quy Hotel	18	C5
Sao Mai Hotel	19	A6
EATING		
A-Mart	(see 32)	
Au Lac	20	C3
Bo De	(see 20)	
Café des Amis	21	B5
Cyclo Café	22	A6
Dam Market	23	C1
La Taverna	(see 29)	
Lac Canh Restaurant	24	C1
Lanterns	25	A6
Le Petit Bistro	26	A6
Mecca	27	B6
Omar's Tandoori Café	28	A5
Same Same But Different Café	29	A6
Thanh Thanh Café	30	C4
DRINKING		
Crazy Kim Bar	31	A5
Guava	32	A5
Louisiane Brewhouse	33	D6
Red Apple Club	(see 12)	
Sailing Club	34	B6
TRANSPORT		
Vietnam Airlines	35	A6

Rainbow Divers (☎ 352 4351; www.divevietnam.com; 90A Hung Vuong) Rainbow Divers is the longest-running dive company in Vietnam, operating out of a popular restaurant and bar.

Sailing Club Diving (☎ 352 2788; www.sailingclubvietnam.com; 72-74 Đ Tran Phu) This is the underwater arm of the famous Sailing Club.

Vietnam Explorer (☎ 352 4490; www.divingvietnam.com; 24 Đ Hung Vuong) Another PADI dive centre with a good reputation in Vietnam.

WATER-BASED FUN

Right on the beach front, **Phu Dong Water Park** (Đ Tran Phu; admission 25,000d; 9am-5pm Sat & Sun) has slides, shallow pools and fountains if salt water is not your thing.

If salt water *is* your thing, check out **Waves Watersports** (☎ 090-544 7393; www.waveswatersports.com; Louisiane Brewhouse, 29 Đ Tran Phu). Offering windsurfing, sea kayaking, wakeboarding and sailing lessons, Waves uses state-of-the-art equipment.

Or get deep down and dirty with muddy waters. **Thap Ba Hot Spring Center** (☎ 383 4939; www.thapbahotspring.com.vn; 25 Ngoc Son; 8am-8pm) is a fun experience. To get here, follow the signpost on the second road to the left past the Po Nagar Cham Towers for 2.5km.

Sleeping

The place is full of guest houses and hotels that offer some of the best value for money in the country. There is a cluster of minihotels in an alleyway at 64 Đ Tran Phu, within striking distance of the beach.

Backpacker's House (☎ 352 3884; www.backpackershouse.net; 54G Đ Nguyen Thien Thuat; dm US$6, s/d US$17-24;) This new flashpacker pad opened in 2008 and is popular with the party set, as it is only a stumble from the nearby Red Apple Club. The dorms are mixed and have four to six beds. The rooms are a smarter choice, but don't check in here for rehab.

Hotel An Hoa (☎ 352 4029; anhoahotel@yahoo.com; 64B/6 Đ Tran Phu; r US$8-12;) A reliable option in the heart of the budget alley, this friendly hostelry has small windowless fan rooms or bigger and better rooms with larger bathrooms and a smarter trim.

our pick **Pho Bien** (☎ 352 4858; phobienhotelint@yahoo.com; 64/1 Đ Tran Phu; r US$8-20;) The Pho Bien is one of the smarter places hiding away down budget alley. It has a big reception area with free internet. Rooms are clean and comfortable and include satellite TV, fridge and hot water. There is also a handy lift these days, helpful after a big night out.

Sao Mai Hotel (☎ 352 6412; saomai2ht@yahoo.com; 99 Đ Nguyen Thien Thuat; r 90,000-180,000d;) This budget crash pad has been around for years, but still offers no-nonsense value for money for those on a budget. The rooms are simple yet clean.

Phu Quy Hotel (☎ 352 1609; phuquyhotel@dng.vnn.vn; 54 Đ Hung Vuong; r US$8-20;) The pad that kick-started the Phu Quy (pronounced Foo-Hwee) empire, there is a great rooftop terrace here that has long lured in backpackers looking to chill out. Rooms are fine for the money, and just US$10 will get a balcony and strained seaview.

56 Hung Vuong Hotel (☎ 352 4584; 56hungvuonghotel@dng.vnn.vn; 56 Đ Hung Vuong; r US$8-15;) Next door to the Phu Quy, this is a friendly pad with expansive, not expensive, rooms and many have a balcony and a sea view (if you are prepared for stairs).

Phong Lan Hotel (☎ 352 2647; orchidhotel2000@yahoo.com; 24/44 Đ Hung Vuong; r US$8-15;) Located in a small alley off Hung Vuong, the Orchid

Hotel, as it translates, is a friendly, family-run place. The clean rooms include TV and fridge.

Blue Star Hotel (☎ 352 5447; quangc@dng.vnn.vn; 1B Đ Biet Thu; r US$8-15; ❄ 💻) When it comes to location, this is one of the better budget places, as it is a stone's throw from the beach (don't try, you might hit someone) and on the doorstep of lots of leading restaurants and bars. The rooms are good value and some have sea views.

Other possible budget options:

62 Tran Phu Hotel (☎ 352 5095; 62 Đ Tran Phu; r US$8-20; ❄) Really run down are the first words that spring to mind, but for the party set who don't care about the room, it has a great seafront location.

Hotel Nhi Hang (☎ 352 5837; www.vngold.com/nt/nhihang; 64B/7 Đ Tran Phu; r US$8-15; ❄) Another little teaser down budget alley, with a similar set-up to An Hoa (see above).

Eating

VIETNAMESE

Café des Amis (☎ 352 1009; 2D Đ Biet Thu; dishes 20,000-70,000d) A traveller fave thanks to cheap eats, fresh seafood and plentiful beer. Look out for local artworks adorning the walls.

Lac Canh Restaurant (☎ 382 1391; 44 Đ Nguyen Binh Khiem; dishes 20,000-100,000d; 🕑 lunch & dinner) Locals flock here in numbers to fire up the tabletop barbecues and grill their own meats, squid, prawns, lobsters and more. Great.

Cyclo Café (☎ 352 4208; 5A Đ Tran Quang Khai; mains 30,000-90,000d) The Cyclo is a lively little place for an inviting blend of Vietnamese and continental dishes. The food is good value, the service is sharp, but the troop of sellers can be tiring.

Mecca (☎ 352 4455; 16 Đ Tran Quang Khai; dishes 30,000-150,000d) Make a pilgrimage to this trendy spot, complete with fresh seafood, local specialities and international offerings. The lush garden is an oasis, by day or night.

our pick **Lanterns** (☎ 352 1674; 72 Đ Nguyen Thien Thuat; dishes 40,000-140,000d) The flavours are predominantly Vietnamese such as braised pork in claypot or fried tofu with lemongrass. The restaurant supports a local orphanage.

As always, taking a meal in the market is a cheap adventure, and **Dam market** (Đ Nguyen Hong Son) in the north end of town has lots of local food stalls, including *com chay* (vegetarian food).

VEGETARIAN

Two places serving excellent vegetarian food of the I-can't-believe-it's-not-meat variety are **Au Lac** (☎ 381 3946; 28C Đ Hoang Hoa Tham; meals from 15,000d) and **Bo De** (☎ 381 0116; 28A Đ Hoang Hoa Tham; meals from 15,000d), neighbouring restaurants near the corner of Đ Nguyen Chanh.

INTERNATIONAL

Same Same But Different Café (☎ 352 4079; 111 Đ Nguyen Thien Thuat; mains 20,000-80,000d; 🕑 breakfast, lunch & dinner) With a name like this, it could only be a backpacker cafe and it's one of the better offerings in town. All the Vietnamese staples are here, plus some Western favourites, including vegie dishes.

Thanh Thanh Cafe (☎ 382 4413; 10 Đ Nguyen Thien Thuat; meals 25,000-95,000d) Another popular backpacker cafe, with Vietnamese dishes and wholesome pizzas.

La Taverna (☎ 352 2259; 115 Đ Nguyen Thien Thuat; mains 32,000-96,000d; 💻) The best-value Italian food in Nha Trang, La Taverna is run by a Swiss-Italian who imports all the homeland ingredients.

Omar's Tandoori Cafe (☎ 352 2459; 89B Đ Nguyen Thien Thuat; dishes 40,000-120,000d) To try an authentic sampling of the subcontinent, look no further than Omar's. It's the venue of choice for curry-craving expats in town.

Le Petit Bistro (☎ 352 7201; 26D Đ Tran Quang Khai; mains 50,000-200,000d; ❄) For an indulgent flirt with French food, this is the place for the *fromage* you have been pining for or a great steak, *bleu* if you dare.

SELF-CATERING

A-Mart (17A Đ Biet Thu; 🕑 6am-10pm) has the ingredients to make snacks or a real meal should you have access to a kitchen.

Drinking

Sailing Club (☎ 382 6528; 72-74 Đ Tran Phu) A Nha Trang institution, this inviting beach bar is where the party crowd ends up at some point. Thumping music, wild dancing, flowing shots and general mayhem. Not forgetting great food by day.

Red Apple Club (☎ 352 5599; 54H Đ Nguyen Thien Thuat; 💻) An old-skool backpacker bar for boat-trip hedonists. Cheap beer, flowing shots, regular promotions and indie anthems ensure that this place is crammed.

Louisiane Brewhouse (☎ 352 1948; 29 Đ Tran Phu; 💻 🏊) Homebrew, Nha Trang-style. Beyond the shiny copper vats lie an inviting swimming pool and a private strip of sand to laze the day away.

Crazy Kim Bar (☎ 352 3072; www.crazykimbar.com; 19 Đ Biet Thu) A reliable party spot, it is also home base for the commendable 'Hands off the Kids!' campaign, which works to prevent paedophilia. Sign up as a volunteer to teach English.

Guava (☎ 352 4140; www.clubnhatrang.com; 17 Đ Biet Thu; 💻) A hip lounge-bar, Guava is a stylin' place. Choose from sunken sofas inside or a leafy garden patio outside.

Shopping

Many restaurants and bars around town display the works of local photographers and artists, which are usually for sale. You'll find a lot of seashells and coral for sale, but their harvesting destroys the beauty and ecology of Nha Trang's reefs.

Check out the hand-painted T-shirts done by a friendly local painter named Kim Quang, who you can find between 2pm and 9pm working from his wheelchair at the Sailing Club (opposite).

Getting There & Away

AIR

Vietnam Airlines (☎ 352 6768; www.vietnamairlines.com; 91 Đ Nguyen Thien Thuat) has flights out of Cam Ranh airport (28km south of Nha Trang) to HCMC, Hanoi and Danang. To get to the airport, catch a shuttle bus (40,000d, 40 minutes) from the old Nha Trang airport terminal, two hours before the flight. **Nha Trang Taxi** (☎ 382 4000) charges 180,000d from town to the airport. Bizarrely, it costs 260,000d from the airport to a downtown destination.

BUS

Minibuses travelling from HCMC to Nha Trang (130,000d, 11 hours) depart from Mien Dong bus station in HCMC. **Lien Tinh bus station** (Ben Xe Lien Tinh; ☎ 382 2192; Đ 23 Thang 10), Nha Trang's main intercity bus terminal, is 500m west of the train station. Regular daily buses head north to Quy Nhon (from 75,000d, five hours), with a few continuing to Danang (140,000d). Regular buses head south to Phan Rang (30,000d, two hours) or into the highlands to Dalat (88,000d, five hours).

Nha Trang is a major stopping point on all of the tourist open-bus tours. These are a good option for accessing Mui Ne, which is not well served by local buses. Open-tour buses also run to Dalat (six hours) and Hoi An (11 hours).

CAR & MOTORCYCLE

A series of roughly parallel roads head inland from near Nha Trang, linking Vietnam's deltas and coastal regions with the Central Highlands.

TRAIN

The **Nha Trang train station** (☎ 382 2113; Đ Thai Nguyen; ⏰ ticket office 7-11.30am, 1.30-5pm & 6-10pm) is down the hill west of the cathedral. Destinations include Danang (220,000d, about 10 hours), Phan Rang (35,000d, about two hours) and HCMC (175,000d, about nine hours).

There is also a luxury train service, **Golden Trains** (☎ 347 1318; www.goldentrains.com.vn). Numbered SN, ticket prices start from 395,000/465,000d for soft seat/soft sleeper between Nha Trang and HCMC.

Getting Around

There is no shortage of motorbikes, taxis and *cyclo* drivers looking for passengers. The old Nha Trang airport, from which buses shuttle passengers to Cam Ranh airport, is on the

OFF THE BEATEN TRACK: BEAUTIFUL BEACHES

It may be that Mui Ne and Nha Trang are the beach babes of the region, but there are many pristine stretches of sand along this coast, some that see very few tourists. Here's our very own favourites from north to south:

- **My Khe** Located near the site of the infamous My Lai Massacre, My Khe (not to be confused with the other My Khe Beach near Danang) is a great beach, with fine white sand and clear water.
- **Quy Nhon** This major transit town between Hoi An and Nha Trang is fast earning a name as an up-and-coming beach destination. Live cheap at **Barbara's: The Kiwi Connection** (☎ 389 2921; nzbarb@yahoo.com; 18 Đ Xuan Dieu; dm 50,000d, r 200,000-300,000d; ❄).
- **Doc Let** Within commuting distance of busy Nha Trang, the beachfront is long and wide, with chalk-white sand and shallow water, and there are several blissful resorts.

southern side of town. *Cyclos* go to both the old airport and the train station for about US$1 or so. **Nha Trang Taxi** (☎ 382 4000) has cars with air-con and meters. Many hotels have bicycle rentals for around US$1 to US$2 per day.

MUI NE

☎ 062

Arguably the best all-round beach in Vietnam, Mui Ne seductively unfurls itself along the coast near Phan Thiet. It is also the 'Sahara' of Vietnam, with the most dramatic sand dunes in the region looming large. Activities abound with the seasonal winds, and kitesurfers come from all over the world to ride the waves. Surf's up from August to December.

Far from the madding crowd of HCMC, yet only three hours away, Mui Ne remains *the beach* to be, despite some stiff competition.

Orientation & Information

Local addresses are designated by a kilometre mark measuring the distance along Rte 706 from Hwy 1 in Phan Thiet. Rte 706 is also known as Đ Nguyen Dinh Chieu.

There are several ATMs along the main drag, plus most hotels offer currency exchange. Internet access is available, plus many places offer wi-fi.

Fami Tour Office (☎ 374 1030; 121 Đ Nguyen Dinh Chieu) Local tours, internet access and cheap international internet calls.

Mui Ne (www.muinebeach.net) A great resource for information.

Sinh Café (☎ 847 542; 144 Đ Nguyen Dinh Chieu) Operates out of its Mui Ne Resort, booking open-tour buses and offering credit-card cash advances.

Sights

Mui Ne is most famous for its fish sauce, but this is more a smell than a sight. There's nothing fishy about the enormous **sand dunes**, which are a lot of fun. To get to the **red dunes** (sometimes called yellow) head east out of town and follow the signs to Pandanus Resort. Pass the resort and soon you'll see the dunes filled with little kids selling rides on plastic sheets down the sandy slopes. The **white dunes** are another 20km after that – definitely more impressive and worth a look. Wear real shoes because even in sandals the dunes are sizzling. Riding the dunes is an art, so try to rent a sheet of plastic from the kids rather than paying for each slide.

It's possible to cycle to the first dunes but start in a cool part of the day and bring plenty of sunscreen. A motorbike-taxi trip to both dunes (from 80,000d) is a better deal than a jeep tour (US$10) because you get dropped off at the same place no matter how you get there. If taking a jeep be careful to agree on an itinerary for the tour, preferably in writing. We've heard complaints, particularly about 'sunset tours' that cut short with the sun high in the sky and the drivers getting aggressive when challenged.

The **Fairy Spring** (Suoi Tien) is a stream that flows through a patch of the dunes and curious rock formations east of town.

On Rte 706 heading towards Phan Thiet, the small **Po Shanu Cham tower** (Km 5; admission 2000d; 🕑 7.30-11.30am & 1.30-4.30pm) occupies a hill with sweeping views of Phan Thiet, the boat-filled estuary and a cemetery filled with candylike tombstones.

Activities

The season for windsurfers runs from late October to late April.

Jibes (☎ 384 7405; www.windsurf-vietnam.com; 90 Đ Nguyen Dinh Chieu; 🕑 7.30am-6pm) rents state-of-the-art gear like windsurfs (one hour/half-day US$12/30), surfboards (one hour/half-day US$7.50/15), and kitesurfs (one hour/half-day US$50/100).

Airwaves (☎ 847 440; www.airwaveskitesurfing.com; 24 Đ Nguyen Dinh Chieu), based at the Sailing Club, is another outfit offering kitesurfing, windsurfing and sailing lessons, plus equipment rentals.

Sleeping

Hai Yen Guesthouse (☎ 384 7243; www.muinebeach.net/haiyen; 132 Đ Nguyen Dinh Chieu; r US$10-20; ❄ 🏊) A little cracker, the friendly Hai Yen has cheap fan rooms, chilled (air-con) rooms and a new swimming pool. There is beachfront access, plus a small restaurant.

our pick **Thai Hoa Mui Ne Resort** (☎ 384 7320; www.thaihoaresort.com; 56 Đ Huynh Thuc Khang; r US$10-25; ❄ 💻) One of the last places on the Mui Ne strip, which also makes it one of the best value. Bungalows front onto a spacious garden and the more expensive ones are up close and personal with the beach. Worth the journey.

Vietnam-Austria House (☎ 384 7047; ngothikimhong@hotmail.com; km 13.5; r US$10-20; ❄ 🏊) One of the old-style places in Mui Ne, the cheapies have share bathrooms. The US$15 price buys some privacy for ablutions, while the most expensive rooms are near the beachfront. Somehow they have squeezed in a pool.

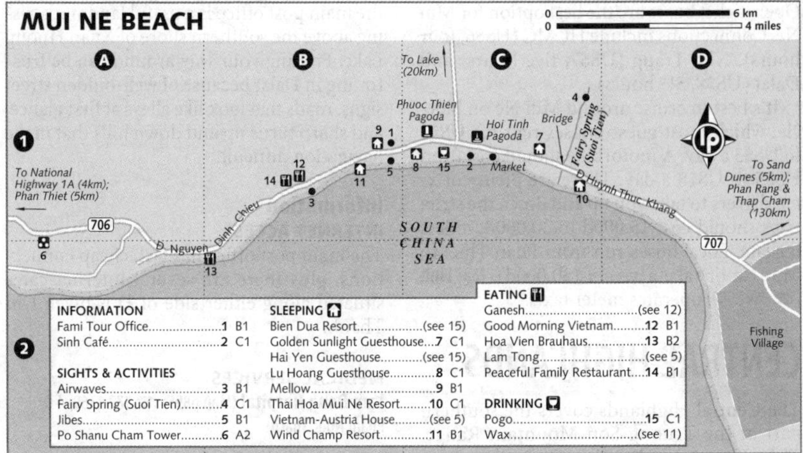

Bien Dua Resort (Coconut Beach; 384 7241; 136 Đ Nguyen Dinh Chieu; r US$10-20;) A small French-run place, the bungalow-style rooms are great value and include some beachfront browsing. All rooms have hot water and TV.

Lu Hoang Guesthouse (350 0060; 106 Đ Nguyen Dinh Chieu; r US$15-20;) This upmarket villa looks more like a swanky private house, but it offers good-value lodgings, including superb bathrooms for this price range. No direct beach access.

Wind Champ Resort (384 7001; www.windchamp.com; 68 Đ Nguyen Dinh Chieu; r US$15-25;) This spacious backpacker resort is reminiscent of Ko Phan Ngan or the way things used to be in Mui Ne before land prices rocketed. Thatched bungalows are set amid coconut palms, and many face the beach.

You want more?

Golden Sunlight Guesthouse (374 3124; hiephoatourism@yahoo.net; 19B Đ Nguyen Dinh Chieu; r US$10) Alright, so it's not on the beach and right at the end of town, but it is a friendly place with clean, airy rooms with fan and attached bathroom.

Mellow (374 3086; 117C Đ Nguyen Dinh Chieu; r US$10-25;) No frills, but some thrills in the attached bar-restaurant. On the 'wrong' (nonbeach) side of town, the cheaper rooms share bathrooms.

Eating & Drinking

our pick **Lam Tong** (384 7598; 92 Đ Nguyen Dinh Chieu; dishes 25,000-75,000d) It doesn't look like much, but this beachfront restaurant serves some of the best seafood in town, with tables right on the sand.

Peaceful Family Restaurant (Yen Gia Quan; 374 1019; 53 Đ Nguyen Dinh Chieu; dishes 30,000-70,000d; lunch & dinner) The family here serve up traditional Vietnamese cuisine under a breezy thatched roof.

Ganesh (374 1330; 57 Đ Nguyen Dinh Chieu; mains 40,000-140,000d; lunch & dinner) A stylish Indian-run restaurant offering authentic flavours from the homeland.

Good Morning Vietnam (384 7585; km 11.8; mains 60,000-140,000d; lunch & dinner) Part of the popular chain of Italian restaurants, this place pioneered the idea of offering free hotel pick-ups to bridge the distance of the strip.

Hoa Vien Brauhaus (374 1383; www.hoavien.vn; 2A Đ Nguyen Dinh Chieu; mains 50,000-150,000d; lunch & dinner) It's not Prague, but then where else can you sup freshly brewed draft Pilsner Urquell overlooking the South China Sea? The food is less impressive.

Pogo (0909-479 346; 138 Đ Nguyen Dinh Chieu) Hop along to Pogo for the chilled atmosphere. The open-air bar features lively decoration, free pool, some sorted sounds and big beanbags for chillin' out.

Wax (384 7001; 68 Đ Nguyen Dinh Chieu) Tucked away on the beachfront in Wind Champ Resort, this is one of the livelier bars in town and stays open late, with good tunes and a mammoth drinks list.

Getting There & Around

From HCMC, the 200km drive to Mui Ne takes three hours, in theory; depending on traffic in HCMC it can take five or more.

Open-ticket buses are the best option for Mui Ne. Connections include HCMC (US$6, four hours), Nha Trang (US$7, five hours) and Dalat (US$8, 5½ hours).

It's best to cruise around Mui Ne on bicycle, which most guest houses rent for US$1 to US$3 a day. A motorbike should cost from US$5 to US$8 a day. There are plenty of *xe om* drivers to take you up and down the strip; trips should cost 15,000d to 30,000d, unless it's late. Local buses run from Phan Thiet to Mui Ne or take a *xe om* (50,000d). **Mai Linh** (☎ 389 8989) operates meter taxis.

CENTRAL HIGHLANDS

The Central Highlands covers the southern part of the Truong Son Mountain Range. This geographical region, home to many Montagnard ethnic groups, is renowned for its cool climate, beautiful mountain scenery and innumerable streams, lakes and waterfalls. For those who can't make it to the far north of the country, this is the place for outdoor adventures.

In early 2001 the government forbade travellers from visiting the central highlands because of unrest among the local tribes. In 2004, there was another brief closure of the area, so check the latest situation before heading to the hills.

DALAT

☎ 063 / pop 190,000

Dalat prides itself on its rebellious spirit. The weather is spring cool instead of tropical hot, the town is dotted with elegant French-colonial villas instead of squat socialist architecture, and the farms around are thick with strawberries and flowers, not rice. As a highland resort it's been welcoming tourists for a century, and it has all the attractions to prove it.

Dotted with lakes and waterfalls and surrounded by evergreen forests, Dalat is nicknamed the City of Eternal Spring. The days are fine and nights frosty at 1475m, but the cool temperatures make trekking or cycling that much easier.

Orientation

Dalat's sights are spread out and the terrain in and around the city is hilly. The central market, set in a bowl, marks the middle of the town. To the southeast, the 'Eiffel Tower' of the main post office is a useful landmark, rising above the southern shore of Xuan Huong Lake. Finding your way around can be frustrating in Dalat because of well-hidden street signs, roads that look like alleys at first glance, and sharp turns up and down hills that make navigation difficult.

Information

INTERNET ACCESS

The main post office has fast, cheap connections, plus there are several internet cafes situated along either side of Đ Nguyen Chi Thanh.

MEDICAL SERVICES

Lam Dong Hospital (Map p895; ☎ 382 1369; 4 Đ Pham Ngoc Thach)

MONEY

The following downtown banks exchange cash and travellers cheques and offer credit-card cash advances and ATMs:

Vietcombank (Map p895; ☎ 351 0586; 6 Đ Nguyen Thi Minh Khai)

Vietinbank (Map p895; ☎ 382 2495; 1 Đ Le Dai Hanh)

POST

Main post office (Map p895; ☎ 382 2586; 14 Đ Tran Phu; 🕒 6.30am-9pm) International phone calls and internet access here.

TRAVEL AGENCIES

There are some great adventure companies based in Dalat offering adrenalin activities as well as the basics.

For information on guided tours by motorbike, see the boxed text, p896.

Dalat Travel Service (Map p895; ☎ 382 2125; dalattravelservice@vnn.vn; 7 Đ 3 Thang 2) Tours and vehicle rentals.

Groovy Gecko Tours (Map p895; ☎ 383 6521; www.groovygeckotours.net; 65 Đ Truong Cong Dinh; 🕒 7.30am-8.30pm) Offers tours, trekking, canyoning and mountain biking.

Phat Tire Ventures (Map p895; ☎ 382 9422; www.phattireventures.com; 73 Đ Truong Cong Dinh) Reputable operator offering trekking, adventures and cycling in the Dalat area.

Sinh Café (☎ 382 2663; www.sinhcafevn.com; 4A Đ Bui Thi Xuan) Tours and open-tour bus bookings.

Sights

Dalat has attractions you won't find elsewhere in Vietnam – and this may be a good thing.

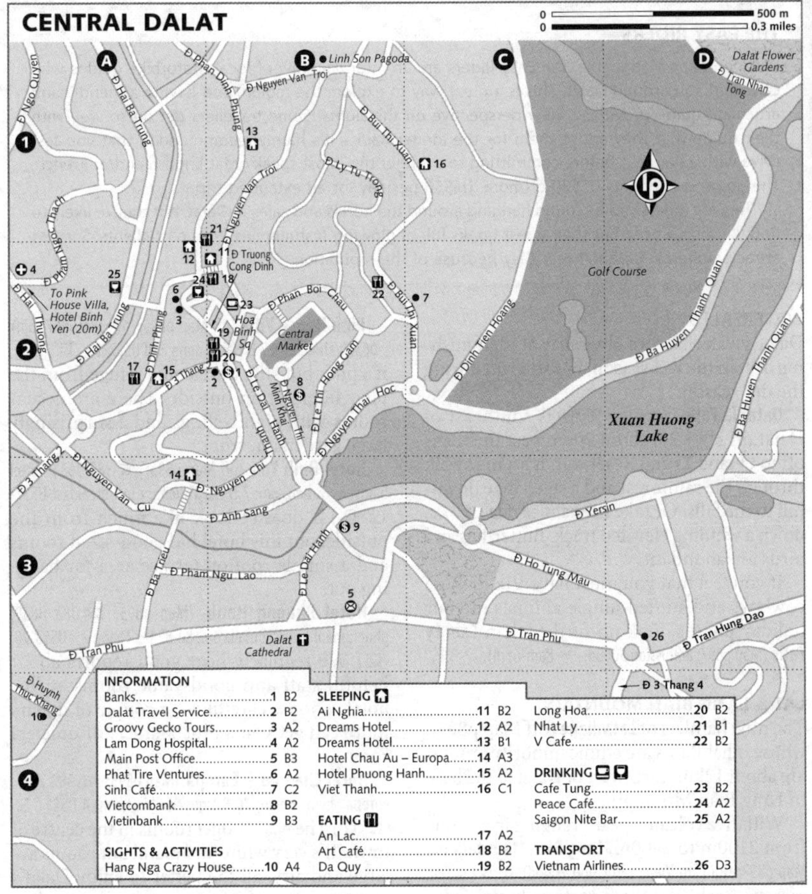

Travel agencies (opposite) offer a range of activities.

The **Crémaillère** (Map p897; ☎ 383 4409; return 80,000d) is a cog railway about 500m east of Xuan Huong Lake that linked Dalat and Thap Cham-Phan Rang from 1928 to 1964. The line has now been partially repaired and you can ride 8km down the tracks to **Trai Mat** village, where you can visit the ornate **Linh Phuoc Pagoda** (off Map p897).

Bao Dai's Summer Palace (Map p897; Đ Le Hong Phong; admission 8000d; 7-11am & 1.30-4pm) is a sprawling villa constructed in 1933. The palace is surrounded by landscaped grounds and decked out in the royal colour yellow.

Southwest of central Dalat, **Hang Nga Crazy House** (Map p895; ☎ 382 2070; 3 Đ Huynh Thuc Khang; admission 12,000d; 8am-7pm) is a funky place that's earned the Crazy House moniker from local residents. It's notable for its *Alice in Wonderland* architecture, where you can perch inside a giraffe or get lost in a giant spider web. You can also stay in one of these kooky, slightly spooky, if grossly overpriced rooms (US$35 to US$110), but book well in advance.

At **Xuan Huong Lake** (Map p897) you can rent a paddleboat that is shaped like a giant swan. About 5km north of Xuan Huong Lake is the **Valley of Love** (Thung Lung Tinh Yeu; Đ Phu Dong Thien Vuong; adult/child 10,000/5000d; 8am-8pm) where you can pose for photos on a pony while accompanied by a Vietnamese dude dressed as a cowboy.

THE EASY RIDERS

Witty and knowledgeable, the Easy Riders are an informal crew of local motorbike guides who can whirl you around Dalat. This is a great way to explore the region, and having a friendly and articulate guide provides a new perspective on the sights. Some travellers get on so well with their guide that they adopt them for the longer haul – it's highly recommended that you test drive with a day tour before committing to a longer trip. Most speak great English and/or French. The going rate now is US$20 or more, US$50 per day for an extended trip.

The Easy Riders can be found hanging around the hotels and cafes in Dalat, but they're likely to find you first. Check out their guest books full of glowing testimonials from past clients. Success attracts imitators so don't rest easy because of the reputation.

WATERFALLS

Dalat's waterfalls are obviously at their gushing best in the wet season, but still run during the dry season.

Datanla Falls (admission 5000d) is southeast of Dalat off Hwy 20, about 200m past the turn-off to Quang Trung Reservoir. It's a nice walk through the rainforest and a steep hike downhill to the falls. Or take the **bobsled ride** (25,000d) down a winding elevated track. Butterflies and birds are abundant.

If you feel that you must have Vietnamese cowboys and stuffed jungle animals in your holiday photos, look no further than **Cam Ly Falls** (Map p897; admission 5000d; 8am-6pm).

LAT & LANG BIAN MOUNTAIN

The nine hamlets of **Lat village** (off Map p897), whose inhabitants are ethnic minority groups, are about 12km northwest of Dalat at the base of Lang Bian Mountain.

With five volcanic peaks ranging in altitude from 2100m to 2400m, **Lang Bian Mountain** (off Map p897; Nui Lam Vien; admission 7000d) makes for a scenic trek (it's three to four hours from Lat village). You might spot some semiwild horses grazing on the side of the mountain, where rhinoceros and tigers lived only half a century ago. The views from the top are tremendous.

Sleeping

Ai Nghia (Map p895; ☎ 352 0529, 80 Đ Dinh Phung; r US$6-14;) Little English is spoken at this minihotel, but rooms are very big, with decent bathrooms.

Viet Thanh (Map p895; ☎ 382 3369; savy@hcm.vnn.vn; 16 Đ Bui Thi Xuan; r US$6-8;) Pick one of the rear rooms here if you want to be near the city centre while waking up to verdant market gardens every morning. They also have motorbikes for rent.

Pink House Villa (off Map p895; ☎ 381 5667; pink_063@yahoo.com; 7 Đ Hai Thuong; s/d US$7/10;) Yes, it's pink but still, a welcome refuge from the busy intersection outside. There are decent rooms with high ceilings and a surprisingly large garden out front.

Hotel Binh Yen (off Map p895; ☎ 382 3631; hotelbinhyen@yahoo.com; 7 Đ Hai Thuong; r incl breakfast US$7-15;) It doesn't look like much from the outside, but this hotel has good-sized rooms and a simple rooftop terrace area for hanging out.

Hotel Phuong Hanh (Map p895; ☎ 383 8839; phuonghanhhotel@gmail.com; 80-82 Đ 3 Thang 2; r US$8-20;) We regularly hear good reports about helpful staff and good-value rooms at this hotel. Choose carefully – a couple of dollars more can get you a much larger (or quieter) room.

Hotel Chau Au – Europa (Map p895; ☎ 382 2870; europa@hcm.vnn.vn; 76 Đ Nguyen Chi Thanh; 4 US$11-20;) The best budget rooms in the centre of town. It's very white and plain, but rooms are large and airy, all the better to enjoy Dalat's climate. The affable owner speaks English and French.

our pick **Dreams Hotel** (Map p895; ☎ 383 3748; dreams@hcm.vnn.vn; 151 Đ Phan Dinh Phung; r US$20-25;) If your stomach and spine could do with a little pampering, fork out a little more cash to stay at this hotel. The buffet breakfast spread is legendary – Vegemite, Marmite and peanut butter are available – and rooms are very comfortable. Owner Mrs Dung is charming and there's no hassle over tours: it doesn't sell any and although it will help you make arrangements, it doesn't take kickbacks. The hotel's latest addition is a sauna, steam room and hot tub, free for guests from 4pm to 7pm. There's a second hotel of the same name down the road (164B Đ Phan Dinh Phung), run on the same principles.

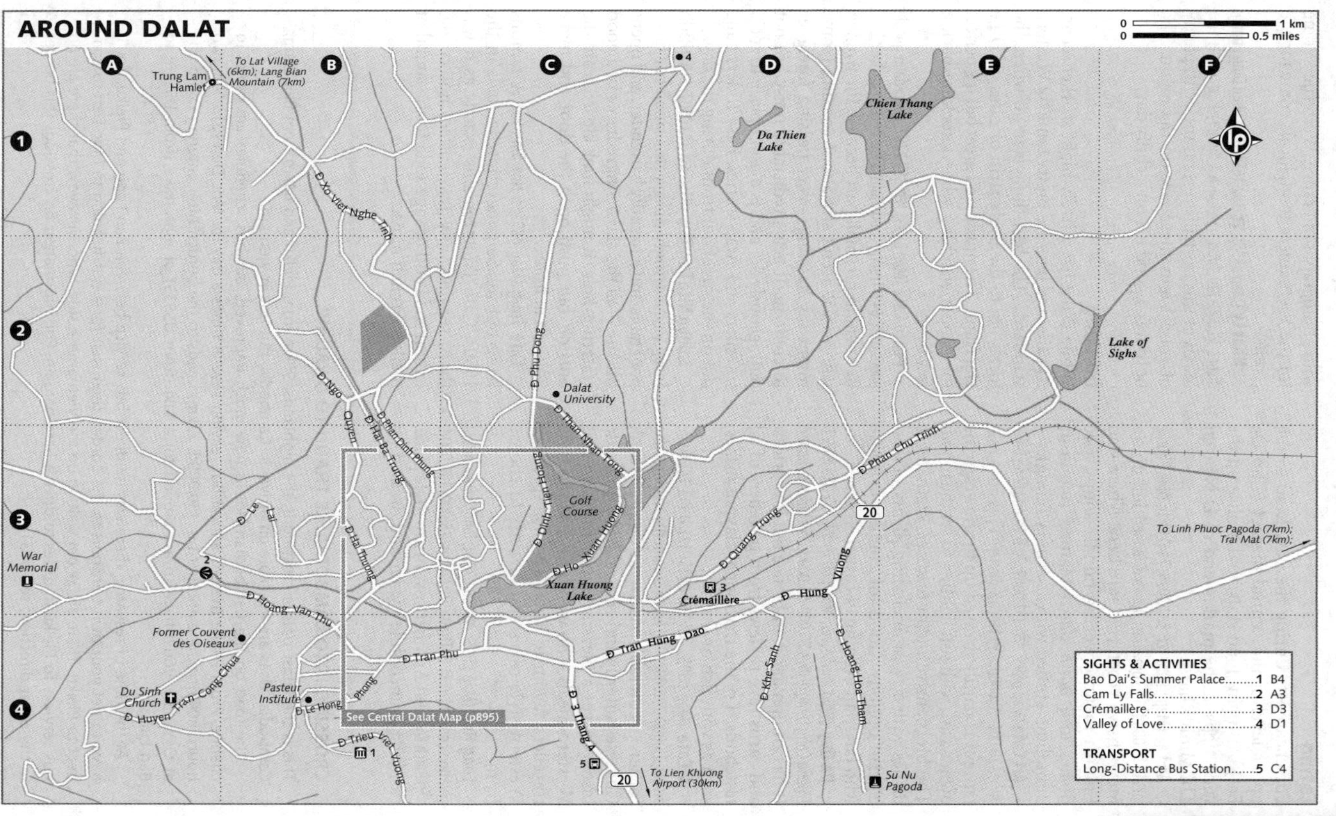
AROUND DALAT
0 1 km
0 0.5 miles
To Lat Village (6km); Lang Bian Mountain (7km)
Trung Lam Hamlet
Chien Thang Lake
Da Thien Lake
Lake of Sighs
Đ Xo Viet Nghe Tinh
Đ Phu Dong
Dalat University
Đ Ngo Quyen
Đ Hai Ba Trung
Đ Phan Dinh Phung
Đ Than Nhan Tong
Đ Dinh Tien Hoang
Golf Course
Đ Ho Xuan Huong
Xuan Huong Lake
Đ Le Lai
Đ Hai Thuong
War Memorial
Đ Hoang Van Thu
Former Couvent des Oiseaux
Du Sinh Church
Đ Tran Cong Chua
Đ Huyen
Pasteur Institute
Đ Le Hong Phong
Đ Tran Phu
See Central Dalat Map (p895)
Đ Trieu Viet Vuong
Đ 3 Thang 4
20
To Lien Khuong Airport (30km)
Đ Phan Chu Trinh
Đ Quang Trung
Crémaillère
Đ Hung Vuong
Đ Tran Hung Dao
Đ Khe Sanh
Đ Hoang Hoa Tham
Su Nu Pagoda
To Linh Phuoc Pagoda (7km); Trai Mat (7km);
SIGHTS & ACTIVITIES
Bao Dai's Summer Palace.........1 B4
Cam Ly Falls.........2 A3
Crémaillère.........3 D3
Valley of Love.........4 D1
TRANSPORT
Long-Distance Bus Station.......5 C4

Eating

For cheap eats during the day, head to the upper level of the central market (Cho Da Lat). At night, food stalls materialise on the wide steps at the market end of Đ Nguyen Thi Minh Khai.

An Lac (Map p895; ☎ 382 2025; 71 Đ Phan Dinh Phung; meals 10,000d; ⏰ breakfast, lunch & dinner) Fill up on inexpensive vegetarian fare here. There's an English menu covering noodle soups, rice dishes and *banh bao* (steamed rice-flour dumplings stuffed with a savoury filling).

Art Café (Map p895; ☎ 351 0089; 70 Đ Truong Cong Dinh; dishes 20,000-70,000d; ⏰ lunch & dinner) This cosy restaurant is nattily dressed up to showcase the owner's art, with soft lighting to set the mood. The inexpensive menu features Vietnamese dishes with a twist, including plenty of vegetarian options. Good for couples or those who fancy an evening of casual elegance.

Da Quy (Wild Sunflower; Map p895; ☎ 351 0883; 49 Đ Truong Cong Dinh; dishes 25,000-55,000d; ⏰ lunch & dinner) It has an upmarket ambience but low prices, and earns rave reviews from travellers of all tastebuds. Try the traditional claypot dishes, such as with fish or shrimp.

V Cafe (Map p895; ☎ 352 0215; 1/1 Đ Bui Thi Xuan; dishes 25,000-79,000d; ⏰ lunch & dinner) Despite the rather predictable decor attempts (think Chinese lanterns and conical hats), this cute bistro serves a pleasing range of Asian and Western meals – no wonder it's a long-time travellers' favourite. There's a small spread of Western-style cakes and desserts to choose from.

Long Hoa (Map p895; ☎ 382 2934; longhoarestaurant@yahoo.com.vn; 6 Đ 3 Thang 2; dishes 25,000-100,000d; ⏰ lunch & dinner) Another cosy bistro-style place, run by a Francophile owner and dressed up with photographs of France. Westerners come for the Vietnamese food, locals come for the steaks.

Nhat Ly (Map p895; ☎ 382 1651; 88 Đ Phan Dinh Phung; dishes 30,000-120,000d; ⏰ lunch & dinner) Eat with the locals at this no-frills restaurant, with plenty of good Vietnamese fare on the menu. The hotpot is a good bet on a chilly day.

Drinking

While Dalat has a lively night market scene, its cafes and bars are pretty tame by Western standards. The best thing is to go where the locals go: to the lively strip of cafes on Đ Le Dai Hanh. The music isn't great but it's perfect for people-watching while knocking back a few beers.

Peace Café (Map p895; ☎ 382 2787; peacedalat.googlepages.com; 64 Đ Truong Cong Dinh) *The* backpacker bar in town, in no small part because the women who run it aren't shy about coaxing (some might say hassling) every passing foreigner to come in. It gets predictably noisy but not outrageously so, and is a good place to meet travellers and swap stories. Easy Riders hang out on the street out front during the day.

Saigon Nite Bar (Map p895; ☎ 382 0007; 11A Đ Hai Ba Trung) Reassuringly dingy, this small bar has a pool table and a friendly bartender, and opens till late – all the classic ingredients of a good watering-hole. It might look closed from the outside, but push open the door and make yourself at home.

Cafe Tung (Map p895; 6 Hoa Binh Sq) A famous hang-out for Saigonese intellectuals in the 1950s, Cafe Tung remains exactly as it was then, serving only tea, coffee, hot cocoa, lemon soda and orange soda to the sound of mellow French music.

CROSSING INTO CAMBODIA: LE THANH TO O YADAW

This is the latest border crossing in the highlands, 90km from Pleiku and 64km from Ban Lung, Cambodia. Visas are available on arrival in Cambodia, but not in Vietnam.

The road on the Cambodian side is now much improved, but bus schedules are prone to change. From Pleiku there is a local bus leaving several times a day for Moc Den (21,000d, two hours, 80km), where another bus (30,000d, 15km) heads to the border. After entering Cambodia at O Yadaw, you'll have to ask around for a taxi (from US$35) or motorbike (from US$10) to Ban Lung.

At the time of research, there was no direct bus service between Ban Lung and Pleiku. You'll have to get your own transport to the border, then wait for a bus heading to Moc Den to connect to Pleiku. There are *xe om* waiting on the Vietnamese side, who will avow that there are no bus services to Pleiku in order to drive a hard bargain. For information on crossings this border in the other direction, see p131.

Shopping

If you can't make it further into the Central Highlands, this is the place to buy tasty Vietnamese coffee. **Hoa Binh Sq** (Map p895) and the market building adjacent to it are the places to go for purchasing ethnic handicrafts from the nearby Montagnard villages and kitschy knick-knacks.

Getting There & Around

Vietnam Airlines (Map p895; ☎ 383 3499; www.vietnamairlines.com; 2 Đ Ho Tung Mau) has daily connections with HCMC and Hanoi. Lien Khuong Airport is 30km south of the city. Vietnam Airlines operates a shuttle bus (35,000d, 30 minutes) timed around flights. Private taxis cost about US$12.

The **long-distance bus station** (Map p897; Đ 3 Thang 2) is about 1km south of the city centre. Services are available to most of the country, including HCMC (110,000d, six to seven hours), Nha Trang (88,000d, seven hours) and Buon Ma Thuot (65,000d, four hours). Open-tour minibuses to Saigon, Mui Ne and Nha Trang can be booked at travellers cafes.

Car rental with a driver starts from about US$40 a day. Full-day tours with local motorbike guides are a great way to see the area, as many of the sights lie outside Dalat's centre. Depending on how far you want to go, expect to pay between US$8 and US$15 for a standard day tour. Many hotels offer bicycle and motorbike hire.

BUON MA THUOT

☎ 050 / pop 312,000

The biggest town in the Central Highlands, Buon Ma Thuot is surrounded by coffee plantations and sells superb coffee at lower prices than in Hanoi or HCMC.

Information

Agribank (☎ 385 3930; 37 Đ Phan Boi Chau) Can change currency and travellers cheques.

DakLak Tourist (☎ 385 8243; daklaktour@dng.vnn.vn; 51 Đ Ly Thuong Kiet) On the ground floor of Thanh Cong Hotel.

Main post office (☎ 385 2612; 1 Đ No Trang Long) Also has internet access.

Vietnam Highland Travel (☎ 385 5009; highlandco@dng.vnn.vn; 24 Đ Ly Thuong Kiet) Located at Thanh Binh Hotel, and has experienced guides who specialise in homestays and trekking trips off the beaten track.

CROSSING INTO LAOS: BO Y TO PHOU KEAU

This crossing at Bo Y–Phou Keau links Pleiku and Quy Nhon with Attapeu and Pakse. Leaving Vietnam, buses depart Pleiku at 8am daily for Attapeu (225,000d, eights hours, 250km), continuing to Pakse (280,000d, 12 hours, 440km). Kon Tum Tourist can arrange tickets to board in Kon Tum at 10am. There are also buses from Quy Nhon to Pakse twice a week. The schedule tends to fluctuate, so inquire at the bus station for the latest details.

For information on crossing this border in the other direction, see p416.

Sights

Places of interest include the **Dak Lak Museum** (☎ 385 0426; 4 Đ Nguyen Du; admission 10,000d; 🕑 7.30-11am & 2-5pm), which has exhibits covering some of the 31 ethnic groups from Dac Lac province. For amazing views from the hills head to Lak Lake, near a M'nong village. Nearby **Yok Don National Park** (Vuon Quoc Gia Yok Don; ☎ 378 3049; yokdonecotourism@vnn.vn) is home to 38 endangered mammal species. Elephant rides and treks can also be arranged. A direct booking at the park costs US$20 per hour per elephant, or US$100 to US$120 for a full-day trek.

Sleeping

Thanh Binh Hotel (☎ 385 3812; 24 Đ Ly Thuong Kiet; r 150,000-180,000d; ❄ 💻) Conveniently located in the middle of the guest-house strip, this hotel has narrow, dark corridors that open up to large, comfortable rooms.

My Linh Hotel (☎ 381 5353; mylinhhotel@yahoo.com; 27-29 Đ Le Dai Hanh; r 150,000-400,000d; ❄ 💻) This minihotel has comfortable rooms and modern decor. The massive, if worn, top-floor suite sleeps 10 and is a bargain at 400,000d.

Thanh Cong Hotel (☎ 858 243; www.daklaktourist.com; 51 Đ Ly Thuong Kiet; r US$15-28; ❄ 💻) One of the nicer places along this stretch, this hotel has a wide range of good rooms, all with bath-tubs.

At the national park headquarters, **Yok Don Guesthouse** (☎ 378 3049; r US$15; ❄) has four basic rooms (cold water only), each with two beds.

Eating

Thanh Loan (☎ 385 4960; 22 Đ Ly Thuong Kiet; meals 15,000d; 🕑 lunch & dinner) There's only one thing

THE HO CHI MINH TRAIL

This legendary route was not one but many paths that formed the major supply link for the North Vietnamese and Viet Cong during the American War. Supplies and troops leaving from the port of Vinh headed inland along inhospitable mountainous jungle paths, crossing in and out of neighbouring Laos, and eventually ending up in southern Vietnam. It's hard to imagine what these soldiers endured – thousands were lost to malaria and American bombs.

While the nature of the trail means that there's no one official route, a widely accepted section follows Hwy 14 north from Kon Tum to Giang, not far from Danang. This exceptionally beautiful track is now served by an excellent road winding along the edge of steep mountains. If you catch a bus between Danang and Kon Tum you'll be following this historic path – albeit in considerably more comfort than the men and women who first trod it.

on the menu: roll-your-own rice-paper rolls, with green vegies and herbs, fried pork, crunchy rice paper and raw garlic.

Dac Biet Bun Bo (☎ 381 0135; 10 Đ Le Hong Phong; meals 15,000d; ⏰ breakfast, lunch & dinner) Another one-dish wonder, this popular eatery serves hearty beef noodles in a spicy broth.

Getting There & Away

Buon Ma Thuot's **bus station** (71 Đ Nguyen Chi Thanh) is about 4km from the centre, with plenty of services to Dalat (65,000d, four hours) and Pleiku (70,000d, four hours). National Hwy 27 from Dalat is best travelled by motorbike or 4WD.

PLEIKU

☎ 059 / pop 236,000

Most travellers prefer to skip the market town of Pleiku in favour of Kon Tum, 49km to the north. Authorities are worried about further unrest among the local ethnic minorities; you need a permit to visit villages in the area and you'll also be required to hire a guide.

Gia Lai Tourist (☎ 874 571; www.gialaitourist.com; 215 Đ Hung Vuong) is located beside the Hung Vuong Hotel; staff can arrange a permit and guide as part of a package.

Pleiku's **bus station** (Ben Xe Duc Long Gia Lai; ☎ 382 9021; 45 Đ Ly Nam De) is 2.5km southeast of town. Regular buses head to Buon Ma Thuot (70,000d, four hours), Kon Tum (15,000d, one hour) and Quy Nhon (70,000d, four hours).

KON TUM

☎ 060 / pop 138,000

Kon Tum seems to hold the most thrall for travellers in the area, especially for cyclists, as motorised traffic is light, the scenery fine and the climate pleasant. No matter how you get around here, the people are among the warmest in Vietnam.

Exchange dollars for dong at **BIDV** (☎ 386 2340; 1 Đ Tran Phu; ⏰ closed Sat). The terrific **Kon Tum Tourist** (☎ 386 1626; ktourist@dng.vnn.vn; 2 Đ Phan Dinh Phung) has its booking office in Dakbla Hotel.

On the edge of town are a couple of **Bahnar villages** within walking distance. Along Đ Nguyen Hue, there's a ceremonial *rong* house – a community hall on stilts – and a **Catholic seminary** with a **hill-tribe museum** on the 2nd floor.

A short walk from the town centre, the **Vinh Son 1** and **Vinh Son 2** orphanages welcome visitors who come to share some time with the adorable multi-ethnic resident children. Donations, canned food, clothing and toys for the kids are much appreciated.

Sleeping & Eating

Viet Tram (☎ 386 9269; 162 Đ Nguyen Hue; r US$10-15; ❄ 💻) A simple family-run minihotel with clean rooms, though it's starting to look a little run down. Room prices can be bargained down if you skip the air-con.

Family Hotel (☎ 386 2448; phongminhkt@yahoo.com; 55 & 61 Đ Tran Hung Dao; r US$10-25; ❄ 💻) This minihotel has a range of good rooms with nice bathrooms, perhaps a touch heavy on the pastels. The real winner is the garden courtyard, where breakfast is served in a peaceful setting.

Nghia II (72 Đ Le Loi; dishes 10,000d; ⏰ lunch & dinner) A casual and cheap eatery serving good vegetarian fare.

Dakbla's (☎ 386 2584; 168 Đ Nguyen Hue; dishes 20,000-80,000d; ⏰ lunch & dinner) Dakbla's has a standard Vietnamese menu spiced up with meats like wild boar and frog. The decor includes tribal artefacts glowering down on diners.

Eva Coffee (☎ 386 2944; evacoffee2002@yahoo.com; 1 Đ Phan Chu Trinh) A cosy neighbourhood cafe with plenty of character, from the treehouse-like setting to the solemn tribal masks overhead. A nice place to unwind with a beer or coffee.

Getting There & Away

Kon Tum's **bus station** (Đ 279 Phan Dinh Phung) has plenty of services to Pleiku (15,000d, one hour) and Danang (130,000d, four hours). It's possible to head for the border with Laos from here (see the boxed text, p899).

HO CHI MINH CITY (SAIGON)

☎ 08 / pop 5.38 million

Fasten your seatbelts as HCMC is a metropolis on the move, and we are not just talking about the motorbikes that throng the streets. Saigon, as it is known to all but the city officials who watch over the place, is Vietnam at its most dizzying, a high-octane city of commerce and culture that has driven the whole country forward with its limitless energy. It is a living organism, breathing life and vitality into all who settle here, and visitors cannot help but come along for the ride.

Saigon is a name so evocative that it conjures up a thousand jumbled images. Wander through timeless alleys to ancient pagodas or teeming markets, past ramshackle wooden shops selling silk and spices, before fast-forwarding into the future beneath sleek skyscrapers and mammoth malls. The ghosts of the past live on in the churches, temples, former GI hotels and government buildings that one generation ago witnessed a city in turmoil.

Despite the apparent chaos, it's easy to fall prey to the charms of this city.

ORIENTATION

A sprawl of 16 urban and five rural *quan* (districts) make up the vast geography of HCMC, though most travellers stick to the centre around the Dong Khoi and Pham Ngu Lao neighbourhoods. Cholon, the city's Chinatown, lies southwest of the centre, and the Saigon River snakes down the eastern side.

The heart of central HCMC beats in Districts 1 and 3, where stately tamarind trees shade fading French colonial buildings and narrow Vietnamese shophouses. High-rise hotels jostle with towers of commerce near the Saigon River.

Street labels are shortened to Đ for *duong* (street) and ĐL for *dai lo* (boulevard).

INFORMATION

For up-to-date information on what's going on in town, check out the **Word HCMC** (www.wordhcmc.com) or **AsiaLIFE HCMC** (www.Asialifehcmc.com), both quality listings magazines.

Bookshops

To find a good read for the bus or beach, just sit down at any traveller hang-out and wait for what looks like an escaped library shelf gone vertical to stagger towards you. For reference, Vietnamese literature or how-to books in French or English consider **Fahasa Bookshop** (Map p906; 🕑 8am-10pm); Đ Dong Khoi (☎ 3822 4670; 185 Đ Dong Khoi); ĐL Nguyen Hue (☎ 3822 5796; 40 ĐL Nguyen Hue).

Cultural Centres

British Council (Map p904; ☎ 3823 2862; www.britishcouncil.org/vietnam; 25 ĐL Le Duan) Attached to the British Consulate.

Idecaf (Institute of Cultural Exchange with France; Map p906; ☎ 3829 5451; 31 Đ Thai Van Lung) Plus Le Jardin, a lovely cafe.

Emergency

Ambulance (☎ 115)
Fire (☎ 114)
Police (☎ 113)

Internet Access

Hundreds of internet cafes thrive in HCMC – in Pham Ngu Lao (Map p910) you can't swing a dead cat without hitting one. Many hotels,

A DAY IN SAIGON

Downtown HCMC can be walked in a day, making a loop from Pham Ngu Lao going via **Ben Thanh Market** (p913), and then walking to the **Reunification Palace** (p905) and the nearby **War Remnants Museum** (p906). Head back to pulsating **Pham Ngu Lao** (p911) to enjoy the nightlife.

A day tour on a *xe om* to points further afield such as **Cholon** (p907) should cost US$7 to US$10.

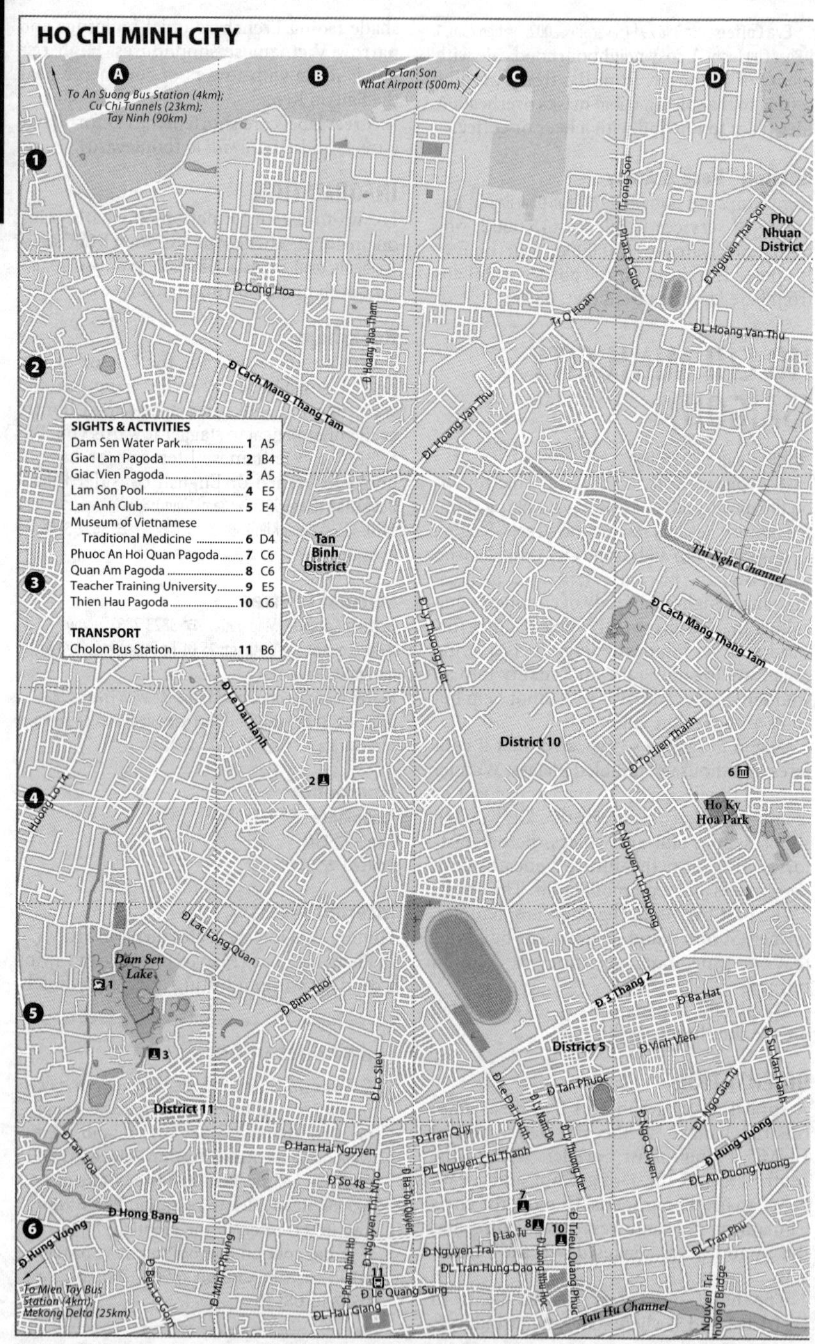
HO CHI MINH CITY
To An Suong Bus Station (4km); Cu Chi Tunnels (23km); Tay Ninh (90km)
To Tan Son Nhat Airport (500m)
SIGHTS & ACTIVITIES
Dam Sen Water Park 1 A5
Giac Lam Pagoda 2 B4
Giac Vien Pagoda 3 A5
Lam Son Pool 4 E5
Lan Anh Club 5 E4
Museum of Vietnamese Traditional Medicine 6 D4
Phuoc An Hoi Quan Pagoda 7 C6
Quan Am Pagoda 8 C6
Teacher Training University 9 E5
Thien Hau Pagoda 10 C6
TRANSPORT
Cholon Bus Station 11 B6
Phu Nhuan District
Tan Binh District
District 10
District 5
District 11
Ho Ky Hoa Park
Dam Sen Lake
Thi Nghe Channel
Tau Hu Channel
Đ Cong Hoa
Đ Hoang Hoa Tham
Đ Cach Mang Thang Tam
ĐL Hoang Van Thu
Tr Q Hoan
Trong Son
Phan Đ Giot
Đ Nguyen Thai Son
Đ Ly Thuong Kiet
Đ Le Dai Hanh
Đ To Hien Thanh
Đ Nguyen Tri Phuong
Huong Lo 14
Đ Lac Long Quan
Đ Binh Thoi
Đ 3 Thang 2
Đ Ba Hat
Đ Vinh Vien
Đ Su Van Hanh
Đ Tan Phuoc
Đ Ngo Gia Tu
Đ Ngo Quyen
Đ Lo Sieu
Đ Ly Nam De
Đ Tan Hoa
Đ Han Hai Nguyen
Đ Tran Quy
ĐL Nguyen Chi Thanh
Đ Hung Vuong
ĐL An Duong Vuong
Đ So 48
Đ Ha Ton Quyen
Đ Hong Bang
Đ Lao Tu
Đ Luong Nhu Hoc
Đ Trieu Quang Phuc
ĐL Tran Phu
Đ Nguyen Trai
ĐL Tran Hung Dao
Đ Nguyen Thi Nho
Đ Pham Dinh Ho
Đ Minh Phung
Đ Ben Lo Gom
Đ Le Quang Sung
ĐL Hau Giang
Nguyen Tri Phuong Bridge
To Mien Tay Bus Station (4km); Mekong Delta (25km)

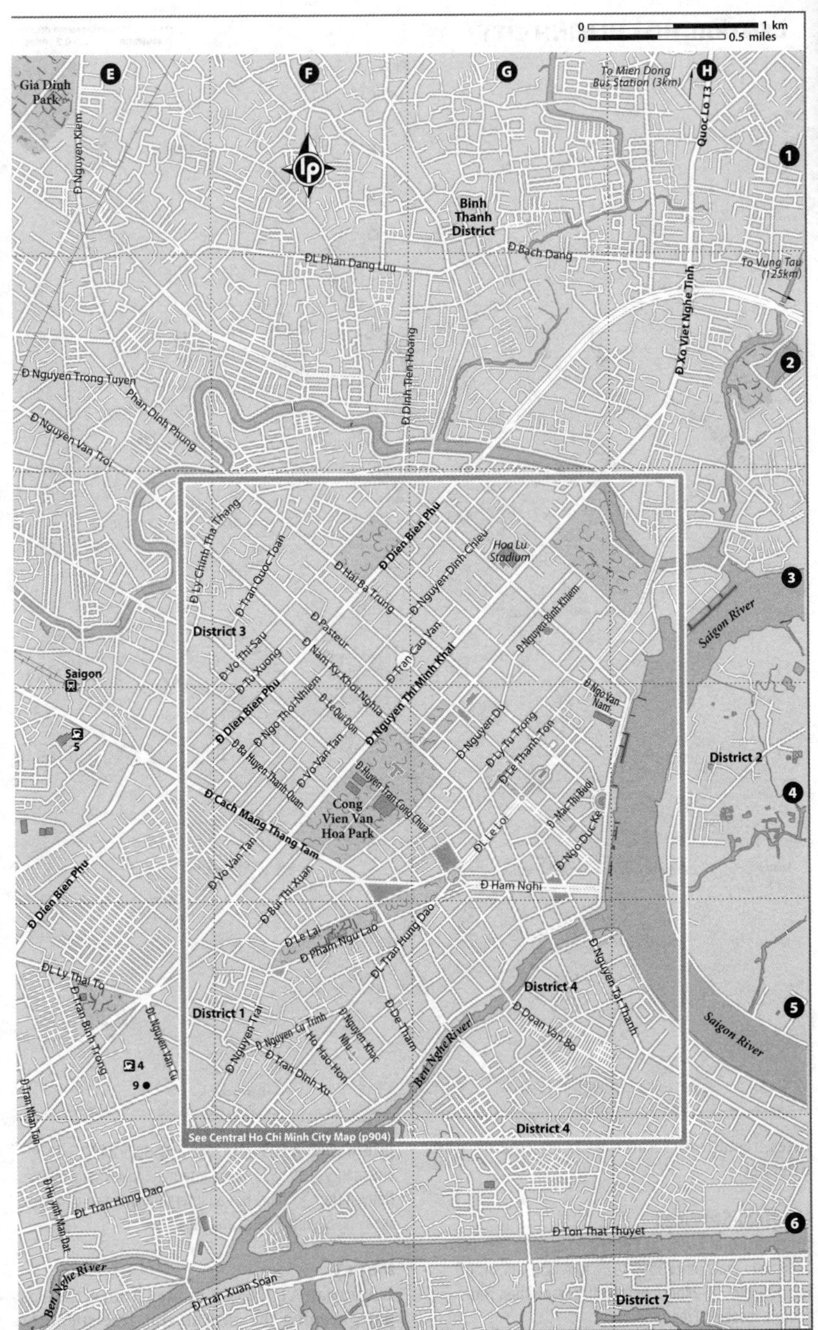
Gia Dinh Park
Đ Nguyen Kiem
Binh Thanh District
Đ Bach Dang
ĐL Phan Dang Luu
To Mien Dong Bus Station (3km)
Quoc Lo 13
To Vung Tau (125km)
Đ Xo Viet Nghe Tinh
Đ Dinh Tien Hoang
Đ Nguyen Trong Tuyen
Phan Dinh Phung
Đ Nguyen Van Troi
Đ Ly Chinh Tha Thang
Đ Tran Quoc Toan
Đ Dien Bien Phu
Đ Hai Ba Trung
Đ Nguyen Dinh Chieu
Hoa Lu Stadium
Saigon River
District 3
Đ Vo Thi Sau
Đ Tu Xuong
Đ Pasteur
Đ Nam Ky Khoi Nghia
Đ Tran Cao Van
Đ Nguyen Binh Khiem
Đ Nguyen Thi Minh Khai
Saigon
Đ Ngo Thoi Nhiem
Đ Le Qui Don
Đ Ngo Van Nam
Đ Ba Huyen Thanh Quan
Đ Vo Van Tan
Đ Huyen Tran Cong Chua
Đ Nguyen Du
Đ Ly Tu Trong
Đ Le Thanh Ton
District 2
Cong Vien Van Hoa Park
Đ Cach Mang Thang Tam
Đ Le Loi
Đ Mac Thi Buoi
Đ Ngo Duc Ke
Đ Ham Nghi
Đ Bui Thi Xuan
Đ Le Lai
Đ Pham Ngu Lao
ĐL Tran Hung Dao
ĐL Ly Thai To
Đ Tran Binh Trong
ĐL Nguyen Van Cu
District 1
Đ Nguyen Trai
Đ Nguyen Cu Trinh
Đ Nguyen Khac Nhu
Ho Hao Hon
Đ De Tham
Đ Tran Dinh Xu
Ben Nghe River
District 4
Đ Doan Van Bo
Đ Nguyen Tat Thanh
Đ Tran Nhan Ton
See Central Ho Chi Minh City Map (p904)
Đ Huynh Man Dat
ĐL Tran Hung Dao
Đ Ton That Thuyet
Đ Tran Xuan Soan
District 7
0 1 km
0 0.5 miles

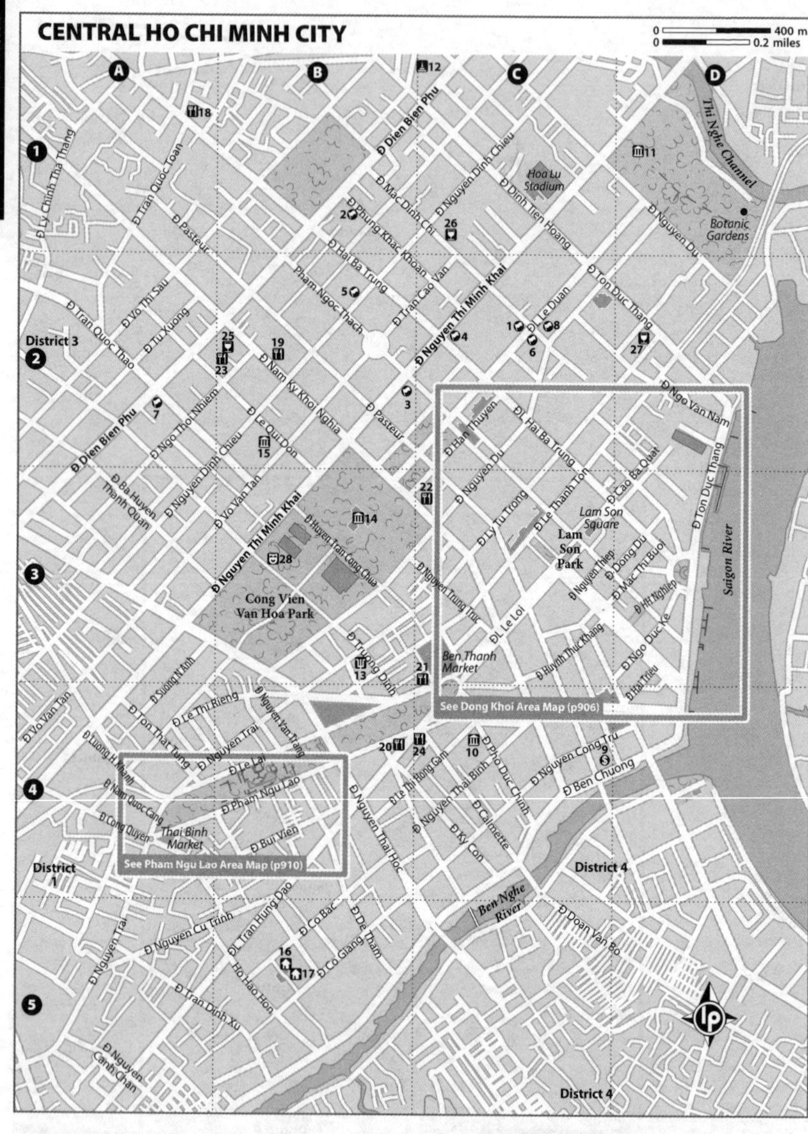

cafes, restaurants and bars offer free wi-fi or internet.

Medical Services

International Medical Centre (Map p906; ☎ 3827 2366, 24hr emergency 3865 4025; fac@hcm.vnn.vn; 1 Đ Han Thuyen; 24hr) A non-profit organisation with English-speaking French doctors.

International SOS (Map p906; ☎ 3929 8424, 24hr emergency 3829 8520; www.internationalsos.com; 65 Đ Nguyen Du; 24hr) Has an international team of doctors speaking English, French and Japanese.

Money

Finding an ATM to get money from is the easy part; keeping the cash in this free-spending

INFORMATION		
American Consulate	1	C2
British Council	(see 8)	
Cambodian Consulate	2	B1
Chinese Consulate	3	B2
French Consulate	4	C2
German Consulate	5	B2
Netherlands Consulate	6	C2
Thai Consulate	7	A2
UK Consulate	8	C2
Vietcombank	9	C4
SIGHTS & ACTIVITIES		
Fine Arts Museum	10	C4
History Museum	11	D1
Jade Emperor Pagoda	12	C1
Mariamman Hindu Temple	13	B3
Reunification Palace	14	B3
War Remnants Museum	15	B2
SLEEPING		
Dan Le Hotel	16	B5
Guest House California	(see 17)	
Miss Loi's Guesthouse	17	B5
Ngoc Son	(see 17)	
EATING		
Banh Xeo 46A	18	A1
Beefsteak Nam Son	19	B2
Falafellim	20	B4
Pho 2000	21	C3
Quan An Ngon	22	C3
Serenata	23	B2
Tin Nghia	24	C4
DRINKING		
Acoustic Bar	25	B2
Hoa Vien	26	C1
Lush	27	D2
ENTERTAINMENT		
Golden Dragon Water Puppet Theatre	28	B3

city is another issue. There are several exchange counters in the hallway of arrivals, just after clearing customs, and most offer the official rates. There are also ATMs available here.

ANZ Bank (Map p906; ☎ 3829 9319; 11 Me Linh Sq) Has a 24-hour ATM.

Sacombank (Map p910; ☎ 3836 4231; 211 Đ Nguyen Thai Hoc) Conveniently located in the backpacker zone, with 24-hour ATM.

Vietcombank (Map p904; ☎ 3829 7245; 29 Đ Ben Chuong; closed Sun & last day of the month) The eastern building is for foreign exchange only, but is also worth a visit just to see the stunningly ornate interior.

Post

Main post office (Buu Dien Thanh Pho Ho Chi Minh; Map p906; ☎ 3829 6555; 2 Cong Xa Paris; 7am-9.30pm) Saigon's French-era post office is next to the Notre Dame Cathedral and offers long-distance and domestic calls in addition to the usual post and parcel services. It's an impressive structure that merits a look.

Tourist Information

Tourist Information Center (Map p906; ☎ 3822 6033; www.vietnamtourism.com; 4G Le Loi; 8am-8pm) This smart information centre distributes city maps and brochures and offers limited advice about goings-on in Saigon.

Travel Agencies

You will find the following budget agencies in the backpacker area of Pham Ngu Lao.

Delta Adventure Tours (Map p910; ☎ 3920 2112; www.deltaadventuretours.com; 267 Đ De Tham)

Handspan Adventure Travel (Map p910; ☎ 3925 7605; www.handspan.com; 7th fl, Titan Bldg, 18A Đ Nam Quoc Cang)

Innoviet (Map p910; ☎ 3295 8840; www.innoviet.com; 158 Đ Bui Vien)

Kim Travel (Map p910; ☎ 3920 5552; www.kimtravel.com; 270 Đ De Tham)

Sinh Cafe (Map p910; ☎ 3836 7338; www.sinhcafevn.com; 246 Đ De Tham)

Sinhbalo Adventures (Map p910; ☎ 3837 6766; www.sinhbalo.com; 283/20 Đ Pham Ngu Lao)

DANGERS & ANNOYANCES

Although travellers very rarely face any physical danger in HCMC (besides the traffic), the city has the most determined thieves in the country. Drive-by 'cowboys' on motorbikes – especially along the riverfront – can steal bags off your arm, and pickpockets work all crowds. Some of the worst perpetrators are the cute children crowding around you, wanting to sell postcards and newspapers with one hand and helping themselves to your valuables with the other. Tourist police in bright green uniforms are increasingly patrolling the streets and might be a source of help if anything goes wrong.

While it's generally safe to take *cyclos* during the day, it is not always safe at night; take a metered taxi instead.

Sometimes *cyclo* and motorbike drivers will demand more than the agreed price after a trip. Be sure to be crystal clear beforehand about whether the fee is per person or the total.

SIGHTS

Reunification Palace

Built in 1966 to serve as South Vietnam's Presidential Palace, today this landmark is known as the **Reunification Palace** (Dinh Thong Nhat; Map p904; ☎ 3829 4117; 106 Đ Nguyen Du; admission 15,000d; 7.30-11am & 1-4pm). The first communist tanks in Saigon crashed through the gates of this building on the morning of 30 April 1975 when Saigon surrendered to the North. The building is a timewarp, having been left just as it looked on that momentous day.

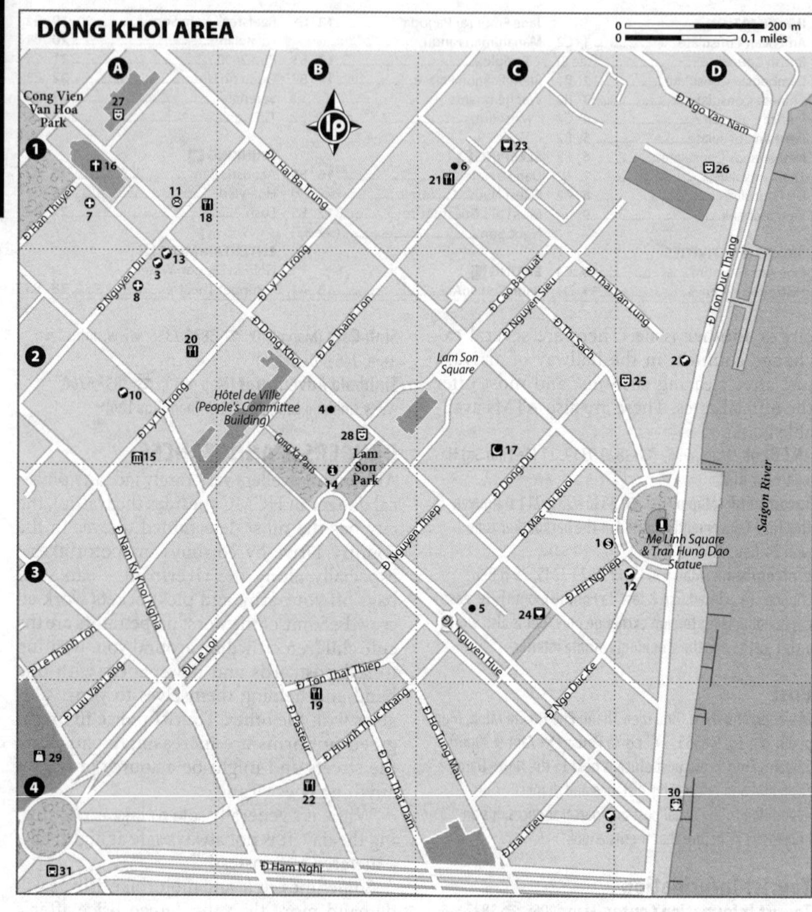

Enter on Đ Nam Ky Khoi Nghia, where English- and French-speaking guides are available.

War Remnants Museum

Documenting the atrocities of war, the **War Remnants Museum** (Bao Tang Chung Tich Chien Tranh; Map p904; ☎ 3930 5587; 28 Đ Vo Van Tan; admission 15,000d; 🕒 7.30am-noon & 1.30-5pm) is unique, brutal and an essential stop. On display are retired artillery pieces, a model of the tiger cages used to house VC prisoners, and an array of photographs of the victims of war – those who suffered torture as well as those who were born with birth defects caused by the use of defoliants. The exhibits are labelled in Vietnamese, English and Chinese, but are rather propagandist in tone.

Other Museums

Housed in a beautiful grey neoclassical structure, the **Museum of Ho Chi Minh City** (Bao Tang Thanh Pho Ho Chi Minh; Map p906; ☎ 3829 9741; 65 Đ Ly Tu Trong; admission 15,000d; 🕒 8am-4pm) was built in 1885 and has displays of artefacts from the various periods of the communist struggle for power in Vietnam.

The impressive collection of HCMC's **History Museum** (Bao Tang Lich Su; Map p904; ☎ 3829 8146; Đ Nguyen Binh Khiem; admission 15,000d; 🕒 8-11am & 1.30-4.30pm Tue-Sun) is housed in a stunning Sino-French building constructed in 1929 by the Société des Études Indochinoises. Displaying artefacts from almost 4000 years of human activity in what is now Vietnam, it's just inside the main entrance to the zoo.

INFORMATION		
ANZ Bank	1	C3
Australian Consulate	2	D2
Canadian Consulate	3	A2
DHL	(see 11)	
Fahasa Bookshop	4	B2
Fahasa Bookshop	5	C3
Idecaf	6	C1
International Medical Centre	7	A1
International SOS	8	A2
Japanese Consulate	9	C4
Lao Consulate	10	A2
Main Post Office	11	A1
Malaysian Consulate	12	D3
New Zealand Consulate	13	A2
Tourist Information Center	14	B3

SIGHTS & ACTIVITIES		
Diamond Superbowl	(see 27)	
Museum of Ho Chi Minh City	15	A2
Notre Dame Cathedral	16	A1
Saigon Central Mosque	17	C2
EATING		
Casbah	18	A1
Fanny	19	B4
Huong Lai	20	A2
Le Jardin	21	C1
X Café	22	B4
DRINKING		
Sheridan's Irish House	23	C1
Underground	24	C3

ENTERTAINMENT		
Apocalypse Now	25	D2
Cage	26	D1
Diamond Plaza Cinema	27	A1
Idecaf	(see 6)	
Opera House	28	B2
SHOPPING		
Ben Thanh Market	29	A4
TRANSPORT		
Bach Dang Jetty (Hydrofoils to Vung Tau)	30	D4
Ben Thanh Local Bus Station	31	A4

The city's **Fine Arts Museum** (Bao Tang My Thuat; Map p904; ☎ 3829 4441; www.baotangmythuattphcm.vn; 97A Đ Pho Duc Chinh; admission 10,000d; 9am-4.30pm Tue-Sun) covers art from the earliest civilisations in Vietnam – Funan and Cham – to contemporary work. The collection represents a good overview of the evolution of Vietnamese aesthetics.

The beautiful **Museum of Vietnamese Traditional Medicine** (Fito Museum; Map pp902-3; ☎ 846 2430; www.fitomuseum.com.vn; 41 Đ Hoang Du Khong St, District 10; admission 32,000d; 8.30am-5.30pm) traces the history of Vietnamese natural remedies from the 2nd century to now. English-speaking guides come with the admission price, and the inside of the building is stunning with massive wood tableaux of scenes from medicinal history. There's a re-creation of a traditional medicine shop and visitors can try their hand (or foot) at the tools used to pulverise healing plants. A short film is the only time the corporate sponsorship of the museum becomes apparent.

Pagodas, Temples & Churches

Whether the traffic has inspired a new religious streak or travellers are just seeking some relative peace, places of worship here tend towards the colourful and architecturally impressive.

CENTRAL HCMC

Built in 1909 by the Cantonese (Quang Dong) Congregation, the **Jade Emperor Pagoda** (Phuoc Hai Tu or Chua Ngoc Hoang; Map p904; 73 Đ Mai Thi Luu; 7.30am-6pm) is a real gem among Chinese temples. Filled with statues of phantasmal divinities and grotesque heroes, the pungent smoke of burning joss sticks fills the air. To get to the pagoda, go to 20 Đ Dien Bien Phu and walk half a block in a northwest direction.

Notre Dame Cathedral (Map p906; Đ Han Thuyen; Mass 9.30am Sun), built between 1877 and 1883, stands regally in the heart of the government quarter. Its red-brick neo-Romanesque form and two 40m-high square towers tipped with iron spires dominate the skyline.

A splash of southern India's colour in Saigon, **Mariamman Hindu Temple** (Chua Ba Mariamman; Map p904; 45 Đ Truong Dinh; 7am-7pm) was built at the end of the 19th century and is dedicated to the Hindu goddess Mariamman.

Constructed by south Indian Muslims in 1935 on the site of an earlier mosque, **Saigon Central Mosque** (Map p906; 66 Đ Dong Du; 9am-5pm) is an immaculately clean and well-kept island of calm in the middle of bustling central Saigon. As at any mosque, remove your shoes before entering.

CHOLON

Cholon has a wealth of wonderful Chinese temples including **Quan Am Pagoda** (Map pp902-3; 12 Đ Lao Tu; 8am-4.30pm), founded in 1816 by the Fujian Chinese congregation. The roof is decorated with fantastic scenes, rendered in ceramic, from traditional Chinese plays and stories. As at most Chinese temples, anyone can buy incense inside and make an offering.

Nearby, **Phuoc An Hoi Quan Pagoda** (Map pp902-3; 184 Đ Hung Vuong; 7am-5.30pm) stands as one of the most beautifully ornamented constructions in the city. To the left of the entrance is a life-size figure of the sacred horse of Quan Cong. Before leaving on a journey, people make offerings to the horse, then stroke its mane and ring the bell around its neck. Behind the main altar is Quan Cong, to whom the pagoda is dedicated.

One of the most active in Cholon, **Thien Hau Pagoda** (Ba Mieu or Pho Mieu; Map pp902-3; 710 Đ Nguyen Trai; 6am-5.30pm) is dedicated to Thien

Hau, the Chinese goddess of the sea. As she protects fisherfolk, sailors, merchants and any other maritime travellers, you might stop by to ask for a blessing for your Mekong Delta journey.

GREATER HCMC

The towering **Giac Lam Pagoda** (Map pp902-3; 118 Đ Lac Long Quan; 6am-9pm) dates from 1744 and is believed to be the oldest in the city. The architecture and ornamentation have not changed since 1900, and the compound is a very meditative place to explore.

In a semirural setting next to Dam Sen Lake, serene **Giac Vien Pagoda** (Map pp902-3; 247 Đ Lac Long Quan; 7am-7pm) was founded by Hai Tinh Giac Vien about 200 years ago and there are literally hundreds if not thousands of Buddha statues inside the well-shaded main building.

ACTIVITIES

Bowling

Diamond Superbowl (Map p906; 3825 7778; Diamond Plaza, 34 ĐL Le Duan; 10-1am) This 32-lane bowling alley is right in the centre of town. It's very popular thanks to fluorescent bowling balls and state-of-the-art scoring.

Massage

Most upmarket hotels offer massage service (some more legitimate than others); the cheapest option is the **Vietnamese Traditional Massage Institute** (Map p910; 3839 6697; 185 Đ Cong Quynh; per hr 40,000-50,000d, sauna 30,000d; 9am-9pm). It offers no-nonsense, muscle-melting massages performed by blind masseurs.

If you're so sore you can't even make it to a real massage place, listen for the metallic clacking sound that signals roving masseurs in the evenings. They'll massage you right in your chair after dinner (30,000d to 50,000d) for 20 minutes or so. Add another 10,000d for 'cupping', the art of applying heated glass cups to the skin that form a seal to supposedly suck out disease. The circular weals would shock the folks back home.

Swimming

Nonguests can pay an admission fee of US$10 to US$20 per day to use the swimming pools at plush hotels. Local clubs with lower fees:

Dam Sen Water Park (Map pp902-3; 3858 8418; www.damsenwaterpark.com.vn; 3 Đ Hoa Binh; 35,000-75,000d; 9am-6pm) It has water slides, a lazy river and a sunbathing area 'for foreigners'.

Lam Son Pool (Map pp902-3; 3835 8028; 342 Đ Tran Binh Trong, District 5; per hr 8000d, after 5pm 10,000d; 8am-8pm) Offering an Olympic-sized pool.

Lan Anh Club (Map pp902-3; 3862 7144; 291 Cach Mang Thang Tam, District 10; gym/pool 50,000d/30,000d; pool 6am-9pm) Good gym here.

COURSES

Cooking

Bi Saigon (Map p910; 3836 0678; www.bisaigon.com; 185/26 Đ Pham Ngu Lao, District 1; per person per dish US$20) Organises private cooking classes on request.

Vietnam Cookery Centre (3512 7246; www.vietnamcookery.com; M1 Cu Xa Tan Tang, Ward 25, Binh Thanh District; per person US$39) Offers a half-day course for lunch or dinner involving five dishes and a souvenir handbook.

Language

Most foreign-language students enrol at the **Teacher Training University** (Dai Hoc Su Pham; Map pp902-3; 3835 5100; ciecer@hcm.vnn.vn; 280 An Duong Vuong, District 5; private/group class US$6/4), which is a department of Ho Chi Minh City University.

SLEEPING

Saigon's backpacker central is known as Pham Ngu Lao. Good deals abound, but some of the most likeable places are on the many little alleys criss-crossing the area.

Pham Ngu Lao

Yellow House (Map p910; 3836 8830; yellowhousehotel@yahoo.com; 31 Đ Bui Vien; dm/s/d US$7/13/17;) One of the few hotels to offer dorm beds, Yellow House has two dormitories (a mixed seven-bed and a three-bed for men or women – whoever arrives first) as well as private rooms. Breakfast included.

Kim's (Map p910; 3836 8584; 91 Đ Bui Vien; r US$10-15;) This small hotel is not part of the Mekong empire that is Kim Café, but an independent family-run pad with good-value rooms. Rates remain mercifully low in these inflationary times.

Ha Vy Hotel (Map p910; 3836 9123; www.havyhotel.com; 16-18 Đ Do Quang Dau; r US$12-17;) Located at the western end of the district, the Ha Vy is a reliable bet thanks to well-kept rooms with a choice of air-con or fan.

Mai Phai Hotel (Map p910; 3836 5868; maiphaihotel@saigonnet.vn; 209 Đ Pham Ngu Lao; r US$14-30;) One place we have stayed in a few times over the years, the service is friendly and rooms are well furnished. Extras include a lift and free wi-fi.

our pick **Madame Cuc's** (madamcuc@hcm.vnn.vn; r US$15-25;) Hotel 127 (Map p910; ☎ 836 8761; 127 Đ Cong Quynh); Hotel 64 (Map p910; ☎ 836 5073; 64 Đ Bui Vien); Hotel MC 184 (Map p910; ☎ 836 1679; 184 Đ Cong Quynh) A three-in-one recommendation here, this trio of places is run by the welcoming Madam Cuc. All the hotels offer clean and spacious rooms with friendly service. There's free tea, coffee and fruit all day; breakfast and a simple dinner are included in the room rates.

Orient Hotel (Map p910; ☎ 3920 3993; www.orienthotel.vn; 274 Đ De Tham; r US$17-40;) One of the biggest hotels on De Tham with 70 rooms, this is heading towards midrange. Smart rooms, breakfast included, free internet and a lift.

Oh yes, plenty more:

Vuong Hoa Hotel (Map p910; ☎ 3836 9491; 36 Đ Bui Vien; dm US$3;) Probably the cheapest beds in town, the dorms here feature six beds per room. Very simple. Downstairs is an internet cafe.

Sao Nam Hotel (Map p910; ☎ 3920 6472; haohiep@yahoo.com; 175/5 Đ Pham Ngu Lao; r US$16-25;) The 'Southern Star' has sparkling bathrooms, plus TV and fridge. Free internet.

Bich Duyen Hotel (Map p910; ☎ 3837 4588; bichduyenhotel@yahoo.com; 283/4 Đ Pham Ngu Lao; r US$18-27;) Very friendly place on a popular alley off Pham Ngu Lao, with free internet.

Co Giang

For a quieter alternative to Pham Ngu Lao, about 10 minutes' walk south there is a string of good guest houses in the quiet alley connecting Đ Co Giang and Đ Co Bac (Map p904). To reach the guest houses, walk southwest on Đ Co Bac and turn left after you pass the *nuoc mam* (fish sauce) shops.

Dan Le Hotel (Map p904; ☎ 3836 9651; 171/10 Đ Co Bac; s/d/vip US$11/16/20;) A smart new minihotel in the midst of these alleys, the Dan Le is cracking value. It is worth being a VIP for the night for more space.

our pick **Miss Loi's Guesthouse** (Map p904; ☎ 3837 9589; missloi@hcm.fpt.vn; 178/20 Đ Co Giang; r US$12-25;) The original Co Giang guest house, we first crashed out here back in 1995 and the homely atmosphere prevails today, although the rooms have definitely been upgraded.

The budget beat goes on:

Ngoc Son (Map p904; ☎ 3836 4717; ngocsonguesthouse@yahoo.com; 178/32 Đ Co Giang; r US$10-15;) Small guest house with good value rooms. Motorbikes for hire.

Guest House California (Map p904; ☎ 3837 8885; guesthousecalifornia-saigon@yahoo.com; 171A Đ Co Bac; r US$15-28;) 'It's such a lovely place…' or so the Eagles might have said. Intimate, friendly and clean.

EATING

Ranging from dirt-cheap, tasty meals at street stalls to upscale epicurean experiences, Saigon has it all.

Markets always have a vast dining area, often on the ground floor or in the basement. Clusters of food stalls can be found in Ben Thanh (Map p904) and Thai Binh (Map p910) Markets. A large bowl of beef noodles costs about 20,000d. Just look for the signs with the words *pho* or *hu tieu*. Don't eat meat? Look for the magic word *chay* (vegetarian) tacked on the end of the sign.

Đ Pham Ngu Lao and Đ De Tham form the axis of Saigon's budget eatery haven, where traveller cafes dish out cuisine that ranges from acceptable to exceptional and book tours on the side.

Vietnamese

Banh Xeo 46A (Map p904; ☎ 3824 1110; 46A Đ Dinh Cong Trang; mains 20,000-40,000d) Locals always hit the restaurants that specialise in a single dish, and this legendary spot has the best *banh xeo* in town.

our pick **Quan An Ngon** (Map p904; ☎ 3825 7179; 138 Đ Nam Ky Khoi Nghia; mains 20,000-90,000d; lunch & dinner) This place positively heaves thanks to the taste of street food in stylish surroundings. Set in a leafy garden ringed by food stalls specialising in a traditional dish.

Beefsteak Nam Son (Map p904; 188 Đ Nam Ky Khoi Nghia; mains 30,000-60,000d; lunch & dinner) Craving a steak and can't afford the fancier places? This is a bargain. Local beef and even some cholesterol-beating ostrich.

Pho 24 (Map p910; ☎ 3821 8122; 271 Đ Pham Ngu Lao; mains from 30,000d) It may be the daddy of noodle-soup chains, but this is no McPho. Enjoy a steaming bowl accompanied by a veritable forest of herbs.

Huong Lai (Map p906; ☎ 3822 6814; 38 Đ Ly Tu Trong; mains 40,000-120,000d; lunch & dinner) A must for beautifully presented traditional Vietnamese food, this is dining with a difference. All staff here are from disadvantaged families or are former street children.

Also recommended:

Pho 2000 (Map p904; ☎ 3822 2788; 1-3 Đ Phan Chu Trinh; pho 30,000d; 6am-2am) Near Ben Thanh Market, Pho 2000 is where former US president Bill Clinton stopped by for a bowl.

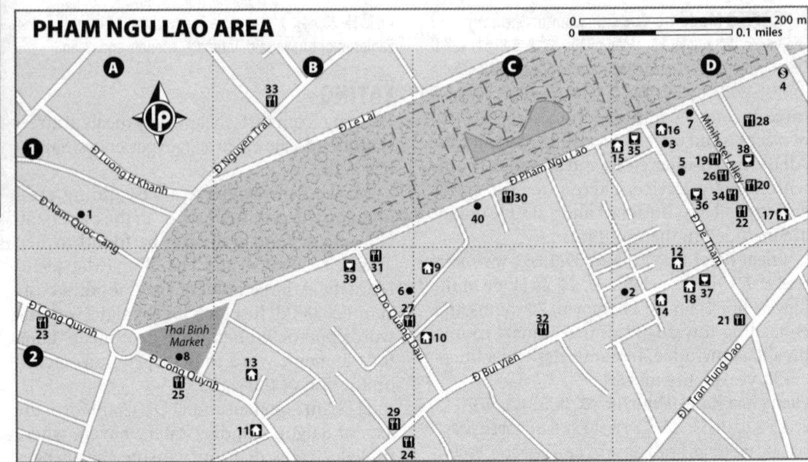

Pho Quynh (Map p910; 323 Đ Pham Ngu Lao; pho from 25,000d) Most of the diners are Vietnamese, which is a good sign. Specialises in *pho bo kho,* a stew-type broth.

Other Asian

Asian Kitchen (Map p910; ☎ 3836 7397; 185/22 Đ Pham Ngu Lao; mains 15,000-60,000d;) A popular Pham Ngu Lao cheapie, the menu here includes some Chinese, Indian and Japanese, plus vegetarian options.

Tan Hai Van (Map p910; ☎ 3925 0824; 162 Đ Nguyen Trai; mains 25,000-75,000d; 24hr) The Chinese place to come if you have an attack of the midnight munchies – it never closes.

our pick **Mumtaz** (Map p910; ☎ 3837 1767; 226 Đ Bui Vien; mains 65,000d; lunch & dinner) It may be the new kid on the block, but everyone is raving about the curries. Try the succulent fish tikka dishes.

Coriander (Map p910; ☎ 3837 1311; 185 Đ Bui Vien; mains 35,000-70,000d; lunch & dinner) One of the smaller Thai restaurants in the city, but it punches above its weight with authentic Siamese delights. Great green curry.

International

Café Zoom (Map p910; 169A Đ De Tham; mains 30,000-70,000d) Paying homage to the classic Vespa, the menu includes great burgers, plus a mix of Italian and Vietnamese favourites.

Chi's Cafe (Map p910; ☎ 3920 4874; 40/27 Đ Pham Ngu Lao; mains 30,000-70,000d; breakfast, lunch & dinner) Chi's is one of the better budget cafes in the area, with big breakfasts, Western favourites and some local dishes.

Bread & Butter (Map p910; ☎ 3836 8452; 40/24 Đ Pham Ngu Lao; mains 40,000-70,000d) Tiny place on hotel alley that is popular with city residents. Pub grub including staples like fish and chips, pies and burgers.

Le Jardin (Map p906; ☎ 3825 8465; 31 Đ Thai Van Lung; mains from 65,000d; lunch & dinner Mon-Sat) Consistently popular with French expats, it has a wholesome bistro-style menu and an outdoor garden.

Saigon has choice:

Falafellim (Map p904; ☎ 3915 1733; 97 Đ Pham Ngu Lao; falafels around 40,000; 10am-10pm) Friends of the falafel should make their way here, a hole-in-the-wall fast-food-style place with bargain bites.

K Cafe (Map p910; ☎ 3913 4673; 28 Đ Do Quang Dau; mains 40,000-195,000d; lunch & dinner) An affordable French bistro that turns out some stylish meats and fish, plus affordable snacks.

Margherita (Map p910; ☎ 3837 0760; 175/1 Đ Pham Ngu Lao; mains 20,000-80,000d) A golden oldie, this place turns out Vietnamese, Italian and Mexican food at a steal.

Vegetarian

Remember that on the 1st and 15th of every month many food stalls go vegie for the day.

Dinh Y (Map p910; ☎ 3836 7715; 171B Đ Cong Quynh; mains from 15,000d) Run by a welcoming Cao Dai family, the food is delicious and cheap, plus there's an English menu.

Tin Nghia (Map p904; ☎ 3821 2538; 9 ĐL Tran Hung Dao; mains from 15,000d; 7am-8.30pm) Opposite Ben Thanh Market, the setting is simple, but the Buddhist owners turn out some traditional treats.

INFORMATION	Madame Cuc's **12** D2	K Cafe **27** B2
Delta Adventure Tours .... (see 35)	Madame Cuc's **13** B2	Margherita **28** D1
Handspan Adventure Travel **1** A1	Kim's **14** D2	Mumtaz **29** B2
Innoviet **2** D2	Mai Phai Hotel **15** D1	Pho 24 .... **30** C1
Kim Travel **3** D1	Orient Hotel **16** D1	Pho Quynh **31** B2
Sacombank **4** D1	Sao Nam Hotel .... (see 28)	Sozo **32** C2
Sinh Cafe **5** D1	Vuong Hoa Hotel **17** D1	Tan Hai Van **33** B1
Sinhbalo Adventures **6** B2	Yellow House **18** D2	Zen **34** D1
	EATING	**DRINKING**
SIGHTS & ACTIVITIES	Asian Kitchen **19** D1	Allez Boo Bar **35** D1
Bi Saigon **7** D1	Bobby Brewers .... (see 18)	Eden **36** D1
Vietnamese Traditional Massage Institute **8** A2	Bread & Butter **20** D1	Go2 .... **37** D2
	Café Zoom **21** D2	Le Pub **38** D1
	Chi's Café **22** D1	Long Phi **39** B2
SLEEPING	Co-op Mart **23** A2	
Bich Duyen Hotel **9** C2	Coriander **24** B2	**TRANSPORT**
Ha Vy Hotel **10** C2	Dinh Y **25** A2	Saigon Railways Tourist Services **40** C1
Madame Cuc's **11** B2	Hong Hoa Mini-Market **26** D1	

Zen (Map p910; ☎ 3837 3713; 185/30 Đ Pham Ngu Lao; mains 20,000-45,000d) Braised mushrooms in claypot, fried tofu with chilli and lemongrass, the menu is packed with goodness at this backpacker favourite.

Cafes

Saigon specialises in cafes, especially around Notre Dame Cathedral.

Serenata (Map p904; ☎ 3930 7436; 6D Đ Ngo Thoi Thien; 7.30am-10pm Mon-Sat) This grand house is the perfect setting for a coffee. The garden is scattered with tables around a pond-filled courtyard.

Our pick **Sozo** (Map p910; ☎ 098 972 2468; 176 Đ Bui Vien; 7.30am-10pm Mon-Sat) A classy little place that features cultured coffee, doughy cinnamon rolls, home-made cookies and various other sweet treats. But best of all, the cafe trains and employs disadvantaged Vietnamese.

Fanny (Map p906; ☎ 3821 1633; 29-31 Đ Ton That Thiep) Set in a lavish French villa, Fanny creates excellent Franco-Vietnamese ice cream in a healthy range of tropical-fruit flavours, including durian and lychee.

Bobby Brewers (Map p910; ☎ 3610 2220; 45 Đ Bui Vien) Contemporary cafe set over three floors, the range of coffees here is professional. Plus movies upstairs.

Other cafes:

Casbah (Map p906; ☎ 090 555 9468; 57 Đ Nguyen Du) Hidden away down an alley near Saigon's main post office, Casbah offers an attractive setting for a coffee or a cocktail.

X Café (Map p906; ☎ 3914 2142; 53 Đ Pasteur) This old colonial-era villa is cool and minimalist downstairs, and relaxed and welcoming upstairs, with regular movies. Great ice-cream.

Self-Catering

Simple, dirt-cheap meals can be cobbled together from street stalls and markets with fresh fruits and vegetables, baguettes baked daily and soft French cheese.

Co-op Mart (Map p910; Đ Cong Quynh; 8am-8pm) A good supermarket west of the traffic circle near Thai Binh Market.

Hong Hoa Mini-Market (Map p910; Đ Pham Ngu Lao; 9am-8pm) Small but packed with toiletries, alcohol and Western snacks.

DRINKING

Saigon's nightlife sometimes grinds to a halt – when officials are in a tizzy about 'social evils' everything closes by midnight. Often enough, though, many of the places below stay open until people stop drinking, which is next to never here.

Pham Ngu Lao Area

Le Pub (Map p910; ☎ 3837 7679; www.lepub.org; 175/22 Đ Pham Ngu Lao) Brit-style pub meets French cafe-bar, and the result is very popular with expats and travellers alike. There are US$1 promotions daily.

Allez Boo Bar (Map p910; ☎ 3837 2505; 187 Đ Pham Ngu Lao) A long-running backpacker bar, it has relocated across the road and gone ever-so-slightly upmarket, but not much. Late, late, late.

Go2 (Map p910; ☎ 3836 9575; 187 Đ De Tham) For all-night action, go to this little club that attracts a fun crowd of drunks and dancers thanks to the party atmosphere upstairs.

Eden (Map p910; ☎ 3836 8154; 185/22 Đ De Tham) A popular place with red lanterns over the bar (no, not those sort of red lights), where the friendly staff are dressed in traditional *ao dai*. Happy hour is 6pm to 9pm.

TIM PAGE

Tim Page experienced a very different Vietnam from the one visitors see today. It was 'Nam, the war was in full flow and he was a war photographer risking all on the frontline. He was the Hunter S Thompson of photojournalists, larger than life and not averse to getting into scrapes, several nearly costing him his life, including taking shrapnel in the brain in 1969 in Vietnam.

We consider the Requiem Exhibition, on permanent show at the War Remnants Museum. 'I was gobsmacked to learn that Requiem is more visited than Reunification Palace,' he laughs. 'We are in discussions to secure a new exhibition space in the main hall, as it's a real shame it is located in an old barracks', he laments.

He reflects nostalgically on the old days: 'Most of the big attractions in Saigon are linked to history, to events from the '60s and '70s, the stuff of folklore and legend,' he states. 'Maybe it's time to turn this into an experience, like the blue plaques in London but for wartime Saigon, covering famous residents and famous events.' No doubt Tim Page himself would be worthy of a plaque or two.

We talk about the ghosts of the past and his old haunts in Saigon. 'Café Brodard is always mentioned, but now it's a Gloria Jean's. That's insulting really,' he says with a hint of mischief. With the Continental Shelf long gone and the Rex 'gone mad', Page finds his Saigon sitting on a plastic stool on the side of the road, the street cafes little changed in four decades. 'Underground is a good meeting place these days,' he offers, 'opposite the old Reuters office during the war. Downstairs was Minh the Tailor who invented the TV anchorman suit.'

We come back to Requiem and discuss the defining shots in the exhibition. 'Larry Burrows was an incredible photographer; his images are almost cinematic in their quality,' he suggests. Burrows was killed in a helicopter crash in 1971 and several of his pictures are in the exhibition. 'Henri Huet's image that looks through the legs of US soldiers at the distressed Vietnamese beyond is very powerful,' he adds, perhaps subconsciously recalling that Huet died in the same helicopter crash as Burrows.

The story of his old friend Sean Flynn resurfaces, the son of Errol Flynn who disappeared in Cambodia in 1970, presumed kidnapped and killed by the Khmer Rouge. 'A lot of people are interested in the story; there are a lot of scripts floating around out there,' he says, although the impression is that he doesn't approve of most of them. Perhaps for Page it is too personal, as the search for Sean Flynn was his 'quest for the holy grail'. He might be too old to play himself in a Hollywood flick about 1970, but don't rule out a film about Tim Page in the next few years, as he has lived more lives than most.

Tim Page is a renowned photojournalist and writer whose work has appeared in magazines, newspapers and exhibitions all over the world. He returned to Vietnam to put together the Requiem Photographic Exhibition at the War Remnants Museum, which chronicles the work of photojournalists on both sides of the conflict. Visit www.timpage.com.au for more on his work or pick up a copy of Page after Page, Derailed in Uncle Ho's Victory Garden *or* Nam.

Long Phi (Map p910; 325 Đ Pham Ngu Lao) One of the PNL originals, this French-run bar stays open late and sometimes hosts live bands. Happy hour is 5pm to 9pm with generous pours of Ricard.

Dong Khoi Area

These bars are generally a notch or two up in price from other parts of town.

Underground (Map p906; ☎ 3829 9079; 69 Đ Dong Khoi; ⏰ 10am-midnight) Going Underground? Expats commute here after work, drawn to the familiar tube sign that lights the way to the never-ending draft-beer happy hour.

Lush (Map p904; ☎ 091 863 0742; 2 Đ Ly Tu Trong) The look is very animé here, with cartoons plastering the walls. Heavy beats, regular DJs and some pool tables hidden out the back.

our pick **Acoustic Bar** (Map p904 ☎ 3930 2239; 6E1 Đ Ngo Thoi Nhiem) The place for live music. Acoustic Bar pays homage to Jimi Hendrix, John Lennon and other legends. Vietnam's leading musicians flock here for creative covers.

Other good spots:

Hoa Vien (Map p904; ☎ 3829 0585; 28 Đ Mac Dinh Chi) An unexpected find in the backstreets of HCMC, this Czech restaurant brews up fresh pilsner.

Sheridan's Irish House (Map p906; ☎ 3823 0793; 17/13 Đ Le Thanh Ton; 🕑 11am-late) This is a pretty authentic Irish pub for anyone yearning for the Emerald Isle.

ENTERTAINMENT

Water puppetry has migrated south thanks to the tourism boom. **Golden Dragon Water Puppet Theatre** (☎ 3930 2196; www.goldendragonwaterpuppet.com; 55B Nguyen Thi Minh Khai; admission 50,000d) has shows at 6.30pm and 8pm.

Theatre, music and films around the Dong Khoi area:

Diamond Plaza Cinema (Map p904; ☎ 3825 7751; Diamond Plaza, 34 Đ Le Duan) Three screens.

Idecaf (Institute of Cultural Exchange with France) (Map p906; ☎ 3829 5451; 31 Đ Thai Van Lung) Screens French-language films.

Opera House (Nha Hat Thanh Pho; Map p906; ☎ 3829 9976; Lam Son Sq) Plays and musical performances.

Nightclubs

Apocalypse Now (Map p906; ☎ 3824 1463; 2C Đ Thi Sach) Others have come and gone, but 'Apo' has been around since the early days. A sprawling place with a big dance floor and an outdoor courtyard, it's quite a circus, with travellers, expats, the beautiful people and not-so-beautiful people.

Cage (Map p906; 3A Đ Ton Duc Thang) The closest thing to an international club, Cage is set in an old warehouse near the Saigon Legend Hotel.

SHOPPING

Boutiques along Đ Le Thanh Ton and Đ Pasteur sell handmade ready-to-wear fashion cheaper than in Hanoi. In Pham Ngu Lao, shops sell fabrics woven by ethnic minorities, as well as handicrafts and T-shirts, while roving salesmen push 'designer' sunglasses and lighters made to look like they once belonged to soldiers. As elsewhere in Vietnam, stores selling communist propaganda are springing up all over. See www.dogmavietnam.com for an idea of what's out there.

Đ Dong Khoi (Map p906) is one big arts-and-crafts tourist shopping haven, but the large number of well-heeled shoppers means prices are high.

Ben Thanh Market (Cho Ben Thanh; Map p906) Stock up on necessities such as soap or find souvenirs at this market, an easy walk from the Pham Ngu Lao area. When night falls the market moves outside and even more food and T-shirt stands sprout up.

GETTING THERE & AWAY

Air

Tan Son Nhat Airport was one of the busiest in the world in the late 1960s. For more details on international air travel, see p839. For domestic flights, see p840.

Boat

Hydrofoils (adult/child 160,000/80,000, 75 minutes) depart for Vung Tau (p915) from the Bach Dang jetty (Map p906) on Đ Ton Duc Thang. Contact **Greenlines** (☎ 3821 5609) or **Petro Express** (☎ 3821 0650).

Bus

Intercity buses operate from several bus stations around HCMC. Local buses (3000d) travelling to the intercity bus stations leave from the local bus station situated opposite Ben Thanh Market (Map p906).

HCMC is one place where the open-tour buses really come into their own, as they depart and arrive in the Pham Ngu Lao area, which saves an extra local bus journey or taxi fare.

GETTING INTO TOWN

Tan Son Nhat airport (off Map pp902–3) is 7km northwest of the city centre. The going rate for taxis between central HCMC and the airport is around 80,000d to 100,000d. There are literally hundreds of taxi drivers waiting outside the airport so be prepared.

Most economical is the airport bus 152 (3000d). Buses leave the airport about every 15 minutes and make regular stops along Đ De Tham (Pham Ngu Lao area) and international hotels along Đ Dong Khoi. Buses are labelled in English, but you might also look for the words 'Xe Buyt San Bay'.

From the Saigon train station (Ga Sai Gon; Map pp902–3), a *xe om* (motorcycle taxi) to Pham Ngu Lao should cost around 15,000d to 30,000d.

From Saigon's intercity bus stations, most fares on a *xe om* should be between 20,000d and 40,000d, but a taxi is more comfortable with a pack. Public buses (3000d) from the stations stop opposite Ben Thanh Market.

GETTING TO CAMBODIA: MOC BAI TO BAVET

Crossing at the Moc Bai–Bavet border is easily done on buses going from Ho Chi Minh City (HCMC) to Phnom Penh (US$12, six hours); there are half a dozen or more companies, and tickets are sold at most traveller cafes and agencies in HCMC. One-month visas (US$20, although minor over-charging is common) are issued on arrival in Cambodia, but require one passport-sized photo. Border formalities can take a few hours around festivals, but bus companies usually fast-track passengers. Many travellers prefer to use one of the Mekong Delta border crossings near Chau Doc or Ha Tien, both covered on p921.

There are four useful bus stations located around the city:

An Suong bus station (off Map pp902-3) Buses to Tay Ninh, Cu Chi and points northeast of HCMC; in District 12, west of the centre.
Cholon bus station (Map pp902-3; Đ Le Quang Trung) Local buses around HCMC; the station is one block north of Binh Tay Market.
Mien Dong bus station (off Map pp902-3; ☎ 3829 4056) Buses heading north of HCMC; in Binh Thanh District, about 5km from downtown on Hwy 13.
Mien Tay bus station (off Map pp902-3; ☎ 3825 5955) Serves the Mekong Delta towns; located about 10km southwest of Saigon in An Lac.

Car & Motorcycle

Hotels and travellers cafes can arrange car rentals from about US$25 per day in town or around US$50 to Cu Chi and Tay Ninh. Pham Ngu Lao is the neighbourhood to look for motorbike rentals (US$7 to US$10 per day) if you fancy an upcountry jaunt.

Train

Saigon Railways Tourist Services (Map p910; ☎ 3836 7640; 275C Đ Pham Ngu Lao) is a convenient place to purchase tickets.
Saigon train station (Ga Sai Gon; Map pp902-3; ☎ 3823 0105; 1 Đ Nguyen Thong) is located in District 3.

GETTING AROUND

Bicycle

Bicycles (US$2) are available for hire from many budget hotels and cafes, especially around Pham Ngu Lao. To deal with HCMC's traffic, glide along the edge of the action and steer clear of big trucks and buses.

Cyclo

Cyclos are the most interesting way of getting around town, but avoid them at night and always agree on fares beforehand. In the eyes of the authorities they slow down traffic – probably true, but a good thing overall – and are being slowly phased out.

Motorcycle & Motorbike Taxi

Motorbikes are available for hire around Pham Ngu Lao for US$7 to US$10 per day. Be sure to have a practice before splashing the cash; you'll usually be asked to leave your passport as collateral. Make sure your health insurance is in order.

Xe om trips in the city centre start at around 10,000d and a trip between the sites in Dong Khoi and Pham Ngu Lao is usually around 15,000d. However, metered taxis aren't much more.

Taxi

Hail taxis on the street. If you don't find one straight away, ring up and one will be dispatched in less time than it takes to say 'Ho Chi Minh'. Note that faulty meters are much less common here than in Hanoi.

Try the following:

Mai Linh Taxi (☎ 3822 6666)
Saigon Taxi (☎ 3823 2323)
Vina Taxi (☎ 3811 1111)

AROUND HO CHI MINH CITY

CU CHI TUNNELS

The **tunnel network** (off Map pp902-3; ☎ 3794 8823; www.cuchitunnel.org.vn; admission 65,000d) at Cu Chi was the stuff of legend during the 1960s for its role in facilitating Viet Cong control of a large rural area 30km from Saigon. At its height, the tunnel system stretched from Saigon to the Cambodian border. In the district of Cu Chi alone, there were over 200km of tunnels. After ineffective ground operations targeting the tunnels claimed large numbers of casualties, the Americans turned their artillery and bombers on the area.

Parts of this remarkable tunnel network have been reconstructed and two sites are open to visitors; one near the village of Ben Dinh and the other at Ben Duoc. During guided tours of the tunnel complex, it's possible to actually descend into the tunnels themselves. Although some sections have been widened, others remain in their original condition. If you can fit into the narrow passageways, you'll gain an empathetic, if claustrophobic, awe for the people who spent months underground.

Day tours operated by traveller cafes charge around US$8 per person (transport only); most include a stop at the Cao Dai Great Temple in Tay Ninh. Private tours are available through hotels and travel agencies.

TAY NINH

☎ 066 / pop 45,000

Tay Ninh town, capital of Tay Ninh Province, serves as the headquarters of one of Vietnam's most interesting indigenous religions. The Cao Dai Great Temple was built between 1933 and 1955. Victor Hugo is among the Westerners especially revered by the Cao Dai; look for his likeness at the Great Temple.

Tay Ninh is 96km northwest of HCMC. The Cao Dai Holy See complex is 4km east of Tay Ninh. Day tours from Saigon, including Tay Ninh and the Cu Chi Tunnels, cost around US$8.

VUNG TAU

☎ 064 / pop 161,300

A popular escape from the city for expats and locals alike, Vung Tau has long been overlooked by travellers as they rush up the coast to Mui Ne or Nha Trang. Perhaps not for much longer thanks to the beautiful new coastal road connecting Vung Tau to Phan Thiet and Mui Ne via some idyllic and empty beaches. Vung Tau rocks at weekends when HCMC exiles descend in numbers, but it is blissfully quiet during the week. Known under the French as Cap St Jacques, Vung Tau sits on a peninsula jutting into the South China Sea.

Orientation & Information

Vung Tau's peninsula is punctuated by Small Mountain (Nui Nho) to the south and Big Mountain (Nui Lon) in the north. Back Beach (Bai Sau) stretches for kilometres, with a wide, sandy beach and a long strip of guest houses and hotels. There are new beach developments beyond here, including Chi Linh and Dong Hai beaches.

International SOS (☎ 385 8776; 1 Đ Le Ngoc Han; 24hr) International standards, international prices.
Main post office (8 Đ Hoang Dieu) Located at the ground level of the Petrovietnam Towers building.
OSC Vietnam Travel (☎ 385 2008; www.oscvietnamtravel.com.vn; 9 Đ Le Loi) Vung Tau's leading travel agency.
Vietcombank (☎ 385 2024; 27-29 Đ Tran Hung Dao) Exchanges cash and travellers cheques, and offers credit-card cash advances.

Sights & Activities

Welcome to Rio di Vietnam, where a **giant Jesus** (admission free, parking 2000d; 7.30-11.30am & 1.30-5pm) stands atop a small mountain. The Vietnamese claim this is the highest Jesus statue in the world at 32m, 6m taller than His illustrious Brazilian cousin. It is possible to ascend to the armpits for a view of Vung Tau.

The nearby 1910 **lighthouse** (admission 2000d; 7am-5pm) boasts a spectacular 360-degree view of Vung Tau. From the ferry dock on Đ Ha Long, take a sharp right on the alley north of the Hai Au Hotel, then roll on up the hill

Pagodas dot the length of Đ Ha Long, but prim **Hon Ba Pagoda** sits offshore on an islet accessible only at low tide.

Sleeping & Eating

There's a string of older midrange hotels on the western side of Small Mountain if you can't find a room on Back Beach.

Song Bien (☎ 352 3311; 131A Đ Thuy Van; d 150,000-300,000d;) One of a cluster of places in this area. The prices here are reasonable and it has a touch more decorative flair than others.

My Tho Guesthouse (☎ 355 1722; 45 Đ Tran Phu, Mulberry Beach; r 150,000-200,000d;) This place is very rough and ready, but has a good location right on the water's edge. Probably only worth it if you can score a seafront room.

Viet An (☎ 385 3735; 1 Đ Hoang Dieu; mains 30,000-100,000d) This shady garden restaurant is located on a peaceful side street and offers an enticing combination of Vietnamese fish and seafood or 100% halal Indian food.

Cay Bang (☎ 383 8522; 69 Đ Tran Phu; mains 30,000-200,000d; 11am-10pm) With a great location on the water, this is one of the most popular seafood restaurants in town and draws a huge crowd at the weekend for the shellfish.

Getting There & Away

From Mien Dong bus station in HCMC, buses leave for Vung Tau (40,000d, two hours, 128km) throughout the day until around 4.30pm.

It's much more memorable to catch a hydrofoil if you have the extra dollars. **Greenlines** (☎ HCMC 08-3821 5609, Vung Tau 351 0720) and **Petro Express** (☎ HCMC 08-3821 0650, Vung Tau 351 5151) both run regular services to HCMC (160,000/80,000d adult/child, 75 minutes). Book ahead at weekends. In Vung Tau the boat leaves from Cau Da pier, opposite the Hai Au Hotel.

Getting Around

Vung Tau is easily traversed on two wheels. Guest houses can arrange bicycle hire (per day US$2); motorbikes cost US$5 to US$10 per day. Or just make eye contact with that *cyclo* or motorbike driver on the corner.

A *xe om* from the **Vung Tau bus station** (192A Đ Nam Ky Khoi Nghia) to Mulberry Beach or Back Beach should cost around 20,000d.

LONG HAI

☎ 064

If Vung Tau is all a bit bling for you, then consider an escape to Long Hai, a somewhat less-commercialised seaside retreat nearby. Long Hai has a pretty white-sand beach and the area benefits from a microclimate that brings less rain than other parts of the south. This is why Bao Đai, the last emperor of Vietnam, built a holiday residence here (now the Anoasis Beach Resort). Long Hai is a peaceful place to visit during the week, but it loses its local character at the weekends when Vietnamese tourists pack the sands.

At Minh Dam, 5km from Long Hai, there are **caves** with historical connections to the Franco–Viet Minh and American Wars. Nearby there's a **mountaintop temple** with great panoramic views of the coastline.

Further north on the new coastal road lie several sublime stretches of sand, including laid back **Loc An**, dune-tastic **Ho Tram** and remote **Ho Coc**, with accommodation offerings for every budget. Rent a motorbike and cruise up the coast for a day.

Sleeping & Eating

Military Guesthouse 298 (Doan an Dieu Duong 298; ☎ 386 8316; Rte 19; r 180,000-250,000d; ❄) Where Rte 19 runs out of road, this spacious complex is run by the navy, helping to explain the prime beachfront location. Some buildings were being upgraded at the time of writing, so prices may rise. Cheaper rooms are fan only.

There's a rustic cluster of thatch-roof beachside restaurants called **Can Tin 1, 2, 3** and **4** (mains around 30,000-90,000d; 🕑 7am-7pm) near Military Guesthouse 298. These serve reliable Vietnamese cuisine, including fresh seafood dishes. Dine, relax in a deckchair and then take a dip.

Getting There & Around

Long Hai is 124km from HCMC and takes about two hours to reach by car. The 15km road between Vung Tau and Long Hai will cost about 50,000 by *xe om* or about 180,000d by meter taxi one-way.

MEKONG DELTA

The 'rice bowl' of Vietnam, the Mekong Delta is an idyllic landscape carpeted in a dizzying display of greens. It is a watery world where boats, houses and even markets float upon the endless rivers, canals and streams that flow like life-giving arteries through this region. The hardy but friendly inhabitants of this region have toiled to tame the nine dragons of Cuu Long, where the Mekong splits into many branches seeking a way to the sea, battling with nature and the seasons to produce one of the most bountiful rice harvests on earth.

After winding its way from its source in Tibet, the Mekong River meets the sea in southernmost Vietnam. This delta-plain is lush with rice paddies and fish farms. Once part of the Khmer kingdom, the Mekong Delta was the last part of modern-day Vietnam to be annexed and settled by the Vietnamese.

By far the easiest and cheapest way to see the delta is by taking a tour (one to three days) with a travel agency in HCMC (p905). Private tours are available, including driver and guide. It is also possible to travel independently. Although sometimes challenging and time-consuming, this option offers maximum flexibility.

MY THO

☎ 074 / pop 180,000

Gateway to the Mekong Delta for whirlwind visitors on a day trip to the region, the slow-paced capital of Tien Giang province is an important market town, but to visit floating markets, you'll need to continue on to Can Tho (p919).

In My Tho, river-boat tours can be booked at the main riverfront office of **Tien Giang Tourist** (Cong Ty Du Lich Tien Giang; ☎ 387 3184; www.tiengiangtourist.com;

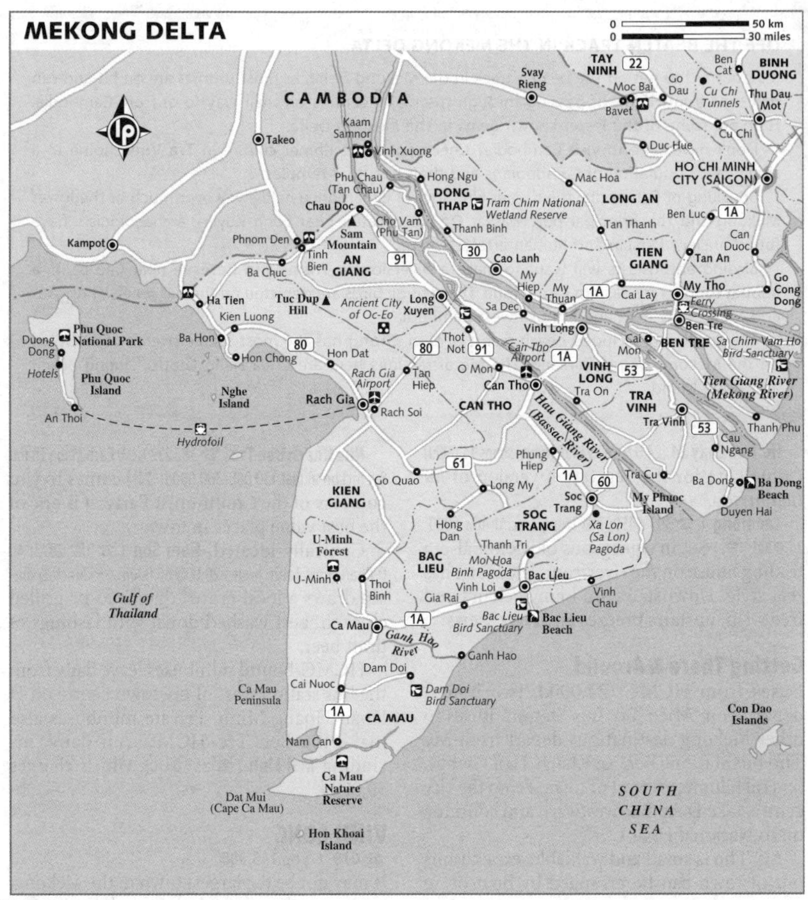

8 Đ 30 Thang 4; 7am-5pm). Boat tours cruise past picturesque rural villages and are the highlight of a visit to My Tho. Depending on what you book, destinations usually include a coconut-candy workshop, a honey-bee farm and an orchid garden. Getting a group together to hire a boat makes these tours economical; otherwise it's US$25 for two hours on the water.

Sleeping & Eating

Trade Union Hotel (Khach San Cong Doan; ☎ 387 4324; congdoantourist@hcm.vnn.vn; 61 Đ 30 Thang 4; r 100,000-220,000d;) This rambling place is good value if you aren't bothered by the creakiness of the rooms.

Rang Dong Hotel (☎ 387 4400; 25 Đ 30 Thang 4; r 130,000-150,000d;) Still popular with budget travellers, this family-run place has good-value rooms, including 3rd-floor offerings that face a terrace with river views.

Rang Dong II Hotel (☎ 397 0085; www.rangdonghotel.net; Đ Le Thi Hong Giam; r US$16-22;) Newer and offers a smarter touch, but is not so central.

Quan Oc 283 (☎ 397 0372; 283 Đ Tet Mau Than; mains 10,000-100,000d; lunch & dinner) Busting with locals, this is the place to come for a bargain seafood barbecue. Point at the platters out front, piled high with clams, scallops and mussels.

Hu Tieu 44 (44 Đ Nam Ky Khoi Nghia; soups 20,000d) Carnivores will enjoy My Tho's special vermicelli soup, *hu tieu mytho*, which is richly garnished with fresh and dried seafood, pork, chicken and fresh herbs.

OFF THE BEATEN TRACK IN THE MEKONG DELTA

It's not hard to get off the beaten track in the Mekong Delta, as most tourists are on hit-and-run day trips from HCMC or passing through the major centres on their way to or from Cambodia. Here are some of the lesser-known gems in the Mekong Delta.

Don't have time to visit Cambodia? Check out some Khmer culture in **Tra Vinh**, home to a significant population of Cambodians and their beautiful temples.

Speaking of Cambodia, the Khmer kingdom of Funan once held sway over much of the lower Mekong and the principal port was at **Oc Eo**. Located near Long Xuyen, archaeologists have found ancient Persian and Roman artefacts here.

Birding enthusiasts will want to make a diversion to **Tram Chin Reserve** near Cao Lanh, a habitat for the rare eastern sarus crane. These huge birds are depicted on the bas reliefs at Angkor and found only here and in northwest Cambodia.

The small and secluded beach resort of **Hon Chong** has the most scenic stretch of coastline on the Mekong Delta mainland. The big attractions here are Chua Hang Grotto, Duong Beach and Nghe Island.

Hu Tieu Chay 24 (24 Đ Nam Ky Khoi Nghia; soups 15,000d) Come here for the vegetarian version of *hu tieu mytho*.

Lac Hong (☎ 397 6459; 3 Đ Trung Trac; drinks 5000-25,000d; wi-fi) Set in a gorgeous old colonial-era trading house on the riverfront, Lac Hong has real style. Downstairs are lounge chairs and free wi-fi, upstairs breezes and river views.

Getting There & Around

Buses from HCMC (24,000d, two hours) depart from Mien Tay Bus Station. Buses to other Mekong destinations depart from My Tho bus station (Ben Xe Khach Tien Giang), several kilometres west of town. From the city centre, take Đ Ap Bac westward and continue on to National Hwy 1.

My Tho is small and walkable; expeditions out of town can be arranged by boat or *xe om*.

BEN TRE

☎ 075 / pop 130,000

Famous for its *keo dua* (coconut candy), Ben Tre is now plugged into the 'mainland' of My Tho thanks to a brand-spanking-new bridge. Located off the main trail, it receives far fewer visitors than My Tho and makes a rewarding stop on a Mekong tour.

There is internet access at the **main post office** (3/1 Đ Dong Khoi; per hr 4000d). Get cash at **Vietinbank** (☎ 382 2507; 42 Đ Nguyen Dinh Chieu).

Phuong Hoang Hotel (☎ 382 1385; 28 Hai Ba Trung; r 50,000-180,000d; air-con) is slightly old and decrepit, but then there is nowhere else in town offering a room for just US$3 with fan. You pays your money, you makes your choice.

Nha Khach Ben Tre (☎ 382 2339; 5 Đ Cach Mang Thang 8; r incl breakfast 130,000-360,000d; air-con) comes to you courtesy of the Communist Party; it is one of the best value places in town.

Centrally located, **Nam Son** (☎ 382 2873; 40 Đ Phan Ngoc Tong; mains 20,000-60,000d; ⏰ lunch & dinner) draws a local crowd thanks to its grilled chicken, best washed down with lashings of draft beer.

HCMC-bound minibuses leave daily from the bus station west of the town centre on Đ Doan Hoang Minh. Private minibuses also make the Ben Tre–HCMC run daily, including **Mai Linh** (☎ 351 0510), which charges 39,000d.

VINH LONG

☎ 070 / pop 145,000

It may not be the largest town in the Mekong, but as a major transit hub it can be noisy and chaotic nonetheless. Escape the mayhem on the riverfront, where there are plenty of cafes and restaurants. Vinh Long is the gateway to island life and some worthwhile sites, including Cai Be floating market, abundant orchards and atmospheric homestays, which can be a highlight of a Mekong journey.

Cuu Long Tourist (☎ 382 3616; www.cuulongtourist.net; 1 Đ 1 Thang 5; ⏰ 7am-5pm) is one of the more capable state-run tour outfits. **Vietcombank** (☎ 382 3109; 143 Đ Le Thai To) can exchange cash and travellers cheques.

What makes a trip to Vinh Long worthwhile are the beautiful islands in the river. Charter a boat through Cuu Long Tourist for around US$10 per person or pay substantially less for a private operator (US$5 per hour).

The bustling **Cai Be floating market** (5am-5pm) is worth including on a boat tour from Vinh Long. Wholesalers on big boats moor here, each specialising in one or a few types of fruit or vegetable.

Don't stay in town, but opt for a homestay: see the boxed text, below for more.

Thien Tan (☎ 382 4001; 56/1 Đ Pham Thai Buong; mains 30,000-80,000d; lunch & dinner), specialising in barbecued dishes, is the best eatery in town. Recommended is the *ca loc nuong tre* (fish cooked in bamboo) and *ga nuong dat set* (chicken cooked in clay).

Frequent buses go between Vinh Long and HCMC (63,000d, three hours). You can also get to Vinh Long by bus from Can Tho (25,000d). Vinh Long's bus station is in the middle of town.

CAN THO

☎ 071 / pop 340,000

The epicentre of the Mekong Delta, Can Tho feels like a veritable metropolis after exploring the backwaters. As the political, economic, cultural and transportation centre of the Mekong Delta, Can Tho hums with activity. It is also the perfect base for nearby floating markets.

Information

Can Tho Tourist (☎ 382 1852; www.canthotourist.com.vn; 20 Đ Hai Ba Trung; 7am-5pm & 6-8pm) Helpful staff speak English and French. Tours available, plus a booking desk for Vietnam Airlines (☎ 382 4088).

Vietcombank (☎ 382 0445; 7 ĐL Hoa Binh) Has foreign-currency exchange and an ATM.

Sights

Cai Rang is the biggest floating market in the Mekong Delta, 6km from Can Tho towards Soc Trang. Although the lively market goes on until around noon daily, show up before 9am for the best photo opportunities. You can hire boats (about US$5 per hour) on the river near the Can Tho market. Cai Rang is one hour away by boat, or you can drive to Cau Dau Sau boat landing, where you can get a rowing boat (per hour around 50,000d) to the market, 10 minutes away.

Less crowded and less motorised is the **Phong Dien market**, with more stand-up rowboats. It's best between 6am and 8am. Twenty kilometres southwest of Can Tho, it's easy to reach by road and you can hire a boat on arrival.

The **Muniransyaram Pagoda** (36 ĐL Hoa Binh) is the one must-see in the city for its impressive Khmer-style architecture.

Activities

Can Tho Water Park (☎ 376 3343; Cai Khe Ward; water park/pool only 40,000/25,000d; 9am-6pm) has water slides and a wave pool where you can cool off. Alternatively, blind massage therapists can help to ease those weary limbs at **Van Tho 2** (☎ 375 2709, 1B Ngo Duc Ke, 25,000-45,000d per hr).

Sleeping & Eating

Hien Guesthouse (☎ 381 2718; hien_gh@yahoo.com; 118/10 Đ Phan Dinh Phung; r US$5-10;) Still a hit with budget travellers, this friendly, family-run place has a local-yokel location down a narrow alley.

A NIGHT ON THE MEKONG

One of the highlights of any Vietnam trip is a homestay with one of the friendly Mekong families. The following places all charge around US$15 per night, which includes dinner, a night's sleep and breakfast the next morning. Vinh Long is the easiest place to arrange a homestay.

Mai Quoc Nam (☎ 070 385 9912; Phuan 1 hamlet, Binh Hoa Phuoc village, Long Ho District) A short hop from Vinh Long, Mai Quoc Nam has attractive wooden bungalows hidden away in the garden. The owners can arrange boat trips around the canals.

Sau Giao (☎ 070 385 9019; Binh Thuan 2 hamlet, Hoa Ninh village, Long Ho district) With the passing of Mr Sau Giao, the traditional wooden house with a pretty bonsai garden is only serving lunch. However, his daughter has kept the homestay tradition alive in a nearby property.

Song Tien (☎ 070 385 8487; An Thanh hamlet, An Binh village, Long Ho District) Across the Co Chien River from Vinh Long, this friendly place offers beds in small bungalows with stop-and-drop toilets. The landscaping here is lush with citrus trees.

Tam Ho (☎ 070 385 9859; info@caygiong.com; Binh Thuan 1 hamlet, Hoa Ninh village, Long Ho district) About 1.5km from Vinh Long, Tam Ho is a working orchard run by a friendly, welcoming family. One of the hosts bears a striking resemblance to Ho Chi Minh.

Huy Hoang Hotel (☎ 382 5833; 35 Đ Ngo Duc Ke; r with fan 100,000-190,000, with air-con 140,000-230,000d; ❄) Friendly and near enough to the riverfront action, this place has good-value rooms with TV and hot shower.

Xuan Mai Mini Hotel (☎ 382 3578; 17 Đ Dien Bien Phu; r US$8-12; ❄) This place has a real local feel, as it is located down a small lane that doubles as An Lac Market by day. It is popular with budget tour groups thanks to spacious, clean rooms.

Tay Ho Hotel (☎ 382 3392; kstayho-ct@hcm.vnn.vn; 31 Đ Hai Ba Trung; r 200,000-280,000d; ❄) Right in the heart of the action, and opposite the 'tin man' statue of Uncle Ho, this budget place has high ceilings and riverfront rooms complete with shuttered doors that open onto the balcony.

Restaurant Alley (Đ Nam Ky Khoi Nghia; mains 15,000-40,000d) If you want to dodge the tourist scene on the riverfront, try this small alley of local joints between Đ Dien Bien Phu and Đ Phan Dinh Phung. Barbecued meats, seafood hotpots and simple vegetables – it's all here.

Cappuccino (☎ 346 1981; 13 Đ Ngo Duc Ke; mains 30,000-75,000d; 🕑 lunch & dinner) The menu here features some pastas, risottos and pizzas at absurdly affordable prices, plus a tempting tiramisu.

Nam Bo (☎ 382 3908; 50 Đ Hai Ba Trung; mains 30,000-90,000d; 🕑 lunch & dinner) Housed in an elegantly restored shophouse overlooking the fruit market, Nam Bo offers well-presented Vietnamese dishes as well as some affordable international offerings. Or just sit on the terrace and enjoy a glass of wine.

You'll find several other popular eateries along the riverfront strip, across from the huge silver Uncle Ho statue, including **Mekong** (☎ 382 1646; 38 Đ Hai Ba Trung; mains 20,000-60,000d; 🕑 8am-2pm & 4-10pm), which is one of the main traveller hang-outs, with a good blend of local and international food at very reasonable prices.

Getting There & Around

Buses and minibuses to Can Tho from Ho Chi Minh City leave the Mien Tay station (from 60,000d, five hours). **Can Tho bus station** (Đ Nguyen Trai & Đ Tran Phu) is about 1km north of town.

Xe loi (motorbikes with two-seater carriages on the back) cost 10,000d or so for rides around town. Most guest houses also hire out bicycles.

CHAU DOC

☎ 076 / pop 100,000

Perched on the banks of the Bassac River, Chau Doc is a charming town near the Cambodian border with sizeable Chinese, Cham and Khmer communities. Thanks to the popular river crossing between Vietnam and Cambodia (see the boxed text, opposite), many travellers now pass through Chau Doc. Nearby Sam Mountain is a holy site with terrific views over Cambodia.

War remnants near Chau Doc include Ba Chuc, the site of a Khmer Rouge massacre with a bone pagoda similar to that of Cambodia's Choeung Ek memorial; and Tuc Dup Hill, where an expensive American bombing campaign in 1963 earned it the nickname Two Million Dollar Hill. It's also possible to visit fish farms set up underneath floating houses on the river.

There's **internet access** (per hr 4000d; 🕑 7am-9pm) in the courtyard of Chau Doc's **main post office** (☎ 869 200; 2 Đ Le Loi). Foreign currency can be exchanged at **Vietinbank** (☎ 386 6497; 68-70 Đ Nguyen Huu Canh). **Delta Adventure** (☎ 356 3810; www.deltaadventuretours.com; 53 Đ Le Loi) and **Mekong Tours** (☎ 386 8222; www.mekongvietnam.com; 14 Đ Nguyen Huu Canh) are reliable travel agents.

Sleeping & Eating

Thuan Loi Hotel (☎ 386 6134; hotelthuanloi@hcm.vnn.vn; 18 Đ Tran Hung Dao; r US$7-10; ❄) The only cheap hotel with a riverside location, it uses it to good effect with a floating restaurant. The rooms are good value, but fairly simple.

Trung Nguyen Hotel (☎ 386 6158; trunghotel@yahoo.com; 86 Đ Bach Dang; r US$12-17; ❄ 💻 📶) Following a facelift, this is the best of the budget places, with a trim and panache that is decidedly more midrange. Added benefits include free wi-fi or internet, plus breakfast.

Good local eateries include **Bay Bong** (☎ 386 7271; 22 Đ Thuong Dang Le; mains from 35,000d) with excellent hotpots and soups, and **Mekong** (☎ 386 7381; 41 Đ Le Loi; mains 30,000-80,000d), set in the grounds of an old villa opposite the posh Victoria Hotel.

Getting There & Around

Buses to Chau Doc depart HCMC's Mien Tay station (95,000d, six hours). For more on the border crossing to Cambodia, see the boxed text, opposite.

Cargo boats run twice weekly between Chau Doc and Ha Tien on the coast via the

GETTING TO CAMBODIA: MEKONG DELTA BORDERS

Vinh Xuong to Kaam Samnor

One of the most enjoyable ways of entering Cambodia is via the Vinh Xuong–Kaam Samnor crossing, which is located just west of Chau Doc along the Mekong River. Numerous agencies in Chau Doc sell boat tickets taking you to Phnom Penh via the Vinh Xuong border. Slow boats for the trip cost around US$15 and take eight hours (leaving around 8am and arriving in Phnom Penh at 4pm).

There are several companies offering fast boats. **Hang Chau** (☎ 076-356 2771; Chau Doc) departs Chau Doc at 8.30am and Phnom Penh at noon, and costs US$15/24 for a slow/fast boat. The more upmarket **Blue Cruiser** (☎ 091-401622; Chau Doc) pulls out at 8.30am and at 1.30pm respectively, costing US$35. It takes about four hours including a slow border check. For information on crossing this border in the other direction, see p85.

Prek Chak to Xa Xia

The Prek Chak–Xa Xia crossing was long anticipated, and connects Ha Tien (and Phu Quoc with a hydrofoil ride from Ha Tien) with Kep and Kampot on Cambodia's south coast. There are currently no cross-border bus services here, but it is simple enough with a combination of local transport. Take a *xe om* from Ha Tien to the border (US$2) and then arrange a *moto* on to Kompong Trach (US$3), Kep (US$6) or Kampot (US$9). It may also possible to charter a taxi from the border to Kampot (US$30 or so), Kep (US$20 or so) or Kompong Trach (US$15). For information on crossing this border in the other direction, see p126. There is also the enticing possibility of fast-boat services between Phu Quoc and both Kep and Sihanoukville in Cambodia some time during the lifetime of this book.

Tinh Bien to Phnom Den

Also nearby is the little used Tinh Bien–Phnom Den crossing, which connects Chau Doc to Takeo Province in Cambodia. Arrange a *xe om* from Chau Doc for about 60,000d or so to the border and then a share taxi (US$3 per seat, US$25 charter) on to Takeo. For information on crossing this border in the other direction, see p85.

Vinh Te Canal (200,000d, eight to 12 hours), which straddles the Cambodian border. Departures are at 5am from a tiny pier (near 60 Đ Trung Hung Dao). There are plans to launch a fast-boat service during the lifetime of this book.

HA TIEN

☎ 077 / pop 93,000

Ha Tien may be part of the Mekong Delta, but lying on the Gulf of Thailand it feels a world away from the rice fields and rivers that typify the region. There are dramatic limestone formations peppering the area, and the town itself has a sleepy charm. Visitor numbers have recently soared thanks to the opening of the border with Cambodia at Xa Xia–Prek Chak (above) and the new fast-boat service to Phu Quoc.

The **post office** (☎ 385 2190; 3 Đ To Chau; ⏰ 7am-10pm) has internet access. **Agribank** (☎ 385 2055; 37 Đ Lam Son) is one block from the waterfront and has an ATM.

Tu Anh Hotel (☎ 385 2622; 170 Đ Mac Thien Tich; r 150,000-250,000d; ❄) is a smart mini-hotel with a good deal, offering a window and air-con in every room. The well-tended rooms include a TV and fridge, plus hot water.

Located in the new part of town near the bridge, **Anh Van Hotel** (☎ 395 9222; www.anhvanhotel.com; Lo 2, Đ Tran Hau; r 150,000-400,000d; ❄ 💻) is one of the best all-rounders in Ha Tien.

It's happy days when shrimp is the cheapest dish on the menu. **Xuan Thanh** (☎ 385 2197; 20 Đ Tran Hau; mains 20,000-60,000d; ⏰ lunch & dinner) has an English menu boasting a range of Vietnamese favourites.

Passenger ferries dock at the ferry terminal, which is opposite the Ha Tien Hotel. There is now a fast-boat service from Ha Tien to Phu Quoc (190,000d one way, 1½ hours), which is operated by **Vinashin** (☎ 395 9060; 11 Đ Tran Hau in Ha Tien, ☎ in Phu Quoc 399 6456). It departs Ha Tien at 8am and returns from Phu Quoc at 2pm.

Buses connect HCMC (from 96,000d, 10 hours) and Ha Tien. Faster express services are operated by Mai Linh costing 132,000d. Ha Tien bus station (Ben Xe Ha Tien) is on the road to Mui Nai Beach and the Cambodian border.

RACH GIA

☎ 077 / pop 200,000

Rach Gia is perched on a river mouth opening onto the Gulf of Thailand, making it a jumping-off point for Phu Quoc Island. It's a prime smuggling hub, due to its proximity to Cambodia, Thailand and the great wide ocean. The centre of town sits on an islet embraced by the two arms of the Cai Lon River; the north side has your getaway options out of town.

Vietcombank (☎ 386 3178; 2 Đ Mac Cuu) has a 24-hour ATM. **Kien Giang Tourist** (Cong Ty Du Lich Kien Giang; ☎ 386 2081; 12 Đ Ly Tu Trong) is the provincial tourism authority.

Sleeping & Eating

Phuong Hong Hotel (☎ 386 6138; 5 Đ Tu Do; r 120,000-200,000d;) A friendly little spot that is conveniently close to the boat pier, the staff speak pretty good English here. Rooms are small but clean.

Kim Co Hotel (☎ 387 9610; 141 Đ Nguyen Hung Son; r 200,000-250,000d;) The most centrally located of the hotels, the rooms are in very good shape, some including decadent bath-tubs.

Than Binh (☎ 387 4780; 2 Đ Nguyen Thai Hoc; mains 15,000-35,000d) The throngs of locals eating at Than Binh attest to the quality of the food, where there are loads of ready-made dishes on display.

Getting There & Away

Vietnam Airlines flies daily between HCMC (536,000d) and Rach Gia, continuing on to Phu Quoc Island (459,000d). The airport is about 10km outside town; taxis cost about 150,000d.

For details on getting to Phu Quoc by hydrofoil, see opposite. Stop by the **Rach Gia hydrofoil terminal** (☎ 3387 9765) the day before, or phone ahead to book a seat.

Buses from HCMC (from 90,000d, six to seven hours) depart for Rach Gia from the Mien Tay bus station. Night buses leave Rach Gia between 7pm and 11pm. The **main bus station** (Ben Xe Rach Soi; 78 Đ Nguyen Trung Truc) is located in Rach Soi, which is 7km south of Rach Gia.

PHU QUOC ISLAND

☎ 077 / pop 90,000

Phu Quoc is the place to take a vacation from your travels. Deserted white-sand beaches wrap around the island and just offshore the untouched reefs will have divers and snorkellers thinking that they have the ocean to themselves. Renting a motorbike and exploring long stretches of empty dirt road through the untouched forest is another way to lose yet one more day to the beauty of this place. However, mass tourism is just gearing up here, with big plans for megaresorts, golf courses and a new international airport on the horizon. Get here before they pave paradise.

Addresses outside of Duong Dong's centre are designated by the kilometre mark south of town. Bring a torch (flash light) to navigate the road and beach at night.

Because almost everything is shipped from the mainland and the island supports very little agriculture, this is one of the pricier destinations in Vietnam but deals can be found; sun bathing is free.

Orientation

The tear-shaped island lies in the Gulf of Thailand, 15km south of the coast of Cambodia. Phu Quoc is Vietnam's largest island but is also claimed by Cambodia; its Khmer name is Koh Tral.

The main shipping port is An Thoi at the southern tip of Phu Quoc Island, but hydrofoils to the mainland now dock at Bai Vong on the east of the island. Most beachside accommodation options are at Long Beach, located on the western side of the island just south of Duong Dong town.

Information

The post office in downtown Duong Dong has internet, plus many hotels and resorts now provide free internet to their guests, either the wired or wireless variety. **Buddy Ice Cream** (☎ 399 4181; 26 Đ Nguyen Trai;) offers free internet and wi-fi to customers. There are plenty of ATMs located in resorts on Long Beach.

Sights & Activities

Deserted white-sand beaches ring the island. Bai Sao and Bai Dam are beautiful beaches on the south end of the island. Long Beach (Bai Truong) is a spectacular stretch of sand from Duong Dong southward along the west coast, almost to An Thoi.

About 90% of Phu Quoc Island is protected forest. The mountainous northern half of the island, where the trees are most dense, has been declared a **national park** (Khu Rung Nguyen Sinh). You'll need a motorbike to get into the reserve and there are no real trekking trails.

The **An Thoi Islands** – 15 islands and islets at the southern tip of Phu Quoc – can be visited by chartered boat and it's a fine area for swimming, snorkelling and fishing.

Diving and snorkelling in Phu Quoc are just taking off, with few crowds and a more pristine marine environment than along the coast. Stop by **Rainbow Divers** (☎ 0913-400 964; www.divevietnam.com; Đ Tran Hung Dao; 🕑 9am-6pm) who offer two dives from US$60.

There are several places to rent **kayaks** (60,000d) along Bai Sao beach, and its protected waters make for a smooth ride.

Sleeping

Accommodation prices on Phu Quoc yo-yo up and down depending on the season and the number of visitors in town, much more than anywhere else in Vietnam.

Thai Tan Tien Guesthouse (☎ 384 7782; r US$10-25) Overlooking a small pond near the beach, this small place is very good value. The fan-cooled bungalows all include a bathroom and fridge.

Luna Resort (☎ 094 968 0801; www.luna-resort.de; bungalows US$10-20) A new budget resort with some beachfront access, these rustic bungalows are good value. The beach bar has quickly earned a name for itself as a lively hang-out.

Lien Hiep Thanh Hotel (☎ 384 7583; r US$10-50; ❄) Also known somewhat more easily as the Family Hotel, this pretty complex includes 21 bungalows and rooms. Rates for beachfront rooms rocket in high season.

Beach Club (☎ 398 0998; www.beachclubvietnam.com; r US$15-28) This chilled retreat has spacious yet simple beachfront bungalows, plus there is a breezy beachside restaurant for stunning sunsets.

our pick **Lam Ha Eco Resort** (☎ 384 7369; r/bungalow US$17-22; ❄) Rooms and bungalows are invitingly set in a lush garden and US$22 buys a mini-suite, complete with kitchen. Nice.

Eating & Drinking

Most guest houses have their own lively cafes or restaurants in-house; wander along Long Beach until you find somewhere appealing.

The night market is one of the most atmospheric (and affordable) places to dine in Duong Dong. Strung out along Đ Vo Thi Sau, there are a dozen or more stalls serving a delicious range of Vietnamese seafood, grills and vegetarian options.

Buddy Ice Cream (☎ 399 4181; 26 Đ Nguyen Trai; 20,000-140,000d) This ice cream shop/information centre is a good stop for budget travellers looking for free internet or impartial advice.

our pick **Le Bistrot** (☎ 398 2200; 118/2 Đ Tran Hung Dao; meals 28,000-120,000d; 🕑 7am-late) This garden restaurant offers French home cooking at a distinctly Vietnamese price, making it a great place. Doubles as a lively bar with pool table.

Ai Xiem (☎ 399 0510; Bai Sao; mains 40,000-100,000d; 🕑 lunch & dinner) Gorgeously located on the inviting white sands of Bai Sao beach, Ai Xiem has succulent barbecued seafood and great fish in claypot.

Pepper's Pizza & Grill (☎ 384 8773; 89 Đ Tran Hung Dao; 40,000-150,000d 🕑 lunch & dinner) Pepper's is home to the best pizzas on the island, according to long-term residents. Other items include steaks, ribs and the like.

Eden (☎ 399 4208) This beach bar has a fine location with tables on the sand and a covered interior with pool tables.

Getting There & Around

Vietnam Airlines (☎ 398 2320; 122 Đ Nguyen Trung Truc) has several daily flights to Phu Quoc from HCMC (820,000d), plus a daily connection to Rach Gia (459,000d). Book ahead in high season.

Numerous companies operate speedy hydrofoils sailing between Rach Gia and Phu Quoc. Boats leave in both directions daily between 7am and 8.30am, and again between 12.30pm and 1.30pm. Ticket prices for the 2½-hour journey are 250,000/170,000d for adults/children. Hydrofoil companies include **Super Dong** (☎ Rach Gia 077-387 8475, Phu Quoc 077-398 0111), **Duong Dong Express** (☎ Rach Gia 077-387 9765, Phu Quoc 077-399 0747) and **Hai Au** (☎ Rach Gia 077-387 9455, Phu Quoc 077-399 0555). For details on the popular fast boat service to Ha Tien, see p921.

From Duong Dong to Bai Vong harbour costs about 20,000/50,000/150,000d by bus/*xe om*/meter taxi. The island's middle road from An Thoi to Duong Dong is paved, but dirt is the shade of the island's other roads. Motorbike rentals are available through guest houses and hotels from US$7 to US$10 per day. **Mai Linh** (☎ 397 9797) has metered taxis.

VIETNAM DIRECTORY

ACCOMMODATION

Accommodation is at a premium during Tet (late January or early February), when the country is on the move and overseas Vietnamese flood back into the country. Prices at this time can rise by 25%. Christmas and New Year is another busy time, but it's less crazy than Tet.

Family-run guest houses usually offer the cheapest rooms, ranging from around US$6 to US$20 per person with private bathroom. Some places offer dorm beds for US$3 to US$6 per person, with shared bathroom. Guesthouse accommodation is generally plentiful, and discounts are negotiable if you plan to stay for a few days or are travelling alone.

A step up from the guest houses, minihotels typically come with more amenities: satellite TV, minifridges and IDD phones. Rates sometimes include breakfast and, as with smaller guest houses, some discounts can be negotiated. Although minihotel rates can be as high as US$20 to US$30, it's still fairly easy to find rooms for around US$15. Rates often decrease with the number of steps to be climbed. Many places now offer free internet for guests in the lobby or wi-fi in the rooms.

Unless otherwise noted, prices in this chapter include private bathrooms.

Homestays

Homestays are a popular option in parts of Vietnam. Homestays were pioneered in the Mekong Delta, but there are also homestays on the island of Cat Ba. Many people like to stay with ethnic minority families in the far north of Vietnam. Sapa (p868) is the number-one destination, but Mai Chau (p867) is another popular place.

ACTIVITIES

Vietnam's roads and rivers, sea and mountains provide ample opportunity for active adventures. Travel agencies and traveller cafes all over the country can arrange local trips, from kayaking on Halong Bay to trekking up Fansipan to kitesurfing in Mui Ne.

Cycling

The flatlands and back roads of the Mekong Delta are wonderful to cycle through and observe the vibrant rural lifestyle. Another spot well away from the insane traffic of National Hwy 1 is the Ho Chi Minh Highway, winding through the central highlands. Arrange mountain-biking tours in the northern mountains at **Handspan Adventure Travel** (Map p850; ☎ 04-3926 0581; www.handspan.com; 80 P Ma May, Hanoi); or stop by **Sinhbalo Adventures** (Map p910; ☎ 08-3837 6766; www.sinhbalo.com; 283/20 Đ Pham Ngu Lao, HCMC) in HCMC if you wish to meander the Mekong Delta or beyond.

Diving & Snorkelling

Vietnam has several great dive destinations. Long established, with many dive sites, is the beachside town of Nha Trang. A notable emerging dive destination is Phu Quoc Island, with fewer visitors and a more pristine environment, and even Hoi An has got in on the underwater action.

Kayaking

For an even closer look at those limestone crags, it's possible to paddle yourself around Halong Bay. Inquire at travel agencies in Hanoi (p846) for more details.

Trekking

The most popular region for trekking in Vietnam is the northwest – most notably around Sapa, which includes Vietnam's tallest mountain, Fansipan. There's also decent trekking through the jungle of Cuc Phuong National Park, and the trekking trails in Bach Ma National Park are also very rewarding. The trek up Lang Bian Mountain (p896) near Dalat also gets good reviews.

Water Sports

Mui Ne (p892) is Vietnam's best shoreline for kitesurfing and windsurfing fiends. Nha Trang (p886) is another good locale for windsurfing, sailing or wakeboarding. The area around China Beach (p880), south of Danang, also gets some serious surf between September and December.

BOOKS

Lonely Planet's *Vietnam* guide provides you with the full scoop on the country. The *Vietnamese Phrasebook* is also practical and will no doubt help you to pass the time on those long bus rides.

For insight into the country's history and juicy stories about political leaders, Robert Templer's *Shadows and Wind* (1999) is a compelling read. *Catfish & Mandala* (1999), by Andrew X Pham, is the author's bicycle journey that wheels from HCMC (Saigon) to Hanoi and far beyond. It's exquisitely intimate but broadly illuminating.

For a human perspective on the North Vietnamese experience during the war, *The Sorrow of War* (1996) is Bao Ninh's poignant tale of love and loss, proving that the boys from the North had the same fears and desires as most American GIs.

Graham Greene's classic novel *The Quiet American* (1955) is the perfect introduction to Vietnam in the 1950s, as the French disengaged and the Americans moved in to take their place.

BUSINESS HOURS

Many small, privately owned shops, restaurants and street stalls stay open seven days a week, often until late at night. Restaurants tend to open very early and serve food all day long.

We only specify business hours in this chapter if they differ from the hours given below; keep in mind the hours given below may vary an hour or so each way.

Banks generally open from 8am to 11am and 2pm to 4pm Monday to Friday, and 8am to 11.30am Saturday.

Government offices open 7.30am to 4.30pm Monday to Friday (with a long lunch from noon), 7.30am to noon Saturday.

Offices and public buildings open 8am to 11am and 2pm to 4pm. Post offices open 6.30am to 9pm

Museums are usually open from 8am to 11am and 2pm to 4pm, but are closed Monday. Most temples are open all day, every day.

CLIMATE

Vietnam's south is tropical but the north can experience chilly winters – in Hanoi, an overcoat might be necessary in January.

The southwestern monsoon blows from April or May to October, bringing warm, damp weather to the whole country, except those areas sheltered by mountains, namely the central part of the coastal strip and the Red River Delta.

Typhoons can strike the central coast especially hard between August and November, and can cause flooding that closes roads for a time and delays flights. Also see the climate charts (p936).

CUSTOMS

Do know that Vietnamese customs may seize suspected antiques or other 'cultural treasures', which cannot legally be taken out of Vietnam. If you do purchase authentic or reproduction antiques, be sure to get a receipt and a customs clearance form from the seller.

DANGERS & ANNOYANCES

Since 1975, many thousands of Vietnamese have been maimed or killed by unexploded rockets, artillery shells, mortars, mines and other ordnance left over from the war. *Never* touch any war relics you come across – such objects can remain lethal for decades, and one bomb can ruin your whole day – or longer.

Violent crime is still relatively rare in Vietnam, but petty theft is definitely not. Drive-by bag snatchers on motorbikes are not uncommon, and thieves on buses, trains and boats stealthily rifle through bags or simply swipe them. Skilled pickpockets work the crowds.

One important suggestion, in particular for HCMC, is to not have anything dangling off your body that you are not ready to part with. This includes cameras and any jewellery. When riding a *xe om*, sling shoulder bags across the front of your body. On public buses, try to stow your bag where you're sitting; on trains, secure it to something if you have to leave it.

DRIVING LICENCE

International driving licences are not valid in Vietnam, so it is not possible to drive a car. When it comes to motorbikes, most foreigners drive without a licence.

SCAMS

Most of the scams in Vietnam are based in a particular town or area, from train-ticket cheats in Sapa to 'English students' in Hanoi. But they all involve either surprise costs or charging for one thing and delivering another. The best thing to do is to buy directly from the source (especially for transport and tours) and to make sure everything is negotiated upfront. The best approach is to stay firm, fair and friendly when doing business.

EMBASSIES & CONSULATES

Visas can be obtained in your home country through the Vietnamese embassy or consulate. See p930 for more information.

Australia (www.ausinvn.com) Hanoi (off Map pp844-5; ☎ 04-3831 7755; 8 Duong Dao Tan, Ba Dinh District); HCMC (Map p906; ☎ 08-3829 6035; 5th fl, 5B Đ Ton Duc Thang)

Cambodia Hanoi (Map pp844-5; ☎ 04-3825 3788; 71A P Tran Hung Dao); HCMC (Map p904; ☎ 08-3827 7696; 41 Đ Phung Khac Khoan)

Canada Hanoi (Map pp844-5; ☎ 04-3823 5500; 31 Đ Hung Vuong); HCMC (Map p906; ☎ 08-3827 9899; 10th fl, 235 Đ Dong Khoi)

China Hanoi (Map pp844-5; ☎ 04-3845 3736; P Hoang Dieu); HCMC (Map p904; ☎ 08-3829 2457; 39 Đ Nguyen Thi Minh Khai)

France Hanoi (Map pp844-5; ☎ 04-3943 7719; P Tran Hung Dao); HCMC (Map p904; ☎ 08-3829 7231; 27 Đ Nguyen Thi Minh Khai)

Germany Hanoi (Map pp844-5; ☎ 04-3845 3836; 29 Đ Tran Phu); HCMC (Map p904; ☎ 08-3822 4385; 126 Đ Nguyen Dinh Chieu)

Indonesia (Map pp844-5; ☎ 04-3825 3353; 50 P Ngo Quyen, Hanoi)

Japan Hanoi (off Map pp844-5; ☎ 04-3846 3000; 27 Pho Lieu Giai, Ba Dinh District); HCMC (Map p906; ☎ 08-3822 5314; 13-17 ĐL Nguyen Hue)

Laos Danang (Map p879; 16 Đ Tran Qui Cap); Hanoi (Map pp844-5; ☎ 04-3825 4576; 22 P Tran Binh Trong); HCMC (Map p906; ☎ 08-3829 7667; 93 Đ Pasteur)

Malaysia Hanoi (off Map pp844-5; ☎ 04-3831 3400; 16th fl, 6B P Lang Ha, Ba Dinh District); HCMC (Map p906; ☎ 08-3829 9023; Ste 1208, Me Linh Point Tower, 2 Đ Ngo Duc Ke)

Myanmar (Map pp844-5; ☎ 04-3845 3369; Bldg A3, Van Phuc Diplomatic Quarter, P Kim Ma, Ba Dinh District, Hanoi)

Netherlands (Map p904; ☎ 04-3823 5932; 29 ĐL Le Duan, HCMC)

New Zealand Hanoi (Map p850; ☎ 04-3824 1481; Level 5, 63 Pho Ly Thai To); HCMC (Map p906; ☎ 08-3822 6907; Ste 909, 235 Đ Dong Khoi)

Philippines (Map pp844-5; ☎ 04-3943 7873; 27B P Tran Hung Dao, Hanoi)

Singapore (Map pp844-5; ☎ 04-3823 3965; 41-43 Đ Tran Phu, Hanoi)

Thailand Hanoi (Map pp844-5; ☎ 04-3823 5092; 63-65 P Hoang Dieu); HCMC (Map p904; ☎ 08-3932 7637; 77 Đ Tran Quoc Thao)

UK (www.uk-vietnam.org) Hanoi (Map p850; ☎ 04-3936 0500; Central Bldg, 31 P Hai Ba Trung); HCMC (Map p904; ☎ 08-3829 8433; 25 ĐL Le Duan)

US (http://usembassy.state.gov/vietnam) Hanoi (off Map pp844-5; ☎ 04-3772 1500; 7 P Lang Ha, Ba Dinh District); HCMC ((Map p904; ☎ 08-3822 9433; 4 ĐL Le Duan)

EMERGENCIES

Ambulance (☎ 115)
Fire (☎ 114)
Police (☎ 113)

FESTIVALS & EVENTS

Vietnam's major festival is Tet – see opposite for details.

Ngay Mot & Ngay Ram Pagodas are packed with Buddhist worshippers on the 1st and 15th days of the lunar month, and tasty, cheap vegetarian meals are served nearby.

Tiet Doan Ngo (Summer Solstice) Human effigies are burnt to satisfy the need for souls to serve in the God of Death's army, on the 5th day of 5th lunar month.

Trung Nguyen (Wandering Souls Day) On the 15th day of the 7th lunar month, offerings are presented to the ghosts of the forgotten dead.

Mid-Autumn Festival On the night of 15 August, children walk the streets carrying glowing lanterns, and people exchange gifts of mooncakes.

FOOD & DRINK

Food

One of the true delights of visiting Vietnam is the cuisine; there are said to be nearly 500 traditional Vietnamese dishes. Generally, the food is fresh, superbly prepared and very cheap…and you never have to go very far to find it.

Pho is the Vietnamese name for the noodle soup that is eaten at all hours of the day, but especially for breakfast. *Com* are rice dishes. You'll see signs saying *pho* and *com* everywhere. Other noodle soups to try are *bun bo Hue* and *hu tieu*.

Spring rolls (known as *nem* in the north, *cha gio* in the south) are a speciality. These are normally dipped in *nuoc mam* (fish sauce), though many foreigners prefer soy sauce (*xi dau* in the north, *nuoc tuong* in the south).

Because Buddhist monks of the Mahayana tradition are strict vegetarians, *an chay* (vegetarian cooking) is an integral part of Vietnamese cuisine.

Street stalls or roaming vendors are everywhere, selling steamed sweet potatoes, rice porridge and ice-cream bars, even in the wee hours. There are many other Vietnamese nibbles to try:

Bap xao Fresh, stir-fried corn, chillies and tiny shrimp.

Bo bia Nearly microscopic shrimp, fresh lettuce and thin slices of Vietnamese sausage rolled up in rice paper and dipped in a spicy-sweet peanut sauce.

Hot vit lon For the brave. Steamed, fertilised duck egg in varying stages of development (all the way up to recognisable duckling), eaten with coarse salt and bitter herb.
Sinh to Shakes made with milk and sugar or yogurt, and fresh tropical fruit.

Vietnamese people don't usually end meals with dessert, which isn't to say they don't have a sweet tooth. Many sticky confections are made from sticky rice, such as *banh it nhan dau,* made with sugar and bean paste and sold wrapped in banana leaf.

Try *che,* a cold, refreshing sweet soup made with sweetened black bean, green bean or corn. It's served in a glass with ice and sweet coconut cream on top.

Aside from the usual delightful Southeast Asian fruits, Vietnam has its own unique *trai thanh long* (green dragon fruit), a bright pink-coloured fruit with green scales. Grown from a cactus along the coastal region near Nha Trang, it has white flesh flecked with edible black seeds, and tastes something like a mild kiwifruit.

Drink

Memorise the words *bia hoi,* which mean 'draught beer'. Similar to this is *bia tuoi,* or 'fresh beer'. Quality varies but it's generally OK and supercheap (from 3000d per litre). Places that serve *bia hoi* usually also have cheap food.

Several foreign labels brewed in Vietnam under licence include Tiger, Fosters, Carlsberg and Heineken. National and regional brands – cheaper, and typically lighter than light – include BGI, Halida, Huda, Saigon and Bia 333 *(ba ba ba).*

Whatever you drink, make sure that it's been boiled or bottled. Ice is generally safe on the tourist trail, but not guaranteed elsewhere.

Vietnamese *ca phe* (coffee) is fine stuff and there is no shortage of cafes in which to sample it. Try seeking out the fairy-lit garden cafes where young couples stake out dark corners for smooch sessions.

Foreign soft drinks are widely available. An excellent local treat is *soda chanh* (carbonated mineral water with lemon and sugar) or *nuoc chanh nong* (hot, sweetened lemon juice).

GAY & LESBIAN TRAVELLERS

Vietnam is pretty hassle-free for gay travellers. There's not much in the way of harassment, nor are there official laws on same-sex relationships (although the government considers homosexuality a 'social evil'). Vietnamese same-sex friends often walk with arms around each other or holding hands, and guest-house proprietors are unlikely to question the relationship of same-sex travel companions. But be discreet – public displays of affection are not socially acceptable whatever your sexual orientation.

Check out **Utopia** (www.utopia-asia.com) to obtain contacts and useful travel information.

HOLIDAYS

The Lunar New Year (Tet) is Vietnam's most important annual festival. The Tet holiday officially lasts three days, but many Vietnamese take the following week off work, so hotels, trains and buses are booked solid – lots of places shut down. If visiting Vietnam during Tet, memorise this phrase: *Chuc mung nam moi* (Happy New Year). Smiles are guaranteed. Other Vietnamese public holidays:

Tet (Tet Nguyen Dan) 14 February 2010 (Year of the Tiger), 3 February 2011 (Year of the Cat).
Liberation Day 30 April; the date Saigon surrendered to the Hanoi-backed forces in 1975.
International Workers' Day 1 May.
Ho Chi Minh's Birthday 19 May.
National Day 2 September; commemorates the proclamation of the Declaration of Independence of the Democratic Republic of Vietnam by Ho Chi Minh in 1945.

INTERNET ACCESS

Internet access is available throughout Vietnam, sometimes in the most surprising backwaters. Faster ADSL connections are becoming more widespread, and wi-fi is common in the bigger cities. USB drives are often available at photography shops and most computers have USB inputs in Vietnam. Travellers can put portable web browsers on their USB drives with all their saved passwords to bypass potential spyware at internet cafes.

PLANET OF THE FAKES

You'll probably notice a lot of cut-price Lonely Planet titles available as you travel around the country. Don't be deceived. These are pirate copies, churned out on local photocopiers. Sometimes the copies are very good, sometimes awful. The only certain way to tell is price. If it's cheap, it's a copy. Look at the print in this copy…if it is faded and the photos are washed out, then this book will self-destruct in five seconds.

The cost for internet access ranges from about 2000d to 20,000d per hour, depending on the location.

INTERNET RESOURCES

Economist.com (www.economist.com/countries/vietnam/index.cfm) A great news source with an in-depth country profile.
Travelfish.org (www.travelfish.org) Well-written and in-depth articles and reviews on the region.
Vietnam Adventures (www.vietnamadventures.com) Full of practical travel information, and features monthly adventures and specials.

LEGAL MATTERS

Most Vietnamese never call the police, preferring to settle legal disputes on the spot (either with cash or fists). If you lose something really valuable such as your passport or visa, you'll need to contact the police. For incidents on the street, seek out the tourist police who patrol the main tourism (and theft) spots in the biggest cities.

The Vietnamese government is seriously cracking down on the burgeoning drug trade. You may face imprisonment and/or large fines for drug offences, and drug trafficking can be punishable by death.

MAPS

Basic road maps of Vietnam and major cities such as Hanoi, HCMC, Hue and Nha Trang are readily available. Vietnam Tourism publishes a handy travel atlas *(ban do du lich)*, available at bigger bookshops.

MEDIA

Vietnam News and the *Saigon Times* are propagandist English-language dailies. Popular listings mags include the *Guide*, which covers listings and info for the whole country, plus the *Word*, which gives the lowdown on HCMC.

Voice of Vietnam hogs the airwaves all day and is pumped through loudspeakers in many smaller towns. Foreign radio services such as the BBC World Service, Radio Australia and Voice of America can be picked up on short-wave frequencies. There are several TV channels and a steady diet of satellite.

MONEY

Vietnam's official currency is the dong (d). Banknotes come in denominations of 200, 500, 1000, 2000, 5000, 10,000, 20,000, 50,000, 100,000 and 500,000. Now that Ho Chi Minh has been canonised (against his wishes), his picture is on *every* banknote. There are also small-denomination coins (from 200d to 5000d). US dollars and euros are the easiest currencies to exchange. Of course, for your own security try to avoid carrying large wads of cash.

ATMs

ATMs are almost everywhere now. All ATMs dispense cash in dong only. The limit per withdrawal is usually two million dong, but multiple withdrawals are allowed. Most banks charge 20,000d a transaction.

Bargaining & Tipping

For *xe om* and *cyclo* trips, as well as anywhere that prices aren't posted, bargaining is possible. In tourist hot spots, you may be quoted as much as five times the going price, but not everyone is trying to rip you off. In less-travelled areas, foreigners are often quoted the Vietnamese price but you can still bargain a little bit.

Bargaining politely usually invites reciprocal good-faith negotiation; getting belligerent gets you nowhere. If you can't agree on a price, thanking the vendor and walking away sometimes brings about a change of heart. When it's a matter of just a few thousand dong, don't drive too hard a bargain.

Tipping isn't expected in Vietnam, but it is enormously appreciated. Many travellers take up a collection (each contributing a few dollars) for their tour guides and drivers, after multiday tours or for outstanding service. For someone making US$100 per month, keep in mind that the cost of your drink can equal half a day's wages.

EXCHANGE RATES

Exchange rates at the time of press were:

Country	Unit	Dong (d)
Australia	A$1	15,644
Cambodia	1000r	4291
Canada	C$1	16,668
Euro zone	€1	26,095
Japan	¥100	19,848
Laos	1000 kip	2082
New Zealand	NZ$1	12,882
Thailand	10B	5340
UK	UK£1	17,836
USA	US$1	17,725

Cash

The US dollar acts as a second local currency. Hotels, airlines and travel agencies all normally quote their prices in dollars, due in part to unwieldy Vietnamese prices (US$100 is around 1.8 million dong). For this reason, we quote some prices in US dollars. For the best prices, pay in dong.

Credit Cards

Visa, MasterCard and American Express (Amex) credit cards are accepted in most cities at a growing number of hotels, restaurants and shops. Getting cash advances on credit cards is also possible, but you'll be charged between 1% and 5% commission.

Exchanging Money

If you need to exchange money after hours, jewellery shops will exchange US dollars at rates comparable to, or even slightly better than, the banks.

Travellers Cheques

Travellers cheques in US dollars can be exchanged for local dong at certain banks; Vietcombank is usually a safe bet, although there is a small commission. Most hotels and airline offices will not accept travellers cheques.

POST

International postal services from Vietnam are reasonably priced when compared with most countries, though parcels mailed from smaller cities and towns may take longer to arrive at their destinations. Be aware that customs will inspect the contents before you ship anything other than documents, so don't show up at the post office with a carefully wrapped parcel ready to go. It will be dissected on the counter.

Poste restante works in the larger cities but don't count on it elsewhere. There is a small surcharge for picking up poste-restante letters. All post offices are marked with the words *buu dien*.

RESPONSIBLE TRAVEL

The tourism industry in Vietnam is very responsive to the desires of travellers; if you make it clear that you'll vote with your dong for businesses and tour operators who do what they can to avoid littering, not harm wildlife, treat animals humanely and act in a generally responsible manner, then hopefully the words 'ecotourism' and 'responsible travel' will become more than marketing buzz.

Buying coral, limestone or dried sea life encourages such harvesting to meet the demand, meanwhile destroying or killing the living ecosystems that travellers visit to enjoy. In the same vein, sampling 'exotic' meats such as muntjac, seahorse or bat may seem culinarily adventurous, but many of these species are endangered. Help preserve vulnerable species by not eating them.

Beggars, especially young ones, are often part of an organised operation run by shady characters. Giving money only perpetuates the exploitation. If nothing else, giving handouts encourages a reliance on begging. Donating to a country-specific development organisation or patronising businesses that provide job training to those in need is a better use of good intentions.

A growing crisis in Vietnam is the accelerating spread of HIV/AIDS. For the protection of others and yourself, practise safe sex.

BEWARE YOUR BLEND

Some consider *chon* to be the highest grade of Vietnamese coffee. It is made of beans fed to a certain species of weasel and later collected from its excrement.

SHOPPING

Vietnam has some fantastic shopping opportunities so it is well worth setting aside half a day or more to properly peruse. Hot spots include Hanoi, Hoi An and HCMC, each of which has a tempting selection of everything from avant-garde art to sumptuous silk suits. Some of the best buys on the block include gorgeous glazed pottery, classic lanterns, 'almost' antiques, embroidered tablecloths, fine furnishings, and lavish silk and linen creations in designer boutiques.

STUDYING

To qualify for a student visa, you need to study at a bona-fide university (as opposed to a private language centre or with a tutor). Universities require that you study 10 hours per week. Lessons usually last for two hours per day, for which you pay tuition of around US$5.

Decide whether you want to study in northern or southern Vietnam, because the regional dialects are very different. See Courses in Hanoi (p849) or HCMC (p908) for school listings.

TELEPHONE

Charges for international calls from Vietnam have dropped significantly and cost less than US$0.50 per minute to most countries. The service is easy to use from any phone in the country; just dial ☎ 17100, the country code and the number.

Many guest houses, hotels and internet cafes offer Voice-over Internet Protocol (VoIP) services, which are very cheap or virtually free if using a service like Skype.

Phone numbers in Hanoi, HCMC and Hai Phong have eight digits. Elsewhere around the country phone numbers have seven digits.

Useful numbers:

Directory assistance (☎ 116)
General information (☎ 1080)
International operator (☎ 110)
International prefix (☎ 00)
Time (☎ 117)

For mobile phones, Vietnam uses GSM 900/1800, which is compatible with most of Southeast Asia, Europe and Australia but not with North America. If your phone has roaming, it is easy enough, if expensive, to make calls in Vietnam. Another option is to buy a SIM card with a local number to use in Vietnam. Mobile-phone service providers such as VinaPhone and MobiFone sell prepaid phonecards.

TOILETS

Most hotels have the familiar Western-style sit-down toilets, but squat toilets in varying states of refinement exist in some cheap hotels and public places such as restaurants and bus stations. Hotels usually supply a roll, but it's wise to keep a stash of toilet paper while travelling.

As public toilets are scarce, ask and ye shall usually receive the blessing to use the toilet at a nearby hotel, restaurant or shop – again, BYOTP (bring your own toilet paper).

TOURIST INFORMATION

Tourist offices in Vietnam have a different philosophy from the majority of tourist offices worldwide. These government-owned enterprises are really travel agencies whose primary interest is turning a profit.

While traveller cafes have a similar agenda, they're generally a better source of information and offer cheaper ways of getting to where you're going. Hitting up your fellow travellers for information is an excellent way to get the latest, greatest scoop on the where and how.

TRAVELLERS WITH DISABILITIES

Vietnam poses many technical challenges for the disabled traveller, including a lack of lifts, a steeplechase of kerbs, steps and uneven pavements, and squat toilets in narrow cubicles.

Disabled Vietnamese get around in hand-pumped vehicles or tricked-out motorbikes, while the poorest of the poor are simply hand-pulled or self-propelled on boards outfitted with wheels. Foreigners can get around in a hired car with driver and/or guide, which is not prohibitively expensive.

Check out Lonely Planet's **Thorn Tree** (http://thorntree.lonelyPlanet.com) to connect with other travellers; search under the Southeast Asia branch.

Vietnam-veteran groups that organise tours to Vietnam might also have some good travel tips, or seek advice from the organisations listed in the Southeast Asia Directory (p943).

VISAS

All visitors require a visa to enter the country, and while Vietnamese bureaucracy is legendary, completing the visa application is pretty painless. You'll need at least one passport-sized photo to accompany the visa application. Travellers shouldn't arrive at a Vietnamese border or airport without a visa; it's necessary to get one in advance from a Vietnamese embassy or consulate abroad. It is possible to arrange a visa on arrival through a Vietnamese travel agent. They will need passport details in advance and will send a confirmation for the visa to be issued at your airport of arrival.

Tourist visas are valid for a single 30-day stay and enable you to enter and exit the country via any international border. Depending on where you acquire it, prices for single-entry tourist visas vary from US$30 to US$60. Cambodia, where your visa application can be processed on the same day, is the most convenient place in Southeast Asia to get a Vietnamese visa. Bangkok is another popular place, as many travel agents offer cheap packages including both an air ticket and a visa.

If you plan to spend more than a month in Vietnam or travel overland between Laos, Vietnam and Cambodia, it's possible to get a three-month multiple-entry visa. These are not available from all Vietnamese embassies but can be picked up for about US$90 in Cambodia.

Business Visas

There are several advantages in having a business visa: such visas are usually valid for three or six months; they can be issued for multiple-entry journeys; you are permitted to work in Vietnam; and the visas can be extended with relative ease. The notable disadvantage is cost, which is about four times as much as a tourist visa.

Getting a business visa tends to be easier once you've arrived in Vietnam; most travel agencies can arrange one for you, sponsor and all.

Visa Extensions

If you've got the dollars, they've got the rubber stamp. Visa extensions cost around US$30, but go to a travel agency to get this taken care of – turning up at the immigration police yourself usually doesn't work. The procedure takes one or two days (your passport is needed) and is readily accomplished in major cities such as Hanoi, HCMC, Danang and Hue.

Official policy is that you are permitted one visa extension only, for a maximum of 30 days. Be on the lookout for sudden changes to these regulations.

VOLUNTEERING

For information on volunteer work opportunities, chase up the full list of non-government organisations (NGOs) at the **NGO Resource Centre** (Map pp844-5; ☎ 04-3832 8570; www.ngocentre.org.vn; Hotel La Thanh, 218 P Doi Can, Hanoi), which keeps a database of all of the NGOs assisting Vietnam. Projects in need of volunteers include the following:

15 May School (www.15mayschool.org) A school in HCMC for disadvantaged children, which provides free education and vocational training.

Friendship Village (www.vietnamfriendship.org) Established by veterans from both sides to help victims of Agent Orange.

Street Voices (www.streetvoices.com.au) Donate your skills, time or money to help give street children career opportunities. Street Voices' primary project is KOTO restaurant (p852).

WOMEN TRAVELLERS

While it always pays to be prudent (avoid dark lonely alleys at night), foreign women have rarely reported problems in Vietnam. As most Vietnamese women do not frequent bars on their own, be aware that you may receive unwanted (though usually harmless) advances if drinking or travelling alone. When travelling on overnight trains it's a good idea to travel with a companion to keep an eye on your bags when you use the toilet, and on each other if you have any overly friendly strangers sharing your compartment.

Some Asian women travelling with Western men have occasionally reported verbal abuse from Vietnamese people who stereotype them as prostitutes. However, with the increase of foreign tourists visiting the country, locals are becoming more accustomed to seeing couples of mixed ethnicity.

Southeast Asia Directory

CONTENTS

This chapter includes general information about Southeast Asia. Specific information for each country is listed in the individual country directories.

ACCOMMODATION

The accommodation listed in this guidebook occupies the low end of the price and amenities scale. Room typically have four walls, a bed and a fan (handy for keeping mosquitoes at bay). In the cheapest instances, the bathroom is shared. Most places geared to foreigners have Western-style toilets, but hotels that cater to locals usually have Asian squat toilets. Air-con, private bathrooms and well-sealed rooms cost more. Camping is not a widespread option.

Be a smart shopper when looking for a room. Always ask for the price first, then ask to see a room to inspect it for cleanliness, comfort and quiet. Don't feel obligated to take a room just because the place is mentioned in Lonely Planet. Sometimes the quality of a guest house plummets after gaining a mention in Lonely Planet, but this can be corrected by diligent travellers who exercise their own judgement.

If the price is too high, ask if they have anything cheaper. We list independent businesses that can alter their prices without notifying us. Unless it is the low season, most rates are non-negotiable. Once you've paid for a room there is no chance of a refund, regardless of the size of the rat that scurried across the floor. It is recommended to pay per day rather than in bulk, but be courteous and pay first thing in the morning to keep staff from resorting to pushiness. Settle your bill the night before if you are catching an early bus out of town; most hotels and guest houses do not staff their desks from midnight to 6am.

Advance reservations (especially with advance deposits) are generally not necessary. If you do make a booking, don't rely on an agent; the price will mysteriously double to pay the extra outstretched hand.

ACTIVITIES

Ocean sports and jungle trips are the major outdoor activities in Southeast Asia. For ocean sports, operators are plentiful and many beach resorts rent out gear. If you're not a beginner, consider bringing the required gear from home as equipment here can be substandard.

Diving & Snorkelling

Southeast Asia is a diving and snorkelling paradise in Thailand, Malaysia, Indonesia and the Philippines. If you've never seen Southeast Asia's jewel-hued waters before, just about anywhere will seem amazing.

BUGGED BY YOUR SLEEPING COMPANION?

Ever noticed a row of welts on your arm that itched with crippling intensity? You've just been feasted upon by bedbugs, nocturnal bloodsuckers about the size and shape of a poppy seed. These critters are superb daytime hiders that infest mattresses in guest houses and hotels. People say that you can inspect the bed sheets and walls looking for small blood stains as evidence of an infestation, but we've been bugged many times and have never noticed any signs until the next itchy morning. Once established, bedbugs are incredibly hard to get rid of and they are keen travellers, hitching rides in luggage and infesting virgin territory. This is why it might seem like every guest house on the trail is a bedbug haven. If you find you've slept tight with the biting bedbugs, wash and seal in plastic all of your clothes and luggage so that you don't become a carrier. Use a little antihistamine cream or all-purpose Tiger balm to reduce the swelling and itching of the bites. And check into another room or guest house hoping that there isn't another buggy night ahead.

In Indonesia, Bali is the diving superstar, but there are countless small islands and reefs between Flores, Timor, Komodo, Maluku and Sulawesi. Pulau Weh, off the coast of Sumatra, has a stunning underwater landscape.

Malaysia's best diving spots are on the east coast, where Pulau Tioman, Pulau Redang and Pulau Perhentian are just some of the possibilities. There are also sites in Malaysian Borneo.

In Thailand, divers who know their coral travel specifically to the world-famous Similan and Surin Islands and the Burma Bank. Most of these sites are visited on live-aboard trips departing from Phuket or Khao Lak. In the Gulf of Thailand, Ko Tao is one of the cheapest places on the planet to get dive certified. In the Philippines, head to the diving hot spot Puerto Galera or to Palawan for wreck dives.

A few noteworthy spots for snorkelling include Lovina in Bali and the Gili Islands, both in Indonesia.

Before scuba diving or snorkelling, obtain reliable information about physical and environmental concerns at the diving or snorkelling site (eg from a reputable local dive operation). If you're diving, make sure you're healthy and that you're diving only at sites within your realm of experience; always engage the services of a competent, professionally trained dive instructor. See the boxed text, p934, for tips on responsible diving.

Surfing

Indonesia is the biggest surfing destination in Asia. For years surfers have been carting their boards to isolated outposts in search of the perfect wave. Kuta in Bali is a famous spot and a good place for beginners. For seasoned wave riders, there's surf right along the south coast of the inner islands – from Sumatra through to Sumbawa, and Sumba across to Papua. Pulau Nias, off the coast of Sumatra, is another beloved spot for its machinelike left break. Indonesia also hosts various surf camps and surf tours. To a lesser degree, Cherating in Malaysia and Phuket in Thailand have a surf season, and Siargao in the Philippines is another good spot.

Trekking

Trekking in mainland Southeast Asia clambers through a diminutive offshoot of the Himalayan range, which is home to many minority hill-tribe villages. The northern Thai cities of Chiang Mai, Mae Hong Son and Chiang Rai are very popular with prospective trekkers. Muang Sing and Luang Nam Tha in Laos have well-regarded ecotrekking tours to ethnic-minority villages. Gunung Rinjani in Indonesia is another area in which you can explore the environment and local culture, while the mountain village of Sapa in Vietnam is also a base for organised hill-tribe journeys.

Malaysia's national parks, including Taman Negara, Gunung Mulu National Park and Kinabalu National Park, offer excellent jungle experiences.

Hiking Southeast Asia's volcanoes is an unbeatable experience. In Indonesia, it's easy to organise volcanic treks in Sumatra, Java and Bali. In Bukit Lawang (Sumatra) the jungle is filled with orang-utan, and Papua and Sulawesi offer adventurous, deep-immersion trekking.

In the Philippines, the volcanic Mt Mayon, Mt Kanlaon and Mt Isarog are interesting

RESPONSIBLE DIVING

Please consider the following tips when diving, and help preserve Southeast Asia's reefs:

- Never use anchors on the reef and take care not to ground boats on coral.
- Avoid touching or standing on living marine organisms or dragging equipment across the reef.
- Be conscious of your fins. The surge from fin strokes can damage delicate organisms. Take care not to kick up clouds of sand, which can smother organisms.
- Practise and maintain proper buoyancy control. Major damage can be done by divers descending too fast and colliding with the reef.
- Spend as little time within underwater caves as possible as your air bubbles may be caught within the roof and thereby leave organisms high and dry. Take turns to inspect the interior of a small cave.
- Resist the temptation to collect or buy coral or shells, or to loot marine archaeological sites (mainly shipwrecks).
- Take home all your rubbish, especially plastics, and other litter you may find as well.
- Do not feed fish.
- Minimise your disturbance of marine animals. Never ride on the backs of turtles.

climbs. There are also some stunning trips in the Cordillera region of North Luzon, including treks around the rice terraces of Banaue and Bontoc.

Before embarking on a trek, make sure you are healthy and feel comfortable walking for a sustained period. Trekking in Southeast Asia requires a guide as trails aren't well marked, transport to the trail-head is difficult to arrange and foreigners are unfamiliar with the region's climate conditions. Hiring a guide also provides income for local villagers who regard the natural areas as their own backyards. You should also be aware of local laws, regulations and etiquette about wildlife and the environment. For more on responsible trekking, see the boxed text, opposite.

BATHING

At the cheaper end of the lodging scale, bathrooms will not have hot-water showers. Instead there will only be cold water showers or even a large basin that is used for bathing. In the latter case, water should be scooped out of the basin with a bowl and poured over the body. Avoid washing directly in the basin or climbing in as this is your source of clean water. Cold-water showers are certainly the more environmental choice but it can be difficult to adequately rinse off soap and shampoo. Consider travelling with an easy-to-rinse soap.

More expensive accommodation, large cities and colder regions will offer hot-water showers, usually point-of-use heaters, for an extra charge.

Many rural people bathe in rivers or streams. If you choose to do the same, be aware that public nudity is not acceptable. Do as the locals do and bathe with some clothing on.

BOOKS

See the country chapters for recommended reading about each country (fiction and nonfiction). For more detailed information on a country, region or city, refer to the large range of travel guidebooks produced by Lonely Planet; see the individual country directories for area-specific titles.

Also of interest to travellers who like to get chatty is Lonely Planet's *Southeast Asia Phrasebook* and the wide-range of country-specific phrasebooks that Lonely Planet produces.

BUSINESS HOURS

In the Buddhist countries of Southeast Asia businesses are typically open seven days a week. In the Muslim countries some businesses close during Friday afternoon prayers. Refer to Business Hours in the individual country directories for more details; in each chapter, opening hours will be listed

RESPONSIBLE TREKKING

To help preserve the ecology and beauty of Southeast Asia, consider the following tips when trekking.

Rubbish

- Carry out all your rubbish. Don't forget cigarette butts, plastic wrappers, sanitary napkins, tampons and condoms. Make an effort to carry out rubbish left by others.
- Never bury your rubbish: digging disturbs soil and ground cover, and encourages erosion. Buried rubbish is likely to be dug up by animals, which may be injured or poisoned by it. It may also take years to decompose.
- Minimise waste by taking minimal packaging and no more food than you will need. Take reusable containers or stuff sacks.

Human Waste Disposal

- Contamination of water sources by human faeces can lead to the transmission of disease. Where there is a toilet, use it. Where there is none, bury your waste. Dig a small hole 15cm (6in) deep and at least 100m (320ft) from any watercourse. Cover the waste with soil and a rock.

Washing

- Don't use detergents or toothpaste in or near watercourses, even if they are biodegradable.
- For personal washing, use biodegradable soap and a water container at least 50m (160ft) away from the watercourse. Disperse the waste water widely to allow the soil to filter it fully.
- Wash cooking utensils 50m (160ft) from watercourses and avoid using detergent.

Erosion

- Hillsides and mountain slopes, especially at high altitudes, are prone to erosion. Stick to existing tracks (even if they're muddy) and avoid short cuts.
- Avoid removing the plant life that keeps topsoils in place.

Fires & Low-Impact Cooking

- Don't depend on open fires for cooking. The cutting of wood for fires can cause deforestation. Cook on a kerosene, alcohol or Shellite (white gas) stove and avoid those powered by disposable butane gas canisters.
- Fires may be acceptable below the tree line in areas that get very few visitors. If you light a fire, use an existing fireplace. Don't surround fires with rocks. Use only dead, fallen wood. Remember the adage 'the bigger the fool, the bigger the fire'. In huts, leave wood for the next person.
- Ensure that you fully extinguish a fire after use. Spread the embers and flood them with water.

only when they diverge from those in these Business Hours sections.

CLIMATE

See p936 for climate charts, and check out individual country directories in this book for country-specific climate information.

CUSTOMS

Customs regulations vary little around the region. Drugs and arms are strictly prohibited – death or a lengthy stay in prison are common sentences. Pornography is also a no no. Check the Customs sections in the directories of the country chapters for further details.

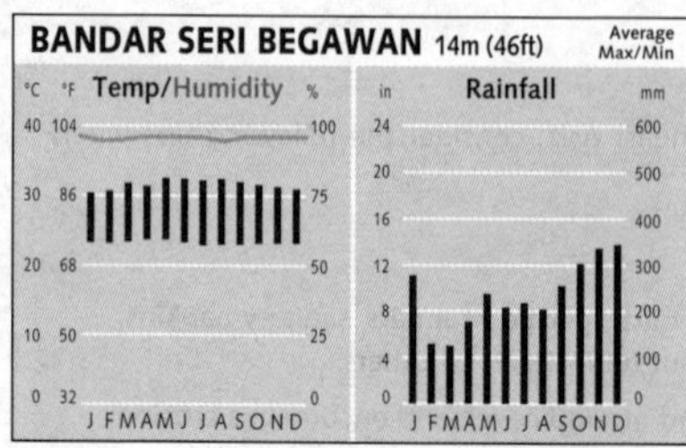
BANDAR SERI BEGAWAN 14m (46ft)
Average Max/Min
Temp/Humidity
Rainfall
J F M A M J J A S O N D

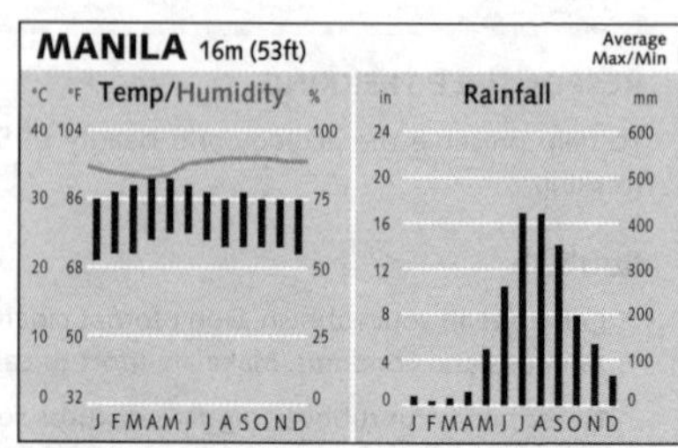
MANILA 16m (53ft)
Average Max/Min
Temp/Humidity
Rainfall
J F M A M J J A S O N D

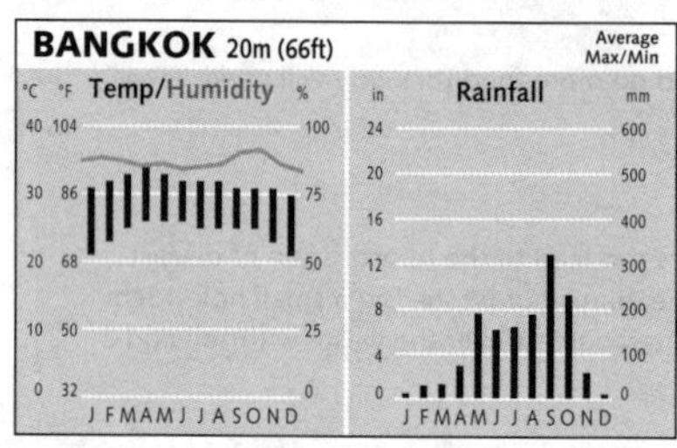
BANGKOK 20m (66ft)
Average Max/Min
Temp/Humidity
Rainfall
J F M A M J J A S O N D

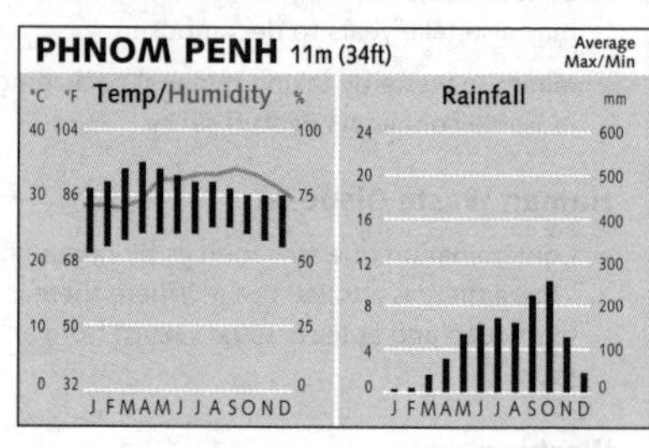
PHNOM PENH 11m (34ft)
Average Max/Min
Temp/Humidity
Rainfall
J F M A M J J A S O N D

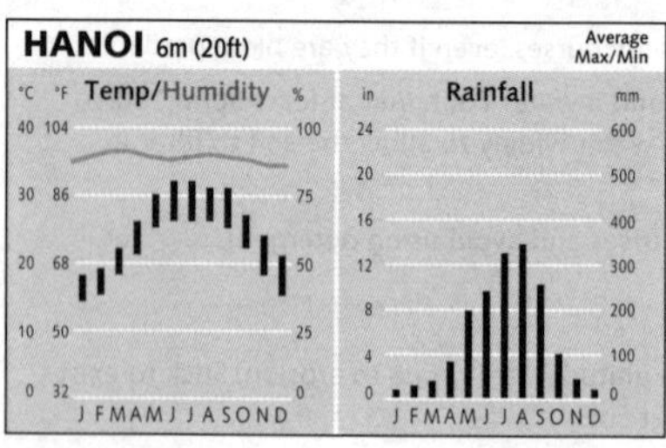
HANOI 6m (20ft)
Average Max/Min
Temp/Humidity
Rainfall
J F M A M J J A S O N D

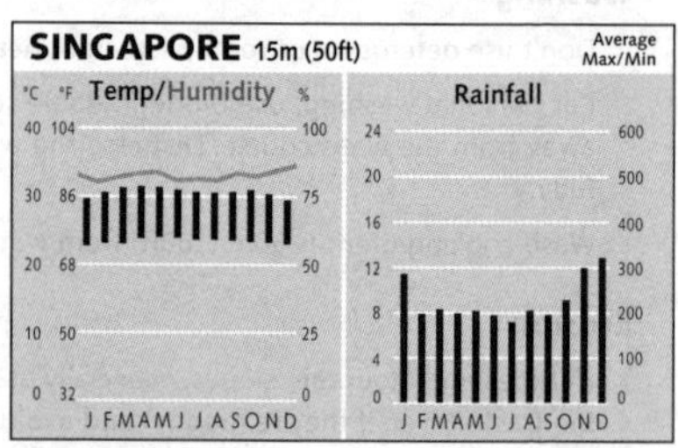
SINGAPORE 15m (50ft)
Average Max/Min
Temp/Humidity
Rainfall
J F M A M J J A S O N D

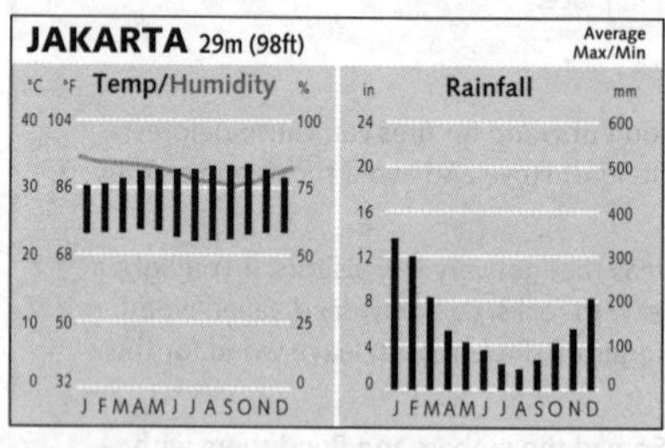
JAKARTA 29m (98ft)
Average Max/Min
Temp/Humidity
Rainfall
J F M A M J J A S O N D

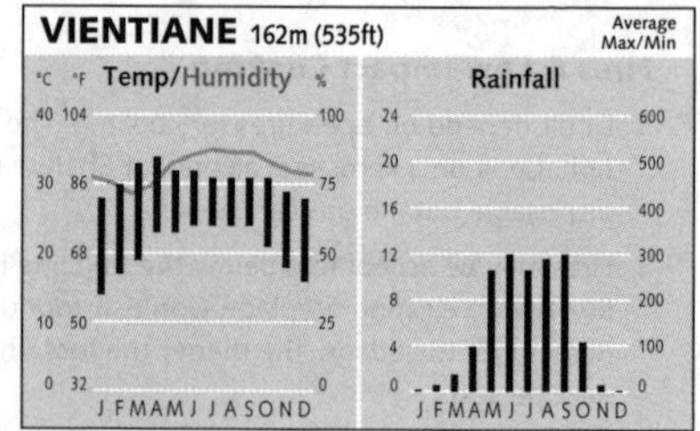
VIENTIANE 162m (535ft)
Average Max/Min
Temp/Humidity
Rainfall
J F M A M J J A S O N D

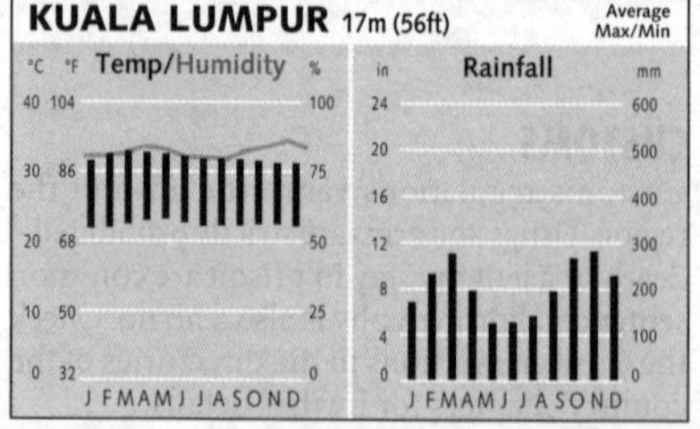
KUALA LUMPUR 17m (56ft)
Average Max/Min
Temp/Humidity
Rainfall
J F M A M J J A S O N D

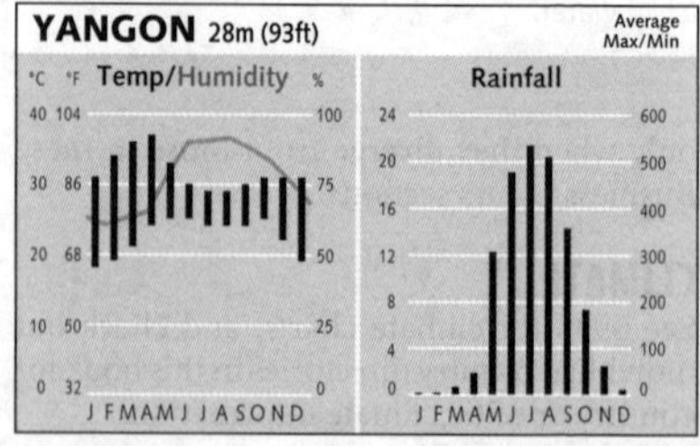
YANGON 28m (93ft)
Average Max/Min
Temp/Humidity
Rainfall
J F M A M J J A S O N D

DANGERS & ANNOYANCES

Drugs

The risks associated with recreational drug use and distribution are serious even in places with illicit reputations; just down the road from Kuta Beach in Bali is a jail where travellers are enjoying the tropical climate for much longer than they had intended. In Indonesia you can be jailed because your travel companions had dope and you didn't report them. A spell in a Thai prison is Third World torture; in Malaysia and Singapore, possession of certain quantities of dope can lead to hanging. With heightened airport security, customs officials are zealous in their screening of both luggage and passengers.

The death penalty, prison sentences and huge fines are given as liberally to foreigners as to locals; no one has evaded punishment because of ignorance of local laws. In Indonesia in 2005, nine Australians (dubbed the 'Bali Nine') were arrested on charges of heroin possession: seven received life sentences and two were sentenced to death by firing squad.

Recreational drug use is often viewed in the same league as drug trafficking and can result in prison terms. In Thailand, sometimes the drug dealers are in cahoots with the police and use a drug transaction as an opportunity to extract a huge bribe. You also never know what you're really getting. In Cambodia, what is sold as methamphetamine is often a homemade concoction of cheap and toxic chemicals and what is sold as cocaine is heavy-duty heroin that is easily consumed in overdose levels.

Mines & Mortars

Cambodia remains one of the most heavily mined countries in the world, especially in the west and northwest, and many mined areas are unmarked. Remember to stay on marked paths and not to touch unexploded devices. The same holds for Vietnam and parts of Laos.

Prostitution & Sex Tourism

Prostitution is usually illegal but common in parts of Southeast Asia. While some sex workers are consenting adults, child prostitutes are often sold and trafficked into the business and forced to work through intimidation and abuse. Sex with minors is a serious offence that is enforced with severe penalties. Many of the Western countries also prosecute and punish citizens for paedophile offences committed abroad.

For more information contact **End Child Prostitution & Trafficking** (Ecpat; www.ecpat.net), a global network that works to stop child prostitution, child pornography and the trafficking of children for sexual purposes.

Scams & Rip-offs

Every year we get letters and emails from travellers reporting that they've been scammed in Southeast Asia. Almost all scams revolve around the scenario of a local presenting you with an opportunity to save or make lots of money. The perennial favourites include card games and gemstones. If someone asks you to join a card game that involves money, walk away – it's rigged.

As for gemstones, if there really were vast amounts of money to be made by selling gems back home, savvy businesspeople would have a monopoly on the market already (oh wait, they already do). See Dangers & Annoyances in the country chapters for local scams.

More common are run-of-the-mill rip-offs in which you pay way more for a ride to the bus station, to exchange money, to buy souvenirs etc than you ought to. Rip-offs are in full force at border crossings, popular tourist attractions, at bus and rail stations and wherever travellers might get confused. Check the destinations' Getting Around sections to figure out a benchmark for the cost of local transport and be suspicious of super-cheap, inclusive tour packages. Southeast Asia operates on a commission basis and too-good-to-be true deals always have hidden costs.

Theft

Theft in Southeast Asia is usually by stealth rather than by force. Keep your money and valuables in a money belt worn underneath your clothes. Be alert to the presence of snatch thieves, who will whisk a camera or a bag off your shoulder. Don't store valuables in easily accessible places such as backpack pockets or packs that are stored in the luggage compartment of buses. Be especially careful about belongings when sleeping in dorm rooms.

Violent theft is rare but usually occurs late at night and after the victim has been drinking. Be careful walking alone at night and don't fall asleep in taxis. When alcohol is involved, avoid getting into heated exchanges with the locals. What might seem like harmless verbal sparring to you might be regarded as so injurious by the local that extreme retribution is required.

Always be diplomatically suspicious of overfriendly locals. However, don't let paranoia ruin your trip. With just a few sensible precautions, most travellers make their way across the region without incident.

Trouble Spots

Militant Islamic groups operating in Southeast Asia include Jemaah Islamiyah (JI), which was formed in the 1990s with the mission of establishing a pan-Islamic state in the region. The group turned to civilian terror tactics in the 2000s and reportedly orchestrated multiple bombing attacks on Western targets in Indonesia during that decade.

Since the 2002 Bali bombings, the most devastating attack in the region, Indonesian security forces have arrested hundreds of JI members and sent others underground. The US State Department believes that some JI fugitives are hiding out in the Sulu archipelago of the Philippines – a lawless area that is used as a smuggling and piracy hideout. In his 2009 *Middle East Quarterly* article titled 'Jemaah Islamiyah Adopts the Hezbollah Model', Zachary Abuza, an analyst and author on Southeast Asian terrorist groups, explains that despite government crackdowns, JI has been working through various Indonesian Muslim charities that received aid money after the 2004 tsunami and earthquake for a massive recruitment effort. In Abuza's opinion, JI will continue to be a regional threat as long as the organisation is allowed to function surreptitiously through social networks.

There is also ongoing militant activity in isolated areas of Thailand and the Philippines, where it is believed that separatist groups unaligned with JI are openly hostile to the respective central governments. Though the violence is largely self-contained, there is always the concern that more densely populated areas or international communities will be targeted to promote the insurgency's cause.

Make sure you get the most up-to-date information on local conditions before setting off (and while you're on the road). The governments of most countries issue travel warnings for their citizens, and the local English-language newspapers available in most parts of Southeast Asia are also good sources of information.

EAST TIMOR

This struggling democracy continues to suffer from mass political unrest that can often turn violent. The best way to avoid trouble is to simply avoid it; if you encounter a political rally, it's best to give it a wide berth. If stones start flying, that's your cue to seek safety.

INDONESIA

The country was on high alert after the 2002 nightclub bombing in Bali (which killed more than 200 people) and was followed by other bombings in Jakarta in 2003 and 2004 and again on Bali in 2005. A period of relative calm in Indonesia was broken in July 2009 when coordinated bombings at Jakarta's JW Marriott and Ritz-Carlton hotels killed nine and wounded 53 people. Indonesian police suspected Noordin Mohamad Top, who had ties to Al-Qaeda and a violent faction of Jemaah Islamiyah, as the ringleader of these post-2002 bombings, including the most recent attack. Top was shot and killed in September 2009 by anti-terrorist police. At the time of writing, it was unclear whether Indonesia had successfully contained its terrorist actors or whether the 2009 Jakarta hotel bombings had marked a renewed period of violence.

PHILIPPINES

Insurgency groups active in the Philippines include the Moro Islamic Liberation Front (MILF) and Abu Sayyaf Group (ASG), both of which are Islamic separatist groups operating in the southern island of Mindanao and the Sulu archipelago. Having orchestrated bombings and kidnappings throughout the region, ASG is the more militant and dangerous of the two. It allegedly has ties to other global Islamic terror networks and espouses a goal of a pan-Islamic state.

In 2008, the US government added to its so-called most wanted list three Philippines-based terrorists who were either ASG members or had links to a series of bombings in Mindanao since 2006. With help from the US government, the Philippine army weakened ASG by killing the group's reported leader, Khadaffy Janjalani, in 2006. But the US State Department still recognises the Sulu archipelago as a safe haven for terrorists and believes that JI fugitives from Indonesia and Malaysia are hiding out there.

Avoid travel in the Sulu archipelago and Mindanao, except for the city of Davao and the areas of northern Mindanao covered in this book.

THAILAND

The predominately Muslim southern provinces of Narathiwat, Yala, Pattani and parts of Songkhla have long experienced periods of unrest between Islamic separatist groups and the central Thai government. Since 2002 violence has re-emerged in the region, and what was a low-wattage war on government targets has steadily escalated into the civilian sector.

After the 2006 coup, it was hoped that the military junta, lead by a Muslim Thai, would be able to broker a peace deal with the southern insurgents. But the death toll has climbed above 3000 since the start of violence and 2008 was a particularly bloody year. The situation is volatile and what was initially deemed an ethno-nationalist struggle appears to have components of random gang-style violence.

It is advised to avoid travel through the Muslim-majority provinces of Narathiwat, Yala and Pattani and to avoid taking the train south to the border crossing of Sungai Kolok. For more information see p805.

Since the fall of 2008, there were minor border conflicts between Cambodian and Thai armies over control of the Angkor ruins of Prasat Preah Vihear (known as Khao Phra Wihan in Thailand). As a result, visa-less cross-border visits from Thailand to the temple have been suspended, though the ruins are accessible from Cambodia. Travellers should inquire about border tensions at this site before making the arduous trip.

DISCOUNT CARDS

The International Student Identity Card (ISIC) is moderately useful in Southeast Asia, with limited success in gaining the holder discounts. Some domestic and international airlines provide discounts to ISIC cardholders, but the cards carry little bargaining power because knock-offs are so readily available.

DISCRIMINATION

Everything is about skin colour in Southeast Asia. White foreigners stand out in a crowd. Children will point, prices will double and a handful of presumptions will precede your arrival. In general, these will seem either minor nuisances or exotic elements of travel. If you are a Westerner of Asian descent, most Southeast Asians will assume that you are a local until the language barrier proves otherwise. With the colour barrier removed, many Western Asians are treated like family and sometimes get charged local prices. Many Asians might mistake people of African heritage with fairly light complexions for locals or at least distant cousins. People with darker complexions will be regarded as foreign as white visitors, but will also be saddled with the extra baggage of Africa's inferior status in the global hierarchy. Mixed Asian and foreign couples will attract some disapproval, especially in Thailand where the existence of a large sex-tourism industry can suggest that the Asian partner is a prostitute. See also p940 for information for gay and lesbian travellers, and p944 for tips for female travellers.

DRIVING LICENCE

Parts of Southeast Asia, including Malaysia, Indonesia and Thailand, are good spots for exploring by car and motorcycle. If you are planning to do any driving, get an International Driving Permit (IDP) from your local automobile association before you leave your home country; IDPs are inexpensive and valid for one year. In some countries (eg Malaysia) your home driving licence is sufficient, but elsewhere (eg Indonesia and Thailand) an IDP is required.

ELECTRICITY

Most countries work on a voltage of 220V to 240V at 50Hz (cycles); note that 240V appliances will happily run on 220V. You should be able to pick up adaptors in electrical shops in most Southeast Asian cities.

EMBASSIES & CONSULATES

It's important to realise what your own embassy – the embassy of the country of which you are a citizen – can and can't do to help you if you get into trouble.

Generally speaking, it won't be much help in emergencies if the trouble you're in is remotely your own fault. You are bound by the laws of the country you are in. Your embassy will not be sympathetic if you end up in jail after committing a crime locally, even if such actions are legal in your own country.

In genuine emergencies you might get some assistance if other channels have been exhausted. For example, if you need to get home urgently, a free ticket home is exceedingly unlikely – the embassy would expect you to have insurance. If you have all your money and documents stolen, it might assist with getting a new passport, but a loan for onward travel is out of the question.

Most travellers should have no need to contact their embassy while in Southeast Asia, although if you're travelling in unstable regions or going into unchartered territory, it may be worth letting your embassy know upon departure and return. In this way valuable time, effort and money won't be wasted looking for you while you're relaxing on the beach somewhere.

For details of embassies in Southeast Asia see Embassies & Consulates in the individual country directories.

FESTIVALS & EVENTS

Most Southeast Asian holidays revolve around religious events. See also Festivals & Events in individual country chapters for country-specific festivals.

January/February

Vietnamese Tet & Chinese New Year Celebrated in Vietnam and in Chinese communities throughout the region with fireworks, temple visits, all-night drumming and two-week vacations in Chinese mercantile shops.

March/April

Easter Week This Christian holiday is observed in the Philippines, Vietnam, Indonesia and East Timor.

Thai, Lao & Cambodian New Year In mid-April these cultures celebrate their interpretation of the lunar new year with displays of religious devotion and symbolic 'water-throwing'. In Thailand, especially in Chiang Mai and Bangkok, this tradition has morphed into water-warfare.

June/July

Buddhist Lent At the start of the monsoonal rains, the Buddhist monks retreat into monasteries in Myanmar, Laos and Thailand. This is the traditional time for young men to enter the monasteries. The ceremonies associated with this period revolve around the temples and have little affect on travel or businesses.

October/November/December

Ramadan Observed in Malaysia, Indonesia, Brunei and southern Thailand during August or September, the Muslim fasting month requires abstinence from food, drink, cigarettes and sex between sunrise and sunset. Non-Muslim restaurants and businesses do open during the day but might appear shut in deference to the observers. Everyone comes out at night to celebrate the breaking of the fast. Travel can be a hassle towards the end of the holiday.

Christmas In December, various local celebrations occur in the Philippines, Vietnam, East Timor and Indonesia.

GAY & LESBIAN TRAVELLERS

Southeast Asia could easily be ranked as one of the most progressive regions regarding homosexuality outside the Western world. In general most urban centres have gay communities, and attitudes towards same-sex relationships are fairly relaxed, though travellers should still mind the region-wide prescription of refraining from public displays of affection.

Utopia Asian Gay & Lesbian Resources (www.utopia-asia.com) has an excellent profile of each country's record on acceptance, as well as short reviews on gay nightspots and handy travel guides to the various Southeast Asian countries. For more details on gay and lesbian travel, see the specific country directories.

INSURANCE

A travel-insurance policy to cover theft, loss and medical problems is a necessity. There's a wide variety of policies available, so check the small print. For more information about the ins and outs of travel insurance, contact a travel agent or travel insurer.

Some policies specifically exclude 'dangerous activities', which can include scuba diving, motorcycling and even trekking. A locally acquired motorcycle licence is also not valid under some policies. Check that the policy covers ambulance rides, emergency flights home and, in the case of death, repatriation of a body.

Also see p955 for further information on health insurance, and for info on car and motorcycle insurance, p953.

INTERNET ACCESS

In metropolitan areas, Southeast Asia is incredibly well wired, with internet cafes, fast connections, cheap prices, Skype headsets and CD burners. Outside the big cities, things start to vary. Good internet connections are usually commensurate with a destination's road system: well-sealed highways usually mean speedy travel through the information superhighway as well.

Wi-fi hotspots are burgeoning but the coverage varies from place to place. In some towns with a strong backpacker presence, businesses will offer free wi-fi, but in other towns the service will charge business-expense rates. Thailand and Singapore have capability to support web-enabled phones.

Censorship of some sites is in effect across the region.

LEGAL MATTERS

Be sure to know the national laws so you don't unwittingly commit a crime. In all of the Southeast Asian countries, using or trafficking drugs carries stiff punishments that are enforced even if you're a foreigner.

If you are a victim of a crime, contact the tourist police, if available; they are usually better trained to deal with foreigners and foreign languages than the regular police force.

MAPS

Country-specific maps are usually sold in English bookstores in capital cities. Local tourist offices and guest houses can also provide maps of smaller cities and towns.

MONEY

Most experienced travellers will carry their money in a combination of cash, credit cards and bank cards. You'll always find situations in which one of these cannot be used, so it pays to carry them all. A few old-timers carry travellers cheques, which provide an alternative should all else fail.

ATMs

In most cities ATMs are widespread and most networks talk to overseas banks, so you can withdraw cash (in the local currency) directly from your home account. But before banking on this option review the Money section in the country directories for specifics: Myanmar, for example, is ATM free.

Use your bank card only when you are dealing with cash machines, not for point-of-sale purchases. Having your card number stolen is a concern, and you will have more consumer protection with a credit card (which is paid after the purchase) than an ATM card (which deducts the cost at the time of purchase). Talk to your bank before heading off about compatibility with foreign ATMs, surcharges and international customer-service phone numbers.

Bargaining & Tipping

Most Southeast Asian countries practise the art of bargaining. Remember that it is an art, not a test of wills, and the trick is to find a price that makes everyone happy. Bargaining is acceptable in markets and in shops where fixed prices aren't displayed. As a beginner, tread lightly by asking the price and then asking if the seller can offer a discount. The price may creep lower if you take your time and survey the object. If the discounted price isn't acceptable give a counter offer but be willing to accept something in the middle. Once you counter you can't name a lower price. Don't start haggling unless you're interested in actually buying it. If you become angry or visibly frustrated then you've lost the game.

Tipping is not standard practice but is greatly appreciated. In some international restaurants in big cities, a service charge or gratuity will be added automatically to the bill.

Cash

Having some cash (preferably US dollars) is handy, but is risky too; if you lose it, it's gone. Try to get crisp, unmarked bills as some money changers can be fickle.

Credit & Bank Cards

For purchases of online airplane tickets, week-long dive trips or Singaporean shopping sprees, a credit card is your best friend; however, keep careful tabs on purchases as fraud is a concern. For credit and bank cards, make sure that your trip doesn't coincide with the expiration date. If so, make arrangements before you leave with your bank to obtain a replacement so that your card doesn't become invalid overseas.

Exchanging Money

Currency exchange is generally straightforward throughout the region. Most banks have exchange counters that offer the market rate; guest houses will exchange currencies often as a courtesy rather than an advertised endeavour, but the rates tend to be lower than businesses dealing in greater volumes of exchanges. See the individual country chapters for more details.

Other major currencies, such as the euro and the Australian dollar, are easy to change in the main centres; it's when you start getting away from regularly visited areas that your currency options become more limited.

Travellers Cheques

Travelling with a stash of travellers cheques can help if you hit an ATM desert. Get your cheques in US dollars and in large denominations, say US$100 or US$50, to avoid heavy per-cheque commission fees. Keep records of which cheques you've cashed, and keep this information separate from your money so you can file a claim if any cheques are lost or stolen.

PASSPORT

To enter most countries your passport must be valid for at least six months from your date of entry, even if you're only staying for a few days. It's probably best to have at least a year left on your passport if you are heading off on a trip around Southeast Asia.

Testy border guards may refuse entry if your passport doesn't have enough blank pages available. Before leaving get more pages added to a valid passport (if this is a service offered by your home country). Once on the road, you can apply for a new passport in most major Southeast Asian cities.

PHOTOGRAPHY

For those travelling with a digital camera, most internet cafes in well-developed countries or cities have fast enough connections for digital uploads; some shops also have CD-burning services. Before leaving home, determine whether your battery charger will require a power adapter by visiting the website of the **World Electric Guide** (www.kropla.com/electric.htm).

Print film is readily available in cities and larger towns across Southeast Asia. When travelling through the airport with sensitive film (1000 ISO and above), it should be checked by hand instead of travelling through the X-ray machines.

The best places to buy camera equipment or have repairs done are Singapore, Bangkok or Kuala Lumpur. Be aware that the more equipment you travel with, the more vulnerable you are to theft.

You should always ask permission before taking a person's photograph. Many hill-tribe villagers seriously object to being photographed, or they may ask for money in exchange; if you want the photo, you should honour the price.

POST

Postal services are generally reliable across the region. There's always an element of risk in sending parcels home by sea, though as a rule they eventually reach their destination. If it's something of value, you're better off mailing home your dirty clothes to make room in your luggage for precious keepsakes. Don't send cash or valuables through government-run postal systems.

Poste restante is widely available throughout the region and is the best way of receiving mail. When getting people to write to you, ask them to leave plenty of time for mail to arrive and to print your name very clearly. Underlining the surname also helps.

SOCIAL PROBLEMS

The disparity between rich and poor is one of Southeast Asia's most pressing social concerns. Few of the region's countries have established social nets to catch people left homeless or jobless by debt mismanagement or larger problems associated with rapid industrialisation. Most destitute people migrate to the cities, doing menial labour for barely subsistence wages, or selling their bodies for more handsome profits. The attendant problems of displaced citizens include drug abuse, HIV/AIDs, and unsanitary and dangerous living conditions. Because of the Buddhist belief in reincarnation, the prevailing political wisdom is that the poor are fated to suffer because of wrongdoings committed in previous lives.

STUDYING

There is a variety of courses available throughout the region, from formal university study to informal cottage classes. See the individual country chapters for specifics.

Council on International Educational Exchange (www.ciee.org/study) arranges study-abroad programs in Thailand, Vietnam and Cambodia. The University of Texas at Austin maintains a useful website, **Study Abroad Asia** (http://asnic.utexas.edu/asnic/stdyabrd/StdyabrdAsia.html), which lists universities that sponsor overseas study programs in Southeast Asia.

TELEPHONE

Phone systems vary widely across Southeast Asia. For international calls, most countries have calling centres (usually in post offices) or public phone booths that accept international phonecards. Each country's system is different, so it's a good idea to check under Telephone in the country directories before making a call.

You can take your mobile phone on the road with you and buy a local SIM card for respectable coverage. However, not all mobile phones are outfitted for international use; this is especially the case for mobile phones from the USA. Check with your service provider for global-roaming fees and other particulars.

Fax services are available in most urban centres across the region.

TOILETS

Across the region, squat toilets are the norm, except in hotels and guest houses geared towards international tourists and business travellers.

Next to the squat toilet is a bucket or cement reservoir filled with water. A plastic bowl usually floats on the water's surface or sits nearby. This water supply has a two-fold function: toilet-goers scoop water from the reservoir with the plastic bowl and use it to clean their nether regions while still squatting over the toilet; and a bowl full of water poured down the toilet takes the place of the automatic flush. More rustic toilets in rural areas may simply consist of a few planks over a hole in the ground.

Even in places where sit-down toilets are installed, the plumbing may not be designed to take toilet paper. In such cases, the usual washing bucket will be standing nearby and there will be a waste basket in which you place used toilet paper.

Public toilets are common in department stores, bus and railway stations, and large hotels. In some cases, they'll be an attendant who collects the nominal toilet fee (usually a few coins).

TOURIST INFORMATION

Most of the Southeast Asian countries have government-funded tourist offices with varying capacities of usefulness. Better information is sometimes available through guest houses and fellow travellers. See Tourist Information in the individual country chapters for contact information.

TRAVELLERS WITH DISABILITIES

Travellers with serious disabilities will likely find Southeast Asia to be a challenging place to travel. Even the more modern cities are very difficult to navigate for mobility- or vision-impaired people. Generally speaking, the various countries' infrastructure is often inadequate for those without disabilities, so it is unrealistic to expect much in the way of public amenities.

International organisations that can provide information on mobility-impaired travel include the following:

Mobility International USA (☎ 541-343-1284; www.miusa.org)

Royal Association for Disability & Rehabilitation (Radar; ☎ 020-7250 3222; www.radar.org.uk)

Society for Accessible Travel & Hospitality (SATH; ☎ 212-447-7284; www.sath.org)

VISAS

Visas are available to people of most nationalities on arrival in most Southeast Asian countries, but rules vary depending on the point of entry. See Visas in the individual country directories.

Depending on the country of entry, it's best get your visas as you go rather than before you leave home; they are often easier and cheaper to get in neighbouring countries. Visas are also only valid within a certain period, which could interfere with an extended trip. Stock up on passport photos as you'll probably need at least two pictures each time you apply for a visa.

Procedures for extending a visa vary from country to country. In some cases, extensions are nearly impossible, in others they're a mere formality. And remember: look smart when you're visiting embassies, consulates and borders.

In some Southeast Asian countries you are required to have an onward ticket out of the country before you can obtain a visa to enter.

VOLUNTEERING

Short-term positions and 'voluntourism' programs can be arranged throughout the region. There are many nongovernment aid groups in northern Thailand working with marginalised communities. In Cambodia, volunteer opportunities help orphans and street children. Malaysia has several environmental conservation programs. For more information, see Volunteering in individual country chapters.

Alternatively, **Global Vision International** (www.gviusa.com, www.gvi.co.uk) organises short-term volunteer opportunities in the region.

For long-term commitments, contact the following organisations working in Southeast Asia:

Australian Volunteers International (www.australianvolunteers.com) Professional contracts for Australians.

Global Volunteers (www.globalvolunteers.org) Professional and paid volunteer work for US citizens.
US Peace Corps (☎ in the USA 800-424-8580; www.peacecorps.gov)
Voluntary Service Overseas (www.vso.org.uk) British overseas volunteer program accepts qualified volunteers from other countries. Branches in Canada (www.vsocanada.org) and the Netherlands (www.vso.nl).
Volunteer Service Abroad (www.vsa.org.nz) Professional contracts for New Zealanders.

WOMEN TRAVELLERS

While travel in Southeast Asia for women is generally safe, solo women should exercise caution when travelling at night or returning home by themselves from a bar. While physical assault is rare, local men often consider foreign women as being exempt from their own society's rules of conduct. Be especially careful in party towns, especially the Thai islands and Bali, where drunken abandon is often exploited by opportunists.

Travelling in Muslim areas introduces some challenges for women. In conservative Muslim areas, local women rarely go out unaccompanied and are usually modestly dressed. Foreign women doing the exact opposite are observed first as strange and secondly as searching for a local boyfriend. While the region is very friendly, be careful about teaming up with young men who may or may not respect certain boundaries.

Keep in mind that modesty in dress is culturally important across all Southeast Asia. Covering past the shoulders and above the knees helps define you as off limits, while spaghetti-strap singlets inadvertently send the message that you're sexually available.

Finally, you can reduce hassles by travelling with other backpackers. This doesn't necessarily mean bringing a friend from home; you can often pair up with other travellers you meet on the way.

WORKING

Teaching English is the easiest way to support yourself in Southeast Asia. For short-term gigs, Bangkok, Ho Chi Minh City (Saigon) and Jakarta have language schools and a high turnover of staff. In the Philippines, English speakers are often needed as language trainers for the call centres. In Indonesia and Thailand you may be able to find some dive-school work.

Payaway (www.payaway.co.uk) provides a handy online list of language schools and volunteer groups looking for recruits for its Southeast Asian programs.

Transitions Abroad (www.transitionsabroad.com) is a web portal that covers all aspects of overseas life, including landing a job in a variety of fields.

Transport

CONTENTS

This chapter gives an overview of the transport options for getting to Southeast Asia, and getting around the region once you're there. For more specific information about getting to (and around) each country, see Transport in the country chapters.

GETTING THERE & AWAY

Step one is to get to Southeast Asia, and flying is the easiest option. The only overland possibilities from outside the region are from Papua New Guinea into Indonesia, an unlikely scenario, and China into Vietnam or Laos.

AIR

Tickets

The major Asian gateways for cheap flights are Bangkok, Kuala Lumpur, Singapore and Denpasar (Bali). Thanks to the proliferation of Asian budget carriers, there are often cheap fares between China and Southeast Asian cities or popular beach resorts. When pricing flights, compare the cost of flying to an East Asian city, like Hong Kong (or even Macau), from your home country, and then connecting to a budget carrier to the cost of flying directly to your Southeast Asian destination on a traditional long-haul airline. Fares on budget carriers don't usually factor into online search engines and their websites tend to be awkward to use. But if you've got more time than money, may the budget forces be with you.

Also be flexible with your travel dates and know when to buy a ticket. Trips that last longer than two weeks tend to be more expensive. Buying a ticket too early or too late before your departure will affect the price as well. The ticket-purchasing sweet spot is 21 to 15 days before departure. When researching airline fares, be sure to dump your computer's cookies, which track your online activity and can sometimes result in a higher fare upon subsequent searches.

The following online resources can help in researching bargain airfares:

Sky Scanner (www.skyscanner.net) Sophisticated fare and airline search engine for budget and traditional carriers.

Attitude Travel (www.attitudetravel.com) Offers a guide to low-cost carriers in Asia, including a list of airlines and destinations.

Lonely Planet (www.lonelyplanet.com) Click on Travel Services to research multidestination trips.

ROUND-THE-WORLD & CIRCLE ASIA TICKETS

If Asia is one of many stops on a worldwide tour, consider a round-the-world (RTW) ticket, which allows a certain number of stops within a set time period as long as you don't backtrack; for more information, talk to a travel agent.

THINGS CHANGE...

The information in this chapter is particularly vulnerable to change. Check directly with the airline or a travel agent to make sure you understand how a fare (and ticket you may buy) works and be aware of the security requirements for international travel. Shop carefully. The details given in this chapter should be regarded as pointers and are not a substitute for your own careful, up-to-date research.

Circle Asia passes are offered by various airline alliances for a circular route originating in the USA, Europe or Australia and travelling to certain destinations in Asia, including Southeast and East Asia. Air Timetable.com (www.airtimetable.com) profiles several of the airlines promotional circle fares under its Air Passes section.

Before committing, check out the fares offered by the budget regional carriers to see if the circle pass provides enough of a saving. Contact the individual airlines or a travel agent for more information.

From Asia

India and China are fused to major Southeast Asian cities through several low-cost airlines. **Air Asia** (code AK; www.airasia.com) does the hop from cities in China, India and Sri Lanka to Kuala Lumpur and sometimes Bangkok. Singapore receives many East Asian and South Asian flights through **Tiger Airways** (code TR; www.tigerairways.com), **Air India Express** (code IX; www.airindiaexpress.in) and **Jetstar Asia** (code 3K; www.jetstar.com). **Bangkok Airways** (code PG; www.bangkokairways.com) doesn't have as competitive fares as the budget airlines but it does have direct service from Bangkok to several Chinese cities, Hiroshima (Japan) and the Maldives, and from Hong Kong to Ko Samui. **Cebu Pacific** (code 5J; www.cebupacificair.com) has direct flights from Hong Kong to Manila and Cebu, and from Manila to many cities in East Asia. In most large cities with a tourist industry, there are also bucket shops that can sell cheap tickets to any destination you can dream of.

From Australia & New Zealand

Jetstar (code JQ; www.jetstar.com) and its sister companies are the biggest budget carriers serving Bangkok, Kuala Lumpur, Ho Chi Minh City (Vietnam), Denpasar (Bali, Indonesia) and Singapore with Australia and New Zealand. **Tiger Airways** (code TR; www.tigerairways.com) flies from Perth to Singapore. **Air Asia** (code AK; www.airasia.com) jumps from the Gold Coast and Perth to Kuala Lumpur.

Pacific Blue (code DJ; www.flypacificblue.com) is an offshoot of Virgin Blue, serving Bali from several Australian and New Zealand cities.

Also look for cheap fares in the travel sections of weekend newspapers such as the *Age* and the *Sydney Morning Herald*. Also try searching **Travel.com** (www.travel.com.au). Two well-known agencies for cheap fares include **Flight Centre** (☎ 133 133; www.flightcentre.com.au) and **STA Travel** (☎ 134 782; www.statravel.com.au), both with offices throughout Australia.

The *New Zealand Herald* has a helpful travel section. **Flight Centre** (☎ 0800 243 544; www.flightcentre.co.nz) and **STA Travel** (☎ 0800 474 400; www.statravel.co.nz) have local offices.

From Canada

Canadian air fares tend to be higher than those sold in the USA, and it is more expensive to fly from the east coast than the west. The *Globe & Mail*, the *Toronto Star*, the *Montreal Gazette* and the *Vancouver Sun* are good places to look for cheap fares. **Travel CUTS** (☎ 1 866 246 9762; www.travelcuts.com) is Canada's national student travel agency and has offices in all major cities.

From Continental Europe

European low-cost carrier **Air Berlin** (code AB; www.airberlin.com) has direct flights from Munich to Phuket (Thailand) and Dusseldorf to Bangkok (Thailand), with connecting flights throughout Europe. Also be creative with your flight route: sometimes there are cheap flights from Europe to the Middle East and the Middle East to Asia, especially if one of the legs is aboard a budget airline.

France has a network of student-travel agencies, including **Voyages Wasteels** (www.wasteels.fr), which can supply discount tickets to travellers of all ages. General travel agencies include **Nouvelles Frontières** (☎ 01 49 20 65 87; www.nouvelles-frontieres.fr) or **Voyageurs du Monde** (☎ 08 92 68 83 63; www.vd m.com).

In Switzerland, **STA Travel** (☎ 0900 450 402; www.statravel.ch) has branches in major Swiss cities.

In the Netherlands, **NBBS Reizen** (☎ 0180 3933 77; www.nbbs.nl) is the official student travel agency.

In Germany, **STA Travel** (☎ 069743 032 92; www.statravel.de) caters for travellers under 26.

From the UK

Air Asia (code D7; www.airasia.com) now operates from London's Stansted airport to Kuala Lumpur.

Check the travel pages of the weekend broadsheets, such as the *Independent* and the *Sunday Times* for travel deals.

For students or travellers under 26, the following are popular travel agencies:

CLIMATE CHANGE & TRAVEL

Climate change is a serious threat to the ecosystems that humans rely upon, and air travel is the fastest-growing contributor to the problem. Lonely Planet regards travel, overall, as a global benefit, but believes we all have a responsibility to limit our personal impact on global warming.

Flying & Climate Change

Pretty much every form of motor travel generates CO_2 (the main cause of human-induced climate change) but planes are far and away the worst offenders, not just because of the sheer distances they allow us to travel, but also because they release greenhouse gases high into the atmosphere. The statistics are frightening: two people taking a return flight between Europe and the US will contribute as much to climate change as an average household's gas and electricity consumption over a whole year.

Carbon Offset Schemes

Climatecare.org and other websites use 'carbon calculators' that allow jetsetters to offset the greenhouse gases they are responsible for with contributions to energy-saving projects and other climate-friendly initiatives in the developing world – including projects in India, Honduras, Kazakhstan and Uganda.

Lonely Planet, together with Rough Guides and other concerned partners in the travel industry, supports the carbon offset scheme run by climatecare.org. Lonely Planet offsets all of its staff and author travel.

For more information check out our website: lonelyplanet.com.

STA Travel (☎ 0871 2300 040; www.statravel.co.uk) Has offices throughout the UK.

Trailfinders (☎ 0845 058 5858; www.trailfinders.co.uk)

From the USA

Ticket promotions frequently connect Asia to Los Angeles, San Francisco, New York and other big cities or airline hubs. The *New York Times,* the *Los Angeles Times,* the *Chicago Tribune* and the *San Francisco Examiner* all produce weekly travel sections in which you will find a number of travel-agency ads and fare promos.

Students and travellers aged under 26 should try the US offices of **STA Travel** (☎ 800 781 4040; www.statr avel.com).

LAND

The land borders between Southeast Asia and the rest of Asia include the border between Myanmar and India and Bangladesh, and the Chinese border with Myanmar, Laos and Vietnam. Of these, it is possible to travel overland from China into Laos and Vietnam. There is also a boat service from Chiang Saen in Thailand to Jinghong in China (see p769). Occasionally the overland route between Myanmar and China is open but this is subject to change. See p403 for the Laos–China border crossing, and p855, p862 and p868 for Vietnam–China border crossings.

Another international crossing is between Indonesia and Papua New Guinea; see p346 for more information.

SEA

Ocean approaches to Southeast Asia from your home continent can be made aboard cargo ships plying various routes around the world. Ridiculously expensive and hopelessly romantic, a trip aboard a cargo ship is the perfect opportunity for you to write that novel that never writes itself. Some freighter ships have space for a few non-crew members, who have their own rooms but eat meals with the crew. Prices vary widely depending on your departure point but costs usually start at around $150 a day plus additional fees.

GETTING AROUND

AIR

Air travel can be a bargain within the region, especially from transit hubs such as Bangkok, Singapore and Kuala Lumpur. No-frills regional carriers have made travelling between capital cities cheaper than taking land transport in some cases. Air routes between Southeast Asian countries are listed in the Transport sections of each country chapter. Some airports in Southeast Asia charge a departure tax, so make sure you have a bit of local currency left.

Approximate intra-Asia fares are shown on the Southeast Asian Air Fares map (p948).

The following airlines often have affordable fares on regional routes:

Air Asia (code AK; www.airasia.com) Links Bangkok, Kuala Lumpur, Bali, Jakarta and Singapore.

Cebu Pacific Air (code; www.cebupacificair.com) Links Manila with Bangkok, Ho Chi Minh City, Kuala Lumpur, Singapore, Jakarta.

Firefly (code FY; www.fireflyz.com.my) Firefly links Sumatra (Indonesia) with Kuala Lumpur and Penang (Malaysia).

Jetstar (www.jetstarasia.com) Links Singapore to Bali through its sister airline ValueAir (code VF), Singapore to Phnom Penh, Manila and Ho Chi Minh with Jetstar Asia (3K).

Tiger Airways (code TR; www.tigerairways.com) Links Singapore to Bangkok, Hanoi, Ho Chi Minh City, Malaysian Borneo, Padang (Sumatra, Indonesia), Jakarta (Java, Indonesia) and Clark (Philippines).

Air Passes

National airlines of Southeast Asian countries frequently run promotional deals from select Western cities or for regional travel. **Airtimetable.com** (www.airtimetable.com) posts seasonal passes and promotions.

BICYCLE

Touring Southeast Asia on a bicycle has long had many supporters. Long-distance cyclists typically start in Thailand and head south through Malaysia to Singapore. Road conditions are good enough for long-haul touring in most places, but mountain bikes are definitely recommended for forays off the beaten track.

Vietnam is a great place to travel by bicycle – you can take bikes on buses, and the entire coastal route is feasible. If flat-land cycling is not your style, then Indonesia might be the challenge you're looking for. Road conditions here are bad and inclines steep, but the Sumatran jungle is still deep and dark. In Laos and Cambodia, road conditions are improving and the traffic is still relatively light.

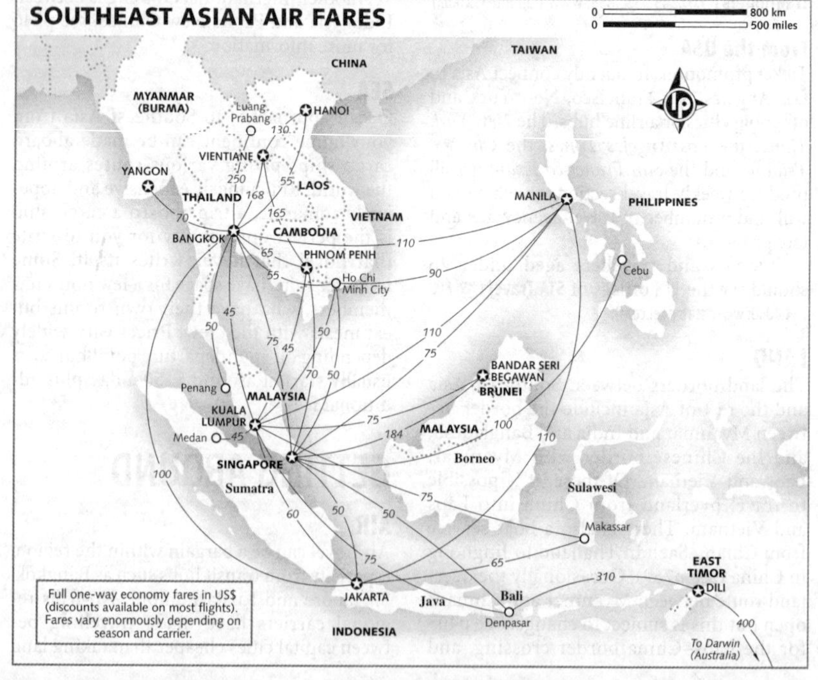

Full one-way economy fares in US$ (discounts available on most flights). Fares vary enormously depending on season and carrier.

Top-quality bicycles and components can be bought in major cities such as Bangkok but, generally, fittings are hard to find. Bicycles can travel by air; check with the airline about extra charges and shipment specifications.

BOAT

Ferries and boats make the trip between Singapore and Indonesia, Malaysia and Indonesia, Thailand and Malaysia and the Philippines and Malaysia. You also have the option of crossing the Mekong River by boat from Thailand to Laos and from Cambodia to Vietnam. Typically, guest houses or travel agents sell tickets and can provide travellers with updated departure times. Do make sure that you check the visa regulations at port cities; some ports do not issue visas on arrival.

BORDER CROSSINGS

Overland travel is easier than ever throughout Southeast Asia, as potholed ditches become major highways and previously closed borders are opening up to foreigners. The border crossings for the region are listed here by country; the following abbreviations are used for convenience: B (Brunei), ET (East Timor), C (Cambodia), I (Indonesia), L (Laos), M (Malaysia), My (Myanmar), P (Philippines), T (Thailand) and V (Vietnam).

Be aware of border closing times, visa regulations and any transport scams by asking your fellow travellers before making a long-distance trip or by referring to the relevant country chapters.

Brunei

The Malaysian states of Sarawak and Sabah form something like a double C clamp around Brunei. All border crossings feed into the Brunei capital of Bandar Seri Begawan (BSB). See p53 for everything you need to know about getting into and out of Brunei.

Cambodia

TO LAOS

The only border passage from Laos to Cambodia is located north of Stung Treng into Laos' Si Phan Don (Four Thousand Islands) region. The crossing is done at Dong Kralor (C), which is sometimes spelt Dom Kralor, to Dong Kalaw (L); see p128, p421 for deatils. In the same vicinity, crossings were once undertaken by boat from Voen Kham, but Cambodia has since closed its border post there.

TO THAILAND

There are five border crossings between Thailand and Cambodia:

- Poipet (C) to Aranya Prathet (T) – popular route linking Siem Reap (C) to Bangkok (T); see p109, p731
- Cham Yeam (C) to Hat Lek (T) – the coastal route from Krong Koh Kong (C) to Trat (T) and Ko Chang (T); see p114, p785
- O Smach (C) to Chong Chom (T) – to/from Surin (T); see p110, p776
- Choam (C) to Chong Sa Ngam (T) – to/from Surin (T); see p112, p776
- Psar Pruhm (C) to Dan Lem (T); see p108, p785

TO VIETNAM

There are now seven border crossings with Vietnam.

- Bavet (C) to Moc Bai (V) – quick passage between Phnom Penh (C) to Ho Chi Minh City (V); see p85, see p914
- Kaam Samnor (C) to Vinh Xuong (V) – scenic route from Phnom Penh (C) to Mekong Delta town of Chau Doc (V); see p85, p921
- Phnom Den (C) to Tinh Bien (V); see p85, p921
- Prek Chak (C) to Xa Xia (V); see p126, p921
- Trapaeng Plong (C) to Xa Mat (V); see p125, p839
- Trapaeng Sre (C) to Loc Ninh (V) see p132, p839
- O Yadaw (C) to Le Thanh (V); see p131, p898

East Timor

Overland travel is a possibility on the divided island of Timor, between independent East Timor and the Indonesian province of West Timor The border crossing is located at Batugade (ET) to Motoain (I); see p155, p314.

Indonesia

TO EAST TIMOR

See above.

TRANSPORT

TO MALAYSIA

High-speed ferries run between Peninsular Malaysia and Sumatra, and the Riau Islands:

- Pulau Penang (M) and Belawan (I) – to/from Medan (I); see p320, p467
- Melaka (M) to Pulau Bengkalis (I); see p320, p455
- Melaka (M) to Dumai (I) – to/from Bukittinggi (I); see p320, p455
- Melaka (M) to Pekanbaru (I); see p320, p455
- Johor Bahru (M) to Riau Islands (I): Tanjung Pinang on Pulau Bintan, and Pulau Batam; see p320, p472

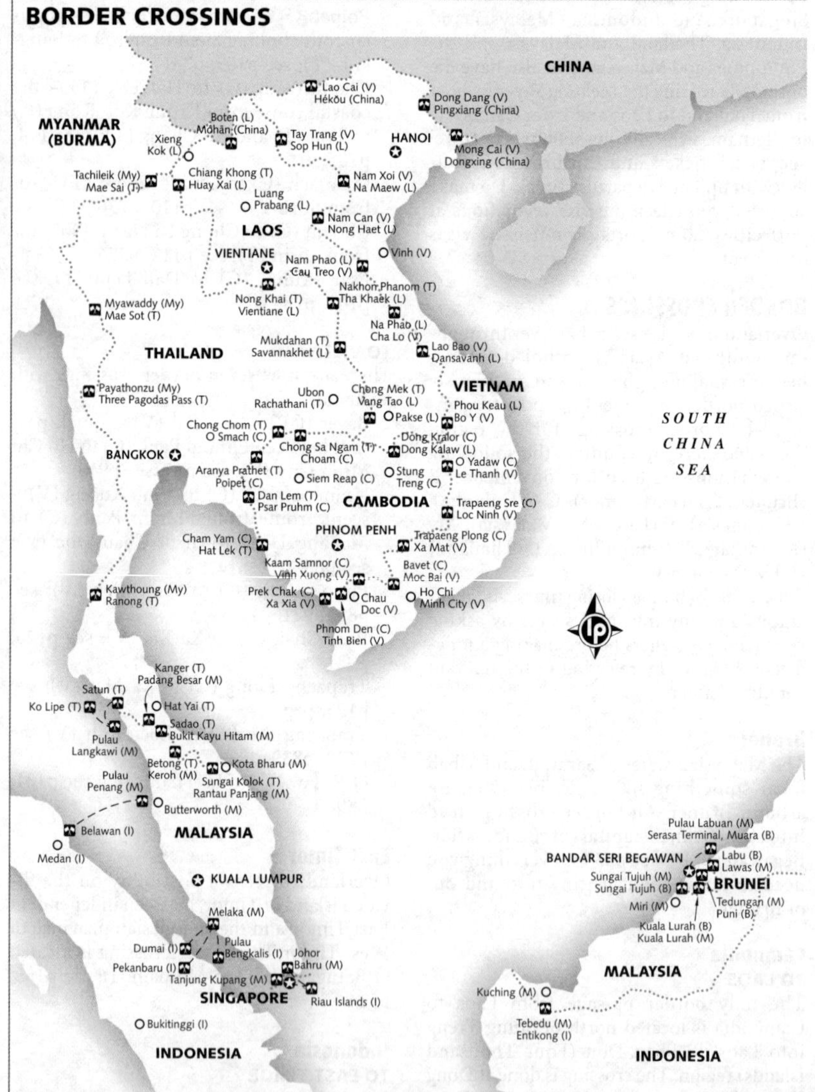

On the island of Borneo, the Indonesia–Malaysia border can be crossed at the following spots:

- Tawau (M) to Nunukan (I) – to/from Tarakan (I) in Kalimantan; see p320
- Tebedu (M) and Entikong (I), which links to Kuching (M); see p320, p511

TO SINGAPORE

Ferries operate from Singapore to several islands in the Riau archipelago (I), including Pulau Bintan (Tanjung Pinang), Pulau Batam, Pulau Kalimun (Tanjung Balai), Pulau Kundur (Tanjung Batu); see p675, p283.

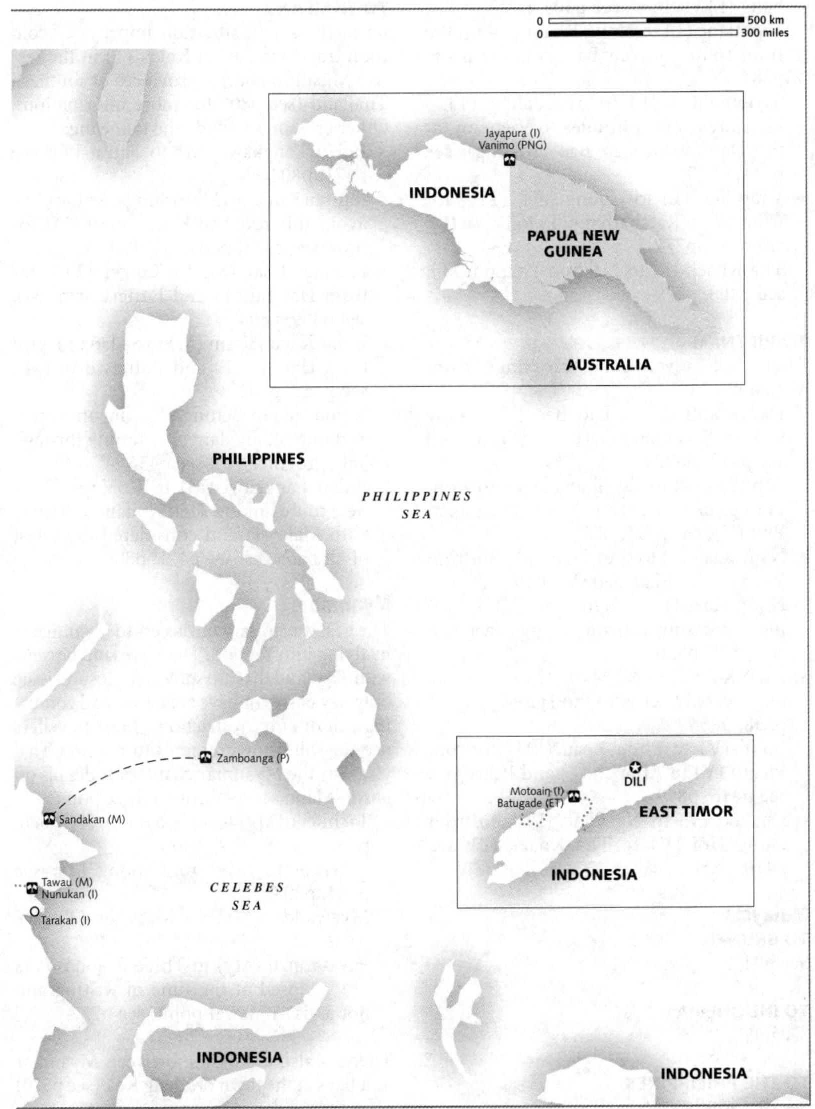

Laos

TO CAMBODIA

See p949.

TO THAILAND

There are five border crossings into Laos:

- Huay Xai (L) to Chiang Khong (T) – to/from northern Thailand to Luang Prabang (L) via boat; see p404, p772
- Vientiane (L) to Nong Khai (T) – on the train route to/from Bangkok; see p376, p781
- Savannakhet (L) to Mukdahan (T) – highway route continues to Vietnam (at the Dansavanh–Lao Bao crossing); see p411, p778
- Vang Tao (L) to Chong Mek (T) – to/from Ubon Ratchathani (T) to Pakse (L); see p415, p777
- Tha Khaek (L) to Nakhon Phanom (T); see p408, p779

TO VIETNAM

There are seven land crossings from Vietnam:

- Dansavanh (L) to Lao Bao (V) – easy link to Savannakhet (L) and Thailand; see p413, p877
- Sop Hun (L) to Tay Trang (V) – to/from Phongsali province (L) and Dien Bien Phu (V); see p393, p856
- Nam Phao (L) to Cau Treo (V) – to/from Vinh (V) and Lak Sao (V); p407, p856
- Nong Haet (L) to Nam Can (V) – a remote crossing to/from Nong Haet (L); see p396, p856
- Nam Xoi (V) to Na Maew (L) – a remote but accessible crossing to Hanoi (V); see p398, p856
- Bo Y (V) to Phou Keau (L) – to/from Pleiku (V) to Attapeu (L) and Pakse (L); see p416, p899
- Cha Lo (V) to Na Phao (L) – to/from Dong Hoi (V) to Tha Khaek (L); see p410, p856

Malaysia

TO BRUNEI

See p949.

TO INDONESIA

See p950.

TO THE PHILIPPINES

See opposite.

TO SINGAPORE

The 1km-long Causeway bridge connects the northern end of Singapore in the suburb of Woodlands to Johor Bahru (M). To the west another bridge connects Singapore in the suburb of Tuas with Tanjung Kupang (M). For details, see p472, p674.

TO THAILAND

Until the safety situation improves, avoid train travel via Sungai Kolok (T) in the restive Muslim-majority provinces of southern Thailand (see p805 for more information). Other crossings include the following:

- Pulau Langkawi (M) to Satun (T); see p471, p804
- Rantau Panjang (M) to Sungai Kolok (T) – avoid this route to Kota Bharu (M) for now; see p485, p804
- Padang Besar (M) to Kanger (T) – to/from Hat Yai (T) and Butterworth (M); see p469, p804
- Bukit Kayu Hitam (M) to Sadao (T) – to/from Hat Yai (T) and Butterworth (M); see p469, p804
- Keroh (M) to Betong (T) – inconvenient and potentially dangerous route through Yala province (T); see p436
- Pulau Langkawi (M) to Ko Lipe (T) – new route linking Thai Andaman islands with Malaysia and considered the safest of all passages; see p471, p804

Myanmar

The best way to gain full access to Myanmar is by flying into Yangon. There are land borders with Thailand that are subject to closure, issue only day passes or have expensive and confusing exit or entry restrictions. Most travellers use the following crossings to renew a Thai visa. See the Myanmar chapter for details on *possible* land access through these points.

- Tachileik (My) to Mae Sai (T); see p570, p767
- Kawthoung (My) to Ranong (T); see p564, p807
- Myawaddy (My) to Mae Sot (T); see p752
- Payathonzu (My) to Three Pagodas Pass (T) – closed at the time of writing and not a visa-renewal point; see p737

There is also a crossing between Myanmar and Laos at the town of Xieng Kok (see p570) accessible with pre-arranged permits.

Philippines

There are infrequent passenger ferries from Zamboanga (P) on Mindanao to Sandakan (M) in Sabah; see p655.

Singapore

Singapore has land crossings into Malaysia and sea crossings into Indonesia; see opposite and opposite, respectively.

Thailand

Thailand has border crossings to/from Cambodia (see p949), Laos (see opposite), Malaysia (see opposite) and Myanmar (see opposite).

Vietnam

Vietnam has open borders with Cambodia (see p949) and Laos (see opposite).

BUS

In most cases, land borders are crossed via bus, which either travels straight through the two countries with a stop for border formalities or requires a change of buses at the appropriate border towns.

Bus travellers will enjoy a higher standard of luxury in Thailand, the Philippines and Malaysia, where roads are well paved, reliable schedules exist and, sometimes, snacks are distributed. Be aware that theft does occur on some long-distance buses, especially those departing from Bangkok's Th Khao San heading south; keep all valuables on your person, not in a stowed locked bag.

Local buses in Laos, Cambodia and Vietnam are like moving sardine cans, but that is part of their charm.

CAR & MOTORCYCLE

What is the sound of freedom in Southeast Asia? The 'put-put' noise of a motorcycle – most Southeast Asians' first and only motorised vehicle. For visitors, motorcycles are convenient for getting around the beaches or touring in the countryside. Car hire is also available in most countries and is handy for local sightseeing or long-haul trips. You could hit Thailand and Malaysia by car pretty easily, enjoying well-signposted, well-paved roads. Road conditions in Laos and Cambodia vary, although sealed roads are becoming the norm. Indonesia and the Philippines have roads that vary between islands but most are in need of repair. Vietnam's major highways are in relatively good health.

See p939 for driving licence laws.

> **MOTORCYCLE TIP**
>
> Most Asians are so adept at driving and riding on motorcycles that they can balance the whole family on the front bumper or even take a quick nap as a passenger. Foreigners unaccustomed to motorcycles are not as graceful. If you're riding on the back of a motorcycle remember to relax. Tall people should keep their long legs tucked in as most drivers are used to shorter passengers. Women wearing skirts should collect loose material so that it doesn't catch in the wheel or drive chain. And watch out for the hot exhaust pipe when riding and disembarking.

Hire

There are Western car-hire chains camped out at Southeast Asian airports, capital cities and major tourist destinations. On many tourist islands, guest houses and locals will hire motorcycles and cars for an affordable rate.

Insurance

Get insurance with a motorcycle if at all possible. The more reputable motorcycle-hire places insure all their motorcycles; some will do it for an extra charge. Without insurance you're responsible for anything that happens to the bike. To be absolutely clear about your liability, ask for a written estimate of the replacement cost for a similar bike – and take photos as a guarantee. Some agencies will accept only the replacement cost of a new motorcycle.

Insurance for a hired car is also necessary. Be sure to ask the car-hire agent about liability and damage coverage.

Road Rules

Drive carefully and defensively; lives are lost at astounding rates on Southeast Asian highways. Remember too that smaller vehicles yield to bigger vehicles regardless of circumstances – on the road, might is right. The middle of the road is typically used as a passing lane, even if there is oncoming traffic, and your horn is used to notify other vehicles that you intend to pass them.

Safety

Always check a machine thoroughly before you take it out. Look at the tyres for treads, check for oil leaks, test the brakes. You may be held liable for any problems that weren't duly noted before your departure.

When riding a motorcycle, wear protective clothing and a helmet; long pants, long-sleeved shirts and shoes are highly recommended as sunburn protection and as a second skin if you fall. If your helmet doesn't have a visor, wear goggles, glasses or sunglasses to keep bugs, dust and other debris out of your eyes.

HITCHING

Hitching is never entirely safe in any country in the world and is not recommended. Travellers who decide to hitch should understand that they are taking a small but potentially serious risk. People who do choose to hitch will be safer if they travel in pairs and let someone know where they are planning to go.

LOCAL TRANSPORT

Because personal ownership of cars in Southeast Asia is limited, local transport within a town is a roaring business. For the right price, drivers will haul you from the bus station to town, around town, around the corner, or around in circles. The bicycle rickshaw still survives in the region, assuming such aliases as sǎamláw in Thailand and *cyclo* in Vietnam. Anything motorised is often modified to carry passengers – from Thailand's obnoxious three-wheeled chariots known as túk-túk to the Philippines' altered US Army jeeps. In large cities, extensive public bus systems either travel on fixed routes or do informal loops around the city, picking up passengers along the way. Bangkok, Kuala Lumpur and Singapore also boast state-of-the-art light-rail systems that make zipping around town feel like time travel.

TRAIN

For intercountry travel, the *International Express* train travels from Thailand all the way through the Malay peninsula, ending its journey in Singapore. Trains also serve Nong Khai, on the Thailand–Cambodia border, and Aranya Prathet, on the Thailand–Laos border.

You'll find that Thailand and then Malaysia have the most extensive intracountry rail systems, although trains rarely run on time.

Health

Dr Trish Batchelor

CONTENTS

Health issues and the quality of medical facilities vary enormously depending on where you travel in Southeast Asia. Many of the major cities are now very well developed, although travel to rural areas can expose you to a variety of health risks and inadequate medical care.

Travellers tend to worry about contracting infectious diseases when in the tropics, but infections are a rare cause of serious illness or death in travellers. Accidental injury (ie traffic accidents) and pre-existing medical conditions account for most life-threatening problems. Becoming ill in some way, however, is relatively common. Fortunately, most common illnesses can be either prevented with some common-sense behaviour or treated easily with a well-stocked traveller's medical kit.

The following advice is a general guide and does not replace the advice of a doctor trained in travel medicine.

BEFORE YOU GO

Pack medications in their original, clearly labelled containers. A signed, dated letter from your physician describing your medical conditions and medications, including generic names, is a good idea. If carrying syringes or needles, have a physician's letter stating their medical necessity. If you have a heart condition, bring a copy of your ECG.

If you take any regular medication, bring a double supply in case of loss or theft. In most Southeast Asian countries, excluding Singapore, you can buy many medications over the counter, but it can be difficult to find some of the newer drugs, particularly the latest antidepressants, blood-pressure medications and contraceptive pills.

INSURANCE

Even if you are fit and healthy, don't travel without health insurance – accidents do happen. Declare any existing medical conditions you have – the insurance company *will* check if your problem is pre-existing and will not cover you if it is undeclared. You may require extra cover for adventure activities such as rock climbing. If your health insurance doesn't cover you for medical expenses abroad, consider getting extra insurance. If you're uninsured, emergency evacuation is expensive – bills of more than US$100,000 are not uncommon.

Find out in advance if your insurance plan will make payments directly to providers or reimburse you later for overseas health expenditures. (In many countries doctors expect payment in cash.) You may prefer a policy that pays doctors or hospitals directly rather than you having to pay on the spot and claim later. If you have to claim later, make sure you keep all documentation. Some policies ask you to call (reverse charges) a centre in your home country, where an immediate assessment of your problem is made. Some policies offer a range of medical-expense options; the higher ones are chiefly for countries that have extremely high medical costs, such as the USA.

VACCINATIONS

Specialised travel medicine clinics are your best source of information; they stock all available vaccines and will be able to give recommendations specifically for you and your trip. The doctors will take into account factors such as past vaccination history, the length of your trip, activities you may be undertaking and underlying medical conditions, such as pregnancy.

RECOMMENDED VACCINATIONS

The World Health Organization (WHO) recommends the following vaccinations for travellers to Southeast Asia:

Adult diphtheria and tetanus Single booster recommended if you haven't had one in the previous 10 years. Side effects include a sore arm and fever.

Hepatitis A Provides almost 100% protection for up to a year; a booster after 12 months provides at least another 20 years' protection. Mild side effects such as a headache and a sore arm occur in 5% to 10% of people.

Hepatitis B Now considered routine for most travellers. Given as three shots over six months. A rapid schedule is also available, as is a combined vaccination with Hepatitis A. Side effects are mild and uncommon, usually a headache and a sore arm. Lifetime protection occurs in 95% of people.

Measles, mumps and rubella (MMR) Two doses of MMR are required unless you have had the diseases. Occasionally a rash and a flulike illness can develop a week after receiving the vaccine. Many young adults require a booster.

Polio Only one booster is required as an adult for lifetime protection. Inactivated polio vaccine is safe during pregnancy.

Typhoid Recommended unless your trip is less than a week long and is only to developed cities. The vaccine offers around 70% protection, lasts for two to three years and comes as a single shot. Tablets are also available. However, the injection is usually recommended as it has fewer side effects. A sore arm and fever may occur.

Varicella If you haven't had chickenpox, discuss this vaccination with your doctor.

The following immunisations are recommended for long-term travellers (more than one month) or those at special risk:

Japanese B Encephalitis Three injections in all. A booster is recommended after two years. A sore arm and headache are the most common side effects, although a rare allergic reaction comprising hives and swelling can occur up to 10 days after any of the three doses.

Meningitis Single injection. There are two types of vaccination: the quadrivalent vaccine gives two to three years' protection, while the meningitis group C vaccine gives around 10 years' protection. Recommended for long-term backpackers aged under 25.

Rabies Three injections in all. A booster after one year will then provide 10 years' protection. Side effects are rare – occasionally a headache and a sore arm.

Tuberculosis (TB) A complex issue. It is usually recommended that long-term adult travellers have a TB skin test before and after travel, rather than vaccination. Only one vaccine is given in a lifetime.

Required Vaccinations

The only vaccine required by international regulations is for yellow fever. Proof of vaccination will be required only if you have visited a country in the yellow-fever zone within the six days before entering Southeast Asia. If you are travelling to Southeast Asia from Africa or South America you should check to see if you require proof of vaccination.

Most vaccines don't produce immunity until at least two weeks after they're given, so visit a doctor four to eight weeks before departure. Ask your doctor for an International Certificate of Vaccination (otherwise known as the yellow booklet), which will list all the vaccinations you've received.

MEDICAL CHECKLIST

Recommended items for a personal medical kit:

- antibacterial cream, eg mupirocin
- antibiotic for skin infections, eg amoxicillin/clavulanate or cephalexin
- antibiotics for diarrhoea, such as norfloxacin or ciprofloxacin; azithromycin for bacterial diarrhoea; tinidazole for giardiasis or amoebic dysentery
- antifungal cream, eg clotrimazole
- antihistamine, such as cetirizine for daytime and promethazine for night
- anti-inflammatory such as ibuprofen
- antiseptic, eg Betadine
- antispasmodic for stomach cramps, eg Buscopan
- contraceptives
- decongestant, eg pseudoephedrine
- DEET-based insect repellent

- diarrhoea treatment; consider bringing an oral rehydration solution (eg Gastrolyte), diarrhoea 'stopper' (eg loperamide) and antinausea medication (eg prochlorperazine)
- first-aid items such as scissors, plasters, bandages, gauze, thermometer (but not one with mercury), sterile needles and syringes, safety pins and tweezers
- indigestion medication, eg Quick Eze or Mylanta
- iodine tablets (unless you are pregnant or have a thyroid problem) to purify water
- laxative, eg Coloxyl
- migraine medication; sufferers should take their personal medicine
- paracetamol
- permethrin to impregnate clothing and mosquito nets
- steroid cream for allergic or itchy rashes, eg 1% to 2% hydrocortisone
- sunscreen and hat
- throat lozenges
- thrush (vaginal yeast infection) treatment, eg Clotrimazole pessaries or Diflucan tablet
- Ural or equivalent if you're prone to urine infections.

INTERNET RESOURCES

There is a wealth of travel-health advice on the internet. For further information, **Lonely Planet** (www.lonelyplanet.com) is a good place to start. The **World Health Organization** (www.who.int/ith) publishes a superb book called *International Travel & Health,* which is revised annually and is available online at no cost. Another website of general interest is **MD Travel Health** (www.mdtravelhealth.com), which provides complete travel-health recommendations for every country and is updated daily. The **Centers for Disease Control & Prevention** (CDC; www.cdc.gov) website also has good general information.

FURTHER READING

Lonely Planet's *Healthy Travel – Asia & India* is a handy pocket-size book that is packed with useful information, including pretrip planning, emergency first aid, immunisation and disease information, and what to do if you get sick on the road. Other recommended references include *Traveller's Health* by Dr Richard Dawood and *Travelling Well* by Dr Deborah Mills – check out www.travellingwell.com.au.

IN TRANSIT

DEEP VEIN THROMBOSIS (DVT)

Deep vein thrombosis (DVT) occurs when blood clots form in the legs during plane flights, chiefly because of prolonged immobility. The longer the flight, the greater the risk. Although most blood clots are reabsorbed uneventfully, some may break off and travel through the blood vessels to the lungs, where they may cause life-threatening complications.

The chief symptom of DVT is swelling of or pain in the foot, ankle or calf, usually but not always on just one side. When a blood clot travels to the lungs, it may cause chest pain and difficulty in breathing. Travellers with any of these symptoms should immediately seek medical attention.

To prevent the development of DVT on long flights walk about the cabin, perform isometric compressions of the leg muscles (ie contract the leg muscles while sitting), drink plenty of fluids and avoid alcohol.

JET LAG & MOTION SICKNESS

Jet lag is common when crossing more than five time zones; it causes symptoms including insomnia, fatigue, malaise or nausea. To avoid jet lag, try drinking plenty of (nonalcoholic) fluids and eating light meals. Upon arrival seek exposure to natural sunlight and readjust your schedule (for meals, sleep etc) as soon as possible.

Antihistamines such as dimenhydrinate (Dramamine) and meclizine (Antivert or Bonine) are usually the first choice for treating motion sickness. Their main side effect is drowsiness. A herbal alternative is ginger, which works like a charm for some people.

IN SOUTHEAST ASIA

AVAILABILITY OF HEALTH CARE

Most capital cities in Southeast Asia now have clinics that cater specifically to travellers and expats. These clinics are more expensive than local medical facilities but offer a superior standard of care. Additionally, they understand the local system and are aware of the safest local hospitals and best specialists. They can also liaise with insurance companies should you require evacuation. Recommended clinics are listed under

Information in the destination sections of country chapters in this book.

It is difficult to find reliable medical care in rural areas. Your embassy and insurance company are good contacts.

Self-treatment may be appropriate if your problem is minor (eg traveller's diarrhoea), you are carrying the appropriate medication and you cannot attend a recommended clinic. If you think you may have a serious disease, especially malaria, do not waste time – travel to the nearest quality facility to receive attention. It is always better to be assessed by a doctor than to rely on self-treatment.

Buying medication over the counter is not recommended, as fake medications and poorly stored or out-of-date drugs are common.

The standard of care in Southeast Asia varies from country to country:

Brunei General care is reasonable. There is no local medical university, so expats and foreign-trained locals run the health-care system. Serious or complex cases are better managed in Singapore, but adequate primary health care and stabilisation is available.

Cambodia There are international clinics in Phnom Penh and Siem Reap and an NGO-run surgical hospital in Battambang that provide primary care and emergency stabilisation. Elsewhere government hospitals should be avoided because they lack properly trained staff, equipment and proper hygiene. For more serious conditions, including dengue fever, it may be advisable to be evacuated to Bangkok.

East Timor No private clinics. The government hospital is basic and should be avoided. Contact your embassy or insurance company for advice.

Indonesia Local medical care in general is not yet up to international standards. Foreign doctors are not allowed to work in Indonesia, but some clinics catering to foreigners have 'international advisers'. Almost all Indonesian doctors work at government hospitals during the day and in private practices at night. This means that private hospitals often don't have their best staff available during the day. Serious cases are evacuated to Australia or Singapore.

Laos There are no good facilities in Laos; the nearest acceptable facilities are in northern Thailand. The Australian Embassy Clinic in Vientiane treats citizens of Commonwealth countries.

Malaysia Medical care in the major centres is good, and most problems can be adequately dealt with in Kuala Lumpur.

Myanmar (Burma) Local medical care is dismal and local hospitals should be used only in desperation. There is an international medical clinic in Yangon (Rangoon). Contact your embassy for advice.

Philippines Good medical care is available in most major cities.

Singapore Has excellent medical facilities, and it acts as the referral centre for most of Southeast Asia.

Thailand There are some very good facilities in Thailand, particularly in Bangkok. After Singapore this is the city of choice for expats living in Southeast Asia who require specialised care.

Vietnam Government hospitals are overcrowded and basic. In order to treat foreigners, the facility needs to obtain a special licence, and so far only a few have been provided. The private clinics in Hanoi and Ho Chi Minh City should be your first port of call. They are familiar with the local resources and can organise evacuations if necessary.

INFECTIOUS DISEASES

Cutaneous Larva Migrans

Risk areas All countries except Singapore.

This disease, caused by dog hookworm, is particularly common on the beaches of Thailand. The rash starts as a small lump, then slowly spreads in a linear fashion. It is intensely itchy, especially at night. It is easily treated with medications and should not be cut out or frozen.

Dengue

Risk areas All countries.

This mosquito-borne disease is becoming increasingly problematic throughout Southeast Asia, especially in the cities. As there is no vaccine available it can be prevented only by avoiding mosquito bites. The mosquito that carries dengue bites day and night, so use insect-avoidance measures at all times. Symptoms include high fever, severe headache and body ache (dengue used to be known as breakbone fever). Some people develop a rash and experience diarrhoea. Thailand's southern islands are particularly high risk. There is no specific treatment, just rest and paracetamol – do not take aspirin as it increases the likelihood of haemorrhaging. See a doctor to be diagnosed and monitored.

Filariasis

Risk areas All countries except Singapore.

This mosquito-borne disease is very common in the local population, yet very rare in travellers. Mosquito-avoidance measures are the best way to prevent this disease.

Hepatitis A

Risk areas All countries.

A problem throughout the region, this food- and waterborne virus infects the liver, causing jaundice (yellow skin and eyes), nausea and

AVIAN INFLUENZA (BIRD FLU)

Six Southeast Asian countries (Cambodia, Indonesia, Laos, Thailand, Vietnam and Myanmar), plus China, Japan and South Korea, have reported outbreaks of avian influenza (bird flu). The strain in question, known as 'Influenza A H5N1' or simply 'the H5N1 virus', is a highly contagious form of avian influenza that has spread as far as Europe to the west. The peak of the outbreaks occurred in 2005 but the virus continues to affect poultry populations in the region as well as individuals who have come in contact with infected animals.

The main risk is to people who directly handle infected birds, or come into contact with contaminated bird faeces or carcasses. Because heat kills the virus, there is no risk of infection from cooked poultry.

There is no clear evidence that the H5N1 virus can be transmitted between humans. However, the main fear is that this highly adaptable virus may mutate and be passed between humans, perhaps leading to a worldwide influenza pandemic. Poultry vaccines are in various states of development and deployment throughout the region, though some have proven ineffective on some strains of the virus. There are also human vaccines with various effectiveness rates that are being stockpiled.

Thus far, however, infection rates are limited and the risk to travellers is low. Travellers to the region should avoid contact with any birds and should ensure that any poultry is thoroughly cooked before consumption.

lethargy. There is no specific treatment for hepatitis A; you just need to allow time for the liver to heal. All travellers to Southeast Asia should be vaccinated against hepatitis A.

Hepatitis B

Risk areas All countries.

The only sexually transmitted disease that can be prevented by vaccination, hepatitis B is spread by body fluids. In some parts of Southeast Asia, up to 20% of the population carry hepatitis B, and usually are unaware of it. The long-term consequences can include liver cancer and cirrhosis.

Hepatitis E

Risk areas All countries.

Hepatitis E is transmitted through contaminated food and water, and has similar symptoms to hepatitis A but is far less common. It is a severe problem in pregnant women, and can result in the death of both mother and baby. There is currently no vaccine, and prevention is by following safe eating and drinking guidelines.

HIV

Risk areas All countries.

HIV is now one of the most common causes of death in people under the age of 50 in Thailand. The Southeast Asian countries with the worst and most rapidly increasing HIV problem are Cambodia, Myanmar, Thailand and Vietnam. Heterosexual sex is now the main method of transmission in these countries.

Influenza

Risk areas All countries.

Present year-round in the tropics, influenza (flu) symptoms include high fever, muscle aches, runny nose, cough and sore throat. It can be very severe in people over the age of 65, and in those with underlying medical conditions such as heart disease or diabetes; vaccination is recommended for these individuals. There is no specific treatment, just rest and paracetamol.

Japanese B Encephalitis

Risk areas All countries except Singapore.

While rare in travellers, this viral disease, transmitted by mosquitoes, infects at least 50,000 locals each year. Most cases of the disease occur in rural areas and vaccination is recommended for travellers spending more than one month outside cities. There is no treatment – a third of infected people will die while another third will suffer permanent brain damage. Highest-risk areas in the region include Vietnam, Thailand and Indonesia.

Leptospirosis

Risk areas Thailand and Malaysia.

Leptospirosis is most commonly contracted after river rafting or canyoning. Early symptoms are very similar to the flu, and include headache and fever. The disease can vary from very mild to fatal. Diagnosis is through blood tests and it is easily treated with doxycycline.

Malaria

Risk areas All countries except Singapore and Brunei.

For such a serious and potentially deadly disease, there is an enormous amount of misinformation concerning malaria. You must get expert advice about whether your trip actually puts you at risk. Many parts of Southeast Asia, particularly city and resort areas, have minimal to no risk of malaria, and the risk of side effects from the prevention tablets may outweigh the risk of getting the disease. For most rural areas, however, the risk of contracting the disease far outweighs the risk of any side effects. Remember that malaria can be fatal. Before you travel, seek medical advice on the right medication and dosage for you.

Malaria is caused by a parasite transmitted by the bite of an infected mosquito. The most important symptom of malaria is fever, but general symptoms such as headache, diarrhoea, cough or chills may also occur. Diagnosis can only be made by taking a blood sample.

Two strategies should be combined to prevent malaria – mosquito avoidance and antimalarial medications. Most people who catch malaria are taking inadequate or no antimalarial medication.

Travellers are advised to prevent mosquito bites by taking the following steps:

- Use an insect repellent containing DEET on exposed skin. Wash this off at night, as long as you are sleeping under a mosquito net. Natural repellents such as citronella can be effective, but must be applied more frequently than products containing DEET.
- Sleep under a mosquito net that is impregnated with permethrin.
- Choose accommodation with screens and fans (if not air-conditioned).
- Impregnate clothing with permethrin when in high-risk areas.
- Wear long sleeves and trousers in light colours.
- Use mosquito coils.
- Spray your room with insect repellent before going out for your evening meal.

There are a variety of medications available. Derivatives of artesunate are not suitable as a preventive medication, although they are useful treatments under medical supervision.

The effectiveness of the chloroquine and paludrine combination is now limited in most of Southeast Asia. Common side effects include nausea (40% of people) and mouth ulcers. The combination is generally not recommended.

The daily doxycycline tablet is a broad-spectrum antibiotic that has the added benefit of helping to prevent a variety of tropical diseases, including leptospirosis, tickborne disease, typhus and meliodosis. The potential side effects include photosensitivity (a tendency to sunburn), thrush in women, indigestion, heartburn, nausea and interference with the contraceptive pill. More serious side effects include ulceration of the oesophagus – you can help prevent this by taking your tablet with a meal and a large glass of water, and by never lying down within half an hour of taking it. It must be taken for four weeks after leaving the risk area.

Lariam (mefloquine) has received much bad press, some of it justified, some not. This weekly tablet suits many people. Serious side effects are rare but include depression, anxiety, psychosis and seizures. Anyone with a history of depression, anxiety, other psychological disorders or epilepsy should not take Lariam. It is considered safe in the second and third trimesters of pregnancy. It is around 90% effective in most parts of Southeast Asia, but there is significant resistance in parts of northern Thailand, Laos and Cambodia. Tablets must be taken for four weeks after leaving the risk area.

Malarone is a combination of atovaquone and proguanil. Side effects are uncommon and mild, most commonly nausea and headache. It is the best tablet for scuba divers and for those on short trips to high-risk areas. It must be taken for one week after leaving the risk area.

A final option is to take no preventive medication but to have a supply of emergency medication should you develop the symptoms of malaria. This is less than ideal, and you'll need to get to a good medical facility within 24 hours of developing a fever. If you choose this option, the most effective and safest treatment is Malarone (four tablets once daily for three days). Other options include mefloquine and quinine, but the side effects of these drugs at treatment doses make them less desirable. Fansidar is no longer recommended.

Measles

Risk areas All countries except Singapore and Brunei.

Measles remains a problem in some parts of Southeast Asia. This highly contagious bacterial infection is spread via coughing and sneezing. Most people born before 1966 are immune as they had the disease during childhood. Measles starts with a high fever and rash, and can be complicated by pneumonia and brain disease. There is no specific treatment.

Meliodosis

Risk areas Thailand only.

This infection is contracted by skin contact with soil. It is rare in travellers, but in some parts of northeast Thailand up to 30% of the local population is infected. The symptoms are very similar to those experienced by tuberculosis sufferers. There is no vaccine but it can be treated with medications.

Rabies

Risk areas All countries except Singapore and Brunei.

Still a common problem in most parts of Southeast Asia, this uniformly fatal disease is spread by the bite or lick of an infected animal, most commonly a dog or monkey. You should seek medical advice immediately after any animal bite and commence postexposure treatment. Having a pretravel vaccination means the postbite treatment is greatly simplified. If an animal bites you, gently wash the wound with soap and water, and apply iodine-based antiseptic. If you are not prevaccinated you will need to receive rabies immunoglobulin as soon as possible.

Schistosomiasis

Risk areas Philippines, Vietnam and Sulawesi (Indonesia).

Schistosomiasis is a tiny parasite that enters your skin after you've been swimming in contaminated water. Travellers usually only get a light infection and hence have no symptoms. If you are concerned, you can be tested three months after exposure. On rare occasions, travellers may develop 'Katayama fever'. This occurs some weeks after exposure, as the parasite passes through the lungs and causes an allergic reaction; symptoms are coughing and fever. Schistosomiasis is easily treated with medications.

STDs

Risk areas All countries.

Sexually transmitted diseases most commonly found in Southeast Asia include herpes, warts, syphilis, gonorrhoea and chlamydia. People carrying these diseases often have no signs of infection. Condoms will prevent gonorrhoea and chlamydia but not warts or herpes. If after a sexual encounter you develop any rash, lumps, discharge or pain when passing urine, seek immediate medical attention. If you have been sexually active during your travels, have an STD check on your return home.

Strongyloides

Risk areas Cambodia, Myanmar and Thailand.

This parasite, transmitted by skin contact with soil, is common in travellers but rarely affects them. It is characterised by an unusual skin rash called *larva currens* – a linear rash on the trunk that comes and goes. Most people don't have other symptoms until their immune system becomes severely suppressed, when the parasite can cause an overwhelming infection. It can be treated with medications.

Tuberculosis

Risk areas All countries.

While TB is rare in travellers, any medical and aid workers and long-term travellers who have significant contact with the local population should take precautions. Vaccination is usually only given to children under five, but it is recommended that adults at risk have pre- and posttravel testing. The main symptoms are fever, cough, weight loss and tiredness.

Typhoid

Risk areas All countries except Singapore.

This serious bacterial infection is spread via food and water. It gives a high and slowly progressive fever and a headache, and may be accompanied by a dry cough and stomach pain. It is diagnosed by blood tests and treated with antibiotics. Vaccination is recommended for all travellers spending more than a week in Southeast Asia, or travelling outside the major cities. Be aware that vaccination is not 100% effective so you must still be careful with what you eat and drink.

DRINKING WATER

- Never drink tap water.
- Bottled water is generally safe – check the seal is intact at purchase.
- Avoid ice.
- Avoid fresh juices – they may have been watered down.
- Boiling water is the most efficient method of purifying it.
- The best chemical purifier is iodine. It should not be used by pregnant women or those with thyroid problems.
- Water filters should also filter out viruses. Ensure your filter has a chemical barrier such as iodine and a small pore size, eg less than four microns.

Typhus

Risk areas All countries except Singapore.

Murine typhus is spread by the bite of a flea, whereas scrub typhus is spread via a mite. These diseases are rare in travellers. Symptoms include fever, muscle pains and a rash. You can avoid these diseases by following general insect-avoidance measures. Doxycycline will also prevent them.

TRAVELLER'S DIARRHOEA

Traveller's diarrhoea is by far the most common problem that affects travellers – between 30% and 50% of people will suffer from it within two weeks of starting their trip. In over 80% of cases, traveller's diarrhoea is caused by bacteria (there are numerous potential culprits), and therefore responds promptly to treatment with antibiotics. Treatment will depend on your situation – how sick you are, how quickly you need to get better, where you are etc.

Traveller's diarrhoea is defined as the passage of more than three watery bowel actions within 24 hours, plus at least one other symptom such as fever, cramps, nausea, vomiting or feeling generally unwell.

Treatment consists of staying well hydrated; rehydration solutions such as Gastrolyte are the best for this. Antibiotics such as norfloxacin, ciprofloxacin or azithromycin will kill the bacteria quickly.

Loperamide is just a 'stopper' and doesn't get to the cause of the problem. It can be helpful, for example, if you have to go on a long bus ride. Don't take loperamide if you have a fever, or blood in your stools. Seek medical attention quickly if you do not respond to an appropriate antibiotic.

Amoebic Dysentery

Amoebic dysentery is very rare in travellers but is often misdiagnosed by poor-quality labs in Southeast Asia. Symptoms are similar to bacterial diarrhoea, ie fever, bloody diarrhoea and generally feeling unwell. You should always seek reliable medical care if you have blood in your diarrhoea. Treatment involves two drugs: tinidazole or metronidazole to kill the parasite in your gut, and then a second drug to kill the cysts. If left untreated, complications such as liver or gut abscesses can occur.

Giardiasis

Giardia lamblia is a relatively common parasite in travellers. Symptoms include nausea, bloating, excess gas, fatigue and intermittent diarrhoea. 'Eggy' burps are often attributed solely to giardiasis, but work in Nepal has shown that they are not specific to this infection. The parasite will eventually go away if left untreated but this can take months. The treatment of choice is tinidazole, with metronidazole being a second option.

ENVIRONMENTAL HAZARDS

Air Pollution

Air pollution, particularly vehicle pollution, is an increasing problem in most of Southeast Asia's major cities. If you have severe respiratory problems, speak with your doctor before travelling to any heavily polluted urban centres. This pollution also causes minor respiratory problems such as sinusitis, dry throat and irritated eyes. If troubled by the pollution, leave the city for a few days and get some fresh air.

Diving

Divers and surfers should seek specialised advice before they travel to ensure their medical kit contains treatment for coral cuts and tropical ear infections, as well as the standard problems. Divers should ensure their insurance covers them for decompression illness – get specialised dive insurance through an organisation such as **Divers Alert Network** (DAN; www.danseap.org). Have a dive medical before you leave your home country; there are certain medical conditions that are incompatible with diving, and economic considerations may override health considerations for some dive operators in Southeast Asia.

Food

Eating in restaurants is the biggest risk factor for contracting traveller's diarrhoea. Ways to avoid diarrhoea include eating only freshly cooked food, and avoiding shellfish and food that has been sitting around in buffets. Peel all fruit, cook vegetables, and soak salads in iodine water for at least 20 minutes. Eat in busy restaurants with a high turnover of customers.

Heat

Many parts of Southeast Asia are hot and humid throughout the year. For most people it takes at least two weeks to adapt to the hot climate. Swelling of the feet and ankles is common, as are muscle cramps caused by excessive sweating. You can prevent these by avoiding dehydration and excessive activity in the heat; you should also take it easy when you first arrive. Don't eat salt tablets (they aggravate the gut), but drinking rehydration solution or eating salty food helps. Treat cramps by stopping activity, resting, rehydrating with double-strength rehydration solution and gently stretching.

Dehydration is the main contributor to heat exhaustion. Symptoms include weakness, headache, irritability, nausea or vomiting, sweaty skin, a fast pulse, and a normal or slightly elevated body temperature. Treatment involves getting out of the heat, fanning the person and applying cool wet cloths to the skin, laying the person flat with their legs raised, and rehydrating them with water containing a quarter of a teaspoon of salt per litre. Recovery is usually rapid, though it is common to feel weak afterwards.

Heat stroke is a serious medical emergency. Symptoms come on suddenly and include weakness, nausea, a hot dry body with a body temperature of over 41°C, dizziness, confusion, loss of coordination, seizures, and eventually collapse and loss of consciousness. Seek medical help and commence cooling by getting the person out of the heat, removing their clothes, fanning them and applying cool wet cloths or ice to their body, especially to the groin and armpits.

Prickly heat is a common skin rash in the tropics caused by sweat being trapped under the skin. The result is an itchy rash of tiny lumps. Treat by moving out of the heat and into an air-conditioned area for a few hours and by having cool showers. Creams and ointments clog the skin so they should be avoided. Locally bought prickly-heat powder can be helpful.

Tropical fatigue is common in long-term expats based in the tropics. It's rarely due to disease and is caused by the climate, inadequate mental rest, excessive alcohol intake and the demands of daily work in a different culture.

Insect Bites & Stings

Bedbugs don't carry disease but their bites are very itchy. They live in the cracks of furniture and walls, and then migrate to the bed at night to feed on you. You can treat the itch with an antihistamine.

Lice inhabit various parts of your body, but most commonly your head and pubic area. Transmission is via close contact with an infected person. Lice can be difficult to treat and you may need numerous applications of an antilice shampoo. Pubic lice are usually contracted from sexual contact.

Ticks are contracted after walking in rural areas. They are commonly found behind the ears, on the belly and in armpits. If you have had a tick bite and experience symptoms such as a rash at the site of the bite or elsewhere, or fever or muscle aches, you should see a doctor. Doxycycline prevents tickborne diseases.

Leeches are found in humid rainforest areas. They do not transmit any disease but their bites are often intensely itchy for weeks afterwards and can easily become infected. Apply an iodine-based antiseptic to any leech bite to help prevent infection.

Bee and wasp stings mainly cause problems for people who are allergic to them. Anyone with a serious bee or wasp allergy should carry an injection of adrenaline (eg an Epipen) for emergency treatment. For others, pain is the main problem – apply ice to the sting and take painkillers.

Most jellyfish in Southeast Asian waters are not dangerous, just irritating. First aid for jellyfish stings involves pouring vinegar onto the affected area to neutralise the poison. Do not rub sand or water onto the stings. Take painkillers, and if you feel ill in any way after being stung seek medical advice. Take local advice if there are dangerous jellyfish around and keep out of the water.

Parasites

Numerous parasites are common in local populations in Southeast Asia; however, most of these are rare in travellers. The two rules for avoiding parasitic infections are to wear shoes and to avoid eating raw food, especially fish, pork and vegetables. A number of parasites are transmitted via the skin by walking barefoot, including strongyloides, hookworm and cutaneous *larva migrans*.

Skin Problems

Fungal rashes are common in humid climates. There are two common fungal rashes that tend to affect travellers. The first occurs in moist areas that get less air, such as the groin, armpits and between the toes. It starts as a red patch that slowly spreads and is usually itchy. Treatment involves keeping the skin dry, avoiding chafing and using an antifungal cream such as clotrimazole or Lamisil. *Tinea versicolor* is also common – this fungus causes small, light-coloured patches, most commonly on the back, chest and shoulders. Consult a doctor.

Cuts and scratches become easily infected in humid climates. Take meticulous care of any cuts and scratches to prevent complications such as abscesses. Immediately wash all wounds in clean water and apply antiseptic. If you develop signs of infection (increasing pain and redness), see a doctor. Divers and surfers should be particularly careful with coral cuts as they can be easily infected.

Snakes

Southeast Asia is home to many species of both poisonous and harmless snakes. Assume that all snakes are poisonous and never try to catch one. Always wear boots and long pants if walking in an area that may have snakes. First aid in the event of a snakebite involves pressure immobilisation using an elastic bandage firmly wrapped around the affected limb, starting at the bite site and working up towards the chest. The bandage should not be so tight that the circulation is cut off, and the fingers or toes should be kept free so the circulation can be checked. Immobilise the limb with a splint and carry the victim to medical attention. Do not use tourniquets or try to suck the venom out. Antivenin is available for most species.

Sunburn

Even on a cloudy day sunburn can occur rapidly. Always use a strong sunscreen (at least factor 30), making sure to reapply after a swim, and always wear a wide-brimmed hat and sunglasses outdoors. Avoid lying in the sun during the hottest part of the day (10am to 2pm). If you become sunburnt, stay out of the sun until you have recovered, apply cool compresses and take painkillers for the discomfort. One per cent hydrocortisone cream applied twice daily is also helpful.

WOMEN'S HEALTH

Pregnant women should receive specialised advice before travelling. The ideal time to travel is in the second trimester (between 16 and 28 weeks), when the risk of pregnancy-related problems is at its lowest and women generally feel at their best. During the first trimester there is a risk of miscarriage and in the third trimester complications such as premature labour and high blood pressure are possible. It's wise to travel with a companion. Always carry a list of quality medical facilities available at your destination and ensure you continue your standard antenatal care at these facilities. Avoid rural travel in areas with poor transport and medical facilities. Most of all, ensure travel insurance covers all pregnancy-related possibilities.

Malaria is a high-risk disease during pregnancy. WHO recommends that pregnant women do *not* travel to areas with chloroquine-resistant malaria. None of the more effective antimalarial drugs are completely safe in pregnancy.

Traveller's diarrhoea can quickly lead to dehydration and result in inadequate blood flow to the placenta. Many of the drugs used to treat various diarrhoea bugs are not recommended in pregnancy. Azithromycin is considered safe.

In the urban areas of Southeast Asia, supplies of sanitary products are readily available. Birth-control options may be limited so bring adequate supplies of your own form of contraception. Heat, humidity and antibiotics can all contribute to thrush. Treatment is with antifungal creams and pessaries such as clotrimazole. A practical alternative is a single tablet of fluconazole (Diflucan). Urinary tract infections can be precipitated by dehydration or long bus journeys without toilet stops; bring suitable antibiotics.

TRADITIONAL MEDICINE

Throughout Southeast Asia, traditional medical systems are widely practised. There is a big difference between these traditional healing systems and 'folk' medicine. Folk remedies should be avoided, as they often involve rather dubious procedures with potential complications. In comparison, healing systems such as traditional Chinese medicine are well respected, and aspects of them are being increasingly utilised by Western medical practitioners.

All traditional Asian medical systems identify a vital life force, and see blockage or imbalance of this force as causing disease. Techniques such as herbal medicines, massage and acupuncture are used to bring this vital force back into balance, or to maintain balance. These therapies are best used for treating chronic disease such as chronic fatigue, arthritis, irritable bowel syndrome and some chronic skin conditions. Traditional medicines should be avoided for treating serious acute infections such as malaria.

Be aware that 'natural' doesn't always mean 'safe', and there can be drug interactions between herbal medicines and Western medicines. If you are using both systems, ensure you inform each practitioner of what the other has prescribed.

Language

CONTENTS

This language guide offers useful words and phrases for basic communication in the nine main languages spoken in the region covered by this book. For more comprehensive coverage of these languages we recommend Lonely Planet phrasebooks: the *Southeast Asia* phrasebook for Burmese, Khmer, Lao, Thai and Vietnamese, and the *East Timor, Filipino, Indonesian* and *Malay* phrasebooks for the other languages.

BAHASA INDONESIA

ACCOMMODATION

bathroom	*kamar mandi*
bed	*tempat tidur*
guesthouse	*losmen*
toilet	*kamar kecil*
Is there a room available?	*Adakah kamar kosong?*
May I see the room?	*Boleh saya melihat kamar?*
one night	*satu malam*
two nights	*dua malam*

CONVERSATION & ESSENTIALS

Good morning.	*Selamat pagi.*
Good day.	*Selamat siang.*
Good afternoon.	*Selamat sore.*
Good evening/night.	*Selamat malam.*
Goodbye. (to person staying)	*Selamat tinggal.*
Goodbye. (to person leaving)	*Selamat jalan.*
How are you?	*Apa kabar?*
I'm fine.	*Kabar baik.*
Please.	*Tolong.*
Thank you (very much).	*Terima kasih (banyak).*
Yes.	*Ya.*
No.	*Tidak/Bukan.*
Excuse me.	*Maaf/Permisi.*
I don't understand.	*Saya tidak mengerti.*
Do you speak English?	*Bisa berbicara bahasa Inggris?*

EMERGENCIES

Help!	*Tolong!*
Call a doctor!	*Panggil dokter!*
Call the police!	*Panggil polisi!*
I'm lost.	*Saya kesasar.*
Go away!	*Pergi!*

FOOD & DRINK

I'm a vegetarian./ I eat only vegetables.	*Saya hanya makan sayuran.*

beef	*daging*
beer	*bir*
chicken	*ayam*
coffee	*kopi*
crab	*kepiting*
drinking water	*air minum/air putih*
egg	*telur*
fish	*ikan*
food	*makanan*
fried noodles	*mie goreng*
fried rice	*nasi goreng*
fried vegetables	*cap cai*
milk	*susu*
mixed vegetables	*sayur-sayuran*
orange juice	*air jeruk*
pork	*babi*
potato	*kentang*
prawns	*udang-udang*
rice with odds & ends	*nasi campur*
soup	*soto*
tea with sugar	*teh manis/teh gula*
tea without sugar	*teh pahit*
white rice	*nasi putih*

NUMBERS

1	*satu*
2	*dua*
3	*tiga*
4	*empat*

5	*lima*
6	*enam*
7	*tujuh*
8	*delapan*
9	*sembilan*
10	*sepuluh*
11	*sebelas*
20	*duapuluh*
21	*duapuluh satu*
30	*tigapuluh*
50	*limapuluh*
100	*seratus*
1000	*seribu*
2000	*duaribu*

SHOPPING & SERVICES

Where is a/the ...? *Dimana ...?*
- **bank** *bank*
- **post office** *kantor pos*
- **public telephone** *telepon umum*
- **public toilet** *WC umum*
- **tourist office** *dinas pariwisata*

How much is it? *Berapa harganya ini?*
expensive *mahal*
open/close *buka/tutup*

TIME & DAYS

When? *Kapan?*
At what time ...? *Pada jam berapa ...?*
yesterday *kemarin*
today *hari ini*
tonight *malam ini*
tomorrow *besok*

Monday *hari Senin*
Tuesday *hari Selasa*
Wednesday *hari Rabu*
Thursday *hari Kamis*
Friday *hari Jumat*
Saturday *hari Sabtu*
Sunday *hari Minggu*

TRANSPORT

What time does the ... leave/arrive? *Jam berapa ... berangkat/tiba?*
- **boat** *kapal*
- **bus** *bis/bus*
- **train** *kereta api*

bus station *setasiun bis*
ticket *karcis/tiket*

Directions

I want to go to ... *Saya mau pergi ke ...*
How far? *Berapa jauh?*
near/far *dekat/jauh*
straight ahead *terus*
left/right *kiri/kanan*

BAHASA MALAYSIA

ACCOMMODATION

bed *tempat tidur*
expensive *mahal*
guesthouse *losmen*
hotel *hotel*
room *bilik*

Is there a room available? *Ada bilik kosong?*
How much is it per night/person? *Berapa harga satu malam/orang?*
May I see the room? *Boleh saya lihat biliknya?*

CONVERSATION & ESSENTIALS

Good morning. *Selamat pagi.*
Good day. (around midday) *Selamat tengah hari.*
Good evening. *Selamat petang.*
Good night. *Selamat malam.*
Goodbye. (to person staying) *Selamat tinggal.*
Goodbye. (to person leaving) *Selamat jalan.*
Yes. *Ya.*
No. *Tidak.*
Please. *Tolong/Silakan.*
Thank you (very much). *Terima kasih (banyak).*
You're welcome. *Kembali.*
Sorry./Pardon. *Maaf.*
Excuse me. *Maafkan saya.*
Do you speak English? *Bolehkah anda berbicara bahasa Inggeris?*
I don't understand. *Saya tidak faham.*

EMERGENCIES

Help! *Tolong!*
Call a doctor! *Panggil doktor!*
Call the police! *Panggil polis!*
I'm lost. *Saya sesat.*
Go away! *Pegi/Belah!*

FOOD & DRINK

I'm a vegetarian./I eat only vegetables. *Saya hanya makan sayuran.*

beef	*daging lembu*
boiled rice	*nasi putih*
chicken	*ayam*
coffee	*kopi*
crab	*ketam*
drinking water	*air minum*
egg	*telur*
fish	*ikan*
fried noodles	*mee goreng*
fried rice	*nasi goreng*
fried vegetables	*cap cai*
milk	*susu*
orange juice	*air jeruk/oren*
pork	*babi*
potatoes	*kentang*
prawns	*udang*
rice with odds & ends	*nasi campur*
soup	*sup*
sugar	*gula*
tea	*teh*
vegetables	*sayur-sayuran*
vegetables only	*sayur saja*

NUMBERS

1	*satu*
2	*dua*
3	*tiga*
4	*empat*
5	*lima*
6	*enam*
7	*tujuh*
8	*delapan*
9	*sembilan*
10	*sepuluh*
11	*sebelas*
12	*dua belas*
13	*tiga belas*
20	*dua puluh*
21	*dua puluh satu*
30	*tiga puluh*
100	*seratus*
1000	*seribu*
2000	*dua ribu*

SHOPPING & SERVICES

Where is a/the ...?	*Di mana ada ...?*
bank	*bank*
hospital	*hospital*
post office	*pejabat pos*
public toilet	*tandas awam*
tourist office	*pejabat pelancong*

What time does it open/close?	*Pukul berapa buka/tutup?*
How much is it?	*Berapa harganya ini?*

TIME & DAYS

When?	*Bila?*
How long?	*Berapa lama?*
yesterday	*kelmarin*
today	*hari ini*
tomorrow	*besok*

Monday	*hari Isnin*
Tuesday	*hari Selasa*
Wednesday	*hari Rabu*
Thursday	*hari Kamis*
Friday	*hari Jumaat*
Saturday	*hari Sabtu*
Sunday	*hari minggu*

TRANSPORT

What time does the ... leave?	*Pukul berapakah ... berangkat?*
boat	*bot*
bus	*bas*
ship	*kapal*
train	*keretapi*

Directions

How can I get to ...?	*Bagaimana saya pergi ke ...?*
Go straight ahead.	*Jalan terus.*
Turn left/right.	*Belok kiri/kanan.*
here/there	*di sini/sana*
near/far	*dekat/jauh*

BURMESE (MYANMAR)

TONES & PRONUNCIATION

Like Thai, Lao and Vietnamese, Burmese is a tonal language, which means that changes in the relative pitch of the speaker's voice can affect the meaning of a word. There are three basic tones in Burmese:

high tone – produced with the voice tense and high-pitched; indicated by an acute accent, eg *ká* (dance)
high falling tone – starts with the voice high, then falls lower; indicated by a grave accent, eg *kà* (car)
low tone – the voice is relaxed and remains low; indicated by no accent, eg *ka* (shield)

Three other features important to Burmese pronunciation are:

a stopped syllable – with a high pitch, the voice is cut off suddenly to produce a glottal stop (similar to the 'non' sound in the middle of the exclamation 'oh-oh'); it's indicated in this guide by a 'q' after the vowel, eg *kaq* (join)

LANGUAGE

a weak syllable – only occurs on the vowel 'a', and is pronounced like the 'a' in 'ago'; indicated by a 'v' accent, eg *ălouk* (work)
aspirated consonants – pronounced with an audible puff of breath; indicated by an apostrophe after the consonant, eg *s'i* (cooking oil)

ACCOMMODATION

guesthouse	*tèh·k'o·gàn*
hotel	*ho·the*
May I see the room?	*ăk'àn cí·bayá·ze?*
How much is ...?	*... beh·lauq·lèh?*
a double room	*hnăyauq·k'an*
a single room	*tăyauq·k'an*
one night	*tăyeq*
two nights	*hnăyeq*

CONVERSATION & ESSENTIALS

Hello.	*min·găla·ba*
How are you?	*k'ămyà* (m)/*shin* (f) *ne·kaùn·yéh·là?*
I'm well.	*ne·kaùn·ba·deh*
Have you eaten?	*t'ămìn sà·pi·bi·là?*
I have eaten.	*sà·pì·ba·bi*
Thanks.	*cè·zù·bèh*
Thank you.	*cè·zù tin·ba·deh*
You're welcome.	*keiq·sá măshí·ba·bù*
Yes.	*houq·kéh*
No.	*măhouq·p'ù*
Do you speak English?	*k'ămyà* (m)/*shin* (f) *in·găleiq·zăgà lo pyàw·daq·thălà?*
I don't understand.	*nà·măleh·ba·bù*

EMERGENCIES

Help!	*keh·ba!*
Call a doctor!	*s'ăya·wun·go k'aw·pè·ba!*
Call an ambulance!	*lu·na·din·gà k'aw·pè·ba!*
I'm lost.	*làn pyauq·thwà·bi*
Go away!	*thwà·zàn!*

FOOD & DRINK

Is there a ... nearby?	*... di·nàh·ma shí·dhălà?*
Chinese restaurant	*tăyouq·s'ain*
food stall	*sà·thauq·s'ain*
noodle stall	*shàn·k'auk·swèh·zain*
restaurant	*sà·daw·s'eq*
breakfast	*măneq·sa*
lunch	*né·leh·za*
dinner	*nyá·za*
snack	*móun*
I can't eat meat.	*ăthà măsà·nain·bù*
beef	*ămèh*
bread	*paun·móun*
butter	*t'àw·baq*
chicken	*ceq·thà*
coffee	*kaw·fi*
egg (boiled)	*ceq·úb·youq*
egg (fried)	*ceq·ú·jaw*
fish	*ngà*
green tea	*lăp'eq·yeh·jàn*
hot (spicy)	*saq·deh*
noodles	*k'auq·s'wèh*
pork	*weq·thà*
rice (cooked)	*t'ămin*
soup	*hìn·jo*
sugar	*thăjà*
toast	*paun·móun·gin*
vegetables	*hìn·dhì·hìn·yweq*
vegetarian	*theq·thaq·luq*
water	*ye*
water (boiled, cold)	*ye·jeq·è*
water (bottled)	*thán·ye*

NUMBERS

1	*tiq/tă*
2	*hniq/hnă*
3	*thòun*
4	*lè*
5	*ngà*
6	*c'auq*
7	*k'ú·hniq/k'ú·hnă*
8	*shiq*
9	*kò*
10	*tă·s'eh*
11	*s'éh·tiq*
12	*s'éh·hniq*
20	*hnăs'eh*
35	*thòun·zéh·ngà*
100	*tăya*
1000	*tă·t'aun*
10,000	*tă·thàun*
100,000	*tă·thèin/lakh*

SHOPPING & SERVICES

Where is a/the ...?	*... beh·hma·lèh?*
bank	*ban·daiq*
hospital	*s'è·youn*
market	*zè*
pharmacy	*s'è·zain*
post office	*sa·daiq*
Where can I buy ...?	*... beh·hma weh·yá·mălèh?*
Do you have ...?	*... shí·là*
How much is ...?	*... beh·lauq·lèh?*
cheap	*zè·pàw·deh*
expensive	*zè·cì·deh*

TIME & DAYS

yesterday	*măné·gá*
today	*di·né*
tomorrow	*măneq·p'yan*
Monday	*tănìn·la·né*
Tuesday	*in·ga·né*
Wednesday	*bouq·dăhù·né*
Thursday	*ca·dhăbădè·né*
Friday	*thauq·ca·né*
Saturday	*săne·né*
Sunday	*tănìn·gănwe·né*

TRANSPORT

Where is the ...?	*... beh·hma·lèh?*
bus station	*baq·săkà·geiq*
railway station	*bu·da·youn*
riverboat jetty	*thìn·bàw·zeiq*
When will the ... leave?	*... be·hăc'ein t'weq mălèh?*
bicycle	*seq·bèin*
bus	*baq·săkà*
motorcycle	*mo·ta s'ain·keh*
rickshaw/sidecar	*s'aiq·kà*
riverboat	*thìn·bàw*
taxi	*ăhngà·kà*
train	*mì·yăt'à*

Directions

How do I get to ...?	*... ko beh·lo thwà·yá·dhălèh?*
Is it far?	*wè·dhălà?*
Is it near?	*di·nà·hma·là?*
straight (ahead)	*téh·déh*
left/right	*beh·beq/nya·beq*

FILIPINO

ACCOMMODATION

camping ground	*kampingan*
cheap hotel	*múrang hotél*
guesthouse	*báhay pára sa nga turist*
price	*halagá*
Do you have any rooms available?	*May bakánte hó ba kayo?*
How much for one night?	*Magkáno hó ba ang báyad pára sa isang gabi?*

CONVERSATION & ESSENTIALS

Hello.	*Haló.*
Good morning.	*Magandáng umága.*
Good evening.	*Magandáng gabí.*
Welcome/Farewell.	*Mabúhay.*
Goodbye.	*Paálam.*
Thank you.	*Salámat hô.*
Excuse me.	*Mawaláng-galang nga hô.*
Yes.	*Oó.*
No.	*Hindí.*
Do you speak English?	*Marunong ba kayóng mag-Inglés?*
I don't understand.	*Hindí ko hô náiintindihán.*

EMERGENCIES

Help!	*Saklolo!*
Where are the toilets?	*Násaán ang kubeta?*
Go away!	*Umalís ka!*
Call ...!	*Tumawag ka ng ...!*
a doctor	*doktór*
the police	*pulís*

FOOD & DRINK

breakfast	*almusal/agahan*
lunch	*tanghalian*
dinner	*hapunan*
snack	*meryenda*
I'm a vegetarian.	*Gulay lamang ang kinákain ko.*
beer	*serbésa*
boiled water	*pinakuluáng túbig*
coffee	*kapé*
food	*pagkaín*
milk	*gátas*
restaurant	*restorán*
salt	*ásin*
sugar	*asúkal*
(cup of) tea	*(isang tásang) tsaá*
vegetables	*gulay*
water	*túbig*

NUMBERS

English numbers are often used for prices.

1	*isá*
2	*dalawá*
3	*tatló*
4	*apát*
5	*limá*
6	*ánim*
7	*pitó*
8	*waló*
9	*siyám*
10	*sampú*

11	*labíng-isá*
12	*labíndalawá*
20	*dalawampû*
30	*tatlumpû*
100	*sandaán*
1000	*isáng libo*

SHOPPING & SERVICES

Where is a/the ...?	*Saán hô may ...?*
bank	*bangko*
market	*palengle*
post office	*pos opis*
public telephone	*telépono*
public toilet	*pálikuran*

How much?	*Magkáno?*
too expensive	*mahál*

TIME & DAYS

What time is it?	*Anong óras na?*
yesterday	*kahápon*
today	*ngayon*
tomorrow	*búkas*

Monday	*Lunes*
Tuesday	*Martes*
Wednesday	*Miyérkolés*
Thursday	*Huwebes*
Friday	*Biyernes*
Saturday	*Sábado*
Sunday	*Linggó*

TRANSPORT

Where is the ...?	*Násaan ang ...?*
bus station	*terminal ng bus*
road to ...	*daan papuntang ...*
train station	*terminal ng tren*

What time does the bus leave/arrive?	*Anong óras áalis/dárating ang bus?*

Directions

Is it far/near from here?	*Maláyó/Malápit ba díto?*
straight ahead	*dirétso lámang*
to the left	*papakaliwá*
to the right	*papakánan*

KHMER (CAMBODIA)

PRONUNCIATION

The pronunciation guide below covers the trickier parts of the transliteration system used in this chapter. It uses the Roman alphabet to give the closest equivalent for the sounds of the Khmer language. The best way to improve your pronunciation is to listen carefully to native speakers.

Vowels

Vowels and diphthongs with an **h** at the end should be pronounced hard and aspirated (with a puff of air).

aa-œ	like a combination of **aa** and **œ**
ae	as the 'a' in 'cat'
ai	as in 'aisle'
am	as the 'um' in 'glum'
ao	as the 'ow' in 'cow'
av	sounds like a very nasal **ao**; the final 'v' is not pronounced
aw	as the 'aw' in 'jaw'
awh	as **aw**, pronounced short and hard
eah	combination of 'e' and 'ah'; pronounced short and hard
eu	like saying 'oo' while keeping the lips spread flat rather than rounded
eua	combination of **eu** and **a**
euh	as **eu**, pronounced short and hard
euv	sounds like a very nasal **eu**; the final 'v' is not pronounced
oam	a combination of 'o' and 'am'
œ	as 'er' in 'her', but more open
oh	as the 'o' in 'hose'; pronounced short and hard
ohm	as the 'ome' in 'home'
ow	as in 'glow'
ua	as the 'ou' in 'tour'
uah	as **ua**, pronounced short and hard
uh	as the 'u' in 'but'

Consonants

Khmer uses some consonant combinations that may sound bizarre to Western ears, such as 'j-r' in *j'rook* (pig), or 'ch-ng' in *ch'ngain* (delicious). In this guide these types of consonant combinations are separated with an apostrophe to make pronunciation easier.

k	as the 'g' in 'go'
kh	as the 'k' in 'kind'
ng	as the 'ng' in 'sing'; practise by repeating 'sing-ing-nging-nging-nging' until you can say 'nging' clearly
ny	as in 'canyon'
p	a hard, unaspirated 'p', as the final 'p' in 'puppy'
ph	as the 'p' in 'pond', never as 'f'

r	as in 'rum', but hard and rolling, with the tongue flapping against the palate; in rapid conversation it is often omitted entirely
t	a hard, unaspirated 't' sound; similar to the 't' in 'stand'
th	as the 't' in 'two', never as the 'th' in 'thanks'
w	as in 'would'; there's no equivalent for the English 'v' sound in Khmer

ACCOMMODATION

Where is a (cheap) hotel?	*ohtail (thaok) neuv ai naa?*
Do you have a room?	*niak mian bantohp tohmne te?*
How much is it per day?	*damlay muy th'ngay pohnmaan?*
I'd like a room ...	*kh'nyohm sohm bantohp ...*
for one person	*samruhp muy niak*
for two people	*samruhp pii niak*
with a bathroom	*dail mian bantohp tuhk*
with a fan	*dail mian dawnghahl*
with a window	*dail mian bawng-uit*

CONVERSATION & ESSENTIALS

Forms of Address

The Khmer language reflects the social standing of the speaker and subject through various personal pronouns and 'politeness words'. These range from the simple *baat* for men and *jaa* for women, placed at the end of a sentence, meaning 'yes' or 'I agree', to the very formal and archaic *Reachasahp* or 'Royal Language', a separate vocabulary reserved for addressing the king and very high officials. Many of the pronouns are determined on the basis of the subject's age and gender. Foreigners are not expected to know all of these forms.

The easiest and most general personal pronoun is *niak* (you), which may be used in most situations and for persons of either gender. Men of your age or older may be called *lowk* (mister). Women of your age or older can be called *bawng srei* (older sister) or, for more formal situations, *lowk srei* (madam). *Bawng* is a good informal, neutral pronoun for men or women who are (or appear to be) older than you. For third person, male or female, singular or plural, the respectful form is *koat* and the common form is *ke*.

Hello.	*johm riab sua*
Goodbye.	*lia suhn hao-y*
See you later.	*juab kh'nia th'ngay krao-y*
Yes.	*baat* (used by men)
	jaa (used by women)
No.	*te*
Please.	*sohm*
Thank you.	*aw kohn*
Excuse me./I'm sorry.	*sohm toh*
Hi, how are you?	*niak sohk sabaay te?*
I'm fine.	*kh'nyohm sohk sabaay*
Where are you going?	*niak teuv naa?* (a very common question used when meeting people, even strangers; an exact answer isn't necessary)
Does any one here speak English?	*tii nih mian niak jeh phiasaa awngle te?*
I don't understand.	*kh'nyohm muhn yuhl te*

EMERGENCIES

Help!	*juay kh'nyohm phawng!*
Call a doctor!	*juay hav kruu paet mao!*
Call the police!	*juay hav polih mao!*
Where are the toilets?	*bawngkohn neuv ai naa?*

FOOD & DRINK

food stall	*kuhnlaing luak m'howp*
market	*p'saa*
restaurant	*resturaan/phowjuhniiyathaan*
I'm a vegetarian.	*kh'nyohm tawm sait*
beef	*sait kow*
boiled water	*tuhk ch'uhn*
chicken	*sait moan*
coffee	*kaafe*
fish	*trei*
milk	*tuhk dawh kow*
sugar	*skaw*
tea	*tai*

NUMBERS & AMOUNTS

Khmers count in increments of five. Thus, after reaching the number five *(bram)*, the cycle begins again with the addition of one, ie 'five-one' *(bram muy)*, 'five-two' *(bram pii)* and so on to 10, which begins a new cycle – for example, the Khmer word for the number 18 consists of three segments: 10, five and three.

There's also a colloquial form of counting that reverses the word order for numbers between 10 and 20 and separates the two words with *duhn: pii duhn dawp* for 12, *bei duhn dawp* for 13, *bram buan duhn dawp* for 19 and so on. This form is often used in markets, so listen keenly.

1	*muy*
2	*pii*
3	*bei*
4	*buan*
5	*bram*
6	*bram muy*
7	*bram pii/puhl*
8	*bram bei*
9	*bram buan*
10	*dawp*
11	*dawp muy*
12	*dawp pii*
16	*dawp bram muy*
20	*m'phei*
21	*m'phei muy*
30	*saamsuhp*
40	*saisuhp*
100	*muy roy*
1000	*muy poan*
1,000,000	*muy lian*

SHOPPING & SERVICES

I'm looking for the …	*kh'nyohm rohk …*
Where is a/the …	*… neuv ai naa?*
bank	*th'niakia*
hospital	*mohntii paet*
market	*p'saa*
police station	*poh polih*
post office	*praisuhnii*
public telephone	*turasahp saathiaranah*
public toilet	*bawngkohn saathiaranah*

How much is it?	*nih th'lay pohnmaan?*
That's too much.	*th'lay pek*

TIME & DAYS

What time is it?	*eileuv nih maong pohnmaan?*
today	*th'ngay nih*
tomorrow	*th'ngay s'aik*

Monday	*th'ngay jahn*
Tuesday	*th'ngay ahngkia*
Wednesday	*th'ngay poht*
Thursday	*th'ngay prohoah*
Friday	*th'ngay sohk*
Saturday	*th'ngay sav*
Sunday	*th'ngay aatuht*

TRANSPORT

What time does the … leave?	*… jein maong pohnmaan?*
boat	*duk*
bus	*laan ch'nual*
plane	*yohn/k'pal hawh*
train	*roht plœng*

airport	*wial yohn hawh*
bus station	*kuhnlaing laan ch'nual*
bus stop	*jamnawt laan ch'nual*
train station	*s'thaanii roht plœng*

Directions

How can I get to …?	*phleuv naa teuv …?*
Is it far?	*wia neuv ch'ngaay te?*
Is it near?	*wia neuv juht nih te?*
Go straight ahead.	*teuv trawng*
Turn left/right.	*bawt ch'weng/s'dam*

LAO

PRONUNCIATION

Vowels

a	as the 'a' in 'about'
aa	as the 'a' in 'father'
aai	as the 'a' in 'father' plus the 'i' in 'pipe'
ae	as the 'a' in 'bad' or 'tab'
aew	as the 'a' in 'bad' plus 'w'
ao	as in 'now' or 'cow'
aw	as in 'jaw'
awy	as the 'oy' in 'boy'
eh	as the 'a' in 'hate'
ehw	as the 'a' in 'care' plus 'w'
eu	as the 'i' in 'sir'
eua	'eu' followed by 'a'
ew	same as **ehw**, but shorter
iaw	a sequence of 'ee-a-oo'
i	as in 'it'
ii	as in 'need'
iu	'i-oo' (as in 'yew')
oe	as the 'u' in 'fur'
oei	'oe-i'
ohy	'oh-i'
u	as in 'flute'
uay	'u-ay-ee'
uu	as in 'food'

Consonants

The consonants in our pronunciation guides are mostly pronounced like in English, with exceptions listed below. An 'aspirated' consonant is produced with no audible puff of air. An 'unvoiced' consonant is produced with no vibration in the vocal chords.

LANGUAGE

j	similar to 'j' in 'join' or, more closely, the second 't' in 'stature' or 'literature' (unaspirated and unvoiced)
k	as the 'k' in 'skin'; similar to the 'g' in 'good', but unaspirated and unvoiced
kh	as the 'k' in 'kite'
ng	as in 'sing'; used as an initial consonant in Lao
ny	as in 'canyon'; used as an initial consonant in Lao
p	a hard 'p' (unaspirated and unvoiced)
ph	'p' as in 'put', never as 'f'
t	a hard 't', unaspirated and unvoiced – a bit like 'd'
th	as in 'tip'

Tones

Lao is a tonal language, meaning that many words are differentiated only by their tone (changes in the pitch of a speaker's voice). The word *sao*, for example, can mean 'girl', 'morning', 'pillar' or 'twenty', depending on the tone. Pitch variations are relative to the speaker's natural vocal range, which means that one person's low tone isn't necessarily the same pitch as another person's.

low tone – produced at the relative bottom of your conversational tonal range, usually flat level, eg *dị* (good)
mid tone – flat like the low tone, but spoken at the relative middle of the speaker's vocal range; no tone mark is used, eg *het* (do)
high tone – flat again, but at the relative top of your vocal range, eg *heúa* (boat)
rising tone – begins a bit below the mid tone and rises to just at or above the high tone, eg *săam* (three)
high falling tone – begins at or above the high tone and falls to the mid level, eg *sâo* (morning)
low falling tone – begins at about the mid level and falls to the level of the low tone, eg *khào* (rice)

ACCOMMODATION

Where's a ...?	*... yùu săi?*
camping ground	*bawn tâng kêm*
guesthouse	*héu-an phak*
hotel	*hóhng háem*

Do you have a ...?	*jâo mii ... wâhng baw?*
double room	*hàwng náwn tiang khuu*
single room	*hàwng náwn tiang diaw*

How much is it per ...?	*... thao dại?*
night	*khéun la*
person	*khón la*

bathroom	*hàwng nâm*
toilet	*sùam*

CONVERSATION & ESSENTIALS

Hello.	*sábạai dii*
Goodbye. (general farewell)	*sábạai dii*
Goodbye. (person leaving)	*láa kawn pại kawn*
Goodbye. (person staying)	*sŏhk dii* (lit: good luck)
See you later.	*phop kạn mai*
Thank you (very much).	*khàwp jại (lăi lăi)*
Excuse me.	*khăw thŏht*
How are you?	*sábạai dii baw?*
I'm fine.	*sábạai dii*
And you?	*jâo dêh?*
Can you speak English?	*jâo pàak pháasăa ạngkít dâi baw?*
I don't understand.	*baw khào jại*

EMERGENCIES

Help!	*suay dae!*
Go away!	*pại dôe!*
I'm lost.	*khàwy lŏng tháang*
Where are the toilets?	*hàwng sùam yùu săi?*
Call a doctor!	*suay tạam hăa măw hài dae!*
Call the police!	*suay ôen tamlùat dae!*

FOOD & DRINK

I eat only vegetables.	*khàwy kịn tae phák*
beer	*bịa*
boiled water	*nâam tọm*
chicken	*kai*
coffee	*kạaféh*
cold water	*nâam yén*
crab	*puu*
fish	*pạa*
fried egg	*khai dạo*
fried potatoes	*mán falang jẹun*
fried rice with ...	*khào ...*
fried spring rolls	*yáw jẹun*
hot Lao tea	*sáa hâwn*
hot water	*nâam hâwn*
ice	*nâam kâwn*
no sugar (a request)	*baw sai nâamtạan*
orange juice/soda	*nâam màak kîang*
plain bread (usually French-style)	*khào jii*
plain milk	*nâam nóm*
plain omelette	*jẹun khai*
pork	*mŭu*
rice whisky	*làoláo*
shrimp/prawns	*kûng*
soda water	*nâam sohdạa*
steamed white rice	*khào nèung*
sticky rice	*khào nĭaw*

weak Chinese tea	*nâam sáa*
yoghurt	*nóm sòm*

NUMBERS

0	*sŭun*
1	*neung*
2	*săwng*
3	*săam*
4	*sii*
5	*hàa*
6	*hók*
7	*jét*
8	*pàet*
9	*kâo*
10	*síp*
11	*síp ét*
12	*síp săwng*
20	*sáo*
21	*sáo ét*
22	*sáo săwng*
30	*săam síp*
100	*hâwy*
200	*săwng hâwy*
1000	*phán*
10,000	*meun*
100,000	*săen*
1,000,000	*lâan*

SHOPPING & SERVICES

Where is the ...?	*... yùu săi?*
I'm looking for a/the ...	*khàwy sâwk hăa ...*
bank	*thanáakháan*
hospital	*hóhng măw*
pharmacy	*hâan khăai yqa*
post office	*pqisánii*
public toilet	*hòrng nâm săathaalànà*
telephone	*thóhlasáp*
How much (for) ...?	*... thao dqi?*
The price is very high.	*láakháa pháeng lăai*

TIME & DATES

What time is it?	*wehláa ják móhng*
At what time?	*tawn ják móhng*
today	*mêu nîi*
tomorrow	*mêu eun*
Monday	*wán jqn*
Tuesday	*wán qngkháan*
Wednesday	*wán phut*
Thursday	*wán phahát*
Friday	*wán súk*
Saturday	*wán săo*
Sunday	*wán qathit*

TRANSPORT

What time will the ... leave?	*... já àwk ják móhng?*
boat	*héua*
bus	*lot*
minivan	*lot tûu*
plane	*héua bĭn*
What time does it arrive there?	*já pai hâwt phûn ják móhng?*
Where is the ...?	*... yùu săi?*
airport	*doen bĭn*
bus station	*sathăanii lot pájqm tháang*
bus stop	*bawn jàwt lot pájqm tháang*

Directions

I want to go to ...	*khàwy yàak pqi ...*
Turn left/right.	*lîaw sâai/khwăa*
Go straight ahead.	*pqi seuseu*
How far?	*kqi thao dqi?*
(not) far	*(baw) kqi*
(not) near	*(baw) kâi*

TETUN (EAST TIMOR)

Tetun is the most widely spoken lingua franca in East Timor. Originally spoken on the south coast of Timor, a form of Tetun was brought to Dili by the Portuguese in the late 18th century. After East Timor gained independence from Indonesia, Tetun became its co-official language, alongside the country's other official language, Portuguese.

PRONUNCIATION

j	as the 's' in 'pleasure'; (sometimes as the 'z' in 'zoo')
r	trilled
x	as the 'sh' in 'ship' (the Portuguese spelling is **ch**); sometimes pronounced as the 's' in 'summer'

ACCOMMODATION

I'm looking for a ...	*Hau buka hela ...*
guesthouse	*losmen/pensaun*
hotel	*otél*
Do you have any rooms available?	*Ita iha kuartu ruma mamuk?*
I'd like ...	*Hau hakarak ...*
a single room	*kuartu mesak ida*
to share a room	*fahe kuartu ida*

CONVERSATION & ESSENTIALS

Hello.	*Haló./Olá.* (pol/inf)
Goodbye.	*Adeus.*
Yes.	*Sin/Diak/Los.*
No.	*Lae.*
Please.	*Favór ida./Halo favór./ Faz favór./Por favór.*
Thank you (very much).	*Obrigadu/a (barak).* (m/f)
You're welcome.	*La iha buat ida./De nada.*
Excuse me.	*Kolisensa.*
What's your name?	*Ita-nia naran sa/saida?*
My name is ...	*Hau-nia naran ...*
Do you speak English?	*Ita koalia Inglés?*
I don't understand.	*Hau la kompriende.*

EMERGENCIES

Help!	*Ajuda!*
Call a doctor!	*Bolu dotór!*
Call the police!	*Bolu polísia!*
I'm lost.	*Hau lakon tiha.*
Where are the toilets?	*Sintina iha nebé?*

FOOD & DRINK

I'm a vegetarian.	*Hau ema vejetarianu.*
beer	*serveja*
boiled water	*be tasak*
bottled water	*ákua*
bread	*paun*
breakfast	*matebixu*
butter	*manteiga*
chicken	*nan manu*
(Timorese) coffee	*kafé (Timór)*
dinner	*jantár*
eggs	*manutolun*
fish	*ikan*
fruit	*aifuan*
lunch	*han meudia*
milk	*susubén*
mineral water	*be minerál*
pepper	*pimenta*
salt	*masin*
sugar	*masin midar* (lit: sweet salt)
tea	*xa*
vegetables	*modo tahan*
water	*be*

NUMBERS

Higher numbers can be given in Tetun, Portuguese or Indonesian.

	Tetun	Portuguese
0	*nol*	*zero*
1	*ida*	*um/uma* (m/f)
2	*rua*	*dois/duas* (m/f)
3	*tolu*	*três*
4	*hat*	*quatro*
5	*lima*	*cinco*
6	*nen*	*seis*
7	*hitu*	*sete*
8	*ualu*	*oito*
9	*sia*	*nove*
10	*sanulu*	*dez*
11	*sanulu-resin-ida*	*onze*
12	*sanulu-resin-rua*	*doze*
20	*ruanulu*	*vinte*
100	*atus ida*	*cem*
1000	*rihun ida*	*mil*

SHOPPING & SERVICES

Where's a/the ...?	*... iha nebé?*
bank	*banku*
general store	*loja*
market	*basar/merkadu*
post office	*koreiu*
public telephone	*wartel*
toilet	*sintina*
What time does ... open/close?	*Tuku hira maka ... loke/taka?*
How much is it?	*Folin hira?*

TIME & DAYS

What time is it?	*Tuku hira ona?*
(It's) one o'clock.	*Tuku ida.*
today	*ohin*
tonight	*ohin kalan*
tomorrow	*aban*
Monday	*segunda*
Tuesday	*tersa*
Wednesday	*kuarta*
Thursday	*kinta*
Friday	*sesta*
Saturday	*sábadu*
Sunday	*dumingu*

TRANSPORT

When does the ... leave/arrive?	*Tuku hira maka ... ba/to?*
bus	*bis/biskota*
minibus	*mikrolet*
plane	*aviaun*
bus station	*terminál bis nian*
road to (Aileu)	*dalan ba (Aileu)*

LANGUAGE

Directions

Go straight ahead.	*Los deit.*
To the left.	*Fila ba liman karuk.*
To the right.	*Fila ba liman los.*
far/near	*dok/besik*

THAI

TONES & PRONUNCIATION

Thai is a tonal language, which means that changes in pitch can affect the meaning of a word. The range of all five tones is relative to each speaker's vocal range, so there's no fixed 'pitch' intrinsic to the language. The five tones of Thai are:

low tone – a flat pitch pronounced at the relative bottom of the vocal range, eg *bàat* (baht – the Thai currency)
level or mid tone – pronounced flat, at the relative middle of the vocal range, eg *dii* (good); no tone mark is used
falling tone – pronounced as if emphasising a word, or calling someone's name from afar, eg *mâi* (no/not)
high tone – pronounced near the relative top of the vocal range, as level as possible, eg *máa* (horse)
rising tone – sounds like the inflection used by English speakers to imply a question, eg *sǎam* (three)

The sounds in Thai that differ from English are pronounced the same as in Lao; see the pronunciation guide on p973.

ACCOMMODATION

I'm looking for a …	*phǒm/dìchǎn kamlang hǎa …* (m/f)
guesthouse	*bâan phák*
hotel	*rohng raem*
youth hostel	*bâan yaowáchon*
Do you have any rooms available?	*mii hâwng wâang mǎi?*
I'd like (a) …	*tâwng kaan …*
bed	*tiang nawn*
double room	*hâwng khûu*
ordinary room (with fan)	*hâwng thammádaa (mii pát lom)*
room with two beds	*hâwng thîi mii tiang sǎwng tua*
single room	*hâwng dìaw*
How much is it …?	*… thâo rai?*
per night	*kheun lá*
per person	*khon lá*

CONVERSATION & ESSENTIALS

When being polite, a male speaker ends his sentence with *khráp* and a female speaker says *khâ*; it's also the common way to answer 'yes' to a question or show agreement.

Hello.	*sàwàtdii (khráp/khâ)*
Goodbye.	*laa kàwn*
Yes.	*châi*
No.	*mâi châi*
Please.	*kàrúnaa*
Thank you.	*khàwp khun*
You're welcome.	*mâi pen rai*
Excuse me.	*khǎw àphai*
Sorry. (forgive me)	*khǎw thôht*
How are you?	*sabai dii rěu?*
I'm fine, thanks.	*sabai dii*
I don't understand.	*mâi khâo jai*
Do you speak English?	*khun phûut phaasǎa angkrìt pen mǎi?*

EMERGENCIES

Help!	*chûay dûay!*
I'm lost.	*chǎn lǒng thaang*
Go away!	*pai sí!*
Call …!	*rîak … nàwy!*
a doctor	*mǎw*
the police	*tamrùat*

FOOD & DRINK

I'd like …	*khǎw …*
I'm allergic to …	*phǒm/dìchǎn pháe …* (m/f)
I don't eat …	*phǒm/dìchǎn kin … mâi dâi* (m/f)
beer	*bia*
chicken	*kài*
coffee	*kaafae*
fish	*plaa*
ice	*náam khǎeng*
meat	*néua sàt*
milk	*nom jèut*
pork	*mǔu*
rice	*khâo*
rice noodles	*kǔaytǐaw*
seafood	*aahǎan tháleh*
tea	*chaa*
water	*náam*

NUMBERS

1	*nèung*	**5**	*hâa*
2	*sǎwng*	**6**	*hòk*
3	*sǎam*	**7**	*jèt*
4	*sìi*	**8**	*pàet*

LANGUAGE

9	*kâo*	30	*săam sìp*
10	*sìp*	100	*nèung ráwy*
11	*sìp èt*	1000	*nèung phan*
12	*sìp săwng*	10,000	*nèung mèun*
20	*yîi sìp*	100,000	*nèung săen*
21	*yîi sìp èt*	1,000,000	*nèung láan*

SHOPPING & SERVICES

I'm looking for a ...	*phŏm/dichăn hăa ...* (m/f)
bank	*thánaakhaan*
market	*talàat*
post office	*praisànii*
public toilet	*hâwng nám săathaaráná*
telephone centre	*sŭun thohrásàp*
tourist office	*sămnák ngaan thâwng thîaw*

When does it open?	*pòet kìi mohng?*
When does it close?	*pìt kìi mohng?*
I'd like to buy ...	*yàak jà séu ...*
How much is it?	*thâo rai?*

TIME & DAYS

What time is it?	*kìi mohng láew?*
It's (eight o'clock).	*(pàet) mohng láew*
When?	*meuarai?*
yesterday	*mêua waan*
today	*wan níi*
tomorrow	*phrûng níi*

Monday	*wan jan*
Tuesday	*wan angkhaan*
Wednesday	*wan phút*
Thursday	*wan pháréuhàt*
Friday	*wan sùk*
Saturday	*wan săo*
Sunday	*wan aathít*

TRANSPORT

What time does the ... leave/arrive?	*... jà àwk/thĕung kìi mohng?*
boat	*reua*
bus	*rót meh/bát*
(intercity) bus	*rót thua*
plane	*khrêuang bin*
train	*rót fai*

I'd like ...	*phŏm/dichăn yàak dâi ...* (m/f)
a one-way ticket	*tŭa thîaw diaw*
a return ticket	*tŭa pai klàp*

airport	*sanăam bin*
bus station	*sathăanii khŏn sòng*
bus stop	*pâai rót meh*
ticket office	*tûu khăi tŭa*
train station	*sathăanii rót fai*

Directions

Where is ...?	*... yùu thîi năi?*
Can you show me (on the map)?	*hâi duu (nai phăen thîi) dâi măi*
How far?	*klai thâo rai?*
near	*klâi*
far	*klai*
(Go) Straight ahead.	*trong pai*
Turn left.	*líaw sáai*
Turn right.	*líaw khwăa*

VIETNAMESE

There are differences between the Vietnamese of the north and the Vietnamese of the south; where different forms are used in this guide, they are indicated by 'N' for the north and 'S' for the south.

TONES & PRONUNCIATION

To help you make sense of the Vietnamese writing system, the words and phrases in this language guide include pronunciations that use a written form more familiar to English speakers. The symbols used for marking the tones are the same as those used in standard written Vietnamese.

SYMBOL		PRONUNCIATION
c, k	ğ	an unaspirated 'k'
-ch	k	as a 'k'
d	z/y	as the 'z' in 'zoo' (N); as the 'y' in 'yes' (S)
đ	đ	as in 'do'
gi-	z/y	as 'z' (N); as 'y' (S)
kh-	ch	as the 'ch' in German *Buch*
ng-	ng	as the '-nga-' sound in 'long ago'
-ng	ng	as the 'ng' in 'long' but with the lips closed sounds like English 'm'
nh-	ny	as the 'ny' in 'canyon'
-nh	ng	as in 'singing'
ph-	f	as in 'farm'
r	z/r	as 'z' (N); as 'r' (S)
s	s/sh	as 's' (N); as 'sh' (S)
th-	t	a strongly aspirated 't'
tr-	ch/tr	as 'ch' (N); as 'tr' (S)
x	s	as an 's'

Vietnamese is a tonal language with six tones, which means that a single syllable can have as many as six different meanings. The word *ma*, for example, can be read to mean 'ghost', 'which', 'mother', 'rice seedling', 'tomb' or 'horse'. The six tones are represented by five accent marks in the

LANGUAGE

written language (the first tone is left unmarked).

ma (ghost) – middle of the vocal range
mà (which) – begins low and falls lower
mả (tomb) – begins low, dips and then rises to higher pitch
mã (horse) – begins high, dips slightly, then rises sharply
mạ (rice seedling) – begins low, falls lower, then stops
má (mother) – begins high and rises sharply

ACCOMMODATION

Where's a (cheap) ...?
Đâu có ... (rẻ tiền)? — đoh ǧó ... (zả đee·ùhn)?
camping ground
nơi cắm trại — ner·ee ǧúhm chại
guesthouse
nhà khách — nyaà kaák
hotel
khách sạn — kaák saạn

I'd like (a) ...
Tôi muốn ... — doy moo·úhn ...
single room
phòng đơn — fòm dern
double-bed room
giường đôi — zuhr·èrng đoy
room with two beds
phòng gồm hai giường ngủ — fòm gàwm hai zuhr·èrng ngoỏ

How much is it ...?
Giá bao nhiêu ...? — zaá bow nyee·oo ...?
per night
một đêm — mạwt đem
per person
một người — mạwt nguhr·eè

air-conditioning	*máy lạnh*	máy laạng
bathroom	*phòng tắm*	fòm dúhm
hot water	*nước nóng*	nuhr·érk nóm
toilet	*nhà vệ sinh*	nyaà vẹ sing

CONVERSATION & ESSENTIALS

There are many different forms of address in Vietnamese. The safest way to address people is using *ông* (for a man of any status), *anh* (for a young man), *bà* (for a middle-aged or older woman), *cô* (for a young woman) and *em* (for a child).

Hello.	*Xin chào.*	sin jòw
Goodbye.	*Tạm biệt.*	dụm bee·ẹt
Please.	*Làm ơn.*	làm ern
Thank you.	*Cảm ơn.*	kảm ern
Excuse me.	*Xin lỗi.*	sin lõ·ee
Yes.	*Vâng.* (N)	vang
	Dạ. (S)	yạ
No.	*Không.*	kom

How are you?
Có khỏe không? — káw kwải kom?
Fine, thank you.
Khỏe, cám ơn. — kwải kảm ern
Do you speak English?
Bạn có nói được tiếng anh không? — Baạn ǧó nóy đuhr·ẹrk díng aang kawm?
I (don't) understand.
Tôi (không) hiểu. — doy (kawm) heẻ·oo

EMERGENCIES

Help!
Cứu tôi! — ǧuhr·oó doy!
I'm lost.
Tôi bị lạc đường. — doi beẹ laạk đuhr·èrng
Leave me alone!
Thôi! — toy!
Where's the toilet?
Nhà vệ sinh ở đâu? — nyaà vẹ sing ẻr doh?

Please call ...
Làm ơn gọi ... — laàm ern gọy ...
a doctor
bác sĩ — baák seẽ
the police
công an — ǧawm aan

FOOD & DRINK

I'm a vegetarian.	*Tôi ăn chay.*	doy uhn jay
beef	*thịt bò*	tịt bò
beer	*bia*	bi·uh
bread	*bánh mì*	baáng mèe
chicken	*thịt gà*	tịt gaà
coffee	*cà phê*	ǧaà fe
fish	*cá*	ǧaá
ice	*đá*	đaá
milk	*sữa*	sũhr·uh
mineral water	*nước khoáng/ suối* (N/S)	nuhr-érk kwaáng/ soo-eé
noodles	*mì*	meè
pork	*thịt heo*	tịt hay-oo
steamed rice	*cơm trắng*	ǧerm chúhng
tea	*chè/trà* (N/S)	jà/chaà
vegetables	*rau sống*	zoh sáwm

NUMBERS

1	*một*	mạwt
2	*hai*	hai

LANGUAGE

3	*ba*	baa
4	*bốn*	báwn
5	*năm*	nuhm
6	*sáu*	sóh
7	*bảy*	bảy
8	*tám*	dúhm
9	*chín*	jín
10	*mười*	muhr·eè
11	*mười một*	muhr·eè mọt
19	*mười chín*	muhr·eè jín
20	*hai mươi*	hai muhr·ee
21	*hai mươi mốt*	hai muhr·ee máwt
22	*hai mươi hai*	hai muhr·ee hai
30	*ba mươi*	ba muhr·ee
90	*chín mươi*	jín muhr·ee
100	*một trăm*	mawt chuhm
200	*hai trăm*	hai chuhm
900	*chín trăm*	jín chuhm
1000	*một nghìn* (N)	mạwt ngyìn
	một ngàn (S)	mọt ngaàn
10,000	*mười nghìn* (N)	muhr·eè ngyìn
	mười ngàn (S)	muhr·eè ngaàn

SHOPPING & SERVICES

I'm looking for a/the ...
Tôi tìm ... doy dìm ...

bank
ngân hàng nguhn haàng
hospital
nhà thương nyaà tuhr·erng
market
chợ jẹr
post office
bưu điện buhr·oo đee·ụhn
public phone
phòng điện thoại fòm đee·ụhn twaị
public toilet
phòng vệ sinh fòm vẹ sing
tourist office
văn phòng hướng dẫn du lịch vuhn fòm huhr·érng zũhn zoo lịk

How much is this?
Cái này giá bao nhiêu? ğaí này zaá bow nyee·oo?
It's too expensive.
Cái này quá mắc. ğaí này gwaá múhk

TIME & DAYS

What time is it?	*Mấy giờ rồi?*	máy zèr zòy?
It's ... o'clock.	*Bây giờ là ... giờ.*	bay zèr laà ... zèr
now	*bây giờ*	bay zèr
today	*hôm nay*	hawm nay
tomorrow	*ngày mai*	ngày mai
Monday	*thứ hai*	túhr hai
Tuesday	*thứ ba*	túhr baa
Wednesday	*thứ tư*	túhr duhr
Thursday	*thứ năm*	túhr nuhm
Friday	*thứ sáu*	túhr sóh
Saturday	*thứ bảy*	túhr bảy
Sunday	*chủ nhật*	jỏo nhụht

TRANSPORT

What time does the (first)... leave?
Chuyến ... (sớm nhất) chạy lúc mấy giờ? jwee·úhn ... (sérm nyúht) jạy lúp máy zèr?

boat
tàu/thuyền dòw/twee·ùhn
bus
xe buýt sa beét
plane
máy bay máy bay
train
xe lửa sa lůhr·uh

Directions

Where is ...?
ở đâu ...? ẻr đoh ...?
I want to go to ...
Tôi muốn đi ... doy moo·úhn đee ...
Go straight ahead.
Thẳng tới trước. tůhng der·eé chuhr·érk
Can you show me (on the map)?
Xin chỉ giùm (trên bản đồ này)? sin jeẻ zùm (chen baản đàw này)?
Turn left.
Sang trái. saang chaí
Turn right.
Sang phải. saang fal
at the corner
ở góc đường ẻr góp đuhr·èrng
at the traffic lights
tại đèn giao tawm dại đèn zow *thông*
far
xa saa
near (to)
gần gùhn

LANGUAGE

Glossary

ABBREVIATIONS

B – Brunei
C – Cambodia
ET – East Timor
I – Indonesia
L – Laos
M – Malaysia
My – Myanmar (Burma)
P – Philippines
S – Singapore
T – Thailand
V – Vietnam

ABC (M) – Air Batang
adat (B, I, M, S) – customary law
alun alun (I) – main public square of a town
amoc/amok (C) – fish baked in banana leaf
andong (I) – four-wheeled horse-drawn cart
angguna (ET) – tray truck where passengers (including the odd buffalo or goat) all pile into the back
angkot (I) – see *bemo*
ao (T) – bay, gulf
ao dai (V) – traditional Vietnamese tunic and trousers
apsara (C) – dancing girl, celestial nymph
argo (I) – taxi meter; 'luxury' class on trains
Asean – Association of Southeast Asian Nations
asura (C) – demon

bâan (T) – house, village; also written as *ban*
Baba Nonya (M) – descendents of Chinese settlers in the Straits settlements (Melaka, Singapore and Penang) who intermarried with Malays and adopted many Malay customs; also written as 'Baba Nyonya'
bajaj (I) – motorised three-wheeled taxi
Bamar (My) – Burmese ethnic group
bangka (P) – local outrigger, pumpboat
barangay (P) – village
baray (C) – Angkorian reservoir
batik (I, M) – cloth coloured by a waxing and dyeing process
BE (L) – Buddhist Era
becak (I) – bicycle rickshaw
bemo (I) – three-wheeled pick-up truck, often with two rows of seats down the side
benteng (I) – fort
bis kota (I) – city bus
bisnis (I) – business class on buses, trains etc
boeng (C) – lake
BSB (B) – Bandar Seri Begawan
bukit (B, I, M, S) – hill
bumboat (S) – motorised *sampan*
bun (L) – festival
butanding (P) – whale shark
buu dien (V) – post office

Cao Daism (V) – Vietnamese religion
CAT (T) – CAT Telecom Public Company Limited (formerly Communications Authority of Thailand or CAT)
Cham (C,V) – ethnic minority descended from the people of Champa, a Hindu kingdom dating from the 2nd century BC
chedi (T) – see *stupa*
chunchiet (C) – ethnolinguistic minorities
cidomo (I) – horse-drawn cart
colt (I) – see *opelet*
CPP (C) – Cambodian People's Party
CTT (My) – Central Telephone & Telegraph
cyclo (C, V) – pedicab

Đ (V) – abbreviation of *duong*
ĐL (V) – abbreviation of *dai lo*
dai lo (V) – boulevard; abbreviated as 'ĐL'
dangdut (I) – Indonesian dance music with strong Arabic and Hindi influences (I)
datu (P) – traditional local chief, head of village
DENR (P) – Department of Environment & Natural Resources
deva (C) – god
devaraja (C) – god-king
DMZ (V) – Demilitarised Zone
dokar (I) – two-wheeled horse-drawn cart
DOT (P) – Department of Tourism
duong (V) – road, street; abbreviated as 'Đ'

Ecpat – End Child Prostitution & Trafficking
ekonomi (I, M) – economy class on buses, trains and other transport
eksekutif (I, M) – executive (ie 1st) class on buses, trains and other transport

falang (L) – Western, Westerner; foreigner
faràng (T) – Western, Westerner; foreigner
FEC (My) – Foreign Exchange Certificate

gamelan (I, M) – traditional Javanese and Balinese orchestra with large xylophones and gongs
gang (I) – alley, lane
gopura (C) – sanctuary
gua (I, M) – cave
gunung (I, M) – mountain

hàat (T) – beach; also written as *hat*
habal-habal (P) – motorcycle taxi
HCMC (V) – Ho Chi Minh City
héua hang nyáo (L) – long-tail boat
héua phai (L) – row boat
héua wái (L) – speedboat
Honda om (V) – see *xe om*
hti (My) – decorated top of a *stupa*

ikat (I) – cloth in which a pattern is produced by dyeing individual threads before the weaving process
istana (B, I, M, S) – palace

jalan (B, ET, I, M, S) – road, street; abbreviated as 'Jl'
JB (M) – Johor Bahru
jeepney (P) – wildly ornamented public transport, originally based on WWII US Army Jeeps
Jl (B, ET, I, M, S) – abbreviation of *jalan*

kaa (My) – city bus
kain songket (M) – fabric woven with gold and/or silver thread
kaki lima (I) – mobile food stall; food court
kalaga (My) – tapestry embroidered with silver threads and sequins
kalesa (P) – two-wheeled horse-drawn cart
kampung (B, I, M, S) – village; also written as *kampong*
kantor pos (I) – post office
kapal biasa (I) – river ferry
karst – limestone region with caves, underground streams, potholes etc
kàthoey (T) – transvestite, transsexual
kedai kopi (M) – coffee shop
khăo (T) – hill, mountain; also written as *khao*
khlong (T) – canal; also written as *khlawng*
khwăn (L) – guardian spirits of the body
KK (M) – Kota Kinabalu
KL (M) – Kuala Lumpur
KLIA (M) – Kuala Lumpur International Airport
klotok (I) – motorised canoe
ko (T) – island
koh (C) – island
kongsi (M) – Chinese clan organisations, also known as ritual brotherhoods, heaven-man-earth societies, triads or secret societies; meeting house for Chinese of the same clan
kota (ET, I, M) – fort, city
krama (C) – checked scarf
kraton (I) – palace
kris (I) – traditional dagger
KTM (M) – Keretapi Tanah Melayu; national rail service
kyaung (My) – Buddhist monastery

labuan (M) – port
lákhon (T) – dance drama
lí-keh (T) – popular form of folk dance-drama; also written as *likay*
longhouse (I, M, My) – enormous wooden structure on stilts that houses a tribal community under one roof
longyi (My) – wraparound garment worn by women and men
losmen (I) – basic accommodation
LRT (M) – Light Rail Transit

macet (I) – gridlock
mae nam (T) – river
mandi (ET, I, M) – large concrete basin from which you scoop water to rinse your body and flush the toilet
masjid (M) – mosque; also written as *mesjid*
merdeka (I, M) – independence
mesjid (I) – mosque; also written as *masjid*
mestizo (ET, P) – person of mixed descent
meuang (T) – city
mikrolet (ET, I) – see *opelet*
MILF (P) – Moro Islamic Liberation Front
Montagnards (V) – highlanders, mountain people; specifically the ethnic minorities that inhabit remote areas of Vietnam
moto (C) – motorcycle taxi
motodup (C) – motorcycle taxi driver
MRT (S) – Mass Rapid Transit; metro system
MTT (My) – Myanmar Travel & Tours
muay thai (T) – Thai boxing
myint hlei (My) – horse cart

nâam (L, T) – water, river
naga (C, L, T) – mythical serpent-being
nákhon (T) – city
năng (T) – shadow play
nat (My) – spirit-being with the power to either protect or harm humans; Myanmar's syncretic Buddhism
Negrito (P) – ancient Asian race whose members are distinguished by their black skin, curly hair and short stature
NLD (My) – National League for Democracy
nop (L) – see *wâi*
NPA (L) – National Protected Area
NPA (P) – New People's Army

ojek (I) – motorcycle taxi
opelet (I) – small minibus
Orang Asli (M) – Original People; Malaysian aboriginal people

P (V) – abbreviation of *pho* (street)
padang (M, S) – open grassy area; town square
pantai (B, ET, I, M) – beach
pasar (I, M) – market
pasar malam (I, M) – night market
paya (My) – holy one; often applied to Buddha figures, *zedi* and other religious monuments

Pelni (I) – national shipping line
pendopo (I) – open-sided pavilion
penginapan (I) – simple lodging house
Peranakan (S) – combination of Malay and Chinese cultures of precolonial Singapore
Ph (C) – abbreviation of *phlauv*
phlauv (C) – road, street; abbreviated as 'Ph'
phleng phêua chii-wít (T) – songs for life; modern Thai folk songs
pho (V) – street; abbreviated as P; also rice-noodle soup
PHPA (I) – Perlindungan Hutan dan Pelestarian Alam; Directorate General of Forest Protection & Nature Conservation
pinisi (I) – fishing boat
polres (I) – local police station
pongyi (My) – Buddhist monk
pousada (ET) – traditional Portuguese lodging
praang (T) – Khmer-style tower structure found on temples; serves the same purpose as a *stupa*
prasat (C, T) – tower, temple
prahoc/prahok (C) – fermented fish sauce
psar (C) – market
pulau (I, M) – island
pwe (My) – show, festival

quan (V) – urban district
quoc ngu (V) – Vietnamese alphabet

raja (B, I, M) – king
Ramakian (T) – Thai version of the *Ramayana*
Ramayana (I, L, M, T) – Indian epic story of Rama's battle with demons
remork (C) – a kind of motorised rickshaw with a motorcycle-pulled trailer; also called 'tuk-tuk'
roi nuoc (V) – water puppetry
rumah makan (I) – restaurant, food stall

săamláw (T) – three-wheeled pedicab; also written as *samlor*
samlor (C) – soup
sai-kaa (My) – bicycle rickshaw
sampan (I, M, S) – small boat
săwngthăew (L, T) – small pick-up truck with two benches in the back; also written as *songthaew*
sima (L) – ordination-precinct marker
Slorc (My) – State Law & Order Restoration Council
soi (T) – lane, small street
STB (S) – Singapore Tourism Board
stung (C) – river
stupa (C, I, L, M, T) – religious monument, often containing Buddha relics
sungai (B, I, M) – river; also written as *sungei*
surat jalan (I) – visitor permit

taman (B, I, M) – park
taman nasional (I) – national park
tambang (M) – double-oared river ferry; small river boat
tamu (B, M) – weekly market
tasik (M) – lake
TAT (T) – Tourism Authority of Thailand
teluk (I, M, S) – bay; also written as *telok*
Tet (V) – lunar New Year
Th (L, T) – abbreviation of *thànŏn*
thâa (T) – ferry, boat pier; also written as *tha*
thâat (L) – Buddhist *stupa*; also written as *that*
thànŏn (L, T) – road, street, avenue; abbreviated as 'Th'
tongkonan (I) – traditional house with roof eaves shaped like buffalo horns
tonlé (C) – river, lake
travel (I) – door-to-door air-con minibus
tukalok (C) – fruit shake made with sweetened condensed milk
túk-túk (L, T) – motorised *săamláw*
tuk-tuk (C) – a kind of motorised rickshaw with a motorcycle-pulled trailer; also called remork

UXO (C, L, V) – unexploded ordnance

vipassana (My, T) – insight-awareness meditation

wâi (L, T) – palms-together greeting
wartel (I) – telephone office
warung (I, M) – food stall
wat (C, L, T) – Buddhist temple-monastery
warnet (I) – public internet facility
wayang golek (I) – wooden puppet
wayang kulit (I) – shadow-puppet play enacting tales from the *Ramayana*
wayang orang (I) – dance-drama enacted by masked performers, recounting scenes from the *Ramayana*
wíhăan (T) – any large hall in a Thai temple, except for the central sanctuary used for official business
wisma (B, I, M, S) – guest house, lodge; office block, shopping centre

xe om (V) – motorbike taxi

yâam (T) – woven shoulder bag
yama (C) – Hindu god of death; crystal meth

zedi (My) – see *stupa*

The Authors

CHINA WILLIAMS

Coordinating Author & Thailand

China has been a Southeast Asia watcher for more than a decade and it just gets better with age. She first arrived as an English teacher in the provincial Thai town of Surin just as the Asian currencies started to crumble in 1997. Since then she's migrated back and forth from the US to find that Thailand is still an old pal with new toys. After years of long-distance commuting for various Lonely Planet titles, China is now mainly a full-time mum with a side job as a guidebook writer and her two-year-old son as her sidekick. She and her family (including hubby, Matt) live in Catonsville, Maryland, near a fantastic Asian supermarket.

GREG BLOOM

Philippines

Greg lived in Manila for almost five years before moving to Phnom Penh with his family in 2008. Travelling the Philippines in the service of Lonely Planet, Greg has fallen off a tricycle, flown out the back of a jeepney, and survived a bus crash on the back roads of Bicol. When not writing about his favourite travel destination, Greg might be found snouting around the former Soviet Union (he once called Kyiv home) or running around Asia's ultimate frisbee fields. His blogs about this and other research trips are at www.mytripjournal.com/bloomblogs.

CELESTE BRASH

Malaysia

Celeste first visited Malaysia while studying at Chiang Mai University, Thailand, in 1993. She's grazed through the hawker capital of the world several times since, travelling on cross-Asia trips and researching for a handful of Lonely Planet titles. When not desensitising her taste buds with sambal, Celeste lives in chilli-challenged French Polynesia with her husband and two children, where her attempts at re-creating Penang street food have earned her the nickname 'Spice Girl'. She's contributed to over a dozen Lonely Planet guidebooks including *Travel with Children*.

ANDREW BURKE

Myanmar

Andrew was first seduced by Myanmar in 1999 when, as a backpacker, he found it beguiling, inspiring and heartbreaking in equal measure. Several trips later and the emotions are still the same, so being able to travel around and write about one of his favourite travel destinations was impossible to resist. Andrew has spent more than 15 years travelling through, photographing, filming and writing about Asia, the Middle East and Africa, including authoring books for Lonely Planet on other personal favourites Iran and Laos. Over the last 10 years he has lived in Hong Kong, Phnom Penh and now Bangkok.

JAYNE D'ARCY

East Timor

In 2003 Jayne signed a nine-week contract to work with East Timor's community radio stations. Over the next 18 months she learnt to live without electricity (and the goodies it powers) and concentrated on other things, like learning Tetun and developing a taste for warm VB beer. Returning after five years to research this chapter, Jayne was blown away by the changes. Many of her radio friends have moved on to bigger and brighter things; Dili now actually resembles a city; and the beer of choice is (cold) Tiger.

SHAWN LOW

Singapore

After 23 hot, sticky and sweaty years in Singapore, Shawn made for the cooler but more temperamental climes of Melbourne in 2001. He found his way into Lonely Planet as a book editor in 2006 (and still constantly pinches himself to see if he's dreaming). Since then, he's done a stint as a commissioning editor and has constantly (sometimes successfully) flirted with Lonely Planet TV. Authoring has always been on his 'to do' list, and if being paid to return home to write the 'definitive' guide to Singapore sounds like a dream job, it probably is. Note: the bruises on his arms are from the constant pinching. OW!

BRANDON PRESSER

Malaysia & Brunei Darussalam

His wanderlust always bigger than his wallet, Brandon has championed the shoestringer lifestyle for almost a decade with myriad treks through Southeast Asia and an epic overland adventure from Morocco to Russia. Brandon holds a degree in art history from Harvard University, but these days he spends his time trotting the globe, pen in hand. He has authored over a dozen Lonely Planet guides including *Thailand, Thailand's Islands & Beaches* and *Malaysia, Singapore & Brunei*. When he's not writing his way around the world, Brandon enjoys scuba diving, crossword puzzles and TV reruns.

NICK RAY

Vietnam

A Londoner of sorts, Nick comes from Watford, the sort of town that makes you want to travel. He has been floating around the Mekong region for a more than a decade now, first as a traveller, later leading people astray as a tour leader for adventure travel companies, and more recently as a location scout for film and TV. Living in Phnom Penh, the Mekong is his backyard of sorts; he has authored several editions of *Cambodia* for Lonely Planet, as well as co-authoring the *Vietnam* book and *Cycling Vietnam, Laos & Cambodia*. While he enjoys Angkor Beer and Larue Export, his tipple of choice is Beer Lao.

DANIEL ROBINSON

Cambodia

Daniel researched the award-winning 1st edition of Lonely Planet's *Cambodia* guide back in 1989, when the ageing Soviet turboprops on the Phnom Penh–Siem Reap run stayed over the middle of the Tonlé Sap to avoid ground fire, and he was Angkor's sole foreign visitor for three whole days. These days his favourite spot for chilling is the (for now) pristine west coast of Koh Kong Island. Daniel is based in Los Angeles and Tel Aviv.

RYAN VER BERKMOES

Indonesia

Ryan first visited Southeast Asia in 1989 as a reporter covering refugee camps on the Thai–Cambodian border. My how things have improved. On visits since he has explored every one of the region's countries, especially Indonesia and especially Bali. But as much as he likes Indonesia, he's yet to find a place with banana pancakes to equal the orgasmic ones from a certain cart on Phuket. Off-island, Ryan lives in Portland, Oregon, and writes about Bali and more at www.ryanverberkmoes.com.

RICHARD WATERS

Laos

A chance visit to Laos in 1999, as the country was still thawing to the West, began a close association that sees Richard returning regularly. His first travels were around Europe as a teenager, then Central America, and the US by campervan. These days he satisfies his itchy-feet cravings by writing for newspapers such as the *Sunday Times*, the *Independent* and the *Observer*, and magazines, *Elle*, *Tatler* and *CNN Traveller*. To read more of his work and articles about Laos visit www.richardwaters.co.uk. He lives with his family in Brighton.

CONTRIBUTING AUTHOR

Dr Trish Batchelor is a general practitioner and travel-medicine specialist who works at the CIWEC Clinic in Kathmandu, Nepal, as well as being a medical adviser to the Travel Doctor New Zealand clinics. Trish teaches travel medicine through the University of Otago, New Zealand, and is interested in underwater and high-altitude medicine, and in the impact of tourism on host countries. She wrote the Health chapter.

Behind the Scenes

THIS BOOK

This is the 15th edition of *Southeast Asia on a Shoestring*. The 1st edition was written by Tony and Maureen Wheeler in 1975, funded by the cult success of their first guidebook, *Across Asia on the Cheap*, a compilation of journey notes put together back in 1973. As the scope of the book grew, so did the need to share the load: this edition is the work of 11 authors. Coordinating author extraordinaire China Williams led a stellar team: Greg Bloom, Celeste Brash, Andrew Burke, Jayne D'Arcy, Shawn Low, Brandon Presser, Nick Ray, Daniel Robinson, Ryan Ver Berkmoes and Richard Waters. Some original research for Vietnam was provided by Yu-Mei Balasingamchow and Iain Stewart. Some original Thailand research was provided by Mark Beales, Tim Bewer, Catherine Bodry, Austin Bush and Brandon Presser.

This guidebook was commissioned in Lonely Planet's Melbourne office, and produced by the following:

Commissioning Editors Kalya Ryan, Tashi Wheeler
Coordinating Editor Katie O'Connell
Coordinating Cartographer David Kemp
Layout Designers Vicki Beale, Frank Deim, Margie Jung, Jacqui Saunders
Managing Editors Sasha Baskett, Liz Heynes, Katie Lynch
Managing Cartographer David Connolly
Assisting Editors Jackey Coyle, Andrea Dobbin, Cathryn Game, Helen Koehne, Kristin Odijk, Fionnuala Twomey, Helen Yeates
Assisting Cartographer Sam Sayer
Cover Research Yukiyoshi Kamimura, lonelyplanet images.com
Internal Image Research Jane Hart, lonelyplanet images.com
Language Content Branislava Vladisavljevic
Project Manager Chris Love

Thanks to Lucy Birchley, Sally Darmody, Bruce Evans, Trent Holden, Laura Jane, Indra Kilfoyle, Yvonne Kirk, Annelies Mertens, Wayne Murphy, Jacqueline Nguyen, Trent Paton, Sarah Sloane, Cara Smith, Laura Stansfeld, Steve Waters

THANKS

CHINA WILLIAMS

Immeasurable thanks to Nong, so glad to have met you. Gratitude to Pong, Pim, Andrew, Alex, Panupan, Pichai, Duen, Sara, Aidan, Olly, Tom and Ken. Also to Joon, Jane and the staff at Buri Gallery for being so sweet to Felix. Thanks in Bangkok to Kaneungnit, Tom, Anne, Ruengsang, Mason, Jane, and the staff at Seven. More thanks to my husband, Matt, who drove the little car that could, and to Felix, my trustworthy, if temperamental, sidekick. And bravo to Tashi Wheeler, the Lonely Planet production team and Southeast Asia's vetted crew of contributing authors.

GREG BLOOM

I couldn't have done it without my gals, wife Karin and daughter Anna. Thanks as always for your love and support. Keen observer of Philippine life Johnny Weekend lent me his crib in Manila, tagged along for various adventures and took two broken ribs for the team on a bike trip in Coron. UDM, bro! I met various random and not-so-random characters along the way who gave me some great tips. A special nod to Andres in Dumaguete, Jonas in Siargao and of course Isabel and Ruth in Palawan.

CELESTE BRASH

Thanks to my family for putting up with my absences, to Peck Choo Ho and all her limes, Yaksa, Joann Khaw for the best ever never-ending Penang info and just for being brilliant, Aril Zainal and Mania, hard-core Amy Wan, Alex Ageev, Rajan Jones, Omar, Kara and Max for the best company, Brandon Presser for endless phone support and happy Borneo coordinating, Simon Richmond and Adam Karlin for kick-ass MSB text, China Williams for putting this huge book together with such finesse and Tashi Wheeler for steady support and clarity.

ANDREW BURKE

I owe a big *chè zù bèh* to the many citizens of Myanmar who helped to make this chapter possible. Alas, naming them all would be tough for me and potentially dangerous for them, but they know my appreciation extends well beyond a name printed in black on a white page. Among the travellers and expats I met on the road, special thanks go to Andrew Dicks, Cinzia Rizzoli, Cristina Majorano and the ever-helpful William. At Lonely Planet, thanks to China Williams, Tashi Wheeler, David Connolly and everyone at LPHQ whose hard work allows me to work in an office where the walls are made of travel stories.

JAYNE D'ARCY

Thanks to Sharik Billington, who embraced East Timor (and karaoke) with such gusto. Thanks to my old radio buddies Antonio Armindo, Julio Cardoso and Maria Bibel for their stories, smiles and laughs. Thanks to Kym Smithies for her diving expertise, Rosalie Sword for her welcome, Tracey Morgan for linking us in (you are a star), Damien Kingsbury for his rapid and knowledgable responses and David Savage for sharing his experiences. A huge thank you to my parents (aka Granny and Papa Houlgate), who did an amazing job looking after my sweet Miles. To think I thought he'd miss me! Ha!

SHAWN LOW

Where do I begin? Thanks to Marg and Errol for graciously picking me for this gig. Tip of the hat to Martin, Melanie and Sasha for dealing with constant changes to my schedules (that damn TV gig!). I'm grateful to the many Singaporeans who showed me a softer side to local life (including an 'auntie' who heaped her food into my bowl. God bless you!). Mum for being Mum and for always believing there was an author in me. And Wency for letting me play for months away from home and appreciating my presence in absence. I love you.

BRANDON PRESSER

At Lonely Planet, thanks to Tashi for CE-ing my journeys through Malaysia, Brunei and Thailand; to Shawn and Carolyn for sending me; to Celeste, my favourite person I've never met; to China for pulling a stellar double shift as CA; to Nigel Chin for editing Thailand while I was lost in Borneo; and to the all-star production staff for putting the finishing touches on a great new guide. In Thailand, *khap khun mahk khrap* to Neal and Rashi, Tash, Songkran, Golf, Wayne Lunt, Hans Ulrich, Robyn Hasson, Rene Balot, Joe Hue, Matt Bolton, Palm on PP, JYSK and TAT. In Sabah and Sarawak, a heartfelt *terima kasih* to Karen Chin, Lillian Agama, Anton and Linn, Frankie and Yanti, I-Gek, Auther, Papa Bear, Lloyd Jones, Big-HeadJer, Melintan, Raddish, Jerome, Philip Yong and everyone else at BA. In Brunei, Irman, Leslie Chiang, Jenny, Amali, Chris and Faten – thank you!

NICK RAY

As always, so many people have been instrumental in helping to put this book together. First thanks to my wonderful wife Kulikar Sotho, who has joined me on many a trip through the Mekong region, sharing boats and bikes the length and breadth of the river. Thanks also to our wonderful young children Julian and Belle for putting up with Daddy's absences along the way. Thanks to Mum and Dad for the support and encouragement that carried me to faraway lands from a young age. There really are too many people to thank on a book like this that covers such an incredible selection of countries. To those of you who have helped, my heartfelt thanks, and I extend an open invitation for a sunset drink on the banks of the Mekong River.

DANIEL ROBINSON

NGO staff who generously shared their time and expertise include Jocelyn Roberts, Ayako Hiwasa, Arnaud Guidal, Seng Bunra, Prum Sitha, Tith Bora, Ben Rawson, Véronique Audibert-Peste, Oran Shapira, Julien Colomer, Anne-Maria Makela, Tommi Tenno, Sok Sophea, Clara Launay, Michael Stimpson, Janet Gracey, Elise Vermeulen, Sarah Galvin, Tania Heath, Nick Butler, Étienne Morin, Xavier Gobin, Kim Dara Chan and Asahel Bush. Also hugely helpful were Toni Curman, Jacob Curman, Duncan Garner, Claire Garner, Scott McKenzee-Lee, Chris Beaven, Henrik Olsson, Jason Webb, Janet Newman, Jean James, Bill Herod, Esther Riepert, Christina Gerth, Dror Marcus, Chamroeun Chhan, Mie Mortensen, Veronica Nordlund, Brad Gordon, and my drivers Srien, Hang Vuthy (Sihanoukville) and Racky Thy (Battambang). It was, as usual, a real pleasure working with Tashi Wheeler, who belongs to the second generation of Wheelers to dispatch me to Cambodia for Lonely Planet, and with Nick Ray. Finally, I'd like to thank my wife Rachel Safman for her backstopping, forbearance and good humour.

RYAN VER BERKMOES

Many thanks to my Indonesia band of contributors: Adam, Celeste, Iain, John, Mark, Steve and Trent. At Lonely Planet, thanks to the entire publishing and production teams for guidance, understanding and the ability to fix a lot of bad syntax. Special thanks to Tashi Wheeler, who I think was born in Southeast Asia or at least hatched there. And to China Williams, who was a great coordinating author and whose work on Sumatra years ago will live forever. Finally, there's Annah who always gives me a welcome 'merp' and Erin Corrigan, who has made Bali her own as well.

RICHARD WATERS

In no particular order I'd like to thank the following for their invaluable help in either getting me on the right bus, boat or plane, or for their helpful insights: Mr Vong at Sabaidee 2 for always being on hand, Matt Verborg for taking me on his boat and giving me the benefits of his island knowledge, Derek Beattie for his useful updates on Luang Prabang politics and coordinates, Mark O, Dr Robert Cooper, the staff at the Gibbon Experience, Thierry at Jules' Classic

BEHIND THE SCENES

Rentals, Chitta at Laos Airlines and Paul McNally for making me see double. Not forgetting the endless warmth and magic of the Lao people, for without this I wouldn't drag myself across their jungles and mountains on a regular basis. And as ever China Williams and Tashi Wheeler for exercising the zen discipline of patience – a prerequisite to work with me!

OUR READERS

Many thanks to the travellers who used the last edition and wrote to us with helpful hints, useful advice and interesting anecdotes:

Elaine Anselmi, Jules Atkins, John Boon, Patrick Bruyere, Bridgette Cole, Laura Crawford, Daniel Darcy, Vincent De Ruiter, Luke Dunn, Don Foster, Pamela Goats, Rachel Henson, Christopher Isele, Greg Jackman, Amanda James, Rachel Jones, Elaine Jones, John Konfusion, Struan L, Megan Mccutchan, Karl Melles, Steven Mendoza, Orion Miller, Jane Noonan, Olesya Novikova, Leo Owen, Ann Persson, Vilja Raatikainen, Don Reynolds, Johanna Rydelius, Mark Simons, Witold Sitko, Tanya Spiteri, James Tennet, Anette Uddqvist, Ana-Maria Udrica, Timmi van Maldegem, Jens Walter, Bill Weir, John Williams

ACKNOWLEDGMENTS

Many thanks to the following for the use of their content:

Globe on title page ©Mountain High Maps 1993 Digital Wisdom, Inc.

Index

000 Map pages
000 Photograph pages

INDEX

D

000 Map pages
000 Photograph pages

INDEX

000 Map pages
000 Photograph pages

INDEX

INDEX

INDEX

000 Map pages
000 Photograph pages

INDEX

THE LONELY PLANET STORY

Fresh from an epic journey across Europe, Asia and Australia in 1972, Tony and Maureen Wheeler sat at their kitchen table stapling together notes. The first Lonely Planet guidebook, *Across Asia on the Cheap*, was born.

Travellers snapped up the guides. Inspired by their success, the Wheelers began publishing books to Southeast Asia, India and beyond. Demand was prodigious, and the Wheelers expanded the business rapidly to keep up. Over the years, Lonely Planet extended its coverage to every country and into the virtual world via lonelyplanet.com and the Thorn Tree message board.

As Lonely Planet became a globally loved brand, Tony and Maureen received several offers for the company. But it wasn't until 2007 that they found a partner whom they trusted to remain true to the company's principles of travelling widely, treading lightly and giving sustainably. In October of that year, BBC Worldwide acquired a 75% share in the company, pledging to uphold Lonely Planet's commitment to independent travel, trustworthy advice and editorial independence.

Today, Lonely Planet has offices in Melbourne, London and Oakland, with over 500 staff members and 300 authors. Tony and Maureen are still actively involved with Lonely Planet. They're travelling more often than ever, and they're devoting their spare time to charitable projects. And the company is still driven by the philosophy of *Across Asia on the Cheap*: 'All you've got to do is decide to go and the hardest part is over. So go!'

Published by Lonely Planet Publications Pty Ltd
ABN 36 005 607 983

Cover montage by Yukiyoshi Kamimura. Photographs by Lonely Planet Images: Austin Bush, Johnny Haglund, Tim Hughes, Dallas Stribley, Jane Sweeney.

Many of the images in this guide are available for licensing from Lonely Planet Images: www.lonelyplanetimages.com.

Printed through Colorcraft Ltd, Hong Kong. Printed in China

LONELY PLANET OFFICES

Australia
Head Office
Locked Bag 1, Footscray, Victoria 3011
☎ 03 8379 8000, fax 03 8379 8111
talk2us@lonelyplanet.com.au

USA
150 Linden St, Oakland, CA 94607
☎ 510 250 6400, toll free 800 275 8555
fax 510 893 8572
info@lonelyplanet.com

UK
2nd fl, 186 City Rd,
London EC1V 2NT
☎ 020 7106 2100, fax 020 7106 2101
go@lonelyplanet.co.uk